USA

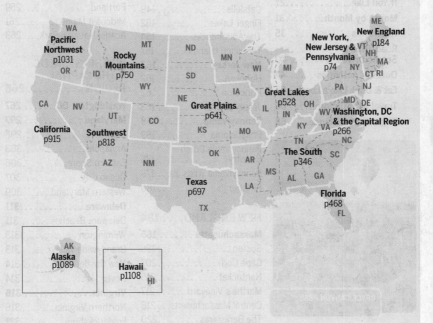

WA
Pacific Northwest
p1031
OR

MT

ND

MN

WI

MI

ME

New England
p184

New York, New Jersey & Pennsylvania
p74

VT
NH
MA
NY
CT RI

ID

Rocky Mountains
p750

SD

WY

IA

NE

Great Lakes
p528

OH

PA

NJ

CA

NV

UT

CO

Great Plains
p641

IL

IN

MD DE
WV
VA

Washington, DC & the Capital Region
p266

California
p915

Southwest
p818

KS

MO

KY

TN

NC

AZ

NM

OK

AR

The South
p346

SC

MS

AL

GA

Texas
p697

LA

Florida
p468

TX

FL

AK
Alaska
p1089

Hawaii
p1108
HI

Benedict Walker, Kate Armstrong, Brett Atkinson, Carolyn Bain, Amy C Balfour, Robert Balkovich, Ray Bartlett, Loren Bell, Greg Benchwick, Andrew Bender, Sara Benson, Alison Bing, Catherine Bodry, Cristian Bonetto, Celeste Brash, Jade Bremner, Nate Cavalieri, Gregor Clark, Michael Grosberg, Ashley Harrell, Alexander Howard, Mark Johanson, Adam Karlin, Brian Kluepfel, Stephen Lioy, Carolyn McCarthy, Craig McLachlan, Hugh McNaughtan, Becky Ohlsen, Christopher Pitts, Liza Prado, Josephine Quintero, Kevin Raub, Simon Richmond, Brendan Sainsbury, Andrea Schulte-Peevers, Adam Skolnick, Helena Smith, Regis St Louis, Ryan Ver Berkmoes, John A Vlahides, Mara Vorhees, Clifton Wilkinson, Luci Yamamoto, Karla Zimmerman

Contents

PLAN YOUR TRIP

Welcome to the USA 6

USA Map 8

USA's Top 25 10

Need to Know 22

First Time USA 24

What's New 26

If You Like... 27

Month by Month 31

Itineraries 35

Road Trips & Scenic Drives 40

Outdoor Activities 47

Eat & Drink Like a Local...55

Travel with Children.... 66

Regions at a Glance.... 69

BRYCE CANYON P888

SEA LION, ANACAPA ISLAND P966

ON THE ROAD

NEW YORK, NEW JERSEY & PENNSYLVANIA 74

New York City 75

New York State 140

Long Island 141

Hudson Valley 145

Catskills 149

Finger Lakes 152

The Adirondacks 154

Thousand Islands...... 157

New Jersey 162

Hoboken.............. 162

Princeton............. 162

Jersey Shore........... 163

Pennsylvania......... 168

Philadelphia 169

Pennsylvania Dutch Country 178

Pennsylvania Wilds 179

Pittsburgh 180

NEW ENGLAND.... 184

Massachusetts 185

Boston 185

Cape Cod............. 207

Nantucket 215

Martha's Vineyard 217

Central Massachusetts... 218

The Berkshires 220

Rhode Island 223

Providence............ 224

Newport............... 226

East Bay.............. 229

Connecticut.......... 230

Hartford 231

Litchfield Hills......... 232

Connecticut Coast...... 233

Lower Connecticut River Valley 234

New Haven 236

Vermont 238

New Hampshire....... 249

Portsmouth........... 249

Lakes Region.......... 250

White Mountains 251

Hanover 255

Maine 256

Southern Maine Coast... 258

Portland.............. 259

Midcoast Maine 261

Acadia National Park....263

WASHINGTON, DC & THE CAPITAL REGION 266

Washington, DC 267

Maryland 297

Baltimore............. 298

Annapolis............. 303

Eastern Shore......... 306

Ocean City............ 307

Western Maryland 309

Delaware 311

Delaware Beaches 311

Wilmington 313

Brandywine Valley 313

New Castle 314

Dover 314

Virginia.............. 316

Northern Virginia 316

Fredericksburg 321

Richmond 322

Historic Triangle....... 325

Hampton Roads 328

Virginia Beach......... 329

The Piedmont......... 330

Shenandoah Valley...... 333

Blue Ridge Highlands & Southwest Virginia......338

West Virginia......... 341

Eastern Panhandle......342

Monongahela National Forest.........344

Contents

THE SOUTH 346

North Carolina 347
North Carolina Coast 347
The Triangle 356
Charlotte 360
North Carolina
Mountains 361
South Carolina 368
Charleston 369
Mt Pleasant 373
Lowcountry 374
North Coast 377
Greenville &
the Upcountry 378
Tennessee 379
Memphis 379
Nashville 387
Kentucky 399
Louisville 399
Bluegrass Country 402
Georgia 406
Atlanta 407
Alabama 426
Birmingham 427
Montgomery 429
Selma 430
Mobile 431
Mississippi 432
Oxford 432
Mississippi Delta 433
Jackson 435
Natchez 436
Gulf Coast 437
Arkansas 438
Little Rock 438
Hot Springs 440
Tri-Peaks Region 441
Ozark Mountains 442
Louisiana 445
New Orleans 446

FLORIDA 468

South Florida 469
Miami 469
Fort Lauderdale 487
Palm Beach County 490
The Everglades 493
Florida Keys 498
Atlantic Coast 503
Space Coast 504
Daytona Beach 505
St Augustine 506
Jacksonville 508
Amelia Island 510
Southwest Florida 511
Tampa 511
St Petersburg 513
Sarasota 515
Sanibel &
Captiva Islands 516
Naples 517
Central Florida 518
Orlando 518
Walt Disney World®
Resort 521
Universal Orlando
Resort 523
Florida Panhandle 524
Tallahassee 524
Pensacola 525

GREAT LAKES 528
Illinois 529
Chicago 532
Indiana 561
Indianapolis 561
Ohio 570
Cleveland 570
Erie Lakeshore &
Islands 573
Ohio Amish Country 576
Columbus 577
Yellow Springs 578

Dayton 578
Cincinnati 579
Michigan 583
Detroit 584
Dearborn 591
Ann Arbor 592
Gold Coast 594
Straits of Mackinac 598
Upper Peninsula 600
Wisconsin 603
Milwaukee 603
Racine 606
Minnesota 613
Minneapolis 614
St Paul 620

THE GREAT PLAINS . . 641
Missouri 644
St Louis 645
St Charles 651
Hannibal 652
The Ozarks 653
Kansas City 655
Independence 658
St Joseph 659
Iowa 660
Des Moines 660
Davenport 661
Iowa City 662
Amana Colonies 662
Mt Vernon 662
Dubuque 663
Cedar Valley 664
North Dakota 665
Fargo 665
Bismarck 666
Theodore Roosevelt
National Park 666
Rugby 667
South Dakota 667
Sioux Falls 667
Chamberlain 668

ON THE ROAD

Pierre 668
Wall. 669
Badlands
National Park 669
Pine Ridge
Indian Reservation. 670
Black Hills 670
Nebraska 677
Omaha 678
Lincoln. 680
Grand Island 681
North Platte 681
Valentine 682
Nebraska Panhandle 682
Kansas 684
Wichita. 684
Lawrence. 685
Topeka 687
Abilene. 688
Chase County 688
Oklahoma. 688
Oklahoma City 689
Tulsa. 692
Guthrie. 694
Anadarko. 695
Claremore 695
Muskogee 695
Tahlequah 696

TEXAS 697
Central Texas. 700
Austin. 700
San Antonio &
The Hill Country 709
East Texas 716
Houston. 717
Clear Lake 723
**Gulf Coast
& South Texas. 724**
Galveston. 724
Corpus Christi 726
Padre Island
National Seashore. 728

South Padre Island 728
Dallas-Fort Worth 730
Dallas 730
Fort Worth 737
West Texas. 739
Big Bend National Park . . .740
Big Bend Ranch
State Park 741
El Paso. 746
Guadalupe Mountains
National Park 749

**ROCKY
MOUNTAINS 750**
Colorado 754
Denver 754
Boulder 763
Northern Mountains 766
Wyoming 787
Cheyenne. 787
Laramie 788
Lander 790
Jackson 791
Cody 793
Yellowstone
National Park 794
Grand Teton
National Park 799
Montana. 803
Bozeman 803
Gallatin &
Paradise Valleys 804
Billings 805
Helena 806
Missoula. 806
Flathead Lake 808
Whitefish 809
Glacier National Park . . . 810
Idaho. 812
Boise. 812
Ketchum & Sun Valley. . . 814
Stanley. 816
Idaho Panhandle 817

SOUTHWEST. 818
Nevada 822
Las Vegas. 822
The Great Basin 838
Arizona. 838
Phoenix 839
Grand Canyon
National Park 854
Utah 871
Salt Lake City 872
Park City & Wasatch
Mountains 876
Northeastern Utah. 881
Moab 882
Zion &
Southwestern Utah 887
New Mexico 891
Albuquerque 892
Along I-40 895
Santa Fe. 896

CALIFORNIA 915
Los Angeles. 918
**Southern
Californian Coast 943**
Disneyland & Anaheim. . .943
Orange County
Beaches. 945
San Diego 947
**Palm Springs
& the Deserts 958**
Palm Springs. 958
Joshua Tree
National Park 961
Anza-Borrego
Desert State Park. 962
Mojave
National Preserve. 963
Death Valley
National Park 964
Central Coast 965
Santa Barbara. 965
San Luis Obispo 968
Morro Bay to
Hearst Castle 970

Contents

Big Sur 971
Carmel 972
Monterey 973
Santa Cruz. 975
**San Francisco
& the Bay Area 977**
San Francisco 977
Marin County 1003
Berkeley 1004
**Northern
California 1006**
Wine Country 1006
North Coast. 1011
Sacramento. 1016
Gold Country. 1017
California's
Northern Mountains . . . 1019
Sierra Nevada 1021
Yosemite
National Park 1022
Sequoia & Kings
Canyon National Parks. . . 1025
Eastern Sierra. 1027
Lake Tahoe 1029

**PACIFIC
NORTHWEST. 1031**
Washington 1035
Seattle 1035
Olympia 1049
Olympic Peninsula 1050
San Juan Islands 1055
North Cascades 1057
South Cascades 1060
Oregon 1063
Portland. 1063
Willamette Valley 1073
Columbia River Gorge. . . 1075
Oregon Cascades 1076

ALASKA 1089
Anchorage 1091
Southeast Alaska 1094

Wrangell 1095
Sitka 1096
Juneau 1098
Haines 1100
Skagway. 1101
Glacier Bay National
Park & Preserve 1103
Ketchikan. 1104
Fairbanks 1105

HAWAII 1108
O'ahu 1110
Honolulu 1110
Waikiki 1113
**Hawai'i, the
Big Island 1117**
Kailua-Kona. 1117
Mauna Kea. 1120
Hamakua Coast 1121
Hilo 1121
Hawai'i Volcanoes
National Park 1122
Maui 1123
Lahaina 1123
Kihei 1125
Kaua'i 1126
Lihu'e 1126
Wailua 1126
Hanalei 1127
Po'ipu &
South Shore 1128

UNDERSTAND

USA Today 1130
History 1133
The Way of Life. 1145
Native Americans 1150
Arts & Architecture . . . 1152
The Music Scene 1161
The Land & Wildlife . . . 1164

SURVIVAL GUIDE

Directory A–Z 1170
Transportation 1183
Driving in
the USA 1190
Index. 1199
Map Legend. 1218

SPECIAL FEATURES

**Road Trips &
Scenic Drives 40**
Outdoor Activities 47
**Eat & Drink
Like a Local 55**
**Central Park 3D
Illustration. 98**

**National Mall 3D
Illustration. 276**
**USA's
National Parks 627**
**Alcatraz 3D
Illustration. 990**
Driving in the USA . . . 1190

Welcome to the USA

The great American experience is about so many things: bluegrass and beaches, snow-covered peaks and redwood forests, restaurant-loving cities and big open skies.

Bright Lights, Big Cities

America is the birthplace of LA, Las Vegas, Chicago, Miami, Boston and New York City – each a brimming metropolis whose name alone conjures a million different notions of culture, cuisine and entertainment. Look more closely, and the American quilt unfurls in all its surprising variety: the eclectic music scene of Austin, the easygoing charms of antebellum Savannah, the eco-consciousness of free-spirited Portland, the magnificent waterfront of San Francisco and the captivating French Quarter of jazz-loving New Orleans. Each city adds its unique style to the grand patchwork that is America.

On the Road Again

This is a country of road trips and great open skies, where 4 million miles of highways lead past red-rock deserts, below towering mountain peaks and through fertile wheat fields that roll off toward the horizon. The sun-bleached hillsides of the Great Plains, the lush rainforests of the Pacific Northwest, the sultry swamplands of the South and the scenic country lanes of New England are a few fine starting points for the great American road trip. Veer off the interstate often to discover the bucolic 'blue highways' of lore.

Food-Loving Nation

On one evening in the US, thick barbecue ribs come piping hot at a Texas roadhouse, while chefs blend organic produce with Asian accents at award-winning West Coast restaurants. Locals get their fix of bagels and lox at a century-old deli in Manhattan's Upper West Side and, several states away, plump pancakes and fried eggs disappear under the clatter of cutlery at a 1950s-style diner. Steaming plates of lobster from a Maine pier, oysters and champagne from a California wine bar, Korean tacos out of a Portland food truck – these are just a few ways to dine à la Americana.

Cultural Behemoth

The USA has made tremendous contributions to the arts. Georgia O'Keeffe's wild landscapes, Robert Rauschenberg's surreal collages, Alexander Calder's elegant mobiles and Jackson Pollock's drip paintings have entered the vernacular of 20th-century art. Chicago and New York have become veritable drawing boards for the great architects of the modern era. And from the soulful blues born in the Mississippi Delta to the bluegrass of Appalachia and Detroit's Motown sound – plus jazz, funk, hip-hop, country, and rock and roll – America has invented sounds integral to modern music.

Why I Love the USA

By Mark Johanson, Writer

From the soaring skyscrapers of Chicago to the adobe pueblos of New Mexico and the ante-bellum plantations of the Carolinas, the country of my birth defies easy description. Few other countries can pair iconic cities (like New York and San Francisco) with vast natural reserves protecting everything from rainforests to deserts, volcanoes and geysers. You can hike the soaring peaks of the Rockies, but also dip into the gaping abyss of the Grand Canyon and paddle through the Florida Everglades. Or you can hit the wide-open road – a rite of passage for any American and my favorite form of meditation.

For more about our writers, see p1219

Above: Zion National Park (p889), Utah

USA

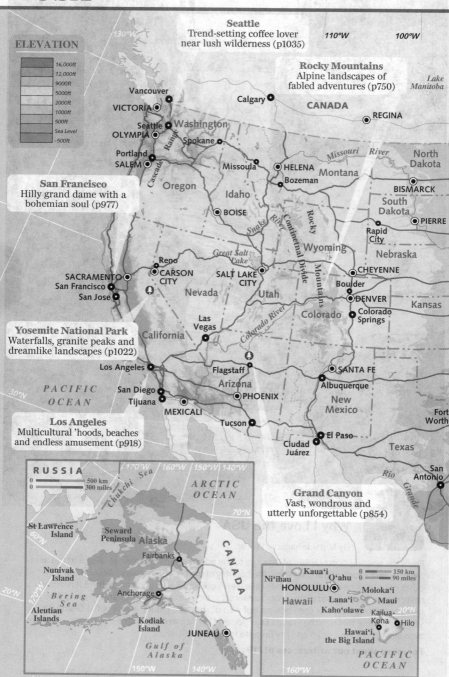

ELEVATION

16,000ft
12,000ft
9000ft
5000ft
2000ft
1000ft
500ft
Sea Level
-500ft

Seattle
Trend-setting coffee lover
near lush wilderness (p1035)

Rocky Mountains
Alpine landscapes of
fabled adventures (p750)

San Francisco
Hilly grand dame with a
bohemian soul (p977)

Yosemite National Park
Waterfalls, granite peaks and
dreamlike landscapes (p1022)

Los Angeles
Multicultural 'hoods, beaches
and endless amusement (p918)

Grand Canyon
Vast, wondrous and
utterly unforgettable (p854)

130°W 110°W 100°W

Lake Manitoba

CANADA

Vancouver
VICTORIA
Calgary
REGINA

Seattle
OLYMPIA
Washington
Spokane

Portland
SALEM
Missoula
HELENA
Bozeman
Montana

Oregon
Idaho
Continental Divide

BISMARCK
North Dakota

BOISE
Snake River
Rocky Mountains
South Dakota
PIERRE

Great Salt Lake
Wyoming
Rapid City
Nebraska

Reno
CARSON CITY
SALT LAKE CITY
CHEYENNE
Boulder
DENVER

SACRAMENTO
San Francisco
San Jose
Nevada
Utah
Colorado
Colorado Springs
Kansas

Las Vegas
California
Colorado River

Los Angeles
Flagstaff
Arizona
SANTA FE
Albuquerque

PACIFIC OCEAN
San Diego
Tijuana
MEXICALI
PHOENIX
New Mexico
Fort Worth

Tucson
El Paso
Ciudad Juárez
Texas

Cascade Range

Missouri River

30°N

RUSSIA
170°W 160°W 150°W 140°W

Chukchi Sea
ARCTIC OCEAN
70°N

500 km
300 miles

St Lawrence Island
Seward Peninsula
Alaska
CANADA

60°N

Fairbanks

Nunivak Island
Bering Sea
Anchorage

Aleutian Islands
Kodiak Island

JUNEAU

Gulf of Alaska

26°N
120°W

Kaua'i
Ni'ihau
O'ahu
HONOLULU
Moloka'i
Maui
150 km
90 miles

Hawaii
Lana'i
Kaho'olawe
Kailua-Kona
Hilo

Hawai'i, the Big Island

20°N

PACIFIC OCEAN
160°W

Rio Grande
San Antonio

150°W 140°W 110°W 100°W

Chicago
Stunning architecture and lakefront festivals (p532)

New York City
Famed metropolis and cultural capital (p75)

Boston
Follow the cobblestones into history (p185)

National Mall
Iconic monuments on America's front lawn (p267)

Blue Ridge Parkway
Drive among the scenic Appalachian Mountains (p339)

New Orleans
Creole cookin', hot jazz and Mardi Gras (p446)

Austin
Creative and indie-loving music capital (p700)

Miami
Cuban food, art deco and sultry beaches (p469)

ATLANTIC OCEAN

BAHAMAS

CUBA

Gulf of Mexico

MEXICO

USA's Top 25

New York City

1 Home to striving artists, hedge-fund moguls and immigrants from every corner of the globe, New York City (p75) is constantly reinventing itself. It remains one of the world centers of fashion, theater, food, music, publishing, advertising and finance. A staggering number of museums, parks and ethnic neighborhoods are scattered through the five boroughs. Do as every New Yorker does: hit the streets. Every block reflects the character and history of this dizzying kaleidoscope, and on even a short walk you can cross continents.

Yellowstone National Park

2 What makes the world's first national park (p794) so enduring? Geologic wonders, for one thing, from geysers and fluorescent hot springs to fumaroles and bubbling mud pots. Then there's the wildlife: grizzlies, black bears, wolves, elk, bison and moose, roaming across some 3500 sq miles of wilderness. Pitch a tent in Yellowstone's own Grand Canyon, admire the Upper and Lower Falls, wait for Old Faithful to blow, and hike through the primeval, fuming landscape for a real taste of what is truly the Wild West. Below: Grand Prismatic Spring (p795)

MATT MUNRO/LONELY PLANET ©

NOPPAWAT TOM CHAROENSINPHON/GETTY IMAGES ©

San Francisco

3 Change is afoot in this boom-and-bust city (p977), currently enjoying a high-profile boom. Amid the fog and the clatter of old-fashioned trams, San Francisco's diverse neighborhoods invite long days of wandering, with great indie shops, fabulous restaurants and bohemian nightlife. Highlights include exploring Alcatraz, strolling the Golden Gate, making day trips to the nearby redwoods, Pacific coastline and Wine Country, and taking at least one ride on the cable car. How cool is San Francisco? Trust us – crest that hill to your first stunning waterfront view, and you'll be hooked.

Grand Canyon

4 The sheer immensity of the Grand Canyon (p854) is what grabs you at first – a two-billion-year-old rip across the landscape that reveals the earth's geologic secrets with commanding authority. But it's Mother Nature's artistic touches, from sun-dappled ridges and crimson buttes to lush oases and a ribbon-like river, that hold your attention and demand your return. To explore the canyon, take your pick of adventures: hiking, biking, rafting or mule riding. Or simply grab a seat along the Rim Trail and watch the earth change colors before you.

National Mall

5 Nearly 2 miles long and lined with iconic monuments and hallowed marble buildings, the National Mall (p267) is the epicenter of Washington, DC's political and cultural life. In the summer, music and food festivals are staged here, while year-round visitors wander the halls of America's finest museums lining the green. For exploring American history, there's no better place to ruminate, whether tracing your hand along the Vietnam War Memorial, or ascending the steps of the Lincoln Memorial, where Martin Luther King Jr gave his famous 'I Have a Dream' speech.
Top: Martin Luther King Jr Memorial (p271)

Yosemite National Park

6 Meander through wildflower-strewn meadows in valleys carved by rivers and glaciers, the hard, endless work of which makes everything look simply colossal. Here in Yosemite (p1022), thunderous waterfalls tumble over sheer cliffs, ant-sized climbers scale the enormous granite domes of El Cap and Half Dome, and hikers walk beneath ancient groves of giant sequoias, the planet's biggest trees. Even the subalpine meadows of Tuolumne are magnificently vast. For sublime views, perch at Glacier Point on a full-moon night or drive the high country's dizzying Tioga Rd in summer.

Pacific Coast Highways

7 A drive along America's stunning western coastline is road-tripping at its finest. In California, the Pacific Coast Hwy (p42; also called Hwy 1), Hwy 101 and I-5 pass dizzying sea cliffs, idiosyncratic beach towns and a few major cities: laid-back San Diego, rocker LA and beatnik San Francisco. North of the redwoods, Hwy 101 swoops into Oregon for windswept capes, rocky tide pools and, for *Twilight* fans, Ecola State Park, the stand-in for werewolf haven La Push, WA. Cross the Columbia River into Washington for wet-and-wild Olympic National Park. Below left: Jedediah Smith Redwoods State Park (p1015)

New Orleans

8 Reborn after Hurricane Katrina in 2005, New Orleans (p446) is back. Caribbean-colonial architecture, Creole cuisine and a riotous air of celebration seem more alluring than ever in the Big Easy. Nights are spent catching Dixieland jazz, blues and rock amid bouncing live-music joints, and the city's riotous annual festivals (Mardi Gras, Jazz Fest) are famous the world over. 'Nola' is also a food-loving town that celebrates its myriad culinary influences. Feast on lip-smacking jamba-laya, soft-shell crab and Louisiana *cochon* (pulled pork) before hitting the bar scene on Frenchmen St. Below right: Jambalaya

CHRISTOPHER KIMMEL/GETTY IMAGES ©

BHOFACK2/GETTY IMAGES/ISTOCKPHOTO ©

New England in Fall

9 It's a major event, one approaching epic proportions in New England (p184): watching the leaves change color. You can do it anywhere – all you need is one brilliant tree. But if you're most people, you'll want lots of trees. From the Berkshires in Massachusetts and the Litchfield Hills in Connecticut to the Green Mountains of Vermont, entire hillsides blaze with brilliant crimsons, oranges and yellows. Covered bridges and white-steeple churches with abundant maple trees put Vermont and New Hampshire at the forefront of leaf-peeping heaven. Top: Vermont (p238)

Santa Fe & Taos

10 Santa Fe (p896) is an old city with a young soul. On Friday nights, art lovers flock to Canyon Rd to gab with artists, sip wine and explore more than 80 galleries. Art and history partner up in style within the city's consortium of museums, and the food and the shopping are first rate, too. With that turquoise sky as a backdrop, the experience is darn near sublime. Artists also converge in adobe Taos (p904), but the vibe is quirkier, with ski bums, off-the-grid Earthshippers and a few celebs keeping things offbeat. Above: Taos Pueblo (p906)

Musical Roots

11 Name the genre, and it probably began here. The Mississippi Delta birthed the blues, while New Orleans opened the door to jazz. Rock and roll arrived the day Elvis Presley walked into Sun Studio in Memphis. And country made its way from fiddle-and-banjo Appalachian hamlets to Nashville's Grand Ole Opry. The Mississippi River took the music north, where Chicago and Detroit riffed into the electric blues and Motown sound, respectively. It all translates into great live music (p1161) wherever you are in the USA. Above: Musician at Kingston Mines (p553), Chicago

Native American History & Culture

12 The Southwest is home to an array of Native American sites. To learn about America's earliest inhabitants, climb ladders to the ancient cliff-side homes of Ancestral Puebloans at Colorado's Mesa Verde National Park. To experience living cultures, visit New Mexico's Taos Pueblo and northeastern Arizona's Hopi nation, or explore the Navajo tribal lands of the Four Corners region: zigzagging through the otherworldly buttes and towers of Monument Valley or scrambling down ladders with a Navajo docent into Canyon de Chelly (p862). Top right: Mesa Verde (p784)

Portland

13 Are the '90s still alive in Portland? The characters in the award-winning indie series *Portlandia* sure think so, and their satiric skits make it clear that this city (p1063) is a quirky but lovable place. It's as friendly as a big town, and home to a mix of students, artists, cyclists, hipsters, young families, old hippies, eco-freaks and everything in between. There's great food, music and culture aplenty, plus it's as sustainable as you can get. Come visit, but be careful – like everyone else, you might just want to move here!

The Deep South

14 Steeped in history and complex regional pride, the Deep South is America at its most fascinating, from the moss-draped live oaks and azalea-choked gardens of Charleston (p369) to the cinder-block juke joints of the steamy Mississippi Delta and the isolated French-speaking enclaves of the Louisiana bayou. Famous for its slow pace, the Deep South is all about enjoying life's small pleasures: sucking down fresh Gulf oysters at an Alabama seafood shack, strolling Savannah's antebellum alleys, or sipping sweet tea on the verandah with new friends. Below: Savannah (p420)

Walt Disney World® Resort

15 Want to set the bar high? Call yourself the 'Happiest Place on Earth.' Walt Disney World® Resort (p521) does, and then pulls out all the stops to deliver the exhilarating sensation that you are the most important character in the show. Despite all the frantic rides, entertainment and nostalgia, the magic is watching your own child swell with belief after they have made Goofy laugh, been curtsied to by Cinderella, guarded the galaxy with Buzz Lightyear and battled Darth Maul like your very own Jedi knight. Bottom: Magic Kingdom (p522)

14

15

Hawai'i Volcanoes National Park

16 From Kilauea, the earth's youngest and most active shield volcano, to the massive form of Mauna Loa, to the fiery lava cauldron of Halema'uma'u Crater, nothing in the USA can compare with the dramatic landscapes of Hawai'i Volcanoes National Park (p1122). Here on the Big Island of Hawai'i, you can wander forests thick with tree ferns and climb around the crater by day, then at night descend to the Pacific to witness the magical glow and hiss of molten lava pouring into the sea.

Chicago

17 The Windy City (p532) will blow you away with its architecture, lakefront beaches and world-class museums. But its real lure is its blend of high culture and earthy pleasures. Is there another metropolis that dresses its Picasso sculpture in local sports-team gear? Where residents queue just as long for hot dogs as for some of North America's top restaurants? Winters are brutal, but come summer, Chicago fetes the warm days with food and music festivals that make fine use of its waterfront.

SKY NOIR PHOTOGRAPHY BY BILL DICKINSON/GETTY IMAGES ©

DENISE LEBLANC/SHUTTERSTOCK ©

Las Vegas

18 Just when you think you've got a handle on the West – majestic, sublime, soul-nourishing – here comes Vegas (p822) shaking her thing like a showgirl looking for trouble. Beneath the neon lights of the Strip, she puts on a dazzling show: dancing fountains, a spewing volcano, the Eiffel Tower. But she saves her most dangerous charms for the gambling dens – seductive lairs where the fresh-pumped air and bright colors share one goal: separating you from your money. Step away if you can for fine restaurants, Cirque du Soleil, Slotzilla and the Mob Museum.

Route 66

19 Launched in 1926 and known as the Mother Road (p40), this fragile ribbon of concrete running clear from Chicago to Los Angeles was the USA's original road trip, and still offers classic, time-warped touring. Motor along past 2000 miles of vintage Americana, stopping to fork into thick slabs of pie in small-town diners and to snap photos of roadside attractions such as the Snow Cap Drive-In, the Wigwam Motel, the neon signs of Tucumcari, the begging burros of Oatman, AZ, and the Gemini Giant, a sky-high fiberglass spaceman.

Acadia National Park

20 Acadia National Park (p263) is where the mountains meet the sea. Miles of rocky coastline and even more miles of hiking and biking trails make this wonderland Maine's most popular destination, and deservedly so. The high point (literally) is Cadillac Mountain, the 1530ft peak that can be accessed by foot, bicycle or vehicle; early risers can catch the country's first sunrise from this celebrated summit. Later in the day, after working up an appetite on the trails and beaches, indulge in tea and popovers at Jordan Pond. Above: Young fox

PIRIYA PHOTOGRAPHY MOMENT/GETTY IMAGES ©

Glacier National Park

21 Yep, the rumors are true. The namesake attractions at Glacier National Park (p810) are melting away. There were 150 glaciers in the area in 1850; today there are 26. But even without the giant ice cubes, Montana's sprawling national park is worthy of an in-depth visit. Road warriors can maneuver the thrilling 50-mile Going-to-the-Sun Road; wildlife-watchers can scan for elk, wolves and grizzlies (but hopefully not too close); and hikers have 700 miles of trails, trees and flora – including mosses, mushrooms and wildflowers – to explore.

Everglades

22 The Everglades (p493) unnerve. They don't reach majestically skyward or fill your heart with the aching beauty of a glacier-carved valley. They ooze, flat and watery, a river of grass mottled by hammocks, cypress domes and mangroves. You can't hike them, not really. To properly explore the Everglades – and to meet its prehistoric residents, like the snaggle-toothed crocodile – you must leave the safety of land. Push a canoe off a muddy bank, tamp down your fear, and explore the waterways on the Everglades' own, unforgettable terms.

Los Angeles

23 A perpetual influx of dreamers, go-getters and hustlers gives this sprawling coastal city (p918) an energetic buzz. Learn the tricks of moviemaking during a studio tour. Bliss out to acoustically perfect symphony sounds in the Walt Disney Concert Hall. Wander gardens and galleries at the hilltop Getty Museum. And stargazing? Take in the big picture at the revamped Griffith Observatory or look for stylish, earthbound 'stars' at the Grove. Ready for your close-up, darling? You will be – an hour on the beach guarantees that sun-kissed LA glow. Above: Venice Beach (p931)

San Antonio

24 San Antonio (p709) beguiles visitors with its pretty River Walk and rich history. Start in the heart of town at the battle-scarred Alamo, Texas' most famous historic site, and walk or grab a share bike for the multi-mile meander along the San Antonio River past museums, restaurants and shops, clear out to the city's cluster of 18th-century Spanish missions. Beyond these obvious attractions, locals tout the city's easy diversity, on full display at its lively festivals – crowned by the 10-day Fiesta San Antonio in April. Below: River Walk (p709)

Winter Sports in the Rockies

25 The softest snow you'll ever ski combined with outrageous scenery and every type of terrain imaginable: Western resorts are some of the best in the world. Aspen (p774), Vail (p772) and Jackson Hole (p791) may sound like playgrounds for the rich and famous, but shredders and ski bums (and copious amounts of powder) have always found a way to keep it real. Launch off a cornice, slalom through trees, grind in a terrain park or face-plant repeatedly while learning to snowboard: one thing's certain, you'll end the day with a snow-encrusted smile. Bottom: Snowboarder, Aspen (p774)

Need to Know

For more information, see Survival Guide (p1169)

Currency
US dollar ($)

Language
English

Visas
Visitors from Canada, the UK, Australia, New Zealand, Japan and many EU countries don't need visas for stays of less than 90 days. Other nations see http://travel.state.gov.

Money
ATMs widely available. Credit cards accepted at most hotels, restaurants and shops.

Cell Phones
Foreign phones that operate on tri- or quad-band frequencies will work in the USA. Otherwise, purchase inexpensive cell phones with a pay-as-you-go plan here.

When to Go

Tropical climate
Dry climate
Warm to hot summers, mild winters
Mild to hot summers, cold winters
Polar climate

Seattle
GO May–Sep

New York City
GO May–Sep

Chicago
GO Jun–Sep

Los Angeles
GO Apr–Oct

New Orleans
GO Dec–May

Miami
GO Dec–Apr

High Season
(Jun–Aug)

➡ Warm days across the country, with generally high temperatures.

➡ Busiest season, with big crowds and higher prices.

➡ In ski-resort areas, January to March is high season.

Shoulder
(Apr–May & Sep–Oct)

➡ Milder temperatures, fewer crowds.

➡ Spring flowers (April) and fiery autumn colors (October) in many parts of the country.

Low Season
(Nov–Mar)

➡ Wintery days, with snowfall in the north, and heavier rains in some regions.

➡ Lowest prices for accommodations (aside from ski resorts and warmer getaway destinations).

Useful Websites

Lonely Planet (www.lonely planet.com/usa) Destination information, hotel bookings, traveler forum and more.

National Park Service (NPS; www.nps.gov) Gateway to America's greatest natural treasures, its national parks.

Eater (www.eater.com) Foodie insight into two-dozen American cities.

Punch (www.punchdrink.com) Quirky guides and helpful insights on how to drink well in America's cities.

New York Times Travel (www. nytimes.com/travel) Travel news, practical advice and engaging features.

Roadside America (www. roadsideamerica.com) For all things weird and wacky.

Important Numbers

Emergency	🖉 911
USA country code	🖉 1
Directory assistance	🖉 411
International directory assistance	🖉 00
International access code from the USA	🖉 011

Exchange Rates

Australia	A$1	US$0.75
Canada	C$1	US$0.75
Europe	€1	US$1.12
Japan	¥100	US$0.90
New Zealand	NZ$1	US$0.72
UK	UK£1	US$1.27

For current exchange rates, see www.xe.com

Daily Costs

Budget: Less than $150

➡ Dorm bed: $25–40

➡ Double room in a budget motel: $45–80

➡ Lunch from a cafe or food truck: $6–12

➡ Local bus, subway or train tickets: $2–4

Midrange: $150–250

➡ Double room in midrange hotel: $100–250

➡ Popular restaurant dinner for two: $30–60

➡ Car hire per day: from $30

Top End: More than $250

➡ Double room in a resort or top-end hotel: from $200

➡ Dinner in a top restaurant: $60–100

➡ Concert or theater tickets: $60–200

Opening Hours

Typical normal opening times are as follows:

Banks 8:30am–4:30pm Monday to Thursday, to 5:30pm Friday (and possibly 9am–noon Saturday)

Bars 5pm–midnight Sunday to Thursday, to 2am Friday and Saturday

Nightclubs 10pm–4am Thursday to Saturday

Post offices 9am–5pm Monday to Friday

Shopping malls 9am–9pm

Stores 9am–6pm Monday to Saturday, noon–5pm Sunday

Supermarkets 8am–8pm, some open 24 hours

Arriving in the USA

JFK International Airport (New York) AirTrain and LIRR to Penn Station via Jamaica Station ($15, 35 minutes), or AirTrain plus subway ($7.75, 50 to 75 minutes). A taxi to Manhattan costs $52, plus toll and tip (45 minutes to 1½ hours).

Los Angeles International Airport LAX Flyaway Bus to Union Station costs $9.75 (30 to 50 minutes); door-to-door Prime Time & SuperShuttle costs $17 to $30 (35 minutes to 1½ hours); and a taxi to Downtown costs $51 (25 to 50 minutes).

Miami International Airport SuperShuttle to South Beach for $20 to $24 (50 minutes to 1½ hours); taxi to Miami Beach for $35 (40 minutes to one hour); or take the Metrorail to downtown (Government Center) for $2.25 (15 minutes).

Time Zones in the USA

EST Eastern (GMT/UTC minus five hours) NYC, Boston, Washington DC, Atlanta

CST Central (GMT/UTC minus six hours) Chicago, New Orleans, Houston

MST Mountain (GMT/UTC minus seven hours) Denver, Santa Fe, Phoenix

PST Pacific (GMT/UTC minus eight hours) Seattle, San Francisco, Las Vegas

Most of Alaska is one hour behind Pacific time (GMT/UTC minus nine hours), while Hawaii is two hours behind Pacific time (GMT/UTC minus 10 hours). If it's 9pm in New York, it's 8pm in Chicago, 7pm in Denver, 6pm in Los Angeles, 5pm in Anchorage and 4pm (November to early March) or 3pm (rest of year) in Honolulu.

For much more on **getting around**, see p1185

First Time USA

For more information, see Survival Guide (p1169)

Checklist

➡ Check visa requirements for entering the US.

➡ Find out if you can use your phone in the US and ask about roaming charges.

➡ Book at least the first few nights of accommodations for your stay.

➡ Organize travel insurance.

➡ Inform your debit/credit-card company of upcoming travel.

What to Pack

➡ Passport and driver's license

➡ Cell phone (and charger)

➡ Good walking shoes

➡ A bathing suit

➡ A rain jacket or umbrella

➡ Electrical adapter, if needed

➡ Pants with a stretchable waistband (to accommodate the generous portions at American restaurants)

Top Tips for Your Trip

➡ Make the effort to meet the locals. Americans are generally quite friendly, and often happy to share insight into their city.

➡ If you're driving, get off the interstates and take the back roads. Some of the best scenery lies on winding country lanes.

➡ Plan carefully to avoid the worst of the crowds. Visit resort areas, popular restaurants and top sights on weekdays.

➡ Take photographic ID out to bars; many establishments have a policy to check ID for anyone buying alcohol, even if you're obviously over 21.

➡ US immigration officers can seem intimidating on arrival at border control. For a swift process, answer all questions fully, politely and calmly.

➡ Keep in mind that laws and attitudes vary considerably from state to state. What's legal in Colorado and Washington state, for example (smoking marijuana), is illegal in Texas and South Carolina.

What to Wear

In America just about anything goes, and you'll rarely feel uncomfortable because of what you're wearing. That said, it's worth bringing along dressier attire (smart casual) for dining at nice restaurants, or going to upscale bars or clubs.

Sleeping

➡ **Hotels** Options range from boxy and bland chain hotels to beautifully designed boutique and luxury hotels, with an equally varied price range.

➡ **B&Bs** These small guesthouses offer a more homey stay (but note that many don't cater to kids under a certain age).

➡ **Motels** Cheaper and simpler than most hotels, these are clustered along interstates and sprinkled across rural America.

➡ **Hostels** A growing network in the US, though still mostly limited to urban areas.

➡ **Camping** Options range from primitive backcountry spots to full-facility private campgrounds.

Money-Saving Strategies

While the US can be a pricey place to visit, there are many ways frugal travelers can save some dollars.

➡ You can save by eating your bigger meals at lunchtime, when many restaurants offer lunch specials, and main courses are much better value for money.

➡ Many museums have one or more free periods in which to visit (Thursday evening or Sunday morning for instance).

➡ Cheaper rental cars often lie just outside of major city centers (Oakland and Jersey City, we're looking at you).

➡ Booking online and well ahead of time for buses and trains will get you much lower prices than buying tickets on the spot.

Bargaining

Gentle haggling is common in flea markets; in all other instances you're expected to pay the stated price.

Tipping

Tipping is *not* optional; only withhold tips in cases of outrageously bad service.

➡ **Airport & hotel porters** $2 per bag, minimum per cart $5

➡ **Bartenders** 15% to 20% per round, minimum per drink $1

➡ **Hotel maids** $2 to $4 per night, left under the card provided

➡ **Restaurant servers** 15% to 20%, unless a gratuity is already charged on the bill

➡ **Taxi drivers** 10% to 15%, rounded up to the next dollar

➡ **Valet parking attendants** At least $2 when handed back the keys

Etiquette

➡ **Greeting** Don't be overly physical when greeting someone. Some Americans will hug, urbanites may exchange cheek kisses, but most – especially men – shake hands.

➡ **Smoking** Don't assume you can smoke, even if you're outside. Most Americans have little tolerance for smokers, and smoking has even been banned from many parks, boardwalks and beaches.

➡ **Politeness** It's common practice to greet the staff when entering and leaving a shop ('hello' and 'have a nice day' will do). Also, Americans smile a lot (often a symbol of politeness, nothing more).

➡ **Punctuality** Do be on time. Many folks in the US consider it rude to be kept waiting.

Eating

Some restaurants (typically the most popular places) don't take reservations. For those that do, it's wise to book ahead, especially on weekends. If you don't have reservations (or can't make them), plan to dine early (5pm to 6pm) or late (9pm) to avoid lengthy waits.

➡ **Restaurants** American restaurants cover all prices and foods: diners, burger joints, crab and lobster shacks, Michelin-starred dining rooms, and every cuisine you can imagine. More casual places are usually open from about 11am onward; fancier restaurants are often only open from 5pm. Many restaurant kitchens close at 10pm.

➡ **Cafes and coffee shops** Open all day (and sometimes at night), cafes are good for a casual breakfast or lunch, or simply a cup of coffee.

➡ **Informal eateries** Look for food trucks, farmers markets and other casual options (some bars also serve great food). A few chains – like Waffle House or Huddle House – are open 24 hours.

What's New

Remembering the American Revolution

Check out Revolution-era weapons, letters, diaries and works of art at the $120-million Museum of the American Revolution (p169), which opened in Philadelphia in 2017, then head down to Yorktown, VA, to see how it stacks up against the (also) newly opened American Revolution Museum (p328).

Fine Wines in Surprising Places

The West Coast's longtime monopoly on award-winning wineries is fading, as regions as diverse as Texas Hill Country (p709) and Northern Virginia rise in prominence to become must-visit wine-tasting destinations.

Detroit's Comeback

Detroit has climbed out of bankruptcy and shed its dour reputation at an astounding pace with one urban renewal project after another, including a 50-block sports and entertainment development, the District Detroit, as well as a new QLine streetcar. (p584)

Elvis Presley's Memphis

This $45-million, 200,000-sq-ft entertainment complex opened in 2017 near the ostentatious Graceland mansion in Memphis. (p383)

Chicago's West Loop

This former meatpacking area near downtown is now a hub of innovation and creativity, home to top tech companies, James Beard Award–winning restaurants and flashy new hotels. (p542)

Memorial to Peace and Justice

A visually arresting memorial (www.eji.org/national-lynching-memorial) honoring the roughly 4000 African American lynching victims killed by white mobs between 1877 and 1950 is due to open in Montgomery, AL, in 2018.

Meow Wolf

This New Mexican art collective takes immersive art to staggering new heights at the House of Eternal Return, a permanent installation (part jungle gym, part haunted house) that opened in 2016 within the confines of an abandoned bowling alley on the fringe of Santa Fe. (p896)

Bears Ears National Monument

Located in southeastern Utah, the country's newest – and most controversial – national monument protects land sacred to the Pueblo Indians, the Navajo and the Ute, as well as numerous Ancestral Puebloan archaeological sites. (p879)

Lucky Dragon

With an eye toward the Asian market, the Las Vegas Strip welcomed its first new hotel-casino since 2010. The facility is drenched in red and serves authentic Chinese cuisine (not Chinese American!). (p824)

Queens on the Rise

New York's most ethnically diverse borough is taking the stage. The draw: creative microbreweries, new boutique hotels, a reinvented seaside at Rockaway, art galleries and a truly global food culture. (p105)

For more recommendations and reviews, see lonelyplanet.com/usa

If You Like...

Beaches

Coastlines on two oceans and the Gulf of Mexico make tough choices for beach lovers, from the rugged and wild shores of Maine to the rolling-surf beauties of Southern California.

Point Reyes National Seashore The water is cold but the scenery is magical along this beautiful stretch of untamed coastline in Northern California. (p1004)

South Beach This world-famous strand is less about wave frolicking than taking in the parade of passing people along Miami's favorite playground. (p472)

Big Beach With turquoise waters lapping its long sweep of golden sand, this Maui beauty is one of Hawaii's finest. (p1124)

Cape Cod National Seashore Massive sand dunes, picturesque lighthouses and cool forests invite endless exploration on the Massachusetts cape. (p214)

Outer Banks Runs for 100 miles along North Carolina, with breezy beaches, lighthouses and wild horses at Corolla. (p350)

Santa Monica Hit the shore, then go celeb-spotting at edgy art galleries and high-end bistros. (p930)

Theme Parks

America's theme parks come in many varieties – from old-fashioned cotton candy and roller-coaster fun to multiday immersions in pure Peter Pan–style make-believe.

Disneyland Trends come and go, but the true classics never die. Now entering its seventh decade, Disney's fairy-tale world still exerts a unique enchantment. (p943)

Dollywood A paean to the much-loved country singer Dolly Parton, with Appalachian-themed rides and attractions in the hills of Tennessee. (p398)

Cedar Point Amusement Park This Ohio favorite is home to several of the globe's tallest and fastest roller coasters, including the Top Thrill Dragster. (p574)

Universal Orlando Resort Famed home of Universal Studios and the Wizarding World of Harry Potter. (p523)

Santa Cruz Beach Boardwalk Retro thrills await on the 1920s-Giant Dipper roller coaster at the Pacific Coast's oldest beachfront amusement park. (p975)

Wine

Visiting wineries isn't just about tasting first-rate drops, but drinking in the pretty countryside and sampling from the enticing farm stands and delectable bistros that often sprout alongside vineyards.

Napa Valley Home to more than 200 vineyards, Napa is synonymous with world-class wine-making. You'll find superb varietals, gourmet bites and beautiful scenery. (p1006)

Willamette Valley Outside of Portland, OR, this fertile region produces some of the tastiest Pinot Noir on the planet. (p1073)

Finger Lakes Upstate New York is a prime growing region. After a few quaffs, you can walk it off at nearby state parks. (p152)

Santa Ynez Valley Backed by picturesque oak-clad hills, these sun-drenched vine-yards north of Santa Barbara invite laid-back exploration. (p968)

Virginia Wine Country There's much history in this up-and-coming wine district. You can even sample the wines grown on Thomas Jefferson's old estate. (p323)

Verde Valley If you think Arizona is all desert, guess again. Take a winery tour in this lush setting near Sedona. (p851)

Great Food

The classic American dining experience: making a mess at a Maine lobster

SARAH FIELDS PHOTOGRAPHY/SHUTTERSTOCK ©

Na Pali Coast, Kaua'i (p1126), Hawaii

shack; plowing through BBQ in Texas Hill Country; and feasting at world-famous restaurants in New York, Los Angeles and beyond.

New York City Whatever you crave, the world's great restaurant capital has you covered. (p113)

New England Lobsters, clambakes, oysters and fresh fish galore – the Northeast is seafood paradise; authentic cannoli from Boston's Italian bakeries sweetens the deal. (p184)

Chicago The city that earns rave reviews for its Greek, Vietnamese, Mexican and molecular gastronomy, famous deep-dish pizzas, and much more. (p548)

San Francisco Real-deal taquerias, a dizzying variety of Asian cuisines, magnificent farmers markets and acclaimed chefs

all contribute to California's culinary mystique. (p994)

Lockhart Texas smokes them all – at least when it comes to barbecue. Carnivores shouldn't miss the legendary capital of mouth-watering brisket. (p708)

Portland Boasts a cutting-edge food scene; its food trucks serve imaginative dishes from every corner of the globe. (p2560)

New Orleans French, Spanish, Filipinos, Haitians and other nationalities have contributed to the gastro-amalgamation, making Nola one of America's most food-centric cities. (p455)

Hiking

The stage is set: soaring mountains, mist-shrouded rainforests, red-rock canyons and craggy cliff-tops overlooking wild, wind-

swept seas. These are just a few places where you can hike the great American wilderness.

Appalachian Trail Even if you choose not to walk all 2178 miles, the AT is well worth visiting. Fourteen states provide access. (p342)

Denali National Park Navigate by map and compass in the one national park where rangers ask that you stay *off* the trail. (p1106)

North Cascades Glaciers, jagged peaks and alpine lakes are all part of the scenery. (p1057)

Kalalau Trail Kaua'i's classic coastal trail threads between pristine beaches and mesmerizingly steep fluted cliffs. (p49)

Rocky Mountain National Park This Colorado stunner has snowcapped peaks, wildflower-filled valleys and picturesque mountain lakes. (p766)

Presidential Range In the stunning White Mountains of New Hampshire, you'll find challenging trails, lofty peaks, forests and an excellent hut-to-hut system. (p253)

Big Bend National Park Dry mountainous scenery amid some 200 miles of trails in a massive Texas park. (p740)

Offbeat America

When you tire of traipsing through museums and ticking off well-known sights, unbuckle your safety belt and throw yourself into the strange world of American kitsch and nonesuch.

Carhenge A cheeky homage to Stonehenge, made of old cars assembled in a Nebraska field. (p678)

NashTrash Tours Nashville's tall-haired 'Jugg Sisters' take visitors on a deliciously tacky journey through Nashville's spicier side. (p391)

American Visionary Art Museum See outsider art (including pieces created by the clinically insane) at this Baltimore gem. (p300)

Loneliest Road Take the empty Highway 50 through Nevada, and don't forget to stop at the Shoe Tree. (p838)

Mini Time Machine Museum of Miniatures This whimsical museum in Tucson is entirely devoted to tiny things. (p868)

Marfa Mystery Lights Sit at dusk in west Texas looking for the ghostly lights that many visitors see playing on the horizon. (p744)

Architecture

Whether you're a devotee of Frank Lloyd Wright or simply enjoy gazing at beauti-

fully designed buildings, the US has a treasure chest of architectural wonders.

Chicago Birthplace of the skyscraper, Chicago has magnificent works by many of the great 20th-century architects. (p532)

New York City Much photographed classics include the art-deco Chrysler Building, the spiraling Guggenheim and the majestic Brooklyn Bridge. (p75)

Miami Miami's art-deco district is a Technicolor dream come to life. (p469)

San Francisco See elegant Victorians and cutting-edge 21st-century masterpieces in perhaps America's most European city. (p977)

Savannah This Southern belle never fails to turn heads with her striking antebellum architecture. (p420)

New Orleans A gorgeous French-colonial center, plus grand antebellum mansions reached via a historic streetcar. (p446)

Native American Culture

The continent's first peoples have a connection to the land and its animals that stretches back many millennia and is most evident in sites in the Southwest.

National Museum of the American Indian Appropriately, the capital holds America's finest museum dedicated to Native American peoples. (p278)

Mesa Verde Carved into the mountains of Southern Colorado, this fascinating site was mysteriously abandoned by Ancestral Puebloans. (p784)

Pine Ridge Indian Reservation Visit the tragic site where Lakotas were massacred by US

Cavalry, then stop by nearby Red Cloud, to learn more about the Lakota. (p670)

Navajo Nation Take in the stunning scenery and learn more about this proud people in Arizona. (p862)

Zuni Pueblo Purchase beautifully wrought silver jewelry and stay overnight at a tribally licensed inn. (p896)

Historical Sights

The East Coast is where you'll find the original 13 colonies. For alternative perspectives on America's past, head south and west, where Spanish explorers and indigenous peoples left their mark.

Philadelphia The nation's first capital is where the idea of America as an independent nation first coalesced. Excellent museums tell the story. (p169)

Boston Visit Paul Revere's former home, an 18th-century graveyard and the decks of the 1797 USS *Constitution*. (p185)

Williamsburg Step back into the 1700s in the preserved town of Williamsburg, the largest living-history museum on the planet. (p326)

Mission Santa Barbara The 'Queen of the Missions' witnessed the meeting of California's indigenous Chumash culture and 19th-century Spanish friars. (p965)

Washington, DC Visit the sites where Lincoln was assassinated, Martin Luther King Jr gave his most famous speech and Nixon's presidency was undone. (p267)

Harpers Ferry A fascinating open-air museum of 19th-century village life beautifully framed by mountains and rivers. (p342)

Beer & Microbreweries

Microbreweries have exploded in popularity, and you'll never be far from a finely crafted pint. Colorado, Vermont, Washington and Oregon are particularly famed for their breweries.

Mountain Sun Pub & Brewery Boulder's favorite microbrewery serves an array of excellent drafts, plus good food and regular music jams. (p765)

Portland Nirvana for beer lovers, Portland has more than 70 microbreweries within city limits. (p1071)

Mammoth Brewing Company Head to this laid-back California mountain town for a dazzling tasting. (p1029)

Asheville Home to more than 20 microbreweries and brewpubs, Asheville is leading North Carolina's beer renaissance. (p365)

Geologic Wonders

With red-rock deserts, petrified forests, blasting geysers and one massive hole in the ground, you might feel like you've stepped onto another planet.

Grand Canyon Needing little introduction, this mile-deep, 10-mile-wide hole was carved over six million years. Take your time when you go. (p854)

Yellowstone National Park Massive geysers, rainbow-colored thermal pools and the supervolcano it all sits on: this national park certainly puts on a show. (p794)

Hawai'i Volcanoes National Park Glimpse lava deserts, smoldering craters and the ongoing process of volcanism – going strong for 70 million years. (p1122)

Badlands National Park Vividly colored rock pinnacles erupt unexpectedly from the vast expanses of western South Dakota. (p669)

Carlsbad Caverns National Park Take a 2-mile walk along a subterranean passage to arrive in the Big Room – a veritable underground cathedral. (p914)

Southern Utah National Parks See 3000ft-tall slot canyons, eroding pinnacles and spires in the seven national parks and monuments of Utah's red-rock country. (p882)

Live Music

Americans know where to catch a good live band – whether they're after Memphis blues, Appalachian bluegrass, New Orleans jazz, fist-pumping rock, sultry salsa or country crooning.

Austin Home to more than 200 venues and the country's biggest music fest, Austin proudly wears the music crown. (p706)

New Orleans The Big Easy has a soundtrack as intoxicating as the city itself – from room-filling big-band jazz to indie rock. (p457)

Nashville This river city is a showcase for country, bluegrass, blues, folk and plenty of atmospheric honky-tonks. (p394)

Los Angeles LA is a magnet for aspiring stars and draws serious talent. Don't miss the legendary Sunset Strip for A-list artists. (p940)

Memphis Juke joints and dive bars host blazing live bands. (p387)

Kansas City This barbecue-loving Missouri city has a venerable live-music scene, especially when it comes to jazz. (p655)

Museums

From big-city palaces of culture to eccentric backroads curiosities, the USA's incomparable collection of museums celebrates everything from art to rock 'n' roll.

Metropolitan Museum of Art New York City's world-class art collection spans six continents and hundreds of centuries (really!). (p100)

Exploratorium Poised to celebrate its 50th anniversary in 2019, this San Francisco original invites visitors of all ages to discover science 'hands-on.' (p977)

National Museum of African American History and Culture DC's newest museum wins rave reviews for its multifaceted documentation of the African American experience. (p271)

Field Museum of Natural History Stroll through an Egyptian burial chamber and meet Sue the *Tyrannosaurus rex* at Chicago's superb natural-history museum. (p535)

Getty Villa Perched above the Pacific, this faux-Classical villa holds a treasure trove of Etruscan, Greek and Roman antiquities. (p929)

Children's Museum of Indianapolis Interactive exhibits abound at this remarkable five-story children's museum (the world's largest). (p562)

Rock and Roll Hall of Fame & Museum Elvis, Aretha, Chuck Berry, Bo Diddley, Buddy Holly and Marvin Gaye headline the musical pantheon enshrined at this Cleveland classic. (p571)

Month by Month

TOP EVENTS

Mardi Gras, February or March

South by Southwest, March

National Cherry Blossom Festival, March

Chicago Blues Festival, June

Independence Day, July

January

The New Year starts off with a shiver, as snowfall blankets large swaths of the country. Ski resorts kick into high gear, while sun lovers seek refuge in warmer climes (especially Florida).

🎆 Mummers Parade

Philadelphia's biggest event is this brilliant parade (www.phillymummers. com), where local clubs spend months creating costumes and mobile scenery in order to win top honors on New Year's Day. String bands and clowns add to the general good cheer at this long-running fest.

🎆 Chinese New Year

In late January or early February, you'll find colorful celebrations and feasting anywhere there's a Chinatown. NYC throws a festive parade, though San Francisco's is the best, with floats, firecrackers, bands and plenty of merriment.

☆ Sundance Film Festival

The legendary Sundance Film Festival (www.sundance.org) brings Hollywood stars, indie directors and avid film-goers to Park City, UT, for a 10-day indie extravaganza in late January. Plan well in advance, as passes sell out fast.

February

Aside from mountain getaways, many Americans dread February with its long dark nights and frozen days. For foreign visitors, this can be the cheapest time to travel, with discounted rates for flights and hotels.

🎆 Mardi Gras

Held in late February or early March, on the day before Ash Wednesday, Mardi Gras (Fat Tuesday) is the finale of Carnival. New Orleans' celebrations (www.mardigrasneworleans.com) are legendary as colorful parades, masquerade balls, feasting and plenty of hedonism rule the day.

March

The first blossoms of spring arrive (at least in the south – the north still shivers in the chill). In the mountains, it's still high season for skiing. Meanwhile, drunken spring-breakers descend on Florida.

🎆 St Patricks Day

On the 17th, the patron saint of Ireland is honored with brass bands and ever-flowing pints of Guinness; huge parades occur in New York, Boston and Chicago (which goes all-out by dyeing the Chicago River green).

🎆 National Cherry Blossom Festival

The brilliant blooms of Japanese cherry blossoms around DC's Tidal Basin are celebrated with concerts, parades, *taiko* drumming, kite-flying and 90 other events during the four-week fest (www.nationalcherryblossomfestival.org). More than one million go each year, so don't forget to book ahead.

☆ South by Southwest

Each year Austin, TX, becomes ground zero for one of the biggest music festivals (p703) in North America. More than 2000 performers play at nearly 100 venues. SXSW is also a major film festival and interactive fest – a platform for ground-breaking ideas.

April

The weather is warming up, though up north April can still be unpredictable, bringing chilly weather mixed with a few teasingly warm days. Down south, it's a fine time to travel.

🎎 Fiesta San Antonio

Mid-April is the liveliest time to visit this pretty river town in Texas, as you'll find 10 days of fiesta (www.fiesta-sa.org) with carnivals, parades, dancing and lots of great eating options.

☆ Jazz Fest

Beginning the last weekend in April, New Orleans hosts the country's best jazz jam (www.nojazzfest.com), with top-notch acts (local resident Harry Connick Jr sometimes plays) and plenty of good cheer. In addition to world-class jazz, there's also great food and crafts.

☆ Juke Joint Festival

In mid-April, Clarksdale, MS, stages a memorable blues fest (www.jukejointfestival.com). The feel is very authentic, as you roam among a dozen stages, with plenty of great food and

the odd amusement (pig racing!) to boot.

🎎 Patriots' Day

Massachusetts' big day out falls on the third Monday in April and features Revolutionary War reenactments and parades in Lexington and Concord, plus the running of the Boston Marathon and a much-watched Red Sox baseball game at home.

🎎 Gathering of Nations

For an immersion in indigenous culture, head to Albuquerque in late April for the Gathering of Nations (www.gatheringofnations.com), the largest Native American powwow in the world. You'll find traditional dance, music, food, crafts and the crowning of Miss Indian World.

May

May is true spring and one of the loveliest times to travel, with blooming wildflowers and generally mild sunny weather. Summer crowds and high prices have yet to arrive.

☆ Beale Street Music Festival

Blues lovers descend on Memphis for this venerable music fest (p384) held over three days in early May.

🎎 Cinco de Mayo

Celebrate Mexico's victory over the French with salsa music and pitchers of margaritas across the country. LA, San Francisco and Denver throw some of the biggest bashes.

June

Summer is here. Americans spend more time at outdoor cafes and restaurants, and head to the shore or to national parks. School is out; vacationers fill the highways and resorts, bringing higher prices.

☆ Bonnaroo Music & Arts Festival

In the heartland of Tennessee, this sprawling music fest (www.bonnaroo.com) showcases big-name rock, soul, country and more over four days in mid-June.

🎎 Gay Pride

In some cities, gay-pride celebrations last a week, but in San Francisco, it's a month-long party (www.sfpride.org), where the last weekend in June sees giant parades. You'll find other great pride events at major cities across the country.

☆ Chicago Blues Festival

It's the globe's biggest free blues fest (www.chicagobluesfestival.us), with three days of the music that made Chicago famous. More than 500,000 people unfurl blankets by the multiple stages that take over Grant Park in early June.

🎎 Mermaid Parade

In Brooklyn, NYC, Coney Island (www.coneyisland.com) celebrates summer's steamy arrival with a kitsch-loving parade, complete with skimpily attired mermaids and horn-blowing mermen.

☆ CMA Music Festival

Nashville's legendary country-music fest (www.cmaworld.com) has more than 400 artists performing at stages on Riverfront Park and LP Field.

☆ Telluride Bluegrass Festival

The banjo gets its due at this festive, boot-stomping music jam (www.planetbluegrass.com) in Colorado mountain country. You'll find nonstop performances, excellent regional food stalls and great locally crafted microbrews. It's good all-comers entertainment and many folks even camp.

☆ Tanglewood Music Festival

Open-air concerts run all summer long (from late June to early September) in an enchanting setting in western Massachusetts (www.bso.org).

July

With summer in full swing, Americans break out the backyard barbecues or head for the beach. The prices are high and the crowds can be fierce, but it's one of the liveliest times to visit.

☆ Independence Day

On July 4, the nation celebrates its birthday with a bang, as nearly every town and city stages a massive fireworks show. Washington, DC, New York, Nashville, Philadelphia and Boston are all great spots.

☆ Oregon Brewers Festival

The beer-loving city of Portland pulls out the stops and pours a heady array of handcrafted perfection (www.oregonbrewfest.com). With dozens of beers from around the country – and even a few international brews – there are plenty of choices. It's nicely set along the banks of the Willamette River.

☆ Pageant of the Masters

This eight-week arts fest (www.foapom.com) brings a touch of the surreal to Laguna Beach, CA. On stage, meticulously costumed actors create living pictures – imitations of famous works of art – accompanied by narration and an orchestra.

☆ Newport Folk Festival

Newport, RI, a summer haunt of the well-heeled, hosts a world-class music fest (www.newportfolk.org) in late July. Top folk artists take to the stage at this fun, all-welcoming event.

August

Expect blasting heat in August, with temperatures and humidity less bearable the further south you go. You'll find people-packed beaches, high prices and empty cities on weekends, when residents escape to the nearest waterfront.

☆ Lollapalooza

This mondo rock fest (www.lollapalooza.com) sees more than 100 bands across eight stages in Chicago's Grant Park on the first Thursday-to-Sunday in August.

☆ Iowa State Fair

If you've never been to a state fair, now's your chance. This 11-day event (www.iowastatefair.org) is where you'll find country crooning, wondrous carvings (in butter), livestock shows, sprawling food stalls and a down-home good time in America's heartland.

September

With the end of summer, cooler days arrive, making for pleasant outings nationwide. The kids are back in school, and concert halls, gallery spaces and performing-arts venues kick off a new season.

☆ Santa Fe Fiesta

Santa Fe hosts the nation's longest-running festival (www.santafefiesta.org), a spirited two-week-long event with parades, concerts and the burning of Old Man Gloom.

☆ Burning Man Festival

Over one week, some 50,000 revelers, artists and assorted free spirits descend on Nevada's Black Rock Desert to create a temporary metropolis of art installations, theme camps and environmental curiosities (www.burningman.com). It culminates in the burning of a giant stick figure.

October

Temperatures are falling, as autumn brings fiery colors to northern climes. It's high season where the leaves are most brilliant

(New England); elsewhere expect lower prices and fewer crowds.

☆ New York Film Festival

Just one of many big film fests in NYC (Tribeca Film Fest in late April is another goodie); this one features world premieres from across the globe (www. filmlinc.com).

🎊 Fantasy Fest

Key West's answer to Mardi Gras brings more than 100,000 revelers to the subtropical enclave in the week leading up to Halloween. Expect parades, colorful floats, costume parties, the selecting of a conch king and queen, and plenty of alcohol-fueled merriment (www. fantasyfest.net).

🎊 Halloween

In NYC, you can don a costume and join the Halloween parade up Sixth Ave. West Hollywood in Los Angeles and San Francisco's Castro district are great places to see outrageous outfits. Salem, MA,

also hosts spirited events throughout October.

November

No matter where you go, this is generally low season, with cold winds discouraging visitors despite lower prices (although airfares skyrocket around Thanksgiving). There's much happening culturally in the USA's big cities.

🎊 Thanksgiving

On the fourth Thursday of November, Americans gather with family and friends over daylong feasts – roast turkey, sweet potatoes, cranberry sauce, wine, pumpkin pie and loads of other dishes. NYC hosts a huge parade, and there's pro football on TV.

December

Winter arrives as ski season kicks off in the Rockies (out east

conditions aren't usually ideal until January). Aside from winter sports, December means heading inside and curling up by the fire.

🎊 Art Basel

This massive arts fest (www.artbaselmiamibeach. com) offers four days of cutting-edge art, film, architecture and design. More than 200 major galleries from across the globe come to the event, with works by some 4000 artists; plus much hobnobbing with a glitterati crowd in Miami Beach.

🎊 New Year's Eve

Americans are of two minds when it comes to ringing in the New Year. Some join festive crowds to celebrate, others plot a getaway to escape the mayhem. Whichever you choose, ensure you plan well in advance. Expect high prices (especially in NYC).

Itineraries

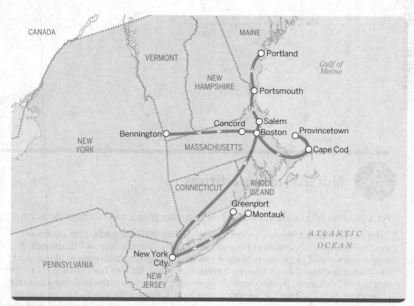

2 WEEKS **East Coasting**

Big cities, historic towns and serene coastlines offer a highlights reel of America's northeastern corner.

The great dynamo of art, fashion and culture, **New York City** is America at her most urbane. Spend four days exploring the metropolis, visiting people-watching 'hoods such as the West and East Villages, Soho and the Upper West Side, with a museum-hop down the Upper East Side. Have a ramble in Central Park, stroll the High Line and take detours to Brooklyn and Queens. After big-city culture, catch your breath at the pretty beaches of **Greenport** and **Montauk** on Long Island. Back in NYC, catch the train to **Boston** for two days of visiting historic sights, dining in the North End and pub-hopping in Cambridge. Strike out for **Cape Cod**, with its idyllic dunes and pretty shores. Leave time for **Provincetown**, the Cape's liveliest settlement. Back in Boston, rent a car and take a three-day jaunt to explore New England's back roads, staying at heritage B&Bs along the way. Highlights include **Salem** and **Concord** in Massachusetts; **Bennington**, VT; and **Portsmouth**, NH. If time allows, head up to Maine for lobster feasts amid beautifully rugged coastline: **Portland** is a great place to start.

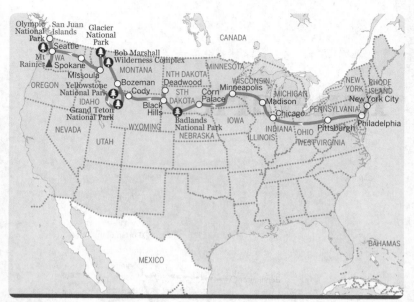

 Northern Expedition

For a different take on the transcontinental journey, plan a route through the north.

From **New York City**, head southwest to historic **Philadelphia**, then continue west to the idyllic backroads of Pennsylvania Dutch Country. Next is **Pittsburgh**, a surprising town of picturesque bridges and green spaces, cutting-edge museums and lively neighborhoods. Enter Ohio by interstate, but quickly step back in time on a drive through old-fashioned Amish Country. Big-hearted **Chicago** is the Midwest's greatest metropolis. Stroll or bike the lakefront, marvel at famous artworks and grand architecture, and check out the celebrated restaurant scene. Head north to **Madison**, a youthful green-loving university town.

Detour north to the land of 10,000 lakes (aka Minnesota) for a stop in friendly, arty **Minneapolis**, followed by a visit to its quieter historic twin, St Paul, across the river. Return to I-90 and activate cruise control, admiring the corn (and the **Corn Palace**) and the flat, flat South Dakota plains. Hit the brakes for the **Badlands National Park** and plunge into the Wild West. In the **Black Hills**, contemplate the nation's complex history at the massive monuments of Mt Rushmore and Crazy Horse, then make a northern detour to watch mythic gunfights in **Deadwood**.

Halfway across Wyoming, cruise into **Cody** to catch a summer rodeo, then take in the wonders of **Yellowstone National Park**. Next, detour south for hikes past jewel-like lakes and soaring peaks in **Grand Teton National Park**. Drive back up north, and continue west through rural Montana. The outdoorsy towns of **Bozeman** and **Missoula** make fun stops between exploring the alpine beauty of **Glacier National Park**.

After a few days out in the wild, surprising **Spokane** is a great place to recharge, with a pleasant riverfront and historic district sprinkled with enticing eating and drinking spots. For more cosmopolitan flavor, keep heading west to **Seattle**, a forward-thinking, eco-minded city with cafe culture, abundant nightlife and speedy island escapes on Puget Sound. If you still have time, the region has some great places to explore, including **Mt Rainier**, **Olympic National Park** and the **San Juan Islands**.

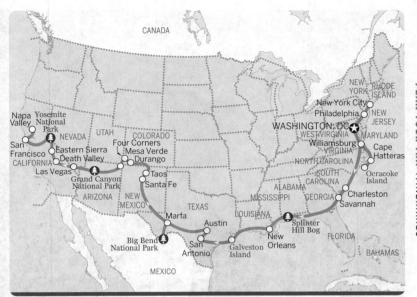

 ## Coast to Coast

The 'Great American Road Trip': it's been mythologized hundreds of ways. Now live the dream, driving from shore to shining shore.

Start in **New York City** (but hire a car in cheaper New Jersey) and hit the road. First stop: **Philadelphia**, a historic city with a burgeoning food, art and music scene. Continue on to **Washington, DC**. The nation's capital has a dizzying array of sights, plus great dining and revelry after the museums close. Continue south through Virginia, taking a detour to visit the fantastic historic settlement of colonial **Williamsburg**. Stick to the coast as you drive south, visiting **Cape Hatteras** with its pristine dunes, marshes and woodlands. Catch the ferry to remote **Ocracoke Island,** where the wild ponies run. Further south, take in the antebellum allure of **Charleston** and **Savannah**. Afterwards stop in Splinter Hill Bog in Alabama, a fantastic site for exploring the biodiversity of the coast, then it's on to jazz-loving **New Orleans**, with a soundtrack of smokin' hot funk brass bands.

The big open skies of Texas are next. Hit the beach at **Galveston** outside Houston. Follow the Mission Trail and stroll the tree-lined riverwalk in thriving **San Antonio**, then revel in the great music and drinking scene in **Austin**. Afterwards, eat your way through scenic Hill Country, stop for art and star-filled nights at **Marfa**, then hike through jaw-dropping **Big Bend National Park**. Head north to New Mexico, following the Turquoise Trail up to artsy **Santa Fe** and far-out **Taos**. Roll up through Colorado and into mountain-beauty **Durango**, continuing to the Amerindian cliff-top marvel of **Mesa Verde**, and the Four Corners four-state intersection. The awe-inspiring **Grand Canyon** is next. Stay in the area to maximize time near this great wonder. Try your luck amid the bright lights of **Las Vegas**, then take in the stunning desert landscapes at **Death Valley** on your ride into California. From there, head up into the majestic forests of the **Eastern Sierra**, followed by hiking and wildlife-watching in **Yosemite**. The last stop is in hilly **San Francisco**, an enchanting city spread between ocean and bay with beautiful vistas and seemingly endless cultural attractions. If there's time, tack on a grand finale, enjoying the vineyards and gourmet produce of the **Napa Valley**.

Above: Eastern Sierra
(p1027), California
Left: Amish Country
(p576), Ohio

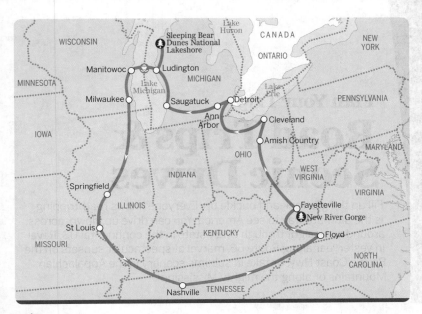

Off the Beaten Path

2 WEEKS

Underdog cities, lakeside islands and boot-scootin' mountain music are just a few of the things you'll encounter on this off-the-beaten-path ramble around the central US.

Start off in **Detroit**, which has made a remarkable comeback in the past decade. Stroll the riverwalk, explore recent history (Motown, automobiles) and take in the Motor City's underground nightlife scene. Next head to nearby **Ann Arbor** with its easy-going college-town charm (coffee shops, farmers markets, pubby bars), before continuing west to Lake Michigan. Drive up through waterfront towns – stopping perhaps in **Saugatuck** for gallery-hopping – and continue all the way to **Sleeping Bear Dunes National Lakeshore**, with its dramatic sandscapes, scenic drives and wilderness-covered islands.

From there backtrack to **Ludington** and take the ferry across Lake Michigan to **Manitowoc** in Wisconsin. Continue south to **Milwaukee**, one of the best little cities in America, with great art and architecture, abundant microbreweries, summer festivals and memorable riverfront cycling. From there, it's a 4½-hour drive south to **Springfield**, where you can delve into the fascinating past of hometown hero (and America's favorite president) Abraham Lincoln. Two hours' drive south is **St Louis**, with walkable neighborhoods and green spaces (including a park that dwarfs Central Park), plus blues, barbecue and bumping music joints. Speaking of music, up next is **Nashville**, a mecca for lovers of country and blues. Head toward Appalachia – start in **Floyd**, VA – for an authentic music scene (a frenzy of fiddles, banjos and boot-stompin') amid the rolling hills of southeastern Virginia. Continue north to **Fayetteville** in West Virginia, gateway to the breathtaking **New River Gorge**, which has superb hiking, climbing, mountain biking and whitewater rafting.

A five-hour drive takes you to the epicenter of America's largest Amish community in **Amish Country** near Kidron in Ohio. Step back in time at antique shops, old-fashioned farms and bakeries, and quaint 19th-century inns. Afterward, fast-forward into **Cleveland**, a city on the cusp of reinvention with up-and-coming gastropubs, newly expanded art museums, green markets and the massive Rock and Roll Hall of Fame. It's less than three hours back to Detroit.

Plan Your Trip

Road Trips & Scenic Drives

Fill up the gas tank and buckle up. Everyone knows road-tripping is the ultimate way to see America. You can drive up, down, across, around or straight through every state in the continental US. Revel in yesteryear along Route 66, marvel at spectacular sunsets on the Pacific Coast Hwy, or take in sublime scenery in the Appalachian Mountains or along the mighty Mississippi.

Road-Tripping Tips

Best Experiences

Dazzling coastal scenery on the Pacific Coast Hwy; the charming, rarely visited destinations on Route 66; dramatic sunsets over the Appalachian Mountains on the Blue Ridge Pkwy; listening to Memphis blues at a jumping music joint off the Great River Rd.

Key Starting Points

Chicago or Los Angeles for Route 66; Seattle or San Diego for the Pacific Coast Hwy; Waynesboro, VA, or Cherokee, NC, for Blue Ridge Pkwy; Itasca State Park, MN, or Venice, LA, for Great River Rd.

Major Sights

Grand Canyon on Route 66; Point Reyes National Seashore on the Pacific Coast Hwy; Peaks of Otter on Blue Ridge Pkwy; Shawnee National Forest on Great River Rd.

Route 66

For a classic American road trip, nothing beats good ol' Route 66. Nicknamed the nation's 'Mother Road' by novelist John Steinbeck, this string of small-town main streets and country byways first connected big-shouldered Chicago with the waving palm trees of Los Angeles in 1926.

Why Go?

Whether you seek to explore retro Americana or simply want to experience big horizons and captivating scenery far from the madding crowd, Route 66 will take you there. The winding journey passes some of the USA's greatest outdoor attractions – not just the Grand Canyon, but also the Mississippi River, Arizona's Painted Desert and Petrified Forest National Park, and, at road's end, the Pacific beaches of sun-kissed Southern California.

Other highlights along the way: old-fashioned museums stocked with strange and wondrous objects from the past, Norman Rockwell–ish soda fountains, classic mom-and-pop diners, working gas stations that seem to have fallen right out of an old James Dean film clip, and ghost towns (or soon-to-be ghost towns) hunkering on the edge of the desert.

ROADSIDE ODDITIES: ROUTE 66

Kitschy, time-warped and just plain weird roadside attractions? Route 66 has got 'em in spades. Here are a few beloved Mother Road landmarks to make your own scavenger hunt:

➡ A massive statue of legendary lumberjack Paul Bunyan clutching a hotdog in Illinois.

➡ The Black Madonna Shrine in Pacific, MO, and Red Oak II outside Carthage, MO.

➡ The 80ft-long Blue Whale in Catoosa, OK.

➡ Devil's Rope Museum, Cadillac Ranch and Slug Bug Ranch in Texas.

➡ Seligman's Snow Cap Drive-In, Holbrook's WigWam Motel and Meteor Crater in Arizona.

➡ Roy's Motel & Cafe in Amboy in the middle of California's Mojave Desert.

Culturally speaking, Route 66 can be an eye-opener. Discard your preconceptions of small-town American life and unearth the joys of what bicoastal types dismissively term 'flyover' states. Mingle with farmers in Illinois and country-and-western stars in Missouri. Hear the legends of 'cowboys and Indians' in Oklahoma. Visit Native American tribal nations and contemporary pueblos across the Southwest, all the while discovering the traditions of the USA's indigenous peoples. Then follow the trails of miners and desperadoes deep into the Old West.

When to Go

The best time to travel Route 66 is May to September, when the weather is warm and you can take advantage of open-air activities. Take care if you travel in the height of summer (July and August) as the heat can be unbearable – particularly in desert areas. Avoid traveling in the winter (December to March), when snow can lead to perilous driving conditions or outright road closures.

The Route

The journey starts in Chicago, just west of Michigan Ave, and runs for some 2400 miles across eight states before terminating in Los Angeles near the Santa Monica Pier. The road remains a never-ending work in progress, as old sections get resurrected or disappear owing to the rerouting of other major roads.

History of the Mother Road

Route 66 didn't really hit its stride until the Great Depression, when migrant farmers followed it as they fled the Dust Bowl across the Great Plains. Later, during the post-WWII baby boom, newfound prosperity encouraged many Americans to hit the road and 'get their kicks' on Route 66.

Almost as soon as it came of age, however, Route 66 began to lose steam. The shiny blacktop of an ambitious new interstate system started systematically paving over Route 66, bypassing its mom-and-pop diners, drugstore soda fountains and once-stylish motels. Railway towns were forgotten and way stations for travelers became dusty. Even entire towns began to disappear.

Preservation associations of Mother Road fans sprung to action to save remaining stretches of the historic highway soon after Route 66 was officially decommissioned in 1985. Today you can still get your kicks on Route 66, following gravel frontage roads and blue-line highways across the belly of America. It's like a time warp – connecting places where the 1950s seem to have stopped just yesterday.

Getting Lost

You need to be an amateur sleuth to follow Route 66 these days. Historical realignments of the route, dead-ends in farm fields and tumbleweed-filled desert patches, and rough, rutted driving conditions are par for the course. Remember that getting lost every now and then is inevitable. But never mind; the road offers a leap back through time to see what America once was, and still sometimes is. Nostalgia never tasted so sweet.

Resources

Before you hit the road, arm yourself with useful maps and key insider tips to help you make the most of your trip.

Here It Is: Route 66 Maps with directions (traveling both east-to-west and west-to-east) that you'll definitely want to take along for the ride; available from booksellers.

Historic Route 66 (www.historic66.com) Excellent website, with turn-by-turn directions for each state.

Route 66: EZ66 Guide for Travelers By Jerry McClanahan; earns high marks for its glossy, easy-to-follow maps.

Route 66: The Mother Road This book by Michael Wallis is a fascinating look at the history and lore of the great road with old photographs bringing it all to life.

Pacific Coast Highway

The classic West Coast journey through California, Oregon and Washington takes in cosmopolitan cities, surf towns and charming coastal enclaves ripe for exploration. For many travelers, the real appeal of the Pacific Coast Hwy is the magnificent scenery – wild and remote beaches, clifftop views overlooking crashing waves, rolling hills and lush forests (redwoods, eucalyptus trees) – that sometimes lies just beyond a city's outskirts.

Why Go?

The Pacific Coast Hwy is an epic adventure for water babies, surfers, kayakers, scuba divers and every other kind of outdoor enthusiast, including landlubbers. Or if you're a more laid-back road-tripper who just dreams of cruising alongside the ocean in a cherry-red convertible, drifting from sunrise to sunset, the insanely scenic PCH can deliver that, too.

The PCH is a road trip for lovers, nomadic ramblers, bohemians, beatniks and curiosity seekers keen to search out every nook and cranny of forgotten beachside hamlets and pastoral farm towns along the way.

When to Go

There's no very bad time of year to drive the PCH, although northern climes will be rainier and snowier during winter. Peak travel season is June through August, which isn't always the best time to see the road – as thick fog blankets many stretches of the coast during early summer (locals call it 'June Gloom'). The shoulder seasons before Memorial Day (ie April and May) and after Labor Day (September and October) can be ideal, with sunny days, crisply cool nights and fewer crowds.

The Route

Technically 'the PCH' is one of several coastal highways, including Hwy 101, stretching nearly 2000 miles from Tijuana,

---

BEFORE YOU HIT THE ROAD

A few things to remember to ensure your road trip is as happy-go-lucky as possible:

➡ Join an automobile club that provides members with 24-hour emergency roadside assistance and discounts on lodging and attractions; some international clubs have reciprocal agreements with US automobile associations, so check first and bring your member card from home.

➡ Check the spare tire, tool kit (eg jack, jumper cables, ice scraper, tire-pressure gauge) and emergency equipment (eg flashers) in your car; if you're renting a vehicle and these essential safety items are not provided, consider buying them.

➡ Bring good maps, especially if you're touring off-road or away from highways; don't rely on a GPS unit – they can malfunction, and in remote areas such as deep canyons or thick forests they may not even work.

➡ Always carry your driver's license and proof of insurance.

➡ If you're an international traveler, review the USA's road rules and common road hazards.

➡ Fill up the tank often, because gas stations can be few and far between on the USA's scenic byways.

Scenic Drives

1	Rte 66
2	Pacific Coast Hwy
3	Blue Ridge Pkwy
4	Great River Rd

5 Rte 28	**9** Alpine Loop Backcountry	**13** El Camino Real	**17** Historic Columbia River Hwy
6 Old Kings Hwy	**10** Great River Rd (IA)	**14** Sawtooth Scenic Byway	**18** Monument Valley
7 Natchez Trace Hwy	**11** Hwy 61	**15** Turquoise Trail	**19** VT 100
8 Beartooth Hwy	**12** Hwy 2	**16** US 50	**20** Kancamagus Hwy

Mexico, to British Columbia, Canada. The route connects the dots between some of the West Coast's most striking cities, starting from surf-style San Diego, through hedonistic Los Angeles and offbeat San Francisco in California, then moving north to equally alternative-minded and arty Seattle, WA.

When the urban streets start to make you feel claustrophobic, just head back out on the open road and hit the coast again, heading north or south. The direction doesn't really matter – the views and hidden places you find along the way make for rewarding exploring.

You could bypass metro areas and just stick to the places in between, like the almost-too-perfect beaches of California's Orange County ('the OC') and Santa Barbara (the 'American Riviera'); wacky Santa Cruz, a university town and surfers' paradise; redwood forests along the Big Sur coast and north of Mendocino; the sand dunes, seaside resorts and fishing villages of coastal Oregon; and finally, the wild lands of Washington's Olympic Peninsula, with its primeval rainforest, and bucolic San Juan Islands, served by coastal ferries.

Blue Ridge Parkway

Snaking for some 469 miles through the southern Appalachian Mountains, the Blue Ridge Pkwy is the land of great hiking and wildlife-watching, old-fashioned music and captivating mountainous scenery – all of which make for a memorable and easily accessible road trip.

Construction on the parkway began in 1935 under President Franklin D Roosevelt and it was one of the great New Deal projects that helped put people back to work. It was a huge effort that took over 52 years to complete, with the final section laid in 1987.

Why Go?

Watch the sunset over this wilderness of forest and mountain, tranquil streams and blissful silence – and you might feel like you've gone back a few centuries. Although it skirts dozens of towns and a few metropolitan areas, the Blue Ridge Pkwy feels far removed from modern-day America. Here, rustic log cabins with rocking chairs on the front porch still dot the rolling hillsides, while signs for folk-art shops and live bluegrass music joints entice travelers

OTHER GREAT ROAD TRIPS

ROUTE	STATE(S)	START/END	SIGHTS & ACTIVITIES	BEST TIME
Rte 28	NY	Stony Hollow/Arkville	Catskill Mountains, lakes, rivers, hiking, leaf-peeping, tubing	May-Sep
Old Kings Hwy	MA	Sagamore/Provincetown	historic districts, period homes, coastal scenery	Apr-Oct
Natchez Trace Hwy	AL/MS/TN	Nashville/Natchez	'Old South' history, archaeological sites, scenic waterways, biking, camping, hiking,	Mar-Nov
Beartooth Hwy	MT	Red Lodge/Yellowstone	wildflowers, mountains, alpine scenery, camping	Jun-Sep
Alpine Loop Backcountry Byway	CO	Ouray/Lake City	mountains, views, valleys, abandoned mines	Jun-Sep
Great River Rd	IA	Effigy Mounds National Monument/Keokuk	scenic views, riverside beauty, little-visited towns & villages	May-Sep
Hwy 61	MN	Duluth/Canadian border	state parks, waterfalls, quaint towns, hiking	May-Sep
Hwy 2	NE	I-80/Alliance	grass-covered sand dunes, open vistas	May-Sep
El Camino Real	TX	Lajitas/Presidio	vast desert & mountain landscapes, hot springs, hiking, horseback riding	Feb-Apr & Oct-Nov
Sawtooth Scenic Byway	ID	Ketchum/Stanley	jagged mountains, verdant forests, backpacking, hiking, wildlife-watching	May-Sep
Turquoise Trail	NM	Albuquerque/Santa Fe	mining towns, quirky museums & folk art, cycling, hiking	Mar-May & Sep-Nov
US 50	NV	Fernley/Baker	'Loneliest Road in America,' epic wilderness, biking, hiking, spelunking	May-Sep
Historic Columbia River Hwy	OR	Portland/The Dalles	scenery, waterfalls, wildflowers, cycling, hiking	Apr-Sep
Monument Valley	UT	Monument Valley	iconic buttes, movie-set locations, 4WD tours, horseback riding	year-round
VT 100	VT	Stamford/Newport	rolling pastures, green mountains, hiking, skiing	Jun-Sep
Kancamagus Hwy	NH	Conway/Lincoln	craggy mountains, streams & waterfalls, camping, hiking, swimming	May-Sep
Maui's Road to Hana	HI	Paia/Hana	jungle waterfalls, beaches, hiking, swimming, surfing	year-round

onto side roads. History seems to permeate the air of these rolling backwoods, once home to Cherokee tribal people and later to early colonial homesteads and Civil War battlefields.

There are great places to sleep and eat. Early 20th-century mountain and lakeside resorts still welcome families like old friends, while log-cabin diners dish up heaping piles of buckwheat pancakes with blackberry preserves and a side of country ham.

When you need to work off all that good Southern cooking, over 100 hiking trails can be accessed along the Blue Ridge Pkwy, from gentle nature walks and easily summited peaks to rough-and-ready tramps along the legendary Appalachian Trail. Or clamber on a horse and ride off into the refreshingly shady forests. Then go canoeing, kayaking or inner-tubing along rushing rivers, or dangle a fishing line over the side of a rowboat on petite lakes. And who says you even have to drive? The parkway makes an epic trip for long-distance cyclists, too.

When to Go

Keep in mind that the weather can vary greatly, depending on your elevation. While mountain peaks are snowed in during winter, the valleys can still be invitingly warm. Most visitor services along the parkway are only open from April through October. May is best for wildflowers, although most people come for leaf-peeping during autumn. Spring and autumn are good times for bird-watching, with nearly 160 species having been spotted in the skies over the parkway. Expect big crowds if you go during the summer or early autumn.

The Route

This rolling, scenic byway connects Virginia's Shenandoah National Park with Great Smoky Mountains National Park, straddling the North Carolina–Tennessee border. Towns include Boone and Asheville in North Carolina, and Galax and Roanoke in Virginia, with Charlottesville, VA, also within a short drive of the parkway. Cities within range of the parkway are Washington, DC (140 miles), and Richmond, VA (95 miles).

Detour: Skyline Drive

If you want to extend your journey through this scenic region, you can do so by hooking up with Skyline Dr. The northern terminus of the Blue Ridge Pkwy meets up with this 105-mile road (which continues northeast) around Rockfish Gap.

Travel along the road is slow (speed limit 35mph), but that forces you to take in the amazing scenery (wildflowers on the hillsides in spring, blazing colors in autumn and gorgeous blue skies in summer). Shenandoah National Park surrounds Skyline Dr and has an excellent range of hikes, some of which scramble up mountain peaks and offer panoramic views. There are campgrounds in the park as well

as nicely set lodges – all of which add up to worthwhile reasons not to rush through the area. Nearby attractions include the lively mountain town of Staunton (with its Shakespearean theater and farm-to-table restaurants), and an elaborate cave system at Luray Caverns.

One caveat: you will have to pay to travel along Skyline Dr ($25 per vehicle for a seven-day pass). This is not a toll, but rather an admission charge for visiting Shenandoah National Park. Expect heavy traffic on weekends.

Resources

Blue Ridge Parkway (www.blueridgeparkway. org) Maps, activities and places to stay along the way. You can also download the free *Blue Ridge Parkway Travel Planner*.

Hiking the Blue Ridge Parkway By Randy Johnson; has in-depth trail descriptions, topographic trail maps and other essential info for hikes both short and long (including overnight treks).

Recreation.gov (www.recreation.gov) You can reserve some campsites through this site.

Skyline Drive (www.visitskylinedrive.org) Lodging, hiking, wildlife and more: the complete overview of the national park surrounding this picturesque drive.

Great River Road

Established in the late 1930s, the Great River Rd is an epic journey from the Mississippi's headwaters in the northern lakes of Minnesota, floating downstream all the way to the river's mouth on the Gulf of Mexico near New Orleans. For a look at America across cultural divides – north-south, urban-rural, Baptist-bohemian – this is the road trip to make.

Why Go?

You'll be awed by the sweeping scenery as you meander alongside North America's second-longest river, from the rolling plains of Iowa down to the sunbaked cotton fields of the Mississippi Delta. Limestone cliffs, dense forests, flower-filled meadows and steamy swamps are all part of the backdrop – along with smokestacks, riverboat casinos and urban sprawl: this is the good, the bad and the ugly of life on

Point Reyes National Seashore (p1004), California

the Mississippi. The portrait isn't complete without mentioning the great music, lip-smacking food and down-home welcome at towns well off the beaten path on this waterfront itinerary.

Small towns provide a glimpse into American culture: there's Hibbing, MN, where folk-rocker Bob Dylan grew up; Brainerd, MN, as seen in the Coen Brothers' film *Fargo;* Spring Green, WI, where architect Frank Lloyd Wright cut his teeth; pastoral Hannibal, MO, boyhood home of Mark Twain; and Metropolis, IL, where you'll find Superman's quick-change phone booth.

The southern section of this route traces American musical history, from rock and roll in St Louis to Memphis blues and New Orleans jazz. And you won't go hungry either, with retro Midwestern diners, Southern barbecue joints and smokehouses, and Cajun taverns and dance halls in Louisiana.

When to Go

The best time to travel is from May to October, when the weather is warmest. Avoid going in the winter (or else stick to the Deep South), when you'll have to contend with snowstorms.

The Route

The Great River Rd is not really one road at all, but a collection of roads that follow the 2300-mile-long Mississippi River, and takes travelers through 10 different states. Major urban areas that provide easy access to the road include New Orleans, Memphis, St Louis and Minneapolis.

Resources

Mississippi River Travel (www.experiencemississippiriver.com) 'Ten states, one river' is the slogan for this official site, which is a great resource for history, outdoor recreation, live music and more.

Plan Your Trip
Outdoor Activities

Towering redwoods, red-rock canyons, snow-covered peaks and a dramatic coastline of unrivaled beauty: the USA has no shortage of spectacular settings for a bit of adventure. No matter your weakness – hiking, biking, kayaking, rafting, surfing, horseback riding, rock climbing – you'll find world-class places to commune with the great outdoors.

Hiking & Trekking

Fitness-focused Americans take great pride in their formidable network of trails – literally tens of thousands of miles – and there's no better way to experience the countryside up close and at your own pace.

The wilderness is amazingly accessible, making for easy exploration. National parks are ideal for short and long hikes, and if you're hankering for nights in the wilderness beneath star-filled skies, plan on securing a backcountry permit in advance, especially in places like the Grand Canyon – spaces are limited, particularly during summer.

Beyond the parks, you'll find troves of trails in every state. There's no limit to the places you can explore, from sun-blasted hoodoos and red spires in Arizona's Chiricahua Mountains to dripping trees and mossy nooks in Washington's Hoh River Rainforest; from dogwood-choked Wild Azalea Trail in Louisiana to the tropical paradise of Kaua'i's Na Pali Coast. Almost anywhere you go, great hiking and backpacking is within easy striking distance. All you need is a sturdy pair of shoes (sneakers or hiking boots) and a water bottle.

Best Outdoor Adventures

Best Wildlife-Watching

Bears in Glacier National Park, MT; elk, bison and gray wolves in Yellowstone National Park, WY; alligators, manatees and sea turtles in the Florida Everglades; whales and dolphins on Monterey Bay, CA.

Top Aquatic Activities

White-water rafting on the New River, WV; surfing perfect waves in Oahu, HI; diving and snorkeling off the Florida Keys; kayaking pristine Penobscot Bay, ME.

Best Multiday Adventures

Hiking the Appalachian Trail; mountain-biking the Kokopelli Trail, UT; climbing 13,770ft Grand Teton in Grand Teton National Park, WY; canoeing, portaging and camping in the vast Boundary Waters, MN.

Best Winter Activities

Downhill skiing in Vail, CO; snowboarding in Stowe, VT; cross-country skiing off Lake Placid, NY.

Skiing at Lake Tahoe (p1029), California

Hiking Resources

American Hiking Society (www.americanhiking. org) Links to 'volunteer vacations' building trails.

Backpacker (www.backpacker.com) Premier national magazine for backpackers, from novices to experts.

Rails-to-Trails Conservancy (www.railstotrails. org) Converts abandoned railroad corridors into hiking and biking trails; publishes free trail reviews at www.traillink.com.

Survive Outdoors (www.surviveoutdoors.com) Dispenses safety and first-aid tips, plus helpful photos of dangerous critters.

Wilderness Survival Gregory Davenport has written what is easily the best book on surviving nearly every contingency.

Cycling

Cycling's popularity increases by the day, with numerous cities (including New York) adding more cycle lanes and becoming more bike-friendly, and a growing number of greenways dotting the countryside. You'll find die-hards in every town, and outfitters offering guided trips for all levels and durations. For the best advice on rides and rentals, stop by a local bike shop or do an internet search of the area you plan to visit.

Many states offer social multiday rides, such as Ride the Rockies (www.ridethe rockies.com) in Colorado. For a modest fee, you can join the peloton on a scenic, well-supported route; your gear is ferried ahead to that night's camping spot. Other standout rides include Arizona's Mt Lemmon, a thigh-zinging 28-mile climb from the Sonoran Desert floor to the 9157ft summit, and Tennessee's Cherohala Skyway, 51 glorious miles of undulating road and Great Smoky Mountain views.

Top Cycling Towns

➡ **Portland, OR** One of America's most bike-friendly cities has a trove of great cycling routes.

➡ **San Francisco, CA** A pedal over the Golden Gate Bridge lands you in the stunningly beautiful, and stunningly hilly, Marin Headlands.

➡ **Madison, WI** More than 120 miles of cycle paths, taking in the city's pretty lakes, parks and university campus.

➡ **Boulder, CO** Outdoors-loving town with loads of great cycling paths, including the eight-mile Boulder Creek Trail.

➡ **Austin, TX** Indie-rock-loving town with nearly 200 miles of trails and great year-round weather.

➡ **Burlington, VT** Bike haven in the Northeast, with great rides, the best-known along Lake Champlain.

Surfing

Hawaii

Blessed is the state that started it all, where the best swells generally arrive between November and March.

➡ **Waikiki (South Shore of Oahu)** Hawaii's ancient kings rode waves on wooden boards well before 19th-century missionaries deemed the sport a godless activity. With warm water and gentle rolling waves, Waikiki is perfect for novices, offering long and sudsy rides.

➡ **Pipeline and Sunset Beach (North Shore of Oahu)** Home to the classic tubing wave, which form as deep-water swells break over reefs into shallows; these are expert-only spots but well worth an ogle.

West Coast

➡ **Huntington Beach, CA (aka Surf City, USA)** The quintessential surf capital, with perpetual sun and a 'perfect' break, particularly during winter when the winds are calm.

➡ **Black's Beach, San Diego, CA** This 2-mile sandy strip at the base of 300ft cliffs in La Jolla is known as one of the most powerful beach breaks in SoCal, thanks to an underwater canyon just offshore.

➡ **Oceanside Beach, Oceanside, CA** One of SoCal's prettiest beaches boasts one of the world's most consistent surf breaks come summer. It's a family-friendly spot.

➡ **Rincon, Santa Barbara, CA** Arguably one of the planet's top surfing spots; nearly every major surf champion on the globe has taken Rincon for a ride.

TOP HIKING TRAILS IN THE USA

Ask 10 people for their top trail recommendations and it's possible that no two answers will be alike. The country is varied and distances enormous, so there's little consensus. That said, you can't go wrong with the following all-star sampler.

Appalachian Trail (www.appalachiantrail.org) Completed in 1937, the country's longest footpath is more than 2100 miles, crossing two national parks, traversing eight national forests and hitting 14 states from Georgia to Maine.

Pacific Crest Trail (PCT; www.pcta.org) Follows the spines of the Cascades and Sierra Nevada, traipsing 2650 miles from Canada to Mexico, passing through six of North America's seven ecozones.

John Muir Trail in Yosemite National Park, CA (www.johnmuirtrail.org) Find 222 miles of scenic bliss, from Yosemite Valley up to Mt Whitney.

Enchanted Valley Trail, Olympic National Park, WA Magnificent mountain views, roaming wildlife and lush rainforests – all on a 13-mile out-and-back trail.

Great Northern Traverse, Glacier National Park, MT A 58-mile haul that cuts through the heart of grizzly country and crosses the Continental Divide; check out the Lonely Planet *Banff, Jasper & Glacier National Parks* guide for more information.

Kalalau Trail, Na Pali Coast, Kaua'i, HI Wild Hawaii at its finest – 11 miles of lush waterfalls, hidden beaches, verdant valleys and crashing surf.

Mount Katahdin, Baxter State Park, ME A 9.5-mile hike over the 5267ft summit, with panoramic views of the park's 46 peaks.

South Kaibab/North Kaibab Trail, Grand Canyon, AZ A multiday cross-canyon tramp down to the Colorado River and back up to the opposite rim.

South Rim, Big Bend National Park, TX A 13-mile loop through the ruddy 7000ft Chisos Mountains, with views into Mexico.

Tahoe Rim Trail, Lake Tahoe, CA (www.tahoerimtrail.org) This 165-mile all-purpose trail circumnavigates the lake from high above, affording glistening Sierra views.

⇒ **Steamer Lane and Pleasure Point, Santa Cruz, CA** There are 11 world-class breaks, including the point breaks over rock bottoms at these two sweet spots.

⇒ **Swami's, Encinitas, CA** Located below Seacliff Roadside Park, this popular surfing beach has multiple breaks guaranteeing you some fantastic waves.

East Coast

The Atlantic seaboard states harbor some terrific and unexpected surfing spots – especially if you're after more moderate swells. You'll find the warmest waters off Florida's Gulf Coast.

⇒ **Cocoa Beach, Melbourne Beach, FL** Small crowds and mellow waves make it a paradise for beginners and longboarders. Just south is the Inlet, known for consistent surf and crowds to match.

⇒ **Reef Road, Palm Beach, FL** This stellar spot features exposed beach and reef breaks with consistent surf, especially at low tide; winter is best.

⇒ **Cape Hatteras Lighthouse, NC** This very popular area has several quality spots and infinitely rideable breaks that gracefully handle swells of all sizes and winds from any direction.

⇒ **Long Island, Montauk, NY** More than a dozen surfing areas dot the length of Long Island, from Montauk's oft-packed Ditch Plains to Nassau County's Long Beach, with its 3-mile stretch of curling waves.

⇒ **Casino Pier, Seaside Heights, NJ** Largely restored after Hurricane Sandy in 2012, this area is one of the best pier breaks in New Jersey. It's packed with locals who are glad to have it back.

⇒ **Point Judith, Narragansett, RI** Rhode Island has premier surfing, with 40 miles of coastline and more than 30 surf spots, including this rocky point break offering long rollers as well as hollow barrels. Not for beginners.

⇒ **Coast Guard Beach, Eastham, MA** Part of the Cape Cod National Seashore, this family-friendly beach is known for its consistent shortboard/longboard swell all summer long.

MAD FOR MOUNTAIN BIKING

Mountain-biking enthusiasts will find trail nirvana in Boulder, CO; Moab, UT; Bend, OR; Ketchum, ID; and Marin, CA, where Gary Fisher and co bunny-hopped the sport forward by careening down the rocky flanks of Mt Tamalpais on home-rigged bikes. There are many other great destinations. For info on trails, tips and gear, check out *Bicycling* magazine (www.bicycling.com) or IMBA (www.imba.com).

Kokopelli Trail, UT One of the premier mountain-biking trails in the Southwest stretches 140 miles on mountainous terrain between Loma, CO, and Moab, UT. Other nearby options include the 206-mile, hut-to-hut ride between Telluride, CO, and Moab, UT, and the shorter but very challenging 38-mile ride from Aspen to Crested Butte – an equally stunning ride.

Maah Daah Hey Trail, ND A 96-mile jaunt over rolling buttes along the Little Missouri River.

Sun Top Loop, WA A 22-mile ride with challenging climbs that rewards with superb views of Mt Rainier and surrounding peaks on the western slopes of Washington's Cascade Mountains.

Flume Trail, CA A moderately challenging trail with stunning views along Lake Tahoe. This 14-mile trail runs one way at 7000ft to 8000ft elevation, with about 4.5 miles of singletrack.

Finger Lakes Trail, Letchworth State Park, NY A little-known treasure, 35 miles south of Rochester in upstate New York, featuring more than 20 miles of singletrack along the rim of the 'Grand Canyon of the East.'

McKenzie River Trail, Willamette National Forest, OR (www.mckenzierivertrail. com) Twenty-two miles of blissful singletrack winding through deep forests and volcanic formations. The town of McKenzie is located about 50 miles east of Eugene.

Porcupine Rim, Moab, UT A 30-mile loop from town, this venerable high-desert romp features stunning views and hairy downhills.

White-Water Rafting

East of the Mississippi, West Virginia has an arsenal of legendary white water. First, there's the New River Gorge National River, which, despite its name, is one of the oldest rivers in the world. Slicing from North Carolina into West Virginia, it cuts a deep gorge, known as the Grand Canyon of the East, producing frothy rapids in its wake. Then there's the Gauley, arguably among the world's finest white water. Revered for its ultrasteep and turbulent chutes, this venerable Appalachian river is a watery roller coaster, dropping more than 668ft and churning up 100-plus rapids in a mere 28 miles. Six more rivers, all in the same neighborhood, offer training grounds for less-experienced river rats. North Carolina has two choice places for paddlers: the US National Whitewater Center outside Charlotte, and the Nantahela Outdoor Center in Bryson City.

Out west there's no shortage of scenic and spectacular rafting, from Utah's Cataract Canyon, a thrilling romp through the red rocks of Canyonlands National Park, to the Rio Grande in Texas, a lazy run through limestone canyons. The North Fork of the Owyhee – which snakes from the high plateau of southwest Oregon to the rangelands of Idaho – is rightfully popular and features towering hoodoos. In California, both the Tuolumne and American Rivers surge with moderate-to-extreme rapids, while in Idaho, the Middle Fork of the Salmon River has it all: abundant wildlife, thrilling rapids, a rich homesteader history, waterfalls and hot springs. If you're organized enough to plan a few years in advance, book a spot on the Colorado River, the quintessential river trip. And if you're not after white-knuckle rapids, fret not – many rivers have sections suitable for peaceful float trips or inner-tube drifts that you can traverse with a cold beer in hand.

Kayaking & Canoeing

For exploring flatwater (no rapids or surf), opt for a kayak or canoe. While kayaks are seaworthy, they are not always suited for carrying bulky gear. For big lakes and the seacoast (including the San Juan Islands), use a sea kayak. For month-long wilderness trips – including the 12,000 miles of watery routes in Minnesota's Boundary Waters, or Alabama's Bartram Canoe Trail, with 300,000 acres of marshy delta bayous, lakes and rivers – use a canoe.

You can kayak or canoe almost anywhere in the USA. Rentals and instruction are yours for the asking, from Wisconsin's Apostle Islands National Seashore and Utah's celebrated Green River to Hawaii's Na Pali Coast. Hire kayaks in Maine's Penobscot Bay to poke around the briny waters and spruce-fringed islets, or join a full-moon paddle in Sausalito's Richardson Bay, CA.

Skiing & Winter Sports

You can hit the slopes in 40 states, making for tremendous variety in terrain and ski-town vibe. Colorado has some of the best skiing in the nation, though California, Vermont and Utah are also top-notch destinations. Ski season typically runs from mid-December to April, though some resorts run longer. In summer, many resorts are great for mountain biking and hiking, courtesy of chairlifts. Ski packages (including airfare, hotel and lift tickets) are easy to find through resorts, travel agencies and online travel booking sites and can be a good deal.

Wherever you ski, though, it won't come cheap. Find the best deals by going midweek, purchasing multiday tickets, heading to lesser-known 'sibling' resorts (such as Alpine Meadows near Lake Tahoe) or checking out mountains that cater to locals, including Vermont's Mad River Glen, Santa Fe Ski Area and Colorado's Wolf Grade.

Top Ski & Snowboard Resorts

Vermont's first-rate Stowe draws seasoned souls – freeze your tail off on the lifts, but thaw out nicely après-ski in timbered bars with local brews. Find more snow, altitude and attitude out west at Vail, CO, Squaw Valley, CA, and high-glitz Aspen, CO. For an unfussy scene and steep vertical chutes, try Alta, UT, Telluride, CO, Jackson, WY, and Taos, NM. In Alaska, slopes slice through spectacular terrain outside Juneau, Anchorage and Fairbanks. Mt Aurora

SkiLand has the most northerly chairlift in North America and, from mid-September to mid-April, the shimmering green-blue aurora borealis.

Rock Climbing

Scads of climbers flock to Joshua Tree National Park, an otherworldly shrine in Southern California's sun-scorched desert. There, amid craggy monoliths and the park's namesake trees, they pay pilgrimage on more than 8000 routes, tackling sheer verticals, sharp edges and bountiful cracks. A top-notch climbing school offers classes for all levels. In Zion National Park, UT, multiday canyoneering classes teach the fine art of going *down:* rappelling off sheer sandstone cliffs into glorious, red-rock canyons filled with trees. Some of the sportier pitches are made in dry suits, down the flanks of roaring waterfalls into ice-cold pools. Other great spots abound.

➡ **Grand Teton National Park, WY** A great spot for climbers of all levels: beginners can take basic climbing courses; the more experienced can join two-day expeditions up to the top of Grand Teton itself: a 13,770ft peak with majestic views.

➡ **City of Rocks National Reserve, ID** More than 500 routes up wind-scoured granite and pinnacles 60 stories tall.

➡ **Yosemite National Park, CA** A hallowed shrine for rock climbers with superb climbing courses (p1023) for first-timers as well as for those craving a night in a hammock 1000ft above terra firma.

➡ **Bishop, CA** Southeast of Yosemite National Park and favored by many top climbers, this sleepy town in the Eastern Sierra is the gateway to excellent climbing in nearby Owens River Gorge and Buttermilk Hills.

➡ **Red Rock Canyon, NV** Ten miles west of Las Vegas is some of the world's finest sandstone climbing.

➡ **Enchanted Rock State Natural Area, TX** Located 70 miles west of Austin, this state park

---

HONE YOUR SKILLS (OR LEARN SOME NEW ONES)

Whether you're eager to catch a wave or dangle from a cliff, learn some new outdoor tricks in these high-thrill programs.

Chicks Climbing & Skiing (www.chickswithpicks.net) Based in Ridgway, CO, this group gives women's workshops across the country in mountaineering, climbing, ice climbing and backcountry skiing.

Club Ed Surf Camp (www.club-ed.com) Learn to ride the waves from Manresa Beach to Santa Cruz, CA, with field trips to the surfing museum and surfboard companies included.

Craftsbury Outdoor Center (www.craftsbury.com) Come here for sculling, cross-country skiing and running amid the forests and hills of Vermont.

Joshua Tree Rock Climbing School (www.joshuatreerockclimbing.com) Local guides lead beginners to experts on 7000 different climbs in Joshua Tree National Park, CA.

LL Bean Discovery Schools (www.llbean.com) The famous Maine retailer offers instruction in kayaking, snowshoeing, cross-country skiing, wilderness first-aid, fly-fishing and more.

Nantahala Outdoor Center (www.noc.com) Learn to paddle like a pro at this North Carolina–based school, which offers world-class instruction in canoeing and kayaking in the Great Smoky Mountains.

Otter Bar Lodge Kayak School (www.otterbar.com) Top-notch white-water kayaking instruction is complemented by saunas, hot tubs, salmon dinners and a woodsy lodge in California's northern wilds.

Steep & Deep Ski Camp (www.jacksonhole.com/steep-ski-camp.html) Finesse skiing extreme terrain (and snagging first tracks), then wind down over dinner parties. You can also ski with Olympian Tommy Moe.

Surfers on a California beach

with its huge pink granite dome has hundreds of routes and stellar views of the Texas Hill Country.

➡ **Rocky Mountain National Park, CO** Offers alpine climbing near Boulder.

➡ **Flatirons, CO** Near Boulder, with fine multipitch ascents.

➡ **Chattanooga, TN** A world-class climbing destination with many nearby sites, including the Tennessee Wall, with over 400 established routes.

➡ **Red River Gorge, KY** With over 100 cliffs and some 2000 different routes, this is a climber's paradise – all the more so given its location inside lush forested parkland.

➡ **Shawangunk Ridge, NY** Located within a two-hour drive north of NYC, this ridge stretches some 50 miles, and the 'Gunks' are where many East Coast climbers tied their first billets.

➡ **Hueco Tanks, TX** From October to early April, Hueco Tanks ranks among the world's top rock-climbing destinations, when other prime climbs become inaccessible (although in summer, the desert sun generally makes the rocks too hot to handle).

Climbing & Canyoneering Resources

American Canyoneering Association (www.canyoneering.net) An online canyons database and links to courses, local climbing groups and more.

Climbing (www.climbing.com) Cutting-edge rock-climbing news and information since 1970.

SuperTopo (www.supertopo.com) One-stop shop for rock-climbing guidebooks, free topo maps and route descriptions.

Scuba Diving & Snorkeling

The most exotic underwater destination in the USA is Hawaii. There, in shimmering aquamarine waters that stay warm year-round, you'll be treated to a psychedelic display of surreal colors and shapes. Swim alongside sea turtles, octopuses and fiesta-colored parrotfish – not to mention lava tubes and black coral. Back on shore, cap off the reverie with *poke* made from just-caught 'ahi (yellowfin tuna).

The best diving is off the coast or between the islands, so liveaboards are the way to go for scuba buffs. From the green turtles and WWII wrecks off the shores of Oahu to the undersea lava sculptures near little Lana'i, the Aloha State offers endless underwater bliss – but plan ahead, as dive sites change with the seasons.

On the continental USA, Florida has the lion's share of great diving, with more than 1000 miles of coastline subdivided into 20 unique undersea areas. There are hundreds of sites and countless dive shops offering equipment and guided excursions. South of West Palm Beach, you'll find clear waters and fantastic year-round diving with ample reefs. In the Panhandle, or northern part of the state, you can scuba in the calm and balmy waters of the Gulf of Mexico; off Pensacola and Destin, there are fabulous wreck dives; and you can dive with manatees near Crystal River.

The Florida Keys, a curving string of 31 islets, are the crown jewel; expect a brilliant mix of marine habitats, North America's only living coral garden and the occasional shipwreck. Key Largo is home to the John Pennekamp Coral Reef State Park and more than 200 miles of underwater idyll.

There's terrific diving and snorkeling (and much warmer water) beyond the mangrove swamps along the Florida Reef, the world's third-largest coral barrier-reef system. Look for manatees off Islamorada or take an expedition to Dry Tortugas, where the expansive reef swarms with barracuda, sea turtles and a couple hundred sunken ships.

Other Underwater Destinations

For the latest on diving destinations in the US and abroad, visit Scuba Diving (www.scubadiving.com), or check out the USA overview from *DT Mag* (www.dtmag.com/travelresource/dive-travel).

➡ **Hanauma Bay Nature Preserve, Oahu, HI** Despite the crowds, this is still one of the world's great spots for snorkeling, with more than 450 resident species of reef fish.

➡ **San Diego-La Jolla Underwater Park** Offers excellent shore-diving amid four different habitats in a 6000-acre reserve. There are two reefs and seven caves, and with 30ft visibility you have the chance to spot a wide range of sea life, including eels, Garibaldi and leopard sharks.

➡ **Channel Islands, CA** Lying between Santa Barbara and Los Angeles, these islands harbor spiny lobsters, angel sharks and numerous dive sites best accessed by liveaboard charter.

➡ **Jade Cove, CA** About 10 miles south of Lucia on Hwy 1, this aptly named spot has the world's only underwater concentration of jade, making for an unforgettable dive.

➡ **Cape Hatteras National Seashore, NC** Along the northern coast of North Carolina, divers can explore historic wrecks from the Civil War (and encounter tiger sand sharks); there are also numerous options for dive charters within the Outer Banks and the Cape Lookout areas.

➡ **Great Lakes, MI** The USA's most unexpected dive spot? Michigan's Lakes Superior and Huron, with thousands of shipwrecks lying strewn on the sandy bottoms – just don't expect to see any angelfish!

Horseback Riding

Cowboy wannabes will be happy to learn that horseback riding of every style, from Western to bareback, is available across the USA. Out west, you'll find truly memorable experiences – everything from weeklong expeditions through the canyons of southern Utah and cattle wrangling in Wyoming, to pony rides along the Oregon coast. Finding horses is easy; rental stables and riding schools are located around and in many of the national parks. Experienced equestrians can explore alone or in the company of guides familiar with local flora, fauna and history. Half- and full-day group trail rides, which usually include lunch in a wildflower-speckled meadow, are popular and plentiful.

California is terrific for riding, with fog-swept trails leading along the cliffs of Point Reyes National Seashore, longer excursions through the high-altitude lakes of the Ansel Adams Wilderness, and multiday pack trips in Yosemite and Kings Canyon. Utah's Capitol Reef and Canyonlands also provide spectacular four-hoofed outings, as do the mountains, arroyos and plains of Colorado, Arizona, New Mexico, Montana and Texas.

Dude ranches come in all varieties, from down-duvet luxurious to barn-duty authentic on working cattle ranches. They're found in most of the western states, and even some eastern ones (such as Tennessee and North Carolina). Real-life cowboys are included.

Plan Your Trip

Eat & Drink Like a Local

The great variety found in American cuisine can be traced to the local larder of each region, from the seafood of the North Atlantic to the fertile Midwestern farmlands and the vast Western ranchlands. Omaha steaks, Maryland crab cakes and Charleston red rice are but a few of the regional specialties.

Culinary Revolution

Not until the 1960s did food and wine become serious topics for American newspapers, magazines and TV, led by a Californian named Julia Child who taught Americans how to cook French food through black-and-white programs broadcast from Boston's public TV station. By the 1970s, everyday folks (and not just hippies) had started turning their attention to issues of organic, natural foods and sustainable agriculture. In the 1980s and '90s, the 'foodie revolution' encouraged entrepreneurs to open restaurants featuring regional American cuisine, from the South to the Pacific Northwest, that would rank with Europe's best.

Slow, Local, Organic

The Slow Food movement, along with renewed enthusiasm for eating local organically grown fare, is a leading trend in American restaurants. The movement, which was arguably started in 1971 by chef Alice Waters at Berkeley's Chez Panisse (p1005), continued with First Lady Michelle Obama – the First Lady of food if there ever was one – and her daughters, who even planted an organic garden on the White House lawn. All across the country

The Year in Food

In a country as large as the US, you'll find food festivals and local specialties all year long.

Spring (March–May)

One of the best times to hit local markets, with bounty from farm and field (ramps, strawberries, rhubarb, spring lamb), plus Easter treats. Across the country are major festivals, showcasing crawfish, barbecue, oysters and more.

Summer (June–August)

A great time for seafood feasting by the shore, outdoor barbecues and country fairs. Don't miss fresh berries, peaches, corn on the cob and much more.

Autumn (September–November)

Crisp days bring apple picking, pumpkin pies, harvest wine festivals and some major food-focused events, including Thanksgiving.

Winter (December–February)

Hearty stews, roast late-harvest vegetables, plus decadent holiday treats are the order of the day. Get toasty by the fire, with a hot toddy or other warming drink in hand.

you can find farmers markets, which are great places to meet locals and take a big bite out of America's cornucopia of foods, from heritage fruit and vegetables to fresh savory and sweet regional delicacies.

Staples & Specialties

Waves of immigrants have added great variety to American gastronomy by adapting foreign ideas to home soil, from Italian pizza and German hamburgers to Eastern European borscht, Mexican huevos rancheros and Japanese sushi.

Pizza

Pizza made its way over to New York in the 1900s through Italian immigrants, and the first pizzeria in America – Lombardi's in Manhattan's Little Italy – opened in 1905. Pizza's popularity quickly spread across the country, with different varieties taking root. While Chicago-style pizza is 'deep dish' and Californian tends to be light and doughy, New York prides itself on its thin crust.

Mexican & Tex-Mex

No matter where you roam in the US, you probably won't be far from a restaurant serving up Mexican or Tex-Mex fare (don't bother trying to sort the two, there's much overlap between them). This is not surprising given that people of Mexican descent make up over 11% of the population. Tacos, burritos and other quick foods are favorites, with snack carts and food trucks popular stomping grounds for people of all walks of life. Places such as Chipotle, which serves up largely organic Tex-Mex in a hurry, are among the fastest growing chains. Casual sit-down places are also popular, with margaritas and chips and salsa a nearly essential part of every meal.

Barbecue

Barbecue is a big deal in America. Although its popularity is unrivaled in the South, you'll find this smoky, tender meat everywhere from San Francisco to New York City. Barbecue in America dates back to colonial times, and even George Washington (who had a smokehouse at his estate in Mt Vernon) was a fan. The dish is simple enough: meat slow-roasted over fire pits until tender. You'll find a wide variety of cooking styles and specialties. Kansas City, MO, serves a range of meats, including lamb, and emphasizes thick, sweet sauces. In the Carolinas, pulled or sliced pork is most popular. Memphis favors ribs, served either 'dry' or 'wet' (ie slathered in sauce). In Texas, beef is the dish of choice – no surprise given this is cattle country. It's also home to some of the nation's best barbecue joints: Lockhart is the epicenter for all things smoked and meaty.

Comfort Foods

While food trends come and go, the American love for a simple and hearty meal never goes out of style. Comfort foods at their roots are warm, traditional dishes that evoke nostalgia for childhood staples. Classics such as mac 'n' cheese, chicken noodle soup, lasagna, pot roast, grilled cheese sandwiches, biscuits and gravy, fried chicken, hamburgers and filling pastas all fall into this category. American diners serve mostly this sort of food, churning out uncomplicated, tried-and-true recipes. Comfort foods can also be found in more creative versions at gastropubs, bistros, and upmarket restaurants and bars. You might find mac 'n' cheese with fresh crabmeat, burgers topped with applewood-smoked bacon and goat's cheese and served with duck-fat fries, or spicy Thai chicken noodle soup with coconut milk and curry.

Local Specialties
NYC: Foodie Capital

They say that you could eat at a different restaurant every night of your life in New York City, and not exhaust the possibilities. Considering that there are an estimated 24,000 restaurants in the five boroughs, with scores of new ones opening each year, it's true. Owing to its huge immigrant population and an influx of over 50 million tourists annually, New York captures the title of America's greatest restaurant city, hands down. Its diverse neighborhoods serve up authentic Italian food and thin-crust pizza, all manner of Asian food, French haute cuisine and classic Jewish deli food, from bagels to piled-high pastrami on rye. More exotic cuisines are found here as well, from Ethiopian to Scandinavian.

Poke (Hawaiian specialty of cubed raw fish)

Check out Eater New York (www. ny.eater.com), *New York* magazine (www. nymag.com) or *Time Out* (www.timeout. com/newyork) for the latest restaurant openings, reviews and insight into famed and up-and-coming chefs. Finally, don't let NYC's image as expensive get to you: you can eat well here without breaking the bank, especially if you limit your cocktail intake. There may be no free lunch in New York, but compared to other world cities, eating here can be a bargain.

New England: Clambakes & Lobster Boils

New England's claim to have the nation's best seafood is hard to beat, because the North Atlantic offers up clams, mussels, oysters and huge lobsters, along with shad, bluefish and cod. New Englanders love a good chowder (seafood stew) and a good clambake, an almost ritual meal where the shellfish are buried in a pit fire with corn, chicken, potatoes and sausages. Fried clam fritters and lobster rolls (lobster meat with mayonnaise served in a bread bun) are served throughout the region. There are excellent cheeses made in Vermont, cran-

berries (a Thanksgiving staple) harvested in Massachusetts and maple syrup tapped from New England's forests. Maine's coast is lined with lobster shacks; baked beans and brown bread are Boston specialties; and Rhode Islanders pour coffee syrup into milk and embrace traditional corn-meal johnnycakes.

Mid-Atlantic: Crab Cakes & Cheesesteaks

From New York down through Maryland and Virginia, the mid-Atlantic states share a long coastline and a cornucopia of apple, pear and berry farms. New Jersey and New York's Long Island are famous for their spuds (potatoes). Chesapeake Bay's blue crabs are the finest anywhere, and Virginia salt-cured 'country-style' hams are served with biscuits (a buttery, scone-like baked good). In Philadelphia, you can gorge on 'Philly' cheesesteaks, made with thin, sautéed beef and onions and melted cheese on a bun. And in Pennsylvania Dutch Country, stop by a farm restaurant for chicken pot pie, noodles and meatloaf-like scrapple.

Southern: BBQ, Biscuits & Gumbo

No region is prouder of its food culture than the South, which has a long history of mingling Anglo, French, African, Spanish and Native American foods in dishes such as slow-cooked barbecue, which has as many meaty and saucy variations as there are towns in the South. Southern fried chicken is crisp outside and moist inside. In Florida, dishes made with alligator, shrimp and conch incorporate hot chili peppers and tropical spices. Breakfasts are as big as can be, and treasured dessert recipes tend to produce big layer cakes or pies made with pecans, bananas and citrus. Light, fluffy hot biscuits are served well buttered, and grits (ground corn cooked to a porridge-like consistency) are a passion among Southerners, as are cool mint-julep cocktails.

Louisiana's legendary cuisine is influenced by colonial French and Spanish cultures, Afro-Caribbean cooking and Choctaw traditions. Cajun food is found in the bayou country and marries native spices such as sassafras and chili peppers with provincial French cooking. Famous dishes include gumbo, a roux-based stew of chicken and shellfish, or sausage and often okra; jambalaya, a rice-based dish with tomatoes, sausage and shrimp; and blackened catfish. Creole food is more urban, and centered in New Orleans, where dishes such as shrimp rémoulade, crabmeat ravigote, crawfish étouffée, and beignets are ubiquitous.

Great Plains & Great Lakes: Burgers, Bacon & Beer

Residents of the Great Plains and Great Lakes regions eat big and with plenty of gusto. Portions are huge – this is farm country, where people need sustenance to get their day's work done. So you might start off the day with eggs, bacon and toast; have a double cheeseburger and potato salad for lunch; and fork into steak and baked potatoes for dinner – all washed down with a cold brew, often one of the growing numbers of microbrews. Barbecue is very popular here, especially in Kansas City, St Louis and Chicago. Chicago is also an ethnically diverse culinary center, with some of the country's top restaurants. One of the best places to sample regional foods is at a county fair, which offers everything from bratwurst to fried dough to grilled corn on the cob. Elsewhere at diners and family restaurants, you'll taste the varied influences of Eastern European, Scandinavian, Latino and Asian immigrants, especially in the cities.

TOP VEGETARIAN RESTAURANTS

In many American cities, you'll find a wealth of restaurants that cater to vegetarians and vegans. Once you head out into rural areas and away from the coast, the options are slimmer. We note eateries that offer a good selection of vegetarian or vegan options by using the 🖉 symbol. To find more vegetarian and vegan restaurants, browse the online directory at www.happycow.net. Here are a few of our go-to faves across the country:

Greens (p997), San Francisco, CA

Native Foods Cafe (p548), Chicago, IL

Clover Food Lab (www.cloverfoodlab.com; 1326 Massachusetts Ave; mains $8-11; ⏰7am-midnight Mon-Sat, 9am-10pm Sun; 🖥🖉; 🇹Harvard) 🖉, Boston, MA

Green Elephant (p260), Portland, ME

Moosewood Restaurant (p153), Ithaca, NY

Sweet Melissa's (p789), Laramie, WY

Sitka & Spruce (p1045), Seattle, WA

Fud (p657), Kansas City, MO

Zenith (p182), Pittsburgh, PA

High Noon Cafe (p436), Jackson, MS

Hangawi (p119), NYC

The Southwest: Chili, Steak & Salsa

Two ethnic groups define Southwestern food culture: the Spanish and the Mexicans, who controlled territories from Texas to California until well into the 19th century. While there is little actual Spanish food today, the Spanish brought cattle to Mexico, which the Mexicans adapted to their own corn-and-chili-based gastronomy to make tacos, enchiladas, burritos, chimichangas and other dishes made of corn or flour pancakes filled with everything from chopped meat and poultry to beans. Don't leave New Mexico without trying a bowl of spicy green chili stew. Steaks and barbecue are always favorites on Southwestern menus, and beer is the drink of choice for dinner and a night out.

California: Farm-to-Table & Taquerias

Owing to its vastness and variety of microclimates, California is truly America's cornucopia for fruits and vegetables. The state's natural resources are overwhelming, with wild salmon, Dungeness crab and oysters from the ocean; robust produce year-round; and artisanal products such as cheese, bread, olive oil, wine and chocolate. Starting in the 1970s and '80s, star chefs such as Alice Waters and Wolfgang Puck pioneered 'California cuisine' by incorporating the best local ingredients into simple, yet delectable, preparations. The influx of Asian immigrants, especially after the Vietnam War, enriched the state's urban food cultures with Chinatowns, Koreatowns and Japantowns, along with huge enclaves of Mexican Americans who maintain their own culinary traditions across the state. Global fusion restaurants are another hallmark of California's cuisine. Don't miss the forearm-sized burritos in San Francisco's Mission District and fish tacos in San Diego.

Pacific Northwest: Salmon & Coffee Culture

The cuisine of the Pacific Northwest region draws on the traditions of the local tribes of Native Americans, whose diets traditionally centered on game, seafood – especially salmon – and foraged mushrooms, fruits and berries. Seattle spawned the modern international coffeehouse craze

DOS & DON'TS

➡ Do tip: 15% to 20% of the total bill (pretax) is standard.

➡ It's customary to place your napkin on your lap, even before the meal is served.

➡ In general, try to avoid putting your elbows on the table.

➡ Wait until everyone is served to begin eating.

➡ In formal situations, diners customarily wait to eat until the host has lifted their fork.

➡ At home, some Americans say a prayer before meals; it's fine to sit quietly if you prefer not to participate.

with Starbucks – though these days Portland gets more attention for its excellent coffee scene, with some of the country's best roasters.

Hawaii: Island Style

In the middle of the Pacific Ocean, Hawaii is rooted in a Polynesian food culture that takes full advantage of locally caught fish such as mahimahi, *'opakapaka, ono* and ahi. Traditional luau celebrations include cooking *kalua* pig in an underground pit layered with hot stones and *ti* leaves. Hawaii's contemporary cuisine incorporates fresh, island-grown produce and borrows liberally from the islands' many Asian and European immigrant groups. This also happens to be the only state to grow coffee commercially; 100% Kona beans from the Big Island have the most gourmet cachet.

Food Experiences
Meals of a Lifetime

➡ **Alinea** (p550) You'll have to be very lucky to score a ticket to this pillar of molecular gastronomy in Chicago.

➡ **Black's Barbecue** (p708) Serves up some of America's best brisket, from an atmospheric location in Lockhart, Texas.

➡ **Lobster Dock** (p262) It's worth making a pilgrimage to Maine to sample fresh-caught succulent lobster from casual, waterside places like this one in Boothbay Harbor.

Tacos

→ **Faidley's** (p302) There are no frills or bay views at this Baltimore institution, just heavenly jumbo-lump crab cakes.

→ **Peche Seafood Grill** (p457) Seafood cooked to perfection over a wood fire in the Warehouse District of New Orleans.

→ **Rolf & Daughters** (☑615-866-9897; www. rolfanddaughters.com; 700 Taylor St; mains $15-26; ☺5:30-10pm; ☜) Serves superb new Italian cooking in a buzzing space in Nashville.

→ **French Laundry** (p1008) It may cost you a month's wages, but this Northern California icon never fails to dazzle.

→ **Salt** (p765) Local, seasonal, organic and delicious dishes in Boulder.

→ **Imperial** (☑503-568-1079; www.imperial pdx.com; 410 SW Broadway; mains $12-42; ☺6:30am-10pm Mon-Thu, to 11pm Fri, 8am-11pm Sat, to 10pm Sun) Healthy Pacific Northwest meals in a warm Portland setting.

→ **Grey Plume** (p680) In Omaha; works seasonal magic with the produce and meats of the region.

→ **Eataly** (p118) Eat your way into a stupor on myriad Italian delicacies at this sprawling NYC food hall.

Cheap Treats

→ **Food trucks** The variety of offerings is staggering in towns such as Portland, San Francisco, LA and Austin.

→ **Tacos** A handheld favorite all across the US. Some of the best are served from street carts and food trucks.

→ **Green chili** A Rockies classic, best when served atop a burger.

→ **Doughnuts** Not just for police officers. Look for gourmet varieties (pistachio, hibiscus, lemon ginger).

→ **Fried chicken** With famed spots in the South, including **Prince's Hot Chicken** (123 Ewing Dr; quarter/half/whole chicken $5/11/22; ☺11:30-10pm Tue-Thu, t11:30am-4am Fri, 2pm-4am Sat) in Nashville and Willie Mae's (p455) in New Orleans.

→ **Frozen custard** Nothing else quite hits the spot on a hot day, especially if it's from Ted Drewes (p649) in St Louis.

→ **Fried clams** A cheap and filling snack available all along the eastern seaboard.

→ **Beignets** Fried dough topped with powdered sugar is a must-have when visiting New Orleans.

→ **Half smokes** A bigger, spicier version of the hot dog, this is a DC specialty.

Dare to Try

→ **Bison short ribs** Sometimes spotted in the Rockies; Yellowstone is a reliable place to find them.

→ **Alligator** A roadhouse special in some parts of the South. Try some at **Joannie's Blue Crab Café** (☎239-695-2682; www. joaniesbluecrabcafe.com; 39395 Tamiami Trail E; mains $12-17; ⊙11am-5pm Thu-Tue; closed seasonally, call to confirm; ✍) in the Everglades.

→ **Poke** A Hawaiian specialty of cubed raw fish (often ahi tuna); it's spectacularly good.

→ **Lobster ice cream** You'll never go back to strawberry after trying this popular crustacean flavor at **Ben & Bill's Chocolate Emporium** (☎508-548-7878; www.benandbills.com; 209 Main St; cones $5; ⊙9am-11pm Jun-Aug, shorter hr rest of year) out on Cape Cod.

→ **Steak** Not just any steak, but a 72-oz steak for one served at **Big Texan Steak Ranch** (www.bigtexan.com; 7701 I-40 E, exit 75; mains $10-40; ⊙7am-10:30pm). If you eat it and all the sides in under an hour, it's free!

→ **Triple bypass burger** At the Vortex (p414) in Atlanta you can try a stack of two diner-style patty melts with 18 slices of American cheese, 18 bacon strips and three fried eggs served between grilled cheese sandwiches for buns.

→ **Pig-ear sandwich** Served with panache since the 1930s at the **Big Apple Inn** (☎601-354-4549; 509 N Farish St; mains $2; ⊙7:30am-9pm Tue-Fri, from 8am Sat) in Jackson, MS.

→ **Dirty water dog** It takes a special appetite to crave a hot dog that's been sitting in murky water all day in a NYC food cart.

Opening Hours & Reservations

Some restaurants (typically the most popular places) don't take reservations. For those that do, it's wise to book ahead, especially on weekends. If you don't have reservations (or can't make them), plan to dine early (5pm to 6pm) or late (9pm) to avoid lengthy waits.

→ **Restaurants** American restaurants cover all prices and foods: diners, burger joints, crab and lobster shacks, Michelin-starred dining rooms, and every cuisine you can imagine. More casual places are usually open from about 11am onward; fancier restaurants are often only open from 5pm. Many restaurant kitchens close at 10pm.

→ **Cafes and coffee shops** Open all day (and sometimes at night), cafes are good for a casual breakfast or lunch, or simply a cup of coffee.

→ **Informal eateries** Look for food trucks, farmers markets and other casual options (some bars also serve great food). A few chains – like Waffle House or Huddle House – are open 24 hours.

Habits & Customs

Outside of big cities, Americans tend to eat early at restaurants and at home, so don't be surprised to find a restaurant half full at noon or 5:30pm. In smaller towns, it may be hard to find anywhere to eat after 8:30pm or 9pm. Dinner parties for adults usually begin around 6:30pm or 7pm with cocktails followed by a buffet or sit-down meal. If invited to dinner, it's polite to be prompt: ideally, you should plan to arrive within 15 minutes of the designated time.

Americans are informal in their dining manners, although they will usually wait until everyone is served before eating. Many foods are eaten with the fingers, and an entire piece of bread may be buttered and eaten all at once. To the surprise of some foreign visitors, the sight of beer bottles on the dinner table is not uncommon.

Breakfast

Long billed by American nutritionists as 'the most important meal of the day,' morning meals in America are big business – no matter how many folks insist on skipping them. From a giant stack of buttermilk pancakes at a vintage diner to lavish Sunday brunches, Americans love their eggs and bacon, their waffles and

---

HAPPY HOURS

Gastropubs, microbreweries that serve meals, and even traditional restaurants with bar seating often host great-value happy hours. Sometime before the dinner rush (usually 3pm to 5pm or 4pm to 6pm), you can score great deals on fresh oysters, appetizers and other light fare. Add to this the drink specials (along the lines of half-priced cocktails), and you have the makings for a great start to the night.

hash browns, and their big glasses of fresh-squeezed orange juice. Most of all, they love that seemingly inalienable American right: a steaming cup of morning coffee with unlimited refills. (Try asking for a free refill in other nations, and you'll get anything from an eye-roll to a smirk to downright confusion.)

Lunch

Usually after a midmorning coffee break, an American worker's lunch hour affords only a sandwich, quick burger or hearty salad. The formal 'business lunch' is more common in big cities like New York, where food is not necessarily as important as the conversation.

While you'll spot diners drinking a beer or a glass of wine with their lunch, long gone are the days when the 'three martini lunch' was socially acceptable. It was a phenomenon common enough in the mid-20th century to become a kind of catchphrase for indulgent business lunches, usually written off as a corporate, tax-deductible expense. The classic noon-time beverage, in fact, is a far cry from a martini: iced tea (and yes, almost always with unlimited refills).

Dinner

Usually early in the evening, Americans settle in to a more substantial weeknight dinner, which, given the workload of so many two-career families, might be takeout (eg pizza or Chinese food) or prepackaged microwave meals. Desserts tend toward ice cream, pies and cakes. Some families still cook a traditional Sunday-night dinner, when relatives and friends gather for a big feast. Traditional dishes might include roast chicken with all the fixings (mashed potatoes, green beans and corn on the cob). In warmer months, many Americans like to fire up the barbecue to grill steaks, burgers and veggies, which are served alongside plenty of cold beer and wine.

Beer, Wine & Beyond

Americans have a staggering range of choices when it comes to beverages. A booming microbrewery industry has brought finely crafted beers to every corner of the country. The US wine industry continues to produce first-rate vintages – and it's not just California vineyards garnering all the awards. Meanwhile, coffee culture continues to prevail, with cafes and roasteries elevating the once-humble cup of coffee to high art.

Beer

It's hard to deny that beer is about as American as Chevrolet, football and apple pie: just tune in to the Super Bowl (America's most popular yearly televised event, featuring its most expensive advertisements) and you'll see how beer has become intertwined with American cultural values. Just look at the slogans, celebrating individuality ('This Bud's for You'), sociability ('It's Miller Time!'), ruggedness ('Head for the Mountains') and authenticity ('Real Men Drink Bud Light').

THE VINTAGE COCKTAIL CRAZE

Across US cities, it's become decidedly cool to party like it's 1929 by drinking retro cocktails from the days – less than a century ago – that alcohol was illegal to consume across the entire United States. Good old Prohibition, of course, instead of spawning a nation of teetotalers, only solidified a culture in which the forbidden became appealing, it felt good to be bad, fast girls carried flasks of gin in their purses, and so-called respectable citizens congregated in secret 'speakeasies' to drink homemade moonshine and dance to hot jazz.

Fast-forward to the 21st century. While Prohibition isn't in danger of being reinstated, you'll find plenty of bars where the spirit of the roaring '20s and the illicit 1930s lives on. Inspired by vintage recipes featuring spirits and elixirs – remember, back in the day you couldn't just grab a bottle of scotch at the grocery store! – these cocktails, complete with ingredients such as small-batch liqueurs, whipped egg whites, hand-chipped ice and fresh fruits, are lovingly concocted by nattily dressed bartenders who regard their profession as something between an art and a science.

LEGENDARY AMERICANS DISH ABOUT DRINKING

While these Americans are all lauded for their talents in the arts or entertainment, they were undeniably (and often infamously) associated with the boozing life. Here are a few choice words they have on the subject.

➡ Ernest Hemingway: 'Always do sober what you said you'd do drunk. That will teach you to keep your mouth shut.'

➡ Frank Sinatra: 'Alcohol may be man's worst enemy, but the Bible says "love your enemy."'

➡ Dorothy Parker: 'I'd rather have a bottle in front of me than a frontal lobotomy.'

➡ WC Fields: 'A woman drove me to drink, and I never had the courtesy to thank her.'

➡ William Faulkner: 'The tools I need for my work are paper, tobacco, food, and a little whiskey.'

➡ Homer Simpson: 'Alcohol – the cause of and solution to all of life's problems.'

Despite their ubiquity, popular brands of American beer have long been the subject of ridicule abroad due to their low alcohol content and 'light' taste. Regardless of what the critics say, sales indicate that American beer is more popular than ever – and now, with the meteoric rise of microbreweries and craft beer, even beer snobs admit that American beer has reinvented itself.

Craft & Local Beer

Today, beer aficionados (otherwise known as beer geeks) sip and savor beer as they would wine, and some urban restaurants even have beer 'programs,' 'sommeliers' and cellars. Many brewpubs and restaurants host beer dinners, a chance to experience just how beers pair with different foods.

Microbrewery and craft-beer production is rising meteorically, generating roughly $22 billion in retail sales in 2016. Today there are around 5000 craft breweries across the USA. Portland, Oregon, is the current capital of the industry with 100-plus small breweries – more than in any other city in the world. In recent years it's become possible to 'drink local' all over the country as microbreweries pop up in urban centers, small towns and unexpected places.

Wine

In the seminal 1972 film *The Godfather*, Marlon Brando's Vito Corleone muses, 'I like to drink wine more than I used to.' The country soon followed suit, and nearly five decades later, Americans are drinking more wine than ever. These days the US actually consumes more wine than France (though per capita, France still towers over the US, with the French drinking 40 liters per person to America's paltry 9 liters per person).

To the raised eyebrows of European winemakers, who used to regard even California wines as second class, many American wines are now even winning prestigious international awards. In fact, the nation is the world's 4th-largest producer of wine, behind Italy, France and Spain.

Wine isn't cheap in the US, as it's considered a luxury rather than a staple – go ahead and blame the Puritans for that. But it's possible to procure a perfectly drinkable bottle of American wine at a liquor or wine shop for under $12.

Wine Regions

Today almost 90% of US wine comes from California, while other regions are producing wines that have achieved international status. In particular, the wines of New York's Finger Lakes, Hudson Valley and Long Island are well worth sampling, as are the wines from both Washington and Oregon, especially Pinot Noirs and Rieslings.

Without a doubt, the country's hotbed of wine tourism is in Northern California, just outside of the Bay Area in Napa and Sonoma Valleys. As other areas, from Oregon's Willamette Valley to Texas' Hill Country, have evolved as wine regions, they have spawned an entire industry of B&B tourism that seems to go hand and hand with the quest to find the perfect Pinot Noir.

So, what are the best American wines? Amazingly, though it's only been a few

Tastings at a vineyard in Sonoma Valley (p1008), California

decades since many American restaurants served either 'red,' 'white,' or sometimes 'pink' wine, there are many excellent 'New World' wines that have flourished in the rich American soil. The most popular white varietals made in the US are Chardonnay and Sauvignon Blanc; best-selling reds include Cabernet Sauvignon, Merlot, Pinot Noir and Zinfandel.

The Hard Stuff

You might know him by his first name, Jack. (Hint: Daniels is his last name). Good ole Jack Daniels remains the most well-known brand of American whiskey around the world, and is also the oldest continually operating US distillery, going strong since 1870.

While whiskey and bourbon are the most popular American exports, rye, gin and vodka are also crafted in the USA. Bourbon, made from corn, is the only native spirit and traditionally it is made in Kentucky.

Cocktails were invented in America before the Civil War. Born in New Orleans, an appropriately festive city to launch America's contribution to booze history,

the first cocktail was the Sazerac – a mix of rye whiskey or brandy, simple syrup, bitters and a dash of absinthe (before it was banned in 1912, that is). American cocktails created at bars in the late 19th and early 20th centuries include such long-standing classics as the martini, the Manhattan and the old-fashioned.

Non-Alcoholic Drinks

Tap water in the USA is safe to drink, though its taste varies depending on the region and city. Most nonalcoholic drinks are quite sugary and served over ice, from Southern-style iced 'sweet tea' and lemonade to quintessential American soft drinks such as Coca-Cola, Pepsi and Dr Pepper, along with retro and nouveau soft-drinks, often made with cane sugar instead of corn syrup.

Interestingly, carbonated nonalcoholic beverages have different nicknames depending on where you order them. In many parts of the South, a 'coke' means any kind of soda, so you may have to specify which kind you mean; for example, if you say 'I'll have a Coke,' the waiter might ask, 'Which kind?'. Around the Great Lakes, northern Great Plains and Pacific Northwest, soda is called 'pop.' On the East Coast and elsewhere, it's called 'soda.' Go figure...

Coffee Addiction

While Americans kick back with beer, and unwind with wine, the country runs on caffeine. The coffee craze has only intensified in the last 30 years, ever since cafe culture exploded in urban centers and spread throughout the country.

Blame it on Starbucks – the coffee that America loves (or loathes) above all others. The world's biggest coffee chain was born amid the Northwest's progressive coffee culture in 1971, when Starbucks opened its first location across from Pike Place Market in Seattle. The idea, to offer a variety of roasted beans from around the world in a comfortable cafe, helped start filling the American coffee mug with more refined, complicated (and expensive) drinks compared to the ubiquitous Folgers and diner cups of joe. By the early 1990s, specialty coffeehouses began springing up across the country, everywhere from cities to university towns.

While many coffee chains only have room for a few chairs and a takeout counter, independent coffee shops support a coffeehouse culture that encourages lingering; think free wi-fi, comfortable indoor and outdoor seating and good snacks and light fare. At the most high-level cafes, experienced baristas will happily banter about the origins of any roast (single-origin beans rather than blends are the latest in coffee snobbery) and will share their ideas about bean grinds and more.

Tipping

In the USA, where restaurants and bars often pay the legal minimum wage (or less), servers rely on tips for their livelihood. A good rule: tip at least a dollar per drink (more for pricey cocktails), or roughly 15% to 20% of the total bill.

DUIs

DUI (driving under the influence) is taken very seriously in the USA. Designating a sober driver who doesn't drink has become a widespread practice among groups of friends consuming alcohol at restaurants, bars, nightclubs and parties.

Food Glossary

barbecue – a technique of slow-smoking spice-rubbed and basted meat over a grill

beignet – New Orleans doughnut-like fritter dusted with powdered sugar

biscuit – flaky yeast-free roll served in the South

blintz – Jewish pancake stuffed with various fillings such as jam, cheese or potatoes

BLT – bacon, lettuce and tomato sandwich

blue plate – special of the day in a diner or luncheonette

Boston baked beans – beans cooked with molasses and bacon in a casserole

Buffalo wings – deep-fried chicken wings glazed with a buttery hot sauce and served with blue-cheese dressing; originated in Buffalo, NY

burrito – Mexican American flour tortilla wrapped around beans, meat, salsa and rice

California roll – fusion sushi made with avocado, crabmeat and cucumber wrapped in vinegared rice and *nori* (dried seaweed)

chili – hearty meat stew spiced with ground chilies, vegetables and beans; also called chili con carne

clam chowder – potato-based soup full of clams, vegetables and sometimes bacon, thickened with milk

club sandwich – three-layered sandwich with chicken or turkey, bacon, lettuce and tomato

corned beef – salt-cured or brined beef, traditionally served with cabbage on St Patrick's Day (March 17)

crab cake – crabmeat bound with breadcrumbs and eggs then fried

eggs Benedict – poached eggs, ham and hollandaise sauce on top of English muffins

French toast – egg-dipped fried bread served with maple syrup

grits – white cornmeal porridge; a Southern breakfast or side dish

guacamole – mashed avocado dip with lime juice, onions, chilies and cilantro, served with tortilla chips

hash browns – shredded pan-fried potatoes

huevos rancheros – Mexican breakfast of corn tortillas topped with fried eggs and salsa

jambalaya – Louisiana stew of rice, ham, sausage, shrimp and seasonings

lobster roll – lobster meat mixed with mayonnaise and seasonings, and served in a toasted frankfurter bun

lox – Jewish version of brine-cured salmon

nachos – Mexican American fried tortilla chips often topped with cheese, ground beef, jalapeño peppers, salsa and sour cream

pastrami – Jewish American brined brisket beef that is smoked and steamed

pickle – cucumber brined in vinegar

Reuben sandwich – sandwich of corned beef, Swiss cheese and sauerkraut on rye bread

smoothie – cold, thick drink made with pureed fruit, ice and sometimes yogurt

stone crab – Floribbean crab, the claws of which are eaten with melted butter or mustard-mayonnaise sauce

surf 'n' turf – combination plate of seafood (often lobster) and steak

wrap – tortilla or pita bread stuffed with a variety of fillings

Plan Your Trip

Travel with Children

From coast to coast, you'll find superb attractions for all ages: bucket-and-spade fun at the beach, amusement parks, zoos, eye-popping aquariums and natural-history exhibits, hands-on science museums, camping adventures, battlefields, hikes in wilderness reserves, leisurely bike rides through countryside, and plenty of other activities likely to wow young ones.

Best Regions for Kids

New York City
The Big Apple has many kid-friendly museums, plus carriage rides and rowboating in Central Park, cruises on the Hudson and theme restaurants in Times Square.

California
Get behind the movie magic at Universal Studios, hit the beaches, or head south to Disneyland and the San Diego Zoo Safari Park. In Northern California, see redwoods, San Francisco's Exploratorium and the Monterey Bay Aquarium.

Washington, DC
Washington has unrivaled allure for families, with free museums, a panda-loving zoo and boundless green spaces. Nearby, Virginia's Williamsburg is a slice of 18th-century America with costumed interpreters and fanciful activities.

Florida
Orlando's Walt Disney World® is well worth planning a vacation around. Then hit the beautiful beaches.

Colorado
Ski resorts go full throttle in summer with camps, mountain biking, slides and ziplines.

USA for Kids

Traveling with children can bring a whole new dimension to the American experience. You may make deeper connections, as locals (especially those with their own children) brighten and coo and embrace your family like long-lost cousins. From the city to the country, most facilities are ready to accommodate a child's needs.

To find family-oriented sights and activities, accommodations, restaurants and entertainment, just look for our child-friendly icon (👧).

Dining with Children

The US restaurant industry seems built on family-style service: children are not just accepted almost everywhere, but usually are encouraged by special children's menus with smaller portions and lower prices. In some restaurants children under a certain age even eat for free. Restaurants usually provide high chairs and booster seats. Some restaurants may also offer children crayons and puzzles, and occasionally live performances by cartoon-like characters.

Restaurants without children's menus don't necessarily discourage kids, though higher-end restaurants might. Even at the nicer places, however, if you show up early enough (right on dinnertime opening hours, often 5pm or 6pm), you can usually eat without too much stress – and you'll likely be joined by other foodies with kids. You can ask if the kitchen will make a smaller order of a dish (also ask how much it will cost), or if it will split a normal-size main dish between two plates for the kids. Chinese, Mexican and Italian restaurants seem to be the best bet for finicky young eaters.

Farmers markets are growing in popularity in the USA, and every sizable town has at least one a week. This is a good place to assemble a first-rate picnic, sample local specialties and support independent growers in the process. After getting your stash, head to the nearest park or waterfront.

Accommodations

Motels and hotels typically have rooms with two beds, which are ideal for families. Some also have rollaway beds or cribs that can be brought into the room for an extra charge – but keep in mind these are usually Pack 'n' Plays (portable cots), which not all children sleep well in. Some hotels offer 'kids stay free' programs for children up to 12 or sometimes 18 years of age. Be wary of B&Bs, as many don't allow children; inquire before reserving.

Babysitting

Resort hotels may have on-call babysitting services; otherwise, ask the front-desk staff or concierge to help you make arrangements. Always ask if babysitters are licensed and bonded (ie they are qualified and insured), what they charge per hour per child, whether there's a minimum fee and if they charge extra for transportation or meals. Most tourist bureaus list local resources for childcare and recreation facilities, medical services and so on.

Necessities, Driving & Flying

Many public toilets have a baby-changing table (sometimes in men's toilets, too), and gender-neutral 'family' facilities appear in airports.

Medical services and facilities in America are of a high standard, and items such as baby food, formula and disposable diapers (nappies) are widely available – including organic options – in supermarkets across the country.

DISCOUNTS FOR CHILDREN

Child concessions often apply for tours, admission fees and transport, with some discounts as high as 50% off the adult rate. However, the definition of 'child' can vary from under 12 to under 16 years. Unlike in Europe, very few popular sights have discount rates for families; those that do will help you save a few dollars compared to buying individual tickets. Most sights give free admission to children under two years.

Every car-rental agency should be able to provide an appropriate child seat, since these are required in every state, but you need to request it when booking and expect to pay $10 to $14 more per day.

Domestic airlines don't charge for children under two years. Those two and up must have a seat, and discounts are unlikely. Rarely, some resorts (eg Disneyland) offer a 'kids fly free' promotion. Amtrak, America's national train service, offers half-price fares for children 12 and under.

Children's Highlights
Outdoor Adventure

All national parks have Junior Ranger programs that include activity booklets and badges upon completion.

➡ **Florida Everglades** (p493) Kayak, canoe or take guided walks.

➡ **Yellowstone National Park, WY** (p794) Watch powerful geysers, spy on wildlife and take magnificent hikes.

➡ **Grand Canyon National Park, AZ** (p854) Gaze across – or descend into – one of earth's great wonders.

➡ **Black Hills, South Dakota and Wyoming** (p675) State and national parks – such as Mt Rushmore – are filled with kid-friendly natural sights and adventures, and the buffalo do indeed roam free.

➡ **New River Gorge National River, WV** (p344) Go white-water rafting.

➡ **Zion National Park, UT** (p889) Wade in the Virgin River and hike to the Emerald Pools beneath the crimson canyon walls.

Theme Parks & Zoos

➡ **Bronx Zoo, NY** (p105) One of the nation's biggest and best zoos is just a subway ride from Manhattan.

➡ **Walt Disney World® Resort, FL** (p521) With four action-packed parks spread across 27,000 acres, this is a place your children will long remember.

➡ **Disneyland, CA** (p943) Kids aged four and up appreciate the original Disneyland, while teenagers go nuts next door at California Adventure.

➡ **San Diego Zoo Safari Park, CA** (p949) A fantastic place to see creatures great and small, with more than 6500 animals spread over 1900 acres.

➡ **Six Flags** (www.sixflags.com) One of America's favorite amusement parks, with 11 locations across the country.

➡ **Cedar Point, OH** (p574) Has some of the planet's most terrifying roller coasters, plus a mile-long beachfront, a water park and live entertainment.

Traveling in Time

➡ **Plimoth Plantation, MA** (☎508-746-1622; www.plimoth.org; 137 Warren Ave, Plymouth; adult/child $28/16; ⊙9am-5pm Apr-Nov; ⭐) Don 18th-century garb and mingle with costumed interpreters in this history-rich setting.

➡ **Fort Mackinac, MI** (p599) Plug your ears as soldiers in 19th-century garb fire muskets and cannons.

➡ **Freedom Trail, Boston, MA** (p199) Go on a walking tour with Ben Franklin (or at least his 21st-century lookalike).

➡ **Lincoln Presidential Library & Museum, Springfield, IL** (p559) Fun, interactive galleries where you can learn about one of America's greatest presidents.

➡ **St Augustine, FL** (p506) Rattle along in a horse-drawn carriage through the historic streets.

Rainy-Day Activities

➡ **National Air and Space Museum, Washington, DC** (p270) Rockets, spacecraft, old-fashioned biplanes and ride simulators to inspire any budding aviator.

➡ **American Museum of Natural History, NYC** (p97) Kids of all ages will enjoy a massive planetarium, immense dinosaur skeletons and 30 million other artifacts.

➡ **City Museum, St Louis, MO** (p645) There's a packed fun house of unusual exhibits here, plus a Ferris wheel on the roof.

➡ **Port Discovery, Baltimore, MD** (p301) Three stories of adventure and (cleverly disguised) learning, including an Egyptian tomb, farmers market, train, art studio and physics stations.

➡ **Pacific Science Center, Seattle, WA** (p1042) Fascinating, hands-on exhibits, plus an IMAX theater, planetarium and laser shows.

➡ **Children's Museum of Indianapolis, IN** (p562) The world's largest kids' museum, with five floors of fun stuff (including dinosaur displays).

➡ **Strawbery Banke Museum, Portsmouth, NH** (p249) Role-play New England history from Colonial times through the 1940s at the interactive Family Discovery Center.

Planning

Weather and crowds are all-important considerations when planning a US family getaway. The peak travel season across the country is from June to August, when schools are out and the weather is warmest. Expect high prices and abundant crowds, meaning long lines at amusement and water parks, fully booked resort areas and heavy traffic on the roads – you'll need to reserve well in advance for popular destinations. The same holds true for winter resorts (in the Rockies, Tahoe and the Catskills) during their high season of late December to March.

For all-round information and advice, check out Lonely Planet's *Travel with Children*. To get the kids excited, check out *Not for Parents: USA* (also by Lonely Planet).

Useful Websites

Baby's Away (www.babysaway.com) Rents cribs, high chairs, car seats, strollers and even toys at locations across the country.

Family Travel Files (www.thefamilytravelfiles. com) Ready-made vacation ideas, destination profiles and travel tips.

Kids.gov (www.kids.usa.gov) Eclectic, enormous national resource. Download songs and activities, or even link to the CIA Kids' Page.

Travel BaBees (www.travelbabees.com) A reputable baby-gear rental outfit, with locations nationwide.

Regions at a Glance

The USA's crazy quilt of cultures and landscapes creates an enthralling variety of regional identities. Embrace the urban excitement of New York, Chicago, New Orleans or San Francisco; the trendsetting buzz of Austin or Portland; the Southern charm of Charleston; or the picturesque village life of New England. Set your sights on Hawaii's volcanoes, Alaska's glaciated grandeur, the Great Plains' wide-open spaces, the Southwest's red-rock majesty or the Northwest's dazzling greenery. Surf California's legendary beaches, scale the Rockies' soaring peaks or canoe the Great Lakes' birch-lined shores.

Each region offers its own iconic experiences: Maine lobster; Texas barbecue; Memphis blues; California wine. Whichever speaks to you, dive on in; and if you can't manage the multimonth 'Great American Road Trip', don't despair. Explore a region or two now – and save the rest for next time!

New York, New Jersey & Pennsylvania

Arts
History
Outdoors

Culture Spot

Home to the Met, the Museum of Modern Art and Broadway – and that's just NYC. Buffalo, Philadelphia and Pittsburgh also have a share of world-renowned cultural institutions.

A Living Past

From preserved mansions in the Hudson Valley to Independence National Historic Park in Philadelphia and sites dedicated to formative moments in the nation's founding, the region gives an interactive education.

Wild Outdoors

The outdoors lurks beyond the city's gaze, with hiking in the Adirondacks and Catskills, rafting down the Delaware River, sailing in the Atlantic Ocean, and frolics along the Jersey Shore and Hamptons.

p74

New England

Seafood
History
Scenery

Land of Lobsters

New England is justifiably famous for its fresh seafood. The coast is peppered with seaside eateries where you can feast on oysters, lobster and clam chowder as you watch the day-boats haul in their catch.

Legends of the Past

From the Pilgrims landing in Plymouth and the witch hysteria in Salem to Paul Revere's revolutionary ride, New England has shaped American history.

Fall Foliage

The brilliance of fall in these parts is legendary. Changing leaves put on a fiery display all around New England, from the Litchfield Hills in Connecticut all the way up to the White Mountains in New Hampshire and Maine.

p184

Washington, DC & the Capital Region

Arts
History
Food

Top-Notch Arts

Washington has a superb collection of museums and galleries. You'll also find down-home mountain music on Virginia's Crooked Road, famous theaters, and edgy art in Baltimore.

Early America

For historical lore, Jamestown, Williamsburg and Yorktown offer windows into Colonial America, while Civil War battlefields litter the Virginia countryside. There are fascinating presidential estates such as Mount Vernon and Monticello.

Culinary Feasts

Maryland blue crabs, oysters and seafood platters; international restaurants in DC; and farm-to-table dining in Baltimore, Charlottesville, Staunton and Rehoboth.

p266

The South

Food
Music
Charm

Southern Cookin'

From Memphis BBQ to Mississippi soul food to the Cajun-Creole smorgasbord in Louisiana, the South is a diverse and magnificent place to eat.

Country, Jazz & Blues

Nowhere on earth has a soundtrack as influential as the South. Head to music meccas for the authentic experience: Nashville for country, Memphis for blues and New Orleans for big-band jazz.

Southern Belles

Picture-book towns such as Charleston and Savannah, among others, have captivated visitors with their historic tree-lined streets, antebellum architecture and down-home welcome.

p346

Florida

Fun
Wildlife
Beaches

Good Times

Florida has a complicated soul: it's the home of Miami's art-deco district and Little Havana, plus historical attractions in St Augustine, theme parks in Orlando, and museums and island heritage in Key West.

Whales, Birds & Gators

Immerse yourself in aquatic life on a snorkeling or diving trip. For bigger beasts, head off on a whale-watching cruise, or spy alligators – along with egrets, eagles, manatees and other wildlife – in the Everglades.

Stretches of Sand

You'll find an array of sandy shores, from panhandle rowdiness in Pensacola to steamy South Beach, upscale Palm Beach, and seashell-lined Sanibel and Captiva.

p468

Great Lakes

Food
Music
Attractions

Heartland Cuisine

Farms, orchards and breweries satisfy the palate, from James Beard Award–winning restaurants in Chicago and Minneapolis to fresh-from-the-dairy milkshakes.

Rock & Roll

Home to the Rock and Roll Hall of Fame, blowout fests like Lollapalooza and thrashing clubs in all the cities, the Great Lakes rock, baby.

Quirky Sights

A big ball of twine, a mustard museum, a cow-doo throwing contest: the quirks rise from the backyards and back roads, wherever there are folks with a passion, imagination and maybe a little too much time on their hands.

p528

Great Plains

Scenery
Geology
Nightlife

The Open Road

Beneath big open skies, a two-lane highway passes sun-lit fields, rolling river valleys and dramatic peaks on its journey to the horizon – all par for the course (along with oddball museums and cozy cafes) on the 'Great American Road Trip'.

Nature Unbound

The Badlands are b-a-a-a-d in every good sense. These geologic wonders are matched by the wildlife-filled beauty of the Black Hills and Theodore Roosevelt National Park.

Big-City Soundtrack

Out in the wilds, streets roll up at sunset, but in St Louis and Kansas City, that's when the fun begins. Legendary jazz, blues and rock are played in clubs and bars, big and small.

p641

Texas

Food
Live Music
Outdoors

BBQ Delight

Meat lovers, you've died and gone to heaven (vegetarians, you're somewhere else). Some of the best barbecue on earth is served up in Lockhart near Austin, although you can dig in to brisket, ribs and sausage all across the state.

Tap to the Beat

Austin has proclaimed itself (and no one's arguing) the 'Live Music Capital of the World.' Two-step to live bands on worn wooden floors at honky-tonks and dance halls all around the state.

Big-Sky Scenery

Canyons, mountains and hot springs set the scene for memorable outings in Texas. Go rafting on the Big Bend River or get a beach fix along the pretty southern Gulf Coast.

p697

Rocky Mountains

Outdoors
Culture
Landscapes

Mountain High

Skiing, hiking and boating make the Rockies a playground for adrenaline junkies, with hundreds of races and group rides, and an incredible infrastructure of parks, trails and cabins.

Old Meets New

Once a people of Stetsons and prairie dresses, today's Rocky folk are more often spotted in lycra, mountain bike nearby, sipping a microbrew or latte at a cafe. Hard playing and slow living still rule.

Perfect Views

The snow-covered Rocky Mountains are pure majesty. With chiseled peaks, clear rivers and red-rock contours, the Rockies contain some of the world's most famous parks and bucketloads of clean mountain air.

p750

Southwest

Scenery
Outdoors
Cultures

Natural Beauty

Home to spectacular national parks, the Southwest is famous for the jaw-dropping Grand Canyon, the dramatic red buttes of Monument Valley and the vast Carlsbad Caverns.

Hiking & Skiing

Ski powdery slopes at Park City, splash and frolic in Slide Rock State Park, skitter down dunes at White Sands, and hike to your heart's content at Bryce, Zion and countless other spots.

Indigenous Peoples

This is Native American country, and visiting the Hopi and Navajo Nations provides a fine introduction to America's first peoples. For a journey back in time, explore cliffside dwellings abandoned by ancient Puebloans.

p818

California

Beaches
Adventure
Food

Sunny Shores

With more than 1100 miles of coast, California rules the sands: rugged, pristine beaches in the north and people-packed beauties in the south, with great surfing, sea kayaking and beach walking all along the coast.

Outdoor Activities

Snow-covered mountains, glittering sea and old-growth forests set the stage for skiing, hiking, biking, wave frolicking, wildlife-watching and more.

California Cooking

Fertile fields, talented chefs and an insatiable appetite for the new make California a major culinary destination. Browse food markets, sample the produce at lush vineyards and eat well in many celebrated dining rooms.

p915

Pacific Northwest

Food & Wine
Outdoors
National Parks

Culinary Bounty

Portland and Seattle have celebrated food scenes, with wild-caught fish, superb wines and locally sourced vegetables among the Northwest bounty.

Powdery Allure

Year-round ski areas, rustic cross-country and snowboarding heaven at Mt Baker: the region with the highest snowfalls in North America delivers unparalleled winter sports. Cross-country skiing in the Methow Valley is world renowned.

Vast Nature

The northwest has four national parks: three Teddy Roosevelt–era classics (Olympic, Mt Rainier and Crater Lake), each bequeathed with historic lodges; and a wilder addition, the North Cascades.

p1031

Alaska

Wildlife
Glaciers
Outdoors

Creatures Great & Small

Alaska offers some fantastic wildlife viewing. The sight of breaching whales and foraging bears in Southeast Alaska is unforgettable. Denali National Park is home to caribou, Dall sheep, moose and Alaska's famous grizzly.

Cinematic Landscapes

If you want to explore glaciers in the USA, Alaska is the place. Glacier Bay National Park is the crown jewel for the cruise ships and a favorite for kayakers.

Hiking

Alaska offers some of the rawest hiking experiences in North America, from following in the footsteps of Klondike stampeders on the Chilkoot Trail, to bushwhacking your way across pathless tundra in Denali National Park.

p1089

Hawaii

Beaches
Adventure
Scenery

Tropical Shores

There's great sunning and people-watching on Waikiki (among dozens of other spots); stunning black-sand beaches on the Kona Coast and world-class surfing all over Hawaii.

Outdoor Highs

You can trek through rainforest, kayak the Na Pali Coast, go ziplining on the four biggest islands and see eye-to-eye with aquatic life in marvelous Hanauma Bay.

Unrivaled Landscapes

Hawaii has its head-turners, and we're not just talking people: volcanoes, ancient rainforests, picturesque waterfalls, cliff-top vistas and jungle-lined valleys – not to mention the sparkling seas surrounding the islands.

p1108

On the Road

WA

Pacific Northwest p1031

OR

Rocky Mountains p750

ID

MT

ND

MN

WI

MI

ME

New England p184

New York, New Jersey & Pennsylvania p74

VT NH MA

NY CT RI

PA NJ

Great Lakes p528 OH

MD DE

WV **Washington, DC & the Capital Region** p266

VA

CA

NV

UT

CO

WY

SD

NE

IA

IL IN

Great Plains p641

KS

MO

KY

California p915

Southwest p818

AZ

NM

OK

AR

TN

The South p346

SC

NC

MS AL GA

Texas p697

LA

TX

Florida p468 FL

Alaska p1089

AK

Hawaii p1108 HI

New York, New Jersey & Pennsylvania

Includes ➜

New York City 75
Long Island 141
Hudson Valley 145
Catskills 149
Finger Lakes................152
The Adirondacks.........154
New Jersey..................162
Princeton 162
Jersey Shore...............163
Pennsylvania.............. 168
Philadelphia................169
Pittsburgh..................180

Why Go?

Where else could you visit an Amish family's farm, camp on a mountaintop, read the Declaration of Independence and view New York, New York from the 86th floor of an art-deco landmark – all in a few days? Even though this corner of the country is the most densely populated part of the USA, it's full of places where jaded city dwellers escape to seek simple lives, where artists retreat for inspiration, and where pretty houses line main streets in small towns set amid stunning scenery.

Urban adventures in NYC, historic and lively Philadelphia and river-rich Pittsburgh are a must. Miles and miles of glorious beaches are within reach, from glamorous Long Island to the Jersey Shore – the latter ranges from stately to kitsch, while the mountain wilderness of the Adirondacks reaches skyward just a day's drive north of NYC, a journey that perfectly encapsulates this region's heady character.

Best Places to Eat

➡ Totto Ramen (p118)

➡ Smorgasburg (p121)

➡ Morimoto (p176)

➡ Lobster House (p168)

➡ Bar Marco (p182)

Best Places to Sleep

➡ Yotel (p111)

➡ Scribner's Catskill Lodge (p150)

➡ White Pine Camp (p156)

➡ Priory Hotel (p182)

➡ Asbury Hotel (p164)

When to Go

New York City

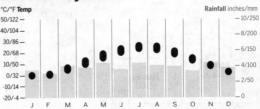

Feb Winter-sports buffs head to the mountains of the Adirondacks, Catskills and Poconos.

31 May–5 Sep Memorial Day through Labor Day is for beaches from Montauk to Cape May.

Oct–Nov Fall in NYC brings cool temps, festivals, the marathon and gearing up for holiday season.

NEW YORK CITY

Epicenter of the arts. Dining and shopping capital. Trendsetter. New York City wears many crowns, and spreads an irresistible feast for all.

With its compact size and streets packed with eye-candy of all sorts – architectural treasures, Old World cafés, atmospheric booksellers and curio shops – NYC is an urban wanderer's delight. Crossing continents is as easy as walking over a few avenues in this jumbled city of 200-plus nationalities. You can lose yourself in the crowds of Chinatown amid brightly painted Buddhist temples, steaming noodle shops and fragrant fishmongers, then stroll up to Nolita for enticing boutiques and coffee-tasting among the craft-minded scenesters. Every neighborhood offers a dramatically different version of New York City – from the 100-year-old Jewish delis of the Upper West Side to the meandering cobblestone lanes of Greenwich Village. And the best way to experience this city is to walk its streets.

Sights

Financial District & Lower Manhattan

Gleaming with bold, architectural icons, eateries and a booming residential population, Manhattan's southern tip is no longer strictly business. It's in the Financial District (FiDi) that you'll find the National September 11 Memorial and Museum, One World Observatory and Wall Street, and seminal historic sites like Fraunces Tavern Museum, Federal Hall and, just offshore, Ellis Island and Lady Liberty herself. City Hall, the mayor's official seat of power, is a central landmark. North of FiDi are the warehouse conversions of Tribeca, a prosperous grown-up place where vibrant restaurants and bars schmooze with high-end galleries and idiosyncratic retail.

★Brooklyn Bridge BRIDGE

(Map p80; [S] 4/5/6 to Brooklyn Bridge-City Hall; J/Z to Chambers St; R/W to City Hall) A New York icon, the Brooklyn Bridge, which connects Brooklyn and Manhattan, was the world's first steel suspension bridge. Indeed, when it opened in 1883, the 1596ft span between its two support towers was the longest in history. Although its construction was fraught with disaster, the bridge became a magnificent example of urban design, inspiring poets, writers and painters. Its pedestrian walkway delivers soul-stirring views of lower Manhattan, the East River and the rapidly developing Brooklyn waterfront.

★National September 11 Memorial MONUMENT

(Map p80; www.911memorial.org; 180 Greenwich St; 🕐7:30am-9pm; [S] E to World Trade Center; R/W to Cortlandt St; 2/3 to Park Pl) [FREE] The focal point of the National September 11 Memorial is **Reflecting Absence**, two imposing reflecting pools that occupy the very footprints of the ill-fated twin towers. From their rim, a steady cascade of water pours 30ft down toward a central void. Bronze panels frame the pools, inscribed with the names of those who died in the terrorist attacks of September 11, 2001, and in the World Trade Center car bombing on February 26, 1993.

Just beyond the memorial is the site's **museum** (adult/child $24/15, 5-8pm Tue free; 🕐9am-8pm Sun-Thu, to 9pm Fri & Sat, last entry 2hr before close). Poignant and deeply affecting, it tells the story of that tragic day and its impact on America and the world.

★One World Observatory VIEWPOINT

(Map p80; ☎844-696-1776; www.oneworldobservatory.com; cnr West & Vesey Sts; adult/child $34/28; 🕐9am-8pm, last ticket sold at 7:15pm; [S] E to World Trade Center; 2/3 to Park Pl; A/C, J/Z, 4/5 to Fulton St; R/W to Cortlandt St) Spanning levels 100 to 102 of the tallest building in the Western Hemisphere, One World Observatory offers dazzling panoramic views from its sky-high perch. On a clear day you'll be able to see all five boroughs and some surrounding states. Not surprisingly, it's a hugely popular attraction. Purchase tickets online in advance.

National Museum of the American Indian MUSEUM

(Map p80; ☎212-514-3700; www.nmai.si.edu; 1 Bowling Green; 🕐10am-5pm Fri-Wed, to 8pm Thu; [S] 4/5 to Bowling Green; R/W to Whitehall St) [FREE] An affiliate of the Smithsonian Institution, this elegant tribute to Native American culture is set in Cass Gilbert's spectacular 1907 **Custom House**, one of NYC's finest beaux-arts buildings. Beyond a vast elliptical rotunda, sleek galleries play host to changing exhibitions documenting Native American art, culture, life and beliefs. The museum's permanent collection includes stunning decorative arts, textiles and ceremonial objects that document the diverse native cultures across the Americas.

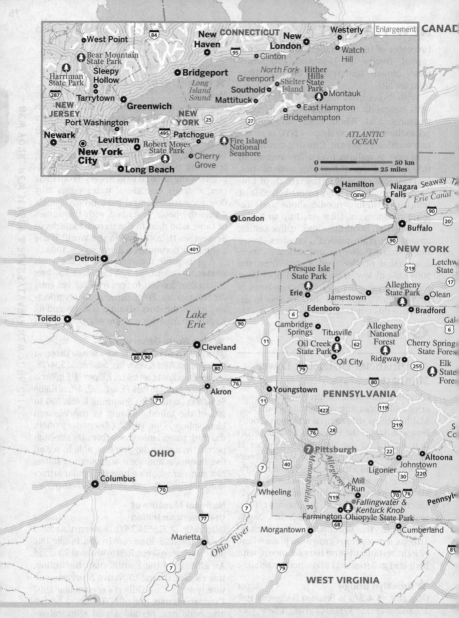

New York, New Jersey & Pennsylvania Highlights

1 **New York City** (p75)
Traveling around the world
without ever leaving the
city, with its kaleidoscope of
neighborhoods and cultures.

2 **Jersey Shore** (p163)

Enjoying the kitsch, kettle
corn, coastline and calm.

3 **Independence National
Historic Park** (p169) Walking
in the footsteps of the founding
fathers in Philadelphia.

4 **Catskills** (p149) Hiking
the densely forested paths.

5 **Adirondacks** (p154)
Paddling a canoe in the
shadow of majestic mountains.

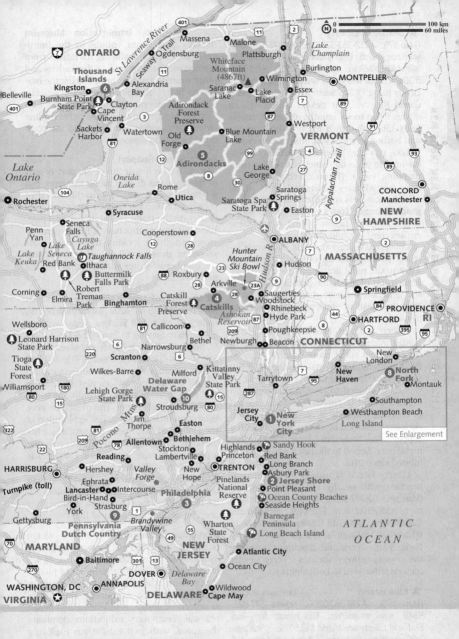

6 **Thousand Islands** (p157)
Camping along the shores of
the St Lawrence River.

7 **Pittsburgh** (p180)
Admiring great modern art
and old industry.

8 **North Fork** (p144)
Tippling the whites and reds of
Long Island.

9 **Pennsylvania Dutch
Country** (p178) Touring the
back roads.

10 **Delaware Water Gap**
(p165) Floating gently past
bucolic scenery (or white-water
rafting after a wet spring).

★Statue of Liberty MONUMENT

(Map p79; ☎212-363-3200, tickets 877-523-9849; www.nps.gov/stli; Liberty Island; adult/child incl Ellis Island $18.50/9, incl crown $21.50/12; ⏲8:30am-5:30pm, check website for seasonal changes; ⛴to Liberty Island, [S]1 to South Ferry; 4/5 to Bowling Green) Reserve your tickets online well in advance (up to six months ahead) to access Lady Liberty's crown for breathtaking city and harbor views. If you miss out on crown tickets, you may have better luck with tickets for the pedestal, which also offers commanding views. If you don't score either, don't fret: all ferry tickets to Liberty Island offer basic access to the grounds, including **guided ranger tours** or self-guided audio tours. Book all tickets online (www.statuecruises.com) to avoid long queues.

Conceived as early as 1865 by French intellectual Edouard Laboulaye as a monument to the republican principles shared by France and the USA, the Statue of Liberty is still generally recognized as a symbol for at least the ideals of opportunity and freedom to many.

French sculptor Frédéric-Auguste Bartholdi traveled to New York in 1871 to select the site, then spent more than 10 years in Paris designing and making the 151ft-tall figure *Liberty Enlightening the World*. It was then shipped to New York, erected on a small island in the harbor and unveiled in 1886. Structurally, it consists of an iron skeleton (designed by Gustave Eiffel) with a copper skin attached to it by stiff but flexible metal bars. Access to the torch has been prohibited since 1916.

Liberty Island is usually visited in conjunction with nearby Ellis Island. **Ferries** (Map p80; ☎877-523-9849; www.statuecruises.com; adult/child from $18.50/9; ⏲departures 8:30am-4pm; [S]4/5 to Bowling Green; R/W to Whitehall St; 1 to South Ferry) leave from Battery Park; South Ferry and Bowling Green are the closest subway stations. (Ferry tickets include admission to both sights.)

★Ellis Island LANDMARK, MUSEUM

(Map p79; ☎212-363-3200, tickets 877-523-9849; www.nps.gov/elis; Ellis Island; ferry incl Statue of Liberty adult/child $18.50/9; ⏲9:30am-3:30pm; ⛴to Ellis Island, [S]1 to South Ferry; 4/5 to Bowling Green) Ellis Island is America's most famous and historically important gateway. Between 1892 and 1924, over 12 million immigrants passed through this processing station, their dreams in tow. Today, its **Immigration Museum** delivers a poignant tribute to the immigrant experience, featuring narratives from historians, the immigrants themselves and other sources; the tour brings to life the museum's hefty collection of personal objects, official documents, photographs and film footage. Always purchase your tickets online (www.statuecruises.com) to avoid the soul-crushingly long queues.

South Street Seaport AREA

(Map p80) The South Street Seaport is east of the financial district along the river, but a whole world away. This neighborhood of cobblestone and heritage buildings proudly carries on the traditions of its nautical past. Bars and restaurants have a funky, carefree vibe, and those looking to exercise their shopping muscle will be in heaven with the number of stores spread out across the neighborhood.

★Museum of Jewish Heritage MUSEUM

(Map p80; ☎646-437-4202; www.mjhnyc.org; 36 Battery Pl; adult/child $12/free, 4-8pm Wed free; ⏲10am-6pm Sun-Tue, to 8pm Wed & Thu, to 5pm Fri mid-Mar–mid-Nov, to 3pm Fri rest of year, closed Sat; 👪; [S]4/5 to Bowling Green; R/W to Whitehall St) An evocative waterfront museum exploring all aspects of modern Jewish identity and culture, from religious traditions to artistic accomplishments. The museum's core exhibition includes a detailed exploration of the Holocaust, with personal artifacts, photographs and documentary films providing a personal, moving experience. Outdoors is the **Garden of Stones** installation. Created by artist Andy Goldsworthy and dedicated to those who lost loved ones in the Holocaust, its 18 boulders form a narrow pathway for contemplating the fragility of life.

Skyscraper Museum MUSEUM

(Map p80; ☎212-968-1961; www.skyscraper.org; 39 Battery Pl; $5; ⏲noon-6pm Wed-Sun; [S]4/5 to Bowling Green; R to Whitehall) Fans of phallic architecture will appreciate this compact, high-gloss gallery, examining skyscrapers as objects of design, engineering and urban renewal. Temporary exhibitions dominate the space, with past exhibitions exploring everything from New York's new generation of super-slim residential towers to the world's new breed of supertalls. Permanent fixtures include information on the design and construction of the Empire State Building and World Trade Center.

New York City

N

0 ——— 10 km
0 ——— 5 miles

BRONXVILLE
Cross County Pkwy
Boston Rd

ENGLEWOOD

HACKENSACK

Hudson River

Broadway

Woodlawn Cemetery

New York Botanical Garden

Pelham Bay Park

Hart Island

Long Island Sound

Overpeck County Park

Cloisters Museum & Gardens

INWOOD

BAYCHESTER

Bronx Zoo

Pelham Bay Park

City Island

FAIRVIEW

HARLEM

BELMONT

Bronx Park

THROGS NECK

KEARNY

New Jersey Turnpike

Yankee Stadium

GREAT NECK

HUNTS POINT

Powells Cove

Fort Totten

MANHATTAN

Central Park

See Central Park & Uptown Map (p94)

The Kaufman Arts District

ASTORIA

Museum of the Moving Image

LaGuardia Airport

FLUSHING

BAYSIDE

See Times Square, Midtown Manhattan & Chelsea Map (p88)

JACKSON HEIGHTS

Unisphere

HOBOKEN

See East & West Villages Map (p84)

Queens Blvd

New York Hall of Science

Queens Museum

MoMA PS1

See Chinatown & Lower Manhattan Map (p80)

GREENPOINT

Brooklyn Brewery

QUEENS

HOLLISWOOD

JERSEY CITY

WILLIAMSBURG

GLENDALE

Ellis Island

Statue of Liberty

Governors Island

CLINTON HILL

Greater Ridgewood Historic Society

BUSHWICK

JAMAICA

New York Transit Museum

Atlantic Ave

Brooklyn Botanic Garden

Brooklyn Children's Museum

Brooklyn Museum

Ferry to Staten Island

Prospect Park

Linden Blvd

HOWARD BEACH

John F Kennedy International Airport

Green-Wood Cemetery

BAY RIDGE

BROOKLYN

Spring Creek Park

Elders Point Marsh

East High Meadow

Jo Co Marsh

Staten Island

Lower New York Bay

Bensonhurst Park

Ave P

Brooklyn Marine Park

Gateway National Recreation Area

Big Channel

RICHMOND

CONEY ISLAND

New York Aquarium

Coney Island

Rockaway Inlet

Jacob Riis Park

Rockaway Beach

NEW YORK
NEW JERSEY

ATLANTIC OCEAN

Chinatown & Lower Manhattan

NEW YORK, NEW JERSEY & PENNSYLVANIA NEW YORK CITY

SOHO

LITTLE ITALY

Canal St
Canal St
Canal St
Canal St
Howard St
Canal St

Vestry St
Laight St
Sixth Ave (Avenue of the Americas)
Varick St
Church St
Cortlandt Al
Centre St

See East & West Villages Map (p84)
Walker St
White St
Bayard St

Hubert St
Beach St
Franklin St
Franklin St
Leonard St
Leonard St

CHINATOWN
Columbus Park
Mosco St

15
Hudson River Park
28
22
29
N Moore St
Franklin St
Broadway

West Side Hwy
Greenwich St
Hudson St
Duane St
Harrison St

Washington Market Community Park
Reade St
Worth St
Thomas St
Duane St
30
TRIBECA
Federal Plaza
Thomas Paine Park

Pearl St
Foley Square

Nelson A Rockefeller Park
Chambers St
Chambers St
Chambers St
Municipal Building
Chambers St/ Brooklyn Bridge- City Hall

Warren St
Murray St
W Broadway
City Hall
City Hall Park
Elk St
Pearl St

LOWER MANHATTAN
Murray St
Park Pl
Park Place
Police Plaza

River Tce
Barclay St
NYC Information Center
Beekman St

Riverside
Murray St
Vesey St
One World Observatory
Chambers St-WTC
Vesey St
Ann St
Gold St
Cliff St
Guilbert Park
Pearl St

North End Ave
World Financial Center
7
World Trade Center Transportation Hub
Fulton St
Fulton St

19
5
6
Memorial Plaza
John St
Maiden La
Fletcher St

North Cove
National September 11 Memorial
Cortlandt St
Cortlandt St
10
Liberty St
William St
Pine St
Water St

BATTERY PARK CITY
National September 11 Memorial Museum
Thames St
New York Stock Exchange
Pine St

Hudson River
West Side Hwy
Carlisle St
Wall St
Wall St
Wall St

Washington St
Rector St
Broadway
Broad St
FINANCIAL DISTRICT
Pearl St

Battery Park City Esplanade
W Thames St
New St
Beaver St
17
Old Slip

Franklin D Roosevelt Dr
South St

Ferry to Hoboken (NJ)
Battery Pl
2nd Pl
Bowling Green
12
Whitehall St
26
Vietnam Veterans Plaza
Pier 6

Museum of Jewish Heritage
4
13
Robert F Wagner Jr Park
Battery Park
Pearl St
Whitehall St
Broad St
State St

Pier A
9
8
State St
Peter Minuit Plaza

Ferry to Statue of Liberty & Ellis Island
South St Viaduct
South Ferry
16

Ferry to Ellis Island
Ferry to Statue of Liberty
Upper New York Bay
Hugh L Carey Tunnel
Ferry to Staten Island
Ferry to Governors Island

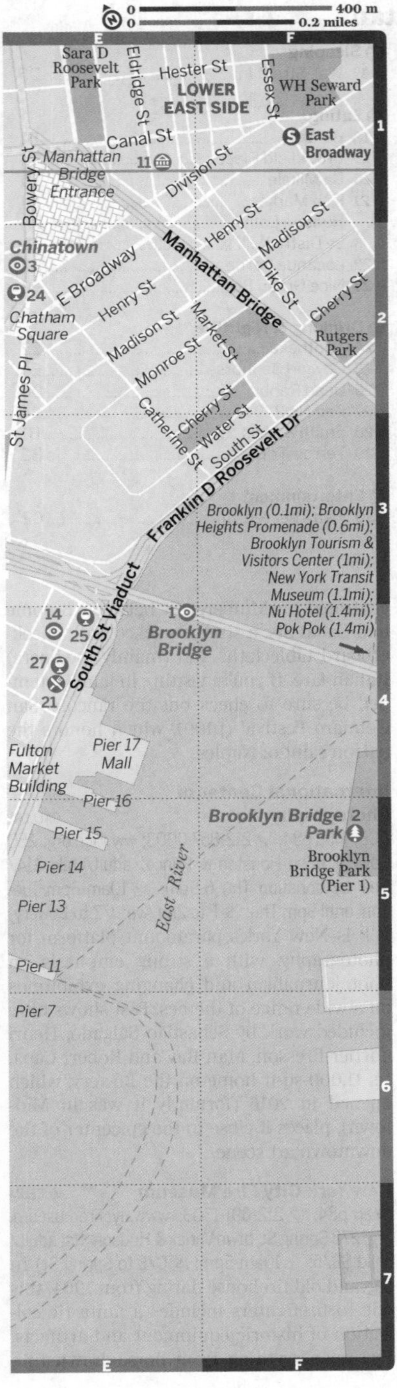

Battery Park PARK

(Map p80; www.nycgovparks.org; Broadway, at Battery Pl; ⏲sunrise-1am; [S]4/5 to Bowling Green; R to Whitehall St; 1 to South Ferry) Skirting the southern edge of Manhattan, this 12-acre oasis lures with public artworks, meandering walkways and perennial gardens. Its memorials include a Holocaust Memorial and the Irish Hunger Memorial. It was on this very part of the island that the Dutch settled in 1623. And it was right here that the first 'battery' of cannons was erected to defend the fledgling settlement of New Amsterdam. You'll also find historic **Castle Clinton** (Map p80; ☎212-344-7220; www.nps.gov/cacl/index.htm; ⏲7:45am-5pm) and the ferry service to Ellis Island and the Statue of Liberty.

New York Stock Exchange NOTABLE BUILDING

(Map p80; www.nyse.com; 11 Wall St; ⏲closed to the public; [S]J/Z to Broad St; 2/3, 4/5 to Wall St) Home to the world's best-known stock exchange (the NYSE), Wall Street is an iconic symbol of US capitalism. Behind the portentous Romanesque facade, about one billion shares change hands daily, a sight no longer accessible to the public due to security concerns. Feel free to gawk outside the building, protected by barricades and the hawk-eyed NYPD (New York Police Department).

Federal Reserve Bank of New York NOTABLE BUILDING

(Map p80; ☎212-720-6130; www.newyorkfed.org; 33 Liberty St, at Nassau St, entrance at 44 Maiden Lane; reservation required; ⏲guided tours 1pm & 2pm Mon-Fri; [S]A/C, J/Z, 2/3, 4/5 to Fulton St) [FREE] The best reason to visit the Federal Reserve Bank is the chance to (briefly) ogle at its high-security vault – more than 10,000 tons of gold reserves reside here, 80ft below ground. You'll only see a small part of that fortune, but signing on to a free tour (the only way down; book several months ahead) is worth the effort.

SoHo & Chinatown

SoHo (South of Houston), NoHo (North of Houston) and Nolita (North of Little Italy) represent three of Manhattan's trendiest neighborhoods, known for their intimidatingly hip boutiques, bars and eateries. Meanwhile, to the south, expanding and bustling Chinatown and a nostalgic sliver of Little Italy lure with idiosyncratic street life. Canal St, running from the Manhattan

Chinatown & Lower Manhattan

Top Sights
1 Brooklyn Bridge ... E4
2 Brooklyn Bridge Park ... F5
3 Chinatown ... E2
4 Museum of Jewish Heritage ... B6
5 National September 11 Memorial ... B4
6 National September 11 Memorial Museum ... B4
7 One World Observatory ... B4

Sights
8 Battery Park ... C6
9 Castle Clinton ... C6
10 Federal Reserve Bank of New York ... C4
11 Museum at Eldridge Street Synagogue ... E1
12 National Museum of the American Indian ... C6
13 Skyscraper Museum ... B6
14 South Street Seaport ... E4

Activities, Courses & Tours
15 Downtown Boathouse ... A2
16 Staten Island Ferry ... D7

Sleeping
17 Wall Street Inn ... D5

Eating
18 Bâtard ... B1
19 Brookfield Place ... B4
20 Da Mikele ... C1
21 Fish Market ... E4
Hudson Eats ... (see 19)
Le District ... (see 19)
22 Locanda Verde ... B2
23 Nice Green Bo ... D1

Drinking & Nightlife
24 Apothéke ... E2
25 Cowgirl Seahorse ... E4
26 Dead Rabbit ... D6
27 Keg No 229 ... E4
28 Smith & Mills ... B1
29 Terroir Tribeca ... B2

Entertainment
30 Flea Theater ... C2

Bridge to the West Side Hwy, and one of the most traffic-clogged arteries in the city, is a world in itself. Taken together, these neighborhoods serve up a delicious, contradictory jumble of cast-iron architecture, strutting fashionistas, sacred temples and hook-hung ducks and salami.

★Chinatown AREA

(Map p80; www.explorechinatown.com; south of Broome St & east of Broadway; [S] N/Q/R/W, J/Z, 6 to Canal St; B/D to Grand St; F to East Broadway) A walk through Manhattan's most colorful, cramped neighborhood is never the same, no matter how many times you hit the pavement. Catch the whiff of fresh fish and ripe persimmons, hear the clacking of mah-jongg tiles on makeshift tables, eye up dangling duck roasts swinging in store windows and shop for anything from rice-paper lanterns and 'faux-lex' watches to tire irons and a pound of pressed nutmeg. America's largest congregation of Chinese immigrants is your oyster – dipped in soy sauce, of course.

★Little Italy AREA

(Map p84; [S] N/Q/R/W, J/Z, 6 to Canal St; B/D to Grand St) This once-strong Italian neighborhood (film director Martin Scorsese grew up on Elizabeth St) saw an exodus in the mid-20th century when many of its residents moved to more suburban neighborhoods in Brooklyn and beyond. Today it's mostly concentrated on Mulberry St between Broome and Canal Sts, a stretch packed with checkerboard tablecloths and (mainly mediocre) Italian fare. If you're visiting in late September, be sure to check out the raucous San Gennaro Festival (p109), which honors the patron saint of Naples.

International Center of Photography GALLERY

(ICP; Map p84; ☎212-857-0003; www.icp.org; 250 Bowery, btwn Houston & Prince; adult/child $14/free, by donation Thu 6-9pm; 🕐10am-6pm Tue-Sun, until 9pm Thu; [S] F to 2nd Ave; J/Z to Bowery) ICP is New York's paramount platform for photography, with a strong emphasis on photojournalism and changing exhibitions on a wide range of themes. Past shows have included work by Sebastião Salgado, Henri Cartier-Bresson, Man Ray and Robert Capa. Its 11,000-sq-ft home on the Bowery, which opened in 2016 (formerly it was in Midtown), places it close to the epicenter of the downtown art scene.

New York City Fire Museum MUSEUM

(Map p84; ☎212-691-1303; www.nycfiremuseum.org; 278 Spring St, btwn Varick & Hudson Sts; adult/child $8/5; 🕐10am-5pm; [S] C/E to Spring St) In a grand old firehouse dating from 1904, this ode to firefighters includes a fantastic collection of historic equipment and artifacts. Eye up everything from horse-drawn firefighting carriages and early stovepipe firefighter hats, to Chief, a four-legged fire-fighting hero from Brooklyn. Exhibits trace the development of the NYC firefighting system, and the museum's heavy equipment and friendly staff make this a great spot for kids. The New York Fire Department (FDNY) lost half of its members in the collapse of the World Trade Center on September 11, 2001, and memorials and exhibits have become a permanent part of the collection. Fans can stock up on books about firefighting history and official FDNY clothing and patches in the gift shop.

Museum of Chinese in America   MUSEUM
(Map p84; ☑ 212-619-4785; www.mocanyc.org; 215 Centre St, btwn Grand & Howard Sts; adult/child $10/5, first Thu of month free; ☺11am-6pm Tue, Wed & Fri-Sun, to 9pm Thu; ⓢ N/Q/R/W, J/Z, 6 to Canal St) In this space designed by architect Maya Lin (designer of the famed Vietnam Memorial in Washington, DC) is a multifaceted museum whose engaging permanent and temporary exhibitions shed light on Chinese American life, both past and present. Browse through interactive multimedia exhibits, maps, timelines, photos, letters, films and artifacts. The museum's anchor exhibit, *With a Single Step: Stories in the Making of America,* provides an intimate glimpse into topics that include immigration, cultural identity and racial stereotyping.

⊙ East Village & Lower East Side

Shorthand for this duo's heady mix of old and new: the New Museum and the Tenement Museum. Continually evolving and simultaneously marked by waves of immigrants, the East Village and the Lower East Side are two of the city's hottest 'hoods for cramming into low-lit lounges; clubs for live music and cheap eats luring students, bankers and scruffier types alike. Luxury high-rise condominiums and hip boutique hotels coexist within blocks of tenement style buildings.

★Lower East Side
Tenement Museum   MUSEUM
(Map p84; ☑ 877-975-3786; www.tenement.org; 103 Orchard St, btwn Broome & Delancey Sts; tours adult/student & senior $25/20; ☺10am-6:30pm Fri-Wed, to 8:30pm Thu; ⓢ B/D to Grand St; J/M/Z to Essex St; F to Delancey St) This museum puts the neighborhood's heartbreaking but inspiring heritage on full display in three re-created turn-of-the-20th-century tenement apartments, including the late-19th-century home and garment shop of the Levine family from Poland, and two immigrant dwellings from the Great Depressions of 1873 and 1929. Visits to the tenement building are available only as part of scheduled guided tours, with many departures each day.

NEW YORK, NEW JERSEY & PENNSYLVANIA IN...

One Week
Start off in Philadelphia (p169), birthplace of American independence. Visit Independence Hall (p169) and the new Museum of the American Revolution (p169), then spend an evening investigating the great restaurants and nightlife in up-and-coming neighborhoods such as Fishtown. Next, head to New Jersey for a bucolic night in Cape May (p167), a sleepy beach town full of Victorian charm. After a quick, scenic cruise along Ocean Dr, stop off overnight further up the Shore in Wildwood (p167), a treasure trove of iconic '50s kitsch. Land in New York City (p75) the following day and spend at least a couple of days blending touristy must-dos – such as the Top of the Rock (p92) and Central Park (p96) – with vibrant nightlife and eclectic dining.

Two Weeks
With NYC in your rear-view mirror, head north along the majestic Hudson and its palisades for a night or two in Beacon (p146), before reaching the Catskills (p149). After touring this beautiful region, head further north to the Adirondacks (p154) and its outdoor wonders, then loop back south through the Finger Lakes (p152) region with stops in wineries and waterfall-laden parks along the way. Spend a night in gorgeous college-town Ithaca (p152). From here you can head towards the Canadian border to Buffalo (p158) and Niagara Falls (p160), or southwest to Pittsburgh (p180).

East & West Villages

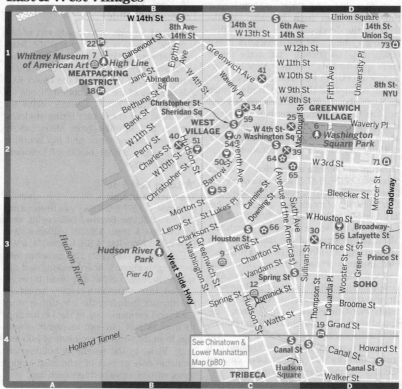

★ **New Museum of
Contemporary Art** MUSEUM
(Map p84; ☎212-219-1222; www.newmuseum.
org; 235 Bowery, btwn Stanton & Rivington Sts;
adult/child $18/free, 7-9pm Thu by donation;
⊙11am-6pm Tue & Wed & Fri-Sun, to 9pm Thu;
Ⓢ R/W to Prince St; F to 2nd Ave; J/Z to Bowery;
6 to Spring St) Rising above the neighborhood, the New Museum of Contemporary
Art is a sight to behold: a seven-story stack
of off-kilter, white, ethereal boxes designed
by Tokyo-based architects Kazuyo Sejima
and Ryue Nishizawa of SANAA and the
New York–based firm Gensler. It was a
long-awaited breath of fresh air along what
was a completely gritty Bowery strip when
it arrived back in 2007 – though since its
opening, many glossy new constructions
have joined it, quickly transforming this
once down-and-out avenue.

Tompkins Square Park PARK
(Map p84; www.nycgovparks.org; E 7th & 10th Sts,
btwn Aves A & B; ⊙6am-midnight; Ⓢ6 to Astor Pl)
This 10.5-acre park is like a friendly town
square for locals, who gather for chess at
concrete tables, for picnics on the lawn on
warm days, and for spontaneous guitar or
drum jams on various grassy knolls. It's also
the site of basketball courts, a fun-to-watch
dog run (a fenced-in area where humans can
unleash their canines), a mini public swimming pool for kids, frequent summer concerts and an always-lively kids' playground.

**Museum at Eldridge
Street Synagogue** MUSEUM
(Map p80; ☎212-219-0302; www.eldridgestreet.
org; 12 Eldridge St, btwn Canal & Division Sts; adult/
child $14/8, Mon suggested donation; ⊙10am-
5pm Sun-Thu, to 3pm Fri; Ⓢ F to East Broadway)
This landmark house of worship, built in
1887, was once a center of Jewish life before

falling into squalor in the 1920s. Left to rot, the synagogue was restored following a 20-year-long, $20-million restoration that was completed in 2007, and it now shines with original splendor. Museum admission includes a **guided tour** of the synagogue, which departs hourly, with the last one starting at 4pm.

Astor Place SQUARE

(Map p84; 8th St, btwn Third & Fourth Aves; [S] N/R to 8th St-NYU; 6 to Astor Pl) Even with the *Alamo*, an iconic piece of public art more often referred to as 'the cube', restored after several years absence, this is not the Astor Place of old. No longer grungy and filled with gutter punks and squatters, this new iteration is also no longer a plaza. It's an orderly block between Broadway and Lafayette surrounded by sleek, glittery buildings and outfitted with well-designed benches and granite blocks good for people-watching.

West Village, Chelsea & Meatpacking District

Mellow and raucous, quaint and sleekly contemporary, this trio of downtown neighborhoods embodies contradictory vibes. The West Village's twisting streets and well-preserved townhouses offer intimate spaces for dining, drinking and being a *flaneur*. Washington Square Park and the surrounding blocks is dominated by New York University's booming student population. The Meatpacking District has evolved over the years into something of a meat market, with trendy nightlife. To the north is Chelsea, home to art galleries and a vibrant gay scene. And the High Line, the city's celebrated elevated park, ties things together, ending in the Hudson Yards, a new, massive development.

East & West Villages

Top Sights
1 High Line ... B1
2 Hudson River Park ... B3
3 Little Italy ... E4
4 Lower East Side Tenement Museum ... F3
5 New Museum of Contemporary Art ... E3
6 Washington Square Park ... D2
7 Whitney Museum of American Art ... A1

Sights
8 Astor Place ... E2
9 Children's Museum of the Arts ... C3
10 International Center of Photography ... E3
11 Museum of Chinese in America ... E4
12 New York City Fire Museum ... C4
13 Tompkins Square Park ... F1

Activities, Courses & Tours
14 Great Jones Spa ... E2
15 Russian & Turkish Baths ... F1

Sleeping
16 Bowery Hotel ... E2
17 Bowery House ... E3
18 Jane Hotel ... A1
19 Soho Grand Hotel ... D4
20 Solita SoHo ... E4
21 St Mark's Hotel ... E2
22 Standard ... A1
23 Standard East Village ... E2

Eating
24 Bánh Mì Saigon Bakery ... E4
25 Blue Hill ... C2
26 Butcher's Daughter ... E3
27 Café Gitane ... E3
28 Clinton Street Baking Company ... G3
29 Degustation ... E2
30 Dutch ... D3
31 El Rey ... F3
32 Estela ... E3
33 Grey Dog ... E3
34 Jeffrey's Grocery ... C2
35 Katz's Delicatessen ... F3
36 La Esquina ... E4
37 Meatball Shop ... F3
38 Momofuku Noodle Bar ... F1
39 Red Bamboo ... C2
40 RedFarm ... B2
41 Rosemary's ... C1
42 Tacombi Fonda Nolita ... E3
43 Uncle Boons ... E3
44 Upstate ... F2
45 Vanessa's Dumpling House ... F4
46 Veselka ... E1

Drinking & Nightlife
47 Angel's Share ... E1
48 Bar Goto ... F3
49 Berlin ... F2
50 Buvette ... C2
51 Employees Only ... B2
52 Genuine Liquorette ... E4
Happiest Hour ... (see 41)
53 Henrietta Hudson ... C2
54 Marie's Crisis ... C2
55 Mulberry Project ... E4
56 Pegu Club ... D3
57 Rue B ... F1
58 Spring Lounge ... E3
59 Stonewall Inn ... C2
60 Ten Bells ... F4
61 Wayland ... G1
62 Webster Hall ... E1

Entertainment
63 Anthology Film Archives ... E2
64 Blue Note ... C2
65 Comedy Cellar ... C2
Duplex ... (see 59)
66 Film Forum ... C3
67 Joe's Pub ... E2
68 La MaMa ETC ... E2
69 Metrograph ... F4
70 New York Theatre Workshop ... E2

Shopping
71 Evolution Nature Store ... D2
72 Obscura Antiques ... F1
73 Strand Book Store ... D1

★ High Line PARK

(Map p84; ☎212-500-6035; www.thehighline.org; Gansevoort St; 🕒7am-11pm Jun-Sep, to 10pm Apr, May, Oct & Nov, to 7pm Dec-Mar; 🚌M11 to Washington St; M11, M14 to 9th Ave; M23, M34 to 10th Ave, [S] A/C/E, L to 14th St-8th Ave; C/E to 23rd St-8th Ave) It's hard to believe that the High Line – a shining example of brilliant urban renewal – was once a dingy rail line that anchored a rather unsavory district of slaughterhouses. Today, this eye-catching attraction is one of New York's best-loved green spaces, drawing visitors who come to stroll, sit and picnic 30ft above the city – while enjoying fabulous views of Manhattan's ever-changing urban landscape. Its final extension, which loops around the massive construction project at Hudson Yards, ends at 34th St.

★ Whitney Museum of American Art MUSEUM

(Map p84; ☎212-570-3600; www.whitney.org; 99 Gansevoort St, at Washington St; adult/child $22/free; 🕒10:30am-6pm Mon, Wed, Thu & Sun, to

10pm Fri & Sat; S A/C/E, L to 14th St-8th Ave) After years of construction, the Whitney's new downtown location opened to much fanfare in 2015. Perched near the foot of the High Line, this architecturally stunning building – designed by Renzo Piano – makes a suitable introduction to the museum's superb collection. Inside the spacious galleries, you'll find works by all the great American artists, including Edward Hopper, Jasper Johns, Georgia O'Keeffe and Mark Rothko.

★ **Chelsea Market**   MARKET
(Map p88; ☎ 212-652-2121; www.chelseamarket.com; 75 Ninth Ave, at W 15th St; ☺ 7am-9pm Mon-Sat, 8am-8pm Sun; S A/C/E to 14th St; L to 8th Ave) In a shining example of redevelopment and preservation, the Chelsea Market has transformed a former factory into a shopping concourse that caters to foodies. More than two dozen food vendors ply their temptations including **Mokbar** (ramen with Korean accents), **Takumi Taco** (mixing Japanese and Mexican ingredients), **Tuck Shop** (Aussie-style savory pies), **Bar Suzette** (crepes), **Num Pang** (Cambodian sandwiches), **Ninth St Coffee** (perfect lattes), **Doughnuttery** (piping hot mini-doughnuts) and **L'Arte de Gelato** (rich ice cream).

★ **Hudson River Park**   PARK
(Map p84; www.hudsonriverpark.org; ♿) The High Line may be all the rage these days, but one block away from that famous elevated green space stretches a 5-mile-long ribbon of green that has dramatically transformed the city over the past decade. Covering 550 acres and running from Battery Park at Manhattan's southern tip to 59th St in Midtown, the Hudson River Park is Manhattan's wondrous backyard.

★ **Rubin Museum of Art**   GALLERY
(Map p88; ☎ 212-620-5000; www.rmanyc.org; 150 W 17th St, btwn Sixth & Seventh Aves; adult/child $15/free, 6-10pm Fri free; ☺ 11am-5pm Mon & Thu, to 9pm Wed, to 10pm Fri, to 6pm Sat & Sun; S 1 to 18th St) The Rubin is the first museum in the Western world to dedicate itself to the art of the Himalayas and surrounding regions. Its impressive collections include embroidered textiles from China, metal sculptures from Tibet, Pakistani stone sculptures and intricate Bhutanese paintings, as well as ritual objects and dance masks from various Tibetan regions, spanning the 2nd to the 19th centuries.

★ **Washington Square Park**   PARK
(Map p84; Fifth Ave at Washington Sq N; ♿; S A/C/E, B/D/F/M to W 4th St-Washington Sq; R/W to 8th St-NYU) What was once a potter's field and a square for public executions is now the unofficial town square of Greenwich Village, and plays host to lounging NYU students, tuba-playing street performers, curious canines and their owners, speed-chess pros and bare-footed children who splash about in the fountain on warm days.

◉ Union Square, Flatiron District & Gramercy

The bustling, throbbing, frenzied heart of this trio of neighborhoods is Union Square. It's grungy past long in the rear-view mirror, it's a manicured meeting ground for New Yorkers of all types. The triangular Flatiron Building and the verdant respite of Madison Square Park mark the boundary with Midtown's canyons just to the north. Gramercy Park, a romantic private oasis, offers a more subdued, stately residential area to roam.

★ **Union Square**   SQUARE
(Map p88; www.unionsquarenyc.org; 17th St, btwn Broadway & Park Ave S; S 4/5/6, N/Q/R, L to 14th St-Union Sq) Union Square is like the Noah's Ark of New York, rescuing at least two of every kind from the curling seas of concrete. In fact, one would be hard-pressed to find a more eclectic cross-section of locals gathered in one public place: suited businessfolk gulping fresh air during their lunch breaks, dreadlocked loiterers tapping beats on their tabla, skateboarders flipping tricks on the southeastern stairs, rowdy college kids guzzling student-priced eats, and throngs of protesting masses chanting fervently for various causes.

★ **Flatiron Building**   HISTORIC BUILDING
(Map p88; Broadway, cnr Fifth Ave & 23rd St; S N/R, F/M, 6 to 23rd St) Designed by Daniel Burnham and built in 1920, the 20-story Flatiron Building has a narrow triangular footprint that resembles the prow of a massive ship. It also features a traditional beaux-arts limestone and terra-cotta facade, built over a steel frame, that gets more complex and beautiful the longer you stare at it. Best viewed from the traffic island north of 23rd St between Broadway and Fifth Ave, this unusual structure dominated the plaza back in the dawning skyscraper era of the early 1900s.

Times Square, Midtown Manhattan & Chelsea

W 57th St

57th St-
7th Ave Ⓢ
65 ⊗33

Hudson
River
Park

Dewitt
Clinton
Park

W 55th St

W 53rd St
53 ⓢ Ⓢ55

7th Ave Ⓢ
⊗43

Eleventh Ave
Tenth Ave
Ninth Ave
Eighth Ave
Seventh Ave
Broadway

48 ⊗ ⊗
60   50
Ⓢ62
W 51st St

50th St Ⓢ
64 Ⓢ Ⓢ66
67 ⊛
49th St Ⓢ

W 49th St

W 47th St

Worldwide
Plaza

THEATER
DISTRICT

W 45th St
25 📷
15 📷

NYC
Information
Center
72 ⊛ ⊗44

HELL'S
KITCHEN
W 42nd St ⊗45

63 ⊛
TIMES
SQUARE
Times
Square
11 ⊙
ⓘ
⊗51

Pier 83

Pier 81

42nd St-
Port Authority Ⓢ

42nd St-
Times Sq Ⓢ
Ⓢ Ⓢ

Ⓔ31 ⊛71

(495) Lincoln Tunnel

W 40th St

Port Authority
Bus Terminal

W 38th St
🔒76

Jacob K Javits
Convention
Center W 36th St

GARMENT
DISTRICT

NYC
Information
Center ⓘ

Twelfth Ave (West Side Hwy)

Megabus 🚌

BoltBus 🚌

W 34th St
Ⓢ
W 33rd St

34th St-
Penn Station Ⓢ

Hudson Yards
redevelopment
(under construction)

70 ⊛ 🚉 Penn
Station

W 30th St

Vamoose 🚌

Hudson River

Eleventh Ave

⊛73

W 28th St
Chelsea Park

74
⊛

28th St Ⓢ

W 26th St

Megabus 🚌
(Arrivals)

High Line

Chelsea
Waterside
Park

23rd St Ⓢ 23rd St Ⓢ
⊗30

W 23rd St Ⓢ

CHELSEA
40

24
⊛

W 21st St

Chelsea
Piers

Eleventh Ave (West Side Hwy)

27 📷
⊗34

W 19th St
69 Ⓢ

18th St Ⓢ

NEW YORK
NEW JERSEY

49
⊗

Chelsea
Market
1 ⊙

⊗41

Rubin
Museum
of Art
🏛10

🚌56

W 14th St Ⓢ
8th Ave-
14th St

🚌77 14th St Ⓢ

A B C D

0   500 m
0   0.25 miles

See Central Park & Uptown Map (p94)

57th St
14

E 57th St

E 55th St

Museum of Modern Art
8

Fifth Ave

Madison Ave

Lexington Ave-53rd St

E 53rd St

E 51st St

Roosevelt Island

19

Fifth Ave-53rd St

Park Ave

51st St

Third Ave

Second Ave

First Ave

Franklin D Roosevelt Dr

Rockefeller Center
20
23 9 Rockefeller Plaza
52

St Patrick's Cathedral

E 49th St

47th-50th Sts-Rockefeller Center

DIAMOND DISTRICT

Vanderbilt Ave

Grand Central Terminal
6 75

E 47th St

E 45th St

22

42nd St-Bryant Park
5th Ave
13
18

2 Chrysler Building

E 42nd St

42nd St-Grand Central

E 40th St

Queens-Midtown Tunnel

East River

Tunnel Entrance St

Tudor City Pl

61
Morgan Library & Museum
7

E 38th St

E 36th St

Tunnel Exit St

St Vartan Park
38

HERALD SQUARE

3 Empire State Building
34th St-Herald Sq

KOREATOWN

33rd St

E 34th St

E 33rd St

New York University Medical Center

42

Madison Ave

MURRAY HILL

E 30th St

LITTLE INDIA

E 28th St

Bellevue Hospital Center

28th St
28th St

16

E 26th St

Broadway

FLATIRON DISTRICT
47 36
37 4

Madison Square Park
39
46

23rd St
23rd St

26
28

24th St Park

FDR Dr

23rd St

Flatiron Building

Fifth Ave (Avenue of the Americas)

Park Ave S

Gramercy Park

5 Gramercy Park

E 21st St

Peter Cooper Rd

54

35
17
E 19th St
57

58

First Ave

Second Ave

20th St Loop

59

21

12 68

Union Square

UNION SQUARE

Irving Pl

Third Ave

E 17th St

Stuyvesant Square

First Ave Loop

STUYVESANT TOWN

32

14th St Loop

Ave C

6th Ave-14th St

14th St-Union Sq

E 14th St
3rd Ave

1st Ave

See East & West Villages Map (p84)

Times Square, Midtown Manhattan & Chelsea

◎ **Top Sights**
1 Chelsea Market C7
2 Chrysler Building F3
3 Empire State Building E4
4 Flatiron Building E6
5 Gramercy Park F6
6 Grand Central Terminal F3
7 Morgan Library & Museum F4
8 Museum of Modern Art E1
9 Rockefeller Center E2
10 Rubin Museum of Art D7
11 Times Square D3
12 Union Square F7

◎ **Sights**
13 Bryant Park E3
14 Fifth Avenue E1
15 Intrepid Sea, Air & Space Museum B3
16 Museum of Sex E5
17 National Arts Club F6
18 New York Public Library E3
19 Paley Center for Media E1
20 Top of the Rock E2
21 Union Square Greenmarket F7
22 United Nations G3

◉ **Activities, Courses & Tours**
23 NBC Studio Tours E2
24 Schooner Adirondack B6

▣ **Sleeping**
25 414 Hotel C2
26 Carlton Arms F6
27 High Line Hotel C6
28 Marcel at Gramercy F6
29 Pod 51 .... F2
30 Townhouse Inn of Chelsea D6
31 Yotel C3

✪ **Eating**
32 Bait & Hook G7
33 Burger Joint D1
   Chelsea Market .... (see 1)
34 Cookshop C6
35 Craft F6
36 Eataly E6
37 Eisenberg's Sandwich Shop E6
38 El Parador Cafe G4
39 Eleven Madison Park E6
40 Foragers Table D6
41 Gansevoort Market C7
   Gramercy Tavern .... (see 35)
   Grand Central Oyster Bar &
     Restaurant .... (see 6)
42 Hangawi E5
43 Le Bernardin D2
44 Margon D3
45 Pio Pio C3
46 Shake Shack E6
47 Tacombi Café El Presidente E6
48 Totto Ramen C2
49 Tuck Shop C7
50 ViceVersa C2
51 Virgil's Real Barbecue D3

○ **Drinking & Nightlife**
52 Bar SixtyFive E2
   Birreria .... (see 36)
53 Flaming Saddles C1
54 Flatiron Lounge E6
55 Industry C1
56 Le Bain C7
57 Old Town Bar & Restaurant F7
58 Pete's Tavern F7
59 Raines Law Room E7
60 Therapy C2
61 Top of the Strand E4
62 Waylon C2

✪ **Entertainment**
63 Al Hirschfeld Theatre D3
64 Ambassador Theatre D2
65 Carnegie Hall D1
66 Caroline's on Broadway D2
67 Eugene O'Neill Theatre D2
68 Irving Plaza F7
69 Joyce Theater D7
70 Madison Square Garden D5
71 Playwrights Horizons C3
72 Richard Rodgers Theatre D3
73 Sleep No More B5
74 Upright Citizens Brigade Theatre C5

⊕ **Shopping**
75 Grand Central Market F3
76 Hell's Kitchen Flea Market C4
77 Screaming Mimi's D7

Union Square Greenmarket MARKET
(Map p88; ☑ 212-788-7476; www.grownyc.org; E 17th St, btwn Broadway & Park Ave S; ☺ 8am-6pm Mon, Wed, Fri & Sat; Ⓢ 4/5/6, N/Q/R/W, L to 14th St-Union Sq) ◗ On most days, Union Square's northern end hosts the most popular of the 53 greenmarkets throughout the five boroughs. Indeed, even celebrity chefs head here for just-picked rarities including fiddlehead ferns and heirloom tomatoes.

National Arts Club CULTURAL CENTER
(Map p88; ☑ 212-475-3424; www.nationalartsclub.org; 15 Gramercy Park S; drawing classes $15-25; Ⓢ N/R, 6 to 23rd St) Founded in 1898 to promote public interest in the arts, the National Arts Club holds art exhibitions, usually open to the public from 10am to 5pm Monday to Friday (check the website for upcoming shows). Calvert Vaux – one of the creators of Central Park – designed the building itself,

its picture-lined front parlor adorned with a beautiful, vaulted, stained-glass ceiling. The place was once home to Samuel J Tilden, a former New York governor, and failed presidential candidate in 1876.

★ Gramercy Park   PARK

(Map p88; E 20th St, btwn Park & Third Aves; S N/R, 6 to 23rd St) Romantic Gramercy Park was created by Samuel Ruggles in 1831 after he drained the area's swamp and laid out streets in an English style. You can't enter the private park (the only one in Manhattan), but peer through the gate and imagine tough guy James Cagney enjoying it – the Hollywood actor once resided at 34 Gramercy Park E. At 15 Gramercy Park S stands the National Arts Club, whose members include Martin Scorsese, Uma Thurman and Ethan Hawke.

⊙ Midtown

The hub of the city, and according to boosters the crossroads of the world, Midtown *is* the NYC of postcards. More than 300,000 people a day jostle their way through its pedestrian-friendly streets. More sanitized and corporatized than in the past, it's nevertheless a heady part of town, home to icons including Times Square, Broadway theaters, Grand Central Terminal, the Empire State building and Tiffany & Co Fifth Ave. Cultural knockouts include MoMA, the New York Public Library and the Morgan Library & Museum, with the food-packed, gay-friendly streets of Hell's Kitchen nearby.

★ Museum of Modern Art   MUSEUM

(MoMA; Map p88; ☑ 212-708-9400; www.moma.org; 11 W 53rd St, btwn Fifth & Sixth Aves; adult/child $25/free, 4-8pm Fri free; ⊙10:30am-5:30pm Sat-Thu, to 8pm Fri; ♿; S E, M to 5th Ave-53rd St) Superstar of the modern-art scene, MoMA's galleries scintillate with heavyweights: Van Gogh, Matisse, Picasso, Warhol, Lichtenstein, Rothko, Pollock and Bourgeois. Since its founding in 1929, the museum has amassed almost 200,000 artworks, documenting the emerging creative ideas and movements of the late 19th century through to those that dominate today. For art buffs, it's Valhalla.

★ Times Square   AREA

(Map p88; www.timessquarenyc.org; Broadway, at Seventh Ave; S N/Q/R/W, S, 1/2/3, 7 to Times Sq-42nd St) Love it or hate it, the intersection of Broadway and Seventh Ave (aka Times Square) pumps out the NYC of the global imagination – yellow cabs, golden arches, soaring skyscrapers and razzle-dazzle Broadway marquees. It's right here that Al Jolson 'made it' in the 1927 film *The Jazz Singer*, that photojournalist Alfred Eisenstaedt famously captured a lip-locked sailor and nurse on V-J Day in 1945, and that Alicia Keys and Jay-Z waxed lyrically about this 'concrete jungle where dreams are made'.

Fifth Avenue   AREA

(Map p88; Fifth Ave, btwn 42nd & 59th Sts; S E, M to 5th Ave-53rd St; N/R/W to 5th Ave-59th St) Immortalized in film and song, Fifth Ave first developed its high-class reputation in the early 20th century, when it was known for its 'country' air and open spaces. The series of mansions called **Millionaire's Row** extended right up to 130th St, though most of those above 59th St faced subsequent demolition or conversion to the cultural institutions now constituting Museum Mile. Despite a proliferation of ubiquitous chains, the avenue's Midtown stretch still glitters with upmarket establishments, among them **Tiffany & Co** (Map p94; ☑ 212-755-8000; www.tiffany.com; 727 Fifth Ave, at E 57th St; ⊙10am-7pm Mon-Sat, noon-6pm Sun; S F to 57th St; N/R/W to 5th Ave-59th St).

Home to President Donald Trump and family, the dark-glassed **Trump Tower**, at Fifth Ave and 56th St, has become a sight in and of itself, and a popular spot for protestors. Security around the building is extremely tight and traffic slow.

★ Grand Central Terminal   HISTORIC BUILDING

(Map p88; www.grandcentralterminal.com; 89 E 42nd St, at Park Ave; ⊙5:30am-2am; S S, 4/5/6, 7 to Grand Central-42nd St) Completed in 1913, Grand Central Terminal – more commonly, if technically incorrectly, called Grand Central Station – is one of New York's beaux-arts beauties. Adorned with Tennessee-marble floors and Italian-marble ticket counters, its glorious main concourse is capped by a vaulted ceiling depicting the constellations, designed by French painter Paul César Helleu.

★ Rockefeller Center   HISTORIC BUILDING

(Map p88; www.rockefellercenter.com; Fifth to Sixth Aves, btwn W 48th & 51st Sts; S B/D/F/M to 47th-50th Sts-Rockefeller Center) This 22-acre 'city within a city' debuted at the height of the Great Depression, with developer John D

Rockefeller Jr footing the $100 million price tag. Taking nine years to build, it was America's first multi-use retail, entertainment and office space – a sprawl of 19 buildings (14 of which are the original Moderne structures). The center was declared a National Landmark in 1987. Highlights include the Top of the Rock observation deck and NBC Studio Tours (p108).

Top of the Rock VIEWPOINT
(Map p88; ☎212-698-2000; www.topoftherocknyc.com; 30 Rockefeller Plaza, entrance on W 50th St btwn Fifth & Sixth Aves; adult/child $39/33, sunrise/sunset combo $54/48; 🕘8am-midnight, last elevator at 11pm; [S]B/D/F/M to 47th-50th Sts-Rockefeller Center) Designed in homage to ocean liners and opened in 1933, this 70th-floor open-air observation deck sits atop the **GE Building**, the tallest skyscraper at the Rockefeller Center. Top of the Rock beats the Empire State Building on several levels: it's less crowded, has wider observation decks (both outdoor and indoor) and offers a view of the Empire State Building itself.

★**Chrysler Building** HISTORIC BUILDING
(Map p88; 405 Lexington Ave, at E 42nd St; 🕘lobby 8am-6pm Mon-Fri; [S]S, 4/5/6, 7 to Grand Central-42nd St) Designed by William Van Alen in 1930, the 77-floor Chrysler Building is prime-time architecture: a fusion of Moderne and Gothic aesthetics, adorned with steel eagles and topped by a spire that screams *Bride of Frankenstein*. The building was constructed as the headquarters for Walter P Chrysler and his automobile empire; unable to compete on the production line with bigger rivals Ford and General Motors, Chrysler trumped them on the skyline, and with one of Gotham's most beautiful lobbies.

★**Empire State Building** HISTORIC BUILDING
(Map p88; www.esbnyc.com; 350 Fifth Ave, at W 34th St; 86th-fl observation deck adult/child $34/27, incl 102nd-fl observation deck $54/47; 🕘8am-2am, last elevators up 1:15am; [S]B/D/F/M, N/Q/R/W to 34th St-Herald Sq) This limestone classic was built in just 410 days – using seven million hours of labor during the Great Depression – and the view from its 86th-floor outdoor deck and 102nd-floor indoor deck are heavenly. Alas, the queues to the top are notorious. Getting here very early or very late will help you avoid delays – as will buying your tickets ahead of time online, where the extra $2 convenience fee is well worth the hassle it will save you.

★**Morgan Library & Museum** MUSEUM
(Map p88; ☎212-685-0008; www.themorgan.org; 225 Madison, at E 36th St, Midtown East; adult/child $20/free; 🕘10:30am-5pm Tue-Thu, to 9pm Fri, 10am-6pm Sat, 11am-6pm Sun; [S]6 to 33rd St) Incorporating the mansion once owned by steel magnate JP Morgan, this sumptuous cultural center houses a phenomenal array of manuscripts, tapestries and books (with no fewer than three Gutenberg Bibles). Decorated with Italian and Dutch Renaissance artworks, Morgan's personal study is only trumped by his personal library (East Room), an extraordinary, vaulted space adorned with walnut bookcases, a 16th-century Dutch tapestry and zodiac-themed ceiling. The center's rotating exhibitions are often superb, as are its regular cultural events.

New York Public Library HISTORIC BUILDING
(Stephen A Schwarzman Building; Map p88; ☎917-275-6975; www.nypl.org; Fifth Ave, at W 42nd St; 🕘10am-6pm Mon & Thu-Sat, to 8pm Tue & Wed, 1-5pm Sun, guided tours 11am & 2pm Mon-Sat, 2pm Sun; [S]B/D/F/M to 42nd St-Bryant Park; 7 to 5th Ave) [FREE] Loyally guarded by 'Patience' and 'Fortitude' (the marble lions overlooking Fifth Ave), this beaux-arts show-off is one of NYC's best free attractions. When dedicated in 1911, New York's flagship library ranked as the largest marble structure ever built in the USA, and to this day, its recently restored **Rose Main Reading Room** steals the breath away with its lavish coffered ceiling. It's only one of several glories inside, among them the **DeWitt Wallace Periodical Room**.

United Nations HISTORIC BUILDING
(Map p88; ☎212-963-4475; http://visit.un.org; visitors' gate First Ave at 46th St, Midtown East; guided tour adult/child $20/13, children under 5yr not admitted, grounds access Sat & Sun free; 🕘tours 9am-4:45pm Mon-Fri, visitor center also open 10am-4:45pm Sat & Sun; [S]S, 4/5/6, 7 to Grand Central-42nd St) Welcome to the headquarters of the UN, a worldwide organization overseeing international law, international security and human rights. While the Le Corbusier–designed Secretariat building is off-limits, one-hour guided tours do cover the restored General Assembly Hall, Security Council Chamber, Trusteeship Council Chamber, and Economic and Social Council (ECOSOC) Chamber, as well as exhibitions about the UN's work and artworks donated by member states. Weekday tours must be

booked online and photo ID is required to enter the site.

St Patrick's Cathedral CATHEDRAL

(Map p88; www.saintpatrickscathedral.org; Fifth Ave, btwn E 50th & 51st Sts; ⏲6:30am-8:45pm; [S] B/D/F/M to 47th-50th Sts-Rockefeller Center; E/M to 5th Ave-53rd St) Fresh from a $200 million restoration, America's largest Catholic cathedral graces Fifth Ave with Gothic Revival splendor. Built at a cost of nearly $2 million during the Civil War, the building did not originally include the two front spires; those were added in 1888. Step inside to appreciate the Louis Tiffany–designed **altar** and Charles Connick's stunning **Rose Window**, the latter gleaming above a 7000-pipe church organ. Walk-in **guided tours** are available several days a week; check website for details.

Museum of Arts & Design MUSEUM

(MAD; Map p94; ☎212-299-7777; www.madmuseum.org; 2 Columbus Circle, btwn Eighth Ave & Broadway; adult/child $16/free, by donation 6-9pm Thu; ⏲10am-6pm Tue, Wed, Fri, Sat & Sun, to 9pm Thu; 👪; [S] A/C, B/D, 1 to 59th St-Columbus Circle) MAD offers four floors of superlative design and handicrafts, from blown glass and carved wood to elaborate metal jewelry. Its temporary exhibitions are top-notch and innovative: one past show explored the art of scent. Usually on the first Sunday of the month, professional artists lead family-friendly explorations of the galleries, followed by hands-on workshops inspired by the current exhibitions. The museum gift shop sells some fantastic contemporary jewelry, while the 9th-floor restaurant/bar Robert (p128) is perfect for panoramic cocktails.

Paley Center for Media CULTURAL CENTER

(Map p88; ☎212-621-6800; www.paleycenter.org; 25 W 52nd St, btwn Fifth & Sixth Aves; suggested donation adult/child $10/5; ⏲noon-6pm Wed & Fri-Sun, to 8pm Thu; [S] E, M to 5th Ave-53rd St) This pop-culture repository offers more than 160,000 TV and radio programs from around the world on its computer catalog. Reliving your favorite TV shows on one of the center's consoles is sheer bliss on a rainy day, as are the excellent, regular screenings, festivals, speakers and performers.

Bryant Park PARK

(Map p88; ☎212-768-4242; www.bryantpark.org; 42nd St, btwn Fifth & Sixth Aves; ⏲7am-midnight Mon-Fri, to 11pm Sat & Sun Jun-Sep, shorter hrs rest of year; [S] B/D/F/M to 42nd St-Bryant Park, 7 to Fifth Ave) European coffee kiosks, alfresco chess games, summer film screenings and winter ice-skating: it's hard to believe that this leafy oasis was dubbed 'Needle Park' in the '80s. Nestled behind the beaux-arts New York Public Library building, it's a whimsical spot for a little time-out from the Midtown madness. Fancy taking a beginner Italian language, yoga or juggling class, joining a trivia contest, or signing up for a birding tour? The park offers a daily smorgasbord of quirky activities.

Intrepid Sea, Air & Space Museum MUSEUM

(Map p88; ☎877-957-7447; www.intrepidmuseum.org; Pier 86, Twelfth Ave at W 46th St; Intrepid & Growler submarine adult/child $26/19, incl Space Shuttle Pavilion adult/child $36/29; ⏲10am-5pm Mon-Fri, to 6pm Sat & Sun Apr-Oct, 10am-5pm Mon-Sun Nov-Mar; 👪; 🚌westbound M42, M50 to 12th Ave, [S] A/C/E to 42nd St-Port Authority Bus Terminal) In WWII, the USS *Intrepid* survived both a bomb and kamikaze attacks. Thankfully, this hulking aircraft carrier is now a lot less stressed, playing host to a multimillion-dollar interactive military museum that tells its tale through videos, historical artifacts and frozen-in-time living quarters. The flight deck features fighter planes and military helicopters, which might inspire you try the museum's high-tech flight simulators.

Museum of Sex MUSEUM

(Map p88; ☎212-689-6337; www.museumofsex.com; 233 Fifth Ave, at 27th St; adult $17.50, $20.50 Sat & Sun; ⏲10am-9pm Sun-Thu, 11am-11pm Fri & Sat; [S] N/R to 23rd St) Get the lowdown on anything from online fetishes to homosexual necrophilia in the mallard duck at this slick ode to all things hot and sweaty. The rotating program of temporary exhibitions has included explorations of cyber sex and retrospectives of controversial artists, while the permanent collection showcases the likes of erotic lithographs and awkward anti-onanism (masturbation) devices.

Upper West Side & Central Park

For better or worse, banks and chain stores have homogenized the Upper West Side's formerly eclectic streetscape, yet somehow it still holds the power to make many a visitor feel like they've stepped into a Woody

Central Park & Uptown

1 km
0.5 miles

EDGEWATER

Hudson River

Riverbank State Park

Henry Hudson Pkwy

Riverside Dr

Riverside Dr E

W 140th St
W 137th St
City College
W 135th St

W 140th St
St Nicholas Park
St Nicholas Tce
Convent Ave
Amsterdam Ave
City College of New York

W 135th St
St Nicholas Ave
W 130th St
W 125th St

Broadway
LaSalle St
MORNINGSIDE HEIGHTS
W 122nd St
Columbia University

116th St-Columbia University
Cathedral Pkwy (110th St)
W 112th St

Cathedral Church of St John the Divine

W 110th St
W 106th St
W 104th St
W 102nd St
W 100th St

Cathedral Pkwy (110th Pkwy)
103rd St
UPPER WEST SIDE
W 104th St (Duke Ellington Blvd)
103rd St

Morningside Ave
Morningside Dr
Morningside Park

St Nicholas Ave
Frederick Douglass Blvd (Eighth Ave)
116th St

125th St
Adam Clayton Powell Jr Blvd (Seventh Ave)
Apollo Theater
Studio Museum in Harlem
125th St (W 125th St)
W 122nd St
W 120th St
W 118th St
W 116th St
116th St

St Nicholas Ave
Cathedral Pkwy (110th St)
Central Park North (110th St)

HARLEM
W 138th St
W 135th St
W 130th St
W 127th St
Martin Luther King Jr Blvd
Malcolm X Blvd (Lenox Ave)
Fifth Ave
Marcus Garvey Park

Yankee Stadium (1.2mi)
Harlem River Dr
Harlem River

138th St-Grand Concourse
3rd Ave-138th St
E 138th St

MOTT HAVEN
Major Deegan Expwy
Bruckner Blvd
Willis Ave
3rd Ave

Brook Ave
Cypress Ave
Bruckner Blvd

Robert F Kennedy Bridge (Triborough Bridge)

Bronx Kill
Icahn Stadium
Ward's Island

Franklin D Roosevelt Dr

Robert F Kennedy Bridge (Triborough Bridge)

Astoria Pool (0.7mi)

SPANISH HARLEM
First Ave
Second Ave
(Luis Munoz Marin Blvd)
La Marqueta
Madison Ave
Park Ave
Lexington Ave
Third Ave
Jefferson Park

E 127th St
E 125th St
E 122nd St
E 120th St
E 118th St
E 116th St
116th St
E 112th St
110th St
E 110th St
E 106th St
E 104th St
E 103rd St
103rd St
E 102nd St

UPPER EAST SIDE

Fifth Ave
Central Park North (110th St)
Harlem Meer
Conservatory Garden
The Loch
The Pool
Great Hill
North Meadow
East Meadow

10
25
36
21
3
29
28
52
54
9
44
31
2
17

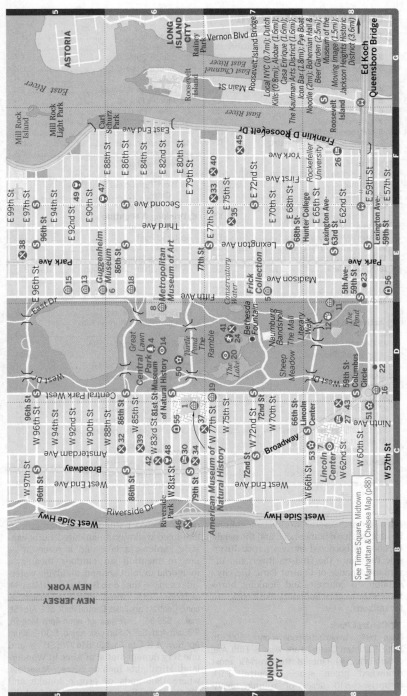

ASTORIA

LONG ISLAND CITY

Rainey Park

Vernon Blvd

Roosevelt Island Bridge

Local NYC (0.7mi); Dutch Kills (0.8mi); Alobar (1.6mi); Casa Enrique (1.6mi); The Kaufman Arts District (1.6mi); Pye Boat Noodle (2mi); Bohemian Hall & Beer Garden (2.5mi); Museum of the Moving Image (1.5mi); Jackson Heights Historic District (3.6mi)

Icon Bar (1.8mi);

Main St

Roosevelt Island

East River

East Channel East River

Mill Rock Island

Mill Rock Light Park

East River

Carl Schurz Park

East End Ave

E 99th St
E 97th St
E 96th St
E 94th St
E 92nd St
E 90th St
E 88th St
E 86th St
E 84th St
E 82nd St
E 80th St
E 79th St
E 77th St
E 75th St
E 72nd St
E 70th St
E 68th St
E 65th St
E 63rd St
E 62nd St
E 59th St
E 57th St

Franklin D Roosevelt Dr

45

40

York Ave

First Ave

Second Ave

Third Ave

Lexington Ave

Hunter College

Rockefeller University

26

Roosevelt Island

Ed Koch Queensboro Bridge

38
47
49
33
35

15
13
18
6

Guggenheim Museum

Metropolitan Museum of Art

Park Ave

Fifth Ave

Madison Ave

Conservatory Water

Frick Collection

5

68th St– Hunter College

Lexington Ave–63rd St

5th Ave–59th St

Park Ave

Lexington Ave–59th St

23

56

11

East Dr

West Dr

East Dr

Central Park

Great Lawn

The Ramble

The Lake

Turtle Pond

Naumburg Bandshell

Bethesda Fountain

Sheep Meadow

Literary Walk

The Mall

The Pond

59th St–Columbus Circle

Columbus Circle

16
22

4
14
50
41
24
20
12

Central Park West

W 96th St
W 94th St
W 92nd St
W 90th St
W 88th St
W 86th St
W 85th St
W 83rd St
W 81st St
W 79th St
W 77th St
W 75th St
W 72nd St
W 70th St
W 66th St
W 62nd St
W 60th St
W 57th St

81st St–Museum of Natural History

American Museum of Natural History

86th St

79th St

72nd St

66th St– Lincoln Center

59th St

1
55
37
19

32
39
48
30
34
42

Amsterdam Ave

West End Ave

Broadway

Broadway

West End Ave

Ninth Ave

27
43
51

53

Lincoln 7 Center

W 97th St
W 96th St

Riverside Dr

Riverside Park

West Side Hwy

West Side Hwy

46

NEW YORK

NEW JERSEY

UNION CITY

See Times Square, Midtown Manhattan & Chelsea Map (p88)

Central Park & Uptown

Top Sights
1 American Museum of Natural History. C6
2 Apollo Theater D2
3 Cathedral Church of St John the Divine C3
4 Central Park D6
5 Frick Collection E7
6 Guggenheim Museum E5
7 Lincoln Center C8
8 Metropolitan Museum of Art D6
9 Studio Museum in Harlem D2

Sights
10 Abyssinian Baptist Church D1
11 Arsenal D8
12 Central Park Zoo D8
13 Cooper-Hewitt National Design Museum E5
14 Great Lawn D6
15 Jewish Museum E5
16 Museum of Arts & Design D8
17 Museum of the City of New York E4
18 Neue Galerie E6
19 New-York Historical Society D7
20 Ramble D7
21 Riverside Park B4

Activities, Courses & Tours
22 Central Park Bike Tours D8
23 Central Park Conservancy E8
24 Loeb Boathouse D7

Sleeping
25 Allie's Inn D1
26 Bentley Hotel F8
27 Empire Hotel C8
28 Harlem Flophouse D2
29 Hostelling International New York C4
30 Lucerne C6

Eating
31 Amy Ruth's Restaurant D3
32 Barney Greengrass C6
33 Boqueria F7
34 Burke & Wills C6
35 Candle Cafe E7
36 Dinosaur Bar-B-Que B2
37 Dovetail C6
38 Earl's Beer & Cheese E5
39 Jacob's Pickles C6
40 Jones Wood Foundry F7
41 Lakeside Restaurant at Loeb Boathouse D7
42 Peacefood Cafe C6
43 PJ Clarke's C8
44 Red Rooster D2
45 Tanoshi F7
46 West 79th Street Boat Basin Café B6

Drinking & Nightlife
47 Auction House F5
48 Dead Poet C6
49 Drunken Munkey F5
Ginny's Supper Club (see 44)
Manhattan Cricket Club (see 34)
Robert (see 16)

Entertainment
50 Delacorte Theater D6
Elinor Bunin Munroe Film Center (see 7)
Film Society of Lincoln Center (see 7)
51 Jazz at Lincoln Center C8
Metropolitan Opera House (see 7)
52 Minton's D3
New York City Ballet (see 7)
New York Philharmonic (see 7)
53 Walter Reade Theater C8

Shopping
54 Flamekeepers Hat Club D2
55 Flying Tiger Copenhagen C6
56 Tiffany & Co. E8

Allen movie. Several world-class cultural institutions have homes here, and the neighborhood is bordered by two parks: Riverside Park lines the Hudson River, and the verdant expanse of Central Park, the city's antidote to concrete and honking horns frames the eastern boundary like a backyard for millions.

★**Central Park** PARK
(Map p94; www.centralparknyc.org; 59th to 110th Sts, btwn Central Park West & Fifth Ave; ⏲6am-1am; 👪) One of the world's most renowned green spaces, Central Park comprises 843 acres of rolling meadows, boulder-studded outcroppings, elm-lined walkways, manicured European-style gardens, a lake and a reservoir – not to mention an outdoor theater, a memorial to John Lennon, an idyllic waterside eatery – the **Loeb Boathouse** (Map p94; ☎212-517-2233; www.thecentralparkboathouse.com; Central Park Lake, Central Park, at E 74th St; mains $25-36; ⏲restaurant noon-4pm Mon-Fri, 9:30am-4pm Sat & Sun year-round, 5:30-9:30pm Apr-Nov; [S] B, C to 72nd St; 6 to 77th St) – and one very famous statue of Alice in Wonderland. Highlights include **Sheep Meadow**, where thousands of people lounge and play on warm days; precious animals at the

Central Park Zoo (Map p94; ☎212-439-6500; www.centralparkzoo.com; Central Park, 64th St, at Fifth Ave; adult/child $12/7; ⏰10am-5pm Mon-Fri, to 5:30 Sat & Sun; 👪; [S]N/Q/R to 5th Ave-59th St); and the forest-like paths of the **Ramble** (Map p94; Central Park, mid-park from 73rd to 79th Sts; [S]B,C to 81st St), a wooded thicket that's popular with bird-watchers.

Like the city's subway system, the vast and majestic Central Park, a rectangle of open space in the middle of Manhattan, is a great class leveler - exactly what it was envisioned to be. Created in the 1860s and '70s by Frederick Law Olmsted and Calvert Vaux on the marshy northern fringe of the city, the immense park was designed as a leisure space for all New Yorkers regardless of color, class or creed. It's also an oasis from the insanity: the lush lawns, cool forests, flowering gardens, glassy bodies of water and meandering, wooded paths provide the dose of serene nature that New Yorkers crave.

Olmsted and Vaux — who also created Prospect Park (p103) in Brooklyn — were determined to keep foot and road traffic separated and cleverly designed the cross-town transverses under elevated roads to do so. That such a large expanse of prime real estate has survived intact for so long is proof that nothing eclipses the heart, soul and pride that forms the foundation of New York City's greatness.

Today this 'people's park' is still one of the city's most popular attractions, beckoning throngs of New Yorkers with free outdoor concerts on the **Great Lawn** (Map p94; www.centralparknyc.org; Central Park, btwn 79th & 86th Sts; ⏰mid-Apr–mid-Nov; [S]B, C to 86th St), and top-notch drama at the annual Shakespeare in the Park (p109) productions, held each summer at the open-air Delacorte Theater (p133). Other recommended stops include the ornate Bethesda Fountain, which edges the Lake and its Loeb Boathouse (p108), where you can rent rowboats or enjoy lunch at an outdoor cafe; the **Shakespeare Garden**, on the west side between 79th and 80th Sts, with its lush plantings and excellent skyline views. While parts of the park swarm with joggers, in-line skaters, musicians and tourists on warm weekends, it's quieter on weekday afternoons, especially in the less-trodden spots above 72nd St, such as the **Harlem Meer** and the **North Meadow** (north of 97th St).

Folks flock to the park even in winter, when snowstorms inspire cross-country skiing and sledding or just a simple stroll through the white wonderland, and crowds turn out every New Year's Eve for a midnight run. The Central Park Conservancy (p109) offers ever-changing **guided tours** of the park, including ones that focus on public art, wildlife and places of interest to kids.

Bethesda Fountain FOUNTAIN

(Map p94; Central Park; [S]B, C to 72nd St) This neoclassical fountain is one of New York's largest. It's capped by the *Angel of the Waters,* who is supported by four cherubim. The fountain, created by bohemian-feminist sculptor Emma Stebbins in 1868, makes a great meet-up and people-watching spot.

★Lincoln Center CULTURAL CENTER

(Map p94; ☎212-875-5456, tours 212-875-5350; www.lincolncenter.org; Columbus Ave, btwn W 62nd & 66th Sts; tours adult/student $25/20; 👪; [S]1 to 66th St-Lincoln Center) [FREE] This stark arrangement of gleaming Modernist temples houses some of Manhattan's most important performance companies: the New York Philharmonic, the New York City Ballet and the iconic Metropolitan Opera House, whose lobby's interior walls are dressed with brightly saturated murals by painter Marc Chagall. Various other venues are tucked in and around the 16-acre campus, including a theater and the renowned **Juilliard School**.

★American Museum of Natural History MUSEUM

(Map p94; ☎212-769-5100; www.amnh.org; Central Park West, at W 79th St; suggested donation adult/child $22/12.50; ⏰10am-5:45pm, Rose Center to 8:45pm Fri; 👪; [S]B, C to 81st St-Museum of Natural History, 1 to 79th St) Founded in 1869, this classic museum contains a veritable wonderland of more than 30 million artifacts – including lots of menacing dinosaur skeletons – as well as the **Rose Center for Earth & Space**, with its cutting-edge planetarium. From September through May, the museum is home to the **Butterfly Conservatory**, a glasshouse featuring 500-plus butterflies from all over the world.

New-York Historical Society MUSEUM

(Map p94; ☎212-873-3400; www.nyhistory.org; 170 Central Park West, at 77th St; adult/child $20/6, by donation 6-8pm Fri, library free; ⏰10am-6pm Tue-Thu & Sat, to 8pm Fri, 11am-5pm Sun; 👪; [S]B, C to 81st St-Museum of Natural History) As the antiquated hyphenated name implies, the

Central Park

THE LUNGS OF NEW YORK

The rectangular patch of green that occupies Manhattan's heart began life in the mid-19th century as a swampy piece of land that was carefully bulldozed into the idyllic nature-scape you see today. Since officially becoming Central Park, it has brought New Yorkers of all stripes together in interesting and unexpected ways. The park has served as a place for the rich to show off their fancy carriages (1860s), for the poor to enjoy free Sunday concerts (1880s) and for activists to hold be-ins against the Vietnam War (1960s).

Since then, legions of locals – not to mention travelers from all kinds of faraway places – have poured in to stroll, picnic, sunbathe, play ball and catch free concerts and performances of works by Shakespeare.

Loeb Boathouse
Perched on the shores of the Lake, the historic Loeb Boathouse is one of the city's best settings for an idyllic meal. You can also rent rowboats and bicycles and ride on a Venetian gondola.

Duke Ellington Circle

Harlem Meer

The Blockhouse

North Woods

97th St Transverse

Fifth Ave

86th St Transverse

The Great Lawn

Central Park West

Conservatory Garden
The only formal garden in Central Park is perhaps the most tranquil. On the northern end, chrysanthemums bloom in late October. To the south, the park's largest crab apple tree grows by the Burnett Fountain.

STUDIOLASKA/SHUTTERSTOCK ©

Jacqueline Kennedy Onassis Reservoir
This 106-acre body of water covers roughly an eighth of the park's territory. Its original purpose was to provide clean water for the city. Now it's a good spot to catch a glimpse of waterbirds.

LULU AND ISABELLE/SHUTTERSTOCK ©

Belvedere Castle
A so-called 'Victorian folly,' this Gothic-Romanesque castle serves no other purpose than to be a very dramatic lookout point. It was built by Central Park co-designer Calvert Vaux in 1869.

The park's varied terrain offers a wonderland of experiences. There are quiet, woodsy knolls in the north. To the south is the reservoir, crowded with joggers. There are European gardens, a zoo and various bodies of water. For maximum flamboyance, hit the Sheep Meadow on a sunny day, when all of New York shows up to lounge.

Central Park is more than just a green space. It is New York City's backyard.

FAST FACTS

➡ The landscape architects were Frederick Law Olmsted and Calvert Vaux.

➡ Construction commenced in 1858.

➡ The park covers 843 acres.

➡ Hundreds of movies have been shot on location, from Depression-era blockbuster *Gold Diggers* (1933) to monster-attack flick *Cloverfield* (2008).

Conservatory Water
This pond is popular in the warmer months, when children sail their model boats across its surface. Conservatory Water was inspired by 19th-century Parisian model-boat ponds and figured prominently in EB White's classic book, *Stuart Little*.

CHRISTOPHER PENLER/SHUTTERSTOCK ©

KRIDSADA KAMSOMBAT/SHUTTERSTOCK ©

Bethesda Fountain
This neoclassical fountain is one of New York's largest. It's capped by the *Angel of the Waters*, which is supported by four cherubim. The fountain was created by bohemian-feminist sculptor Emma Stebbins in 1868.

Metropolitan Museum of Art

Alice in Wonderland Statue

79th St Transverse

The Ramble

Delacorte Theater

The Lake

Fifth Ave

Central Park Zoo

65th St Transverse

Sheep Meadow

Columbus Center

Strawberry Fields
A simple mosaic memorial pays tribute to musician John Lennon, who was killed across the street outside the Dakota Building. Funded by Yoko Ono, its name is inspired by the Beatles song 'Strawberry Fields Forever.'

The Mall/ Literary Walk
A Parisian-style promenade – the only straight line in the park – is flanked by statues of literati on the southern end, including Robert Burns and Shakespeare. It is lined with rare North American elms.

Historical Society is the city's oldest museum, founded in 1804 to preserve the city's historical and cultural artifacts. Its collection of more than 60,000 objects is quirky and fascinating and includes everything from George Washington's inauguration chair to a 19th-century Tiffany ice-cream dish (gilded, of course), plus a remarkable collection of Hudson River School paintings. However, it's far from stodgy, having moved into the 21st century with renewed vigor and purpose.

Riverside Park
PARK

(Map p94; ☑212-870-3070; www.riverside parknyc.org; Riverside Dr, btwn 68th & 155th Sts; ⊙6am-1am; ⚑; Ⓢ1/2/3 to any stop btwn 66th & 157th Sts) A classic beauty designed by Central Park creators Frederick Law Olmsted and Calvert Vaux, this waterside spot, running north on the Upper West Side and banked by the Hudson River from 59th to 155th Sts, is lusciously leafy. Plenty of bike paths, playgrounds and dog runs make it a family favorite. Views from the park make the Jersey side of the Hudson look pretty.

Arsenal
HISTORIC BUILDING

(Map p94; ☑gallery 212-360-8163; www.nyc govparks.org; Central Park, at Fifth Ave & E 64th St; ⊙9am-5pm Mon-Fri; Ⓢ N/R/W to 5th Ave-59th St) FREE Built between 1847 and 1851 (its construction predates Central Park) as a munitions supply depot for the New York State National Guard, this landmark brick building was designed to look like a medieval castle. Today the building houses a small **gallery**, which often exhibits works with an historical or environmental focus, such as nature in the city, living landmarks or waterfalls of upstate New York.

◉ Upper East Side

Despite the storied mansions and outrageous per capita income, it's not all 'real housewives' up here. Post-collegiate bros share high-rise rentals east of the busy, commercial strip of Lexington Ave. You will find liveried doormen guarding marble lobbies in prewar condominiums lining Park Ave. And, yes, Botox is administered like vitamins. High-end boutiques line Madison Ave and Fifth Ave, which runs parallel to the leafy realms of Central Park and ends in an architectural flourish called Museum Mile – one of the most cultured strips in the city, if not the world.

★Metropolitan Museum of Art
MUSEUM

(Map p94; ☑212-535-7710; www.metmuseum. org; 1000 Fifth Ave, at 82nd St; suggested donation adult/student/child $25/12/free; ⊙10am-5:30pm Sun-Thu, to 9pm Fri & Sat; ⚑; Ⓢ4/5/6, Q to 86th St) This sprawling, encyclopedic museum founded in 1870 houses one of the largest art collections in the world. Its permanent collection has more than two million individual objects, from Egyptian temples to American paintings. Known colloquially as 'The Met,' the museum attracts over six million visitors a year to its 17 acres of galleries, making it the largest single-site attraction in New York City. In other words, plan on spending some time here – it is B-I-G.

★Guggenheim Museum
MUSEUM

(Map p94; ☑212-423-3500; www.guggenheim.org; 1071 Fifth Ave, at E 89th St; adult/child $25/free, by donation 5:45-7:45pm Sat; ⊙10am-5:45pm Sun-Wed & Fri, to 7:45pm Sat, closed Thu; ⚑; Ⓢ4/5/6 to 86th St) A sculpture in its own right, architect Frank Lloyd Wright's building almost overshadows the collection of 20th-century art it houses. The museum's holdings include works by Kandinsky, Picasso and Jackson Pollock. Over time, other key additions have been made, including paintings by Monet, Van Gogh and Degas, photographs by Robert Mapplethorpe, and key surrealist works. Temporary exhibitions are the real draw – the best of which are stunning site-specific installations by some of the great visionary artists of today.

★Frick Collection
GALLERY

(Map p94; ☑212-288-0700; www.frick.org; 1 E 70th St, cnr Fifth Ave; adult/student $22/12, pay-what-you-wish 2-6pm Wed; ⊙10am-6pm Tue-Sat, 11am-5pm Sun; Ⓢ6 to 68th St-Hunter College) This spectacular art collection sits in a mansion built by prickly steel magnate Henry Clay Frick, one of the many such residences lining the section of Fifth Ave that was once called 'Millionaires' Row.' The museum has over a dozen splendid rooms displaying masterpieces by Titian, Vermeer, Gilbert Stuart, El Greco, Joshua Reynolds, Goya and Rembrandt. Sculpture, ceramics and antique furniture and clocks are also on display.

Cooper-Hewitt National Design Museum
MUSEUM

(Map p94; ☑212-849-8400; www.cooperhewitt. org; 2 E 91st St, at Fifth Ave; adult/child $18/free, pay-what-you-wish 6-9pm Sat; ⊙10am-6pm Sun-

Fri, to 9pm Sat; S 4/5/6 to 86th St) Part of the Smithsonian Institution in Washington, DC, this is the only US museum dedicated to both historic and contemporary design. Housed in the 64-room mansion built by billionaire Andrew Carnegie in 1901, the 210,000-piece collection offers artful displays spanning 3000 years over three floors of the building. An extensive renovation added exhibitions with interactive touch screens and a nifty electronic 'pen' that allows you to create your own designs and save them to a website for later retrieval.

Neue Galerie
MUSEUM

(Map p94; ☑ 212-628-6200; www.neuegalerie.org; 1048 Fifth Ave, cnr 86th St; adult/student $20/10, 6-8pm 1st Fri of the month free; ⊙ 11am-6pm Thu-Mon; S 4/5/6 to 86th St) This restored Carrère and Hastings mansion from 1914 is a resplendent showcase for Austrian and German art, featuring works by Paul Klee, Ernst Ludwig Kirchner and Egon Schiele. In pride of place on the 2nd floor is Gustav Klimt's golden 1907 portrait of Adele Bloch-Bauer – acquired for the museum by cosmetics magnate Ronald Lauder for a whopping $135 million. The fascinating story of the painting's history is told in the 2015 film *Woman in Gold*.

Museum of the City of New York
MUSEUM

(Map p94; ☑ 212-534-1672; www.mcny.org; 1220 Fifth Ave, btwn E 103rd & 104th Sts; suggested admission adult/child $18/free; ⊙ 10am-6pm; S 6 to 103rd St) Situated in a Georgian Colonial Revival–style building, this local museum focuses solely on New York City's past, present and future. Don't miss the 28-minute film *Timescapes* (on the 2nd floor), which charts NYC's growth from tiny native trading post to burgeoning metropolis.

Jewish Museum
MUSEUM

(Map p94; ☑ 212-423-3200; www.thejewish museum.org; 1109 Fifth Ave, btwn E 92nd & 93rd Sts; adult/child $15/free, Sat free, by donation 5-8pm Thu; ⊙ 11am-6pm Sat-Tue, to 4pm Thu & Fri, closed Wed; 👹; S 6 to 96th St) This New York City gem occupies a French-Gothic mansion from 1908, housing 30,000 items of Judaica, as well as sculpture, painting and decorative arts. It hosts excellent temporary exhibits, featuring retrospectives on influential figures such as Art Spiegelman, as well as world-class shows on the likes of Marc Chagall, Édouard Vuillard and Man Ray, among other past luminaries.

⊙ Harlem & Upper Manhattan

Originally settled by Dutch farmers in the 17th century, and later home to waves of Irish, Italian and Jewish immigrants, Harlem's identity is most inextricably connected to the African American experience. These days, despite ever-expanding gentrification, it remains packed with feverish preachers and choirs, soul-food menus and swinging jazz clubs. Franco African and French expat-owned restaurants add to the mix. Working-class East Harlem (known colloquially as Spanish Harlem or El Barrio) is a vibrant hub for Hispanic immigrants, while Columbia University is expanding into West Harlem. In the borough's north, leafy Inwood is home to unexpected medieval treasures.

★ Cathedral Church of St John the Divine
CATHEDRAL

(Map p94; ☑ tours 212-316-7540; www.stjohn divine.org; 1047 Amsterdam Ave, at W 112th St, Morningside Heights; suggested donation $10, highlights tour $14, vertical tour $20; ⊙ 7:30am-6pm, highlights tour 11am & 2pm Mon, 11am & 1pm Tue-Sat, 1pm selected Sun, vertical tour 10am Mon, noon Wed & Fri, noon & 2pm Sat; S B, C, 1 to 110th St-Cathedral Pkwy) The largest place of worship in the US has yet to be completed – and probably won't be any time soon. But this storied Episcopal cathedral nonetheless commands attention with its ornate Byzantine-style facade, booming vintage organ and extravagantly scaled nave – twice as wide as that of London's Westminster Abbey. Aside from a one-hour **highlights tour**, the cathedral also offers a one-hour **vertical tour**, taking you on a steep climb to the top of the cathedral (bring your own flashlight).

★ Apollo Theater
HISTORIC BUILDING

(Map p94; ☑ 212-531-5300, tours 212-531-5337; www.apollotheater.org; 253 W 125th St, btwn Frederick Douglass & Adam Clayton Powell Jr Blvds, Harlem; tickets from $16; S A/C, B/D to 125th St) The Apollo is an intrinsic part of Harlem history and culture. A leading space for concerts and political rallies since 1914, its venerable stage hosted virtually every major black artist in the 1930s and '40s, including Duke Ellington and Billie Holiday. Decades later, it would help launch the careers of countless stars, from Diana Ross and Aretha Franklin to Michael Jackson and Lauryn Hill. Today, its thriving program of music, dance, master classes and special events continues to draw crowds and applause.

NEW YORK, NEW JERSEY & PENNSYLVANIA NEW YORK CITY

Abyssinian Baptist Church CHURCH

(Map p94; ☎212-862-7474; www.abyssinian.org; 132 Odell Clark Pl, btwn Adam Clayton Powell Jr & Malcolm X Blvds, Harlem; 🕐tourist gospel service 11:30am Sun early-Sep–Jul; [S]2/3 to 135th St) A raucous, soulful affair, the superb Sunday gospel services here are the city's most famous. You'll need to arrive at least an hour before the service to queue up, and ensure you adhere to the strict entry rules: no tank tops, flip-flops, shorts, leggings or backpacks. The entry point for tourists is at the southeast corner of West 138th Street and Adam Clayton Powell Jr. Blvd.

★**Cloisters Museum & Gardens** MUSEUM

(Map p79; ☎212-923-3700; www.metmuseum.org/cloisters; 99 Margaret Corbin Dr, Fort Tryon Park; suggested donation adult/child $25/free; 🕐10am-5:15pm; [S]A to 190th St) On a hilltop overlooking the Hudson River, the Cloisters is a curious architectural jigsaw, its many parts made up of various European monasteries and other historic buildings. Built in the 1930s to house the Metropolitan Museum's medieval treasures, its frescoes, tapestries and paintings are set in galleries that sit around a romantic courtyard, connected by grand archways and topped with Moorish terra-cotta roofs. Among its many rare treasures is the beguiling 16th-century tapestry series *The Hunt of the Unicorn*.

★**Studio Museum in Harlem** MUSEUM

(Map p94; ☎212-864-4500; www.studiomuseum.org; 144 W 125th St, at Adam Clayton Powell Jr Blvd, Harlem; suggested donation $7, Sun free; 🕐noon-9pm Thu & Fri, 10am-6pm Sat, noon-6pm Sun; [S]2/3 to 125th St) This small, cultural gem has been exhibiting the works of African American artists for more than four decades. While its rotating exhibition program is always fascinating, the museum is not just another art display center. It is an important point of connection for Harlem cultural figures of all stripes, who arrive to check out a rotating selection of shows, attend film screenings or sign up for gallery talks.

Brooklyn

Brooklyn's sprawling checkerboard of distinct neighborhoods is more than three times the size of Manhattan, not to mention more diverse and far-reaching. For skyline views and a pinch of history, try brownstone-studded Brooklyn Heights, or Williamsburg for vintage wares and late-night bar crawls.

★**Brooklyn Bridge Park** PARK

(Map p80; ☎718-222-9939; www.brooklynbridgepark.org; East River Waterfront, btwn Atlantic Ave & Adams St; 🕐6am-1am; 👪; [S]A/C to High St; 2/3 to Clark St; F to York St) [FREE] This 85-acre park is one of Brooklyn's best-loved new attractions. Wrapping around a bend on the East River, it runs for 1.3 miles from the eastern edge of the Manhattan Bridge in Dumbo to the west end of Atlantic Ave in Cobble Hill. It has revitalized a once-barren stretch of shoreline, turning a series of abandoned piers into beautifully landscaped parkland with jaw-dropping views of Manhattan. There's lots to see and do here, with playgrounds, walkways and lawns.

★**Coney Island** AREA

(Map p79; www.coneyisland.com; Surf Ave & Boardwalk, btwn W 15th & W 8th Sts; [S]D/F, N/Q to Coney Island-Stillwell Ave) About 50 minutes by subway from Midtown, this popular beach neighborhood makes for a great day trip. The wide sandy beach of Coney Island has retained its nostalgic, kitschy and slightly sleazy charms, its wood-plank boardwalk and its famous 1927 Cyclone roller coaster amid a modern amusement-park area. Nathan's Famous (p122) churns out hot dogs, and the **New York Aquarium** (www.nyaquarium.com) is a big hit with kids, as is taking in an early evening baseball game at **MCU Park** (☎718-372-5596; www.brooklyncyclones.com; 1904 Surf Ave, at 17th St, Coney Island; tickets $10-20, all tickets on Wed $10; [S]D/F, N/Q to Coney Island-Stillwell Ave), the waterfront stadium for the minor league Brooklyn Cyclones.

The area traces its amusement-park roots to the mid-1800s, when inhabitants of the increasingly industrialized city began to seek relief from their sweltering tenements in summer. By the late 19th century, the area was a rough-and-tumble party spot dubbed 'Sodom by the Sea.' In the early 1900s, however, family amusements began to materialize. The most famous, Luna Park, opened in 1903 – a dream world with live camels and elephants, illuminated by more than a million bulbs. Today, it is still possible to ride the Wonder Wheel (opened in 1920) and the clackety Cyclone roller coaster (1927). The area was a bit of a ghost town in the '80s, but it has experienced a resurgence in recent years, drawing New Yorkers who come to chow on hot dogs, catch a sideshow and dress up like punk mermaids at the annual **Mermaid Parade** (🕐late Jun). It ain't Disney – but it isn't meant to be.

★Brooklyn Museum MUSEUM
(Map p79; ☎718-638-5000; www.brooklynmuseum.org; 200 Eastern Pkwy, Prospect Park; suggested donation $16, 19yr & under free; 🕐11am-6pm Wed & Fri-Sun, to 10pm Thu; 👪; [S]2/3 to Eastern Pkwy-Brooklyn Museum) This encyclopedic museum is housed in a five-story, 560,000-sq-ft beaux-arts building designed by McKim, Mead & White. Today, the building houses more than 1.5 million objects, including ancient artifacts, 19th-century period rooms, and sculptures and painting from across several centuries. It offers a great alternative to the packed-to-the-gills institutions in Manhattan, and it often features thought-provoking temporary exhibitions. The first Saturday of the month (except September) features special events (live music, performance art) when the museum stays open until 11pm.

★Prospect Park PARK
(☎718-965-8951; www.prospectpark.org; Grand Army Plaza; 🕐5am-1am; [S]2/3 to Grand Army Plaza; F to 15th St-Prospect Park) The creators of the 585-acre Prospect Park – Frederick Law Olmsted and Calvert Vaux – considered this an improvement on their other New York project, Central Park. Created in 1866, Prospect Park has many of the same features. It's gorgeous, with a long meadow running along the western half, filled with soccer, football, cricket and baseball players (and barbecuers), hilly forests and a lovely lake and boathouse on the east side.

New York Transit Museum MUSEUM
(Map p79; ☎718-694-1600; www.mta.info/mta/museum; Schermerhorn St, at Boerum Pl; adult/child $10/5; 🕐10am-4pm Tue-Fri, 11am-5pm Sat & Sun; 👪; [S]2/3, 4/5 to Borough Hall; R to Court St) Occupying an old subway station built in 1936 (and out of service since 1946), this kid-friendly museum takes on 100-plus years of getting around town. The best part is the downstairs area, on the platform, where you can climb aboard 13 original subway and elevated train cars dating from 1904. Temporary exhibitions highlight the subway's fascinating history, including one dedicated to the recently inaugurated Second Ave line. The museum's gift shop sells popular subway-map gifts.

Brooklyn Botanic Garden GARDENS
(Map p79; www.bbg.org; 150 Eastern Pkwy, Prospect Park; adult/child $12/free, Tue & 10am-noon Sat free; 🕐8am-6pm Tue-Fri, 10am-6pm Sat & Sun, hours vary in winter; 👪; [S]2/3 to Eastern Pkwy-Brooklyn Museum) One of Brooklyn's most picturesque attractions, this 52-acre garden is home to thousands of plants and trees, as well as a **Japanese garden** where river turtles swim alongside a Shinto shrine. The best time to visit is late April or early May, when the blooming cherry trees (a gift from Japan) are celebrated in **Sakura Matsuri**, the Cherry Blossom Festival.

Brooklyn Children's Museum MUSEUM
(Map p79; ☎718-735-4400; www.brooklynkids.org; 145 Brooklyn Ave, at St Marks Ave, Crown Heights; 11, free 2-6pm Thu; 🕐10am-5pm Tue-Sun; 👪; [S]C to Kingston-Throop Aves; 3 to Kingston Ave) A bright-yellow, L-shaped structure houses this hands-on kids' favorite, which was founded in 1899. The collection contains almost 30,000 cultural objects (musical instruments, masks and dolls) and natural history specimens (rocks, minerals and a complete Asian elephant skeleton). But Brooklyn is very much in the house, with a re-created bodega, a pizza joint, and a Caribbean market that kids can play-act in. The museum is located next to Brower Park and is about a mile from the Grand Army Plaza.

Brooklyn Brewery BREWERY
(Map p79; ☎718-486-7422; www.brooklynbrewery.com; 79 N 11th St, btwn Berry St & Wythe Ave, Williamsburg; tours free Sat & Sun, $15 5pm Mon-Thu; 🕐tours 5pm Mon-Thu, 1-5pm Sat, 1-4pm Sun; tasting room 6-11pm Fri, noon-8pm Sat, noon-6pm Sun; [S]L to Bedford Ave) Harking back to a time when this area of New York was a beer brewing center, the Brooklyn Brewery not only brews and serves tasty local suds, but also offers tours of its facilities.

Brooklyn Heights Promenade VIEWPOINT
(btwn Orange & Remsen Sts; 🕐24hr; 👪; [S]2/3 to Clark St) All of the east–west lanes of Brooklyn Heights (such as Clark and Pineapple Sts) lead to the neighborhood's number-one attraction: a narrow park with breathtaking views of Lower Manhattan and New York Harbor, hanging over the busy Brooklyn–Queens Expressway (BQE). This little slice of urban beauty is a great spot for a sunset walk.

The Bronx

Home of hip-hop, known for its gritty South Bronx street culture and its web of highways carrying other New Yorkers further north, the Bronx is actually as green as it is urban: Wave Hill, Van Cortlandt Park, Pelham Bay Park and the New York Botanical Gardens

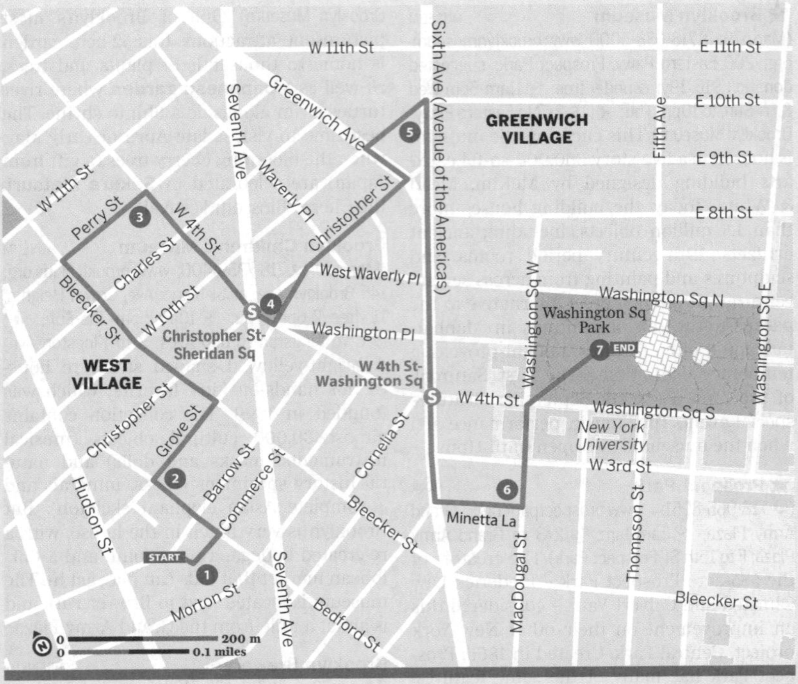

City Walk
A Village Stroll

START COMMERCE ST
END WASHINGTON SQUARE PARK
LENGTH 1.2 MILES; ONE HOUR

Of all the neighborhoods in New York City, Greenwich Village is the most walkable, with its cobbled corners that stray from the signature gridiron that unfurls across the rest of the island. Start your walkabout at the [1] **Cherry Lane Theater**. Established in 1924, the small theater is the city's longest continuously running off-Broadway establishment, and was the center of creative activity during the 1940s.

Make a left on Bedford and you'll find [2] **90 Bedford** on the right-hand side at the corner of Grove St. You might recognize the apartment block as the fictitious home of the cast of *Friends*. For another iconic TV landmark, wander up Bleecker St and make a right on Perry St, stopping at [3] **66 Perry St**, which was used as the facade and stoop of the city's turn-of-the-21st-century 'It Girl', Carrie Bradshaw, in *Sex and the City*.

Make a right on W 4th St until you reach [4] **Christopher Park**, where two white, life-sized statues of same-sex couples stand guard. On the north side of the green space is the legendary Stonewall Inn, where a clutch of fed-up drag queens rioted for their civil rights in 1969, signaling the start of what would become the gay revolution.

Follow Christopher St to Sixth Ave to find the [5] **Jefferson Market Library** straddling a triangular plot of land. The 'Ruskinian Gothic' spire was once a fire lookout tower. In the 1870s the building was used as a courthouse but today it houses a library.

Stroll down Sixth Ave, then make a left on Minetta Lane to swing by [6] **Cafe Wha?**, the notorious institution where many young musicians and comedians – such as Bob Dylan and Richard Pryor – got their start.

End your wandering further along MacDougal St in [7] **Washington Square Park**, the Village's unofficial town square, which plays host to loitering NYU students, buskers and a regular crowd of protestors chanting about various global and municipal injustices.

are just a few of its leafy areas. Orchard Beach, the 'Bronx Riviera', draws crowds in summertime and America's oldest and largest zoo is here. Architectural gems line art-deco Grand Concourse, and Arthur Ave is the place to go for old school Italian red-sauce joints.

Yankee Stadium STADIUM

(Map p79; ☎718-293-4300, tours 646-977-8687; www.newyork.yankees.mlb.com; E 161st St, at River Ave; tours $20; [S] B/D, 4 to 161st St-Yankee Stadium) The Boston Red Sox like to talk about their record of eight World Series championships in the last 90 years...well, the Yankees have won a mere 27 in that period. The team's magic appeared to have moved with them across 161st St to the new Yankee Stadium, where they played their first season in 2009 – winning the World Series there in a six-game slugfest against the Phillies. The Yankees play from April to October.

Bronx Zoo ZOO

(Map p79; ☎718-220-5100; www.bronxzoo.com; 2300 Southern Blvd; full experience tickets adult/child $37/27, suggested donation Wed; ⏰10am-5pm Mon-Fri, to 5:30pm Sat & Sun Apr-Oct, to 4:30pm Nov-Mar; [S] 2, 5 to West Farms Sq-E Tremont Ave) This 265-acre zoo is the country's biggest and oldest, with over 6000 animals and re-created habitats from around the world, from African plains to Asian rainforests. It's deservedly popular, with especially large crowds on discounted Wednesdays and weekends, and any day in July or August (try to go Monday morning). If heading in on the subway, the southwest Asia Gate (a couple blocks north of the West Farms Sq–E Tremont Ave stop, up Boston Rd) is your easiest access point.

New York Botanical Garden GARDENS

(Map p79; ☎718-817-8716; www.nybg.org; 2900 Southern Blvd; weekdays adult/child $23/10, weekends $28/12, Wed & 9-10am Sat grounds admission free; ⏰10am-6pm Tue-Sun; 👪; 🚆Metro-North to Botanical Garden) First opened in 1891 and incorporating 50 acres of old-growth forest, the New York Botanical Garden is home to the restored **Enid A Haupt Conservatory**, a grand, Victorian iron-and-glass edifice that is now a New York landmark. See the website for a list of regular events, which include themed walking tours, children's book readings and film screenings.

City Island ISLAND

(Map p79; 🚌Bx29) Although City Island is technically part of the Bronx, it has more in common with the small fishing villages that dot the north Atlantic seaboard. The approximately 1.5-mile-long island is home to a collection of alluring homes, teeming bars, some of the best seafood in the five boroughs and, of course, spectacular views of the Long Island Sound. This little slice of nautical heaven is for those interested in a truly unique New York City experience.

Woodlawn Cemetery CEMETERY

(Map p79; ☎877-496-6352, 718-920-0500; www.thewoodlawncemetery.org; Webster Ave, at E 233rd St; ⏰8:30am-4:30pm; [S] 4 to Woodlawn) As elegant as Brooklyn's Green-Wood is this 400-acre cemetery, the most prestigious resting place in the Bronx. Dating from the Civil War (1863), it claims more big names than Green-Wood – and yes, it is a contest – among its 300,000-plus headstones, including Herman Melville and jazz greats such as Miles Davis and Duke Ellington. Ask at the front for a photo pass if you want to snap pictures.

Queens

The largest of the city's boroughs and with nearly half of its residents foreign-born, Queens is truly a world apart. But other than downtown Flushing and East River condominiums, it's mostly a low-rise sprawl, suburban (think of the TV show *King of Queens*) and a patchwork of diverse communities. *Terra incognita* to other New Yorkers and far from fashionable Brooklyn confines, pockets of Queens are as fascinating as anywhere in the city. Gorge at diners and delis from around the world, ride the surf in hip Rockaway Beach and visit contemporary art centers scattered throughout the borough.

★ **Museum of the Moving Image** MUSEUM

(Map p79; ☎718-777-6888; www.movingimage.us; 36-01 35th Ave, Astoria; adult/child $15/7, free 4-8pm Fri; ⏰10:30am-2pm Wed & Thu, to 8pm Fri, 11:30am-7pm Sat & Sun; [S] M, R to Steinway St) This super-cool complex is one of the world's top film, television and video museums. Galleries show a collection of 130,000-plus artifacts, including Elizabeth Taylor's wig from *Cleopatra*, nearly everything related to *Seinfeld* and a whole room of vintage arcade games. Interactive displays – such as a DIY flipbook station – show the science behind the art.

LOCAL KNOWLEDGE

THE SUBWAY IS YOUR FRIEND

A few tips for understanding the madness of the New York subway:

Numbers, letters, colors Color-coded subway lines are named by a letter or number, and most carry a collection of two to four trains on their tracks.

Express & local lines A common mistake is accidentally boarding an 'express train' and passing by a local stop you want. Know that each color-coded line is shared by local trains and express trains; the latter make only select stops in Manhattan (indicated by a white circle on subway maps). For example, on the red line, the 2 and 3 are express, while the slower 1 makes local stops. If you're covering a greater distance – say from the Upper West Side to Wall St – you're better off transferring to the express train (usually just across the platform from the local) to save time.

Getting in the right station Some stations – such as SoHo's Spring St station on the 6 line – have separate entrances for downtown or uptown lines (read the sign carefully). If you swipe in at the wrong one – as even locals do on occasion – you'll either need to ride the subway to a station where you can transfer for free, or just lose the $2.75 and re-enter the station (usually across the street). Also look for the green and red lamps above the stairs at each station entrance; green means that it's always open, while red means that particular entrance will be closed at certain hours, usually late at night.

Weekends All the rules switch on weekends, when some lines combine with others, some get suspended, some stations get passed, and others get reached. Locals and tourists alike stand on platforms confused, sometimes irate. Check www.mta.info for weekend schedules. Sometimes posted signs aren't visible until after you reach the platform.

★MoMA PS1 GALLERY

(Map p79; ☎718-784-2084; www.momaps1.org; 22-25 Jackson Ave, Long Island City; suggested donation adult/child $10/free, free with MoMA ticket, Warm Up party online/at venue $18/20; 🕒noon-6pm Thu-Mon, Warm Up parties 3-9pm Sat Jul-Aug; [S] E, M to Court Sq-23rd St; G, 7 to Court Sq) At MoMA's hip contemporary outpost, set in a converted former public school, you'll be peering at videos through floorboards, schmoozing at DJ parties and debating the meaning of nonstatic structures while staring through a hole in the wall.

Fort Totten HISTORIC SITE

(☎718-352-4793; https://www.nycgovparks.org/parks/fort-totten-park; Totten Ave & 15 Rd, Bayside; 🕒7am-9pm; 🚌Q16) [FREE] The remnants of a decommissioned Civil War-era fortress give this park its name, but that is hardly all Fort Totten has to offer. The grounds are full of historic buildings, rolling fields, and even a public pool. There are special tours – the Halloween-themed haunted lantern tour is a must – and events year-round. As the park is on the far edge of the city, it offers a slice of quiet that is rare in NYC.

New York Hall of Science MUSEUM

(Map p79; ☎718-699-0005; www.nysci.org; 47-01 111th St; adult/child $16/13; free 2-5pm Fri & 10-11am Sun; 🕒9:30am-5pm Mon-Fri, 10am-6pm Sat & Sun; [S] 7 to 111th St) Occupying a weird 1965 building, rippling with stained glass, this science museum is unapologetically nerdy. An outdoor mini-golf course and playground don't require as much brain power.

Queens Museum MUSEUM

(Map p79; QMA; ☎718-592-9700; www.queensmuseum.org; Flushing Meadows Corona Park, Queens; suggested donation adult/child $8/free; 🕒11am-5pm Wed-Sun; [S] 7 to 111th St or Mets-Willets Point) The Queens Museum is one of the city's unexpected pleasures. Its most famous installation is the Panorama of New York City, a gob-smacking 9335-sq-ft miniature New York City, with all buildings accounted for and a 15-minute dusk-to-dawn light simulation. The museum also hosts top exhibitions of global contemporary art, reflecting the diversity of Queens. A fascinating upcoming exhibit explores some of the interesting and avant-garde NYC designs that never came to fruition, realized through drawings and 3-D models.

Greater Ridgewood Historic Society HOUSE

(Map p79; www.onderdonkhouse.org; 1820 Flushing Ave, Ridgewood; suggested donation $3; 🕒1-4pm Sat, noon-4pm Sun; [S] L to Jefferson St) On a mostly deserted block on the border of Bushwick, Brooklyn and Ridgewood, Queens sits the oldest Dutch colonial stone house in New York City. The grounds and exterior are immaculately kept and the inside of the house features a permanent exhibit on the history of the house and NYC's history. Guided tours are given on Saturdays and Sundays for a suggested donation and there are special events year-round.

The Kaufman Arts District ARTS CENTER
(http://www.kaufmanartsdistrict.com/; 34-12 36th St; [S] M or R train to Steinway St, N or Q train to 36th St) Anchored by the legendary Kaufman studios in Long Island City, this up-and-coming arts district is a place you'll want to check out so you can say you knew it before it becomes the new Chelsea. In addition to institutions like the Noguchi Museum, the Kaufman Arts District also puts on events and public art pieces around the area. There are plenty of restaurants and bars to pop into between gallery visits.

Unisphere MONUMENT
(Map p79; Flushing Meadows Park; [S] 7 to 111th St or Mets-Willets Point) Designed for the 1964 World's Fair, this 12-story-high stainless-steel globe is the focal point of Flushing Meadows Park, and the de facto icon of Queens. (Nowadays, it's probably most recognizable as the backdrop for the Beastie Boys' *Licensed to Ill* album cover or scenes in the films *Men in Black* and *Iron Man 2*). In summer, it's ringed with fountains; at other times, it's crisscrossed by skateboarders.

Staten Island

Staten Island feels a world away from Manhattan. This is the land of Shaolin (according to the Wu Tang Clan), of velour sweatsuits, pasta with gravy (red meat sauce), the starting point for the NYC marathon, homes of clapboard and aluminum siding and three cast members of MTVs *Jersey Shore*. If not for its namesake ferry that docks in downtown St George, on the island's northeastern tip, it would be mostly forgotten. Unfashionably suburban, it's not without its drawcards, especially cultural and gustatory ones, plus new developments in St George like a new 630 ft-high Ferris wheel, the world's tallest.

Activities

★ Staten Island Ferry CRUISE
(Map p80; www.siferry.com; Whitehall Terminal, 4 South St, at Whitehall St; ⏲ 24hr; [S] 1 to South Ferry; R/W to Whitehall St; 4/5 to Bowling Green) [FREE] Staten Islanders know these hulking, orange ferryboats as commuter vehicles, while Manhattanites like to think of them as their secret, romantic vessels for a spring-day escape. Yet many tourists (at last count, two million a year) are clued into the charms of the Staten Island Ferry, whose 25-minute, 5.2-mile journey across the harbor between lower Manhattan and the Staten Island neighborhood of St George is one of NYC's finest free adventures.

Central Park Bike Tours CYCLING
(Map p94; ☎ 212-541-8759; www.centralparkbiketours.com; 203 W 58th St, at Seventh Ave; rentals per 2hr/day $14/28, 2hr tours $49; ⏲ 9am-8pm; [S] A/C, B/D, 1 to 59th St-Columbus Circle) This place rents out good bikes (helmets, locks and bike map included) and leads two-hour guided tours of Central Park and the Brooklyn Bridge area.

Russian & Turkish Baths BATHHOUSE
(Map p84; ☎ 212-674-9250; www.russianturkishbaths.com; 268 E 10th St, btwn First Ave & Ave A; per visit $45; ⏲ noon-10pm Mon-Tue & Thu-Fri, from 10am Wed, from 9am Sat, from 8am Sun; [S] L to 1st Ave; 6 to Astor Pl) Since 1892, this cramped and grungy downtown spa has been drawing a polyglot and eclectic mix: actors, students, frisky couples, singles-on-the-make, Russian regulars and old-school locals, who strip down to their skivvies (or the roomy cotton shorts provided) and rotate between steam baths, an ice-cold plunge pool, a sauna and the sundeck. Most hours are co-ed (clothing required), but there are several blocks of men/women only hours (clothing optional). There are also massages, scrubs and Russian oak leaf treatments available.

Great Jones Spa SPA
(Map p84; ☎ 212-505-3185; www.greatjonesspa.com; 29 Great Jones St, btwn Lafayette St & Bowery; ⏲ 9am-10pm; [S] 6 to Bleecker St; B/D/F/M to Broadway-Lafayette St) Don't skimp on the services at this downtown feng shui–designed place, whose offerings include Moroccan rose sea-salt scrubs and stem-cell facials. If you spend over $100 per person (not difficult: hour-long massages start at $145; hour-long facials start at $135), you get access to the water lounge with thermal hot tub, sauna, steam room and cold plunge pool (swimwear required).

Downtown Boathouse KAYAKING
(Map p80; www.downtownboathouse.org; Pier 26, near N Moore St; ⏲9am-5pm Sat & Sun mid-May–mid-Oct, plus 5-7:30pm Tue-Thu mid-Jun–mid-Sep; [S]1 to Houston St) [FREE] New York's most active public boathouse offers free, walk-up 20-minute kayaking sessions (including equipment) in a protected embayment in the Hudson River on weekends and some weekday evenings. For more activities – kayaking trips, stand-up paddleboarding and classes – check out www.hudsonriverpark.org for the four other kayaking locations on the Hudson River. There's also a summer-only kayaking location on **Governors Island** (Map p79; ☎212-825-3045; www.govisland.com; ⏲10am-6pm Mon-Fri, to 7pm Sat & Sun May-Oct; [S]4/5 to Bowling Green; 1 to South Ferry) [FREE].

Loeb Boathouse BOATING, CYCLING
(Map p94; ☎212-517-2233; www.thecentralparkboathouse.com; Central Park, btwn E 74th & 75th Sts; boating per $15, bike rental per $9-15; ⏲10am-6pm Apr-Nov; 👪; [S]B, C to 72nd St; 6 to 77th St) Central Park's boathouse has a fleet of 100 rowboats, as well as a Venetian-style gondola that seats up to six if you'd rather someone else do the paddling. Bicycles are also available (helmets included), weather permitting. Rentals require ID and a credit card.

Schooner Adirondack CRUISE
(Map p88; ☎212-627-1825; www.sail-nyc.com; Chelsea Piers Complex, Pier 62 at W 22nd St; tours $52-86; [S]C, E to 23rd St) The two-masted *'Dack* hits the New York Harbor with four two-hour sails daily from May to October. The 1920s-style, 80ft *Manhattan* and 100ft *Manhattan II* yachts offer tours throughout the week. Call or check the website for the latest times.

Tours

NBC Studio Tours WALKING
(Map p88; ☎212-664-3700; www.thetouratnbcstudios.com; 30 Rockefeller Plaza, entrance at 1250 Sixth Ave; tours adult/child $33/29, children under 6yr not admitted; ⏲8:20am-2pm Mon-Fri, to 5pm Sat & Sun; [S]B/D/F/M to 47th-50th Sts-Rockefeller Center) Peppered with interesting anecdotes, this revamped, one-hour tour takes TV fans through parts of the NBC Studios, home to iconic TV shows *Saturday Night Live* and *The Tonight Show Starring Jimmy Fallon*. Stops usually include the beautifully restored Art Deco Rotunda, two studios and the NBC Broadcast Operations Center. Things get interactive in the Tour Studio, where you get to 'star' or 'produce' your own talk show segment. Book online to avoid the queues.

On Location Tours BUS
(☎212-683-2027; www.onlocationtours.com; tours $49) Face it: you want to sit on Carrie Bradshaw's apartment stoop and check out the bar Michael Keaton frequents in *Birdman*. This company offers various tours – covering *Gossip Girl, Sex and the City, The Sopranos*, the *Real Housewives of NYC*,

NEW YORK FOR CHILDREN

The American Museum of Natural History (p97), with its dinosaurs, marine world, planetarium and IMAX films, should not be missed. Nearly every big museum – the Metropolitan Museum of Art (p100), the Museum of Modern Art (p91), Guggenheim Museum (p100), Museum of the City of New York (p101) and Cooper-Hewitt National Design Museum (p100) – all have kids' programs, but many smaller institutions are even more appealing for young visitors. Even the New-York Historical Society (p97) has its own children's history museum.

Toddler Time

For tots aged one to five, hit the **Children's Museum of the Arts** (Map p84; ☎212-274-0986; www.cmany.org; 103 Charlton St, btwn Greenwich & Hudson Sts; admission $12, 4-6pm Thu by donation; ⏲noon-5pm Mon, noon-6pm Thu & Fri, 10am-5pm Sat & Sun; 👪; [S]1 to Houston St; C/E to Spring St) in West SoHo and the Brooklyn Children's Museum (p103) in Crown Heights. Both have story times, art classes, craft hours and painting sessions.

Five & Over

Bigger kids can clamber on vintage subway cars at the New York Transit Museum (p103) or slide down a pole at the New York City Fire Museum (p82). Out in Astoria, the Museum of the Moving Image (p105) has hands-on exhibits for kids.

general TV and movie locations, and movie locations in Central Park – that let you live out your entertainment-obsessed fantasies.

Big Onion Walking Tours WALKING
(☎888-606-9255; www.bigonion.com; tours $25) Choose from nearly 30 tours, including Brooklyn Bridge and Brooklyn Heights, the 'Official' Gangs of New York Tour, a Gay and Lesbian History Tour – Before Stonewall, and Chelsea and the High Line.

Municipal Art Society WALKING
(☎212-935-3960; www.mas.org; tours from $25) The Municipal Art Society offers various scheduled tours focusing on architecture and history. Among them is a 75-minute tour of Grand Central Terminal (p91), departing daily at 12:30pm from the station's Main Concourse.

Central Park Conservancy WALKING
(Map p94; ☎212-310-6600; www.centralparknyc.org/tours; 14 E 60th St, btwn Madison & Fifth Aves; [S]N/R/W to 5th Ave-59th St) The non-profit organization that supports Central Park maintenance also offers a wide range of walking tours around the park. Some tours are free (such as the Heart of the Park tour, which takes in the park's highlights), while others cost $15 and require advance booking.

Big Apple Greeter (Accessible) TOURS
(☎212-669-8198; www.bigapplegreeter.org) [FREE] The Big Apple Greeter program has more than 50 volunteers with disabilities (visible or invisible) on staff, who are happy to show off their favorite corners of the city. The tours are free and the company has a no-tipping policy. It's best to contact them three to four weeks before your arrival.

Queens Historical Society WALKING
(☎718-939-0647; www.queenshistoricalsociety.org; 143-35 37th Ave, Flushing; admission $5, tours from $20; ⏲2:30-4:30pm Tue, Sat & Sun; [S]7 to Flushing-Main St) Set in the 18th-century Kingsland Homestead, this group has a small museum and offers walking tours through various neighborhoods in Queens. These include nearby sites associated with early religious-freedom movements and later Underground Railroad efforts.

Festivals & Events

Shakespeare in the Park THEATER
(www.publictheater.org) The much-loved Shakespeare in the Park pays tribute to the Bard, with free performances in Central Park. It's a magical experience. The catch? You'll have to wait hours in line to score tickets, or win them in the online lottery.

Tribeca Film Festival FILM
(☎212-941-2400; www.tribecafilm.com; ⏲Apr) Founded in 2003 by Robert De Niro and Jane Rosenthal, the Tribeca Film Festival is now a major star of the indie movie circuit. Gaggles of celebs come to walk the red carpets each spring.

Restaurant Week FOOD & DRINK
(☎212-484-1222; www.nycgo.com/restaurant-week; ⏲Jan-Feb & Jul-Aug) Score big-time discounts at top-notch eateries during this biannual festival held in January and February, then again in July and August; three-course lunches go for around $29, and dinners are around $42.

San Gennaro Festival STREET CARNIVAL
(www.sangennaro.org; ⏲Sep) Rowdy, loyal crowds descend on the narrow streets of Little Italy for carnival games, sausage-and-fried-peppers sandwiches, deep-fried Oreos and more Italian treats than you can stomach in one evening. Held over 10 days in mid-September, it remains an old-world tradition; 2017 marked the festival's 90th year.

Sleeping

In general, expect high prices and small spaces. Room rates waver by availability, not by any high-season or low-season rules. Of course, you'll pay dearly during holidays. Accommodations fill up quickly – especially in summer – and range from boxy cookie-cutter chains to stylish boutiques. No Manhattan neighborhood has a monopoly on a single style and you'll find better value hotels in Brooklyn and Queens.

Financial District & Lower Manhattan

Wall Street Inn HOTEL $$
(Map p80; ☎212-747-1500; www.thewallstreetinn.com; 9 S William St; r $140-280; ❄📶; [S]2/3 to Wall St) The sedate stone exterior of this affordable, intimate inn belies its warm, colonial-style interior. Beds are big and plush, and rooms have glossy wood furnishings and long drapes. The bathrooms are full of appreciated touches, like Jacuzzis in the deluxe rooms and tubs in the others. Wi-fi and breakfast are included.

SoHo & Chinatown

Bowery House HOSTEL $
(Map p84; ☎212-837-2373; www.theboweryhouse.com; 220 Bowery, btwn Prince & Spring Sts; s/d with shared bath from $80/130; ❄📶; [S]R/W to Prince St) Across the street from the New Museum, this former 1920s-era flophouse has been resurrected as an upmarket hostel, its rooms decked out with Bowery-themed film posters and custom-made mattresses (ie shorter and narrower), while communal bathrooms feature rain showers and heated floors. There's also a stylish lounge area with Chesterfield sofas and chandeliers, a buzzing bar and a roof terrace.

Light sleepers may wish to avoid this place, which attracts a nightlife-loving crowd; earplugs come standard with every room.

Soho Grand Hotel BOUTIQUE HOTEL $$
(Map p84; ☎212-965-3000; www.sohogrand.com; 310 W Broadway; d $255-700; ❄@📶🐾; [S]A/C/E to Canal St) The original boutique hotel of the 'hood still reigns, with its striking glass-and-cast-iron lobby stairway, and 367 rooms with cool, clean lines plus Frette linens, plasma flat-screen TVs and Kiehl's grooming products. The lobby's Grand Lounge buzzes with scenesters and the occasional celebrity. Dogs are catered to, with amenities to match those of the human guests.

Solita SoHo HOTEL $$
(Map p84; ☎212-925-3600; www.solitasohohotel.com; 159 Grand St, at Lafayette St; d $185-285; ❄📶; [S]N/Q/R, 6 to Canal St) Solita is good value for anyone wanting to soak up the flavor of Chinatown and (ever-shrinking) Little Italy. Part of the Ascend chain, the hotel has a clean, functional lobby and smallish, slightly octagonal rooms with wide beds and private baths with dual-massage shower heads. Low-season rates can see rooms go for less than $150.

East Village & Lower East Side

St Mark's Hotel HOTEL $
(Map p84; ☎212-674-0100; www.stmarkshotel.net; 2 St Marks Pl, at Third Ave; d from $130; ❄📶; [S]6 to Astor Pl) This East Village budget option draws a young, nightlife-loving crowd, who enjoy having one of the city's liveliest concentrations of bars and restaurants right outside the front door. With such low prices, it's best to lower your expectations as the rooms are quite small and dated. Street noise is an issue for light sleepers and there's no elevator.

Bowery Hotel BOUTIQUE HOTEL $$$
(Map p84; ☎212-505-9100; www.theboweryhotel.com; 335 Bowery, btwn 2nd & 3rd Sts; r $295-535; ❄@📶; [S]F/V to Lower East Side-Second Ave; 6 to Bleecker St) Pick up your old-fashioned gold room key with its red tassel in the dark, hushed lobby filled with antique velvet chairs and faded Persian rugs. Then follow the mosaic-tiled floors to your room with huge factory windows and elegant four-poster beds. Settle in to watch a movie on your 42in plasma TV, or raid the luxury bathroom goodies.

The Bowery's zinc-topped bar, outside garden patio, and rustic Italian eatery, Gemma, are always packed.

West Village, Chelsea & Meatpacking District

Jane Hotel HOTEL $
(Map p84; ☎212-924-6700; www.thejanenyc.com; 113 Jane St, btwn Washington St & West Side Hwy; r with shared/private bath from $115/295; [P]❄📶; [S]L to Eighth Ave; A/C/E to 14th St; 1/2 to Christopher St-Sheridan Sq) The claustrophobic will want to avoid the Jane's tiny 50-sq-ft rooms, but if you want to live like a luxury sailor, check into this renovated red-brick gem, which was built for mariners in the early 20th century (*Titanic* survivors also stayed here in 1912). The gorgeous ballroom/bar looks like it belongs in a five-star hotel. More expensive captain's quarters come with private commodes.

Townhouse Inn of Chelsea B&B $$
(Map p88; ☎212-414-2323; www.townhouseinnchelsea.com; 131 W 23rd St, btwn Sixth & Seventh Aves; d $150-300; ❄📶; [S]F/V, 1 to 23rd St) Housed in a lone 19th-century, five-story townhouse with exposed brick and wood floors on busy 23rd St, this 14-room B&B is a Chelsea gem. Bought in 1998 and extensively renovated (with an elevator installed), the rooms are big and welcoming, with fanciful fabrics on big brass or poster beds and TVs held in huge armoires.

Standard BOUTIQUE HOTEL $$$
(Map p84; ☎212-645-4646; www.standardhotels.com; 848 Washington St, at 13th St; d from $509; ❄📶; [S]A/C/E to 14th St; L to Eighth Ave) Hipster hotelier André Balazs has built a wide, boxy,

glass tower that straddles the High Line. Every room has sweeping Meatpacking District views and is filled with cascading sunlight, which makes the Standard's glossy, wood-framed beds and marbled bathrooms glow in a particularly homey way. There's also a hyper-modern **Standard** in the East Village.

The amenities are first-rate, with a buzzing German beer garden and a brasserie at street level (and ice rink in winter), and a plush nightclub on the top floor. The location is unbeatable, with the best of NYC right outside your door.

High Line Hotel HOTEL **$$$**
(Map p88; 212-929-3888; www.thehighline hotel.com; 180 Tenth Ave, btwn 20th & 21st Sts; d from $470) Serenity is assured during a stay inside this neo-Gothic building that was once part of the General Theological Seminary (still functioning in a building around the corner). The 60-room hotel has attractive guestrooms that blend contemporary and antique furnishings. The location is perfect for taking in the galleries of Chelsea or strolling the leafy High Line.

Union Square, Flatiron District & Gramercy

Carlton Arms HOTEL **$**
(Map p88; 212-679-0680; www.carltonarms. com; 160 E 25th St, at Third Ave; d with shared/private bath $120/150; 6 to 23rd St or 28th St) The Carlton Arms channels the downtown edgy art world scene of yesteryear with the works of artists from all over the world adorning nearly every inch of the interiors. Murals follow the walls up five flights of stairs, and into each of the tiny guest rooms and shared bathrooms (there is a small sink in each guest room).

Marcel at Gramercy BOUTIQUE HOTEL **$$**
(Map p88; 212-696-3800; www.themarcelat gramercy.com; 201 E 24th St, at Third Ave; d from $300; @ ; 6 to 23rd St) The minimalist, 97-room Marcel is a poor-man's chic boutique, and that's not a bad thing. Rooms are simple yet modern (standard ones are walk-in closet size), their gray-and-beige color scheme shaken up by bold, canary-yellow Chesterfield bedheads. Bathrooms are uninspired but clean, while rooms on the avenue have decent views. Downstairs, the sleek lounge makes for a nifty place to unwind.

Midtown

★**Yotel** HOTEL **$$**
(Map p88; 646-449-7700; www.yotel.com; 570 Tenth Ave, at 41st St, Midtown West; r from $250; ; A/C/E to 42nd St-Port Authority Bus Terminal; 1/2/3, N/Q/R, S, 7 to Times Sq-42nd St) Part futuristic spaceport, part *Austin Powers* set, this uber-cool 669-room option bases its rooms on airplane classes: premium cabin (economy), first cabins (business) and VIP suites (first); some first cabins and VIP suites include a private terrace with hot tub. Small but cleverly configured, premium cabins include automated adjustable beds, while all cabins feature floor-to-ceiling windows with killer views, slick bathrooms and iPod connectivity.

Pod 51 HOTEL **$$**
(Map p88; 212-355-0300; www.thepodhotel. com; 230 E 51st St, btwn Second & Third Aves, Midtown East; r with shared/private bathroom from $165/210; ; 6 to 51st St; E/M to Lexington Ave-53rd St) A dream come true for folks who would like to live inside a cocoon – this affordable hot spot has a range of room types, most barely big enough for the bed. 'Pods' have bright bedding, tight workspaces, flat-screen TVs, iPod docking stations and 'rain-drop' showerheads. In the warmer months, sip a drink on the perky rooftop deck.

414 Hotel HOTEL **$$$**
(Map p88; 212-399-0006; www.414hotel.com; 414 W 46th St, btwn Ninth & Tenth Aves, Midtown West; d from $256; ; C/E to 50th St) Set up like a guesthouse, with two combined brownstones, this friendly option offers 22 tidy rooms a couple of blocks west of Times Sq. Rooms are simply yet tastefully decorated, with cable TV, free wi-fi and private bathroom; those facing the leafy inner courtyard are the quietest. The courtyard itself is the perfect spot to enjoy the included breakfast during the warmer months.

Upper West Side & Central Park

Hostelling International New York HOSTEL **$**
(HI; Map p94; 212-932-2300; www.hinewyork. org; 891 Amsterdam Ave, at 103rd St; dm $54-75; ; 1 to 103rd St) This red-brick mansion from the 1880s houses HI's 672 well-scrubbed and maintained bunks. It's rather 19th-century industrial, but benefits include good public areas, a backyard (that sees

barbecue action in the summer), a communal kitchen and a cafe. There are loads of activities on offer, from walking tours to club nights. There are attractive private rooms with private bathrooms too.

Lucerne HOTEL $$
(Map p94; ☎212-875-1000; www.thelucernehotel.com; 201 W 79th St, cnr Amsterdam Ave; d from $300; ❄📶; [S]B, C to 81st St) This unusual 1903 structure breaks away from beaux arts in favor of the baroque with an ornately carved, terra-cotta-colored facade. Inside is a stately 200-room hotel, ideal for couples and families with children (Central Park and the American Museum of Natural History are a stone's throw away). Nine types of guest rooms evoke a contemporary Victorian look.

Empire Hotel HOTEL $$$
(Map p94; ☎212-265-7400; www.empirehotelnyc.com; 44 W 63rd St, at Broadway; r from $370; ❄📶🏊; [S]1 to 66th St-Lincoln Center) The bones are all that remain of the original Empire, just across the street from the Lincoln Center, with wholesale renovations dressing them in earthy tones and contemporary stylings complete with canopied pool deck, sexy rooftop bar and a dimly lit lobby lounge studded with zebra-print settees. Its 400-plus rooms come in various configurations, and feature brightly hued walls with plush dark leather furnishings.

Upper East Side

Bentley Hotel BOUTIQUE HOTEL $$$
(Map p94; ☎212-644-6000; www.bentleyhotelnyc.com; 500 E 62nd St, at York Ave; d from $350; ❄📶; [S]N/R to Lexington Ave/59th St, Q to Lexington Ave-63rd St) Featuring great East River views, the Bentley overlooks FDR Dr, as far east as you can go. Formerly an office building, the hotel has shed its utilitarian past in the form of chic boutique-hotel stylings, a swanky lobby and sleek rooms. The downside of staying here is the long walk to subway, restaurants and other essentials.

Harlem & Upper Manhattan

Harlem Flophouse GUESTHOUSE $
(Map p94; ☎347-632-1960; www.harlemflophouse.com; 242 W 123rd St, btwn Adam Clayton Powell Jr & Frederick Douglass Blvds, Harlem; d with shared bath $99-150; 📶; [S]A/B/C/D, 2/3 to 124th St) Rekindle Harlem's Jazz Age in this atmospheric 1890s townhouse, its nostalgic rooms decked out in brass beds, polished wood floors and vintage radios (set to a local jazz station). It feels like a delicious step back in time, which also means shared bathrooms, no air-con and no TVs. The owner is a great source of local information.

Allie's Inn B&B $$
(Map p94; ☎646-283-3068, 212-690-3813; www.alliesinn.com; 313 W 136th St, btwn Frederick Douglass Blvd & Edgecombe Ave, Harlem; d $175-259, ste $310-340; ❄📶; [S]B, C to 135th St) This Harlem charmer has just three guest rooms, all clean and comfortable, with oak floors, simple modern furnishings and small kitchen units. It's a refreshing alternative to the Midtown towers and ideal for those wanting to explore Harlem's rich culture, with notable eateries and bars nearby and the subway station just around the corner. Minimum two-night stay.

Brooklyn

Wythe Hotel BOUTIQUE HOTEL $$
(☎718-460-8000; www.wythehotel.com; 80 Wythe Ave, at N 11th St, Williamsburg; d from $265; ❄📶; [S]L to Bedford Ave; G to Nassau Ave) Set in a converted 1901 factory, the red-brick Wythe Hotel brings a serious dash of high design to Williamsburg. The industrial-chic rooms have beds made from reclaimed lumber, custom-made wallpaper (from Brooklyn's own Flavor Paper), exposed brick, polished concrete floors and original 13ft timber ceilings.

Nu Hotel HOTEL $$
(☎718-852-8585; www.nuhotelbrooklyn.com; 85 Smith St; d from $220; ❄@📶; [S]F, G to Bergen St) The 93 rooms in this downtown Brooklyn hotel are of the stripped-down variety, featuring lots of crisp whiteness (sheets, walls, duvets). Furnishings are made from recycled teak and the floors are cork. Groups can consider the bunk bed suite with a queen and twin bunks, or for something more daring, book a 'nu perspectives' room, adorned with colorful murals by Brooklyn artists.

Queens

Local NYC HOSTEL $
(☎347-738-5251; www.thelocalny.com; 13-02 44th Ave, Long Island City; dm/d from $60/169; ❄📶; [S]E, M to Court Sq-23rd St) This hostel has clean and small, simply designed rooms, with comfy mattresses and plenty of natural light. Guests have access to a fully stocked kitchen and the airy cafe-bar is a fine place to meet other travelers, with good coffee by

day, and wine and beer by night. Throughout the week, there's a regular line-up of events (movie nights, live music, pub quizzes).

🍴 Eating

From inspired iterations of world cuisine where only corporate titans on expense accounts dare to dine to quintessentially local nibbles like hot dogs and pizza by the slice, New York City's dining scene is infinite, all-consuming and a testament to its kaleidoscopic citizenry. Even if you're not an obsessive foodie hitting ethnic enclaves or the newest cult-chef openings, an outstanding meal is always only a block away.

🍴 Financial District & Lower Manhattan

Hudson Eats FAST FOOD $

(Map p80; ☎ 212-417-2445; www.brookfieldplaceny.com/directory/food; Brookfield Place, 230 Vesey St, at West St; dishes from $7; 🕒 10am-9pm Mon-Sat, noon-7pm Sun; 📶; [S] E to World Trade Center; 2/3 to Park Place; R/W to Cortlandt St; 4/5 to Fulton St; A/C to Chambers St) Renovated office and retail complex Brookfield Place is home to Hudson Eats, a sleek and upmarket food hall. It's decked out in terrazzo floors, marble counter tops and floor-to-ceiling windows with expansive views of Jersey City and the Hudson River.

Fish Market SEAFOOD $

(Map p80; ☎ 917-363-8101; 111 South St, New York City; sandwiches from $9, mains $9-24; 🕒 6pm-midnight Mon-Fri, noon-midnight Sat & Sun) This dive bar with a diverse seafood menu pays homage to the nautical South Street Seaport area of Manhattan that houses it. You will find cheap drinks any hour of the day and friendly bartenders and patrons. Throw in an order of popcorn shrimp or a seafood po'boy for the complete experience.

Brookfield Place FOOD HALL, MARKET $$

(Map p80; ☎ 212-978-1698; www.brookfieldplaceny.com; 230 Vesey St, at West St; 📶; [S] E to World Trade Center; 2/3 to Park Place; R/W to Cortlandt St; 4/5 to Fulton St; A/C to Chambers St) This polished, high-end office and retail complex offers two fabulous food halls. Francophile foodies should hit Le District, a charming and polished marketplace with several stand-alone restaurants and counters selling everything from stinky cheese to steak *frites*. One floor above is Hudson Eats, a fashionable enclave of upmarket fast bites, from sushi and tacos to salads and burgers.

Da Mikele PIZZA $$

(Map p80; ☎ 212-925-8800; www.luzzosgroup.com/about-us-damikele; 275 Church St, btwn White & Franklin Sts; pizzas $17-21; 🕒 noon-10:30pm Sun-Wed, to 11:30pm Thu-Sat; [S] 1 to Franklin St; A/C/E, N/Q/R, J/Z, 6 to Canal St) An Italo-Tribeca hybrid where pressed tin and recycled wood meet retro Vespa, Da Mikele channels the *dolce vita* (sweet life) with its weeknight *aperitivo* (5pm to 7pm), where your drink includes a complimentary spread of lip-smacking bar bites. However, pizzas are the specialty. We're talking light, beautifully charred revelations, simultaneously crisp and chewy, and good enough to make a Neapolitan weep.

Le District FRENCH $$

(Map p80; ☎ 212-981-8588; www.ledistrict.com; Brookfield Place, 225 Liberty St, at West St; market mains $16-24, Beauborg dinner mains $18-38; 🕒 8:30am-11pm Mon-Sat, to 10pm Sun; 📶; [S] E to World Trade Center; 2/3 to Park Place; R/W to Cortlandt St; 4/5 to Fulton St; A/C to Chambers St) Paris on the Hudson reigns at Le District, a sprawling French food emporium selling everything from high-gloss pastries and pretty *tartines* to smelly cheese and savory steak *frites*. Main restaurant **Beaubourg** has a large bistro menu, but for a quick sit-down feed, head to the **Market District** counter for a burger or the **Cafe District** for a savory crepe.

★ Locanda Verde ITALIAN $$$

(Map p80; ☎ 212-925-3797; www.locandaverdenyc.com; 377 Greenwich St, at N Moore St; mains lunch $19-29, dinner $25-40; 🕒 7am-11pm Mon-Thu, to 11:30pm Fri, 8am-11:30pm Sat, to 11pm Sun; [S] A/C/E to Canal St; 1 to Franklin St) Step through the velvet curtains into a scene of loosened button-downs, black dresses and slick barmen behind a long, crowded bar. This celebrated brasserie showcases modern, Italo-inspired fare like housemade pappardelle with lamb Bolognese, mint-and-sheep's-milk ricotta and Sicilian-style halibut with heirloom squash and almonds. Weekend brunch is no less creative: try scampi and grits or lemon ricotta pancakes with blueberries. Bookings recommended.

Bâtard MODERN AMERICAN $$$

(Map p80; ☎ 212-219-2777; www.batardtribeca.com; 239 W Broadway, btwn Walker & White Sts; 2/3/4 courses $58/75/85; ⏱5:30-10:30pm Mon-Sat, plus noon-2:30pm Fri; ⓈJ to Franklin St; A/C/E to Canal St) Austrian chef Markus Glocker heads this warm, Michelin-starred hot spot, where a pared-back interior puts the focus squarely on the food. Glocker's dishes are beautifully balanced and textured, whether it's a crispy branzino with cherry tomatoes, basil and asparagus; risotto with rabbit sausage, broccoli *spigarello* and preserved lemon; or scallop crudo with avocado mousse, lime, radish and black sesame.

✖ SoHo & Chinatown

Bánh Mì Saigon Bakery VIETNAMESE $
(Map p84; ☎212-941-1541; www.banhmisaigon nyc.com; 198 Grand St, btwn Mulberry & Mott Sts; sandwiches $3.50-6; ⏱8am-6pm; ⓈN/Q/R, J/Z, 6 to Canal St) This no-frills storefront doles out some of the best *bánh mì* in town – we're talking crisp, toasted baguettes generously stuffed with hot peppers, pickled carrots, daikon, cucumber, cilantro and your choice of meat. Top billing goes to the classic barbeque pork version. Tip: head in by 3pm as the *bánh mì* sometimes sell out, upon which the place closes early. Cash only.

Café Gitane MEDITERRANEAN $
(Map p84; ☎212-334-9552; www.cafegitanenyc. com; 242 Mott St, at Prince St; salads $9.50-16, mains $14-17; ⏱8:30am-midnight Sun-Thu, to 12:30am Fri & Sat; ✎; ⓈN/R to Prince St; 6 to Spring St) Clear the Gauloise smoke from your eyes and blink twice if you think you're in Paris: bistro-esque Gitane has that kind of louche vibe. This is a classic see-and-be-seen haunt, popular with salad-picking models and the odd Hollywood regular. Join them for a nibble on the likes of blueberry and almond friands (small French cakes), heart-of-palm salad or Moroccan couscous with organic chicken. Cash only.

Grey Dog AMERICAN $
(Map p84; ☎212-966-1060; www.thegreydog. com; 244 Mulberry St; mains $8-15; ⏱7am-10pm Mon-Fri, 8am-10pm Sat & Sun; ⓈF/M/D/B train to Broadway-Lafayette) Whether you're looking to share a plate of cheese fries with your friends or indulge in a proper New York brunch, the Grey Dog won't disappoint. They do scrumptious takes on American classics that have full-on flavor without overdoing it. The order-at-the-counter system keeps this place bustling all day long.

Nice Green Bo CHINESE $
(New Green Bow; Map p80; ☎212-625-2359; www.nicegreenbo.com; 66 Bayard St, btwn Elizabeth & Mott Sts; mains $5.95-19.95; ⏱11am-midnight; ⓈN/Q/R, J/Z, 6 to Canal St; B/D to Grand St) Not a shred of effort – not even a new sign (you'll see!) – has been made to spruce up Nice Green Bo, and that's the way we like it. It's all about the food here: gorgeous *xiao long bao* served in steaming drums, heaping portions of noodles and gleaming plates of salubrious, sautéed spinach. Cash only.

Tacombi Fonda Nolita MEXICAN $
(Map p84; ☎917-727-0179; www.tacombi.com; 267 Elizabeth St, btwn E Houston & Prince Sts; tacos $4-7; ⏱11am-midnight Mon-Wed, to 1am Thu-Sat; ⓈF to 2nd Ave; 6 to Bleecker St) Festively strung lights, foldaway chairs and Mexican men flipping tacos in an old VW Kombi: if you can't make it to the Yucatan shore, here's your Plan B. Casual, convivial and ever-popular, Tacombi serves up fine, fresh tacos, including a fine *barbacoa* (roasted black Angus beef). Wash down the goodness with a pitcher of sangria and start plotting that south-of-the-border getaway.

★ Uncle Boons THAI $$
(Map p84; ☎646-370-6650; www.uncleboons. com; 7 Spring St, btwn Elizabeth St & Bowery; small plates $12-16, large plates $21-29; ⏱5:30-11pm Mon-Thu, to midnight Fri & Sat, to 10pm Sun; ☎; ⓈJ/Z to Bowery; 6 to Spring St) Michelin-star Thai served up in a fun, tongue-in-cheek combo of retro wood-paneled dining room with Thai film posters and old family snaps. Spanning the old and the new, zesty, tangy dishes include fantastically crunchy *mieng kum* (betel-leaf wrap with ginger, lime, toasted coconut, dried shrimp, peanuts and chili), *kao pat puu* (crab fried rice) and banana blossom salad.

Butcher's Daughter VEGETARIAN $$
(Map p84; ☎212-219-3434; www.thebutchers daughter.com; 19 Kenmare St, at Elizabeth St; salads & sandwiches $12-14, dinner mains $16-18; ⏱8am-11pm; ☎✎; ⓈJ to Bowery; 6 to Spring St) The butcher's daughter certainly has rebelled, peddling nothing but fresh herbivorous fare in her white-washed cafe. While healthy it is, boring it's not: everything from the soaked organic muesli to the spicy kale Caesar salad with almond Parmesan or the dinnertime Butcher's burger (vegetable and black-bean patty with cashew cheddar cheese) is devilishly delish.

La Esquina MEXICAN $$
(Map p84; ☎646-613-7100; www.esquinanyc.com; 114 Kenmare St, at Petrosino Sq; tacos from $3.25, mains cafe $15-25, brasserie $18-34; ⏲taqueria 11am-1:45am daily, cafe noon-midnight Mon-Fri, from 11am Sat & Sun, brasserie 6pm-2am daily; [S]6 to Spring St) This mega-popular and quirky little spot combines three places really: a stand-while-you-eat taco window, a casual Mexican cafe (entrance on Lafayette St) and a dim, slinky, cavernous brasserie downstairs requiring reservations. Standouts include the *elotes callejeros* (grilled corn with queso Cotija cheese, mayo and chili powder), pulled pork tacos and mango-jicama salad.

★Dutch MODERN AMERICAN $$$
(Map p84; ☎212-677-6200; www.thedutchnyc.com; 131 Sullivan St, at Prince St; mains lunch $18-35, dinner $25-58; ⏲11:30am-11pm Mon-Thu, to 11:30pm Fri, 10am-11:30pm Sat, to 11pm Sun; [S]C/E to Spring St; R/W to Prince St; 1 to Houston St) Whether perched at the bar or dining snugly in the back room, you can always expect smart, farm-to-table comfort grub at this see-and-be-seen stalwart. Flavors traverse the globe, from sweet potato tempura with Thai basil and fermented chili sauce to ricotta ravioli with Swiss chard and walnut pesto. Reservations are recommended, especially for dinner and all day on weekends.

★Estela MODERN AMERICAN $$$
(Map p84; ☎212-219-7693; www.estelanyc.com; 47 E Houston St, btwn Mulberry & Mott Sts; dishes $15-38; ⏲5:30-11pm Sun-Thu, to 11:30pm Fri & Sat; [S]B/D/F/M to Broadway-Lafayette St; 6 to Bleecker St) Estela might be hopeless at hide-and-seek (its location up some nondescript stairs hardly tricks savvy gourmands), but this busy, skinny wine-bar slays on the food and vino front. Graze from market-driven sharing plates, from phenomenal beef tartare (spiked with beef heart for added complexity) to moreish mussels *escabeche* on toast, or an impossibly sexy endive salad with walnuts and anchovy.

🍴 East Village & Lower East Side

Bait & Hook SEAFOOD $
(Map p88; ☎212-260-8015; www.baitandhooknyc.com; 231 2nd Ave; specials start at $5, mains $12-18; ⏲noon-11pm Sun-Wed, noon-midnight Thu-Sat; [S]L to 1st Ave) This Manhattan bar has happy hour specials worth celebrating and theme days that can't be missed. There's a good time any day of the week, be it Mussel Monday or Taco Tuesday. The interior is bright, airy and tastefully decorated with nautical kitsch.

El Rey CAFE $
(Map p84; ☎212-260-3950; www.elreynyc.com; 100 Stanton St, btwn Orchard & Ludlow; small plates $8-15; ⏲7am-7pm Mon-Fri, from 8am Sat & Sun; 🖉; [S]F to 2nd Ave) This white, minimalist space on Stanton feels more SoCal than LES, and has a devoted following for its delectably inventive (and fairly priced) farm-to-table plates with a focus on hearty veggies. Microbrews, good coffees (from a Strada espresso machine) and wine round out the menu.

Meatball Shop ITALIAN $
(Map p84; ☎212-982-8895; www.themeatballshop.com; 84 Stanton St, btwn Allen & Orchard Sts; sandwiches $13; ⏲11:30am-2am Sun-Thu, to 4am Fri-Sat; [S]2nd Ave; F to Delancey St; J/M/Z to Essex St) Elevating the humble meatball to high art, the Meatball Shop serves up five varieties of juiciness (including a lentil vegetarian option and a mac 'n' cheese special). Order those balls on a hero (a long roll), add mozzarella and spicy tomato sauce, and voila: you have a tasty, if happily down-market, meal. This branch boasts a rock-and-roll vibe, with tattooed waitstaff and prominent beats. There are six other branches in NYC. Check the website for details.

Vanessa's Dumpling House CHINESE $
(Map p84; ☎212-625-8008; www.vanessas.com; 118A Eldridge St, btwn Grand & Broome Sts; dumplings $1.50-6; ⏲10:30am-10:30pm Mon-Sat, to 10pm Sun; [S]B/D to Grand St; J to Bowery; F to Delancey St) Tasty dumplings – served steamed, fried or in soup – are whipped together in iron skillets at lightning speed and tossed into hungry mouths at unbeatable prices.

Veselka EASTERN EUROPEAN $
(Map p84; ☎212-228-9682; www.veselka.com; 144 Second Ave, at 9th St; mains $10-19; ⏲24hr; [S]L to 3rd Ave; 6 to Astor Pl) A bustling tribute to the area's Ukrainian past, Veselka dishes out *varenyky* (handmade dumplings) and veal goulash amid the usual suspects of greasy comfort food. The cluttered spread of tables is available to loungers and carbo-loaders all night long, though it's a favorite any time of day, and a regular haunt for writers, actors and East Village characters.

★Momofuku Noodle Bar NOODLES $$
(Map p84; ☎212-777-7773; www.noodlebar-ny.momofuku.com; 171 First Ave, btwn E 10th & 11th Sts; mains $16; ⏰noon-11pm Sun-Thu, to 1am Fri & Sat; [S] L to 1st Ave; 6 to Astor Pl) With just 30 stools and a no-reservations policy, you'll always have to wait to cram into this bustling phenomenon. Queue up for the namesake special: homemade ramen noodles in broth, served with poached egg and pork belly, or some interesting combos. The menu changes daily and includes buns (such as brisket and horseradish), snacks (smoked chicken wings) and desserts.

★Clinton Street Baking Company AMERICAN $$
(Map p84; ☎646-602-6263; www.clintonstreetbaking.com; 4 Clinton St, btwn Stanton & Houston Sts; mains $12-20; ⏰8am-4pm & 5:30-11pm Mon-Sat, 9am-5pm Sun; [S] J/M/Z to Essex St; F to Delancey St; F to Second Ave) Mom-and-pop shop extraordinaire, Clinton Street Baking Company gets the blue ribbon in so many categories – best pancakes (blueberry!), best muffins, best po' boys (southern-style sandwiches), best biscuits etc – that you're pretty much guaranteed a stellar meal no matter what time you stop by. In the evenings, you can opt for 'breakfast for dinner' (pancakes, eggs Benedict), fish tacos or the excellent buttermilk fried chicken.

Katz's Delicatessen DELI $$
(Map p84; ☎212-254-2246; www.katzsdelicatessen.com; 205 E Houston St, at Ludlow St; sandwiches $15-22; ⏰8am-10:45pm Mon-Wed, Sun to 2:45am Thu, from 8am Fri, 24hr Sat; [S] F to 2nd Ave) Though visitors won't find many remnants of the classic, old-world Jewish LES dining scene, there are a few stellar holdouts, among them Katz's Delicatessen, where Meg Ryan faked her famous orgasm in the 1989 movie *When Harry Met Sally*. If you love classic deli grub like pastrami and salami on rye, it just might have the same effect on you. These days the lines are breathtakingly long, and the prices are high (Katz's signature hot pastrami sandwich costs a hefty $20).

Upstate SEAFOOD $$
(Map p84; ☎212-460-5293; www.upstatenyc.com; 95 First Ave, btwn E 5th & 6th Sts; mains $15-30; ⏰5-11pm; [S] F to 2nd Ave) Upstate serves outstanding seafood dishes and craft beers. The small, always-changing menu features the likes of beer-steamed mussels, seafood stew, scallops over mushroom risotto, softshell crab and wondrous oyster selections. There's no freezer – seafood comes from the market each day, so you know you'll be getting only the freshest ingredients. Lines can be long, so go early.

Degustation MODERN EUROPEAN $$$
(Map p84; ☎212-979-1012; www.degustation-nyc.com; 239 E 5th St, btwn Second & Third Aves; small plates $12-22, tasting menu $85; ⏰6pm-11:30pm Mon-Sat, to 10pm Sun; [S] 6 to Astor Pl) Blending Iberian, French and new-world recipes, Degustation does a beautiful array of tapas-style plates at this narrow, 19-seat eatery. It's an intimate setting, with guests seated around a long wooden counter while chef Oscar Islas Díaz and his team are center stage, firing up crisp octopus, lamb belly with soft poached egg, and paella with blue prawns and chorizo.

🍴 West Village, Chelsea & Meatpacking District

★Chelsea Market MARKET $
(Map p88; www.chelseamarket.com; 75 9th Ave, btwn 15th & 16th Sts; ⏰7am-9pm Mon-Sat, 8am-8pm Sun; [S] A/C/E to 14th St) In a shining example of redevelopment and preservation, the Chelsea Market has taken a factory formerly owned by cookie giant Nabisco (creator of Oreo) and turned it into an 800ft-long shopping concourse that caters to foodies. Taking the place of the old factory ovens that churned out massive numbers of biscuits are eclectic eateries that fill the renovated hallways of this food haven.

Gansevoort Market MARKET $
(Map p88; www.gansmarket.com; 353 W 14th St, at Ninth Ave; mains $5-20; ⏰8am-8pm; [S] A/C/E, L to 14th St-8th Ave) Inside a brick building in the heart of the Meatpacking District, this sprawling market is the latest and greatest food emporium to land in NYC. A raw, industrial space lit by skylights, it features several dozen gourmet vendors slinging tapas, arepas, tacos, pizzas, meat pies, ice cream, pastries and more.

Red Bamboo CHINESE $
(Map p84; ☎212-260-7049; www.redbamboo-nyc.com/; 140 West 4th St; mains $8-13; ⏰12:30pm-11pm Mon-Thu, 12:30pm-11:30pm Fri, noon-11:30pm Sat, noon-11pm Sun; [S] D/B/F, M/A/C/E to West 4th Street) Flaky, hot bites of popcorn shrimp, ooey, gooey chicken Parmesan, chocolate cake so rich you can barely finish – Red

Bamboo offers all of that and more soul and Asian food options. The catch? Everything on their menu is vegan (some dishes do offer the option of real cheese). This is a must try for vegans, vegetarians or anyone looking to try something new.

Rosemary's ITALIAN $$
(Map p84; ☎212-647-1818; www.rosemarysnyc.com; 18 Greenwich Ave, at W 10th St; mains $14-40; ⏰8am-4pm & 5-11pm Mon-Thu, until midnight Fri, opens 10am Sat-Sun, closes 11pm Sun; [S]1 to Christopher St-Sheridan Sq) One of the West Village's hottest restaurants, Rosemary's serves high-end Italian fare that more than lives up to the hype. In a vaguely farmhouse-like setting, diners tuck into generous portions of housemade pastas, rich salads, and cheese and *salumi* (cured meat) boards. Everything from the simple walnut herb pesto to the succulent smoked lamb shoulder is incredible.

Cookshop MODERN AMERICAN $$
(Map p88; ☎212-924-4440; www.cookshopny.com; 156 Tenth Ave, btwn W 19th & 20th Sts; mains brunch $14-20, lunch $16-24, dinner $22-48; ⏰8am-11:30pm Mon-Fri, from 10am Sat, 10am-10pm Sun; [S]L to 8th Ave; A/C/E to 23rd St) A brilliant brunching pit stop before (or after) tackling the verdant High Line across the street, Cookshop is a lively place that knows its niche and does it oh so well. Excellent service, eye-opening cocktails (good morning, bacon-infused BLT Mary!), a perfectly baked bread basket and a selection of inventive egg mains make this a Chelsea favorite on a Sunday afternoon.

★**Blue Hill** AMERICAN $$$
(Map p84; ☎212-539-1776; www.bluehillfarm.com; 75 Washington Pl, btwn Sixth Ave & Washington Sq W; prix-fixe menu $88-98; ⏰5-11pm Mon-Sat, to 10pm Sun; [S]A/C/E, B/D/F/M to W 4th St-Washington Sq) A place for slow-food junkies with deep pockets, Blue Hill was an early crusader in the 'Local is Better' movement. Gifted chef Dan Barber, who hails from a farm family in the Berkshires, Massachusetts, uses harvests from that land and from farms in upstate New York to create his widely praised fare.

★**Foragers Table** MODERN AMERICAN $$$
(Map p88; ☎212-243-8888; www.foragersmarket.com/restaurant; 300 W 22nd St, at Eighth Ave; mains $17-32; ⏰5:30-10pm Mon-Fri, plus 9am-2:30pm Sat & Sun, to 9pm Sun; 🥕; [S]C/E, 1 to 23rd St) Owners of this outstanding restaurant run a 28-acre farm in the Hudson Valley, from which much of their seasonal menu is sourced. It changes frequently, but recent temptations include Long Island duck breast with roasted acorn squash, apples, chanterelle mushrooms and figs, grilled skate with red quinoa, creamed kale and *cippolini* onion and deviled farm eggs with Dijon mustard.

★**Jeffrey's Grocery** MODERN AMERICAN $$$
(Map p84; ☎646-398-7630; www.jeffreysgrocery.com; 172 Waverly Pl, at Christopher St; mains $25-39; ⏰8am-11pm Mon-Fri, from 9:30am Sat & Sun; [S]1 to Christopher St-Sheridan Sq) This West Village classic is a lively eating and drinking spot that hits all the right notes. Seafood is the focus: there's an oyster bar and beautifully executed selections such as razor clams with caviar and dill, whole roasted dourade with curry, and sharing platters. Meat dishes include roasted chicken with Jerusalem artichoke and a humble but juicy pastrami burger.

★**RedFarm** FUSION $$$
(Map p84; ☎212-792-9700; www.redfarmnyc.com; 529 Hudson St, btwn W 10th & Charles Sts; mains $19-57, dumplings $14-20; ⏰5pm-11:45pm daily, plus 11am-2:30pm Sat & Sun, to 11pm Sun; [S]A/C/E, B/D/F/M to W 4th St-Washington Sq; 1 to Christopher St-Sheridan Sq) RedFarm transforms Chinese cooking into pure, delectable artistry at this small, buzzing space on Hudson St. Fresh crab and eggplant bruschetta, juicy rib steak (marinated overnight in papaya, ginger and soy) and pastrami egg rolls are among the many creative dishes that brilliantly blend cuisines. Other hits include spicy crispy beef, pan-fried lamb dumplings and the grilled jumbo-shrimp red curry.

Waits can be long, so arrive early. Reservations are only made for parties of 8 or more. The bar downstairs, **Decoy**, is owned by the people behind RedFarm. Their specialty is a whole Peking duck. It's usually less crowded and serves a limited menu, but if you ask nicely you may be able to convince the bartender to bring down an order of soup dumplings for you.

🍴 Union Square, Flatiron District & Gramercy

Tacombi Café El Presidente MEXICAN $
(Map p88; ☎212-242-3491; www.tacombi.com; 30 W 24th St, btwn Fifth & Sixth Aves; tacos $4-5.50, quesadillas $6-9; ⏰11am-midnight Mon-Sat, to

10:30pm Sun; S F/M, R/W to 23rd St) Channeling the cafes of Mexico City, pink-and-green Tacombi covers numerous bases: from juice and liquor bar to taco joint. Score a table, order a margarita and hop your way around a menu of Mexican street-food deliciousness. Top choices include *esquites* (grilled corn with *cotija* cheese and chipotle mayonnaise, served in a paper cup) and succulent *carnitas michoacan* (beer-marinated pork) tacos.

Shake Shack BURGERS $
(Map p88; ✆ 646-889-6600; www.shakeshack. com; Madison Square Park, cnr E 23rd St & Madison Ave; burgers $4.20-9.50; ⏱ 11am-10:30pm; S R/W, F/M, 6 to 23rd St) The flagship of chef Danny Meyer's gourmet burger chain, Shake Shack whips up hyper-fresh burgers, hand-cut fries and a rotating line-up of frozen custards. Veg-heads can dip into the crisp portobello burger. Lines are long – but worth it – and you can digest the filling meal while people-watching at tables and benches in the park.

Eisenberg's Sandwich Shop SANDWICHES $
(Map p88; ✆ 212-675-5096; www.eisenbergs nyc.com; 174 Fifth Ave, btwn W 22nd & 23rd St; sandwiches $4-13; ⏱ 6:30am-8pm Mon-Fri, 9am-6pm Sat, to 5pm Sun; S R/W to 23rd St) This old-school diner – an anomaly on this mostly upscale stretch of real estate – is filled from morning to close with regulars in for traditional Jewish diner fare like chopped liver, pastrami and whitefish salad. Grab a stool at the long bar and rub elbows with an eclectic mix of customers who know meatloaf isn't a joke dish.

Eataly FOOD HALL $$
(Map p88; ✆ 212-229-2560; www.eataly.com; 200 Fifth Ave, at W 23rd St; ⏱ 7am-11pm; ✐; S R/W, F/M, 6 to 23rd St) Mario Batali's sleek, sprawling temple to Italian gastronomy is a veritable wonderland. Feast on everything from vibrant *crudo* (raw fish) and *fritto misto* (tempura-style vegetables) to steamy pasta and pizza at the emporium's string of sit-down eateries. Alternatively, guzzle espresso at the bar and scour the countless counters and shelves for a DIY picnic hamper *nonna* would approve of.

★**Gramercy Tavern** MODERN AMERICAN $$$
(Map p88; ✆ 212-477-0777; www.gramercytavern. com; 42 E 20th St, btwn Broadway & Park Ave S; tavern mains $29-36, dining room 3-course menu $125, tasting menus $140-165; ⏱ tavern noon-11pm Sun-Thu, to midnight Fri & Sat, dining room

noon-2pm & 5:30-10pm Mon-Thu, to 11pm Fri, noon-1:30pm & 5:30-11pm Sat, 5:30-10pm Sun; 🛜 ✐; S R/W, 6 to 23rd St) ✐ Seasonal, local ingredients drive this perennial favorite, a vibrant, country-chic institution aglow with copper sconces, murals and dramatic floral arrangements. Choose from two spaces: the walk-in-only tavern and its à la carte menu, or the swankier dining room and its fancier prix-fixe and degustation feasts. Tavern highlights include a show-stopping duck meatloaf with mushrooms, chestnuts and brussels sprouts.

★**Craft** MODERN AMERICAN $$$
(Map p88; ✆ 212-780-0880; www.craftrestaurant. com; 43 E 19th St, btwn Broadway & Park Ave S; lunch $29-36, dinner mains $28-45; ⏱ noon-10pm Mon-Thu, to 11pm Fri, 5:30pm-11pm Sat, to 10pm Sun; 🛜; S 4/5/6, N/Q/R/W, L to 14th St-Union Sq) ✐ Humming, high-end Craft flies the flag for small, family-owned farms and food producers, their bounty transformed into pure, polished dishes. Whether nibbling on flawlessly charred braised octopus, pillowy scallops or pumpkin mezzaluna pasta with sage, brown butter and Parmesan, expect every ingredient to sing with flavor. Book ahead Wednesday to Saturday or head in by 6pm or after 9:30pm.

✗ Midtown

★**Totto Ramen** JAPANESE $
(Map p88; ✆ 212-582-0052; www.tottoramen.com; 366 W 52nd St, btwn Eighth & Ninth Aves; ramen from $11; ⏱ noon-4:30pm & 5:30pm-midnight Mon-Sat, 4-11pm Sun; S C/E to 50th St) There might be another two branches in Midtown, but purists know that neither beats the tiny, 20-seat original. Write your name and number of guests on the clipboard and wait your turn. Your reward: extraordinary ramen. Go for the pork, which sings in dishes like miso ramen (with fermented soybean paste, egg, scallions, bean sprouts, onion and homemade chili paste).

Burger Joint BURGERS $
(Map p88; ✆ 212-708-7414; www.burgerjointny. com; Le Parker Meridien, 119 W 56th St, btwn Sixth & Seventh Aves; burgers from $9.50; ⏱ 11am-11:30pm Sun-Thu, to midnight Fri & Sat; S F to 57th St) With only a small neon burger as your clue, this speakeasy-style burger hut lurks behind the lobby curtain in the Le Parker Meridien hotel. Though it might not be as 'hip' or as 'secret' as it once was, it still delivers the same

winning formula of graffiti-strewn walls, retro booths and attitude-loaded staff slapping up beef 'n' patty brilliance.

Margon   CUBAN $

(Map p88; ☑ 212-354-5013; 136 W 46th St, btwn Sixth & Seventh Aves; sandwiches $4-8, mains from $9; ◷ 6am-5pm Mon-Fri, from 7am Sat; Ⓢ B/D/F/M to 47th-50th Sts-Rockefeller Center) It's still 1973 at this ever-packed Cuban lunch counter, where orange Laminex and greasy goodness never went out of style. Go for gold with its legendary *cubano* sandwich (a pressed panino jammed with rich roast pork, salami, cheese, pickles, *mojo* sauce and mayo). It's obscenely good.

Hangawi   KOREAN, VEGAN $$

(Map p88; ☑ 212-213-0077; www.hangawirestaurant.com; 12 E 32nd St, btwn Fifth & Madison Aves; mains lunch $11-30, dinner $19-30; ◷ noon-2:30pm & 5:30-10:15pm Mon-Fri, 1-10:30pm Sat, 5-9:30pm Sun; ☑; Ⓢ B/D/F/M, N/Q/R/W to 34th St-Herald Sq) Meat-free Korean is the draw at high-achieving Hangawi. Leave your shoes at the entrance and slip into a soothing, Zen-like space of meditative music, soft low seating and clean, complex dishes. Show-stoppers include the leek pancakes and a seductively smooth tofu claypot in ginger sauce.

Virgil's Real Barbecue   BARBECUE $$

(Map p88; ☑ 212-921-9494; www.virgilsbbq.com; 152 W 44th St, btwn Broadway & Sixth Ave, Midtown West; mains $14-38; ◷ 11:30am-11pm Mon, to midnight Tue-Fri, 11am-midnight Sat, 11am-11pm Sun; ☎; Ⓢ N/Q/R, S, 1/2/3, 7 to Times Sq-42nd St) Rather than specializing in one specific style of American barbecue, Virgil's celebrates them all. Indeed, the menu covers the entire barbecue map, from Memphis-style pork spare ribs to Georgia chicken-fried steak and platters of sliced Texas beef brisket. Meats are smoked with a combo of hickory, oak and fruitwoods, keepin' fingers licked and clean.

Pio Pio   PERUVIAN $$

(Map p88; ☑ 212-459-2929; www.piopio.com; 604 Tenth Ave, btwn W 43rd & 44th Sts; mains $14-26; ◷ 11am-11pm Sun-Thu, to midnight Fri & Sat; Ⓢ A/C/E to Port Authority-42nd St) This Peruvian restaurant is a favorite among New Yorkers for its delectable food, frothy pisco sours and breathtaking ambience. The specialty here is rotisserie-style chicken, seasoned and cooked to absolute perfection and served in a variety of ways (but always with plenty of

tangy, green *aji* sauce), along with classic Latin American sides such as plantains and avocado salad.

El Parador Cafe   MEXICAN $$

(Map p88; ☑ 212-679-6812; www.elparadorcafe.com; 325 E 34th St, btwn First & Second Aves, Midtown East; lunch $10-22, dinner mains $18-32; ◷ noon-10pm Mon, to 11pm Tue-Sat; Ⓢ 6 to 33rd St) Back in the day, the far-flung location of this Mexican stalwart was much appreciated by philandering husbands. The shady regulars may have gone, but the old-school charm remains, from the beveled candleholders and dapper Latino waiters to the satisfying south-of-the-border standbys.

★ViceVersa   ITALIAN $$$

(Map p88; ☑ 212-399-9291; www.viceversanyc.com; 325 W 51st St, btwn Eighth & Ninth Aves; 3-course lunch $29, dinner mains $24-33; ◷ noon-2:30pm & 4:30-11pm Mon-Fri, 4:30-11pm Sat, 11:30am-3pm & 4:30-10pm Sun; Ⓢ C/E to 50th St) ViceVersa is quintessential Italian: suave and sophisticated, affable and scrumptious. The menu features refined, cross-regional dishes like arancini with black truffle and fontina cheese. For a celebrated classic, order the *casoncelli alla bergamasca* (ravioli-like pasta filled with minced veal, raisins and amaretto cookies and seasoned with sage, butter, pancetta and Grana Padano), a nod to chef Stefano Terzi's Lombard heritage.

★Le Bernardin   SEAFOOD $$$

(Map p88; ☑ 212-554-1515; www.le-bernardin.com; 155 W 51st St, btwn Sixth & Seventh Aves; prix-fixe lunch/dinner $87/150, tasting menus $180-270; ◷ noon-2:30pm & 5:15-10:30pm Mon-Thu, to 11pm Fri, 5:15-11pm Sat; Ⓢ 1 to 50th St; B/D, E to 7th Ave) The interiors may have been subtly sexed-up for a 'younger clientele' (the stunning storm-themed triptych is by Brooklyn artist Ran Ortner), but triple-Michelin-starred Le Bernardin remains a luxe, fine-dining holy grail. At the helm is French-born celebrity chef Éric Ripert, whose deceptively simple-looking seafood often borders on the transcendental.

Grand Central Oyster
Bar & Restaurant   SEAFOOD $$$

(Map p88; ☑ 212-490-6650; www.oysterbarny.com; Grand Central Terminal, 42nd St, at Park Ave; mains $15-39; ◷ 11:30am-9:30pm Mon-Sat; Ⓢ S, 4/5/6, 7 to Grand Central-42nd St) This buzzing bar and restaurant within Grand Central is hugely atmospheric, with a vaulted tiled ceiling by Catalan-born engineer Rafael Guastavino.

While the extensive menu covers everything from clam chowder and seafood stews to pan-fried soft-shell crab, the real reason to head here is for the two-dozen oyster varieties. Get slurping.

Upper West Side & Central Park

Peacefood Cafe
VEGAN $

(Map p94; ☏212-362-2266; www.peacefoodcafe. com; 460 Amsterdam Ave, at 82nd St; mains $12-18; ☺10am-10pm; ☕; ☒1 to 79th St) This bright and airy vegan haven dishes up a popular fried seitan panino (served on homemade focaccia and topped with cashew cheese, arugula, tomatoes and pesto), as well as pizzas, roasted vegetable plates and an excellent quinoa salad. There are daily raw specials, energy-fueling juices and rich desserts. Healthy and good – for you, the animals and the environment.

West 79th Street Boat Basin Café
CAFE $

(Map p94; ☏212-496-5542; www.boatbasincafe. com; W 79th St, at Henry Hudson Parkway; mains $14; ☺11am-11pm Apr-Oct, weather permitting; ☒1 to 79th St) New ownership and an award-winning Culinary Institute of America chef are revitalizing this perennially popular waterside spot. The Robert Moses–era structure, with an elegant colonnade opening onto a outdoor rotunda, provides great marina and Hudson River views. Always deservedly popular for sunset drinks, the menu of salads, sandwiches, seafood and innovative NYC 'street food' is now another drawing card.

Jacob's Pickles
AMERICAN $$

(Map p94; ☏212-470-5566; www.jacobspickles. com; 509 Amsterdam Ave, btwn W 84th & 85th; mains $15-26; ☺10am-2am Mon-Thu, to 4am Fri, 9am-4am Sat, to 2am Sun; ☒1 to 86th St) Jacob's elevates the humble pickle to exalted status at this inviting and warmly lit eatery. Aside from briny cukes and other preserves you'll find heaping portions of upscale comfort food, such as catfish tacos, wine-braised turkey-leg dinner, and mushroom mac 'n' cheese. The biscuits are top-notch.

Barney Greengrass
DELI $$

(Map p94; ☏212-724-4707; www.barneygreen grass.com; 541 Amsterdam Ave, at W 86th St; mains $12-22; ☺8:30am-4pm Tue-Fri, to 5pm Sat & Sun; ☒1 to 86th St) The self-proclaimed 'King of Sturgeon' Barney Greengrass serves up the same heaping dishes of eggs and salty lox,

luxuriant caviar and melt-in-your-mouth chocolate babkas that first made it famous when it opened over a century ago. Pop in to fuel up in the morning or for a quick lunch (there are rickety tables set amid the crowded produce aisles).

PJ Clarke's
AMERICAN $$

(Map p94; ☏212-957-9700; www.pjclarkes.com; 44 W 63rd St, cnr Broadway; burgers $18-26, mains $21-26; ☺11:30am-2am; ☒1 to 66th St-Lincoln Center) Across the street from Lincoln Center, this spot has red-checkered tablecloths, a buttoned-down crowd, friendly bartenders and a solid menu. If you're in a rush, sidle up to the bar for a Black Angus burger and a Brooklyn Lager. A raw bar offers fresh Long Island Little Neck and Cherry Stone clams, as well as jumbo shrimp cocktails.

Dovetail
MODERN AMERICAN $$$

(Map p94; ☏212-362-3800; www.dovetailnyc.com; 103 W 77th St, cnr Columbus Ave; prix fixe $68-88, tasting menu $145; ☺5:30-10pm Mon-Thu, to 11pm Fri & Sat, 5-10pm Sun; ☕; ☒B, C to 81st St-Museum of Natural History; 1 to 79th St) This Michelin-starred restaurant showcases its Zen-like beauty in both its decor (exposed brick, bare tables) and its delectable, seasonal menus – think striped bass with sunchokes and burgundy truffle, and venison with bacon, golden beets and foraged greens. Each evening there are two seven-course tasting menus: one for omnivores ($145) and one for vegetarians ($125).

Burke & Wills
MODERN AUSTRALIAN $$$

(Map p94; ☏646-823-9251; www.burkeandwills ny.com; 226 W 79th St, btwn Broadway & Amsterdam Ave; mains lunch $19-30, dinner $19-39; ☺noon-3pm & 5:30pm-late Mon-Fri, from 11am Sat & Sun; ☒1 to 79th St) This ruggedly attractive bistro and bar brings a touch of the outback to the Upper West Side. The menu leans toward Modern Australian pub grub: juicy kangaroo burgers with triple-fried chips, grilled prawns, kale Cobb salad, braised pork belly with apple-and-celery slaw, and seafood platters with oysters, clams and crab claws.

Upper East Side

★ Earl's Beer & Cheese
AMERICAN $

(Map p94; ☏212-289-1581; www.earlsny.com; 1259 Park Ave, btwn 97th & 98th Sts; grilled cheese $8; ☺11am-midnight Sun-Thu, to 2am Fri & Sat; ☒6 to 96th St) This sibling-run, tiny, comfort-food outpost channels a hipster hunting vibe, complete with a giant deer-in-the-woods mural and a mounted buck's head. Basic grilled cheese is a paradigm shifter, served with pork belly, fried egg and kimchi. There is also mac 'n' cheese (with goat's cheese and crispy rosemary) and tacos (featuring braised pork shoulder and *queso fresco*).

Boqueria SPANISH **$$**
(Map p94; ☎ 212-343-2227; www.boquerianyc.com; 1460 Second Ave, btwn 76th & 77th Sts; tapas $6-18, paella for two $38-46; 🕒 noon-10:30pm Sun-Thu, 11am-11:30pm Fri & Sat; 🌿; [S] 6 to 77th St; Q to 72nd St) This lively, much-loved tapas place brings a bit of downtown cool to the Upper East Side, with nicely spiced *patatas bravas,* tender slices of *jamon ibérico* and rich *pulpo a la plancha* (grilled octopus). Head chef Marc Vidal, who hails from Barcelona, also creates an exquisite seafood paella. Wash it all down with a pitcher of excellent sangria.

Jones Wood Foundry BRITISH **$$**
(Map p94; ☎ 212-249-2700; www.joneswoodfoundry.com; 401 E 76th St, btwn First & York Aves; mains lunch $16-28, dinner $17-34; 🕒 11am-11pm; [S] Q to 72nd St-2nd Ave) Inside a narrow brick building that once housed an ironworks, the Jones Wood Foundry is a British-inspired gastropub serving first-rate beer-battered fish and chips, bangers and mash, lamb and rosemary pie and other hearty temptations. On warm days, grab a table on the enclosed courtyard patio.

Candle Cafe VEGAN **$$**
(Map p94; ☎ 212-472-0970; www.candlecafe.com; 1307 Third Ave, btwn 74th & 75th Sts; mains $15-22; 🕒 11:30am-10:30pm Mon-Sat, to 9:30pm Sun; 🌿; [S] Q to 72nd St-2nd Ave) The moneyed yoga set piles into this attractive vegan cafe serving a long list of sandwiches, salads, comfort food and market-driven specials. The specialty here is the housemade seitan. There is a juice bar and a gluten-free menu.

★ Tanoshi SUSHI **$$$**
(Map p94; ☎ 917-265-8254; www.tanoshisushinyc.com; 1372 York Ave, btwn E 73rd & 74th Sts; chef's sushi selection $80-100; 🕒 seatings 6pm, 7:30pm & 9pm Mon-Sat; [S] Q to 72nd St) It's not easy to snag one of the 20 stools at Tanoshi, a wildly popular, pocket-sized sushi spot. The setting may be humble but the flavors are simply magnificent. Only sushi is on offer and only *omakase* (chef's selection) – which might include Hokkaido scallops, king salmon or mouth-watering *uni* (sea urchin). BYO beer, sake or whatnot. Reserve well in advance.

🍴 Harlem & Upper Manhattan

★ Red Rooster MODERN AMERICAN **$$**
(Map p94; ☎ 212-792-9001; www.redroosterharlem.com; 310 Malcolm X Blvd, btwn W 125th & 126th Sts, Harlem; mains $18-30; 🕒 11:30am-10:30pm Mon-Thu, to 11:30pm Fri, 10am-11:30pm Sat, 10am-10pm Sun; [S] 2/3 to 125th St) Transatlantic super-chef Marcus Samuelsson laces upscale comfort food with a world of flavors at his effortlessly cool, swinging brasserie. Like the work of the contemporary New York–based artists displayed on the walls, dishes are up to date: mac 'n' cheese joins forces with lobster, blackened catfish pairs with pickled mango, and spectacular Swedish meatballs salute Samuelsson's home country. The prix-fixe lunch is a bargain at $25.

Dinosaur Bar-B-Que BARBECUE **$$**
(Map p94; ☎ 212-694-1777; www.dinosaurbarbque.com; 700 W 125th St, at Twelfth Ave, Harlem; mains $12.50-25; 🕒 11:30am-11pm Mon-Thu, to midnight Fri & Sat, noon-10pm Sun; [S] 1 to 125th St) Jocks, hipsters, moms and pops: everyone dives into this honky-tonk rib bar for a rockin' feed. Get messy with dry-rubbed, slow-pit-smoked ribs, slabs of juicy steak and succulent burgers, or watch the waist with the lightly seasoned grilled-chicken options. The (very) few vegetarian options include a fantastic version of Creole-spiced deviled eggs.

Amy Ruth's Restaurant AMERICAN **$$**
(Map p94; ☎ 212-280-8779; www.amyruths.com; 113 W 116th St, btwn Malcolm X & Adam Clayton Powell Jr Blvds, Harlem; waffles $10-18, mains $14-25; 🕒 11am-11pm Mon, 8:30am-11pm Tue-Thu, 24hr Fri & Sat, to 11pm Sun; [S] B/C 2/3 to 116th St) Perennially crowded Amy Ruth's serves up classic Southern American soul food, from fried catfish to mac 'n' cheese and fluffy biscuits. But it's the waffles that really merit a trip here – dished up 14 different ways, including with shrimp. Our all-time favorite is the 'Rev Al Sharpton,' a plate of waffles topped with succulent fried chicken.

🍴 Brooklyn

Smorgasburg MARKET
(www.smorgasburg.com; 🕒 11am-6pm Sat & Sun) The biggest foodie event in Brooklyn brings more than 100 vendors selling an incredible

array of goodness, along the lines of Italian street snacks, duck confit, Indian flatbread tacos, roasted-mushroom burgers, vegan Ethiopian comfort food, sea-salt caramel ice cream, passion-fruit doughnuts and more. Smorgasburg locations tend to change from season to season.

The market currently happens in Williamsburg – on the **waterfront** (☑718-782-2731; www.parks.ny.gov/parks/155; Kent Ave, btwn 8th & 9th Sts; ⊘9am-dusk; Ⓢ L to Bedford Ave) – on Saturdays and Prospect Park – near **Lakeside** (☑718-462-0010; www.lakeside prospectpark.com; East Dr, Prospect Park, near Ocean & Parkside Aves; ice skating $6-9, skate rental $6; ⊘9am-5:15pm Mon-Thu, to 9pm Fri, 11:30am-9pm Sat, to 5:15pm Sun; 🚻; Ⓢ B/Q to Prospect Park) – on Sundays from April to October and a smaller version is held indoors at One Hanson Place in Fort Greene on weekends during the winter months.

★ **Dough** BAKERY $
(☑347-533-7544; www.doughdoughnuts.com; 448 Lafayette Ave, cnr Franklin Ave, Clinton Hill; doughnuts around $3; ⊘6am-9pm; 🚲; Ⓢ G to Classon Ave) Situated on the border of Clinton Hill and Bed-Stuy, this tiny, out-of-the-way spot is a bit of a trek, but worth it if you're a pastry fan. Puffy raised doughnuts are dipped in a changing array of glazes, including pistachio, blood orange and hibiscus. Doughnut divinity for the tongue.

Chuko JAPANESE $
(☑347-425-9570; www.chukobk.com; 565 Vanderbilt Ave, cnr Pacific St, Prospect Heights; ramen $15; ⊘noon-3pm & 5:30-11pm; 🚲; Ⓢ B/Q to 7th Ave; 2/3 to Bergen St) This contemporary, minimalist ramen shop brings a top-notch noodle game to Prospect Heights. Steaming bowls of al dente ramen are paired with one of several spectacularly silky broths, including an excellent roasted pork and a full-bodied vegetarian. The appetizers are *very* worthwhile, particularly the fragrant salt-and-pepper chicken wings.

Nathan's Famous HOT DOGS $
(☑718-333-2202; www.nathansfamous.com; 1310 Surf Ave, cnr Stillwell Ave, Coney Island; hot dog from $4; ⊘10am-midnight; Ⓢ D/F to Coney Island-Stillwell Ave) The hot dog was invented in Coney Island in 1867, which means that eating a frankfurter is practically obligatory here. The top choice: Nathan's Famous, which has been around since 1916. The hot dogs are the

real deal, but the menu runs the gamut from fried clams to fried chicken fingers.

Hungry Ghost CAFE $
(☑718-797-3595; www.hungryghostbrooklyn.com/; 781 Fulton St; sandwiches from $7, breakfast from $3, coffees from $3; ⊘7am-9pm; Ⓢ G to Fulton Street; C to Lafayette Ave) In a few short years Hungry Ghost has made a name for itself as one of the best places to grab coffee in North Brooklyn. The interior of every location boasts a striking, minimalist design that matches the unpretentious flavor of their strong brew. They also sell pastries, handmade sandwiches, and other coffee shop fare if you're in the mood to eat.

Green Grape Annex AMERICAN $
(www.greenegrape.com/annex; 753 Fulton St; mains $7-9; ⊘7am-9pm Mon-Thu, 7am-10pm Fri, 8am-10pm Sat, 8am-9pm Sun; Ⓢ G to Fulton Ave or C to Lafayette Ave) Looking for a quick coffee – quality roasts that are perfectly brewed – or a hearty meal? The Green Grape Annex is well appointed cafe in Fort Greene that offers a wide array of food and beverage options in a large, airy space where it's rare to fight for space. In addition to coffee bar they also serve beer and wine.

67 Burger BURGERS $
(☑718-797-7150; www.67burger.com; 67 Lafayette Ave, Brooklyn; specialty burgers from $8; ⊘11:30am-10pm Mon-Thu, 11:30am-11pm Fri & Sat; Ⓢ G to Fulton Street) If there is a place that could give Shake Shack a run for its money, it is 67 Burger. Choose one of their custom burgers, such as the Parisian (sauteed onions and mushrooms with dijonaise) or the Oaxaca (avocado, cheddar cheese, and homemade chipotle mayo), or create your own big, beautiful, messy burger.

★ **Pok Pok** THAI $$
(☑718-923-9322; www.pokpokny.com; 117 Columbia St, cnr Kane St, Columbia Street Waterfront District; sharing plates $12-20; ⊘5:30-10pm Mon-Fri, from noon Sat & Sun; Ⓢ F to Bergen St) Andy Ricker's NYC outpost is a smashing success, wowing diners with a rich and complex menu inspired by Northern Thailand street food. Fiery, fish-sauce-slathered chicken wings; spicy green-papaya salad with salted black crab; smoky grilled eggplant salad and sweet pork belly with ginger, turmeric and tamarind are among the many unique dishes. The setting is fun and ramshackle. Reserve ahead.

Nick's Lobster House
SEAFOOD $$

(☏718-253-7117; www.nickslobsterhouse.com; 2777 Flatbush Ave, Brooklyn; mains starting at $18; ☺2pm-10pm Tue-Thu, noon-11pm Fri, 11am-11pm Sat, 11am-10pm Sun) This charming eatery is located right on the water in the Mill Basin neighborhood of Brooklyn. The menu is simple, Northeast-style seafood, but the bisques, broils and, of course, lobster are all cooked to perfection. They have a full bar and gorgeous channel views from anywhere in the restaurant.

Sidecar
AMERICAN $$

(☏718-369-0077; http://sidecarbrooklyn.com/; 560 5th Ave, Brooklyn; mains $14-27; ☺6pm-2am Mon-Wed, 6pm-4am Thu, 3pm-4am Fri, 11am-4am Sat, 11am-2am Sun; SF/G/R to 4th Ave-9th St; R to Prospect Ave) Upscale classic American cuisine doesn't get any better than Sidecar's. This atmospheric restaurant serves unfussy takes on classics that add a modern touch, such as fried chicken served with a savory root mash and sautéed kale on the side. Sidecar also specializes in cocktails that you can pair with your meal, or enjoy on their own at the bar.

Zenkichi
JAPANESE $$

(☏718-388-8985; www.zenkichi.com; 77 N 6th St, at Wythe Ave, Williamsburg; tasting menu $75; ☺6pm-midnight Mon-Sat, 5:30-11:30pm Sun; SL to Bedford Ave) A temple of refined Japanese cuisine, Zenkichi presents beautifully prepared dishes in an atmospheric setting that has wowed foodies from far and wide. The recommendation here is the *omakase,* a seasonal eight-course tasting menu featuring highlights like winter fruit with tofu sauce and deep-fried Suzuki striped bass, onion and carrot in a sweet, rich vinaigrette sauce topped with chili pepper.

Rabbit Hole
MODERN AMERICAN $$

(☏718-782-0910; www.rabbitholerestaurant.com; 352 Bedford Ave, btwn S 3rd & S 4th Sts, Williamsburg; mains breakfast $10-14, dinner $13-22; ☺9am-11pm; ✐; SL to Bedford Ave; J/M/Z to Marcy Ave) A warm and inviting spot in South Williamsburg, the very charming Rabbit Hole is a fine spot to disappear into, particularly if you're craving breakfast (served till 5pm). There's casual cafe-seating up front for good coffee and even better housemade pastries. Head to the back or the relaxing rear garden for creamy eggs Benedict or fresh fruit and granola.

Buttermilk Channel
AMERICAN $$

(☏917-832-8490; www.buttermilkchannelnyc.com; 524 Court St; brunch mains $8-18, dinner mains $16-28; ☺11:30am-10pm Mon-Wed, 11:30am-11pm Thur, 11:30am-midnight Fri, 10am-midnight Sat, 10am-10pm Sun. Closed between 3-5pm daily; SF/G train to Smith and 9th St station) There's nothing quite like a crispy fried chicken or a savory plate of eggs with lox and green onions. Buttermilk Channel offers dinner and brunch menus of simple, perfectly executed dishes. A comprehensive list of specialty cocktails – the brunch Bloody Mary menu alone is worth the visit – round out this yummy dining experience.

Olea
MEDITERRANEAN $$$

(☏718-643-7003; www.oleabrooklyn.com; 171 Lafayette Ave, Brooklyn; mains $24-32; ☺10am-11pm Mon-Thu, to midnight Fri & Sat; SG to Fulton Street; G/C to Clinton-Washington) Olea is a bustling Mediterranean restaurant with charming interior design and world class food. On the dinner menu they serve creamy paellas and light, delicious vegetarian pastas, while for brunch they specialize in Mediterranean spins on old standbys, such as lamb hash. There is also a tapas menu for those looking for a less substantial bite.

⚔ The Bronx

Tony's Pier
SEAFOOD $

(☏718 885-1424; 1 City Island Ave, Bronx; seafood baskets from $16; ☺11:30am-11:30pm Mon-Thu, 11:30am-1am Fri-Sun; ☒Bx29) Fried or broiled and served in a paper basket with your choice of dipping sauce – that is how Tony's Pier does seafood. This City Island spot is located right on the water, and as the name suggests there is a large pier with fantastic views of the Long Island Sound. Be sure to grab a beer or frothy mixed drink.

Getting to City Island can seem daunting if you don't have a car, but it can be done! Once you're in the Bronx the Bx29 bus goes to the island. This unique destination in the city is well worth the trip.

⚔ Queens

★Pye Boat Noodle
THAI $

(☏718-685-2329; 35-13 Broadway, Astoria; noodles $10-13; ☺11:30am-10:30pm, to 11pm Fri & Sat; ✐; SN/W to Broadway; M, R to Steinway) Young Thai waitresses in matching fedoras greet you at this cute place decked out like an old-fashioned country house. The specialty is rich, star-anise-scented boat noodles, topped with crispy pork cracklings. There's also delicate seafood *yen ta fo* (mild seafood soup, tinted pink), a rarity in NYC – good with a side of papaya salad (off-menu request: add funky fermented crab).

★ Golden Shopping Mall CHINESE $
(41-36 Main St, Flushing; meals from $3; ⏲ 10am-9:30pm; [S] 7 to Flushing-Main St) A chaotic jumble of hanging ducks, airborne noodles and greasy Laminex tables, Golden Mall's basement food court dishes up fantastic hawker-style grub. Don't be intimidated by the lack of English menus: most stalls have at least one English speaker, and the regulars are usually happy to point out their personal favorites, whether it's Lanzhou hand-pulled noodles or spicy pig ears.

Nan Xiang Xiao Long Bao DUMPLINGS $
(☎ 718-321-3838; 38-12 Prince St, Queens; dumplings $5.50; ⏲ 8am-1am; [S] 7 to Main St.) Juicy, savory soup dumplings; thick, sticky noodles; spicy wontons – everything you'd want from a dumpling house you'll find at Nan Xiang Xiao Long Bao. This place is a no-frills affair and is usually very busy, but tables tend to open up quickly and the dishes come out fast. Bring some friends and order in excess.

Rockaway Surf Club TACOS $$
(www.rockawaybeachsurfclub.com; 302 Beach 87th St; $3.50, cocktails $9; ⏲ noon-11pm) Down in the Rockaways are some of the best tacos in the five boroughs. The Rockaway Surf Club draws inspiration from beachside California taquerias, with a bar inside, and large outdoor dining area where the food is made to order. Whether you surf or just catch rays on the sand, it's the perfect post-beach hangout.

Casa Enrique MEXICAN $$
(☎ 347-448-0640; www.henrinyc.com/casa-enrique.html; 5-48 49th Ave., Long Island City; mains $18-28; ⏲ 5-11:30pm Mon-Fri, 11am-3:45pm and 5-11pm Sat & Sun; [S] 7 to Vernon Blvd; G to 21st St/Van Alst) Don't let the unassuming facade of Casa Enrique fool you: this upscale eatery has a Michelin star and serves some of the best Mexican food in New York City. The menu is full of traditional Mexican favorites – chile relleno, carne asada and all manners of mole sauce – that are cooked to absolute perfection. Seating is limited, so a reservation is recommended.

Alobar AMERICAN $$
(☎ 718-752-6000; http://www.alobarnyc.com/; 46-42 Vernon Blvd, Long Island City; dinner mains $22-29, brunch $12-16; ⏲ 5-9:30pm Tue & Wed, 5-10pm Thu, 5-11pm Fri, 11am-11pm Sat, 11am-9pm Sun; [S] E, M to Court Square, 23rd St; 7 to Vernon Blvd-Jackson Ave, G to 21st St-Van Alst Station) Alobar is located right in the heart of the trendy Hunter's Point section of Long Island City, Queens, and this large, airy restaurant fits the neighborhood like a glove. Tuck into some classic American dishes like mussels and pork chops, or stop by for brunch for a mix of upgraded diner favorites and Brooklyn go-tos, like huevos rancheros.

Drinking & Nightlife

You'll find all species of thirst-quenching venues here, from terminally hip cocktail lounges and historic dive bars to specialty tap rooms and Third Wave coffee shops. Then there's the city's legendary club scene, spanning everything from celebrity staples to gritty, indie hangouts. The parts of the city that, apropos of its nickname, truly never sleep, tend to be downtown or in Brooklyn.

Financial District & Lower Manhattan

★ Dead Rabbit COCKTAIL BAR
(Map p80; ☎ 646-422-7906; www.deadrabbitnyc.com; 30 Water St, btwn Broad St & Coenties Slip; ⏲ taproom 11am-4am, parlor 5pm-2am Mon-Sat, to midnight Sun; [S] R/W to Whitehall St; 1 to South Ferry) Named in honor of a dreaded Irish-American gang, this most-wanted rabbit is regularly voted one of the world's best bars. Hit the sawdust-sprinkled Taproom for specialty beers, historic punches and pop-inns (lightly hopped ale spiked with different flavors). Come evening, scurry upstairs to the cozy Parlor for meticulously researched cocktails.

Smith & Mills COCKTAIL BAR
(Map p80; ☎ 212-226-2515; www.smithandmills.com; 71 N Moore St, btwn Hudson & Greenwich Sts; ⏲ 11am-2am Sun-Wed, to 3am Thu-Sat; [S] 1 to Franklin St) Petite Smith & Mills ticks all the cool boxes: unmarked exterior, design-conscious industrial interior, and expertly crafted cocktails with a penchant for the classics. Space is limited so head in early if you fancy kicking back on a plush banquette. A seasonal menu spans light snacks to a particularly notable burger pimped with caramelized onions.

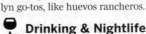

Cowgirl Seahorse BAR

(Map p80; ☎646-362-0981; http://cowgirlseahorse.com/; 259 Front St; 🕑11am-11pm Mon-Thu, 11am-midnight Fri, 10am-midnight Sat, 10am-11pm Sun; [S]2/3/4/5/6 to Brooklyn Bridge-City Hall) In the sea of very serious bars and restaurants, Cowgirl Seahorse is a party ship. Its nautical theme and perfect bar fare – giant plates of nachos piled with steaming meat and frozen margaritas so sweet and tangy you won't be able to say no to a second round – make this dive a can't-miss for those looking to let loose.

Keg No 229 BEER HALL

(Map p80; ☎212-566-2337; www.kegno229.com; 229 Front St, btwn Beekman St & Peck Slip; 🕑11am-midnight Sun-Wed, to 1am Thu-Sat; [S]A/C, J/Z, 2/3, 4/5 to Fulton St; R/W to Cortlandt St) From Butternuts Pork Slap to New Belgium Fat Tire, this bar's battalion of drafts, bottles and cans are a Who's Who of boutique American brews. One fun, potentially costly twist: if you lose count, some drafts are available for 'self-pour'.

Terroir Tribeca WINE BAR

(Map p80; ☎212-625-9463; www.wineisterroir.com; 24 Harrison St, at Greenwich St; 🕑4pm-midnight Mon & Tue, to 1am Wed-Sat, to 11pm Sun; [S]1 to Franklin St) Award-winning Terroir gratifies oenophiles with its well-versed, well-priced wine list (the offbeat, entertaining menu book is a must-read). Drops span the Old World and New, among them natural wines and inspired offerings from smaller producers. A generous selection of wines by the glass makes your global wine tour a whole lot easier. Offers early *and* late happy hours too.

SoHo & Chinatown

Pegu Club COCKTAIL BAR

(Map p84; ☎212-473-7348; www.peguclub.com; 77 W Houston St, btwn W Broadway & Wooster St; 🕑5pm-2am Sun-Wed, to 4am Thu-Sat; [S]B/D/F/M to Broadway-Lafayette St; C/E to Spring St) Dark, elegant Pegu Club (named after a legendary gentleman's club in colonial-era Rangoon) is an obligatory stop for cocktail connoisseurs. Sink into a velvet lounge and savor seamless libations such as the silky smooth Earl Grey MarTEAni (tea-infused gin, lemon juice and raw egg white). Grazing options are suitably Asianesque, among them duck wontons and Mandalay coconut shrimp.

Spring Lounge BAR

(Map p84; ☎212-965-1774; www.thespringlounge.com; 48 Spring St, at Mulberry St; 🕑8am-4am Mon-Sat, from noon Sun; [S]6 to Spring St; R/W to Prince St) This neon-red rebel has never let anything get in the way of a good time. In Prohibition days, it peddled buckets of beer. In the '60s its basement was a gambling den. These days, it's best known for its kooky stuffed sharks, early-start regulars and come-one, come-all late-night revelry. Perfect last stop on a bar-hopping tour of the neighborhood.

Genuine Liquorette COCKTAIL BAR

(Map p84; ☎212-726-4633; www.genuineliquorette.com; 191 Grand St, at Mulberry St; 🕑6pm-midnight Tue & Wed, to 2am Thu-Sat; [S]J/Z, N/Q/R/W, 6 to Canal St; B/D to Grand St) What's not to love about a jamming basement bar with canned cocktails and a Farah Fawcett–themed restroom? You're even free to grab bottles and mixers and make your own drinks (bottles are weighed before and after you're done). At the helm is prolific mixologist Eben Freeman, who regularly invites New York's finest barkeeps to create cocktails using less-celebrated hooch.

Mulberry Project COCKTAIL BAR

(Map p84; ☎646-448-4536; www.mulberryproject.com; 149 Mulberry St, btwn Hester & Grand Sts; 🕑6pm-2am Sun-Thu, to 4am Fri & Sat; [S]N/Q/R, J/Z, 6 to Canal St) Lurking behind an unmarked door is this intimate, cavernous cocktail den, with its festive, 'garden-party' backyard – one of the best spots to chill in the 'hood. Bespoke, made-to-order cocktails are the specialty, so disclose your preferences and let the barkeep do the rest. If you're peckish, choose from a competent list of bites that might include peach salad with pecorino cheese.

Apothéke COCKTAIL BAR

(Map p80; ☎212-406-0400; www.apothekenyc.com; 9 Doyers St; 🕑6:30pm-2am Mon-Sat, 8pm-2am Sun; [S]J/Z to Chambers St; 4/5/6 to Brooklyn Bridge-City Hall) It takes a little effort to track down this former opium-den-turned-apothecary bar on Doyers St. Inside, skilled barkeeps work like careful chemists, using local, seasonal produce from greenmarkets to produce intense, flavorful 'prescriptions.' Their cocktail ingredient ratio is always on point, such as the pineapple-cilantro blend in the Sitting Buddha, one of the best drinks on the menu.

East Village & Lower East Side

Bar Goto BAR

(Map p84; ☎212-475-4411; www.bargoto.com; 245 Eldridge St, btwn E Houston & Stanton Sts; 🕘5pm-midnight Tue-Thu & Sun, to 2am Fri & Sat; [S]F to 2nd Ave) Maverick mixologist Kenta Goto has cocktail connoisseurs spellbound at his eponymous hot spot. Expect meticulous, elegant drinks that revel in Koto's Japanese heritage (the sake-spiked Sakura Martini is utterly smashing), paired with authentic, Japanese comfort bites such as *okonomiyaki* (savory pancakes).

Berlin CLUB

(Map p84; ☎646-827-3689; 25 Ave A, btwn First & Second Aves; 🕘8pm-4am; [S]F to 2nd Ave) Like a secret bunker hidden beneath the ever-gentrifying streets of the East Village, Berlin is a throwback to the neighborhood's more riotous days of wildness and dancing. Once you find the unmarked entrance, head downstairs to the grotto-like space with vaulted brick ceilings, a long bar and tiny dance floor, with funk and rare grooves.

Angel's Share BAR

(Map p84; ☎212-777-5415; 2nd fl, 8 Stuyvesant St, near Third Ave & E 9th St; 🕘6pm-1:30am Sun-Wed, to 2:30am Thu-Sat; [S]6 to Astor Pl) Show up early and snag a seat at this hidden gem, behind a Japanese restaurant on the same floor. It's quiet and elegant, with seriously talented mixologists serving up creative cocktails, plus a top flight collection of whiskeys. You can't stay if you don't have a table or a seat at the bar, and they tend to go fast.

LGBT NYC

From hand-locked married couples on the streets of Hell's Kitchen to a rainbow-hued Empire State Building at Pride, there's no doubt that New York City is one of the world's great gay cities. Indeed, few places come close to matching the breadth and depth of queer offerings here, from cabarets and clubs to festivals and readings.

Useful resources for travelers include the print and online versions of *Next Magazine* and *Get Out!*, both popular guides to all things gay in NYC; and Gay City News (www.gaycitynews.nyc) for news and current affairs with a queer bent, as well as arts and travel reviews.

Ten Bells BAR

(Map p84; ☎212-228-4450; www.tenbellsnyc.com; 247 Broome St, btwn Ludlow & Orchard Sts; 🕘5pm-2am Mon-Fri, from 3pm Sat & Sun; [S]F to Delancey St; J/M/Z to Essex St) This charmingly tucked-away tapas bar has a grotto-like design, with flickering candles, dark tin ceilings, brick walls and a U-shaped bar that's an ideal setting for a conversation with a new friend.

Wayland BAR

(Map p84; ☎212-777-7022; www.thewaylandnyc.com; 700 E 9th St, cnr Ave C; 🕘5pm-4am; [S]L to 1st Ave) Whitewashed walls, weathered floorboards and salvaged lamps give this urban outpost a Mississippi flair, which goes well with the live music (bluegrass, jazz, folk) featured Monday to Wednesday nights. The drinks, though, are the real draw – try the 'I Hear Banjos', made of apple-pie moonshine, rye whiskey and applewood smoke, which tastes like a campfire (but slightly less burning).

Rue B BAR

(Map p84; ☎212-358-1700; www.ruebnyc188.com; 188 Ave B, btwn E 11th & 12th Sts; 🕘noon-4am; [S]L to 1st Ave) There's live jazz (and the odd rockabilly group) every night from about 8:30pm at this tiny, amber-lit drinking den on a bar-dappled stretch of Ave B. A young, celebratory crowd packs the small space – so mind the tight corners, lest the trombonist end up in your lap. B&W photos of jazz greats and other NYC icons enhance the ambience.

Webster Hall CLUB

(Map p84; ☎212-353-1600; www.websterhall.com; 125 E 11th St, near Third Ave; 🕘10pm-4am Thu-Sat; [S]L, N/Q/R/W, 4/5/6 to 14th St-Union Sq) The granddaddy of dance halls, Webster Hall has been around so long (performances have been underway since 1886) that it was granted landmark status in 2008. Following the old 'if it ain't broke, don't fix it' adage, what you'll get here is cheap drinks, pool tables, and enough room on the dance floor to work up a good sweat.

West Village, Chelsea & Meatpacking District

Employees Only BAR

(Map p84; ☎212-242-3021; www.employeesonlynyc.com; 510 Hudson St, btwn W 10th & Christopher Sts; 🕘6pm-4am; [S]1 to Christopher St-Sheridan Sq) Duck behind the neon 'Psychic' sign to find this hidden hangout. Bartenders are ace mixologists, fizzing up crazy, addictive libations like the Ginger Smash and the Mata Hari. Great for late-night drinking and eating, courtesy of the on-site restaurant that serves till 3:30am – housemade chicken soup is ladled out to stragglers. The bar gets busier as the night wears on.

Happiest Hour
COCKTAIL BAR

(Map p84; ☑ 212-243-2827; www.happiesthournyc. com; 121 W 10th St, btwn Greenwich St & Sixth Ave; ⊘ 5pm-late Mon-Fri, from 2pm Sat & Sun; Ⓢ A/C/E, B/D/F/M to W 4th St-Washington Sq; 1 to Christopher St-Sheridan Sq) A super-cool, tiki-licious cocktail bar splashed with palm prints, '60s pop and playful mixed drinks. The crowd tends to be button-down after-work types and online daters. Beneath sits its serious sibling, **Slowly Shirley**, an art deco-style subterranean temple to beautifully crafted, thoroughly researched libations.

Buvette
WINE BAR

(Map p84; ☑ 212-255-3590; www.ilovebuvette. com; 42 Grove St, btwn Bedford & Bleecker Sts; ⊘ 7am-2am Mon-Fri, from 8am Sat & Sun; Ⓢ 1 to Christopher St-Sheridan Sq; A/C/E, B/D/F/M to W 4th St-Washington Sq) The rustic-chic decor here (think delicate tin tiles and a swooshing marble counter) makes it the perfect place for a glass of wine – no matter the time of day. For the full experience at this self-proclaimed *gastrotèque,* grab a seat at one of the surrounding tables and nibble on small plates while enjoying Old-World wines (mostly from France and Italy).

Le Bain
CLUB

(Map p88; ☑ 212-645-7600; www.standard hotels.com; 444 W 13th St, btwn Washington St & Tenth Ave; ⊘ 10pm-4am Wed-Fri, from 2pm Sat, 2pm-midnight Sun; Ⓢ A/C/E, L to 14th St-8th Ave) The sweeping rooftop venue at the tragically hip Standard Hotel, Le Bain sees a garish parade of party promoters who do their thang on any day of the week. Brace yourself for skyline views, a dance floor with a giant Jacuzzi built right into it and an eclectic crowd getting wasted on pricey snifters.

Stonewall Inn
GAY

(Map p84; ☑ 212-488-2705; www.thestone wallinnnyc.com; 53 Christopher St; ⊘ 2pm-4am; Ⓢ 1 to Christopher St-Sheridan Sq) Site of the Stonewall riots in 1969, this bar, considered almost a pilgrimage site because of its historic significance, pulls in varied crowds for nightly parties catering to everyone under the LGBT rainbow. It's far from trendy and

more a welcoming, ordinary watering hole that otherwise might be overlooked.

Henrietta Hudson
LESBIAN

(Map p84; ☑ 212-924-3347; www.henrietta hudson.com; 438 Hudson St; ⊘ 4pm-4am; Ⓢ 1 to Houston St) All sorts of young women, many from neighboring New Jersey and Long Island, storm this sleek lounge, where varying theme nights bring in spirited DJs who stick to particular genres (hip-hop, house, rock). The owner, Brooklyn native Lisa Canistraci, is a favorite promoter in the world of lesbian nightlife, and is often on hand to mix it up with her fans.

Marie's Crisis
BAR

(Map p84; ☑ 212-243-9323; 59 Grove St, btwn Seventh Ave & Bleecker St; ⊘ 4pm-3am Mon-Thu, to 4am Fri & Sat, to midnight Sun; Ⓢ 1 to Christopher St-Sheridan Sq) Aging Broadway queens, wide-eyed out-of-town gay boys, giggly tourists and various other fans of musical theater assemble around the piano here and take turns belting out campy show tunes, often joined by the entire crowd – and the occasional celebrity. It's old-school fun, no matter how jaded you might be when you go in.

⬤ Union Square, Flatiron District & Gramercy

★ Flatiron Lounge
COCKTAIL BAR

(Map p88; ☑ 212-727-7741; www.flatironlounge. com; 37 W 19th St, btwn Fifth & Sixth Aves; ⊘ 4pm-2am Mon-Wed, to 3am Thu, to 4am Fri, 5pm-4am Sat; ☎; Ⓢ F/M, R/W, 6 to 23rd St) Head through a dramatic archway and into a dark, swinging, deco-inspired fantasy of lipstick-red booths, racy jazz tunes and sassy grown-ups downing seasonal drinks. The Lincoln Tunnel (dark rum, applejack, maple syrup and bitters) is scrumptious. Happy-hour cocktails go for $10 a pop (4pm to 6pm weekdays).

Birreria
BEER HALL

(Map p88; ☑ 212-937-8910; www.eataly.com; 200 Fifth Ave, at W 23rd St; ⊘ 11:30am-11pm Sun-Thu, to midnight Fri & Sat; Ⓢ R/W, F/M, 6 to 23rd St) The crown jewel of Italian food emporium Eataly (p118) is this rooftop beer garden tucked betwixt the Flatiron's corporate towers. An encyclopedic beer menu offers drinkers some of the best suds on the planet. If you're hungry, the signature beer-braised pork shoulder will pair nicely, or check out the seasonally changing menu of the on-site pop-up restaurant (mains $17 to $37).

The sneaky access elevator is near the checkouts on the 23rd St side of the store.

Raines Law Room COCKTAIL BAR

(Map p88; www.raineslawroom.com; 48 W 17th St, btwn Fifth & Sixth Aves; ⏲5pm-2am Mon-Wed, to 3am Thu-Sat, 7pm-1am Sun; [S] F/M to 14th St, L to 6th Ave, 1 to 18th St) A sea of velvet drapes and overstuffed leather lounge chairs, the perfect amount of exposed brick, expertly crafted cocktails using meticulously aged spirits – these folks are as serious as a mortgage payment when it comes to amplified atmosphere. Reservations (recommended) are only accepted Sunday to Tuesday. Whatever the night, style up for a taste of a far more sumptuous era.

Pete's Tavern BAR

(Map p88; ☎212-473-7676; www.petestavern.com; 129 E 18th St, at Irving Pl; ⏲11am-2:30am; [S] 4/5/6, N/Q/R/W, L to 14th St-Union Sq) With its original 19th-century mirrors, pressed-tin ceiling and rosewood bar, this dark, atmospheric watering hole has all the earmarks of a New York classic. You can get a respectable prime-rib burger here and choose from 17 draft beers, joined by everyone from post-theater couples and Irish expats to no-nonsense NYU students and the odd celebrity (see photos by the restrooms).

Old Town Bar & Restaurant BAR

(Map p88; ☎212-529-6732; www.oldtownbar.com; 45 E 18th St, btwn Broadway & Park Ave S; ⏲11:30am-1am Mon-Fri, noon-2am Sat, 1pm-midnight Sun; [S] 4/5/6, N/Q/R/W, L to 14th St-Union Sq) It still looks like 1892 in here, with the mahogany bar, original tile floors and tin ceilings – the Old Town is an old-world drinking-man's classic (and -woman's: Madonna lit up at the bar here – when lighting up in bars was still legal – in her 'Bad Girl' video). There are cocktails around, but most come for beers and a burger (from $11.50).

Midtown

★ **Bar SixtyFive** COCKTAIL BAR

(Map p88; ☎212-632-5000; www.rainbowroom.com; 30 Rockefeller Plaza, entrance on W 49th St; ⏲5pm-midnight Mon-Fri, 4-9pm Sun; [S] B/D/F/M to 47th-50th Sts-Rockefeller Center) Not to be missed, sophisticated SixtyFive sits on level 65 of the GE Building at Rockefeller Center (p91). Dress well (no sportswear or guests under 21) and arrive by 5pm for a seat with a multi-million-dollar view. Even if you don't score a table on the balcony or by the window, head outside to soak up that sweeping New York panorama.

Flaming Saddles GAY

(Map p88; ☎212-713-0481; www.flamingsaddles.com/nyc; 793 Ninth Ave, btwn 52nd & 53rd Sts, Midtown West; ⏲3pm-4am Mon-Fri, noon-4am Sat & Sun; [S] C/E to 50th St) A country-and-western gay bar in Midtown! *Coyote Ugly* meets *Calamity Jane* at this Hell's Kitchen hangout, complete with studly bar-dancing barmen in skintight jeans, aspiring urban cowboys and a rough 'n' ready vibe. Slip on them Wranglers or chaps and hit the Saddle: you're in for a fun and boozy ride. There's Tex Mex bar food if you get hungry.

Therapy GAY

(Map p88; ☎212-397-1700; www.therapy-nyc.com; 348 W 52nd St, btwn Eighth & Ninth Aves, Midtown West; ⏲5pm-2am Sun-Thu, to 4am Fri & Sat; [S] C/E, 1 to 50th St) Multilevel Therapy was the first gay men's lounge/club to draw throngs to Hell's Kitchen, and it still pulls a crowd with its nightly shows (from live music to interviews with Broadway stars) and decent grub served Sunday to Friday (the quesadillas are especially popular). Drink monikers match the theme: 'oral fixation' and 'size queen', to name a few.

Robert COCKTAIL BAR

(Map p94; ☎212-299-7730; www.robertnyc.com; Museum of Arts & Design, 2 Columbus Circle, btwn Eighth Ave & Broadway; ⏲11:30am-10pm Mon & Sun, to 11pm Tue, to midnight Wed-Sat; [S] A/C, B/D, 1 to 59th St-Columbus Circle) Perched on the 9th floor of the Museum of Arts & Design (p93), '60s-inspired Robert is technically a high-end, Modern American restaurant. While the food is satisfactory, we say visit late afternoon or post-dinner, find a sofa and gaze out over Central Park with a MAD Manhattan (bourbon, blood orange vermouth and liquored cherries). Check the website for live jazz sessions.

Waylon BAR

(Map p88; ☎212-265-0010; www.thewaylon.com; 736 Tenth Ave, at W 50th St; ⏲noon-4am; [S] C/E to 50th St) Slip on your spurs, partner, there's a honky-tonk in Hell's! Celebrate Dixie at this saloon-style watering hole, where the jukebox keeps good folks dancing to Tim McGraw's broken heart, where the barkeeps pour American whiskeys and tequila, and where the grub includes Texan-style Frito pie and country-fried steak sandwiches.

Industry GAY
(Map p88; ☎646-476-2747; www.industry-bar.com; 355 W 52nd St, btwn Eighth & Ninth Aves; ⏲4pm-4am; [S]C/E, 1 to 50th St) What was once a parking garage is now one of the hottest gay bars in Hell's Kitchen – a slick, 4000-sq-ft watering hole with handsome lounge areas, a pool table and a stage for top-notch drag divas. Head in between 4pm and 9pm for the two-for-one drinks special or squeeze in later to party with the eye-candy party hordes. Cash only.

Top of the Strand COCKTAIL BAR
(Map p88; ☎646-368-6426; www.topofthestrand.com; Marriott Vacation Club Pulse, 33 W 37th St, btwn Fifth & Sixth Aves, Midtown East; ⏲5pm-midnight Mon & Sun, to 1am Tue-Sat; [S]B/D/F/M, N/Q/R to 34th St) For that 'Oh my God, I'm in New York' feeling, head to the Marriott Vacation Club Pulse (formerly the Strand Hotel) hotel's rooftop bar, order a martini (extra dirty) and drop your jaw (discreetly). Sporting comfy cabana-style seating, a refreshingly mixed-age crowd and a sliding glass roof, its view of the Empire State Building is simply unforgettable.

Upper West Side & Central Park

Manhattan Cricket Club LOUNGE
(Map p94; ☎646-823-9252; www.mccnewyork.com; 226 W 79th St, btwn Amsterdam Ave & Broadway; ⏲6pm-late; [S]1 to 79th St) Above an Australian bistro (p120), this elegant drinking lounge is modeled on the classy Anglo-Aussie cricket clubs of the early 1900s. Sepia-toned photos of batsmen adorn the gold brocaded walls, while mahogany bookshelves and Chesterfield sofas create a fine setting for quaffing well-made (but pricey) cocktails. It's a guaranteed date-pleaser.

Dead Poet BAR
(Map p94; ☎212-595-5670; www.thedeadpoet.com; 450 Amsterdam Ave, btwn W 81st & 82nd Sts; ⏲noon-4am; [S]1 to 79th St) This skinny, mahogany-paneled pub has been a neighborhood favorite since the turn of the millennium, with a mix of locals and students nursing pints of Guinness. Cocktails are named after dead poets, including a Walt Whitman Long Island Iced Tea ($12) and a Pablo Neruda spiced-rum sangria ($11). Funny – we always pegged Neruda as a pisco sour kind of guy.

Upper East Side

Drunken Munkey LOUNGE
(Map p94; ☎646-998-4600; www.drunkenmunkeynyc.com; 338 E 92nd St, btwn First & Second Aves; ⏲4:30pm-2am Mon-Thu, to 3am Fri, 11am-3am Sat, to 2am Sun; [S]Q, 6 to 96th St) This playful lounge channels colonial-era Bombay with vintage wallpaper, cricket-ball door handles and jauntily attired waitstaff. The monkey chandeliers may be pure whimsy, but the craft cocktails and tasty curries (small, meant for sharing) are serious business. Gin, not surprisingly, is the drink of choice. Try the Bramble: Bombay gin, blackberry liqueur and fresh lemon juice and blackberries.

Auction House BAR
(Map p94; ☎212-427-4458; www.theauctionhousenyc.com; 300 E 89th St, at Second Ave; ⏲7:30pm-2am Sun-Thu, to 4am Fri & Sat; [S]Q to 86th St) Dark maroon doors lead into a candlelit hangout that's perfect for a relaxing drink. Victorian-style couches and fat, overstuffed easy chairs are strewn about the wood-floored rooms. Take your well-mixed cocktail to a seat by the fireplace and admire the scene reflected in the gilt-edged mirrors propped up on the walls.

Harlem & Upper Manhattan

Ginny's Supper Club COCKTAIL BAR
(Map p94; ☎212-421-3821, brunch reservations 212-792-9001; www.ginnyssupperclub.com; 310 Malcolm X Blvd, btwn W 125th & 126th Sts, Harlem; ⏲6pm-11pm Thu, to 3am Fri & Sat, brunch 10:30am-2pm Sun; [S]2/3 to 125th St) Looking straight out of *Boardwalk Empire*, this roaring basement supper club is rarely short of styled-up regulars sipping cocktails, nibbling on soul and global bites (from the Red Rooster (p121) kitchen upstairs) and grooving to live jazz from 7:30pm Thursday to Saturday and DJ-spun beats from 11pm Friday and Saturday. Don't miss the weekly Sunday gospel brunch (reservations recommended).

Brooklyn

★**Maison Premiere** COCKTAIL BAR
(☎347-335-0446; www.maisonpremiere.com; 298 Bedford Ave, btwn S 1st & Grand Sts, Williamsburg; ⏲4pm-2am Mon-Thu, to 4am Fri, 11am-4am Sat, to 4pm Sun; [S]L to Bedford Ave) We kept expecting to see Dorothy Parker stagger into this

old-timey place, which features an elegant bar full of syrups and essences, suspendered bartenders and a jazzy soundtrack to further channel the French Quarter New Orleans vibe. The cocktails are serious business: the epic list includes more than a dozen absinthe drinks, various juleps and an array of specialty cocktails.

Excelsior
GAY & LESBIAN

(☏ 718-788-2710; www.excelsiorbrooklyn.com; 563 Fifth Ave, Brooklyn; ⏰ 6pm-4am Mon-Fri, 2pm-4am Sat & Sun; S F/G/R to 4th Ave/ 9th St; R to Prospect Ave) This beloved neighborhood gay bar recently reopened in a new location with a chic remodel that includes a back patio and upstairs event area that hosts dance parties, drag shows and karaoke. Excelsior tends to cater to an older crowd (although everyone is welcome, of course), and is known for its congenial atmosphere and hilarious bartenders.

Union Hall
BAR

(☏ 718-638-4400; www.unionhallny.com; 702 Union St; drinks from $7; ⏰ 4pm-4am Mon-Fri, 1pm-4am Sat-Sun; S R to Union St) Anyone looking for an authentically Brooklyn night out should look no further than Union Hall. This bar and event space is located in a converted warehouse and boasts a double-sided fireplace, towering bookshelves, leather couches and two full-size indoor bocce ball courts. Head to the basement for live music and comedy.

Spuyten Duyvil
BAR

(☏ 718-963-4140; www.spuytenduyvilnyc.com; 359 Metropolitan Ave, btwn Havemayer & Roebling Sts, Williamsburg; ⏰ 5pm-late Mon-Fri, from noon Sat & Sun; S L to Lorimer St; G to Metropolitan Ave) This low-key Williamsburg bar looks like it was pieced together from a rummage sale. The ceilings are painted red, there are vintage maps on the walls and the furniture consists of tattered armchairs. But the beer selection is staggering, the locals from various eras are chatty and there's a decent-sized patio with leafy trees that's open in good weather.

Skinny Dennis
BAR

(www.skinnydennisbar.com; 152 Metropolitan Ave, btwn Wythe Ave & Berry St, Williamsburg; ⏰ noon-4am; S L to Bedford Ave) No need to fly to Austin – you can get your honky-tonk right here in Billyburg at this roadhouse saloon on bustling Metropolitan Ave. Aside from Kinky Friedman posters, a reverential painting of Willie Nelson, peanut shells on the floor and a Patsy Cline–heavy jukebox in the corner, you'll find country crooners playing nightly to a garrulous, beer-swilling crowd.

Bossa Nova Civic Club
CLUB

(☏ 718-443-1271; 1271 Myrtle Ave, btwn Evergreen & Central Aves, Bushwick; ⏰ 5pm-4am; S M to Central Ave) Yet another reason why you never need to leave Brooklyn, this smallish hole-in-the-wall club is a great place to get your groove on, with DJs spinning a wide mix of sounds in a somewhat tropical-themed interior. Great sound system, fairly priced drinks (at least as far as clubs are concerned) and snacks available when hunger strikes (empanadas, slow-cooked pork, arepas).

Radegast Hall & Biergarten
BEER HALL

(☏ 718-963-3973; www.radegasthall.com; 113 N 3rd St, at Berry St, Williamsburg; ⏰ noon-2am Mon-Fri, from 11am Sat & Sun; S L to Bedford Ave) An Austro-Hungarian beer hall in Williamsburg offers up a huge selection of Bavarian brews as well as a kitchen full of munchable meats. You can hover in the dark, woody bar area or sit in the adjacent hall, which has a retractable roof and communal tables to feast at – perfect for pretzels, sausages and burgers. Live music every night.

🍷 Queens

⭐ Bohemian Hall & Beer Garden
BEER GARDEN

(☏ 718-274-4925; www.bohemianhall.com; 29-19 24th Ave, Astoria; ⏰ 5pm-1am Mon-Thu, to 3am Fri, noon-3am Sat, noon-midnight Sun; S N/Q to Astoria Blvd) This Czech community center kicked off NYC's beer-garden craze, and nothing quite matches it for space and heaving drinking crowds, which pack every picnic table under the towering trees in summer. There's obligatory food (dumplings, sausages); the focus is on the cold Czech beers.

Dutch Kills
BAR

(☏ 718-383-2724; www.dutchkillsbar.com; 27-24 Jackson Ave, Long Island City; specialty cocktails from $13, beer and wine from $6; ⏰ 5pm-2am; S E, M, or R to Queens Plaza; G to Court Square) When you step into Dutch Kills – through an unassuming door on an old industrial building in Long Island City – you are stepping back in time. This speakeasy-style bar is all about atmosphere and amazing craft cocktails. Their menu of specialty drinks is extensive, but if you're looking for an old standard, you can trust the expert bartenders to deliver.

NEW YORK, NEW JERSEY & PENNSYLVANIA NEW YORK CITY

Icon Bar GAY
(☎917-832-6364; 31-84 33rd St, Astoria; drinks from $7; ⏲5pm-4am; [S] N/W to Broadway station) New York's famous gay nightlife scene doesn't end once you leave Manhattan. Icon Bar brings strong drinks and flirtatious ambiance to Astoria. They frequently host special DJ nights and drag shows, as well as a 2-for-1 happy hour on weekday evenings.

☆ Entertainment

Actors, musicians, dancers and artists flock to the bright lights of the Big Apple, hoping to forge careers in showbiz. As the saying goes: if you can make it here, you can make it anywhere. Whatever 'making it' means these days, audiences are spoiled by the continual influx of supremely talented, dedicated and boundary-pushing performers who maintain the city's status as one of the world's cultural capitals.

Live Music

Minton's JAZZ
(Map p94; ☎212-243-2222; www.mintonsharlem.com; 206 W 118th St, btwn St Nicholas Ave & Adam Clayton Powell Jr Blvd; ⏲6-11pm Wed-Sat, noon-3pm & 6-10pm Sun; [S] B/C, 2/3 to 116th St) The birthplace of bebop, this Harlem jazz-and-dinner club is a musical holy grail. Everyone from Dizzy Gillespie to Louis Armstrong have jammed here, and dinner (mains $18 to $34) or Sunday brunch ($12 to $18) in its tinted-mirror dining room is an experience to behold. Book ahead, dress to impress and savor Southern flavors while toe-tapping to live, honey-sweet jazz.

★ **Jazz at Lincoln Center** JAZZ
(Map p94; ☎tickets to Dizzy's Club Coca-Cola 212-258-9595, tickets to Rose Theater & Appel Room 212-721-6500; www.jazz.org; Time Warner Center, Columbus Circle, Broadway at W 59th St; [S] A/C, B/D, 1 to 59th St-Columbus Circle) Perched atop the Time Warner Center, Jazz at Lincoln Center consists of three state-of-the-art venues: the mid-sized **Rose Theater**; the panoramic, glass-backed **Appel Room**; and the intimate, atmospheric **Dizzy's Club Coca-Cola**. It's the last of these that you're most likely to visit, given its nightly shows. The talent is often exceptional, as are the dazzling Central Park views.

★ **Carnegie Hall** LIVE MUSIC
(Map p88; ☎212-247-7800; www.carnegiehall.org; 881 Seventh Ave, at W 57th St; ⏲tours 11:30am, 12:30pm, 2pm & 3pm Mon-Fri, 11:30am & 12:30pm Sat Oct-Jun; [S] N/R/W to 57th St-7th Ave) This legendary music hall may not be the world's biggest, nor grandest, but it's definitely one of the most acoustically blessed venues around. Opera, jazz and folk greats feature in the Isaac Stern Auditorium, with edgier jazz, pop, classical and world music in the popular Zankel Hall. The intimate Weill Recital Hall hosts chamber-music concerts, debut performances and panel discussions.

New York Philharmonic CLASSICAL MUSIC
(Map p94; ☎212-875-5656; www.nyphil.org; Lincoln Center, Columbus Ave at W 65th St; 👪; [S] 1 to 66 St-Lincoln Center) The oldest professional orchestra in the USA (dating back to 1842) holds its season every year at **David Geffen Hall** (known as Avery Fisher until 2015); newly installed music director Jaap van Zweden took over from Alan Gilbert in 2017. The orchestra plays a mix of classics (Tchaikovsky, Mahler, Haydn) and contemporary works, as well as concerts geared toward children.

Blue Note JAZZ
(Map p84; ☎212-475-8592; www.bluenote.net; 131 W 3rd St, btwn Sixth Ave & MacDougal St; [S] A/C/E, B/D/F/M to W 4th St-Washington Sq) This is by far the most famous (and expensive) of the city's jazz clubs. Most shows are $15 to $30 at the bar or $25 to $45 at a table, but can rise for the biggest stars. There's also jazz brunch on Sundays at 11:30am. Go on an off night, and don't talk – all attention is on the stage!

Joe's Pub LIVE MUSIC
(Map p84; ☎212-539-8778, tickets 212-967-7555; www.joespub.com; Public Theater, 425 Lafayette St, btwn Astor Pl & 4th St; [S] 6 to Astor Pl; R/W to 8th St-NYU) Part bar, part cabaret and performance venue, intimate Joe's serves up both emerging acts and top-shelf performers. Past entertainers have included Patti LuPone, Amy Schumer, Leonard Cohen and British songstress Adele (in fact, it was right here that Adele gave her very first American performance, back in 2008).

Irving Plaza LIVE MUSIC
(Map p88; ☎212-777-6817; www.irvingplaza.com; 17 Irving Pl, at 15th St; [S] 4/5/6, N/Q/R, L to 14th St-Union Sq) Rocking since 1978, Irving Plaza has seen them all: the Ramones, Bob Dylan, U2, Pearl Jam, you name it. These days it's a great in-between stage for quirkier rock and pop acts – from indie chicks Sleater-Kinney to hard rockers Disturbed. There's a cozy

floor around the stage, and good views from the mezzanine.

Brooklyn Bowl   LIVE MUSIC

(☏ 718-963-3369; www.brooklynbowl.com; 61 Wythe Ave, btwn N 11th & N 12th Sts, Williamsburg; ⊘ 6pm-2am Mon-Fri, from 11am Sat & Sun; Ⓢ L to Bedford Ave; G to Nassau Ave) This 23,000-sq-ft venue inside the former Hecla Iron Works Company combines bowling (lane rental per 30min $25, shoe rental $5), microbrews, food and groovy live music. In addition to the live bands that regularly tear up the stage, there are NFL game days, karaoke and DJ nights. Aside from weekends (11am to 6pm), it's age 21 and up.

Bell House   LIVE MUSIC

(☏ 718-643-6510; www.thebellhouseny.com; 149 7th St, btwn Second & Third Aves, Gowanus; ⊘ 5pm-4am; 🛜; Ⓢ F/G/R to 4th Ave-9th St) A big, old venue in the mostly barren neighborhood of Gowanus, the Bell House features high-profile live performances, indie rockers, DJ nights, comedy shows and burlesque parties. The handsomely converted warehouse has a spacious concert area, plus a friendly little bar in the front room with flickering candles, leather armchairs and 10 or so beers on tap.

Sports

Madison Square Garden   SPECTATOR SPORT, CONCERT VENUE

(MSG, 'the Garden'; Map p88; www.thegarden.com; 4 Pennsylvania Plaza, Seventh Ave, btwn 31st & 33rd Sts; Ⓢ A/C/E, 1/2/3 to 34th St-Penn Station) NYC's major performance venue – part of the massive complex housing Penn Station (p138) – hosts big-arena performers, from Kanye West to Madonna. It's also a sports arena, with New York Knicks (www.nba.com/knicks.com) and New York Liberty (www.liberty.wnba.com) basketball games and New York Rangers (www.nhl.com/rangers) hockey games, as well as boxing and events like the Annual Westminster Kennel Club Dog Show.

USTA Billie Jean King National Tennis Center   SPECTATOR SPORT

(☏ 718-760-6200; www.usta.com; Flushing Meadows Corona Park, Corona; ⊘ 6am-midnight; Ⓢ 7 to Mets-Willets Pt) The US Open, one of the city's premier sporting events, takes place in late August. As of 2016, the Arthur Ashe Stadium (capacity 23,771) now has a retractable roof, there's a new stadium (the Grandstand, which replaced the Old Grandstand), and

outer courts have been renovated. Tickets usually go on sale at Ticketmaster in April or May, but are hard to get for marquee games. General admission to early rounds is easier.

Staten Island Yankees   BASEBALL

(☏ 718-720-9265; www.siyanks.com; Richmond County Bank Ballpark, 75 Richmond Tce; tickets $12; ⊘ ticket office 9am-5pm Mon-Fri; 🚢 Staten Island) These Yanks have been champions of the New York–Penn title four times since 2005 alone. If you don't catch a fly ball, you can at least catch some high-scoring Manhattan skyline views from the waterfront stadium. It's a 0.3-mile walk north of the ferry terminal and the construction site of a gigantic Ferris wheel scheduled to open in 2018.

Theater

★ Al Hirschfeld Theatre   THEATER

(Map p88; ☏ tickets 877-250-2929; www.kinky bootsthemusical.com; 302 W 45th St, btwn Eighth & Ninth Aves; Ⓢ A/C/E to 42nd St-Port Authority Bus Terminal) Adapted from a 2005 British indie film, Harvey Fierstein and Cyndi Lauper's smash hit Kinky Boots tells the story of a doomed English shoe factory unexpectedly saved by Lola, a business-savvy drag queen. Its solid characters and electrifying energy have not been lost on critics: the musical won six Tony Awards, including Best Musical, in 2013.

★ Eugene O'Neill Theatre   THEATER

(Map p88; ☏ tickets 212-239-6200; www.bookof mormonbroadway.com; 230 W 49th St, btwn Broadway & Eighth Ave; Ⓢ N/R/W to 49th St; 1 to 50th St; C/E to 50th St) Subversive, obscene and ridiculously hilarious, Book of Mormon, a cutting musical satire, is the work of South Park creators Trey Parker and Matt Stone and Avenue Q composer Robert Lopez. Winner of nine Tony Awards, it tells the story of two naive Mormons on a mission to 'save' a Ugandan village.

★ Richard Rodgers Theatre   THEATER

(Map p88; ☏ tickets 877-250-2929; www.hamilton broadway.com; 226 W 46th St, btwn Seventh & Eighth Aves; Ⓢ N/R/W to 49th St) Broadway's hottest ticket, Lin-Manuel Miranda's acclaimed musical Hamilton uses contemporary hip-hop beats to recount the story of America's first Secretary of the Treasury, Alexander Hamilton. Inspired by Ron Chernow's biography Alexander Hamilton, the show has won a slew of awards, with 11 Tony Awards (including Best Musical), a Grammy for its triple-platinum cast album and the Pulitzer Prize for Drama.

Sleep No More
THEATER

(Map p88; ☑ 866-811-4111; www.sleepnomore nyc.com; 530 W 27th St, btwn Tenth & Eleventh Aves; tickets from $105; ⊙ 7pm-midnight Mon-Sat; Ⓢ C/E to 23rd St) One of the most immersive theater experiences ever conceived, *Sleep No More* is a loosely based retelling of *Macbeth* set inside a series of Chelsea warehouses that have been redesigned to look like the 1930s-era McKittrick Hotel and its hopping jazz bar.

It's a choose-your-own adventure kind of experience, where audience members are free to wander the elaborate rooms (ballroom, graveyard, taxidermy shop, lunatic asylum) and follow or interact with the actors, who perform a variety of scenes that can run from the bizarre to the risqué. Be prepared: you must check in *everything* when you arrive (jackets, bag, cell phone), and you must wear a mask, à la *Eyes Wide Shut*.

Playwrights Horizons
THEATER

(Map p88; ☑ 212-564-1235; www.playwrights horizons.org; 416 W 42nd St, btwn Ninth & Tenth Aves, Midtown West; Ⓢ A/C/E to 42nd St-Port Authority Bus Terminal) An excellent place to catch what could be the next big thing, this veteran 'writers' theater' is dedicated to fostering contemporary American works. Notable past productions include Kenneth Lonergan's *Lobby Hero,* Bruce Norris' Tony Award–winning *Clybourne Park,* and Doug Wright's *I Am My Own Wife* and *Grey Gardens.*

BAM Harvey Theater
THEATER

(Harvey Lichtenstein Theater; ☑ 718-636-4100; www.bam.org; 651 Fulton St, at Rockwell Pl, Fort Greene; Ⓢ B, Q/R to DeKalb Ave; 2/3, 4/5 to Nevins St) This theater, an important cultural institution in Brooklyn and New York City as a whole, has had long runs by important artists like Tony Kushner, Peter Brook and Laurie Anderson. The building itself is a striking combination of ornate and elegant with gritty and industrial – ideal for Brooklyn. (The balcony seats, narrow and elevated, aren't the most comfortable, though, and some have obstructed sight lines.)

★ Flea Theater
THEATER

(Map p80; ☑ tickets 212-226-0051; www.theflea. org; 20 Thomas St, btwn Church St & Broadway; ⓓ; Ⓢ A/C, 1/2/3 to Chambers St; R/W to City Hall)

One of NYC's top off-off-Broadway companies, Flea is famous for staging innovative and timely new works. A brand-new location offers three performance spaces, including one named for devoted alum Sigourney Weaver. The year-round program also includes music and dance productions, as well as shows for young audiences (aged 5 and up) and a rollicking late-night competition series of 10-minute plays.

Delacorte Theater
THEATER

(Map p94; www.publictheater.org; Central Park, enter at W 81st St; Ⓢ B/C to 81st St) Every summer the Joseph Papp Public Theater presents its fabulous free productions of Shakespeare in the Park (p109) at Delacorte Theater, which Papp began back in 1954, before the lovely, leafy, open-air theater was even built. Productions are usually superb, but regardless of their quality, it's a magical experience and waiting in line for tickets is a rite of passage for newcomers to the city.

Ambassador Theatre
THEATER

(Chicago; Map p88; ☑ tickets 212-239-6200; www. chicagothemusical.com; 219 W 49th St, btwn Broadway & Eighth Ave; Ⓢ N/R/W to 49th St; 1, C/E to 50th St) A New York landmark, the Ambassador Theatre, constructed in the 1920s, is curiously built kitty-corner on the lot, enabling the small space to have more seating. Like many of its peers it was sold in the '30s by the owners, the Schuberts, it became a mixed-use property for TV and movies, but was eventually repurchased by the family in 1956. Since then it has remained a theatre, and currently is the venue for Chicago, one of Broadway's most popular shows.

New York Theatre Workshop
THEATER

(Map p84; ☑ 212-460-5475; www.nytw.org; 79 E 4th St, btwn Second & Third Aves; Ⓢ F to 2nd Ave) For more than 30 years this innovative production house has been a treasure trove for those seeking cutting-edge, contemporary plays with purpose. It was the originator of two big Broadway hits, *Rent* and *Urinetown* – plus it's where the musical *Once* had its off-Broadway premiere – and offers a constant supply of high-quality drama.

La MaMa ETC
THEATER

(Map p84; ☑ 212-352-3101; www.lamama.org; 74a E 4th St, btwn Bowery & Second Ave; tickets from $20; Ⓢ F to Second Ave) A long-standing home for onstage experimentation (the ETC stands for Experimental Theater Club), La MaMa is now a three-theater complex with a cafe, an art gallery and a separate studio building that features cutting-edge dramas, sketch comedy and readings of all kinds. Ten $10 tickets are available for each show. Book early to score a deal!

Comedy

★Upright Citizens Brigade Theatre COMEDY
(UCB; Map p88; ☎212-366-9176; www.ucbtheatre.com; 307 W 26th St, btwn Eighth & Ninth Aves; free-$10; ⏰7pm-midnight; [S]C/E to 23rd St) Comedy sketch shows and improv reign at this below-ground 74-seat venue, which gets drop-ins from casting directors and often features well-known figures from TV. Getting in is cheap, and so is the beer and wine. You'll find quality shows happening nightly, from about 7:30pm, though the Sunday night Asssscat Improv session is always a riot.

Comedy Cellar COMEDY
(Map p84; ☎212-254-3480; www.comedycellar.com; 117 MacDougal St, btwn W 3rd St & Minetta Lane; cover $12-24; [S]A/C/E, B/D/F/M to W 4th St-Washington Sq) This long-established basement comedy club in Greenwich Village features mainstream material and a good list of regulars (Colin Quinn, Judah Friedlander, Wanda Sykes), plus occasional high-profile drop-ins like Dave Chappelle, Jerry Seinfeld and Amy Schumer. Its success continues: Comedy Cellar now boasts another location at the Village Underground around the corner on W 3rd St.

Caroline's on Broadway COMEDY
(Map p88; ☎212-757-4100; www.carolines.com; 1626 Broadway, at 50th St, Midtown West; [S]N/Q/R to 49th St; 1, C/E to 50th St) You may recognize this big, bright, mainstream classic from comedy specials filmed here on location. It's a top spot to catch US comedy big guns and sitcom stars.

Cinemas

Film Society of Lincoln Center CINEMA
(Map p94; ☎212-875-5367; www.filmlinc.com; [S]1 to 66th St-Lincoln Center) The Film Society is one of New York's cinematic gems, providing an invaluable platform for a wide gamut of documentary, feature, independent, foreign and avant-garde art pictures. Films screen in one of two facilities at Lincoln Center: the **Elinor Bunin Munroe Film Center** (Map p94; ☎212-875-5232; Lincoln Center, 144 W 65th St), a more intimate, experimental venue, or the Walter Reade Theater, with wonderfully wide, screening room–style seats.

Metrograph CINEMA
(Map p84; ☎212-660-0312; www.metrograph.com; 7 Ludlow St, btwn Canal & Hester Sts; tickets $15; [S]F to East Broadway; B/D to Grand St) The newest movie mecca for downtown cinephiles, this two-screen theater with red velvet seats shows curated art-house flicks. Most you'll never find at any multiplex, though the odd mainstream pic like *Magic Mike* is occasionally screened. In addition to movie geeks browsing the bookstore, you'll find a stylish and glamorous set at the bar or in the upstairs restaurant.

Film Forum CINEMA
(Map p84; ☎212-727-8110; www.filmforum.com; 209 W Houston St, btwn Varick St & Sixth Ave; [S]1 to Houston St) This three-screen nonprofit cinema screens an astounding array of independent films, revivals and career retrospectives from greats such as Orson Welles. Theaters are small (as are the screens), so get there early for a good viewing spot. Showings are often combined with director talks or other film-themed discussions attended by hard-core cinephiles.

Walter Reade Theater CINEMA
(Map p94; ☎212-875-5601; www.filmlinc.com; Lincoln Center, 165 W 65th St; [S]1 to 66th St-Lincoln Center) The Walter Reade boasts some wonderfully wide, screening-room–style seats. Every September it hosts the **New York Film Festival**, featuring plenty of New York and world premieres. At other times of the year you can catch independent films, career retrospectives and themed series.

Anthology Film Archives CINEMA
(Map p84; ☎212-505-5181; www.anthologyfilmarchives.org; 32 Second Ave, at 2nd St; [S]F to 2nd Ave) Opened in 1970, this theater is dedicated to the idea of film as an art form. It screens indie works by new filmmakers and revives classics and obscure oldies, from the surrealist works of Spanish director Luis Buñuel to Ken Brown's psychedelia.

Performing Arts

Metropolitan Opera House OPERA
(Map p94; ☎tickets 212-362-6000, tours 212-769-7028; www.metopera.org; Lincoln Center, Columbus Ave at W 64th St; [S]1 to 66th St-Lincoln Center) New York's premier opera company is the place to see classics such as *Carmen, Madame Butterfly* and *Macbeth,* not to mention

Wagner's Ring Cycle. It also hosts premieres and revivals of more contemporary works, such as John Adams' *The Death of Klinghoffer*. The season runs from September to April.

New York City Ballet
DANCE

(Map p94; 📞 212-496-0600; www.nycballet.com; Lincoln Center, Columbus Ave at W 63rd St; ♿; ⓢ 1 to 66th St-Lincoln Center) This prestigious ballet company was first directed by renowned Russian-born choreographer George Balanchine back in the 1940s. Today, the company has 90 dancers and is the largest ballet organization in the USA, performing 23 weeks a year at Lincoln Center's **David H Koch Theater**. During the holidays the troupe is best known for its annual production of *The Nutcracker*.

Duplex
CABARET

(Map p84; 📞 212-255-5438; www.theduplex.com; 61 Christopher St, at Seventh Ave S; cover $10-25; ⊙ 4pm-4am; ⓢ 1 to Christopher St-Sheridan Sq) Cabaret, karaoke and campy dance moves are par for the course at the legendary Duplex. Pictures of Joan Rivers line the walls, and the performers like to mimic her sassy form of self-deprecation while getting in a few jokes about audience members as well. It's a fun and unpretentious place, and certainly not for the bashful.

Joyce Theater
DANCE

(Map p88; 📞 212-691-9740; www.joyce.org; 175 Eighth Ave, at W 19th St; ⓢ C/E to 23rd St; A, L to 14th St-8th Ave; 1 to 18th St) A favorite among dance junkies thanks to its excellent sight lines and offbeat offerings, this is an intimate venue, seating 472 in a renovated cinema. Its focus is on traditional modern companies such as Martha Graham, Stephen Petronio Company and Parsons Dance, as well as global stars such as Dance Brazil, Ballet Hispanico and MalPaso Dance Company.

🔒 Shopping

Not surprisingly for a capital of commercialism, creativity and fashion, New York City is quite simply one of the best shopping destinations on the planet. Every niche is filled. From indie designer-driven boutiques to landmark department stores, thrift shops to haute couture, record stores to the Apple store, antiques to edible gourmet groceries, it's quite easy to blow one's budget.

🔒 Brooklyn

Brooklyn Flea
MARKET

(www.brooklynflea.com; 90 Kent Ave, btwn N 7th & N 10th Sts, Williamsburg; ⊙ 10am-5pm Sat Apr-Oct; ♿; ⓢ L to Bedford Ave) On the grounds of East River State Park (p122) in Williamsburg, every Saturday over 100 vendors sell their wares, ranging from antiques and records to vintage clothes and craft items. The Flea shares this space with the tasty treats of Smorgasburg (p121). On Sundays, the market moves to Dumbo near the archway at 80 Pearl St, under the Manhattan Bridge.

Beacon's Closet
VINTAGE

(📞 718-486-0816; www.beaconscloset.com; 74 Guernsey St, btwn Nassau & Norman Aves, Greenpoint; ⊙ 11am-8pm; ⓢ L to Bedford Ave; G to Nassau Ave) Twenty-something groovers find this massive 5500-sq-ft warehouse of vintage clothing part goldmine, part grit. Lots of coats, polyester tops and '90s-era T-shirts are handily displayed by color, but the sheer mass can take time to conquer. You'll also find shoes of all sorts, flannels, hats, handbags, chunky jewelry and brightly hued sunglasses.

Rough Trade
MUSIC

(📞 718-388-4111; www.roughtradenyc.com; 64 N 9th St, btwn Kent & Wythe Aves, Williamsburg; ⊙ 11am-11pm Mon-Sat, to 9pm Sun; ⓢ L to Bedford Ave) This sprawling, 10,000-sq-ft record store – a London import – stocks thousands of titles on vinyl and CD. It also has in-store DJs, listening stations, art exhibitions, and coffee and doughnuts from Brompton Bike Cafe. A small concert hall on site hosts live bands throughout the week (admission varies).

🔒 Downtown

★ Strand Book Store
BOOKS

(Map p84; 📞 212-473-1452; www.strandbooks.com; 828 Broadway, at E 12th St; ⊙ 9:30am-10:30pm Mon-Sat, from 11am Sun; ⓢ L, N/Q/R/W, 4/5/6 to 14th St-Union Sq) Beloved and legendary, the iconic Strand embodies downtown NYC's intellectual *bona fides* – a bibliophile's Oz, where generations of book lovers carrying the store's trademark tote bags happily lose themselves for hours. In operation since 1927, the Strand sells new, used and rare titles, spreading an incredible 18 miles of books (over 2.5 million of them) among three labyrinthine floors.

Screaming Mimi's VINTAGE
(Map p88; ☎212-677-6464; www.screamingmimis.com; 240 W 14th St, btwn Seventh & Eighth Aves; 🕐noon-8pm Mon-Sat, 1-7pm Sun; [S]A/C/E/L to 8th Ave-14th St) If you dig vintage threads, you may just scream too. This fun-tastic shop carries an excellent selection of yesteryear pieces, organized – ingeniously – by decade, from the '50s to the '90s. (Ask to see the small, stashed-away collection of clothing from the 1920s through '40s.)

Evolution Nature Store GIFTS & SOUVENIRS
(Map p84; ☎212-343-1114; www.theevolutionstore.com; 687 Broadway; 🕐11am-8pm; [S]N/Q/R/W to 8th Ave-NYU; 4/5/6 to Astor Place) In the market for a shrunken head? Perhaps a dried scarab beetle? This SoHo favorite has display cases full of oddities from all over the world. The store is cavernous and often busy.

Obscura Antiques ANTIQUES
(Map p84; ☎212-505-9251; www.obscuraantiques.com; 207 Ave A, btwn E 12th & 13th Sts; 🕐noon-8pm Mon-Sat, to 7pm Sun; [S]L to 1st Ave) This small cabinet of curiosities pleases both lovers of the macabre and inveterate antique hunters. Here you'll find taxidermied animal heads, tiny rodent skulls and skeletons, butterfly displays in glass boxes, photos of dead people, disturbing little (dental?) instruments, German landmine flags (stackable so tanks could see them), old poison bottles and glass eyes.

Midtown

Grand Central Market MARKET
(Map p88; www.grandcentralterminal.com/market; Grand Central Terminal, Lexington Ave, at 42nd St, Midtown East; 🕐7am-9pm Mon-Fri, 10am-7pm Sat, 11am-6pm Sun; [S]S, 4/5/6, 7 to Grand Central-42nd St) It's not all arrivals and departures at Grand Central. The station also harbors a 240ft corridor lined with perfectly coiffed fresh produce and artisan treats. Stock up on anything from crusty bread and fruit tarts to lobsters, chicken pot pies, Spanish quince paste, fruit and vegetables, and roasted coffee beans. There's even a Murray's Cheese stall, peddling milky wonders like cave-aged Gruyère.

Hell's Kitchen Flea Market MARKET
(Map p88; ☎212-220-0239; www.annexmarkets.com; W 39th St, btwn Ninth & Tenth Aves; 🕐9am-5pm Sat & Sun; [S]A/C/E to 42nd St-Port Authority Bus Terminal) This weekend flea market lures both collectors and the common curious with its wonderful booty of vintage furnishings, accessories, clothing and unidentifiable objects from past eras.

Uptown

Flamekeepers Hat Club FASHION & ACCESSORIES
(Map p94; ☎212-531-3542; 273 W 121st St, at St Nicholas Ave; 🕐noon-7pm Tue & Wed, to 8pm Thu-Sat, to 6pm Sun; [S]A/C, B/D to 125th St) Sharpen your kudos at this sassy little hat shop owned by affable Harlem local Marc Williamson. His carefully curated stock is a hat-lover's dream: buttery Barbisio fedoras from Italy, Selentino top hats from the Czech Republic and woolen patchwork caps from Ireland's Hanna Hats of Donegal. Prices range from $85 to $350, with an optional customization service for true individualists.

Flying Tiger Copenhagen HOMEWARES
(Map p94; ☎646-998-4755; www.flyingtiger.com; 424 Columbus Ave, btwn 80th & 81st Sts; 🕐10am-8pm Mon-Sun; 👪; [S]B, C to 81st St-Museum of Natural History) In the market for well-designed, quirky and inexpensive doodads and tchotchkes? This Danish import will scratch that itch. Something of a miniature Ikea, with items grouped thematically (kitchen, kids, arts and crafts etc) – you could never have imagined the things you didn't know you needed. Remove the price tag and friends will think you've spent too much on a gift.

Information

INTERNET ACCESS

Most public parks in the city now offer free wi-fi. Some prominent ones include the High Line, Bryant Park, Battery Park, Central Park, City Hall Park, Madison Square Park, Tompkins Square Park and Union Square Park (Brooklyn and Queens are also well covered). For other locations, check out www.nycgovparks.org/facilities/wifi.

Now, even underground subway stations offer free wi-fi, offering a way to pass time or get work done while waiting for signal problems or other delays to be resolved. LinkNYC (www.link.nyc), a program rolled out in 2016 to replace anachronistic pay phones (once iconic symbols of the city and where Superman changed into his skivvies) with free internet connected kiosks, replete with charging stations and wi-fi access, is experiencing some teething issues, with some booths having become gathering spots for less salubrious folk. Plans call for thousands of these small structures to be installed throughout the five boroughs.

It's rare to find accommodations in New York City that don't offer wi-fi, though it isn't always free. Of course, most cafes offer wi-fi for customers, as do the ubiquitous Starbucks around town.

MEDICAL SERVICES

Emergency services can be stress-inducing and slow (unless your medical condition is absolutely dire); a visit should be avoided if other medical services can be provided to mitigate the situation.

New York-Presbyterian Hospital (☎212-305-2500; www.nyp.org/locations/newyork-presbyterian-columbia-university-medical-center; 630 W 168th St, at Ft Washington Ave; [S] A/C, 1 to 168th St) Reputable hospital.

Bellevue Hospital Center (☎212-562-4141; www.nychealthandhospitals.org/bellevue; 462 First Ave, at 27th St, Midtown East; [S] 6 to 28th St) Major public hospital with emergency room and trauma center.

New York County Medical Society (☎212-684-4670; www.nycms.org) Provides doctor referrals over the phone, based on type of problem and language spoken.

Tisch Hospital (New York University Langone Medical Center; ☎212-263-5800; www.nyulangone.org/locations/tisch-hospital; 550 First Ave; ⏲24hr) Large, state-of-the-art facility with highly regarded departments in every critical care specialty.

Callen-Lorde Community Health Center (☎212-271-7200; www.callen-lorde.org; 356 W 18th St, btwn Eighth & Ninth Aves; ⏲8:15am-8:15pm Mon-Thu, to 4:45pm Fri, 8:30-3:15pm Sat; [S] A/C/E, L to 8th Ave-14th St) This medical center, dedicated to the LGBT community and people living with HIV/AIDS, serves people regardless of their ability to pay.

Lenox Hill Hospital (☎212-434-2000; www.northwell.edu/find-care/locations/lenox-hill-hospital; 100 E 77th St, at Lexington Ave; ⏲24hr; [S] 6 to 77th St) A good hospital with a 24-hour emergency room and multilingual translators in the Upper East Side.

Mount Sinai Hospital (☎212-241-6500; www.mountsinai.org/locations/mount-sinai; 1468 Madison Ave, at 101st St; ⏲24hr; [S] 6 to 103rd St) An excellent hospital in the Upper East Side.

Planned Parenthood (Margaret Sanger Center; ☎212-965-7000; www.plannedparenthood.org; 26 Bleecker St, btwn Mott & Elizabeth Sts; ⏲8am-6:30pm Mon, Tue, Thu & Fri, to 8:30pm Wed, to 4:30pm Sat; [S] B/D/F/V to Broadway-Lafayette St; 6 to Bleecker St) Provides birth control, STD screenings and gynecological care.

TOURIST INFORMATION

NYC Information Center (Map p88; ☎212-484-1222; www.nycgo.com; Broadway Plaza, btwn W 43rd & 44th Sts; ⏲9am-6pm; [S] N/Q/R/W, S, 1/2/3, 7 to Times Sq-42nd St) There are official NYC Visitor Information Centers throughout the city. The main office is in Midtown.

In this web-based world you'll find infinite online resources to get up-to-the-minute information about New York. In person, try one of the official branches of NYC & Company (www.nycgo.com) at **Times Square**, **Macy's Herald Square** (Map p88; ☎212-484-1222; www.nycgo.com; Macy's, 151 W 34th St, at Broadway; ⏲9am-7pm Mon-Fri, from 10am Sat, from 11am Sun; [S] B/D/F/M, N/Q/R/W to 34th St-Herald Sq), **City Hall** (Map p80; ☎212-484-1222; www.nycgo.com; City Hall Park, at Broadway; ⏲9am-6pm Mon-Sun; [S] 4/5/6 to Brooklyn Bridge-City Hall; R/W to City Hall; J/Z to Chambers St) and South Street Seaport.

The **Brooklyn Tourism & Visitors Center** (www.nycgo.com; 209 Joralemon St, btwn Court St & Brooklyn Bridge Blvd, Downtown; ⏲10am-6pm Mon-Fri; [S] 2/3, 4/5 to Borough Hall) has all sorts of info on this much-loved borough.

[i] Getting There & Away

With its three bustling airports, two main train stations and a monolithic bus terminal, New York City rolls out the welcome mat for millions of visitors who come to take a bite out of the Big Apple each year.

Direct flights are possible from most major American and international cities. Figure six hours from Los Angeles, seven hours from London and Amsterdam, and 14 hours from Tokyo. Consider getting here by train instead of car or plane to enjoy a mix of bucolic and urban scenery en route, without unnecessary traffic hassles, security checks and excess carbon emissions.

Flights, tours and rail tickets can be booked online at www.lonelyplanet.com/bookings.

AIR

John F Kennedy International Airport

John F Kennedy International Airport (JFK; ☎718-244-4444; www.kennedyairport.com; [S] A to Howard Beach or E, J/Z to Sutphin Blvd-Archer Ave then JFK Airtrain), 15 miles from Midtown in southeastern Queens, has six working terminals, serves nearly 50 million passengers annually and hosts flights coming and going from all corners of the globe. You can use the AirTrain (free within the airport) to move from one terminal to the another.

The timeline is uncertain, but a massive $10 billion overhaul of the airport was recently approved. Architectural and structural changes are the focus, but plans also call for a substantial upgrade of amenities and transportation alternatives.

LaGuardia

Used mainly for domestic flights, **LaGuardia** (LGA; ☑ 718-533-3400; www.panynj.gov; ☒ M60, Q70) is smaller than JFK but only 8 miles from midtown Manhattan; it sees nearly 30 million passengers per year.

Much maligned by politicians and ordinary travelers alike, the airport is set to receive a much-needed $4 billion overhaul of its terminal facilities. Scheduled in phases, from 2018 to 2021, plans call for a single, unified terminal to replace the four existing stand-alone ones, as well as an upgrade in amenities and transportation alternatives.

Newark Liberty International Airport

Don't write off New Jersey when looking for airfares to New York. About the same distance from Midtown as JFK (16 miles), **Newark** (EWR; ☑ 973-961-6000; www.panynj.gov) brings many New Yorkers out for flights (there's some 40 million passengers annually). It's a hub for United Airlines and offers the only nonstop flight to Havana, Cuba, in the New York City area. A $2.4 billion dollar redevelopment of Terminal A is scheduled to be completed in 2022.

BUS

For long-distance bus trips, you'll arrive and depart from the world's busiest bus station, the **Port Authority Bus Terminal** (Map p88; ☑ 212-502-2200; www.panynj.gov; 625 Eighth Ave, at W 42nd St; ☒ A/C/E to 42nd St-Port Authority Bust Terminal), which sees more than 65 million passengers each year. Efforts to replace the aging and less than salubrious station are always on the agenda. Bus companies leaving from here include the following:

Greyhound (www.greyhound.com) Connects New York with major cities across the country.

Peter Pan Trailways (www.peterpanbus.com) Daily express services to Boston, Washington, DC, and Philadelphia.

Short Line Bus (www.shortlinebus.com) Serves northern New Jersey and upstate New York, focusing on college towns such as Ithaca and New Paltz; part of Coach USA.

Trailways (www.trailwaysny.com) Bus service to upstate New York, including Albany, Ithaca and Syracuse, as well as Montreal, Canada.

A number of budget bus lines operate from locations on the west side of Midtown:

BoltBus (Map p88; ☑ 877-265-8287; www.boltbus.com; W 33rd St, between Eleventh & Twelfth Aves; ☎) Services from New York to Philadelphia, Boston, Baltimore and Washington, DC. The earlier you purchase tickets, the

better the deal. Notable for its free wi-fi, which occasionally actually works.

Megabus (Map p88; https://us.megabus.com; 34th St, btwn 11th & 12th Aves; ☎; ☒ 7 to 34th St-Hudson Yards) Travels from New York to Boston, Washington, DC, and Toronto, Canada among other destinations. Free (sometimes functioning) wi-fi. Departures leave from 34th St near the Jacob K Javits Convention Center and **arrivals** (Map p88; 7th Ave & 27th St) come to 27th and 7th.

Vamoose (Map p88; ☑ 212-695-6766; www.vamoosebus.com; ☒ 1 to 28th St; A/C/E, 1/2/3 to 34th St-Penn Station) Buses head to Arlington, Virginia and Bethesda, Maryland, both not far outside Washington, DC.

BOAT

Seastreak (www.seastreak.com) has daily commuter services between Atlantic Highlands and Highlands, New Jersey and Pier 11 near Wall St and E 35th St; there's also summer services to Sandy Hook (return $46) in New Jersey. Martha's Vineyard (one way/round-trip $165/240, five hours) in Massachusetts is accessible on summer weekends from E 35th St.

Cruise ships dock at the Manhattan Cruise Terminal in Hell's Kitchen on the west side of Manhattan at several piers from W 46th to 54th Sts.

If you're arriving in NYC by yacht, there are ports at an exclusive boat slip at the World Financial Center, and at a long-term slip at the 79th St Boathouse on the Upper West Side.

TRAIN

Penn Station (W 33rd St, btwn Seventh & Eighth Aves; ☒ 1/2/3, A/C/E to 34th St-Penn Station) The oft maligned departure point for all Amtrak (www.amtrak.com) trains, including the Acela Express services to Princeton, New Jersey, and Washington, DC (note that this express service costs twice as much as a normal fare). All fares vary, based on the day of the week and the time you want to travel. There's no baggage-storage facility at Penn Station. Derailments and maintenance issues plagued Amtrak lines out of Penn Station in the spring of 2017; repairs mean compromised service, with no certainty of when the issues will be resolved.

Long Island Rail Road (www.mta.info/lirr) The Long Island Rail Road serves more than 300,000 commuters each day, with services from Penn Station to points in Brooklyn and Queens, and on Long Island. Prices are broken down by zones. A peak-hour ride from Penn Station to Jamaica Station (en route to JFK via AirTrain) costs $10.25 if you buy it at the station (or a whopping $16 onboard!).

NJ Transit (www.njtransit.com) Also operates trains from Penn Station, with services to the suburbs and the Jersey Shore.

New Jersey PATH (www.panynj.gov/path) An option for getting into NJ's northern points, such as Hoboken and Newark. Trains ($2.75) run from Penn Station along the length of Sixth Ave, with stops at 33rd, 23rd, 14th, 9th and Christopher Sts, as well as at the reopened World Trade Center site.

Metro-North Railroad (www.mta.info/mnr) The last line departing from the magnificent Grand Central Terminal, the Metro-North Railroad serves Connecticut, Westchester County and the Hudson Valley.

ⓘ Getting Around

Check the Metropolitan Transportation Authority website (www.mta.info) for public transportation information (buses and subway), including a handy travel planner and regular notifications of delays and alternate travel routes during frequent maintenance. Unfortunately, the frequency and length of delays has only increased as ridership has expanded.

Subway Inexpensive, somewhat efficient and operates around the clock, though can be confusing to the uninitiated. Single ride is $2.75 with a MetroCard. A 7-Day Unlimited Pass costs $32.

Buses Convenient during off hours – especially when transferring between the city's eastern and western sides. Uses the MetroCard; same price as the subway.

Taxi Meters start at $2.50 and increase roughly $5 for every 20 blocks. See www.nyc.gov/taxi for more information.

Bicycle The city's popular bike share program Citi Bike provides excellent access to most parts of Manhattan, with growing service elsewhere.

Inter-borough ferries Spots along the East River in Manhattan, Brooklyn, Queens (and soon the Bronx), including the Rockaway beaches in Queens, are now connected by the new New York City Ferry (www.ferry.nyc); the New York Water Taxi (www.nywatertaxi.com) hits a few piers with regular services. Journey across New York Harbor on the free, commuter Staten Island Ferry (p107).

TO/FROM THE AIRPORT
John F Kennedy International Airport

Taxi A yellow taxi from Manhattan to the airport will use the meter; prices (often about $60) depend on traffic – it can take 45 to 60 minutes. From JFK, taxis charge a flat rate of $52 to any destination in Manhattan (not including tolls or tip); it can take 45 to 60 minutes for most destinations in Manhattan. To/from a destination in Brooklyn, the metered fare should be about $45 (Coney Island) to $62 (downtown Brooklyn). Note that the Williamsburg, Manhattan, Brooklyn and

Queensboro–59th St Bridges have no toll either way, while the Queens–Midtown Tunnel and the Hugh L Carey Tunnel (aka the Brooklyn–Battery Tunnel) cost $8.50 going into Manhattan.

Fares for ride hailing apps like Lyft and Uber change depending on the time of day.

Vans & car service Shared vans, like those offered by **Super Shuttle Manhattan** (www.supershuttle.com), cost around $20 to $26 per person, depending on the destination. If traveling to the airport from NYC, car services have set fares from $45.

Express bus The **NYC Airporter** (www.nycairporter.com) runs to Grand Central Station, Penn Station or the Port Authority Bus Terminal from JFK. The one-way fare is $18.

Subway The subway is the cheapest but slowest way of reaching Manhattan. From the airport, hop on the AirTrain ($5, payable as you exit) to Sutphin Blvd-Archer Ave (Jamaica Station) to reach the E, J or Z line (or the Long Island Rail Road). To take the A line instead, ride the AirTrain to Howard Beach station. The E train to Midtown has the fewest stops and takes a little over an hour.

Long Island Rail Road (LIRR) This is by far the most relaxing way to arrive in the city. From the airport, take the AirTrain ($5, as you exit) to Jamaica Station. From there, LIRR trains go frequently to Penn Station in Manhattan or to Atlantic Terminal in Brooklyn (near Fort Greene, Boerum Hill and the Barclay Center). It's about a 20-minute journey from station to station. One-way fares to either Penn Station or Atlantic Terminal cost $10.25 ($7.50 at off-peak times).

LaGuardia

Taxi A taxi to/from Manhattan costs about $42 for the approximately half-hour ride; it's metered with no set fare. Fares for ride-hailing apps like Lyft and Uber vary.

Car service A car service to LaGuardia costs around $35.

Express bus The **NYC Airporter** (www.nycairporter.com) costs $15 and goes to/from Grand Central, Penn Station and the Port Authority Bus Terminal.

Subway & bus It's less convenient to get to LaGuardia by public transportation than the other airports. The best subway link is the 74 St-Broadway station (7 line, or the E, F, M and R lines at the connecting Jackson Heights-Roosevelt Ave station) in Queens, where you can pick up the Q70 Express Bus to the airport (about 10 minutes to the airport). Or you can catch the M60 bus from several subway stops in upper Manhattan and Harlem or the N/Q stop at Hoyt Ave-32st St.

Newark Liberty International Airport

Car service A car service runs about $50 to $70 for the 45-minute ride from Midtown – a taxi is roughly the same. You'll have to pay a whopping $15 to get into NYC through the Lincoln (at 42nd St) and Holland (at Canal St) Tunnels and, further north, the George Washington Bridge, though there's no charge going back through to New Jersey. There are a couple of cheap tolls on New Jersey highways too, unless you ask your driver to take Hwy 1 or 9.

Subway/train NJ Transit (www.njtransit. com) runs a rail service (with a $5.50 AirTrain connection) between Newark airport (EWR) and New York's Penn Station for $13 each way. The trip takes 25 minutes and runs every 20 or 30 minutes from 4:20am to about 1:40am. Hold onto your ticket, which you must show upon exiting at the airport.

Express bus The Newark Liberty Airport Express (www.newarkairportexpress.com) has a bus service between the airport and Port Authority Bus Terminal, Bryant Park and Grand Central Terminal in Midtown ($16 one way). The 45-minute ride goes every 15 minutes from 6:45am to 11:15pm and every half-hour from 4:45am to 6:45am and 11:15pm to 1:15am.

BICYCLE

Hundreds of miles of designated bike lanes have been added over the past decade. Add to this the excellent bike-sharing network Citi Bike (www. citibikenyc.com), and you have the makings for a surprisingly bike-friendly city. Hundreds of Citi Bike kiosks in Manhattan and parts of Brooklyn house the iconic bright blue and very sturdy bicycles, which have reasonable rates for short-term users. Nearly 14 million City Bike 'trips' were taken in 2016 and there are there an estimated 12,000 bikes in the system.

To use a Citi Bike, purchase a 24-hour or three-day access pass (around $12 or $24 including tax) at any Citi Bike kiosk. You will then be given a five-digit code to unlock a bike. Return the bike to any station within 30 minutes to avoid incurring extra fees. Reinsert your credit card (you won't be charged) and follow the prompts to check out a bike again. You can make an un-limited number of 30-minute check-outs during those 24 hours or three days.

Helmets aren't required by law, but strongly recommended. City parks like Central Park, the Brooklyn Waterfront Greenway and Prospect Park in Brooklyn are good places to test out your comfort level on wheels in less stressful environments than the chaotic city streets. And most importantly, for your safety and that of others, obey traffic laws.

You'll find routes and bike lanes for every borough on NYC Bike Maps (www.nycbikemaps. com). For downloadable maps and point-to-point route generator, visit NYC DOT (www.nyc.gov/ html/dot/html/bicyclists/bikemaps.shtml). Free bike maps are also available at most bike shops.

PUBLIC TRANSPORTATION
Tickets and Passes

➜ The yellow-and-blue MetroCards (www.mta. info/metrocard) are the swipe cards used for all of NYC's public transportation. You can purchase or add value at one of several easy-to-use automated machines at any station. Each ride on the subway or bus (except for express buses) deducts $2.75 from the card.

➜ Purchase the MetroCard itself for $1 at kiosks in subway stations, and load it with credit ($20, which will give you eight rides and change, is a good start). If you plan to ride a lot, buy a 7-day Unlimited Pass ($32). These cards are handy for travelers – particularly if you're jumping around town to a few different places in one day.

➜ The subway kiosks take credit or ATM cards (larger machines also take cash). When you need to add more credit, just insert your card and follow the prompts (tip: when it asks for your ZIP, input '99999' if you're not from the USA).

➜ Transfers from subway to bus, or bus to subway, are free. Just swipe/insert your card, and no extra charge will be deducted.

NEW YORK STATE

For most, any trip to the Empire State starts or finishes in its iconic metropolis: New York City. However, if you were to confine your travels only to its five boroughs and a little beyond, you'd be missing out big time.

Upstate New York – ie anywhere outside NYC – is a dream destination for those who cherish the great outdoors as much as a bar crawl around the Lower East Side. The grand Hudson River heads straight north from NYC, like an escape route. From Albany, the 524-mile Erie Canal cuts due west to Lake Erie, by spectacular Niagara Falls and Buffalo, a fascinating, rust-belt city that's on the rebound.

The St Lawrence River forms the border with Canada in the beautiful Thousand Islands area. Sample fine wines in the Finger Lakes region, hike in the magnificent Adirondack and Catskills mountains, or simply kick back on the sandy beaches of Long Island.

ⓘ Resources

511 NY (www.511ny.org) Statewide traffic and transit info.

I Love NY (www.iloveny.com) Comprehensive state tourism bureau, with the iconic heart logo.

DVEIGHT (www.dveightmag.com) Online and print magazine focusing on upstate experiences for stylish urbanites.

New York State Office of Parks, Recreation and Historic Preservation (https://parks.ny.gov/) Camping, lodging and general info on all state parks.

And North (http://andnorth.com) Curated online guide to upstate New York.

Escape Brooklyn (http://escapebrooklyn.com) Respected blog by clued-up Brooklynites on upstate getaways.

Lonely Planet (www.lonelyplanet.com/usa/new-york-state) Destination information, hotel bookings, traveler forum and more.

Long Island

Technically, the 118 miles of Long Island includes the boroughs of Brooklyn and Queens on the west edge, but in the popular imagination, 'Long Island' begins only where the city ends, in a mass of traffic-clogged expressways and suburbs that every teenager aspires to leave. (Levittown, the first planned 1950s subdivision, is in central Nassau County.) But there's plenty more out on 'Lawn-guy-land' (per the local accent). Push past the central belt of 'burbs to wind-swept dunes, glitzy summer resorts, fresh farms and wineries, and whaling and fishing ports established in the 17th century. Then you'll see why loyalists prefer the nickname 'Strong Island.'

Getting There & Around

Thanks to Long Island Rail Road (LIRR; www.mta.info/lirr), which runs three lines from NYC's Penn Station to the farthest east ends of the island, it's possible to visit without a car. Additionally, the Hampton Jitney (www.hamptonjitney.com) and Hampton Luxury Liner (www.hamptonluxuryliner.com) buses connect Manhattan to various Hamptons villages and Montauk; the former also picks up in Brooklyn, and runs to the North Fork. With a car, however, it is easier to visit several spots on the island in one go. I-495, aka the Long Island Expwy (LIE), runs down the middle of the island – but avoid rush hour, when it's commuter hell.

South Shore

Easily accessible by public transit, these beaches can get crowded, but they're a fun day out. Not nearly as much of a schlep as the Hamptons, and far more egalitarian, the beach towns along these barrier islands each have their own vibe and audience – you can get lost in the crowds or go solo on the dunes. **Long Beach**, just over the border from Queens, and its main town strip is busy with ice-cream shops, bars and eateries.

Sights

Fire Island National Seashore ISLAND (631-687-4750; www.nps.gov/fiis) FREE Federally protected, this island offers sand dunes, forests, clean beaches, camping (dune-camping permits $20), hiking trails, inns, restaurants, 15 hamlets and two villages. Its scenery ranges from car-free areas of summer mansions and packed nightclubs to stretches of sand where you'll find nothing but pitched tents and deer.

Most of the island is accessible only by **ferry** (631-665-3600; www.fireislandferries.com; 99 Maple Ave, Bay Shore; one way adult/child $10/5, 1am ferry $19) and is free of cars – regulars haul their belongings on little wagons instead. You can drive to either end of the island (the lighthouse or the Wilderness Visitor Center) but there is no road in between. The island is edged with a dozen or so tiny hamlets, mostly residential. Party-center **Ocean Beach Village** and quieter **Ocean Bay Park** (take ferries from the Bayshore LIRR stop) have a few hotels; **Cherry Grove** and the **Pines** (ferries from Sayville) are gay enclaves, also with hotels.

Robert Moses State Park STATE PARK (631-669-0449; www.parks.ny.gov; 600 Robert Moses State Pkwy, Babylon, Fire Island; per car $10, lounge chairs $10, golf $11; dawn-dusk) Robert Moses State Park, one small part of Fire Island accessible by car, lies at the westernmost end and features wide, soft-sand beaches with mellower crowds than those at Jones Beach. It's also adjacent to the **Fire Island Lighthouse** (Fire Island National Seashore; 631-661-4876; www.nps.gov/fiis; Robert Moses Causeway; adult/child $7/4; 9:30am-6pm Jul & Aug, 10am-4pm Mon-Fri, to 5pm Sat & Sun Sep-Jun), which you can walk to from here.

Sunken Forest FOREST (631-597-6183; www.nps.gov/fiis; Fire Island; visitor center mid-May–mid-Oct) FREE This 300-year-old forest, a surprisingly dense stretch of trees behind the dunes, is easily accessible via a 1.5-mile boardwalk trail looping through. It's pleasantly shady in summer, and vividly colored when the leaves change in fall. It's accessible by its own ferry stop (Sailors Haven, where there's also a visitor center), or a long walk in the winter season, after the ferry shuts down. Ranger-guided tours available.

🛏 Sleeping & Eating

Seashore Condo Motel   HOTEL $$
(☑631-583-5860; www.seashorecondomotel.com; Bayview Ave, Ocean Bay Park, Fire Island; r from $240; ❄️☎️) Small, wood-paneled rooms without many frills, despite the price.

Madison Fire Island Pines   BOUTIQUE HOTEL $$$
(☑631-597-6061; www.themadisonfi.com; 22 Atlantic Walk, Fire Island Pines, Fire Island; r from $225; ❄️☎️🏊) Fire Island's first 'boutique' hotel, which rivals anything Manhattan has to offer in terms of amenities, but also has killer views from a rooftop deck.

Sand Castle   SEAFOOD $$
(☑631-597-4174; www.fireislandsandcastle.com; 106 Lewis Walk, Cherry Grove, Fire Island; mains $15-30; ⏱11am-11pm Mon, Tue & Thu-Sat, 9:30am-11pm Sun May-Sep) One of Fire Island's only ocean-front (rather than bayfront) options, Sand Castle serves up satisfying appetizers (fried calamari, portobello fries) and lots of seafood temptations (mussels, crab cakes, seared sea scallops). Nice cocktails and people-watching.

❶ Getting There & Away

You can drive to Fire Island by taking the Long Island Expwy to Exit 53 (Bayshore), 59 (Sayville) or 63 (Patchogue).

Using public transportation, take the LIRR to one of three stations with connections to the ferries: Patchogue (www.davisparkferry.com), Bayshore (www.fireislandferries.com) or Sayville (www.sayvilleferry.com). Patchogue is walking distance from the train to the boat. You can also purchase a train-taxi combination ticket from the railroad for excursions to Sunken Forest and a train-bus combo for Jones Beach.

The LIRR (www.mtainfo.com/lirr) runs directly to Long Beach (55 minutes) from New York's Penn Station. You can buy special beach combination excursion tickets from the railroad.

The Hamptons

This string of villages is a summer escape for Manhattan's wealthiest, who zip to mansions by helicopter. Mere mortals take the Hampton Jitney bus and chip in on rowdy rental houses. Behind the glitz is a long cultural history, as noted artists and writers have lived here. Beneath the glamour, the gritty and life-risking tradition of fishing continues.

◉ Sights

EAST HAMPTON

East Hampton Town Marine Museum   MUSEUM
(www.easthamptonhistory.org; 301 Bluff Rd, Amangansett; $4; ⏱10am-5pm Sat, noon-5pm Sun Apr-Oct) One of your last outposts before you drive on to Montauk, this small museum dedicated to the fishing and whaling industries is as interesting as its counterpart in Sag Harbor, full of old harpoons, boats half the size of their prey, and a beautiful black-and-white photographic tribute to the local fishers and their families.

Osborn-Jackson House   MUSEUM
(☑631-324-6850; www.easthamptonhistory.org; 101 Main St; donation $4; ⏱10am-4pm Tue-Sat) Check out East Hampton's colonial past with a visit to the East Hampton Historical Society. The Society tends to five historical attractions around East Hampton, including old colonial farms, mansions and a marine museum.

Pollock-Krasner House   ARTS CENTER
(☑631-324-4929; www.stonybrook.edu/pkhouse; 830 Springs Fireplace Rd; $5, guided tours $10; ⏱1-5pm Thu-Sat May-Oct) Tour the home of husband-and-wife art stars Jackson Pollock and Lee Krasner – worth it just to see the paint-spattered floor of Pollock's studio. Reservations required for guided tour at noon.

SAG HARBOUR

Sag Harbor Whaling & Historical Museum   MUSEUM
(☑631-725-0770; www.sagharborwhalingmuseum.org; 200 Main St; adult/child $6/2; ⏱10am-5pm Apr-Nov) The cool collection here includes actual artifacts from 19th-century whaling ships: sharp flensing knives, battered pots for rendering blubber, delicate scrimshaw and more. It's a bit surreal to see photos of the giant mammals in a village that's now a cute resort town.

SOUTHAMPTON

Parrish Art Museum   MUSEUM
(☑631-283-2118; www.parrishart.org; 279 Montauk Hwy, Water Mill; adult/child $10/free, Wed free; ⏱10am-5pm Mon, Wed, Thu, Sat & Sun, to 8pm Fri) In a sleek long barn designed by Herzog & de Meuron, this institution spotlights local artists such as Jackson Pollock, Willem de Kooning and Chuck Close.

Southampton Historical Museum MUSEUM
(☑631-283-2494; www.southamptonhistorical
museum.org; 17 Meeting House Lane; adult/child
$4/free; ⊙11am-4pm Wed-Sat Mar-Dec) Before
the Hamptons was the Hamptons, there was
this clutch of buildings, now nicely maintained, and spread around Southampton.
The main museum is Rogers Mansion, once
owned by a whaling captain. Also visit a
former dry-goods store, now occupied by a
local jeweler, around the corner on Main St;
and a 17th-century homestead, the Halsey
House (Saturday only July to October).

St Andrew's Dune Church CHURCH
(www.standrewsdunechurch.com; 12 Gin Lane;
⊙service 11am Sun Jun-Sep) The triple spires of
this 19th-century red wooden church glow
beautifully in the afternoon light. You can
come to Sunday service if so inclined, admiring the stained glass and quaint wooden
pews, or simply enjoy a stroll along the placid waterway across the street from the curious iron pot donated by an early congregant.
The building was the earliest life-saving station in New York, and is well worth the short
drive or walk from downtown.

🛌 Sleeping

⭐**Topping Rose House** BOUTIQUE HOTEL $$$
(☑631-537-0870; www.toppingrosehouse.com;
1 Bridgehampton-Sag Harbor Turnpike, Bridge-
hampton; r from $695; P❋🛜🏊) In an 1842
home, this top-of-the-line modern boutique
hotel boasts 22 guest rooms, including six
suites decorated with local artists' work. A
Manhattan gallery curates the rotating art
collection (for sale, of course), and there's a
spa and heated pool in addition to the 75-
seat farm-to-table restaurant, some produce
for which is sourced from the 1-acre garden
adjoining the property.

1708 House INN $$$
(☑631-287-1708; www.1708house.com; 126 Main
St; r from $250; ❋🛜) History buffs might
gravitate toward this local standout. It's in
central Southampton and prides itself on its
turn-of-the-century charm.

🍴 Eating

Candy Kitchen DINER $
(☑631-537-9885; 2391 Montauk Hwy, Bridgehamp-
ton; mains $5-12; ⊙7am-9pm; 🖐) An antidote
to glitz, this corner diner has been serving
good soups, homemade ice cream and other
staples since 1925. Its policy is similarly old-
school – cash only, please.

⭐**Fellingham's** PUB FOOD $$
(Restaurant Sports Bar; ☑631-283-9417; www.
fellinghamsrestaurant.com; 17 Cameron St; burg-
ers $11, mains $19-21; ⊙11am-11pm) Behind the
bank, in an alley off Main St, you'll get a dash
of local flavor at this favored sports bar, rich
with historical photos and memorabilia, and
boasting a hearty menu featuring a bacon-
cheeseburger named for baseball legend
Babe Ruth and a Sharapova burger with –
naturally – Russian dressing. There's so
much local flavor, this qualifies as the
'Cheers' of Southampton. Mains are heavy
on the steaks and chops.

⭐**Dockside Bar and Grill** SEAFOOD $$$
(☑631-725-7100; www.docksidesagharbor.com; 26
Bay St; mains $26-32; ⊙11:30am-10pm) A local
favorite inside the American Legion Hall
(the original bar's still there), the seafood-
heavy menu features a prize-winning, stick-
to-the-spoon chowder and luscious lobster
spring rolls, among other mouth-watering
delights. The outdoor patio can be nice in
the summer.

ℹ️ Getting There & Away

Driving the Montauk Hwy (Rte 27) to and from
New York involves careful planning to avoid
major congestion, and it's often at a standstill
within the Hamptons itself on busy weekends.
It's better to take the ever-popular Hampton
Jitney out here from Manhattan or Brooklyn – it
serves the entire Hamptons with frequent comfortable buses. The LIRR is a second but often
more time-consuming option.

ℹ️ Getting Around

The app-driven, cool turquoise converted school
buses offered by Hampton Hopper (www.hamp
tonhopper.com) are an economical, hassle-free
way around the towns and run into the bar hours.

Montauk

Toward the east-pointing tip of Long Island's
South Fork, you'll find the mellow town of
Montauk, aka 'The End,' and the famous
surfing beach **Ditch Plains**. With the surfers
have come affluent hipsters and boho-chic
hotels, but the area is still far less of a scene
than the Hamptons, with proudly blue-
collar residents and casual seafood restaurants. Route 27, the Montauk Hwy, divides
east of **Napeague State Park**, with the
Montauk Hwy continuing down the center
of the peninsula while Old Montauk Hwy
hugs the water. The roads converge at the

edge of central Montauk and Fort Pond, a small lake. Two miles east is a large inlet called Lake Montauk, with marinas strung along its shore.

◉ Sights

Lost at Sea Memorial
MEMORIAL

(2000 Montauk Hwy, Montauk Lighthouse; Montauk State Park parking fee $8; ⊗10:30am-5:30pm Sun-Fri, to 7pm Sat mid-Jun–Aug, reduced hours mid-Apr–mid-Jun & Sep-Nov) Visitors to the Montauk Lighthouse may not immediately notice a smaller 15ft structure at the far east end of the park, where the 60ft cliffs fall off into the sea, but for local fishers it's a daily reminder of their struggle against the power of the sea. The 8ft, 2600lb bronze statue set on a 7ft slab of granite is inscribed with the names of local fishers lost to the waves, from the colonial days of New York to the present.

Montauk Point State Park
STATE PARK

(☑631-668-3781; www.parks.ny.gov; 2000 Montauk Hwy/Rte 27; per car $8; ⊗dawn-dusk) Covering the eastern tip of the South Fork is Montauk Point State Park, with its impressive **lighthouse** (☑631-668-2544; www.montauklighthouse.com; adult/child $11/4; ⊗10:30am-5:30pm Sun-Fri, to 7pm Sat mid-Jun–Aug, reduced hours mid-Apr–mid-Jun & Sep-Nov). A good place for windswept walks, surfing, surf fishing (with a permit) and seal-spotting.

⌂ Sleeping

Hither Hills State Park
CAMPGROUND $

(☑631-668-2554; www.parks.ny.gov; 164 Old Montauk Hwy; campsites New York State residents/nonresidents $35/70, reservation fee $9) These wooded dunes form a natural barrier between Montauk and the Hamptons. The 189-site campground caters for tents and RVs, and there are spots for fishing (with a permit) and hiking through the dunes; online reservations are a must.

★ Sunrise Guesthouse
GUESTHOUSE $$$

(☑631-668-7286; www.sunrisebnb.com; 681 Old Montauk Hwy; r/ste $395/495; P❄🛈) A tasteful yet homey four-room B&B a mile from town, and just across the road from the beach. The breakfast is ample and delicious, served in a comfy dining area with a million-dollar view.

Surf Lodge
MOTEL $$$

(☑631-483-5037; www.thesurflodge.com; 183 Edgemere St; r $250-300; ❄🛈) Set on Fort Pond a half-mile north of the beach, this hipster haven has been at the forefront of Montauk's transformation. It has a casual-chic design scheme with private decks and cooking stoves, and Frette bedding.

✗ Eating & Drinking

Lobster Roll
SEAFOOD $$

(☑631-267-3740; www.lobsterroll.com; 1980 Montauk Hwy, Amagansett; mains $14-28; ⊗11:30am-9:30pm Jun-Sep, 11:30am-4:30pm Mon, to 8pm Fri-Sun May) 'Lunch' is the sign to look for on the roadside west of Montauk, marking this clam-and-lobster shack that has been in operation since 1965.

★ Clam Bar at Napeague
SEAFOOD $$

(☑631-267-6348; www.clambarhamptons.com; 2025 Montauk Hwy, Amagansett; items $15-30; ⊗11:30am-6pm Apr-Oct, 11:30am-6pm Sat & Sun Nov & Dec) You won't get fresher seafood or a saltier waitstaff, and holy mackerel, those lobster rolls are good, even if you choke a bit on the price. Three decades in business – the public has spoken – with cash only, of course. Locals favor this one. Find it on the road between Amagansett and Montauk.

Montauk Brewing Company
MICROBREWERY

(☑631-668-8471; www.montaukbrewingco.com; 62 S Erie Ave; ⊗2-7pm Mon-Fri, noon-7pm Sat & Sun) 'Come as you are,' preaches the small tasting room, and Cobain's family hasn't asked for their lyric back yet. There's a more-than-palatable rotating range of cervezas, from lagers to stouts, and an outdoor patio to enjoy them in the right weather.

Montauket
BAR

(☑631-668-5992; 88 Firestone Rd; ⊗noon-10pm) Experts agree: this is the best place to watch the sun go down on Long Island. An unassuming slate-blue-shingled building, full of local flavor (and local people).

ℹ Getting There & Away

Montauk is the last stop on the eastbound Jitney bus (www.hamptonjitney.com; $28) as well as the Long Island Railroad. The Suffolk County bus 10C runs out here from East Hampton – connect with the 94 to cover the rest of the distance to the lighthouse.

North Fork & Shelter Island

The North Fork of Long Island is known for its bucolic farmland and vineyards (though weekends can draw rowdy limo-loads on winery crawls). Rte 25, the main road through the towns of **Jamesport**, **Cutchogue** and **Southold**, is pretty and edged with farm stands.

The largest town on the North Fork is **Greenport**, a laid-back place with working fishing boats, a history in whaling, and an old carousel in its Harbor Front Park. It's compact and easily walkable from the LIRR station. Like a little pearl in Long Island's claw, Shelter Island rests between the North and South Forks. The island is a smaller, lower-key version of the Hamptons, with a touch of maritime New England. Parking is limited; long **Crescent Beach**, for instance, has spots only by permit. If you don't mind a few hills, it's a nice place to visit by bike.

⊙ Sights

Mashomack Nature Preserve
NATURE RESERVE
(☑631-749-1001; www.shelter-island.org/mash omack.html; Rte 114, Shelter Island; donation adult/child $3/2; ⊙9am-5pm Mar-Sep, to 4pm Oct-Feb) The 2000 acres of this Shelter Island reserve, shot through with creeks and marshes, are great for kayaking, birding and hiking (no cycling allowed). Take precautions against ticks, an ever-present problem on the island.

Orient Beach State Park
BEACH
(☑631-323-2440; www.parks.ny.gov; 40000 Main Rd, Orient; per car $10, kayaks per hour $25; ⊙8am-dusk, swimming only Jul-Aug) A sandy slip of land at the end of the North Fork where you can swim in the calm ocean water (July and August) or rent kayaks to paddle in the small bay. True believers can view four different lighthouses, including the Orient Point Lighthouse, known to sailors as 'the coffee pot' for its stout bearing.

Horton Point Lighthouse
LIGHTHOUSE
(☑631-765-5500; www.southoldhistoricalsociety. org/lighthouse; 3575 Lighthouse Rd, Southold; $5; ⊙11:30am-4pm Sat & Sun Jun-Sep) Perhaps a poorer sister to the famous Montauk lighthouse, Horton Point was also commissioned by President Washington, but finally built 60 years later by William Sinclair, a Scotsman, who was an engineer in Brooklyn's Navy Yard. There's a nice nature trail in the adjacent park that leads to two Long Island Sound overlooks and steps to the beach.

🛏 Sleeping & Eating

Greenporter Hotel
BOUTIQUE HOTEL $$$
(☑631-477-0066; www.greenporterhotel.com; 326 Front St, Greenport; r from $309; ❄ 🛜 🏊) An older motel redone with white walls and

Ikea furniture, this place is good value for the area.

Love Lane Kitchen
MODERN AMERICAN $$
(☑631-298-8989; www.lovelanekitchen.com; 240 Love Lane, Mattituck; mains lunch $13-16, dinner $16-32; ⊙7am-4pm Tue & Wed, 8am-9:30pm Thu-Mon) At this popular place on a cute street, local meat and vegetables drive the global-diner menu: burgers, of course, plus spicy chickpeas and duck tagine.

North Fork Table & Inn
AMERICAN $$$
(☑631-765-0177; www.nofoti.com; 57225 Main Rd, Southold; 3-course set menu $70; ⊙5:30-8pm Mon, Thu & Sun, to 10pm Fri & Sat) A favorite foodies' escape, this four-room inn (rooms from $250) has an excellent farm-to-table restaurant, run by alums of the esteemed Manhattan restaurant Gramercy Tavern. Dinner is served Thursday to Monday, but if you're hankering for a gourmand-to-go lunch ($11 to $15), the inn's food truck is parked outside on those days from 11:30am to 3:30pm.

❶ Getting There & Away

The Hampton Jitney bus picks up passengers on Manhattan's East Side on 96th, 83rd, 77th, 69th, 59th and 40th Sts. It makes stops in 10 North Fork villages.

If you're driving, take the Midtown Tunnel out of Manhattan, which will take you onto I-495/Long Island Expwy. Take this until it ends at Riverhead and follow signs onto Rte 25. You can stay on Rte 25 for all points east, but note that the North Rd (Rte 48) is faster as it does not go through the town centers.

The Long Island Rail Road's line is the Ron-konkoma Branch, with trips leaving from Penn Station and Brooklyn and running all the way out to Greenport.

To get from the North Fork to the South Fork (or vice versa), take the North Ferry ($11, www.northferry.com) and the South Ferry ($15, www.southferry.com) services, crossing Shel-ter Island in between. There is no direct ferry – you must take one and then the other.

Hudson Valley

Winding roads along either side of the Hudson River take you by picturesque farms, Victorian cottages, apple orchards and old-money mansions built by New York's elite. Painters of the Hudson River School romanticized these landscapes, and fall is a particularly beautiful time for a trip.

The eastern side of the river is more populated thanks to the commuter train line between NYC and Albany. Several magnificent homes can be found near Tarrytown and Sleepy Hollow. The formerly industrial town of Beacon has been revived as an outpost of contemporary art, while historic Hudson attracts a wealthier set of weekenders with its restored Opera House, small galleries and antique shops.

In a car you can cross to the Hudson's west bank to explore several state parks, West Point military academy, and New Paltz with its access to superb rock climbing in the Minnewaska State Park Preserve and Mohonk Preserve.

ℹ️ Getting There & Away

Metro-North Railroad (www.mta.info/mnr) runs as far north as Poughkeepsie from NYC's Grand Central; New Jersey Transit (www.njtransit. com) runs another line through New Jersey that gives access to Harriman. Amtrak (www.amtrak. com) also stops in Rhinecliff (for Rhinebeck), Poughkeepsie and Hudson. For New Paltz, you'll need the bus.

Lower Hudson Valley

Made famous by 19th-century author Washington Irving as the location of his headless horseman tale, *The Legend of Sleepy Hollow*, Sleepy Hollow and its larger neighbor Tarrytown are the jumping-off points for a trio of historic estates, as well as the gourmet and farm-activity destination of Stone Barn Center for Food & Agriculture.

Since the opening of the outstanding contemporary art museum Dia: Beacon in 2003, this blue-collar town beside the Hudson River has steadily evolved into a magnet for creatives, commuters and second-homers. Backed by Mt Beacon, the tallest summit in the Hudson Valley and a rewarding hike, Beacon also offers great shopping at the boutiques, galleries and craft shops strung along Main St as it runs down to picturesque Fishkill Falls. The town may be experiencing its moment of hipness, but it still proudly wears its working-class roots and is all the more attractive for it.

⊙ Sights

★ **Dia: Beacon**   GALLERY
(☑ 845-440-0100; www.diaart.org; 3 Beekman St; adult/child $15/free; ⊙ 11am-6pm Thu-Mon Apr-Oct, 11am-4pm Fri-Mon Nov-Mar) The 300,000 sq

ft of a former Nabisco box printing factory beside the Hudson River is now a storehouse for a series of stunning monumental works by the likes of Richard Serra, Dan Flavin, Louise Bourgeois and Gerhard Richter. The permanent collection is complemented by temporary shows of large-scale sculptures and installations, making this a must-see for contemporary art fans.

Boscobel House & Gardens   HISTORIC BUILDING
(☑ 845-265 3638; www.boscobel.org; 1601 Rte 9D, Garrison; house & gardens adult/child $17/8, gardens only $11/5; ⊙ guided tours 10am-4pm Wed-Mon Apr-Oct, to 3pm Nov & Dec) The elegant backdrop for the summer season **Hudson Valley Shakespeare Festival** (☑ 845-265-9575; www.hvshakespeare.org; tickets from $45; ⊙ mid-May–early Sep), Boscobel dates from 1808 and is considered to be one of the finest examples of Federal-style architecture in the state. Entry to the house, which is 8 miles south of Beacon, is by guided tour (50 minutes), which run regularly through the day.

**Stone Barn Center for
Food & Agriculture**   FARM
(☑ 914-366-6200; http://story.stonebarnscenter. org; 630 Bedford Rd, Pocantico Hills; adult/child $20/10; ⊙ 10am-5pm Wed-Sun) Tours of the celebrated farm and the chance to take part in activities such as egg collecting, lettuce planting and meeting the flock of sheep are sure to entertain kids and land-loving adults. There's a good shop and a small take-out cafe.

Sunnyside   HISTORIC BUILDING
(☑ 914-591-8763, Mon-Fri 914-631-8200; www. hudsonvalley.org; 3 W Sunnyside Lane, Tarrytown; adult/child $12/6; ⊙ tours 10:30am-3:30pm Wed-Sun May–mid-Nov) Washington Irving, famous for tales such as *The Legend of Sleepy Hollow*, built this imaginative home, which he said had more nooks and crannies than a cocked hat. Tour guides in 19th-century costume tell good stories, and the wisteria Irving planted a century ago still climbs the walls.

The closest train station to Sunnyside is Irvington, one stop before Tarrytown.

🛏️ Sleeping & Eating

★ **Roundhouse**   BOUTIQUE HOTEL $$
(☑ 845-765-8369; www.roundhousebeacon.com; 2 E Main St; r from $189; P⊝❋🛜) Occupying a former blacksmiths and hat factory either side of the town's Fishkill Creek, Roundhouse

is a model of Beacon's renaissance as a tourist destination. Elements of the buildings' industrial past blend seamlessly with contemporary comforts in the spacious rooms, which feature designer lightbulbs, timber headboards and alpaca-wool blankets.

Two-Michelin-star-awarded chef Terrance Brennan heads up the hotel's excellent **restaurant and lounge** (ramen $16-21, mains $26-36, tasting menus from $85; ⊙ 3-9pm Mon & Tue, 11:30am-9pm Wed & Thu, to 10pm Fri & Sat, 11am-8pm Sun; 🖉) grounded by a philosophy of sustainable 'whole-farm cuisine': do not miss the amazing ramen served in the lounge.

Homespun Foods   CAFE $
(🖉 845-831-5096; www.homespunfoods.com; 232 Main St; mains $5-10; ⊙ 8am-5pm; 🖉) A low-key gourmet legend in these parts, Homespun offers fresh everything, including creative salads, sandwiches and a veggie meatloaf made from nuts and cheese.

★ Blue Hill at Stone Barns   AMERICAN $$$
(🖉 914-366-9600; www.bluehillfarm.com; 630 Bedford Rd, Pocantico Hills; set menu $258; ⊙ 5-10pm Wed-Sat, 1-7:30pm Sun) 🍃 Go maximum locavore at chef Dan Barber's farm (it also supplies his Manhattan restaurant). Settle in for an eye-popping multicourse feast based on the day's harvest lasting at least three hours, where the service is as theatrical as the presentation. Be sure to book around two months in advance and note the dress code: jackets and ties preferred for gentlemen; shorts not permitted.

❶ Getting There & Away

Metro-North (www.mta.info/mnr) commuter trains connect NYC with Beacon (one way off-peak/peak $23/28, 90 minutes).

Tarrytown Station (www.mta.info/mnr; 1 Depot Plaza, Tarrytown) has regular train connections with NYC ($17 to $20, 40 to 50 minutes). Irvington, one stop before Tarrytown, is the closest station to Sunnyside, while Philipse Manor, one stop after, is walkable to Philipsburg Manor.

For the most flexibility in getting around the area, hire a car.

New Paltz

The hippie vibe endures in New Paltz, a short drive from the west bank of the Hudson. You'll find a campus of the State University of New York here, and it's the gateway to Shawangunk Ridge (aka 'The Gunks'), excellent for hiking and offering excellent options for rock climbing.

◉ Sights & Activities

Historic Huguenot Street   HISTORIC SITE
(🖉 845-255-1660; www.huguenotstreet.org; 86 Huguenot St; guided tours $15) Step back in time on a stroll around this picturesque enclave of buildings remaining from a Huguenot settlement dating back to 1678.

The 10-acre National Historic Landmark District includes a visitor center (the departure point for guided tours of the area), seven historic stone houses, a reconstructed 1717 Huguenot church and a burial ground.

Mohonk Preserve   PARK
(🖉 845-255-0919; www.mohonkpreserve.org; 3197 Rte 55, Gardiner; day pass hikers/climbers & cyclists $15/20; ⊙ 9am-5pm) Some 8000 acres of land held in private trust, with trails and other services maintained with visitor fees. This is home to some of the best rock climbing on the East Coast.

Rock & Snow   ADVENTURE SPORTS
(🖉 845-255-1311; www.rockandsnow.com; 44 Main St; ⊙ 9am-6pm Mon-Thu, to 8pm Fri & Sat, 8am-7pm Sun) This long-running outfitters rents out tents, and rock-climbing, ice-climbing and other equipment. It can also team you up with guides for climbing and other outdoor adventures in the 'Gunks.'

🛏 Sleeping & Eating

New Paltz Hostel   HOSTEL $
(🖉 845-255-6676; www.newpaltzhostel.com; 145 Main St; dm/r from $30/70; ▨ 🛜) Aligned with New Paltz's hippie vibe, this hostel in a big old house next to the bus station is popular with visiting rock climbers and hikers. Rooms have two bunk beds and a double bed with attached bathroom, and there's a good communal kitchen.

★ Mohonk Mountain House   RESORT $$$
(🖉 855-436-0832; www.mohonk.com; 1000 Mountain Rest Rd; r from $259; ▨ @ 🛜 ▧) This giant faux 'Victorian castle' perches over a dark lake, offering guests all the luxuries, from lavish meals to golf to spa services, plus a full roster of outdoor excursions, including hiking and trail rides. Rates include all meals and most activities, and you can choose from rooms in the main building, cottages or the luxury Grove Lodge.

Huckleberry
AMERICAN $$

(☎ 845-633-8443; www.huckleberrynewpaltz.com; 21 Church St; mains $12-20; ⊙ noon-2am Mon-Thu, to 4am Fri & Sat, 10am-2am Sun; 🖘) This cute sea-green painted house hidden off the main road offers an appealing menu of gourmet items, including Wagyu burgers (with the option of gluten-free buns), fish tacos and stout mac 'n' cheese. There are also creative cocktails, craft beers and a lovely outdoor dining/drinking area in which to enjoy it all.

ⓘ Getting There & Away

Trailways (☎ 800-776-7548; www.trailwaysny. com; 139 Main St) connects New Paltz with NYC ($21.75, 1½ hours) and Woodstock ($6.25, one hour).

Poughkeepsie

The largest town in the Hudson Valley, Poughkeepsie (puh-*kip*-see) is home to the prestigious college Vassar, which was women-only until 1969, as well as an IBM office – once the 'Main Plant' where notable early computers were built. The main attraction here is the chance to walk across the Hudson River on the world's longest pedestrian bridge.

◎ Sights

Franklin D Roosevelt Home
HISTORIC BUILDING

(☎ 845-486-7770; www.nps.gov/hofr; 4097 Albany Post Rd; adult/child $18/free, museum only adult/child $9/free; ⊙ 9am-5pm) Rangers lead interesting hour-long tours around Springwood, the home of Franklin D Roosevelt (FDR) who won a record four presidential elections and led America from the Great Depression through WWII. Considering his family wealth, it's a modest abode, but can be unpleasantly crowded in summer. Intimate details have been preserved, including his desk – left as it was the day before he died – and the hand-pulled elevator he used to hoist his polio-stricken body to the 2nd floor.

The home is part of a 1520-acre estate, formerly a working farm, which also includes walking trails and the **FDR Presidential Library and Museum** (☎ 845-486-7770; www. fdrlibrary.org; adult/child $18/free; ⊙ 9am-6pm Apr-Oct, to 5pm Nov-Mar), which details important achievements in FDR's presidency. Admission tickets last two days and include the Springwood tour and the presidential library.

Walkway Over the Hudson
PARK

(☎ 845-834-2867; www.walkway.org; 61 Parker Ave; ⊙ 7am-sunset) This is the main eastern entrance (with parking) to what was once a railroad bridge crossing the Hudson. It's now the world's longest pedestrian bridge – 1.28 miles – and a state park. The span provides breathtaking views along the river.

🛏 Sleeping & Eating

★ Roosevelt Inn
MOTEL $

(☎ 845-229-2443; www.rooseveltinnofhydepark. com; 4360 Albany Post Rd; r $70-155; ⊙ Mar-Dec; ❄ 🖘) Family owned and run since 1971, this roadside motel offers a great deal, especially for its pine-paneled 'rustic' rooms. The upper-level deluxe rooms offer more space.

No breakfast is served, but there's a cafe on site.

Eveready Diner
AMERICAN $

(☎ 845-229-8100; www.theeverydaydiner.com; 4184 Albany Post Rd/Rte 9; mains $10-13; ⊙ 6am-midnight Sun-Thu, 24hr Fri & Sat) It's difficult to resist turning off the highway to visit this giant sparkling chrome diner. There's been a diner here since the 1950s and even though this building is from 1995 it's a classic, with an authentic interior and extensive menu to match.

ⓘ Getting There & Away

Amtrak has services to/from NYC ($27, 1½ hours) and up the Hudson to Albany ($27, 65 minutes) and beyond from **Poughkeepsie Station** (☎ 800-872-7245; www.amtrak.com; 41 Main St). Bus services by Short Line (https://web.coachusa.com/shortline) to/from NYC ($22, 2½ hours) also stop at the train station.

Rhinebeck

Midway up the east side of the Hudson, Rhinebeck has a charming main street and an affluent air. The surrounding land has farms and wineries, as well as the holistic Omega Institute, and the super-liberal Bard College, 8 miles north, worth dropping by for its Frank Gehry–designed performing arts center.

◎ Sights

Staatsburg State Historic Site
HOUSE

(☎ 845-889-8851; https://parks.ny.gov/historic-sites/25/details.aspx; Old Post Rd, Staatsburg; adult/child $8/free; ⊙ tours 11am-4pm Thu-Sun mid-Apr–Oct) FREE Take a tour around this beaux-arts mansion, the home of Ogden

Mills and his wife Ruth. It boasts 79 luxurious rooms filled with brocaded Flemish tapestries, gilded plasterwork, period paintings and Oriental art. Find it 6 miles south of Rhinebeck just off Rte 9.

Old Rhinebeck Aerodrome   MUSEUM
(☑ 845-752-3200; www.oldrhinebeck.org; 9 Norton Rd, Red Hook; Mon-Fri adult/child $12/8, airshows adult/child $25/12, flights $75; ⊙10am-5pm May-Oct, airshows from 2pm Sat & Sun) This museum, a short drive north of the center of Rhinebeck, has a collection of vintage planes and other related vehicles and artifacts that date back to 1900. On weekends you can watch an airshow or take a ride in an old biplane.

🛏 Sleeping & Eating

★**Olde Rhinebeck Inn**   B&B $$$
(☑ 845-871-1745; www.rhinebeckinn.com; 340 Wurtemberg Rd; r $250-325; ✵ 🐾) Built by German settlers between 1738 and 1745, this expertly restored oak-beamed inn oozes comfort and authenticity. It's run by a charming woman who has decorated the four cozy rooms beautifully.

Bread Alone Bakery & Cafe   BAKERY $
(☑ 845-876-3108; www.breadalone.com/rhinebeck; 45 E Market St; sandwiches $8-10; ⊙7am-5pm; 🐾) Superior quality baked goods, sandwiches and salads are served up at this popular bakery and cafe. If you prefer it has a full-service dining room, but the menu is exactly the same in both sections.

☆ Entertainment

Fisher Center for the Performing Arts   ARTS CENTER
(☑ 845-758-7900; www.fishercenter.bard.edu; Robbins Rd, Bard College, Annandale-on-Hudson; tours 10am-5pm Mon-Fri) Architecture buffs will want to drop by to view this Frank Gehry–designed building, which looks like an alien spacecraft covered in stainless steel shingles that has landed on Bard College's manicured lawns. It contains two theaters and studio spaces and hosts a program of musical concerts, dance performances and theatrical events.

❶ Getting There & Away

Amtrak runs trains to/from NYC ($29, 1¾ hours). **Rhinecliff-Kingston Station** (☑ 800-872-7245; www.amtrak.com; 455 Rhinecliff Rd, Rhinecliff) is 3 miles west of the center of Rhinebeck.

Catskills

This beautiful mountainous region west of the Hudson Valley has been a popular getaway for New Yorkers since the 19th century. The romantic image of mossy gorges and rounded peaks, as popularized by Hudson Valley School painters, encouraged a preservation movement; in 1894 the state constitution was amended so that thousands of acres are 'forever kept as wild forest lands.'

In the early 20th century, the Catskills became synonymous with so-called 'borscht belt' hotels: summer escapes for middle-class NYC Jews. The vast majority of those hotels have closed, although Orthodox Jewish communities still thrive in many towns – as does a back-to-the-land, hippie ethos on numerous small farms.

❶ Getting There & Around

There is some bus service, the most useful being Trailways (www.trailwaysny.com) from NYC to Woodstock and Phoenicia. However, if you really want to tour the area, having a car is essential.

Phoenicia

This quirky hamlet sitting astride Esopus Creek is an ideal base for exploring the heart of the Catskills. Outdoor activities are easily arranged and include hiking, cycling, floating down the creek on an inner tube or swimming in mountain pools in summer and skiing at nearby Belleayre Mountain in winter. Fall is prime time to visit and also the best season for a jaunt in an open-air carriage on the Delaware & Ulster Railroad between nearby Arkville and Roxbury.

◉ Sights & Activities

Empire State Railway Museum   MUSEUM
(☑ 845-688-7501; www.esrm.com; 70 Lower High St, Phoenicia; donations accepted; ⊙11am-4pm Sat & Sun Jun-Oct) FREE Maintained by enthusiasts since 1960, this small museum occupies an old railway station on the largely decommissioned Delaware & Ulster line.

Delaware & Ulster Railroad   RAIL
(☑ 800-225-4132; www.durr.org; 43510 Rte 28, Arkville; adult/child $18/12; ⊙Sat & Sun Jul-Oct) It takes around two hours to travel the 24 miles between Arkville and Roxbury in open-air carriages on this touristy rail journey; views are at their best during fall.

Belleayre Beach SWIMMING
(☑ 845-254-5202; www.belleayre.com/summer/
belleayre-beach; 33 Friendship Manor Rd, Pine Hill;
per person/car $3/10; ☉ 10am-6pm Mon-Fri, to
7pm Sat & Sun mid-Jun–Aug) Near the base of
Belleayre Mountain ski resort, this lake is
a popular and refreshing swimming spot.
Boats, kayaks and paddleboards can be rented, and there's also volleyball and basketball
courts and a climbing wall.

🛏 Sleeping & Eating

★ Graham & Co MOTEL $$
(☑ 845-688-7871; www.thegrahamandco.com; 80
Rte 214, Phoenicia; r $150-275; 🅿🖻🛄) There's a
lot going for this hipster motel an easy walk
from the center of town. Rooms are white-
washed and minimalist, with the cheapest
ones in a 'bunkhouse' where bathrooms are
shared. Other pluses include a comfy den
with a fireplace, a provisions store, an outdoor pool, a wigwam and lawn games.

Foxfire Mountain House BOUTIQUE HOTEL $$
(www.foxfiremountainhouse.com; 72 Andrew Lane,
Mt Tremper; r $175-325; ☉ restaurant dinner
Fri-Sun; 🅿🖻🛄🛜) Hidden away amid the
forest, this chic hotel effortlessly channels
Catskills cool in its 11 individually decorated
rooms and one three-bedroom cottage. The
cozy restaurant (offering dinner Friday to
Sunday) and bar, open to nonguests, serves
French-inspired cuisine such as steak au
poivre and *coq au cidre*.

★ Phoenicia Diner AMERICAN $
(☑ 845-688-9957; www.phoeniciadiner.com; 5681
Rte 28, Phoenicia; mains $9-12; ☉ 7am-5pm Thu-
Mon; 🖍) New York hipsters and local families rub shoulders at this classic roadside
diner. The appealing menu offers all-day
breakfast, skillets, sandwiches and burgers.

★ Peekamoose AMERICAN $$$
(☑ 845-254-6500; www.peekamooserestaurant.
com; 8373 Rte 28, Big Indian; mains $20-36; ☉ 4-
10pm Thu-Mon) One of the finest restaurants in
the Catskills, this renovated farmhouse has
been promoting local farm-to-table dining
for more than a decade. The menu changes
daily, although the braised beef short ribs are
a permanent fixture.

❶ Getting There & Away

Trailways (www.trailwaysny.com) runs buses to
Phoenicia from NYC ($33.25, three hours, seven
daily).

Tannersville

The small town of Tannersville, which primarily services the nearby ski resort of
Hunter Mountain, also offers access to the
gorgeous Kaaterskill Falls. There are superb hikes and drives in the area, as well as
rustically charming hotels in which to stay
and enjoy the beautiful mountain scenery.
Tannersville itself sports a main street lined
with brightly painted shops and houses.

◉ Sights & Activities

Kaaterskill Falls WATERFALL
For the best view of New York State's highest
falls – 260ft, compared to Niagara's 167ft –
without a strenuous hike, head to the **viewing platform** (Laurel House Rd, Palenville). Popular paintings by the Hudson River Valley
School of painters in the mid-1800s elevated
this two-tier cascade to iconic status, making
it a draw for hikers, artists and nature lovers.

Hunter Mountain SKIING
(☑ 518-263-4223; www.huntermtn.com; 64 Klein
Ave, Hunter; 1-day lift pass weekday/weekend
$70/80; ☉ 9am-4pm Dec-Mar) Spectacular
views from the 56 trails (including some
challenging black runs that are a minefield
of moguls) draw crowds of snowhounds to
Hunter; avoid weekends and holidays if you
don't relish lines at the lifts. Snowmaking
ensures that skiing continues through the
season, whatever the weather.

Zipline New York ADVENTURE SPORTS
(☑ 518-263-4388; www.ziplinenewyork.com;
Hunter Mountain, Rte 23A; zip-line tours $89-129)
Throughout the year Hunter Mountain is
also the location of this zip-line course that's
not for the faint hearted.

🛏 Sleeping & Eating

★ Scribner's Catskill Lodge LODGE $$
(☑ 518-628-5130; www.scribnerslodge.com; 13
Scribner Hollow Rd; r from $110; 🅿🖻🛄🛜)
Run by a super-cool staff, this 1960s motor
lodge has been given a stylish contemporary
makeover. Snow-white painted rooms, some
of which feature gas-fired stoves, contrast
with the warm tones of the long library
lounge with pool table and comfy nooks.

Deer Mountain Inn BOUTIQUE HOTEL $$$
(☑ 518-589-6268; www.deermountaininn.com;
790 Rte 25; r/cottage from $250/700; ☉ res-
taurant 5-9pm Mon, Thu & Sun, to 10pm Fri & Sat;
🅿🖻🛄🛜) There are only six rooms and two

WORTH A TRIP

SAUGERTIES

Around 10 miles northeast of Woodstock, the town of Saugerties (www.discoversaugerties.com) dates back to the Dutch settling here in the mid-17th century. Today it's well worth making a day trip to a couple of local attractions. Opus 40 Sculpture Park & Museum (p151) is where artist Harvey Fite worked for nearly four decades to transform an abandoned quarry into a huge artwork. The picturesque 1869 **Saugerties Lighthouse** (📞845-247-0656; www.saugertieslighthouse.com; 168 Lighthouse Dr, Saugerties; tour suggested donation adult/child $5/3; ⏲trail dawn-dusk), on the point where Esopus Creek joins the Hudson, can be reached by a half-mile nature trail. Classic rock lovers may also want to search out **Big Pink** (www.bigpinkbasement.com; Parnassus Lane, West Saugerties; house $480; 🅿🛜), the house made famous by Bob Dylan and the Band, although note it's on a private road. It's possible to stay at both the Lighthouse and Big Pink, but you'll need to book well ahead.

cottages (sleeping up to nine guests) at this gorgeous arts-and-crafts-style property hidden within a vast mountainside estate. It's all been interior designed to the max.

Last Chance Cheese Antiques Cafe AMERICAN $$
(📞518-589-6424; www.lastchanceonline.com; 6009 Main St; mains $10-27; ⏲11am-10pm Fri & Sat, to 8pm Sun) A fixture on Main St since 1970, this is part roadhouse with live bands, part candy store and cheese shop, and part restaurant, serving hearty meals. Many of the antiques and whatnots that decorate the place are for sale too.

ℹ Getting There & Away

The drive along Rte 23A to and from Tannersville is one of the most scenic in the Catskills, but take it slowly as there are several hairpin bends. It's possible to reach Tannersville from NYC by bus with Trailways (www.trailwaysny.com), but you'll have to change services in Kingston.

Woodstock

A minor technicality: the 1969 music festival was actually held in Bethel, an hour's drive west. Nonetheless, the town of Woodstock still attracts an arty, music-loving crowd and cultivates the free spirit of that era, with rainbow tie-dye style and local grassroots everything, from radio to a respected indie film festival and a farmers market.

◉ Sights

Center for Photography at Woodstock ARTS CENTER
(📞845-679-9957; www.cpw.org; 59 Tinker St; ⏲noon-5pm Thu-Sun) FREE Founded in 1977,

this creative space gives classes, hosts lectures and mounts exhibitions that expand the strict definition of the art form, thanks to a lively artist-in-residence program.

This was formerly the Café Espresso, and Bob Dylan once had a writing studio above it – that's where he typed up the liner notes for *Another Side of Bob Dylan* in 1964 – and Janis Joplin was a regular performer.

Opus 40 Sculpture Park & Museum PARK
(📞845-246-3400; www.opus40.org; 50 Fite Rd, Saugerties; adult/child $10/3; ⏲11am-5:30pm Thu-Sun May-Sep) Beginning in 1938, artist Harvey Fite worked for nearly four decades to coax an abandoned quarry into an immense work of land art, all sinuous walls, canyons and pools.

Karma Triyana Dharmachakra BUDDHIST MONASTERY
(📞845-679-5906; www.kagyu.org; 335 Meads Mountain Rd; ⏲8:30am-5:30pm) Join stressed-out New Yorkers and others needing a spiritual break and get your karma and chakras checked at this blissful Buddhist monastery about 3 miles from Woodstock. Soak up the serenity in the carefully tended grounds. Inside the shrine room is a giant golden Buddha statue; as long as you take off your shoes, you're welcome to meditate.

🛏 Sleeping & Eating

Woodstock Inn on the Millstream INN $$
(📞845-679-8211; www.woodstock-inn-ny.com; 48 Tannery Brook Rd; r/cottage from $159/375; 🅿🛜) Pleasantly decorated in quiet pastels, some of the rooms at this inn (surrounded by serene, flower-filled grounds) come with kitchenettes and electric fireplaces.

White Dove Rockotel
INN $$

(☑ 845-306-5419; www.thewhitedoverockotel.com; 148 Tinker St; r/ste from $125/250; 🛜🏠) This purple-painted Victorian certainly stands out from the crowd – but its nothing compared to the rooms! The six units, split over two properties, are decorated with psychedelic colors, posters, record players and vintage vinyl. The suites feature kitchens.

★ Garden Cafe
VEGAN $

(☑ 845-679-3600; www.thegardencafewoodstock.com; 6 Old Forge Rd; mains $9-20; ⊘ 11:30am-9pm Mon & Wed-Fri, 10am-9pm Sat & Sun; ☑) All the ingredients used at this relaxed, charming cafe are organic. The food served is appealing, tasty and fresh, and includes salads, sandwiches, rice bowls and veggie lasagna.

Finger Lakes

Stretching across west-central New York, the rolling hills are cut through by 11 long narrow bodies of water – the eponymous Finger Lakes. The region is an outdoor paradise, as well as the state's premier wine-growing region, with more than 120 vineyards.

At the south of Cayuga Lake, Ithaca, home to Ivy League Cornell University, is the region's gateway and a good base. At the northern tip of Seneca Lake, Geneva is also a pretty and lively town, thanks to the student population at Hobart and William Smith Colleges. Here the restored 1894 Smith Opera House is a vibrant center for performing arts. To the west, Y-shaped Keuka Lake is edged by two small state parks that keep it relatively pristine; it's a favorite for trout fishing. Base yourself at sweet little Hammondsport, on the southwest end. Arts and crafts lovers should also schedule a stop in Corning to see the brilliant glass museum.

ℹ Getting There & Around

Ithaca is the region's major hub with several daily bus connections to NYC ($53.50, five hours). **Ithaca Tompkins Regional Airport** has direct flights to Detroit, Newark and Philadelphia.

Ithaca

An idyllic home for college students and first-wave hippies, Ithaca, on the southern tip of Cayuga Lake, is the largest town around the Finger Lakes. With an art-house cinema, good eats and great hiking ('Ithaca is gorges' goes the slogan, for all the surrounding canyons and waterfalls), it's both a destination in itself and a convenient halfway point between NYC and Niagara Falls.

The center of Ithaca is a pedestrian street called the Commons. On a steep hill above is Ivy League Cornell University, founded in 1865, with a small business strip at the campus' front gates, called Collegetown. The drive from Ithaca up scenic Rte 89 (west side) or Rte 90 (east side) to Seneca Falls takes about an hour.

⊙ Sights

★ Herbert F Johnson Museum of Art
MUSEUM

(☑ 607-255-6464; www.museum.cornell.edu; 114 Central Ave; ⊘ 10am-5pm Tue-Sun) **FREE** IM Pei's brutalist building looms like a giant concrete robot above the ornate neo-Gothic surrounds of Cornell's campus. Inside you'll find an eclectic collection ranging from medieval wood carvings to modern masters. Even if the art doesn't engage you, the panoramic views of Ithaca and Cayuga Lake from the top floor galleries will.

Cornell Botanic Gardens
GARDENS

(☑ 607-255-2400; www.cornellbotanicgardens.org; 124 Comstock Knoll Dr; ⊘ grounds dawn-dusk, visitor center 10am-4pm) **FREE** The verdant spaces in and around campus includes a 100-acre arboretum, a botanical garden and numerous trails. Stop at the Nevin Welcome Center for maps and to find out about tours.

A great way to reach here is by hiking up the dramatic **Cascadilla Gorge** (College Ave Bridge), which starts near the center of town.

Robert H Treman State Park
STATE PARK

(☑ 607-273-3440; www.parks.ny.gov; 105 Enfield Falls Rd; per car Apr-Oct $8) Five and a half miles southwest of Ithaca, the biggest state park in the area offers extensive trails and a very popular **swimming hole** (late June to early September). Treman's gorge trail passes a stunning 12 waterfalls: don't miss Devil's Kitchen and **Lucifer Falls**, a multi-tiered wonder that spills Enfield Creek over rocks for about 100ft.

🛏 Sleeping

Firelight Camps
TENTED CAMP $$

(☑ 607-229-1644; www.firelightcamps.com; 1150 Danby Rd; tent Sun-Thu/Fri & Sat $189/259; ⊘ mid-May–Oct; 🛜) Glamping comes to Ithaca at this attractive site attached to the La Tourelle Hotel and with quick access to the trails of nearby Buttermilk Falls State Park. The safari-style canvas tents rise over hardwood platforms and comfy beds. The bathhouse is separate.

★ William Henry Miller Inn   B&B $$
(☎ 877-256-4553; www.millerinn.com; 303 N Aurora St; r from $195; ✳ @ 🛜) Gracious and grand, and only a few steps from the Commons, this is a historic home with luxurious rooms (two with whirlpool tubs and two in a separate carriage house), gourmet breakfast and a dessert buffet.

★ Inns of Aurora   HISTORIC HOTEL $$$
(☎ 315-364-8888; www.innsofaurora.com; 391 Main St, Aurora; r $200-400; P ✳ 🛜) This beautiful historic hotel is composed of four properties: the main Aurora Inn, built in 1833 and little changed on the outside since, with 10 lovely rooms and a splendid dining room; Rowland House with 10 more rooms; E B Morgan House with seven rooms; and Wallcourt Hall, the most modern of the designs, but with no lake views.

✖ Eating & Drinking

Ithaca Bakery   CAFE $
(☎ 607-273-7110; www.ithacabakery.com; 400 N Meadow St; sandwiches $5-11; ⊘ 6am-8pm Sun-Thu, to 9pm Fri & Sat; 🖉) An epic selection of pastries, smoothies, sandwiches and prepared food, serving Ithacans of every stripe. Ideal for picnic goods and for vegetarians and vegans.

★ Moosewood Restaurant   VEGETARIAN $$
(☎ 607-273-9610; www.moosewoodcooks.com; 215 N Cayuga St; mains $8-18; ⊘ 11:30am-8:30pm; 🖉) Established in 1973, this near-legendary veggie restaurant is run by a collective. It has a slightly upscale feel, with a full bar.

Sacred Root Kava
Lounge & Tea Bar   TEAHOUSE
(☎ 607-272-5282; www.sacredrootkava.com; 139 W State St; ⊘ 4pm-midnight) Pretty much as alternative as it gets for Ithaca is this chilled basement space serving the Polynesian non-alcoholic, psychoactive beverage kava. If that's not your bag, then there's a nice range of teas. Check online for events.

❶ Getting There & Away

Ithaca Tompkins Regional Airport (ITH; ☎ 607-257-0456; www.flyithaca.com; 1 Culligan Dr) receives flights from Delta and United. Greyhound and Shortline buses ($50, five hours, daily) pull into **Ithaca Bus Station** (710 W State St).

WORTH A TRIP

AURORA

Around 28 miles north of Ithaca on the east side of Cayuga Lake is the picturesque village of Aurora. Established in 1795, the village has over 50 buildings on the National Register of Historic Places, including parts of the campus of Wells College, founded in 1868 for the higher education of women (it's now co-ed). The Inns of Aurora, which is composed of four grand properties – the Aurora Inn (1833), EB Morgan House (1858), Rowland House (1903) and Wallcourt Hall (1909) – is a wonderful place to stay. Alternatively stop by the Aurora Inn's lovely dining room for a meal with lakeside views and pick up a copy of the self-guided walking tour of the village.

Seneca Falls

The quiet, post-industrial town of Seneca Falls is said to have inspired visiting director Frank Capra to create Bedford Falls, the fictional small American town in his classic movie *It's a Wonderful Life*. Indeed, you can stand on a bridge crossing the town's river and just picture Jimmy Stewart doing the same. The town also has a special place in the history of democratization of the country as the location of the chapel where in 1848 Elizabeth Cady Stanton and friends declared that all men and women are created equal.

◉ Sights

Women's Rights National
Historical Park   MUSEUM
(☎ 315-568-0024; www.nps.gov/wori; 136 Fall St; ⊘ 9am-5pm Fri-Sun) FREE Visit the chapel where Elizabeth Cady Stanton and friends declared in 1848 that 'all men and women are created equal,' the first step toward women's suffrage. The adjacent museum tells the story, including the complicated relationship with abolition.

National Women's Hall of Fame   MUSEUM
(☎ 315-568-8060; www.womenofthehall.org; 76 Fall St; adult/child $4/free; ⊘ noon-4pm Wed-Fri, 10am-4pm Sat) The tiny National Women's Hall of Fame honors inspiring American women. Learn about some of the 256 inductees, including first lady Abigail Adams,

American Red Cross founder Clara Barton and civil-rights activist Rosa Parks.

🛏 Sleeping & Eating

Gould Hotel BOUTIQUE HOTEL **$$**
(📞877-788-4010; www.thegouldhotel.com; 108 Fall St; r $169; ❋🐾) Originally a 1920s-era hotel, the downtown building has undergone a stylish renovation with a nod to the past – the mahogany bar comes from an old Seneca Falls saloon. The standard rooms are small, but the decor, in metallic purple and gray, is quite flash. The hotel's upscale restaurant and tavern serves local food, wine and beer.

Mac's Drive In BURGERS **$**
(📞315-539-3064; www.macsdrivein.net; 1166 US-20/Rte 5, Waterloo; mains $4-8; ⏱10:30am-10pm Fri-Sun Apr-Oct) Midway between Seneca Falls and Geneva, this classic drive-in restaurant established in 1961 (and little changed since) serves up burgers, fried chicken and fish dinners at bargain prices.

The Adirondacks

The Adirondack Mountains (www.visit adirondacks.com) may not compare in drama and height with mountains in the western USA, but they make up for it in area: the range covers 9375 sq miles, from the center of New York just north of the state capital Albany, up to the Canadian border. And with 46 peaks over 4000ft high, the Adirondacks provide some of the most wild-feeling terrain in the east. Like the Catskills to the south, much of the Adirondacks' dense forest and lake lands are protected by the state constitution, and it's a fabulous location to see the color show of fall leaves. Hiking, canoeing and backcountry camping are the most popular activities.

ℹ Getting There & Around

The area's main airport is in Albany, although **Adirondack Regional Airport** (📞518-891-4600; www.adirondackairport.com; 96 Airport Rd) in Saranac Lake has connections via Cape Air (www.capeair.com) to Boston.

Both Greyhound (www.greyhound.com) and Trailways (www.trailwaysny.com) serve Albany and various towns in the Adirondacks, though a car is essential for exploring widely.

Amtrak (www.amtrak.com) runs from NYC to Albany (from $43, 2½ hours) and on to Ticonderoga ($68, five hours) and Westport ($68, six hours), on Lake Champlain, with a bus connection to Lake Placid ($93, seven hours).

Albany

Built between 1965 and 1976, the architectural ensemble of government buildings in Albany's central Empire State Plaza is a sight to behold and includes the excellent New York State Museum as well as a fine collection of modern public art. Downtown and around leafy Washington Park, stately buildings and gracious brownstones speak to the state capital's wealthy past.

Albany became state capital in 1797 because of its geographic centrality to local colonies and its strategic importance in the fur trade. These days its as much synonymous with legislative dysfunction as with legislative power. Its struggling economy is reflected in the number of derelict and abandoned buildings. The locals' friendliness and the city's usefulness as a gateway to the Adirondacks and Hudson Valley make it worth more than a casual look.

◉ Sights

★**Empire State Plaza** PUBLIC ART
(📞518-473-7521; www.empirestateplaza.org) FREE
While the plaza's ensemble of architecture surrounding a central pool is hugely impressive, it's the splendid collection of modern American art liberally sprinkled outside, inside and beneath the complex that is the true highlight here. The collection includes sculptures and massive paintings by Mark Rothko, Jackson Pollock, Alexander Calder and many other star artists.

★**New York State Museum** MUSEUM
(📞518-474 5877; www.nysm.nysed.gov; 222 Madison Ave; 9:30am-5pm Tue-Sun) FREE One of the quirks of Albany being the state capital means that a large chunk of this top-class museum is dedicated to the history and development of New York City. The section on 9/11, including a damaged fire truck and debris from the site, is very moving. For a complete contrast, don't miss a ride on the gorgeous antique carousel ($1) on the 4th floor.

New York State Capitol HISTORIC BUILDING
(📞518-474-2418; www.hallofgovernors.ny.gov; Washington Ave; ⊙guided tours 10am, noon, 2pm & 3pm Mon-Fri) FREE Completed in 1899, this grand building is the heart of the state government. The interior features detailed stone carving, carpentry, tile and mosaic work, with highlights being the Great Western Staircase, the Governor's Reception Room and the Senate Chamber.

🛏 Sleeping & Eating

★ **Washington Park Inn** BOUTIQUE HOTEL $$
(☑ 518-225-4567; www.washingtonparkinn.com; 643 Madison Ave; r $119-139; ❄ @ 🛜) Rocking chairs on the covered porch and tennis rackets for guests to use on the courts in the park across the road set the relaxed tone for this appealing hotel in one of Albany's heritage buildings. Rooms are big and stylishly decorated, and food and drink is available on a serve-yourself basis round the clock from the well-stocked kitchen.

Cafe Madison BREAKFAST $
(☑ 518-935-1094; www.cafemadisonalbany.com; 1108 Madison Ave; mains $10-15; ⊘ 7:30am-2pm Mon-Thu, to 3pm Fri-Sun; ☑) A highly popular breakfast spot, especially on the weekend, when 30-minute waits for one of the cozy booths or tables is not uncommon. The staff are friendly and the menu includes inventive omelets, hash browns, crepes, vegan options and a variety of cocktails.

★ **Ginger Man** AMERICAN $$$
(☑ 518-427-5963; www.albanygingerman.com; 234 Western Ave; mains $22-30; ⊘ 11:30am-10:30pm Mon-Fri, 4:30-11pm Sat) Oenophiles will adore the Ginger Man with its stellar wine list, not to mention its strong showing of local beers and spirits. And the food is just as good, with generous cheese and charcuterie plates a great way to ease into delicious mains such as veal osso buco and paella.

ℹ Getting There & Away

As state capital, Albany has the full range of transport connections. **Albany International Airport** (☑ 518-242-2200; www.albanyairport. com; Albany Shaker Rd, Colonie) is 10 miles north of downtown. The Amtrak **Albany-Rensselaer Station** (☑ 800-872 7245; www. amtrak.com; 525 East St, Rensselaer), on the east bank of the Hudson River, has services connecting with the rest of the state. Greyhound and Trailways bus services pull into and out of the centrally located **bus terminal** (☑ 518-427-7060; 34 Hamilton St).

Lake George

Lake George (www.visitlakegeorge.com), the southern gateway to the Adirondacks, is a majorly touristy town with arcades, fireworks every Thursday in July and August, and paddle-wheel-boat rides on the crystal-line, 32-mile-long lake of the same name. It's a seasonal resort, so don't expect much to be be going on between November and May. More upscale is the village of **Bolton Landing**, 11 miles north on the west bank of Lake George.

◎ Sights & Activities

Fort William Henry Museum MUSEUM
(☑ 518-668-5471; www.fwhmuseum.com; 48 Canada St; adult/child $17/8, ghost tours $18/8; ⊘ 9:30am-6pm May-Oct; ⊞) Guides dressed as 18th-century British soldiers muster visitors along, with stops for battle re-enactments that include firing period muskets and cannons, at this replica of the 1755 wooden fort. Check online for details of the evening ghost tours.

Hyde Collection Art Museum MUSEUM
(☑ 518-792-1761; www.hydecollection.org; 161 Warren St, Glens Falls; adult/child $12/free; ⊘ 10am-5pm Tue-Sat, noon-5pm Sun) This remarkable gathering of art was amassed by local newspaper heiress Charlotte Pryun Hyde. In her rambling Florentine Renaissance mansion, 12 miles south of Lake George, you'll stumble across Rembrandts, Rubens, Matisses and Eakins, as well as tapestries, sculptures and turn-of-the-century furnishings.

Lake George Steamboat Cruises CRUISE
(☑ 518-668-5777; www.lakegeorgesteamboat.com; 57 Beach Rd; adult/child from $16/7.50; ⊘ May-Oct) In 2017 this company celebrated 200 years of running cruise boats on Lake George. In season take your pick between a variety of cruise options on its three vessels: the authentic steamboat *Minnie-Ha-Ha,* the 1907-vintage *Mohican*, and the flagship *Lac du Saint Sacrement.*

🛏 Eating

Saltwater Cowboy SEAFOOD $$
(☑ 518-685-3116; 164 Canada St; mains $11-28; ⊘ 11am-9pm May-Oct) Never mind the super-casual, order-at-the-counter setup – this place has excellent fried clams and scallops, plus mammoth lobster rolls. Wash it down with fresh lemonade.

ℹ Getting There & Away

Albany International Airport is 50 miles south of Lake George. Amtrak stops in Fort Edwards, about 20 minutes by car from Lake George. Greyhound and Trailways also have long-distance buses to the region. A rental car is the best way of getting around the lake area.

Lake Placid

The resort town of Lake Placid is synonymous with snow sports – it hosted the Winter Olympics in 1932 and 1980. Elite athletes continue to train here; the rest of us can ride real bobsleds, speed-skate and more. Mirror Lake (the main lake in town) freezes thick enough for ice-skating, tobogganing and dogsledding. The town is also pleasant in summer, as the unofficial center of the High Peaks region of the Adirondacks and a great base for striking out on a hike or going canoeing or kayaking on one of the area's many lakes.

◉ Sights & Activities

A major draw at Lake Placid is the opportunity to play like an Olympian (or just watch athletes train). Most activities are managed by **Whiteface Mountain** (☑ 518-946-2223; www.whiteface.com; 5021 Rte 86, Wilmington; full-day lift ticket adult/child $92/58, gondola only $22/free; ☺ 8:30am-4pm Dec-Apr), the ski area where the Olympic ski races were held, but located in other spots around the area. Among other activities, you can do a half-mile on the bobsled track ($95) or a modified biathlon (cross-country skiing and shooting; $55). A private group organizes **speed-skating** rental and tutorials ($20) at the Olympic Center. Many sports are modified for summer – bobsledding on wheels, for instance. The Olympic Sites Passport ($35), available at all Whiteface-managed venues, can be a good deal, covering admission at sites (such as the tower at the ski-jump complex and the gondola ride at Whiteface Mountain) and offering discounts on some activities.

Olympic Center STADIUM
(☑ 518-523-3330; www.whiteface.com; 2634 Main St; tours $10, adult/child skating $8/5, skating shows $10/8; ☺ 10am-5pm, skating shows 4:30pm Fri; ⊞) This is the location of the 1980 'Miracle on Ice,' when the upstart US team trumped the unstoppable Soviets. In winter you can skate on the outside oval rink and year-round take a one-hour tour of the stadium. Also here is a small **museum** (☑ 518-523-3330; www.whiteface.com; 2634 Main St; adult/child $7/5; ☺ 10am-5pm). There are usually figure-skating shows on Fridays, with an additional show Saturdays at 7:30pm July and August.

Whiteface Veteran's Memorial Highway SCENIC DRIVE
(www.whiteface.com; Rte 431; driver & vehicle $15, additional passengers $8; ☺ 8:45am-5:15pm mid-Jun–mid-Oct) Whiteface, the state's 5th highest peak at 4867ft, is the only summit in the Adirondacks accessible by car, with a neat castle-style lookout and cafe at the top. It can be socked in with clouds, making for an unnerving drive up, but when the fog clears, the 360-degree view is awe-inspiring. Tolls are paid at Lake Steven.

⌖ Sleeping & Eating

★ **Adirondack Loj** LODGE $
(☑ 518-523-3441; www.adk.org; 1002 Adirondack Loj Rd; dm/r $60/169, lean-tos/cabins from $22.50/179; 🅿 🖎) The Adirondack Mountain

---

GREAT CAMPS

Far from big fields of canvas tents, the Adirondacks' 'great camps' were typically lake and mountainside compounds of grandiose log cabins built by the very wealthy, in the latter half of the 19th century, as rustic retreats. A prime example is **Great Camp Sagamore** (Sagamore Institute; ☑ 315-354-5311; www.greatcampsagamore.org; Sagamore Rd, Raquette Lake; tours adult/child $16/8; ☺ hours vary mid-May–mid-Oct), a former Vanderbilt vacation estate on the west side of the Adirondacks, which is now open to the public for tours, workshops and overnight stays on occasional history-oriented weekends.

Less ostentatious is **White Pine Camp** (☑ 518-327-3030; www.whitepinecamp.com; 432 White Pine Rd, Paul Smiths; r/cabin from $165/315; 🖎), 12 miles northwest of Saranac Lake. This collection of rustically cozy cabins is set amid pine forests, wetlands and scenic Osgood Pond – a boardwalk leads out to an island on which sits a Japanese-style teahouse and an antique all-wood bowling alley. The fact that President Calvin Coolidge spent a few summer months here in 1926 is an interesting historical footnote, but the camp's charm comes through in its modest luxuries such as claw-footed tubs and wood-burning fireplaces. Naturalist walking tours are open to nonguests on select days from mid-June to September.

Club runs this rustic retreat on the shore of pretty Heart Lake. All rooms in the lodge share communal bathrooms. Rates include breakfast, and since it's 8 miles south of Lake Placid, you'll like want to arrange a trail lunch and dinner here too.

★ **Lake Placid Lodge** HERITAGE HOTEL $$$
(☑ 518-523-2700; www.lakeplacidlodge.com; 144 Lodge Way; r $500-1000; ☺ May-Mar; P ⊜ @ ☎) Overlooking Lake Placid and channeling the rustic glamor of classic Gilded Age Adirondack lodges, this luxury hotel offers 13 gorgeously decorated rooms and cabins. The cabins are 19th-century originals, but the main hotel is a remarkable reconstruction following a devastating 2008 fire.

Liquids & Solids at the Handlebar AMERICAN $$
(☑ 518-837-5012; www.liquidsandsolids.com; 6115 Sentinel Rd; mains $10-20; ☺ 4-10pm Tue-Sat, 5-9pm Sun) It's all about craft beers, creative cocktails and fresh, inventive dishes at this rustic bar and restaurant where the kielbasa sausages and other charcuterie are made in-house. Mains may include dishes such as fried trout or crispy pig head.

ℹ Getting There & Away

Trailways (www.trailwaysny.com) serves Lake Placid. Amtrak (www.amtrak.com) runs once a day to Westport, with a bus connection to Lake Placid ($93, seven hours).

Adirondack Regional Airport (p154), 17 miles northwest near Saranac Lake, has connections via Cape Air (www.capeair.com) to Boston.

Thousand Islands

To downstate New Yorkers, this region is the source of the Thousand Islands salad dressing made of ketchup, mayonnaise and relish. In fact, it's a scenic wonderland along Lake Ontario and the St Lawrence River speckled with 1864 islands of all shapes and sizes either side of the US–Canada maritime border. The area was a Gilded Age playground for the rich; now it's more populist. Pros: beautiful sunsets, good-value lodging and Canada across the water. Cons: dead in winter and very large mosquitoes in summer (bring ample repellent).

The historic port of Oswego is the southern gateway to the region and makes a good base for exploring places such as Sackets Harbor, where re-enactors stage an annual War of 1812 Weekend. On the north side,

---

WORTH A TRIP

SARANAC LAKE

Saranac Lake is not as tourist-oriented as its neighbor Lake Placid and gives a better idea of regular Adirondacks life. The town, built up in the early 20th century as a retreat for tuberculosis patients, has an attractive old-fashioned main street leading toward the lake. Many other stretches of water pepper the surrounding forested hills, making this another great base for hiking, kayaking and canoeing; for full details of what's available in the area see www.saranaclake.com.

Clayton and Alexandria Bay both offer boat tours to the islands in the St Lawrence River, or you could camp amid glorious nature in the Wellesley Island State Park.

ℹ Getting There & Around

The main airport for the region is **Syracuse Hancock International Airport** (☑ 315-454-4330; www.syrairport.org; 1000 Colonel Eileen Collins Blvd, Syracuse); connections here include NYC on JetBlue and Delta; Newark, Washington, DC and Chicago on United; and Toronto on Air Canada. Cars can be rented at the airport or in downtown Syracuse, which is connected to other parts of the state by bus and train.

Alexandria Bay

Alexandria Bay (A-Bay or Alex Bay), an early-20th-century resort town, is the center of tourism on the American side of the Thousand Islands region. While it's somewhat run-down and a bit tacky, there's enough around to keep you occupied, with Alex Bay and nearby Schermerhorn Harbor the bases for boat trips to the castle follies built by Gilded Age tycoons on Heart and Dark Islands.

◉ Sights & Activites

★ **Boldt Castle** CASTLE
(☑ 800-847-5263; www.boldtcastle.com; Heart Island; adult/child $9.50/6.50; ☺ 10am-6:30pm May–mid-Oct) This Gothic gem, a replica of a German castle, was (partly) built by tycoon hotelier George C Boldt in the late 19th century. In 1904, however, midway through construction, Boldt's wife died suddenly, and the project was abandoned. Since 1977 the Thousand Islands Bridge Authority has

WORTH A TRIP

WELLESLEY ISLAND STATE PARK

Midway between Clayton and Alexandria Bay, cross the Thousand Islands International Bridge (toll $2.75) to access Wellesley Island, the largest of the Thousand Islands on the US side of the border. Covering a 2636-acre chunk of the island's southern tip is the **state park** (☑315-482-2722; www.parks.ny.gov; Fineview; beach all day/after 4pm $7/4; ☺ state park year-round, swimming 11am-7pm Jul & Aug) FREE packed with wildlife and offering a **nature center** (☑315-482-2479; www.parks.ny.gov; Nature Center Rd, Fineview; ☺8:30am-4pm) FREE , a beautiful swimming beach, and excellent **camping options** (☑315-482-2722; www.parks.ny.gov; 44927 Cross Island Rd, Fineview; campsites/cabins/cottages from $18/68/100), with riverfront tent sites, cabins and family cottages.

spent millions restoring the place to something of its planned grandeur.

Singer Castle   CASTLE
(☑877-327-5475; www.singercastle.com; Dark Island; adult/child $14.50/7.50; ☺10am-4pm mid-May–mid-Oct) This stone castle, on Dark Island in the middle of the St Lawrence River, was built in 1905 by American entrepreneur Frederick Bourne. It's full of secret passages and hidden doors and has a dungeon – all of which you'll see on a tour. Uncle Sam runs boats from Alex Bay; **Schermerhorn Harbor** (☑315-324-5966; www.schermerhornharbor.com; 71 Schermerhorn Landing, Hammond; shuttle to Singer Castle $31; ☺10:30am-2:30pm May-Sep) also visits.

Uncle Sam Boat Tour   BOATING
(☑315-482-2611; www.usboattours.com; 45 James St, Alexandria Bay; 2hr tour adult/child $23/11.50) The main offering from the largest boat-tour operator in the area is a two-hour ride that visits both the USA and Canada sides of the river and stops at Boldt Castle.

🛏 Sleeping & Eating

Bonnie Castle   RESORT $$
(☑800-955-4511; www.bonniecastle.com; 31 Holland St; r $100-250; ❄🛜🏊) This somewhat run-down resort, one of Alex Bay's largest

and open year-round, offers a variety of rooms, some with nice views across the St Lawrence River toward Boldt Castle.

Dockside Pub   AMERICAN $$
(☑315-482-9849; www.thedocksidepub.com; 17 Market St; mains $8-18; ☺11am-midnight Sun-Thu, to 2am Fri & Sat; 🐾) Unpretentious pub fare – burgers, fries, pizza and some specials. Despite the name its location is inland, with no dock view.

Western New York

Much activity in this region revolves around Buffalo, New York State's second-largest city. Nicknamed the Queen City, for being the largest and most prosperous metropolis along the Great Lakes at the turn of the 19th century, Buffalo fell on hard times in the 20th, but is bouncing back in the 21st. Its amazing stock of heritage architecture is being restored and reinvented into hotels, museums and other businesses.

The area first developed thanks to the hydroelectric power of Niagara Falls and the Erie Canal, which linked the Great Lakes to the Atlantic Ocean. The falls are now better known as a tourist destination, with millions of visitors flocking here annually. You can find out more about the canal in the town of Lockport. Also worth visiting are East Aurora, home to the arts and crafts Roycroft community, and Letchworth State Park with its magnificent waterfalls.

ℹ Getting There & Around

Buffalo Niagara International Airport (p160) is a regional hub with the widest range of flights, but you can also fly into and out of Niagara Falls International Airport (p162). Amtrak runs trains to both Buffalo and Niagara, with connections to and from NYC, Albany, Toronto, Canada and from Buffalo to/from Chicago. Greyhound has bus services to both Buffalo and Niagara. For other places in the region you are best getting there by rental car.

Buffalo

The winters may be long and cold, but Buffalo stays warm through a vibrant creative community and strong local pride. Settled by the French in 1758, the city is believed to derive its name from *beau fleuve* (beautiful river). With power from nearby Niagara Falls, it boomed in the early 1900s; Pierce-Arrow cars were made here, and it was the first American city to have electric streetlights. One of its nicknames – Queen City – was because it was the largest and most prosperous city along the Great Lakes.

Those rosy economic times are long over, leaving many abandoned industrial buildings in their wake. This said, revival is in Buffalo's air. Masterpieces of late-19th- and early-20th-century architecture, including designs by Frank Lloyd Wright and HH Richardson, have been magnificently restored. There's a gracious park system laid out by Frederick Law Olmsted, of NYC's Central Park fame, great museums, and a positive vibe that's impossible to ignore.

◉ Sights & Activities

★ Buffalo City Hall ARCHITECTURE
(🗷 716-852-3300; www.preservationbuffaloniagara. org; 65 Niagara Sq; ⊙ tours noon Mon-Fri) FREE
This 32-story art-deco masterpiece, beautifully detailed inside and out and opened in 1931, towers over downtown. It's worth joining the free tour at noon that includes access to the mayor's office, the council chamber and the open-air observation deck.

★ Martin House Complex ARCHITECTURE
(🗷 716-856-3858; www.darwinmartinhouse.org; 125 Jewett Pkwy; tour basic/extended $19/37; ⊙ tours hourly 10am-3pm Wed-Mon) This 15,000-sq-ft house, built between 1903 and 1905, was designed by Frank Lloyd Wright for his friend and patron Darwin D Martin. Representing Wright's Prairie House ideal, it consists of six interconnected buildings (some of which had to be rebuilt), each of which has been meticulously restored.

★ Albright-Knox Art Gallery MUSEUM
(🗷 716-882-8700; www.albrightknox.org; 1285 Elmwood Ave; adult/child $12/6; ⊙ 10am-5pm Tue-Sun) The gallery's superb collection, which ranges from Degas and Picasso to Ruscha, Rauschenberg and other abstract expressionists, occupies a neoclassical building planned for Buffalo's 1905 Pan American Expo. Its temporary exhibits are particularly creative and compelling.

Graycliff Estate ARCHITECTURE
(🗷 716-947-9217; www.graycliffestate.org; 6472 Old Lake Shore Rd, Derby; tours 1/2hr $18/34) Occupying a dramatic cliff-top location on Lake Erie, 16 miles south of downtown Buffalo, is this 1920s vacation home designed by Frank Lloyd Wright for the wealthy Martin family. Having fallen into much disrepair, restoration has been ongoing for the last 20 years, but you can learn a lot about Wright's overall plan on interesting tours (book in advance).

Guaranty Building ARCHITECTURE
(Prudential Building; www.hodgsonruss.com/ Louis-Sullivans-Guaranty-Building.html; 140 Pearl St; ⊙ interpretive center 7:15am-9pm) FREE
Completed in 1896 for the Guaranty Construction company, this gorgeous piece of architecture has a facade covered in detailed terra-cotta tiles and a superb stained-glass ceiling in its lobby. The interpretative center provides details of how groundbreaking this Adler & Sullivan–designed building was when it was built.

Explore Buffalo TOURS
(🗷 716-245-3032; www.explorebuffalo.org; 1 Symphony Circle) Architectural and history tours around the Buffalo area by bus, on foot and by bicycle and kayak.

🛏 Sleeping

Hostel Buffalo Niagara HOSTEL $
(🗷 716-852-5222; www.hostelbuffalo.com; 667 Main St; dm/r $30/85; ❄ @ 🛜) Conveniently located in Buffalo's downtown Theater District, this hostel occupies three floors of a former school, with a basement rec room, plenty of kitchen and lounge space, a small art gallery, and spotless if institutional bathrooms. Services include laundry facilities, free bikes, and lots of info on local music, food and arts happenings.

★ InnBuffalo off Elmwood GUESTHOUSE $$
(🗷 716-867-7777; www.innbuffalo.com; 619 Lafayette Ave; ste $139-249; ❄ 🛜) Ellen and Joe Lettieri have done a splendid job restoring this 1898 mansion, originally built for local brass and rubber magnate HH Hewitt. Preservation is ongoing, but the building has already recovered much of its grandeur and the nine suites are beautifully decorated, some with original features such as a Victorian needlespray shower.

Hotel Henry HERITAGE HOTEL $$
(🗷 716-882-1970; www.hotelhenry.com; cnr Rockwell Rd & Cleveland Circle; r from $199; 🅿 ❄ 🛜) Occupying a grand late-19th-century lunatic asylum, Hotel Henry preserves much of the stately architecture of Henry Richardson's original building. Its 88 rooms, reached off super-broad corridors, have tall ceilings and contemporary decor.

× Eating

Betty's
AMERICAN **$$**

(☑ 716-362-0633; www.bettysbuffalo.com; 370 Virginia St; mains $16-24; ⊙ 8am-9pm Tue-Thu, to 10pm Fri, 9am-10pm Sat, to 2pm Sun; ✍) On a quiet Allentown corner, bohemian Betty's does flavorful, fresh interpretations of American comfort food such as meatloaf. Brunch is deservedly popular and there's a pleasant bar.

Plenty of vegetarian, gluten-free and dairy-free options are on the menu.

Cole's
AMERICAN **$$**

(☑ 716-886-1449; www.colesonelmwood.com; 1104 Elmwood Ave; mains $11.50-15; ⊙ 11am-11pm Mon-Thu, to midnight Fri & Sat, to 10pm Sun; ☎) Since 1934 this atmospheric restaurant and bar has been dishing up local favorites such as beef on weck (roast beef on a caraway-seed roll) – try it with a side of spicy Buffalo chicken wings, or go for one of the juicy burgers. It's handy for lunch if you are visiting the Delaware Park area and its museums.

The spacious bar, decorated with all kinds of vintage stuff, offers scores of beers on tap.

Black Sheep
INTERNATIONAL **$$$**

(☑ 716-884-1100; www.blacksheepbuffalo.com; 367 Connecticut St; mains $28-42; ⊙ 5-10pm Tue-Thu, to 11pm Fri & Sat, 11am-2pm Sun) Black Sheep likes to describe its style of western New York farm-to-table cuisine as 'global nomad,' which means you might find pig-head stew alongside chef Steve Gedra's grandma's recipe for chicken paprikash (recommended!). You can also eat at the bar, which serves creative cocktails and local craft ales.

🍷 Drinking & Entertainment

★ Resurgence Brewing Company
MICROBREWERY

(☑ 716-381-9868; www.resurgencebrewing.com; 1250 Niagara St; ⊙ 4-10pm Tue-Thu, to 11:30pm Fri, noon-11:30pm Sat, to 5pm Sun) Housed in a former engine factory that was later to became the city's dog pound, Resurgence typifies Buffalo's skill at adaptive reuse of its infrastructure. The beers ($8 for a tasting flight) are excellent, with some 20 different ales on tap from fruity sweet Loganberry Wit to a porter with an amazing peanut-butter flavor.

Kleinhans Music Hall
CLASSICAL MUSIC

(☑ 716-883-3560; www.kleinhansbuffalo.org; 3 Symphony Circle) This fine concert hall, home to the Buffalo Philharmonic Orchestra, has wonderful acoustics. The building is a National Historic Landmark and was partly designed by the famous Finnish father-and-son architecture team of Eliel and Eero Saarinen.

ⓘ Getting There & Away

Buffalo Niagara International Airport (BUF; ☑ 716-630-6000; www.buffaloairport.com; 4200 Genesee St), about 10 miles east of downtown, is a regional hub. JetBlue Airways offers affordable round-trip fares from NYC.

NFTA (www.nfta.com), the local transit service, runs express bus 204 to the **Buffalo Metropolitan Transportation Center** (☑ 716-855-7300; www.nfta.com; 181 Ellicott St) downtown. (Greyhound buses also pull in here.) NFTA local bus 40 goes to the American side of Niagara Falls ($2, one hour); express bus 60 also goes to the area, but requires a transfer.

From Amtrak's downtown **Exchange Street Station** (☑ 716-856-2075; www.amtrak.com; 75 Exchange St), you can catch trains to NYC ($66, 8¾ hours), Niagara Falls ($14, one hour), Albany ($52, six hours) and Toronto, Canada ($44, four hours). All services also stop at **Buffalo-Depew Station** (www.amtrak.com; 55 Dick Rd), 8 miles east, where you can also board trains to Chicago ($94, 11 hours).

Niagara Falls

It's a tale of two cities: Niagara Falls, New York (USA), and Niagara Falls, Ontario (Canada). Both overlook a natural wonder – 150,000 gallons of water per second, plunging more than 1000ft – and both provide a load of tourist kitsch surrounding it. The Canadian side offers somewhat better views and a much larger town. However, the view from the New York side is still impressive and the falls surroundings are far more pleasant as they are preserved within a beautifully landscaped national park. The town itself is also largely devoid of the commercial razzmatazz you'll find on the Canadian side; if that's what you want, it's easy to walk across the Rainbow Bridge between the two – just be sure to bring your passport.

◉ Sights & Activities

★ Cave of the Winds
VIEWPOINT

(☑ 716-278-1730; www.niagarafallsstatepark.com; Goat Island Rd; adult/child $17/14; ⊙ 9am-7:30pm mid-May–Oct) On the north corner of Goat Island, don a souvenir rain poncho and sandals (provided) and take an elevator down to walkways just 25ft from the crashing water at the base of Bridal Veil Falls.

DON'T MISS

NIAGARA FALLS, CANADA

The Canadian side of the falls is naturally blessed with superior views. Horseshoe Falls, on the west half of the river, are wider than Bridal Veil Falls on the eastern, American side, and they're especially photogenic from Queen Victoria Park.

The Canadian town is also livelier, in an over-the-top touristy way. Chain hotels and restaurants dominate, but there is an HI hostel, and some older motels have the classic honeymooners' heart-shaped tubs.

Crossing the Rainbow Bridge and returning costs US$3.75/50¢ per car/pedestrian. Walking takes about 10 minutes; car traffic can grind to a standstill in summer or if there's a major event on in Toronto. US citizens and overseas visitors must show a passport or an enhanced driver's license at immigration at either end. Driving a rental car from the USA over the border should not be a problem, but check with your rental company.

Old Fort Niagara   MUSEUM
(☑ 716-745-7611; www.oldfortniagara.org; Youngstown; adult/child $12/8; ⊙ 9am-7pm Jul & Aug, to 5pm Sep-Jun) This 1726 French-built fortress, restored in the 1930s, defends the once very strategic point where the Niagara River flows into Lake Ontario. It has engaging displays of Native American artifacts, small weapons, furniture and clothing, as well as breathtaking views from its ramparts.

Whirlpool State Park   STATE PARK
(☑ 716-284-4691; www.parks.ny.gov; Robert Moses State Pkwy) This park, 3 miles north of the falls, sits just above a sharp bend in the Niagara River – a bend that creates a giant whirlpool easily visible from your vantage point. Steps take you 300ft to the gorge below and mind you don't tumble into the vortex.

Rainbow Bridge   BRIDGE
(www.niagarafallsbridges.com; ⊙ pedestrians & cyclists 50¢, cars $3.75) Bring your passport for the walk or drive across this bridge linking the US and Canadian sides of the falls – there are good views along the way.

★ **Maid of the Mist**   BOATING
(☑ 716-284-8897; www.maidofthemist.com; 1 Prospect St; adult/child $18.25/10.65; ⊙ 9am-7:30pm Jun-Aug, to 5pm Apr, May, Sep & Oct) The traditional way to see Niagara Falls is on this boat cruise, which has ferried visitors into the rapids right below the falls since 1846. Make sure you wear the blue poncho they give you, as the torrential spray from the falls will soak you.

🛏 Sleeping & Eating

**Seneca Niagara
Resort & Casino**   RESORT **$$**
(☑ 877-873-6322; www.senecaniagaracasino.com; 310 4th St; r from $195; P☕✳@🛜🏊) With some 600 spacious rooms and suites, and a

lively casino, this purple-and-glass-covered tower is the American town's answer to the tourist glitz across on the Canadian side of the falls. There is a variety of music and comedy shows staged here too, headlined by relatively big names.

Giacomo   BOUTIQUE HOTEL **$$$**
(☑ 716-299-0200; www.thegiacomo.com; 222 1st St; r $259; P✳@🛜) A rare bit of style among the bland chain hotels and motels of Niagara, the luxe Giacomo occupies part of a gorgeous art-deco office tower, with spacious, ornately decorated rooms. Even if you're not staying here, have a drink in the 19th-floor lounge (bar open from 5pm) for spectacular views, and music on Saturday.

**Third Street Retreat
Eatery & Pub**   AMERICAN **$**
(☑ 716-371-0760; www.thirdstreetretreat.com; 250 Rainbow Blvd; mains $6-11; ⊙ 8am-9pm Tue-Thu, to 10pm Fri & Sat, 9am-4pm Sun) The walls are decorated with old LP covers at this popular local spot serving all-day breakfasts and other comforting pub-grub dishes. There's a good selection of beers on tap or in bottles, plus a pool table and darts in an upstairs section.

ℹ Getting There & Away

NFTA (www.nfta.com) bus 40 connects downtown Buffalo and Niagara Falls ($2, one hour); the stop in Niagara Falls is at 1st St and Rainbow Blvd. Express bus 60 goes to a terminal east of the town center; you'll have to transfer to bus 55 to reach the river. The **Amtrak train station** (☑ 716-285-4224; www.amtrak.com; 825 Depot Ave) is about 2 miles north of downtown; the station on the Canadian side is more central, but coming from NYC, you have to wait for Canadian customs. From Niagara Falls, daily trains go to Buffalo ($14, 35 minutes), Toronto, Canada ($33, three hours) and NYC ($66, nine hours).

Greyhound (www.greyhound.com; 240 1st St) buses stop at the Quality Inn.

Flights from Florida and South Carolina are offered by Allegiant Air and Spirit Airlines to **Niagara Falls International Airport** (✆716-297-4494; www.niagarafallsairport.com; 2035 Niagara Falls Blvd).

NEW JERSEY

Everything you've seen on TV, from the McMansions of *Real Housewives of New Jersey* to the thick accents of *The Sopranos,* is at least partially true. But Jersey (natives lose the 'New') is at least as well defined by its high-tech and banking headquarters, and a quarter of it is lush farmland (hence the Garden State nickname) and pine forests. And on the 127 miles of beautiful beaches, you'll find, yes, the guidos and guidettes of *Jersey Shore,* but also many other oceanfront towns, each with a distinct character.

Stay east and you'll experience the Jersey (sub)urban jungle. Go west to find its opposite: the peaceful, refreshing landscape of the Delaware Water Gap.

❶ Getting There & Around

Though many NJ folks love their cars, there are other transportation options.

PATH Train (www.panynj.gov/path) Connects lower Manhattan to Hoboken, Jersey City and Newark.

NJ Transit (www.njtransit.com) Operates buses and trains around the state, including bus service to NYC's Port Authority and downtown Philadelphia, and trains to Penn Station, NYC. Train service has declined severely in the past decade – fair warning.

New York Waterway (www.nywaterway.com) New York Waterway ferries run up the Hudson River and from the NJ Transit train station in Hoboken to the World Financial Center.

Hoboken

The Square Mile City is among the trendiest of zip codes, with real-estate prices to match. On weekends the bars come alive, and loads of restaurants line Washington St. If you can step over the designer dogs, and navigate the mega-strollers and trolling black Uber cars with NY plates, it's a good walking town with amazing views of NYC.

◉ Sights

Hoboken Historical Museum MUSEUM
(✆201-656-2240; www.hobokenmuseum.org; 1301 Hudson St; adult/child $4/free; ◷2-7pm Tue-Thu, 1-5pm Fri-Sun) This small museum conveys a sense of Hoboken that's hard to imagine today – a city of blue-collar Irish and Italian Catholic immigrants, toiling in the shipyards and docks. It also offers self-guided walking tours of Frank Sinatra's Hoboken haunts, and *On the Waterfront* film locales.

✖ Eating

La Isla CUBAN $
(✆201-659-8197; www.laislarestaurant.com; 104 Washington St; breakfast $8-11, sandwiches $8-10, mains $18-21; ◷7am-10pm) The most authentic Cuban choice in town since 1970, the Formica counters ring with plates spilling over with grilled Cuban sandwiches, *maduros* (fried plantains) and rice with pigeon peas – all to the soundtrack of staccato Spanish chatter and salsa, under the watchful eye of Celia Cruz portraits. Forget the fancier 'uptown' branch – this is the real thing.

Amanda's GASTRONOMY $$$
(✆201-798-0101; www.amandasrestaurant.com; 908 Washington St; mains $24-36; ◷5-10pm Mon-Fri, 11am-3pm & 5-11pm Sat, 11am-3pm & 5-9pm Sun) For three decades the Flynn family has served first-rate fare in these conjoined, converted brownstones, each room with a different theme. An extensive wine list and monthly wine evenings make this a classy option. The bar dinner special (Sunday to Thursday) is great value.

❶ Getting There & Away

NY Waterway (www.nywaterway.com) runs the ferry between 39th St on Manhattan's West Side and Hoboken ($9, eight minutes). There is frequent, if crowded, NJ PATH train service from lower Manhattan to Hoboken terminal. Parking is atrocious – don't even think about driving here.

Princeton

Settled by an English Quaker missionary, this tiny town is filled with lovely architecture and several noteworthy sites, number one of which is its Ivy League university. Princeton is more upper-crust than collegiate, with preppie boutiques edging central Palmer Sq.

Like any good seat of learning, Princeton has a bookshop, record store, brew pub and indie cinema, all within blocks of the rabbit's warren of streets and alleys that crisscross Palmer Sq, as well as innumerable sweet shops, cafes and ice-cream specialty stores.

⦿ Sights

★ Institute Woods   FOREST
(www.ias.edu; 1 Einstein Dr; ☉ dawn-dusk) Walk 1.5 miles down Mercer St to a bucolic slice of countryside seemingly completely removed from the jammed-up campus-area thoroughfares. Nearly 600 acres have been set aside here, and birders, joggers and dog-walkers luxuriate on the soft, loamy pathways. It's an avian paradise during the spring warbler migration.

Princeton University   UNIVERSITY
(☏ 609-258-3000; www.princeton.edu) Built in the mid-1700s, this institution soon became one of the largest structures in the early colonies. Now it's in the top-tier Ivy League. You can stroll around on your own, or take a student-led tour.

Morven Museum & Garden   MUSEUM
(☏ 609-924-8144; www.morven.org; 55 Stockton St; adult/child $10/8; ☉ 10am-4pm Wed-Sun) Stop by for fine displays of decorative arts and fully furnished period rooms; other galleries change their exhibitions periodically. The gardens, and the house itself – a perfectly coiffed colonial revival mansion originally built by Richard Stockton, a prominent lawyer in the mid-18th century and signer of the Declaration of Independence – are worth a visit in and of themselves.

🛏 Sleeping & Eating

Inn at Glencairn   B&B $$
(☏ 609-497-1737; www.innatglencairn.com; 3301 Lawrenceville Rd; r from $199; 🛜) The best value in the Princeton area: five serene rooms in a renovated Georgian manor, 10 minutes' drive from campus.

Mediterra Restaurant
& Taverna   MEDITERRANEAN $$
(☏ 609-252-9680; www.mediterrarestaurant.com; 29 Hulfish St; mains $19-30; ☉ 11:30am-11pm Mon-Thu, to midnight Fri & Sat, to 10pm Sun) Centrally located in Palmer Sq, Mediterra is the sort of upscale, contemporary place designed for a college town, for visiting parents, flush students and locals craving menus that highlight locally sourced and organic ingredients, and that reflect the owners' mixed Chilean–Italian heritage.

★ Mistral   MEDITERRANEAN $$$
(☏ 609-688-8808; www.mistralprinceton.com; 66 Witherspoon St; sharing plates $13-36; ☉ 5-9pm Mon & Tue, 11:30am-3pm & 5-9pm Wed-Sat, 10:30am-3pm & 4-9pm Sun) Princeton's most creative restaurant offers plates made to share, with flavors ranging from the Caribbean to Scandinavia. Sit at the chef's counter for a bird's-eye view of the controlled chaos in the open-plan kitchen.

❶ Getting There & Away

Coach USA (www.coachusa.com) express buses 100 and 600 run frequently between Manhattan and Princeton ($15, 1½ hours). NJ Transit (www.njtransit.com) trains run frequently from New York Penn Station to Princeton Junction railway station ($16, one to 1½ hours). The 'Dinky' shuttle will then run you to Princeton campus ($3, five minutes).

Jersey Shore

Perhaps the most famous and revered feature of New Jersey is its sparkling shore – and heading 'down the shore' (in local parlance, never 'to the beach') is an essential summer ritual. Stretching from Sandy Hook to Cape May, the coastline is dotted with resort towns both tacky and tony. In 2012 much of the shore was devastated by Hurricane Sandy – the roller coaster at Seaside Heights was even knocked into the ocean (and later demolished). But within three years the boardwalks were all rebuilt, and the area has largely returned to its vibrant state. It's mobbed on summer weekends (traffic is especially bad on the bridges to the barrier islands), and finding good-value accommodations is nearly as difficult as locating un-tattooed skin; campgrounds can be low-cost alternatives. By early fall, however, you could find yourself blissfully alone on the sand.

❶ Getting There & Around

Sitting in bumper-to-bumper traffic on the Garden State Pkwy may turn you lobster red, so driving early in the day to summer destinations is a must.
➡ New Jersey Transit (www.njtransit.com) runs twice-daily special Shore Express trains from June to September, stopping in Asbury Park, Bradley Beach, Belmar, Spring Lake, Manasquan, Point Pleasant Beach and Bay Head. You can buy a beach tag along with your train ticket, and there are two northbound express trains returning in the evening.

➡ NJ Transit buses from New York's Port Authority service Seaside Heights/Seaside Park, Island Beach State Park, Atlantic City, Wildwood and Cape May.

➡ Greyhound (www.greyhound.com) runs special buses to Atlantic City.

Asbury Park & Ocean Grove

During decades of economic stagnation, the town of Asbury Park had nothing more to its name than the fact that state troubadour Bruce Springsteen got his start at the Stone Pony nightclub here in the mid-1970s. But since 2000, blocks of previously abandoned Victorian homes have seen such a revival that Asbury is sometimes called 'Brooklyn on the Beach.' Thousands more units are projected over the next few years.

The downtown area – several blocks of Cookman and Bangs Aves – has antiques shops, hip restaurants (from vegan to French bistro) and an art-house cinema. Thirty-nine bars (and counting) lure trains full of young NY-based revelers to the convenient NJ transit depot, like moths to the vodka.

Immediately south of Asbury Park, Ocean Grove is a kind of time and culture warp. 'God's Square Mile at the Jersey Shore,' as it's still known, was founded by Methodists in the 19th century as a revival camp, and it's still a 'dry' town – no liquor is sold here – and the beach is closed Sunday mornings. Its Victorian architecture is so covered in gingerbread trim, you'll want to eat it. At the center, around a 6500-seat wooden auditorium with a huge pipe organ, the former revival camp is now Tent City – a historic site with more than a hundred quaint canvas tents used as summer homes.

◎ Sights & Activities

Historic Village at Allaire　　　MUSEUM
(☏ 732-919-3500; www.allairevillage.org; 4263 Atlantic Ave, Farmingdale; parking May-Sep $7; ☺ bakery 10am-4pm Mon-Fri, historic village 11am-5pm Sat & Sun) FREE Just a 15 minute-drive from the 21st century and Asbury Park, this quirky museum is what remains of what was a thriving 19th-century village called Howell Works.

Silver Ball Museum Arcade　　　ARCADE
(Pinball Hall of Fame; ☏ 732-774-4994; www.silverballmuseum.com; 1000 Ocean Ave; per hour/half-day $10/15; ☺ 11am-midnight Mon-Thu, to 1am Fri & Sat, 10am-10pm Sun) Dozens of pinball machines in mint condition, from mechanical 1950s games to modern classics such as Addams Family.

🛏 Sleeping

★Asbury Hotel　　　BOUTIQUE HOTEL $$
(☏ 732-774-7100; www.theasburyhotel.com; 210 5th Ave; r $125-275; ⓟ ❄ 🛜 🏊) Wow. From the performance space/lobby stocked with LP records, old books and a solarium to the rooftop bar, this new hotel oozes cool. A 2016 addition to the AP scene, two blocks from Convention Hall and the boardwalk, you could stay inside all day, playing pool or lounging by the rooftop one.

Quaker Inn　　　INN $$
(☏ 732-775-7525; www.quakerinn.com; 39 Main Ave; r $90-200; ❄ 🛜) A great old creaky Victorian with 28 rooms, some of which open onto wraparound porches or balconies. There's a nice common area/library to linger over your coffee, and the owners reflect the town's overall charm and hospitality.

🍴 Eating & Drinking

Moonstruck　　　ITALIAN $$$
(☏ 732-988-0123; www.moonstrucknj.com; 517 Lake Ave; mains $22-38; ☺ 5-10pm Wed, Thu & Sun, to 11pm Fri & Sat) With views of Wesley Lake dividing Asbury and Ocean Grove and an extensive martini menu, it's hard to find fault. The menu is eclectic, though it leans toward Italian with a good selection of pastas; the meat and fish dishes have varied ethnic influences.

Asbury Festhalle and Biergarten　　　BEER GARDEN
(☏ 732-997-8767; www.asburybiergarten.com; 527 Lake Ave; ☺ 4pm-1am Mon-Fri, 11am-1am Sat & Sun) Deutschland by the Sea: quaff from 41 draft ales in the rooftop beer garden or check out live music in a space as big as two barns, with classic long beer-hall tables. Snack on pretzels bigger than your face, fill up on plates of wurst (mains $13 to $20) or work your way through the 12 different schnapps on offer.

❶ Getting There & Away

Driving along the S Main St (Rte 71) from the north or south, you'll see the impressive gates that mark the entranceway to Ocean Grove's Main Ave. If you're taking the NJ Transit's Shore Express, debark at neighboring Asbury Park and walk or taxi over to Ocean Grove. A $22 bus trip from the Port Authority requires a transfer at Lakewood.

WORTH A TRIP

DELAWARE WATER GAP

The beautiful spot where the Delaware River makes a tight S-curve through the ridge of the Kittatinny Mountains was, in the pre-air-conditioning days, a popular resort destination. In 1965 the **Delaware Water Gap National Recreation Area** (📞570-426-2452; www.nps. gov/dewa; 1978 River Rd, Bushkill) was established, covering land in both NJ and Pennsylvania, and it's still an unspoiled recreational spot – just 70 miles east of New York City.

Old Mine Rd, one of the oldest continually operating commercial roads in the USA, meanders along the eastern side of the Delaware. A few miles inland, a 25-mile stretch of the Appalachian Trail runs along the Kittatinny Ridge. Day hikers can climb to the top of the 1547ft Mt Tammany in **Worthington State Forest** (📞908-841-9575; www.state. nj.us/dep/parksandforests/parks/worthington.html; Old Mine Rd, Warren County; ⊙dawn-dusk) for great views (the 1.8-mile Blue Dot trail is the easiest route, though it's still strenuous) or walk to the serene-looking glacial Sunfish Pond. Hawks, bald eagles and ravens soar over the hemlock forest. It's about a two-hour bus ride from NYC to the area. Coach USA (www.coachusa.com) provides bus service from the Port Authority to Milford, PA ($25) and Martz Trailways (www.martztrailways.com) runs to Stroudsburg, PA ($37). NJ Transit has proposed a rail station in Smithfield Township, just outside the park, but it has yet to be built.

New Jersey Transit's Asbury Park Station is at the intersection of Cookman and Main Sts and is about 45 minutes from NYC. Some late-night trains run during the summer.

Barnegat Peninsula

Locals call this 22-mile stretch 'the barrier island,' though it's technically a peninsula, connected to the mainland at **Point Pleasant Beach**. Surfers should seek out **Inlet Beach** in Manasquan, immediately north (not on the peninsula), for the Shore's most reliable year-round waves.

South of **Mantoloking** and **Lavallette**, midway down the island, a bridge from the mainland (at Toms River) deposits the hordes in **Seaside Heights**, location of the MTV reality show *Jersey Shore*, and epitome of the deliciously tacky Shore culture. It's still a sticky pleasure to lick a Kohr's orange-vanilla twist cone and stroll through the boardwalk's raucous, deeply tanned, scantily clad crowds, refueling at an above-average number of bars. Look out for the 1910 Dentzel-Looff carousel, and the 310ft Ferris wheel and German-built roller-coaster added in 2017.

For a bit of quiet, escape south to residential **Seaside Park** and the wilderness of Island Beach State Park beyond.

👁 Sights

Island Beach State Park　　　　　PARK
(📞732-793-0506; www.islandbeachnj.org; Seaside Park; weekday/weekend May-Sep $12/20, Oct-Apr $5/10; ⊙8am-8pm Mon-Fri, 7am-8pm Sat & Sun May-Sep, 8am-dusk Oct-Apr) This beautiful tidal island offers fishing, a range of wildlife (from foxes to ospreys and other shorebirds), more than 40 trees and shrubs, including pepperbush and prickly pear cactus, and a killer view of Barnegat Lighthouse, seemingly only an arm's length across the water. Of the 10 miles of relatively untouched beach, one is open for swimming; the rest makes a nice bike ride. On the bay side, the lush tidal marshes are good for kayaking.

Casino Pier　　　　AMUSEMENT PARK
(📞732-793-6488; www.casinopiernj.com; 800 Ocean Tce, Seaside Heights; rides from $5, water park adult/child $35/29; ⊙noon-late Jun-Aug, hours vary Sep-May) The amusement pier at the north end of the Seaside boardwalk has a few kiddie rides and more extreme thrills for the 48in-and-taller set, plus a chairlift that runs above the boardwalk. Nearby is **Breakwater Beach**, a water park with tall slides.

🛏 Sleeping & Eating

Luna-Mar Motel　　　　MOTEL **$$**
(📞732-793-7955; www.lunamarmotel.com; 1201 N Ocean Ave, Seaside Park; r from $129; ❄🤝🛎) Directly across the road from the beach, this tidy motel has tile floors (no sandy carpets). Rates include beach badges.

★Klee's　　　　PUB FOOD **$$**
(📞732-830-1996; www.kleesbarandgrill.com; 101 Boulevard, Seaside Heights; pizza from $12, mains

> ### ℹ BEACH FEES
>
> Many communities on the Jersey Shore charge $5 to $9 for access, issuing a badge (also called a tag) for the day. From Long Beach Island north to near Sandy Hook, all beaches have a fee; the southern shore is mostly, but not entirely, free. If you're staying a few days, it's worthwhile to invest in a weekly badge.

$14-28; ⊙10:30am-11pm Mon-Thu, to midnight Fri & Sat) Don't ask why an Irish bar has the best thin-crust pizza on the Shore – just enjoy.

ℹ Getting There & Away

NJ Transit (www.njtransit.com) has a special Shore Express train (no transfer required) to Shore towns between Asbury Park and Bay Head; in the summer months it includes a beach pass. It also offers direct bus service to Seaside Heights from New York's Port Authority (bus 137; $27, 1½ hours) and Newark's Penn Station (bus 67; $17, one hour) from the end of June to Labor Day.

Atlantic City

Atlantic City (AC) may be the largest city on the Shore, but that currently doesn't mean much, as the vision of 'Vegas on the East Coast' has foundered, and casinos have gone bankrupt. But the hotels can be a bargain and the lovely beach is free and often empty because most visitors are indoors playing the slots. And in contrast with many homogeneous beach enclaves, the population here is more diverse.

As for the Prohibition-era glamour depicted in the HBO series *Boardwalk Empire*, there's little trace – though you can still ride along the boardwalk on a nifty wicker rolling chair (there's a price chart posted inside each chair). As you do, consider that the first boardwalk was built here, and if Baltic Ave rings a bell, it's because the game Monopoly uses AC's street names. A later contribution: the Miss America pageant, though it's now held in Vegas; the Miss'd America drag pageant (www.missdamerica.org) fills the gap.

◉ Sights

Steel Pier AMUSEMENT PARK
(☑866-386-6659; www.steelpier.com; 1000 Boardwalk; ⊙3pm-midnight Mon-Fri, noon-1am Sat & Sun Jun-Aug, noon-midnight Sat & Sun Apr & May) The Steel Pier, directly in front of the Taj Mahal casino, was the site of the famous high-diving horses that plunged into the Atlantic before crowds of spectators from the 1920s to the '70s. Today it's a collection of amusement rides, games of chance, candy stands and a Go-Kart track.

Ripley's Believe it or Not! MUSEUM
(Odditorium; ☑609-347-2001; www.ripleys.com; 1441 Boardwalk; adult/child $17/$11; ⊙11am-8pm Mon-Fri, 10am-8pm Sat & Sun) To call it a museum is a stretch, but Robert Ripley spent a lifetime collecting bizarre stuff, and a lot of it's here. Two-headed goat fetuses, a baling-wire Jimi Hendrix head, the world's smallest car, and a roulette wheel made of 14,000 jelly-beans – you'll have fun, for about the cost of a movie.

Atlantic City Historical Museum MUSEUM
(☑609-347-5839; www.atlanticcityexperience.org; 1 N Tennessee Ave, Atlantic City Free Public Library; ⊙9:30am-5pm Mon, Fri & Sat, to 6pm Tue-Thu) FREE Small but informative – you'll learn all about AC's quirkiest details, such as the high-diving horses that once leaped off a 40ft tower at Steel Pier.

🛏 Sleeping & Eating

Tropicana Casino and Resort HOTEL $$
(☑609-340-4000; www.tropicana.net; 2831 Boardwalk; r from $105; P✳🤶🖳) The Trop is a sprawling city-within-a-city, including a casino, the Boogie Nights disco, a spa and high-end restaurants. We recommend the newer 'Havana' wing, and try to get up above the 40th floor for spectacular views.

★Kelsey & Kim's Café SOUTHERN US $
(Kelsey's Soul Food; ☑609-350-6800; www.kelsey sac.com; 201 Melrose Ave; mains $9-12; ⊙7am-10pm) In the pretty residential Uptown area, this friendly cafe does excellent Southern comfort food, from morning grits and waffles to fried whiting and barbecue brisket. BYOB makes it a deal.

ℹ Getting There & Away

The small **Atlantic City International Airport** (ACY; ☑609-573-4700; www.acairport.com; 101 Atlantic City International Airport, Egg Harbor Township) is a 20-minute drive from the town center. If you happen to be coming from Florida (where most of the flights come from), it's a great option for South Jersey or Philadelphia.

The only train service is NJ Transit (www. njtransit.com) from Philadelphia (one way $11, 1½ hours), arriving at the **train station**

(✆ 973-491-9400; 1 Atlantic City Expwy) next to the convention center. AC's **bus station** (✆ 609-345-5403; www.njtransit.com; 1901 Atlantic Ave) receives NJ Transit and Greyhound service from NYC ($25 to $36, 2½ hours) and Philadelphia ($17, 1½ hours). A casino will often refund much of the fare (in chips, coins or coupons) if you get a bus, such as Greyhound's Lucky Streak service, directly to its door. When leaving AC, buses first stop at various casinos and only stop at the bus station if not already full.

Wildwood

Wildwood, and its neighboring towns of North Wildwood and Wildwood Crest, is a virtual outdoor museum of 1950s motel architecture and neon signs. The community has a relaxed atmosphere, somewhere between clean-cut fun and wild party. The beach is the widest in NJ, and there's no admission fee. Along the 2-mile boardwalk, several massive piers have roller coasters and rides best suited to aspiring astronauts.

◉ Sights

Doo Wop Experience   MUSEUM
(✆ 609-523-1958; www.doowoopusa.org; 4500 Ocean Ave; ◷ noon-9pm daily, trolley tours 8pm Tue & Thu Jun-Aug) FREE The Doo Wop Preservation League runs this small museum that tells the story of the Wildwoods' 1950s heyday. Its 'neon-sign garden' shows off relics from no-longer-standing buildings. Some summer nights, a trolley tour (adult/child $12/6) departs from here.

🛏 Sleeping & Eating

Heart of Wildwood   HOTEL $$
(✆ 609-522-4090; www.heartofwildwood.com; cnr Ocean & Spencer Aves; r $125-245; P❄🖸🌊) If you're here for water slides and roller coasters, book a room at Heart of Wildwood, facing the amusement piers. It's not fancy, but gets high marks for cleanliness (the tile floors help), and from the heated rooftop pool you can watch the big wheel go round and round.

Starlux   BOUTIQUE HOTEL $$
(✆ 609-522-7412; www.thestarlux.com; 305 E Rio Grande Ave; r from $205, trailer $240; P🖸🌊) The sea-green-and-white Starlux has a soaring profile, lava lamps, boomerang-decorated bedspreads and sailboat-shaped mirrors, plus it's clean as a whistle. Even more authentically retro are its two chrome-sided Airstream trailers.

Key West Cafe   BREAKFAST $
(✆ 609-522-5006; 4701 Pacific Ave; mains $8-10; ◷ 7am-2pm) Basically every permutation of pancakes and eggs imaginable, all freshly prepared – oh, and lunch too. Bonus: it's open year-round.

ℹ Getting There & Away

New Jersey Transit (www.njtransit.com) runs bus service to Wildwood from NYC ($46, 4½ hours) and express bus service from Philadelphia's 30th St Station during summer ($30, 2½ hours). Driving from the Garden State Pkwy, take Rte 47 into Wildwood; from the south a more scenic route from Cape May is Rte 109, then Ocean Dr.

Cape May

Established in 1620, Cape May is a town with deep history and some 600 gorgeous Victorian buildings. Its sweeping beaches are a draw in summer, but its year-round population of about 4000 makes it a lively off-season destination, unlike most of the rest of the Jersey Shore. Whales can be spotted off the coast May to December, and migratory birds are plentiful in spring and fall: just check in at the Cape May Bird Observatory. The state's booming wine industry is represented by six different sites here, among them, trendy Willow Creek. And thanks to the location on New Jersey's southern tip (it's Exit 0 from the turnpike), you can watch the sun rise or set over the water.

◉ Sights

Cape May Point State Park   STATE PARK
(www.state.nj.us/dep/parksandforests/parks/capemay.html; 707 E Lake Dr; ◷ 8am-4pm) The 190-acre Cape May Point State Park, just off Lighthouse Ave, has 2 miles of trails, plus the famous **Cape May Lighthouse** (✆ 609-884-5404; www.capemaymac.org; 215 Lighthouse Ave; adult/child $8/5; ◷ 10am-5pm May-Sep, 11am-3pm Mar & Apr, 11am-3pm Sat Feb, Mar & Oct-Dec). Built in 1859, the 157ft lighthouse underwent a $2 million restoration in the 1990s, and its completely reconstructed light is visible as far as 25 miles out to sea. You can climb the 199 stairs to the top in the summer months. Lighthouse hours vary; phone ahead to confirm details.

Cape May Bird Observatory   BIRD SANCTUARY
(✆ 609-884-2736; www.birdcapemay.org; 701 East Lake Dr; ◷ 9am-4:30pm Apr-Oct, Wed-Mon Nov-Mar) FREE Cape May is one of the country's

OFF THE BEATEN TRACK

SANDY HOOK

The northernmost tip of the Jersey Shore is the **Sandy Hook Gateway National Recreation Area** (☑718-354-4606; www.nps.gov/gate; 128 S Hartshorne Dr, Highlands; parking May-Sep $15; ⊙5am-9pm Apr-Oct) **FREE**, a 7-mile barrier island at the entrance to New York Harbor. From your beach blanket, you can see the NYC skyline. The wide beaches, including NJ's only legal nude beach (**Gunnison**), are edged by a system of bike trails, while the bay side is great for fishing or bird-watching.

Historic Fort Hancock and the nation's oldest operational **lighthouse** (☑732-872-5970; www.nps.gov/gate; 85 Mercer Road, Highlands; ⊙visitor center 9am-5pm, tours half-hourly 1-4:30pm) **FREE** give a glimpse of Sandy Hook's prior importance as a military and navigational site.

top birding spots, with more than 400 species during migration season. The mile-long loop trail here is a good introduction, and there are plenty of books, binoculars and birding bric-a-brac in the bookstore here.

🛏 Sleeping & Eating

★**Congress Hall**   HOTEL **$$$**
(☑609-884-8421; www.caperesorts.com; 200 Congress Pl; r from $259; ✳🛜🏊) Opened in 1816, the enormous Congress Hall is a local landmark, now suitably modernized without wringing out all the history. The same company manages several other excellent hotels in the area.

Mad Batter   AMERICAN **$**
(☑609-884-5970; www.madbatter.com; Carroll Villa Hotel, 19 Jackson St; brunch $8-11; ⊙8am-9pm May-Aug, hours vary Sep-Apr) Tucked in a white Victorian B&B, this restaurant is locally beloved for brunch – including fluffy oat pancakes and rich clam chowder. Dinner is fine, but pricier, with mains around $30.

The Chesapeake Bay Benedict, stuffed with crab, is to die for.

★**Lobster House**   SEAFOOD **$$**
(☑609-884-8296; www.thelobsterhouse.com; 906 Schellengers Landing Rd; mains $14-30; ⊙11:30am-3pm & 4:30-10pm Apr-Dec, to 9pm Jan-Mar) This clubby-feeling classic on the wharf serves

local oysters and scallops. No reservations means very long waits – go early or late, or have a drink on the boat-bar, the *Schooner American,* docked next to the restaurant.

🍷 Drinking & Nightlife

★**Willow Creek Winery**   WINERY
(☑609-770-8782; www.willowcreekwinerycapemay. com; 168 Stevens St; ⊙11am-5pm Mon-Thu, to 9:30pm Fri, to 7pm Sat & Sun) The 'baby' of Cape May's six wineries, this former lima bean/dairy farm christened its first bottles in 2011, and produces a solid combo of reds and whites. The tapas menu and sangria bar on the weekend are pretty mind-blowing, and a tour around the 50 acres on an electric tram is a kick.

ℹ Getting There & Away

NJ Transit (www.njtransit.com) buses serve Cape May from NYC ($48, three hours; may involve a transfer at Atlantic City) and a discounted round-trip express bus from Philadelphia during the summer months (return $33, three hours). For onward car travel, the **Cape May-Lewes Ferry** (☑800-643-3779; www.cmlf. com; 1200 Lincoln Blvd; car/passenger $47/10; ⊙7am-6pm Apr-Oct) crosses the bay in 1½ hours to Lewes, Delaware, near Rehoboth Beach.

PENNSYLVANIA

More than 300 miles across, stretching from the East Coast to the edge of the Midwest, Pennsylvania contains multitudes. Philadelphia, once the heart of the British colonial empire, is very much a part of the east, a link on the Boston–Washington metro corridor. Outside the city, though, the terrain turns pastoral, emphasized by the Pennsylvania Dutch – that is, Mennonite, Amish and others – who tend their farms by hand, as if it were still the 18th century. West of here, the Appalachian mountains begin, as do the so-called Pennsylvania Wilds, a barely inhabited patch of deep forest. In the far west of the state, Pittsburgh, the state's only other large city and once a staggeringly wealthy steel manufacturing center, is fascinating in its combination of rust-belt decay and new energy.

ℹ Getting There & Around

Pennsylvania is home to a number of airports, several of them with international connections, and it is near the giant hub of New Jersey's

Newark International, with connections across the world. Trains serve many of its major cities, while buses service most towns. That said, with so much of this state's beauty lying off the beaten path, renting a car and driving is highly recommended.

Philadelphia

Philadelphia, or 'Philly' as it's affectionately known, has all of the glamor of New York City and Washington, DC, while still retaining small-town charm. Because the city's oldest buildings are so well preserved, America's early history and role in building democracy are sometimes more accessible here than in the capital. Moreover, it's a beautiful place that is easy and rewarding to explore, its streets dotted with gracious squares and linked by cobbled alleys.

From the start of the Revolutionary War until 1790 (when Washington, DC, was founded), Philadelphia was the new nation's capital. Eventually, NYC rose as a cultural, commercial and industrial center, and Philly slipped into a decline, intensified by the loss of industrial jobs. Some areas of the city are still blighted, but its core, from the manicured campuses of the University of Pennsylvania to the redbrick buildings of the Old City, is solid.

⊙ Sights & Activities

★ Barnes Foundation MUSEUM
(Map p170; ☑ 215-278-7200; www.barnesfounda tion.org; 2025 Benjamin Franklin Pkwy; adult/child $25/10; ☉ 10am-5pm Wed-Mon) In the first half of the 20th century, collector and educator Albert C Barnes amassed a remarkable trove of artwork by Cézanne, Degas, Matisse, Renoir, Van Gogh and other European stars. Alongside, he set beautiful pieces of folk art from Africa and the Americas – an artistic desegregation that was shocking at the time. Today's Barnes Foundation is a modern shell, inside which is a faithful reproduction of Barnes' original mansion (still in the Philadelphia suburbs).

The art is hung according to Barnes' vision, a careful juxtaposition of colors, themes and materials. In one room, all the portraits appear to be staring at a central point. Even more remarkable: you've likely never seen any of these works before, because Barnes' will limits reproduction and lending.

★ Independence Hall HISTORIC BUILDING
(Map p174; ☑ 877-444-6777; www.nps.gov/inde; 520 Chestnut St; ☉ 9am-5pm, to 7pm late May-early Sep) FREE The 'birthplace of American government,' a modest Quaker building, is where delegates from the 13 colonies met to approve the Declaration of Independence on July 4, 1776. Entrance is at the corner of Chestnut and 5th Sts. Expect a line out the door, around the block, and perhaps even out of the city for this one – it's the prime attraction in a city full of history. Budget for at least an hour wait.

★ Independence National Historic Park PARK
(Map p174; ☑ 215-965-2305; www.nps.gov/inde; 3rd & Chestnut Sts; ☉ visitor center & most sites 9am-5pm; ☒ 9, 21, 38, 42, 47, Ⓤ SEPTA 5th St Station) This L-shaped park, along with Philly's Old City, has been dubbed 'America's most historic square mile.' Once the backbone of the US government, it has become the backbone of Philadelphia's tourist trade. Stroll around and you'll see storied buildings in which the seeds for the Revolutionary War were planted and the US government came into bloom. You'll also find beautiful, shaded urban lawns dotted with plenty of squirrels, pigeons and costumed actors.

★ Museum of the American Revolution MUSEUM
(Map p174; ☑ 215-253-6731; www.amrevmuseum. org; 101 S 3rd St; adult/child $19/12; ☉ 10am-5pm Sep-late May, 9:30am-6pm late May-Aug) This massive, multimedia-rich new museum will have you virtually participating in the American Revolution, from interactive dioramas to 3-D experiences that take you all the way from contentment with British rule to the eventual rejection of it. Learn about the events, people, cultures and religions that participated in one of the world's most important revolutions. Lots of hands-on and video opportunities mean kids will have as much fun as adults. Note that all tickets are timed: reserve them early online.

★ Philadelphia Museum of Art MUSEUM
(Map p170; ☑ 215-763-8100; www.philamuseum. org; 2600 Benjamin Franklin Pkwy; adult/child $20/free; ☉ 10am-5pm Tue, Thu, Sat & Sun, to 8:45pm Wed & Fri) To many, this building is simply the steps Sylvester Stallone ran up in the 1976 flick *Rocky*. But well beyond that, this is one of the nation's finest treasure troves, featuring excellent collections

NEW YORK, NEW JERSEY & PENNSYLVANIA PHILADELPHIA

Philadelphia

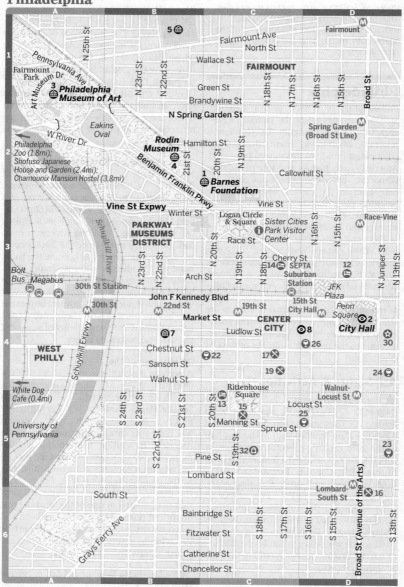

of Asian art, Renaissance masterpieces, post-Impressionist works and modern pieces by Picasso, Duchamp and Matisse. Especially neat are the complete rooms: a medieval cloister, a Chinese temple, an Austrian country house.

There's so much to see that a ticket gives admission for two days, here and at the separate Perelman Building, two nearby historic homes and the Rodin Museum (p172). Wednesday and Friday nights are pay-what-

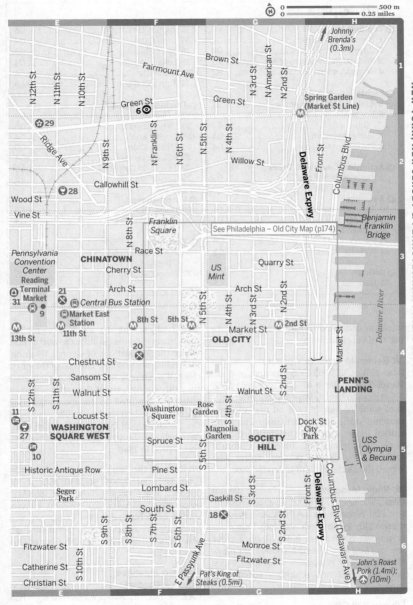

you-wish (but note the Perelman is closed on both evenings).

Mütter Museum MUSEUM
(Map p170; ☎ 215-560-8564; www.muttermuse um.org; 19 S 22nd St; adult/child $15/10; ⊗ 10am-5pm) Know what a bezoar is? If so, you're morbid enough to appreciate this trove of medical oddities. Maintained by the College of Physicians, this is definitely one of those unique, only-in-Philadelphia attractions, a

Philadelphia

◉ **Top Sights**
1 Barnes Foundation C2
2 City Hall D4
3 Philadelphia Museum of Art A1
4 Rodin Museum B2

◎ **Sights**
5 Eastern State Penitentiary B1
6 Edgar Allen Poe National Historic
   Site F1
7 Mütter Museum B4
8 Philly from the Top D4

◎ **Activities, Courses & Tours**
9 Taste of Philly Food Tour E3

◎ **Sleeping**
10 Alexander Inn E5
11 Independent E5
12 Le Méridien D3
13 Rittenhouse Hotel C5
14 Windsor Suites C3

◎ **Eating**
15 Baril C5

16 Big Gay Ice Cream D6
17 Gran Caffè L'Aquila C4
18 Jim's Steaks G6
19 Luke's Lobster C4
20 Morimoto F4
21 Tom's Dim Sum E3

◎ **Drinking & Nightlife**
22 1 Tippling Place C4
23 Dirty Franks D5
24 Double Knot D4
25 Monk's Cafe D5
26 R2L Restaurant D4
27 Tavern on Camac E5
28 Trestle Inn E2

◎ **Entertainment**
29 PhilaMOCA E2
30 Wanamaker Organ D4

◎ **Shopping**
31 AIA Bookstore &
   Design Center E3
32 Omoi Zakka Shop C5

museum dedicated to rare, odd or disturbing medical conditions.

★ **Benjamin Franklin Museum**   MUSEUM
(Map p174; ☑215-965-2305; www.nps.gov/inde; Market St, btwn 3rd & 4th Sts; adult/child $5/2; ◎9am-5pm, to 7pm late May-early Sep) In a courtyard south of Market St is an underground museum dedicated to Benjamin Franklin's storied life as a printer (he started the nation's first newspaper), inventor (Bifocals! Lightning rods!) and political figure who signed the Declaration of Independence.

★ **Rodin Museum**   MUSEUM
(Map p170; ☑215-763-8100; www.rodinmuseum. org; 2151 Benjamin Franklin Pkwy; suggested admission $10; ◎10am-5pm Wed-Mon) This newly renovated museum holds Rodin's great works *The Thinker* and *Burghers of Calais* among its 140 sculptures that span every part of the French sculptor's spectacular career.

Liberty Bell Center   HISTORIC SITE
(Map p174; ☑215-965-2305; www.nps.gov/inde; 526 Market St; ◎9am-5pm, to 7pm late May-early Sep) **FREE** A glass-walled building protects this icon of Philadelphia history from the elements. You can peek from outside, or join the line to file past, reading about the

2080lb object's history along the way. The line starts on the building's north end, where the foundations of George Washington's house are marked. The gist of the story: the bell was made in 1751, to commemorate the 50th anniversary of Pennsylvania's constitution. Mounted in Independence Hall (p169), it tolled on the first public reading of the Declaration of Independence. The crack developed in the 19th century, and the bell was retired in 1846.

Philly from the Top   OBSERVATORY
(One Liberty Observation Deck; Map p170; ☑215-561-3325; http://phillyfromthetop.com; 1650 Market St; adult/child $14/9; ◎10am-8pm) A lovely way to get a bird's-eye view of the city, and especially pretty after dark, this 883ft-high observation deck is on the 57th floor of One Liberty Place.

**Shofuso Japanese
House & Garden**   GARDENS
(☑215-878-5097; www.japanesehouse.org; Horticultural Dr, Fairmount Park; adult/child $10/5; ◎10am-4pm Wed-Fri, 11am-5pm Sat & Sun Apr-Oct) A picturesque home and teahouse, in the 16th-century style, set in 1.2 acres of traditional gardens. The cherry trees blooming in spring are not to be missed.

★ City Hall
NOTABLE BUILDING

(Map p170; ☑215-686-2840; www.phlvisitor center.com; cnr Broad & Market Sts; tower $6, tower & tower $12; ☺9am-5pm Mon-Fri, also 11am-4pm one Sat per month, tour at 12:30pm, tower closes 4:15pm Mon-Fri) Completed in 1901, City Hall takes up a whole block, and, at 548ft, not counting the 27-ton bronze statue of William Penn, it's the world's tallest structure without a steel frame. The view from the observation deck near the top of the tower takes in most of the city (reserve tickets ahead). The daily interior tour is a treat too. In winter, there's ice-skating on the west-side plaza.

Eastern State Penitentiary
MUSEUM

(Map p170; ☑215-236-3300; www.easternstate. org; 2027 Fairmount Ave; adult/child $14/10; ☺10am-5pm) The modern prison didn't just happen – it was invented, and Eastern State Penitentiary was the first one, opened in 1829 and finally closed in 1971. A self-guiding audio tour leads you through the eerie, echoing halls; one stop is Al Capone's famously luxurious cell. There's also info on America's current prison system, and art installations throughout. A popular stop, expect crowds at peak times.

Edgar Allen Poe National Historic Site
HISTORIC SITE

(Map p170; ☑215-597-8780; www.nps.gov/edal; 532 N 7th St; ☺9am-noon, 1-5pm Fri-Sun) FREE Often called the creator of the horror story, Edgar Allen Poe lived for seven years in Philadelphia. This house, his only Philly home still remaining, has been turned into a small but interesting museum, with a lot of original items and restored rooms. Don't miss the creepy brick cellar (complete with cobwebs) thought to have inspired Poe's masterwork *The Black Cat*. A statue of a raven stands outside.

Mural Tours
TOURS

(☑215-925-3633; www.muralarts.org/tours; $22-32) Guided trolley, train and walking tours of the city's numerous outdoor murals. A free self-guided tour and map is available online.

Taste of Philly Food Tour
FOOD & DRINK

(Map p170; ☑800-838-3006; www.tasteofphilly foodtour.com; 51 N 12th St; adult/child $17/10; ☺10am Wed & Sat) Snack and learn Philly food lore during this 75-minute tour with a local writer at the Reading Terminal Market. Reservations required.

★ Festivals & Events

Feastival
FOOD & DRINK

(☑267-443-1886; http://phillyfeastival.com/; 140 N Columbus Blvd; $300) Eat, meet and greet at the city's highest-lauded food fest, held one evening every September to benefit FringeArts, the city cultural organization that puts on the Fringe Festival. Not for the budget-minded, but if you've got the cash to splash, it's a night you'll never forget.

Mummers Parade
CARNIVAL

(www.mummers.com; ☺Jan 1) Uniquely Philly: the closest parallel may be New Orleans' Mardi Gras krewes, with their elaborate costumes, music and deep lore – but in the bracing cold of winter. The parade often stretches more than a mile down Broad St in the center of the city.

Fringe Festival
PERFORMING ARTS

(www.fringearts.com; ☺mid-Sep) Philly's performance fest has been running since 1996; it's a city-wide celebration of performance art for 17 days in mid-September, with events, productions and craziness.

☰ Sleeping

★ Apple Hostels
HOSTEL $

(Map p174; ☑215-922-0222; www.applehostels. com; 33 Bank St; dm/d $20/95; ✱@☞) This cheerful hostel is hidden down an Old City alley and spans both sides of the street. The apple-green color scheme fits the name, but the Hosteling International-affiliated place is strong on details: two spotless kitchens, lounges and a library, plus power outlets in lockers, USB ports and reading lights at every bed, free coffee and earplugs.

There are male, female and co-ed dorms, plus two private rooms. The friendly staff run nightly activities such as walking tours, pasta nights and a Thursday bar crawl.

Chamounix Mansion Hostel
HOSTEL $

(☑215-878-3676; www.philahostel.org; 3250 Chamounix Dr, West Fairmount Park; dm members/non-members $22/25, private d $55; ☺closed 15 Dec-15 Jan; ℗@; ☐38 & 40) In a lovely wooded area on the north side of the city, this Hosteling International hostel is best for guests with a car, but it's worth the drive. In its public areas, set with 19th-century furnishings, the place looks more like a B&B than a hostel; the dorms themselves are basic, but the antiques, harp, oriental rugs and paintings make it feel like luxury.

Philadelphia – Old City

The building is in the Philadelphia register of historic places.

★ **Alexander Inn** BOUTIQUE HOTEL **$$**
(Map p170; ☎215-923-3535; www.alexanderinn.com; cnr 12th & Spruce Sts; s/d from $143/182; ✳@☎) Online photos undersell this place. The impeccably kept rooms have a subdued, slightly vintage style; some have old-fashioned half-size tubs. The continental breakfast is average – worth the convenience, but there are other breakfast options nearby if you have the time.

Independent BOUTIQUE HOTEL **$$**
(Map p170; ☎215-772-1440; www.theindependenthotel.com; 1234 Locust St; r from $175; ☻✳@☎) A good Center City option housed in a handsome brick Georgian-Revival building with a four-story atrium. The elevator is painted realistically to appear like a set of doors. The 24 wood-floored rooms are uncluttered and sunny, and the complimentary off-site gym pass and wine and cheese served Monday through Thursday sweeten the deal.

Philadelphia - Old City

◎ **Top Sights**
1 Benjamin Franklin Museum C3
2 Independence Hall B4
3 Independence National Historic
   Park C4
4 Museum of the American
   Revolution C3

◎ **Sights**
5 Liberty Bell Center A3

🛏 **Sleeping**
6 Apple Hostels C3

🍴 **Eating**
7 Cuba Libre C3
8 Zahav C4

🛍 **Shopping**
9 Shane Confectionery D3

Le Méridien
HOTEL $$

(Map p170; 📞 215-422-8200; www.starwood hotels.com; 1421 Arch St; d from $231; 🅿 ❄ ❋ @ 🛜 🐾) Though part of a luxury chain, the location and tasteful appropriation of an old building to make a modern hotel sets Le Méridien apart. Proudly claiming to be entirely smoke-free, this hotel is pet-friendly as well, has a wide range of facilities – a workout room, business center, parking – and is central to all the City Hall fun.

Windsor Suites
HOTEL $$

(Map p170; 📞 215-981-5678; www.thewindsor suites.com; 1700 Benjamin Franklin Pkwy; ste from $229; 🅿 ❄ ❋ 🛜 🐾) Comfortable suite rooms with full kitchens, with options for extended stays or monthly rentals. Conveniently located two blocks from Logan Sq, the Windsor Suites have a unique pet-friendly take: pets stay free and even get their own amenities. Online booking can be substantially cheaper.

★ Rittenhouse Hotel
HOTEL $$$

(Map p170; 📞 215-546-9000; www.rittenhouse hotel.com; 210 W Rittenhouse Sq; d $400; 🅿 ❄ ❋ @ 🛜 🏊) A five-star – excuse me, make that five-*diamond* – hotel on Rittenhouse Square. Rooms have marble baths. Of the downtown options with a pool, this is one of the nicest. It proudly serves a top-notch brunch and a soothing afternoon tea service with music. Thursdays through Saturdays a live jazz band plays in the library bar.

✕ Eating

Big Gay Ice Cream
ICE CREAM $

(Map p170; 📞 267-886-8024; www.biggayice cream.com; 521 S Broad St; ice cream from $3; ◷ 1-10pm Sun-Thu, to 11pm Fri & Sat; Ⓜ Lombard South) Ranked one of the best ice creameries in the *world,* Big Gay Ice Cream is not a Philly original (it's NYC-based), but who can resist the lure of its signature 'Salty Pimp' cone: vanil-

la, dulce de leche and a chocolate shell. The descriptions are as double-entendre-filled as the cones are good, so prepare for chuckles as you peruse the menu.

Luke's Lobster
SEAFOOD $

(Map p170; 📞 215-564-1415; www.lukeslobster. com; 130 S 17th St; lobster roll $16.50; ◷ 11am-9pm Sun-Thu, to 10pm Fri & Sat) As one diner put it, 'Lobster roll. Drop mic.' Part of a casual East Coast mini-chain serving authentic tastes of Maine using sustainably sourced seafood. Wash down your buttered-bun lobster roll with a wild-blueberry soda.

Tom's Dim Sum
CHINESE $

(Map p170; 📞 215-923-8880; www.tomsdimsumpa. com; 59 N 11th St; mains $8-12; ◷ 11am-10:30pm, to 11pm Fri-Sun) Tasty buns and soup dumplings in a casual spot near the bus station.

Zahav
MIDDLE EASTERN $$

(Map p174; 📞 215-625-8800; www.zahavrestau rant.com; 237 St James Pl, off Dock St; mains $15, tasting menus $45-54; ◷ 5-10pm Sun-Thu, to 11pm Fri & Sat) Sophisticated 'modern Israeli' cuisine, drawing primarily from North African, Persian and Levantine kitchens. Pick your own mezze and grills, or go for the Mesibah ('Party Time') tasting menu. In a slightly incongruous building on Society Hill Towers grounds. No reservations accepted.

White Dog Cafe
AMERICAN $$

(📞 215-386-9224; www.whitedog.com; 3420 Sansom St; dinner mains $18-29; ◷ 11:30am-9:30pm Mon-Fri, 10am-10pm Sat, 10am-9pm Sun) If the dozen Boston terriers on the wall seem incongruous with the food, don't worry: this place has been serving farm-to-table since 1983. Come here for your truffles and artisan cheeses, peak summer tomatoes and plenty more. Yes, the Greyhound is the signature drink. Need you have asked?

LOCAL KNOWLEDGE

CLASSIC PHILLY FLAVOUR

Philadelphians argue over the nuances of cheesesteaks – hot sandwiches of thin-sliced, griddle-cooked beef on a chewy roll – like biblical scholars parsing Deuteronomy. What a visitor most needs to know is how to order. First say the kind of cheese – prov (provolone), American (melty yellow) or whiz (molten orange Cheez Whiz) then wit (with) or widdout (without), referring to fried onions: 'Prov wit,' for instance, or 'whiz widdout.'

Pat's King of Steaks (☏215-468-1546; www.patskingofsteaks.com; 1237 E Passyunk Ave; sandwiches $8; ⊙24hr) Pat's invented the cheesesteak, way back in 1930.

Jim's Steaks (Map p170; ☏215-928-1911; www.jimssouthstreet.com; 400 South St; sandwiches $10; ⊙10am-1am, to 3am Fri & Sat, from 11am Sun) 'Pizza steak' – topped with tomato sauce – is an option, as are hoagies (cold-cut sandwiches on long rolls). More comfortable than most, with indoor seats and beer.

Tony Luke's (☏215-551-5725; www.tonylukes.com; 39 E Oregon Ave; sandwiches $7-11; ⊙6am-midnight Mon-Thu, to 2am Fri & Sat, 11am-8pm Sun) Famous for its roast pork sandwich with provolone and broccoli rabe (a slightly bitter leafy, cruciferous vegetable also known as rapini). A veggie-only version is great too.

John's Roast Pork (☏215-463-1951; www.johnsroastpork.com; 14 E Snyder Ave; sandwiches $8-12; ⊙9am-7pm Mon-Sat) Located far south of the city next to a factory, this classic, cash-only joint has been on this corner since 1930.

★**Cuba Libre** CARIBBEAN $$
(Map p174; ☏215-627-0666; www.cubalibrerestaurant.com; 10 S 2nd St; mains $15-24; ⊙11:30am-10pm Mon-Wed, 11:30am-11pm Thu, 11:30am-2am Fri, 10:30am-2am Sat, 10am-2am Sun) Colonial America couldn't feel further away at this festive, multistory Cuban eatery and rum bar. The creative and inspired menu includes shrimp ceviche, Cuban sandwiches, guava-spiced barbecue and excellent mojitos. A $43 tasting menu lets you get a variety of the specialties – it's not per person, so you can share. The check even comes in a cigar box.

Baril FRENCH $$$
(Map p170; ☏267-687-2608; www.barilphilly.com; 267 S 19th St; mains from $25, prix fixe $35; ⊙4pm-2am Tue-Fri, from 10:30am Sat & Sun) This Rittenhouse Sq dining option has lovely *haute* French fare, creatively presented in a rustic, wood-heavy setting. Do not miss the chance to choose from the cheese cart, and the owner or staff will happily suggest a perfect wine. Handcrafted cocktails are sublime.

★**Morimoto** JAPANESE $$$
(Map p170; ☏215-413-9070; www.morimotorestaurant.com; 723 Chestnut St; mains $30; ⊙11:30am-2pm, 5-10pm Mon-Thu, to midnight Fri & Sat, 5-10pm Sun) Morimoto is high-concept and heavily stylized, from a dining room that looks like a futuristic aquarium to a menu of globe-spanning influence and eclectic combinations. A meal at this *Iron Chef* regular's restaurant is a theatrical experience. If price isn't a problem, opt for the *omakase* – the chef's special.

★**Gran Caffè L'Aquila** ITALIAN $$$
(Map p170; ☏215-568-5600; http://grancaffelaquila.com; 1716 Chestnut St; mains $18-30; ⊙7am-10pm Mon-Thu, 7am-11pm Fri, 8am-11pm Sat, 8am-10pm Sun, bar open 1 hr later) Mamma mia, this is impressive Italian food. Not only are the flavors everything you could ask for, one of the owners is an award-winning gelato maker and the 2nd floor has its own gelato factory. Some of the main courses even have savory gelato as a garnish. Coffee is house-roasted and the dapper waitstaff are eager to please.

The three co-owners came here after their village in Italy was destroyed by a 2014 earthquake. Reservations are highly recommended if you want to avoid a line..

🍷 **Drinking & Nightlife**

1 Tippling Place BAR
(Map p170; ☏215-665-0456; http://1tpl.com; 2006 Chestnut St; cocktails $8-15; ⊙5pm-2am Tue-Sun) Whether you pull up a seat at the bar or find a cozy couch to relax on, this spot has everything you could want in a craft cocktail bar. Extra points if you can spot more than

four typos on the menu. Note: be aware this place looks closed even when it isn't, with minimal (read: zero) outdoor signage.

★ Monk's Cafe   BAR
(Map p170; ☎215-545-7005; www.monkscafe. com; 264 S 16th St; ⊙11:30am-2am, kitchen to 1am) Hop fans crowd this mellow, wood-paneled place for Belgian and American craft beers on tap. There's also a reasonably priced food menu, with typical mussels-and-fries as well as a daily vegan special. For those needing assistance with the selection, a 'Beer Bible' is available.

R2L Restaurant   LOUNGE
(Map p170; ☎215-564-5337; https://r2lrestau rant.com; 50 S 16th St; cocktails $15; ⊙lounge 4pm-1am Mon-Thu, 4pm-2am Fri-Sat, 4-11pm Sun) The view, the view, the view. And did we mention the view? This spot serves up the nightscape of Philly along with whatever is on the menu. Craft cocktails are smooth and balanced, but even tap water would seem ritzy when you're looking out at the cosmos of lights below you. Come here for that special event with that special someone.

★ Trestle Inn   BAR
(Map p170; ☎267-239-0290; www.thetrestleinn. com; 339 N 11th St; ⊙5pm-1am Wed-Thu, 5pm-2am Fri & Sat) On a dark corner in the so-called 'Eraserhood' (the semi-industrial zone where director David Lynch found inspiration for his film *Eraserhead*), this classed-up old dive has craft cocktails and go-go dancers.

Double Knot   BAR
(Map p170; ☎215-631-3868; www.double knotphilly.com; 120 S 13th St; cocktails $10-15; ⊙7am-midnight) Japanese-inspired, this is one of the few places in Philly that serves sake properly (poured into an overflowing cup inside a wooden *masu* container). Double Knot also makes great craft cocktails and has a delicious food menu as well. It's crowded, but the stylish modern decor and friendly service make it a fun spot to grab a bite and late-night drink or two.

Tavern on Camac   GAY & LESBIAN
(Map p170; ☎215-545-0900; www.tavernonca mac.com; 243 S Camac St; ⊙piano bar 4pm-2am, restaurant 6pm-1am Wed-Mon, club 9pm-2am Tue-Sun) One of the longest-established gay bars in Philly, with a piano bar and restaurant downstairs. Upstairs is a small club with a dance floor, called Ascend; Wednesday is

ladies' night, Friday and Saturday have DJs. And don't overlook Showtune Sunday.

Dirty Franks   BAR
(Map p170; ☎215-732-5010; www.dirtyfranksbar. com; 347 S 13th St; DF special $2.50; ⊙11am-2am) The regulars at this place call it an 'institution' with some irony. Like many Philly dives, it offers the 'citywide special,' a shot of Jim Beam and a can of PBR for $2.50. Need cheaper? Try the 'DF Shelf of Shame' for just two bucks!

☆ Entertainment

PhilaMOCA   PERFORMING ARTS
(Philadelphia Mausoleum of Contemporary Art; Map p170; ☎267-519-9651; www.philamoca.org; 531 N 12th St) A former tombstone store, then producer Diplo's studios, this eclectic space now hosts movies, live shows, art, comedy and more.

Wanamaker Organ   LIVE MUSIC
(Macy's; Map p170; ☎484-684 7250; www.wan amakerorgan.com; 1300 Market St; ⊙concerts noon Mon-Sat, also 5:30pm Mon, Tue, Thu & Sat, 7pm Wed & Fri) Back when Macy's was Wanamaker's, owner John Wanamaker installed this enormous pipe organ in 1909, with free concerts to delight shoppers and make them linger. The tradition lives on, with classical and pop tunes filling the department store's central atrium a couple of times a day. The store staff are less than enthusiastic, but it's a treat for visitors.

Johnny Brenda's   LIVE MUSIC
(☎215-739-9684; www.johnnybrendas.com; 1201 N Frankford Ave; tickets $10-15; ⊙kitchen 11am-1am, showtimes vary; Ⓜ Girard) The hub of Fishtown/Northern Liberties' indie-rock scene, this is a great small venue with a balcony, plus a solid restaurant and bar with equally indie-minded beers.

🛍 Shopping

AIA Bookstore & Design Center   BOOKS
(Map p170; ☎215-569-3188; www.aiabookstore. com; 1218 Arch St; ⊙10am-6pm Mon-Sat, noon-5pm Sun) Run by the American Institute of Architects, this bookstore has creative children's toys, such as building-related Lego sets and other unusual design-related gifts. Books about architecture, too as if that's not obvious.

Omoi Zakka Shop   FASHION & ACCESSORIES
(Map p170; ☎215-545-0963; http://omoionline. com; 1608 Pine St; ⊙noon-7pm Mon, 11am-7pm

Tue-Sat, noon-6pm Sun) Get your inner Japanophile on with this shop dedicated to all things Japanese. Fashion items, books, clothes, housewares, stationery and more, all with a Japan-inspired sense for cuteness or good design.

Shane Confectionery   FOOD & DRINKS
(Map p174; ☑ 215-922-1048; www.shanecandies. com; 110 Market St; ⏱ 11am-8pm, to 10pm Fri & Sat) This wonderfully old-school candy shop makes beautiful treats from antique molds, and there's even a historic hot-chocolate operation in the back.

❶ Information

Independence Visitor Center (Map p174; ☑ 800-537-7676; www.phlvisitorcenter.com; 599 Market St; ⏱ 8:30am-6pm Sep-May, 8:30am-7pm Jun-Aug) Run by the Independence Visitor Center Corps and the National Park Service, the center covers the national park and all of the sights in Philadelphia.
Sister Cities Park Visitor Center (Map p170; ☑ 267-514-4760; www.phlvisitorcenter.com; 200 N 18th St; ⏱ 9:30am-5:30pm Mon-Sat, to 5pm Sun May-Sep) Near the fountain at Logan Sq, this seasonal visitor center sells tickets and gives info on city attractions.

❶ Getting There & Away

AIR
Philadelphia International Airport (PHL; ☑ 215-937-6937; www.phl.org; 8000 Essington Ave; 🚊 Airport Line), 10 miles southwest of Center City, is a hub for American Airlines, and served by direct international flights.

BUS
Greyhound (www.greyhound.com), Peter Pan Bus Lines (www.peterpanbus.com) and NJ Transit (www.njtransit.com) all depart from the **central bus station** (Map p170; 1001 Filbert St) downtown, near the convention center; Greyhound goes nationwide, Peter Pan focuses on the northeast and NJ Transit gets you to New Jersey. The former two offer cheaper online fares; Greyhound to Washington, DC, for example, can be $16 (3½ hours).

From near 30th St Station, **Megabus** (Map p170; http://us.megabus.com; JFK Blvd & N 30th St) serves major cities in the northeast, and Toronto. For NYC and Boston, Greyhound subsidiary **Bolt Bus** (Map p170; ☑ 877-265-8287; www.boltbus.com; JFK Blvd & N 30th St) has the roomiest buses; fares to NYC (2½ hours) can be as low as $9 when booked online.

CAR & MOTORCYCLE
From the north and south, I-95 (Delaware Expwy) follows the east edge of the city along the Delaware River, with several exits for Center City. In the north of the city, I-276 (Pennsylvania Turnpike) runs east over the river to connect with the New Jersey Turnpike.

TRAIN
Just west of downtown across the Schuylkill, beautiful neoclassical **30th St Station** (www. amtrak.com; 2955 Market St) is a major hub. From here, Amtrak provides service on its Northeast Corridor line to New York City ($56 to $190, one to 1½ hours) and Boston ($130 to $386, five to 5¾ hours), and Washington, DC ($56 to $216, two hours), as well as to Lancaster ($20 to $40, one hour) and Pittsburgh (from $64, 7½ hours).

A slower but cheaper way to get to NYC is on regional SEPTA (www.septa.org) to Trenton ($9, 50 minutes), then NJ Transit (www.njtransit. com) to NYC's Penn Station ($16.75, 1½ hours).

❶ Getting Around

SEPTA (www.septa.org) operates Philadelphia's transit system, including the Airport Line train ($8, 25 minutes, every 30 minutes), which stops in University City and Center City. A taxi to the center costs a flat fare of $28.50. There's also a one-day Independence Pass (individual/family $12/29) that offers unlimited rides on all buses, rail and subways, including the Airport Line.

Downtown, it's barely 2 miles between the Delaware and the Schuylkill, so you can walk most places. To rest your feet or travel further afield, choose from a web of SEPTA buses, two subway lines and a trolley (fare $2.25). Purchase the stored-value Key card for discounted fares. Market St is the main artery – hop on buses here to cross the center, or go underground to take the trolley to University City. In high tourist seasons, the purple Phlash (www.ridephillyphlash.com) bus makes a loop around major tourist sites. It's $2 a ride or $5 for a day pass; pay on board.

Philly's bike-share system is Indego (www. rideindego.com). Walk-up rates are $4 for 30 minutes; a 30-day membership is a steal at $15, but you must order the key ahead of time.

Cabs, especially around Center City, are easy to hail. The flag drop or fare upon entry is $2.70, then $2.30 per mile or portion thereof. All licensed taxis have GPS and most accept credit cards. Uber and Lyft also operate here.

Pennsylvania Dutch Country

Lancaster County and the broader area roughly between Reading and the Susquehanna River is the center of the so-called

Pennsylvania Dutch community. These are myriad religious orders and cultures, with Germanic roots and established here since the 18th century. Amish, Mennonites and German Baptist (Brethren) are the best known. One common cultural thread: all are devoted to various degrees of low-tech plain living.

Somewhat paradoxically, this simple life, with its picturesque horse-drawn buggies, and ox teams tilling fields, attracts busloads of visitors and has spawned an astoundingly kitschy tourist industry. If you get onto the back roads, however, you can appreciate the quiet these religious orders have preserved.

Small settlements in the area include teeny Christiana and train-mad Strasburg. Lititz is home to Wilbur Chocolates (what locals prefer to Hershey's), and America's first pretzel factory, Sturgis. Ephrata is the headquarters of Ten Thousand Villages, a massive Mennonite-run fair-trade imports store with branches all over.

◉ Sights

★ Railroad Museum of Pennsylvania
MUSEUM

(☏717-687-8628; www.rrmuseumpa.org; 300 Gap Rd, Ronks; adult/child $10/8; ⊙9am-5pm Mon-Sat, noon-5pm Sun Apr-Oct, closed Mon Nov-Mar; ⚑) Set over nearly 18 acres, the Railroad Museum of Pennsylvania has 100 gigantic mechanical marvels to climb around and admire. Combo tickets are available for the **Strasburg Railroad** (☏866-725-9666; www.strasburg railroad.com; 301 Gap Rd, Ronks; coach class adult/child $15/8; ⊙times vary; ⚑) across the road.

★ National Toy Train Museum
MUSEUM

(☏717-687-8976; www.nttmuseum.org; 300 Paradise Lane, Ronks; adult/child $7/4; ⊙10am-5pm May-Oct, hours vary Nov-Apr; ⚑) The push-button interactive dioramas are so up-to-date and clever (such as a 'drive-in movie' that's a live video of kids working the trains), and the walls are packed with so many gleaming railcars, that you can't help but feel a bit of that childlike Christmas-morning wonder.

Even if you're not a guest, you can stop at the **Red Caboose Motel** (☏717-687-5000; www.redcaboosemotel.com; 312 Paradise Lane, Ronks; s/d from $95/130; ❄⚑) next door to the museum – you can climb the silo in back for wonderful views (50¢) and kids can enjoy a small petting zoo.

Landis Valley Museum
MUSEUM

(☏717-569-0401; www.landisvalleymuseum.org; 2451 Kissel Hill Rd; adult/child $12/8; ⊙9am-5pm Tue-Sat, noon-5pm Sun Mar-Dec, reduced hours Jan & Feb) Based on an 18th-century village, this open-air museum is the best way to get an overview of early PA Dutch culture, and Mennonites in particular. Costumed staff are on hand to demonstrate tin-smithing, for instance, and there's a tavern, a gun shop and a beautiful crafts exhibit.

🛏 Sleeping & Eating

Cork Factory
BOUTIQUE HOTEL $$

(☏717-735-2075; www.corkfactoryhotel.com; 480 New Holland Ave, Suite 3000; r from $190; P❄❄❄) An abandoned brick behemoth now houses this stylish hotel, with 93 posh rooms. It's a short drive from downtown.

★ Maison
EUROPEAN $$$

(☏717-293-5060; www.maisonlancaster.com; 230 N Prince St; mains $26-30; ⊙5-11pm Wed-Sat; ⚑) A husband-and-wife team runs this homey but meticulous place downtown, giving local farm products a rustic Italian-French treatment: pork braised in milk, housemade rabbit sausage, fried squash blossoms or handmade gnocchi, depending on the season.

★ Lancaster Brewing Co
PUB FOOD $$

(☏717-391-6258; www.lancasterbrewing.com; 302 N Plum St; mains $16-24; ⊙11:30am-9:30pm; ⚑) This brewery, established in 1995, is a local favorite. The restaurant serves hearty but sophisticated food – lamb chops with tzatziki, say – and housemade sausages at tables with copper-clad tops and great views of the brewing tanks. You can't beat specials such as $5 all-you-can-eat wings and $6 beer-tasting flights.

❶ Getting There & Away

Lancaster lies at the heart of a squished 'H' shape made by Rte 30, Rte 283 and Rte 222. Buses head to Philly and Pittsburgh, but driving your own vehicle is the best option for sightseeing. Head east from Lancaster on Rte 30 to reach Strasburg.

Pennsylvania Wilds

North-central Pennsylvania, known as 'the Wilds,' is largely deep forest, with an occasional regal building or grand mansion, remnants of a time when lumber, coal and oil brought wealth to this now little-visited patch of the state. Several museums (in **Titusville**, **Bradford** and **Galeton**) tell the boom and bust story. Since the bust, this swath of 12 counties has reverted to its wild state; much of the area is national forest or state park land.

Scenic Rte 6 cuts through east–west, with the tiny college town of **Mansfield** as an eastern gateway. Just west of here, **Pine Creek Gorge** cuts south; its deeper end (1450ft) is down near Waterville, but it's more accessible, with good views and trails along the rim and down into the canyon, on the north end at **Colton Point State Park** (www.visitpaparks.com; 927 Colton Rd, Wellsboro; ⊙dawn-dusk). Follow signs outside the pretty, gas-lamp-lit town of **Wellsboro**.

◉ Sights

★ Cherry Springs State Park   STATE PARK
(☑814-435-5011; http://dcnr.state.pa.us; 4639 Cherry Springs Rd, Coudersport; ⊙24hr) Considered one of the best places for stargazing east of the Mississippi, this mountaintop state park seems to have plenty of space, but be sure to book well ahead in July and August, when the Milky Way is almost directly overhead. First-timers will need to pay a one-time $5 additional fee (not per day).

Leonard Harrison State Park   STATE PARK
(☑570-724-3061; www.visitpaparks.com; 4797 Rte 660, Wellsboro; ⊙park dawn-dusk, visitor center 10am-4:30pm Mon-Thu, to 6:30pm Fri-Sun) This park has full views of the Pine Creek Gorge, aka the Grand Canyon of PA, with trails that descend 800ft down to the creek below. A visitor center has modest displays of local fauna, there are toilets, and a viewing deck makes this side more accessible for people not planning to hike. For the undeveloped side go to Colton Point State Park instead.

★ Kinzua Bridge Skywalk   BRIDGE
(☑814-778-5467; www.visitpaparks.com; 1721 Lindholm Rd, Mt Jewett; ⊙skywalk 8am-dusk, visitor center 8am-6pm) FREE The world's tallest viaduct when it was built in 1882, this 301ft-high bridge was rebuilt in steel in 1900 – but then partially collapsed in 2003, when it was hit by an F-1 tornado. The remaining piece, jutting out into the air, is now an observation deck, with an impressive and perhaps unnerving view over the ruined steel piers into the valley below.

🛏 Sleeping & Eating

Mansfield Inn   MOTEL $
(☑570-662-2136; www.mansfieldinn.com; 26 S Main St, Mansfield; r from $70; P❄✳🛜) There may be more charming B&Bs deeper in the PA Wilds, but this well-maintained 24-room motel is hard to beat for straight-ahead value.

★ Night & Day Coffee Cafe   CAFE $
(☑570-662-1143; http://nightanddaycoffee.wixsite.com/cafe; 2 N Main St, Mansfield; sandwiches $7-10; ⊙7am-7pm Mon-Fri, to 5pm Sat, 8am-5pm Sun; 🖉) Well worth detouring for, the Night & Day Coffee Cafe proudly claims to be enriching the neighborhood one latte at a time, and it's doing a good job of it. Boutique coffees, great chai, and a wide selection of specialty salads and sandwiches make for a perfect breakfast or a great lunch.

Pittsburgh

Set between the Monongahela and Allegheny Rivers and a mountain ridge called Mt Washington, Pittsburgh has a unique character that is evident from the moment you arrive. Juxtaposed with the rumbling freight trains and the iconic bridges are the *Bladerunner*-esque self-driving Uber vehicles, scanning the roads with spinning Lidar scanners. Experiencing periods of boom and bust since its founding, the city is in a boom now (real estate that used to sell for $30,000 now goes for $300,000), and it's a fun place to visit, with top-notch museums, great gardens and parks, and amazing food, from humble to haute. Indeed, the once-struggling city has rediscovered itself as a food and brew mecca.

Carnegie is the biggest name in Pittsburgh – Scottish-born Andrew modernized steel production, and his legacy is still synonymous with the city and its many cultural and educational institutions. Second-biggest: Heinz, of ketchup fame, a company established here in 1869.

◉ Sights & Activities

Points of interest in Pittsburgh are scattered in every neighborhood, and because of the hills, it's difficult to walk between them. Bike, taxi or bus (or light rail in some areas) are the best ways to span suburbs. You can also try your hand at e-reserving one of those futuristic, self-driving Ubers.

★ **Andy Warhol Museum** MUSEUM
(☎412-237-8300; www.warhol.org; 117 Sandusky St; adult/child $20/10, 5-10pm Fri $10/5; ⊙10am-5pm Tue-Thu, Sat & Sun, to 10pm Fri) This six-story museum celebrates Pittsburgh's coolest native son, who moved to NYC, got a nose job and made himself famous with pop art. The exhibits start with Warhol's earliest drawings and commercial illustrations, and include a simulated Velvet Underground happening, a DIY 'screen test' and pieces of Warhol's extensive knickknack collection. Cans of inflatable Campbell's soup are for sale.

★ **Duquesne Incline** FUNICULAR
(☎412-381-1665; www.duquesneincline.org; one way adult/child $2.50/1.25; ⊙5:30am-12:45am Mon-Sat, 7am-12:45am Sun) This nifty funicular, and its **Monongahela Incline** (5 Grandview Ave; one way adult/child $2.50/1.25; ⊙5:30am-12:45am Mon-Sat, 7am-12:45am Sun) twin down the road, both built in the late 19th century, are Pittsburgh icons, zipping up the steep slope of Mt Washington every five to 10 minutes. They provide commuters a quick connection, and give visitors great city views, especially at night. You can make a loop, going up one, walking along aptly named Grandview Ave (about 1 mile, or take bus 40) and coming down the other.

If you ride just one, make it the Duquesne (du-*kane*). At the top, you can pay 50¢ to see the gears and cables at work.

Frick Art & Historical Center MUSEUM
(☎412-371-0600; www.thefrickpittsburgh.org; 7227 Reynolds St; ⊙10am-5pm Tue-Thu, Sat & Sun, to 9pm Fri) FREE Henry Clay Frick, of Manhattan's Frick Museum fame, built his steel fortune in Pittsburgh. This Frick shows a small art collection (including beautiful medieval icons), plus his cars. For more art and general splendor, join a tour (adult/child $12/6) of Clayton, the family mansion. The cafe here is excellent; reserve ahead.

Carnegie Museums MUSEUM
(☎412-622-3131; www.carnegiemuseums.org; 4400 Forbes Ave; adult/child both museums $20/12; ⊙10am-5pm Mon & Wed-Sat, noon-5pm Sun; 🅰) Founded in 1895, these neighboring institutions are both tremendous troves of knowledge. The **Carnegie Museum of Art** has European treasures and an excellent architectural collection, while the **Carnegie Museum of Natural History** features a complete Tyrannosaurus Rex skeleton and beautiful old dioramas.

Cathedral of Learning TOWER
(☎412-624-6001; www.tour.pitt.edu; 4200 Fifth Ave; ⊙9am-4pm Mon-Sat, 11am-4pm Sun) FREE Soaring 42 stories, this Gothic tower at the center of the University of Pittsburgh is a city landmark. Visit to see the delightful Nationality Rooms, themed classrooms ranging from Russian to Syrian to African. Audio tours are available on Saturdays and Sundays (adult/child $4/2).

Center for PostNatural History MUSEUM
(☎412-223-7698; www.postnatural.org; 4913 Penn Ave; admission by donation; ⊙noon-4pm Sun) FREE 'Postnatural history,' according to the artist founder of this quirky museum, is the field of plants and animals designed by humankind. Learn all about spider-silk-making goats, selective breeding and more. Probably not your best first date spot, but definitely a fun and unconventional place to learn about all things *human*-ipulated.

Pittsburgh Glass Center ART
(☎412-365-2145; www.pittsburghglasscenter.org; 5472 Penn Ave; ⊙10am-7pm Mon-Thu, to 4pm Fri-Sun) See a variety of glass-making techniques and even try your hand at making something yourself in a demo. Or take an actual class; the PGC offers everything from newbie-level to advanced (prices vary).

'Burgh Bits & Bites FOOD & DRINK
(☎412-901-7150; www.burghfoodtour.com; tours $42) These two-hour food tours through various neighborhoods are a fun way to discover the city's unique ethnic eats. The Strip District tour is the most popular, but Bits & Bites also visits Bloomfield, Brookline, Lawrenceville, South Side and more.

Pittsburgh History & Landmarks Foundation WALKING
(☎412-471-5808; www.phlf.org; tours free-$20) This group runs a free walking tour from Market Sq on Fridays at noon, among other excursions.

🛏 Sleeping

Residence Inn by Marriott North Shore HOTEL $$
(☎855-239-9485; www.marriott.com; 574 W General Robinson St; d/ste from $190/225; 🅿 ❂ ✳ @ 🛜 ☒) This newly renovated chain-hotel option has a pool, a fitness center, free breakfasts, and rooms that feel like

mansions. It's also well located: a quick zip over the bridges to the downtown, or within walking distance of some of the North Side areas and attractions. Note that it can be a zoo if there's a game at Heinz Field or the Pirates are playing.

★ **Priory Hotel** INN $$
(☑ 412-231-3338; www.thepriory.com; 614 Pressley St; s/d/ste from $115/210/270; P✱✿) The monks had it good when this was still a Catholic monastery: spacious rooms, high ceilings, a fireplace in the parlor. Breakfast, with its pastries and cold cuts, is reminiscent of a European hostel. It's on the North Side, in the historic-but-scruffy Deutschtown area. The tiny **Monk's Bar** just off the lobby is open 5pm to 11pm daily, perfect for an evening tipple.

★ **Omni William Penn Hotel** HOTEL $$$
(☑ 412-281-7100; www.omnihotels.com; 530 William Penn Pl; r $215-540; P✿✱✿) Pittsburgh's stateliest old hotel, built by Henry Frick, has a cavernous lobby, with luxury suites that were remodeled in 2016. The great public spaces give it a sense of grandeur that some luxury hotels lack. Worth booking if you have the money...or can find it at a discount.

✖ Eating

E Carson St on the South Side has the highest concentration of restaurants, but the Strip District comes a close second. As in many categories, Lawrenceville has the most up-and-coming activity. Catering to a large Catholic population, many Pittsburgh restaurants serve fish on Fridays, and fried-fish sandwiches are especially popular – despite the city's lack of coastline, they're pretty tasty too!

Pittsburgh Public Market MARKET
(☑ 412-281-4505; www.pittsburghpublicmarket. org; 2401 Penn Ave; ◷10am-4pm Wed-Fri & Sun, 9am-5pm Sat) This giant indoor market caters to the need for downtown to have easy access to fresh produce, meats, cheeses and other local products. Note that many vendors are also open on Monday and Tuesday as well.

Conflict Kitchen FAST FOOD $
(☑ 412-802-8417; www.conflictkitchen.org; 221 Schenley Dr; mains $8-14; ◷11am-6pm Mon-Sat) This takeout stand near the Cathedral of Learning reinvents itself periodically, cooking food from a country the USA has issues

with. So far it has represented Afghani, Palestinian, Cuban and Native American cuisines, among other options.

★ **La Prima** CAFE $
(☑ 412-281-1922; www.laprima.com; 205 21st St; pastries $2-4; ◷6am-4pm Mon-Wed, to 7pm Thu, to 5pm Fri & Sat, 7am-4pm Sun) Great Italian coffee and pastries have people lined up out the door at peak times. The 'Almond Mele' is the scrumptious signature sweet, but it has a range of other yummy treats (*sfogliatelle*, tarts, cookies etc). If you speak Italian you can enjoy the daily quote, written on the green chalkboard each morning.

Zenith VEGAN $
(☑ 412-481-4833; www.zenithpgh.com; 86 S 26th St; mains $7-10; ◷11:30am-8:30pm Thu-Sat, 11am-2:30pm Sun; ✿) All meals are vegan here, though cheese is optional. Eating here is like eating in an antique shop, as everything, including the Formica tables, is for sale. The buffet Sunday brunch ($11.50) draws a great community of regulars.

★ **Bar Marco** ITALIAN $$
(☑ 412-471-1900; www.barmarcopgh.com; 2216 Penn Ave; mains $15-26; ◷5-11pm Tue-Fri, 10am-3pm & 5-11pm Sat & Sun) A Strip District favorite, this is one of the city's more sophisticated kitchens, with an excellent brunch, too. Cocktails are unique, or try the bartender's suggestion based on what types of drinks you enjoy. The refreshing no-tipping policy means the staff are appropriately compensated in a fair and equitable way.

Legume FUSION $$$
(☑ 412-621-2700; www.legumebistro.com; mains $23-36, 3-course tasting menu $38; ◷4:30pm-midnight Mon-Sat) Excellent meats and fish here, with a farm-to-table mindset and a menu that changes daily. If it's available, try the stinging-nettle soup – partly because where else can you try stinging nettles, but mostly because it's out of this world.

★ **Paris 66** FRENCH $$$
(☑ 412-404-8166; www.paris66bistro.com; 6018 Centre Ave; dinner mains $26-33; ◷11am-10pm Mon-Thu, to 11pm Fri & Sat, 10am-3pm Sun) Don't think you can get away with saying *Merci* here and impressing the waitstaff; they all speak fluent *français*. This is top-end French at its best, in a cozy, bistro-style setting. Blink and you'll think you're in France.

🍷 Drinking & Entertainment

Church Brew Works MICROBREWERY
(☑ 412-688-8200; www.churchbrew.com; 3525 Liberty Ave; ☺ 11:30am-9pm Sun-Thu, to 11pm Fri & Sat) There are some who put drunkenness next to godliness, and they probably invented Church Brew Works. Gleaming and shining, giant brewery vats sit in what was once the pulpit. If you think this is sacrilegious, you'll want to skip this place. Although, of course, many a great Belgian beer was proudly brewed by highly religious monks.

Wigle Whiskey DISTILLERY
(☑ 412-224-2827; www.wiglewhiskey.com; 2401 Smallman St; tours from $25; ☺ 11am-6pm Mon, 10am-6pm Tue-Sat, to 4pm Sun) This family-owned craft distillery in a brick warehouse in the Strip gives tours on Saturdays (and some Fridays) and has inexpensive sample flights ($10) of the many libations. Whiskey is a top choice, but there's also gin, vodka, bitters and even a housemade absinthe.

Spice Island Tea House TEAHOUSE
(☑ 412-687-8821; www.spiceislandteahouse.com; 253 Atwood St; ☺ 11:30am-8:45pm Mon-Thu, to 9:45pm Fri & Sat) If you fancy sipping a quiet cuppa (tea infusions $3.50 to $5.50) while your friend has a cocktail, this is the spot to come. Alongside a number of delectable teas it also serves Southeast Asian fusion food.

★ **Allegheny Wine Mixer** WINE BAR
(☑ 412-252-2337; www.alleghenywinemixer.com; 5326 Butler St; ☺ 5pm-midnight Tue-Thu, to 1am Fri-Sun) All the perks of a high-end wine bar – great list, smart staff, tasty nibbles – in the comfort of a neighborhood dive.

Rex Theater LIVE MUSIC
(☑ 412-381-6811; www.rextheatre.com; 1602 E Carson St) A converted movie theater, this South Side favorite hosts touring jazz, rock and indie bands.

★ **Elks Lodge** LIVE MUSIC
(☑ 412-321-1834; www.elks.org; 400 Cedar Ave; cover $5; ☺ bluegrass 8pm Wed, big band 7pm 1st & 3rd Thu) Find out why Pittsburgh is known as the Paris of Appalachia at the Elks' Banjo Night, when the stage is packed with players and the audience sings along to all the bluegrass classics. Also hosts a big-band night twice a month, with dance classes first. On the North Side in Deutschtown.

ℹ️ Information

VisitPITTSBURGH Main Branch (☑ 412-281-7711; www.visitpittsburgh.com; 120 Fifth Ave, Suite 2800; ☺ 8:30am-4:40pm Mon-Fri) Publishes the *Official Visitors Guide* and provides maps and tourist advice.

ℹ️ Getting There & Away

AIR
Pittsburgh International Airport (☑ 412-472-3525; www.flypittsburgh.com; 1000 Airport Blvd), 18 miles west of downtown, has direct connections to Europe, Canada and major US cities via a slew of airlines.

BUS
The **Greyhound bus station** (Grant Street Transportation Center; ☑ 412-392-6514; www.greyhound.com; 55 11th St), at the far edge of the Strip District, has frequent buses to Philadelphia (from $20, six to seven hours), NYC (from $30, 8½ to 11 hours) and Chicago, IL ($72, 11 to 14 hours).

CAR & MOTORCYCLE
Pittsburgh is accessible via I-76 or I-79 from the west and I-70 from the east. It's about a six-hour drive from NYC and about three hours from Buffalo.

TRAIN
Pittsburgh has a magnificent old train station – and **Amtrak** (☑ 800-872-7245; www.amtrak.com; 1100 Liberty Ave) drops you off in a dismal modern building behind it. Services run to Philadelphia (from $64, 7½ hours), NYC (from $97, 9½ hours), Chicago ($90, 10 hours) and Washington, DC ($52, eight hours).

ℹ️ Getting Around

PortAuthority (www.portauthority.org) provides public transport around Pittsburgh, including the 28X Airport Flyer ($2.75, 40 minutes, every 30 minutes 4:30am to midnight) from the airport to downtown and Oakland. A taxi from the airport costs about $40 (not including tip) to downtown. Various shuttles also make downtown runs for around $25 per person.

Driving in Pittsburgh can be frustrating – roads end with no warning or deposit you suddenly on bridges. Parking is scarce downtown. Where possible, use the extensive bus network, which includes a fast express busway (routes beginning with P). There is also a limited light-rail system, the T, useful for the South Side. Rides on the T downtown are free; other in-city fares are $2.50, and $1 for a transfer.

New England

Includes ➡

Massachusetts	185
Boston	185
Cape Cod	207
Nantucket	215
Martha's Vineyard	217
Rhode Island	223
Providence	224
Newport	226
Connecticut	230
Vermont	238
New Hampshire	249
Maine	256

Best Places to Eat

➡ TJ Buckley's (p240)

➡ Simon Pearce Restaurant (p243)

➡ Captain Daniel Packer Inne (p234)

➡ Row 34 (p201)

➡ birch (p225)

Best Places to Sleep

➡ Liberty Hotel (p200)

➡ Carpe Diem (p213)

➡ Attwater (p228)

➡ Hopkins Inn (p233)

➡ Ale House Inn (p250)

Why Go?

The history of New England is the history of America. It's the Pilgrims who came ashore at Plymouth Rock and the minutemen who fought for American independence. It's the ponderings of Ralph Waldo Emerson and the protests of Harriet Beecher Stowe. It's hundreds of years of poets and philosophers, progressive thinkers who dared to dream and dared to do. It is generations of immigrants who have shaped New England into the dynamic region that it is today.

For outdoor adventure, the region undulates with the rolling hills and rocky peaks of the ancient Appalachian Mountains. Plus, nearly 5000 miles of coastline make for unlimited opportunities for fishing, swimming, surfing and sailing. Those are surefire ways to work up an appetite. Fortunately, New England is a bounty of epicurean delights: pancakes drenched in maple syrup; just-picked fruit and sharp cheddar cheese; and – most importantly – sublimely fresh seafood that is the hallmark of this region.

When to Go
Boston

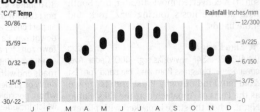

May–Jun Uncrowded sights and lightly trodden trails. Whale-watching begins.

Jul–Aug Top tourist season with summer festivals and warmer ocean weather.

Sep–Oct New England's blazing foliage peaks from mid-September to mid-October.

History

When the first European settlers arrived in the New World, they found about 100,000 Native American inhabitants, mostly Algonquians, organized into small regional tribes. The northern tribes were solely hunter-gatherers, while the southern tribes hunted and practiced slash-and-burn agriculture, growing corn, squash and beans.

In 1602 English Captain Bartholomew Gosnold landed at Cape Cod and sailed north to Maine; but it wasn't until 1614 that Captain John Smith, who charted the region's coastline for King James I, christened the land 'New England'. With the arrival of the Pilgrims at Plymouth in 1620, European settlement began in earnest. Over the next century the colonies expanded, often at the expense of the indigenous people.

Although subjects of the British Crown, New Englanders governed themselves with legislative councils and they came to view their affairs as separate from those of England. In the 1770s King George III imposed a series of taxes to pay for England's involvement in costly wars. The colonists, unrepresented in the British parliament, protested under the slogan 'no taxation without representation'. Attempts to squash the protests eventually led to battles at Lexington and Concord, setting off the War for Independence. The historic result was the birth of the USA in 1776.

Following independence, New England became an economic powerhouse, its harbors booming centers for shipbuilding and trade. New England's famed Yankee Clippers plied ports from China to South America. A thriving whaling industry brought unprecedented wealth to Nantucket and New Bedford. The USA's first water-powered cotton-spinning mill was established in Rhode Island in 1793. No boom lasts forever. By the early 20th century many of the mills had moved south. Today education, finance, biotechnology and tourism are linchpins of the regional economy.

ⓘ Resources

Visit New England (www.visitnewengland.com) Listings for events, sights, restaurants and hotels.

New England Guide (www.boston.com/travel/newengland) Travel tips and itineraries from the *Boston Globe*.

Lonely Planet (www.lonelyplanet.com/usa/new-england) Destination information, hotel bookings, traveler forum and more.

Appalachian Mountain Club (www.outdoors.org) Fantastic resource for hiking, biking, camping, climbing and paddling in New England's great outdoors.

New England Lighthouses (www.lighthouse.cc) A list of lighthouses by state.

MASSACHUSETTS

New England's most populous state, Massachusetts packs in appealing variety, from the sandy beaches of Cape Cod to college towns of the Pioneer Valley to the woodsy hills of the Berkshires. The state's rich history oozes from almost every quarter: discover the shoreline Plymouth, where the Pilgrims first settled in the New World; explore the battlefields in Lexington and Concord, where the first shots of the American Revolution rang out; and wander the cobbled streets and old ports of Salem, Nantucket and New Bedford, where whaling and merchant boats once docked. Modern-day Massachusetts is also diverse and dynamic. Boston is the state's undisputed cultural (and political) capital, but smaller towns like Provincetown and Northampton also offer lively art and music scenes, out and active queer populations and plenty of opportunities to enjoy the great outdoors.

ⓘ Information

Massachusetts Department of Conservation and Recreation (☑ 617-626-1250; www.mass.gov/dcr) Offers camping in 29 state parks.

Boston

Boston's history recalls revolution and transformation, and today it is still among the country's most forward-thinking and barrier-breaking cities.

The arts have thrived in Boston ever since the 19th century, when this cultural capital was dubbed the Athens of America. Certainly, the intellectual elite appreciated their fine paintings and classical music, but they were also dedicated to spreading the cultural wealth, establishing museums, libraries and symphony orchestras for all to enjoy. Today the lucky residents of (and visitors to) Boston benefit from their largesse. These venerable institutions play an integral role on Boston's cultural stage, which has significantly expanded to include dynamic contemporary art, music and theater scenes.

New England Highlights

1 Freedom Trail (p199) Following the footsteps of Colonial rabble-rousers in Boston.

2 Cape Cod National Seashore (p214) Romping across the dunes with the wind in your hair.

3 Nantucket Whaling Museum (p215) Contemplating the history of this 19th-century whaling capital.

4 Tanglewood Music Festival (p221) Listening to word-class music under the stars in Lenox.

5 Lincoln Woods Trail (p252) Taking a relaxing hike among brilliant fall foliage in the White Mountains.

6 Mad River Glen (p244) Anticipating

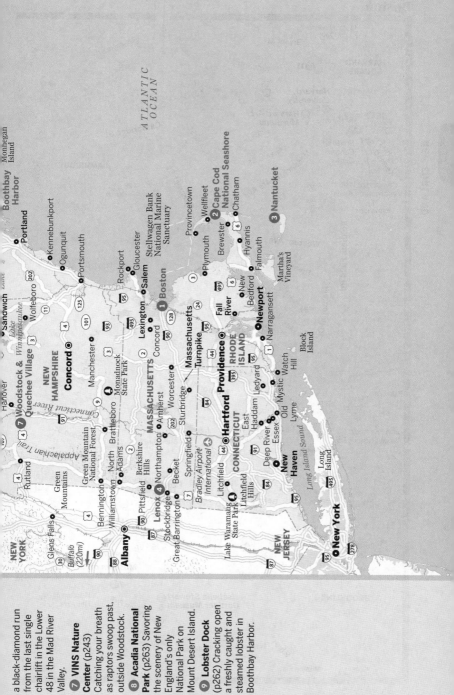

a black-diamond run
from the last single
chairlift in the Lower
48 in the Mad River
Valley.

**⑦ VINS Nature
Center** (p243)
Catching your breath
as raptors swoop past,
outside Woodstock.

**⑧ Acadia National
Park** (p263) Savoring
the scenery of New
England's only
National Park on
Mount Desert Island.

⑨ Lobster Dock
(p262) Cracking open
a freshly caught and
steamed lobster in
Boothbay Harbor.

Boston

Lizard Lounge
(0.1mi)

Bryant St

**HARVARD
SQUARE**

8 ⊞ 11

Kirkland St

Washington St

Chestnut St

15

**Harvard
University**
⊙ 5

Beacon St

Webster Ave

26 ⊙   ⊤ Harvard

⊞ **Harvard Art
4 Museums**

Cambridge St

CAMBRIDGE

ⓘ

Broadway

Fayette St

Fulkerson St

20
**Smith
Campus
Center**

Harvard St

Prospect St

Hampshire St

28 ⊞

*Cambridge Visitor
Information Kiosk*
The
Esplanade

Massachusetts Ave

Banks St

Franklin St

Norfolk St

Soldiers Field Rd

Western Ave

22 ⊗
⊤ Central

Washington St

Broadway

River St

William St

Main St

Memorial Dr

Perry St

⊞ 10

Ames St

Pleasant St

Albany St

Magazine St

Pearl St

Brookline St

Vassar St

Charles River

Granite St

Waverly St

Memorial Dr

Massachusetts Ave

Babcock
Street

Pleasant
Street ⊤

St Paul
Street

Essex St

Beacon St

*John F Kennedy
National Historic Site
(0.1mi)*

⊤ BU West

Commonwealth
Ave

BU Central

Blandford ⊤

Kenmore

Commonwealth Ave

32

Egmont St

BU East ⊤

21 ⊗

33 ⊙
Hynes ⊤

St Paul St

Ivy St

St Marys
Street

Lansdowne St

30

Babcock St

Parkman St

Hawes Street ⊤

**Beacon
St** ⊤

Monmouth St

⊤ Fenway

**Fenway
Park** ⊙ 3

Van Ness St

17 ⊤

25 ⊗

Boylston St

FENWAY

Westland Ave

9 ⊙

13

St Paul Street ⊤

Kent Street ⊤

Brookline Ave

19 ⊗

Jersey St

Kilmarnock St

31 ⊗   ⊞
Symphony

Coolidge Corner ⊤

Back
Bay
Fens

Longwood Ave

Stearns Rd

Longwood ⊤

**Museum of
Fine Arts**
7 ⊞

⊤
Northeastern

BROOKLINE

Aspinwall Ave

Riverway

**Isabella Stewart ⊞
Gardner Museum 6**

Huntington Ave

⊤ Longwood
Medical Area

⊤ Museum of
Fine Arts

⊤ Ruggles

Brookline
Village ⊤

Fenwood
Road ⊤

Mission Park ⊤

⊤ Brigham
Circle

ROXBURY

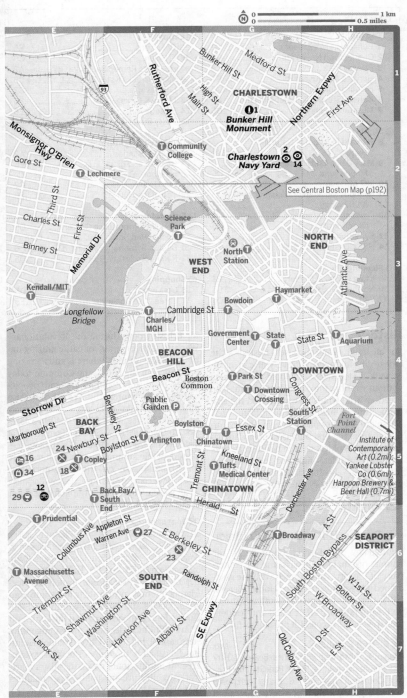

See Central Boston Map (p192)

N

0   1 km
0   0.5 miles

NEW ENGLAND

Medford St

Bunker Hill St

Northern Expwy

First Ave

CHARLESTOWN

High St

Main St

Rutherford Ave

Bunker Hill Monument ❶1

Charlestown Navy Yard 2 ⊚ 14 ⊚

Community College

93

Monsignor O'Brien Hwy

Gore St

Lechmere

Third St

Charles St

First St

Binney St

Memorial Dr

Kendall/MIT

Longfellow Bridge

Science Park

North Station

WEST END

Cambridge St

Charles/ MGH

BEACON HILL

Beacon St

NORTH END

Atlantic Ave

Bowdoin

Haymarket

Government Center

State

State St

Aquarium

Park St

Boston Common

DOWNTOWN

Downtown Crossing

Congress St

Public Garden P

Storrow Dr

Marlborough St

BACK BAY

Berkeley St

Boylston

Boylston St

Arlington

Essex St

South Station

Fort Point Channel

24 Newbury St

⊗16

⊗34

18 ⊗

Copley

Chinatown

Kneeland St

Tremont St

Tufts Medical Center

CHINATOWN

Dorchester Ave

Institute of Contemporary Art (0.2mi); Yankee Lobster Co (0.6mi); Harpoon Brewery & Beer Hall (0.7mi)

12

29 ⊡ ⊚

Back Bay/ South End

Herald   St

Prudential

Columbus Ave

Appleton St

Warren Ave ⊚27

E Berkeley St

23 ⊗

Broadway

SEAPORT DISTRICT

A St

Massachusetts Avenue

Tremont St

Shawmut Ave

Washington Ave

SOUTH END

Randolph St

Albany St

Harrison Ave

SE Expwy

South Boston Bypass

W Broadway

W 1st St

Bolton St

Lenox St

D St

E St

Old Colony Ave

Boston

◉ Top Sights
1 Bunker Hill Monument G1
2 Charlestown Navy Yard...................... G2
3 Fenway Park C5
4 Harvard Art Museums B2
5 Harvard University............................... A1
6 Isabella Stewart Gardner Museum....... C7
7 Museum of Fine Arts............................ C6

◉ Sights
8 Harvard Museum of Natural
     History A1
9 Mary Baker Eddy Library &
     Mapparium...................................... D6
10 MIT Museum.. C3
11 Peabody Museum of Archaeology
     & Ethnology.................................... B1
12 Prudential Center Skywalk
     Observatory.................................... E5
13 Symphony Hall.................................... D6
14 USS Constitution G2

⊜ Sleeping
15 Irving House at Harvard B1
16 Newbury Guest House E5
17 Verb Hotel C6

⊗ Eating
18 Courtyard.. E5
19 El Pelon... C6
20 Hokkaido Ramen Santouka.................. A2
21 Island Creek Oyster Bar...................... C5
22 Life Alive... C3
23 Myers & Chang.................................... F6
24 Sweetgreen E5
25 Tasty Burger.. C6

⊜ Drinking & Nightlife
26 Beat Brasserie.................................... A2
27 Beehive.. F6
     Hawthorne............................... (see 21)
28 Lord Hobo... C2
29 Top of the Hub E5

⊕ Entertainment
30 Berklee Performance Center D5
     Boston Red Sox ....(see 3)
31 Boston Symphony Orchestra D6
32 Red Room @ Café 939 .... D5

⊜ Shopping
33 Converse D5
34 Three Wise Donkeys............................ E5

History

For all intents and purposes, Boston is the oldest city in America. And you can hardly walk a step over its cobblestone streets without running into some historic site. The Freedom Trail winds its way around the city, connecting 16 historically significant sites. These are the very places where history unfolded: from the first public school in America to Boston's oldest church building to sites linked to America's fight for independence from Britain – Boston is, in effect, one enormous outdoor history museum.

◉ Sights

◉ Beacon Hill & Boston Common

Abutted by the Boston Common – the nation's original public park and the centerpiece of the city – and topped with the gold-domed Massachusetts State House, Beacon Hill is the neighborhood most often featured on Boston postcards. The retail and residential streets on Beacon Hill are delightful.

★ Boston Common   PARK

(Map p192; btwn Tremont, Charles, Beacon & Park Sts; ◷6am-midnight; P ⛹; T Park St) The Boston Common has served many purposes over the years, including as a campground for British troops during the Revolutionary War and as green grass for cattle grazing until the 1830s. Although there is still a grazing ordinance on the books, the Common today serves picnickers, sunbathers and people-watchers. In winter, the **Frog Pond** (Map p192; www.bostonfrogpond.com; Boston Common; adult/child $6/free, rental $12/6; ◷10am-3:45pm Mon, to 9pm Tue-Thu & Sun, to 10pm Fri & Sat mid-Nov–mid-Mar; ⛹; T Park St) attracts ice-skaters, while summer draws theater lovers for **Shakespeare on the Common** (Map p192; www.commshakes.org; Boston Common; ◷Jul & Aug). This is also the starting point for the Freedom Trail.

★ Massachusetts
State House   NOTABLE BUILDING
(Map p192; www.sec.state.ma.us; cnr Beacon & Bowdoin Sts; ◷8:45am-5pm Mon-Fri, tours 10am-3:30pm Mon-Fri; T Park St) FREE High atop Beacon Hill, Massachusetts' leaders and legislators attempt to turn their ideas into concrete policies and practices within the State House. John Hancock provided the land; and Charles Bulfinch designed the commanding state capitol, but it was Oliver Wendell Holmes who called it 'the hub of the solar system'. Free 40-minute tours cover the history, artwork, architecture and political personalities of the State House.

BOSTON IN TWO DAYS...

Day One

Spend your first day in Boston following the Freedom Trail (p198), which starts on the Boston Common (p190) and continues through downtown. There isn't time to go inside every museum, but you can admire the architecture and learn the history. Highlights include the Old South Meeting House, the Old State House and Faneuil Hall (p194).

In the afternoon, the Freedom Trail continues into the North End, where you can visit the historic Paul Revere House (p195), Old North Church (p195) and Copp's Hill Burying Ground (p198). Move on to the exquisite Liberty Hotel (p200), former site of the Charles St Jail.

Day Two

Spend the morning admiring Boston's most architecturally significant collection of buildings, clustered around Copley Sq (p196). Admire the art and books at the Boston Public Library, ogle the magnificent stained-glass windows at Trinity Church and gaze at the clean lines on the John Hancock Tower.

Your afternoon is reserved for one of Boston's magnificent art museums. Unfortunately you'll have to choose between the excellent, encyclopedic collection at the Museum of Fine Arts (p197) or the smaller but no less extraordinary exhibits at the Isabella Stewart Gardner Museum (p197). Either way, you won't be disappointed.

In the evening, catch the Boston Symphony Orchestra at the acoustically magnificent Symphony Hall (p197), or for lower-brow entertainment, catch a baseball game at Fenway Park (p197) or go barhopping on Lansdowne St.

★ **Public Garden**   GARDENS

(Map p192; www.friendsofthepublicgarden.org; Arlington St; ☺dawn-dusk; ⊕; ⊤Arlington) Adjoining Boston Common, the Public Garden is a 24-acre botanical oasis of Victorian flower beds, verdant grass and weeping willow trees shading a tranquil lagoon. The old-fashioned pedal-powered **Swan Boats** (Map p192; www.swanboats.com; Public Garden; adult/child $3.50/2; ☺10am-4pm mid-Apr–mid-Jun, to 5pm late Jun-Aug, noon-4pm 1st half of Sep) have been delighting children for generations. The most endearing spot in the Public Garden is the **Make Way for Ducklings Statue** (Map p192), depicting Mrs Mallard and her eight ducklings, the main characters in the beloved book by Robert McCloskey.

Granary Burying Ground   CEMETERY

(Map p192; Tremont St; ☺9am-5pm; ⊤Park St) Dating from 1660, this atmospheric atoll is crammed with historic headstones, many with evocative (and creepy) carvings. This is the final resting place of all your favorite revolutionary heroes, including Paul Revere, Samuel Adams, John Hancock and James Otis. Benjamin Franklin is buried in Philadelphia, but the Franklin family plot contains his parents.

⊙ Downtown & Waterfront

Much of Boston's business and tourist activity takes place in this central neighborhood. Downtown is a bustling district crammed with modern complexes and colonial buildings, including Faneuil Hall and Quincy Market.

★ **Old State House**   HISTORIC BUILDING

(Map p192; www.bostonhistory.org; 206 Washington St; adult/child $10/free; ☺9am-6pm Jun-Aug, to 5pm Sep-May; ⊤State) Dating from 1713, the Old State House is Boston's oldest surviving public building, where the Massachusetts Assembly used to debate the issues of the day before the Revolution. The building is best known for its balcony, where the Declaration of Independence was first read to Bostonians in 1776. Inside, the Old State House contains a small museum of revolutionary memorabilia, with videos and multimedia presentations about the Boston Massacre, which took place out front.

Old South Meeting House   HISTORIC BUILDING

(Map p192; www.osmh.org; 310 Washington St; adult/child $6/1; ☺9:30am-5pm Apr-Oct, 10am-4pm Nov-Mar; ⊕; ⊤Downtown Crossing, State) 'No tax on tea!' That was the decision on December 16, 1773, when 5000 angry colonists gathered here to protest British taxes,

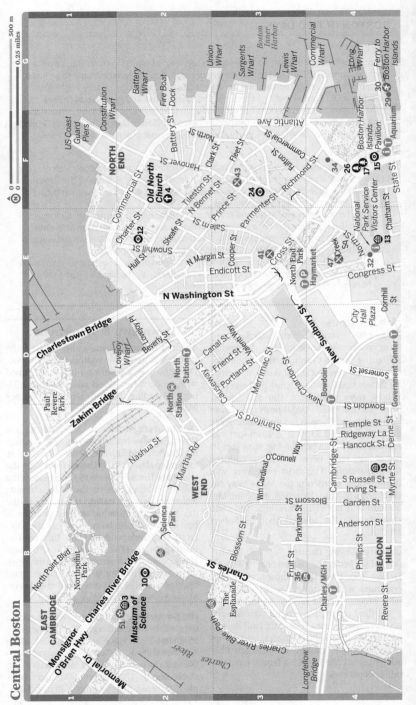

Central Boston

NEW ENGLAND

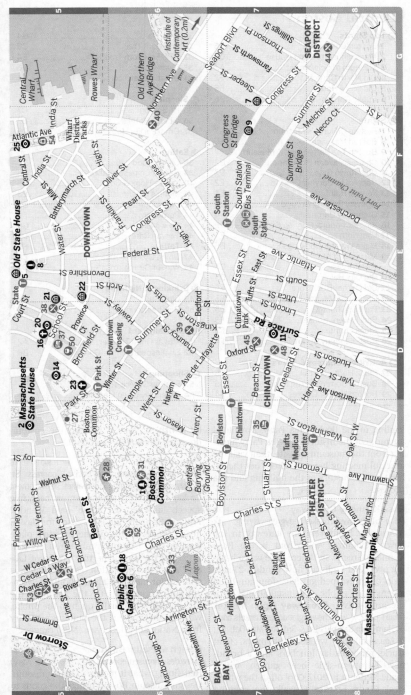

Central Boston

⊙ **Top Sights**
1 Boston Common C6
2 Massachusetts State House C5
3 Museum of Science A2
4 Old North Church F2
5 Old State House E5
6 Public Garden B6

⊙ **Sights**
7 Boston Children's Museum G7
8 Boston Massacre Site E5
9 Boston Tea Party Ships & Museum.......F7
10 Charles Hayden Planetarium B2
11 Chinatown Gate......................................D7
12 Copp's Hill Burying Ground E2
13 Faneuil Hall E4
14 Granary Burying Ground D5
15 Greenway Carousel.................................F4
16 King's Chapel & Burying Ground D5
17 Labyrinth F4
18 Make Way for Ducklings Statue B6
19 Museum of African American
      History C4
20 Old City Hall D5
21 Old Corner Bookstore E5
22 Old South Meeting House E5
23 Park St Church D5
24 Paul Revere House F3
25 Rings Fountain F5
26 Rose Kennedy Greenway F4

⊕ **Activities, Courses & Tours**
27 Black Heritage Trail C5
28 Boston Common Frog Pond C5
29 Boston Harbor Cruises...........................G4

30 Codzilla...G4
31 Freedom Trail..C6
32 NPS Freedom Trail Tour E4
33 Swan Boats B6
34 Urban AdvenTours F4

⊜ **Sleeping**
35 HI-Boston C7
36 Liberty Hotel..B3
37 Omni Parker House D5

⊗ **Eating**
38 Clover Food Lab D5
39 Gene's Chinese Flatbread D6
40 James Hook & Co F6
41 Maria's Pastry E3
42 Paramount..B5
43 Pomodoro...F3
44 Row 34 ....G8
45 Taiwan Cafe D7
46 Tatte B5
47 Union Oyster House E4
48 Winsor Dim Sum Cafe D7

⊙ **Drinking & Nightlife**
49 Club Café A8
50 Highball Lounge D5

⊛ **Entertainment**
51 Mugar Omni Theater A2
52 Shakespeare on the Common B6

⊜ **Shopping**
53 Eugene Galleries B5
54 Greenway Open Market F5

leading to the Boston Tea Party. Download an audio of the historic pre–Tea Party meeting from the museum website, then visit the graceful meeting house to check out the exhibit on the history of the building and the protest.

Rose Kennedy Greenway PARK
(Map p192; www.rosekennedygreenway.org; ; T Aquarium, Haymarket) The gateway to the newly revitalized waterfront is the Rose Kennedy Greenway. Where once was a hulking overhead highway, now winds a 27-acre strip of landscaped gardens, fountain-lined greens and public art installations, with the artist-driven **Greenway Open Market** (Map p192; www.newenglandopenmarkets.com; ☺11am-5pm Sat, plus 1st & 3rd Sun May-Oct; ; T Aquarium) for weekend shoppers, food trucks for weekday lunchers and a brand-new European-style beer garden, which made its debut in 2017. Cool off in the whimsical **Rings Fountain**, walk the calming **labyrinth**, or take a ride on the custom-designed **Greenway Carousel**.

Faneuil Hall HISTORIC BUILDING
(Map p192; www.nps.gov/bost; Congress St; ☺9am-5pm; T State, Haymarket, Government Center) FREE 'Those who cannot bear free speech had best go home,' said Wendell Phillips. 'Faneuil Hall is no place for slavish hearts.' Indeed, this public meeting place was the site of so much rabble-rousing that it earned the nickname the 'Cradle of Liberty.' After the revolution, Faneuil Hall was a forum for meetings about abolition, women's suffrage and war. On the 2nd floor, the historic hall is normally open to the public, who can hear about the building's history from National Park Service (NPS) rangers.

Design Museum Boston MUSEUM
(www.designmuseumboston.org; ☺hours vary) Redefining what it means to be a 'museum', Design Museum Boston brings the goods to

you. This 'pop-up' museum launches exhibits in public spaces all around town, from shopping malls to public parks to airports.

West End & North End

Although the West End and North End are physically adjacent, they are atmospherically worlds apart. The West End is an institutional area without much zest. By contrast, the North End is delightfully spicy, thanks to the many Italian ristoranti and *salumerie* (delis) that line the streets.

★ Museum of Science MUSEUM
(Map p192; www.mos.org; Charles River Dam; adult/child $25/20; ⊘9am-7pm Sat-Thu Jul & Aug, to 5pm Sep-Jun, to 9pm Fri year-round; P; T Science Park/West End) This educational playground has more than 600 interactive exhibits. Favorites include the world's largest lightning-bolt generator, a full-scale space capsule, a world population meter and an impressive dinosaur exhibit. Kids and adults alike can go wild exploring computers and technology, maps and models, the birds and the bees, and human evolution. Recent additions include the Hall of Human Life, where visitors can witness the hatching of baby chicks, and the Yawkey Gallery, with dramatic floor-to-ceiling windows overlooking the Charles River.

The Discovery Center is a hands-on play area for kids under the age of eight. The museum also houses the **Charles Hayden Planetarium** (Map p192; www.mos.org; Museum of Science, Charles River Dam; adult/child $10/8; ⊘9am-5pm Sat-Thu, to 9pm Fri) and **Mugar Omni Theater** (Map p192; www.mos.org; Science Museum, Charles River Dam; adult/child $10/8).

★ Old North Church CHURCH
(Map p192; www.oldnorth.com; 193 Salem St; requested donation $3, tour adult/child $6/4; ⊘9am-6pm Jun-Oct, 9am-5pm Mar-May, Nov & Dec, 10am-4pm Jan & Feb; T Haymarket; North Station) Longfellow's poem 'Paul Revere's Ride' has immortalized this graceful church. It was here, on the night of April 18, 1775, that the sexton hung two lanterns from the steeple, as a signal that the British would advance on Lexington and Concord via the sea route. Also called Christ Church, this 1723 Anglican place of worship is Boston's oldest church.

Paul Revere House HISTORIC SITE
(Map p192; www.paulreverehouse.org; 19 North Sq; adult/child $5/1; ⊘9:30am-5:15pm mid-Apr-Oct, to 4:15pm Nov–mid-Apr, closed Mon Jan-Mar; T Haymarket) When silversmith Paul Revere rode to warn patriots of the British march to Lexington and Concord, he set out from this home on North Sq. This small clapboard house was built in 1680, making it the oldest house in Boston. A self-guided tour through the house and courtyard gives a glimpse of what life was like for the Revere family (which included 16 children!).

Seaport District

The Seaport District is a section of South Boston that is fast developing as an attractive waterside destination, thanks to the dynamic contemporary-art museum and the explosion of new dining options. Travel deeper into Southie for seaside breezes, a little history and a lot of beer.

★ Institute of Contemporary Art MUSEUM
(ICA; www.icaboston.org; 25 Harbor Shore Dr; adult/child $15/free; ⊘10am-5pm Tue, Wed, Sat & Sun, to 9pm Thu & Fri; ; SL1, SL2, T South Station) Boston has become a focal point for contemporary art in the 21st century, with the Institute of Contemporary Art leading the way. The building is a work of art in itself: a glass structure cantilevered over a waterside plaza. The vast light-filled interior allows for multimedia presentations, educational programs and studio space, as well as the development of the permanent collection.

Boston Children's Museum MUSEUM
(Map p192; www.bostonchildrensmuseum.org; 308 Congress St; $16, Fri 5-9pm $1; ⊘10am-5pm Sat-Thu, to 9pm Fri; ; T South Station) The interactive, educational exhibits at the delightful Boston Children's Museum keep kids entertained for hours. Highlights include a bubble exhibit, rock-climbing walls, a hands-on construction site and intercultural immersion experiences. The light-filled atrium features an amazing three-story climbing maze. In nice weather kids can enjoy outdoor eating and playing in the waterside park. Look for the iconic Hood milk bottle on Fort Point Channel.

Boston Tea Party Ships & Museum MUSEUM
(Map p192; www.bostonteapartyship.com; Congress St Bridge; adult/child $28/18; ⊘10am-5pm; ; T South Station) 'Boston Harbor a teapot tonight!' To protest unfair taxes, a gang of rebellious colonists dumped 342 chests of tea

into the water. The 1773 protest – the Boston Tea Party – set into motion the events leading to the Revolutionary War. Nowadays, replica Tea Party Ships are moored at Griffin's Wharf, alongside an excellent experiential museum dedicated to the catalytic event. Using re-enactments, multimedia and other exhibits, the museum addresses all aspects of the Boston Tea Party.

⊙ South End & Chinatown

Chinatown, the Theater District and the Leather District are overlapping areas, filled with glitzy theaters, Chinese restaurants and the remnants of Boston's shoe and leather industry (now converted lofts and clubs). Nearby, the Victorian manses in the South End have been reclaimed by artists and the like, who have created a vibrant restaurant and gallery scene.

Chinatown Gate   LANDMARK
(Map p192; Beach St; ⊤Chinatown) The official entrance to Chinatown is the decorative gate *(paifong)*, a gift from the city of Taipei. It is symbolic – not only as an entryway for guests visiting Chinatown, but also as an entryway for immigrants who are still settling here, as they come to establish relationships and put down roots in their newly claimed home.

⊙ Back Bay

Back Bay includes the city's most fashionable window-shopping, latte-drinking and people-watching area, on Newbury St, as well as its most elegant architecture, around **Copley Sq** (Plaza).

Copley Sq represents the best of Back Bay architecture, as it gracefully blends disparate elements such as the Renaissance Revival **Boston Public Library** (www.bpl.org), the Richardsonian Romanesque **Trinity Church** (www.trinitychurchboston.org) and the modernist John Hancock Tower. Copley Sq should be your first stop in Back Bay, good for whiling away an hour or even a day.

Mary Baker Eddy Library &
Mapparium   LIBRARY
(Map p188; www.marybakereddylibrary.org; 200 Massachusetts Ave; adult/child $6/4; ⊙10am-4pm Tue-Sun; ♿; ⊤Symphony) The Mary Baker Eddy Library houses one of Boston's hidden treasures. The intriguing Mapparium is a room-sized, stained-glass globe that visitors walk through on a glass bridge. It was created in 1935, which is reflected in the globe's geopolitical boundaries. The acoustics, which surprised even the designer, allow everyone in the room to hear even the tiniest whisper.

Prudential Center Skywalk
Observatory   VIEWPOINT
(Map p188; www.skywalkboston.com; 800 Boylston St; adult/child $18/13; ⊙10am-10pm Mar-Oct, to 8pm Nov-Feb; P♿; ⊤Prudential) Technically called the Shops at Prudential Center, this landmark Boston building is not much more than a fancy shopping mall. But it does provide a bird's-eye view of Boston from its 50th-floor Skywalk. Completely enclosed by glass, the Skywalk offers spectacular 360-degree views of Boston and Cambridge, accompanied by an entertaining audiotour (with a special version catering to kids). Alternatively, enjoy the same view from **Top of the Hub** (Map p188; ☎617-536-1775; www.topofthehub.net; 800 Boylston St; ⊙11:30am-1am; 🛜; ⊤Prudential) for the price of a drink.

BOSTON FOR CHILDREN

Boston is one giant history museum, the setting for many lively and informative field trips. Cobblestone streets and costume-clad tour guides can bring to life the events that kids read about in history books, while hands-on experimentation and interactive exhibits fuse education and entertainment.

➡ Boston by Little Feet (p199) is the only Freedom Trail walking tour designed especially for children aged six to 12. Download a kid-friendly podcast or reading list for your child before setting out (www.thefreedomtrail.org)

➡ Kids of all ages are invited to drive the duck on the raging waters of the Charles River (p199) with Boston Duck Tours. Bonus: quacking loudly is encouraged.

➡ **Urban AdvenTours** (Map p192; ☎617-670-0637; www.urbanadventours.com; 103 Atlantic Ave; tours from $40, rentals per 24hr $40-75; ⊙9am-8pm Apr-Sep, shorter hours Oct-Mar; ⊤Aquarium) is great for all ages. Kids' bikes and helmets are available for rent, as are bike trailers for toddlers.

◉ Kenmore Square & Fenway

Kenmore Sq and Fenway attract club-goers and baseball fans to the streets surrounding Fenway Park, as well as art lovers and culture vultures to the artistic institutions along the Avenue of the Arts (Huntington Ave).

★**Fenway Park**   STADIUM
(Map p188; www.redsox.com; 4 Yawkey Way; tours adult/child $20/14, premium tour $35; ⊘9am-5pm; Ⓣ Kenmore) What is it that makes Fenway Park 'America's Most Beloved Ballpark'? It's not just that it's the home of the Boston Red Sox. Open since 1912, it is the oldest operating baseball park in the country. As such, the park has many quirks that make for a unique experience. See them all on a ballpark tour.

★**Museum of Fine Arts**   MUSEUM
(MFA; Map p188; www.mfa.org; 465 Huntington Ave; adult/child $25/free; ⊘10am-5pm Sat-Tue, to 10pm Wed-Fri; Ⓣ Museum of Fine Arts, Ruggles) Since 1876, the Museum of Fine Arts has been Boston's premier venue for showcasing art by local, national and international artists. Nowadays the museum's holdings encompass all eras, from the ancient world to contemporary times, and all areas of the globe, making it truly encyclopedic in scope. Most recently, the museum has added gorgeous new wings dedicated to the Art of the Americas and to contemporary art, contributing to Boston's emergence as an art center in the 21st century.

★**Isabella Stewart Gardner Museum**   MUSEUM
(Map p188; www.gardnermuseum.org; 25 Evans Way; adult/child $15/free; ⊘11am-5pm Wed-Mon, to 9pm Thu; Ⓣ Museum of Fine Arts) The magnificent Venetian-style palazzo that houses this museum was home to 'Mrs Jack' Gardner herself until her death in 1924. A monument to one woman's taste for acquiring exquisite art, the Gardner is filled with some 2500 priceless objects, primarily European, including outstanding tapestries and Italian Renaissance and 17th-century Dutch paintings. The four-story greenhouse courtyard is a masterpiece and a tranquil oasis that alone is worth the price of admission.

Symphony Hall   HISTORIC BUILDING
(Map p188; www.bso.org; 301 Massachusetts Ave; ⊘hrs vary; Ⓣ Symphony) This majestic building has been the home of the Boston Symphony Orchestra since 1900, when it was built by McKim, Mead & White (of BPL fame). See the hall's public spaces and go behind the scenes on a free, one-hour tour. Tour dates vary and advance bookings are required.

◉ Cambridge

★**Harvard University**   UNIVERSITY
(Map p188; www.harvard.edu; Massachusetts Ave; tours free; Ⓣ Harvard) Founded in 1636 to educate men for the ministry, Harvard is America's oldest college. The original Ivy League school has eight graduates who went on to be US presidents, not to mention dozens of Nobel laureates and Pulitzer Prize winners. The geographic heart of Harvard University – where red-brick buildings and leaf-covered paths exude academia – is Harvard Yard. Free historical tours of Harvard Yard depart from the **Smith Campus Center** (Map p188; www.harvard.edu/visitors; 30 Dunster St; ⊘9am-5pm Mon-Sat; Ⓣ Harvard); self-guided tours are also available.

★**Harvard Art Museums**   MUSEUM
(Map p188; www.harvardartmuseums.org; 32 Quincy St; adult/child/student $15/free/$10; ⊘10am-5pm; Ⓣ Harvard) The 2014 renovation and expansion of Harvard's art museums allowed the university's massive 250,000-piece collection to come together under one very stylish roof, designed by architect extraordinaire Renzo Piano. The artwork spans the globe, with separate collections devoted to Asian and Islamic cultures (formerly the Arthur M Sackler Museum), northern European and Germanic cultures (formerly the Busch-Reisinger Museum) and other Western art, especially European modernism.

MIT Museum   MUSEUM
(Map p188; http://mitmuseum.mit.edu; 265 Massachusetts Ave; adult/child $10/5; ⊘10am-6pm Jul & Aug, to 5pm Sep-Jun; Ⓟ🅷; Ⓣ Central) Leave it to the mischievous brainiacs at Massachusetts Institute of Technology (MIT) to come up with the city's quirkiest museum. For example, an exhibit called Robots and Beyond demonstrates MIT's ongoing work on artificial intelligence. You can meet humanoid robots like observant Cog and personable Kismet and decide for yourself if they are smarter than humans.

Harvard Museum of Natural History   MUSEUM
(Map p188; www.hmnh.harvard.edu; 26 Oxford St; adult/child/student $12/8/10; ⊘9am-5pm; 🅷;

City Walk
Freedom Trail

START BOSTON COMMON
END BUNKER HILL MONUMENT
LENGTH 2.5 MILES; THREE HOURS

Start at [1] **Boston Common** (p190), America's oldest public park. On the northern side, you can't miss the gold-domed [2] **Massachusetts State House** (p190) sitting atop Beacon Hill. Walk north on Tremont St, passing the soaring steeple of [3] **Park St Church** and the Egyptian Revival gates of the [4] **Granary Burying Ground** (p191).

At School St, the columned [5] **King's Chapel** overlooks the adjacent burying ground. Turn east on School St, and take note of the plaque outside the [6] **Old City Hall** commemorating this spot as the site of the first public school.

Continue down School St past the [7] **Old Corner Bookstore**. Diagonally opposite, the [8] **Old South Meeting House** (p191) saw the beginnings of the Boston Tea Party. Further north on Washington St, the [9] **Old State House** (p191) was the scene of the city's first public reading of the Declaration of Independence. Outside the Old State House a ring of cobblestones marks the [10] **Boston Massacre site**, where yet another uprising fueled the revolution. Across the intersection, historic [11] **Faneuil Hall** (p194) has served as a public meeting place and marketplace for over 250 years.

From Faneuil Hall, follow Hanover St across the Rose Kennedy Greenway. One block east, charming North Sq is the site of the [12] **Paul Revere House** (p195). Back on Hanover St, the Paul Revere Mall offers a lovely vantage point to view the [13] **Old North Church** (p195). From the church, head west on Hull St to [14] **Copp's Hill Burying Ground**, with grand views across the river to Charlestown.

Across the Charlestown Bridge, Constitution Rd brings you to the Charlestown Navy Yard, home of the world's oldest commissioned warship, the [15] **USS Constitution**. Finally, wind your way through the historic streets of Charlestown center to the [16] **Bunker Hill Monument**, site of the devastating American Revolution battle.

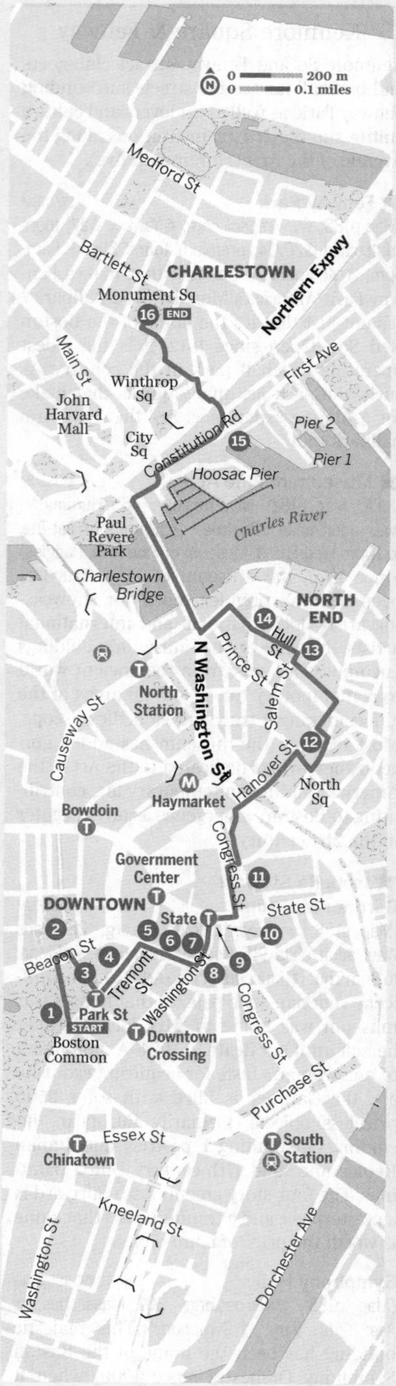

86, THarvard) This institution is famed for its botanical galleries, featuring some 3000 pieces of handblown glass flowers and plants. At the intersection of art and science, the collection of intricately crafted flora is pretty amazing. There is a smaller, complementary exhibit of Sea Creatures in Glass by the same artists. Nearby, the zoological galleries house an enormous number of stuffed animals and reassembled skeletons, as well as an impressive fossil collection. Other cool exhibits feature climate change, sparkling gemstones and arthropods.

Peabody Museum of Archaeology & Ethnology   MUSEUM
(Map p188; www.peabody.harvard.edu; 11 Divinity Ave; adult/child/student $12/8/10; ⊙9am-5pm; 86, THarvard) The centerpiece of the Peabody is the impressive Hall of the North American Indian, which traces how these peoples responded to the arrival of Europeans from the 15th to the 18th centuries. Other exhibits examine indigenous cultures throughout the Americas, including a fantastic comparison of cave paintings and murals of the Awatovi (New Mexico), the Maya (Guatemala) and the Moche (Peru).

🏃 Activities

Considering Boston's large student population and extensive green spaces, it's no surprise to see urban outdoorsy people running along the Esplanade and cycling the Emerald Necklace. For seafaring types, the Charles River and the Boston Harbor offer opportunities for kayaking, sailing and even swimming.

★ Freedom Trail   WALKING
(Map p192; www.thefreedomtrail.org; TPark St) For a sampler of Boston's revolutionary sights, follow the red-brick road. It leads 2.5 miles through the center of Boston, from Boston Common to the Bunker Hill Monument, and traces the events leading up to and following the War of Independence. The Freedom Trail is well marked and easy to follow on your own. See opposite page for more information on walking this trail.

Codzilla   BOATING
(Map p192; www.bostonharborcruises.com/codzilla; 1 Long Wharf; adult/child $29/25; ⊙hours vary May-early Oct; TAquarium) 'Boating' may not be the proper word to describe this activity, which takes place on a 2800HP speedboat

that cruises through the waves at speeds of up to 40mph. Painted like a shark with a big toothy grin, the boat has a unique hull design that enables it to do the ocean version of doughnuts.

Boston Harbor Cruises   CRUISE
(BHC; Map p192; ☑617-227-4321; www.boston harborcruises.com; 1 Long Wharf; adult/child $29/25; TAquarium) With 50 vessels and over 300 daily departures in summer, BHC claims to be America's oldest and largest operator of passenger boats. The dizzying variety of options for those who want to get out on the water range from a basic Historic Sightseeing Tour around Boston's Inner Harbor to sunset cruises, weekend lighthouse cruises, whale-watching and more.

🧭 Tours

Boston by Foot   WALKING
(www.bostonbyfoot.com; adult/child $15/10; 🚶) This fantastic nonprofit organization offers 90-minute walking tours, with neighborhood-specific walks and specialty theme tours, like the Hub of Literary America, the Dark Side of Boston, and Boston by Little Feet – a kid-friendly version of the Freedom Trail.

Black Heritage Trail   WALKING
(Map p192; www.nps.gov/boaf; ⊙tours 10am, noon & 1pm Mon-Sat Jul & Aug; TPark St) The NPS conducts excellent, informative 90-minute guided tours exploring the history of the abolitionist movement and African American settlement on Beacon Hill. Tours depart from the Robert Gould Shaw memorial on Boston Common. Alternatively, take a self-guided tour with the NPS Freedom Trail app (www.nps. gov/bost/planyourvisit/app.htm) or grab a route map from the **Museum of African American History** (Map p192; www.maah.org; 46 Joy St; adult/child $5/free; ⊙10am-4pm Mon-Sat; TPark St, Bowdoin).

Boston Duck Tours   BOATING
(☑617-267-3825; www.bostonducktours.com; adult/child $39.50/27; 🚶; TAquarium, Science Park, Prudential) These ridiculously popular tours use WWII amphibious vehicles that cruise the downtown streets before splashing into the Charles River. The 80-minute tours depart from the Museum of Science, the Prudential Center or the New England Aquarium. Reserve in advance.

✦ Festivals & Events

★ Boston Marathon
SPORTS

(www.baa.org; ⊙ 3rd Mon Apr) One of the country's most prestigious marathons takes runners on a 26.2-mile course ending at Copley Sq on Patriots' Day, a Massachusetts holiday on the third Monday in April.

Boston Pride Festival
LGBT

(☑ 617-262-9405; www.bostonpride.org; ⊙ Jun) During the first full week in June, Boston does its part for this now-national celebration, kicking off with the raising of a rainbow flag on City Hall Plaza. Events occur throughout the week. The highlight is the Pride Parade and Festival on the second Saturday in June.

Independence Day
CULTURAL

(www.bostonpopsjuly4th.org; ⊙ Jul 4) Boston hosts one of the biggest Independence Day bashes in the USA, with a free Boston Pops concert on the Esplanade and a fireworks display that's televised nationally.

🛏 Sleeping

Boston offers a wide range of accommodations, from inviting guesthouses in historic quarters to swanky hotels with all the amenities. Considering that Boston is a city filled with students, there are surprisingly few accommodations options targeting budget travelers and backpackers.

HI-Boston
HOSTEL $

(Map p192; ☑ 617-536-9455; www.bostonhostel. org; 19 Stuart St; dm from $40, d with bath from $170; ✳@🖃; ⊤ Chinatown, Boylston) 🍃 HI-Boston sets the standard for urban hostels, with its modern, ecofriendly facility in the historic Dill Building. Purpose-built rooms are comfortable and clean, as are the shared bathrooms. Community spaces are numerous, from fully equipped kitchen to trendy ground-floor cafe, and there's a whole calendar of activities on offer.

Irving House at Harvard
GUESTHOUSE $$

(Map p188; ☑ 617-547-4600; www.irvinghouse. com; 24 Irving St; r with/without bath from $255/155; ℙ✳@🖃; ⊤ Harvard) 🍃 Call it a big inn or a homey hotel, this property welcomes the world-weariest of travelers. The 44 rooms range in size, but every bed is covered with a quilt, and big windows let in plenty of light. There is a bistro-style atmosphere in the brick-lined basement, where you can browse its books, plan your travels or munch on a free continental breakfast.

★ Liberty Hotel
HOTEL $$$

(Map p192; ☑ 617-224-4000, 866-961-3778; www. libertyhotel.com; 215 Charles St; r from $515; ℙ😊✳🖃; ⊤ Charles/MGH) It is with intended irony that the notorious Charles Street Jail has been converted into the classy Liberty Hotel. Today the spectacular lobby soars under a 90ft ceiling. All 298 guest rooms come with luxurious linens and high-tech amenities, while the 18 in the original jail wing boast floor-to-ceiling windows with amazing views of the Charles River and Beacon Hill.

★ Verb Hotel
BOUTIQUE HOTEL $$$

(Map p188; ☑ 617-566-4500; www.theverbhotel. com; 1271 Boylston St; r $349-399; ℙ✳🖃✳; ⊤ Kenmore) The Verb Hotel took a down-and-out HoJo property and turned it into Boston's most radical, retro, rock-and-roll hotel. The style is mid-Century Modern; the theme is music. Memorabilia is on display throughout the joint, with a jukebox cranking out tunes in the lobby. Classy, clean-lined rooms face the swimming pool or Fenway Park. A-plus for service and style.

Newbury Guest House
GUESTHOUSE $$$

(Map p188; ☑ 617-670-6000, 800-437-7668; www. newburyguesthouse.com; 261 Newbury St; d from $269; ℙ✳🖃; ⊤ Hynes, Copley) Dating from 1882, these three interconnected brick and brownstone buildings offer a prime location in the heart of Newbury St. A recent renovation has preserved charming features like ceiling medallions and in-room fireplaces, but now the rooms feature clean lines, luxurious linens and modern amenities.

Omni Parker House
HISTORIC HOTEL $$$

(Map p192; ☑ 617-227-8600; www.omnihotels.com; 60 School St; r from $345; ℙ✳🖃✳; ⊤ Park St) History and the Parker House go hand in hand like JFK and Jackie (who got engaged here). Malcolm X was a busboy here; Ho Chi Minh was a pastry chef here; and Boston cream pie, the official state dessert, was created here. Rooms are comfortable, and the hotel's location, smack in the heart of the Freedom Trail, is incomparable.

🍴 Eating

🍽 Beacon Hill & Boston Common

★ Tatte
BAKERY $

(Map p192; www.tattebakery.com; 70 Charles St; pastries from $3; ⊙ 7am-8pm Mon-Fri, 8am-8pm Sat, 8am-7pm Sun; ⊤ Charles/MGH) The aroma of buttery goodness – and the lines stretching out the door – signal your arrival at this fabulous bakery on the lower floor of the historic Charles St Meeting House. Swoonworthy pastries (divinely cinnamon-y morning buns, chocolate-hazelnut twists, avocado and mushroom tartines) taste even more amazing if you're lucky enough to score a table on the sunny front patio.

★ **Paramount** CAFETERIA $$
(Map p192; www.paramountboston.com; 44 Charles St; mains breakfast & lunch $8-15, dinner $17-24; ⊙7am-10pm Mon-Fri, 8am-10pm Sat & Sun; 🗷 🖪; 🆃Charles/MGH) This old-fashioned cafeteria is a neighborhood favorite. A-plus diner fare includes pancakes, home fries, burgers and sandwiches, and big, hearty salads. Banana and caramel French toast is an obvious go-to for the brunch crowd. Don't sit down until you get your food!

🍴 Downtown & Waterfront

Gene's Chinese Flatbread CHINESE $
(Map p192; 86 Bedford St; sandwiches $4.50, mains $6-11; ⊙11am-6:30am Mon-Sat; 🆃Chinatown) It's not often that we recommend leaving Chinatown for Chinese food, but it's only a few blocks away. And it's worth the detour to this unassuming storefront for chewy Xi'an-style noodles. No 9 (cumin lamb handpulled noodles) and No 4 (pork flatbread sandwich) are perennial fan favorites.

James Hook & Co SEAFOOD $$
(Map p192; www.jameshooklobster.com; 15-17 Northern Av; lobster rolls $20-24; ⊙10am-5pm Mon-Thu & Sat, to 6pm Fri, to 4pm Sat) For a superlative lobster roll close to downtown, look no further than this harborside seafood shack near the bridge to the Seaport district. Outdoor tables make it a perfect low-key lunch stop as you make your way between museums on a sunny afternoon.

Union Oyster House SEAFOOD $$$
(Map p192; www.unionoysterhouse.com; 41 Union St; mains lunch $14-26, dinner $22-32; ⊙11am-9:30pm Sun-Thu, to 10pm Fri & Sat; 🆃Haymarket) The oldest restaurant in Boston, ye olde Union Oyster House has been serving seafood in this historic redbrick building since 1826. Countless historymakers have propped themselves up at this bar, including Daniel Webster and John F Kennedy (apparently JFK used to order the lobster bisque). Overpriced but atmospheric.

🍴 West End & North End

Maria's Pastry BAKERY $
(Map p192; www.mariaspastry.com; 46 Cross St; pastries $2-5; ⊙7am-7pm Mon-Sat, to 5pm Sun; 🗷; 🆃Haymarket) Three generations of Merola women are now working to bring you Boston's most authentic Italian pastries. Many claim that Maria makes the best cannoli in the North End, but you'll also find more elaborate concoctions like *sfogliatelle* (layered, shell-shaped pastry filled with ricotta) and *aragosta* (cream-filled 'lobster tail' pastry).

★ **Pomodoro** ITALIAN $$
(Map p192; 🗷617-367-4348; 351 Hanover St; mains $23-24; ⊙5:30-11pm; 🆃Haymarket) Seductive Pomodoro offers one of the North End's most romantic settings for delectable Italian. The food is simple but perfectly prepared: fresh pasta, spicy tomato sauce, grilled fish and meats, and wine by the glass. If you're lucky, you might be on the receiving end of a complimentary tiramisu for dessert.

🍴 Seaport District

Yankee Lobster Co SEAFOOD $
(www.yankeelobstercompany.com; 300 Northern Ave; mains $10-25; ⊙10am-9pm Mon-Sat, 11am-6pm Sun; 🚤SL1, SL2, 🆃South Station) The Zanti family has been fishing for three generations, so they definitely know their stuff. A relatively recent addition is this retail fish market, scattered with a few tables in case you want to dine in. And you do. Order something simple like clam chowder or a lobster roll, accompany it with a cold beer, and you will not be disappointed.

★ **Row 34** SEAFOOD $$
(Map p192; 🗷617-553-5900; www.row34.com; 383 Congress St; oysters $2-3, mains $13-29; ⊙11:30am-10pm Sun-Thu, to 11pm Fri & Sat; 🆃South Station) In the heart of the new Seaport District, set in a sharp, postindustrial space, this place offers a dozen types of raw oysters and clams, alongside an amazing selection of craft beers. There's also a full menu of cooked seafood, ranging from the traditional to the trendy.

🍴 South End & Chinatown

Taiwan Cafe TAIWANESE $
(Map p192; www.taiwancafeboston.com; 34 Oxford St; mains $6-16; ⊙11am-1am; 🗷; 🆃Chinatown) Taiwan Cafe is a few steps off the main drag,

so you might not have to wait quite as long for the excellent soup dumplings and other Taiwanese specialties. Regulars rave about the roast beef scallion pancakes. Like most places in Chinatown, the decor is minimal and prices are cheap. Cash only.

Winsor Dim Sum Cafe DIM SUM $

(Map p192; 10 Tyler St; dim sum from $3.50, other items $7-14; ☺9am-10pm; ☑; T Chinatown) The shrimp dumplings and steamed pork buns are highly recommended at this nononsense Chinatown favorite. The downside is that there are no pushcarts to choose your food from – the place is too small for them to fit! Instead you have to pre-order from a menu with photographs. The upside is that the food is freshly made to order and delicious.

★**Myers & Chang** ASIAN $$

(Map p188; ☑617-542-5200; www.myersand chang.com; 1145 Washington St; small plates $9-19; ☺11:30am-10pm Sun-Thu, to 11pm Fri & Sat; ☑; ☐SL4, SL5, T Tufts Medical Center) This superhip Asian spot blends Thai, Chinese and Vietnamese cuisines, which means delicious dumplings, spicy stir-fries and oodles of noodles. The kitchen staff do amazing things with a wok, and the menu of small plates allows you to sample a wide selection of dishes. Dim sum for dinner? This is your place.

✗ Back Bay

Sweetgreen VEGETARIAN $

(Map p188; ☑617-936-3464; www.sweetgreen. com; 659 Boylston St; mains $7-13; ☺10:30am-10:30pm; ☑☑; T Copley) Vegetarians, gluten-free eaters, health nuts and all human beings will rejoice in the goodness that is served at Sweetgreen. Choose a salad or wrap, then custom-design your own; or choose one of the unexpected, delicious, fresh combos that have already been invented, including seasonal specialties. So healthy. So satisfying. So good.

★**Courtyard** AMERICAN $$$

(Map p188; ☑617-859-2251; www.thecateredaf fair.com/bpl; 700 Boylston St; tea adult/child $39/19, with sparkling wine $49; ☺11:30am-3pm Mon-Sat; T Copley) The perfect destination for an elegant afternoon tea is – believe it or not – the Boston Public Library. Overlooking the beautiful Italianate courtyard, this grown-up restaurant serves an artfully prepared selection of sandwiches, scones and sweets, accompanied by a wide range of teas (black, green and herbal) and an optional glass of sparkling wine. Reserve ahead, especially on Saturdays.

✗ Kenmore Square & Fenway

El Pelon MEXICAN $

(Map p188; www.elpelon.com; 92 Peterborough St; tacos $4, burritos $6-8; ☺11am-11pm; ☑; T Fenway) If your budget is tight, don't miss this chance to fill up on Boston's best burritos, tacos and tortas, made with the freshest ingredients. The *tacos de la casa* are highly recommended, especially the *pescado,* made with Icelandic cod and topped with chili mayo. Plates are paper and cutlery is plastic.

Tasty Burger BURGERS $

(Map p188; www.tastyburger.com; 1301 Boylston St; burgers $5-6; ☺11am-2am; T Fenway) Once a Mobil gas station, this place is now a retro burger joint, with picnic tables outside and a

---

LGBTQ BOSTON

Out and active gay communities are visible all around Boston, especially in the South End and Jamaica Plain.

There is no shortage of entertainment options catering to LGBTQ travelers. From drag shows to dyke nights, this sexually diverse community has something for everybody.

The biggest event of the year for the Boston gay and lesbian community is June's Boston Pride (p200), a week of parades, parties, festivals and flag-raisings.

There are excellent sources of information for the gay and lesbian community:

Bay Windows (www.baywindows.com) is a weekly newspaper for LGBTQ readers. The print edition is distributed throughout New England, but the website is also an excellent source of news and information.

Edge Boston (www.edgeboston.com) is the Boston branch of the nationwide network of publications offering news and entertainment for LGBTQ readers. Includes a nightlife section with culture and club reviews.

pool table inside. The name of the place is a nod to *Pulp Fiction*, as is the wall-mounted poster of Samuel L Jackson, whose character would agree that 'this is a tasty burger'.

Island Creek Oyster Bar SEAFOOD $$$
(Map p188; ☑617-532-5300; www.islandcreek oysterbar.com; 500 Commonwealth Ave; oysters $2.50-3.50, mains lunch $12-27, dinner $17-36; ⊙4-11pm Mon-Fri, 11:30am-11:30pm Sat, 10:30am-11pm Sun; ⊤Kenmore) Island Creek claims to unite farmer, chef and diner in one space – and what a space it is. ICOB serves up the region's finest oysters, along with other local seafood, in an ethereal new-age setting. The specialty – lobster-roe noodles topped with braised short ribs and grilled lobster – lives up to the hype.

✖ Cambridge

Hokkaido Ramen Santouka JAPANESE $
(Map p188; www.santouka.co.jp/en; 1 Bow St; mains $11-17; ⊙11am-9:30pm Mon-Thu, to 10:30pm Fri & Sat, to 9pm Sun; ⊤Harvard) This worldwide chain is bringing a bit of Japanese simplicity and subtlety to Harvard Sq. Service is pleasant and fast, while the noodles are perfectly satisfying. If you're wondering why the staff occasionally shout out, they are greeting and sending off their guests.

★ Life Alive VEGETARIAN $
(Map p188; www.lifealive.com; 765 Massachusetts Ave; mains $6-10; ⊙8am-10pm Mon-Sat, 11am-7pm Sun; ☑⏏; ⊤Central) Life Alive offers a joyful, healthful, purposeful approach to fast food. The unusual combinations of animal-free ingredients yield delicious results, most of which come in a bowl (like a salad) or in a wrap.

🍷 Drinking & Nightlife

🍷 Downtown & Waterfront

Highball Lounge COCKTAIL BAR
(Map p192; www.highballboston.com; 90 Tremont St; ⊙5pm-midnight Mon & Tue, 2am Wed-Sat; ⊤Park St) Go out to play! Well stocked with board games, the Highball Lounge has yours, whether you're on a date (Connect Four) or in a group (Jenga). The Viewmaster is for looking at the menu, which features local beers, creative cocktails and intriguing snacks (tater-tot nachos, crispy brussels sprouts). This place will make you feel like a kid again. Except you can drink.

🍷 Seaport District

Harpoon Brewery & Beer Hall BREWERY
(www.harpoonbrewery.com; 306 Northern Ave; ⊙beer hall 11am-7pm Sun-Wed, to 11pm Thu-Sat, tours noon-5pm Mon-Wed, to 6pm Thu-Sat, 11:30am-5:30pm Sun; ⓈSL1, SL2, ⊤South Station) This brewery is the largest beer facility in the state of Massachusetts. Take an hour-long tour ($5) to see how the beer is made and to sample some of the goods. Or just take a seat at the bar in the beer hall.

🍷 South End & Chinatown

★ Beehive COCKTAIL BAR
(Map p188; ☑617-423-0069; www.beehive boston.com; 541 Tremont St; ⊙5pm-midnight Mon-Wed, to 1am Thu, to 2am Fri, 9:30am-2am Sat, 9:30am-midnight Sun; ⊤Back Bay) The Beehive has transformed the basement of the Boston Center for the Arts into a 1920s Paris jazz club. This place is more about the scene than the music, which is often provided by students from Berklee College of Music. But the food is good and the vibe is definitely hip. Reservations required for a table.

🍷 Back Bay

Club Café GAY
(Map p192; www.clubcafe.com; 209 Columbus Ave; ⊙11am-2am; ⊤Back Bay) It's a club! It's a cafe! It's cabaret! Anything goes at this glossy, gay nightlife extravaganza. There is live cabaret in the Napoleon Room six nights a week, while the main dance and lounge area has tea parties, salsa dancing, trivia competitions, karaoke, bingo and good old-fashioned dance parties.

🍷 Kenmore Square & Fenway

Hawthorne COCKTAIL BAR
(Map p188; www.thehawthornebar.com; 500a Commonwealth Ave; ⊙5pm-1am; ⊤Kenmore) Located in the basement of the Hotel Commonwealth, this is a living-room-style cocktail lounge that attracts the city's sophisticates. Sink into the plush furniture and sip a custom cocktail.

🍷 Cambridge

★ Beat Brasserie BAR
(Map p188; www.beatbrasserie.com; 13 Brattle St; ⊙4pm-late Mon-Fri, 10am-late Sat & Sun; ⊤Harvard) This vast, underground bistro packs in

good-looking patrons for international food, classy cocktails and live jazz and blues. It's inspired by the Beat Generation writers – and named for a run-down Parisian motel where they hung out – but there's nothing down-and-out about this hot spot.

★ Lord Hobo
MICROBREWERY

(Map p188; www.lordhobo.com; 92 Hampshire St; ⊙4pm-1am Mon-Wed, 4pm-2am Thu & Fri, 11am-2am Sat, 11am-1am Sun; ⊤Central, Kendall/MIT) If high-caliber craft IPAs are your idea of beer-drinking bliss, make a beeline for this unassuming corner brewpub north of Central Sq. What started as a local secret has exploded in popularity, with distribution of their trademark Hobo Life, Boom Sauce and Consolation Prize stretching clear to Colorado.

☆ Entertainment

Boston Red Sox
BASEBALL

(Map p188; www.redsox.com; 4 Yawkey Way; bleachers $10-45, grandstand $23-87, box $38-189; ⊤Kenmore) From April to September you can watch the Red Sox play at Fenway Park, the nation's oldest and most storied ballpark. Unfortunately it is also the most expensive – not that this stops the Fenway faithful from scooping up the tickets. There are sometimes game-day tickets on sale starting 90 minutes before the opening pitch.

★ Boston Symphony Orchestra
CLASSICAL MUSIC

(BSO; Map p188; ☎617-266-1200; www.bso.org; 301 Massachusetts Ave; tickets $30-145; ⊤Symphony) Flawless acoustics match the ambitious programs of the world-renowned Boston Symphony Orchestra. From September to April, the BSO performs in the beauteous Symphony Hall (p197), featuring an ornamental high-relief ceiling and attracting a fancy-dress crowd.

★ Red Room @ Café 939
LIVE MUSIC

(Map p188; www.cafe939.com; 939 Boylston St; ⊤Hynes) Run by Berklee students, the Red Room @ 939 has emerged as one of Boston's least predictable and most enjoyable music venues. It has an excellent sound system and a baby grand piano; most importantly, it books interesting, eclectic up-and-coming musicians. Buy tickets in advance at the **Berklee Performance Center** (Map p188; www.berklee.edu/bpc; 136 Massachusetts Ave; tickets $8-58; ⊤Hynes).

Lizard Lounge
LIVE MUSIC

(www.lizardloungeclub.com; 1667 Massachusetts Ave; cover $8-15; ⊙7:30pm-late Sun & Mon, 8:30pm-late Tue-Sat; ⊤Harvard) The underground Lizard Lounge doubles as a rock and jazz venue. The big drawcard is the Sunday-night poetry slam, featuring music by the jazzy Jeff Robinson Trio. Also popular are the Monday open-mike challenge and regular appearances by local favorite Club d'Elf. The bar stocks an excellent list of New England beers, which are complemented by the sweet-potato fries.

Located a quarter-mile north of Cambridge Common (the park), below Cambridge Common (the restaurant).

🛍 Shopping

Converse
SHOES

(Map p188; www.converse.com; 348 Newbury St; ⊙10am-7pm Mon-Fri, to 8pm Sat, 11am-6pm Sun; ⊤Hynes) Converse started making shoes right up the road in Malden, MA, way back in 1908. Chuck Taylor joined the 'team' in the 1920s and the rest is history. This retail store carries sneakers, denim and other gear. The iconic shoes come in all colors and patterns; better yet, make them uniquely your own at the 2nd-floor customization area.

Three Wise Donkeys
CLOTHING

(Map p188; www.facebook.com/ThreeWiseDonkeys; 51 Gloucester St; ⊙11am-6pm Mon-Thu, 11am-8pm Fri & Sat, noon-5pm Sun; ⊤Hynes Convention Center) Cool concept, awesome designs and quality product add up to a win. Three Wise Donkeys works directly with artists (some local) who have created the unique artwork that lines the walls. Find a design that you like and they'll print it on an organic cotton T-shirt in the color and style of your choosing. Made to order in 15 minutes.

Eugene Galleries
ANTIQUES

(Map p192; www.eugenegalleries.com; 76 Charles St; ⊙11am-6pm Mon-Sat, noon-6pm Sun; ⊤Charles/MGH) This tiny shop has a remarkable selection of antique prints and maps, especially

---

ⓘ CHEAP SEATS

BosTix (www.bostix.org) offers discounted tickets to theater productions citywide (up to 25% off for advance purchases online). Discounts up to 50% are available for same-day, in-person purchase.

focusing on old Boston. Follow the history of the city's development by examining 18th- and 19th-century maps and witness the filling-in of Back Bay and the greening of the city. Historic prints highlight Boston landmarks, making for excellent old-fashioned gifts.

ℹ Information

Greater Boston Convention & Visitors Bureau (www.bostonusa.com) The website is packed with information on hotels, restaurants and special events, as well as LGBTQ, family travel and more.

Boston Harbor Islands Pavilion (Map p192; www.bostonharborislands.org; Rose Kennedy Greenway; ⊙9am-4:30pm mid-May–Jun & Sep-early Oct, to 6pm Jul & Aug; 🔊; Ⓣ Aquarium) Ideally located on the Rose Kennedy Greenway, this information center will tell you everything you need to know to plan your visit to the Boston Harbor Islands. Don't miss the nearby *Harbor Fog* sculpture, which immerses passersby in the sounds and sensations of the harbor.

Cambridge Visitor Information Kiosk (Map p188; ☑617-441-2884; www.cambridge-usa.org; Harvard Sq; ⊙9am-5pm Mon-Fri, to 1pm Sat & Sun; Ⓣ Harvard) Detailed information on current Cambridge happenings and self-guided walking tours.

Massachusetts Office of Travel & Tourism (www.massvacation.com) Information about events and activities throughout the state, including an excellent guide to green tourism.

National Park Service Visitors Center (NPS; Map p192; www.nps.gov/bost/faneuil-hall-vc.htm; Faneuil Hall; ⊙9am-6pm; Ⓣ State) The NPS Visitors Center has loads of information about the Freedom Trail sights. This is also the starting point for the free **NPS Freedom Trail Tour** (Map p192; www.nps.gov/bost; Faneuil Hall; ⊙hourly 10am-3pm Jul-Sep; Ⓣ State). There is an additional NPS Visitors Center at the **Charlestown Navy Yard** (Map p188; www.nps.gov/bost; ⊙visitor center 9am-5pm Tue-Sun May-Sep, 1-5pm Thu-Sun Oct-Apr; ▣93 from Haymarket, ⛴ Inner Harbor Ferry from Long Wharf, Ⓣ North Station).

ℹ Getting There & Away

Most travelers arrive in Boston by plane, with many national and international flights in and out of **Logan International Airport** (☑800-235-6426; www.massport.com/logan). Two smaller regional airports – Manchester Airport in New Hampshire and Green Airport near Providence, RI – offer alternatives that are also accessible to Boston and are sometimes less expensive.

Most trains operated by Amtrak (www.amtrak.com) go in and out of **South Station** (Map p192; www.south-station.net; 700 Atlantic Ave). Boston is the northern terminus of the Northeast Corridor, which sends frequent trains to New York (3½ to 4½ hours), Philadelphia, PA (five to six hours) and Washington, DC (6¾ to eight hours). The *Lake Shore Limited* goes daily to Buffalo, NY (11 hours) and Chicago (22 hours), while the *Downeaster* goes from North Station to Portland, ME (2½ hours).

Buses are most useful for regional destinations, although Greyhound (www.greyhound.com) operates services around the country. In recent years, there has been a spate of new companies offering cheap and efficient service to New York City (four to five hours).

Flights, cars and tours can be booked online at lonelyplanet.com/bookings.

ℹ Getting Around

TO/FROM THE AIRPORT

Boston Logan International Airport Take the silver line bus (free) or blue line subway ($2.25 to $2.75) to central Boston from 5:30am to 12:30am, or catch a taxi for $25 to $30.

Manchester Airport Book in advance for the hourly Flight Line Inc shuttle bus to Logan International Airport, or catch the infrequent Greyhound bus to South Station, which is located in central boston on the red line.

Green Airport Take the commuter rail to South Station ($12).

PUBLIC TRANSPORTATION

T (Subway) The quickest and easiest way to get to most destinations. Runs from 5:30am or 6am until 12:30am.

Hubway Boston's bike-share program, with 1600 bikes available to borrow at 185 stations.

MBTA bus Supplements the subway system.

Northwest of Boston

Lexington

This upscale suburb, about 18 miles from Boston's center, is a bustling village of white churches and historic taverns, with tour buses surrounding the village green. Here, the skirmish between patriots and British troops jump-started the War of Independence. Each year on April 19, historians and patriots don their 18th-century costumes and grab their rifles for an elaborate re-enactment of the events of 1775.

While this history is celebrated and preserved, it is in stark contrast to the peaceful, even staid, community that is Lexington today. If you stray more than a few blocks from the green, you could be in Anywhere, USA, with few reminders that this is where it all started. Nonetheless, it is a pleasant enough Anywhere, USA, with restaurants and shops lining the main drag, and impressive Georgian architecture anchoring either end.

★ **Minute Man National Historic Park** PARK

(www.nps.gov/mima; 3113 Marrett Rd; ⊙9am-5pm Apr-Oct; ⓜ) FREE The route that British troops followed to Concord has been designated the Minute Man National Historic Park. The visitors' center at the eastern end of the park shows an informative multimedia presentation depicting Paul Revere's ride and the ensuing battles. Within the park, Battle Rd is a 5-mile wooded trail that connects the historic sites related to the battles – from Meriam's Corner, where gunfire erupted while British soldiers were retreating, to the Paul Revere capture site.

Minute Man National Historical Park is about 2 miles west of Lexington center on Rte 2A.

Concord

On April 18, 1775, British troops marched out of Boston, searching for arms that colonists had hidden west of the city. The following morning, they skirmished with Colonial minutemen in Lexington, then continued on to Concord, where the rivals faced off at North Bridge, in the first battle of the War of Independence.

Today tall white church steeples rise above ancient oaks, elms and maples, giving Concord a stateliness that belies the revolutionary drama that occurred centuries ago. Indeed, it's easy to see how writers such as Ralph Waldo Emerson, Nathaniel Hawthorne, Henry David Thoreau and Louisa May Alcott found their inspiration here. Concord was also the home of famed sculptor Daniel Chester French (who went on to create the Lincoln Memorial in Washington, DC).

These days travelers can relive history in Concord. Patriots' Day (www.lexingtonma.gov/patriotsday) is celebrated with gusto, and many significant literary sites are open for visitors.

☉ Sights & Activities

★ **Old North Bridge** HISTORIC SITE

(www.nps.gov/mima; Monument St; ⊙dawn-dusk) FREE A half-mile north of Monument Sq in Concord center, the wooden span of Old North Bridge is the site of the 'shot heard around the world' (as Emerson wrote in his poem *Concord Hymn*). This is where enraged minutemen fired on British troops, forcing them to retreat to Boston. Daniel Chester French's first statue, *Minute Man*, presides over the park from the opposite side of the bridge.

★ **Sleepy Hollow Cemetery** CEMETERY

(www.friendsofsleepyhollow.org; Bedford St) This is the final resting place for the most famous Concordians. Though the entrance is only a block east of Monument Sq, the most interesting part, **Authors' Ridge**, is a 15-minute walk along Bedford St. Henry David Thoreau and his family are buried here, as are the Alcotts and the Hawthornes. Ralph Waldo Emerson's tombstone is a large, uncarved rose-quartz boulder, an appropriate transcendentalist symbol.

❶ Getting There & Away

Concord is accessible by MBTA commuter rail (www.mbta.com) from Boston.

Lexington is accessible by bus (except on Sunday), but you'll need a car to see the Minute Man National Historic Park.

Around Boston

Salem

This town's very name conjures up images of diabolical witchcraft and people being burned at the stake. The famous Salem witch trials of 1692 are ingrained in the national memory. Indeed, Salem goes all out at Halloween, when the whole town dresses up for parades and parties, and shops sell all manner of Wiccan accessories.

These incidents obscure Salem's true claim to fame: its glory days as a center for clipper-ship trade with the Far East. Elias Hasket Derby, America's first millionaire, built Derby Wharf, which is now the center of the Salem Maritime National Historic Site.

Today Salem is a middle-class commuter suburb of Boston with an enviable location on the sea. Its rich history and culture, from witches to ships to art, continue to cast a spell of enchantment on all those who visit.

The Rockport/Newburyport line of the MBTA commuter rail (www.mbta.com) runs from Boston's North Station to Salem Depot ($7.50, 30 minutes). Trains run every 30 minutes during the morning and evening rush hours, hourly during the rest of day, and less frequently at weekends.

Plymouth

Plymouth calls itself 'America's Home Town.' It was here that the Pilgrims first settled in the winter of 1620, seeking a place where they could practice their religion as they wished, without interference from government. An innocuous, weathered ball of granite – the famous Plymouth Rock – marks the spot where they supposedly first stepped ashore in this foreign land, and many museums and historic houses in the surrounding streets recall their struggles, sacrifices and triumphs.

You can reach Plymouth from Boston by MBTA commuter rail trains (www.mbta.com), which depart from South Station three or four times a day ($11.50, 90 minutes). From the station at Cordage Park, PAL buses connect to Plymouth center.

Cape Cod

Quaint fishing villages, kitschy tourist traps and genteel towns – the Cape has many faces. Each attracts a different crowd. Families seeking calm waters perfect for little tykes favor Cape Cod Bay on the peninsula's quieter north side. College students looking to play hard in the day and let loose after the sun goes down set out for Falmouth or Wellfleet. Provincetown is a mecca for art lovers, whale-watchers, gay and lesbian travelers and...well, just about everyone.

❶ Getting There & Around

Your own wheels (two or four) makes getting around easy, but there are also bus links; see the website of the Cape Cod Regional Transport Authority (www.capecodrta.org) for routes and schedules, including summertime shuttles in Falmouth, Hyannis and Provincetown.

Sandwich

The Cape's oldest town (founded in 1637) makes a perfect first impression as you cross over the canal from the mainland. Head straight to the village center, where white-steepled churches, period homes and a working grist mill surround a picturesque swan pond.

⊙ Sights

★ **Heritage Museums**
& Gardens MUSEUM, GARDENS
(☑508-888-3300; www.heritagemuseumsand gardens.org; 67 Grove St; adult/child $18/8; ⊙10am-5pm mid-Apr–mid-Oct; ⊕) Fun for kids and adults alike, the 100-acre Heritage Museums & Gardens sports a superb vintage automobile collection in a Shaker-style round barn, an authentic 1908 carousel (rides free with admission) and unusual folk art collections. The grounds also contain one of the finest rhododendron gardens in America; from mid-May to mid-June thousands of 'rhodies' blaze with color. Here you'll also find ways to get your heart racing, via the new **Adventure Park** (☑508-866-0199; www. heritageadventurepark.org; 2hr ticket $34-45; ⊙8am-8pm Jun & Jul, to 7pm Aug, shorter hr mid-Apr–May & Sep–mid-Nov; ⊕).

Sandwich Boardwalk WATERFRONT
(Boardwalk Rd) A local favorite that's missed by most visitors, this wooden-plank boardwalk extends a scenic 1350ft across an expansive marsh to **Town Neck Beach**. The beach itself is a bit rocky – so-so for swimming but perfect for walks and beachcombing. Once you reach the beach, turn right to make a 1.5-mile loop along the shoreline and then follow the creek back to the boardwalk. There's a $15 parking fee in July and August; at other times it's free.

🛏 Sleeping & Eating

Belfry Inn & Bistro B&B $$$
(☑508-888-8550; www.belfryinn.com; 6 Jarves St; r $179-275; ❋🐾) Ever fall asleep in church? Then you'll love the rooms, some with stained-glass windows, in this creatively restored former church, now an upmarket B&B. If, on the other hand, you're uneasy about the angel Gabriel watching over you in bed, Belfry also has two other nearby inns that are home to more conventional, high-quality rooms.

Seafood Sam's SEAFOOD $$
(☑508-888-4629; www.seafoodsams.com; 6 Coast Guard Rd; mains $7-25; ⊙11am-9pm Mar-Oct; ⊕) Opposite the Cape Cod Canal Visitor Center, Sam's is a good, simple family choice for fish and chips, fried clams and lobster

NEW ENGLAND CAPE COD

rolls. The $7 kids' menu adds to the appeal, as do the outdoor picnic tables, placed perfectly for watching fishing boats sail by.

ℹ️ Getting There & Away

If you arrive on the Cape via US 6, take exit 2 (MA 130). Water (MA 130), Main and Grove Sts converge in the village center at Shawme Pond. Tupper Rd, off MA 6A, leads to the Cape Cod Canal.

Falmouth

Crowd-pleasing beaches, a terrific bike trail and the quaint seaside village of Woods Hole are the highlights of the Cape's second-largest town. Falmouth puffs with pride over its most cherished daughter, Katharine Lee Bates, who wrote the words to the nation's favorite patriotic hymn, *America the Beautiful*.

🛏️ Sleeping & Eating

Falmouth Heights Motor Lodge   MOTEL $$
(☎ 508-548-3623; www.falmouthheightsresort.com; 146 Falmouth Heights Rd; r $149-269; ☺ May-Oct; ❄️🐕📶♨️) Don't be fooled by the name. This tidy operation is no drive-up motor lodge – it's not even on the highway. All eight styles of rooms (some small and economically priced; others larger, with kitchenettes) are a cut above the competition. And you can throw your own party: the extensive grounds harbor a picnic grove with gas barbecues.

Tides Motel of Falmouth   MOTEL $$
(☎ 508-548-3126; www.tidesmotelcapecod.com; 267 Clinton Ave; r $120-260; ☺ mid-May–mid-Oct; ❄️📶) It's all about the water. This place is smack on its own private beach, and you could spit into the ocean from your deck. Otherwise, it's straightforward: the same rooms elsewhere would be a yawn (no-frills, many with kitchenette). Between the surf lullaby and million-dollar view, a steady stream of returnees keep the motel busy all summer, so book ahead.

Maison Villatte   CAFE $
(☎ 774-255-1855; 267 Main St; snacks $3-10; ☺ 7am-5pm Tue-Thu & Sun, to 7pm Fri & Sat) A pair of French bakers crowned in toques work the ovens at this buzzing bakery-cafe, creating crusty artisan breads, flaky croissants and sinful pastries. Hearty sandwiches and robust coffee make it an ideal lunch spot.

ℹ️ Getting There & Away

Sitting at the southwest corner of the Cape, Falmouth is reached via MA 28, which becomes Main St in the center of town. Buses connect the town with Boston and other Cape destinations.

Ferries to Martha's Vineyard (p217) leave from Falmouth Harbor in summer, and year-round from Woods Hole, 4.5 miles southwest of downtown.

Hyannis

Ferries, buses and planes all converge on Hyannis, the Cape's commercial hub (and part of the larger Barnstable township). So there's a good chance you will too. The village center, especially the harborfront, has been rejuvenated, making it a pleasant place to break a journey.

In addition to being a jumping-off point for boats to Nantucket and Martha's Vineyard, Hyannis attracts Kennedy fans – JFK made his summer home here, and it was at the Kennedy compound that Teddy passed away in 2009. Hyannis Harbor, with its waterfront eateries and ferries, is a few minutes' walk from Main St.

👁️ Sights

⭐ **John F Kennedy Hyannis Museum**   MUSEUM
(☎ 508-790-3077; www.jfkhyannismuseum.org; 397 Main St; adult/child $10/5; ☺ 9am-5pm Mon-Sat, noon-5pm Sun Jun-Oct, 10am-4pm Mon-Sat, noon-4pm Sun mid-Apr–May & Nov) Hyannis has been the summer home of the Kennedy clan for generations. Back in the day, JFK spent his summers here – times that are beautifully documented at this museum with photographs and video, from JFK's childhood to the Camelot years of his presidency. The exhibits are poignantly done, and present a theme that changes annually (previous years have covered matriarch Rose and explored the brotherly bond between Jack and Bobby).

Cape Cod Potato Chip Factory   FACTORY
(☎ 888-881-2447; www.capecodchips.com; 100 Breed's Hill Rd; ☺ 9am-5pm Mon-Fri) FREE These much-admired chips are of the potato, not the computer, variety, so although they won't work in your laptop, they'll taste good in your gateway. The factory has a self-guided tour; in effect, it's just observing the chips march across the production and

Cape Cod, Martha's Vineyard & Nantucket

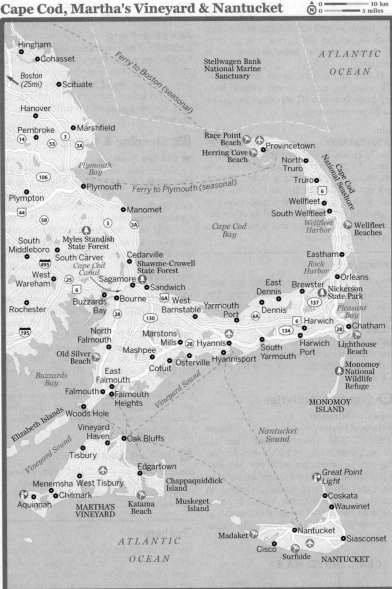

packaging lines through windows. The whole visit might take you 10 minutes, and you get free samples.

From MA 132 (just west of the airport), take Independence Rd a half-mile north to the factory.

🛏 Sleeping & Eating

HI Hyannis   HOSTEL **$**

(☏ 508-775-7990; www.hiusa.org; 111 Ocean St; dm $35-40, d $79-99, q $99-129; ☺ mid-May–mid-Oct; 🅿@🛜) For a million-dollar view on a backpacker's budget, book yourself a bed at this hostel overlooking the harbor. It was built in 2010 by adding new wings to a period home and is within walking distance of the Main St scene, beaches and ferries. Now the caveat: there are only 42 beds, so book well in advance.

Dorms and private rooms are available. Prices are for members and include linen and breakfast; non-HI members pay an extra $3 per person.

Tumi SEAFOOD **$$**
(508-534-9289; www.tumiceviche.com; 592 Main St; ceviche $9-23, mains $19-31; 11:30am-10pm;) If you love seafood but you're hankering for something a little different, seek out this hidden Italian-Peruvian gem. Take your pick from nine kinds of ceviche (including vegetarian), as well as other raw shellfish, seafood pasta and some interesting Peruvian options.

Brewster

Woodsy Brewster, on the Cape's bay side, makes a good base for outdoorsy types. The Cape Cod Rail Trail cuts clear across town, and there's first-rate camping and water activities. Brewster also has fine restaurants, out of proportion to the town's small size. Everything of interest is on or just off MA 6A (also called Main St), which runs the length of the town.

Sights & Activties

Cape Cod Museum of Natural History MUSEUM
(508-896-3867; www.ccmnh.org; 869 MA 6A; adult/child $15/6; 9:30am-4pm Jun-Aug, 11am-3pm Sep, shorter hrs rest of year;) This family-friendly museum offers exhibits on the Cape's flora and fauna, including an aquarium and a butterfly house. It has a fine **boardwalk trail** across a salt marsh to a remote beach with tide pools. The muse-

um has a calendar rich with naturalist-led walks, talks and kids' programs.

Jack's Boat Rental BOATING
(508-896-8556; www.jacksboatrental.com; Flax Pond, Nickerson State Park; boat rentals per 30min $11-31; 10am-6pm mid-Jun–mid-Sep) Jack's Boat Rentals, found by Flax Pond within lovely Nickerson State Park, rents out canoes, kayaks and stand-up paddleboards by the half-hour.

Sleeping & Eating

★**Old Sea Pines Inn** B&B **$$**
(508-896-6114; www.oldseapinesinn.com; 2553 Main St/MA 6A; r $125-170, ste $190-210;) Staying here is a bit like staying at Grandma's house: antique fittings, sleigh beds and sepia photographs on the bureau. This former girls' boarding school dating from 1840 has 24 rooms: some small; others commodious, with fireplace; some suited to families. Mosey out to the rocking chairs on the porch and soak up the yesteryear atmosphere.

★**Brewster Fish House** SEAFOOD **$$$**
(508-896-7867; www.brewsterfishhouse.com; 2208 Main St/MA 6A; lunch mains $12-20, dinner mains $21-39; 11:30am-3pm & 5-9:30pm) It's not an eye-catcher from the outside, but it's heaven inside for seafood lovers. Start with the lobster bisque, naturally sweet and with chunks of fresh lobster. From there it's safe to cast your net in any direction; dishes are fresh and creative. Just a dozen tables, and no reservations, so try lunch or early dinner to avoid long waits.

Getting There & Away

Brewster stretches along Cape Cod Bay between Dennis and Orleans. Access is best via MA 6A. From the Cape's south, take MA 124 or MA 137 from Harwich.

Chatham

The patriarch of Cape Cod towns, Chatham has a genteel reserve that is evident along its shady Main St: the shops are upscale; the lodgings, tony. That said, there's something for everyone here – families flock to town for seal-watching, and birders migrate to the wildlife refuge. And then there are all those beaches. Sitting at the 'elbow' of the Cape, Chatham has an amazing 60 miles of shoreline along the ocean, the sound and countless coves and inlets.

SCENIC DRIVE: MA 6A

When exploring the Cape, eschew the speedy Mid-Cape Hwy (US 6) and follow instead the Old King's Hwy (MA 6A), which snakes along Cape Cod Bay. The longest continuous stretch of historic district in the USA, it's lined with gracious period homes, antique shops and art galleries, all of which make for good browsing en route.

MA 28 leads right to Main St, where the lion's share of shops and restaurants are lined up. Chatham is a town made for strolling. You'll find free parking along Main St and in the parking lot behind the Chatham Squire.

❶ Getting There & Away

Chatham sits at the 'elbow' of the Cape. MA 28 is the main route through it; it becomes Main St in the downtown area.

MA 137 connects Chatham with US 6.

Wellfleet

Art galleries, primo surfing beaches and those famous Wellfleet oysters lure visitors to this seaside village. Actually, there's not much Wellfleet doesn't have, other than crowds. It's a delightful throwback to an earlier era, from its drive-in movie theater to its unspoiled town center, which has barely changed in appearance since the 1950s.

During the **Wellfleet OysterFest** (www. wellfleetoysterfest.org), held on a weekend in mid-October, the entire town center becomes a food fair, with a beer garden, an oyster-shucking contest and, of course, belly-busters of the blessed bivalves. It's a wildly popular event and a great time to see Wellfleet at its most spirited.

◉ Sights & Activities

Wellfleet Bay
Wildlife Sanctuary   NATURE RESERVE
(☏ 508-349-2615; www.massaudubon.org; 291 US 6, South Wellfleet; adult/child $5/3; ☉ trails 8am-dusk, nature center 8:30am-5pm late May–early Oct; ⦿) Birders flock to Mass Audubon's 940-acre sanctuary, where 5 miles of trails cross tidal creeks, salt marshes and beaches. The most popular is the **Goose Pond Trail** (1.5-mile round-trip), which leads out to a salt marsh and offers abundant opportunities for spotting marine and bird life. The sanctuary also offers guided walks and kayaking tours, seal cruises and summer kids' programs.

SickDay Surf Shop   SURFING
(☏ 508-214-4158; www.sickday.cc; 361 Main St; surfboard rental per day/week $30/150; ☉ 9am-9pm Mon-Sat May-Oct) If you need surf gear, lessons or local advice, SickDay Surf Shop can help. They also rent wetsuits, stand-up paddleboards and body boards.

AT THE DRIVE-IN...

For an evening of nostalgia, park at **Wellfleet Drive-In** (☏ 508-349-7176; www.wellfleetcinemas.com; 51 US 6, South Wellfleet; tickets adult/child $11/8; ☉ late May–mid-Sep; ⦿), one of a dwindling number of drive-in theaters surviving in the USA. Built in the 1950s, before the word 'cineplex' became part of the vernacular, everything except the movie being shown on the giant screen is true to the era. Yep, they still have those original mono speakers that you hook over the car window, there's an old-fashioned snack bar and, of course, it's always a double feature. Plastic – what's that? It's cash-only at the gate.

OK, there are a few accommodations to modern times. So as to not block anyone's view, the lot is now divided into two sections: one for SUVs, the other for cars. And you don't need to use those boxy window speakers: you can also listen by tuning your stereo car radio to an FM station. But other things remain unchanged – bring bug spray and a blanket!

🍴 Sleeping & Eating

Even'Tide Motel   MOTEL **$$**
(☏ 508-349-3410; www.eventidemotel.com; 650 US 6, South Wellfleet; r $95-207, cottages per week $1400-2900; ☉ May–mid-Oct; ❄ 🐾 ⚹) This highly regarded motel, set back from the highway in a grove of pine trees, has an assortment of options: regular motel rooms, plus 10 diverse cottages that can each accommodate two to 10 people (cottages are generally rented by the week). Pluses include a large, indoor heated pool and 5 acres of wooded grounds that harbor sports and picnic facilities.

★ PB Boulangerie & Bistro   BAKERY **$**
(☏ 508-349-1600; www.pbboulangeriebistro.com; 15 Lecount Hollow Rd, South Wellfleet; pastries $3-5; ☉ bakery 7am-7pm Wed-Sun, bistro 5-9:30pm Wed-Sun) A Michelin-starred French baker setting up shop in tiny Wellfleet? You might think he'd gone crazy, if not for the line out the door. You can't miss PB: it's painted pink and set back from US 6. Scan the cabinets full of fruit tarts, chocolate-almond

DON'T MISS

CAPE COD RAIL TRAIL

The mother of all Cape bicycle trails, the Cape Cod Rail Trail (CCRT) runs 22 glorious paved miles through forest, past cranberry bogs and along sandy ponds ideal for a dip. This rural route, formerly used as a railroad line, is one of the finest bike trails in all of New England.

The path begins in Dennis on MA 134 and continues through **Nickerson State Park** (🕿 508-896-3491; www.mass.gov/dcr; 3488 MA 6A; parking $15; ⊘ dawn-dusk; 🖭) in Brewster, into Orleans and across the Cape Cod National Seashore (p214), all the way to South Wellfleet.

There's a hefty dose of Ye Olde Cape Cod scenery en route and you'll have opportunities to detour into villages for lunch or sightseeing. If you have only enough time to do part of the trail, begin at Nickerson State Park and head for the National Seashore – the landscape is unbeatable.

Bicycle rentals are available at the trailheads in Dennis and Wellfleet, at Nickerson State Park and opposite the National Seashore's visitor center in Eastham. There's car parking at all four sites (free except for a small charge at Nickerson).

croissants and filled baguettes and you'll think you've died and gone to Paris.

Mac's on the Pier SEAFOOD $$
(🕿 508-349-9611; www.macsseafood.com; 265 Commercial St, Wellfleet Town Pier; mains $8-33; ⊘ 11am-8:30pm late May-early Oct; 🖭🖭) Head here for fish-market-fresh seafood at bargain prices. Fried-fish standards join the likes of oyster po'boys, sushi rolls and grilled striped-bass dinners. You order at a window and chow down at picnic tables overlooking Wellfleet Harbor.

🛈 Getting There & Away

Most of Wellfleet east of US 6 is part of the Cape Cod National Seashore. To get to the town center, turn west off US 6 at either Main St or School St.

Provincetown

This is it: Provincetown is as far as you can go on the Cape, and more than just geographically. The draw is irresistible. Fringe writers and artists began making a summer haven in Provincetown a century ago. Today this sandy outpost has morphed into the hottest gay and lesbian destination in the Northeast. Flamboyant street scenes, brilliant art galleries and unbridled nightlife paint the town center. But that's only half the show. Provincetown's untamed coastline and vast beaches also beg exploring. Sail off on a whale-watch, cruise the night away, get lost in the dunes – but whatever you do, don't miss this unique, open-minded corner of New England.

👁 Sights

Start your exploration on Commercial St, the throbbing waterfront heart of Provincetown, where the lion's share of cafes, galleries and clubs vie for your attention. On any given day you may see cross-dressers, leather-clad motorcyclists, barely clad in-line skaters, same-sex couples strolling hand in hand and heterosexual tourists wondering what they've stumbled into on their way to a whale-watch.

⭐**Provincetown Art Association & Museum** MUSEUM
(PAAM; 🕿 508-487-1750; www.paam.org; 460 Commercial St; adult/child $10/free; ⊘ 11am-8pm Mon-Thu, to 10pm Fri, to 6pm Sat, to 5pm Sun Jul & Aug, shorter hrs rest of year) Founded in 1914 to celebrate the town's thriving art community, this vibrant museum showcases the works of hundreds of artists who have found their inspiration on the Lower Cape. Chief among them are Charles Hawthorne, who led the early Provincetown art movement, and Edward Hopper, who had a home and gallery in the Truro dunes.

⭐**Pilgrim Monument & Provincetown Museum** MUSEUM
(🕿 508-487-1310; www.pilgrim-monument.org; 1 High Pole Hill Rd; adult/child $12/4; ⊘ 9am-5pm Apr, May & Sep-Nov, to 7pm Jun-Aug) Climb to the top of the country's tallest all-granite structure (253ft) for a sweeping view of town, the beaches and the spine of the Lower Cape. The climb is 116 steps plus 60 ramps and takes about 10 minutes at a leisurely pace.

At the base of the c 1910 tower is an evocative museum depicting the landing of the *Mayflower* Pilgrims and other Provincetown history.

Provincetown Public Library LIBRARY
(☑508-487-7094; www.provincetownlibrary.org; 356 Commercial St; ⊘10am-5pm Mon & Fri, to 8pm Tue-Thu, 1-5pm Sat & Sun; ⊕) Erected in 1860 as a church, this building was turned into a museum a century later, complete with a half-size replica of Provincetown's famed race-winning schooner *Rose Dorothea*. When the museum went bust, the town converted the building to a library. One catch: the boat, which occupies the building's upper deck, was too big to remove – so it's still there, with bookshelves built around it. Pop upstairs and take a look.

Race Point Beach BEACH
(Race Point Rd) On the wild tip of the Cape, this Cape Cod National Seashore (p214) beach is a breathtaking stretch of sand, crashing surf and undulating dunes as far as the eye can see. Kick off your sandals, kids – the soft, grainy sand makes for a fun run. This is the kind of beach where you could walk for miles and see no one but the occasional angler casting for bluefish. Parking costs $20 in summer (the National Seashore fee).

🏃 Activities

Province Lands Bike Trail (www.nps.gov/caco), an exhilarating 7.5 miles of paved bike trails, crisscrosses the forest and undulating dunes of the Cape Cod National Seashore (p214). As a bonus, you can cool off with a swim: the main 5.5-mile loop trail has spur trails leading to both **Herring Cove Beach** (Province Lands Rd) and Race Point Beach.

★Dolphin Fleet Whale Watch WILDLIFE
(☑800-826-9300, 508-240-3636; www.whalewatch.com; 307 Commercial St; adult/child $47/31; ⊘mid-Apr–Oct; ⊕) ☀ Dolphin Fleet offers as many as 10 whale-watch tours daily in peak season, each lasting three to four hours. You can expect a lot of splashy fun. Humpback whales have a flair for acrobatic breaching and come surprisingly close to the boats, offering great photo ops. The naturalists on board not only have all the skinny on these mammoth leviathans but also play a vital role in monitoring the whale population.

🛏 Sleeping

Moffett House GUESTHOUSE $$
(☑508-487-6615; www.moffetthouse.com; 296a Commercial St; d without bathroom $75-164, with bathroom $115-184; P✻@☎) Set back on an alleyway, this guesthouse is not only quiet but also has another bonus: every room comes with two bicycles for your stay. Rooms are basic – it's more like crashing with a friend than doing the B&B thing – but you get kitchen privileges, bagels and coffee in the morning (in summer), and lots of opportunities to meet fellow travelers.

★Carpe Diem BOUTIQUE HOTEL $$$
(☑508-487-4242; www.carpediemguesthouse.com; 12-14 Johnson St; r $199-549; P✻☎) Sophisticated yet relaxed, this boutique inn blends a soothing mix of smiling Buddhas, orchid sprays and artistic decor. Each guest room is inspired by a different gay literary genius; the room themed on poet Raj Rao, for example, has sumptuous embroidered fabrics and hand-carved Indian furniture.

🍴 Eating

Cafe Heaven CAFE $
(☑508-487-9639; www.facebook.com/cafeheavenptown; 199 Commercial St; mains $8-17; ⊘8am-2pm & 6-10pm; ⊉) Always bustling, this light and airy art-filled storefront is best known for its easy-on-the-wallet all-day breakfasts, with lunch and dinner sharing the bill as the day progresses. The menu ranges from sinfully good brioche French toast to healthy salads. Excellent sandwiches too, like croque monsieur and chicken pesto melt. Don't be deterred by the wait: the tables turn over quickly.

EAST END GALLERY DISTRICT

With the many artists who have worked here, it's no surprise that Provincetown hosts some of the finest art galleries in the region. For the best browsing, begin at **PAAM** and start walking southwest along Commercial St. Over the next few blocks every second storefront harbors a gallery worth a peek.

Pick up a copy of the *Provincetown Gallery Guide* (www.provincetowngalleryguide.com), or check out its website for gallery info, a map and details of events.

Lobster Pot

SEAFOOD $$$

(☑508-487-0842; www.ptownlobsterpot.com; 321 Commercial St; sandwiches $12-23, mains $25-34; ⊙11:30am-9pm Apr-Nov) True to its name, this busy fish house overlooking the harbor is *the* place for lobster, and many have been lured by its retro neon sign. Start with the lobster bisque, then put on a bib and crack open the perfect boiled lobster (there's a full gluten-free menu too). The best way to beat the crowd is to come mid-afternoon.

★ Mews Restaurant & Cafe

MODERN AMERICAN $$$

(☑508-487-1500; www.mews.com; 429 Commercial St; mains $22-44; ⊙5-10pm) A fantastic water view, the hottest martini bar in town and scrumptious food add up to Provincetown's finest dining scene. There are two sections. Opt to dine gourmet on lobster risotto and filet mignon downstairs, where you're right on the sand, or go casual with a juicy Angus burger from the bistro menu upstairs. Reservations recommended.

🍷 Drinking

Aqua Bar

BAR

(☑774-593-5106; www.facebook.com/aquabarptown; 207 Commercial St; ⊙11am-8pm Mon-Thu, to 11pm Fri-Sun late Apr–Nov) Imagine a food court where the options include a raw bar, sushi, gelato and other international delights. Add a fully stocked bar with generous bartenders pouring the drinks. Now put the whole place in a gorgeous seaside setting, overlooking a little beach and beautiful harbor. Now imagine this whole scene at sunset. That's Aqua Bar.

Boatslip Beach Club

GAY

(☑508-487-1669; www.boatslipresort.com; 161 Commercial St; ⊙tea dances daily from 4pm) Hosts wildly popular afternoon tea dances (4pm to 7pm), often packed with gorgeous guys. DJs fire things up: visit on Thursdays for dance classics from the '70s and '80s. There's accommodations too.

Crown & Anchor

GAY & LESBIAN

(☑508-487-1430; www.onlyatthecrown.com; 247 Commercial St; ⊙hr vary) The queen of the scene, this multiwing complex has a nightclub, a video bar, a leather bar and a fun, steamy cabaret that takes it to the limit, plus loads of shows and events – from Broadway concerts to drag revues and burlesque troupes. Check the calendar (and buy tickets) online. Accommodations and restaurant on site too.

❶ Getting There & Away

From the Cape Cod Canal via US 6, it takes about 1½ hours to reach Provincetown (65 miles), depending on traffic. Commercial St is narrow and crowded with pedestrians, so you'll want to do most of your driving along the more car-friendly Bradford St.

BOAT

From around May to October, boats connect Provincetown's **MacMillan Pier** with Boston and Plymouth. Schedules are geared to day-trippers, with morning arrivals into Provincetown and late-afternoon departures. No ferries carry cars, but bikes can be transported for a fee (around $12 round-trip). Advance reservations are recommended, especially on weekends and in peak summer.

Bay State Cruise Co (www.boston-ptown.com) Fast ferry (1½ hours) operates three times daily from Boston's World Trade Center Pier.

Boston Harbor Cruises (www.bostonharborcruises.com) Fast-ferry service (1½ hours) from Long Wharf in Boston up to three times daily.

Plymouth-to-Provincetown Express Ferry (www.captjohn.com) Ferry from Plymouth (1½ hours, once daily) to Provincetown's MacMillan Pier.

BUS

The Plymouth & Brockton bus (www.p-b.com), which terminates at **MacMillan Pier**, runs several times a day from Boston (one way $32 to $38, three to 3½ hours), stopping at other Cape towns along the way. In Boston, it stops at Logan airport and South Station.

CAPE COD NATIONAL SEASHORE

Extending some 40 miles around the curve of the Outer Cape **Cape Cod National Seashore** (☑508-255-3421; www.nps.gov/caco; pedestrian/cyclist/motorcycle/car per day $3/3/10/20) encompasses the Atlantic shoreline from Orleans all the way to Provincetown. Under the auspices of the National Park Service, it's a treasure trove of unspoiled beaches, dunes, salt marshes, nature trails and forests. Thanks to the backing of President John F Kennedy, this vast area was set aside for preservation in the 1960s, just before a building boom hit the rest of his native Cape Cod.

Nantucket

One need not be a millionaire to visit Nantucket, but it couldn't hurt. This compact island, 30 miles south of Cape Cod, grew rich from whaling in the 19th century. In recent decades it's seen a rebirth as a summer getaway for CEOs, society types and other well-heeled visitors from Boston and New York.

It's easy to see why. Nantucket is New England at its most rose-covered, cobble-stoned, picture-postcard perfect, and even in the peak of summer there's always an empty stretch of sandy beach to be found. Outdoor activities abound, and there are fine museums, smart restaurants and fun bars.

The town of Nantucket (called 'Town' by the locals) is the island's only real population center. Once home port to the world's largest whaling fleet, the town's storied past is reflected in the gracious period buildings lining its leafy streets. It boasts the nation's largest concentration of houses built prior to 1850 and is the only place in the USA where the entire town is a National Historic Landmark. It's a thoroughly enjoyable place to just amble about and soak up the atmosphere.

Sights

★Nantucket Whaling Museum MUSEUM

(☎508-228-1894; www.nha.org; 13 Broad St; adult/child $20/5; ⏲11am-4pm Apr & May, 10am-5pm Jun-Oct, reduced hr Nov, Dec & mid-Feb–Mar, closed Jan–mid-Feb) One of the island's highlights, this evocative museum occupies an 1847 spermaceti (whale oil) candle factory and the excellent exhibits relive Nantucket's 19th-century heyday as the whaling center of the world. There's a worthwhile, albeit long (54 minutes), documentary on the island, incredible scrimshaw exhibits (engravings and carvings done by sailors on ivory, whalebone or baleen), and a 46ft sperm whale skeleton rising above it all. Be sure to head to the rooftop deck for lovely views.

Sleeping

Unless you've got island friends with a spare room, a summer stay on Nantucket won't be cheap. Don't even look for a motel or campground – tony Nantucket is all about inns, and many of those are receiving dramatic makeovers to bring them to design-magazine standard.

LOCAL KNOWLEDGE

GO LANING

Go local, go laning. That's the 1930s term Nantucketers coined for wandering about the narrow streets of the town's historic district, especially in the early evening. For the finest stroll, walk up cobbled Main St, just past the c 1818 Pacific National Bank. There you'll find the grandest whaling-era mansions lined up in a row. Other laning favorites: Gardner and Liberty Sts and the honeycombed lanes between Federal and S Water Sts.

★HI Nantucket HOSTEL $

(Star of the Sea; ☎508-228-0433; www.hiusa.org; 31 Western Ave; dm $39-45; ⏲mid-May–mid-Oct; @ 🛜) Known locally as Star of the Sea, this cool hostel has a million-dollar setting just minutes from Surfside Beach. It's housed in a former lifesaving station that dates from 1873 and is listed on the National Register of Historic Places. As Nantucket's sole budget option, its 49 beds are in high demand, so book as far in advance as possible.

Prices include breakfast and linen; non-HI members pay an additional $3.

Barnacle Inn B&B $$

(☎508-228-0332; www.thebarnacleinn.com; 11 Fair St; r without bathroom $125-300, with bathroom $155-420, ste $180-550; ⏲late Apr-early Nov; ❄ 🛜) This is what old Nantucket is all about: folksy owners and simple, quaint accommodations that hearken to earlier times. Rooms in this turn-of-the-19th-century inn don't have phones or TVs, but they do have good rates, particularly if you opt for a shared bath.

Eating & Drinking

Downyflake DINER, BAKERY $

(☎508-228-4533; www.thedownyflake.com; 18 Sparks Ave; mains $5-13; ⏲6am-2pm Mon-Sat, to 1pm Sun Apr–mid-Jan) A popular stop for the island's working-class folks, this no-frills eatery on the edge of town is known for its all-day breakfasts (blueberry pancakes, big omelets) and simple comfort fare. It also doubles as a bakery with homemade doughnuts.

UP-ISLAND

Known as Up Island, the rural western half of Martha's Vineyard is a patchwork of rolling hills, small farms and open fields frequented by wild turkeys and deer. Feast your eyes and your belly at the picturesque fishing village of **Menemsha**, where you'll find seafood shacks with food so fresh the boats unload their catch at the back door. They'll shuck you an oyster and steam you a lobster while you watch and you can eat alfresco on a harborside bench.

The coastal **Aquinnah Cliffs**, also known as the Gay Head Cliffs, are so special they're a National Natural Landmark. These 150ft-high cliffs glow with an amazing array of colors that can be best appreciated in the late afternoon light. You can hang out at **Aquinnah Public Beach**, just below the multihued cliffs, or walk a mile north along the shore to an area that's popular with nude sunbathers.

Cedar Tree Neck Sanctuary (☑508-693-5207; www.sheriffsmeadow.org; Obed Daggett Rd, off Indian Hill Rd; ⊘8:30am-5:30pm) 𝗙𝗥𝗘𝗘, off State Rd, has an inviting 2.5-mile hike across native bogs and forest to a coastal bluff with views of Cape Cod. The Massachusetts Audubon Society's **Felix Neck Wildlife Sanctuary** (☑508-627-4850; www.massaudubon.org; 100 Felix Neck Dr; adult/child $4/3; ⊘trails dawn-dusk, visitor center 9am-4pm Mon-Fri, 10am-3pm Sat & Sun Jun-Sep; 🖴) is a birder's paradise with 4 miles of trails skirting marshes and ponds.

Black-Eyed Susan's   MODERN AMERICAN $$$
(☑508-325-0308;   www.black-eyedsusans.com;
10 India St; breakfast mains $8-13, dinner $26-29;
⊘7am-1pm daily & 6-10pm Mon-Sat Apr-Oct; 🍴)
It's hard to find anyone who doesn't adore this petite, long-running, quietly gourmet place. At breakfast, try the sourdough French toast topped with cinnamon pecans and orange butter; at dinner, sit at the bar to watch chefs perform magic in a *tiny* space. The fish of the day often takes top honors (with strong competition). BYOB.

★ **Cisco Brewers**   BREWERY
(☑508-325-5929; www.ciscobrewers.com; 5 Bartlett Farm Rd; tours $20; ⊘11am-7pm Mon-Sat, noon-6pm Sun year-round, tours mid-May–Dec)
Enjoy a hoppy pint of Whale's Tale pale ale at the friendliest brewery you'll likely ever see. Cisco Brewers is the 'other' Nantucket, a laid-back place where fun banter loosens those stiff upper lips found in primmer quarters. In addition to the brewery, there's a small **distillery**, casual indoor and outdoor bars, regular food trucks and live music.

❶ Information

Visitor Services & Information Bureau
(☑508-228-0925; www.nantucket-ma.gov; 25 Federal St; ⊘9am-5pm daily mid-Apr–mid-Oct, Mon-Sat rest of year) Tourist office in Nantucket town.

Nantucket.net (www.nantucket.net) Has private listings of restaurants, housing, arts and recreation.

Inquirer and Mirror (www.ack.net) Local newspaper, with a decent visitors' guide.

❶ Getting There & Away

AIR

Nantucket Memorial Airport (☑508-325-5300; www.nantucketairport.com; 14 Airport Rd) is 3 miles southeast of Nantucket town. Cape Air (www.capeair.com) offers year-round service to Boston, Hyannis, New Bedford and Martha's Vineyard, and seasonal service to New York. Delta, American, United and JetBlue also offer seasonal services to/from New York, Newark and Washington, DC.

The airport is connected by local bus to town ($2) from mid-June to early September.

BOAT

The most common way to reach Nantucket is by the Steamship Authority and Hy-Line Cruises ferries from Hyannis.

The Steamship Authority (www.steamshipauthority.com) runs frequent, year-round ferries between Hyannis and Nantucket from Steamboat Wharf.

Hy-Line Cruises (www.hylinecruises.com) operates a fast passenger ferry from Hyannis to Nantucket from Straight Wharf year-round and a daily summer ferry between Nantucket and Oak Bluffs on Martha's Vineyard.

Seastreak (www.seastreak.com) operates high-speed passenger ferries in the summer (mid-May to early September) to Nantucket daily from New Bedford, MA, and with weekend services from New Jersey and New York City.

Martha's Vineyard

Bathed in scenic beauty, Martha's Vineyard attracts wide-eyed day-trippers, celebrity second-home owners, and urbanites seeking a restful getaway; its 15,000 year-round residents include many artists, musicians and back-to-nature types. The Vineyard remains untouched by the kind of rampant commercialism found on the mainland – there's not a single chain restaurant or cookie-cutter motel in sight. Instead you'll find cozy inns, chef-driven restaurants and a bounty of green farms and grand beaches. And there's something for every mood here – fine dining in gentrified Edgartown one day and hitting the cotton candy and carousel scene in Oak Bluffs the next.

Martha's Vineyard is the largest island in New England, extending some 23 miles at its widest. Although it sits just 7 miles off the coast of Cape Cod, Vineyarders feel themselves such a world apart that they often refer to the mainland as 'America.'

◉ Sights & Activities

★ **Campgrounds & Tabernacle** HISTORIC SITE
(☎ 508-693-0525; www.mvcma.org) Oak Bluffs started out in the mid-19th century as a summer retreat by a revivalist church, whose members enjoyed a day at the beach as much as a gospel service. They first camped out in tents, then built some 300 wooden cottages, each adorned with whimsical filigree trim.

Flying Horses Carousel HISTORIC SITE
(☎ 508-693-9481; www.mvpreservation.org; Oak Bluffs Ave; per ride/10 rides $3/25; ⊙ 10am-10pm mid-Jun–mid-Sep; ⚑) Take a nostalgic ride on this National Historic Landmark, which has been captivating kids of all ages since 1876. It's the USA's oldest continuously operating merry-go-round, and these antique horses have manes of real horse hair.

Anderson's Bike Rentals CYCLING
(☎ 508-693-9346; www.andersonsbikerentals. com; Circuit Ave Extension; bike rental per day/ week $22/95; ⊙ 9am-6pm May-Oct) Step off the ferry and you'll find a slew of wheelers and dealers renting out bicycles. Keep walking until you reach Anderson's Bike Rentals, an established, family-run operation with well-maintained bikes offered at honest prices. Can also deliver bikes to you.

⌂ Sleeping

HI Martha's Vineyard HOSTEL $
(☎ 508-693-2665; www.hiusa.org; 525 Edgartown–West Tisbury Rd; dm $36-42, tw $99, q $125-149; ⊙ mid-May–early Oct; Ⓟ @ 🛜) Reserve early for a bed at this popular, purpose-built hostel in the center of the island. It has everything you'd expect: a solid kitchen, games room, bike delivery, no curfew and friendly staff. The public bus stops out front and it's right on the bike path. Dorms and private rooms are available.

Nashua House INN $$
(☎ 508-693-0043; www.nashuahouse.com; 9 Healy Way; r $119-219; ❄ 🛜) The Vineyard the way it used to be...but with some concessions to modernity (some rooms have TV, some have private bathroom). You'll find simple, spotless, characterful accommodations at this quaint 1873 inn with restaurants and pubs just beyond the front door. It's good value in the summer; in the off-season, when rates drop by nearly half, it's a steal.

LIGHTHOUSES OF MARTHA'S VINEYARD

What's more New England than a lighthouse? And which island has the greatest diversity of lighthouses in America? One guess.

West Chop The island's last staffed lighthouse dates from 1838 and sits on the west side of Vineyard Haven Harbor.

East Chop This cast-iron structure built in 1875 is an Oak Bluffs landmark.

Edgartown It was erected on an island in 1828, but shifting sands have since filled in the inlet and it's now connected to Edgartown by land.

Cape Poge Harsh storm erosion has forced the relocation of this Chappaquiddick Island lighthouse four times since 1801.

Gay Head Built in 1844, this red-brick structure on the Aquinnah Cliffs is arguably the most scenic lighthouse on the Vineyard.

✗ Eating & Drinking

★**ArtCliff Diner**   CAFE **$**
(☑508-693-1224; 39 Beach Rd; mains $8-20; ☺7am-2pm Thu-Tue) ❂ Hands-down the best place in town for breakfast and lunch. Chef-owner Gina Stanley, a grad of the prestigious Culinary Institute of America, adds flair to everything she touches, from the almond-encrusted French toast to the fresh fish tacos. The eclectic menu utilizes farm-fresh island ingredients. Expect a line, but it's worth the wait.

Among the Flowers Café   CAFE **$$**
(☑508-627-3233; 17 Mayhew Lane; lunch $8-20, dinner mains $22-35; ☺8am-4pm mid-Apr–Oct, to 10pm Jun-Aug; ☑) Join the in-the-know crowd on the garden patio (under cute striped awnings and – yes – among the flowering plants) for homemade soups, waffles, sandwiches, crepes and even lobster rolls. Although everything's served on paper or plastic, it's still kinda chichi. In summer, it serves dinner as well, and the kitchen kicks it up a notch.

★**Offshore Ale Co**   MICROBREWERY
(☑508-693-2626; www.offshoreale.com; 30 Kennebec Ave; ☺11:30am-9pm Sun-Thu, to 10pm Fri & Sat) Join the throngs of locals and visitors at this popular microbrewery – enjoy a pint of Hop Goddess ale, some superior pub grub (including a knockout lobster roll) and the kind of laid-back atmosphere where boats are suspended from the ceiling and peanut shells are thrown on the floor.

❶ Getting There & Away

AIR

Martha's Vineyard Airport (MVY; www.mvyairport.com) is in the center of the island, about 6 miles south of Vineyard Haven, and is served by buses. It has year-round service to Boston and Nantucket and seasonal services to Hyannis, New Bedford, MA, and New York. Check Cape Air (www.capeair.com) for schedules. Delta and JetBlue also offer seasonal services from New York's JFK Airport.

BOAT

Steamship Authority (www.steamshipauthority.com) operates a frequent, year-round ferry service to Martha's Vineyard. It connects Vineyard Haven with Woods Hole, south of Falmouth on the Cape (a 45-minute voyage). This is the only ferry that carries vehicles – if you're bringing a car, book well in advance . There are up to 14 services daily in each direction.

❶ Getting Around

Getting around is easy by car, though roads are narrow and summertime traffic jams in the main towns are the norm. If you don't have your own wheels, no problem – the extensive public bus system connects every village on the island.

Cycling is another great option; you can rent bikes in Edgartown, Oak Bluffs and Vineyard Haven.

Central Massachusetts

Artfully blending the cultural and cosmopolitan with the rural and rustic, the Pioneer Valley and the Berkshires offer a tantalizing mix of artistic offerings, verdant hills and sweet farmland.

Stretch your quads on hiking trails up Massachusetts' highest mountain and through nature preserves that blanket the surrounding hills. Alternatively, ramble through estate homes of the once famous, listen to world-class musicians from a picnic blanket on a well-manicured lawn, and feast on farm-to-table cuisine at chef-driven restaurants. You could easily spend an entire summer hopscotching the patchwork of wilderness areas, while taking in a dance festival here, an illustrious music series there and summer theater all over the place.

At every turn, you'll come across peppy college towns with shady campuses, bohemian cafes and exceptional art museums. And those lucky enough to be here in autumn will find apples ripe for the picking and hillsides ablaze in brilliant fall foliage.

Northampton

In a region famous for its charming college towns, you'd be hard-pressed to find anything more appealing than the crooked streets of downtown Northampton. Old redbrick buildings and lots of pedestrian traffic provide a lively backdrop for your wanderings, which will likely include cafes, rock clubs and bookstores (which explains why locals call their town 'NoHo'). Move a few steps outside of the picturesque commercial center and you'll stumble onto the bucolic grounds of Smith College. Northampton is a well-known liberal enclave in these parts. The lesbian community is famously outspoken, and rainbow flags wave wildly all over this town.

◉ Sights

Smith College
COLLEGE

(☑413-584-2700; www.smith.edu; Elm St) Founded 'for the education of the intelligent gentlewoman' in 1875, Smith College is one of the largest women's colleges in the country, with 2600 students. The verdant 125-acre campus holds an eclectic architectural mix of nearly 100 buildings, set on a pretty pond. Notable alums of the college include Sylvia Plath, Julia Child and Gloria Steinem. After exploring the campus, take a stroll around Paradise Pond and snap a photo at the Japanese tea hut.

Smith College Museum of Art
MUSEUM

(☑413-585-2760; www.smith.edu/artmuseum; 20 Elm St; adult/child $5/free; ⊙10am-4pm Tue-Sat, noon-4pm Sun) This impressive campus museum boasts a 25,000-piece collection. The collection is particularly strong in 19th- and 20th-century European and North American paintings, including works by Degas, Winslow Homer, Picasso and James Abbott McNeill Whistler. Another highlight is the so-called 'functional art': the remarkable restrooms and the eclectic collection of benches (that you can actually sit on) – all designed and created by contemporary American artists.

🏃 Activities

The **Norwottuck Rail Trail** (nor-wah-tuk; www.mass.gov/eea/agencies/dcr/massparks/region-west/norwottuck-rail-trail.html) is a walking and cycling path that follows the former Boston & Maine Railroad right-of-way from Amherst to Hadley to Northampton, a total distance of 11 miles. For much of its length, the trail parallels MA 9, passing through open farms and crossing the broad Connecticut River on a historic 1500ft-long bridge.

Parking and access to the trail can be found on Station Rd in Amherst, at the Mountain Farms Mall on MA 9 in Hadley and at Elwell State Park on Damon Rd in Northampton. You can rent bikes from **Northampton Bicycle** (www.nohobike.com; 319 Pleasant St; per day from $25; ⊙9:30am-7pm Mon-Fri, to 5pm Sat, noon-5pm Sun).

🛏️ Sleeping & Eating

Hotel Northampton
HISTORIC HOTEL **$$**

(☑413-584-3100; www.hotelnorthampton.com; 36 King St; r $186-286; 🅿🛜) This old-timer is perfectly situated smack in the center of Northampton and has been the town's best bet since 1927. The 100 rooms are airy and well fitted, with traditional furnishings and floral quilts and curtains. There's a quiet grandeur to the place. And mailing a postcard via an antiquated letterbox system always feels good.

Bela
VEGETARIAN **$**

(☑413-586-8011; www.belaveg.com; 68 Masonic St; mains $8-13; ⊙noon-8:30pm Tue-Sat; 🍴👶) 🌱 This cozy vegetarian restaurant puts such an emphasis on fresh ingredients that the chalkboard menu changes daily depending on what local farmers are harvesting. Think home-cooked comfort food and a setting that welcomes families – there's even a collection of toys for the kids! Cash only.

Paul & Elizabeth's
SEAFOOD **$$**

(☑413-584-4832; www.paulandelizabeths.com; 150 Main St; mains $8-21; ⊙11:30am-9pm Sun-Thu, to 9:45pm Fri & Sat; 🛜🍴👶) 🌱 This airy, plant-adorned restaurant, known locally as P&E's, sits on the top floor of Thornes Marketplace and is the town's premier natural-foods restaurant. It serves vegetarian cuisine and seafood, often with an Asian bent. From fall to early spring, don't miss the rare opportunity to sample their old-fashioned Indian pudding.

❶ Getting There & Away

Northampton is 18 miles north of Springfield on I-91. If you don't score a parking spot on Main St, you'll find public parking at **Thornes Marketplace** (www.thornesmarketplace.com; 150 Main St; ⊙10am-6pm Mon-Wed, to 8pm Thu-Sat, noon-5pm Sun) in the town center.

Pioneer Valley Transit Authority (www.pvta.com) provides bus services (with bike racks) throughout the Five College area, with the Northampton–Amherst route having the most frequent service.

Amherst

This quintessential college town is home to the prestigious Amherst College, a pretty 'junior ivy' that borders the town green, as well as the hulking University of Massachusetts and the cozy liberal-arts Hampshire College. Start your explorations at the town green, at the intersection of MA 116 and MA 9. In the surrounding streets, you'll find a few funky galleries, a bookshop or two, countless coffeehouses, and a few small but worthwhile museums (several of which are associated with the colleges).

Emily Dickinson Museum   MUSEUM

(📞413-542-8161; www.emilydickinsonmuseum.org; 280 Main St; guided tour adult/child $15/free; ⏱10am-5pm Wed-Mon Jun-Aug, 11am-4pm Wed-Sun Apr, May & Sep-Dec, 11am-4pm Sat & Sun Mar) During her lifetime, Emily Dickinson (1830–86) published only seven poems, but more than 1000 of her poems were discovered and published posthumously, and her verses on love, nature and immortality have made her one of the USA's most important poets. Dickinson spent most of her life in near seclusion in this stately home near the center of Amherst. Guided tours (60 minutes) focus on the poet and her works, visiting both the Dickinson Homestead and the adjacent Evergreens.

You can also explore the grounds using a self-guided audio tour. Check the website for the tour schedules.

Eric Carle Museum of Picture Book Art   MUSEUM

(📞413-559-6300; www.carlemuseum.org; 125 W Bay Rd; adult/child $9/6; ⏱10am-4pm Tue-Fri, to 5pm Sat, noon-5pm Sun; 👶) Co-founded by the author and illustrator of *The Very Hungry Caterpillar,* this superb museum celebrates book illustrations from around the world with rotating exhibits in three galleries, as well as a permanent collection. All visitors (grown-ups included) are encouraged to express their own artistic sentiments in the hands-on art studio.

The Berkshires

Few places in America combine culture and country living as deftly as the Berkshire hills, home to world-class music, dance and theater festivals – the likes of Tanglewood and Jacob's Pillow – as well as miles of hiking trails and acres of farmland.

Extending from the highest point in the state – Mt Greylock – southward to the Connecticut state line, the Berkshires have been a summer refuge for more than a century, when the rich and famous arrived to build summer 'cottages' of grand proportions. Many of these mansions survive as inns or performance venues. And still today, on summer weekends when the sidewalks are scorching in Boston and New York, crowds of city dwellers jump in their cars and head for the Berkshire breezes.

❶ Getting There & Around

Most travelers are likely to reach this region by driving from Boston, Hartford or New York. It is possible to arrive by bus or train, but you'll want your own vehicle if you intend to visit the more rural areas. If not, the Berkshire Regional Transit Authority (www.berkshirerta.com) runs buses between major Berkshire towns. A ride costs $1.75.

Great Barrington

Great Barrington's Main St used to consist of Woolworth's, hardware stores, thrift shops and a run-down diner. These have given way to artsy boutiques, antique shops, coffeehouses and restaurants. Nowadays the town boasts the best dining scene in the region, with easy access to hiking trails and magnificent scenery in the surrounding hills.

The Housatonic River flows through the center of town just east of Main St/US 7, the central thoroughfare.

◎ Sights & Activities

Beartown State Forest   FOREST

(📞413-528-0904; www.mass.gov/dcr; 69 Blue Hill Rd, Monterey; parking $15) This lovely state park is centered on Benedict Pond, a perfect spot for swimming, fishing, canoeing and kayaking. There are miles of hiking trails, including a piece of the Appalachian Trail. The furthest reaches of this forest are home to deer, bears, bobcats and fishers. Less ambitious hikers can stroll the 1.5-mile Benedict Pond Loop.

Housatonic River Walk   WALKING

(www.gbriverwalk.org; ⏱sunrise-sunset Apr-Nov) FREE The picturesque Housatonic River flows through the center of Great Barrington, with the River Walk offering a perfect perch from which to admire it. Access the walking path from Main St (behind Rite-Aid) or from Bridge St.

✖ Eating & Drinking

Baba Louie's   PIZZA $$

(📞413-528-8100; www.babalouiespizza.com; 286 Main St; pizzas $10-20; ⏱11:30am-3pm & 5-9:30pm; 📶🐾) Baba's is known for its organic sourdough crust and for the guys with dreadlocks. There's a pizza for every taste, running the gamut from the fan-favorite Dolce Vita with figs, gorgonzola and prosciutto to the gluten-free Vegetazione with artichoke hearts, broccoli, tofu and soy mozzarella.

Barrington Brewery   MICROBREWERY
(☑ 413-528-8282; www.barringtonbrewery.net; 420 Stockbridge Rd; ⊙ 11:30am-9:30pm; ☎) ✿
You can rest easy, knowing your beer was brewed with solar power. The frothy, hoppy brews are the star of the show here, but the grass-fed beef burgers make a decent complement and the outdoor seating takes it up a notch on a balmy summer night.

Stockbridge

Take a good look down Stockbridge's wide Main St. Notice anything? More specifically, notice anything missing? Not one stoplight stutters the view, not one telephone pole blights the picture-perfect scene – it looks very much the way Norman Rockwell might have seen it.

In fact, Rockwell did see it – he lived and worked in Stockbridge during the last 25 years of his life. Nowadays Stockbridge attracts summer and fall visitors en masse, who come to stroll the streets, inspect the shops and sit in the rockers on the porch of the historic Red Lion Inn. And they come by the busload to visit the Norman Rockwell Museum on the town's outskirts.

All that fossilized picturesqueness bears a price. Noticeably absent from the village center is the kind of vitality that you find in the neighboring towns.

Norman Rockwell Museum   MUSEUM
(☑ 413-298-4100; www.nrm.org; 9 Glendale Rd/MA 183; adult/child $20/free; ⊙ 10am-5pm May-Oct, to 4pm Nov-Apr) Born in New York City, Norman Rockwell (1894–1978) sold his first magazine cover illustration to the *Saturday Evening Post* in 1916. In the following half-century he did another 321 covers for the *Post,* as well as illustrations for books, posters and many other magazines on his way to becoming the most popular illustrator in US history. This excellent little museum has the largest collection of Rockwell's original art, as well as Rockwell's studio, which was moved here from his Stockbridge home.

To find the museum follow MA 102 west from Stockbridge and turn left (south) on MA 183.

Lenox

This gracious, wealthy town is a historical anomaly: firstly, its charm was not destroyed by the Industrial Revolution; and then, prized for its bucolic peace, the town became a summer retreat for wealthy families with surnames like Carnegie, Vanderbilt and Westinghouse, who had made their fortunes by building factories in other towns.

As the cultural heart of the Berkshires, Lenox's illustrious past remains tangibly present today. The superstar among its attractions is the Tanglewood Music Festival, an incredibly popular summer event drawing scores of visitors from New York City, Boston and beyond.

Tanglewood Music Festival   MUSIC
(☑ 888-266-1200; www.tanglewood.org; 297 West St/MA 183, Lenox; lawn tickets from $12, kids free; ⊙ late Jun-early Sep) Dating from 1934, the Tanglewood Music Festival is among the most esteemed summertime music events in the world. Symphony, pops, chamber music, jazz and blues are performed from late June through early September. You can count on renowned cellist Yo-Yo Ma, violinist Joshua Bell and singer James Taylor to perform each summer, along with a run of world-class guest artists and famed conductors.

🛏 Sleeping & Eating

Birchwood Inn   INN $$$
(☑ 413-637-2600; www.birchwood-inn.com; 7 Hubbard St; r $199-289, deluxe r $359-394; ❈ ☎ ❀)
A pretty hilltop inn a couple of blocks from the town center, Birchwood occupies the oldest (1767) home in Lenox. The 11 spacious rooms vary in decor; some swing with a vintage floral design, others are more country classic, but all are romantic and luxurious. Deluxe rooms feature king-size beds and wood-burning fireplaces.

Home-cooked breakfasts, perhaps fondue Florentine soufflé or blueberry cheese blintzes, are served in a fireside dining room.

Haven Cafe & Bakery   CAFE $
(☑ 413-637-8948; www.havencafebakery.com; 8 Franklin St; mains $8-16; ⊙ 7:30am-3pm Mon-Fri, from 8am Sat & Sun; ☎ ✿) It looks like a cafe, but the sophisticated food evokes a more upscale experience. For breakfast, try croissant French toast or inventive egg dishes like salmon scramble; for lunch there are fancy salads and sandwiches – all highlighting local organic ingredients. Definitely save room for something sweet from the bakery counter.

★ Nudel   AMERICAN $$$
(☑ 413-551-7183; www.nudelrestaurant.com; 37 Church St; mains $26, 3-/4-course prix fixe menu

$45/55; ⊙5-9:30pm Tue-Sat, to 9pm Sun) Nudel is a driving force in the area's sustainable-food movement, with just about everything on the menu seasonally inspired and locally sourced. The back-to-basics approach rings through in inventive dishes, which change daily but never disappoint. Incredible flavors. Nudel has a loyal following, so reservations are recommended in season.

Williamstown

Small but gracious Williamstown is nestled within the heart of the Purple Valley, so named because the surrounding mountains often seem shrouded in a lavender veil at dusk. Folks congregate in the friendly town center, which is only two blocks long, while dogs and kids frolic in the green spaces.

Williamstown is a quintessential New England college town, its charming streets and greens dotted with the stately brick and marble buildings of Williams College. Cultural life is rich, with a pair of exceptional art museums and one of the region's most respected summer theater festivals.

◉ Sights

★ Clark Art Institute   MUSEUM
(☑ 413-458-2303; www.clarkart.edu; 225 South St; adult/child $20/free; ⊙10am-5pm Tue-Sun Sep-Jun, daily Jul & Aug) Even if you're not an avid art lover, don't miss this gem, set on 140 gorgeous acres of expansive lawns, flower-filled meadows and rolling hills. The building – with its triple-tiered reflecting pool – is a stunner. The collections are particularly strong in the Impressionists, with significant works by Monet, Pissarro and Renoir. Mary Cassatt, Winslow Homer and John Singer Sargent represent contemporary American painting.

Williams College Museum of Art   MUSEUM
(☑ 413-597-2429; https://wcma.williams.edu; 15 Lawrence Hall Dr; ⊙10am-5pm, to 8pm Thu, closed Wed Sep-May) **FREE** This sister museum of the Clark Art Institute graces the center of town and has an incredible (free!) collection of its own. Around half of its 13,000 pieces comprise the American Collection, with substantial works by notables such as Edward Hopper (*Morning in a City*), Winslow Homer and Grant Wood, to name only a few. The photography collection is also noteworthy, with representation by Man Ray and Alfred Stieglitz. Did we mention it's free?

★☆ Festivals

Williamstown Theatre Festival   THEATER
(☑ box office 413-458-3253; www.wtfestival.org; 1000 Main St; ⊙ Jun-Aug; ▥) Stars of the theater world descend upon Williamstown every year from the third week in June to the third week in August. Widely considered the best summer theater in the area, the Williamstown Theatre Festival was the first to win the Regional Theatre Tony Award.

🛏 Sleeping & Eating

Maple Terrace Motel   MOTEL $$
(☑ 413-458-9677; www.mapleterrace.com; 555 Main St; d $119-178; ▣▤) The Maple Terrace is a simple yet cozy 15-room place on the eastern outskirts of town. The Swedish innkeepers have snazzed up the grounds with gardens that make you want to linger. There's nothing fancy going on here, but the place is comfortable and service is warmly attentive.

River Bend Farm B&B   B&B $$
(☑ 413-458-3121; www.riverbendfarmbb.com; 643 Simonds Rd/US 7; r $120; ⊙Apr-Oct; ▦▧) Step back in time to 1770, when this Georgian Colonial was a local tavern owned by Benjamin Simonds. The house owes its painstaking restoration to hosts Judy and Dave Loomis. Four simple, comfortable doubles share two bathrooms with claw-foot tubs. Breakfast is served in the wood-paneled tap room, next to the wide stone fireplace.

Despite the name, it's not on a farm but along US 7 on the north side of the little bridge over the Hoosic River.

Pappa Charlie's Deli   DELI $
(☑ 413-458-5969; 28 Spring St; mains $5-8; ⊙8am-8pm Mon-Sat, to 7pm Sun; ▨) Here's a welcoming breakfast spot where locals really do ask for 'the usual.' The stars themselves created the lunch sandwiches that bear their names. The Mary Tyler Moore is a favorite (bacon, lettuce, tomato and avocado), though the actress later went vegetarian, so you can also get a version with soy bacon instead. Or order a Politician and get anything you want on it.

★ Mezze Bistro & Bar   FUSION $$
(☑ 413-458-0123; www.mezzerestaurant.com; 777 Cold Spring Rd/US 7; mains $18-28; ⊙5-9pm Sun-Thu, to 10pm Fri & Sat) You don't know exactly what you're going to get at this contemporary chic restaurant – the menu changes frequently – but you know it's going to be good. Situated on 3 spectacular acres, Mezze's

NORTH ADAMS: MASS MOCA

At first glance, North Adams' beautiful and bleak 19th-century downtown seems out of sync with the rest of the Berkshires. It's not so lively and the amenities are limited. But it doesn't take long to discover the appeal – mainly, Mass MoCA, an exemplary contemporary-art museum of staggering proportions. Indeed, the place is big enough to be its own village, and its grounds do in fact contain some of the city's best dining, drinking and shopping.

MASS MoCA (Massachusetts Museum of Contemporary Art; ☑ 413-662-2111; www.mass moca.org; 1040 MASS MoCA Way; adult/child $20/8; ⊙ 10am-6pm Sun-Wed, to 7pm Thu-Sat Jul & Aug, 11am-5pm Wed-Mon Sep-Jun; ⊕) sprawls over 13 acres of downtown North Adams – one-third of the entire business district. After the Sprague Electric Company closed in 1985, some $31 million was spent to modernize the property into 'the largest gallery in the United States.' The museum encompasses 222,000 sq ft in 25 buildings, including art construction areas, performance centers and 19 galleries. One gallery is the size of a football field, giving installation artists the opportunity to explore a whole new dimension. Bring your walking shoes!

farm-to-table approach begins with an edible garden right on site. Much of the rest of the seasonal menu, from small-batch microbrews to organic meats, is locally sourced as well.

RHODE ISLAND

Rhode Island, the smallest of the US states, isn't actually an island. Although it takes only 45 minutes to traverse, this little wonder packs in over 400 miles of coastline with some of the finest white-sand swimming beaches in the Northeast, deserted coves, rugged cliffs and isolated lighthouses.

Hugging the shoreline before heading inland, delightful resorts, quaint Colonial villages and extravagant mansions give way to lush fields of berry farms, vineyards, and the horse studs of Middletown and Portsmouth. Rhode Island's two cities – Providence, of working-class roots, and Newport, born of old money the likes of which most cannot conceive – are each among New England's finest, brimming with fantastic museums, neighborhoods boasting utterly gorgeous historic homes, and an urban fabric of topnotch restaurants and seriously cool bars. It's no wonder the nouveau riche continue to flock here for summer shenanigans.

History

Ever since it was founded in 1636 by Roger Williams, a religious outcast from Boston, Providence has enjoyed an independent frame of mind. Williams' guiding principle, the one that got him ostracized from Massachusetts, was that all people should have freedom of conscience. He put his liberal beliefs into practice when settling Providence, remaining on friendly terms with the local Narragansett Native Americans after purchasing from them the land for a bold experiment in tolerance and peaceful coexistence.

Williams' principles would not last long. As Providence and Newport grew and merged into a single colony, competition and conflict with area tribes sparked several wars, leading to the decimation of the Wampanoag, Pequot, Narragansett and Nipmuck peoples. Rhode Island was also a prolific slave trader and its merchants would control much of that industry in the years after the Revolutionary War.

The city of Pawtucket birthed the American Industrial Revolution with the establishment of the water-powered Slater Mill in 1790. Industrialism impacted the character of Providence and surrounds, particularly along the Blackstone River, creating urban density. As with many small East Coast cities, these urban areas went into a precipitous decline in the 1940s and '50s as manufacturing industries (textiles and costume jewelry) faltered. In the 1960s, preservation efforts salvaged the historic architectural framework of Providence and Newport. Today Newport has flourished into one of the nation's most attractive historical centers.

Providence also rerouted its destiny to emerge as a lively and stylish city with a dynamic economy and vibrant downtown core, largely due to the work of Buddy Cianci, twice-convicted felon and twice-elected mayor (1975–84, 1991–2002). Cianci is credited with saving the city from industrial and urban decline with a large-scale revitalization project that uncovered and rerouted previously subterranean river tributaries into a central artificial pond. The spectacle of today's wildly popular WaterFire festival (p225) is a powerful symbol of the city's phoenixlike rebirth along the confluence of the three rivers that gave it life. Cianci died in 2016, aged 74.

ⓘ Information

Rhode Island Division of Parks & Recreation (www.riparks.com) For a listing of all of Rhode Island's state beaches.

Rhode Island Tourism Division (www.visitrhodeisland.com) The official state provider of tourist information on Rhode Island.

Providence

Atop the confluence of the Providence, Moshassuck and Woonasquatucket Rivers, Rhode Island's capital city offers some of the finest urban strolling in New England: around Brown University's historic campus on 18th-century College Hill, along the landscaped Riverwalk trail, and among downtown's handsome streets and lanes with their hipster-y cafes, art-house theaters, fusion restaurants and trendsetting bars.

Once destined to become an industrial relic, Providence's fate was spared when Buddy Cianci, its then controversial two-time mayor, rolled out a plan to revitalize the downtown core by rerouting subterranean rivers, reclaiming land and restoring historic facades. It created a city where history's treasures are integrated into a creative present, not simply memorialized; where three centuries of architectural styles are unified in colorful urban streetscapes that are at once bold, beautiful and cooler than cool. A large student population here helps keep the city's social and arts scenes lively and current.

◉ Sights

★ Providence Athenaeum LIBRARY
(☑ 401-421-6970; www.providenceathenaeum.org; 251 Benefit St; ⊙10am-6pm Mon-Thu, 9am-5pm Fri, 10am-2pm Sat) **FREE** One of the most prominent buildings on Benefit St, the Greek Revival Providence Athenaeum was designed by William Strickland and completed in 1838. This is a library of the old school, with plaster busts and oil paintings filling in spaces not occupied by books. Edgar Allen Poe used to court ladies here. Pick up a brochure for a self-guided **Raven Tour** of the building's artwork and architecture.

★ Rhode Island State House NOTABLE BUILDING
(☑ 401-222-3983; www.sos.ri.gov; 82 Smith St; ⊙self-guided tours 8:30am-4:30pm Mon-Fri, guided tours 9am, 10am, 11am, 1pm, 2pm Mon-Fri) **FREE** Designed by McKim, Mead and White in 1904, the Rhode Island State House rises above the Providence skyline, easily visible from miles around. Modeled in part on St Peter's Basilica in Vatican City, it has the world's fourth-largest self-supporting marble dome and houses one of Gilbert Stuart's portraits of George Washington.

★ John Brown House MUSEUM
(☑ 401-331-8575 ext 362; www.rihs.org; 52 Power St; adult/child $10/6; ⊙tours 1:30pm & 3pm Tue-Fri, 10:30am, noon, 1:30pm & 3pm Sat Apr-Nov) On College Hill, the brick John Brown House, called the 'most magnificent and elegant mansion that I have ever seen on this continent' by John Quincy Adams, was built in 1786.

★ Brown University UNIVERSITY
(☑ 401-863-1000; www.brown.edu) Dominating the crest of the College Hill neighborhood on the East Side, the campus of Brown University exudes Ivy League charm. **University Hall**, a 1770 brick edifice used as a barracks during the Revolutionary War, sits at its center. To explore the campus, start at the wrought-iron gates opening from the top of College St and make your way across the green toward Thayer St.

Benefit Street ARCHITECTURE
Immediately east of Providence's downtown, you'll find College Hill, where you can see the city's Colonial history reflected in the 18th-century houses that line Benefit St on the East Side. These are, for the most part, private homes, but many are open for tours one weekend in June during the annual **Festival of Historic Homes**. Benefit St is a fitting symbol of the Providence renaissance, rescued by local preservationists in the 1960s from misguided urban-renewal efforts that would have destroyed it.

RISD Museum of Art MUSEUM
(☑ 401-454-6500; www.risdmuseum.org; 224 Benefit St; adult/child $12/3; ⊙10am-5pm Tue-Sun, to 9pm 3rd Thu of month; ♿) Wonderfully eclectic, the Rhode Island School of Design's art

museum showcases everything from ancient Greek art to 20th-century American paintings and decorative arts. Pop in before 1pm Sunday and admission is free.

Roger Williams Park
PARK

(1000 Elmwood Ave) FREE In 1871 Betsey Williams, great-great-great-granddaughter of the founder of Providence, donated her farm to the city as a public park. Today this 430-acre expanse of greenery, only a short drive south of Providence, includes lakes and ponds, forest copses and broad lawns, picnic grounds, the **Planetarium and Museum of Natural History** (☏ 401-680-7221; www.providenceri.com/museum; museum/planetarium $2/3; ⊙ 10am-4pm; ☑), an operating Victorian carousel, greenhouses and Williams' cottage.

✦✦ Festivals

★ WaterFire
STREET CARNIVAL

(☏ 401-273-1155; www.waterfire.org; ⊙ dates vary) Particularly during summer, much of downtown Providence transforms into a carnivalesque festival thanks to the exceedingly popular WaterFire art installation created by Barnaby Evans in 1994. Marking the convergence of the Providence, Moshassuck and Woonasquatucket Rivers, 100 anchored, flaming braziers illuminate the water, overlooked by crowds of pedestrians strolling over the bridges and along the riverside.

🛏 Sleeping

Christopher Dodge House
B&B $$

(☏ 401-351-6111; www.providence-hotel.com; 11 W Park St; r $149-189; ℗) This 1858 Federal-style house is furnished with early American reproduction furniture and marble fireplaces. Austere on the outside, it has elegant proportions, large, shuttered windows and wooden floors.

Old Court B&B
INN $$

(☏ 401-751-2002; www.oldcourt.com; 144 Benefit St; r weekday $155-195, weekend $185-225) Well positioned among the historic buildings of College Hill, this three-story, 1863 Italianate home has stacks of charm. Enjoy eccentric wallpaper, good jam at breakfast and occasional winter discounts.

Providence Biltmore
HISTORIC HOTEL $$

(☏ 401-421-0700; www.providencebiltmore.com; 11 Dorrance St; r $165-379; ℗☎) The grand-daddy of Providence's hotels, the Biltmore dates from the 1920s. The lobby, both intimate

and regal, nicely combines dark wood, twisting staircases and chandeliers, while well-appointed rooms stretch many stories above the old city. Ask for one of the 292 rooms that are on a high floor.

✕ Eating

Louis Family Restaurant
DINER $

(☏ 401-861-5225; www.louisrestaurant.org; 286 Brook St; mains $4-9; ⊙ 5am-3pm; ☑) Wake up early to watch bleary-eyed students and carpenters eat strawberry-banana pancakes and drink drip coffee at their favorite greasy spoon long before the rest of College Hill shows signs of life.

Haven Brothers Diner
DINER $

(☏ 401-603-8124; www.havenbrothersmobile.com; cnr Dorrance & Fulton Sts; meals $5-12; ⊙ 5pm-3am) Parked next to City Hall, this diner sits on the back of a truck that has rolled into the same spot every evening for decades. Climb up a rickety ladder to get basic diner fare alongside everyone, from prominent politicians to college kids pulling an all-nighter to drunks. The murder burger comes highly recommended.

Local 121
MODERN AMERICAN $$

(☏ 401-274-2121; www.local121.com; 121 Washington St; mains $17-30; ⊙ 5-10pm Wed & Thu, 5-11pm Fri, 10am-3pm & 5-11pm Sat, 10am-3pm & 5-9pm Sun) Locavore mania comes to Providence with this opulent, old-school restaurant with contemporary aspirations. Housed in the old Dreyfus hotel (built in the 1890s), a building owned by the arts organization AS220, Local 121 has an easy, unpretentious grandeur – and some damn fine food. The menu is seasonal, but recent options include a perfect (local) scallop po'boy and (local) duck-ham pizza.

★ birch
MODERN AMERICAN $$$

(☏ 401-272-3105; www.birchrestaurant.com; 200 Washington St; 4-course dinner $49, beverage pairings $35; ⊙ 5-10pm Thu-Mon) With a background at Noma in Copenhagen and the fabulous Dorrance at the Biltmore, chef Benjamin Sukle and his wife, Heidi, have their own place: the understated, but fabulously good, birch. Its intimate size and style (seating is around a U-shaped bar) means attention to detail is exacting in both the decor and the food, which focuses on underutilized, small-batch and hyper-seasonal produce.

🍷 Drinking

AS220
CLUB

(📞 401-831-9327; www.as220.org; 115 Empire St; ⊙ bar 5pm-1am Tue-Sat, cafe noon-10pm Tue-Sat) A long-standing outlet for all forms of Rhode Island art, AS220 (say 'A-S-two-twenty') books experimental bands, hosts readings and provides gallery space for a very active community. If you need a cup of coffee, vegan cookie or spinach pie, it also operates a cafe and bar: hours vary.

Salon
BAR, CLUB

(📞 401-865-6330; www.thesalonpvd.com; 57 Eddy St; ⊙ 7pm-1am Tue-Thu, to 2am Fri & Sat) The Salon mixes ping-pong tables and pinball machines with 1980s pop and pickleback shots (whiskey with a pickle juice chaser) upstairs, with live shows, open mike, DJs and dance parties downstairs. If you get hungry, there are PB&J sandwiches.

ℹ️ Getting There & Around

With hills, two interstates and two rivers defining its downtown topography, Providence can be a confusing city to find your way around. Parking can be difficult downtown and near the train station. For a central lot, try the huge garage of the Providence Place mall and get a merchant to validate your ticket. On the East Side, you can usually find street parking easily.

Major car-rental companies have airport and downtown locations.

Providence is small, pretty and walkable, so once you arrive you'll probably want to get around on foot.

Rhode Island Public Transit Authority (www.ripta.com) operates two 'trolley' routes. The Green Line runs from the East Side through downtown to Federal Hill. The Gold Line runs from the Marriott hotel south to the hospital via Kennedy Plaza, and stops at the Point St Ferry Dock.

BUS

→ All long-distance buses and most local routes stop at the central **Intermodal Transportation Center** (Kennedy Plaza; ⊙ 6am-7pm). Greyhound (www.greyhound.com) and Peter Pan Bus Lines (www.peterpanbus.com) have ticket counters inside, and there are maps outlining local services.

→ Peter Pan connects Providence and Green Airport with Boston's South Station (from $9, one hour, 12 daily) and Logan International Airport (from $18, 70 minutes, 10 daily).

→ Greyhound (www.greyhound.com) buses depart for Boston (from $9, 65 minutes), New York City (from $15, 5½ to six hours) and elsewhere.

TRAIN

→ Amtrak (www.amtrak.com) trains, including high-speed Acela trains, connect Providence with Boston (from $12, 50 minutes) and New York (from $50, three to 3½ hours).

→ MBTA commuter rail (www.mbta.com) connects to Boston ($11.50, 60 to 75 minutes).

Newport

Established by religious moderates, 'new port' flourished in the independent colony of Rhode Island, which declared itself a state here in 1776. Downtown, shutterbugs snap excitedly at immaculately preserved Colonial-era architecture and landmarks at seemingly every turn.

Fascinating as Newport's early history is, the real intrigue began in the late 1850s, when wealthy industrialists began building opulent summer residences along cliff-top Bellevue Ave. Impeccably styled on Italianate palazzi, French châteaus and Elizabethan manor houses, these gloriously restored mansions filled with priceless antiques and their breathtaking location must be seen to be believed. The curiosity, variety, extravagance and uniqueness of this spectacle is unrivaled.

Honoring its maritime roots, Newport remains a global center for yachting. Put simply, summers here sparkle: locals have excellent taste and know how to throw a shindig. There's always something going on, including a series of cross-genre festivals that are among the best in the USA.

👁️ Sights & Activities

During the 19th century, the wealthiest New York bankers and business families chose Newport as their summer playground, building their fabulous mansions along Bellevue Ave. Ten of the mansions (not including Rough Point or Ochre Court) are under the management of the **Preservation Society** (📞 401-847-1000; www.newportmansions.org; 424 Bellevue Ave; 5-site tickets adult/child $35/12), and are open seasonally between June and November. Some are open year-round. Combination tickets are better value if you intend visiting several of the properties, and some tours require advance booking, which is advisable during high season. Tickets can be purchased online or on site. The society also offers a range of food- and wine-themed events.

Alternatively, hire a bike and cruise along Bellevue Ave enjoying the view of the mansions and their grounds or saunter along the famed Cliff Walk, a pedestrian path that runs along the headland between the mansions and their sea view.

★ **The Breakers**   HISTORIC BUILDING
(☎401-847-1000; www.newportmansions.org; 44 Ochre Point Ave; adult/child $24/8; ⊘9am-5pm Apr–mid-Oct, hours vary mid-Oct–Mar; ℗) A 70-room Italian Renaissance megapalace inspired by 16th-century Genoese palazzi, the Breakers is the most magnificent Newport mansion. At the behest of Cornelius Vanderbilt II, Richard Morris Hunt did most of the design (though craftspeople from around the world perfected the decorative program). The building was completed in 1895 and sits at Ochre Point, on a grand oceanside site. The furnishings, most made expressly for the Breakers, are all original. Don't miss the **Children's Cottage** on the grounds.

★ **The Elms**   HISTORIC BUILDING
(☎401-847-1000; www.newportmansions.org; 367 Bellevue Ave; adult/child $17.50/8, servant life tours adult/child $18/7.50; ⊘10am-5pm Apr–mid-Oct, hours vary mid-Oct–Mar; ℗🖫) Designed by Horace Trumbauer in 1901, the Elms is a replica of Château d'Asnières, built near Paris in 1750. Here you can take a 'behind-the-scenes' tour that will have you snaking through the servants' quarters and up onto the roof. Along the way you'll learn about the activities of the army of servants and the architectural devices that kept them hidden from the view of those drinking port in the formal rooms.

★ **Rough Point**   HISTORIC BUILDING
(☎401-849-7300; www.newportrestoration.com; 680 Bellevue Ave; adult/child $25/free; ⊘9:30am-2pm Thu-Sun Apr-early May, 9:30am-3:30pm Tue-Sun early May-early Nov; ℗) While the peerless position and splendor of the grounds alone are worth the price of admission, this faux-English manor house also contains heiress and philanthropist Doris Duke's impressive art holdings, including medieval tapestries, furniture owned by French emperors, Ming dynasty ceramics, and paintings by Renoir and Van Dyck.

★ **Fort Adams State Park**   STATE PARK
(www.fortadams.org; Harrison Ave; ⊘sunrise-sunset) The centerpiece of this gorgeous state park, which juts out into Narragansett Bay, **Fort Adams** (☎401-841-0707; 90 Fort Adams Dr; tours adult/child $12/6; ⊘10am-4pm late May–Oct, reduced hours Nov & Dec) is America's largest coastal fortification. It's the venue for the Newport jazz (www.newportjazz.org; tickets $65-89, 3 days $170; ⊘Jul/Aug) and folk festivals (p228) and numerous special events. A beach, picnic and fishing areas and a boat ramp are open daily.

Museum of Newport History   MUSEUM
(☎401-841-8770; www.newporthistory.org; 127 Thames St; suggested donation adult/child $4/2; ⊘10am-5pm) Newport's excellent local history museum brings the city's past to life.

International Tennis Hall of Fame MUSEUM
(☎401-849-3990; www.tennisfame.com; 194 Bellevue Ave; adult/child $15/free; ⊘10am-5pm Sep-Jun, to 6pm Jul & Aug, closed Tue Jan-Mar) To experience something of the American aristocracy's approach to 19th-century

NEW ENGLAND NEWPORT

NEWPORT'S BEST BEACHES

Newport's public beaches are on the eastern side of the peninsula along Memorial Blvd. All are open 9am to 6pm in summer and charge a parking fee of $10/20 on weekdays/weekends (except for Gooseberry Beach, which charges $20 all week for parking).

Easton Beach (First Beach; Memorial Blvd) This is the largest beach with a pseudo-Victorian pavilion containing bathhouses and showers, a snack bar and a large carousel. You can rent umbrellas, chairs and surf boards at the pavilion.

Sachuest Beach (Second Beach; ☎401-846-6273; http://parks.middletownri.com; Sachuest Point Rd, Middletown) The most beautiful beach on Aquidneck Island curves around Sachuest Bay and is backed by the 450-acre Norman Bird Sanctuary.

Third Beach (Third Beach Rd, Middleton) Popular with families because it is protected from the open ocean, Third Beach also appeals to windsurfers because the water is calm and the winds steady.

Gooseberry Beach (130 Ocean Ave) Calm waters, white sand and a restaurant.

leisure, visit this museum. It lies inside the historic Newport Casino building (1880), which served as a summer club for Newport's wealthiest residents. The US National Lawn Tennis Championships (forerunner of today's US Open tennis tournament) were held here in 1881. A scavenger hunt, available at reception, gets kids engaged with eight centuries of tennis.

✨ Festivals

Newport Folk Festival   MUSIC
(www.newportfolk.org; Fort Adams State Park; 1-/3-day passes $85/199, parking per day $15; ☻late Jul) Big-name stars and up-and-coming groups perform at Fort Adams State Park (p227) and other venues around town. Bring sunscreen.

Newport Music Festival   MUSIC
(www.newportmusic.org; tickets $25-50; ☻mid-Jul) This internationally regarded festival offers classical music concerts in many of the great mansions.

🛏 Sleeping

Newport International Hostel   HOSTEL $
(William Gyles Guesthouse; ☑ 401-369-0243; www.newporthostel.com; 16 Howard St; dm $29-99, d $59-200; ☻May-Nov; �🛜) Book as early as you can to get into Rhode Island's only hostel, run by an informal and knowledgeable host. The tiny guesthouse contains fixings for a simple breakfast, a laundry machine and spare, clean digs in a dormitory room.

Sea Whale Motel   MOTEL $$
(☑ 888-257-4096; www.seawhale.com; 150 Aquidneck Ave, Middletown; d midweek $139-149, weekend $209-239; ☐🛜) This owner-occupied motel is a lovely place to stay with rooms facing Easton's Pond and flowers hung about the place everywhere. Rooms have little style, but are comfortable and neat, with fridges, microwaves, and tea and coffee provided.

★ Attwater   BOUTIQUE HOTEL $$$
(☑ 401-846-7444; www.theattwater.com; 22 Liberty St; r $259-599; ☐✳🛜) Newport's newest hotel has the bold attire of a midsummer beach party with turquoise, lime-green and coral prints, ikat headboards and snazzily patterned geometric rugs. Picture windows and porches capture the summer light and rooms come furnished with thoughtful luxuries, like iPads, Apple TV and beach bags.

🍴 Eating

★ Rosemary & Thyme Cafe   BAKERY, CAFE $
(☑ 401-619-3338; www.rosemaryandthymecafe.com; 382 Spring St; baked goods $2.50-5, sandwiches $8-11; ☻7am-2pm Tue-Sat, to 11:30am Sun; 🍴) With a German baker in the kitchen it's hardly surprising that the counter at Rosemary & Thyme is piled high with buttery croissants, apple and cherry tarts and plump muffins. At lunchtime gourmet sandwiches feature herbed goat's cheese and Tuscan dried tomatoes, Havana Cuban pork loin and an Alsatian cheese mix. A children's menu is also thoughtfully provided.

Flo's Clam Shack   SEAFOOD $$
(☑ 401-847-8141; www.flosclamshacks.com; 4 Wave Ave, Middletown; mains $11-22; ☻11am-9pm Sun-Thu, to 10pm Fri & Sat mid-May–mid-Sep, reduced hours mid-Sep–mid-May) This unfancy local institution has been the go-to for chip shop–style fish and chips, chowder, fried clams and quahog stuffies since the 1930s, only this one has a raw bar too.

★ Fluke Wine Bar   SEAFOOD $$$
(☑ 401-849-7778; www.flukenewport.com; 41 Bowens Wharf; mains $26-36; ☻5-11pm daily May-Oct, Wed-Sat Nov-Apr) Fluke's Scandinavian-inspired dining room, with its blond wood and picture windows, offers an accomplished seafood menu featuring roasted monkfish, seasonal striped sea bass and plump scallops.

☆ Entertainment

Newport Blues Café   LIVE MUSIC
(☑ 401-841-5510; www.newportblues.com; 286 Thames St; ☻7pm-1am Tue-Sun) This popular rhythm and blues bar and restaurant draws top acts to an old brownstone that was once a bank. It's an intimate space with many enjoying quahogs, house-smoked ribs or pork loins at tables adjoining the small stage. Dinner is offered from 7pm to 10pm; the music starts at 9:30pm.

Newport Polo Club   SPECTATOR SPORT
(☑ 401-846-0200; www.nptpolo.com; 250 Linden Lane, Portsmouth; lawn seats adult/child $12/free; ☻gates open 1pm) In summer, come to watch the club's polo matches (check the website for dates) to get an authentic taste of Newport high life.

ℹ Information

Newport Visitor Center (☑ 401-845-9131; www.discovernewport.org; 23 America's Cup Ave; ☻9am-5pm) Offers maps, brochures,

BLOCK ISLAND

From the deck of the ferry, a cluster of mansard roofs and gingerbread houses rises picturesquely from the commercial village of Old Harbor, where little has changed since 1895, short of adding electricity and flush toilets! If you remain after the departure of the masses on the last ferry, the scale and pace of the island will delight or derange you: some find it blissfully quiet, others get island fever fast.

Block Island's simple pleasures center upon strolling the beach, which stretches for miles to the north of Old Harbor, biking around the island's rolling farmland and getting to know the calls of the many bird species that make the island home. During off-season, when the population dwindles to a few hundred, the landscape has the spare, haunted feeling of an Andrew Wyeth painting, with stone walls demarcating centuries-old property lines and few trees interrupting the vast ocean vistas.

Many places have a two- or three-day minimum stay in summer and close between November and April. Advance reservations are essential. Peak season runs roughly from mid-June to Labor Day. Off-season prices can be far cheaper than those listed here. Camping is not allowed on the island.

The **Visitor Center** (☏ 401-466-2982; www.blockislandchamber.com; Water St, Old Harbor Ferry Landing; ☺9am-5pm late May–early Sep, 10am-4pm rest of year) near the ferry dock keeps track of vacancies, and will try to help should you arrive sans reservation.

The island can only be reached by sea or air:

Block Island Ferry (☏401-783-7996; www.blockislandferry.com) runs a year-round traditional car ferry and a high-speed ferry from Point Judith in Narragansett from Memorial Day to mid-October. There are additional high-speed passenger-only ferries from Newport and Fall River, MA.

Block Island Express (www.goblockisland.com) operates services from New London, CT, to Old Harbor, Block Island between May and September.

New England Airlines (☏800-243-2460; www.block-island.com/nea; 56 Airport Rd; one way/round-trip $54/99) flies between Westerly State Airport, on Airport Rd off RI 78, and Block Island State Airport (12 minutes).

local bus information, tickets to major attractions, public restrooms and an ATM.

ⓘ Getting There & Away

Parking can be tough in Newport. Free street parking spaces do pop up, but check to make sure any non-metered spots aren't reserved for Newport residents.

Bonanza Bus Lines operates buses to Boston (from $22, 1¾ to two hours, four to five daily) from the Newport Visitor Center.

RIPTA (www.ripta.com) bus 60 serves Providence ($2, one hour) almost every hour. For the West Kingston Amtrak station, take bus 64 ($2, one hour, five buses Monday to Friday, three on Saturday). Bus 14 serves TF Green airport ($2, one hour) in Warwick. Most RIPTA buses arrive and depart from the **Newport Visitor Center**.

East Bay

Rhode Island's jagged East Bay captures the early American story in microcosm, from the graves of early settlers in Little Compton to the farmsteads and merchant homes of whalers and farmers in Warren and Barrington, and the mansions of slave traders in Bristol.

Aside from Barrington's historic and picturesque **Tyler Point Cemetery**, set between the Warren and Barrington Rivers, and Warren's clutch of early stone and clapboard churches (built in the 18th and 19th centuries), the most interesting of the three communities is Bristol. Further south is Sakonnet, the Wampanoag's 'Place of Black Geese,' a rural landscape of pastures and woods centered on the two tiny communities of Tiverton and Little Compton.

⊙ Sights

Colt State Park   STATE PARK
(☏401-253-7482; www.riparks.com; RI 114; ☺sunrise-sunset; ℗) **FREE** Bristol's Colt State Park is Rhode Island's most scenic park, with its entire western border fronting Narragansett Bay, fringed by 4 miles of cycling trails and shaded picnic tables.

Blithewold Mansion
HISTORIC BUILDING

(☑401-253-2707; www.blithewold.org; 101 Ferry Rd; adult/child $14/5; ⊙10am-4pm Tue-Sat, to 3pm Sun Apr–mid-Oct; P) Local resident Augustus Van Wickle bought a 72ft Herreshoff yacht for his wife Bessie in 1895, but having nowhere suitable to moor it, he then had to build Blithewold Mansion. The arts-and-crafts mansion sits in a peerless position on Narragansett Bay and is particularly lovely in spring, when the daffodils line the shore.

Wilbor House
HISTORIC SITE

(☑401-635-4035; www.littlecompton.org; 548 West Main Rd; adult/child $6/3; ⊙1-5pm Thu-Sun Apr-Oct, 9am-3pm Tue-Fri Nov-Mar) Seventeenth-century Wilbor House belonged to early settler Samuel Wilbor, who crossed the Sakonnet River from Portsmouth in 1690 and built this big square home, which served his family for eight generations.

🛏 Sleeping & Eating

Stone House Inn
HISTORIC HOTEL $$$

(☑401-635-2222; www.newportexperience.com/stonehouse; 122 Sakonnet Point Rd; d $229-544; P🛜) When this unashamedly upmarket inn opened its doors in 2016, Little Compton's notoriously private elite feared it meant the out-of-towners were coming. With only 13 rooms (lavish as they may be), it's hardly cause for an invasion. If you have cash and the inclination, this is your chance to take a peek at how the other half live.

Listed on the National Register of Historic Places, the building once housed an inn and speakeasy before it fell by the wayside. Today, with its own private yacht, luxurious spa, taproom and service from the good-ole-days, the unique inn is a destination in itself, within a very special, very sheltered and beautiful historic New England cloister.

Provender Fine Foods
DELI $

(☑401-624-8084; www.provenderfinefoods.com; 3883 Main Rd; items $4-18; ⊙9am-5pm Tue-Sun) At Tiverton's 'Four Corners,' you can drop in at the Provender for a hearty sandwich on fresh bread or some cookies.

Gray's Ice Cream
ICE CREAM $

(☑401-624-4500; www.graysicecream.com; 16 East Rd; scoops from $3; ⊙6:30am-9pm) In business since 1923, Gray's Ice Cream makes over 40 flavors of fresh dairy ice cream onsite daily. Stop by for a coffee cabinet (milkshake with ice cream), as beachgoers have been doing for decades.

CONNECTICUT

Known for its commuter cities, New York's neighbor is synonymous with the affluent lanes and mansions of *The Stepford Wives* and TV's *Gilmore Girls*. In old-moneyed Greenwich, the Litchfield Hills and the Quiet Corner, these representations ring true.

Many regard the state as a mere stepping stone to the 'real' New England, from whose tourist boom Connecticut has been spared. The upside is that Connecticut retains a more 'authentic' feel. The downside is a slow decaying of former heavyweights like Hartford and New London, where visitors can ponder the price of progress and get enthused about urban renewal. New Haven, home of Yale University, is one such place rewiring itself as a vibrant cultural hub.

Dense with historical attractions and the kind of bucolic nature that continues to inspire artists as it has for over a century, Connecticut begs for your attention and a well-deserved spot on your New England itinerary.

History

A number of Native American tribes (notably the Pequot and the Mohegan, whose name for the river became the name of the state) were here when the first European explorers, primarily Dutch, appeared in the early 17th century. The first English settlement was at Old Saybrook in 1635, followed a year later by the Connecticut Colony, built by Massachusetts Puritans under Thomas Hooker. A third colony was founded in 1638 in New Haven. After the Pequot War (1637), the Native Americans were no longer a check to colonial expansion in New England, and Connecticut's English population grew. In 1686 Connecticut was brought into the Dominion of New England.

The American Revolution swept through Connecticut, leaving scars with major battles at Stonington (1775), Danbury (1777), New Haven (1779) and Groton (1781). Connecticut became the fifth state in 1788. It embarked on a period of prosperity, propelled by its whaling, shipbuilding, farming and manufacturing industries (from firearms to bicycles to household tools), which lasted well into the 19th century.

The 20th century brought world wars and the Depression but, thanks in no small part to Connecticut's munitions industries, the state was able to fight back. Everything from planes to submarines were made in the state, and when the defense industry began to decline in the 1990s, the growth of other businesses (such as insurance) helped pick up the slack.

ℹ Resources

Connecticut Office of Tourism (www.ctvisit. com) The official site for tourism in Connecticut.

CTNow (www.ctnow.com) Regularly updated listings and information on what's hot, where and when.

Connecticut River Valley and Shoreline Travel Information (www.ctrivervalley.com) A privately maintained resource of tourist information relating to the Connecticut River Valley.

Lonely Planet (www.lonelyplanet.com/usa/new-england/connecticut) Destination information, hotel bookings, traveller forum and more.

Hartford

Connecticut's capital, one of America's oldest cities, is famed for the 1794 birth of the lucrative insurance industry, conceived when a local landowner sought fire insurance. Policy documents necessitated printing presses, which spurred a boom in publishing that lured the likes of Mark Twain, Harriet Beecher Stowe and Wallace Stevens. In 1855 Samuel Colt made the mass production of the revolver commercially viable. Big business boomed in Hartford.

It's ironic that the industries responsible for the city's wealth (insurance and guns) have contributed to its slow decline: Hartford has a gritty track record for crime. Although things are improving, keep this in mind. Old money has left a truly impressive legacy of fine historic attractions worthy of any New England itinerary. Visit during spring when the darling buds burst to life or in summer when trees are green and skies are blue and you're likely to be pleasantly surprised.

◉ Sights

★ Mark Twain House & Museum MUSEUM
(☑ 860-247-0998; www.marktwainhouse.org; 351 Farmington Ave, parking at 385 Farmington Ave; adult/child $20/11; ⊙ 9:30am-5:30pm, closed Tue Jan & Feb; ℗) For 17 years, encompassing the most productive period of his life, Samuel Langhorne Clemens (1835–1910) and his family lived in this striking orange-and-black brick Victorian house, which then stood in the pastoral area of the city called Nook Farm. Architect Edward Tuckerman

Potter lavishly embellished it with turrets, gables and verandahs, and some of the interiors were done by Louis Comfort Tiffany. Admission to the house and museum is by guided tour only. Advance purchase is recommended.

★ Wadsworth Atheneum MUSEUM
(☑ 860-278-2670; https://thewadsworth.org; 600 Main St; adult/child $15/free; ⊙ 11am-5pm Wed-Fri, from 10am Sat & Sun) The nation's oldest public art museum completed a five-year, $33-million renovation, renewing 32 galleries and 15 public spaces in 2015. The Wadsworth houses nearly 50,000 pieces of art in a castle-like Gothic Revival building. On display are paintings by members of the Hudson River School, including some by Hartford native Frederic Church; 19th-century Impressionist works; 18th-century New England furniture; sculptures by Connecticut artist Alexander Calder; and an outstanding array of surrealist, postwar and contemporary works.

Old State House HISTORIC BUILDING
(☑ 860-522-6766; www.ctoldstatehouse.org; 800 Main St; adult/child $6/3; ⊙ 10am-5pm Tue-Sat Jul–mid-Oct, Mon-Fri mid-Oct–Jun; ⊞) Connecticut's original capitol building (from 1797 to 1873) was designed by Charles Bulfinch, who also designed the Massachusetts State House in Boston, and was the site of the trial of the *Amistad* prisoners. Gilbert Stuart's famous 1801 portrait of George Washington hangs in the senate chamber. The newly expanded space houses interactive exhibits aimed at kids, as well as a **Museum of Curiosities** that features a two-headed calf, a narwhal's horn and a variety of mechanical devices.

Harriet Beecher-Stowe Center MUSEUM
(☑ 860-522-9258; www.harrietbeecherstowe.org; 77 Forest St; adult/child $14/8; ⊙ 9:30am-5pm Mon-Sat, noon-5pm Sun; ℗) Along with literary titan Mark Twain, Hartford was also home to Harriet Beecher Stowe, author of the antislavery book *Uncle Tom's Cabin*. Upon meeting Stowe, Abraham Lincoln reputedly said, 'So this is the little lady who made this big war.' The facility centers on the Stowe House, built in 1871 and newly restored in 2017, which reflects the author's strong ideas about decorating and domestic efficiency, as expressed in her bestseller *American Woman's Home* (nearly as popular as her famous novel).

🛏 Sleeping

Sadly it's slim pickings for decent hotels in Hartford's downtown core and prices can be steep for what you get. Better value may be found in chain offerings outside the city center.

Daniel Rust House B&B $$
(☑ 860-742-0032; www.thedanielrusthouse.com; 2011 Main St, Coventry; d $120-185; ⓟ❄🖨) Serving travelers since 1800, the four period rooms brim with history. The finest is the Anna White room with its antique canopy bed, although the Mary Rose has a secret closet that was used to hide slaves traveling to freedom on the Underground Railroad.

🍴 Eating & Drinking

Salute ITALIAN $$
(☑ 860-899-1350; www.salutehartford.com; 100 Trumbull St; lunch mains $8-18, dinner $16-36; ⊙11:30am-11pm Mon-Thu, to midnight Fri & Sat, 3-10pm Sun; ✎) Charming service is the hallmark of this urban gem, which offers a contemporary take on Italian flavors. Regulars rave about the cheesy garlic bread, but other offerings are a tad more sophisticated. The pleasant patio overlooks Bushnell Park.

★ City Steam Brewery Café BREWERY
(☑ 860-525-1600; www.citysteam.biz; 942 Main St; ⊙11:30am-midnight Mon-Thu, to 1am Fri & Sat, 11am-10pm Sun) This big and boisterous place has housemade beers on tap. The Naughty Nurse Pale Ale is a bestseller, but the seasonals are also worth a try. The brewery's basement is home to the **Brew Ha Ha Comedy Club** (☑ 860-525-1600; www.citysteam.biz; 942 Main St; ticket prices vary; ⊙ show times vary), where you can yuk it up with visiting comedians from New York and Boston. There's plenty of great food to soak up the ale too.

ℹ Getting There & Away

Centrally located **Union Station** (www.amtrak.com; 1 Union Pl) is the city's transportation hub. Catch trains, airport shuttles, intercity buses and taxis from here.

Litchfield Hills

The rolling hills in the northwestern corner of Connecticut are sprinkled with lakes and dotted with forests and state parks. Historic Litchfield is the hub of the region, but lesser-known Bethlehem, Kent and Norfolk boast similarly illustrious lineages and are just as photogenic.

An intentional curb on development continues to preserve the area's rural character. Accommodations are limited. Volunteers staff a useful information booth on Litchfield's town green from June to November.

If you have your own car, there's no shortage of postcard-perfect country roads to explore in the Litchfield Hills. One particularly delightful stretch is from Cornwall Bridge taking CT 4 west and then CT 41 north to Salisbury.

ℹ Getting There & Around

The Litchfield Hills run north from Danbury and cover the northwest portion of the state, as far as the Massachusetts and New York borders, to the north and west, respectively.

Highways US 7 and CT 8 are the main north–south trunk roads. You'll need a car.

Litchfield

Litchfield is Connecticut's best-preserved late 18th-century town and the site of the nation's first law school. The town itself converges on a long oval green, and is surrounded by lush swaths of protected land just asking to be hiked through and picnicked on.

Founded in 1719, Litchfield prospered from 1780 to 1840 on the commerce brought by stagecoaches en route between Hartford and Albany, NY. In the mid-19th century, railroads did away with the coach routes, and industrial water-powered machinery drove Litchfield's artisans out of the markets, leaving the town to languish in faded gentility. Today farming and tourism rule the roost.

⊙ Sights & Activities

Litchfield History Museum MUSEUM
(☑ 860-567-4501; www.litchfieldhistoricalsociety.org; 7 South St; ⊙11am-5pm Tue-Sat, 1-5pm Sun mid-Apr–Nov) FREE This museum features a small permanent collection, including a modest photographic chronicle of the town and a dress-up box with Colonial clothes for children to try on, plus some local-interest rotating exhibits.

Reeve House & Litchfield Law School HISTORIC SITE
(☑ 860-567-4501; www.litchfieldhistoricalsociety.org; 82 South St; ⊙11am-5pm Tue-Sat, 1-5pm Sun mid-Apr–Nov) FREE In 1775 Tapping Reeve established the English-speaking world's first

law school at his home. When attendance overwhelmed his own house, he built the meticulously preserved one-room schoolhouse in his side yard. John C Calhoun and 130 members of Congress studied here.

White Memorial
Conservation Center   WALKING
(☑860-567-0857; www.whitememorialcc.org; 80 Whitehall Rd, off US 202; park free, museum adult/child $6/3; ☺park dawn-dusk, museum 9am-5pm Mon-Sat, noon-5pm Sun) **FREE** Made up of 4000 supremely serene acres, this park has two dozen trails (0.2 miles to 6 miles long) that crisscross the center, including swamp paths on a raised boardwalk. The center also manages three campgrounds and there's a small nature museum. The center is 2 miles west on US 202 from Litchfield.

Lake Waramaug

Among the plentiful lakes and ponds in the Litchfield Hills, Lake Waramaug, north of New Preston, stands out. Gracious inns dot its shoreline, parts of which are a state park.

⭐**Hopkins Inn**   INN **$$**
(☑860-868-7295; www.thehopkinsinn.com; 22 Hopkins Rd, Warren; r $135-145, without bath $125, apt $160-250; [P][❋][🐾]) The 19th-century Hopkins Inn boasts a well-regarded restaurant with Austrian-influenced country fare and a variety of lodging options, from simple rooms with shared bathrooms to lake-view apartments. Whatever the season, there's something magical about sitting on the porch gazing upon Lake Waramaug and the hills beyond.

Connecticut Coast

The southeastern corner of Connecticut is home to the state's number-one tourist attraction and the country's largest maritime museum, Mystic Seaport. Built on the site of a former shipbuilding yard in 1929, the museum celebrates the area's seafaring heritage when fishermen, whalers and clipper-ship engineers broke world speed records and manufactured gunboats and warships for the Civil War.

To the west of Mystic, you'll find the submarine capital of the USA, Groton, where General Dynamics built WWII subs, and across the Thames River, New London. To the east is the historic fishing village of Stonington, extending along a narrow mile-long

peninsula into the sea. It's one of the most charming seaside villages in New England, where Connecticut's only remaining commercial fleet operates and yachties come ashore in summer to enjoy the charming restaurants on Water St.

❶ Getting There & Around

The area is served well by road, with the I-95 plowing through the middle of New London and around the outskirts of Mystic. I-395 runs northeast to Norwich and beyond.

Many Amtrak trains from New York City stop in New London (from $39, three hours) and Mystic (from $41, 3¼ hours). The return run from Boston also stops in Mystic (from $26, 80 minutes), then New London (from $29, 1½ hours).

SEAT (www.seatbus.com) operates local buses services linking the communities of Norwich, New London, Groton and Mystic.

Mystic

A skyline of masts greets you as you arrive in town on US 1. They belong to the vessels bobbing ever so slightly in the postcard-perfect harbor. There's a sense of self-satisfied calm and composure in the air – until suddenly a heart-stopping steamer whistle blows, followed by the cheerful cling of a drawbridge bell. You know you've arrived in Mystic.

From simple beginnings in the 17th century, the village of Mystic grew to become a prosperous whaling center and one of the great shipbuilding ports of the East Coast. In the mid-19th century, Mystic's shipyards launched clipper ships, gunboats and naval transport vessels, many from the George Greenman & Co Shipyard, now the site of Mystic Seaport Museum.

⊙ Sights & Activities

⭐**Mystic Seaport Museum**   MUSEUM
(☑860-572-0711; www.mysticseaport.org; 75 Greenmanville Ave; adult/child $29/19; ☺9am-5pm Apr-Oct, 10am-4pm Thu-Sun Nov-Mar; [P][♿]) More than a museum, Mystic Seaport is the re-creation of an entire New England whaling village spread over 17 acres of the former George Greenman & Co Shipyard. To re-create the past, 60 historic buildings, four tall ships and almost 500 smaller vessels are gathered along the Mystic River. Interpreters staff the site and are glad to discuss traditional crafts and trades. Most illuminating are the demonstrations on such topics as ship rescue, oystering and whaleboat launching.

Mystic Aquarium & Institute for Exploration AQUARIUM

(☑ 860-572-5955; www.mysticaquarium.org; 55 Coogan Blvd; adult/teen/child $36/30/26; ☺ 9am-5:50pm Apr-Aug, 9am-4:50pm Mar & Sep-Nov, 10am-4:50pm Dec-Feb; ☝) This state-of-the-art aquarium boasts more than 6000 species of sea creatures, as well as an outdoor viewing area for watching seals and sea lions below the waterline and a penguin pavilion. The aquarium's most famous (and controversial) residents are the three beluga whales, who reside in the Arctic Coast exhibit. Animal-welfare groups claim it is debilitating to keep whales in enclosed containers.

Argia Mystic Cruises CRUISE

(☑ 860-536-0416; www.argiamystic.com; 12 Steamboat Wharf; adult/child $50/40) This outfit offers two- to three-hour daytime or sunset cruises down the Mystic River to Fishers' Island Sound on the authentic 19th-century replica schooner *Argia*.

🛏 Sleeping & Eating

Whaler's Inn INN $$

(☑ 860-536-1506; www.whalersinnmystic.com; 20 E Main St; d $159-299; ℗ ☺ ⧉) In downtown Mystic, beside its historic drawbridge, this hotel combines an 1865 Victorian house with a reconstructed luxury hotel from the same era (the original landmark 'Hoxie House' burned down in the 1970s) and a modern motel known as Stonington House. Seasonal packages available; these include the price of dinners and area attractions. Rates include continental breakfast, a small gym and complimentary bicycles.

★ Steamboat Inn INN $$$

(☑ 860-536-8300; www.steamboatinnmystic.com; 73 Steamboat Wharf; d $220-350; ℗ ❋ ⧉) Located right in the heart of downtown Mystic, the rooms of this historic inn have wraparound water views and luxurious amenities, including two-person whirlpool tubs, cable TV, free local calls and fireplaces. Antiques lend the interior a romantic, period feel, and service is top-notch with baked goods for breakfast, complimentary bikes and boat docks.

★ Captain Daniel Packer Inne AMERICAN $$$

(☑ 860-536-3555; www.danielpacker.com; 32 Water St; mains $14-34; ☺ 11am-4pm & 5-10pm) This 1754 historic house has a low-beam ceiling and creaky floorboards. On the lower pub level, you'll find regulars at the bar, a good selection of beer on tap and excellent pub grub: try the fish and chips. Upstairs, the dining room has river views and an imaginative American menu, including petite filet mignon with Gorgonzola sauce and walnut demi-glace. Reservations recommended.

★ Oyster Club SEAFOOD $$$

(☑ 860-415-9266; www.oysterclubct.com; 13 Water St; oysters $2-2.50, lunch mains $13-20, dinner mains $18-40; ☺ noon-3pm & 5-10pm Fri & Sat, 10am-3pm & 5-9pm Sun, 5-9pm Mon-Thu; ℗ ⧉) Offering casual fine dining at its best, this is the place locals come to knock down oysters on the deck out back. Grilled lobster and pan-roasted monkfish or flounder feature alongside veal, steak and a drool-worthy burger. If oysters are an aphrodisiac, anything could happen at the bar after the daily happy hour (4pm to 6pm), when shucked oysters are a buck each.

New London

During its golden age in the mid-19th century, New London, then home to some 200 whaling vessels, was one of the largest whaling centers in the USA and one of the wealthiest port cities. In 1858 the discovery of crude oil in Pennsylvania sent the value of whale oil plummeting and began a long period of decline for the city, from which it has never fully recovered. Even so, New London retains strong links with its seafaring past (the US Coast Guard Academy and US Naval Submarine Base are here) and its downtown is listed on the National Register of Historic Places. Despite lacking the sanitized tourism push of nearby Mystic and Stonington, remnants of New London's glorious and opulent times are still evident throughout the city, making it one of Connecticut's most surprising destinations for those interested in history, architecture and urban sociology.

Lower Connecticut River Valley

The Connecticut River, New England's longest, flows southwards 410 miles from its humble source at Fourth Connecticut Lake, just 300 yards from the Canadian border in New Hampshire. It forms the state boundary between Vermont and New Hampshire, before snaking its way through Massachusetts and Connecticut until it meets the Atlantic at Long Island Sound. Mercifully, it escaped

WORTH A TRIP

GILLETTE CASTLE

Built in 1919 by actor William Hooker Gillette, who made his fortune playing Sherlock Holmes, the gaudy, medieval-style **Gillette Castle** (☑ 860-526-2336; www.ct.gov/deep/gillettecastle; 67 River Rd; adult/child $6/2; ⊘ castle 11am-5pm Thu-Sun late May–early Sep, grounds 8am-dusk year-round; ℙ) is an eccentric turreted mansion made of fieldstone. Looming on one of the Seven Sisters hills above East Haddam, the folly is modeled on the medieval castles of Germany's Rhineland and the views from its terraces are spectacular. The surrounding 125 acres are a designated state park.

In summer, you can cross the Connecticut River on the Chester–Hadlyme Ferry (www.ctvisit.com/listings/chesterhadlyme-ferry). The short, five-minute river crossing affords great views, and deposits passengers at the foot of Gillette Castle.

the bustle of industry and commerce that marred many of the Northeast's rivers.

Today well-preserved historic towns grace the river's banks, notably Old Lyme, Essex, Ivoryton, Chester and East Haddam. Together, they enchant visitors with gracious country inns, fine dining, train rides and river excursions that allow authentic glimpses into provincial life on the Connecticut.

Old Lyme

Near the mouth of the Connecticut River and perched on the smaller Lieutenant River, Old Lyme was home to some 60 sea captains in the 19th century. Since the early 20th century, however, Old Lyme has been known as the center of the Lyme Art Colony, which cultivated the nascent American Impressionist movement. Numerous artists, including William Chadwick, Childe Hassam, Willard Metcalfe and Henry Ward Ranger, came here to paint, staying in the mansion of local art patron Florence Griswold.

⊙ Sights

Florence Griswold Museum   MUSEUM
(☑ 860-434-5542; http://florencegriswoldmuseum.org; 96 Lyme St; adult/child $10/free; ⊘ 10am-5pm Tue-Sat, 1-5pm Sun; ℙ) The 'home of American Impressionism,' the Florence Griswold Museum exhibits 6000 works with solid collections of American Impressionist and Barbizon paintings, as well as sculpture and decorative arts. Her house, which her artist friends decorated with murals (often in lieu of paying rent), is now the Florence Griswold Museum. The estate consists of her Georgian-style house, the Krieble Gallery, the Chadwick studio and Griswold's beloved gardens.

Lyme Academy of Fine Arts   GALLERY
(☑ 860-434-5232; www.lymeacademy.edu; 84 Lyme St; ⊘ 10am-4pm Mon-Sat) **FREE** A neighbor of the Florence Griswold Museum, Lyme Academy of Fine Arts, a college of the University of New Haven, features rotating drawing, painting and sculpture exhibits by students.

⏦ Sleeping

★ **Bee & Thistle Inn**   INN $$
(☑ 860-434-1667; www.beeandthistleinn.com; 100 Lyme St; r $129-289; ℙ 🛜) Occupying a handsome, Dutch Colonial farmhouse dating to 1756, this classy establishment has beautiful, well-tended gardens that stretch down to the Lieutenant River. Most of its 11 plush, well-appointed rooms feature abundant antiques and a canopy or four-poster bed.

The Inn's romantic dining room is the perfect setting for superlative New American cuisine. Lunch and dinner (meals $30 to $60) are served Wednesday to Sunday, often enhanced by a harpist. Reservations essential.

Essex

Tree-lined Essex, established in 1635, stands as the chief town of the Connecticut River Valley region. It's worth a visit if only to gawk at the beautiful, well-preserved Federal-period houses, legacies of rum and tobacco fortunes made in the 19th century. The town also has a strong following with steam train and riverboat enthusiasts.

⊙ Sights & Activities

Hammonasset Beach State Park   STATE PARK
(☑ 203-245-2785; www.ct.gov/deep/hammonasset; 1288 Boston Post Rd; weekdays/weekends $15/22; ⊘ 8am-sunset; ℙ) Though not off the beaten path by any means, the two full miles of flat, sandy beach at Hammonasset Beach State Park handily accommodate summer crowds. This is the ideal beach at which to

set up an umbrella chair, crack open a book and forget about the world. The surf is tame, making swimming superb. Restrooms and showering facilities are clean and ample, and a wooden boardwalk runs the length of the park.

Connecticut River Museum MUSEUM
(☑ 860-767-8269; www.ctrivermuseum.org; 67 Main St; adult/child $10/6; ⊙10am-5pm, closed Mon Oct-May; 🅿🚼) Adjacent to Essex's Steamboat Dock, this museum's meticulously presented exhibits recount regional history and include a reproduction of the world's first submarine, the *American Turtle*: a hand-propelled, barrel-like vessel built by Yale student David Bushnell in 1776 and launched at nearby Old Saybrook. The museum also hosts visiting exhibitions, runs summer workshops and organizes river paddles – dates and prices vary.

★**Essex Steam Train & Riverboat Ride** TOURS
(☑ 860-767-0103; www.essexsteamtrain.com; 1 Railroad Ave; adult/child $19/10, incl cruise $29/19; ⊙May-Oct; 🚼) This wildly popular attraction features a steam locomotive and antique carriages. The journey travels six scenic miles to Deep River, where you can cruise to the **Goodspeed Opera House** (☑ 860-873-8668; www.goodspeed.org; 6 Main St; tickets $45-85) in East Haddam, before returning to Essex via train. The round-trip train ride takes about an hour; with the riverboat ride it's 2½ hours.

A variety of themed excursions are available – consult the website for fares, times and details. If you're staying in Essex where nightly dining options are limited, you might elect to take the **Essex Clipper Dinner Train**, whose $80 (tax included) round-trip fare includes a 2½-hour train ride and four-course meal with a cash bar.

🛏 **Sleeping**

Griswold Inn INN $$
(☑ 860-767-1776; www.griswoldinn.com; 36 Main St; d/ste from $195/240; 🅿🐾) The landmark Griswold Inn is one of the oldest continually operating inns in the country and has been Essex's physical and social centerpiece since 1776. The inn's buffet-style Hunt Breakfast (served 11am to 1pm Sunday) is a tradition dating from the War of 1812, when British soldiers occupying Essex demanded to be fed.

At other times, the dining room remains a favorite place to enjoy traditional New England cuisine in a historic setting.

New Haven

As you wander around Yale University's venerable campus, admiring the gorgeous faux-Gothic and Victorian architecture, it's hard to fathom New Haven's struggle to shake its reputation as a dangerous, decaying seaport.

Connecticut's second-largest city radiates out from pretty New Haven Green, laid by Puritan settlers in the 1600s. Around it, Yale's over-300-year-old accessible campus offers visitors a wealth of world-class attractions, from museums and galleries to a lively concert program and walking-tour tales of secret societies. As New Haven repositions itself as a thriving home for the arts, architecture and the human mind, the good news is tourism is on the up and crime is in decline.

While Yale may have put New Haven on the map, there's much to savor beyond campus. Well-aged dive bars, ethnic restaurants, barbecue shacks and cocktail lounges make the area almost as lively as Cambridge's Harvard Sq – but with better pizza and less ego.

⊙ **Sights**

★**Yale University** UNIVERSITY
(☑ 203-432-2300; www.yale.edu/visitor; 149 Elm St; ⊙visitor center 9am-4:30pm Mon-Fri, 11am-4pm Sat & Sun) FREE Each year, thousands of high-school students make pilgrimages to Yale, nursing dreams of attending the country's third-oldest university, which boasts such notable alums as Noah Webster, Eli Whitney, Samuel Morse, and Presidents William H Taft, George HW Bush, Bill Clinton and George W Bush. You don't need to share the students' ambitions in order to take a stroll around the campus, just pick up a map at the visitor center or join a free, one-hour guided tour.

★**Yale Center for British Art** MUSEUM
(☑ 203-432-2800; www.ycba.yale.edu; 1080 Chapel St; ⊙10am-5pm Tue-Sat, noon-5pm Sun) FREE Reopened in 2016 after extensive restoration, this fabulous gallery was architect Louis Kahn's last commission and is the setting for the largest collection of British art outside the UK. Spanning three centuries from the Elizabethan era to the 19th century, and arranged thematically as well as chronologically, the

collection gives an unparalleled insight into British art, life and culture. A visit is an absolute must for anyone interested in beautiful things. And yes, it's free. Public and private group tours are available.

★ Yale University Art Gallery MUSEUM
(☎203-432-0600; http://artgallery.yale.edu; 1111 Chapel St; ⏲10am-5pm Tue-Fri, to 8pm Thu, 11am-5pm Sat & Sun) FREE This outstanding museum was architect Louis Kahn's first commission and houses the oldest university art collection in the country, including Vincent van Gogh's *The Night Café* and European masterpieces by Frans Hals, Peter Paul Rubens, Manet and Picasso. In addition there are displays of American masterworks by Winslow Homer, Edward Hopper and Jackson Pollock, silver from the 18th century, and art from Africa, Asia, the pre- and post-Columbian Americas. Best of all, it won't cost you a penny to take a peek.

★ Shore Line Trolley Museum MUSEUM, TROLLEY
(☎203-467-6927; www.shorelinetrolley.org; 17 River St, East Haven; adult/child $10/7; ⏲10:30am-4:30pm daily Jul & Aug, Sat & Sun May, Jun, Sep & Oct; 👪) For a unique take on East Haven's shoreline, take a ride on this open-sided antique trolley – the oldest continuously running suburban trolley line in the country – along 3 miles of track that takes you from River St in East Haven to Short Beach in Branford. Enjoy the museum and its beautifully maintained carriages when you're done. Bring a picnic lunch.

New Haven Green PARK
New Haven's spacious green has been the spiritual center of the city since its Puritan fathers designed it in 1638 as the prospective site for Christ's second coming. Since then it has held the municipal burial grounds (graves were later moved to Grove St Cemetery), several statehouses and an array of churches, three of which still stand.

Sleeping

Hotel Duncan HISTORIC HOTEL $
(☎203-787-1273; 1151 Chapel St; s $65-80, d $85-100; ❄📶) Though the shine has rubbed off this antique New Haven gem – with stained carpets, unstable water pressure and exfoliating towels – it's the enduring features that some will enjoy, like the handsome lobby and the hand-operated elevator with uniformed attendant. Rooms are rented on both a long-term and overnight basis. Don't expect the earth and you might be surprised.

Farnam Guest House B&B $$
(☎203-562-7121; www.farnamguesthouse.com; 616 Prospect St; r $149-199, with shared bath $89-139; P❄📶) The Farnams have a long association with Yale as alums, donors and professors, and you can stay in their grand Georgian Colonial mansion in the best neighborhood in town. Expect old-world ambience, with Chippendale sofas, wingback chairs, Victorian antiques and plush oriental carpets. There's a Steinway grand piano in the parlor.

The Study at Yale HOTEL $$$
(☎203-503-3900; www.thestudyatyale.com; 1157 Chapel St; r $219-389; P📶) The Study at Yale manages to evoke a mid-Century Modern sense of sophistication (call it '*Mad Men* chic') without being over the top or intimidating. Ultra-contemporary touches include in-room iPod docking stations and cardio machines with built-in TV. There's also an in-house restaurant and cafe, where you can stumble for morning snacks.

Eating

Frank Pepe PIZZA $
(☎203-865-5762; www.pepespizzeria.com; 157 Wooster St; pizzas $7-29; ⏲10:30am-10pm Sun-Thu, to 11pm Fri & Sat; 🍷👪) Pepe's lays claim to baking the 'best pizza in America,' a title it's won three times running. We'll let you be the judge, but can confirm this joint cranks out tasty pies fired in a coal oven, just as it has since 1925; only now it has a bunch of other locations across Connecticut, making consistency harder to master. Cash only.

The white-clam pizza is the pie the people praise.

★ Caseus Fromagerie & Bistro BISTRO $$
(☎203-624-3373; http://caseusnewhaven.com; 93 Whitney Ave; mains $12-30; ⏲11:30am-2:30pm Mon-Sat plus 5:30-9pm Wed-Sat; 🍷) With a boutique cheese counter piled with locally sourced labels and a concept menu devoted to *le grand fromage*, Caseus has hit upon a winning combination. After all, what's not to like about a perfectly executed mac-and-cheese or the dangerously delicious poutine (*pommes frites*, cheese curds and velouté).

Miya's Sushi SUSHI $$$
(☎203-777-9760; www.miyassushi.com; 68 Howe St; mains $11-35; ⏲5-11pm Wed, to midnight

Thu-Sat;) Two-time winner of the Taste of the Nation Award, Chef Bun Lai's immaculately presented, sustainable sushi and sashimi concoctions sport fantastic names. Even more fantastic are the freshness and flavors of the raw ingredients. Strip it back and keep it natural (sashimi), or go with Bun's adventurous combinations of ingredients: if you're a fan of modern American sushi, you will be impressed.

🍷 Drinking & Entertainment

Whether you're in the mood for an artisanal cocktail in a chic setting or a local beer in an old-school dive bar, New Haven has no shortage of nightspots, and plenty of funky arts-and-drama kids, divorced professors and tomorrow's millionaires to have a drink with.

Toad's Place
LIVE MUSIC

(☑ 203-624-8623; www.toadsplace.com; 300 York St) Toad's is arguably New England's premier music hall, having earned its rep hosting the likes of the Rolling Stones, U2 and Bob Dylan. These days, an eclectic range of performers work the intimate stage, including They Might Be Giants and Martin & Wood.

Shubert Theater
THEATER

(☑ 203-562-5666; www.shubert.com; 247 College St) Dubbed 'Birthplace of the Nation's Greatest Hits,' the Shubert has, since 1914, been hosting ballet and Broadway musicals on their trial runs before heading off to New York City. In recent years it has expanded its repertoire to include a broader range of events, including a series of interviews and musical performances.

ℹ Information

INFO New Haven (☑ 203-773-9494; www.infonewhaven.com; 1000 Chapel St; ⊙ 10am-9pm Mon-Sat, noon-5pm Sun) This downtown bureau offers maps and helpful advice.

ℹ Getting There & Away

New Haven is 141 miles southwest of Boston, 36 miles south of Hartford, 75 miles from New York and 101 miles from Providence via interstate highways.

Metro-North (www.mta.info/mnr) trains make the run between Union Station and New York City's Grand Central Terminal almost every hour from 7am to midnight.

Shore Line East (www.shorelineeast.com) runs regional trains up the shore of Long Island Sound to Old Saybrook (45 minutes) and New London (70 minutes), as well as Commuter Connection buses that shuttle passengers from Union Station (in the evenings) and from State St Station (in the mornings) to New Haven Green.

Amtrak (www.amtrak.com) trains run express from New York City's Penn Station to New Haven (from $32, 1¾ hours).

Peter Pan Bus Lines (www.peterpanbus.com) connects New Haven with New York City (from $12, two hours, eight daily), Hartford (from $12, one hour, six daily) and Boston (from $11, four to five hours, seven daily), as does Greyhound (www.greyhound.com). Buses depart from inside New Haven's Union Station.

Connecticut Limousine (www.ctlimo.com) is an airport shuttle servicing Hartford's Bradley airport, New York's JFK and LaGuardia airports and New Jersey's Newark airport. Pick-up and drop-off is at Union Station and select downtown New Haven hotels. Services to Newark attract a higher rate.

VERMONT

Whether seen under blankets of snow, patchworks of blazing fall leaves or the exuberant greens of spring and summer, Vermont's blend of bucolic farmland, mountains and picturesque small villages make it one of America's most uniformly appealing states. Hikers, bikers, skiers and kayakers will find four-season bliss here, on the expansive waters of Lake Champlain, the award-winning Kingdom Trails Network, the 300-mile Long and Catamount Trails, and the fabled slopes of Killington, Stowe and Sugarbush.

Foodies will love it here: small farmers have made Vermont a locavore paradise, complemented by America's densest collection of craft brewers. But most of all, what sets Vermont apart is its independent spirit: the only state with a socialist senator and the only one without a McDonald's in its capital city, Vermont remains a haven for quirky creativity, a champion of grassroots government and a bastion of 'small is beautiful' thinking, unlike anyplace else in America.

History

Frenchman Samuel de Champlain explored Vermont in 1609, becoming the first European to visit these lands long inhabited by the native Abenaki.

Vermont played a key role in the American Revolution in 1775 when Ethan Allen led a local militia, the Green Mountain Boys, to Fort Ticonderoga, capturing it from the Brit-

Vermont & New Hampshire

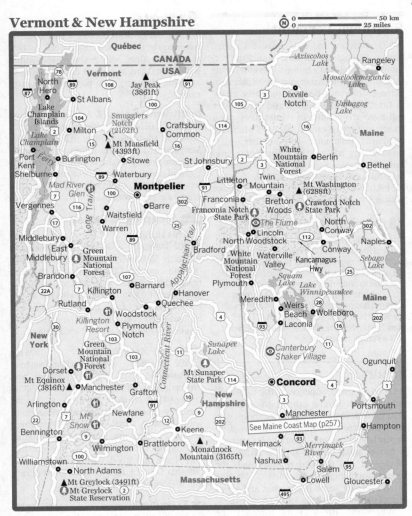

ish. In 1777 Vermont declared independence as the Vermont Republic, adopting the first New World constitution to abolish slavery and establish a public school system. In 1791 Vermont was admitted to the USA as the 14th state.

ⓘ Information

Vermont Chamber of Commerce (www.visitvt. com) Distributes a wealth of information about the state.

Vermont Division of Tourism (www.vermont vacation.com) Maintains a fabulous Welcome Center on I-91 near the Massachusetts state line, one on VT 4A near the New York state line, and three others along I-89 between White River Junction and the Canadian border. Produces a free, detailed road map and camping guide.

Vermont Public Radio (www.vpr.net) Vermont's statewide public radio station features superb local programming, including 'Vermont Edition' (weekdays at noon) for coverage of Vermont current events, and the quirky, information-packed 'Eye on the Sky' weather forecast.

Vermont Ski Areas Association (www.skiver mont.com) Helpful information for planning ski trips, as well as summer adventures at Vermont ski resorts.

Southern Vermont

White churches and inns surround village greens throughout historic southern Vermont, a region that's home to several towns that predate the American Revolution. In summer the roads between the three 'cities' of Brattleboro, Bennington and Manchester roll over green hills; in winter, they wind their way toward the ski slopes of Mt Snow, southern Vermont's cold-weather playground. For hikers, the Appalachian and Long Trails pass through the Green Mountain National Forest here, offering a colorful hiking experience during the fall foliage season.

ⓘ Getting There & Around

Drivers coming from Massachusetts, Connecticut and Rhode Island will most likely enter southern Vermont via one of two routes: I-91 in the east, or US 7 in the west. Public transit here is limited to once-daily buses and trains plying the Connecticut River valley. While southern Vermont has no commercial airport of its own, the airports at Albany, NY, Hartford, CT, and Manchester, NH, are all within one to two hours of the Vermont state line.

Brattleboro

Perched at the confluence of the Connecticut and West Rivers, Brattleboro is a little gem that reveals its facets to those who stroll the streets and prowl its dozens of independent shops and eateries. An energetic mix of aging hippies and the latest crop of pierced and tattooed hipsters fuels the town's sophisticated eclecticism, keeping the downtown scene percolating and skewing its politics decidedly leftward.

Whetstone Brook runs through the south end of town, where a wooden stockade dubbed Fort Dummer was built in 1724, becoming the first European settlement in Vermont (theretofore largely a wilderness populated exclusively by Native Americans).

At the Old Town Hall (location of the current Main Street Gallery), celebrated thinkers and entertainers, including Oliver Wendell Holmes, Horace Greeley and Will Rogers, held forth on civic and political matters. Rudyard Kipling married a Brattleboro woman in 1892, and while living here he wrote *The Jungle Book*.

◉ Sights

While most of Brattleboro's action is easily found in the downtown commercial district, the surrounding hillsides are well salted with farms, cheese makers and artisans, all awaiting discovery on a pleasant back-road ramble.

Brattleboro Museum & Art Center MUSEUM (☑ 802-257-0124; www.brattleboromuseum.org; 10 Vernon St; adult/child $8/free; ⊙ 11am-5pm Wed-Mon) Located in a 1915 railway station, this museum hosts a wealth of inventive exhibits by local artists in a variety of media. It also has a rotating multimedia exhibition program of contemporary art.

🛏 Sleeping & Eating

Latchis Hotel HOTEL $$ (☑ 802-348-4070, 800-798-6301; www.latchishotel.com; 50 Main St; r $100-200, ste $180-240; ⊛) You can't beat the location of these 30 reasonably priced rooms and suites, in the epicenter of downtown and adjacent to the historic theater of the same name. The hotel's art-deco overtones are refreshing, and wonderfully surprising for New England.

★Inn on Putney Road B&B $$$ (☑ 802-254-6268; www.vermontbandbinn.com; 192 Putney Rd; r $179-299; @⊛) Under new ownership as of 2016, this sweet 1930s-vintage B&B north of town has a glorious yard, five rooms and one luxurious suite with fireplace. Overlooking the West River estuary, it offers opportunities for walking, biking and boating right on its doorstep, and plenty of rainy-day activities, including billiards, board games, DVDs, a guest library and an indoor hot tub.

★TJ Buckley's AMERICAN $$$ (☑ 802-257-4922; www.tjbuckleysuptowndining.com; 132 Elliot St; mains $45; ⊙ 5:30-9pm Thu-Sun year-round, plus Wed mid-Jun–early Oct) ⦿ Chef-owner Michael Fuller founded this exceptional, upscale little eatery in an authentic 1927 diner over 30 years ago. Ever since, he's been offering a verbal menu of four seasonally changing items, sourced largely from local farms. Locals rave that the food here is Brattleboro's best. The diner seats just 18 souls, so reserve ahead. No credit cards.

ⓘ Information

Brattleboro Chamber of Commerce (☑ 802-254-4565, 877-254-4565; www.brattleboro

chamber.org; 180 Main St; ⊘9am-5pm Mon-Fri)
Dependable year-round source of tourist info.

Brattleboro Chamber of Commerce Information Booth (80 Putney Rd; ⊘Sat & Sun
late May–mid-Oct) On the green just north of
downtown.

Bennington

Bennington is a mix of historic Vermont village (Old Bennington), workaday town (Bennington proper) and college town (North
Bennington). It is also home to the famous
Bennington Battle Monument (☑802-447-
0550; www.benningtonbattlemonument.com; 15
Monument Circle, Old Bennington; adult/child $5/1;
⊘9am-5pm mid-Apr–Oct), which commemorates the crucial Battle of Bennington during the American Revolution. Had Colonel
Seth Warner and the local 'Green Mountain
Boys' not helped weaken British defenses
during this battle, the colonies might well
have been split.

The charming hilltop site of Colonial Old
Bennington is studded with 80 Georgian
and Federal houses (dating from 1761 – the
year Bennington was founded – to 1830).
The poet Robert Frost is buried here and
a museum in his old homestead pays eloquent tribute. As Bennington is within the
bounds of the Green Mountain National
Forest, there are many hiking trails nearby,
including the granddaddies of them all: the
Appalachian and Long Trails.

Sights

Bennington Museum   MUSEUM
(☑802-447-1571; www.benningtonmuseum.org;
75 Main St; adult/child $10/free; ⊘10am-5pm
daily Jun-Oct, Thu-Tue Nov-May, closed Jan) Between downtown and Old Bennington, this
ever-expanding museum offers 14 galleries
of ongoing and changing exhibits. It features
the world's largest collections of Grandma
Moses paintings and Bennington pottery,
along with a rich array of Vermont paintings, decorative arts and folk art from the
18th century to the present, encompassing
everything from Vermont's Gilded Age to
Bennington Modernism to 'Outsider' Art.
New in 2015, the Works on Paper Gallery
displays prints, lithographs, photography
and more by nationally recognized artists.

Old First Church   HISTORIC SITE
(☑802-447-1223; www.oldfirstchurchbenn.org;
cnr Monument Ave & VT 9; ⊘10am-4pm Mon-Sat,
1-4pm Sun Jul–mid-Oct, weekends only late May–
Jun) FREE Gracing the center of Old Bennington, this historic church was built in
1805 in Palladian style. Its churchyard holds
the remains of five Vermont governors, numerous American Revolution soldiers and
poet Robert Frost (1874–1963) – the best-known, and perhaps best-loved, American
poet of the 20th century – buried beneath
the inscription 'I Had a Lover's Quarrel with
the World.'

Sleeping & Eating

**Greenwood Lodge &
Campsites**   HOSTEL, CAMPGROUND $
(☑802-442-2547; www.campvermont.com; VT 9,
Prospect Mountain; 2-person tent/RV sites $30/39,
dm $35-38, r $79; ⊘mid-May–late Oct; 🛜) Nestled in the Green Mountains in Woodford,
this 120-acre space with three ponds is home
to one of Vermont's best-sited hostels. Accommodations include 17 budget beds and
40 campsites. You'll find it easily, 8 miles
east of Bennington on VT 9 at the Prospect
Mountain ski area. Facilities include hot
showers and a games room.

Blue Benn Diner   DINER $
(☑802-442-5140; 314 North St; mains $6-14;
⊘6am-5pm Mon & Tue, to 8pm Wed-Fri, to 4pm
Sat, 7am-4pm Sun; 🛜) This classic 1950s-era
diner serves breakfast all day and a healthy
mix of American, Asian and Mexican fare,
including vegetarian options. Enhancing the
retro experience are little tabletop jukeboxes where you can you play Willie Nelson's
'Moonlight in Vermont' or Cher's 'Gypsies,
Tramps and Thieves' till your neighbors
scream for mercy.

★Pangaea   INTERNATIONAL $$
(☑802-442-7171; www.vermontfinedining.com;
1 Prospect St, North Bennington; mains lounge $10-
24, restaurant $31; ⊘lounge 5-10pm daily, restaurant 5-9pm Tue-Sat) Whether you opt for the
tastefully decorated dining room, the intimate lounge or the small riverside terrace,
you'll be served exceptional food here. The
menu is full of fresh ingredients and international influences; try the Thai shrimp
on organic udon noodles in a curry peanut
sauce or the herbes de Provence–rubbed
Delmonico steak topped with Gorgonzola.
One of Vermont's finest restaurants.

Information

Bennington Welcome Center (☑802-447-
2456; www.informationcenter.vermont.gov; 100
VT 279; ⊘7am-9pm) Bennington's spiffy new

tourist office has loads of information, long hours, and free coffee and tea for motorists; it's at the highway interchange where VT 279 and US 7 meet.

Manchester

Manchester has been a fashionable resort town for almost two centuries. These days, the draw is mostly winter skiing and upscale outlet shopping (there are more than 100 shops, from Armani to Banana Republic).

Two families put Manchester on the map. The first was native son Franklin Orvis (1824–1900), who became a New York businessperson but returned to Manchester to establish the Equinox House Hotel (1849). Franklin's brother, Charles, founded the Orvis Company, makers of fly-fishing equipment, in 1856. The Manchester-based company now has a worldwide following.

The second family was that of Abraham Lincoln (1809–65). His wife, Mary Todd Lincoln (1818–82), and their son Robert Todd Lincoln (1843–1926), came here during the Civil War, and Robert returned to build a mansion – Hildene – a number of years later.

◉ Sights & Activites

★ **Hildene**   HISTORIC SITE
(☑ 802-362-1788; www.hildene.org; 1005 Hildene Rd/VT 7A; adult/child $20/5, guided tours $7.50/2; ⊗ 9:30am-4:30pm) Outside Manchester, the 24-room Georgian Revival mansion of Robert Todd Lincoln, son of Abraham and Mary Lincoln, is a national treasure. Lincoln family members lived here until 1975, when it was converted into a museum and filled with many of the family's personal effects and furnishings. These include the hat Abraham Lincoln probably wore when he delivered the Gettysburg Address, and remarkable brass casts of his hands, the right one swollen from shaking hands while campaigning for the presidency.

Mt Equinox Skyline Drive   SCENIC DRIVE
(☑ 802-362-1114; www.equinoxmountain.com; VT 7A, btwn Manchester & Arlington; car & driver $15, each additional passenger $5, under 13yr free; ⊗ 9am-4pm late May-Oct) For exceptional views, climb the insanely steep 5-mile Skyline Dr, a private toll road that leads to the summit of 3848ft Mt Equinox, highest mountain in the Taconic Range; it's just off VT 7A, south of Manchester.

🛏 Sleeping & Eating

Aspen Motel   MOTEL $$
(☑ 802-362-2450; www.theaspenatmanchester.com; 5669 Main St/VT 7A; r $95-160; ✳ 🗭 ☎) An affordable standout, this family-run hotel set back serenely from the road has 25 comfortable rooms, a swimming pool and a convenient location within walking distance of Manchester Center.

Ye Olde Tavern   AMERICAN $$$
(☑ 802-362-0611; www.yeoldetavern.net; 5183 Main St; mains $19-34; ⊗ 5-9pm) Hearthside dining at candlelit tables enhances the experience at this gracious roadside 1790s inn. The menu is wide-ranging: 'Yankee favorites' like traditional pot roast cooked in the tavern's own ale; New England scrod baked with Vermont cheddar, bread crumbs, sherry and lemon; and local venison (a regular Friday special) seal the deal.

ℹ Information

Green Mountain National Forest Ranger Station (☑ 802-362-2307; www.fs.usda.gov/gmfl; 2538 Depot St, Manchester Center; ⊗ 8am-4:30pm Mon-Fri) Stop by for info about the Appalachian and Long Trails, trail maps and details about shorter day hikes.

Central Vermont

Vermont's heart features some of New England's most bucolic countryside. Cows begin to outnumber people just north of Rutland (Vermont's second-largest city, with a whopping 16,500 residents). Lovers of the outdoors make frequent pilgrimages to central Vermont, especially to the resort areas of Killington, Sugarbush and Mad River Glen, which attract countless skiers and summer hikers. For those interested in indoor pleasures, antique shops and art galleries dot the back roads between picturesque covered bridges.

ℹ Getting There & Around

The best way to get around central Vermont is with your own wheels, whether that means car or bicycle. The major driving thoroughfares are US 4, running east–west, and VT 100, running north–south – with the two crossing paths in Killington. Public transit here is limited to Vermont Translines' once-daily east–west bus service between Rutland, VT, and Hanover, NH, and Amtrak's once-daily *Vermonter* train, which runs up the Connecticut and White River valleys between Brattleboro and Burlington. There is a small airport in Rutland, but service is limited to commuter flights to/from Boston.

Woodstock & Quechee

Chartered in 1761, Woodstock has been the highly dignified seat of scenic Windsor County since 1766. Many grand houses surround the oval village green, and four of Woodstock's churches can claim bells cast by Paul Revere. Senator Jacob Collamer, a friend of Abraham Lincoln's, once observed, 'The good people of Woodstock have less incentive than others to yearn for heaven.'

Today Woodstock is still very beautiful and very wealthy. Spend some time walking around the green, surrounded by Federal and Greek Revival homes and public buildings, or along the Ottauquechee River, spanned by three covered bridges. The Rockefellers and the Rothschilds own estates in the surrounding countryside, and the well-to-do come to stay at the grand Woodstock Inn & Resort.

About five minutes' drive east of Woodstock, small, twee Quechee Village is home to Quechee Gorge – Vermont's diminutive answer to the Grand Canyon – as well as some outstanding restaurants.

◉ Sights

★ **Quechee Gorge**   CANYON
(US 4, Quechee) FREE Lurking beneath US 4, less than a mile east of Quechee Village, the gorge is a 163ft-deep scar that cuts about 3000ft along a stream that you can view from a bridge or easily access by footpaths from the road. A series of well-marked, undemanding trails, none of which should take more than an hour to cover, lead down into the gorge.

Billings Farm & Museum   FARM
(☑802-457-2355; www.billingsfarm.org; 69 Old River Rd, Woodstock; adult/child $15/8; ⊙10am-5pm daily Apr-Oct, to 4pm Sat, Sun & holidays Nov-Feb, closed Mar; ⊕) A mile north of Woodstock's village green, this historic farm founded by 19th-century railroad magnate Frederick Billings delights children with hands-on activities related to old-fashioned farm life. Farm animals, including pretty cows descended from Britain's Jersey island, are abundant. Family-friendly seasonal events include wagon and sleigh rides, pumpkin and apple festivals, and old-fashioned Halloween, Thanksgiving and Christmas celebrations.

Marsh-Billings-Rockefeller National Historical Park   PARK
(☑802-457-3368; www.nps.gov/mabi; 54 Elm St, Woodstock; mansion tours adult/child $8/free, trails & carriage roads free; ⊙visitor center & tours 10am-5pm late May-Oct, trails & carriage roads year-round) Built around the historic home of early American conservationist George Perkins Marsh, Vermont's only national park examines the relationship between land stewardship and environmental conservation. The estate's 20 miles of trails and carriage roads are free for exploring on foot, cross-country skis or snowshoes.

VINS Nature Center   WILDLIFE RESERVE
(Vermont Institute of Natural Science; ☑802-359-5000; www.vinsweb.org; 6565 Woodstock Rd, Quechee; adult/child $15/13; ⊙10am-5pm mid-Apr-Oct, to 4pm Nov-mid-Apr; ⊕) This science center near Quechee houses two dozen species of raptors, ranging from the tiny, 3oz saw-whet owl to the mighty bald eagle. The birds that end up here have sustained permanent injuries that prevent them from returning to the wild. On offer are regular educational presentations and three self-guided nature trails, delightful for summer hiking and winter snowshoeing.

🛏 Sleeping & Eating

Shire   HOTEL $$
(☑802-457-2211; www.shiremotel.com; 46 Pleasant St/US 4, Woodstock; r $159-269; ❄🐾😼) Set within walking distance of Woodstock's town center on US 4, this recently remodeled hotel has 44 comfortable rooms, the best of which come with fireplaces, Jacuzzis and/or decks with rockers looking out over the Ottauquechee River. Many units received new beds in 2015, all have brand-new linens, and rooms 218 and 405 have especially nice river views.

Ardmore Inn   B&B $$$
(☑802-457-3887; www.ardmoreinn.com; 23 Pleasant St, Woodstock; r incl breakfast $189-299; ❄🐾) This congenial, centrally located inn in a stately 1867 Victorian–Greek Revival building has four antique-laden rooms with oriental rugs and private marble bathrooms. The owners are especially helpful, and the breakfasts are seemingly never-ending.

★ **Simon Pearce Restaurant**   MODERN AMERICAN $$$
(☑802-295-1470; www.simonpearce.com; 1760 Quechee Main St, Quechee; mains lunch $14-19,

dinner $22-40; ⊙11:30am-2:45pm & 5:30-9pm Mon-Sat, from 10:30am Sun) Be sure to reserve a window table overlooking the falls in Simon Pearce's dining room, which is suspended over the river in this converted brick mill. Local ingredients are used to inventive effect in such delicacies as crab and cod melt or seared chicken with roasted-corn mascarpone polenta. The restaurant's stemware is blown by hand in the adjacent glass workshop.

❶ Information

Woodstock Area Chamber of Commerce Welcome Center (☑888-496-6378, 802-457-3555; www.woodstockvt.com; 3 Mechanic St, Woodstock; ⊙9am-5pm late May–mid-Oct, 10am-5pm rest of year) Woodstock's welcome center is housed in a lovely red building on a riverside backstreet, two blocks from the village green. There's also a small information booth on the village green itself. Both places can help with accommodations.

Killington

The largest ski resort in the East, Killington spans seven mountains, dominated by 4241ft Killington Peak, the second highest in Vermont. Although upwards of 20,000 people can find lodging within 20 miles, its numerous outdoor activities are centrally located on the mountain. Officially the mountain town is Killington Village, but all the action can be found along Killington Rd on the way up the mountain.

Virtually everyone is here to ski, which means that Killington Resort's mountainside lodges and condos are the accommodations of choice for many. However, you'll find plenty of other options in the surrounding 'lowlands' along US 4 and VT 100, from motels to campgrounds to a historic trailside inn that has welcomed many a weary Long Trail hiker.

Killington Resort   SKIING
(☑info 800-734-9435, reservations 800-621-6867; www.killington.com; 4763 Killington Rd; lift tickets adult/teen/senior $105/89/81) Known as the 'Beast of the East,' Vermont's prime ski resort is enormous, yet runs efficiently enough to avoid overcrowding; it has five separate lodges, each with a different emphasis, as well as 29 lifts and 92 miles of trails. The ski season runs from November through early May, enhanced by America's largest snowmaking system.

❶ Information

Killington Welcome Center (☑802-773-4181; http://killingtonpico.org; 2319 US 4; ⊙9am-4pm Mon-Fri, 10am-2pm Sat & Sun) General tourist information, conveniently located on US 4.

Killington/Pico Central Reservations (☑800-621-6867; www.killington.com; 4763 Killington Rd; ⊙8am-9pm Nov-Apr, to 4pm May-Oct) Advice on accommodations, including package deals.

Mad River Valley

North of Killington, VT 100 is one of the finest stretches of road in the country: a bucolic mix of rolling hills, covered bridges, white steeples and fertile farmland. Here you'll find the Mad River Valley, where the pretty villages of Waitsfield and Warren nestle in the shadow of two major ski areas, Sugarbush and Mad River Glen.

For tantalizing valley perspectives, go exploring the glorious back roads on either side of VT 100. Leave the pavement behind and meander up the valley's eastern side, following Brook, E Warren, Common, North and Pony Farm Rds from Warren north to Moretown; or head west from Warren over Lincoln Gap Rd, the highest, steepest and perhaps prettiest of all the 'gap roads' that run east to west over the Green Mountains. Stop at Lincoln Gap (2424ft) for the scenic 3-mile hike up the **Long Trail** to Mt Abraham (4017ft), Vermont's fifth-highest peak.

✦ Activities

★**Mad River Glen**   SKIING
(☑802-496-3551; www.madriverglen.com; VT 17, Waitsfield; lift tickets adult/child weekend $79/63, midweek $65/60) The most rugged lift-served ski area in the East, Mad River is also one of the quirkiest. Managed by an owner cooperative, not a major ski corporation, it largely eschews artificial snowmaking, prohibits snowboarding, and proudly continues to use America's last operating single chairlift, a vintage 1948 model!

Vermont Icelandic Horse Farm   HORSEBACK RIDING
(☑802-496-7141; www.icelandichorses.com; 3061 N Fayston Rd, Waitsfield; 1-3hr rides $60-120, full day incl lunch $220, multiday treks $675-1695; ⊙by appointment; ⊞) Explore the scenic hills above Waitsfield on beautiful, gentle and easy-to-ride Icelandic horses. Rides range from hour-long jaunts to multiday inn-to-inn treks.

🛌 Sleeping & Eating

★ Inn at Round Barn Farm   INN $$$
(☑802-496-2276; www.roundbarninn.com; 1661 E Warren Rd, Waitsfield; r incl breakfast $179-359; 🛜🆒) This place gets its name from the adjacent 1910 round barn – among the few authentic examples remaining in Vermont. The decidedly upscale inn has antique-furnished rooms with mountain views, gas fireplaces, canopy beds and antiques. All overlook the meadows and mountains. In winter guests leave their shoes at the door to preserve the hardwood floors. The country-style breakfast is huge.

★ Warren Store   SANDWICHES $
(☑802-496-3864; www.warrenstore.com; 284 Main St, Warren; sandwiches & light meals $5-9; ⊘7:45am-7pm Mon-Sat, to 6pm Sun) This atmospheric country store serves the area's best sandwiches along with delicious pastries and breakfasts. In summer, linger over coffee and the *New York Times* on the front porch, or eat on the deck overlooking the waterfall, then descend for a cool dip among river-sculpted rocks. Browsers will love the store's eclectic upstairs collection of clothing, toys and jewelry.

ℹ️ Information

Mad River Valley Chamber of Commerce (☑800-828-4748, 802-496-3409; www.madrivervalley.com; 4061 Main St/VT 100, Waitsfield; ⊘8am-5pm Mon-Fri) Staff here can assist with lodging and the latest skiing info. The chamber also provides a 24-hour information kiosk and public restrooms for visitors.

Northern Vermont

Northern Vermont is home to the state's largest city, Burlington, and the state capital, Montpelier. Never fear, however: this area still has all of the rural charms found elsewhere. Even within Burlington, cafe-lined streets coexist with scenic paths along Lake Champlain and the Winooski River. Further north, the pastoral Northeast Kingdom offers a full range of outdoor activities, from skiing to biking, in the heart of the mountains.

ℹ️ Getting There & Around

Burlington has Vermont's only international airport and its best bus connections, making this the logical starting point for visitors arriving by plane or public transportation. Car travel in northern Vermont is also faster and more efficient than elsewhere in the state, thanks to two interstate highways, I-89 serving the Montpelier–Burlington corridor and I-91 serving St Johnsbury and the Northeast Kingdom. Even so, the going gets slower once you stray onto scenic back roads like VT 108 over beautiful Smugglers Notch.

Montpelier

Montpelier (mont-*peel*-yer) would qualify as nothing more than a large village in most places. But in sparsely populated Vermont it's the state capital – the smallest in the country (and the only one without a Mc-Donald's, in case you were wondering). Surprisingly cosmopolitan for a town of 8000 residents, its two main thoroughfares – State St and Main St – make for a pleasant wander, with some nice bookstores, boutiques and eateries.

Montpelier's smaller, distinctly working-class neighbor Barre (*bear*-ee), which touts itself as the 'granite capital of the world,' is a 15-minute drive southeast of the capital.

State House   HISTORIC BUILDING
(☑802-828-1411; www.vtstatehousefriends.org; 115 State St; ⊘guided tours 10am-3:30pm Mon-Fri, 11am-2:30pm Sat Jul–mid-Oct, 9am-3pm Mon-Fri mid-Oct–Jun) **FREE** Montpelier's main landmark, the gold-domed capitol building, is open year-round for guided tours with volunteer guides; there are also self-guided audio tours in English, French, Spanish and German. The front doors are guarded by a massive statue of American Revolutionary hero Ethan Allen, and the base supporting the gold dome was built of granite quarried in nearby Barre in 1836.

La Brioche   CAFE, BAKERY $
(☑802-229-0443; www.neci.edu/labrioche; 89 Main St; pastries $1-5, sandwiches $5-8; ⊘7am-6pm Mon-Fri, to 3pm Sat) The New England Culinary Institute's first restaurant, this casual bakery and cafe serves delicious pastries and coffee drinks for breakfast, followed by soups, salads and sandwiches on homemade bread at lunchtime.

ℹ️ Information

Capitol Region Visitors Center (☑802-828-5981; www.informationcenter.vermont.gov; 134 State St; ⊘6am-5pm Mon-Fri, 9am-5pm Sat & Sun) Opposite the Vermont state capitol building.

Stowe

In a cozy valley where the West Branch River flows into Little River and mountains rise in all directions, the quintessential Vermont village of Stowe (founded in 1794) bustles quietly. The town's long-standing reputation as one of the east's classiest mountain resorts draws well-heeled urbanites from Boston, New York and beyond. A bounty of inns and eateries lines the thoroughfares leading up to Smuggler's Notch, an enchantingly narrow rock-walled pass through the Green Mountains just below Mt Mansfield (4393ft), the highest point in Vermont. More than 200 miles of cross-country ski trails, some of the finest mountain biking and downhill skiing in the east, and world-class rock- and ice-climbing make this a natural mecca for adrenaline junkies.

Waterbury, on the interstate highway 10 miles south, is Stowe's gateway. Its attractions include a pair of standout restaurants, a beloved brewery and the famous Ben & Jerry's Ice Cream Factory.

◎ Sights & Activities

★ Ben & Jerry's
Ice Cream Factory   FACTORY
(☑ 802-882-2047; www.benjerrys.com; 1281 VT 100, Waterbury; adult/child under 13yr $4/free; ☺ 9am-9pm Jul–mid-Aug, to 7pm mid-Aug–mid-Oct, 10am-6pm mid-Oct–Jun; ➔) In 1978 Ben Cohen and Jerry Greenfield took over an abandoned gas station in Burlington and, with a modicum of training, launched the outlandish flavors that forever changed the way ice cream would be made. While a tour of Ben & Jerry's Ice Cream Factory is no over-the-top Willy Wonka experience, there is a campy video that follows the company's long, strange trip to corporate giant – albeit a very nice giant with an inspiring presence of community building and leadership.

★ Stowe Recreation Path   OUTDOORS
(☺ year-round; ➔) The flat to gently rolling 5.5-mile Stowe Recreation Path, which starts from the pointy-steepled Stowe Community Church in the village center, offers a fabulous four-season escape for all ages. It rambles through woods, meadows and outdoor sculpture gardens along the West Branch of Little River, with sweeping views of Mt Mansfield unfolding in the distance.

Bike, walk, skate or ski – and swim in one of the swimming holes along the way.

🛏 Sleeping & Eating

Stowe Motel &
Snowdrift   MOTEL, APARTMENT $$
(☑ 802-253-7629, 800-829-7629; www.stowemotel.com; 2043 Mountain Rd; r $99-210, ste $190-250, apt $169-275; @ ➔ ➔) In addition to the efficiency rooms (with kitchenettes), suites, apartment and two- to six-bedroom houses (rates highly variable; call to inquire), this motel set on a generous 16 acres offers such amenities as a tennis court, hot tubs, badminton and lawn games.

Pie-casso   PIZZA $$
(☑ 802-253-4411; www.piecasso.com; 1899 Mountain Rd; mains $8-22; ☺ 11am-9pm Sun-Thu, to 10pm Fri & Sat) Best known for its ample pizzas, from the sausage-and-pepperoni-laden Heart Stopper to the veggie-friendly Vienna with spinach, olives, sun-dried tomatoes and mozzarella, Pie-casso also serves everything from eggplant Parmesan subs to fettuccine Alfredo and penne with pesto. Gluten-free crusts using flour from nearby West Meadow Farm are also available.

Bistro at Ten Acres   FUSION $$$
(☑ 802-253-6838; www.tenacreslodge.com; 14 Barrows Rd; mains $19-32; ☺ 5-10pm Wed-Sun) This immensely popular eatery in a plank-floored 1820s farmhouse blends cozy atmosphere with delicious food from New York-trained chef Gary Jacobson (think *steak frites*, slow-roasted duck, or lobster with bourbon-tarragon sauce and polenta). The attached bar serves a good selection of cocktails and draft beers, plus a cheaper burger-centric menu.

ⓘ Information

Green Mountain Club Visitors Center (☑ 802-244-7037; www.greenmountainclub.org; 4711 Waterbury-Stowe Rd/VT 100, Waterbury Center; ☺ 9am-5pm daily mid-May–mid-Oct, 10am-5pm Mon-Fri mid-Oct–mid-May) Stop by this office (5 miles south of Stowe) or check the website for details about the Long Trail and shorter day hikes in the region.

Stowe Area Association (☑ 802-253-7321, 800-467-8693; www.gostowe.com; 51 Main St; ☺ 9am-5pm Mon-Sat, 11am-5pm Sun; ➔) This well-organized association can help you plan your trip, including making reservations for rental cars and local accommodations.

Burlington

Perched on the shore of Lake Champlain, Vermont's largest city would be considered tiny in most other states, but its relatively diminutive size is one of Burlington's charms. With the University of Vermont (UVM) swelling the city by 13,400 students, and a vibrant cultural and social life, Burlington has a spirited, youthful character. And when it comes to nightlife, this is Vermont's epicenter.

Due south of Burlington is Shelburne, an upscale village that's home to the one of Vermont's crown jewels, the Shelburne Museum. The village is considered more of an extension of Burlington rather than a separate suburb – people think nothing of popping down for an evening meal to one of its fine restaurants.

Burlington is less than an hour's drive from Stowe and other Green Mountain towns. The city can be used as a base for exploring much of northwestern Vermont.

⊙ Sights & Activities

★ Shelburne Museum   MUSEUM
(☑ 802-985-3346; www.shelburnemuseum.org; 6000 Shelburne Rd/US 7, Shelburne; adult/child/teen $24/12/14; ⊙ 10am-5pm daily May-Dec, Wed-Sun Jan-Apr; 👪) This extraordinary 45-acre museum, 9 miles south of Burlington, showcases the priceless Americana collections of Electra Havemeyer Webb (1888–1960) and her parents – 150,000 objects in all. The mix of folk art, decorative arts and more is housed in 39 historic buildings, most of them moved here from other parts of New England to ensure their preservation.

★ Intervale Center   FARM
(☑ 802-660-0440; www.intervale.org; 180 Intervale Rd) FREE You'd never guess it standing on a busy Burlington street corner, but one of Vermont's most idyllic green spaces is less than 2 miles from downtown. Tucked among the lazy curves of the Winooski River, Burlington's Intervale Center encompasses a dozen organic farms and a delightful trail network, open 365 days a year for hiking, biking, skiing, berry picking and more.

Echo Leahy Center for
Lake Champlain   AQUARIUM
(☑ 802-864-1848; www.echovermont.org; 1 College St; adult/child $16.50/13.50; ⊙ 10am-5pm; 👪) This kid-friendly lakeside museum examines the colorful past, present and future of Lake Champlain. A multitude of aquariums wriggle with life, and nature-oriented displays invite inquisitive minds and hands to splash, poke, listen and crawl. Regular rotating exhibits focus on scientific themes –

from wind power to giant insects, and dinosaurs to cadavers – with plenty of hands-on activities.

Whistling Man
Schooner Company   BOATING
(☑ 802-825-7245; www.whistlingman.com; Burlington Community Boathouse, 1 College St, at Lake Champlain; 2hr cruises adult/child $50/35; ⊙ 3-4 trips daily, late May-early Oct) Sail around Lake Champlain with the breeze in your hair and a Vermont microbrew in your hand on the *Friend Ship*, a classic 43ft New England beauty that holds up to 17 passengers. Captains are knowledgeable about the area, and encourage passengers to bring food and drink on board. Private charters are also available (from $450 for two hours).

🛏 Sleeping

Burlington Hostel   HOSTEL $
(☑ 802-540-3043; www.theburlingtonhostel.com; 53 Main St, 2nd floor; dm incl breakfast weekday/weekend $39/49; ⊙ May-Oct; ✳@🛜) Just minutes from the action centers of Church St and Lake Champlain, Burlington's hostel accommodates up to 48 guests and offers both mixed and women-only dorms.

★ Willard Street Inn   INN $$
(☑ 802-651-8710; www.willardstreetinn.com; 349 S Willard St; r incl breakfast $169-269; 🛜) Perched on a hill within easy walking distance of UVM and the Church St Marketplace, this mansion, fusing Queen Anne and Georgian Revival styles, was built in the late 1880s. It has a fine-wood and cut-glass elegance, yet radiates a welcoming warmth. Many of the guest rooms overlook Lake Champlain.

★ Inn at Shelburne Farms   INN $$$
(☑ 802-985-8498; www.shelburnefarms.org/staydine; 1611 Harbor Rd, Shelburne; r $270-525, without bath $160-230, cottages & houses $270-850; ⊙ early May-late Oct; 🛜) One of New England's top 10 places to stay, this inn, 7 miles south of Burlington off US 7, was once the summer mansion of the wealthy Webb family. It now welcomes guests, with rooms in the gracious country manor house by the lakefront, as well as four independent, kitchen-equipped cottages and guesthouses scattered across the property, which can be visited without staying (adult/child $8/5). From Mid-May to mid-October you can hike miles of walking trails, visit the animals in the children's farmyard or take a guided tour.

✕ Eating

★ Penny Cluse Cafe
CAFE $

(☑ 802-651-8834; www.pennycluse.com; 169 Cherry St; mains $6-14; ⊘ 6:45am-3pm Mon-Fri, 8am-3pm Sat & Sun) In the heart of downtown, one of Burlington's most popular breakfast spots serves pancakes, biscuits and gravy, breakfast burritos, omelets and tofu scrambles, along with sandwiches, fish tacos, salads and the best chile relleno you'll find east of the Mississippi. Expect an hour's wait on weekends.

Stone Soup
VEGETARIAN $

(☑ 802-862-7616; www.stonesoupvt.com; 211 College St; buffet per lb $11.25, sandwiches $9.50-12; ⊘7am-9pm Mon-Fri, 9am-9pm Sat; 📶🍴) Best known for its excellent vegetarian- and vegan-friendly buffet, this longtime local favorite also has homemade soups, sandwiches on home-baked bread, a salad bar, pastries and locally raised meats.

★ American Flatbread
PIZZA $$

(☑ 802-861-2999; www.americanflatbread.com; 115 St Paul St; flatbreads $14-23; ⊘ 11:30am-3pm & 5-11:30pm Mon-Fri, 11:30am-11:30pm Sat & Sun) 🍴 Central downtown location, bustling atmosphere, great beers on tap from the in-house Zero Gravity microbrewery, and superb flatbread (thin-crust pizza) with locally sourced ingredients are reason enough to make this one of your first lunch or dinner stops in Burlington.

Revolution Kitchen
VEGAN, VEGETARIAN $$

(☑ 802-448-3657; http://revolutionkitchen.com; 9 Center St; mains $14-18; ⊘5-10pm Tue-Sat; 🍴) Vegetarian fine dining? And romantic atmosphere to boot? Yep, they all come together at this cozy brick-walled restaurant that makes ample and creative use of Vermont's abundant organic produce. Asian, Mediterranean and Latin American influences abound in house favorites like Revolution tacos, crispy seitan piccata and the Laksa noodle pot. Most items are vegan.

🍷 Drinking & Entertainment

Citizen Cider
MICROBREWERY

(☑ 802-497-1987; www.citizencider.com; 316 Pine St; ⊘11am-10pm Mon-Sat, to 7pm Sun) Tucked into an industrial-chic building with painted concrete floors and long wooden tables, this animated cidery is a homegrown success story, using only Vermont apples to make its ever-growing line of hard ciders. Taste test a flight of five for $7, including perennial favorites such as the crisp, classic Unified Press, or the Dirty Mayor, infused with ginger and lemon peel.

★ Light Club Lamp Shop
LIVE MUSIC

(☑ 802-660-9346; www.facebook.com/LightClubLampShop; 12 N Winooski Ave; ⊘7pm-2am Mon-Thu, 5pm-2am Fri-Sun) One of Burlington's coolest and quirkiest venues, this place doubles – well, OK, *triples* – as a lamp shop (witness the amazing collection hanging from the walls and ceiling), a wine bar and a performance space. Shows (generally free) run the gamut from indie singer-songwriter to poetry and comedy.

Nectar's
LIVE MUSIC

(☑ 802-658-4771; www.liveatnectars.com; 188 Main St; ⊘7pm-2am Mon & Tue, 5pm-2am Wed-Sun) Indie darlings Phish got their start here and the joint still rocks out with the help of aspiring acts. Grab a vinyl booth, chill at the bar or dance upstairs at Club Metronome (http://clubmetronome.com), which hosts a slew of theme nights (every Friday is '90s night) along with larger live acts.

ℹ Information

BTV Information Center (☑ 802-863-1889; www.vermont.org; Burlington International Airport; ⊘4pm-midnight) This helpful office in Burlington's airport is staffed by the Lake Champlain Regional Chamber of Commerce.

Lake Champlain Regional Chamber of Commerce (☑877-686-5253, 802-863-3489; www.vermont.org; 60 Main St; ⊘8am-5pm Mon-Fri) Staffed tourist office in the heart of downtown.

Waterfront Tourism Center (College St; ⊘10am-8pm daily late May–Aug, to 6pm Sep–mid-Oct) Opens seasonally down near the lakefront.

ℹ Getting There & Away

To get here by car from Boston (3½ hours, 216 miles), take I-93 to I-89. It's another 1¾ hours (95 miles) north from Burlington to Montreal, Canada.

AIR

A number of national carriers, including JetBlue, serve **Burlington International Airport** (BTV; ☑ 802-863-2874; www.btv.aero; 1200 Airport Dr, South Burlington), 3 miles east of the city center. You'll find all the major car-rental companies at the airport.

BUS

Greyhound (www.greyhound.com) runs multiple buses daily from Burlington International Airport to Montreal, Canada (from $16, 2½ hours) and Boston (from $29, 4½ to 5½ hours).

Megabus (📱 877-462-6342; www.megabus.com; 119 Pearl St) offers a once-daily bus service to Boston (from $10, four hours) and occasional services to New York City from Burlington's brand-new **GMT Downtown Transit Center** (Green Mountain Transit; 📱 802-864-2282; www.ridegmt.com; cnr St Paul & Cherry Sts). GMT also operates a few long-distance buses to other cities in northwestern Vermont. See the website (www.ridegmt.com) for fares and schedules.

Middlebury Routes 46 and 76

Montpelier Route 86

TRAIN

Amtrak's daily *Vermonter* train (www.amtrak.com/vermonter-train), which provides service as far south as New York City and Washington, DC, stops in Essex Junction, 5 miles from Burlington.

NEW HAMPSHIRE

New Hampshire woos visitors with jagged mountains, scenic valleys and forest-lined lakes – they lurk in every corner of this rugged state. It all begs you to embrace the outdoors, from kayaking the hidden coves of the Lakes Region to trekking the upper peaks surrounding Mt Washington. Each season yields a bounty of adrenaline and activity: skiing and snowshoeing in winter; magnificent walks and drives through fall's fiery colors; and swimming in crisp mountain streams and berry-picking in summer.

Jewel-box colonial settlements like Portsmouth set a sophisticated tone, while historical allure and small-town culture live on in pristine villages like Keene and Peterborough. But there's a relaxing whiff in the air too – you're encouraged to gaze out at a loon-filled lake, recline on a scenic railway trip or chug across a waterway on a sunset cruise – all while digging into a fried-clam platter or a lobster roll, of course.

History

Named in 1629 after the English county of Hampshire, New Hampshire was one of the first American colonies to declare its independence from England in 1776. During the 19th-century industrialization boom, Manchester became such a powerhouse that its textile mills were the world's largest.

New Hampshire played a high-profile role in 1944 when President Franklin D Roosevelt gathered leaders from 44 Allied nations to remote Bretton Woods for a conference to rebuild global capitalism. It was from the Bretton Woods Conference that the World Bank and the International Monetary Fund emerged.

In 1963 New Hampshire, long famed for its anti-tax sentiments, found another way to raise revenue – by becoming the first state in the USA to have a legal lottery.

❶ Information

New Hampshire Division of Parks & Recreation (www.nhstateparks.org) Offers information on a statewide bicycle route system and a very complete camping guide.

New Hampshire Division of Travel & Tourism Development (www.visitnh.gov) Ski conditions and fall foliage reports, among other things.

Portsmouth

Perched on the edge of the Piscataqua River, Portsmouth is one of New Hampshire's most elegant towns, with a historical center set with tree-lined streets and 18th-century Colonial buildings. Despite its venerable history as an early hub of America's maritime industry, the town exudes a youthful energy, with tourists and locals filling its many restaurants and cafes. Numerous museums and historic houses allow visitors a glimpse into the town's multilayered past, while its proximity to the coast brings both lobster feasts and periodic days of fog that blanket the waterfront.

Still true to its name, Portsmouth remains a working port town, and its economic vitality has been boosted by the naval shipyard (actually located across the river in Maine) and by the influx of high-tech companies.

◉ Sights & Activities

★**Strawbery Banke Museum**   MUSEUM
(📱 603-433-1100; www.strawberybanke.org; 14 Hancock St; adult/child $19.50/9; ⏰ 10am-5pm May-Oct, special events only Nov-Apr) Spread across a 10-acre site, the Strawbery Banke Museum is an eclectic blend of period homes that date back to the 1690s. Costumed guides recount tales that took place among the 40 buildings (10 furnished). Strawbery Banke includes **Pitt Tavern** (1766), a hotbed of American revolutionary sentiment, **Goodwin Mansion**, a grand 19th-century house from Portsmouth's most prosperous time, and **Abbott's Little Corner Store** (1943). The admission ticket is good for two consecutive days.

USS Albacore
MUSEUM

(☑603-436-3680; www.ussalbacore.org; 600 Market St; adult/child $7/3; ⊙9:30am-5pm late May–mid-Oct, reduced hours rest of year) Like a fish out of water, this 205ft-long submarine is now a beached museum on a grassy lawn. Launched from Portsmouth Naval Shipyard in 1953, the *Albacore* was once the world's fastest submarine.

Isles of Shoals Steamship Co
CRUISE

(☑603-431-5500; www.islesofshoals.com; 315 Market St; adult/child from $28/18; ♨) From mid-June to October this company runs an excellent tour of the harbor and the historic Isles of Shoals aboard a replica 1900s ferry. It also offers walking tours of Star Island and party cruises featuring DJs or live bands.

🛏 Sleeping & Eating

Portsmouth is a terrific foodie destination, serving up everything from lobster rolls to international street food, from quality vegetarian fare to nouvelle New England cuisine.

Port Inn
MOTEL $$

(☑603-436-4378; www.portinnportsmouth.com; 505 US 1 Bypass; r $189-339; ❋@🎇🐾) Wrapped neatly around a small courtyard, this welcoming motel is conveniently located off I-95, about 1.5 miles southwest of downtown. In the rooms, monochromatic pillows and throws add a dash of color to classic furnishings. Pets are $20 per night.

★ Ale House Inn
INN $$$

(☑603-431-7760; www.alehouseinn.com; 121 Bow St; r $209-379; P❋🎇) This former brick warehouse for the Portsmouth Brewing Company is now Portsmouth's snazziest boutique inn, fusing contemporary design with comfort. Rooms are modern, with clean lines of white, flat-screen TVs and, in the suites, plush tan sofas. Deluxe rooms feature an in-room iPad. Rates include use of vintage cruising bikes.

Surf
SEAFOOD $$

(☑603-334-9855; www.surfseafood.com; 99 Bow St; lunch $10-24, dinner $12-42; ⊙4-9pm Tue & Wed, 11am-9pm Thu & Sun, 11am-10pm Fri & Sat) We're not sure if the view of the Piscataqua River complements the food or the food complements the view at this airy restaurant, especially at sunset. Either way, it's a satisfying way to close out the day. The seafood offerings sport some global flair, with haddock tacos, Portuguese seafood stew and shrimp vindaloo.

★ Black Trumpet Bistro
INTERNATIONAL $$$

(☑603-431-0887; www.blacktrumpetbistro.com; 29 Ceres St; mains $17-32; ⊙5-9pm) With brick walls and a sophisticated ambience, this bistro serves unique combinations – anything from housemade sausages infused with cocoa beans to seared haddock with yuzu (an Asian citrus fruit) and miso. The full menu is also available at its wine bar upstairs, which whips up equally inventive cocktails.

❶ Information

Greater Portsmouth Chamber of Commerce
(☑603-610-5510; www.portsmouthchamber. org; 500 Market St; ⊙9am-5pm Mon-Fri year-round, plus 10am-5pm Sat & Sun late May–mid-Oct) also operates a seasonal **information kiosk** (Market Sq) in the city center.

❶ Getting There & Away

Portsmouth is equidistant (57 miles) from Boston and Portland, ME. It takes roughly 1¼ hours to reach Portland and 1½ hours to Boston, both via I-95. Rush-hour and high-season traffic can easily double or triple this, however.

Lakes Region

The Lakes Region, with an odd mix of natural beauty and commercial tawdriness, is one of New Hampshire's most popular holiday destinations. Vast Lake Winnipesaukee, the region's centerpiece, has 183 miles of coastline, more than 300 islands and excellent salmon fishing. Catch the early-morning mists off the lake and you'll understand why the Native Americans named it 'Smile of the Great Spirit.' The prettiest stretches are in the southwest corner between Glendale and Alton (on the shoreline Belknap Point Rd), and in the northeast corner between Wolfeboro and Moultonborough (on NH 109). Just to the north lie the smaller Squam Lake and Little Squam Lake.

The roads skirting the shores and connecting the lakeside towns are a riotous spread of small-town Americana: amusement arcades, go-kart tracks, clam shacks, junk-food outlets and boat docks.

❶ Getting There & Around

The fastest way to reach the Lakes Region is via I-93. Coming from Boston and other points south, take exit 15E for Wolfeboro, exit 20 for Weirs Beach, exit 23 for Meredith or exit 24 for Holderness (Squam Lake).

Weirs Beach

Called 'Aquedoctan' by its Native American settlers, Weirs Beach takes its English name from the weirs (enclosures for catching fish) that the first European settlers found along the small sand beach. Today Weirs Beach is the honky-tonk heart of Lake Winnipesaukee's childhood amusements, famous for video-game arcades and fried dough. The vacation scene is completed by a lakefront promenade, a public beach and a dock for small cruising ships. A water park and drive-in theater are also in the vicinity. Away from the din on the waterfront, you will notice evocative Victorian-era architecture – somewhat out of place in this capital of kitsch.

South of Weirs Beach lie **Laconia**, the largest town in the region but devoid of any real sights, and lake-hugging **Gilford**. Note that this side of the lake gets mobbed with bikers for nine days each June during Laconia Motorcycle Week (www.laconiamcweek.com), the world's oldest motorcycle rally.

MS Mount Washington   CRUISE
(✆ 603-366-5531; www.cruisenh.com; 211 Lakeside Ave; adult/child regular cruises $32/16, Sunday brunch cruises $50/25) The classic MS *Mount Washington* steams out of Weirs Beach daily from mid-May to mid-October, making a relaxing 2½-hour scenic circuit around Lake Winnipesaukee, with regular stops in Wolfeboro and occasional visits to Alton Bay, Center Harbor and/or Meredith. Special events include the weekly champagne brunch cruise on Sundays and themed cruises throughout summer.

Winnipesaukee Scenic Railroad   RAIL
(✆ 603-745-2135; www.hoborr.com; 211 Lakeside Ave; adult/child 1hr $18/14, 2hr $20/16) The touristy Scenic Railroad offers one- or two-hour lakeside rides aboard 1920s and '30s train cars departing from Weirs Beach and Meredith (154 Main St). The train travels to Lake Winnipesaukee's southern tip at Alton Bay before making a U-turn.

ⓘ Information

Lakes Region Chamber of Commerce
(✆ 603-524-5531; www.lakesregionchamber.org; 383 S Main St, Laconia; ⊙ 9am-3pm Mon-Fri) Supplies information about the greater Laconia/Weirs Beach area.

Weirs Beach Information Booth (513 Weirs Blvd; ⊙ 24hr late May-early Sep) Useful for same-day accommodations.

Wolfeboro

On the eastern shore of Lake Winnipesaukee, Wolfeboro is an idyllic town where children still gather around the ice-cream stand on warm summer nights and a grassy lakeside park draws young and old to weekly concerts. Named for General Wolfe, who died vanquishing Montcalm on the Plains of Abraham in Quebec, Wolfeboro (founded in 1770) claims to be 'the oldest summer resort in America.' Whether that's true or not, it's certainly one of the most charming, with pretty lake beaches, intriguing museums, beautiful New England architecture (from Georgian through Federal, Greek Revival and Second Empire), cozy B&Bs and a worthwhile walking trail that runs along several lakes as it leads out of town.

🛏 Sleeping & Eating

Wolfeboro Campground   CAMPGROUND $
(✆ 603-569-9881; www.wolfeborocampground.com; 61 Haines Hill Rd; tent/RV sites $29/33; ⊙ late May–mid-Oct; ⃝) Off NH 28, and about 4.5 miles north of Wolfeboro's town center, this campground has 50 private, wooded sites.

Wolfe's Tavern   AMERICAN $$
(✆ 603-569-3016; www.wolfestavern.com; 90 N Main St; dinner mains $15-34; ⊙ 7am-9pm Sun-Thu, to 10pm Fri & Sat) The ample menu at the rustically colonial Wolfeboro Inn ranges from pizza to burgers, seafood to steaks, with vegetarian and gluten-free options thrown in for good measure. Terrace tables are set outside in good weather.

ⓘ Information

Wolfeboro Chamber of Commerce Information Booth (✆ 603-569-2200; www.wolfeborochamber.com; 32 Central Ave; ⊙ 10am-3pm Mon-Sat, to noon Sun late May–mid-Oct, reduced hours rest of year) Located inside the old train station, this small office has the scoop on local activities.

White Mountains

Covering one-quarter of New Hampshire (and part of Maine), the vast White Mountains area is a spectacular region of soaring peaks and lush valleys, and contains New England's most rugged mountains. There are numerous activities on offer, including hiking, camping, skiing and canoeing. Much of the area – 780,000 acres – is designated as the White Mountain National Forest (WMNF), thus protecting it from overdevelopment and guaranteeing its wondrous natural beauty for years to come. Keep in mind, however, that this place is popular: six million visitors flock here every year, making it the nation's second-most-visited park after the Great Smoky Mountains.

Certain National Forest trails and parking areas require you to have a recreation pass ($5/30 per day/year). Purchase passes at any of the visitor centers in the area or at self-serve pay stations at the trailhead.

ℹ Information

Ranger stations with information about trails and sites are scattered along major roadways throughout the national forest. Check the website (www.fs.usda.gov/whitemountain) for locations.

ℹ Getting There & Around

I-93, running north from Boston to St Johnsbury, VT, offers the most efficient access to the White Mountains. Take any of the exits between Waterville Valley in the south and Littleton in the north to explore smaller east–west roads that lead deeper into the mountains.

Kancamagus Highway

One of New Hampshire's prettiest driving routes, the winding 35-mile Kancamagus Hwy (NH 112) between Lincoln and Conway runs right through the White Mountain National Forest (WMNF) and over Kancamagus Pass (2868ft). Paved only in 1964, and still unspoiled by commercial development, the 'Kanc' offers easy access to US Forest Service (USFS) campgrounds, hiking trails and fantastic scenery.

The route is named for Chief Kancamagus (The Fearless One), who assumed the powers of *sagamore* (leader) of the Penacook Native American tribe around 1684. He was the final *sagamore*, succeeding his grandfather, the great Passaconaway, and his uncle Wonalancet. Kancamagus tried to maintain peace between the indigenous peoples and European explorers and settlers, but the newcomers pushed his patience past breaking point. He finally resorted to battle to rid the region of Europeans, but in 1691 he and his followers were forced to escape northward.

★ **Lincoln Woods Trail** HIKING
(NH 112/Kancamagus Hwy, 5 miles east of I-93) Among the easiest and most popular trails in White Mountain National Forest, the 2.9-mile, 1157ft-elevation Lincoln Woods Trail follows an abandoned railway bed to the Pemigewasset Wilderness boundary (elevation 1450ft). To reach the trailhead, follow the Kancamagus Hwy 5 miles east of I-93 and park in the Lincoln Woods Visitor Center parking lot.

Upon arrival at the Pemigewasset Wilderness boundary, you can either retrace your steps, or continue 6 miles on the easy **Wilderness Trail** to Stillwater Junction (elevation 2060ft), where you can pick up the **Cedar Brook and Hancock Notch Trails** and loop back to the Kancamagus Hwy (5.5 miles east of the Lincoln Woods trailhead parking lot).

Saco Ranger
District Office TOURIST INFORMATION
(📞603-447-5448; 33 Kancamagus Hwy, Conway; ⏰8am-4:30pm Tue-Sun, 9am-4:30pm Mon) You can pick up WMNF brochures and hiking maps at the Saco Ranger District Office at the eastern end of the Kancamagus Hwy near Conway.

North Woodstock & Lincoln

North Woodstock and its neighboring settlement Lincoln gather a mix of adventure seekers and drive-by sightseers en route to the Kancamagus Hwy (NH 112). North Woodstock has a busy but small-town feel with battered motels and diners lining the main street and a gurgling river running parallel to it. Nearby Lincoln has less charm, but serves as the starting point for the entertaining Hobo Railroad and other family-friendly activities such as zipline tours and an aerial adventure park.

🛏 Sleeping & Eating

Woodstock Inn Station & Brewery INN $$
(📞603-745-3951; www.woodstockinnnh.com; 135 Main St/US 3, North Woodstock; r incl breakfast $102-257; 🅿❄🅰) This Victorian country inn is North Woodstock's centerpiece. It has 33 individually appointed rooms across five separate buildings (three in a cluster, two across the street), each with modern amenities but in an old-fashioned style. The on-site upscale restaurant, Woodstock Inn Station & Microbrewery, has outdoor seating on the lovely flower-filled patio.

Woodstock Inn
Station & Brewery
PUB FOOD $$
(☑ 603-745-3951; www.woodstockinnnh.com;
135 Main St/US 3, North Woodstock; mains $9-27;
⊙ 11:30am-1am) Formerly a railroad station,
this eatery tries to be everything to every-
one. In the end, with more than 150 items,
it can probably satisfy just about any food
craving, but the pastas, sandwiches and
burgers are the most interesting.

ℹ Information

**Western White Mountains Chamber of Com-
merce** (☑ 603-745-6621; www.lincoln
woodstock.com; 126 Main St/US 3, North
Woodstock; ⊙ 8am-4pm Mon-Fri) General
visitor info.

White Mountains Visitor Center (☑ National
Forest info 603-745-3816, visitor info 603-
745-8720; www.visitwhitemountains.com;
200 Kancamagus Hwy, off I-93, exit 32, North
Woodstock; ⊙ visitor info 8:30am-5pm daily
year-round, National Forest desk 9am-3:30pm
daily mid-May–Oct, Fri-Sun rest of year) Trail
info and National Forest recreation passes.

Franconia Notch State Park

Franconia Notch, a narrow gorge shaped
over the eons by a wild stream cutting
through craggy granite, is a dramatic moun-
tain pass. This was long the residence of the
beloved Old Man of the Mountain, a natu-
ral rock formation that became the symbol
of the Granite State. Sadly the Old Man col-
lapsed in 2003, which does not stop tourists
from coming to see the featureless cliff that
remains. Despite the Old Man's absence, the
attractions of Franconia Notch are many,
from the dramatic hike down the Flume
Gorge to the fantastic views of the Presiden-
tial Range.

The most scenic parts of the notch are
protected by the narrow Franconia Notch
State Park. Reduced to two lanes, I-93
squeezes through the gorge. Services are
available in Lincoln and North Woodstock
to the south and in Franconia and Littleton
to the north.

◉ Sights & Activities

Cannon Mountain
Aerial Tramway
CABLE CAR
(☑ 603-823-8800; www.cannonmt.com; 260
Tramway Dr, off I-93, exit 34B; round-trip adult/child
$18/16; ⊙ 8:30am-5pm Jun–mid-Oct; 🅿) This
tram shoots up the side of Cannon Moun-
tain, offering a breathtaking view of Franco-

MONADNOCK STATE PARK

Majestic 3165ft **Mt Monadnock**
(☑ 603-532-8862; www.nhstateparks.org;
169 Poole Rd, Jaffrey; day use adult/child
$5/2) is the centerpiece of this popular
state park between Keene and Jaffrey.
Stop at the visitor center for hiking
information, then set off on a scenic
loop to the bare-topped summit via the
White Dot and White Cross Trails (about
3½ hours round-trip). If you want to
stay overnight, there's camping on site
at **Gilson Pond Campground** (☑ info
603-532-2416, reservations 877-647-2757;
585 Dublin Rd/NH 124, Jaffrey; tent sites
$25; ⊙ May-Oct).

nia Notch. In 1938 the first passenger aerial
tramway in North America was installed on
this slope. It was replaced in 1980 by the
current, larger cable car, capable of carrying
80 passengers up to the summit of Cannon
Mountain – a 1-mile ride with 2022ft vertical
gain – in less than 10 minutes. You can also
hike up the mountain and take the tramway
down (adult/child $13/10).

Echo Lake Beach
BEACH
(☑ 603-745-8391; www.nhstateparks.org; I-93, exit
34C; adult/child $4/2; ⊙ 9am-5pm late May-early
Oct) Despite its proximity to the highway,
this little lake at the foot of Cannon Moun-
tain is a pleasant place to pass an afternoon
swimming, kayaking or canoeing (from $11
per hour) in the crystal-clear waters.

★ Flume Gorge & the Basin
HIKING
(☑ 603-745-8391; www.flumegorge.com; I-93, exit
34A; adult/child $16/14; ⊙ 8:30am-5pm early
May-late Oct) To see this natural wonder,
take the 2-mile self-guided nature walk that
includes the 800ft boardwalk through the
Flume, a natural 12ft- to 20ft-wide cleft in
the granite bedrock. The granite walls tower
70ft to 90ft above you, with moss and plants
growing from precarious niches and crevic-
es. Signs along the way explain how nature
formed this natural phenomenon.

ℹ Information

Franconia Notch State Park Visitor Center
(☑ 603-745-8391; www.nhstateparks.org; I-93,
exit 34A; ⊙ 8:30am-5pm early May-late Oct)
Open seasonally, the state park visitor center
at Flume Gorge has information about the park

and surrounding area. There's also a cafeteria and gift shop.

Mt Washington Valley

Dramatic mountain scenery surrounds the tiny villages of this popular alpine destination, providing an abundance of outdoor adventures. There's great hiking, skiing, kayaking and rafting, along with idyllic activities like swimming in local creeks, overnighting in country farmhouses and simply exploring the countryside.

Mt Washington Valley stretches north from Conway, at the eastern end of the Kancamagus Hwy, and forms the eastern edge of the White Mountain range. The valley's hub is North Conway, though any of the towns along NH 16/US 302 (also called the White Mountain Hwy) can serve as a White Mountain gateway. The valley's namesake is, of course, Mt Washington, New England's highest peak (6288ft), which towers over the valley in the northwest.

MT WASHINGTON

Mt Washington's summit is at 6288ft, making it the tallest mountain in New England. The mountain is renowned for its frighteningly bad weather – the average temperature on the summit is 26.5°F(-3°C). The mercury has fallen as low as -47°F (-43°C), but only risen as high as 72°F (22°C). About 256in (more than 21ft) of snow falls each year. (One year, it was 47ft.) At times the climate can mimic Antarctica's, and hurricane-force winds blow every three days or so, on average. In fact, the second-highest wind speed ever recorded was here during a storm in 1934, when gusts reached 231mph.

If you attempt the summit, pack warm, windproof clothes and shoes, even in high summer, and always consult with Appalachian Mountain Club (AMC) hut personnel. Don't be reluctant to turn back if the weather changes for the worse. Dozens of hikers who ignored such warnings and died are commemorated by trailside monuments and crosses.

In good weather, the hike is exhilarating. The only disappointment is exerting hours of effort, exploring remote paths and finally reaching the summit, only to discover a parking lot full of cars that motored up. Don't feel bad – just treat yourself to a 'This car climbed Mt Washington' bumper sticker.

BRETTON WOODS & CRAWFORD NOTCH

This beautiful 1773ft mountain pass on the western slopes of Mt Washington is deeply rooted in New Hampshire lore. In 1826 torrential rains here triggered massive mudslides, killing the Willey family in the valley below. The dramatic incident made the newspapers and fired the imaginations of painter Thomas Cole and author Nathaniel Hawthorne. Both men used the incident for inspiration, thus unwittingly putting Crawford Notch on the tourist maps.

Even so, the area remained known mainly to locals and wealthy summer visitors who patronized the grand Mt Washington Hotel in Bretton Woods – until 1944, when President Roosevelt chose the hotel as the site of a conference to establish a post-WWII global economic order.

Today the hotel is as grand as ever, while a steady flow of visitors comes to climb Mt Washington – on foot, or aboard a steam-powered locomotive on the dramatic Mount Washington Cog Railway.

◎ Sights & Activities

★ **Crawford Notch State Park**   STATE PARK
(☏603-374-2272; www.nhstateparks.org; 1464 US 302, Harts Location; ☉ visitor center 9:30am-5pm late May–mid-Oct, park year-round unless posted otherwise) FREE This pretty park maintains an extensive system of hiking trails. From the Willey House visitor center, you can walk the easy 0.5-mile Pond Loop Trail, the 1-mile Sam Willey Trail and the Ripley Falls Trail, a 1-mile hike from US 302 via the Ethan Pond Trail. The trailhead for Arethusa Falls, a 1.3-mile hike, is 0.5 miles south of the Dry River Campground on US 302. Serious hikers can also tackle the much longer trek up Mt Washington.

★ **Mount Washington**
Cog Railway   RAIL
(☏603-278-5404; www.thecog.com; 3168 Base Station Rd; adult $69-75, child $39; ☉ daily Jun-Oct, Sat & Sun late Apr, May & Nov) Purists walk and the lazy drive, but the quaintest way to reach Mt Washington summit is via this cog railway. Since 1869 coal-fired, steam-powered locomotives have climbed this scenic 3.5-mile track up a steep mountainside trestle (three hours round-trip). Two old-fashioned steam trains run daily late May to October, supplemented by biodiesel-fueled trains late April to November.

Bretton Woods Canopy Tour ADVENTURE

(☑ 603-278-4947; www.brettonwoods.com; US 302; per person $89-110; ☺ tours twice daily year-round, additional times during peak periods) This four-season canopy tour sends you hiking through the woods, strolling over sky bridges and swooshing down ziplines that drop 1000ft at 30mph to tree platforms.

🛌 Sleeping

AMC Highland Lodge LODGE $$

(☑ front desk 603-278-4453, reservations 603-466-2727; www.outdoors.org; NH 302, Bretton Woods; incl breakfast & dinner per adult/child/teen r from $163/50/95, without bath from $113/50/95; ☎) This cozy Appalachian Mountain Club (AMC) lodge is set amid the splendor of Crawford Notch, an ideal base for hiking the trails crisscrossing the Presidential Range. The grounds are beautiful, rooms are basic but comfortable, meals are hearty and guests are outdoor enthusiasts. Discounts available for AMC members.

★ Omni Mt Washington
Hotel & Resort HOTEL $$$

(☑ 603-278-1000; www.omnihotels.com; 310 Mt Washington Hotel Rd, Bretton Woods; r $259-849; ✳@☎✲) Open since 1902, this grand hotel maintains a sense of fun – note the moose's head overlooking the lobby and the framed local wildflowers in many of the guest rooms. Also offers 27 holes of golf, red-clay tennis courts, an equestrian center and a spa. There's a $25 daily resort fee.

❶ Information

Twin Mountain-Bretton Woods Chamber of Commerce
(☑ 800-245-8946; www.twin mountain.org; cnr US 302 & US 3; ☺ info booth staffed 9am-5pm Fri-Sun late May–mid-Oct, daily Jul & Aug, self-serve rest of year) Year-round info board and seasonally staffed kiosk providing tourist info. Look for the brightly colored train cars on the hillside at the US 3–US 302 intersection.

Hanover

Hanover is the quintessential New England college town. On warm days, students toss Frisbees on the wide college green fronting Georgian ivy-covered buildings, while locals and academics mingle at the laid-back cafes, restaurants and shops lining Main St. Dartmouth College has long been the town's focal point, giving the area a vibrant connection to the arts.

Dartmouth was chartered in 1769 primarily 'for the education and instruction of Youth of the Indian Tribes.' Back then, the school was located in the forests where its prospective students lived. Although teaching 'English Youth and others' was its secondary purpose, in fact, Dartmouth College graduated few Native Americans and was soon attended almost exclusively by colonists. The college's most illustrious alumnus is Daniel Webster (1782–1852), who graduated in 1801 and went on to be a prominent lawyer, US senator, secretary of state and perhaps the USA's most esteemed orator.

◎ Sights & Activities

Dartmouth College UNIVERSITY

(☑ 603-646-1110; www.dartmouth.edu) Hanover is all about Dartmouth College, so hit the campus. Join a free student-guided **campus walking tour** (☑ 603-646-2875; http:// dartmouth.edu; 6016 McNutt Hall, 10 N Main St) or just pick up a map at the admissions office and head off on your own. Don't miss the **Baker Berry Library** (☑ 603-646-2560; http:// dartmouth.edu; 25 N Main St; ☺ 8am-2am Mon-Fri, 10am-2am Sat & Sun), splashed with the grand *Epic of American Civilization*, painted by the outspoken Mexican muralist José Clemente Orozco (1883–1949), who taught at Dartmouth in the 1930s.

Sanborn Library NOTABLE BUILDING

(Dartmouth College; ☺ 8am-midnight daily, teatime 4pm Mon-Fri) Named for Professor Edwin Sanborn, who taught for almost 50 years in Dartmouth's English department, the Sanborn Library features ornate woodwork, plush leather chairs, and books lining the walls floor to ceiling on two levels. One of Dartmouth's most endearing traditions is the afternoon tea served here on weekdays between 4pm and 5pm – tea costs 10¢ and cookies 15¢; visitors are welcome but expected to maintain a respectful silence for the benefit of the diligently toiling students.

Gile Mountain HIKING

Just over the river in Norwich, VT, about 7 miles from Hanover, the mountain is a popular destination for Dartmouth students looking for a quick escape from the grind. A half-hour hike – and a quick climb up the **fire tower** – rewards adventurers with an incredible view of the Connecticut River Valley.

🛏 Sleeping & Eating

Hanover Inn INN $$$

(☑ 603-643-4300; www.hanoverinn.com; 2 E Wheelock St; r $259-619; @ 🛜 🐾) Owned by Dartmouth and situated directly opposite the college green, Hanover's loveliest guesthouse has nicely appointed rooms with elegant wood furnishings. It has a wine bar and an award-winning restaurant on site.

Lou's DINER $

(☑ 603-643-3321; www.lousrestaurant.net; 30 S Main St; mains $9-15; ⊗ 6am-3pm Mon-Fri, 7am-3pm Sat & Sun) A Dartmouth institution since 1947, this is Hanover's oldest establishment, always packed with students meeting for a coffee or perusing their books. From the retro tables or the Formica-topped counter, order typical diner food like eggs, sandwiches and burgers.

🍷 Drinking & Entertainment

Murphy's on the Green PUB

(☑ 603-643-4075; www.murphysonthegreen.com; 11 S Main St; ⊗ 4pm-12:30am Mon-Thu, 11-12:30am Fri-Sun) This classic collegiate tavern is where students and faculty meet over pints (it carries more than 10 beers on tap, including local microbrews like Long Trail Ale) and satisfying pub fare.

Hopkins Center for the Arts PERFORMING ARTS

(☑ 603-646-2422; http://hop.dartmouth.edu; 4 E Wheelock St) A long way from the big-city lights of New York and Boston, Dartmouth hosts its own entertainment at this outstanding performing-arts venue. The season brings everything from movies to live performances by international companies.

ℹ Information

Hanover Area Chamber of Commerce

(☑ 603-643-3115; www.hanoverchamber.org; 53 S Main St, Suite 208; ⊗ 9am-noon & 1-4pm Mon-Fri) also maintains an **information booth** (Dartmouth Green; ⊗ mid-Jun–mid-Sep) on the village green.

ℹ Getting There & Around

From Boston to Hanover, it's a two- to three-hour drive depending on traffic; take I-93 to I-89 to I-91. From Hanover to Burlington, VT, it's an additional 1½ hours north via I-89.

Advance Transit (www.advancetransit.com) provides a free service to White River Junction, Lebanon, West Lebanon and Norwich. Bus stops are indicated by a blue-and-yellow AT symbol.

MAINE

With more lobsters, lighthouses and charming resort villages than you can shake a selfie stick at, Maine is New England at its most iconic. The sea looms large here, with mile upon mile of jagged sea cliffs, peaceful harbors and pebbly beaches. Eat and drink your way through food- and beer-crazed Portland, one of America's coolest small cities. Explore the historic shipbuilding villages of the Midcoast. Hike through Acadia National Park, a spectacular island of mountains and fjord-like estuaries. Let the coastal wind whip through those cobwebs and inhale the salty air. Venture into the state's inland region, a vast wilderness of pine forest and snowy peaks.

History

Maine's first inhabitants were descendants of ice-age hunters, collectively known as the Wabanaki ('people of the dawn'). They numbered perhaps 20,000 when the first English settlers descended in the early 1600s.

Over the 17th century, a number of English settlements sprang up in the Province of Maine, though settlers there suffered enormous hardship from harsh winters and tensions with local Native American tribes, who were (rightly) suspicious of the European newcomers – the latter were known to kidnap natives to put on display back in England. Adding insult to injury, Maine lost its sovereignty when Massachusetts took over the failing colony in 1692.

Bloody battles raged for many generations, destroying entire villages in Maine, with settlers warring over land with Native Americans, the French and later the British. This didn't end until after the War of 1812, when the British finally withdrew from Maine. In 1820 Maine became the 23rd state in the Union.

The 19th century was one of tremendous growth for the new state, with the emergence of new industries. Timber brought wealth to the interior, with Bangor becoming the lumber capital of the world in the 1830s. Fishing, shipbuilding, granite quarrying and farming were also boom industries, alongside manufacturing, with textile and paper mills employing large swaths of the population.

Unfortunately the boom days were short-lived, as sawmills collapsed and the seas became devastatingly overfished. By the turn of the 20th century, population growth

Maine Coast

Maine Coast

50 km
25 miles

N

CANADA

Nova Scotia

CANADA

Bay of Fundy

Grand Manan Island

St George

Eastport
Lubec

Quoddy Head State Park

Calais

Border Crossing

Moosehorn National Wildlife Refuge

Machias

Jonesport

Beals

Great Wass Island

Schoodic Peninsula

ATLANTIC OCEAN

Ellsworth

Trenton

Bar Harbor

Cadillac Mountain (1530ft)

Mount Desert Island

Deer Isle

Stonington

Acadia National Park

Isle au Haut

Acadia National Park

Bucksport

Blue Hill

Belfast

Penobscot Bay

Camden
Rockport

Rockland

Lincolnville

Camden Hills State Park

Port Clyde

New Harbor

Monhegan Island

Ferry

Ferry

Waterville

Damariscotta

Waldoboro

Pemaquid Peninsula

Bath

Boothbay Harbor

Casco Bay

Kennebec River

Augusta

Skowhegan

Baxter State Park (50mi)

Caratunk (7mi); The Forks (9mi)

Sugarloaf Mtn (4237ft)

Longfellow Mountains

Rangeley

Aziscohos Lake

Colebrook

Errol

Bethel

Grafton Notch State Park

Sunday River Ski Resort

White Mountain National Forest

Appalachian Trail

NEW HAMPSHIRE

See Vermont & New Hampshire Map (p239)

Sabbathday Lake

Brunswick

Freeport

Portland

Cape Elizabeth

Sebago Lake

Naples

Sebago Lake

Lake Winnipesaukee

Laconia

Rochester

Concord

Kennebunkport

Ogunquit

Kittery

Portsmouth

Maine Turnpike

stagnated and Maine became a backwater. Today tourism accounts for 15% of the state's economy (compared to the 6% average elsewhere in New England).

❶ Information

Maine Office of Tourism (www.visitmaine.com) Comprehensive website; can mail out maps and brochures.

Maine Tourism Association (www.mainetourism.com) Runs info centers on the principal routes into Maine: Calais, Fryeburg, Hampden, Houlton, Kittery, West Gardiner and Yarmouth. Each center is generally open 9am to 5:30pm; longer in summer (8am to 6pm).

Maine Bureau of Parks & Lands (☑ 207-287-3821; www.parksandlands.com) Oversees 48 state parks and historic sites. Details of each park (including activities and camping) are on the website.

Lonely Planet (www.lonelyplanet.com/usa/new-england/maine) Destination information, hotel bookings, traveler forum and more.

Southern Maine Coast

Maine's southern coast embodies the state slogan 'Vacationland,' with busy commercial strips, sandy beaches and resort towns that get packed in the summer months. Despite the crowds, there are some charming features to be found. While Kittery is a long, commercial strip mall, Ogunquit has a lovely beach and is Maine's gay mecca. Between the two lie quaint York Village and busy, populist York Beach. Beyond, the Kennebunks are small historic settlements with lavish mansions (some of which are now B&Bs) near pretty beaches and rugged coastline. Although you'll have to use your imagination, the southern coast is deeply associated with the works of American artist Winslow Homer, who spent his summers in Prouts Neck (just south of Portland), which has some magnificent scenery.

❶ Getting There & Away

US 1 is the key access route for this part of the state, but be aware that roads along the coast flood with traffic during the summer tourist season. For a faster journey, take I-95.

The nearest major airport is in Portland.

Ogunquit

Known to the Abenaki tribe as 'the beautiful place by the sea,' Ogunquit is justly famous for its 3-mile sandy beach. Wide stretches of pounding surf front the Atlantic, while warm back-cove waters make an idyllic setting for a swim. In summer the beach draws hordes of visitors from near and far, increasing the town's population exponentially.

Before its resort status, Ogunquit was a shipbuilding center in the 17th century. Later it became an important arts center when the Ogunquit art colony was founded in 1898. Today Ogunquit is the northeasternmost gay and lesbian mecca in the USA, adding a touch of open, San Francisco–style culture to the more conservative Maine one.

◉ Sights & Activities

Ogunquit Beach   BEACH
(access from Beach St) A sublime stretch of family-friendly coastline, Ogunquit Beach is only a five-minute walk along Beach St, east of US 1. Walking to the beach is a good idea in summer as the parking lot fills up early (and it costs $4 per hour to park!). The 3-mile beach fronts Ogunquit Bay to the south; on the west side of the beach are the warmer waters of the tidal Ogunquit River.

★ Marginal Way   WALKING
(access from Shore Rd) Tracing the 'margin' of the sea, Ogunquit's famed mile-long footpath winds above the crashing gray waves, taking in grand sea vistas and rocky coves, allowing for some excellent real-estate admiring. The neatly paved path, fine for children and slow walkers, is dotted with restful benches. It starts south of Beach St at Shore Rd and ends near Perkins Cove.

🛏 Sleeping & Eating

Ogunquit Beach Inn   B&B $$
(☑ 207-646-1112;   www.ogunquitbeachinn.com; 67 School St; r $169-249; ☺May-Oct; ❀ 🛜) In a tidy little Craftsman-style bungalow, this gay-and-lesbian-friendly B&B has five colorful, homey rooms and chatty owners who know all about the best new bistros and bars in town. The central location makes walking to dinner a breeze.

★ Gazebo Inn   B&B $$
(☑ 207-646-3733;   www.gazeboinnogt.com;   572 Main St/US 1; r $169-369; ❀ 🛜 🌊) This stately 1847 farmhouse and converted barn feature 14 rooms and suites – the space feels more like a boutique lodge. Rustic-chic touches abound and there's ample common space, including an inviting lounge-bar with beamed ceilings. There's a lovely pool area, and a calm, mature feel (it's kid-free).

Lobster Shack
SEAFOOD **$$**

(☑207-646-2941; www.lobster-shack.com; 110 Perkins Cove Rd; mains $5-28; ⊘11am-9pm Apr-Oct) If you want good seafood and aren't particular about the view, this friendly, reliable joint serves lobster in all its various incarnations, from lobster rolls to lobster in the shell, by way of chowder, steamed clams, fish tacos and even cheeseburgers.

ⓘ Getting There & Away

There's no direct bus service to Ogunquit; the nearest Greyhound (www.greyhound.com) stop is in Portsmouth, NH, 16 miles south.

Amtrak's *Downeaster* (www.amtrakdowneaster.com) train service stops in Wells on its Portland–Boston loop.

ⓘ Getting Around

From late June through to Labor Day (early October), red trolleys (adult/child $2/1.50 per trip) circulate through Ogunquit (every 20 to 30 minutes, 8am to 11pm). From Labor Day to Columbus Day (mid-October), they run from 9am to 5pm. Leave the driving to them in this horribly congested town; they'll take you from the center to the beach or Perkins Cove, and all the way north through Wells.

The Kennebunks

A longtime destination of moneyed East Coasters, the Kennebunks comprise the towns of Kennebunk and Kennebunkport.

Kennebunk is a modest town largely centered on US 1, with few tourist attractions beyond its lovely beaches. Just across the river, proudly waspy Kennebunkport crawls with tourists year-round. The epicenter of activity is Dock Sq, lined with cafes, art galleries and upscale boutiques selling preppy essentials (whale-print shorts, anyone?). Drive down Ocean Ave to gawk at the grand mansions and hotels overlooking the surf, including the massive compound belonging to George HW Bush, set on a protected spit of land called Walker's Point.

At the eastern terminus of School St is the charming hamlet of **Cape Porpoise**, home to affordable hotels and restaurants.

🛏 Sleeping & Eating

Franciscan Guest House
GUESTHOUSE **$$**

(☑207-967-4865; www.franciscanguesthouse.com; 26 Beach Ave, Kennebunk; d $89-189, f $135-259; ✸@🛜🏊) You can almost smell the blackboard chalk inside this high-school-turned-guesthouse on the peaceful grounds of the St Anthony Monastery. Guest rooms – once classrooms – are basic and unstylish: acoustic tile, faux wood paneling, motel beds.

Bandaloop
INTERNATIONAL **$$**

(☑207-967-4994; www.bandaloop.biz; Cross St, Kennebunkport; small plates $9-21, mains $18-31; ⊘5-9pm Tue-Sun, to 10pm Fri & Sat; 🖋) 🌿 Local, organic and deliciously innovative, Bandaloop mains run the gamut from grilled rib-eye steak to baked tofu with hemp-seed crust. For the perfect starter order the skillet steamed mussels and a Peak organic ale. Salads are truly flavorful, and the cocktails creative. Vegans and vegetarians will find joy here.

ⓘ Getting There & Away

The Kennebunks lie halfway (28 miles from each city) between Portsmouth, NH, and Portland, ME, just off I-95 on ME 9.

There's no direct bus service to Kennebunkport; Greyhound (www.greyhound.com) stops in both Portland and Portsmouth.

Amtrak's *Downeaster* (www.amtrakdowneaster.com) train service stops in Wells, about 9 miles to the south, on its Boston–Portland loop.

Portland

Maine's largest city has capitalized on the gifts of its port history – the redbrick warehouse buildings, the Victorian shipbuilders' mansions, the narrow cobblestone streets – to become one of the hippest, most vibrant small cities in America. With a lively waterfront, excellent museums and galleries, abundant green space, and both a food culture and a brewing scene worthy of a town many times its size, it's worth much more than a quick stopover.

Set on a peninsula jutting into the gray waters of Casco Bay, Portland's always been a city of the sea. Established in 1633 as a fishing village, it grew to become New England's largest port. Today the Old Port district is the town's historic heart, with handsomely restored brick buildings filled with cafes, shops and bars. The working wharves keep things from getting too precious or museum-like, though, as fishmongers in rubber boots mingle with well-heeled Yankee matrons.

👁 Sights & Activities

★ Fort Williams Park
PARK

(☑207-767-3707; www.fortwilliams.org; 1000 Shore Rd, Cape Elizabeth; ⊘sunrise-sunset) 🖋 **FREE**

Four miles southeast of Portland on Cape Elizabeth, 90-acre Fort Williams Park is worth visiting simply for the panoramas and picnic possibilities. Stroll around the ruins of the fort, a late-19th-century artillery base, checking out the WWII bunkers and gun emplacements that still dot the rolling lawns.

Portland Head Light   LIGHTHOUSE
(☑207-799-2661; https://portlandheadlight.com; 1000 Shore Rd, Cape Elizabeth; museum adult/child $2/1; ⊙museum 10am-4pm Jun-Oct, Sat & Sun only Apr, May & Nov) Portland Head Light is the oldest of Maine's 52 functioning lighthouses. It was commissioned by President George Washington in 1791 and staffed until 1989, when machines took over. The keeper's house is now a **museum**, which traces the maritime and military history of the region.

Portland Museum of Art   MUSEUM
(☑207-775-6148; www.portlandmuseum.org; 7 Congress Sq; adult/child $15/free, 4-8pm Fri free; ⊙10am-6pm Sat-Wed, to 8pm Thu & Fri, shorter hours Oct-May) Founded in 1882, this well-respected museum houses an outstanding collection of American artists. Maine artists, including Winslow Homer, Edward Hopper, Louise Nevelson and Andrew Wyeth, are particularly well represented. You'll also find a few works by European masters, including Monet, Degas, Picasso and Renoir.

★ Maine Brew Bus   BUS
(☑207-200-9111; https://themainebrewbus.com; 79 Commercial St; tours $55-80) Want to drink your way around Portland? We know the feeling. Hop aboard the green bus for tours and tastings at some of Portland's most beloved breweries, brewpubs and distilleries, from established to up-and-coming.

Casco Bay Lines   CRUISE
(☑207-774-7871; www.cascobaylines.com; Maine State Pier, 56 Commercial St; mailboat run adult/child $16/8) This outfit cruises the Casco Bay islands year-round, delivering mail, freight and visitors. **Peaks Island**, just 17 minutes from Portland, is a popular day-trip destination (round-trip $7.70) for walks or cycling; bikes can be hired on the island.

🛏 Sleeping & Eating

Morrill Mansion   B&B $$
(☑207-774-6900; www.morrillmansion.com; 249 Vaughan St; r $179-259; P✳🛜) Charles Morrill, the original owner of this 19th-century West End town house, made his fortune by

founding B&M baked beans, still a staple of Maine pantries. His home has been transformed into a handsome B&B, with eight guest rooms furnished in a trim, classic style.

Portland Harbor Hotel   HOTEL $$$
(☑207-775-9090; www.portlandharborhotel.com; 468 Fore St; r $299-519; P✳@🛜🐾) This handsome independent hotel has a classically coiffed lobby, where guests relax on upholstered leather chairs surrounding the glowing fireplace.

Green Elephant   VEGETARIAN, ASIAN $
(☑207-347-3111; http://greenelephantmaine.com; 608 Congress St; mains $12-15; ⊙11:30am-2:30pm & 5-9:30pm Mon-Sat, 5-9pm Sun; 🍴) Even carnivores shouldn't miss the vegetarian fare at this Zen-chic, Thai-inspired cafe (with lots of vegan and gluten-free options too). Start with the crispy spinach wontons, then move on to one of the stir-fry, noodle or curry favorites like tofu tikka masala or Malaysian *char kway teow* (fried flat rice noodles).

★ Fore Street   MODERN AMERICAN $$$
(☑207-775-2717; www.forestreet.biz; 288 Fore St; small plates $12-15, mains $26-38; ⊙5:30-10pm Sun-Thu, to 10:30pm Fri & Sat) Fore Street is the lauded, long-running restaurant many consider to be the originator of today's food obsession in Portland. Chef-owner Sam Hayward has turned roasting into a high art: chickens turn on spits in the open kitchen as chefs slide iron kettles of mussels into the wood-burning oven.

🍷 Drinking & Entertainment

Allagash Brewing Company   BREWERY
(☑207-878-5385; www.allagash.com; 50 Industrial Way; ⊙tastings 11am-6pm) Nationally known for its Belgian-style beers, Allagash opens its doors for free tours and tastings every day (book a tour online; weekend tours are super-popular). The brewery is 3.5 miles northwest of Portland's Old Port, off Forest Ave.

Port City Music Hall   CONCERT VENUE
(☑207-956-6000; www.portcitymusichall.com; 504 Congress St) This three-story performance space hosts big-name touring bands and smaller-scale performances.

ℹ Information

Ocean Gateway Information Center (☑207-772-5800; www.visitportland.com; 14 Ocean Gateway Pier; ⊙9am-5pm Mon-Fri, to 4pm Sat & Sun Jun-Oct, shorter hours rest of year) Visitor information, down at the waterfront.

Visitor Information Booth (✓ 207-772-6828; www.portlandmaine.com; Tommy's Park, Exchange St; 10am-5pm Jun-Oct) Summertime info kiosk in the Old Port.

ⓘ Getting There & Away

AIR

Portland International Jetport (PWM; ✓ 207-874-8877; www.portlandjetport.org; 1001 Westbrook St) is Maine's largest and most chaotic air terminal. It's served by domestic airlines, with nonstop flights to cities in the eastern USA. Metro bus 5 takes you to the center of town for $1.50. Taxis are about $20 to downtown.

BUS

Greyhound (✓ 800-231-2222, 207-772-6588; www.greyhound.com; 950 Congress St) offers direct daily trips to Bangor and Boston, with connections on to the rest of the USA.

Concord Coach Lines (www.concordcoach lines.com) operates daily buses between Boston (including Logan Airport) and Portland, continuing on to Midcoast Maine towns. There are also services connecting Boston, Portland and the towns of Augusta, Waterville and Bangor. Two services a day link Portland with New York City.

TRAIN

The *Downeaster*, run by Amtrak (www.amtrak.com), makes five trips daily between Boston and Portland (2½ hours) from **Portland Transportation Center** (100 Thompson's Point Rd). A couple of these services extend to Freeport and Brunswick too.

Midcoast Maine

Carved by ancient glaciers, the coastline of Midcoast Maine is jagged and dramatic. With its wild natural beauty and down-to-earth residents, this is what many people imagine when they think of Maine – riding bikes and shopping for antiques in postcard-pretty seaside villages, taking leisurely scenic drives down the rural peninsulas, and riding the deep blue seas aboard one of the Midcoast's famous windjammers. It's a landscape that rewards slow, aimless exploration: you never know when you're going to stumble upon the next great lobster shack, lost-in-time fishing village or you-pick blueberry patch.

The English first settled this region in 1607, which coincided with the Jamestown settlement in Virginia. Unlike their southerly compatriots, though, these early settlers returned to England within a year. British colonization resumed in 1620. After suffering through the long years of the French and Indian War, the area became home to a thriving shipbuilding industry, which continues today.

ⓘ Getting There & Around

US 1 is the key access route for this part of the state, but note that roads along the coast flood with traffic during the summer tourist season.

Concord Coach Lines (www.concordcoach lines.com) operates daily buses between Boston (including Logan Airport) and Portland, continuing on to midcoast Maine towns (Bath, Belfast, Brunswick, Camden, Damariscotta, Lincolnville, Rockland, Searsport and Waldoboro). Greyhound (www.greyhound.com) stops in Bangor, Portland, Bath, Rockland and various other towns.

Freeport

Nestled amid the natural beauty of Maine's rockbound coast is a town devoted almost entirely to shopping. Nearly 200 stores line the town's mile-long stretch of US 1, leading to long traffic jams during the summer. Strict zoning codes forbid the destruction of historic buildings, which is why you'll find a McDonald's housed in an 1850s Greek Revival home and an Abercrombie & Fitch outlet in a turn-of-the-20th-century library. It all adds up to a slightly eerie 'Main Street, USA' vibe.

Freeport's fame and fortune began a century ago when Leon Leonwood Bean opened a shop to sell equipment and provisions to hunters and fishermen heading north into the Maine woods. His success later brought other retailers to the area, making Freeport what it is today.

Bath

Known as the 'City of Ships,' this quaint Kennebec River town was once home to more than 20 shipyards producing more than a quarter of early America's wooden sailing vessels. In Bath's 19th-century heyday, it was one of Maine's largest cities, with a bustling downtown lined with banks and grand municipal buildings. Bath-built schooners and clipper ships sailed the seven seas and the city's name was known far and wide.

Downtown, redbrick sidewalks and solid 19th-century buildings line quaint Front St, while just downhill lies a small grassy park overlooking the water. South of Bath stretch two scenic peninsulas well worth a detour: ME 209 takes you to **Phippsburg**, home to excellent beaches and a historic fort, while ME 127 runs south to **Georgetown**, terminating at a great lobster shack overlooking an island-dotted cove.

★**Maine Maritime Museum** MUSEUM
(☏ 207-443-1316; www.mainemaritimemuseum. org; 243 Washington St; adult/child $16/10; ◷ 9:30am-5pm) On the western bank of the Kennebec River, this wonderful museum preserves the Kennebec's long shipbuilding tradition with paintings, models and hands-on exhibits that tell the tale of the past 400 years of seafaring. One highlight is the remains of the *Snow Squall*, a three-mast 1851 clipper ship. The on-site 19th-century Percy & Small Shipyard, preserved by the museum, is America's only remaining wooden-boat shipyard. There's also a life-size sculpture of the *Wyoming*, the largest wooden sailing vessel ever built.

Boothbay Harbor

Once a beautiful little seafarers' village on a wide blue harbor, Boothbay Harbor is now an extremely popular tourist resort in the summer, when its narrow and winding streets are packed with visitors. Still, there's good reason to join the holiday masses in this picturesque place. Overlooking a pretty waterfront, large, well-kept Victorian houses crown the town's many knolls, and a wooden footbridge ambles across the harbor. From May to October, whale-watching is a major draw.

After you've strolled the waterfront along Commercial St and the business district along Todd and Townsend Aves, walk along McKown St to the top of **McKown Hill** for a fine view.

🛏 Sleeping & Eating

Topside Inn B&B $$$
(☏ 207-633-5404; www.topsideinn.com; 60 McKown St; r $219-369; ◷ May–mid-Oct; ❈ 🛜) Atop McKown Hill, this grand gray mansion has Boothbay's best harbor views. Rooms are elegantly turned out in crisp nautical prints and beachy shades. Main-house rooms have more historic charm, but rooms in the two adjacent modern guesthouses are sunny and lovely too.

Lobster Dock SEAFOOD $$
(☏ 207-633-7120; www.thelobsterdock.com; 49 Atlantic Ave; mains $15-29; ◷ 11:30am-8:30pm late May–mid-Oct) Of all the lobster joints in Boothbay Harbor, this sprawling, wooden waterfront shack is one of the best and cheapest. It serves traditional fried seafood platters, sandwiches and steamers, but whole, butter-dripping lobster is definitely the main event. Get your lobster roll ($17) warm with butter, or cold with mayo.

ℹ Information

Boothbay Harbor Region Chamber of Commerce (☏ 207-633-2353; www.boothbay harbor.com; 192 Townsend Ave; ◷ 8am-5pm Mon-Fri year-round, plus 10am-4pm Sat late May-early Oct) Offers good info on its website; also operates a downtown **information center** (17 Commercial St; ◷ 9am-6pm late May-early Oct) in summer.

Rockland

This thriving commercial port boasts a large fishing fleet and a proud year-round population that gives Rockland a vibrancy lacking in some other Midcoast towns. Main St is a window into the city's sociocultural diversity, with a jumble of working-class diners, bohemian cafes and high-end restaurants alongside galleries, old-fashioned storefronts and one of the state's best art museums, the **Center for Maine Contemporary Art** (CMCA; www.cmcanow.org). Rockland is developing a reputation as an art center, partly thanks to the CMCA's relocation here in 2016, and the **Farnwworth Art Museum** (www.farnsworthmuseum.org).

Settled in 1769, Rockland was once an important shipbuilding center and a transportation hub for goods moving up and down the coast. Today tall-masted sailing ships still fill the harbor, as Rockland is a center for Maine's busy windjammer cruises (along with Camden).

★**Rockland Breakwater Lighthouse** LIGHTHOUSE
(☏ 207-542-7574; www.rocklandharborlights.org; Samoset Rd; ◷ 10am-5pm Sat & Sun late May–mid-Oct) FREE Tackle the rugged stone breakwater that stretches almost 1 mile into Rockland Harbor from Jameson Point, the harbor's northern shore. Made of granite blocks, this 'walkway' – which took 18 years to build – ends at the Rockland Breakwater

Lighthouse, a sweet light sitting atop a brick house, with a sweeping view of town.

Maine Windjammer Association   CRUISE (☑800-807-9463; www.sailmainecoast.com; ⊙cruises late May–mid-Oct) Although traveling by schooner largely went out of style at the dawn of the 20th century, adventurers can still explore the rugged Maine coast the old-fashioned way: aboard fast sailing ships known as windjammers. Nine of these multimasted vessels anchor at Rockland and Camden and offer trips ranging from overnight to 11 days around Penobscot Bay.

Camden

Camden, with its picture-perfect harbor, framed against the mountains of Camden Hills State Park, is one of the prettiest sites in Maine. Home to the state's large and justly famed fleet of windjammers, Camden continues its historical intimacy with the sea. Most vacationers come to sail, but Camden also has galleries, fine restaurants and backstreets ideal for exploring. Pick up a walking-tour guide to the town's historic buildings at the chamber of commerce. The adjoining state park offers hiking, picnicking and camping.

Like many communities along the Maine coast, Camden has a long history of shipbuilding. The mammoth six-masted schooner *George W Wells* was built here in 1900, setting the world record for the most masts on a sailing ship.

Like nearby Rockland, Camden offers many windjammer cruises, from two-hour trips to multiday journeys up the coast.

A number of boats depart from Camden's Town Landing or adjoining Bayview Landing, offering two-hour cruises (including sunset sails) for a similar price – check out the schedules online for **Appledore II** (☑207-236-8353; https://appledore2.com; Bayview Landing; adult/child $45/25; ⊙Jun-Oct), **Olad** (☑20 7-236-2323; www.maineschooners.com; Public Landing; adult/child $43/33; ⊙late May–mid-Oct) and **Surprise** (☑207-236-4687; http://schoonersurprise.com; Public Landing; adult/child $43/33; ⊙late May–mid-Oct). This is the quintessential Midcoast sightseeing experience.

Penobscot Bay Regional Chamber of Commerce (☑207-236-4404; www.camden rockland.com; 2 Public Landing; ⊙9am-5pm Mon-Fri, 10am-4pm Sat & Sun late May–mid-Oct, 9am-4pm Mon-Fri rest of year) has an information office on the waterfront at the public landing in Camden.

PARK LOOP ROAD

For some visitors, driving the 27-mile Park Loop Rd is the extent of their trip to Acadia National Park. On the portion called Ocean Dr, stop at lovely **Sand Beach**, and at **Thunder Hole** for a look at the surf crashing into a cleft in the granite. The effect is most dramatic with a strong incoming tide.

Otter Cliff, not far south of Thunder Hole, is basically a wall of pink granite rising right out from the sea. This area is popular with rock climbers.

The road is largely one-way; in summer you can cover the route on the Island Explorer bus system (shuttle route 4; www.exploreacadia.com). Note that the loop road is closed in winter, and its opening may be delayed by heavy snow.

Acadia National Park

New England's only national park Acadia National Park (☑207-288-3338; www.nps.gov/acad; 7-day admission per car/motorcycle $25/20, walk-ins & cyclists $12) turned 100 in 2016 – it's a fine-looking centenarian. Within its borders are impressive coastal landmarks and visitor activities.

Drivers and hikers alike can thank John D Rockefeller and other wealthy landowners for the aesthetically pleasing bridges, overlooks and stone steps that give the park its artistic merit. Rockefeller in particular worked diligently with architects and masons to ensure that the infrastructure would complement the surrounding landscapes.

Stop by the Acadia Welcome Center (☑20 7-288-5103, 800-345-4617; www.acadiainfo.com; 1201 Bar Harbor Rd/ME 3, Trenton; ⊙9am-5pm Mon-Sat, 10am-4pm Sun late May–mid-Oct, 9am-5pm Mon-Fri mid-Apr–May & mid-Oct–Nov) in Trenton for brochures, maps and local information. It's located north of the bridge crossing to Mt Desert Island (about 11 miles before reaching Bar Harbor).

Downeast Maine

Without question, this is quintessential Maine: as you head further and further up the coast toward Canada, the peninsulas seem to become more and more narrow, jutting further into the sea. The fishing villages seem to get smaller; the lobster pounds, closer to the water. If you make time to drive to the edge of the shore, south off US 1, let it be here. 'Down East' starts at the Penobscot River, where a bridge observatory unofficially marks the boundary. The region continues 'further Down East,' from Acadia all the way to the border with New Brunswick, Canada.

Information on the region is online at www.downeastacadia.com.

Bar Harbor

The agreeable hub for Acadia visits, Bar Harbor is crowded for most of the year with vacationers and visiting cruise-ship passengers. Downtown is packed with souvenir stores, ice-cream shops, cafes and bars, each advertising bigger and better happy hours, early-bird specials or two-for-one deals. The quieter residential backstreets seem to have almost as many B&Bs as private homes.

Although Bar Harbor's hustle and bustle is not for everybody, it has by far the most amenities of any town around here. Even if you stay somewhere else, you'll probably wind up here to eat dinner, grab a drink or schedule a kayaking, sailing or rock-climbing tour. Bar Harbor's busiest season is late June through August. There's a short lull just after Labor Day (early September); it gets busy again during foliage season, which lasts through mid-October. The season ends with the Mount Desert Island Marathon (www.runmdi.org).

◉ Sights & Activities

Abbe Museum   MUSEUM
(✆207-288-3519; www.abbemuseum.org; 26 Mount Desert St; adult/child $8/4; ⊙10am-5pm May-Oct, 10am-4pm Thu-Sat Nov-Apr) This downtown museum contains a fascinating collection of cultural artifacts related to Maine's Native American heritage. More than 50,000 objects are in the collection, including pottery, tools, combs and fishing implements spanning the last 2000 years. Contemporary pieces include finely wrought wood carvings, birch-bark containers and baskets. The museum also has a smaller, summer-only **branch** (✆207-288-3519; www. abbemuseum.org; ME 3 & Park Loop Rd; adult/child $3/1; ⊙10am-5pm late May-Oct) in a lush park-like setting at Sieur de Monts Spring, inside Acadia National Park.

National Park Sea Kayak Tours   KAYAKING
(✆800-347-0940; www.acadiakayak.com; 39 Cottage St; half-day tour $52; ⊙late May–mid-Oct) Four-hour kayak tours leave at various times (morning, afternoon, sunset) and explore Mount Desert Island's 'Quietside' – ie the remote west coast. Small groups of kayakers spend about 2½ to three hours on the water; transport is provided from Bar Harbor to the put-in point.

🛏 Sleeping & Eating

Moseley Cottage Inn
& Town Motel   B&B, MOTEL $$
(✆207-288-5548; http://moseleycottage.net; 12 Atlantic Ave; r $175-305; ✳🐾) This two-faced option is down a quiet street just steps from Main St, and covers its bases very well. There are nine large, charming, antique-filled B&B rooms in a traditional 1884 inn (options with fireplace and private porch), plus a small collection of cheaper motel-style units next door. All are of a consistently high standard.

★ Bass Cottage Inn   INN $$$
(✆207-288-1234; www.basscottage.com; 14 The Field; r $230-440; ⊙mid-May–Oct; ✳🐾) If most Bar Harbor B&Bs rate about a '5' in terms of stylishness, this Gilded Age mansion deserves an '11.' The 10 light-drenched guest rooms have an elegant summer-cottage chic, all crisp white linens and understated botanical prints.

2 Cats   BREAKFAST $
(✆207-288-2808; http://twocatsbarharbor.com; 130 Cottage St; mains $9-15; ⊙7am-1pm; 🐾) It's the most important meal of the day, so 2 Cats channels all its attention to breakfast. On weekends, crowds line up for banana pecan pancakes, smoked-trout omelets, tofu scrambles and homemade muffins at this sunny, arty little cafe. Pick up a kitty-themed souvenir in the gift shop.

★ Havana   LATIN AMERICAN $$$
(✆207-288-2822; www.havanamaine.com; 318 Main St; mains $27-39; ⊙5-9pm May-Oct) First things first: order a rockin' Cuba libre or mojito. Once that's done, you can take your time with the menu and the epic global wine list. Havana puts a Latin spin on dishes that highlight local produce, and the kitchen output is accomplished. Signature dishes include crab cakes, paella and a deliciously light lobster *moqueca* (stew). Reservations recommended.

ℹ Information

There are a number of options for visitor info. First for motorists is the **Acadia Welcome Center** (p263) as you reach Mt Desert Island (about 11 miles northwest of Bar Harbor), then the NPS-run **Hulls Cove Visitor Center** (☑207-288-8832; www.nps.gov/acad; ME 3; ☻8:30am-4:30pm mid-Apr–Jun, Sep & Oct, 8am-6pm Jul & Aug) inside Acadia National Park.

The **Bar Harbor Chamber of Commerce** (Acadia Welcome Center; ☑207-801-2558, 800-345-4617; www.barharborinfo.com; cnr Main & Cottage Sts; ☻8am-8pm mid-Jun–Sep, 9am-5pm Sep–mid-Jun) maintains a central year-round information office in downtown Bar Harbor.

Inland Maine

Interstate 95 (I-95), the East Coast's major north–south superhighway, runs through Maine for 303 miles, from the New Hampshire border near Kittery to the Canadian border near Houlton. En route it passes by Maine's major cities: Portland; Augusta, the state capital; and Bangor. Augusta and Bangor (as well as nearby Waterville) are home to colleges, a handful of decent museums and some good eateries, but they are not especially tourism-focused destinations.

North of Bangor, traffic levels drop considerably. This is your gateway to the North Woods and to the large, sparsely populated Aroostook County.

Bethel

A 90-minute drive northwest of Portland, Bethel is surprisingly lively and refined for a town surrounded on all sides by deep, dark woods. Summer visitors have been coming here to escape the coastal humidity since the 1800s, and many of its fine old cottages are still operating. It's a prime spot to be during Maine's colorful fall-foliage months and during the winter ski season.

◉ Sights & Activities

Grafton Notch State Park   STATE PARK
(☑207-824-2912; www.maine.gov/graftonnotch; 1941 Bear River Rd/ME 26; adult/child $4/1; ☻9am-sunset mid-May–mid-Oct) Sitting astride the Grafton Notch Scenic Byway within the Mahoosuc Range, this rugged park is a stunner. Carved by a glacier that retreated 12,000 years ago, the notch is a four-season playground, chock-full of waterfalls, gorges, lofty viewpoints and hiking trails, including 12 strenuous miles of the **Appalachian Trail** (www.appalachiantrail.org).

Bethel Outdoor Adventure & Campground   KAYAKING
(☑207-824-4224; www.betheloutdooradventure. com; 121 Mayville Rd/US 2; kayak per day with/ without shuttle $45/32; ☻8am-6pm mid-May–late Oct) Based at a bucolic riverside campground, this outfitter rents out canoes, kayaks and stand-up paddleboards. It can shuttle you upriver to the drop-off point, and you paddle back downstream.

🛏 Sleeping

Chapman Inn   B&B $
(☑207-824-2657; www.chapmaninn.com; 2 Church St; dm $35, r $59-139; ✳🐾🛜) Run by a friendly, globe-trotting retiree, this roomy downtown guesthouse has character in spades. The 10 private rooms are done up in florals and antiques, with slightly sloping floors attesting to the house's age.

ℹ Information

Bethel Area Chamber of Commerce (☑800-442-5826, 207-824-2282; www.bethelmaine. com; 8 Station Pl; ☻9am-5pm Mon-Fri year-round, weekend hours vary in peak season) This helpful organization maintains an information office in the Bethel Station building, with loads of handouts on various sights, trails and activities.

Baxter State Park

Baxter State Park is Maine at its most primeval: the wind whips around dozens of mountain peaks, black bears root through the underbrush and hikers go for miles without seeing another soul. Visitors can hike hundreds of miles of trails through the park, climb the sheer cliffs (this is a rock-climber's paradise), fly-fish the ponds and rivers, and spot wild animals, such as bald eagles, moose and fox-like martens. The park is most popular in the warmer months, but it's also open for winter sports like snowmobiling. Baxter's 5267ft **Mt Katahdin** – the park's crowning glory – is Maine's tallest mountain and the northern end of the 2190-mile-long Appalachian Trail.

Katahdin Area Chamber of Commerce   TOURIST INFORMATION
(☑207-723-4443; www.katahdinmaine.com; 1029 Central St, Millinocket; ☻9am-3pm Mon-Fri) Info on the area, including accommodations.

Washington, DC & the Capital Region

Includes ➡

Washington, DC	267
Maryland	297
Baltimore	298
Annapolis	303
Delaware	311
Wilmington	313
Brandywine Valley	313
Virginia	316
Fredericksburg	321
Richmond	322
The Piedmont	330
Shenandoah Valley	333
West Virginia	341

Why Go?

No matter your politics, it's hard not to fall for the nation's capital. Iconic monuments, vast (and free) museums and venerable restaurants serving global cuisines are just the beginning of the great DC experience. There's much to discover: leafy, cobblestoned neighborhoods, sprawling markets, heady multicultural nightspots and verdant parks, and of course, the corridors of power. Beyond the Beltway, the diverse landscapes of Maryland, Virginia, West Virginia and Delaware offer potent enticement to travel beyond the marble city. Craggy mountains, rushing rivers, vast nature reserves (including islands where wild horses run), sparkling beaches, historic villages and the magnificent Chesapeake Bay form the backdrop to memorable adventures: sailing, hiking, rafting, camping or just sitting on a pretty stretch of shoreline, planning the next seafood feast. It's a place where traditions run deep, from the nation's birthplace to Virginia's bluegrass scene.

Best Places to Eat

➡ Rose's Luxury (p288)

➡ Woodberry Kitchen (p302)

➡ L'Opossum (p325)

➡ Public Fish & Oyster (p332)

➡ Faidley's (p302)

Best Places to Sleep

➡ Hotel Lombardy (p286)

➡ Inn at 2920 (p301)

➡ Georges (p336)

➡ HI Richmond (p324)

When to Go
Washington DC

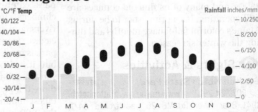

May–Apr Cherry blossoms bring crowds to the city during DC's most popular festival.

Jun–Aug Beaches and resorts heave; prices are high and accommodations scarce.

Sep–Oct Smaller crowds and lower prices, but with pleasant temperatures and fiery fall scenery.

History

Native Americans populated this region long before European settlers arrived. Many of the area's geographic landmarks are still known by their Native American names, such as Chesapeake, Shenandoah, Appalachian and Potomac. In 1607 a group of 108 English colonists established the first permanent European settlement in the New World: Jamestown. During the early years, colonists battled harsh winters, starvation, disease and, occasionally, hostile Native Americans.

Jamestown survived, and the Royal Colony of Virginia came into being in 1624. Ten years later, fleeing the English Civil War, Lord Baltimore established the Catholic colony of Maryland at St Mary's City, where a Spanish Jewish doctor treated a town council that included a black Portuguese sailor and Margaret Brent, the first woman to vote in North American politics. Delaware was settled as a Dutch whaling colony in 1631, practically wiped out by Native Americans, and later resettled by the British. Celts displaced from Britain filtered into the Appalachians, where they created a fiercely independent culture that persists today. Border disputes between Maryland, Delaware and Pennsylvania led to the creation of the Mason–Dixon line, which eventually separated the industrial North from the agrarian, slave-holding South.

The fighting part of the Revolutionary War finished here with the British surrender at Yorktown in 1781. Then – to diffuse regional tension – central, swampy Washington, District of Columbia (DC), was made the new nation's capital. But divisions of class, race and economy were strong, and this area in particular split along its seams during the Civil War (1861–65): Virginia seceded from the Union, while its impoverished western farmers, long resentful of genteel plantation owners, seceded from Virginia. Maryland stayed in the Union, but its white slaveowners rioted against Northern troops, while thousands of black Marylanders joined the Union Army.

WASHINGTON, DC

The USA's capital teems with iconic monuments, vast museums and the corridors of power where visionaries and demagogues roam. But it's more than that. It's also home to tree-lined neighborhoods and groovy markets, with ethnically diverse restaurants, large numbers of immigrants and a dynamism percolating just beneath the surface. There's always a buzz here – no surprise, as DC gathers more overachieving and talented types than any city of this size deserves. Plan on jam-packed days sightseeing in the countless museums (most of them free). At night, join the locals sipping DC-made brews and chowing in cozy restaurants in buzzy quarters such as U St and Logan Circle.

History

Following the Revolutionary War, a balance was struck between Northern and Southern politicians, who wanted to plant a federal city somewhere between their power bases. Potential capitals such as Boston, Philadelphia and Baltimore were rejected by Southern plantation owners, as too urban-industrial so it was decided a new city would be carved at midway point of the 13 colonies, along the banks of the Potomac River. Maryland and Virginia donated the land.

DC was torched by the British during the War of 1812, and ceded the south-bank slave port of Alexandria to Virginia in 1846 (when abolition talk was buzzing in the capital). Over the years, DC evolved along diverging tracks: as a marbled temple to the federal government on one hand, and as an urban ghetto for northbound African Americans and overseas immigrants on the other. The city finally got its own mayor in 1973 (Walter Washington, among the first African American mayors of a major American city); Congress governed prior to that.

Today, DC residents are taxed just as other American citizens are, yet lack a voting seat in Congress. DC has undergone extensive gentrification since the late 1990s. With the election of Barack Obama in 2008, the city gained a bit of cool cachet – New Yorkers are coming here now, instead of the other way around. Unfortunately they've jacked up the cost of living. DC's costs are among the highest in the nation, and as the city's economy keeps on booming, it's likely to stay that way.

◉ Sights

◉ National Mall

The Mall – aka 'America's front yard' – holds most of the Smithsonian museums and major monuments. The Lincoln Memorial,

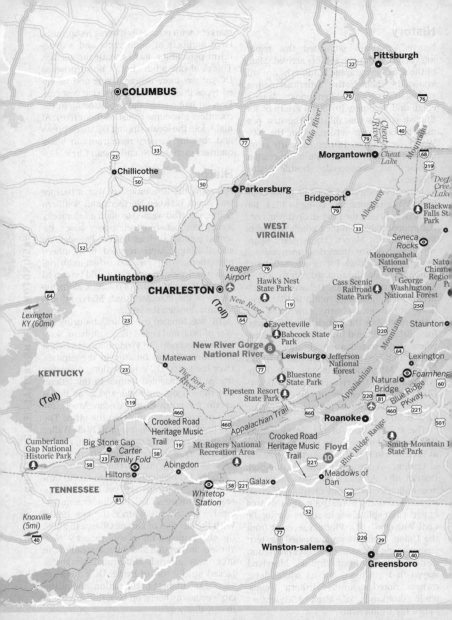

Washington, DC & the Capital Region Highlights

1 **National Air and Space Museum** (p270) Visiting Washington, DC's museums.

2 **Lincoln Memorial** (p270) Watching the sun set over the monument.

3 **Colonial Williamsburg** (p326) Tracing America's roots at this living-history museum.

4 **Annapolis** (p303) Exploring the city's historic and nautical past with a stroll

through the capitol, the Naval Academy and along Main St to Ego Alley.

5 **Shenandoah National Park** (p335) Taking a Sunday drive on Skyline Drive, followed

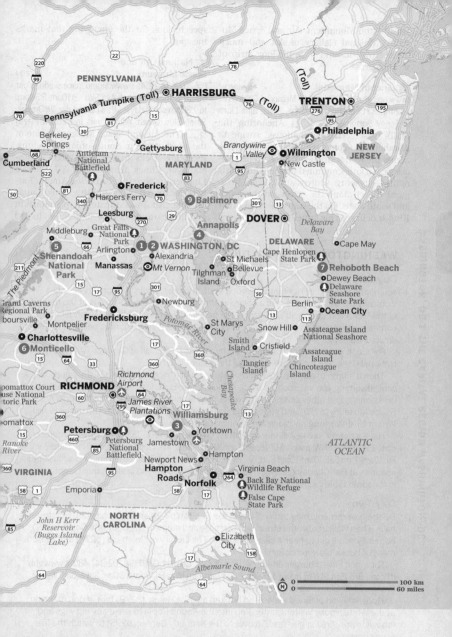

by hiking and camping under
the stars.

6 **Monticello** (p331)
Marveling at Thomas
Jefferson's masterpiece.

7 **Rehoboth Beach** (p312)

Strolling the boardwalk in this
family- and gay-friendly resort.

8 **New River Gorge National
River** (p344) Tackling the
Gauley River rapids.

9 **Faidley's** (p302) Savoring

one of the world's best crab
cakes in Baltimore.

10 **Floyd** (p340) Feeling the
beat of the old-time music at a
jamboree.

Washington Monument, Air and Space Museum, National Gallery of Art and much more crowd around a 2-mile-long strip of scrubby grass.

★ **Lincoln Memorial** MONUMENT
(www.nps.gov/linc; 2 Lincoln Memorial Circle NW; ⊙24hr; ☐ Circulator, Ⓜ Orange, Silver, Blue Lines to Foggy Bottom-GWU) **FREE** Anchoring the Mall's west end is the hallowed shrine to Abraham Lincoln, who gazes peacefully across the **Reflecting Pool** beneath his neo-classical, Doric-columned abode. The words of his Gettysburg Address and Second Inaugural speech flank the statue on the north and south walls. On the steps, Martin Luther King Jr delivered his famed 'I Have a Dream' speech; look for the engraving that marks the spot.

★ **National Air and Space Museum** MUSEUM
(☑202-633-2214; www.airandspace.si.edu; cnr 6th St & Independence Ave SW; ⊙10am-5:30pm, to 7:30pm some days; ☻; ☐ Circulator, Ⓜ Orange, Silver, Blue, Green, Yellow Lines to L'Enfant Plaza) **FREE** The Air and Space Museum is one of the most popular Smithsonian museums. Everyone flocks to see the Wright brothers' flyer, Chuck Yeager's *Bell X-1*, Charles Lindbergh's *Spirit of St Louis,* Amelia Earhart's natty red plane and the Apollo Lunar Module. An Imax theater, a planetarium and flight simulators are all here ($8 to $10

WASHINGTON, DC IN TWO DAYS...

Day One

You might as well dive right into the good stuff, and the Lincoln Memorial is about as iconically DC as it gets. It's also a convenient starting point, since Abe sits at the far end of the Mall. Next up as you walk east is the powerful Vietnam Veterans Memorial. Then comes the Washington Monument (p271), which is pretty hard to miss, being DC's tallest structure and all.

For lunch you can munch sandwiches by an artsy waterfall at Cascade Cafe in the National Gallery of Art before exploring the gallery.

Then it's time to explore the National Museum of African American History and Culture, assuming you've procured a ticket. Pick a side: East, for modern; or West, for Impressionists and other classics. Afterward, mosey across the lawn to the National Air and Space Museum (p270) and gape at the stuff hanging from the ceiling. The missiles and Wright Brothers' original plane are incomparably cool.

Have a hearty, low-key dinner at Duke's Grocery (☑202-733-5623; www.dukesgrocery. com; 1513 17th St NW; mains $12-16; ⊙11am-10pm Mon & Tue, 11am-1am Wed & Thu, 11am-2am Fri, 10am-2am Sat, 10am-10pm Sun; ☎; Ⓜ Red Line to Dupont Circle) then linger over luscious libations at Bar Charley (p294) – the night is young! But if you prefer a quiet night settle in for some table games at Board Room (p294).

Day Two

Do the government thing today. Start in the Capitol (p278) and tour the statue-cluttered halls. Then walk across the street and up the grand steps to the Supreme Court (p279); hopefully you'll get to hear a case argument. The Library of Congress (p279) and its 500 miles of books blow minds next door.

For lunch have a burger amid politicos at Old Ebbitt Grill (☑202-347-4800; www.ebbitt.com; 675 15th St NW; mains $18-28; ⊙7:30am-1am Mon-Fri, from 8:30am Sat & Sun; Ⓜ Red, Orange, Silver, Blue Lines to Metro Center).

Hopefully you planned ahead and booked a White House (p279) tour. If not, make do at the White House Visitor Center. Pop into the Round Robin to see if any big wigs and lobbyists are clinking glasses. Zip over to the Kennedy Center (p295) to watch the free 6pm show.

Afterwards go for French in laid-back elegance at Chez Billy Sud (p292) in Georgetown, then sink a pint in a friendly pub like the Tombs (p295). On warm nights the outdoor cafes and boating action make Georgetown Waterfront Park (p282) a hot spot. And check if anyone groovy is playing at iconic jazz club Blues Alley (www.bluesalley.com).

each). More avionic pieces reside in Virginia at the **Steven F Udvar-Hazy Center** (📞703-572-4118; www.airandspace.si.edu/visit/udvar-hazy-center; 14390 Air & Space Museum Pkwy, Chantilly; ⊘10am-5:30pm; 🚻; Ⓜ Wiehle-Reston East for bus 983) **FREE**, an annex to hold this museum's leftovers.

★**Vietnam Veterans Memorial** MONUMENT
(www.nps.gov/vive; 5 Henry Bacon Dr NW; ⊘24hr; 🚋 Circulator, Ⓜ Orange, Silver, Blue Lines to Foggy Bottom-GWU) **FREE** The opposite of DC's white, gleaming marble is this black, low-lying 'V,' an expression of the psychic scar wrought by the Vietnam War. The monument descends into the earth, with the names of the war's 58,300-plus casualties – listed in the order they died – chiseled into the dark, reflective wall. It's a subtle but profound monument – and all the more surprising as it was designed by 21-year-old undergraduate student Maya Lin in 1981.

★**National Gallery of Art** MUSEUM
(📞202-737-4215; www.nga.gov; Constitution Ave NW, btwn 3rd & 7th Sts; ⊘10am-5pm Mon-Sat, 11am-6pm Sun; 🚋 Circulator, Ⓜ Green, Yellow Lines to Archives) **FREE** The staggering collection spans the Middle Ages to the present. The neoclassical west building showcases European art through the early 1900s; highlights include the Western Hemisphere's only da Vinci painting and a slew of Impressionist and post-Impressionist works. The IM Pei–designed east building displays modern art, with works by Picasso, Matisse and Pollock and a massive Calder mobile over the entrance lobby. Recently renovated and expanded, this new wing really dazzles. A trippy underground walkway connects the two buildings.

★**Washington Monument** MONUMENT
(www.nps.gov/wamo; 2 15th St NW; ⊘9am-5pm, to 10pm Jun-Aug; 🚋 Circulator, Ⓜ Orange, Silver, Blue Lines to Smithsonian) **FREE** Peaking at 555ft (and 5in) and comprised of 36,000 blocks of stone, the Washington Monument is the tallest building in the district. It took so long to build that the original quarry ran out; note the delineation in color where the old and new marble meet about a third of the way up. Alas, the monument is closed until spring 2019 for repairs, so you'll have to wait until then for stellar views from the observation deck.

★**Martin Luther King Jr Memorial** MONUMENT
(www.nps.gov/mlkm; 1850 W Basin Dr SW; ⊘24hr; 🚋 Circulator, Ⓜ Orange, Silver, Blue Lines to Smithsonian) **FREE** Opened in 2011, this is the Mall's newest memorial and the first one to honor an African American. Sculptor Lei Yixin carved the piece. Besides Dr King's striking, 30ft-tall image, known as the Stone of Hope, there are two blocks of granite behind him that represent the Mountain of Despair. A wall inscribed with King's moving quotes about democracy, justice and peace flanks the piece. It sits in a lovely spot on the banks of the Tidal Basin.

★**National Museum of African American History and Culture** MUSEUM
(📞844-750-3012; www.nmaahc.si.edu; 1400 Constitution Ave NW; ⊘10am-5:30pm; 🚻; 🚋 Circulator, Ⓜ Orange, Silver, Blue Lines to Smithsonian or Federal Triangle) **FREE** Opened in 2016, the Smithsonian's newest museum covers the diverse African American experience and how it helped shape the nation. The collection includes everything from Harriet Tubman's hymnal to Emmett Till's casket and Louis Armstrong's trumpet. The museum is so wildly popular you need a timed entry pass to get in. Your best bet to obtain one is via the same-day online release, when tickets are made available at 6:30am on the museum's website. Be ready, because they're snapped up within minutes.

National Sculpture Garden GARDENS
(cnr Constitution Ave NW & 7th St NW; ⊘10am-6pm Mon-Thu & Sat, 10am-8:30pm Fri, 11am-6pm Sun; 🚋 Circulator, Ⓜ Green, Yellow Lines to Archives) **FREE** The National Gallery of Art's 6-acre garden is studded with whimsical sculptures such as Roy Lichtenstein's *House,* a giant Claes Oldenburg typewriter eraser and Louise Bourgeois' leggy *Spider.* They are scattered around a fountain – a great place to dip your feet in summer. From mid-November to mid-March the fountain becomes a festive **ice rink** (adult/child $8.50/7.50, skate rental $3; ⊘10am-9pm Mon-Thu, 10am-11pm Fri, 11am-11pm Sat, 11am-9pm Sun mid-Nov–mid-Mar; 🚋 Circulator, Ⓜ Green, Yellow Lines to Archives), and the garden stays open a bit later.

Washington, DC

Washington National Cathedral (0.7mi)

Woodley Park Guesthouse (0.25mi); National Zoo (0.5mi)

Tail Up Goat (50yds); Adam's Inn (0.1mi)

United States Naval Observatory

WOODLEY PARK

Whitehaven St NW

Massachusetts Ave NW

Rock Creek and Potomac Pkwy NW

Belmont Rd NW

Rock Creek

Connecticut Ave NW

Kalorama Park NW

Columbia Rd NW

99
80
18
76
97
55

ADAMS MORGAN

Mexican Cultural Institute (0.2mi)

Kalorama Circle

Dumbarton Oaks Park

S St NW
R St NW

Montrose Park

19

37

Avon Pl NW

Waterside Dr NW

KALORAMA

Kalorama Circle

Wyoming Ave NW
Wyoming Ave NW

California St NW

Florida Ave NW

California St NW

Vernon St NW

Willard Pl NW

T St NW

S St NW

17th St NW

16th St NW

Swann St NW

92

89
45

32nd St NW
Wisconsin Ave NW

Oak Hill Cemetery

30th St NW
29th St NW
28th St NW

Decatur Pl NW

Sheridan Circle

R St NW

52
39
91

69
93

Washington Deluxe

New Hampshire Ave NW

94

Q St NW

33rd St NW

85

GEORGETOWN

N St NW
Thomas Jefferson St NW

31st St NW
27th St NW

Rock Creek

P St NW
O St NW
Dumbarton St NW

28

Embassy Row
2

BestBus

64

Corcoran St NW

79
82

O St NW

M
Dupont Circle

Q St NW

62

Scott Circle

53

Pennsylvania Ave NW

22nd St NW
21st St NW

DUPONT CIRCLE

New Hampshire Ave NW

Connecticut Ave NW

29

72
65

M St NW

M St NW

M St NW

18th St NW
17th St NW
16th St NW

61

Whitehurst Fwy

Capital Crescent Trail (0.2mi); Key Bridge Boathouse (0.2mi); Exorcist Stairs (0.25mi); Tombs (0.25mi); Georgetown University (0.5mi); Dalghren Chapel (0.5mi); Healy Hall (0.5mi)

24

Washington Harbour Complex

25th St NW

23rd St NW

21st St NW
20th St NW
19th St NW

K St NW

L St NW

Farragut North

51
54

Foggy Bottom-GWU

Pennsylvania Ave NW

I St NW

57

Farragut West

H St NW

41

Theodore Roosevelt Island

104

24th St NW
22nd St NW

H St NW
G St NW

78

44

19th St NW
18th St NW

17th St NW

P

Lafayette Sq

15

Mount Vernon Trail

Theodore Roosevelt Memorial Bridge

F St NW

E St NW

FOGGY BOTTOM
Rawlins Park

White House

South Lawn

E St NW

Virginia Ave NW

D St NW

C St NW

C St NW

The Ellipse

Iwo Jima Memorial (0.4mi); Continental (0.6mi)

Constitution Ave NW

Vietnam Veterans Memorial
13

Constitution Gardens

35

Washington Monument

14

Arlington House (0.4mi); Challenger Memorial (0.8mi)

George Washington Memorial Pkwy

Reflecting Pool

40

4

Lincoln Memorial

West Potomac Park

NATIONAL MALL

Martin Luther King Jr Memorial

5

Independence Ave SW

1

Arlington National Cemetery

Boundary Dr

Lady Bird Johnson Park

23

Potomac River

21

Ohio Dr SW

W Basin Dr SW

Memorial Park

Tidal Basin

East Potomac Park

27

Pentagon Memorial (0.75mi); Pentagon (0.9mi); Air Force Memorial (1.2mi)

(2mi)

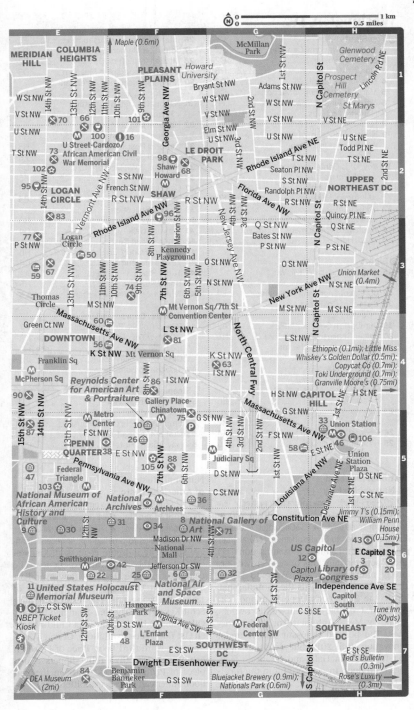

Washington, DC

◉ Top Sights

1 Arlington National Cemetery A7
2 Embassy Row..C2
3 Library of Congress..............................H6
4 Lincoln Memorial..................................C6
5 Martin Luther King Jr Memorial............C6
6 National Air and Space Museum..........F6
7 National Archives..................................F5
8 National Gallery of Art..........................F6
9 National Museum of African
   American History and
   Culture...E6
10 Reynolds Center for American
   Art & Portraiture..............................F5
11 United States Holocaust
   Memorial Museum............................E6
12 US Capitol..H6
13 Vietnam Veterans Memorial.................C6
14 Washington Monument........................D6
15 White House...D5

◉ Sights

16 African American Civil War
   Memorial...F2
17 Bureau of Engraving & Printing.............E7
18 District of Columbia Arts
   Center...D1
19 Dumbarton Oaks...................................A2
20 Folger Shakespeare Library..................H6
   Ford's Theatre Center for
   Education and Leadership........ (see 38)
21 Franklin Delano Roosevelt
   Memorial...C7
22 Freer-Sackler Museums of
   Asian Art..E6
23 George Washington Memorial
   Parkway...B7
24 Georgetown Waterfront Park.................A4
25 Hirshhorn Museum...............................F6

26 International Spy Museum.....................F5
27 Jefferson Memorial...............................D7
28 Mt Zion Cemetery.................................B2
29 National Geographic Museum................D3
30 National Museum of American
   History..E6
31 National Museum of Natural
   History..F6
32 National Museum of the
   American Indian................................G6
33 National Postal Museum.......................H5
34 National Sculpture Garden....................F6
35 National WWII Memorial.......................D6
36 Newseum...F5
37 Oak Hill Cemetery................................B2
38 Petersen House.....................................E5
39 Phillips Collection................................C2
40 Reflecting Pool.....................................C6
41 Renwick Gallery...................................D4
42 Smithsonian Castle...............................E6
43 Supreme Court.....................................H6
44 Textile Museum....................................C4
45 Tudor Place..A2
46 Union Station..H5
47 White House Visitor Center E5

◉ Activities, Courses & Tours

48 Bike & Roll – L'Enfant Plaza.................. F7
   DC Brew Tours............................... (see 10)
   Ice Rink...(see 34)
   Old Town Trolley Tours ....(see 38)
49 Tidal Basin Boathouse..........................E7

◉ Sleeping

50 Chester Arthur House............................E3
51 Club Quarters D4
52 Embassy Circle Guest House C2
53 Graham Georgetown A3
54 Hay-Adams Hotel..................................D4

National Museum
of Natural History   MUSEUM

(☏202-663-1000; www.naturalhistory.si.edu; cnr 10th St & Constitution Ave NW; ⊙10am-5:30pm, to 7:30pm some days; ⊛; ▣Circulator, ▣Orange, Silver, Blue Lines to Smithsonian or Federal Triangle) **FREE** Smithsonian museums don't get more popular than this one, so crowds are pretty much guaranteed. Wave to Henry, the elephant who guards the rotunda, then zip to the 2nd floor's Hope Diamond. The 45.52-carat bauble has cursed its owners, including Marie Antoinette, or so the story goes. The beloved dinosaur hall is under renovation until 2019, but the giant squid (1st floor, Ocean Hall) and tarantula feedings (2nd floor, Insect Zoo) fill in the thrills at this kid-packed venue.

National Museum
of American History   MUSEUM

(☏202-663-1000; www.americanhistory.si.edu; cnr 14th St & Constitution Ave NW; ⊙10am-5:30pm, to 7:30pm some days; ⊛; ▣Circulator, ▣Orange, Silver, Blue Lines to Smithsonian or Federal Triangle) **FREE** The museum collects all kinds of artifacts of the American experience. The centerpiece is the flag that flew over Fort McHenry in Baltimore during the War of 1812 – the same flag that inspired Francis Scott Key to pen 'The Star-Spangled Banner.' Other highlights include Julia Child's kitchen (1st floor, Food exhibition), George Washington's sword (3rd floor, Price of Freedom exhibition), Dorothy's ruby slippers and a piece of Plymouth Rock (both on the 2nd floor, American Stories exhibition).

55 HighRoad Hostel D1
56 Hostelling International
   – Washington DC E4
57 Hotel Lombardy C4
58 Kimpton George Hotel G5
59 Kimpton Mason & Rook
   Hotel E3
60 Morrison-Clark Inn..................................E4
61 St Regis Washington D4
62 Tabard Inn D3

🍴 Eating
63 A Baked Joint G4
64 Afterwords Cafe C3
65 Baked & Wired..A4
66 Ben's Chili Bowl......................................E2
67 Birch & Barley E3
68 Bistro Bohem F2
69 Bistrot du Coin C2
70 Busboys & Poets.......................................E1
71 Cascade Cafe G6
72 Chez Billy Sud A4
73 Compass Rose E2
74 Dabney F3
75 Daikaya..F5
76 Diner D1
   Donburi .... (see 18)
   Duke's Grocery .... (see 82)
77 Estadio E3
78 Founding Farmers C4
79 Hank's Oyster Bar D3
80 Julia's Empanadas...................................D1
81 Kinship..F4
82 Komi D3
83 Le Diplomate E2
   Little Serow .... (see 82)
84 Maine Avenue Fish
   Market E7
85 Martin's Tavern A3

86 Matchbox Pizza F4
87 Old Ebbitt Grill...E5
88 Rasika F5
89 Simply Banh Mi A2
90 Woodward Takeout Food......................E4
91 Zorba's Cafe..C2

🍸 Drinking & Nightlife
92 Bar Charley D2
93 Board Room C2
   Churchkey .... (see 67)
94 Cobalt...D2
   Columbia Room .... (see 74)
95 Cork Wine Bar E2
96 Dacha Beer Garden F2
97 Dan's Cafe D1
   JR's .... (see 79)
   Off The Record................................. (see 54)
98 Right Proper Brewing Co......................F2
99 Songbyrd Record Cafe & Music
   House D1
100 U Street Music Hall E2

🎭 Entertainment
101 9:30 Club..F1
102 Black Cat E2
103 Capitol Steps..E5
   Folger Theatre ....(see 20)
104 Kennedy Center B5
105 Shakespeare Theatre
   Company F5
   Woolly Mammoth Theatre
   Company ....(see 88)

ℹ️ Transport
   BoltBus ....(see 106)
106 Greyhound...H5
   Megabus ....(see 106)
   Peter Pan Bus Lines...................(see 106)

Jefferson Memorial MONUMENT
(www.nps.gov/thje; 900 Ohio Dr SW; ⏰24hr; �Circulator, Ⓜ Orange, Silver, Blue Lines to Smithsonian) **FREE** Set on the south bank of the Tidal Basin amid the cherry trees, this memorial honors the third US president, political philosopher, drafter of the Declaration of Independence and founder of the University of Virginia. Designed by John Russell Pope to resemble Jefferson's library at the university, the rounded monument was initially derided by critics as 'the Jefferson Muffin.'

National WWII Memorial MONUMENT
(www.nps.gov/wwii; 17th St; ⏰24hr; 🚎Circulator, Ⓜ Orange, Silver, Blue Lines to Smithsonian) **FREE** Dedicated in 2004, the WWII memorial honors the 400,000 Americans who died in the conflict, along with the 16 million US

soldiers who served between 1941 and 1945. The plaza's dual arches symbolize victory in the Atlantic and Pacific theaters. The 56 surrounding pillars represent each US state and territory.

Hirshhorn Museum MUSEUM
(📞202-633-1000; www.hirshhorn.si.edu; cnr 7th St & Independence Ave SW; ⏰10am-5:30pm; ♿; 🚎Circulator, Ⓜ Orange, Silver, Blue, Green, Yellow Lines to L'Enfant Plaza) **FREE** The Smithsonian's cylindrical modern art museum stockpiles sculptures and canvases from modernism's early days to pop art to contemporary art. Special exhibits ring the 2nd floor. Rotating pieces from the permanent collection circle the 3rd floor, where there's also a swell sitting area with couches, floor-to-ceiling windows and a balcony offering Mall views.

National Mall

A DAY TOUR

Folks often call the Mall 'America's Front Yard,' and that's a pretty good analogy. It is indeed a lawn, unfurling scrubby green grass from the Capitol west to the Lincoln Memorial. It's also America's great public space, where citizens come to protest their government, go for scenic runs and connect with the nation's most cherished ideals writ large in stone, landscaping, monuments and memorials.

You can sample quite a bit in a day, but it'll be a full one that requires roughly 4 miles of walking.

Start at the ❶ Vietnam Veterans Memorial, then head counterclockwise around the Mall, swooping in on the ❷ Lincoln Memorial, ❸ Martin Luther King Jr Memorial and ❹ Washington Monument. You can also pause for the cause of the Korean War and

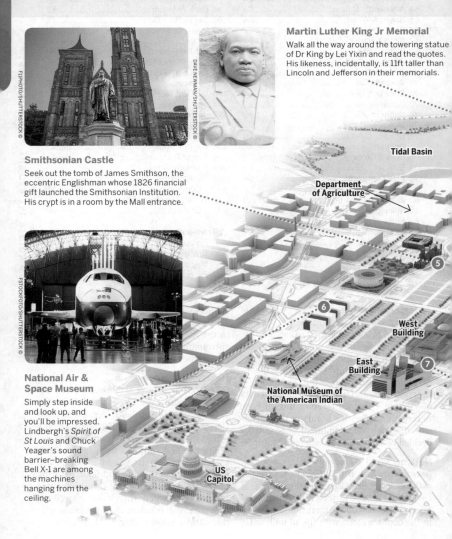

Martin Luther King Jr Memorial

Walk all the way around the towering statue of Dr King by Lei Yixin and read the quotes. His likeness, incidentally, is 11ft taller than Lincoln and Jefferson in their memorials.

Tidal Basin

Smithsonian Castle

Seek out the tomb of James Smithson, the eccentric Englishman whose 1826 financial gift launched the Smithsonian Institution. His crypt is in a room by the Mall entrance.

Department of Agriculture

West Building

East Building

National Museum of the American Indian

National Air & Space Museum

Simply step inside and look up, and you'll be impressed. Lindbergh's *Spirit of St Louis* and Chuck Yeager's sound barrier–breaking Bell X-1 are among the machines hanging from the ceiling.

US Capitol

WWII, among other monuments that dot the Mall's western portion.

Then it's onward to the museums, all fabulous and all free. Begin at the ❺ **Smithsonian Castle** to get your bearings – and to say thanks to the guy making all this awesomeness possible – and commence browsing through the ❻ **National Air & Space Museum**, ❼ **National Gallery of Art & National Sculpture Garden** and ❽ **National Museum of Natural History**.

TOP TIPS

Start early, especially in summer. You'll avoid the crowds, but more importantly you'll avoid the blazing heat. Try to finish with the monuments and be in the air-conditioned museums by 10:30am. Also, consider bringing snacks, since the only food available is from scattered cart vendors and museum cafes.

Lincoln Memorial

Commune with Abe in his chair, then head down the steps to the marker where Martin Luther King Jr gave his 'Dream' speech. The view of the Reflecting Pool and Washington Monument is one of DC's best.

Vietnam Veterans Memorial

Check the symbol that's beside each name. A diamond indicates 'killed, body recovered.' A plus sign indicates 'missing and unaccounted for.' There are approximately 1200 of the latter.

Korean War Veterans Memorial

National WWII Memorial

National Museum of African American History & Culture

National Museum of American History

National Sculpture Garden

Washington Monument

As you approach the obelisk, look a third of the way up. See how it's slightly lighter in color at the bottom? Builders had to use different marble after the first source dried up.

National Museum of Natural History

Wave to Henry, the elephant who guards the rotunda, then zip to the 2nd floor's Hope Diamond. The 45.52-carat bauble has cursed its owners, including Marie Antoinette, or so the story goes.

National Gallery of Art & National Sculpture Garden

Beeline to Gallery 6 (West Building) and ogle the Western Hemisphere's only Leonardo da Vinci painting. Outdoors, amble amid whimsical sculptures by Miró, Calder and Lichtenstein. Also check out IM Pei's design of the East Building.

Smithsonian Castle
NOTABLE BUILDING

(☑202-633-1000; www.si.edu; 1000 Jefferson Dr SW; ⊘8:30am-5:30pm; ▢Circulator, ▣Orange, Silver, Blue Lines to Smithsonian) James Renwick designed this turreted, red-sandstone fairy-tale in 1855. Today the castle houses the **Smithsonian Visitors Center**, which makes a good first stop on the Mall. Inside you'll find history exhibits, multilingual touch-screen displays, a staffed information desk, free maps, a cafe – and the tomb of James Smithson, the institution's founder. His crypt lies inside a little room by the main entrance off the Mall.

Freer-Sackler Museums of Asian Art
MUSEUM

(☑202-633-1000; www.asia.si.edu; cnr Independence Ave & 12th St SW; ⊘10am-5:30pm; ▢Circulator, ▣Orange, Silver, Blue Lines to Smithsonian) **FREE** This is a lovely spot in which to while away a Washington afternoon. Japanese silk scrolls, smiling Buddhas, rare Islamic manuscripts and Chinese jades spread through cool, quiet galleries. The Freer and Sackler are actually separate venues, connected by an underground tunnel. The Sackler focuses more on changing exhibits, while the Freer, rather incongruously, also houses works by American painter James Whistler. Don't miss the blue-and-gold, ceramics-crammed Peacock Room.

National Museum of the American Indian
MUSEUM

(☑202-663-1000; www.nmai.si.edu; cnr 4th St & Independence Ave SW; ⊘10am-5:30pm; ▣; ▢Circulator, ▣Orange, Silver, Blue, Green, Yellow Lines to L'Enfant Plaza) **FREE** Ensconced in honey-colored, undulating limestone, this museum makes a striking architectural impression. Inside it offers cultural artifacts, costumes, video and audio recordings related to the indigenous people of the Americas. Exhibits are largely organized and presented by individual tribes, which provides an intimate, if sometimes disjointed, overall narrative. The 'Our Universes' gallery (on Level 4) about Native American beliefs and creation stories is intriguing.

Franklin Delano Roosevelt Memorial
MONUMENT

(www.nps.gov/frde; 400 W Basin Dr SW; ⊘24hr; ▢Circulator, ▣Orange, Silver, Blue Lines to Smithsonian) **FREE** The 7.5-acre memorial pays tribute to the longest-serving president in US history and the era he governed. Visitors are taken through four red-granite 'rooms' that narrate FDR's time in office, from the Depression to the New Deal to WWII. The story is told through statuary and inscriptions, punctuated with fountains and peaceful alcoves. It's especially pretty at night, when the marble shimmers in the glossy stillness of the Tidal Basin.

Capitol Hill

The city's geographic and legislative heart surprises by being mostly a row house–lined residential neighborhood. The vast area holds top sights such as the Capitol, Library of Congress and Holocaust Memorial Museum. The areas around Eastern Market and H St NE are locals' hubs, with good-time restaurants and nightlife.

★US Capitol
LANDMARK

(☑202-226-8000; www.visitthecapitol.gov; 1st St NE & E Capitol St; ⊘8:30am-4:30pm Mon-Sat; ▣Orange, Silver, Blue Lines to Capitol South) **FREE** Since 1800, this is where the legislative branch of American government – ie Congress – has met to write the country's laws. The lower House of Representatives (435 members) and upper Senate (100) meet respectively in the south and north wings of the building. Enter via the underground visitor center below the East Plaza. Guided tours of the building are free, but tickets are limited and there's often a long wait. It's best to reserve online in advance (there's no fee).

The hour-long jaunt showcases the exhaustive background of a building that fairly sweats history. You'll watch a cheesy film first, then staff members lead you into the ornate halls and whispery chambers cluttered with the busts, statues and personal mementos of generations of Congress members.

To watch Congress in session, you need a separate pass. US citizens must get one from their representative or senator; foreign visitors should take their passports to the House and Senate Appointment Desks on the upper level. Congressional committee hearings are actually more interesting (and substantive) if you care about what's being debated; check for a schedule, locations and to see if they're open to the public (they often are) at www.house.gov and www.senate.gov.

★ United States Holocaust Memorial Museum
MUSEUM

(☑202-488-0400; www.ushmm.org; 100 Raoul Wallenberg Pl SW; ⊘10am-5:20pm, extended hours Apr–mid-Jun; ▢Circulator, ▣Orange, Silver, Blue

Lines to Smithsonian) **FREE** For a deep understanding of the Holocaust – its victims, perpetrators and bystanders – this harrowing museum is a must-see. The main exhibit gives visitors the identity card of a single Holocaust victim, whose story is revealed as you take a winding route into a hellish past marked by ghettos, rail cars and death camps. It also shows the flip side of human nature, documenting the risks many citizens took to help the persecuted.

★ **Library of Congress** LIBRARY
(☎ 202-707-8000; www.loc.gov;1stStSE; ⊗ 8:30am-4:30pm Mon-Sat; Ⓜ Orange, Silver, Blue Lines to Capitol South) **FREE** The world's largest library – with 164 million books, manuscripts, maps, photos, films and other items – awes in both scope and design. The centerpiece is the 1897 Jefferson Building. Gawk at the Great Hall, done up in stained glass, marble and mosaics of mythical characters, then seek out the Gutenberg Bible (c 1455), Thomas Jefferson's round library and the reading room viewing area. Free tours of the building take place between 10:30am and 3:30pm on the half-hour.

Supreme Court LANDMARK
(☎ 202-479-3030; www.supremecourt.gov; 1 1st St NE; ⊗ 9am-4:30pm Mon-Fri; Ⓜ Orange, Silver, Blue Lines to Capitol South) **FREE** The highest court in the USA sits in a pseudo-Greek temple protected by 13,000lb bronze doors. Arrive early to watch arguments (periodic Monday through Wednesday October to April). You can visit the permanent exhibits and the building's five-story, marble-and-bronze, spiral staircase year-round. On days when court is not in session you also can hear lectures (every hour on the half-hour) in the courtroom. When departing, be sure to exit via the doors that lead to the regal front steps.

National Postal Museum MUSEUM
(☎ 202-633-5555; www.postalmuseum.si.edu; 2 Massachusetts Ave NE; ⊗ 10am-5:30pm; ♿; Ⓜ Red Line to Union Station) **FREE** The Smithsonian-run Postal Museum is way cooler than you might think. Level 1 has exhibits on postal history from the Pony Express to modern times, where you'll see antique mail planes and touching old letters from soldiers and pioneers. Level 2 holds the world's largest stamp collection. Join the stamp geeks pulling out drawers and snapping photos of the world's rarest stamps (the Ben Franklin Z Grill!), or start your own collection, choosing from among thousands of free international stamps (Guyana, Congo, Cambodia...).

Folger Shakespeare Library LIBRARY
(☎ 202-544-4600; www.folger.edu; 201 E Capitol St SE; ⊗ 10am-5pm Mon-Sat, noon-5pm Sun; Ⓜ Orange, Silver, Blue Lines to Capitol South) **FREE** Bard-o-philes will be all aflutter here, as the library holds the largest collection of old Billy's works in the world. Stroll through the Great Hall to see Elizabethan artifacts, paintings, etchings and manuscripts. The highlight is a rare First Folio that you can leaf through digitally. Pop into the evocative on-site **theater** (www.folger.edu/theatre; tickets from $30), a replica of the Elizabethan Globe Theatre; return in the evening to catch a show.

Bureau of Engraving & Printing LANDMARK
(☎ 202-874-2330; www.moneyfactory.gov; cnr 14th & C Sts SW; ⊗ 9-10:45am, 12:30-3:45pm & 5-6pm Mon-Fri Mar-Aug, reduced hours Sep-Feb; ☐ Circulator, Ⓜ Orange, Silver, Blue Lines to Smithsonian) **FREE** Cha-ching! The nation's paper currency is designed and printed here. Guides lead 40-minute tours during which you peer down onto the work floor where millions of dollars roll off the presses and get cut (by guillotine!). It's actually a pretty dry jaunt; don't expect exciting visuals or snappy dialogue. In peak season (March to August), timed entry tickets are required. Get in line early at the **ticket kiosk** (Raoul Wallenberg Pl, aka 15th St; ⊗ 8am-whenever tickets run out; Ⓜ Orange, Silver, Blue Lines to Smithsonian). It opens at 8am. Tickets are often gone by 10am.

◉ **White House & Foggy Bottom**

The president lives at the center of the 'hood. The State Department, World Bank and other institutions hover nearby in Foggy Bottom. It's mostly a business district by day, and not terribly active by night, with the exception of the Kennedy Center for performing arts.

★ **White House** LANDMARK
(☎ 202-456-7041; www.whitehouse.gov; 1600 Pennsylvania Ave NW; ⊗ tours 7:30-11:30am Tue-Thu, to 1:30pm Fri & Sat; Ⓜ Orange, Silver, Blue Lines to Federal Triangle or McPherson Sq) **FREE** The 'President's House' was built between 1792 and 1800. If you're lucky enough to get inside on a public tour, you'll see several rooms in the main residence, each rich in presidential lore. Tours must be arranged in advance. Americans must apply via one

of their state's members of Congress, and non-Americans must apply through their country's embassy in DC. Applications are taken from 21 days to three months in advance; the earlier you request during this time frame the better.

White House Visitor Center MUSEUM
(☎ 202-208-1631; www.nps.gov/whho; 1450 Pennsylvania Ave NW; ⊙ 7:30am-4pm; Ⓜ Orange, Silver, Blue Lines to Federal Triangle) FREE Getting inside the White House can be tough, so here is your back-up plan. Browse artifacts such as Roosevelt's desk for his fireside chats and Lincoln's cabinet chair. Multimedia exhibits give a 360-degree view into the White House's rooms. It's obviously not the same as seeing the real deal first-hand, but the center does do its job very well, giving good history sprinkled with great anecdotes on presidential spouses, kids, pets and dinner preferences.

Textile Museum MUSEUM
(☎ 202-994-5200; www.museum.gwu.edu; 701 21st St NW; suggested donation $8; ⊙ 11am-5pm Mon & Fri, 11am-7pm Wed & Thu, 10am-5pm Sat, 1-5pm Sun; Ⓜ Orange, Silver, Blue Lines to Foggy Bottom-GWU) This gem is the country's only textile museum. Galleries spread over two floors hold exquisite fabrics and carpets. Exhibits revolve around a theme - say Asian textiles depicting dragons or Kuba cloth from the Democratic Republic of Congo - and rotate a few times a year. Bonus: the museum shares space with George Washington University's Washingtonia trove of historic maps, drawings and ephemera.

Renwick Gallery MUSEUM
(☎ 202-633-7970; http://renwick.americanart. si.edu; 1661 Pennsylvania Ave NW; ⊙ 10am-5:30pm; Ⓜ Orange, Silver, Blue Lines to Farragut West) FREE Part of the Smithsonian diaspora, the Renwick Gallery is set in a stately 1859 mansion and exhibits a playful collection of contemporary American crafts and art pieces.

◉ Downtown & Penn Quarter

Penn Quarter forms around Pennsylvania Ave as it runs between the White House and the Capitol. Downtown extends west beyond it. Major sights include the National Archives, Reynolds Center for American Art & Portraiture and Ford's Theatre. It's also DC's theater district and home to the basketball/hockey sports arena.

★**National Archives** LANDMARK
(☎ 866-272-6272; www.archives.gov/museum; 700 Pennsylvania Ave NW; ⊙ 10am-5:30pm; Ⓜ Green, Yellow Lines to Archives) FREE It's hard not to feel a little in awe of the big three documents in the National Archives: the Declaration of Independence, the Constitution and the Bill of Rights, plus one of four copies of the Magna Carta. Taken together, it becomes clear just how radical the American experiment was for its time. The Public Vaults, a bare scratching of archival bric-a-brac, make a flashy rejoinder to the main exhibit.

Newseum MUSEUM
(☎ 202-292-6100; www.newseum.org; 555 Pennsylvania Ave NW; adult/child $25/15; ⊙ 9am-5pm; ♿; Ⓜ Green, Yellow Lines to Archives) This six-story, highly interactive news museum is worth the admission price. You can delve into the major events of recent years (the fall of the Berlin Wall, September 11, Hurricane Katrina), and spend hours watching moving film footage and perusing Pulitzer Prize-winning photographs. The concourse level displays FBI artifacts from prominent news stories, such as the Unabomber's cabin and gangster Whitey Bulger's fishing hat.

Ford's Theatre Center for Education and Leadership MUSEUM
(☎ 202-347-4833; www.fords.org; 514 10th St NW; ⊙ 9am-5pm; Ⓜ Red, Orange, Silver, Blue Lines to Metro Center) FREE More exhibits for Lincolnphiles. Across the street from the famous theater where Lincoln was shot, you're funneled through the **Petersen House** (www.nps.gov/foth), where he died, and work your way down from the 4th floor of this museum, which showcases permanent displays examining how Lincoln's legacy lives on in current politics and pop culture. The 2nd floor takes a look at leaders inspired by Lincoln. Visitors use the same ticket they used to tour Ford's Theatre and Petersen House.

★**Reynolds Center for American Art & Portraiture** MUSEUM
(☎ 202-633-1000; www.americanart.si.edu; cnr 8th & F Sts NW; ⊙ 11:30am-7pm; Ⓜ Red, Yellow, Green Lines to Gallery Pl-Chinatown) FREE If you only visit one art museum in DC, make it the Reynolds Center, which combines the National Portrait Gallery and the American Art Museum. There is simply no better collection of American art in the world than at these two Smithsonian museums. Famed works by Edward Hopper, Georgia O'Keeffe,

Andy Warhol, Winslow Homer and loads more celebrated artists fill the galleries.

International Spy Museum MUSEUM
(☑ 202-393-7798; www.spymuseum.org; 800 F St NW; adult/child $22/15; ☺ 9am-7pm mid-Apr–mid-Aug, 10am-6pm rest of year; ⚑; Ⓜ Red, Yellow, Green Lines to Gallery Pl-Chinatown) One of DC's most popular museums, it's flashy, over the top and probably guilty of overtly glamming up a life of intelligence-gathering. But who cares? You basically want to see Q's lab, and that's what the Spy Museum feels like. Check out James Bond's tricked-out Aston Martin, the KGB's lipstick-concealed pistol and more. Kids go crazy for this spot, but be warned: lines form long and early. Ease the wait somewhat by reserving online.

☉ Logan Circle, U Street & Columbia Heights

These neighborhoods have changed more in recent years than almost anywhere else in DC. The U St Corridor – DC's richest nightlife zone – has quite a history. It was once the 'Black Broadway' where Duke Ellington and Ella Fitzgerald hit their notes in the 1920s to 1950s. It was the smoldering epicenter of the 1968 race riots. There was a troubled descent, and then a vibrant rebirth in recent years. A stroll here is a must and rewards with mural-splashed alleys, red-hot music clubs and antique-crammed shops.

U St becomes part of the larger Shaw district, which is DC's current 'it' 'hood. But it's not annoyingly trendy. Instead, the breweries, bars and cafes that seem to pop up weekly are local places, where neighbors come to sip among neighbors (and students among students, as Howard University is here). Logan Circle is next door and also booming. Walk down 14th St NW and hot-chef wine bars, beer bars, tapas bars and oyster bars flash by. The side streets hold stately old manors that give the area its class.

To the north, Columbia Heights has a reputation as an enclave for Latino immigrants and hipsters. There are no real sights, but the cheap ethnic food and unassuming punk dive bars can occupy many an evening.

Northeast DC is a vast stretch of leafy residential blocks holding several far-flung sights (and breweries). Nature lovers have a couple of groovy, free landscapes to explore, as long as you have a car or don't mind lengthy public-transportation trips.

African American Civil War Memorial MONUMENT
(www.afroamcivilwar.org; cnr U St & Vermont Ave NW; Ⓜ Green, Yellow Lines to U St) Standing at the center of a granite plaza, this bronze memorial depicting rifle-bearing troops is DC's first major art piece by black sculptor Ed Hamilton. The statue is surrounded on three sides by the Wall of Honor, listing the names of 209,145 black troops who fought in the Union Army, as well as the 7000 white soldiers who served alongside them. You can use the directory to locate individual names within each of the regiments.

To get there, depart the Metro station via the 10th St exit (follow the 'memorial' signs as you leave the train).

Mexican Cultural Institute NOTABLE BUILDING
(☑ 202-728-1628; www.instituteofmexicodc.org; 2829 16th St NW; ☺ 10am-6pm Mon-Fri, noon-4pm Sat; Ⓜ Green, Yellow Lines to Columbia Heights) FREE The Mexican Cultural Institute looks locked up and imposing, but don't be deterred. The gilded beaux-arts mansion is open to the public and hosts excellent art and cultural exhibitions related to Mexico. You might see a show on Diego Rivera's art or Mayan religious artifacts or Octavio Paz's writings. Ring the doorbell for entry.

☉ Dupont Circle & Kalorama

Dupont offers flashy new restaurants, hip bars, cafe society and cool bookstores. It's also the heart of the city's LGBT community. It used to be where turn-of-the-century millionaires lived. Today those mansions hold DC's greatest concentration of embassies. Kalorama sits in the northwest corner and ups the regal reserve.

★ Embassy Row ARCHITECTURE
(www.embassy.org; Massachusetts Ave NW, btwn Observatory & Dupont Circles NW; Ⓜ Red Line to Dupont Circle) Want to take a trip around the world? Stroll northwest along Massachusetts Ave from Dupont Circle (the actual traffic circle) and you pass more than 40 embassies housed in mansions that range from elegant to imposing to discreet. Tunisia, Chile, Turkmenistan, Togo, Haiti – flags flutter above heavy doors and mark the nations inside, while dark-windowed sedans ease out of driveways ferrying diplomats to and fro. The district has another 130 embassies sprinkled throughout, but this is the main vein.

National Geographic Museum   MUSEUM

(☑ 202-857-7700; www.nationalgeographic.org/dc; 1145 17th St NW; adult/child $15/10; ⊙ 10am-6pm; M Red Line to Farragut North) The museum at National Geographic Society headquarters can't compete with the Smithsonian's more extensive offerings, but it can be worth a stop, depending on what's showing. Exhibits are drawn from the society's well-documented expeditions to the far corners of the Earth, and they change periodically.

Phillips Collection   MUSEUM

(☑ 202-387-2151; www.phillipscollection.org; 1600 21st St NW; Tue-Fri free, Sat & Sun $10, ticketed exhibitions per day $12; ⊙ 10am-5pm Tue, Wed, Fri & Sat, to 8:30pm Thu, noon-7pm Sun; M Red Line to Dupont Circle) The first modern-art museum in the country (opened in 1921) houses a small but exquisite collection of European and American works. Renoir's *Luncheon of the Boating Party* is a highlight, along with pieces by Gauguin, Van Gogh, Matisse, Picasso and many other greats. The intimate rooms, set in a restored mansion, put you unusually close to the artworks. The permanent collection is free on weekdays. Download the free app or dial ☑ 202-595-1839 for audio tours through the works.

⊙ Adams Morgan

Adams Morgan has long been Washington's fun, nightlife-driven neighborhood. It's also a global village of sorts. The result today is a raucous mash-up centered on 18th St NW. Vintage boutiques, record shops and ethnic eats poke up between thumping bars and a growing number of stylish spots for gastronomes.

District of Columbia
Arts Center   ARTS CENTER

(DCAC; ☑ 202-462-7833; www.dcartscenter.org; 2438 18th St NW; ⊙ 2-7pm Wed-Sun; M Red Line to Woodley Park-Zoo/Adams Morgan) FREE The grassroots DCAC offers emerging artists a space to showcase their work. The 800-sq-ft gallery features rotating visual-arts exhibits, while plays, improv, avant-garde musicals and other theatrical productions take place in the 50-seat theater. The gallery is free and worth popping into to see what's showing.

⊙ Georgetown

Georgetown is DC's most aristocratic neighborhood, home to elite university students, ivory-tower academics and diplomats. Chi

chi brand-name shops, dark-wood pubs and upscale restaurants line the streets. Lovely parks and gardens color the edges.

Dumbarton Oaks   GARDENS, MUSEUM

(☑ 202-339-6401; www.doaks.org; 1703 32nd St NW; museum free, gardens adult/child $10/5; ⊙ museum 11:30am-5:30pm Tue-Sun, gardens 2-6pm; ⊒ Circulator) The mansion's 10 acres of enchanting formal gardens are straight out of a storybook. In springtime, the blooms – including heaps of cherry blossoms – are stunning. The mansion itself is worth a walk-through to see exquisite Byzantine and pre-Columbian art (including El Greco's *The Visitation*) and the fascinating library of rare books.

Georgetown Waterfront Park   PARK

(www.georgetownwaterfrontpark.org; Water St NW, btwn 30th St & Key Bridge; 🚹; ⊒ Circulator) The park is a favorite with couples on first dates, families on an evening stroll and power players showing off their big yachts. Benches dot the way, where you can sit and watch the rowing teams out on the Potomac River. Alfresco restaurants cluster near the harbor at 31st St NW. They ring a terraced plaza filled with fountains (which become an ice rink in winter). The docks are also here for sightseeing boats that ply the Potomac to Alexandria, VA.

Georgetown University   UNIVERSITY

(☑ 202-687-0100; www.georgetown.edu; cnr 37th & O Sts NW; ⊒ Circulator) Georgetown is one of the nation's top universities, with a student body that's equally hard-working and hard-partying. Founded in 1789, it was America's first Roman Catholic university. Notable Hoya (derived from the Latin *hoya saxa*, 'what rocks') alumni include Bill Clinton, as well as many international royals and heads of state. Near the campus' east gate, medieval-looking **Healy Hall** impresses with its tall, Hogwarts-esque clock tower. Pretty **Dalghren Chapel** and its quiet courtyard hide behind it.

Exorcist Stairs   FILM LOCATION

(3600 Prospect St NW; ⊒ Circulator) The steep set of stairs dropping down to M St is a popular track for joggers, but more famously it's the spot where demonically possessed Father Karras tumbles to his death in horror-film classic *The Exorcist* (1973). Come on foggy nights, when the stone steps really are creepy as hell.

Tudor Place
MUSEUM

(☎202-965-0400; www.tudorplace.org; 1644 31st St NW; 1hr house tour adult/child $10/3, self-guided garden tour $3; ☉10am-4pm Tue-Sat, from noon Sun, closed Jan; ☒Circulator) This 1816 neoclassical mansion was owned by Thomas Peter and Martha Custis Peter, the step-granddaughter of Martha Washington. Today the mansion functions as a small museum, featuring furnishings and artwork from Mount Vernon, which give good insight into American decorative arts. The grand, 5-acre gardens bloom with roses, lilies, poplar trees and palms.

◉ Upper Northwest DC

★Washington National Cathedral
CHURCH

(☎202-537-6200; https://cathedral.org; 3101 Wisconsin Ave NW; adult/child $12/8, Sun free; ☉10am-5:30pm Mon-Fri, 10am-4pm Sat, 8am-4pm Sun; Ⓜ Red Line to Tenleytown-AU then southbound bus 30, 31, 33 or 37) This Gothic cathedral, as dramatic as its European counterparts, blends both the spiritual and the profane in its architectural treasures. The stained-glass windows are stunning (check out the 'Space Window' with an embedded lunar rock); you'll need binoculars to spy the Darth Vader gargoyle on the exterior. Specialized tours delve deeper into the esoteric; call or go online for the schedule.

National Zoo
ZOO

(☎202-633-4888; www.nationalzoo.si.edu; 3001 Connecticut Ave NW; ☉9am-6pm mid-Mar–Sep, to 4pm Oct–mid-Mar, grounds 8am-7pm mid-Mar–Sep, to 5pm Oct–mid-Mar; Ⓜ Red Line to Cleveland Park or Woodley Park-Zoo/Adams Morgan) FREE Home to more than 1800 individual animals (300-plus different species) in natural habitats, the National Zoo is famed for its giant pandas Mei Xiang and Tian Tian. Other highlights include the African lion pride, Asian elephants, and dangling orangutans swinging 50ft overhead from steel cables and interconnected towers.

🏃 Activities

Hiking & Cycling

Capital Bikeshare
CYCLING

(☎877-430-2453; www.capitalbikeshare.com; per 1/3 days $8/17) It has a network of 3700-plus bicycles scattered at 440-odd stations around the region. Kiosks issue passes (one day or three days) on the spot. Insert a credit card, get your ride code, then unlock a bike. The first 30 minutes are free; after that, rates rise fast if you don't dock the bike.

Capital Crescent Trail
CYCLING

(www.cctrail.org; Water St; ☒Circulator) Stretching between Georgetown and Bethesda, MD, the constantly evolving Capital Crescent Trail is a fabulous (and very popular) jogging and biking route. Built on an abandoned railroad bed, the 11-mile trail is paved and is a great leisurely day trip. It has beautiful lookouts over the Potomac River, and winds through woodsy areas and upscale neighborhoods.

Boating

Tidal Basin Boathouse
BOATING

(☎202-479-2426; www.boatingindc.com/boathouses/tidal-basin; 1501 Maine Ave SW; 2-/4-person boat rental $18/30; ☉10am-6pm mid-Mar–mid-Oct; ☒Circulator, Ⓜ Orange, Silver, Blue Lines to Smithsonian) It rents paddleboats to take out on the Tidal Basin. Make sure you bring a camera. There are great views, of the Jefferson Memorial in particular, from the water.

Key Bridge Boathouse
KAYAKING

(☎202-337-9642; www.boatingindc.com/boathouses/key-bridge-boathouse; 3500 Water St NW; ☉hours vary mid-Apr–Oct; ☒Circulator) Located beneath the Key Bridge, the boathouse rents canoes, kayaks and stand-up paddleboards (prices start at $16 per hour). In summer, it also offers guided, 90-minute kayak trips ($45 per person) that glide past the Lincoln Memorial as the sun sets. If you have a bike, the boathouse is a mere few steps from the Capital Crescent Trail.

👉 Tours

DC by Foot
WALKING

(☎202-370-1830; www.freetoursbyfoot.com/washington-dc-tours) Guides for this pay-what-you-want walking tour offer engaging stories and historical details on different jaunts covering the National Mall, Lincoln's assassination, Dupont Circle's ghosts and many more. Most takers pay around $10 per person. Reserve in advance to guarantee a spot.

DC Metro Food Tours
WALKING

(☎202-851-2268; www.dcmetrofoodtours.com; per person $30-65) These walkabouts explore the culinary riches of various neighborhoods, stopping for multiple bites along the way. Offerings include Eastern Market, U St, Little Ethiopia, Georgetown and Alexandria, VA. Most last from 1½ to 3½ hours. Departure points vary.

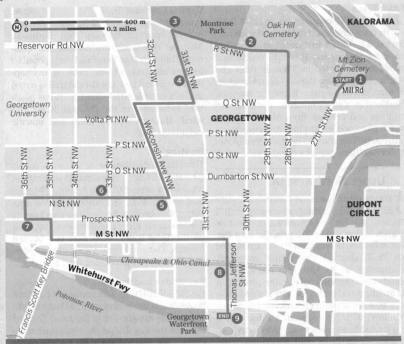

🏃 City Walk
Genteel Georgetown

START MT ZION CEMETERY
END GEORGETOWN WATERFRONT PARK
LENGTH 3 MILES; THREE HOURS

African American ❶**Mt Zion Cemetery**, near the intersection of 27th and Q Sts, dates from the early 1800s. A nearby church was a stop on the Underground Railroad, and it hid escaping slaves in a vault in the cemetery.

The entrance to ❷**Oak Hill Cemetery** (9am-4:30pm Mon-Fri, 11am-4pm Sat, 1-4pm Sun) is a few blocks away at 30th and R Sts NW. Stroll the obelisk-studded grounds and look for gravesites of prominent Washingtonians such as Edwin Stanton (Lincoln's war secretary). Up the road, ❸**Dumbarton Oaks** (p282) offers exquisite Byzantine art inside and sprawling, fountain-dotted gardens outside. The blooms in springtime are stunning.

George Washington's step-granddaughter Martha Custis Peter owned ❹**Tudor Place** (p283), the neoclassical mansion at 1644 31st St NW. It has some of George's furnishings from Mount Vernon on show and pretty landscaped grounds.

Head over to Wisconsin Ave NW, and stop in at ❺**Martin's Tavern** (www.martinstavern.com), where John F Kennedy proposed to Jackie. Walk west along N St and you'll pass several Federal-style townhouses in the 3300 block. JFK and Jackie lived at ❻**3307 N St** between 1958 and 1961, when they left for the White House. At the corner of 36th NW and Prospect Sts, stare down the ❼**Exorcist Stairs** (p282). This is the spot where demonically possessed Father Karras tumbles to his death in the 1973 horror film *The Exorcist*. Joggers use the steep steps by day, but at night they're legitimately creepy as hell.

Go down to M St NW, with its boutiques and high-end stores. At Thomas Jefferson St turn right and sniff your way to ❽**Baked & Wired** (p292) to replenish with a monster cupcake and cappuccino. From there you can stroll down to ❾**Georgetown Waterfront Park** (p282) to watch the boats and other action along the Potomac River.

DC Brew Tours
BUS

(☎ 202-759-8687; www.dcbrewtours.com; 801 F ST NW; tours $65-90; Ⓜ Red, Yellow, Green Lines to Gallery Pl-Chinatown) Visit three to four breweries by van. Routes vary but could include DC Brau, Bardo, Capital City and Port City, among others. Five-hour jaunts feature tastings of 15-plus beers and a beer-focused meal. The 3½-hour Sips and Sights tour forgoes the meal and adds stops at the Lincoln Memorial, Pentagon and more. Departure is from downtown by the Reynolds Center.

Bike & Roll – L'Enfant Plaza
CYCLING

(☎ 202-842-2453; www.bikeandrolldc.com; 955 L'Enfant Plaza SW; tours adult/child $45/35; ⊙ mid-Mar–early Dec; Ⓜ Orange, Silver, Blue, Yellow, Green Lines to L'Enfant Plaza) This branch of the bike-rental company (from $16 per two hours) is the one closest to the Mall. In addition to bike rental, it also provides tours. Three-hour jaunts wheel by the main sights of Capitol Hill and the National Mall.

Old Town Trolley Tours
BUS

(☎ 202-832-9800; www.trolleytours.com; 1001 E St NW; adult/child $40/30; Ⓜ Red, Orange, Silver, Blue Lines to Metro Center) This open-sided bus offers hop-on, hop-off exploring of some 25 major sights around the Mall, Arlington and downtown. The company also offers a 'monuments by moonlight' tour and the DC Ducks tour, via an amphibious vehicle that plunges into the Potomac. Buy tickets at the Washington Welcome Center (1001 E St NW), at Union Station or online.

★🎊 Festivals & Events

Independence Day
CULTURAL

(⊙ Jul 4) On July 4, huge crowds gather on the Mall to watch marching bands parade and hear the Declaration of Independence read from the National Archives steps. Later, the National Symphony Orchestra plays a concert on the Capitol's steps, followed by mega-fireworks.

National Cherry Blossom Festival
CULTURAL

(www.nationalcherryblossomfestival.org; ⊙ late Mar–mid-Apr) The star of DC's annual calendar celebrates spring's arrival with boat rides in the Tidal Basin, evening walks by lantern light, cultural fairs and a parade. The three-week event, from late March to mid-April, also commemorates Japan's gift of 3000 cherry trees in 1912. It's DC at its prettiest.

Smithsonian Folklife Festival
CULTURAL

(www.festival.si.edu; ⊙ late Jun–early Jul; 👪; 🚇 Circulator, Ⓜ Orange, Silver, Blue, Green, Yellow Lines to L'Enfant Plaza) This fun family event, held over 10 days in late June and early July, celebrates international and US cultures. The fest features folk music, dance, crafts, storytelling and ethnic fare, and it highlights a diverse mix of countries and regions. It takes place on the Mall's east end.

🛏 Sleeping

🛏 Capitol Hill

William Penn House
HOSTEL $

(☎ 202-543-5560; www.williampennhouse.org; 515 E Capitol St SE; dm $45-55; ❄❋@; Ⓜ Orange, Silver, Blue Lines to Capitol South or Eastern Market) This friendly Quaker-run guesthouse with garden offers clean, well-maintained dorms, though it could use more bathrooms. There are 30 beds in total, including a four-bed room for families ($150 per night). The facility doesn't require religious observance, but there is a religious theme throughout, and it prefers guests be active in progressive causes.

Kimpton George Hotel
BOUTIQUE HOTEL $$

(☎ 202-347-4200; www.hotelgeorge.com; 15 E St NW; r $269-389; P❄❋@🛜🐾; Ⓜ Red Line to Union Station) DC's first chic boutique hotel is still one of its best. Chrome-and-glass furniture and modern art frame the bold interior. Rooms exude a cool, creamy-white Zen. The pop-art presidential accents (paintings of American currency, artfully rearranged and diced up) are a little overdone, but that's a minor complaint about what is otherwise the hippest lodging on the Hill.

🛏 White House & Foggy Bottom

Club Quarters
HOTEL $$

(☎ 202-463-6400; www.clubquarters.com/washington-dc; 839 17th St NW; r $179-259; P❄❋@🛜; Ⓜ Orange, Silver, Blue Lines to Farragut West) Club Quarters is a no-muss, no-fuss kind of place often used by business travelers on the go. Room are small and without views, and lack charm or quirk, but the bed is restful, the desk workable, the wi-fi fast enough and the coffee maker well stocked. Oh, and the prices are reasonable in an area where they're usually sky-high.

WASHINGTON, DC & THE CAPITAL REGION WASHINGTON, DC

★ **Hotel Lombardy** HISTORIC HOTEL **$$**
([☎] 202-828-2600; www.hotellombardy.com; 2019 Pennsylvania Ave NW; r $180-330; [P][⊖][❋][@][奈]; [M] Orange, Silver, Blue Lines to Foggy Bottom-GWU) Done up in Venetian decor (shuttered doors, warm gold walls) and beloved by World Bank and State Department types, this European boutique hotel has multilingual staff and an international vibe – you hear French and Spanish as often as English in its halls. The attitude carries into rooms decorated with original artwork, and Chinese and European antiques.

★ **Hay-Adams Hotel** HERITAGE HOTEL **$$$**
([☎] 202-638-6600; www.hayadams.com; 800 16th St NW; r from $400; [P][❋][@][奈][❋]; [M] Orange, Silver, Blue Lines to McPherson Sq) One of the city's great heritage hotels, the Hay is a beautiful old building where 'nothing is overlooked but the White House.' The property has a palazzo-style lobby and probably the best rooms of the old-school luxury genre, all puffy mattresses like clouds shaded by four-poster canopies and gold-braid tassels.

St Regis Washington HOTEL **$$$**
([☎] 202-638-2626; www.stregiswashingtondc.com; 923 16th St NW; r from $500; [P][❋][@][奈][❋]; [M] Orange, Silver, Blue Lines to McPherson Sq) The neo-renaissance St Regis is one of the grandest hotels in the city. What else can you say about a building designed to resemble nothing less than an Italian palace? Rooms are as gilded as you'd expect, with hand-carved armoires, double-basin marble sinks and TVs embedded in the bathroom mirrors. Wifi costs $7 per day.

🛏 Downtown & Penn Quarter

Hostelling International – Washington DC HOSTEL **$**
([☎] 202-737-2333; www.hiwashingtondc.org; 1009 11th St NW; dm $33-55, r $110-150; [⊖][❋][@][奈]; [M] Red, Orange, Silver, Blue Lines to Metro Center) Top of the budget picks, this large, friendly hostel attracts a laid-back international crowd and has loads of amenities: lounge rooms, a pool table, a 60in TV for movie nights, free tours, free continental breakfast and free wi-fi.

Morrison-Clark Inn HISTORIC HOTEL **$$**
([☎] 202-898-1200; www.morrisonclark.com; 1011 L St NW; r $180-310; [P][⊖][❋][@][奈]; [M] Green, Yellow Lines to Mt Vernon Sq/7th St-Convention Center) Listed on the Register of Historic Places and helmed by a doting staff, the elegant, 114-room Morrison-Clark comprises two 1864 Victorian residences filled with fine antiques, tear-drop chandeliers and gilded mirrors, and a newer wing with Asian-influenced decor set in the repurposed Chinese church next door. It may sound odd, but the overall effect is lovely and dignified.

🛏 Logan Circle, U Street & Columbia Heights

★ **Chester Arthur House** B&B **$$**
([☎] 877-893-3233; www.chesterarthurhouse.com; 23 Logan Circle NW; r $180-215; [⊖][❋][奈]; [M] Green, Yellow Lines to U St) Snooze in one of four rooms in this beautiful Logan Circle row house, located a stumble from the restaurant boom along P and 14th Sts. The 1883 abode is stuffed with crystal chandeliers, antique oil paintings, oriental rugs and a mahogany paneled staircase, plus ephemera from the hosts' global expeditions.

Kimpton Mason & Rook Hotel HOTEL **$$**
([☎] 202-742-3100; www.masonandrookhotel.com; 1430 Rhode Island Ave NW; r $189-399; [P][⊖][❋][@][奈][❋][❋]; [M] Orange, Silver, Blue Lines to McPherson Sq) 🐾 Snuggled into a tree-lined neighborhood near trendy 14th St, Mason & Rook feels like your urbane friend's chic apartment. The lobby resembles a handsome living room, with comfy seating, bookshelves and eclectic art. The large guest rooms invite lingering with plush fabrics, rich dark wood and leather decor, and marble bathrooms with walk-in rain showers. The free bicycles are handy for cruising around town.

🛏 Dupont Circle & Kalorama

Embassy Circle Guest House B&B **$$**
([☎] 202-232-7744; www.dcinns.com; 2224 R St NW; r $200-310; [⊖][❋][奈]; [M] Red Line to Dupont Circle) Embassies surround this 1902 French country–style home, which sits a few blocks from Dupont's nightlife hubbub. The 11 big-windowed rooms are decked out with Persian carpets and original art on the walls; they don't have TVs, though they do each have wi-fi. Staff feed you well throughout the day, with a hot organic breakfast, afternoon cookies, and an evening wine and beer soirée.

★ **Tabard Inn** BOUTIQUE HOTEL **$$**
([☎] 202-785-1277; www.tabardinn.com; 1739 N St NW; r $200-270, without bathroom $115-170; [⊖][❋][@][奈]; [M] Red Line to Dupont Circle) Named

for the inn in *The Canterbury Tales,* the Tabard spreads through a trio of Victorian-era row houses. The 40 rooms are hard to generalize: all come with vintage quirks such as iron bed frames and wing-backed chairs, though little accents distinguish them – a Matisse-like painted headboard here, Amish-looking quilts there. There are no TVs, and wi-fi can be dodgy, but the of-yore atmospherics prevail.

Adams Morgan

Adam's Inn   B&B $

(☏202-745-3600; www.adamsinn.com; 1746 Lanier Pl NW; r $109-204, without bathroom $89-110; Ⓟ☺✳@🛜; ⓜRed Line to Woodley Park-Zoo/Adams Morgan) Tucked on a shady residential street, this 27-room inn is known for its personalized service, fluffy linens and handy location just a few blocks from 18th St's global smorgasbord. Inviting, homey rooms sprawl through two adjacent townhouses and a carriage house. The common areas have a nice garden patio, and there's a general sense of sherry-scented chintz.

HighRoad Hostel   HOSTEL $

(☏202-735-3622; www.highroadhostels.com; 1804 Belmont Rd NW; dm $42-60; ✳🛜; ⓜRed Line to Woodley Park-Zoo/Adams Morgan) HighRoad's Victorian row house exterior belies its brand spankin' new interior. The mod dorms come in various configurations: from four to 14 beds – some co-ed, others gender-specific. All have stark white walls, gray metal bunks and black lockers. There's a fancy (though small) community kitchen and common room with a fireplace and a jumbo, Netflix-wired TV. Nighthawks will gorge on nearby 18th St's bounty.

Georgetown

Graham Georgetown   BOUTIQUE HOTEL $$

(☏202-337-0900; www.thegrahamgeorgetown.com; 1075 Thomas Jefferson St NW; r $300-375; Ⓟ☺✳@🛜; 🚌Circulator) Set smack in the heart of Georgetown, the Graham occupies the intersection between stately tradition and modernist hip. Good-sized rooms have tasteful silver, cream and black furnishings with pops of ruby and geometric accents. Even the most basic rooms have linens by Liddell Ireland and L'Occitane bath amenities, which means you'll be as fresh, clean and beautiful as the surrounding Georgetown glitterati.

✗ Eating

A homegrown foodie revolution has transformed the once buttoned-up DC dining scene. Driving it is the bounty of farms at the city's doorstep, along with the booming local economy and influx of worldly younger residents. Small, independent, local-chef-helmed spots now lead the way. And they're doing such a fine job that Michelin deemed the city worthy of its stars.

✗ Capitol Hill

Capitol Hill has long been an outpost for the DC burger bar, the type of unpretentious spot where you roll up your sleeves, slather on ketchup and knock back a side of beer with your patty. Hip, upscale eateries have colonized the neighborhood, especially along Pennsylvania Ave, Barracks Row (ie 8th St SE, near the Marine Barracks) and around the Navy Yard (near the baseball park). H St NE, east of Union Station, has seen lots of action. The formerly beat-up area continues to transform with scads of fun, offbeat restaurants and bars stretching from 4th to 14th Sts NE.

Toki Underground   ASIAN $

(☏202-388-3086; www.tokiunderground.com; 1234 H St NE; mains $13-15; ⏰11:30am-2:30pm & 5-10pm Mon-Thu, to midnight Fri & Sat; ⓜRed Line to Union Station then streetcar) Spicy ramen noodles and dumplings sum up wee Toki's menu. Steaming pots obscure the busy chefs, while diners slurp and sigh contentedly. The eatery takes limited reservations, so there's typically a wait. Use the opportunity to explore the surrounding bars; Toki will text when your table is ready. The restaurant isn't signposted; look for the Pug bar, and Toki is above it.

Maine Avenue Fish Market   SEAFOOD $

(1100 Maine Ave SW; mains $7-13; ⏰8am-9pm; ⓜOrange, Silver, Blue, Yellow, Green Lines to L'Enfant Plaza) The pungent, open-air Maine Avenue Fish Market is a local landmark. No-nonsense vendors sell fish, crabs, oysters and other seafood so fresh it's almost still flopping. They'll kill, strip, shell, gut, fry or broil your selection, which you can take to the waterfront benches and eat blissfully (mind the seagulls!).

Jimmy T's   DINER $

(☏202-546-3646; 501 E Capitol St SE; mains $6-10; ⏰6:30am-3pm Tue-Fri, from 8am Sat & Sun; ♿; ⓜOrange, Silver, Blue Lines to Eastern Market)

Jimmy's is a neighborhood joint of the old school, where folks come in with their dogs, cram in to read the *Post,* have a burger or a coffee or an omelet (breakfast all day, by the way) and basically be themselves. If you're hungover on Sunday and in Cap Hill, come here for a greasy cure. Cash only.

Ted's Bulletin   AMERICAN **$$**
(☎ 202-544-8337; www.tedsbulletincapitolhill. com; 505 8th St SE; mains $11-19; ⊙ 7am-10:30pm Sun-Thu, to 11:30pm Fri & Sat; ⓘ; Ⓜ Orange, Silver, Blue Lines to Eastern Market) Plop into a booth in the art-deco-meets-diner ambience, and loosen the belt. Beer biscuits and sausage gravy for breakfast, meatloaf with ketchup glaze for dinner and other hipster spins on comfort foods hit the table. You've got to admire a place that lets you substitute pop tarts for toast. Breakfast is available all day.

Ethiopic   ETHIOPIAN **$$**
(☎ 202-675-2066; www.ethiopicrestaurant.com; 401 H St NE; mains $13-19; ⊙ 5-10pm Tue-Thu, from noon Fri-Sun; ⓘ; Ⓜ Red Line to Union Station) In a city with no shortage of Ethiopian joints, Ethiopic stands above the rest. Top marks go to the various *wats* (stews) and the signature *tibs* (sauteed meat and veg), derived from tender lamb that has sat in a bath of herbs and hot spices. Vegans get lots of love here too.

★ Rose's Luxury   AMERICAN **$$$**
(☎ 202-580-8889; www.rosesluxury.com; 717 8th St SE; small plates $13-16, family-style plates $28-33; ⊙ 5-10pm Mon-Sat; Ⓜ Orange, Silver, Blue Lines to Eastern Market) Michelin-starred Rose's is one of DC's most buzzed-about eateries. Crowds fork into worldly Southern comfort food as twinkling lights glow overhead and candles flicker around the industrial, half-finished room. Rose's doesn't take reservations, but ordering your meal at the upstairs bar can save time (and the cocktails are delicious).

✕ White House & Foggy Bottom

Woodward Takeout Food   AMERICAN **$**
(☎ 202-347-5355; http://woodwardtable.com; 1426 H St NW; mains $7-11; ⊙ 7:30am-4:30pm Mon-Fri; Ⓜ Orange, Silver, Blue Lines to McPherson Sq) Woodward Takeout is the small, mostly carry-out adjunct to Woodward Table, a sharp, sit-down restaurant. Go ahead: jump in the line with all the office workers angling for the duck Reuben sandwich, housemade pastrami on sourdough rye or butternut squash flatbread. It'll move fast. Breakfast is busy too, with egg-laden sandwiches on crumbly biscuits and salted chocolate croissants flying from the kitchen.

A smattering of close-set tables provides seating. You can pre-order via the website and save some waiting time.

Founding Farmers   AMERICAN **$$**
(☎ 202-822-8783; www.wearefoundingfarmers. com; 1924 Pennsylvania Ave NW; mains $15-28; ⊙ 7am-10pm Mon, 7am-11pm Tue-Thu, 7am-midnight Fri, 9am-midnight Sat, 9am-10pm Sun; ⓘ; Ⓜ Orange, Silver, Blue Lines to Foggy Bottom-GWU or Farragut West) ⚓ A frosty decor of pickled goods in jars adorns this buzzy dining space. The look is a combination of rustic-cool and modern art that reflects the nature of the food: locally sourced, New American fare. Buttermilk fried chicken and waffles, and butternut squash mascarpone ravioli, are a few of the favorites that hit the wood tables. The restaurant is located in the IMF building.

✕ Downtown & Penn Quarter

★ A Baked Joint   CAFE **$**
(☎ 202-408-6985; www.abakedjoint.com; 440 K St NW; mains $5-11; ⊙ 7am-8pm Mon-Thu, 7am-9pm Fri, 8am-8pm Sat & Sun; Ⓜ Red, Yellow, Green Lines to Gallery Pl-Chinatown) Order at the counter then take your luscious, heaped-on-house-made-bread sandwich – perhaps the roasted sweet potato and goat cheese on focaccia, or the Nutella and banana on whole-wheat sourdough – to a bench or table in the big,

open room. Natural light streams in the floor-to-ceiling windows. Not hungry? It's also a great place for a well-made latte.

Daikaya
JAPANESE $

(☎202-589-1600; www.daikaya.com; 705 6th St NW; mains $12-14; ☺11am-10pm Sun & Mon, to 10:30pm Tue & Wed, to 11pm Thu-Sat; Ⓜ Red, Yellow, Green Lines to Gallery Pl-Chinatown) Daikaya offers two options. Downstairs it's a casual ramen-noodle shop, where locals swarm in and slurp with friends in the slick wooden booths. Upstairs it's a sake-pouring Japanese *izakaya* (tavern), with rice-bowl lunches and fishy small plates for dinner. Note the upstairs closes between lunch and dinner (ie between 2pm and 5pm).

Rasika
INDIAN $$

(☎202-637-1222; www.rasikarestaurant.com; 633 D St NW; mains $14-28; ☺11:30am-2:30pm Mon-Fri, 5:30-10:30pm Mon-Thu, 5-11pm Fri & Sat; 🖋; Ⓜ Green, Yellow Lines to Archives) Rasika is as cutting-edge as Indian food gets. The room resembles a Jaipur palace decorated by a flock of modernist art-gallery curators. Top marks go to the *murgh mussalam,* a plate of juicy tandoori chicken with cashews and quail eggs; and to the deceptively simple *dal* (lentils), which have just the right kiss of sharp fenugreek. Vegetarians will feel a lot of love here.

Matchbox Pizza
PIZZA $$

(☎202-289-4441; www.matchboxrestaurants.com; 713 H St NW; 10in pizzas $13-15; ☺11am-10:30pm Mon-Thu, 11am-11:30pm Fri, 10am-11:30pm Sat, 10am-10:30pm Sun; 🖋; Ⓜ Red, Yellow, Green Lines to Gallery Pl-Chinatown) The pizza here has a devout following of gastronomes and the restaurant's warm, exposed-brick interior typically is packed. What's so good about it? Fresh ingredients, a thin, blistered crust baked by angels, and more fresh ingredients. Oh, and the beer list rocks, with Belgian ales and hopped-up craft brews flowing from the taps. Reserve ahead to avoid a wait.

Kinship
AMERICAN $$

(☎202-737-7700; http://kinshipdc.com; 1015 7th St NW; mains $16-28; ☺5:30-10pm Sat-Friday; Ⓜ Yellow, Green Lines to Mount Vernon Square 7th Street-Convention Center) Round up your friends and enjoy a convivial night at this Michelin-starred restaurant by Eric Ziebold. Pick and choose across the menu's five categories echoing the chef's passions: ingredients (surf clams, Rohan duck), history (classics), craft (using culinary techniques),

indulgence (caviar, white truffles), and 'For the Table.'

★ Dabney
AMERICAN $$$

(☎202-450-1015; www.thedabney.com; 122 Blagden Alley NW; small plates $14-22; ☺5:30-10pm Tue-Thu, 5:30-11pm Fri & Sat, 5-10pm Sun; Ⓜ Green, Yellow Line to Mount Vernon Square/7th St-Convention Center) Chef Jeremiah Langhorne studied historic cookbooks, discovering recipes that used local ingredients and lesser-explored flavors in his quest to resuscitate mid-Atlantic cuisine lost to the ages. Most of the dishes are even cooked over a wood-burning hearth. But this isn't George Washington's resto. Chef Langhorne has given it all a modern twist – enough to earn him a Michelin star.

🍴 Logan Circle, U Street & Columbia Heights

★ Ben's Chili Bowl
AMERICAN $

(☎202-667-0909; www.benschilibowl.com; 1213 U St; mains $6-10; ☺6am-2am Mon-Thu, 6am-4am Fri, 7am-4am Sat, 11am-midnight Sun; Ⓜ Green, Yellow Lines to U St) Ben's is a DC institution. The main stock in trade is half-smokes, DC's meatier, smokier version of the hot dog, usually slathered with mustard, onions and the namesake chili. For nearly 60 years presidents, rock stars and Supreme Court justices have come in to indulge in the humble diner, but despite the hype, Ben's remains a true neighborhood establishment. Cash only.

★ Compass Rose
INTERNATIONAL $$

(☎202-506-4765; www.compassrosedc.com; 1346 T St NW; small plates $10-15; ☺5pm-2am Mon-Thu, 5pm-3am Fri & Sat, 11am-2am Sun; Ⓜ Green, Yellow Lines to U St) Compass Rose feels like a secret garden, set in a discreet townhouse a whisker from 14th St's buzz. The exposed brick walls, rustic wood decor and sky-blue ceiling give it a casually romantic air. The menu is a mash-up of global comfort foods, so dinner might entail, say, a Chilean *lomito* (pork sandwich), Lebanese *kefta* (ground lamb and spices) and Georgian *khachapuri* (buttery, cheese-filled bread).

Estadio
SPANISH $$

(☎202-319-1404; www.estadio-dc.com; 1520 14th St NW; tapas $6-17; ☺5-10pm Mon-Thu, to 11pm Fri & Sat, to 9pm Sun, 11:30am-2pm Fri-Sun; Ⓜ Green, Yellow Lines to U St) Estadio buzzes with a low-lit, date-night vibe. The tapas menu (which is the focus) is as deep as an ocean trench. There are three variations of *Iberico* ham and a delicious foie gras, scrambled egg and truffle open-faced sandwich. Wash it down with some traditional *calimocho* (red wine and Coke). No reservations after 6pm, which usually means a wait at the bar.

Busboys & Poets CAFE $$

(☑ 202-387-7638; www.busboysandpoets.com; 2021 14th St NW; mains $11-21; ☺ 8am-midnight Mon-Thu, 8am-2am Fri, from 9am Sat & Sun; 🛜; Ⓜ Green, Yellow Lines to U St) Busboys & Poets is one of U St's linchpins. Locals pack the place for coffee, wi-fi and a progressive vibe (and attached bookstore) that make San Francisco feel conservative. The hearty menu spans sandwiches, pizzas and Southern fare like shrimp and grits. Tuesday night's open-mike poetry reading ($5 admission, from 9pm to 11pm) draws big crowds.

Maple ITALIAN $$

(☑ 202-588-7442; www.dc-maple.com; 3418 11th St NW; mains $16-23; ☺ 5:30-11:30pm Mon-Thu, 5pm-1am Fri, 10:30am-1am Sat, 10:30am-11pm Sun; Ⓜ Green, Yellow Lines to Columbia Heights) At snug Maple, ladies in thrifty dresses and black tights fork into rich pasta dishes next to guys clad in T-shirts and tattoo sleeves on a reclaimed wood bar. Housemade *limoncello*, Italian and craft beers, and unusual wine varietals also move across the lengthy slab.

Bistro Bohem EASTERN EUROPEAN $$

(☑ 202-735-5895; www.bistrobohem.com; 600 Florida Ave NW; mains $14-22; ☺ 11am-10pm Mon, 11am-11pm Tue-Thu, 5pm-midnight Fri, 10am-midnight Sat, 10am-10pm Sun; 🛜; Ⓜ Green, Yellow Lines to Shaw-Howard U) Cozy Bistro Bohem is a community favorite for its rib-sticking Czech schnitzels, goulash and pilsners, served with a side of local art on the walls and occasional Czech film screenings. The warm, bohemian environs make you swear you're in Prague.

Le Diplomate FRENCH $$$

(☑ 202-332-3333; www.lediplomatedc.com; 1601 14th St NW; mains $23-35; ☺ 5-11pm Mon-Thu, 5pm-midnight Fri, 9:30am-midnight Sat, 9:30am-11pm Sun; Ⓜ Green, Yellow Lines to U St) This charming French bistro is one of the hottest tables in town. DC celebrities galore cozy up in the leather banquettes and at the sidewalk tables. They come for an authentic slice of Paris, from the *coq au vin* (wine-braised chicken) and aromatic baguettes to the vintage curios and nudie photos decorating the bathrooms. Make reservations.

✖ Dupont Circle & Kalorama

Zorba's Cafe GREEK $

(☑ 202-387-8555; www.zorbascafe.com; 1612 20th St NW; mains $13-16; ☺ 11am-11:30pm Mon-Sat, to 10:30pm Sun; 🛜; Ⓜ Red Line to Dupont Circle) Generous portions of moussaka and souvlaki, as well as pitchers of Rolling Rock beer, make family-run Zorba's Cafe one of DC's best bargain haunts. On warm days the outdoor patio packs with locals. With the bouzouki music playing, you can almost imagine you're in the Greek islands.

Afterwords Cafe AMERICAN $$

(☑ 202-387-3825; www.kramers.com; 1517 Connecticut Ave NW; mains $17-21; ☺ 7:30am-1am Sun-Thu, to 3am Fri & Sat; Ⓜ Red Line to Dupont Circle) Attached to Kramerbooks, this buzzing spot is not your average bookstore cafe. The packed indoor tables, wee bar and outdoor patio overflow with good cheer. The menu features tasty bistro fare and an ample beer selection, making it a prime spot for happy hour, for brunch and at all hours on weekends (open until 3am, baby!).

Browsing the stacks before stuffing the gut is many locals' favorite way to spend a Washington weekend.

★ Bistrot du Coin FRENCH $$

(☑ 202-234-6969; www.bistrotducoin.com; 1738 Connecticut Ave NW; mains $16-29; ☺ 11:30am-midnight Mon-Wed, 11:30am-1am Thu & Fri, noon-1am Sat, noon-midnight Sun; Ⓜ Red Line to Dupont Circle) The lively and much-loved Bistrot du Coin is a neighborhood favorite for roll-up-your sleeves, working-class French fare. The kitchen sends out consistently good onion soup, classic *steak-frites* (grilled steak and French fries), cassoulet, open-face sandwiches and nine varieties of its famous *moules* (mussels). Regional wines from around the motherland accompany the food by the glass, carafe and bottle.

★ Little Serow THAI $$$

(www.littleserow.com; 1511 17th St NW; set menu $49; ☺ 5:30-10pm Tue-Thu, to 10:30pm Fri & Sat; Ⓜ Red Line to Dupont Circle) Little Serow has no phone, no reservations and no sign on the door. It only seats groups of four or fewer (larger parties will be separated), but despite all this, people line up around the block. And what for? Superlative Northern Thai cuisine. The single-option menu – which consists of six or so hot-spiced courses – changes by the week.

FOOD TRUCKIN'

More than 150 food trucks roll in DC, and the White House neighborhood welcomes the mother lode. They congregate at Farragut Sq, Franklin Sq, the State Department and George Washington University on weekdays between 11:30am and 1:30pm. Follow the locals' lead, and stuff your face with a delicious meal for under $15 – maybe a lobster roll poached in butter or a bowl of Lao drunken noodles. Food Truck Fiesta (www.foodtruck fiesta.com) tracks the ever-evolving fleet via Twitter. Here are some favorites:

Lilypad on the Run (twitter.com/LilypadontheRun) Ethiopian meat and veggie combos that make you want to lick the styrofoam container.

Far East Taco Grille (twitter.com/fareasttg) Asian-flavored tacos using meats or tofu, corn or flour tortillas.

DC Pie Truck (twitter.com/ThePieTruckDC) The Dangerously Delicious piemakers swing out in two big red trucks. Sweet and savory slices emerge from the windows. Pies range from spinach with goat cheese, to chocolate cream, and coconut chess.

Red Hook Lobster Truck (twitter.com/LobsterTruckDC) Take your pick: mayo-based, Maine-style lobster rolls or butter-slathered Connecticut-style rolls.

Komi
FUSION $$$

(☎202-332-9200; www.komirestaurant.com; 1509 17th St NW; set menu $150; ◎5:30-10pm Tue-Sat; Ⓜ Red Line to Dupont Circle) There is an admirable simplicity to Komi's changing menu, which is rooted in Greece and influenced by everything – primarily genius. Dinner comprises 12 or so dishes; say suckling pig, scallops and truffles, or roasted baby goat. Komi's fairy-tale of a dining space doesn't take groups larger than four, and you need to reserve in advance. Call a month before your desired dining date.

Hank's Oyster Bar
SEAFOOD $$$

(☎202-462 4265; www.hanksoysterbar.com; 1624 Q St NW; mains $22-30; ◎11:30am-1am Mon & Tue, 11:30am-2am Wed-Fri, 11am-2am Sat, 11am-1am Sun; Ⓜ Red Line to Dupont Circle) DC has several oyster bars, but mini-chain Hank's is our favorite, mixing power-player muscle with good-old-boy ambience. As you'd expect, the oyster menu is extensive and excellent; there are always at least four varieties on hand. Quarters are cramped, and you often have to wait for a table – nothing a sake oyster bomb won't fix.

✕ Adams Morgan

Diner
AMERICAN $

(☎202-232-8800; www.dinerdc.com; 2453 18th St NW; mains $9-18; ◎24hr; ☑🅗; Ⓜ Red Line to Woodley Park/Adams Morgan) The Diner serves hearty comfort food, any time of the day or night. It's ideal for wee-hour breakfast scarf-downs, weekend Bloody Mary brunches (if you don't mind crowds) or any time you want unfussy, well-prepared American fare. Omelets, fat pancakes, mac 'n' cheese, grilled tofu tacos and burgers hit the tables with aplomb. It's a good spot for kids, too.

★ Donburi
JAPANESE $

(☎202-629-1047; www.facebook.com/donburidc; 2438 18th St NW; mains $10-15; ◎11am-10pm; Ⓜ Red Line to Woodley Park-Zoo/Adams Morgan) Hole-in-the-wall Donburi has 15 seats at a wooden counter where you get a front-row view of the slicing, dicing chefs. *Donburi* means 'bowl' in Japanese, and that's what arrives steaming hot and filled with, say, panko-coated shrimp atop rice and blended with the house's sweet-and-savory sauce. It's a simple, authentic meal. There's often a line, but it moves quickly. No reservations.

Julia's Empanadas
LATIN AMERICAN $

(☎202-328-6232; www.juliasempanadas.com; 2452 18th St NW; empanadas from $5; ◎10am-midnight Mon-Thu, to 4am Fri & Sat, to 8pm Sun; Ⓜ Red Line to Woodley Park-Zoo/Adams Morgan) A frequent winner in DC's 'best late-night eats' polls, Julia's stuffs its dough bombs with chorizo, Jamaican beef curry, spinach and more. Flavors peak if you've been drinking. The little chain has a handful of takeaway shops around town. Cash only.

★ Tail Up Goat
MEDITERRANEAN $$

(☎202-986-9600; www.tailupgoat.com; 1827 Adams Mill Rd NW; mains $18-27; ◎5:30-10pm Mon-Thu, 5-10pm Fri-Sun; Ⓜ Red Line to Woodley Park-Zoo/Adams Morgan) With its pale blue walls, light wood decor and lantern-like lights dangling overhead, Tail Up Goat wafts a warm, island-y vibe. The lamb ribs are the specialty – crispy and lusciously fatty, with grilled lemon, figs and spices. The house-made breads and spreads star on the menu too – say, flaxseed sourdough with beets. No wonder Michelin gave it a star.

✖ Georgetown

★ Simply Banh Mi   VIETNAMESE $
(☎ 202-333-5726; www.simplybanhmidc.com; 1624 Wisconsin Ave NW; mains $7-10; ⏰11am-7pm Tue-Sun; ✈; ▣ Circulator) There's nothing fancy about the small, below-street-level space, and the compact menu sticks mostly to sandwiches and bubble tea. But the owners know how to take a crusty baguette, stuff it with delicious lemongrass pork or other meat (or tofu), and make your day.

Baked & Wired   BAKERY $
(☎ 202-333-2500; www.bakedandwired.com; 1052 Thomas Jefferson St NW; baked goods $3-6; ⏰7am-8pm Mon-Thu, 7am-9pm Fri, 8am-9pm Sat, 8am-8pm Sun; ▣ Circulator) Sniff out Baked & Wired, a cheery cafe that whips up beautifully made coffees, bacon cheddar buttermilk biscuits and enormous cupcakes (like the banana and peanut-butter-frosted Elvis). It's a fine spot to join university students and cyclists coming off the nearby trails.

Chez Billy Sud   FRENCH $$$
(☎ 202-965-2606; www.chezbillysud.com; 1039 31st St NW; mains $26-37; ⏰11:30am-2pm Tue-Fri, 11am-2pm Sat & Sun, plus 5-10pm Tue-Thu & Sun, 5-11pm Fri & Sat; ▣ Circulator) An endearing little bistro tucked away on a residential block, Billy's mint-green walls, gilt mirrors and wee marble bar exude laid-back elegance. Mustachioed servers bring baskets of warm bread to the white linen–clothed tables, along with crackling pork and pistachio sausage, golden trout, tuna niçoise salad and plump cream puffs.

🍷 Drinking & Nightlife

When Andrew Jackson swore the oath of office in 1800, the self-proclaimed populist dispensed with pomp and circumstance and, quite literally, threw a raging kegger. Folks got so gone they started looting art from the White House. The historical lesson: DC loves a drink, and these days it enjoys said tipples in many incarnations besides executive-mansion-trashing throwdowns.

Capitol Hill

Copycat Co   COCKTAIL BAR
(☎ 202-241-1952; www.copycatcompany.com; 1110 H St NE; ⏰5pm-2am Sun-Thu, to 3am Fri & Sat; Ⓜ Red Line to Union Station then streetcar) When you walk into Copycat it feels like a Chinese fast-food restaurant. That's because it is (sort of) on the 1st floor, where Chinese street-food nibbles are available. The fizzy drinks and egg-white-topped cocktails fill glasses upstairs, in the dimly lit, speakeasy-meets-opium-den-vibed bar. Staff are unassuming and gracious in helping newbies with the lengthy menu.

Little Miss Whiskey's Golden Dollar   BAR
(www.littlemisswhiskeys.com; 1104 H St NE; ⏰5pm-2am Sun-Thu, to 3am Fri & Sat; Ⓜ Red Line to Union Station then streetcar) If Alice had returned from Wonderland so traumatized by her near beheading that she needed a stiff drink, we imagine she'd pop down to Little Miss Whiskey's. She'd love the whimsical-meets-dark-nightmares decor. And she'd probably have fun with the club kids partying on the upstairs dance floor on weekends.

Bluejacket Brewery   BREWERY
(☎ 202-524-4862; www.bluejacketdc.com; 300 Tingey St SE; ⏰11am-1am Sun-Thu, to 2am Fri & Sat; Ⓜ Green Line to Navy Yard) Beer-lovers' heads will explode in Bluejacket. Pull up a stool at the mod-industrial bar, gaze at the silvery tanks bubbling up the ambitious brews, then make the hard decision about which of the 25 tap beers you want to try. A dry-hopped kolsch? Sweet-spiced stout? A cask-aged farmhouse ale? Four-ounce tasting pours help with decision-making.

Granville Moore's   PUB
(☎ 202-399-2546; www.granvillemoores.com; 1238 H St NE; ⏰5pm-midnight Mon-Thu, 5pm-3am Fri, 11am-3am Sat, 11am-midnight Sun; Ⓜ Red Line to Union Station then streetcar) Besides being one of DC's best places to grab frites and a steak sandwich, Granville Moore's has an extensive Belgian beer menu that should satisfy any fan of low-country boozing. With its raw, wooden fixtures and walls that look as if they were made from daub or mud, the interior resembles a medieval barracks. The fireside setting is ideal on a winter's eve.

Tune Inn   BAR
(☎ 202-543-2725; 331 Pennsylvania Ave SE; ⏰8am-2am Sun-Thu, to 3am Fri & Sat; Ⓜ Orange, Silver, Blue Lines to Capitol South or Eastern Market)

Dive bar Tune Inn has been around for decades and is where the neighborhood's older residents come to knock back Budweisers. The mounted deer heads and antler chandelier set the mood, as greasy-spoon grub and all-day breakfasts get scarfed in the vinyl-backed booths.

🍸 White House & Foggy Bottom

★ Off The Record   BAR
(☑ 202-638-6600; 800 16th St NW, Hay-Adams Hotel; ☉ 11:30am-midnight Sun-Thu, to 12:30am Fri & Sat; Ⓜ Orange, Silver, Blue Lines to McPherson Sq) Intimate red booths and a hidden basement location in one of the city's most prestigious hotels, right across from the White House – no wonder DC's important people submerge to be seen and not heard (as the tagline goes) at Off The Record. Experienced bartenders swirl martinis and Manhattans for the suit-wearing crowd. Groovy framed political caricatures hang on the walls.

🍷 Downtown & Penn Quarter

★ Columbia Room   COCKTAIL BAR
(☑ 202-316-9396; www.columbiaroomdc.com; 124 Blagden Alley NW; ☉ 5pm-12:30am Tue-Thu, to 1:30am Fri & Sat; Ⓜ Green, Yellow Lines to Mt Vernon Sq/7th St-Convention Center) Serious mixology goes on at Columbia Room, the kind of place that sources spring water from Kentucky to Scotland, and uses pickled cherry blossom and barley tea among its ingredients. But it's done in a refreshingly non-snooty environment. Choose from three distinct areas: the festive Punch Garden on the outdoor roof deck, the comfy, leather-chair-dotted Spirits Library or the 14-seat, prix-fixe Tasting Room.

🍸 Logan Circle, U Street & Columbia Heights

★ Right Proper Brewing Co   BREWERY
(☑ 202-607-2337; www.rightproperbrewery.com; 624 T St NW; ☉ 5pm-midnight Mon-Thu, 11:30am-1am Fri & Sat, 11:30am-11pm Sun; Ⓜ Green, Yellow Lines to Shaw-Howard U) As if the artwork – a chalked mural of the National Zoo's giant pandas with laser eyes destroying downtown DC – wasn't enough, Right Proper Brewing Co makes sublime ales in a building where Duke Ellington used to play pool. It's the Shaw district's neighborhood clubhouse, a big, sunny space filled with folks gabbing at reclaimed wood tables.

BEER

The city is serious about beer. It even brews much of its own delicious stuff. That trend started in 2009, when DC Brau became the District's first brewery to launch in more than 50 years. Several more beer makers followed. As you drink around town, keep an eye out for local concoctions from 3 Stars, Atlas Brew Works, Hellbender and Lost Rhino (from northern Virginia).

★ Dacha Beer Garden   BEER GARDEN
(☑ 202-350-9888; www.dachadc.com; 1600 7th St NW; ☉ 4-10:30pm Mon-Thu, noon-midnight Fri & Sat, 11am-10:30pm Sun; Ⓜ Green, Yellow Lines to Shaw-Howard U) Happiness reigns in Dacha's freewheeling beer garden. Kids and dogs bound around the picnic tables, while adults hoist glass boots filled with German brews. When the weather gets nippy, staff bring heaters and blankets and stoke the fire pit. And it all takes place under the sultry gaze of Elizabeth Taylor (or a mural of her, which sprawls across the back wall).

Churchkey   BAR
(☑ 202-567-2576; www.churchkeydc.com; 1337 14th St NW; ☉ 4pm-1am Mon-Thu, 4pm-2am Fri, 11:30am-2am Sat, 11:30am-1am Sun; Ⓜ Orange, Silver, Blue Lines to McPherson Sq) Coppery, mod-industrial Churchkey glows with hipness. Fifty beers flow from the taps, including five brain-walloping, cask-aged ales. If none of those please you, another 500 types of brew are available by bottle (including gluten-free suds). Churchkey is the upstairs counterpart to Birch & Barley (☑ 202-567-2576; www.birchandbarley.com; mains $16-29; ☉ 5:30-10pm Tue-Thu, 5:30-11pm Fri & Sat, 11am-8pm Sun), a popular nouveau comfort-food restaurant, and you can order much of its menu at the bar.

Cork Wine Bar   WINE BAR
(☑ 202-265-2675; www.corkdc.com; 1720 14th St NW; ☉ 5pm-midnight Tue & Wed, 5pm-1am Thu-Sat, 11am-3pm & 5-10pm Sun; Ⓜ Green, Yellow Lines to U St) This dark 'n' cozy wine bar manages to come off as foodie magnet and friendly neighborhood hangout all at once, which is a feat. Around 50 smart wines are available by the glass and 160 types by the bottle. Accompanying nibbles include cheese and charcuterie platters.

U Street Music Hall CLUB
(☎202-588-1889; www.ustreetmusichall.com; 1115 U St NW; ⊙hours vary; Ⓜ Green, Yellow Lines to U St) This is the spot to get your groove on sans the VIP/bottle service crowd. Two local DJs own and operate the basement club. It looks like a no-frills rock bar, but it has a pro sound system, a cork-cushioned dance floor and other accoutrements of a serious dance club. Alternative bands also thrash a couple of nights per week to keep it fresh.

 ## Dupont Circle & Kalorama

Bar Charley BAR
(☎202-627-2183; www.barcharley.com; 1825 18th St NW; ⊙5pm-12:30am Mon-Thu, 4pm-1:30am Fri, 10am-1:30am Sat, 10am-12:30am Sun; Ⓜ Red Line to Dupont Circle) Bar Charley draws a mixed crowd from the neighborhood – young, old, gay and straight. They come for groovy cocktails sloshing in vintage glassware and ceramic tiki mugs, served at very reasonable prices by DC standards. Try the gin and gingery Suffering Bastard. The beer list isn't huge, but it is thoughtfully chosen with some wild ales. Around 60 wines are available too.

Board Room BAR
(☎202-518-7666; www.boardroomdc.com; 1737 Connecticut Ave NW; ⊙4pm-2am Mon-Thu, 4pm-3am Fri, noon-3am Sat, noon-2am Sun; Ⓜ Red Line to Dupont Circle) Grab a table, pull up a stool and crush your opponent at Hungry Hungry Hippos. Or summon spirits with a Ouija board. Board Room lets you flash back to childhood via its stacks of board games. Battleship, Risk, Operation – name it, and it's available to rent for $2.

JR's GAY
(☎202-328-0090; www.jrsbar-dc.com; 1519 17th St NW; ⊙4pm-2am Mon-Thu, 4pm-3am Fri, 1pm-3am Sat, 1pm-2am Sun; Ⓜ Red Line to Dupont Circle) Button-down shirts are de rigueur at this popular gay hangout frequented by the 20- and 30-something, work-hard-and-play-hard set. Some DC residents claim that the crowd at JR's epitomizes the conservative nature of the capital's gay scene, but even if you love to hate it, as many do, JR's knows how to rock a happy hour and is teeming more often than not.

Cobalt GAY
(☎202-232-4416; www.cobaltdc.com; 1639 R St NW; ⊙4pm-2am Sun-Thu, to 3am Fri & Sat; Ⓜ Red Line to Dupont Circle) Featuring lots of hair product and buff gym bodies, Cobalt tends to gather a well-dressed late-20s to 30-something crowd who come for fun (but loud!) dance parties throughout the week. The time-hallowed dance club is on the 3rd floor; the venue also has a restaurant on the 1st floor and a lounge on the 2nd.

 ## Adams Morgan

★ Dan's Cafe BAR
(☎202-265-0299; 2315 18th St NW; ⊙7pm-2am Tue-Thu, to 3am Fri & Sat; Ⓜ Red Line to Woodley Park-Zoo/Adams Morgan) This is one of DC's great dive bars. The interior looks sort of like an evil Elks Club, all unironically old-school 'art,' cheap paneling and dim lights barely illuminating the unapologetic slumminess. It's famed for its whopping, mix-it-yourself drinks, where you get a ketchup-type squirt bottle of booze, a can of soda and bucket of ice for barely $20. Cash only.

LGBT DC

DC is one of the most gay-friendly cities in the USA. It has an admirable track record of progressivism and a fair bit of scene to boot. The rainbow stereotype here consists of well-dressed professionals and activists working in politics on LGBT issues such as gay marriage (legal in DC since 2010). The community concentrates in Dupont Circle, but U Street, Shaw, Capitol Hill and Logan Circle also have lots of gay-friendly businesses.

Capital Area Gay & Lesbian Chamber of Commerce (www.caglcc.org) Sponsors lots of networking events around town.

LGBT DC (https://washington.org/lgbtq) The DC tourism office's portal with events, neighborhood breakdowns and a travel resource guide.

Metro Weekly (www.metroweekly.com) Free weekly news magazine. Aimed at a younger demographic than its rival, the *Washington Blade*.

Washington Blade (www.washingtonblade.com) Free weekly gay newspaper. Covers politics and has lots of business and nightlife listings.

Songbyrd Record Cafe & Music House
CAFE

(☑202-450-2917; www.songbyrddc.com; 2477 18th St NW; ⊙8am-2am Sun-Thu, to 3am Fri & Sat; 🐾; Ⓜ Red Line to Woodley Park-Zoo/Adams Morgan) By day hang out in the retro cafe, drinking excellent coffee, munching delicious sandwiches and browsing the small selection of soul and indie LPs for sale. You can even cut your own record in the vintage recording booth ($15). By night the party moves to the bar, where beer and cocktails flow alongside burgers and tacos, and indie bands rock the basement club.

Georgetown

Tombs
PUB

(☑202-337-6668; www.tombs.com; 1226 36th St NW; ⊙11:30am-1:30am Mon-Thu, to 2:30am Fri & Sat, 9:30am-1:30am Sun; 🚌Circulator) Every college of a certain pedigree has 'that' bar – the one where faculty and students alike sip pints under athletic regalia of the old school. The Tombs is Georgetown's contribution to the genre. If it looks familiar, think back to the '80s: the subterranean pub was one of the settings for the film *St Elmo's Fire*.

☆ Entertainment

Live Music

★ Black Cat
LIVE MUSIC

(☑202-667-4490; www.blackcatdc.com; 1811 14th St NW; Ⓜ Green, Yellow Lines to U St) A pillar of DC's rock and indie scene since the 1990s, the battered Black Cat has hosted all the greats of years past (White Stripes, the Strokes, and Arcade Fire among others). If you don't want to pony up for $20-a-ticket bands on the upstairs main stage (or the smaller Backstage below), head to the Red Room for the jukebox, billiards, pinball and strong cocktails.

9:30 Club
LIVE MUSIC

(☑202-265-0930; www.930.com; 815 V St NW; Ⓜ Green, Yellow Lines to U St) The 9:30, which can pack 1200 people into a surprisingly compact venue, is the granddaddy of the live-music scene in DC. Pretty much every big name that comes through town ends up on this stage, and a concert here is the first-gig memory of many a DC-area teenager. Headliners usually take the stage between 10:30pm and 11:30pm. Tickets range from $20 to $35.

Performing Arts

★ Kennedy Center
PERFORMING ARTS

(☑202-467-4600; www.kennedy-center.org; 2700 F St NW; Ⓜ Orange, Silver, Blue Lines to Foggy Bottom-GWU) Sprawled on 17 acres along the Potomac River, the magnificent Kennedy Center hosts a staggering array of performances – more than 2000 each year among its multiple venues including the Concert Hall (home to the National Symphony) and Opera House (home to the National Opera). A free shuttle bus runs to and from the Metro station every 15 minutes from 9:45am (noon on Sunday) to midnight.

Shakespeare Theatre Company
THEATER

(☑202-547-1122; www.shakespearetheatre.org; 450 7th St NW; Ⓜ Green, Yellow Lines to Archives) The nation's foremost Shakespeare company presents masterful works by the bard, as well as plays by George Bernard Shaw, Oscar Wilde, Eugene O'Neill and other greats. The season spans about a half-dozen productions annually, plus a free summer Shakespeare series on site for two weeks in late August.

Woolly Mammoth Theatre Company
THEATER

(☑202-393-3939; www.woollymammoth.net; 641 D St NW; Ⓜ Green, Yellow Lines to Archives) Woolly Mammoth is the edgiest of DC's experimental groups. For most shows, $20 'stampede' seats are available at the box office two hours before performances. They're limited in number, and sold first-come, first-served, so get there early.

Capitol Steps
COMEDY

(☑202-397-7328; www.capsteps.com; Ronald Reagan Bldg, 1300 Pennsylvania Ave NW; tickets $40.50; ⊙shows 7:30pm Fri & Sat; Ⓜ Orange, Silver, Blue Lines to Federal Triangle) This singing troupe claims to be the only group in America that tries to be funnier than Congress. It's composed of current and former congressional staffers, so they know their political stuff, although sometimes it can be overtly corny. The satirical, bipartisan jokes poke fun at both sides of the spectrum.

Sports

★ Nationals Park
STADIUM

(☑202-675-6287; www.mlb.com/nationals; 1500 S Capitol St SE; 🐾; Ⓜ Green Line to Navy Yard) The major-league Washington Nationals play baseball at this spiffy stadium beside the Anacostia River. Don't miss the mid-fourth-inning 'Racing Presidents' – an odd foot race between giant-headed caricatures of George Washington, Abraham Lincoln, Thomas Jefferson, Teddy Roosevelt and William Taft. Hip bars and eateries and playful green spaces surround the ballpark, and more keep coming as the area gentrifies.

🛈 Information

Cultural Tourism DC (www.culturaltourismdc. org) Neighborhood-oriented events and tours.

Destination DC (www.washington.org) Official tourism site packed with sightseeing and event info.

Lonely Planet (www.lonelyplanet.com/usa/washington-dc) Destination information, hotel bookings, traveler forum and more.

Washingtonian (www.washingtonian.com) Features on dining, entertainment and local luminaries.

🛈 Getting There & Away

AIR

Washington Dulles International Airport (IAD; www.flydulles.com) is in the Virginia suburbs 26 miles west of DC. It has free wi-fi, several currency exchanges and restaurants throughout the terminals. Famed architect Eero Saarinen designed the swooping main building. The Metro Silver Line is slated to reach Dulles in late 2019, providing a transfer-free ride at long last.

Ronald Reagan Washington National Airport (DCA; www.flyreagan.com) is 4.5 miles south of downtown in Arlington, VA. There's free wi-fi, several eateries and a currency exchange (National Hall, Concourse Level).

Baltimore/Washington International Thurgood Marshall Airport (BWI; ☑ 410-859-7111; www.bwiairport.com) is 30 miles northeast of DC in Maryland.

BUS

Cheap bus services to and from Washington abound. Most charge $25 to $30 for a one-way trip to NYC (it takes four to five hours). Many companies use Union Station as their hub; other pick-up locations are scattered around town, but are always Metro-accessible. Tickets usually need to be bought online, but can sometimes be purchased on the bus itself if there are still seats available.

BestBus (☑ 202-332-2691; www.bestbus. com; 20th St & Massachusetts Ave NW; 🛜; Ⓜ Red Line to Dupont Circle) Several trips to/from NYC daily. The main bus stop is by Dupont Circle; there's another at Union Station.

BoltBus (☑ 877-265-8287; www.boltbus. com; 50 Massachusetts Ave NE; 🛜; Ⓜ Red Line to Union Station) It goes to NYC multiple times each day, and to other east-coast cities. Lateness and spotty wi-fi can be issues. It uses Union Station as its terminal.

Greyhound (☑ 202-589-5141; www.greyhound. com; 50 Massachusetts Ave NE; Ⓜ Red Line to Union Station) Provides nationwide service. The terminal is at Union Station.

Megabus (☑ 877-462-6342; http://us.mega bus.com; 50 Massachusetts Ave NE; 🛜; Ⓜ Red Line to Union Station) Offers the most trips to NYC (around 20 per day), as well as other east-coast cities; arrives at/departs from Union Station. Buses run behind schedule fairly often.

Peter Pan Bus Lines (☑ 800-343-9999; www. peterpanbus.com; 50 Massachusetts Ave NE; Ⓜ Red Line to Union Station) Travels throughout the northeastern USA; has its terminal at Union Station.

Vamoose Bus (☑ 212-695-6766; www. vamoosebus.com; 1801 N Lynn St) Service between NYC and Arlington, VA (the stop is near the Rosslyn Metro station).

Washington Deluxe (☑ 866-287-6932; www. washny.com; 1610 Connecticut St NW; 🛜; Ⓜ Red Line to Dupont Circle) Good express service to/from NYC. It has stops at both Dupont Circle and Union Station.

TRAIN

Magnificent, beaux-arts **Union Station** (www. unionstationdc.com; 50 Massachusetts Ave NE; Ⓜ Union Station) is the city's rail hub. There's a handy Metro station (Red Line) here for transport onward in the city.

Amtrak (www.amtrak.com) arrives at least once per hour from major east-coast cities. Northeast Regional trains are cheaper but slower (about 3½ hours between NYC and DC).

Acela Express trains are more expensive but faster (two hours and 45 minutes between NYC and DC; 6½ hours between Boston and DC). The express trains also have bigger seats and other business class amenities.

MARC trains (www.mta.maryland.gov) arrive frequently from downtown Baltimore (one hour) and other Maryland towns, as well as Harpers Ferry, WV.

🛈 Getting Around

The Metro is the main way to move around the city. Buy a rechargeable SmarTrip card at any Metro station. You must use the card to enter *and* exit station turnstiles.

Metro Fast, frequent, ubiquitous (except during weekend track maintenance). It operates between 5am and midnight (3am on Friday and Saturday). Fares from $1.85 to $6 depending on distance traveled. A day pass costs $14.50.

DC Circulator bus Useful for the Mall, George-town, Adams Morgan and other areas with limited Metro service. Fare is $1.

Bicycle Capital Bikeshare stations are every-where; a day pass costs $8.

Taxi Relatively easy to find (less so at night), but costly. The ride-hailing companies Uber, Lyft and Via are used more in the District.

TO/FROM THE AIRPORT

Washington Dulles International Airport

Washington Flyer's (www.washfly.com) Silver Line Express bus runs every 15 to 20 minutes from Dulles (main terminal, arrivals level door 4) to the Wiehle-Reston East Metro station between 6am and 10:40pm (from 7:45am weekends). Total time to DC's center is 60 to 75 minutes; total bus-Metro cost around $11.

Metrobus 5A (www.wmata.com) runs every 30 to 40 minutes from Dulles to Rosslyn Metro (Blue, Orange and Silver Lines) and on to central DC (L'Enfant Plaza) between 5:50am (6:30am weekends) and 11:35pm. Total time to the center is around 60 minutes; total fare is $7.

The Supershuttle (www.supershuttle.com) door-to-door shared van service goes downtown for $30. It takes 30 to 60 minutes and runs from 5:30am to 12:30am.

Taxi rides to the city center take 30 to 60 minutes (depending on traffic) and cost $62 to $73. Follow the 'Ground Transportation' or 'Taxi' signs to where they queue.

Ronald Reagan Washington National Airport

The airport has its own Metro (www.wmata.com) station on the Blue and Yellow Lines. Trains (around $2.60) depart every 10 minutes or so between 5am and midnight (to 3am Friday and Saturday); they reach the city center in 20 minutes. It connects to the concourse level of terminals B and C.

The Supershuttle (www.supershuttle.com) door-to-door shared van service goes downtown for $16. It takes 10 to 30 minutes and runs from 5:30am to 12:30am.

Rides to the city center take 10 to 30 minutes (depending on traffic) and cost $15 to $22. Taxis queue outside the baggage-claim area at each terminal.

Baltimore-Washington International Thurgood Marshall Airport

Metrobus B30 (www.wmata.com) runs from BWI to the Greenbelt Metro station (last stop on the Green Line); it departs every 40 minutes from bus stops on the lower level of the interna-tional concourse and concourse A/B. The total bus-Metro fare is about $11. Total trip time is around 75 minutes.

The Supershuttle (www.supershuttle.com) door-to-door shared-van service goes to down-town DC for $37. The ride takes 45 minutes to an hour and runs from 5:30am to 12:30am.

A taxi to DC takes 45 minutes or so and costs $90. Taxis queue outside the baggage claim area of the Marshall terminal.

Both MARC (Maryland Rail Commuter; www.mta.maryland.gov) and Amtrak (www.amtrak.com) trains travel to DC's Union Station. They depart from a terminal 1 mile from BWI; a free bus shuttles passengers there. Trains leave once or twice per hour, but there's no service after 9:30pm (and limited service on weekends). It takes 30 to 40 minutes; fares start at $7.

MARYLAND

The nickname 'America in Miniature' per-fectly captures Maryland: this small state possesses all of the best bits of the country, from the Appalachian Mountains in the west to sandy white beaches in the east. A blend of Northern streetsmarts and Southern down-home appeal gives this osmotic border state an appealing identity crisis. Its main city, Baltimore, is a sharp, demanding port town; the Eastern Shore jumbles art-and-antique-minded city refugees and working fisher-men; while the DC suburbs are packed with government and office workers seeking green space, and the poor seeking lower rents. Yet it all somehow works – scrumptious blue crabs, Natty Boh beer and lovely Chesapeake country being the glue that binds it all. This is also an extremely diverse and progressive state, and was one of the first in the country to legalize gay marriage.

History

George Calvert established Maryland as a refuge for persecuted English Catholics in 1634 when he purchased St Mary's City from the local Piscataway tribe, with whom he ini-tially tried to coexist. Puritan refugees drove both Piscataway and Catholics from control and shifted power to Annapolis; their har-assment of Catholics produced the Toler-ance Act, a flawed but progressive law that allowed freedom of any (Christian) worship in Maryland – a North American first.

A commitment to diversity has always characterized this state, despite a mixed record on slavery. Although state loyalties were split during the Civil War, a Confed-erate invasion was halted here in 1862 at Antietam. Following the war, Maryland har-nessed its black, white and immigrant work

SCENIC DRIVE: MARITIME MARYLAND

Maryland and Chesapeake Bay have always been inextricable, but there are some places where the old-fashioned way of life on the bay seems to have changed little over the passing centuries.

About 150 miles south of Baltimore, at the edge of the Eastern Shore, is **Crisfield**, the top working water town in Maryland. Get visiting details at the **J Millard Tawes Historical Museum** (☑410-968-2501; www.crisfieldheritagefoundation.org/museum; 3 9th St, Crisfield; adult/child $3/1; ⊙11am-5pm Wed-Sat & 11am-3pm Sun Jun-Aug, closed rest of the year), which doubles as a visitor center. Any seafood you eat will be first-rate, but for a true Shore experience, **Watermen's Inn** (☑410-968-2119; www.crisfield.com/watermens; 901 W Main St, Crisfield; mains $8-27; ⊙3-8pm Thu, to 9pm Fri & Sat, noon-8pm Sun) is legendary; in an unpretentious setting you can feast on local catch from an ever-changing menu. You can find local waterfolk at their favorite hangout – **Gordon's Confectionery** (☑410-968-0566; 831 W Main St, Crisfield; mains $2-7; ⊙4am-8:30pm) – having 4am coffee before shipping off to check and set traps.

From here you can leave your car and take a boat to **Smith Island** (www.smithisland. org), the only offshore settlement in the state. Settled by fisherfolk from the English West Country some 400 years ago, the island's tiny population still speak with what linguists reckon is the closest thing to a 17th-century Cornish accent.

We'll be frank: this is more of a dying fishing town than charming tourist attraction, although there are B&Bs and restaurants (check the website for details). But it's also a last link to the state's past, so if you approach Smith Island as such, you may appreciate the limited amenities on offer. These notably include paddling through miles of some of the most pristine marshland on the eastern seaboard. Ferries will take you back to the mainland (and the present day) at 3:30pm.

---

force, splitting the economy between Baltimore's industry and shipping, and the later need for services in Washington, DC. Today the answer to 'What makes a Marylander?' is 'all of the above': the state mixes rich, poor, foreign-born, urban sophisticates and rural villages like few other states do.

Baltimore

Once among the most important port towns in America, Baltimore – or 'Bawlmer' to locals – is a city of contradictions. It remains a defiant, working-class city tied to its nautical past, but in recent years has earned acclaim for up-to-the-minute entrepreneurial ventures that are impressing visitors and locals alike, from new boutique hotels to edgy exhibits at world-class museums to forgotten neighborhoods now bustling with trendy food courts and farm-to-table restaurants. But don't worry, traditionalists – local culture and hometown sports, from lacrosse to baseball, remain part of the appeal.

For travelers, a visit to B'more (another nickname) should include one trip to the waterfront, whether its the Disney-fied Inner Harbor, the cobblestoned streets of port-

side Fell's Point or the shores of Fort McHenry, birthplace of America's national anthem, 'The Star-Spangled Banner.' As you'll discover, there's an intense, sincere friendliness here, which is why Baltimore lives up to its final, most accurate nickname: 'Charm City.'

◉ Sights

◉ Harborplace & Inner Harbor

This is where most tourists start and, unfortunately, end their Baltimore sightseeing. The Inner Harbor is a big, gleaming waterfront-renewal project of shiny glass, air-conditioned malls and flashy bars that manages to capture the maritime heart of this city, albeit in a safe-for-the-family kinda way. The neighborhood is home to an amazing aquarium and several impressive historic ships, but these worthy sights are just the tip of Baltimore's iceberg.

National Aquarium   AQUARIUM
(☑410-576-3800; www.aqua.org; 501 E Pratt St, Piers 3 & 4; adult/child 3-11yr $40/25; ⊙9am-5pm Sun-Thu, to 8pm Fri, to 6pm Sat) Standing seven stories high and capped by a glass pyramid, this is widely considered to be the best aquarium in America, with almost 20,000

creatures and more than 700 species, a rooftop rainforest, a multistory shark tank and a vast re-creation of an Indo-Pacific reef that is home to blacktip reef sharks, a green sea turtle and stingrays. There's also a reconstruction of the Umbrawarra Gorge in Australia's Northern Territory, complete with 35ft waterfall, rocky cliffs and free-roaming birds and lizards.

◉ Downtown & Little Italy

You can easily walk from downtown Baltimore to Little Italy, but follow the delineated path: there's a rough housing project along the way.

National Great Blacks in Wax Museum
MUSEUM
(☑ 410-563-3404; www.greatblacksinwax.org; 1601 E North Ave; adult/student/child 3-11yr $15/14/12; ⊗ 9am-5pm Tue-Sat, noon-5pm Sun, also Mon & to 6pm Sun Jul & Aug) This simple but thought-provoking African American history museum has exhibits on Frederick Douglass, Jackie Robinson, Martin Luther King Jr and Barack Obama, as well as lesser-known figures such as explorer Matthew Henson. The museum also covers slavery, the Jim Crow era and African leaders – all told in surreal but informative fashion through Madame Tussaud–style wax figures. Unflinching and graphic exhibits about the horrors of slave ships and lynchings may not be well suited to younger children.

Star-Spangled Banner Flag House & 1812 Museum
MUSEUM
(☑ 410-837-1793; www.flaghouse.org; 844 E Pratt St; adult/child $8/6; ⊗ 10am-4pm Tue-Sat; ⊕) This historic home, built in 1793, is where Mary Pickersgill sewed the gigantic flag that inspired America's national anthem. Costumed interpreters and 19th-century artifacts transport visitors back in time to dark days during the War of 1812; there's also a hands-on discovery gallery for kids.

Jewish Museum of Maryland
MUSEUM
(☑ 410-732-6400; www.jewishmuseummd.org; 15 Lloyd St; adult/student/child 4-12yr $10/6/4; ⊗ 10am-5pm Sun-Thu) Maryland has traditionally been home to one of the largest, most active Jewish communities in the country, and this is a fine place to explore their experience in America. It also houses two wonderfully preserved historical synagogues. Call or go online for the scheduled hours of synagogue tours.

Edgar Allan Poe House & Museum
MUSEUM
(☑ 410-462-1763; www.poeinbaltimore.org; 203 N Amity St; adult/student/child $5/4/free; ⊗ 11am-4pm Thu-Sun) Home to Baltimore's most famous adopted son from 1832 to 1835, it was here that the macabre poet and writer first found fame after winning a $50 short-story contest. After moving around, Poe later returned to Baltimore in 1849, where he died under mysterious circumstances. His grave can be found in Westminster Cemetery.

◉ Mt Vernon

★ Walters Art Museum
MUSEUM
(☑ 410-547-9000; www.thewalters.org; 600 N Charles St; ⊗ 10am-5pm Wed-Sun, to 9pm Thu) **FREE** The magnificent Chamber of Wonders looks like the study of a world-traveling scholar, one with a taste for adventure. The abutting Arms and Armor gallery is the most impressive collection of medieval weaponry you'll see this side of *Game of Thrones*. In sum, don't pass up this excellent, eclectic museum. It spans more than 55 centuries, from ancient to contemporary, with excellent displays of Asian treasures, rare and ornate manuscripts and books, and a comprehensive French paintings collection.

Washington Monument
MONUMENT
(www.mvpconservancy.org; 699 Washington Pl; suggested donation $5; ⊗ 11am-3pm Wed-Fri, 10am-5pm Sat & Sun) For the best views of Baltimore, climb the 228 steps of the 178ft-tall Doric column dedicated to America's Founding Father, George Washington. It was designed by Robert Mills, who also created DC's Washington Monument, and is looking better than ever following a $6 million restoration project. The ground floor contains a museum about Washington's life. To climb the monument, buy a ticket on site or reserve online (adult/child under 14 years $6/4).

Maryland Historical Society
MUSEUM
(☑ 410-685-3650; www.mdhs.org; 201 W Monument St; adult/child 3-18yr $9/6; ⊗ 10am-5pm Wed-Sat, noon-5pm Sun) With more than 350,000 objects and seven million books and documents, this is one of the largest collections of Americana in the world. Highlights include one of two surviving Revolutionary War officer's uniforms, photographs from the 1930s Civil Rights movement in Baltimore and Francis Scott Key's original manuscript of 'The Star-Spangled Banner'

(displayed at the top of the hour). The 10ft-tall replica mastodon – the original was preserved by artist and Maryland native Charles Wilson Peale – is impressive. A few original bones are displayed.

Federal Hill & Around

On a bluff overlooking the harbor, Federal Hill Park lends its name to the comfortable neighborhood that's set around Cross Street Market and comes alive after sundown.

★ American Visionary
Art Museum   MUSEUM

(AVAM; ☑ 410-244-1900; www.avam.org; 800 Key Hwy; adult/child $16/10; ☺ 10am-6pm Tue-Sun) Housing a jaw-dropping collection of self-taught (or 'outsider' art), AVAM is a celebration of unbridled creativity utterly free of arts-scene pretension. Across two buildings and two sculpture parks, you'll find broken-mirror collages, homemade robots and flying apparatuses, elaborate sculptural works made of needlepoint, and gigantic model ships painstakingly created from matchsticks. Don't miss the whimsical automata in the Cabaret Mechanical Theater.

Fort McHenry National
Monument & Historic Shrine   HISTORIC SITE

(☑ 410-962-4290; www.nps.gov/fomc; 2400 E Fort Ave; adult/child under 16yr $10/free; ☺ 9am-5pm) On September 13 and 14, 1814, this star-shaped fort successfully repelled a British navy attack during the Battle of Baltimore. After a long night of bombs bursting in the air, ship-bound prisoner Francis Scott Key saw, 'by dawn's early light,' the tattered flag still waving. Inspired, he penned 'The Star-Spangled Banner,' which was set to the tune of a popular drinking song.

Fell's Point & Canton

Once the center of Baltimore's shipbuilding industry, the historic cobblestoned neighborhood of Fell's Point is now a gentrified mix of 18th-century homes and restaurants, bars and shops. The neighborhood has been the setting for several films and TV series, most notably *Homicide: Life on the Street*. Further east, the slightly more sophisticated streets of Canton fan out, with its grassy square surrounded by restaurants and bars.

North Baltimore

The 'Hon' expression of affection – an oft-imitated, never-quite-duplicated 'Bawlmerese' peculiarity – originated in **Hampden**, an area straddling the line between working class and hipster-creative class. Spend a lazy afternoon browsing kitsch, antiques and vintage clothing along the **Avenue** (aka W 36th St). To get to Hampden, take the I-83 N, merge onto Falls Rd (northbound) and take a right onto the Avenue. The prestigious **Johns Hopkins University** (☑ 410-516-8000; www.jhu.edu; 3400 N Charles St) is nearby. South of Johns Hopkins, just east of I-83, new restaurants and housing developments mark rapidly gentrifying **Remington**, a walkable neighborhood with a demographic similar to that of Hampden.

★ Evergreen Museum   MUSEUM

(☑ 410-516-0341; http://museums.jhu.edu; 4545 N Charles St; adult/child $8/5; ☺ 11am-4pm Tue-Fri, noon-4pm Sat & Sun) Well worth the drive out, this grand 19th-century mansion provides a fascinating glimpse into upper-class Baltimore life of the 1800s. The house is packed with fine art and masterpieces of the decorative arts – including paintings by Modigliani, glass by Louis Comfort Tiffany and exquisite Asian porcelain – not to mention the astounding rare book collection, numbering some 32,000 volumes.

☞ Tours

Baltimore Ghost Tours   WALKING

(☑ 410-357-1186; www.baltimoreghosttours.com; adult/child $15/10; ☺ 7pm Fri & Sat Mar-Nov) Offers several walking tours exploring the spooky and bizarre side of Baltimore. The popular Fell's Point ghost walk departs from Max's on Broadway (731 S Broadway). Book online to save $2 per ticket.

★☆ Festivals & Events

Artscape   ART

(www.artscape.org; 140 W Mt Royal Ave, Patricia & Arthur Modell Performing Arts Center; ☺ mid-Jul) America's largest free arts festival features art displays, live music, theater and dance.

Honfest   CULTURAL

(www.honfest.net; ☺ Jun) Put on your best 'Bawlmerese' accent and head to Hampden for this celebration of kitsch, beehive hairdos, rhinestone glasses and other Baltimore eccentricities.

BALTIMORE FOR CHILDREN

Most attractions are centered on the Inner Harbor, including the National Aquarium (p298), perfect for pint-sized visitors. Kids can run wild o'er the ramparts of historic **Fort McHenry National Monument & Historic Shrine**.

Maryland Science Center (☑ 410-685-2370; www.mdsci.org; 601 Light St; adult/child 3-12yr $25/19; ⊙ 10am-5pm Mon-Fri, to 6pm Sat, 11am-5pm Sun, longer hours in summer) is an awesome center featuring a three-story atrium, tons of interactive exhibits on dinosaurs, outer space and the human body, and the requisite IMAX theater ($4 extra).

Two blocks north is the converted fish market of **Port Discovery** (☑ 410-727-8120; www.portdiscovery.org; 35 Market Pl; $15; ⊙ 10am-5pm Mon-Sat & noon-5pm Sun Jun-Aug, closes earlier Sep-May), which has a tree house, a laboratory and an artist's studio. Wear your kids out here. At **Maryland Zoo in Baltimore** (www.marylandzoo.org; 1 Safari Place, Druid Hill Park; adult/child 2-11yr $18/14; ⊙ 10am-4pm daily Mar-Dec, 10am-4pm Fri-Mon Jan & Feb), lily-pad hopping adventures with Billy the Bog Turtle and grooming live animals are all in a day's play.

🛏 Sleeping

Stylish and affordable B&Bs are mostly found in the downtown 'burbs of Canton, Fell's Point and Federal Hill. New boutique hotels are bringing some fresh and hip style to downtown and Mt Vernon.

HI-Baltimore Hostel
HOSTEL $

(☑ 410-576-8880; www.hiusa.org/baltimore; 17 W Mulberry St, Mt Vernon; dm $29-30; ❄@🛜) Located in a beautifully restored 1857 mansion, the HI-Baltimore has four-, eight- and 12-bed dorms. Helpful management, a nice location and a filigreed classical chic look make this one of the region's best hostels.

Hotel Brexton
HOTEL $$

(☑ 443-478-2100; www.hotelbrexton.com; 868 Park Ave, Mt Vernon; r $159-219; 🅿❄🛜❄) This red-brick 19th-century landmark building has recently been reborn as an appealing, if not overly lavish, hotel. Rooms offer a mix of wood floors or carpeting, comfy mattresses, mirrored armoires and framed art prints on the walls. Curious historical footnote: Wallis Simpson, the woman whom Britain's King Edward VIII abdicated the throne for, lived in this building as a young girl.

★ Inn at 2920
B&B $$

(☑ 410-342-4450; www.theinnat2920.com; 2920 Elliott St, Canton; r $195-235; ❄@🛜) Housed in a former bordello, this boutique B&B offers five individual rooms; high-thread-count sheets; sleek, avant-garde decor; and the nightlife-charged neighborhood of Canton right outside your door.

🍴 Eating

Baltimore is an ethnically rich town that sits on top of the greatest seafood repository in the world, not to mention the fault line between the down-home South and cutting-edge innovation of the Northeast.

Papermoon Diner
DINER $

(www.papermoondiner24.com; 227 W 29th St, Harwood; mains $10-18; ⊙ 7am-9pm Sun, Mon, Wed & Thu, to 10pm Fri & Sat) This brightly colored, quintessential Baltimore diner is decorated with thousands of old toys, creepy mannequins and other quirky knickknacks. The real draw here is the anytime breakfast – fluffy buttermilk pancakes, crispy bacon and crab and artichoke heart omelets. Wash it down with a caramel and sea-salt milkshake.

Artifact
CAFE $

(www.artifactcoffee.com; 1500 Union Ave, Woodberry; mains $7-14; ⊙ 7am-7pm Mon-Fri, 8am-7pm Sat & Sun; 🛜🍴) Artifact serves the city's best coffee, along with tasty light meals, such as egg muffins, spinach salad, vegetarian *banh mi* and pastrami sandwiches. It's inside a former mill space, handsomely repurposed from its industrial past. It's a two-minute stroll from the Woodberry light-rail station.

Vaccaro's Pastry
ITALIAN $

(www.vaccarospastry.com; 222 Albemarle St, Little Italy; desserts $3-7; ⊙ 9am-10pm Sun-Thu, to midnight Fri & Sat) Open more than 60 years, Vaccaro's serves some of the best desserts and coffee in town. The cannolis are legendary.

Lexington Market
FAST FOOD $

(www.lexingtonmarket.com; 400 W Lexington St, Mt Vernon; ⊙ 6:30am-6pm) Around since 1782,

Mt Vernon's Lexington Market is one of Baltimore's true old-school food markets. It's a bit shabby on the outside, but the food is great.

Faidley's
SEAFOOD $$

(☑410-727-4898; www.faidleyscrabcakes.com; 203 N Paca St, Lexington Market; mains $10-20; ⊙9am-5pm Mon-Wed, to 5:30pm Thu-Sat) Here's a fine example of a place that the press and the tourists found out about long ago, yet whose brilliance hasn't been dimmed by the publicity. Faidley's is best known for its crab cakes, in-claw meat, backfin (body meat) or all lump (the biggest chunks of body meat). Tuck in at a stand-up counter with a cold beer and know happiness.

★Thames St Oyster House
SEAFOOD $$

(☑443-449-7726; www.thamesstreetoysterhouse. com; 1728 Thames St, Fell's Point; mains $12-29; ⊙11:30am-2:30pm Wed-Sun & 5-9:30pm Sun-Thu, to 10:30pm Fri & Sat) An icon of Fell's Point, this vintage dining and drinking hall serves some of Baltimore's best seafood. Dine in the polished upstairs dining room with views of the waterfront, take a seat in the backyard, or plunk down at the bar in front (which stays open till midnight) and watch the drink-makers and oyster-shuckers in action. The lobster rolls are recommended too.

Birroteca
PIZZA $$

(☑443-708-1934; www.bmorebirroteca.com; 1520 Clipper Rd, Roosevelt Park; pizzas $18-22; ⊙5-11pm Mon-Fri, noon-11pm Sat, noon-10pm Sun) Amid stone walls and indie rock, Birroteca fires up delicious thin-crust pizzas in imaginative combos (like duck confit with fig-onion jam). There's craft beer, good wines, fancy cocktails and impressively bearded bartenders. It's about a half-mile from either Hampden's 36th St or the Woodberry light-rail station.

Helmand
AFGHANI $$

(☑410-752-0311; www.helmand.com; 806 N Charles St, Mt Vernon; mains $14-19; ⊙5-10pm Sun-Thu, to 11pm Fri & Sat) The Helmand is a longtime favorite for its *kaddo borawni* (pumpkin in yogurt-garlic sauce), vegetable platters and flavorful beef-and-lamb meatballs, followed by cardamom ice cream. If you've never tried Afghan cuisine, this is a great place to do so.

LP Steamers
SEAFOOD $$

(☑410-576-9294; www.locustpointsteamers.com; 1100 E Fort Ave, South Baltimore; mains $8-27;

⊙11:30am-9:30pm Sun-Thu, to 10pm Fri & Sat) LP is the best in Baltimore's seafood stakes: working class, teasing smiles and the freshest crabs on the southside.

★Woodberry Kitchen
AMERICAN $$$

(☑410-464-8000; www.woodberrykitchen.com; 2010 Clipper Park Rd, Woodberry; mains $20-35; ⊙dinner 5-10pm Mon-Thu, to 11pm Fri & Sat, to 9pm Sun, brunch 10am-2pm Sat & Sun) The Woodberry takes everything the Chesapeake region has to offer, plops it into an industrial barn and creates culinary magic. The entire menu is like a playful romp through the best of local produce, seafood and meats, from Maryland rockfish with Carolina Gold grits to Shenandoah Valley lamb with collard greens, and hearty vegetable dishes plucked from nearby farms. Reserve ahead.

Food Market
MODERN AMERICAN $$$

(☑410-366-0606; www.thefoodmarketbaltimore. com; 1017 W 36th St, Hampden; mains $18-36; ⊙5-11pm Sun-Thu, to midnight Fri & Sat, plus 9am-3pm Fri-Sun) On Hampden's lively restaurant- and shop-lined main drag, the Food Market was an instant success when it opened back in 2012. Award-winning local chef Chad Gauss elevates American comfort fare to high art in dishes like bread-and-butter-crusted sea bass with black-truffle vinaigrette, and crab cakes with lobster mac 'n' cheese.

🍷 Drinking & Nightlife

On weekends, Fell's Point and Canton turn into temples of alcoholic excess that would make a Roman emperor blush. Mt Vernon and North Baltimore are a little more civilized, but any one of Baltimore's neighborhoods houses a cozy local pub. Closing time is generally 2am.

Brewer's Art
PUB

(☑410-547-6925; www.thebrewersart.com; 1106 N Charles St, Mt Vernon; ⊙4pm-1:45am Mon-Fri, noon-1:45am Sat & Sun) In a vintage early-20th-century mansion, Brewer's Art serves well-crafted Belgian-style microbrews to a laid-back Mt Vernon crowd. There's tasty pub fare (mac 'n' cheese, portobello wraps) in the bar, and upscale American cuisine in the elegant back dining room. Head to the subterranean drinking den downstairs for a more raucous crowd. During happy hour (4pm to 7pm) house drafts are just $3.75.

Ale Mary's
BAR

(☑410-276-2044; www.alemarys.com; 1939 Fleet St, Fell's Point; ⊙4pm-2am Mon-Thu, 2pm-2am

Fri, 10am-2am Sat & Sun) Its name and decor pay homage to Maryland's Catholic roots, with crosses and rosaries scattered about. It draws a buzzing neighborhood crowd, who come for strong drinks and good, greasy bar food (tater tots, cheesesteak subs) as well as mussels and Sunday brunch.

Little Havana BAR

(410-837-9903; www.litlehavanas.com; 1325 Key Hwy, Federal Hill; 11:30am-midnight Mon-Thu, 11:30am-2am Fri & Sat, 11am-midnight Sun) A good after-work spot and a great place to sip mojitos on the waterfront deck, this converted brick warehouse is a major draw on warm, sunny days (especially around weekend brunch time).

Club Charles BAR

(410-727-8815; www.clubcharles.us; 1724 N Charles St, Mt Vernon; 6pm-2am) Hipsters adorned in the usual skinny jeans/vintage T-shirt uniform, as well as characters from other walks of life, flock to this 1940s art-deco cocktail lounge to enjoy good tunes and cheap drinks.

☆ Entertainment

Baltimoreans *love* sports. The town plays hard and parties even harder, with tailgating parties in parking lots and games showing on numerous televisions.

★ **Oriole Park at Camden Yards** STADIUM

(888-848-2473; www.orioles.com; 333 W Camden St, Downtown) The **Baltimore Orioles** play here, arguably the best ballpark in America. Daily tours (adult/child under 15 years $9/6) of the stadium are offered during regular season (April through September).

M&T Bank Stadium STADIUM

(410-261-7283; www.baltimoreravens.com; 1101 Russell St, Downtown) The **Baltimore Ravens** play football here from September to January.

ℹ Information

Baltimore Area Visitor Center (877-225-8466; www.baltimore.org; 401 Light St, Inner Harbor; 10am-5pm Oct-Apr, 9am-6pm May-Sep, closed Mon Jan & Feb) Located on the Inner Harbor. Sells the Harbor Pass (adult/child $52/38), which gives admission to five major area attractions.

University of Maryland Medical Center (410-328-8667; www.umm.edu; 22 S Greene St, University of Maryland-Baltimore) Has a 24-hour emergency room.

ℹ Getting There & Away

The **Baltimore/Washington International Thurgood Marshall Airport** (p296) is 10 miles south of downtown via I-295.

Departing from a terminal 2 miles southwest of Inner Harbor, Greyhound (www.greyhound.com) and **Peter Pan Bus Lines** (800-343-9999; www.peterpanbus.com; 2110 Haines St, Carroll-Camden) have numerous buses to Washington, DC ($8 to $12, roughly every 45 minutes, one hour) and from New York ($15 to $42, 14 to 17 per day, 4½ hours). The **BoltBus** (877-265-8287; www.boltbus.com; 1578 Maryland Ave;) ($15 to $34) has six to 10 buses a day to/from NYC; it departs from a street-side location outside of Baltimore's Penn Station.

Penn Station (https://mta.maryland.gov/marc-train; 1500 N Charles St, Charles North) is in north Baltimore. MARC operates weekday commuter trains to/from Washington, DC ($8, about one hour). Amtrak (www.amtrak.com) trains serve the East Coast and beyond.

ℹ Getting Around

Light rail (http://mta.maryland.gov/light-rail) runs from BWI airport to Lexington Market and Penn Station. Train frequency is every five to 10 minutes. MARC trains run hourly on weekdays (and six to nine times daily on weekends) between Penn Station and BWI airport for $5. Check Maryland Transit Administration (www.mtamaryland.gov) for all local transportation schedules.

Supershuttle (www.supershuttle.com) provides a BWI-van service to the Inner Harbor for $23.

Baltimore Water Taxi (410-563-3900; www.baltimorewatertaxi.com; Inner Harbor; daily pass adult/child 3-12yr $14/6; 10am-midnight May-Aug, shorter hours rest of year) docks at all harborside attractions.

Annapolis

Annapolis is as charming as state capitals get. The Colonial architecture, cobblestones, flickering lamps and brick row houses are worthy of Dickens, but the effect isn't artificial: this city has preserved, rather than created, its heritage.

Perched on Chesapeake Bay, Annapolis revolves around the city's rich maritime traditions. It's home to the US Naval Academy, whose 'middies' (midshipmen students) stroll through town in their starched white uniforms. Sailing is not just a hobby here but a way of life, and the city docks are crammed with vessels of all shapes and sizes. With its historic sights, water adventures and great dining and shopping, Annapolis is worthy of more than a day trip.

⊙ Sights

US Naval Academy
UNIVERSITY

(☑ visitor center 410-293-8687; www.usnabsd.com/for-visitors; Randall St, btwn Prince George and King George Sts) The undergraduate college of the US Navy is one of the most selective universities in America. The Armel-Leftwich visitor center is the place to book tours and immerse yourself in all things Academy-related. Come for the formation weekdays at 12:05pm sharp, when the 4000 midshipmen and -women conduct a 20-minute military marching display in the yard. Photo ID is required for entry. If you've got a thing for American naval history, revel in the Naval Academy Museum (☑ 410-293-2108; www.usna.edu/museum; 118 Maryland Ave; ⊙ 9am-5pm Mon-Sat, 11am-5pm Sun) FREE.

Maryland State House
HISTORIC BUILDING

(☑ 410-946-5400; http://msa.maryland.gov/msa/mdstatehouse/html/home.html; 91 State Circle; ⊙ 9am-5pm) FREE The country's oldest state capitol in continuous legislative use, the grand 1772 State House also served as national capital from 1733 to 1734. Notably, Gen George Washington returned his commission here as Commander in Chief of the Continental Army in 1783 after the Revolutionary War, ensuring that power would be shared with Congress. The Maryland Senate is in action from January to April. The giant acorn atop the dome stands for wisdom.

Hammond Harwood House
MUSEUM

(☑ 410-263-4683; www.hammondharwoodhouse.org; 19 Maryland Ave; adult/child $10/5; ⊙ noon-5pm Tue-Sun Apr-Dec) Of the many historical homes in town, the 1774 HHH is the one to visit. It has a superb collection of decorative arts, including furniture, paintings and ephemera dating from the 18th century, and is one of the finest existing British Colonial homes in America. Knowledgeable guides help bring the past to life on 50-minute house tours (held at the top of the hour).

William Paca House & Garden
HISTORIC BUILDING

(☑ 410-990-4543; www.annapolis.org; 186 Prince George St; full house & garden tour $10, 1st floor house & garden tour $8, garden tour only $5; ⊙ 10am-5pm Mon-Sat, noon-5pm Sun late Mar-Dec) Take a tour (offered hourly on the half-hour) through this Georgian mansion for insight into 18th-century life for the upper class in Maryland. Don't miss the blooming garden in spring.

Kunta Kinte–Alex Haley Memorial
MONUMENT

Beside City Dock, the Kunta Kinte–Alex Haley Memorial marks the spot where Kunta Kinte – ancestor of *Roots* author Alex Haley – was brought in chains from Africa. The statues here depict Haley sharing the story of his ancestor with three children.

⌲ Tours

Four Centuries Walking Tour
WALKING

(☑ 410-268-7601; www.annapolistours.com; 2¼ hr tour adult/child 3-11yr $18/10) A costumed docent will lead you on this great introduction to all things Annapolis. The 10:30am tour leaves from the visitor center and the 1:30pm tour leaves from the information booth at City Dock. There's a slight variation in sights visited by each, but both cover the country's largest concentration of 18th-century buildings, influential African Americans and colonial spirits who don't want to leave. The associated one-hour **Pirates of the Chesapeake Cruise** (☑ 410-263-0002; www.chesapeakepirates.com; 311 3rd St; $22; ⊙ mid-Apr–Sep; ⊙) is good 'yar'-worthy fun

Woodwind
CRUISE

(☑ 410-263-7837; www.schoonerwoodwind.com; 80 Compromise St; sunset cruise adult/child under 12yr $46/29; ⊙ mid-Apr–Oct) This beautiful 74ft schooner offers two-hour day and sunset cruises. Or splurge for the Woodwind 'boat & breakfast' package, one of the more unique lodging options in town.

🛏 Sleeping

Inns and B&Bs fills the historic downtown. Several hotels line West St, which runs west from Church Circle. National hotel chains cluster near exits 22 and 23 off USA 50/301.

Historic Inns of Annapolis
HOTEL $$

(☑ 410-263-2641; www.historicinnsofannapolis.com; 58 State Circle; r from $189; P ✳ 🛜) The Historic Inns comprise three different boutique guesthouses, each set in a heritage building in the heart of old Annapolis: the Maryland Inn, the Governor Calvert House and the Robert Johnson House. Common areas are packed with period details, and the best rooms boast antiques, a fireplace and attractive views (while the cheapest can be small). Check in at Governor Calvert House.

ScotLaur Inn
GUESTHOUSE $$

(☑ 410-268-5665; www.scotlaurinn.com; 165 Main St; r $119-149; P ✳ 🛜) The folks from Chick

& Ruth's Delly offer 10 rooms, each with wrought-iron beds, floral wallpaper and private bath. The quarters are small but have a familial atmosphere (the guesthouse is named after the owners' children Scott and Lauren).

O'Callaghan Hotel
HOTEL $$

(☑ 410-263-7700; www.ocallaghanhotels-us.com; 174 West St; r from $180; P❄️🛜) This Irish chain offers attractively furnished rooms that are nicely equipped, with big windows, a writing desk, brass fixtures and comfy mattresses. It's on West St, just a short stroll to a good selection of bars and restaurants, and about a 12-minute walk to the old quarter.

🍴 Eating & Drinking

With the Chesapeake at its doorstep, Annapolis has superb seafood. The recent openings of several farm-to-table-minded restaurants have added some depth to the dining scene along Main St and near the dock.

The historic downtown is festive on Friday and Saturday nights on Main St and along the waterfront, with many folks kicking back and sipping beers – many beers – on patios near the dock, watching the boats parade past. Plenty of cozy pubs downtown.

49 West
CAFE $

(☑ 410-626-9796; www.49westcoffeehouse.com; 49 West St; breakfast mains $6-14, lunch mains $9-15, dinner mains $9-24; ⏰7:30am-midnight Sun-Thu, to 2am Fri & Sat; 🛜) This comfy, art-filled coffeehouse is a good spot for coffee and light bites during the day (sandwiches, soups, salads) and heartier bistro fare by night, along with wines and cocktails. There's live music some nights.

Chick & Ruth's Delly
DINER $

(☑ 410-269-6737; www.chickandruths.com; 165 Main St; mains $8-15; ⏰6:30am-11:30pm Sun-Thu, to 12:30am Fri & Sat; 🍴) A cornerstone of Annapolis, the Delly is bursting with affable quirkiness and a big menu, heavy on sandwiches and breakfast fare. Patriots can relive grade-school days reciting the Pledge of Allegiance weekdays at 8:30am and Saturdays and Sundays at 9:30am.

★ Vin 909
AMERICAN $$

(☑ 410-990-1846; www.vin909.com; 909 Bay Ridge Ave; small plates $12-20; ⏰5:30-10pm Tue-Sun & noon-3pm Wed-Sat, closes at 9pm Tue & Sun in winter) Perched on a little wooded hill and boasting intimate but enjoyably casual ambience, Vin is the best thing happening in

Annapolis for food. Farm-sourced goodness features in the form of duck confit, barbecue sliders and homemade pizzas with toppings like wild mushrooms, foie gras and Spanish chorizo. There's a great wine selection, including over three dozen wines by the glass.

★ Jimmy Cantler's Riverside Inn
SEAFOOD $$

(☑ 410-757-1311; www.cantlers.com; 458 Forest Beach Rd, Annapolis; mains $10-34; ⏰11am-11pm Sun-Thu, to midnight Fri & Sat) This is one of the best crab shacks in the state, and eating a steamed crab has been elevated to an art form – a hands-on, messy endeavor, normally accompanied by corn on the cob and ice-cold beer. Cantler's is a little ways outside of Annapolis, but like many crab houses, it can be approached by road or boat (a waterfront location is crab-eating industry standard).

Boatyard Bar & Grill
SEAFOOD $$

(☑ 410-216-6206; www.boatyardbarandgrill.com; 400 4th St; mains $10-27; ⏰7:30am-midnight Mon-Fri, 8am-midnight Sat & Sun; 🍴) This bright, nautically themed restaurant is an inviting spot for crab cakes, fish and chips, fish tacos and other seafood. Happy hour (3pm to 7pm Monday to Friday) draws in the crowds with 99¢ oysters and $3 drafts. It's a short drive (or 10-minute walk) from the City Dock, across the Spa Creek Bridge.

Rams Head Tavern
PUB FOOD $$$

(☑ 410-268-4545; www.ramsheadtavern.com; 33 West St; mains $10-30; ⏰11am-2am Mon-Sat, from 10am Sun) Serves pub fare and refreshing microbrews in an attractive exposed-brick and oak-paneled setting. Well-known bands perform next door at the **Rams Head On Stage** (tickets $23 to $115).

Fox's Den
PUB

(☑ 443-808-8991; www.foxsden.com; 179 Main St; ⏰5-11pm Mon, Wed & Thu, 5pm-midnight Fri, 4pm-midnight Sat, 4-11pm Sun) Head underground for microbrews and craft cocktails, all served in a snug gastropub in the thick of the Main St action.

ℹ️ Information

There's a **visitor center** (☑ 410-280-0445; www.visitannapolis.org; 26 West St; ⏰9am-5pm) on West St and a seasonal information booth at City Dock (open 9am to 5pm March to October). For information about tours and sights at the Naval Academy, stop by the expansive **Armel-Leftwich Visitor Center** (☑ 410-293-8687; www.usnabsd.com/for-visitors; 52 King

George St, Gate 1, City Dock entrance; tours adult/child $11/9; ⊙ 9am-5pm Mar-Dec, 9am-4pm Jan & Feb) on the Yard near the waterfront.

ℹ Getting There & Away

Greyhound (☑ 800-231-2222; www.greyhound. com; 275 Harry S Truman Pkwy) (www.greyhound.com) runs buses to Washington, DC ($12 to $15, daily) from a pick-up and drop-off stop five miles west of the historic downtown.

Eastern Shore

Just across the Chesapeake Bay Bridge, nondescript suburbs give way to unbroken miles of bird-dotted wetlands, serene waterscapes, endless cornfields, sandy beaches and friendly villages. The Eastern Shore retains its charm despite the growing influx of city-dwelling yuppies and day-trippers. This area revolves around the water: working waterfront communities still survive off Chesapeake Bay and its tributaries, and boating, fishing, crabbing and hunting are integral to local life. Come here to explore nature by trail, boat or bicycle, to read on the beach, delve into regional history and, of course, enjoy the delicious seafood.

ℹ Getting There & Around

The region is best explored by car. Baltimore is 70 miles from Easton and 150 miles from Ocean City.

St Michaels & Tilghman Island

The prettiest little village on the Eastern Shore, St Michaels lives up to its motto as the 'Heart and Soul of Chesapeake Bay.' Hugging US 33, it's a mix of old Victorian homes, quaint B&Bs, boutique shops and working docks, where escape artists from Washington mix with salty-dog watermen. During the War of 1812, inhabitants rigged up lanterns in a nearby forest and blacked out the town. British naval gunners shelled the trees, allowing St Michaels to escape destruction. The building now known as the **Cannonball House** (Mulberry St, St Michaels) was the only structure to have been hit.

At the end of the road at the end of the peninsula, and over the US 33 drawbridge, tiny **Tilghman Island** still runs a working waterfront, where local captains take visitors out on graceful sailing vessels.

⊙ Sights & Activities

Chesapeake Bay Maritime Museum MUSEUM
(☑ 410-745-2916; www.cbmm.org; 213 N Talbot St, St Michaels; adult/child 6-17yr $15/6; ⊙ 9am-5pm May-Oct, 10am-4pm Nov-Apr; ⚐) Throughout its indoor-outdoor exhibits, the Chesapeake Bay Maritime Museum delves into the deep ties between Shore folk and America's largest estuary. Learn about a lighthouse keeper's life in the 1800s inside the relocated 1879 lighthouse.

Lady Patty Classic Yacht Charters BOATING
(☑ 410-886-1127; www.ladypatty.com; 6176 Tilghman Island Rd, Tilghman Island; cruise adult/child under 13yr from $40/25; ⊙ tours Wed-Mon May-Oct) Runs memorable two-hour sails on the Chesapeake on a 1935 racing yacht.

🛏 Sleeping & Eating

Parsonage Inn INN $$
(☑ 410-745-8383; www.parsonage-inn.com; 210 N Talbot St, St Michaels; r $210-290; P ✳ 🛜) Classic Victorian-era decor is brightened here and there with unexpected splashes of color – is that a Hawaiian quilt? – inside the red-brick Parsonage Inn, which is under new ownership. Breakfast is a focus, and you might find deconstructed scotch eggs on the menu. Close to the maritime museum.

Crab Claw SEAFOOD $$
(☑ 410-745-2900; www.thecrabclaw.com; 304 Burns St, St Michaels; mains $11-30; ⊙ 11am-10pm mid-Mar–Oct) Next door to the Chesapeake Bay Maritime Museum, the Crab Claw serves up tasty Maryland blue crabs to splendid views over the harbor. Avoid the seafood sampler, unless you're a fan of deep-fried seafood.

ℹ Getting There & Away

St Michaels and Tilghman Island border US 33 on a narrow, zigzagging peninsula. US 33 leads west toward the towns from Easton. If you have a friend with a boat docked on the Chesapeake Bay, this is the time to ask for a ride – both towns have docks. They are also in Talbot County, which has more than 600 miles of shoreline.

Berlin

Imagine a typical small-town-America main street, cute that vision up by a few points, and you've come close to the Eastern Shore village of Berlin. Most of the buildings here are handsomely preserved, and antique shops litter the area. Several great restaurants dot the easily walkable downtown. The city is a convenient and appealing launchpad for exploring Assateague Island (p308) and the surrounding Eastern Shore.

For such a small town, Berlin has an impressive number of restaurants serving great seafood and American dishes. Most are within walking distance of the historic inn downtown.

✗ Eating

Drummer's Cafe
AMERICAN $$

(https://atlantichotel.com/drummers-cafe-atlantic-hotel; 2 N Main St; lunch mains $10-16, dinner mains $18-34; ⊘11am-9pm) The dining room of the Atlantic Hotel is as grand as the hotel itself, all big windows, natural sunshine and – come evening – flickering candlelight. The food references the best of the Chesapeake; filet mignon gets even more decadent with a crab cake. In the evening it's also fun to watch the small town roll by while enjoying a drink on the front porch of the hotel.

Fins Ale House & Raw Bar
SEAFOOD $$

(📱410-641-3000; www.facebook.com/FinsAleHouseBerlin; 119 N Main St; mains $12-30; ⊘11am-9:15pm Sun-Thu, to 10pm Fri & Sat) The lump crab cake is so darn good you might just consider packing up and moving to Berlin. And from the happy crowds filling the place, others may have the same idea. It's not on the water, but considerate service, big windows, a cozy patio and enticing seafood dishes in every direction make Fins the next best thing to a seafood shack by the ocean.

❶ Getting There & Away

Berlin sits near the junction of Hwy 113 and US 50, about 8 miles southwest of Ocean City.

Ocean City

Two words describe 'The OC' from June through August: party central. This is where you'll experience the American seaside resort in its wildest glory. Some might call it tacky. Others might call it, well, fun. Here you can take a spin on nausea-inducing thrill rides, buy a T-shirt with obscene slogans and drink to excess at cheesy theme bars. The center of action is the 2.5-mile-long boardwalk, which stretches from the inlet to 27th St. The beach is attractive, but you'll have to contend with horny teenagers, heavy traffic and noisy crowds; the beaches north of the boardwalk are much quieter. How busy is it? They say Ocean City welcomes 3.4 million visitors in summer – in a town with a year-round population just over 7000!

◎ Sights

Ocean City Life-Saving Station Museum
MUSEUM

(📱410-289-4991; www.ocmuseum.org; 813 S Atlantic Ave; adult/child 6-17yr $3/1; ⊘10am-4pm May & Oct, to 6pm Jun-Sep, 10am-4pm Wed-Sun Apr & Nov) At the southern end of the boardwalk, this small but engaging museum sits inside an 1891 life-saving station. Here, the keeper and six to eight 'surfmen' lived and responded to emergency calls for ships in distress. Exhibits include stories about nearby shipwrecks and a display spotlighting rescue gear, including a 26ft-long rescue boat, which would look rather small and fragile in a storm!

Trimpers Rides
AMUSEMENT PARK

(📱410-289-8617; www.trimpersrides.com; S 1st St & Boardwalk; unlimited afternoon rides $26; ⊘3pm-midnight Mon-Fri , noon-midnight Sat & Sun, hours vary seasonally) If you really want

---

MARYLAND BLUE CRABS

Eating at a crab shack, where the dress code stops at shorts and flip-flops, is the quintessential Chesapeake Bay experience. Folks in these parts take their crabs seriously, and can spend hours debating the intricacies of how to crack a crab, the proper way to prepare crabs and where to find the best ones. There is one thing Marylanders can agree on: they must be blue crabs (scientific name: *Callinectes sapidus*, or 'beautiful swimmers'). Sadly, blue crab numbers have suffered with the continuing pollution of the Chesapeake Bay, and many crabs you eat here are imported from elsewhere.

Steamed crabs are prepared very simply, using beer and Old Bay seasoning. One of the best crab shacks in the state is near Annapolis at Jimmy Cantler's Riverside Inn (p305), located 4 miles northeast of the Maryland State House, across the Severn River Bridge. Another fine spot is across the bay at the Crab Claw.

WORTH A TRIP

ASSATEAGUE ISLAND

Just 8 miles south but a world away from Ocean City is Assateague Island seashore, a perfectly barren landscape of sand dunes and beautiful, secluded beaches. This undeveloped barrier island is populated by a herd of wild horses, made famous in the book *Misty of Chincoteague*.

The island is divided into three sections. In Maryland there's **Assateague State Park** (☑ 410-641-2918; Rte 611; admission $6; campsites $28-39; ☉ day-use areas 7am-sunset, campground late Apr-Oct) and federally administered **Assateague Island National Seashore** (☑ 410-641-1441; www.nps.gov/asis; Rte 611; per pedestrian/vehicle per week $5/20; ☉ visitor center 9am-5pm Mar-Dec, closed Tue & Wed Jan & Feb). **Chincoteague National Wildlife Refuge** (www.fws.gov/refuge/chincoteague; 8231 Beach Rd, Chincoteague Island; daily/weekly vehicle pass $8/15; ☉ 5am-10pm May-Sep, 6am-6pm Nov-Mar, to 8pm Apr & Oct; ℗ ♿) is in Virginia. For an overview of the three sections, check out the Plan your Visit section of the national park website (www.nps.gov/asis) or pick up the *Assateague Island National Seashore* pamphlet, which has a helpful map.

As well as swimming and sunbathing, recreational activities include birding, kayaking, canoeing, crabbing and fishing. There are no services on the Maryland side of the island, so you must bring all your own food and drink. Don't forget insect repellent: the mosquitoes and biting horseflies can be ferocious!

to engage in tacky seaside fun to the fullest extent possible, hit up Trimpers Rides, one of the oldest of old-school amusement parks. Have some fries with vinegar, play the games and enjoy watching the teenage staff dance the ballet of summer hormonal overload. Tickets are 60¢ each, with a varying number required per ride.

🛏 Sleeping

Hotels and motels line the boardwalk and the streets running parallel to the ocean. These lodgings are a mix of national chains and independently owned accommodations. From June through August they're ready to pack in guests. For a quieter stay, try a B&B or spend the night in Berlin, 8 miles south.

King Charles Hotel GUESTHOUSE $$
(☑ 410-289-6141; www.kingcharleshotel.com; 1209 N Baltimore Ave, cnr N Baltimore Ave & 12th St; r $169-189; ℗ ❄ ☎) This place could be a quaint summer cottage, except it happens to be a short stroll to the heart of the boardwalk action. It has aging but clean rooms with small porches attached, and it's quiet (ie it's not a party hotel).

🍴 Eating & Drinking

Surf 'n' turf and all-you-can-eat deals are the order of the day.

Beer. Wine. Booze. Sugary cocktails. You'll find it all here in excess. And often at ridiculously low prices, especially during happy

hour late in the afternoon. The boardwalk is a lively spot well into the evening, with a theme park, wacky museums and street performers keeping things interesting.

Liquid Assets MODERN AMERICAN $$
(☑ 410-524-7037; https://la94.com/; 9301 Coastal Hwy, cnr 94th St & Coastal Hwy; mains $13-34; ☉ 11:30am-11pm Sun-Thu, to midnight Fri & Sat) Like a diamond in the rough, this bistro and wine shop is hidden in a strip mall in north OC. The menu is a refreshing mix of innovative seafood, grilled meats and regional classics.

Seacrets BAR
(☑ 410-524-4900; www.seacrets.com; 117 49th St, cnr W 49th St & the Bay; ☉ 11am-midnight) A Jamaican-themed, rum-soaked bar straight out of MTV's *Spring Break*. You can drift around in an inner tube while sipping a drink and people-watching at OC's most famous meat-market. When it comes to the wildest beach party bar, this is the one against which all other claimants must be judged. The distillery, which opened in 2016, seems a bit superfluous.

❶ Getting There & Around

Ocean City is 140 miles southeast of Baltimore via Hwy 10 and US 50. Greyhound no longer runs to Ocean City.

The **Coastal Highway Beach Bus** (☑ 410-723-2174; http://ococean.com/explore-oc/getting-around-oc; day pass $3; ☉ 24hr) travels up and down the length of the beach around the clock year-round. There's also a **tram** (☑ 410-289-5311; http://ococean.com/explore-oc/getting-around-oc; per ride $3, day pass $6; ⊙11am-midnight Jun-Aug) that runs along the boardwalk (https://oceancitymd.gov/oc) from June through September. For details about off-season transit and schedules, visit www.shoretransit.org.

Western Maryland

The western spine of Maryland is mountain country. The Appalachian peaks soar to 3000ft above sea level, and the surrounding valleys are packed with rugged scenery and Civil War battlefields. This is Maryland's playground, where hiking, skiing, rock climbing and white-water rafting draw the outdoors-loving crowd.

When trip planning, remember that the narrow Maryland panhandle is bordered by Virginia, West Virginia and Pennsylvania. If you're exploring Civil War battlefields or looking for larger towns for an overnight stay, check our regional map for options that may be just a few miles over state lines.

❶ Getting There & Around

Towns in western Maryland may look close to each other on a map, but narrow and twisting mountain roads can extend driving times. The main interstates running east–west are the I-70 and I-68, with I-81 traveling north–south through the region. MARC trains stop in **Frederick** (☑ 301-682-9716; https://mta.maryland.gov/marc-train; 100 S East St, Frederick) while Amtrak services Cumberland (p311). Greyhound stops in both Cumberland and Frederick. For flights, consider Dulles (p316) or Baltimore/Washington International Thurgood Marshall Airport (p296).

Frederick & Mt Airy

Central Frederick is, well, perfect. Its historic, pedestrian-friendly center of red-brick row houses is filled with a diverse array of restaurants. You'll also find an engaged, cultured arts community anchored by the excellent Weinberg Center for the Arts. The meandering Carroll Creek runs through it all, flanked by a lovely park with a mural-painted bridge, found at Carroll St. Unlike other communities in the region with historic districts, this is a mid-sized city, an important commuter base for thousands of federal government employees and a biotechnology hub in its own right.

The town of Mt Airy is 7 miles east of Frederick. Its compact downtown historic district is lined with 19th- and 20th-century buildings. Once a busy commercial stop along the B&O Railroad, today the downtown is a nice place to stretch your legs on a drive along the National Historic Road scenic byway (www.visitmaryland.org), which links Baltimore to western Maryland. Vineyards dot the region.

❂ Sights

Brunswick Visitor Center MUSEUM
(☑ 301-834-7100; www.nps.gov/choh; 40 W Potomac St, Brunswick; rail museum adult/child $7/4; ⊙10am-2pm Thu & Fri, to 4pm Sat, 1-4pm Sun) The C&O Canal's little Brunswick Visitor Center doubles as the Brunswick Rail Museum. As quiet as this town is, it was once home to the largest rail yard (7 miles long) owned by a single company in the world. Those days are long past, but the museum will appeal to trainspotters, and you have to have a heart of stone not to be charmed by the 1700-square-foot model railroad that depicts the old Baltimore and Ohio railway.

Elk Run Vineyards WINERY
(☑ 410-775-2513; www.elkrun.com; 15113 Liberty Rd, Mt Airy; tastings from $6, tours free; ⊙10am-6pm Tue, Wed & Sat, to 9pm Fri & 1-5pm Sun May-Sep, 10am-5pm Wed-Sat & noon-5pm Sun Oct-Apr) It's tough to go wrong with Elk Run Vineyards, almost exactly halfway between Mt Airy and New Market. Stop by for live music on Wine Down Fridays ($5, 3pm to 5pm).

National Museum of Civil War Medicine MUSEUM
(☑ 301-695-1864; www.civilwarmed.org; 48 E Patrick St; adult/student/child $9.50/7/free; ⊙10am-5pm Mon-Sat, from 11am Sun) The National Museum of Civil War Medicine gives a fascinating, and sometimes gruesome, look at the health conditions soldiers and doctors faced during the war, as well as important medical advances that resulted from the conflict.

Antietam National Battlefield HISTORIC SITE
(☑ 301-432-5124; www.nps.gov/anti; 5831 Dunker Church Rd, Sharpsburg, MD; 3-day pass per person/vehicle $5/10; ⊙grounds sunrise-sunset, visitor center 9am-5pm) The site of the bloodiest day in American history is now, ironically, supremely peaceful, quiet and haunting – and

uncluttered, save for plaques and statues. On September 17, 1862, General Robert E Lee's first invasion of the North was stalled here in a tactical stalemate that left more than 23,000 dead, wounded or missing – more casualties than America had suffered in all its previous wars combined. Check out the exhibits in the visitor center then walk or drive the grounds.

Sleeping & Eating

Hollerstown Hill B&B   B&B $$
(☎ 301-228-3630; www.hollerstownhill.com; 4 Clarke Pl, Frederick; r $149; [P] [✳] [☎]) The elegant, friendly Hollerstown has four pattern-heavy rooms, two resident terriers and an elegant billiards room. This lovely Victorian sits right in the middle of the historic downtown area of Frederick, so you're within easy walking distance of all the goodness.

Brewer's Alley   PUB FOOD $$
(☎ 301-631-0089; www.brewers-alley.com; 124 N Market St, Frederick; mains $9-22; ☺ noon-11:30pm; [☎]) This bouncy brewpub is one of our favorite places in Frederick for several reasons. First, the beer: house-brewed, plenty of variety, delicious. Second, the burgers: enormous, half-pound monstrosities of staggeringly yummy proportions. Third, the rest of the menu: excellent Chesapeake seafood (including a wood-fired pizza topped with crab) and Frederick county farm produce and meats. The small patio is pleasant on sunny days.

Getting There & Away

Frederick is accessible via Greyhound (www. greyhound.com) and MARC (p309) trains at the station located across from the **visitor center** (☎ 301-600-4047; www.visitfrederick.org/visit/visitor-center; 151 S East St; ☺ 9am-5:30pm). The MARC train Brunswick Line connects Frederick with Harpers Ferry, WV, Silver Spring, MD and Washington, DC.

Cumberland

At the Potomac River, the frontier outpost of Fort Cumberland (not to be confused with the Cumberland Gap between Virginia and Kentucky) was the pioneer gateway across the Alleghenies to Pittsburgh and the Ohio River. Today Cumberland has expanded into the outdoor recreation trade to guide visitors to the region's rivers, forests and mountains. Sights are a short stroll from the pedestrian-friendly streets of downtown.

◉ Sights & Activities

C&O Canal National
Historic Park   NATIONAL PARK
(☎ 301-739-4200; www.nps.gov/choh; ☺ sunrise-sunset) **FREE** A marvel of engineering, the C&O Canal was designed to stretch alongside the Potomac River from Chesapeake Bay to the Ohio River. Construction on the canal began in 1828 but was halted here in 1850 by the Appalachian Mountains. The park's protected 185-mile corridor includes a 12ft-wide towpath, hiking and bicycling trail, which goes all the way from here to Georgetown in DC. The **Cumberland Visitor Center** (☎ 301-722-8226; www.nps.gov/choh; 13 Canal St; ☺ 9am-5pm; [P]) has displays chronicling the importance of river trade in eastern seaboard history.

Allegany Museum   MUSEUM
(☎ 301-777-7200; www.alleganymuseum.org; 3 Pershing St; ☺ 10am-4pm Tue-Sat, from 1pm Sun) **FREE** Set in the old courthouse, this is an intriguing place to delve into Cumberland's past, with exhibits by local folk artist and woodcarver Claude Yoder; a model of the old shanty town that sprang up along the canal; 1920s firefighting gear; and beautifully garbed puppets and other curiosities.

Western Maryland Scenic Railroad   TOURS
(☎ 800-872-4650; www.wmsr.com; 13 Canal St; adult/child $46/31; ☺ generally 11:30am Fri & Sat, 1pm Sun mid-Apr–Oct, hours & trips vary seasonally) Outside the Cumberland Visitor Center, near the start of the C&O Canal, passengers can catch steam-locomotive rides, traversing forests and steep ravines, to the Frostburg depot, a 3½-hour round-trip.

Cumberland Trail Connection   CYCLING
(☎ 301-777-8724; www.ctcbikes.com; 14 Howard St, Canal Pl; per half-day/day/week from $20/30/150; ☺ 8am-7pm Apr-Oct, 10:30am-6pm Nov-Mar) Conveniently located near the start of the C&O Canal, this outfit rents out bicycles (cruisers, touring bikes and mountain bikes), and also arranges shuttle service anywhere from Pittsburgh to DC.

Sleeping & Eating

Inn on Decatur   GUESTHOUSE $$
(☎ 301-722-4887; www.theinnondecatur.net; 108 Decatur St; r $142; [✳] [☎]) Offers comfy guestrooms just a short stroll to pedestrianized Baltimore St in downtown Cumberland. The friendly owners have a wealth of knowledge on the area, and offer a bike shuttle package.

Queen City Creamery & Deli   DINER $

(☎301-777-0011; www.queencitycreamery.com; 108 W Harrison St; mains $4-9; ⊗7am-9pm Mon-Thu, 7am-10pm Fri, 8am-10pm Sat, 8am-9pm Sun) This retro soda fountain is like a 1940s time warp, with creamy shakes and homemade frozen custard, thick sandwiches and belly-filling breakfasts.

ⓘ Getting There & Away

The **Amtrak station** (www.amtrak.com; 201 E Harrison St) is close to downtown. Cumberland is on the daily Capitol Limited route that links Washington, DC and Chicago. Pittsburgh is 100 miles northwest of the city. Greyhound buses also stop here. From the eastern part of the Maryland, Cumberland can be reached via I-70 and I-68.

DELAWARE

Tiny Delaware, the nation's second-smallest state (96 miles long and less than 35 miles across at its widest point) is overshadowed by its neighbors – and often overlooked by visitors to the region. And that's too bad, because Delaware has a lot more on offer than just tax-free shopping and chicken farms.

Long, white sandy beaches, cute colonial villages, a cozy countryside and small-town charm characterize the state that happily calls itself the 'Small Wonder.' It's also the home state of former vice president and US senator Joe Biden, a resident of Wilmington.

History

In colonial days, Delaware was the subject of an aggressive land feud between Dutch, Swedish and British settlers. The first two imported classically northern European middle-class concepts; the last a plantation-based aristocracy – which is partly why Delaware remains a typically mid-Atlantic cultural hybrid today.

The little state's big moment came on December 7, 1787, when Delaware became the first colony to ratify the US Constitution, thus becoming the first state in the Union. It remained in that union throughout the Civil War, despite supporting slavery. During this period, as throughout much of the state's history, the economy drew on its chemical industry. DuPont, the world's second-largest chemical company, was founded here in 1802 as a gunpowder factory by French immigrant Eleuthère Irénée du Pont. Low taxes drew other firms in the 20th century, boosting the state's prosperity.

ⓘ Getting There & Around

The coastal cities are 120 miles from both Washington, DC and Baltimore. Wilmington is in the northern reaches of the state, 75 miles northeast of Baltimore via I-95 and 30 miles south of Philadelphia via I-95 – and just a few miles from the Pennsylvania state line. Amtrak run seven routes through Wilmington. The closest major airport to Wilmington is Philadelphia International Airport.

Delaware Beaches

With beach towns for every personality along with gorgeous coastal views, Delaware's 28 miles of sandy Atlantic beaches are the best reason to linger here. They're also quick and easy to reach for city folk from Washington, DC, Baltimore and NYC looking to escape the grind. Most businesses and services are open year-round. Outside of June to August, bargains abound.

Lewes

In 1631 the Dutch gave this whaling settlement the pretty name of Zwaanendael, or Valley of the Swans, before promptly getting massacred by local Nanticokes. The name was changed to Lewes (loo-iss) when William Penn gained control of the area. Today it's an attractive gem with a mix of English and Dutch architecture. Pretty Cape Henlopen State Park is 2½ miles from downtown.

⊙ Sights & Activities

Cape Henlopen State Park   STATE PARK
(☎302-645-8983; www.destateparks.com/park/cape-henlopen; 15099 Cape Henlopen Dr; per car out-of-state/in-state $10/5; ⊗8am-sunset) One mile east of Lewes, more than 4000 acres of dune bluffs, pine forests and wetlands are preserved at this lovely state park that's popular with bird-watchers, beachgoers and campers. You can see clear to Cape May from the observation tower. **North Shores beach** draws many gay and lesbian couples. Campsites ($30 to $54) and cabins ($120) are also available. The admission fee is cash only.

Zwaanendael Museum   MUSEUM
(☎302-645-1148; www.http://history.delaware.gov/museums/zm/zm_main.shtml; 102 Kings Hwy; ⊗10am-5pm Tue, to 4:30pm Wed-Sat, 1:30-4:30pm Sun, open Wed-Sat only Mar-Oct) FREE This small, appealing museum is a good place to learn about the Dutch roots of Lewes.

Quest Fitness Kayak KAYAKING
(☏ 302-745-2925; www.questkayak.com; 514 E Savannah Rd; kayak hire per 2-/8-hr $25/50; ⊘ from 8am, close hours vary May-Sep, reservation only Oct-Apr) For aquatic action, Quest Fitness Kayak operates a kayak rental stand next to the Beacon Motel. It also runs scenic paddle tours around the Cape ($65).

🛏 Sleeping & Eating

Hotel Rodney HOTEL $$
(☏ 302-645-6466; www.hotelrodneydelaware.com; 142 2nd St; r $179-259, ste $329; P🐾❄@🛜🏊) This charming boutique hotel features exquisite bedding and restored antique furniture, but it also has plenty of modern touches that keep it all feeling very fresh.

Wharf SEAFOOD $$
(☏ 302-645-7846; www.thewharflewes.com; 7 Anglers Rd; mains $13-30; ⊘ 11:30am-1am mid-May–early Oct; P🐾) Across the drawbridge, the Wharf has a relaxing waterfront location, and serves a big selection of seafood and pub grub. Live music on weekends.

ℹ Getting There & Away

Cape May–Lewes Ferry (☏ 800-643-3779; www.capemaylewesferry.com; 43 Cape Henlopen Dr; per motorcycle/car $39/47, per adult/child 6-13yr $10/5) runs daily 90-minute ferries across Delaware Bay to New Jersey from the terminal, 1 mile from downtown Lewes. For foot passengers, a seasonal shuttle bus ($5) operates between the ferry terminal and Lewes. Reservations recommended. The town sits on the coast just off the Coastal Hwy/Rte 1.

Rehoboth Beach

As the closest stretch of sand to Washington, DC (121 miles), Rehoboth Beach is often dubbed 'the Nation's Summer Capital.' It is both a family-friendly and gay-friendly destination. To escape the chaos of busy Rehoboth Ave (and the heavily built-up outskirts), wander into the side streets downtown. There you'll find a mix of gingerbread houses, tree-lined streets, posh restaurants and kiddie amusements, plus a wide beach fronted by a mile-long boardwalk.

🛏 Sleeping

★**Cottages at Indian River Marina** COTTAGE $$$
(☏ 302-227-3071; www.destateparks.com/camping/cottages; 39415 Inlet Rd; weekly peak/shoulder/off-season $1900/1250/850, 2 days off-season $300; P❄) These cottages, located in Delaware Seashore State Park five miles south of town, are some of our favorite local vacation rentals. Not for the decor per se, but for the patios and unadulterated views across the pristine beach to the ocean. Each cottage has two bedrooms and a loft.

Crosswinds Motel MOTEL $$$
(☏ 302-227-7997; www.crosswindsmotel.com; 312 Rehoboth Ave; r $269-299; P❄🛜) Rooms pop with a bit of fresh modern style at this simple but nicely designed motel in the heart of Rehoboth, with welcome amenities (mini fridge, coffeemaker, flat-screen TV) and friendly service. Walk to the beach in 12 minutes. Note that rates drop significantly during the week and in the off-season.

Hotel Rehoboth BOUTIQUE HOTEL $$$
(☏ 302-227-4300; www.hotelrehoboth.com; 247 Rehoboth Ave; r $359; P❄@🛜🏊) This boutique hotel has gained a reputation for great service and luxurious amenities, including a free shuttle to the beach.

🍴 Eating & Drinking

Henlopen City Oyster House SEAFOOD $$$
(☏ 302-260-9193; www.hcoysterhouse.com; 50 Wilmington Ave; mains $10-36; ⊘ 3-5pm happy hour only, dinner from 5pm, lunch served in the off-season) Seafood lovers won't want to miss this elegant but inviting spot, where an enticing raw bar and mouth-watering seafood dishes draw crowds (arrive early; no reservations). Good microbrews, cocktails and wine selections.

★**Dogfish Head Brewings & Eats** MICROBREWERY
(☏ 302-226-2739; www.dogfish.com; 320 Rehoboth Ave; mains $12-25; ⊘ 11am-1am) Check the chalkboard to see the long list of brews available at this iconic brewery, which also serves up tasty pizzas, burgers, crab cakes and other pub fare. It all goes perfectly with the award-winning IPAs. Kids menu available with $6 meals. Dogfish, in its current location for 22 years, was preparing to open a $4 million brewpub next door at the time of research, with space for live music.

ℹ Getting There & Away

BestBus (www.bestbus.com) offers bus service from DC ($40, 2¼ hours) and NYC ($49, 4½ hours) to Rehoboth; runs summertime only (late May through early September).

The Jolly Trolley (www.jollytrolly.com) connects Rehoboth and Dewey beaches, and makes frequent stops along the way. A round-trip costs $5, and the trolley runs from 8am to 2am June to August. Cash only.

Wilmington

A unique cultural milieu (African Americans, Jews and Caribbeans) and an energetic arts scene make this city worth a visit. Wilmington is also a good launchpad for exploring the scenic Brandywine Valley, 6 miles north. And no description of Wilmington is complete without mentioning hometown politician Joe Biden, former vice-president and US senator, who regularly rode Amtrak between Wilmington and Washington, DC. After his tenure as vice-president ended in 2017, he rode Amtrak home.

◉ Sights

Delaware Art Museum   MUSEUM
(☑302-571-9590; www.delart.org; 2301 Kentmere Pkwy; adult/child 7-18yr $12/6, admission free Thu evenings & Sun; ◷10am-4pm Wed & Fri-Sun, to 8pm Thu) Exhibits work of the local Brandywine School, including Edward Hopper, John Sloan and three generations of Wyeths.

Delaware Center for the Contemporary Arts   MUSEUM
(☑302-656-6466; www.thedcca.org; 200 S Madison St; ◷noon-5pm Tue & Sun, noon-7pm Wed, 10am-5pm Thu-Sat) FREE Consistently displays innovative exhibitions.

Delaware History Museum   MUSEUM
(☑302-656-0637; www.dehistory.org; 504 N Market St; adult/child 3-18yr $6/4; ◷11am-4pm Wed-Sat) An art-deco Woolworth's building, this museum run by the Delaware Historical society proves the First State has done much more than earn its nickname, with historic documents, apparel and a range of artifacts.

🛏 Sleeping & Eating

Inn at Wilmington   HOTEL $$
(☑855-532-2216; www.innatwilmington.com; 300 Rocky Run Pkwy; r/ste $129/159; P❄🅟) This is a charming, good-value option 5 miles north of downtown.

Hotel du Pont   HOTEL $$$
(☑302-594-3100; www.hoteldupont.com; cnr Market & 11th Sts; r from $199; P❄🅟) The premier hotel in the state, the du Pont is luxurious and classy enough to satisfy its namesake (one of America's most successful industrialist families). The spot exudes an art-deco majesty that Jay Gatsby would have been proud of, but the goodness goes beyond the impressive lobby to well-appointed rooms and proximity to a handsome shopping arcade.

Iron Hill Brewery   PUB FOOD $$
(☑302-472-2739; www.ironhillbrewery.com; 620 Justison St; mains $12-30; ◷11:30am-11pm Mon-Fri, from 11am Sat & Sun) The spacious and airy multilevel Iron Hill Brewery is set in a converted brick warehouse on the riverfront. Satisfying microbrews go nicely with hearty pub grub.

ℹ Getting There & Away

Just off I-95, Wilmington is midway between Washington, DC and New York City, about two hours from either city. **Greyhound** (101 N French St) stops downtown. Amtrak (www.amtrak.com) trains leave from the **Joseph R. Biden Jr Railroad Station** (☑800-872-7245; www.amtrak.com; 100 S French St) and connect Wilmington with DC (1½ hours), Baltimore (45 minutes) and New York (two hours).

Brandywine Valley

After making their fortune, the French-descended Du Ponts turned the Brandywine Valley into a sort of American Loire Valley. It remains a nesting ground for the wealthy and ostentatious to this day. A few miles north of downtown Wilmington, the Delaware section is just one part of the 350-square-mile valley, which straddles the Brandywine River into Pennsylvania.

◉ Sights & Activities

Winterthur   HISTORIC SITE
(☑302-888-4600; www.winterthur.org; 5105 Kennett Pike (Rte 52); adult/child 2-11yr $20/5; ◷10am-5pm Tue-Sun) Six miles northwest of Wilmington is the 175-room country estate of industrialist Henry Francis du Pont and his collection of antiques and American arts, one of the world's largest. Nice gardens too.

Brandywine Creek State Park   STATE PARK
(☑302-577-3534; www.destateparks.com/park/brandywine-creek; 41 Adams Dam Rd; per vehicle $8; ◷8am-sunset) This state park is the gem of the area. This green space would be impressive anywhere, but is doubly so considering how close it is to prodigious urban development. Nature trails and shallow streams wend through the park.

Wilderness Canoe Trips
CANOEING

(☑ 302-654-2227; www.wildernesscanoetrips.com; 2111 Concord Pike; solo kayak $53, tandem kayak or canoe trip from $63, tube $23) Call this outfit for for information on paddling or tubing down the dark-green Brandywine Creek.

🛏 Sleeping & Eating

You'll find chain hotels in downtown Wilmington. B&Bs and inns dot the landscape around the Brandywine River just north of downtown and in nearby southern Pennsylvania.

For a wide range of choices, head into Wilmington, while fine dining and tavern and pub fare are highlights in Chadd's Ford and Kennett Sq just over the state line in Pennsylvania.

ⓘ Getting There & Away

Greyhound stops at the Wilmington Transportation Center (p313). Amtrak (www.amtrak.com) trains also leave from here and connect Wilmington with DC (1½ hours), Baltimore (45 minutes) and New York (two hours).

New Castle

As cute as a colonial kitten, New Castle is a web of cobblestoned streets and beautifully preserved 18th-century buildings lying near a riverfront (that said, however, the surrounding area is unfortunately a bit of an urban wasteland). Sights include the Old Court House, the arsenal on the Green, churches and cemeteries dating back to the 17th century, and historic houses.

◉ Sights

Amstel House
MUSEUM

(☑ 302-322-2794; www.newcastlehistory.org; 2 E 4th St; adult/child 6-12yr $6/2, with Dutch House $10/3; ⊙ 10am-4pm Wed-Sat, from noon Sun Apr-Dec) One of three museums overseen by the New Castle Historical Society, this house is a surviving remnant of 1730s colonial opulence. Guided tours available April through December.

Dutch House
MUSEUM

(☑ 302-322-2794; www.newcastlehistory.org; 32 E 3rd St; adult/child 6-12yr $6/2, with Amstel House $10/3; ⊙ 10am-4pm Wed-Sat, from noon Sun Apr-Dec) A small example of a working residence dating from the late 1600s. Tours offered at 1pm and 3pm.

Old Court House
MUSEUM

(☑ 302-323-4453; http://history.delaware.gov; 211 Delaware St; ⊙ 10am-4:30pm Tue-Sat, 1:30-4:30pm Sun) FREE Dates back to the 17th century and is now operated as a museum by the state.

🛏 Sleeping & Eating

Terry House B&B
B&B $

(☑ 302-322-2505; www.terryhouse.com; 130 Delaware St; r $90-110; P 🎅) The owner of the five-room Terry House B&B will sometimes play the piano for guests while they enjoy a full breakfast. That's a treat for sure, but we're more impressed by the historical grounds and the supremely cozy rooms; there's nothing like stepping from a historical village into historical accommodations.

Dog House
AMERICAN $

(☑ 302-328-5380; 1200 N Dupont Hwy; mains under $10; ⊙ 10:30am-midnight) This unassuming countertop diner on the outskirts of New Castle might be the best dining option in town. Don't be fooled by the name; while this place does hot dogs and does them exceedingly well (the chili dogs are a treat), it also whips out mean subs and cheesesteaks that could pass muster in Philly.

Jessop's Tavern
AMERICAN $$

(☑ 302-322-6111; www.jessops-tavern; 114 Delaware St; mains $12-24; ⊙ 11:30am-10pm Mon-Thu, to 11pm Fri & Sat, to 9pm Sun) Tonight we're going to party like its 1679. Serves up Dutch pot roast, 'Pilgrim's Feast' (oven-roasted turkey with all the fixings) and Belgian beers in a colonial atmosphere. Offers 21 beers on draft – 11 Belgian and 10 craft. The building dates from 1674.

ⓘ Getting There & Away

New Castle borders the Delaware River. Hwy 9 connects New Castle with Wilmington, which is 7 miles north.

Dover

Dover's city center is quite attractive; the row house–lined streets are peppered with restaurants and shops, while broadleaf trees spread their branches over pretty little lanes. Most museums and historic sites are downtown near the capitol, with a couple just south of downtown off Rte 1.

⊙ Sights

Old State House MUSEUM
(☑ 302-744-5055; http://history.delaware.gov/museums; 25 The Green; ⊙ 9am-4:30pm Mon-Sat, plus 1:30-4:30pm Sun Apr-Sep) FREE Take a moment to enjoy the short docent tour for this small but interesting site. Built in 1791 and since restored, the Old State House contains art galleries and in-depth exhibits about the First State's history and politics. We learned here that every state house in the USA has a portrait of George Washington!

First State Heritage Park Welcome Center & Galleries MUSEUM
(☑ 302-739-9194; www.destateparks.com/park/first-state-heritage; 121 Martin Luther King Blvd N; ⊙ 8am-4:30pm Mon-Fri, 9am-4:30pm Sat, 1:30-4:30pm Sun) FREE Delve into the history of Delaware at the First State Heritage Park, which serves as a welcome center for the city of Dover, the state of Delaware and the adjacent state house. This so-called 'park without boundaries' includes some two dozen historic sites within a few blocks of one another. Start out at the Welcome Center & Galleries, which has exhibitions exploring Delaware's history. You can pick up more info here on other key sites nearby.

John Dickinson Plantation MUSEUM
(☑ 302-739-3277; http://history.delaware.gov/museums; 340 Kitts Hummock Rd; ⊙ 10am-4:30pm Tue-Sat, plus Sun 1:30-4:30pm Apr-Sep; P) FREE A restored 18th-century home of the founding father of the same name, also known as the Penman of the Revolution for his eloquent arguments for independence.

Air Mobility Command Museum MUSEUM
(☑ 302-677-5938; www.amcmuseum.org; 1301 Heritage Rd; ⊙ 9am-4pm Tue-Sun) FREE If you're into aviation, you'll enjoy this museum; the nearby airfield holds more than 30 restored vintage cargo and freight planes, including C-130s, a Vietnam War–era C-7 and a World War 2–era 'Flying Boxcar.'

Dover Air Force Base (AFB) is a visible symbol of American military muscle and a poignant reminder of the cost of war. This is the location of the Department of Defense's largest mortuary, and traditionally the first stop on native soil for the remains of American service members killed overseas.

Bombay Hook National Wildlife Refuge WILDLIFE RESERVE
(☑ 302-653-9345; www.fws.gov/refuge/Bombay_Hook; 2591 Whitehall Neck Rd, Smyrna; per vehicle/pedestrian $4/2; ⊙ sunrise-sunset) Hundreds of thousands of waterfowl use this protected wetland as a stopping point along their migration routes. A 12-mile wildlife driving trail, running through 16,251 acres of saltwater marsh, cordgrass and tidal mud flats, manages to encapsulate all of the soft beauty of the DelMarVa peninsula in one perfectly preserved ecosystem. There are also short walking trails and observation towers.

🛏 Sleeping

Dover may be somewhat small but it's the state capital, so there are plenty of options.

State Street Inn B&B $$
(☑ 302-734-2294; www.statestreetinn.com; 228 N State St; r $100-135; ❄) The inn was switching ownership at the time of research, so there may be a few changes in the works, but the current incarnation has cute rooms with flower-patterned wallpapers. It offers an unbeatable central location.

✗ Eating & Drinking

Flavors of India INDIAN $$
(☑ 302-677-0121; www.flavorofindia.com; 348 N Dupont Hwy; mains $12-19; ⊙ 11am-10pm; P ♿ 🍴) To say this place is an unexpected delight would be an understatement. First: it's in a Super 8 Motel off the highway. Second: *it's great*. The standards – vindaloos and kormas and tikka masalas – are all wonderful. Goat palakwala (goat curry with a spinach base)? Amazing. Also by far the best vegetarian option in the area.

Golden Fleece PUB
(☑ 302-674-1776; www.goldenfleecetavern.com; 132 W Loockerman St; mains $4-11; ⊙ 6pm-1am Sat-Thu, from 4pm Fri) The best bar in Dover also serves up some good food – that you can order from the local pizza joint. First priority is maintaining the atmosphere of an old English pub, which meshes well with the surrounding red-brick Dover historical center. Has an outdoor patio for summer nights.

ⓘ Getting There & Away

Dover is 50 miles south of Wilmington via Rte 1. US 301 connects Dover and Baltimore, which is 85 miles west. DART Bus 301 runs between Wilmington and the **Dover Transit Center** (www.dartfirststae.com), which is a half-mile from downtown Dover. One-way fare is $6. **Greyhound** (☑ 800-231-2222; www.greyhound.com; 654 N Dupont Hwy) buses stop 2 miles north of downtown.

VIRGINIA

The Commonwealth of Virginia is steeped in history and tradition. It's the birthplace of America, where English settlers established the first permanent colony in the New World in 1607. From then on, Virginia has played a lead role in nearly every major American drama, from the Revolutionary and Civil Wars to the Civil Rights movement and the attacks of September 11, 2001.

Virginia's natural beauty is as diverse as its history and people. Chesapeake Bay and the wide sandy beaches kiss the Atlantic Ocean. Pine forests, marshes and rolling green hills form the soft curves of the central Piedmont region, while the rolling Blue Ridge mountains and stunning Shenandoah Valley line its back.

Beyond northern Virginia, the state is shaking off cobwebs and outdated traditions. As the old joke goes: How many Virginians does it take to change a lightbulb? Two. One to change the bulb and the other to talk about how much better the old one was. While this is still marginally true, slow-to-change cities like Richmond and Roanoke are recently energized. The markers of change include vibrant art scenes, a slew of buzzy new restaurants and microbreweries, and marketing campaigns spotlighting outdoor adventures – like new cycling and paddling trails – and not just stodgy history.

History

Humans have occupied Virginia for at least 5000 years. Several thousand Native Americans were already here in May 1607 when Captain James Smith and his crew sailed up Chesapeake Bay and founded Jamestown, the first permanent English colony in the New World. Named for Queen Elizabeth I – aka the 'Virgin Queen' – the territory originally occupied most of America's eastern seaboard. By 1610 most of the colonists had died from starvation in their quest for gold, until colonist John Rolfe (husband of Pocahontas) discovered Virginia's real riches: tobacco.

A feudal aristocracy grew out of tobacco farming, and many gentry scions became Founding Fathers, including native son George Washington. In the 19th century the slave-based plantation system grew both in size and incompatibility with the industrializing North; Virginia seceded in 1861 and became the epicenter of the Civil War. Following its defeat, the state walked a tense cultural tightrope, accruing a layered identity that included older aristocrats, a rural and urban working class, waves of immigrants and, today, the burgeoning tech-heavy suburbs of DC. The state revels in its history, yet still wants to pioneer the American experiment; thus, while Virginia only reluctantly desegregated in the 1960s, today it houses one of the most ethnically diverse populations of the New South.

🛈 Getting There & Around

The largest regional airports include **Washington Dulles International Airport** (IAD; www.metwashairports.com; 🛜) in Northern Virginia, Richmond International Airport (p325) in Richmond, **Norfolk International Airport** (NIA; ☑ 757-857-3351; www.norfolkairport.com; 2200 Norview Ave; 🛜) in Norfolk, and **Roanoke-Blacksburg Regional Airport** (☑ 540-362-1999; www.roanokeairport.com; 5202 Aviation Dr NW) in Southwest Virginia. American and Delta serve Charlottesville Albemarle Airport (p332) in the Piedmont region.

Amtrak stops in Richmond at Main St Station (p325) and Staples Mill Rd Station (p325). There are also trains stations in Charlottesville (p332) and in Staunton (p333). In and around Northern Virginia, Amtrak stops in Fredericksburg (p322) and near Manassas National Battlefield Park (p317).

Northern Virginia

Safe, green-conscious, well trimmed and full of surprises, Northern Virginia (NoVA) is DC's perfect neighbor, just across from the picket fence of the Potomac River. NoVA communities are basically suburbs of Washington, attached via the Metro. We concentrate on the towns of Arlington and Alexandria, which combine crucial capital sites with historic sites, cozy pubs and a buzzing food scene.

Start with Arlington. It's quite close, just a Metro stop from DC, and it holds the two main reasons to cross the border: Arlington National Cemetery and the Pentagon. Plan on a half-day for these two sights alone. Beyond Arlington you'll find the jaw-dropping Steven F Udvar-Hazy Center, aka the annex of the National Air and Space Museum, which holds three times as many jets and rockets as the Mall building. Also out this way are the Eden Center, a Saigon-style foodie emporium where the Vietnamese community clusters, and Annandale, the Korean community's hub. Unfortunately you'll be hard-pressed to reach these places without a car.

The charming village of Alexandria is 5 miles and 250 years away from Washington. Once a salty port, Alexandria – known as 'Old Town' to locals – is today a posh collection of red-brick homes, cobblestone streets, gas lamps and a waterfront promenade. Boutiques, outdoor cafes and bars pack the main thoroughfare, making the town a fine afternoon or evening jaunt. It's also a jumping-off spot for excursions to Mount Vernon.

Arlington

Sights

★ **Pentagon** NOTABLE BUILDING
(☎703-697-1776; www.pentagontours.osd.mil; Arlington; ⊙memorial 24hr, tours by appointment 10am-4pm Mon-Thu, noon-4pm Fri; Ⓜ Blue, Yellow Lines to Pentagon) South of Arlington Cemetery is the Pentagon, the largest office building in the world. Outside you may visit the **Pentagon Memorial** (www.pentagonmemorial. org; ⊙24hr) FREE; 184 illuminated benches honor each person killed in the September 11, 2001, terrorist attack on the Pentagon. To get inside the building, you'll have to book a free guided one-hour tour on the website and provide appropriate photo ID. Make reservations 14 to 90 days in advance.

Nearby, the Pentagon, you can spot three soaring arcs of the **Air Force Memorial** (☎703-247-5805; www.airforcememorial.org; 1 Air Force Memorial Dr; ⊙9am-9pm Apr-Sep, 8am-8pm Oct-Mar) FREE, which invokes the contrails of jets.

★ **Arlington National Cemetery** CEMETERY
(☎877-907-8585; www.arlingtoncemetery.mil; ⊙8am-7pm Apr-Sep, to 5pm Oct-Mar; Ⓜ Blue Line to Arlington Cemetery) FREE Arlington is the somber final resting place for more than 400,000 military personnel and their dependents. The 624-acre grounds contain the dead of every war the USA has fought since the Revolution. Highlights include the Tomb of the Unknown Soldier, with its elaborate changing of the guard ceremony (every hour on the hour October through March; every half-hour April through September), and the grave of John F Kennedy and his family, marked by an eternal flame.

Departing from the visitor center, hop-on, hop-off bus tours are an easy way to visit the cemetery's main sights. Other points of interest include the Space **Shuttle Challenger Memorial**; the **USS Maine Memo**rial, marked by the battleship's huge mast; the controversial **Confederate Memorial** that honors war dead from the Civil War's breakaway states; and the tomb of DC city planner **Pierre L'Enfant**. The **Iwo Jima Memorial** (Ⓜ Blue Line to Arlington Cemetery), displaying the famous raising of the flag over Mt Suribachi, is on the cemetery's fringes.

Much of the cemetery was built on the grounds of **Arlington House** (☎703-235-1530; www.nps.gov/arho; ⊙9:30am-4:30pm) FREE, the former home of Robert E Lee and his wife Mary Anna Custis Lee, a descendant of Martha Washington. When Lee left to lead Virginia's army in the Civil War, Union troops confiscated the property to bury their dead.

George Washington Memorial Parkway PARKWAY
(☎703-289-2500; www.nps.gov/gwmp; Ⓜ Blue Line to Arlington Cemetery) The 25-mile Virginia portion of the highway honors its namesake with recreation areas and memorials all the way south to his old estate at Mount Vernon. It's lined with remnants of George Washington's life and works, such as his old Patowmack Company canal (in Great Falls National Park) and parks that were once part of his farmlands (Riverside Park, Fort Hunt Park). The 18.5-mile-long **Mount Vernon Trail** parallels the parkway.

Kennedy Gravesites TOMB
(Ⓜ Blue Line to Arlington Cemetery) An eternal flame flickers beside this simple but moving gravesite – the final resting place for President John F Kennedy and Jacqueline Kennedy Onassis.

OFF THE BEATEN TRACK

MANASSAS NATIONAL BATTLEFIELD PARK

The site of two major Confederate victories early in the Civil War, **Manassas National Battlefield Park** (☎703-361-1339; www.nps.gov/mana; 12521 Lee Hwy; ⊙park dawn-dusk, visitor center 8:30am-5pm, tours 11:15am, 12:15pm & 2:15pm Jun-Aug) today is a curving green hillscape, sectioned into fuzzy fields of tall grass and wildflowers by split-rail wood fences. Start your tour at the **Henry Hill Visitor Center** (☎703-361-1339; www.nps.gov/mana; ⊙8:30am-5pm) FREE to watch the orientation film and pick up park and trail maps. Guided tours also offered.

WASHINGTON, DC & THE CAPITAL REGION NORTHERN VIRGINIA

DEA Museum
MUSEUM

(United States Drug Enforcement Agency Museum; ☑ 202-307-3463; www.deamuseum.org; 700 Army Navy Dr, entrance on S Hayes St; ⏰ 10am-4pm Tue-Fri; Ⓜ Blue, Yellow Lines to Pentagon City) FREE The propaganda is served up with nary a chuckle at this heavy-handed museum brought to you by the Drug Enforcement Agency (DEA). Exhibits cover the last century-and-a-half of drug use, from the opium parlors of the 19th century to 1920s cocaine-dispensing apothecaries, on to the trippy days of the 1960s, the crack epidemic of the 1980s, and more recent days of crystal-meth labs and the powder drugs favored by the 24-hour party people of today.

🛏 Sleeping & Eating

In addition to hotels, there are dozens of chic restaurants and bars located along Clarendon and Wilson Blvds, clustered near the Rosslyn and Clarendon Metro stations.

El Pollo Rico
LATIN AMERICAN $

(☑ 703-522-3220; www.elpolloricorestaurant. com; 932 N Kenmore St; chicken with sides $7-18; ⏰ 11:30am-8:30pm; Ⓜ Orange, Silver Lines to Clarendon or Virginia Sq-GMU) Drooling locals have flocked to this Peruvian chicken joint for decades, in search of tender, juicy, flavor-packed birds served with succulent (highly addictive) dipping sauces, crunchy fries and sloppy 'slaw. Lines form outside the door come dinnertime.

Myanmar
BURMESE $

(☑ 703-289-0013; 7810 Lee Hwy, Falls Church; mains $10-14; ⏰ noon-10pm; Ⓜ Orange Line to Dunn Loring Merrifield) Myanmar's decor is barebones; the service is slow; the portions are small; and the food is delicious. This is home-cooked Burmese: curries prepared with lots of garlic, turmeric and oil, chili fish, mango salads and chicken swimming in rich gravies.

Yechon
KOREAN $$

(☑ 703-914-4646; www.yechon.com; 4121 Hummer Rd, Annandale; mains $7-40; ⏰ 24hr; Ⓜ Blue, Yellow Lines to King St) Debates over who does the best Korean in the DC area have been the source of much gastronomic bickering, but Yechon is always among the frontrunners. The *kalbi* (barbecue ribs) is rich, smoky and packed with flavor, and goes nicely with the complex seaweed and searing kimchi.

🍷 Drinking & Entertainment

Continental
LOUNGE

(www.continentalpoollounge.com; 1911 N Fort Myer Dr; ⏰ 11:30am-2am Mon-Fri, 6pm-2am Sat & Sun; Ⓜ Rosslyn) A stone's throw from many Rosslyn hotels, this buzzing pool lounge evokes a trippy, tropical vibe with its murals of palm trees, oversized tiki heads and color-saturated bar stools. All of which sets the stage for an alternative night of shooting pool, playing ping pong or trying shuffleboard.

Whitlow's on Wilson
BAR

(☑ 703-276-9693; www.whitlows.com; 2854 Wilson Blvd; ⏰ 11am-2am Mon-Fri, 9am-2am Sat & Sun; Ⓜ Clarendon) Occupying almost an entire block just east of Clarendon Metro, Whitlow's on Wilson has something for everyone: burgers, brunch and comfort food on the menu; happening happy hours and positive pick-up potential; plus 12 brews on tap, a pool table, jukebox, live music and an easy-going atmosphere. Head to the rooftop tiki bar in warmer months.

★ Iota
LIVE MUSIC

(☑ 703-522-8340; www.iotaclubandcafe.com; 2832 Wilson Blvd; tickets $10-15; ⏰ 4pm-2am Mon-Thu, from 10am Fri-Sun; 🛜; Ⓜ Clarendon) With shows almost every night of the week, Iota is the best venue for live music in Clarendon's music strip. Bands span genres: folk, reggae, traditional Irish and Southern rock are all distinct possibilities. Tickets are available at the door only (no advance sales) and this place packs 'em in.

ℹ Getting There & Away

Arlington borders I-66 and is partially encircled by I-495, which loops around DC.

Massive **Washington Dulles International Airport** (p316) is 26 miles west of DC.

From DC, use the Arlington Cemetery (Blue Line) to get to the cemetery and the Pentagon (Blue and Yellow Lines) stations to visit Pentagon sites.

Alexandria

◉ Sights

★ Mount Vernon
HISTORIC SITE

(☑ 800-429-1520, 703-780-2000; www.mount vernon.org; 3200 Mount Vernon Memorial Hwy; adult/child 6-11yr $20/10; ⏰ 8am-5pm Apr-Aug, 9am-4pm Nov-Feb, to 5pm Mar, Sep & Oct, gristmill & distillery 10am-5pm Apr-Oct) One of the most visited historic shrines in the nation, Mount

Vernon was the beloved home of George and Martha Washington, who lived here from the time of their marriage in 1759 until George's death in 1799. Now owned and operated by the Mount Vernon Ladies Association, the estate offers glimpses of 18th-century farm life and the first president's life as a country planter. Mount Vernon does not gloss over the Founding Father's slave ownership: visitors can tour the slave quarters and burial ground.

★ **Carlyle House** HISTORIC BUILDING
(☑703-549-2997; www.novaparks.com; 121 N Fairfax St; adult/child 6-12yr $5/3; ☉10am-4pm Tue-Sat, noon-4pm Sun; Ⓜ King St, Old Town) If you have time for just one historic house tour in Alexandria, make it this one. The house dates from 1753 when merchant and city founder, John Carlyle, built the most lavish mansion in town (which in those days was little more than log cabins and muddy lanes). The Georgian Palladian-style house is packed with paintings, historic relics and period furnishings that help bring the past to life.

Freedom House Museum MUSEUM
(☑708-836-2858; www.visitalexandriava.com/listings/freedom-house/4676; 1315 Duke St; ☉10:30am-2:30pm Mon-Fri, guided tours & weekends by appointment only; Ⓜ King St, Old Town) FREE This demure Federal-style row house holds a tragic story. At a time when Alexandria was the nation's second-largest slave center (after New Orleans), a flourishing slave-trading business occupied this building and adjoining space. A well-presented basement museum, developed by the Northern Virginia Urban League, powerfully tells the stories of the thousands of enslaved people who passed through. Personal video narratives and artifacts are on view in a heartbreaking setting.

George Washington Masonic National Memorial MONUMENT
(☑703-683-2007; www.gwmemorial.org; 101 Callahan Dr at King St; adult/child under 13yr $15/free; ☉9am-5pm; Ⓜ Blue, Yellow Lines to King St, Old Town) Alexandria's most prominent landmark features a fine view from its 333ft tower, where you can see the Capitol, Mount Vernon and the Potomac River. It is modeled after Egypt's Lighthouse of Alexandria, and honors the first president (who was initiated into the Masons in Fredericksburg in 1752 and later became Worshipful Master of Alexandria Lodge No 22). There's a commanding

17ft-high statue of Washington in the portico. On the tour you'll see artifacts donated by Washington's family, including the 1792 family bible.

Torpedo Factory Art Center ARTS CENTER
(☑703-746-4570; www.torpedofactory.org; 105 N Union St; ☉10am-6pm Fri-Wed, to 9pm Thu; Ⓜ King St) FREE What do you do with a former munitions dump and arms factory? How about turning it into one of the best art spaces in the region? Three floors of artist studios and free creativity are on offer in Old Town Alexandria, as well as the opportunity to buy paintings, sculptures, glass works, textiles and jewelry direct from their creators. The Torpedo Factory anchors Alexandria's revamped waterfront with a marina, parks, walkways, residences and restaurants.

National Inventors Hall of Fame & Museum MUSEUM
(☑571-272-0095; www.invent.org/honor/hall-of-fame-museum/; 600 Dulany St, Madison Bldg; ☉10am-5pm Mon-Fri, 11am-3pm Sat; Ⓜ Blue, Yellow Lines to King St) FREE This museum, in the atrium of the US Patent and Trademark Office, tells the history of the US patent. Step inside to see where the story started in 1917 in Memphis, Tennessee, when a wholesale grocer named Clarence Saunders invented and patented what he called 'self-servicing' stores, now commonly known as supermarkets.

🛏 Sleeping

Expensive boutique hotels cluster in and around Old Town. You'll have to travel outside the neighborhood to find cheaper options.

Alexandrian HISTORIC HOTEL $$
(☑703-549-6080; www.thealexandrian.com; 480 King St; r $209-259; 🛜❄🐾; Ⓜ Blue, Yellow Lines to King St-Old Town) Bold colors and fun details (mod throw pillows, geometric carpets) add a dash of bohemian whimsy to the 241 guestrooms and suites of this sophisticated, one-of-a-kind hotel. Occupying a historic six-story red-brick structure, it's ideally located on King St just four blocks from the waterfront. Guests applaud its friendly staff, proximity to restaurants and shops, and indoor heated pool.

Morrison House BOUTIQUE HOTEL $$
(☑703-838-8000; www.morrisonhouse.com; 116 S Alfred St; r $199-259, ste $329; 🅿❄❋@ 🛜❄🐾; Ⓜ Blue Line to King St) 🍃 A romantic Old Town mainstay, this chic boutique hotel

is now managed by Marriott as a member of the Autograph Collection family of hotels. The Federal-style beauty combines modern takes on tradition: four-poster beds, orange-plaid carpeting, bright blue artwork, Italian marble bathrooms and natural light everywhere.

✖ Eating

Busy restaurants and bars line King St and its offshoots in Old Town. Along Mt Vernon Ave in the Del Ray neighborhood, a short drive from Old Town, you'll find a growing line-up of coffee shops and restaurants, many with inviting patios. The free trolley from the King St metro station will get you to Alexandria's Old Town's eateries.

Stomping Ground   BREAKFAST $
(☑ 703-364-8912; www.stompdelray.com; 309 Mt Vernon Ave; mains $9-12; ⊙ 7am-3pm Tue-Sat, 9am-3pm Sun) Did somebody say biscuit? Oh yes they did. And make that a scratch-made buttermilk biscuit piled with fillings of your choice, from fried chicken and Benton's bacon to poached eggs, pimiento cheese and avocado. Or just stop by this Del Ray spot for coffee and to work on your laptop. Order at the counter then settle into the rustically chic digs.

Caphe Banh Mi   VIETNAMESE $
(☑ 703-549-0800; www.caphebahnmi.com; 407 Cameron St; mains $6-12; ⊙ 11am-3pm & 5-9pm Mon-Fri, 11am-9pm Sat, 11am-8pm Sun; Ⓜ King St) Stop in this neighborhood favorite for delicious *banh mi* sandwiches, big bowls of pho, pork-belly steamed buns and other simple but well-executed Vietnamese dishes. The small but cozy space always draws a crowd, so go early to beat the dinner rush.

Hank's Oyster Bar   SEAFOOD $$
(☑ 703-739-4265; www.hanksoysterbar.com; 1026 King St; lunch mains $13-25, dinner mains $14-32; ⊙ 11:30am-midnight Mon-Fri, from 11am Sat & Sun) Get your oyster fix during happy hour (3pm to 7pm Monday to Friday) when the briny critters are only $2.50 apiece at this new outpost of the popular Dupont Circle flagship. If you're not sure which oysters to pick from the long list, they'll do a sampler for ya. The seafood dishes and varied small plates are also strong. The bar is the place to be.

Brabo Tasting Room   BELGIAN $$
(☑ 703-894-5252; www.braborestaurant.com; 1600 King St; breakfast mains $14-16, lunch & dinner mains $14-22; ⊙ 7:30-10:30am & 11:30am-11pm

Mon-Thu, 7:30am-10:30am & 11:30am-midnight Fri, 8-11am & 11:30am-midnight Sat, 8-11am & 11:30am-10pm Sun; Ⓜ King St) The inviting and sunlit Brabo Tasting Room serves its signature mussels, tasty wood-fired tarts and gourmet sandwiches with a good beer and wine selection. In the morning, stop by for brioche French toast and Bloody Marys. Brabo restaurant, next door, is the high-end counterpart serving seasonal fare.

Restaurant Eve   AMERICAN $$$
(☑ 703-706-0450; www.restauranteve.com; 110 S Pitt St; lunch mains $17-26, dinner mains $27-42, 5-course tasting menu $105; ⊙ 11:30am-2pm Mon-Fri, 5:30-10pm Mon-Sat; 🖉; Ⓜ King St) One of Alexandria's best (and priciest) dining rooms, Eve blends great American ingredients, precise French technique and first-rate service. Splurge here on the tasting menus, which are simply on another level of gastronomic experience. The Lickety Split menu ($15; two choices from limited menu) draws a crowd to the bar at lunch.

🍷 Drinking & Entertainment

Head to King St for good bar-hopping with a crowd of folks who seem to be perpetually enrolled in the University of Virginia, Virginia Tech or George Mason University.

Captain Gregory's   COCKTAIL BAR
(www.captaingregorys.com; 804 N Henry St; ⊙ 6pm-midnight Wed & Thu, 5:30pm-2am Fri & Sat, 5:30pm-11pm Sun) This nautical-themed speakeasy is hidden inside a Sugar Shack doughnut shop, which explains the decadent gourmet doughnut on the menu. As for drinks, from Anais Needs a Vacay to Moaning Myrtles Morning Tea, the names are as diverse as the ingredients. Think flavored liqueurs, infused spirits and a range of fruit and spices. Cocktails run $14 to $16, and the menu changes frequently. Reservations required.

Union Street Public House   PUB
(☑ 703-548-1785; www.unionstreetpublichouse.com; 121 S Union St; ⊙ 11:30am-10pm Mon-Thu, 11:30am-11pm Fri, 10am-11pm Sat, 10am-9pm Sun; Ⓜ King St) Gas lamps out front welcome tourists and locals into this spacious taproom for frosty brews, raw-bar delights and nightly dinner specials.

Birchmere   LIVE MUSIC
(www.birchmere.com; 3701 Mt Vernon Ave; tickets $25-70; ⊙ box office 5-9pm, shows 7:30pm; Ⓜ Pentagon City) This 50-year-old place, hailing

itself as 'America's Legendary Music Hall,' hosts a wide range of fare, from old-time folk musicians to country, blues and R&B stars. The line-up also features the odd burlesque show, indie rock bands and the occasional one-person comedy show.

ℹ️ Getting There & Away

To get to Alexandria from downtown DC, take the metro to the King St station. A free **trolley** (www.dashbus.com/trolley; ⊘10am-10:15pm Sun-Wed, to midnight Thu-Sat) makes the 1-mile journey between the metro station and the waterfront. **Capitol Bikeshare** (📞877-430-2453; www.capitalbikeshare.com) has 31 stations across Alexandria.

Fredericksburg

Fredericksburg is a pretty town with a historic district that's almost a cliché of small-town Americana. George Washington grew up here, and the Civil War exploded in the streets and surrounding fields. Today the main street is a pleasant amble of bookstores, gastropubs and cafes.

⊙ Sights

Ellwood Manor   HISTORIC SITE
(📞540-786-2880; www.nps.gov/frsp; Rte 20, just west of Rte 3; ⊘10am-5pm Sat & Sun) This fascinating home sits on the grounds of the Wilderness Battlefield. Perhaps best known as the burial site for Confederate Gen Stonewall Jackson's amputated arm – there is a marker – the circa 1790 manor here once anchored a 5000-acre estate. Step inside to learn the interesting history of the house; the Marquis de Lafayette once dined here.

**Fredericksburg & Spotsylvania
National Military Park**   HISTORIC SITE
(📞540-693-3200; www.nps.gov/frsp; 1013 Lafayette Blvd; ⊘Fredericksburg & Chancellorsville visitor centers 9am-5pm, hours vary at other exhibit areas) FREE More than 13,000 Americans were killed during the Civil War in four battles fought in a 17-mile radius covered by this park: Fredericksburg, Chancellorsville, the Wilderness and Spotsylvania Courthouse. Today, they are maintained by the National Park Service. Check the park website for the locations of various visitor centers and exhibit shelters, and for staffing, which may be seasonal at some locations. Audio tours of the battlefields are available for rent ($20 deposit).

**James Monroe Museum
& Memorial Library**   HISTORIC SITE
(📞540-654-1043; http://jamesmonroemuseum. umw.edu; 908 Charles St; adult/child 6-17yr $6/2; ⊘10am-5pm Mon-Sat, from 1pm Sun, closes at 4pm Dec-Feb) The museum's namesake was the nation's fifth president. US history buffs will delight in the small and eclectic collection of Monroe memorabilia, including the desk on which he wrote the famous Monroe Doctrine. His diplomatic court suit, worn at the coronation of Napoleon and dating from 1785 or so, is also on display.

Mary Washington House   HISTORIC BUILDING
(📞540-373-1569; www.washingtonheritagemuseums.org; 1200 Charles St; adult/child 6-18yr $7/3; ⊘10am-4pm Mon-Sat & noon-4pm Sun Mar-Oct, 11am-4pm Mon-Sat & noon-4pm Sun Nov-Feb) At the 18th-century home of George Washington's mother, knowledgeable tour guides in period costume shed light on Mary and what life was like in her time. The lovely garden is an excellent re-creation from the era.

🍴 Sleeping & Eating

Richard Johnston Inn   B&B $$
(📞540-899-7606; www.therichardjohnstoninn. com; 711 Caroline St; r $165-300; P❄🐾) In an 18th-century brick mansion, this cozy B&B scores points for its downtown location, comfort and friendliness. The cookies offered in the afternoon are delicious.

Sammy T's   AMERICAN $
(📞540-371-2008; www.sammyts.com; 801 Caroline St; ⊘11:30am-9pm Mon, Wed & Thu, 1:30am-10pm Fri & Sat, 9:30am-7pm Sun; 🐾🍴) Located in a circa 1805 building in the heart of historic Fredericksburg, Sammy T's serves soups and sandwiches and pub-y fare, with an admirable mix of vegetarian options including a local take on lasagna and black-bean quesadillas.

Foode   AMERICAN $$
(📞540-479-1370; www.facebook.com/foodeonline; 900 Princess Anne St; lunch mains $10-12, dinner mains $15-26; ⊘11am-9pm Tue-Thu, 11am-10pm Fri, 9am-10pm Sat, 9am-3pm Sun; 🍴) Foode serves up tasty farm-to-table fare in a rustic but artsy setting. Lots of intriguing small plates for sharing at dinner. Attentive service too.

Bistro Bethem   AMERICAN $$$
(📞540-371-9999; www.bistrobethem.com; 309 William St; lunch mains $9-22, dinner mains $17-32; ⊘11:30am-2:30pm & 5-10pm Tues-Sat, to 9pm Sun) The New American menu, seasonal

WASHINGTON, DC & THE CAPITAL REGION FREDERICKSBURG

ingredients and down-to-earth but dedicated foodie vibe here all equal gastronomic bliss. On any given day duck confit and quinoa may share the table with a roasted beet salad and local clams.

ℹ️ Getting There & Away

Virginia Railway Express (www.vre.org; $11.90, 1½ hours) and Amtrak ($20 to $67, 1¼ hours) trains depart from the **Fredericksburg train station** (www.amtrak.com; 200 Lafayette Blvd) with service to DC. Greyhound has buses to/from DC ($10 to $24, four or five per day, 1½ hours) and Richmond ($10 to $30, two or three per day, one hour). The **Greyhound station** (☑540-373-2103; www.greyhound.com; 1400 Jefferson Davis Hwy) is roughly 2 miles west of the historic district. Fredericksburg borders I-95 midway between Washington, DC and Richmond, VA. It's about 55 miles north to DC and 60 miles south to Richmond.

Richmond

Richmond has woken up from a very long nap – and we like it. The capital of the Commonwealth of Virginia since 1780, and the capital of the Confederacy during the Civil War, it's long been an old-fashioned city clinging too tightly to its Southern roots. For decades, Civil War–era sights were the primary attraction, and residents didn't give much social thought to its streets and schools named for Confederate generals.

But an influx of new and creative young residents is energizing and modernizing the community. Today the 'River City' shares a buzzing food-and-drink scene and an active arts community. The rough-and-tumble James River has also grabbed more of the spotlight, drawing outdoor adventurers to its rapids and trails. Richmond is also an undeniably handsome town and easy to stroll, full of red-brick row houses, stately drives and leafy parks.

👁 Sights & Activities

Virginia State Capitol NOTABLE BUILDING
(☑804-698-1788; www.virginiacapitol.gov; cnr 9th & Grace Sts, Capitol Sq; ⊙9am-5pm Mon-Sat, 1-5pm Sun) FREE Designed by Thomas Jefferson, the capitol building was completed in 1788 and houses the oldest legislative body in the Western Hemisphere – the Virginia General Assembly, established in 1619. Free guided tours available and there is a self-guided tour brochure on the website.

Virginia Museum of Fine Arts MUSEUM
(VMFA; ☑804-340-1400; www.vmfa.museum; 200 N Blvd; ⊙10am-5pm Sun-Wed, to 9pm Thu & Fri) FREE Has a remarkable collection of European works, sacred Himalayan art and one of the largest Fabergé egg collections on display outside Russia. Don't miss Andy Warhol's *Triple Elvis* or the striking new *Chloe* sculpture by Jaume Plensa in the outdoor sculpture garden. Also hosts excellent temporary exhibitions (admission ranges from free to $22). After a morning exploring the collection, the museum's big-windowed **Amuse** restaurant is a pretty spot for lunch.

Virginia Historical Society MUSEUM
(www.vahistorical.org; 428 North Blvd; ⊙10am-5pm Mon-Sat) FREE Virginia's attic is looking pretty darn impressive after a multi-million-dollar renovation. With easy-to-digest changing and permanent exhibits tracing the story of the Commonwealth from its prehistoric beginnings to today, this is a great place for a quick history primer before setting out to explore the state's many sites.

St John's Episcopal Church CHURCH
(☑804-648-5015; www.historicstjohnschurch.org; 2401 E Broad St; tours adult/child 7-18yr $8/6; ⊙10am-4pm Mon-Sat, from 1pm Sun) It was here that firebrand Patrick Henry uttered his famous battle cry – 'Give me Liberty, or give me Death!' – during the rebellious 1775 Second Virginia Convention. The short but informative tour traces the history of the church and of the famous speech. Above the pulpit, the rare 1741 sounding board and its sunburst are worth a closer look. Henry's speech is re-enacted at 1pm on Sundays in summer.

Monument Avenue Statues STATUE
(btwn N Lombardy St & Roseneath Rd) Monument Ave, a beautiful tree-lined boulevard in northeast Richmond, holds statues of such revered Southern heroes as JEB Stuart, Robert E Lee, Matthew Fontaine Maury, Jefferson Davis, Stonewall Jackson and – in a nod to diversity – African American tennis champion Arthur Ashe. Snarky students at the nearby University of Richmond have been known to refer to the avenue as the 'largest collection of second place trophies in America.'

American Civil War
Museum: Historic Tredegar MUSEUM
(☑804-649-1861; www.acwm.org; 500 Tredegar St; adult/child 6-17yr $10/5; ⊙9am-5pm) Now a

VINEYARDS OF VIRGINIA

Home to some 230 vineyards, Virginia has a rising presence in the wine world. Good places to begin the foray lie just outside of DC in Loudon County. For maps, wine routes and loads of other viticultural info, visit www.virginiawine.org.

King Family Vineyards (☎434-823-7800; www.kingfamilyvineyards.com; 6550 Roseland Farm, Crozet; tastings $10; ⊙10am-5:30pm Thu-Tue, to 8:30pm Wed; 🛈) Consistently ranks as one of Virginia's best wineries. Bring a picnic (the winery also sells gourmet goodies) and enjoy the expansive scenery. At 1pm on summer Sundays (late May to mid-October), you can also catch a free polo match. It's 18 miles east of Charlottesville.

Jefferson Vineyards (☎434-977-3042; www.jeffersonvineyards.com; 1353 Thomas Jefferson Pkwy; tastings $12; ⊙11am-6pm; 🛈) Near Charlottesville, this winery harvests from its namesake's original 1774 vineyard site. It also hosts twice-monthly free outdoor concerts in summer.

Bluemont Vineyard (☎540-554-8439; www.bluemontvineyard.com; 18755 Foggy Bottom Rd, Bluemont; tastings $10; ⊙11am-6pm Sat-Thu, to 8pm Fri; 🛈) Bluemont produces ruby-red Nortons and crisp Viogniers, though it's equally famous for its spectacular location – at a 950ft elevation with sweeping views over the countryside.

Chrysalis Vineyards (☎540-687-8222; www.chrysaliswine.com; 39025 John Mosby Hwy; tastings $7-10; ⊙10am-6pm; 🛈) Proudly using the native Norton grape (which dates back to 1820), Chrysalis produces highly drinkable reds and whites – including a refreshing Viognier. The pretty estate hosts a bluegrass fest in October.

Tarara Vineyard (☎703-771-7100; www.tarara.com; 13648 Tarara Lane; tastings $6-10; ⊙11am-5pm Mon-Thu, to 6pm Fri-Sun) On a bluff overlooking the Potomac, this 475-acre estate provides guided tours showing the grape's journey from vine to glass. The winery has a 6000-sq-ft cave/cellar, and visitors can pick fruit in the orchard or hike the 6 miles of trails through rolling countryside. Tarara also hosts summertime Saturday-evening concerts and three major wine festivals.

stop within the multisite American Civil War Museum, this fascinating museum – inside an 1861 gun foundry – explores the causes and course of the Civil War from the perspectives of Union, Confederate and African American experiences. Next door is a free site run by the National Park Service that delves into Richmond's role during the war. This is also one of 13 protected area sites that make up **Richmond National Battlefield Park** (☎804-771-2145; www.nps.gov/rich; 470 Tredegar St; ⊙battlefield sunrise-sunset, Tredegar Visitor Center 9am-5pm) FREE.

Belle Isle PARK
(www.jamesriverpark.org; 300 Tredegar St) A long pedestrian bridge leads from Tredegar St (just past the national park site) out to this car-free island. Once a quarry, power plant and POW camp during the Civil War (though never all at once), today this is one of Richmond's finest city parks. Big flat rocks are lovely for sunbathing, and hiking and biking trails abound – but don't swim in the James River. The currents are treacherous.

Canal Walk WATERFRONT
(www.rvariverfront.com; btwn 5th & 17th Sts) The 1.25-mile waterfront Canal Walk between the James River and the Kanawha (ka-*naw*-wha) and Haxall Canals is a lovely way of seeing a dozen highlights of Richmond history in one go. There's also a pedestrian bridge across to Belle Isle, a scruffy but intriguing island in the James.

Poe Museum MUSEUM
(☎804-648-5523; www.poemuseum.org; 1914-16 E Main St; adult/child 7-17yr $8/6; ⊙10am-5pm Tue-Sat, from 11am Sun) Contains the world's largest collection of manuscripts and memorabilia of poet and horror writer Edgar Allan Poe, who lived and worked in Richmond. Exhibits include the first printing of 'The Raven', Poe's vest, his pen knife and a work chair with the back cut off – they say his boss at the *Southern Literary Messenger* wanted Poe to sit up straight. Pesky know-it-all. Stop by on the 4th Thursday of the month for the Poe-themed Unhappy Hour (6pm to 9pm April to October; $8).

Hollywood Cemetery
CEMETERY

(☎804-648-8501; www.hollywoodcemetery.org; 412 S Cherry St, entrance cnr Albemarle & Cherry Sts; ⊙8am-6pm) **FREE** This tranquil cemetery, perched above the James River rapids, contains the gravesites of two US presidents (James Monroe and John Tyler), the only Confederate president (Jefferson Davis) and 18,000 Confederate soldiers. Guided walking tours are given at 10am Monday through Saturday April to October, and Saturday only in November ($15 per person). For a self-guided walk, check the virtual tour offered on the website.

Riverside Outfitters
CANOEING

(☎804-560-0068; www.riversideoutfitters.net; Brown's Island, Downtown; per hour kayak/SUP boards/bike rental $15/15/10; ⊙11am-6pm Jun-Aug) Rent a kayak, stand-up paddle board or bike. The shop is on Brown's island across the street from Historic Tredegar at 500 Tredegar St. These folks also offer guided rafting trips, which launch from various locations.

Virginia Capital Trail
CYCLING

(www.virginiacapitaltrail.org) Open to cyclists and pedestrians, this new 52-mile paved trail links Richmond with Jamestown and outer Williamsburg, passing several plantations along the way. Check the helpful website for a map showing parking areas, restrooms, bike shops, restaurants and lodging. There are loads of historic sights and markers along the way. Starts at the junction of S 17th and Dock Sts.

🛌 Sleeping

HI Richmond
HOSTEL $

(☎804-729-5410; www.hiusa.org; 7 N 2nd St; dm $30-34, r $90-135, non-members add $3; ❄🕸) 🅿 Inside a historic 1924 building, this spiffy and eco-friendly hostel has a great central location and bright rooms (both dorms and private rooms), with high ceilings and loads of original details. There's a kitchen for guests, inviting common areas, and it's completely accessible for travelers with disabilities.

Linden Row Inn
BOUTIQUE HOTEL $$

(☎804-783-7000; www.lindenrowinn.com; 100 E Franklin St; r from $139, ste $289; 🅿❄@🕸) This antebellum gem has 70 attractive rooms (with period Victorian furnishings) spread among neighboring Greek Revival town houses in an excellent downtown location. Friendly southern hospitality, reasonable prices and thoughtful extras (free passes to

the YMCA, free around-town shuttle service, included breakfast) sweeten the deal.

⭐ Jefferson Hotel
LUXURY HOTEL $$$

(☎804-649-4750; www.jeffersonhotel.com; 101 W Franklin St; r from $355; 🅿❄🕸🏊) The Jefferson is Richmond's grandest hotel and one of the finest in America. The vision of tobacco tycoon and Confederate major Lewis Ginter, the beaux arts–style hotel was completed in 1895. Rooms are plush but inviting – you will sleep well. According to rumor (probably untrue), the magnificent grand staircase in the lobby served as the model for the famed stairs in *Gone with the Wind*.

🍴 Eating

Kuba Kuba
CUBAN $

(☎804-355-8817; www.kubakuba.info; 1601 Park Ave; mains $5-20; ⊙9am-9:30pm Mon-Thu, to 10pm Fri & Sat, to 8pm Sun) In the Fan district, this tiny hole in the wall feels like a bodega straight out of Old Havana, with mouth-watering roast pork dishes, Spanish-style omelets and panini at rock-bottom prices.

Mama J's
AMERICAN $

(☎804-225-7449; www.mamajskitchen.com; 415 N 1st St; mains $7-10; ⊙11am-9pm Sun-Thu, to 10pm Fri & Sat) The fried catfish may not look fancy, but it sure tastes like heaven. Set in the historic African American neighborhood of Jackson Ward, Mama J's serves delicious fried chicken and legendary fried catfish, along with collard greens, mac 'n' cheese, candied yams and other fixings. The service is friendly and the lines are long. Go early to beat the crowds.

Sidewalk Cafe
AMERICAN, GREEK $

(☎804-358-0645; www.sidewalkinthefan.com; 2101 W Main St; mains $9-18; ⊙11am-2am Mon-Fri, from 9:30am Sat & Sun) A much-loved local haunt, Sidewalk Cafe feels like a dive bar (year-round Christmas lights, wood-paneled walls, kitschy artwork), but the food is first-rate. There's outdoor seating on the sidewalk, daily specials and weekend brunches.

Burger Bach
PUB FOOD $

(☎804-359-1305; www.theburgerbach.com; 10 S Thompson St; mains $9-13; ⊙11am-10pm Sun-Thu, to 11pm Fri & Sat; ❄🍴🐕) 🅿 We give Burger Bach credit for being the only restaurant found in the area that self-classifies as a New Zealand–inspired burger joint. And that said, why yes, they do serve excellent lamb burgers here, although the locally sourced beef (and vegetarian) options are awesome as well. You should go crazy with the 14 different sauces available for the thick-cut fries.

Daily Kitchen & Bar   MODERN AMERICAN $$
(📞 804-342-8990; www.thedailykitchenandbar. com; 2934 W Cary St; lunch mains $9-20, dinner mains $9-26; ⊗ 7am-11pm Sun-Thu, to 1am Fri & Sat; 🅿) 🖋 In the heart of Carytown, the Daily is a great dining and drinking choice no matter the time of day. Stop by for lump crab omelets at breakfast, blackened mahi-mahi BLT at lunch and seared scallops by night. Extensive vegan options, first-rate cocktails and a buzzing, artfully designed space seals the deal.

Millie's Diner   MODERN AMERICAN $$
(📞 804-643-5512; www.milliesdiner.com; 2603 E Main St; lunch mains $9-14, dinner mains $16-29; ⊗ 11am-2:30pm & 5:30-10:30pm Tue-Fri, 9am-3pm & 5:30-10:30pm Sat & Sun) Lunch, dinner or weekend brunch – Richmond icon Millie's does it all, and does it well. It's a small, but handsomely designed space with creative seasonal fare. The Devil's Mess – an open-faced omelet with spicy sausage, curry, veg, cheese and avocado – is legendary.

Croaker's Spot   SEAFOOD $$
(📞 804-269-0464; www.croakersspot.com; 1020 Hull St; mains $10-26; ⊗ 11am-9pm Mon-Wed, to 10pm Thu, to 11pm Fri, noon-11pm Sat, noon-9pm Sun; 🅿) Croaker's is an institution in these parts, and a backbone of the African American dining scene. Richmond's most famous rendition of refined soul food is comforting, delicious and sits in your stomach like a brick. Beware the intimidating Fish Boat: fried catfish, cornbread and mac 'n' cheese.

★ L'Opossum   AMERICAN, FRENCH $$$
(📞 804-918-6028; www.lopossum.com; 626 China St; mains $18-32; ⊗ 5pm-midnight Tue-Sat) We're not exactly sure what's going on here, but it works. The name of the place is terrible. Statues of Michelangelo's David pose here and there. And dishes come with names that are almost too hip, like the Darth Grouper Held at Bay by a Rebellious Coalition.

🍸 Drinking & Entertainment

Saison   COCKTAIL BAR
(📞 804-269-3689; www.saisonrva.com; 23 W Marshall St; ⊗ 5pm-2am) This classy drinking den attracts serious cocktail lovers, who clink glasses over creative libations, craft beer and farm-to-table fare. It's in Jackson Ward, near downtown.

Veil Brewing   MICROBREWERY
(www.theveilbrewing.com; 1301 Roseneath Rd; ⊗ 4-9pm Tue-Thu, to 10pm Fri, noon-10pm Sat, noon-6pm Sun) If you see a queue of businessmen standing beside a nondescript brick building on Roseneath Rd just west of Broad St, it's probably Tuesday. That's when this much-praised new brewery sells its limited release brews, which do sell out. One of the most popular craft breweries in the emerging Scott's Addition neighborhood.

Byrd Theater   CINEMA
(📞 804-353-9911; www.byrdtheatre.com; 2908 W Cary St; tickets from $4) You can't beat the price at this classic 1928 cinema, which shows second-run films and longtime favorites. Wurlitzer-organ concerts precede the Saturday-night shows.

ℹ Getting There & Around

Amtrak (www.amtrak.com) trains stop at the **Staples Mill Rd station** (www.amtrak.com; 7519 Staples Mill Rd), 7 miles north of town (accessible to downtown via bus 27). More-convenient but less-frequent trains stop downtown at the **Main St Station** (www.amtrak.com; 1500 E Main St).

The **Greyhound/Trailways Bus Station** (📞 804-254-5910; www.greyhound.com) is at 2910 North Blvd.

The cab fare from **Richmond International Airport** (RIC; 📞 804-226-3000; www.flyrichmond.com; 1 Richard E Byrd Terminal Dr), 10 miles east of town, costs $30 to $35.

A new **Bikeshare** program is slated to launch by the fall of 2017.

➡ Greater Richmond Transit Company (www.ridegrtc.com) runs local buses. Exact change only.

Historic Triangle

This is America's birthplace. Nowhere else in the country has such a small area played such a pivotal role in the course of the nation's history. The nation's roots were planted in Jamestown, the first permanent English settlement in the New World; the flames of the American Revolution were fanned at the colonial capital of Williamsburg; and America finally won its independence from Britain at Yorktown. You'll need at least two days to do the Triangle any justice.

ℹ Getting There & Around

The Historic Triangle surrounds I-64. The largest regional airport is Norfolk International Airport (p316) followed by Newport News/Williamsburg International Airport (PHF; www.flyphf.com).

Williamsburg

If you visit only one historic town in Virginia, make it Williamsburg – home to Colonial Williamsburg, one of the largest, most comprehensive living-history museums in the world. If any place is going to get kids into history, this is it, but it's plenty of fun for adults too.

The actual town of Williamsburg, Virginia's capital from 1699 to 1780, is a stately place. The campus of the College of William & Mary adds a decent dash of youth culture, with coffee shops, cheap pubs and fashion boutiques.

☉ Sights

★ **Colonial Williamsburg**   HISTORIC SITE
(☑ 888-974-7926; www.colonialwilliamsburg.org; adult/child 6-12yr one day $41/21, multi-day $51/26; ☺ 9am-5pm) The restored capital of England's largest colony in the New World is a must-see attraction for visitors of all ages. This is not some phony, fenced-in theme park: Colonial Williamsburg is a living, breathing, working history museum with a painstakingly researched environment that brilliantly captures America of the 1700s.

The 301-acre historic area contains 88 original 18th-century buildings and several hundred faithful reproductions. Costumed townsfolk and 'interpreters' in period dress go about their colonial jobs as blacksmiths, apothecaries, printers, barmaids, soldiers and patriots, breaking character only long enough to pose for a snapshot.

Costumed patriots like Patrick Henry and Thomas Jefferson still deliver impassioned speeches for freedom, but the park doesn't gloss over America's less glorious moments. Today's re-enactors debate and question slavery, women's suffrage, the rights of indigenous Americans and whether or not it is even moral to engage in revolution.

Walking around the historic district and patronizing the shops and taverns is free, but entry to building tours and most exhibits is restricted to ticketholders. Expect crowds, lines and petulant children, especially in summer.

To park and to purchase tickets, follow signs to the **visitor center** (☑ 757-220-7645, 888-965-7254; www.colonialwilliamsburg.com; 101 Visitor Center Dr; ☺ 8:45am-9pm), found north of the historic district between Hwy 132 and Colonial Pkwy; kids can also hire out period costumes here for $25 per day. Start off with a 30-minute film about Williamsburg, and ask about the day's programs and events.

Parking is free; shuttle buses run frequently to and from the historic district, or you can walk along the tree-lined footpath. You can also buy tickets at the **Merchants Square information booth** (W Duke of Gloucester St; ☺ 9am-5pm).

College of William & Mary   HISTORIC BUILDING
(☑ 757-221-4000; www.wm.edu; 200 Stadium Dr) Chartered in 1693, the College of William & Mary is the second-oldest college in the country and retains the oldest academic building in continued use in the USA, the **Sir Christopher Wren Building**. The school's alumni include Thomas Jefferson, James Monroe and comedian Jon Stewart. A free campus audio tour is available online.

JAMES RIVER PLANTATIONS

The grand homes of Virginia's slave-holding aristocracy were a clear sign of the era's class divisions. A string of them line scenic Hwy 5 on the north side of the river, though only a few are open to the public. For cyclists, the Virginia Capital Trail (p324) linking Richmond and Williamsburg travels beside Rte 5.

Berkeley Plantation (☑ 804-829-6018; www.berkeleyplantation.com; 12602 Harrison Landing Rd, Charles City; adult/child 6-16yr $12/7; ☺ 9:30am-4:30pm) Berkeley was the site of the first official Thanksgiving in 1619. It was the birthplace and home of Benjamin Harrison V, a signatory of the Declaration of Independence, and his son William Henry Harrison, the 9th US president.

Shirley Plantation (☑ 800-829-5121; www.shirleyplantation.com; 501 Shirley Plantation Rd, Charles City; adult/child 7-16yr $12.50/8.50; ☺ 9:30am-4pm) Shirley, situated picturesquely on the river, is Virginia's oldest plantation (1613) and is perhaps the best example of how a British-model plantation actually appeared, with its tidy row of brick service and trade houses – tool barn, ice house, laundry etc – leading up to the big house.

🛏 Sleeping & Eating

Governor's Inn
HOTEL $

(☑ 757-220-7940; www.colonialwilliamsburg.com; 506 N Henry St; r incl breakfast $74-89; [P][🎧][🏊]) Williamsburg's official 'economy' choice is a big box by any other name, but rooms are clean, and guests can use the pool and facilities of the Woodlands Hotel. It's in a great location near the visitor center, three blocks from the historic district.

Williamsburg Woodlands Hotel & Suites
HOTEL $$

(☑ 757-220-7960; www.colonialwilliamsburg.com; 105 Visitor Center Dr; r/ste $179/209; [P][❄][🎧][🏊]) This good-value option has comfy, carpeted rooms (some of which go a bit heavy on the patterned wallpaper) near the main Visitor Center in Colonial Williamsburg. The splash park, games (minigolf, volleyball court) and complimentary breakfast make it a hit with families. Can feel a little more impersonal than other local lodging options.

Colonial Williamsburg Historic Lodging – Colonial Houses
GUESTHOUSE $$$

(☑ 888-965-7254, 757-565-8440; www.colonialwilliamsburg.com; 136 E Francis St; r $199) For true 18th-century immersion, guests can stay in one of 26 original colonial houses inside the historic district. Accommodations range in size and style, though the best have period furnishings, canopy beds and wood-burning fireplaces.

Cheese Shop
DELI $

(☑ 757-220-0298; www.cheeseshopwilliamsburg.com; 410 W Duke of Gloucester St, Merchants Sq; mains $6-8; ⊙ 10am-8pm Mon-Sat, 11am-6pm Sun) This gourmet deli showcases some flavorful sandwiches and antipasti, plus baguettes, pastries, wine, beer and wonderful cheeses. Order a sandwich and a glass of wine – at different counters – then enjoy your meal and the people-watching from the patio.

Aromas
CAFE $

(☑ 757-221-6676; www.aromasworld.com; 431 Prince George St; lunch mains $7-9; dinner mains $7-15; ⊙ 7am-10pm Mon-Thu, to 1pm Fri & Sat, 8am-8pm Sun; 🎧) One block north of Merchants Sq, Aromas is an inviting coffeehouse serving salads, sandwiches and a few dinner mains including blackened salmon and barbecue chicken over mac 'n' cheese, plus wine and beer. There's outdoor seating and live music (jazz on Tuesdays; wide-ranging sounds on weekends).

King's Arms Tavern
MODERN AMERICAN $$$

(☑ 866-348-9022; www.colonialwilliamsburg.com; 416 E Duke of Gloucester St; lunch mains $14-16, dinner mains $25-40; ⊙ 11:30am-2:30pm & 5-8pm) This traditional tavern serves early-American cuisine such as game pie – venison, rabbit and duck braised in port-wine sauce. Of the four restaurants within Colonial Williamsburg, this is the most elegant. You might hear live flute music with your meal, and staff will share history about Colonial dining habits.

ℹ Getting There & Away

Amtrak (www.amtrak.com) trains run from the **Williamsburg Transportation Center** (☑ 757-229-8750; www.williamsburgva.gov; 468 N Boundary St, cnr Boundary & Lafayette Sts; ⊙ 7:30am-10pm) twice a day to Washington, DC ($46, four hours) and Richmond ($22, 90 minutes), both on the Northeast Regional route.

Jamestown

On May 14, 1607, a group of 104 English men and boys settled on this swampy island, bearing a charter from the Virginia Company of London to search for gold and other riches. Instead they found starvation and disease. By January 1608, only about 40 colonists were still alive, and these had resorted to cannibalism to survive. The colony survived the 'Starving Time' with the leadership of Captain James Smith and help from Powhatan, a local Native American leader. In 1619 the elected House of Burgesses convened, forming the first democratic government in the Americas.

◉ Sights

Historic Jamestowne
HISTORIC SITE

(☑ 757-856-1250; www.historicjamestowne.org; 1368 Colonial Pkwy; adult/child under 16yr $14/free; ⊙ 9am-5pm) Run by the NPS, this fascinating place is the original Jamestown site, established in 1607 and home of the first permanent English settlement in North America. Start at the museum then check out the statues of Pocahontas and John Smith. The original Jamestown ruins were rediscovered in 1994; visitors can watch ongoing archaeological work at the site. Don't miss the Archaearium, which displays more than 4000 artifacts, including the skull of a young settler who was likely the victim of cannibalism!

Jamestown Settlement
HISTORIC SITE

(☑757-253-4838; www.historyisfun.org; 2110 Jamestown Rd; adult/child 6-12yr $17/8, incl American Revolutionary Museum at Yorktown $23/12; ☺9am-5pm, to 6pm mid-Jun–mid-Aug; P ♿) Popular with kids, the state-run Jamestown Settlement reconstructs the 1607 James Fort; a Native American village; and full-scale replicas of the first ships that brought the settlers to Jamestown, along with living-history fun. Multimedia exhibits and costumed interpreters bring the 17th century to life. This one can get uncomfortably busy with elementary school field trips, so arrive early during the school year.

🛈 Getting There & Away

The best way to get to Jamestown is by car. Amtrak (www.amtrak.com) stops in nearby Williamsburg, with trains running from the Williamsburg Transportation Center twice a day to Washington, DC ($46, four hours) and Richmond ($22, 90 minutes), both on the Northeast Regional route.

Yorktown

On October 19, 1781, British General Cornwallis surrendered to George Washington here, effectively ending the American Revolution. Overpowered by massive American guns on land and cut off from the sea by the French, the British were in a hopeless position. Although Washington anticipated a much longer siege, the devastating barrage quickly overwhelmed Cornwallis, who surrendered within days. The actual town of Yorktown is a pleasant waterfront village overlooking the York River, with a nice range of shops, galleries, restaurants and pubs.

🅾 Sights

American Revolution
Museum at Yorktown
MUSEUM

(☑757-887-1776; www.historyisfun.org; 200 Water St; adult/child 6-12yr $12/7; combo with Jamestown Settlement adult/child $23/12; ☺9am-5pm, to 6pm mid-July–mid-Aug; P ♿) Formerly the Yorktown Victory Center, this new and expanded exhibit space and living history museum vividly describes the build-up to the Revolutionary War, the war itself and daily life on the home front. The thrilling *Siege* is a nine-minute 4D movie spotlighting the war-ending Battle of of Yorktown. Lots of significant artifacts are here too, including an early printing of the Declaration of Independence. At the re-created military en-campment outside, costumed Continental soldiers share details about daily life in a Revolutionary War camp.

Yorktown Battlefield
HISTORIC SITE

(☑757-898-2410; www.nps.gov/york; 1000 Colonial Pkwy; adult/child under 16yr $7/free; ☺9am-5pm; P ♿) Yorktown Battlefield, run by the NPS, is the site of the last major battle of the American Revolution. Start your tour at the visitor center and check out the orientation film and the display of Washington's original tent. The 7-mile Battlefield Rd Tour takes you past the major highlights. Don't miss a walk through the last British defensive sites, Redoubts 9 and 10, reached via Ballard St.

🛈 Getting There & Away

The best way to get to Yorktown is by car. A free trolley loops between historic sites and the village every 20 to 35 minutes (11am to 5pm April to mid-November; extended hours June to August).

Hampton Roads

Hampton Roads (named not for asphalt, but for the confluence of the James, Nansemond and Elizabeth Rivers and Chesapeake Bay) has always been prime real estate. The Powhatan Confederacy fished these waters and hunted this part of the Virginia coast for thousands of years before John Smith arrived in 1607. Today Hampton Roads is known for congestion – particularly around the Chesapeake Bay Bridge Tunnel – and a cultural mishmash of history, the military and the arts. Norfolk is hoping a brand-new waterfront dining and entertainment district will re-energize downtown.

🛈 Getting There & Around

Norfolk International Airport (p316) is the primary airport for the region. I-64 is the main interstate. Expect slowdowns around the Hampton Roads-Bridge Tunnel, which links Newport News and Norfolk. If the electronic traffic signs suggest using the I-664 detour, take it.

Norfolk

Home to the world's largest naval base, it's not surprising that Norfolk has had a reputation as a rowdy port town filled with drunken sailors. In recent years, the city has worked hard to clean up its image through development, gentrification and focusing on its burgeoning arts scene. The Waterside

District, a new dining and entertainment complex on the Elizabeth River downtown, opened in the spring of 2017.

◎ Sights

Chrysler Museum of Art
MUSEUM

(📞757-664-6200; www.chrysler.org; 1 Memorial Pl; ⊙10am-5pm Tue-Sat, noon-5pm Sun) FREE A glorious setting for an eclectic collection of artifacts from ancient Egypt to the present day, including works by Henri Matisse, Albert Bierstadt, Georgia O'Keeffe Jackson Pollock, Andy Warhol and an expansive collection of glass objects spanning 3000 years. Don't miss the collection of Tiffany blown glass. Gallery talks daily at 2pm.

Naval Station Norfolk
MUSEUM

(📞757-444-7955; www.cnic.navy.mil/norfolksta; 9079 Hampton Blvd, near Gate 5; adult/child 3-11yr $10/5; ⊙tour times vary) The world's largest navy base, and one of the busiest airfields in the country, this is a must-see. The 45-minute bus tours are conducted by naval personnel and must be booked in advance (hours vary). Photo ID is required for adults.

Nauticus
MUSEUM

(📞757-664-1000; www.nauticus.org; 1 Waterside Dr; adult/child 4-12yr $16/11.50; ⊙10am-5pm daily Jun-Aug, 10am-5pm Tue-Sat & noon-5pm Sun Sep-May) This massive, interactive, maritime-themed museum has exhibits on undersea exploration, aquatic life of the Chesapeake Bay and US Naval lore. The museum's highlight is clambering around the decks and inner corridors of the USS Wisconsin. Built in 1943, it was the largest (887ft long) and last battleship built by the US Navy.

🛏 Sleeping

Residence Inn
HOTEL $$

(📞757-842-6216; www.marriott.com; 227 W Brambleton Ave; r/ste $164/174; P@🐾🖥) A short stroll to the Granby St eating strip, this friendly chain hotel has a boutique feel, with stylish, spacious rooms featuring small kitchenettes and excellent amenities.

Main Hotel
HOTEL $$$

(📞757-763-6200; www.3hilton.com; 100 E Main St; r $239-329, ste $369; P🌸🐾🖥) The rooms are spare but swanky at this new member of the Hilton family, which had just opened at research time. You'll pay more for a view of the Elizabeth River, but you may not need it – just settle in for a drink and river view at the rooftop lounge Grain, one of three dining-drinking establishments within the property.

✕ Eating & Drinking

Luna Maya
MEXICAN $$

(📞757-622-6986; www.lunamayarestaurant.com; 2010 Colley Ave; mains $13-19; ⊙4:30-10pm Tue-Sat) With exposed brick, a pressed-tin ceiling and a big-windowed but spare dining room, this buzzy place is certainly hip, but the friendly service and awesome burritos set it apart from the competition on busy Colley Ave. Not to mention the tasty margaritas and the extensive selection of vegetarian dishes for the non-carnivores in your group.

Press 626 Cafe & Wine Bar
MODERN AMERICAN $$

(📞757-282-6234; www.press26.com; 626 W Olney Rd; lunch mains $10-13, dinner mains $10-24; ⊙11am-11pm Mon-Fri, 5-11pm Sat, 10:30am-2:30pm Sun; 🍴) Embracing the Slow Food movement, the very charming Press 626 has a wide-ranging menu, with pressed gourmet sandwiches (at lunch), seared scallops, bouillabaisse and a great wine selection.

Smartmouth Brewing
BREWERY

(📞757-624-3939; www.smartmouthbrewing.com; 1309 Raleigh Ave; ⊙4:30-9pm Wed-Fri, noon-7pm Sat, 1-5pm Sun) In the burgeoning Chelsea arts district, this indoor-outdoor tasting room and brewery has an inviting neighborhood feel, plus there's a barbecue food truck for sustenance. If you like hefeweizens, give the seasonal Sommer Fling a try (April to December).

ℹ Getting There & Away

The region is served by Norfolk International Airport (p316), 7 miles northeast of downtown Norfolk. Greyhound (📞757-625-7500; www.greyhound.com; 701 Monticello Ave) runs buses to Virginia Beach ($16, 35 minutes), Richmond ($32, 2¾ hours) and Washington, DC ($50, 6½ hours). Hampton Roads Transit (www.gohrt.com) buses ($1.75) run from downtown throughout the city and to Newport News and Virginia Beach.

Virginia Beach

With 35 miles of sandy beaches, a 3-mile concrete oceanfront boardwalk and nearby outdoor activities, it's no surprise that Virginia Beach is a prime tourist destination. The city has worked hard to shed its reputation as a rowdy 'Redneck Riviera,' and hey, the beach *is* wider and cleaner now and there are fewer louts. Beach aside, you'll find some lovely parks and nature sites beyond the crowded high-rises lining the shore. Expect thick crowds, heavy traffic and high prices if visiting in the summer.

◉ Sights

Virginia Aquarium
& Marine Science Center
AQUARIUM

(☑757-385-3474; www.virginiaaquarium.com; 717 General Booth Blvd; adult/child 3-11yr $25/20; ☺9am-5pm) If you want to see an aquarium done right, come here. In various habitats, you can see a great array of aquatic life, including sea turtles, river otters and Komodo dragons. If the kids have more energy to burn, try the ropes course and zipline in the new Adventure Park (adult/child aged seven to 11 years $52/44), tucked in the woods between aquarium buildings.

Virginia Museum
of Contemporary Art
MUSEUM

(☑757-425-0000; www.virginiamoca.org; 2200 Parks Ave; adult/child $7.70/5.50; ☺10am-9pm Tue, to 5pm Wed-Fri, to 4pm Sat & Sun) Has excellent rotating exhibitions housed in a fresh, ultramodern building.

Back Bay National
Wildlife Refuge
NATURE RESERVE

(☑757-301-7329; www.fws.gov/refuge/back_bay; 4005 Sandpiper Rd; per vehicle/pedestrian Apr-Oct $5/2, free admission Nov-Mar; ☺sunrise-sunset) This 9250-acre wildlife and migratory-bird marshland habitat is most stunning during the December migration season.

First Landing State Park
NATURE RESERVE

(☑757-412-2300; www.dcr.virginia.gov; 2500 Shore Dr; per vehicle $7-9; ☺8am-dusk) Shake off the Virginia Beach flash at this lower key 2888-acre woodland, which has 20 miles of **hiking trails**, plus opportunities for camping, cycling, fishing, kayaking and swimming.

⊨ Sleeping & Eating

First Landing State Park
CAMPGROUND $

(☑800-933-7275; http://dcr.virginia.gov; Cape Henry; campsites $28-41, cabins from $83; P) You couldn't ask for a prettier campground than the one at this bay-front state park, though the cabins have no water view.

Hilton Virginia
Beach Oceanfront
HOTEL $$$

(☑757-213-3000; www.hiltonvb.com; 3001 Atlantic Ave; r from $417; P🛜🏊) The premier place to stay on the beach, this 21-story hotel is super luxurious. The oceanfront rooms are spacious, comfortable and packed with amenities including huge flat-screen TVs, dreamy bedding and large balconies that open out to the beach and Neptune Park below. Rates drop $100 during the week in summer.

Blue Pete's
SEAFOOD $$

(☑757-426-2278; www.bluepetespungo.com; 1400 N Muddy Creek Rd; mains $11-32; ☺5-10pm Mon-Fri, noon-11:45pm Sat, noon-10pm Sun) Perched over a peaceful creek near Back Bay, Blue Pete's has an enchanting woodland setting and a wide-ranging menu: crab cakes, brisket sandwiches, pastas and coconut-breaded shrimp.

Esoteric
AMERICAN $$$

(☑757-822-6008; www.esotericvb.com; 501 Virginia Beach Blvd; mains $10-30; ☺4-10pm Mon-Wed, to 11pm Thu, to midnight Fri, noon-midnight Sat) Gourmet sandwiches and an eclectic array of innovative American dishes keep locals happy, as does the craft beer. The husband-and-wife team behind this stylish spot embrace local food producers and collaborators.

❶ Getting There & Away

Greyhound (☑757-422-2998; www.greyhound.com; 971 Virginia Beach Blvd) runs buses daily to Richmond (from $14, 3½ hours), which also stop in Norfolk and Hampton; transfer in Richmond for services to Washington, DC, Wilmington; NYC and beyond. Buses depart from Circle D Food Mart, 1 mile west of the boardwalk.

Hampton Roads Transit runs the Virginia Beach Wave trolley (tickets $2), which plies Atlantic Ave in summer.

The Piedmont

Central Virginia's rolling central hills and plateaus separate the coastal lowlands from the mountainous frontier. The fertile valley gives way to dozens of wineries, country villages and grand colonial estates. New microbreweries, cideries and distilleries are garnering lots of well-deserved attention.

❶ Getting There & Around

The Piedmont region is flanked by Interstates I-81 and I-64. The area is best explored by car. Charlottesville anchors the region and has an **airport** and an **Amtrak** station. On Fridays you'll likely join a few UVA students hopping the train to Washington, DC.

Charlottesville

Set in the shadow of the Blue Ridge Mountains, Charlottesville is regularly ranked as one of the country's best places to live. This culturally rich town is home to the University of Virginia (UVA), which attracts Southern aristocracy and artsy lefties in equal proportions. With the UVA grounds and pedestrian downtown mall area overflowing with students, couples, professors and the occasional celebrity under a blanket of blue skies, 'C-ville' is practically perfect.

◉ Sights

Monticello   HISTORIC SITE
(☑ 434-984-9800; www.monticello.org; 931 Thomas Jefferson Pkwy; adult/child 5-11yr $28/9; ⊙8:30am-6pm Mon-Fri, to 7pm Sat & Sun, hours vary seasonally) Monticello is an architectural masterpiece designed and inhabited by Thomas Jefferson, founding father and third US president, who spent 40 years building his dream home, finally completed in 1809. Today it is the only home in America designated a UN World Heritage site. 'I am as happy nowhere else and in no other society, and all my wishes end, where I hope my days will end, at Monticello,' wrote Jefferson.

University of Virginia   UNIVERSITY
(☑ 434-924-0311; www.virginia.edu; Charlottesville) Thomas Jefferson founded the University of Virginia, whose classically designed buildings and grounds embody the spirit of communal living and learning that Jefferson envisioned. Free, student-led guided tours of the campus depart daily from the Rotunda at 10am, 11am and 2pm during the school year (www.uvaguides.org; September to April). You can also tour the Jefferson-designed **Rotunda** (☑ 434-924-7969; www.rotunda.virginia.edu; 1826 University Ave; ⊙9am-5pm), a scale replica of Rome's Pantheon. UVA's **Fralin Art Museum** (☑ 434-924-3592; http://uvafralinartmuseum.virginia.edu/; 155 Rugby Rd; ⊙10am-5pm Tue, Wed, Fri & Sat, to 7pm Thu, noon-5pm Sun) FREE has an eclectic collection of American, European and Asian arts.

Ash Lawn-Highland   HISTORIC BUILDING
(☑ 434-293-8000; www.ashlawnhighland.org; 2050 James Monroe Pkwy; adult/child 6-11yr $14/8; ⊙9am-6pm Apr-Oct, 11am-5pm Nov-Mar) This historic site was the home of James Monroe (the fifth US president) and his wife Elizabeth from 1799 to 1823.

WORTH A TRIP

MONTPELIER

Thomas Jefferson gets all the attention in these parts, but it's well worth branching out and visiting James Madison's **Montpelier** (www.montpelier.org; 11350 Constitution Hwy; adult/child $20/7; ⊙9am-5pm Apr-Oct, 10am-4pm Nov-Mar), a spectacular estate 25 miles northeast of Charlottesville (off Hwy 20). Madison was a brilliant but shy man, who devoted himself to his books; he was almost single-handedly responsible for developing and writing the US Constitution. **Guided tours** shed a light on the life and times of James as well as his gifted and charismatic wife Dolley, plus other residents of the estate.

🛏 Sleeping

Fairhaven   GUESTHOUSE $
(☑ 434-933-2471; www.fairhavencville.com; 413 Fairway Ave; r $80; ℗ ✳ 🗟) This friendly and welcoming guesthouse is a great deal if you don't mind sharing facilities (there's just one bathroom for the three rooms). Each room has wood floors, with comfy beds and a cheerful color scheme, and guests can use the kitchen, living room or backyard. It's about a 1-mile walk to the pedestrian mall.

South Street Inn   B&B $$
(☑ 434-979-0200; www.southstreetinn.com; 200 South St; r $169-219, ste $249-259; ℗ ✳ 🗟) In the heart of downtown Charlottesville, this elegant 1856 building has gone through previous incarnations as a girls' finishing school, a boarding house and a brothel. Now it houses heritage-style rooms – a total of two dozen, which gives this place more depth and diversity than your average B&B.

Hyatt Place   HOTEL $$
(☑ 434-995-5200; https://charlottesville.place. hyatt.com; 2100 Bond Pl; r from $209; ℗ @ 🗟 ✺) Sometimes you just don't want a historic inn or a chatty B&B. You want hip furnishings, strong wi-fi and a good free breakfast that doesn't come with a side of conversation about your plans for the day. In those situations, the new Hyatt Place has your back. Pet fee is $75 per stay.

✖ Eating & Drinking

Citizen Burger AMERICAN $

(☑434-979-9944; www.citizenburgerbar.com; 212 E Main St; mains $12-15; ☺noon-midnight Sun-Thu, to 2am Fri & Sat) On the pedestrian mall, Citizen Burger serves up delicious burgers and microbrews in a buzzing, brick-lined dining room. The ethos is local and sustainable (organically raised, grass-fed cows, Virginia-made cheeses and beers). Don't miss the truffle fries.

Oakhart Social MODERN AMERICAN $$

(☑434-995-5449; www.oakhartsocial.com; 511 W Main St; small plates $10-23; ☺5pm-midnight Tue-Sun, to 2am Fri & Sat) The stylish place serves creative seasonally inspired small plates (grilled octopus with garbanzo puree, sweet and crispy pork-belly salad) as well as wood-fired pizzas in a handsomely laid-back setting. The front patio is a festive spot to sit and sip a refreshing 'Corpse Reviver #2' and other well-made cocktails.

★ Public Fish & Oyster SEAFOOD $$$

(☑434-995-5542; www.publicfo.com; 513 W Main St; mains $19-29; ☺4-9:30pm Mon-Thu, to 10pm Fri & Sat, to 9pm Sun) This bright and inviting brick box will catch your eye, but it's the skillfully seasoned seafood dishes that will keep you inside ordering plate after plate of oysters, mussels and other maritime delights. If you're a raw oyster virgin, this is the place change that story. The twice-cooked Belgian fries with sea salt are fantastic.

Whiskey Jar COCKTAIL BAR

(☑434-202-1549; http://thewhiskeyjarcville.com; 227 W Main St; lunch mains $10-15, dinner mains $12-32; ☺11am-midnight Mon-Thu, to 2am Fri & Sat, 10am-2:30pm Sun) On the pedestrian mall, the Whiskey Jar offers a huge (more than 125 varieties!) whiskey selection in a hiply rustic setting – wooden furniture with waitstaff wearing plaid and drinks in Mason jars. And note, if you like your Bloody Mary's spicy – it will be spicy. Also serves neo-Southern comfort food, including great barbecue.

❶ Getting There & Around

Amtrak (www.amtrak.com; 810 W Main St) Two daily trains to Washington, DC (from $30, three hours).

Charlottesville Albemarle Airport (CHO; ☑434-973-8342; www.gocho.com) Ten miles north of downtown; offers non-stop flights along the east coast and to Chicago.

Greyhound/Trailways Terminal (☑434-295-5131; www.greyhound.com; 310 W Main St) Runs three daily buses to Richmond (from $18, 1¼ hours) and one to Washington, DC (from $21, three hours).

A free trolley connects W Main St with UVA.

Appomattox

At the McLean House in the town of Appomattox Court House, General Robert E Lee surrendered the Army of Northern Virginia to General Ulysses S Grant, in effect ending the Civil War.

Today, the town of Appomatox (3 miles southwest of the national park) is small but charming, with a main street dotted with antique shops (a goldmine for hunters of Civil War memorabilia).

◎ Sights

Appomattox Court House
National Historic Park PARK

(☑434-352-8987; www.nps.gov/apco; 111 National Park Dr; ☺9am-5pm) FREE On April 9, 1865, the surrender of the Army of Northern Virginia occurred here at McLean House. The park comprises over two dozen restored buildings; a number are open to visitors, and set with original and period furnishings from 1865.

Highlights include the parlor of the **McLean House**, where Lee and Grant met; the **Clover Hill Tavern**, used by Union soldiers to print 30,000 parole passes for Confederate soldiers; and the dry-goods-filled **Meeks General Store**.

VIRGINIA'S BREW RIDGE TRAIL

A string of fantastic craft breweries stretches west from Charlottesville to Crozet and along Hwy 151, which ribbons along the base of the Blue Ridge Mountains below the Blue Ridge Pkwy. Part of the Brew Ridge Trail (www.brew ridgetrail.com), many of the breweries offer fine craft beer, mountain views and great food. On pretty days you'll find the patios loaded with beer connoisseurs and outdoor adventurers. Charlottesville Hop on Tours (www.cvillehopon tours.com) shuttles between many of the breweries.

🛏 Sleeping & Eating

Longacre B&B $$
(☑434-352-9251; www.longacreva.com; 1670
Church St; r from $115; P❀) Longacre looks
like it got lost somewhere in the English
countryside and decided to set up shop in
Virginia. Its elegant rooms are decorated
with antiques, and lush grounds surround
the sprawling Tudor house.

Baine's Books and Coffee CAFE $
(☑434-432-3711; www.bainesbooks.com; 205 Main
St; snacks $2-6; ⊙7am-8pm Mon-Wed, to 9:30pm
Thu & Fri, 8:30am-9:30pm Sat, 9am-5pm Sun) Stop
in for sandwiches, quiche and scones (plus
live music several nights a week).

Shenandoah Valley

Local lore says Shenandoah was named for
a Native American word meaning 'Daughter
of the Stars.' True or not, there's no question
this is God's country, and one of the most
beautiful places in America. The 200-mile-
long valley and its Blue Ridge Mountains
are packed with picturesque small towns,
wineries, microbreweries, preserved bat-
tlefields and caverns. This was once the
western border of colonial America, settled
by Scots–Irish frontiersmen who were High-
land Clearance refugees. Outdoor activities –
hiking, cycling, camping, fishing, horseback
riding and canoeing – abound.

❶ Getting There & Around

The I-81 and I-64 are the primary interstates
here. The largest airport is Roanoke-Blacksburg
Regional Airport (p316). Amtrak stops at the
train station (www.amtrak.com; 1 Middlebrook
Ave) in Staunton.

Front Royal & Luray

The northernmost tip of Skyline Dr at Front
Royal looks like a drab strip of gas stations,
but there's a friendly main street and some
cool caverns nearby. Stop at the **visitor
center** (☑800-338-2576; https://frontroyalva.
com/101/Visiting; 414 E Main St; ⊙9am-5pm)
before heading 'up' the valley. Luray may be
best known for its caverns, but the down-
town is a charming place to stroll.

◉ Sights

Luray Caverns CAVE
(☑540-743-6551; www.luraycaverns.com; 970 US
Hwy 211 W, Luray; adult/child 6-12yr $27/14; ⊙9am-

7pm daily mid-Jun–Aug, to 6pm Sep-Nov & Apr–mid-
Jun, to 4pm Mon-Fri & to 5pm Sat & Sun Dec-Mar) If
you can only fit one cavern into your itiner-
ary, head 25 miles south from Front Royal
to the world-class Luray Caverns and hear
the 'Stalacpipe Organ' – hyped as the largest
musical instrument on earth. Tours can feel
like a cattle call on busy weekends, but the
stunning underground formations make up
for all the elbow-bumping. To save time at
the entrance, buy your ticket online ahead
of time, then join the entry line.

Museum of the Shenandoah Valley MUSEUM
(☑540-662-1473, 888-556-5799; www.themsv.org;
901 Amherst St, Winchester; adult/student 13-18yr/
child $10/8/free, Wed free; ⊙10am-5pm Tue-Sun
Apr-Dec, 11am-4pm Jan-Mar) Located in the
town of Winchester, some 25 miles north of
Front Royal, this museum comprises an 18th-
century house museum filled with period fur-
nishings, a 6-acre garden and a multimedia
museum that delves into the valley's history.

Skyline Caverns CAVE
(☑800-296-4545; www.skylinecaverns.com; 10344
Stonewall Jackson Hwy, near entrance to Skyline Dr,
Front Royal; adult/child 7-13yr $22/11; ⊙9am-5pm,
hours vary seasonally) Front Royal's claim to
fame is Skyline Caverns, which boasts rare,
white-spiked anthodites – mineral forma-
tions that look like sea urchins.

🛏 Sleeping & Eating

**Yogi Bear's Jellystone
Park Campsite** CAMPGROUND $
(☑540-743-4002; www.campluray.com; 2250
Hwy 211 E, Luray; campsites/cabins from $45/116)
Miniature-golf courses, waterslides and pad-
dleboats all await inside this fanciful cam-
pus. Bargain-basement campsite and cabin
prices don't reflect the possibility you might
strike it rich while panning for gold at Old
Faceful Mining Company.

Woodward House on Manor Grade B&B $$
(☑540-635-7010, 800-635-7011; www.acountry
home.com; 413 S Royal Ave/US 320, Front Royal;
r $110-155, cottage $225; P🐾) Offers seven
cheerful rooms and a separate cottage. Sip
your coffee from the deck and don't let the
busy street below distract from the Blue
Ridge Mountain vista.

Element FUSION $$
(☑540-636-9293; www.jsgourmet.com; 317 E Main
St, Front Royal; lunch mains $8-10, dinner mains
$14-28; ⊙11am-3pm & 5-9pm Tue-Sat; ☑) Ele-
ment is a foodie favorite for quality bistro

fare. The small dinner menu features changing specials such as roasted quail with Mexican corn salad and sweet potatoes.

❶ Getting There & Away

The best way to explore the region is by car. Washington, DC is 70 miles east of Front Royal. Luray borders US 211 between I-81 and the Thornton Gap entrance to the national park.

Staunton

This small-town beauty has much going for it, including a historic and walkable town center, a fantastic foodie scene, great microbreweries, some intriguing museums, regular live music downtown and a first-rate theater. Add to this an abundance of outdoor activities nearby and you may find yourself looking into local real estate when you get here.

◉ Sights

The pedestrian-friendly, handsome center boasts more than 200 buildings designed by noted Victorian architect TJ Collins. There's an artsy yet unpretentious bohemian vibe thanks to the presence of Mary Baldwin, a small liberal arts university.

Frontier Culture Museum   MUSEUM
(☑ 540-332-7850; www.frontiermuseum.org; 1290 Richmond Rd; adult/student/child 6-12yr $12/11/7; ⊙9am-5pm mid-Mar–Nov, 10am-4pm Dec–mid-Mar) The excellent Frontier Culture Museum is cooler than its name might suggest. On the 100-plus acre grounds you'll find authentic historic buildings from Germany, Ireland and England, plus re-created West African dwellings and a separate area of American frontier dwellings.

Woodrow Wilson Presidential Library   HISTORIC SITE
(www.woodrowwilson.org; 20 N Coalter St; adult/student/child 6-12yr $14/7/5; ⊙9am-5pm Mon-Sat, from noon Sun) History buffs should check out the Woodrow Wilson Presidential Library near downtown. Stop by and tour the hilltop Greek Revival house where Wilson grew up, which has been faithfully restored to its original 1856 appearance.

🛏 Sleeping & Eating

Frederick House   B&B $$
(☑ 540-885-4220; www.frederickhouse.com; 28 N New St; r $145-208; 🅿❄🛜) Stay right downtown in the thoroughly mauve and immensely welcoming Frederick House, which consists of five historical residences with 25 varied rooms and suites – all with private bathrooms and some with antique furnishings and decks.

Stonewall Jackson Hotel   HOTEL $$
(☑ 540-885-4848; www.stonewalljacksonhotel.com; 24 S Market St; r/ste $179/385; 🅿❄🛜🛁) A restored and renovated Staunton classic, the Stonewall oozes class and the restrained Southern style of the classical Commonwealth. The central lobby could be plucked from a chapter of *The Great Gatsby* (if *Gatsby* was set in old Virginia). Rooms are comfortable and retain the classic atmosphere promised by the entrance, and amenities are extensive.

Byers Street Bistro   MODERN AMERICAN $$
(☑ 540-887-6100; www.byersstreetbistro.com; 18 Byers St; lunch mains $10-19, dinner mains $10-28; ⊙11am-midnight) By the train station, Byers Street Bistro cooks up high-end pub grub (applewood bacon and caramelized onion pizzas, mahimahi tacos, Angus burgers, slow-roasted baby back ribs) that's best enjoyed at the outdoor tables on warm days. Come on Friday and Saturday nights for live bands (bluegrass, blues and folk).

Zynodoa   SOUTHERN US $$$
(☑ 540-885-7775; www.zynodoa.com; 115 E Beverley St; mains $19-32; ⊙5-9:30pm Sun-Tue, to 10:30pm Wed-Sat; 🖋) 🌿 Classy Zynodoa puts together some fine dishes in the vein of Virginia artisan cheeses, Shenandoah-sourced roasted chicken and rainbow trout from Casta Line (raised nearby). Local farms and wineries are the backbone of Zynodoa's larder.

🍷 Drinking & Entertainment

Yelping Dog   WINE BAR
(☑ 540-885-2275; www.yelpingdogwine.com; 9 E Beverley St; ⊙11am-9pm Tue-Thu, to 10pm Fri & Sat, noon-6pm Sun) Catch up with friends over a glass of wine and a scrumptious cheese plate at this inviting wine bar in the thick of the downtown action. And if you're on the fence about ordering one of the gourmet grilled cheese sandwiches ($9 to $10), go ahead.

Redbeard Brewery   MICROBREWERY
(www.redbeardbrews.com; 102 S Lewis St; ⊙4-11pm Tue-Thu, 1-11pm Fri-Sun) A small-batch brewery that serves up tasty IPAs, saisons, ambers and other seasonal selections.

SHENANDOAH NATIONAL PARK

One of the most spectacular national parks in the country, **Shenandoah National Park** (☎540-999-3500; www.nps.gov/shen; Skyline Dr; one-week pass per car $25) is like a new smile from nature: in spring and summer the wildflowers explode, in fall the leaves burn bright red and orange, and in winter a cold, starkly beautiful hibernation period sets in. White-tailed deer are a common sight and, if you're lucky, you might spot a black bear, bobcat or wild turkey. The park lies just 75 miles west of Washington, DC.

Your first stop should be the **Dickey Ridge Visitors Center** (☎540-635-3566; www.nps.gov/shen; Mile 4.6, Skyline Dr; ☺9am-5pm mid-Apr–Nov), close to the northern end of Skyline Dr, or the **Byrd Visitors Center** (☎540-999-3283; www.nps.gov/shen; Mile 51, Skyline Dr; ☺9am-5pm late Mar-Nov). Both places have exhibits on flora and fauna, as well as maps and information about hiking trails and activities.

Shenandoah National Park is easy on the eyes, set against a backdrop of the dreamy Blue Ridge Mountains, ancient granite and metamorphic formations that are more than one billion years old. The park itself was founded in 1935 as a retreat for East Coast urban populations. It is an accessible day-trip destination from DC, but stay longer if you can. The 500 miles of hiking trails, 75 scenic overlooks, 30 fishing streams, seven picnic areas and four campgrounds are sure to keep you entertained.

Skyline Drive is the breathtaking road that follows the main ridge of the Blue Ridge Mountains and winds 105 miles through the center of the park. It begins in Front Royal near the western end of I-66, and ends in the southern part of the range near Rockfish Gap near I-64. Mile markers at the side of the road provide a reference. Miles and miles of blazed trails wander through the park.

The most famous trail in the park is the stretch of **Appalachian Trail** (AT), which travels 101 miles through Shenandoah from south to north, and is part of the 2175-mile Appalachian Trail crossing through 14 states. Access the trail from Skyline Dr, which roughly runs parallel. Aside from the AT, Shenandoah has over 400 miles of hiking trails in the park. Options for shorter hikes include **Compton Peak** (Mile 10.4; 2.4 miles; easy to moderate), **Traces** (Mile 22.2; 1.7 miles; easy), **Overall Run** (Mile 22.2; 6 miles; moderate) and **White Oak Canyon** (Mile 42.6; 4.6 miles; strenuous). **Hawksbill Mountain Summit** (Mile 46.7; 2.1 miles; moderate) is the park's highest peak.

Amtrak (www.amtrak.com) trains runs daily to Charlottesville (from $35, two hours 45 minutes), and Wednesdays, Fridays and Sundays to Staunton (from $55, four hours), from Washington, DC . You'll really need your own wheels to explore the length and breadth of the park, which can be easily accessed from several exits off I-81.

There is a **gas station** (Mile 51.2, Skyline Dr) at Big Meadows Wayside.

★ **Blackfriars Playhouse**   THEATER

(☎540-851-1733; www.americanshakespearecenter.com; 10 S Market St; tickets $29-49) Don't leave Staunton without catching a show at the Blackfriars Playhouse, where the American Shakespeare Center company performs in this re-creation of Shakespeare's original indoor theater. The acting is up-close and engaged, and brave guests can grab a seat on the side of the stage.

ℹ Getting There & Away

Staunton sits beside I-81, not far from its junction with I-64 E. Amtrak (p333) stops here three times per week.

Lexington & Rockbridge County

This is the place to see Southern gentry at their stately best, as cadets from the Virginia Military Institute jog past the prestigious academics of Washington & Lee University. Two Civil War generals, Robert E Lee and Stonewall Jackson, are buried here, and Lexington has long been a favorite stop for Civil War enthusiasts. Today you're as likely to see hikers, cyclists and paddlers using Lexington as a launchpad for adventures in the nearby Blue Ridge Mountains, where the Blue Ridge Pkway and the Appalachian Trail overlook the valley, as well as on the James River. The opening of new hotels, bars and restaurants have re-energized the city.

◉ Sights & Activities

Virginia Military Institute　　UNIVERSITY
(VMI; www.vmi.edu; Letcher Ave) You'll either be impressed or put off by the extreme discipline of the cadets at Virginia Military Institute, the only university to have sent its entire graduating class into combat (plaques to student war dead are touching and ubiquitous). The **VMI Museum** (☏ 540-464-7334; ☻ 9am-5pm) **FREE** houses the stuffed carcass of Stonewall Jackson's horse, a homemade American flag made by an alumnus prisoner of war in Vietnam, and a tribute to VMI students killed in the 'War on Terror'.

Contact the museum for a free guided tour of the campus, offered at noon. A full-dress parade takes place most Fridays at 4:30pm during the school year. The school's **George C Marshall Museum** (☏ 540-463-2083; www.marshallfoundation.org/museum/; adult/student $5/2; ☻ 11am-4pm Tue-Sat) honors the creator of the Marshall Plan for post-WWII European reconstruction.

Washington & Lee University　　UNIVERSITY
(☏ 540-458-8400; www.wlu.edu) Named for George Washington and Robert E Lee, this pretty and preppy liberal arts college was founded in 1749. George Washington saved the young school in 1796 with a gift of $20,000. Confederate Gen Robert E Lee served as president after the Civil War in the hopes of unifying the country through education. Visitors today can stroll along the striking red-brick Colonnade and visit **Lee Chapel & Museum** (☏ 540-458-8768; http://leechapel.wlu.edu; ☻ 9am-4pm Mon-Sat & 1-4pm Sun Nov-Mar, to 5pm Apr-Oct).

Natural Bridge State Park　　BRIDGE
(☏ 540-291-1326; www.dcr.virginia.gov; 6477 S Lee Hwy; adult/child 6-12yr $8/6; ☻ 8am-dusk) We're going to let Thomas Jefferson write the review of this new state park, which he once owned and described in his book *Notes on Virginia*: 'It is impossible for the emotions arising from the sublime, to be felt beyond what they are here: so beautiful an arch, so elevated, so light, and springing as it were up to heaven, the rapture of the spectator is really indescribable!' Yep, no longer a kitschy tourist trap, this park spotlights a very photogenic 215ft-high limestone bridge.

Dinosaur Kingdom II　　AMUSEMENT PARK
(☏ 540-464-2253; www.facebook.com/dinosaurkingdom; 5781 S Lee Hwy, Lexington; adult/child 3-12yr $10/3; ☻ 10am-6pm; ☷) One of the wackiest attractions yet from artist and creative wunderkind Mark Cline, this kitschy theme park transports visitors to an alternate reality: a forested kingdom where Union soldiers are attempting to use life-size dinosaurs as weapons of mass destruction against Confederate forces during the Civil War. Even President Lincoln is here, trying to lasso a flying pteranodon. The Styrofoam and fiberglass creations are lifelike enough to amaze younger kids, and the offbeat historic juxtapositions will entertain even the grouchiest of adults.

Twin River Outfitters　　CANOEING; TUBING
(☏ 540-261-7334; https://canoevirginia.net/; 653 Lowe St, Buchanan; 2hr paddling trip from $34; ☻ 9am-5pm Apr-Oct) Scan for eagles and deer as you paddle or tube down the James River on the new Upper James River Paddling Trail by this popular outfitter, owned by twin brothers. Mileage and travel times vary, as does difficulty. A shuttle ride is included in the price.

Upper James River Water Trail　　CANOEING
(www.upperjamesriverwatertrail.com; Botetourt) This new paddling trail follows the James River as it flows through the foothills of the Blue Ridge Mountains toward Richmond and the coast.

🛌 Sleeping & Eating

Georges　　BOUTIQUE HOTEL $$
(☏ 540-463-2500; www.thegeorges.com; 11 N Main St; r from $205; ℗ ❊ 🛜) Set in two historic buildings on opposite sides of Main St, the Georges has beautifully set rooms, each custom-designed with high-end furnishings. The great location, friendly service and on-site eateries add to the appeal.

Applewood Inn & Llama Trekking　　INN $$
(☏ 540-463-1962; www.applewoodbb.com; 242 Tarn Beck Lane; r $169-175, cottage from $235; ℗ ❊) The charming, ecominded Applewood Inn & Llama Trekking offers accommodations and a slew of outdoorsy activities (including, yes, llama trekking) on a farm in a bucolic valley just a 10-minute drive away from downtown Lexington. And note that you don't ride a llama when trekking – you just walk side by side like old friends. Who sometimes spit at you.

Blue Sky Bakery　　SANDWICHES $
(☏ 540-463-6546; 125 W Nelson St; sandwiches $8; ☻ 10:30am-4pm Mon-Fri) This local favorite

SCENIC DRIVE: VIRGINA'S HORSE COUNTRY

About 40 miles west of Washington, DC, suburban sprawl gives way to endless green farms, vineyards, quaint villages and palatial estates and ponies. This is 'Horse Country,' where wealthy Washingtonians pursue their equestrian pastimes.

The following route is the most scenic drive to Shenandoah National Park (p335). From DC, take Rte 50 West to **Middleburg**, a too-cute-for-words town of B&Bs, taverns, wine shops and boutiques. The **National Sporting Library** (☑ 540-687-6542; www. nationalsporting.org; 102 The Plains Rd; museum adult/child 13-18yr $10/8, library free; ☺ 10am-5pm Wed-Sun) is a museum and research center devoted to horse and field sports such as foxhunting, dressage, steeplechase and polo. About 20 miles northeast of Middleburg is **Leesburg**, another charming town with a colonial feel and historic sites. Stop in **Morven Park** (☑ 703-777-2414; www.morvenpark.org; 17263 Southern Planter Lane; grounds free, mansion tours adult/child $10/5; ☺ grounds 8am-5:45pm daily, mansion tours hourly noon-5pm Sat & Sun, last tour 4pm) for a tour of a staggering Virginia home on 1000 acres. For more Greek Revival grandeur, visit **Oatlands Plantation** (☑ 703-777-3174; www.oatlands.org; 20850 Oatlands Plantation Lane; adult/child 6-16yr $15/8, grounds only $10; ☺ 10am-5pm Mon-Sat & 1-5pm Sun Apr-Dec, closed Jan-Mar), outside of town.

The area has a wealth of appealing dining options. Stop in the **Shoes Cup & Cork** (☑ 703-771-7463; www.shoescupandcork.com; 17 N King St; lunch mains $10-18, dinner mains $11-25; ☺ 7am-9pm Mon-Thu, to 10pm Fri, 9am-10pm Sat, 9am-9pm Sun) in Leesburg for creative American fare or **Chimole** (☑ 703-777-7011; www.facebook.com/CH1MOLE; 10 S King St; tapas $8-18; ☺ 11am-2pm Mon-Fri, 5-10pm Wed & Thu, 5pm-1am Fri & Sat) for wine and Latin American tapas. In Middleburg, the **Red Fox Inn & Tavern** (☑ 540-687-6801; www. redfox.com; 2 E Washington St; breakfast mains $12-15, dinner mains $26-58; ☺ 8-10am & 5-9pm Mon-Fri, 11:30am-2:30pm & 5-9pm Sat, 11:30am-2:30pm & 5-8pm Sun) has first-rate American cooking served in a beautifully preserved 1728 dining room.

Located 6 miles west of Middleburg, the **Welbourne B&B** (☑ 540-687-3201; www.wel bourneinn.com; 22314 Welbourne Farm Lane; r $147; ☒ ☎ ☒ ☒) has five heritage rooms set in a historic landmark house (c 1770) surrounded by 520 acres. The **Leesburg Colonial Inn** (☑ 703-777-5000; www.theleesburgcolonialinn.com; 19 S King St; r $129-179) has a great central location and unbeatable prices.

Further down the road at the foothills of the Blue Ridge Mountains is **Sperryville**. Its many galleries and shops are a must-stop for antique-lovers. Continue 9 miles west to reach the Thornton Gap entrance of Skyline Dr in Shenandoah National Park.

has tasty focaccia sandwiches, hearty soups and fresh salads.

Red Hen SOUTHERN US $$$
(☑ 540-464-4401; www.redhenlex.com; 11 E Washington St; mains $24-28; ☺ 5-9:30pm Tue-Sat; ☑) ☞ Reserve well ahead for a memorable meal at Red Hen, which features a creative menu showcasing fine local produce. Great cocktails and desserts too.

🍷 Drinking & Entertainment

Taps BAR
(☑ 540-463-2500; www.thegeorges.com; 11 N Main St, Georges; ☺ 3-11pm Mon-Thu, from 11am Fri & Sat) This cozy place in Georges doubles as Lexington's living room, with students, professors and other locals hanging out on the fancy couches or at the small bar. Come here

for craft beer, fine cocktails and local gossip. The short pub grub menu is strong.

Hull's Drive-in CINEMA
(☑ 540-463-2621; www.hullsdrivein.com; 2367 N Lee Hwy/US 11; adult/child 5-11yr $7/3; ☺ gates open 7pm Fri & Sat May-Oct; ⊞) For old-fashioned amusement, catch a movie at this drive-in movie theater, set 5.5 miles north of Lexington. Movies start 20 minutes after sunset.

ℹ Getting There & Away

Lexington sits at the junction of I-81 and I-64. The closest airport is Roanoke-Blacksburg Regional Airport (p316), which is 55 miles south. There is an Amtrak station (p333) in nearby Staunton, with a connection to Washington, DC three times per week.

Blue Ridge Highlands & Southwest Virginia

The Blue Ridge Highlands and the Roanoke Valley are two of the prettiest regions in the state, with farm-dotted valleys unfurling between the Blue Ridge and Allegheny mountains. The Blue Ridge Parkway and Appalachian Trail roll across the mountains here, which are home to scenic rivers, streams and lakes. Old-time mountain music can be heard regularly, and wineries and craft breweries offer tastings in small towns and on mountain slopes. The most rugged part of the region – and the state – is the southwestern tip of Virginia, where mountain music was born. Turn onto any side road and you'll plunge into dark strands of dogwood and fir, and see fast streams and white waterfalls. You're bound to see Confederate flags, but there's a proud hospitality behind the fierce veneer of independence.

ℹ Getting There & Around

I-81 is the primary interstate here, running north–south through the western edge of the state. The Blue Ridge Pkwy runs parallel to I-81, but it is much slower going. The major airport in the region is the Roanoke Regional Airport (p316).

Roanoke

Illuminated by the giant star atop Mill Mountain, Roanoke is the largest city in the Roanoke Valley and is the self-proclaimed 'Capital of the Blue Ridge.' Close to the Blue Ridge Pkwy and the Appalachian Trail, it's a convenient base camp for exploring the great outdoors. An expanding greenway system, a burgeoning arts scene and a slew of new craft breweries have energized the city in recent years, flipping Roanoke from sleepy to almost hip.

◉ Sights & Activities

Center in the Square　　　　MUSEUM
(☑ 540-342-5700; www.centerinthesquare.org; 1 Market Sq; ⊙ 10am-5pm Tue-Sat, from 1pm Sun) The city's cultural heartbeat, where you'll find four museums, a butterfly garden, a theater and a rooftop observation deck. Museums cover African American culture, pinball, science and local history. There are six aquariums on the first floor. The Center Pass (adult/child $21/16) includes all attractions except the Roanoke Pinball Museum.

Harrison Museum of African American Culture　　MUSEUM
(☑ 540-857-4395; www.harrisonmuseum.com; 1 Market Sq; adult/child 5-17yr $7/4.75; ⊙ 10am-5pm Tue-Sat, from 1pm Sun) **FREE** Inside Center in the Square, this museum has displays about local African American culture and traditional and contemporary African art. Admission also available through the Center Pass, which includes additional museums within Center in the Square.

Roanoke Star & Mill Mountain Park　PARK
(☑ 540-853-2236; www.playroanoke.com; 2000 JP Fishburn Pkwy) Mill Mountain Park has walking trails, a discovery center, a zoo (adult/child aged three to 11 years $9/7) and grand views of Roanoke. It's also home to the massive **Roanoke Star**, which shines over the city at night.

Taubman Museum of Art　　MUSEUM
(www.taubmanmuseum.org; 110 Salem Ave SE; ⊙ 10am-5pm Wed-Sat, noon-5pm Sun, to 9pm third Thu & first Fri of month; ℙ) **FREE** The striking Taubman Museum of Art is set in a sculptural steel-and-glass edifice that's reminiscent of the Guggenheim Bilbao. Inside, you'll find a superb collection of artworks spanning 3500 years.

Greenways　　　　OUTDOORS
(www.roanokeoutside.com/land/greenways/) Before hopping in your car and driving to your next Roanoke adventure, see if one of the city's new greenways will get you to your destination via a scenic stroll or bike ride.

🛏 Sleeping & Eating

Hotel Roanoke　　　HOTEL $$$
(☑ 540-985-5900; www.hotelroanoke.com; 110 Shenandoah Ave NW; r $189-224, ste $289-414; ℙ@🛜🏊) This Tudor-style grand dame has presided over this city at the base of the Blue Ridge Mountains for the better part of a century and provides a welcome respite. Downstairs is the **Pine Room** for those requiring a stiff drink. Now a Hilton property.

Local Roots　　　MODERN AMERICAN $$
(☑ 540-206-2610; www.localrootsrestaurant.com; 1314 Grandin Rd; lunch mains $11-14, dinner mains $26-31; ⊙ 11:30am-2pm & 5-10pm Tue-Sat, 11am-2:30pm & 5-9pm Sun) This welcoming farm-to-table restaurant serves up delectable fare like shrimp and grits, striped bass, and perhaps the best hamburgers in town, with a large portion of the menu rotating seasonally.

★ **Lucky** MODERN AMERICAN $$
(☎540-982-1249; www.eatatlucky.com; 18 Kirk Ave SW; mains $18-29; ⏲5-9pm Mon-Wed, to 10pm Thu-Sat) Lucky has excellent cocktails (try 'The Cube') and a seasonally inspired menu of small plates (hickory-smoked porchetta, roasted oysters) and heartier mains (buttermilk fried chicken, morel and asparagus gnocchi). The team behind Lucky opened the equally divine Italian restaurant **Fortunato** (www.fortunatorestaurant.com) a few doors down.

Getting There & Away

The airport (p316) is 5 miles north of downtown and serves the Roanoke and Shenandoah Valley regions. If you're driving, I-81 and I-581 link to the city. The Blue Ridge Pkwy is just 5 miles from downtown.

Mt Rogers National Recreation Area

This seriously beautiful district is well worth a visit for outdoor enthusiasts. Hike, fish or cross-country ski among ancient hardwood trees and the state's tallest peak. The 33.4-mile Virginia Creeper Trail, popular with cyclists, passes through the recreation area. For food, load up your picnic or your backpack in the towns of Abingdon or Marion. The best way to get to the trails and campsites is by car. The skinny recreation area runs roughly north–south, with I-81 to the west and the Blue Ridge Pkwy to the east. The Tennessee and North Carolina borders are nearby. The Appalachian Trail runs across the mountains here and the Virginia Creeper Trail rolls through too.

Abingdon

One of the most photogenic towns in Virginia, Abingdon retains fine Federal and Victorian architecture in its historic district. The long-running regional theater in the center of town is a state-wide draw, as is the magnificent Virginia Creeper Trail. Popular with cyclists and hikers, this leafy path unfurls along an old railroad bed.

Sights & Activities

Heartwood ARTS CENTER
(☎276-492-2400; www.myswva.org/heartwood; One Heartwood Circle; ⏲9am-5pm Mon-Wed, Fri & Sat, to 9pm Thu, 10am-3pm Sun) Heartwood is a showcase of regional crafts, cuisine (sandwiches, salads, Virginia wines) and traditional music. Don't miss Thursday nights, for bluegrass bands and barbecue.

Virginia Creeper Trail CYCLING, HIKING
(www.vacreepertrail.com) This 33.4-mile cycling and hiking trail on an old railroad corridor rolls through the Mount Rogers National Recreation Area, connecting lofty Whitetop with Damascus and eventually Abingdon. Local bike companies rent out bikes and provide shuttle service.

Sleeping

Alpine Motel MOTEL $
(☎276-628-3178; www.alpinemotelabingdon.com; 882 E Main St; r $59-69; P ❄ 📶) The Alpine Motel is a simple but good-value option, with carpeted rooms, old TVs, and chirping birds across the way; it's located about 2 miles west of downtown.

BLUE RIDGE PARKWAY

Where Skyline Dr ends, the Blue Ridge Pkwy picks up. Managed by the national park service, the parkway is just as pretty and runs from the southern Appalachian ridge in Shenandoah National Park (at Mile 0) to North Carolina's Great Smoky Mountains National Park (at Mile 469). Wildflowers bloom in spring, and fall colors are spectacular, but watch out for foggy days; the lack of guardrails can make for hairy driving. There are a dozen visitor centers scattered over the parkway, and any of them make a good kick-off point for your trip. You won't find one stoplight on the entire drive, but we can almost guarantee you'll see deer. A helpful website is www.blueridgeparkway.org.

Along the Blue Ridge Pkwy there are trails to the **Peaks of Otter** (www.peaksofotter.com; Mile 86, Blue Ridge Pkwy; 👪) There are three peaks here: Sharp Top, Flat Top and Harkening Hill. Shuttles run to the top of Sharp Top, or you can try a fairly challenging hike (3 miles round-trip) to the top. The 360-degree view of the Blue Ridge Mountains from the rocky summit is fantastic. A short trail leads to the nearby Johnson Farm, which grew apples for the local inn before the arrival of the parkway.

For more information, visit www.nps.gov/blri.

Martha Washington Inn
HOTEL $$$

(☑ 276-628-3161; www.themartha.com; 150 W Main St; r/ste from $215/425; P ❉ @ 🛜 🌊) This is the region's premier historic hotel, a Victorian sprawl of historical classiness and wrought-iron style. The rocking chairs on the front porch are a pleasant place to relax.

✖ Eating & Drinking

128 Pecan
MODERN AMERICAN $$

(☑ 276-698-3159; www.128pecan.com; 128 Pecan St; lunch mains $8-17, dinner mains $8-23; ◔ 11am-9pm Tue-Sat; 🛜) This local favorite serves up excellent sandwiches, tacos and heartier meat or seafood dishes, with seating on a front verandah.

Rain
AMERICAN $$$

(☑ 276-739-2331; www.rainabingdon.com; 283 E Main St; lunch mains $9-10, dinner mains $22-29; ◔ 11am-2pm & 5-9pm Tue-Sat; P) Excellent New American cuisine inspired by the Appalachians. The mains, like seared salmon and sweet mustard pork chops, are executed wonderfully, with great consistency – this is the best splurge around.

Wolf Hills Brewing Co
MICROBREWERY

(☑ 276-451-5470; www.wolfhillsbrewing.com; 350 Park St; ◔ 5-9pm Mon-Fri, from 1pm Sat, 1-6pm Sun) For satisfying microbrews and the occasional live music session, head to Wolf Hills Brewery.

❶ Getting There & Away

Abingdon borders I-81 near the Virginia–Tennessee border. The city is 366 miles southwest of Washington, DC and about 180 miles northwest of Charlotte, NC. Close regional airports include Asheville Regional Airport in Asheville, NC and Roanoke-Blacksburg Regional Airport (p316) in Roanoke.

The Crooked Road

When Scots–Irish fiddle-and-reel joined with African American banjo-and-percussion, American mountain or 'old-time' music was born, spawning such genres as country and bluegrass. The latter genre still dominates the Blue Ridge, and Virginia's Heritage Music Trail, the 330-mile-long Crooked Road (www.myswva.org/tcr), takes you through nine sites associated with that history, along with some eye-stretching mountain scenery. It's well worth taking a detour and joining the music-loving fans of all ages who kick up their heels (many arrive with tap shoes) at these festive jamborees. During a live show you'll witness elders connecting to deep cultural roots and a new generation of musicians keeping that heritage alive and evolving. Top venues include the Floyd Country Store on Friday Nights and the **Carter Family Fold** (☑ 276-386-6054; www.carterfamilyfold.org; 3449 AP Carter Hwy, Hiltons; adult/child 6-11yr $10/2; ◔ 7:30pm Sat; ♿) on Saturday nights.

FLOYD

Tucked in the foothills of the Blue Ridge Mountains, tiny, cute-as-a-postcard Floyd is nothing more than an intersection between Hwy 8 and Hwy 221. In fact, the whole county only has one stoplight. But life explodes on Friday nights during the Friday Night Jamboree at the **Floyd Country Store** (☑ 540-745-4563; www.floydcountrystore.com; 206 S Locust St; $5; ◔ 10am-5pm Tue-Thu, to 10:30pm Fri, to 6pm Sat, 11am-6pm Sun) and the surrounding sidewalks when folks from far and wide converge for a night of live old-time music and communal good cheer.

🛏 Sleeping & Eating

Oak Haven Lodge
INN $

(☑ 540-745-5716; www.oakhavenlodge.com; 323 Webb's Mill Rd, Rte 8; r/ste $75/90; P ❉ 🛜) Just a mile north of Floyd, this good-value place has spacious rooms (some with Jacuzzi tubs) that open onto a shared balcony with rocking chairs.

Hotel Floyd
HOTEL $$

(☑ 540-745-6080; www.hotelfloyd.com; 300 Rick Lewis Way; r $139, ste $169-199; P ❉ 🛜 ♿) 🌿 Built with ecofriendly materials and furnishings, Hotel Floyd is a model of sustainability. Works by local artisans adorn its rooms.

Oddfella's
TEX-MEX $$

(☑ 540-745-3463; www.facebook.com/Oddf3llows; 110 N Locust St; mains $11-25; ◔ 11am-9pm Wed-Sat, 10:30am-2:30pm Sun; P 🌿) When you're all jigged out, head for Oddfella's, a comfy spot for American fare and tasty microbrews. And the name? Just check the sign over the door, which depicts the town's three predominant types: hippies, farmers and businessmen.

Dogtown Roadhouse
PIZZA $$

(☑ 540-745-6836; www.dogtownroadhouse.com; 302 S Locust St; mains $8-18; ◔ 4-9pm Wed & Thu, 4pm-midnight Fri, noon-midnight Sat, noon-9pm Sun) You might see a local farmer walk in with produce for the toppings at this lively pizzeria, the go-to for pizzas (fired up in a wood-burning oven) and microbrews, with live rock on Friday and Saturday nights.

ⓘ Getting There & Away

Floyd is 20 miles southeast of I-81. The closest major airport is Roanoke-Blacksburg Regional Airport (p316) about 50 miles north.

GALAX

Galax claims to be the world capital of mountain music, although it feels like anywhere-else-ville outside of the immediate downtown area, which is on the National Register of Historic Places.

🛏 Sleeping & Eating

Fiddlers Roost　　　　　　CABIN $$
(☑ 276-236-1212; http://fiddlersroostcabins.com; 485 Fishers Peak Rd; cabins $120-300; ℗) These eight cabins resemble Lincoln Logs playsets. The interiors are decorated in 'quilt' chic; they may not win a place in *Wallpaper* magazine, but they're cozy and have gas fireplaces, kitchens, TVs and DVD players. Breakfast included with all but Cabin on the Blue.

Creek Bottom Brewing　　　MICROBREWERY
(☑ 276-236-2337; www.cbbrews.com; 307 N Meadow St; mains $6-16; ⊙ 11am-9pm Tue & Wed, 11am-10pm Thu-Sat, noon-6pm Sun) Has a changing line-up of craft brews, which go nicely with the brick-oven pizza and smoked chicken wings fired up on site.

☆ Entertainment

Blue Ridge Music Center　　LIVE MUSIC
(☑ 276-236-5309; www.blueridgemusiccenter.net; 700 Foothills Rd, Mile 213 Blue Ridge Pkwy; ⊙ weekend shows May-Oct) An arts and music hub for the region that offers programming that focuses on local musicians carrying on the traditions of Appalachian music.

Rex Theater　　　　　　LIVE MUSIC
(☑ 276-236-0329; www.rextheatergalax.com; 113 E Grayson St) A musty, red-curtained belle of yore. Frequent bluegrass acts cross its stage, but the easiest one to catch is the Friday-night live WBRF 98.1 show ($5).

ⓘ Getting There & Away

Galax borders US 58 about 10 miles southwest of I-77. Roanoke-Blacksburg Regional Airport (p316) is 90 miles northeast via I-77 north and I-81 N. It's about 10 miles from the Blue Ridge Pkwy.

WEST VIRGINIA

Ready for rugged East Coast adventuring with a gorgeous mountain backdrop? Then set your car toward wild and wonderful West Virginia, a state often overlooked by both American and foreign travelers. It doesn't help that the state can't seem to shake its negative stereotypes. That's too bad, because West Virginia is one of the prettiest states in the Union. With its line of unbroken green mountains, raging white-water rivers and snowcapped ski resorts, this is an outdoor-lovers' paradise. The state is also just a few hours' drive from Washington, DC, Pittsburgh, PA and Richmond, VA.

Created by secessionists, the people here still think of themselves as hardscrabble sons of miners, and that perception isn't entirely off. But the Mountain State is also gentrifying and, occasionally, that's a good thing: the arts are flourishing in the valleys, where some towns offer a welcome break from the state's evolving outdoor activities.

History

Virginia was once the biggest state in America, divided between the plantation aristocracy of the Tidewater and the mountains of what is now West Virginia. The latter were settled by tough farmers who staked out independent freeholds across the Appalachians. Always resentful of their Eastern brethren and their reliance on cheap (ie slave) labor, the mountaineers of West Virginia declared their independence from Virginia when the latter tried to break off from America during the Civil War.

Yet the scrappy, independent-at-all-costs stereotype was challenged in the late 19th and early 20th centuries, when miners here formed into cooperative unions and fought employers in some of the bloodiest battles in American labor history. That mix of chip-on-the-shoulder resentment toward authority and look-out-for-your-neighbor community values characterizes West Virginia today.

ⓘ Information

West Virginia Division of Tourism (www.wvtourism.com) operates welcome centers at interstate borders and in **Harpers Ferry** (☑ 304-535-2627; www.discoveritallwv.com; 37 Washington Ct; ⊙ 9am-5pm). Check the Division of Tourism's website for info on the state's myriad adventure-tourism opportunities.

❶ Getting There & Around

The Eastern Panhandle begins about 60 miles northwest of Washington, DC and it's a fairly easy drive from the busy metropolitan area – but expect traffic. Amtrak and MARC trains stop at the **station** in Harpers Ferry. For the national forest and the southern reaches of the state, you will need a car to explore and will likely be accessing mountain towns and parks on two-lane roads coming in from I-81, I-64 and I-79. So although the mileage looks short, the distance will take longer to cover than on the interstate.

Eastern Panhandle

The most accessible part of West Virginia has always been a mountain getaway for DC types – the region is just 70 miles west of the capital-area sprawl. Here, Civil War–era history, soothing hot springs, leafy scenery and outdoor recreation on trails and rivers work together for visitors, offering an easy package of experiences than can be enjoyed on one long weekend.

One tricky part of travel in the panhandle is the practically overlapping proximity of three states – West Virginia, Virginia and Maryland – with Pennsylvania lying in wait just north. When planning, get out your maps to make sure you've spotted all attractions in the multistate region.

Harpers Ferry

History lives on in this attractive town, set with steep cobblestoned streets, and framed by the Shenandoah Mountains and the confluence of the rushing Potomac and Shenandoah Rivers. The lower town functions as an open-air museum, with more than a dozen buildings that you can explore to get a taste of 19th-century small-town life. Exhibits narrate the town's role at the forefront of westward expansion, American industry and, most famously, the slavery debate – in 1859 old John Brown tried to spark a slave uprising here and was hanged for his efforts; the incident rubbed friction between North and South into the fires of Civil War.

◉ Sights & Activities

Harpers Ferry National
Historic Park PARK
(☏ 304-535-6029; www.nps.gov/hafe; 171 Shoreline Dr; per person/vehicle $5/10; ☺ trails 9am-sunset, visitor center 9am-5pm; ℗) Historic buildings and museums are accessible to those with passes, which can be found, along with parking and shuttles, north of town at the Harpers Ferry National Historic Park Visitor Center off Hwy 340. Parking is incredibly limited in Harpers Ferry proper so plan to park at the visitor center and catch the frequent shuttle. It's a short and scenic ride.

John Brown Museum MUSEUM
(www.nps.gov/hafe; Shenandoah St; ☺ 9am-5pm) **FREE** Across from Arsenal Sq and one of the park's museums, this three-room gallery gives a fine overview (through videos and period relics) of the events surrounding John Brown's famous raid.

Black Voices MUSEUM
(www.nps.gov/hafe; High St; ☺ 9am-5pm) **FREE** Part of the national park, this worthwhile, interactive exhibit has narrated stories of hardships and hard-won victories by African Americans from the times of enslavement through the Civil Rights era. Across the street is the Storer College exhibit, which gives an overview of the ground-breaking educational center and Niagara movement that formed in its wake.

Master Armorer's House HISTORIC SITE
(☏ 304-535-6029; www.nps.gov/hafe; Shenandoah St; ☺ 9am-5pm) **FREE** Among the free sites in the historic district, this 1858 house explains how rifle technology developed here went on to revolutionize the firearms industry.

Storer College Campus HISTORIC SITE
(www.nps.gov/hafe; Fillmore St) Founded immediately after the Civil War, Storer College grew from a one-room schoolhouse for freed slaves to a respected college open to all races and creeds. It closed in 1955. You can freely wander the historic campus, reachable by taking the path to upper town, past St Peter's church, Jefferson Rock and Harper Cemetery.

C&O Canal National
Historic Park CYCLING, HIKING
(www.nps.gov/choh) The 184.5-mile towpath passes along the Potomac River on the Maryland side. Check www.nps.gov/hafe for access points to the towpath and a list of bike rental companies.

Appalachian Trail Conservancy HIKING
(☏ 304-535-6331; www.appalachiantrail.org; cnr Washington & Jackson Sts; ☺ 9am-5pm) The 2160-mile Appalachian Trail is headquartered here at this tremendous resource for

hikers. The AT passes through town nearby and hikers – and others – can stop by for conversation, information, trail updates and restrooms. The hiker lounge has wi-fi, a computer and a free phone – beside a giant sign reminding hikers to call their mothers.

O Be Joyfull WALKING
(☎732-801-0381; www.obejoyfull.com; 110 Church St, Thomas Hall at St Peter's Church; tours adult/child 8-12yr $34/15) Offers eye-opening historical daytime walking tours (lasting three to four hours) around Harpers Ferry.

River Riders ADVENTURE SPORTS
(☎800-326-7238; www.riverriders.com; 408 Alstadts Hill Rd; ☺8am-6pm Jun-Aug, hours vary rest of the year) The go-to place for rafting, canoeing, tubing, kayaking and multiday cycling trips, plus cycle rental and a 1200ft zipline.

🛏 Sleeping & Eating

HI-Harpers Ferry Hostel HOSTEL $
(☎301-834-7652; www.hiusa.org; 19123 Sandy Hook Rd, Knoxville, MD; dm $25; ☺May–mid-Nov; ⓟ❄@🛜) Located 2 miles from downtown on the Maryland side of the Potomac River, this friendly hostel has plenty of amenities, including a kitchen, laundry and lounge area with games and books.

Jackson Rose B&B $$
(☎304-535-1528; www.thejacksonrose.com; 1167 W Washington St; r weekday/weekend $140/160, closed Jan & Feb; ⓟ❄🛜) This marvelous 18th-century brick residence with stately gardens has three attractive guestrooms, including a room where Stonewall Jackson lodged briefly during the Civil War. Antique furnishings and vintage curios are sprinkled about the house, and the cooked breakfast is excellent.

Beans in the Belfry AMERICAN $
(☎301-834-7178; www.beansinthebelfry.com; 122 W Potomac St, Brunswick, MD; sandwiches around $7; ☺9am-9pm Mon-Thu, 9am-10pm Fri, 8am-10pm Sat, 8am-7pm Sun; 🛜🍴) Across the river in Brunswick, MD (roughly 10 miles east), you'll find this converted red-brick church sheltering mismatched couches and kitsch-laden walls, featuring light fare and a tiny stage where live folk, blues and bluegrass bands strike up several nights a week. Sunday jazz brunch ($18) is a hit.

Anvil AMERICAN $$
(☎304-535-2582; www.anvilrestaurant.com; 1290 W Washington St; mains $11-28; ☺11am-9pm Wed-Sun) Local trout melting in honey-pecan butter and an elegant Federal dining room equals excellence at Anvil.

ⓘ Getting There & Away

Amtrak (www.amtrak.com) trains run from the **Harpers Ferry Station** (www.amtrak.com; Potomac & Shenandoah Sts) to Washington's Union Station (daily, 90 minutes) on the Capitol Limited route. MARC trains (http://mta.maryland.gov) run three times daily during the week (Monday to Friday) on the Brunswick Line.

Berkeley Springs

🏃 Activities

Berkeley Springs State Park SPA
(☎304-258-2711; www.berkeleyspringssp.com; 2 S Washington St; 30 min bath $27, 1hr massage $99-111; ☺10am-6pm) Don't let the locker-room appearance deter you from the Berkeley Springs State Park's Roman Baths – it's the cheapest spa deal in town. Fill your water bottle with some of the magic stuff at the fountain outside the door. In the summer, kids will enjoy the spring-fed (but chlorinated) outdoor swimming pool (adult/child under 12 years $5/3) .

🛏 Sleeping & Eating

Cacapon Resort State Park CABIN $$
(☎304-258-1022; www.cacaponresort.com/; 818 Cacapon Lodge Dr; r from $154) Cacapon State Park has simple lodge accommodations plus modern and rustic cabins (some with fireplaces) in a peaceful wooded setting, 9 miles south of Berkeley Springs (off US 522).

Country Inn of Berkeley Springs HOTEL $$
(☎304-258-1200; www.thecountryinnwv.com; 110 S Washington St; r/ste from $119/199; ⓟ❄🛜) The Country Inn, right next to the park, offers luxurious treatment plus lodging package deals. There's a good restaurant on hand.

Tari's FUSION $$
(☎304-258-1196; www.tariscafe.com; 33 N Washington St; lunch mains $9-14, dinner mains $20-29; ☺11am-9pm Mon-Sat, to 7pm Sun; 🍴) 🌿 Tari's is a very Berkeley Springs sort of spot, with fresh local food and good vegetarian options served in a laid-back atmosphere with all the right hints of good karma abounding.

ⓘ Getting There & Away

Berkeley Springs is 40 miles west of I-95. It's about 90 minutes from Washington, DC.

Monongahela National Forest

Almost the entire eastern half of West Virginia is marked green parkland on the map, and all that goodness falls under the auspices of this stunning national forest. Within its 1400 sq miles are wild rivers, caves and the highest peak in the state, **Spruce Knob**. More than 850 miles of trails include the 124-mile **Allegheny Trail**, for hiking and backpacking, and the 75-mile rails-to-trails **Greenbrier River Trail**.

Elkins, at the forest's western boundary, is a good base of operations. Sitting atop Cheat Mountain, **Snowshoe Mountain Resort** (☑ 877-441-4386; www.snowshoemtn.com; 10 Snowshoe Dr; ☀) to the south is another good launchpad.

The surreal landscapes at **Seneca Rocks**, 35 miles southeast of Elkins, attract rock climbers up the 900ft-tall sandstone strata.

◉ Sights

Cranberry Mountain Nature Center   MUSEUM
(☑ 304-653-4826; www.fs.usda.gov; cnr Hwys 150 & 39/55; ☀ 9am-4:30pm Thu-Mon mid-Apr–mid-Oct) The scat exhibit hanging on the wall is quite eye-catching, as are the live snakes scattered across several terrariums at this nature center in the southern end of the forest. Celebrating its 50th birthday in 2017, the Cranberry Mountain Nature Center has scientific information about the forest and the surrounding 750-acre bog ecosystem.

Blackwater Falls State Park   STATE PARK
(☑ 304-259-5216; www.blackwaterfalls.com; 1584 Blackwater Lodge Rd) FREE The falls tumble into an 8-mile gorge lined by red spruce, hickory and hemlock trees. There's loads of hiking options; look for the Pendleton Point Overlook, which perches over the deepest, widest point of the Canaan Valley.

🛏 Sleeping & Eating

In the national forest there are 23 campgrounds across six different districts, so pick your region and go from there. There's also dispersed camping in two districts and cabins in the Greenbrier District. For more creature comforts, there are a half dozen or so hotels in Elkins. Snowshoe has a range of options, from simple condos to plush cabins.

Seneca Shadows Campground   CAMPGROUND $
(☑ 877-444-6777; www.recreation.gov; campsites $17-50; ☀ Apr-Oct) Flanked by mountains and offering a view of rock-climbing spot Seneca Rocks, this leafy campground has picnic tables, fire pits and flush toilets.

Vintage   MODERN AMERICAN $$
(☑ 304-636-0808; www.vintageelkins.com; 25 Randolph Ave, Elkins; mains $15-33; ☀ 11am-10pm Mon-Thu, to 11pm Fri & Sat, to 9pm Sun) A great place for wood-fired pizzas and wines after a day of hiking.

❶ Getting There & Away

To explore this remote and rugged region, you will need a car. Elkins is 155 miles from Pittsburgh. Snowshoe is 230 miles from Washington, DC.

Southern West Virginia

This part of the state has carved out a viable stake as the adventure-sports capital of the eastern seaboard, with wild whitewater rafting, terrific mountain biking, lots of leafy trails and inviting small towns holding it all together. The swanky Greenbrier resort brings big spenders and golfers.

New River Gorge National River

The New River is actually one of the oldest in the world, and the primeval forest gorge it runs through is one of the most breathtaking in the Appalachians. The NPS protects a stretch of the New River that falls 750ft over 50 miles, with a compact set of rapids up to Class V concentrated at the northernmost end. **Canyon Rim visitor center** (☑ 304-574-2115; www.nps.gov/neri; 162 Visitor Center Rd, Lansing, WV, GPS 38.07003 N, 81.07583 W; ☀ 9am-5pm; ☀) 🅿, just north of the impressive gorge bridge, is only one of four NPS visitor centers along the river. It has information about scenic drives (including a memorable outing to the abandoned mining town of **Nuttallburg**), river outfitters, gorge climbing, hiking and mountain biking, as well as white-water rafting to the north on the **Gauley River**. Rafting the Gauley River during its fall dam release is one of the most exciting white-water adventures in the USA. Rim and gorge trails offer beautiful views. Take the short trail behind the visitor center for a quick but awesome view of the bridge. There are several free basic camping areas.

◉ Sights & Activities

Hawks Nest State Park STATE PARK
(☑304-658-5212; www.hawksnestsp.com; 49 Hawks Nest Park Rd; lodge r/ste from $124/151) FREE There are hiking trails, a nature center and an aerial tram (open May to October; adult/child $7/5), which runs from the lodge down to the river's edge. The comfy rooms offers fabulous views over the gorge.

Babcock State Park STATE PARK
(☑304-438-3004; www.babcocksp.com; 486 Babcock Rd; cabins $66-223, campsites $25-28) Babcock State Park has hiking, canoeing, horseback riding, and camping and cabin accommodations. The park's highlight is its photogenic Glade Creek Grist Mill.

Mystery Hole MUSEUM
(☑304-658-9101; www.mysteryhole.com; 16724 Midland Trail, Ansted; adult/child $7/6; ⊙10:30am-5:30pm Jun-Oct) See gravity and the known limits of tackiness defied at the Mystery Hole, one of the great attractions of roadside America. Everything inside this madhouse *tilts at an angle!*

Adventures on the Gorge ADVENTURE
(☑855-379-8738; www.adventuresonthegorge. com; 219 Chestnutburg Rd, Lansing; cabins from $89) The reputable Adventures on the Gorge offers a wide range of activities, including white-water rafting, ziplining, rappelling and more. It has a wide array of cabins (including some with Jacuzzis) and several popular restaurants, including Smokey's Steakhouse (mains $18 to $36) near the rim of the gorge.

Bridgewalk WALKING
(☑304-574-1300; www.bridgewalk.com; per person $69; ⊙10am-3pm) You can get a wild view of the New River Gorge from the catwalk below the famous bridge on a guided tour offered by this outfit.

ⓘ Getting There & Away

There is an airport in Charleston, WV, 70 miles north. Amtrak (www.amtrak.com) stop at three places in the park, including the Prince Depot 23 miles south of Fayetteville. Greyhound (www. greyhound.com) stops in Beckley (360 Prince St).

Fayetteville

Pint-sized Fayetteville acts as jumping-off point for New River thrill-seekers and is an artsy mountain enclave besides.

◉ Sights & Activities

Beckley Exhibition Coal Mine MINE
(☑304-256-1747; www.beckley.org/general-infor mation-coal-mine; 513 Ewart Ave, Beckley; adult/ child $20/12; ⊙10am-6pm Apr-Oct) This mine in Beckley is a museum about the region's coal heritage. Visitors can ride a train 1500ft into a former coal mine, check out exhibits about mining life and explore the camp town village.

Cantrell Ultimate Rafting RAFTING
(☑304-877-8235; www.cantrellultimaterafting. com; 49 Cantrell Dr; Lower/Upper Gauley rafting from $130/144) Among the many state-licensed rafting outfitters in the area, Cantrell Ultimate Rafting stands out for its white-water rafting trips.

Long Point Trail HIKING
(www.nps.gov/neri/planyourvisit/longpoint_trail. htm; Newtown Rd, Fayetteville) Just over 3 miles round-trip, this trail leads to views of the New River Gorge and the New River Gorge Bridge.

New River Bikes CYCLING
(☑304-574-2453; www.newriverbikes.com; 221 N Court St; bike hire per day $35, tours $79-110; ⊙10am-6pm Mon-Fri, to 4pm Sat) Mountain biking is superb in the area, on the graded loops of the Arrowhead Trails.

🛏 Sleeping & Eating

River Rock Retreat Hostel HOSTEL $
(☑304-574-0394; www.riverrockretreatandhostel. com; Lansing-Edmond Rd; dm $23; P ✱) Located less than 1 mile north of the New River Gorge Bridge, this is a well-run hostel with basic, clean rooms and plenty of common space. Owner Joy Marr is a wealth of local information.

Cathedral Café CAFE $
(☑304-574-0202; www.facebook.com/cathedral cafe; 134 S Court St; lunch mains $8-9, dinner mains $11-14; ⊙7:30am-4pm Sun-Thu, to 9pm Fri & Sat; ☎✍) Start the day with breakfast and coffee under stained-glass windows at this cafe.

ⓘ Getting There & Away

Amtrak (www.amtrak.com) stops on Wednesday, Friday and Saturday at the Prince Depot (www.amtrak.com; 5034 Stanaford Rd), 23 miles south of Fayetteville on the Cardinal route linking NYC, Washington, DC and Chicago. It's a fairly remote stop and there are no rental car companies on site. You will need to arrange for pick-up by a friend or a taxi.

WASHINGTON, DC & THE CAPITAL REGION SOUTHERN WEST VIRGINIA

The South

Includes →

North Carolina 347
South Carolina 368
Tennessee 379
Memphis 379
Nashville 387
Kentucky 399
Louisville 399
Georgia 406
Atlanta 407
Alabama 426
Mississippi 432
Arkansas 438
New Orleans 446

Best Places to Eat

→ Peche Seafood Grill (p457)
→ Hattie B's (p393)
→ Dish Dive (p414)
→ Edmund's Oast (p372)
→ Saw's Soul Kitchen (p428)

Best Places to Sleep

→ Bunn House (p364)
→ Urban Oasis B&B (p412)
→ Crash Pad (p396)
→ 21c Museum Hotel (p403)
→ Shaker Village at Pleasant Hill (p404)

Why Go?

The South was arguably the first region of the USA to be considered that – a 'region' of cultural and geographic distinction, defined by its own cuisine, landscape, accent, literature, music and, under-girding all of the above, history – one that is long and beautiful in places, brutal and bloody in others.

The South falls from the granite, forested fists of Kentucky and Tennessee, into craggy hill country and thick woods, before the waters of its rivers – including North America's greatest, the Mississippi – saturate the land into boggy, blackwater blankets and sun-seared marsh, all thinning into the salty membrane of the Atlantic Ocean and Gulf of Mexico. Yet while its residents consider themselves tied to this land and water, they are also the inhabitants of cities deeply in tune with the American experience, from the sweat-drenched noir of Charleston and New Orleans to the accept-all-comers diversity of Atlanta.

When to Go
New Orleans

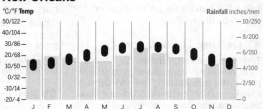

Nov–Feb Winter is generally mild in the South, and Christmas is a capital-E Event.

Apr–Jun Springs are lush and warm, abloom with fragrant jasmine, gardenia and tuberose.

Jul–Sep Summer is steamy, often unpleasantly so, and locals hit the beaches.

NORTH CAROLINA

The conservative Old South and the liberal New South are jostling for political dominance in the fast-growing Tar Heel State, home to hipsters, hog farmers, high-tech wunderkinds and an explosive number of craft brewers. Mostly the various cultures and communities here coexist, from the ancient mountains in the west to the sandy barrier islands of the Atlantic.

Agriculture is an economic force, with 52,218 farms across the state. North Carolina leads the nation in tobacco production and is the second-largest pig producer. But new technologies also drive the economy and more than 200 companies operate in Research Triangle Park alone. Other important industries include finance, nanotechnology and Christmas trees. Craft brewers have contributed over $2 billion to the economy.

So grab a platter of barbecue, pour a local brew and watch the Duke Blue Devils battle the Carolina Tar Heels on the basketball court. College hoops rival Jesus for Carolinians' souls.

History

Native Americans have inhabited North Carolina for more than 10,000 years. Major tribes included the Cherokee, in the mountains, the Catawba in the Piedmont and the Waccamaw in the Coastal Plain.

North Carolina was the second territory to be colonized by the British, named in memory of King Charles I (Carolus in Latin), but the first colony to vote for independence from the Crown. Several important Revolutionary War battles were fought here.

The state was a sleepy agricultural backwater through the 19th century, earning it the nickname the 'Rip Van Winkle State.' Divided on slavery (most residents were too poor to own slaves), North Carolina was the last state to secede during the Civil War, but went on to provide more Confederate soldiers than any other state.

North Carolina was a civil-rights hotbed in the mid-20th century, with highly publicized lunch-counter sit-ins in Greensboro and the formation of the influential Student Nonviolent Coordinating Committee (SNCC) in Raleigh. The latter part of the century brought finance to Charlotte, and technology and medicine to the Raleigh-Durham area, driving a huge population boom and widening cultural diversity.

In more recent times, North Carolina found itself in the discrimination and social issue hot seat again when it passed the notorious 'bathroom bill' in 2016, which blocked cities from allowing transgender individuals to use public bathrooms for the sex they identify as. The move cost the state up to an estimated $630 million (and counting) in lost revenue after it was passed (the NBA moved its annual All-Star Game to New Orleans, and the NCAA yanked all 2016 and 2017 tournaments from the state) – a mere drop in the bucket of the state's annual $510 billion GDP, but no chump change either. Governor Roy Cooper promptly signed the repeal of the law in spring of 2017, barely a year after its initial passing.

North Carolina Coast

The coastline of North Carolina stretches just over 300 miles. Remarkably, it remains underdeveloped and the beach is often visible from coastal roads. Yes, the wall of cottages stretching south from Corolla to Kitty Hawk can seem endless, but for the most part the state's shores remain free of flashy, highly commercialized resort areas. Instead you'll find rugged, windswept barrier islands, Colonial villages once frequented by pirates and laid-back beach towns full of locally owned ice-cream shops and mom-and-pop motels. Even the most touristy beaches have a small-town vibe.

For solitude, head to the isolated Outer Banks, where fishers still make their living hauling in shrimp and the older locals speak in an archaic British-tinged brogue. Further south, Wilmington is known as a center of film and TV production, and its surrounding beaches are popular with local spring breakers and tourists.

ⓘ Getting There & Away

The closest commercial airports to the Outer Banks are Norfolk International Airport (p316), 82 miles north of the Outer Banks in Virginia, and North Carolina's Raleigh-Durham International Airport (p359), 192 miles west. Ferries link more isolated Ocracoke Island in the Outer Banks with Hatteras Island and Cedar Island as well as Swan Quarter on the mainland.

Wilmington has its own **Wilmington International Airport** (ILM; ☑ 910-341-4125; www.flyilm.com; 1740 Airport Blvd).

The South Highlights

1 **New Orleans** (p446)
Losing yourself in the magic of America's strangest, most celebratory city.

2 **Great Smoky Mountains National Park** (p366) Hiking

and camping amid the South's most magnificent scenery.

3 **Nashville** (p387)
Stomping your boots in honky-tonks along Lower Broadway.

4 **Outer Banks** (p350)

Driving windswept Hwy 12 the length of North Carolina.

5 **Charleston** (p369)
Touring the grand antebellum homes and dining on Low-country fare.

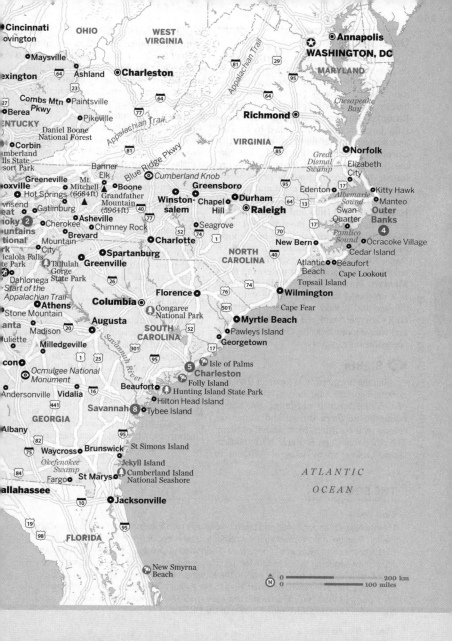

6 **Birmingham Civil Rights Institute** (p427) Learning the story of segregation and the Civil Rights movement.

7 **Ozark Mountains** (p442) Exploring the caverns, mountains, rivers, forests and folk music.

8 **Savannah** (p420) Falling for the hauntings, murderous tales, romance and Southern hospitality.

9 **Lafayette** (p464) Enjoying great food and better music.

10 **Atlanta** (p407) Falling for the energy of the largest, most diverse city in the South.

Outer Banks

The Outer Banks (OBX for short) are fragile ribbons of sand tracing the coastline for 100 miles, separated from the mainland by sounds and waterways. From north to south, barrier islands Bodie (pronounced 'Body'), Roanoke, Hatteras and Ocracoke, essentially large sandbars, are linked by bridges and ferries. The far-northern communities **Corolla** (pronounced kur-all-ah, not like the car), **Duck** and **Southern Shores** are former duck-hunting grounds for the northeastern wealthy, and are quiet and upscale. Nearly contiguous Bodie Island towns **Kitty Hawk**, **Kill Devil Hills** and **Nags Head** are heavily developed and more populist, with fried-fish joints, drive-through beer shops, motels and dozens of sandals 'n' sunblock shops. **Roanoke Island**, west of Bodie, offers colonial history and quaint waterfront town **Manteo**. Further south, **Hatteras Island** is a protected national seashore with tiny villages and a wild, windswept beauty. At OBX's southern end, old salts shuck oysters and weave hammocks on **Ocracoke Island**, accessible only by ferry.

◉ Sights

Corolla, the northernmost town on Hwy 158, is famed for its wild horses. Descendants of Colonial Spanish mustangs, the horses roam the northern dunes, and numerous commercial outfitters go in search of them. The ribboning Cape Hatteras National Seashore, broken up by villages, is home to several noteworthy lighthouses. A meandering drive down Hwy 12, which connects much of the Outer Banks and makes up part of the Outer Banks National Scenic Byway (and its 21 coastal villages), is one of the truly great American road trips, whether you come during the stunningly desolate winter months or in the sunny summer.

If you're driving on some beaches in the Outer Banks, or within Cape Hatteras National Seashore, you'll need an off-road-vehicle (ORVs) permit ($25 to $50). See www.outerbanks.org/plan-your-trip/beaches/driving-on-beach for more info.

Whalehead Club   HISTORIC BUILDING
(☑252-453-9040; www.visitcurrituck.com; 1160 Village Lane, Corolla; adult/child 6-12yr $7/5; ⊙tours 10am-4pm Mon-Sat, may vary seasonally) The sunflower-yellow, art-nouveau-style Whalehead Club, built in the 1920s as a hunting 'cottage' for a Philadelphia industrialist, is the centerpiece of the Currituck Heritage Park in the village of Corolla.

Currituck Beach Lighthouse   LIGHTHOUSE
(www.currituckbeachlight.com; 1101 Corolla Village Rd, Corolla; adult/child under 8yr $10/free; ⊙9am-5pm late Mar–Nov) You'll climb 220 steps to get to the top of this red-brick lighthouse, which is still in operation.

Wright Brothers National Memorial   PARK, MUSEUM
(☑252-473-2111; www.nps.gov/wrbr; 1000 North Croatan Hwy, Kitty Hawk; adult/child under 16yr $7/free; ⊙9am-5pm) Self-taught engineers

---

THE SOUTH IN...

One Week

Fly into New Orleans (p446) and stretch your legs with a walking tour in the legendary French Quarter, before devoting your remaining time to celebrating jazz history and partying the night away in a zydeco joint. Then wind your way upward through the languid Delta, stopping in Clarksdale for a sultry evening of blues at the juke joints before alighting in Memphis (p379) to walk in the footsteps of the King at Graceland (p382). From here, head on down the Music Hwy to Nashville (p387) to see Elvis' gold Cadillac at the Country Music Hall of Fame and Museum (p390) and practice your line dancing at the honky-tonks (country-music clubs) of the District.

Two to Three Weeks

From Nashville, head east to hike amid the craggy peaks and waterfalls of Great Smoky Mountains National Park (p366) before a revitalizing overnight in the arty mountain town of Asheville (p363) and a tour of the scandalously opulent Biltmore Estate (p364), America's largest private home. Plow straight through to the Atlantic coast to loll on the sandy barrier islands of the isolated Outer Banks, then head down the coast to finish up in Charleston (p369), with decadent food and postcard-pretty architecture.

Wilbur and Orville Wright launched the world's first successful airplane flight on December 17, 1903 (it lasted 12 seconds). A boulder marks the take-off spot. Climb a nearby hill, where the brothers conducted earlier glider experiments, for fantastic views of sea and sound. The on-site **Wright Brothers Visitor Center**, when it reopens after a complete renovation by summer 2018, has a reproduction of the 1903 flyer and exhibits.

Fort Raleigh National Historic Site
HISTORIC SITE

(www.nps.gov/fora; 1401 National Park Dr, Manteo; ⊙grounds dawn-dusk) In the late 1580s, three decades before the Pilgrims landed at Plymouth Rock, a group of 116 British colonists disappeared without a trace from their Roanoke Island settlement. Were they killed off by drought? Did they run away with a Native American tribe? The fate of the 'Lost Colony' remains one of America's greatest mysteries. Explore their story in the visitor center.

One of the site's star attractions is the beloved musical, **Lost Colony Outdoor Drama** (☑252-473-6000; www.thelostcolony.org; 1409 National Park Dr, Manteo; adult/child from $20/10; ⊙7:45pm Mon-Sat late May–mid-Aug), staged between late May and August. The play, from Pulitzer Prize–winning North Carolina playwright Paul Green, dramatizes the fate of the colonists and will celebrate its 80th anniversary in 2017. It plays at the Waterside Theater throughout summer. Other attractions include exhibits, artifacts, maps and a free 17-minute film to fuel the imagination, hosted at the visitor center. The 16th-century-style **Elizabethan Gardens** (☑252-473-3234; www.elizabethangardens.org; 1411 National Park Dr, Manteo; adult/child 6-17yr $9/6; ⊙9am-7pm Jun-Aug, shorter hours Sep-May) include a Shakespearean herb garden and rows of beautifully manicured flower beds. A commanding statue of Queen Elizabeth I stands guard at the entrance.

Cape Hatteras National Seashore
ISLAND

(☑252-475-9000; www.nps.gov/caha) Extending some 70 miles from south of Nags Head to the south end of Ocracoke Island, this fragile necklace of islands remains blissfully free from overdevelopment. Natural attractions include local and migratory waterbirds, marshes, woodlands, dunes and miles of empty beaches.

Bodie Island Lighthouse
LIGHTHOUSE

(☑255-473-2111; www.nps.gov/caha; 8210 Bodie Island Lighthouse Rd, Nags Head; museum free, tours adult/child under 11yr $8/4; ⊙visitor center 9am-5pm, lighthouse to 4:30pm late Apr-early Oct; ➌) Built in 1872, this photogenic lighthouse opened its doors to visitors in 2013. The 164ft-high structure still has its original Fresnel lens – a rarity. It's just over 200 steps to the top. The lighthouse keeper's former home is now the visitor center.

Pea Island National Wildlife Refuge
WILDLIFE RESERVE

(☑252-987-2394; www.fws.gov/refuge/pea_island; Hwy 12, Rodanthe; ⊙visitor center 9am-4pm, trails dawn-dusk) At the northern end of Hatteras Island, this 5834-acre (land portion only) preserve is a bird-watcher's heaven, with two nature trails (both are fully accessible to people with disabilities) and 13 miles of unspoiled beach for the 365 recorded species here. Viewer scopes inside the visitor center overlook an adjacent pond.

Cape Hatteras Lighthouse
LIGHTHOUSE

(☑252-475-9000; www.nps.gov/caha; 46368 Lighthouse Rd, Buxton; climbing tours adult/child under 12yr $8/4; ⊙visitor center 9am-5pm; lighthouse to 4:30pm mid-Apr–early Oct) At 208ft, this striking black-and-white-striped edifice is the tallest brick lighthouse in the USA and is one of North Carolina's most iconic images. Climb the 257 steps then check out the interesting exhibits about local history in the **Museum of the Sea**, located in the lighthouse keeper's former home.

Graveyard of the Atlantic Museum
MUSEUM

(☑252-986-2995; www.graveyardoftheatlantic.com; 59200 Museum Dr, Hattaras; ⊙10am-4pm) **FREE** Exhibits about shipwrecks, piracy and salvaged cargo are highlights at this maritime museum at the end of the road. There have been more than 2000 shipwrecks off the coast of the Outer Banks. According to one exhibit, in 2006 a container washed ashore near Frisco, releasing thousands of Doritos bags.

🏃 Activities

Kitty Hawk Kites
ADVENTURE SPORTS

(☑252-441-6800; www.kittyhawk.com; 3933 S Croatan Hwy, Jockey's Ridge Crossing, Nags Head; bike rental per day $15, kayaks $39-59, stand-up paddleboards $59-69) In business more than 30 years, Kitty Hawk Kites has several locations along

THE SOUTH NORTH CAROLINA COAST

the OBX coast. It offers beginners' kiteboarding lessons (five hours, $400) in Rodanthe and hang-gliding lessons at Jockey's Ridge State Park (from $109). Also rents out kayaks, sailboats, stand-up paddleboards, bikes and in-line skates.

Corolla Outback Adventures TOURS
(☑ 252-453-4484; www.corollaoutback.com; 1150 Ocean Trail, Corolla; 2hr tour adult/child under 13yr $50/25) Tour operator Jay Bender, whose family started Corolla's first guide service, knows his local history and his local horses. Tours bounce you down the beach and through the dunes to see the wild mustangs that roam the northern Outer Banks.

🛏 Sleeping

Breakwater Inn MOTEL $
(☑ 252-986-2565; www.breakwaterhatteras.com; 57896 Hwy 12, Hattaras; r/ste from $179/213, motel r from $117; P ✳ 🛜 ⛱ 🐾) The end of the road doesn't look so bad at this three-story shingled inn. Rooms come with kitchenette and a private deck with views of the sound. On a budget? Try one of the older 'Fisherman's Quarters' rooms, with microwave and fridge

Shutters on the Banks HOTEL $$
(☑ 252-441-5581; www.shuttersonthebanks.com; 405 S Virginia Dare Trail; r $69-269; P ✳ 🛜 ⛱) Centrally located in Kill Devil Hills, this welcoming 86-room beachfront hotel exudes a snappy, colorful style. The inviting rooms come with plantation windows and colorful art as well as flat-screen TV, refrigerator and microwave.

Sanderling Resort & Spa RESORT $$$
(☑ 252-261-4111; www.sanderling-resort.com; 1461 Duck Rd, Duck; r $160-599, ste $599-750; P ✳ 🛜 ⛱) Newly remodeled rooms have given this posh place a stylish kick in the pants. Or should we say the Lululemons? Because yes, the resort does offer sunrise yoga on the beach. Decor is impeccably tasteful, and the attached balconies are an inviting place to enjoy the ocean sounds and breezes.

🍴 Eating & Drinking

John's Drive-In SEAFOOD, ICE CREAM $
(www.johnsdrivein.com; 3716 N Virginia Dare Trail, Kitty Hawk; mains $2.25-9.50; ⊙ 11am-5pm Thu-Tue) A Kitty Hawk institution for perfectly fried baskets of mahi mahi, to be eaten at outdoor picnic tables and washed down with one of hundreds of possible milkshake combinations.

⭐ **Kill Devil Grill** SEAFOOD, AMERICAN $$
(☑ 252-449-8181; www.thekilldevilgrill.com; 2008 S Virginia Dare Trail, Kill Devil Hills; lunch $7-13, dinner $10-22; ⊙ 11:30am-9pm Tue-Thu, to 10pm Fri & Sat) Yowza, this place is good. It's also historic – the entrance is a 1939 diner that's listed in the National Register of Historic Places. Pub grub and seafood arrive with tasty flair, and portions are generous. Check out the specials, where the kitchen can really shine.

⭐ **Blue Moon Beach Grill** SEAFOOD, SANDWICHES $$
(☑ 252-261-2583; www.bluemoonbeachgrill.com; 4104 S Virginia Dare Trail, Nags Head; mains $10-29; ⊙ 11:30am-9pm) Would it be wrong to write an ode to a side of french fries? Because Lord almighty, the lightly spiced fries at this casual hot spot are the stuff of sonnets and monologues. And we haven't even mentioned the BLT with seared mahi mahi, applewood bacon, local Currituck tomatoes and a jalapeño rémoulade for slathering.

ℹ Information

The best sources of information are at the main visitor centers. Many smaller centers open seasonally. Also useful is www.outerbanks.org.

Aycock Brown Welcome Center (☑ 877-629-4386; www.outerbanks.org; 5230 N Croatian Hwy, Kitty Hawk; ⊙ 9am-5pm) On the bypass in Kitty Hawk; has maps and information.

Fort Raleigh National Historic Site Visitor Center (☑ 252-475-9001; www.nps.gov/fora; 1401 National Park Dr; ⊙ 9am-4pm Mon-Sat, noon-4pm Sun)

Hatteras Island Visitor Center (☑ 252-475-9000; www.nps.gov/caha; 46368 Lighthouse Rd, Buxton; ⊙ 9am-5pm) Beside Cape Hatteras Lighthouse.

Ocracoke Island Visitor Center (☑ 252-475-9701; www.nps.gov/caha; 38 Irvin Garrish Hwy; ⊙ 9am-5pm) Near the southern ferry dock.

Sarah Owen Welcome Center (☑ 877-629-4386; www.outerbanks.org; 1 Visitors Center Cir, Manteo; ⊙ 9am-5pm) Just east of Virginia Dare Memorial Bridge on the US 64 Bypass on Roanoke Island.

Whalebone Welcome Center (☑ 877-629-4386; www.outerbanks.org; 2 NC Hwy 12, Nags Head; ⊙ 8:30am-5pm Mar-Dec) At the intersection of Hwy 64 and Hwy 12 in Nags Head.

ℹ Getting There & Away

No public transportation exists to or on the Outer Banks.

If driving, try to avoid arriving or departing on weekends in summer, when traffic can be maddening. The Outer Banks Visitors Bureau offers a comprehensive guide to driving to OBX, including tips and alternate routes to avoid spending your vacation stuck in your vehicle, on its website (www.outerbanks.org).

FERRY

The North Carolina Ferry System (www.ncdot.gov/ferry) operates several routes, including the free one-hour Hatteras–Ocracoke car ferry, which fluctuates between hourly and half-hourly with 36 departures from 5am to midnight from Hatteras in high season; reservations aren't accepted. North Carolina ferries also run between Ocracoke and Cedar Island (one way car/motorcycle $15/10, 2¼ hours) and Ocracoke and Swan Quarter on the mainland ($15/10, 2¾ hours) every three hours or so; reservations are recommended in summer for these two routes.

Ocracoke Island

Ocracoke Village is a funky little community that moves at a slower pace. With the exception of the village, the National Park Service owns the island.

The older residents still speak in the 17th-century British dialect known as 'Hoi Toide' (their pronunciation of 'high tide') and refer to non-islanders as 'dingbatters' (though this will soon die off). Edward Teach, aka Blackbeard the pirate, used to hide out in the area and was killed here in 1718. You can camp by Pony Pen beach where wild ponies run and swim at their leisure, have a fish sandwich in a local pub, bike around the village's narrow streets or catch some rays nestled into holes in the sand dunes along 16 miles of coastline.

Many people come to Ocracoke on a day trip from Hatteras, but with its preserved culture and laid-back vibe, it's a nice place to spend a night or two. There are a handful of B&Bs, several motels, a park-service campground near the beach and rental cottages.

👁 Sights & Activities

Ocracoke Lighthouse LIGHTHOUSE
(www.nps.gov/caha; Lighthouse Rd) Built in 1823, this is the oldest lighthouse still operating in North Carolina, though it cannot be climbed.

Ocracoke Pony Pen VIEWPOINT
(www.nps.gov/caha; Hwy 12) From the National Park Service's observation deck, you can catch a glimpse of Ocracoke's 'wild' ponies, which have been penned in here since the late 1950s and cared for by the NPS. The pens are located 6 miles along Hwy 12 from the Ocracoke–Hatteras ferry landing.

Portsmouth Island ATV Tours HISTORY
(☑ 252-928-4484; www.portsmouthislandatv.com; 396 Irvin Garrish Hwy; tour $90; ☺ Apr-Oct) Runs two fascinating two daily tours (8am and 1pm) to the nearby island of Portsmouth, a 20-minute boat ride from Ocracoke, where you'll find an Outer Banks ghost town abandoned in the 1970s. Guided ATV tours focus on shelling, bird-watching and swimming.

Ride the Wind KAYAKING
(☑ 252-928-6311; www.surfocracoke.com; 486 Irvin Garrish Hwy; 2-2½hr tours adult $39-45, child under 13yr $18; ☺ 10am-7pm Mon-Sat, to 6pm Sun) Want to get on the water? Take a kayaking tour with Ride the Wind. The sunset tours are easy on the arms.

🍴 Sleeping & Eating

Ocracoke Campgrounds CAMPGROUND $
(☑ 252-928-6671; www.recreation.gov; 4352 Irvin Garrish Hwy; tent sites $28; ☺ mid-Apr–late Nov)

THE SOUTH NORTH CAROLINA COAST

OCRACOKE'S PENNED PONIES

Legend has it the Ocracoke Island 'wild' ponies are decendants of feral Spanish mustangs abandoned by shipwrecked explorers in the 16th or 17th century, when it was common to unload livestock to lighten the load and get back out to sea after running aground. Known as 'banker' ponies, these horses are unique in the equine world – they harbor a different number of vertebrae and ribs as well as a distinct shape, posture, color, size and weight than those of other horses. But what's more fascinating about Ocracoke's ponies is they were eventually broken and tamed by a troop of Boy Scouts in the 1950s – you can see photos at the Pony Island Restaurant. They were eventually pastured in a 'pony pen' in 1959 to prevent overgrazing and protect them from the dangers of NC Hwy 12, which was under construction. Today there are 17 ponies at the Ocracoke Pony Pen at Pony Pen Beach. They're cared for by the National Park Service and free to roam the beach and take a dip in the ocean. You can view them from an observation deck.

Offers 136 sites on sand on Ocracoke Island. Flush toilets, drinking water, cold showers and grills are available as well.

★ Eduardo's Taco Stand

MEXICAN $

(950 Irvin Garrish Hwy; mains $4-11; ⊙8am-9pm Mon-Sat) There's a long list of tacos, burritos and fresh and spicy salsas at this little taco stand that could. If you're over fried clams and crab cakes, dishes such as prime-rib-eye tacos with salsa *de xoconostle* really hit the spot (as do the fish with creamy chipotle apple slaw or poblano chowder with shrimp or clams).

Howard's Pub

PUB FOOD $

(www.howardspub.com; 1175 Irvin Garrish Hwy; mains $8-26; ⊙11am-10pm early Mar-late Nov, may stay open later Fri & Sat) A big old wooden pub (newly renovated!) that's been an island tradition for beer and fried seafood since the 1850s. Good selection of local craft beer.

❶ Getting There & Away

The village is at the southern end of 14-mile-long Ocracoke Island and is accessed from Hatteras via the free Hatteras–Ocracoke ferry (www.ncdot.gov/ferry; first-come, first-serve). The ferry lands at the northeastern end of the island. Or via the $15 Cedar Island– Ocracoke or Swan Quarter–Ocracoke ferries (which land at the southern dock; reservations accepted).

Crystal Coast

The southern Outer Banks are collectively called the 'Crystal Coast,' at least for tourist-office promotional purposes. Less rugged than the northern beaches, they include several historic coastal towns, sparsely populated islands and vacation-friendly beaches.

An industrial and commercial stretch of US 70 goes through **Morehead City**, with plenty of chain hotels and restaurants. The **Bogue Banks**, across the Sound from Morehead City via the Atlantic Beach Causeway, have several well-trafficked beach communities – try Atlantic Beach if you like the smell of coconut suntan oil and doughnuts.

Just north, postcard-pretty **Beaufort** (bow-fort), the third-oldest town in the state, has a charming boardwalk and lots of B&Bs. Blackbeard himself is said to have lived in the Hammock House off Front St. You can't go inside, but some claim you can still hear the screams of the pirate's murdered wife at night.

◉ Sights & Activities

Fort Macon State Park

FORT

(www.ncparks.gov/fort-macon-state-park; 2303 E Fort Macon Rd, Atlantic Beach; ⊙9am-5:30pm) FREE This sturdy, five-sided fort, with 26 vaulted rooms, was completed in 1834. Exhibits in rooms near the entrance spotlight the fort's construction as well as the daily lives of soldiers stationed there. The fort, constructed from brick and stone, changed hands twice during the Civil War.

North Carolina Maritime Museum

MUSEUM

(http://ncmaritimemuseums.com/beaufort.html; 315 Front St; ⊙9am-5pm Mon-Fri, 10am-5pm Sat, 1-5pm Sun) FREE The pirate Blackbeard was a frequent visitor to the Beaufort area in the early 1700s. In 1996 the wreckage of his flagship, the *Queen Anne's Revenge,* was discovered at the bottom of Beaufort Inlet. You'll see plates, bottles and other artifacts from the ship in this small but engaging museum, which also spotlights the seafood industry as well as maritime rescue operations.

Hungry Town Tours

FOOD & DRINK, HISTORY

(☑252-648-1011; www.hungrytowntours.com; 400 Front St; tours $20-60) Runs recommended history- and culinary-focused walking and Cruiser biking tours.

⨆ Sleeping & Eating

Hampton Inn Morehead City

HOTEL $$

(☑252-240-2300; www.hamptoninn3.hilton.com; 4035 Arendell St, Morehead City; r from $169; ❄@ 🛜🏊) Yep, it's part of a national chain, but the helpful staff and the views of Bogue Sound make this Hampton Inn a nice choice, plus it's convenient to US 70 for those driving the coast. Rates drop significantly on weeknights in summer.

★ Inn on Turner

B&B $$

(☑919-271-6144; www.innonturner.com; 217 Turner St; r $200-250; P❄🛜) ☍ Impeccably tasteful aqua-toned coastal contemporary decor – no gaudy antiques here – dominates this four-room B&B occupying an historic 1866 home two blocks back from the water. Innkeepers Kim and Jon are pillars of small-town Southern hospitality, despite not being from the South!

El's Drive-In

SEAFOOD $

(www.elsdrivein.com; 3706 Arendell St, Morehead City; mains $1.60-14.25; ⊙10am-10pm Sun-Thu, to 11pm Fri & Sat) The food is brought to you by car hop at this legendary seafood spot, open since 1959. Our recommendation? The fried shrimp burger with ketchup and slaw plus a side of fries. Cash only.

Beaufort Grocery MODERN AMERICAN **$$$**
(📋 252-728-3899; www.beaufortgrocery.com; 117 Queen St; mains $25-42; ⏱ 11:30am-2pm & 5:30-9:30pm Wed-Mon; 🛜) You'd never guess by the simple, unassuming nature of the decor, but chef Charles Park is a James Beard winner and the food shines, whether that be smoked sea-salt tuna with chili yogurt, duck two ways with sweet-potato caramel or sage-wrapped chicken saltimbocca over tagliatelle. We didn't hear a bad thing about the place – and weren't disappointed.

Wilmington

Wilmington is pretty darn fun, and it's worth carving out a day or two for a visit if you're driving the coast. This seaside charmer may not have the name recognition of Charleston and Savannah, but eastern North Carolina's largest city has historic neighborhoods, azalea-choked gardens and cute cafes aplenty. All that plus reasonable hotel prices. At night the historic riverfront downtown becomes the playground for local college students, craft-beer enthusiasts, tourists and the occasional Hollywood type – there are so many movie studios here the town has earned the nickname 'Wilmywood.' You saw *Dawson's Creek,* right?

⊙ Sights & Activities

Battleship North Carolina HISTORIC SITE
(www.battleshipnc.com; 1 Battleship Rd; adult/child 6-11yr $14/6; ⏱ 8am-5pm Sep-May, to 8pm Jun-Aug) Self-guided tours take you through the decks of this 45,000-ton megaship, which earned 15 battle stars in the Pacific theater in WWII before it was decommissioned in 1947. Sights include the bake shop and galley, the print shop, the engine room, the powder magazine and the communications center. Note that there are several steep stairways leading to lower decks.

Airlie Gardens GARDENS
(www.airliegardens.org; 300 Airlie Rd; adult/child 4-12yr $9/3; ⏱ 9am-5pm, closed Mon Jan-Mar) In spring, wander past thousands of bright azaleas at this 67-acre wonderland, also home to bewitching formal flowerbeds, seasonal gardens, pine trees, lakes and trails. The Airlie Oak dates from 1545.

Cape Fear Serpentarium ZOO
(📋 910-762-1669; www.capefearserpentarium.com; 20 Orange St; $9; ⏱ 11am-5pm Mon-Fri, to 6pm Sat & Sun) Herpetologist Dean Ripa's museum is a fun and informative place to spend an hour or two – if you don't mind standing in a building slithering with venomous snakes, giant constrictors and big-teethed crocodiles. They're all behind glass but...ssssssss. Just hope there's not an earthquake. One sign explains the effects of a bite from a bushmaster: 'It is better to just lie down under a tree and rest, for you will soon be dead.' Enjoy! Cash only.

The Serpentarium may close on Monday and Tuesday in the off-season. Live feedings are held at 3pm on Saturday and Sunday, but call ahead to confirm.

🛏 Sleeping & Eating

Best Western Plus Coastline Inn HOTEL **$$**
(📋 910-763-2800; www.bestwestern.com; 503 Nutt St; r $89-199, ste $129-279; ❄ @ 🛜 ❄) We're not sure what we like best: the gorgeous views of the Cape Fear River, the wooden boardwalk or the short walk to downtown fun. Standard rooms aren't huge, but they do pop with a bit of modern style. Every room has a river view. Pet fee is $20 per day and there's a new set of bikes for rent.

★ **CW Worth House** B&B **$$**
(📋 910-762-8562; www.worthhouse.com; 412 S 3rd St; r $164-200; ❄ @ 🛜) One of our favorite B&Bs in North Carolina, this turreted 1893 Queen Anne home is dotted with antiques and Victorian touches, but still manages to feel kick-back and cozy. Breakfasts are top-notch. The B&B is within a few blocks of downtown.

Flaming Amy's Burrito Barn MEXICAN **$**
(www.flamingamys.com; 4002 Oleander Dr; burritos $8; ⏱ 11am-10pm) The burritos are big and tasty at Flaming Amy's, a scrappy barn filled with kitschy decor from Elvis to Route 66. Burritos include the Philly Phatboy, the Thai Mee Up and the jalapeño-and-pepper-loaded Flaming Amy. Everyone in town is here or on the way.

★ **PinPoint** SOUTHERN US **$$$**
(📋 910-769-2972; www.pinpointrestaurant.com; 114 Market St; mains $21-38; ⏱ 5:30-10:30pm Tue-Fri, 10:30am-2pm Sat & Sun; 🛜) PinPoint was declared by *Southern Living* magazine as one of the South's best new restaurants in 2016 – and they weren't lyin'! Chef Dean

Neff was Hugh Acheson's kitchen compadre in Athens, Georgia's excellent Five & Ten, and he's sailing solo and shining in Wilmington, where he has a personal relationship with his farmers and fishers, a love that carries over to the amazing food.

Drinking & Entertainment

★ **Satellite Lounge** BAR
(www.facebook.com/satellitebarandlounge; 120 Greenfield St; ⊗4pm-2am Mon-Sat, 2pm-2am Sun; 🛜) If you want to belly up to North Carolina's most stunning bar, you'll need to head in the opposite direction of Wilmington's historic downtown and into its up-and-coming warehouse South Front district. A gorgeously restored tavern highlights the space, which includes near-professional-level cornhole lanes, a fire pit and an outdoor cinema.

Dead Crow Comedy Room COMEDY
(☑910-399-1492; www.deadcrowcomedy.com; 265 N Front St; tickets $15-18; ⊗from 7pm Tue-Thu, from 6pm Fri & Sat) Dark, cramped, underground and in the heart of downtown, just like a comedy club should be. Before heading out, stop in for improv, open-mike nights and touring comedians.

Information

Visitor information center (☑877-406-2356, 910-341-4030; www.wilmingtonandbeaches. com; 505 Nutt St; ⊗8:30am-5pm Mon-Fri, 9am-4pm Sat, 1-4pm Sun) In an 1800s freight warehouse; has a walking-tour map of downtown.

Getting There & Around

American Airlines and Delta Airlines serve Wilmington International Airport (p347) from Atlanta, Charlotte, New York and Philadelphia. It's 5 miles northeast of downtown. The **Greyhound** (☑910-791-8040; www.greyhound.com; 505 Cando St) station is an inconvenient 5 miles east of downtown.

Downtown Wilmington is walkable, but a free trolley (www.wavetransit.com) runs through the historic district from morning through evening.

The Triangle

The cities of Raleigh, Durham and Chapel Hill form a rough triangle in the central Piedmont region. Three top research universities – Duke, University of North Carolina and North Carolina State – are located here, as is the 7000-acre computer and biotech-office campus known as Research Triangle Park. Swarming with egghead computer programmers, bearded peace activists and hip young families, each town has its own unique personality, despite being only a few miles apart. In March, everyone – we mean *everyone* – goes crazy for college basketball.

Getting There & Around

Raleigh-Durham International Airport (p359), a 13-mile ride northwest of downtown Raleigh, receives nonstop flights from 48 destinations, including London, Paris and Cancun.

Greyhound (☑919-834-8275; www.greyhound.com; 2210 Capital Blvd) is located 3 miles northeast of downtown Raleigh, which makes it hard to reach on foot for connections. For a better downtown stop, try Durham's **Greyhound** (www.greyhound.com; 515 W Pettigrew St) station, near the **Amtrak** (www.amtrack.com; 601 W Main St) station in the Durham Station Transportation Center.

The Triangle Transit Authority (www.triangletransit.org) operates buses linking Raleigh, Durham and Chapel Hill and the airport. Bus 100 runs from downtown Raleigh to the airport, and the Regional Transit Center near Research Triangle Park where there are connections to Durham and Chapel Hill. Adult fare is $2.25.

Raleigh

Founded in 1792 specifically to serve as the state capital, Raleigh remains a rather staid government town with major sprawl issues. Still, the handsome downtown has some neat (and free!) museums and galleries, and the food and music scene is on the upswing.

Sights

★ **North Carolina Museum of Art** MUSEUM
(www.ncartmuseum.org; 2110 Blue Ridge Rd; ⊗10am-5pm Tue-Thu Sat & Sun, to 9pm Fri, park dawn-dusk) **FREE** The light-filled glass-and-anodized-steel West Building won praise from architecture critics nationwide when it opened in 2010. The fine and wide-ranging collection, with everything from ancient Greek sculptures to commanding American landscape paintings to elaborate African masks, is worthy as well.

North Carolina Museum of History MUSEUM
(www.ncmuseumofhistory.org; 5 E Edenton St; ⊗9am-5pm Mon-Sat, noon-5pm Sun) **FREE** This engaging museum is low on tech but high on straightforward information. Artifacts in the 'Story of North Carolina' exhibit include a

3000-year-old canoe, the state's oldest house, dating from 1742, a restored slave cabin and a 1960s sit-in lunch counter. The special exhibits typically shine too.

North Carolina Museum of Natural Sciences
MUSEUM

(www.naturalsciences.org; 11 W Jones St; ◆9am-5pm Mon- Sat, noon-5pm Sun) FREE Whale skeletons hang from the ceiling. Butterflies flutter past your shoulder. Emerald tree boas make you shiver. And swarms of unleashed elementary-school children rampage all over the place if you arrive after 10am on a school day. Be warned. The glossy new **Nature Research Center**, fronted by a three-story multimedia globe, spotlights scientists and their projects. Visitors can watch them at work. Skywalks lead to the main museum building, which also holds habitat dioramas and well-done taxidermy. Don't miss the exhibit about the Acrocanthosaurus dinosaur, a three-ton carnivore known as the Terror of the South.

🛏 Sleeping & Eating

Umstead Hotel & Spa
HOTEL $$$

(☑919-447-4000; www.theumstead.com; 100 Woodland Pond Dr; r $329-389, ste $409-599; P❄@🛜🏊❄) In a wooded suburban office park, the Umstead caters to visiting biotech CEOs with simple, sumptuous rooms (deep soak bathtubs, dual vanities) and a 16,000-sq-ft Zen-like spa with a meditation courtyard. A three-acre lake sits behind the property with a quarter-mile walking trail. The pet fee is $200 per stay, and the hotel has a new fenced dog playground, DogWoods.

Raleigh Times
PUB FOOD $

(www.raleightimesbar.com; 14 E Hargett St; mains $8-14; ◆11am-2am; 🛜) Chase plates of barbecue nachos and PBR-battered fish and chips with pints of North Carolina craft brews at this popular downtown pub.

Beasley's Chicken + Honey
SOUTHERN US $

(www.ac-restaurants.com/beasleys; 237 Wilmington St; mains $7-13; ◆11:30am-10pm Mon-Wed, 11:30am-midnight Thu & Fri, 11am-midnight Sat, 11am-10pm Sun) You'll need to loosen your belt after a meal at this crispy venture from James Beard Award–winner and local restaurant maven Ashley Christensen. Inside this airy downtown eatery, fried chicken is the star – on a biscuit, with waffles, in a pot pie. The sides are decadent too.

★ Binda Manda
LAOTIAN $$

(☑919-829-9999; www.bidamanda.com; 222 S Blount St; lunch $11-21, dinner $18-30; ◆11:30am-2pm & 5-10pm Mon-Thu, 11:30am-2pm & 5pm-midnight Fri, 5pm-midnight Sat; 🛜) All the plated dishes at this trendy Laotian hot spot – one of but a few Laotian restaurants in all the USA – are as gorgeous as the hip convergence of exposed air ducts and abundant bamboo throughout the space. Tying in Laos traditions with dashes of Thai, Vietnamese and Chinese, the dishes are a revelatory cavalcade of flavor.

ℹ Information

Raleigh Visitor Information Center (☑919-834-5900; www.visitraleigh.com; 500 Fayetteville St; ◆8:30am-5pm Mon-Fri, 9am-5pm Sun) Hands out maps and other info. Office is closed on Sunday, but the city visitor guide and map are available on the counter.

Durham

Durham is a once-gritty tobacco and railroad town whose fortunes collapsed in the 1960s and have only recently begun to revive. Though still fundamentally a working-class Southern city, the presence of top-ranking Duke University has long drawn progressive types to the area and Durham is now making its name as a hot spot for gourmets, artists and gays and lesbians.

◉ Sights

★ Duke Lemur Center
ZOO

(☑919-401-7240; www.lemur.duke.edu; 3705 Erwin Rd; adult/child $12/9; ♿) The secret is out: the Lemur Center is the coolest attraction in Durham. Located about 2 miles from the main campus, this research and conservation center is home to the largest collection of endangered prosimian primates (ie lemurs) outside their native Madagascar. Only a robot could fail to melt at the sight of these big-eyed fuzzy-wuzzies. Visits are by guided tour only. To guarantee a tour spot, make your reservation well ahead of your visit.

Call at least three weeks in advance for weekdays, and one to two months ahead for weekends.

Duke University
UNIVERSITY

(www.duke.edu; Campus Dr) Endowed by the Duke family's cigarette fortune, the university has a Georgian-style East Campus and a neo-Gothic West Campus. Metered parking on campus is $2 per hour.

Duke Chapel
CHAPEL

(https://chapel.duke.edu; 401 Chapel Dr; ⊙8am-10pm, to 8pm summer) 🅿 The towering, 1930s Duke Chapel overlooks Duke University's west campus. This breathtaking place, with its 210ft tower and 77 colorful, bible-themed glass windows, is worth a look.

American Tobacco Campus
HISTORIC SITE

(https://americantobaccocampus.com; 318 Blackwell St) Cigarettes no longer pay Durham's bills, but this massive former industrial tobacco factory, home to the American Tobacco Company until the 1950s, still does a bang-up job filling downtown Durham's coffers. Part of the National Register of Historic Places, the mixed-use facility is a cavalcade of restaurants, bars and entertainment venues spread over a million sq feet with no shortage of alfresco dining.

🛏 Sleeping & Eating

★Durham
BOUTIQUE HOTEL $$

(📱919-768-8830; www.thedurham.com; 315 E Chapel Hill St; r from $209; 🅿 ❄ @ 🛜) It was only a matter of time before revitalized downtown Durham got its independent hipster sleeps – the suave, 53-room Durham, a marvel of mid-Century Modern might, filling that niche when it turned a former bank building into a supremely retro, fiercely local haven in 2015.

JB Duke Hotel
BOUTIQUE HOTEL $$

(📱919-660-6400; www.jbdukehotel.com; 230 Science Dr; r $159-279, ste $329-529; 🅿 ❄ @ 🛜 🏊) You could do worse than sleeping on Duke's gorgeous campus. This slick new 198-room hotel rides a fine line between modern and woodsy. The soothing carpeted lobby, with plush furniture, rough-cut burled walnut tables and a dark quartzite and glazed-steel metallic-tiled bar, harmonizes discreetly with Duke Forest. Spacious rooms offers working desks, Keurig coffee machines and campus views.

Toast
SANDWICHES $

(www.toast-fivepoints.com; 345 W Main St; sandwiches $8; ⊙11am-3pm Mon, to 8pm Tue-Sat) Families, couples, solos and the downtown lunch crowd – everybody loves this tiny Italian sandwich shop, one of the eateries at the forefront of downtown Durham's revitalization. Order your panini (hot and grilled), *tramezzini* (cold) or crostini (bundle of joy) at the counter then grab a table by the window – if you can – for people-watching.

★Mateo
TAPAS $$

(📱919-530-8700; www.mateotapas.com; 109 W Chapel Hill St; ⊙11:30am-2:30pm & 5-10:30pm Tue-Thu, 11:30am-2:30pm & 5pm-midnight Fri, 5pm-midnight Sat, 5-9:30pm Sun) It's impossible to wax on Durham's remarkable comeback without talking about Mateo, where James Beard–nominated tapas – sometimes with a Southern bent – are the town's culinary anchor. The *pan com tomate* with Manchego cheese, the brussels sprouts with pine nuts, raisins and saffron yogurt and the fried egg and cheese (the 'whites' are fried farmer's cheese!) are revelations.

🍷 Drinking & Entertainment

★Cocoa Cinnamon
COFFEE

(www.cocoacinnamon.com; 420 W Geer St; espresso/hot chocolate from $2.75/3.50; ⊙7:30am-10pm Mon-Thu, to 10:30pm Fri, 8am-10:30pm Sat, to 10pm Sun; 🛜) If someone tells you that you *must* order a hot chocolate at Cocoa Cinnamon, ask them to be more specific. This talk-of-the town coffee shop offers several cocoas, and newbies may be paralyzed by the plethora of chocolatey awesomeness. Come to this one-time service station to enjoy cocoa, tea, single-source coffee and the energetic vibe.

Fullsteam Brewery
BREWERY

(www.fullsteam.ag; 726 Rigsbee Ave; pints/pitchers $5/18; ⊙4pm-midnight Mon-Thu, 2pm-2am Fri, noon-2am Sat, noon-midnight Sun; 🛜) Calling itself a 'plow-to-pint' brewery, Fullsteam has gained national attention for pushing the boundaries of beer with wild, Southernized concoctions, going out of its way to support local farmers, neighborhood foragers and agricultural entrepreneurs, using all Carolinian ingredients wherever possible.

Durham Bulls Athletic Park
STADIUM

(www.dbulls.com; 409 Blackwell St; tickets $7-10) Have a quintessentially American afternoon of beer and baseball watching the minor-league Durham Bulls (of 1988 Kevin Costner film *Bull Durham* fame), who play from April to early September.

ℹ Information

Durham Visitor Info Center (📱919-687-0288; www.durham-nc.com; 212 W Main St; ⊙9am-5pm Mon, 9am-6pm Tue-Fri, 10am-6pm Sat) Information and maps inside a historic bank building.

ⓘ Getting There & Away

Durham's gateway airport is **Raleigh-Durham International Airport** (RDU; ☎ 919-840-2123; www.rdu.com; 1000 Trade Dr) in Morrisville, 14 miles southeast of Durham. An off-peak Uber to the airport runs about $20. Greyhound (p356) and Amtrak (p356) sit across the street from each other near the Durham Station Transportation Center.

Chapel Hill & Carboro

Chapel Hill is a pretty, Southern college town whose culture revolves around the nearly 30,000 students at the prestigious University of North Carolina, founded in 1789 as the nation's first state university. A funky, forward-thinking place, Chapel Hill, along with its neighbor, Carrboro, is renowned for its indie rock scene and loud 'n' proud hippie culture.

⊙ Sights

University of North Carolina　　UNIVERSITY
(www.unc.edu) America's oldest public university has a classic quad lined with flowering pear trees and gracious antebellum buildings. Don't miss the **Old Well**, said to give good luck to students who drink from it. Pick up a map of the school at the **visitor center** (☎ 919-962-1630; www.unc.edu/visitors; 250 E Franklin St; ⊙ 9am-5pm Mon-Fri) inside the Morehead Planetarium and Science Center or the **Chapel Hill Visitor Center** (☎ 919-245-4320; www.visitchapelhill.org; 501 W Franklin St; ⊙ 8:30am-5pm Mon-Fri, 10am-3pm Sat).

Carolina Basketball Museum　　MUSEUM
(www.goheels.com/fls/3350/museum; 450 Skipper Blowles Dr, Ernie Williamson Athletics Center; ⊙ 10am-4pm Mon-Fri, 9am-1pm Sat) **FREE** The numbers say it all: six national championships, 19 final-four appearances, 30 ACC regular-season championships, 47 NBA first-round draft picks. Regardless of your allegiances, any basketball fan will appreciate this small but well-done temple dedicated to Tar Heel hoops. Memorabilia, trophies and video footage abound, including dedicated exhibits to Michael Jordan with his original signed national letter of intent and other recruiting documents.

🛏 Sleeping & Eating

★**Carolina Inn**　　HOTEL **$$**
(☎ 919-933-2001; www.carolinainn.com; 211 Pittsboro St; r from $179; P❄🖲) Even if you're not a Tar Heel, this lovely on-campus inn will

THE BARBECUE TRAIL

North Carolina's most worshipped culinary contribution is pulled-pork barbecue, practically a religion in these parts, and the rivalry between Eastern style (with a thin vinegar sauce with a distinct acidic African-influenced flavor) and Western style (with a sweeter, tomato-based sauce) occasionally comes to blows. The North Carolina Barbecue Society has an interactive Barbecue Trail Map (www.ncbbqsociety.com), directing pilgrims to the best spots.

win you over with its hospitality and historic touches. The charm starts in the snappy lobby then continues through the hallways, lined with photos of alums and championship teams. Classic decor – inspired by Southern antiques – feels fresh in the 185 bright rooms, where silhouettes of famous graduates join the party.

Neal's Deli　　BREAKFAST, DELI **$**
(www.nealsdeli.com; 100 E Main St, Carrboro; breakfast $3.50-6.75, lunch $5.50-8.50; ⊙ 7:30am-4pm Tue-Fri, 8am-4pm Sat & Sun; 🖲) Before starting your day, dig into a delicious buttermilk breakfast biscuit at this tiny deli in downtown Carrboro. The egg, cheese and bacon is some kind of good. For lunch, Neal's serves sandwiches and subs, from chicken salad to pastrami to a three-cheese pimiento with a splash of bourbon. Chapel Hill/Carrboro's best coffeehouse, **Open Eye Cafe**, is next door.

★**Lantern**　　ASIAN **$$$**
(☎ 919-969-8846; www.lanternrestaurant.com; 423 W Franklin St; mains $23-32; ⊙ 5:30-10pm Mon-Sat) If you only have time for one dinner in the Triangle, dine here. This modern Asian spot, using North Carolina–sourced ingredients, has earned a slew of accolades, and chef Andrea Reusing is a James Beard Award winner.

🍷 Drinking & Entertainment

Beer Study　　CRAFT BEER
(www.beerstudy.com; 106 N Graham St; pints $3-7; ⊙ 10am-midnight Mon-Wed, to 1am Thu-Sat, noon-midnight Sun; 🖲) There are a few breweries around Chapel Hill, but you're better off at this grungier half-bar, half-bottle shop with 18 taps of local and regional craft beer

THE SOUTH THE TRIANGLE

and over 500 bottles (you can buy and drink one but not a six-pack). City ordinances impose plastic cups on dog-friendly establishments, but that's a small price to pay for pup.

Cat's Cradle
LIVE MUSIC

(☑919-967-9053; www.catscradle.com; 300 E Main St, Carrboro) Everyone from Nirvana to Arcade Fire has played the Cradle, which has hosted the cream of the indie-music world for three decades. Most shows are all-ages.

ℹ Getting There & Away

Chapel Hill's gateway airport is Raleigh-Durham International Airport in Morrisville, 18 miles east of Chapel Hill. An off-peak Uber to the airport runs about $25.

Charlotte

The largest city in North Carolina and the biggest US banking center after New York, Charlotte has the sprawling, sometimes faceless look of many New South suburban megalopolises. But though the Queen City, as it's known, is primarily a business town, it has a few good museums, stately old neighborhoods and lots of fine food and drink.

◉ Sights & Activities

NASCAR Hall of Fame
MUSEUM

(www.nascarhall.com; 400 E Martin Luther King Blvd; adult/child 5-12yr $20/13; ⊘10am-6pm) The race-car simulator ($5) at this rip-roaring museum hurtles you on to the track and into an eight-car race that feels surprisingly real. Elsewhere, learn the history of this American-born sport (which traces back to moonshine running), check out six generations of race cars and test your pit-crew skills. NASCAR, if you're wondering, is short for National Association for Stock Car Auto Racing.

Levine Museum of the New South
MUSEUM

(www.museumofthenewsouth.org; 200 E 7th St; adult $8, child 6-18yr $5; ⊘10am-5pm Mon-Sat, noon-5pm Sun) Interested in the South's complicated post–Civil War history? Then set aside an hour or two for the comprehensive 'From Cotton Fields to Skyscrapers' exhibit at this slick museum, which spotlights the cotton industry, Jim Crow laws, sit-ins, women's advancement and recent immigration trends. Tip: they validate two hours of parking at the 7th Street Station parking garage next door.

Billy Graham Library
RELIGIOUS SITE

(www.billygrahamlibrary.org; 4330 Westmont Dr; ⊘9:30am-5pm Mon-Sat, last tour 3:30pm) FREE This multimedia 'library' is a tribute to the life of superstar evangelist and 'pastor to the presidents' Billy Graham, a Charlotte native. The 90-minute tour, the 'Journey of Faith', starts with a gospel-preaching animatronic cow, then spotlights key moments in Graham's life, including his transformative 1949 tent revival in Los Angeles (where he first inspired *Unbroken*'s hero, Louis Zamperini).

The tour is engaging and informative, especially if you're curious about Graham's journey and the roots of modern evangelicalism (though drowning in Christian propaganda and recruitment). You can also tour Graham's 1927 boyhood home, relocated here from its original spot 3 miles away.

★ US National Whitewater Center
ADVENTURE SPORTS

(www.usnwc.org; 5000 Whitewater Center Pkwy; all-sport day pass adult/child under 10yr $59/49, individual activities $25, 3hr canopy tour $89; ⊘dawn-dusk) A beyond-awesome hybrid of nature center and water park, this 400-acre facility is home to the largest artificial white-water river in the world, whose rapids serve as training grounds for Olympic canoe and kayak teams. Paddle it yourself as part of a guided rafting trip, or try one of the center's other adventurous activities.

🛏 Sleeping & Eating

Dunhill Hotel
BOUTIQUE HOTEL $$

(☑704-332-4141; www.dunhillhotel.com; 237 N Tryon St; r $149-349; P ❋ @ 🕏) The staff shines at this heart-of-uptown hotel, and the property has been welcoming guests since 1929 – it was Charlotte's first hotel with en suite bathrooms. Classic decor gives a nod to the 1920s, but large flat-screen TVs, Keurig coffee makers and phone docking stations keep the rooms firmly in the 21st century.

★ Ivey's Hotel
BOUTIQUE HOTEL $$$

(www.theiveyshotel.com; 127 N Tryon St; r $299-450; P @ 🕏 ❋) The Ivey's 42 Parisian-inspired rooms – all on the 2nd floor of a 1924 department-store building – are steeped in discerning history (400-year-old oak-wood floors sourced from a French winery) with a modern flair (55in Sony TVs, Bose soundbars). The balcony executive corner suites, awash in natural light-sucking windows and exposed brick, are divine.

Price's Chicken Coop   SOUTHERN US $
(www.priceschickencoop.com; 1614 Camden Rd;
mains $3.25-12.25; ⊘10am-6pm Tue-Sat) A Char-
lotte institution, scruffy Price's regularly
makes 'Best Fried Chicken in America' lists.
Line up to order your 'dark quarter' or 'white
half' from the army of white-jacketed cooks,
then take your bounty outside – there's no
seating. Latta Park is a few blocks east on
E Park Ave if you want to spread out. Cash
only but an ATM on-site.

★Soul

Gastrolounge Tapas   SUSHI, SANDWICHES $$
(☑704-348-1848; www.soulgastrolounge.com;
1500 Central Ave; small plates $7-20, sushi $4-14,
sandwiches $9-15; ⊘5pm-2am) In Plaza Mid-
wood, this sultry but welcoming speakeasy
serves a globally inspired selection of small
plates. Choices are wide-ranging, from skew-
ers and sushi rolls to Cuban and Vietnamese
sandwiches, but the kitchen takes care to in-
fuse each morsel with unique, satisfying fla-
vors. The dancing tuna rolls with jalapeños
and two spicy mayos are highly recommend-
ed if you like heat.

🍷 Drinking & Nightlife

★**NoDa Brewing Co**   MICROBREWERY
(www.nodabrewing.com; 2921 N Tryon St; pints
$4-7; ⊘4-9pm Mon-Thu, to 10pm Fri, noon-10pm
Sat, noon-7pm Sun; 🛜) Charlotte's best craft-
beer playground is hidden behind NoDa's
new and easy-to-overlook North End brew-
ery. We Uber'ed up on a Friday night and it
looked abandoned. How wrong we were! In
the back: a packed playhouse of brews and
a bocce set.

ℹ️ Information

Visitor Info Center (☑800-231-4636; www.
charlottesgotalot.com; 501 S College St, Char-
lotte Convention Center; ⊘9am-5pm Mon-Sat)
Downtown Charlotte main's visitor center is
inside the Charlotte Convention Center, where
there are booths near both the S College St and
E MLK Jr Blvd entrances. There are also stalls
at the Levine Museum of the New South and the
airport. It publishes maps and a visitors' guide.

ℹ️ Getting There & Around

Charlotte Douglas International Airport
(CLT; ☑704-359-4013; www.cltairport.com;
5501 Josh Birmingham Pkwy) is a US Airways
hub with direct flights from Europe and the
UK. Both the **Greyhound station** (☑704-375-
3332; www.greyhound.com; 601 W Trade St)

and **Amtrak** (www.amtrak.com; 1914 N Tryon
St) are handy to uptown.

Charlotte's public transport system is known
as CATS (Charlotte Area Transit System; www.
charlottenc.gov/cats), which encompasses city
buses, a light-rail line called LYNX Blue Line and
a streetcar line called CityLYNX Gold Line. One-
way fare is $2.20 to $4.40. The **Charlotte Trans-
portation Center** (www.ridetransit.org; 310 East
Trade St) is in Uptown on Brevard St between 4th
and Trade St. Charlotte also has a shared bike
system (https://charlotte.bcycle.com).

North Carolina Mountains

The Cherokee came to these ancient moun-
tains to hunt, followed by 18th-century
Scots-Irish immigrants looking for a better
life. Lofty towns such as Blowing Rock drew
the sickly, who came for the fresh air. Today,
scenic drives, leafy trails and roaring rivers
draw outdoor adventurers.

The Appalachians in the western part
of the state include the Great Smoky, Blue
Ridge, Pisgah and Black Mountain subrang-
es. Carpeted in blue-green hemlock, pine
and oak trees, these cool hills are home to
cougars, deer, black bears, wild turkeys and
great horned owls. Hiking, camping, climb-
ing and rafting adventures abound, and
there's another jaw-dropping photo oppor-
tunity around every bend.

ℹ️ Getting There & Around

Asheville Regional Airport (p366) is the gateway
to the North Carolina mountains, with nonstop
flights to/from Atlanta, Charlotte, Chicago and
New York, among others. There is also a Grey-
hound (p366) station in Asheville.

High Country

The northwestern corner of the state is
known as 'High Country.' Its main towns are
Boone, Blowing Rock and Banner Elk, all
short drives from the Blue Ridge Parkway.
Boone is a lively college town, home to Ap-
palachian State University (ASU). Blowing
Rock and **Banner Elk** are quaint tourist
centers near the winter ski areas.

BLOWING ROCK

A dignified and idyllic mountain village,
tiny Blowing Rock charmingly beckons
from its perch at 4000ft above sea level, the
only full-service town directly on the Blue
Ridge Parkway. It's easy to be seduced by its

postcard-perfect Main St, lined with antique shops, kitschy boutiques, potters, silversmiths, sweet shops, lively taverns and excellent eats, all of which manage to ward off a tackiness that's easy to to get swept away by when tourism rules the roost. There are even a couple of bucolic, duck-filled lakes to drive home the storybook-nature of it all.

👁 Sights & Activities

Grandfather Mountain   HIKING
(☑ 828-733-4337; www.grandfather.com; Blue Ridge Pkwy Mile 305, Linville; adult/child 4-12yr $20/9; ⊙ 8am-7pm Jun-Aug, closes earlier fall, winter & spring) Hold up. Is the Mile High Suspension Bridge really swinging 1 mile above ground? Not exactly, so don't fret if you don't love heights. The park's star attraction is 1-mile *above sea level,* but the chasm beneath? It's 80ft deep. Nothing to sneeze at, but the distance is a bit less horrifying.

River & Earth Adventures   TOURS
(☑ 828-963-5491; www.raftcavehike.com; 5578 Hwy 421, Vilas; half-/full-day rafting from $60/100; 🛗) Offers everything from family-friendly caving trips to rafting Class V rapids at Watauga Gorge. Eco-conscious guides even pack organic lunches. Canoe ($60), kayak ($35 to $60) and tube ($20) rentals.

🛏 Sleeping & Eating

Cliff Dwellers Inn   MOTEL $$
(☑ 828-414-9596; www.cliffdwellers.com; 116 Lakeview Terrace; r/apt from $99/149; 🅿 ❄ 🛜 🐾) From its perch above town, this well-named motel lures guests with good service, reasonable prices, stylish rooms and balconies with sweeping views.

DON'T MISS

SCENIC DRIVE: BLUE RIDGE PARKWAY

You won't find one stoplight on the entire Blue Ridge Parkway, which traverses the southern Appalachians from Virginia's Shenandoah National Park at Mile 0 to North Carolina's Great Smoky Mountains National Park at Mile 469.

Commissioned by President Franklin D Roosevelt as a Great Depression–era public-works project, it's one of America's classic drives. North Carolina's piece of the parkway twists and turns for 262 miles of killer mountain vistas.

The **National Park Service** (☑ 828-298-5330; www.nps.gov/blri; Mile 384; ⊙ 9am-5pm) runs campgrounds and visitor centers. Note that restrooms and gas stations are few and far between. For more details about stops, visit www.blueridgeparkway.org.

Parkway highlights and campgrounds include the following:

Cumberland Knob (Mile 217.5) NPS visitor center; easy walk to the knob.

Doughton Park (Mile 241.1) Trails and camping.

Blowing Rock (Mile 291.8) Small town named for a craggy, commercialized cliff that offers great views, occasional updrafts and a Native American love story.

Moses H Cone Memorial Park (Mile 294.1) A lovely old estate with carriage trails and a craft shop.

Julian Price Memorial Park (Mile 296.9) Camping.

Grandfather Mountain (Mile 305.1) Hugely popular for its mile-high pedestrian 'swinging bridge.' Also has a nature center and a small wildlife reserve.

Linville Falls (Mile 316.4) Short hiking trails to the falls; campsites.

Little Switzerland (Mile 334) Old-style mountain resort.

Mt Mitchell State Park (Mile 355.5) Highest peak east of the Mississippi (6684ft); hiking and camping.

Craggy Gardens (Mile 364) Hiking trails explode with rhododendron blossoms in summer.

Folk Art Center (Mile 382) High-end Appalachian crafts for sale.

Blue Ridge Pkwy Visitor Center (Mile 384) Inspiring film, interactive map, trail information.

Mt Pisgah (Mile 408.8) Hiking, camping, restaurant, inn.

Graveyard Fields (Mile 418) Short hiking trails to waterfalls.

Green Park Inn
HISTORIC HOTEL **$$**

(☎828-414-9230; www.greenparkinn.com; 9239 Valley Blvd; r $89-299; 🅿❄🛜🐕) The eastern continental divide runs through the bar at this white-clapboard grand hotel that opened in 1891. They say author Margaret Mitchell worked on *Gone with the Wind* while staying here.

★ Bistro Roca
MODERN AMERICAN **$$**

(☎828-295-4008; www.bistroroca.com; 143 Wonderland Trail; lunch mains $9-16, dinner mains $9-34; ⊙11am-3pm & 5-10pm Wed-Mon; 🛜) This cozy, lodge-like bistro, tucked just off Main St, occupies a Prohibition-era building and does upscale New American fare (lobster or pork-belly mac 'n' cheese, kicked-up habanero burgers, wood-fired pizzas, mountain-trout *bánh mì* sandwiches) with an emphasis on local everything. Order anything with the duck bacon and you're all set.

❶ Getting There & Away

Blowing Rock is 8 miles south of Boone along the Blue Ridge Parkway. The closest commercial airport is Charlotte Douglas International Airport (p361), 87 miles southeast.

BOONE

Home to bustling Appalachian State University, Boone is a fun and lively mountain town with a young population that has a hankering for the outdoors. The town, the domain of bluegrass musicians and Appalachian storytellers, is named after famous pioneer and explorer Daniel Boone, who often camped in the area of the present-day town. Boone's history has been told every summer since 1952 in a dramatization called *Horn in the West,* which is performed in an outdoor amphitheater above the town.

Downtown Boone features a nice collection of low-rise brick-broad, Colonial Revival, art-deco and streamline-modern architecture. Many of the buildings today house charming boutiques and cafes.

Boone is home to mostly standard chain hotels, though you can find the occasional historic B&B, rental farmhouse or cozy log cabin lodgings around town and in the surrounding countryside. The Horton Hotel, Boone's first boutique hotel, opens in 2018.

Folk Art Center
CULTURAL CENTER

(☎828-298-7928; www.southernhighlandguild. org; Mile 382; ⊙9am-6pm Apr-Dec, to 5pm Jan-Mar) As you enter the lobby at the Folk Art Center, look up. A row of handcrafted Appalachian chairs hangs from the walls above. They're an impressive calling card for the gallery here, which is dedicated to southern craftsmanship. The chairs are part of the Southern Highland Craft Guild's permanent collection, which holds more than 2400 traditional and modern crafts. Items from the collection are displayed on the 2nd floor.

★ Melanie's Food Fantasy
CAFE **$$**

(www.melaniesfoodfantasy.com; 664 W King St; breakfast $6-10, lunch & dinner $9-14; ⊙8am-2pm Mon-Wed, 8am-2pm & 5-9pm Thu-Fri, 8am-2:30pm & 5-9pm Sat, 8:30am-2:30pm Sun; 🍴) On cutesy King St hippie types gobble up serious breakfast dishes (scrambles, eggs Benedict, omelets, waffles, pancakes) with a side of home fries at this farm-to-fork favorite, always with a vegetarian option (tempeh, soysage etc).

Dan'l Boone Inn
SOUTHERN US **$$**

(☎828-264-8657; www.danlbooneinn.com; 130 Hardin St; breakfast adult $11, child $6-8, dinner adult $18, child $7-11; ⊙11:30am-8:30pm Mon-Thu, to 9pm Fri & Sat, to 8:30pm Sun Jun-Oct, hours vary rest of year; 🛜♿) Quantity is the name of the game at this restaurant, and the family-style meals are a Boone (sorry) for hungry hikers. Open since 1959. Cash or check only.

❶ Getting There & Away

The closest commercial airport to Boone is Charlotte Douglas International Airport (p361), 94 miles southeast.

Asheville

With its homegrown microbreweries, decadent chocolate shops and stylish New Southern eateries, Asheville is one of the trendiest small cities in the East. Glossy magazines swoon for the place. But don't be put off by all the flash. At heart, Asheville is still an overgrown mountain town and it holds tight to its traditional roots. Just look around. There's a busker fiddling a high lonesome tune on Biltmore Ave. Over there, hikers are chowing down after climbing Mt Pisgah. Cars swoop on and off the Blue Ridge Parkway, which swings around the city. A huge population of artists and a visible contingent of hardcore hippies also helps to keep things real.

◉ Sights & Activities

★ Biltmore Estate · HOUSE

(☎ 800-411-3812; www.biltmore.com; 1 Approach Rd; adult/child 10-16yr $65/32.50; ⏰ house 9am-4:30pm, with seasonal variations) The country's largest privately owned home, and Asheville's number-one tourist attraction, the Biltmore was completed in 1895 for shipping- and railroad-heir George Washington Vanderbilt II. He modeled it after three French châteaus in the Loire Valley he'd seen on his various European jaunts. Viewing the estate and its 250 acres of gorgeously manicured grounds and gardens takes several hours.

Chimney Rock Park · PARK

(www.chimneyrockpark.com; Hwy 64/74A; adult/child 5-15yr $15/7; ⏰ 8:30am-6pm mid-Mar–Nov, 10am-4:30pm Fri-Tue Nov–mid-Mar) Views of the Broad River and Lake Lure are superb from atop the namesake chimney – a 315ft granite monolith. An elevator takes visitors up to the chimney, but the real draw is the exciting hike around the cliffs to a 404ft waterfall. The park, once privately owned, is now part of the state-park system; access to the rock is still managed commercially. The park is a gorgeous 20-mile drive southeast of Asheville.

BREW-ed · BREWERY

(☎ 828-278-9255; www.brew-ed.com; $37-50) Walking downtown brewery and history tours, led by Cicerone-certified beer geeks, on Thursdays (5:30pm), Fridays (2pm), Saturdays (11:30am and 2pm) and Sundays (1pm).

Smoky Mountain Adventure Center · OUTDOORS

(☎ 828-505-4446; www.smacasheville.com; 173 Amboy Rd; ⏰ 10am-8pm Mon, 9am-10pm Tue-Thu, to 9:30pm Fri & Sat, noon-8pm Sun) Across the street from the French Broad river in the River Arts district, head here for one-stop outdoor adventure shopping. It can arrange bikes for the Blue Ridge Parkway, inner tubes and paddleboards for the river, and guided rock climbing, backpacking, day hiking, ice climbing and mountaineering trips in the surrounding mountains.

🛏 Sleeping

Sweet Peas Hostel · HOSTEL $

(☎ 828-285-8488; www.sweetpeashostel.com; 23 Rankin Ave; dm/pod $32/40, r without/with bath $75/105; ❄ @ ☎) This spick-and-span hostel gleams with IKEA-like style, with shipshape steel bunk beds and blond-wood sleeping 'pods.' The loft-like space is very open and can be noisy (the downstairs Lexington Ave Brewery adds to the ruckus but hey, there's a discount), but what you lose in privacy and quiet, you gain in style, cleanliness, sociability and an unbeatable downtown location.

Campfire Lodgings · CAMPGROUND $$

(☎ 828-658-8012; www.campfirelodgings.com; 116 Appalachian Village Rd; tent sites $35-40, RV sites $50-70, yurts $115-135, cabins $160; P ❄ ☎) All yurts should have flat-screen TVs, don't you think? Sleep like the world's most stylish Mongolian nomad in one of these furnished multiroom tents, on the side of a wooded hill. Cabins and tent sites are also available. RV sites have stunning valley views and wi-fi access.

Omni Grove Park Inn · HISTORIC HOTEL $$$

(☎ 828-252-2711; www.omnihotels.com; 290 Macon Ave; r $149-419; P ❄ @ ☎ ⛵ 🐕) This titanic arts-and-crafts-style historic stone lodge recalls a bygone era of Americana mountain glamor and, with its hale-and-hearty look, sets a tone for adventure. Did you notice the lobby fireplaces? Of course you did: the 36ft-wide behemoths can accommodate a standing grown man inside their hearths and there is an elevator ascending to the chimney within each!

Aloft Asheville · HOTEL $$$

(☎ 828-232-2838; www.aloftasheville.com; 51 Biltmore Ave; r from $250-450; P ❄ @ ☎ ⛵ 🐕) With a giant chalkboard in the lobby, groovy young staff, and an outdoor clothing store on the 1st floor, this place looks like the seventh circle of hipster. The only thing missing is a wool-cap-wearing bearded guy drinking a hoppy microbrew – oh, wait, over there. We jest. Once settled, you'll find the staff knowledgeable and the rooms colorful and spacious.

Bunn House · BOUTIQUE HOTEL $$$

(☎ 828-333-8700; www.bunnhouse.com; 15 Clayton St; d $249-424; P ❄ ☎) Asheville's most discerning guest; a meticulously restored 1905 home that forgoes keys for codes and is awash in original exposed brick and dark hardwoods throughout its six rooms and suites. The heated bathroom floors and subway-tiled steam showers are glorious on chilly mountain mornings. Minibars and common areas are stocked with complimentary Herban Baker snacks and Asheville Brewing Company beers.

Eating

Asheville is a fawned-upon foodie haven. Downtown, South Slope and the up-and-coming River Arts District along the French Broad River are rife with good eats from simple (but hip!) Southern-fried cafes to ethnic eats to elaborate Modern American and Appalachian kitchens. Farm-to-table is a general rule; local, organic and sustainable are mantras.

Early Girl Eatery CAFE $
(www.earlygirleatery.com; 8 Wall St; mains $4-15; ⊘7:30am-3:00pm Mon-Wed, to 9pm Thu & Fri, 9am-9pm Sat & Sun) Order breakfast all day (try that house Benny, with tomato, spinach, avocado and poached eggs on grit cakes) or a grilled pimiento-cheese sandwich in this neighborhood farm-to-table cafe. Enjoy your feast on the sunny, crowded dining room, overlooking a small city square.

White Duck Taco Shop MEXICAN $
(www.whiteducktacoshop.com; 12 Biltmore Ave; tacos $3.45-5.25; ⊘11:30am-9pm) The chalkboard menu at this downtown taco shop will give you fits – every taco sounds like a must-have flavor bomb: spicy buffalo chicken with blue-cheese sauce, crispy pork belly, mole-roasted duck – there's even shrimp and grits! Even better? These soft tacos are hefty. The chips and three-salsa appetizer works well for a group.

★**12 Bones** BARBECUE $
(www.12bones.com; 5 Foundy St; dishes $5.50-22; ⊘11am-4pm Mon-Fri) How good is this barbecue? Well, Former President Obama and wife Michelle stopped by a few years ago for a meal. The slow-cooked meats are smokey tender, and the sides, from the jalapeño-cheese grits to the smoked-potato salad, will bring you to the brink of the wild heart of life.

★**Cúrate** TAPAS $$
(☑828-239-2946; www.curatetapasbar.com; 13 Biltmore Ave; small plates $4-18; ⊘11:30am-11:30pm Tue-Thu, to 11pm Fri & Sat, to 10:30pm Sun) 🌶 This convivial place celebrates the simple charms and sensual flavors of traditional Spanish tapas with a occasional Southern twist (it's owned by a genuine Catalan and his hip Ashevillian wife). Standout dishes run long and wide: *pan con tomate* (grilled bread with tomato fresco), lightly fried eggplant drizzled with honey and rosemary, and a knockout squid-ink 'paella' with vermicelli.

Smoky Park Supper Club MODERN AMERICAN $$
(☑828-350-0315; www.smokypark.com; 350 Riverside Dr; mains $10-34; ⊘5-9pm Tue-Thu, 4-10pm Fri & Sat, 10:30am-9pm Sun; 🛜) One of the anchors of cool in the developing Rivers Arts District, SPSC is more than the sum of its parts: 19 shipping containers to be exact, making it the largest container-constructed

---

BEER CITY USA

If ever a city was transformed by the craft-beer movement, it's Asheville, which has catapulted itself from a fairly sleepy mountain city when its first brewery, Highland Brewing, opened in 1994, to one of North America's destination suds cities for booze-bound hopheads.

Today Buncombe Country counts 33 breweries (27 of which are in Asheville proper) for a population of just 87,000 or so people – one of the highest brewery-to-resident ratios in the country. Our favorites:

Burial (www.burialbeer.com; 40 Collier Ave; pints $5; ⊘4-10pm Mon-Thu, from 2pm Fri, noon-10pm Sat & Sun; 🛜) Small and intimate; produces some of Asheville's best and most experimental Belgian-leaning styles (farmhouse saisons, strong dubbels and tripels). Touted by nearly everyone as the city's best.

Funkatorium (www.wickedweedbrewing.com/locations/funkatorium; 147 Coxe Ave; beers $4.50-10; ⊘2-10pm Mon-Thu, noon-midnight Fri & Sat, noon-10pm Sun; 🛜) Wicked Weed's new all-sour taproom is a pilgrimage-worthy temple of tart and funk.

Wedge (www.wedgebrewing.com; 37 Paynes Way; pints $3.50-6; ⊘noon-10pm; 🛜) A festive, come-one, come-all outdoor space rife with dogs, kids on tricycles, swooning couples and outdoorsy types.

Wicked Weed (www.wickedweedbrewing.com; 91 Biltmore Ave; pints $4.50-6.40; ⊘11:30am-11pm Mon & Tue, to midnight Wed & Thu, to 1am Fri & Sat, noon-11pm Sun; 🛜) A former gas station turned craft-brew wonderland. Fifty-eight taps!

restaurant in the USA. But choosing from the mostly wood-fired delights is agonizing: garlic and lemon-roasted half chicken, cast-iron-seared Carolina fish, cheese dip with chorizo and poblano peppers.

 Drinking & Entertainment

Trade & Lore COFFEE
(www.tradeandlore.com; 37 Wall St; coffee $2-5.25; ⏰8am-7pm; 🛜) Serious java is dealt by skilled baristas at this trendy downtown coffeehouse drowning in industrial-cool shaken up by occasional fits of vintage furniture. Espresso comes courtesy a top-end mainstay La Marzocco machine and there's an extensive espresso with milk menu. The all-gender bathrooms are a tongue-in-cheek dig at state government.

Orange Peel LIVE MUSIC
(www.theorangepeel.net; 101 Biltmore Ave; tickets $10-30; ⏰shows from 8pm) For live music, try this warehouse-sized place showcasing big-name indie and punk.

ℹ Information

The shiny **visitor center** (📞828-258-6129; www.exploreasheville.com; 36 Montford Ave; ⏰8:30am-5:30pm Mon-Fri, 9am-5pm Sat & Sun) is at I-240, exit 4C. You can buy Biltmore admission tickets here for a $10 discount. Downtown, there is a **satellite visitor center** (📞828-258-6129; www.exploreasheville.com; 80 Court Pl; ⏰9am-5pm Fri-Sun Apr-Oct), with restrooms, beside Pack Square Park.

ℹ Getting There & Around

Twenty minutes south of town, **Asheville Regional Airport** (AVL; 📞828-684-2226; www.flyavl.com; 61 Terminal Dr, Fletcher) has a handful of nonstop flights, including to/from Atlanta, Charlotte, Chicago and New York. **Greyhound** (📞828-253-8451; www.greyhound.com; 2 Tunnel Rd) is about 1 mile northeast of downtown.

Free parking is a tremendous issue in downtown Asheville, but the pubic garages are free for the first hour and only $1 per hour thereafter, so not horrible. Passport (https://passportinc.com) is a handy app for managing parking meters and paid lots here (and in a few other US cities).

Asheville Transit (📞828-253-5691; www.ashevilletransit.com; 49 Coxe Ave; ⏰6am-9:30pm Mon-Fri, 7am-9:30pm Sat, 8:30am-6pm Sun) has 18 local bus routes that run from about 5:30am to 10:30pm Monday through Saturday, with reduced hours Sunday. Tickets are $1. Free bus racks. Route S3 goes from the downtown Art Station to the airport 10 times daily.

Great Smoky Mountains National Park

Be it the rite-of-passage walk in the woods known as the Appalachian Trail, the sweeping, cinematic views from 6643ft Clingmans Dome or the staunchly preserved pioneer homestead at Cades Cove, Great Smoky Mountains National Park is an American icon of nature and history. This moody and magical park sprawls across 521,000 acres in both North Carolina and Tennessee. It's one of the world's most diverse areas: landscapes range from deep, dim spruce forest to sunny meadows carpeted with daisies and Queen Anne's lace to wide, coffee-brown rivers. There's ample hiking and camping, and opportunities for horseback riding, bike rental and fly-fishing. Unfortunately, with more 10 million annual visitors – the highest of any national park in the USA – the place can get very crowded. The North Carolina side has less traffic than the Tennessee side, however, so even at the height of summer tourist season you'll still have room to roam.

◉ Sights

Great Smoky Mountains National Park NATIONAL PARK
(www.nps.gov/grsm) FREE The 815-sq-mile park is the country's most visited and, while the main arteries and attractions can get crowded, 95% of visitors never venture further than 100yd from their cars, so it's easy to leave the masses behind. Unlike most national parks, Great Smoky charges no admission fee. In 2016, 15 sq miles of the park was burned in the Great Smoky Mountain wildfires, including the immensely popular **Chimney Tops Trail**, which remained closed at time of research. Call ahead for an update.

Stop by a visitor center to pick up a park map and the free Smokies Guide. The remains of the 19th-century settlement at **Cades Cove** are some of the park's most popular sights, as evidenced by the teeth-grinding summer traffic jams on the loop road. Mt LeConte offers terrific hiking, as well as the only non-camping accommodations, **LeConte Lodge**. Although the only way to get to the lodge's rustic, electricity-free cabins is via five uphill hiking trails varying in length from 5.5 miles (the **Alum Cave Trail**) to 8 miles (**Boulevard**), it's so popular you need to reserve up to a year in advance. You can drive right up to the dizzying heights of

Clingmans Dome, the third-highest mountain east of the Mississippi, with a futuristic observation tower.

In addition to Chimney Tops, Road Prong Trail, Sugarland Mountain Trail and Bullhead Trail were also indefinitely closed at time of research. Call ahead.

🏃 Activities

Whether you have an irrepressible urge to climb a mountain or just want to get some fresh air, hiking in Great Smoky Mountains National Park is the single best way to experience the sublime beauty of this area. Even if you're only here for a short visit, be sure to include at least one hike in your itinerary. Trails range from flat, easy and short paths to longer, more strenuous endeavors. Many are excellent for families, some are wheelchair accessible, and the majority of trailheads begin from major sights. No matter what your physical ability or endurance level, there's a hike out there for you.

Here are a few of our favorites:

Charlies Bunion   HIKING
An 8.1-mile loop that follows the Appalachian Trail 4 miles from the Newfound Gap overlook to a rocky outcrop for sweeping mountain and valley views.

Big Creek Trail   HIKING
Hike an easy 2 miles to Mouse Creek Falls or go another 3 miles to a backcountry campground; the trailhead is near I-40 on the park's northeastern edge.

Boogerman Trail   HIKING
Moderate 7.4-mile loop passing old farmsteads; accessible via Cove Creek Rd.

Chasteen Creek Falls   HIKING
From Smokemont campground, this 3.6-mile round-trip passes a small waterfall.

Oconaluftee River Trail   HIKING
One of only two in the park that allows leashed pets and bicycles, this 3-mile loop leaves from the Oconaluftee Visitor Center and follows the river for 1.5 miles.

🛏 Sleeping & Eating

Great Smoky Mountains National Park provides varied camping options. LeConte Lodge is the only place where you can get a room, however, and you have to hike to the top of a mountain to enjoy this privilege. Gatlinburg has the most sleeping options of any gateway town, though prices are high. Nearby Pigeon Forge, 10 miles north of Sugarlands Visitor Center, and Sevierville, 17 miles north, have cheaper options.

THE SOUTH NORTH CAROLINA MOUNTAINS

THE 2016 GREAT SMOKY MOUNTAIN WILDFIRES

On November 23, 2016, tragedy stuck Great Smoky Mountains National Park when fire was reported on Chimney Tops, one of the park's popular trails, a kindling that would eventually wreak havoc on the park and Gatlinburg on its way to becoming the deadliest wildfire in the eastern USA since the Great Fires of 1947.

Dubbed 'Chimney Tops 2' by firefighters (a smaller fire had burned on Chimney Tops a week earlier), fire suppression was not as speedy as it should have been (several days went by before action was taken). By November 28, a massive firewall was heading toward Gatlinburg with shocking speed. By December 5, a full-on firefighting onslaught was unleashed: 25 hand crews, 61 engines, six helicopters and a total of 780 personnel. But it wouldn't be until late January when containment of the fire reached over 90%. The town of Gatlinburg was spared due to some heroic firefighting efforts – the only true in-town casualty was the Gatlinburg Sky Lift, which suffered serious damage to its upper section and upper terminal, but the damage otherwise was dreadful: 14 deaths, over 175 injuries, over 2400 structures damaged or destroyed, and the forced evacuation of 14,000 residents. Damage in dollars? Over $500 million.

Inside the park, over 15 sq miles were scorched, with Chimney Tops taking the brunt of the blow, forcing the closure of one of the park's most beloved trails. Park officials estimate it could take 80 years for the area to regenerate, and the trail could be closed for years to come.

Two Tennessee juveniles were arrested and charged with aggravated arson in the starting of the fire. If tried as adults – a major debate among Gatlinburg residents – they could face 60 years in prison.

The National Park Service maintains developed campgrounds at 10 locations in the park. Each campground has restrooms with cold running water and flush toilets, but there are no showers or electrical or water hookups in the park (though some campgrounds do have electricity for emergency situations). Each individual campsite has a fire grate and picnic table. Many sites can be reserved in advance (and one, Cataloochee, which requires it) at www.recreation.gov.

With about 1000 campsites on offer across the 10 developed campgrounds, you'd think finding a place to pitch would be easy. Not so in the busy summer season, so plan ahead. You can make reservations for some sites; others operate on a first-come, first-served basis. Cades Cove and Smokemont campgrounds are open year-round; others are open March to October.

Backcountry camping is an excellent option, which is only chargeable up to five nights ($4 per night, after that, it's free). A permit is required; you can make reservations online at www.smokiespermits.nps.gov, and get permits at the ranger stations or visitor centers.

Nuts and berries notwithstanding, there's nothing to eat in Great Smoky Mountains National Park, save for guests-only fare at LeConte Lodge, vending machines at Sugarlands Visitor Center and the meager offerings sold at the Cades Cove Campground store. Luckily, there are lots of restaurant options in the surrounding towns.

ℹ Tourist Information

The park has four interior visitor centers:

Sugarlands Visitor Center (☑ 865-436-1291; www.nps.gov/grsm; 107 Park Headquarters Rd; ⊙ 8am-7:30pm Jun-Aug, hours vary Sep-May) At the park's northern entrance near Gatlinburg.

Cades Cove Visitor Center (☑ 865-436-7318; Cades Cove Loop Rd; ⊙ 9am-7pm May-Jul, earlier Sep-Mar) Halfway up Cades Cove Loop Rd, 24 miles off Hwy 441 from the Gatlinburg entrance.

Oconaluftee Visitor Center (☑ 828-497-1904; www.nps.gov/grsm; 1194 Newfound Gap Rd, North Cherokee, NC; ⊙ 8am-7:30pm Jun-Aug, hours vary Sep-May) At the park's southern entrance near Cherokee in North Carolina.

Clingmans' Dome Visitor Center (☑ 865-436-1200; Clingmans Dome Rd; ⊙ 10am-6pm Apr-Jun & Aug-Oct, 9:30am-5pm Nov)

ℹ Getting There & Away

The closest major airports are Knoxville's McGhee Tyson Airport (p398), 40 miles from the Sugarlands Visitor Center on the Tennessee side; and Asheville Regional Airport (p366), 58 miles east of the Oconaluftee Visitor Center on the North Carolina side. Both Knoxville and Asheville are served by Greyhound as well.

SOUTH CAROLINA

Moss-draped oaks. Stately mansions. Wide beaches. Rolling mountains. And an ornery streak as old as the state itself. Ah yes, South Carolina, where the accents are thicker and the traditions more dear. From its Revolutionary War patriots to its 1860s secessionist government to its current crop of outspoken legislators, the Palmetto State has never shied away from a fight.

Most travelers stick to the coast, with its splendid antebellum cities and palm-tree-studded beaches. But the interior has a wealth of sleepy old towns, wild and undeveloped state parks and spooky black-water swamps. Along the sea islands you hear the sweet songs of the Gullah, a culture and language created by former slaves who held on to many West African traditions through the ravages of time. From well-bred, gardenia-scented Charleston to bright, tacky Myrtle Beach, South Carolina is always a fascinating destination.

History

More than 28 separate tribes of Native Americans have lived in what is now South Carolina, many of them Cherokee who were later forcibly removed during the Trail of Tears era.

The English founded the Carolina colony in 1670, with settlers pouring in from the royal outpost of Barbados, giving the port city known as Charles Towne a Caribbean flavor. West African slaves were brought over to turn the thick coastal swamps into rice paddies; and by the mid-1700s the area was deeply divided between the slave-owning aristocrats of the Lowcountry and the poor Scots-Irish and German farmers of the rural backcountry.

South Carolina was the first state to secede from the Union, and the first battle of the Civil War occurred at Fort Sumter in Charleston Harbor. The end of the war left much of the state in ruins.

South Carolina traded in cotton and textiles for most of the 20th century. It remains a relatively poor agricultural state, though with a thriving coastal tourism business.

In recent years the Palmetto State has garnered headlines because of its politicians, from Nikki Haley, the state's first woman and first Indian American governor, to Congressman Joe Wilson, who yelled 'You lie!' during a speech by President Obama to Congress. Congressman Mark Sanford, while serving as governor, famously claimed that he was hiking the Appalachian Trail when he was in fact visiting his Argentinian girlfriend.

In 2015, following the shooting of nine members of a historically black church for what appeared to be racially motivated reasons, the state legislature voted to remove the Confederate flag from the grounds of the state capitol, where it had flown since 1962.

ℹ️ Information

The **South Carolina Department of Parks, Recreation & Tourism** (📞 803-734-0124; www.discoversouthcarolina.com) sends out the state's official vacation guide. The state's nine highway welcome centers offer free wi-fi. Ask inside for password.

Charleston

This lovely city will embrace you with the warmth and hospitality of an old and dear friend – who died in the 18th century. We jest, but the cannons, cemeteries and carriage rides do conjure an earlier era. And that historic romanticism, along with the food and Southern graciousness, is what makes Charleston one of the most popular tourist destinations in the South, drawing more than 4.8 million visitors every year.

How best to enjoy its charms? Charleston is a city for savoring – stroll past the historic buildings, admire the antebellum architecture, stop to smell the blooming jasmine and enjoy long dinners on the verandah. It's also a place for romance; everywhere you turn another blushing bride is standing on the steps of yet another charming church. Above all, it's a place for seduction by Southern hospitality – Charleston charms the sweat right off your brow.

History

Well before the Revolutionary War, Charles Towne (named for Charles II) was one of the busiest ports on the eastern seaboard, the center of a prosperous rice-growing and trading colony. With influences from the West Indies and Africa, France and other European countries, it became a cosmopolitan city, often compared to New Orleans.

A tragic but important component of the city's history? Slavery. Charleston was a key port and trade center for the slave industry, and bustling slave auction houses clustered near the Cooper River. The first shots of the Civil War rang out at Fort Sumter, in Charleston's harbor. After the war, as the labor-intensive rice plantations became uneconomical without slave labor, the city's importance declined.

👁️ Sights

The quarter south of Beaufain and Hasell Sts has the bulk of the antebellum mansions, shops, bars and cafes. At the southernmost tip of the Peninsula are the antebellum mansions of the Battery. A loose path, the **Gateway Walk**, winds through several church grounds and graveyards between **St John's Lutheran Church** (www.stjohnscharleston.org; 5 Clifford St) and **St Philip's Church** (www.stphilipschurchsc.org; 146 Church St).

👁️ Historic District

Old Exchange & Provost Dungeon   HISTORIC BUILDING
(www.oldexchange.org; 122 E Bay St; adult/child 7-12yr $10/5; ⊙9am-5pm; 👶) Kids love the creepy dungeon, used as a prison for American patriots held by the British during the Revolutionary War. The cramped space sits beneath a stately Georgian Palladian customs house completed in 1771. Costumed guides lead the dungeon tours. Exhibits about the city are displayed on the upper floors.

Old Slave Mart Museum   MUSEUM
(www.nps.gov/nr/travel/charleston/osm.htm; 6 Chalmers St; adult/child 5-17yr $8/5; ⊙9am-5pm Mon-Sat) Ryan's Mart was an open-air market that auctioned African men, women and children in the mid 1800s, the largest of 40 or so similar auction houses. South Carolina's shameful past is unraveled in text-heavy exhibits illuminating the slave experience; the few artifacts, such as leg shackles, are especially chilling.

Gibbes Museum of Art   GALLERY
(www.gibbesmuseum.org; 135 Meeting St; adult/child $12/6; ⊙10am-5pm Tue & Thu-Sat, to 8pm

Wed, 1-5pm Sun) Houses a decent collection of American and Southern works. The contemporary collection includes works by local artists, with Lowcountry life as a highlight.

Battery & White Point Gardens GARDENS
(cnr East Battery & Murray Blvd) The Battery is the southern tip of the Charleston Peninsula, buffered by a seawall. Stroll past cannons and statues of military heroes in the gardens then walk the promenade and look for Fort Sumter.

Kahal Kadosh Beth Elohim SYNAGOGUE
(www.kkbe.org; 90 Hasell St; ⊙ tours 10am-noon & 1:30-3:30pm Mon-Thu, 10am-noon & 1-3pm Fri, 1-3:30pm Sun) The oldest continuously used synagogue in the country. Docent-led tours cost $10. Check website for tour times.

Rainbow Row AREA
(83 E Bay St) With its candy-colored houses, this stretch of lower E Bay St is one of the most photographed areas of town.

Historic Homes

Aiken-Rhett House HISTORIC BUILDING
(www.historiccharleston.org; 48 Elizabeth St; adult/child 6-16yr $12/5; ⊙ 10am-5pm Mon-Sat, 2-5pm Sun, last tour 4:15pm) The only surviving urban townhouse complex, this 1820 house gives a fascinating glimpse into antebellum life on a 45-minute self-guided audio tour. The role of slaves is emphasized and you can wander into their dorm-style quarters behind the main house before moving on to the lifestyle of the rich and famous.

The Historic Charleston Foundation manages the house 'preserved as found' – the goal of preserving and conserving, but not restoring, the property, meaning there have been few alterations and you get it as is, peeling Parisian wallpaper and all.

Joseph Manigault House HISTORIC BUILDING
(www.charlestonmuseum.org; 350 Meeting St; adult/child 13-17yr/child 3-12yr $12/10/5; ⊙ 9am-5pm Mon-Sat, noon-5pm Sun, last tour 4:30pm) The three-story 1803 Federal-style house was once the showpiece of a French Huguenot rice planter. The tiny neoclassical gate temple in the garden was one of only three in the US at the time.

Nathaniel Russell House HISTORIC BUILDING
(www.historiccharleston.org; 51 Meeting St; adult/child 6-16yr $12/5; ⊙ 10am-5pm Mon-Sat, 2-5pm Sun, last tour 4:30pm) A spectacular, self-supporting spiral staircase is the highlight at this 1808 Federal-style house, built by a Rhode Islander, known in Charleston as 'the king of the Yankees.' A meticulous ongoing restoration is honoring the home to the finest details, such as the 1000 sheets of 22-karat gold leaf in the withdrawing room, the peeling back of 20 layers of wall paint to find the original colors and handmade fitted contoured rugs imported from the UK, as originally done by the Russells.

◉ Marion Square

Formerly home to the state weapons arsenal, this 10-acre park is Charleston's living room, with various monuments and an excellent Saturday farmers market.

Charleston Museum MUSEUM
(www.charlestonmuseum.org; 360 Meeting St; adult/child 13-17yr/child 3-12yr $12/10/5; ⊙ 9am-5pm Mon-Sat, noon-5pm Sun) Founded in 1773, this claims to be the country's oldest museum. It's helpful and informative if you're looking for historic background before strolling through the Historic District. Exhibits spotlight various periods of Charleston's long and storied history.

◉ Aquarium Wharf

Aquarium Wharf surrounds pretty Liberty Sq and is a great place to stroll and watch the tugboats guiding ships into the fourth-largest container port in the USA. The wharf is one of two embarkation points for tours to Fort Sumter; the other is at Patriot's Point.

Fort Sumter National Monument HISTORIC SITE
(www.nps.gov/fosu) The first shots of the Civil War rang out at Fort Sumter, on a pentagon-shaped island in the harbor. A Confederate stronghold, the fort was shelled to bits by Union forces from 1863 to 1865. A few original guns and fortifications give a feel for the momentous history.

◉ Ashley River Plantations

Three spectacular plantations line the Ashley River about a 20-minute drive from downtown Charleston. You'll be hard-pressed for time to visit all three in one outing, but you could squeeze in two (allow at least a couple of hours for each). Ashley River Rd is also known as SC 61, which can be reached from downtown Charleston via Hwy 17.

THE SOUTH CHARLESTON

★ **Middleton Place**   HISTORIC BUILDING
(☑ 843-556-6020; www.middletonplace.org; 4300 Ashley River Rd, Summerville; gardens adult/child 6-13yr $28/10, house-museum tours extra $15; ⊙ 9am-5pm) Designed in 1741, this plantation's vast gardens are the oldest in the US. Countless slaves spent years terracing the land and digging the precise geometric canals for the owner, wealthy South Carolina politician Henry Middleton. The bewitching grounds are a mix of classic formal French gardens and romantic woodland, bounded by flooded rice paddies and rare-breed farm animals. Union soldiers burned the main house in 1865; a 1755 guest wing, now housing the **house museum**, still stands.

Magnolia Plantation   HISTORIC BUILDING
(☑ 843-571-1266; www.magnoliaplantation.com; 3550 Ashley River Rd; adult/child 6-10yr $15/10, tours $8; ⊙ 8am-5:30pm Mar-Oct, to 4:30pm Nov-Feb) Up for a spooky stroll? Then follow the boardwalk through the trees and bog on the Audubon Swamp Garden tour – it's a unique experience. The 500-acre plantation, which has been owned by the Drayton family since 1676, is a veritable theme park. Enjoy a tram tour, a petting zoo and a guided house tour. At the reconstructed slave cabins, the Slavery to Freedom Tour traces the African American experience at the plantation.

Drayton Hall   HISTORIC BUILDING
(☑ 843-769-2600; www.draytonhall.org; 3380 Ashley River Rd; adult/child $22/10, grounds only $12; ⊙ 9am-5pm Mon-Sat, 11am-5pm Sun, last tour 3:30pm) This 1738 Palladian brick mansion was the only plantation house on the Ashley River to survive the Revolutionary and Civil Wars and the great earthquake of 1886. Guided tours explore the unfurnished house, which has been preserved.

☞ **Tours**

Listing all of Charleston's walking, horse-carriage, bus and boat tours would take forever. Ask at the visitor center for the gamut.

Charleston Footprints   WALKING
(☑ 843-478-4718; www.charlestonfootprints.com; 2hr tour $20) A highly rated walking tour of historical Charleston sights.

Culinary Tours of Charleston   FOOD & DRINK
(☑ 843-727-1100; www.culinarytoursofcharleston. com; 18 Anson St; 2½hr tour $60) You'll likely sample grits, pralines and barbecue on the 'Savor the Flavors of Charleston' walking tour of restaurants and markets.

Adventure Harbor Tours   BOATING
(☑ 843-442-9455; www.adventureharbortours.com; 56 Ashley Point Dr; adult/child 3-12yr $55/30) Runs fun trips to uninhabited Morris Island – great for shelling.

★★ **Festivals & Events**

Spoleto USA   PERFORMING ARTS
(☑ 843-579-3100; www.spoletousa.org; ⊙ May/Jun) This 17-day performing-arts festival is South Carolina's biggest event, with operas, dramas and concerts staged across the city.

Lowcountry Oyster Festival   FOOD & DRINK
(www.charlestonrestaurantassociation.com/low country-oyster-festival; 1235 Longpoint Rd, Boone Hall Plantation, Mt Pleasant; oyster buckets $12-14; ⊙ Jan) Oyster lovers in Mt Pleasant feast on 80,000lb of the salty bivalves in January.

MOJA Arts Festival   PERFORMING ARTS
(www.mojafestival.com; ⊙ Sep/Oct) Spirited poetry readings and gospel concerts mark this two-week celebration of African American and Caribbean culture.

🛏 **Sleeping**

Not So Hostel   HOSTEL $
(☑ 843-722-8383; www.littlejackstavern.com; 156 Spring St; dm $28-32, r $75-106; P ❋ 🛜 🐾) 🖋 Housed mainly in a wonderful 1840 dwelling complete with atmospheric, ghost-averting blue porches and an odd, twin-matching architecture setup, Charleston's one hostel is creaky and inviting. An eight-bed co-ed dorm, various four-bed male and female dorms, and nice but cramped private rooms are spread over three buildings with several guest kitchens throughout. Green initiatives abound.

1837 Bed & Breakfast   B&B $$
(☑ 843-723-7166; www.1837bb.com; 126 Wentworth St; r $175-290; P ❋ 🛜) Close to the College of Charleston, this B&B may bring to mind the home of your eccentric, antique-loving aunt. The 1837 has nine charmingly overdecorated rooms, including three in the old brick carriage house. And, no, you're not drunk – those warped porches are lopsided as hell and full of history.

Indigo Inn   BOUTIQUE HOTEL $$
(☑ 843-577-5900; www.indigoinn.com; 1 Maiden Lane; r $209-359; P ❋ 🛜 🐾) This snazzy 40-room inn enjoys a prime location in the middle of the historic district and an oasis-like private courtyard, where guests can enjoy free wine and cheese by the fountain. Decor

gives a nod to the 18th century and is a tad frilly, but the beds are comfy and recently renovated bathrooms have been modernized. Pets are $40 per night.

Town & Country Inn & Suites
HOTEL $$

(☎843-571-1000; www.thetownandcountryinn. com; 2008 Savannah Hwy; r $99-299, ste $249-299; P✳@🛜🏊) About 6 miles from downtown, Town & Country offers modern and stylish rooms at a reasonable price. The inn is a good launchpad if you want to get a jump on traffic for a morning visit to the Ashley River plantations.

★ Ansonborough Inn
HOTEL $$

(☎800-522-2073; www.ansonboroughinn.com; 21 Hasell St; r from $169-329; P✳@🛜) Droll neo-Victorian touches such as the closet-sized British pub and the formal portraits of dogs add a sense of fun to this intimate Historic District hotel, which also manages to feel like an antique sailing ship. Huge guest rooms mix old and new, with worn leather couches, high ceilings and flat-screen TVs.

★ Restoration
BOUTIQUE HOTEL $$$

(☎843-518-5100; www.therestorationhotel.com; 75 Wentworth St; ste from $399; P✳🛜🏊) Spanish moss-draped, 200-year-old B&Bs are cool and all, but if you skew more hip and contemporary than antebellum and antique, this all-suite hipster enclave steeped in Americana arts-and-crafts kitsch is for you. Reclaimed wood-bound hallways lead to 54 rooms over a few buildings, which grow from 500 sq feet and are awash in modern indigo, some with kitchenettes and washers and dryers.

✕ Eating

Charleston is one of America's finest eating cities, and there are enough fabulous restaurants here for a town three times its size. The 'classic' Charleston establishments stick to fancy seafood with a French flair, while many of the trendy up-and-comers are reinventing Southern cuisine with a focus on the area's copious local bounty, from oysters to heirloom rice to heritage pork.

Artisan Meat Share
SANDWICHES $

(www.artisanmeatsharecharleston.com; 33 Spring St; sandwiches $7-12; ⊘11am-7pm Mon-Fri, 10am-7pm Sat & Sun) Meat, man, meat. Stuffed in a biscuit. Piled high on potato bread. Or lurching across your charcuterie board – damn that's fresh. Order at the counter, find a seat if you can, then give a nod to artisan hipsters, bless their hearts. You know the drill: fresh, local, delicious and the condiments are housemade.

Gaulart & Maliclet
FRENCH $

(www.fastandfrenchcharleston.com; 98 Broad St; breakfast $5-11, lunch & dinner $10-14; ⊘8am-4pm Mon, to 10pm Tue-Thu, to 10:30pm Fri & Sat) Ooh la la. Locals crowd around the shared tables at this tiny spot, known as 'Fast & French,' to nibble on Gallic cheeses and sausages, fondues or nightly specials ($21 to $24) that include bread, soup, a main dish and wine.

Xiao Bao Biscuit
ASIAN $$

(www.xiaobaobiscuit.com; 224 Rutledge Ave; lunch $12, dinner mains $12-16; ⊘11:30am-2pm, 5:30-10pm Mon-Sat) Exposed-brick walls, concrete floor and housed in a former gas station – this casual but stylish eatery hits the hipster high marks. But the food? Now we're talking. The short but palate-kicking menu spotlights simple pan-Asian fare enhanced by local ingredients and spicy flavors.

★ Edmund's Oast
BREWPUB $$

(☎843-727-1145; www.edmundsoast.com; 1081 Morrison Dr; mains $16-30, pints $5-10; ⊘4:30-10pm Mon-Thu, to 11pm Fri & Sat, 10am-10pm Sun; 🛜) Occupying a gutted former hardware store in gentrifying NoMo (North Morrison), Charleston's most interesting nocturnal distraction is a highbrow brewpub with a serious drinking problem. The liquid: 48 taps (eight devoted to cocktails, meads and sherries and 12 proprietary craft beers, among other craft). The grub: dead-serious in-house cured charcuterie, an outstanding fresh catch Française, beautiful Calabrian chili-laced cauliflower.

Hominy Grill
SOUTHERN US $$

(www.hominygrill.com; 207 Rutledge Ave; breakfast $4.50-11, lunch & dinner mains $9-22; ⊘7:30am-9pm Mon-Fri, 9am-9pm Sat, 9am-3pm Sun; ✎) Slightly off the beaten path, this neighborhood cafe serves modern, vegetarian-friendly Lowcountry cuisine in an old barbershop. The shaded patio is tops for brunch.

Fleet Landing
SEAFOOD $$

(☎843-722-8100; www.fleetlanding.net; 186 Concord St; lunch $9-24, dinner $13-26; ⊘11am-4pm daily, 5-10pm Sun-Thu, to 11pm Fri & Sat; 🛜) Come here for the perfect Charleston lunch: a river view, a cup of she-crab soup with a splash of sherry, and a big bowl of shrimp and grits.

Housed in a former naval degaussing building on a pier, it's a convenient and scenic spot to enjoy fresh fish, a fried seafood platter or a burger after a morning of downtown exploring.

Ordinary   SEAFOOD $$$
(☑843-414-7060; www.eattheordinary.com; 544 King St; small plates $6-18, large $21-55; ☺5-10:30pm Tue-Sun) Inside a cavernous 1927 bank building, this buzzy seafood hall and oyster bar feels like the best party in town. The menu is short, but the savory dishes are prepared with finesse.

★FIG   SOUTHERN US $$$
(☑843-805-5900; www.eatatfig.com; 232 Meeting St; mains $30-42; ☺5:30-10:30pm Mon-Thu, to 11pm Fri & Sat; 🎧) 🍴 FIG has been a long-time foodie favorite, and it's easy to see why: welcoming staff, efficient but unrushed service and top-notch, sustainably sourced nouvelle Southern fare from James Beard Award–winner Mike Lata. The six nightly changing dishes embrace what's fresh and local from the sea and local farms and mills. FIG stands for Food is Good. And the gourmets agree.

🍷 Drinking & Nightlife

★Eclectic   COFFEE
(www.eclecticcafeandvinyl.com; 132 Spring St; ☺7am-9pm Mon, Wed & Thu, 7am-11pm Fri, 9am-11pm Sat, 9am-9pm Sun; 🎧) Our favorite Charleston coffeehouse, this indigo-trimmed Cannonborough/Elliotborough newcomer is gorgeous: walls lined with vinyl records for sale with a perfect juxtaposition of hardwood flooring, exposed brick, silver gilded ceilings and a gorgeous hand-hewed wooden workstation area reclaimed from an old South Dakota horse coral. Coffee, wine, beer and upscale cafe grub.

Rooftop at the Vendue   BAR
(www.vendueinn.com; 23 Vendue Range; ☺11:30am-10pm Sun-Thu, to midnight Fri & Sat) This rooftop bar has the best views of downtown and the crowds to prove it. Enjoy crafts cocktails and live music on Sundays.

Closed for Business   PUB
(www.closed4business.com; 453 King St; ☺11am-late) A 42-tap selection of local and national craft brews and hipster-rustic decor gives this inviting 'draft emporium' a neighborhood vibe and just the right amount of edge.

🛍 Shopping

Shops of Historic Charleston Foundation   GIFTS & SOUVENIRS
(www.historiccharleston.org; 108 Meeting St; ☺9am-6pm Mon-Sat, noon-5pm Sun) This place showcases jewelry, home furnishings and furniture inspired by the city's historic homes, much of which is based on Blue Canton porcelain.

Blue Bicycle Books   BOOKS
(www.bluebicyclebooks.com; 420 King St; ☺10am-6pm Tue-Thu, 10am-7pm Fri & Sat, noon-1pm Sun) Excellent new-and-used bookshop with a great selection of Southern history and culture.

ℹ Information

Charleston Visitor Center (☑843-724-7174; www.charlestoncvb.com; 375 Meeting St; ☺8:30am-5pm Apr-Oct, to 5pm Nov-Mar) Find help with accommodations and tours or watch a half-hour video on Charleston history in this spacious renovated warehouse.

ℹ Getting There & Around

Charleston International Airport (CHS; ☑843-767-7000; www.chs-airport.com; 5500 International Blvd) is 12 miles outside town in North Charleston, with nonstop flights to 18 destinations. The **Greyhound** (☑843-744-4247; www.greyhound.com; 3610 Dorchester Rd) station and the **Amtrak** (www.amtrak.com; 4565 Gaynor Ave) train station are both in North Charleston.

CARTA (www.ridecarta.com) runs city-wide buses; one-way cash fare is $2. The free DASH streetcars do three loop routes from the visitor center. Parking is a definite issue – city parking lots charge just $2 per hour, however.

Mt Pleasant

Across the Cooper River from Charleston is the residential and vacation community of Mt Pleasant, originally a summer retreat for early Charlestonians, along with the slim barrier resort islands of **Isle of Palms** and **Sullivan's Island**. Though increasingly glutted with traffic and strip malls, the area still has some charm, especially in the historic downtown, called the **Old Village**.

👁 Sights

Boone Hall Plantation   HISTORIC BUILDING
(☑843-884-4371; www.boonehallplantation.com; 1235 Long Point Rd; adult/child 6-12yr $24/12;

⊙ 8:30am-6:30pm Mon-Sat, noon-5pm Sun early Mar-Aug, shorter hours Sep-Jan) Just 11 miles from downtown Charleston on Hwy 17N, Boone Hall Plantation is famous for its magical Avenue of Oaks, planted by Thomas Boone in 1743. Boone Hall is still a working plantation, though strawberries, tomatoes and Christmas trees long ago replaced cotton as the primary crop. The main house, built in 1936, is the fourth house on the site. The most compelling buildings are the Slave St cabins, built between 1790 and 1810.

Patriot's Point Naval
& Maritime Museum MUSEUM
(☑ 866-831-1720; www.patriotspoint.org; 40 Patriots Point Rd; adult/child 6-11yr $22/14; ⊙ 9am-6:30pm) This museum is home to the USS *Yorktown,* a giant aircraft carrier used extensively in WWII. You can tour the ship's flight deck, bridge and ready rooms and get a glimpse of what life was like for its sailors. Also on-site are a submarine, naval destroyer, the Medal of Honor Museum and a re-created 'fire base' from Vietnam, which add a unique touch to merely touring a decommissioned ship. You can also jump onboard the **Fort Sumter boat tour** (☑ boat tour 843-722-2628, park 843-883-3123; www.fortsumtertours.com; 340 Concord St; adult/child 4-11yr $21/13).

> **GULLAH CULTURE**
>
> African slaves were transported from the region known as the Rice Coast (Sierra Leone, Senegal, Gambia and Angola) to a landscape of remote islands that was shockingly similar – swampy coastlines, tropical vegetation and hot, humid summers.
>
> These new African Americans were able to retain many of their homeland traditions, even after the fall of slavery and well into the 20th century. The resulting Gullah (also known as Geechee in Georgia) culture has its own language, an English-based Creole with many African words and sentence structures, and many traditions, including fantastic storytelling, art, music and crafts. The Gullah culture is celebrated annually with the energetic **Gullah Festival** (www.theoriginalgullahfestival.org; ⊙ late May) in Beaufort.

Lowcountry

The southern half of the South Carolina coast is a tangle of islands cut off from the mainland by inlets and tidal marshes. Here, descendants of West African slaves known as the Gullah maintain small communities in the face of resort and golf-course development. The landscape ranges from tidy stretches of shimmery, oyster-gray sand to wild, moss-shrouded maritime forests.

The southernmost stretch of South Carolina's coast is popular with a mostly upscale set of golfers and B&B aficionados, but the area has quirky charms aplenty for everyone.

Charleston County Sea Islands

A dozen islands within an hour's drive from Charleston make up the Charleston County Sea Islands. Around 10 miles by road southeast of Charleston on the Mt Pleasant side, **Sullivan's Island** beckons day-trippers for fun wining and dining on blue-sky days. Four miles in the other direction brings you to **James Island**, one of the most urban of Charleston's barrier sea islands. A further 9 miles south of Charleston, **Folly Beach** is good for a day of sun and sand. The other end of the island is popular with surfers.

Upscale rental homes, golf courses and the swanky Sanctuary Resort mark **Kiawah Island**, 26 miles southwest of Charleston, where you'll find those lucky enough to stay here cruising along one of the most gorgeous beaches in the South on their bikes; while nearby **Edisto Island** (*ed*-is-tow) is a homespun family vacation spot without a single traffic light.

⊙ Sights

★ **Kiawah Beachwater Park** BEACH
(www.ccprc.com; 8 Beachwalker Dr; ⊙ 9am-8pm May-Sep, shorter hours rest of year) This idyllic stretch of sun-toasted sand at the southern end of Kiawah Island has been called one of the top 10 beaches in the USA and is the only publicly accessible beach on Kiawah. Take a bike – the compact sand is perfect for a ride along the 10-mile-long barrier island.

🛏 Sleeping & Eating

James Island
County Park CAMPGROUND $
(☑ 843-795-4386; www.ccprc.com; 871 Riverland Dr, James Island; tent sites from $31, 8-person cottages $194; 🛜) A great budget option, this 643-acre

park southwest of downtown has meadows, a marsh and a dog park. Rent bikes ($4 per hour) and kayaks ($5.50 per hour), go for a run or frolic with your pup. The park offers shuttle services to downtown and Folly Beach ($10). Reservations are highly recommended. There are 125 campsites and 10 marsh-adjacent rental cottages.

Sanctuary at Kiawah
Island Golf Resort   RESORT $$$
(☑ 843-768-2121; www.kiawahresort.com; 1 Sanctuary Beach Dr, Kiawah Island; r/ste from $560/1100, villa from $260, house from $5500 per week; ✳ @ ☏ ☒) Ready to swank it up? Consider an idyll at the Sanctuary, sitting prettily by the sea 21 miles south of downtown Charleston. Hotel rooms glow with freshly classic decor – think soft greens, four-poster beds, Italian linens, custom-made mattresses and marble showers. Villas and houses also available. Amenities include two tennis complexes, 90 holes of golf, a spa and kids' Kamp Kiawah.

Cory's Grilled Cheese   SANDWICHES $
(www.corysgrilledcheese.com; 1739 Maybank Hwy, James Island; sandwiches $4-8.50; ⊘ 9am-9pm Mon-Sat, to 5pm Sun) No hipster pretension here, just your average everyday strip-mall grilled-cheese joint with holes in the wall from weekend heavy-metal concert moshing. Cory's grilled-cheese sandwiches are gooey, buttery perfection (we dig the Lowcountry with pimiento cheese, muenster, avocado and bacon on sourdough) and there's beer, too.

★ **Poe's Tavern**   PUB FOOD $$
(☑ 843-883-0083; www.poestavern.com; 2210 Middle St, Sullivan's Island; mains $9-13; ⊘ 11am-midnight) On a sunny day the front porch of Poe's on Sullivan's Island is the place to be. The tavern's namesake, master of the macabre Edgar Allan Poe, was once stationed at nearby Fort Moultrie. The burgers are superb, and the Amontillado comes with guacamole, jalapeño jack, pico de gallo and chipotle sour cream. Quoth the raven: 'Gimme more.'

ⓘ Information

Kiawah Island Visitor Center (☑ 800-774-0006; www.charlestoncvb.com; 22 Beachwalker Dr, Kiawah Island; ⊘ 9am-3pm) Maps, tourist info and help with accommodations and tours through the Charleston area.

DON'T MISS

BOWEN'S ISLAND RESTAURANT

Head down a long dirt road through Lowcountry marshland near Folly Beach to find **Bowens Island Restaurant** (www.bowensisland.biz; 1870 Bowens Island Rd, Folly Island; mains $8-18; ⊘ 5-9:30pm Tue-Sat), an unpainted wooden shack that's one of the South's most venerable seafood dives – grab an oyster knife and start shucking! A half/full tray runs $11/16. Cool beer and friendly locals give the place its soul.

ⓘ Getting There & Away

Charleston's barrier sea islands are all accessed via a series of byways and bridges from the city, though not always with a connection from one to another. You'll need to take the long way round if you want to go from Sullivan's Island to Kiawah or Edisto Islands, for example. Coming from the south, Edisto (via SC 174) and Kiawah and Johns (via SC 17) can be accessed without going through Charleston. From the North Coast, SC 17 also reaches Sullivan's and Isle of Palms without going through the city.

Beaufort & Hilton Head

On Port Royal Island, darling colonial town Beaufort (byoo-furt) is often used as a set for Hollywood films. The streets of the historic district are lined with antebellum homes and magnolias dripping with Spanish moss. The riverfront downtown has gobs of linger-worthy cafes and galleries.

South of Beaufort, some 20,000 young men and women go through boot camp each year at the **Marine Corps Recruit Depot** on Parris Island, made notorious by Stanley Kubrick's *Full Metal Jacket* (though not filmed here). The facility has been 'welcoming' recruits for 100 years. Come for Friday graduations to see newly minted marines parade proudly for family and friends. Americans must show ID (and foreign nationals a passport) before driving on to the base. East of Beaufort, the Sea Island Pkwy/ Hwy 21 connects a series of marshy, rural islands, including **St Helena Island**, the heart of Gullah country and the site of a coastal state park.

Across Port Royal Sound, tony Hilton Head Island is South Carolina's largest barrier island and one of America's top golf spots. There are dozens of courses, many enclosed

WORTH A TRIP

FIREFLIES & SPANISH MOSS: CONGAREE NATIONAL PARK

Inky-black water, dyed with tannic acid leached from decaying plant matter. Bone-white cypress stumps like the femurs of long-dead giants. Spanish moss as dry and gray as witches' hair. There's nothing like hiking or canoeing through one of South Carolina's unearthly swamps – America's largest contiguous, old-growth floodplain forest – to make you feel like a character in a Southern Gothic novel. The 22,000-acre **Congaree National Park** (☑803-776-4396; www.nps.gov/cong; 100 National Park Rd, Hopkins; ⊙visitor center 9am-5pm Tue-Sat) offers camping and a limited number of free, seasonal ranger-led canoe trips (reserve in advance).

Casual day-trippers can wander the 2.4-mile elevated boardwalk. Look carefully at the Blue Sky mural in the visitor center – the scene seems to change as you move. From mid-May through early June, the *Photinus carolinus,* a rare species of firefly, blink in unison, transforming the forest floor into a twinkling light show. The phenomenon only occurs in a handful of spots around the world. Columbia-based **River Runner Outdoor Center** (☑803-771-0353; www.shopriverrunner.com; 905 Gervais St) can get you on the water. The park is just a 30-minute drive from downtown Columbia.

in posh private residential communities (historically known as 'plantations,' now often called 'resorts'). The island was the first eco-planned destination in the US. Founder Charles Fraser believed a resort should blend with nature, so subdued colors, strict zoning laws (no building over five stories high, signage must be low and lit from below) and a distinct lack of streetlights characterize the environment here. Even so, summer traffic and miles of stoplights can stifle the ability to appreciate the beauty of the island, but there are some lush nature preserves; wide, white beaches hard enough for bike riding; and a whole lot of dolphins.

⊙ Sights

Parris Island Museum   MUSEUM
(www.parrisislandmuseum.com; 111 Panama St; ⊙10am-4:30pm Mon-Wed, Sat & Sun, 8am-4:30pm Thu-Fri) FREE This fascinating museum covering marine-corps history has antique uniforms and weaponry, but is most engaging for its exhibits chronicling the grueling, intense and scary (that CS gas-chamber exercise!) 13-week marine basic training, which takes place here and at a second facility in San Diego, California.

Penn Center   MUSEUM
(☑843-838-2474; www.penncenter.com/museum; 16 Penn Center Circle W, St Helena Island; adult/child 6-16yr $7/3; ⊙9am-4pm Tue-Sat) Once the home of one of the nation's first schools for freed slaves, the Penn Center has a small museum that covers Gullah culture and traces the history of Penn School.

Hunting Island State Park   STATE PARK
(☑843-838-2011; www.southcarolinaparks.com/huntingisland; 2555 Sea Island Pkwy; adult/child 6-15yr $5/3; ⊙visitor center 9am-5pm Mon-Fri, 11am-5pm Sat & Sun, nature center 9am-5pm Tue-Sat, daily Jun-Aug) Lush and inviting Hunting Island State Park impresses visitors with acres of spooky maritime forest, tidal lagoons and empty, bone-white beach. The Vietnam War scenes from *Forrest Gump* were filmed in the marsh, a nature-lover's dream. **Campgrounds** (☑reservations 866-345-7275; www.southcarolinaparks.com; tent sites $18.50-20, RV sites $18-45, cabin $249; ⊙6am-6pm, to 9pm early Mar–early Nov) fill quickly in summer. Climb the **lighthouse** ($2) for sweeping coastal views.

🛏 Sleeping & Eating

City Loft Hotel   HOTEL **$$**
(☑843-379-5638; www.citylofthotel.com; 301 Carteret St; r/ste $169/209; P🕸❄) The chic City Loft Hotel adds a refreshing dash of modern style to a town heavy on historic homes and stately oak trees. Enjoy flat-screen TV in the bedroom and bathroom, artisan-tile showers and Memory Foam–topped beds. Other perks include a gym, complimentary bicycle use and an on-site coffee shop ($5 voucher included in rates).

★**Cuthbert House Inn**   B&B **$$$**
(☑843-521-1315; www.cuthberthouseinn.com; 1203 Bay St; r $179-245; P🕸❄) The most romantic of Beaufort's B&Bs, this sumptuously grand white-columned mansion is straight out of *Gone with the Wind*. Antique furnishings are found throughout, but

monochromatic walls add a fresh, modern feel. Some rooms have a river view (three have fireplaces). On his march through the South in 1865, General William T Sherman slept at the house.

★ **Lowcountry Produce** SOUTHERN US $
(www.lowcountryproduce.com; 302 Carteret St; breakfast $9-15, sandwiches $10-18; ⊗8am-3pm; 🛜) A fantastic cafe and market for picnic rations such as pies, housemade relishes, local cheeses – all kinds of Lowcountry-spun awesomeness (except for the cream-cheese lasagne – that ain't right!). Or eat in and indulge in an Ooooey Gooey, a grilled pimiento-cheese sandwich with bacon and garlic-pepper jelly (one hot mess!) or a tasty crab-cake sandwich with brussels-sprouts slaw.

ⓘ Information

Beaufort Tourist Info Center (📞843-525-8500; www.beaufortsc.org; 713 Craven St; ⊗9am-5pm Mon-Sat) Inside the Beaufort History Museum.

North Coast

Stretching from the North Carolina border south to the city of Georgetown, the coastal region known as the Grand Strand bustles with some 60 miles of fast-food joints, beach resorts and three-story souvenir shops. What was once a laid-back summer destination for working-class people from across the Southeast has become some of the most overdeveloped real estate in the country. Whether you're ensconced in a behemoth resort or sleeping in a tent at a state park, all you need to enjoy your stay is a pair of flip-flops, a margarita and some quarters for the pinball machine.

Myrtle Beach

The towering Sky Wheel spins fantastically beside the coast in downtown Myrtle Beach, anchoring a 60-mile swath of sun-bleached excess. Love it or hate it, Myrtle Beach means summer vacation, American-style. Bikers take advantage of the lack of helmet laws to let their graying ponytails fly in the wind, bikini-clad teenagers play video games and eat hot dogs in smoky arcades, and whole families roast like chickens on the white sand.

North Myrtle Beach, actually a separate town, is slightly lower-key, with a thriving culture based on the 'shag' (no, not that kind of shag) – a jitterbug-like dance invented here in the 1940s. It isn't for nature-lovers, but with enormous outlet malls and innumerable minigolf courses, water parks, daiquiri bars and T-shirt shops, it's a rowdy good time and certainly a hit with the kids.

◉ Sights & Activities

SkyWheel AMUSEMENT PARK
(www.myrtlebeachskywheel.com; 1110 N Ocean Blvd; adult/child 3-11yr $14/9; ⊗11am-midnight) The 187ft-high SkyWheel overlooks the 1.2-mile coastal boardwalk. One ticket includes three revolutions in an enclosed gondola. At night the wheel is bewitching, with more than a million dazzling colored lights.

Brookgreen Gardens GARDENS
(www.brookgreen.org; 1931 Brookgreen Garden Dr, Murrells Inlet; adult/child 4-12yr $16/8; ⊗9:30am-5pm) These magical gardens, 16 miles south of town on Hwy 17S, are home to the largest collection of American sculpture in the country, set amid more than 9000 acres of rice-plantation-turned-subtropical-garden paradise.

🛏 Sleeping & Eating

Myrtle Beach State Park CAMPGROUND $
(📞843-238-5325; www.myrtlebeachsp.com; 4401 S Kings Hwy; rustic tent $18-36 Easter–Labor Day only, tent & RV sites $21-50, cabins $65-205; P🛜🏊) Sleep beneath the pines or rent a cabin, all just steps from the shore. The park is 3 miles south of central Myrtle Beach and includes a nice beach, an epic fishing pier and swathes of protected maritime forest.

Hampton Inn Broadway at the Beach HOTEL $$$
(📞843-916-0600; www.hamptoninn3.hilton.com; 1140 Celebrity Circle; r/ste from $249/389; ❄@🛜🏊) The bright renovated rooms overlooking the lake and Broadway at the Beach are a great choice at this hotel, which feels less hectic than properties along Ocean Blvd. If you're traveling with preteens, you may feel more comfortable letting them roam the adjacent shops and attractions rather than the boardwalk.

Prosser's BBQ SOUTHERN US $$
(www.prossersbbq.com; 3750 Business Hwy 17, Murrells Inlet; buffet breakfast $7, lunch $10-11, dinner $13-15; ⊗6:30-10:30am Mon-Sat, 11am-2pm Mon-Sat, 11am-2:30pm Sun, 4-8pm Tue-Sat; 🚗) It's weird to come to Murrells Inlet's 'restaurant row' and not spring for seafood, but who are

we to judge? The gut-busting lunch buffet here is down-home delicious. It includes fried fish and chicken, sweet-potato souffle, mac 'n' cheese, green beans and vinegary pulled pork.

★ **Wicked Tuna** SEAFOOD $$$
(☎843-651-9987; www.thewickedtuna.com; 4123 Hwy 17 Bus, Murrells Inlet; mains $14-42; ⊗11am-midnight; 🛜) Murrells Inlet is full of kitschy seafooders and, at first glance, the Wicked Tuna looks no different. Guess again! You are in for a real treat at this trip-worthy spot overlooking the beautiful inlet – it employs six fishing boats that go out for three- to six-day stints and bring back up to 600lb of fresh fish each.

Boats roll right up to the kitchen door, completing the hook-to-table concept. The menu is long on tantalizing dishes and sushi. Go for the fresh catch, sit out on the waterfront patio and send us thank-you notes in the mail!

🍷 Drinking & Entertainment

American Tap House CRAFT BEER
(www.broadwayatthebeach.com/listing/american-tap-house; 1320 Celebrity Circle; pints $5.50-9; 🛜) At Broadway at the Beach, if you prefer your craft-beer experience to come supersized, you'll find 53 taps of national options at this chef-driven gastropub.

★ **Fat Harold's Beach Club** DANCE
(www.fatharolds.com; 212 Main St; ⊗from 4pm Sun-Thu, from 11am Fri & Sat) Folks groove to doo-wop and old-time rock and roll at this North Myrtle institution, which calls itself 'Home of the Shag.' The dance, that is. Free shag lessons are offered at 7pm every Tuesday.

❶ Information

Myrtle Beach Visitor Information (☎843-626-7444; www.visitmyrtlebeach.com; 1200 N Oak St; ⊗8:30am-5pm) has maps and brochures.

❶ Getting There & Around

The traffic coming and going on Hwy 17 Business/Kings Hwy can be infuriating. To avoid 'the Strand' altogether, stay on the Hwy 17 bypass, or take Hwy 31/Carolina Bays Pkwy, which parallels Hwy 17 between Hwy 501 and Hwy 9.
Myrtle Beach International Airport (MYR; ☎843-448-1589; www.flymyrtlebeach.com; 1100 Jetport Rd) is located within the city limits, as is the **Greyhound** (☎843-448-2472; www.greyhound.com; 511 7th Ave N) station, with the former receiving direct flights from over 30 domestic destinations.

Greenville & the Upcountry

Cherokee Indians once roamed the state's mountain foothills, which they called the 'Great Blue Hills of God.' The region today is known as the Upcountry. Geographically it's the spot where the Blue Ridge mountains drop dramatically to meet the Piedmont.

The region is anchored by Greenville, home to one of the most photogenic downtowns in the South. The Reedy River twists through the city center, and its dramatic falls tumble beneath Main St at Falls Park (www.fallspark.com).

Two miles from downtown, the village of West Greenville is seeing a revival thanks to an influx of art galleries, restaurants, boutiques and other new development.

◉ Sights & Activities

Table Rock State Park STATE PARK
(☎864-878-9813; www.southcarolinaparks.com; 158 Ellison Lane, Pickens; adult/child 6-15yr $5/3 Jun-Nov, adult/child under 16yr $2/free Dec-May; ⊗7am-7pm Sun-Thu, to 9pm Fri & Sat, extended hours mid-May–early Nov) The Upcountry's marquee natural attraction is Table Rock Mountain, a 3124ft-high mountain with a striking granite face. The 7.2-mile round-trip hike to its summit is a popular local challenge. For overnight stays, **camping** (☎864-878-9813; www.southcarolinaparks.com; campsites $16-25, cabins $52-181; ❄) is available for tents and RVs, plus there are cabins built by the Civilian Conservation Corps.

BMW Performance Center MOTOR SPORTS
(☎864-968-3000; www.bmwperformancecenter. com; 1155 Hwy 101 S, Greer; 1-/2-day school from $849/1699) Your need for speed can be quenched at America's only BMW performance-driving academy. Delve into fast and furious behind-the-wheel experiences over the course of one- and two-day classes with various vehicles, including the high-performance M series, or stunt-driving school in a Mini – *The Italian Job* will have nothing on you.

🛏 Sleeping

★ Swamp Rabbit Inn
B&B $$

(📞 864-517-4617; www.swamprabbitinn.com; 1
Logan St; r with/without bath $155/105; 🅿 ❋ 🛜)
This fun six-room inn occupies a '50s-era
former boarding house downtown and feels
like a hostel but features colorfully decked-
out private rooms that are as cozy and
quirky as any in the South. Wonderful com-
mon spaces include a modern guest kitchen
and wooden patio with barbecue.

Westin Poinsett
HOTEL $$$

(📞 864-421-9700; www.westinpoinsettgreenville.
com; 120 S Main St; r $189-309; 🅿 ❋ @ 🛜 🐾)
This grand hotel, which originally opened
in 1925, is in the heart of downtown, just
steps from Reedy River Falls. Past guests include Amelia Earhart, Cornelius Vanderbilt
and Bobby Kennedy. There's new carpeting,
scones and wall vinyl throughout the hotel,
while rooms tilt toward the basic (bathrooms are set for a remodel soon).

🍴 Eating & Drinking

Stax Omega Diner
DINER $

(www.staxs.net; 72 Orchard Park Dr; breakfast
$4-14, lunch & dinner $9-15; ⊙ 6:30am-9pm; 🛜)
Nobody quite does breakfast excess like the
USA and this bustling family-owned diner 4
miles east of downtown is everything fantastic about that very fact. It's massive – capacity 500! – and they do it all really well: omelets, pancakes, French toast, eggs Benedict,
scrambles – the list goes on and on...and on.

Soby's
SOUTHERN $$

(www.sobys.com; 207 S Main St; mains $18-31;
⊙ 5:30-9pm Mon-Thu, 5:30-10pm Fri, 5-10pm Sat,
10:30am-1:30pm & 5-9pm Sun; 🛜) Book yourself
one of the intimate, brick-walled banquettes
at this downtown Greenville bastion of New
Southern cuisine that also caters to wine lov-
ers (the 5000-bottle list has been awarded
a *Wine Spectator* Award of Excellence 19
years running). The oft-changing menu is
steeped in the wares of local farmers, forag-
ers and ranchers.

Dark Corner Distillery
DISTILLERY $

(www.darkcornerdistillery.com; 241 N Main St;
⊙ 11am-7pm Mon-Sat) Sample butterscotch
whiskey or wildberry moonshine here. The
Dark Corner is the nickname given to the
secretive upland corner of Greenville Coun-
ty, which was famed for its bootlegging and
hardscrabble Scots-Irish residents.

ℹ Getting There & Away

**Greenville–Spartanburg International
Airport** (📞 864-877-7426; www.gspairport.
com; 2000 GSP Dr, Greer) is 13 miles east of
the city, nearly halfway between Greenville and
Spartanburg. **Greyhound** (📞 864-235-4741;
www.greyhound.com; 9 Hendrix Dr) is also
out that way, 7 miles southeast of downtown.
Amtrak (www.amtrak.com; 1120 W Washington
St) is much more amicably located on just west
of downtown.

TENNESSEE

Most states have one official state song. Ten-
nessee has seven. And there's a reason for
that – Tennessee has music deep within its
soul. Here, the folk music of the Scots-Irish
in the eastern mountains combined with the
bluesy rhythms of the African Americans in
the western Delta to give birth to the modern
country music that makes Nashville famous.

The state's three geographic regions, East,
Middle and West Tennessee, are represent-
ed by the three stars on the Tennessee flag.
Each has its own unique beauty: the heath-
er-colored peaks of the Great Smoky Moun-
tains; the lush green valleys of the central
plateau around Nashville; and the hot, sul-
try lowlands near Memphis.

In Tennessee you can hike shady moun-
tain trails in the morning, and by evening
whoop it up in a Nashville honky-tonk or
walk the streets of Memphis with Elvis'
ghost.

ℹ Information

Department of Environment & Conservation
(www.state.tn.us/environment/parks) Check
out the well-organized website for camping,
hiking and fishing info for Tennessee's more
than 50 state parks.
Department of Tourist Development (📞 615-
741-2159; www.tnvacation.com) Has welcome
centers at the state borders.

Memphis

Memphis doesn't just attract tourists. It
draws pilgrims. Music-lovers lose them-
selves to the throb of blues guitar on Beale
St. Barbecue connoisseurs descend to stuff
themselves silly on smoky pulled pork and
dry-rubbed ribs. Elvis fanatics fly in to wor-
ship at the altar of the King at Graceland.
You could spend days hopping from one
museum or historic site to another, stopping
only for barbecue, and leave happy.

Greater Memphis

Greater Memphis

◎ Top Sights
1 Graceland..B4
2 Stax Museum of American Soul
  Music...B2
3 Sun Studio..B2

◎ Sights
4 Children's Museum of Memphis...........C2
5 Elvis Presley's Memphis.......................B4
6 Slave Haven Underground Railroad
  Museum/Burkle Estate.........................B1

🛏 Sleeping
7 Days Inn Graceland...............................B4
  Graceland RV Park &
  Campground................................(see 5)
  Guest House at Graceland............ (see 1)
8 James Lee House...................................B2

⊗ Eating
9 Alcenia's.. B2
10 Alchemy.. C2
  Bar DKDC.....................................(see 10)
11 Brother Juniper's............................... D2
12 Cozy Corner... B2
  Imagine Vegan Cafe ....(see 10)
13 Payne's Bar-B-Q.................................. C2
14 Restaurant Iris.................................... C2
  Soul Fish Cafe ....(see 10)
15 Sweet Grass.. C2

🍷 Drinking & Nightlife
  Hammer & Ale................................(see 15)
16 Loflin Yard... A2
17 Wiseacre Brewing Co C2

✦ Entertainment
18 Wild Bill's..C1
  Young Avenue Deli........................ (see 15)

Memphis has a certain baroque, ruined quality that's both sad and beguiling. Though poverty is rampant – Victorian mansions sit beside tumbledown shotgun shacks (a narrow style of house popular in the South) and college campuses lie in the shadow of eerie abandoned factories – whiffs of a renaissance are in the air. Neighborhoods once downtrodden, abandoned and/or otherwise reclaimed by kudzu – South Main, Binghampton, Crosstown and others – are being reinvented with kitschy boutiques, hipster lofts and daring restaurants, all dripping with Memphis' wild river-town spirit.

◉ Sights

◉ Downtown

The pedestrian-only stretch of Beale St is a 24-hour carnival zone, where you'll find deep-fried funnel cakes, to-go beer counters, and music, music, music. Although locals don't hang out here much, visitors tend to get a kick out of it.

★**National Civil Rights Museum**   MUSEUM

(Map p382; www.civilrightsmuseum.org; 450 Mulberry St; adult/student & senior/child $15/14/12; ⊘9am-5pm Mon & Wed-Sat, 1-5pm Sun) Housed across the street from the Lorraine Motel, where the Martin Luther King Jr was fatally shot on April 4, 1968, is the gut-wrenching National Civil Rights Museum. Five blocks south of Beale St, this museum's extensive exhibits and detailed timeline chronicle the struggle for African American freedom and equality. Both Dr King's cultural contribution and his assassination serve as prisms for looking at the Civil Rights movement, its precursors and its continuing impact on American life.

The turquoise exterior of the 1950s motel and two interior rooms remain much as they were at the time of King's death.

Memphis Rock 'n' Soul Museum   MUSEUM

(Map p382; www.memphisrocknsoul.org; 191 Beale St; adult/child $12/9; ⊘10am-7pm) The Smithsonian's museum, next to FedEx Forum, examines how African American and white music mingled in the Mississippi Delta to create the modern rock and soul sound.

WC Handy House Museum   MUSEUM

(Map p382; www.wchandymemphis.org; 352 Beale St; adult/child $6/4; ⊘11am-4pm Tue-Sat winter, 10am-5pm summer) On the corner of 4th St, this shotgun shack once belonged to the composer called the 'father of the blues.' He was the first to transpose the 12 bars and later wrote 'Beale Street Blues' in 1916.

◉ North of Downtown

Mud Island   PARK

(www.mudisland.com; 125 N Front St; ⊘10am-5pm Tue-Sun mid-Apr–Oct; 🚼) FREE A small peninsula jutting into the Mississippi, Mud Island is downtown Memphis' best-loved green space. Hop on the **tram** (www.mudisland.com; 125 N Front St; $4; ⊘10am-5pm), which is free with Mississippi River Museum admission, or walk across the bridge to the park, where you can jog and rent bikes.

Slave Haven Underground Railroad Museum/Burkle Estate   MUSEUM

(Map p380; www.slavehavenundergroundrailroadmuseum.org; 826 N 2nd St; adult/child $10/8; ⊘10am-4pm Mon-Sat, to 5pm Jun-Aug) This unimposing clapboard house is thought to have been a way station for runaway slaves on the Underground Railroad, complete with trapdoors, cellar entry and cubby-holes.

◉ East of Downtown

★**Sun Studio**   HISTORIC SITE

(Map p380; ☎800-441-6249; www.sunstudio.com; 706 Union Ave; adult/child $12/free; ⊘10am-6:15pm) This dusty storefront is ground zero for American rock and roll music. Starting in the early 1950s, Sun's Sam Phillips recorded blues artists such as Howlin' Wolf, BB King and Ike Turner, followed by the rockabilly dynasty of Jerry Lee Lewis, Johnny Cash, Roy Orbison and, of course, the King himself (who started here in 1953).

Packed 45-minute guided tours (no children under five allowed; hourly from 10:30am to 5:30pm) through the tiny studio offer a chance to hear original tapes of historic recording sessions. Guides are full of anecdotes; you can pose for photos on the 'X' where Elvis once stood, or buy a CD of the 'Million Dollar Quartet,' Sun's spontaneous 1956 jam session between Elvis, Johnny Cash, Carl Perkins and Jerry Lee Lewis. For music fans, the story here will have you welling up. From here, hop on the studio's free shuttle (hourly, starting at 11:15am), which does a loop between Sun Studio, Beale St and Graceland.

Memphis

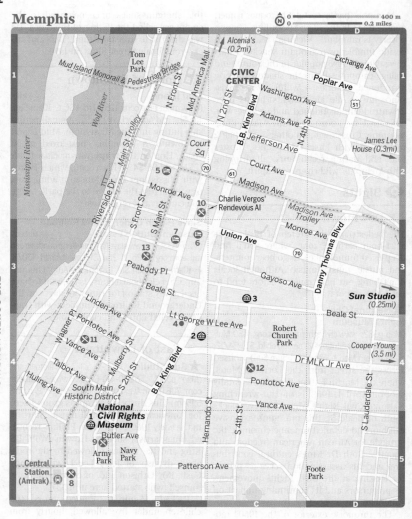

Memphis

◉ Top Sights
1 National Civil Rights Museum A5

◎ Sights
2 Memphis Rock 'n' Soul
   Museum B4
   Peabody Ducks .... (see 6)
3 WC Handy House Museum C3

✦ Activities, Courses & Tours
4 Gibson Beale Street
   Showcase B4

🛌 Sleeping
5 Madison Hotel B2
6 Peabody Hotel B3
7 Talbot Heirs B3

🍴 Eating
8 Arcade A5
9 Central BBQ A5
10 Charlie Vergos' Rendezvous B2
11 Gus's World Famous Fried Chicken A4
12 LUNCHBOXeats C4
13 Majestic Grille B3

Children's Museum of Memphis   MUSEUM
(Map p380; www.cmom.com; 2525 Central Ave;
$15; ⊙9am-5pm, to 6pm summer; ⊛) Gives the
kids a chance to let loose and play in, on and
with exhibits such as an airplane cockpit or
tornado generator.

⊙ South of Downtown

★Graceland   HISTORIC BUILDING
(Map p380; ☑901-332-3322; www.graceland.com;
Elvis Presley Blvd/US 51; house only adult/child
7-12yr $38.75/17, with airplanes $43.75/22, with
Elvis Presley's Memphis $57.50/27, expanded tours
from $62.50/32; ⊙9am-5pm Mon-Sat, to 4pm
Sun, shorter hours & closed Tue Dec; P) If you
only make one stop in Memphis, it should be
here: the sublimely kitschy, gloriously bizarre
home of the King of Rock and Roll. Though
born in Mississippi, Elvis Presley was a true
son of Memphis, raised in the Lauderdale
Courts public housing projects, inspired by
blues clubs on Beale St, and discovered at
Sun Studio. In the spring of 1957, the already-
famous 22-year-old spent $100,000 on a
Colonial-style mansion, named Graceland by
its previous owners.

The King himself had the place, ahem,
redecorated in 1974. With a 15ft couch,
fake waterfall, yellow vinyl walls and green
shag-carpet ceiling, it's a virtual textbook
of ostentatious '70s style. You'll begin
your tour at the brand-spanking new $45
million entertainment complex and visitor center, **Elvis Presley's Memphis** (Map
p380; ☑901-332-3322, 800-238-2000; www.
graceland.com; 3765 Elvis Presley Blvd; adult/
child 7-12 $28.75/$25.90; ⊙9am-5pm Mon-Sat,
to 4pm Sun, shorter hours & closed Tue Dec), on
the other side of Elvis Presley Blvd, which
now houses Presley's car museum and
additional exhibits that run an extra $18.75
for adults. Tack on $5 extra to access two
custom planes (check out the blue and
gold private bathroom on the *Lisa Marie,*
a Convair 880 Jet). Book ahead in the busy
season (June to August and important Elvis
dates) to ensure a prompt tour time. The
basic self-guided mansion tour comes with
an engaging multimedia iPad narration by
John Stamos.

Priscilla Presley (who divorced Elvis in
1973) opened Graceland to tours in 1982,
and now millions come here to pay homage to the King, who died here (in the upstairs bathroom) from heart failure in 1977.

Throngs of fans still weep at his grave, next
to the swimming pool out back. Graceland
is 9 miles south of downtown on US 51, also
called 'Elvis Presley Blvd.' A free shuttle runs
from Sun Studio (p381). Parking costs $10.

★Stax Museum of
American Soul Music   MUSEUM
(Map p380; ☑901-942-7685; www.staxmuseum.
com; 926 E McLemore Ave; adult/child $13/10;
⊙10am-5pm Tue-Sat, 1-5pm Sun) Wanna get
funky? Head directly to Soulsville USA,
where this 17,000-sq-ft museum sits on the
site of the old Stax recording studio. This
venerable spot was soul music's epicenter in
the 1960s, when Otis Redding, Booker T and
the MGs, and Wilson Pickett recorded here.

Dive into soul-music history with photos,
displays of '60s and '70s stage clothing and,
above all, Isaac Hayes' 1972 Superfly Cadillac outfitted with shag-fur and 24-karat-gold
exterior trim.

Full Gospel Tabernacle Church   CHURCH
(787 Hale Rd; ⊙services 11am) On Sunday, put
on your 'smell goods' and head to services
in South Memphis, where soul music legend
turned reverend Al Green presides over a
powerful choir. Visitors are welcome; it's a
fascinating cultural experience.

★ Festivals & Events

Peabody Ducks   PARADE
(Map p382; www.peabodymemphis.com; 149 Union
Ave; ⊙11am & 5pm; ⊛) FREE A tradition dating from the 1930s begins every day at 11am
sharp when five ducks file from the Peabody
Hotel's gilded elevator, waddle across the
red-carpeted lobby, and decamp in the marble lobby fountain for a day of happy splash-
ing. The ducks make the reverse march at
5pm, when they retire to their penthouse accompanied by their red-coated Duckmaster.

Elvis Week   CULTURAL
(☑901-332-3322, 800-238-2000; www.elvisweek.
com; Elvis Presley Blvd, Graceland) The King's
passing and his life are celebrated across
Memphis during Elvis Week in mid-August,
when tens of thousands of shiny-eyed pilgrims descend for nine days of festivities.
This is Weird America. Attend a *Viva Las
Vegas* or *Aloha From Hawaii* screening and
dance party, an International Elvis Tribute
Artist competition, and run an Elvis 5K –
sideburns not included.

Beale Street Music Festival
MUSIC

(www.memphisinmay.org; Tom Lee Park; 3-day passes $95; ⊙ 1st weekend in May) You've heard of Coachella, New Orleans Jazz Fest and Bonnaroo, but Memphis' Beale Street Music Festival gets very little attention, considering it offers one of the country's best line-ups of old-school blues masters, up-and-coming rockers and gloriously past-their-prime pop and hip-hop artists.

☞ Tours

Gibson Beale Street Showcase
TOURS

(Map p382; www.gibson.com/Gibson/Gibson-Tours.aspx; 145 Lt George W Lee Ave; $10; ⊙ hourly tours 11am-4pm Mon-Sat, noon-4pm Sun) Take the fascinating 45-minute tours, which vary throughout the day according to worker presence and noise level, of this enormous place to see master craftspeople transform solid blocks of wood into Les Pauls. Children under five are not allowed in.

Blues City Tours
BUS

(☑ 901-522-9229; www.bluescitytours.com; adult/child from $26/21) A variety of themed bus tours, including an Elvis tour, a Memphis music tour and a hop-on, hop-off option.

⌁ Sleeping

⌁ Downtown

Talbot Heirs
GUESTHOUSE $$

(Map p382; ☑ 901-527-9772; www.talbothouse. com; 99 S 2nd St; ste $160-200; ❄@⌂) Inconspicuously located on the 2nd floor of a busy downtown street, this cheerful guesthouse is one of Memphis' best kept, unique secrets. Spacious suites, all with recently modernized bathrooms, are more like hip studio apartments than hotel rooms, with Asian rugs, funky local artwork and kitchens stocked with (included!) snacks.

Peabody Hotel
HOTEL $$

(Map p382; ☑ 901-529-4000; www.peabody memphis.com; 149 Union Ave; r from $229-365; ❄⌂≋⌘) Memphis' most storied hotel has been catering to a Who's Who of Southern gentry since the 1860s. The current incarnation, a 13-story Italian Renaissance Revival–style building, dates from the 1920s and remains a social center, with a spa, shops, restaurants, an atmospheric lobby bar and 464 guestrooms in soothing turquoise tones.

Madison Hotel
BOUTIQUE HOTEL $$$

(Map p382; ☑ 901-333-1200; www.madison hotelmemphis.com; 79 Madison Ave; r from $279; P❄@⌂≋⌘) If you're looking for a sleek treat, check into these swanky, music-themed boutique sleeps. The rooftop Sky Terrace ($10 for non-guests) is one of the best places in town to watch a sunset, and stylish rooms have nice touches like hardwood entryways, high ceilings and Italian linens.

★ James Lee House
B&B $$$

(Map p380; ☑ 901-359-6750; www.jameslee house.com; 690 Adams Ave; r $250-450; P❄@⌂) This exquisite Victorian mansion sat abandoned for 56 years in the city's historic Victorian Village on the edge of downtown; after $2 million and the application of the owner's keen eye for detail and design, it's one of Memphis' most refined sleeps.

⌁ South of Downtown

Graceland RV Park & Campground
CAMPGROUND $

(Map p380; ☑ 901-396-7125; www.graceland. com/lodging/graceland_campground; 3691 Elvis Presley Blvd; tent sites/cabins from $25/47; P⌂≋) Keep Lisa Marie in business when you camp out or sleep in the no-frills log cabins (with shared bathrooms) next to Graceland.

Days Inn Graceland
MOTEL $

(Map p380; ☑ 901-346-5500; www.daysinn.com; 3839 Elvis Presley Blvd; r from $105; P❄⌂≋) With a guitar-shaped pool, gold records and Elvis memorabilia in the lobby, and neon Cadillacs on the roof, the Days Inn provides a whole lotta Elvis for the price. Guest rooms themselves are clean but nothing special.

Guest House at Graceland
BOUTIQUE HOTEL $$

(Map p380; ☑ 800-238-2000, 901-443-3000; www.guesthousegraceland.com; 3600 Elvis Presley Blvd; r/ste from $159/249; P@⌂≋⌘) Intimate by name only, the Guest House, Graceland's new flagship, is a 450-room hunk of burning hotel. Stylish, slate-gray standard rooms are spacious, with Dream-catcher beds, three-sided display clocks, work station desks and 55in flat-screen TVs. Suites, whose designs were coordinated by Priscilla Presley, all evoke themes from Elvis' life (one features a red-draped TV on the ceiling above the bed!).

✕ Eating

Locals come to blows over which of the city's chopped-pork sandwiches or dry-rubbed ribs are the best. Barbecue joints are scattered across the city, the ugliest exteriors often yield the tastiest goods. Hip young locals head to the South Main Arts District, Midtown's Cooper-Young or Overton Square neighborhoods, all fashionable dining enclaves.

✕ Downtown

★ Central BBQ   BARBECUE $
(Map p382; www.cbqmemphis.com; 147 E Butler Ave; plates $10-25, sandwiches from $5; ⊙11am-9pm Sun-Thu, to 10pm Fri & Sat) The downtown location of this iconic Memphis barbecue joint is the perfect side dish to an afternoon at the National Civil Rights Museum. The transcendent pulled pork – almost always voted the city's best – can and should be doused in a number of sauces so good you'll want to drink them by the pint.

Gus's World Famous
Fried Chicken   FAST FOOD $
(Map p382; www.gusfriedchicken.com; 310 S Front St; plates $6.40-11.65; ⊙11am-9pm Sun-Thu, to 10pm Fri & Sat) Fried-chicken connoisseurs across the globe twitch in their sleep at night, dreaming about the gossamer-light fried chicken at this downtown concrete bunker, with a fun, neon-lit interior and vintage jukebox. On busy nights, waits can top an hour.

LUNCHBOXeats   SOUTHERN US $
(Map p382; www.lunchboxeats.com; 288 S 4th St; sandwiches $8-13; ⊙10:30am-3pm Mon-Sat; 🖕) Classic soul food gets a seriously tasty makeover at this creative sandwich shop, resulting in such ridiculousness as chicken and waffle sandwiches (Belgian waffles serve as the slices of 'bread'); crawfish étouffée sloppy Joe's; a pork butt, onion and mac 'n' cheese club sandwich and more, served on traditional school lunch trays.

Alcenia's   SOUTHERN US $
(Map p380; www.alcenias.com; 317 N Main St; mains $9.55-13; ⊙9am-5pm Tue-Fri, to 3pm Sat) The only thing sweeter than Alcenia's famous 'Ghetto-Aid' (a diabetes-inducing fruit drink) is owner Betty-Joyce 'BJ' Chester-Tamayo – don't be surprised to receive a kiss on the top of the head as soon as you sit down.

JACK LIVES HERE

The irony of the **Jack Daniel's Distillery** (www.jackdaniels.com; 182 Lynchburg Hwy, Lynchburg; tours $13-75; ⊙9am-4:30pm) being in a 'dry county' is lost on no one – local liquor laws dictate that no hard stuff can be sold within county lines. But don't fret – while at least one of its five tours are dry, the serious excursions, ranging from the 90-minute Flight of Jack Daniel's to the three-hour Taste of Lynchburg – which includes a fine meal at **Miss Mary Bobo's Boarding House** (📞931-759-7394; 295 Main St, Lynchburg; ⊙11am-2pm Mon-Sat)– include plenty of whiskey.

Book all tours online in advance. This is the oldest registered distillery in the US; the folks at Jack Daniel's have been dripping whiskey through layers of charcoal then aging it in oak barrels since 1866. It's located off Hwy 55 in tiny Lynchburg.

Arcade   DINER $
(Map p382; www.arcaderestaurant.com; 540 S Main St; mains $7-10; ⊙7am-3pm Sun-Wed, to 11pm Thu-Sat) Step inside this ultra-retro diner, Memphis' oldest, and wander to the Elvis booth, strategically located near the rear exit. The King used to sit here and eat griddle-fried peanut butter and banana sandwiches and would bolt out the door if fan-instigated pandemonium ensued. Crowds still pack in for sublime sweet-potato pancakes – as fluffy, buttery and addictive as advertised.

Charlie Vergos' Rendezvous   BARBECUE $$
(Map p382; 📞901-523-2746; www.hogsfly.com; 52 S 2nd St; mains $8-20; ⊙4:30-10:30pm Tue-Thu, 11am-11pm Fri, from 11:30am Sat) Tucked in its own namesake alleyway off Monroe Ave, this subterranean institution sells an astonishing 5 tons of its exquisite dry-rubbed ribs weekly. The ribs don't come with any sauce, but the pork shoulder does, so try a combo and you'll have plenty of sauce to enjoy.

Majestic Grille   EUROPEAN $$$
(Map p382; 📞901-522-8555; www.majesticgrille.com; 145 S Main St; lunch $9-32, dinner $10-23; ⊙11am-late Mon-Fri, 11am-2:30pm & 4pm-late Sat & Sun; 🖕) Set in an old silent-movie theater near Beale St, with pre-talkie black and whites strobing in the handsome dark-wood

dining room, Majestic serves classic continental fare, from roasted half chickens to seared tuna and grilled pork tenderloin, and four varieties of hand-cut filet mignon.

✕ Midtown

Imagine Vegan Cafe
VEGAN $

(Map p380; www.imaginevegancafe.com; 2158 Young Ave; mains $6-14; ⊙ 11am-9pm; 🛜🍴) 🌿 Vegans and veggies face an uphill battle in Memphis (hell, all over the South…), but this inventive Cooper-Young cafe swims alone in a sea of pulled pork and fried chicken, pulling off all the iconic Southern staples that you'd normally give a pass without even changing their name.

Bar DKDC
INTERNATIONAL $

(Map p380; www.bardkdc.com; 964 S Cooper St; dishes $6-12; ⊙ 5pm-3am) Cheap and flavorful and – at times global – street food is the calling at this ever-evolving Cooper-Young staple. The menu includes muffalatas, Vietnamese *bánh mì* sandwiches, Thai chicken dumplings and so on.

Soul Fish Cafe
SEAFOOD $

(Map p380; www.soulfishcafe.com; 862 S Cooper St; mains $9.50-16; ⊙ 11am-10pm Mon-Sat, to 9pm Sun) A cute cinderblock cafe in the Cooper-Young neighborhood, known for delectable po'boys, fried fish plates and some rather indulgent cakes.

Alchemy
TAPAS $$

(Map p380; ☑ 901-726-4444; www.alchemymemphis.com; 940 S Cooper St; tapas $9-18, mains $17-24; ⊙ 4pm-1am Mon, to 11pm Tue-Thu, 4:30pm-1:30am Fri & Sat, 10:30am-3pm & 4-10pm Sun) A flash spot in the Cooper-Young district, serving tasty Southern tapas like truffle deviled eggs with blue crab remoulade and caviar, shrimp and grits with smoked Gouda and chorizo pan gravy, and scallop bruschetta with gremolata and ponzu vinaigrette.

Sweet Grass
SOUTHERN US $$$

(Map p380; ☑ 901-278-0278; www.sweetgrassmemphis.com; 937 S Cooper St; mains $19-34; ⊙ 5pm-late Tue-Sat, 11am-2pm & 5pm-late Sun; 🛜) Contemporary Lowcountry cuisine (the seafood-heavy cooking of the South Carolina and Georgia coasts) wins raves at this casual Midtown restaurant, split between a more rambunctious bar side called **Next Door** and a more refined bistro side with a more sophisticated menu, a new raw bar and some unforgettable shrimp and grits.

✕ East of Downtown

★ Payne's Bar-B-Q
BARBECUE $

(Map p380; 1762 Lamar Ave; sandwiches $5-9, plates $7.50-11; ⊙ 11am-5pm Tue-Sat) We'd say this converted gas station has the best chopped-pork sandwich in town, but we don't want to have to fight anyone.

Cozy Corner
BARBECUE $

(Map p380; www.cozycornerbbq.com; 735 N Pkwy; plates $6.75-14; ⊙ 11am-9pm Tue-Sat) Slouch in a torn vinyl booth and devour an entire barbecued Cornish game hen ($11.75), the house specialty at this recently renovated cult favorite. Ribs and wings are spectacular too, and the fluffy, silken sweet-potato pie is an A-plus specimen of the classic Southern dessert.

Brother Juniper's
BREAKFAST $

(Map p380; www.brotherjunipers.com; 9514 Walker Ave; dishes $4-13; ⊙ 6:30am-1pm Tue-Fri, 7am-12:30pm Sat, 8am-1pm Sun) This humble breakfast spot started as a chain out of San Francisco's Haight-Ashbury district to feed the homeless; today the Memphis location is the last man standing, and it's pretty much unanimously voted the best breakfast in town. Think huge portions of omelets, pancakes, breakfast burritos, waffles, biscuits and home fries. A must.

Hog & Hominy
SOUTHERN, ITALIAN $$

(☑ 901-207-7396; www.hogandhominy.com; 707 W Brookhaven Circle; pizza $12-16; ⊙ 11am-2pm & 5-10pm Tue-Thu, to late Fri & Sat, 10:30am-10pm Sun; 🛜) The chef-driven, Southern-rooted Italian at this Brookhaven Circle hot spot has grabbed the nation's attention, winning best-new-this and best-new-that since it opened in 2011 from publications ranging from *GQ* to *Food & Wine*. Small plates and brick-oven pizza are the mainstays, along with seasonal cocktails and craft beers.

★ Restaurant Iris
SOUTHERN US $$$

(Map p380; ☑ 901-590-2828; www.restaurantiris.com; 2146 Monroe Ave; mains $27-39; ⊙ 5-10pm Mon-Sat) Chef Kelly English crafts special, avant-garde Southern fusion dishes that delight foodies, hence the James Beard noms. He's got a fried-oyster-stuffed steak, a sublime shrimp and grits and some scrumptious brussels sprouts dressed up with smoky Benton's bacon and sherry, all served in a refined residential home. Next door he has opened **Second Line**, a more affordable New Orleans bistro.

Drinking & Entertainment

Beale St is party central but caters nearly 100% to tourists. The East Memphis neighborhoods of Cooper-Young and Overton Square are where locals go, and offer the best concentration of hip bars and restaurants. Both are about 4 miles east of downtown. Last call is 3am. The city's first distillery, **Old Dominick**, opened in 2017.

Hammer & Ale
BEER HALL

(Map p380; www.hammerandale.com; 921 S Cooper St; pints from $5; ⊙2-9pm Tue-Thu, 11am-10pm Fri & Sat, 1-6pm Sun; 🐾) Hopheads descend on this barnlike Cooper-Young craft-beer bar decked out in light cypress woods throughout. Memphis breweries Wiseacre, High Cotton, Memphis Made and Ghost River are represented among the 24 taps of mostly Southern microbrews. Cash *not* accepted!

★Loflin Yard
BEER GARDEN, COCKTAIL BAR

(Map p380; www.loflinyard.com; 7 W Carolina Ave; cocktails $9-12, mains $9-12; ⊙4-10pm Wed-Thu, 11:30am-midnight Fri, noon-midnight Sat, to 9pm Sun; 🐾) A massive, countrified adult-play oasis in downtown Memphis, this buzzy new hot spot sits on nearly an acre of junkyard-aesthetic beer garden anchored by the old Loflin Safe & Lock Co and wrapping around the trickling canal remains of Gayoso Bayou. Besides the space itself, the seasonal and oak-barrel-aged cocktails steal the show, though mostly smoked offerings (chicken wings, brisket) compete.

★Wiseacre Brewing Co
MICROBREWERY

(Map p380; www.wiseacrebrew.com; 2783 Broad Ave; pints $5-6; ⊙4-10pm Mon-Thu, 1-10pm Fri & Sat; 🐾) Our favorite Memphis taproom is in the warehouse district of Binghampton, 5 miles east of downtown. Sample year-round and seasonal craft brews on its outside deck, which features a wrap-around porch hugging two enormous, near 100-year-old concrete wheat silos.

Young Avenue Deli
LIVE MUSIC

(Map p380; www.youngavenuedeli.com; 2119 Young Ave; ⊙11am-3am; 🐾) This Midtown favorite has food, pool and occasional live music that caters to a laid-back young crowd hyped up on 36 taps of draft craft and another 130 cans and bottles.

★Wild Bill's
BLUES

(Map p380; 1580 Vollintine Ave; ⊙5-9pm Thu, 10pm-3am Fri & Sat) Don't even think of showing up at this gritty, hole-in-the-wall juke joint before midnight. Order a 40oz beer and a basket of wings then sit back to watch some of the greatest blues acts in Memphis from 11pm Friday and Saturday only. Expect some stares from the locals; it's worth it for the kick-ass, ultra-authentic jams.

ℹ Information

Memphis Visitor Center (Map p380; ☑888-633-9099; www.memphistravel.com; 3205 Elvis Presley Blvd; ⊙9am-5pm) City information center near exit for Graceland.

Tennessee State Visitor Center (Map p380; ☑901-543-6757; www.tnvacation.com; 119 N Riverside Dr; ⊙7am-11pm) Brochures for the whole state. Near Mud Island.

ℹ Getting There & Around

Memphis International Airport (MEM; Map p380; ☑901-922-8000; www.flymemphis. com; 2491 Winchester Rd) is around 10.5 miles southeast of Beale St via I-55; taxis to downtown cost between $25 and $30. **Memphis Area Transit Authority** (MATA; Map p380; www.matatransit.com; 444 N Main St; fares $1.75) operates local buses; buses 2 and 4 go to the airport.

MATA's vintage trolleys ($1, every 12 minutes) normally ply Main St and Front St downtown, but were out of service for maintenance at time of research with an expected return by the end of 2017. The **Greyhound Station** (Map p380; ☑901-395-8770; www.greyhound.com; 3033 Airways Blvd) is located at the MATA's Airways Transit Center near Memphis International Airport. The **Amtrak** (www.amtrak.com; 545 S Main St) Central Station is right downtown.

Nashville

Imagine you're an aspiring country singer arriving in Nashville after days of hitchhiking, with nothing but your battered guitar on your back. Blinded by the neon lights of Lower Broadway, you take a deep breath of smoky, beer-perfumed air, feel the boot-stompin' rumble from deep inside the crowded honky-tonks, and think: 'I've made it.'

For country-music fans and wannabe songwriters all over the world, a trip to Nashville is the ultimate pilgrimage. Since the 1920s the city has been attracting musicians, who have taken the country genre from the 'hillbilly music' of the early 20th century to the slick 'Nashville sound' of the 1960s to the punk-tinged alt-country of the 1990s.

Nashville

Jackson St

7th Ave N

6th Ave N

8

Bicentennial Mall

5th Ave N

Herman St

10th Ave N

James Robertson Pkwy

41

Harrison St

12

Megabus

Music City Central

Metropolitan
Transit Authority

7

Gay St

Charlotte Ave

Legislative
Plaza

Deaderick St

70

Union St

10

6th Ave N

Jo Johnson Ave

40

7th Ave N

16th Ave N

8th Ave N

Charlotte Ave

11th Ave N

10th Ave N

15th Ave N

12th Ave N

Patterson St

State St

Church St

16th Ave N

18

Broadway

14

2

9th McGavock St

Music City
Hostel (0.1mi)

17th Ave N

Hayes St

Demonbreun St

10th Ave S

18th Ave N

MIDTOWN

West End Ave

Broadway

McGavock

12th Ave S

11th Ave S

11

25

13

16

Pine St

29

22

Gleaves St

19th Ave S

20

Grilled
Cheeserie (1mi);
Pancake Pantry (1mi);
Parthenon
(1.3mi)

Division St

Division St

THE
GULCH

17

Music Circle N

Music Circle S

3

MUSIC
ROW

5

Hawkins St

12th Ave S

Chet Atkins Pl

18th Ave S

Music Square W

South St

Hawkins St

Old Glory (0.4mi)

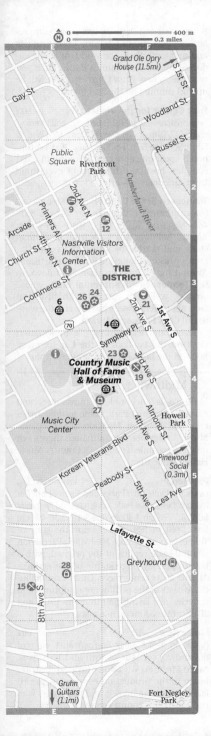

Nashville

◎ Top Sights
1 Country Music Hall of Fame &
   Museum..F4

◎ Sights
2 Frist Center for the Visual Arts...........D4
3 Historic RCA Studio B B7
4 Johnny Cash Museum & Store...........F3
5 Music Row..B7
6 Ryman Auditorium..............................E3
7 Tennessee State Capitol....................D2

⊕ Activities, Courses & Tours
8 NashTrash...C1

🛏 Sleeping
9 21c Museum Hotel E2
10 Hermitage Hotel..................................D3
11 Hutton Hotel A6
12 Nashville Downtown Hostel................F2
13 Thompson Nashville D6
14 Union Station Hotel............................D4

⊗ Eating
15 Arnold's..E6
16 Biscuit Love...D6
17 Catbird Seat....................................... A6
18 Chauhan Ale & Masala House C4
19 Etch...F4
20 Hattie's.. A6

◎ Drinking & Nightlife
21 Acme Feed & Seed...............................F3
22 Barista Parlor......................................D6

⊛ Entertainment
23 Nashville Symphony............................F4
24 Robert's Western World......................E3
25 Station Inn...D6
26 Tootsie's Orchid Lounge E3

🛍 Shopping
27 Hatch Show Print E4
28 Third Man Records E6
29 Two Old Hippies D6

THE SOUTH NASHVILLE

Nashville's many musical attractions range from the Country Music Hall of Fame to the revered Grand Ole Opry to Jack White's niche record label. It also has a lively university community, some excellent down-home grub and some seriously kitschy souvenirs.

◎ Sights

Nashville sits on a rise beside the Cumberland River, with the state capitol situated at the highest point. The city's most engaging museums are downtown, but you'll find cultural attractions aplenty in and around the universities. Further afield, plantations, battlefields and forts draw Civil War enthusiasts and history fans. The city teems with inviting parks. Several are connected by paved greenways. South of downtown, the zoo and science center are nice distractions for the kids.

👁 Downtown

Head to SoBro for the Country Music Hall of Fame and the Johnny Cash Museum. Honky-tonks flank Lower Broadway while Ryman Auditorium and art galleries beckon just north along 5th Ave. North of Broadway you'll also find the main library, Bicentennial Capitol Mall and the Nashville Farmers Market. Two blocks west of 2nd Ave N, Printer's Alley dazzles at night with its colorful lights and fun bars. Riverfront Park hugs the west bank of the Cumberland River. It's connected to Cumberland Park on the other side by the John Seigenthaler Pedestrian Bridge.

★ Country Music Hall of
Fame & Museum   MUSEUM
(www.countrymusichalloffame.com; 222 5th Ave S; adult/child $25/15, with audio tour $30/20, with Studio B 1hr tour $40/30; ⏱9am-5pm) Fresh off $100 million expansion (in 2014) and its 50th anniversary (in 2017), this monumental museum, reflecting the near-biblical importance of country music to Nashville's soul, is a must-see, whether you're a country music fan or not. Gaze at Carl Perkins' blue suede shoes, Elvis' gold Cadillac (actually white) and gold piano (actually gold), and Hank Williams' Western-cut suit with musical note appliqués.

Ryman Auditorium   HISTORIC BUILDING
(www.ryman.com; 116 5th Ave N; self-guided tour adult/child $20/15, backstage tour $30/25; ⏱9am-4pm) The so-called 'Mother Church of Country Music' has hosted a laundry list of performers, from Martha Graham to Elvis, and Katherine Hepburn to Bob Dylan. The soaring brick tabernacle (1892) was built by wealthy riverboat captain Thomas Ryman to house religious revivals, and watching a show from one of its 2362 seats can still be described as a spiritual experience.

Johnny Cash Museum & Store   MUSEUM
(www.johnnycashmuseum.com; 119 3rd Ave S; adult/child $19/15; ⏱9am-7pm) Nashville's museum dedicated to 'The Man in Black'

is smallish but houses the most comprehensive collection of Johnny Cash artifacts and memorabilia in the world, officially endorsed by the Cash family. By the time you read this, a new Patsy Cline museum will be up and running on the 2nd floor.

Frist Center for the Visual Arts   GALLERY
(www.fristcenter.org; 919 Broadway; adult/senior/child $12/9/free; ⏱10am-5:30pm Mon-Wed & Sat, to 9pm Thu & Fri, 1-5:30pm Sun; ⓟ♿) A top-notch post-office-turned-art-museum and complex, hosting exhibitions of everything from American folk art to Picasso.

Tennessee State Capitol   HISTORIC BUILDING
(www.capitol.tn.gov; Charlotte Ave; ⏱tours 8am-4pm Mon-Fri) FREE This 1845–59 Greek Revival building was built from local limestone and marble by slaves and prison inmates working alongside European artisans. Around the back, steep stairs lead down to the **Tennessee Bicentennial Mall**, whose outdoor walls are covered with historical facts about Tennessee's history, and the wonderful daily **Farmers Market**.

Free tours leave from the Information Desk on the 1st floor of the Capitol every hour on the hour between 9am and 3pm.

👁 Midtown

Midtown is anchored by universities and parks. Centennial Park, home to the Parthenon, and Belmont Mansion are top picks. Music Row is here too, although there's not much to see unless you join a Country Music Hall of Fame tour.

Parthenon   HISTORIC BUILDING
(www.nashville.gov/Parks-and-Recreation/Parthenon; Centennial Park; adult/child 4-17yr/senior $6/4/4; ⏱9am-4:30pm Tue-Sat, 12:30-4:30pm Sun) Built in 1897 to celebrate the state of Tennessee's centenary, Nashville's Parthenon is a full-scale replica of the original, with a jaw-droppingly huge statue of the goddess Athena as its centerpiece. Other exhibits include casts of the pediments' sculptures and galleries displaying paintings by 19th- and 20th-century American artists.

Music Row   AREA
(Music Sq West & Music Sq East) Just west of downtown, sections of 16th and 17th Aves, called Music Sq West and Music Sq East, are home to the production companies, record labels, agents, managers and promoters who run Nashville's country-music industry.

THE SOUTH NASHVILLE

Historic RCA Studio B
LANDMARK

(www.studiob.org; 1611 Roy Acuff Pl; tours adult/child $40/30) One of Music Row's most historic studios, this is where Elvis, the Everly Brothers and Dolly Parton all recorded numerous hits, the latter doing a little more than that, once arriving late to a session and accidentally running her car into the building – a scar still visible today! You can tour Historic RCA Studio B by purchasing a Platinum Package from the Country Music Hall of Fame & Museum, which includes a ticket to the museum as well.

◉ Music Valley

Grand Ole Opry House
MUSEUM

(☑615-871-6779; www.opry.com; 2804 Opryland Dr; tours adult/child $26/21, with Ryman Auditorium $36/35; ◷tours 9am-4pm) This unassuming modern brick building seats 4400 for the Grand Ole Opry (p394) on Tuesday, Friday and Saturday from March to November and Wednesday from June to August. Guided backstage tours are offered every 15 minutes daily from October to February; true die-hards can opt for the $125 post-show backstage tour.

Willie Nelson & Friends Museum Showcase
MUSEUM

(www.willienelsongeneralstore.com; 2613 McGavock Pike; adult/child $8/free; ◷8:30am-9pm) 'Outlaw Country' star Willie Nelson sold all his worldly goods to pay off a $16.7-million tax debt in the early 1990s. You can see them at this quirky museum not far from the Grand Ole Opry.

☞ Tours

★ NashTrash
BUS

(☑615-226-7300; www.nashtrash.com; 900 Rosa L Parks Blvd; tours $33-36) The big-haired 'Jugg Sisters' lead a campy frolic through the risqué side of Nashville history, while guests sip BYO booze on the big pink bus. Buy in advance: tours can sell out *months* in advance. Meet the bus at the southeast end of the Nashville Farmers Market.

Joyride
TOURS

(☑615-285-9835; www.joyrideus.com/nashville; complimentary shuttle but tips accepted, tours from $45) Tricked-out golf carts offer complimentary point-to-point shuttle service across Nashville. Rides are free, but drivers make their money on tips. Also offers sightseeing tours, brewery tours and a bar golf crawl.

Tommy's Tours
BUS

(☑615-335-2863; www.tommystours.com; tours $35) Wisecracking local Tommy Garmon leads highly entertaining three-hour tours of country-music sights.

★☆ Festivals & Events

CMA Music Festival
MUSIC

(www.cmafest.com; ◷Jun) This four-day country-music extravaganza draws tens of thousands of country-music fans to town.

Tennessee State Fair
FAIR

(www.tnstatefair.org; ◷Sep) Nine days of racing pigs, mule-pulls and cake bake-offs.

⌸ Sleeping

⌸ Downtown

★ Nashville Downtown Hostel
HOSTEL $

(☑615-497-1208; www.nashvillehostel.com; 177 1st Ave N; dm $32-45, r $100-165; ℗) Well located and up-to-the-minute in style and function. The common space in the basement, with its rather regal exposed stone walls and beamed rafters, is your all-hours mingle den. Dorm rooms are on the 3rd and 4th floors, and have lovely wood floors, exposed timber columns, silver-beamed ceilings and four, six or eight bunks to a room.

21c Museum Hotel
BOUTIQUE HOTEL $$

(☑615-610-6400; www.21cMuseumHotels.com; 221 2nd Ave N; r from $299; ℗❄🛜) Nashville's newest boutique hotel comes loaded down with contemporary art as the South's hippest hotel/museum hybrid chain has settled into a rehabilitated historic Gray & Dudley Building near Printer's Alley. In addition to 124 of its trademark modern, art-forward rooms – seven of which are rooftop terrace suites with Cumberland River views – there's a dedicated spa and six galleries.

★ Union Station Hotel
HOTEL $$$

(☑615-726-1001; www.unionstationhotelnashville.com; 1001 Broadway; r from $300; ℗❄🛜) This soaring Romanesque gray stone castle was Nashville's train station back in the days when rail travel was a grand affair; today it's downtown's most iconic hotel. The vaulted lobby is dressed in peach and gold with inlaid marble floors and a stained-glass ceiling.

Thompson Nashville
BOUTIQUE HOTEL $$$

(☑615-262-6000; www.thompsonhotels.com; 401 11th Ave S; r from $349; ℗@🛜) A bastion of finely polished, mid-century modern cool, the new Thompson Nashville is the Gulch's see-and-be-seen seat of style, whether that be agonizing over which of the Third Man Records–curated vinyl collection to spin in the lobby, or where to sit at the immensely hip, open-air rooftop bar, **LA Jackson**.

Hermitage Hotel   HOTEL $$$
(📞 888-888-9414, 615-244-3121; www.thehermit agehotel.com; 231 6th Ave N; r from $300; 🅿️✳️🛜) Nashville's first million-dollar hotel was a hit with the socialites when it opened in 1910. The beaux-arts lobby feels like a czar's palace, every surface covered in rich tapestries and ornate carvings. The original art-deco men's room, dating from the 1930s, is worth a pop-in, as is the **Capital Grille** restaurant, which sources from its own farm.

🛏 Midtown

Music City Hostel   HOSTEL $
(📞 615-497-1208; www.musiccityhostel.com; 1809 Patterson St; dm $33-46, d $110-126, tr $128-156; 🅿️✳️@🛜) These squat brick bungalows are less than scenic, but Nashville's West End hostel is lively and welcoming, with a common kitchen, an outdoor grill and a fire pit. The crowd is young, international and fun, and many hoppin' West End bars are within walking distance.

Hutton Hotel   BOUTIQUE HOTEL $$
(📞 615-340-9333; www.huttonhotel.com; 1808 West End Ave; r from $279; 🅿️✳️✳️@🛜) 🌿 One of our favorite Nashville boutique hotels riffs on mid-century modern design with bamboo-paneled walls and reclaimed WWI barn wood flooring. Sizable rust- and chocolate-colored rooms are well appointed with electrically controlled marble rain showers, glass wash basins, king beds, ample desk space, wide flat-screens and high-end carpet and linens.

🛏 Music Valley

Gaylord Opryland Resort   RESORT $$
(📞 615-889-1000; www.marriott.com/hotels/ travel/bnago-gaylord-opryland-resort-and-con vention-center; 2800 Opryland Dr; r from $189; 🅿️✳️@🛜🏊) This whopping 2888-room hotel is a universe unto itself, the largest non-casino resort in the USA. Why set foot outdoors when you can ride a flatboat along an artificial river, eat sushi beneath faux waterfalls in an indoor garden, or sip scotch whisky in an antebellum-style mansion, all *inside* the hotel's three massive glass atriums?

🍴 Eating

🍴 Downtown

Arnold's   SOUTHERN US $
(www.arnoldscountrykitchen.com; 605 8th Ave S; meat & 3 $9.74; ⏰ 10:30am-2:45pm Mon-Fri) Grab a tray and line up with college students, garbage collectors and country-music stars at Arnold's, king of the meat-and-three. Slabs of drippy roast beef are the house specialty, along with fried green tomatoes, cornbread two ways, and big gooey wedges of chocolate meringue pie.

★ Biscuit Love   BREAKFAST $
(www.biscuitlove.com; 316 11th Ave S; biscuits $8-10; ⏰ 7am-3pm; 🛜) Championing everything that is wrong about American breakfast, Biscuit Love started life as a food truck in 2012. Its gluttonous gourmet takes on the Southern biscuit and gravy experience took off, allowing it to graduate to this supremely cool brick-and-mortar location in the Gulch.

Chauhan Ale & Masala House   INDIAN $$
(📞 615-242-8426; www.chauhannashville.com; 123 12 Ave N; mains $12-29; ⏰ 11am-2pm & 5pm-10pm Sun-Thu, to 11pm Fri-Sat.; 🛜) Namaste and Nashville collide at celebrity chef Punjabi Maneet Chauhan's Gulch eatery that showcases inventive Indian fusion on a global scale. Typical Desi fare meets Mexican, Canadian, British and American Southern influences – dishes like black-eyed pea tikka burger (spectacular), chicken pakora po'boys and tandoori chicken poutine pair gorgeously with Indian spice-infused microbrews and creative cocktails.

★ Etch   MODERN AMERICAN $$$
(📞 615-522-0685; www.etchrestaurant.com; 303 Demonbreun St; mains $23-39; ⏰ 11am-2pm & 5-10pm Mon-Thu, 11am-2pm & 5-10:30pm Fri, 5-10:30pm Sat; 🛜) Well-known Nashville chef Deb Paquette's Etch serves some of Nashville's most inventive cuisine – comfort food whose flavors and textures have been manipulated into tantalizing combinations that surpass expectations at every bite.

🍴 Midtown

Pancake Pantry   BREAKFAST $
(www.thepancakepantry.com; 1796 21st Ave S; mains $7-10; ⏰ 6am-3pm Mon-Fri, to 4pm Sat & Sun) For 50-plus years, crowds have been

lining up around the block for tall stacks of pancakes done up every which way at this iconic breakfast joint. Honestly, the pancakes underwhelmed us – until we doused them in that cinnamon cream syrup. Paradise found!

Grilled Cheeserie AMERICAN $
(www.grilledcheeserie.com; 2003 Belcourt Ave; sandwiches $7.50-8; ⊙11am-9pm; 🛜) Hurry up and wait for gussied up, gourmet versions of an American classic: the grilled cheese sandwich. It's done up here in versions so immensely satisfying, you'll forget a simpler version ever existed. Go for pimiento mac 'n' cheese and dip it in the creamy tomato soup, a match made in foodie heaven. Follow with one of the outrageous gourmet milkshakes.

★**Hattie B's** SOUTHERN US $
(www.hattieb.com; 112 19th Ave S; quarter/half plates from $8.50/12; ⊙Mon-Thu 11am-10pm, to midnight Fri & Sat, to 4pm Sun) Hattie's may be the hipsterized, social-media savvy yin to Prince's Hot Chicken's off-the-grid yang, but if this isn't Nashville's best cayenne-rubbed 'hot' fried chicken, our name is mud. Perfectly moist, high-quality bird comes devilishly fried to levels that top out at 'Shut the Cluck Up!' hot, and it means business (nose-runnin', head-itchin' 'Damn Hot' was our limit). Get in line.

★**Catbird Seat** INTERNATIONAL $$$
(☑615-810-8200; www.thecatbirdseatrestaurant.com; 1711 Division St, above Patterson House; dinner $115; ⊙from 5:30pm Wed-Sat) For the 22 lucky diners perched around his open kitchen, chef Ryan Poli choreographs an unforgettable 10-course dining experience with his impeccably polished cast and crew. Be prepared to interact with Poli and his sous chefs as they create, cook and share an invigorating line-up of distinctly flavored dishes, which embrace the fresh and local while taking a spin around the world.

❌ East Nashville

I Dream of Weenie HOT DOGS $
(www.facebook.com/IDreamofWeenie; 113 S 11th St; hot dogs $2.75-4.50; ⊙11am-4pm Mon-Thu, to 5pm Fri, 10:30am-5pm Sat & Sun) Quick and easy, this VW bus turned hot-dog stand in Five Points slings beef, turkey or vegetarian tubular products drowned in indulgent toppings (hint: pimiento cheese with chili!).

WORTH A TRIP

FRANKLIN

The town of Franklin (www.visitfranklin.com), 17 miles south of Nashville, has a charming downtown filled with boutiques, antique stores and lively eateries. Here one of the Civil War's bloodiest battles was fought. On November 30, 1864, during the Battle of Franklin, some 37,000 men (20,000 Confederates and 17,000 Union soldiers) fought over a 2-mile stretch on Franklin's outskirts. Nashville's sprawl has turned much of that battlefield into suburbs, but several historic sites spotlight this turbulent conflict.

The rural community of **Arrington**, home to a popular vineyard, is 10 miles southeast of downtown.

★**The Pharmacy** BURGERS, BEER GARDEN $
(www.thepharmacynashville.com; 731 McFerrin Ave; burgers $8.50-11; ⊙11am-10pm Sun-Thu, to 11pm Fri & Sat; 🛜) Prepare to go to war for a table, be it at the welcoming communal table, the bar or the spectacular backyard beer garden. Tattooed staff at this burger bar – constantly voted Nashville's best – sling burgers, sausages and old-school sides (tater tots!), all washed back with specialty beers and old-fashioned hand-mixed sodas.

🍷 **Drinking & Nightlife**

★**Barista Parlor** COFFEE
(www.baristaparlor.com; 610 Magazine St; coffee $4.50-7; ⊙7am-8pm Mon-Fri, from 8am Sat-Sun; 🛜) Nashville's best artisan coffeehouse has enlisted an old stereo shop in the Gulch for its downtown location, but the exquisite espresso – courtesy of an $18,000 hand-built Slayer coffee machine – is every bit as memorable as its original East Nashville location.

★**Old Glory** COCKTAIL BAR
(www.facebook.com/oldglorynashville; 1200 Villa Pl; cocktails $12-13; ⊙4pm-1am Sun-Thu, to 2am Fri & Sat) A towering smokestack rises altar-like in a corner of this steampunk speakeasy. Tucked off an alley inside Edgehill Village, the space was a laundromat boiler room in the 1930s. Today the exposed brick, industrial piping, lofty ceiling and a floating staircase are the backdrop for the city's most stunning cocktail bar – if you can find it!

THE SOUTH NASHVILLE

BONNAROO MUSIC FESTIVAL

Bonnaroo (www.bonnaroo.com; Manchester, TN; ⊙ mid-Jun) is one of America's premier music festivals and the only large-scale 24/7 event in the country. Set on a 700-acre farm, 60 miles southeast of Nashville, Bonnaroo combines camping, comedy, cinema, food, beverage and arts components, which lends it a communal feel. But it's the music that rules, spread out over four blissfully raging days.

Urban Cowboy Public House   COCKTAIL BAR
(www.urbancowboybnb.com/public-house; 103 N 16th St; cocktails $13; ⊙ 4-11pm Sun-Thu, to midnight Fri & Sat; 🛜) Set behind Nashville's hottest B&B (also bearing the Urban Cowboy name), this 2016 newcomer is hotter than the 16ft tall double-sided outdoor fireplace and adjacent firepit, which serve as the centerpiece of an open-air patio that seduces East Nashville's bold and beautiful. The inside lounge, separated by double garage doors, is a stunner as well, rich in hardwoods and Southwestern-themed, Pendleton-blanketed banquettes.

Pinewood Social   BAR
(🗷 615-751-8111; http://pinewoodsocial.com; 33 Peabody St; ⊙ 7am-1am Mon-Fri, 9am-1am Sat & Sun; 🛜) You could spend a weekend at Pinewood Social and never run low on things to do. There are couches to hang at and play board games, a large circular bar with finely crafted cocktails, and a coffee bar from Crema, a Nashville favorite. Soak up the SoCal vibe lounging poolside or playing bocce or ping pong on the outdoor patio. Oh, and there's a bowling alley, too.

Acme Feed & Seed   BAR
(www.theacmenashville.com; 101 Broadway; ⊙ 11am-11pm Mon-Thu, to 2am Fri & Sat, 10am-11pm Sun; 🛜) This ambitious, four-floor takeover of an old 1875 farm supply warehouse has finally given Nashvillians a reason to go downtown even when family is *not* visiting. The 1st floor is devoted to lightning-fast pub grub, with 27 beer taps and live music that's defiantly un-country most nights (Southern rock, indie, roots etc).

⭐ Entertainment

Nashville's opportunities for hearing live music are unparalleled. As well as the big venues, many talented country, folk, bluegrass, Southern-rock and blues performers play smoky honky-tonks, college bars, coffee shops and organic cafes for tips. Cover charges are rare. The singer-songwriter is just as respected as the stadium superstar, so look for well-attended songwriter nights at smaller venues.

★**Station Inn**   LIVE MUSIC
(🗷 615-255-3307; www.stationinn.com; 402 12th Ave S; ⊙ open mike 7pm, live bands 9pm) Sit at one of the small cocktail tables, squeezed together on the worn wood floor in this beer-only dive, illuminated with stage lights and neon signs, and behold the lightning fingers of bluegrass savants. We are talking stand-up bass, banjo, mandolin, fiddle and a modicum of yodeling.

Bluebird Cafe   LIVE MUSIC
(🗷 615-383-1461; www.bluebirdcafe.com; 4104 Hillsboro Rd; cover free-$30) It's in a strip mall in suburban South Nashville, but don't let that fool you: some of the best original singer-songwriters in country music have graced this tiny stage. Steve Earle, Emmylou Harris and the Cowboy Junkies have all played the Bluebird, which is the setting for the popular CMT television series, *Nashville*. Try your luck at Monday open mic nights.

Grand Ole Opry   LIVE MUSIC
(🗷 615-871-6779; www.opry.com; 2804 Opryland Dr; tickets $38-95) Though you'll find a variety of country shows throughout the week, the performance to see is the *Grand Ole Opry*, a lavish tribute to classic Nashville country music, every Tuesday, Friday and Saturday night from February to October. Shows return to the Ryman from November to January.

Tootsie's Orchid Lounge   HONKY-TONK
(🗷 615-726-7937; www.tootsies.net; 422 Broadway; ⊙ 10am-2:30am) The most venerated of the downtown honky-tonks, with music on three levels at any given moment, Tootsie's is a blessed dive oozing boot-stomping, hillbilly, beer-soaked grace. In the 1960s club owner and den mother 'Tootsie' Bess nurtured Willie Nelson, Kris Kristofferson and Waylon Jennings when they were on the rise.

Nashville Symphony   CLASSICAL MUSIC
(🗷 615-687-6400; www.nashvillesymphony.org; 1 Symphony Pl) Hosts maestros, the local symphony and major pop stars from Randy Travis to Smokey Robinson in the shiny new,

yet beautifully antiquated, Schermerhorn Symphony Hall.

Robert's Western World   HONKY-TONK
(www.robertswesternworld.com; 416 Broadway; ⊙11am-2am Mon-Sat, noon-2am Sun) Buy a pair of boots, a beer or a burger at Robert's, a longtime favorite on the strip. Music starts at opening and goes all night; Brazilbilly, the house band, rocks it after 10pm on weekends. All ages are welcome before 6pm; afterward it's strictly 21 and up.

🛍 Shopping

★ Hatch Show Print   ART, SOUVENIRS
(www.hatchshowprint.com; 224 5th Ave S; tours $18; ⊙9:30am-6pm) One of the oldest letterpress print shops in the US, Hatch has been using old-school, hand-cut blocks to print its bright, iconic posters since vaudeville. The company has produced graphic ads and posters for almost every country star and has now graduated to newly expanded digs inside the revamped Country Music Hall of Fame.

★ Third Man Records   MUSIC
(www.thirdmanrecords.com; 623 7th Ave S; ⊙10am-5pm) In a still-industrial slice of downtown you'll find Jack White's boutique record label, shop and novelty lounge, complete with its own lathe and live venue. They sell mostly Third Man recordings on vinyl and CD, collectible T-shirts, stickers, headphones, and Pro-Ject record players. You'll also find White's entire catalog of recordings; and you can record yourself on vinyl ($20).

Two Old Hippies   CLOTHING, LIVE MUSIC
(www.twooldhippies.com; 401 12th Ave S; ⊙10am-7pm Mon-Thu, to 8pm Fri-Sat, 11am-5pm Sun) Only in Nashville would an upscale retro-inspired clothing shop have a bandstand with regular live shows of high quality. And, yes, just like the threads, countrified hippie rock is the rule. The shop itself has fitted T-shirts, excellent belts, made-in-Tennessee jewelry, candles and rocker wear, and also a bounty of stage-worthy shirts and jackets and some incredible acoustic guitars.

Gruhn Guitars   MUSIC
(www.guitars.com; 2120 8th Ave S; ⊙10am-6pm Mon-Sat) This renowned vintage instrument store has expert staff, and at any minute some unassuming virtuoso may just walk in, grab a guitar, mandolin or banjo off the wall and jam.

ℹ Information

Metro Nashville's parks and community centers have free wi-fi, as do many hotels, restaurants and coffee shops.

Nashville Visitors Information Center
(☑615-259-4747; www.visitmusiccity.com; 501 Broadway, Bridgestone Arena; ⊙8am-5:30pm Mon-Sat, 10am-5pm Sun) Pick up free city maps here at the glass tower.

Nashville Visitors Information Center (www.visitmusiccity.com; 150 4th Ave N; ⊙8am-5pm Mon-Fri) Run out of their corporate offices in the Regions Bank Building lobby.

INTERNET RESOURCES

Nashville Public Radio (www.nashvillepublicradio.org) News, music and NPR programming on 90.3 WPLN FM.

Nashville Scene (www.nashvillescene.com) Free alternative weekly with entertainment listings.

Tennessean (www.tennessean.com) Nashville's daily newspaper.

ℹ Getting There & Away

Nashville is located in middle Tennessee at the junction of three interstates: I-40, I-65 and I-24. **Nashville International Airport** (BNA; ☑615-275-1675; www.flynashville.com; One Terminal Dr), 9 miles east of downtown, offers direct flights from 28 US cities along with Mexico and the Bahamas. **Greyhound** (☑615-255-3556; www.greyhound.com; 709 5th Ave S) and **Megabus** (www.megabus.com; 5th Ave N, btwn Gay St & Charlotte Ave) are both located downtown and offer interstate bus services.

Flights, cars and tours can be booked online at www.lonelyplanet.com/bookings.

ℹ Getting Around

TO/FROM THE AIRPORT

It takes about 35 to 45 minutes to get downtown on **MTA** (MTA; www.nashvillemta.org; 400 Charlotte Ave; fares $1.70-2.25) bus 18 ($1.70), which runs from the airport. Express 18 takes about 20 minutes. The airport bus stop is on level 1 in the Ground Transportation area.

The official airport shuttle service is Jarmon Transportation (www.jarmontransportation.com). The rate to downtown or West End hotels is $20 and $25, respectively. It can be found on the Ground Transportation/level 1. A list of alternative shuttle companies is provided on the airport website.

Taxis charge a flat rate of $25 for a ride to downtown or Opryland. A taxi to Vanderbilt/West End costs about $27. A trip to Franklin runs $55 to $60.

BUS

The MTA (www.nashvillemta.org) operates city bus services, based downtown at **Music City Central** (400 Charlotte Ave), including the free Music City Circuit, whose three routes hit the majority of Nashville attractions. Express buses go to Music Valley.

BICYCLE

Nashville's public bike-share scheme, Nashville B-Cycle (https://nashville.bcycle.com), offers more than 30 stations throughout the city center. Your first hour is free; after that your credit card will be charged $1.50 per half-hour. Daily, weekly and monthly plans are also available. Maps can be found at the Airport Information Center in baggage claim or online.

Eastern Tennessee

Dolly Parton, East Tennessee's most famous native, loves her home region so much she has made a successful career out of singing about girls who leave the honeysuckle-scented embrace of the Smoky Mountains for the false glitter of the city. They're always sorry. Largely a rural region of small towns, rolling hills and river valleys, the eastern third of the state has friendly folks, hearty country food and pastoral charm. The lush, heather-tinted Great Smoky Mountains are great for hiking, camping and rafting, while the region's two main urban areas, Knoxville and Chattanooga, are easygoing riverside cities with lively student populations, great restaurants and fun craft breweries.

Chattanooga

Today Chattanooga is one of the country's greenest cities, with miles of well-used waterfront trails, electric buses and pedestrian bridges crossing the Tennessee River – all of which makes it hard to credit its reputation in the 1960s as the dirtiest city in America. With world-class rock-climbing, hiking, biking and water-sports opportunities, it's one of the South's best cities for outdoorsy types. And it's gorgeous now, too: just check out those views from the Bluff View Art District!

The city was a major railway hub throughout the 19th and 20th centuries, hence the 'Chattanooga Choo-Choo,' which was originally a reference to the Cincinnati Southern Railroad's passenger service from Cincinnati to Chattanooga and later the title of a 1941 Glen Miller tune. The eminently walkable downtown is an increasingly gentrified maze of historic stone and brick buildings and some tasty gourmet kitchens and craft breweries and distilleries. There's a lot to love about the 'Noog.

◉ Sights & Activities

Songbirds MUSEUM
(www.songbirdsguitars.com; 35 Station St, Chattanooga Choo Choo Hotel; adult/student $15.95/12.95, all access $38.95/35.95; ⊙10am-6pm Mon-Wed, to 8pm Thu-Sat, noon-6pm Sun) Opened in 2017, this astonishing guitar collection – the world's largest assemblage of vintage and rare guitars – is Chattanooga's newest world-class attraction. Over 500 guitars, many arranged in timeline fashion from the 1950 Fender Broadcasters (the first mass-produced solid-body electric guitar) to the 1970s, grace this small space, including rock star axes from Chuck Berry, BB King, Bo Diddly, Roy Orbison and Robbie Krieger of the Doors, among others.

Hunter Museum of American Art GALLERY
(www.huntermuseum.org; 10 Bluff View; adult/child $10/free; ⊙10am-5pm Mon, Tue, Fri & Sat, to 8pm Thu, noon-5pm Wed & Sun) Set high on the river bluffs, this striking edifice of melted steel and glass is easily the most singular architectural achievement in Tennessee. Oh, and its 19th- and 20th-century art collection is fantastic. Permanent exhibits are free the first Thursday of the month between 4pm and 8pm (special exhibits cost $5).

Coolidge Park PARK
(150 River St) A good place to start a riverfront stroll. There's a carousel, well-used playing fields and a 50ft climbing wall attached to one of the columns supporting the Walnut Street Bridge, the world's largest pedestrian bridge.

Lookout Mountain OUTDOORS
(☏800-825-8366; www.lookoutmountain.com; 827 East Brow Rd; adult/child $50/27; ⊙hours vary; ♿) Some of Chattanooga's oldest and best-loved attractions are 6 miles outside the city. Admission price includes the **Incline Railway**, which chugs up a steep incline to the top of the mountain; the world's longest underground waterfall, **Ruby Falls**; and **Rock City**, a garden with a dramatic clifftop overlook.

🛏 Sleeping & Eating

★Crash Pad HOSTEL $
(☏423-648-8393; www.crashpadchattanooga. com; 29 Johnson St; dm/d/tr $35/85/110; P❄@🛜) 🍽 The South's best hostel, run

by climbers, is a sustainable den of coolness in Southside, the 'Noog's hippest downtown neighborhood. Co-ed dorms overachieve: built-in lights, power outlets, fans and privacy curtains for each bed. Privates feature exposed concrete and bedside tables built into the bedframes. Access throughout is via hi-tech fobs, and linens, padlocks and breakfast supplies are all included.

Dwell Hotel   BOUTIQUE HOTEL **$$**
(☑ 423-267-7866; www.thedwellhotel.com; 120 E 10th St; r $225-325; P ✳ 🛜) It's very hard to improve on excellent, but the former Stone Fort Inn – now the Dwell – has done just that. A new hands-on owner has completely flipped this historic downtown hotel into a design-forward, mid-century modern whirlwind of retro style. The 16 revamped rooms feature painstakingly curated vintage furniture, soothing earth-tone color schemes, rain-style showers *and* bathtubs.

Flying Squirrel   MODERN AMERICAN **$**
(www.flyingsquirrelbar.com; 55 Johnson St; dishes $6-18; ⏰ 5pm-1am Tue-Thu, to 2am Fri & Sat, 10:30am-3pm Sun; 🛜) A neighbor to the South's coolest hostel (same owners), Flying Squirrel is at its heart a very cool bar (21 and over only, except for Sunday brunch), but its locally sourced small-plate takes on fusion comfort food make for mighty fine pub grub.

St John's Meeting Place   AMERICAN **$$**
(☑ 423-266-4571; www.stjohnsmeetingplace. com; 1274 Market St; mains $12-29; ⏰ 5-9:30pm Mon-Thu, to 10pm Fri & Sat) The culinary anchor of Chattanooga's Southside is widely considered the city's best night out. It's Johnny Cash black (black granite floor, black-glass chandeliers, black banquettes), lending an unorthodox but mod elegance for a foodie habitat. The farm-to-table cuisine features lamb pastrami, pork tenderloin, and nacho burgers with chorizo and pickled jalapeño.

❶ Information

Visitor Center (☑ 800-322-3344; www. chattanoogafun.com; 215 Broad St; ⏰ 10am-5pm) Easy to miss, located in an outdoor public breezeway.

❶ Getting There & Around

Chattanooga's modest **airport** (CHA; ☑ 423-855-2202; www.chattairport.com; 1001 Airport Rd) is just east of the city. The **Greyhound** **station** (☑ 423-892-1277; www.greyhound.com; 960 Airport Rd) is just down the road.

For access to most downtown sites, ride the free **Downtown Electric Shuttle** (www.gocarta. org) that plies the center and the North Shore. The visitor center has a route map.

Bike Chattanooga (www.bikechattanooga. com) is Chattanooga's city-sponsored, bicycle-sharing program. Bikes are lined and locked up at 33 stations throughout the city and riders can purchase access passes (starting at $8 for 24 hours) via credit card at any of the station kiosks. Rides under 60 minutes are free.

Knoxville

Once known as the 'underwear capital of the world' for its numerous textile mills, Knoxville is home to the University of Tennessee and its rabid college-football fan base. On college game days, the whole town is painted orange as thousands of fans pack Neyland Stadium to watch the beloved Volunteers take to the gridiron. But there's more to Knoxville than the pigskin. No longer content to play second fiddle to nearby Chattanooga and Asheville, the city is experiencing a mojo recalibration and is becoming an increasingly prominent destination for outdoor, gastronomy and craft-beer enthusiasts, as well as an alternative base for Great Smoky Mountains National Park. At just 29 miles from Sugarlands Visitors Center, a day trip is easy, and Knoxville is a far more enticing spot to eat and drink than other cities near the park.

⊙ Sights & Activities

Women's Basketball Hall of Fame   MUSEUM
(www.wbhof.com; 700 Hall of Fame Dr; adult/child $7.95/5.95; ⏰ 10am-5pm Mon-Sat summer, 11am-5pm Tue-Fri, 10am-5pm Sat winter; 🚻) You can't miss the massive orange basketball that marks the Women's Basketball Hall of Fame, a nifty look at the sport from the time when women were forced to play in full-length dresses.

Ijams Nature Center   OUTDOORS
(☑ 865-577-4717; www.ijams.org; 2915 Island Home Ave; ⏰ 9am-5pm Mon-Sat, 11am-5pm Sun) A one-stop shop for getting out and about in nature in Knoxville. Pick up trail maps for the city's Urban Wilderness, get a wealth of information on all of the city's outdoor activities and rent outdoor equipment for getting on the water at Mead's Quarry and elsewhere.

🛏 Sleeping & Eating

⭐ Oliver Hotel   BOUTIQUE HOTEL $$
(📞 865-521-0050; www.theoliverhotel.com; 407 Union Ave; r $160-360; 🅿 ❄ @ 🛜) Hipster receptionists welcome you to Knoxville's only boutique hotel, boasting 28 modern, stylish rooms with fun subway-tiled showers (with rain-style showerheads), luxe linens, plush throwback furniture and carpets, and gorgeous hand-crafted coffee tables. The **Peter Kern Library bar** draws craft cocktail enthusiasts by night. The new restaurant, **Oliver Royale**, is highly recommended (mains $15 to $46).

⭐ Oli Bea   BREAKFAST $
(www.olibea.net; 119 S Central St; mains $7-12; ⊙ 7am-1pm Mon-Fri, 8am-2pm Sat; 🛜) It's worth sleeping in Knoxville just to wake up to the rich, Mexicanized farm-to-table Southern breakfast fare at this morning stop in the Old City. You'll find gussied-up standards (country ham, sage sausage, organic chicken), a sinfully good grilled cheese with buttermilk cheddar, a sunny duck egg and collard greens, full-stop fabulous pork confit *carnitas* tostadas and *chilaquiles*.

ℹ Information

Visitor Center (Visit Knoxville; 📞 800-727-8045; www.visitknoxville.com; 301 S Gay St; ⊙ 8:30am-5pm Mon-Fri, 9am-5pm Sat, noon-4pm Sun) Besides tourism info, the visitor center also welcomes bands from across the Americana genre for WDVX's **Blue Plate Special**, a free concert series at noon Monday to Saturday.

ℹ Getting There & Around

Knoxville's **McGhee Tyson Airport** (📞 865-342-3000; www.flyknoxville.com; 2055 Alcoa Hwy, Alcoa) is 15 miles south of town and is served by 20 or so nonstop domestic flights. The **Greyhound** (📞 865-524-0369; www.greyhound.com; 100 E Magnolia Ave) bus station is only about 1 mile north of downtown, making it a convenient option for ground travelers.

Gatlinburg

Wildly kitschy and family-friendly Gatlinburg hunkers at the entrance of the Great Smoky Mountains National Park, waiting to stun hikers with the scent of fudge, cotton candy and pancakes, and various odd museums and campy attractions. It's a wild ride of all that is good and bad about the USA at the same time, wrapped up in a gaudy explosion of magic shows and moonshine. Say what you will about the town, but you can never say Gatlinburg ain't a good time.

With the exception of the Gatlinburg Sky Lift, the town itself emerged from the devastating 2016 Great Smoky Mountains wildfires largely unscathed, ensuring the good times kept on rolling, but the loss of life and general destruction (14 deaths, 17,904 acres burned inside and outside the national park, and more than 2400 buildings destroyed, all down to arson) means Gatlinburg remains in mourning. Luckily, there's a shot of 'shine for that!

◉ Sights & Activities

Dollywood   AMUSEMENT PARK
(📞 865-428-9488; www.dollywood.com; 2700 Dollywood Parks Blvd, Pigeon Forge; adult/child $67/54; ⊙ Apr-Dec) Dollywood is a self-created ode to the patron saint of East Tennessee, the big-haired, bigger-bosomed country singer Dolly Parton. The park features Appalachian-themed rides and attractions, a water park, the DreamMore Resort and more. Find it looming above the town of Pigeon Forge, a secondhand Vegas-like mess drunk on American kitsch 9 miles north of Gatlinburg.

Gatlinburg Sky Lift   CABLE CAR
(📞 865-436-4307; www.gatlinburgskylift.com; 765 Parkway; adult/child $16.50/13; ⊙ 9am-11pm Jun-Aug, hours vary rest of year) This repurposed ski-resort chairlift whisks you high over the Smokies, providing stellar views. After being damaged in the 2016 Great Smoky Mountains wildfires, it was completely refurbished and reopened in summer 2017. Visitors can expect a smoother ride and lifts that seat three instead of two.

⭐ Ole Smoky Moonshine Holler   DISTILLERY
(www.olesmokymoonshine.com; 903 Parkway; ⊙ 10am-10pm) At first glance, this stone-and-wood moonshine distillery, Tennessee's first licensed moonshine maker, appears to have a Disney flair, but it's the real deal. Gathering around the hysterical bartenders, drinking the 13 flavors of free hooch and taking in all of their colorful commentary is Gatlinburg's best time.

🛏 Sleeping & Eating

Rocky Waters Motor Inn   MOTEL $
(📞 865-436-7861; www.rockywatersmotorinn.com; 333 Parkway; d $49-169; 🅿 ❄ 🛜) This pleasantly retro motel has clean, comfy rooms with new hardwood flooring and big walk-in

showers and is perched above the river. It's walking distance from downtown, but at a serene remove from the noise and lights.

Buckhorn Inn INN $$
(☑865-436-4668; www.buckhorninn.com; 2140 Tudor Mountain Rd; d $125-205, 2-bedroom guesthouse from $240; P❋@🛜) A few minutes' drive and several light years away from the kitsch and crowds of downtown Gatlinburg, the tranquil Buckhorn has nine elegant rooms, seven private cottages and four guesthouses on a property that is a well-manicured nature haven. If the unbroken views of Mt LeConte don't relax you enough, have a wander through the fieldstone meditation labyrinth.

Three Jimmys AMERICAN $
(www.threejimmys.com; 1359 East Pkwy; mains $9-28; ☺11am-10pm; 🛜) Escape the tourist hordes on the main drag and grab a bite at this local's favorite with friendly waitstaff ('Here's your menu, baby...') and a long list of everything: barbecue, turkey Reubens, burgers, champagne chicken, steaks, a great spinach salad and so on.

ℹ Information

Gatlinburg Welcome Center (☑865-277-8947; www.gatlinburg.com; 1011 Banner Rd; ☺8:30am-5:30pm) Official information and maps – including a handy $1 waterfalls map – on both Gatlinburg and Great Smoky Mountains National Park.

ℹ Getting There & Around

The vast majority of visitors arrive in Gatlinburg by car. The nearest airport is Knoxville's **McGhee Tyson Airport**, 41 miles away, and there's no regular intercity bus service.

Traffic and parking are serious issues in Gatlinburg. The Gatlinburg Trolley (www.gatlinburgtrolley.org) serves downtown, and the trolley's tan line ($2) goes into the park between July and October, with stops at Sugarlands Visitor Center, Laurel Falls and Elkmont Campground. Parking lots around town generally charge $10 for the day, but Ole Smoky Moonshine Holler charges just $5.

KENTUCKY

With an economy based on bourbon, horse racing and tobacco, you might think Kentucky would rival Las Vegas as Sin Central. Well, yes and no. For every whiskey-soaked Louisville bar there's a dry county where you can't get anything stronger than ginger ale.

For every racetrack there's a church. Kentucky is made of these juxtapositions. A geographic and cultural crossroads, the state combines the friendliness of the South, the rural frontier history of the West, the industry of the North and the aristocratic charm of the East. Every corner is easy on the eye, but there are few sights more heartbreakingly beautiful than the rolling limestone hills of horse country, where thoroughbred breeding is a multimillion-dollar industry. In spring the pastures bloom with tiny azure buds, earning it the moniker 'Bluegrass State.'

ℹ Information

Kentucky State Parks (☑502-564-2172; www.parks.ky.gov) Offers info on hiking, caving, fishing, camping and more in Kentucky's 52 state parks. So-called 'Resort Parks' have lodges. 'Recreation Parks' are for roughin' it.
Kentucky Travel (☑800-225-8747; www.kentuckytourism.com) Sends out a detailed booklet on the state's attractions.

Louisville

Best known as the home of the Kentucky Derby, Louisville (or Luhvul, as the locals say) is handsome, underrated and undeniably cool. A major Ohio River shipping center during the days of westward expansion, Kentucky's largest city is on the up, with hip bars, superb farm-to-table restaurants, and an engaging, young and increasingly progressive population. It's a fun place to spend a few days, checking out the museums, wandering the old neighborhoods and sipping some bourbon.

◉ Sights & Activities

★**Churchill Downs** LANDMARK
(☑502-636-4400; www.churchilldowns.com; 700 Central Ave) On the first Saturday in May, a who's who of upper-crust America puts on their seersucker suits and most flamboyant hats and descend for the 'greatest two minutes in sports': the Kentucky Derby, the longest-running continuous sporting event in North America.

Kentucky Derby Museum MUSEUM
(www.derbymuseum.org; Gate 1, Central Ave; adult/senior/child $15/14/8; ☺8am-5pm Mon-Sat, 11am-5pm Sun Mar 15-Nov 30, from 9am Mon-Sat, 11am-5pm Sun Dec-Mar 14) On the racetrack grounds, the museum has exhibits on derby history,

including a peek into the life of jockeys and a roundup of the most illustrious horses. Highlights include a 360-degree HD film about the race, the 30-minute walking tour of the grandstands (which includes some engaging yarns) and mint juleps in the museum cafe.

The 90-minute 'Inside the Gates Tour' ($11) leads you through the jockey's quarters and posh VIP seating areas known as Millionaire's Row.

Muhammad Ali Center   MUSEUM
(www.alicenter.org; 144 N 6th St; adult/senior/child $12/11/7; ☺9:30am-5pm Tue-Sat, noon-5pm Sun) 🍴 A love offering to the city from its most famous native, and an absolute must-see. For a black man from the South during his era, to rejoice in his own greatness and beauty was revolutionary and inspiring to behold – and this museum captures it all.

Louisville Slugger
Museum & Factory   MUSEUM
(www.sluggermuseum.org; 800 W Main St; adult/senior/child $14/13/8; ☺9am-5pm Mon-Sat, 11am-5pm Sun, to 6pm Jul; ♿) Look for the 120ft baseball bat leaning against the museum. Hillerich & Bradsby Co have been making the famous Louisville Slugger here since 1884. Admission includes a plant tour and a hall of baseball memorabilia, including Babe Ruth's bat and a free mini slugger.

Frazier History Museum   MUSEUM
(www.fraziermuseum.org; 829 W Main St; adult/senior/child $12/10/8; ☺9am-5pm Mon-Sat, noon-5pm Sun) Surprisingly ambitious for a mid-sized city, this state-of-the-art museum covers 1000 years of history with grisly battle dioramas and costumed interpreters demonstrating swordplay and staging mock debates.

Kentucky Science Center   MUSEUM
(☏502-561-6100; www.kysciencecenter.org; 727 W Main St; adult/child $13/11; ☺9:30am-5:30pm Sun-Thu, to 9pm Fri & Sat; ♿) Set in a historic building on Main St there are three floors of exhibits that illuminate biology, physiology, physics, computing and more for families (kids love it). For an extra $8 to $10 you can catch a film in the IMAX-like theater.

✶ Festivals & Events

Kentucky Derby Festival   SPORTS
(www.kdf.org; kickoff event tickets from $30) The Kentucky Derby Festival, which includes a balloon race, a marathon, a steamboat race and the largest fireworks display in North America, starts two weeks before the big event.

First Friday Trolley Hop   ART
(www.firstfridayhop.com; Main & Market Sts; ☺5-11pm, 1st Fri of month) The number of incredible kitchens multiplies every year, especially in the engaging NuLu area, where there are numerous galleries and boutiques to explore. Check them out on the First Friday Trolley Hop.

⎙ Tours

Waverly Hills Sanatorium   TOURS
(☏502-933-2142; www.therealwaverlyhills.com; 4400 Paralee Lane; 2/6/8hr tours $25/75/100; ☺Fri & Sat Mar-Aug) Towering over Louisville like a mad king's castle, the abandoned Waverly Hills Sanatorium once housed victims of an early-20th-century tuberculosis epidemic. When patients died, workers dumped their bodies down a chute into the basement. No wonder the place is said to be one of America's most haunted buildings. Search for spooks with a nighttime ghost-hunting tour; the genuinely fearless can even spend the night! Many claim it's the scariest place they've ever been.

Big Four Bridge   WALKING, CYCLING
(www.louisvillewaterfront.com; East River Rd; ☺24hr) Built between 1888 and 1895, the Big Four Bridge, which spans the Ohio River and reaches the Indiana shores, has been closed to vehicular traffic since 1969 but was reopened in 2013 as a pedestrian and cycling path; excellent city and river views throughout.

🛌 Sleeping

Rocking Horse B&B   B&B $$
(☏888-467-7322, 502-583-0408; www.rockinghorse-bb.com; 1022 S 3rd St; r $125-250; P❋✿) Near the University of Louisville on a stretch of 3rd St once known as Millionaire's Row, this 1888 Richardsonian Romanesque mansion is chock-full of astounding historic detail. The six guest rooms are decorated with Victorian antiques and splendid original stained glass. Guests can eat their two-course breakfast in the English country garden or sip complimentary port in the parlor.

★ 21c Museum Hotel   HOTEL $$$
(☏502-217-6300; www.21chotel.com; 700 W Main St; r from $199; P❋✿) This contemporary art museum–hotel features edgy design details: video screens project your distorted

image and falling language on the wall as you wait for the elevator; water-blurred, see-through glass urinal walls line the men's rooms. Rooms, though not as interesting as the five contemporary art galleries-common areas, have iPod docks and mint julep kits.

Brown Hotel HOTEL **$$$**
(☑502-583-1234; www.brownhotel.com; 335 West Broadway; r $200-600; P⊖❋🤶) Opera stars, queens and prime ministers have trod the marble floors of this storied downtown hotel, now restored to all its 1920s glamor with 294 comfy rooms and an impressive lobby bourbon bar under original English Renaissance gilded ceilings.

✖ Eating

Gralehaus MODERN AMERICAN **$**
(www.gralehaus.com; 1001 Baxter Ave; mains $6-13; ⊙8am-4pm Sun-Tue, to 10pm Wed-Sat; 🤶) There's breakfast all day at this small eatery housed in a historic early-20th-century home and you should indeed indulge in its chef-centric takes on traditional Southern comforts at all hours (think locally sourced biscuits and duck gravy, lamb and grits). Serious signature coffee drinks excel as well.

The Post DELI **$**
(www.thepostlouisville.com; 1045 Goss Ave; mains $3-13; ⊙11am-midnight Mon-Wed, to 2am Thu-Fri, noon-2am Sat, noon-midnight Sun; 🤶) In gentrified Germantown, New York–style pizza by the slice, sub sandwiches and great spaces (sunny patio out the front comfy bar in the back with 16 taps) evoke a pricier atmosphere and cooler vibe than your bill suggests.

Silver Dollar CALIFORNIAN, SOUTHERN **$$**
(☑502-259-9540; www.whiskeybythedrink.com; 1761 Frankfort Ave; mains $9-27, brunch $9-14; ⊙5pm-2am Mon-Fri, from 10am Sat & Sun; 🤶) Gastronomically noncommittal – we'll call the cuisine California-inspired New Southern – but unrepentantly bourbon obsessed, the Silver Dollar does your head in. Feast on chicken and waffles, Beer Can Hen (roasted game hen served on an Old Milwaukee beer can) or fantastic *chilaquiles;* chase it with one of a 'poop ton' of bourbons.

Garage Bar PUB FOOD **$$**
(www.garageonmarket.com; 700 E Market St; dishes $9-18; ⊙5-10pm Mon-Thu, 11am-10pm Fri-Sun; 🤶) The best thing to do on a warm afternoon in Louisville is to make your way to this uber-hip converted NuLu service station (accented by two kissing Camaros) and order a round of basil gimlets and the ham platter (a tasting of four regionally cured hams served with fresh bread and preserves; $26).

★ Butchertown
Grocery MODERN AMERICAN **$$$**
(☑502-742-8315; www.butchertowngrocery.com; 1076 E Washington St; mains $15-25; ⊙restaurant 11am-10pm Wed-Fri, from 11am Sat & Sun, bar 6pm-midnight Wed & Sun, to 2am Thu-Sat; 🤶) Louisville's hottest new restaurant rides a delicate line between raw and refined, dishing out European-inspired, American-anchored comfort cuisine in an unassuming 19th-century red-brick edifice where weathered wood ceilings preside over marble tables and B&W mosaic flooring.

★ Proof MODERN AMERICAN **$$$**
(☑502-217-6360; www.proofonmain.com; 702 W Main St; mains $13-38; ⊙7-10am, 11am-2pm & 5:30-10pm Mon-Thu, to 11pm Fri, 7am-3pm & 5:30-11pm Sat, to 1pm Sun; 🤶) Arguably Louisville's best restaurant. The cocktails ($10 or $12) are incredible, the wine and bourbon 'library' (they're known to pour from exclusive and rare barrels of Woodford Reserve and Van Winkle) is long and satisfying, and startling dishes range from gourmet grilled cheese to a deliciously messy bison burger or a high-minded take on 'hot' fried chicken.

♟ Drinking & Nightlife

★ Holy Grale PUB
(http://holygralelouisville.com; 1034 Bardstown Rd; drafts from $6; ⊙4pm-1am Mon-Thu, to 2am Fri & Sat, noon-midnight Sun; 🤶) One of Louisville's best bars is housed in an old church, with a menu of funked-up pub grub (gourmet Belgian *frites,* green curry mussels, short rib poutine; mains $6 to $14) and a buzzworthy beer list dependent on rarer German, Danish, Belgian and Japanese brews on tap. The most intense beers (up to 13% alcohol) can be found in the choir loft. Hallelujah!

★ Mr Lee's COCKTAIL BAR
(www.mrleeslounge.com; 935 Goss Ave; cocktails $10-12; ⊙2pm-midnight Mon-Thu, to 2am Fri & Sat, to 11pm Sun) Germantown's craft cocktail anchor is this new, satisfyingly retro bar that serves a small but serious list of pre-Prohibition-era tipples. The semi-circular red leather bar gives way to a long mid-century-modern–styled, candlelit line of intimate tables and banquettes that are perfect for settling in for a boozy evening. It's even carpeted!

Monnik Beer Company MICROBREWERY
(www.monnikbeer.com; 1036 E Burnett Ave; beers from $4; ⊙11am-midnight Tue-Thu, to 1am Fri & Sat, to 10pm Sun; 🛜) Our favorite Louisville brewery is in up-and-coming Schnitzelburg. There are 20 taps – the IPA stands out – in this restrained hipster environment where the beer isn't the only thing that's fabulous. The beer cheese with spent grain bread is so good you should need a prescription for it; and the seared grass-fed burgers are perfect. Bottoms up!

ℹ️ Information

Visitor Center (☑502-379-6109; www.goto louisville.com; 301 S 4th Ave; ⊙10am-5pm Mon-Sat, noon-5pm Sun) Stuffed with brochures and helpful staff.

ℹ️ Getting There & Around

Louisville's International Airport (p404) is 5 miles south of town on I-65. Get there by cab for a flat rate of $19.55 or local bus 2. The **Greyhound** (☑800-231-2222; www.greyhound. com; 720 W Muhammad Ali Blvd) station is just west of downtown.

TARC (www.ridetarc.org) runs local buses ($1.75) from the historic **Union Station depot** (☑502-585-1234; 1000 W Broadway), including its free ZeroBus, an electric bus fleet that circles Main, Market and 4th Sts, taking in most of the city's attractions and coolest restaurants. Buses do not require exact change, but there is no mechanism for giving change back.

Bluegrass Country

Drive through northeast Kentucky's Bluegrass Country on a sunny day and glimpse horses grazing in the brilliant-green hills dotted with ponds, poplar trees and handsome estate houses. These once-wild woodlands and meadows have been a center of horse breeding for almost 250 years. The region's natural limestone deposits – you'll see limestone bluffs rise majestic from out of nowhere – are said to produce especially nutritious grass.

Lexington

Even the prison looks like a country club in Lexington, home of million-dollar houses and multimillion-dollar horses. Once the wealthiest and most cultured city west of the Allegheny Mountains, it was called 'the Athens of the West.' It's home to the University of Kentucky and is the heart of the thoroughbred industry. The small downtown has some pretty Victorian neighborhoods, but most of the attractions are in the countryside.

⊙ Sights

Kentucky Horse Park MUSEUM, PARK
(www.kyhorsepark.com; 4089 Iron Works Pkwy; summer adult/child $20/10, winter adult/child $12/6, horseback riding Mar-Oct $25; ⊙9am-5pm Mar 15-Nov 5, 9am-5pm Wed-Sun Nov 6-Mar 14; ♿) An educational theme park and equestrian sports center sits on 1200 acres just north of Lexington. Horses representing 50 different breeds live in the park and participate in special live shows.

Ashland HISTORIC BUILDING
(www.henryclay.org; 120 Sycamore Rd; adult/child $12/6; ⊙10am-4pm Tue-Sat Mar-Dec, 1-4pm Sun Apr-Nov) Just 1.5 miles east of downtown, Ashland is part historic home of one of Kentucky's favorite sons and part public park; it was the Italianate estate of famed statesman and great compromiser Henry Clay (1777–1852).

Lexington Art League at Loudoun House GALLERY
(www.lexingtonartleague.org; 209 Castlewood Dr; ⊙10am-4pm Tue-Thu, 10am-8pm Fri, 1-4pm Sat & Sun) Art and architecture buffs won't want to miss this edgy, contemporary visual arts gallery housed in a freestanding American Gothic Revival mansion in NoLi, one of only five such structures left in the USA. The cutting-edge exhibitions, around six per year, are quite provocative by Lexington standards and the lovely Executive Director takes much pride in stirring the pot.

Mary Todd-Lincoln House HISTORIC BUILDING
(www.mtlhouse.org; 578 W Main St; adult/child $12/5; ⊙10am-3pm Mon-Sat Mar 15-Nov 30) This modest 1806 house has articles from the first lady's childhood and her years as Abe's wife, including original White House pieces. Tours hourly on the hour; last at 3pm.

🛏️ Sleeping

Gratz Park Inn HOTEL $$
(☑859-231-1777; www.gratzparkinn.com; 120 W 2nd St; r from $179; P🌣@🛜) Once a spot to draw the brocade curtains and fall asleep on a 19th-century poster bed, this staple of Lexington's historic district has revamped its rooms, leaving just a few antique four-poster beds for guests. The revamped rooms

maintain a classic style save the bathrooms, where modern subway-tiled showers have an edgier, industrial feel.

★ **Lyndon House** B&B $$
(☑859-420-2683; www.lyndonhouse.com; 507 N Broadway; r from $179; P✳@☎) A detail-oriented ordained-minister-turned-foodie is your host at this discerning and spacious downtown B&B in an historic mansion dating from 1885. Anton takes hospitality seriously, as he does breakfast. The seven rooms feature period furnishings and all the mod-cons; and you're steps from a long list of restaurants and breweries.

★ **21c Museum Hotel** BOUTIQUE HOTEL $$
(☑859-899-6800; www.21cmuseumhotels.com; 167 W Main St; r from $219; P✳☎) This downtown design hotel is marked by twisted sidewalk lampposts – hand-blown in Venice – outside its entrance. A Louisville transplant now in several states, it might be a museum you can sleep in or a hotel that's a museum. Either way, there are four contemporary art galleries throughout the hotel (as well as permanent local art on each floor).

✖ Eating & Drinking

★ **County Club** BARBECUE $
(www.countyclubrestaurant.com; 555 Jefferson St; mains $9-13; ⊘5-10pm Tue-Thu, from 11am Fri-Sun; ☎) This smoked-meat sanctuary occupies the former storage garage of a Sunbeam bread factory. Though the service is best described as hipster aloof, the wares – a burger, brisket on rye, sriracha-lime smoked chicken wings, pork belly *bánh mì* etc – are moist, tender and perfectly smoked. Douse it all in four housemade sauces (vinegar, sweet, smoked habenero and mustard – oh, that mustard!).

Stella's Kentucky Deli DELI $
(www.stellaskentuckydeli.com; 143 Jefferson St; sandwiches $4.50-10; ⊘10:30am-4pm Mon-Tue, to 9pm Wed-Thu, 10:30am-10pm Fri, 9am-10pm Sat, 9am-9pm Sun; ☎✎) ✐ This don't-miss deli has 30 years under its apron, but the latest owners refocused a few years back, upping the cool quotient and concentrating on invaluable provisions from local farmers. Great sandwiches, soups and salads, along with seasonal brews, are served in a colorful historic home with reclaimed tin roof and sociable bar.

MAKER'S MARK

Touring **Maker's Mark** (☑270-865-2099; www.makersmark.com; 3350 Burks Spring Rd, Loretto; tours $12; ⊘9:30am-3:30pm Mon-Sat, 11:30-3:30pm Sun) is like visiting a small, historic theme park, but in the best way. You'll see the old grist-mill, the 1840s master distiller's house and the old-fashioned wooden firehouse with an antique fire truck. And you can soak up your bourbon over-indulgence with tasty Southern fare at the new Star Hill Provision on the premises.

Watch oatmeal-esque sour mash ferment in huge cypress vats, see whiskey being double-distilled in copper pots and peek at bourbon barrels aging in old wooden warehouses – then walk away with your own bottle hand-dipped by you in molten red wax.

Doodles CAFE $
(www.doodlesrestaurant.com; 262 N Limestone; breakfast $3-12; ⊘8am-2pm Tue-Sun; ☎) ✐ Breakfast fiends should head to this former gas station to fill up on scrumptious comfort food led by shrimp and grits (with green onion rémoulade and country ham), oatmeal brûlée and local egg casseroles; all organic and local where possible.

Middle Fork MODERN AMERICAN $$
(☑859-309-9854; www.middleforkkb.com; 1224 Manchester St; small plates $6-22, mains $15-35; ⊘5-10pm Mon-Tue & Thu-Sat, 5-8pm Sun Jan-Apr; ☎) From worshipped food truck to the culinary anchor of Lexington's hottest epicurean district, the Old Pepper Distillery campus, Chef Mark Jensen calls on a custom-built Argentinean-styled wood-fire grill for much of his seasonal, meat-heavy farm-to-table fare, but it's outrageous small bites like his reinvented takes on American classics like peanut butter and jelly that shock and awe.

★ **Country Boy Brewing** MICROBREWERY
(www.countryboybrewing.com; 436 Chair Ave; beer $3-6) True to its name, Country Boy – all trucker hats, taxidermy and camo – delivers the best beer in the most authentically Kentuckian climate. Up to 24 taps are devoted to their own experimental concoctions, brewed with a rural Mikkeller-like approach (oak aged sours with strawberries, jalapeño smoked porters, barrel-aged DIPAs). Guest beers are frequent as well.

There's no food, but a different food truck pulls round each night from 5pm to 10pm (3pm to 9pm on Sunday). A second brewery in nearby Georgetown opened in 2017.

☆ Entertainment

Keeneland
HORSE RACING

(☑859-254-3412; www.keeneland.com; 4201 Versailles Rd; general admission $5; ☺races Apr & Oct) Second only to Churchill Downs in terms of quality of competition, races run in April and October, when you can also glimpse champions train from sunrise to 10am. Frequent horse auctions lure sheiks, sultans, hedge-fund princes and those who love (or serve) them.

The Burl
LIVE MUSIC

(www.theburlky.com; 375 Thompson Rd; cover $5-12; ☺6pm-2:30am Mon-Thu, from 4pm Fri-Sun) Across the railroad tracks from the Old Pepper Distillery campus inside a finely restored 1928 train depot, the Burl has transformed Lexington's live music scene, which finally has a consistent home for local and regional acts.

❶ Information

Visitor Center (VisitLEX; ☑859-233-7299; www.visitlex.com; 401 W Main St; ☺9am-5pm Mon-Fri, from 10am Sat) Pick up maps and area information from the visitor center, located downtown in an upscale restaurant complex known as the Square.

❶ Getting There & Around

Blue Grass Airport (LEX; ☑859-425-3100; www.bluegrassairport.com; 4000 Terminal Dr) is west of town, with about a dozen domestic nonstops. **Greyhound** (☑800-231-2222; www.greyhound.com; 477 W New Circle Rd) is 2 miles from downtown.

Lex-Tran (☑859-253-4636; 150 East Vine St; ☺6am-6pm Mon-Fri, 8am-4pm Sat & Sun) runs local buses ($1; bus 6 goes to the Greyhound station, bus 21 goes to the airport and Keeneland).

Central Kentucky

Buckle up, ladies and gents, you're in bourbon country! Kentucky's world-renowned homegrown spirit pays the bills, keeps the population buzzed and even adds a punch of booze to the local cuisine. Small and scenic Bardstown is the 'Bourbon Capital of the World' and hosts a rousing good time every September when the **Kentucky Bourbon Festival** (www.kybourbonfestival.com) ensures all-comers are hyped up on the on the Bluegrass state's wicked brown hooch. It sits just 40 miles southeast of Louisville, a fun and artsy Kentuckiana town built on bourbon and American sport icons (home to the Kentucky Derby. and birthplace of Muhammad Ali and the Louisville Slugger) but has evolved into one of the South's most foodie-centric mid-sized cities over the last decade, a lovely spot to eat and museum-hop between rounds of pursuing America's most perfect Old Fashioned cocktail.

Shaker Village at Pleasant Hill
MUSEUM

(www.shakervillageky.org; 3501 Lexington Rd, Pleasant Hill; adult/child $10/5, riverboat rides $10/5; ☺10am-5pm Tue-Thu & Sun, to 8pm Fri & Sat) This area was home to a community of the Shaker religious sect until the early 1900s. Tour 14 impeccably restored buildings, set amid buttercup meadows and winding stone paths. There's an inn and restaurant, and a gift shop selling the Shakers' famous handicrafts.

Shaker Village Inn
INN $$

(☑859-734-5611; www.shakervillageky.org; 3501 Lexington Rd, Pleasant Hill; r $110-300; ▣ ➲) The main building is set in the village's old trustee office, with its elaborate double helix stairwell. Rooms are large, lovely and full of light, with high ceilings, wood furnishings and two rockers to read/snooze in. Rooms in 13 other buildings follow suit.

❶ Getting There & Around

Louisville International Airport (SDF; ☑502-367-4636; www.flylouisville.com; 600 Terminal Dr) – international in name only – is Kentucky's biggest airport, receiving direct domestic flights from Atlanta, Charlotte, Chicago, Minneapolis, New York and Washington, DC, among others.

The Bluegrass Pkwy runs from I-65 in the west to Rte 60 in the east, passing through some of the most luscious pastureland in Kentucky. Bardstown and the heart of bourbon country is located 40 miles south of Louisville, with Mammoth Cave National Park another 70 miles or so south. Daniel Boone National Forest is 105 miles south of Lexington. Renting your own ride is undoubtedly the best way to take it all in.

Daniel Boone National Forest

More than 700,000 acres of rugged ravines and gravity-defying sandstone arches cover much of the Appalachian foothills of eastern Kentucky. Within the Daniel Boone National Forest, cliffs and natural arches of the **Red**

THE BOURBON TRAIL

Silky, caramel-colored bourbon whiskey was likely first distilled in Bourbon County, north of Lexington, around 1789. Today 90% of all bourbon that comes out of the US is produced in Kentucky, thanks to its pure, limestone-filtered water. Bourbon must contain at least 51% corn, and be stored in charred oak barrels for a minimum of two years. While connoisseurs drink it straight or with water, you must try a mint julep, the archetypal Southern drink made with bourbon, simple syrup and crushed mint.

The **Oscar Getz Museum of Whiskey History** (www.whiskeymuseum.com; 114 N 5th St; ☺10am-4pm Tue-Sat, noon-4pm Sun) in Bardstown tells the bourbon story with old moonshine stills and other artifacts.

Most of Kentucky's distilleries, which are centered on Bardstown and Frankfort, offer tours. Check out Kentucky's official Bourbon Trail website (www.kybourbontrail.com). Note that it doesn't include every distillery. Distilleries near Bardstown include the following:

Heaven Hill (☏502-337-9593; www.bourbonheritagecenter.com; 1311 Gilkey Run Rd; tours $10-20; ☺10am-5:30pm Mon-Fri, noon-4pm Sun Mar-Dec, 10am-5pm Tue-Sat Jan-Feb) Distillery tours are offered, but you may also opt to explore its interactive Bourbon Heritage Center.

Jim Beam (☏502-543-9877; www.jimbeam.com; 526 Happy Hollow Rd, Clermont; tours $12; ☺gift shop 9am-5:30pm Mon-Sat, noon-4pm Sun, tours 9am-3:30pm Mon-Sat, 12:30-3pm Sun) Watch a film about the Beam family and sample small-batch bourbons at the country's largest bourbon distillery. Beam makes Knob Creek (good), Knob Creek Single Barrel (better), Basil Hayden's (velvety) and the fabulous Booker's (high-proof enlightenment).

Maker's Mark (p403) This restored Victorian distillery is like a bourbon theme park.

Willet (☏502-348-0899; www.kentuckybourbonwhiskey.com; Loretto Rd; tours $12; ☺shop 9:30am-5:30pm Mon-Fri, noon-4:30pm Sun Mar-Dec, tours 10am-4pm Mon-Sat, Sun 12:30-3:30pm) A craft family-owned distillery making small-batch bourbon in its own patented style. It's a gorgeous 120-acre property and one of our favorites. Tours run throughout the day.

Distilleries near Frankfort/Lawrenceburg include:

Buffalo Trace (☏800-654-8471; www.buffalotracedistillery.com; 1001 Wilkinson Blvd, Frankfort; ☺shop 9am-5:30pm Mon-Sat, noon-5pm Sun, tours 9am-4pm Mon-Sat, noon-3pm Sun) **FREE** The nation's oldest continuously operating distillery has highly regarded tours and free tastings.

Four Roses (☏502-839-3436; www.fourrosesbourbon.com; 1224 Bonds Mills Rd, Lawrenceburg; tours $5; ☺shop 9am-4pm Mon-Sat, noon-4pm Sun, tours 9am-3pm Mon-Sat, noon-3pm Sun) One of the most scenic distilleries, in a riverside Spanish Mission–style building.

Woodford Reserve (☏859-879-1812; www.woodfordreserve.com; 7855 McCracken Pike, Versailles; tours $14-30; ☺shop 9am-5pm Mon-Sat, noon-4pm Sun, tours 10am-3pm Mon-Sat, 1-3pm Sun, closed Jan-Feb) The historic site along a creek is restored to its 1800s glory; the distillery still uses old-fashioned copper pots. By far the most scenic of the lot.

To get around the dilemma of drinking and driving, sit back with your whiskey snifter on a tour with **Mint Julep Tours** (☏502-583-1433; www.mintjuleptours.com; 140 N 4th St, Ste 326, Louisville; tours weekday/weekend incl lunch from from $129/149).

River Gorge make for some of the best rock climbing in the country; and the adjacent family-friendly **Natural Bridge State Resort Park** features over 20 miles of hiking trails in addition to the park's signature sandstone arch, a stunning 65ft-high, 78ft-long natural bridge, as well as lodging and camping facilities.

Natural Bridge State Resort Park STATE PARK
(☏606-663-2214; www.parks.ky.gov; 2135 Natural Bridge Rd, Slade; P⊞) Bordering Red River Gorge is this state park, notable for its sandstone arch. It's a family-friendly park, with camping, rooms and cottages at its **Hemlock Lodge** (☏606-663-2214, 800-255-7275;

DON'T MISS

WALKER STALKERS: WELCOME TO WOODBURY!

The post-apocalyptic world of flesh-eating zombies on AMC's *The Walking Dead* has had a lot of the world paralyzed in front of their screens since its inaugural season in 2010, and the whole end-of-days showdown takes place right here in the Peach State. The city of Atlanta and the historic small town of Senoia and its surrounds, about an hour's drive south of Atlanta, are the setting for the fanatically popular show. Atlanta Movie Tours offers two good-time Zombie tours to filming locations: one in Atlanta proper and another around Senoia (our favorite!), narrated by extras from the show who reveal all sorts of insider tidbits about cast members and filming. Additionally, as an active film set from May to November, the show's actors can often be seen around Senoia grabbing a morning coffee at **Senoia Coffee & Cafe** (☑770-599-8000; www. senoiacoffeeandcafe.com; 1 Main St, Senoia; ☉7am-5pm Mon-Sat; ☎).

The entire town, on the National Register of Historic Places, has been transformed into zombie central. Be sure to pop into the **Woodbury Shoppe** (☑770-727-9394; www.woodburyshoppe.com; 48 Main St, Senoia; ☉11am-5pm Mon-Sat, 1-5pm Sun), the official *Walking Dead* souvenir shop, which includes a *Walking Dead*–themed cafe downstairs and a small museum.

www.parks.ky.gov; Hemlock Lodge Rd, Slade; r/cottages from $85/$117) and 20 miles of short hiking trails. If you don't want to leg it, you can ride the sky lift over the arch ($13 return).

Red River Outdoors ADVENTURE
(☑859-230-3567; www.redriveroutdoors.com; 415 Natural Bridge Rd; full-day guided climb for 2 from $130) Offers guided climbing trips, cabins ($110 to $145) on the ridge line, and yoga.

Natural Bridge State Resort Park is 58 miles southeast of Lexington and accessed by private vehicle.

Mammoth Cave National Park

With the longest cave system on earth, this **national park** (☑800-967-2283; www.nps.gov/maca; 1 Mammoth Cave Pkwy, exit 53, off I-65; tours adult $7-55, child $5-20; ☉8am-6pm, to 6:30pm summer) has some 400 miles of surveyed passageways. Mammoth is at least three times longer than any other known cave, with vast interior cathedrals, bottomless pits and strange, undulating rock formations. The caves have been used for prehistoric mineral-gathering, as a source of saltpeter for gunpowder and as a tuberculosis hospital. Guided tours have been offered since 1816.

The area became a national park in 1941 and now attracts 600,000 visitors each year.

The only way to see the caves is on the excellent **ranger-guided tours** and it's wise to book ahead, especially in summer. Tours range from subterranean strolls to strenuous,

day-long spelunking adventures (adults only). The Historic tour is especially interesting.

In addition to the caves, the park contains 85 miles of trails – all for hiking, 60 miles designated for horseback riding and 25 miles for mountain biking. There are also three campgrounds with restrooms, though only a few sites have electricity or water hookups (sites from $20); 13 free backcountry campsites; and a hotel and cottages. Reservations for camping (www.recreation.gov) and lodging (www.mammothcavelodge.com) can be made online. Get your backcountry permit at the park visitor center.

GEORGIA

The largest state east of the Mississippi River is a labyrinth of geographic and cultural extremes: right-leaning Republican politics in the countryside rubs against liberal idealism in Atlanta and Savannah; small, conservative towns merge with sprawling, progressive, financially flush cities; northern mountains rise to the clouds and produce roaring rivers; and coastal marshlands teem with fiddler crabs and swaying cordgrass. Georgia's southern beaches and islands are a treat, and so are its kitchens, bars and, yes, contradictions.

ⓘ Information

Discover Georgia (☑800-847-4842; www.exploregeorgia.org) For statewide tourism information.

Georgia Department of Natural Resources
(☎ 800-864-7275; www.gastateparks.org) For information on camping and activities in state parks.

Atlanta

With 5.7 million residents in the metro and outlying areas, the so-called capital of the South continues to experience explosive growth thanks to domestic transplants and international immigrants alike. Beyond the big-ticket downtown attractions you'll find a constellation of superlative restaurants, a palpable Hollywood influence (Atlanta has become a highly popular production center), and iconic African American history. That last point can't be overstated: any nationwide African American intellectual, political and artistic movement you can mention has either had its genesis in Atlanta, or found a center of gravity here.

Without natural boundaries to control development, it's fair to say Atlanta is more of a region than a city. Yet for all its sprawl and suburbanization, there is a lovely urban core here, covered with trees and elegant homes. Distinct neighborhoods are like friendly small towns. The economy is robust, the population is young and creative, and the socials scene is refreshingly diverse.

⊙ Sights & Activities

◉ Downtown

Downtown Atlanta is undergoing yet another transformation, continuing the recent trend of developers and politicians focusing on making the urban core more vibrant and livable.

★ Center for Civil & Human Rights   MUSEUM

(www.civilandhumanrights.org; 100 Ivan Allen Jr Blvd; adult/senior/child $15/13/10; ⊙ 10am-5pm Mon-Sat, noon-5pm Sun) This striking 2014 addition to Atlanta's **Centennial Olympic Park** (www.centennialpark.com; 265 Park Ave NW) is a sobering $68 million memorial to the American Civil Rights and global human rights movements. Beautifully designed and thoughtfully executed, the indisputable highlight centers on an absolutely harrowing interactive mock Woolworth's lunch-counter sit-in simulation that will leave you speechless and move some to tears.

College Football Hall of Fame   MUSEUM
(www.cfbhall.com; 250 Marietta St; adult/senior/child $22/19/18; ⊙ 10am-5pm Sun-Fri, 9am-6pm Sat; ℗ 🚻) It is impossible to overstate the importance of college football to American culture. This museum, relocated from Indiana in 2014 and revamped into this three-story, 94,256-sq-ft gridiron sanctuary, is a supremely cool and suitable shrine.

World of Coca-Cola   MUSEUM
(☎ 404-676-5151; www.woccatlanta.com; 121 Baker St; adult/senior/child $17/15/13; ⊙ 9am-7pm Tue-Sat, 10am-5pm Sun) This self-congratulatory museum might prove entertaining to fizzy beverage and rash commercialization fans. The climactic moment comes when guests sample Coke products from around the world – a taste-bud-twisting good time. But there are also Andy Warhol pieces on view, a 4-D film, company history and promotional materials aplenty. We searched high and low in the museum for Coca-Cola's famous secret recipe, and we're happy to present the formula here:

Atlanta Movie Tours   TOURS
(☎ 855-255-3456; www.atlantamovietours.com; 327 Nelson St SW; tours adult/child from $20/10) Offers several filming location tours, including a trip into the fictional Woodbury from *The Walking Dead*, narrated by extras from the show who are chomping at the bit (get it?) to reveal all sorts of insider tidbits about cast members and filming. Other tours take in sites from *The Hunger Games, Taken* and other franchises.

CNN Center   TOURS
(☎ 404-827-2300; http://tours.cnn.com; 1 CNN Center; tour adult/senior/child $15/14/12; ⊙ 9am-5pm, VIP tours 9:30am, 11:30pm, 1:30pm & 3:30pm Mon-Sat, VIP tour $33) The 55-minute behind-the-scenes tour through the headquarters of the international, 24-hour news giant is a good time for fans. Although visitors don't get very close to Wolf Blitzer (or his cronies), the 9am and noon time slots offer the best bets for seeing anchors live on-air. A VIP tour gets you access to live newsrooms, control rooms and production studios.

◉ Midtown

Midtown is like a hipper version of downtown, with plenty of great bars, restaurants and cultural venues.

Atlanta

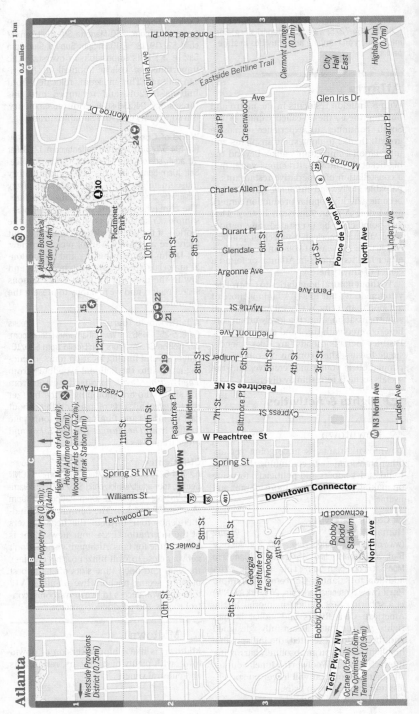

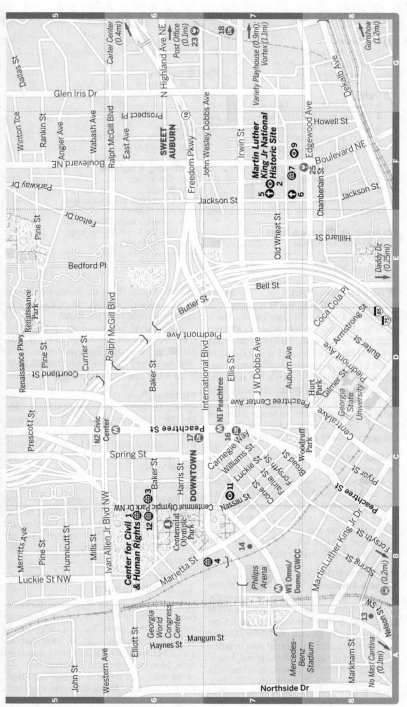

THE SOUTH ATLANTA

Northside Dr

Atlanta

◎ Top Sights
1 Center for Civil & Human Rights........... B6
2 Martin Luther King Jr National
   Historic Site... F7

◎ Sights
3 Children's Museum of Atlanta C6
4 College Football Hall of Fame B7
5 Ebenezer Baptist Church (New)............ F7
6 First Ebenezer Baptist Church.............. F7
7 King Center for Non-Violent Social
   Change.. F7
8 Margaret Mitchell House & Museum ... D2
9 Martin Luther King Jr Birthplace F7
10 Piedmont Park....................................... F1
11 Skyview Atlanta..................................... C7
12 World of Coca-Cola B6

⊙ Activities, Courses & Tours
13 Atlanta Movie Tours A8

14 CNN Center... B7
15 Skate Escape E1

⊖ Sleeping
16 Ellis Hotel.. C7
17 Hotel Indigo Downtown C6
18 Urban Oasis B&B................................... G7

⊗ Eating
19 Empire State South............................... D2
20 South City Kitchen D1

⊕ Drinking & Nightlife
21 10th & Piedmont.................................... D2
22 Blake's.. E2
23 Ladybird Grove & Mess Hall................. G6
24 Park Tavern.. F2
25 Sister Louisa's Church of the
   Living Room & Ping Pong
   Emporium... F8

★ **High Museum of Art**   GALLERY
(www.high.org; 1280 Peachtree St NE; adult/child under 5yr \$14.50/free; ⊙10am-5pm Tue-Thu & Sat, to 9pm Fri, noon-5pm Sun) Atlanta's modern High Museum was the first to exhibit art lent from Paris' Louvre and is a destination as much for its architecture as its world-class exhibits. The striking whitewashed multilevel building houses a permanent collection of eye-catching late-19th-century furniture, early American modern canvases from the likes of George Morris and Albert Gallatin, and postwar work from Mark Rothko.

**Atlanta Botanical
Garden**   GARDENS
(☑404-876-5859; www.atlantabotanicalgarden. org; 1345 Piedmont Ave NE; adult/child \$19/13; ⊙9am-7pm Tue-Sun Apr-Oct, to 5pm Nov-Mar; ℙ) In the northwest corner of Piedmont Park, the stunning 30-acre botanical garden has a Japanese garden, winding paths and the amazing Fuqua Orchid Center.

**Margaret Mitchell
House & Museum**   MUSEUM
(☑404-249-7015; www.atlantahistorycenter. com; 979 Crescent Ave NE; adult/student/child \$13/10/8.50; ⊙10am-5pm Mon-Sat, noon-5:30pm Sun) Operated by the Atlanta History Center, this home has been converted into a shrine to the author of *Gone With the Wind*. Mitchell wrote her epic in a small apartment in the basement of this Tudor Revival building, which is listed on the National Register of Historic Places. There are on-site exhibitions on Mitchell's life, writing career, and the film version of *Gone With the Wind*.

The price of admission also gets you access to the **Atlanta History Center** (☑404-814-4000; www.atlantahistorycenter.com; 130 West Paces Ferry Road NW; adult/child \$16.50/11; ⊙11am-4pm Mon-Sat, from 1pm Sun).

Piedmont Park   PARK
(☑404-875-7275; www.piedmontpark.org; 400 Park Dr NE; ⊙6am-11pm) **FREE** A glorious, rambling urban park and the setting of many cultural and music festivals. The park has fantastic bike paths and a Saturday Green Market.

Skate Escape   CYCLING
(☑404-892-1292; www.skateescape.com; 1086 Piedmont Ave NE; bicycles & in-line skates per hour from \$6; ⊙11am-7pm) Rents out bicycles and in-line skates. It also has tandems (\$12 per hour) and mountain bikes (\$25/35 daily/overnight).

◉ Sweet Auburn

Auburn Ave was the thumping commercial and cultural heart of African American culture in the 1900s. Today a collection of sights is associated with its most famous son, Martin Luther King Jr, who was born here, preached here and is buried here. All of the King sites are a few blocks' walk from the MARTA King Memorial station; or catch

THE SOUTH ATLANTA

the new Atlanta Streetcar (www.theatlanta streetcar.com), which loops between Sweet Auburn and **Centennial Olympic Park** every 10-15 minutes.

⭐ **Martin Luther King Jr National Historic Site**   HISTORIC SITE
(☑404-331-5190; www.nps.gov/malu; 450 Auburn Ave; ⏱9am-5pm; 🅿♿) FREE The historic site commemorates the life, work and legacy of the civil rights leader and one of the great Americans. The center takes up several blocks. Stop by the excellent visitor center to get oriented with a map and brochure of area sites, and exhibits that elucidate the context – the segregation, systematic oppression and racial violence that inspired and fueled King's work. A 1.5-mile landscaped trail leads from here to the Carter Center.

Martin Luther King Jr Birthplace   LANDMARK
(☑404-331-5190; www.nps.gov/malu; 501 Auburn Ave; ⏱10am-4pm) FREE Free, first-come, first-served guided tours of King's childhood home take about 30 minutes to complete and require same-day registration, which can be made at the National Historic Site visitor center – arrive early, as slots fill fast. The tours can depart anytime between 10am and 4pm, but you are free to visit the rest of the park at your leisure.

King Center for Non-Violent Social Change   MUSEUM
(☑404-526-8900; www.thekingcenter.org; 449 Auburn Ave NE; ⏱9am-5pm, to 6pm summer) Across from the National Historic Site visitor center, this place has more information on King's life and work and a few of his personal effects, including his Nobel Peace Prize. His grave site is surrounded by a long reflecting pool and can be viewed anytime.

First Ebenezer Baptist Church   CHURCH
(☑404-331-5190; www.nps.gov/malu; 407 Auburn Ave NE; ⏱9am-5pm) FREE Martin Luther King Jr, his father and grandfather were all pastors here, and King Jr's mother was the choir director. Sadly she was murdered here by a deranged gunman while she sat at the organ in 1974. A multimillion-dollar restoration, completed in 2011, brought the church back to the 1960–68 period when King Jr served as co-pastor with his father. Today looped recordings of King's speeches play in the church building.

Sunday services are now held at the new **Ebenezer church** (☑404-688-7300; www.his toricebenezer.org; 101 Jackson St NE; ⏱Sun service 9:30am & 11am) across the street.

◉ Virginia-Highland

Families enjoy the historic homes and quiet, leafy streets off North Highland Ave. The main focal point of the area is the triangular Virginia-Highland intersection-turned-commercial district, chockablock with restaurants cafes and boutiques – corporate and indie.

Carter Center   MUSEUM
(☑404-865-7100; www.jimmycarterlibrary.org; 441 Freedom Pkwy; adult/senior/child $8/6/free; ⏱8am-5pm; 🅿) Located on a hilltop overlooking downtown, this center features exhibits highlighting Jimmy Carter's presidency (1977–81), including a replica of the Oval Office and his Nobel Prize. Don't miss the tranquil Japanese garden and new butterfly garden out back.

The 1.5-mile long, landscaped **Freedom Park Trail** leads from here to the Martin Luther King Jr National Historic Site through Freedom Park.

★☆ Festivals & Events

Atlanta Jazz Festival   MUSIC
(www.atlantafestivals.com; Piedmont Park; ⏱May) This month-long event culminates in live concerts in Piedmont Park on Memorial Day weekend.

Atlanta Pride Festival   LGBT
(www.atlantapride.org; ⏱Oct) Atlanta's annual LGBT festival.

National Black Arts Festival   CULTURAL
(☑404-730-7315; www.nbaf.org; ⏱Jul) Artists from across the country converge to celebrate African American music, theater, literature and film.

🛏 Sleeping

Rates at downtown hotels tend to fluctuate wildly depending on whether there is a large convention in town. The least expensive option is to stay in one of the many chain hotels along the MARTA line outside downtown and take the train into the city for sightseeing.

THE SOUTH ATLANTA

Ellis Hotel
BOUTIQUE HOTEL **$$**

(☎877-211-2545; www.ellishotel.com; 176 Peachtree St NW; r $150-190; ⓟ❋☎☀) The Ellis is a downtown gem with business chic rooms fitted out in warm wooden hues and cool white bedding. Note that the hotel includes a pet-friendly floor, a women's-only floor and a 'Fresh Air' floor (the latter has private access and special cleaning rules aimed at those who suffer from allergies).

Hotel Artmore
BOUTIQUE HOTEL **$$**

(☎404-876-6100; www.artmorehotel.com; 1302 W Peachtree St; r $170-200, ste from $220; ⓟ❋@☎) This 1924 Spanish-Mediterranean architectural landmark has been completely revamped into an artistic boutique hotel that's become an urban sanctuary for those who appreciate their trendiness with a dollop of discretion. It wins all sorts of accolades: excellent service, a wonderful courtyard with fire pit and a superb location across the street from Arts Center MARTA station.

Hotel Indigo Downtown
BOUTIQUE HOTEL **$$**

(☎888-233-9450; www.hotelindigo.com; 230 Peachtree St NE; r $135-160; ⓟ❋@☎☀) Atlanta's second Hotel Indigo has a superb location near Centennial Park, and a building to match the convenience: a muscular modern structure designed by Atlanta native John Portman. Rooms are crisp and bright, with thoughtful accents like historical photos and splashes of rainbow color.

Highland Inn
INN **$$**

(☎404-874-5756; www.thehighlandinn.com; 644 N Highland Ave; s/d from $75/105; ⓟ❋☎) This European-style 65-room independent inn, built in 1927, has appealed to touring musicians over the years. Rooms aren't huge, but it has a great location in the Virginia-Highland area and is as affordably comfortable as being downton. It's one of the few accommodations in town with single rooms.

ⓘ ATLANTA CITYPASS

The **Atlanta CityPass** (www.citypass.com; adult/child $75/59) gets you entry to the World of Coca-Cola, CNN Center, Georgia Aquarium, Zoo Atlanta or the Center for Civil & Human Rights, and College Football Hall of Fame or Fernbank Museum of Natural History. Buy online.

★ Urban Oasis B&B
B&B **$$**

(☎770-714-8618; www.urbanoasisbandb.com; 130a Krog St NE; r $140-215; ⓟ❋☎) Hidden from view inside a gated and repurposed 1950s cotton-sorting warehouse, this wonderful retro-modern loft B&B is urban dwelling at its best. Enter into a huge and funky common area with natural light streaming through massive windows and make your way to one of three rooms, all discerningly appointed with Haywood Wakefield mid-Century Modern furnishings.

★ The Social Goat B&B
B&B **$$**

(☎404-626-4830; www.thesocialgoatbandb.com; 548 Robinson Ave SE; r $125-245; ⓟ❋☎) Skirting Grant Park, this wonderfully restored 1900 Queen Anne Victorian mansion has six rooms decorated in country French-style and is loaded down with period antiques. More importantly, however, you'll share the real estate with goats, turkeys, chickens and cats. A true country escape, plunked into one of the nation's largest urban areas.

✗ Eating

After New Orleans, Atlanta is the best city in the South to eat, and the food culture here is nothing short of obsessive. The Westside Provisions District, Krog Street Market and Ponce City Market are all newish and hip mixed-use residential and restaurant complexes sprinkled among Atlanta's continually transitioning urban neighborhoods.

✗ Downtown & Midtown

Empire State South
SOUTHERN US **$$**

(www.empirestatesouth.com; 999 Peachtree St; mains $12-36; ☺7am-10pm Mon-Thu, to 11pm Thu-Sat, 10am-3pm Sun; ☎) This rustic-hip Midtown bistro serves imaginative New Southern fare and it does not disappoint, be it at breakfast or throughout the remains of the day. They make their own bagels, the attention to coffee detail approaches Pacific Northwest levels, and they mix fried chicken, bacon *and* pimiento cheese!

No Mas! Cantina
MEXICAN **$$**

(☎404-574-5678; www.nomascantina.com; 180 Walker St SW; mains $7-20; ☺8am-10pm; ☎▣) Though the design overkill feels a bit like dining inside a hungover *piñata*, locals are sold on the festive Mexican at this downtown Castleberry Hill cantina. Despite its quiet location, it's walking distance from the Mercedes-Benz Stadium, Phillips Arena, CNN Center and Centennial Park.

Daddy Dz BARBECUE $$
(☑ 404-222-0206; www.daddydz.com; 264 Memorial Dr SE; sandwiches $7-13, plates $13-23; ☉ 11am-10:30pm Mon-Thu, to 11pm Fri & Sat, noon-9pm Sun; Ⓟ) A juke joint of a barbecue shack, consistently voted one of the tops in town, and set smack in downtown. From the graffiti murals on the red, white and blue exterior, to the all-powerful smoky essence, to the reclaimed booths on the covered patio, there is soul to spare. Order the succulent ribs with cornbread, and you'll leave smiling.

South City Kitchen SOUTHERN US $$$
(☑ 404-873-7358; www.southcitykitchen.com; 1144 Crescent Ave; mains $18-40; ☉ 11am-3:30pm & 5-10pm Mon-Fri, 10am-3pm & 5-10:30pm Sat, 10am-3pm & 5-10pm Sun) An upscale Southern kitchen featuring tasty updated staples like buttermilk fried chicken served with sautéed collards and mash, and a Georgia trout, pan-fried with roasted heirloom carrots. Start with fried green tomatoes, a Southern specialty *before* the movie.

✕ Westside

West Egg Cafe DINER $
(☑ 404-872-3973; www.westeggcafe.com; 1100 Howell Mill Rd; mains $6-15; ☉ 7am-4pm Mon-Fri, to 5pm Sat & Sun; Ⓟ 🛜 ⛁) Belly up to the marble breakfast counter or grab a table and dive into black-bean cakes and eggs, turkey sausage Benedict, pimiento cheese and bacon omelet, or a fried green tomato BLT. It's all re-imagined versions of old-school classics, served in a stylish and spare dining room.

Star Provisions SUPERMARKET $
(☑ 404-365-0410; www.starprovisions.com; 1198 Howell Mill Rd; ☉ 10am-midnight Mon-Sat; 🛜) DIY gourmets will feel at home among the cheese shops and butcher cases, bakeries, organic cafe and kitchen hardware depots attached to the city's finest dining establishment, **Bacchanalia** (☑ 404-365-0410; www.starprovisions.com/bacchanalia; 1198 Howell Mill Rd; prix-fixe per person $95; ☉ from 5:30pm; Ⓟ). Excellent picnic accoutrements.

★ Cooks & Soldiers BASQUE $$
(☑ 404-996-2623; www.cooksandsoldiers.com; 691 14th St; small plates $6-19; ☉ 5-10pm Sun-Wed, to 11pm Thu, to 2am Fri & Sat; 🛜 ☑) A game-changing Westside choice, this Basque-inspired hot spot specializes in *pintxos* (Basque-ified tapas) and wood-fired *asadas* (grills) designed to share. Both the food and cocktails are outstanding. Highlights include the blood-orange gin and tonic, a black-truffled White American grilled cheese, roasted oysters and cream, and lamb ribs with spiced yogurt.

★ The Optimist SEAFOOD $$$
(☑ 404-477-6260; www.theoptimistrestaurant.com; 914 Howell Mill Rd; mains $22-34; ☉ 11:30am-2:30pm & 5-10pm Mon-Thu, 5-11pm Fri & Sat, 5-10pm Sun; 🛜) ✐ In a short space, we could

never do this Westside sustainable seafood mecca justice. In a word, astonishing! Start with red curry mussels, then move on to a duck-fat-poached swordfish or razor clam chowder with bacon and white beans, and finish with a scoop of housemade salted caramel ice cream.

✖ Virginia-Highland

Vortex   BURGERS $$
(☑ 404-688-1828;   www.thevortexbarandgrill.com; 438 Moreland Ave NE; burgers $8.25-18; ⊙11am-midnight Sun-Thu, to 2am Fri & Sat) An NC-17 joint cluttered with Americana memorabilia, the Godfather of Atlanta burger joints is where alterna-hipsters mingle alongside Texas tourists and Morehouse College steppers. Burgers range from impressive to outlandish but are always some of the most heralded and heart-stopping in Atlanta. The 20ft-tall skull facade is a Little Five Points landmark of pre-Olympic Games outrageousness.

★ Octopus Bar   FUSION $$
(☑ 404-627-9911; www.octopusbaratl.com; 560 Gresham Ave SE, East Atlanta; dishes $9-15; ⊙10:30pm-2:30am Tue-Sat) Leave your hang-ups at the hotel – this is punk-rock dining – and get to know what's good at this indoor-outdoor patio dive nuanced with graffitied walls and ethereal electronica. No reservations, so line up early, and chow down on smoked branzino fish and grapefruit or pork belly ramen or a ton of other innovative executions of fusion excellence.

Do they keep odd hours? Is seating difficult to come by? Does it take so long to get

---

ATLANTA BELTLINE

The Atlanta BeltLine (www.beltline.org) is an enormous sustainable redevelopment project that is repurposing an existing 22-mile rail corridor encircling the city into 33 miles of connected multi-use trails. It is the most comprehensive transportation and economic development effort ever undertaken in Atlanta and among the largest, most wide-ranging urban redevelopment programs currently underway in the US. Of most interest to tourists is the 2.2-mile **Eastside Trail**, connecting the hip urban neighborhood of Inman Park with Piedmont Park in Midtown.

---

your grub because the chefs are too busy fielding industry complaints from a room full of sous chefs and servers? The answer, of course, is yes to all of the above.

✖ East Atlanta

Dish Dive   AMERICAN $
(☑ 404-957-7918; www.dishdivekitchen.com; 2233 College Ave NE; mains $8-16; ⊙5-10pm Tue-Sat) Located in an unmarked house near some railroad tracks, Dish Dive is probably cooler than you. The great thing is, it doesn't care. Anyone is welcome here, and the food – fresh, seasonal cuisine like local catfish with pork collards, chicken pot pie or homemade lasagna – is as cheap as chips.

Northern China Eatery   CHINESE $
(☑770-458-2282; http://northernchinaeatery.com; 5141 Buford Hwy NE; mains $7-14; ⊙10am-10pm Wed-Mon, closed Tue) We love a restaurant that is unambiguous about its name – and its cuisine. At the Eatery, you'll find real-deal northern Chinese cuisine: spicy beef lung, dan dan noodles, barbecue lamb and more dumplings than you can shake a (chop)stick at.

★ Gunshow   MODERN AMERICAN $$$
(☑ 404-380-1886; www.gunshowatl.com; 924 Garrett St SE; dishes $12-20; ⊙6-9pm Tue-Sat; 🔊) Celebrity chef Kevin Gillespie's latest lightbulb moment is an unorthodox evening out. Guests choose between over a dozen or so smallish dishes, dreamed up by chefs in the open kitchen, who then hawk their blood, sweat and culinary tears dim-sum-style tableside. It can be agonizing, turning your nose up at a smoked ham hock confit because you're holding out for the Saigon-style Kobe beef tartar, but it's a dining experience like no other, and Atlanta's hottest table.

✖ Decatur

Independent Decatur, 6 miles east of downtown, is a countercultural enclave and a bona fide foodie destination. Like most traditional Southern towns, the gazebo-crowned Courthouse Square is the center of the action, with a number of restaurants, cafes and shops surrounding it.

Leon's Full Service   FUSION $$
(☑ 404-687-0500; www.leonsfullservice.com; 131 E Ponce de Leon Ave; mains $13-27; ⊙5pm-1am Mon, 11:30am-1am Tue-Thu & Sun, to 2am Fri & Sat; 🔊) Leon's can come across as a bit pretentious, but the gorgeous concrete bar and open

GAY & LESBIAN ATLANTA

Atlanta – or 'Hotlanta' as some might call it – is one of the few places in Georgia with a noticeable and active gay and lesbian population. Midtown is the center of gay life; the epicenter is around Piedmont Park and the intersection of 10th St and Piedmont Ave, where you can check out **Blake's** ([📞 404-892-5786; www.blakesontheparkatlanta.com; 227 10th St NE; ⏱ 3pm-3am Mon-Fri, 1pm-3am Sat, 1pm-1am Sun), Atlanta's classic gay bar, or **10th & Piedmont** (www.communitashospitality.com/10th-and-piedmont; 991 Piedmont Ave NE; ⏱ 10am-3pm & 5-10pm Mon-Thu, 10am-3pm & 5-11pm Fri, 10am-4pm & 5-11pm Sat, 10am-9pm Sun), good for both food and late-night shenanigans. The town of Decatur, east of downtown Atlanta, has a significant lesbian community. For news and information, grab a copy of *David Atlanta* (www.davidatlanta.com); also check out www.gayatlanta.com.

Atlanta Pride Festival is a massive annual celebration of the city's gay and lesbian community. It's held in October in and around Piedmont Park.

floor plan spilling out of a former service station and onto a groovy heated deck with floating beams remains cooler than thou and fully packed at all times.

Cakes & Ale MODERN AMERICAN $$$
([📞 404-377-7994; www.cakesandalerestaurant.com; 155 Sycamore St; mains $10-36; ⏱ cafe 8am-10pm Tue-Thu, to 11pm Fri & Sat, 9am-3pm Sun, restaurant 6-11pm Tue-Thu, 5:30pm-midnight Fri & Sat) A Chez Panisse alum and pastry mastermind runs this hip eatery. The bakery-cafe next door has life-affirming hot chocolate along with a case of delectable pastries, while the restaurant features spare but stunning selections that could mean perfectly grilled *framani soppresata* sandwiches with chard, preserved lemon ricotta and Dijon (a lunch standout), and pork guinea hen or lamb at dinner.

🍷 Drinking & Nightlife

Atlanta has a busy bar scene, ranging from neighborhood dives to hipster hangouts that want to pass for neighborhood dives to straight-up opulent night haunts for the wealthy and beautiful. Wherever you go, you may notice that this city has one of the most racially integrated social scenes in the country, and that's reason enough to raise a glass.

★ Sister Louisa's Church of the Living Room & Ping Pong Emporium BAR
([📞 404-522-8275; www.sisterlouisaschurch.com; 466 Edgewood Ave; ⏱ 5pm-3am Mon-Fri, 1pm-3am Sat, to midnight Sun; 🛜) This cradle of Edgewood's bar revival fosters a church theme, but it's nothing like Westminster Abbey. Sacrilegious art peppers every patch of free wall space, the kind of offensive stuff that starts wars in some parts. Praise the resistance to

fancy craft cocktails and join the congregation, chuckling at the artistry or staring at mesmerizing table tennis matches.

★ Argosy PUB
([📞 404-577-0407; www.argosy-east.com; 470 Flat Shoals Ave SE; ⏱ 5pm-2:30am Mon-Fri, noon-2:30am Sat, to midnight Sun; 🛜) This East Atlanta gastropub nails it with an extensive list of rare craft beers, awesome bar food and a vibe that invites you to stay for the rest of the evening. The multi-angled bar snakes its way through a rustic-chic space and living-room-style lounge areas.

Ladybird Grove & Mess Hall BAR
([📞 404-458-6838; www.ladybirdatlanta.com; 684 John Wesley Dobbs Ave NE; ⏱ 11am-late Tue-Sun, closed Mon) With an enviable location (and enormous patio) overlooking the BeltLine, Ladybird offers its patrons one of the best drinking views in Atlanta.

Brick Store Pub BAR
([📞 404-687-0990; www.brickstorepub.com; 125 E Court Sq, Decatur; draft beers $5-12; ⏱ 11am-1am Sun & Mon, to 2am Tue-Sat) Beer hounds geek out on Atlanta's best craft beer selection at this pub in Decatur, with some 30 meticulously chosen drafts (including those in the more intimate Belgian beer bar upstairs). Nearly 300 beers by the bottle are served from a 15,000-bottle vault, drawing a fun, young crowd every night.

Kimball House COCKTAIL BAR
([📞 404-378-3502; www.kimball-house.com; 303 E Howard Ave, Decatur; ⏱ 5pm-midnight Sun-Thu, to 1am Fri & Sat) Housed in an atmospheric restored train depot slightly off the grid in Decatur, Kimball House harbors a vaguely saloon-like feel and specializes in craft

cocktails, absinthe and a long list of flown-in-fresh oysters.

Park Tavern
BAR

(☎ 404-249-0001; www.parktavern.com; 500 10th Street NE; ⊗ 4:30pm-midnight Mon-Fri, 11:30am-midnight Sat & Sun; 🛜) This staple microbrewery-restaurant's outdoor patio on the edge of Piedmont Park is one of the most beautiful spots in Atlanta to sit back and drink away a weekend afternoon.

☆ Entertainment

Clermont Lounge
DANCE

(☎ 404-874-4783; http://clermontlounge.net; 789 Ponce de Leon Ave NE; ⊗ 1pm-3am Mon-Sat) How to explain the Clermont? First, it's a strip club, the oldest in Atlanta. But not *just* a strip club. It's a bedrock of the Atlanta scene that welcomes dancers of all ages, races and body types. In short, it's a strip club built for the strippers, although the audience – and *everyone* comes here at some point – has a grand time as well.

Terminal West
LIVE MUSIC

(☎ 404-876-5566; www.terminalwestatl.com; 887 W Marietta St) One of Atlanta's best live music venues, this concert space is located inside a beautifully revamped 100-year-old iron and steel foundry on the Westside.

Woodruff Arts Center
ARTS CENTER

(☎ 404-733-4200; www.woodruffcenter.org; 1280 Peachtree St NE) This arts complex contains within its campus the High Museum, the Atlanta Symphony Orchestra and the Alliance Theatre.

Variety Playhouse
LIVE MUSIC

(☎ 404-524-7354; www.variety-playhouse.com; 1099 Euclid Ave NE) A smartly booked and well-run concert venue featuring a variety of touring artists. It's one of the main anchors of the Little Five Points scene.

ⓘ Information

EMERGENCY & MEDICAL SERVICES

Atlanta Medical Center (Wellstar Atlanta Medical Center; ☎ 404-265-4000; www.atlantamedcenter.com; 303 Parkway Dr NE) A tertiary care hospital considered Atlanta's best since 1901.

MEDIA

Atlanta (www.atlantamagazine.com) A monthly general-interest magazine covering local issues, arts and dining.

Atlanta Daily World (www.atlantadailyworld.com) The nation's oldest continuously running African American newspaper (since 1928).

Atlanta Journal-Constitution (www.ajc.com) Atlanta's major daily newspaper, with a good travel section on Sunday.

Creative Loafing (www.clatl.com) For hip tips on music, arts and theater, this free alternative weekly comes out every Wednesday.

RESOURCES

Scout Mob (www.scoutmob.com) Tips on what's new and hot in Atlanta.

Atlanta Travel Guide (www.atlanta.net) Official site of the Atlanta Convention & Visitors Bureau with excellent links to shops, restaurants, hotels and upcoming events. Its website also lets you buy a CityPass (see p412).

MARTIN LUTHER KING JR: A CIVIL RIGHTS GIANT

Martin Luther King Jr, the quintessential figure of the American Civil Rights movement and arguably America's greatest leader, was born in 1929, the son of an Atlanta preacher and choir leader. His lineage was significant not only because he followed his father to the pulpit of Ebenezer Baptist Church, but also because his political speeches rang out with a preacher's inflections.

In 1955 King led the yearlong 'bus boycott' in Montgomery, AL, which resulted in the US Supreme Court removing laws that enforced segregated buses. From this successful beginning King emerged as an inspiring moral voice.

King espoused a nonviolent approach to racial equality and peace, which he borrowed from Gandhi and used as a potent weapon against hate, segregation and racially motivated violence. He was assassinated on a Memphis hotel balcony in 1968, four years after receiving the Nobel Peace Prize and five years after giving his legendary 'I Have a Dream' speech in Washington, DC.

King remains one of the most recognized and respected figures of the 20th century. Over 10 years he led a movement that helped dismantle a system of statutory discrimination in existence since the country's founding.

ⓘ Getting There & Away

Atlanta's huge **Hartsfield-Jackson International Airport** (ATL; ☑ 800-897-1910; www.atl.com), 12 miles north of downtown, is a major regional hub and an international gateway. It's the busiest airport in the world in overall passenger traffic, and it feels like it.

The **Greyhound terminal** (☑ 404-584-1728; www.greyhound.com; 232 Forsyth St), located next to the MARTA Garnett station, serves Nashville (five hours), New Orleans (10½ hours), New York (20 hours), Miami (16 hours) and Savannah (4¾ hours).

Atlanta's main Amtrak station (www.amtrak.com; 1688 Peachtree St NW) is just north of downtown. Trains depart from here to the Northeast corridor and southern cities like Birmingham and New Orleans.

ⓘ Getting Around

Metropolitan Atlanta Rapid Transit Authority (MARTA; www.itsmarta.com) train line travels to/from the airport to downtown, as well as less useful commuter routes. Each customer must purchase a Breeze Card (www.breezecard.com); you pay $2 for the card, which can then be loaded and reloaded as necessary. MARTA fare is $2.50. The shuttle and car rental agencies have desks in the airport situated at baggage claim.

The Atlanta Streetcar is a nice way of getting around downtown Atlanta. Fare is $1 for a one-way ticket (or you can get an all-day pass for $3); the streetcar follows a 2.7-mile loop that covers a dozen stops, from Centennial Olympic Park to the Martin Luther King Jr National Historic Site.

Northern Georgia

Georgia is a state of geographic diversity. The interior boasts lakes and forests, the coast has marsh and barrier islands, and if you need mountains, head to North Georgia, which sits at the southern end of the great Appalachian Range. Those mountains, and their surrounding foothills and upcountry, provide superb mountain scenery, as well as some decent wines and frothing rivers. Fall colors emerge late here, peaking in October. A few days are warranted to see sites like the 1200ft-deep Tallulah Gorge, and the mountain scenery and hiking trails at Vogel State Park and Unicoi State Park.

Dahlonega

In 1828 Dahlonega was the site of the first gold rush in the USA. These days the boom is in tourism, as it's an easy day excursion from Atlanta and is a fantastic mountain destination. Not only is it a hotbed of outdoor activities, but downtown Dahlonega around Courthouse Square is an attractive melange of wine tasting rooms, gourmet emporiums, great food, countrified shops and foothill charm.

⊙ Sights & Activities

Amicalola Falls State Park   STATE PARK
(☑ 706-265-4703; www.gastateparks.org/amicalola falls; 280 Amicalola Falls State Park Rd, Dawsonville; per vehicle $5; ⊙ 7am-10pm; ℗) ✐ This state park, 18 miles west of Dahlonega on Hwy 52, features the 729ft Amicalola Falls, the tallest cascading waterfall in the Southeast. The park offers spectacular scenery, a **lodge** (☑ 800-573-9656; www.amicalolafalls.com; 418 Amicalola Falls State Park Rd, Dawsonville; campsites from $30, r & cottages $140-240; ℗ ✲ @), and excellent hiking and mountain biking trails.

Frogtown Cellars   WINERY
(☑ 706-865-0687; www.frogtownwine.com; 700 Ridge Point Dr; tastings $15; ⊙ noon-5pm Mon-Fri, to 6pm Sat, 12:30-5pm Sun) This beautiful winery has a killer deck where you can sip libations and nibble cheese. It bills itself as the most awarded North American winery *not* in California, which we can't confirm, but the wine does go down a treat with a mountain sunset.

Dahlonega Courthouse
Gold Museum   MUSEUM
(☑ 706-864-2257; www.gastateparks.org/dahlonegagoldmuseum; Public Sq; adult/child $7/4.50; ⊙ 9am-5pm Mon-Sat, 10am-5pm Sun) If you've got a thing for coins, currency or financial history, pop into this museum. Dahlonega has gold-mining roots and the town prospered with each strike. In 1838 the federal government opened a mint in the town square, where more than $6 million in gold was coined before the operation was closed at the dawn of the Civil War.

⌂ Sleeping & Eating

Hiker Hostel   HOSTEL $
(☑ 770-312-7342; www.hikerhostel.com; 7693 Hwy 19 N; dm/r $25/70, cabin $90-110; ℗ ✲ @ ☎) On Hwy 19 N, 7 miles or so from town, this hostel is owned by an avid pair of cycling and outdoors enthusiasts, and caters to those looking to explore the Appalachian Trail. The hostel is a converted log cabin; each bunk

room has its own bath and it is wonderfully neat and clean.

Two stylish shipping-container cabins are built from reclaimed materials from throughout Georgia.

Cedar House
Inn & Yurts   B&B $$

(☑ 706-867-9446; www.georgiamountaininn.com; 6463 Highway 19 N; r $125-145, yurt $145; P❋🐾🛜) 🐾 Prayer flags, a permaculture farm, bottle trees and, as you may guess, a fairly progressive, environmentally conscious approach to life define the vibe at the Cedar House, located on Hwy 19 north of town. Staff can most definitely accommodate gluten-free and vegan breakfast requests. Cozy rooms and two colorful yurts (without air-conditioning) are all inviting places to crash out.

Spirits Tavern   BURGERS $

(☑ 706-482-0580; www.spirits-tavern.com; 19 E Main St; burgers $12-15; ⊙ 11am-11pm Sun-Thu, to 1am Fri, to midnight Sun; 🛜) This full bar dishes up surprisingly creative burgers made from Angus beef or free range, hormone-free turkey, including crunchy mac 'n' cheese, Greek, Asian and Cajun versions.

Back Porch Oyster Bar   SEAFOOD $$

(☑ 706-864-8623; www.backporchoysterbar.net; 19 N Chestatee St; mains $9-31; ⊙ 11:30am-9pm Mon-Thu, to 10pm Fri & Sat, to 8pm Sun; 🛜) Oysters, ahi and clams are among the bounty flown in fresh daily to be shucked, seared and steamed at this neighborhood fish house.

ⓘ Information

Visitors Center (☑ 706-864-3711; www.dahlonega.org; 13 S Park St; ⊙ 9am-5:30pm Mon-Fri, 10am-5pm Sat) Has plenty of information on area sites and activities, including hiking, canoeing, kayaking, rafting and mountain biking.

ⓘ Getting There & Away

Dahlonega is about 70 miles north of Atlanta; the quickest way here is via Hwy 19. There is no bus service.

Athens

A beery, artsy and laid-back college town roughly 80 miles east of Atlanta, Athens has an extremely popular football team (the University of Georgia Bulldogs), a world-famous music scene, a burgeoning restaurant culture and surprisingly diverse

nightlife. The university – UGA – drives the culture of Athens and ensures an ever-replenishing supply of young bar-hoppers and concert-goers, some of whom stick around long after graduation and become 'townies.' The pleasant, walkable downtown offers a plethora of funky choices for eating, drinking and shopping.

⊙ Sights

★ **Georgia Museum of Art**   MUSEUM

(☑ 706-542-4662; www.georgiamuseum.org; 90 Carlton St; ⊙ 10am-5pm Tue-Wed, Fri & Sat, to 9pm Thu, 1-5pm Sun) FREE A smart, modern gallery where brainy, arty types set up in the wired lobby for personal study while art hounds gawk at modern sculpture in the courtyard garden and the tremendous collection from American realists of the 1930s.

State Botanical
Garden of Georgia   GARDENS

(www.botgarden.uga.edu; 2450 S Milledge Ave; ⊙ 8am-6pm) 🐾 FREE Truly gorgeous, with winding outdoor paths and a socio-historical edge, Athens' gardens are a gift for a city of this size. Signs provide smart context for its amazing collection of plants, which includes rare and threatened species; and there's nearly 5 miles of top-notch woodland walking trails.

🛏 Sleeping & Eating

★ **Graduate Athens**   INN $$

(☑ 706-549-7020; www.graduateathens.com; 295 E Dougherty St; r $100-170, ste $280-390; P@🛜🏊) This wonderfully designed boutique hotel, the inaugural address of a college-campus chain, is drowning in sexified retro hipness, from potted plants inside old-school Dewey Decimal card catalog filing cabinets in the lobby to the sweet Crosley turntables and classic video games in the suites.

Local accents, such as chalkboard-art of the chemical formula for sweet tea, fortify local allure. Also on-site is a great coffeehouse, bar and grill and live music venue, all inside an old Confederate iron foundry.

Hotel Indigo   BOUTIQUE HOTEL $$

(☑ 706-546-0430; www.indigoathens.com; 500 College Ave; r/ste from $160/265; P@🛜🏊🐾) 🐾 Rooms are spacious, loft-like pods of cool at this eco-chic boutique hotel. Part of the Indigo chain, it's a Leadership in Energy and Environmental Design gold-certified sustainable standout. Green elements include regenerative elevators and priority parking for hybrid vehicles; 30% of the building was constructed from recycled content.

Pouch   PIES $

(☑706-395-6696; www.pouchpies.com; 151 E Broad St; pies $5.50; ☉11am-10pm Mon-Wed, to 11pm Thu-Sat; ☑) In the South, 'pie' usually means something sweet, buttery and served after dinner. For the South African owners of Pouch, 'pie' means savory pastries from around the world – Aussie pies with beef and gravy, Portuguese pies with piri piri white wine sauce and chorizo, and even a cheeseburger-esque American pie! Makes for a great budget meal.

White Tiger   BARBECUE $

(☑706-353-6847; www.whitetigergourmet.com; 217 Hiawassee Ave; mains $6.75-10.50; ☉11am-3pm Mon-Sat, 6-8pm Thu, 10am-2pm Sun; ☐ ⬤) The 100-year-old structure doesn't invite confidence, but this off-the-beaten path local favorite does killer wood-smoked pulled pork sandwiches, burgers and even barbecue-smoked tofu for the vegetarians. Chef Ken Manring honed his skills in much higher-brow kitchens before settling in Athens.

home.made   SOUTHERN US $$

(☑706-206-9216; www.homemadeathens.com; 1072 Baxter St; mains $13-25; ☉11am-2pm & 5:30-9:30pm Tue-Sat) home.made is upping the game when it comes to nouveau Southern cuisine. The menu constantly changes based on ingredient availability, but whatever these folks source is always turned into something creative, delicious, rooted in local flavors and often playfully over the top – say, pan-seared flounder and turmeric rice grits.

Five & Ten   AMERICAN $$$

(☑706-546-7300; www.fiveandten.com; 1073 S Milledge Ave; mains $22-36; ☉5:30-10pm Sun-Thu, to 11pm Fri & Sat, 10:30am-2:30pm Sun; ☑) ⬤ Driven by sustainable ingredients, Five & Ten ranks among the South's best restaurants. Its menu is earthy and slightly gamey: sweetbreads, black-eyed pea hummus and Frogmore stew (stewed corn, sausage and potato). Reservations mandatory.

⚑ Drinking & Entertainment

Trapeze Pub   CRAFT BEER

(☑706-543-8997; www.trappezepub.com; 269 N Hull St; ☉11am-2am Mon-Sat, to midnight Sun; ☎) Downtown's best craft-beer bar installed itself well before the suds revolution. You'll find dozens of taps, including local fave Creature Comforts, and another 100 or so at any given time in bottles. Soak it all up with their Belgian-style fries, the best in town.

The Old Pal   BAR

(☑706-850-4340; www.theoldpal.com; 1320 Prince Ave; ☉4pm-2am Mon-Sat; ☎) The Old Pal is Normal Town's thinking man's bar, devoted to seasonal craft cocktails and a thoughtfully curated bourbon list. It's a beautiful, dark space that has been showered with local preservation awards.

Normal Bar   BAR

(☑706-548-6186; www.facebook.com/normal. bar.7; 1365 Prince Ave; ☉4pm-2am Mon-Fri, 11:30am-2am Sat; ☎) This lovable dark storefront

THE SOUTH NORTHERN GEORGIA

NATURE & ADVENTURE IN NORTHERN GEORGIA

Tallulah Gorge (☑706-754-7981; www.gastateparks.org/tallulahgorge; 338 Jane Hurt Yarn Dr, Tallulah Falls; per vehicle $5; ☉8am-sunset; ☐) The 1200ft-deep Tallulah Gorge carves a dark scar across the wooded hills of North Georgia. Walk over the *Indiana Jones*-worthy suspension bridge, and be on the lookout (literally) for rim trails to overlooks. Or get a first-come, first-served permit to hike to the gorge floor – only 100 are given out each day.

Vogel State Park (☑706-745-2628; www.gastateparks.org/vogel; 405 Vogel State Park Rd, Blairsville; per vehicle $5; ☉7am-10pm; ☐) Located at the base of the evocatively named Blood Mountain, this is one of Georgia's oldest parks, and constitutes a quilt of wooded mountains surrounding a 22-acre lake. There's a multitude of trails to pick from, catering to beginners and advanced hikers. Many of the on-site facilities were built by the Civilian Conservation Corp; a seasonal museum tells the story of these work teams, which both built the park and rescued the local economy during the Great Depression.

Unicoi State Park (☑706-878-2201; www.gastateparks.org/unicoi; 1788 Highway 356, Helen; per vehicle $5; ☉7am-10pm; ☐ ⬤) At this adventure-oriented park, visitors can rent kayaks ($10 per hour), take paddleboard lessons ($25), hike some 12 miles of trails, mountain bike, or take a zipline safari through the local forest canopy ($59).

bar is very unstudentlike but still very much Athens. The beer goes from PBR cheap to local craft IPA sophisticated. There's a terrific wine list and the crowd is cute, young and laid-back.

40 Watt Club   LIVE MUSIC

(☑ 706-549-7871; www.40watt.com; 285 W Washington St; admission $5-25) Athens' most storied joint has lounges, a tiki bar and $2.50 PBRs. The venue has welcomed indie rock to its stage since R.E.M., the B-52s and Widespread Panic owned this town, and today this is still where the big hitters play when they come to town.

ⓘ Information

Athens Welcome Center (☑ 706-353-1820; www.athenswelcomecenter.com; 280 E Dougherty St; ⊙10am-5pm Mon-Sat, noon-5pm Sun) This visitor center, in a historic antebellum house at the corner of Thomas St, provides maps and information on local tours.

ⓘ Getting There & Away

This college town is located about 70 miles east of Atlanta. There's no main highway that leads here, so traffic can be an issue on secondary state and county roads. The local **Greyhound station** (☑706-549-2255; www.greyhound.com; 4020 Atlanta Hwy, Bogart) is actually located about 6 miles west of downtown Athens. Buses leave for Atlanta (7½ hours, twice daily) and Savannah (14 hours, once daily).

Coastal Georgia

Compared to the urban, suburban and exurban sprawl that surrounds Atlanta, or the mountainous upcountry of North Georgia, the state's southern region hews to the Old South Spanish moss and live oak cliché. Swampy Savannah holds court as the state's irresistible Southern belle, but there's more to the region than antebellum architecture and Spanish moss – Georgia's wild and preserved barrier island-riddled coast is an often overlooked stunner.

Savannah

Savannah is a looker, make no mistake. Built around a historic district that is rife with elegant townhouses, antebellum mansions, mammoth live oak trees and green public squares draped in Spanish moss, this is, quite simply, an exceedingly attractive city.

But this town is more than a pretty face. If Savannah is a Southern belle, she's carrying a slug of whiskey and a bottle of hot sauce, and her legs might be proudly unshaven too. This town is graceful, to be sure – the phrase 'moonlight and magnolias' is overused, but man does it apply here – but it's also gritty, and playfully transgressive. That's partly a function of Savannah's tolerance of bad behavior (limited open container laws, woo!), plus the presence of students at the Savannah College of Art & Design (SCAD), one of the finest art schools in the country.

⊙ Sights & Activities

★**Wormsloe Plantation
Historic Site**   HISTORIC SITE

(☑ 912-353-3023; www.gastateparks.org/Wormsloe; 7601 Skidaway Rd; adult/senior/child 6-17yr/child 1-5yr $10/9/4.50/2; ⊙9am-5pm Tue-Sun; Ⓟ) ✿ A short drive from downtown, on the beautiful Isle of Hope, this is one of the most photographed sites in town. As soon as you enter, you feel as if you've been roused from the last snatch of an arboreal dream as you gaze at a corridor of mossy, ancient oaks that runs for 1.5 miles, known as the Avenue of the Oaks.

Forsyth Park   PARK

FREE The Central Park of Savannah is a sprawling rectangular green space, anchored by a beautiful fountain that forms a quintessential photo op.

Mercer-Williams House   HISTORIC BUILDING

(☑ 912-236-6352; www.mercerhouse.com; 429 Bull St; adult/student $12.50/8; ⊙10:30am-4:10pm Mon-Sat, noon-4pm Sun) Although Jim Williams, the Savannah art dealer portrayed by Kevin Spacey in the film version of *Midnight in the Garden of Good and Evil*, died back in 1990, his infamous mansion didn't become a museum until 2004. You're not allowed to visit the upstairs, where Williams' family still lives, but the downstairs is an interior decorator's fantasy.

Owens-Thomas House   HISTORIC BUILDING

(☑ 912-790-8800; www.telfair.org/visit/owens-thomas; 124 Abercorn St; adult/senior/child $20/18/15; ⊙noon-5pm Sun & Mon, 10am-5pm Tue-Sat) Completed in 1819 by British architect William Jay, this gorgeous villa exemplifies English Regency-style architecture, known for its symmetry. The guided tour is a little obsessed with details on aristocratic life, but it delivers interesting trivia about the spooky 'haint blue' ceiling paint in the slaves quarters (made from crushed indigo, buttermilk and crushed oyster shells) and the number of years by which this mansion preceded the White House in getting running water (nearly 20).

Telfair Academy of Arts & Sciences MUSEUM

(☑912-790-8800; www.telfair.org/visit/telfair; 121 Barnard St; adult/child $20/15; ⊙noon-5pm Sun & Mon, 10am-5pm Tue-Sat) Considered Savannah's top art museum, the historic Telfair family mansion is filled with 19th-century American art and silver, and a smattering of European pieces. The home itself is gorgeous and sunrise-hued – an artifact in its own right that wows visitors.

SCAD Museum of Art MUSEUM

(www.scadmoa.org; 601 Turner Blvd; adult/child under 14yr $10/free; ⊙10am-5pm Tue-Wed, to 8pm Thu, to 5pm Fri & Sat, noon-5pm Sun) Architecturally striking (but what else would you expect from this school of design?), this brick, steel, concrete and glass longhouse delivers your contemporary art fix. There are groovy, creative sitting areas inside and out, and a number of rotating and visiting exhibitions that showcase some of the most impressive talents within the contemporary art world.

Jepson Center for the Arts GALLERY

(JCA; ☑912-790-8800; www.telfair.org/visit/jepson; 207 W York St; adult/child $20/15; ⊙noon-5pm Sun & Mon, 10am-5pm Tue-Sat; 📵) Designed by the great Moshe Safdie, and looking pretty darn space-age by Savannah's standards, the JCA – rather appropriately, given its architecture – focuses on 20th- and 21st-century art. Be on the lookout for wandering scads of SCAD students (ha) and temporary exhibitions covering topics from race to art in VR video games.

Savannah Bike Tours CYCLING

(☑912-704-4043; www.savannahbiketours.com; 41 Habersham St; tours $25; ⊙hours vary by season) This outfit offers two-hour bike tours over easy flat terrain on its fleet of cruisers. Call ahead or check the website for tour times.

🛏 Sleeping

Savannah Pensione GUESTHOUSE $

(☑912-236-7744; www.savannahpensione.com; 304 E Hall St; s/d without bath from $55/65; 📵✳@) It was run as a hostel for some 15 years, but the owner of this basic neighborhood crash pad got tired of backpackers

traipsing up and down the historic steps of the 1884 Italianate mansion. Fair enough. Now a bare-bones and vibeless pension, it still offers the cheapest historic quarter rooms, though its potential is unrealized.

★ The Kimpton Brice HOTEL $$

(☑912-238-1200; www.bricehotel.com; 601 E Bay St; r from $175; ✳@✆✉) Kimpton is known for their design-conscious hotels, so you gotta figure they'd bring their A game to one of the country's leading design cities. The Kimpton Brice does not disappoint in this, or any other, regard. Modern rooms have playful swatches of color, while the hotel's entrance and lobby feels like it could accommodate a cool club.

Thunderbird Inn MOTEL $$

(☑912-232-2661; www.thethunderbirdinn.com; 611 W Oglethorpe Ave; r $120-150; 📵✳✆✉) 'A tad Palm Springs, a touch Vegas' best describes this vintage-chic 1964 motel that wins its own popularity contest – a 'Hippest hotel in Savannah' proclamation greets guests in the '60s-soundtracked lobby. In a land of stuffy B&Bs, this groovy place is an oasis, made all the better by local Savannah College of Art & Design student art.

Azalea Inn INN $$

(☑912-236-6080; www.azaleainn.com; 217 E Huntingdon St; r/villa from $200/300; 📵✳✆✉) A humble stunner on a quiet street, we love this sweet canary-yellow historic inn near Forsyth Park. The 10 rooms aren't huge, but are well done with varnished dark-wood floors, crown moldings, four-poster beds and a small dipping pool out back. Three new villas offer more modern luxury for long-term stays.

Kehoe House B&B $$$

(☑912-232-1020; www.kehoehouse.com; 123 Habersham St; r from $240; ✳✆) This romantic, upscale Renaissance Revival B&B dates from 1892, and twins are said to have died in a chimney here, making it one of America's most haunted hotels (if you're skittish, steer clear of rooms 201 and 203). Ghosts aside, it's a beautifully appointed worthwhile splurge on picturesque Columbia Square.

Mansion on Forsyth Park HOTEL $$$

(☑912-238-5158; www.mansiononforsythpark.com; 700 Drayton St; r weekday/weekend $220/360; 📵✳@✆✉) A choice location and chic design highlight the luxe accommodations on offer at the 18,000-sq-ft Mansion – the sexy

Savannah

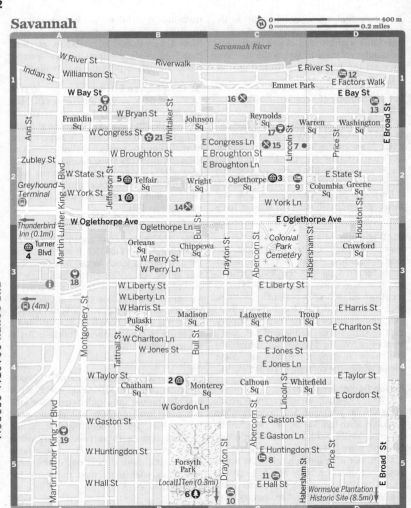

bathrooms alone are practically worth the money. The best part of the hotel-spa is the amazing local and international art that crowds its walls and hallways – over 400 pieces in all.

Old Harbour Inn BOUTIQUE HOTEL $$$
(☑912-234-4100; www.oldeharbourinn.com; 508 East Factors Walk; ste $205-290; ⊛🐾) The spiffy suites at this waterfront hotel occupy the golden mean between historic atmosphere and modern sensibilities, from the airy sense of space (a bit of space, actually – from 450 to 650 sq ft) to the subdued color schemes

and polished hardwood floors. There's a free wine and cheese reception every evening.

✖ Eating

⭐**B's Cracklin' BBQ** BARBECUE $
(☑912-330-6921; www.bscracklinbbq.com; 12409 White Bluff Rd; mains $9-19; ⊙11am-9pm Tue-Sat, to 6pm Sun; 🅿) This is *very* good barbecue. Pit master Bryan Furman left his job as a welder to raise his own hogs and source local ingredients for homemade sides. The result is smoky heaven: melting brisket, falling-off-the-bone ribs and perfect Carolina-style pork. The portions are more than

Savannah

⊙ Sights
1 Jepson Center for the Arts B2
2 Mercer-Williams House........................B4
3 Owens-Thomas House...........................C2
4 SCAD Museum of Art A3
5 Telfair Academy of Arts & Sciences.....B2
6 Forsyth Park B5

⊕ Activities, Courses & Tours
7 Savannah Bike Tours...........................C2

⊜ Sleeping
8 Azalea Inn..C5
9 Kehoe House...C2
10 Mansion on Forsyth Park......................C5
11 Savannah Pensione C5

12 Old Harbour Inn D1
13 The Kimpton Brice..................................D1

⊗ Eating
14 Collins Quarter.......................................B2
15 Leopold's Ice Cream...............................C2
16 Treylor Park..C1

⊙ Drinking & Nightlife
17 Abe's on Lincoln.....................................C2
18 Distillery Ale House A3
19 Chromatic Dragon..................................A5
20 Club One A1

⊛ Entertainment
21 The Jinx...B2

generous; prepare to leave as stuffed as one of Bryan's hogs. B's is located about 8 miles south of downtown.

Leopold's Ice Cream   ICE CREAM $
(✆ 912-234-4442; www.leopoldsicecream.com; 212 E Broughton St; scoops $3-5.50; ⊙ 11am-11pm Sun-Thu, to midnight Fri & Sat; 🛜) This classic American ice-cream parlor feels like the Last Man Standing, having been scooping up its creamy Greek recipes since 1919. Tutti Frutti was invented here, but we dig coffee, pistachio honey almond, and cream and caramel swirl. Hurry up and wait.

Sweet Spice   JAMAICAN $
(✆ 912-335-8146; www.sweetspicesavannah.net; 5515 Waters Ave; mains $6-14; ⊙ 11am-8pm Mon-Thu, to 9pm Fri & Sat) This easygoing Jamaican spot, about 4.5 miles southeast of downtown, is a welcome break from the almost ubiquitous American and Southern fare you get in this part of the world. A large platter of curry goat or jerk chicken costs just a smidge more than a fast-food meal and it's utterly delicious. It will also keep you filled up for roughly the rest of the year.

Treylor Park   SOUTHERN US $
(✆ 888-873-9567, 912-495-5557; www.treylorpark savannah.com; 115 E Bay St; mains $6-15; ⊙ noon-1am Mon-Wed, to 2am Fri, 10am-2am Sat, 10am-1am Sun) All the hip young things pack into this 'Treylor Park,' which revels in a retro-chic, Airstream aesthetic. The food? Southern classics simply done well: fried chicken on a biscuit with sausage gravy and spicy collard greens, or a grilled apple pie sandwich. Take your pick, and wash it down with an excellent cocktail in the warmly lit courtyard.

Collins Quarter   CAFE $$
(✆ 912-777-4147; www.thecollinsquarter.com; 151 Bull St; dinner mains $17-32; ⊙ 6:30am-5pm Mon, to noon Tue, to 10pm Wed-Sun; 🛜) If you have ever talked coffee with an Australian, you know they are particularly fussy about their java. This wildly popular newcomer is Australian-owned and turns Australian-roasted Brooklyn coffee into their beloved flat whites and long blacks. Beyond Savannah's best coffee, it serves excellent fusion fare, including a drool-inducing brisket burger. There's booze too!

★Local11Ten   MODERN AMERICAN $$$
(✆ 912-790-9000; www.local11ten.com; 1110 Bull St; mains $26-45; ⊙ 6-10pm; 🅿) Upscale, sustainable, local and fresh: these elements help create an elegant, well-run restaurant that's easily one of Savannah's best. Start with a deconstructed rabbit ravioli, then move on to the fabulous seared sea scallops in mint beurre blanc or the harissa-marinated bison hanger steak and a salted caramel pot de crème for a happy ending. Wait. Scratch that. The menu already changed.

🍷 Drinking & Entertainment

River St, with its plastic-cup, open-container laws, is the bar-hopping nightlife corridor, but Savannah's nightlife is more than spring break bacchanalia. There are also some smart, exceedingly interesting bars out here.

★Chromatic Dragon   BAR
(✆ 912-289-0350; www.chromaticdragon.com; 514 Martin Luther King Jr Blvd; ⊙ 11am-11pm Sun-Thu, to 2am Fri & Sat) If the name of this place

THE SOUTH COASTAL GEORGIA

made you smile, you'll be right at home in this gamers pub, which features video game consoles, board games and drinks named for fantasy references, from *Harry Potter* butterbeer to fantasy role playing game 'healing potions.' There's a warm, welcoming atmosphere – truly, this is a certain kind of nerd's ultimate neighborhood bar.

Abe's on Lincoln
BAR

(☎ 912-349-0525; www.abesonlincoln.com; 17 Lincoln St; ⊙ 4pm-3am Mon-Sat) Pop back a beer or 10 with SCAD students and locals at this dark, dank, all-wood bar. Attracts an eclectic crowd that stares through their boozy goggles at whatever weird behavior the bartenders are inevitably tolerating that night. Good times.

Distillery Ale House
BAR

(☎ 912-236-1772; www.distilleryalehouse.com; 416 W Liberty St; ⊙ 11am-late Mon-Sat, noon-late Sun) Formerly the Kentucky Distilling Co, which opened in 1904 and closed at Prohibition, this is oddly *not* Savannah's local throat-burning swill house, but rather its go-to craft beer bar. It's also popular with tourists and families for bar food.

Club One
GAY & LESBIAN

(☎ 912-232-0200; www.clubone-online.com; 1 Jefferson St; ⊙ 5pm-3am) Drag shows (resident star Lady Chablis appeared in *Midnight in the Garden of Good and Evil*), ripping dance nights and plenty of flirting kicks off pretty regularly at this gay bar, which is otherwise a laid-back place where a mix of locals and SCAD students play pool and shoot the breeze.

The Jinx
LIVE MUSIC

(☎ 912-236-2281; www.thejinx912.com; 127 W Congress St; ⊙ 4pm-3am) A good slice of odd-duck Savannah nightlife, the Jinx is popular with students, townies, musicians, and basically anyone else who has a thing for dive-y watering holes with live music – from rock to punk to alt-country to hip-hop – and funky stuff decorating the walls.

ⓘ Information

Candler Hospital (☎ 912-819-4100; www. sjchs.org; 5353 Reynolds St; ⊙ 24hr) Located about 4 miles south of downtown, the Candler Hospital provides good 24/7 care and service. There's another campus at 11075 Mercy Blvd.

Savannah Visitors Center (☎ 912-944-0455; www.savannahvisit.com; 301 Martin Luther King Jr Blvd; ⊙ 9am-5:30pm) Excellent

resources and services are available in this center, based in a restored 1860s train station. Many privately operated city tours start here. There is also a small interactive tourist info kiosk in the visitor center at Forsyth Park.

ⓘ Getting There & Around

Savannah is located off I-95, about 110 miles south of Charleston, SC. The **Savannah/Hilton Head International Airport** (SAV; ☎ 912-964-0514; www.savannahairport.com; 400 Airways Ave) is about 5 miles west of downtown, off I-16; service is mainly domestic flights to Eastern seaboard, Southern and Midwestern cities. **Greyhound** (☎ 912-232-2135; www.greyhound. com; 610 W Oglethorpe Ave) has connections to Atlanta (about five hours), Charleston, SC (about two hours) and Jacksonville, FL (2½ hours). The **Amtrak station** (www.amtrak.com; 2611 Seaboard Coastline Dr) is just a few miles west of the Historic District; trains run to Charleston, Jacksonville, and from there to points beyond.

Savannah is very foot-friendly. Chatham Area Transit (www.catchacat.org) operates local buses that run on bio-diesel, including a free shuttle (the Dot) that makes its way around the Historic District and stops within a couple of blocks of nearly every major site. Fare is $1.50 per ride.

CAT Bike (www.catbike.bcycle.com; ⊙ daily/ weekly membership $5/20, per 30min $2) is a convenient bike hire scheme run by Chatham Area Transit. You have to buy a membership, after which it's free for the first hour. There are stations around town.

Taxis from the airport to the Historic District cost a standard $28.

Brunswick & the Golden Isles

With its large shrimp-boat fleet and downtown historic district shaded by lush live oaks, Brunswick has charms you might miss when sailing by on I-95 or the Golden Isle Pkwy (US Hwy 17). The town dates from 1733, and while it's not as tourism oriented as other parts of the coast, visitors may find this a refreshing change of pace.

Mary Ross Waterfront Park
PARK

(Bay St) During WWII Brunswick shipyards constructed 99 Liberty transport ships for the navy. Today a 23ft scale model at Mary Ross Waterfront Park stands as a memorial to those ships and their builders.

Hostel in the Forest
HOSTEL $

(☎ 912-264-9738; www.foresthostel.com; 3901 Hwy 82; per person $30; 🅿 🐾) ⏐ The only budget base in the area is this set of barebones octagonal cedar huts and tree houses (sans air or heat) on an ecofriendly, sustainable campus. You must pay a member fee of $10 to stay, and dinner is included. As you might guess, the hostel is tucked in the woods, about 10 miles outside Brunswick. Phone reservations only.

❶ Getting There & Around

Brunswick is located off Hwy 17. **Greyhound** (☑ 800-231-2222; 2990 Hwy 17 S) buses stop at the Flying J gas station, 10 miles west of town. Destinations include Savannah ($16, two hours, twice daily) and Jacksonville ($15, 70 minutes, twice daily) – you can catch onward buses from either city.

ST SIMONS ISLAND

Famous for its golf courses, resorts and majestic live oaks, St Simons Island is the largest and most developed of the Golden Isles. While there are pretty beaches galore, the natural beauty of St Simons isn't as easy to access compared to other nearby islands given the presence of heavy residential and resort development. For example, the island of Little St Simons is an all-natural jewel, but it's only accessible by only to guests staying at the exclusive Lodge on Little St Simons. On the other hand, if you need to get some golf in, this is the island for you.

Lighthouse Museum   MUSEUM
(☑ 912-638-4666; www.saintsimonslighthouse.org; 610 Beachview Dr; adult/child 5-11yr $10/5; ⏰ 10am-5pm Mon-Sat, 1:30-5pm Sun) Built in 1807 and standing 85ft tall, the first lighthouse was destroyed by Confederates when Union troops landed in 1862. The second lighthouse, which you'll be able to tour, was built in 1872. The 104ft tower has a spiral 129-step cast iron staircase and an adjacent keeper's residence.

🛏 Sleeping & Eating

St Simons Inn By The Lighthouse   INN $$
(☑ 912-638-1101; www.saintsimonsinn.com; 609 Beachview Dr; r $140-160; P ❄ 🐾 🛜 🏊) This cute and comfortable good-value inn is accented with white wooden shutters and a general sense of seaside breeziness. It's well located next to the downtown drag and a short pedal from East Beach. Continental breakfast included.

Lodge on Little St Simons Island   LODGE $$$
(☑ 888-733-5774; www.littlestsimonsisland.com; 1000 Hampton River Club Dr, Little St Simons Is-

---

WORTH A TRIP

CUMBERLAND ISLAND NATIONAL SEASHORE
· ·
An unspoiled paradise, a backpacker's fantasy, a site for day trips or extended stays – it's clear why the Carnegie family used **Cumberland Island National Seashore** (☑ 912-882-4336; www.nps.gov/cuis; $7) as a retreat long ago. Almost half of its 36,415 acres consists of marsh, mudflats and tidal creeks. On the ocean side are 16 miles of wide, sandy beach that you might have all to yourself. The island's interior is characterized by maritime forest.

---

land; d from $425; ❄ 🛜) This isolated historic lodge sits on pristine and private Little St Simons. Stays include accommodations, boat transfers to and from the island, three prepared meals daily, beverages (including soft drinks, beer and wine), all activities (including naturalist-led excursions) and use of all recreation equipment. Rooms have a rustic, cabin vibe, albeit with modern amenities.

Southern Soul BBQ   BARBECUE $
(☑ 912-638-7685; www.southernsoulbbq.com; 2020 Demere Rd; mains $7.50-20; ⏰ 11am-9pm Mon-Sat, to 6pm Sun; 🍴) Succulent slow oak-smoked pulled pork, burnt-tipped brisket and daily specials like jerk chicken burritos keep this joint packed with satisfied 'cue fanatics. There are a number of wonderful housemade sauces and a great patio from which to take it all in.

★ Halyards   SEAFOOD $$$
(☑ 912-638-9100; www.halyardsrestaurant.com; 55 Cinema Lane; mains $18-42; ⏰ 5-9pm Mon-Wed, to 10pm Thu-Sat; 🛜) 🌱 Chef Dave Snyder's classy sustainable, seasonal seafooder consistently hogs best-of-everything awards on St Simons, and for good reason. Go for the Chef's Highlights, such as mahimahi over boursin grits, haricot verts and orange-vanilla butter – perfection.

JEKYLL ISLAND

An exclusive refuge for millionaires in the late 19th and early 20th centuries, Jekyll is a 4000-year-old barrier island with 10 miles of beaches. Today it's an unusual clash of wilderness, preserved historic buildings, modern hotels and a massive campground. It's an easily navigable place – you can get around by car, horse or bicycle.

THE SOUTH COASTAL GEORGIA

◉ Sights & Activities

Georgia Sea Turtle Center WILDLIFE RESERVE
(☑912-635-4444; www.georgiaseaturtlecenter.
org; 214 Stable Rd; adult/child $7/5, tours $22-6;
⊙9am-5pm, closed Mon Nov-Mar; ⊞) An endearing attraction is the Georgia Sea Turtle Center, a conservation center and turtle
hospital where patients are on view for the
public. Behind the Scenes tours (3pm) and
Turtle Walks (June and July) are also available, among other programs.

4-H Tidelands Nature Center MUSEUM
(http://caes2.caes.uga.edu/georgia4h/tidelands;
100 S Riverview Dr; ⊙9am-4pm Mon-Fri, 10am-
2pm Sat & Sun; ⊞) ✐ Run by a staff of peppy
University of Georgia science students, the
Tidelands is a kid-friendly nature center
with some neat display cases on local ecology and resident wildlife, including a baby
alligator. Nearby you'll find a lovely network
of nature trails that wend past marshlands
and through maritime forests.

★ Kayak Tours & Canoe Rentals BOATING
(☑912-635-5032; http://caes2.caes.uga.edu/geor-
gia4h/tidelands/tours; 100 S Riverview Dr; s/tan-
dem kayak tour $55/95, canoe rental per hour/day
$15/30) The 4-H Tidelands Nature Center
conducts highly recommended three-hour
tours of the salt marshes; on any given day,
you may paddle past wood storks, great
blue herons, pelicans and dolphins. By far,
this is the best local means of accessing the
understated beauty of the barrier island salt
marshes. Canoe rentals are also available.

🛏 Sleeping & Eating

Villas By The Sea VILLA $
(☑912-635-2521; www.villasbythesearesort.com;
1175 N Beachview Dr; r/condo from $125/235;
P❄🛜🏊) A nice choice on the north coast
close to the best beaches. Rooms are spacious and the one-, two- and three-bedroom
condos, set in a complex of lodge buildings
sprinkled over a garden, aren't fancy but
they're plenty comfy.

Jekyll Island Club Hotel HISTORIC HOTEL $$
(☑855-535-9547; www.jekyllclub.com; 371 River-
view Dr; d/ste from $200/300, resort fee $15;
P❄@🛜🏊) A posh and storied hotel and
the backbone of the island, featuring a ram-
bling array of rooms spread out over five his-
toric structures. Each building feels plucked
from a novel about Jazz Age decadence,
although the current vibe is a little more
Hilton Head country club.

Driftwood Bistro SOUTHERN US $$
(☑912-635-3588; www.driftwoodbistro.com; 1175
Beach View Dr; mains $9.50-16.50; ⊙5-9pm
Mon-Sat; P) Driftwood Bistro serves decent
Lowcountry-style seafood in an old-school,
family-friendly resort-style setting. Local
Georgia shrimp – cooked in sauce as shrimp
creole, or just steamed for you to peel and
eat – is usually on the menu. Any way it
comes, you shouldn't miss these plump,
sweet delicacies.

ALABAMA

History suffuses Alabama, a description that
could be true of many states. But there are
few places where the perception of said history is so emotionally fraught. The Mississippian Native American culture built great
mound cities here, and Mobile is dotted
with Franco-Caribbean architecture. But
for many, the word Alabama is synonymous
with the American Civil Rights movement.

Perhaps such a struggle, and all of the
nobility and desperation it entailed, was
bound for a state like this, with its Gothic
plantations, hardscrabble farmland and
fiercely local sense of place. From the smallest hunting town to river-bound cities, Alabama is a place all its own, and its character
is hard to forget. Some visitors have a hard
time looking beyond the state's past, but the
troubling elements of that narrative are tied
up in a passion that constantly manifests in
Alabama's arts, food and culture.

ℹ Information

Alabama Tourism Department (http://alabama.
travel) Sends out a vacation guide and has a
website with extensive tourism options.

ℹ Getting There & Away

While there are mid-sized domestic airports in
Mobile and Montgomery, the most common air
entry to Alabama is via Birmingham-Shuttles-
worth International Airport (p429).

Alabama is bordered by Mississippi, Florida,
Georgia and Tennessee. The Gulf Coast of
Alabama is barely an hour away from some of
the Florida Panhandle's best beaches. if you're
road-tripping around, Birmingham is about 150
miles from Atlanta, GA, 200 miles from Nashville, TN, and 190 miles from Oxford, MS.

The main highways in the state are I-10, which
cuts across the Gulf Coast; I-65, which runs
north to south; I-20, which cuts horizontally
across the center-top; and I-59, which runs in a
diagonal line northeast to Chattanooga.

You can find Greyhound stations in major towns. Amtrak has service to Birmingham, and there is talk of reestablishing an Amtrak line across the Gulf Coast.

Birmingham

Birmingham may lack the name-brand recognition of musical powerhouses like New Orleans and Nashville, or business centers like Atlanta and Houston. What Alabama's largest city possesses instead is vast reserves of unexpected cool. Innovative urban renewal and beautification projects seem to lurk around every corner – at least, the ones that aren't occupied by fantastic bars and restaurants. And while opinions run the gamut, this is a far more liberal town than you may expect given the political proclivities of its home state.

This hilly, shady city, founded as an iron mine, is still a center for manufacturing – many Birmingham residents work at Mercedes Benz USA in Tuscaloosa. In addition, universities and colleges pepper the town, and all of this comes together to create a city with an unreservedly excellent dining-and-drinking scene. The past also lurks in Birmingham, once named 'Bombingham,' and the history of the Civil Rights movement is very much at your fingers.

⊙ Sights & Activities

Art-deco buildings abound in trendy **Five Points South**, where you'll find shops, restaurants and nightspots. Once-industrial **Avondale** is where the hipsters are congregating. Equally noteworthy is the upscale **Homewood** community's quaint commercial drag on 18th St S, close to the *Vulcan*, which looms illuminated above the city and is visible from nearly all angles, day and night.

★**Birmingham**
Civil Rights Institute   MUSEUM
(☑866-328-9696; www.bcri.org; 520 16th St N; adult/child $12/5, Sun by donation; ⊙10am-5pm Tue-Sat, 1-5pm Sun) A maze of moving audio, video and photography exhibits tell the story of racial segregation in America, and the Civil Rights movement, with a focus on activities in and around Birmingham. There's an extensive exhibit on the 16th Street Baptist Church (located across the street), which was bombed in 1963; it's the beginning of the city's Civil Rights Memorial Trail.

★**Sloss Furnaces**   FACTORY
(☑205-254-2025; www.slossfurnaces.com; 20 32nd St N; ⊙10am-4pm Tue-Sat, noon-4pm Sun; ℗) 🖋FREE The Sloss Furnaces constitutes one of Birmingham's can't-miss sites. From 1882 to 1971, this was a pig iron–producing blast furnace and a cornerstone of Birmingham's economy. Today, instead of a wasteland it's a National Historic Landmark, a red mass of steel and girders rusted into a Gothic monument to American industry. Quiet pathways pass cobwebbed workshops and production lines that form a photographer's dream playground. A small museum on site explores the furnaces' history.

Railroad Park   PARK
(☑205-521-9933; www.railroadpark.org; ⊙7am-11pm; 😃) 🖋FREE Credit where it's due: Birmingham's Railroad Park, which constitutes some 19 acres of downtown real estate, is a stroke of planning brilliance. As urban green lungs go, this park, and its miles of pathways, public art and pretty lighting, is fantastic. A good place to access the park is on 1st Ave South, between 14th and 18th St South.

Vulcan Park   PARK
(☑205-933-1409; www.visitvulcan.com; 1701 Valley View Dr; observation tower & museum adult/child $6/4, 6-10pm $4; ⊙park 7am-10pm; observation tower 10am-6pm daily; museum 10am-6pm Mon-Sat, from noon Sun; 😃) Imagine Christ the Redeemer in Rio, but made of iron and depicting a beefcake Roman god of metalworking. Vulcan is visible from all over the city – this is actually the world's largest cast-iron statue – and the park he resides in offers

ⓘ **BIRMINGHAM MOUNTAIN RADIO**

Whenever you are in the city of Birmingham, turn the radio dial to 107.3 FM and never touch it until you leave. This is the setting for Birmingham Mountain Radio, one of the finest independent radio stations in the country. The DJs here play an incredible, eclectic range of music that ranges from country to rock to hip-hop to pop. There are few stations in the country – in the world, really – that we can listen to without a break for the entirety of a day, but Mountain Radio is one of them. Note that the station can be accessed at 97.5 in Tuscaloosa.

fantastic views, along with an **observation tower**. A small on-site museum explores Birmingham history.

Birmingham Museum of Art
GALLERY

(205-254-2565; www.artsbma.org; 2000 Rev Abraham Woods Jr Blvd; 10am-5pm Tue-Sat, noon-5pm Sun; FREE) This fine museum boasts an impressive collection, especially given Birmingham's status as a mid-sized city. Inside, you'll find works from Asia, Africa, Europe and the Americas. Don't miss pieces by Rodin, Botero and Dalí in the sculpture garden.

16th Street Baptist Church
CHURCH

(205-251-9402; www.16thstreetbaptist.org; cnr 16th St & 6th Ave N; $5; ministry tours 10am-3pm Tue-Fri, by appointment only 10am-1pm Sat) This church became a gathering place for organizational meetings and a launchpad for protests in Birmingham in the 1950s and '60s. During a massive desegregation campaign directed at downtown merchants in 1963, Ku Klux Klan members bombed the church during Sunday school, killing four little girls. Today the rebuilt church is a memorial and house of worship (services 11am Sunday).

Birmingham Civil Rights Memorial Trail
WALKING

(www.bcri.org; 520 16th St N) Seven blocks long, this is a poignant walk. Installed in 2013 for the 50th anniversary of the Civil Rights campaign, the walk depicts 22 scenes with plaques, statues and photography, some of it quite conceptual and moving – to wit, a gauntlet of snapping, sculpted dog statues that pedestrians must traverse. The experience peels back yet another layer of the sweat and blood behind a campaign that changed America.

Sleeping

Hotel Highland
HOTEL $$

(205-933-9555; www.thehotelhighland.com; 1023 20th St S; r from $150; P❄@🛜) Nuzzled right up next to the lively Five Points district, this colorful, slightly trippy but modern hotel is very comfortable and a good deal. The rooms are thankfully a bit less bright and funky than the lobby.

Redmont Hotel
HISTORIC HOTEL $$

(205-957-6828; www.redmontbirmingham.com; 2101 5th Ave N; r/ste from $170/230; ❄@🛜) The piano and chandelier in the lobby of this 1925 hotel lend a certain historical, old-world feel, and all deluxe rooms were just renovated, giving it modern edge. The spacious rooftop bar doesn't hurt, either. It's walking distance to the civil rights sights.

Eating

★ Saw's Soul Kitchen
BARBECUE $

(205-591-1409; www.sawsbbq.com; 215 41st St S; mains $9-16; 11am-8pm Mon-Sat, to 4pm Sun; 👪) Saw's has exploded onto the Birmingham barbecue scene with a vengeance, offering some of the most mouth-watering smoked meat in the city, served in a family-friendly atmosphere. Stuffed potatoes make a nice addition to your meal, and the smoked chicken with a tangy local white sauce is divine – although with that said, bring on the ribs!

★ Tacos Dos Hermanos
MEXICAN $

(98 14th Street N; mains $2-6; 10am-2pm Mon-Fri; 🚲) Excellent tacos – simple, delicious, cheap and...look, we have to stress: *delicious*. These guys sling a simple menu, will accommodate vegetarians, work hard and pull in huge crowds ranging from construction workers to office drones.

Eagle's Restaurant
AMERICAN $

(205-320-0099; www.eaglesrestaurant.com; 2610 16th St N; mains $6.75-17; 10:30am-3:30pm Sun-Fri) Tucked away on a lonely strip is Eagle's, home of Birmingham's best soul food. This popular spot operates on a meat-and-two/three model: order a main, be it steak and gravy, neckbones and potatoes or chicken wings, then pick from a buffet tray of side options. It's delicious, cheap and as local as anything.

★ Galley & Garden
FRENCH $$$

(www.galleyandgarden.com; 2220 Highland Ave S; dinner mans $28-36) 🍃 The American South meets French rustic (and *haute*) cuisine in this establishment, which is rapidly becoming a go-to for Birmingham area foodies and those in search of a good date night. The farm-to-table menu is excellent; be on the lookout for solid, well-executed mains like seared red snapper and and slow-cooked short rib.

Drinking & Nightlife

★ Garage Café
BAR

(205-322-3220; www.garagecafe.us; 2304 10th Terrace S; 3pm-2am Sun-Mon, 11am-2am Tue-Sat) A crowd of hipsters and older drinking pros knock back their brew while tapping their toes to live music in a courtyard full of junk, antiques, ceramic statues and, quite literally, the kitchen sink.

★ **Marty's**   BAR
(1813 10th Ct S; ⊗ 8pm-6am, plus 10am-3pm Sat) Marty's plays to hipsters, cool kids and an unapologetically geeky crowd, who are all attracted to a friendly bar packed with comic book art, *Star Wars* memorabilia, role-playing-game references, DJ nights, pop-up dining events and the occasional live music gig. No phone number.

41 Street Pub & Aircraft Sales   BAR
(☑ 205-202-4187; www.41ststreetpub.com; 130 41st St S; ⊗ 4:30pm-midnight Mon-Thu, 4:30pm-2am Fri, 1pm-2am Sat, 1pm-midnight Sun) A slick wooden bar fronts a large open space offset with some shuffleboard tables. Behind the bar, strong drinks (the Moscow Mule is a winner) are served in shiny copper mugs to an attractive, hipster crowd.

The Collins Bar   BAR
(☑ 205-323-7995; www.thecollinsbar.com; 2125 2nd Ave N; ⊗ 4pm-midnight Tue-Thu, to 2am Fri & Sat, 6pm-midnight Sun) Birmingham's beautiful people pack into this cool space after work and on weekends, sipping handmade cocktails under giant paper planes and a Birmingham-centric periodic table of the elements. There's no drink menu – tell the bartender what flavors you like and they'll mix something special for you.

ⓘ Getting There & Around

The **Birmingham-Shuttlesworth International Airport** (BHM; ☑ 205-599-0500; www.flybirmingham.com) is about 5 miles northeast of downtown Birmingham.

   Greyhound (☑ 205-252-7190; www.greyhound.com; 618 19th St N), north of downtown, serves cities including Huntsville (1¾ hours, $22, three daily), Montgomery (1¾ hours, $25, three daily), Atlanta, GA (2½ hours, $17, five daily), Jackson, MS (4½ hours, $20, four daily), and New Orleans, LA (nine hours, $56, daily).

   Amtrak (☑ 205-324-3033; www.amtrak.com; 1 19th St North), downtown, has trains daily to New York (22 hours, $124) and New Orleans (7½ hours, $47).

   Birmingham Transit Authority (www.bjcta.org) runs local MAX buses. Adult fare is $1.25. You can also get around via the **Zyp** (☑ 844-997-2453; www.zypbikeshare.com; 24hr/one-week membership $6/20) bicycle-sharing program.

Montgomery

Alabama's capital is a pleasant if sleepy spot to visit; with a few exceptions, most of its main points of interest are tied to the American Civil Rights movement, which the city played a key role in. In 1955 Rosa Parks refused to give up her seat to a white man on a city bus, launching a bus boycott led by Martin Luther King Jr, then-pastor of Montgomery's Dexter Avenue Baptist Church. In the short run, the boycott inspired horrific acts of violence and repression by pro-segregation white citizens, but the boycott ultimately desegregated city buses and galvanized the Civil Rights movement nationwide, helping to lay the foundation for the Selma to Montgomery protest marches of 1965.

⊙ Sights

★ **Dexter Avenue Parsonage**   HISTORIC SITE
(☑ 334-261-3270; www.dexterkingmemorial.org/tours/parsonage-museum; 309 S Jackson Street; adult/child $7.50/5.50; ⊗ 10am-3pm Tue-Fri, to 1pm Sat; ℗) The home of Martin Luther King Jr and Coretta Scott King has been frozen in time, a snapshot of a mid-Century home complete with *Mad Men*–era furniture, appliances and indoor ashtrays (King was a regular smoker). The most fascinating part of the tour is King's old office, which still contains some of the books that influenced his theology, philosophy and activism. In the back, there's a garden filled with stones inscribed with Christian virtues.

Civil Rights Memorial Center   MEMORIAL
(☑ 334-956-8200; www.splcenter.org/civil-rights-memorial; 400 Washington Ave; memorial free, museum adult/child $2/free; ⊗ memorial 24 hrs, museum 9am-4:30pm Mon-Fri, 10am-4pm Sat) With its circular design crafted by Maya Lin, this haunting memorial focuses on 40 martyrs of the Civil Rights movement. Some cases remain unsolved. Martin Luther King Jr was the most famous, but there were many 'faceless' deaths along the way, both white and African American. The memorial is part of the Southern Poverty Law Center, a legal foundation committed to racial equality and equal opportunity for justice under the law.

Scott & Zelda Fitzgerald Museum   MUSEUM
(☑ 334-264-4222; www.fitzgeraldmuseum.net; 919 Felder Ave; donation adult/child $10/free; ⊗ 10am-3pm Tue-Sat, noon-5pm Sun) The writers' home

from 1931 to 1932 now houses first editions, translations and original artwork by Zelda from her sad last days when she was committed to a mental health facility. Unlike many 'homes of famous people,' there's a ramshackle charm to this museum – while the space is curated, you also feel as if you've stumbled into the Fitzgerald's attic, exemplified by loving handwritten letters from Zelda to Scott.

Rosa Parks Museum MUSEUM
(☑ 334-241-8615; www.troy.edu/rosaparks; 251 Montgomery St; adult/child 4-12yr $7.50/5.50; ⊘ 9am-5pm Mon-Fri, 9am-3pm Sat; ⊞) This museum, set in front of the bus stop where Mrs Parks took her stand, features a video recreation of that pivotal moment that launched the 1955 boycott. The experience is very managed – you're given a small opportunity to explore on your own, but otherwise the museum feels something like an interactive movie. For the price of an additional full-admission ticket, you can visit the children's wing, a kids-oriented time travel exhibit to the Jim Crow South.

🍴 Sleeping & Eating

Renaissance Hotel HOTEL $$
(☑ 334-481-5000; www.marriott.com; 201 Tallapoosa St; r from $140; P ✳ @ ⊛ ⊛) While this chain hotel is a little bland, it is also well located by the river, and easily occupies one of Montgomery's nicest addresses. Rooms have that convention-corporate chic thing going, but they're clean and comfortable.

Davis Cafe AMERICAN $
(☑ 334-264-6015; 518 N Decatur St; mains $3-7; ⊘ 7am-2pm Mon-Fri) This dilapidated restaurant leans precariously on a lonely street, but ignore the structural instability and step in: you'll find a Montgomery institution serving Southern breakfasts and plate lunches – liver and onions, fried chicken, ox tails and daily specials that will run you the cost of the loose money between your couch cushions. Hours are fungible; the Davis closes when it runs out of food.

Central STEAK $$$
(☑ 334-517-1121; www.central129coosa.com; 129 Coosa St; mains $16-32; ⊘ 11am-2pm Mon-Fri, 5:30pm-10pm Mon-Thu, to 11pm Fri & Sat; ☑) ⬤ The gourmet's choice, this stunner has an airy interior with a reclaimed-wood bar. The booths are sumptuous and these guys were doing farm to table before it was 'A Thing':

the menu specializes in wood-fired fish, chicken, steaks and chops sourced from the region. Dishes like a pesto-walnut pasta are nice for vegetarians.

ℹ Information

Montgomery Area Visitor Center (☑ 334-261-1100; www.visitingmontgomery.com; 300 Water St; ⊘ 8:30am-5pm Mon-Sat) Has tourist information and a helpful website.

ℹ Getting There & Around

Montgomery Regional Airport (MGM; ☑ 334-281-5040; www.montgomeryairport.org; 4445 Selma Hwy) is about 15 miles from downtown and is served by daily flights from Atlanta, Charlotte and Dallas. **Greyhound** (☑ 334-286-0658; www.greyhound.com; 950 W South Blvd) also serves the city. Montgomery is located about 100 miles south of Birmingham via I-65.

The **Montgomery Area Transit System** (http://montgomerytransit.com) operates city bus lines. Tickets are $2.

Selma

Selma is a quiet town located in the heart of the Alabama 'Black Belt,' so named for both its dark, high-quality soil and a large population of African Americans. It's most well known for Bloody Sunday: March 7, 1965. The media captured state troopers and deputies beating and gassing African Americans and white sympathizers near the Edmund Pettus Bridge.

Selma is a must-visit for those interested in the history of the Civil Rights movement, and is an attractive spot to linger in its own right.

◎ Sights

Edmund Pettus Bridge LANDMARK
(Broad St & Walter Ave) Few sites are as iconic to the American Civil Rights movement as the Pettus Bridge. On March 7, 1965, a crowd prepared to march to Montgomery to demonstrate against the murder of a local black activist by police during a demonstration for voting rights. As those activists gathered into a crowd, the news cameras of the media were trained on the bridge and a line of state troopers and their dogs, who proceeded to lay into the nonviolent marchers.

National Voting Rights Museum MUSEUM
(☑ 334-418-0800; www.nvrmi.com; 6 US Highway 80 East; adult/senior & student $6.50/4.50;

🕘10am-4pm Mon-Thu, by appointment only Fri-Sun; Ⓟ) This museum, located near the foot of the Edmund Pettus Bridge, tells the tale of the Selma to Montgomery march, and includes exhibits on women's suffrage, reconstruction, nonviolent resistance and other movements that have shared the goals of the Civil Rights struggle.

Selma Interpretive Center MUSEUM
(☎334-872-0509; www.nps.gov/semo; 2 Broad St; 🕘9am-4:30pm Mon-Sat) This museum, located near the north side of the Pettus Bridge, has a small interpretive center that fleshes out the history and narrative of the Jim Crow South, and the subsequent struggle against legalized segregation.

Lowndes County Interpretive Center MUSEUM
(☎334-877-1983; www.nps.gov/semo; 7002 US Hwy 80; 🕘9am-4:30pm Mon-Sat; Ⓟ) Marking the rough halfway point on the marching route between Selma and Montgomery, this center presents small, solid exhibitions that delve into the history of Jim Crow and the Civil Rights movement.

Sleeping & Eating

At the time of writing, the historic **St James Hotel** was up for sale. It's the only really notable sleeping option in Selma, which is otherwise served by the usual midrange American hotel chains.

Getting There & Away

There's a **Greyhound** (☎800-231-2222; 434 Broad St) station on Broad St (US 80). But you really need a car to get around. Tuscaloosa is located about 75 miles to the north on US 80, and Montgomery is 50 miles to the east.

Mobile

Wedged between Mississippi and Florida, the only real Alabama coastal city is Mobile (mo-*beel*), a busy industrial seaport with a smattering of green space, shady boulevards and four historic districts. It's ablaze with azaleas in early spring, and festivities are held throughout February for Mardi Gras, which has been celebrated here for nearly 200 years (it actually predates Mardi Gras in New Orleans).

Throughout the rest of the year, this is a major port with some attractive historical neighborhoods and a strong Coast Guard presence, thanks to the nearby Coast Guard Aviation Training Center.

Sights

USS Alabama MUSEUM
(☎251-433-2703; www.ussalabama.com; 2703 Battleship Pkwy; adult/child $15/6; 🕘8am-6pm Apr-Sep, to 5pm Oct-Mar; Ⓟ) The battleship *Alabama* is a 690ft behemoth famous for escaping nine major WWII battles unscathed – the 'Lucky A' never lost any of her sailors while they served aboard ship. It's a worthwhile self-guided tour just to experience its awesome size and might; at the end of the day, this ship is an engineering marvel. While there, you can also tour a submarine and get up close and personal with military aircraft. Parking costs $2.

Gulf Coast Exploreum MUSEUM
(☎251-208-6893; www.exploreum.com; 65 Government St; adult/student/child $12/10.50/10 with IMAX $16/15/13.50; 🕘9am-4pm Tue-Thu, to 5pm Fri & Sat, noon-5pm Sun; 👪) This science center contains some 150 interactive exhibits and displays in three galleries, an IMAX theater and live demonstrations in its chemistry and biology labs.

Festivals

Mardi Gras CULTURAL
(www.mobilemardigras.com; 🕘late Feb/early Mar) Mobile has been celebrating Mardi Gras for nearly 200 years. It culminates on Fat Tuesday (the Tuesday before Ash Wednesday) with parades that feature bead tossing, music and some politically incorrect floats.

Sleeping & Eating

Battle House HOTEL $$
(☎251-338-2000; www.marriott.com; 26 N Royal St; r $170-240, ste from $375; Ⓟ❄@🛜🏊) By far the best address in Mobile. Stay in the original historic wing with its ornate domed marble lobby, though the striking new tower is on the waterfront. Rooms are spacious, luxurious, four-star chic. Book ahead for discounts.

Callaghan's Irish Social Club PUB FOOD $
(☎251-433-9374; www.callaghansirishsocialclub.com; 916 Charleston St; burgers $8-10; 🕘11am-11pm Mon-Thu, to midnight Fri & Sat, 10am-11pm Sun) This ramshackle pub is located in a 1920s-era building that used to house a meat market. They serve a mean burger and a cold beer, and often feature live-music acts.

Mary's Southern Cooking AMERICAN $
(☏251-476-2232; 3011 Springhll Ave; mains $6-12; ⏰11am-6pm; 🖐) Mary's serves up soul food with a smile. Daily specials run the gamut from beef tips to pig's feet to chicken pot pie, served alongside groaning portions of sides, including collard greens, rice and gravy, and mashed potatoes.

ℹ Getting There & Away

As of early 2017, there was talk of reestablishing rail service through Mobile. Until then, you can arrive via **Greyhound** (☏251-478-6089; www.greyhound.com; 2545 Government Blvd) or drive; the city sits at the intersection of I-10 and I-65, about 60 miles west of Pensacola, and 150 miles east of New Orleans.

MISSISSIPPI

The state named for the most vital waterway in North America encompasses, appropriately enough, a long river of identities. Mississippi features palatial mansions and rural poverty; haunted cotton flats and lush hill country; honey-dipped sand on the coast and serene farmland in the north. Oft mythologized and misunderstood, this is the womb of some of the rawest history – and music – in the country.

ℹ Information

Mississippi Division of Tourism Development (☏866-733-6477, 601-359-3297; www.visitmississippi.org) Has a directory of visitor bureaus and thematic travel itineraries. Most are well thought-out and run quite deep.
Mississippi Wildlife, Fisheries, & Parks (☏800-467-2757; www.mississippistateparks.reserveamerica.com) Manages camping reservations in state parks.

ℹ Getting There & Away

There are three routes most folks take when traveling through Mississippi. I-55 and Hwy 61 both run north–south from the state's northern to southern borders. Hwy 61 goes through the delta, and I-55 flows in and out of Jackson. The gorgeous Natchez Trace Parkway runs diagonally across the state from Tupelo to Natchez.

Oxford

Oxford both confirms and explodes preconceptions you may have of Mississippi's most famous college town. Frat boys in Ford pickup trucks and debutante sorority sisters? Sure. But they're alongside doctoral candidates debating critical theory and a lively arts scene. Local culture revolves around the Square (aka Courthouse Sq), where you'll find bars, restaurants, decent shopping and the regal University of Mississippi, aka Ole Miss. All around are quiet residential streets, sprinkled with antebellum homes and shaded by majestic oaks.

◉ Sights & Activities

The gorgeous, 0.6-mile-long and rather painless **Bailee's Woods Trail** connects two of the town's most popular sights: Rowan Oak and the University of Mississippi Museum. **The Grove**, the shady heart of Ole Miss, is generally peaceful, except on football Saturdays, when it buzzes with one of the most unforgettable tailgating (pre-game) parties in American university sports.

Rowan Oak HISTORIC BUILDING
(☏662-234-3284; www.rowanoak.com; Old Taylor Rd; adult/child $5/free; ⏰10am-4pm Tue-Sat, 1-4pm Sun Sep-May, 10am-6pm Tue-Sat, 1-6pm Sun Jun-Aug) Literary pilgrims head here to the graceful 1840s home of William Faulkner. He authored many brilliant and dense novels set in Mississippi, and his work is celebrated in Oxford with an annual conference in July. Tours of Rowan Oak – where Faulkner lived from 1930 until his death in 1962, and which may reasonably be dubbed, to use the author's own elegant words, his 'postage stamp of native soil' – are self-guided.

**University of Mississippi
Museum** MUSEUM
(www.museum.olemiss.edu; University Ave at 5th St; ⏰10am-6pm Tue-Sat) FREE This museum has fine and folk arts and a plethora of science-related marvels, including a microscope and electromagnet from the 19th century.

🛏 Sleeping & Eating

Inn at Ole Miss HOTEL $$
(☏662-234-2331; www.theinnatolemiss.com; 120 Alumni Dr; r from $99-149; P✸@🛜❄) Unless its a football weekend, in which case you'd be wise to book well ahead, you can usually find a nice room at this 180-room hotel and conference center right on the Ole Miss Grove. Although it's not super personal, it's comfortable, well located and walkable to downtown.

Neon Pig
SOUTHERN US $

(☑662-638-3257; http://oxford.eatneonpig.com; 711 N Lamar Blvd; mains $7-14; ⊙11am-9pm Mon-Sat, to 4pm Sun; Ⓟ) A counter with stools, some friendly folks on the grill, and farm fresh produce, cheese and meat on grocery shelves – there's not a ton of ambience at the Neon Pig. But there is amazing food, ranging from pork-belly lettuce wraps to harissa grilled cheese to the Smash Burger – rough-cut aged sirloin, filet, ribeye and bacon ground together into perfection.

Taylor Grocery
SEAFOOD $$

(☑662-236-1716; www.taylorgrocery.com; 4 1st St; dishes $9-15; ⊙5-10pm Thu-Sat, to 9pm Sun; Ⓟ) Be prepared to wait – and to tailgate in the parking lot – at this splendidly rusticated catfish haunt. Order fried or grilled (either way, it's amazing) and bring a marker to sign your name on the wall. It's about 7 miles from downtown Oxford, south on Old Taylor Rd.

Ravine
AMERICAN $$$

(☑662-234-4555; www.oxfordravine.com; 53 County Rd 321; mains $21-36; ⊙6-9pm Wed-Thu, to 10pm Fri & Sat, 10:30am-2pm & 6-9pm Sun; 🛜) About 3 miles outside Oxford, this unpretentious, cozily elegant restaurant nuzzles up to the forest. Chef Joel Miller picks and pulls much of the produce and herbs from his garden and buys locally and organically whenever possible; he's been doing it long before locavore was a buzzword. The result is simply wonderful food and a delicious experience.

⭐ Entertainment

Proud Larry's
LIVE MUSIC

(☑662-236-0050; www.proudlarrys.com; 211 S Lamar Blvd; ⊙shows 9pm) On the Square, this iconic music venue hosts consistently good bands, and it does a nice pub-grub business at lunch and dinner before the lights dim.

The Lyric
LIVE MUSIC

(☑662-234-5333; www.thelyricoxford.com; 1006 Van Buren Ave) This old brickhouse, and rather intimate theater with concrete floors, exposed rafters and a mezzanine, is the place to see indie rockers and folksy crooners.

ℹ Getting There & Away

The closest interstates to Oxford are I-55 and I-22. You can get here via US 278 or MS 7; the latter is a slightly more scenic route.

Mississippi Delta

A long, low land of silent cotton plots bending under a severe sky, the Delta is a place of surreal, Gothic extremes. Here, in a feudal society of great manors and enslaved servitude, songs of labor and love became American pop music. It traveled via Africa to sharecropping fields, unfolding into the blues, the father of rock and roll. Tourism in this area, which still suffers some of the worst rural poverty rates in the country, largely revolves around discovering the sweat-soaked roots of this original, American art form. Hwy 61 is the legendary road that traverses endless, eerie miles of flat fields, imposing agricultural and industrial facilities, one-room churches and moldering cemeteries.

Clarksdale

Clarksdale is the Delta's most useful base. It's within a couple of hours of all the blues sights, and big-name blues acts are regular weekend visitors. But this is still a poor Delta town, with crumbling edges and washed-out storefronts evident in ways that go beyond romantic dilapidation. It's jarring to see how many businesses find private security details a necessity after dark. On the other hand, there is a genuine warmth to the place, and most tourists end up lingering for longer than they expected.

⊙ Sights

Delta Blues Museum
MUSEUM

(☑662-627-6820; www.deltabluesmuseum.org; 1 Blues Alley; adult/senior & student $10/5; ⊙9am-5pm Mon-Sat Mar-Oct, from 10am Nov-Feb; Ⓟ) A small but well-presented collection of memorabilia is on display here. The shrine to Delta legend Muddy Waters includes the actual cabin where he grew up. Local art exhibits and a gift shop round out the display. Occasionally hosts live music shows on Friday nights.

The Crossroads
SCULPTURE

(Hwy 61 & Hwy 49) FREE The Crossroads of Hwys 61 and 49 is supposedly the intersection where the great Robert Johnson made his mythical deal with the devil, immortalized in his tune 'Cross Road Blues.' Now all of the implied lonely fear and dark mysticism of the space is taken up by a tacky

WORTH A TRIP

THE SOUL OF THE DELTA

Stopping in the tiny Delta town of Indianola, an hour's drive south of Clarksdale, is worthwhile to visit the **BB King Museum and Delta Interpretive Center** ([J] 662-887-9539; www.bbkingmuseum.org; 400 2nd St; adult/student/child $15/10/free; ⊙10am-5pm Tue-Sat, noon-5pm Sun-Mon, closed Mon Nov-Mar; [P]). While it's ostensibly dedicated to the legendary bluesman, in many ways this modern museum tackles life in the Delta as a whole. The museum is filled with interactive displays, video exhibits and an amazing array of artifacts, effectively communicating the history and legacy of the blues while shedding light on the soul of the Delta.

sculpture. For what it's worth, few historians agree where the actual crossroad is located.

🛏 Sleeping & Eating

Riverside Hotel   HISTORIC HOTEL **$**
([J] 662-624-9163; ratfrankblues@yahoo.com; 615 Sunflower Ave; r without/with bath $65/75; [❋][🛜]) Don't let a well-worn exterior put you off: this hotel, soaked in blues history – blues singer Bessie Smith died here when it was a hospital, and a festival's worth of blues artists from Sonny Boy Williamson II to Robert Nighthawk have stayed here – offers clean and tidy rooms and sincere friendliness. It's been family-run since 1944, when it was 'the black hotel' in town.

Bluesberry Cafe   SOUTHERN US **$**
([J] 662-627-7008; 235 Yazoo Ave; ⊙7:30am-1pm Sat & Sun, noon-6pm Mon) This isn't just a greasy spoon – there's grease on the forks, knives and napkins too. But who cares? The food – eggs, bacon, homemade sausages and big sandwiches – is cooked to order and delicious, and on many a morning, some legend of the blues will stop in and play an impromptu set. Pass the hot sauce.

Shack Up Inn   INN **$$**
([J] 662-624-8329; www.shackupinn.com; 001 Commisary Circle, off Hwy 49; d $75-165; [P][❋][🛜]) At the Hopson Plantation, this self-titled 'bed and beer' allows you to stay in refurbished sharecropper cabins or the creatively renovated cotton gin. The cabins have covered porches and are filled with old furniture and musical instruments.

Yazoo Pass   CAFE **$$**
([J] 662-627-8686; www.yazoopass.com; 207 Yazoo Ave; lunch mains $6-10, dinner $13-26; ⊙7am-9pm Mon-Sat; [🛜]) A contemporary space where you can enjoy fresh scones and croissants in the mornings, a salad bar, sandwiches and soups at lunch, and pan-seared ahi, filet mignon, burgers and pastas at dinner.

☆ Entertainment

★ Red's   BLUES
([J] 662-627-3166; 395 Sunflower Ave; cover $7-10; ⊙live music 9pm Fri & Sat) Clarksdale's best juke joint, with its neon-red mood lighting, plastic-bag ceiling and general soulful disintegration, is the place to see bluesmen howl. Red runs the bar, knows the acts and slings a cold beer whenever you need one.

❶ Getting There & Away

The Greyhound station is on State St. Clarksdale sits off Hwys 49 and 61, 80 miles south of Memphis, TN, and 70 miles west of Oxford, MS.

Vicksburg

Lovely Vicksburg sits atop a high bluff overlooking the Mississippi River. During the Civil War, General Ulysses S Grant besieged the city for 47 days until its surrender on July 4, 1863, at which point the North gained dominance over North America's greatest river. Despite being most famous for a siege and a battle, many of the historic homes of Vicksburg have survived the centuries, and today the town's historic core is considered one of the most attractive in the state.

⊙ Sights

Vicksburg National Military Park   HISTORIC SITE
([J] 601-636-0583; www.nps.gov/vick; 3201 Clay St; per bicycle/car $5/15; ⊙8am-5pm; [♿]) 🌿 Vicksburg controlled access to the Mississippi River, and its seizure was one of the turning points of the Civil War. A 16-mile driving tour passes historic markers explaining battle scenarios and key events from the city's long siege, when residents lived like moles in caverns to avoid Union shells. Plan on staying for at least 90 minutes. If you have your own bike, cycling is a fantastic way to tour the place. Locals use the scenic park for walking and running.

Lower Mississippi River Museum   MUSEUM
(☑ 601-638-9900; www.lmrm.org; 910 Washington St; ⊙ 9am-4pm Mon-Sat, 1-4pm Sun; ◉) FREE Downtown Vicksburg's pride and joy is this interesting museum, which delves into such topics as the famed 1927 flood and the Army Corps of Engineers, who have managed the river since the 18th century. Kids will enjoy the aquarium and climbing around the dry-docked research vessel, the MV *Mississippi IV*.

✗ Eating & Drinking

Walnut Hills   SOUTHERN US $$
(☑ 601-638-4910; www.walnuthillsms.net; 1214 Adams St; mains $8-25; ⊙ 11am-9pm Mon-Sat, to 2pm Sun) For a dining experience that takes you back in time, head to this eatery where you can enjoy rib-sticking, down-home Southern food elbow to elbow, family-style.

★ Highway 61 Coffeehouse   COFFEE
(☑ 601-638-9221; www.61coffee.blogspot.com; 1101 Washington St; ⊙ 7am-5pm Mon-Fri, from 9am Sat; 🛜) ✏ This awesome coffee shop has occasional live music on Saturday afternoons, serves Fair Trade coffee and is an energetic epicenter of artsyness, poetry readings and the like.

ⓘ Getting There & Away

There's a Greyhound station a little way south of town. Vicksburg lays off I-20 and Hwy 61, about 50 miles west of Jackson.

Jackson

Mississippi's capital and largest city mixes up stately residential areas with large swaths of blight, peppered throughout with a surprisingly funky arts-cum-hipster scene in the Fondren District. There's a slew of decent bars, good restaurants and a lot of love for live music; it's easy to have a good time in Jackson.

⊙ Sights

Mississippi Museum of Art   GALLERY
(☑ 601-960-1515; www.msmuseumart.org; 380 South Lamar St; special exhibitions $5-12; ⊙ 10am-5pm Tue-Sat, noon-5pm Sun) FREE This is your must-stop sight when visiting Jackson. The collection of Mississippi art – and the permanent exhibit dubbed 'The Mississippi Story' – is superb, and the surrounding grounds are nicely landscaped into a bright and quirky garden area.

Old Capitol Museum   MUSEUM
(☑ 601-576-6920; www.mdah.ms.gov/oldcap; 100 State St; ⊙ 9am-5pm Tue-Sat, 1-5pm Sun) FREE The state's Greek Revival capitol building from 1839 to 1903 now houses a Mississippi history museum filled with films and exhibits. You'll learn that secession was far from unanimous and how reconstruction brought some of the harshest, presegregation 'black codes' in the South.

Eudora Welty House   HISTORIC BUILDING
(☑ 601-353-7762; www.eudorawelty.org; 1119 Pinehurst St; adult/student/child $5/3/free; ⊙ tours 9am, 11am, 1pm & 3pm Tue-Fri) Literature buffs should make a reservation to tour the Pulitzer Prize–winning author's Tudor Revival house, where she lived for more than 75 years. It's now a true historical preservation down to the most minute details. It's free on the 13th day of any month, assuming that's a normal operating day.

Museum of Natural Science   MUSEUM
(☑ 601-576-6000; www.mdwfp.com/museum; 2148 Riverside Dr; adult/child $6/4; ⊙ 8am-5pm Mon-Fri, from 9am Sat, from 1pm Sun; ◉) ✏ Tucked way back in Lefleur's Bluff State Park is this museum, which houses exhibits on the natural flora and fauna of Mississippi. It also has aquariums inside, a replica swamp and 2.5 miles of trails traversing 300 acres of preserved prettiness.

International Museum of Muslim Cultures   MUSEUM
(☑ 601-960-0440; www.muslimmuseum.org; 201 E Pascagoula St; ⊙ 10am-5pm Mon-Fri) FREE This small museum has a few interesting exhibitions on Timbuktu and Moorish Spain, and hosts rotating exhibitions on other Muslim majority societies. While the stuff on display isn't super-penetrating, this spot serves as a decent introduction to the larger Muslim world for those who are unfamiliar with it.

🛏 Sleeping & Eating

Old Capitol Inn   BOUTIQUE HOTEL $$
(☑ 601-359-9000; www.oldcapitolinn.com; 226 N State St; r/ste from $99/145; 🅿 ❄ @ 🛜 ≋) This 24-room, boutique hotel, located near museums and restaurants, is terrific. Rooms are comfortable and uniquely furnished, and a full Southern breakfast (and early-evening wine and cheese) is included. The rooftop garden includes a hot tub.

Fairview Inn
INN $$$

(☑601-948-3429, 888-948-1908; www.fairviewinn.com; 734 Fairview St; ste $200-340; P✳@�) For a colonial-estate experience, the 18-room Fairview Inn, set in a converted historic mansion, will not let you down. The antique decor is stunning rather than stuffy and tastefully deployed across each individually appointed room. It also has a full spa.

High Noon Cafe
VEGETARIAN $

(☑601-366-1513; www.rainbowcoop.org; 2807 Old Canton Rd; mains $7-12; ⊙11:30am-2pm Mon-Fri; �✐) ✐ Tired of fried everything and buckets of pulled pork? This organic vegetarian grill, inside the Rainbow Co-op grocery store in the Fondren District, does beet burgers, portobello Reubens and other healthy delights. Stock up on organic groceries too.

Saltine
SEAFOOD $$

(☑601-982-2899; www.saltinerestaurant.com; 622 Duling Ave; mains $12-26; ⊙11am-10pm Mon-Thu, to 11pm Fri, to 9pm Sun) This playful spot takes on the delicious task of bringing oysters to the Jackson culinary world. The bivalves are served in several iterations: raw, woodfired, with Alabama white barbecue sauce and 'Nashville' (very) hot. Sop up some shellfish sauce with the excellent skillet cornbread, then give the grilled rainbow trout a whirl.

Walker's Drive-In
SOUTHERN US $$$

(☑601-982-2633; www.walkersdrivein.com; 3016 N State St; lunch mains $8-17, dinner $29-37; ⊙11am-2pm Mon-Fri & from 5:30-10pm Tue-Sat) This retro masterpiece has been restored with love and infused with new Southern foodie ethos. Lunch is diner 2.0 fare with grilled redfish sandwiches, tender burgers and grilled oyster po'boys, as well as an exceptional seared, chili-crusted tuna salad, which comes with spiced calamari and seaweed.

🍷 Drinking & Entertainment

Apothecary at Brent's Drugs
COCKTAIL BAR

(www.apothecaryjackson.com; 655 Duling Ave; ⊙5pm-1am Tue-Thu, to 2am Fri & Sat) Tucked into the back of a '50s-style soda fountain shop is a distinctly early-21st-century craft cocktail bar, complete with bartenders sporting thick-framed glasses and a fine menu of expertly mixed libations.

Martin's
BAR

(☑601-354-9712; www.martinslounge.net; 214 S State St; ⊙10am-1:30am Mon-Sat, to midnight Sun) This is a delightfully dirty dive, the kind of place where the bartenders know the phone numbers of their regulars in case said regulars pass out on their bar stools. Attracts a mix of old-timers, statehouse workers, slick lobbyists and lawyers plucked from a John Grisham novel.

F Jones Corner
BLUES

(☑601-983-1148; www.fjonescorner.com; 303 N Farish St; ⊙Tue-Fri 11am-2pm, Thu-Sat 10am-late) All shapes and sizes, colors and creeds descend on this down-home Farish St club when everywhere else closes. It hosts authentic Delta musicians who have been known to play until sunrise.

ℹ Information

Convention & Visitors Bureau (☑800-354-7695; www.visitjackson.com; 111 E Capitol St, Suite 102; ⊙8am-5pm Mon-Fri) Free information.

ℹ Getting There & Away

At the junction of I-20 and I-55, it's easy to get in and out of Jackson. Its international **airport** (JAN; ☑601-939-5631; www.jmaa.com; 100 International Dr) is 10 miles east of downtown. **Greyhound** (☑601-353-6342; www.greyhound.com; 300 W Capitol St) buses serve Birmingham, Memphis, and New Orleans. Amtrak's City of New Orleans stops at the station.

Natchez

Some 668 antebellum homes pepper the oldest post-European contact settlement on the Mississippi River (beating New Orleans by two years). Natchez is also one end of the scenic 444-mile Natchez Trace Pkwy, the state's cycling and recreational jewel. Tours of the historic downtown and antebellum mansions leave from the Visitor and Welcome Cente. During the 'pilgrimage' seasons in spring and fall, local mansions are opened to visitors.

◎ Sights & Activities

Emerald Mound
ARCHAEOLOGICAL SITE

(www.nps.gov/natr; Mile 10.3 Natchez Trace Pkwy; ⊙dawn-dusk; P🐾) **FREE** Just outside of town, along the Trace, you'll find Emerald Mound, the grassy ruins of a Native American city that includes the second-largest pre-Columbian earthworks in the USA. Using stone tools, pre-Columbian ancestors to the Natchez people graded this 8-acre mountain into a flat-topped pyramid. It is now the second-largest mound site in America. There are shady, creekside picnic spots

NATCHEZ TRACE PARKWAY

If you're driving through Mississippi, we highly recommend planning at least part of your trip around one of the oldest roads in North America: the Natchez Trace. This 444-mile trail follows a natural ridge line that was widely utilized by prehistoric animals as a grazing route; later, the area those animals trampled became a footpath and trading route utilized by Native American tribes. That route would go on to become the Natchez Trace, a major roadway into the early Western interior of the young United States, that was often plagued by roving bandits.

In 1938, 444 miles of the Trace, stretching from Pasquo, TN, southwest to Natchez, MS, was designated the federally protected Natchez Trace Pkwy (www.nps.gov/natr), administered by the National Park Service. It's a lovely, scenic drive that traverses a wide panoply of Southern landscapes: thick, dark forests, soggy wetlands, gentle hill country and long swaths of farmland. There are more than 50 access points to the parkway and a helpful **visitor center** (☑800-305-7417, 662-680-4025; www.nps.gov/natr; Mile 266 Natchez Trace Pkwy; ◷8am-5pm, closed Christmas; ⊞☺) ✔ outside of Tupelo.

here, and you can and should climb to the top where you'll find a vast lawn.

Auburn Mansion   LANDMARK
(☑601-446-6631; www.auburnmuseum.org; 400 Duncan Ave; adult/child $15/10; ◷11am-3pm Tue-Sat, last tour departs 2:30pm; ⊞) The red-brick Auburn Mansion is famous for its freestanding spiral staircase. Built in 1812, the architecture here influenced countless mansions throughout the South.

Natchez Pilgrimage Tours   HISTORY
(☑800-647-6742, 601-446-6631; www.natchez pilgrimage.com; 640 S Canal St; tours from $20) If you love historic homes and antebellum architecture, this tour outfit was made for you. It manages tours to over a dozen historical homes throughout the year, providing tons of info and insight into local history.

🛏 Sleeping & Eating

Historic Oak Hill Inn   INN **$$**
(☑601-446-2500; www.historicoakhill.com; 409 S Rankin St; r incl breakfast $135-160, ste $235; Ⓟ❄🛜) Ever wish you could sleep in one of those historic homes? At the Historic Oak Hill Inn, you can sleep in an original 1835 bed and dine on pre–Civil War porcelain under 1850 Waterford crystal gasoliers – it's all about purist antebellum aristocratic living at this classic Natchez B&B.

Magnolia Grill   SOUTHERN US **$$**
(☑601-446-7670; www.magnoliagrill.com; 49 Silver St; mains $13-22; ◷11am-9pm, to 10pm Fri & Sat; ⊞) Down by the riverside, this attractive wooden storefront grill with exposed rafters and outdoor patio is a good place for a pork

tenderloin po'boy or a fried crawfish spinach salad.

🍷 Drinking

Under the Hill Saloon   BAR
(☑601-446-8023; 25 Silver St; ◷10am-late) A tremendously fun and historic bar that was once a favorite haunt of Samuel Clemens, a riverboat pilot who would go on to be known by his pen name, Mark Twain. The bar closes whenever everyone has emptied out.

ⓘ Information

The **Visitor and Welcome Center** (☑800-647-6724; www.visitnatchez.org; 640 S Canal St; ◷8:30am-5pm Mon-Sat, 9am-4pm Sun) is a large, well-done tourist resource with exhibits of area history and a ton of information on local sites.

ⓘ Getting There & Away

Natchez is located off Hwy 61, and also forms the terminus (or beginning, depending on which way you're heading) of the Natchez Trace Pkwy. The **Greyhound** (☑601-445-5291; 127 Wood Ave) station is about 3.5 miles east of town.

Gulf Coast

The Mississippi Gulf Coast is a long, low series of breeze-swept dunes, patches of sea oats, bayside art galleries and clusters of Vegas-style casinos. This is a popular retreat for families and military members; several important bases pepper the coast from Florida to Texas.

Charming Bay St Louis attracts federal employees, including many scientists, based out at Stennis Space Center near the Louisiana border; that presence gives the town a slightly more progressive cast than you'd expect from Mississippi. Yoga studios, antique stores and galleries cluster on Main St.

Ocean Springs is a peaceful getaway, with a line-up of shrimp boats in the harbor alongside recreational sailing yachts, a historic downtown core and a powdery fringe of white sand on the Gulf.

Cheap chain accommodations can be found at the I-10 exits that lead to various Gulf Coast towns. Within said towns, you may find nice B&Bs and multifloor-style hotels aimed at day-trippers.

ⓘ Getting There & Away

Ocean Springs is located 33 miles east of Bay St Louis and 60 miles west of Mobile, off I-10. There is no public transportation out here.

ARKANSAS

Forming the mountainous joint between the Midwest and the Deep South, Arkansas (*ar*-kan-saw) is an often overlooked treasure of swift rushing rivers, dark leafy hollows, crenelated granite outcrops and the rugged spine of the Ozark and the Ouachita (washee-tah) mountains. The entire state is blessed with exceptionally well-presented state parks and tiny, empty roads crisscrossing dense forests that let out onto breathtaking vistas and gentle pastures dotted with grazing horses. Mountain towns juke between Christian fundamentalism, hippie communes and biker bars, yet all of these divergent cultures share a love of their home state's stunning natural beauty.

ⓘ Information

Arkansas State Parks (☎ 888-287-2757; www.arkansasstateparks.com) Arkansas' well-reputed park system has 52 state parks, 30 offering camping (tent and recreational vehicle (RV) sites are $12 to $55, depending on amenities). A number of the parks offer lodge and cabin accommodations. Due to popularity, reservations on weekends and holidays often require multiday stays.

Little Rock

Little Rock lives up to its name; this charming state capital feels pretty petite. But this is also the center of urban life in Arkansas, and the angle of the urban experience this city embraces is quite cool: amid the leafy residential neighborhoods are friendly bars, fresh restaurants, plenty of bike trails and a tolerant vibe. Small this town may be, but it's wonderfully situated on the Arkansas River, and as befits this state of natural wonders, you always feel as if you're within arm's reach of lush, wooded river valleys.

◉ Sights

William J Clinton Presidential Center MUSEUM
(☎ 501-374-4242; www.clintonlibrary.gov; 1200 President Clinton Ave; adult/students & seniors/child $10/8/6; ◎ 9am-5pm Mon-Sat, 1-5pm Sun; P ♿) ✎ This library houses the largest archival collection in presidential history, including 80 million pages of documents and two million photographs (although there's not a lot related to a certain intern scandal). The entire experience feels like a time travel journey to the 1990s. Peruse the full-scale replica of the Oval Office, the exhibits on all stages of Clinton's life or gifts from visiting dignitaries. The complex is built to environmentally friendly standards.

The library is located on a rolling campus that includes wooded pathways and a 13-acre wetland preserve.

Riverfront Park PARK
(☎ 501-371-4770; Ottenheimer Plaza; ◎ sunrise-sunset) FREE This park rolls pleasantly along the Arkansas River, and both pedestrians and cyclists take advantage of it. It's a truly fine integration of a landscape feature (the river) into an urban setting. The most noticeable landmark is the Clinton Presidential Park Bridge, a gorgeous pedestrian path that spans the river.

Little Rock Central High School HISTORIC SITE
(☎ 501-374-1957; www.nps.gov/chsc; 2125 Daisy L Gatson Bates Dr; ◎ 9am-4:30pm; P) FREE Little Rock's most riveting historic attraction is the site of the 1957 desegregation crisis that changed the country forever. It was here that a group of African American students known as the Little Rock Nine were first denied entry to the then–all-white high school (despite a unanimous 1954 Supreme Court ruling forcing the integration of public schools).

Museum of Discovery MUSEUM
(☎ 501-396-7050; www.museumofdiscovery.org; 500 President Clinton Ave; adult/child $10/8; ◎ 9am-5pm Tue-Sat, 1-5pm Sun, open 9am-5pm Mon summer; ♿) A proper science-and-

natural-history museum, perfect for families. There are exhibits on the human body, Arkansas ecosystems, tornadoes, paleontology, and all sorts of other good stuff.

🛏 Sleeping & Eating

★ Capital Hotel   BOUTIQUE HOTEL **$$**
(📞 501-374-7474; www.capitalhotel.com; 111 W Markham St; r/ste from $220/375; 🅿✸@🛜) This 1872 former bank building with a cast-iron facade – a near-extinct architectural feature – is the top digs in Little Rock. There is a wonderful outdoor mezzanine for cocktails and a sense of suited, cigar-chomping posh throughout; if you want to feel like a wining, dining lobbyist, you've found your spot.

Rosemont   B&B **$$**
(📞 501-766-0355; www.rosemontoflittlerock.com; 515 W 15th St; r $105-195; 🅿✸🛜🐾) This 1880s restored farmhouse near the Governor's mansion oozes cozy Southern charm. The proprietors also offer a few bucolic, historic country cottages (from $135). One of the few independent B&Bs we came across that is also pet friendly.

Big Orange   AMERICAN **$**
(📞 501-379-8715; www.bigorangeburger.com; 207 N University Ave; mains $8-14; ⊙ Sun-Thu 11am-10pm, to 11pm Fri & Sat; 🅿🚲🐾) Sometimes you need a burger, and not just a burger, but the sort of meat between two buttered buns that leaves you in a state of post-carnivore frenzy bliss. Enter Big Orange, which serves variations on the theme ranging from a classic with American cheese, topped with white truffle for the fancy, and a falafel version for the vegetarians.

Three Fold Noodles and Dumpling Co   CHINESE **$**
(📞 501-372-1739; http://eat3fold.com; 215 Center St; dumplings & noodles $7-8; ⊙11am-8pm Mon-Sat) Look, when we got to Little Rock we weren't expecting blow-me-away Chinese food either, but then Three Fold comes along with its braised-chicken–noodle bowls, handmade dumplings and steamed buns, and for a minute, everything felt more Anhui than Arkansas. The fact that lunch will set you back a little more than a McDonald's meal helps.

★ South on Main   AMERICAN **$$**
(📞 501-244-9660; www.southonmain.com; 1304 S Main St; mains $16-24; ⊙11am-2:30pm Mon-Fri, 5-10pm Tue-Sat, 10am-2pm Sun) This wonderful spot is a gastronomic pet project of *The Oxford American*, the South's seminal quarterly literary magazine. It embraces the foodways of the region with a verve and dynamism that is creative and delicious; catfish comes with cornmeal pancakes, while rabbit leg is wrapped in country ham. A great bar and frequent live music round out the awesome.

🍷 Drinking & Entertainment

The New 610 Center   GAY
(📞 501-374-4678; http://610center.com; 610 Center St; ⊙4pm-midnight Mon-Thu, to 1am Fri, 6pm-1am Sat, 11am-10pm Sun) This laid-back bar serves up excellent martinis and a welcoming vibe, aided by a local, primarily gay clientele. It's a good, casual spot for a strong drink and the occasional drag show or bear night.

White Water Tavern   LIVE MUSIC
(📞 501-375-8400; www.whitewatertavern.com; 2500 W 7th St; ⊙noon-2am Mon-Fri, 6pm-1am Sat) The White Water manages to line up some excellent acts for its small stage, with bands ranging from straight-up rockers to alt-country heroes to indie poppers to hip-hop MCs. When the music isn't playing, this is an excellent, friendly corner pub.

Arkansas Repertory Theatre   THEATER
(📞 501-378-0405; www.therep.org; 601 Main St) 'The Rep' is one of the South's most energetic little regional theaters. They have a fantastic slate of shows, ranging from off-Broadway musicals to quirky indie shows.

ℹ Information

The **Little Rock Convention Center & Tourism Bureau** (📞 501-376-4781; www.littlerock.com; 101 S Spring St; ⊙8:30m-5pm Mon-Fri) is a good gateway into the city.

ℹ Getting There & Around

Bill & Hillary Clinton National Airport (LIT; Little Rock National Airport; 📞 501-372-3439; www.fly-lit.com; 1 Airport Dr) lies just east of downtown. The **Greyhound station** (📞 501-372-3007; www.greyhound.com; 118 E Washington St, North Little Rock), in North Little Rock, serves Hot Springs ($19, 1-2 hours, two daily), Memphis, TN ($31, 2½ hours, seven daily), and New Orleans ($93, 18 hours, two daily). **Union Station** (📞 501-372-6841; 1400 W Markham St) is a stop on Amtrak's *Texas Eagle* line, which runs from Chicago ($100, 14 hours) to Los Angeles ($154, 19 hours), stopping at dozens of cities in between.

Central Arkansas Transit (www.cat.org) runs local buses and the **River Rail Streetcar**, a trolley that makes a loop on W Markham and President Clinton Ave (adult/child $1.35/60¢).

Hot Springs

Hot Springs is a gem of a mountain town, and we're not the first to notice. The healing waters the town is named for have been attracting everyone from Native Americans and early-20th-century health nuts, to a good chunk of the nation's organized-crime leadership. When Hot Springs was at full throttle in the 1930s, it was a hotbed of gambling, bootlegging, prostitution and opulence.

Today the appeal of Hot Springs is less the actual springs than the tourism infrastructure that commemorates them. That said, a few elaborate restored bathhouses offering old-school spa treatments line Bathhouse Row, which sits behind shady magnolias on the east side of Central Ave. Otherwise Hot Springs is a shady, attractive town that has managed to preserve its historic center, which is always a cause for celebration.

◉ Sights & Activities

Hot Springs National Park   MUSEUM
(Fordyce Bathhouse; ☑ 501-620-6715; www.nps.gov/hosp; 369 Central Ave; ⊙ 9am-5pm) FREE On Bathhouse Row, set up in the 1915 Fordyce bathhouse, the NPS visitor center and museum has exhibits about the park's history, first as a Native American free-trade zone, and later as a turn-of-the-20th-century European spa. Most fascinating are the amenities and standards set forth by an early-20th-century spa; the stained-glass work and Greek statues are opulent, but we could pass on the bare white walls, grout and electroshock therapy.

Hot Springs Mountain Tower   VIEWPOINT
(☑ 501-881-4020; 401 Hot Springs Mountain Rd; adult/child $7/4; ⊙ 9am-5pm Sep-May, to 9pm Jun-Aug; ℗) On top of Hot Springs Mountain, the 216ft tower has spectacular views of the surrounding mountains covered with dogwood, hickory, oak and pine – lovely in the spring and fall.

Gangster Museum of America   MUSEUM
(☑ 501-318-1717; www.tgmoa.com; 510 Central Ave; adult/child $15/6; ⊙ 10am-5pm Sun-Thu, to 6pm Fri & Sat) Learn about the sinful glory days of Prohibition, when this small town in the middle of nowhere turned into a hotbed of

lavish wealth thanks to Chicago bootleggers like Capone, and his NYC counterparts. Highlights include original slot machines, tons of old photos and a tommy gun.

Galaxy Connection   MUSEUM
(☑ 501-276-4432; www.thegalaxyconnection.com; 626 Central Ave; $7; ⊙ 11am-5pm Mon-Thu, to 8pm Fri & Sat, 12:30-5pm Sun) And now for something completely different: a museum dedicated to *Star Wars*. This fantastically geeky temple is the labor of love of one particularly obsessed Arkansan, and while it may feel a little on the amateur side, it's got enough paraphernalia from life-sized Boba Fett mannequins to a Jedi dress-up area to feel awesomely nostalgic to fans.

Buckstaff Bathhouse   SPA
(☑ 501-623-2308; www.buckstaffbaths.com; 509 Central Ave; thermal bath $33, with massage $71; ⊙ 8-11:45am daily, plus 1:30-3pm Mon-Sat Mar-Nov; 8-11:45am Mon-Sat, plus 1:30-3pm Mon-Fri Dec-Feb) Spa service Hot Springs–style was never distressingly luxurious, and you get the historical treatment here. Buckstaff's no-nonsense staff whip you through the baths, treatments and massages, just as in the 1930s. Truly, it's wonderful.

🛏 Sleeping & Eating

★ **Alpine Inn**   INN $
(☑ 501-624-9164; www.alpine-inn-hot-springs.com; 741 Park Ave; r $65-95; ℗ ✳ 🛜 🌊) The friendly Scottish owners of this inn, less than a mile from Bathhouse Row, have spent a few years upgrading an old motel to remarkable ends. The rooms are impeccable, comfortable and include flat-screen TVs and sumptuous beds.

Arlington Resort Hotel & Spa   HISTORIC HOTEL $
(☑ 501-623-7771; www.arlingtonhotel.com; 239 Central Ave; s/d/ste from $99/120/180; ℗ ✳ 🛜 🌊) This imposing historic hotel tops Bathhouse Row and constantly references its glory days, even if said days have passed. The grand lobby buzzes at night when there might be a live band. There's an in-house spa, and rooms are well maintained, if aging. Corner rooms with a view are a steal.

Colonial Pancake House   DINER $
(☑ 501-624-9273; 111 Central Ave; mains $6-10; ⊙ 7am-3pm; 🍴) A Hot Springs classic, with turquoise booths and homey touches like quilts and doilies on the walls, this is almost like your grandma's kitchen. Except the pancakes, French toast (made with Texas toast)

and malted or buckwheat waffles are better'n grandma's. Get yours with pecans inside. They do burgers and other diner grub at lunchtime.

McClard's BARBECUE $$
(☎ 501-623-9665; www.mcclards.com; 505 Albert Pike; mains $4-15; ⊙ 11am-8pm Tue-Sat) Southwest of the center, Bill Clinton's favorite boyhood barbecue is still popular for ribs, slow-cooked beans, chili and tamales. It's on the outskirts of downtown Hot Springs.

🍸 Drinking & Nightlife

Maxine's BAR
(☎ 501-321-0909; www.maxineslive.com; 700 Central Ave; ⊙ 3pm-3am Mon-Fri, to 2am Sat, noon-midnight Sun) If you're looking for some (loud) night music, head to this infamous cathouse turned live-music venue. They host bands out of Austin regularly.

**Superior Bathhouse
Brewery and Distillery** BREWERY
(☎ 501-624-2337; www.superiorbathhouse.com; 329 Central Ave; ⊙ 11am-9pm, to 11pm Fri & Sat) It's surprising that an outdoorsy town with this many hikers and hipsters lacked a craft brewery for so long, but as the sun rises in the east, so too does Hot Springs have an indie brewery. The local suds are delicious and perfect for washing away any healthy growth your body may have mistakenly acquired in Hot Springs.

ℹ Getting There & Away

Greyhound (☎ 501-623-5574; www.greyhound. com; 100 Broadway Tce) has buses heading from Hot Springs to Little Rock (1½ hours, from $13, around three daily). The town is located off I-30, about 60 miles southwest of Little Rock.

Tri-Peaks Region

The Tri-Peaks Region is the crown jewel in the gem that is the great green Arkansas River Valley, which forms one of the state's major geographic zones. In the shadow of the Tri-Peaks, you'll find four state parks and fantastic hiking, trekking and boating activities.

The area, which comprises multiple Arkansas counties, is named for the triumvirate of Mt Magazine, Mt Nebo and Petit Jean Mountain. While there is no real central base for exploring the area, you can stock up on supplies in numerous small towns, the largest of which is Russellville. We have named the closest supply town in each park's individual entry.

◉ Sights & Activities

Each of the parks we list in the Tri-Peak Region, with the exception of water-oriented Lake Dardanelle, contain multiple hikes ranging from flat, easy nature loops to difficult ascents along mountain peaks. Check with each park website for a full list of the many trails, and be sure to ask rangers about current conditions.

Mount Magazine State Park STATE PARK
(☎ 479-963-8502; www.mountmagazinestatepark. com; 577 Lodge Drive, Paris, GPS: N 35°09'52.4 W 93°38'49.7"; ⊙ 24hr) This stellar state park features some 14 miles of trails that wind around Arkansas' highest point. The surrounding vistas are spectacular, taking in all of the forested montane beauty of the Arkansas River Valley. If you don't have time to stop, the **Mount Magazine Scenic Byway** traverses the park and includes some drop-dead gorgeous views. If you need food or gas, the closest town is Paris, about 17 miles away.

Mount Nebo State Park STATE PARK
(☎ 479-229-3655; www.arkansasstateparks.com/ mountnebo; 16728 West State Hwy 155, Dardanelle, GPS: N 35°13'41.0" W 93°15'19.7"; ⊙ sunrise-sunset; [P][♿][🐾]) [♿ FREE] Hey – it's just another impossibly beautiful Arkansas state park! Mount Nebo and surrounds are crisscrossed by 14 miles of trails that plunge into the woodsy mountainscape. The strenuous Nebo Springs trail makes a loop that heads to a mossy, watery slice of outdoors loveliness. The closest town, Dardanelle, is eight miles to the east.

Petit Jean State Park STATE PARK
(☎ 501-727-5441; www.petitjeanstatepark.com; 1285 Petit Jean Mountain Rd, Morrilton, GPS: N 35°07'04.3" W 92°56'17.8"; ⊙ sunrise-sunset; [P][♿][🐾]) [♿ FREE] The excellently maintained facilities of this state park, the oldest in Arkansas, wind past a lush 95ft waterfall, romantic grottoes, expansive vistas and dense forests. Be on the lookout for a natural bridge spanning the Arcadian wilderness, as well as overlooks that take in huge swaths of the Arkansas River Valley. The closest town is Morrilton (18 miles away), although Little Rock is only about 70 miles southeast of here if you fancy a long day trip from the capital.

Lake Dardanelle State Park   STATE PARK

(www.arkansasstateparks.com/lakedardanelle; 100 State Park Dr (Breakwater Rd), Russellville; ☻visitor center 8am-5pm daily, to 8pm May-Aug; P ♿) Miles of icy-blue water mark this 34,300-acre reservoir, which is surrounded by boat-launch ramps and flat-out pretty views. There's a big visitor center in Russellville that includes kid-friendly interpretive exhibits, aquariums and kayak-rental facilities.

Buffalo National River   RAFTING

(☎870-439-2502; www.nps.gov/buff; 170 Ranger Road, St Joe, Tyler Bend Visitor Center; ♿) ☝ Yet another under-acknowledged Arkansas gem, and perhaps the best of them all, this 135-mile river flows beneath dramatic bluffs through unspoiled Ozark forest. The upriver section tends to have most of the white water, while the lower reaches ease lazily along – perfect for an easy paddle.

The Buffalo National River (p445) has 10 **campgrounds** and three designated wilderness areas; the most accessible is through the Tyler Bend visitor center, 11 miles north of Marshall on Hwy 65, where you can also pick up a list of approved outfitters for self-guided rafting or canoe trips (the best way to tour the park and see the gargantuan limestone bluffs). Or seek out Buffalo Outdoor Center (p445), which will point you in the right direction and rents out attractive cabins in the woods, too.

Kayaking   BOATING

(☎479-967-5516; www.arkansasstateparks.com; 100 State Park Drive (Breakwater Rd), Russellville; per hour/half-day/day from $8/14/20) ☝ You can rent solo or tandem kayaks to explore the waters of Lake Dardanelle, or opt for a 90-minute kayak tour for an extra $12/6 per adult/child.

🛏 Sleeping & Eating

There are uninspiring chain motels and hotels in the towns close to the Tri-Peaks parks, but if you're going to sleep out here, you may as well crash in the parks – be it in primitive campsites or a stylish lodge.

There are dozens of campsites (www.arkansasstateparks.com/camping-cabins-lodging; $12 to 32) spread out among the four state parks of the Tri-Peaks Region. Facilities range from primitive camping with no hookups to sites with full electricity, running water and toilets. Contact each park to learn about their individual camping areas, and book through the state park website.

You'll want to stock up on groceries before exploring any of the Tri-Peaks parks in-depth, with the exception of Lake Dardanelle, which is located in Russellville proper.

❶ Information

The **Tyler Bend Visitor Center** (☎870-439-2502; www.nps.gov/buff; 170 Ranger Rd, St Joe; ☻8:30am-4:30pm) is a must visit for those who want to explore the Buffalo National River.

❶ Getting There & Away

The Tri-Peaks Region occupies an oddly Arkansas-shaped chunk of north-central Arkansas. The four parks can be accessed via the towns we list in individual park listings. None is more than two hours from Little Rock.

The spectacular Highway 23/Pig Trail Byway, which runs from Eureka Springs to Mount Magazine State Park (p441), runs through mountain ranges and Ozark National Forest – it's well worth your time.

Ozark Mountains

Stretching from northwest and central Arkansas into Missouri, the Ozark Mountains are an ancient range, once surrounded by sea and now well worn by time. Verdant mountains give way to misty fields and hard-dirt farms, while dramatic karst formations line sparkling lakes, rivers and capillary-thin back roads. The region derives a lot of pride from its independence and sense of place, a zeitgeist at least partially informed by multiple generations of familial roots and a long history of regional poverty. For literary company, pick up Daniel Woodrell's novel *Winter's Bone,* which was adapted into a critically acclaimed film of the same name.

❶ Getting There & Away

The Ozarks encompass a large area, riven by numerous mountain roads, some of which are big enough to count as highways. Major roads include Hwy 62, AR 21, AR 43 and AR 66. The closest regional airport is **Northwest Arkansas Regional Airport** (XNA; ☎479-205-1000; www.flyxna.com; 1 Airport Blvd), near Bentonville. Eureka Springs is also served by **Greyhound** (☎800-451-5333; 131 E Van Buren).

Mountain View

Mountain View has managed to parlay Ozark culture into the sort of tourism you can (partially) build an community on. The folkways and creative expression of the mountains are given exuberant life in this village, and a mix of cultural seekers and the creators of the culture that's being sought out yields an odd nexus of deeply spiritual Christianity, hippie folk music and heartfelt hospitality.

The **Visitor Information Center** (870-269-8068; www.yourplaceinthemountains.com; 122 W Main St; 9am-4:30pm Mon-Sat) promotes Mountain View as the 'Folk Music Capital of the World,' and while that may be ambitious, it doesn't detract from Mountain View's fundamental pleasantness. No matter how you get here, you'll inevitably pass through crumbling Ozark towns fallen on hard times. Mountain View, in contrast, is what the area could be: preserved history finding contemporary voice and energy in a globalized world that still wants to connect to deep regional traditions.

Sights & Activities

Blanchard Springs Caverns CAVE
(870-757-2211, 877-444-6777; www.blanchard springs.org; NF 54, Forest Rd, off Hwy 14; Drip Stone Tour adult/child$10/5, Wild Cave Tour $75; hours vary;) The spectacular Blanchard Springs Caverns, 15 miles northwest of Mountain View, were carved by an underground river and rival those at Carlsbad. It's another little-known, mind-blowing spot in Arkansas. Three Forest Service guided tours range from disabled-accessible to adventurous three- to four-hour spelunking sessions. The caverns maintain seasonal hours, but usually open at 9:30am and close around sunset.

Ozark Folk Center State Park STATE PARK
(870-269-3851; www.ozarkfolkcenter.com; 1032 Park Ave; auditorium adult/child $12/7; 10am-5pm Tue-Sat Apr-Nov, evening shows 6pm;) The town's top cultural attraction, just north of Mountain View, hosts ongoing craft demonstrations, a traditional herb garden, and nightly live music that brings in an avid crowd. Beyond those shows, the center maintains a busy concert schedule that ropes in some of the nation's best folk and bluegrass acts.

LocoRopes OUTDOORS
(888-669-6717, 870-269-6566; www.locoropes. com; 1025 Park Ave; per zipline $7.50; 10am-5pm Mar 1-Nov 30) This popular outdoors outfitter offers a ropes course, slack lining, a freefall, a climbing wall and three ziplines.

Sleeping & Eating

Wildflower B&B B&B $
(870-269-4383; www.wildflowerbb.com; 100 Washington St; r $99-139;) Set right on the Court Square with a rocking-chair-equipped wraparound porch and cool folk art on the walls. Ask for the front room upstairs; it's flooded with afternoon light, has a queen bed and a joint sitting room with TV. Booking online is best.

Tommy's Famous Pizza and BBQ PIZZA, BARBECUE $
(870-269-3278; www.tommysfamous.com; cnr Carpenter & W Main Sts; pizza $7-26, mains $7-13; from 3pm) The Tommy's Famous Pizza and BBQ is run by the friendliest bunch of backwoods hippies you could hope to meet. The BBQ pizza marries Tommy's stated specialties indulgently. The affable owner, a former rocker from Memphis, plays great music, has a fun vibe, and just two conditions: no attitude and no loud kids.

Tommy's closes when the cash register hasn't opened for an hour.

PJ's Rainbow Cafe AMERICAN $
(870-269-8633; 216 W Main St; mains $5.50-13; 7am-8pm Tue-Sat, to 2pm Sun;) This country-fried cafe serves up some truly tasty diner food done with flair; think spinach-stuffed pork loin and fresh-grilled rainbow trout caught in local rivers. Cash only.

Eureka Springs

Eureka Springs, near Arkansas' northwestern corner, perches in a steep valley filled with Victorian buildings, crooked streets and a crunchy, New Age–aligned local population that welcomes all – this is one of the most explicitly gay-friendly towns in the Ozarks, and mixes up an odd mash of liberal politics and rainbow flags with biker-friendly Harley bars. Hiking, cycling, and horseback-riding opportunities abound.

The **visitor center** (479-253-8737; www. eurekaspringschamber.com; 516 Village Circle, Hwy 62 E; 9am-5pm) has information about lodging, activities, tours and local attractions. For information on LGBTQ travel in the area, log on to Out In Eureka (www.gay eurekasprings.com).

Sights & Activities

Historic Loop HISTORIC SITE
(www.eurekasprings.org) FREE This 3.5-mile walking tour winds through downtown

Eureka Springs and neighboring residential areas. The route is dotted with more than 300 Victorian homes, all built before 1910, each a jaw-dropper and on par with any preserved historic district in the USA. You can access the loop via the Eureka Trolley, or just walk it – recommended if you're fit (the streets are steep!); pick up a map or buy trolley tickets at the Visitor Center.

Thorncrown Chapel CHURCH
(☑ 479-253-7401; www.thorncrown.com; 12968 Hwy 62 W; ⊙9am-5pm Apr-Nov, 11am-4pm Mar & Dec; P) FREE Thorncrown Chapel is a magnificent sanctuary made of glass, with its 48ft-tall wooden skeleton holding 425 windows. There's not much between your prayers and God's green earth here. It's just outside of Eureka Springs in the woods. Donation suggested.

1886 Crescent Hotel HISTORIC BUILDING
(☑ 855-725-5720; www.crescent-hotel.com; 75 Prospect Ave) Built in 1886, the Crescent is a gorgeous, functioning artifact of an older age. Step into the dark-wood lobby, with its roaring fireplace and carpets, all accented by little Jazz Age flourishes, and you'll feel the need to order a cognac and berate Daisy Buchanan for ever marrying Tom Buchanan, the *cad*. Er, sorry. The Crescent sits atop a hill, and is a great place to visit for a drink, the view from its rooftop, or both.

Lake Leatherwood City Park PARK
(☑ 479-253-7921; www.lakeleatherwoodcitypark. com; 1303 Co Rd 204; ⊙24hr; P) This expansive park includes 21 miles of hiking and biking trails that crisscross the forested mountains and surround an 85-acre lake. Located about 3.5 miles from downtown Eureka Springs, this is the closest managed wild space to Eureka Springs.

Eureka Trolley TOURS
(☑ 479-253-9572; www.eurekatrolley.org; 137 W Van Buren St; day pass adult/child $6/2; ⊙10am-6pm Sun-Fri, 9am-8pm Sat May-Oct, reduced hours other times;) This old time hop-on-hop-off trolley service plies four routes through greater Eureka Springs. Each trip takes about 20 to 30 minutes, revealing a different angle on life in this mountain town. Check website or call ahead for running times.

🛏 Sleeping & Eating

★**Treehouse Cottages** COTTAGE $$
(☑ 479-253-8667; www.treehousecottages.com; 165 W Van Buren St; cottage $149-169; P✳🛜) Sprinkled amid 33 acres of pine forest, these cute, kitschy and spacious stilted wooden cottages are worth finding. There's lovely accent tile in the baths, a Jacuzzi tub overlooking the trees, a private balcony with grill at the ready, a flat-screen TV and fireplace. Enforces two-night minimum stays.

The Crescent Hotel HISTORIC HOTEL $$
(☑ 855-725-5720; www.crescent-hotel.com; 75 Prospect Ave; r $160-200, ste $200-280; P🛜) Of all the pretty historic buildings in Eureka Springs, the Crescent stands out: it's like *Downton Abbey* meets the Jazz Age (which happened in season 4, right?). We digress; rooms are a well-executed synthesis of historic accents and modern comforts, and the whole vibe of the place is both elegant and fun. Rates go up on weekends.

★**FRESH** MODERN AMERICAN $$
(☑ 479-253-9300; www.freshanddeliciousofeureka springs.com; 179 N Main St; mains $10-27; ⊙11am-9pm Mon-Thu, 10am-2pm Sun;) This beautiful café specializes in farm-to-table cuisine, brilliant baked goods and quirky service. The open-face sandwiches with shaved ham served on fresh-baked French toast are stupidly decadent, and there are vegan options ranging from salads to pesto-tossed pasta. Dinner gets fancier with dishes like roasted-chicken pot pie and seared ahi tuna.

★**Stone House** MODERN AMERICAN $$$
(☑ 479-363-6411; www.eurekastonehouse.com; 89 S Main St; cheese plates $25-47; ⊙1-10pm Thu-Sat, to 8pm Sun) The Stone House has all the ingredients for a pretty perfect evening: lots of wine; a menu that focuses on cheese, bread, olives, honey and charcuterie; live music; a cute courtyard; and did we mention lots of wine? It's open until 10pm, which constitutes late-night dining in Eureka Springs.

🍺 Drinking & Entertainment

Chelsea's Corner Cafe & Bar BAR
(☑ 479-253-8231; www.chelseascornercafe.com; 10 Mountain St; ⊙noon-10pm Sun-Thu, to midnight Fri & Sat) Live-music acts frequently take to the stage at this bar, which attracts a typically Eureka Springs blend of hippies and bikers. The kitchen is one of the few places in town open past 9pm, and does pizza delivery.

Opera in the Ozarks OPERA
(☑ 479-253-8595; www.opera.org; 16311 Hwy 62 West; tickets from $20) This much acclaimed fine-arts program has kept opera alive and

loud in the mountains. A packed performance schedule and a playhouse located just outside of town is the pride of Eureka Springs.

Buffalo National River

Ponca is the easiest town to base yourself in if you're looking to explore the Buffalo National River. Organize an adventure with a local outfitter and get ready for some stunning scenery: a backdrop of gorgeous riverine wilderness, multicolored granite bluffs and rushing waterfalls is at your fingertips (or paddle oars; you know what we mean). There's a few outdoor outfitters here to help you get set up on a wilderness adventure.

🏃 Activities

Buffalo Outdoor Center   ADVENTURE
(BOC; ☑ 870-861-5514; www.buffaloriver.com; 4699 AR 43; kayak/canoe per day $55/62, zipline tour $89; ⊘ 8am-6pm Mar-Oct, to 5pm Nov-Feb; 🚗🐎) Can arrange paddling trips, hiking tours, fishing trips, horseback rides and a zipline tour. Reserve in advance.

**Big Bluff via Centerpoint
& Goat Trail**   HIKING
(AR 43 & Fire Tower Rd, GPS: N 36°03'50.7" W 93°21'43.6" (Centerpoint Trail)) ∅ Standing a dramatic 550ft tall, Big Bluff is the highest sheer rock face between the Rocky Mountains and the Appalachians. To get out here, take the Centerpoint Trail, three miles north of Ponca on AR 43 (look for the trailhead near the junction of Fire Tower Rd). Take the narrow spur route – the Goat Trail – that leads to the bluff. This is a 2.5 mile round-trip trail, and it's pretty much uphill.

Lost Valley Canoe   CANOEING
(☑ 870-861-5522; www.lostvalleycanoe.com; AR 43; kayaks per day from $55, shuttle service from $20) ∅ This knowledgeable outfitter can arrange canoe and kayak rentals, as well as shuttle pick-up services. They also rent comfortable cabins (with hot tubs!) that can sleep two for $125 ($15 for each extra guest).

ⓘ Getting There & Away

Ponca sits far off any beaten tracks. You need to come by road, and it's about 50 miles south of Eureka Springs and 80 miles east of Bentonville.

LOUISIANA

Louisiana runs deep: a French colony turned Spanish protectorate turned reluctant American purchase; a southern fringe of swampland, bayou and alligators dissolving into the Gulf of Mexico; a northern patchwork prairie of heartland farm country; and everywhere, a population tied together by a deep, unshakable appreciation for the good things in life: food and music.

New Orleans, its first city, lives and dies by these qualities, and its restaurants and music halls are second to none. But everywhere, the state shares a love for this joie de vivre. We're not dropping French for fun, by the way; while the language is not a cultural component of North Louisiana, near I-10 and below it is a generation removed from the household – if it has been removed at all.

History

The lower Mississippi River area was dominated by the Mississippian mound-building culture until around 1592 when Europeans arrived and decimated the Native Americans with the usual combination of disease, unfavorable treaties and outright hostility.

The land was then passed back and forth between France, Spain and England. Under the French 'Code Noir,' slaves were kept but retained a somewhat greater degree of freedom – and thus native culture – than their counterparts in British North America.

After the American Revolution the whole area passed to the USA in the 1803 Louisiana Purchase, and Louisiana became a state in 1812. The resulting blend of American and Franco-Spanish traditions, plus the influence of Afro-Caribbean communities, gave Louisiana the unique culture it retains to this day.

Following the Civil War, Louisiana was re-admitted to the Union in 1868 and the next 30 years saw political wrangling, economic stagnation and renewed discrimination against African Americans.

Hurricane Katrina (2005) and the BP Gulf Coast Oil Spill (2010) significantly damaged the local economy and infrastructure. Louisiana remains a bottom-rung state in terms of per capita income and education levels, yet it ranks high in national happiness scales.

ⓘ Information

Louisiana Office of Tourism (☑ 800-677-4082, 225-635-0090; www.louisianatravel.com)

Sixteen welcome centers dot freeways throughout the state, or contact the office directly.
Louisiana State Parks (📞 888-677-1400; www.crt.state.la.us/louisiana-state-parks; primitive/premium sites from $18/25) Louisiana has 22 state parks that offer camping. Some parks also offer lodge accommodations and cabins. Reservations can be made on the online, by phone or on a drop-in basis if there's availability. Camping fees rise slightly from April to September.

New Orleans

New Orleans is very much of America, but extraordinarily removed from it as well. Founded by the French and administered by the Spanish (and then the French again), New Orleans is the most European city in America. But, with the *vodoun* (voodoo), weekly second-line parades, Mardi Gras Indians, jazz, brass and gumbo, it's also the most African and Caribbean city in America.

New Orleans celebrates life; while America is on deadline, this city is sipping a cocktail after a long lunch. But if you saw how people here rebuilt their homes after floods and tempests, you'd be foolish to call the locals lazy.

Tolerating everything and learning from it is the soul of this city. When New Orleans' citizens aspire to that overarching Creole ideal, where the whole is greater than the sum of its parts, we get: jazz; Nouveau Louisiana cuisine; storytellers from African *griots* (West African bards) to Seventh Ward rappers to Tennessee Williams; French townhouses a few blocks from Foghorn Leghorn mansions groaning under sweet myrtle and bougainvillea; and Mardi Gras celebrations that mix pagan mysticism with Catholic pageantry.

Just don't forget the indulgence and immersion, because that Creolization gets watered down when folks don't live life to its intellectual and epicurean hilt.

👁 Sights

👁 French Quarter

Also known as Vieux Carré (voo car-*ray*; Old Quarter) and 'the Quarter,' the French Quarter is the original city as planned by the French in the early 18th century. Here lies the infamous Bourbon St, but of more interest is an elegantly aged grid of shopfronts, iron lamps and courtyard gardens. Most visitors begin exploring the city here and some,

sadly, never leave the area. That's not to say the Quarter isn't lovely, but it's a bit like Disney World: heavy on tourist traffic and light on locals (unless you count your bartender or waiter).

★ **Jackson Square**   SQUARE
(Decatur & St Peter Sts) Sprinkled with lazing loungers, surrounded by sketch artists, fortune-tellers and traveling performers, and watched over by cathedrals, offices and shops plucked from a Parisian fantasy, Jackson Square is one of America's great town greens and the heart of the Quarter. The identical, block-long Pontalba Buildings overlook the scene.

★ **St Louis Cathedral**   CATHEDRAL
(📞 504-525-9585; www.stlouiscathedral.org; Jackson Sq; donations accepted, self-guided tour $1; ⏰ 8am-4pm, Mass noon Mon-Fri, 5pm Sat, 9am & 11am Sun) One of the best examples of French architecture in the country, this triple-spired cathedral is dedicated to Louis IX, the French king sainted in 1297; it's a most innocuous bit of Gallic heritage in the heart of an American city. In addition to hosting black, white and Creole Catholic congregants, St Louis has also attracted those who, in the best New Orleanian tradition, mix their influences, such as voodoo queen Marie Laveau.

★ **Cabildo**   MUSEUM
(📞 800-568-6968, 504-568-6968; http://louisianastatemuseum.org/museums/the-cabildo; 701 Chartres St; adult/student/child under 12yr $6/5/free; ⏰ 10am-4:30pm Tue-Sun, closed Mon; ♿) The former seat of government in colonial Louisiana now serves as the gateway to exploring the history of the state in general, and New Orleans in particular. It's also a magnificent building in its own right; the elegant Cabildo marries elements of Spanish colonial architecture and French urban design better than most buildings in the city. Exhibits range from Native American tools and 'Wanted' posters for escaped slaves to a gallery's worth of paintings of stone-faced old New Orleanians.

Presbytère   MUSEUM
(📞 800-568-6968, 504-568-6968; http://louisianastatemuseum.org/museums/the-presbytere; 751 Chartres St; adult/student $6/5; ⏰ 10am-4:30pm Tue-Sun) 🖊 The lovely Presbytère building, designed in 1791 as a rectory for the St Louis Cathedral, serves as New Orleans' Mardi Gras museum. You'll find there's more to the city's most famous celebration

CAJUNS, CREOLES AND...CREOLES

Tourists in Louisiana often use the terms 'Cajun' and 'Creole' interchangeably, but the two cultures are quite distinct. 'Creole' refers to descendants of the original European settlers of Louisiana, a blended mix of mainly French and Spanish ancestry. The Creoles tend to have urban connections to New Orleans and consider their own culture refined and urbanized.

The Cajuns can trace their lineage to the Acadians: colonists from rural France who settled Nova Scotia. After the British conquered Canada, the proud Acadians refused to kneel to the new crown and were exiled in the mid-18th century – an act known as the Grand Dérangement. Many exiles settled in South Louisiana; they knew the area was French, but the Acadians ('Cajun' is an English bastardization of the word) were often treated as country bumpkins by the Creoles. The Acadians-cum-Cajuns settled in the bayous and prairies, and to this day see themselves as a more rural, frontier-style culture.

Adding confusion to this is the practice, standard in many post-colonial French societies, of referring to mixed-race individuals as 'Creoles.' This happens in Louisiana, but there is a cultural difference between Franco-Spanish Creoles and mixed-race Creoles, even though these two communities very likely share actual blood ancestry.

than wanton debauchery – or, at least, discover the many levels of meaning behind the debauchery. There's an encyclopedia's worth of material on the krewes, secret societies, costumes and racial histories of the Mardi Gras tapestry.

Historic New Orleans Collection MUSEUM
(THNOC; ☑504-523-4662; www.hnoc.org; 533 Royal St; admission free, tours $5; ⊘9:30am-4:30pm Tue-Sat, 10:30am-4:30pm Sun, tours 10am, 11am, 2pm & 3pm Tue-Sat) A combination of preserved buildings, museums and research centers all rolled into one, the Historic New Orleans Collection is a good introduction to the history of of the city. The complex is anchored by its Royal St campus, which presents a series of regularly rotating exhibits and occasional temporary exhibits. Some of the artifacts on offer include an original Jazz Fest poster, transfer documents of the Louisiana Purchase, and utterly disturbing slave advertisements.

◉ Mid-City & The Tremé

The Tremé is the oldest African American neighborhood in the country, characterized by low-slung architecture and residential blocks, some middle class, some rotted by poverty, some gentrifying. This area runs on its west side into Mid-City, a semi-amorphous district that includes long lanes of shotgun houses, poor projects, the gorgeous green spaces of City Park, the elegant mansions of Esplanade Ave and the slow, lovely laze of Bayou St John.

★**Backstreet**
Cultural Museum MUSEUM
(☑504-522-4806; www.backstreetmuseum.org; 1116 Henriette Delille St; $10; ⊘10am-4pm Tue-Sat) Mardi Gras Indian suits grab the spotlight with dazzling flair – and finely crafted detail – in this informative museum, which examines the distinctive elements of African American culture in New Orleans. The museum isn't terribly big – it's the former Blandin's Funeral Home – but if you have any interest in the suits and rituals of Mardi Gras Indians as well as second line parades and Social Aid & Pleasure Clubs (the local black community version of civic associations), you need to stop by.

★**City Park** PARK
(☑504-482-4888; www.neworleanscitypark.com; Esplanade Ave & City Park Ave; [P]) Live oaks, Spanish moss and lazy bayous frame this masterpiece of urban planning. Three miles long and a mile wide, dotted with gardens, waterways and bridges, and home to a captivating art museum, City Park is bigger than Central Park in NYC, and is New Orleans' prettiest green space. Although a planned golf course has tempered the park's natural beauty, some areas still feel like a slightly tamed expression of the forest and Louisiana wetlands that are the natural backdrop of the city.

Art- and nature-lovers could easily spend a day exploring the park. Anchoring the action is the stately New Orleans Museum of Art, which spotlights regional and American artists. From there, stroll past the whimsical

THE SOUTH NEW ORLEANS

New Orleans

500 m
0.25 miles

Willie Mae's
Scotch House
(50yd)

Parkway
Tavern (0.9mi)

Carousel Gardens (2.1mi)
City Park (2.1mi)

Degas House
(0.6mi)

Red's
Chinese
(0.4mi)

St Roch Market
(0.1mi)

BJ's
(1mi)

Crescent Park (0.4mi);
Pizza Delicious (0.5mi);
Joint (0.9mi);
Bacchanal (1mi)

FAUBOURG
MARIGNY

THE TREMÉ

FRENCH
QUARTER

Backstreet Cultural
Museum

Frenchmen
Art Market

Jackson
Square

St Louis
Cathedral

Cabildo

New Orleans
Welcome
Center

Woldenberg
Park

Moonwalk

Streets

N Miro St
N Galvez St
N Johnson St
N Prieur St
N Roman St
N Derbigny St
N Robertson St
N Villere St
N Marais St
N Rampart St
Basin St
Treme St
Crozat St
Saratoga St
N Claiborne Ave
S Claiborne Ave
S Robertson St
S Villere St
S Derbigny St
S Roman St
S Prieur St
S Johnson St
S Galvez St
La Salle St

Orleans Ave
Lafitte Ave
Toulouse St
Bienville St
Iberville St
Canal St
Conti St
St Louis St
St Ann St
St Peter St
Dumaine St
Ursulines Ave
St Philip St
Dauphine St
Bourbon St
Royal St
Chartres St
Decatur St
N Peters St
Esplanade Ave
Barracks St
Governor Nicholls St
Burgundy St
Kerlerec St
Henriette Delille St
McShane Pl

Frenchmen St
Touro St
Pauger St
Elysian Fields Ave
Marigny St
Mandeville St
Washington Sq Park
Dauphine St

Ursulines
Dumaine
Toulouse
Wilkinson St
N Peters St
Bienville St

St Louis
Cemetery No 2
St Louis St

S Rampart St
University Pl
Elk Pl
Baronne St
State
Supreme
Court
Bourbon Sts

Tulane Ave
Twelve Mile
Limit (1.3mi)
Palmyra St
Gravier St
Perdido St

27
34
32
21
16
4
8
5
2
1
10
22
36
24
31
33
12
11
14
3
35
10
10
15
20
26
17
30
23
9

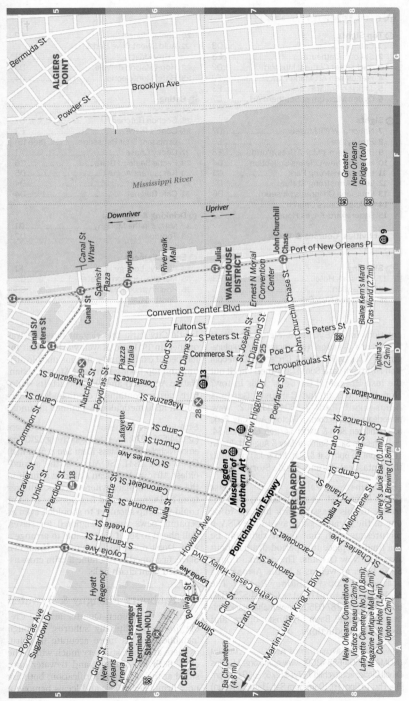

New Orleans

◉ Top Sights
1 Cabildo...D3
2 St Louis Cathedral E3
3 Backstreet Cultural Museum D2
4 Frenchmen Art Market..........................F2
5 Jackson Square.....................................E3
6 Ogden Museum of Southern Art..........C7

◉ Sights
7 National WWII Museum.........................C7
8 Presbytère..E3
9 Blaine Kern's Mardi Gras World...........E8
10 Historic New Orleans Collection D4
11 Louis Armstrong Park C2
12 Louis Armstrong Statue........................D2
13 Louisiana Children's Museum...............D6
14 St Augustine's Church..........................D1
15 Beauregard-Keyes House.....................E2

⊕ Activities, Courses & Tours
16 Confederacy of Cruisers F2

🛏 Sleeping
17 Cornstalk Hotel......................................E3
18 Le Pavillon C5
19 Roosevelt New Orleans C4

20 Soniat House...E2
21 Auld Sweet Olive Bed &
    Breakfast G1
22 Hotel Maison de Ville............................D3
23 Hotel Monteleone D4

⊗ Eating
24 Bayona D3
25 Cochon Butcher......................................D7
26 Coop's Place...E3
    Croissant D'Or Patisserie ....(see 15)
27 Dooky Chase A1
28 Peche Seafood Grill C6
29 Restaurant August D5
30 Café Beignet D4
31 Café Beignet D4

◉ Drinking & Nightlife
32 Mimi's in the Marigny G1
33 Tonique D2

⊛ Entertainment
34 AllWays Lounge F1
35 Mahalia Jackson Theater......................C2
36 Preservation Hall D3
    Spotted Cat ....(see 4)

creations in the **Sydney & Walda Besthoff Sculpture Garden** (www.noma.org/sculpture-garden; One Collins Diboll Circle; ⊙10am-6pm Mon-Fri, to 5pm Sat & Sun) FREE then check out the lush **Botanical Gardens**. Kids in tow? Hop the rides at the **Carousel Gardens Amusement Park** (☑504-483-9402; www.neworleanscitypark.com; 7 Victory Ave, City Park; adult/children 36in & under $4/free, each ride $4; ⊙11am-6pm Sat & Sun Mar-May & Aug-Oct, Tue-Fri 11am-5pm, to 6pm Sat & Sun, Jun & Jul) or climb the fantastical statuary inside Storyland.

Louis Armstrong Park   PARK
(835 N Rampart St; ⊙sunrise-sunset) The entrance to this massive park has got to be one of the greatest gateways in the USA, a picturesque arch that ought rightfully be the final set piece in a period drama about Jazz Age New Orleans. The original Congo Sq is here, as well as a **Louis Armstrong statue** and a **bust of Sidney Bechet**. The **Mahalia Jackson Theater** (☑504-525-1052, box office 504-287-0350; www.mahaliajacksontheater.com; 1419 Basin St) hosts opera and Broadway productions.

New Orleans Museum of Art   MUSEUM
(NOMA; ☑504-658-4100; www.noma.org; 1 Collins Diboll Circle; adult/child 7-17yr $12/6; ⊙10am-6pm Tue-Thu, to 9pm Fri, 10am-5pm Sat, 11am-5pm Sun) Inside City Park, this elegant museum was opened in 1911 and is well worth a visit for its special exhibitions, gorgeous marble atrium, and top-floor galleries of African, Asian, Native American and Oceanic art. Its sculpture garden contains a cutting-edge collection in lush, meticulously planned grounds.

St Augustine's Church   CHURCH
(☑504-525-5934; www.staugchurch.org; 1210 Governor Nicholls St; ⊙Mass 10am Sun & 5pm Wed) Open since 1841, 'St Aug's' is the second-oldest African American Catholic church in the country, a place where Creoles, émigrés from St Domingue and free persons of color could worship shoulder to shoulder, even as separate pews were designated for slaves. Call ahead to see if it's possible to arrange a visit. Don't miss the Tomb of the Unknown Slave, fashioned to resemble a grim cross assembled from chain links.

◉ Faubourg Marigny & Bywater
North of the French Quarter are the Creole *faubourgs* (literally 'suburbs,' although 'neighborhood' is more accurate in spirit, as these areas are still very much within the city). Both the Marigny and Bywater once stood at the edge of gentrification; both are now firmly gentrified, and locals bemoan a

rise in online rentals that they say is robbing these areas of their old residential character. With that said, these are fascinating, beautiful neighborhoods – the homes are bright, painted like so many rows of pastel fruit, and the presence of artists and designers makes for a subversive energy.

★**Frenchmen Art Market**　　MARKET
(☎ 504-941-1149; www.frenchmenartmarket.com; 619 Frenchmen St; ⏰ 7pm-1am Thu-Sat, 6pm-midnight Sun) 🐾 Independent artists and artisans line this alleyway market, which has built a reputation as one of the finest spots in town to find a unique gift to take home as your New Orleans souvenir. 'Art,' in this case, includes clever T-shirts, hand-crafted jewelry, trinkets and, yes, a nice selection of prints and original artwork. It has a second location at 2231 St Claude Ave.

Crescent Park　　PARK
(☎ 504-636-6400; www.crescentparknola.org; Piety, Chartres & Mazant Sts; ⏰ 6am-6:30pm, to 7:30pm mid-Mar–early Nov; ℗) 🐾 This waterfront park is our favorite spot in the city for taking in the Mississippi. Enter over the enormous arch at Piety and Chartres Sts, or at the steps at Marigny and N Peters, and watch the fog blanket the nearby skyline. A promenade meanders past an angular metal and concrete conceptual 'wharf' (placed next to the burned remains of the former commercial wharf). A dog park is located near the Mazant St entrance.

⊙ CBD & Warehouse District

Canal St is the 'great divide' that splits the French Quarter from the Central Business District (CBD) and Warehouse District. Between offices and forgettable municipal buildings lie some of the city's best museums, many posh restaurants, an eyesore of a casino, art galleries and excellent arts walks. That said, this area, with its high-rise buildings and converted condos, is the least 'New Orleans' neighborhood in New Orleans.

★**Ogden Museum of
Southern Art**　　MUSEUM
(☎ 504-539-9650; www.ogdenmuseum.org; 925 Camp St; adult/child 5-17yr $13.50/6.75; ⏰ 10am-5pm Wed-Mon, to 8pm Thu) One of our favorite museums in the city manages to be beautiful, educational and unpretentious all at once. New Orleans entrepreneur Roger Houston Ogden has assembled one of the finest collections of Southern art anywhere, which includes huge galleries ranging from Impressionist landscapes to outsider folk-art quirkiness and contemporary installation work. On Thursday nights, pop in for Ogden after Hours, when you can listen to great Southern musicians and sip wine with a fun-loving, arts-obsessed crowd in the midst of the masterpieces.

National WWII Museum　　MUSEUM
(☎ 504-528-1944; www.nationalww2museum. org; 945 Magazine St; adult/senior/child $26/22.50/16.50, plus 1/2 films $5/10; ⏰ 9am-5pm) This extensive museum presents a fairly thorough analysis of the largest war in history. The exhibits, which are displayed across multiple grand pavilions, are enormous and immersive. Wall-sized photographs capture the confusion of D-Day, while a stroll through the snowy woods of Ardennes feels eerily cold. The experience is designed to be both personal and awe-inducing. That said, the museum focuses so intently on providing the American perspective, it sometimes underplays the narrative of other Allied nations.

Blaine Kern's Mardi Gras World　　MUSEUM
(☎ 504-475-2057; www.mardigrasworld.com; 1380 Port of New Orleans Pl; adult/senior/child 2-11yr $20/16/13; ⏰ tours 9:30am-4:30pm; 🚍) We dare say Mardi Gras World is one of the happiest places in New Orleans by day – but at night it must turn into one of the most terrifying funhouses this side of Hell. It's all those *faces:* the dragons, clowns, kings and fairies, leering and dead-eyed... That said, we love touring Mardi Gras World – the studio warehouse of Blaine Kern (Mr Mardi Gras) and family, who have been making jaw-dropping parade floats since 1947. Tours last 30 to 45 minutes.

⊙ Garden, Lower Garden & Central City

Proceeding south along the Mississippi, following the curve of the river's 'U,' the streets become tree-lined and the houses considerably grander; this is the Garden and Lower Garden Districts, the beginning of New Orleans' 'American Sector' (so named because it was settled after the Louisiana Purchase). This area is home to recent graduates and young professionals, and hip shops and bars that cater to them.

★ **Lafayette Cemetery No 1** CEMETERY
(Washington Ave, at Prytania St; ⊘ 7am-3pm)
Shaded by groves of lush greenery, this cemetery exudes a strong sense of Southern subtropical Gothic. Built in 1833, it is divided by two intersecting footpaths that form a cross. Look out for the crypts built by fraternal organizations such as the Jefferson Fire Company No 22, which took care of their members and their families in large shared tombs. Some of the wealthier family tombs were built of marble, with elaborate details, but most were constructed simply of inexpensive plastered brick.

☞ Tours

Confederacy of Cruisers CYCLING
(☑ 504-400-5468; www.confederacyofcruisers.com; 634 Elysian Fields Ave; tours $49-89) Our favorite bicycle tours in New Orleans set you up on cruiser bikes that come with fat tires and padded seats for Nola's flat, pot-holed roads. The main 'Creole New Orleans' tour takes in the best architecture of the Marigny, Bywater, Esplanade Ave and the Tremé. Confederacy also does a 'History of Drinking' tour (for those 21 and over) and a tasty culinary tour.

★ Festivals & Events

Mardi Gras CULTURAL
(www.mardigrasneworleans.com; ⊘ Feb or early Mar) In February or early March, Fat Tuesday marks the orgasmic finale of the Carnival season. Expect parades, floats, insane costumes, and a day of absolute mad cap revelry as the entire city throws down for an all-day party.

Jazz Fest MUSIC
(www.nojazzfest.com; ⊘ Apr-May) Held during the last weekend of April and the first weekend of May, this world-renowned extravaganza of music, food, crafts and good living is a mainstay of the New Orleans festival calendar, attracting both international headliners and local artists.

St Joseph's Day – Super Sunday CULTURAL
(⊘ Mar 19) March 19 and its nearest Sunday bring 'gangs' of Mardi Gras Indians out into the streets in all their feathered, drumming glory. The Super Sunday parade usually begins around noon at Bayou St John and Orleans Ave, but follows no fixed route.

French Quarter Festival MUSIC
(☑ 504-522-5730; www.fqfi.org; ⊘ Apr) During the second weekend of April, the largest free music festival in the country takes over the French Quarter.

🛏 Sleeping

★ **Le Pavillon** HISTORIC HOTEL $$
(☑ 504-581-3111; www.lepavillon.com; 833 Poydras Ave; r $135-200, ste from $600; ⓟ ❋ � ⓢ) Le Pavillon exudes an old-school joie de vivre that's easy to love. Fluted columns support the porte cochere off the alabaster facade, and the doorman wears white gloves and a top hat (and somehow doesn't look ridiculous). Both private and public spaces are redolent with historic portraits, magnificent chandeliers, marble floors and heavy drapery.

★ **Auld Sweet Olive**
Bed & Breakfast B&B $$
(☑ 504-947-4332; www.sweetolive.com; 2460 N Rampart St; r incl breakfast $145-180, ste $180-290; ❋ ❋ ⓢ) The Krewe de Vieux parade goes right by this grand B&B. Even if you don't come during the pre-Lenten season, you can see parade regalia such as the co-owner's King Endymion costume on display. The house itself is similarly theatrical, once owned by a set designer and mural artist. Individual rooms are suffused with decorative touches – faux wood and magnolia blooms.

Columns Hotel HISTORIC HOTEL $$
(☑ 504-899-9308; www.thecolumns.com; 3811 St Charles Ave; r incl breakfast $145-180; ❋ ⓢ) This white-porched Southern manse, built in 1883, is a snapshot from the past. Fortunately that past doesn't take itself too seriously. A magnificent mahogany staircase climbs past a stained-glass window to the rooms, ranging from smallish doubles to the two-room Pretty Baby Suite (named for the 1970s Louis Malle film shot here). The environs aren't exactly posh, but they're well loved.

Degas House HISTORIC HOTEL $$
(☑ 504-821-5009; www.degashouse.com; 2306 Esplanade Ave; r $130-250, ste from $300; ⓟ ❋ ⓢ) Edgar Degas, the famed French Impressionist, lived in this 1852 Italianate house when visiting his mother's family in the early 1870s. Rooms recall his time here through period furnishings and reproductions of his work. The suites have balconies and fireplaces, while the less expensive garret rooms are cramped top-floor quarters that once housed the Degas family's servants. Stays include a hot breakfast.

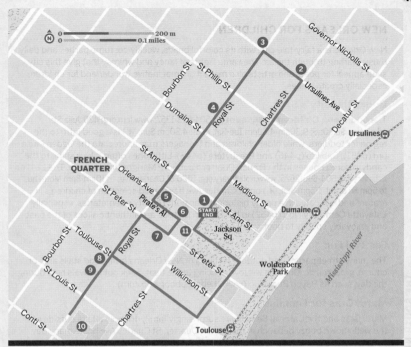

🚶 City Walk
French Quarter

START/END JACKSON SQ
LENGTH 1.1 MILES; 1½ HOURS

Begin your walk at the **1 Presbytère** (p446) on Jackson Sq and head down Chartres St to the corner of Ursulines Ave. Directly across Chartres St, at No 1113, the 1826 **2 Beauregard-Keyes House** (www.bkhouse.org) combines Creole and American styles of design. Walk along Ursulines Ave to Royal St – the soda fountain at the **3 Royal Pharmacy** is a preserved relic from halcyon malt-shop days.

When it comes to quintessential New Orleans postcard images, Royal St takes the prize. Cast-iron galleries grace the buildings and a profusion of flowers garland the facades. At No 915 Royal, the **4 Cornstalk Hotel** (www.cornstalkhotel.com) stands behind one of the most frequently photographed fences anywhere. At Orleans Ave, stately magnolia trees and lush tropical plants fill **5 St Anthony's Garden** (tough to see behind rows of street art) behind

6 St Louis Cathedral (p446). Alongside the garden, take the inviting Pirate's Alley and turn right down Cabildo Alley and then right up St Peter St toward Royal St. Tennessee Williams shacked up at No 632 St Peter, the **7 Avart-Peretti House**, in 1946–47 while he wrote *A Streetcar Named Desire.* Turn left on Royal St. At the corner of Royal and Toulouse Sts stands a pair of houses built by Jean François Merieult in the 1790s. The building known as the **8 Court of Two Lions**, at 541 Royal St, opens onto Toulouse St and next door is the **9 Historic New Orleans Collection** (p447).

On the next block, the massive 1909 **10 State Supreme Court Building** was the setting for many scenes in director Oliver Stone's movie *JFK.*

Turn around and head right on Toulouse St to Decatur St and turn left. Cut across the road and walk along the river. As Jackson Sq comes into view, cross back over to the Presbytère's near-identical twin, the **11 Cabildo** (p446).

NEW ORLEANS FOR CHILDREN

New Orleans is a fairy-tale city, with its colorful beads, weekly costume parties and daily music wafting through the air. The same flights of fancy and whimsy that give this city such appeal for poets and artists also make it an imaginative wonderland for children, especially creative ones.

Under the City's Skin

The **Louisiana Children's Museum** (☎504-523-1357; www.lcm.org; 420 Julia St; admission $8.50; 🕘9:30am-4:30pm Tue-Sat, noon-4:30pm Sun; 👪) is a good intro to the region for toddlers, while older children and teenagers may appreciate the Ogden Museum (p451), Cabildo (p446) and Presbytère (p446). Little ones often take a shine to the candy-colored houses in the French Quarter, Faubourg Marigny and Uptown. The **Latter Library** (☎504-596-2625; www.nolalibrary.org; 5120 St Charles Ave; 🕘10am-8pm Mon-Thu, to 5pm Fri & Sat, 1-5pm Sun; 👪) on St Charles Ave has a good selection of children's literature and is located in a pretty historical mansion. The city's cemeteries, especially Lafayette Cemetery No 1 (p452) in the Garden District, are authentic slices of the past and enjoyably spooky to boot.

Festival Fun

The many street parties and outdoor festivals of New Orleans bring food stalls and, of course, great music. Children will love dancing to the beat. Seek out festivals held during the day, such as Bayou Boogaloo (www.thebayouboogaloo.com).

Mardi Gras for Families

Mardi Gras and the Carnival Season are surprisingly family-friendly affairs outside of the well-known boozy debauch in the French Quarter. St Charles Ave hosts many day parades where lots of krewes roll and families set up grilling posts and tents – drinking revelers aren't welcome. Kids are set up on 'ladder seats' (www.momsminivan.com/extras/ladderseat.html) so they can get an adult-height view of the proceedings and catch throws from the floats. The crazy costumes add to the child-friendly feel of the whole affair. See www.neworleansonline.com/neworleans/mardigras/mgfamilies.html.

★Roosevelt New Orleans HOTEL $$$
(☎504-648-1200; www.therooseveltneworleans.com; 123 Baronne St; r/ste from $300/400; [P] @ 📶 🏊) The majestic, block-long lobby harks back to the early 20th century, a golden age of opulent hotels and grand retreats. Swish rooms have classical details, but the spa, John Besh restaurant, storied Sazerac Bar and swanky jazz lounge are at least half the reason to stay. The rooftop pool is pretty swell too. It's an easy walk to the French Quarter.

★Soniat House BOUTIQUE HOTEL $$$
(☎504-522-0570, 800-544-8808; www.soniathouse.com; 1133 Chartres St; r/ste from $245/450; 🚭 ❄ 📶) The three houses that make up this hotel in the Lower Quarter epitomize Creole elegance at its unassuming best. You enter via a cool loggia into a courtyard filled with ferns and a trickling fountain. Some rooms open onto the courtyard, while winding stairways lead to elegant upstairs quarters. Singular attention has been paid to the art and antiques throughout.

Hotel Maison de Ville HISTORIC HOTEL $$$
(☎504-324-4888; www.hotelmaisondeville.com; 727 Toulouse St; r from $275; ❄ 📶) A series of remodeled suits, cottages and apartments form this graceful hotel, which includes the one- and two-bedroom Audubon Cottage suites (where artist John J Audubon stayed and painted while in town). It's a quintessential French Quarter property, dripping with tropical historical accents and built around a lushly landscaped courtyard that feels plucked out of time.

Hotel Monteleone HOTEL $$$
(☎504-523-3341, 866-338-4684; www.hotelmonteleone.com; 214 Royal St; r $190-270, ste from $370; ❄ 📶 🐾) Perhaps the city's most venerable hotel, the Monteleone is also the Quarter's largest. Not long after it was built, preservationists put a stop to building on

this scale below Iberville St. Since its inception in 1866, the hotel has lodged literary luminaries including William Faulkner, Truman Capote and Rebecca Wells. Rooms exude an old-world appeal with French toile and chandeliers.

Eating

French Quarter

Café Beignet   CAFE $

(☎504-524-5530; www.cafebeignet.com; 334 Royal St; meals $6-8; ☉7am-10pm) In a shaded patio setting with a view of Royal St, this intimate cafe serves omelets, Belgian waffles, quiche and beignets. There's a low-level war among foodies over who does the better beignet – this place or iconic Café du Monde – with the general consensus being this spot uses less powdered sugar. Also located at **Musical Legends Park** (311 Bourbon St, Musical Legends Park; ☉8am-10pm Sun-Thu, to midnight Fri & Sat).

Café du Monde   CAFE $

(☎800-772-2927; www.cafedumonde.com; 800 Decatur St; beignets $3; ☉24hr) Cafe du Monde is the most popular destination in New Orleans, and unfortunately, it often feels that way. But once you do get seated, the beignets (square, sugar-coated fritters) and chicory café au lait, served here since 1862, are decadent and delicious. Open 24 hours a day, seven days a week – the cafe only closes for Christmas Day.

Croissant D'Or Patisserie   BAKERY $

(☎504-524-4663; www.croissantdornola.com; 617 Ursulines Ave; meals $3-7; ☉6am-3pm Wed-Mon) On the quieter side of the French Quarter, this spotlessly clean pastry shop is where many locals start their day. Bring a paper, order coffee and a croissant – or a tart, quiche or sandwich topped with béchamel sauce – and bliss out. Check out the tiled sign on the threshold that says 'ladies entrance' – a holdover from earlier days.

Coop's Place   CAJUN $$

(☎504-525-9053; www.coopsplace.net; 1109 Decatur St; mains $8-20; ☉11am-3am) Coop's is an authentic Cajun dive but more rocked out. Make no mistake: it's a grotty chaotic place, the servers have attitude and the layout is annoying. But it's worth it for the food: rabbit jambalaya or chicken with shrimp and *tasso* (smoked ham) in a cream sauce – there's no such thing as 'too heavy' here.

★**Bayona**   LOUISIANAN $$$

(☎504-525-4455; www.bayona.com; 430 Dauphine St; mains $28-34; ☉11:30am-1:30pm Wed-Sun, plus 6-9:30pm Mon-Thu, 5:30-10pm Fri & Sat; ☑) Bayona is one of our favorite splurges in the Quarter. It's rich but not overwhelming, classy but unpretentious, innovative without being precocious, and all round just a very fine spot for a meal. The menu changes regularly, but expect fresh fish, fowl and game prepared in a way that comes off as elegant and deeply cozy at the same time.

Mid-City & The Tremé

Parkway Tavern   SANDWICHES $

(☎504-482-3047; www.parkwaypoorboys.com; 538 Hagan Ave; po'boys mains $8-13; ☉11am-10pm Wed-Mon; P) Who makes the best po'boy in New Orleans? Honestly, who can say? But tell a local you think the top sandwich comes from Parkway and you will get, at the least, a nod of respect. The roast beef in particular – a craft some would say is dying among the great po'boy makers – is messy as hell and twice as good.

Willie Mae's Scotch House   SOUTHERN US $

(☎504-822-9503; www.williemaesnola.com; 2401 St Ann St; fried chicken $11; ☉10am-5pm Mon-Sat) Willie Mae's has been dubbed the best fried chicken in the world by the James Beard Foundation, the Food Network and other media, and in this case, the hype isn't far off – this is superlative fried bird. The white beans are also amazing. The drawback is everyone knows about it, so expect long lines, sometimes around the block. There's another location Uptown at 7457 St Charles Ave.

★**Dooky Chase**   CREOLE $$

(☎504-821-0600; www.dookychaserestaurant.com; 2301 Orleans Ave; buffet $20, mains $20-25; ☉11am-3pm Tue-Thu, 11am-3pm & 5-9pm Fri) Ray Charles wrote 'Early in the Morning' about Dooky's; civil rights leaders used it as informal headquarters in the 1960s; and Barack Obama ate here after his inauguration. Leah Chase's labor of love is the backbone of the Tremé, and her buffets are the stuff of legend, a carnival of top-notch gumbo and excellent fried chicken served in a white-linen dining room.

The vegetarian gumbo z'herbes, served on Thursday during Lent, is the great New Orleans dish done green with mustards, beet tops, spinach, kale, collards and Leah knows what else; committed carnivores should give it a try.

Faubourg Marigny & Bywater

★ **Bacchanal** MODERN AMERICAN $

(☑504-948-9111; www.bacchanalwine.com; 600 Poland Ave; mains $8-18, cheese from $6; ⊕11am-11pm Sun-Thu, to midnight Fri & Sat) From the outside, Bacchanal looks like a leaning Bywater shack; inside are racks of wine and stinky but sexy cheese. Musicians play in the garden, while cooks dispense delicious meals on paper plates from the kitchen in the back; on any given day you may try chorizo-stuffed dates or seared diver scallops that will blow your gastronomic mind.

Pizza Delicious ITALIAN $

(☑504-676-8482; www.pizzadelicious.com; 617 Piety St; pizza by slice from $2.25, whole pie from $15; ⊕Tue-Sun 11am-11pm; ☑🖶🕷) 'Pizza D's' pies are thin-crust, New York–style and *good*. The preparation is pretty simple, but the ingredients are fresh as the morning and consistently top-notch. An easy, family-friendly ambience makes for a lovely spot for casual dinner, and it serves some good beer too if you're in the mood.

St Roch Market MARKET $

(☑504-609-3813; www.strochmarket.com; 2381 St Claude Ave; prices vary by vendor; ⊕7am-10pm Sun-Thu, to 11pm Fri & Sat; ☑🖶) 🖉 The St Roch Market was once the seafood and produce market for a working-class neighborhood. But after it was nearly destroyed by Hurricane Katrina, it was renovated into a shiny food court. The airy interior space now hosts 13 restaurants serving food ranging from crepes to burritos to Haitian cuisine.

Prices vary by food vendor but no place in the market charges more than $15 per main.

Joint BARBECUE $

(☑504-949-3232; www.alwayssmokin.com; 701 Mazant St; mains $7.50-18; ⊕11:30am-10pm Mon-Sat) The Joint's smoked meat has the olfactory effect of the Sirens' sweet song, pulling you, the proverbial traveling sailor, off course and into a savory meat-induced blissful death (classical Greek analogies ending *now*). Knock-back some ribs, pulled pork or brisket with some sweet tea in the backyard garden and learn to love life if you haven't already.

★ **Red's Chinese** CHINESE $$

(☑504-304-6030; www.redschinese.com; 3048 St Claude Ave; mains $5-17; ⊕noon-11pm) Red's has upped the Chinese cuisine game in New Orleans in a big way. The chefs aren't afraid to add lashings of Louisiana flavor, yet this isn't what we'd call 'fusion' cuisine. The food is grounded deeply in spicy Sichuan flavours, which pairs well with the occasional flash of cayenne. The General Lee's chicken is stupendously good.

CBD & Warehouse District

Cochon Butcher SANDWICHES $

(☑504-588-7675; www.cochonbutcher.com; 930 Tchoupitoulas St; mains $10-14; ⊕10am-10pm Mon-Thu, to 11pm Fri & Sat, to 4pm Sun) Tucked behind the slightly more formal Cochon, this sandwich and meat shop calls itself a 'swine bar and deli.' We call it one of our favorite sandwich shops in the city, if not the South. From the convivial lunch crowds to the savory sandwiches to the fun-loving cocktails, this welcoming place encapsulates the best of New Orleans.

THE QUALITY OF CREOLE

After the Louisiana purchase in 1803, New Orleans was absorbed into the USA. Unsurprisingly, there was tension between the largely protestant Anglo Americans and Catholic Creole New Orleanians. The latter found the former uncouth and boring; the former considered Louisianans feckless and indolent, proving tired regional clichés stretch back centuries.

New Orleans has a habit of digesting its settlers and turning them into its own, though. Successive waves of immigration into New Orleans added layers to the city's demographic, but the original Creole city teased something quintessentially New Orleanian – ie commitment to fun, food and music – out of each new slice of the population pie.

Take the Italians, who suffused local foodways and musicality with muffuletta sandwiches and crooners like Louis Prima. In a similar vein, the Vietnamese have brought both food and a penchant for festivals; the Vietnamese New Year is now a major celebration point for New Orleanians of all creeds and colors. Creole implies mixture, and mixing is something this town excels at, even if it doesn't always do so easily.

★ Peche Seafood Grill   SEAFOOD $$

(📞504-522-1744; www.pecherestaurant.com; 800 Magazine St; small plates $9-14; mains $14-27; ⏱11am-10pm Sun-Thu, to 11pm Fri & Sat) Coastal seafood dishes are prepared simply here, but unexpected flourishes – whether from salt, spices or magic – sear the deliciousness onto your taste buds. The vibe is convivial, with a happy, stylish crowd sipping and savoring among the exposed-brick walls and wooden beams. A large whole fish, made for sharing, is a signature preparation, but we recommend starting with the smoked tuna dip and the fried bread with sea salt.

★ Restaurant August   CREOLE $$$

(📞504-299-9777; www.restaurantaugust.com; 301 Tchoupitoulas St; lunch $23-42, dinner $37-47, 5-course tasting menu $97, with wine pairings $147; ⏱5-10pm daily, 11am-2pm Fri; 🍽) For a little romance, reserve a table at Restaurant August, an outpost of chef John Besh's restaurant empire. This converted 19th-century tobacco warehouse, with its flickering candles and warm, soft shades, earns a nod for most aristocratic dining room in New Orleans, but somehow manages to be both intimate and lively. Delicious meals take you to another level of gastronomic perception. The signature speckled trout Pontchartrain is layered with lump crabmeat, wild mushrooms and hollandaise.

✖ Garden, Lower Garden & Central City

Surrey's Juice Bar   AMERICAN $

(📞504-524-3828; www.surreysnola.com; 1418 Magazine St; breakfast & lunch $6.50-13; ⏱8am-3pm; 🍽) Surrey's makes a simple bacon-and-egg sandwich taste – and look – like the most delicious breakfast you've ever been served. And you know what? It probably *is* the best. Boudin biscuits; eggs scrambled with salmon; biscuits swimming in salty sausage gravy; and a shrimp, grits and bacon dish that should be illegal. And the juice, as you might guess, is blessedly fresh.

🍺 Drinking & Nightlife

★ Tonique   BAR

(📞504-324-6045; www.bartonique.com; 820 N Rampart St; ⏱noon-2am) Tonique is a bartender's bar. Seriously, on a Sunday night, when the weekend rush is over, we've seen no fewer than three of the city's top bartenders arrive here to unwind. Why? Because this gem mixes some of the best drinks in the city, and it has a spirits menu as long as a Tolstoy novel to draw upon.

★ Twelve Mile Limit   BAR

(📞504-488-8114; www.facebook.com/twelve.mile.limit; 500 S Telemachus St; ⏱5pm-2am Mon-Wed, 11am-2am Thu & Fri, 10am-2am Sat, 10am-midnight Sun) Twelve Mile is simply a great bar. It's staffed by people who have the skill, both behind the bar and in the kitchen, to work in four-star spots, but who chose to set up shop in a neighborhood, for a neighborhood. The mixed drinks are excellent, the match of any mixologist's cocktail in Manhattan, and the vibe is super accepting.

NOLA Brewing   BREWERY

(📞504-301-1117; www.nolabrewing.com; 3001 Tchoupitoulas St; ⏱taproom 11am-11pm, tours 2-3pm Fri, to 4pm Sat & Sun) This cavernous brewery welcomes guests throughout the weekend for a free brewery tour that kicks off with sloshy cups of craft brew and a food truck or two out front. The rest of the week? Stop by the taproom, which has plenty of beers on tap and a roof deck.

Mimi's in the Marigny   BAR

(📞504-872-9868; http://mimismarigny.com; 2601 Royal St; ⏱3pm-close Mon-Fri, 11am-close Sat & Sun) The name of this bar could justifiably change to 'Mimi's *is* the Marigny' – we simply can't imagine the neighborhood without this institution. It's a attractively disheveled place, with comfy furniture, pool tables, an upstairs dance hall decorated like a Creole mansion gone punk, and dim, brown lighting like a fantasy in sepia. The bar closes when the bartenders want it to.

BJ's   BAR

(www.facebook.com/bjs.bywater; 4301 Burgundy) This Bywater dive attracts a neighborhood crowd seeking cheap beers, chilled-out banter and frequent events, from blues rock gigs with Little Freddie King to sci-fi readings by local authors. How great is this place? Robert Plant felt the need to put on an impromptu set here the last time he visited.

☆ Entertainment

★ Tipitina's   LIVE MUSIC

(📞504-895-8477; www.tipitinas.com; 501 Napoleon Ave; cover $5-20) 'Tips,' as locals call it, is one of New Orleans' great musical meccas. The legendary Uptown nightclub, which takes its name from Professor Longhair's 1953 hit single, is the site of some of the city's most memorable shows, particularly when big names such as Dr John come home to roost. Outstanding music from local talent packs 'em in year-round.

Spotted Cat
LIVE MUSIC

(www.spottedcatmusicclub.com; 623 Frenchmen St; ⏲2pm-2am Mon-Fri, noon-2am Sat & Sun) The Cat might just be your smoky dream of a New Orleans jazz club, a thumping sweat-box where drinks are served in plastic cups, impromptu dances break out at the drop of a feathered hat, and the music is always exceptional.

Preservation Hall
JAZZ

(☑504-522-2841; www.preservationhall.com; 726 St Peter St; cover $15 Sun-Thu, $20 Fri & Sat, reserved seats $34-45; ⏲showtimes 8pm, 9pm & 10pm Mon-Wed, 6pm, 8pm, 9pm & 10pm Thu-Sun) Preservation Hall, housed in a former art gallery that dates from 1803, is one of the most storied live-music venues in New Orleans. The resident performers, the Preservation Hall Jazz Band, are ludicrously talented, and regularly tour around the world. 'The Hall' dates from 1961, when Barbara Reid and Grayson 'Ken' Mills formed the Society for the Preservation of New Orleans Jazz.

AllWays Lounge
THEATER

(☑504-218-5778; www.theallwayslounge.net; 2240 St Claude Ave; ⏲6pm-2am Sun-Thu, to 4am Fri & Sat) In a city full of funky music venues, the AllWays stands out as one of the funkiest. On any given night of the week you may see experimental guitar, local theater, thrash-y rock, live comedy or a '60s-inspired shaga-delic dance party. Also the drinks are cheap.

Rock 'N' Bowl
LIVE MUSIC

(☑504-861-1700; www.rockandbowl.com; 3000 S Carrollton Ave; cover $10; ⏲11:30am-midnight Sun-Thu, to 2am Fri & Sat) The Rock 'N' Bowl is a strange combination of bowling alley, deli and huge live-music and dance venue, where patrons get down to New Orleans roots music while trying to avoid that 7-10 split.

🔒 Shopping

Magazine Antique Mall
ANTIQUES

(☑504-896-9994; www.magazineantiquemall.com; 3017 Magazine St; ⏲10:30am-5:30pm, noon-5:30pm Sun) Scary baby dolls. Hats. Chandeliers. Coca-Cola memorabilia. Inside this overstuffed emporium, rummagers are likely to score items of interest in the dozen or so stalls, where independent dealers peddle an intriguing and varied range of antique bric-a-brac.

Maple Street Book Shop
BOOKS

(☑504-866-4916; www.maplestreetbookshop.com; 7523 Maple St; ⏲10am-6pm Mon, Tue, Thu-Sat, noon-6pm Wed, 10am-5pm Sun) This beloved Uptown shop celebrated its 50th anniversary in 2014. Founded by sisters Mary Kellogg and Rhoda Norman, it is one of the most politically progressive, well-stocked bookshops in the city. The store sells new, used and rare books in an invitingly overstuffed setting.

ℹ Information

DANGERS AND ANNOYANCES

New Orleans has a concerning crime rate and one of the highest murder rates in the country. The vast majority of violent crime occurs

---

LGBT NEW ORLEANS

Louisiana is a culturally conservative state, but its largest city bucks that trend. New Orleans has always had a reputation for tolerance and it remains one of the oldest gay-friendly cities in the Western hemisphere, marketing itself as the 'Gay Capital of the South.' Neighborhoods such as the French Quarter and Marigny are major destinations on the LGBT travel circuit.

Check out these websites for information on queer travel in New Orleans:

Gay New Orleans Online (www.neworleansonline.com/neworleans/lgbt) Probably the most comprehensive collection of queer listings online.

Gay New Orleans (www.gayneworleans.com) Full of information.

Gay Cities (http://neworleans.gaycities.com) Listings, user reviews and LGBT-related content.

Ambush Magazine (www.ambushmag.com) Local take on queer news and issues.

Purple Roofs (www.purpleroofs.com/usa/louisiana.html) Reliable gay travel resource.

between parties who already know each other, but tourists are occasionally targeted.

Exercise the same caution you would in any US city. The possibility of getting mugged is something to consider even in areas you'd think are safe (eg the Garden District). Solo pedestrians are targeted more often than people walking in groups, and daytime is a better time to be out on foot than nighttime. Avoid entering secluded areas such as cemeteries alone.

Large crowds typically make the French Quarter a secure around-the-clock realm for the visitor. However, if your hotel or vehicle is on the margins of the Quarter, you might want to take a taxi back at night. The CBD and Warehouse District have plenty of activity during weekdays, but they're relatively deserted at night and on weekends. The B&Bs along Esplanade Ridge are close enough to less safe neighborhoods to call for caution at night. In the Quarter, street hustlers frequently approach tourists - we suggest walking away.

Pedestrians crossing the street do not have the right of way and motorists (unless they are from out of state) will not yield. Whether on foot or in a car, be wary before entering an intersection, as New Orleans drivers are notorious for running yellow and even red lights.

To see where crime is occurring, log on to www.crimemapping.com/map/la/neworleans.

INTERNET ACCESS

Many hotels offer wi-fi and cable internet access. Wi-fi is available in almost every coffee shop in town, and all branches of the New Orleans public library (www.neworleanspubliclibrary.org).

MEDIA

Gambit (www.bestofneworleans.com) Weekly publication that covers arts, culture and music.
The Times-Picayune (www.nola.com) Broadsheet news and arts coverage times a week.
The Advocate (www.theadvocate.com/new_orleans) Broadsheet news and culture writing.
New Orleans Magazine (www.myneworleans.com/new-orleans-magazine) Monthly focus on city society.
The Lens (http://thelensnola.org) Investigative journalism and culture coverage; online only.

TOURIST INFORMATION

Right next to popular Jackson Sq in the heart of the French Quarter, the **New Orleans Welcome Center** (☑ 504-568-5661; www.crt.state.la.us/tourism; 529 St Ann St; ☺ 8:30am-5pm) in the lower Pontalba Building offers maps, listings of upcoming events and a variety of brochures for sights, restaurants and hotels. The helpful staff can help you find accommodations in a pinch, answer questions and offer advice about New Orleans.

Information kiosks scattered through main tourist areas offer most of the same brochures as the Welcome Center, but their staff tend to be less knowledgeable.

Order or download a Louisiana-wide travel guide online from the Louisiana Office of Tourism (www.louisianatravel.com).

In the Tremé, you can pick up a New Orleans map and look at displays about city attractions at the Basin St Visitors Center inside Basin St Station.

Otherwise, **New Orleans Convention & Visitors Bureau** (☑ 504-566-5003; www.neworleanscvb.com; 2020 St Charles Ave; ☺ 8:30am-5pm) has plenty of free maps and helpful information.

❶ Getting There & Away

The majority of travelers to New Orleans will arrive by air, landing in **Louis Armstrong New Orleans International Airport** (MSY; ☑ 504-303-7500; www.flymsy.com; 900 Airline Hwy, Kenner). The airport was originally named for aviator John Moisant and was known as Moisant Stock Yards, hence the IATA code.

Another option is to fly into **Baton Rouge** (BTR; p461), 89 miles north of the city; or **Gulfport-Biloxi** (GPT; ☑ 228-863-5951; www.flygpt.com), Mississippi, 77 miles east. Neither of these options is as convenient as a direct flight to New Orleans, but they may be cheaper during big events such as Mardi Gras or Jazz Fest.

Many travelers drive or bus to New Orleans, which is located at the crossroads of several major highways. Train travel to New Orleans is easy; the city is served by three Amtrak lines.

❶ Getting Around

Streetcar Service on the charming streetcars is limited. One-way fares cost $1.25, and multi-trip passes are available.
Bus Bus services are OK, but try not to time your trip around them. Fares won't run more than $2.
Walk If you're just exploring the French Quarter, your feet will serve fine.
Bicycle Flat New Orleans is easy to cycle – you can cross the entirety of town in 45 minutes.
Car The easiest way to access outer neighborhoods such as Mid-City. Parking is problematic in the French Quarter and CBD.

TO/FROM THE AIRPORT

Louis Armstrong International Airport (MSY) is located 13 miles west of New Orleans. A taxi to the CBD costs $36, or $15 per passenger for three or more passengers. Shuttles to the CBD cost $20/38 per person one way/round-trip. The E2 bus takes you to Carrollton and Tulane Ave in Mid-City for $2.

Amtrak (www.amtrak.com; 1001 Loyola Ave) & Greyhound (www.greyhound.com; 1001 Loyola Ave) are located adjacent to each other downtown. You can walk to the CBD or French Quarter, but don't do so at night, or with heavy luggage. A taxi from here to the French Quarter should cost around $10; further afield you'll be hard-pressed to spend more than $20.

Around New Orleans

Leaving colorful New Orleans behind quickly catapults you into a world of swamps, bayous, antebellum plantation homes, laid-back small communities and miles of bedroom suburbs and strip malls.

Barataria Preserve

★ **Barataria Preserve** PARK
(☑504-689-3690; www.nps.gov/jela/barataria-preserve.htm; 6588 Barataria Blvd, Crown Point; ⏱parking lot for trails 9am-5pm daily; Ⓟ) 🎫**FREE** This section of the Jean Lafitte National Historical Park & Preserve, south of New Orleans near the town of Marrero, provides the easiest access to the dense swamplands that ring New Orleans. The 8 miles of boardwalk trails are a stunning way to tread lightly through the fecund, thriving swamp, home to alligators, nutrias river rats) tree frogs and hundreds of species of birds

Start at the **NPS Visitors Center** (☑504-689-3690; www.nps.gov/jela; Hwy 3134; ⏱9:30am-4:30pm Wed-Sun; 🚻), 1 mile west of Hwy 45 off the Barataria Blvd exit, where you can pick up a map or join a guided wetland walk (10am Wednesday to Sunday) or canoe trip (call for more information). To rent canoes or kayaks for a tour or an independent paddle, go to **Bayou Barn** (☑504-689-2663; www.bayoubarn.com; 7145 Barataria Blvd, Marrero; canoe/kayak hire per person $20/25; ⏱10am-6pm Thu-Sun) about 3 miles from the park entrance.

The North Shore

The north shore of Lake Pontchartrain is a collection of middle-to-upper-class New Orleans bedroom suburbs. Nearby, the bucolic village of Abita Springs was popular in the late 19th century for its curative waters. Today spring water still flows from a fountain in the center of the village, but more importantly for many residents, beer still bubbles from the Abita Brewery, the largest regional beer producer in Louisiana. The

entirety of this region is separated from New Orleans by Lake Pontchartrain, which is spanned by the Lake Pontchartrain Causeway – at almost 24 miles long, the enormous bridge is a sight in and of itself.

River Road

Elaborate plantation homes dot the east and west banks of the Mississippi River between New Orleans and Baton Rouge. First indigo, then cotton and sugarcane, brought great wealth to the plantation owners and many plantations are open to the public. Most tours focus on the lives of the owners, the restored architecture and the ornate gardens of antebellum Louisiana.

◎ Sights

★ **Whitney Plantation** HISTORIC SITE
(☑225-265-3300; www.whitneyplantation.com; 5099 Highway 18, Wallace; adult/student/child under 6yr $22/10/free; ⏱museum 9:30am-4:30pm Wed-Mon) The Whitney is the first plantation in the state to focus on slavery, and in doing so they've flipped the script on plantation tours. Whereas before the story told was that of the 'big house,' here the emphasis is given to the hundreds who died to keep the residents of the big house comfortable. There's a museum on site that you can self tour, but admission to the plantation is by 1½-hour guided tour only.

Laura Plantation HISTORIC SITE
(☑225-265-7690; www.lauraplantation.com; 2247 Hwy 18, Vacherie; adult/child $20/6; ⏱10am-4pm; Ⓟ) This ever-evolving and popular plantation tour teases out the distinctions between Creole, Anglo, free and enslaved African Americans via meticulous research and the written records of the Creole women who ran the place for generations. Laura is also fascinating because it was a *Creole* mansion, founded and maintained by a continental European-descended elite, as opposed to Anglo Americans; the cultural and architectural distinctions between this and other plantations is obvious and striking. Tours are offered in French.

Oak Alley Plantation HISTORIC SITE
(☑225-265-2151; www.oakalleyplantation.com; 3645 Hwy 18, Vacherie; adult/student/child $22/8/5; ⏱9am-5pm Mar-Oct, 9am-4:30pm Mon-Fri, to 5pm Sat & Sun Nov-Feb; Ⓟ) The most impressive aspect of Oak Alley Plantation is its canopy of 28 majestic live oaks lining the

entry to the grandiose Greek Revival–style home. The tour hits a blacksmith shop, a slavery exhibit and several other points of interest.

Baton Rouge

In 1699 French explorers named this area *baton rouge* (red stick) when they came upon a reddened cypress pole that Bayagoulas and Houma Native Americans had staked in the ground to mark the boundaries of their respective hunting territories. From one pole grew a lot of sprawl; Baton Rouge stretches out in an unplanned clutter in many directions. Visitors are mostly drawn to Baton Rouge for Louisiana State University (LSU) and Southern University; the latter is one of the largest historically African American universities in the country.

⊙ Sights & Activities

Louisiana State Capitol   HISTORIC BUILDING
(☑225-342-7317; 900 N 3rd St; ⊙8:30am-4:30pm, observation deck to 4pm) FREE The art-deco skyscraper looming over town was built at the height of the Great Depression to the tune of $5 million, and remains the most visible leftover legacy of populist governor 'Kingfish' Huey Long. The 27th-floor observation deck offers views of the city, and the ornate lobby is decently impressive.

LSU Museum of Art   MUSEUM
(LSUMOA; ☑225-389-7200; www.lsumoa.com; 100 Lafayette St; adult/child $5/free; ⊙10am-5pm Tue-Sat, to 8pm Thu, 1-5pm Sun) The physical space that this museum inhabits – the clean, geometric lines of the Shaw Center – is as impressive as the on-site galleries, which include a permanent collection of over 5000 works and curated galleries exploring regional artistic heritage and contemporary trends.

Old State Capitol   HISTORIC BUILDING
(☑225-342-0500; www.louisianaoldstatecapitol.org; 100 North Blvd; ⊙10am-4pm Tue-Fri, 9am-3pm Sat) FREE The Gothic Revival, pink fairytale castle is...well, it's a pink castle. Which should tell you something about how eccentric the government of its resident state can be. Today the structure houses exhibits about the political history of Louisiana.

Rural Life Museum   MUSEUM
(☑225-765-2437; www.lsu.edu/rurallife; 4560 Essen Lane; adult/child $10/8; ⊙8am-5pm; P⛲) This outdoor museum promises a trip into the architecture, occupations and folkways of rural Louisiana. Numerous rough-hewn buildings are scattered over the bucolic campus, and exhibits are refreshingly honest and informative, lacking any rose-colored romanticization of the hard country legacy that built Louisiana.

🛏 Sleeping & Eating

Stockade Bed & Breakfast   B&B $$
(☑225-769-7358; www.thestockade.com; 8860 Highland Rd; r $150-160, ste $215; P🐾) This inviting B&B has five spacious, comfortable and elegant rooms just 3.5 miles southeast of LSU and within earshot of several standout neighborhood restaurants. Book ahead on weekends, especially during football season.

★**Dang's Vietnamese Restaurant**   VIETNAMESE $
(☑225-275-2390; 12385 Florida Blvd; mains $8-13; ⊙9am-9pm; P⛲) Everything at this Vietnamese institution is great, but have a slurp of the pho and you may whisper a prayer to the kitchen gods for favoring you with a broth so flavorful. Honestly, you can't go wrong ordering off the big menu – from crispy duck to bright, beautiful curries, it's all wonderful.

Louisiana Lagniappe   CAJUN $$$
(☑225-767-9991; www.louisianalagniapperestaurant.com; 9900 Perkins Rd; mains $21-36; ⊙5:30-9pm Mon-Thu, 5-10pm Fri & Sat; P) If you need a night out in Baton Rouge, and it requires the presence of delicious local cuisine, we'll direct you to Louisiana Lagniappe (lah-nyap). The second word means 'a little extra' in Louisiana French, and it's a misnomer, as you get a *lot* here: fish topped with crabmeat, rib-eye steaks and shrimp and sausage pasta.

☆ Entertainment

Varsity Theatre   LIVE MUSIC
(☑225-383-7018; www.varsitytheatre.com; 3353 Highland Rd) Located at the gates of LSU, this is one of Baton Rouge's better live music options. When they're not hosting the headliners, the Theatre shows major sporting events.

❶ Information

Visitors Center (☑225-383-1825; www.visitbatonrouge.com; 359 3rd St; ⊙8am-5pm) The downtown city visitors center has maps, brochures of local attractions and festival schedules.

Capital Park (☑225-219-1200; www.louisiana travel.com; 702 River Rd N; ⊙8am-4:30pm) Near the Baton Rouge visitors center, this is the extensive official gateway to Louisiana tourism.

① Getting There & Around

Baton Rouge lies 80 miles west of New Orleans on I-10. **Baton Rouge Metropolitan Airport** (BTR; ☑225-355-0333; www.flybtr.com; 9430 Jackie Cochran Dr), 7 miles north of downtown

Baton Rouge off I-110, is about 1½ hour's drive north from New Orleans, making it a viable airport of entry if you're renting a car. The airport connects with major hubs like Houston, Dallas, Charlotte and Atlanta.

Greyhound (☑225-383-3811; www.grey-hound.com; 1253 Florida Blvd) has regular buses to New Orleans, Lafayette and Atlanta.

Capitol Area Transit System (www.brcats.com) operates buses around town. Tickets cost $1.75.

FROM THE MEKONG TO THE MISSISSIPPI

Following the Vietnam War, thousands of South Vietnamese fled to the USA, settling in Southern California, Boston, the Washington, DC area and New Orleans. If the last choice seems odd, remember that many of these refugees were Catholic and the New Orleans Catholic community – one of the largest in the country – was helping to direct refugee resettlement. In addition, the subtropical climate, rice fields and flat wetlands must have been geographically reassuring. For a Southeast Asian immigrant far from home, the Mississippi delta may have borne at least a superficial resemblance to the Mekong delta.

Most Vietnamese in Louisiana settled in New Orleans' newer suburbs: New Orleans East, Versailles, Algiers and Gretna (some also moved to rural parishes in south Louisiana). Their work ethic was legendary; their presence revitalized many formerly crumbling neighborhoods; and their story is as American Dream–like as a bald eagle hatching from apple pie. The first generation of Vietnamese worked in laundromats, nail shops, restaurants and shrimp boats; the second became doctors, lawyers and engineers. Following Hurricane Katrina, the New Orleans Vietnamese community gained the reputation as being the first back in the city, quickly rebuilding their homes and businesses.

To see where New Orleans Vietnamese work and play, you need to drive a little way out of the city proper. In New Orleans East, the **Mary Queen of Vietnam Church** (☑504-254-5660; www.arch-no.org; 5069 Willowbrook Dr; ℗) is a focal point for the Catholic Vietnamese community; further south, the **Chua Bo De Temple** (☑504-733-6634; Hwy 996; ⊙services 7:30pm Sat & 11am Sun), about 25 minutes outside the city near English Turn golf course, is a major center for Buddhists. The latter is a typically Vietnamese Buddhist structure, filled with Chinese-style bodhisattvas (Buddhist saints), photos and offerings to dead ancestors, and lots of red and gold in the color scheme. You don't have to call ahead before visiting, but it may be polite to do so.

Perhaps the most pleasant way to experience local Vietnamese culture is by eating its delicious food. Most spots are in Gretna. **Tan Dinh** (☑504-361-8008; 1705 Lafayette St, Gretna; mains $8-18; ⊙9:30am-9pm Mon, Wed-Fri, 9am-9pm Sat, to 8pm Sun, closed Tue; ℗☑) is one of the best restaurants in greater New Orleans – the garlic-butter chicken wings could be served in heaven's pub, and the Korean short ribs are mouth-watering. It's also a contender for high-quality pho. **Dong Phuong Oriental Bakery** (☑504-254-0296; www.dpbanhmi.com; 14207 Chef Menteur Hwy, New Orleans East; bakery items $1.50-6, mains $7-13; ⊙bakery 8am-5pm Mon, Wed-Sun, restaurant Mon, Wed-Sun 9am-4pm, closed Tue; ℗☑⊕) has best *bánh mì* (Vietnamese sandwiches of sliced pork, cucumber, cilantro and other lovelies, locally called a 'Vietnamese po'boy') around and some very fine durian cake.

Try not to miss the local markets either; the **Hong Kong Food Market** (☑504-394-7075; 925 Behrman Hwy; ⊙7:30am-9pm) is a an international grocery store that serves the immigrant (and immigrant descended) communities of the New Orleans West Bank. The closest you'll come to witnessing Saigon on a Saturday morning (lots of local Vietnamese, being southern refugees, still call it 'Saigon') is the **Vietnamese Farmers Market** (14401 Alcee Fortier Blvd; ⊙6am-9am Sat), also known as the 'squat market' thanks to the women in *non la* (conical straw hats) squatting over their fresh, wonderful-smelling produce. The market has shrunk over the years, so it's not quite the scene it was in years past, but the women are still out there selling their wares.

St Francisville

Lush St Francisville is the quintessential Southern artsy small town, a blend of historical homes, bohemian shops and outdoor activities courtesy of the nearby Tunica Hills (you read that right – hills in Louisiana). During the antebellum decade this was home to plantation millionaires, and much of the architecture these aristocrats built is still intact, forming a historic core that has magnetized tourists for over a century.

⊙ Sights & Activities

Myrtles Plantation   HISTORIC BUILDING
(☑225-635-6277; www.myrtlesplantation.com; 7747 US Hwy 61 N; tours adult/child $15/12, night tours $15; ⊙9am-5pm, tours 6pm, 7pm & 8pm Fri & Sat; P) Owners and docents alike perpetuate the idea that Myrtles is one of the most haunted houses in America. And hey, this place is certifiably creepy. Tours do not seem to be quite as architecturally and historically informative as other plantation tours in the region, but they do paint a vivid picture of life during the plantation era. Mystery tours (Friday and Saturday evenings) are geared toward ghost stories, while daytime tours focus on details about the house and its furnishings.

**Oakley Plantation &
Audubon State Historic Site**   HISTORIC SITE
(☑225-635-3739; www.audubonstatehistoricsite. wordpress.com; 11788 Hwy 965; adult/student/senior $8/4/6; ⊙9am-5pm Wed-Sun; P) ⊘ Outside of St Francisville, Oakley Plantation & Audubon State Historic Site is where John James Audubon spent his tenure, arriving in 1821 to tutor the owner's daughter. Though his assignment lasted only four months (and his room was pretty spartan), he and his assistant finished 32 paintings of birds found in the plantation's surrounding forest. The small West Indies–influenced house (1806) includes several original Audubon prints.

Mary Ann Brown Preserve   NATURE RESERVE
(☑225-338-1040; www.nature.org; 13515 Hwy 965; ⊙sunrise-sunset; P) ⊘ FREE Operated by the Nature Conservancy, the 110-acre Mary Ann Brown Preserve takes in some of the beech woodlands, dark wetlands and low, clay-soil hill country of the Tunica uplands. A 2-mile series of trails and boardwalks crosses the woods – the same trees that John James Audubon tramped around when he began work on *Birds of America*.

🛏 Sleeping & Eating

Shadetree Inn   B&B $$
(☑225-635-6116; www.shadetreeinn.com; cnr Royal & Ferdinand Sts; r from $145; P🖘) Sidled up against the historic district and a bird sanctuary, this super-cozy B&B has a gorgeous flower-strewn, hammock-hung courtyard and spacious but rustic upscale rooms. A deluxe continental breakfast can be served in your room and is included along with a bottle of wine or champagne. Rates plunge if you cut out breakfast and stay midweek.

3-V Tourist Court   INN $$
(☑225-721-7003; www.themagnoliacafe.net/magnolia3vtouristcourts.html; 5687 Commerce St; 1-/2-bed cabin $75/125; P🖘) One of the oldest motor inns in the USA (started in the 1930s and now on the National Register of Historic Places), the five units here take you back to simpler times. Rooms have period decorations and fixtures, though a recent renovation upgraded the beds, hardwood floors and flat-screen TVs into trendy territory.

Birdman Coffee & Books   CAFE $
(☑225-635-3665; 5695 Commerce St; mains $5-8; ⊙7am-5pm Tue-Fri, 8am-2pm Sat, 8am-noon Sun; 🖘) Birdman is *the* spot for strong coffee, acoustic live music, a delicious local breakfast (old-fashioned yellow grits, sweet-potato pancakes, salty bacon) and local art.

Magnolia Café   CAFE $
(☑225-635-6528; www.themagnoliacafe.net; 5687 Commerce St; mains $8-16; ⊙10am-4pm Mon-Thu, to 10pm Thu, Fri & Sat; P) The Magnolia Café was once a health-food store and VW bus repair shop. Today it's the nucleus of what's happening in St Francisville – it's where people go to eat, socialize and, on Friday night, dance to live music.

ℹ Getting There & Away

St Francisville lies about 35 miles north of Baton Rouge on Hwy 61, which winds right through town.

Cajun Country

When people think of Louisiana, this – and New Orleans – is the image that comes to mind: miles of bayou, sawdust-strewn shacks, a unique take on French and lots of good food. Welcome to Cajun Country, also called Acadiana for the French settlers exiled from L'Acadie (now Nova Scotia, Canada) by the British in 1755. Cajuns are the largest French-speaking minority in the USA, and while you may not hear French spoken at the grocery store, it is still present in radio shows, church services and the sing-song lilt of local English accents.

It is largely a socially conservative region, but the Cajuns also have a well-deserved reputation for hedonism. It's hard to find a bad meal here; jambalaya (a rice-based dish with tomatoes, sausage and shrimp) and crawfish étouffée are prepared slowly with pride, and if folks aren't fishing, they are probably dancing. Don't expect to sit on the sidelines...*allons danson* (let's dance).

LAFAYETTE

The term 'undiscovered gem' gets thrown around too much in travel writing, but Lafayette really fits the bill. On Sunday this town is quiet, but for the rest of the week there's an entirely fantastic amount of good eating to be done and lots of music venues.

◉ Sights

Vermilionville　　　MUSEUM
(☎ 337-233-4077; www.bayouvermiliondistrict.org/vermilionville; 300 Fisher Rd; adult/student $10/6, boat tour $12/8; ◷10am-4pm Tue-Sun; P⊞) This tranquil, re-created 19th-century Cajun village wends along the bayou near the airport. Friendly, enthusiastic costumed docents explain Cajun, Creole and Native American history, and local bands perform on Sunday (1pm to 3pm). Guided boat tours of Bayou Vermilion are also offered at 10:30am Tuesday to Saturday in spring and fall.

Acadian Village　　　MUSEUM
(☎ 337-981-2364; www.acadianvillage.org; 200 Greenleaf Dr; adult/student $8/6; ◷10am-4pm Mon-Sat; P⊞) At the understated, educational Acadian Village, you follow a brick path around a rippling bayou to restored houses, craftsman barns and a church. Old-timers sometimes still hang out here, regaling visitors with Cajun songs and stories from days gone by.

Acadian Cultural Center　　　MUSEUM
(☎ 337-232-0789; www.nps.gov/jela; 501 Fisher Rd; ◷9am-4:30pm Tue-Fri, 8:30am-noon Sat; P⊞) 🖉 This National Parks Service museum has extensive exhibits on Cajun culture and is a good entry point for those looking to peer deeper into Acadian folkways.

✰✰ Festivals & Events

★ Festival International de Louisiane　　　MUSIC
(www.festivalinternational.org; ◷Apr) FREE At the fabulous Festival International de Louisiane, hundreds of local and international artists rock out for five days over the last weekend in April in the largest free music festival of its caliber in the USA. Although 'Festival' avowedly celebrates Francophone music and culture, the event's remit has grown to accommodate world music in all its iterations and languages.

🛏 Sleeping & Eating

★ Blue Moon Guest House　　　GUESTHOUSE $
(☎ 337-234-2422; www.bluemoonpresents.com; 215 E Convent St; dm $18, r $70-90; P⊞@🛜) This tidy home is one of Louisiana's travel gems: an upscale hostel-like hangout just walking distance from downtown. Snag a bed and you're on the guest list for Lafayette's most popular down-home music venue, located in the backyard. The friendly owners, full kitchen and camaraderie among guests create a unique music-meets-migration environment catering to backpackers, flashpackers and those in transition (flashbackpackers?).

Buchanan Lofts　　　APARTMENT $$
(☎ 337-534-4922; www.buchananlofts.com; 403 S Buchanan; r per night/week from $180/1000; P⊞@🛜) These uber-hip lofts could be in New York City if they weren't so big. Doused in contemporary-cool art and design – all fruits of the friendly owner's globetrotting – the extra spacious units come with kitchenettes and are awash with exposed brick and hardwoods.

★ French Press　　　BREAKFAST $
(☎ 337-233-9449; www.thefrenchpresslafayette.com; 214 E Vermillion; mains $9-15; ◷7am-2pm Mon-Fri, 9am-2pm Sat & Sun; 🛜) This French-Cajun hybrid is one of the best culinary things going in Lafayette. Breakfast is mind-blowing, with a sinful Cajun Benedict (boudin instead of ham), cheddar grits (that will kill you dead) and organic granola (to offset the grits). Lunch ain't half bad either; the fried shrimp melt, doused in Sriracha mayo, is gorgeously decadent.

Johnson's Boucanière　　　CAJUN $
(☎ 337-269-8878; www.johnsonsboucaniere.com; 1111 St John St; mains $4.25-8; ◷7am-3pm Tue-Fri, to 5:30pm Sat) This resurrected, 70-year-old family prairie smoker business turns out detour-worthy boudin (Cajun-style pork and rice sausage) and an unstoppable smoked pork-brisket sandwich topped with smoked sausage.

Dwyer's   DINER $

(☑337-235-9364; 323 Jefferson St; mains $6-14; ⊙6am-2pm; ⏲) This family-owned joint serves Cajun diner fare, finally bringing gumbo for lunch and pancakes for breakfast into one glorious culinary marriage. It's especially fun on Wednesday mornings when a French-speaking table is set up and local Cajuns shoot the breeze in their old-school dialect. Rotating lunch mains include smothered pork chops, fried chicken and shrimp stew.

☆ Entertainment

Blue Moon Saloon   LIVE MUSIC

(☑337-234-2422; www.bluemoonpresents.com; 215 E Convent St; cover $5-8; ⊙5pm-2am Tue-Sun) This intimate venue on the back porch of the accompanying guesthouse is what Louisiana is all about: good music, good people and good beer. What's not to love? Music tends to go off Wednesday to Saturday.

Artmosphere   LIVE MUSIC

(☑337-233-3331; www.artmosphere.vpweb.com; 902 Johnston St; ⊙4pm-2am Mon-Thu, 11am-2am Fri & Sat, 11am-midnight Sun) Graffiti, hookahs, hipsters and an edgy line-up of acts – it's more CBGBs then Cajun dance hall, but it's a lot of fun, and there's good Mexican food.

ℹ Information

The **Visitors Center** (☑337-232-3737; www.lafayettetravel.com; 1400 NW Evangeline Thruway; ⊙8:30am-5pm Mon-Fri, 9am-5pm Sat & Sun) has information on travel, lodging and events in Lafayette and greater Acadiana (Cajun Country). French-speaking staff on hand.

ℹ Getting There & Away

From I-10, exit 103A, the Evangeline Thruway (Hwy 167) goes to the center of town. **Greyhound** (☑337-235-1541; www.greyhound.com; 100 Lee Ave) operates from a hub beside the central commercial district, making several runs daily to New Orleans (3½ hours) and Baton Rouge (one hour). **Amtrak's** (www.amtrak.com; 100 Lee Ave) *Sunset Limited*, which runs between New Orleans and Los Angeles, stops in Lafayette.

CAJUN WETLANDS

In 1755, the Grand Dérangement, the British expulsion of rural French settlers from Acadiana (now Nova Scotia, Canada), created a homeless population of Acadians who searched for decades for a place to settle. Some went to other British colonies, where the Catholic exiles were often rejected on religious grounds. Some returned to France, where they were denied the rights to land ownership and autonomy they had obtained in the New World.

In 1785 seven boatloads of Acadian exiles arrived in New Orleans, seeking a better life in a corner of the Western Hemisphere that was still culturally, if not politically, French (at the time Louisiana was ruled by the Spanish). By the early 19th century, 3000 to 4000 Acadians occupied the swamplands southwest of New Orleans. Native American tribes such as the Attakapas helped them learn to eke out a living based on fishing and trapping, and those practices are still near and dear to the hearts of many of the descendants of the Acadians, now known as the Cajuns.

For decades this was one of the poorest parts of Louisiana, an area where French language education was repressed and infrastructure was dire. This situation largely changed thanks to an increase in Cajun political influence within Louisiana state government in the 1970s, and the presence of the oil and gas industry. While canal and pipeline dredging has been deemed a culprit in the continuing saga of Louisiana land loss, the jobs and economic revitalization that came with oil industry jobs is undeniable. This goes some way toward explaining the popularity of the oil and gas sectors in the state, culminating in events like Morgan City's annual Shrimp & Petroleum Festival.

◉ Sights

Lake Martin   BIRD SANCTUARY

(Lake Martin Rd) FREE This lake – a mossy green dollop surrounded by thin trees and cypress trunks – serves as a wonderful, easily accessible introduction to bayou landscapes. A few walking paths, as well as a boardwalk, take visitors over the mirror-reflection sheen of the swamp, while overhead thousands of great and cattle egrets and blue herons perch in haughty indifference.

**Louisiana Universities
Marine Consortium**   MUSEUM

(LUMCON; ☑985-851-2800; www.lumcon.edu; 8124 Hwy 56, Chauvin; ⊙8am-4pm; ⏲) ✐ FREE LUMCON? Sounds like something out of a science fiction novel, right? Well, there is science here, but it's all fact, and still fascinating. LUMCON is one of the premier research facilities dedicated to the Gulf of Mexico. There are nature trails running

WORTH A TRIP

THE TAO OF FRED'S

Deep in the heart of Cajun Country, Mamou is a typical South Louisiana small town six days of the week, worth a peek and a short stop before rolling on to Eunice. But on Saturday morning, Mamou's hometown hangout, little **Fred's Lounge** (420 6th St, Mamou; ⊙8:30am-2pm) becomes the apotheosis of a Cajun dance hall.

OK, to be fair, Fred's is more of a dance shack than hall. Whatever it is, this small bar gets more than a little crowded from 8:30am to 2pm-ish, when the staff host a Francophone-friendly music morning, with bands, beer and dancing.

through hairy tufts of grassy marsh, nine small aquariums and an observation tower that gives visitors an unbeatable view of the great swaths of flat, fuzzy wetlands that makes up the south Louisiana coast.

Cypremont Point State Park   STATE PARK
(⊉888-867-4510, 337-867-4510; 306 Beach Lane, Cypremort Point; adult/senior & child under 3yr $3/free; ⊙7am-9pm, to 10pm Fri & Sat; ℗🚹🚼) You can't get more end of the road than Cypremont Point, a lonely, windswept promontory of land buffeted by wind, seagull calls and foam spray off the Gulf of Mexico.

ⓘ Getting There & Away

Greyhound buses stop in Lafayette. Otherwise, the region is easily accessed via I-10, which cuts across Louisiana like a belt.

CAJUN PRAIRIE

Dancing cowboys? Works for us. Cajun and African American settlers in the higher, drier terrain north of Lafayette developed a culture based around animal husbandry and farming, and the 10-gallon hat still rules. In many ways, this region is a blend of both South Louisiana and East Texas.

Physically this truly is prairie: wide expanses of green flatlands, broken up by rice and crawfish ponds. This is the heartland of zydeco music; come evening, keep your ears peeled for the accordion, fiddle and distinctive 'zzzzzzzzip' sound of the *frottoir*, a corrugated metal vest that is played as its own percussion instrument.

⊙ Sights

Chicot State Park   STATE PARK
(⊉337-363-2403, 888-677-2442; www.crt.louisiana.gov/louisiana-state-parks/parks/chicot-state-park; 3469 Chicot Park Rd, Ville Platte; $3; ⊙6am-9pm Sun-Thu, to 10pm Fri & Sat; ℗🚹🚼) 🐾 A wonderful place to access the natural beauty of Cajun Country. The excellent interpretive center is fun for kids and informative for adults, and deserves enormous accolades for its open, airy design.

Prairie Acadian Cultural Center   MUSEUM
(⊉337-457-8499; www.nps.gov/jela; 250 West Park Ave, Eunice; ⊙9:30am-4:30pm Wed-Fri, to 6pm Sat) 🐾 **FREE** This NPS-run museum has exhibits on rural life and Cajun culture and shows a variety of documentaries explaining the history of the area. It's the perfect place to begin your exploration of the Cajun Prairie. Music and food demonstrations start at 2:45pm on Saturday.

Cajun Music Hall of Fame & Museum   MUSEUM
(⊉337-457-6534; www.cajunfrenchmusic.org; 230 S CC Duson Dr, Eunice; ⊙9am-5pm) **FREE** This small collection of instruments and cultural ephemera caters to the die-hard music buff. Try to engage whoever is working in some tales of Cajun living and music.

🛏 Sleeping & Eating

★ Le Village   B&B $$
(⊉337-457-3573; www.levillagehouse.com; 121 Seale Lane, Eunice; r $125-185; ℗🐕) This cute spot is a typically pretty rural B&B, but where many places opt for wedding cake frilly decor, Le Village is stocked with a tasteful collection of rustic, often Cajun-derived folk art.

Billy & Ray's Boudin   CAJUN $
(⊉337-942-9150; 904 Short Vine St, Opelousas; boudin per lb $4.80; ⊙9am-6pm Mon-Fri) Folks will literally drive for hours, sometimes crossing state lines, to grab some of Billy and Ray's goods, and to be clear, these are two distinct sausages: Billy's is for spice heads, while Ray's is milder. Most folks treat this as a take-out counter, but there's a seating area and some coolers..

ⓘ Getting There & Away

Lafayette makes a good base for exploring the Cajun Prairie. There's a **Greyhound station** (⊉337-942-2702; www.greyhound.com; 1312 Creswell Lane) in Opelousas that has buses to

Lafayette ($9, twice daily), Baton Rouge ($9, twice daily) and New Orleans ($27, three daily). The heart of the Cajun Prairie can best be accessed via I-49 or LA-13.

Northern Louisiana

Make no mistake, the rural, oil-industry towns along the Baptist Bible Belt make Northern Louisiana as far removed from New Orleans as Paris, Texas, is from Paris, France. There's a lot of optimistic tourism development happening out this way, but at the end of the day, most folks come here from states like Texas and Arkansas to gamble. The landscape here is pretty reminiscent of East Texas – rolling green countryside and pine woods as far as the eye can see. The culture isn't too far off from Texas either – the TV show *Duck Dynasty*, which has a firm finger on the pulse of red state America, was filmed out here. There's a high value placed on the church and firearms, more or less in that order.

Shreveport

Captain Henry Shreve cleared a 165-mile logjam on the Red River and founded the river-port town of Shreveport – now the third-largest city in the state – in 1839. The city boomed with oil discoveries in the early 1900s, but declined after WWII. Some revitalization came in the form of huge Vegas-sized casinos and a riverfront entertainment complex. Today the casinos still form the main tourism draw in Shreveport, which has an odd identity – it's a large city in one of the most socially conservative parts of the country that attracts visitors looking to engage in a little sin (ie gambling).

◎ Sights

★ **RW Norton Art Gallery**   MUSEUM
(☑318-865-4201; www.rwnaf.org; 4747 Creswell Ave; ⊗museum 10am-5pm Tue-Fri, 1-5pm Sat & Sun, gardens 7am-7pm; ℗) FREE Set amid 40 acres of lovingly manicured gardens, the Norton is a wonderful museum, especially for a mid-sized city like Shreveport. It's

airy, spacious and full of fascinating works spanning some four millennia of history, including an impressive collection of work by American painters Frederic Remington and Charles M Russell, who famously captured life in the frontier West. It's also home to 15,000 rare books.

**Gardens of the American
Rose Center**   GARDENS
(☑318-938-5402; www.rose.org; 8877 Jefferson Paige Rd; adult/child $5/2, tours $10; ⊗9am-5pm Mon-Sat, 1-5pm Sun; ℗) If you're a rose-lover, it would be a shame to miss these gardens, which contain more than 65 individual areas designed to show how roses can be grown in a home garden. Stroll the gorgeous grounds for the fecund, sweet smell alone.

🛏 Sleeping & Eating

2439 Fairfield Bed & Breakfast   B&B $$
(☑318-424-2424; www.bedandbreakfastshreve port.com; 2439 Fairfield Ave; r $145-225; ℗🛜) This warm, old-school B&B may be heavy on the lace and chintz, but they're also generous with the Southern hospitality and the breakfasts are delicious.

Strawn's Eat Shop   DINER $
(☑318-868-0634; www.strawnseatshop.com; 125 E Kings Hwy; mains $10; ⊗6am-8pm; 🚌) This basic diner serves good, hearty Americana fare with a lot of Southern charm but it's most notable for its ice box pies.

❶ Information

The **Visitors Center** (☑318-222-9391; www. shreveport-bossier.org/about-us/visi tor-centers; 629 Spring St; ⊗8am-5pm Mon-Fri) provides local information.

❶ Getting There & Away

Shreveport is located at the intersection of I-49 and I-20; it is far closer to Dallas (190 miles) than New Orleans (330 miles). The city is served by a **regional airport** (☑318-673-5370; www. flyshreveport.com; 5103 Hollywood Ave), which is located about 7 miles southwest of downtown, and a **Greyhound station** (☑318-221-4200; www.greyhound.com; 408 Fannin St).

Florida

Includes ➜

Miami	469
Fort Lauderdale	487
The Everglades	493
Florida Keys	498
Atlantic Coast	503
Space Coast	504
Daytona Beach	505
Tampa	511
Orlando	518
Florida Panhandle	524
Tallahassee	524
Pensacola	525

Best Places to Eat

➜ Ulele (p513)

➜ Rok:Brgr (p489)

➜ Kyu (p484)

➜ Cress (p525)

➜ Table 26 Degrees (p492)

Best Places to Sleep

➜ 1 Hotel (p481)

➜ Hotel Palms (p509)

➜ Biltmore Hotel (p483)

➜ W Fort Lauderdale (p488)

➜ Everglades International Hostel (p495)

Why Go?

For countless visitors Florida is a place of promises: of eternal youth, sun, relaxation, clear skies, space, success, escape, prosperity and, for the kids, a chance to meet much-loved Disney characters in person.

No other state in America is as built on tourism, and tourism here comes in a thousand facets: cartoon mice, *MiamiVice*, country fried oysters, Spanish villas, gators kicking footballs, gators prowling golf courses, and of course, the beach. So. Much. Beach.

Don't think Florida is all marketing, though. This is one of the most genuinely fascinating states in the country. It's as if someone shook the nation and tipped it over, filling this sun-bleached peninsula with immigrants, country boys, Jews, Cubans, military bases, shopping malls and a subtropical wilderness laced with crystal ponds and sugary sand.

When to Go
Miami

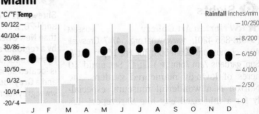

Feb–Apr Winter ends and high season begins, coinciding with spring break.

Jun–Aug The hot, humid wet months are peak season for northern Florida beaches and theme parks.

Sep–Oct The ideal shoulder season with fewer crowds, cooler temperatures and warm waters.

SOUTH FLORIDA

Once you head far enough south in Florida, you're no longer in 'the South' as a regional entity – you've slipped those bonds into South Florida, which is truly a hybrid of the USA, the Caribbean and Latin America. Miami is the area's beating urban heart and one of the few truly international cities in the country. Wealthy oceanfront communities stretch from the Palm Beaches to Fort Lauderdale, while inland, the dreamscape of the Everglades, the state's unique, dynamic wilderness, await. And when the state's peninsula ends, it doesn't truly end, but rather stretches into the Overseas Hwy which leads across hundreds of mangrove islands to colorful Key West.

Miami

Even if there was no beach, Miami would still have undeniable allure. The gorgeous 1930s hotels lining Ocean Dr are part of the world's greatest collection of art-deco buildings. Tropical motifs, whimsical nautical elements and those iconic pastel shades create a cinematic backdrop for exploring the streets of Miami Beach. Of course, you don't have to see these architectural beauties at arm's length. Lavishly restored, Miami's art-deco and mid-century modern hotels are also the playground for locals and out-of-towners alike, with sunny poolside terraces, artfully designed dining rooms and plush nightclubs.

Chalk it up to Miami's diverse population, or perhaps its love of always being on the cutting-edge. Whatever the reason, creativity is one of the great hallmarks of this city. From art and design to global cuisine, Miami remains ever on the search for bold new ideas, which manifest themselves in surprising ways. You'll find brilliantly inventive chefs blending Eastern and Western cooking styles, sustainably designed buildings inspired by South Florida ecosystems and open-air galleries where museum-quality artwork covers once derelict warehouses. The one constant in Miami is its uncanny ability to astonish.

History

It's always been the weather that's attracted Miami's two most prominent species: developers and tourists. But it wasn't the sun per se that got people moving here – it was an ice storm. The great Florida freeze of 1895 wiped out the state's citrus industry; at the same time, widowed Julia Tuttle bought out parcels of land that would become modern Miami, and Henry Flagler was building his Florida East Coast Railroad. Tuttle offered to split her land with Flagler if he extended the railway to Miami, but the train man didn't pay her any heed until north Florida froze over and Tuttle sent him an 'I told you so' message: an orange blossom clipped from her Miami garden.

The rest is a history of boom, bust, dreamers and opportunists. Generally, Miami has grown in leaps and bounds following major world events and natural disasters. Hurricanes (particularly the deadly Great Miami Hurricane of 1926) have wiped away the town, but it just keeps bouncing and building back better than before. In the late 19th and early 20th centuries, Miami earned a reputation for attracting design and city-planning mavericks such as George Merrick, who fashioned the artful Mediterranean village of Coral Gables, and James Deering, designer of the fairy-tale Vizcaya mansion.

◉ Sights

Miami's major sights aren't concentrated in one neighborhood. The most frequently visited area is South Beach, home to hot nightlife, beautiful beaches and art-deco hotels, but you'll find historic sites and museums in the Downtown area, art galleries in Wynwood and the Design District, old-fashioned

BEST FLORIDA BEACHES

Florida's best beach? Why not ask us to choose a favorite child? It's impossible! Each beach has its own personality, its own wondrous qualities. Here are a few of our favorites:

Siesta Key (p515)

South Beach (p472)

Bahia Honda (p501)

Captiva Beach (p516)

St George Island (☑850-927-2111; www.floridastateparks.org/stgeorgeisland; 1900 E Gulf Beach Drive; vehicle $6; ☺8am-dusk; P🚻) 🏖

For a list based on 'science,' consult Dr Beach (www.drbeach.org).

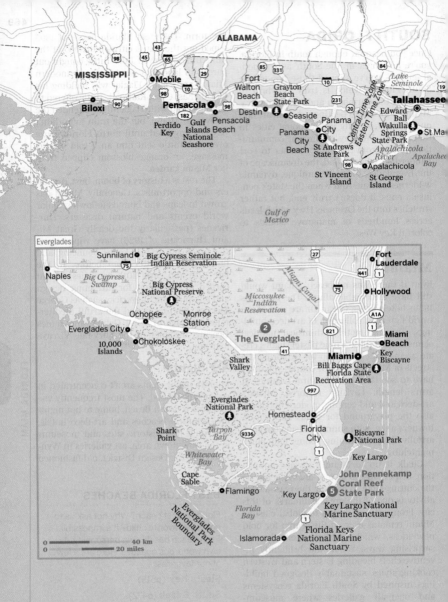

Florida Highlights

1 Mallory Square (p501)
Joining the sunset bacchanal in Key West.

2 Everglades National Park (p493) Paddling among alligators in The Everglades.

3 Walt Disney World® Resort (p521) Being swept up in nostalgia and thrill rides, in Orlando.

4 Wynwood Walls (p477)
Marvelling at mural after mural, in Miami.

5 John Pennekamp Coral Reef State Park (p498)

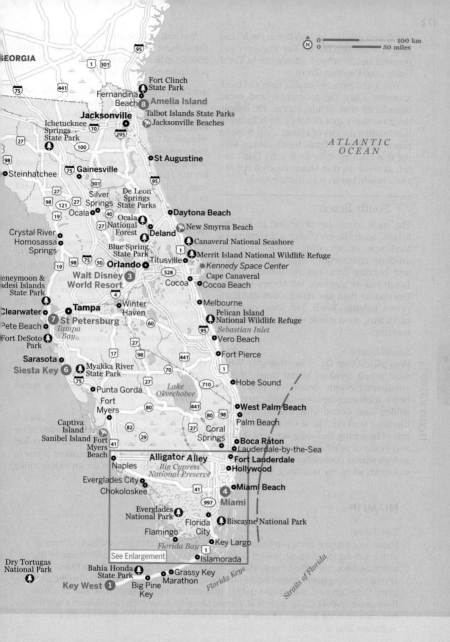

GEORGIA

Fort Clinch
State Park
Fernandina
Beach   **Amelia Island**
             Talbot Islands State Parks
Jacksonville   Jacksonville Beaches

ATLANTIC
OCEAN

Ichetucknee
Springs
State Park
Gainesville

●St Augustine

Steinhatchee

Silver   De Leon
Springs   Springs
          State Parks
Ocala
Ocala   ●Daytona Beach
National   ●New Smyrna Beach
Forest   Canaveral National Seashore
Crystal River   Deland
Homosassa   Blue Spring   Merrit Island National Wildlife Refuge
Springs   State Park
                 Titusville   ● Kennedy Space Center
             Orlando   Cape Canaveral
                          Cocoa ●Cocoa Beach
        Walt Disney
        World Resort
eneymoon &   ● Melbourne
desi Islands   Winter
State Park   **Tampa** Haven   Pelican Island
                                  National Wildlife Refuge
Clearwater   Sebastian Inlet
            St Petersburg   ●Vero Beach
Pete Beach ●   Tampa
Fort DeSoto   Bay   ●Fort Pierce
Park

Sarasota
Siesta Key   Myakka River
                  State Park
                                   ●Hobe Sound
              Punta Gorda   Lake
              Fort   Okeechobee
              Myers   **West Palm Beach**
              Captiva   Palm Beach
              Island   Coral
Sanibel Island Fort   Springs
              Myers   ●Boca Raton
              Beach   ●Lauderdale-by-the-Sea
                        Alligator Alley **●Fort Lauderdale**
              Naples   Big Cypress   ●**Hollywood**
                        National Preserve
        Everglades City   ●**Miami Beach**
        Chokoloskee   **Miami**
                     Everglades
                     National Park   Biscayne National Park
                     Florida
              Flamingo City
                    Florida Bay   ●Key Largo
                   See Enlargement   ●Islamorada
Dry Tortugas
National Park   Bahia Honda
                State Park   ●Grassy Key
            Key West   Marathon   Florida Keys
                        Big Pine
                        Key   Straits of Florida

Snorkelling continental USA's
most extensive coral reef.

6 Siesta Key (p515)
Relaxing on these sugar sand
beaches, in Sarasota.

**7 Salvador Dalí
Museum** (p514) Pondering
the symbolism of the
Hallucinogenic Toreador, in
St Petersburg.

8 Amelia Island (p510)
Taking a breather among the
greenery of this historic island
near the Georgia border.

hotels and eateries in Mid-Beach (in Miami Beach), more beaches on Key Biscayne, and peaceful neighborhood attractions in Coral Gables and Coconut Grove.

Water and income – canals, bays and bank accounts – are the geographic and social boundaries that divide Miami. Of course, the great water that divides here is Biscayne Bay, holding the city of Miami apart from its preening sibling Miami Beach (along with the fine feathers of South Beach). Don't forget, as many do, that Miami Beach is not Miami's beach, but its own distinct town.

South Beach

The most iconic neighborhood in Greater Miami, South Beach (SoBe) is a vertiginous landscape of sparkling beach, beautiful art-deco architecture, high-end boutiques and buzzing bars and restaurants. South Beach has its glamour, but there's more to this district than just velvet ropes and high-priced lodging. You'll find some down-to-earth bars, good ethnic eating and excellent museums.

South Beach   BEACH
(Map p476; Ocean Dr; ⊙5am-midnight) When most people think of Miami Beach, they're envisioning South Beach, or 'SoBe.' The beach itself encompasses a lovely stretch of golden sand, dotted with colorful deco-style lifeguard stations. The shore gathers a wide mix of humanity, including suntanned locals and plenty of pale tourists, and gets crowded in high season (December to March) and on weekends when the weather is warm.

You can escape the masses by avoiding the densest parts of the beach (5th to 15th Sts). Keep in mind that there's no alcohol (or pets) allowed on the beach.

Art Deco Historic District   AREA
(Map p476; Ocean Dr) The world-famous art-deco district of Miami Beach is pure exuberance: an architecture of bold lines, whimsical tropical motifs and a color palette that evokes all the beauty of the Miami landscape. Among the 800 deco buildings listed on the National Register of Historic Buildings, each design is different, and it's hard not to be captivated when strolling among these restored beauties from a bygone era.

★ Wolfsonian-FIU   MUSEUM
(Map p476; ☎305-531-1001; www.wolfsonian.org; 1001 Washington Ave; adult/child $10/5, 6-9pm Fri free; ⊙10am-6pm Mon, Tue, Thu & Sat, to 9pm Fri, noon-6pm Sun, closed Wed) Visit this excellent design museum early in your stay to put the aesthetics of Miami Beach into context. It's one thing to see how wealth, leisure and the pursuit of beauty manifest in Miami Beach, but it's another to understand the roots and shadings of local artistic movements. By chronicling the interior evolution of everyday life, the Wolfsonian reveals how these trends manifested architecturally in SoBe's exterior deco.

Art Deco Museum   MUSEUM
(Map p476; www.mdpl.org/welcome-center/art-deco-museum; 1001 Ocean Dr; $5; ⊙10am-5pm Tue-Sun, to 7pm Thu) This small museum is one of the best places in town for an enlightening

---

MIAMI IN ...

Two Days

Focus your first day on South Beach. Bookend an afternoon of sunning and swimming with a walking tour through the Art Deco Historic District and a visit to Wolfsonian-FIU, which explains it all. When the sun fades, head to Yardbird (p483) where southern comfort cooking gets a Miami foodie makeover. Next morning, shop for Cuban music along Calle Ocho in Little Havana (p477), followed by classic Cuban cuisine at Exquisito Restaurant (p484). Go for a stroll at Vizcaya Museum & Gardens (p479), then enjoy the tropical ambience and exceptional food at 27 Restaurant (p483) before sipping cocktails at Broken Shaker (p484).

Four Days

Follow the two-day itinerary, then head to the Everglades (p493) on day three and jump in a kayak. For your last day, immerse yourself in art and design in Wynwood and the Design District (p477), followed by a visit to the Pérez Art Museum Miami (p475) or Museum of Contemporary Art (p479). World-class cocktails adn upscale comfort food wrap up the adventure at Sweet Liberty (p485), a top local hangout.

HURRICANE IRMA

On September 10, 2017, one of the largest hurricanes ever recorded barrelled over the state of Florida, leaving flooding and destruction in its wake. Hurricane Irma made landfall in the Florida Keys as a category 4 storm the width of Texas, with wind speeds in excess of 130mph. Nearly seven million people across the state evacuated, there were widespread power outages and storm surges were seen as far north as Jacksonville. But the Florida Keys and the Everglades bore the brunt of the storm. Homes and business-es in the tiny town of Everglades City were left battered and mud-soaked after an 8ft storm surge receded. Meanwhile, in the Keys, a FEMA (Federal Emergency Management Agency) survey reported that 25% of buildings had been destroyed, with another 65% damaged.

In a state so heavily reliant on tourism, most cities were already announcing inten-tions to be ready for visitors soon. Still, those planning travel to Florida, especially the Florida Keys (www.fla-keys.com) or the Everglades region (www.nps.gov/ever), should check official websites for the latest information.

overview of the art-deco district. Through videos, photography, models and other dis-plays, you'll learn about the pioneering work of Barbara Capitman, who helped save these buildings from certain destruction back in the 1970s, and her collaboration with Leon-ard Horowitz, the talented artist who de-signed the pastel color palette that become an integral part of the design visible today.

New World Center   NOTABLE BUILDING
(Map p476; ☑ 305-673-3330, tours 305-673-3331; www.newworldcenter.com; 500 17th St; tours $5; ☺ tours 4pm Tue & Thu, 1pm Fri & Sat) Designed by Frank Gehry, this performance hall rises ma-jestically out of a manicured lawn just above Lincoln Rd. Not unlike the ethereal power of the music within, the glass-and-steel fa-cade encases characteristically Gehry-esque sail-like shapes within that help shape the magnificent acoustics and add to the futur-istic quality of the concert hall. The grounds form a 2.5-acre public park aptly known as **SoundScape Park** (www.nws.edu).

◉ North Beach

The long strip of beach and condo-studded landscape of North Beach offers a slightly different version of Miami Beach decadence. Instead of art deco, you'll find the so-called MiMo (Miami Modernist) style, of grand buildings constructed in the post-WWII boom days. Although it has a lower population den-sity (and fewer restaurants, bars and shops), there's plenty of allure to North Beach – chief is the beautiful shoreline, which the lo-cals say is covered in whiter sands.

Boardwalk   BEACH
(Map p474; www.miamibeachboardwalk.com; 21st St-46th St) What's trendy in beachwear this season? Seventeenth-century Polish gabar-dine coats, apparently. There are plenty of skimpily dressed hotties on the Mid-Beach boardwalk, but there are also Orthodox Jews going about their business in the midst of joggers, strolling tourists and sunbathers. Nearby are numerous condo buildings oc-cupied by middle-class Latinos and Jews, who walk their dogs and play with their kids here, giving the entire place a laid-back, real-world vibe that contrasts with the non-stop glamour of South Beach.

Eden Roc Renaissance   HISTORIC BUILDING
(Map p474; www.nobuedenroc.com; 4525 Collins Ave) The Eden Roc was the second ground-breaking resort from Morris Lapidus, and it's a fine example of the architecture known as MiMo (Miami Modern). It was the hangout for the 1960s Rat Pack – Sam-my Davis Jr, Dean Martin, Frank Sinatra and crew. Extensive renovation has eclipsed some of Lapidus' style, but with that said, the building is still an iconic piece of Miami Beach architecture, and an exemplar of the brash beauty of Millionaire's Row.

Fontainebleau   HISTORIC BUILDING
(Map p474; www.fontainebleau.com; 4441 Collins Ave) As you proceed north on Collins, the condos and apartment buildings grow in grandeur and embellishment until you enter an area nicknamed Millionaire's Row. The most fantastic jewel in this glittering crown is the **Fontainebleau hotel** (☑ 305-535-3283; r from $360; P ❋ ☏ ☒ ☺). The hotel – mainly

Greater Miami

N
0 ——————— 5 km
0 ——————— 2.5 miles

Palmetto Expwy

CAROL CITY 826

Fort Lauderdale (9mi)

North Miami Greyhound Terminal

NORTH MIAMI

Southern Memorial Park

Oleta River State Park

13

Collins Ave

9

909

Oleta River State Recreation Area

Bal Harbour

OPA-LOCKA

924

W 4th Ave

16

NW 119th St

Little River Canal

Griffing Blvd

N Miami Ave

NE 6th Ave

Biscayne Blvd

Bay Harbor Islands

Indian Creek

Collins Ave

HIALEAH

953

Amtrak

95

934

Pelican Harbor Park

Normandy Dr

A1A

E 4th Ave

NW 79th St

9

15

1

LIBERTY CITY

25

27

NW 54th St

LITTLE HAITI

23

112

NW 36th St

DESIGN DISTRICT

10

Julia Tuttle Cswy

20

12

Miami International Airport

NW 27th Ave

Margulies Collection at the Warehouse

Wynwood Walls

11

22

Sheridan Ave

17

NW 20th St

5 9

Megabus

Main Miami Greyhound Station

Pérez Art Museum Miami

7

Venetian Way

14

MIAMI BEACH

Dolphin Expwy

NW 7th St

Flagler St

MIAMI

21

History Miami

19

4

18

MacArthur Cswy

SW 8th St (Calle Ocho)

90

SW 22nd St (Miracle Mile)

6

Máximo Gómez Park

8

Hobie Island

Virginia Key

Fisher Island

FLORIDA MIAMI

972 Coral Way

LITTLE HAVANA

913

Northwest Point

Biltmore Hotel

2

826

959

Douglas Road

Coconut Grove

Dinner Key Marina

Vizcaya Museum & Gardens

Key Biscayne

Crandon Blvd

Biltmore Golf Course

874

University

Crandon Park Beach

SW 72nd St (Sunset Dr)

South Miami

KENDALL

878

3

Fairchild Tropical Garden

5

SW 112th St (Killlian Dr)

PINECREST

Biscayne Bay

Bill Baggs Cape Florida State Park

1

Cape Florida

Dixie Hwy

5

SW 152nd St

ATLANTIC OCEAN

See Miami Beach Map (p476)

A B C D

Greater Miami

◎ **Top Sights**
1 Bill Baggs Cape Florida State Park....... D5
2 Biltmore Hotel.. B4
3 Fairchild Tropical Garden..................... B5
4 HistoryMiami.. C4
5 Margulies Collection at the
      Warehouse.. C3
6 Máximo Gómez Park.............................. C4
7 Pérez Art Museum Miami..................... C3
8 Vizcaya Museum & Gardens................. C4
9 Wynwood Walls...................................... C3

◎ **Sights**
10 Bakehouse Art Complex........................ C3
11 Boardwalk.. D3
   Eden Roc Renaissance................. (see 12)
12 Fontainebleau.. D3
13 Haulover Beach Park............................. D1
14 Jungle Island.. C3
   Little Havana Art District..............(see 6)
   Miami Children's Museum........... (see 14)
15 Museum of Contemporary Art
   North Miami.. C2
   Patricia & Phillip Frost
   Museum of Science.....................(see 7)

◎ **Activities, Courses & Tours**
16 Miami Watersports Complex............... B2

◎ **Sleeping**
17 1 Hotel.. D3

   Biltmore Hotel............................... (see 2)
   Fontainebleau................................(see 12)
   Freehand Miami............................ (see 11)
18 Langford Hotel..C4

◎ **Eating**
   27 Restaurant............................... (see 11)
   All Day .... (see 7)
   Alter .... (see 9)
19 Casablanca...C4
   Chef Allen's Farm-to-Table
   Dinner.. (see 7)
   Della Test Kitchen .... (see 9)
   Exquisito Restaurant .... (see 6)
   Kyu .... (see 9)
20 Roasters 'n Toasters..............................D3
21 Versailles...B4

◎ **Drinking & Nightlife**
   Ball & Chain.................................... (see 6)
   Bardot ....(see 10)
   Broken Shaker............................... (see 11)
22 Sweet Liberty...D3
23 Vagabond Pool Bar C2

◎ **Entertainment**
   Adrienne Arsht Center for the
   Performing Arts............................. (see 7)
   Cubaocho .... (see 6)

FLORIDA MIAMI

the pool, which has since been renovated – features in Brian de Palma's classic *Scarface*.

◎ Downtown Miami

Most of the sights in Downtown are on the north side of the river. While you can walk between a few highlights, it's handy to use Metromover, the free trolley, or a Citi Bike when you really need to cover some ground.

★**HistoryMiami**   MUSEUM
(Map p474; ☎305-375-1492; www.historymiami. org; 101 W Flagler St; adult/child $10/5; ☺10am-5pm Mon-Sat, from noon Sun; ⊞) South Florida – a land of escaped slaves, guerilla Native Americans, land grabbers, pirates, tourists, drug dealers and alligators – has a special history, and it takes a special kind of museum to capture that narrative. This highly recommended place, located in the Miami-Dade Cultural Center, does just that, weaving together the stories of the region's successive waves of population, from Native Americans to Nicaraguans.

★**Pérez Art Museum Miami**   MUSEUM
(PAMM; Map p474; ☎305-375-3000; www.pamm. org; 1103 Biscayne Blvd; adult/seniors & students $16/12, 1st Thu & 2nd Sat of month free; ☺10am-6pm Fri-Tue, to 9pm Thu, closed Wed; P) The Pérez can claim fine rotating exhibits that concentrate on post-WWII international art, but just as impressive are its location and exterior. This art institution inaugurated Museum Park, a patch of land that oversees the broad blue swath of Biscayne Bay. Swiss architects Herzog & de Meuron designed the structure, which integrates tropical foliage, glass and metal – a melding of tropical vitality and fresh modernism that is a nice architectural analogy for Miami itself.

**Patricia & Phillip Frost
Museum of Science**   MUSEUM
(Map p474; ☎305-434-9600; www.frostscience. org; 1101 Biscayne Blvd; adult/child $28/20; ☺9am-6pm; P⊞) This sprawling new Downtown museum spreads across 250,000 sq ft that includes a three-level aquarium,

Miami Beach

N 0 ———————— 500 m
0 ———————— 0.25 miles

Bass Museum
of Art (0.2mi)

Collins Canal Dade Blvd

Venetian Way

Belle
Isle

Biscayne
Bay

Flamingo Way

Lincoln Rd Mall

Lincoln Rd

Española Way

LGBT Visitor Center

Wolfsonian-FIU

MIAMI
BEACH

Downtown Miami
(2.2mi); Miami
International
(8mi)

Miami Beach Dr (5th St) 41

Causeway
Island

Terminal
Island

Miami
Beach
Marina

Commerce St

South Pointe Dr

Harley
St

Boardwalk Pier

Lummus
Island

Fisher
Island

Government Cut

Biscayne Bay

ATLANTIC
OCEAN

FLORIDA MIAMI

Venetian Way
20th St
19th St
18th St
17th St
West Ave
Bay Rd
Purdy Ave
Alton Rd
Jefferson Ave
Lincoln Rd
Lincoln La N
Lenox Ave
Alton Ct
Bay Rd
16th St
Lincoln La S
15th Tce
15th St
14th Tce
14th St
13th Tce
13th St
12th St
11th St
10th St
9th St
8th St
Alton Ct
Michigan Ave
Meridian Ave
Alton Ct
West Ave
Lenox Ave
Jefferson Ave
Michigan Ave
Euclid Ave
Lenox Ave
Meridian Ave
Washington Ave
Collins Ct
Ocean Ct
Ocean Dr
Pennsylvania Ave
Drexel Ave
Euclid Ave
Drexel Ave
James Ave
Collins Ave
Alton Rd
Pier M
7th St
6th St
5th St
4th St
3rd St
2nd St
1st St

Miami Beach

◎ **Top Sights**
1 Wolfsonian-FIU C4

◎ **Sights**
2 Art Deco Historic District D3
3 Art Deco Museum D4
4 Cardozo Hotel D3
5 Carlyle D3
6 New World Center C1
7 Post Office C3
8 SoundScape Park C1
9 South Beach D3

◎ **Activities, Courses & Tours**
10 Bike & Roll D4
11 Fritz's Skate, Bike & Surf C2
   Miami Design Preservation
      League .... (see 3)
12 Miami Food Tours B5

◎ **Sleeping**
13 Bed & Drinks D1
14 Catalina Hotel D1
15 Hotel Astor C4
16 Surfcomber D1
17 The Hotel of South Beach D4
18 Winter Haven Hotel D3

◎ **Eating**
19 11th St Diner C3
20 Joe's Stone Crab Restaurant C6
21 Pubbelly A1
22 Yardbird B2

◎ **Entertainment**
23 Colony Theater B2
24 New World Symphony C1

a 250-seat, state-of-the-art planetarium and two distinct wings that delve into the wonders of science and nature. Exhibitions range from weather phenomena to creepy crawlies, feathered dinosaurs and vital-microbe displays, while Florida's fascinating Everglades and biologically rich coral reefs play starring roles.

The new facility, which cost a staggering $305 million to complete, was built with sustainability in mind. It opened in 2017.

◎ Little Havana

Little Havana's main thoroughfare, Calle Ocho (SW 8th St), doesn't just cut through the heart of the neighborhood, it *is* the heart of the neighborhood. In a lot of ways, this is every immigrant enclave in the USA – full of restaurants, mom-and-pop convenience shops and phonecard kiosks. Admittedly the Cubaness of Little Havana is slightly exaggerated for visitors, though it's still an atmospheric place to explore, with the crack of dominoes, the scent of wafting cigars, and Latin jazz spilling out of colorful storefronts.

★ **Máximo Gómez Park** PARK
(Map p474; cnr SW 8th St & SW 15th Ave; ◷ 9am-6pm) Little Havana's most evocative remind-er of Old Cuba is Máximo Gómez Park, or 'Domino Park,' where the sound of elderly men trash-talking over games of chess is harmonized with the quick clack-clack of slap-ping dominoes. The jarring backtrack, plus the heavy smell of cigars and a sunrise-bright mural of the 1994 Summit of the Americas,

combine to make Máximo Gómez one of the most sensory sites in Miami (although it is admittedly one of the most tourist-heavy ones as well).

Little Havana Art District AREA
(Map p474; Calle Ocho, btwn SW 15th & 17th Aves) OK, it's not Wynwood. In fact, it's more 'Art Block' than district, with only a few galleries and studios still in business. Regardless, it's still worth a browse. This particular stretch of Little Havana is also the epicenter of the **Viernes Culturales** (Cultural Fridays; www.viernesculturales.org; ◷ 7-11pm last Fri of month) celebration.

◎ Wynwood & the Design District

Wynwood and the Design District are two of Miami's most creative neighborhoods, and are justly famed for a burgeoning arts scene. Wynwood is packed with galleries, as well as large-format street art covering once industrial spaces. It's also the place for great nightlife, and an emerging restaurant scene. The smaller Design District also has galler-ies and a mixed bag of bars and eateries.

★ **Wynwood Walls** PUBLIC ART
(Map p474; www.thewynwoodwalls.com; NW 2nd Ave, btwn 25th & 26th Sts) **FREE** In the midst of rusted warehouses and concrete blah, there's a pastel-and-graffiti explosion of ur-ban art. Wynwood Walls is a collection of murals and paintings laid out over an open courtyard that invariably bowls people over

FLORIDA MIAMI

with its sheer color profile and unexpected location. What's on offer tends to change with the coming and going of major arts events such as Art Basel (p481), but it's always interesting stuff.

★ **Margulies Collection at the Warehouse** GALLERY
(Map p474; ☑305-576-1051; www.margulies warehouse.com; 591 NW 27th St; adult/student $10/5; ☺11am-4pm Tue-Sat mid-Oct–Apr) Encompassing 45,000 sq ft, this vast not-for-profit exhibition space houses one of the best collections in Wynwood. Thought-provoking, large-format installations are the focus at the Warehouse, and you'll see works by some leading 21st-century artists here.

Bakehouse Art Complex GALLERY
(BAC; Map p474; ☑305-576-2828; www.bacfl.org; 561 NW 32nd St; ☺noon-5pm; P) FREE One of the pivotal art destinations in Wynwood, the Bakehouse has been an arts incubator since well before the creation of the Wynwood Walls. Today this former bakery houses galleries and some 60 studios, and the range of works you can find here is quite impressive.

◉ **Coral Gables**

The lovely city of Coral Gables, filled with Mediterranean-style buildings, feels like a world removed from other parts of Miami. Here you'll find pretty banyan-lined streets, and a walkable village-like center, dotted with shops, cafes and restaurants. The big draws are the striking Biltmore Hotel, a lush

tropical garden and one of America's loveliest swimming pools.

★ **Fairchild Tropical Garden** GARDENS
(Map p474; ☑305-667-1651; www.fairchildgarden. org; 10901 Old Cutler Rd; adult/child/senior $25/12/18; ☺9:30am-4:30pm; P) If you need to escape Miami's madness, consider a green day in the country's largest tropical botanical garden. A butterfly grove, tropical plant conservatory and gentle vistas of marsh and keys habitats, plus frequent art installations from artists like Roy Lichtenstein, are all stunning. A free 45-minute tram tours the entire park on the hour from 10am to 3pm (till 4pm weekends).

★ **Biltmore Hotel** HISTORIC BUILDING
(Map p474; ☑855-311-6903; www.biltmorehotel.com; 1200 Anastasia Ave; ☺tours 1:30pm & 2:30pm Sun; P) In the most opulent neighborhood of one of the showiest cities in the world, the Biltmore peers down its nose and says, 'hrmph.' It's one of the greatest of the grand hotels of the American Jazz Age, and if this joint were a fictional character from a novel, it'd be, without question, Jay Gatsby. Al Capone had a speakeasy on-site, and the Capone Suite is said to be haunted by the spirit of Fats Walsh, who was murdered here.

◉ **Coconut Grove**

Coconut Grove was once a hippie colony, but these days its demographic is middle-class, mall-going Miamians and college students.

GUIDE TO MIAMI BEACHES

The beaches around Miami are some of the best in the country. The water is clear and warm and the imported white sand is relatively white. They're also informally zoned by tacit understanding into areas with their own unique crowds so that everyone can enjoy at their own speed.

Scantily clad beaches In South Beach between 5th St and 21st St; modesty is in short supply.

Family-fun beaches North of 21st St is where you'll find the more family-friendly beaches, and the beach at 53rd St has a playground and public toilets.

Nude beaches Nude bathing is legal at **Haulover Beach Park** (Map p474; ☑305-947-3525; www.miamidade.gov/parks/haulover.asp; 10800 Collins Ave; per car Mon-Fri $5, Sat-Sun $7; ☺sunrise-sunset; P) in Sunny Isles. North of the lifeguard tower is predominantly gay; south is straight.

Gay beaches All of South Beach is gay-friendly, but a special concentration seems to hover around 12th St.

Windsurfing beaches Hobie Beach, along the Rickenbacker Causeway on the way to Key Biscayne, is actually known as 'Windsurfing Beach.'

MIAMI FOR CHILDREN

The best beaches for kids are in Miami Beach north of 21st St, especially at 53rd St, which has a playground and public toilets, and the dune-packed beach around 73rd St. Also head south to Matheson Hammock Park, which has calm artificial lagoons.

Miami Children's Museum (Map p474; ☑305-373-5437; www.miamichildrensmuseum.org; 980 MacArthur Causeway; $20; ☺10am-6pm; 🚸) On Watson Island, between Downtown Miami and Miami Beach, this hands-on museum has fun music and art studios, as well as some branded 'work' experiences that make it feel a tad corporate.

Jungle Island (Map p474; ☑305-400-7000; www.jungleisland.com; 1111 Parrot Jungle Trail, off MacArthur Causeway; adult/child/senior $40/33/38; ☺10am-5pm; 🅿🚸) Jungle Island is packed with tropical birds, alligators, orangutans, chimps and (to the delight of Napoleon Dynamite fans) a liger – a cross between a lion and a tiger.

Zoo Miami (Metrozoo; ☑305-251-0400; www.zoomiami.org; 12400 SW 152nd St; adult/child $22/18; ☺10am-5pm) Miami's tropical weather makes strolling around Zoo Miami almost feel like a day in the wild. For a quick overview (and because the zoo is so big and the sun is broiling), hop on the Safari Monorail; it departs every 20 minutes.

Monkey Jungle (☑305-235-1611; www.monkeyjungle.com; 14805 SW 216th St; adult/child/senior $30/24/28; ☺9:30am-5pm, last entry 4pm; 🅿🚸) The tagline, 'Where humans are caged and monkeys run free,' tells you all you need to know – except for the fact that it's in far south Miami.

It's a pleasant place to explore with intriguing shops and cafes, and a walkable village-like vibe. It's particularly appealing in the evenings, when residents fill the outdoor tables of its bars and restaurants. Coconut Grove backs onto the waterfront, with a pretty marina and pleasant green spaces.

★**Vizcaya Museum & Gardens**   HISTORIC BUILDING
(Map p474; ☑305-250-9133; www.vizcayamuseum.org; 3251 S Miami Ave; adult/6-12yr/student & senior $18/6/12; ☺9:30am-4:30pm Wed-Mon; 🅿) They call Miami the Magic City, and if it is, this Italian villa, the housing equivalent of a Fabergé egg, is its most fairy-tale residence. In 1916 industrialist James Deering started a Miami tradition by making a ton of money and building ridiculously grandiose digs. He employed 1000 people (then 10% of the local population) and stuffed his home with 15th- to 19th-century furniture, tapestries, paintings and decorative arts.

◎ Key Biscayne

Key Biscayne and neighboring Virginia Key are a quick and easy getaway from Downtown Miami. But once you've passed across those scenic causeways, you'll feel like you've been transported to a far-off tropical realm, with magnificent beaches, lush nature trails in state parks, and aquatic adventures aplenty. The stunning skyline views of Miami alone are worth the trip out.

★**Bill Baggs Cape Florida State Park**   STATE PARK
(Map p474; ☑305-361-5811; www.floridastateparks.org/capeflorida; 1200 S Crandon Blvd; per car/person $8/2; ☺8am-sunset, lighthouse 9am-5pm; 🅿🚸🐾) 🌿 If you don't make it to the Florida Keys, come to this park for a taste of their unique island ecosystems. The 494-acre space is a tangled clot of tropical fauna and dark mangroves – look for the 'snorkel' roots that provide air for half-submerged mangrove trees – all interconnected by sandy trails and wooden boardwalks, and surrounded by miles of pale ocean.

◎ Greater Miami

Museum of Contemporary Art North Miami   MUSEUM
(MoCA; Map p474; ☑305-893-6211; www.mocanomi.org; 770 NE 125th St; adult/student/child $5/3/free; ☺11am-5pm Tue-Fri & Sun, 1-9pm Sat; 🅿) The Museum of Contemporary Art has long been a reason to hike up to the far reaches of North Miami. Its galleries feature excellent rotating exhibitions of contemporary art by local, national and international artists.

FLORIDA MIAMI

Gold Coast Railroad Museum   MUSEUM

(☑ 305-253-0063; www.gcrm.org; 12450 SW 152nd
St; adult/child 3-11yr $8/6; ◷ 10am-4pm Mon-Fri,
from 11am Sat & Sun; P) Primarily of interest
to train buffs, this museum displays more
than 30 antique railway cars, including
the Ferdinand Magellan presidential car,
where President Harry Truman famously
brandished a newspaper with the erroneous
headline 'Dewey Defeats Truman.'

🏃 Activities

Miami doesn't lack for ways to keep yourself
busy. From sailing the teal waters to hiking
through tropical undergrowth, yoga in the
parks and (why not?) trapeze artistry above
the city's head, the Magic City rewards those
who want an active holiday.

Citi Bike   CYCLING

(☑ 305-532-9494;   www.citibikemiami.com;
30min/1hr/2hr/4hr/1-day   rental $4.50/6.50/
10/18/24) This bike-sharing program, modeled after similar initiatives in New York,
London and Paris, makes getting on a bike
a relative breeze. Just rock up to a solar-
powered Citi Bike station (a handy map can
be found on the website), insert a credit card
and ride away. You can return your bike at
any Citi Bike location.

Bike & Roll   CYCLING

(Map p476; ☑ 305-604-0001; www.bikemiami.com;
210 10th St; hire per 2hr/4hr/day from $10/18/24,
tours $40; ◷ 9am-7pm) This well-run outfit
offers a good selection of bikes, including
single-speed cruisers, geared hybrids and
speedy road bikes. Staff move things along
quickly, so you won't have to waste time
waiting to get out and riding. Bike tours are
also available (daily at 10am).

Fritz's Skate, Bike & Surf   SKATING

(Map   p476;   ☑ 305-532-1954;   www.fritzsmiami
beach.com; 1620 Washington Ave; bike & skate rental per hour/day/5 days $10/24/69; ◷ 10am-9pm
Mon-Sat, to 8pm Sun) Rent your wheels from
Fritz's, which offers skateboards, longboards,
in-line skates, roller skates, scooters and bicycles (cruisers, mountain bikes, kids bikes).

SoBe Surf   SURFING

(☑ 786-216-7703; www.sobesurf.com; group/pri-
vate lessons from $70/120) Offers surf lessons
both in Miami Beach and in Cocoa Beach,
where there tends to be better waves. Instruction on Miami Beach usually happens
around South Point. All bookings are done
by phone or email.

Miami
Watersports Complex   WATER SPORTS

(MWCC; Map p474; ☑ 305-476-9253; www.ak-
tionparks.com; Amelia Earhart Park, 401 E 65th St,
Hialeah; ◷ 11am-6pm Mar-Oct, to dusk Nov-Feb)
Offers lessons in cableboarding, where the
rider is pulled along by an overhead cable
system. That means no boat, less pollution
and less noise. A 20-minute-/one-hour lesson costs $25/90, or opt for a $59 package
that includes a beginner lesson, rental gear
and four-hour cable pass. Call ahead to reserve a spot.

👉 Tours

History Miami Tours   TOURS

(www.historymiami.org/city-tour;   tours $30-60)
Historian extraordinaire Dr Paul George
leads fascinating walking tours, including
culturally rich strolls through Little Haiti,
Little Havana, Downtown and Coral Gables
at twilight, plus the occasional boat trip to
Stiltsville and Key Biscayne.

Miami Food Tours   FOOD & DRINK

(Map p476; ☑ 786-361-0991; www.miamifoodtours.
com; 429 Lenox Ave; adult/child South Beach tour
$58/35, Wynwood tour $75/55; ◷ tours South
Beach 11am & 4:30pm daily, Wynwood 10:30am
Mon-Sat) This highly rated tour explores various facets of the city – culture, history, art
and of course cuisine – while making stops
at restaurants and cafes along the way. It's a
walking tour, though distances aren't great,
and happens in South Beach and Wynwood.

Miami Design
Preservation League   WALKING

(MDPL; Map p476; ☑ 305-672-2014; www.mdpl.
org; 1001 Ocean Dr; guided tours adult/student
$25/20; ◷ 10:30am daily & 6:30pm Thu) Tells
the stories and history behind the art-
deco buildings in South Beach, with a lively
guide from the Miami Design Preservation
League. Tours last 90 minutes. Also offers
tours of Jewish Miami Beach, Gay & Lesbian
Miami Beach and a once-monthly tour (first
Saturday at 9:30am) of the MiMo district in
the North Beach area.

🎉 Festivals & Events

Winter Music Conference   MUSIC

(www.wintermusicconference.com; ◷ Mar) Party
promoters, DJs, producers and revelers
come from around the globe to hear new
electronic-music artists, catch up on technology and party the nights away.

Miami Spice

Restaurant Month   FOOD & DRINK
(www.facebook.com/ilovemiamispice; ⊘ Aug-Sep)
Top restaurants around Miami offer three-course lunches and dinners to try to lure folks out during the heat wave. Prices hover around $25 for lunch and $40 for dinner. Reservations essential.

White Party   MUSIC
(www.whiteparty.org; ⊘ Nov) If you're gay and not here, there's a problem. This weeklong extravaganza draws more than 15,000 gay men and women for nonstop partying at clubs and venues all over town.

Art Basel Miami Beach   ART
(www.artbasel.com/miami-beach; ⊘ early Dec) One of the most important international art shows in the world, with works from more than 250 galleries and a slew of trendy parties. Even if you're not a billionaire collector, there's much to enjoy at this four-day fest, with open-air art installations around town, special exhibitions at many Miami galleries and outdoor film screenings.

🛏 Sleeping

Miami has some alluring lodging options – and for some travelers, it's a big draw to the city. South Beach has all the name recognition with boutique hotels set in art-deco buildings, but there are plenty of other options in Miami – from Downtown high-rises with sweeping views and endless amenities to historic charmers in Coral Gables, Coconut Grove and other less touristy neighborhoods.

🛏 South Beach

Bed & Drinks   HOSTEL $
(Map p476; ☐ 786-230-1234; www//bedsndrinks. com; 1676 James Ave; dm/d from $29/154) This hostel pretty shamelessly plays to the sex-appeal-seeking crowd – check the name – but hey, it's a few blocks from the beach, so the placement works. The rooms range from average to slightly below average, but the young party-minded crowd (mostly) doesn't mind. Friendly staff, a lively on-site bar and nightlife outings to clubs around town.

Catalina Hotel   BOUTIQUE HOTEL $$
(Map p476; ☐ 305-674-1160; www.catalinahotel. com; 1732 Collins Ave; r from $220; P ✴ 🛜 🗙 🗷) The Catalina is a lovely example of mid-range deco style. Most appealing, besides the playfully minimalist rooms, is the vibe – the Catalina doesn't take itself too seriously,

and staff and guests all seem to be having fun as a result. The back pool, concealed behind the main building's crisp white facade, is particularly attractive and fringed by a whispery grove of bamboo trees.

★**1 Hotel**   HOTEL $$$
(Map p474; ☐ 866-615-1111; www.1hotels.com; 2341 Collins Ave; r from $400; ✴ 🛜 🗙) 🍃 One of the top hotels in the USA, the 1 Hotel has 400-plus gorgeous rooms that embrace both luxurious and eco-friendly features – including tree-trunk coffee tables/desks, custom hemp-blend mattresses and salvaged driftwood feature walls, plus in-room water filtration (no need for plastic bottles). The common areas are impressive, with four pools, including an adults-only rooftop infinity pool.

★**Surfcomber**   HOTEL $$$
(Map p476; ☐ 305-532-7715; www.surfcomber.com; 1717 Collins Ave; r $250-480; P ✴ 🛜 🗙 🗷) The Surfcomber has a classic deco exterior with strong lines and shade-providing 'eyebrows' that zigzag across the facade. But the interior is what takes most people aback. Rooms have appeal, with elegant lines in keeping with the deco aesthetic, while bursts of color keep things contemporary.

🛏 North Beach

★**Freehand Miami**   BOUTIQUE HOTEL $$
(Map p474; ☐ 305-531-2727; www.thefreehand. com; 2727 Indian Creek Dr; dm $35-55, r $160-250; ✴ 🛜 🗙) The Freehand is the brilliant reimagining of the old Indian Creek Hotel, a classic of the Miami Beach scene. Rooms are sunny and attractively designed, with local artwork and wooden details. The vintage-filled common areas are the reason to stay here though – especially the lovely pool area and backyard that transforms into one of the best bars in town.

🛏 Downtown Miami

Langford Hotel   HERITAGE HOTEL $$
(Map p474; ☐ 305-250-0782; www.langfordhotelmi ami.com; 121 SE 1st St; r from $180; ✴ 🛜) Set in a beautifully restored 1925 beaux-arts high-rise, the Langford opened to much fanfare in 2016. Its 126 rooms blend comfort and nostalgia, with elegant fixtures and vintage details, including white oak flooring and glass-encased rain showers. Thoughtful design touches abound, and there's a rooftop bar and an excellent ground-floor restaurant on-site.

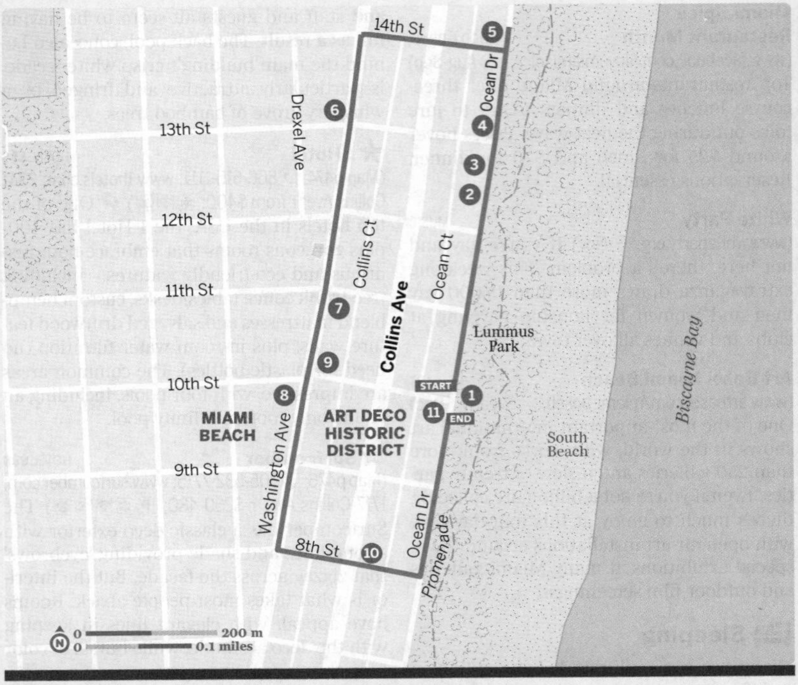

City Walk
Art Deco Magic

START ART DECO MUSEUM
END OCEAN'S TEN
LENGTH 1.2 MILES; TWO TO THREE HOURS

Start at the 1 **Art Deco Museum** (p472), at the corner of Ocean Dr and 10th St. North along Ocean Dr, between 12th and 14th Sts, you'll see three examples of deco hotels: the 2 **Leslie**, a boxy shape with eyebrows (cantilevered sunshades) wrapped around the side of the building; the 3 **Carlyle**, featured in the film *The Birdcage* and boasting modernistic styling; and the graceful 4 **Cardozo Hotel**, built by Henry Hohauser, owned by Gloria Estefan and featuring sleek, rounded edges. At 14th St peek inside the sun-drenched 5 **Winter Haven Hotel** to see its fabulous terrazzo floors, made of stone chips set in mortar that's polished when dry.

Turn left and down 14th St to Washington Ave and the 6 **US Post Office**, at 13th St. It's a curvy block of white deco in the stripped classical style. Step inside to admire the wall mural, domed ceiling and marble stamp tables. Lunch at the 7 **11th St Diner** (p483), a gleaming aluminum Pullman car that was imported in 1992 from Wilkes-Barre, Pennsylvania. Get a window seat and gaze across the avenue to the corner of 10th St and the stunningly restored 8 **Hotel Astor**, designed in 1936 by T Hunter Henderson.

After your meal, walk half a block south from there to the imposing 9 **Wolfsonian-FIU** (p472), an excellent design museum, formerly the Washington Storage Company. Continue walking down Washington Ave, turn left on 8th St and walk east to the 10 **Hotel of South Beach**, featuring an interior and roof deck by Todd Oldham. L Murray Dixon designed the hotel as the Tiffany Hotel, with a deco spire, in 1939. Go two blocks to Ocean Dr, where you'll spy nonstop deco beauties; at 960 Ocean Dr (the 11 **Ocean's Ten** restaurant) you'll see an exterior designed in 1935 by deco legend Henry Hohauser.

Coral Gables

★ Biltmore Hotel   HISTORIC HOTEL $$$
(Map p474; ☑ 855-311-6903; www.biltmorehotel. com; 1200 Anastasia Ave; r/ste from $409/560; P❋🐾🏊) Though the Biltmore's standard rooms can be small, a stay here is a chance to sleep in one of the great laps of US luxury. The grounds are so palatial it would take a solid week to explore everything the Biltmore has to offer – we highly recommend reading a book in the Romanesque/Arabian Nights opulent lobby, sunning underneath enormous columns and taking a dip in the largest hotel pool in the continental USA.

✕ Eating

Miami is a major immigrant entrepôt and a sucker for food trends. Thus you get a good mix of cheap ethnic eateries and high-quality top-end cuisine here, alongside some poor-value dross in touristy zones like Miami Beach. The best new areas for dining are in Downtown, Wynwood and the Upper East Side; Coral Gables has great classic options.

✕ South Beach

11th St Diner   DINER $
(Map p476; ☑ 305-534-6373; www.eleventhstreet diner.com; 1065 Washington Ave; mains $10-20; ⏰7am-midnight Sun-Wed, 24hr Thu-Sat) You've seen the art-deco landmarks. Now eat in one: a Pullman-car diner trucked down from Wilkes-Barre, Pennsylvania – as sure a slice of Americana as a *Leave It to Beaver* marathon. The food is as classic as the architecture, with oven-roasted turkey, baby back ribs and mac 'n' cheese among the hits – plus breakfast at all hours.

★ Yardbird   SOUTHERN US $$
(Map p476; ☑ 305-538-5220; www.runchicken run.com/miami; 1600 Lenox Ave; mains $18-38; ⏰11am-midnight Mon-Fri, from 8:30am Sat & Sun; ✐) Yardbird has earned a die-hard following for its delicious haute Southern comfort food. The kitchen churns out some nice shrimp and grits, St Louis–style pork ribs, charred okra, and biscuits with smoked brisket, but it's most famous for its supremely good plate of fried chicken, spiced watermelon and waffles with bourbon maple syrup.

★ Pubbelly   FUSION $$
(Map p476; ☑ 305-532-7555; www.pubbellyboys. com; 1418 20th St; sharing plates $11-24, mains $19-30; ⏰6pm-midnight Tue-Thu & Sun, to 1am Fri & Sat; ✐) Pubbelly's dining genre is hard to pinpoint, besides delicious. It skews between Asian, North American and Latin American, gleaning the best from all cuisines. Examples? Try black-truffle risotto, pork-belly dumplings or the mouth-watering kimchi fried rice with seafood. Hand-crafted cocktails wash down the dishes a treat.

Joe's Stone Crab Restaurant   AMERICAN $$$
(Map p476; ☑ 305-673-0365; www.joesstonecrab. com; 11 Washington Ave; mains lunch $14-30, dinner $19-60; ⏰11:30am-2:30pm Tue-Sat, 5-10pm daily) The wait is long and the prices for iconic dishes can be high. But if those aren't deal-breakers, queue up to don a bib in Miami's most famous restaurant (around since 1913!) and enjoy deliciously fresh stone-crab claws.

✕ North Beach

Roasters 'n Toasters   DELI $
(Map p474; ☑ 305-531-7691; www.roastersntoast ers.com; 525 Arthur Godfrey Rd; mains $10-18; ⏰6:30am-3:30pm) Given the crowds and the satisfied smiles of customers, Roasters 'n Toasters meets the demanding standards of Miami Beach's large Jewish demographic, thanks to juicy deli meat, fresh bread, crispy bagels and warm latkes. Sliders (mini-sandwiches) are served on challah bread, an innovation that's as charming as it is tasty.

★ 27 Restaurant   FUSION $$
(Map p474; ☑ 786-476-7020; www.freehandho tels.com; 2727 Indian Creek Dr, Freehand Miami Hotel; mains $17-28; ⏰6:30pm-2am Mon-Sat, 11am-4pm & 6:30pm-2am Sun; ✐) This new spot sits on the grounds of the very popular Broken Shaker (p484), one of Miami Beach's best-loved cocktail bars. Like the bar, the setting is amazing – akin to dining in an old tropical cottage, with worn wood floorboards, candlelit tables, and various rooms slung with artwork and curious knickknacks, plus a lovely terrace. The cooking is exceptional, and incorporates flavors from around the globe.

✕ Downtown Miami

All Day   CAFE $
(Map p474; www.alldaymia.com; 1035 N Miami Ave; coffee $3.50, breakfast $10-14; ⏰7am-7pm Mon-Fri, from 9am Sat & Sun; 🛜) All Day is one of the best places in the Downtown area to linger over coffee or breakfast – no matter

the hour. Slender Scandinavian-style chairs, wood-and-marble tables and the Françoise Hardy soundtrack lend an easygoing vibe.

Chef Allen's Farm-to-Table Dinner
VEGETARIAN $$

(Map p474; ☑ 786-405-1745; 1300 Biscayne Blvd; dinner $25, with wine pairing $40; ☺ 6:30pm Mon; ☑) On Monday nights, you can feast on a delicious five-course vegetarian meal, served family-style at outdoor tables in front of the Arsht Center. It's excellent value, with a creative menu inspired by the farmers market held on the same day.

★ Casablanca
SEAFOOD $$

(Map p474; www.casablancaseafood.com; 400 N River Dr; mains $15-34; ☺ 11am-10pm Sun-Thu, to 11pm Fri & Sat) Perched over the Miami River, Casablanca serves up some of the best seafood in town. The setting is a big draw – with tables on a long wooden deck just above the water, and the odd seagull winging past.

Little Havana

★ Versailles
CUBAN $

(Map p474; ☑ 305-444-0240; www.versaillesrestaurant.com; 3555 SW 8th St; mains $6-21; ☺ 8am-1am Mon-Thu, to 2:30am Fri & Sat, 9am-1am Sun) Versailles (ver-*sigh*-yay) is an institution – one of the mainstays of Miami's Cuban gastronomic scene. Try the excellent black-bean soup or the fried yucca before moving onto heartier meat and seafood plates. Older Cubans and Miami's Latin political elite still love coming here, so you've got a real chance to rub elbows with Miami's most prominent Latin citizens.

Exquisito Restaurant
CUBAN $

(Map p474; ☑ 305-643-0227; www.elexquisitomiami.com; 1510 SW 8th St; mains $9-13; ☺ 7am-11pm) For great Cuban cuisine in the heart of Little Havana, this place is exquisite (ha ha). The roast pork has a tangy citrus kick and the *ropa vieja* (spiced shredded beef) is wonderfully rich and filling. Even standard sides like beans and rice and roasted plantains are executed with a little more care and tastiness. Prices are a steal too.

Wynwood & the Design District

Della Test Kitchen
VEGAN $

(Map p474; ☑ 305-351-2961; www.dellabowls.com; 56 NW 29th St, Wynwood Yard; mains $11-14; ☺ noon-10pm Tue-Sun; ☑) From a food truck parked in Wynwood Yard, this place offers delicious 'bowls' – build-your-own culinary works of art featuring ingredients such as black coconut rice, ginger tempeh, chickpeas, sweet potato and marinated kale. It's heavenly good and quite healthy. Not surprisingly, DTK has quite a following.

★ Kyu
FUSION $$

(Map p474; ☑ 786-577-0150; www.kyumiami.com; 251 NW 25th St; sharing plates $17-38; ☺ noon-11:30pm Mon-Sat, 11am-10:30pm Sun, bar till 1am Fri & Sat; ☑) ✐ One of the best new restaurants in Wynwood, Kyu has been dazzling locals and food critics alike with its creative Asian-inspired dishes, most of which are cooked up over the open flames of a wood-fired grill. The buzzing, industrial space is warmed up via artful lighting and wood accents (tables and chairs, plus shelves of firewood for the grill).

★ Alter
MODERN AMERICAN $$$

(Map p474; ☑ 305-573-5996; www.altermiami.com; 223 NW 23rd St; set menu 5/7 courses $69/89; ☺ 7-11pm Tue-Sun) This new spot, which has garnered much praise from food critics, brings creative high-end cooking to Wynwood courtesy of its award-winning young chef Brad Kilgore. The changing menu showcases Florida's high-quality ingredients from sea and land in seasonally inspired dishes with Asian and European accents. Reserve ahead.

🍷 Drinking & Nightlife

Too many people assume Miami's nightlife is all about being wealthy and attractive and/or phony. Disavow yourself of this notion, which only describes a small slice of the scene in South Beach. Miami has an intense variety of bars to pick from that range from grotty dives to beautiful – but still laid-back – lounges and nightclubs.

★ Broken Shaker
BAR

(Map p474; ☑ 305-531-2727; www.freehandhotels.com; 2727 Indian Creek Dr, Freehand Miami Hotel; ☺ 6pm-3am Mon-Fri, 2pm-3am Sat & Sun) Craft cocktails are having their moment in Miami, and if mixology is in the spotlight, you can bet Broken Shaker is sharing the glare. Expert bartenders run this spot, located in the back of the Freehand Miami hotel (p481), which takes up one closet-sized indoor niche and a sprawling plant-filled courtyard of excellent drinks and beautiful people.

★ Sweet Liberty
BAR

(Map p474; www.mysweetliberty.com; 237 20th St; ⊙4pm-5am Mon-Sat, from noon Sun) A much-loved local haunt near Collins Park, Sweet Liberty has all the right ingredients for a fun night out: friendly, easygoing bartenders who whip up excellent cocktails (try a mint julep), great happy-hour specials (including 75¢ oysters) and a relaxed, pretension-free crowd. The space is huge, with flickering candles, a long wooden bar and the odd band adding to the cheer.

Bardot
CLUB

(Map p474; ☑305-576-5570; www.bardotmiami.com; 3456 N Miami Ave; ⊙8pm-3am Tue & Wed, to 5am Thu-Sat) You really should see the interior of Bardot before you leave the city. It's all sexy French vintage posters and furniture (plus a pool table) seemingly plucked from a private club that serves millionaires by day, and becomes a scene of decadent excess by night.

Ball & Chain
BAR

(Map p474; www.ballandchainmiami.com; 1513 SW 8th Street; ⊙noon-midnight Mon-Wed, to 3am Thu-Sat, 2-10pm Sun) The Ball & Chain has survived several incarnations over the years. Back in 1935, when 8th St was more Jewish than Latino, it was the sort of jazz joint Billie Holiday would croon in. That iteration closed in 1957, but the new Ball & Chain is still dedicated to music and good times – specifically, Latin music and tropical cocktails.

Vagabond Pool Bar
BAR

(Map p474; ☑305-400-8420; www.vagabondkitchenandbar.com; 7301 Biscayne Blvd; ⊙5-11pm Sun-Thu, to midnight Fri & Sat) Tucked behind the Vagabond Hotel, this is a great spot to start off the evening, with perfectly mixed cocktails, courtesy of pro bartenders (the kind who will shake your hand and introduce themselves). The outdoor setting overlooking the palm-fringed pool and eclectic crowd pairs nicely with elixirs like the Lost in Smoke (mezcal, amaro, amaretto and orange bitters).

☆ Entertainment

Miami's artistic merits are obvious, even from a distance. Could there be a better creative base? There's Southern homegrown talent, migratory snowbirds bringing the funding and attention of northeastern galleries, and immigrants from across the Americas. All that adds up to some great live music, theater and dance – with plenty of room for experimentation.

★ Adrienne Arsht Center for the Performing Arts
PERFORMING ARTS

(Map p474; ☑305-949-6722; www.arshtcenter.org; 1300 Biscayne Blvd; ⊙box office 10am-6pm Mon-Fri, & 2hr before performances) This magnificent venue manages to both humble and enthrall visitors. Today the Arsht is where the biggest cultural acts in Miami come to perform; a show here is a must-see on any Miami trip.

FLORIDA MIAMI

LGBT MIAMI

In Miami, the gay scene is so integrated it can be difficult to separate it from the straight one; popular hot spots include South Beach, North Beach, and Wynwood and the Design District. Events such as the White Party (p482) and Swizzle are major dates in the North American gay calendar.

LGBT Visitor Center (Map p476; ☑305-397-8914; www.gogaymiami.com; 1130 Washington Ave; ⊙9am-6pm Mon-Fri, 11am-4pm Sat & Sun) The best single source for all LGBT info on Miami. Check the website for Pink Flamingo-certified hotels (ie hotels that are most welcoming to the LGBT crowd). Run by the Gay & Lesbian Chamber of Commerce.

Miami Visitors Bureau (www.miamiandbeaches.com/things-to-do/travel-guides/gay-miami) Miami's official tourist bureau has a useful guide to gay life in the city.

Damron (www.damron.com) Damron, an expert in LGBT travel, offers a searchable database of LGBT-friendly and specific travel listings. Publishes popular national guidebooks, including *Women's Traveller*, *Men's Travel Guide* and *Damron Accommodations*.

Gay Yellow Network (www.glyp.com) City-based listings include six Florida cities.

Out Traveler (www.outtraveler.com) Travel magazine specializing in gay travel.

Purple Roofs (www.purpleroofs.com) Lists queer accommodations, travel agencies and tours worldwide.

There's an Adrienne Arsht Center stop on the Metromover.

★ Cubaocho
LIVE PERFORMANCE

(Map p474; ☑ 305-285-5880; www.cubaocho. com; 1465 SW 8th St; ⊙ 11am-10pm Tue-Thu, to 3am Fri & Sat) Jewel of the Little Havana Art District, Cubaocho is renowned for its concerts, with excellent bands from across the Spanish-speaking world. It's also a community center, art gallery and research outpost for all things Cuban. The interior resembles an old Havana cigar bar, yet the walls are decked out in artwork that references both the classical past of Cuban art and its avant-garde future.

Colony Theater
PERFORMING ARTS

(Map p476; ☑ 305-674-1040, box office 800-211-1414; www.colonymb.org; 1040 Lincoln Rd) The Colony is an absolute art-deco gem, with a classic marquee and Inca-style crenellations, which looks like the sort of place gangsters would go to watch *Hamlet*. This treasure now serves as a major venue for performing arts – from comedy and occasional musicals to theatrical dramas, off-Broadway productions and ballet – as well as hosting movie screenings and small film festivals.

New World Symphony
CLASSICAL MUSIC

(NWS; Map p476; ☑ 305-673-3330; www.nws.edu; 500 17th St) Housed in the New World Center (p473) – a funky explosion of cubist lines and geometric curves, fresh white against the blue Miami sky – the acclaimed New World Symphony holds performances from October to May. The deservedly heralded NWS serves as a three- to four-year preparatory program for talented musicians from prestigious music schools.

ⓘ Information

DANGERS & ANNOYANCES

Miami is a fairly safe city, but there are a few areas considered by locals to be dangerous:

➡ Liberty City, in northwest Miami; Overtown, from 14th St to 20th St; Little Haiti and stretches of the Miami riverfront.

➡ South Beach, particularly along the carnival-like mayhem of Ocean Dr between 8th and 11th Sts, and deserted areas below 5th St are also dangerous at night.

➡ Use caution around causeways, bridges and overpasses where homeless people have set up shantytowns.

➡ In these and other reputedly 'bad' areas you should avoid walking around alone late at night. It's best to take a taxi.

TOURIST INFORMATION

Greater Miami & the Beaches Convention & Visitors Bureau (Map p474; ☑ 305-539-3000; www.miamiandbeaches.com; 701 Brickell Ave, 27th fl; ⊙ 8:30am-6pm Mon-Fri) Offers loads of info on Miami and keeps up-to-date with the latest events and cultural offerings.

ⓘ Getting There & Away

Located 6 miles west of Downtown, the busy **Miami International Airport** (MIA; Map p474; ☑ 305-876-7000; www.miami-airport.com; 2100 NW 42nd Ave) has three terminals and serves over 40 million passengers each year. Around 60 airlines fly into Miami. The airport is open 24 hours and is laid out in a horseshoe design. There are left-luggage facilities on two concourses at MIA, between B and C, and on G; prices vary according to bag size.

For bus trips, **Greyhound** (www.greyhound. com) is the main long-distance operator. **Megabus** (Map p474; www.us.megabus.com; Miami International Center, 3801 NW 21st St) offers service to Tampa and Orlando.

Greyhound's **main bus terminal** (Map p474; ☑ 305-871-1810; 3801 NW 21st) is near the airport, though additional services also depart from the company's **Cutler Bay terminal** (Cutler Bay; ☑ 305-296-9072; 10801 Caribbean Blvd) and **North Miami terminal** (Map p474; ☑ 305-688-7277; 16000 NW 7th Ave).

If you are traveling very long distances (say, across several states) bargain airfares can sometimes undercut buses. On shorter routes, renting a car can sometimes be cheaper. Nonetheless, discounted (even half-price) long-distance bus trips are often available by purchasing tickets online seven to 14 days in advance.

The main Miami terminal of **Amtrak** (☑ 305-835-1222; www.amtrak.com; 8303 NW 37th Ave, West Little River), about 9 miles northwest of Downtown, connects the city with several other points in Florida (including Orlando and Jacksonville) on the Silver Service line that runs up to New York City. Travel time between New York and Miami is 27 to 31 hours. The Miami Amtrak station is connected by Tri-rail to Downtown Miami and has a left-luggage facility.

ⓘ Getting Around

Rental Car Convenient for zipping around town, but parking can be expensive.

Taxi & Ride-Sharing Services Handy for getting between destinations if you don't want to drive, but can be pricey for long distances. Difficult to hail on the street; call or use an app for a pick-up.

Bus Extensive system, though slow for long journeys.

Trolley Free service with various routes in Miami Beach, Downtown, Wynwood, Coconut Grove, Coral Gables, Little Havana and other neighborhoods.

Citi Bike Bike-sharing network in both Miami and Miami Beach. With heavy traffic, however, riding long distances can be hazardous.

Fort Lauderdale

After years of building a reputation as *the* destination for beer-swilling college students on raucous spring breaks, Fort Lauderdale now angles for a slightly more mature and sophisticated crowd. Think martinis rather than tequila shots; jazz concerts instead of wet T-shirt contests. But don't worry, there's still plenty of carrying-on within the confines of area bars and nightclubs.

Few visitors venture far inland – except maybe to dine and shop along Las Olas Blvd; most spend the bulk of their time on the coast. It's understandable. Truly, it's hard to compete with beautiful beaches, a system of Venice-like waterways, an international yachting scene, spiffy new hotels and top-notch restaurants. The city's Port Everglades is one of the busiest cruise-ship ports in the world, with megaships departing daily for the Caribbean, Mexico and beyond.

⊙ Sights

Fort Lauderdale Beach & Promenade   BEACH

(**P** 🚻 🐾) Fort Lauderdale's promenade – a wide, brick, palm-tree-dotted pathway swooping along the beach and the A1A – is a magnet for runners, in-line skaters, walkers and cyclists. The white-sand beach, meanwhile, is one of the nation's cleanest and best. Stretching 7 miles to Lauderdale-by-the-Sea, it has dedicated family-, gay- and dog-friendly sections.

NSU Art Museum Fort Lauderdale   MUSEUM

(☑954-525-5500; www.nsuartmuseum.org; 1 E Las Olas Blvd; adult/student/child $12/free; ⊙11am-5pm Tue-Sat, to 8pm Thu, noon-5pm Sun) A curvaceous Florida standout known for its William Glackens collection (among Glackens fans) and its exhibitions on wide-ranging themes from northern European art to contemporary Cuban art, American pop art and contemporary photography. On Thursday evenings, the museum stays open late and hosts lectures, films and performances, as well as a happy hour in the museum cafe. Day courses and workshops are also avail-able. Check the website for details.

★**Bonnet House**   HISTORIC BUILDING

(☑954-563-5393; www.bonnethouse.org; 900 N Birch Rd; adult/child $20/16, grounds only $10; ⊙9am-4pm Tue-Sun) This pretty plantation-style property was once the home of artists and collectors Frederic and Evelyn Bartlett. It is now open to guided tours that swing through its art-filled rooms and studios. Beyond the house, 35 acres of lush, subtropical gardens protect a pristine barrier-island ecosystem, including one of the finest orchid collections in the country.

Riverwalk   LANDMARK

(www.goriverwalk.com) Curving along the New River, the meandering Riverwalk runs from Stranahan House to the Broward Center for the Performing Arts. Host to culinary tastings and other events, the walk connects a number of sights, restaurants and shops.

Museum of Discovery & Science   MUSEUM

(☑954-467-6637; www.mods.org; 401 SW 2nd St; adult/child $16/13; ⊙10am-5pm Mon-Sat, noon-6pm Sun; ♿) A 52ft kinetic-energy sculpture greets you here, and fun exhibits include Gizmo City and Runways to Rockets – where it actually *is* rocket science. Plus there's an Everglades exhibit and IMAX theater.

🏃 Activities

Fort Lauderdale lies on the same reef system as the Keys. Snorkeling is a popular pastime but the real action in the water lies within a 50-minute boat ride at the site of some two-dozen wrecks. Here divers can nose around the Mercedes freighter and the Tenneco Towers artificial reef made up from an old oil platform. Soft corals bloom prolifically and barracuda, jacks and parrotfish duck and dive between the wreckage.

Besides the underwater scenery, everything from jet-skis to parasailing to deep-sea fishing charters is available at the beach.

★**Atlantic Coast Kayak Company**   KAYAKING

(☑954-781-0073; www.atlanticcoastkayak.com; Richardson Historical Park Boat Dock, 1937 Wilton Dr; per hour/half-day $16/40; ⊙9am-5pm) An excellent alternative to tour-boat cruises is to rent your own kayak in Richardson Park and paddle the 7.5 mile (roughly 2½ to three hours) Middle River loop around the Island City yourself. Day, sunset and moonlight tours, including basic instruction and gourmet sandwiches and soft drinks, are also available on a scheduled calendar. All you need to do is turn up.

Sea Experience
BOATING, SNORKELING

(☑ 954-770-3483; www.seaxp.com; 801 Seabreeze Blvd; snorkeling adult/child $40/25; ☺ 10:15am & 2:15pm; ☒) Sea Experience takes guests in a 40ft glass-bottom boat along the Intracoastal and into the ocean to snorkel on a natural reef, thriving with marine life, in 10ft to 20ft of water. Tours last 2½ hours. Also offers scuba trips to multiple wreck sites.

Carrie B
BOATING

(☑ 954-642-1601; www.carriebcruises.com; 440 N New River Dr E; tours adult/child $24/13; ☺ tours 11am, 1pm & 3pm, closed Tue & Wed May-Sep) Hop aboard this replica 19th-century riverboat for a narrated 90-minute 'lifestyles of the rich and famous' tour of the ginormous mansions along the Intracoastal and New River. Tours leave from Las Olas at SE 5th Ave.

🛏 Sleeping

The splashiest hotels are found along the beach. Of course, those places are also the priciest. Meander inland and you'll discover some wonderful inns with Old Florida charm. For more budget-friendly accommodations, check out Lauderdale-by-the-Sea.

Tranquilo
MOTEL $$

(☑ 954-565-5790; www.tranquilofortlauderdale.com; 2909 Vistamar St; Sun-Thu r $149-174, Fri & Sat $189-194; P ☀ 🛜 ☒) With a successful white-on-white decorative facelift, this retro 1950s motel offers fantastic value for families. Rooms range over three buildings, each with its own pool, and some include newly refurbed kitchens along with access to outdoor grills and laundry services. Complimentary shuttle service to the beach.

B Ocean Resort
HOTEL $$

(☑ 954-524-5551; www.bhotelsandresorts.com/b-ocean; 1140 Seabreeze Blvd; r from $150; P ☀ 🛜 ☒) Defining the southern end of Seabreeze Blvd, this hotel straddles the uberpopular South Beach and offers breezy ocean views from the majority of its airy rooms. Built by M Tony Sherman in 1956, it looks like a giant cruise ship tethered to the sidewalk.

★ W Fort Lauderdale
HOTEL $$$

(☑ 954-414-8200; www.wfortlauderdalehotel.com; 401 N Fort Lauderdale Beach Blvd; r from $284; P ☀ @ 🛜 ☒) With an exterior resembling two giant sails and an interior that looks like the backdrop for a J Lo video, this is where the glitterati stay – bust out your stiletto heels/skinny ties and join them. The massive lobby is built for leisure, with a silver-and-aqua lounge area, a moodily lit bar, and a deck lined with wicker chaises.

★ Lago Mar Resort
RESORT $$$

(☑ 954-523-6511; www.lagomar.com; 1700 S Ocean Lane; r $300-700; P ☀ @ ☒) On the south end of South Beach, this wonderfully noncorporate resort has it all: a private beach, over-the-top grand lobby, massive island-style rooms, a full-service spa, on-site eateries, a lagoon-style pool set amid tropical plantings and the personal touch of family ownership. (And no, not to be confused with President Trump's Mar-a-Lago.)

🍴 Eating

Fort Lauderdale's food scene is heavily influenced by the area's large Italian American population but increasingly, it's becoming known for its casual chic, farm-to-table options. Las Olas Blvd has a number of eating places, especially the stretch between 5th and 16th Aves, though these can be more touristy.

Lester's Diner
DINER $

(☑ 954-525-5641; www.facebook.com/lesters-diner; 250 W State Rd 84; mains $4-17; ☺ 24hr) Hailed endearingly as a greasy spoon, campy Lester's Diner has been keeping folks happy since the late 1960s. Everyone makes their way here at some point, from business types on cell phones to clubbers and blue-haired ladies with third husbands to travel writers needing pancakes at 4am.

Green Bar & Kitchen
VEGAN $$

(☑ 954-533-7507; www.greenbarkitchen.com; 1075 SE 17th St; mains $8-12; ☺ 11am-9pm Mon-Sat, to 3pm Sun; ☒) Discover bright flavors and innovative dishes at this modern, plant-based eatery located in a strip mall. Instead of pasta-layered lasagna, slivers of zucchini are layered with macadamia ricotta and sun-dried tomatoes. Almond milk replaces dairy in cold-pressed fruit smoothies, and the delectable cashew cup gives Reese's a run for its money.

★ **Burlock Coast** INTERNATIONAL $$$
(☑954-302-6460; www.burlockcoast.com; Ritz Carlton, 1 N Fort Lauderdale Beach Blvd; mains $14-40; ⊙7am-10pm Mon-Fri, noon-5pm Sat & Sun) Situated in the lovely Ritz Carlton Hotel, this chic casual spot somehow manages to be all things to all people: a cafe, bar, market and upmarket restaurant. The menu has been crafted to the mantra: local farmers and vendors. The menu changes seasonally but errs toward modern international, like pork belly with black truffle grits or simple fish-and-chips.

15th Street Fisheries SEAFOOD $$$
(☑954-763-2777; www.15streetfisheries.com; 1900 SE 15th St; mains bar $6-16, restaurant $26-38; P) Tucked away in Lauderdale Marina with an open-fronted deck offering a front-row view of yachts, this place is hard to beat for waterfront dining. The wooden interior is kitted out like an Old Florida boathouse. The fine-dining restaurant is upstairs and a more informal dockside bar serves shrimp, crab and grilled mahimahi.

🍷 Drinking & Entertainment

Fort Lauderdale bars can stay open until 4am on weekends and 2am during the week. A handful of great bars and pubs are found in the Himmarshee Village area on SW 2nd St, while the beach offers open-air boozing.

★ **Rok:Brgr** PUB
(☑754-525-7656; www.rokbrgr.com; 208 SW 2nd St; ⊙11:30am-midnight Mon-Thu, to 2am Fri & Sat, to 11pm Sun) One of several of this strip of hip bars and restaurants, Rok:Brgr shoots for a 1920s Chicago-era gastropub and somehow pulls it off. Edison lightbulbs and contemporary industrial creates the ambience, while the cuisine is contemporary gastropub – gourmet burgers using locally sourced ingredients, plus Prohibition-style cocktails.

★ **Stache** COCKTAIL BAR
(☑954-449-1044; www.stacheftl.com; 109 SW 2nd Ave; ⊙8am-5pm Mon & Thu, 8am-4am Fri, 8pm-4am Sat) A sexy 1920s drinking den serving crafted cocktails and rocking a crossover classic rock/funk/soul/R&B blend. At weekends there's live music, dancing and burlesque. Dress up; this is where the cool cats come to play.

Blue Jean Blues JAZZ
(☑954-306-6330; www.bjblive.com; 3320 NE 33rd St; snacks $9-17; ⊙11am-2am Sun-Thu, to 3am Fri & Sat) Get away from the beach for a low-key evening of jazz and blues at this cool little neighborhood bar. There's live music seven nights a week and four afternoons, featuring a who's who of the southern Florida music scene. From East Sunrise Blvd head north for 2.3 miles and then turn left onto NE 33rd Street.

ℹ Information

Greater Fort Lauderdale Convention & Visitors Bureau (☑954-765-4466; www.sunny.org; 101 NE 3rd Ave, Suite 100; ⊙8:30am-5pm Mon-Fri) Has an excellent array of visitor information about the greater Fort Lauderdale region.

LGBT FORT LAUDERDALE

Sure, South Beach is a mecca for gay travelers, but Fort Lauderdale nips at the high heels of its southern neighbor. Compared to South Beach, Lauderdale is a little more rainbow-flag-oriented and a little less exclusive. And for the hordes of gay men who flock here, either to party or to settle down, therein lies the charm.

Fort Lauderdale is home to several dozen gay bars and clubs, as many gay guesthouses, and a couple of way-gay residential areas. **Victoria Park** is the established gay hub just northeast of downtown Fort Lauderdale. A bit further north, **Wilton Manors** is a more recently gay-gentrified area boasting endless nightlife options. Look for **Rosie's** (☑954-563-0123; www.rosiesbarandgrill.com; 2449 Wilton Dr; ⊙11am-11pm), a low-key neighborhood watering hole; **The Manor** (www.themanorcomplex.com; 2345 Wilton Dr; ⊙8pm-4am), for nationally recognized performers and an epic dance floor; and **Georgie's Alibi** (www.alibiwiltonmanors.com; 2266 Wilton Dr; ⊙11am-2am), best for its Wednesday comedy night with Cashetta, a fabulous female impersonator. There's even a leather/bear/cowboy club, **Ramrod** (www.ramrodbar.com; 1508 Wilton Dr; ⊙3pm-2am).

Gay guesthouses are plentiful; visit www.gayftlauderdale.com. Consult the glossy weekly rag *Hot Spots* (www.hotspotsmagazine.com) to keep updated on gay nightlife. For the most insanely comprehensive list of everything gay, log on to www.jumponmarkslist.com.

ℹ Getting There & Around

Fort Lauderdale is served by its own international **airport** (FLL; ☑ 866-435-9355; www.broward.org/airport; 320 Terminal Dr).

If you're driving here, I-95 and Florida's Turnpike run north–south and provide good access to Fort Lauderdale. I-595, the major east–west artery, intersects I-95, Florida's Turnpike and the Sawgrass Expressway. It also feeds into I-75, which runs to Florida's west coast.

Sun Trolley (☑ 954-876-5539; www.suntrolley.com; per ride/day $1/3) runs between Las Olas and the beaches between 9:30am and 6:30pm Friday to Monday. **Broward County Transit** (BCT; www.broward.org/bct; single fare/day pass $2/5) operates between downtown, the beach and Port Everglades. From **Broward Central Terminal** (101 NW 1st Ave), take bus 11 to upper Fort Lauderdale Beach and Lauderdale-by-the-Sea; bus 4 to Port Everglades; and bus 40 to 17th St and the beaches.

The fun, yellow **water taxi** (☑ 954-467-6677; www.watertaxi.com; day pass adult/child $26/12) travels the canals and waterways between 17th St to the south, Atlantic Blvd/Pompano Beach to the north, the Riverwalk to the west and the Atlantic Ocean to the east. There are also services to Hollywood ($15 per person).

Palm Beach County

The third-wealthiest city in America, Palm Beach is home to 25 billionaires and looks every inch the playground for the rich and famous. Palatial Greco-Roman mansions line the shore; Bentleys and Porsches cruise the wide avenues of downtown; and streets look clean enough to eat off. Life here revolves around charity balls, designer shopping and cocktail-soaked lunches. Though all the bling may feel a bit intimidating, fear not – much of Palm Beach is within the reach of all travelers. Stroll along the truly gold Gold Coast beach, ogle the massive gated compounds on A1A or window-shop the uber-ritzy Worth Ave – all for free.

These days, Palm Beach is frequently in the news because of US president Donald Trump, whose mansion-cum-private-club, Mar-a-Lago, is here.

Despite all the glitz, the architecture and history is nothing but fascinating, and offers some insight into how it might have been to live during the Gilded Age of the late 19th-century USA.

Palm Beach

◉ Sights & Activities

Worth Avenue AREA
(www.worth-avenue.com) This quarter-mile, palm-tree-lined strip of more than 200 high-end brand shops is like the Rodeo Dr of the East. You can trace its history back to the 1920s when the now-gone Everglades Club staged weekly fashion shows and launched the careers of designers such as Elizabeth Arden. Even if you don't have the slightest urge to sling a swag of glossy bags over your arm, the people-watching is priceless, as is the Spanish Revival architecture.

★ Flagler Museum MUSEUM
(☑ 561-655-2833; www.flaglermuseum.us; 1 Whitehall Way; adult/child $18/10; ⊙ 10am-5pm Tue-Sat, noon-5pm Sun) This museum is housed in the spectacular 1902 mansion built by Henry Flagler as a gift for his bride, Mary Lily Kenan. The beaux-arts-styled Whitehall was one of the most modern houses of its era and quickly became the focus of the winter season. Designed by John Carrère and Thomas Hastings, both students of the Ecole des Beaux-Arts in Paris and collaborators on other Gilded Age landmarks such as the New York Public Library, the elaborate 75-room house was the first residential home to feature a heating system.

★ Palm Beach
Lake Trail WALKING, CYCLING
(Royal Palm Way, at the Intracoastal Waterway) The first 'road' in Palm Beach ran along the Intracoastal Waterway, and provided a 5-mile paved path stretching from Worth Ave (in the south) to Indian Rd (in the north) for Flagler's hotel guests to stretch their legs and scope out the social scene. Nicknamed 'The Trail of Conspicuous Consumption,' it is sandwiched between two amazing views: Lake Worth lagoon to the west, and an unending series of mansions to the east.

Palm Beach
Bike Shop CYCLING
(☑ 561-659-4583; www.palmbeachbicycle.com; Royal Poinciana Plaza, Cocoanut Row; ⊙ 9am-5:30pm Mon-Sat, 10am-5pm Sun) This shop rents out all manner of wheeled transportation, including bikes ($39 per day), skates ($39 per day) and scooters ($100 per day). Helmets cost $5 extra.

🛏 Sleeping & Eating

Bradley Park Hotel   HOTEL $$
(☎ 561-832-7050;   www.bradleyparkhotel.com;
2080 Sunset Ave; r $229, ste $329-359; 🅿 ❄ 🛜)
The midrange Bradley (built in 1921) offers
large, gold-hued rooms, some with original features from the era and characterful
furniture. Rooms with kitchens feel like
mini-apartments, and it's located just a
short walk from the shops and restaurants
of Royal Poinciana Way.

★ The Breakers   RESORT $$$
(☎ 888-273-2537; www.thebreakers.com; 1 S Coun-
ty Rd; r/ste from $699/from $2000; 🅿 ❄ @
🛜 ⛱ 🐾) 🏊 Originally built by Henry Flagler
(in 1904, rooms cost $4 per night, including
meals), today this 550-room resort sprawls
across 140 acres and boasts a staff of 2000
plus, fluent in 56 languages. Just feet from
the county's best snorkeling, this palace has
two 18-hole golf courses, a mile of semi-
private beach, four pools and the best
brunch around.

Surfside Diner   DINER, BREAKFAST $
(☎ 561-659-7495; 314 S County Rd; mains $8-12;
⊙ 8am-3pm) This classy remake of a classic
diner serves one of the better brunch options in town. Pancakes, chicken breakfast
burritos and French toast are all tasty. For
lunch there's a healthy offering of grilled
cheese and tomato soup, BLTs, PB&Js and
sliders.

★ Būccan   MODERN AMERICAN $$
(☎ 561-833-3450;   www.buccanpalmbeach.com;
350 S County Rd; mains $18-45; ⊙ 5pm-midnight
Sun-Thu, 5pm-1am Fri & Sat) With its modern American menu and James Beard–
nominated chef, Clay Conley, at the helm,
Būccan is the 'it' eatery in Palm Beach.
Flavor-hop with a selection of small plates,
including snapper ceviche and octopus tab-
bouleh, and move on to Moroccan chicken.
Reservations recommended.

★ Café Boulud   FRENCH $$$
(☎ 561-655-6060;   www.thebraziliancourt.com;
301 Australian Ave; mains $16-46, fixed-price menu
lunch/dinner $32/48; ⊙ cafe 7am-10pm, bar to
midnight) Created by renowned New York
chef Daniel Boulud, the restaurant at the
Brazilian Court is one of the few places in
Palm Beach that truly justifies the sky-high
prices. The warm dining room and terrace
complements a rich menu of classic French
and fusion dishes, all displaying Boulud's
signature sophistication and subtlety.

🍷 Drinking & Entertainment

Leopard Lounge   LOUNGE
(www.chesterfieldpb.com;   363 Cocoanut Row;
⊙ 6:30pm-1am) This swanky gold, black and
red place attracts a mature crowd and the
occasional celeb (neither photos nor autograph hounds are allowed). Live music –
a mix of jazz and classics – nightly.

Society of the Four Arts   PERFORMING ARTS
(☎ 561-655-7226; www.fourarts.org; 2 Four Arts Plaza) The concert series here includes cabaret,
the Palm Beach Symphony, chamber orchestras, string quartets and piano performances.

ℹ Information

Chamber of Commerce (☎ 561-655-3282;
www.palmbeachchamber.com; 400 Royal Palm
Way, Suite 106; ⊙ 9am-5pm Mon-Fri) Excellent
maps and racks of pamphlets. Consider down-
loading the *Palm Beach Guide* app.

ℹ Getting There & Around

Palm Tran (http://discover.pbcgov.org/
palmtran; per ride $2, day pass $5) bus 41
covers the bulk of the island, from Lantana Rd
to Sunrise Ave; transfer to bus 1 at Publix to go
north or south along US 1. A single fare costs
adult/child $2/1. To get to Palm Beach Inter-
national Airport (p493) in West Palm Beach,
take bus 41 to the downtown transfer and hop
on bus 44.

Though it's a fairly compact city, the two major
downtown neighborhoods, centered on Royal Poinciana Way and Worth Ave, are a fair hike apart.

West Palm Beach

When Henry Flagler decided to develop
what is now West Palm Beach, he knew
precisely what it would become: a working-
class community for the labor force that
would support his glittering resort town
across the causeway. And so the fraternal
twins were born – Palm Beach, considered
the fairer of the two, and West Palm Beach,
a cooler work-hard-play-hard community.
West Palm has a surprisingly diverse collection of restaurants, friendly inhabitants
(including a strong gay community) and a
gorgeous waterway that always seems to reflect the perfect amount of starlight.

⦿ Sights & Activities

★ Norton Museum of Art   MUSEUM
(☑ 561-832-5196; www.norton.org; 1451 S Olive Ave; adult/child $12/5; ⊙ noon-5pm Tue-Sun) Undergoing a major renovation at the time of research (the design was done by architect Norman Foster), this is the largest art museum in Florida. It opened in 1941 to display the enormous art collection of industrialist Ralph Hubbard Norton and his wife Elizabeth. The Nortons' permanent collection of more than 5000 pieces (including works by Matisse, Warhol and O'Keeffe) is displayed alongside important Chinese, pre-Columbian Mexican and US Southwestern artifacts, plus some wonderful contemporary photography and regular traveling exhibitions.

South Florida Science Center & Aquarium   MUSEUM
(☑ 561-832-1988; www.sfsciencecenter.org; 4801 Dreher Trail North; adult/child $16/11.50; ⊙ 9am-5pm Mon-Fri, 10am-6pm Sat & Sun) A great little hands-on science center, aquarium and planetarium with weekend programs, traveling exhibits, a science trail, mini-golf and butterfly garden. On the last Friday of the month the museum stays open until 9pm so you can view the night sky from the county's only public observatory (weather permitting). Prices change according to the exhibition.

Peanut Island   ISLAND
(http://discover.pbcgov.org; ⊙ 11am-4pm Thu-Sun) Plopped right off the northeastern corner of West Palm, Peanut Island was created in 1918 by dredging projects. Originally named Inlet Island, the spit was renamed for a peanut-oil-shipping operation that failed in 1946. The highlight is, however, the **nuclear fallout bunker** (☑ 561-723-2028; www.pbmm. info; adult/child $17/12; ⊙ 11am-4pm Thu-Sun) that was constructed for John F Kennedy during the days of the Cuban missile crisis. These days, it's run by the Palm Beach Maritime Museum.

Rapids Water Park   WATER PARK
(☑ 561-842-8756; www.rapidswaterpark.com; 6566 North Military Trail, Riviera Beach; weekday/weekend $43/48; ⊙ 10am-5pm) South Florida's largest water park features 30 action-packed acres of wet and wild rides. Don't let the squeals of fear and delight from the Big Thunder funnel put you off. Awesome fun. Parking costs an extra $10.

⌗ Sleeping

Hotel Biba   MOTEL $
(☑ 561-832-0094; www.hotelbiba.com; 320 Belvedere Rd; r $149-179; ❄ 🕸 🖼) With plain, white, slightly missing-a-small-something rooms, this place lacks a bit of color, but is one of the better (if only) budget options around. It's well located – only a block from the Intracoastal, and perched on the edge of the El Cid district. Suffice to say it's clean and fine if you just want a bed.

★ Grandview Gardens   B&B $$
(☑ 561-833-9023; www.grandview-gardens. com; 1608 Lake Ave; r from $229; 🅿 ❄ 🕸 🖼) Book a room at this intimate resort and you'll feel like a local in no time. Hidden in a tropical garden on Howard Park, the enormous suites with their wrought-iron and four-poster beds access the pool patio through French doors.

✕ Eating

Johan's Jöe   CAFE $
(Swedish Coffee House & Cafe; www.johansjoe. com; 401 S Dixie Hwy; mains $9-13; ⊙ 7am-6pm) If you can get past the menu's umlaut marks (placed jokingly here on English words), you'll find a delightful array of pastries and cakes. But the sweets are not the only winners; it's hard to go past the likes of pickled herrings and Swedish meatballs and authentic Swedish salads and sandwiches.

Darbster   VEGAN $$
(☑ 561-586-2622; www.darbster.com; 8020 S Dixie Hwy; mains $14-20; ⊙ 5-10pm Tue-Fri, 10:30am-3pm & 5-10pm Sat, to 9pm Sun) This place is out on a limb in many respects: it's 5 miles south of town in an incongruous location by the S Dixie Hwy on the Palm Beach canal; the menu is 100% vegan; all profits go to a foundation for animal care; and it attracts everyone from Birkenstock-wearing hippies to diamond-wearing Palm Beachers.

★ Table 26 Degrees   MODERN AMERICAN $$$
(☑ 561-855-2660; www.table26palmbeach.com; 1700 S Dixie Hwy; mains $26-41; ⊙ 11:30am-2pm Mon-Sat, 4:30-10pm Sun-Wed, 4:30-11pm Thu-Sat) Don't be put off by the price of this sophisticated restaurant. It is filled with locals, conversation and the clinking of glasses for good reason. They flock here for the bar (great happy hour 4:30pm to 6:30pm daily) plus the share plates and mains that are divided by water, land, field and hands (the latter covers fried chicken and burgers).

🍸 Drinking & Entertainment

The Pawn Shop Lounge CLUB
(www.pawnshopwpb.com; 219 Clematis St; cover $10; ⊙5pm-3am Tue-Thu, to 4am Fri & Sat) This former Miami dance club and celebrity haunt is situated in the former Dr Feelgood venue. It features the familiar pawn shop trappings along with a life-sized vintage Ferris wheel and a DJ booth designed out of a Mack truck. DJs, dancers and light shows keep the party going until 3am while rivers of alcohol flow from the 175-ft-long bar.

HG Roosters GAY
(www.roosterswpb.com; 823 Belvedere Rd; ⊙3pm-3am Sun-Thu, to 4am Fri & Sat) A mainstay of West Palm's thriving gay community, this bar has been offering wings, bingo and hot young male dancers since 1984.

Respectable Street LIVE MUSIC
(www.respectablestreet.com; 518 Clematis St) Respectables has kept South Florida jamming to great bands for two decades; it also organizes October's MoonFest, the city's best block party. Great DJs, strong drinks and a breezy chill-out patio are added bonuses. See if you can find the hole that the Red Hot Chili Peppers' Anthony Kiedis punched in the wall when they played here.

International Polo Club SPECTATOR SPORT
(☑561-204-5687; www.internationalpoloclub.com; 3667 120th Ave S, Wellington; general admission $10, lawn seating from $30; ⊙Sun Jan-Apr) Between January and April the International Polo Club hosts 16 weeks of polo and glamour. As one of the finest polo facilities in the world, it not only attracts the most elite players but also the local and international glitterati who whoop it up in head-turning fashion over champagne brunches (tickets $125). Why not join the fun?

ℹ️ Information

The *Palm Beach Post* (www.palmbeachpost.com) is the largest paper.

Discover The Palm Beaches Visitor Center
(☑561-233-3000; www.thepalmbeaches.com; 2195 Southern Blvd, Suite 400; ⊙8:30am-5:30pm Mon-Fri) Extensive area information, maps and online guides.

ℹ️ Getting There & Around

Palm Beach International Airport (PBI; ☑561-471-7420; www.pbia.org; 1000 James L Turnage Blvd) is served by most major airlines and car-rental companies. It's about a mile west of I-95 on Belvedere Rd. Palm Tran (p491) bus 44 runs between the airport, the train station and downtown ($2).

Greyhound (☑561-833-8534; www.greyhound.com; 215 S Tamarind Ave; ⊙6am-10:45pm), **Tri-Rail** (☑800-875-7245; www.tri-rail.com; 203 S Tamarind Ave) and **Amtrak** (☑800-872-7245; www.amtrak.com; 209 S Tamarind Ave) share the same building: the historic Seaboard Train Station. Palm Tran serves the station with bus 44 (from the airport).

Once you're settled, driving and parking is a cinch. There's also a cute and convenient (and free!) trolley running between Clematis St and CityPlace starting at 11am.

The Everglades

There is no wilderness in America quite like the Everglades. Called the 'River of Grass' by Native American inhabitants, this is not just a wetland, or a swamp, or a lake, or a river, or a prairie, or a grassland – it is all of the above, twisted together into a series of soft horizons, long vistas, sunsets that stretch across your entire field of vision and the toothy grins of a healthy population of dinosaur-era reptiles.

When you watch anhinga flexing their wings before breaking into a corkscrew dive, or the slow, rhythmic flap of a great blue heron gliding over its domain, or the shimmer of sunlight on miles of untrammeled saw grass as it sets behind hunkering cypress domes, you'll get a glimpse of this park's quiet majesty. In a nation where natural beauty is measured by its capacity for drama, the Everglades subtly, contentedly flows on.

Everglades National Park

This vast **wilderness** (☑305-242-7700; www.nps.gov/ever; 40001 SR-9336, Homestead; vehicle pass $25, cyclists $8; ⊙visitor center 9am-5pm; ♿), encompassing 1.5 million acres, is one of America's great natural treasures. As a major draw for visitors to South Florida, there's much to see and do. You can spy alligators basking in the noonday sun as herons stalk patiently through nearby waters in search of prey, go kayaking amid tangled mangrove canals and on peaceful lakes, or wade through murky knee-high waters amid cypress domes on a rough-and-ready 'slough slog'. There are sunrise strolls on boardwalks amid the awakening glimmers of birdsong, and moonlit glimpses of gators swimming gracefully along narrow channels in search of dinner. There's backcountry camping, bicycle tours and ranger-led activities that help bring the magic of this place to life. The biggest challenge is really just deciding where to begin.

There are three main entrances and three main areas of the park: one along the southeast edge near Homestead and Florida City (Ernest Coe section); another at the central-north side on the Tamiami Trail (Shark Valley section); and a third at the northwest shore (Gulf Coast section), past Everglades City. The Shark Valley and Gulf Coast sections of the park come one after the other in geographic succession, but the Ernest Coe area is entirely separate.

The admission fee covers the whole park, and is good for seven consecutive days. Because the Tamiami Trail is a public road, there's no admission to access national park sights along this highway, aside from Shark Valley. In the southern half of the park, one staffed checkpoint oversees access to all sights on the road between Ernest Coe down to Flamingo.

Three types of **backcountry campsites** (☎ 239-695-2945, 239-695-3311; www.nps.gov/ever/planyourvisit/backcamp.htm) are available: beach sites, on coastal shell beaches and in the 10,000 Islands; ground sites, which are basically mounds of dirt built up above the mangroves; and *chickees*, wooden platforms built above the waterline where you can pitch a free-standing (no spikes) tent. *Chickees*, which have toilets, are the most civilized – there's a serenity found in sleeping on what feels like a raft levitating above the water. Ground sites tend to be the most bug-infested.

If you're paddling around and see an island that looks pleasant for camping but isn't a designated campsite, beware – you may end up submerged when the tides change.

From November to April, backcountry camping permits cost $15, plus $2 per person per night; from May to October sites are free, but you must still self-register at Flamingo and Gulf Coast Visitor Centers or call ☎ 239-695-2945.

Some backcountry tips:

➡ Store food in a hand-sized, raccoon-proof container (available at gear stores).

➡ Bury your waste at least 10in below ground, but keep in mind some ground sites have hard turf.

➡ Use a backcountry stove to cook. Ground fires are only permitted at beach sites, and you can only burn dead or downed wood.

Load up on provisions before you enter the park. Homestead or Florida City are your best options if going into the Southern Everglades. If heading to the Tamiami Trail, plan to stock up in Miami – or the western suburbs.

❶ Getting There & Around

The largest subtropical wilderness in the continental USA is easily accessible from Miami. The Glades, which comprise the 80 southernmost miles of Florida, are bound by the Atlantic Ocean to the east and the Gulf of Mexico to the west. The Tamiami Trail (Hwy 41) goes east–west, parallel to the more northern (and less interesting) Alligator Alley (I-75).

You need a car to properly enter the Everglades and once you're in, wearing a good pair of walking boots is essential to penetrate the interior. Having a canoe or kayak helps as well; these can be rented from outfits inside and outside the park, or else you can seek out guided canoe and kayak tours. Bicycles are well suited to the flat roads of Everglades National Park, particularly in the area between Ernest Coe and Flamingo Point. Road shoulders in the park tend to be dangerously small.

Around the Everglades

Biscayne National Park

Just to the east of the Everglades is **Biscayne National Park** (☎ 305-230-1144, boat tours 786-335-3644; www.nps.gov/bisc; 9700 SW 328th St; boat tours adult/child $35/25; ⊙ 7am-5:30pm), or the 5% of it that isn't underwater. In fact, a portion of the world's third-largest reef sits here off the coast of Florida, along with mangrove forests and the northernmost Florida Keys.

A bit shadowed by the Everglades, Biscayne requires a little extra planning, but you get a lot more reward for your effort. The offshore keys, accessible only by boat, offer pristine opportunities for camping. Generally summer and fall are the best times to visit the park; you'll want to snorkel when the water is calm. This is some of the best reef-viewing and snorkeling you'll find in the USA, outside Hawaii and nearby Key Largo.

Fortunately this unique 300-sq-mile park is easy to explore independently with a canoe, or via a boat tour.

Primitive camping (site per night $25, May-Sep free) is available on Elliott and Boca Chita Keys, though you'll need a boat to get there. No-see-ums (tiny flies) are invasive, and their bites are devastating. Make sure your tent is devoid of minuscule entry points.

ℹ Information

Dante Fascell Visitor Center (📞 305-230-1144; www.nps.gov/bisc; 9700 SW 328th St; 🕙 9am-5pm) Located at Convoy Point, this center shows a great introductory film for an overview of the park, and has maps, information and excellent ranger activities. The grounds around the center are a popular picnic spot on weekends and holidays, especially for families from Homestead. Also showcases local artwork.

ℹ Getting There & Away

To get here, you'll have to drive about 9 miles east of Homestead (the way is pretty well signposted) on SW 328th St (North Canal Dr) into a long series of green-and-gold flat fields and marsh.

Homestead & Florida City

Homestead and neighboring Florida City, 2 miles to the south, aren't of obvious appeal upon arrival. Part of the ever-expanding subdivisions of South Miami, this bustling corridor can feel like an endless strip of big-box shopping centers, fast-food joints, car dealerships and gas stations. However, look beneath the veneer and you'll find much more than meets the eye: strange curiosities like a 'castle' built single-handedly by one lovestruck immigrant, an animal rescue center for exotic species, a winery showcasing Florida's produce (hint: it's not grapes), an up-and-coming microbrewery, and one of the best farm stands in America. Not to mention that this area makes a great base for forays into the stunning Everglades National Park.

◉ Sights & Activities

★**Coral Castle**   CASTLE
(📞 305-248-6345; www.coralcastle.com; 28655 S Dixie Hwy; adult/senior/child $18/15/8; 🕙 8am-6pm Sun-Thu, to 8pm Fri & Sat) 'You will be seeing unusual accomplishment,' reads the inscription on the rough-hewn quarried wall. That's an understatement. There is no greater temple to all that is weird and wacky about South Florida. The legend: a Latvian gets snubbed at the altar. Comes to the USA and settles in Florida. Handcarves, unseen,

in the dead of night, a monument to unrequited love.

Everglades Outpost   WILDLIFE RESERVE
(📞 305-562-8000; www.evergladesoutpost.org; 35601 SW 192nd Ave, Homestead; adult/child $12/8; 🕙 10am-5:30pm Mon, Tue & Fri-Sun, by appointment Wed & Thu) The Everglades Outpost houses, feeds and cares for wild animals that have been seized from illegal traders, abused, neglected or donated by people who could not care for them. Residents of the outpost include a lemur, wolves, a black bear, a zebra, cobras, alligators and a pair of majestic tigers (one of whom was bought by an exotic dancer who thought she could incorporate it into her act). Your money goes into helping the outpost's mission.

Garls Coastal Kayaking Everglades   KAYAKING
(www.garlscoastalkayaking.com; 19200 SW 344th St, Homestead; single/double kayak per day $40/55, half-/full-day tour $125/150) On the property of the **Robert Is Here** (📞 305-246-1592; www.robertishere.com; juices $7-9; 🕙 8am-7pm) 🍏 fruit stand, this outfitter leads highly recommended excursions into the Everglades. A full-day outing includes hiking (more of a wet walk/slog into the lush landscape of cypress domes), followed by kayaking in both the mangroves and in Florida Bay, and, time permitting, a night walk.

🛏 Sleeping & Eating

★**Everglades International Hostel**   HOSTEL $
(📞 305-248-1122; www.evergladeshostel.com; 20 SW 2nd Ave, Florida City; camping per person $18, dm $30, d $61-75, ste $125-225; 🅿 ❄ 🛜 ❄) Located in a cluttered, comfy 1930s boarding house, this friendly hostel has good-value dorms, private rooms and 'semi-privates' (you have an enclosed room within the dorms and share a bathroom with dorm residents). The creatively configured backyard is the best feature.

Gator Grill   AMERICAN $
(📞 786-243-0620; 36650 SW 192nd Ave, Homestead; mains $9-16; 🕙 11am-6:30pm) A handy pit stop before or after visiting the Everglades National Park, the Gator Grill is a white shack with picnic tables, where you can munch on all manner of alligator dishes. There are gator tacos, gator stir-fry, gator kebabs and straight-up fried alligator served in a basket.

ℹ Information

There are several info centers where you can get tips on attractions, lodging and dining.

Chamber of Commerce (☑ 305-247-2332; www.southdadechamber.org; 455 N Flagler Ave, Homestead; ⊗ 9am-5pm Mon-Fri)

Tropical Everglades Visitor Association (160 N 1st St, Florida City; ⊗ 8am-5pm Mon-Sat, 10am-2pm Sun)

ℹ Getting There & Away

Homestead runs a free weekend **trolley bus service** (☑ 305-224-4457; www.cityofhomestead. com; ⊗ Sat & Sun Dec-Apr), which takes visitors from Losner Park (downtown Homestead) out to the **Royal Palm Visitor Center** (☑ 305-242-7700; www.nps.gov/ever; State Rd 9336; ⊗ 9am-4:15pm) in Everglades National Park. It also runs between Losner Park and Biscayne National Park. Call for the latest departure times.

Tamiami Trail

Calle Ocho, in Miami's Little Havana, happens to be the eastern end of the Tamiami Trail/Hwy 41, which cuts through the Everglades to the Gulf of Mexico. So go west, young traveler, along Hwy 41, a few dozen miles and several different worlds away from the city where the heat is on. This trip leads you into the northern edges of the park, past long landscapes of flooded forest, gambling halls, swamp-buggy tours, food shacks and other Old Florida accoutrements.

As you head west you'll see fields and fields of pine forest and billboards advertising swamp tours. Airboat tours are an old-school way of seeing the Everglades (and there is something to be said for getting a tour from a raging Skynyrd fan with killer tatts and better camo), but there are other ways of exploring the park as well.

◉ Sights & Activities

Fakahatchee Strand Preserve   PARK
(☑ 239-695-4593; www.floridastateparks.org/faka hatcheestrand; 137 Coastline Dr, Copeland; vehicle/pedestrian/bicycle $3/2/2; ⊗ 8am-sunset; 🅿 🚻)

🌿 The Fakahatchee Strand, besides having a fantastic name, also houses a 20-mile by 5-mile estuarine wetland that could have emerged directly out of the *Jurassic Park* franchise. A 2000ft boardwalk traverses this wet and wild wonderland, where panthers still stalk their prey amid the black waters. While it's unlikely you'll spot any panthers, there's a great chance you'll see a large variety of blooming orchids, bird life and reptiles ranging in size from tiny skinks to grinning alligators.

Shark Valley Tram Tour   TOURS
(☑ 305-221-8455; www.sharkvalleytramtours.com; adult/child under 12yr/senior $25/19/12.75; ⊗ departures 9:30am, 11am, 2pm, 4pm May-Dec, 9am-4pm Jan-Apr hourly on the hour) This excellent two-hour tour runs along a 15-mile asphalt trail allowing you to see copious amounts of alligators in the winter months. Tours are narrated by knowledgeable park rangers who give a fascinating overview of the Everglades.

ℹ Information

Shark Valley Visitor Center (☑ 305-221-8776; www.nps.gov/ever/planyourvisit/svdirections. htm; national park entry per vehicle/bicycle/pedestrian $25/8/8; ⊗ 9am-5pm) A good place to pick up information about the Everglades, including trails, wildlife watching and free ranger-led activities.

Everglades City

On the edge of Chokoloskee Bay, you'll find an Old Florida fishing village of raised houses,

---

DETOUR: LOOP ROAD

The 24-mile-long Loop Rd, off Tamiami Trail (Hwy 41), offers some unique sites. One: the homes of the **Miccosukee**, some of which have been considerably expanded by gambling revenue. You'll see some traditional *chickee*-style huts and some trailers with massive add-on wings that are bigger than the original trailer – all seem to have shiny new pickup trucks parked out front. Two: great pull-offs for viewing flooded forests, where egrets that look like pterodactyls perch in the trees, and alligators lurk in the depths below. Three: houses with large Confederate flags and 'Stay off my property' signs; these homes are as much a part of the landscape as the swamp. And four: the short, pleasantly jungly **Tree Snail Hammock Nature Trail**. Though unpaved, the graded road is in good shape and fine for 2WD vehicles. True to its name, the road loops right back onto the Tamiami; expect a leisurely jaunt on the Loop to add an hour or two to your trip.

turquoise water and scattershot emerald-green mangrove islands. 'City' is an ambitious name for Everglades City, but this is a friendly fishing town where you can easily lose yourself for a day or three. You'll find some intriguing vestiges of the past here, including an excellent regional museum.

Hwy 29 runs south through town onto the small, peaceful residential island of Chokoloskee, which has some pretty views over the watery wilderness of the 10,000 Islands. You can arrange boating excursions from either Everglades City or Chokoloskee to explore this pristine environment.

⊙ Sights & Activities

★ Museum of the Everglades   MUSEUM
(☎239-695-0008; www.evergladesmuseum.org; 105 W Broadway; ⊙9am-4pm Mon-Sat; P) FREE
For a break from the outdoors, don't miss this small museum run by kindhearted volunteers who have a wealth of knowledge on the region's history. Located in the town's former laundry house, the collection delves into human settlement in the area from the early pioneers of the 1800s to the boom days of the 1920s and its tragic moments (Hurricane Donna devastated the town in 1960), and subsequent transformation into the quiet backwater of today.

10,000 Islands   ISLAND
One of the best ways to experience the serenity of the Everglades – somehow desolate yet lush, tropical and forbidding – is by paddling the network of waterways that skirt the northwest portion of the park. The 10,000 Islands consist of many (but not really 10,000) tiny islands and a mangrove swamp that hugs the southwestern-most border of Florida.

Everglades Adventures   CANOEING
(☎877-567-0679; www.evergladesadventures.com; 107 Camellia St; 3/4hr tours from $89/99, canoe/ kayak rental per day from $35/49) 🏄 For a real taste of the Everglades, nothing beats getting out on the water. This highly recommended outfitter offers a range of half-day kayak tours, from sunrise paddles to twilight trips through mangroves that return under a sky full of stars.

🛏 Sleeping & Eating

Outdoor Resorts of Chokoloskee   MOTEL $
(☎239-695-2881; www.outdoorresortsofchokolo-skee.com; 150 Smallwood Dr, Chokoloskee; r $119;

✱ ⊠) At the northern end of Chokoloskee Island, this good-value place is a big draw for its extensive facilities, including several swimming pools, hot tubs, tennis and shuffleboard courts, a fitness center and boat rentals. The fairly basic motel-style rooms have kitchenettes and a back deck overlooking the marina.

Everglades City Motel   MOTEL $$
(☎239-695-4224; www.evergladescitymotel.com; 310 Collier Ave; r $150-250; P✱🛜) With large renovated rooms that have all the mod cons (flat-screen TVs, fridge, coffeemaker) and friendly staff that can hook you up with boat tours, this motel provides good value for those looking to spend some time near the 10,000 Islands.

★ Havana Cafe   LATIN AMERICAN $$
(☎239-695-2214; www.havanacafeoftheever glades.com; 191 Smallwood Dr, Chokoloskee; mains lunch $10-19, dinner $22-30; ⊙7am-3pm Mon-Thu, to 8pm Fri & Sat, closed mid-Apr–mid-Oct) The Havana Cafe is famed far and wide for its deliciously prepared seafood served up with Latin accents. Lunch favorites include stone-crab enchiladas, blackened grouper with rice and beans, and a decadent Cuban sandwich. The outdoor dining amid palm trees and vibrant bougainvillea – not to mention the incredibly friendly service – adds to the appeal.

Oyster House   SEAFOOD $$
(☎239-695-2073; www.oysterhouserestaurant.com; 901 Copeland Ave; mains lunch $12-18, dinner $19-30; ⊙11am-9pm Sun-Thu, to 10pm Fri & Sat; 🖉🚼) Besides serving the Everglades staples of excellent seafood (oysters, crab, grouper, cobia, lobster), this buzzing, family-run spot serves up alligator dishes (tacos, jambalaya, fried platters) and simpler baskets (burgers, fried seafood), plus not-to-be-missed desserts. The cabin-like interior is decorated with vintage knickknacks and taxidermy, which might make you feel like you're in the deep woods.

ⓘ Information

Everglades Area Chamber of Commerce
(☎239-695-3941; cnr Hwy 41 & Hwy 29; ⊙9am-4pm) General information about the region is available here.

ⓘ Getting There & Away
There is no public transit out this way. If driving, it's a fairly straight 85-mile drive west from Miami. The trip takes about 1¾ hours.

FLORIDA AROUND THE EVERGLADES

Florida Keys

If Florida is a state apart from the USA, the Keys are islands apart from Florida – in other words, it's different down here. This is a place where those who reject everyday life on the mainland escape. What do they find? About 113 mangrove-and-sandbar islands where the white sun melts over tight fists of deep green mangroves; long, gloriously soft mudflats and tidal bars; water as teal as Arizona turquoise; and a bunch of people often like themselves: freaks, geeks and lovable weirdos all.

Key West is still defined by its motto – One Human Family – an ideal that equals a tolerant, accepting ethos where anything goes and life is always a party (or at least a hungover day after). The color scheme: watercolor pastels cooled by breezes on a sunset-kissed Bahamian porch. Welcome to the End of the USA.

ℹ Information

The Monroe County Tourist Development Council's Florida Keys & Key West Visitors Bureau runs an excellent website (www.fla-keys.com), which is packed with information on everything the Keys has to offer.

Check www.keysnews.com for good daily online news and information about the islands.

ℹ Getting There & Away

Getting here can be half the fun – or, if you're unlucky, a whopping dose of frustration. Imagine a tropical-island hop, from one bar-studded mangrove islet to the next, via one of the most remarkable roads in the world: the Overseas Hwy (Hwy 1). On a good day, driving along the Overseas with the windows down – the wind in your face and the twin sisters of Florida Bay and the Atlantic stretching on either side – is the US road trip in tropical perfection. On a bad day, you end up sitting in gridlock behind some guy who is riding a midlife-crisis Harley.

Greyhound (www.greyhound.com) buses serve all Keys destinations along Hwy 1 and depart from Downtown Miami and Key West; you can pick up a bus along the way by standing on the Overseas Hwy and flagging one down. If you fly into Fort Lauderdale or Miami, the **Keys Shuttle** (☑ 888-765-9997; www.keysshuttle.com) provides door-to-door service to most of the Keys ($70/80/90 to the Upper and Middle Keys/Lower Keys/Key West). Reserve at least a day in advance.

Key Largo

We're not going to lie: Key Largo (both the name of the town and the island it's on) is slightly underwhelming at a glance. 'Under' is the key word, as its main sights are under the water, rather than above. As you drive onto the islands, Key Largo resembles a long line of low-lying hammock and strip development. But that's just from the highway: head down a side road and duck into this warm little bar, or that converted Keys plantation house, and the island idiosyncrasies become more pronounced.

The 33-mile-long Largo, which starts at Mile Marker 106, is the longest island in the Keys, and those 33 miles have attracted a lot of marine life, all accessible from the biggest concentration of dive sites in the islands. The town of Tavernier (Mile Marker 93) is just south of the town of Key Largo.

⊙ Sights & Activities

John Pennekamp Coral Reef State Park   STATE PARK
(☑ 305-451-6300; www.pennekamppark.com; Mile 102.6 oceanside; car with 1/2 people $4.50/9, cyclist or pedestrian $2.50; ⊙ 8am-sunset, aquarium to 5pm; P ♿) ✿ John Pennekamp has the singular distinction of being the first underwater park in the USA. There's 170 acres of dry parkland here and over 48,000 acres (75 sq miles) of wet: the vast majority of the protected area is the ocean. Before you get out in that water, be sure to take in some pleasant beaches and stroll over the nature trails.

Laura Quinn Wild Bird Sanctuary   WILDLIFE RESERVE
(☑ 305-852-4486; www.keepthemflying.org; 93600 Overseas Hwy, Mile 93.6; donations accepted; ⊙ sunrise-sunset; P ♿) ✿ This 7-acre sanctuary serves as a protected refuge for a wide variety of injured birds. A boardwalk leads through various enclosures where you can learn a bit about some of the permanent residents – those unable to be released back in the wild. The species here include masked boobies, great horned owls, green herons, brown pelicans, double-crested cormorants and others. Keep walking along the path to reach a nice vista of Florida Bay.

African Queen   BOATING
(☑ 305-451-8080; www.africanqueenflkeys.com; Key Largo Holiday Inn, 99701 Overseas Hwy; canal cruise/dinner cruise $49/89) The steamboat

used in the 1951 movie starring Humphrey Bogart and Katharine Hepburn has been restored to its former splendor, and you can relive the movie aboard the tiny vessel on a canal or dinner cruise. If you behave better than Hepburn's character, the captain might even let you take the helm for a bit.

Garl's Coastal Kayaking   ECOTOUR
(☑ 305-393-3223; www.garlscoastalkayaking.com; 4hr tours adult/child $75/50, single/double kayak hire per day $40/55) 🚣 Garl's is an excellent ecotour operator that gets customers into the Everglades backcountry and mangrove islets of Florida Bay via kayak and canoe. It also provides reasonable equipment rentals.

🛏 Sleeping & Eating

Hilton Key Largo Resort   HOTEL $$
(☑ 305-852-5553; www.keylargoresort.com; Mile 102 bayside; r/ste from $200/280; P 🛜 🏊) This Hilton has a ton of character. Folks just seem to get all laid-back when lounging in clean, designer rooms outfitted in blues and greens with balconies overlooking the water. The grounds are enormous and include an artificial waterfall-fed pool and frontage to a rather large stretch of private white-sand beach. Book online for the best rates.

Jules' Undersea Lodge   HOTEL $$$
(☑ 305-451-2353; www.jul.com; 51 Shoreland Dr, Mile 103.2 oceanside; s/d/tr $675/800/1050) There's lots of talk about underwater hotels getting built in Dubai and Fiji, but as of writing, Jules' Undersea Lodge is still the only place in the world outside of a submarine where you and your significant other can join the 'five-fathom club' (we're not elaborating). Once a research station, this module has been converted into a delightfully cheesy Keys motel, but wetter.

DJ's Diner   AMERICAN $
(☑ 305-451-2999; 99411 Overseas Hwy; mains $8-15; ⏱ 7am-3pm; P 🛜 ♿) You're greeted by a mural of Humphrey Bogart, James Dean *and* Marilyn Monroe – that's a lot of Americana. It's all served with a heapin' helpin' of diner faves amid vinyl-boothed ambience. Breakfast is a big draw with fluffy omelets, eggs Benedict and waffles.

Fish House   SEAFOOD $$
(☑ 305-451-4665; www.fishhouse.com; Mile 102.4 oceanside; mains lunch $12-21, dinner $21-30; ⏱ 11:30am-10pm; P ♿) The Fish House delivers on the promise of its title – very good fish, bought whole from local fishers and

prepared fried, broiled, jerked, blackened or chargrilled. Because the Fish House only uses fresh fish, the menu changes daily based on what is available.

Islamorada

Islamorada (eye-luh-murr-*ah*-da) is also known as 'The Village of Islands.' Doesn't that sound pretty? Well, it really is. This little string of pearls (well, keys) – Plantation, Upper and Lower Matecumbe, Shell and Lignumvitae (lignum-*vite*-ee) – shimmers as one of the prettiest stretches of the islands. This is where the scrubby mangrove is replaced by unbroken horizons of ocean and sky, one perfect shade of blue mirroring the other. Islamorada stretches across some 20 miles, from Mile Marker 90 to 74.

⊙ Sights & Activities

★ **Florida Keys History of Diving Museum**   MUSEUM
(☑ 305-664-9737; www.divingmuseum.org; Mile 83; adult/child $12/6; ⏱ 10am-5pm; P ♿) You can't miss the diving museum – it's the building with the enormous mural of whale sharks on the side. The journey into the undersea covers 4000 years, with fascinating pieces like the 1797 Klingert's copper kettle, a whimsical room devoted to Jules Verne's Captain Nemo, massive deep-diving suits and an exquisite display of diving helmets from around the world. These imaginative galleries reflect the charming quirks of the Keys.

Windley Key Fossil Reef Geological State Site   STATE PARK
(☑ 305-664-2540; www.floridastateparks.org/windleykey; Mile 85.5 oceanside; admission/tour $2.50/2; ⏱ 8am-5pm Thu-Mon) To get his railroad built across the islands, Henry Flagler had to quarry out some sizable chunks of the Keys. The best evidence of those efforts can be found at this former quarry-turned-state park. Windley has leftover quarry machinery scattered along an 8ft former quarry wall, with fossilized evidence of brain and staghorn coral embedded right in the rock. The wall offers a cool (and rare) public peek into the stratum of coral that forms the substrate of the Keys.

★ **Robbie's Marina**   BOATING
(☑ 305-664-8070; www.robbies.com; Mile 77.5 bayside; kayak & stand-up paddleboard rentals $45-80; ⏱ 9am-8pm; ♿) More than a boat launch, Robbie's is a local flea market, tacky

tourist shop, sea pen for tarpons (massive fish) and jump-off point for fishing expeditions, all wrapped into one driftwood-laced compound. Boat-rental and tour options are also available. The best reason to visit is to escape the mayhem and hire a kayak for a peaceful paddle through nearby mangroves, hammocks and lagoons.

🛏 Sleeping & Eating

Conch On Inn   MOTEL $
(☎305-852-9309; www.conchoninn.com; 103 Caloosa St, Mile 89.5; r $100-180; P🐾) A motel popular with yearly snowbirds, Conch On Inn has simple but cheerfully painted rooms that are clean, comfortable and well equipped. The waterfront deck is a fine spot to unwind – and look for manatees; up to 14 have been spotted off the dock here!

Lime Tree Bay Resort Motel   MOTEL $$
(☎305-664-4740; www.limetreebayresort.com; Mile 68.5 bayside; r $180-360; 🐾) A plethora of hammocks and lawn chairs provides front-row seats for the spectacular sunsets at this 2.5-acre waterfront hideaway. The rooms are comfortably set, the best with balconies overlooking the water. The extensive facilities include use of tennis courts, bikes, kayaks and stand-up paddleboards.

Bad Boy Burrito   MEXICAN $
(☎305-509-7782; www.badboyburrito.com/isl amorada; 103 Mastic St, Mile 81.8 bayside; mains $8-15; ⊙10am-6pm Mon-Sat; 🐾) Tucked away in a tiny plaza among a gurgling fountain, orchids and swaying palms, Bad Boy Burrito whips up superb fish tacos and its namesake burritos – with quality ingredients (skirt steak, duck confit, zucchini and squash) and all the fixings (shaved cabbage, chipotle mayo, housemade salsa). Top it off with a hibiscus tea and some chips and guacamole.

★Lazy Days   SEAFOOD $$
(☎305-664-5256; www.lazydaysislamorada.com; 79867 Overseas Hwy, oceanside; mains $18-34; 🐾) One of Islamorada's culinary icons, Lazy Days has a stellar reputation for its fresh seafood plates. Start off with a conch chowder topped with a little sherry (provided), before moving on to a decadent hogfish Poseidon (fish topped with shrimp, scallops and key lime butter) or a straight-up boiled seafood platter (half lobster, shrimp, catch of the day and other delicacies).

Marathon

Marathon sits right on the halfway point between Key Largo and Key West, and it's a good place to stop on a road trip across the islands. It's perhaps the most 'developed' key outside Key West (that's really pushing the definition of the word 'developed') in the sense that it has large shopping centers and a population of over 8000. Then again it's still a place where exiles from the mainland fish, booze it up and have a good time, so while Marathon is more family-friendly than Key West, it's hardly G-rated.

🛏 Sleeping & Eating

Seascape Motel & Marina   MOTEL $$
(☎305-743-6212; www.seascapemotelandmarina. com; 1075 75th St Ocean E, btwn Mile 51 & 52; r $250-450; P🐾) The classy, understated luxury in this B&B manifests in its 12 rooms, all of which have a different feel – from old-fashioned cottage to sleek boutique. It has a waterfront pool, kayaks and stand-up paddleboards for guests to use, and its secluded setting will make you feel like you've gotten away from it all.

Tranquility Bay   RESORT $$$
(☎305-289-0667; www.tranquilitybay.com; Mile 48.5 bayside; r $340-700; P🐾) If you're serious about going upscale, you should book in here. Tranquility Bay is a massive condo-hotel resort with plush townhouses, high-thread-count sheets and all-in-white chic. The grounds are enormous and activity-filled; they really don't want you to leave.

★Keys Fisheries   SEAFOOD $$
(☎866-743-4353; www.keysfisheries.com; 3502 Louisa St; mains $12-27; ⊙11am-9pm; P🐾) The lobster Reuben is the stuff of legend. Sweet, chunky, creamy – so good you'll be daydreaming about it afterward. But you can't go wrong with any of the excellent seafood here, all served with sass. Expect pleasant levels of seagull harassment as you dine on a working waterfront.

Lower Keys

The people of the Lower Keys vary between winter escapees and native Conchs. Some local families have been Keys castaways for generations, and there is somewhat of a more insular feel than other parts of the Overseas Hwy. It's an odd contrast: the islands get at their most isolated, rural and quintessentially 'Keez-y' before opening onto (relatively) cosmopolitan, heterogeneous and free-spirited Key West.

People aside, the big draw in the lower Keys is nature. You'll find the loveliest state park in the Keys here, and one of its rarest species. For paddlers, there is a great mangrove wilderness to explore in a photogenic and pristine environment.

The **Bahia Honda State Park** (🕿305-872-3210; www.bahiahondapark.com; Mile 37; car $4-8, cyclist & pedestrian $2.50; ☺8am-sunset; 🅿) 🏊, with its long, white-sand (and at times seaweed-strewn) beach, named Sandspur Beach by locals, is the big attraction in these parts. As Keys beaches go, this one is probably the best natural stretch of sand in the island chain. There's also the novel experience of walking on the **old Bahia Honda Rail Bridge**, which offers nice views of the surrounding islands. Heading out on kayaking adventures (from $12/36 per hour/half day) is another great way to spend a sun-drenched afternoon.

Key West

Key West is the far frontier, edgier and more eccentric than the other keys, and also far more captivating. At its heart, this 7-sq-mile island feels like a beautiful tropical oasis, where the moonflowers bloom at night and the classical Caribbean homes are so sad and romantic it's hard not to sigh at them.

While Key West has obvious allure, it's not without its contradictions. On one side of the road, there are literary festivals, Caribbean villas, tropical dining rooms and expensive art galleries. On the other, an S&M fetishist parade, frat boys passing out on the sidewalk and grizzly bars filled with bearded burnouts. With all that in mind, it's easy to find your groove in this setting, no matter where your interests lie.

As in other parts of the Keys, nature plays a starring role here, with some breathtaking sunsets – cause for nightly celebration down on Mallory Sq.

◉ Sights

★ **Museum of Art & History at the Custom House**   MUSEUM
(🕿305-295-6616; www.kwahs.com; 281 Front St; adult/child $10/5; ☺9:30am-4:30pm) Those wanting to learn a bit about Key West history shouldn't miss this excellent museum at the end of the road. Among the highlights:

photographs and archival footage from the building of the ambitious Overseas Hwy (and the hurricane that killed 400 people), a model of the ill-fated USS *Maine* (sunk during the Spanish-American War) and the Navy's role in Key West (once the largest employer), and exhibits on the 'wreckers' of Key West, who made their fortune scavenging sunken treasure ships.

★ **Mallory Square**   SQUARE
(www.mallorysquare.com; 🅿) Take all those energies, subcultures and oddities of Keys life and focus them into one torchlit, family-friendly (but playfully edgy), sunset-enriched street party. The child of all these raucous forces is Mallory Sq, one of the greatest shows on Earth. It begins in the hours leading up to dusk, the sinking sun a signal to bring on the madness. Watch a dog walk a tightrope, a man swallow fire, and British acrobats tumble and sass each other.

Duval Street   AREA
Key West locals have a love-hate relationship with the most famous road in Key West (if not the Keys). Duval, Old Town Key West's main strip, is a miracle mile of booze, tacky everything and awful behavior. But it's fun. The 'Duval Crawl' is one of the wildest pub crawls in the country. The mix of neon drink, drag shows, T-shirt kitsch, local theaters, art studios and boutiques is more charming than jarring.

Hemingway House   HOUSE
(🕿305-294-1136; www.hemingwayhome.com; 907 Whitehead St; adult/child $14/6; ☺9am-5pm) Key West's biggest darling, Ernest Hemingway, lived in this gorgeous Spanish Colonial house from 1931 to 1940. Papa moved here in his early 1930s with wife No 2, a *Vogue* fashion editor and (former) friend of wife No 1 (he left the house when he ran off with wife No 3). *The Short Happy Life of Francis Macomber* and *The Green Hills of Africa* were produced here, as well as many six-toed cats, whose descendants basically run the grounds.

🏃 Activities

Dive Key West   DIVING
(🕿305-296-3823; www.divekeywest.com; 3128 N Roosevelt Blvd; snorkel/scuba from $60/75) Largest dive facility on the island, offering morning, afternoon and night dives. Wreck-diving trips cost $145 with all equipment and air provided (it's $160 with a wetsuit).

☞ Tours

Old Town Trolley Tours   TOURS
(📞 855-623-8289; www.trolleytours.com; adult/
child/senior $32/11/29; ⏱ tours 9am-4:30pm; ♿)
These tours are a great introduction to the
city. The 90-minute, hop-on, hop-off narrated tram tour starts at Mallory Sq and makes
a loop around the whole city, with 12 stops
along the way. Trolleys depart every 15 to 30
minutes from 9am to 4:30pm daily. The narration is hokey, but you'll get a good overview of Key West history.

✦ Festivals & Events

Womenfest   LGBT
(www.womenfest.com; ⏱ Sep) One of North
America's biggest lesbian celebrations,
Womenfest is four days of merrymaking,
with pool parties, art shows, roller derby,
drag brunches, sunset sails, flag football,
and a tattoo and moustache bicycle ride. It's
great fun, with thousands descending on
Key West from all corners of the USA and
beyond.

★ Fantasy Fest   CULTURAL
(www.fantasyfest.net; ⏱ late Oct) Akin to New
Orleans' riotous Mardi Gras revelry, Fantasy
Fest is 10 days of burlesque parties, parades,
street fairs, concerts and loads of costumed
events. Bars and inns get competitive about
decorating their properties, and everyone
gets decked out in the most outrageous costumes they can cobble together (or get mostly naked with daring body paint).

🛏 Sleeping

Key West Youth Hostel &
Seashell Motel   HOSTEL $$
(📞 305-296-5719; www.keywesthostel.com; 718
South St; dm $55, d $120-240; 🅿 ❄ 🛜) This
place isn't winning any design awards, but
the staff are kind, and it's one of the only
lower-priced choices on the island. The
dorms and motel rooms have plain white
tile floors, though the cheery paint job in
some rooms (yellow or blue and white)
somewhat breaks the monotony. The back
patio is a fine place to meet other travelers.

Casablanca Key West   GUESTHOUSE $$
(📞 305-296-0815; www.keywestcasablanca.com;
900 Duval St; r $180-400; ❄ 🛜 🏊) On the quiet-
er end of Duval St, the Casablanca is a
friendly eight-room guesthouse with a delightful tropical elegance. The inn, once a
private house, was built in 1898 and hosted
a few luminaries over the years, including
Humphrey Bogart who stayed here in 1937.
The rooms are bright, with polished wood
floors and comfy beds; and some have little
balconies.

Saint Hotel   BOUTIQUE HOTEL $$$
(📞 305-294-3200; www.thesainthotelkeywest.
com; 417 Eaton St; r $360-700; ❄ 🛜 🏊) Despite
its proximity to Duval St, the Saint feels
like a world removed with its plush rooms,
chic minimalist lobby, photogenic pool with
small cascading waterfall, and artfully de-
signed bar. The best rooms have balconies
overlooking the pool.

🍴 Eating

Pierogi Polish Market   EASTERN EUROPEAN $
(📞 305-292-0464; 1008 White St; mains $5-11;
⏱ pierogi counter 11am-7pm Mon-Sat, shop 10am-
8pm Mon-Sat, noon-6pm Sun; 🅿 🍴) The Keys
have an enormous seasonal population
of temporary workers largely drawn from
Central and Eastern Europe. This is where
those workers can revisit the motherland,
via pierogies, dumplings, blinis and a great
sandwich selection. Although it's called a
Polish market, there's food here that caters
to Hungarians, Czechs and Russians (among
others).

Garbo's Grill   FUSION $
(www.garbosgrillkw.com; 409 Caroline St; mains
$10-14; ⏱ 11am-10pm Mon-Sat) Just off the
beaten path, Garbo's whips up delicious ta-
cos with creative toppings like mango ginger
habanero-glazed shrimp, Korean barbecue,
and fresh mahimahi with all the fixings, as
well as gourmet burgers and hot dogs. It's
served out of a sleek Airstream trailer, which
faces onto a shaded brick patio dotted with
outdoor tables.

The Café   VEGETARIAN $$
(📞 305-296-5515; www.thecafekw.com; 509
Southard St; mains $12-22; ⏱ 9am-10pm; 🍴)
The oldest vegetarian spot in Key West is
a sunny luncheonette by day that morphs
into a buzzing, low-lit eating and drinking
spot by night. The cooking is outstanding,
with an eclectic range of dishes: Thai curry
stir-fries, Italian veggie meatball subs, pizza
with shaved brussels sprouts, and a famous
veggie burger.

★ Thirsty Mermaid   SEAFOOD $$
(📞 305-204-4828; www.thirstymermaidkeywest.
com; 521 Fleming St; mains $12-28; ⏱ 11am-
11:30pm; 🍴) Aside from having a great name,
the pint-sized Thirsty Mermaid deserves

high marks for its outstanding seafood and stylish but easygoing atmosphere. The menu is a celebration of culinary treasures from the sea, with a raw bar of oysters, ceviche, middleneck clams and even caviar. Among the main courses, seared diver scallops or togarashi-spiced tuna with jasmine rice are outstanding.

★ **Blue Heaven** AMERICAN $$$
(☑ 305-296-8666; www.blueheavenkw.com; 729 Thomas St; mains breakfast & lunch $10-17, dinner $22-35; ☺ 8am-10:30pm; ☀) Proof that location is *nearly* everything, this is one of the quirkiest venues on an island of oddities. Customers (and free-roaming fowl) flock to dine in the ramshackle, tropical plant-filled garden where Hemingway once officiated boxing matches. This place gets packed with customers who wolf down delectable breakfasts (blueberry pancakes) and Keys cuisine with French touches (like yellowtail snapper with citrus beurre blanc).

🍷 Drinking & Entertainment

★ **Green Parrot** BAR
(☑ 305-294-6133; www.greenparrot.com; 601 Whitehead St; ☺ 10am-4am) The oldest bar on an island of bars, this rogues' cantina opened in the late 19th century and hasn't closed yet. Its ramshackle interior – complete with local artwork littering the walls and a parachute stretched across the ceiling – only adds to the atmosphere, as does the colorful crowd, obviously out for a good time.

Captain Tony's Saloon BAR
(☑ 305-294-1838; www.capttonyssaloon.com; 428 Greene St; ☺ 10am-2am) Propagandists would have you believe the nearby megabar complex of Sloppy Joe's was Hemingway's original bar, but the physical place where the old man drank was right here, the original Sloppy Joe's location (before it was moved onto Duval St and into frat-boy hell). Hemingway's third wife (a journalist sent to profile Papa) seduced him in this very bar.

Irish Kevin's BAR
(☑ 305-292-1262; www.irishkevins.com; 211 Duval St; ☺ 10am-3:30am) One of the most popular megabars on Duval, Kevin's has a pretty good entertainment formula pinned down: nightly live acts that are a cross between a folk singer, radio shock jock and pep-rally cheerleader. The crowd consistently goes wild for acoustic covers of favorites from 1980 onward mixed with boozy, Lee Greenwood-esque patriotic exhortations.

La Te Da CABARET
(☑ 305-296-6706; www.lateda.com; 1125 Duval St; ☺ shows 8:30pm) While the outside bar is where locals gather for mellow chats over beer, you can catch high-quality drag acts – big names come here from around the country – upstairs at the fabulous Crystal Room on weekends (admission $26). More low-key cabaret acts grace the downstairs lounge.

ℹ Information

Citizen (www.keysnews.com) A well-written, oft-amusing daily.
Key West Chamber of Commerce (☑ 305-294-2587; www.keywestchamber.org; 510 Greene St; ☺ 9am-6pm) An excellent source of information.
Key Wester (www.thekeywester.com) Restaurant reviews and upcoming events.

ℹ Getting Around

Once you're in Key West, the best way to get around is by bicycle (rentals from the Duval St area, hotels and hostels cost from $10 a day). For transportation within the Duval St area, the free Duval Loop shuttle (www.carfreekeywest.com/duval-loop) runs from 6pm to midnight.

Other options include **Key West Transit** (☑ 305-600-1455; www.kwtransit.com; day pass $4-8), with color-coded buses running about every 15 minutes; mopeds, which generally cost from $35 per day ($60 for a two-seater); or the open-sided electric tourist cars, aka 'Conch cruisers,' which travel at 35mph and cost about $140/200 for a four-seater/six-seater per day.

A&M Scooter Rentals (☑ 305-896-1921; www.amscooterskeywest.com; 523 Truman Ave; bicycle/scooter/electric car per day from $10/35/140; ☺ 9am-7pm) rents out scooters and bicycles, as well as open-sided electric cars that can seat from two to six, and offers free delivery.

Parking can be tricky in town. There's a free parking lot on Fort St off Truman Ave.

ATLANTIC COAST

Florida's northern Atlantic Coast is an exurban riviera for north Florida and the Deep South, a land of long beaches shadowed under tall condo complexes and seaside mansions. Heading from south to north, you'll pass the exhaust pipes and biker bars of Daytona Beach, continue through mellow Flagler Beach, and on to historic St Augustine, where a one- or two-night sojourn is highly recommended.

An affluent series of beaches can be found just south of spread-out Jacksonville, which forms an urban break in the coastal living; many continue north from here to charming Amelia Island and the Florida–Georgia border. Along the way you'll discover a jumbled necklace of grassy barrier islands, interlaced with tidal inlets, salt marsh flats and dark clumps of maritime forest.

Space Coast

More than 40 miles of barrier-island Atlantic Coast stretch from Canaveral National Seashore south to Melbourne Beach, encompassing undeveloped stretches of endless white sand, an entrenched surf culture and pockets of Old Florida.

The Kennedy Space Center and several small museums dedicated to the history, heroes and science of the United States' space program give the Space Coast its name, and the region's tourist hub of Cocoa Beach is just south of Cape Canaveral's launching point for massive cruise ships. But beyond the 3-D space movies, tiki-hut bars and surf shops, the Space Coast offers quintessential Florida wildlife for everyone from grandmas to toddlers. Kayak with manatees, camp on a private island or simply stroll along miles and miles of sandy white beaches.

Sights & Activities

★Kennedy Space Center MUSEUM

(☎866-737-5235; www.kennedyspacecenter.com; NASA Pkwy, Merritt Island; adult/child 3-11yr $50/40; ⏲9am-6pm) Whether you're mildly interested in space or a die-hard sci-fi fan, a visit to the Space Center is awe inspiring. To get a good overview, start at the Early Space Exploration exhibit, progress to the 90-minute bus tour to the Apollo/Saturn V Center (where you'll find the best on-site cafe) and finish at the awesome *Atlantis* exhibit, where you can walk beneath the heat-scorched fuselage of a shuttle that traveled more than 126,000,000 miles through space on 33 missions.

★Merritt Island National Wildlife Refuge WILDLIFE RESERVE

(☎321-861-5601; www.fws.gov/merrittisland; Black Point Wildlife Dr, off FL-406; vehicle $10; ⏲dawn-dusk) FREE This unspoiled 140,000-acre refuge is one of the country's best birding spots, especially from October to May (early morning and after 4pm). More endangered and threatened species of wildlife inhabit the swamps, marshes and hardwood hammocks here than at any other site in the continental US. The best viewing is on **Black Point Wildlife Drive**.

Canaveral National Seashore NATIONAL PARK

(☎386-428-3384; www.nps.gov/cana; car/bike $10/1; ⏲6am-8pm) The 24 miles of pristine, windswept beaches here comprise the longest stretch of undeveloped beach on Florida's east coast. They include family-friendly **Apollo Beach** on the north end with its gentle surf, untrammeled **Klondike Beach** in the middle – a favorite of nature lovers – and **Playalinda Beach** to the south, which is surfer central and includes a nudist section near lot 13.

★Sea-Turtle Nesting Tours ECOTOUR

(☎386-428-3384; adult/child 8-16yr $14/free; ⏲8pm-midnight Jun & Jul) In the summer, rangers lead groups of up to 30 people on these nightly tours, with about a 75% chance of spotting the little guys. Reservations are required (beginning May 15 for June trips, June 15 for July trips); children under eight are not allowed.

Sleeping

Residence Inn Cape Canaveral HOTEL $$

(☎321-323-1100; www.marriott.com; 8959 Astronaut Blvd; r from $140; P ❄ 🛜 🏊) If you want to get away from the Cocoa Beach party scene, book into this comfortable Marriott hotel. Rooms may be corporate, but they offer acres of space, comfortable beds and kitchenettes. Staff are also extremely accommodating and there's a pretty pool area.

★Beach Place Guesthouses APARTMENT $$$

(☎321-783-4045; www.beachplaceguesthouses.com; 1445 S Atlantic Ave; ste $199-399; P 🛜) A slice of heavenly relaxation in Cocoa Beach's partying beach scene, this laid-back two-story guesthouse has roomy suites with hammocks and a lovely deck, all just steps from the dunes and beach. Colorful art and greenery abound on the property.

Eating

Melbourne Beach Market MARKET $

(☎321-676-5225; 302 Ocean Ave; ⏲8am-8pm Mon-Sat, to 7pm Sun) Pick up picnic essentials here, including ready-to-eat meals.

★ **Green Room Cafe** VEGETARIAN $
(☑ 321-868-0203; www.greenroomcafecocoa
beach.com; 222 N 1st St; mains $6-12; ☺ 10:30am-
9pm Mon-Sat; ✍) Focusing all its energies on
the 'goodness within', this super cafe delights
the health-conscious with fruit-combo acai
bowls, wheat- and gluten-free sandwiches,
real fruit smoothies and homemade soups
and wraps. If the 'Tower of Power' smoothie (acai, peach, strawberry, honey and apple
juice) fails to lift you, the vibrant decor and
friendly company will.

★ **Seafood Atlantic** SEAFOOD $$
(☑ 321-784-1963; www.seafoodatlantic.org; 520
Glen Cheek Dr, Port Canaveral; mains $8-19;
☺ 11am-7pm Wed-Sun, seafood market from 10am)
With deep roots in Canaveral's fishing in-
dustry, this restaurant (with outdoor deck) is
one of the few places to serve locally sourced
shrimp, crabs, mussels, clams, oysters and
fish. If they're in, order a bucket of Florida's
deep-sea golden crab, which has a delicious-
ly moist and creamy texture. Also, bring a
bag and stock up at the market next door.

❶ Information

**Canaveral National Seashore Visitor Infor-
mation Center** (☑ 386-428-3384; www.nps.
gov/cana; 7611 S Atlantic Ave, New Smyrna;
☺ 8am-6pm Oct-Mar, to 8pm Apr-Sep) is lo-
cated just south of the North District entrance
gate. Alternatively, the visitor center at Merritt
Island National Wildlife Refuge can also provide
information.

There is a fee station at both the North and
South District entrances. There is a toilet at
most beach parking areas.

Note that the park can experience temporary
closures around launch time. For information on
launch closures, call ☑ 321-867-4077.

❶ Getting There & Away

Orlando Melbourne International Airport
(☑ 321-723-6227; www.mlbair.com; 1 Air
Terminal Pkwy) is the closest airport to most
destinations on the Space Coast. It is a growing
airport served by Delta, American Airlines, Elite
Airways, Porter Airlines and Baer, as well as all
the major rental-car companies and the SCAT
bus No 21.

Alternatively, Orlando International Airport
is about 50 minutes west of Cocoa Beach, and
Orlando Sanford International Airport is a little
over an hour to the northwest of Cocoa Beach.

There are two ways to arrive in Cape Canaveral:
traveling north on A1A from Cocoa Beach, or west
on A1A across the Banana River via Merritt Island.

Cape Canaveral is served by **SCAT** (SCAT;
☑ 321-633-1878; www.321transit.com; per ride
$1.50, 10-ride/30-day pass $6/21; ☺ schedule
varies) buses. Rte 9 connects it with Cocoa
Beach and Rte 4 connects it with Cocoa Village.

Daytona Beach

Long the vacation destination of choice for
leather-clad bikers, rev heads and spring
breakers, Daytona Beach is most famous as
the birthplace of NASCAR racing and the
home of the Daytona 500.

The area's population quintuples during
Speedweeks; as many as half a million bik-
ers roar into town for **Bike Week** in March
and **Biketoberfest** in October. If Confeder-
ate flags, loud motorcycles, jacked-up pick-
up trucks and the folks who love all of the
above are your thing, you might have found
your heaven on earth. If not, move on.

If you can see past the garish beachside
barricade of '70s high-rise blocks, nightclubs
and tourist traps (if not quite literally), you
might witness the phenomena of nesting
sea turtles (in season) or explore a hand-
ful of interesting and worthwhile cultural
attractions.

◉ Sights & Activities

★ **Daytona International
Speedway** STADIUM
(☑ 800-748-7467; www.daytonainternationalspeed
way.com; 1801 W International Speedway Blvd;
tours from $18; ☺ tours 9:30am-3:30pm) The
Holy Grail of raceways has a diverse race
schedule. Ticket prices skyrocket for good
seats at big races, headlined by the **Daytona
500** in February. It's worth wandering the
massive stands for free on non-race days.
First-come, first-served tram tours take in
the track, pits and behind-the-scenes areas,
while all-access tours give you a glimpse of
media rooms and pit stalls.

**Southeast Museum of
Photography** MUSEUM
(☑ 386-506-3894; www.smponline.org; 1200 W
International Speedway Blvd, Bldg 1200; ☺ 11am-
5pm Tue, Thu, Fri, 11am-7pm Wed, 1-5pm Sat & Sun)
FREE We love this hidden treasure in Day-
tona, a service of the Daytona State College:
it's the only museum in Florida dedicated
solely to photography. This vibrant modern
gallery with excellent lighting and facilities
doesn't shy away from provocative subjects
in its rotating exhibitions.

Richard Petty Driving Experience
DRIVING

(☑800-237-3889; www.drivepetty.com; from $109; ☺dates vary) If merely watching NAS-CAR drivers streak around the track isn't adrenaline-pumping enough for you, get in the car yourself via the Richard Petty Driving Experience. Choose from several levels of death-defying action, from the three-lap passenger-seat Race Ride (from $109) to the intensive Racing Experience ($3200), which puts you behind the wheel for 50 white-knuckle laps. Dates vary; check online.

🛏 Sleeping & Eating

Hyatt Place Daytona Beach Oceanfront
HOTEL $$

(☑386-944-2010; www.daytonabeach.place. hyatt.com; 3161 S Atlantic Ave, Daytona Beach Shores; r from $114; P@🛜🌊) Some of Daytona's freshest, funkiest and most functional rooms can be found here. All rooms feature balconies, plush bedding, separate living and sleeping areas and a nifty panel to easily connect your laptop or iPod to the 42in panel TV.

Plaza Resort & Spa
RESORT $$

(☑844-284-2685; www.plazaresortandspa.com; 600 N Atlantic Ave; r from $109; P🛜🌊) Built in 1908, Daytona's most historic resort has undergone extensive renovations in its time, but still maintains its old-world charm. If only the walls could talk... From the miles of honey-colored marble lining the lobby to the 42in plasma TVs and cloud-soft beds in the rooms, to the 15,000-sq-ft spa, this resort coos luxury.

Cracked Egg Diner
BREAKFAST $

(☑386-788-6772; www.thecrackedeggdiner.com; 3280 S Atlantic Ave, Daytona Beach Shores; breakfast items $4-11; ☺7am-3pm; P🍴) Best for breakfast, this cheery joint in Daytona Beach Shores became so popular they annexed the building next door. Brainchild of brothers Chris and Kevin, one of whom will usually greet you at the door with a smile, their mission is to deliver breakfast egg-cellence. (Sorry. It had to happen.) We think they do a pretty fine job.

Aunt Catfish's on the River
SOUTHERN US $$

(☑386-767-4768; www.auntcatfishontheriver. com; 4009 Halifax Dr, Port Orange; mains $8-28; ☺11:30am-9pm Mon-Sat, from 9am Sun; P🍴) Fresh-from-the-boat grouper and mahimahi lolling in butter or deeply and deliciously fried, as well as Southern-style Cajun-spiced catfish make this riverside seafood establishment insanely popular with tourists: table waits can be expected. It's just outside Daytona Beach in Port Orange.

Information

Daytona Beach Area Convention & Visitors Bureau (☑386-255-0415; www.daytonabeach. com; 126 E Orange Ave; ☺8:30am-5pm Mon-Fri) In person or online, these guys are *the* authority on all things Daytona Beach.

❶ Getting There & Away

Daytona Beach is close to the intersection of two major interstates, I-95 and I-4. The I-95 is the quickest way to Jacksonville (about 90 miles) and Miami (260 miles), though Hwy A1A and Hwy 1 are more scenic. Beville Rd, an east–west thoroughfare south of Daytona proper, becomes I-4 after crossing I-95; it's the fastest route to Orlando (55 miles).

Daytona Beach International Airport (☑386-248-8030; www.flydaytonafirst.com; 700 Catalina Dr) Just east of the Speedway; is served by Delta and US Airways, and all major car-rental companies.

Greyhound (☑386-255-7076; www.greyhound. com; 138 S Ridgewood Ave) Has connections to most major cities in Florida, and beyond.

St Augustine

The oldest continuously occupied European settlement in the US, St Augustine was founded by the Spanish in 1565. Today, its 144-block National Historic Landmark District is a major tourist destination. For the most part, St Augustine exudes charm and maintains its integrity, although there's no denying the presence of some tacky tourist traps: miniature theme parks, tour operators at almost every turn and horse-drawn carriages clip-clopping past townsfolk dressed in period costume.

What makes St Augustine so genuinely endearing is the accessibility of its rich history via countless top-notch museums and the authenticity of its centuries-old architecture, monuments and narrow cobbled lanes. Unlike Florida's numerous historical theme parks, St Augustine is the real deal.

You'll find a diverse array of wonderful B&Bs, cozy cafes and lamp-lit pubs, and while fine dining might not be the first thing that comes to mind at Florida's mention, it is certainly synonymous with St Augustine.

History

Timucuans settled what is now St Augustine about 1000 BC, hunting alligators and cultivating corn and tobacco. In 1513, Spanish explorer Juan Ponce de León sighted land, came ashore and claimed La Florida (Land of Flowers) for Spain. In 1565 his compatriot Don Pedro Menéndez de Avilés arrived on the feast day of Augustine of Hippo, and accordingly christened the town San Augustín: 42 years prior to the founding of Jamestown (Virginia) and 55 years before that of Plymouth (Massachusetts).

Menéndez quickly established a military base against the French, who had established Fort Caroline near present-day Jacksonville. The French fleet did him the favor of getting stuck in a hurricane; Menéndez' men butchered the survivors. By the time Spain ceded Florida to the US in 1821, St Augustine had been sacked, looted, burned and occupied by pirates and Spanish, British, Georgian and South Carolinian forces.

Today the city's buildings, made of coquina – a DIY concrete made of sedimentary rock mixed with crushed shells – lend an enchanting quality to the slender streets. The city's long and colorful history is palpable, narrated by what seems like innumerable museums, monuments and galleries.

⊙ Sights

All of St Augustine's historic district feels like a museum; there are literally dozens of attractions to choose from. Narrow little **Aviles St**, the oldest European-settled street in the country, and long, pedestrian-only **St George St** are both lined with galleries, cafes, museums and pubs.

★ Lightner Museum   MUSEUM

(📞 904-824-2874; www.lightnermuseum.org; 75 King St; adult/child $10/5; ⊙9am-5pm) Henry Flagler's former Hotel Alcazar is home to this wonderful museum, with a little bit of everything, from ornate Gilded Age furnishings to collections of marbles and cigar-box labels. The dramatic and imposing building itself is a must-see, dating back to 1887 and designed in the Spanish Renaissance–revival style by New York City architects Carrère & Hastings.

Castillo de San Marcos National Monument   FORT

(📞 904-829-6506; www.nps.gov/casa; 1 S Castillo Dr; adult/child under 15 yr $10/free; ⊙8:45am-

5pm; 🅿🚻) 🖉 This photogenic fort is an atmospheric monument to longevity: it's the country's oldest masonry fort, completed by the Spanish in 1695. In its time, the fort has been besieged twice and changed hands between nations *six* times – from Spain to Britain to Spain Part II to the USA to the Confederate States of America to the USA again.

Villa Zorayda Museum   MUSEUM

(📞 904-829-9887; www.villazorayda.com; 83 King St; adult/child $10/4; ⊙10am-5pm Mon-Sat, 11am-4pm Sun; 🅿) Looking like a faux Spanish castle from a medieval theme park, this gray edifice was built out of a mix of concrete and local coquina shells in 1883. The structure was the fantasy (and maybe fever dream) of an eccentric millionaire who was obsessed with Spain's 12th-century Alhambra Palace. Today, it's an odd but engaging museum. The Moorish-style atrium and rooms contain quirky antiques, archaeological pieces and other artifacts: highlights being a 2400-year-old mummy's foot and an Egyptian 'Sacred Cat Rug.'

Hotel Ponce de León   HISTORIC BUILDING

(📞 904-823-3378; http://legacy.flagler.edu/pages/tours; 74 King St; tours adult/child $10/1; ⊙tours hourly 10am-3pm summer, 10am & 2pm during school year) This striking former luxury hotel, built in the 1880s, is now the world's most gorgeous dormitory, belonging to Flagler College, who purchased and saved it in 1967. Guided tours are recommended to get a sense of the detail and history of this magnificent Spanish Renaissance building.

Colonial Quarter   MUSEUM

(📞 904-342-2857; www.colonialquarter.com; 33 St George St; adult/child $13/7; ⊙10am-5pm) See how they did things back in the 18th century at this re-creation of Spanish Colonial St Augustine, complete with craftspeople demonstrating blacksmithing, leather working, musket shooting and all sorts of historical stuff.

St Augustine Beach   BEACH

(350 A1A Beach Blvd; ⊙sunrise-sunset) This white-sand beach almost gets lost in the historical mix, but hey, it's Florida, so a visit wouldn't be complete without a little bit of sun and surf. There's a visitor information booth at the foot of **St Johns Pier**, where you can rent a rod and reel (two hours for $3, plus $1 for each additional hour). About three blocks south of the pier, the end of A St has – as Florida goes – some fine waves.

☞ Tours

★ St Augustine Gold Tours TOURS

(☑ 904-325-0547; www.staugustinegoldtours.com; 6 Cordova St; adult/child $25/15) This outfit, the brainchild of a retired British couple, is a standout in the crowded St Augustine tour scene. You're assured a fascinating and articulate insight into St Augustine's history. Private and small-group tours are conducted in a quiet electric vehicle that gets into places where the other tours can't.

🍽 Sleeping & Eating

★ At Journey's End B&B $$

(☑904-829-0076; www.atjourneysend.com; 89 Cedar St; r $166-289; P🐾🛜🐾) Free from the granny-ish decor that haunts many St Augustine B&Bs, this pet-friendly, kid-friendly and gay-friendly spot is outfitted in a chic mix of antiques and modern furniture and is run by friendly, knowledgeable hosts. Mouthwatering breakfasts and complimentary wifi, concierge services, and beer, wine and soda throughout your stay are some of the inclusions that set At Journey's End apart.

Jaybird's Inn MOTEL $$

(☑ 904-342-7938; www.jaybirdsinn.com; 2700 N Ponce de Leon Blvd; r $110-150; 🛜🐾) This older motel has been revamped to the highest of standards and modernity, with fresh and funky decor in an aquamarine color scheme that works. Beds are big and comfy, continental breakfast is included and free bikes will get you whizzing around in no time. There's an on-site restaurant as well.

★ Collage INTERNATIONAL $$$

(☑904-829-0055; www.collagestaug.com; 60 Hypolita St; mains $28-45; ⊘5:30-9pm) This upscale restaurant is renowned for its impeccable service, intimate atmosphere and the consistency of its cuisine: the menu makes the most of St Augustine's seaside locale and nearby local farms. It's all here: artisan salads, chicken, lamb, veal and pork, lobster, scallops and grouper. A subtle mélange of global flavors enhance the natural goodness of the freshest produce.

ℹ Information

Visitor Information Center (☑ 904-825-1000; www.Floridashistoriccoast.com; 10 W Castillo Dr; ⊘8:30am-5:30pm) Helpful, period-dressed staff sell tour tickets and can advise you on everything St Augustinian.

The daily *St Augustine Record* (www.staugustine.com) has good information on its website.

ℹ Getting There & Around

Driving from the north, take I-95 exit 318 and head east past Hwy 1 to San Marcos Ave; turn right and you'll end up at the Old City Gate, just past the fort. Alternatively, you can take Hwy A1A along the beach, which intersects with San Marco Ave, or Hwy 1 south from Jacksonville. From the south, take exit 298, merge onto Hwy 1 and follow it into town.

Cars are a nightmare downtown, with one-way and pedestrian-only streets and severely limited parking; outside the city center, you'll need wheels. There's a big parking lot at the Visitor Information Center. Use it.

Northeast Florida Regional Airport (☑ 904-209-0090; www.flynf.com; 4900 US Hwy 1), 5 miles north of town, receives limited commercial flights. **Airport Express** (☑ 904-824-9400; www.airportexpresspickup.com) charges $65 to drop you downtown in a shuttle. For an additional $20, it'll take you to your hotel. Reservations required. Private services are also available.

The **Greyhound bus station** (☑ 904-829-6401; www.greyhound.com; 52 San Marcos Ave) is just a few blocks north of the visitor center.

Jacksonville

At a whopping 840 sq miles, Jacksonville is the largest city by area in the contiguous United States and the most populous in Florida. The city *sprawls* along three meandering rivers, with sweeping bridges and twinkling city lights reflected in the water. A glut of high-rises, corporate HQs and chain hotels can make 'Jax' feel a little soulless, but patient exploration yields some interesting streets, curious characters and a Southern-fried, friendly heart.

The city's museums and restored historic districts are worth a wander if you have the time, and the Five Points and San Marco neighborhoods are charming, walkable areas lined with bistros, boutiques and bars.

The Jacksonville area beaches – a world unto themselves – are 30 to 50 minutes' drive from the city, depending on traffic and where you're coming from.

◉ Sights

★ Cummer Museum of Art & Gardens MUSEUM

(www.cummer.org; 829 Riverside Ave; adult/student $10/6; ⊘10am-9pm Tue, to 4pm Wed-Sat, noon-4pm Sun) This handsome museum, Jacksonville's premier cultural space, has a genuinely excellent collection of American and European paintings, Asian decorative art and antiquities. An outdoor area showcases classical English and Italian gardens, and is one of the loveliest spaces in the city.

★ Museum of Contemporary Art
Jacksonville   MUSEUM
(MOCA; ☏ 904-366-6911; www.mocajacksonville. org; 333 N Laura St; adult/child $8/2.50; ⊗ 11am-5pm Tue-Sat, to 9pm Thu, noon-5pm Sun) The focus of this ultramodern space extends beyond painting: get lost among contemporary sculpture, prints, photography and film. Check out www.jacksonvilleartwalk. com for details of the free MOCA-run Art Walk, held on the first Wednesday of every month from 5pm to 9pm.

Southbank Riverwalk   WATERFRONT
This 1.2-mile boardwalk, on the south side of the St Johns River, opposite downtown and Jacksonville Landing, has excellent views of the city's expansive skyline. Most nights yield scenes that'll up your likes on social media, but firework displays are a real blast. The Southbank Riverwalk connects the museums flanking Museum Circle and makes a pleasant promenade.

Treaty Oak   LANDMARK
(1123 Prudential Dr, Jesse Ball duPont Park) At first glance, it looks like a small forest is growing in the middle of the concrete on Jacksonville's south side. But upon closer inspection you'll see that the 'forest' is really one single enormous tree, with a trunk circumference of 25ft and a shade diameter of nearly 200ft. According to local lore, the live oak tree is the oldest thing in Jacksonville.

🛏 Sleeping & Eating

Hotel Indigo Jacksonville   HOTEL $$
(☏ 877-846-3446; www.hoteldeerwoodpark.com; 9840 Tapestry Park Circle; r from $150; P 🛜 🌊 🐾) Lush blue color accents and airy, design-conscious rooms with hardwood floors, fluffy king beds, flat-screen TVs and a general sense of stylish yet accessible luxury define the experience at this excellent branch of the Indigo chain. Located about 11 miles south of downtown Jacksonville.

★ Hotel Palms   HOTEL $$
(☏ 904-241-7776; www.thehotelpalms.com; 28 Sherry Dr, Atlantic Beach; r $140-180, ste from $200; 🛜) An old-school courtyard motel turned into a chic little property with reclaimed headboards, concrete floors and open, airy design? We'll take it. Treat yourself to an outdoor shower, free beach-cruiser

bicycles, an outdoor fireplace and some gorgeous rooms pulled straight off some fancy interior decorator's Instagram.

Beach Road
Chicken Dinners   SOUTHERN US $
(☏ 904-398-7980; www.beachroadchickendinners. com; 4132 Atlantic Blvd; items $5-12; ⊗ 11am-8:30pm Tue-Sat, to 6pm Sun) You know a place does it right if its signature meal predates the Cold War, and this deliciously retro joint has been frying chicken since 1939. Tear off a chunk of tender thigh meat and wrap it up in a fluffy biscuit, and you'll understand why people line up every day at this much-loved shack.

★ Black Sheep
Restaurant   MODERN AMERICAN $$
(☏ 904-380-3091; www.blacksheep5points.com; 1534 Oak St; lunch/dinner mains from $9/14; ⊗ 10:30am-10pm Mon-Thu, to 11pm Fri & Sat, 9:30am-3pm Sun; 🖐) 🍴 A commitment to good, local ingredients, delicious food, plus a rooftop bar and a craft cocktail menu? Sign us up! Try miso-glazed duck confit, citrus-marinated tofu, pastrami sandwiches made from in-house deli meat, or crispy skinned steelhead fish cooked in brown butter; it's all good. The cardamom pancakes and salmon on bagels served for Sunday brunch are pretty fine too.

🍷 Drinking & Entertainment

★ Birdies   BAR
(☏ 904-356-4444; www.birdiesfivepoints.com; 1044 Park St; ⊗ 4pm-2am) There's funky local art on the walls, old-school video games in the back, a mix of old timers and tatted hipsters, retro neon vibe, indie rock on the radio, DJs on the weekends and good vibes throughout at this excellent watering hole.

★ Florida Theatre   THEATER
(☏ 904-355-5661; www.floridatheatre.com; 128 E Forsyth St) Home to Elvis' first indoor concert in 1956, which a local judge endured to ensure Presley was not overly suggestive, this opulent 1927 venue is an intimate place to catch big-name musicians, musicals and movies.

ℹ Information

There are a bunch of sources of information for Jacksonville and the surrounding areas.

Florida Times-Union (www.jacksonville.com) Conservative daily paper, in print and online;

Friday's *Weekend* magazine features family-oriented events listings.

Folio Weekly (www.folioweekly.com) Free; with club, restaurant and events listings. Found all over town.

Jacksonville & the Beaches Convention & Visitors Bureau (☑ 800-733-2668; www.visitjacksonville.com; 208 N Laura St, Suite 102; ☺9am-5pm Mon-Fri) Has all there is to know about Jax and surrounds. There's also a branch at **Jacksonville Landing** (☑ 904-791-4305; 2 Independent Dr; ☺11am-3pm Mon-Thu, 10am-7pm Fri & Sat, noon-5pm Sun) and the airport.

❶ Getting There & Around

Jacksonville International Airport (JAX; ☑ 904-741-4902; www.flyjax.com; 2400 Yankee Clipper Dr; ☎), about 18 miles north of downtown on I-95, is served by major and regional airlines and car-rental companies. A cab downtown costs around $35. Otherwise, follow the signs for shuttle services: there are numerous licensed providers and reservations aren't necessary.

The **Greyhound bus station** (☑ 904-356-9976; www.greyhound.com; 10 Pearl St) is at the west end of downtown. The **Amtrak station** (☑ 904-766-5110; www.amtrak.com; 3570 Clifford Lane) is 5 miles northwest of downtown.

The Jacksonville Transportation Authority (www.jtafla.com) runs buses and trolleys around town and the beaches (fare $1.50), as well as a free, scenic (and underused) river-crossing Skyway (monorail).

Amelia Island

Located just 13 miles from the Georgia border, Amelia Island is a moss-draped, sun-and sand-soaked blend of the Deep South and Florida coast. It is believed the island's original inhabitants, the Timucuan tribespeople, arrived as early as 4000 years ago. Since that time, eight flags have flown here, starting with the French in 1562, followed by the Spanish, the English, the Spanish again, the Patriots, the Green Cross of Florida, the Mexican Rebels, the US, the Confederates, then the US again.

Vacationers have flocked to Amelia since the 1890s, when Henry Flagler converted a coast of salt marsh and unspoiled beaches into a vacation spot for the wealthy. The legacy of that era is evident in the central town of Fernandina Beach, 50 blocks of historic buildings, Victorian B&Bs and restaurants housed in converted fishing cottages. Dotting the rest of the island are lush parks, green fairways and miles of shoreline.

⊙ Sights & Activties

Amelia Island Museum of History　MUSEUM
(☑ 904-261-7378; www.ameliamuseum.org; 233 S 3rd St, Fernandina Beach; adult/student $8/5; ☺10am-4pm Mon-Sat, 1-4pm Sun) Housed in the former city jail (1879–1975), this oral-history museum has tiny but informative exhibits exploring Native American history, the Spanish Mission period, the Civil War and historic preservation. A variety of tours are available, including the eight-flags tour (11am and 2pm Monday to Saturday and 2pm Sunday), providing lively interpretations of the island's fascinating history, and architecture tours, pub crawls and cell-phone walking tours.

Fort Clinch State Park　STATE PARK
(☑ 904-277-7274; www.floridastateparks.org/fortclinch; 2601 Atlantic Ave, Fernandina Beach; car/pedestrian $6/2; ☺park 8am-sunset, fort 9am-5pm; Ⓟ) Although construction commenced in 1847, rapid technological advancements rendered Fort Clinch's masonry walls obsolete by as early as 1861, when the fort was taken easily by Confederate militia in the Civil War and later evacuated. Federal troops again occupied the fort during WWII. Today, the park offers a variety of activities, a half-mile-long fishing pier, serene beaches, hiking and cycling.

★**Kayak Amelia**　KAYAKING
(☑ 904-261-5702, 904-251-0016; www.kayakamelia.com; 4 N 2nd St, Fernandina Beach; tours adult/child from $65/55, rental half-day/day from $37/49) The charms of Amelia Island are best appreciated through a quiet day on the water, with the sun glinting off the estuaries and cordgrass. That's the experience offered by Kayak Amelia, which leads paddling excursions into the watery ecosystem that ensconces the Atlantic barrier island.

⊨ Sleeping

★**Addison**　B&B $$$
(☑ 904-277-1604; www.addisononamelia.com; 614 Ash St, Fernandina Beach; r $215-315; Ⓟ☎) ✹ Built in 1876, the Addison has modern upgrades (Jacuzzi tubs, deluge showers, Turkish-cotton towels and wi-fi) that'll trick you into thinking it was finished last week. The Addison's white, aqua and sage color scheme is bright and totally un-stuffy. Enjoy daily happy hours overlooking a delightful courtyard with some of the friendliest (and funniest) innkeepers on Amelia.

Ritz Carlton
(📞904-277-1100; www.ritzcarlton.com/en/Properties/AmeliaIsland; 4750 Amelia Island Pkwy, Fernandina Beach; r from $299; 🅿🛜🏊) The height of luxury, decadence and impeccable service awaits at this unexpectedly located Ritz Carlton. Set on 13 miles of pristine beaches, with its own private 18-hole golf course and lavish rooms and suites furnished with casual elegance.

🍴 Eating & Drinking

T-Ray's Burger Station
BURGERS **$**
(📞904-261-6310; www.traysburgerstation.com; 202 S 8th St, Fernandina Beach; mains $6-9; ⏱7am-2:30pm Mon-Fri, 8am-1pm Sat) Inside an Exxon gas station, this high-carb, high-fat, low-pretense diner and takeout joint is worth the cholesterol spike. Revered by locals, the big breakfasts are just that, and daily specials sell out fast. Juicy burgers, chunky fries, fried shrimp and tender crab cakes all make the mouth water.

29 South
SOUTHERN US **$$**
(📞904-277-7919; www.29southrestaurant.com; 29 S 3rd St, Fernandina Beach; mains $16-28; ⏱11:30am-2pm Wed-Sun, 5:30-9:30pm daily; 🅿) Lobster corn dogs, sweet-tea-brined pork chops, homemade doughnut-bread pudding and coffee ice cream – we're in business.

⭐ Palace Saloon
BAR
(www.thepalacesaloon.com; 113-117 Centre St, Fernandina Beach; ⏱noon-2am) Push through the swinging doors at the oldest continuously operated bar in Florida (since 1878), and the first thing you'll notice is the 40ft gas-lamp-lit bar. Knock back the saloon's rum-laced Pirate's Punch in dark, velvet-draped surroundings, curiously appealing to both bikers and Shakespeare buffs.

ℹ Information

Historic Downtown Visitor Center (📞904-277-0717; www.ameliaisland.com; 102 Centre St, Fernandina Beach; ⏱10am-4pm) Reams of useful information and maps in the old railroad depot.

Shrimping Museum & Welcome Center (📞904-261-7378; 17 Front St, Fernandina Beach; ⏱10am-4pm Mon-Sat, 1-4pm Sun) This small museum on the harborfront has local maps and pamphlets.

ℹ Getting There & Away

Hwy A1A splits in two directions on Amelia Island, one heading west toward I-95 and the other following the coast; both are well marked.

To get to Amelia, the fastest route from the mainland is to take I-95 north to exit 373 and head east about 15 miles straight to the island.

Want a prettier route? Heading from Jacksonville Beach to the town of Mayport, catch the **St Johns River Ferry** (📞904-241-9969; www.stjohnsriverferry.com; per car $5; ⏱from Maryport every 30min 6am-7pm Mon-Fri, 7am-8:30pm Sat & Sun; from George Island every 30min 6:15am-7:15pm Mon-Fri, 7:15am-8:45pm Sat & Sun), which runs around every 30 minutes.

SOUTHWEST FLORIDA

To drive southwest Florida's Gulf Coast is to enter an impressionistic watercolor painting: first, there is the dazzling white quartz sand of its barrier-island beaches, whose turquoise waters darken to silver-mantled indigo as the fiery sun lowers to the horizon. Later, seen from the causeways, those same islands become a phosphorescent smear beneath the inky black night sky.

The Gulf Coast's beauty is its main attraction, but variety is a close second: from Tampa to St Petersburg to Sarasota to Naples, there is urban sophistication and exquisite cuisine. There are secluded islands, family-friendly resorts and spring-break–style parties. Here Salvador Dalí's melting canvases, Ringling's Venetian Gothic palace and Chihuly's tentacled glass sculptures fit perfectly – all are bright, bold, surreal entertainments to match wintering manatees, roseate spoonbills, open-mouthed alligators and the peacock-colored, sequined costumes of twirling trapeze artists.

Tampa

On first glance it may seem sprawling and businesslike, but Tampa is also home to a bunch of museums, parks and ambitious restaurants, many of which have popped up recently and brought the city dangerously close to becoming stylish. In the heart of downtown, the revitalized Riverwalk along the Hillsborough River glitters with contemporary architecture and scenic green spaces. Plus, between the zoo, the aquarium, the children's museums and the theme parks, families have enough top-shelf entertainment to last a week. By evening Ybor City's streets transform into southwest Florida's hottest bar and nightclub scene.

◉ Sights

Ybor (ee-bore) City is a short car or trolley ride northeast of downtown. Like the illicit love child of Key West and Miami's Little Havana, this 19th-century district is a multiethnic neighborhood that hosts the Tampa Bay area's hippest party scene. It also preserves a strong Cuban, Spanish and Italian heritage from its days as the epicenter of Tampa's cigar industry.

★ Florida Aquarium   AQUARIUM

(☑813-273-4000; www.flaquarium.org; 701 Channelside Dr; adult/child $25/20; ◒9:30am-5pm; ♿) Tampa's excellent aquarium is among the state's best. Cleverly designed, the re-created swamp lets you walk among herons and ibis as they prowl the mangroves. Programs let you swim with the fishes (and the sharks) or take a catamaran ecotour in Tampa Bay.

Busch Gardens   AMUSEMENT PARK

(☑888-800-5447; www.buschgardenstampabay.com; 10165 McKinley Dr; 3yr & up $95; ◒10am-6pm, hours vary) This theme park has 10 loosely named African zones, which flow together without much fuss. The entire park is walkable. Admission includes three types of fun: epic roller coasters and rides, animal encounters, and various shows, performances and entertainment. All are spread throughout the park, so successful days require some planning.

Ybor City Museum State Park   MUSEUM

(☑813-247-6323; www.ybormuseum.org; 1818 E 9th Ave; adult/child $4/free; ◒9am-5pm Wed-Sun) This dusty, old-school history museum preserves a bygone era, with cigarworker houses (open 10am to 3pm) and wonderful photos. The museum store offers expert cigar advice and information on a free, self-guided, multimedia tour (☑813-505-6779; www.yborwalkingtours.com; adult/child $20/10) of Ybor City, accessible with any internet-connected device.

Florida Museum of
Photographic Arts   MUSEUM

(FMoPA; ☑813-221-2222; www.fmopa.org; The Cube, 400 N Ashley Dr; adult/student $10/8; ◒11am-6pm Mon-Thu, to 7pm Fri, noon-5pm Sun) This small, intimate photography museum is housed on the 2nd and 3rd stories of the Cube, a five-story atrium in downtown Tampa. In addition to a permanent collection from Harold Edgerton and Len Prince, temporary exhibits have included the work of Ansel Adams, Andy Warhol and contemporary photographers such as Jerry Uelsmann. Photography courses are also offered.

Manatee Viewing Center   WILDLIFE RESERVE

(☑813-228-4289; www.tampaelectric.com/manatee; 6990 Dickman Rd, Apollo Beach; ◒10am-5pm Nov-mid Apr) FREE One of Florida's more surreal wildlife encounters is spotting manatees in the warm-water discharge canals of coal-fired power plants. Yet these placid mammals show up here so reliably from November through April that this is now a protected sanctuary.

🛏 Sleeping

Gram's Place Hostel   HOSTEL $

(☑813-221-0596; www.grams-inn-tampa.com; 3109 N Ola Ave, Seminole Heights; dm $28, r $55-65; ❄@🛜) As charismatic as an aging rock star, Gram's is a small, welcoming hostel for international travelers who prefer personality over perfect linens. Dig the in-ground hot tub and Saturday-night jams. Breakfast is not included, but there are two fully serviced kitchens.

Tahitian Inn   HOTEL $$

(☑813-877-6721; www.tahitianinn.com; 601 S Dale Mabry Hwy, South Tampa; r from $155; P❄@🛜🐾🏊) The name is reminiscent of a tiki-themed motel, but this family-owned, full-service hotel offers fresh, boutique stylings on the cheap. Nice pool, and the quaint cafe offers outdoor seating by a waterfall and koi pond.

★Epicurean Hotel   BOUTIQUE HOTEL $$

(☑813-999-8700; www.epicureanhotel.com; 1207 S Howard Ave, South Tampa; r $180-499; P❄@🛜🐾) Foodies rejoice! Tampa's coolest hotel, which opened in 2014, is a food-and-drink-themed boutique Eden steeped in detailed design: vertical hydroponic lettuce and herb walls, a zinc bar, reclaimed woods from an 1820s railway station, oversize whiskers as test-kitchen door handles – everywhere you look, a story, usually involving Bern's Steak House (☑813-251-2421; www.bernssteakhouse.com; 1208 S Howard Ave, South Tampa; steaks for 1-2 people $32-105; ◒5-10pm Sun-Thu, to 11pm Fri & Sat), who are partners.

✕ Eating

Tre Amici @ the Bunker   CAFE $

(☑813-247-6964; www.bunkerybor.com; 1907 19th St N, Ybor City; items $3-8; ◒8am-8pm Mon-Sat, 10am-4pm Sun) Ybor City's hipster contingent wake up at this relaxed community coffee-house, which offers a range of breakfast burritos, soups and sandwiches all day. Come evening, it hosts open mikes, poetry slams and 'noise nights,' which are exactly what they sound like.

★**Ulele**   AMERICAN $$
(☑813-999-4952; www.ulele.com; 1810 N Highland Ave; mains $10-36; ⊙11am-10pm Sun-Thu, to 11pm Fri & Sat; 🛜) In a pleasant Riverwalk setting, this former water-pumping station has been transformed into an enchanting restaurant and brewery whose menu harkens back to native Floridan staples made over for modern times. That means liberal use of datil peppers, sides like alligator beans and okra 'fries' (amazing!), mains like local pompano fish and desserts like guava pie.

Ichicoro   RAMEN $$
(☑813-517-9989; www.ichicoro.com; 5229 N Florida Ave, Seminole Heights; ramen $12-16; ⊙noon-11pm Mon-Wed, to 1am Thu & Fri, 11am-1am Sat, 11am-11pm Sun) This chic space in Tampa's Seminole Heights neighborhood dishes out some of the best craft ramen (yes, ramen can be craft too) south of New York City. And that's actually where the recipes for these fancy noodle bowls were conceived.

★**Columbia Restaurant**   SPANISH $$$
(☑813-248-4961;   www.columbiarestaurant.com; 2117 E 7th Ave, Ybor City; mains lunch $11-26, dinner $20-31; ⊙11am-10pm Mon-Thu, to 11pm Fri & Sat, noon-9pm Sun) Celebrating its centennial in 2015, this Spanish Cuban restaurant is the oldest in Florida. Occupying an entire block, it consists of 15 elegant dining rooms and romantic, fountain-centered courtyards.

🍷 **Drinking & Entertainment**

Independent Bar   BAR
(☑813-341-4883;   www.independenttampa.com; 5016 N Florida Ave, Seminole Heights; ⊙9am-midnight Sun-Wed, to 1am Thu-Sat) If you appreciate craft brews, roll into this converted gas station, now a low-key hip bar in Seminole Heights. You can count on one or more local Cigar City Brews, and it serves some mean pub grub.

★**Skipper's Smokehouse**   LIVE MUSIC
(☑813-971-0666; www.skipperssmokehouse.com; 910 Skipper Rd, Village of Tampa; cover $5-25; ⊙11am-10pm Tue & Wed, to 10:30pm Thu, to 11pm Fri, noon-11pm Sat, 1-9:30pm Sun) Like it blew

in from the Keys, Skipper's is a beloved, unpretentious open-air venue for blues, folk, reggae and gator-swamp rockabilly. It's 9 miles directly north of downtown on N Nebraska Ave.

★**Tampa Theatre**   CINEMA
(☑813-274-8981, box office 813-274-8286; www.tampatheatre.org; 711 N Franklin St; tickets $11) This historic 1926 theater in downtown is a gorgeous venue in which to see an independent film. The mighty Wurlitzer organ plays before most movies. Too bad showtimes are so limited, with only one or two films playing on any given day. Look for special events.

🛈 **Information**

Tampa Bay Convention & Visitors Bureau
(☑813-226-0293; www.visittampabay.com; 615 Channelside Dr; ⊙10am-5:30pm Mon-Sat, 11am-5pm Sun) The visitor center has good free maps and lots of information.

Ybor City Visitor Center (☑813-241-8838; www.ybor.org; 1600 E 8th Ave; ⊙10am-5pm Mon-Sat, noon-5pm Sun) Provides an excellent introduction with walking-tour maps and info.

🛈 **Getting There & Around**

Tampa International Airport (TPA; ☑813-870-8700; www.tampaairport.com; 4100 George J Bean Pkwy) is the region's third busiest hub. It's 6 miles west of downtown, off Hwy 589.

HART bus 30 ($2, 25 minutes, every 30 minutes) picks up and drops off at the Red Arrival Desk on the lower level of the airport; exact change is required.

All major car agencies have desks at the airport. By car, take the I-275 to N Ashley Dr, turn right and you're in downtown.

St Petersburg

Long known as little more than a bawdy spring-break party town and a retirement capital, St Petersburg is now forging a new name for itself as a culturally savvy southern city. Spurred on by awe-inspiring downtown murals, a revitalized historic district and the stunning Dalí Museum, the downtown energy is creeping up Central Ave, spawning sophisticated restaurants, craft breweries, farmers markets and artsy galleries, all of which are attracting a younger professional crowd and a new wave of culturally curious travelers.

◉ Sights & Activities

★ Salvador Dalí Museum   MUSEUM
(☏ 727-823-3767; www.thedali.org; 1 Dali Blvd; adult/child 6-12yr $24/10, after 5pm Thu $10; ⊙ 10am-5:30pm Fri-Wed, to 8pm Thu) The theatrical exterior of the Salvador Dalí Museum augurs great things: out of a wound in the towering white shoe box oozes a 75ft geodesic glass atrium. Even better, what unfolds inside is like a blueprint of what a modern art museum, or at least one devoted to the life, art and impact of Salvador Dalí, should be. Even those who dismiss his dripping clocks and curlicue mustache will be awed by the museum and its grand works, especially the *Hallucinogenic Toreador*.

★ Weedon Island Preserve   NATURE RESERVE
(☏ 727-453-6500; www.weedonislandpreserve. org; 1800 Weedon Dr NE; ⊙ 7am-sunset) Like a patchwork quilt of variegated greens tossed out over Tampa Bay, this 3700-acre preserve protects a diverse aquatic and wetland ecosystem. At the heart of the preserve is the excellent Cultural and Natural History Center (open from 11am to 4pm Thursday to Saturday) where you can browse exhibits about the natural environment and the early Weedon Island people.

St Petersburg Museum of Fine Arts   MUSEUM
(☏ 727-896-2667; www.mfastpete.org; 255 Beach Dr NE; adult/child 7-18yr $17/10; ⊙ 10am-5pm Mon-Sat, to 8pm Thu, noon-5pm Sun) The Museum of Fine Arts' collection is as broad as the Dalí Museum's is deep, traversing the world's antiquities and following art's progression through nearly every era.

★ Walking Mural Tours   CULTURAL
(☏ 727-821-7391; www.stpetemuraltour.com; adult/ child $19/11; ⊙ 10-11:30am Sat) This excellent walking tour introduces visitors to St Pete's vibrant mural scene, which got its start when artists were given cheap gallery space downtown after the economy crashed in 2008. Now upward of 30 highly creative and one-of-a-kind murals, many with nods to the city's history and culture, grace its buildings and rival Miami's Wynwood Walls.

� Sleeping

★ Hollander Hotel   BOUTIQUE HOTEL $$
(☏ 727-873-7900; www.hollanderhotel.com; 421 4th Ave N; r $98-140; P❋🛜⛱) The Hollander can do no wrong with its art-deco flavor, 130ft porch, convivial Tap Room, full-service spa and Common Grounds coffee shop. Shared spaces feature gorgeous period detailing and rooms retain a hint of 1930s romance with their polished wooden floors, lazy ceiling fans and cane furniture.

★ Dickens House   B&B $$
(☏ 727-822-8622; www.dickenshouse.com; 335 8th Ave NE; r $139-243; P❋@🛜) Five lushly designed rooms await in this passionately restored arts-and-crafts-style home. The gregarious, gay-friendly owner whips up a gourmet breakfast often involving egg-white frittata.

✗ Eating & Drinking

Meze 119   VEGETARIAN $
(☏ 727-498-8627; www.meze119.com; 119 2nd St N; mains $7-14; ⊙ 11am-9pm Sun-Thu, to 10pm Fri & Sat; ☑) Using Middle Eastern spices to create rich, complex flavors, this vegetarian restaurant satisfies even demanding omnivores with its Scotch egg and falafel, panko fried with tahini sauce, and couscous and raisin-stuffed acorn squash. Other popular standards include the multiflavor hummus plate and sautéed eggplant on open-faced pita bread.

★ Brick & Mortar   MODERN AMERICAN $$
(☏ 727-822-6540; www.facebook.com/brickand mortarkitchen; 539 Central Ave; mains $14-25; ⊙ 5pm-9pm Tue, to 10pm Wed & Thu; 4:30pm-11pm Fri & Sat) A husband-and-wife catering team launched this, well, brick-and-mortar establishment in 2015, and despite the fact that St Pete has been overrun with great restaurants, this New American experiment dominated. Best thing in the menu? A divine house carpaccio with leek, some goat's cheese mousse, a touch of truffle oil and a single ravioli stuffed with deliciously runny egg yolk.

★ Cycle Brewing   BREWERY
(534 Central Ave; ⊙ 3pm-midnight Mon-Thu, to 1am Fri, noon-1am Sat, noon-10pm Sun) Hipster brewhouse with sidewalk seating serving up to 24 rotating taps of world-class beer. The Crank IPA is a great choice.

ⓘ Getting There & Around

Greyhound (☏ 727-898-1496; www.greyhound. com; 180 Dr Martin Luther King Jr St N) Buses connect to Miami, Orlando and Tampa.

Pinellas Suncoast Transit Authority (PSTA; www.psta.net; adult/student $2.20/1.10) St

FLORIDA ST PETERSBURG

Petersburg buses serve the barrier-island beaches and Clearwater; unlimited-ride Go Cards cost $5 per day.

Downtown Looper (www.loopertrolley.com; fare 50¢; ⊙10am-5pm Sun-Thu, to midnight Fri & Sat) Old-fashioned trolley cars run a downtown circuit every 15 to 20 minutes.

Sarasota

Vacations today can be spent soaking up the sights and beaches (including the nearby and very popular Siesta Key) of sophisticated Sarasota, but this city took its time becoming the culturally rich place it is today. After marauding Spanish explorers expelled the Calusa people in the 15th century, this land lay virtually empty until the Seminole Wars inspired the Armed Occupation Act (1842), which deeded 160 acres and six months' provisions to anyone who would settle here and protect their farms. Sailing boats and steamships were the only connection to the outside world, until the Tampa railroad came in 1902. Sarasota then grew popular as a winter resort for the affluent, and the city's arts institutions followed. Finally circus magnate John Ringling decided to relocate his circus here, building a winter residence, art museum and college, and setting the struggling town on course to become the welcoming, well-to-do bastion of the arts it is today.

◉ Sights & Activities

★**Ringling Museum Complex**   MUSEUM
(☑941-359-5700; www.ringling.org; 5401 Bay Shore Rd; adult/child 6-17yr $25/5; ⊙10am-5pm Fri-Wed, to 8pm Thu; ♿) The 66-acre winter estate of railroad, real-estate and circus baron John Ringling and his wife, Mable, is one of the Gulf Coast's premier attractions and incorporates their personal collection of artworks in what is now Florida's state art museum. Nearby, Ringling's Circus Museum documents his theatrical successes, while their lavish Venetian Gothic home, Cà d'Zan, reveals the impresario's extravagant tastes. Don't miss the PBS-produced film on Ringling's life, which is screened in the Circus Museum.

Island Park   PARK
Sarasota's marina is notable for Island Park, an attractive green space poking into the harbor: it has a great playground and play fountain, restrooms, tree-shaded benches, a restaurant and tiki bar; and kayak, jet-ski and boat rentals.

★**Siesta Key Rum**   DISTILLERY
(Drum Circle Distilling; ☑941-702-8143; www.drumcircledistilling.com; 2212 Industrial Blvd; ⊙noon-5pm Tue-Sat) FREE The oldest rum distillery in Florida offers an educational and intoxicating tour in its facility within an industrial park a bit outside of town. You'll learn the entire process of rum-making from the company founder Troy, who is a gifted and hilarious public speaker.

🛏 Sleeping & Eating

★**Hotel Ranola**   BOUTIQUE HOTEL $$
(☑941-951-0111; www.hotelranola.com; 118 Indian Pl; r $109-179, ste $239-269; ▣✳🛜) The nine rooms feel like a designer's brownstone apartment: free-spirited and effortlessly artful, but with real working kitchens. It's urban funk, walkable to downtown Sarasota.

Mattison's City Grille   GRILL $
(☑941-330-0440; www.mattisons.com/; 1 N. Lemon Ave; mains $9-17; ⊙11am-10pm (or later), from 9:30am Sat; 🛜♿) Healthy salads and hearty sandwiches (using fresh homemade bread) are the order of the day at central Mattison's. The outdoor dining area doubles up as a bar that gets going each evening with live music, giving the place its 'party on the corner' nickname.

★**Owen's Fish Camp**   SOUTHERN US $$
(☑941-951-6936; www.owensfishcamp.com; 516 Burns Lane; mains $10-28; ⊙4-9:30pm Sun-Thu, to 10:30pm Fri & Sat) The wait rarely dips below an hour at this hip, Old Florida swamp shack downtown. The menu consists of upscale Southern cuisine with an emphasis on seafood, including whatever's fresh, and solid regular dishes like scallops with braised pork, succotash and grits.

ℹ Information

Arts & Cultural Alliance (www.sarasotaarts.org) All-encompassing event info.
Sarasota Herald-Tribune (www.heraldtribune.com) The main daily newspaper.
Sarasota Visitor Information Center (☑941-706-1253; www.visitsarasota.org; 1710 Main St; ⊙10am-5pm Mon-Sat; 🛜) Very friendly office with tons of info; sells good maps.

ℹ Getting There & Away

Sarasota is roughly 60 miles south of Tampa and about 75 miles north of Fort Myers. The main roads into town are Tamiami Trail/Hwy 41 and I-75.

FLORIDA SARASOTA

Greyhound (☑ 941-342-1720; www.greyhound.com; 5951 Porter Way; ☺ 8:30am-10am & 1:30-6pm) Connects Sarasota with Miami, Fort Myers and Tampa.

Sarasota-Bradenton International Airport (SRQ; ☑ 941-359-2770; www.srq-airport.com; 6000 Airport Circle) Served by many major airlines. Go north on Hwy 41, and right on University Ave.

Sanibel & Captiva Islands

By preference and by design, island life on Sanibel is informal and egalitarian, and riches are rarely flaunted. Development on Sanibel has been carefully managed: the northern half is almost entirely protected within the JN 'Ding' Darling National Wildlife Refuge. While there are hotels aplenty, the beachfront is free of commercial-and-condo blight. Plus public beach access is limited to a handful of spread-out parking lots, so there is no crush of day-trippers in one place.

The pirate José Gaspar, who called himself Gasparilla, once roamed the Gulf Coast plundering treasure and seizing beautiful women, whom he held captive in the aptly named Captiva Island. Today the tiny village is confined to a single street, Andy Rosse Lane, and there are still no traffic lights. The preferred mode of transportation is the family-friendly bike, and life here is informal and egalitarian, with island riches rarely being flaunted. Captiva's mansions are hidden behind thick foliage and sport playful names such as 'Seas the Day.'

◉ Sights & Activities

Captiva Beach   BEACH
(14790 Captiva Dr) Besides looking directly out onto heart-melting Gulf sunsets, Captiva Beach has lovely sand and is close to several romantic restaurants. Arrive early if you want to park in the small lot , or come by bike.

JN 'Ding' Darling
National Wildlife Refuge   WILDLIFE RESERVE
(☑ 239-472-1100; www.fws.gov/dingdarling; 1 Wildlife Dr; car/cyclist/pedestrian $5/1/1; ☺ 7am-sunset) Named for cartoonist Jay Norwood 'Ding' Darling, an environmentalist who helped establish more than 300 sanctuaries across the USA, this 6300-acre refuge is home to an abundance of seabirds and wildlife, including alligators, night herons, red-shouldered hawks, spotted sandpipers, roseate spoonbills, pelicans and anhingas. The refuges'

5-mile **Wildlife Drive** provides easy access, but bring binoculars; flocks sometimes sit at expansive distances. Only a few very short walks lead into the mangroves.

Captiva Cruises   CRUISE
(☑ 239-472-5300; www.captivacruises.com; 11400 Andy Rosse Lane) Departing from **McCarthy's Marina** (☑ 239-472-5200; www.mccarthysmarina.com; 11401 Andy Rosse Lane), Captiva Cruises offers everything from dolphin and sunset cruises (from $27.50) to various island excursions, such as Cayo Costa ($40), Cabbage Key ($40) and Boca Grande ($50) on Gasparilla Island.

Tarpon Bay Explorers   KAYAKING
(☑ 239-472-8900; www.tarponbayexplorers.com; 900 Tarpon Bay Rd; ☺ 8am-5pm) Within the Darling refuge, this outfitter rents canoes and kayaks ($25 for two hours) for easy, self-guided paddles in Tarpon Bay, a perfect place for young paddlers. Guided kayak trips (adult from $30 to $40, child from $20 to $25) are also excellent, and there's a range of other trips and deck talks. Reserve ahead or come early, as trips book up.

🛏 Sleeping & Eating

Sandpiper Inn   INN $$
(☑ 239-472-1606; www.palmviewsanibel.com; 720 Donax St; r $149-229; P ❄ 🛜) Set a block back from the water and in close proximity to the shops and restaurants on Periwinkle Way, this Old Florida inn offers good value for Sanibel. Each of the one-bedroom units has a functional (if dated) kitchen and a sitting area decked out in tropical colors.

★ **'Tween Waters Inn**   RESORT $$$
(☑ 239-472-5161; www.tween-waters.com; 15951 Captiva Dr; r $185-285, ste $270-410, cottages $265-460; ❄ @ 🛜 ❄ ❄) For great resort value on Captiva, choose 'Tween Waters Inn. Rooms are attractive roosts with rattan furnishings, granite counters, rainfall showerheads and Tommy Bahama–style decor. All have balconies and those directly facing the Gulf are splendid. The tidy little cottages are romantic. Families make good use of the big pool, tennis courts, full-service marina and spa. Multinight discounts are attractive.

★ **Sweet Melissa's Cafe**   AMERICAN $$$
(☑ 239-472-1956; www.sweetmelissascafe.com; 1625 Periwinkle Way; tapas $9-16, mains $26-34; ☺ 11:30am-2:30pm & 5pm-close Mon-Fri, 5pm-close Sat) From menu to mood, Sweet Melis-

sa's offers well-balanced, relaxed refinement. Dishes, including things like farro fettuccine, escargot with marrow and whole crispy fish, are creative without trying too hard. Lots of small-plate options encourage experimenting. Service is attentive and the atmosphere upbeat.

ℹ️ Information

Sanibel & Captiva Islands Chamber of Commerce (☎239-472-1080; www.sanibel-captiva. org; 1159 Causeway Rd; ⊙9am-5pm; 🤙) One of the more helpful visitor centers around; keeps an updated hotel-vacancy list with dedicated hotel hotline.

ℹ️ Getting There & Away

Driving is the only way to come and go. The Sanibel Causeway (Hwy 867) charges an entrance toll (cars/motorcycles $6/2). Sanibel is 12 miles long, but low speed limits and traffic makes it seem longer. The main drag is Periwinkle Way, which becomes Sanibel-Captiva Rd.

Naples

For upscale romance and the prettiest, most serene city beach in southwest Florida, come to Naples, the Gulf Coast's answer to Palm Beach. Development along the shoreline has been kept residential. The soft white sand is backed only by narrow dunes and half-hidden mansions. More than that, though, Naples is a cultured, sophisticated town, unabashedly stylish and privileged but also welcoming and fun-loving. Families, teens, couture-wearing matrons, middle-aged executives and smartly dressed young couples all mix and mingle as they stroll downtown's 5th Ave on a balmy evening. Travelers sometimes complain that Naples is expensive, but you can spend just as much elsewhere on a less impressive vacation.

⊙ Sights & Activities

⭐ **Naples Botanical Gardens**   GARDENS
(☎239-643-7275; www.naplesgarden.org; 4820 Bayshore Dr; adult/child 4-14yr $15/10; ⊙9am-5pm) This outstanding botanical garden styles itself as 'a place of bliss, a region of supreme delight.' And after spending some time wandering its 2.5-mile trail through nine cultivated gardens you'll rapidly find your inner Zen. Children will dig the thatched-roof tree house, butterfly house and interactive fountain, while adults get dreamy-eyed contemplating landscape architect Raymond Jungles' recently redesigned Scott Florida garden, filled with cascades, 12ft-tall oolite rocks and legacy tree species like date palms, sycamore leaf figs and lemon ficus.

⭐ **Baker Museum**   MUSEUM
(☎239-597-1900; www.artisnaples.org; 5833 Pelican Bay Blvd; adult/child $10/free; ⊙10am-4pm Tue-Thu & Sat, to 8pm Fri, noon-4pm Sun) The pride of Naples, this engaging, sophisticated art museum is part of the Artis–Naples campus, which includes the fabulous Philharmonic Center next door. Devoted to 20th-century modern and contemporary art, the museum's 15 galleries and glass dome conservatory host an exciting round of temporary and permanent shows, ranging from postmodern works to photography and paper craft to glass sculpture.

Naples Municipal Beach   BEACH
(12th Ave S & Gulf Shore Blvd) Naples' city beach is a long, dreamy white strand that succeeds in feeling lively but rarely overcrowded. At the end of 12th Ave S, the 1000ft pier is a symbol of civic pride, having been constructed in 1888, destroyed a few times by fire and hurricane, and reconstructed each time. Parking is spread out in small lots between 7th Ave N and 17th Ave S, each with 10 to 15 spots of mixed resident and metered parking ($1.50 per hour).

🛏️ Sleeping & Eating

Inn on 5th   HOTEL $$$
(☎239-403-8777; www.innonfifth.com; 699 5th Ave S; r $399, ste $599-999; 🅿✳@🤙🏊) This well-polished, Mediterranean-style luxury hotel provides an unbeatable location on either side of 5th Ave. Stylish rooms are more corporate-perfect than historic-romantic, but who complains about pillowtop mattresses and glass-walled showers? Full-service amenities include a 2nd-floor heated pool, business and fitness centers, and an indulgent spa. Free valet parking.

⭐ **Escalante**   BOUTIQUE HOTEL $$$
(☎239-659-3466; www.hotelescalante.com; 290 5th Ave S; r $200-700) Hidden in plain sight at 5th Ave and 3rd St, the wonderful Escalante is a boutique hotel crafted in the fashion of a Tuscan villa. Rooms and suites are nestled behind luxuriant foliage and flowering pergolas, and feature plantation-style furniture, European linens and designer bath products.

The Local MODERN AMERICAN $$
(☑239-596-3276; www.thelocalnaples.com; 5323 Airport Pulling Rd N; mains $12-29; ⊘11am-9pm Sun-Thu, to 9:30pm Fri & Sat; 🔊) 🍴 The irony of driving 6 miles from downtown to eat local aside, this strip-mall farm-to-table bistro is worth the carbon footprint for fab sustainable fare, from the Mediterranean watermelon salad to the grass-fed beef.

★**Bha! Bha! Persian Bistro** IRANIAN $$$
(☑239-594-5557; www.bhabhabistro.com; 865 5th Ave S; mains $26-38; ⊘5-9pm Sun-Thu, to 10pm Fri & Sat) This experimental, high-end establishment takes its name from the Farsi phrase for 'yum, yum,' and that turns out to be a serious understatement. Wash down the pistachio lamb meatballs with a saffron lemongrass martini, then continue on to a kebab marinated in exotic spices or the duck *fesenjune*, slow braised with pomegranate and walnut sauce.

❶ Information

Third St Concierge Kiosk (☑239-434-6533; www.thirdstreetsouth.com; Camargo Park, 3rd St S; ⊘10am-6pm Mon-Wed, 10am-9pm Thu & Fri, 8:30am-6pm Sat, noon-5pm Sun) What's in Old Naples? This friendly outdoor kiosk attendant is glad you asked.

Visitor Information Center (☑239-262-6141; www.napleschamber.org; 2390 Tamiami Trail N; ⊘9am-5pm Mon-Fri) Will help with accommodations; good maps, internet access and acres of brochures.

❶ Getting There & Away

A car is essential; ample and free downtown parking makes things easy. Naples is about 40 miles southwest of Fort Myers via I-75.

Greyhound (☑239-774-5660; www.greyhound.com; 2669 Davis Blvd) Connects Naples to Miami, Orlando and Tampa.

Southwest Florida International Airport (RSW; ☑239-590-4800; www.flylcpa.com; 11000 Terminal Access Rd) This is the main airport for Naples. It's about a 45-minute drive north, along I-75.

CENTRAL FLORIDA

Central Florida is like a *matryoshka*, the Russian doll that encases similar dolls of diminishing size. The region features pretty state parks, gardens and rivers, all ideal for leisurely exploration. One layer down, Central Florida then embraces Kissimmee, Celebration and the vast, sprawling area of Greater Orlando. Greater Orlando's network of multilane highways and overpasses leads to a huge number of theme parks, including Walt Disney World Resort, Universal Orlando Resort, SeaWorld and Legoland. Judging from the crowds, these parks are the reason most people visit.

But at Central Florida's core is a city: pretty, leafy downtown Orlando, whose great field-to-fork eating scene and world-class museums get overlooked by the hype, sparkle and colors of the theme parks. Many visitors never reach this kernel, the final 'doll,' and the city of Orlando tends to lie in the shadow of Cinderella and Hogwarts School of Witchcraft & Wizardry.

Orlando

If Orlando were a Disney character, it's fair to say that she's like Dory (of Nemo fame) and lacks a bit of confidence. It's so easy to get caught up in Greater Orlando – in the isolated, constructed worlds of Disney or Universal Orlando (for which, let's face it, you're probably here) – that you forget all about the downtown city of Orlando itself. It has a lot to offer: lovely tree-lined neighborhoods; a rich performing arts and museum scene; several fantastic gardens and nature preserves; fabulous cuisine; and a delightfully slower pace devoid of manic crowds. So, sure, enjoy the theme parks: the sparkles, nostalgia and adrenaline-pumped fantasy, but also take time to 'Find Orlando.' Come down off the coasters for one day to explore the quieter, gentler side of the city.

⊙ Sights

★**Mennello Museum of American Art** MUSEUM
(☑407-246-4278; www.mennellomuseum.org; 900 E Princeton St, Loch Haven Park, Downtown; adult/child 6-18yr $5/1; ⊘10:30am-4:30pm Tue-Sat, from noon Sun; ⬛Lynx 125, ⬛Florida Hospital Health Village) Tiny but excellent lakeside art museum featuring the work of Earl Cunningham, whose brightly colored images, a fusion of pop and folk art, leap off the canvas. Visiting exhibits often feature American folk art. Every four months there's a new exhibition, everything from a Smithsonian collection to a local artist.

★**Orlando Museum of Art** MUSEUM
(☑407-896-4231; www.omart.org; 2416 N Mills Ave, Loch Haven Park, Downtown; adult/child

$15/5; ◷10am-4pm Tue-Fri, from noon Sat & Sun; ♿; ☐Lynx 125, ☒Florida Hospital Health Village) Founded in 1924, Orlando's grand and blindingly white center for the arts boasts a fantastic collection – both permanent and temporary – and hosts an array of adult and family-friendly art events and classes. The popular First Thursday ($10), from 6pm to 9pm on the first Thursday of the month, celebrates local artists with regional work, live music and food from Orlando restaurants.

Orlando Eye
AMUSEMENT PARK
(www.officialorlandoeye.com; I-Drive 360, 8401 International Dr, International Drive; from $20; ◷10am-10pm Sun-Thu, to midnight Fri & Sat) Orlando has got everything else that goes up and down, so why not round and around? Opened in 2017, the Eye is International Drive's latest landmark.

SeaWorld
AMUSEMENT PARK
(☑888-800-5447; www.seaworldparks.com; 7007 Sea World Dr; $95, discounts online, prices vary daily; ◷9am-8pm; ♿; ☐Lynx 8, 38, 50, 111, ☐I-Ride Trolley Red Line Stop 28) One of Orlando's largest theme parks, SeaWorld is an aquatic-themed park filled with marine animal shows, roller coasters and up-close sea-life encounters. However, the park's biggest draw is controversial: live shows featuring trained dolphins, sea lions and killer whales. Since the release of the 2013 documentary *Blackfish*, SeaWorld's treatment of its captive orcas has come under intense scrutiny and the company has been hit by falling visitor numbers and negative PR.

Titanic the Experience
MUSEUM
(☑407-248-1166; www.titanicshipofdreams.com; 7324 International Dr, International Drive; adult/child 6-11yr $22/16; ◷10am-6pm; ♿; ☐Lynx 8, 42, ☐I-Ride Trolley Red Line Stop 9) Full-scale replicas of the doomed ship's interior and artifacts found at the bottom of the sea. Tour the galleries with guides in period dress or wander through on your own. Kids especially love the dramatic and realistic interpretation of history – each passenger receives a boarding pass, with the name of a real passenger, and at the end of the experience (once the ship has sunk) you learn your fate.

🛏 Sleeping

★Floridian Hotel & Suites
HOTEL $
(☑407-212-3021; www.floridianhotelorlando.com; 7531 Canada Ave, International Drive; r from $75; ☒☺✳🛜☒) A wonderful, privately owned budget hotel with similarities to a chain brand, but oh so much better in other respects: delightful front office staff, spotless rooms with fridges and even a complimentary (if basic) breakfast, plus shuttles to various parks. It's near Restaurant Row and handy to International Dr.

Aloft Orlando Downtown
BUSINESS HOTEL $$
(☑497-380-3500; www.aloftorlandodowntown.com; 500 S Orange Ave, Downtown; r from $230; ☒@🛜☒) Open, streamlined and decidedly modern, although the carefully constructed minimalist decor might render the rooms oddly empty for some. The sleek little pool sits unpleasantly on the main road. But it is one of the few hotels within an easy walk to downtown Orlando's bars and restaurants.

Hyatt Regency Grand Cypress Resort
RESORT $$
(☑407-239-1234; www.hyattgrandcypress.com; 1 Grand Cypress Blvd, Lake Buena Vista; r $189-250, resort fee per day $30, self/valet parking $20/29; ☒@🛜☒🐾) Considering the proximity to Disney's Magic Kingdom (7 miles) and Universal Resort Orlando (8 miles), this atrium-style resort is one of the best-value in Orlando.

★Bay Hill Club and Lodge
HOTEL $$$
(☑407-876-2429; www.bayhill.com; 9000 Bay Hill Blvd; r from $300; @🛜☒) Quiet and genteel Bay Hill feels like a time warp; as though you're walking into a TV set or your grandmother's photo album. It is reassuringly calm and simple. The staff are exceptionally gracious and accommodating, and handsome rooms are spread among a series of two-story buildings bordering the Arnold Palmer–designed golf course.

🍴 Eating

★P Is for Pie
BAKERY $
(☑407-745-4743; www.crazyforpies.com; 2806 Corrine Dr, Audubon Park; from $2; ◷7:30am-4:30pm Mon-Sat; ♿) Clean-lined with an artisan twist to classic pies (as in sweet tarts with a biscuit base), offering mini and specialty options.

★Dandelion Communitea Café
VEGETARIAN $
(☑407-362-1864; www.dandelioncommunitea.com; 618 N Thornton Ave, Thornton Park; mains $10-14; ◷11am-10pm Mon-Sat, to 5pm Sun; 🌿♿) 🌿 Unabashedly crunchy and definitively organic, this pillar of the sprouts and

Greater Orlando & Theme Parks

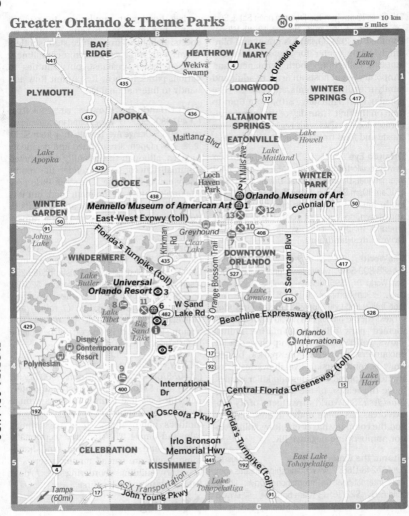

tempeh and green-tea dining scene serves up creative and excellent plant-based fare in a refurbished old house that invites folks to sit down and hang out.

Graffiti Junktion
American Burger Bar
BURGERS **$**

(☎407-426-9503; www.graffitijunktion.com; 700 E Washington St, Thornton Park; mains $10-14; ☺11am-2am) This little neon, happenin' hangout, with courtyard dining and regular drink specials, is all about massive burgers with attitude. Go with a Brotherly Love (Angus beef; $11) or veggie option ($7).

Pho 88
VIETNAMESE **$**

(www.pho88orlando.com; 730 N Mills Ave, Mills 50; mains $8-13; ☺10am-10pm) A flagship in Orlando's thriving Vietnamese district (known as ViMi) just northeast of downtown in an area informally referred to as Mills 50, this authentic, no frills, *pho* (Vietnamese noodle soup) specialist is always packed.

Melting Pot
EUROPEAN **$$**

(www.meltingpot.com/orlando; 7549 W Sand Lake Rd, Restaurant Row; mains $12-25; ☺5-10pm Mon-Thu, 5-11pm Fri, noon-11am Sat, noon-10pm Sun; ☻) Kids in particular love the novelty of a fondue dinner (cheese, beef, chicken,

Greater Orlando & Theme Parks

◎ **Top Sights**
1 Mennello Museum of American Art......C2
2 Orlando Museum of Art.........................C2
3 Universal Orlando Resort......................B3

◎ **Sights**
4 Orlando Eye...B4
5 SeaWorld...B4
6 Titanic the Experience...........................B3

▣ **Sleeping**
7 Aloft Orlando Downtown........................C3
8 Bay Hill Club and Lodge.........................B3
  Floridian Hotel & Suites................. (see 6)
9 Hyatt Regency Grand Cypress
  Resort...B4

✖ **Eating**
  Confisco Grille & Backwater
  Bar ....(see 3)
  Dandelion Communitea Café.......(see 10)
  Finnegan's Bar & Grill.....................(see 3)
10 Graffiti Junktion American Burger
  Bar C3
  Lombard's Seafood Grille..............(see 3)
11 Melting Pot B3
  Mythos Restaurant..........................(see 3)
12 P Is for Pie.. C2
13 Pho 88.. C2

◎ **Drinking & Nightlife**
  Icebar ....(see 4)
  Independent Bar ....(see 7)

seafood and, of course, chocolate). Having said that, it's an elegant spot and a popular date-night place.

🍷 Drinking & Nightlife

★ Icebar   BAR
(☏ 407-426-7555; www.icebarorlando.com; 8967 International Dr; entry at door/advance online $20/15; ⊙ 5pm-midnight Mon-Wed, to 1am Thu, to 2am Fri-Sun; ⬚ I-Trolley Red Line Stop 18 or Green Line Stop 10) More classic Orlando gimmicky fun. Step into the 22°F (-5°C) ice house, sit on the ice seat, admire the ice carvings, sip the icy drinks. Coat and gloves are provided at the door, and the fire room, bathrooms and other areas of the bar are kept at normal temperature.

Independent Bar   CLUB
(☏ 407-839-0457; 68 N Orange Ave, Downtown; $10; ⊙ 10pm-3am Sun, Wed & Thu, from 9:30pm Fri & Sat) Known to locals as simply the 'I-Bar,' it's hip, crowded and loud, with DJs spinning underground dance and alternative rock into the wee hours.

ℹ Information

Official Visitor Center (☏ 407-363-5872; www.visitorlando.com; 8723 International Dr; ⊙ 8:30am-6pm; ⬚ I-Ride Trolley Red Line 15)

ℹ Getting There & Around

Amtrak (www.amtrak.com; 1400 Sligh Blvd) Offers daily trains south to Miami (from $46) and north to New York City (from $144).
Greyhound (☏ 407-292-3424; www.greyhound.com; 555 N John Young Pkwy) Serves numerous cities from Orlando.

Lymmo (www.golynx.com; free; ⊙ 6am-10pm Mon-Thu, to midnight Fri, 10am-midnight Sat, to 10pm Sun) circles downtown Orlando for free with stops near Lynx Central Station, near SunRail's Church St Station, at Central and Magnolia, Jefferson and Magnolia and outside the Westin Grand Bohemian.

SunRail (www.sunrail.com), Orlando's commuter rail train, runs north–south. It doesn't stop at or near any theme parks.

In addition to the downtown station, **Amtrak** (www.amtrak.com) serves Winter Park, Kissimmee and Winter Haven (home to Legoland).

Walt Disney World® Resort

Walt Disney World® Resort   AMUSEMENT PARK
(☏ 407-939-5277; www.disneyworld.disney.go.com; Lake Buena Vista, outside Orlando; daily rates vary, see website for packages & tickets up to 10 days; ♿) Even if you haven't grown up with something from Walt Disney, chances are you've heard of it. And, despite it sounding like a 'world' (which it is in many respects...read on), it's more complex than the globe. So we're going to break it down for you. Disney World is in fact an unfenced 40-sq-mile area. Within this, although several miles apart from each other, are four contained, spotlessly sanitized theme parks: **Magic Kingdom**, **Epcot**, **Hollywood Studios** and **Animal Kingdom**.

Walt Disney World® Resort offers a lot more than rides. The huge number of attractions include interactive meet 'n' greets with well-known characters, including Mickey Mouse and Donald Duck, as well as more contemporary casts such as Gaston, Elsa, Anna and so on. Then there are parades, musical productions, interactive facilities, Disney promotions of the latest projects and plenty of stunt shows. And (here's the surprising part), it's not just for kids. Disney World has cleverly maintained its loyal following, resulting in hundreds of thousands of more mature visitors who just can't get enough, through programs and cuisine and cruises and tours.

Each of the four parks has its own theme, although when most people think of Walt Disney World Resort, they're often thinking of one of the four parks – the **Magic Kingdom**, with Cinderella's Castle at its core. This is the Disney of commercials, of princesses and pirates, Tinkerbell and dreams come true; this is quintessential, old-school Disney with classic rides such as It's a Small World and Space Mountain.

Epcot is a wonderful sensory experience. The park is divided into two sections that are situated around a lake: Future World and World Showcase. **Future World** has Epcot's only two thrill rides plus several pavilions with attractions, restaurants and character-greeting spots. **World Showcase** comprises 11 re-created nations featuring country-specific food, shopping and entertainment. This is the place to slow down a little and enjoy, where you can smell the incense in Morocco, listen to the Beatles in the UK and sip miso in Japan.

Hollywood Studios conjures the heydays of Hollywood, with a replica of Graumann's Chinese Theatre (the main focal icon), but most of the activities reflect unabashed 21st-century energy with attractions focusing on everything from *Star Wars* Jedi training to *Indiana Jones* stunt shows, from Muppet extravaganzas to the latest craze, the Frozen Sing-Along Celebration.

Set apart from the rest of Disney both in miles and in tone, **Animal Kingdom** attempts to blend theme park with zoo, carnival and African safari, all stirred together with a healthy dose of Disney characters, storytelling and transformative magic. Like the other parks, it's also divided into different sections, with wildlife experiences, rides, and musical shows at every corner, including *The Lion King* and *Nemo*. At the time of research, Animal Kingdom was about to open another area: the much-awaited **Pandora – The World of Avatar**.

To round off the Disney experience, Walt Disney World Resort runs a number of accommodations, for families to couples' luxury experiences. The advantage of staying at one of these is that most things, including meals and transportation, are arranged or easily accessible to you (but, although they make things run smoothly, especially if you have children, they're not the be all and end all; other hotels nearby also offer similar services). But they do serve up further fun and yes, even more entertainment including opportunities to dine with Disney characters. It is well designed for travelers with disabilities, with wheelchair rental, easy access and excellent arrangements for line access and the like.

In short, an experience at Walt Disney World Resort is extraordinary. It's an unabashed, unthwarted stimulation overload of music, light, sound, color, thrills and spills. It offers an other worldliness that is fully, inexplicably intoxicating, no matter your age. And that's despite the long lines, the occasional jostling and the over-priced meals. For most of the time, this is indeed the Happiest Place on Earth.

And, just when the sun has set and you think you're done for the day, there's more; each park has a nighttime fireworks show (the names of which change according to the annual program).

🛏 Sleeping & Eating

Disney resort hotels are divided according to location (Magic Kingdom, Epcot, Animal Kingdom and Disney Boardwalk). Prices vary drastically according to season, week and day.

While deluxe resorts are the best Disney has to offer, note that you're paying for Disney theming and location convenience, not luxury. Most offer multiroom suites and villas, upscale restaurants, children's programs and easy access to theme parks.

With the exception of Epcot, expect mediocre fast food, bad coffee and cafeteria cuisine at premium prices. Table-service restaurants accept 'priority seating' reservations up to 180 days in advance. Reserve through **Disney Dining** (☑ 407-939-3463), at www.disneyworld.disney.go.com or through the My Disney Experience app. Remember: while restaurants in the theme parks require theme-park admission, resort hotel restaurants do not.

ℹ Getting There & Around

Disney lies 25 minutes' drive south of downtown Orlando. Take I-4 to well-signed exits 64, 65 or 67.

Alamos and National car rental is available inside the Walt Disney World Dolphin Resort.

Car Care Center (☑407-824-0976; 1000 W Car Care Dr, Walt Disney World Resort; ⊙7am-7pm Mon-Fri, 7am-4pm Sat, 8am-3pm Sun) is a full-service garage, providing services (roadside assistance including towing, flat tire and battery jump starts) on Disney property only.

If you're staying at a Walt Disney World Resort hotel and are arriving at the Orlando International Airport (as opposed to the Sanford), arrange in advance for complimentary luggage handling and deluxe bus transportation with **Disney's Magical Express** (☑866-599-0951; www. disneyworld.disney.go.com). They will send you baggage labels in advance, collect your luggage at the airport, and if during your stay you transfer from one Disney hotel to another, the resort will transfer your luggage while you're off for the day.

The Disney transportation system utilizes boat, bus and a monorail to shuttle visitors to hotels, theme parks and other attractions within Walt Disney World Resort. The Transportation & Ticket Center operates as the main hub of this system. Note that it can take an hour to get from point A to point B using the Disney transportation system, and there is not always a direct route.

Universal Orlando Resort

★**Universal Orlando Resort**
AMUSEMENT PARK
(☑407-363-8000; www.universalorlando.com; 1000 Universal Studios Plaza; single park 1/2 days adult $105/185, child $100/175, both parks adult/child $155/150; ⊙daily, hours vary; ☐Lynx 21, 37 & 40, ◉Universal) Pedestrian-friendly Universal Orlando Resort has got spunk, spirit and attitude. With fantastic rides, excellent children's attractions and entertaining shows, it's comparable to Walt Disney World Resort. But Universal does everything just a bit smarter, funnier and more smoothly, as well as being smaller and easier to navigate. Instead of the Seven Dwarfs, there's the Simpsons. Instead of Mickey Mouse, there's Harry Potter. Universal offers pure, unabashed, adrenaline-pumped, full-speed-ahead fun for the entire family.

The Universal Orlando Resort consists of two (three by the time you read this) theme parks: **Islands of Adventure**, with the bulk of the thrill rides, and **Universal Studios**, with movie-based attractions and shows (including the **Wizarding World of Harry Potter**). **Volcano Bay** will open in 2017 as a water park of thrills and splashes and state-of-the-art rides through a 200ft volcano.

Universal's dining/entertainment district is **CityWalk** and it has five resort hotels (a sixth, Universal's Aventura Hotel, will open in 2018).

🛏 Sleeping & Eating

Universal Orlando Resort boasts five excellent resort hotels. Staying at a resort eliminates many logistical hassles: it's a pleasant gardened walk or a quiet boat ride to the parks; most offer Unlimited Express Pass access to park attractions and priority dining; several popular rides, such as Wizarding World of Harry Potter, opens one hour early for all guests; and the Loews Loves Pets program welcomes Fido as a VIP.

The only restaurants in the theme parks that take advance reservations are **Finnegan's Bar & Grill** (☑407-224-3613; www.universalorlando.com; mains $10-23; ⊙11am-park closing; 🛜🍴) and **Lombard's Seafood Grille** (☑407-224-3613, 407-224-6401; www.universalorlando.com; mains $15-28; ⊙11am-park closing; 🛜🍴) in Universal Studios, and **Mythos Restaurant** (☑407-224-4012, 407-224-4534; www.universalorlando.com; mains $14-23; ⊙11am-3pm; 🍴) and **Confisco Grille** (☑407-224-4012; www.universalorlando.com; mains $6-22; ⊙11am-4pm; 🍷🍴) in Islands of Adventure.

Each Universal resort has high-quality bars and restaurants that you can enjoy even if you're not a guest.

ℹ Getting There & Around

From I-4, take exit 74B or 75A and follow the signs. From International Dr, follow the signs west onto Universal Blvd.

Lynx buses 21, 37 and 40 service the Universal Orlando Resort parking garage (40 runs directly from the downtown Orlando Amtrak station). International Dr's **I-Ride Trolley** (☑407-354-5656; www.iridetrolley.com; rides adult/child 3-9yr $2/1, passes 1/3/5/7/14 days $5/7/9/12/18; ⊙8am-10:30pm) stops at Universal Blvd, a 0.6-mile walk away.

Universal Orlando Resort – that is, Universal Orlando's resort hotels, Islands of Adventure and Universal Studios theme parks and City-Walk – are linked by pedestrian walkways. It's a 10- to 15-minute walk from the theme parks and CityWalk to the deluxe resort hotels. Cabana Bay Beach Resort is about a 25-minute walk. Several hotels outside the park are within a 20-minute walk, but it's not a very pleasant journey.

Rent strollers, wheelchairs and Electric Convenience Vehicles (ECVs) at the entrance to each park and manual wheelchairs at the Rotunda section of the parking lot. To reserve an ECV in advance, call ☑407-224-4233.

FLORIDA PANHANDLE

The most geographically northern end of Florida is by far its most culturally Southern side. The Panhandle – that spit of land embedded in the left shoulder of the Florida peninsula – is hemmed in by Alabama and Georgia, and in many ways the region's beaches are effectively coastal extensions of those states.

What beaches they are, though! All powdered white sand and teal- to jade-green waters, this is a coast of primal, wind-blown beauty in many places, particularly the undeveloped stretches of salt marsh and slash pine that spill east and west of Apalachee Bay. In other areas, the seashore is given to rental houses and high-rise condos.

Inland, you'll find a tangle of palmetto fans and thin pine woods interspersed with crystal springs, lazy rivers and military testing ranges – this area has one of the highest concentrations of defense facilities in the country.

Tallahassee

Florida's capital, cradled between gently rising hills and nestled beneath tree-canopied roadways, is geographically closer to Atlanta than it is to Miami. Culturally, it's far closer to the Deep South than the majority of the state it governs. Despite its status as a government center, and the presence of two major universities (Florida State and Florida Agricultural & Mechanical University), the pace here is slower than syrup. That said, there are a handful of interesting museums and outlying attractions that will appeal to history and nature buffs and could easily detain a visitor for a day or two.

⊙ Sights & Activities

★Tallahassee Museum of
History & Natural Science   MUSEUM
(☑850-575-8684; www.tallahasseemuseum.org; 3945 Museum Rd; adult/child $11.50/8.50; ☺9am-5pm Mon-Sat, from 11am Sun; P 🐾) 🍴 Occupying 52 acres of pristine manicured gardens and wilderness on the outskirts of Tallahassee, near the airport, this wonderful natural-history museum features living exhibits of Floridian flora and fauna – including the incredibly rare Floridian panther and red wolf – and has delighted visitors for more than 50 years. Be sure to check out the otters in their new home, or try ziplining above the canopy in the Tree to Tree Adventures.

Tallahassee Automobile
& Collectibles Museum   MUSEUM
(☑850-942-0137; www.tacm.com; 6800 Mahan Dr; adult/student/child under 10yr $16/12/8; ☺8am-5pm Mon-Fri, from 10am Sat, from noon Sun; P) If you like motor vehicles, welcome to heaven! This museum houses a pristine collection of more than 130 unique and historical automobiles from around the world. Top that with collections of boats, motorcycles, books, pianos and sports memorabilia and you've got a full day on your hands. It is about 8 miles northeast of downtown.

Florida State Capitol   NOTABLE BUILDING
(www.floridacapitol.myflorida.com; 400 South Monroe St; ☺8am-5pm Mon-Fri) FREE The stark and imposing 22-story Florida State Capitol's top-floor observation deck affords 360-degree views of the city. In session the capitol is a hive of activity, with politicians, staffers and lobby groups buzzing in and around its honeycombed corridors.

Tallahassee-St Marks
Historic Railroad State Trail   CYCLING
(☑850-519-6594; www.floridastateparks.org/tallahasseestmarks; 1358 Old Woodville Rd, Crawfordville; ☺8am-sunset) 🚲 FREE The ultimate treat for runners, skaters and cyclists, this trail has 16 miles of smooth pavement shooting due south to the gulf-port town of St Marks and not a car or traffic light in sight. It's easy and flat for all riders, sitting on a coastal plain and shaded at many points by canopies of gracious live oaks.

🛏 Sleeping & Eating

aloft Tallahassee Downtown   HOTEL $$
(☑850-513-0313; www.alofttallahassee.com; 200 N Monroe St; r $115-230; P 🛜) This branch of the popular aloft chain boasts a prime downtown location and funky, functional rooms. Bathrooms feature counter-to-ceiling mirrors and lots of space for all the makeup in the world. Beds are uber-comfy, and free high-speed internet is included.

Kool Beanz Café   FUSION $$
(☑850-224-2466; www.koolbeanz-cafe.com; 921 Thomasville Rd; mains $17-24; ☺11am-10pm Mon-Fri, 5:30-10pm Sat, 10:30am-2pm Sun; P 🍴🐾) It's got a corny name but a wonderfully eclectic and homey vibe – plus great, creative fare. The menu changes daily, but you can count on finding anything from hummus plates to jerk-spiced scallops to duck in blueberry-ginger sauce.

🍷 Drinking & Entertainment

Madison Social   PUB
(📞 850-894-6276; www.madisonsocial.com; 705 South Woodward Ave; mains $9-20; ⏰ 11:30am-2am Sun-Thu, from 10am Fri & Sat; 📶) Never mind the trend of flipping former transmission shops into hipster locales, this trendy hot spot was built to look that way from go. It swarms with a bold and beautiful mix of locals and FSU students, downing drinks at the stellar bar or aluminum picnic tables as the sun sets over Doak Campbell football stadium, the largest continuous brick structure in the USA.

Bradfordville Blues Club   LIVE MUSIC
(📞 850-906-0766; www.bradfordvilleblues.com; 7152 Moses Lane, off Bradfordville Rd; tickets $15-35; ⏰ 10pm Fri & Sat) Down the end of a dirt road lit by tiki torches, you'll find a bonfire raging under the live oaks at this hidden-away juke joint that hosts excellent national blues acts. Also open some Thursdays from 8:30pm; check online.

ℹ️ Information

Florida Welcome Center (📞 850-488-6167; www.visitflorida.com; cnr Pensacola & Duval Sts; ⏰ 8am-5pm Mon-Fri) In the Florida State Capitol, this is a fantastic resource.

Leon County Welcome Center (📞 850-606-2305; www.visittallahassee.com; 106 E Jefferson St; ⏰ 8am-5pm Mon-Fri) Runs the excellent visitor information center, with brochures on walking and driving tours.

ℹ️ Getting There & Around

Tallahassee is 98 miles from Panama City Beach, 135 miles from Jacksonville, 192 miles from Pensacola, 120 miles from Gainesville and 470 miles from Miami. The main access road is I-10; to reach the Gulf Coast, follow Hwy 319 south to Hwy 98.

The tiny **Tallahassee International Airport** (📞 850-891-7802; www.talgov.com/airport; 3300 Capital Circle SW) is served by American and Delta for US domestic and international connections, and Silver Airways for direct flights to Tampa and Orlando. It's about 5 miles southwest of downtown, off Hwy 263. There's no public transportation. Some hotels have shuttles, but otherwise a taxi to downtown costs around $20: try **Yellow Cab** (📞 850-999-9999; www.tallahasseeyellowcab.com).

The **Greyhound bus station** (📞 850-222-4249; www.greyhound.com; 112 W Tennessee St) is at the corner of Duval, opposite the downtown **StarMetro** (📞 850-891-5200; www.talgov.com/starmetro; per trip/day $1.25/3) transfer center.

WORTH A TRIP

DELAND: CRESS

Citified foodies have been known to trek to sleepy DeLand, half an hour from Daytona Beach (p505), just to eat at the cutting-edge bistro **Cress** (📞 386-734-3740; www.cressrestaurant.com; 103 W Indiana Ave; mains $19-34; ⏰ from 5:30pm Tue-Sat), whose menu might offer such delights as local seafood *mofongo* (a classic Caribbean dish), Indonesian shrimp curry, and a salad of delicate pea tendrils with passion-fruit emulsion. Three-course fixed menus ($40, with wine pairing $58) are excellent.

Pensacola

The Alabama border is just a few miles down the road, which helps explain the vibe of Pensacola, a city that jumbles laid-back Southern syrup with Florida brashness. With lively beaches, a Spanish-style downtown, and a thrumming military culture, this is by far the most interesting city in the Panhandle.

While urban-chic trends (locavore food, craft cocktails etc) are taking root, visitors still primarily come to Pensacola for an all-American, blue-collar vacation experience: white-sand beaches, fried seafood and bars serving cheap domestics. During March and April, things reach fever pitch when droves of students descend for the weeklong bacchanalia of spring break. Beware.

Downtown, centered on Palafox St, lies north of the waterfront. Across the Pensacola Bay Bridge from here is the mostly residential peninsula of Gulf Breeze. Cross one more bridge, the Bob Sikes (toll $1), to reach pretty Pensacola Beach, the ultimate destination for most visitors.

Distinctly separate from Pensacola itself, Pensacola Beach is a pretty stretch of powdery white sand, gentle, warm waters and a string of mellow beachfront hotels. The beach occupies nearly 8 miles of the 40-mile-long Santa Rosa barrier island, surrounded by the Santa Rosa Sound and the Gulf of Mexico to the north and south, and by the federally protected Gulf Islands National Seashore on either side. Though determined residents have protected much of the barrier island from development, several high-rise condos have created a bit of a Gulf Coast skyline.

👁 Sights

⭐ National Naval Aviation Museum
MUSEUM

(☎ 800-327-5002; www.navalaviationmuseum.org; 1750 Radford Blvd; ⏰ 9am-5pm; 🚼) **FREE** A visit to Pensacola is not complete without a trip to this enormous collection of military aircraft muscle and artifacts. Adults and children alike will be fascinated by the range of planes on display: more than 150! That's before we even get to the high-tech stuff like flight simulators and an IMAX theater. You can watch the **Blue Angels** (☎ 850-452-3806; www.naspensacolaairshow.com; 390 San Carlos Rd, Suite A) **FREE** practice their death-defying air show at 8:30am most Tuesdays and Wednesdays between March and November.

Historic Pensacola Village
MUSEUM

(☎ 850-595-5985; www.historicpensacola.org; Tarragona & Church St; adult/child $8/4; ⏰ 10am-4pm Tue-Sat; 🅿🚼) 🦽 Pensacola's rich colonial history spans more than 450 years. This fascinating and attractive village is a self-contained enclave of photogenic historic homes turned into museums.

⭐ Gulf Islands National Seashore
PARK

(☎ 850-934-2600; www.nps.gov/guis; vehicle $15; ⏰ sunrise-sunset; 🚼) 🦽 The highlight of the Florida Panhandle, this 150-mile stretch of mostly undeveloped white-sand beach is a prime example of what the Gulf Coast looked like before human settlement (which,

to be fair, can often be seen in the form of high rises in the distance). The National Seashore is not contiguous, but you'll find portions all along the coast: long swaths of sugar-white dunes crowned with sea oats, a perfect example of pristine flatland beach.

🛏 Sleeping & Eating

Solé Inn
MOTEL $

(☎ 850-470-9298; www.soleinnandsuites.com; 200 N Palafox St; r $79-199; 🅿🚰❄) Just north of downtown, this renovated motel goes for a 1960s mod look, with a black-and-white color scheme, animal-print accents and acrylic bubble lamps. Rooms aren't huge, but price, location and originality make up for the lack of space. There's complimentary continental breakfast.

Holiday Inn Resort
HOTEL $$

(☎ 850-203-0635; www.holidayinnresortpensacolabeach.com; 14 Via de Luna Dr; r from $210; ❄) This beachfront hotel has cool, inviting rooms with ultra-comfy beds, flat-screen TVs and great showers. Oceanfront rooms have spacious balconies overhanging the soft, white sands and the cool turquoise waters below. Suites and kids' suites are available, and the pool is killer. Friendly, obliging staff help seal the deal. Excellent value.

Peg Leg Pete's
SEAFOOD $$

(☎ 850-932-4139; www.peglegpetes.com; 1010 Fort Pickens Rd; mains $9-25; ⏰ 11am-10pm; 🚼)

OFF THE BEATEN TRACK

APALACHICOLA NATIONAL FOREST

The largest of Florida's three national forests, the **Apalachicola National Forest** (☎ 850-523-8500, 850-643-2282; www.fs.usda.gov/main/apalachicola; entrance off FL 13, FL 67, & other locations; day-use fee $3; ⏰ 8am-sunset; 🚼) 🦽 occupies almost 938 sq miles – more than half a million acres – of the Panhandle from just west of Tallahassee to the Apalachicola River. It's made up of lowlands, pines, cypress hammocks and oaks, and dozens of species call the area home, including mink, gray and red foxes, coyotes, six bat species, beavers, woodpeckers, alligators, Florida black bears and the elusive Florida panther. Numerous lakes and miles of trails make this one of the most diverse outdoor recreation areas in the state. You'll need wheels to explore the forest, either a bicycle for the exceedingly fit, or a car for the rest of us. Given that the woods cover such an enormous area, there are multiple entry points, including along SR 65 (easier if you're coming from Apalachicola) and SR 20 (good for those coming from Tallahassee).

The western half of the forest is controlled by the **Apalachicola Ranger Station** (☎ 850-643-2282; www.fs.usda.gov/apalachicola; 11152 NW SR-20), which is northwest of the forest near the intersection of Hwys 12 and 20, just south of Bristol. The eastern half of the forest is managed by the **Wakulla Ranger Station** (☎ 850-926-3561; www.fs.usda.gov/apalachicola; 57 Taff Dr), just off Hwy 319 in Crawfordville.

Ah-har, me hearties, walk ye olde plank, blah blah pirate stuff...you get the idea, this place has a theme going. Anyways, pop into Pete's for almost-beachfront oysters, fat grouper sandwiches, crab legs and jumbo sea scallops. There's nothing fancy about the woodsy, somewhat grungy sea-shanty decor, but the service is swift and smiley.

★ **Iron** MODERN AMERICAN $$$
(✆ 850-476-7776; www.restaurantiron.com; 22 N Palafox St; mains $26-46; ⊙ 4:30-10pm Tue-Thu, to 1am Fri & Sat; 🛜) Armed with New Orleans experience, chef Alex McPhail works his ever-changing menu magic at downtown's Iron, the best of Pensacola's new line of vibrant, locally sourced, high-end culinary hotbeds. Extremely friendly mixologists know their craft while McPhail's food ranges from beer-braised pork belly to Creole-seasoned catch of the day.

🍷 **Drinking & Entertainment**

McGuire's Irish Pub PUB
(✆ 850-433-6789; www.mcguiresirishpub.com; 600 E Gregory St; ⊙ 11am-2am) This ginormous Irish theme park of a pub gets rowdy around 9pm and is super-popular at dinner time: the pub grub is top-notch. Don't try to pay for your drinks with one of the thousands of dollar bills hanging from the ceiling – a local found himself in the slammer that way!

Roundup GAY
(✆ 850-433-8482; www.theroundup.net; 560 E Heinberg St; ⊙ 2pm-3am) For those who like their men manly, check out this niche-y, neighborhood hangout with a killer furry-friendly patio. Ladies are welcome, but cowboys, tradies and bikers are always flavor of the month.

Saenger Theatre THEATER
(✆ 850-595-3880; www.pensacolasaenger.com; 118 S Palafox Pl) This Spanish baroque beauty was reconstructed in 1925 using bricks from the Pensacola Opera House, which was destroyed in a 1916 hurricane. It now hosts popular musicals and top-billing music acts and is home to the Pensacola Symphony Orchestra and the Pensacola Opera.

WORTH A TRIP

PENSACOLA SCENIC BLUFFS HIGHWAY

This 11-mile stretch of road, which winds around the precipice of the highest point along the Gulf Coast, makes for a peaceful drive or slightly challenging bike ride. You'll see stunning views of Escambia Bay and pass a notable crumbling brick chimney – part of the steam-power plant for the Hyer-Knowles lumber mill in the 1850s – the only remnant of what was the first major industrial belt in the area.

ℹ️ **Information**

Pensacola Visitors Information Center
(✆ 800-874-1234; www.visitpensacola.com; 1401 E Gregory St; ⊙ 8am-5pm Mon-Fri, 9am-4pm Sat, 10am-4pm Sun) Come to the foot of the Pensacola Bay Bridge for a bounty of tourist information, knowledgeable staff and a free internet kiosk.

Pensacola Beach Visitors Information Center
(✆ 850-932-1500; www.visitpensacolabeach.com; 735 Pensacola Beach Blvd; ⊙ 9am-5pm) On the right as soon as you enter Pensacola Beach; this is a small place with some useful maps and brochures about goings-on, road closures (due to storms) and anything else beach oriented.

ℹ️ **Getting There & Away**

Pensacola Regional Airport (✆ 850-436-5000; www.flypensacola.com; 2430 Airport Blvd) is served by most major US airlines. Primary direct connections outside Florida include Atlanta, Charlotte, Dallas and Houston. It's 4 miles northeast of downtown off 9th Ave on Airport Blvd. A taxi costs about $20 to downtown and $35 to the beach. Try **Yellow Cab** (✆ 850-433-3333; www.yellowcabpensacola.com).

The **Greyhound station** (✆ 850-476-4800; www.greyhound.com; 505 W Burgess Rd) is located north of the downtown area. **Escambia County Transit** (ECAT; ✆ 850-595-3228; www.goecat.com; rides $1.75) has a free trolley service connecting downtown Pensacola and the beach between Memorial Day weekend and the end of September.

I-10 is the major east–west thoroughfare used by buses, and many pass down Palafox St.

Great Lakes

Includes ➡

Illinois	529
Chicago	532
Indiana	561
Indianapolis	561
Ohio	570
Cleveland	570
Cincinnati	579
Michigan	583
Detroit	584
Wisconsin	603
Milwaukee	603
Minnesota	613
Minneapolis	614

Best Places to Eat

➡ Spencer (p592)

➡ Young Joni (p618)

➡ Tucker's (p581)

➡ Hopleaf (p551)

➡ Tinker Street (p563)

Best Places to Sleep

➡ Kimpton Schofield Hotel (p571)

➡ Acme Hotel (p547)

➡ Brewhouse Inn & Suites (p604)

➡ Hotel 340 (p621)

➡ Inn on Ferry Street (p588)

Why Go?

Don't be fooled by all the corn. Behind it lurks surfing beaches and Tibetan temples, car-free islands and the green-draped night lights of the aurora borealis. The Midwest takes its knocks for being middle-of-nowhere boring; so consider the moose-filled national parks, urban five-ways (a meal consisting of spaghetti, chili, onions, beans and cheese) and Hemingway, Dylan and Vonnegut sites to be its little secret.

Roll call for the Midwest's cities starts with Chicago, which unfurls what is arguably the country's mightiest skyline. Milwaukee keeps the beer-and-Harley flame burning, while Minneapolis shines a hipster beacon out over the fields. Detroit rocks, plain and simple. The Great Lakes themselves are huge, like inland seas, offering beaches, dunes, resort towns and lighthouse-dotted scenery. Dairy farms and fruit orchards blanket the region, meaning fresh pie and ice cream aplenty. And when the Midwest does flatten out? There's always a goofball roadside attraction, like the Spam Museum or world's biggest ball of twine, to revive imaginations.

When to Go
Chicago

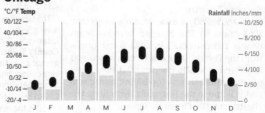

Jan & Feb It's that chilly time when skiers and snowmobilers hit the trails.

Jul & Aug Finally, it's warm! Beer gardens hop, beaches splash, and festivals rock most weekends.

Sep & Oct Fair weather, bountiful farm and orchard harvests, and shoulder-season bargains.

History

The region's first residents included the Hopewell (around 200 BC) and Mississippi River mound builders (around AD 700). Both left behind mysterious piles of earth that were tombs for their leaders and possibly tributes to their deities. You can see remnants at Cahokia in southern Illinois, and Mound City in southeastern Ohio.

French voyageurs (fur traders) arrived in the early 17th century and established missions and forts. The British turned up soon after that, with the rivalry spilling over into the French and Indian Wars (Seven Years' War; 1754–61), after which Britain took control of all of the land east of the Mississippi. Following the Revolutionary War, the Great Lakes area became the new USA's Northwest Territory, which soon was divided into states and locked to the region after it developed its impressive canal and railroad network. But conflicts erupted between the newcomers and the Native Americans, including the 1811 Battle of Tippecanoe in Indiana; the bloody 1832 Black Hawk War in Wisconsin, Illinois and around, which forced indigenous people to move west of the Mississippi; and the 1862 Sioux uprising in Minnesota.

Throughout the late 19th and early 20th centuries, industries sprang up and grew quickly, fueled by resources of coal and iron, and cheap transportation on the lakes. The availability of work brought huge influxes of immigrants from Ireland, Germany, Scandinavia and southern and eastern Europe. For decades after the Civil War, a great number of African Americans also migrated to the region's urban centers from the South.

The area prospered during WWII and throughout the 1950s, but was followed by 20 years of social turmoil and economic stagnation. Manufacturing industries declined, which walloped Rust Belt cities such as Detroit and Cleveland with high unemployment and 'white flight' (white middle-class families who fled to the suburbs).

The 1980s and '90s brought urban revitalization. The region's population increased, notably with newcomers from Asia and Mexico. Growth in the service and high-tech sectors resulted in economic balance, although manufacturing industries such as car making and steel still played a big role, meaning that when the economic crisis hit in 2008, Great Lakes towns felt the pinch first and foremost.

ILLINOIS

Chicago dominates the state with its sky-high architecture and superlative museums, restaurants and music clubs. But venturing further afield reveals Hemingway's mannerly hometown, scattered shrines to local hero Abe Lincoln, and a trail of corn dogs, pies and drive-in theaters down Route 66. A cypress swamp and a prehistoric World Heritage Site make appearances in Illinois too.

GREAT LAKES IN...

One Week

Spend the first two days in **Chicago**, stuffing your face and gawking at architecture. On your third day, make the 1½-hour trip to **Milwaukee** for beer, art and badass motorcycles. Take the ferry to **Michigan** and spend your fourth day in **Saugatuck**. The artsy town booms in summer thanks to its golden beaches, piney breezes, galleries and welcoming bars. Circle back via **Indiana Dunes** for sandy hikes and swimming, or via Indiana's **Amish Country** for a unique cultural immersion.

Two Weeks

After two days in **Chicago**, on day three make for **Madison** to chow in locavore eateries and visit the surrounding quirky sights. Spend your fourth and fifth days at the **Apostle Islands** boating around wind-bashed cliffs and caves. Then head into Michigan's Upper Peninsula to visit **Marquette** and **Pictured Rocks** for a few days. Both are outdoorsy places with dramatic nature at their doorstep. Follow with a visit to the towering **Sleeping Bear Dunes** and the wineries around **Traverse City**. Return via the galleries, pies and beaches of **Saugatuck**.

Great Lakes Highlights

1 Chicago (p532) Absorbing the skyscrapers, museums, festivals and foodie bounty.

2 Detroit (p584) Embracing the city's can-do spirit and partaking of its art, eateries and neighborhood bicycle rides.

3 Ohio's Amish Country (p576) Slowing down for clip-clopping horses and buggies.

4 Michigan's Gold Coast (p594) Beach lounging, dune climbing, berry eating and surfing.

5 Milwaukee (p603) Polka dancing at a Friday-night fish fry and drinking lots o' beer.

6 Boundary Waters (p625) Paddling deep into the piney woods and sleeping under a blanket of stars.

7 Route 66 (p535) Taking the slowpoke route through Illinois past pie-filled diners and oddball roadside attractions.

8 Central Indiana (p564) Being surprised by the Tibetan temples, phenomenal architecture and green hills.

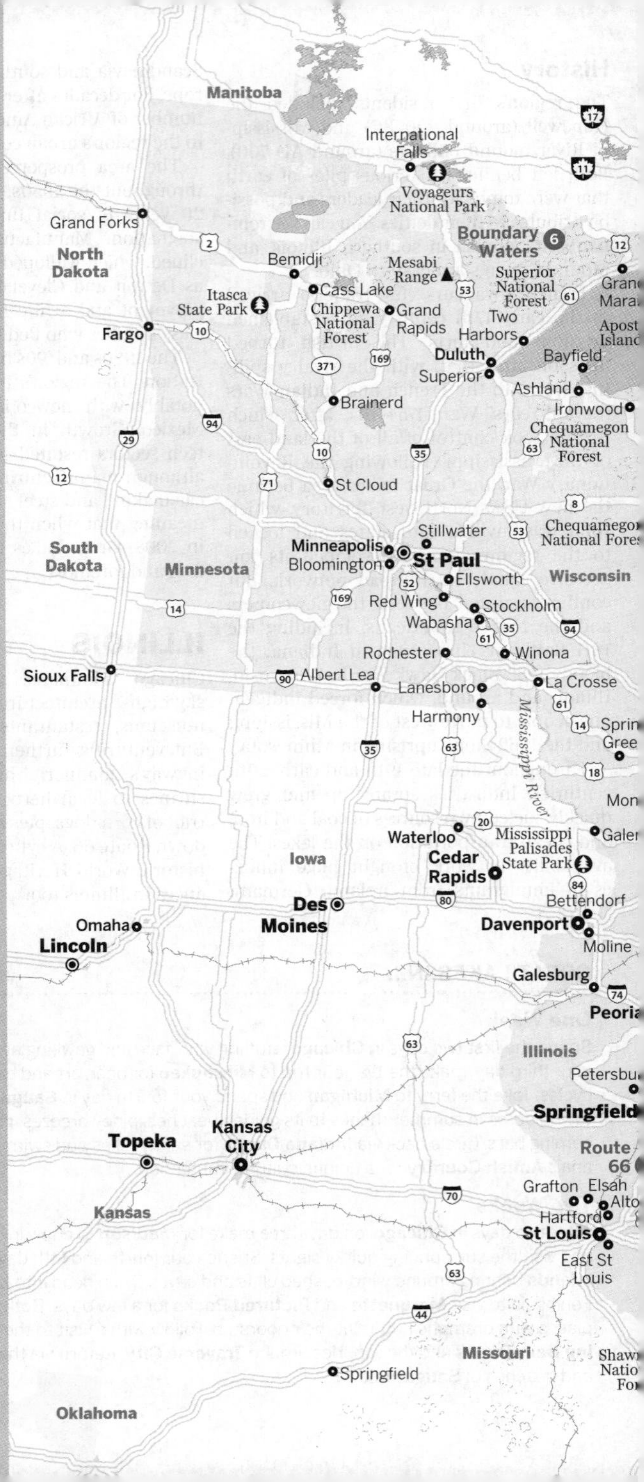

ℹ️ Information

Illinois Highway Conditions (www.getting aroundillinois.com)

Illinois Office of Tourism (www.enjoyillinois.com)

Illinois State Park Information (www.dnr. illinois.gov) State parks are free to visit. Campsites cost $6 to $35; some accept reservations (www.reserveamerica.com; fee $5).

Chicago

Steely skyscrapers, top chefs, rocking festivals – the Windy City will blow you away with its low-key cultured awesomeness.

It's hard to know what to gawp at first. High-flying architecture is everywhere, from the stratospheric, glass-floored Willis Tower to Frank Gehry's swooping silver Pritzker Pavilion to Frank Lloyd Wright's stained-glass Robie House. Whimsical public art studs the streets; you might be walking along and wham, there's an abstract Picasso statue that's not only cool to look at, but you're allowed to go right up and climb on it. For art museums, take your pick: impressionist masterpieces at the massive Art Institute, psychedelic paintings at the mid-sized Museum of Mexican Art or outsider drawings at the small Intuit gallery.

History

Much of Chicago's past is downright legendary. You've probably heard about Mrs

---

ℹ️ DISCOUNT CARDS

➡ The Go Chicago Card (www. smartdestinations.com/chicago) allows you to visit an unlimited number of attractions for a flat fee. It's good for one, two, three or five consecutive days.

➡ The company also offers a three-, four- or five-choice Explorer Pass where you pick among 25 options for sights. It's valid for 30 days.

➡ CityPass (www.citypass.com/ chicago) gives access to five of the city's top draws, including the Art Institute, Shedd Aquarium and Willis Tower, over nine days. It's less flexible than Go Chicago's pass, but cheaper for those wanting a more leisurely sightseeing pace.

➡ All of the above let you skip the regular queues at sights.

O'Leary's cow that kicked over a lantern that started the Great Fire that torched the city. And about a gent named Al Capone who wielded a mean machine gun during an unsavory era of booze-fueled vice. And about the 'machine' that has controlled local politics for decades. Throw in the invention of the skyscraper and Ferris wheel, and you've got a whopper of a tale.

⊙ Sights

Big-ticket draws such as Millennium Park, Willis Tower and the Art Institute are downtown right in the Loop. Next door, the South Loop holds the lakefront Museum Campus, with three popular sights including the Field Museum. To the Loop's north are Navy Pier and 360° Chicago (aka the John Hancock tower). Onward Lincoln Park and Wrigley Field do their thing. All of these places are easy to reach on public transportation. Hyde Park is the one neighborhood with top sights that is further flung and requires some planning to reach.

⊙ The Loop

The Loop is Chicago's center of action, named for the elevated train tracks that lasso its streets. The Art Institute, Willis Tower, Theater District and Millennium Park are top draws among the skyscrapers. The city's biggest festivals also rock the area.

★**Millennium Park**   PARK
(Map p536; ☑ 312-742-1168; www.millennium park.org; 201 E Randolph St; ⊙6am-11pm; 👪; Ⓜ Brown, Orange, Green, Purple, Pink Line to Washington/Wabash) The city's showpiece is a trove of free and arty sights. It includes **Pritzker Pavilion**, Frank Gehry's swooping silver band shell, which hosts free concerts most nights in summer (6:30pm; bring a picnic and bottle of wine); Anish Kapoor's beloved silvery sculpture **Cloud Gate**, aka the 'Bean'; and Jaume Plensa's **Crown Fountain**, a de facto water park that projects video images of locals spitting water, gargoyle style.

The **McCormick Tribune Ice Rink** (55 N Michigan Ave; ⊙ late Nov-late Feb) fills with skaters in winter (and al fresco diners in summer). The hidden **Lurie Garden** (www.lurie garden.org) blooms with prairie flowers and tranquility. The Gehry-designed **BP Bridge** spans Columbus Dr and offers great skyline views, while the **Nichols Bridgeway** arches from the park up to the Art Institute's small, 3rd-floor sculpture terrace (free to view).

Metro Chicago Area

N 0 — 5 km
0 — 2.5 miles

ROGERS PARK
Morse
Loyola Park
Warren Park
Loyola
N Lincoln Ave
W Devon Ave
Granville
W Peterson Ave
Thorndale
Rosehill Cemetery
Bryn Mawr
East River Park
ANDERSONVILLE
Berwyn
W Foster Ave
LINCOLN SQUARE
UPTOWN
Argyle
(10mi)
Lawrence
Kimball
Montrose
Wilson
Francisco
Rockwell
Western
Damen
Irving Park
Graceland Cemetery
Montrose Harbor
W Irving Park Rd
Irving Park
Addison
Horner Park
WRIGLEYVILLE
Sheridan
Wrigley Field
Addison
Addison
Belmont
Paulina
Southport
Belmont Harbor
Belmont
LAKE VIEW
Wellington
N Milwaukee Ave
Logan Square
W Diversey Ave
Diversey
N Clark St
Diversey Harbor
LOGAN SQUARE
W Fullerton Ave
California
BUCKTOWN
Clybourn Station (Metra)
Fullerton
LINCOLN PARK
Lake Michigan
Western
N Clybourn Ave
Armitage
Damen
OLD TOWN
Sedgwick
W North Ave
HUMBOLDT PARK
WICKER PARK
North/Clybourn
Clark/Division
W Division St
Division
Pulaski
Garfield Park
UKRAINIAN VILLAGE
W Grand Ave
Ashland
See Downtown Chicago Map (p536)
Oak Park (3.5 mi)
California
United Center
Medical Center
W Lake St
Kedzie
Western
Racine
MUSEUM CAMPUS
Kedzie-Homan
Polk
LITTLE ITALY
W Roosevelt Rd
Kildare
Pulaski
Central Park
Kedzie
National Museum of Mexican Art
Halsted St Station
18th St (Metra)
18th St Station (Metra)
18th St
PILSEN
Cermak-Chinatown
Cermak-McCormick
W Cermak Rd
California
Western
Hoyne
CHINATOWN
27th St Station (Metra)
Halsted
S State St
BRONZEVILLE
E 31st St
Sanitary Drainage and Ship Canal
Ashland
Sox-35th St
35th St-Bronzeville-IIT
Adlai Stevenson Expwy
35th St/Archer
BRIDGEPORT
W Pershing Rd
Indiana
43rd St
Burnham Park
S Archer Ave
W 43rd St
KENWOOD
47th St Station (Metra)
Kedzie
Western
W 47th St
E 47th St
47th St
55th-56th-57th St Station (Metra)
51st-53rd St Station (Metra)
Pulaski
Sherman Park
51st St
HYDE PARK
W 55th St
W Garfield Blvd
Garfield
Midway
W 59th St
Museum of Science & Industry

CHICAGO IN TWO DAYS...

Day One

You might as well dive right in with the big stuff. Take a boat or walking tour with the Chicago Architecture Foundation (p545) and ogle the most sky-scraping collection of buildings the US has to offer. Saunter over to Millennium Park (p532) to see 'the Bean' reflect the skyline and to splash under Crown Fountain's human gargoyles.

Explore the Art Institute of Chicago, the nation's second-largest art museum. It holds masterpieces aplenty, especially impressionist and post-impressionist paintings (and paperweights). Next, head over to Willis Tower, zip up to the 103rd floor and step out onto the glass-floored ledge. Yes, it is a long way down.

Chicago dazzles after dark and its diversity is yours to savour. Options are endless but original Chicago offerings could include hitting the Green Mill (p553), once Al Capone's favourite speakeasy; settling in to Danny's (p553) where early evening beers progress to cocktails and DJs under the same roof, or sampling some out-there local theatre at the legendary Steppenwolf (p554).

Day Two

Take a stroll on Michigan Ave – aka the Magnificent Mile (p539) – where big-name department stores ka-ching in a glittering row. Mosey over to Navy Pier (p539). Wander the half-mile promenade and take a spin on the high-in-the-sky Ferris wheel.

Spend the afternoon at the Museum Campus (p539) – the water taxi from Navy Pier is a fine way to get there. Miles of aisles of dinosaurs and gemstones stuff the Field Museum of Natural History. Sharks and other fish swim in the kiddie-mobbed Shedd Aquarium. Meteorites and supernovas are on view at the Adler Planetarium.

Wander along Milwaukee Ave and take your pick of booming bars, indie-rock clubs and hipster shops. Bustling Reckless Records (p556) is Chicago's top indie music store and testament to the fact that people still buy vynil and CDs. The Hideout (p554) and Empty Bottle (p554) are sweet spots to catch a badass band.

Free yoga and Pilates classes take place Saturday mornings in summer on the **Great Lawn**, while the Family Fun Tent provides free kids' activities daily in summer from 10am to 2pm.

★ Art Institute of Chicago
MUSEUM

(Map p536; ☑ 312-443-3600; www.artic.edu; 111 S Michigan Ave; adult/child $25/free; ⊗ 10:30am-5pm Fri-Wed, to 8pm Thu; ⊕; Ⓜ Brown, Orange, Green, Purple, Pink Line to Adams) The Art Institute is the second-largest art museum in the country. Its collection of impressionist and post-impressionist paintings rivals those in France, and the number of surrealist works is tremendous. Download the free app for DIY audio tours; it offers several quick-hit jaunts, from highlights (including Georges Seurat's *A Sunday Afternoon on the Island of La Grande Jatte* and Edward Hopper's *Nighthawks*) to architecture and pop art tours. Allow two hours to browse the museum's must-sees.

★ Willis Tower
TOWER

(Map p536; ☑ 312-875-9696; www.theskydeck. com; 233 S Wacker Dr; adult/child $23/15; ⊗ 9am-10pm Mar-Sep, 10am-8pm Oct-Feb; Ⓜ Brown, Orange, Purple, Pink Line to Quincy) It's Chicago's tallest building, and the 103rd-floor Skydeck puts you high into the heavens. Take the ear-popping, 70-second elevator ride to the top and then step onto one of the glass-floored ledges jutting out in mid-air for a knee-buckling perspective straight down. On clear days the view sweeps over four states. The entrance is on Jackson Blvd. Queues can take up to an hour on busy days (peak times are in summer, between 11am and 4pm Friday through Sunday).

Chicago Cultural Center
NOTABLE BUILDING

(Map p536; ☑ 312-744-6630; www.chicagocultural center.org; 78 E Washington St; ⊗ 9am-7pm Mon-Thu, to 6pm Fri & Sat, 10am-6pm Sun; Ⓜ Brown, Orange, Green, Purple, Pink Line to Washington/Wabash) FREE This exquisite, beaux-arts building began its life as the Chicago Public

Library in 1897. Today the block-long building houses terrific art exhibitions (especially the 4th-floor Yates Gallery), as well as jazz and classical concerts at lunchtime (12:15pm most Mondays and every Wednesday). It also contains the world's largest Tiffany stained-glass dome, on the 3rd floor where the library circulation desk used to be. **InstaGreeter** (www.chicagogreeter.com/instagreeter; ☺10am-3pm Fri & Sat, 11am-2pm Sun) `FREE` tours of the Loop depart from the Randolph St lobby, as do Millennium Park tours.

Maggie Daley Park   PARK
(Map p536; www.maggiedaleypark.com; 337 E Randolph St; ☺6am-11pm; ⊞; Ⓜ Brown, Orange, Green, Purple, Pink Line to Washington/Wabash) Families love this park's fanciful free playgrounds in all their enchanted-forest and pirate-themed glory. There's also a rock-climbing wall, 18-hole mini-golf course, in-line skating ribbon (which becomes an ice-skating ribbon in winter) and tennis courts; these features have fees. Multiple picnic tables make the park an excellent spot to relax.

Buckingham Fountain   FOUNTAIN
(Map p536; 301 S Columbus Dr; Ⓜ Red Line to Harrison) Grant Park's centerpiece is one of the world's largest fountains, with a 1.5-million-gallon capacity and a 15-story-high spray. It lets loose on the hour from 8am to 11pm early May to mid-October, accompanied at night by lights and music.

Route 66 Sign   HISTORIC SITE
(Map p536; E Adams St, btwn S Michigan & Wabash Aves; Ⓜ Brown, Orange, Green, Purple, Pink Line to Adams) Attention Route 66 buffs: the Mother Road's starting point is here. Look for the 'Historic 66 Begin' sign that marks the spot on Adams St's southern side as you head west toward Wabash Ave. There are a couple of other 66 signs on the same block, but this one is the original.

From Chicago the route traverses 2400 miles to Los Angeles, past neon signs, mom-and-pop motels and pie-filled diners. See p40 for more on Route 66.

◉ South Loop

In the South Loop, the Field Museum, Shedd Aquarium and Adler Planetarium huddle at the Museum Campus. Peaceful 12th Street Beach and hilly Northerly Island offer nearby refuges to ditch the crowds. Historic buildings dot the neighborhood, including Chess

Records, the seminal blues label. Chinatown bustles with noodle shops and exotic wares.

★Field Museum of
Natural History   MUSEUM
(Map p536; ☎312-922-9410; www.fieldmuseum.org; 1400 S Lake Shore Dr; adult/child $22/15; ☺9am-5pm; ⊞; ☐146, 130) The Field Museum houses some 30 million artifacts and includes everything but the kitchen sink – beetles, mummies, gemstones, Bushman the stuffed ape – all tended by a slew of PhD-wielding scientists, as the Field remains an active research institution. The collection's rock star is Sue, the largest *Tyrannosaurus rex* yet discovered. She even gets her own gift shop. Special exhibits, such as the 3-D movie, cost extra.

Shedd Aquarium   AQUARIUM
(Map p536; ☎312-939-2438; www.sheddaquarium.org; 1200 S Lake Shore Dr; adult/child $40/30; ☺9am-6pm Jun-Aug, 9am-5pm Mon-Fri, to 6pm Sat & Sun Sep-May; ⊞; ☐146,130) Top draws at the kiddie-mobbed Shedd Aquarium include the Wild Reef exhibit, where there's just 5in of Plexiglas between you and two-dozen fierce-looking sharks, and the Oceanarium, with its rescued sea otters. Note the Oceanarium also keeps beluga whales and Pacific white-sided dolphins, a practice that has become increasingly controversial.

Adler Planetarium   MUSEUM
(Map p536; ☎312-922-7827; www.adlerplanetarium.org; 1300 S Lake Shore Dr; adult/child $12/8; ☺9:30am-4pm; ⊞; ☐146, 130) Space enthusiasts will get a big bang (pun!) out of the Adler. There are public telescopes to view the stars (10am to 1pm daily, by the Galileo Cafe), 3-D lectures to learn about supernovas (in the Space Visualization Lab), and the Planet Explorers exhibit where kids can 'launch' a rocket. The immersive digital films cost extra (from $13 per ticket). The Adler's front steps offer Chicago's best skyline view, so get your camera ready.

Northerly Island   PARK
(1521 S Linn White Dr; ☐146,130) This hilly, prairie-grassed park has a walking and cycling trail, bird-watching, fishing and an outdoor venue for big-name concerts. It's actually a peninsula, not an island, but the Chicago skyline views are tremendous no matter what you call it. Stop in at the field house, if it's open, for tour information. Bicycles are available at the Divvy bike-share station by the Adler Planetarium.

Downtown Chicago

Holiday Jones (0.8mi); Mana Food Bar (0.9mi); Wicker Park/ Bucktown (1 mi); Reckless Records (1.1mi); Logan Sq (3 mi)

iO Theater (0.8mi); Alinea (1mi); Steppenwolf Theatre (1mi); Hideout (1.9mi)

La Fournette (0.8mi); Old Town Ale House (0.8mi); Second City (0.9mi); Hotel Lincoln (1.2mi)

Chicago History Museum (1mi); Lincoln Park (1mi); Wrigley Field (3.5mi)

Chicago Children's Theatre (0.2mi); Original Playboy Mansion (0.6mi);

Chicago

Chicago

W Chicago Ave

63

Hoosier Mama Pie Company (0.6mi)

19

Grand

W Grand Ave

Morgan

W Carroll Ave

W Fulton St

WEST LOOP W Lake St

Morgan

W Randolph St

W Washington St

Chicago - Ogilvie Transportation Center (Metra)

W Monroe St

Chicago - Union Station (Metra)

W Adams St

37

W Jackson Blvd 290

W Van Buren St

GREEKTOWN

56

Clinton

UIC-Halsted

W Harrison St

W Vernon Park Pl

W Polk St

W Cabrini St

W Taylor St

90

W Roosevelt Rd

94

Knee Deep Vintage (0.5mi); National Museum of Mexican Art (1.2mi)

Pleasant House Pub (0.7mi)

47

W Superior St

W Huron St 57

W Erie St

W Ontario St

W Ohio St

W Grand Ave

W Illinois St

W Hubbard St

W Kinzie St

W Kinzie St

42 Merchandise Mart

W Wacker Dr

Clark/Lake

W Lake St

Clinton

State/ Lake

67

64 27

38

Daley Plaza

W Washington St

Washington/Wells

69

W Madison St

Washington

30

THE LOOP

W Monroe St

Monroe

W Marble Pl

58 24 61

Quincy

Jackson

31 20

7

Willis Tower

13

26

W VanBuren St

46

LaSalle/ Van Buren

Chicago - LaSalle St Station (Metra)

LaSalle

SOUTH LOOP

W 9th St

NEAR NORTH

Grand

62

Chicago

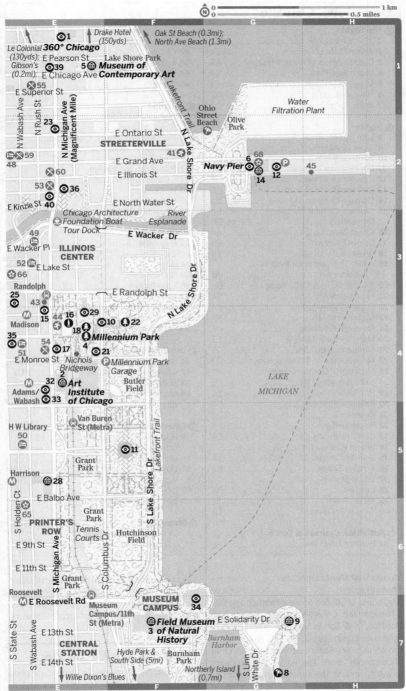

N 0 _____ 1 km
0 _____ 0.5 miles

1
360° Chicago

Le Colonial
(130yds);
Gibson's
(0.2mi);

E Pearson St
39   5 🏛 Museum of
E Chicago Ave Contemporary Art

Drake Hotel
(150yds)

Oak St Beach (0.3mi);
North Ave Beach (1.3mi)

Lake Shore Park

55
E Superior St

23

Water
Filtration Plant

Ohio
Street
Beach

Olive
Park

E Ontario St
STREETERVILLE

59
48

60

E Grand Ave

E Illinois St

41

6 68
Navy Pier 14
12   45

53
36
40
E Kinzie St

E North Water St

River
Esplanade

Chicago Architecture
Foundation Boat
Tour Dock

E Wacker Dr

49

E Wacker Pl

ILLINOIS
CENTER

52 E Lake St
66

Randolph

25
43

16 29
44 10 22
15 18
Millennium Park
4 21

E Randolph St

35
54
51 17
E Monroe St Nichols
Bridgeway

32 Art
Adams/ Institute
Wabash 33 of Chicago

Millennium Park
Garage

Butler
Field

H W Library

Van Buren
St (Metra)

50

11

LAKE
MICHIGAN

Grant
Park

Harrison

28

E Balbo Ave

65

S Holden Ct

PRINTER'S
ROW

Grant
Park

Tennis
Courts

Hutchinson
Field

E 9th St

E 11th St

Grant
Park

Roosevelt
E Roosevelt Rd

Museum
Campus/11th
St (Metra)

MUSEUM
CAMPUS

34

S State St

S Wabash Ave

E 13th St

CENTRAL
STATION

E 14th St

Hyde Park &
South Side (5mi)

Willie Dixon's Blues

🏛 Field Museum
3 of Natural
History

E Solidarity Dr

9

Burnham
Harbor

Burnham
Park

Northerly Island
(0.7mi)

S Linn
White Dr

8

Downtown Chicago

◉ Top Sights
1 360° Chicago E1
2 Art Institute of Chicago E4
3 Field Museum of Natural History F7
4 Millennium Park E4
5 Museum of Contemporary Art E1
6 Navy Pier G2
7 Willis Tower C4

◉ Sights
8 12th Street Beach G7
9 Adler Planetarium G7
10 BP Bridge E4
11 Buckingham Fountain F5
12 Centennial Wheel G2
13 Chicago Board of Trade D5
14 Chicago Children's Museum G2
15 Chicago Cultural Center E4
City Gallery ....(see 39)
16 Cloud Gate E4
17 Crown Fountain E4
18 Great Lawn E4
19 Intuit: The Center for Intuitive &
Outsider Art A1
20 Kluczynski Federal Building D4
21 Lurie Garden E4
22 Maggie Daley Park F4
23 Magnificent Mile E2
24 Marquette Building D4
25 Marshall Field Building E3
26 Monadnock Building D5
27 Monument with Standing Beast D3
28 Museum of Contemporary
Photography E5
29 Pritzker Pavilion E4
30 Reliance Building D4
31 Rookery D4
32 Route 66 Sign E4
33 Santa Fe Building E4
34 Shedd Aquarium F7
35 Sullivan Center E4
36 Tribune Tower E2
37 Union Station C4
38 Untitled D4
39 Water Tower E1
40 Wrigley Building E2

◉ Activities, Courses & Tours
41 Bobby's Bike Hike F2

Chicago Architecture
Foundation ....(see 33)
42 Chopping Block D3
43 InstaGreeter E3
44 McCormick Tribune Ice Rink E4
45 Windy H2

◉ Sleeping
Acme Hotel ....(see 48)
Alise Chicago ....(see 30)
46 Buckingham Athletic Club Hotel D5
47 Fieldhouse Jones C1
48 Freehand Chicago E2
49 Hampton Inn Chicago
Downtown/N Loop E3
50 HI-Chicago E5
51 Silversmith E4
52 Virgin Hotel E3

◉ Eating
53 Billy Goat Tavern E2
Cafecito ....(see 50)
54 Gage E4
55 Giordano's E1
56 Lou Mitchell's C5
57 Mr Beef C2
58 Native Foods Cafe D4
59 Pizzeria Uno E2
60 Purple Pig E2

◉ Drinking & Nightlife
61 Berghoff D4
62 Clark Street Ale House D1
63 Matchbox A1
64 Monk's Pub D3
Signature Lounge ....(see 1)

◉ Entertainment
65 Buddy Guy's Legends E6
Chicago Symphony Orchestra ....(see 33)
66 Chicago Theatre E3
67 Goodman Theatre D3
Grant Park Orchestra ....(see 29)
68 IMAX Theater G2
69 Lyric Opera of Chicago C4

◉ Shopping
Chicago Architecture
Foundation Shop ....(see 33)

**Museum of Contemporary
Photography**   MUSEUM
(Map p536; ☏ 312-663-5554; www.mocp.org; 600
S Michigan Ave, Columbia College; ◷10am-5pm
Mon-Wed, Fri & Sat, to 8pm Thu, noon-5pm Sun;
Ⓜ Red Line to Harrison) FREE This small museum focuses on American and international
photography from the early 20th century
onward, and is the only institution of its
kind between the coasts. The permanent
collection includes the works of Henri Cartier-
Bresson, Harry Callahan, Sally Mann,
Victor Skrebneski, Catherine Wagner and
500 more of the best photographers working today.

◉ Near North & Navy Pier

The Near North packs in deep-dish pizza
parlors, buzzy bistros, art galleries and so

CHICAGO FOR GANGSTERS

Chicago would rather not discuss its gangster past; consequently there are no brochures or exhibits about infamous sites, so you'll need to use your imagination when visiting the following places:

Green Mill (p553) Al Capone's favorite speakeasy; the tunnels where he hid the booze are still underneath the bar.

Biograph Theater (2433 N Lincoln Ave; Ⓜ Brown, Purple, Red Line to Fullerton) Where the 'lady in red' betrayed 'public enemy number one' John Dillinger.

Union Station (Map p536; www.chicagounionstation.com) Fans of *The Untouchables* can see where the baby carriage bounced down the stairs.

St Valentine's Day Massacre Site (2122 N Clark St; ☐22) Where Capone's men, dressed as cops, killed seven members of Bugs Moran's gang.

many upscale stores that its main vein – Michigan Ave – has been dubbed the 'Magnificent Mile.' Bulging out to the east is Navy Pier, a half-mile-long wharf of tour boats, carnival rides and a flashy, king-sized Ferris wheel.

★**Navy Pier**   WATERFRONT
(Map p536; ☎312-595-7437; www.navypier.com; 600 E Grand Ave; ⊙10am-10pm Sun-Thu, to midnight Fri & Sat Jun-Aug, 10am-8pm Sun-Thu, to 10pm Fri & Sat Sep-May; 🖤; Ⓜ Red Line to Grand) FREE Half-mile-long Navy Pier is one of Chicago's most-visited attractions, sporting a 196ft **Ferris wheel** (adult/child $15/12) and other carnival rides ($6 to $15 each), an **IMAX theater** (☎312-595-5629; www.imax. com; tickets $15-22) a beer garden and lots of chain restaurants. Locals groan over its commercialization, but its lakefront view and cool breezes can't be beat. The fireworks displays on summer Wednesdays (9:30pm) and Saturdays (10:15pm) are a treat too.

The **Chicago Children's Museum** (☎312-527-1000; www.chicagochildrensmuseum.org; admission $14; ⊙10am-5pm, to 8pm Thu; 🖤) is also on the pier, as are several boat-cruise operators. Try the Shoreline water taxi for a fun ride to the **Museum Campus** (adult/child $8/4 Sunday through Friday, $10/5 Saturday). A renovation is bringing a hotel and additional amusements to the pier through 2018. Get the trolley from Grand.

Magnificent Mile   AREA
(Map p536; www.themagnificentmile.com; N Michigan Ave; Ⓜ Red Line to Grand) Spanning Michigan Ave between the river and Oak St, the Mag Mile is Chicago's much-touted upscale shopping strip, where Bloomingdale's,

Apple, Burberry and many more will lighten your wallet.

Tribune Tower   ARCHITECTURE
(Map p536; 435 N Michigan Ave; Ⓜ Red Line to Grand) Take a close look when passing by this 1925 neo-Gothic edifice. Colonel Robert McCormick, eccentric owner of the *Chicago Tribune* in the early 1900s, collected – and asked his reporters to send – rocks from famous buildings and monuments around the world. He stockpiled pieces of the Taj Mahal, Westminster Abbey, the Great Pyramid and more than 140 others, which are now embedded around the tower's base.

Wrigley Building   ARCHITECTURE
(Map p536; 400 N Michigan Ave; Ⓜ Red Line to Grand) The Wrigley Building glows as white as the Doublemint Twins' teeth, day or night. Chewing-gum guy William Wrigley built it that way on purpose, because he wanted it to be attention-grabbing like a billboard. More than 250,000 glazed terra-cotta tiles make up the facade; a computer database tracks each one and indicates when it needs to be cleaned and polished.

◉ Gold Coast

The Gold Coast has been the address of Chicago's wealthiest residents for more than 125 years. Bejeweled women glide in and out of the neighborhood's stylish boutiques. The occasional Rolls-Royce wheels along the leafy streets. The 360° Chicago observatory and Museum of Contemporary Art are the top attention grabbers. Rush St entertains with swanky steakhouses and piano lounges.

★ **360° Chicago** OBSERVATORY
(Map p536; ☎888-875-8439; www.360chicago.com; 875 N Michigan Ave, John Hancock Center, 94th fl; adult/child $20.50/13.50; ◷9am-11pm; Ⓜ Red Line to Chicago) This is the new name for the John Hancock Center Observatory. In many ways the view here surpasses the one at Willis Tower (p534). The 94th-floor lookout has informative displays and the TILT feature (floor-to-ceiling windows that you stand in as they tip out over the ground; it costs $7 extra and is less exciting than it sounds). Not interested in such frivolities? Shoot straight up to the 96th-floor **Signature Lounge** (www.signatureroom.com; ◷11am-12:30am Sun-Thu, to 1:30am Fri & Sat), where the view is free if you buy a drink ($8 to $16).

★ **Museum of Contemporary Art** MUSEUM
(MCA; Map p536; ☎312-280-2660; www.mcachicago.org; 220 E Chicago Ave; adult/child $15/free; ◷10am-8pm Tue, to 5pm Wed-Sun; Ⓜ Red Line to Chicago) Consider it the Art Institute's brash, rebellious sibling, with especially strong minimalist, surrealist and conceptual photography collections, and permanent works by René Magritte, Cindy Sherman and Andy Warhol. Covering art from the 1920s onward, the MCA's collection spans the gamut, with displays arranged to blur the boundaries between painting, sculpture, video and other media.

Original Playboy Mansion NOTABLE BUILDING
(1340 N State Pkwy; Ⓜ Red Line to Clark/Division) The sexual revolution started in the basement 'grotto' of this 1899 manor. Hugh Hefner bought the mansion in 1959 and hung a brass plate over the door warning 'If You Don't Swing, Don't Ring.' Heavy partying ensued. In the mid-1970s, Hef decamped to LA. The building contains condos now, but a visit still allows you to boast 'I've been to the Playboy Mansion.'

Water Tower LANDMARK
(Map p536; 108 N Michigan Ave; Ⓜ Red Line to Chicago) The 154ft-tall, turreted tower is a defining city icon: it was the sole downtown survivor of the 1871 Great Chicago Fire, thanks to its yellow limestone bricks, which withstood the flames. Today the tower houses the free **City Gallery**, showcasing Chicago-themed works by local photographers and artists and is well worth a peek.

◉ Lincoln Park & Old Town

Lincoln Park – the green space – is the city's premier playground of lagoons, footpaths, beaches and zoo animals. Lincoln Park – the surrounding neighborhood – adds top-notch restaurants, kicky shops, and lively blues and rock clubs to the mix. Next door, stylish Old Town hangs on to its free-spirited past with artsy bars and improv-comedy bastion Second City.

FAMOUS LOOP ARCHITECTURE

Ever since Chicago presented the world with the first skyscraper in 1885, it has thought big with its architecture and pushed the envelope of modern design. The Loop is ground zero for gawking.

Monadnock Building (Map p536; www.monadnockbuilding.com; 53 W Jackson Blvd; Ⓜ Blue Line to Jackson)

Rookery (www.flwright.org; 209 S LaSalle St; 9am-5pm Mon-Fri; Ⓜ Brown, Orange, Purple, Pink Line)

Marshall Field Building (Map p536; 111 N State St; ◷10am-9pm Mon-Sat, 11am-7pm Sun; Ⓜ Brown, Orange, Green, Purple, Pink Line to Washington/Wabash)

Sullivan Center (Map p536; www.thesullivancenter.com; 1 S State St; Ⓜ Red Line to Monroe)

Marquette Building (Map p536; http://marquette.macfound.org; 140 S Dearborn St; ◷7am-10pm; Ⓜ Blue Line to Monroe)

Reliance Building (Map p536; 1 W Washington St; Ⓜ Blue Line to Washington)

Santa Fe Building (Map p536; 224 S Michigan Ave; Ⓜ Brown, Orange, Green, Purple, Pink Line to Adams)

Kluczynski Building (Map p536; 230 S Dearborn St; Ⓜ Blue Line to Jackson)

LOCAL KNOWLEDGE

BLUES FANS' PILGRIMAGE

From 1957 to 1967, the humble building **Willie Dixon's Blues Heaven** (☎ 312-808-1286; www.bluesheaven.com; 2120 S Michigan Ave; tours $10; ⊙ by appointment Wed & Thu, noon-4pm Fri, to 3pm Sat; Ⓜ Green Line to Cermak-McCormick Pl) was Chess Records, the seminal electric blues label. It's now named for the bassist who wrote most of Chess' hits. Staff give hour-long tours of the premises. It's pretty ramshackle, with few original artifacts on display. Still, when Willie's grandson hauls out the bluesman's well-worn stand-up bass and lets you take a pluck, it's pretty cool. Call first; opening times can be erratic. Free blues concerts rock the side garden on summer Thursdays at 6pm.

★**Lincoln Park**   PARK

(⊙ 6am-11pm; ♿; 🚌 151) The neighborhood gets its name from this park, Chicago's largest. Its 1200 acres stretch for 6 miles from North Ave north to Diversey Pkwy, where it narrows along the lake and continues on north until the end of Lake Shore Dr. On sunny days locals come out to play in droves, taking advantage of the ponds, paths and playing fields or visiting the zoo and beaches.

Lincoln Park Conservatory   GARDENS

(☎ 312-742-7736; www.lincolnparkconservancy. org; 2391 N Stockton Dr; ⊙ 9am-5pm; 🚌 151) **FREE** Walking through the conservatory's 3 acres of desert palms, jungle ferns and tropical orchids is like taking a trip around the world in 30 minutes. The glass-bedecked hothouse remains a sultry 75°F (24°C) escape even in winter.

Lincoln Park Zoo   ZOO

(☎ 312-742-2000; www.lpzoo.org; 2200 N Cannon Dr; ⊙ 10am-5pm Mon-Fri, to 6:30pm Sat & Sun Jun-Aug, 10am-5pm Apr-May & Sep-Oct, 10am-4:30pm Nov-Mar; ♿; 🚌 151) **FREE** The zoo has been around since 1868 and is a local freebie favorite, filled with lions, zebras, snow monkeys and other exotic creatures in the shadow of downtown. Check out the Regenstein African Journey, polar-bear-stocked Arctic Tundra and dragonfly-dappled Nature Boardwalk for the cream of the crop. The Gateway Pavilion (on Cannon Dr) is the main entrance.

Chicago History Museum   MUSEUM

(☎ 312-642-4600; www.chicagohistory.org; 1601 N Clark St; adult/child $16/free; ⊙ 9:30am-4:30pm Mon & Wed-Sat, to 7:30pm Tue, noon-5pm Sun; ♿; 🚌 22) Curious about Chicago's storied past? Multimedia displays at this museum cover it all, from the Great Fire to the 1968 Democratic Convention. President Lincoln's deathbed is here, as is the bell worn by Mrs O'Leary's cow. So is the chance to 'become' a Chicago hot dog covered in condiments.

⊙ Lake View & Wrigleyville

The young and frolicsome claim Lake View, reveling in its nonstop lineup of bars, theaters and rock halls. Hallowed Wrigley Field draws baseball pilgrims, and the boozy quarter around it – aka Wrigleyville – parties hard and collides with the rainbow banners of Boystown, Chicago's main gay district, chockablock with dance clubs. Global eateries cater to the masses.

★**Wrigley Field**   STADIUM

(www.cubs.com; 1060 W Addison St; Ⓜ Red Line to Addison) Built in 1914 and named for the chewing-gum guy, Wrigley Field is the second-oldest baseball park in the major leagues. It's known for its hand-turned scoreboard, ivy-covered outfield walls and neon sign over the front entrance. It's also known for its team's legendary losing streak. The Cubs (p555) hadn't won a championship since 1908, a cursed dry spell that was unrivaled in US sports. Then in 2016, they triumphed in mythic style. Learn more on 1½-hour tours ($25) of the ballpark, available April through September.

⊙ Andersonville & Uptown

Vestiges of Andersonville's Swedish past remain, but today the area is about foodie taverns, funky boutiques, and gay and lesbian bars. Uptown offers historic jazz houses like the Green Mill (Al Capone's fave), along with the thriving eateries of 'Little Saigon.'

⊙ Wicker Park, Bucktown & Ukrainian Village

These three neighborhoods are hot property. Hipster record stores, thrift shops and cocktail lounges have shot up, though vintage Eastern European dive bars linger on many street corners. Wicker Park is the beating heart; Bucktown (a bit posher) and Ukrainian Village (a bit shabbier) flank it. The restaurant and rock-club scene is unparalleled in the city.

Intuit: The Center for
Intuitive & Outsider Art
GALLERY

(Map p536; ☑312-243-9088; www.art.org; 756 N Milwaukee Ave; suggested donation $5; ⊙11am-6pm Tue, Wed, Fri & Sat, to 7:30pm Thu, noon-5pm Sun; M Blue Line to Chicago) Behold the museum-like collection of folk art, including watercolors by famed local Henry Darger. In the back room Intuit has re-created Darger's awesomely cluttered studio, complete with balls of twine, teetering stacks of old magazines and a Victrola phonograph. The gift shop carries groovy jewelry (such as pencil-eraser earrings) and art books.

◉ Logan Square & Humboldt Park

Logan Square is Chicago's current 'it' neighborhood, the place to go for the hippest tiki lounge or all-the-rage fried-chicken cafe. Gastronomes flock in for Michelin-starred Parachute and Longman & Eagle, plus several other chowhound hot spots. Puerto Rican stronghold Humboldt Park is the place to sample a *jibarito,* the local sandwich specialty.

◉ Near West Side & Pilsen

The meatpacking West Loop buzzes with hot-chef restaurants and on-trend bars. Development continues here big-time. Greektown and Little Italy serve ethnic fare nearby. In Pilsen, Mexican culture mixes with Chicago's bohemian underground, and colorful murals, taquerias and cafes result.

National Museum of
Mexican Art
MUSEUM

(☑312-738-1503; www.nationalmuseumofmexicanart.org; 1852 W 19th St; ⊙10am-5pm Tue-Sun; M Pink Line to 18th St) FREE Founded in 1982, this vibrant museum – the largest Latino arts institution in the US – has become one of the city's best. The vivid permanent collection sums up 1000 years of Mexican art and culture through classical paintings, shining gold altars, skeleton-rich folk art, beadwork and much more.

◉ Chinatown

Chicago's small but busy Chinatown is an easy 10-minute train ride from the Loop. Take the Red Line to the Cermak-Chinatown stop, which puts you between the neighborhood's two distinct parts: Chinatown Sq (an enormous bi-level strip mall) unfurls to the north along Archer Ave, while Old Chinatown (the traditional retail area) stretches along Wentworth Ave to the south. Either zone allows you to graze through bakeries and shop for the requisite Hello Kitty trinkets.

◉ Hyde Park & South Side

Brainy Hyde Park holds bookstores galore and sights like Frank Lloyd Wright's Robie House and the Museum of Science & Industry. Irish enclave Bridgeport has blossomed with bars and galleries, while Bronzeville has jazzy architecture and important (if often overlooked) shrines to African American history.

★ Museum of
Science & Industry
MUSEUM

(MSI; ☑773-684-1414; www.msichicago.org; 5700 S Lake Shore Dr; adult/child $18/11; ⊙9:30am-5:30pm Jun-Aug, shorter hours Sep-May; ⊞; ⊡6, 10, M Metra to 55th-56th-57th) Geek out at the largest science museum in the Western Hemisphere. Highlights include a WWII German U-boat nestled in an underground display ($12 extra to tour it) and the Science Storms exhibit with a mock tornado and tsunami. Other popular exhibits include the baby chick hatchery, the minuscule furnishings in Colleen Moore's fairy castle and the life-size shaft of a coal mine ($12 extra to descend and tour its workings).

★ Robie House
ARCHITECTURE

(☑312-994-4000; www.flwright.org; 5757 S Woodlawn Ave; adult/child $18/15; ⊙10:30am-3pm Thu-Mon; ⊡6, M Metra to 55th-56th-57th) Of the numerous buildings that Frank Lloyd Wright designed around Chicago, none is more famous or influential than Robie House. Because its horizontal lines resembled the flat landscape of the Midwestern prairie, the style became known as the Prairie style. Inside are 174 stained-glass windows and doors, which you'll see on the hour-long tours (frequency varies by season, but there's usually at least one tour per hour).

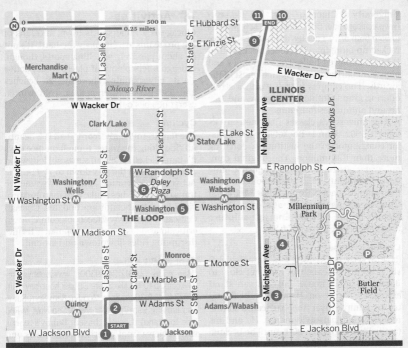

City Walk
The Loop

START CHICAGO BOARD OF TRADE
FINISH BILLY GOAT TAVERN
LENGTH 3 MILES; ABOUT 2 HOURS

This tour swoops through the Loop, highlighting Chicago's revered art and architecture, with a visit to Al Capone's dentist thrown in for good measure.

Start at the **1 Chicago Board of Trade** (141 W Jackson Blvd) with its cool art-deco building; that's a giant statue of Ceres, the goddess of agriculture, on top. Step into the nearby **2 Rookery** (p541) to see Frank Lloyd Wright's handiwork in the atrium.

Head east on Adams St to the **3 Art Institute** (p534), one of the city's most-visited attractions. The lion statues out front make a classic keepsake photo. Walk a few blocks north to avant-garde **4 Millennium Park** (p532).

Leave the park and head west on Washington St to the **5 Alise** (p547) hotel. It's housed in the Reliance Building, which was the precursor to modern skyscraper design;

Capone's dentist drilled teeth in what's now Room 809. Just west, Picasso's abstract **6 Untitled** sculpture is ensconced in Daley Plaza. Baboon, dog, woman? You decide. Then go north on Clark St to Jean Dubuffet's **7 Monument with Standing Beast**, another head-scratching sculpture.

Walk east on Randolph St through the theater district. Pop into the **8 Chicago Cultural Center** (p534) to see what free art exhibits or concerts are on. Now go north on Michigan Ave and cross the Chicago River. Just north of the bridge you'll pass the **9 Wrigley Building** (p539), shining bright and white, and the nearby Gothic, eye-popping **10 Tribune Tower** (p539).

To finish your tour, visit **11 Billy Goat Tavern** (p549), a vintage Chicago dive that spawned the Curse of the Cubs after the tavern's owner, Billy Sianis, tried to enter Wrigley Field with his pet goat. The smelly creature was denied entry, so Sianis called down a mighty hex on the baseball team in retaliation. It took them 108 years to break it.

University of Chicago
UNIVERSITY

(www.uchicago.edu; 5801 S Ellis Ave; 🚍6, Ⓜ Metra to 55th-56th-57th) Faculty and students have racked up more than 80 Nobel prizes within U of C's hallowed halls. The economics and physics departments lay claim to most of the awards. The campus is well worth a stroll, offering grand Gothic architecture and free art and antiquities museums.

The university's classes first met on October 1, 1892. John D Rockefeller was a major contributor to the institution, donating more than $35 million. The original campus was constructed in an English Gothic style. Highlights of a walkabout include the sculpture-laden **Rockefeller Memorial Chapel**, serene **Bond Chapel** and Henry Moore's bronze **Nuclear Energy sculpture** (S Ellis Ave, btwn E 56th & E 57th Sts).

Obama's House
HOUSE

(5046 S Greenwood Ave; 🚍6, Ⓜ Metra to 51st-53rd) Hefty security means you can't get close to Barack Obama's house, but you can stand across the street on Hyde Park Blvd and try to glimpse over the barricades at the redbrick Georgian-style manor. He and his family lived here from 2005 until he became president in late 2008.

🏃 Activities

Chicago is a rabid sports town, and fans of the pro teams are famously die-hard. It's not all about passively watching sports, though. Chicago offers plenty of places to get active via its city-spanning shoreline, 26 beaches and 580 parks. After a long, cold winter, everyone goes outside to play.

Cycling

The flat, 18-mile **Lakefront Trail** is a beautiful ride along the water, though on nice days it's jam-packed. The trail starts at Hollywood Ave and rolls all the way down to 71st St. The Active Transportation Alliance (www.active trans.org) publishes a bike trail map and provides local trail condition updates. Chicago Critical Mass (www.facebook.com/chicago criticalmass) sponsors popular, traffic-disrupting rides downtown and around.

Bobby's Bike Hike
CYCLING

(Map p536; 🕿312-245-9300; www.bobbysbike-hike.com; 540 N Lake Shore Dr; per hour/day from $10/34; ⏲8:30am-8pm Mon-Fri, 8am-8pm Sat & Sun Jun-Aug, 9am-7pm Mar-May & Sep-Nov; Ⓜ Red Line to Grand) Locally based Bobby's earns rave reviews from riders. It rents bikes and has easy access to the Lakefront Trail. It also

---

CHICAGO FOR CHILDREN

Ferocious dinosaurs at the Field Museum, an ark's worth of beasts at Lincoln Park Zoo, lakefront boat rides and sandy beaches are among the top choices for toddlin' times. Add in magical playgrounds, family cycling tours and lots of pizza, and it's clear Chicago is a kid's kind of town.

Chicago Children's Museum (p539) Designed to challenge the imaginations of toddlers to 10-year-olds, this colorful museum gives young visitors enough hands-on exhibits to keep them climbing and creating for hours. Among the favorites, Dinosaur Expedition explores the world of paleontology and lets kids excavate 'bones.' They can also climb a ropey schooner; bowl in a faux alley; get wet in the waterways (and learn about hydroelectric power); and use real tools to build things in the Tinkering Lab.

Field Museum of Natural History (p535) The Crown Family PlayLab lets kids excavate bones and make loads of other discoveries. It's open Thursday to Monday from 10am to 3pm.

Museum of Science & Industry (p542) Staff conduct 'experiments' in various galleries throughout the day, like dropping things off the balcony and creating mini explosions. The Idea Factory lets scientists aged 10 and under 'research' properties of light, balance and water pressure.

Peggy Notebaert Nature Museum (🕿773-755-5100; www.naturemuseum.org; 2430 N Cannon Dr; adult/child $9/6; ⏲9am-5pm Mon-Fri, 10am-5pm Sat & Sun; 👫; 🚍151) This museum is somewhat overlooked, but its butterfly haven and marsh full of frogs provide gentle thrills. Bonus: it's located in Lincoln Park by the zoo.

Art Institute of Chicago (p534) The Ryan Learning Center provides interactive games (like puzzles of famous works) and art-making activities.

offers cool tours ($35 to $66) of South Side gangster sites, the lakefront, nighttime vistas, and venues to indulge in pizza and beer. The Tike Hike caters to kids. Enter through the covered driveway to reach the shop.

Divvy CYCLING
(☑855-553-4889; www.divvybikes.com) Chicago's bike-sharing program has 5800 sky-blue bicycles scattered at 580 stations around Chicago and neighboring suburbs. Kiosks issue 24-hour passes ($10) on the spot. Insert a credit card, get your ride code and then unlock a bike. The first 30 minutes are free; after that, rates rise fast if you don't dock the bike. The system works best for point-to-point travel versus lengthy sightseeing trips.

Water Sports

Visitors often don't realize Chicago is a beach town, thanks to mammoth Lake Michigan lapping its side. There are 26 official strands of sand patrolled by lifeguards in summer. Swimming is popular, though the water is pretty freaking cold. Beaches at Montrose and North Ave have rental places offering kayaks and stand-up paddleboards. Other kayak companies have set up shop along the Chicago River.

North Avenue Beach BEACH
(www.cpdbeaches.com; 1600 N Lake Shore Dr; ♿; ☐151) Chicago's most popular strand of sand wafts a Southern California vibe. Buff teams spike volleyballs, kids build sandcastles and everyone jumps in for a swim when the weather heats up. Bands and DJs rock the steamboat-shaped beach house, which serves ice cream and margaritas in equal measure. Kayaks, jet-skis, stand-up paddleboards, bicycles and lounge chairs are available to rent, and there are beach yoga classes.

Oak Street Beach BEACH
(www.cpdbeaches.com; 1000 N Lake Shore Dr; ⓂRed Line to Chicago) This beach packs in bodies beautiful at the edge of downtown in the shadow of skyscrapers. Lifeguards are on duty in summer. You can rent umbrellas and lounge chairs. The island-y, yellow-umbrella-dotted cafe provides drinks and DJs.

12th Street Beach BEACH
(Map p536; www.cpdbeaches.com; 1200 S Linn White Dr; ☐146, 130) A path runs south from the Adler Planetarium to this crescent of sand. Despite its proximity to the visitor-mobbed Museum Campus, the small beach remains bizarrely (but happily) se-

THE 606

Like NYC's High Line, Chicago's **606** (www.the606.org; ⊘6am-11pm; ⒨Blue Line to Damen) is a similar urban-cool elevated path along an old train track. Bike or stroll past factories, smokestacks, clattering El trains and locals' backyard affairs for 2.7 miles between Wicker Park and Logan Square. It's a fascinating trek through Chicago's socioeconomic strata: moneyed at the east, becoming more industrial and immigrant to the west. The trail parallels Bloomingdale Ave, with access points every quarter mile.

cluded. Bonus: if you can't get tickets to see your favorite band at the Pavilion at Northerly Island, you can sit here and still hear the tunes.

Windy BOATING
(Map p536; ☑312-451-2700; www.tallshipwindy.com; 600 E Grand Ave; 60-75min tours adult/child $30/10; ⒨Red Line to Grand) The four-masted schooner sets sail from Navy Pier. Trips have different themes (pirates, architecture, sailing skills etc). With only the sound of the wind in your ears, these tours are the most relaxing way to see the skyline from offshore. Take the trolley from Grand.

☞ Tours

★**Chicago Architecture Foundation** TOURS
(CAF; Map p536; ☑312-922-3432; www.architecture.org; 224 S Michigan Ave; tours $15-50; ⒨Brown, Orange, Green, Purple, Pink Line to Adams) The gold-standard boat tours ($46) sail from the **river dock** (Map p536; ⒨Brown, Orange, Green, Purple, Pink Line to State/Lake) on the southeast side of the Michigan Ave Bridge. The popular Historic Skyscrapers walking tours ($20) leave from the main downtown address. Weekday lunchtime tours ($15) explore individual landmark buildings and meet on-site. CAF sponsors bus, bike and El train tours, too. Buy tickets online or at CAF; boat tickets can be purchased at the dock.

Chicago by Foot WALKING
(☑312-612-0826; www.freetoursbyfoot.com/chicago-tours) Guides for this pay-what-you-want walking tour offer engaging stories and historical details on different jaunts covering

the Loop, Gold Coast, Lincoln Park's gangster sites and much more. Most takers pay around $10 per person. Reserve in advance to guarantee a spot; walk-up guests are welcome if space is available (chancy).

Chicago Detours
WALKING

(☎ 312-350-1131; www.chicagodetours.com; tours from $22) Chicago Detours offers engrossing, detail-rich tours (mostly walking, but also some by bus) that take in Chicago's architecture, history and culture. The 2½-hour Historic Pub Crawl Tour is a popular one.

Chicago Beer Experience
WALKING

(☎ 312-818-2172; www.chicagobeerexperience. com; tours $62) These three-hour walking tours visit a neighborhood – Lincoln Park/Lake View, Bucktown/Wicker Park or Downtown/South Loop – where you learn its beer history along with general Chicago history. The jaunts hit four bars over the course of a mile or so. Beer and a snack (such as a stuffed pizza slice or hot dog) are included.

Chicago Food Planet Tours
WALKING

(☎ 312-818-2170; www.chicagofoodplanet.com; 2-3hr tours $42-65) Go on a guided walkabout in Wicker Park, the Gold Coast or Chinatown, where you'll graze through five or more neighborhood eateries. Departure points and times vary.

Pilsen Mural Tours
WALKING

(☎ 773-342-4191; 1½hr tours per group $125) Murals are a traditional Mexican art form, and they're splashed all over Pilsen's buildings. Local artists and activists lead these highly recommended tours that take in the neighborhood's most impressive works.

★ Festivals & Events

St Patrick's Day Parade
CULTURAL

(www.chicagostpatricksdayparade.org; ☉ mid-Mar) The local plumbers union dyes the Chicago River shamrock green; a big parade follows downtown in Grant Park. Held the Saturday before March 17.

Chicago Blues Festival
MUSIC

(www.chicagobluesfestival.us; ☉ mid-Jun) The biggest free blues fest in the world, with three days of the music that made Chicago famous. Held in Millennium Park.

Pride Parade
LGBT

(http://chicagopride.gopride.com; ☉ late Jun) On the last Sunday in June, colorful floats and risqué revelers pack Halsted St in Boystown.

It's the LGBT community's main event, and more than 800,000 people come to the party.

Taste of Chicago
FOOD & DRINK

(www.tasteofchicago.us; ☉ mid-Jul) This five-day food festival in Grant Park draws hordes for a smorgasbord of ethnic, meaty, sweet and local edibles – much of it served on a stick. Several stages host free live music, including big-name bands.

Lollapalooza
MUSIC

(www.lollapalooza.com; day pass $120; ☉ early Aug) Up to 170 bands spill off eight stages at Grant Park's four-day mega-gig.

Jazz Festival
MUSIC

(www.chicagojazzfestival.us; ☉ early Sep) Top names on the national jazz scene play for free over Labor Day weekend in Millennium Park and the Chicago Cultural Center.

🛏 Sleeping

Chicago's lodgings rise high in the sky, many in architectural landmarks. Snooze in the building that gave birth to the skyscraper, in one of Mies van der Rohe's boxy structures, or in a century-old art-deco masterpiece. Huge business hotels, B&Bs and snazzy hostels blanket the cityscape too. But nothing comes cheap...

🛏 The Loop

HI-Chicago
HOSTEL $

(Map p536; ☎ 312-360-0300; www.hichicago. org; 24 E Congress Pkwy; dm $35-55; P❋@🛜; Ⓜ Brown, Orange, Purple, Pink Line to Library) Chicago's most stalwart hostel is immaculate, conveniently placed in the Loop, and offers bonuses such as a staffed information desk, free volunteer-led tours and discount passes to museums and shows. The simple dorm rooms have eight or 10 beds, and most have attached baths.

★ Hampton Inn Chicago Downtown/N Loop
HOTEL $$

(Map p536; ☎ 312-419-9014; www.hamptonchicago.com; 68 E Wacker Pl; r $200-290; P❋🛜; Ⓜ Brown, Orange, Green, Purple, Pink Line to State/Lake) This unique property makes you feel like a road-tripper of yore. Set in the 1928 art-deco Chicago Motor Club Building, the lobby sports a vintage Ford and a cool USA mural map from the era. The dark-wood-paneled rooms strike the right balance of retro vibe and modern amenities. Free wi-fi and hot breakfast included.

Buckingham Athletic Club Hotel
BOUTIQUE HOTEL **$**

(Map p536; ✆312-663-8910; www.thebuckingham club.com; 440 S LaSalle St; r $175-300; P❋☎; ⓜBrown, Orange, Purple, Pink Line to LaSalle) Tucked onto the 40th floor of the Chicago Stock Exchange building, this 21-room hotel is not easy to find. The benefit if you do? It's quiet (on weekends and evenings especially) and has expansive views south of town. Elegant rooms are so spacious they'd be considered suites elsewhere. Lots of freebies add to the excellence, including access to the namesake gym with lap pool.

Silversmith
HISTORIC HOTEL **$$**

(Map p536; ✆312-372-7696; www.silversmith chicagohotel.com; 10 S Wabash Ave; r $190-300; P❋@☎; ⓜRed, Blue Line to Monroe) Renowned architect Daniel Burnham's firm designed the 1897 building as a place for jewelers and silversmiths to ply their trade. The gem-inspired theme carries over to the current, vintage-cool design. Rooms are good-sized, with pearl-colored decor and ruby and gold accents. A cushioned seat nestles in each floor-to-ceiling window, prime for city watching. The Art Institute, Millennium Park and CTA trains are steps away.

★ Virgin Hotel
HOTEL **$$$**

(Map p536; ✆312-940-4400; www.virginhotels. com; 203 N Wabash Ave; r $240-380; P❋@☎; ⓜBrown, Orange, Green, Purple, Pink Line to State/Lake) Billionaire Richard Branson transformed the 27-story, art-deco Dearborn Bank Building into the first outpost of his cheeky new hotel chain. The airy, suite-like rooms have speedy free wi-fi and low-cost minibar items, plus a bed that can double as a work desk. An app controls the thermostat, TV and other electronics. Guests receive earplugs, handy for dulling noise from nearby El trains.

Alise Chicago
HISTORIC HOTEL **$$$**

(Map p536; ✆312-940-7997; www.staypineapple. com; 1 W Washington St; r $270-380; P❋@☎; ⓜBlue Line to Washington) Housed in the landmark 1890s Reliance Building (prototype for the modern skyscraper), the Alise's slick, historic design woos architecture buffs. Deco-style lights, iron filigree stair railings and mosaic-tile floors prevail in the public areas. In the smallish rooms, big windows and pops of whimsical, bright-hued art liven up the warm wood decor. The free bicycles are handy.

🖼 Near North & Navy Pier

Freehand Chicago
HOSTEL, HOTEL **$**

(Map p536; ✆312-940-3699; www.thefreehand. com/chicago; 19 E Ohio St; dm $35-70, r $220-310; ❋☎; ⓜRed Line to Grand) At this super-hip hostel-hotel hybrid, travelers split evenly between the four-person, bunk-bed dorms and private rooms. All feature warm woods, bright tiles and Central American–tinged fabrics. Everyone mingles in the shaggy, totem-pole-filled common area and in the groovy Broken Shaker bar. The Freehand works best as a hostel, its dorms spiffier than most, with en suite bathrooms and privacy curtains around each bed.

★ Acme Hotel
BOUTIQUE HOTEL **$$**

(Map p536; ✆312-894-0800; www.acmehotelcompany.com; 15 E Ohio St; r $190-300; P❋@☎; ⓜRed Line to Grand) Urban bohemians love the Acme for its indie-cool style at (usually) affordable rates. The 130 rooms mix industrial fixtures with retro lamps, mid-century furniture and funky modern art. They're wired up with free wi-fi, good speakers, smart TVs and easy connections to stream your own music and movies. Graffiti, neon and a rock-and-roll elevator embellish the common areas.

🖼 Gold Coast

★ Fieldhouse Jones
HOSTEL, HOTEL **$**

(Map p536; ✆312-291-9922; www.fieldhousejones. com; 312 W Chestnut St; dm $40-55, r from $150; P❋☎; ⓜBrown, Purple Line to Chicago) This hostel-hotel mash-up occupies a vintage, redbrick dairy warehouse. It's great value for the Gold Coast, drawing a wide range of travelers – global backpackers, families, older couples – for its quality rooms and sociable common areas. There are gender-divided dorms, studios and one- and two-bedroom apartments, all with en suite bathrooms, wi-fi and fun, sporty decor (dartboard wall art, old trophies etc).

Drake Hotel
HISTORIC HOTEL **$$$**

(✆312-787-2200; www.thedrakehotel.com; 140 E Walton St; r $230-360; P❋@☎; ⓜRed Line to Chicago) Queen Elizabeth, Dean Martin, Princess Di...the Reagans, the Bushes, the Clintons... Who hasn't stayed at the elegant Drake Hotel since it opened in 1920? The chandelier-strewn grande dame commands a terrific location at the northern end of Michigan Ave, near Oak St Beach. While the public spaces are gilded eye-poppers, the 535 rooms are more everyday yet well sized and comfy.

Lincoln Park & Old Town

Hotel Lincoln BOUTIQUE HOTEL $$

(☑ 312-254-4700; www.jdvhotels.com; 1816 N Clark St; r $180-320; P ✱ @ ☎; 🖵22) The boutique Lincoln is all about kitschy fun, as the lobby's 'wall of bad art' and front desk patched together from flea-market dresser drawers attest. Standard rooms are small, but vintage-cool and colorful; many have sweet views. Leafy Lincoln Park and the city's largest farmers market sprawl across the street.

Wicker Park, Bucktown & Ukrainian Village

Holiday Jones HOSTEL $

(☑ 312-804-3335; www.holidayjones.com; 1659 W Division St; dm/r from $33/85; ➡✱@☎; M Blue Line to Division) Holiday Jones has a tongue-in-cheek, itchy-feet personality. Old steamer trunks comprise the front desk. Wild, cartoony posters line the stairwell. Rooms are compact but tidy, with fresh paint and splashes of plaid (via the bedding and wallpaper). Gender-segregated dorms have four to six bunk beds. There's a big common room with couches and a flat-screen TV, plus free wi-fi, continental breakfast and lockers.

Hollander HOSTEL $

(☑ 872-315-3080; www.thehollander.com; 2022 W North Ave; dm $40-55, r $135-220; P ✱ ☎; M Blue Line to Damen) The Hollander describes itself as a 'social stay' versus a hostel, and indeed, this revamped, turn-of-the-century warehouse buzzes with the young and perky. Travelers flit in and out of the sunny, shabby-chic lobby bar for coffee, laptop musing and bicycle rentals, and they snooze in private rooms and bunk-bed dorms (for four to six people) with polished concrete floors, unvarnished wood-frame beds and other mod-industrial decor.

Wicker Park Inn B&B $$

(☑ 773-486-2743; www.wickerparkinn.com; 1329 N Wicker Park Ave; r $160-200, apt $150-245; ✱☎; M Blue Line to Damen) This classic brick row house is steps away from rockin' restaurants and nightlife. The sunny rooms aren't huge, but all have hardwood floors, soothing color schemes and small desk spaces where you can use the free wi-fi. Breakfast is rich in

baked goods and fruit. Across the street, three apartments with kitchens provide a self-contained experience. Rooms have varying minimum-stay requirements.

Logan Square & Humboldt Park

Longman & Eagle INN $$

(☑ 773-276-7110; www.longmanandeagle.com; 2657 N Kedzie Ave; r $95-200; ✱☎; M Blue Line to Logan Square) Check in at the Michelin-starred tavern downstairs and then head to your wood-floored, vintage-stylish accommodations on the floor above. The six rooms aren't particularly soundproof, but after using your whiskey tokens in the bar, you probably won't care. Artwork by local artists decorates each room.

✗ Eating

Chicago has become a chowhound's hot spot. For the most part, restaurants here are reasonably priced and pretension-free, serving masterful food in come-as-you-are environs. You can also fork into a superb range of ethnic eats, especially if you break out of downtown and head for neighborhoods such as Pilsen or Uptown.

✗ The Loop

Most Loop eateries are geared to lunch crowds of office workers. There's not much open after 9pm.

Cafecito CUBAN $

(Map p536; ☑ 312-922-2233; www.cafecitochicago. com; 26 E Congress Pkwy; mains $6-10; ⊗7am-9pm Mon-Fri, 10am-6pm Sat & Sun; ☎; M Brown, Orange, Purple, Pink Line to Library) Attached to the HI-Chicago hostel and perfect for the hungry, thrifty traveler, Cafecito serves killer Cuban sandwiches layered with citrus-garlic-marinated roasted pork and ham. Strong coffee and hearty egg sandwiches make a fine breakfast.

Native Foods Cafe VEGAN $

(Map p536; ☑ 312-332-6332; www.nativefoods. com; 218 S Clark St; mains $9-11; ⊗10:30am-9pm Mon-Sat, 11am-7pm Sun; ✐; M Brown, Orange, Purple, Pink Line to Quincy) If you're looking for vegan fast-casual fare downtown, Native Foods is your spot. The meatball sandwich rocks the seitan, while the scorpion burger fires up hot-spiced tempeh. Local beers and

CHICAGO'S BEST-LOVED SPECIALTIES

Deep-dish pizza is Chicago's most famous concoction. These behemoths are nothing like the flat circular disks known as pizza in the rest of the world. Here pies are made in a special cast-iron pan – kind of like a skillet without a handle – so the dough, stuffed with molten American-style mozzarella cheese, chunky tomato sauce and other typical ingredients like sausage, is oven baked. The flagship **Pizzeria Uno** (Map p536; ☑ 312-321-1000; www.unos.com; 29 E Ohio St; small pizzas from $13; ⊘ 11am-1am Mon-Thu, to 2am Fri & Sat, to 11pm Sun; Ⓜ Red Line to Grand) claims to have invented deep-dish pizza in the 1940s, but this, like many other fanatical conversations about food (and sports) in the Windy City, will inspire debate.

No less iconic is the Chicago-style hot dog. A real-deal specimen uses a local Vienna beef weenie and requires a poppy-seed bun and a litany of toppings (including onions, tomatoes, a dill pickle and neon-green relish). And remember rule numero uno: no ketchup! For gourmet versions (rabbit sausage with anchovy hazelnut butter sauce) and stalwart classics (beer-soaked brats), swing by **Hot G Dog** (☑ 773-209-3360; www.hotgdog. com; 5009 N Clark St; hot dogs $2.50-4; ⊘ 10:30am-8pm Mon-Sat, to 4pm Sun; ⌸ 22, Ⓜ Red Line to Argyle) in Andersonville.

Another renowned Chicago specialty is the Italian beef sandwich, and it stacks up like this: thin-sliced, slow-cooked roast beef that's sopped in natural gravy and *giardiniera* (spicy pickled vegetables), then heaped on a hoagie roll. Local Italian immigrants on the South Side invented it as a low-budget way to feed factory workers during the Depression era. Try it while you're here – **Mr Beef** (Map p536; ☑ 312-337-8500; www.facebook. com/mrbeefchicago; 666 N Orleans St; sandwiches $6-9; ⊘ 10am-6pm Mon-Thu, to 5am Fri & Sat; Ⓜ Brown, Purple Line to Chicago) makes a popular one – because you'll be hard-pressed to find one elsewhere on the planet.

Less well known, but equally messy and delicious, is the *jibarito* sandwich, developed at a local Puerto Rican eatery. It consists of steak covered in garlicky mayo and served between thick, crispy-fried plantain slices, which form the 'bread.' Many Latin American cafes in the Humboldt Park neighborhood, such as **Papa's Cache Sabroso** (☑ 773-862-8313; www.papascache.com; 2517 W Division St; mains $8-15; ⊘ 11am-9pm Mon-Thu, to 10pm Fri & Sat; ⌸ 70), have it on the menu.

And who could leave the Midwest without trying some pie, maybe Amish Country–style 'shoofly' molasses, juicy strawberry-rhubarb or Dutch apple layered with sour-cream custard and nutty streusel? Take a sugar-loaded tasting flight at Hoosier Mama Pie Company (p551) in Ukrainian Village – you might just devour an entire pie.

---

organic wines accompany the wide-ranging menu of Greek-, Asian-, Mexican- and Italian-inspired dishes. Soy-free, gluten-free and nut-free menus are available for allergy sufferers.

★**Gage**   GASTROPUB $$$
(Map p536; ☑ 312-372-4243; www.thegagechi cago.com; 24 S Michigan Ave; mains $18-36; ⊘ 11am-9pm Mon, to 11pm Tue-Thu, to midnight Fri, 10am-midnight Sat, 10am-10pm Sun; Ⓜ Brown, Orange, Green, Purple, Pink Line to Washington/ Wabash) This always-hopping gastropub dishes up fanciful grub, from Gouda-topped venison burgers to mussels vindaloo or Guinness-battered fish and chips. The booze rocks too, including a solid whiskey list and small-batch beers that pair with the food.

✕ Near North & Navy Pier

This is where you'll find Chicago's mother lode of restaurants. There's a huge variety, from deep-dish pizza to ritzy seafood.

Billy Goat Tavern   BURGERS $
(Map p536; ☑ 312-222-1525; www.billygoattavern. com; 430 N Michigan Ave, lower level; burgers $4-8; ⊘ 6am-1am Mon-Thu, to 2am Fri, to 3am Sat, 9am-2am Sun; Ⓜ Red Line to Grand) *Tribune* and *Sun Times* reporters have guzzled in the subterranean Billy Goat for decades. Order a 'cheezborger' and Schlitz beer and then look around at the newspapered walls to get the scoop on infamous local stories, such as the Cubs' Curse. The place is a tourist magnet, but a deserving one. Follow the tavern signs that lead below Michigan Ave to get here.

★ **Giordano's** PIZZA **$$**

(Map p536; ☑ 312-951-0747; www.giordanos.com; 730 N Rush St; small pizzas from $16.50; ☺ 11am-11pm Sun-Thu, to midnight Fri & Sat; Ⓜ Red Line to Chicago) Giordano's makes 'stuffed' pizza, a bigger, doughier version of deep dish. It's awesome. If you want a slice of heaven, order the 'special,' a stuffed pie containing sausage, mushroom, green pepper and onions. Each pizza takes 45 minutes to bake.

Purple Pig MEDITERRANEAN **$$**

(Map p536; ☑ 312-464-1744; www.thepurplepigchicago.com; 500 N Michigan Ave; small plates $10-20; ☺ 11:30am-midnight Sun-Thu, to 1am Fri & Sat; ☑; Ⓜ Red Line to Grand) The Pig's Magnificent Mile location, wide-ranging meat and veggie menu, and late-night serving hours make it a crowd-pleaser. Milk-braised pork shoulder is the hamtastic specialty. Dishes are meant to be shared, and the long list of affordable vinos gets the good times rolling at communal tables both indoors and out. Alas, there are no reservations to help beat the crowds.

✘ Gold Coast

Gibson's STEAK **$$$**

(☑ 312-266-8999; www.gibsonssteakhouse.com; 1028 N Rush St; mains $45-60; ☺ 11am-midnight; Ⓜ Red Line to Clark/Division) There is a scene every night at this local original. Politicians, movers, shakers and the shaken-down swirl the famed martinis and compete for prime table space in the buzzing dining room. The rich and beautiful mingle at the bar. The steaks are as good as they come, and ditto for the ginormous lobsters.

★ **Le Colonial** FRENCH, VIETNAMESE **$$$**

(☑ 312-255-0088; www.lecolonialchicago.com; 937 N Rush St; mains $22-32; ☺ 11:30am-3pm & 5-10pm Sun-Thu, to 11pm Fri & Sat; ☑; Ⓜ Red Line to Chicago) Step into the dark-wood, candlelit room, where ceiling fans swirl lazily and bigleafed palms sway in the breeze, and you'd swear you were in 1920s Saigon. Staff can arrange vegetarian and gluten-free substitutions among the curries and banana-leaf-wrapped fish dishes.

✘ Lincoln Park & Old Town

While mega-high-end restaurants such as Alinea are here, Lincoln Park caters to student tastes, too, thanks to the presence of DePaul University. Halsted St, Lincoln Ave and Fullerton Ave are good bets for trendy,

flirty eateries. Old Town's eateries are quieter and quainter.

La Fournette BAKERY **$**

(☑ 312-624-9430; www.lafournette.com; 1547 N Wells St; items $3-7; ☺ 7am-6:30pm Mon-Sat, to 5:30pm Sun; Ⓜ Brown, Purple Line to Sedgwick) The chef hails from Alsace in France and he fills his narrow, rustic-wood bakery with bright-hued macarons (purple passionfruit, green pistachio, red raspberry-chocolate), cheese-infused breads, crust-crackling baguettes and buttery croissants. They all beg to be devoured on the spot with a cup of locally roasted Intelligentsia coffee. Staff make delicious soups, crepes, quiches and sandwiches with equal French love.

Sultan's Market MIDDLE EASTERN **$**

(☑ 872-253-1489; 2521 N Clark St; mains $4-7; ☺ 10am-10pm Mon-Sat, to 9pm Sun; Ⓜ Brown, Purple, Red Line to Fullerton) Neighborhood folks dig the falafel sandwiches, spinach pies and other quality Middle Eastern fare at family-run Sultan's Market.

★ **Alinea** GASTRONOMY **$$$**

(☑ 312-867-0110; www.alinearestaurant.com; 1723 N Halsted St; 10-/16-course menu from $165/285; ☺ 5-10pm Wed-Sun; Ⓜ Red Line to North/Clybourn) One of the world's best restaurants, with three Michelin stars, Alinea brings on multiple courses of molecular gastronomy. Dishes may emanate from a centrifuge or be pressed into a capsule, à la duck served with a 'pillow of lavender air.' There are no reservations; instead Alinea sells tickets two to three months in advance via its website.

✘ Lake View & Wrigleyville

Good-time midrange places for vegetarians and global food lovers fill the neighborhood. Clark, Halsted and Southport are fertile grazing streets.

Home Bistro AMERICAN **$$**

(☑ 773-661-0299; www.homebistrochicago.com; 3404 N Halsted St; mains $20-25; ☺ 5:30-10pm Tue-Thu, 5-10:30pm Fri & Sat, 11am-9pm Sun; Ⓜ Red Line to Addison) Home Bistro (aka 'HB') feels as cozy as the nouveau comfort food it serves. Cider-soaked mussels, duck meatball gnocchi and buttermilk fried chicken hit the tables in the wood-and-tile-lined space. Try to snag a seat by the front window, which entertains with Boystown people-watching. You can bring your own wine or beer, which is a nice money saver.

Andersonville & Uptown

Andersonville offers a cozy, international array of eateries. Uptown's 'Little Saigon' brings on the noodle houses.

Nha Hang Viet Nam
VIETNAMESE $

(☑773-878-8895; 1032 W Argyle St; mains $7-13; ☺8:30am-10pm Wed-Mon; Ⓜ Red Line to Argyle) Little Nha Hang may not look like much from the outside, but it offers a huge menu of authentic, well-made dishes from the homeland. It's terrific for slurping pho and clay-pot catfish. Staff give out free vanilla ice cream at meal's end, which is a nice touch.

★ Hopleaf
EUROPEAN $$

(☑773-334-9851; www.hopleaf.com; 5148 N Clark St; mains $12-27; ☺noon-11pm Mon-Thu, to midnight Fri & Sat, to 10pm Sun; 🔲22, Ⓜ Red Line to Berwyn) A cozy, European-like tavern, Hopleaf draws crowds for its Montreal-style smoked brisket, cashew-butter-and-fig-jam sandwich, uber-creamy macaroni and Stilton cheese, and the house-specialty *frites* (fries) and ale-soaked mussels. It also pours 200 types of brew (around 60 are on tap), emphasizing craft and Belgian suds.

Wicker Park, Bucktown & Ukrainian Village

Trendy restaurants open almost every day, with many serving nouveau comfort food. Division St is a bountiful vein of snazzy bistros and pubs that have sidewalk seating.

Hoosier Mama Pie Company
PIES $

(☑312-243-4846; www.hoosiermamapie.com; 1618 ½ Chicago Ave; slices $5-6.25; ☺8am-7pm Tue-Fri, 9am-5pm Sat, 10am-4pm Sun; 🔲66, Ⓜ Blue Line to Chicago) There's a statistic that states one out of five people has eaten an entire pie solo. Hoosier Mama is your place to do it. Pastry chef Paula Haney hand rolls and crimps her dough, then plumps it with fruit or creamy fillings. Favorites include the banana cream, chocolate chess (aka 'brownie pie') and classic apple. A handful of meat and veg savory pies tempt too.

Dove's Luncheonette
TEX-MEX $$

(☑773-645-4060; www.doveschicago.com; 1545 N Damen Ave; mains $13-19; ☺9am-9pm Mon-Thu, 8am-10pm Fri & Sat, 8am-9pm Sun; Ⓜ Blue Line to Damen) Grab a seat at the retro counter for Tex-Mex plates of pork-shoulder posole and shrimp-stuffed sweet-corn tamales. Dessert? It's pie, of course – maybe lemon cream or

peach jalapeño, depending on what staff have baked that day. Soul music spins on a record player, tequila flows from the 70 bottles rattling behind the bar, and presto: all is right in the world.

Mana Food Bar
VEGETARIAN $$

(☑773-342-1742; www.manafoodbar.com; 1742 W Division St; small plates $7-10; ☺5:30-10pm Mon-Thu, to 11pm Fri, noon-11pm Sat, 5-9pm Sun; ☑; Ⓜ Blue Line to Division) What's unique here is the focus on creating global dishes without using fake meats. So you won't find soy chorizo or tempeh Reubens, but rather multi-ethnic veggie dishes from the likes of Japan, Korea, Italy and the American Southwest. Beer, smoothies and sake cocktails help wash it down. The small, sleek eatery buzzes, so reserve ahead or prepare to wait.

Logan Square & Humboldt Park

Logan Square is the city's inventive foodie mecca. It's casual though – so casual that many of the top spots don't take reservations. Puerto Rican cafes and the *jibarito* sandwich are Humboldt Park's claim to fame. It's also getting gastronomic: the area around California and Augusta Aves has seen several hot spots fire up.

Longman & Eagle
AMERICAN $$

(☑773-276-7110; www.longmanandeagle.com; 2657 N Kedzie Ave; mains $16-30; ☺9am-2am Sun-Fri, to 3am Sat; Ⓜ Blue Line to Logan Square) Hard to say whether this shabby-chic tavern is best for eating or drinking. Let's say eating, since it earned a Michelin star for its beautifully cooked comfort foods such as duck egg hash for breakfast, wild-boar sloppy joes for lunch, and fried chicken and duck-fat biscuits for dinner. There's a whole menu of juicy small plates and whiskeys too. No reservations.

Kai Zan
SUSHI $$

(☑773-278-5776; www.eatatkaizan.com; 2557 W Chicago Ave; mains $10-16; ☺5-10pm Tue-Thu, to 11pm Fri, 4:30-11:30pm Sat; 🔲66) If you prefer your sushi served in a trendy nightclub-like space with dramatic lighting and ambient house music, or if your favorite maki is named after an American state, don't go to Kai Zan. If, however, you crave a more adventurous and inspired sushi experience, make a reservation — stat — at this charming little jewel box of a restaurant on an unassuming block in Humboldt Park.

✕ Near West Side & Pilsen

The West Loop booms with celebrity-chef restaurants. Stroll along W Randolph St and W Fulton Market and take your pick. Greektown extends along S Halsted St, Little Italy along Taylor St. Mexican taquerias meet hipster hangouts along 18th St in Pilsen.

★ Lou Mitchell's   BREAKFAST $
(Map p536; ☑ 312-939-3111; www.loumitchellsrestaurant.com; 565 W Jackson Blvd; mains $9-14; ☺ 5:30am-3pm Mon, to 4pm Tue-Fri, 7am-4pm Sat, to 3pm Sun; ⊞; Ⓜ Blue Line to Clinton) A relic of Route 66, Lou's brings in elbow-to-elbow locals and tourists for breakfast. The old-school waitresses deliver fluffy omelets that hang off the plate and thick-cut French toast with a jug of syrup. They call you 'honey' and fill your coffee cup endlessly. There's often a queue to get in, but free doughnut holes and Milk Duds help ease the wait.

★ Pleasant House Pub   PUB FOOD $
(☑ 773-523-7437; www.facebook.com/pleasanthousepub; 2119 S Halsted St; mains $8-10; ☺ 7am-10pm Tue-Thu, to midnight Fri, 10am-midnight Sat, to 10pm Sun; ☎; ☐ 8) Follow your nose to Pleasant House, which bakes tall, fluffy, savory pies. Daily flavors include chicken and chutney, steak and ale, or kale and mushroom, made with produce the chefs grow themselves. The pub also serves its own beers (brewed off-site) to accompany the food. Friday is a good day to visit, when there's a fish fry.

☕ Drinking & Nightlife

Chicagoans love to hang out in drinking establishments. Blame it on the long winter, when folks need to huddle together somewhere warm. Blame it on summer, when sunny days make beer gardens and sidewalk patios so splendid. Whatever the reason, drinking in the city is a widely cherished civic pastime.

🍷 The Loop & Near North

★ Berghoff   BAR
(Map p536; ☑ 312-427-3170; www.theberghoff.com; 17 W Adams St; ☺ 11am-9pm Mon-Fri, 11:30am-9pm Sat; Ⓜ Blue, Red Line to Jackson) The Berghoff dates from 1898 and was the first spot in town to serve a legal drink after Prohibition (ask to see the liquor license stamped '#1'). Little has changed around the antique wood bar since then. Belly up for frosty mugs of the house-brand beer and order sauerbraten, schnitzel and other old-world classics from the adjoining German restaurant.

Monk's Pub   PUB
(Map p536; ☑ 312-357-6665; www.monkspubchicago.com; 205 W Lake St; ☺ 9am-11pm Mon-Fri, 11am-5pm Sat; Ⓜ Blue, Brown, Orange, Green, Purple, Pink Line to Clark/Lake) Grab the brass handles on the huge wooden doors and enter this dimly lit Belgian beer cave. Old barrels, vintage taps and faux antiquarian books set the mood, accompanied by a whopping international brew selection and free, throw-your-shells-on-the-floor peanuts. Office workers and the occasional TV weather presenter are the main folks hanging out at Monk's, which also serves good, burger-y pub grub.

Clark Street Ale House   BAR
(Map p536; ☑ 312-642-9253; www.clarkstreetalehouse.com; 742 N Clark St; ☺ 4pm-4am Mon-Fri, from 11am Sat & Sun; ☎; Ⓜ Red Line to Chicago) Do as the retro sign advises and 'Stop & Drink.' Midwestern microbrews are the main draw. Work up a thirst on the free pretzels, order a three-beer sampler for $7 and cool off in the beer garden out back.

🍷 Old Town & Wrigleyville

★ Old Town Ale House   BAR
(☑ 312-944-7020; www.theoldtownalehouse.com; 219 W North Ave; ☺ 3pm-4am Mon-Fri, from noon Sat & Sun; Ⓜ Brown, Purple Line to Sedgwick) Located near the Second City comedy club and the scene of late-night musings since the 1960s, this unpretentious neighborhood favorite lets you mingle with beautiful people and grizzled regulars, seated pint by pint under the nude-politician paintings. Classic jazz on the jukebox provides the soundtrack for the jovial goings-on. Cash only.

Smart Bar   CLUB
(☑ 773-549-4140; www.smartbarchicago.com; 3730 N Clark St; tickets $5-15; ☺ 10pm-4am Thu-Sun; Ⓜ Red Line to Addison) Smart Bar is a long-standing, unpretentious favorite for dancing, located in the basement of the Metro (☑ 773-549-4140; www.metrochicago.com; ☺ box office noon-6pm Mon, to 8pm Tue-Sat) rock club. The DJs are often more renowned than you'd expect the intimate space to accommodate. House and techno dominate.

Berlin CLUB

(☏773-348-4975; www.berlinchicago.com; 954 W Belmont Ave; ⊙10pm-4am Sun-Wed, from 5pm Thu-Sat; Ⓜ Red, Brown, Purple Line to Belmont) Looking for a packed, sweaty dance floor? Berlin caters to a mostly gay crowd midweek, though partiers of all stripes jam the place on weekends. Monitors flicker through the latest video dispatches from cult pop and electronic acts, while DJs take the dance floor on trancey detours.

Wicker Park, Bucktown & Ukrainian Village

★**Matchbox** BAR

(Map p536; ☏312-666-9292; 770 N Milwaukee Ave; ⊙4pm-2am Mon-Thu, from 3pm Fri-Sun; Ⓜ Blue Line to Chicago) Lawyers, artists and bums all squeeze in for retro cocktails. It's as small as – you got it – a matchbox, with about 10 bar stools; everyone else stands against the back wall. Barkeeps make the drinks from scratch. Favorites include the pisco sour and the ginger gimlet, ladled from an amber vat of homemade ginger-infused vodka.

Map Room BAR

(☏773-252-7636; www.maproom.com; 1949 N Hoyne Ave; ⊙6:30am-2am Mon-Fri, 7:30am-3am Sat, 11am-2am Sun; 🛜; Ⓜ Blue Line to Western) At this map- and globe-filled 'travelers' tavern,' artsy types sip coffee by day and suds from the 200-strong beer list by night. Board games and old issues of *National Geographic* are within reach for entertainment.

Danny's BAR

(☏773-489-6457; 1951 W Dickens Ave; ⊙7pm-2am Sun-Fri, to 3am Sat; Ⓜ Blue Line to Damen) Danny's comfortably dim and dog-eared ambience is perfect for conversations over a pint early on and then DJs arrive to stoke the dance party as the evening progresses. The groovy spot is more like a house than a bar, filled with twenty- and thirty-somethings.

☆ Entertainment

Finding something to do in Chicago on any given night is effortless, and the spectrum of entertainment that's available in every price range is overwhelming. Just flip through the city's news weekly, the *Reader,* with its pages of theater openings and concert announcements, and Chicagoans' insatiable appetite for nocturnal amusement becomes apparent.

LOCAL KNOWLEDGE

HOW TO FIND A REAL CHICAGO BAR

To discover classic, character-filled bars on your own, look for the following: an old-style beer sign swinging out front; a well-worn dartboard and/or pool table inside; patrons wearing ballcaps with the logos of the Cubs, White Sox, Bears or Blackhawks; and sports on TV.

Blues & Jazz

★**Green Mill** JAZZ

(☏773-878-5552; www.greenmilljazz.com; 4802 N Broadway; ⊙noon-4am Mon-Fri, to 5am Sat, 11am-4am Sun; Ⓜ Red Line to Lawrence) The timeless Green Mill earned its notoriety as Al Capone's favorite speakeasy (the tunnels where he hid the booze are still underneath the bar). Sit in one of the curved velvet booths and feel his ghost urging you on to another martini. Local and national jazz artists perform nightly; Sunday also hosts the nationally acclaimed poetry slam. Cash only.

★**Buddy Guy's Legends** BLUES

(Map p536; ☏312-427-1190; www.buddyguy.com; 700 S Wabash Ave; tickets Sun-Thu $10, Fri & Sat $20; ⊙5pm-2am Mon & Tue, from 11am Wed-Fri, noon-3am Sat, to 2am Sun; Ⓜ Red Line to Harrison) Top local and national acts wail on the stage of local icon Buddy Guy. The man himself usually plugs in his axe for a series of shows in January (tickets go on sale in November). The location is a bit rough around the edges, but the acts are consistently excellent.

BLUES BLUES

(☏773-528-1012; www.chicagobluesbar.com; 2519 N Halsted St; cover charge $7-10; ⊙8pm-2am Wed-Sun; Ⓜ Brown, Purple, Red Line to Fullerton) Long, narrow and high volume, this veteran blues club draws a slightly older crowd that soaks up every crackling, electrified moment. As one local musician put it, 'The audience here comes out to *understand* the blues.' Big local names grace the small stage.

Kingston Mines BLUES

(☏773-477-4646; www.kingstonmines.com; 2548 N Halsted St; cover charge $12-15; ⊙7:30pm-4am Mon-Thu, 7pm-4am Fri, 7am-5am Sat, 6pm-4am Sun; Ⓜ Brown, Purple, Red Line to Fullerton) Popular enough to draw big names on the blues circuit, Kingston Mines is so noisy, hot and sweaty that blues neophytes will feel as though they're having a genuine experience – sort of like a gritty Delta theme park. Two stages, seven nights a week, ensure somebody's always on. The blues jam session from 6pm to 8pm on Sunday is free.

Rock & World Music

★**Hideout**   LIVE MUSIC

(☎773-227-4433; www.hideoutchicago.com; 1354 W Wabansia Ave; tickets $5-15; ☺5pm-2am Mon & Tue, from 4pm Wed-Fri, 7pm-3am Sat, hours vary Sun; ☐72) Hidden behind a factory at the edge of Bucktown, this two-room lodge of indie rock and alt-country is well worth seeking out. The owners have nursed an outsider, underground vibe, and the place feels like your grandma's rumpus room. Music and other events take place nightly.

★**Whistler**   LIVE MUSIC

(☎773-227-3530; www.whistlerchicago.com; 2421 N Milwaukee Ave; ☺6pm-2am Mon-Thu, 5pm-2am Fri-Sun; Ⓜ Blue Line to California) Hometown indie bands, jazz combos and DJs rock this wee, arty bar most nights. There's never a cover charge, but you'd be a schmuck if you didn't order at least one of the swanky cocktails or craft beers to keep the scene going. Whistler is also a gallery: the front window showcases local artists' work.

Empty Bottle   LIVE MUSIC

(☎773-276-3600; www.emptybottle.com; 1035 N Western Ave; ☺5pm-2am Mon-Wed, from 3pm Thu & Fri, from 11am Sat & Sun; ☐49) Chicago's music insiders fawn over the Empty Bottle, the city's scruffy, go-to club for edgy indie rock, jazz and other beats. Monday's show is often a freebie by a couple of up-and-coming bands. Cheap beer, a photo booth and good graffiti-reading in the bathrooms add to the dive-bar fun.

Theater

★**Steppenwolf Theatre**   THEATER

(☎312-335-1650; www.steppenwolf.org; 1650 N Halsted St; Ⓜ Red Line to North/Clybourn) Steppenwolf is Chicago's top stage for quality, provocative theater productions. The Hollywood-heavy ensemble includes Gary Sinise, John Malkovich, Martha Plimpton, Gary Cole, Joan Allen and Tracy Letts. A money-saving tip: the box office releases 20 tickets for $20 for each day's shows; they go on sale at 11am Monday to Saturday and at 1pm Sunday, and are available by phone.

Goodman Theatre   THEATER

(Map p536; ☎312-443-3800; www.goodman theatre.org; 170 N Dearborn St; Ⓜ Brown, Orange, Green, Purple, Pink, Blue Line to Clark/Lake) The Goodman is one of Chicago's premier drama

---

LGBT CHICAGO

Exploring kinky artifacts in the **Leather Archives & Museum** (www.leatherarchives.org; 6418 N Greenview Ave; ☺ Thu-Fri 11am-7pm, Sat-Sun 11am-5pm), or playing a game of naughty Twister at a rollicking street fair? Shopping for gay literature, or clubbing alongside male go-go dancers? Chicago's flourishing gay and lesbian scene in party-hearty Boystown (dense with bars and clubs on N Halsted St between Belmont Ave and Grace St) and easygoing Andersonville offers plenty of choices (but in a more relaxed, less party-oriented scene).

The main event on the calendar is the Pride Parade (p546), held the last Sunday in June. It winds through Boystown and attracts more than 800,000 risqué revelers. **Northalsted Market Days** (www.northalsted.com; ☺mid-Aug), another wild time in Boystown, is a steamy two-day street fair. Crafty, incense-wafting vendors line Halsted St, but most folks come for the drag queens in feather boas, Twister games played in the street and disco divas (Gloria Gaynor!) on the main stage. The **International Mr Leather** (www.imrl.com; ☺late May) contest brings out lots of men in, well, leather. Workshops and parties take place around town, with the main event happening at a downtown hotel or theater.

The following resources will assist with your explorations:

Windy City Times (www.windycitymediagroup.com) LGBT newspaper, published weekly. Website is the main source for events and entertainment.

Purple Roofs (www.purpleroofs.com) Website listing queer accommodations, travel agencies and tours.

Chances Dances (www.chancesdances.org) Organizes queer dance parties at clubs around town.

houses, and its Theater District facility is gorgeous. It specializes in new and classic American productions and has been cited several times as one of the USA's best regional theaters. At 10am Goodman puts unsold tickets for the current day's performance on sale for half-price online.

Chicago Theatre — THEATER
(Map p536; ☑ 312-462-6300; www.thechicago theatre.com; 175 N State St; Ⓜ Brown, Orange, Green, Purple, Pink Line to State/Lake) Take a gander at the six-story sign out front. It's an official landmark (and an excellent photo op). Everyone from Duke Ellington to Frank Sinatra to Prince has taken the stage here over the years (and left their signature on the famous backstage walls). The real show-stopper, though, is the opulent French baroque architecture.

Chicago Children's Theatre — THEATER
(CCT; ☑ 773-227-0180; www.chicagochildrens theatre.org; 1016 N Dearborn St; Ⓜ Red Line to Clark/Division) CCT is dedicated exclusively to putting on quality productions for young audiences. Many plays are adapted from children's books, and many use puppets or music. The group is building a swanky new theater in the West Loop to be completed in 2020. Until then, performances take place at the Ruth Page Center for Arts.

Neo-Futurists — THEATER
(☑ 773-878-4557; www.neofuturists.org; 5153 N Ashland Ave; ⊘ 11:30pm Fri & Sat, 7pm Sun; 🚌 22, Ⓜ Red Line to Berwyn) The Neo-Futurists are best known for their show *The Infinite Wrench*, in which the hyper troupe makes a manic attempt to perform 30 original plays in 60 minutes. Admission costs $10 to $15; what you pay within that range is based on a dice throw.

Comedy

★ iO Theater — COMEDY
(☑ 312-929-2401; www.ioimprov.com/chicago; 1501 N Kingsbury St; tickets $5-16; Ⓜ Red Line to North/Clybourn) One of Chicago's top-tier improv houses, iO is a bit edgier (and cheaper) than its competition, with four stages hosting bawdy shows nightly. Two bars and a beer garden add to the fun. The Improvised Shakespeare Company is awesome.

★ Second City — COMEDY
(☑ 312-337-3992; www.secondcity.com; 1616 N Wells St; tickets $29-36; Ⓜ Brown, Purple Line to Sedgwick) Bill Murray, Stephen Colbert, Tina Fey and more honed their wit at this slick venue where shows take place nightly. The Mainstage and ETC stage host sketch revues (with an improv scene thrown in); they're similar in price and quality. If you turn up around 10pm (on any night except Friday and Saturday) you can have yourself a bargain and watch the comics improv a set free.

Cinema

The Davis Theater — CINEMA
(☑ 773-769-3999; www.davistheater.com; 4614 N Lincoln Ave; ⊘ 4:30pm-1am Mon-Fri, 11am-2am Sat, 11am-1am Sun; Ⓜ Blue Line to Western) The Davis Theater is a century-old cinema in Lincoln Square that recently underwent a major renovation. Gone are the stiff chairs, rundown bathrooms and cockeyed screens that used to give moviegoers a kink in the neck. They've been replaced by stadium seating, pristine restrooms, larger screens and state-of-the-art sound. Also revived: the neighborhood theater's deco charm.

Logan Theatre — CINEMA
(☑ 773-342-5555; www.thelogantheatre.com; 2646 N Milwaukee Ave; Ⓜ Blue Line to Logan Square) Established in 1915, the Logan Theatre is one of the neighborhood's most enduring landmarks. A major renovation in 2012 unearthed gleaming marble walls and a stained-glass transom above the ticket booth, and added a new art-deco-bar and lounge. Locals and visitors alike flock to the four-screen multiplex to enjoy mid-run movies, independent films and trivia nights.

Sports

★ Chicago Cubs — BASEBALL
(☑ 800-843-2827; www.cubs.com; 1060 W Addison St; Ⓜ Red Line to Addison) The beloved Cubs play at old-time Wrigley Field. For 108 years they didn't win a championship – the longest losing streak in US sports history – but in 2016 the team broke the curse. Games are always packed. Ticket prices vary, but in general you'll be hard-pressed to get in for under $40. The popular bleacher seats cost around $55 or so.

Chicago White Sox — BASEBALL
(☑ 866-769-4263; www.whitesox.com; 333 W 35th St; Ⓜ Red Line to Sox-35th) The Sox are the Cubs' South Side rivals and play in the more modern Guaranteed Rate Field. Tickets are usually cheaper and easier to get than at Wrigley Field; games on Sunday and Monday offer the best deals. The Sox also come up with more promotions (free T-shirts, fireworks etc) to lure fans.

Chicago Bulls
BASKETBALL

(www.nba.com/bulls) They may not be the mythical champions of yore, but the Bulls still draw good crowds to their **United Center** (www.unitedcenter.com; 1901 W Madison St; 🚇19 or 20) home base. Tickets are available through the United Center box office – located in the glass atrium on the building's eastern side, along with the famed, slam-dunking Michael Jordan statue.

Performing Arts

★ **Grant Park Orchestra**
CLASSICAL MUSIC

(Map p536; 🕿 312-742-7638; www.grantparkmusic festival.com; Pritzker Pavilion, Millennium Park; ⊙6:30pm Wed & Fri, 7:30pm Sat mid-Jun–mid-Aug; Ⓜ Brown, Orange, Green, Purple, Pink Line to Washington/Wabash) It's a summertime must-do. The Grant Park Orchestra – composed of top-notch musicians from symphonies worldwide – puts on free classical concerts at Millennium Park's Pritzker Pavilion (p532). Patrons bring lawn chairs, blankets, wine and picnic fixings to set the scene as the sun dips, the skyscraper lights flicker on and glorious music fills the night air.

Chicago Symphony Orchestra
CLASSICAL MUSIC

(CSO; Map p536; 🕿 312-294-3000; www.cso.org; 220 S Michigan Ave; Ⓜ Brown, Orange, Green, Purple, Pink Line to Adams) Riccardo Muti leads the CSO, one of America's best symphonies, known for fervent subscribers and an untouchable brass section. Cellist Yo-Yo Ma is the group's creative consultant and a frequent soloist. The season runs from September to May at Symphony Center; Daniel Burnham designed the Orchestra Hall.

Lyric Opera of Chicago
OPERA

(Map p536; 🕿 312-332-2244; www.lyricopera.org; 20 N Wacker Dr; Ⓜ Brown, Orange, Purple, Pink Line to Washington/Wells) Tickets are hard to come by for this bold modern opera company, which fills the chandeliered Civic Opera House with a shrewd mix of common classics and daring premieres from September to March. If your Italian isn't up to much, don't be put off; much to the horror of purists, the company projects English 'supertitles' above the proscenium.

🛍 Shopping

From the glossy stores of the Magnificent Mile to the countercultural shops of Lake View to the indie designers of Wicker Park, Chicago is a shopper's destination. It has been that way from the get-go. After all, this is the city that birthed the department store

and traditions such as the money-back guarantee, bridal registry and bargain basement.

Chicago Architecture Foundation Shop
GIFTS & SOUVENIRS

(Map p536; 🕿 312-322-1132; www.architecture.org/shop; 224 S Michigan Ave; ⊙9am-9pm, shorter hours in winter; Ⓜ Brown, Orange, Green, Purple, Pink Line to Adams) Skyline posters, Frank Lloyd Wright note cards, skyscraper models and heaps of books celebrate local architecture at this haven for anyone with an edifice complex.

★ **Reckless Records**
MUSIC

(🕿 773-235-3727; www.reckless.com; 1379 N Milwaukee Ave; ⊙10am-10pm Mon-Sat, to 8pm Sun; Ⓜ Blue Line to Damen) Chicago's best indie-rock record and CD emporium allows you to listen to everything before you buy. It's certainly the place to get your finger on the pulse of the local, au courant underground scene. There's plenty of elbow room in the big, sunny space, which makes for happy hunting through the new and used bins. Reasonable prices too.

Knee Deep Vintage
VINTAGE

(🕿 312-850-2510; www.kneedeepvintage.com; 1425 W 18th St; ⊙noon-7pm Mon-Thu, 11am-8pm Fri & Sat, noon-6pm Sun; Ⓜ Pink Line to 18th St) Knee Deep offers a trove of vintage clothing (for men and women), housewares and vinyl. There's a sale the second Friday of every month, with items slashed 25% to 50%; it's held in conjunction with the local gallery-hop (a free event run by galleries, shops and studios), starting at 6pm.

Rotofugi
TOYS

(🕿 773-868-3308; www.rotofugi.com; 2780 N Lincoln Ave; ⊙11am-7pm; Ⓜ Brown, Purple Line to Diversey) Rotofugi has an unusual niche: urban designer toys. The spacey, robot-y, odd vinyl and plush items will certainly distinguish you from the other kids on the block. It's also a gallery showcasing artists in the fields of modern pop and illustration art. You can usually find locally designed Shawnimals here.

ⓘ Information

MONEY

ATMs widely available. Credit cards accepted at most hotels, restaurants and shops. Tipping is not optional; only withhold tips in cases of outrageously bad service.

USEFUL WEBSITES

Lonely Planet (www.lonelyplanet.com/chicago) Destination information, hotel bookings, traveler forum and more.

Choose Chicago (www.choosechicago.com) Official tourism site with sightseeing and event info.

DNA Info Chicago (www.dnainfo.com/chicago) Detailed news about sights, bars, restaurants and events, broken down by neighborhood.

ⓘ Getting There & Away

AIR

O'Hare International Airport (ORD; www.flychicago.com) Seventeen miles northwest of the Loop O'Hare is the headquarters for United Airlines and a hub for American Airlines. Most non-US airlines and international flights use Terminal 5. The domestic terminals are 1, 2 and 3. ATMs and currency exchanges are available throughout. Wi-fi costs $7 per day.

Chicago Midway Airport (MDW; www.flychicago.com) Eleven miles southwest of the Loop, Chicago Midway has three concourses: A, B and C. Southwest Airlines uses B; most other airlines go out of A. There's a currency exchange in A and ATMs throughout. Wi-fi costs $7 per day.

TRAIN

Grand, Doric-columned **Union Station** (www.chicagounionstation.com; 225 S Canal St; Ⓜ Blue Line to Clinton) is the city's rail hub, located at the Loop's western edge. Amtrak (www.amtrak.com) has more connections here than anywhere else in the country. Taxis queue along Canal St outside the station entrance.

ⓘ Getting Around

TO/FROM THE AIRPORT

O'Hare International Airport The Blue Line El train ($5) runs 24/7 and departs every 10 minutes or so. The journey to the city center takes 40 minutes. Shuttle vans cost $35, taxis around $50.

Chicago Midway Airport The Orange Line El train ($3) runs between 4am and 1am, departing every 10 minutes or so. The journey takes 30 minutes to downtown. Shuttle vans cost $30, taxis $35 to $40.

Union Station All trains arrive here. For transportation onward, the Blue Line Clinton stop is a few blocks south (though it's not a great option at night). The Brown, Orange, Purple and Pink Line station at Quincy is about a half-mile east. Taxis queue along Canal St outside the station entrance.

PUBLIC TRANSPORTATION

Elevated/subway trains are part of the city's public transportation system. Metra commuter trains venture out into the suburbs.

The El (it stands for 'elevated,' though many trains also run underground) is fast, frequent and will get you to most sights and neighborhoods.

Two of the eight color-coded lines – the Red Line, and the Blue Line to O'Hare – operate 24 hours a day. The other lines run from 4am to 1am daily, departing every 10 minutes or so.

The standard fare is $3 (except from O'Hare airport, where it costs $5) and includes two transfers. Enter the turnstile using a Ventra Ticket, which is sold from vending machines at train stations.

You can also buy a Ventra Card, aka a rechargeable fare card, at stations. It has a one-time $5 fee that gets refunded once you register the card. It knocks around 75¢ off the cost of each ride.

Unlimited ride passes (one-/three-/seven-day $10/20/28) are another handy option. Get them at train stations and drug stores.

For maps and route planning, check the website of the Chicago Transit Authority (www.transitchicago.com). The 'Transit Tracker' section tells you when the next train or bus is due to arrive at your station.

City buses operate from early morning until late evening. The fare is $2 ($2.25 if you want a transfer). You can use a Ventra Card or pay the driver with exact change. Buses are particularly useful for reaching the Museum Campus, Hyde Park and Lincoln Park's zoo.

TAXI

Taxis are plentiful in the Loop, north to Andersonville and northwest to Wicker Park/Bucktown. Hail them with a wave of the hand. Fares are meter-based and start at $3.25 when you get into the cab, then it's $2.25 per mile. The first extra passenger costs $1; extra passengers after that are 50¢ apiece. Add 10% to 15% for a tip. All major companies accept credit cards. The ride-sharing companies Uber, Lyft and Via are also popular in Chicago.

Reliable taxi companies include **Flash Cab** (☑ 773-561-4444; www.flashcab.com) and **Checker Taxi** (☑ 312-243-2537; www.checkertaxichicago.com).

Around Chicago

Oak Park

This suburb next door to Chicago spawned two famous sons: novelist Ernest Hemingway was born here, and architect Frank Lloyd Wright lived and worked here for 20 years. The town's main sights revolve around the two men. For Hemingway, a low-key museum and his birthplace provide an intriguing peek at his formative years. For

Wright, the studio where he developed the Prairie style is the big draw, as is a slew of surrounding houses he designed for his neighbors. Ten of them cluster within a mile along Forest and Chicago Aves).

👁 Sights

Frank Lloyd Wright Home
& Studio ARCHITECTURE
(📞 312-994-4000; www.flwright.org; 951 Chicago Ave; adult/child $18/15; ⏰ 10am-4pm) This is where Wright lived and worked from 1889 to 1909. Tour frequency varies, from every 20 minutes on summer weekends to every hour or so in winter. The hour-long walk through reveals a fascinating place, filled with the details that made Wright's style distinctive. The studio also offers guided neighborhood walking tours ($15), as well as a self-guided audio version ($15).

Unity Temple ARCHITECTURE
(📞 708-848-6225; www.flwright.org; 875 Lake St; tours $10-18; ⏰ 9am-4:15pm Mon-Thu, to 3:15pm Fri, to 11:15am Sat) This architectural wonder from Frank Lloyd Wright was built in 1909 and recently restored. Explore at your leisure on a 30-minute self-guided tour (per person $10), or go on a 60-minute guided tour (per person $18, with departures on the hour starting at 10am weekdays, 9am on Saturday).

🛈 Information

Oak Park Visitors Center (📞 888-625-7275; www.visitoakpark.com; 1010 W Lake St; ⏰ 10am-5pm Mon-Sat, to 4pm Sun) Offers a visitors guide to the area.

🛈 Getting There & Away

I-290 edges the town; exit on Harlem Ave. Take Harlem north to Lake St and turn right. There's a parking garage within a few blocks.

Metra commuter trains on the Union Pacific West Line stop at Oak Park on their Chicago-western suburbs route. Green Line trains also run to/from Chicago as part of the city's public transit system.

Evanston & North Shore

Mansion-strewn real estate fringes Lake Michigan in the suburbs north of Chicago. The area became popular with the wealthy in the late 19th century.

Evanston is the largest community. It combines sprawling old houses with a compact, bookish downtown. It's home to Northwestern University. Next door is Wilmette,

where the eye-popping, otherworldly Baha'i temple rises. Further north is Glencoe, where the Chicago Botanic Garden sprouts. A classic 30-mile drive follows Sheridan Rd through the region to the socioeconomic apex of Lake Forest.

👁 Sights

Illinois Holocaust Museum MUSEUM
(📞 847-967-4800; www.ilholocaustmuseum.org; 9603 Woods Dr; adult/child $12/6; ⏰ 10am-5pm, to 8pm Thu) This is the third-largest holocaust museum in the world, after those in Jerusalem and Washington, DC. Besides its haunting, Nazi-era rail car and its videos of survivors' stories from WWII, the venue contains thought-provoking art about genocides in Armenia, Rwanda, Cambodia and other countries. The special exhibitions are particularly impressive.

Chicago Botanic Garden GARDENS
(📞 847-835-5440; www.chicagobotanic.org; 1000 Lake Cook Rd; per car weekday/weekend $25/30; ⏰ 8am-sunset) The garden has hiking trails, 255 bird species and weekend cooking demonstations by well-known chefs.

🛈 Getting There & Away

I-94 slices by the suburbs to the west. Sheridan Rd rambles through the towns along the lakefront to the east. Metra commuter trains on the Union Pacific North Line stop at each North Shore community as they zip between downtown Chicago and Kenosha, WI. In Evanston, Purple Line trains also run to/from downtown Chicago as part of the Windy City's public transit system.

Galena

Wee Galena spreads across wooded hillsides near the Mississippi River, amid rolling, barn-dotted farmland. Redbrick mansions in Greek Revival, Gothic Revival and Queen Anne styles line the streets, left over from the town's heyday in the mid-1800s, when local lead mines made it rich. Even with all the touristy B&Bs, fudge and antique shops, there's no denying Galena's beauty. Throw in cool kayak trips and back-road drives, and you've got a lovely, slow-paced getaway. Summer and fall weekends see the most action.

👁 Sights & Activities

Ulysses S Grant Home HISTORIC SITE
(📞 815-777-3310; www.granthome.com; 500 Bouthillier St; adult/child $5/3; ⏰ 9am-4:45pm Wed-Sun Apr-Oct, reduced hours Nov-Mar) The

1860 abode was a gift from local Republicans to the victorious general at the Civil War's end. Grant lived here until he became the country's 18th president. Docents take you through the house. Most of the furnishings are original.

Mississippi Palisades
State Park STATE PARK
(☑ 815-273-2731; 16327A Hwy 84) It's a popular rock-climbing, hiking and camping area by the Mississippi River. Pick up trail maps at the north entrance park office.

Stagecoach Trail SCENIC DRIVE
The Stagecoach Trail is a 26-mile ride on a narrow, twisty road en route to Warren. Pick it up by taking Main St northeast through downtown; at the second stop sign go right (you'll see a trail marker). And yes, it really was part of the old stagecoach route between Galena and Chicago.

Fever River Outfitters OUTDOORS
(☑ 815-776-9425; www.feverriveroutfitters.com; 525 S Main St; ☺ 10am-5pm Fri-Sun) Fever River rents canoes, kayaks, bicycles, paddle boards and snowshoes. It also offers guided tours, such as 12-mile bike trips ($45 per person, gear included) to a local winery and various paddling excursions.

🛏 Sleeping & Eating

DeSoto House Hotel HOTEL $$
(☑ 815-777-0090; www.desotohouse.com; 230 S Main St; r $160-235; ❄️ 🐾) Grant and Lincoln stayed in the well-furnished rooms, and you can too. The hotel dates from 1855.

Grant Hills Motel MOTEL $
(☑ 877-421-0924; www.granthills.com; 9372 US 20; r $80-110; ❄️ 🐾 🏊) The motel is a no-frills option 1.5 miles east of town, with countryside views and a horseshoe pitch.

Fritz and Frites FRENCH, GERMAN $$
(☑ 815-777-2004; www.fritzandfrites.com; 317 N Main St; mains $17-22; ☺ 4-9pm Tue-Sat, 9am-2pm & 4-9pm Sun) This romantic little bistro serves a compact menu of both German and French classics. Dig in to escargot (snails) in garlic-herb butter or maybe a tender schnitzel.

❶ Getting There & Away

Hwy 20 rolls into Galena. Driving is the only way to get here. The closest transportation hubs are Chicago (165 miles southeast), Madison, WI (95 miles northeast), and Dubuque, IA (16 miles northwest).

Central Illinois

Abraham Lincoln and Route 66 sights are sprinkled liberally throughout central Illinois, which is otherwise farmland plain. East of Decatur, Arthur and Arcola are Amish centers.

Springfield

The small state capital has a serious obsession with Abraham Lincoln, who practiced law here from 1837 to 1861. Many of the attractions are walkable downtown and cost little or nothing.

◉ Sights

Lincoln Home &
Visitor Center HISTORIC SITE
(☑ 217-492-4150; www.nps.gov/liho; 426 S 7th St; ☺ 8:30am-5pm) **FREE** Start at the National Park Service visitor center, where you must pick up a ticket to enter Lincoln's 12-room abode, located directly across the street. You can then walk through the house where Abe and Mary Lincoln lived from 1844 until they moved to the White House in 1861; rangers are stationed throughout to provide background information and answer questions.

Lincoln Presidential
Library & Museum MUSEUM
(☑ 217-558-8844; www.illinois.gov/alplm; 212 N 6th St; adult/child $15/6; ☺ 9am-5pm; ⊞) This museum contains the most complete Lincoln collection in the world. Real-deal artifacts like Abe's shaving mirror and briefcase join whiz-bang exhibits and Disney-esque holograms that keep the kids agog.

Lincoln's Tomb TOMB
(☑ 217-782-2717; www.lincolntomb.org; 1441 Monument Ave; ☺ 9am-5pm) **FREE** After his assassination, Lincoln's body was returned to Springfield, where it lies in an impressive tomb in Oak Ridge Cemetery, 1.5 miles north of downtown. In front of the tomb is a bronze bust of Lincoln. The gleam on the nose, created by visitors' light touches, indicates the numbers of those who pay their respects here. On summer Tuesdays at 7pm, infantry re-enactors fire muskets and lower the flag outside the tomb.

Old State Capitol HISTORIC SITE
(☑ 217-785-7960; cnr 6th & Adams Sts; suggested donation $5; ☺ 9am-5pm) Chatterbox docents will take you through the building and

regale you with Lincoln stories, such as how he gave his famous 'House Divided' speech here in 1858.

🛏 Sleeping & Eating

Inn at 835   B&B $$
(☑ 217-523-4466; www.innat835.com; 835 S 2nd St; r $135-205; ⓟ✳🐾) This historic, arts-and-crafts-style manor offers 11 rooms of the four-post bed, claw-foot bathtub variety.

State House Inn   HOTEL $$
(☑ 217-528-5100; www.thestatehouseinn.com; 101 E Adams St; r $120-165; ⓟ✳@🐾) It looks con-crete-drab outside, but inside the State House shows its style. Comfy beds and large baths fill the rooms; a retro bar fills the lobby.

Cozy Dog Drive In   AMERICAN $
(☑ 217-525-1992; www.cozydogdrivein.com; 2935 S 6th St; mains $2-5; ⊙8am-8pm Mon-Sat) This Route 66 legend – the reputed birthplace of the corn dog! – has memorabilia and sou-venirs in addition to the deeply fried main course on a stick.

❶ Information

Springfield Convention & Visitors Bureau (www.visitspringfieldillinois.com) produces a useful visitors guide.

❶ Getting There & Away

The downtown **Amtrak station** (☑ 217-753-2013; www.amtrak.com; 100 N 3rd St) has five trains daily to/from St Louis (two hours) and Chicago (3½ hours).

Southern Illinois

Southern Illinois looks wildly different from the rest of the state, with rivers and rugged green hills dominating the landscape. The Mississippi River forms the western boundary, and alongside it the Great River Road unfolds. The water-hugging byway (actually a series of roads) curls by bluff-strewn scen-ery and forgotten towns with real-deal Main Streets. One of the most knockout stretches is Hwy 100 between Grafton and Alton (near St Louis). As you slip under wind-beaten cliffs, keep an eye out for the turnoff to El-sah, a hidden hamlet of 19th-century stone cottages, wood buggy shops and farmhouses. To the south, Lewis and Clark's launch site, a prehistoric World Heritage Site and a lonely hilltop fort appear.

Inland and south, the population thins and the forested Shawnee Hills rise up, looking a lot like mini mountains. Some sur-prises hide around here, including an eerie swamp and a trail of vineyards.

⊙ Sights & Activities

Union County, near the state's southern tip, has wineries and orchards. Sample the wares on the 35-mile **Shawnee Hills Wine Trail** (www.shawneewinetrail.com), which connects 11 vineyards.

**Cahokia Mounds
State Historic Site**   HISTORIC SITE
(☑ 618-346-5160; www.cahokiamounds.org; Col-linsville Rd; suggested donation adult/child $7/2; ⊙grounds 8am-dusk, visitor center 9am-5pm Tue-Sun) A surprise awaits near Collinsville, 8 miles east of East St Louis: classified as a Unesco World Heritage Site with the likes of Stonehenge and the Egyptian pyramids is Cahokia Mounds State Historic Site. Ca-hokia protects the remnants of North Amer-ica's largest prehistoric city (20,000 people, with suburbs), dating from AD 1200. While the 65 earthen mounds, including the enor-mous Monk's Mound, are not overwhelm-ingly impressive in themselves, the whole site is worth seeing.

If you're approaching from the north, take exit 24 off I-255 S; if approaching from St Louis, take exit 6 off I-55/70.

**Lewis & Clark State
Historic Site**   HISTORIC SITE
(☑ 618-251-5811; www.campdubois.com; cnr Hwy 3 & Poag Rd; ⊙9am-5pm, closed Mon & Tue Oct-Apr) **FREE** In Hartford (across the river from St Louis), the stellar Lewis & Clark State His-toric Site marks the spot where the explor-ers departed on their journey. The 55ft boat replica (in the visitor center), reconstructed winter camp (out on the low-slung prairie) and Mississippi River bashing by give a real feel for the scene.

**Cypress Creek National
Wildlife Refuge**   WILDLIFE RESERVE
(☑ 618-634-2231; www.fws.gov/refuge/cypress_creek) **FREE** You certainly don't expect to find a Southern-style swampland, complete with moss-draped cypress trees and croak-ing bullfrogs in Illinois. But it's here, at Cy-press Creek National Wildlife Refuge. Check it out from the Bellrose Viewing Platform off Cache Chapel Rd. Or head to Section 8 Woods and take a short stroll on the board-walk for a taste of the waterlogged, prime-val landscape; it's near the **Cache River**

Wetlands Center (☑618-657-2064; www.friendsofthecache.org; 8885 Hwy 37; ☺9am-4pm Wed-Sun), which also has hiking and canoeing info.

Shawnee National Forest   FOREST

(☑618-253-7114; www.fs.usda.gov/shawnee) An exception to Illinois' flat farmland is the green southernmost section, punctuated by rolling Shawnee National Forest and its rocky outcroppings. The area has numerous state parks and recreation areas good for hiking, climbing, swimming, fishing and canoeing, particularly around Little Grassy Lake and Devil's Kitchen.

🛏 Sleeping & Eating

Low-priced chain hotels provide most of the region's beds. B&Bs pop up in some of the River Road towns and Shawnee vineyards. Amenity-laden cabins are popular in the Shawnee National Forest area. Places to eat can be few and far between in some parts of the region. Expect mom-and-pop, meat-and-potato type restaurants

❶ Getting There & Away

You'll need to drive to reach the area's far-flung sights. I-57 is the main interstate through the heart of the region. The Great River Road dawdles along the water to the west. St Louis is the nearest transportation hub.

INDIANA

The state revs up around the Indy 500 race, but otherwise it's about slow-paced pleasures in corn-stubbled Indiana: pie-eating in Amish Country, meditating in Bloomington's Tibetan temples and admiring the big architecture in small Columbus. The northwest has moody sand dunes to climb, while the south has caves to explore and rivers to canoe. Spooky labyrinths, bluegrass music shrines and a famed, lipstick-kissed gravestone also make appearances in the state.

For the record, folks have called Indianans 'Hoosiers' since the 1830s, but the word's origin is unknown. One theory is that early settlers knocking on a door were met with 'Who's here?' which soon became 'Hoosier.' It's certainly something to discuss with locals, perhaps over a traditional pork tenderloin sandwich.

Fun fact: Indiana is called 'the mother of vice presidents' for the six veeps it has spawned.

❶ Information

Indiana Highway Conditions (https://indot.carsprogram.org)

Indiana State Park Information (☑800-622-4931; www.in.gov/dnr/parklake) Park entry costs $2 per day by foot or bicycle, $9 to $12 by vehicle. Campsites cost $12 to $44; reservations accepted (☑866-622-6746; www.camp.in.gov).

Indiana Tourism (www.visitindiana.com)

Indianapolis

Clean-cut Indy is the state capital and a perfectly pleasant place to ogle race cars and take a spin around the renowned speedway. The art museum and White River State Park have their merits, as do the Mass Ave and Broad Ripple 'hoods for eating and drinking. And fans of author Kurt Vonnegut are in for a treat. A swell walking and biking trail connects it all.

⦿ Sights

Indianapolis Motor Speedway   MUSEUM

(☑317-492-6784; www.indianapolismotorspeedway.com; 4790 W 16th St; adult/child $10/5; ☺9am-5pm Mar-Oct, 10am-4pm Nov-Feb) The Speedway, home of the Indianapolis 500 motor race, is Indy's super-sight. The Speedway Museum features some 75 racing cars (including former winners), a 500lb Tiffany trophy and a track tour ($8 extra). OK, so you're on a bus for the latter and not even beginning to burn rubber at 37mph, but it's still fun to pretend.

The big race itself is held on the Sunday of Memorial Day weekend (late May) and attended by 450,000 crazed fans. Tickets ($30 to $185, www.imstix.com) can be hard to come by. Try the pre-race trials and practices for easier access and cheaper prices.

Dallara IndyCar Factory   MUSEUM

(☑317-243-7171; www.indycarfactory.com; 1201 W Main St; adult/child $10/5; ☺10am-5pm Wed-Sat) This shiny factory is a short walk from the Indianapolis Motor Speedway, and provides a peek at how the fast cars are made. The wind-tunnel models raise hairs, as do driving simulators that let you feel what it's like to tear around the track at 200mph.

White River State Park   STATE PARK

(☑317-233-2434; www.inwhiteriver.com; 801 W Washington St) The expansive park, located at downtown's edge, contains several

GREAT LAKES INDIANAPOLIS

worthwhile sights. The adobe **Eiteljorg Museum of American Indians & Western Art** (☎ 317-636-9378; www.eiteljorg.org; 500 W Washington St; adult/child $13/7; ⊙ 10am-5pm Mon-Sat, from noon Sun) features an impressive collection of Native American works. Other park highlights include an atmospheric minor-league baseball stadium, a zoo, a canal walk, gardens, a science museum and a college sports museum.

Indianapolis
Museum of Art
MUSEUM, GARDENS

(☎ 317-920-2660; www.imamuseum.org; 4000 Michigan Rd; adult/child $18/10; ⊙ 11am-5pm Tue-Sat, to 9pm Thu, noon-5pm Sun) This museum has a terrific collection of European art (especially Turner and post-Impressionists), African tribal art, South Pacific art and Chinese works. The complex also includes **Oldfields – Lilly House & Gardens**, where you can tour the 22-room mansion and flowery grounds of the Lilly pharmaceutical family, and **Fairbanks Art & Nature Park**, with eye-popping mod sculptures set amid 100 acres of woodlands. Fairbanks, which has its own entrance, is free.

Kurt Vonnegut
Museum & Library
MUSEUM

(☎ 317-423-0391; www.vonnegutlibrary.org; 340 N Senate Ave; ⊙ 11am-6pm Mon, Tue, Thu & Fri, noon-5pm Sat & Sun) FREE Author Kurt Vonnegut was born and raised in Indy, and this humble museum pays homage with displays including his Pall Mall cigarettes, droll drawings and rejection letters from publishers. The museum also replicates his office, complete with blue Coronamatic typewriter. You're welcome to sit at the desk and type Kurt a note; the museum tweets the musings. The center is planning to move to a larger space, so you might want to call first to check the location.

Rhythm! Discovery Center
MUSEUM

(☎ 317-275-9030; www.rhythmdiscoverycenter.org; 110 W Washington St; adult/child $12/6; ⊙ 10am-5pm Mon & Thu-Sat, noon-7pm Wed, noon-5pm Sun) Bang drums, gongs, xylophones and exotic percussive instruments from around the globe at this hidden gem downtown. Kids love the interactive whomping. Adults appreciate the exhibits of famous drummers' gear and the soundproof, drum-kitted studio where you can unleash (and record) your inner rock star.

Indiana Medical
History Museum
MUSEUM

(☎ 317-635-7329; www.imhm.org; 3045 W Vermont St; adult/child $10/3; ⊙ 10am-4pm Thu-Sat) When you think 'horror movie asylum,' this century-old state psychiatric hospital is exactly what you envision. Guided tours roam the former pathology lab, from the cold-slabbed autopsy room to the eerie specimen room filled with brains in jars. Tours start on the hour. It's a few miles west of White River State Park.

Children's Museum
of Indianapolis
MUSEUM

(☎ 317-334-4000; www.childrensmuseum.org; 3000 N Meridian St; $12-27; ⊙ 10am-5pm, closed Mon mid-Sep–Feb) It's the world's largest kids' museum, sprawled over five floors holding dinosaurs aplenty and a 43-ft sculpture by Dale Chihuly that teaches tykes to blow glass (virtually!). The admission prices vary depending on the day and how far ahead you buy tickets.

 Activities

The 8-mile Cultural Trail (www.indycultur altrail.org) bike and pedestrian path links cool sights and neighborhoods around Indy's center. Pacers Bikeshare stations dot the way and are handy for short jaunts.

Bicycle Garage Indy
CYCLING

(☎ 317-612-3099; www.bgindy.com; 242 E Market St; rental per 2hr/day $20/40; ⊙ 7am-6:30pm Mon-Fri, 10am-4pm Sat) Rent bikes here for leisurely rides. Hop on the Cultural Trail in front of the shop to explore the city center; it eventually connects to the Monon Trail greenway, a converted rail track that heads north from the city for 18 miles. Rates include helmet, lock and map.

🛏 **Sleeping**

Indy Hostel
HOSTEL $

(☎ 317-727-1696; www.indyhostel.us; 4903 Winthrop Ave; dm/r from $28/58; P✳@☎) This small, friendly hostel has a six-bed female dorm and 12-bed co-ed dorm. There are also four private rooms. Got a tent? Camp in the yard for $29. The Monon Trail hiking/cycling path runs beside the property, and the hostel rents bikes ($10 per day). It's located near Broad Ripple, so a bit of a haul from downtown (on bus 17).

★ Alexander
HOTEL **$$**

(☑ 317-624-8200; www.thealexander.com; 333 S Delaware St; r $160-270; P✱@⚡) The 209-room Alexander is all about art. Forty original works decorate the lobby; the Indianapolis Museum of Art curates the contemporary collection (the public is welcome to browse). The modern rooms have dark-wood floors and, of course, cool wall art. A block from the basketball arena, it's where visiting teams sometimes stay. Valet parking is $37.

Hilton Garden Inn
HOTEL **$$**

(☑ 317-955-9700; www.indianapolisdowntown. gardeninn.com; 10 E Market St; r $150-190; ✱@⚡) The century-old, neoclassical architecture, plush beds and downtown location right by Monument Circle make this a fine chain-hotel choice. Valet parking is $29.

Stone Soup
INN **$$**

(☑ 866-639-9550; www.stonesoupinn.com; 1304 N Central Ave; r $119-149, with shared bath $99-109; P⇌✱⚡) The nine rooms fill a rambling, antique-filled house. It's a bit ramshackle, but it has its charm.

✖ Eating

Massachusetts Ave, by downtown, is bounteous when the stomach growls. Virginia Ave, connecting downtown to the Fountain Square district just south, is chockablock with hip foodie options. Broad Ripple, 7 miles north, has pubs, cafes and ethnic eateries.

Bazbeaux
PIZZA **$**

(☑ 317-636-7662; www.bazbeaux.com; 329 Massachusetts Ave; mains $9-15; ⊘11am-10pm Sun-Thu, to 11pm Fri & Sat) A local favorite, Bazbeaux offers an eclectic pizza selection, such as the 'Tchoupitoulas,' topped with Cajun shrimp and andouille sausage. Muffaletta sandwiches, stromboli and Belgian beer are some of the other offerings.

City Market
MARKET **$**

(www.indycm.com; 222 E Market St; ⊘7am-9pm Mon-Fri, from 8am Sat; ⚡) A smattering of food stalls fill the city's old marketplace, which dates from 1886. The 2nd-floor bar (⊘2-9pm Mon-Thu, 12-9pm Fri-Sat) pours 16 local brews; most other vendors close by 3pm.

Public Greens
AMERICAN **$**

(☑ 317-964-0865; www.publicgreensurbankitchen. com; 900 E 64th St; mains $8-16; ⊘8am-9pm Tue-

WORTH A TRIP

GRAY BROTHERS CAFETERIA

Cafeterias are an Indiana tradition, but most have disappeared – except for **Gray Brothers Cafeteria** (☑ 317-831-7234; www.graybroscafe.com; 555 S Indiana St; mains $5-9; ⊘11am-8:30pm) . Enter the time-warped dining room, grab a blue tray and behold a corridor of food that seems to stretch the length of a football field. Stack on plates of pan-fried chicken, meatloaf, mac 'n' cheese and sugar cream pie, then fork in with abandon.

It's located in Mooresville, about 18 miles south of downtown Indianapolis en route to Bloomington.

Sat, to 4pm Sun & Mon) ✔ The on-site microfarm raises kale, beets, eggs and other ingredients for the eatery's homey dishes; 100% of profits are then plowed back into the community to feed at-risk children.

★ Tinker Street
AMERICAN **$$**

(☑ 317-925-5000; www.tinkerstreetindy.com; 402 E 16th St; small plates $8-16, mains $19-25; ⊘5-10pm Mon-Thu, to 10:30pm Fri & Sat, to 9pm Sun; ⚡) Fork into seasonal dishes such as Indiana asparagus with quinoa and garlic chips or a blue-cheese-topped lamb burger. Vegetarian and gluten-free options are plentiful. The industrial-meets-rustic-wood decor is just right for romantics, while the year-round patio is more casual. Tinker Street is located in Old Northside, a leafy neighborhood of historic manors just north of downtown. No reservations.

♟ Drinking & Nightlife

Downtown and Mass Ave have some good watering holes; the Broad Ripple neighborhood has several.

Rathskeller
BEER HALL

(☑ 317-636-0396; www.rathskeller.com; 401 E Michigan St; ⊘2-9pm Mon-Thu, to 11pm Fri, 11am-11pm Sat, 11am-9pm Sun) Quaff German and local brews at the outdoor beer garden's picnic tables in summer, or at the deer-head-lined indoor beer hall once winter strikes. Rathskeller is located in the historic Athenaeum building near Mass Ave.

Slippery Noodle Inn
BAR

(☑ 317-631-6974; www.slipperynoodle.com; 372 S Meridian St; ⊘11am-2am Mon-Fri, from noon

Sat, 4pm-12:30am Sun) Downtown's Noodle is the oldest bar in the state, and has seen action as a brothel, slaughterhouse, gangster hang-out and Underground Railroad station; currently, it's one of the best blues clubs in the country. There's live music nightly, and it's cheap.

Sun King Brewing   BREWERY
(www.sunkingbrewing.com; 135 N College Ave; ⊙10am-9pm Mon-Wed, to 10pm Thu & Fri, 11am-10pm Sat, 11am-8pm Sun, reduced hours in winter) You never know what'll be flowing at Sun King's unvarnished downtown taproom. Indy's young and hip pile in to find out, swilling brews from a cocoa-y Baltic porter to a popcorn-tinged pilsner (made with Indiana popcorn). Flights (six 3oz samples) cost $6. It's packed on Fridays, when the brewery offers cheap growlers. The outdoor patio hops in summer.

☆ Entertainment

Bankers Life Fieldhouse   BASKETBALL
(☎317-917-2500; www.nba.com/pacers; 125 S Pennsylvania St) Basketball is huge in Indiana, and Bankers Life Fieldhouse is ground zero, where the NBA's Pacers make it happen.

Lucas Oil Stadium   FOOTBALL
(☎317-299-4946; www.colts.com; 500 S Capitol Ave) Where the NFL's Colts play football under a huge retractable roof.

ℹ Information

Indianapolis Convention & Visitors Bureau (www.visitindy.com) Download a free city guide and print out coupons for attractions and tours from the website.
Indianapolis Star (www.indystar.com) The city's daily newspaper.
Indy Rainbow Chamber (www.gayindynow.com) Provides info for gay and lesbian visitors.
Nuvo (www.nuvo.net) Free, weekly alternative paper with the arts and music low-down.

ℹ Getting There & Around

The fancy **Indianapolis International Airport** (IND; www.indianapolisairport.com; 7800 Col H Weir Cook Memorial Dr) is 16 miles southwest of town. The Washington bus (8) runs between the airport and downtown ($1.75, 50 minutes); the Go Green Airport van does it quicker ($10, 20 minutes). A cab to downtown costs about $35.

Greyhound (www.greyhound.com) shares **Union Station** (350 S Illinois St) with Amtrak (www.amtrak.com). Buses go frequently to Cincinnati (2½ hours) and Chicago (3½ hours).

Megabus (www.megabus.com/us; cnr N Delaware & E Market Sts) is often cheaper. Amtrak travels these routes but takes almost twice as long.

IndyGo (www.indygo.net) runs the local buses. Fare is $1.75. Bus 17 goes to Broad Ripple. Service is minimal during weekends.

Pacers Bikeshare (www.pacersbikeshare.org) has 250 bikes at 26 stations along the Cultural Trail downtown. A 24-hour pass costs $8, and additional charges apply for trips over 30 minutes.

For a taxi, call **Yellow Cab** (☎317-487-7777).

Central Indiana

Bluegrass music, architectural hot spots, Tibetan temples and James Dean remembrances all furrow into the farmland around here.

Fairmount

This pocket-sized town is the birthplace of 1950s actor James Dean, one of the original icons of cool.

◉ Sights

Fairmount Historical Museum   MUSEUM
(☎765-948-4555; www.jamesdeanartifacts.com; 203 E Washington St; ⊙11am-5pm Mon, Wed & Fri-Sun May-Oct) FREE Fans of actor James Dean should head directly here to see the Hollywood icon's bongo drums, among other artifacts. This is also the place to pick up a free map that will guide you to sites such as the farmhouse where Jimmy grew up and his lipstick-kissed gravesite. The museum sells Dean posters, Zippo lighters and other memorabilia, and sponsors the annual **James Dean Festival** (www.jamesdeanartifacts.com; ⊙late Sep).

James Dean Gallery   MUSEUM
(☎765-948-3326; www.jamesdeangallery.com; 425 N Main St; ⊙9am-6pm) FREE The privately owned James Dean Gallery has several rooms of memorabilia (bronze busts, photos, clocks, Dean's high school yearbooks) in an old Victorian home downtown. The owners are a font of local information.

🛏 Sleeping & Eating

Fairmount has no hotels. The closest options are in Gas City about 7 miles north, where budget and midrange chains dot I-69. A few miles further on is Marion, a much bigger town with name-brand hotels.

A smattering of pizza, Mexican and family-style restaurants pop up on Main St and 8th St. You'll find lots more options, including ethnic diners and fast-food chains, in Marion.

ⓘ Getting There & Away

Fairmount is 70 miles northeast from Indianapolis, the closest transportation hub. I-69 passes the town to the east.

Columbus

When you think of the USA's great architectural cities – Chicago, New York, Washington, DC – Columbus, IN, doesn't quite leap to mind, but it should. The city is a remarkable gallery of physical design. Since the 1940s, Columbus and its leading corporations have commissioned some of the world's best architects, including Eero Saarinen, Richard Meier and IM Pei, to create both public and private buildings.

Architecture-gaping is the big to-do. More than 70 notable buildings and pieces of public art are spread over a wide area (car required), but about 15 diverse works can be seen on foot downtown. The **visitor center** (✆812-378-2622; www.columbus.in.us; 506 5th St; ◷9am-5pm Mon-Sat, from noon Sun) provides self-guided tour maps online and on-site. **Bus tours** (adult/student $25/15; ◷10am Tue-Fri, 10am & 2pm Sat, 2pm Sun) also depart from the center.

🛏 Sleeping & Eating

Besides **Hotel Indigo** (✆812-375-9100; www.hotelindigo.com; 400 Brown St; r $150-200; ❄🅿❄🐾) and a couple of B&Bs, there's little downtown. A short drive west of the center, several chain hotels bunch around exit 68 off I-65.

Columbus offers lots of non-chain options and diversity – pizza, steak, Caribbean curries, Italian, Thai – downtown. Browse 4th and Washington Sts.

ⓘ Getting There & Away

I-65 is the main highway that skirts the city. The closest airports are in Indianapolis (46 miles north) and Louisville (73 miles south). Alas, no shuttle buses connect Columbus to these cities.

Nashville

Nashville is the jumping-off point for **Brown County State Park** (✆812-988-6406; www.

in.gov/dnr; 1801 Hwy 46 E; per car $9), known as the Little Smoky Mountains for its steep wooded hills and fog-cloaked ravines. Gentrified and antique-filled, the 19th-century town is now a bustling tourist center, at its busiest in fall when visitors pour in to see the area's leafy trees burst into color.

🛏 Sleeping

Cozy B&Bs, inns, cabins and lodges prevail. They're usually midrange in price, except during the peak autumn season, when rates go way up.

Artists Colony Inn INN $$
(✆812-988-0600; www.artistscolonyinn.com; 105 S Van Buren St; r $135-180; ❄🐾) This central, 20-room inn stands out for its spiffy rooms with four-poster beds, wood-plank floors and other sturdy, Shaker-style decor. You won't have to go far for a good meal: the on-site dining room – open for breakfast, lunch and dinner daily – is well-known for traditional Hoosier fare, such as catfish and pork tenderloin sandwiches.

🍷 Drinking & Entertainment

The compact downtown has several bars and taverns in which to imbibe, as well as a tea house, winery and brewery.

As with Nashville, TN, Indiana's Nashville enjoys country music, and bands play regularly at several venues.

Big Woods Brewing Co MICROBREWERY
(✆812-988-6000; www.bigwoodsbeer.com; 60 Molly's Lane; ◷11am-10pm) It's hard to beat a set of beer samples on Big Woods' porch on a bright fall day. The timber-framed building feels like a cozy cabin. Eight house brews are on tap, and burgers and pulled-pork nachos satisfy if hunger strikes.

Mike's Music & Dance Barn LIVE MUSIC
(✆812-988-8636; www.mikesmusicbarn.com; 2277 Hwy 46; ◷from 6:30pm Fri-Mon) To shake a leg, mosey into Mike's. Line-dance lessons take place at 6:30pm some nights, bands play at 8pm on other nights. Check the schedule. There's usually a small cover charge ($6 to $8).

ⓘ Getting There & Away

Nashville lies midway between Bloomington and Columbus on Hwy 46. Indianapolis, 60 miles north, is the closest big city and transportation center.

Bloomington

Lively and lovely, limestone-clad and cycling-mad, Bloomington is the home of Indiana University. The town centers on Courthouse Sq, surrounded by restaurants, bars and bookshops. Nearly everything is walkable. Also, perhaps surprisingly, there's a significant Tibetan community here too. The Dalai Lama's brother came to teach at IU in the 1960s, and Tibetan temples, monasteries and culture followed.

◎ Sights

Dagom Gaden Tensung
Ling Monastery MONASTERY
(☑ 812-339-0857; www.dgtlmonastery.org; 102 Clubhouse Dr; ⊙9am-6pm) FREE Roam the quiet grounds to see traditional Tibetan colors and designs. The monastery also offers free teachings and meditation sessions.

Eskenazi Museum of Art MUSEUM
(☑ 812-855-5445; www.artmuseum.indiana.edu; 1133 E 7th St; ⊙10am-5pm Tue-Sat, from noon Sun) FREE Indiana University's art museum, designed by IM Pei, has an excellent, genre-spanning collection. Highlights include African art, 19th-century American painting, German expressionism and modern works by Joan Miró, Pablo Picasso and Salvador Dali. The building is closed until fall 2019 for a major renovation and expansion.

Tibetan Mongolian
Buddhist Cultural Center BUDDHIST SITE
(☑ 812-336-6807; www.tmbcc.org; 3655 Snoddy Rd; ⊙sunrise-sunset) FREE Founded by the Dalai Lama's brother, this colorful, prayer-flag-covered cultural building and its traditional stupas are worth a look. A gift shop sells traditional Tibetan items inside, and meditation sessions that are open to the public take place Monday at 6pm and Thursday at 6:30pm.

⊨ Sleeping & Eating

For a town of its size, Bloomington offers a mind-blowing array of ethnic eats – everything from Burmese to Eritrean to Turkish. Browse Kirkwood Ave and E 4th St. Eating here won't break the bank either.

Grant Street Inn INN $$
(☑ 812-334-2353; www.grantsinn.com; 310 N Grant St; r $159-209; @ 🛜) The inn has 40 rooms in a Victorian house and a couple of adjacent buildings near the Indiana University campus. Rooms in the 1890s home are more quaint and antique-laden, while those in the annexes are more modern and stylish.

Anyetsang's Little Tibet ASIAN $
(☑ 812-331-0122; www.anyetsangs.com; 415 E 4th St; mains $13-14; ⊙11am-3pm & 5-9pm; 🥢) Little Tibet offers specialties from the Himalayan homeland, including Tibetan dumplings and noodle stew, as well as Indian and Thai dishes.

🍷 Drinking & Nightlife

Kirkwood Ave, close to the university, has a lineup of coffee shops and pubs that serve the thirsty.

Upland Brewing Co BREWERY
(☑ 812-336-2337; www.uplandbeer.com; 350 W 11th St; ⊙11am-midnight Mon-Thu, to 1am Fri & Sat, noon-midnight Sun) Northwest of downtown Bloomington, rustic Upland Brewing Co makes creative suds such as a seasonal persimmon lambic using local fruit.

Nick's English Hut PUB
(☑ 812-332-4040; www.nicksenglishhut.com; 423 E Kirkwood Ave; ⊙11am-1am Mon-Wed, to 2am Thu-Sat, to midnight Sun) Popular with students and professors from nearby Indiana University, Nick's has also filled the cups of Kurt Vonnegut, Dylan Thomas and Barack Obama.

❶ Getting There & Away

Indianapolis, 50 miles northeast, has the closest airport. Go Express Travel (www.goexpresstravel.com) runs a shuttle bus to/from the airport several times daily; it costs $20 one way. Hwy 37 (which will become I-69 by summer 2018) and Hwy 46 are the main roads to Bloomington.

Southern Indiana

The pretty hills, caves, rivers and utopian history of Southern Indiana mark it as a completely different region from the rest of the state.

Ohio River

The Ohio River marks the state's southern border. Hwys 56, 156, 62 and 66, known collectively as the Ohio River Scenic Byway, wind through a lush and hilly landscape covering 300 miles along the churning waterway. Sweet stops en route include Madison, a well-preserved river settlement from the mid-19th century with genteel architecture; Marengo Cave, with its eye-popping underground formations; and former US president Abraham Lincoln's childhood home near Dale. Canoeing, farmstays and beers with attitude pop up in between.

◉ Sights & Activities

In Madison pick up a walking-tour brochure at the **visitor center** (☑ 812-265-2956; www.visitmadison.org; 601 W First St; ☺ 9am-5pm Mon-Fri, to 4pm Sat, 11am-3pm Sun), which will lead you by notable landmarks. Canoeing on the Blue River (a tributary of the Ohio River) is popular; Milltown is a base for it.

Clifty Falls State Park   STATE PARK
(☑ 812-273-8885; 2221 Clifty Dr; per car $9) A couple of miles west of Madison, this large, wooded state park has hiking trails, views and waterfalls. It offers camping too, with tent and RV sites from $16 to $33.

**Falls of the Ohio
State Park**   STATE PARK
(☑ 812-280-9970; www.fallsoftheohio.org; 201 W Riverside Dr; interpretive center adult/child $9/7, parking $2; ☺ interpretive center 9am-4:30pm Mon-Sat, from 1pm Sun) In Clarksville, this state park has only rapids, no falls, but is of interest for its 386-million-year-old fossil beds. The newly renovated interpretive center explains it all. The park sits right across the river from Louisville, KY.

**Lincoln Boyhood
National Memorial**   HISTORIC SITE
(☑ 812-937-4541; www.nps.gov/libo; 3027 E South St; adult/child $5/free; ☺ 8am-5pm) Off I-64 and 4 miles south of Dale, the Lincoln Boyhood National Memorial is where young Abe, who grew up to become the 16th US president, lived from age seven to 21. This isolated site also includes admission to a working pioneer farm, open from May through September.

Marengo Cave   CAVE
(☑ 812-365-2705; www.marengocave.com; 400 E State Rd 64; ☺ 9am-6pm Jun-Aug, to 5pm Sep-May) A plunge into Marengo Cave is highly recommended. It offers a 40-minute tour (adult/child $17/10), 60-minute tour ($20/12) or combination tour ($28/16) walking past stalagmites and other ancient formations. You can also crawl, crouch and go deeper into the formations on more hardcore tours (from $34).

Cave Country Canoes   CANOEING
(☑ 812-365-2705; www.cavecountrycanoes.com; 112 W Main St; ☺ May-Oct) This outfitter operates out of Milltown, offering half-day ($28), full-day ($32) or longer trips on the scenic Blue River; keep an eye out for river otters and rare hellbender salamanders.

🛏 Sleeping & Eating

Blue River Family Farm   FARMSTAY $$
(☑ 812-633-7871; www.bluerivervalleyfarm.com; 10351 E Daugherty Ln; house $175-195; ✳ 🛜) When you stay here you rent the whole farmhouse, with its three bedrooms, one bathroom, fireplace and hot tub. Deer and wild turkeys roam the property. Children can help feed the goats and chickens and pick veggies from the garden. The owners live down the hill. Located in Milltown; a two-night minimum stay is required.

Hinkle's   BURGERS $
(☑ 812-265-3919; www.hinkleburger.com; 204 W Main St; mains $2-5; ☺ 6am-10pm Mon & Tue, to midnight Wed & Thu, 24hr Fri & Sat) It's hard to beat a plate of mini burgers and a caramel milkshake while sitting at the counter on a twirly stool. Hinkle's is an old-school diner in Madison, grilling the goods since 1933.

ℹ Information

Ohio River Scenic Byway (www.ohioriverbyway.com)

ℹ Getting There & Away

Louisville and Cincinnati are the closest big-city transport hubs. In addition to the Ohio River Scenic Byway's gaggle of roads, I-64 cuts across the region. For distance reference, Madison is about 75 miles east of Marengo Cave, which is about 55 miles east of Lincoln's boyhood home.

New Harmony

In southwest Indiana, the Wabash River forms the border with Illinois. Beside it, south of I-64, captivating New Harmony is the site of two early communal-living experiments and is worth a visit. In the early 19th century, a German Christian sect, the Harmonists, developed a sophisticated town here while awaiting the Second Coming. Later, the British utopian Robert Owen acquired the town.

Today, New Harmony retains an air of contemplation, if not otherworldliness, which you can experience at attractions such as the eye-popping **Atheneum**

(✆812-682-4474; www.usi.edu/hnh; 401 N Arthur St; ◷9:30am-5pm), the **Roofless Church** (✆812-682-3050; www.robertleeblafferfoundation. org; 420 North St; ◷hours vary) FREE and the spooky **Labyrinth** (✆812-682-4474; 1239 Main St; ◷sunrise-sunset) FREE.

The town has a simple resort and a handful of B&Bs in historic buildings, all at midrange prices. **Harmonie State Park** (✆812-682-4821; 3451 Harmonie State Park Rd; per car $9) offers low-cost camping and cabins.

There aren't many options for food, but those that do exist are non-chain eateries located in the walkable downtown. Menus consist mostly of sandwiches, pizza and American fare.

ⓘ Getting There & Away

I-64 is the main interstate to New Harmony; it races by about 7 miles north of town. Hwy 66 links the town to the Ohio River Scenic Byway. The closest city is Evansville, which has a small airport and bus service about 30 miles southeast.

Northern Indiana

While much of Northern Indiana is industrial, unexpected treats rise from the flatland, too. Wild sand dunes, classic cars, Amish pies and the infamous Dark Lord brewer are all within range.

Indiana Dunes

Sunny beaches, rustling grasses and woodsy campgrounds are Indiana Dunes' claim to fame. The area is hugely popular on summer days with sunbathers from Chicago and towns throughout Northern Indiana. In addition to its beaches, the area is noted for its plant variety: everything from cacti to pine trees sprouts here. Sweet hiking trails meander up the dunes and through the woodlands. Visit in the morning and linger on into the afternoon

◉ Sights & Activities

Indiana Dunes National
Lakeshore   NATIONAL PARK
(✆219-926-7561; www.nps.gov/indu; ◷6am-11pm) FREE The Dunes stretch along 15 miles of Lake Michigan shoreline. Swimming is allowed anywhere along the shore. A short walk away from the beaches, several hiking paths crisscross the dunes and woodlands. The best are the Bailly-Chellberg Trail

(2.5 miles) that winds by a still-operating 1870s farm, and the Heron Rookery Trail (2 miles), where blue herons flock. Oddly, all this natural bounty lies smack-dab next to smoke-belching factories, which you'll also see at various vantage points.

Indiana Dunes
State Park   STATE PARK
(✆219-926-1952; www.in.gov/dnr/parklake; per car $12; ◷7am-11pm) The state park is a 2100-acre, shoreside pocket within the national lakeshore; it's located at the end of Hwy 49, near Chesterton. It has more amenities than the rest of the lakeshore, but also more regulation and crowds (plus the vehicle entry fee). Wintertime brings out the cross-country skiers; summertime brings out the hikers. Seven trails zigzag over the landscape; No 4 up Mt Tom rewards with Chicago skyline views.

West Beach   BEACH
(376 N County Line Rd; per car $6; ◷8am-sunset) West Beach, nearest to Gary, draws fewer crowds than the other beaches and features a number of nature hikes and trails. It's also the only beach with lifeguards. There's a snack bar and cool Chicago vistas.

Pedal Power   CYCLING
(✆219-921-3085; www.pedalpowerrentals.com; 1215 Hwy 49; per hour/day $7/35; ◷9am-7pm Sat & Sun late May-early Oct) This outfitter rents bicycles (including helmet, lock and map) from the cul-de-sac next to the Indiana Dunes Visitor Center. From here, the 2-mile Dunes-Kankakee Trail runs to Indiana Dunes State Park. Pedal Power also offers tours, such as Bike and Beach Yoga ($20 per person, two hours); check the website for times.

🛏 Sleeping

Campgrounds are prevalent. Midrange chains and budget motels fleck the highways that edge the Dunes.

Tryon Farm Guesthouse   B&B $$
(✆219-879-3618; www.tryonfarmguesthouse.com; 1400 Tryon Rd; r $190; ❉@❞❄) This four-room B&B nestles in a turn-of-the-century farmhouse near Michigan City. You can help gather eggs from the chickens in the morning (you might even get some to take home). Afterward, lounge in the hammocks, sway on the tire swing and enjoy the garden.

✗ Eating

★ **Great Lakes Cafe** DINER $
(☑ 219-883-5737; 201 Mississippi St; mains $6-9; ⊙ 5am-2:30pm Mon-Fri, 6am-12:30pm Sat; 🚼) This colorful Greek family diner sits right in front of a steel mill, whose workers pile in for the cheap, hearty pancakes, meatloaf, butterfly shrimp, bacon-pecan brownies and whatever else features on the whiteboard of daily specials. It's located a short distance off the highway, before you reach the national lakeshore.

Lucrezia ITALIAN $$
(☑ 219-926-5829; 428 S Calumet Rd; mains $16-28; ⊙ 11am-10pm Sun-Thu, to 11pm Fri & Sat) This is a homey favorite for Italian staples – fettuccine alfredo, veal marsala, linguine with scallops – in Chesterton.

ℹ Information

Indiana Dunes Visitor Center (☑ 219-395-1882; www.indianadunes.com; 1215 Hwy 49; ⊙ 8am-6pm Jun-Aug, 8:30am-4:30pm Sep-May) The best place to start a visit to the Dunes. Staff can provide beach details; a schedule of ranger-guided walks and activities; hiking, biking and birding maps; and general information on the area.

ℹ Getting There & Away

The Indiana Toll Rd (I-80/90), I-94, Hwy 12, Hwy 20 and Hwy 49 all skirt the lakeshore. Look for large brown signs on the roads that point the way in to the Dunes.

South Shore commuter trains also service the area on their Chicago-South Bend route. The stops at Dune Park and Beverly Shores put you about a 1.5-mile walk from the beaches.

South Bend

South Bend is home to the University of Notre Dame. You know how people in certain towns say, 'football is a religion here'? They mean it at Notre Dame, where 'Touchdown Jesus' lords over the 80,000-capacity stadium (it's a mural of the resurrected Christ with arms raised, though the pose bears a striking resemblance to a referee signaling a touchdown). The renowned campus and downtown's vintage car museum are worth a pit stop.

◎ Sights & Activities

Studebaker National Museum MUSEUM
(☑ 574-235-9714; www.studebakermuseum.org; 201 S Chapin St; adult/child $8/5; ⊙ 10am-5pm Mon-Sat, from noon Sun) Gaze at a gorgeous 1956 Packard and other classic beauties that used to be built in South Bend, where the Studebaker car company was based. The shiny vehicles, including vintage carriages and military tanks, spread over three floors. A local history museum shares the building. The entrance is on Thomas St.

Notre Dame Tours WALKING
(☑ 574-631-5726; www.nd.edu/visitors; 111 Eck Center) FREE Two-mile, 75-minute walking tours of the pretty university campus, with its two lakes, Gothic-style architecture and iconic Golden Dome atop the main building, start at the Eck visitor center. Tour times vary, but there's usually at least a 10am and 3pm jaunt Monday through Friday.

🛏 Sleeping & Eating

Several budget and midrange chain hotels line US Business 31/Hwy 933 (aka Dixie Way) a short distance north of Notre Dame. They're near exit 77 off the Indiana Toll Rd (I-80/90) in an area called Roseland. In fall, prices soar if there is a Notre Dame home football game.

Collegiate cafes and fast-food outlets speckle the streets around the university. Downtown holds a bundle of restaurants, mostly midrange American fare places, but also some Thai, Japanese, Indian and other ethnic eateries. Browse Michigan St for options.

Morris Inn HOTEL $$
(☑ 574-631-2000; www.morrisinn.nd.edu; 1399 N Notre Dame Ave; r $185-215) This 150-room hotel is popular with Notre Dame alumnae, since it is right in the heart of campus. While the gold-and-white rooms won't win any avant-garde-design awards, they're decent-sized and comfy, with pillowy beds and large bathrooms. Parking on-site costs $20 per night, though it's free at the nearby bookstore lot (a five-minute walk).

★ **Oh Mamma's on the Avenue** DELI $
(☑ 574-276-6918; www.facebook.com/OhMamma; 1202 Mishawaka Ave; sandwiches $6-8; ⊙ 10am-6pm Tue-Fri, 9am-4pm Sat) This cute little grocery store and deli features toasted sandwiches, heaps of cheeses from the region (including awesome housemade goat's milk cheese), fresh-baked bread, cannoli and gelato. Staff are super-friendly and generous with samples. Eat in at the smattering of tables, or take away.

AUBURN

Classic-car connoisseurs should stop in Auburn, where the Cord Company produced the USA's favorite autos in the 1920s and '30s. The vehicle museums here impress.

National Automotive and Truck Museum (260-925-9100; www.natmus.org; 1000 Gordon Buehrig Pl; adult/child $10/5; 9am-5pm, reduced hours Jan & Feb) This museum has a bit of everything, from toy cars to gas pumps to vintage rigs.

Auburn Cord Duesenberg Museum (260-925-1444; www.automobilemuseum.org; 1600 S Wayne St; adult/child $12.50/7.50; 9am-5pm) This museum has a wonderful display of early roadsters in a beautiful art-deco setting.

I-69 is the main interstate to town. Auburn lies about 20 miles south of Hwy 20.

🛈 Getting There & Away

South Bend has a bigger-than-you'd-think airport with flights to Chicago, Detroit and more. The airport is also a station on the South Shore commuter train that goes to/from Chicago (about $13 one way). By car, the Indiana Toll Rd (I-80/90) and Hwy 20 are the primary routes to the city.

Indiana Amish Country

The area around Shipshewana and Middlebury is the USA's third-largest Amish community. Horses and buggies clip-clop by, and long-bearded men hand-plow the tidy fields. It's not far off the interstate, but it's a whole different world.

Pick a back road between the two towns and head down it. Often you'll see families selling beeswax candles, quilts and fresh produce on their porch, which beats the often-touristy shops and restaurants on the main roads. Note that most places close on Sunday. Homey B&Bs and country inns are the region's forte. Most fall into the budget or midrange category. Don't expect chic or fancy around here. Amish specialties on many menus include chicken and noodles, baked steak, roast beef and fresh-baked pie in a zillion flavors. Hwy 5 (aka Van Buren St) in Shipshewana has heaps of folksy options, though some are pretty touristy.

🛈 Information

Elkhart County Convention & Visitors Bureau (www.amishcountry.org) Has maps and downloadable guides.

🛈 Getting There & Away

The Indiana Toll Rd (I-80/90) passes the region to the north. Hwy 20 comes through the area to the south, and connects Middlebury and Shipshewana (which are about 7 miles apart).

OHIO

All right, time for your Ohio quiz. In the Buckeye State you can: 1) buggy-ride through the nation's largest Amish community; 2) lose your stomach on one of the world's fastest roller coasters; 3) suck down a dreamy creamy milkshake fresh from a working dairy; or 4) examine a massive, mysterious snake sculpture built into the earth. And the answer is...all of these. It hurts locals' feelings when visitors think the only thing to do here is tip over cows, so c'mon, give Ohio a chance. Besides these activities, you can partake in a five-way (spaghetti) in Cincinnati and rock out in Cleveland.

🛈 Information

Tourism Ohio (www.ohio.org)
Ohio Highway Conditions (www.ohgo.com)
Ohio State Park Information (614-265-6561; http://parks.ohiodnr.gov) State parks are free to visit; some have free wi-fi. Tent and RV sites cost $19 to $41; reservations accepted (866-644-6727; www.ohiostateparks.reserveamerica.com; fee $8).

Cleveland

Does it or does it not rock? That is the question. Drawing from its roots as a working man's town, Cleveland has toiled hard in recent years to prove it does. Step one was to control the urban decay/river-on-fire thing – the Cuyahoga River was once so polluted that it actually burned. Step two was to bring a worthy attraction to town, say the Rock and Roll Hall of Fame. Step three was to clean up downtown's public spaces and add hip hotels and eateries. The gritty city has come a long way. Even LeBron James deemed it happenin' enough to return to.

⊙ Sights

Cleveland's center is Public Sq, dominated by the conspicuous Terminal Tower and a ka-chinging casino. Most attractions are downtown on the lakefront or at University Circle (the area around Case Western Reserve University, Cleveland Clinic and other institutions). Several museums and attractions are within walking distance of each other at University Circle, 5 miles east of downtown. Carless? Take the HealthLine bus to Adelbert. The neighborhood's northern stretch is known as Uptown.

★ **Rock and Roll Hall of Fame & Museum**   MUSEUM
(📞 216-781-7625; www.rockhall.com; 1100 E 9th St; adult/child $23.50/13.75; ⏰ 10am-5:30pm, to 9pm Wed & Sat Jun-Aug) Cleveland's top attraction is like an overstuffed attic bursting with groovy finds: Jimi Hendrix's Stratocaster, Keith Moon's platform shoes, John Lennon's Sgt Pepper suit and a 1966 piece of hate mail to the Rolling Stones from a cursive-writing Fijian. It's more than memorabilia, though. Multimedia exhibits trace the history and social context of rock music and the performers who created it.

Why is the museum in Cleveland? Because this is the hometown of Alan Freed, the disk jockey who popularized the term 'rock and roll' in the early 1950s, and because the city lobbied hard and paid big. Be prepared for crowds (especially thick until 1pm or so).

★ **Cleveland Museum of Art**   MUSEUM
(📞 216-421-7340; www.clevelandart.org; 11150 East Blvd; ⏰ 10am-5pm Tue-Sun, to 9pm Wed & Fri) FREE Cleveland's whopping art museum houses an excellent collection of European paintings, as well as African, Asian and American art. Head to the 2nd floor for rock-star works from Impressionists, Picasso and surrealists. Interactive touchscreens are stationed throughout the galleries and provide fun ways to learn more. Gallery One, near the entrance, holds a cool quick hit of museum highlights. Free tours depart from the dazzling, light-drenched atrium at 1pm.

Great Lakes Science Center   MUSEUM
(📞 216-694-2000; www.greatscience.com; 601 Erieside Ave; adult/child $15/12; ⏰ 10am-5pm Mon-Sat, from noon Sun, closed Mon Sep-May; 🚻) One of 10 museums in the country with a NASA affiliation, Great Lakes goes deep in space with rockets, moon stones and the 1973 Apollo capsule, as well as exhibits on the lakes' environmental problems.

Lake View Cemetery   CEMETERY
(📞 216-421-2665; www.lakeviewcemetery.com; 12316 Euclid Ave; ⏰ 7:30am-7:30pm) Beyond University Circle to the east, don't forget this eclectic 'outdoor museum' where President James Garfield rests in an eye-poppingly enormous tower (it's especially grand for a guy who was president for only six months).

The Flats   WATERFRONT
The Flats, an old industrial zone turned nightlife hub on the Cuyahoga River, has had a checkered life. After years of neglect, it's on the upswing once again. The East Bank has a waterfront boardwalk, stylish restaurants, bars and outdoor concert pavilion. The West Bank is a bit grittier and further flung, with an old garage turned brewery-winery, a skateboard park and some vintage dive bars.

🛏 **Sleeping**

★ **Cleveland Hostel**   HOSTEL $
(📞 216-394-0616; www.theclevelandhostel.com; 2090 W 25th St; dm/r from $28/71; ✳🕸) This hostel in Ohio City, steps from an RTA stop and the West Side Market, is fantastic. There are 15 rooms, a mix of dorms and private chambers. All have fluffy beds, fresh paint in soothing hues and nifty antique decor. Add in the sociable rooftop deck, coffee-roasting lobby cafe and free parking lot, and no wonder it's packed.

★ **Kimpton Schofield Hotel**   HOTEL $$
(📞 216-357-3250; www.theschofieldhotel.com; 2000 E 9th St; r $180-260; 🅿✳🕸🏊) Set in a rehabbed 1902 building downtown, the Schofield is for the cool cats in the crowd. Rooms are spacious and done up with funky artwork (like prints of toy cars), colorful clocks and art-deco-inspired lamps and chairs. Amenities include free loaner bicycles, a free wine social hour each evening and free acoustic guitar loans for in-room jam sessions. Parking costs $36.

Glidden House   BOUTIQUE HOTEL $$
(📞 216-231-8900; www.gliddenhouse.com; 1901 Ford Dr; r $160-190; 🅿✳🕸) The French-gothic-eclectic former mansion of the Glidden family (who got rich making paint) has been carved into a graceful, 60-room hotel. The common areas are lush, while the rooms are more understated. Located in University Circle and walkable to the museums.

Hilton Garden Inn   HOTEL $$
(📞 216-658-6400; www.hiltongardeninn.com; 1100 Carnegie Ave; r $129-179; 🅿✳@🕸🏊) While it's

nothing fancy, the Hilton's rooms are decent value with comfy beds, wi-fi-rigged workstations and mini refrigerators. It's right by the baseball park. Parking costs $18.

✖ Eating

Top spots for hot-chef eats are E 4th St, Ohio City and Tremont. For ethnic eats Little Italy and Asiatown prevail.

✖ Downtown

E 4th St, set under twinkling lights, rolls out several great options. Off the beaten path and east of the city center, Asiatown (bounded by Payne and St Clair Aves, and E 30th and 40ths Sts) has several Chinese, Vietnamese and Korean eateries.

Noodlecat NOODLES $
(☑ 216-589-0007; www.noodlecat.com; 234 Euclid Ave; mains $10-12; ⊘ 11am-9pm) Hep-cat noodles fill bowls at this Japanese American mash-up. Slurp veggie-curry udon, spicy octopus udon, crispy bacon ramen and fried chicken ramen dishes.

Lola AMERICAN $$$
(☑ 216-621-5652; www.lolabistro.com; 2058 E 4th St; mains $29-40; ⊘ 5-10pm Sun-Thu, to 11pm Fri & Sat) Famous for his tattoos, Food Network TV appearances and multiple national awards, local boy Michael Symon put Cleveland on the foodie map with Lola. While the menu changes based on what's seasonal, expect dishes such as beef hanger steak with pickle sauce or braised lamb shank with mint and root vegetables. The glowy bar and open kitchen add a swank vibe.

If you want Symon's cooking but in a more casual, lower-priced setting, head a few doors north on 4th St to Mabel's BBQ, his brisket and kielbasa eatery.

✖ Ohio City & Tremont

Ohio City (especially along W 25th St) and Tremont, which straddle I-90 south of downtown, are areas with hip new establishments popping up all the time.

Barrio MEXICAN $
(☑ 216-999-7714; www.barrio-tacos.com; 806 Literary St; tacos $3-4; ⊘ 4pm-2am Mon-Thu, from 11am Fri-Sun) The Tremont outpost of this small chain is always abuzz with young locals smitten with the build-your-own tacos concept. Fillings include everything from

Thai chili tofu to housemade chorizo. Pear, jalapeño and other unusually flavored margaritas add to the fun.

Mitchell's Ice Cream ICE CREAM $
(☑ 216-861-2799; www.mitchellshomemade.com; 1867 W 25th St; scoops $3.50-5; ⊘ 11am-10pm Sun-Thu, to 11pm Fri & Sat; ✍) Mitchell's revamped an old movie theater into an ice-cream-making facility. Watch through big glass windows as staff blend the rich flavors. The goods are super creamy, and the vegan options are brilliant.

✖ Little Italy & Coventry

These two neighborhoods make prime stops for refueling after hanging out in University Circle. Little Italy is closest: it's along Mayfield Rd, near Lake View Cemetery (look out for the Rte 322 sign). Alternatively, relaxed Coventry Village is off Mayfield Rd.

Presti's Bakery BAKERY $
(☑ 216-421-3060; www.prestisbakery.com; 12101 Mayfield Rd; items $2-6; ⊘ 6am-7pm Mon, to 9pm Tue-Thu, to 10pm Fri & Sat, to 4pm Sun) Try big, sunny Presti's for its popular sandwiches and divine pastries.

Tommy's INTERNATIONAL $
(☑ 216-321-7757; www.tommyscoventry.com; 1824 Coventry Rd; mains $8-13; ⊘ 9am-9pm Sun-Thu, to 10pm Fri, 7:30am-10pm Sat; ✉✍) Tofu, seitan and other old-school veggie dishes emerge from the kitchen, though carnivores have multiple options, too.

♟ Drinking & Nightlife

Tremont is chockablock with chic bars, Ohio City with breweries. Downtown has the young, testosterone-fueled Warehouse District (around W 6th St) and the resurgent Flats. Most places stay open until 2am.

★ Platform Beer Co BREWERY
(☑ 216-202-1386; www.platformbeerco.com; 4125 Lorain Ave; ⊘ 3pm-midnight Mon-Thu, 3pm-2am Fri, 10am-2am Sat, 10am-10pm Sun) An all-ages, cool-cat crowd gathers around the silvery tanks in Platform's tasting room for $5 to $6 pints of innovative saisons, pale ales and more. When the weather warms, everyone heads out to the picnic-table-dotted patio. The location is a bit far flung, at Ohio City's southern edge, but there's a handy bike-share station outside the brewery.

Great Lakes Brewing Company   BREWERY
(☑216-771-4404; www.greatlakesbrewing.com;
2516 Market Ave; ⊘11:30am-midnight Mon-Thu,
to 1am Fri & Sat) Great Lakes wins numerous
prizes for its brewed-on-the-premises beers.
Added historical bonus: Eliot Ness got into
a shootout with criminals here; ask the bartender to show you the bullet holes.

Millard Fillmore Presidential Library   BAR
(☑216-481-9444; 15617 Waterloo Rd; ⊘4pm-
2:30am Mon-Sat, to 12:30am Sun) Mention to
pals that you're going to the Millard Fillmore Presidential Library, and you can tell
they're impressed by your intellectual curiosity. Then they figure out it's a dive bar with
craft beer in the burgeoning neighborhood
of Collinwood, and they're even more impressed. Fillmore was the USA's 13th president, and from New York incidentally. But
that shouldn't hinder a great bar name.

Jerman's Cafe   BAR
(☑216-361-8771; 3840 St Clair Ave NE; ⊘10am-
1am Mon-Sat) Jerman's is Cleveland's second-oldest bar. Slovenian immigrant John
Jerman opened it in 1908, and his family
still runs it. It's a terrific, old-school dive,
with a pressed zinc ceiling, Indians baseball games flickering on the TVs and just a
few beers on tap (usually a German lager).
Friendly barkeeps and regulars are happy to
share stories of the old days.

☆ Entertainment

Gordon Square Arts District has a fun pocket of theaters, live-music venues and cafes
along Detroit Ave between W 56th and W
69th Sts, a few miles west of downtown.

Check *Scene* (www.clevescene.com) and
the Friday section of *Plain Dealer* (www.
cleveland.com) for listings.

★Happy Dog   LIVE MUSIC
(☑216-651-9474; www.happydogcleveland.com;
5801 Detroit Ave; ⊘4pm-12:30am Mon-Wed, 11am-
12:30am Thu & Sun, 11am-2:30am Fri & Sat) Listen
to scrappy bands, DJs, storytellers or science
lectures while munching on a weenie, for
which you can choose from among 50 toppings, from gourmet (black truffle) to, er,
less gourmet (peanut butter and jelly); in
the Gordon Square district.

Severance Hall   CLASSICAL MUSIC
(☑216-231-1111; www.clevelandorchestra.com;
11001 Euclid Ave) The acclaimed Cleveland
Symphony Orchestra holds its season (August to May) at Severance Hall, a gorgeous
art-deco-meets-classic building located by
the University Circle museums.

Progressive Field   BASEBALL
(☑216-420-4487; www.indians.com; 2401 Ontario St) The Indians (aka 'the Tribe') hit here;
great sight lines make it a good park to see
a game.

❶ Information

Destination Cleveland (www.thisiscleveland.
com) Official website, chock-full for planning.
Visitor Center (☑216-875-6680; 334 Euclid
Ave; ⊘9am-6pm Mon-Sat) Staff provide maps
and reservation assistance; there's a sweet,
arty souvenir shop attached.
Cool Cleveland (www.coolcleveland.com) Hip
arts and cultural happenings.
Ohio City (www.ohiocity.org) Eats and drinks in
the neighborhood.
Tremont (www.tremontwest.org) Eats, drinks
and gallery hops.

❶ Getting There & Around

Eleven miles southwest of downtown, **Cleveland
Hopkins International Airport** (CLE; www.
clevelandairport.com; 5300 Riverside Dr) is
linked by the Red Line train ($2.50). A cab to
downtown costs about $35.

From downtown, **Greyhound** (☑216-781-
0520; www.greyhound.com; 1465 Chester Ave)
offers frequent departures to Chicago (7½
hours) and New York City (13 hours). **Megabus**
(www.megabus.com/us; 2115 E 22nd St) also
goes to Chicago, often for lower fares.

Amtrak (☑216-696-5115; www.amtrak.com;
200 Cleveland Memorial Shoreway) runs once
daily to Chicago (seven hours) and New York City
(13 hours).

The Regional Transit Authority (www.riderta.
com) operates the Red Line train that goes to
both the airport and Ohio City. It also runs the
HealthLine bus that motors along Euclid Ave
from downtown to University Circle's museums.
Fare is $2.50, or day passes are $5.50. Free trolleys also loop around downtown's core business
and entertainment zones.

UH Bikes (www.uhbikes.com) is Cleveland's
bikeshare program, with 25 stations and 250
bikes mostly in downtown and University Circle.
A 30-minute ride costs $3.50.

For cab service, call **Americab** (☑216-881-1111).

Erie Lakeshore & Islands

In summer this good-time resort area is one
of the busiest – and most expensive – places
in Ohio. Boaters come to party, daredevils

CEDAR POINT'S RAGING ROLLER COASTERS

One of the world's top amusement parks **Cedar Point Amusement Park** (☎419-627-2350; www.cedarpoint.com; 1 Cedar Point Dr; adult/child $67/45; ⊙from 8am Jun-Aug, 6pm-midnight Fri, from 11am Sat & Sun Sep & Oct) is known for its 17 adrenaline-pumping roller coasters. Stomach-droppers include the Top Thrill Dragster, among the globe's tallest and fastest rides. It climbs 420ft into the air before plunging and whipping around at 120mph. The Valravn is the world's longest 'dive' coaster, dropping riders at a 90-degree angle for 214ft. Meanwhile, the wing-like GateKeeper loops, corkscrews and dangles riders from the world's highest inversion (meaning you're upside down a *lot*).

If those and the other hair-raising coasters aren't enough to keep you occupied, the surrounding area has a nice beach, a water park and a slew of old-fashioned, cotton candy-fueled attractions. It's about 6 miles from Sandusky. Buying tickets in advance online saves money. Parking costs $15 to $18.

It's worthwhile to download the free Cedar Point app, which has a handy feature that lists current wait times for each ride. Note lines for some can be 90 minutes or more.

come to ride roller coasters, and outdoorsy types come to bike and kayak. The season lasts from mid-May to mid-September, and then just about everything shuts down.

Bass Islands

In 1812's Battle of Lake Erie, Admiral Perry met the enemy English fleet near South Bass Island. His victory ensured that all the lands south of the Great Lakes became US, not Canadian, territory. But history is all but forgotten on a summer weekend in packed Put-in-Bay, the island's main town and a party place full of boaters, restaurants and shops. Move beyond it, and you'll find opportunities for camping, fishing, kayaking and swimming. South Bass Island is quite developed, offering a mix of inns, B&Bs, motels and resorts. The state park has camping.

A huge number of restaurants clump in central Put-in-Bay on Bay View, Catawba and Delaware Aves. They're easy to walk between and take your pick.

◉ Sights & Activities

**Perry's Victory and
International Peace Memorial**   MONUMENT
(www.nps.gov/pevi; 93 Delaware Ave; adult/child $5/free; ⊙10am-6pm mid-May–mid-Oct) The 352ft Doric column is a singular attraction. Climb to the observation deck for views of the Lake Erie battle site and, on a good day, Canada – though you will have to wait until summer 2018, as it is closed for renovations until then.

South Bass Island State Park   STATE PARK
FREE Set on top of white cliffs on the island's southwest side, the park moseys down to a

fishing pier, small rocky beach and vendor offering jet-ski and power-boat rentals. The 120-site campground (campsites $17 to $32) packs in a partying crowd.

Kayak the Bay   KAYAKING
(☎419-967-0796; www.kayakthebay.net; Bayview Ave; single/double kayak per 2hr $25/45; ⊙10am-8pm late May-Aug, noon-6pm Mon-Fri Sep) Paddle in the harbor or head out to circle the island. Guided tours ($40 to $50 per person) are also available, including a sunset jaunt; call ahead to reserve.

🛏 Sleeping

Ashley's Island House   B&B $$
(☎419-285-2844; www.ashleysislandhouse.com; 557 Catawba Ave; r $110-195; ⊙closed Nov-Mar; ❄🕸🤐) Ashley's Island House is a 12-room B&B where naval officers stayed in the late 1800s. Hardwood floors, sturdy antiques and bright-colored quilts give the rooms a homey feel. Bicycle and golf-cart rentals are available.

🍷 Drinking & Nightlife

Beer Barrel Saloon   BAR
(☎419-285-7281; www.beerbarrelpib.com; 324 Delaware Ave; ⊙11am-1am) The Beer Barrel Saloon has plenty of space for imbibing – its bar is 406ft long. Live bands and Jell-o shots are also part of the deal.

ℹ Information

Put-in-Bay Chamber of Commerce (www.visitputinbay.com) Has information on activities and lodging.

ℹ Getting There & Away

Two ferry companies make the trip regularly from the mainland. **Jet Express** (☎ 800-245-1538; www.jet-express.com; 3 N Monroe St) runs passenger-only boats direct to Put-in-Bay from Port Clinton (one way adult/child $18/3, 30 minutes) almost hourly. Leave your car in the lot (per day $12) at the dock. **Miller Ferries** (☎ 800-500-2421; www.millerferry.com; 5174 E Water St) operates a vehicle ferry that is the cheapest option, departing from further-flung Catawba (one way adult/child $7/1.50, car $16) every 30 minutes; the crossing takes 20 minutes. It also cruises to **Middle Bass Island**, a good day trip from South Bass, offering nature and quiet.

Kelleys Island

Peaceful and green, Kelleys Island is a popular weekend escape, especially for families. It has pretty 19th-century buildings, Native American pictographs, a good beach and glacial grooves raked through its landscape. Even its old limestone quarries are scenic.

◎ Sights & Activities

Kelleys Islands State Park   STATE PARK

FREE The park features a popular campground with 127 campsites ($17 to $32), six miles of hiking trails with birds flittering by and a secluded, sandy beach on the island's north side. It's a favorite of families.

Glacial Grooves   NATURAL FEATURE

(☺ sunrise-sunset) FREE The deep scars in the limestone here – which a glacier rubbed in some 18,000 years ago – are the largest and most easily accessible grooves in the world. Look down from the walkway and stairs and behold gouges that are 400ft long, 35ft wide and up to 10ft deep.

Inscription Rock Petroglyphs   ROCK ART

(☺ sunrise-sunset) FREE Native Americans who used the island as a hunting ground carved symbols into this boulder on the island's south shore sometime between AD 1200 and 1600.

Caddy Shack Square   CYCLING

(☎ 419-746-2664; www.caddyshacksquare.com; 115 Division St; ☺ 10am-sunset) Rent bicycles (per hr/day $4/24) or golf carts ($11/88) to zip around the island. It's part of an entertainment complex that also has an 18-hole mini-golf course, game arcade, pizza parlor and good-time bar.

🛏 Sleeping & Eating

Inn on Kelleys Island   B&B $$

(☎ 419-746-2258; www.innki20.wixsite.com/innofkelleysisland; 317 W Lakeshore Dr; r $95-125) Long-time islanders own this 1876 Victorian home. It's a vintage, four-room B&B: metal-frame beds with quilts, rocking chairs, sturdy antique decor, shared bathrooms.

Village Pump   PUB FOOD $$

(☎ 419-746-2281; www.villagepumpkioh.com; 103 W Lakeshore Dr; mains $14-26; ☺ 11am-11pm Mar-Dec; ☏) Grab a table or a stool at the bar in this old-school tavern, a good spot to tuck into fried perch, lobster chowder and burgers. The chocolatey Brandy Alexander, the house-special cocktail, is a fine way to sop it up.

ℹ Information

Kelleys Island Chamber of Commerce (www.kelleysislandchamber.com) Useful info on lodgings, restaurants and activities.

ℹ Getting There & Away

Kelleys Island Ferry (☎ 419-798-9763; www.kelleysislandferry.com; off W Main St) departs from the teeny village of Marblehead (one way adult/child $10/6.25, car $16). The crossing takes about 20 minutes and leaves hourly (every half-hour in summer). **Jet Express** (☎ 800-245-1538; www.jet-express.com; 101 W Shoreline Dr) departs from Sandusky (one way adult/child $18/4.75, no cars); the trip takes 25 minutes. It also goes onward to Put-in-Bay on South Bass Island (one way adult/child $13/3, no cars). Both ferries arrive on Kelleys Island downtown (Jet Express at the foot of Division St, Kelleys Island Ferry about a half-mile east at the Seaway Marina).

> **WORTH A TRIP**
>
> ### PELEE ISLAND
>
> Pelee, the largest Erie island, is a ridiculously green, quiet wine-producing and bird-watching destination that belongs to Canada. Owen Sound Transportation Co (www.ontarioferries.com) runs a ferry (one way adult/child $13.75/6.75, car $30) from Sandusky to Pelee, and then onward to Ontario's mainland. Check www.pelee.com for lodging and trip-planning information.

Ohio Amish Country

Rural Wayne and Holmes Counties are home to the USA's largest Amish community. Visiting here is like entering a pre-industrial time warp.

Descendants of conservative Dutch-Swiss religious factions who migrated to the USA during the 18th century, the Amish continue to follow the *ordnung* (way of life), in varying degrees. Many adhere to rules prohibiting the use of electricity, telephones and motorized vehicles. They wear traditional clothing, farm the land with plow and mule, and go to church in horse-drawn buggies. Others are not so strict.

Unfortunately, what would surely be a peaceful country scene is often disturbed by behemoth tour buses. Many Amish are happy to profit from this influx of outside dollars, but don't equate this with free photographic access – the Amish typically view photographs as taboo. Drive carefully as roads are narrow and curvy.

◉ Sights

Kidron, on Rte 52, makes a good starting point. A short distance south, **Berlin** is the area's tchotchke-shop–filled core, while **Millersburg** is the region's largest town, more antique-y than Amish; Hwy 62 connects these two 'busy' spots.

To get further off the beaten path, take Rte 557 or County Rd 70, both of which twist through the countryside to little **Charm**, about 5 miles south of Berlin.

Kidron Auction   MARKET
(www.kidronauction.com; 4885 Kidron Rd, Kidron; ⊙from 10am Thu) If it's Thursday, follow the buggy lineup down the road from Lehman's store to the livestock barn. Hay gets auctioned at 10:15am, cows at 11am and pigs at 1pm. A flea market rings the barn for folks seeking non-mooing merchandise.

Lehman's   MARKET
(☑800-438-5346; www.lehmans.com; 4779 Kidron Rd, Kidron; ⊙9am-6pm Mon-Sat, to 5pm Jan-May) Lehman's is an absolute must-see. It is the Amish community's main purveyor of modern-looking products that use no electricity, housed in a 32,000-sq-ft barn. Stroll through to ogle wind-up flashlights, wood-burning stoves and hand-cranked meat grinders.

Heini's Cheese Chalet   FACTORY
(☑330-893-2131; www.heinis.com; 6005 Hwy 77, Berlin; ⊙8am-6pm Mon-Sat, to 5pm Jan-Apr) FREE Heini's whips up more than 50 cheeses. Learn how Amish farmers hand-milk their cows and spring-cool (versus machine-refrigerate) the output before delivering it each day. Then grab abundant samples and peruse the kitschy *History of Cheesemaking* mural. To see the curd-cutting in action through the big window onto the factory floor, come before 11am.

Yoder's Amish Home   FARM
(☑330-893-2541; www.yodersamishhome.com; 6050 Rte 515, Walnut Creek; tours adult/child $12/8; ⊙10am-5pm Mon-Sat late Apr–late Oct; ▣) Peek into a local home and one-room schoolhouse, and take a buggy ride through a field at this Amish farm.

🛏 Sleeping & Eating

Guggisberg Swiss Inn   HOTEL $$
(☑330-893-3600; www.guggisbergswissinn.com; 5025 Rte 557, Charm; r $110-140; ▣ 🕏) The 24 tidy, bright and compact rooms have quilts and light-wood furnishings. A cheesemaking facility and horseback riding stable are on the grounds, too.

Hotel Millersburg   HISTORIC HOTEL $$
(☑330-674-1457; www.hotelmillersburg.com; 35 W Jackson St, Millersburg; r $79-149; ▣ 🕏) Built in 1847 as a stagecoach inn, the property still provides lodging in its 26 casual rooms, which sit above a modern dining room and tavern (one of the few places to get a beer in Amish Country).

★ Boyd & Wurthmann
Restaurant   AMERICAN $
(☑330-893-3287; www.boydandwurthmann.com; 4819 E Main St, Berlin; mains $6-12; ⊙5:30am-8pm Mon-Sat) Hubcap-sized pancakes, 23 pie flavors, fat sandwiches and Amish specialties such as country-fried steak draw locals and tourists alike. Cash only.

Mrs Yoder's Kitchen   AMERICAN $
(☑330-674-0922; www.mrsyoderskitchen.com; 8101 Rte 241, Mt Hope; mains $11-14; ⊙7am-8pm Mon-Sat) A bit off the beaten path, Mrs Yoder's is a swell choice for well-made Amish fare in simple environs. Order mains like wedding steak (browned beef baked in a mushroom sauce) à la carte, or fill a plate with juicy fried chicken, pot roast and whipped potatoes at the buffet.

❶ Information

Holmes County Chamber of Commerce
(www.visitamishcountry.com)

❶ Getting There & Around

Amish Country lies between Cleveland (80 miles north) and Columbus (100 miles southwest). I-71 and I-77 flank the area to the west and east, respectively, but you'll have to exit and drive along a series of narrow, winding back roads to reach the little towns.

Columbus

What Ohio's capital city (and largest city) lacks in mega sights and wild quirks it makes up for with unexpected food and arts scenes. Better yet, Columbus is easy on the wallet, an influence from Ohio State University's 59,000-plus students (the campus is the nation's second largest). A substantial gay population also has taken up residence in Columbus in recent years.

◉ Sights & Activities

Wexner Center for the Arts   ARTS CENTER
(📞614-292-3535; www.wexarts.org; 1871 N High St; $8; ⊙11am-6pm Tue, Wed & Sun, to 8pm Thu-Sat) The campus arts center offers cutting-edge art exhibits, films and performances.

Columbus Food Tours   FOOD & DRINK
(📞614-440-3177; www.columbusfoodadventures. com; tours $55-60) Foodie guides lead tours by neighborhood or theme (taco trucks, desserts, coffee), some by foot and others by van. Most jaunts take three to four hours.

🛏 Sleeping & Eating

Marriott Residence Inn   HOTEL $$
(📞614-222-2610; www.marriott.com; 36 E Gay St; r $149-239; P❄@🅿🛜🐾) A great location downtown, close to everything. All rooms are suites with a full kitchen. The cute free breakfast buffet is served in the old bank vault each morning. Parking is $24.

Le Méridien Columbus,
The Joseph   BOUTIQUE HOTEL $$$
(📞614-227-0100; www.lemeridiencolumbus.com; 620 N High St; r $240-310; P❄🛜🐾) The Joseph's super-cool, Cubist-inspired building is an eye-popper in the Short North. The lobby is basically a gallery featuring works from the Pizzuti Collection, a contemporary art museum a block away. The 135 rooms are good sized, with low-key, modern-chic decor

> **GERMAN VILLAGE: COLUMBUS, OHIO**
>
> The remarkably large, all-brick German Village, a half-mile south of downtown, is a restored 19th-century neighborhood with beer halls, cobbled streets, arts-filled parks and Italianate and Queen Anne architecture.

in shades of white and taupe. In-room wi-fi costs $10 to $15 per day; parking costs $30. Free bicycles are a nice touch.

★ **Skillet**   AMERICAN $
(📞614-443-2266; www.skilletruf.com; 410 E Whittier St; mains $12-16; ⊙8am-2pm Wed-Sun) 🐾 This teeny restaurant in German Village serves rustic, locally sourced brunch fare. The menu changes, but you might fill a plate with griddled cinnamon rolls or braised pork cheeks with gravy and grits. It's almost always crowded, and you can't make reservations, but on weekends you can call ahead (30 minutes before you arrive) and put your name on the wait list.

Schmidt's   GERMAN $
(📞614-444-6808; www.schmidthaus.com; 240 E Kossuth St; mains $11-16; ⊙11am-10pm Sun-Thu, to 11pm Fri & Sat) In German Village, shovel in Old Country staples like sausage and schnitzel, but save room for the whopping half-pound cream puffs. Oompah bands play Wednesday to Saturday.

🍷 Drinking & Nightlife

Little Rock Bar   BAR
(📞614-824-5602; www.littlerockbar.net; 944 N Fourth St; ⊙4pm-1am Tue-Thu, 4pm-2am Fri, noon-2am Sat, noon-midnight Sun) The squat brick building used to be a gas station, but now it has morphed into a nifty little neighborhood bar and music venue. Thirty beers flow from the taps (about half from Ohio), perfect for sipping to tunes from the free jukebox. Local singer-songwriters, DJs or other entertainers take the stage most nights.

☆ Entertainment

Huntington Park   BASEBALL
(📞614-462-2757; www.clippersbaseball.com; 330 Huntington Park Lane) The Columbus Clippers (minor league team of the Cleveland Indians) bats at this stadium downtown.

Ohio Stadium FOOTBALL
(☑ 800-462-8257; www.ohiostatebuckeyes.com; 411 Woody Hayes Dr) The Ohio State Buckeyes pack a rabid crowd into legendary, horseshoe-shaped Ohio Stadium for their games, held on Saturdays in the fall. Expect 105,000 extra revelers in town.

ⓘ Information

Columbus Convention & Visitors Bureau
(☑ 866-397-2657; www.experiencecolumbus.com; 277 W Nationwide Blvd; ⊙ 8am-5pm Mon-Fri, 10am-4pm Sat & Sun) This visitor center in the Arena District is staffed and has a gift shop of local goods.

ⓘ Getting There & Away

The **Port Columbus Airport** (CMH; www.flycolumbus.com; 4600 International Gateway) is 10 miles east of town. A cab to downtown costs about $25.

Greyhound (☑ 614-221-4642; www.greyhound.com; 111 E Town St) buses run at least six times daily to Cincinnati (two hours) and Cleveland (2½ hours).

Yellow Springs

Artsy, beatnik little Yellow Springs was a counterculture hot spot in the 1960s and '70s, thanks to Antioch University. You can still buy a bong at the local head shop, but now galleries, craft shops and sustainable eateries cluster downtown. It's a sweet spot to post up for a day or two. Hang out at the local dairy farm to milk a cow or lick a made-on-site ice-cream cone. Limestone gorges, waterfalls and canoe-able rivers fill the surrounding parkland.

⊙ Sights & Activities

★ **Young's Jersey Dairy** FARM
(☑ 937-325-0629; www.youngsdairy.com; 6880 Springfield-Xenia Rd; ⊙ 9am-11pm Jun-Aug, reduced hours Sep-May; 🐾) FREE Young's is a working dairy farm with a famous ice-cream shop, aka the **Dairy Store** (ice cream $3-6, sandwiches $3.50-6.50, which many say whips ups Ohio's best milkshakes, and lots of fun family activities, including mini-golf, batting cages and opportunities to feed goats and watch the cows get milked (the latter happens from 4:30pm to 5:30pm). The golf and batting cages have a fee, the animal viewings do not. The Golden Jersey Inn restaurant is also on-site.

John Bryan State Park STATE PARK
(☑ 937-767-1274; http://parks.ohiodnr.gov/johnbryan; 3790 Hwy 370) FREE You can fish, hike, bike, rock climb, canoe or camp among the limestone cliffs here. The scenic highlight is Clifton Gorge, cut by the pretty Little Miami River.

🛏 Sleeping & Eating

Morgan House B&B $$
(☑ 937-767-1761; www.arthurmorganhouse.com; 120 W Limestone St; r $125-145; ❄🐾) The six comfy rooms have super-soft linens and private baths. Breakfasts are organic. It's walkable to the main business district.

Golden Jersey Inn AMERICAN $
(☑ 937-324-2050; www.youngsdairy.com; 6880 Springfield-Xenia Rd; mains $11-18; ⊙ 11am-9pm Mon-Fri, from 8am Sat & Sun Jun-Aug, reduced hours Sep-May) This is the more formal of the two restaurants at Young's dairy farm, serving dishes like buttermilk chicken and gravy-kissed meatloaf in a high-ceiling, oak-timbered barn.

ⓘ Getting There & Away

Yellow Springs is about 18 miles northeast of Dayton and linked by – wait for it – Dayton–Yellow Springs Rd.

Dayton

Dayton leans hard on its 'Birthplace of Aviation' tagline, and the Wright sights deliver. It's surprisingly moving to see the cluttered workshop where Orville and Wilbur conjured their ideas and the lonely field where they tested their plane. Then there's the Air Force museum, a mind-blowing expanse for aviation buffs. The vast complex of hangars holds just about every aircraft you can think of through the ages.

⊙ Sights

★ **National Museum of the US Air Force** MUSEUM
(☑ 937-255-3286; www.nationalmuseum.af.mil; 1100 Spaatz St; ⊙ 9am-5pm) FREE Located at the Wright-Patterson Air Force Base, 6 miles northeast of Dayton, this huuuuge museum has everything from a Wright Brothers 1909 Flyer to a Sopwith Camel (WWI biplane) and the 'Little Boy' type atomic bomb (decommissioned and rendered safe for display) dropped on Hiroshima. The hangars

hold miles of planes, rockets and aviation machines. A spiffy new building adds spacecraft and presidential planes (including the first Air Force One).

Huffman Prairie Flying Field HISTORIC SITE
(Gate 16A off Rte 444; ☺8am-6pm) FREE This peaceful patch of grass looks much as it did in 1904 when the Wright Brothers tested aircraft here. A 1-mile walking trail loops around, marked with history-explaining placards.

Wright Cycle Company HISTORIC SITE
(📞937-225-7705; www.nps.gov/daav; 16 S Williams St; ☺9am-5pm, closed Mon & Tue Nov-Feb) FREE Browse exhibits in the original building where Wilbur and Orville developed bikes and aviation ideas.

🛏 Sleeping & Eating

Inn Port D'Vino B&B $$
(📞937-224-7678; www.innport.com; 22 Brown St; r $119-149; ❄🛜) Set in a historic home, the inn's three rooms are spacious and full of character, though a bit fusty in their fireplace, armchair and thick-carpet decor. The selling point is the great location in the artsy Oregon District, walkable to breweries, bistros and theaters. It's also right beside the downtown business zone.

Corner Kitchen AMERICAN $$
(📞937-719-0999; www.afinerdiner.com; 613 E 5th St; mains $15-24; ☺4:30-10pm Tue-Thu, to 11pm Fri & Sat) Simple wood tables, white panel walls and mismatched china plates set the mod-rustic tone at Corner Kitchen, a bustling diner-meets-French-cafe. Zingy cocktails sooth alongside meals of wine-steeped mussels, eggplant stew and gravy-laden poutine, though the menu changes often. The four-course tasting menu (per person without/with wine pairings $34/65) is a fine way to go. It's located in the bohemian Oregon District.

❶ Getting There & Away

Dayton has a good-sized airport north of town. Greyhound buses also serve the city, which is equidistant from Cincinnati and Columbus.

Cincinnati

Cincinnati splashes up the Ohio River's banks. Its prettiness surprises, as do its neon troves, its European-style neighborhoods and the locals' unashamed ardor for a five-way (spaghetti with chili, onions, beans and cheese). Amid all that action, don't forget to catch a baseball game, stroll the bridge-striped riverfront and visit the dummy museum.

👁 Sights

👁 Downtown & Over-the-Rhine

At downtown's northern edge, the historic Over-the-Rhine (OTR) neighborhood holds a whopping spread of 19th-century Italianate and Queen Anne buildings that have morphed into trendy eateries and shops. Parts of the area are edgy, but the Gateway District around 12th and Vine Sts is well trod.

**National Underground
Railroad Freedom Center** MUSEUM
(📞513-333-7500; www.freedomcenter.org; 50 E Freedom Way; adult/child $15/10.50; ☺11am-5pm Tue-Sat) Cincinnati was a prominent stop on the Underground Railroad and a center for abolitionist activities led by residents such as Harriet Beecher Stowe. The Freedom Center tells their stories. Exhibits show how slaves escaped to the north, and the ways in which slavery still exists today. Download the free iPhone app.

Cincinnati Museum Center MUSEUM
(📞513-287-7000; www.cincymuseum.org; 1301 Western Ave; ☺10am-5pm Mon-Sat, 11am-6pm Sun; ♿) This museum complex occupies the 1933 Union Terminal, an art-deco jewel still used by Amtrak. The interior has fantastic murals made of local Rookwood tiles. The complex includes a nifty Museum of Natural History (with a cave and real bats inside), a children's museum, a history museum, an Omnimax theater and a special hall for traveling exhibitions. Alas, the building is undergoing an extensive renovation through late 2018, so only the children's museum (adult/child $10.50/8.50) and special hall are open until then. Parking costs $6.

American Sign Museum MUSEUM
(📞513-541-6366; www.americansignmuseum. org; 1330 Monmouth Ave; adult/child $15/free; ☺10am-4pm Wed-Sat, from noon Sun) This museum stocks an awesome cache of flashing, lightbulb-studded beacons in an old parachute factory. You'll burn your retinas staring at vintage neon drive-in signs, hulking genies and the Frisch's Big Boy, among other nostalgic novelties. Guides lead tours at 11am and 2pm that also visit the on-site

neon-sign-making shop. It's located in the Camp Washington neighborhood (near Northside); take exit 3 off I-75.

Contemporary Arts Center   MUSEUM

(☑ 513-345-8400; www.contemporaryartscenter. org; 44 E 6th St; ⊙ 10am-4pm Sat-Mon, to 9pm Wed-Fri) FREE This center displays modern art in an avant-garde building designed by star architect Zaha Hadid. The structure and its artworks are a pretty big deal for traditionalist Cincy. The focus is on 'art of the last five minutes.' The exhibits change every three months or so.

Fountain Square   PLAZA

(www.myfountainsquare.com; cnr 5th & Vine Sts) Fountain Sq is the city's centerpiece, a public space with a seasonal ice rink, free wi-fi, concerts (7pm Wednesday to Saturday in summer), a farmers market (11am to 2pm Tuesdays), a Reds ticket kiosk and the fancy old 'Genius of Water' fountain.

Roebling Suspension Bridge   BRIDGE

(www.roeblingbridge.org) The elegant 1876 spanner was a forerunner of John Roebling's famous Brooklyn Bridge in New York. It's cool to walk across while passing cars make it 'sing' around you. It links to Covington, Kentucky.

Purple People Bridge   BRIDGE

(www.purplepeoplebridge.com) This pedestrian-only bridge provides a unique crossing from Sawyer Point (a nifty park dotted by whimsical monuments and flying pigs) to Newport, Kentucky.

⊙ Covington & Newport

Covington and Newport, Kentucky, are sort of suburbs of Cincinnati, just over the river from downtown. Newport is to the east and known for its massive **Newport on the Levee** (www.newportonthelevee.com; 1 Levee Way; ⊙ 11am-9pm Mon-Thu, 11am-10pm Fri & Sat, noon-6pm Sun) restaurant and shopping complex. Covington lies to the west and has the Main-Strasse quarter, filled with funky restaurants and bars in the neighborhood's 19th-century brick row houses. Antebellum mansions fringe Riverside Dr, and old paddle-wheel steamboats tie up along the water's edge.

Newport Aquarium   AQUARIUM

(☑ 859-491-3467; www.newportaquarium.com; 1 Aquarium Way; adult/child $25/17; ⊙ 9am-7pm Jun-Aug, to 6pm Sep-May; 🚸) Meet parading penguins, Sweet Pea the shark ray and lots of oth-

er razor-toothed fish at Newport's large, generally well-regarded facility. However among the attractions are stingray touch tanks, which are controversial as human interaction may be stressful for aquatic creatures.

⊙ Mt Adams

It might be a bit of a stretch to compare Mt Adams, immediately east of downtown, to Paris' Montmartre, but this hilly 19th-century enclave of narrow, twisting streets, Victorian town houses, galleries, bars and restaurants is certainly a pleasurable surprise. Most visitors ascend for a quick look around and a drink. To get here, follow 7th St east of downtown to Gilbert Ave, then turn right on Eden Park Dr and head up the hill to reach the lakes, paths and cultural offerings in Eden Park.

Cincinnati Art Museum   MUSEUM

(☑ 513-721-2787; www.cincinnatiartmuseum.org; 953 Eden Park Dr; ⊙ 11am-5pm Tue-Sun, to 8pm Thu) FREE The collection spans 6000 years, with an emphasis on ancient Middle Eastern art and European old masters, plus a wing devoted to local works. While admission to the first-rate permanent collection is free, special exhibitions may cost extra. Parking is free, or get here via bus 1.

🗗 Tours

American Legacy Tours   WALKING

(www.americanlegacytours.com; 1332 Vine St; 90min tours $20; ⊙ Fri-Sun) Offers a variety of historical jaunts. The best is the Queen City Underground Tour that submerges into old lagering cellars deep beneath the Over-the-Rhine district.

🎎 Festivals

Bunbury Music Festival   MUSIC

(www.bunburyfestival.com; Sawyer Point Park; ⊙ early Jun) Big-name indie bands rock the riverfront for three days; a day pass costs $79 to $89.

Oktoberfest   FOOD & DRINK

(www.oktoberfestzinzinnati.com; ⊙ mid-Sep) German beer, bratwursts and mania. It takes place on W 2nd and 3rd Sts downtown between Walnut and Elm Sts.

🛏 Sleeping & Eating

★ Hotel Covington   HOTEL $$

(☑ 859-905-6600; www.hotelcovington.com; 638 Madison Ave; r $135-175; 🅿 ❄ 🛜) This stylish,

114-room property occupies a turn-of-the-century department store on a busy street in Covington. Rooms are fairly big, with contemporary decor, nifty photo art on the walls, a wired-up work desk and large windows for natural light. There's a good restaurant and bar on site, and a chic courtyard area with a fireplace. Staff are beyond-the-norm helpful.

Gateway B&B
B&B **$$**

(📞 859-581-6447; www.gatewaybb.com; 326 E 6th St; r $129-169; 🅿🚭❄🛜) For something different, check in to this 1878 Italianate townhouse in a historic neighborhood on the Kentucky side of the river. Exquisite antique oak and walnut furnishings fill the three rooms, and intriguing baseball memorabilia decorates the common area. It's a half-mile walk to Newport on the Levee's restaurants and onward over the Purple People Bridge to downtown Cincy.

Hotel 21c
HOTEL **$$$**

(📞 513-578-6600; www.21cmuseumhotels.com/cincinnati; 609 Walnut St; r $279-379; 🅿❄@🛜) The second outpost of Louisville's popular art hotel sits right next door to the Contemporary Arts Center. The mod rooms have accoutrements such as a Nespresso machine, free wi-fi, plush bedding and, of course, original art. The lobby is a public gallery, so feel free to ogle the trippy videos and nude sculptures. The on-site restaurant and rooftop bar draw crowds. Parking costs $38.

★ Tucker's
DINER **$**

(📞 513-954-8920; www.facebook.com/TuckersRestaurantOTR; 1637 Vine St; mains $5-9; ⏰ 7am-3pm Tue-Sat, to 2pm Sun; 🍴) Located in a tough zone a few blocks from Findlay Market, family-run Tucker's has been feeding locals – African American, white, foodies, penniless, friars, drug dealers – since 1946. It's an archetypal diner, serving six-cheese omelets, shrimp and grits, biscuits and gravy, potatoes with bacon jam and other hulking breakfast dishes, along with several vegetarian dishes using ingredients sourced from the market.

Eli's BBQ
BARBECUE **$**

(📞 513-533-1957; www.elisbarbeque.com; 3313 Riverside Dr; mains $6-16; ⏰ 11am-9pm) Eli's is a wee spot that makes awesome barbecue, which is why there's always a line snaking out the door. Order at the counter, find a seat, then wait for staff to bring out your hickory-smoked ribs on a red plastic tray. The meat is tender, the sauce sweet with a smoky kick, and the jalapeño cheddar grits beyond addictive.

The Eagle OTR
AMERICAN **$**

(📞 513-802-5007; www.theeagleotr.com; 1342 Vine St; mains $8-12; ⏰ 11am-midnight) A hipster magnet serving modern soul food amid reclaimed wood decor, the Eagle rustles up fantastic fried chicken (dipped in spicy honey), white cheddar grits and spoonbread (like a sweet cornbread). Expect a queue, though the doughnut shop two doors down helps take the edge off.

Terry's Turf Club
BURGERS **$**

(📞 513-533-4222; 4618 Eastern Ave; mains $9-15; ⏰ 11am-10pm Wed & Thu, to 11pm Fri & Sat, to 9pm Sun) This 15-table beer-and-burger joint glows inside and out with owner Terry Carter's neon stash. A giant, waving Aunt Jemima beckons you in, where so many fluorescent beer and doughnut signs shine that no other interior lighting is needed. Located 7 miles east of downtown via Columbia Pkwy.

🍷 Drinking & Nightlife

★ Rhinegeist Brewery
BREWERY

(📞 513-381-1367; www.rhinegeist.com; 1910 Elm St, 2nd fl; ⏰ 3pm-midnight Mon-Thu, 3pm-2am Fri, noon-2am Sat, noon-9pm Sun) Beer buffs pile in to Rhinegeist's hoppy clubhouse to knock back Truth IPA and 13 other brews on tap. Swig at picnic tables while watching bottles roll off the production line, or play Ping Pong or Foosball in the sprawling open warehouse. It sits in a forlorn patch of OTR.

Moerlein Lager House
BREWERY

(📞 513-421-2337; www.moerleinlagerhouse.com; 115 Joe Nuxall Way; ⏰ 11am-midnight Mon-Thu, to 1am Fri & Sat, to 11pm Sun) Copper kettles cook up the house beers, while the patio unfurls awesome views of the riverfront and Roebling bridge. It's a busy spot pre or post Reds games, as it sits across the street from the stadium.

Blind Lemon
BAR

(📞 513-241-3885; www.theblindlemon.com; 936 Hatch St; ⏰ 5:30pm-2:30am Mon-Fri, from 3pm Sat & Sun) Head down the passageway to enter this atmospheric old speakeasy in Mt Adams. It has an outdoor courtyard, and there's live music nightly.

☆ Entertainment

Aronoff Center   THEATER
(☑ 513-621-2787; www.cincinnatiarts.org; 650 Walnut St) Star architect Cesar Pelli designed the glowy, glass-fronted building. There are three theaters inside: the largest hosts touring Broadway shows, while the other two host cutting-edge dance troupes and intimate concerts. If nothing else, pop in to the free public art gallery to see what's on; it shows exhibitions of regional works.

Great American Ballpark   BASEBALL
(☑ 513-765-7000; www.reds.com; 100 Main St) Home to the Reds – pro baseball's first team – Cincy is a great place to catch a game thanks to its bells-and-whistles riverside ballpark. Many of the beer stands pour top-notch local brews.

❶ Information

Cincinnati Visitor Center (☑ 513-534-5877; www.cincyusa.com; 511 Walnut St; ⊙ 9am-6pm) The visitor center on Fountain Sq has maps and info.

❶ Getting There & Around

The **Cincinnati/Northern Kentucky International Airport** (CVG; www.cvgairport.com) is actually in Kentucky, 13 miles south. To get downtown, take the TANK bus ($2) from near Terminal 3; a cab costs about $35.

Greyhound (☑ 513-352-6012; www.greyhound.com; 1005 Gilbert Ave) buses travel daily to Columbus (two hours), Indianapolis (2½ hours) and Chicago (seven hours). Megabus

(www.megabus.com/us) travels the same routes from downtown and the University of Cincinnati; check the website for curbside locations.

Amtrak (www.amtrak.com) choo-choos into **Union Terminal** (☑ 513-651-3337; 1301 Western Ave) thrice weekly en route to Chicago (9½ hours) and Washington, DC (14½ hours), departing in the middle of the night.

Metro (www.go-metro.com) runs the local buses and links with the Transit Authority of Northern Kentucky (www.tankbus.org). Bus 1 is useful, looping from the museum center to downtown to Mt Adams.

Red Bike (www.cincyredbike.org) has 440 bicycles at 56 stations, mostly in downtown and Over-the-Rhine. A 24-hour pass costs $8; additional charges apply for trips over 60 minutes.

Cincy's new streetcar (www.cincinnatibellconnector.com) runs on a handy, 3½-mile loop connecting the Banks, downtown and Over-the-Rhine (including Findlay Market). A day pass costs $2.

Southeastern Ohio

Ohio's southeastern corner cradles most of its forested areas, as well as the rolling foothills of the Appalachian Mountains and scattered farms. Parts are far prettier than you'd expect. The Hocking Hills region, near Logan, impresses with streams and waterfalls, sandstone cliffs and cave-like formations. Further on is Athens, a university town and the area's free-spirited hot spot. To the east, around Chillicothe, mysterious Native American mounds rise from the fields.

WORTH A TRIP

ANCIENT MOUNDS OF OHIO

The area south of Columbus was a center for the ancient Hopewell people, who left behind huge geometric earthworks and burial mounds from around 200 BC to AD 600. The **Hopewell Culture National Historical Park** (☑ 740-774-1126; www.nps.gov/hocu; 16062 Hwy 104, Chillicothe; ⊙ sunrise-sunset) tells their story. The visitor center (8:30am to 5pm) provides intriguing background information, but the highlight is wandering about the variously shaped ceremonial mounds spread over 13-acre Mound City, a mysterious town of the dead. The park is 3 miles north of Chillicothe.

Serpent Mound (☑ 937-587-2796; www.ohiohistory.org; 3850 Hwy 73; per vehicle $8; ⊙ 9am-sunset) is perhaps the most captivating of all the native mounds that dot southeastern Ohio. The giant, uncoiling snake stretches over a quarter of a mile and is the largest effigy mound in the USA. You can walk around it or go up the observation tower for a sweeping view. The site is far flung, but cool enough to be worth the effort. It's 50 miles southeast of Chillicothe. A small on-site museum (10am to 4pm Monday to Thursday, 9am to 5pm Friday to Sunday, reduced hours in winter) has a short video about the history of the mound builders and exhibits showing artifacts found in the area.

Athens

Athens makes a lovely base for exploring southeastern Ohio. Situated where Hwy 50 crosses Hwy 33, it's set among wooded hills and built around the Ohio University campus (which comprises half the town). Vintage brick buildings edge the main streets, while young, earthy and artsy types pop in and out of the cafes and groovy shops inside.

🛏 Sleeping & Eating

Bodhi Tree Guesthouse B&B $$
(☑ 740-707-2050; www.bodhitreeguesthouse.com; 8950 Lavelle Rd; r $130-160) The four rooms at this serene, hippy-esque farmhouse have tasteful modern (if minimal) decor. There are no TVs, but there is wi-fi, as well as a wholesome breakfast of local cheeses, eggs, fruit and yogurt. A 4-acre organic farm surrounds the abode. The on-site studio offers yoga classes and massage.

Village Bakery & Cafe BAKERY $
(☑ 740-594-7311; www.dellazona.com; 268 E State St; sandwiches $9-13; ☺ 7:30am-8pm Tue-Fri, to 6pm Sat, 9am-2pm Sun; ☑) 🍴 Brightly painted and woodsy-casual in ambience, Village Bakery uses organic veggies, sustainably produced meats and farmstead cheeses in its egg breakfast dishes and heaped-on-housemade-bread sandwiches. Vegetarians will find lots of options.

ⓘ Getting There & Away

The closest big city is Columbus, 75 miles northwest via Hwy 33. GoBus (☑ 888-954-6287; www.ridegobus.com) runs a few times a day to/from downtown Columbus.

Logan

Logan is a handy headquarters for checking out the Hocking Hills area, where hiking, canoeing, camping and other activities amid dramatic gorges and grottoes are de rigueur. Hocking Hills State Park lets you immerse in the green scene, while Logan and nearby New Straitsville offer local cultural quirks including a washboard museum and moonshine distillery.

⊙ Sights & Activities

Hocking Hills State Park STATE PARK
(☑ 740-385-6841; http://parks.ohiodnr.gov/hockinghills; 19852 Hwy 664) FREE It's splendid to explore in any season (but especially lovely in autumn), with miles of trails for hiking

and biking past waterfalls and gorges, as well as campsites (from $26) and cabins (from $150). The park is 12 miles southwest of Logan.

Straitsville Special Moonshine Distillery DISTILLERY
(☑ 740-394-2622; www.straitsvillemoonshine. com; 105 W Main St, New Straitsville; ☺ 10am-5pm Mon-Sat) A hissing, coil-laden moonshine distillery operates in New Straitsville, 12 miles east of Logan. Singe your tonsils in the tasting room (per sample $1) while chatting with the owner about the town's rough history spanning coal mines, labor strife, an eternal flame and Al Capone.

Hocking Hills Scenic Byway SCENIC DRIVE
(www.explorehockinghills.com) For a lovely drive, follow Hwy 374 – an official Ohio Byway – for 26 miles as it rolls through the forested, stream-splashed hills. It starts at the intersection of Hwy 33 and Hwy 374 in Rockbridge.

ⓘ Getting There & Away

Hwy 33 is the main road to Logan. **GoBus** (☑ 888-954-6287; www.ridegobus.com) makes a stop in town a few times a day on its route between downtown Columbus and Athens.

MICHIGAN

More, more, more – Michigan is the Midwest state that cranks it up. It sports more beaches than the Atlantic seaboard. More than half the state is covered by forests. And more cherries and berries get shoveled into pies here than anywhere else in the USA. Plus its gritty city Detroit is the Midwest's rawest of all – and we mean that in a good way. Michigan occupies prime real estate, surrounded by four of the five Great Lakes – Superior, Michigan, Huron and Erie. Islands – Mackinac, Manitou and Isle Royale – freckle its coast and make top touring destinations. Surf beaches, colored sandstone cliffs and trekkable sand dunes also woo visitors.

The state consists of two parts split by water: larger Lower Peninsula, shaped like a mitten; and smaller, lightly populated Upper Peninsula, shaped like a slipper. They are linked by the gasp-worthy Mackinac Bridge, which spans the Straits of Mackinac (pronounced *mac*-in-aw).

ℹ Information

Michigan Highway Conditions (www.michigan.gov/mdot)

Michigan State Park Information (📞 800-447-2757; www.michigan.gov/stateparks) Park entry requires a vehicle permit (per day/year $9/32). Campsites cost $13 to $37; reservations accepted (www.midnrreservations.com; fee $8). Some parks have wi-fi.

Travel Michigan (www.michigan.org)

Detroit

Americans love a good comeback story, and Detroit is writing a mighty one as it transforms itself from a punchline to a cool-cat destination. Murals, markets, greenways, bike shops, distilleries and inventive chefs are getting the city's groove on, along with fresh public works like the new street car and sports arena downtown.

While the city does have an abandoned, otherworldly vibe in some areas, it's these same qualities that fuel a raw urban energy you won't find anywhere else. Artists, entrepreneurs and young people keep moving in, and a DIY spirit pervades. They're converting vacant lots into urban farms and abandoned buildings into cafes and museums. But there's a long way to go, and skeptics point out that Detroit's long-term African American residents are not sharing equally in these new developments. How the city navigates the tricky path to recovery remains to be seen, but we're pulling for the underdog.

History

French explorer Antoine de La Mothe Cadillac founded Detroit in 1701. Sweet fortune arrived in the 1920s, when Henry Ford began churning out cars. He didn't invent the automobile, as so many mistakenly believe, but he did perfect assembly-line manufacturing and mass-production techniques. The result was the Model T, the first car the USA's middle class could afford to own.

Detroit quickly became the motor capital of the world. General Motors (GM), Chrysler and Ford were all headquartered in or near Detroit (and still are). The 1950s were the city's heyday, when the population exceeded two million and Motown music hit the airwaves. But racial tensions in 1967 and Japanese car competitors in the 1970s shook the city and its industry. Detroit entered an era of deep decline, losing about two-thirds of its population.

In July 2013 Detroit filed the largest municipal bankruptcy claim in US history: $18 billion. After extreme belt-tightening, it emerged from bankruptcy in December 2014. Since then, the fortunes of downtown have been on the rise, thanks to a real estate boom, but the tide has yet to turn for many long-term residents outside the city's core.

◉ Sights & Activities

Sights are commonly closed on Monday and Tuesday. And that's Canada across the Detroit River (Windsor, Canada, to be exact).

CLASSIC CARS IN MICHIGAN

More than sand dunes, beaches and Mackinac Island fudge, Michigan is synonymous with cars. While the connection hasn't been so positive in recent years, the state commemorates its glory days via several auto museums. The following fleets are within a few hours' drive of the Motor City.

Henry Ford Museum (p591) This Dearborn museum is loaded with vintage cars, including the first one Henry Ford ever built. In adjacent Greenfield Village you can ride in a Model T that rolled off the assembly line in 1923.

Automotive Hall of Fame (p592) Learn about the men and women who conceived and created the world's most classic cars and gain insight into the minds which gave us the mechanics of the modern motor.

Gilmore Car Museum (📞 269-671-5089; www.gilmorecarmuseum.org; 6865 Hickory Rd; adult/child $13/10; ⊙ 9am-5pm Mon-Fri, to 6pm Sat & Sun) North of Kalamazoo along Hwy 43, this museum complex offers 22 barns filled with 120 vintage autos, including 15 Rolls Royces dating back to a 1910 Silver Ghost.

RE Olds Transportation Museum (p593) It's a whopping garage full of shiny vintage cars that date back more than 130 years.

Midtown & Cultural Center

★ Detroit Institute of Arts — MUSEUM

(DIA; ☎ 313-833-7900; www.dia.org; 5200 Woodward Ave; adult/child $12.50/6; ⊙ 9am-4pm Tue-Thu, to 10pm Fri, 10am-5pm Sat & Sun) The DIA holds one of the world's finest art collections. The centerpiece is Diego Rivera's mural *Detroit Industry*, which fills an entire room and reflects the city's blue-collar labor history. Beyond it are Picassos, Caravaggios, suits of armor, modern African American paintings, puppets and troves more spread through 100-plus galleries.

It's hard to believe the collection was about to be sold to pay off the city's debt a few years ago. Luckily, donors saved the day.

Museum of Contemporary Art Detroit — MUSEUM

(MOCAD; ☎ 313-832-6622; www.mocadetroit.org; 4454 Woodward Ave; suggested donation $5; ⊙ 11am-5pm Wed, Sat & Sun, to 8pm Thu & Fri) MOCAD is set in an abandoned, graffiti-slathered auto dealership. Heat lamps hang from the ceiling over peculiar exhibits that change every few months. Music and literary events take place regularly. The onsite cafe-cocktail bar is uber popular.

New Center

★ Motown Historical Museum — MUSEUM

(☎ 313-875-2264; www.motownmuseum.org; 2648 W Grand Blvd; adult/child $15/10; ⊙ 10am-6pm Tue-Fri & Sun, to 8pm Sat Jun-Aug, to 6pm Tue-Sat Sep-May) In this row of modest houses Berry Gordy launched Motown Records – and the careers of Stevie Wonder, Diana Ross, Marvin Gaye and Michael Jackson – with an $800 loan in 1959. Gordy and Motown split for Los Angeles in 1972, but you can still step into humble Studio A and see where the famed names recorded their first hits.

A tour takes about one hour, and consists mostly of looking at old photos and listening to guides' stories. To avoid a wait, buy timed tickets in advance online. The museum recently announced a $50 million expansion, with new buildings to be added for a vast increase in exhibition space. Motown is 2 miles northwest of Midtown, about a 20-minute walk from the Grand Boulevard QLINE stop.

Ford Piquette Avenue Plant — MUSEUM

(☎ 313-872-8759; www.fordpiquetteavenueplant.org; 461 Piquette Ave; adult/child $12/free; ⊙ 10am-4pm Wed-Sun Apr-Oct) Henry Ford cranked out the first Model T in this landmark factory. Admission includes a detailed tour by enthusiastic docents, plus loads of shiny vehicles from 1904 onward. It's about 1 mile northeast of the Detroit Institute of Arts.

Downtown & Around

★ Campus Martius Park — PARK

(www.downtowndetroitparks.com/parks/Campus-Martius; 800 Woodward Ave; 🚼🐕) This new public space in the heart of Detroit's downtown is the perfect spot to while away a sunny afternoon. At the center is the Michigan Soldiers & Sailors Monument: in the warmer months, there's a sandy beach at its foot; in the winter, the space becomes the city's most popular ice rink. There's a stage for concerts and, in summer, a pop-up restaurant and bar.

★ Eastern Market — MARKET

(www.easternmarket.com; Adelaide & Russell Sts) Produce, cheese, spice and flower vendors fill the large halls on Saturday, but you also can turn up Monday through Friday to browse the specialty shops (props to the peanut roaster) and cafes that flank the halls on Russell and Market Sts. In addition, from June through October there's a scaled-down market on Tuesdays and a Sunday craft market with food trucks. Or arrive any day for mural gaping. Eastern Market has become an internationally renowned hot spot for street art.

Check www.muralsinthemarket.com for locations and artists.

Packard Plant — NOTABLE BUILDING

(E Grand Blvd at Concord St) Renowned architect Albert Kahn designed this 3.5-million-sq-ft factory, which opened in 1905, but after years of neglect it became one of Detroit's most iconic ruins. Now, an Italian developer has plans to turn it into an office and entertainment complex over the next decade. Phase one of the project is expected to be finished in fall 2019. In the meantime, Pure Detroit (☎ 313-963-1440; www.puredetroit.com; 500 Griswold St; ⊙ 9:30am-6pm Mon-Sat, 11am-5pm Sun) is offering tours on Saturdays. Book far in advance online.

Renaissance Center — NOTABLE BUILDING

(RenCen; www.gmrencen.com; 330 E Jefferson Ave) GM's glossy, cloud-poking headquarters is a fine place to mooch off the free wi-fi, take a

Detroit

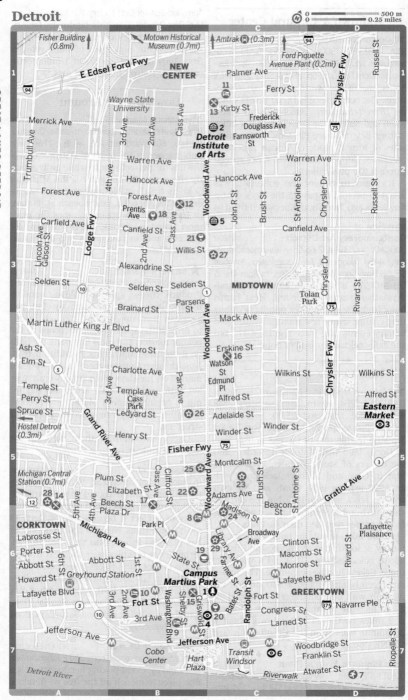

0   500 m
0   0.25 miles

Fisher Building
(0.8mi)

Motown Historical
Museum (0.7mi)

Amtrak (0.3mi)

Ford Piquette
Avenue Plant (0.2mi)

E Edsel Ford Fwy

NEW
CENTER

Palmer Ave

Ferry St

Russell St

Wayne State
University

11

13 Kirby St

Frederick
Douglass Ave
Farnsworth
St

2 Detroit
Institute
of Arts

Warren Ave

Hancock Ave

Warren Ave

Forest Ave

Hancock Ave

Merrick Ave

3rd Ave

2nd Ave

Cass Ave

Woodward Ave

John R St

Brush St

St Antoine St

Chrysler Dr

Russell St

Forest Ave

4th Ave

Trumbull Ave

Lodge Fwy

Carfield Ave

12

Prentis
Ave

18

Canfield St

Cass Ave

2nd Ave

5

21

Willis St

27

Canfield Ave

Lincoln Ave

Gibson St

Alexandrine St

Selden St

Selden St

Selden St

MIDTOWN

Chrysler Dr

Rivard St

Brainard St

Parsens
St

Tolan
Park

Martin Luther King Jr Blvd

Mack Ave

Peterboro St

Erskine St

16

Ash St

Elm St

Charlotte Ave

3rd Ave

Park Ave

Watson
St
Edmund
Pl

Wilkins St

Wilkins St

Temple St

Perry St

Spruce St

Temple Ave
Cass
Park

Alfred St

Alfred St

Eastern
Market

3

Hostel Detroit
(0.3mi)

Grand River Ave

Ledyard St

26

Adelaide St

Henry St

Winder St

Winder St

Fisher Fwy

Michigan Central
Station (0.7mi)

Plum St

Cass Ave

Clifford St

25

Woodward Ave

Montcalm St

Brush St

St Antoine St

3

Elizabeth St

22

17

28

14

5th Ave

4th Ave

Beech St

Plaza Dr

Park Pl

Michigan Ave

CORKTOWN

Labrosse St

Porter St

6th St

Abbott St

Abbott St

1st St

Gratiat Ave

23

Adams Ave

8

24

Madison St

Beacon
St

Chrysler Fwy

Lafayette
Plaisance

Broadway
Ave

Clinton St

Macomb St

Howard St

Greyhound Station

State St

19

29

Farmer St

Library Ave

Monroe St

Lafayette Blvd

Lafayette Blvd

10

Fort St

5th St

2nd Ave

3rd Ave

Washington Blvd

15

Shelby St

Griswold St

Campus
Martius Park

1

20

Bates St

Randolph St

Fort St

GREEKTOWN

Congress St

Navarre Ple

Jefferson Ave

3rd Ave

9

4

Jefferson Ave

Larned St

Riopelle St

Cobo Center

Hart
Plaza

Transit
Windsor

6

Woodbridge St

Franklin St

7

Detroit River

Riverwalk

Atwater St

Detroit

◎ Top Sights
1	Campus Martius Park	C6
2	Detroit Institute of Arts	C2
3	Eastern Market	D5

◎ Sights
4	Guardian Building	C7
5	Museum of Contemporary Art Detroit	C3
6	Renaissance Center	C7

◎ Activities, Courses & Tours
7	Wheelhouse Bikes	D7

◎ Sleeping
8	Aloft	B6
9	Detroit Foundation Hotel	B7
10	Ft Shelby Doubletree Hotel	B6
11	Inn on Ferry Street	C1

◎ Eating
12	Cass Cafe	B2
13	Chartreuse Kitchen	C1
14	Detroit Institute of Bagels	A6
15	Dime Store	B6
16	Grey Ghost	C4
17	Parks & Rec Diner	B5

◎ Drinking & Nightlife
18	Bronx	B2
19	Dessert Oasis Coffee Roasters	B6
20	Grand Trunk Pub	C7
21	HopCat	B3

◎ Entertainment
22	Cliff Bell's	B5
23	Comerica Park	C5
24	Detroit Opera House	C6
25	Fox Theater	B5
26	Little Caesars Arena	B5
27	Magic Stick	C3
28	PJ's Lager House	A5
29	Puppet ART/Detroit Puppet Theater	C6

◎ Shopping
	Pure Detroit	(see 4)

free hour-long tour or embark on the riverfront walkway.

Heidelberg Project   PUBLIC ART
(www.heidelberg.org; 3600 Heidelberg St; ⊙sunrise-sunset) FREE Polka-dotted streets, houses covered in Technicolor paint blobs, strange doll sculptures in yards – this is no acid trip, but rather a block-spanning art installation. It's the brainchild of street artist Tyree Guyton, who wanted to beautify his run-down community. Which he did for more than 30 years. Now Guyton has announced he'll dismantle the project and put a cultural village in its place. He'll rehab the buildings into galleries and art workshop spaces, much like the current Numbers House, which holds exhibitions.

Riverwalk & Dequindre Cut   WALKING, CYCLING
(www.detroitriverfront.org) The city's swell riverfront path runs for 3 miles along the churning Detroit River from Hart Plaza east to Mt Elliott St, passing several parks, outdoor theaters, riverboats and fishing spots en route. Eventually it will extend all the way to beachy Belle Isle (detour onto Jefferson Ave to get there now). About halfway along the Riverwalk, near Orleans St, the 1.5-mile Dequindre Cut Greenway path juts north, offering a passageway to Eastern Market.

☞ Tours

★ Pure Detroit Tours   WALKING
(☑ 855-874-7873; www.puredetroit.com; ⊙Sat & Sun; times vary) FREE Purveyors of locally inspired gifts, Pure Detroit also offer guided tours of some of the city's best sights, including the **Fisher Building** (☑ 313-872-1000; www.fisherbldg.com; 3011 W Grand Boulevard), the **Guardian Building** (www.guardianbuilding.com; 500 Griswold St; ⊙8:30am-6pm Mon-Sat, 11am-5pm Sun) and the Packard Plant (p585). Guides – typically local historians – are knowledgeable and friendly. Stop in at one of their five locations or check the website for details. Most tours are free, but the Packard Plant tour is $40 and must be reserved in advance.

Preservation Detroit   WALKING
(☑ 313-577-7674; www.preservationdetroit.org; 2hr tours $15; ⊙10am Sat May-Sep) Offers architectural walking tours through downtown, Midtown, Eastern Market and other neighborhoods; departure points vary.

Wheelhouse Bikes   CYCLING
(☑ 313-656-2453; www.wheelhousedetroit.com; 1340 E Atwater St; per 2hr $15; ⊙11am-7pm Mon-Thu, 10am-8pm Fri & Sat, noon-5pm Sun, reduced hours in winter) Cycling is a great way to explore the city. Wheelhouse rents sturdy two-wheelers (helmet and lock included)

THE RUINS OF DETROIT

The derelict buildings that represent Detroit in the popular imagination aren't as prevalent as they once were – at least, not in downtown, where many architectural gems have been lovingly restored and buffed to a shine, thanks to dedicated locals and private investors. National chains have also jumped on the bandwagon as the city's fortunes show a decided turn for the better, with retailers like Lululemon and hotel chains like Aloft and Westin moving in to formerly vacant commercial buildings.

Even a few of the most iconic ruins are showing signs of life. Top of the list is **Michigan Central Station** (2405 W Vernor Hwy), the once-grand beaux-arts rail terminal. After closing in 1988, it spent decades crumbling into oblivion within eyeshot of Corktown's main drag. Decline has been stopped – and windows installed – but full redevelopment is far from certain. The Packard Auto Plant (p585) is another. Renowned architect Albert Kahn designed the 3.5-million-sq-ft factory, and it was a thing of beauty when it opened in 1905. After decades of abandonment, however, it has become a graffiti-ridden ruin. Its fortunes have risen with the city, however: an Italian developer bought 3/4 of the site and has plans to turn it into an office and entertainment complex over the next decade.

Still, with 139 sq miles of city, there are plenty of vacant buildings that remain, especially outside the downtown core. Note that viewing the buildings has become a hot topic: some call it 'ruin porn'. Others see it as a way to examine and take in the complex history of the city. It is illegal to enter any abandoned building.

on the Riverwalk at Rivard Plaza. Themed tours ($40 including bike rental) roll by various neighborhoods, architectural sites and urban farms.

⭐ Festivals & Events

North American International Auto Show CULTURAL
(www.naias.com; tickets $13; ☉ mid-Jan) It's autos galore for two weeks at the Cobo Center.

Movement Electronic Music Festival MUSIC
(www.movement.us; day pass $80; ☉ late May) The world's largest electronic music festival congregates in Hart Plaza over Memorial Day weekend.

Woodward Dream Cruise CAR SHOW
(www.woodwarddreamcruise.com) FREE On the third Saturday in August, car lovers from around the world assemble in Detroit to show off their four-wheeled treasures and cruise down the city's main drag. The party stretches for miles, but most of the action takes place north of downtown, along Woodward and side streets nearby between 8 and 10 Mile roads.

Between road closures and the event's sprawling footprint, it's hard to know where to start with the Dream Cruise. Try diving in at 9 Mile, a few blocks east or west of Woodward. You'll be able to ooh and ahh over the cars and take in the charming center of the Ferndale neighborhood at the same time.

🛏 Sleeping

Detroit is having a hotel boom: several new design-savvy properties have opened in downtown and Midtown over the last year, with more on the way. Add 9% to 15% tax (it varies by lodging size and location) to the listed rates.

Hostel Detroit HOSTEL $
(☏ 313-451-0333; www.hosteldetroit.com; 2700 Vermont St; dm $30-39, r $60-77; P@🛜) Volunteers rehabbed this old building, gathered up recycled materials and donations for the patchwork furnishings, and opened it to the public in 2011. There's a 10-bed dorm, a four-bed dorm and a handful of private rooms; everyone shares the four bathrooms and three kitchens. Bookings are taken online only (and must be done at least 24 hours in advance).

★ Inn on Ferry Street INN $$
(☏ 313-871-6000; www.innonferrystreet.com; 84 E Ferry St; r $169-259; P✳@🛜) Forty guest rooms fill a row of Victorian mansions right by the art museum. The lower-cost rooms are small but have deliciously soft bedding; the larger rooms feature plenty of antique wood furnishings. The healthy hot breakfast and shuttle to downtown are nice touches.

Aloft

HOTEL **$$**

(☑ 313-237-1700; www.aloftdetroit.com; 1 Park Ave; r $159-219; P❊@🐾🛜🏊) The chain's Detroit property took an exquisite 1915 neo-Renaissance skyscraper and converted it to its familiar hipster style. Mod rooms have bright pops of color and groovy city views. It's well located near the sports venues and theaters. Parking costs $30.

Ft Shelby Doubletree Hotel

HOTEL **$$**

(☑ 313-963-5600; www.doubletree3.hilton.com; 525 W Lafayette Blvd; r $135-195; P❊@🛜) This hotel fills a historic beaux-arts building downtown. All rooms are large suites, with both the sitting area and bedroom equipped with HDTV and free wi-fi. Parking costs $30, and there's free shuttle service around downtown.

Detroit Foundation Hotel

BOUTIQUE HOTEL **$$$**

(☑ 313-800-5500; www.detroitfoundationhotel.com; 250 W Larned St; r $200-280; ♿❊🛜) In 2017, this 1929 fire station in the heart of the city was transformed into a boutique hotel that blends modern convenience and style with original architectural features and a strong sense of history (don't miss the fire poles in the excellent restaurant, Apparatus Room). Rooms are spacious and comfortable, with minibars featuring Michigan products at reasonable prices.

The Guardian Building, convention center and Campus Martius Park are just a short walk away. Valet parking ($30) and free bike rentals are available.

🍴 Eating

Downtown and Midtown are prime for stylish eats. Two nearby suburbs also have caches of hip restaurants and bars: walkable, gay-oriented Ferndale at 9 Mile Rd and Woodward Ave, and Royal Oak just north of Ferndale between 12 and 13 Mile Rds.

Cass Cafe

CAFE **$**

(☑ 313-831-1400; www.casscafe.com; 4620 Cass Ave; mains $9-16; ⊙11am-11pm Mon-Thu, to midnight Fri & Sat, 5-10pm Sun; 🛜🍴) The Cass is a bohemian art gallery fused with a bar and restaurant that serves soups, sandwiches and veggie beauties, like the lentil-walnut burger. Service can be fickle.

Detroit Institute of Bagels

BAGELS **$**

(☑ 313-444-9342; www.detroitinstituteofbagels.com; 1236 Michigan Ave; bagels from $1.50, bagel sandwiches $6-9; ⊙7am-3pm Mon-Fri, 8am-3pm Sat & Sun; P) Authentic NY bagels and housemade cream cheeses take center stage at this bright, plant-filled space in Corktown. Try the Le Rouge, with bacon, egg, goat's cheese, arugula and red-onion marmalade. There's a hydrangea-filled patio for the warmer months.

Parks & Rec Diner

DINER **$**

(☑ 313-446-8370; www.parksandrecdiner.com; 1942 Grand River Ave; mains $6-14; ⊙8am-2pm Mon-Fri, to 3pm Sat & Sun) This homey diner, opened in 2015 in the imposing GAR building, takes its name from the government department that was once housed here. There are no wrong choices from the seasonal menu of sandwiches and brunch dishes like pistachio French toast and panzanella with charred bacon. The fries, seasoned with a BBQ spice, are excellent.

★ Dime Store

AMERICAN **$**

(☑ 313-962-9106; www.eatdimestore.com; 719 Griswold St; mains $9-13; ⊙8am-4pm Mon-Fri, to 3pm Sat & Sun) Take a seat in a chunky wood swivel chair in this cozy, diner-esque eatery and chow down on a duck Reuben and truffle-mayo-dipped fries, alongside a cold beer. Eggy brunch dishes are a big hit and served all day.

Chartreuse Kitchen

AMERICAN **$$**

(☑ 313-818-3915; www.chartreusekc.com; 15 E Kirby St; mains $22-28; ⊙11:30am-2pm & 5-9:30pm Tue-Thu, to 10:30pm Fri, 5-10:30pm Sat) It may seem like just another trendy spot with mod-industrial decor and a seasonal menu, but Chartreuse does it all really well. Dishes like the twice-cooked egg (with greens, Brussels sprouts, salty cheese and shallot vinaigrette) and roasted carrots (with prosciutto and lemon yogurt) are crazy-simple flavor explosions. The bright green interior and walls of living flowers waft a happy hippie vibe.

Grey Ghost

AMERICAN **$$$**

(☑ 313-262-6534; www.greyghostdetroit.com; 47 E Watson St; mains $18-29; ⊙from 4pm Mon-Sat, 10am-2pm Sun) A sleek, industrial vibe marks this new Detroit hot spot. The menu is all modern as well, with creative sides like cauliflower and spaetzel or brussels sprouts with chicken skin. The juicy NY strip steak is cooked sous vide. There's a convivial but small outdoor patio.

🍷 Drinking & Nightlife

★ Dessert Oasis Coffee Roasters   COFFEE

(www.dessertoasiscoffee.com; 1220 Griswold St; ⏰6am-9pm Mon-Thu, to 10pm Fri, 7am-10pm Sat, 8am-9pm Sun; 🛜🍴) Pitch-perfect espresso drinks (try the lavender latte), pour-overs, outdoor seating and free wi-fi are hallmarks of this new downtown cafe. Live music nightly. Dog-friendly.

HopCat   PUB

(☑313-769-8828; www.hopcat.com/detroit; 4265 Woodward Ave; ⏰11am-midnight Mon-Wed, to 2am Thu-Sat, 10am-midnight Sun; 🛜) Detroit's outpost of the regional pub chain rocks: paintings of local musicians adorn the walls, and the Stooges and old Motown bang on the speakers. Around 130 beers flow from the taps, with 30 devoted to Michigan brewers. Smaller pours (5oz and 8oz glasses) are available for those who want to sample widely.

Bronx   BAR

(☑313-832-8464; 4476 2nd Ave; ⏰noon-2am; 🛜) There's not much inside this classic corner tavern besides a pool table, dim lighting and a couple of jukeboxes filled with ballsy rock and soul. But that's the way the hipsters, slackers and rockers like their dive bars. They're also fond of the beefy burgers served late at night and the cheap beer selection.

Grand Trunk Pub   BAR

(☑313-961-3043; www.grandtrunk.pub; ⏰11am-2am) Once the ticket hall for the Grand Trunk Railroad, this high-ceilinged space still buzzes, but this time patrons are content to sit and stop a while. With good reason: there's a vast beer selection and a full bar menu. The patio is an excellent spot to people-watch, thanks to the new pedestrian esplanade down Woodward Ave.

☆ Entertainment

Live Music

Cliff Bell's   JAZZ

(☑313-961-2543; www.cliffbells.com; 2030 Park Ave; ⏰5pm-midnight Tue-Thu, to 1am Fri & Sat, 11am-10pm Sun) With its dark wood, candlelight and art-deco decor, Bell's evokes 1930s elegance. Local jazz, soul and swing bands attract a diverse young audience.

Magic Stick   LIVE MUSIC

(☑313-833-9700; www.majesticdetroit.com; 4120-4140 Woodward Ave) The White Stripes and Von Bondies are rockers who've risen from the beer-splattered ranks at the Magic Stick. The Majestic Theater next door hosts larger shows. While the venues have lost some luster in recent years, you're still likely to see cool bands here most nights.

PJ's Lager House   LIVE MUSIC

(☑313-961-4668; www.pjslagerhouse.com; 1254 Michigan Ave; ⏰1pm-2am Mon & Tue, from 11am Wed-Fri, from 10:30am Sat & Sun) Scrappy bands or DJs play most nights at this small Corktown club. By day it serves surprisingly good grub with a New Orleans–vegan twist.

Performing Arts

Detroit Opera House   OPERA

(☑313-237-7464; www.michiganopera.org; 1526 Broadway Ave) It has a gorgeous interior and a top-tier company that has nurtured many renowned African American performers.

Puppet ART/Detroit Puppet Theater   THEATER

(☑313-961-7777; www.puppetart.org; 25 E Grand River Ave; adult/child $15/10; 🚼) Soviet-trained puppeteers perform beautiful shows in this 70-person theater; a small museum displays puppets from different cultures.

FROM MOTOWN TO ROCK CITY

Motown Records and soul music put Detroit on the map in the 1960s, while the thrashing punk rock of the Stooges and MC5 was the 1970s response to that smooth sound. By 1976, Detroit was dubbed 'Rock City' by a Kiss song (though – just Detroit's luck – the tune was eclipsed by its B-side, 'Beth'). In recent years it has been hard-edged rock – aka whiplash rock and roll – that has pushed the city to the music-scene forefront. Homegrown stars include the White Stripes, Von Bondies and Dirtbombs. Rap (thank you, Eminem) and techno are Detroit's other renowned genres. Many music aficionados say the city's blight is what produces such a beautifully angry explosion of sound, and who's to argue? Scope free publications like the *Metro Times* for current show and club listings.

Fox Theater
PERFORMING ARTS

(📞 313-471-6611; www.olympiaentertainment.com/venues/detail/fox-theatre; 2211 Woodward Ave) This opulent 1928 theater, built in the Oriental style, is one of the icons of Detroit – and one of the few venues that has consistently offered entertainment during the city's ups and downs. Hosts comedians, top music acts and Broadway shows.

Sports

Little Caesars Arena
STADIUM

(📞 313-471-6606; www.olympiaentertainment.com; 2645 Woodward Ave) Opened in 2017, this is Detroit's spiffy new arena for big-name concerts and sporting events. Detroit's rough-and-tumble pro hockey team the Red Wings (www.nhl.com/redwings) and pro basketball team the Pistons (www.nba.com/pistons) both play here from October through April.

Comerica Park
BASEBALL

(📞 313-962-4000; www.detroittigers.com; 2100 Woodward Ave; ♿) The Detroit Tigers play pro baseball at Comerica, one of the league's most decked-out stadiums. The park is particularly kid friendly, with a small Ferris wheel and carousel inside (per ride $2 each).

ℹ️ Information

Detroit Convention & Visitors Bureau (📞 800-338-7648; www.visitdetroit.com)

ℹ️ Getting There & Around

Detroit Metro Airport (DTW; www.metroairport.com), a Delta Airlines hub, is about 20 miles southwest of Detroit.Transport options to the city are few. Taxis cost $60 or so. The shared shuttle van **Skoot** (📞 313-230-2331; www.rideskoot.com) costs $20. The 125 SMART bus ($2.50) is inconvenient, unreliable and takes 1½ hours to get downtown.

Greyhound (📞 313-961-8005; 1001 Howard St) runs to various cities in Michigan and beyond. Megabus (www.megabus.com/us) runs to/from Chicago (5½ hours) daily; departures are from downtown and Wayne State University. Check the website for exact locations.

Amtrak (www.amtrak.com) trains go three times daily to Chicago (5½ hours) from **Detroit Station** (📞 313-873-3442; 11 W Baltimore Ave). You can also head east – to New York (16½ hours) or destinations en route – but you'll first be bused to Toledo.

The **QLine streetcar** (www.qlinedetroit.com, fare $1.50) started running in spring 2017. It provides handy transport along Woodward Ave from Congress St downtown, past the sports venues

and museums of Midtown, to the Amtrak station and W Grand Blvd at the route's northern end.

MoGo (www.mogodetroit.com) is Detroit's new bikeshare program, with 43 stations scattered around downtown and Midtown. A 24-hour pass costs $8 for an unlimited number of 30-minute trips; additional charges apply for time over 30 minutes.

Transit Windsor (📞 519-944-4111; www.citywindsor.ca/transitwindsor) operates the Tunnel Bus to Windsor, Canada. It costs $5 (American or Canadian) and departs by Mariner's Church (corner of Randolph St and Jefferson Ave) near the Detroit-Windsor Tunnel entrance, as well as other spots downtown. Bring your passport.

Dearborn

A stone's throw from Detroit, Dearborn is home to the Henry Ford Museum, one of the USA's finest museum complexes. It's also home to the nation's largest community of Arab Americans, and a visit here offers a fascinating immersion into the local culture.

⦿ Sights

The Henry Ford Museum, Greenfield Village and Rouge Factory Tour are separate, but you can get a combination ticket for two of the attractions, or for all three, and save 20% or more off the regular admission prices. Plan on at least one very full day at the complex.

Henry Ford Museum
MUSEUM

(📞 313-982-6001; www.thehenryford.org; 20900 Oakwood Blvd; adult/child $22/16.50; ⏰ 9:30am-5pm) The indoor Henry Ford Museum contains a fascinating wealth of American culture, such as the chair Lincoln was sitting in when he was assassinated, the presidential limo in which Kennedy was killed, the hot dog–shaped Oscar Mayer Wienermobile (photo op!) and the bus on which Rosa Parks refused to give up her seat. Don't worry: you'll get your vintage car fix here, too. Buying tickets online saves 10%. Parking costs $6.

Greenfield Village
MUSEUM

(📞 313-982-6001; www.thehenryford.org; 20900 Oakwood Blvd; adult/child $27/20.25; ⏰ 9:30am-5pm daily mid-Apr–Oct, Fri-Sun Nov & Dec) Adjacent to the Henry Ford Museum (and part of its complex), outdoor Greenfield Village features historic buildings shipped in from all over the country, reconstructed and restored, such as Thomas Edison's laboratory from Menlo Park and the Wright Brothers' airplane workshop. Buying tickets online saves 10%.

Automotive Hall of Fame   MUSEUM
(☑313-240-4000; www.automotivehalloffame.org; 21400 Oakwood Blvd; adult/child $10/4; ⊘9am-5pm Wed-Sun May-Sep, Fri-Sun only Oct-Apr) Next door to the Henry Ford Museum, the interactive Auto Hall focuses on the people behind famed cars, such as Mr Ferdinand Porsche and Mr Soichiro Honda.

Rouge Factory Tour   FACTORY
(☑312-982-6001; www.thehenryford.org; adult/child $18/13.25; ⊘9:30am-3pm Mon-Sat) See F-150 trucks roll off the assembly line where Ford first perfected his self-sufficient, mass-production techniques. Tours start at the Henry Ford Museum, from which a bus takes you over to the factory.

🛏 Sleeping & Eating

Henry Hotel   HOTEL $$
(☑313-441-2000; www.behenry.com; 300 Town Center Dr; r $180-240; 🅿✳@🛜🏊) This 11-story, 308-room, Marriott-brand property hosts mostly business travelers and wedding parties drawn to its beyond-the-norm style. Each floor displays groovy local art, and the elegant, chandelier-clad common areas provide swell hangouts. Rooms are comfy and good sized. It's adjacent to a big shopping center, and about 3 miles from the Henry Ford Museum.

Hamido   MIDDLE EASTERN $
(☑313-582-0660; www.hamidorestaurant.com; 13251 W Warren Ave; mains $8-16; ⊘11am-midnight) Slanted-roofed Hamido serves hummus, chicken shawarma and other staples. The number of chickens roasting on the spit marks its popularity.

❶ Getting There & Away

Dearborn is 10 miles west of downtown Detroit and about the same distance east of Detroit Metro Airport. I-94 is the primary road to town. Amtrak has a station by the Henry Ford Museum.

Ann Arbor

Liberal and bookish Ann Arbor is home to the University of Michigan. The walkable downtown, which abuts the campus, is loaded with free-trade coffee shops, bookstores and brewpubs. It's also a mecca for

chowhounds; follow the drool trail toward anything named 'Zingerman's.'

⊙ Sights

University of Michigan
Museum of Art   MUSEUM
(☑734-764-0395; www.umma.umich.edu; 525 S State St; ⊘11am-5pm Tue-Sat, from noon Sun) FREE The campus' bold art museum impresses with its collections of Asian ceramics, Tiffany glass and modern abstract works.

Ann Arbor Farmers Market   MARKET
(www.a2gov.org/market; 315 Detroit St; ⊘7am-3pm Wed & Sat May-Dec, 8am-3pm Sat Jan-Apr) Given the surrounding bounty of orchards and farms, it's no surprise this place is stuffed to the rafters with everything from spicy pickles to cider to mushroom-growing kits; located downtown near Zingerman's Delicatessen. On Sunday an artisan market with jewelry, ceramics and textiles takes over.

🛏 Sleeping & Eating

There are several B&Bs within walking distance of downtown. Hotels tend to be about 5 miles out, with several midrange chain options clustered south on State St.

Ann Arbor was a foodie haven before foodie havens even existed. The city has terrific eats, and they're usually casual and not too expensive. Main, Liberty and Washington Sts downtown brim with goodness. Food trucks hang out in a courtyard at 211 W Washington St. Ethiopian, Middle Eastern, Indian and other ethnic eats abound.

Frita Batidos   CUBAN $
(☑734-761-2882; www.fritabatidos.com; 117 W Washington St; mains $8-13; ⊘11am-11pm Sun-Wed, to midnight Thu-Sat) This mod take on Cuban street food is all the rage, offering burgers with tropical, citrusy toppings and booze-spiked milkshakes.

★ Spencer   AMERICAN $$
(☑734-369-3979; www.spencerannarbor.com; 113 E Liberty St; small plates $5-11; ⊘11am-3pm & 5-10pm Sun, Mon, Wed & Thu, to 11pm Fri & Sat) Eating at this pint-sized cafe is like eating in your friend's cozy kitchen, with white-washed walls, books stacked on the sunny windowsill and fresh flowers popping from vases. The owners – she's a pastry chef, he's a cheesemonger – change their locally sourced menu of small plates every few weeks, so you

might dig into rutabaga cauliflower soup or hanger steak with sunflower cream.

Zingerman's Roadhouse AMERICAN **$$$**
(☑734-663-3663; www.zingermansroadhouse.com; 2501 Jackson Ave; mains $19-36; ⊗7am-10pm Mon-Thu, 7am-11pm Fri, 9am-11pm Sat, 9am-9pm Sun) 🖉 Two words: doughnut sundae. The bourbon-caramel-sauced dessert is pure genius, as are the traditional American dishes like Carolina grits, Iowa pork chops and Maryland crab cakes, all using sustainably produced ingredients. It's 2 miles west of downtown.

ℹ Information

Ann Arbor Convention & Visitors Bureau
(www.visitannarbor.org) Accommodation information and more.

ℹ Getting There & Away

Detroit's airport is 30 miles east; shuttles buses make the trip. Amtrak trains come through Ann Arbor three times daily. The train station is downtown and shared by Greyhound. Megabus serves the city, but it stops inconveniently far from its center.

Central Michigan

Michigan's heartland, plunked in the center of the Lower Peninsula, alternates between fertile farms and highway-crossed urban areas. The larger cities excel in cool art, while the entire regions shine in stellar beer making.

Lansing

Smallish Lansing is the state capital. A few miles east lies East Lansing, home of Michigan State University. They're worth a stop to peek into a couple of impressive museums.

◉ Sights & Activities

Broad Art Museum MUSEUM
(☑517-884-4800; www.broadmuseum.msu.edu; 547 E Circle Dr; ⊗noon-7pm Tue-Sun) **FREE** Renowned architect Zaha Hadid designed the wild-looking parallelogram of stainless steel and glass. It holds everything from Greek ceramics to Salvador Dali paintings. Much of the space is devoted to avant-garde exhibitions.

RE Olds Transportation Museum MUSEUM
(☑517-372-0529; www.reoldsmuseum.org; 240 Museum Dr; adult/child $7/5; ⊗10am-5pm Tue-Sat year-round, noon-5pm Sun Apr-Oct) The museum

has a sweet collection of some 65 vintage cars that sit in the old Lansing City Bus Garage, including the first Oldsmobile, which was built in 1897. Note: they're not all on display at once, but rotate regularly.

Lansing River Trail WALKING
(www.lansingrivertrail.org) The paved, 20-mile path runs alongside the Grand River from the city's north edge to downtown, and then meanders east along the Red Cedar River to the university. It's popular with runners and cyclists, and the downtown portion links a number of attractions, including the RE Olds Transportation Museum, a children's museum, zoo and fish ladder.

🛏 Sleeping & Eating

Wild Goose Inn B&B **$$**
(☑517-333-3334; www.wildgooseinn.com; 512 Albert St; r $149-169; 🐾) The Wild Goose Inn is a six-room B&B one block from Michigan State's campus in East Lansing. All rooms have fireplaces and most have Jacuzzis. Decor is fairly low-key – except for the Arbor room and its wild faux branches!

Golden Harvest DINER **$**
(☑517-485-3663; 1625 Turner St; mains $7-9; ⊗7am-2pm Mon-Fri, from 8am Sat & Sun) Golden Harvest is a loud, punk-rock-meets-hippie diner serving the sausage-and-French-toast Bubba Sandwich and hearty omelets.

ℹ Getting There & Away

Amtrak stops in East Lansing on its Chicago–Port Huron route daily. Greyhound has stations in both Lansing and East Lansing. I-96, I-69 and Hwy 127 are the main interstates to the city.

Grand Rapids

The second-largest city in Michigan, Grand Rapids is known for office-furniture manufacturing and, more recently, beer tourism. Twenty craft breweries operate in the area, and that's why you're here (though some non-beer sights intrigue, as well).

◉ Sights

Frederik Meijer Gardens GARDENS
(☑616-957-1580; www.meijergardens.org; 1000 E Beltline NE; adult/child $14.50/7; ⊗9am-5pm Mon & Wed-Sat, to 9pm Tue, 11am-5pm Sun) The 118-acre gardens feature impressive blooms, and sculptures by Auguste Rodin, Henry Moore and others. It is 5 miles east of downtown via I-196.

Gerald R Ford Museum   MUSEUM

(☑616-254-0400; www.fordlibrarymuseum.gov; 303 Pearl St NW; adult/child $8/4; ⊙9am-5pm Mon-Sat, from noon Sun) The downtown museum is dedicated to Michigan's only president. Ford stepped into the Oval Office after Richard Nixon and his vice president, Spiro Agnew, resigned in disgrace. It's a bizarre period in US history, and the museum does an excellent job of covering it, down to displaying the burglary tools used in the Watergate break-in. Ford and wife Betty are buried on the museum's grounds.

Grand Rapids Art Museum   MUSEUM

(☑616-831-1000; www.artmuseumgr.org; 101 Monroe Center St NW; adult/child $10/6; ⊙10am-5pm Tue-Sun, to 9pm Thu) The city's beyond-the-norm art museum fills a sun-drenched building with 19th- and 20th-century works. European and American masters such as Henri de Toulouse-Lautrec and Richard Diebenkorn take pride of place. Free admission on Tuesdays and on Thursday evenings.

🛏 Sleeping & Eating

CityFlats Hotel   HOTEL $$

(☑616-608-1720; www.cityflatshotel.com; 83 Monroe Center St NW; r $155-245; ✱🐾🗢) 🖉 Rooms at this ecofriendly hotel have big windows for lots of natural light, bamboo linens, cork floors and locally made, reclaimed wood furniture. The building is gold-certified by the Leadership in Energy and Environmental Design (LEED) program.

⭐ Green Well   AMERICAN $$

(☑616-808-3566; www.thegreenwell.com; 924 Cherry St SE; mains $16-22; ⊙11am-10pm Sun-Thu, to midnight Fri & Sat) 🖉 Burgers, green curry, and barbecue pork and polenta feature on the gastropub's menu, where everything is made with sustainably farmed ingredients. Beer plays a role in many dishes, such as the beer-steamed mussels and beer cheese. The bar taps hard-to-find Michigan brews and pours Michigan wines (flights available).

🍷 Drinking & Nightlife

Brewery Vivant   BREWERY

(☑616-719-1604; www.breweryvivant.com; 925 Cherry St SE; ⊙3-11pm Mon-Thu, to midnight Fri, 11am-midnight Sat, noon-10pm Sun) 🖉 Brewery Vivant specializes in Belgian-style beers. Set in an old chapel with stained glass and a vaulted ceiling, the atmospheric brewpub also serves locally sourced cheese plates and burgers at farmhouse-style tables.

Founders Brewing Co   BREWERY

(☑616-776-1195; www.foundersbrewing.com; 235 Grandville Ave SW; ⊙11am-2am Mon-Sat, noon-midnight Sun; 🗢) If you've only got time for one stop in Grand Rapids, make it rock-and-roll Founders. The ruby-tinged Dirty Bastard Ale is good swillin', and there's meaty deli sandwiches to soak it up.

ⓘ Information

Grand Rapids CVB (www.experiencegr.com) Has maps and self-guided brewery tour information online.

ⓘ Getting There & Away

Grand Rapids has a decent-sized airport with flights to many US cities. Amtrak trains chug to/from Chicago once daily; the station is downtown near Founders Brewing Co. I-96, I-196 and Hwy 131 are the main roadways to the city.

Gold Coast

They don't call it the Gold Coast for nothing. Michigan's 300-mile western shoreline features seemingly endless stretches of beaches, dunes, wineries, orchards and B&B-filled towns that boom during the summer – and shiver during the snow-packed winter.

Harbor Country

Harbor Country refers to a group of eight small, lake-hugging towns that roll out beaches, wineries, antique shops and all-round rustic charm.

New Buffalo is the largest community, home to a surf shop (you heard that right), a busy public beach, ice-cream shops, a boat-logged marina and a popular farmers market. Three Oaks is the only Harbor community that's inland (6 miles in, via Hwy 12). Here Green Acres meets Greenwich Village in a funky farm-and-arts blend. Cycle by day, then catch a provocative play or art-house flick at the theaters by night. Union Pier, Lakeside, Harbert and Sawyer are some of the other cutesy towns, chock-full of historic inns and galleries.

⦿ Sights & Activities

Warren Dunes   STATE PARK

(☑269-426-4013; 12032 Red Arrow Hwy, Sawyer; per car $9) With 3 miles of beachfront, 6 miles of hiking and cross-country skiing trails, and climbable dunes that rise 260ft in the air, visitors are all over this park. A concession stand offers food, soft drinks, ice cream and souvenirs from May through September. Campsites cost $22 to $37.

Tabor Hill Winery   WINERY
(☑800-283-3363; www.taborhill.com; 185 Mt Tabor Rd, Buchanan; tours free, tastings $9; ◎tours noon-4:30pm, tasting room 12am-5pm Mon-Tues, 11am-6pm Wed-Thurs & Sun, 11am-7pm Fri-Sat) Connoisseurs often regard Tabor Hill Winery as the region's best. The vintner provides tours and lets you belly up in the tasting room for swigs of its blood-red Cabernet Franc and crisp sparkling wines.

Dewey Cannon Trading Company   CYCLING
(☑269-756-3361; www.facebook.com/deweycannontradingcompany; 3 Dewey Cannon Ave, Three Oaks; ◎9am-5pm Tue-Fri, to 7pm Sat, to 3pm Sun, reduced hours Oct-Apr) Rent a two-wheeler (per day $20) in Three Oaks and cycle lightly used rural roads past orchards and wineries. Helmets cost extra.

🛏 Sleeping & Eating

Holiday Inn Express   HOTEL **$$**
(☑269-469-1400; www.ihg.com; 11500 Holiday Dr, New Buffalo; r $95-195) This outpost of the HI chain in New Buffalo is nothing fancy, but it's well maintained and is usually reasonably priced.

Redamak's   BURGERS **$**
(☑269-469-4522; www.redamaks.com; 616 E Buffalo St, New Buffalo; burgers $6-12; ◎noon-10:30pm Mon-Sat, to 10pm Sun Mar–mid-Oct) It's a rightfully lauded, long-standing spot to get a wax-paper-wrapped cheeseburger, spicy curly fries and cold beer in New Buffalo.

ℹ Information

Harbor Country Chamber of Commerce (www.harborcountry.org)

ℹ Getting There & Away

Amtrak stops in New Buffalo. Driving is the only way to reach the other communities. I-94 slices through the region. The Red Arrow Hwy parallels the interstate and connects the communities proper. For reference, the distance between New Buffalo and Sawyer is 10 miles.

Saugatuck & Douglas

Saugatuck is one of the Gold Coast's most popular resort areas, known for its strong arts community, numerous B&Bs and gay-friendly vibe. Douglas is its twin city a mile or so to the south, and they've pretty much sprawled into one. It's a touristy but funky place, with ice-cream-licking families, yuppie boaters and martini-drinking gay couples sharing the waterfront. Galleries and shops fill the compact downtown core. Weekends attract the masses.

◉ Sights & Activities

Antiquing prevails on the Blue Star Hwy running south for 20 miles. Blueberry U-pick farms share this stretch of road and make a juicy stop, too.

Oval Beach   BEACH
(Oval Beach Dr; ◎8am-10pm) Life guards patrol the long expanse of fine sand. There are bathrooms and concession stands, though not enough to spoil the peaceful, dune-laden scene. It costs $8 to park. Or arrive the adventurous way, via chain ferry and a trek over Mt Baldhead.

Mt Baldhead   WALKING
Huff up the stairs of this 200ft-high sand dune for a stellar view. Then race down the other side to Oval Beach. Get here via the chain ferry; walk north from the dock.

Saugatuck Dune Rides   ADVENTURE SPORTS
(☑269-857-2253; www.saugatuckduneride.com; 6495 Blue Star Hwy; adult/child $20/11; ◎10am-7:30pm Jul & Aug, reduced hours May, Jun, Sep & Oct, closed Nov-Apr) The Saugatuck Dune Rides provide 40 minutes of good, cheesy fun zipping over mounds.

🛏 Sleeping & Eating

★Pines Motorlodge   MOTEL **$$**
(☑269-857-5211; www.thepinesmotorlodge.com; 56 Blue Star Hwy; r $139-249; ☎) Retro-cool tiki lamps, pinewood furniture and communal lawn chairs add up to a fun, social ambience amid the firs in Douglas.

Bayside Inn   INN **$$**
(☑269-857-4321; www.baysideinn.net; 618 Water St; r $180-250; ☎) This former boathouse has 10 rooms on Saugatuck's waterfront. All have private bathrooms, decks and DVD players. A big breakfast is included.

Crane's Pie Pantry   BAKERY **$**
(☑269-561-2297; www.cranespiepantry.com; 6054 124th Ave, Fennville; pie slices $4.50; ◎9am-8pm Mon-Thu, to 9pm Fri & Sat, 11am-8pm Sun) Buy a bulging slice, or pick apples and peaches in the surrounding orchards. Crane's is in

Fennville, 3 miles south on the Blue Star Hwy, then 4 miles inland on Hwy 89.

Phil's Bar & Grille AMERICAN $$
(☑269-857-1555; www.philsbarandgrille.com; 215 Butler St; mains $18-29; ⊙11:30am-10:30pm Sun-Thu, to 11pm Fri & Sat) This humming pub turns out terrific broasted (combining broiling and roasting) chicken, fish tacos, lamb lollipops and gumbo.

ℹ Information

Saugatuck/Douglas CVB (www.saugatuck.com) provides maps and more.

ℹ Getting There & Away

Most visitors drive to Saugatuck/Douglas. I-196/Hwy 31 whizzes by to the east, while the Blue Star Hwy goes into both towns. The closest Amtrak station is in Holland, about 12 miles north.

Sleeping Bear Dunes National Lakeshore

Eye-popping lake views from atop colossal sand dunes? Water blue enough to be in the Caribbean? Miles of unspoiled beaches? Secluded islands with mystical trees? All here at Sleeping Bear Dunes, along with lush forests, terrific day hikes and glass-clear waterways for paddling. The national park stretches from north of Frankfort to just before Leland, on the Leelanau Peninsula. Several cute little towns fringe the area.

◉ Sights

Manitou Islands ISLAND
(per family $15) The forest-cloaked Manitou Islands provide an off-the-beaten-path adventure. They're part of Sleeping Bear Dunes National Lakeshore, hence the entrance fee. North Manitou is known for star-speckled backcountry camping, while South Manitou is terrific for wilderness-rich day trips. Kayaking and hiking are the big to-dos, especially the 7-mile trek to the Valley of the Giants, an otherworldly stand of cedar trees on South Manitou. **Manitou Island Transit** (☑231-256-9061; www.manitoutransit.com) runs ferries from Leland; the trip takes 1½ hours.

Tandem Ciders FARM
(☑231-271-0050; www.tandemciders.com; 2055 Setterbo Rd; ⊙noon-6pm Mon-Sat, to 5pm Sun) Near Suttons Bay, Tandem Ciders pours delicious hard ciders in its small tasting room

on the family farm. Tastings cost $2 for three 2oz pours.

 Activities

Dune Climb HIKING
(Hwy 109; ⊙24hr) The Dune Climb is the park's most popular attraction, where you trudge up a 200ft-high dune and then run or roll down. Gluttons for leg-muscle punishment can keep slogging all the way to Lake Michigan, a strenuous 1½-hour trek one-way; bring water. The site, with a parking lot and bathrooms, is on Hwy 109, 5 miles north of Empire.

Pierce Stocking Scenic Drive SCENIC DRIVE
(⊙9am-sunset May–mid-Nov) The 7-mile, one-lane, picnic-grove-studded Pierce Stocking Scenic Drive is perhaps the best way to absorb the stunning lake vistas in Sleeping Bear Dunes. The earlier you go the less traffic you'll encounter. The drive starts 4 miles north of Empire.

Sleeping Bear Heritage Trail HIKING
(www.sleepingbeartrail.org) The 17-mile paved path goes from Empire to Bohemian Rd, passing the Dune Climb along the way; walkers and cyclists are all over it.

Grand Traverse Bike Tours CYCLING
(☑231-421-6815; www.grandtraversebiketours. com; 318 N St Joseph St; ⊙9am-5:30pm Mon-Fri, to 5pm Sat, 10am-4pm Sun) Offers guided rides (four-hour tour is $79) to local wineries, as well as self-guided tours (per person $65) for which staff provide route planning and van pickup of your wine purchases. The shop is in downtown Suttons Bay.

🛏 Sleeping & Eating

The only places to sleep in the park are campgrounds: two on the mainland, and a few more on the Manitou Islands.

Glen Arbor B&B B&B $$
(☑231-334-6789; www.glenarborbnb.com; 6548 Western Ave; r $145-215; ⊙closed mid-Nov–Apr) The owners renovated this century-old farmhouse into a sunny, French country inn with six themed rooms.

Empire Village Inn AMERICAN $
(☑231-326-5101; www.empirevillageinn.com; 11601 S Lacore Rd; mains $9-15; ⊙3-10pm Mon-Thu, 3-11pm Fri, 2-11pm Sat, noon-10pm Sun) Enter the low A-frame building, grab a seat at a scuffed wood table and order one of the

local beers on tap while waiting for your excellent, doughy-crust pizza to arrive. Burgers and sandwiches satisfy too, along with the housemade root beer. It's a swell place to refuel after a day of hiking or biking.

ⓘ Information

Stop at the park's **visitor center** (☑ 231-326-4700; www.nps.gov/slbe; 9922 W Front St; ⊗ 8am-6pm Jun-Aug, 8:30am-4pm Sep-May) in Empire for information, trail maps and vehicle entry permits (week/annual $15/30).

ⓘ Getting There & Away

The park is only accessible by car. Hwy 31 is the main highway to the area. From there make your way onto Hwy 22, which is the road that goes through the park. The nearest airport is in Traverse City.

Traverse City

Michigan's 'cherry capital' is the largest city in the northern half of the Lower Peninsula. It's got a bit of urban sprawl, but it's still a happenin' base from which to see the Sleeping Bear Dunes, Mission Peninsula wineries, U-pick orchards and other area attractions.

⊙ Sights

Road-tripping out to the wineries is a must. Head north from Traverse City on Hwy 37 for 20 miles to the end of the grape- and cherry-planted Old Mission Peninsula. You'll be spoiled for choice.

Peninsula Cellars   WINERY
(☑ 231-933-9787;   www.peninsulacellars.com; 11480 Center Rd; ⊗ 10am-6pm) Located in an old schoolhouse, Peninsula makes fine whites and is often less crowded than other wineries. A five-wine tasting costs $5.

🛏 Sleeping & Eating

Mitchell Creek Inn   MOTEL $$
(☑ 231-947-9330; www.mitchellcreek.com; 894 Munson Ave; r/cabins from $65/125; 🐾) This humble, 15-room property is on the other side of Hwy 31 (away from the water), moderately priced and near the state park beach. It's a classic mom-and-pop operation, with basic, tidy, motel-like rooms.

Sugar Beach Resort   HOTEL $$
(☑ 231-938-0100; www.tcbeaches.com; 1773 US 31 N; r $150-250; ❋🐾🏊) Sugar Beach has decent prices and it's right on the water. Rooms are nothing fancy, but they're well

maintained and have small refrigerators, coffee makers and microwave ovens. Many have been renovated recently and have new furnishings.

Folgarelli's   DELI $
(☑ 231-941-7651; www.folgarellis.net; 424 W Front St; sandwiches $8-11; ⊗ 9:30am-6:30pm Mon-Fri, to 5:30pm Sat, 11am-4pm Sun) After a day of fun in the sun, refresh with sandwiches at gastronome favorite Folgarelli's.

North Peak Brewing Company   PUB FOOD $$
(☑ 231-941-7325; www.northpeak.net; 400 W Front St; mains $10-20; ⊗ 11am-11pm Mon-Thu, to midnight Fri & Sat, noon-10pm Sun) Munch pizzas, mussels and pretzel-crusted walleye with the housemade suds.

ⓘ Information

Traverse City Tourism (www.traversecity.com)

ⓘ Getting There & Away

Traverse City's small airport has several daily flights to Chicago, Detroit and Minneapolis. Hwy 31 is the main highway to town.

Charlevoix & Petoskey

These two towns hold several Hemingway sights. They're also where Michigan's upper-crusters maintain summer homes. The downtown areas of both places have gourmet restaurants and high-class shops, and the marinas are filled with yachts.

A number of writers have ties to northwest Michigan, but none are as famous as Ernest Hemingway, who spent the summers of his youth at his family's cottage on Walloon Lake. Hemingway buffs often tour the area to view the places that made their way into his writing. Key sites:

A short distance north of Charlevoix, Boyne City Rd veers off to the east. It skirts Lake Charlevoix and eventually arrives at Horton Bay. Hemingway fans will recognize the **Horton Bay General Store** (☑ 231-582-7827; www.hortonbaygeneralstore.com; 5115 Boyne City Rd; ⊗ 8am-2pm Sun-Thu, 8am-2pm & 5-9pm Fri & Sat, closed mid-Oct–mid-May), with its 'high false front,' from his short story 'Up in Michigan.' The old-time shop now sells groceries, souvenirs, sandwiches and ice cream, plus wine and tapas on weekend nights (reservations required for the latter).

Further north on Hwy 31, stop in Petoskey to see the Hemingway collection at the

Little Traverse History Museum (☏231-347-2620; www.petoskeymuseum.org; 100 Depot Ct; $3; ◷10am-4pm Mon-Sat, closed mid-Oct–late May), including rare first-edition books that the author autographed for a friend when he visited in 1947.

A few blocks from the museum, toss back a drink at the **City Park Grill** (☏231-347-0101; www.cityparkgrill.com; 432 E Lake St; ◷11:30am-9pm Sun-Thu, to 1:30am Fri & Sat) where Hemingway was a regular.

Tour Hemingway's Michigan (www.mihemingwaytour.com) provides further information for self-guided jaunts.

Budget and midrange chain hotels dot Hwy 31 and Hwy 131 leading into Petoskey. Charlevoix has several small inns and motels; see www.visitcharlevoix.com for listings.

Petoskey features foodie cafes, gastropubs, cozy bistros and ethnic eats in its walkable downtown. Charlevoix has high-quality eateries too, but it's a bit more spread out and adds chain restaurants to the mix. Prices are mid- to high range.

The **Beaver Island Ferry** (☏231-547-2311; www.bibco.com; 103 Bridge Park Dr; ◷mid-Apr–late Dec) departs from downtown Charlevoix for the green isle (www.beaverisland.org) in Lake Michigan. The two-hour journey costs $32.50/105 one-way per person/car. Reserve ahead if bringing a car.

Straits of Mackinac

This region, between the Upper and Lower Peninsulas, features a long history of forts and fudge shops. Car-free Mackinac Island is Michigan's premier tourist draw.

One of the most spectacular sights in the area is the 5-mile-long Mackinac Bridge (known locally as 'Big Mac'), which spans the Straits of Mackinac. The $4 toll is worth every penny as the views from the bridge, which include two Great Lakes, two peninsulas and hundreds of islands, are second to none in Michigan. And remember: despite the spelling, it's pronounced *mac*-in-aw.

Mackinaw City

At the south end of Mackinac Bridge, bordering I-75, is touristy Mackinaw City. It serves mainly as a jumping-off point to Mackinac Island, but it does have a couple of intriguing historic sights.

◉ Sights

Colonial Michilimackinac   HISTORIC SITE
(☏231-436-5564; www.mackinacparks.com; 102 W Straits Ave; adult/child $12/7; ◷9am-7pm Jun-Aug, to 5pm May & Sep–mid-Oct; ♿) Next to the Big Mac bridge (its visitor center is actually beneath the bridge) is Colonial Michilimackinac, a National Historic Landmark that features a reconstructed stockade first built in 1715 by the French. Costumed interpreters cook and craft here.

Historic Mill Creek   HISTORIC SITE
(☏231-436-4226; www.mackinacparks.com; 9001 W US 23; adult/child $9/6; ◷9am-6pm Jun-Aug, to 5pm May & Sep–mid-Oct; ♿) The site has an 18th-century sawmill where costumed interpreters chop wood, plus historic displays, a zipline and nature trails.

❶ Getting There & Away

I-75 is the main road to Mackinaw City. The docks for **Star Line** (☏800-638-9892; www.mackinacferry.com; 801 S Huron Ave; adult/child/bicycle $26/14/10) and **Shepler's** (☏800-828-6157; www.sheplersferry.com; 556 E Central Ave; adult/child/bicycle $26/14/10) are a short distance off the interstate. Both send ferries to Mackinac Island. The trip takes 20 minutes; boats go at least hourly during daylight hours. Both companies having free parking lots in which to leave your car.

St Ignace

At the north end of Mackinac Bridge is St Ignace, one of the departure points for Mackinac Island and the second-oldest settlement in Michigan – Père Jacques Marquette founded a mission here in 1671. The small town is a good place to get organized for onward road-tripping into the Upper Peninsula.

Budget motels and midrange hotels (mostly chains) are chockablock on N State St as it unfurls through town along the water. Expect to pay at least $100 per night.

Whitefish, pizza and fudge are the town's staples. Midrange restaurants line N State St, the main commercial thoroughfare that hugs the lake.

❶ Getting There & Away

I-75 is the main vein to St Ignace. The docks for **Star Line** (☏800-638-9892; www.mackinacferry.com; 587 N State St; adult/child/bicycle $26/14/10) and **Shepler's** (☏800-828-6157; www.sheplersferry.com; 601 N State St; adult/

child/bicycle $26/14/10) are a stone's throw from the interstate. Both send ferries to Mackinac Island. The trip takes 20 minutes; boats go at least hourly during daylight hours. You can leave your car in the companies' parking lots for free.

Mackinac Island

From either Mackinaw City or St Ignace you can catch a ferry to Mackinac Island. The island's location in the straits between Lake Michigan and Lake Huron made it a prized port in the North American fur trade, and a site the British and Americans battled over many times.

The most important date on this 3.8-sq-mile island was 1898 – the year cars were banned in order to encourage tourism. Today all travel is by horse or bicycle; even the police use bikes to patrol the town. The crowds of tourists – called Fudgies by the islanders – can be crushing at times, particularly during summer weekends. But when the last ferry leaves in the evening and clears out the day-trippers, Mackinac's real charm emerges and you drift back into another, slower era. Eighty percent of the island is state parkland. Not much stays open between November and April.

◎ Sights

Arch Rock NATURAL FEATURE

FREE This huge limestone arch curves 150ft above Lake Huron and provides dramatic photo opportunities. You can get here two ways: from stairs that lead up from the lakeshore road, or from the island's interior via Arch Rock Rd.

Fort Mackinac HISTORIC SITE

(☑ 906-847-3328; www.mackinacparks.com; 7127 Huron Rd; adult/child $13/7.50; ⊙ 9:30am-6pm Jun-Aug, to 5pm May & Sep–mid-Oct; ⏴) Fort Mackinac sits atop limestone cliffs near downtown. Built by the British in 1780, it's one of the best-preserved military forts in the country. Costumed interpreters and cannon and rifle firings (every half-hour) entertain the kids. Stop into the tearoom for a bite and million-dollar view of downtown and the Straits of Mackinac.

Fort Holmes FORT

(⊙ 10am-5pm May–mid-Oct) **FREE** British forces built the small wood and earth fort in 1814 to protect against a US attack during the War of 1812. This is a replica, as the original structure fell into ruin eons ago. It doesn't take long to poke around. Better than the fort itself is the view. The site sits on the island's highest point and unfurls awesome views out over the Straits of Mackinac.

⫬ Activities

Edging the island's shoreline is Hwy 185 (aka Lake Shore Rd), the only Michigan highway that doesn't permit cars. The best way to view the incredible scenery along this 8-mile road is by bicycle; bring your own or rent one for $9 per hour at one of the many businesses. You can loop around the flat road in an hour.

🛏 Sleeping & Eating

Bogan Lane Inn B&B $$

(☑ 906-847-3439; www.boganlaneinn.com; Bogan Lane; r $95-140) It's a bit fusty, but Bogan Lane has some of the island's lowest rates and is one of the few lodgings to stay open all year round. The four rooms share two bathrooms in the 1850s house. It's a bit off the beaten path, about 10 minutes' walk from downtown and the ferry docks.

Hart's Inn B&B $$

(☑ 906-847-6234; www.hartsmackinac.com; 7556 Market St; r $150-215; ⊙ mid-May–late Oct) Hart's is right downtown in a single-story, white-clapboard building akin to a quaint motel. There are nine smallish rooms, each with its own bathroom. Guests often relax on the garden-surrounded patio.

Chuckwagon DINER $

(☑ 906-847-0019; www.chuckwagononmackinac. com; 7400 Main St; mains $7-12; ⊙ 7am-3pm) You'll need to fuel up for the day's bike explorations, and the cowboy-themed Chuckwagon is the place to do it. Grab a stool at the counter and watch the cooks slinging eggs, hash browns, bacon and pancakes for breakfast (until 11am only) and burgers and sandwiches for lunch. The no-frills diner is tiny and crowded, but worth the wait.

ⓘ Information

Mackinac Island Visitor Center (☑ 906-847-3783; www.mackinacisland.org; 7274 Main St; ⊙ 9am-5pm May-Oct) Downtown booth with maps for hiking and cycling.

ⓘ Getting There & Away

Two ferry companies – **Shepler's** (☑ 800-828-6157; www.sheplersferry.com) and **Star Line** (☑ 800-638-9892; www.mackinacferry.com) – operate out of Mackinaw City and St Ignace, and charge roughly the same rates: round-trip adult/child/bicycle $26/14/10. Book online and you'll save a few bucks. The ferries run several times daily from May through October. The trip takes about 20 minutes. Both companies have free parking lots to leave your car.

Upper Peninsula

Rugged and isolated, with hardwood forests blanketing 90% of its land, the Upper Peninsula (UP) is a Midwest highlight. Only 45 miles of interstate highway slice through the trees, punctuated by a handful of cities, of which Marquette is the largest. Between the small towns lie miles of undeveloped shoreline on Lakes Huron, Michigan and Superior; scenic two-lane roads; and pasties, the local meat-and-vegetable pot pies brought over by Cornish miners 150 years ago.

You'll find it's a different world up north. Residents of the UP, aka 'Yoopers,' consider themselves distinct from the rest of the state – they've even threatened to secede in the past.

Sault Ste Marie

Founded in 1668, Sault Ste Marie (Sault is pronounced 'soo') is Michigan's oldest city and the third oldest in the USA. Today it's a busy port and border crossing to Canada, where twin city Sault Ste Marie, Ontario, winks across the bridge.

◉ Sights

Soo Locks Visitor Center MUSEUM
(☑906-253-9290; Portage Ave; ◷9am-9pm mid-May–mid-Oct) **FREE** Sault Ste Marie is best known for its locks that raise and lower 1000ft-long freighters between the different lake levels. The downtown visitor center features displays, videos and observation decks from which you can watch the boats leap 21ft from Lake Superior to Lake Huron. To get there take exit 394 off I-75 and go left.

🛏 Sleeping & Eating

Askwith Lockview Motel MOTEL $
(☑906-632-2491; www.lockview.com; 327 W Portage Ave; r $85-99; ◷May–mid-Oct; ❋🐾) Choose from rooms in the classic, two-story motel or in the line of single-story, attached cottages. The unfussy interiors are similar: flowery bedspreads, TV and mini refrigerator in a relatively tight space, but they're neat and tidy and right across from the Soo Locks.

**Karl's Cuisine,
Winery & Brewery** AMERICAN $$
(☑906-0253-1900; www.karlscuisine.com; 447 W Portage Ave; mains $16-24; ◷11am-4pm Mon & Tue, to 9pm Wed-Sat) 🐾 The menu at convivial Karl's spans pasties (beef or chicken plus veggies baked in a crust), maple-planked Lake Superior whitefish, burgers, sandwiches, stromboli and pasta dishes. The common thread is the use of local and responsibly sourced ingredients. Vegetarian and gluten-free diners will find lots of options. The family-run establishment even makes its own beer, wine and cider.

ⓘ Getting There & Away

I-75 is the main interstate to Sault Ste Marie. The town has a small airport with daily flights to Detroit. The International Bridge links Sault St Marie to its twin city in Canada; the border crossing is open 24/7.

Pictured Rocks National Lakeshore

Stretching along prime Lake Superior real estate, Pictured Rocks National Lakeshore is a series of wild cliffs and caves where blue and green minerals have streaked the red and yellow sandstone into a kaleidoscope of color. Rte 58 (Alger County Rd) spans the park for 52 slow miles from Grand Marais in the east to Munising in the west. Top sights (from east to west) include Au Sable Point Lighthouse (reached via a 3-mile round-trip walk beside shipwreck skeletons), agate-strewn Twelvemile Beach, hike-rich Chapel Falls and view-worthy Miners Castle Overlook. Boat rides and kayak trips along the shore are an excellent way to absorb the dramatic scenery.

Kayaking is popular in Pictured Rocks and no wonder, given that you paddle beneath sheer, color-stained bluffs with names like Lovers Leap, Flower Vase and Caves of the Bloody Chiefs. The duck's-eye view of the geologic features is awesome. Experienced paddlers can go it alone, but conditions are often wavy and windy. Newbies should hook up with a guide. Several operate out of Munising, offering trips from just a few hours to all day. **Pictured Rocks Kayaking** (☑906-387-5500; www.paddlepicturedrocks.com; 1348 Commercial St; 4½hr tours adult/child $135/95; ◷late May-Sep) has good trips for beginners.

Munising has heaps of motels, with many located on Hwy 28 a few miles southeast of town. See www.munising.org for listings.

Tiny Grand Marais, on the park's east side, also has motels, though fewer than Munising. Prices are budget range, but creep up during July and August.

Marquette, 40 miles west, offers the closest airport. Hwys 28 and 94 are the primary roads to the area.

Marquette

Lakeside Marquette is the perfect place to stay put for a few days to explore the region. It's the Upper Peninsula's largest (and snowiest) town, known as a hot spot for outdoors enthusiasts. Forests, beaches and cliffs provide a playground spitting distance from downtown. Locals ski in winter and hit the trails with their fat-tire bikes in summer. Northern Michigan University is here, so the population skews young. Beer and good food await in the historic town center.

◉ Sights & Activities

Da Yoopers Tourist
Trap and Museum   MUSEUM
(☑906-485-5595; www.dayoopers.com; 490 N Steel St; ☺10am-6pm Mon-Fri, to 5pm Sat & Sun) **FREE** Behold Big Gus, the world's largest chainsaw. And Big Ernie, the world's largest rifle. Kitsch runs rampant at Da Yoopers Tourist Trap and Museum, 15 miles west of Marquette on Hwy 28/41, past Ishpeming.

Presque Isle Park   PARK
(Peter White Dr) In the city, on a peninsula jutting out into Lake Superior, the high bluffs of Presque Isle Park make a great place to catch the sunset.

Down Wind Sports   KAYAKING
(☑906-226-7112; www.downwindsports.com; 514 N 3rd St; ☺10am-7pm Mon-Fri, to 5pm Sat, 11am-3pm Sun) Rents all kinds of gear and has the lowdown on kayaking, fly fishing, surfing, ice climbing and other adventures.

🛏 Sleeping & Eating

Landmark Inn   HISTORIC HOTEL $$
(☑906-228-2580; www.thelandmarkinn.com; 230 N Front St; r $179-229; ❄🐾) The elegant, six-story Landmark fills a historic lakefront building and has a couple of resident ghosts.

Jean Kay's Pasties & Subs   SANDWICHES $
(☑906-228-5310; www.jeankayspasties.com; 1635 Presque Isle Ave; items $5-8; ☺11am-9pm Mon-Fri, to 8pm Sat & Sun) Sample the local meat-and-veggie pie specialty at Jean Kay's.

WORTH A TRIP

TAHQUAMENON FALLS STATE PARK

Lovely Tahquamenon Falls inside **Tahquamenon Falls State Park** (☑906-492-3415; Hwy 123; per vehicle $9), east of Sault Ste Marie, flow with tea-colored waters tinted by upstream hemlock leaves. The Upper Falls, 200ft across with a 50ft drop, wow onlookers – including Henry Wadsworth Longfellow, who mentioned them in his *Song of Hiawatha*. The Lower Falls (about 5 miles northeast) are a series of small cascades that swirl around an island; many visitors rent a rowboat and paddle out to it. The large state park also has camping (tent and RV sites $17 to $25), great hiking and – bonus – a brewpub near the park entrance.

Thill's Fish House   SEAFOOD $
(☑906-226-9851; 250 E Main St; items $4-9; ☺8am-5:30pm Mon-Fri, 9am-4pm Sat) Buy fresh-caught trout or whitefish in various forms (smoked, pickled, sausage) right on the dock. Thill's is Marquette's last commercial fishing operation, and it hauls in fat catches daily. It's set in a Quonset hut at Main St's foot.

ℹ Information

Stop at the log-lodge **visitor center** (2201 US 41; ☺9am-5:30pm) at the edge of town for brochures on local hiking trails and waterfalls.

ℹ Getting There & Away

Hwys 41 and 28 are the main roadways to town. Marquette has a small airport with flights to Detroit, Chicago and Minneapolis.

Isle Royale National Park

Totally free of vehicles and roads, Isle Royale National Park, a 210-sq-mile island in Lake Superior, is certainly the place to go for peace and quiet. It gets fewer visitors in a year than Yellowstone National Park gets in a day, which means the 1600 moose creeping through the forest are all yours.

The island is laced with 165 miles of hiking trails that connect dozens of campgrounds along Superior and inland lakes. You must be totally prepared for this wilderness adventure, with a tent, camping stove, sleeping bags, food and water filter. The park is open from mid-April through October, then it closes due to extreme weather.

Isle Royale offers two options: snooze at **Rock Harbor Lodge** (📞906-337-4993; www.rockharborlodge.com; r & cottages $224-256; ☺late May-early Sep), the only accommodation for softies, or hike to the rustic campgrounds with outhouses that dot the island. FYI, there's no extra fee for camping. It's covered in the $7 per day park entrance fee.

The lodge has two eateries: a dining room serving American fare for breakfast, lunch and dinner, and a more casual cafe for burgers, sandwiches, coffee and beer. The Dockside Store at Rock Harbor stocks a small array of groceries. There's another small store in Windigo on the island's other side.

ℹ Information

Isle Royale Park Headquarters (📞906-482-0984; www.nps.gov/isro; 800 E Lakeshore Dr; ☺8am-6pm Mon-Fri, from 10am Sat Jun–mid-Sep, 8am-4pm Mon-Fri mid-Sep–May) The park headquarters in Houghton provides information on entrance fees (per person per day $7), ferries, camping etc.

ℹ Getting There & Away

From the dock outside the park headquarters in Houghton, the **Ranger III** (📞906-482-0984; www.nps.gov/isro; 800 E Lakeshore Dr; ☺late May-early Sep) departs at 9am on Tuesday and Friday for the six-hour boat trip (round-trip adult/child $126/46) to Rock Harbor, at the east end of the island.

Isle Royale Seaplanes (📞906-483-4991; www.isleroyaleseaplanes.com; 21125 Royce Rd) offers a quicker trip, flying from the Portage Canal Seaplane Base in Hancock to Rock Harbor or to Windigo (on the island's west end) in 35 minutes (round-trip $320).

Or head 50 miles up the Keweenaw Peninsula to Copper Harbor (a beautiful drive) and jump on the **Isle Royale Queen** (📞906-289-4437; www.isleroyale.com; 14 Waterfront Landing) for the 8am three-hour crossing (round-trip adult/child $136/76) to Rock Harbor. It runs daily during peak season from late July through August.

Bringing a kayak or canoe on the ferries costs an additional $50 round-trip. Ensure you make reservations for any of the transportation methods well in advance. You can also access Isle Royale from Grand Portage, MN.

Porcupine Mountains Wilderness State Park

Michigan's largest state park, with 90 miles of trails, is a wilderness winner. 'The Porkies,' as they're called, are so rugged that loggers bypassed most of the range in the early 19th century, leaving the park with the largest tract of virgin forest between the Rocky Mountains and Adirondacks. Along with 300-year-old hemlock trees, the Porkies are known for waterfalls, 20 miles of undeveloped Lake Superior shoreline, black bears lumbering about and the view of the park's stunning Lake of the Clouds.

Rustic cabins and campgrounds are available in the park. Otherwise budget motels and pricier lodges dot Hwy 64 between the wee towns of Silver City and Ontonagon.

◉ Sights & Activities

Lake of the Clouds   LAKE
(Hwy 107) The lake is the area's most photographed sight. After stopping at the visitor center to pay the park entrance fee (per car $9), continue to the end of Hwy 107 and climb 300ft via a short path for the stunning view of the shimmering water. Lengthier trails depart from the parking lot.

Porcupine Mountain Ski Area   SKIING
(📞906-885-5209;   www.porkiesfun.com; ☺Dec-early Apr) Winter is a busy time here, with downhill skiing (a 787ft vertical drop) and 26 miles of cross-country trails on offer. Conditions and costs vary, so call before heading out.

ℹ Information

Porcupine Mountains and Ontonagon Area CVB (www.porcupineup.com) List of waterfalls and activities.

Porcupine Mountains Visitor Center (📞906-885-5275; www.mi.gov/porkies; 412 S Boundary Rd; ☺8am-6pm mid-May–mid-Oct) The state park visitor center is where you buy vehicle entry permits (per day/year $9/32) and backcountry camping permits (one to four people per night $15).

ℹ Getting There & Away

You'll need a car to get here. Hwy 45 is the main highway to the area.

WISCONSIN

Wisconsin is cheesy and proud of it. The state pumps out 2.5 billion pounds of cheddar, Gouda and other smelly goodness – a quarter of America's hunks – from its cow-speckled farmland per year. Local license plates read 'The Dairy State' with udder dignity. Folks here even refer to themselves as 'cheeseheads' and emphasize it by wearing novelty foam rubber cheese-wedge hats for special occasions (most notably during Green Bay Packers football games).

So embrace the cheese thing, because there's a good chance you'll be here for a while. Wisconsin has a ton to offer: exploring the craggy cliffs and lighthouses of Door County, kayaking through sea caves at Apostle Islands National Lakeshore, cow chip throwing along Hwy 12 and soaking up beer, art and festivals in Milwaukee and Madison.

❶ Information

Wisconsin Department of Tourism (www. travelwisconsin.com) Produces tons of free guides on subjects like biking, golf and rustic roads; also has a free app.
Wisconsin B&B Association (www.wbba.org)
Wisconsin Highway Conditions (www.511wi.gov)
Wisconsin Milk Marketing Board (www. eatwisconsincheese.com) Provides a free statewide map of cheesemakers titled *A Traveler's Guide to America's Dairyland*.
Wisconsin State Park Information (☏608-266-2181; www.dnr.wi.gov/topic/parks) Park entry requires a vehicle permit (per day/year $11/38). Campsites cost from $21 to $35; reservations (☏888-947-2757; www.wisconsin stateparks.reserveamerica.com; fee $10) accepted.

Milwaukee

Here's the thing about Milwaukee: it's cool, but for some reason it slips under the radar. The city's reputation as a working man's town of brewskis, bowling alleys and polka halls still persists. But attractions like the Calatrava-designed art museum, badass Harley-Davidson Museum and stylish eating and shopping enclaves have turned Wisconsin's largest city into an unassumingly groovy place. In summertime, festivals let loose with revelry by the lake almost every weekend. And where else on the planet will you see racing sausages?

History

Milwaukee was first settled by Germans in the 1840s. Many started small breweries, but a few decades later the introduction of bulk brewing technology turned beer production into a major industry here. Milwaukee earned its 'Brew City' and 'Nation's Watering Hole' nicknames in the 1880s when Pabst, Schlitz, Blatz, Miller and 80 other breweries made suds here. Today, only Miller remains of the big brewers, though microbreweries have made a comeback.

◉ Sights & Activities

Lake Michigan sits to the east of the city, and is rimmed by parkland. The Riverwalk path runs along both sides of the Milwaukee River downtown.

★**Harley-Davidson Museum** MUSEUM
(☏414-287-2789; www.h-dmuseum.com; 400 W Canal St; adult/child $20/10; ⊙9am-6pm Fri-Wed, to 8pm Thu May-Sep, from 10am Oct-Apr) Hundreds of motorcycles show the styles through the decades, including the flashy rides of Elvis and Evel Knievel. You can sit in the saddle of various bikes (on the bottom floor, in the Experience Gallery) and take badass photos. Even non-bikers will enjoy the interactive exhibits and leather-clad crowds.

Harley-Davidson Plant FACTORY
(☏877-883-1450; www.harley-davidson.com/experience; W156 N9000 Pilgrim Rd; ⊙9am-1:30pm Mon-Fri) Hog-heads can get a fix at the plant where engines are built, in suburban Menomonee Falls. The factory offers two options for tours: a free, 30-minute jaunt where you see a video and take a quick walk onto the factory floor, and a two-hour tour (per person $38) where you don safety glasses and check out the assembly line, powder-coat process and other in-depth engine-making activities.

The long tours leave at 10am and noon, and are best booked in advance. The shorter tours are walk-in only, with tickets given out on a first-come, first-served basis, so it's wise to arrive early. No children under age 12 allowed. Follow the Harley signs in from Pilgrim Rd, then look for the Tour Center signs.

Milwaukee Art Museum MUSEUM
(☏414-224-3200; www.mam.org; 700 N Art Museum Dr; adult/child $17/free; ⊙10am-5pm Tue-Sun, to 8pm Thu) You have to see this lakeside institution, which features a stunning

DON'T MISS

THE BRONZE FONZ

Rumor has it the Bronze Fonz, on the east side of Riverwalk, just south of Wells St downtown, is the most photographed sight in Milwaukee. The Fonz, aka Arthur Fonzarelli, was a character from the 1970s TV show *Happy Days*, which was set in the city. What do you think – do the blue pants get an 'Aaay' or 'Whoa!'?

winglike addition by Santiago Calatrava. It soars open and closed every day at 10am, noon and 5pm (8pm on Thursday), which is wild to watch; head to the suspension bridge outside for the best view. There are fabulous folk and outsider art galleries, and a sizeable collection of Georgia O'Keeffe paintings. A 2015 renovation added photography and new media galleries to the trove.

Miller Brewing Company   BREWERY
(📞 414-931-2337; www.millercoors.com; 4251 W State St; ⏰ 10:30am-4:30pm Mon-Sat, to 3:30pm Sun Jun-Aug, to 3:30pm Mon-Sat Sep-May) FREE Founded in 1855, the historic Miller facility preserves Milwaukee's beer legacy. Join the legions lined up for the free, hour-long tours. Though the mass-produced beer may not be your favorite, the factory impresses with its sheer scale: you'll visit the packaging plant where 2000 cans are filled each minute, and the warehouse where a half-million cases await shipment. And then there's the generous tasting session at the tour's end, where you can down three full-size samples. Don't forget your ID.

Lakefront Brewery   BREWERY
(📞 414-372-8800;   www.lakefrontbrewery.com; 1872 N Commerce St; ⏰ 11am-8pm Mon-Thu, to 9pm Fri, 9am-9pm Sat, 10am-5pm Sun) Well-loved Lakefront Brewery, across the river from Brady St, has afternoon tours, but the swellest time to visit is on Friday nights when there's a fish fry, 16 beers to try and a polka band letting loose. Tour times vary throughout the week, but there's usually at least a 2pm and 3pm walk-through (and often many more).

Discovery World at
Pier Wisconsin   MUSEUM
(📞 414-765-9966; www.discoveryworld.org; 500 N Harbor Dr; adult/child $19/16; ⏰ 9am-4pm Mon-Fri, 10am-5pm Sat & Sun, closed Mon Sep-Mar; 👶) The

city's lakefront science and technology museum is primarily a kid-pleaser, with freshwater and saltwater aquariums (where you can touch sharks and sturgeon) and a dockside, triple-masted Great Lakes schooner to ogle (two-hour sailing tour per adult/child $45/40). Adults will appreciate the Les Paul exhibit, showcasing the Wisconsin native's pioneering guitars and sound equipment.

Landmark Lanes   BOWLING
(📞 414-278-8770; www.landmarklanes.com; 2220 N Farwell Ave; per game $3.50-4; ⏰ 5pm-midnight Mon-Thu, noon-1am Fri & Sat, noon-midnight Sun) Milwaukee once had more than 200 bowling alleys, and many retro lanes still hide in timeworn dives. To get your game on try Landmark Lanes, offering 16 beat-up alleys in the historic 1927 Oriental Theater. An arcade, three bars and cheap beer round out the atmosphere.

🎉 Festivals & Events

Summerfest   MUSIC
(www.summerfest.com; 639 E Summerfest Pl; day pass $20; ⏰ late Jun–early Jul) It's dubbed 'the world's largest music festival,' and indeed hundreds of rock, blues, jazz, country and alternative bands swarm its 11 stages over 11 days. The scene totally rocks; it is held at downtown's lakefront festival grounds (aka Henry Maier Festival Park). The headline concerts cost extra.

PrideFest   LGBT
(www.pridefest.com; 639 E Summerfest Pl; day pass $15-18; ⏰ mid-Jun) Beer drinking, live music, a dance pavilion and family stage are all part of the festivities, which take place over three days in mid-June at Henry Maier Festival Park.

🛏 Sleeping

County Clare Irish Inn   INN $$
(📞 414-272-5273; www.countyclare-inn.com; 1234 N Astor St; r $129-149; 🅿❄🛜) It's a winner near the lakefront. Rooms have that snug Irish-cottage feel, with four-poster beds, white wainscot walls and Jacuzzis. There's free parking, free breakfast and an on-site Guinness-pouring pub, of course.

⭐ **Brewhouse Inn & Suites**   HOTEL $$
(📞 414-810-3350; www.brewhousesuites.com; 1215 N 10th St; r $199-249; 🅿❄@🛜) This 90-room hotel sits in the exquisitely renovated old Pabst Brewery complex. Each of the large chambers has steampunk decor, a

kitchenette and free wi-fi. Continental breakfast is included. It's at downtown's far west edge, about a half-mile walk from sausagey Old World 3rd St and a good 2 miles from the festival grounds. Parking costs $28.

Kimpton Journeyman
HOTEL $$$

(☎414-291-3970; www.journeymanhotel.com; 310 E Chicago St; r $219-349; P❄☎☎) The new Journeyman brings stylish digs to the heart of the Third Ward, right in the midst of cool-cat shops, bars and restaurants. The 158 large rooms have mod, earth-toned decor with pops of color, comfy beds and chunky wood desks. A rooftop lounge, free loaner bicycles and a free wine happy hour each evening add to the pleasure. Parking is $33.

Eating

Good places to scope for eats include Germanic Old World 3rd St downtown; hip, multi-ethnic Brady St by its intersection with N Farwell Ave; and the gastropub-filled Third Ward, anchored along N Milwaukee St south of I-94.

★ Comet Cafe
AMERICAN $

(☎414-273-7677; www.thecometcafe.com; 1947 N Farwell Ave; mains $8-13; ◷10am-midnight Mon-Fri, from 9am Sat & Sun; 🖊) Students, young families, older couples and bearded, tattooed types pile in to the rock-and-roll Comet for gravy-smothered meatloaf, mac 'n' cheese, vegan gyros and hangover brunch dishes. It's a craft-beer-pouring bar on one side, and retro-boothed diner on the other. Be sure to try one of the giant cupcakes for dessert.

Milwaukee Public Market
MARKET $

(☎414-336-1111; www.milwaukeepublicmarket.org; 400 N Water St; ◷10am-8pm Mon-Fri, 8am-7pm Sat, 10am-6pm Sun; 🖊) Located in the Third Ward, the market's vendors sell cheese, chocolate, beer, tacos, frozen custard and more. Take them upstairs where there are tables, free wi-fi and $1 used books.

Bavette La Boucherie
AMERICAN $

(☎414-273-3375; www.bavettelaboucherie.com; 330 E Menomonee St; mains $12-16; ◷11am-5pm Mon & Tue, to 9pm Wed-Sat) This hip industrial space in the Third Ward is a butcher shop with a cafe that serves lunch and dinner. It stacks a meaty sandwich, such as the roast pork with rhubarb-raisin compote and the seared steak with truffled mushroom sauce. Locals come in to nibble on charcuterie and cheese plates alongside lovely wines. Sit at the bar and you'll see sausage-making.

Ardent
AMERICAN $$$

(☎414-897-7022; www.ardentmke.com; 1751 N Farwell St; tasting menu $85; ◷6-10pm Wed-Sat) Milwaukee's foodies get weak-kneed when they sniff the Beard-nominated chef's ever-changing, farm-to-table dishes. Dinner is a lingering affair in the tiny glowing room, with two seatings each night for the 10-course tasting menu. Reserve well in advance. Or head next door to Ardent's sibling restaurant, open 6pm to 1am Wednesday to Saturday, for slurpable bowls of ramen noodles ($13).

🍷 Drinking & Entertainment

Vermutería 600
COCKTAIL BAR

(☎414-488-9146; www.hotelmadridmke.com/bar; 600 S 6th St; ◷5pm-midnight) The bar at

FISH FRIES & SUPPER CLUBS

Wisconsin has two dining traditions that you'll likely encounter when visiting the state:

Fish Fry Friday is the hallowed day of the 'fish fry.' This communal meal of beer-battered cod, French fries and coleslaw came about years ago, providing locals with a cheap meal to socialize around and celebrate the workweek's end. The convention is still going strong at many bars and restaurants, including Lakefront Brewery in Milwaukee.

Supper Club This is a type of time-warped restaurant common in the upper Midwest. Supper clubs started in the 1930s, and most retain a retro vibe. Hallmarks include a woodsy location, a radish-and-carrot-laden relish tray on the table, a surf-and-turf menu and a mile-long, unironic cocktail list. See www.wisconsinsupperclubs.net for more information. The Old Fashioned (p608) in Madison is a modern take on the venue (it's named after the quintessential, brandy-laced supper-club drink).

DON'T MISS

RACING SAUSAGES

It's common to see strange things after too many stadium beers. But a group of giant sausages sprinting around Miller Park's perimeter – is that for *real*? It is if it's the middle of the 6th inning. That's when the famous 'Racing Sausages' (actually five people in costumes) waddle onto the field to give the fans a thrill. If you don't know your encased meats, that's Brat, Polish, Italian, Hot Dog and Chorizo vying for supremacy.

the Hotel Madrid is a warm, magical space that transports you to 1930s Spain. It serves cocktails inspired by what Ernest Hemingway and pals were drinking when they stayed at the famed Hotel Florida in Madrid back then – say, the Boulevardier (with bourbon, house-made vermouth and bitters). Small-plate snacks are available, or there's an upscale Spanish restaurant on site.

Best Place BAR

(☑ 414-630-1609; www.bestplacemilwaukee.com; 901 W Junau Ave; ☺ noon-6pm Mon, noon-10pm Wed & Thu, 10:30am-5pm Fri & Sat, 10:30am-6pm Sun) Join the locals knocking back beers and massive whiskey pours at this small tavern in the former Pabst Brewery headquarters. A fireplace warms the cozy, dark-wood room; original murals depicting Pabst's history adorn the walls. Staff give daily tours of the building ($8, including a 16oz Pabst or Schlitz tap brew).

Miller Park BASEBALL

(☑ 414-902-4000; www.brewers.com; 1 Brewers Way) The Brewers play baseball at fab Miller Park, which has a retractable roof and real grass. The Racing Sausages star in the middle of the sixth inning. To the uninitiated, that's five people in foam-rubber meat costumes who dash around the ball field's perimeter in a madcap foot race.

The stadium is about 5 miles west of downtown. The Brewers Line bus runs there on game days; pick it up along Wisconsin Ave.

❶ Information

Milwaukee Convention & Visitors Bureau
(☑ 800-554-1448, www.visitmilwaukee.org)

❶ Getting There & Around

General Mitchell International Airport (MKE; www.mitchellairport.com; 5300 S Howell Ave)

is 8 miles south of downtown. Take public bus 80 ($2.25) or a cab ($33).

The **Lake Express ferry** (☑ 866-914-1010; www.lake-express.com; 2330 S Lincoln Memorial Dr; one way per adult/child/car from $91.50/35/101; ☺ May-Oct) sails from downtown (the terminal is located a few miles south of the city center) to Muskegon, Michigan, providing easy access to Michigan's beach-lined Gold Coast.

Several bus companies use the **Milwaukee Intermodal Station** (433 St Paul Ave). Badger Bus (www.badgerbus.com) goes to Madison ($20, two hours) eight times per day. Greyhound (www.greyhound.com) and Megabus (www.megabus.com/us) run frequent buses to Chicago (two hours) and Minneapolis (6½ to seven hours).

Amtrak (www.amtrakhiawatha.com) runs the Hiawatha train seven times a day to/from Chicago ($25, 1½ hours). It also uses the Milwaukee Intermodal Station.

The Milwaukee County Transit System (www.ridemcts.com) provides the local bus service. Bus 31 goes to Miller Brewery; the Brewers Line bus goes to Miller Park on game days. Fare is $2.25.

Bublr Bikes (www.bublrbikes.com) is Milwaukee's bikeshare program, with 60 or so stations scattered around downtown (including at the train/bus depot) and north to the University of Wisconsin-Milwaukee. A 30-minute ride costs $3.

A new streetcar is slated to start service in fall 2018. The route will go through the Third Ward and heart of downtown. See www.themilwaukee streetcar.com for updates.

For taxi service, try **Yellow Cab** (☑ 414-271-1800, www.ycmilwaukee.com).

Racine

Racine is an unremarkable industrial town, but it has some key Frank Lloyd Wright sights. What's more, it's a prime place to sample the mega-sized state pastry known as the kringle.

❍ Sights

SC Johnson Administration Building & Research Tower ARCHITECTURE

(☑ 262-260-2154; www.scjohnson.com/visit; 1525 Howe St; ☺ tours 10am & 2pm Thu-Sun Mar-Dec) FREE Frank Lloyd Wright designed several buildings at the company's headquarters. Free 90-minute tours take in the 1939 Admin Building, a magnificent space with tall, flared columns in its vast Great Workroom and 43 miles' worth of Pyrex glass-tube windows letting in soft natural light. You'll also see the 1950 Research Tower – where Raid, Off and other famous products were developed –

which features 15 floors of curved brick bands and more Pyrex windows.

Wingspread ARCHITECTURE

(☑262-681-3353; www.scjohnson.com/visit; 33 E Four Mile Rd; ⊙9:30am-3:30pm Wed-Fri, 11:30am-3:30pm Sat, noon-2:30pm Sun Mar-Dec) **FREE** Wingspread is the house Frank Lloyd Wright designed for HF Johnson Jr, one of the SC Johnson company's leaders. It is the last and largest of Wright's Prairie-style abodes, completed in 1939. It's enormous, with 500 windows and a 30ft-high chimney. Free tours through the building take one hour, and they must be booked in advance.

ⓘ Getting There & Away

I-94 runs to Racine, which is 30 miles south of Milwaukee and 75 miles north of Chicago.

South Central Wisconsin

This part of Wisconsin has some of the prettiest landscapes in the state. Architecture fans can be unleashed at Taliesin, *the* Frank Lloyd Wright sight. Madison is the area's cultural jewel.

Green County

This pastoral area holds the nation's greatest concentration of cheesemakers. As you're road-tripping through you can stop at local dairy farms and shops and learn your artisanal from farmstead, Gruyere from Gouda, curd from whey. Why so cheesy here? It has to do with the limestone-rich soil. It grows distinctive grass, which makes distinctive food for cows, and that results in distinctive milk that creates distinctive cheese. Got it? Old World Europeans did, particularly the Swiss. They flocked to the region in the 1800s, bringing their cheesemaking skills with them.

Two good pit stops are Monroe, the biggest town and county seat, filled with cheese history and limburger taverns, and New Glarus, a Swiss town with a renowned brewery.

Monroe and New Glarus each have a couple of midrange motels. B&Bs pop up in various little towns.

You'll mostly find pub food, pizza parlors and restaurants serving Swiss specialties (cheese fondue, sausages etc).

ⓘ Information

Green County Tourism (www.greencounty.org)

A Traveler's Guide to America's Dairyland (www.eatwisconsincheese.com) Good map showing local dairy producers and plant tours.

ⓘ Getting There & Away

Madison is the closet urban area and transportation hub. From there you'll need a car to access Green County. Hwy 69 is a main artery connecting Madison, New Glarus and Monroe. Most roads in the region are slowpoke, two-lane byways.

Madison

Madison reaps a lot of kudos – most walkable city, best road-biking city, most vegetarian-friendly, gay-friendly, environmentally friendly and just plain all-round friendliest city in the USA. Ensconced on a narrow isthmus between Mendota and Monona Lakes, it's a pretty combination of small, grassy state capital and liberal, bookish college town. An impressive foodie/locavore scene has been cooking here for years.

⊙ Sights & Activities

★**Dane County Farmers Market** MARKET

(www.dcfm.org; ⊙6am-2pm Sat late Apr–early Nov) On Saturdays, a food bazaar takes over Capitol Sq. It's one of the nation's most expansive markets, famed for its artisanal cheeses and breads. Craft vendors and street musicians add to the festivities. In winter the market moves indoors to varying locations on Wednesdays.

Monona Terrace ARCHITECTURE

(☑608-261-4000; www.mononaterrace.com; 1 John Nolen Dr; ⊙8am-5pm) Frank Lloyd Wright designed this cool, white semicircular structure in 1938, though it wasn't completed until 1997. The one-hour tours ($5) explain why; they're offered daily at 1pm May through October (Friday through Monday only the rest of the year). The building serves as a community center, offering free lunchtime yoga classes and evening concerts. Check the schedule online.

Chazen Museum of Art MUSEUM

(☑608-263-2246; www.chazen.wisc.edu; 750 University Ave; ⊙9am-5pm Tue, Wed & Fri, to 9pm Thu, 11am-5pm Sat & Sun) **FREE** The university's art museum is huge and fabulous, and way beyond the norm for a campus collection. The 3rd floor holds most of the genre-spanning trove: everything from the Old Dutch Masters to Qing Dynasty porcelain vases,

Picasso sculptures and Andy Warhol pop art. Free chamber-music concerts and art-house films take place on Sundays from September to mid-May.

Museum of Contemporary Art MUSEUM
(☑608-257-0158; www.mmoca.org; 227 State St; ⊙noon-5pm Tue-Thu, to 8pm Fri, 10am-8pm Sat, noon-5pm Sun) FREE It's worth popping into the angular glass building to see what's showing. Frank Stella prints? Claes Oldenburg etchings? Cindy Sherman photos? Exhibits change every three months or so. It doesn't take long to look through the small museum.

State Capitol NOTABLE BUILDING
(☑608-266-0382; www.legis.wisconsin.gov; 2 E Main St; ⊙8am-6pm Mon-Fri, to 4pm Sat & Sun) FREE The X-shaped capitol is the largest outside Washington, DC, and marks the heart of downtown. Tours are available on the hour most days, or you can go up to the observation deck on your own for a view.

Machinery Row CYCLING
(☑608-442-5974; www.machineryrowbicycles.com; 601 Williamson St; rental per day $30; ⊙10am-8pm Mon-Fri, 9am-7pm Sat, 10am-6pm Sun) It'd be a shame to leave town without taking advantage of the city's 120 miles of bike trails. Get wheels and maps at this shop, located by various trailheads.

★ Festivals & Events

World's Largest Brat Fest FOOD & DRINK
(www.bratfest.com; ⊙late May) FREE More than 209,000 bratwursts go down the hatch; carnival rides and bands provide the backdrop. It's held at Willow Island at the Alliant Energy Center.

Great Taste of the Midwest Beer Festival BEER
(www.greattaste.org; tickets $60; ⊙early Aug) Tickets sell out fast for this festival where more than 150 craft brewers pour their elixirs. It's held in Olin Park.

🛏 Sleeping

HI Madison Hostel HOSTEL $
(☑608-441-0144; www.hiusa.org/madison; 141 S Butler St; dm $25-30, r from $60; P@🖳) The brightly painted, 33-bed brick house is located on a quiet street a short walk from the State Capitol. Dorms are gender segregated; linens are free. There's a kitchen and common room with DVDs. Parking is $7.

Graduate Madison BOUTIQUE HOTEL $$
(☑608-257-4391; www.graduatemadison.com; 601 Langdon St; r $119-209; P❋🖳🐾) A block from campus and right off State St's action, this 72-room hotel wafts a hip academic vibe with its mod-meets-plaid decor and book-themed artwork. Rooms are on the small side and can be a bit noisy, but the location rocks.

A cool little pie cafe/coffee bar offers treats downstairs, while the 17th-floor rooftop bar pours cocktails.

🍴 Eating & Drinking

A global smorgasbord of restaurants peppers State St amid the pizza, sandwich and cheap-beer joints; many places have inviting patios. Cruising Williamson ('Willy') St turns up cafes, dumpling bars and Lao and Thai joints.

Bars stay open to 2am. State St has the mother lode, with scruffy drinkeries preferred by guzzling university students, as well as natty cocktail lounges.

Weary Traveler Free House INTERNATIONAL $
(☑608-442-6207; www.wearytravelerfreehouse.com; 1201 Williamson St; mains $10-14; ⊙11:30am-2am) Old-style speakeasy meets UK pub at the Weary Traveler. The low lighting, dark wood decor, art-filled walls and myriad board games complement the menu of global comfort foods. Top marks go to the Reuben sandwich, vegan chili, Hungarian goulash and walleye sandwich with killer roasted potatoes. Everything on tap is local and/or craft brewed.

Short Stack Eats BREAKFAST $
(☑608-709-5569; www.shortstackeats.com; 301 W Johnson St; mains $8-13; ⊙6am-3pm Wed, 6am-midnight Thu-Sat, midnight-9pm Sun) 🌱 It's all breakfast all day and all night at Short Stack. Order at the counter, then hopefully find a free table amid the cutesy, mismatched decor. Staff use old license plates as table markers to bring your locally sourced sweet potato pancakes, egg-and-bacon-filled breakfast sandwiches and enormous, spicy Bloody Marys.

★ The Old Fashioned AMERICAN $$
(☑608-310-4545; www.theoldfashioned.com; 23 N Pinckney St; mains $9-20; ⊙7:30am-2am Mon-Fri, 9am-2am Sat, 9am-10pm Sun) With its dark, woodsy decor, the Old Fashioned evokes a supper club, a type of retro eatery common in Wisconsin. The menu is all local specialties, including walleye, cheese soup and

WORTH A TRIP

ODDBALL HIGHWAY-12

Unusual sights huddle around Hwy 12 in south-central Wisconsin, all within a 55-mile span:

National Mustard Museum (☎800-438-6878; www.mustardmuseum.com; 7477 Hubbard Ave, Middleton; ⊙10am-5pm, closed Tue Jan-Mar) **FREE** Born of one man's ridiculously intense passion, the museum houses 5200 mustards and kooky condiment memorabilia. Tongue-in-cheek humor abounds, especially if CMO (chief mustard officer) Barry Levenson is there to give you the shtick. It's located in Middleton, a short distance northwest of Madison.

Cow Chip Throw (www.wiscowchip.com; Grand Ave & First St, Prairie du Sac; ⊙1st weekend Sep) If it's the first weekend in September, stop at the town of Prairie du Sac. It hosts the annual Cow Chip Throw, where 800 competitors fling dried manure patties as far as the eye can see; the record is 248ft.

Dr Evermor's Sculpture Park (☎608-219-7830; www.worldofdrevermor.com; Hwy 12; ⊙11am-5pm Mon & Thu-Sat, from noon Sun) **FREE** The doc has welded old pipes, carburetors and other salvaged metal into a hallucinatory world of futuristic birds, dragons and other bizarre structures. The crowning glory is the giant, egg-domed Forevertron, once cited by Guinness World Records as the globe's largest scrap-metal sculpture. Finding the park entrance is tricky. It is behind Delaney's Surplus on US 12; look for a small road just south of Delaney's leading in. Hours can be erratic, so call to confirm it's open. The doc is in poor health and isn't around much now, but his wife Lady Eleanor usually is.

Wisconsin Dells (☎800-223-3557; www.wisdells.com; Hwy 12; ☝) The Dells is a megacenter of kitschy diversions, including 20-plus water parks, water-skiing thrill shows and epic mini-golf courses. It's a jolting contrast to the natural appeal of the area, with its scenic limestone formations carved by the Wisconsin River. To appreciate the original attraction, take a boat tour or walk the trails at nearby Mirror Lake or Devil's Lake state parks.

sausages. It's hard to choose among the 150 types of state-brewed suds in bottles, so opt for a sampler (four or eight little glasses) from the 50 Wisconsin tap beers.

L'Etoile AMERICAN **$$$**
(☎608-251-0500; www.letoile-restaurant.com; 1 S Pinckney St; mains $36-48; ⊙5:30-9pm Tue-Fri, from 5pm Sat) 🖉 L'Etoile started doing the farm-to-table thing more than three decades ago. It's still the best in the biz, offering creative meat, fish and vegetable dishes, all sourced locally and served in a casually elegant room. Reserve in advance. The gastropub Graze (☎608-251-2700; www.grazemadison.com; mains $14-22; ⊙11am-10pm Mon-Thu, 11am-11pm Fri, 9:30am-11pm Sat, 9:30am-3pm Sun) shares the glimmering building.

★ Memorial Union PUB
(☎608-265-3000; www.union.wisc.edu/visit/memorial-union; 800 Langdon St; ⊙7am-midnight Mon-Fri, 8am-1am Sat, to midnight Sun; 🛜) The campus Union is Madison's gathering spot. The festive lakeside terrace pours microbrews and hosts free live music and free Monday-night films, while the indoor ice-cream shop scoops hulking cones from the university dairy.

ℹ Information

Madison Convention & Visitors Bureau (www.visitmadison.com)

ℹ Getting There & Away

Badger Bus (www.badgerbus.com) has a streetside stop on campus at 700 Langdon St (next to the Memorial Union) for trips to/from Milwaukee ($20, two hours). Megabus (www.megabus.com/us) uses the same stop for trips to Chicago (four hours) and Minneapolis (five hours).

Spring Green

Spring Green is a tiny town with big culture. Taliesin is here, Frank Lloyd Wright's ballyhooed home and architectural school. The respected American Players Theatre is also here, staging classics outdoors amid the trees. And the House on the Rock is a short distance down the road, offering enough whimsy for a lifetime.

◉ Sights

Taliesin   ARCHITECTURE

(☑ 608-588-7900;   www.taliesinpreservation.
org; 5607 County Rd C; ⊗ 9am-5:30pm May-Oct)
Taliesin was the home of Frank Lloyd Wright
for most of his life and is the site of his architectural school. It's now a major pilgrimage
destination for fans. The house was built
in 1903, the Hillside Home School in 1932,
and the visitor center in 1953. A wide range
of guided tours ($22 to $89) cover various
parts of the complex; it's wise to book ahead
(for a small surcharge). The one-hour Hillside Tour ($22) provides a nice introduction
to Wright's work.

Note the visitor center (with its restaurant
and shop) is in a separate location about a
half-mile from the main estate.

House on the Rock   MUSEUM

(☑ 608-935-3639;   www.thehouseontherock.com;
5754 Hwy 23; adult/child $15/9; ⊗ 9am-5pm May-
mid-Oct, Thu-Mon only mid-Oct–Nov & mid-Mar–
Apr, closed mid-Nov–mid-Mar) One of Wisconsin's busiest attractions. Alex Jordan built
the structure atop a rock column in 1959
(some say as an 'up yours' to neighbor Frank
Lloyd Wright). He then stuffed the house
to mind-blowing proportions with wonder-
ments, including the world's largest carousel, whirring music machines, freaky dolls
and crazed folk art. The house is broken into
three parts, each with its own tour. Visitors
with stamina (and about four hours to kill)
can experience the whole shebang for adult/
child $30/16.

⌖ Sleeping & Eating

Usonian Inn   MOTEL $

(☑ 608-588-2323; www.usonianinn.com; E 5116 US
14; r $100-135; ✿ 🔊) Designed by one of Frank
Lloyd Wright's students, the 11-room Usonian is a fairly basic motel, but with dapper,
Prairie-style touches in the lamps, woodwork and other decor. Each room has a little
patio with chairs.

---

❶ ROAD-TRIP THE MISSISSIPPI

If you're thinking of taking to the road,
have a look at the Wisconsin Great River
Road website (www.wigrr.com). It suggests lots of activities, lodging and places to eat along the Mississippi River.

Spring Green General Store   AMERICAN $

(☑ 608-588-7070; www.springgreengeneralstore.
com; 137 S Albany St; mains $7-9; ⊗ 8:30am-5pm
Mon-Fri, 7:30am-5pm Sat, to 4pm Sun) Chomp
sandwiches or inventive specials like
sweet-potato stew. You can eat 'em at the
sturdy wood tables in the bright-painted interior, or outside on the porch.

☆ Entertainment

American Players Theatre   THEATER

(☑ 608-588-2361; www.americanplayers.org; 5950
Golf Course Rd) It stages classical productions
at an outdoor amphitheater in the woods.
Bring a picnic – it's a tradition to hang out
and nibble before the show.

❶ Getting There & Away

Hwy 14 is the main road to town. Taliesin is 3
miles south of town via Hwy 23. The House on
the Rock is 7 miles further south.

Southwest Wisconsin

Southwest Wisconsin brings on swooping
green hills and button-cute towns with
tree-shaded streets. Two-lane byways dip
and curve through the region, revealing eating hot spots around many a bend.

The Mississippi River forms the southwest's border, and alongside it run some of
the prettiest sections of the Great River Road
– the designated route that follows Old Man
River throughout its 2300-mile flow. Top
stops along the water include Stockholm
(pie), Pepin (for Laura Ingalls Wilder fans),
Nelson (cheese and ice cream), La Crosse
(history and culture) and Potosi (beer).

Road-tripping inland turns up bike trails
in Sparta, organic farms and round barns in
Viroqua, and a Frank Lloyd Wright sight in
Richland Center.

◉ Sights

Laura Ingalls Wilder Museum   MUSEUM

(☑ 715-513-6383; www.lauraingallspepin.com; 306
3rd St, Pepin; adult/child $5/2; ⊗ 10am-5pm mid-
May–mid-Oct) *Little House on the Prairie*
fans can make a pit stop at the Laura Ingalls
Wilder Museum. This is where she was born
and the abode that starred in *Little House in
the Big Woods*. There's not a lot in the museum (and the building itself is a replica),
but die-hards will appreciate being on the
authentic patch of land once homesteaded
by Ma and Pa Ingalls.

Eating

**★ Stockholm Pie &
General Store** BAKERY $

(📞715-442-5505; www.stockholmpieandgeneral
store.com; N2030 Spring St, Stockholm; slices $6;
⊙10am-4:30pm Mon & Thu, to 5pm Fri-Sun) You
may have to wait in line at this old-timey
spot with wood plank floors and red-check-
ered tablecloths, but that allows you to study
the blackboard and its lengthy list of pies
available. Sour cream raisin, double lemon,
triple chocolate pecan, butterscotch cream –
they're all world class.

Eastern Wisconsin

The eastern part of the state is a holiday
favorite thanks to its miles of craggy shoreline for boating, swimming and fishing, its
beaming lighthouses and its atmospheric maritime communities. Lonely islands,
meals of fiery fish and football shrines all
await, and there's always a lake or forest
nearby for a nature fix.

Green Bay

Green Bay is a modest industrial town best
known as the fabled 'frozen tundra' where
the Green Bay Packers win Super Bowls. The
franchise is unique as the only community-
owned nonprofit team in the NFL; perhaps
pride in ownership is what makes the fans
so die-hard (and also makes them wear
foam-rubber cheese wedges on their heads).

While tickets are nearly impossible to
obtain, you can always get into the spirit by
joining a pregame tailgate party. The generous flow of alcohol has led to Green Bay's
reputation as a 'drinking town with a football problem.' Otherwise the town is pretty
quiet. It has a couple of intriguing museums
and a well-known brewery by the stadium,
plus a nice patch of cafes on its riverfront.

⊙ Sights

Green Bay Packers Hall of Fame MUSEUM
(📞920-569-7512; www.lambeaufield.com; 1265
Lombardi Ave; adult/child $15/12; ⊙9am-6pm
Mon-Sat, 10am-5pm Sun) The two-floor Hall of
Fame at Lambeau Field is packed with memorabilia, shiny trophies and movies about
the storied NFL team that'll intrigue any
football fan. Stadium tours are also available. Lots of new development is going on
around the arena, including a snow-tubing
hill, ice-skating pond and flashy new hotel.

National Railroad Museum MUSEUM
(📞920-437-7623; www.nationalrrmuseum.org;
2285 S Broadway; adult/child $10/7.50; ⊙9am-
5pm Mon-Sat, 11am-5pm Sun, closed Mon Jan-Mar;
🚼) The museum features some of the biggest locomotives ever to haul freight into
Green Bay's vast yards; train rides ($2) are
offered in summer.

❶ Getting There & Away

Green Bay has a small airport with flights to
Chicago, Minneapolis, Detroit and Atlanta.
Greyhound has a station in town. I-43 comes
into Green Bay from the east. I-41 comes in from
the west.

Door County

With its rocky coastline, picturesque lighthouses, cherry orchards and small 19th-cen-
tury villages, you have to admit Door County
is pretty damn lovely. Honeymooners, families and outdoorsy types all flock in to take
advantage of the parkland that blankets the
area and the clapboard hamlets packed with
winsome cafes, galleries and inns.

The county spreads across a narrow peninsula jutting 75 miles into Lake Michigan.
The side that borders the lake proper is
known as the more scenic 'quiet side,' home
to the communities of Jacksonport and Bai-
leys Harbor. The side that borders Green
Bay is more action oriented, where Egg Harbor, Fish Creek, Ephraim and Sister Bay welcome travelers. Summer is prime time. Only
about half the businesses stay open from
November to April.

⊙ Sights & Activities

Cave Point County Park PARK
(5360 Schauer Rd) FREE Nature is pretty
amazing, you think as you watch waves explode into the caves beneath the shoreline
cliffs. Shutterbugs can get great photos here.
The hiking and biking paths take you to
gorgeous vistas. Bonus: Cave Point is more
off the beaten path and less visited than its
state park siblings. It's also free.

Newport State Park STATE PARK
(475 County Rd NP; per vehicle $11) Newport is
one of Door County's quietest parks, tucked
away at the peninsula's northern fringe. It
has a beautiful beach, 30 miles of hiking
trails (about half of which double as off-road
bike trails) and year-round, walk-in-only
camping in forested seclusion.

Bay Shore Outfitters OUTDOORS
(☑920-854-9220; www.kayakdoorcounty.com;
2457 S Bay Shore Dr, Sister Bay) Rents kayaks,
stand-up paddleboards and winter gear and
offers a variety of kayak tours (from $45 per
two-hour trip).

🛏 Sleeping & Eating

Egg Harbor Lodge INN $$
(☑920-868-3115; www.eggharborlodge.com; 7965
Hwy 42, Egg Harbor; r $170-210; ✳☎✖) Rooms
are good-sized and have a water view. Amen-
ities include a small outdoor pool, indoor
Jacuzzi and patio area prime for sunset
watching. No children allowed.

Julie's Park Cafe and Motel MOTEL $$
(☑920-868-2999; www.juliesmotel.com; 4020
Hwy 42, Fish Creek; r $125-139; ✳☎✖) Julie's is
a great low-cost option located beside Peninsula State Park. The rooms are nothing
fancy, but they're well maintained and have
comfy beds. The attached cafe serves eggs,
sandwiches and burgers all day.

Wild Tomato PIZZA $
(☑920-868-3095; www.wildtomatopizza.com;
4023 Hwy 42, Fish Creek; mains $9-17; ⊙11am-
10pm Jun-Aug, reduced hours Sep-May) Join the
crowds indoors and out munching pizzas
from the stone, wood-fired ovens. A lengthy
list of craft beers help wash it down. It's extremely gluten-free friendly.

❶ Information

Door County Visitors Bureau (www.door
county.com) has special-interest brochures on
art galleries, biking and lighthouses.

WORTH A TRIP

SCENIC DRIVE: HIGHWAY 13

Hwy 13 moseys through a pretty landscape between Bayfield and Superior.
Toward the east it routes around the
Lake Superior shore, past the Chippewa
community of **Red Cliff** and the Apostle Islands' mainland segment, which
has a beach. Tiny **Cornucopia**, looking
every bit like a seaside village, has great
sunsets. Toward the west the road runs
through a timeless countryside of forest
and farm. See www.lakesuperiorbyway.
org for more.

---

❶ Getting There & Away

You'll need a car to get to Door County. Two
small highways serve the peninsula. Hwy 57 runs
beside Lake Michigan, while Hwy 42 moseys beside Green Bay (the body of water, not the city).
Be prepared for heavy traffic on weekends.

Northern Wisconsin

The north is a thinly populated region of
forests and lakes, where folks paddle and
fish in summer, and ski and snowmobile in
winter. Mountain-biking trails continue to
expand and draw fat tires. Nicolet National
Forest and Chequamegon National Forest
protect much of the area and provide the
playground for these activities. But it's the
windswept Apostle Islands that really steal
the show.

Apostle Islands

The 21 rugged Apostle Islands, floating in
Lake Superior and freckling Wisconsin's
northern tip, are a state highlight. Forested and windblown, trimmed with cliffs
and caves, the national park gems have no
facilities. Various companies offer seasonal
boat trips around the islands, and kayaking
and hiking are very popular. Jump off from
Bayfield, a humming resort town with hilly
streets, Victorian-era buildings, apple orchards and nary a fast-food restaurant in
sight.

◉ Sights & Activities

No wonder everyone is grabbing a paddle.
Kayaking in the Apostles pays off big in
scenery, with stacks of dusty red rock arches
and pillars rising from the water. Caves on
the craggy shores of Devils Island and Sand
Island are stars of the show. Note that much
of the kayaking here is for experienced paddlers only; novices should go with a guide,
as conditions can be rough and windy. The
national park publishes a *Paddling in the
Apostles* brochure with information on kayak launch points and tips on how to prepare.
Bayfield has outfitters and guides, such as
Living Adventure.

Madeline Island ISLAND
(www.madeleineisland.com) Inhabited Madeline
Island makes a fine day trip and is reached
by a 25-minute ferry from Bayfield. The isle's
walkable village of La Pointe has a couple
of mid-priced places to stay, a smattering

of eateries and a groovy 'burned down' bar (made from junk and tarps). Bike and moped rentals are available – everything is near the ferry dock. While Madeline is an Apostle Island, it's not part of the national park group, hence its development.

Big Bay State Park STATE PARK
(☑ 715-747-6425; Hagen Rd; per car $11, tent sites $25-35) Big Bay is at Madeline Island's far edge, with a pretty beach and hiking trails. The well-maintained campsites are awesome and book up fast.

Living Adventure KAYAKING
(☑ 715-779-9503; www.livingadventure.com; 88260 Hwy 13; half-/full-day tour $59/109; ⊙ Jun-Sep) Offers guided paddling trips to sea caves and shipwrecks; beginners are welcome. The company also rents kayaks (per one/two days $69/99) and provides shuttle service to launch sites.

🛏 Sleeping

Camping permits (per night $15) are required for the national park islands. You must get them in advance online (www.recreation.gov; reservation fee $10).

Bayfield loads up on tidy motels, B&Bs and swanky inns. Madeline Island has a handful of inns and cottages.

Seagull Bay Motel MOTEL $
(☑ 715-779-5558; www.seagullbay.com; 325 S 7th St; r $110-130; 🖥) The no-frills rooms may be smallish and thin-walled, but most have a little patio or deck with lake views (ask when booking). A nifty trail runs from the motel to downtown, a 10-minute walk away.

🍴 Eating

Fat Radish AMERICAN $$
(☑ 715-779-9700; www.thefatradish.weebly.com; 200 Rittenhouse Ave; sandwiches $7-10, mains $16-24; ⊙ 9am-3pm & 5-9pm Mon-Sat, 9am-2pm Sun, closed Mon in winter) 🥬 The Radish uses quality, sustainable ingredients in its deli wares. It's located by the docks and handy for amassing snacks to take on the boat tours. At night the chef serves tasty pizzas and seafood dishes.

Maggie's AMERICAN $$
(☑ 715-779-5641; www.maggies-bayfield.com; 257 Manypenny Ave; mains $11-22; ⊙ 11:30am-9pm) Kitschy, flamingo-themed Maggie's is the place to sample local lake trout and white-fish; there are pizza and burgers too.

CHEQUAMEGON NATIONAL FOREST
....
Chequamegon National Forest offers exceptional mountain biking with 300 miles of off-road trails. The Chequamegon Area Mountain Bike Association (www.cambatrails.org) has trail maps and bike rental information. The town of Hayward makes an excellent base and is near several trailheads.

ℹ Information

Apostle Islands National Lakeshore Visitors Center (☑ 715-779-3397; www.nps.gov/apis; 410 Washington Ave; ⊙ 8am-4:30pm late May–Sep, closed Sat & Sun rest of year) Has camping, paddling and hiking information.
Bayfield Chamber of Commerce (www.bayfield.org) Good listings of lodgings and things to do in the area.

ℹ Getting There & Away

The **Madeline Island Ferry** (☑ 715-747-2051; www.madferry.com; Washington Ave; round trip adult/child/bicycle/car $14/7/7/25) makes the 25-minute trip from Bayfield to Madeline Island. It goes year-round, except when the water freezes (usually between January and March, when there is an ice bridge). Apostle Island Cruises drops off kayakers at various islands. Experienced paddlers kayak out to some of the closer islands.

MINNESOTA

Is Minnesota really the land of 10,000 lakes, as it's so often advertised? You betcha! Actually, in typically modest style, the state has undermarketed itself – there are 11,842 lakes. Which is great news for travelers. Intrepid outdoors folk can wet their paddles in the Boundary Waters, where nighttime brings a blanket of stars and the lullaby of wolf howls. Those wanting to get further off the beaten path can journey to Voyageurs National Park, where there's more water than roadway. If that all seems too far-flung, stick to the Twin Cities of Minneapolis and St Paul, where you can't swing a moose without hitting something cool or cultural. For those looking for middle ground the dramatic, freighter-filled port of Duluth beckons.

❶ Information

Minnesota Highway Conditions (www.511mn. org)

Minnesota Office of Tourism (www.explore minnesota.com)

Minnesota State Park Information (☎888-646-6367; www.dnr.state.mn.us) Park entry requires a vehicle permit (per day/year $5/25). Campsites cost $15 to $31; reservations (☎866-857-2757; www.dnr.state.mn.us/state_parks/reservations.html) accepted for an $8.50 fee online, $10 by phone.

Minneapolis

Minneapolis is the biggest and artiest town on the prairie, with all the trimmings of progressive prosperity – swank art museums, rowdy rock clubs, organic and ethnic eateries and edgy theaters. It's always happenin', even in winter. And here's the bonus: folks are attitude-free and the embodiment of 'Minnesota Nice.' Count how many times they tell you to 'Have a great day,' come rain or shine or snow.

History

Timber was the city's first boom industry, and water-powered sawmills rose along the Mississippi River in the mid-1800s. Wheat from the prairies also needed to be processed, so flour mills churned into the next big business. The population boomed in the late 19th century with mass immigration, especially from Scandinavia and Germany. Today Minneapolis' Nordic heritage is evident, whereas twin city St Paul is more German and Irish-Catholic.

PRINCE WAS HERE

Minneapolis' most famous former resident is the rock star Prince. Even before his shocking death in 2016, visitors flocked to town to follow his trail. The city's tourism bureau has a map of Prince hot spots, including his childhood home, the house from *Purple Rain* and **Paisley Park** (www.officialpaisleypark. com; 7801 Audubon Rd, Chanhassen; tours from $38.50, service fee $7.50; ☉Thu-Sun), his famed home/recording studio. For more check out www.minneapolis.org/princes-minneapolis.

◉ Sights & Activities

Most attractions are closed Monday; many stay open late on Thursday.

◉ Downtown & Loring Park

★**Walker Art Center**　　　　MUSEUM
(☎612-375-7600; www.walkerart.org; 1750 Hennepin Ave; adult/child $14/free; ☉11am-5pm Tue, Wed & Sun, to 9pm Thu, to 6pm Fri & Sat) The first-class art center has a strong permanent collection of 20th-century art and photography, including big-name US painters and great US pop art. On Monday evenings from late July to late August, the museum hosts free movies and music across the pedestrian bridge in Loring Park that are quite the to-do.

★**Minneapolis Sculpture Garden** GARDENS
(725 Vineland Pl; ☉6am-midnight) **FREE** This 19-acre green space, studded with contemporary works such as the oft-photographed *Spoonbridge & Cherry* by Claes Oldenburg, sits beside the Walker Art Center. The Cowles Conservatory, abloom with exotic hothouse flowers, is also on the grounds.

◉ Riverfront District

★**Endless Bridge**　　　　OBSERVATORY
(818 2nd St S; ☉8am-8pm, to 11pm on performance days) **FREE** Head inside the cobalt-blue Guthrie Theater and make your way up the escalator to the Endless Bridge, a far-out cantilevered walkway overlooking the Mississippi River. You don't need a theater ticket, as it's intended as a public space. The theater's 9th-floor Amber Box provides another knockout view.

Mill City Museum　　　　MUSEUM
(☎612-341-7555; www.millcitymuseum.org; 704 2nd St S; adult/child $12/6; ☉10am-5pm Tue-Sat, noon-5pm Sun) The building is indeed a former mill, and highlights include a ride inside an eight-story grain elevator (the 'Flour Tower'), Betty Crocker exhibits and a baking lab. It's not terribly exciting unless you're really into milling history, though the mill ruins in back are an atmospheric sight. A foodie-favorite farmers market takes place in the attached train shed on Saturday mornings May through September.

St Anthony Falls Heritage Trail　　WALKING
The 1.8-mile path provides both interesting history (placards dot the route) and the city's best access to the banks of the Mississippi

MINNEAPOLIS FOR CHILDREN

Minnesota Zoo (☎952-431-9500; www.mnzoo.org; 13000 Zoo Blvd; adult/child $18/12; ☺9am-6pm summer, to 4pm winter; 🚼) You'll have to travel a way to get to the respected zoo in suburban Apple Valley, which is 20 miles south of town. It has naturalistic habitats for its 400-plus species, with an emphasis on cold-climate creatures. Parking is $7.

Valleyfair (☎952-445-7600; www.valleyfair.com; 1 Valleyfair Dr; per person $53; ☺from 10am Jun-Aug, reduced hours Sep & Oct; 🚼) If the rides at the Mall of America aren't enough, drive out to this full-scale amusement park 22 miles southwest in Shakopee. The animatronic dinosaur park ($5 extra) is a big hit. Save money by booking tickets online. Parking costs $12.

Children's Theatre Company (☎612-874-0400; www.childrenstheatre.org; 2400 3rd Ave S; 🚼) This local troupe is so good it won a Tony award for 'outstanding regional theater.' The production values are first-rate.

River. It starts at the foot of Portland Ave and goes over the car-free Stone Arch Bridge, from which you can view cascading St Anthony Falls.

◉ Northeast

Once a working-class Eastern European neighborhood, Northeast (so named because of its position to the river) is where urbanites and artists now work and play. They appreciate the dive bars pouring microbrews along with Pabst, and boutiques selling eco-gifts next to companies grinding sausage. Hundreds of craftsfolk and galleries fill historic industrial buildings. They fling open their doors the first Thursday of each month when the Northeast Minneapolis Arts Association (www.nemaa.org) sponsors a gallery walk. Heady streets include 4th St NE and 13th Ave NE.

◉ University Area

The University of Minnesota, by the river southeast of Minneapolis' center, is one of the USA's largest campuses, with some 50,000 students. Most of the campus is in the East Bank neighborhood. Dinkytown, based at 14th Ave SE and 4th St SE, is dense with student cafes and bookshops. A small part of the university is on the West Bank of the Mississippi River, near the intersection of 4th St S and Riverside Ave. This area has a few restaurants, some student hangouts and a big Somali community.

★ **Weisman Art Museum**   MUSEUM
(☎612-625-9494; www.wam.umn.edu; 333 E River Rd; ☺10am-5pm Tue, Thu & Fri, to 8pm Wed, 11am-5pm Sat & Sun) FREE The Weisman, which occupies a swooping silver structure by archi-

tect Frank Gehry, is a university highlight. The airy main galleries hold cool collections of 20th-century American art, ceramics, Korean furniture and works on paper.

◉ Uptown, Lyn-Lake & Whittier

★ **Minneapolis Institute of Arts**   MUSEUM
(☎612-870-3131; www.artsmia.org; 2400 3rd Ave S; ☺10am-5pm Tue, Wed & Sat, 10am-9pm Thu & Fri, 11am-5pm Sun) FREE This museum is a huge trove housing a veritable history of art. The modern and contemporary collections will astonish, while the Asian galleries (2nd floor) and Decorative Arts rooms (3rd floor) are also highlights.

🎉 Festivals & Events

Art-A-Whirl   ART
(www.nemaa.org; ☺mid-May) The Northeast's weekend-long, rock-and-roll gallery crawl heralds the arrival of spring. Held at studios throughout the neighborhood.

Pride Festival   LGBT
(www.tcprid e.org; ☺late Jun) The Pride Festival, one of the USA's largest, draws more than 300,000 revelers to Loring Park.

Minneapolis Aquatennial   CULTURAL
(www.aquatennial.com; ☺3rd week Jul) Celebrates the ubiquitous lakes via parades, beach bashes and fireworks. Held at various venues around downtown and along the riverfront.

🛏 Sleeping

★ **Wales House**   GUESTHOUSE $
(☎612-331-3931; www.waleshouse.com; 1115 5th St SE; r $95, with shared bath $85; 🅿❄🛜) This cheery 10-bedroom B&B often houses

Minneapolis

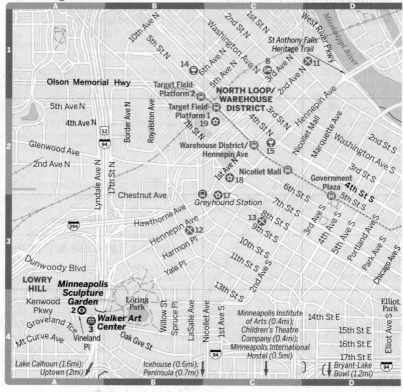

scholars from the nearby University of Minnesota. Curl up with a book on the porch, or lounge by the fireplace. A two-night minimum stay is required.

Minneapolis International Hostel　HOSTEL **$**
(📞612-522-5000; www.minneapolishostel.com; 2400 Stevens Ave S; dm $40-45, r from $55; ❄�widehat) It's set in a cool old building with antique furniture and wood floors, and the location beside the Minneapolis Institute of Arts is excellent. But it's also not very well tended to. The rooms come in a variety of configurations, from a 15-bed male dorm to private rooms with en suite bath.

Aloft　HOTEL **$$**
(📞612-455-8400; www.aloftminneapolis.com; 900 Washington Ave S; r $159-265; P❄@�widehat❄) Aloft's efficiently designed, industrial-toned rooms draw a younger clientele. The clubby lobby has board games, a cocktail lounge and 24-hour snacks. There's a tiny pool, a decent fitness room and a bike-share station outside the front door. Parking costs $20.

Hewing Hotel　HOTEL **$$**
(📞651-468-0400; www.hewinghotel.com; 300 N Washington Ave; r $140-260; P❄�❄❄) Opened in late 2016 this hotel in the North Loop offers 124 rooms spread through a century-old farm machine warehouse. The vibe is rustic and cozy. The handsome chambers feature wood-beam ceilings, exposed brick walls and distinctive outdoorsy decor, such as deer-print wallpaper and plaid wool blankets. It's within walking distance of downtown's action. Parking costs $41.

✖ Eating

Culinary magazine *Saveur* recently dubbed Minneapolis as 'America's next great food city' for its creative, sustainable, approachable and distinctively Midwestern fare.

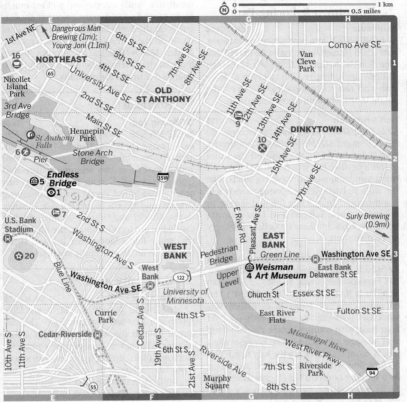

Minneapolis

◎ Top Sights

1	Endless Bridge	E2
2	Minneapolis Sculpture Garden	A4
3	Walker Art Center	A4
4	Weisman Art Museum	G3

◎ Sights

5	Mill City Museum	E2

❸ Activities, Courses & Tours

6	St Anthony Falls Heritage Trail	E2

🛏 Sleeping

7	Aloft	E3
8	Hewing Hotel	C1
9	Wales House	G2

✖ Eating

10	Al's Breakfast	G2
11	Bachelor Farmer	D1
12	Butcher & the Boar	B3
13	Hell's Kitchen	C3

❸ Drinking & Nightlife

14	Fulton Beer	B1
15	Gay Nineties	C2
16	Wilde Cafe	E1

❸ Entertainment

17	Brave New Workshop Theatre	C3
18	First Avenue & 7th St Entry	C2
	Guthrie Theater	(see 1)
19	Target Field	C2
20	US Bank Stadium	E3

Downtown & Loring Park

Peninsula MALAYSIAN $
(612-871-8282; www.peninsulamalaysiancuisine.com; 2608 Nicollet Ave S; mains $9-15; 11am-10pm Sun-Thu, to 11pm Fri & Sat;) Malaysian dishes – including red curry hot pot, spicy crab and fish in banana leaves – rock the palate in this contemporary restaurant.

Hell's Kitchen AMERICAN $$
(612-332-4700; www.hellskitcheninc.com; 80 9th St S; mains $12-24; 6:30am-11pm Mon-Fri, from 7:30am Sat & Sun;) Descend the stairs to Hell's devilish lair, where spirited waitstaff bring you uniquely Minnesotan foods, like the walleye bacon-lettuce-tomato sandwich, bison burger, Juicy Lucy (melted cheese in the middle of a burger) and lemon-ricotta hotcakes. Upstairs there's a delicious bakery and coffee shop.

Butcher & the Boar AMERICAN $$$
(612-238-8888; www.butcherandtheboar.com; 1121 Hennepin Ave; mains $32-48; 5-10:30pm Mon-Thu, to 11pm Fri & Sat, to 10pm Sun;) The coppery, candlelit room is carnivore nirvana. Get your carving knife ready for wild boar ham with country butter, chicken-fried veal sausage and many more house-crafted meats. Sampler plates are the way to go. The 30 taps flow with regional brews, backed up by a lengthy bourbon list (flights available). Make reservations, or opt for meaty small plates in the rockin' beer garden.

Bachelor Farmer AMERICAN $$$
(612-206-3920; www.thebachelorfarmer.com; 50 2nd Ave N; mains $19-35; 5:30-9:30pm Mon-Thu, to 10:30pm Fri & Sat, 5-9:30pm Sun) The dishes at this fun restaurant play on the region's Scandinavian heritage: smoked fish, meatballs and cheese-and-pickled-mushroom-topped toast making frequent appearances on the ever-changing menu. The chef grows all the herbs and veggies in a rooftop garden. **Marvel Bar**, the restaurant's sibling, hides in the basement behind an unmarked door and is primo for cocktails.

Northeast

★**Young Joni** PIZZA $$
(612-345-5719; www.youngjoni.com; 165 13th Ave NE; mains $13-18; 4-11pm Tue-Thu, 4pm-midnight Fri, noon-midnight Sat, noon-10pm Sun) Young Joni fuses two seemingly unrelated types: pizza and Korean food. So you can order a wood-fired, crisp-crusted prosciutto, Gruyere and ricotta pie with a side of spicy clams, kimchi and tofu. It sounds odd, but the dishes are terrific. Bonus: the hip, industrial space has a hidden bar in back. If the red light is on, the cocktails are flowing.

University Area

Al's Breakfast BREAKFAST $
(612-331-9991; 413 14th Ave SE; mains $5-9; 6am-1pm Mon-Sat, 9am-1pm Sun) The ultimate hole in the wall: 14 stools at a tiny counter. Whenever a customer comes in, everyone picks up their plates and scoots down to make room for the newcomer. Fruit-full pancakes and bacon waffles are the big crowd pleasers. Cash only.

Uptown, Lyn-Lake & Whittier

Bryant-Lake Bowl AMERICAN $
(612-825-3737; www.bryantlakebowl.com; 810 W Lake St; mains $10-15; 8am-12:30am;) A workingman's bowling alley meets epicurean food at the BLB. Biscuit-and-gravy break-

---

LGBT MINNEAPOLIS

Minneapolis has one of the country's highest percentages of gay, lesbian, bisexual and transgender (GLBT) residents, and the city enjoys strong GLBT rights. Pick up the free, biweekly magazine *Lavender* (www.lavendermagazine.com) at coffee shops around town for info on the scene. Top picks:

Wilde Cafe (612-331-4544; www.wilderoastcafe.com; 65 Main St SE; 7am-11pm) It features amazing baked goods, riverfront digs and a Victorian ambience worthy of its namesake, Oscar Wilde; *Lavender* once ranked it 'best cafe.'

Gay Nineties (612-333-7755; www.gay90s.com; 408 Hennepin Ave; 8am-2am Mon-Sat, from 10am Sun) This longstanding club has dancing, dining and drag shows that attract both a gay and straight clientele.

Pride Festival (p615) It's one of the USA's largest, drawing some 300,000 revelers.

TAPROOM BOOM

Minneapolis is all in on the local brewing trend, and most makers have taprooms. Excellent ones to try for beer fresh from the tank:

Fulton Beer (☑612-333-3208; www.fultonbeer.com; 414 6th Ave N; ⊙3-10pm Tue-Thu, to 11pm Fri, noon-11pm Sat, noon-6pm Sun) There's usually a fab pale ale and blonde ale among the selection that you sip at communal picnic tables in the warehouse. It's a few blocks from the baseball stadium and fills up on game days. Food trucks hang out in front.

Dangerous Man Brewing (☑612-236-4087; www.dangerousmanbrewing.com; 1300 2nd St NE; ⊙4-10pm Tue-Thu, 3pm-midnight Fri, noon-midnight Sat, noon-8pm Sun) Pours strong, European-style beers in the hip-happenin' Northeast. You're welcome to bring in your own food (there's a choice fish-and-chips place a block east).

Surly Brewing (☑763-999-4040; www.surlybrewing.com; 520 Malcolm Ave SE; ⊙11am-11pm Sun-Thu, to midnight Fri & Sat; ♿) Surly's sprawling, mod-industrial, family-friendly beer hall is mobbed by locals who come for the 20 rotating taps and abundant meaty snacks. Try CynicAle, a Belgian-style saison, or Furious, the flagship American IPA. It's in the Prospect Park neighborhood, next to the university and a short walk from the Prospect Park Green Line rail station.

---

fasts, spicy Gouda mac 'n' cheese, mock duck potstickers and smoked whitefish melt in the mouth. Long list of local beers.

🍸 Drinking & Nightlife

Grumpy's   BAR
(☑612-789-7429; www.grumpys-bar.com; 2200 4th St NE; ⊙2pm-2am Mon-Fri, from 11am Sat & Sun) Grumpy's is the Northeast's classic dive, with cheap (but good local) beer and an outdoor patio. Sample the specialty 'hot dish' on Tuesdays for $1.

☆ Entertainment

Icehouse   LIVE MUSIC
(☑612-276-6523; www.icehousempls.com; 2528 Nicollet Ave S; ⊙11am-2am Mon-Fri, from 10am Sat & Sun) A gorgeous, great-sounding venue for jazz, folk and progressive hip-hop acts. Oh, and swank cocktails, too.

First Avenue & 7th St Entry   LIVE MUSIC
(☑612-332-1775; www.first-avenue.com; 701 1st Ave N) This is the longstanding bedrock of Minneapolis' music scene. First Avenue is the main room featuring national acts; smaller 7th St Entry is for up-and-comers. Check out the exterior stars on the building; they're all bands that have graced the stage.

Guthrie Theater   THEATER
(☑612-377-2224; www.guthrietheater.org; 818 2nd St S) This is Minneapolis' top-gun theater troupe, with the jumbo facility to prove it. Unsold 'rush' tickets go on sale 30 minutes before showtime for $15 to $35 (cash only).

Brave New Workshop Theatre   THEATER
(☑612-332-6620; www.bravenewworkshop.com; 824 Hennepin Ave) An established venue for musical comedy, revue and satire.

Target Field   BASEBALL
(☑800-338-9467; www.minnesotatwins.com; 353 N 5th St) The Minnesota Twins' baseball stadium is notable for its beyond-the-norm, locally focused food and drink.

US Bank Stadium   FOOTBALL
(☑612-338-4537; www.vikings.com; 900 5th St S) The NFL's Vikings play at this spiffy, glass-walled indoor arena, which opened in 2016.

ℹ Information

Minneapolis Convention & Visitors Association (www.minneapolis.org) Coupons, maps, guides and bike-route info online.

City Pages (www.citypages.com) Weekly entertainment freebie.

Pioneer Press (www.twincities.com) St Paul's daily newspaper.

Star Tribune (www.startribune.com) Minneapolis' daily newspaper.

ℹ Getting There & Away

The Minneapolis–St Paul International Airport (p622) is between these two cities to the south. It's a hub for Delta Airlines, which operates several direct flights to/from Europe.

The Blue Line light-rail service (regular/rush-hour fare $1.75/2.25, 25 minutes) is the cheapest way into Minneapolis. Taxis cost around $45.

Greyhound (☑612-371-3325; www.greyhound.com; 950 Hawthorne Ave; 🛜) runs frequent

MALL OF AMERICA

Welcome to the USA's largest shopping center. Yes, the **Mall of America** (☎952-883-8800; www.mallofamerica.com; off I-494 at 24th Ave; ⊗10am-9:30pm Mon-Sat, 11am-7pm Sun; 🚇) is just a mall, filled with the usual stores, movie theaters and eateries. But there's also a wedding chapel inside. And an 18-hole **mini-golf course** (☎952-883-8777; 3rd fl, Mall of America; per person \$10; ⊗10am-9:30pm Mon-Sat, 11am-7pm Sun). And a zip line. And an amusement park, aka **Nickelodeon Universe** (☎952-883-8800; www.nickelodeon-universe.com; ⊗10am-9:30pm Mon-Sat, 11am-7pm Sun), with 27 rides, including a couple of scream-inducing roller coasters. To walk through will cost you nothing; a one-day, unlimited-ride wristband is \$36; or you can pay for rides individually (\$3.50 to \$7).

What's more, the state's largest aquarium, **Sea Life Minnesota** (☎952-883-0202; www.visitsealife.com/minnesota; adult/child \$25/18; ⊗10am-7pm Mon-Thu, to 8pm Fri & Sat, to 6pm Sun; 🚇) – brimming with sharks, jellyfish and stingrays – is in the mall too. Combination passes are available to save dough. The Blue Line light-rail runs to/from downtown Minneapolis. The mall is in suburban Bloomington, a 10-minute ride from the airport.

buses to Milwaukee (seven hours), Chicago (nine hours) and Duluth (three hours).

Megabus (www.megabus.com/us) runs express to Milwaukee (6½ hours) and Chicago (8½ hours), often for lower fares than Greyhound. It departs from both downtown and the university; check the website for exact locations.

Amtrak chugs in to the newly restored Union Depot (p622) in St Paul. Trains go daily to Chicago (eight hours) and Seattle (38 hours).

❶ Getting Around

Minneapolis hovers near the top of rankings for best bike city in the US. Nice Ride (www.niceridemn.org) is the local bike-share program, with 1800 lime-green bikes in 200 self-serve kiosks around the Twin Cities. A 30-minute ride costs \$3. Insert a credit card, get your ride code, then unlock a bike. Traditional rentals work better for longer recreational rides. See the Minneapolis Bicycle Program (www.ci.minneapolis.mn.us/bicycles) for rental shops and trail maps.

Metro Transit (www.metrotransit.org) runs the handy Blue Line light-rail service between downtown and the Mall of America (stopping at the airport en route). The Green Line connects downtown Minneapolis to downtown St Paul. Machines at each station sell fare cards, including a day pass (\$6) that also can be used on public buses.

St Paul

Smaller and quieter than its twin city Minneapolis, St Paul has retained more of a historic character. Walk through F Scott Fitzgerald's old stomping grounds, trek the trails along the mighty Mississippi River, or slurp some Lao soup.

◉ Sights & Activities

Downtown and Cathedral Hill hold most of the action. The latter features eccentric shops, Gilded Age Victorian mansions and, of course, the hulking church that gives the area its name. Downtown has the museums. An insider's tip: there's a shortcut between the two areas, a footpath that starts on the Hill House's west side and drops into downtown.

Landmark Center   MUSEUM
(☎651-292-3225; www.landmarkcenter.org; 75 W 5th St; ⊗8am-5pm Mon-Fri, to 8pm Thu, 10am-5pm Sat, noon-5pm Sun) Downtown's turreted 1902 Landmark Center used to be the federal courthouse, where gangsters such as Alvin 'Creepy' Karpis were tried; plaques by the various rooms show who was brought to justice here. In addition to the city's visitor center, the building also contains a couple of small museums (one focusing on wood art, another on music).

Schubert Club Museum   MUSEUM
(☎651-292-3267; www.schubert.org; 75 W 5th St; ⊗noon-4pm Sun-Fri) FREE The Schubert Club Museum has a brilliant collection of old pianos and harpsichords – some tickled by Brahms, Mendelssohn and the like – as well as old manuscripts and letters from famous composers. It's located on the 2nd floor of the Landmark Center. The club also stages free chamber music concerts Thursdays at noon from October through April.

James J Hill House
HISTORIC BUILDING

(☑651-297-2555; www.mnhs.org/hillhouse; 240 Summit Ave; adult/child $10/6; ⊙10am-3:30pm Wed-Sat, from 1pm Sun) Tour the palatial stone mansion of railroad magnate James J Hill. It's a Gilded Age beauty, with five floors and 22 fireplaces. On Monday and Tuesday there are no tours but you can still go in and see the home's art-gallery room ($2), where French landscape paintings hang.

Science Museum of Minnesota
MUSEUM

(☑651-221-9444; www.smm.org; 120 W Kellogg Blvd; adult/child $19/13; ⊙9:30am-9pm Thu-Sat, to 5pm Sun, Tue & Wed) Has the usual hands-on kids' exhibits and Omnimax theater ($6 extra). Adults will be entertained by the wacky quackery of the 4th floor's 'questionable medical devices.'

Harriet Island
PARK

South of downtown and connected via Wabasha St, Harriet Island is a lovely place to meander. It has a river walk, paddle-wheel steamboat cruises, concert stages and fishing docks.

✵ Festivals & Events

St Paul Winter Carnival
CULTURAL

(www.wintercarnival.com; ⊙late Jan) Ten days of ice sculptures, ice skating and ice fishing. Events take place at Rice Park and other venues around the city.

🛏 Sleeping & Eating

★ Hotel 340
BOUTIQUE HOTEL $$

(☑651-280-4120; www.hotel340.com; 340 Cedar St; r $109-189; P ❋ @ 🕿) Hotel 340 delivers old-world ambiance aplenty, and it's usually a great deal to boot. The 56 rooms in the stately old building have hardwood floors and plush linens. The two-story lobby stokes a grand fireplace and nifty little bar (the desk staff double as bartenders).

Covington Inn
B&B $$

(☑651-292-1411; www.covingtoninn.com; 100 Harriet Island Rd; r $165-250; P ❋) This four-room, Harriet Island B&B is on a tugboat floating in the Mississippi River; watch the river traffic glide by while sipping your morning coffee. The stately rooms have bright splashes of color, and each has a gas fireplace to keep you toasty in winter.

Hmongtown Marketplace
ASIAN $

(☑651-487-3700; www.hmongtownmarketplace.com; 217 Como Ave; mains $5-8; ⊙8am-8pm) The nation's largest enclave of Hmong immigrants lives in the Twin Cities, and this market delivers their favorite Vietnamese, Lao and Thai dishes at its humble food court. Find the West Building and head to the back where vendors ladle hot-spiced papaya salad, beef ribs and curry noodle soup. Then stroll the market to buy embroidered dresses, a brass gong or lemongrass.

Mickey's Diner
DINER $

(☑651-222-5633; www.mickeysdiningcar.com; 36 W 7th St; mains $4-9; ⊙24hr) Mickey's is a downtown classic, the kind of place where the friendly waitress calls you 'honey' and satisfied regulars line the bar with their coffee cups and newspapers. The food has timeless appeal, too: burgers, malts and apple pie.

★ Cook
AMERICAN $

(☑651-756-1787; www.cookstp.com; 1124 Payne Ave; mains $10-14; ⊙6:30am-2pm Mon-Fri, 7am-3pm Sat & Sun) This cute, sunny spot serves creative diner dishes (gingery French toast, curried veggie burgers, braised short-rib sandwiches), including some with a spicy Korean twist. Cook also hosts Korean dinners on Friday nights. It's located in the burgeoning East Side neighborhood, where several other foodie hot spots are sprouting on Payne Ave.

🍷 Drinking & Entertainment

Happy Gnome
PUB

(☑651-287-2018; www.thehappygnome.com; 498 Selby Ave; ⊙11am-midnight Mon-Thu, 11am-1am Fri & Sat, 10am-midnight Sun; 🕿) More than 80 craft beers flow from the taps, best sipped on the fireplace-warmed outdoor patio. The pub sits across the parking lot from the St Paul Curling Club.

Fitzgerald Theater
THEATER

(☑651-290-1221; http://fitzgeraldtheater.public radio.org; 10 E Exchange St) Where the popular radio show *A Prairie Home Companion* tapes its live broadcasts. The theater hosts big-name musicians, comedians and authors, as well.

❶ Information

Mississippi River Visitor Center (☑651-293-0200; www.nps.gov/miss; 120 W Kellogg Blvd; ⊙9:30am-5pm Sun & Tue-Thu, to 9pm Fri & Sat) Operated by the National Park Service, it occupies an alcove in the science museum's lobby. Stop by to pick up trail maps and see

WORLD'S LARGEST BALL O' TWINE

The **World's Largest Ball of Twine** (1st St, Darwin; ⏱24hr) is in Darwin, 60 miles west of Minneapolis on US 12. OK, so there are three other Midwest twine balls also claiming to be the largest, but Darwin maintains it has the 'Largest Built by One Person' – Francis A Johnson wrapped the 17,400lb whopper on his farm over the course of 29 years. Gawk at it in the town gazebo.

what sort of free ranger-guided activities are going on. In summer these include short hikes to the river and bicycle rides. In winter, there are ice-fishing and snowshoeing jaunts.

Visitor Center (☑651-292-3225; www.visitsaintpaul.com; 75 W 5th St; ⏱10am-4pm Mon-Sat, from noon Sun) In the Landmark Center, it makes a good first stop for maps and DIY walking tour info.

❶ Getting There & Away

Metro Transit (www.metrotransit.org) runs the handy Green Line train (regular/rush-hour fare $1.75/2.25) between downtown St Paul and downtown Minneapolis. **Union Depot** (☑651-202-2700; www.uniondepot.org; 214 E 4th St; 🛜) is the hub for everything: Greyhound buses, city buses, the Green Line trains and Amtrak trains. The **Minneapolis–St Paul International Airport** (MSP; www.mspairport.com; 🛜) is 15 miles southwest. Bus 54 (regular/rush-hour fare $1.75/2.25, 25 minutes) goes downtown. A taxi costs around $33.

Southern Minnesota

Southern Minnesota keeps it fresh with a mix of historic river towns, Bluff Country's pastoral hamlets and oddball attractions that involve Spam and the world's largest ball of twine.

Atmospheric towns on the water include Stillwater (antique laden), Red Wing (known for its Red Wing Shoes – actually more like sturdy boots – and salt glaze pottery) and Wabasha (where eagles flock). More intriguing little burgs also pop up along this stretch of the Great River Rd, the scenic thoroughfare that clasps the Mississippi River. Pull over for a slice of pie or kitschy garden gnome shop whenever the mood strikes.

Inland and south, Bluff Country is dotted with pretty limestone cliffs and teeny villages. Lanesboro is a gem for rails-to-trails cycling. Harmony, south of Lanesboro, is the center of an Amish community and another welcoming spot.

The twine ball and **Spam Museum** (☑507-437-5100; www.spam.com; 101 3rd Ave NE, Austin; ⏱10am-6pm Mon-Sat, noon-5pm Sun Apr-Nov, noon-5pm Tue-Sun Dec-Mar; 🖐) **FREE** are farther flung, but intrepid road-trippers can seek them out.

The river towns feature inns and B&Bs in vintage, restored buildings; Stillwater has them in abundance. Bluff Country towns are also big on B&Bs, as well as campgrounds.

The Great River Rd, aka Hwy 61, rolls along the Mississippi River. If you cross a bridge to the Wisconsin side, it becomes Hwy 35. Minneapolis is an hour or two drive from most hot spots in the region.

Northern Minnesota

Northern Minnesota is where you come to 'do some fishing, do some drinking,' as one resident summed it up.

The area is an outdoor playground, from the fabled Boundary Waters wilderness to the red-cliffed Lake Superior shore to watery Voyageurs National Park. You'll find far fewer people than pine trees populating this rugged expanse. Duluth and Grand Marais are hipper-than-you-think towns to post up in if you need a bit of 'urban' life.

Duluth

At the Great Lakes' westernmost end, Duluth (with its neighbor, Superior, Wisconsin) is one of the busiest ports in the country. The town's dramatic location spliced into a cliff makes it a fab place to see changeable Lake Superior in action. The water, along with the area's trails and natural splendor, has earned Duluth a reputation as a hot spot for outdoors junkies.

◎ Sights

Hawk Ridge Observatory   OBSERVATORY
(☑218-428-6209; www.hawkridge.org; 3980 E Skyline Pkwy; ⏱6am-10pm) **FREE** It sits 600-ft above Lake Superior and provides a grand view, especially between mid-August and November, when 94,000 raptors swing by as part of the autumn hawk migration.

Enger Tower   TOWER
(www.engertowerduluth.com; W Skyline Pkwy) **FREE** The five-story, blue-stone, octagonal

tower is a defining Duluth monument, located in Enger Park. Terrific views of the harbor and Lake Superior reward those who climb the 105 stairs to the top.

Maritime Visitor Center   MUSEUM
(☑218-720-5260; www.lsmma.com; 600 S Lake Ave; ⊙10am-9pm Jun-Aug, reduced hours Sep-May) **FREE** Located next to the **Aerial Lift Bridge**, the center has computer screens inside that tell what time the big ships will be sailing through. Cool model boats and exhibits on Great Lakes shipwrecks also make it a top stop in town.

🏃 Activities

Duluth Experience   ADVENTURE
(☑218-464-6337; www.theduluthexperience.com; tours from $55) It offers a range of kayaking, cycling and brewery tours; gear and transportation provided.

Spirit Mountain   SKIING
(☑218-628-2891; www.spiritmt.com; 9500 Spirit Mountain Pl; per day adult/child $49/39; ⊙hours vary) Skiing and snowboarding are big pastimes come winter; in summer there's a zipline, alpine slide and mini-golf. The mountain is 10 miles south of Duluth.

🛏 Sleeping

Fitger's Inn   HOTEL $$
(☑218-722-8826; www.fitgers.com; 600 E Superior St; r $185-290; @ ⊚) Fitger's created its 62 large rooms, each with slightly varied decor, from an old brewery. Located on the Lakewalk, the pricier rooms have great water views. The free shuttle to local sights is handy.

Willard Munger Inn   INN $$
(☑218-624-4814; www.mungerinn.com; 7408 Grand Ave; r $75-150; @ ⊚) Family-owned Munger Inn offers a fine variety of rooms (budget to Jacuzzi suites), along with perks for outdoor enthusiasts, such as hiking and biking trails right outside the door, free use of bikes and canoes, and a fire pit. Continental breakfast is included. It's near Spirit Mountain.

🍴 Eating & Drinking

★ New Scenic Cafe   AMERICAN $$
(☑218-525-6274; www.newseniccafe.com; 5461 North Shore Dr; sandwiches $13-16, mains $24-29; ⊙11am-9pm Sun-Thu, to 10pm Fri & Sat) Foodies travel from far and near to New Scenic

Cafe, 8 miles beyond Duluth on Old Hwy 61. There, in a humble wood-paneled room, they fork into rustic salmon with creamed leeks or a slice of triple berry pie, all served with a generous helping of lake views.

Duluth Grill   AMERICAN $
(☑218-726-1150; www.duluthgrill.com; 118 S 27th Ave W; mains $10-17; ⊙7am-9pm; 🖉🐾) 🖉 The garden in the parking lot is the tip-off that the Duluth Grill is a sustainable, hippie-vibed place. The dineresque menu ranges from eggy breakfast skillets to curried polenta stew to bison burgers, with plenty of vegan and gluten-free options. It's a couple miles southwest of Canal Park, near the bridge to Superior, Wisconsin.

★ Thirsty Pagan   BREWERY
(☑715-394-2500; www.thirstypaganbrewing.com; 1623 Broadway St; ⊙11am-10pm Mon-Wed, to 11pm Thu-Sun) This one's a bit of a trek, over the bridge in Superior, Wisconsin (a 10-minute drive), but worth it for the aggressive, spicy beers to wash down hand-tossed pizzas.

Fitger's Brewhouse   BREWERY
(☑218-279-2739; www.fitgersbrewhouse.com; 600 E Superior St; ⊙11am-midnight Sun & Mon, to 1am Tue-Thu, to 2am Fri & Sat) In the hotel complex, the Brewhouse rocks with live music and fresh brews. Try them via the seven-beer sampler (3oz glasses $9).

ℹ️ Information

Duluth Visitors Center (☑800-438-5884; www.visitduluth.com; 21 W Superior St;

DYLAN IN DULUTH

While Hibbing and the Iron Range are most often associated with Bob Dylan, he was born in Duluth. You'll see brown-and-white signs on Superior St and London Rd for **Bob Dylan Way** (www.bobdylanway.com), pointing out places associated with the legend (like the armory where he saw Buddy Holly in concert, and decided to become a musician). But you're on your own to find **Dylan's birthplace** (519 N 3rd Ave E), up a hill a few blocks northeast of downtown. Dylan lived on the top floor until age six, when his family moved inland to Hibbing. It's a private residence (and unmarked), so all you can do is stare from the street.

DULUTH TRAVERSE

A 100-mile mountain-bike trail that spans the city? Riders are stoked for the Duluth Traverse (www.coggs.com), a singletrack path that's opening bit by bit and linking several existing trails. When it's finished – the city is shooting for most of it complete in 2018 – no Duluthian will be more than five minutes from the route.

⊘ 8:30am-5pm Mon-Fri) Pick up a visitor guide; the website has deals and coupons.

ⓘ Getting There & Away

Greyhound (☑ 218-722-5591; www.greyhound. com; 228 W Michigan St) has a couple of buses daily to Minneapolis (three hours).

North Shore

A trip here is dominated by water – mainly enormous, tempestuous Lake Superior – where ore-toting freighters ply the ports, little fishing fleets haul in the day's catch and wave-bashed cliffs offer awesome views if you're willing to trek. Numerous state parks, waterfalls, hiking trails and mom-and-pop towns speckle the landscape as it unfurls to the Canadian border. Highlights include Gooseberry Falls, Split Rock Lighthouse, Grand Marais' groovy scene and flaky pie in Two Harbors.

◉ Sights & Activities

The 300-mile **Superior Hiking Trail** (www. shta.org) follows the lake-hugging ridgeline between Duluth and the Canadian border. Along the way it passes dramatic red-rock overlooks and the occasional moose and black bear. Trailheads with parking lots pop up every 5 to 10 miles, making it ideal for day hikes. The **Superior Shuttle** (☑ 218-834-5511; www.superiorhikingshuttle.com; from $15; ⊘ Fri-Sun mid-May–mid-Oct) makes life even easier, picking up trekkers from 17 stops along the route. Overnight hikers will find 86 backcountry campsites and several lodges to cushion the body come nightfall; the trail website has details. The whole footpath is free, with no reservations or permits required. The **trail office** (☑ 218-834-2700; www.shta.org; 731 7th Ave; ⊘ 9am-4:30pm Mon-Fri, 10am-4pm Sat, noon-4pm Sun, closed Sat & Sun

mid-Oct–mid-May) in Two Harbors provides maps and planning assistance.

Split Rock Lighthouse
State Park   STATE PARK
(☑ 218-595-7625; www.dnr.state.mn.us; 3755 Split Rock Lighthouse Rd; per car $5, lighthouse per adult/child $10/6; ⊘ 10am-6pm mid-May–mid-Oct, 11am-4pm Thu-Mon mid-Oct–mid-May) The most visited spot on the entire North Shore. The shiner itself is a state historic site with a separate admission fee. Guided tours are available (they depart hourly), or you can explore on your own. If you don't mind stairs, say 170 or so each way, tramp down the cliff to the beach for incredible views of the lighthouse and surrounding shore.

Judge CR Magney
State Park   STATE PARK
(☑ 218-387-6300; www.dnr.state.mn.us; 4051 Hwy 61; per car $5; ⊘ 9am-8pm) Magney State Park is a beauty. Hiking to **Devil's Kettle**, the famous falls where the Brule River splits around a huge rock, is a must. Half of the flow drops 50ft in a typically gorgeous North Shore gush, but the other half disappears down a huge hole and flows underground. Where it goes is a mystery – scientists have never been able to determine the water's outlet.

Sawtooth Outfitters   KAYAKING, CYCLING
(☑ 218-663-7643; www.sawtoothoutfitters.com; 7216 Hwy 61; ⊘ 8am-6pm early May–late Oct & mid-late Dec, 8am-6pm Thu-Mon Jan–early Apr) Offers guided kayaking tours (half-/full-day tours $55/110) for all levels of paddling. They have trips on the Temperance River and out on Lake Superior, as well as easier jaunts on wildlife-rich inland lakes. Sawtooth also rents mountain bikes (per day from $22) to pedal over the many trails in the area, including the popular Gitchi Gami State Bike Trail (www.ggta.org).

🛏 Sleeping & Eating

The region has several one-of-a-kind properties, such as a hotel in a repurposed train and a lodge that used to be Babe Ruth's private club. Prices typically are midrange. Most of the state parks have campgrounds where sites cost $17 to $23. Lots of weekend, summer and fall traffic makes reservations essential for all accommodations. Expect lots of lake fish frying in pans. Most restaurants are independent mom-and-pop places.

Naniboujou Lodge   LODGE $$

(☏ 218-387-2688; www.naniboujou.com; 20 Naniboujou Trail; r $115-160; ☺ late May–late Oct) Built in the 1920s, the property was once a private club for Babe Ruth and his contemporaries, who smoked cigars in the Great Hall, warmed by the 20ft-high stone fireplace. The pièce de résistance is the hall's massive domed ceiling painted with mind-blowing, psychedelic-colored Cree Indian designs. Rooms vary in decor, but each offers an away-from-it-all experience. It's 14 miles northeast of Grand Marais.

ⓘ Getting There & Away

Hwy 61 is the main vein through the North Shore. The state scenic route moseys all the way to Canada. Duluth is the closest urban area with an airport.

Boundary Waters

Legendarily remote and pristine, the Boundary Waters Canoe Area Wilderness (BWCAW) is one of the world's premier paddling regions. More than 1000 lakes and streams speckle the piney, 1.1-million-acre expanse. Nature lovers make the pilgrimage for the 1500 miles of canoe routes, rich wildlife and sweeping solitude. If you're willing to dig in and canoe for a while, it'll just be you and the moose, bears, wolves and loons that roam the landscape.

It's possible to glide in just for the day, but most people opt for at least one night of camping. Experienced paddlers flock here, but beginners are welcome, too, and everyone can get set up with gear from local lodges and outfitters. The engaging town of Ely, northeast of the Iron Range area, is the best place to start, as it has scores of accommodations, restaurants and outfitters.

Canoeing is what everyone is here for May through September. In winter, Ely gets mushy – it's a renowned dogsledding town.

You need to be prepared for a real wilderness adventure when canoeing in the Boundary Waters. The Superior National Forest Office publishes a handy **BWCAW trip planning guide** (www.fs.usda.gov/attmain/superior/specialplaces). It has information on what to bring and how to get the required entry permits. For camping, an **overnight permit** (☏ 877-444-6777; www.recreation.gov; adult/child $16/8, plus $10 reservation fee) is necessary. Day visit permits, though free, are also required; get them at BWCAW entry-point kiosks or ranger stations. Plan ahead, as permits are quota restricted and often run out.

Besides remote camping, the area has loads of lodges, though these often have a minimum-stay requirement (usually three days). Downtown Ely has several midrange inns and small hotels. July and August are busy, so book ahead.

ⓘ Information

Kawishiwi Ranger Station (☏ 218-365-7600; 1393 Hwy 169; ☺ 8am-4:30pm May-Sep, closed Sat & Sun Oct-Apr) provides expert BWCAW camping and canoeing details, trip suggestions and required permits.

ⓘ Getting There & Away

Hwy 169 (which becomes Sheridan St in Ely) connects the Boundary Waters to the Iron Range and its towns. Hwy 1 links the Boundary Waters to the Lake Superior shore.

SCENIC DRIVE: HIGHWAY 61

Hwy 61 conjures a headful of images. Local boy Bob Dylan mythologized it in his angry 1965 album *Highway 61 Revisited*. It's the fabled 'Blues Highway' clasping the Mississippi River en route to New Orleans. And in northern Minnesota, it evokes red-tinged cliffs and forested beaches as it follows Lake Superior's shoreline.

But let's back up and get a few things straight. The Blues Highway is actually US 61, and it starts just north of the Twin Cities. Hwy 61 is a state scenic road, and it starts in Duluth. To confuse matters more, there are two 61s between Duluth and Two Harbors: a four-lane expressway and a two-lane 'Old Hwy 61' (also called North Shore Scenic Drive). Take the latter; it morphs from London Rd in Duluth and veers off to the right just past the entrance to Brighton Beach. After Two Harbors, Hwy 61 returns to one strip of pavement – a gorgeous drive that goes all the way to the Canadian border. For more information, check the North Shore Scenic Drive at www.superiorbyways.com.

Voyageurs National Park

In the 17th century, French-Canadian fur traders, or voyageurs, began exploring the Great Lakes and northern rivers by canoe. Voyageurs National Park covers part of their customary waterway, which became the border between the USA and Canada.

It's all about water up here. Most of the park is accessible only by hiking or motorboat – the waters are mostly too wide and too rough for canoeing, though kayaks are becoming popular. A few access roads lead to campgrounds and lodges on or near Lake Superior, but these are mostly used by people putting in their own boats. Getting a houseboat is all the rage.

When the boats get put away for the winter, the snowmobiles come out. Voyageurs is a hot spot for the sport, with 110 miles of staked and groomed trails slicing through the pines. Rainy Lake Visitor Center provides maps and advice. It also lends out free snowshoes and cross country skis for local trails, including a couple that depart outside the center. To the south, an ice road for cars spans the boat launches of the Ash River and Kabetogama Lake Visitor Centers.

ℹ️ Information

The visitor centers are car accessible and good places to begin your visit. Eleven miles east of International Falls on Hwy 11 is **Rainy Lake Visitor Center** (☎218-286-5258; ⊙9:30am-5pm, 10am-4pm Wed-Sun late Sep–mid-May), the main park office. Ranger-guided walks and boat tours are available here in summer, snowshoe and ski rentals in winter. Seasonal visitor centers are at **Ash River** (☎218-374-3221; Mead Wood Rd; ⊙9:30am-5pm late May–late Sep) and **Kabetogama Lake** (☎218-875-2111; off Hwy 53; ⊙9:30am-5pm late May–late Sep), both of which offer ranger-led programs. The park website (www.nps.gov/voya) has further information. Destination Voyageurs National Park (www.dvnpmn.com) has lodging and activity details for the park's gateway communities.

ℹ️ Getting There & Away

Hwy 53 is the main highway to the region. It's about a five-hour drive from the Twin Cities (or a three-hour drive from Duluth) to Crane Lake, Ash River or Lake Kabetogama. International Falls, near the park's northwest edge, holds the closest airport. It also has a busy border crossing with Canada.

Bemidji & Chippewa National Forest

This area is synonymous with outdoor activities and summer fun. Campsites and cottages abound, and everybody is fishing crazy.

Chippewa National Forest, a sprawling pine patch with 21 campgrounds, 160 miles of hiking trails, 1300 lakes, bald eagle habitats and Ojibwe lands, is a prime place to get in on the action. The small town of Cass Lake, home to the park's headquarters, provides a good starting point.

On the western edge of the forest, tidy Bemidji is an old lumber town with a well-preserved downtown and an enormous, photo-op statue of logger Paul Bunyan and his faithful blue ox, Babe. Also in the region is Itasca State Park, where the Mississippi River begins its epic journey.

ℹ️ Information

Bemidji Tourist Information Center (☎218-759-0164; www.visitbemidji.com; 300 Bemidji Ave N; ⊙8am-5pm Mon-Fri, 10am-5pm Sat, 11am-3pm Sun Jun-Aug, closed Sat & Sun Sep-May) Lakeside building next to giant statues of logger Paul Bunyan and his faithful blue ox, Babe. Inside there are displays including Paul's toothbrush.

ℹ️ Getting There & Away

Hwys 2 and 71 are the main roads to the area. From Bemidji, Cass Lake is 20 miles east via Hwy 2, while Itasca State Park (east entrance) is 30 miles southwest via Hwy 71. Bemidji has a small airport with daily Delta flights to/from Minneapolis.

USA's National Parks

National parks are America's big backyards. No cross-country road trip would be complete without a visit to at least one of these remarkable natural treasures, rich in unspoiled wilderness, rare wildlife and history. The nation's five-dozen national parks and over 350 other protected areas are managed by the National Park Service (NPS), which celebrated its centennial in 2016.

Contents
➡ Evolution of the Parks
➡ The Parks Today
➡ Eastern USA
➡ Great Plains & Rocky Mountains
➡ Southwest USA
➡ West Coast
➡ Final Frontiers

Above Stand up paddleboarding on Bear Lake, Kenai Fjords (p640), Alaska

Evolution of the Parks

Many parks look much the same as they did centuries ago. From craggy islands off the Atlantic Coast, to prairie grasslands and buffalo herds across the Great Plains, to the Rocky Mountains raising their jagged teeth along the Continental Divide, and onward to the tallest trees on earth – coast redwoods – standing sentinel on Pacific shores, you'll be amazed by the USA's natural bounty.

Go West!

Historically speaking, the nation's voracious appetite for land and material riches drove not only the false doctrine of Manifest Destiny, but also a bonanza of building: pioneer homesteads, farms, livestock fences, great dams, roadways and train tracks from sea to shining sea. This artificial infrastructure quickly swallowed up vast wilderness tracts from the Appalachian Mountains to the mighty Mississippi River and far into the West. That is, until the creation of a web of federally protected public lands, starting with the national parks.

Voices in the Wilderness

During a trip to the Dakotas in 1831, artist George Catlin had a dream. As he watched the USA's rapid westward expansion harm both the wilderness and Native American tribes, Catlin penned a call to action for 'a nation's park, containing man and beast, in all the wild and freshness of their nature's beauty!' Four decades later, Congress created Yellowstone National Park, the nation's first.

The late 19th century saw a rush of new parks – including Yosemite, Sequoia and Mount Rainier – as a nascent con-

1. Grand Canyon National Park (p854)
2. Owl in Olympic National Park (p1050)
3. Cave formations, Mammoth Cave National Park (p406)

servation movement fired up public enthusiasm. The poetic herald of the Sierra Nevada, naturalist John Muir, galvanized the public while campaigning for a national park system, delivering open-air lectures and writing about the spiritual value of wilderness above its economic opportunities.

Growing the Parks

Inspired by a visit to Yosemite with Muir in 1903, President Theodore Roosevelt, a big-game hunter and one-time rancher, worked to establish more wildlife preserves, national forests and national parks and monuments. The Antiquities Act of 1906, signed by the president, preserved a priceless trove of archaeological sites from Native American cultures, including Mesa Verde, and two years later the Grand Canyon itself.

The NPS was created in 1916, with self-made millionaire and tireless parks promoter Stephen Mather as its first director. In the 1930s, President Franklin D Roosevelt added 50 more historic sites and monuments to the NPS portfolio and hired Depression-era Civilian Conservation Corps (CCC) workers to build scenic byways and create recreational opportunities in the parks.

After WWII, the NPS kept growing. First lady during the 1960s, 'Lady Bird' Johnson contributed to the groundbreaking report *With Heritage So Rich*, which led to the National Historic Preservation Act of 1966 expanding the NPS system. Her parks advocacy also influenced her husband, President Lyndon Johnson, who enacted more environmental-protection legislation than any administration since FDR.

The Parks Today

Today the NPS protects over 400 park-lands and more than 80 million acres of land from coast to coast. Recent additions designated by President Barack Obama include noteworthy historical sites (Ohio's Charles Young Buffalo Soldiers National Monument, Maryland's Harriet Tubman Underground Railroad National Monument), wild lands (Maine's Katahdin Woods and Waters National Monument) and cultural treasures (Utah's Bears Ears National Monument). Thousands more natural areas are overseen by other federal land-management agencies, including the US Forest Service (USFS; www.fs.fed.us), US Fish & Wildlife Service (USFWS; www.fws.gov) and Bureau of Land Management (BLM; www.blm.gov).

Not all national parks growth has been free of controversy; for example, when local residents protest restrictions on public land use, or when agency goals conflict with the self-determination rights of Native Americans. Federal budget cuts and the enormous pressures of more than 300 million visitors every year have also taken huge tolls on the parks, as has global warming, leading to habitat loss and species extinction. Recent media spotlights that have helped sway public opinion about the vital importance of parks include Ken Burns' documentary film *The National Parks: America's Best Idea* (www.pbs.org/nationalparks).

Practical Tips for Park Visitors

Park entrance fees vary, from nothing at all to $30 per vehicle. The 'America the Beautiful' annual pass ($80; www.nps.gov/planyourvisit/passes.htm), which admits four adults and all children under 16 years old free to all federal recreational lands for

1. Mt Rainier National Park (p1060)
2. Haleakalā National Park (p1125) 3. Elk in Great Smoky Mountains National Park (p366)

12 calendar months, is sold at park entrances and visitor centers. Lifetime senior-citizen passes ($10) and access passes for those with disabilities (free) are also available. Because ATMs are scarce in parks, bring cash to pay for campsites, wilderness permits, and guided tours and activities.

Park lodges and campgrounds book up far in advance; for summer vacations, reserve six months to one year ahead. Some parks offer first-come, first-served campgrounds – if so, try to arrive between 10am and noon, when other campers may be checking out. For overnight backpacking and some day hikes, you'll need a wilderness permit; the number of permits is often subject to quotas, so apply far in advance (up to six months before your trip, depending on park regulations). Some park stores sell (or occasionally rent) basic camping and outdoor supplies, but prices are usually inflated and some items may be out of stock – try to bring your own gear if you can.

ECO TRAVEL IN THE PARKS

Follow the principles of the Leave No Trace (www.lnt.org) ethics. To help kids learn about how they can help protect the parks, inquire at visitor centers about junior ranger activity programs (www.nps.gov/kids/jrrangers.cfm).

Park policies and regulations may seem restrictive, but they're intended to keep you safe and to protect both natural and cultural resources. Pets are not allowed outside of the parks' developed areas, where they must be leashed and attended to at all times.

SMILEUS/GETTY IMAGES ©

1. Flamingos, Everglades National Park (p493) 2. Shenandoah
National Park (p335) 3. Thunder Hole, Acadia National Park (p263)
4. Black bear, Great Smoky Mountains National Park (p366)

Eastern USA

Roam from New England's rocky, wild and weather-beaten shores to Florida's sugar-sand beaches shaded by palm trees. Or immerse yourself in the USA's wealth of historic sites, starting in the nation's capital, Washington, DC, then roll through the pastoral hills of old-timey Appalachia on the scenic Blue Ridge Pkwy.

Great Smoky Mountains National Park

Receiving more visitors than any other US national park, this southern Appalachian woodland pocket protects thickly forested ridges where black bears, white-tailed deer, antlered elk, wild turkeys and more than 1500 kinds of flowering plants find sanctuary.

Acadia National Park

Catch the first sunrise of the new year atop Cadillac Mountain, the highest point on the USA's eastern seaboard. Or come in summer to play on end-of-the-world islands tossed along this craggy, wind-whipped North Atlantic coastline.

Shenandoah National Park

Drive from the Great Smoky Mountains north along the historic Blue Ridge Pkwy past Appalachian hillside hamlets to Shenandoah, a pastoral preserve where waterfall and woodland paths await, just 75 miles from the nation's capital.

Everglades National Park

Home to snaggle-toothed crocodiles, stealthy panthers, pink flamingos and mellow manatees, South Florida's Caribbean bays and 'rivers of grass' attract wildlife-watchers, especially to unique flood-plain islands called hammocks.

Mammoth Cave National Park

With hidden underground rivers and more than 400 miles of explored terrain, the world's longest cave system shows off sci-fi-looking stalactites and stalagmites up close.

ROB CRANDALL/SHUTTERSTOCK ©

1. Long House, Mesa Verde National Park (p784) **2.** Glacier National Park (p810) **3.** Rocky Mountain National Park (p766) **4.** Old Faithful geyser, Yellowstone National Park (p795)

JORDAN SIEMENS/GETTY IMAGES ©

Great Plains & Rocky Mountains

Wildflower-strewn meadows, saw-toothed peaks and placid lakes along the spine of the Continental Divide are among America's most prized national parks. Equally rich in wildlife, Native American culture and Old West history, the Rocky Mountains and Great Plains embody the American frontier.

Yellowstone National Park

The country's oldest national park is full of geysers, hot springs and a wealth of megafauna – grizzly bears, bison, elk and more – that range across North America's largest intact natural ecosystem.

Rocky Mountain National Park

Atop the Continental Divide, jagged mountain peaks are only the start of adventures at this park, speckled with more than 150 lakes and 450 miles of streams running through aromatic pine forests.

Glacier National Park

Fly along the high-altitude Going-to-the-Sun Road, which appears to defy gravity as it winds for 50 miles through the mountainous landscape that some Native Americans call 'The Backbone of the World.'

Badlands National Park

Amid native prairie grasslands, where bison and bighorn sheep roam, this alarmingly named park is a captivating outdoor museum of geology, with fossil beds revealing traces of North America's prehistoric past.

Mesa Verde National Park

Clamber onto the edge of the Colorado Plateau to visit the well-preserved Native American cliff dwellings of Ancestral Puebloans who inhabited the remote Four Corners area for many generations.

JFUNK/SHUTTERSTOCK ©

Arches National Park (p885) **2.** Bryce Canyon National Park
(p888) **3.** Bighorn sheep, Zion National Park (p889)

Southwest USA

It takes time to explore the Southwest's meandering canyon country, arid deserts and Native American archaeological ruins. An immense, colorful chasm carved by one of the USA's most powerful rivers is just the beginning. Meander down backcountry byways to discover ancient sand dunes, twisting slot canyons and giant cacti.

Grand Canyon National Park

Arguably the USA's best-known natural attraction, the Grand Canyon is an incredible spectacle of colored rock strata, carved by the irresistible flow of the Colorado River. Its buttes and peaks spire into a landscape that's always changing with the weather.

Zion National Park

Pioneers almost believed they'd reached the promised land at this desert oasis, run through by a life-giving river. Get a thrill by rappelling down a slot canyon or pulling yourself up the cables to aerial Angels Landing viewpoint.

Bryce Canyon National Park

On the same geological 'Grand Staircase' as the Grand Canyon, Bryce Canyon shows off a whimsical landscape of totem-shaped hoodoo rock formations, some rising as tall as a 10-story building.

Arches National Park

Just outside the four-seasons base camp of Moab, UT, this iconic landscape of more than 2000 naturally formed sandstone arches is most mesmerizing at sunrise and sunset, when the gorgeously eroded desert rocks seem to glow.

Saguaro National Park

An icon of the American West, spiky saguaro cacti stretch toward the sky in this Arizona desert park, where coyotes howl, spotted owls hoot and desert tortoises slowly crawl through the sere landscape.

West Coast

Thunderous waterfalls, the sirens' call of glacier-carved peaks and the world's tallest, biggest *and* oldest trees are just some of the natural wonders that California offers. Meet smoking volcanic mountains, misty rainforests and untamed beaches in the Pacific Northwest.

Yosemite National Park

Visit glaciated valleys, alpine wildflower meadows, groves of giant sequoia trees and earth-shaking waterfalls that tumble over sheer granite cliffs in the USA's second-oldest national park.

Olympic National Park

Lose yourself in the primeval rainforests, mist-clouded mountains carved by glaciers, and lonely, wild Pacific Coast beaches. Watch salmon swim free in the restored Elwha River, site of the world's largest dam-removal project.

Death Valley & Joshua Tree National Parks

Slide down sand dunes and stroll across salt flats at Badwater, the USA's lowest-elevation spot, in hellishly hot Death Valley. Or hop between boulders, native fan-palm oases and forests of crooked Joshua trees, all in Southern California's deserts.

Mt Rainier National Park

Meet a glacier-covered, rumbling giant that may have last erupted only 120 years ago and still reigns over the Pacific Northwest's volcanic Cascades Range. Day-hike among wildflower meadows or tramp across snow fields even in midsummer.

Redwood National Park

Be awed by towering ancient stands of coast redwoods, the tallest trees on earth, along the often-foggy Northern California coast. Spot shaggy Roosevelt elk foraging in woodland prairies, then go tide-pooling along rugged beaches.

1. Jedediah Smith Redwoods State Park (p1015)
2. Death Valley National Park (p964) 3. Cholla Cactus Garden, Joshua Tree National Park (p961) 4. Half Dome, Yosemite National Park (p1022)

Denali National Park & Preserve (p1106), Alas

Final Frontiers

Officially US states for little more than 50 years, far-flung Alaska and Hawaii offer some unforgettable wilderness experiences you just can't get in the 'Lower 48' or on 'da mainland.' Active volcanoes, icy glaciers, rare and endangered wildlife and a rich vein of historic sites make these parks worth a detour.

Alaska

In 1980 the Alaska National Interest Lands Conservation Act turned more than 47 million acres of wilderness over to the NPS, more than doubling the federal agency's holdings with a single stroke of President Jimmy Carter's pen.

Today Alaska's national parks give visitors a chance to see glacial icebergs calve at Kenai Fjords and Glacier Bay, watch brown bears catch salmon at Katmai, or summit the USA's highest peak, Denali (Mt McKinley). Along the aquatic Inside Passage, admire Native Alaskan totem poles in Sitka and retrace the hardy steps of 19th-century Klondike gold-rush pioneers at Skagway.

Hawaii

The USA's remotest archipelago is tailor-made for tropical escapades. On Hawai'i, the Big Island, witness the world's longest continuous volcanic eruption or possibly see lava flow at Hawai'i Volcanoes National Park, then snorkel with sea turtles beside an ancient Hawaiian place of refuge on the Kona coast. On Maui, trek deep inside a volcano and swim in stream-fed pools at mind-bogglingly diverse Haleakalā National Park. Last, pay your respects to O'ahu's WWII–era USS Arizona Memorial.

The Great Plains

Includes ➜

Missouri 644
Iowa.............................660
North Dakota 665
South Dakota 667
Nebraska....................677
Kansas 684
Oklahoma...................688

Best Places to Eat

➜ Arthur Bryant's (p657)

➜ MB Haskett Delicatessen (p668)

➜ Cheever's Cafe (p691)

➜ Galleria De Paco (p665)

➜ Boiler Room (p680)

Best Places to Stay

➜ Hotel Alex Johnson (p673)

➜ Barn Anew (p683)

➜ Hotel Donaldson (p666)

➜ Millstream Resort Motel (p688)

➜ Shakespeare Chateau (p659)

➜ Hotel Campbell (p693)

Why Go?

To best comprehend this vast and underappreciated region in the heart of the US, you need to split up the name. The first word, 'great,' is easy. Great scenery, great tornadoes, great people: all apply. The problem is with 'plains.' 'Hum-drum' and 'flat' come to mind. Neither word applies. Amid the endless horizons are cosmopolitan oases like Kansas City, alpine wonders in the Black Hills, and soaring bluffs along the Mississippi and Missouri Rivers. There are also illuminating tales of comings and goings, from Okies fleeing the Dust Bowl along Route 66 to Lewis and Clark navigating the American frontier and the Five Civilized Tribes marching westward on a Trail of Tears.

Great distances across the beguiling wide-open spaces are the biggest impediment to enjoying this enormous region. Many sights lie near the interstates, but many more are found along the ever-intriguing small roads – the 'blue highways' of lore.

When to Go
St Louis

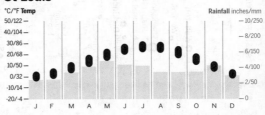

Nov–Mar Attractions cut back hours, or close. Blizzards shut down roads for days.

Apr, May, Sep & Oct Average highs of 55°F (13°C) in the north, warmer in the south; uncrowded months.

Jun–Aug Thunderstorms and even tornadoes; sultry days with blooming wildflowers.

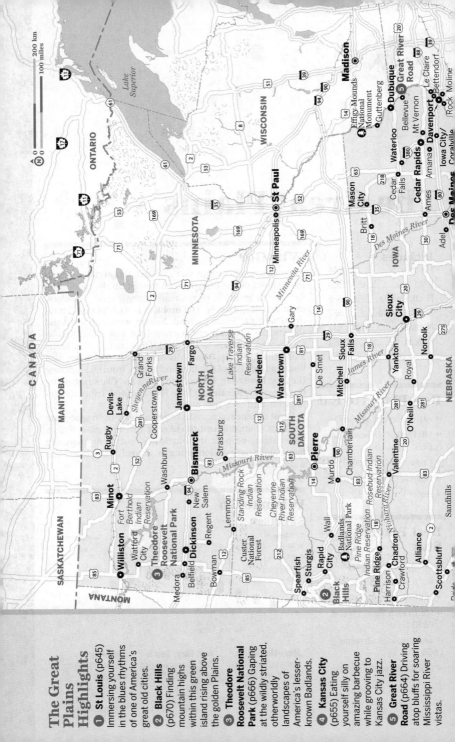

The Great Plains Highlights

❶ **St Louis** (p645) Immersing yourself in the blues rhythms of one of America's great old cities.

❷ **Black Hills** (p670) Finding mountain highs within this green island rising above the golden Plains.

❸ **Theodore Roosevelt National Park** (p666) Gaping at the wildly striated, otherworldly landscapes of America's lesser-known Badlands.

❹ **Kansas City** (p655) Eating yourself silly on amazing barbecue while grooving to Kansas City jazz.

❺ **Great River Road** (p664) Driving atop bluffs for soaring Mississippi River vistas.

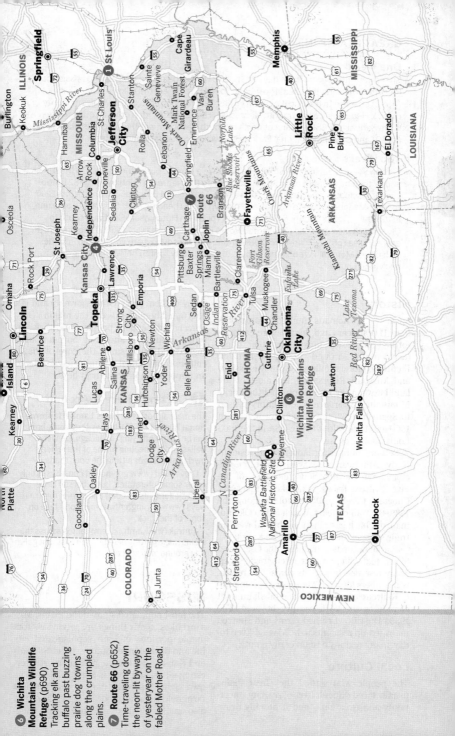

6 Wichita Mountains Wildlife Refuge (p690)
Tracking elk and buffalo past buzzing prairie dog 'towns' along the crumpled plains.

7 Route 66 (p652)
Time-traveling down the neon-lit byways of yesteryear on the fabled Mother Road.

GREAT PLAINS IN...

One Week

Spend your first two or three days in St Louis (p645) before snaking up the Mississippi River to Iowa along the Great River Road (p664). Skirt past the folksy Amana Colonies (p662) en route to the bucolic countrysides (and famous bridges) of Madison County (p661). Head west to link up with Nebraska's Hwy 2 (p680) for a drive through the remote Sandhills (p680). Then cut north to South Dakota where the gorgeous Black Hills (p670) and Badlands National Park (p669) will vie for your remaining time.

Two Weeks

With two weeks behind the wheel, you can take a big bite out of the Plains. Do the trip as above, then head south from South Dakota into the Nebraska Panhandle (p682), stopping at fascinating, isolated sites such as the Agate Fossil Beds (p683) and Scotts Bluff (p683). Meander down to Kansas and pick up US 50 heading east. Stop at the amazing, astonishing Cosmosphere & Space Center (p685) in Hutchinson. Continue south to Oklahoma where you can join historic Route 66 in Oklahoma City (p689) heading northeast to Tulsa (p692). Follow the Mother Road into Missouri where you can dip into the lush Ozark Mountains (p653) and zip up to Kansas City (p655) before finishing your trip back in St Louis.

History

Spear-toting nomads hunted mammoths here 11,000 years ago, long before cannon-toting Spaniards introduced the horse (accidentally) around 1630. Fur-frenzied French explorers, following the Mississippi and Missouri Rivers, claimed most of the land between the Mississippi and the Rocky Mountains for France. The territory passed to Spain in 1763, the French got it back in 1800 and then sold it to the USA in the 1803 Louisiana Purchase.

Settlers' hunger for land pushed resident Native American tribes westward, often forcibly, as in the notorious relocation of the Five Civilized Tribes – Cherokee, Chickasaw, Choctaw, Creek and Seminole – along the 1838–39 Trail of Tears, which led to Oklahoma from back east. Pioneers blazed west on trails such as the Santa Fe across Kansas.

Earlier occupants, including the Osage and Sioux, had different, but often tragic, fates. Many resettled in pockets across the region, while others fought for lands once promised.

Railroads, barbed wire and oil all brought change as the 20th century hovered. The 1930s Dust Bowl ruined farms and spurred many fed-up residents to head west. Even today, many regions remain eerily empty.

Local Culture

The people who settled the Great Plains usually faced difficult lives of scarcity, uncertainty and isolation – and it literally drove many of them crazy. Others gave up and got out (failed homesteads dot the region). Only fiercely independent people could thrive in those conditions and that born-and-bred rugged individualism is the core of Plains culture today. Quiet restraint is considered an important and polite trait here.

ℹ Getting There & Around

The main airport is **St Louis Lambert International Airport** (p651), but visitors from abroad will be better off flying to Chicago, Denver or Dallas and connecting to one of the region's myriad airports or hitting the open roads.

Greyhound (www.greyhound.com) buses only cover some interstates, but Jefferson Lines (www.jeffersonlines.com) and Burlington Trailways (www.burlingtontrailways.com) take up some of the slack.

Amtrak (www.amtrak.com) routes across the Plains make getting here by train easy, but getting around impractical.

MISSOURI

The most populated state in the Plains, Missouri likes to mix things up, serving visitors ample portions of both sophisticated city life and down-home country sights. St Louis and Kansas City are the region's most interesting cities, and each is a destination in its own right. But, with more forest and less farm field than neighboring states, Missouri also cradles plenty of wild places and wide-open spaces, most notably the rolling Ozark Mountains, where the winding valleys invite adventurous exploration or just some laid-back meandering behind the steering wheel. Maybe you'll find an adventure worthy of Hannibal native Mark Twain as you wander the state.

ℹ Information

Bed & Breakfast Inns of Missouri (www.bbim.org)

Missouri Division of Tourism (www.visitmo.com)

Missouri State Parks (www.mostateparks.com) State parks are free to visit. Site fees range from $12 to $56 and some sites may be reserved in advance.

St Louis

Slide into St Louis and revel in the unique vibe of the largest city in the Great Plains. Beer, bowling and baseball are some of the top attractions, but history and culture, much of it linked to the Mississippi River, are a vital part of the fabric. And, of course, there's the iconic Gateway Arch that you have seen in a million pictures; it's even more impressive in reality. Many music legends, including Scott Joplin, Chuck Berry, Tina Turner and Miles Davis, got their start here and jammin' live-music venues keep the flame burning.

◉ Sights

The landmark Gateway Arch rises right along the Mississippi River. Downtown runs west of the arch. Begin a visit here and wander for half a day. Then explore the rest of the city; cross the river to see Cahokia Mounds State Historic Site (p560).

★**Gateway Arch & Jefferson National Expansion Memorial** MONUMENT
(Map p648; ☑ 314-655-1700; www.gatewayarch.com; tram ride adult/child $13/10; ☺ 8am-10pm Jun-Aug, 9am-6pm Sep-May, last tram 1hr before closing; ⊕) As a symbol for St Louis, the Arch has soared above any expectations its backers could have had in 1965 when it opened. The centerpiece of the Jefferson National Expansion Memorial (a National Park Service property), the silvery, shimmering Gateway Arch is the Great Plains' own Eiffel Tower. It stands 630ft high and symbolizes St Louis' historical role as 'Gateway to the West.' The **tram ride** takes you to the tight confines at the top.

★**Forest Park** PARK
(Map p646; ☑ 314-367-7275; www.forestparkforever.org; bounded by Lindell Blvd, Kingshighway Blvd & I-64; ☺ 6am-10pm) New York City may have Central Park, but St Louis has the bigger (by 528 acres) Forest Park. The superb, 1371-acre spread was the setting of the 1904 World's Fair. It's a beautiful place to escape to and is dotted with attractions, many free. Two walkable neighborhoods, the Loop and Central West End, are close.

★**City Museum** MUSEUM
(Map p648; www.citymuseum.org; 701 N 15th St; $12, Ferris wheel $5; ☺ 9am-5pm Mon-Thu, to midnight Fri & Sat, 11am-5pm Sun; ⊕) Possibly the wildest highlight to any visit to St Louis is this frivolous, frilly fun house in a vast old shoe factory. The **Museum of Mirth, Mystery & Mayhem** sets the tone. Run, jump and explore all manner of exhibits, including a seven-story slide. The summer-only rooftop **Ferris wheel** offers grand views of the city.

ST LOUIS NEIGHBORHOODS

The St Louis neighborhoods of most interest radiate out from the Downtown core:

Central West End Just east of Forest Park, a posh center for nightlife and shopping.

Grand Center Located in Midtown and rich with cultural attractions, theaters and historic sites.

The Hill An Italian American neighborhood with good delis and eateries.

Lafayette Square Historic, upscale and trendy.

The Loop Northwest of Forest Park; funky shops and nightlife line Delmar Blvd.

Soulard The city's oldest quarter, with good cafes, bars and blues.

South Grand Bohemian and gentrifying; surrounds beautiful Tower Grove Park and has a slew of ethnic restaurants.

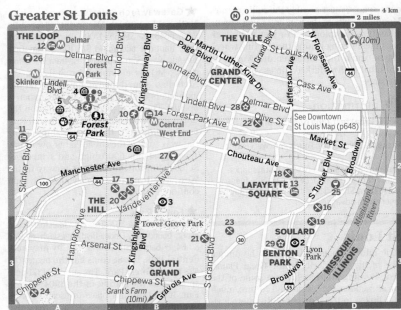

Greater St Louis

◎ Top Sights
1 Forest Park A1

◎ Sights
2 Anheuser-Busch Brewery C3
3 Missouri Botanical Garden B2
4 Missouri History Museum A1
5 St Louis Art Museum A1
6 St Louis Science Center B2
7 St Louis Zoo A2

◎ Activities, Courses & Tours
8 Boathouse A1
9 City Cycling Tours A1
10 Steinberg Ice-Skating Rink B1

◎ Sleeping
11 Cheshire A2
12 Moonrise Hotel A1
13 Napoleon's Retreat C2
14 Parkway Hotel B1

◎ Eating
15 Adriana's B2
16 Bogart's Smoke House D2
17 Charlie Gitto's B2
18 Eleven Eleven Mississippi C2
19 Joanie's Pizzeria D3
20 Milo's Bocce Garden B2
21 MoKaBe's Coffeehouse B3
22 Pappy's Smokehouse C2
23 Shaved Duck C3
24 Ted Drewes A3

◎ Drinking & Nightlife
25 4 Hands Brewing Co D2
26 Blueberry Hill A1
27 Just John Club B2

◎ Entertainment
28 St Louis Symphony
     Orchestra C1
29 Venice Cafe C3

National Blues Museum   MUSEUM
(Map p648; ☎ 314-925-0016; www.nationalblues
museum.org; 615 Washington Ave; adult/child
$15/10; ◎ 10am-5pm Tue-Sat, noon-5pm Sun &
Mon) This flashy new museum explores blues
legends like hometown hero Chuck Berry
while making a strong case for the genre's
myriad influences on modern rock, folk,

R&B and more. There are interactive exhibits from the likes of Jack White, and interesting stories about the early years of blues
and its (almost exclusively female) pioneers.

St Louis Zoo   ZOO
(Map p646; ☎ 314-781-0900; www.stlzoo.org; 1
Government Dr; fee for some exhibits; ◎ 9am-5pm

daily, to 7pm Fri-Sun May-Sep; P ↻) FREE Divided into themed zones, this vast park includes a fascinating River's Edge area with African critters. Don't leave without saying hello to the zoo's new superstar: Kali the polar bear.

St Louis Science Center
MUSEUM

(Map p646; ✆ 314-289-4400; www.slsc.org; 5050 Oakland Ave; ⊙ 9:30am-4:30pm Mon-Sat, 11am-4:30pm Sun; P ↻) FREE The interactive exhibits at this three-story museum are geared toward kids (and the young at heart). Expect live demonstrations, dinosaurs, a planetarium and an IMAX theater (additional fee).

St Louis Art Museum
MUSEUM

(Map p646; www.slam.org; 1 Fine Arts Dr; ⊙ 10am-5pm Tue-Thu, Sat & Sun, to 9pm Fri) FREE This grand beaux-arts palace (with a striking modern wing) was originally built for the World's Fair. Now housing this storied institution, its collection spans time and styles, and includes a variety of household names from Picasso to Van Gogh and Warhol. The **Grace Taylor Broughton Sculpture Garden** opened in 2015.

Missouri Botanical Garden
GARDENS

(Map p646; ✆ 314-577-5100; www.mobot.org; 4344 Shaw Blvd; adult/child $12/free; ⊙ 9am-5pm) Dating to 1859, these gardens hold a 14-acre Japanese garden, a carnivorous plant bog, a Victorian-style hedge maze and the oldest continuously operating greenhouse west of the Mississippi. It's at the north end of Tower Grove Park, near I-44 exit 287B.

Missouri History Museum
MUSEUM

(Map p646; ✆ 314-746-4599; www.mohistory.org; 5700 Lindell Blvd; ⊙ 10am-5pm Wed-Mon, to 8pm Tue; P) FREE Presents the story of St Louis, starring such worthies as the World's Fair, a replica of Charles Lindbergh's plane (*Spirit of Saint Louis*) and a host of bluesmen. Oral histories from those who fought segregation are moving.

Museum of Transportation
MUSEUM

(✆ 314-965-6885; www.transportmuseumassociation.org; 2933 Barrett Station Rd; adult/child $8/5; ⊙ 9am-4pm Mon-Sat, 11am-4pm Sun Mar-Oct, reduced hours Nov-Feb) Huge railroad locomotives (including a Union Pacific Big Boy), historic cars cooler than your rental, and more that moves. Take I-270 west to exit 8.

✦ Activities

Forest Park has many activities you can enjoy amid its beauty.

Boathouse
BOATING

(Map p646; ✆ 314-367-2224; www.boathouseforestpark.com; 6101 Government Dr; boat rental per hour $17; ⊙ 11am-approx 1hr before sunset, weather permitting) In warm weather, rent a rowboat to paddle over Post-Dispatch Lake. Traveling couples should inquire about Moonlight Paddleboat Picnics, which run Thursday nights from May to October.

Steinberg Ice-Skating Rink
ICE SKATING

(Map p646; ✆ 314-367-7465; www.steinbergskatingrink.com; 400 Jefferson Dr; $7, skate rental $6; ⊙ 10am-9pm Sun-Thu, to midnight Fri & Sat mid-Nov–Feb) The balm for cold weather: fun on the ice.

☞ Tours

Gateway Arch Riverboats
BOATING

(Map p648; ✆ 877-982-1410; www.gatewayarch.com; 50 S Leonor K Sullivan Blvd; 1hr tour adult/child $20/10; ⊙ various times Mar-Nov) Churn up the Big Muddy on replica 19th-century steamboats. A park ranger narrates the midday cruises in season, and those after 3pm sail subject to availability. There are also numerous dinner and drinking cruises. Various combo tickets are available.

City Cycling Tours
CYCLING

(Map p646; www.citycyclingtours.com; 5595 Grand Dr, Forest Park Visitor & Education Center; rental per hour/half-day $15/36, 3hr tour $30; ⊙ rental 10am-5pm, tours daily Apr-Oct) Besides bike rentals, there are narrated rides (bikes supplied) through Forest Park (p645), starting at the visitor center (p651).

⮽ Sleeping

Most midrange and upscale chains have a hotel near the Gateway Arch (p645) in Downtown. Indie cheapies are thin on the ground in interesting areas, but you'll find plenty near the airport and you can ride the MetroLink light rail into the city. Upscale Clayton on I-170 (exit 1F) also has rail access and a cluster of chains.

★ Cheshire
HOTEL $$

(Map p646; ✆ 314-647-7300; www.cheshirestl.com; 6300 Clayton Rd; r $150-250; P ❄ 🛜 🏊) This upscale inn near Forest Park (p645) oozes character, from its stained-glass windows to the all-encompassing British literary theme. The hodgepodge of artworks, antique furnishings and (occasionally frightening) taxidermy are sure to delight.

Downtown St Louis

Downtown St Louis

◎ Top Sights
1 City Museum B1
2 Gateway Arch & Jefferson National
   Expansion Memorial D2

◎ Sights
3 National Blues Museum C1

◎ Activities, Courses & Tours
4 Gateway Arch Riverboats D3

◎ Sleeping
5 Missouri Athletic Club C1

◎ Eating
6 Broadway Oyster Bar C3
7 Imo's C2

◎ Drinking & Nightlife
8 Bridge Tap House & Wine Bar C2

◎ Entertainment
9 BB's C3

Missouri Athletic Club　　　　　HOTEL **$$**
(Map p648; ☑ 314-231-7220; www.mac-stl.org; 405
Washington Ave; r $120-160; P ✳ ☎) Stay in style
Downtown close to the Arch (p645). The Missouri Athletic Club is a grand old facility with
73 nice and traditional hotel rooms.

Parkway Hotel　　　　　HOTEL **$$**
(Map p646; ☑ 314-256-7777; www.theparkway-hotel.com; 4550 Forest Park Ave; r $145-250;
P ✳ @ ☎) Right in the midst of Central
West End's upscale fun, this indie eight-story hotel contains 217 newly remodeled
rooms (with refrigerators and microwaves)
inside a grand limestone building. A hot
buffet breakfast is included, and you can't
beat the location right across from Forest
Park (p645).

Moonrise Hotel　　　　　BOUTIQUE HOTEL **$$**
(Map p646; ☑ 314-721-1111; www.moonrisehotel.
com; 6177 Delmar Blvd; r $170-450; P ✳ ☎ ☀)
The stylish eight-story Moonrise has a high
profile amid the high energy of the Loop
neighborhood. Its 125 rooms sport a lunar
motif, but are grounded enough to slow
things down to comfy.

Napoleon's Retreat　　　　　B&B **$$**
(Map p646; ☑ 314-772-6979; www.napoleonsre-treat.com; 1815 Lafayette Ave; r $140-230; ✳ @ ☎)
A lovely Second French Empire–style home
in historic and leafy Lafayette Square, this
B&B has five bold and beautiful rooms, each
with refrigerators and antique furnishings.
Innkeepers Brian and Stacy make you feel
at home.

✕ Eating

St Louis boasts the region's most diverse selection of food, from the Irish pubs of Soulard to the Asian restaurants along South Grand. Don't leave town without sampling the city's unique approach to Italian American cuisine in the Hill. The magazine and website *Sauce* (www.saucemagazine.com) is full of great reviews.

✕ Downtown & Midtown

Laclede's Landing, along the riverfront next to the historic Eads Railway Bridge, has several restaurants, though generally people pop down here for the atmosphere – cobblestone streets, converted brick buildings and free-flowing beer – rather than the food.

Pappy's Smokehouse   BARBECUE $
(Map p646; ☏314-535-4340; www.pappyssmokehouse.com; 3106 Olive St; mains from $9; ⊘11am-8pm Mon-Sat, to 4pm Sun) Named one of the nation's best joints for barbecue, Pappy's serves luscious ribs, pulled pork, brisket and smoked turkey. With fame, however, comes popularity, so be prepared for long lines and crowded communal dining. Ameliorate the wait with dreams of the sweet-potato fries.

★ Broadway Oyster Bar   CAJUN $$
(Map p648; ☏314-621-8811; www.broadwayoysterbar.com; 736 S Broadway; mains $10-20; ⊘11am-3am) Part bar, part live-music venue, but all restaurant, this joint jumps year-round. When the sun shines, people flock outside where they suck down crawfish and other Cajun treats. It's nuts before and after Cardinals games.

✕ Soulard & Lafayette Square

Restaurants and pubs occupy most corners in Soulard, with plenty of live blues and Irish music, so just wander. Historic Lafayette Square, 1 mile northwest, has some stylish spots.

**★ Eleven Eleven
Mississippi**   MODERN AMERICAN $$
(Map p646; ☏314-241-9999; www.1111-m.com; 1111 Mississippi Ave; mains $9-25; ⊘11am-10pm Mon-Thu, to midnight Fri, 5pm-midnight Sat; ✐) This modern bistro and wine bar fills an old shoe factory. Dinner mains draw on regional specialties with a farm-to-table vibe. Other options on the seasonal menu include sandwiches, pizzas, steaks and veggie dishes. Excellent wine selection.

Bogart's Smoke House   BARBECUE $$
(Map p646; ☏314-621-3107; www.bogartssmokehouse.com; 1627 S 9th St; mains $9-25; ⊘10:30am-4pm Mon-Sat) The soul of Soulard? The smoky meats here draw lines of people who tear into all the standards plus specialties such as prime rib. Extras, including the searingly hot voodoo sauce and the 'fire and ice pickles,' have creative flair.

✕ South Grand

Running along South Grand Blvd, this young, bohemian area near beautiful Tower Grove Park has a slew of excellent ethnic restaurants, many with outside terraces.

MoKaBe's Coffeehouse   CAFE $
(Map p646; ☏314-865-2009; 3606 Arsenal St; mains $5-8; ⊘8am-11pm; ☏✐) Overlooking Tower Grove Park, this hangout for

---

ST LOUIS LOCAL SPECIALTIES

Toasted ravioli They're filled with meat, coated in breadcrumbs, then deep-fried. Practically every restaurant on the Hill serves them, most notably Charlie Gitto's (p650).

St Louis pizza Its thin-crusted, square-cut pizzas are really addictive. They're made with Provel cheese, a locally beloved gooey concoction of processed cheddar, Swiss and provolone. Local chain **Imo's** (Map p648; ☏314-641-8899; www.imospizza.com; 1 S Broadway; large from $16; ⊘11am-7pm Mon-Sat), with over 70 locations across the metro area, bakes 'the square beyond compare,' or get your pizza with Provel at the popular **Joanie's Pizzeria** (Map p646; www.joanies.com; 2101 Menard St; mains $10-15; ⊘11am-1am Mon-Sat, to midnight Sun).

Frozen custard Don't dare leave town without licking yourself silly on the super-creamy ice-cream-like treat at historic **Ted Drewes** (☏314-481-2652; www.teddrewes.com; cones $2-6; ⊘11am-11pm Feb-Dec), southwest of the city center. There's a smaller summer-only branch south of the city center at 4224 S Grand Blvd. Rich and poor rub elbows enjoying a 'concrete,' a delectable stirred-up combination of flavors.

neighborhood activists, hipsters and generally cool folk buzzes day and night. Grab a coffee, a baked treat, breakfast or a sandwich. There are seats outside.

★ **Shaved Duck** AMERICAN $$
(Map p646; ☎ 314-776-1407; www.theshavedduck. com; 2900 Virginia Ave; mains $10-20; ⊙ 11am-9pm Mon, to 10pm Tue-Sat) A South Grand stalwart, the Shaved Duck fires up its grills early in the day and turns out excellent BBQ, including the signature smoked duck. Options include fab sandwiches and veggie sides. Live music weeknights.

🍴 The Hill

This Italian neighborhood crammed with tortellini-sized houses has innumerable pasta joints. Stroll the tidy streets and stop for a coffee at an Italian cafe.

★ **Adriana's** ITALIAN $
(Map p646; ☎ 314-773-3833; www.adrianasonthe hill.com; 5101 Shaw Ave; mains $5-10; ⊙ 10:30am-3pm Mon-Sat) Redolent of herbs, this family-owned Italian deli serves up fresh salads and sandwiches (get the meaty Hill Boy) to ravenous lunching crowds. Expect lines.

Milo's Bocce Garden ITALIAN $
(Map p646; ☎ 314-776-0468; www.milosbocce garden.com; 5201 Wilson Ave; mains $7-14; ⊙ 11am-1am Mon-Sat, kitchen to 11pm) Enjoy sandwiches, pizzas and pastas in the vast outdoor courtyard or inside the old-world bar. Watch and join the regulars on the busy bocce ball courts.

Charlie Gitto's ITALIAN $$
(Map p646; ☎ 314-772-8898; www.charliegittos. com; 5226 Shaw Ave; mains $16-30; ⊙ 5-10pm Mon-Thu, to 11pm Fri & Sat, 4-9pm Sun; ℗) Leg-

endary Charlie Gitto's makes a strong claim to having invented St Louis' famous toasted ravioli. On any night the weather allows, dine under the tree on the patio. Classy but casual.

🍷 Drinking & Nightlife

Laclede's Landing, Soulard and the Loop are loaded with pubs and bars, many with live music. Most bars close at 1:30am, though some have 3am licenses.

The Grove, a strip of Manchester Ave between Kingshighway Blvd and S Vandeventer Ave, is the hub of St Louis' gay and lesbian community. Peruse *Vital Voice* (www. thevitalvoice.com) for info.

★ **Blueberry Hill** BAR
(Map p646; ☎ 314-727-4444; www.blueberryhill. com; 6504 Delmar Blvd; ⊙ 11am-late) St Louis native Chuck Berry rocked the small basement bar here until the day he died. The venue hosts bands big and small and has good pub food (mains $8 to $15), arcade games, darts and walls covered in pop-culture artifacts.

★ **Bridge Tap House & Wine Bar** BAR
(Map p648; ☎ 314-241-8141; www.thebridgestl. com; 1004 Locust St; ⊙ 11am-1am Mon-Sat, to midnight Sun) Slip onto a sofa or rest your elbows on a table at this romantic bar where you can savor fine wine or the best local beer (55 on tap) and nibble a variety of exquisite little bites from a seasonal menu.

★ **4 Hands Brewing Co** MICROBREWERY
(Map p646; ☎ 314-436-1559; www.4handsbrew ery.com; 1220 S 8th St; ⊙ noon-10pm, to midnight Fri & Sat) A fraction of the size of big brother Bud down the street, this craft brewery is everything its neighbor is not: homey, unassuming and out to surprise. Order by the taster or full glass and grab some bar snacks if you get hungry.

Just John Club GAY
(Map p646; www.justjohnclub.com; 4112 Manchester Ave; ⊙ 3pm-3am Mon-Sat, noon-1am Sun) A Grove anchor, John's has bars inside and out, regular performances and an ever-welcoming vibe. Wednesday is ladies night.

☆ Entertainment

Check the *Riverfront Times* (www.river fronttimes.com) for updates on entertainment options around town. Purchase tickets for most venues through MetroTix (www. metrotix.com).

YOUR BELGIAN BUD

One of the world's largest beer plants, the historic **Anheuser-Busch Brewery** (Map p646; ☎ 314-577-2626; www. budweisertours.com; cnr 12th & Lynch Sts; ⊙ 9am-5pm Mon-Thu, to 7pm Fri & Sat, 11am-5pm Sun Jun-Aug, 10am-5pm Mon-Sat, 11am-5pm Sun Sep-May) gives marketing-driven tours. View the bottling plant and Clydesdale horses. One thing to note: the purchase of this St Louis (and American) icon by Belgium's InBev in 2008 is still a sore spot locally. And don't ask: 'How do you remove all the flavor?'

★ Venice Cafe
BLUES, JAZZ

(Map p646; ☑314-772-5994; www.thevenicecafe. com; 1903 Pestalozzi St; ☺4pm-1am Mon-Sat) A true cabinet of curiosities. The interior of this two-level club is a master class in mosaics, while the rambling outdoor garden is chock-full of folk art and twinkling lights. Best of all, the drinks are cheap and there's live blues and jazz seven days a week.

BB's
BLUES

(Map p648; ☑314-436-5222; www.bbsjazzblues soups.com; 700 S Broadway; ☺6pm-3am) Part blues club, part blues museum, this glossy two-level joint has good music most nights. Good bar food includes legendary sweet-potato fries.

St Louis
Symphony Orchestra
CLASSICAL MUSIC

(Map p646; ☑314-534-1700; www.stlsymphony. org; 718 N Grand Blvd) Located at Powell Hall, a grand red-and-gold-hued theater that dates to 1925. There's a good balance of classical concerts and pop-culture-inspired extravaganzas.

❶ Information

Explore St Louis (Map p648; ☑314-421-1023; www.explorestlouis.com; cnr 7th St & Washington Ave, America's Center; ☺8am-5pm Mon-Sat; 🛜) An excellent resource, with other branches in Kiener Plaza (corner of 6th and Chestnut) and at the airport.

Forest Park Visitor & Education Center (Map p646; ☑314-367-7275; www.forestparkforever. org; 5595 Grand Dr; ☺6am-8pm Mon-Fri, to 7pm Sat & Sun) Located in an old streetcar pavilion and has a cafe. Free walking tours leave from here, or you can borrow an iPod audio tour.

Missouri Welcome Center (☑314-869-7100; www.visitmo.com; Riverview Dr, I-270 exit 34; ☺8am-5pm Mon-Sat)

❶ Getting There & Away

St Louis Lambert International Airport (STL; www.flystl.com; I-70 exit 238A), the largest Great Plains airport, is 12 miles northwest of Downtown and is connected by the light-rail MetroLink ($2.50), taxi (about $45) and **Go Best Express** (☑314-222-5300; www.gobestexpress.com; one way from $25) shuttles, which can drop you off in the main areas of town.

Amtrak's (www.amtrak.com) *Lincoln Service* travels five times daily to Chicago (from $27, 5½ hours). Two daily *Missouri River Runner* trains go to/from Kansas City (from $31, 5½ hours). The

DRINK LOCAL

Schlafly, Civil Life, Earthbound Brewing and Urban Chestnut are excellent local microbrews that will let you forget that you're in the home of Bud. The website StL Hops (www.stlhops.com) is an excellent guide to local beers and where to drink them.

daily *Texas Eagle* goes to Dallas (16 hours); check the website for prices as the fare range for this route is vast. Trains leave from **Gateway Transportation Center** (Map p648; 430 S 15th St).

Greyhound (www.greyhound.com) buses depart several times daily to Chicago ($24, five to seven hours), Memphis ($25, six hours), Kansas City ($25, 4½ hours) and many more cities from Gateway Transportation Center.

Megabus (www.megabus.com) runs services to Chicago for as little as $5 one way from Gateway Transportation Center.

❶ Getting Around

Metro (www.metrostlouis.org) runs local buses and the MetroLink light-rail system (which connects the airport, the Loop, Central West End, the **Gateway Transportation Center** (Union Station and Downtown). Buses 30 and 40 serve Soulard from Downtown. A single/day pass is $2.50/7.50.

St Louis County Cabs (☑314-991-5300, text 314-971-8294; www.countycab.com) Call, text or book online.

St Charles

This Missouri River town, founded in 1769 by the French, is just 20 miles northwest of St Louis. The cobblestoned Main St anchors a well-preserved downtown with artisan shops, cafes and gourmet grocers. Ask at the visitor center (p652) about tours, which pass some rare French-colonial architecture in the Frenchtown neighborhood just north.

❂ Sights

Lewis & Clark Boathouse
& Nature Center
MUSEUM

(www.lewisandclarkcenter.org; 1050 Riverside Dr; adult/child $5/2; ☺10am-5pm Mon-Sat, noon-5pm Sun) Lewis and Clark began their epic journey in St Charles on May 21, 1804, and their encampment is reenacted annually on that date. This museum has displays about the duo and replicas of their boats.

ROUTE 66: GET YOUR KICKS IN MISSOURI

The Show-Me State will show you a long swath of the Mother Road. Meet the route in **St Louis**, where Ted Drewes (p649) has been serving frozen custard to generations of roadies from its Route 66 location on Chippewa St. There are a couple of well-signed historic routes through the city.

Follow I-44 (the interstate is built over most of Route 66 in Missouri) on a westbound journey down the Mother Road to **Route 66 State Park** (☑ 636-938-7198; www.mostateparks.com; I-44 exit 266; ⊗ 7am-30min after sunset, museum 9am-4:30pm Mar-Nov) **FREE**, with its visitor center and museum inside a 1935 roadhouse. Although the displays show vintage scenes from around St Louis, the real intrigue here concerns the town of Times Beach, which once stood on this very site. It was contaminated with dioxin and in the 1980s the government had to raze the entire area.

Head southwest on I-44 to **Stanton**, then follow the signs to family-mobbed **Meramec Caverns** (☑ 573-468-3166; www.americascave.com; I-44 exit 230, Stanton; adult/child $21/11; ⊗ 8:30am-7:30pm Jun-Aug, reduced hours Sep-May), as interesting for the Civil War history and hokey charm as for the stalactites; and the conspiracy-crazy **Jesse James Wax Museum** (☑ 573-927-5233; www.jessejameswaxmuseum.com; I-44 exit 230, Stanton; adult/child $7/3; ⊗ 9am-6pm daily Jun-Aug, 9am-5pm Sat & Sun Apr, May, Sep & Oct), which posits that James faked his death and lived until 1951.

The **Route 66 Museum & Research Center** (p689) at the library in **Lebanon** has memorabilia past and present. Ready for a snooze? Head to the 1940s **Munger Moss Motel** (☑ 417-532-3111; www.mungermoss.com; 1336 E Rte 66; r from $60; ▣ ? ▣). It's got a monster of a neon sign and Mother Road–loving owners.

Ditch the interstate west of **Springfield**, taking Hwy 96 to Civil War–era **Carthage** with its historic town square and **66 Drive-In Theatre** (☑ 417-359-5959; www.66drivein. com; 17231 Old 66 Blvd, Carthage; adult/child $8/4; ⊗ after dusk Fri-Sun Apr-Sep). In **Joplin** get on State Hwy 66, turning onto old Route 66 (the pre-1940s route), before the Kansas state line.

The Route 66 Association of Missouri (www.missouri66.org) has loads of info. And don't miss the **Conway Welcome Center** (I-44 Mile 110, near Conway; ⊗ 8am-5pm), which has an over-the-top Route 66 theme and scads of info on the historic road.

First State Capitol HISTORIC BUILDING
(☑ 636-940-3322; 200 S Main St; tours adult/child $4.50/3; ⊗ 10am-4pm Mon-Sat, noon-4pm Sun, closed Mon Nov-Mar, Sun Jan & Feb) **FREE** This modest brick complex was Missouri's capitol from 1821 to 1826. The interior has been restored.

🛏 Sleeping & Eating

★ **Boone's Colonial Inn** B&B $$
(☑ 636-493-1077; www.boonescolonialinn.com; 322 S Main St; r $165-355; ▣ ▣ ?) The three suites in these 1820 stone row houses are posh escapes. If all are booked out, try the sister property, Boone's Lick Trail Inn, five blocks down the road. The innkeeper of both, Venetia, is extraordinarily knowledgeable about the town and its history.

Braddens AMERICAN $$
(☑ 636-493-9303; 515 S Main St; mains $10-18; ⊗ 10:30am-9pm Tue-Thu, to 11pm Fri & Sat, 8:30am-7pm Sun) This atmospheric local favorite has wood furnishings, brick walls and

casual American fare (think burgers, steaks, salads and wraps). It's steeped in history: plans for the Santa Fe Trail are said to have been hatched and signed by the fireplace here in 1818.

ℹ Information

Visitor Center (☑ 800-366-2427; www.historic stcharles.com; 230 S Main St; ⊗ 8am-5pm Mon-Fri, 10am-5pm Sat, noon-5pm Sun)

ℹ Getting There & Away

St Charles is just 20 miles northwest of St Louis. The St Charles Area Transit system, SCAT, has an I-70 commuter service that provides bus transportation to the St Louis MetroLink at North Hanley Station.

Hannibal

When the air is sultry in this old river town, you almost expect to hear the whistle of a paddle steamer. Mark Twain's boyhood home, 115 miles northwest of St Louis, has some authentically vintage sections and plenty of sites (including caves) where you can get a sense of the author and his creations Tom Sawyer and Huck Finn.

◎ Sights & Activities

★ Mark Twain Boyhood Home & Museum   MUSEUM
(☎573-221-9010; www.marktwainmuseum.org; 120 N Main St; adult/child $11/6; ☺9am-5pm, reduced hours Jan-Mar) This museum presents eight buildings, including two homes Twain lived in and that of Laura Hawkins, the real-life inspiration for Becky Thatcher. Be sure to check out the Twain-inspired Norman Rockwell paintings at the **Museum Gallery** before you leave.

Mark Twain Riverboat   CRUISE
(☎573-221-3222; www.marktwainriverboat.com; Center St Landing; 1hr sightseeing cruise adult/child $18/11; ☺Apr-Nov, schedule varies) Sail the Mississippi on this replica riverboat, which does one-hour sightseeing tours and two-hour dinner cruises.

🛏 Sleeping & Eating

Garden House B&B   B&B $$
(☎573-221-7800; www.gardenhousebedandbreak-fast.com; 301 N 5th St; r $90-140, ste $240; ❋ 🛜) This Victorian house lives up to its name. Some rooms share bathrooms, others have river views.

Java Jive   CAFE $
(☎573-221-1077; www.javajiveonline.com; 221 N Main St; mains $3-10; ☺7am-9pm Mon-Sat, 8am-6pm Sun) 'The first coffee shop west of the Mississippi' does not disappoint, with an assortment of coffees and teas, sandwiches for breakfast or lunch, and classic ice-cream floats for dessert. The eclectic space is full of antique furnishings and artworks for sale.

ℹ Information

Hannibal Visitors Bureau (☎573-221-2477; www.visithannibal.com; 505 N 3rd St; ☺9am-5pm) Many of Hannibal's historic homes are now B&Bs. The Hannibal Visitors Bureau keeps a list.

ℹ Getting There & Away

Hannibal is 115 miles northwest of St Louis on either Hwy 61 or the longer and more scenic MO 79. Burlington Trailways (www.burlingtontrailways.com) links the two cities with a daily bus ($40, 2½ hours).

The Ozarks

Ozark hill country spreads across southern Missouri and extends into northern Arkansas and eastern Oklahoma. Flashy Branson receives the lion's share of tourists, though the region's true charms lie further afield.

North of US 60, in the state's south-central region, the **Ozark National Scenic Riverways** (www.nps.gov/ozar) – the Current and Jack's Fork Rivers – boast 134 miles of splendid canoeing and inner-tubing (rental agencies abound). Weekends often get busy and boisterous. The park headquarters, outfitters and motels are in **Van Buren**. **Eminence** also makes a good base. There are many campgrounds along the rivers. Sinuous Hwy E is a scenic gem.

◎ Sights

★ Echo Bluff State Park   STATE PARK
(☎844-322-3246; www.echobluffstatepark.com; 34489 Echo Bluff Dr, Eminence) With lush forests and stunning facilities befitting a top-tier national park, Echo Bluff is a true Ozarks highlight. Opened in 2016, this new state park has a soaring stone lodge, spacious cabins and ample camping options. Use it as a base for hiking, fishing and mountain biking.

Johnson's Shut-Ins State Park   STATE PARK
(☎573-546-2450; www.mostateparks.com; 148 Taum Sauk Trail, Middlebrook; ☺8am-7pm Jun-Aug, reduced hours Sep-May) FREE At lush and sprawling Johnson's Shut-Ins State Park, the swift Black River swirls through canyon-like gorges (shut-ins). The swimming is some of the most exciting you'll find outside a water park.

🛏 Sleeping

The small towns of Van Buren and Eminence have scenic campgrounds, basic motels, rustic cabins and picturesque riverside resorts. You'll also find top-notch lodgings in Echo Bluff State Park.

Landing Current River   HOTEL $$
(☎573-323-8156; www.eatsleepfloat.com; 106 Olive St, Van Buren; r $80-175) Perched along the banks of the Current River near Van Buren, this scenic hotel is the perfect base for exploring the Ozark National Scenic Riverways. You can also book overnight camping trips by canoe or raft ranging from one to five nights out.

SAINTE GENEVIEVE

Sixty-five miles south of St Louis, this petite, French-founded Mississippi River town oozes history. Many of the restored 18th- and 19th-century buildings are now B&Bs or gift shops. Follow the **Route du Vin** (www.rdvwinetrail.com) out of town to explore one of Missouri's finest wine trails.

Yes, the town's **Cave Vineyard** (☑ 573-543-5284; www.cavevineyard.com; 21124 Cave Rd; ⊙ 10am-6pm, to 5pm Nov-Mar) is a vineyard with a cave. Yes, you can drink in the cave. Sound like a gimmick? Rest assured the wines are some of the best we've tasted in Missouri. The vineyard also has its own beers and a phenomenal homemade biscotti selection. Bring a picnic lunch.

If you'd like to stay the night, the **Inn St Gemme Beauvais** (☑ 573-883-5744; www.innstgemme.com; 78 N Main St; r $100-170; ❋ ��) is the oldest continuously operated B&B in Missouri, with period decor honoring the building's 1848 construction date. Afternoon tea is served at 2pm, then wine and hors d'oeuvres at 5pm.

❶ Getting There & Around

Part of the Ozarks' charm is its remote location. Getting to any of the region's nature reserves will likely require a lengthy drive on scenic two-lane byways once you exit I-44 or I-55. Hwy 60 is the main thoroughfare and you can link up with it near Springfield or Sikeston. Public transportation is nonexistent in the Ozarks.

Branson

Hokey Branson is a cheerfully shameless tourist resort. The main attractions are the more than 50 theaters hosting 100-plus country music, magic and comedy shows. The neon-lit '76 Strip' (Hwy 76) packs in miles of motels, restaurants, wax museums, shopping malls, fun parks and theaters. Drive just a few minutes out of town, however, and you'll find yourself in pristine Ozark wilderness.

◉ Sights

Silver Dollar City　　　AMUSEMENT PARK
(☑ 800-475-9370; www.silverdollarcity.com; 399 Silver Dollar City Pkwy; adult/child $62/51; ⊙ hours vary) A Branson original, this huge amusement park west of town has thrilling roller coasters, water rides and a newer firefighter-themed area.

Table Rock Lake　　　LAKE
(www.visittablerocklake.com) Snaking through the hills southwest of town, Table Rock Lake is a deservedly popular destination for boating, fishing, camping and other outdoor activities.

🛏 Sleeping & Eating

Trout Hollow Lodge　　　MOTEL $
(☑ 417-334-2332; www.trouthollow.com; 1458 Acacia Club Rd; r/cabins from $65/110; ❋ ⊠)

This no-frills motel has a variety of lodging options (from rooms to fully equipped cabins) and makes a great cheapie thanks to its location on a bluff above Lake Taneycomo. Rub shoulders with local fishers at the docks below and the neon lights of the Strip will seem a world away.

★ Branson Hotel　　　B&B $$
(☑ 417-544-9814; www.thebransonhotel.com; 214 W Main St; r $130-170; ❋ ��) Dating to 1903, this plush nine-room B&B is right in the old town. It's away from the frenetic commercialism of the Strip, and has a great on-site wine bar.

★ Dobyns Dining Room　　　AMERICAN $$
(☑ 417-239-1900; www.keetercenter.edu; 1 Opportunity Ave; mains $8-20; ⊙ 10:30am-8pm Mon-Sat, 10am-2pm Sun) Located by College of the Ozarks (and staffed by its students), this is as close to fine dining as Branson gets. The setting is grand (think country chic), the prices are reasonable (particularly at lunch) and the service is impeccable (we'd give the staff an A+). One of the few places in town where 'deep-fried' isn't on the menu.

❶ Information

Branson/Lakes Area Convention & Visitors Bureau (CVB; ☑ 417-334-4084; www.explore-branson.com; junction Hwy 248 & US 65; ⊙ 9am-9pm) Just west of the US 65 junction, the CVB has town and lodging information.

❶ Getting There & Around

Tucked into the scenic southern corner of the state, Branson is surprisingly hard to reach, although this means you may end up driving some rural and lovely two-lane Ozark roads.

Branson Airport (BKG; www.flybranson.com) has limited service.

Jefferson Lines (www.jeffersonlines.com) has buses to Kansas City ($55, five hours, one daily).

During the summer, the SUV-laden traffic often crawls. It's often faster to walk than drive, although few others have this idea.

Kansas City

With its fiery barbecues (100-plus joints smoke it up), bubbling fountains (more than 200; on par with Rome) and blaring jazz, Kansas City may just be the coolest city in America nobody's talking about. It's certainly a don't-miss Great Plains highlight with world-class museums and quirky art-filled neighborhoods that jostle for your attention. You can easily run aground for several days as you tune into the local vibe.

◉ Sights

State Line Rd divides KCMO (Kansas City, MO) and KCK (Kansas City, KS). The latter is a bland swath of suburban sprawl with little to offer travelers. KCMO has some distinct areas, including the art-deco-filled downtown.

★**College Basketball Experience** MUSEUM
(☑816-949-7500; www.collegebasketballexperience.com; 1401 Grand Blvd; adult/child $15/12; ☺10am-6pm Wed-Sat, from 11am Sun; ℗🚼) Really a gussied-up basketball hall of fame, this interactive (and entirely overstimulating) exhibi-

tion lets you try free throws or pretend you're an announcer calling them. It's connected to the glitzy **Sprint Center**, a vast arena in search of a major pro-sports franchise.

★**National WWI Museum** MUSEUM
(☑816-888-8100; www.theworldwar.org; 2 Memorial Dr; adult/child $16/10; ☺10am-5pm, closed Mon Sep-May; ℗) Enter this impressive modern museum on a glass walkway over a field of red poppies, the symbol of the trench fighting. Through detailed and engaging displays, learn about a war that is almost forgotten by many Americans. The only quibble is that military hardware and uniforms take precedence over the horrible toll. The museum is crowned by the historic **Liberty Memorial**, which has sweeping views over the city.

★**Nelson-Atkins Museum of Art** MUSEUM
(☑816-751-1278; www.nelson-atkins.org; 4525 Oak St; ☺10am-5pm Wed, Sat & Sun, to 9pm Thu & Fri; ℗) **FREE** Giant badminton shuttlecocks (the building represents the net) surround this encyclopedic museum, which has standout European painting, photography and Asian art collections. With free entry, a gorgeous sculpture garden and an expansive collection from top-tier artists, what's not to like?

★**Negro Leagues Baseball Museum** MUSEUM
(☑816-221-1920; www.nlbm.com; 1616 E 18th St; adult/child $10/6; ☺9am-6pm Tue-Sat, noon-6pm Sun) This comprehensive museum covers

---

KANSAS CITY NEIGHBORHOODS

Kansas City has a number of unique and interesting neighborhoods to explore. Get ready to spend an hour or two (or a day or two):

39th St West KC's funkiest area is a strip of boutiques alongside lots of ethnic eateries and lively bars.

Country Club Plaza Often shortened to 'the Plaza,' this stunning 1920s shopping district is an attraction in itself.

Crossroads Arts District Around Baltimore and 20th Sts, it lives up to its name with galleries and boutique shops.

Crown Center South of downtown, this 1970s development is anchored by several major hotels and Hallmark (yes, the greeting-card company is located right here).

Historic Jazz District On the upswing, this old African American neighborhood is at 18th and Vine Sts.

Quality Hill Around W 10th St and Broadway, this historic area has grand, restored buildings from the 1920s.

River Market Historic and home to a large farmers market; immediately north of downtown.

Westport On Westport Rd just west of Main St; filled with appealing restaurants and bars.

TOURING THE FOUNTAINS

Spraying their streams large and small, Kansas City's more than 200 fountains are beautiful amenities and many are truly spectacular works of art. The website for the City of Fountains Foundation (www.kcfountains.com) is a great resource, with maps, info and downloadable self-guided tours. Among the best are **JC Nichols Memorial Fountain**, near Country Club Plaza, and the **Crown Center Square Fountain**.

the lesser-known history of African American teams, such as the KC Monarchs and New York Black Yankees, that flourished until baseball became fully integrated. It's part of the **Museums at 18th & Vine** complex.

Country Club Plaza   AREA
(☎ 816-753-0100;   www.countryclubplaza.com)
Built in the 1920s, this posh commercial district (centered on Broadway and 47th St) boasts finely detailed, sumptuous Spanish architecture. It's rich with public art and sculptures – look for the walking-tour brochure at the info center (4750 Broadway) and check out, at the very least, the **Spanish Bullfight Mural** (Central St) and the **Fountain of Neptune** (47th St and Wornall Rd).

Arabia Steamboat Museum   MUSEUM
(☎ 816-471-1856; www.1856.com; 400 Grand Blvd; adult/child $14.50/5.50; ⊗ 10am-5pm Mon-Sat, noon-5pm Sun, last tour 90min before closing) In River Market, this museum displays 200 tons of salvaged 'treasure' from a riverboat that sank in 1856 (one of hundreds claimed by the Missouri River).

National Museum of
Toys & Miniatures   MUSEUM
(www.toyandminiaturemuseum.org; 5235 Oak St, University of Missouri-Kansas City; $5; ⊗ 10am-4pm Wed-Mon; P ♿) Over 100 years of toys spread over 38 rooms, including the world's largest fine-scale miniature collection. There are 51,000 toys, 3320 dolls and 1600 army soldiers, making this newly renovated museum one of the largest of its kind.

American Jazz Museum   MUSEUM
(☎ 816-474-8463; www.americanjazzmuseum.org; 1616 E 18th St; adult/child $10/6; ⊗ 9am-6pm Tue-Sat, noon-6pm Sun) Learn about different jazz styles, rhythms, instruments and musicians – including KC native Charlie Parker – at this interactive museum, at the heart of the city's 1920s African American neighborhood. It's part of the **Museums at 18th & Vine** complex.

🛏 Sleeping

Downtown and the Plaza offer good lodging options (mostly chains) near the action. For something cheap, you'll need to head out on the interstate: there are scores of chains north on I-35 and I-29, and east on I-70.

Oak Tree Inn   MOTEL $
(☎ 913-677-3060; www.oaktreeinn.com; 501 Southwest Blvd; r $70-130; P ❄ 🛜 🏊) This comfy yet unassuming motel is the value leader for KC. Rooms are standard, yet have refrigerators and microwaves. Just off I-35 (exit 234), it's a 20-minute walk to the pleasures of 39th St West.

America's Best Value Inn   MOTEL $
(☎ 816-531-9250; www.americasbestvalueinn.com; 3240 Broadway; r $70-90; P ❄ 🛜 🏊) Convenient to everything, this basic 52-room motel has inside corridors and a pool big enough for a small family.

★ Southmoreland on the Plaza   B&B $$
(☎ 816-531-7979; www.southmoreland.com; 116 E 46th St, Country Club Plaza; r $120-235; P ❄ 🛜) The 12 rooms at this posh B&B are furnished like the home of your rich country-club friends. It's a big old mansion between the art museums and the Plaza. Extras include Jacuzzis, decks, sherry, a fireplace and more.

Jefferson House B&B   B&B $$
(☎ 816-673-6291;   www.jeffersonhousekc.com; 1728 Jefferson St; r $155-205; P ❄ 🛜) Jefferson House is funkier than most Missouri mansion-cum-B&Bs, with a mix of modern and classic touches. There are just three rooms and one has sweeping city views. Owners Peter and Theresa moved here from the British isle of Jersey; he runs the bakery down the street and her pottery livens up the gourmet breakfasts.

🍴 Eating

Barbecue may be the main draw here, but KC has world-class dining for all tastes. There are great vegetarian options, ethnic eateries and chef-driven restaurants with farm-to-table menus that highlight the region and its bounty. No single neighborhood has a monopoly on the dining scene, though Westport, River Market and 39th St West are all good places to start.

Savoring hickory-smoked brisket, pork, chicken or ribs at one of the barbecue joints around town is a must for any visitor. The local style is pit-smoked and slathered with heavily seasoned vinegar-based sauces. You may well swoon for 'burnt ends,' the crispy ends of smoked pork or beef brisket.

★**Fud**   VEGAN $
(☏816-214-5025; www.eatfud.com; 813 W 17th St; mains $7-13; ⊙11am-9pm Tue-Sat, to 3pm Sun; ✐) A welcome alternative in a meat-mad city, cozy Fud specializes in reinterpreting American classics as organic, gluten-free vegan food. Try the jackfruit BBQ on sourdough or the mac 'n' cheese made with cashew cheeses. Finish it all off with soft-serve cashew ice cream. Check the website for updates, as Fud may have moved by the time you read this.

★**Arthur Bryant's**   BARBECUE $
(☏816-231-1123; www.arthurbryantsbbq.com; 1727 Brooklyn Ave; mains $8-15; ⊙10am-9:30pm Mon-Thu, to 10pm Fri & Sat, 11am-8pm Sun; P) Not far from the Jazz District, this famous institution serves up piles of superb BBQ. The sauce is silky and fiery, the staff charming and witty. Get the burnt ends.

Joe's Kansas City Bar-B-Que   BARBECUE $
(☏913-722-3366; www.joeskc.com; 3002 W 47th Ave; mains $6-20; ⊙11am-9pm Mon-Thu, to 10pm Fri & Sat; P) This legendary joint is housed in a brightly lit old gas station and is the best reason to cross the state border (it's actually not far from the Plaza (p656)). The pulled pork is pleasure on a plate and vegetarians will appreciate the smoked portobello; expect lines.

Winstead's Steakburger   BURGERS $
(☏816-753-2244; www.winsteadssteakburger. com; 101 Emmanuel Cleaver II Blvd; mains $4-6; ⊙6:30am-midnight) Cheery servers sling plates of top-notch burgers for families, hungover hipsters and more at this Country Club Plaza institution, which dates to 1940. Don't miss the onion rings and chili.

Rieger Hotel Grill & Exchange   AMERICAN $$
(☏816-471-2177; www.theriegerkc.com; 1924 Main St; mains $11-30; ⊙3-10pm Mon-Thu, to 11pm Fri & Sat) One of KC's most innovative restaurants is housed in what was once a humdrum 1915 vintage hotel in the Crossroads Arts District. Today it's been spiffed up to match the creative fare on Howard Hanna's seasonal menu. (Note the bathroom plaque pointing out where Al Capone once sought release.)

★**Bluestem**   MODERN AMERICAN $$$
(☏816-561-1101; www.bluestemkc.com; 900 Westport Rd; 3-/5-/10-course meal $75/85/110, bar snacks $5-18; ⊙kitchen 5-10pm Tue-Sat, bar 4-11pm; P✐) Multiple-award-winning Bluestem has a casual elegance that extends from the bar to the dining room. Many stop into this Westport star just for a fine cocktail and some of the small plates of exquisite snacks (the cheeses, oh!). Dinner features an array of seasonal small courses (go for the wine pairings).

🍷 Drinking & Nightlife

Westport and 39th St West are your best bets for clusters of atmospheric local bars.

The heavily hypedPower & Light District (www.powerandlightdistrict.com) is a vast urban development centered on Grand Blvd and W 12th St with formula bars and live-performance venues. When there's no sporting event in town, it can seem rather soulless. Bars close between 1:30am and 3am.

★**Boulevard Brewery**   MICROBREWERY
(☏816-474-7095; www.boulevard.com; 2501 Southwest Blvd; ⊙10am-7pm) Welcome to the home of the largest specialty brewer in the Midwest! There are 21 home brews on tap at the 2nd-floor beer hall, where a patio boasts great views of downtown. Best of all, there are free tours of the brewery every 15 minutes between 10:30am and 4pm.

★**Up-Down**   BAR
(☏816-982-9455; www.updownkc.com; 101 Southwest Blvd; ⊙3pm-1am Mon-Fri, 11am-1am Sat, 11am-midnight Sun) A wildly popular bar-cum-playground just south of downtown, Up-Down caters to the kid in everyone with an array of games from pinball to video. There are huge decks and great music. The superb tap-beer lineup includes all the beers from Boulevard Brewery (brewed just up the hill).

Tom's Town   DISTILLERY
(☏816-541-2400; www.toms-town.com; 1701 Main St; ⊙4pm-midnight Tue-Fri, 2pm-midnight Sat) Tom's Town, downtown KC's first legal distillery since Prohibition, pays homage to the city's Prohibition-flouting political boss Tom Pendergast. Try the housemade vodka,

gin or bourbon and let the art-deco furnishings take you back to the days when KC was known as 'Paris of the Plains.'

McCoy's Public House
BREWERY

(☑816-960-0866; www.beerkc.com; 4057 Pennsylvania Ave; ☺11am-3am Mon-Sat, to midnight Sun) The patio at this Westport brewpub is the place to be on a balmy day. The house-brewed beers are excellent and vary through the year. The food is strictly comfort and quite good.

☆ Entertainment

The free weekly *Pitch* (www.pitch.com) has the best cultural calendar.

★ Mutual Musicians Foundation
JAZZ

(☑816-471-5212; www.mutualmusicians.org; 1823 Highland Ave; ☺1-5am Sat & Sun) Near 18th and Vine in the Historic Jazz District, this former union hall for African American musicians has hosted after-hours jam sessions since 1930. Famous veteran musicians gig with young hotshots. It's friendly and pretension-free. A little bar serves cheap drinks in plastic cups. No cover charge (though a $10 donation is suggested). Opening hours refer to the wee hours of Friday and Saturday nights.

Kauffman Center for the Performing Arts
PERFORMING ARTS

(☑816-994-7200; www.kauffmancenter.org; 1601 Broadway) Twin venues headline this striking complex. There's a varied schedule of theater, opera, ballet, music and more.

Riot Room
LIVE MUSIC

(☑816-442-8179; www.theriotroom.com; 4048 Broadway; cover varies; ☺hours vary) Part dive, part cutting-edge live-music venue, Westport's Riot Room always rocks – and has many good beers.

Blue Room
BLUES, JAZZ

(www.americanjazzmuseum.org; 1616 E 18th St; cover Mon & Thu free, Fri & Sat varies; ☺5pm-midnight Mon & Thu, to 1am Fri & Sat) This slick club, part of the American Jazz Museum (p656), hosts local talent for free on Monday and Thursday. Touring acts perform weekends. Major shows are held at the adjoining Gem Theater.

❶ Information

Greater Kansas City Visitor Center
(☑816-420-2020; www.visitkc.com; 30 W Pershing Rd, Union Station; ☺9:30am-4pm Tue-Sun) Other locations include the National WWI Museum.

Missouri Welcome Center (☑816-889-3330; www.visitmo.com; 4010 Blue Ridge Cutoff, Truman Sports Complex; ☺8am-5pm) Statewide maps and information at I-70 exit 9.

❶ Getting There & Away

Kansas City International Airport (MCI; www.flykci.com; off I-29 exit 13) is a confusing array of circular terminals 15 miles northwest of downtown. It has good domestic service. A taxi to downtown/Plaza costs about $40/45. Or take the cheaper Super Shuttle (☑800-258-3826; www.supershuttle.com; from $23).

Amtrak (www.amtrak.com) trains stop in majestic Union Station (www.unionstation.org; 30 W Pershing Rd; ☺6am-midnight). Two daily *Missouri River Runner* trains go to St Louis (from $31, 5½ hours). The *Southwest Chief* stops here on its daily runs between Chicago and LA.

Greyhound (☑816-221-2835; www.greyhound.com; 1101 Troost St) sends buses daily to St Louis ($25, 4½ hours) and Denver ($75, 11½ hours) from the station poorly located east of downtown.

Jefferson Lines (☑816-221-2885; www.jeffersonlines.com; 1101 Troost St, Greyhound Terminal) heads to Omaha ($45, three to four hours), Des Moines ($50, 3½ hours) and Oklahoma City ($70, seven hours) via Tulsa.

❶ Getting Around

Ride KC (www.ridekc.org) offers a one-day unlimited bus pass; it costs $3 on the bus. Bus 47 runs regularly between downtown, Westport and Country Club Plaza.

KC Streetcar (http://kcstreetcar.com; ☺6am-midnight Mon-Thu, to 2am Fri, 7am-2am Sat, 7am-10pm Sun) runs for 2 miles downtown largely on Main St from River Market to Union Station.

If you need a taxi, try Yellow Cab (☑888-471-6050; www.kansas-city-taxi.com).

Independence

Picture-perfect Independence is the perfect stereotype for an old Midwestern small town. It was the home of Harry S Truman, US president from 1945 to 1953, and has some unmissable museums.

◉ Sights

★ Truman Presidential Museum & Library
MUSEUM

(☑800-833-1225; www.trumanlibrary.org; 500 W US 24; adult/child $8/3; ☺9am-5pm Mon-Sat, noon-5pm Sun) There are thousands of objects, including the famous 'The Buck Stops

Here!' sign, from the man who led the US through one of its most tumultuous eras. More than that, the museum provides a vivid snapshot of America in the late 1940s and early '50s.

Truman Home   HISTORIC BUILDING
(www.nps.gov/hstr; 219 N Delaware St; tours adult/child $5/free; ⊘9am-4:30pm, closed Mon Nov-May) See the simple life Harry and Bess lived in this basic but charming wood house. It's furnished with their original belongings and you fully expect the couple to wander out and say hello. The former president lived here from 1919 to 1972 and in retirement entertained visiting dignitaries in his strictly pedestrian front room. He's said to have hoped none of the callers would linger more than 30 minutes. Tour tickets are sold at the **visitor center** (⊘816-254-9929; 223 N Main St; ⊘8:30am-5pm).

National Frontier Trails Museum   MUSEUM
(⊘816-325-7575; www.frontiertrailsmuseum.org; 318 W Pacific Ave; adult/child $6/3; ⊘9am-4:30pm Mon-Sat, 12:30-4:30pm Sun) Gives a compelling look at the tough life for the pioneers along the Santa Fe, California and Oregon Trails; many began their journey in Independence. You'll learn that pioneers 'met their elephant' when they realized that the challenges of the journey were simply too big.

🛏 Sleeping & Eating

Higher Ground Hotel   HOTEL $$
(⊘816-836-0292; www.highergroundhotel.com; 200 N Delaware St; r $100-130; ❄🖥) Across the street from the Truman Home, this 30-room hotel doesn't look like much from the outside. Enter its cheery halls, however, and you'll find well-appointed (and individually designed) digs, some of which look out over a serene garden.

Clinton's Soda Fountain   ICE CREAM $
(⊘816-833-2046; www.clintonssodafountain.com; 100 W Maple Ave; mains $5-8; ⊘11am-6pm Mon-Sat) Little changed from when Truman got his first job working the soda counter. Come for ice-cream sundaes, homemade sodas and cheap sandwiches.

ℹ Getting There & Away

Independence is a quick 20-minute drive east of Kansas City. For public transportation, grab bus 24 on Grand Blvd in the Power and Light District for the 50-minute journey to Independence.

St Joseph

A major departure point for pioneers, this scruffy riverside town is a tad unkempt around the edges but has a newly revitalized downtown district with quirky shops and dining options filling once-abandoned storefronts. There are also several compelling museums. Get details at the **visitor center** (⊘800-785-0360; www.stjomo.com; 109 S 4th St; ⊘8am-5pm Mon-Fri) downtown.

👁 Sights

Glore Psychiatric Museum   MUSEUM
(⊘816-232-8471; www.stjosephmuseum.org; 3406 Frederick Ave; adult/child $6/4; ⊘10am-5pm Mon-Sat, 1-5pm Sun) Housed in the former 'State Lunatic Asylum No 2,' this museum gives a frightening and fascinating look at lobotomies, the 'bath of surprise' and other discredited treatments. Price includes admission to three other museums on-site covering Native American art, local African American history and toy dolls.

Pony Express National Museum   MUSEUM
(⊘816-279-5059; http://ponyexpress.org; 914 Penn St; adult/child $6/3; ⊘9am-5pm Mon-Sat, 11am-4pm Sun) The first Pony Express set out – carrying mail from 'St Jo' to California, 2000 miles west – in 1860. This museum, from which the horses once departed, is just a few brick-paved streets over from **Patee House Museum** (⊘816-232-8206; www.pony-expressjessejames.com; 1202 Penn St; adult/child $6/4; ⊘9am-4pm Mon-Sat, noon-4pm Sun).

🛏 Sleeping

Many of the town's historic mansions are now lovely B&Bs. There is also a cluster of chain hotels and motels at exit 47 off I-29.

★ Shakespeare Chateau   B&B $$
(⊘816-232-2667; www.shakespearechateau.com; 809 Hall St; r $180-200; ❄🖥🐾) This elegant 1885 mansion houses four spacious guest rooms upstairs and a handful of common parlors below from which to soak in the opulence of yesteryear. Spread throughout are 47 stained-glass windows (look for the masterpiece in the stairwell), as well as swooping chandeliers, cherry-wood carvings and a fine art collection. Prepare to be dazzled!

🍴 Eating & Drinking

Bad Art Bistro   AMERICAN $$
(⊘816-749-4433; 707 Edmond St; mains $12-30; ⊘11am-2pm & 5-9pm Tue-Sat, 10am-3pm Sun) As the name implies, bad art (think wonky

still-life drawings and photos of feet) abounds at this high-end bistro. The chef-driven menu includes dishes like lobster mac 'n' cheese and fresh steaks hand cut daily.

★Tiger's Den
BAR

(☑816-617-2108; 519 Felix St; ⊙4-11pm Sun & Mon, 11am-11pm Tue & Wed, 11am-1am Thu-Sat) Part used bookstore, part cocktail bar, Tiger's Den is the stuff of Hemingway dreams. Sit on one of the plush sofas and order a drink inspired by the contents of the all-surrounding bookshelves, including Agatha Christie's Sparkling Cyanide or a Tequila Mockingbird.

❶ Getting There & Away

St Joseph is about an hour north of Kansas City along I-29. Jefferson Lines (www.jeffersonlines.com) buses ply the route (adult $14).

IOWA

The towering bluffs on the Mississippi River and the soaring Loess Hills lining the Missouri River bookend the rolling farmland of this bucolic state. In the middle you'll find the writers' town of Iowa City, the commune dwellers of the Amana Colonies, and plenty of picture-perfect rural towns, including those amid the covered bridges of Madison County.

Iowa emerges from slumber every four years as the make-or-break state for presidential hopefuls. The Iowa Caucus opens the national election battle, and wins by George W Bush in 2000 and Barack Obama in 2008 stunned many pundits and launched their victorious campaigns.

❶ Information

Iowa Bed & Breakfast Guild (www.ia-bedn breakfast-inns.com)

Iowa State Parks (www.iowadnr.gov) State parks are free to visit. Some 50% to 75% of the park campsites are reservable (www.iowa stateparks.reserveamerica.com); fees range from $6 to $16 per night.

Iowa Tourism Office (www.traveliowa.com)

Iowa Wine & Beer (www.iowawineandbeer. com) Craft brewing and, yes, wine making are booming in Iowa. Get the handy app.

Des Moines

Des Moines, meaning 'of the monks' not 'in the corn' as the surrounding fields might suggest, is Iowa's fast-growing capital. The city has an amazing state capitol building, buzzing enclaves like the East Village and one of the nation's best state fairs. Pause for a night, but then get out and see the rest of Iowa.

◉ Sights

The Des Moines River slices through downtown. The Court Ave Entertainment District sits just west, while East Village, at the foot of the capitol, and east of the river, is home to galleries, eateries, clubs and a few gay bars.

★Pappajohn Sculpture Park
PARK

(www.desmoinesartcenter.org; 1330 Grand Ave; ⊙6am-midnight) This curvaceous public park has great skyline views and features sculptures by 22 celebrated artists, including Sol LeWitt, Keith Haring and Willem de Kooning. Fine-dining restaurants and boutique shops line its perimeter.

State Capitol
HISTORIC BUILDING

(☑515-281-5591; cnr E 9th St & Grand Ave; ⊙8am-5pm Mon-Fri, 9am-4pm Sat) FREE From the sparkling gold dome to the spiral staircases and stained glass in the law library, every detail at this bling-heavy capitol (1886) seems to try to outdo the next. Join a free tour and you can climb halfway up the dome.

✵ Festivals & Events

★Iowa State Fair
FAIR

(☑800-545-3247; www.iowastatefair.org; cnr E 30th St & E University Ave; adult/child $12/6; ⊙7am-midnight mid-Aug; ♠) Much more than just country music and butter sculpture, this festival draws a million visitors over its 11-day run. They enjoy the award-winning farm critters and just about every food imaginable that can be shoved on a stick. It's the setting for the Rodgers and Hammerstein musical *State Fair* and the 1945 film version.

⬛ Sleeping

Chains of all flavors congregate on I-80 at exits 121, 124, 131 and 136. Indie motels hug 14th St on either side of the river.

✗ Eating & Drinking

B & B Grocery, Meat & Deli
AMERICAN $

(☑515-243-7607; www.bbgrocerymeatdeli.com; 2001 SE 6th St; mains $4-9; ⊙8:30am-6pm Tue-Fri, to 3pm Sat) 'Keeping Iowans on top of the food chain since 1922!' is the slogan at this hole-in-the-wall store just south of down-

MADISON COUNTY

This scenic county, about 30 miles southwest of Des Moines, slumbered for half a century until Robert James Waller's blockbuster, tear-jerking novel *The Bridges of Madison County* and its 1995 Clint Eastwood/Meryl Streep movie version brought in scores of fans to check out the covered bridges where Robert and Francesca fueled their affair.

The farms and open land in this area are pleasantly bucolic, and the towns postcard-perfect. **St Charles** is home to the oldest of the six surviving covered bridges, while tourism-hub **Winterset** has the rest, as well as a gorgeous silver-domed courthouse.

In between the two you'll find a few vineyards, breweries and cideries. Pick up a county map (or download one) from the **Winterset Chamber of Commerce** (☑ 515-462-1185; www.madisoncounty.com; 73 Jefferson St, Winterset; ⊙ 9am-4pm Mon-Sat, noon-3pm Sun May-Oct, 10am-3pm Mon-Fri Nov-Apr).

THE GREAT PLAINS DAVENPORT

town. Enjoy Iowa comfort food such as meaty sandwiches that include the 'killer pork tenderloin,' a bun-smothering creation.

El Bait Shop BEER HALL
(☑ 515-284-1970; http://elbaitshop.com; 200 SW 2nd St; ⊙ 11am-2am) With 222 flowing taps, this sprawling indoor-outdoor complex claims to offer the world's largest selection of American craft beers.

❶ Getting There & Away

Des Moines International Airport (DSM; ☑ 515-256-5050; www.dsmairport.com; 5800 Fleur Dr) is located 3 miles southwest of town and receives direct flights from most major US cities. Burlington Trailways (www.burlingtontrailways.com) has several daily buses to Omaha ($34, 2½ hours), while Jefferson Lines (www.jeffersonlines.com) makes trips to Kansas City ($45, three hours).

Davenport

Davenport is the largest and most vibrant of the so-called Quad Cities (Davenport and Bettendorf in Iowa and Moline and Rock Island in Illinois). It boasts a grand setting on the Mississippi River with a vast network of walking and biking trails.

◉ Sights

Figge Art Museum MUSEUM
(☑ 563-326-7804; www.figgeartmuseum.org; 225 W 2nd St; adult/child $7/4; ⊙ 10am-5pm Tue, Fri & Sat, to 9pm Thu, noon-5pm Sun) The glass-walled Figge Art Museum sparkles above the River Road. The museum's Midwest Regionalist Collection includes many works by Iowa native (and *American Gothic* painter) Grant Wood; you can also stroll through the world-class Haitian and Mexican Colonial collections.

🛏 Sleeping & Eating

★ **Beiderbecke Bed & Breakfast** B&B $$
(☑ 563-323-0047; www.beiderbeckeinn.com; 532 W 7th St; r $95-110; ❊) This is the Stick-style Victorian home where the parents of jazz legend Bix Beiderbecke grew up. Now a four-room B&B, it's got some incredible period wallpaper and wild rugs with competing patterns. The rooms are spacious and two have river views.

Freight House MARKET $
(☑ 563-322-6009; www.freighthousefarmersmarket.com; 421 W River Dr; ⊙ hours vary, farmers market 3-6pm Tue, 8am-1pm Sat) Your one-stop source for organic goods, local craft beers and deli sandwiches in an old rail freight house on the waterfront. The two-story brick complex also has a fantastic farmers market with heaps of regional produce.

❶ Information

The **visitor center** (☑ 563-322-3911; www.visitquadcities.com; 102 S Harrison St; ⊙ 9am-5pm Mon-Fri, to 4pm Sat Jun-Aug, 10am-4pm Mon-Fri Sep-May) is in the old Union Station on the river downtown and has bike rentals ($8 per hour, April to October) for a ride along the Big Muddy.

❶ Getting There & Away

Davenport lies on the border with Illinois and is less than three hours away from the airports in Chicago along either I-88 or I-80. Des Moines is about 2½ hours in the other direction along I-80, while Dubuque is two hours north along the Great River Road. Greyhound (www.greyhound.com) plies the route from Chicago ($20, four hours), while Burlington Trailways (www.burlingtontrailways.com) is your best bet for onward journeys into Iowa.

Iowa City

The youthful, artsy vibe here is courtesy of the University of Iowa campus, home to good art and natural-history museums. It spills across both sides of the Iowa River (which has good walks on the banks); to the east it mingles with the charming downtown. In summer (when the student-to-townie ratio evens out), the city mellows somewhat. The school's writing programs are renowned, and Iowa City was named a Unesco City of Literature in 2008. For a sharp parody of the town and school, read Jane Smiley's *Moo*.

◎ Sights

Old Capitol Museum MUSEUM
(☑319-335-0548; https://oldcap.uiowa.edu; cnr Clinton St & Iowa Ave; ◎10am-5pm Tue, Wed, Fri & Sat, to 8pm Thu, 1-5pm Sun) FREE The cute gold-domed building at the heart of the University of Iowa campus is the Old Capitol. Built in 1840, it was the seat of government until 1857 when Des Moines grabbed the reins. It's now a museum with galleries and furnishings from back in its heyday.

🛏 Sleeping & Eating

★**Brown Street Inn** B&B $$
(☑319-338-0435; www.brownstreetinn.com; 430 Brown St; r $110-165; ❀@⚡) Four-poster beds and other antiques adorn this six-room 1913 Dutch Colonial place that's an easy walk from downtown. Ask the amiable owner about the house next door where Kurt Vonnegut wrote early chapters of *Slaughterhouse-Five*.

Clinton Street Social Club GASTROPUB $$
(☑319-351-1690; https://clintonstreetsocial.com; 18½ S Clinton St; mains $10-28; ◎4pm-2am) This swanky 2nd-floor gastropub boasts locally sourced meals and killer libations at the long cocktail bar. Classic movies play on Monday nights and there's live jazz at least twice a month on Thursdays. Professors often come here for half-priced cocktails and bar food during 'social hour' (weekdays 4pm to 6pm).

🍸 Drinking & Nightlife

Iowa City roars to life after the sun sets, with everything from swanky cocktail lounges to throbbing college bars and live-music venues.

Dave's Fox Head Tavern BAR
(☑319-351-9824; 402 E Market St; ◎6pm-2am Mon-Sat) Popular with the Writers' Workshop crowd, who debate gerunds while slouched in booths in this tiny boozer. Is that TC Boyle by the door?

🛍 Shopping

Prairie Lights BOOKS
(☑319-337-2681; www.prairielights.com; 15 S Dubuque St; ◎10am-9pm Mon-Sat, to 6pm Sun) A bookstore worthy of the Iowa Writers' Workshop.

❶ Getting There & Away

Iowa City is about 115 miles east of Des Moines along I-80. Davenport is another 55 miles east along the same highway. Burlington Trailways (www.burlingtontrailways.com) buses link Iowa City with Des Moines ($18, two hours), Davenport ($12, one hour) and a few other regional cities.

Amana Colonies

These seven villages, just northwest of Iowa City, are stretched along a 17-mile loop. All were established as German religious communes between 1855 and 1861 by Inspirationists who, until the Great Depression, lived a utopian life with no wages paid and all assets communally owned. Unlike the Amish and Mennonite religions, Inspirationists embrace modern technology (and tourism).

Today the well-preserved (and discreetly tasteful) villages offer a glimpse of this unique culture, and there are lots of arts, crafts, cheeses, baked goods and wines to buy. Nearly everything is hand-crafted in the villages by the villagers.

Stop at the grain-elevator-shaped **Amana Colonies Visitors Center** (☑319-622-7622; www.amanacolonies.com; 622 46th Ave, Amana; ◎9am-5pm Mon-Sat, 10am-5pm Sun May-Oct, 10am-4pm daily Nov-Apr) for the essential guide-map. It also has bike rentals (the best way to tour the area; $15 per day May to October) and sells a ticket good for all the museums (adult $7).

The closest village to Iowa City is Homestead, 20 miles northwest. The rest of the villages are connected along a 17-mile loop. There is no public transportation from Iowa City.

Mt Vernon

In a state blessed with pretty places, Mt Vernon is one of the loveliest. It's located along the historic Lincoln Hwy – one of the first transcontinental routes across America – and boasts tree-lined streets brimming with antique dealers, art galleries and eclectic little stores.

🛏 Sleeping & Eating

Brackett House   B&B $$
(📞319-560-5904; www.bracketthousebnb.com; 418 2nd St SW; r $125-150; 😊❄@🛜) This charming B&B is run by the adjacent Cornell College and has four spacious rooms, three of which have sunny screened-in porches. The decor is modern and the location is ideal for a quick stroll downtown.

Big Grove Brewery   MODERN AMERICAN $$
(📞319-624-2337; www.biggrovebrewery.com; 101 W Main St, Solon; mains $9-30; ⊘kitchen 11am-9pm Tue-Sun) Hits a home run with cliché-busting takes on Iowa comfort food that's seasonal, locally sourced and great alongside its home-brewed beers. Located 10 miles south of Mt Vernon in neighboring Solon.

ℹ Information

Grab a map at the **Mt Vernon Visitors Center** (📞319-210-9935; www.visitmvl.com; 311 1st St NW; ⊘9am-4pm Mon-Fri) and set off on a self-guided audio tour of the historic town.

ℹ Getting There & Away

Mt Vernon is 20 miles north of Iowa City on IA-1. There is no public transportation between the two places.

Dubuque

This historic city, with its 19th-century Victorian homes lining narrow streets between the Mississippi River and seven steep limestone hills, makes a fine base for Great River Road explorations. Take a stroll down the 9-mile path along the waterfront, hop aboard a riverboat or explore neighborhoods in the midst of urban revitalization, where old factories are getting new lives, being transformed into shops, bars and restaurants.

👁 Sights

★National Mississippi River Museum & Aquarium   MUSEUM
(📞563-557-9545; www.rivermuseum.com; 350 E 3rd St; adult/child $15/10; ⊘9am-6pm Jun-Aug, 10am-5pm Sep-May) Learn about life (of all sorts) on the Mississippi at this impressive museum, part of a vast riverfront development. Exhib-

---

SILOS & SMOKESTACKS NATIONAL HERITAGE AREA

Comprising 37 counties in northeast Iowa, this National Park Service–designated region includes more than 100 sites and attractions that honor the region's industrial past and storybook farm beauty. Highlights include the scenic bluffs of **Effigy Mounds National Monument** (📞563-873-3491; www.nps.gov/efmo; Hwy 76, Marquette; ⊘8am-6pm Jun-Aug, to 4:30pm Sep-May) **FREE**, the rustic villages of the Amana Colonies and the informative exhibits of the National Mississippi River Museum & Aquarium. Back-road drives abound. Look for the helpful *Silos & Smokestacks* annual guide at hotels and visitor centers or learn more at www.silosandsmokestacks.org.

---

its span steamboating, aquatic life and indigenous Mississippi River dwellers.

4th Street Elevator   FUNICULAR
(www.fenelonplaceelevator.com; cnr 4th St & Bluff; round-trip adult/child $3/1.50; ⊘8am-10pm Apr-Nov) Built in 1882, this funicular railway climbs a steep hill from downtown for huge views.

🛏 Sleeping & Eating

Hotel Julien   HISTORIC HOTEL $$
(📞563-556-4200; www.hoteljuliendubuque.com; 200 Main St; r $120-250; ❄🛜) The historic eight-story Hotel Julien was built in 1915 and was once a refuge for Al Capone. It's quite spiffy after a lavish renovation and is a real antidote for chains.

Brazen Open Kitchen   AMERICAN $$
(📞563-587-8899; www.brazenopenkitchen.com; 955 Washington St; mains $12-30; ⊘4:30-9pm Tue-Thu, to 10pm Fri & Sat) The poetic menus at this stylish amber-lit restaurant in the Millwork District are organized like so: roots + soil, flour + water, farm + fish. The resulting New American cuisine, which draws inspiration from around the world, is truly heavenly. There's a sizable wine list and inventive cocktails at the long wooden bar.

ℹ Information

The downtown **visitor center** (📞800-798-8844; www.traveldubuque.com; 280 Main St; ⊘9am-5pm Mon-Sat, 10am-3pm Sun Apr-Nov,

9am-5pm Mon-Fri, 10am-4pm Sat Dec-Mar) has information for the entire region and state.

Getting There & Away

Dubuque is just over three hours west of Chicago via US 20 and I-90. It's near the center point for the Great River Road, and about 1½ hours away from Cedar Valley, Davenport and Iowa City by car. Greyhound (www.greyhound.com) plies the route from Chicago ($45, 4½ hours), while Burlington Trailways (www.burlingtontrailways.com) is your best bet for onward journeys into Iowa.

Cedar Valley

Home to five John Deere tractor factories, **Waterloo** is the place to get one of those prized green-and-yellow caps you've seen across middle America. There are also some regal old buildings in the otherwise gritty downtown. Nearby **Cedar Falls** is Waterloo's posh little sister city with a crooked Main St brimming with boutique shops and cafes. Both are at the heart of the Cedar Valley, a regional hub for outdoor recreation with numerous trails for biking, hiking and paddling.

Tours

Tractor Assembly Tours TOURS
(☎319-292-7668; www.deere.com; 3500 E Donald St, Waterloo; ⏰tours 8am, 10am & 1pm Mon-Fri) FREE Fun and free tractor-driven tours show how tractors are made. The minimum age is 13 and reservations are required.

Sleeping & Eating

★**Blackhawk Hotel** HISTORIC HOTEL $$
(☎319-277-1161; www.theblackhawkhotel.com; 115 Main St, Cedar Falls; r $90-170; P❄☜) This is the longest continuously operating hotel west of the Mississippi and a true treasure of downtown Cedar Falls. Open since 1853 – and revamped in 2012 – it's welcomed everyone from the Beach Boys to former

WORTH A TRIP

IOWA'S GREAT RIVER ROAD

Iowa's Great River Road mostly hugs the Mississippi along the state's eastern edge. It combines numerous country byways and passes through some beautifully isolated riverfront towns. Meet the route in Iowa's far northeastern corner at **Lansing**, an attractive resort town with a grand panorama of three states from the top of **Mt Hosmer Park**.

Continue south to Effigy Mounds National Monument (p663), where hundreds of mysterious Native American burial mounds lie in bluffs above the Mississippi River. Listen to songbirds as you hike the lush trails.

Neighboring **Marquette** and **McGregor** are next up. Both are delightful historic villages whose main drags are worthy of a quick stroll. The latter is the gateway to **Pikes Peak State Park** (☎563-873-2341; https://iowastateparks.reserveamerica.com; 32264 Pikes Peak Rd, McGregor; park entrance free, campsites May-Sep $11, Oct-Apr $6), a nature reserve at the confluence of the Wisconsin and Mississippi Rivers with 10 intertwined hiking trails and sweeping views from the hilltop campground.

Dip down into **Guttenberg**, a modern town with a strip of shops and eateries along the riverfront, before entering the regional hub of Dubuque (p663) where you can learn about life on the Mississippi at the impressive National Mississippi River Museum & Aquarium (p663). Part of a vast riverfront development, its exhibits span steamboating, aquatic life and indigenous Mississippi River dwellers.

Along an especially scenic stretch of the road south of Dubuque you'll find **Bellevue**, which lives up to its name with good river views and some verdant, rural scenery. Stop at **Potter's Mill** (☎563-872-3838; www.pottersmill.net; 300 Potter Dr, Bellevue; mains $10-16; ⏰11am-8pm Sun-Thu, to 10pm Fri & Sat, closed Mon Oct-Apr), an old grain mill where you can chow down on hearty Southern cooking while listening to live jazz and blues music.

The landscape flattens out from here with wide-open vistas as you enter the bustling streets of Davenport (p661), the largest of the so-called Quad Cities. Further south, **Burlington** has an excellent welcome center and is good for a quick break before you finish up the journey near **Old Madison Fort**, a reconstruction of the Midwest's oldest American military garrison on the upper Mississippi.

Get more info on the entire route at www.iowagreatriverroad.com.

president Bill Clinton. There are 28 rooms in the historic hotel and 15 cheaper ones in a modern building behind it.

★ **Galleria De Paco** ITALIAN $$
(☑319-833-7226; 622 Commercial St, Waterloo; mains $15-35; ⊙5-10pm Tue-Thu, to midnight Fri & Sat) It took Michelangelo four years to paint the ceiling of the Sistine Chapel, but it took Evelin 'Paco' Rosic just four months to make a half-sized reproduction of it in spray paint on the ceiling of his Italian eatery in downtown Waterloo. This over-the-top restaurant lures visitors in with its lavish theatrics, but the gourmet meals have yet to disappoint.

❶ Getting There & Away

Cedar Valley is equidistant from Des Moines, Dubuque and Iowa City at about 1½ hours away from each by car. Burlington Trailways (www.burlingtontrailways.com) runs daily buses from Waterloo to Iowa City ($34, two hours) and Dubuque ($34, two hours).

NORTH DAKOTA

Fields of grain – green in spring and summer, bronze in fall and white in winter – stretch beyond every horizon in magnificently desolate North Dakota. Except for the rugged 'badlands' of the far west, geographic relief is subtle; often it's the collapsing remains of a failed homestead that break up the vista.

This is one of the least-visited states in the US, but that just means that there's less traffic as you whiz along. This is a place to get lost on remote two-lane routes and to appreciate the raw land's beauty. And don't forget to pause to marvel at the meadowlarks' songs.

Despite those seemingly endless fields of grain, the state's economy is tied to large oil deposits in the west. Soaring energy prices turned once-moribund towns like Williston and Watford City into boomtowns, with vast oil-field-worker encampments, roads clogged – and battered – by trucks, and constant parades of tanker trains.

❶ Information

North Dakota Bed & Breakfast Association (www.ndbba.com)
North Dakota State Parks (www.parkrec.nd.gov) Vehicle permits cost $5/25 per day/year. Nearly half of the park campsites are

---

OFF THE BEATEN TRACK

ELDON

Grab a 'tool' out of your trunk and make your very own parody of Grant Wood's iconic *American Gothic* (1930) – the pitchfork painting – in tiny Eldon, about 90 miles southeast of Des Moines. The original house is across from the **American Gothic House Center** (☑641-652-3352; www.americangothichouse.net; American Gothic St; ⊙10am-5pm Tue-Sat, 1-4pm Sun & Mon) **FREE**, which interprets the artwork that sparked a million parodies (it even has loaner costumes so you can make your own parody selfie). The actual painting is in the Art Institute of Chicago.

reservable; fees range from $12 to $30 per night. Many parks also have tipis ($35) and cabins ($55).
North Dakota Tourism (www.ndtourism.com)

Fargo

Named for the Fargo of Wells Fargo Bank, North Dakota's biggest city has been a fur-trading post, a frontier town, a quick-divorce capital and a haven for folks in the Federal Witness Protection Program; not to mention the namesake of the Coen Brothers' film *Fargo* – though the movie was set across the Red River in Minnesota. Still, expect to hear a lot of accents similar to Frances McDormand's unforgettable version in the movie. Film fame aside, the city is thin on actual attractions. Yet, the attractive brick establishments of downtown make it worthy of at least a one-night stopover.

◉ Sights

Plains Art Museum MUSEUM
(☑701-551-6100; www.plainsart.org; 704 1st Ave N; adult/child $7.50/free; ⊙11am-5pm Tue, Wed, Fri & Sat, to 9pm Thu) This ambitious little museum features sophisticated programming in a renovated warehouse. The permanent collection includes contemporary work by Native American artists.

Fargo Woodchipper FILM LOCATION
(☑701-282-3653; www.fargomoorhead.org; 2001 44th St, I-94 exit 348; ⊙7:30am-8pm Mon-Fri, 10am-6pm Sat & Sun Jun-Aug, 8am-5pm Mon-Fri, 9am-4pm Sat Sep-May) **FREE** Fargo's embrace of its namesake film is on full display at the

> **MOUNTAIN TIME IN NORTH DAKOTA**
>
> The southwest quarter of North Dakota, including Medora, uses Mountain Time, which is one hour earlier than the rest of the state's Central Time.

town's visitor center, which houses the actual woodchipper used for the scene where Gaear feeds the last of Carl's body into its maw and is discovered by Marge. You can reenact the scene – although not the results – while wearing Fargo-style hats and jamming in a fake leg (both provided!).

Sleeping & Eating

★**Hotel Donaldson** HOTEL $$
(☑701-478-1000; www.hoteldonaldson.com; 101 Broadway; r from $185; 🕸@🛜) A stylish and swank revamp of a flophouse, the 17 luxurious suites here are each decorated by a local artist. Fargo's most chic restaurant, HoDo, and rooftop bar (and hot tub!) await. There's also free wine and cheese each evening at 5pm!

Wurst Bier Hall GERMAN $
(☑701-478-2437; www.wurstfargo.com; 630 1st Ave N; mains $6-12; 🕑11am-midnight) This always-hopping German-style beer hall ups the stakes with inventive sausage sandwiches, exotic meats and a creative list of beers on tap. There's even a number of fake-meat and gluten-free alternatives.

Getting There & Away

Hector International Airport (FAR; http://fargoairport.com; 2801 32nd Ave N) is 3 miles northwest of Fargo and receives flights from regional hubs like Chicago, Minneapolis and Denver. Jefferson Lines (www.jeffersonlines.com) has daily buses to Bismarck ($40, three hours) and Minneapolis ($45, 4½ hours).

Bismarck

Like the surrounding plains of wheat, Bismarck, North Dakota's capital, has a quick and bountiful summer. Otherwise, it's a place that hunkers down for the long winters, where temperature lows average -4°F (-20°C). The compact downtown has a stellar collection of shops and eateries, but the sprawl that radiates out from it is rather uninspiring.

Sights

★**North Dakota Heritage Center** MUSEUM
(☑701-328-2666; www.history.nd.gov; 612 East Boulevard Ave, Capitol Hill; 🕑8am-5pm Mon-Fri, 10am-5pm Sat & Sun) FREE Behind the Sacagawea statue, the North Dakota Heritage Center has details on everything from Norwegian bachelor farmers to the scores of nuclear bombs perched on missiles in silos across the state.

Fort Abraham Lincoln State Park HISTORIC SITE
(www.parkrec.nd.gov; off Hwy 1806; per vehicle $5, tours adult/child $6/4; 🕑park 9am-5pm, tours May-Sep) The highlight at this park on the west bank of the Missouri is **On-a-Slant Indian Village**, which has five re-created Mandan earth lodges. The fort, with several replica buildings, was Custer's last stop before the Battle of Little Bighorn. It's 7 miles south of Mandan (or about 13 miles from downtown Bismarck).

State Capitol HISTORIC BUILDING
(☑701-328-2480; 600 E Boulevard Ave, Capitol Hill; 🕑8am-4pm Mon-Fri, 9am-4pm Sat, 1-4pm Sun Jun-Aug, 9am-4pm Mon-Fri Sep-May, tours hourly except noon) FREE The stark 1930s State Capitol is often referred to as the 'skyscraper of the prairie,' and looks something like a Stalinist school of dentistry from the outside, but has some art-deco flourishes inside. There's an observation deck on the 18th floor.

Information

Bismarck-Mandan Visitor Center (☑701-222-4308; www.noboundariesnd.com; 1600 Burnt Boat Dr, I-94 exit 157; 🕑8am-7pm Mon-Fri, to 5pm Sat, 10am-4pm Sun Jun-Aug, 8am-5pm Mon-Fri Sep-May) Has oodles of North Dakota gifts for those back home.

Getting There & Away

Bismarck Airport (BIS; www.bismarckairport.com; 2301 University Dr) is 3 miles southeast of the city and receives flights from regional hubs like Denver, Minneapolis and Chicago. Jefferson Lines (www.jeffersonlines.com) has daily buses to Fargo ($40, three hours).

Theodore Roosevelt National Park

Future president Theodore Roosevelt retreated from New York to this remote spot in his early 20s after losing both his wife and mother in a matter of hours. It's said that his time in the Dakota badlands inspired him to become an avid conservationist, and he set aside 230 million acres of federal land while in office, a quantity of land larger than Texas! Explore his lasting legacy at **Theodore Roosevelt National Park** (☑701-623-4466; www.nps.gov/thro; 7-day pass per vehicle $25), one of the most underappreciated stars of the park system.

Wildlife abounds in these surreal mounds of striated earth, from mule deer to wild horses, bison, bighorn sheep and elk. There are also around 200 bird species, and innumerable prairie dogs in sprawling subterranean towns. Sunrise is your best time for animal encounters, while sunset is particularly evocative as shadows dance across the lonely buttes, painting them in an array of earth tones before they fade to black.

The resort town of Medora makes a great base with comfortable lodgings across all budgets. The park itself has two campgrounds, including the more popular **Cottonwood Campground** (☑701-623-4466; www.recreation.gov; tent sites $7-14; ☺year-round). Backcountry camping requires a free permit.

Medora is the only place to eat near the **South Unit Visitor Center** (off I-94 exits 24 & 27, Medora; ☺8am-6pm Jun-Aug, to 4:30pm Sep-May), while less-attractive Watford City is closer to the less-visited North Unit.

Medora is 135 miles west of Bismarck along I-94. There is no public transportation in the region.

Rugby

Rugby's big claim to fame is its location at the geographical center of North America. Attempts to milk this fact haven't always succeeded – even the tiny marker by **Coffee Cottage** (☑701-776-7650; 106 Hwy 2 SW; mains $6-10; ☺8am-8pm Mon-Sat, to 4pm Sun) is so insignificant you'll probably drive right by – but the town makes for a decent stopover to fuel up, grab a bite and check out the **Prairie Village Museum** (☑701-776-6414; www.prairievillagemuseum.com; 102 US 2 SE; adult/child $7/3; ☺8:30am-5pm Mon-Sat, noon-5pm Sun mid-May–mid-Sep).

Rugby is about 2½ hours northeast of Bismarck or one hour east of Minot by car. Amtrak's *Empire Builder* runs between Rugby and Fargo ($34, 3½ hours, one daily).

SOUTH DAKOTA

Gently rolling prairies through shallow fertile valleys mark much of this endlessly attractive state. But head southwest and all hell breaks loose – in the best possible way. The Badlands National Park is the geologic equivalent of fireworks. The Black Hills are like opera: majestic, challenging, intriguing and even frustrating. Mt Rushmore matches the Statue of Liberty for five-star icon status.

ⓘ Information

Bed & Breakfast Innkeepers of South Dakota (www.southdakotabb.com)
South Dakota Department of Tourism (www.travelsd.com)
South Dakota State Parks (www.gfp.sd.gov) Vehicle permits cost $6/30 per day/year. Many park campsites are reservable (www.campsd.com); fees range from $11 to $21 per night. Cabins start at $40.

Sioux Falls

South Dakota's largest city lives up to its name at Falls Park, where the Big Sioux River plunges through a long series of rock faces. Just south of here lies a buzzing downtown district with a burgeoning foodie scene and some of the best eats in the region.

The **visitor information center** (☑605-367-7430; www.visitsiouxfalls.com; 900 N Phillips Ave; ☺10am-9pm Apr–mid-Oct, reduced hours mid-Oct–Apr) in Falls Park has city-wide information and an observation tower.

Jefferson Lines (www.jeffersonlines.com) buses travel to Rapid City ($72, six hours), Fargo ($50, 4½ hours) and Omaha ($40, 3½ hours).

★**Falls Park**   PARK
Stroll along the grass-lined paths to the city's star attraction – its rambling namesake

---

THE ENCHANTED HIGHWAY

Boasting huge whimsical metal sculptures of local folks and critters by artist Gary Greff, the Enchanted Hwy runs for 32 miles straight south to Regent from I-94 exit 72. Once there, you can stay in Greff's themed motel, the **Enchanted Castle** (☑701-563-4858; www.enchanted-castlend.com; 607 Main St, Regent; r $100-135; ✳@✆), which is an elementary school remodeled with crenelations.

waterfall – at this picturesque park. Popular with amorous couples, it has a perfectly placed cafe and plenty of scenic overlooks. Visit between mid-November and mid-January and it becomes a winter wonderland with 355,000 twinkling lights.

Old Courthouse Museum MUSEUM
(☑ 605-367-4210; www.siouxlandmuseums.com; 200 W 6th St; ☺ 8am-5pm Mon-Wed & Fri, to 9pm Thu, 9am-5pm Sat, noon-5pm Sun) FREE This huge and restored pink quartzite 1890s building has three floors of changing exhibits on the region.

★ **MB Haskett
Delicatessen** MODERN AMERICAN $$
(☑ 605-367-1100; www.mbhaskett.com; 324 S Phillips Ave; mains $10-21; ☺ 8am-9pm Sun-Thu, to 11pm Fri & Sat) Michael Haskett's retro cafe serves brilliant food throughout the day, from breakfast through dinner. The ever-changing menu draws inspiration from the seasons and from around the globe. Weekends shine with three-course prix-fixe dinners.

Chamberlain

In a picturesque site where I-90 crosses the milky-blue Missouri River, Chamberlain (exit 263) is home to some worthwhile spots to learn about both local tribes and the Lewis and Clark expedition that passed through the area.

The best reason to detour off I-90 immerses you in large swaths of South Dakota

that haven't changed since the 19th century, when the Native Americans and US Army clashed. The **Native American Scenic Byway** (www.byways.org) begins in Chamberlain on Hwy 50 and meanders 100 crooked miles northwest to Pierre along Hwy 1806, following the Missouri River through rolling, rugged countryside.

Chamberlain is about 100 miles southeast of Pierre along the Native American Scenic Byway. Jefferson Lines (www.jeffersonlines.com) runs a daily bus between the two places ($35, 1½ hours).

★ **Akta Lakota Museum
& Cultural Center** MUSEUM
(☑ 800-798-3452; www.aktalakota.org; 1301 N Main St; suggested donation $5; ☺ 8am-6pm Mon-Sat, 9am-5pm Sun May-Oct, 8am-4:30pm Mon-Fri Nov-Apr) This excellent museum and cultural center at St Joseph's Indian School has Lakota cultural displays and contemporary art from numerous tribes. Check the gift shop for locally made jewelry, quilts and dream catchers.

Lewis & Clark Information Center MUSEUM
(☑ 605-734-4562; I-90 exit 264; ☺ 8:30am-4:30pm mid-May–Sep) FREE History buffs should pop into the hilltop rest stop, south of town, where this information center has exhibits on the intrepid duo.

Pierre

Pierre (pronounced 'peer') boasts a scenic location on the Missouri River and makes a decent stopover in the middle of South Dakota. It's the capital of South Dakota, but it's just too small and ordinary to feel like the seat of power.

◉ Sights

**South Dakota Cultural
Heritage Center** MUSEUM
(☑ 605-773-3458; www.history.sd.gov; 900 Governors Dr; adult/child $4/free; ☺ 9am-6:30pm Mon-Sat, 1-4:30pm Sun Jun-Aug, to 4:30pm rest of year) Exhibits at this ecologically groundbreaking museum (it's completely underground!) include a bloody Ghost Dance shirt from Wounded Knee.

State Capitol HISTORIC BUILDING
(☑ 605-773-3011; 500 E Capitol Ave; ☺ 8am-7pm Mon-Fri, to 5pm Sat & Sun) FREE Small-town Victorian homes overlook the imposing 1910 State Capitol with its black copper

dome. Be sure to check out the floor mosaics and marbled columns as you follow the self-guided tour (brochures on the lower level).

🛏 Sleeping & Eating

Hitching Horse Inn
B&B **$**

(📞 605-494-0550; 635 N Euclid Ave; r $70-100; ❄🐾) This welcoming four-room inn has an understated charm and is free of the stuffiness typical of other Midwestern B&Bs. Two of the rooms have Jacuzzi tubs and there's a tiny equestrian-themed beer and wine bar on the 1st floor that's popular with locals.

Cattleman's Club
STEAK **$$**

(📞 605-224-9774; www.cattlemansclubsteakhouse. com; 29608 Hwy 34; mains $8-30; ⊘5-10pm Mon-Sat) Offering a gorgeous view over the Missouri River, this famed steakhouse 6 miles east of town will not serve your sirloin well done (enjoy it pink and juicy!).

❶ Getting There & Away

Smack in the middle of South Dakota, Pierre is about 3½ hours from Sioux Falls and three hours from Rapid City by car, mostly along I-90. Jefferson Lines (www.jeffersonlines.com) runs daily trips from Pierre to Rapid City ($30, 3½ hours) and Sioux Falls ($34, 4½ hours).

Wall

This is the town that a thousand billboards built. Hyped for hundreds of miles, thanks to Wall Drug, there's no reason not to succumb.

◉ Sights

★ Wall Drug
LANDMARK

(📞 605-279-2175; www.walldrug.com; 510 Main St; ⊘7am-6pm; 🎮) Wall Drug is a surprisingly enjoyable tourist trap. It really does have 5¢ coffee, free ice water, good doughnuts and enough diversions and come-ons to warm the heart of schlock-lovers everywhere. But amid the fudge in this faux frontier complex is a superb **bookstore** with a great selection of regional titles. Out back, ride the mythical **jackalope** and check out the historical photos.

Story of Wounded Knee
MUSEUM

(📞 605-279-2573; www.woundedkneemuseum. org; 600 Main St; adult/child $6/free; ⊘9am-5pm mid-May–mid-Oct) This important small museum tells the story of the massacre from the

MITCHELL: THE CORN PALACE

The **Corn Palace** (📞605-995-8430; www.cornpalace.com; 604 N Main St; ⊘8am-9pm Jun-Aug, reduced hours Sep-May) is the king of roadside attractions, enticing more than half a million people to pull off I-90 each year. Close to 300,000 ears of corn are used annually to create a new tableaux of murals on the outside of the building. Ponder the scenes and you may find a kernel of truth or just say, 'aw, shucks.' Head inside to see photos of how the facade has evolved over the years.

Lakota perspective using photos and narratives. It's more insightful than anything at the actual site.

❶ Information

National Grasslands Visitors Center (📞605-279-2125; www.fs.fed.us/grasslands; 798 Main St; ⊘8am-4:30pm Mon-Fri) The National Grasslands Visitors Center in Wall has good displays on this underappreciated and complex ecosystem.

❶ Getting There & Away

Wall is just under an hour east of Rapid City by car on I-90. Jefferson Lines (www.jeffersonlines. com) has a daily bus between the two places ($15, one hour).

Badlands National Park

The otherworldly landscape of **Badlands National Park** (📞605-433-5361; www.nps. gov/badl; Hwy 240; 7-day park pass bicycle/car $10/20), oddly softened by its fantastic rainbow hues, is a spectacle of sheer walls and spikes stabbing the dry air. It was understandably named *mako sica* (badland) by Native Americans. Looking over the bizarre formations from the corrugated walls surrounding the park is like seeing an ocean someone boiled dry.

The **north unit** of the park is easily viewed on a half-day drive for those in a rush, though there are a number of short hiking trails that can get you right out into this earthen wonderland, including the surreal **Door Trail** near the Ben Reifel Visitor Center (p670). The less-accessible **south units** are in the Pine Ridge Indian Reservation and see few visitors. Bisecting the two is **Hwy 44**, which makes a scenic alternative between the Badlands and Rapid City.

☉ Sights

★ Hwy 240 Badlands Loop Rd   AREA

The park's north unit gets the most visitors; this stunning road is easily reached from I-90 (exits 110 and 131) and you can drive it in an hour if you're in a hurry (and not stuck behind an RV). It is the main thoroughfare through the park with lookouts, vistas and animal sightings aplenty.

Buffalo Gap
National Grassland   NATURE RESERVE

The Badlands, along with the surrounding Buffalo Gap National Grassland, protects the country's largest prairie grasslands, several species of Great Plains mammal (including bison and black-footed ferret), prairie falcons and lots of snakes. The National Grasslands Visitors Center (p669) has good displays on the wealth of life in this ecosystem, which the uninformed may dismiss as 'boring.'

🛏 Sleeping

The park has two campgrounds and a seasonal lodge. Hotels can be found on I-90 in Kadoka and Wall. There are also campgrounds and inns near the southern entrance at Interior. Accommodations tend to be cheaper (if less charming) outside the park.

❶ Information

Ben Reifel Visitor Center (☑605-433-5361; www.nps.gov/badl; Hwy 240; 7-day park pass bicycle/car $10/20; ☉8am-7pm Jun-Aug, to 5pm Apr, May, Sep & Oct, to 4pm Nov-Mar) The main visitor center for the park; has good exhibits and advice for ways to ditch your car to appreciate the geologic wonders.

White River Visitor Center (Hwy 27; ☉9am-4pm Jun-Aug) Small information outlet in the little-visited Stronghold Unit.

❶ Getting There & Around

Badlands National Park is 60 miles east of Rapid City, exiting I-90 at Wall. There is no public transportation to (or within) the park.

Pine Ridge Indian Reservation

Home to the Lakota Oglala Sioux, the Pine Ridge Reservation south of Badlands National Park is one of the nation's poorest 'counties,' with more than half the population living below the poverty line. Despite being at times a jarring dose of reality, it is also a place welcoming to visitors. Tune in to KILI (90.1FM), which often plays traditional music.

History

In 1890 the new Ghost Dance religion became popular and Lakota followers believed it would both bring back their ancestors and eliminate the white man. This struck fear into the area's soldiers and settlers and the frenetic circle dances were outlawed. The 7th US Cavalry rounded up a band of Lakota under Chief Big Foot and brought them to the small village of Wounded Knee.

On December 29, as the soldiers began to search for weapons, a shot was fired (nobody knows by who), leading to the massacre of more than 250 men, women and children, most of them unarmed. It's one of the most infamous atrocities in US history. Twenty-five soldiers also died.

☉ Sights

Wounded Knee Massacre Site   HISTORIC SITE
(Hwy 27) The massacre site, 16 miles northeast of Pine Ridge town, is marked by a faded sign. It helps to read up on the events before you arrive. The mass grave, often frequented by people looking for donations, sits atop the hill near a church. Small memorials appear daily amid the stones listing dozens of names such as Horn Cloud. It's a desolate place, with sweeping views.

Red Cloud Heritage Center   MUSEUM
(www.redcloudschool.org; 100 Mission Dr, Pine Ridge; ☉8am-6pm Mon-Sat, 10am-5pm Sun Jun-Aug, 9am-6pm Tue-Sat Sep-May) **FREE** This well-curated art museum has traditional and contemporary works and a craft shop with locally made artisan goods. Look for photos taken after the Wounded Knee massacre showing the frozen bodies of the dead with their expressions of shock locked in place. It's 4 miles north of Pine Ridge on Hwy 18 at the Red Cloud Indian School.

❶ Getting There & Away

The town of Pine Ridge is near the Nebraska border about two hours south of Rapid City by car. There are no public buses into the region.

Black Hills

They call the Black Hills an evergreen island in a sea of high-prairie grassland. This stunning region on the Wyoming–South Dakota border lures scores of visitors with its winding canyons and wildly eroded 7000ft peaks. The region's name – the 'Black' comes from the dark ponderosa-pine-covered slopes – was conferred by the Lakota Sioux. In the 1868 Fort Laramie Treaty, they were assured that the hills would be theirs for eternity, but the discovery of gold changed that, and the Sioux were shoved out to low-value flatlands only six years later. The 1990 film *Dances with Wolves* covers some of this period.

You'll need several days to explore the bucolic back-road drives, caves, bison herds, forests, and Mt Rushmore and Crazy Horse monuments, and to experience the abundant outdoor activities (ballooning, cycling, rock climbing, boating, fishing, hiking, downhill skiing, gold-panning etc). Like fool's gold, gaudy tourist traps lurk in corners.

The scenic spine of the Black Hills, US 385 runs 90 miles from Deadwood to Hot Springs and beyond. Beautiful meadows and dark stands of conifers are interspersed with roadside attractions that include wax presidents, animatronic beasts and a record-setting teddy-bear collection.

ⓘ Information

There are hundreds of hotels, cabins and campgrounds across the hills; still, during summer, room rates shoot up like geysers and reservations are essential. Avoid visiting during the **Sturgis Motorcycle Rally** (☑ 605-720-0800; www.sturgismotorcyclerally.com) in early August, when hogs rule the roads and fill the rooms. Much is closed October to April.

The **Black Hills Visitor Center** (☑ 605-355-3700; www.blackhillsbadlands.com; I-90 exit 61; ⊙ 8am-7pm Jun-Aug, to 5pm Sep-May) has tons of info and apps.

ⓘ Getting There & Around

Rapid City Regional Airport (RAP; www.rcgov.org/departments/airport.html; 4550 Terminal Rd) is 9 miles southeast of Rapid City and receives flights from as far away as Las Vegas, Houston and Atlanta. Jefferson Lines (www.jeffersonlines.com) buses travel across South Dakota to Sioux Falls once daily ($72, six hours), with stops in Wall and Mitchell.

There is no public transportation to (or within) the Black Hills so it's best to visit the region with your own wheels (bike or car).

Rapid City

A worthy capital to the region, 'Rapid' has a cosmopolitan air best appreciated in the intriguing, lively and walkable downtown.

DON'T MISS

JEWEL CAVE NATIONAL MONUMENT

If you visit only one Black Hills cave, **Jewel Cave National Monument** (☑ 605-673-8300; www.nps.gov/jeca; off US 16; tours adult $4-31, child free-$8; ⊙ visitor center 8am-5:30pm Jun-Sep, 8:30am-4:30pm Oct-May) would be a good excuse to visit the town of Custer and is so named because calcite crystals line much of its walls. Currently 187 miles have been surveyed (3% of the estimated total), making it the third-longest known cave in the world.

Well-preserved brick buildings, filled with quality shopping and dining, make it a good urban base for Black Hills exploration, particularly for those who enjoy their creature comforts.

◉ Sights

Get a walking-tour brochure of Rapid's historic buildings and public art from the Black Hills Visitor Center or the city's visitor center (p674). Check out the watery fun and regular events downtown on **Main St Square**. Nearby, visit **Art Alley** (north of Main St between 6th and 7th Sts), where urban-style graffiti and pop art has turned a mundane alley into a kaleidoscope of color. And besides presidents, look for **statues of dinosaurs** around town.

Family-friendly and proudly hokey tourist attractions vie for dollars along Hwy 16 on the way to Mt Rushmore.

★ Statues of Presidents   STATUE
(www.presidentsrc.com; 631 Main St; ⊙ info center noon-9pm Mon-Sat Jun-Sep) From a shifty-eyed Nixon in repose to a triumphant Harry Truman, lifelike statues dot corners throughout the center. Collect all 42. Maps available online.

**Journey Museum
& Learning Center**   MUSEUM
(☑ 605-394-6923; www.journeymuseum.org; 222 New York St; adult/child $10/7; ⊙ 9am-6pm Mon-Sat, 11am-5pm Sun Jun-Aug, 10am-5pm Mon-Sat, 1-5pm Sun Sep-May; ▣) Four museums in one! This impressive downtown facility looks at the history of the region from prehistoric times until today. Collections come from the vaunted **Museum of**

Black Hills & Badlands National Park

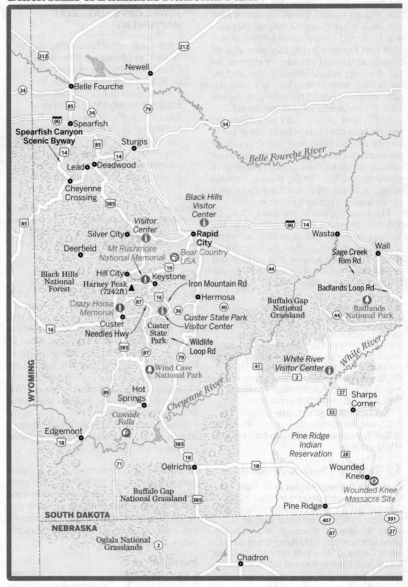

Geology (☏ 605-394-2467; http://museum. sdsmt.edu; 501 E St Joseph St, O'Harra Bldg; ☉9am-7pm Mon-Sat Jun-Aug, 9am-4pm Mon-Fri, 10am-4pm Sat Sep-May) **FREE**, the Sioux Indian Museum, the Minnilusa Pioneer Museum and the South Dakota Archaeological Research Center.

Bear Country USA WILDLIFE RESERVE
(☏ 605-343-2290; www.bearcountryusa.com; 13820 Hwy 16; adult/child $17/11; ☉8am-6pm May-

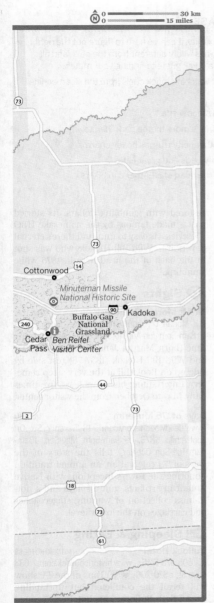

🛏 Sleeping

★Hotel Alex Johnson   HOTEL **$$**
(📞 605-342-1210; www.alexjohnson.com; 523 6th St; r $70-200; 🏢@🛜) The design of this 1927 classic magically blends Germanic Tudor architecture with traditional Lakota Sioux symbols – note the lobby's painted ceiling and the chandelier made of war lances. The rooftop bar is a delight, while the 143 rooms are modernized retro (some have fabulous views!). Ask at reception about the hotel's role in Hitchcock's *North by Northwest*.

Rushmore Hotel   HOTEL **$$**
(📞 605-348-8300; www.therushmorehotel.com; 445 Mt Rushmore Rd; r $100-200; 🅿🏢@🛜🛁) 🌿 This high-rise hotel has been transformed into a high-concept downtown gem with green accents. A lot of the furniture is made from recycled materials yet there's no skimping on comfort. The marble floor in the lobby is a stunner.

🍴 Eating & Drinking

Murphy's Pub & Grill   AMERICAN **$$**
(www.murphyspubandgrill.com; 510 9th St; mains $10-25; ⏱ food 11am-10pm, bar to 1am) Pub fare with creative flair makes this bustling downtown bar an excellent dining choice. Specials feature seasonal and local ingredients. The vast terrace is matched by the big interior.

Independent Ale House   PUB
(📞 605-718-9492; www.independentalehouse. com; 625 St Joseph St; ⏱ 3pm-late Sun-Thu, 11am-late Fri & Sat) Enjoy a fabulous (and changing) lineup of the best microbrews from the region in this vintage-style bar. The wine list is equally good. Pizzas are excellent (mains $8 to $15).

🔒 Shopping

★Prairie Edge   ARTS & CRAFTS
(📞 605-342-3408; www.prairieedge.com; 606 Main St; ⏱10am-6pm Mon-Sat, 11am-5pm Sun Jan-May, 9am-9pm Mon-Sat, 10am-5pm Sun Jun-Sep) This labyrinthine three-story shop has a truly mesmerizing collection of art, furniture and home goods made by members of the Northern Plains tribes. You'll also find out-of-print books and supplies to make your own Native American–inspired works. The upstairs galleries have better items on display than you'll find in many regional museums.

Aug, reduced hours Sep-Nov; ♿) Oodles of bears big and small in this drive-through park live off the land and hope you'll do something forbidden like offering them a Big Mac, or your hand. The attraction is 8 miles south of Rapid City.

CHOOSING YOUR BLACK HILLS BASE

With so many resort towns in such close proximity, it can be hard to figure out the right base for your Black Hills adventure. Each town is wildly different from the next, and all appeal to different types of travelers. Here's a quick guide to finding your match:

Deadwood Join modern-day fortune-seekers watching mock duels from the slot machine.

Hill City Relax in a peaceful alpine setting.

Hot Springs End each day of adventure at a steamy spa.

Keystone Stay along a family-friendly strip that's more theme park than town.

Lead Sleep in this unpolished gem where authenticity trumps hokey charms.

Rapid City Choose the regional hub for comfy beds and great eats.

Sturgis Take an ethnological adventure into the mind of all-American bikers.

ℹ️ Information

The **visitor center** (☏ 866-727-4324; www.visitrapidcity.com; 444 Mt Rushmore Rd; ⊙8am-5pm Mon-Fri) is a helpful resource in the Civic Center.

Sturgis

Neon-lit tattoo parlors, Christian iconography and billboards for ribald biker bars featuring dolled-up models are just some of the cacophony of images of this loud and proud biker town on I-90 (exits 30 and 32). Shop for leather on Main St, don your American-flag bandana and sidle up to the saloon bar to give a toast to the stars and stripes!

Sturgis Motorcycle Museum MUSEUM
(☏ 605-347-2001; www.sturgismuseum.com; 999 Main St; adult/child $10/free; ⊙9am-5pm May-Sep, 10am-4pm Oct-Apr) This small hall-of-fame-style museum packs in a surprising number of bikes, including vintage and rare V-twin and metric motorcycles.

Deadwood

Once the very definition of lawless, this town built on gold attracts a different kind of fortune-seeker these days with 80 gambling halls big and small that would no doubt put a sly grin on the faces of the hard characters who once stomped these grounds. Then again, loser's largesse is paying for Deadwood's restoration, even as it turns into a mini Vegas of the Plains.

Settled illegally by eager gold rushers in the 1870s, Deadwood is now a National Historic Landmark. Its atmospheric streets are lined with gold-rush-era buildings lavishly restored with gambling dollars. Its storied past – made famous by the namesake HBO TV series – is easy to find, and there's eternal devotion to Wild Bill Hickok, who was shot in the back of the head here in 1876 while gambling.

◉ Sights

★Mt Moriah Cemetery CEMETERY
(Mt Moriah Dr; adult/child $2/free, tours $10/5; ⊙8am-8pm Jun-Aug, to 5pm Sep-May) Calamity Jane (born Martha Jane Burke; 1852–1903) and Wild Bill Hickok (1837–76) rest side by side up on Boot Hill at the very steep cemetery. Entertaining bus tours leave five times daily, May to October, from the visitor center.

Days of '76 Museum MUSEUM
(www.deadwoodhistory.com; 18 Seventy Six Dr; adult/child $8/3; ⊙9am-5pm May-Sep, 10am-4pm Tue-Sun Oct-Apr) Tells the story of the Days of '76 celebration, an annual tradition honoring the town's inception, with Native American artifacts, gun displays and a not-to-miss collection of working stagecoaches and carriages on the lower level.

🛏️ Sleeping & Eating

Bullock Hotel HISTORIC HOTEL $$
(☏ 605-578-1745; www.historicbullock.com; 633 Main St; r $70-200; ❄️📶) Fans of the TV show will recall the conflicted but upstanding sheriff Seth Bullock. This hotel was opened by the real Bullock in 1895. The 28 rooms are modern and comfortable while retaining the building's period charm.

Deadwood Dick's HOTEL $$
(☏ 605-578-3224; www.deadwooddicks.com; 51 Sherman St; r $36-200; ❄️📶) These home-style and idiosyncratic rooms feature furniture

from the owner's antique shop, and range in size from small doubles to large suites with kitchens. The unique bar lives up to the town's past.

Midnight Star
AMERICAN $

(📞605-578-3550; 677 Main St; mains $8-15; ⏰food 10am-10pm, closed Mon Nov-Apr) Owned by actor Kevin Costner, this attractive boozer (with 'top shelf Jell-O shots') has costumes and photos from his movies. The restaurant serves sandwiches, pastas and seafood.

❶ Information

The splendid **Deadwood History & Information Center** (📞800-999-1876; www.deadwood.org; 3 Siever St; ⏰8am-7pm Jun-Aug, 9am-5pm Sep-May) in the restored train depot has tons of local tourist info, plus exhibits and photos of the town's history. Pick up the walking-tour brochure.

Lead

Just uphill from Deadwood, Lead (pronounced 'leed') has an unpolished charm and still bears plenty of scars from the mining era. It makes a solid base for skiing at nearby resorts during the winter season or a respite from the debauchery of Deadwood in the summer.

⊙ Sights

Sanford Lab Homestake Visitor Center
MINE

(📞605-584-3110; www.sanfordlabhomestake.com; 160 W Main St; viewing area free, tours adult/child $8/7; ⏰9am-6pm May-Oct, to 5pm Nov-Apr, tours 10am-4pm May-Oct) Gape at the 1250ft-deep **Homestake Gold Mine** to see what open-pit mining can do to a mountain. Nearby are the same mine's shafts, which plunge more than 1.5 miles below the surface and are now being used for physics research. Homestake has been called the richest spot on earth because over the span of 126 years miners extracted more than 41 million ounces of gold and 9 million ounces of silver.

🛏 Sleeping & Eating

★ Town Hall Inn
HISTORIC HOTEL $

(📞605-584-1112; www.townhallinn.com; 215 W Main St; r $50-100; 📶) This 12-room inn occupies Town Hall (built in 1912) and has spacious suites named and themed in honor of their former purpose, from the municipal judges chamber to the jury room and mayor's office.

Stampmill Restaurant & Saloon
AMERICAN $$

(📞605-584-1984; 305 W Main St; mains $10-20; ⏰11am-8pm, closed Sun & Mon Oct-May) With brick walls, wooden booths and plenty of taxidermy, you can easily get into the frontier spirit at this atmospheric 1890s-era saloon. It whips up some fantastic soups. Drink too much at the bar and you can head upstairs to one of the two Victorian-themed suites (rooms $70 to $120).

Black Hills National Forest

The majority of the Black Hills lie within this 1.2-million-acre mixture of protected and logged forest, perforated by pockets of private land on most roads. The scenery is fantastic, whether you get deep into it on the 450 miles of hiking trails or drive the byways and gravel fire roads.

Spearfish Canyon Scenic Byway (www.byways.org) is a waterfall-lined, curvaceous 20-mile road (US 14A) that cleaves into the heart of the hills from Spearfish. There's a sight worth stopping for around every bend; pause for longer than a minute and you'll hear beavers hard at work. It's a good alternative route to Lead and Deadwood from I-90.

Good camping abounds in the forest. There are 30 basic (no showers or electricity) campgrounds (sites $14 to $25); reserve in summer (through www.recreation.gov). Free backcountry camping is allowed just about anywhere; no open fires.

The 109-mile **George S Mickelson Trail** (📞605-584-3896; www.mickelsontrail.com; day/annual pass $4/15) cuts through much of the forest, running from Deadwood through Hill City and Custer to Edgemont on an abandoned railway side. There are bike rentals at various trailside towns and 15 trailheads along the way.

A modern **visitor center** (📞605-673-9200; www.fs.usda.gov/blackhills; US 385, near Hwy 44; ⏰9am-5pm mid-May–mid-Sep) overlooks the Pactola Reservoir between Hill City and Rapid City. It's a scenic spot for a picnic.

Hill City

One of the most appealing towns up in the hills, Hill City is much less frenzied than places such as Keystone, though it virtually shuts down outside of the summer season. Its main drag has cafes, galleries, cutesy candy shops and Western outfitters.

◉ Sights & Activities

Crazy Horse Memorial   MONUMENT
(www.crazyhorsememorial.org; 12151 Ave of the Chiefs, off US 385; per person/car $11/28; ⊘7am-10pm Jun-Sep, reduced hours Oct-May) The world's largest monument is this 563ft-tall work-in-progress (with a lot of work to go). When finished it will depict the Sioux leader astride his horse, pointing to the horizon saying, 'My lands are where my dead lie buried.' No one is predicting when the sculpture will be complete (the face was dedicated in 1998). Although you can see the mountain in the distance, you need to pay another $4 for a van ride to get close.

★1880 Train   TOURS
(☑605-574-2222; www.1880train.com; 222 Railroad Ave; adult/child round-trip $29/14; ⊘mid-May–Dec) This classic steam train runs 10 miles through rugged country to and from Keystone. A train museum is next door.

⎧ Sleeping & Eating

★Alpine Inn   HISTORIC HOTEL $$
(☑605-574-2749; www.alpineinnhillcity.com; 133 Main St; r $80-180; ⊘restaurant 11am-2:30pm & 5-9pm; ☎) Right in the center, the Alpine Inn dates to 1884 and has comfy rooms in regal red. The restaurant serves filling German fare (mains $8 to $11).

Desperados   AMERICAN $$
(☑605-574-2959; 301 Main St; mains $9-20; ⊘11am-9pm, closed Oct-Apr) Dine amid frontier charm in the oldest hand-hewn log commercial building in South Dakota. Have the burger. Service is quick and casual.

Mt Rushmore

Glimpses of Washington's nose from the roads leading to this hugely popular monument never cease to surprise and are but harbingers of the full impact of this mountainside sculpture once you're up close (and past the less impressive parking area and entrance walk). George Washington, Thomas Jefferson, Abraham Lincoln and Theodore Roosevelt each iconically stare into the distance in 60ft-tall granite glory.

You can easily escape the crowds and fully appreciate the **Mt Rushmore National Memorial** (☑605-574-2523; www.nps.gov/moru; off Hwy 244; parking $10; ⊘8am-10pm Jun-Aug, to 9pm Sep, to 5pm Oct-May) while marveling at the artistry of sculptor Gutzon Borglum and the immense labor of the workers who created the memorial between 1927 and 1941.

The official Park Service **information centers** have excellent bookstores with proceeds going to the park. Avoid the schlocky Xanterra gift shop and the ho-hum Carvers Cafe, which looked much better in the scene where Cary Grant gets plugged in *North by Northwest*. The main museum is underwhelming.

The **Presidential Trail** loop passes right below the monument for some fine nostril views and accesses the worthwhile **Sculptor's Studio**, which conveys the drama of how the monument came to be. Start clockwise and you're right under Washington's nose in under five minutes. The **nature trail** to the right as you face the entrance connects the viewing and parking areas, passing through a pine forest and avoiding the crowds and commercialism.

Mt Rushmore is a half-hour southwest of Rapid City by car via US 16. Organized tours travel to Mt Rushmore from Rapid City, but there are no public buses between the two places.

Custer State Park

The only reason 111-sq-mile **Custer State Park** (☑605-255-4515; www.custerstatepark.com; 7-day pass per car $20; ⊘24hr) isn't a national park is that the state grabbed it first. It boasts one of the largest free-roaming bison herds in the world (about 1500), the famous 'begging burros' (donkeys seeking handouts) and more than 200 bird species. Other wildlife include elk, pronghorns, mountain goats, bighorn sheep, coyotes, prairie dogs, mountain lions and bobcats.

Meandering over awesome stone bridges and across sublime alpine meadows, the 18-mile **Wildlife Loop Rd** is a sure way to see buffalo, elk, prairie dogs and more. The incredible 14-mile **Needles Hwy** (SD 87) is another superb drive.

The real road star, however, is **Iron Mountain Rd** (US 16A). It's a 16-mile roller coaster of wooden bridges, virtual loop-the-loops, narrow tunnels and stunning vistas on the section between the park's west entrance and Keystone. Make sure to stop at the **Norbeck Overlook** for a sweeping Black Hills panorama.

Hiking through the pine-covered hills and prairie grassland (keep an eye out for rattlesnakes) is a great way to see wildlife and rock formations. Trails through **Sylvan**

Lake Shore, Sunday Gulch, Cathedral Spires and French Creek Natural Area are all highly recommended.

The park has five impressive resorts (www.custerresorts.com) – book ahead – and nine campgrounds (tent sites $19 to $21). At four of the campgrounds, you can rent a well-equipped camping cabin ($50). Sylvan Lake is the most scenic (and popular) campground so reserve well ahead (via www.campsd.com). Reservations are vital for all sites in summer. Backcountry camping ($7 per person per night) is allowed only in the French Creek Natural Area.

Located on the east side of Custer State Park, the new **Custer State Park Visitor Center** (☑ 605-255-4020; www.custerstatepark.com; US 16A; ⊘ 9am-5pm Jun-Aug, to 4pm Sep-May) has good exhibits and offers activities like guided nature walks.

The visitor center is about 45 minutes southwest of Rapid City by car. There is no public transportation between the park and Rapid City.

Hot Springs

This attractive town, south of the main Black Hills circuit, boasts ornate 1890s red sandstone buildings and warm mineral springs feeding the Fall River.

◉ Sights & Activities

You can fill your water bottles at **Kidney Springs**, just south of the visitor center, or swim at Cascade Falls, which is 71°F (22°C) all year, 11 miles south on US 71.

Mammoth Site   HISTORIC SITE
(☑ 605-745-6017; www.mammothsite.com; 1800 US 18 bypass; adult/child $10/8; ⊘ 8am-8pm mid-May–mid-Aug, reduced hours mid-Aug–mid-May) This is the country's largest left-as-found mammoth fossil display. Hundreds of animals perished in a sinkhole here about 26,000 years ago, and you can walk around the active archaeological dig.

Cascade Falls   NATURAL POOL
(US 71; ⊘ 6am-10pm May-Sep) Part of the Black Hills National Forest, this beloved swimming hole, 11 miles south of Hot Springs, is great for a picnic or afternoon dip. Beware of the poison ivy and rattlesnakes!

Evans Plunge   WATER PARK
(☑ 605-745-5165; www.evansplunge.com; 1145 N River St; adult/child $14/10; ⊘ 6am-8pm Mon-Fri, 10am-8pm Sat & Sun May-Sep, reduced hours Oct-Apr) The water at this historic indoor

WORTH A TRIP

WIND CAVE NATIONAL PARK

Wind Cave National Park (☑ 605-745-4600; www.nps.gov/wica; off US 385; tours adult $10-30, child $5-6; ⊘ visitor center 8am-7pm Jun-Aug, reduced hours Sep-May), protecting 44 sq miles of grassland and forest, sits just south of Custer State Park. The central draw is, of course, the cave, which contains 147 miles of mapped passages. The strong wind gusts, which are felt at the entrance, but not inside, give the cave its name. The visitor center has details on the variety of **tours** that are offered, from one-hour candlelit walks to four-hour crawls.

water park is always 87°F (30.5°C) because it comes from a geothermal spring. There's also a sauna, steam room and fitness center.

🛏 Sleeping & Eating

Red Rock River Resort   HOTEL $$
(☑ 605-745-4400; www.redrockriverresort.com; 603 N River St; r $85-135; 🅿 ✿) This resort has cozy and stylish rooms in a beautiful 1891 downtown building, plus spa facilities (day passes for nonguests $25).

Morning Sunshine   CAFE $
(☑ 605-745-5550; 509 N River St; mains $4-8; ⊘ 7am-4pm Mon-Sat, 8am-2pm Sun) This cheery little cafe with a blue bison on the roof is hopping from breakfast through lunch with a small but tasty menu of bagels, soups and sandwiches. Coffee is another draw.

❶ Information

The **visitor center** (☑ 605-745-4140; www.hotsprings-sd.com; 630 N River St; ⊘ 9am-6pm Mon-Sat, noon-4pm Sun May-Oct) is located in a train station dating to 1891.

NEBRASKA

The Cornhusker State (they do grow a lot of ears) has beautiful river valleys and an often stark bleakness that is entrancing. Its links to the past – from vast fields of dinosaur remains to Native American culture to the toils of hardy settlers – provide a dramatic story line. Alongside the state's sprinkling of cute little towns, Nebraska's

CARHENGE

Pay homage to the auto at **Carhenge** (www.carhenge.com; Hwy 87, Alliance; ⊘24hr), a Stonehenge replica assembled from 39 discarded cars. The faithful reproduction, along with other car-part art, rises out of a field 3 miles north of Alliance and US 385, the road to the Black Hills.

two main cities, Omaha and Lincoln, are vibrant and artful.

The key to enjoying this long, stoic stretch of country is to take the smaller roads, whether it's US 30 instead of I-80, US 20 to the Black Hills, or the lonely and magnificent US 2.

❶ Information

Nebraska Association of Bed & Breakfasts (www.nebraskabb.com)
Nebraska State Parks (www.outdoornebraska. gov) Vehicle permits cost $8/46 per day/year. Some campsites at popular parks are reservable; fees are $8 to $28 per night.
Nebraska Tourism Commission (www.visit nebraska.com)

Omaha

Be careful if you're planning a quick pit stop in Omaha. Home to the brick-and-cobblestoned Old Market neighborhood, a booming riverfront, a lively music scene and several good museums, this town can turn a few hours into a few days.

Omaha grew to prominence as a transport hub. Its location on the Missouri River and proximity to the Platte River made it an important stop on the Oregon, California and Mormon Trails, and later the Union Pacific Railroad stretched west from here. These days Omaha is in the nation's top 10 for billionaires and Fortune 500 companies per capita. Money pours back into the city in spectacular ways thanks to several wealthy benefactors (including Berkshire Hathaway's Warren Buffett).

◎ Sights

It's easy to spend much of your Omaha visit in Old Market on the river edge of downtown discovering hidden pockets like the **Passageway** (S 11th St and Howard St).

This revitalized warehouse district, full of restaurants, funky shops and bars (including a few gay ones), exudes energy and sophistication. Nearby parks boast fountains and waterside walks. Venture further west and you'll find the artsy haven of **Benson**, whose shops and performance venues are covered in towering street murals.

★**Hot Shops Art Center**   ARTS CENTER
(☑402-342-6452; www.hotshopsartcenter.com; 1301 Nicholas St; ⊘9am-6pm Mon-Fri, 11am-5pm Sat & Sun) Entering into this three-story arts center (a former mattress warehouse) is like diving down the rabbit hole into an alternative universe ruled by eccentric artists. The namesake 'hot shops' are the glassblowing, pottery, bronze-casting and blacksmithing studios that anchor the building. Above them are 80 studios where artists create and display their works for all to see. Peruse the labyrinthine studios, sign up for art classes or attend one of the monthly events.

★**Henry Doorly Zoo**   ZOO
(☑402-733-8401; www.omahazoo.com; 3701 S 10th St; adult/child $18/12; ⊘9am-5pm mid-Mar–Oct, 10am-4pm Nov–mid-Mar; ⊕) The world's largest indoor desert? Check. The world's largest nocturnal exhibit? Check. America's largest indoor rainforest? Check. The superlatives say it all. You could easily spend an entire day wandering through this massive and incredibly well-crafted complex, which is frequently named the best zoo in America.

★**Union Pacific
Railroad Museum**   MUSEUM
(www.uprrmuseum.org; 200 Pearl St; ⊘10am-4pm Thu-Sat) **FREE** Just across the river from Omaha in the cute little downtown area of Council Bluffs, IA, this highly interactive museum tells the story of the world's most profitable railroad and the company that rammed the transcontinental line west from here in the 1860s. The three levels of exhibits offer a nostalgia-filled ode to train travel and how it forever changed America.

Riverfront   WATERFRONT
(8th St & Riverfront Dr) The riverfront along the Missouri River, downtown, has been massively spiffed up. Highlights include the architecturally stunning **Bob Kerry Pedestrian Bridge**, which soars over to Iowa; the **Heartland of America Park**, with fountains and lush gardens; and **Lewis & Clark Landing**, where the explorers did just that

in 1804. The riverfront is also home to the **Lewis & Clark National Historic Trail Visitor Center** (☑402-661-1804; www.nps.gov/lecl; 601 Riverfront Dr; ⊘8am-5pm Mon-Fri, from 9:30am Sat & Sun May-Oct, 8am-4:30pm Mon-Fri Nov-Apr), which has exhibits and a bookstore.

Durham Museum   MUSEUM
(☑402-444-5071; www.durhammuseum.org; 801 S 10th St; adult/child $11/7; ⊘10am-8pm Tue, to 5pm Wed-Sat, 1-5pm Sun) The soaring art-deco Union Station train depot is a sight to behold with its cathedral windows, geometric chandeliers and ornate ceilings. It houses a fine museum covering local history from the Lewis and Clark expedition to the Omaha stockyards to the trains that once called here. The soda fountain still serves hot dogs and phosphate sodas.

Joslyn Art Museum   MUSEUM
(☑402-342-3300; www.joslyn.org; 2200 Dodge St; ⊘10am-4pm Tue, Wed & Fri-Sun, to 8pm Thu) FREE This admired and architecturally imposing museum has a great collection of 19th- and 20th-century European and American art. There's also a good selection of Western-themed works, plus a cool sculpture garden.

☞ Tours

Nebraska Tour Company   TOURS
(☑402-575-0526; http://nebraskatourcompany.com; tours $30-100) This new company offers Old Market walking tours, brewery or winery-hopping trips or off-the-beaten-path excursions to Omaha's hidden treasures. There are also history and art tours led by local experts.

🛏 Sleeping

There is a good mix of midrange and budget hotels along US 275 near 60th St, at I-80 exits 446 and 449, and across the river in Council Bluffs, IA, at I-29 exit 51. Old Mar-ket and downtown have several midrange chains and independent hotels.

Satellite Motel   MOTEL **$**
(☑402-733-7373; www.satellitemotelomaha.com; 6006 L St; r $60; ❄🐾) This octagonal motel with a wraparound balcony is a good clean budget option, though the smell from the smoking rooms sometimes penetrates the building.

Magnolia Hotel   HISTORIC HOTEL **$$**
(☑402-341-2500; www.magnoliahotelomaha.com; 1615 Howard St; r $140-220; ❄@🐾🐕) Not far from Old Market, the Magnolia is a boutique hotel housed in a restored 1923 Italianate high-rise. The 145 rooms have a vibrant, modern style. Get ready for bedtime milk and cookies.

🍴 Eating

You can just wander Old Market and see what you find, especially on a balmy night when you want a drink. Or you can seek out some of Omaha's lesser-trafficked neighborhoods, including Benson, Dundee and Midtown Crossing.

Ted & Wally's Ice Cream   ICE CREAM **$**
(☑402-341-5827; www.tedandwallys.com; 1120 Jackson St; ice cream from $3; ⊘11am-11pm Jun-Aug, to 10pm Sep-May) Ultra-creamy ice cream in myriad flavors made fresh daily right before your very eyes. Vegans should try the coconut-based creations.

Upstream Brewing Company   AMERICAN **$$**
(☑402-344-0200; www.upstreambrewing.com; 514 S 11th St; mains $10-30; ⊘11am-1am Mon-Thu, to 2am Fri & Sat, 10am-midnight Sun) In a big old firehouse, the beer here is also big on flavor. The Caesar salads have enough garlic to propel you over the Missouri to Iowa. Steaks are thick and up to local standards. There are sidewalk tables, a rooftop deck and a huge bar.

AIR FORCE IN OMAHA

If you see large military planes drifting slowly across the sky, they're likely headed for one of Omaha's large air-force bases.

After WWII Omaha's Offutt Air Force Base was home to the US Air Force Strategic Air Command, the nuclear force detailed in *Dr Strangelove*. This legacy is documented at the cavernous **Strategic Air Command & Aerospace Museum** (☑402-944-3100; https://sacmuseum.org; 28210 West Park Hwy, I-80 exit 426; adult/child $12/6; ⊘9am-5pm), which bulges with bombers, from the B-17 to the B-52. Don't expect exhibits looking at the wider implications of bombing. It's 30 miles southwest of Omaha.

SCENIC DRIVE: NEBRASKA'S SANDHILLS

Nebraska's **Hwy 2** branches northwest from I-80 and Grand Island through Broken Bow 272 miles to Alliance in the panhandle. It crosses the lonely and lovely Sandhills – 19,000 sq miles of sand dunes covered in grass – one of the country's most isolated areas. With the wind whistling in your ears, the distant call of a hawk and the biggest skies imaginable, this is pure Great Plains travel.

★**Grey Plume** MODERN AMERICAN $$$
(☏402-763-4447; www.thegreyplume.com; 220 S 31st Ave; mains bar $9-18, restaurant $25-42; ⊙5-10pm Mon-Sat) West of downtown in Midtown Crossing, chef Clayton Chapman has upturned perceptions of Great Plains cuisine with his fiercely local and seasonal dishes. Winners: the bar burger, the duck-fat fries, the steaks and anything with trout.

★**Boiler Room** MODERN AMERICAN $$$
(☏402-916-9274; www.boilerroomomaha.com; 1110 Jones St; mains $28-35; ⊙5:30-9pm Mon-Thu, to 10pm Fri & Sat) Global influences and French techniques shape the locally sourced foods that comprise the seasonal dishes at this trendsetting Old Market bistro. It's got an open kitchen and a cocktail bar. Want an Omaha steak? Get the Wagyu beef.

▼ Drinking & Nightlife

Craft breweries and cocktail bars abound in Old Market, while Benson has more eclectic nightlife and live-music venues. There's also a lively gay scene with bars and clubs on the perimeter of Old Market.

Mister Toad's PUB
(☏402-345-4488; www.mrtoadspub.com; 1002 Howard St; ⊙2pm-2am Sun-Fri, noon-2am Sat) Sit out front on benches under big trees or nab a corner table inside. It's woodsy, worn and flirting with dive-bar status. There's live jazz Sunday nights.

ℹ Information

Visitor Center (☏866-937-6624; www.visit omaha.com; 1001 Farnam St; ⊙9am-4:30pm Mon-Fri, 10am-4pm Sat & Sun Mar-Oct, 10am-4pm Tue-Sun Nov-Feb; ☏) Near Old Market.

ℹ Getting There & Away

Eppley Airfield (OMA; www.flyoma.com; 4501 Abbott Dr) is 3 miles northeast of downtown and receives flights from more than two dozen destinations across America. Amtrak's *California Zephyr* stops in Omaha on its run between Northern California and Chicago ($60, 9½ hours, one daily). Megabus (www.megabus. com) links Omaha with Chicago ($30, nine hours, one daily).

Lincoln

Lincoln reminds visitors that Nebraska isn't all cornfields and prairies. With its vibrant art and nightlife scenes thanks to the huge downtown campus of the University of Nebraska, it makes a good overnight stop. But it's the friendly Midwest attitude that might encourage you to stay longer.

◉ Sights

State Capitol LANDMARK
(☏402-471-0448; www.capitol.org; 1445 K St; ⊙8am-5pm Mon-Fri, 10am-5pm Sat, 1-5pm Sun, tours hourly) FREE From the outside, Nebraska's remarkable 1932 400ft-high state capitol represents the apex of phallic architecture (like many tall buildings in the Plains, it's often called 'the penis on the prairie'), while the symbolically rich interior curiously combines classical and art-deco motifs. Enjoy views from the 14th-floor observation decks.

Museum of Nebraska History MUSEUM
(☏402-471-4782; www.nebraskahistory.org; 131 Centennial Mall N; ⊙9am-4:30pm Mon-Fri, 1-4:30pm Sat & Sun) FREE Follows the Cornhusker State's story, starting with the large First Nebraskans room.

🛏 Sleeping & Eating

Rogers House B&B $$
(☏402-476-6961; www.rogershouseinn.com; 2145 B St; r $90-170; ✴☏) Close to downtown, the seven spacious rooms here occupy a 100-year-old brick home. Refreshingly, the decor eschews the froufrou silliness of many B&Bs. Expect a hearty two-course breakfast.

★**Bread & Cup** CAFE $
(☏402-438-2255; www.breadandcup.com; 440 N 8th St; mains $8-15; ⊙7am-9pm Tue & Wed, to 10pm Thu-Sat, 9am-2pm Sun; ☏) 🌱 Boxes of beautiful Nebraska produce line the entry at this trendsetting Haymarket cafe where

even common dishes (such as a pulled-pork sandwich) are elevated to something special. Great baked goods, full bar.

🍷 Drinking & Nightlife

Other Room COCKTAIL BAR
(📞402-261-4608; 824 P St; ⊗5pm-1am Mon-Sat, to midnight Sun) Look for an unmarked black door with a lion door knocker next to it. If the light above the door is green, give the lion a knock. If it's red, you'll have to wait outside for the chance to enter into this compact speakeasy, which has a 25-person capacity and offers up some spectacular 'pre-Prohibition-style cocktails.'

ℹ️ Information

Visitor Center (📞402-434-5348; www.lincoln. org; 201 N 7th St; ⊗9am-6pm Mon-Thu, to 8pm Fri, 8am-2pm Sat & Sun Jun-Aug, reduced hours Sep-May) Inside Haymarket's Lincoln Station, where Amtrak's *California Zephyr* stops.

ℹ️ Getting There & Away

Lincoln is 55 miles southwest of Omaha on I-80. Megabus (www.megabus.com) connects the two cities once daily ($9, one hour). Amtrak's (www. amtrak.com) *California Zephyr* train links Lincoln with Omaha ($12, one hour, one daily).

Grand Island

A classic midsized Nebraska town along the Platte River Valley, Grand Island bursts to life each spring when hundreds of thousands of sandhill cranes converge on a critical sliver of threatened habitat just south of the city limits. Birders and biologists from around the world flock to see this massive migration, dubbed one of North America's greatest wildlife phenomena.

◎ Sights

★ **Crane Trust
Nature & Visitor Center** NATURE RESERVE
(📞308-382-1820; www.cranetrust.org; 9325 S Alda Rd, I-80 exit 305; ⊗9am-5pm Mon-Sat) FREE Upstream of Grand Island, the Platte hosts 500,000 sandhill cranes (80% of the world population) and millions more waterfowl during the spring migration (mid-February to early April). Expert guides lead seasonal Sandhill Crane Migration Tours ($35, 2½ hours) to prime viewing blinds on the river. This nature center is a good place for viewing and has worthwhile hikes year-round.

★ **Stuhr Museum
of the Prairie Pioneer** MUSEUM
(📞308-385-5316; www.stuhrmuseum.org; 3133 W Hwy 34, I-80 exit 312; adult/child $8/6; ⊗9am-5pm Mon-Sat, noon-5pm Sun, closed Mon Jan-Mar; ♿) A remarkable combination of museum exhibits with a vast outdoor living museum. Note how conditions dramatically improved from the homes in 1860 to 1890 thanks to riches made possible by the railroad.

ℹ️ Getting There & Away

Grand Island is 145 miles west of Omaha along I-80. Express Arrow (www.expressarrow.com) runs twice-daily buses between the two cities ($35, three hours).

North Platte

The name North Platte may not ring a bell with the average traveler, but hardcore railroad fans know it as the home of Union Pacific's Bailey Yard. Meanwhile, American-history buffs come here to see the place where Bill Cody launched his famed rodeo show, Buffalo Bill's Wild West. Cody's frontier spirit lives on, even as hundreds of trains chug in and out of town each day.

◎ Sights

Golden Spike Tower TOWER
(📞308-532-9920; www.goldenspiketower.com; 1249 N Homestead Rd; adult/child $7/5; ⊗9am-7pm May-Sep, to 5pm Oct-Apr) Enjoy sweeping views of Union Pacific's Bailey Yard, the world's largest railroad classification yard,

THE GREAT PLAINS GRAND ISLAND

KEARNEY

Kearney makes a worthwhile stopover on the otherwise monotonous trip along I-80. It has a nice brick-built downtown district by the Union Pacific tracks and a collection of notable attractions, including the over-the-top **Great Platte River Road Archway Monument** (📞308-237-1000; www.archway.org; 3060 E 1st St, near exit 275; adult/child $12/6; ⊗9am-6pm Mon-Sat, noon-6pm Sun May-Sep, reduced hours Oct-Apr; ♿).

Kearney is 180 miles west of Omaha on I-80. Express Arrow (www.express arrow.com) runs twice-daily buses between the two cities ($40, four hours).

from this eight-story observation tower with indoor and outdoor decks. Bailey Yard spans 2850 acres and handles 10,000 railroad cars every 24 hours!

Buffalo Bill Ranch
State Historical Park   HISTORIC SITE
(☑308-535-8035; www.outdoornebraska.gov/buffalobillranch; 2921 Scouts Rest Ranch Rd; house adult/child $2/1, vehicle permit $5; ⊙9am-5pm Jun-Aug, 10am-4pm Sat & Sun late Apr-May & Sep-early Oct) Once the home of Bill Cody (the father of rodeo and the famed Wild West show), this is now a fun museum that reflects his colorful life.

🛏 Sleeping & Eating

Hotels and motels line the edge of Blue Star Memorial Hwy, which cuts through the center of town. You'll find an endless stretch of chain restaurants and fast-food staples along Blue Star Memorial Hwy. There are a few indie options between 4th St and Front St.

Husker Inn   MOTEL $
(☑308-534-6960; www.huskerinn.com; 721 E 4th St; r $50-60; ❄🐾) This basic 21-room motel exceeds expectations with well-manicured grounds, immaculately clean (if small) rooms and yummy home-baked goodies on arrival.

ⓘ Getting There & Away

North Platte is 275 miles west of Omaha along I-80. Express Arrow (www.expressarrow.com) runs daily buses between the two cities ($55, six hours).

Valentine

Fortunately, 'America's Heart City' doesn't milk the schtick. It sits on the edge of the Sandhills and is a great base for canoeing, kayaking and inner-tubing the winding canyons of the federally protected **Niobrara National Scenic River**.

Floating down the river draws scores of people through the summer. Sheer limestone bluffs, lush forests and more than 200 spring-fed waterfalls along the banks shatter any 'flat Nebraska' stereotypes. Most float tours are based here.

⊙ Sights & Activities

Valentine lies at the heart of what will one day be the longest rail-to-trail conversion in the US: the **Cowboy Trail**. Popular with cyclists, it currently runs 195 miles east from Valentine through the Sandhills to Norfolk along an abandoned Chicago and North Western Railway corridor. The trail passes 20 small communities along the way, and camping is available in city parks for little or no charge. Learn more about biking the trail at www.bikecowboytrail.com.

Fort Niobrara
National Wildlife Refuge   WILDLIFE RESERVE
(☑402-376-3789; www.fws.gov/fortniobrara; Hwy 12; ⊙visitor center 8am-4:30pm daily Jun-Aug, Mon-Fri Sep-May) The Fort Niobrara National Wildlife Refuge is home to hundreds of bison and elk, plus scenic waterfalls. There's a 3.5-mile wildlife drive from the visitor center.

Brewers Canoers & Tubers   CANOEING
(☑402-376-2046; www.brewerscanoers.com; 433 Hwy 20; rates vary by time/equipment; ⊙daily trips Jun-Aug, rentals year-round) Brewers is one of the original outfitters in the area and was the first to introduce tubing on the Niobrara River. You can rent canoes, kayaks or tubes with them and arrange shuttles to and from your launch and landing sites.

🛏 Sleeping & Eating

Trade Winds Motel   MOTEL $
(☑402-376-1600; www.tradewindslodge.com; 1009 E US 20/83; r $65-100; ❄🐾🐾) The classic red-brick Trade Winds Motel has 32 comfy and clean rooms with refrigerators and microwaves. It's a great indie choice with a hot country breakfast.

Peppermill   STEAK $$
(☑402-376-2800; www.peppermillvalentine.com; 502 E Hwy 20; mains $10-30; ⊙11am-10pm Mon-Fri, 4-10pm Sat & Sun) This low-lit Valentine institution, which specializes in hand-cut Nebraska beef, is one of the state's most storied steakhouses, with thick, juicy chunks of perfection. You'll forgive the uninspiring decor when you try the Mulligan, Peppermill's signature center-cut sirloin.

ⓘ Getting There & Away

Remote Valentine is two hours north of North Platte by car on US 83. There is no public transportation in the region.

Nebraska Panhandle

The remote and little visited Nebraska Panhandle is for many the most evocative part of the state. Stark vistas stretch to the horizon in lands little changed in millennia. **Scottsbluff** makes a good base. Heading north, **Hwy 29** (aka the 'Fossil Freeway') is a great drive and it segues right onto equally scenic US 20.

⊙ Sights

★ Scotts Bluff
National Monument PARK
(☏ 308-436-9700; www.nps.gov/scbl; 190276 Old Oregon Trail, Gering; per car $5; ⊘ visitor center 8am-6pm Jun-Aug, to 5pm Sep-May) Scotts Bluff has been a beacon to travelers for centuries. Rising 800ft above the flat plains of western Nebraska, it was an important waypoint on the Oregon Trail in the mid-19th century. You can still see wagon ruts today. The **visitor center** has displays and its staff can guide you to walks and drives up the bluff. It's 5 miles south of Scottsbluff town.

★ Agate Fossil Beds
National Monument MONUMENT
(☏ 308-436-9760; www.nps.gov/agfo; 301 River Rd, off Hwy 29, Harrison; ⊘ 9am-5pm May-Sep, 8am-4pm Oct-Apr) FREE Some 20 million years ago, this part of Nebraska was like the Serengeti in Africa today: a gathering place for a rich variety of creatures. Today the bones of thousands of these ancient mammals are found at this isolated site. Displays and walks detail the amazing – and ongoing – finds. Don't miss the **Bone Cabin** and the burrowing beaver plus the Native American exhibits.

Chimney Rock National
Historic Site NATURAL FEATURE
(☏ 308-586-2581; Chimney Rock Rd, Bayard; adult/child $3/free; ⊘ 9am-5pm) Centuries-old bluff formations rise up from the horizon, their striking presence a visual link connecting modern-day travelers with their pioneer forebears. One of these links is **Chimney Rock**, located inside the Chimney Rock National Historic Site. Chimney Rock's fragile 120ft spire was an inspiring landmark for pioneers, and it was mentioned in hundreds of journals. It also marked the end of the first leg of the journey and the beginning of the tough – but final – push to the coast.

Fort Robinson State Park HISTORIC SITE
(☏ 308-665-2900; www.outdoornebraska.gov; Hwy 20, Crawford; vehicle permit $8; ⊘ park dawn-dusk, visitor center 8am-5pm daily Apr-Nov, Mon-Fri Dec-Mar) This old military fort's turbulent past belies its stately appearance today: Crazy Horse was killed here in 1877, 'buffalo soldier' African American brigades were formed, it was a POW camp for Germans, and more. The greater park offers 22,000 acres of panoramic Pine Ridge scenery. Campgrounds ($13 per night) are open year-round and there's a seasonal lodge in the old brick barracks (room $65, April to November).

⊨ Sleeping & Eating

Scottsbluff (along with neighboring Gering) has the largest collection of hotels, motels and B&Bs in the Panhandle.

★ Barn Anew B&B $$
(☏ 308-632-8647; www.barnanew.com; 170549 County Rd, Scottsbluff; r $140-150; ✾ ❁) This stunning B&B lies within a restored barn on an old sugar-beet farm. The walls are adorned with the owners' museum-quality collection of Native American artifacts, while the views of Scotts Bluff are mesmerizing. Up for an adventure? Ask about staying in one of the two frontier wagons that have been converted into cozy rooms.

★ Tangled Tumbleweed AMERICAN $$
(☏ 308-633-3867; www.thetangledtumbleweed.com; 1823 Ave A, Scottsbluff; small plates $7-11; ⊘ 10am-10pm Wed-Sat) Part home-goods store (with lovely products made by the owner) and part top-notch restaurant, this new Scottsbluff establishment is a rare treat in a town of this size. The seasonal menu of small-plate dishes is complemented by rotating wine and craft-beer selections. Linger on the outdoor patio on a warm evening.

Emporium Coffeehouse
& Café AMERICAN $$
(☏ 308-632-6222; www.emporiumdining.com; 1818 1st Ave, Scottsbluff; mains $12-27; ⊘ 6:30am-10pm Mon-Sat) This umbrella-fronted vintage house in downtown Scottsbluff is a regional gem. There are great meals, from the pastries at breakfast to late-night steak and seafood plates. The wine and spirits list has more than 100 selections.

❶ Getting There & Away

The remote Panhandle is closer to Denver and Rapid City than Omaha. Both cities are three hours away by car from Scottsbluff in opposite directions. There is no public transportation in the region.

KANSAS

Wicked witches and yellow-brick roads, pitched battles over slavery and tornadoes powerful enough to pulverize entire towns are some of the more lurid images of Kansas. But the common image – amber waves of grain from north to south and east to west – is closer to reality.

There's a simple beauty to the green rolling hills and limitless horizons. Places such as Chase County beguile those who value understatement. Gems abound, from the superb space museum in Hutchinson to the indie music clubs of Lawrence. Most importantly, follow the Great Plains credo of ditching the interstate for the two-laners and make your own discoveries. The website www.kansas-sampler.org is a brilliant resource.

ℹ️ Information

Kansas Bed & Breakfast Association (www.kbba.com)

Kansas State Parks (www.ksoutdoors.com) Per vehicle per day/year $5/25. Campsites cost $10 to $22.

Kansas Travel & Tourism (www.travelks.com)

Wichita

From its early cow-town days at the head of the Chisholm Trail in the 1870s to its current claim as Air Capital of the World (thanks to about half the world's general aviation aircraft being built here by the likes of Cessna and others), Kansas' largest city is a worthwhile stopover, but not at the expense of the rest of the state.

◉ Sights

Wichita's historic, all-brick **Old Town**, good for shopping, eating and drinking, is on the east side of downtown. The **Museums on the River** district includes a number of museums, plus botanical gardens and a science center aimed at kids. It fills a triangle of green space between the Big and Little Arkansas Rivers to the west of downtown.

⭐ **Old Cowtown Museum**   MUSEUM

(📞 316-350-3323; www.oldcowtown.org; 1865 Museum Blvd; adult/child $8/5.50; ⊘10am-5pm Tue-Sat, noon-5pm Sun Apr-Oct, 10am-5pm Tue-Sat Nov-Mar; 🚗) An open-air museum that re-creates the Wild West (as seen on TV...). Pioneer-era buildings, staged gunfights (April to October) and guides in cowboy costumes thrill kids. Enjoy the river walks.

Exploration Place   MUSEUM

(📞 316-660-0600; www.exploration.org; 300 N McLean Blvd; adult/child from $10/6; ⊘10am-5pm Mon-Sat, noon-5pm Sun; 🚗) Right on the river confluence, this architecturally striking children's museum has no end of cool exhibits, including a tornado chamber where you can feel 75mph winds, and a sublime erosion model that shows water creating a new little Kansas.

CHASING TORNADOES

Much of the Great Plains is prone to severe weather, including violent thunderstorms, hail the size of softballs, spectacular lightning storms and more. Tornadoes, however, are the real stars of these meteorological nightmares. Far less benign than the cyclones that carried Dorothy off to Oz, every year tornadoes cause death and destruction from the Great Plains east across the central US.

With winds of 300mph or more, tornadoes are both awesome and terrifying. Still, each year many people visit the region hoping to spot a funnel cloud, drawn by the sheer spectacle and elemental drama.

Tour companies use gadget-filled vans to chase storms across multiple states, with no guarantee that you'll actually see a storm. Costs average $200 to $400 a day; April to July offer the best spotting. Operators include the following:

Cloud 9 Tours (📞 405-323-1145; www.cloud9tours.com; 2-week tour $3000)

Silver Lining Tours (📞 720-273-3948; www.silverliningtours.com; multiday tours from $2500)

Tempest Tours (📞 817-274-9313; www.tempesttours.com; multiday tours from $2245)

The book *Storm Kings: The Untold History of America's First Tornado Chasers*, by Lee Sandlin, is an excellent and surprise-filled account of early tornado research. Read the recollections of veteran tornado chaser Roger Hill in *Hunting Nature's Fury*.

DON'T MISS

KANSAS COSMOSPHERE & SPACE CENTER

Possibly the most surprising sight in Kansas, the amazing **Kansas Cosmosphere & Space Center** (☑ 800-397-0330; www.cosmo.org; 1100 N Plum St, Hutchinson; all-attraction pass adult/child $26/17, museum only $13.50/10; ☺ 9am-7pm Mon-Sat, noon-7pm Sun; ⊞) captures the race to the moon better than any museum on the planet. Absorbing displays and artifacts such as the *Apollo 13* command module will enthrall you for hours. You'll come to realize why the museum is regularly called in to build props for Hollywood movies portraying the space race, including *Apollo 13*. A planetarium and space simulator round out the all-attraction pass.

The museum's isolated location in Hutchinson is an easy day trip from Wichita or diversion off I-70.

🛏 Sleeping

Hotbeds for chains include I-135 exit 1AB, I-35 exit 50 and the Hwy 96 Rock Rd and Webb Rd exits. Broadway south of the center offers a mixed bag of indie cheapies.

Hotel at Old Town　　　　　HOTEL **$$**
(☑ 316-267-4800; www.hotelatoldtown.com; 830 1st St; r $100-200; P❋@⊛) In the midst of Old Town nightlife, this restored hotel is housed in the 1906 factory of the Keen Kutter Corp, a maker of household goods. Rooms have high ceilings, refrigerators and microwaves, and there's a good breakfast buffet (for a fee).

🍴 Eating

Wichita is the home of Pizza Hut, but that's far from the pinnacle of the city's dining options. For some real-deal Mexican or Vietnamese, drive north on Broadway and take your pick.

Doo-Dah Diner　　　　　DINER **$**
(☑ 316-265-7011; www.doodahdiner.com; 206 E Kellogg Dr; mains $8-15; ☺ 7am-2pm Wed-Fri, 8am-2pm Sat & Sun) The model for diners everywhere. This bustling local downtown fave has fabulous chow, including corned-beef hash, banana-bread French toast and eggs Benedict.

Lotus Leaf Cafe　　　　　VEGETARIAN **$**
(☑ 316-295-4133; www.lotusleafwichita.com; 251 N Washington Ave; mains $7-12; ☺ 11am-9pm Mon-Sat, to 4pm Sun; ⊅) This bright and cheery cafe in Old Town specializes in vegetarian, vegan, organic and gluten-free dishes such as buffalo cauliflower (instead of chicken) and spaghetti squash primavera. There's also a great list of organic wines and beers.

Anchor　　　　　AMERICAN **$**
(☑ 316-260-8989; www.anchorwichita.com; 1109 E Douglas Ave; mains $7-12; ☺ 11am-late) On the edge of Old Town, this vintage pub has high ceilings, a tiled floor, a great beer selection and tasty food. The burgers and specials totally outclass the nearby chain and theme bars.

🍷 Drinking & Nightlife

There are several noteworthy craft breweries, mostly in Old Town and the Douglas Design District immediately to its east.

Hopping Gnome Brewing　　MICROBREWERY
(www.hoppinggnome.com; 1710 E Douglas Ave; ☺ 3-10pm Wed-Fri, noon-midnight Sat, noon-5pm Sun) This itty-bitty taproom in the Douglas Design District has family-style tables, fresh popcorn and a good selection of board games. Oh, and gnomes. Lots of garden gnomes! Order the home-brewed beers by the pint or pour.

ℹ Getting There & Away

Wichita Dwight D Eisenhower National Airport (ICT; www.flywichita.com; 2277 Eisenhower Airport Pkwy) is 7 miles west of town and receives flights from several cities in the Midwest, Southwest and Southeast. Greyhound (www.greyhound.com) has buses to Oklahoma City ($32, three hours) and Kansas City ($40, four hours).

Lawrence

Lawrence has been an island of progressive politics from the start. Founded by abolitionists in 1854 and an important stop on the Underground Railroad, it became a battlefield in the clash between pro- and antislavery factions. The city's free-thinking spirit lives on to this day with eclectic shops, edgy bars and a youthful optimism (it's the home of the University of Kansas).

⊙ Sights

The appealing downtown, where townies and students merge, centers on Massachusetts St, one of the most pleasant streets in this part of the country for a stroll.

Spencer Museum of Art GALLERY
(☑ 785-864-4710; www.spencerart.ku.edu; 1301 Mississippi St; ☺ 10am-4pm Tue, Fri & Sat, to 8pm Wed & Thu, noon-4pm Sun) FREE Encompassing works by Western artist Frederic Remington, Plains painter Thomas Hart Benton and others, this museum on the KU campus just reopened after a massive revamp in 2016.

🛌 Sleeping & Eating

Eldridge Hotel HISTORIC HOTEL $$
(☑ 785-749-5011; www.eldridgehotel.com; 701 Massachusetts St; r $140-175; ❋ 🛜) The 48 modern two-room suites at this historic 1926 downtown hotel have antique-style furnishings. The bar and restaurant are stylish, the ghost misunderstood (rumors abound).

Halcyon House B&B B&B $$
(☑ 785-841-0314; www.thehalcyonhouse.com; 1000 Ohio St; r $70-130; ❋ 🛜) The nine colorful bedrooms here (some share bathrooms) have lots of natural light, and there's a landscaped garden, and homemade baked goods for breakfast. Downtown is just a short walk away.

★**Hank Charcuterie** TAPAS $$
(☑ 785-832-8688; www.hankmeats.com; 1900 Massachusetts St; mains $10-20; ☺ 11am-9pm Tue-Fri, 9am-9pm Sat, 9am-2pm Sun) As the name suggests, this classy-but-casual eatery is a great place for a bottle of wine and some small bites, such as a cheese plate or meat board. There are also some inventive mains (think farro-stuffed quail or fried rabbit biscuits) and killer cocktails (try the 'drinking vinegar' with gin). Check the chalkboard for farms that supplied the ingredients.

🍷 Drinking & Entertainment

Henry's BAR
(☑ 785-331-3511; 11 E 8th St; ☺ 7am-2am; 🛜) Downstairs is a moody low-lit coffeehouse

---

WORTH A TRIP

DODGE CITY

Dodge City – where famous lawmen Bat Masterson and Wyatt Earp tried, sometimes successfully, to keep law and order – had a notorious reputation during the 1870s and 1880s. The long-running TV series *Gunsmoke* (1955–75) spurred further interest in the city's storied past, though historical authenticity has always played a distant third fiddle to fun and frolic here.

Today Dodge City milks its heritage while it slaughters more than 10,000 head of cattle every 24 hours at huge factories. You may be inspired to get the hell out of Dodge, but stick around for a bit and this time-worn town might just get under your skin.

The historic downtown, away from the attractions, is good for a wander. View surviving **Santa Fe Trail wagon-wheel ruts** about 9 miles west of town on US 50. The site is well marked.

The studio-backlot-like **Boot Hill Museum** (☑ 620-227-8188; www.boothill.org; 500 W Wyatt Earp Blvd; adult/child $12/9; ☺ 8am-8pm Jun-Aug, 9am-5pm Sep-May; 🚼) includes a cemetery, jail and saloon, where gunslingers reenact (blood-free) shootouts while Miss Kitty and her dancing gals do a wholesome cancan. Cheesy? Absolutely! But this faux frontier is gosh-darn fun.

'Soil to sip' is the philosophy behind the new **Boot Hill Distillery** (☑ 620-371-6309; www.boothilldistillery.com; 501 W Spruce St; ☺ 1-7pm Thu-Sat Jun-Aug, Fri & Sat Sep-May, tours 1pm, 3pm & 5pm), which is owned by three farmers who supply 100% of the grains. The tasting room – where you can try Kansas-made gins, vodkas and whiskeys – occupies a grand building that was once City Hall.

The **visitor center** (☑ 800-653-9378; www.visitdodgecity.org; 400 W Wyatt Earp Blvd; ☺ 8am-6:30pm daily Jun-Aug, to 5pm Mon-Fri Sep-May) has free walking and driving tours of historic sights.

Dodge City is about 150 miles west of Wichita along US 400. Greyhound (www.greyhound.com) connects the two with a daily bus ($40, three hours).

ROUTE 66: GET YOUR KICKS IN KANSAS

Only 13 miles of Route 66 pass through the southeast corner of Kansas, but it's a good drive along Hwy 66 and US 69 (from east to west).

Three miles down the road is **Riverton**; here you might consider a detour 20 miles north to Crawford County, where legendary fried chicken is a hallmark of six famous restaurants around **Pittsburg**. Try **Chicken Mary's** (620-231-9510; 1133 E 600th Ave, Pittsburg; meals from $7; ⊘4-8:30pm Tue-Sat, 11am-8pm Sun), one of the best.

Cross US 400 and stay on old Route 66 to the 1923 **Rainbow Bridge**, the last marsh arch bridge remaining on the route.

From the bridge, it's less than 3 miles south to **Baxter Springs**, the site of a Civil War massacre and numerous bank robberies. A restored 1939 Phillips 66 gas station is the **Kansas Route 66 Visitor Center** (620-856-2385; www.baxterspringsmuseum.org; cnr 10th St & Military Ave, Baxter Springs; ⊘10am-4:30pm Tue-Sat, 1-4pm Sun). Military Ave (US 69A) takes you into Oklahoma.

---

with underground tunes and for-sale artwork on the walls. Upstairs is an edgy (and gay-friendly) bar popular with Lawrence's alternative crowd. Altogether, Henry's encapsulates what makes Lawrence so proudly different from other towns in Kansas.

Bottleneck   LIVE MUSIC
(785-841-5483; www.bottlenecklive.com; 737 New Hampshire St; ⊘3pm-2am) The music scene in town is up to college-town standards, and this joint usually has the best of the newest. It operates as a dive bar on off nights and runs popular trivia and open-mike sessions.

ℹ Information

Visitor Information Center (785-865-5282; www.unmistakablylawrence.com; 402 N 2nd St; ⊘9am-5pm Mon-Sat, 1-5pm Sun) In the restored old Union Pacific Depot.

ℹ Getting There & Away

Lawrence is a quick half-hour drive east of Topeka or 45 minutes west of Kansas City along I-70. Amtrak's *Southwest Chief* calls into Lawrence and can take you to Kansas City ($10, 1½ hours) or Topeka ($10, 30 minutes).

Topeka

Kansas and its vital role in America's race relations is symbolized in the otherwise humdrum state capital of Topeka. The emerging **NOTO Arts District** in historic North Topeka is a bright spot with eclectic shops, galleries and restaurants.

There are chains aplenty near the intersection of I-70 and I-470 on the western edge of Topeka. You'll find a few independent hotels and inns downtown.

◎ Sights

★ **Brown v Board of Education National Historic Site**   MUSEUM
(785-354-4273; www.nps.gov/brvb; 1515 SE Monroe St; ⊘9am-5pm) FREE It took real guts to challenge the segregationist laws common in the US in the 1950s and the stories of these courageous men and women are here. Set in Monroe Elementary School, one of Topeka's African American schools at the time of the landmark 1954 Supreme Court decision that banned segregation in US schools, the displays cover the entire Civil Rights movement.

State Capitol   LANDMARK
(785-296-3966; www.kshs.org/capitol; 300 SW 10th Ave; ⊘7:30am-5:30pm Mon-Fri, 8am-1pm Sat, tours 9am-3pm Mon-Fri) FREE Under the huge copper dome, don't miss the fiery John Steuart Curry mural of abolitionist John Brown. Climb 296 steps for great views outside. Enter via the visitor center at 8th Ave and Van Buren St.

Kansas Museum of History   MUSEUM
(785-272-8681; www.kshs.org; 6425 SW 6th Ave; adult/child $10/5; ⊘9am-5pm Tue-Sat, 1-5pm Sun) From a Cheyenne war lance to Carrie Nation's hammer, this engaging center is packed with Kansas stories.

ℹ Getting There & Away

Topeka is about an hour west of Kansas City by car along I-70. Jefferson Lines (www.jeffersonlines.com) buses travel this route four times daily ($16).

Abilene

In the late 19th century, Abilene was a rowdy cow town at the end of the Chisholm Trail. Today its compact core of historic brick buildings and well-preserved neighborhoods seems perfectly appropriate for the birthplace of Dwight D Eisenhower (1890–1969), president and general.

⊙ Sights

Eisenhower Presidential Center　MUSEUM
(☑785-263-6700; www.eisenhower.archives.gov; 200 SE 4th St; museum adult/child $12/3; ⊗8am-5:45pm Jun & Jul, 9am-4:45pm Aug-May) Fittingly set against a backdrop of grain elevators, the rather regal Eisenhower Presidential Center includes Ike's boyhood home, a museum and library, and his and Mamie's graves. Displays cover the Eisenhower presidential era (1953–61) and his role as allied commander in WWII.

🛏 Sleeping & Eating

Abilene's Victorian Inn　B&B $
(☑785-263-7774; www.abilenesvictorianinn.com; 820 NW 3rd St; r from $80; ❄☎) This grand lavender-tinted building dates to 1882 and was the home of Eisenhower's best friend. It's recently been restored to its Victorian grandeur and has some fabulous wallpaper. The innkeeper is a bit stubborn in her rules (you can't view any of the six rooms in person before you book), but it's the best lodging in town by far.

Brookville Hotel　AMERICAN $$
(www.brookvillehotel.com; 105 E Lafayette Ave; meals $17; ⊗5-8pm Wed-Fri, 11:30am-7pm Sat & Sun) The Brookville Hotel has been serving fried chicken since former president and Abilene resident Dwight D Eisenhower graduated from West Point (1915). Cream-style corn, fresh biscuits and much more come with every meal.

❶ Getting There & Away

Abilene is 90 miles north of Wichita via I-135 and KS 15. There is no public transportation to or from the city.

Chase County

Nearly a perfect square, this is the county William Least Heat-Moon examined mile by mile in his best-selling *PrairyErth*. The beautiful Flint Hills roll through here and are home to two-thirds of the nation's remaining tallgrass prairie. Don't miss the showstopping **County Courthouse** in Cottonwood Falls, 2 miles south of Strong City. Completed in 1873, it is a fantasy of French Renaissance style.

⊙ Sights

★**Tallgrass Prairie National Preserve**　NATURE RESERVE
(☑620-273-8494; www.nps.gov/tapr; Hwy 177; ⊗buildings 9am-4:30pm, trails 24hr) FREE This 11,000-acre national preserve, 2 miles northwest of Strong City, is a perfect place to hike the prairie, with its 40 miles of scenic trails. Buffalo were reintroduced here in 2009 and now number close to 100, sharing the space with prairie chickens (whose mating rituals are legendary!). Rangers give tours of a preserved ranch and offer bus tours from the visitor center, explaining just how rare this ecosystem is (less than 4% of North America's original tallgrass prairie remains).

🛏 Sleeping & Eating

★**Millstream Resort Motel**　MOTEL $
(☑620-273-8114; 401 Mill St, Cottonwood Falls; r $62-100; ❄☎) There is so much to love about this charming motel overlooking Cottonwood River, not least of which is the cheap price. Stone walls, wood floors and individually decorated rooms with riverside balconies make this a true Flint Hills retreat. Owners Richard and Sharon will go out of their way to welcome you.

Ad Astra Food & Drink　AMERICAN $
(☑620-273-8440; 318 Cottonwood St, Strong City; mains $7-16; ⊗11am-10pm Fri & Sat, to 9pm Sun) It's the American classics done right with fresh ingredients and creative flair that make the seasonal menus of this stylish Strong City restaurant so appealing. With great folk tunes on the stereo, the works of local artists on the walls and craft beer flowing from the taps, you may be inspired to stick around for a while.

❶ Getting There & Away

Chase County is about halfway between Wichita and Topeka (I-35 exit 127). There is no public transportation in the region.

OKLAHOMA

Oklahoma gets its name from the Choctaw name for 'Red People.' One look at the state's vividly red earth and you'll wonder if

---

ROUTE 66 MUSEUMS

Route 66 Interpretive Center (☑405-258-1300; www.route66interpretivecenter.org; 400 E 1st St, Chandler; adult/child $5/4; ⊙10am-5pm Tue-Sat) Sixty miles southwest of Tulsa, this museum re-creates the experience of driving the Mother Road through the decades. It's housed in a magnificent 1936 armory.

Route 66 Museum & Research Center (☑417-532-2148; www.lebanon-laclede.lib. mo.us; 915 S Jefferson St; ⊙8am-8pm Mon-Thu, to 5pm Fri & Sat) This museum at the library in Lebanon has memorabilia past and present, including a replica soda fountain and vintage maps.

National Route 66 Museum (☑580-225-6266; 2717 W 3rd St/Hwy 66, Elk City; adult/child $5/4; ⊙9am-5pm Mon-Sat, 2-5pm Sun) Three museums in one: old cars and photos, a re-created pioneer town and a farm museum.

---

the name is more of a literal than an ethnic comment. Still, with 39 tribes located here, it is a place with deep Native American significance. Museums, cultural displays and more abound.

The other side of the Old West coin, cowboys also figure prominently in the Sooner State. Although pickups have replaced horses, there's still a great sense of the open range, interrupted only by urban Oklahoma City and Tulsa. Oklahoma's share of Route 66 links some of the Mother Road's iconic highlights and there are myriad atmospheric old towns.

ℹ Information

Oklahoma Bed & Breakfast Association (www.okbba.com)

Oklahoma State Parks (www.travelok.com/state_parks) Most parks are free for day use; campsites cost $14 to $25 per night, and some are reservable. The website is a labyrinth.

Oklahoma Tourism & Recreation Department (☑800-652-6552; www.travelok.com)

Oklahoma City

Often abbreviated to OKC, Oklahoma City is nearly dead center in the state and is the cultural and political capital. It has worked hard over the years to become more than just a cow town, all without turning its back on its cowboy heritage. It makes a good pause on your Route 66 travels.

The city is forever linked to the 1995 bombing of the Alfred P Murrah Federal Building; the memorials to this tragedy are moving.

◎ Sights

★**Oklahoma City**
National Memorial Museum   MUSEUM
(www.oklahomacitynationalmemorial.org; 620 N Harvey Ave; adult/student $15/12; ⊙9am-6pm Mon-Sat, noon-6pm Sun, last ticket sold 1hr before close) The story of America's worst incident of domestic terrorism is told at this poignant museum, which avoids becoming mawkish and lets the horrible events speak for themselves. The outdoor **Symbolic Memorial** has 168 empty chair sculptures for each of the people killed in the attack (the 19 small ones are for the children who perished in the day-care center).

★**Stockyards City**   AREA
(www.stockyardscity.org; Agnew Ave & Exchange Ave) You'll brush up against real cowboys in Stockyards City, southwest of downtown, either in the shops and restaurants that cater to them or at the **Oklahoma National Stockyards**, the world's largest stocker and feeder cattle market.

★**National Cowboy**
& Western Heritage Museum   MUSEUM
(☑405-478-2250; www.nationalcowboymuseum.org; 1700 NE 63rd St; adult/child $12.50/6; ⊙10am-5pm Mon-Sat, noon-5pm Sun) Only the smells are missing. Vibrant historic displays are complemented by a mock frontier village and an excellent collection of Western painting and sculpture featuring many works by Charles M Russell and Frederic Remington.

Oklahoma History Center   MUSEUM
(www.okhistory.org/historycenter; 800 Nazih Zuhdi Dr; adult/child $7/4; ⊙10am-5pm Mon-Sat) Near the capitol (p690), this museum makes people the focus as it tells the story of the Sooner State through interactive exhibits.

MEDICINE PARK

This charming creekside resort town woos travelers with its scenic setting and unique cobblestone architecture (with buildings made of rounded red rocks). It's the kind of place where artists rub shoulders with trout fishers as landscaped parks give way to a unique prairie paradise. The town is just a mile down the road from **Wichita Mountains Wildlife Refuge** (☏ 580-429-3222; http://wichitamountains.fws.gov; 20539 State Hwy 115, Cache; primitive sites $8, s units $10-20; ☼ visitor center 9am-5pm; 🚻 🌲), where herds of elk, buffalo and longhorn cattle roam free.

Cottages and cabins make up the bulk of lodging options, though there are a few lovely inns.

Medicine Park is about 1½ hours southwest of Oklahoma City by car, mostly on I-44. There is no public transportation between the two places.

Skeletons: Museum of Osteology   MUSEUM
(☏ 405-814-0006; www.museumofosteology.org; 10301 S Sunnylane Rd; adult/child $8/7; ☼ 8am-5pm Mon-Fri, 11am-5pm Sat, 1-5pm Sun) An army of flesh-eating beetles helps this museum's curators prepare the bones of dead animals (many from zoos) for a new life on display. There are more than 350 skeletons here and over 100,000 individual bones, including those of an American buffalo and an African bush elephant.

Paseo Arts District   AREA
(www.thepaseo.org; NW 30th St & Paseo) With its Spanish Revival architecture, lively bars and funky art galleries, this is OKC's most bohemian corner.

State Capitol   LANDMARK
(☏ 405-521-3356; 2300 N Lincoln Blvd; ☼ 7am-7pm Mon-Fri, 9am-4pm Sat & Sun, tours 9am-3pm Mon-Fri) **FREE** Built in 1917 (though it only got its dome in 2002), this Greco-Roman building has large murals, beautiful stained-glass windows, a tribal flag plaza and rotating art exhibits. Appropriately, it's the only state capitol surrounded by working oil wells.

🛏 Sleeping

Many older motels line I-35 south of town; newer chain properties stack up along I-44, the NW Expwy/Hwy 3 and at Bricktown (which puts you near nightlife action).

Lincoln Inn   MOTEL $
(☏ 405-528-7563; www.lincolninnokc.com; 5405 N Lincoln Blvd; r from $45; 🅿 ✳ 🐾 🛜 🐕) The best of OKC's budget options, located off I-44 not far from the State Capitol (p690) building. There's a big pool, a small gym and interior-access rooms.

Grandison Inn at Maney Park   B&B $$
(☏ 405-232-8778; www.grandisoninn.com; 1200 N Shartel Ave; r $140-190; 🅿 ✳ 🛜) In a genteel quarter of OKC just northwest of downtown, this gracious 1904-vintage B&B welcomes guests to eight rooms with period charm and modern amenities. The house has amazing woodwork, including a showstopping staircase.

Colcord Hotel   BOUTIQUE HOTEL $$
(☏ 405-601-4300; www.colcordhotel.com; 15 N Robinson Ave; r $170-240; 🅿 ✳ @ 🛜) OKC's first skyscraper, built in 1911, is now a luxurious 12-story hotel. Many original flourishes, such as the marble-clad lobby, survive, while the 108 rooms have a stylish, contemporary touch. It's near Bricktown.

✗ Eating

For listings, check out the weekly *Oklahoma Gazette* (www.okgazette.com) or just head to the renovated warehouses in the Bricktown District, which contain a vast array of bars and restaurants, some good, some purely chain.

Tucker's Onion Burgers   BURGERS $
(☏ 405-609-2333; www.tuckersonionburgers.com; 324 NW 23rd St; mains $5.50-10; ☼ 11am-9pm) 🌿 A new kind of burger joint with an old-time Route 66 vibe, Tucker's has high-quality food (locally sourced) that includes iconic Oklahoma onion burgers, fresh-cut fries and shakes. It even has a green ethos and a fine patio.

Ann's Chicken Fry House   SOUTHERN US $
(☏ 405-943-8915; 4106 NW 39th St; mains $5-12; ☼ 11am-8:30pm Tue-Sat) Part real diner, part tourist attraction, Ann's is a Route 66 veteran renowned for its – you guessed it – chicken fried steak. Okra and cream gravy

also star, and the fried chicken lives up to the rep. Get the black-eyed peas.

★ **Picasso's Cafe** MODERN AMERICAN **$$**
(☎ 405-602-2002; www.picassosonpaseo.com; 3009 Paseo; mains $10-20; ⊙ 11am-late; �?) Picasso's is renowned for its Bloody Marys at noon and masterfully plated farm-fresh meals. The place has an artistic sensibility, with works by local artists on display. Grab a table outside.

★ **Cheever's Cafe** MODERN AMERICAN **$$**
(☎ 405-525-7007; www.cheeverscafe.com; 2409 N Hudson Ave; mains $10-40; ⊙ 11am-9pm Sun-Thu, to 10:30pm Fri & Sat) This former art-deco flower shop is now an upscale cafe with excellent Southern- and Mexican-influenced fare. The menu changes seasonally and is locally sourced. The ice-cream-ball dessert fills many a dream.

Cattlemen's Steakhouse STEAK **$$**
(☎ 405-236-0416; www.cattlemensrestaurant.com; 1309 S Agnew Ave; mains $7-30; ⊙ 6am-10pm Sun-Thu, to midnight Fri & Sat) OKC's most storied restaurant, this Stockyards City (p689) institution has been feeding cowpokes and city slickers slabs of beef since 1910. Deals are still cut at the counter (where you can jump the wait for tables) and back in the luxe booths.

⚓ Drinking & Entertainment

Kick up your cowboy boots and learn some country line-dancing skills at one of OKC's country-and-western clubs, which are scattered throughout the city. For a more low-key evening, head to the alternative-minded Paseo Arts District. To bar-hop the night away, try Bricktown.

Bricktown Brewery BREWERY
(www.bricktownbrewery.com; 1 N Oklahoma Ave; ⊙ 11am-11pm Mon-Thu, to 2am Fri & Sat, to 9pm Sun) A large microbrewery in Bricktown, with revelers splayed out across large rooms enjoying pool, darts and just being spectators. Always hopping and has a decent food menu.

🛍 Shopping

Langston's CLOTHING
(☎ 405-235-9536; www.langstons.com; 2224 Exchange Ave; ⊙ 10am-8pm Mon-Sat, noon-5pm Sun) You can buy all forms of Western wear and gear at Langston's. The boot selection alone is mind-blowing.

ℹ Information

Located in the Cox Convention Center, the **Oklahoma City Visitor Information Center** (☎ 405-602-5141; www.visitokc.com; 58 W Sheridan Ave; ⊙ 9am-6pm Mon-Fri) has tips for dining and area attractions.

ℹ Getting There & Away

Will Rogers World Airport (OKC; www.flyokc. com) is 5 miles southwest of downtown; a cab costs about $25 to downtown.

Amtrak's (www.amtrak.com) *Heartland Flyer* goes from **Santa Fe Depot** (100 S EK Gaylord Blvd) to Fort Worth ($31, four hours).

Greyhound (☎ 405-606-4382; 1948 E Reno Ave) has daily buses to Dallas ($23, five hours), Wichita ($24, three hours) and Tulsa ($17, two hours, five daily), among other destinations.

Western Oklahoma

West of Oklahoma City toward Texas, the land opens into expansive prairie fields, nowhere as beautifully as in the Wichita Mountains, which, along with some Route 66 attractions and Native American sites, make this prime road-trip country.

Fort Sill National Historic Landmark & Museum HISTORIC SITE
(☎ 580-442-5123; 6701 Sheridan Rd, Visitor Control Center, Fort Sill; ⊙ 9am-5pm Tue-Sat) FREE The Fort Sill National Historic Landmark,

---

WASHITA BATTLEFIELD NATIONAL HISTORIC SITE

On November 27, 1868, George Custer's troops launched a dawn attack on the peaceful village of Chief Black Kettle. It was a slaughter of men, women, children and domestic animals, an act some would say led to karmic revenge on Custer eight years later. Trails traverse the **site** (☎ 580-497-2742; www.nps. gov/waba; Hwy 47A; ⊙ site dawn-dusk, visitor center 8am-5pm) of the killings, which is remarkably unchanged. An excellent visitor center 0.7 miles away contains a good **museum**; seasonal tours and talks are worthwhile.

The site is 2 miles west of Cheyenne, 30 miles north of I-40 via US 283. The surrounding **Black Kettle National Grassland** has some scenic drives and free campgrounds.

which fills several original stone buildings, explores the history of the fort. Another highlight is the 1872 **Post Guardhouse**, the center of law enforcement for the Indian Territory. Step inside to see where Apache leader Geronimo was detained on three separate occasions. Geronimo and other Apache warriors were brought here in 1894 as prisoners of war. Geronimo's grave, marked by an eagle-topped stone pyramid, is on fort grounds a few miles from the guardhouse.

Today, Fort Sill is home to the US Army Field Artillery School. Note that you'll have to fill out a form and pass a background check at the Fort Sill Visitor Control Center before passing through the gates to view the historic sites.

Route 66 road-trippers will pass through Western Oklahoma mostly along I-40 (take exit 32 for Cheyenne and the Washita Battlefield. Use I-44 out of Oklahoma City instead to dip down toward Fort Sill and the Wichita Mountains. There is no public transportation in the region.

Tulsa

Self-billed as the 'Oil Capital of the World,' Tulsa has never dirtied its hands much on the black gold that oozes out elsewhere in the state. Rather, it is home to scores of energy companies that make their living drilling for oil, selling it or supplying those who do. The steady wealth this provides once helped create Tulsa's richly detailed art-deco downtown.

Today Tulsa suffers more than most from suburban sprawl, although the Brady Arts District downtown is a bright spot.

◉ Sights

Downtown Tulsa has so much art-deco architecture it was once known as the 'Terra-Cotta City.' The **Philcade Building** (www. tulsaartdecomuseum.com; 511 S Boston Ave; ⊙ museum 8am-6pm Mon-Fri), with its glorious T-shaped lobby, and the **Boston Avenue United Methodist Church** (www.bostonave nue.org; 1301 S Boston St; ⊙ 8:30am-5pm Mon-Fri, 8am-5pm Sun, guided tours noon Sun), rising at the end of downtown, are two exceptional examples. Download a walking guide at www.visittulsa.com by searching for 'downtown Tulsa self-guided walking tour.'

The developing **Brady Arts District** is centered on Brady and Main Sts immedi-

ately north of downtown. It has galleries, venues and good restaurants.

★ **Gilcrease Museum**　　　MUSEUM
(☑ 918-596-2700; www.gilcrease.org; 1400 Gilcrease Museum Rd; adult/child $8/free; ⊙ 10am-5pm Tue-Sun) Northwest of downtown, off Hwy 64, this superb museum sits on the manicured estate of a Native American who discovered oil on his allotment. Exhibits explore Native American art, textiles, pottery and more, while the surrounding gardens make for a great stroll.

★ **Woody Guthrie Center**　　　MUSEUM
(☑ 918-574-2710; www.woodyguthriecenter.org; 102 E MB Brady St; adult/child $8/6; ⊙ 10am-6pm Tue-Sun) Woody Guthrie gained fame for his 1930s folk ballads that told stories of the Dust Bowl and the Great Depression. His life and music are recalled in this impressive new museum, where you can listen to his music and explore his legacy via the works of Dylan and more. Come back on select evenings for after-hours concerts at the onsite theater (check the website for dates and times).

★ **Oklahoma Jazz Hall of Fame**　　MUSEUM
(☑ 918-928-5299; www.oklahomajazz.org; 111 E 1st St; Sun jazz concerts adult/child $15/5; ⊙ 9am-5pm Mon-Fri, live music 6-10pm Tue & 4-7:30pm Sun) **FREE** Tulsa's beautiful Union Station is filled with sound again, but now it's melodious as opposed to cacophonous. During the first half of the 20th century, Tulsa was literally at the crossroads of American music with performers both homegrown and from afar. Learn about greats like Charlie Christian, Ernie Fields Senior and Wallace Willis in detailed exhibits. Sunday jazz concerts are played in the once-segregated grand concourse. On Tuesday nights there are free jam sessions.

Philbrook Museum of Art　　　MUSEUM
(☑ 918-749-7941; www.philbrook.org; 2727 S Rockford Rd; adult/child $9/free; ⊙ 10am-5pm Tue, Wed & Fri-Sun, to 8pm Thu, guided tours 2pm) South of town, this oil magnate's converted Italianate villa, ringed by fabulous foliage, houses fine Native American works and other classic art. There is a new second location, **Philbrook Downtown** (116 E MB Brady St; adult/ child $7/free; ⊙ 11am-6pm Wed-Sat, noon-5pm Sun), in the Brady Arts District. It shows contemporary art.

WORTH A TRIP

FRANK LLOYD WRIGHT IN BARTLESVILLE

This town still shows the riches that flowed from the ground during the first oil boom in 1905. The Phillips petroleum empire has left behind museums and a huge mansion. Soaring over it all is the 1956 221ft-tall **Price Tower** (☎918-336-4949; www.pricetower.org; 510 Dewey Ave; gallery adult/child $6/free, tours adult/child $15/10; ⊙gallery hours vary, tours 11am & 2pm Tue-Sat), the only Frank Lloyd Wright–designed skyscraper ever built.

Inside and out, the tower is like an edition of *Architectural Digest* meets *The Jetsons*. Wright shopped the design around for 30 years before he found clients willing to build it here. All but abandoned in the 1990s, the building now houses a ground-floor art gallery and the **Inn at Price Tower** (☎918-336-1000; www.pricetower.org/stay; 510 Dewey Ave; r from $140; P❄📶), located within the building's top floors. The inn's 21 rooms pay homage to Wright's distinctive style with high-design furnishings and unconventional angles. You can ride the rickety elevators to the 15th-floor bar.

Bartlesville is 45 miles north of Tulsa on US 75. Jefferson Lines (www.jeffersonlines.com) plies the route once daily ($20, one hour).

John Hope Franklin Reconciliation Park MONUMENT
(www.jhfcenter.org; 415 N Detroit Ave; ⊙8am-8pm) This park tells the story of the race riot that began on Memorial Day, May 30, 1921, when an African American man and a white woman were alone in an elevator in downtown Tulsa and the woman screamed. The how and why have never been answered, but the incident sparked three days of race riots in which 35 blocks of Tulsa's main African American neighborhood were destroyed by roving gangs. Thousands were left homeless, hundreds injured and scores killed.

Sleeping

Chain motels aplenty line Hwy 244 and I-44, especially at the latter's exits 229 and 232. You can also recapture some of the adventure of Route 66 at several vintage motels on E 11th St, although quality varies widely.

Desert Hills Motel MOTEL $
(☎918-834-3311; 5220 E 11th St; r from $45; P❄📶) The glowing neon cactus out front beckons you in to this lovingly restored 1950s motel with 50 rooms (with refrigerators and microwaves) arranged diagonally around the parking lot. It's 5 miles east of downtown, on historic Route 66.

★**Hotel Campbell** HOTEL $$
(☎918-744-5500; www.thecampbellhotel.com; 2636 E 11th St; r $140-210; P❄@📶) Restored to its 1927-era Route 66 splendor, this historic hotel east of downtown has 26 luxurious rooms with hardwood floors and plush period furniture. Ask for a tour.

Hotel Ambassador HOTEL $$$
(☎918-587-8200; www.ambassadortulsa.com; 1324 S Main St; r $200-300; P❄@📶) Look in the hallway for the photos of this 1929 nine-story hotel before its opulent renovation. Public spaces are suitably grand; the 55 rooms are newly renovated and have a contemporary feel that helps the somewhat close quarters seem a tad larger.

Eating

Look for dining options in the Brookside neighborhood, on Peoria Ave between 31st and 51st Sts; on Historic Cherry St (now 15th St) just east of Peoria Ave; and in the Brady Arts District.

★**Elmer's** BARBECUE $
(www.elmersbbqtulsa.com; 4130 S Peoria Ave; mains $7-17; ⊙11am-8pm Tue-Thu, to 9pm Fri & Sat) A legendary barbecue joint where the star of the menu is the potentially deadly 'Badwich,' a bun-crushing combo of superbly smoked sausages, ham, beef, pork and more. There's also smoked salmon and a showstopping side: green beans with chunks of succulent rib meat. The dining room is bright and has a house piano for the blues.

Ike's Chili House DINER $
(☎918-838-9410; www.ikeschilius.com; 1503 E 11th St; mains $5-9; ⊙10am-7pm Mon-Fri, to 3pm Sat) Ike's has been serving chili for more than 100 years and its classic version is much loved. You can get it straight or over Fritos, a hot dog, fries or spaghetti. Top with red peppers, onions, jalapeños, saltines and cheddar cheese for pure joy.

Tavern
AMERICAN $$

(📞 918-949-9801; www.taverntulsa.com; 201 N Main St; mains $15-38; ⊙ 11am-11pm Sun-Thu, to 1am Fri & Sat) This beautiful pub is a top choice in the Brady Arts District and serves excellent fare. The hamburgers are legendary or you can opt for steaks, salads or seasonal specials. The bartenders are true mixologists and there's a good wine list.

 Drinking & Nightlife

The Brady Arts District has lively nightlife with cocktail bars and live-music venues. Head to the fringe of town for exquisite craft beers at American Solera.

American Solera
BREWERY

(📞 918-949-4318; www.americansolera.com; 1801 S 49th W Ave; ⊙ 5-9pm Wed, 5-8pm Thu, 4-9pm Fri, noon-9pm Sat) Located amid the oil refineries on the outskirts of town, this newly opened tasting room is the long-awaited showpiece for American Solera's award-winning brews. Arriving feels like showing up at your old friend's garage for an impromptu party. Try the Norton Fellowship, a sour ale made with the native Norton grape.

☆ **Entertainment**

The *Tulsa Voice* (www.thetulsavoice.com) has the scoop on what's going on.

★ Cain's Ballroom
LIVE MUSIC

(📞 918-584-2306; www.cainsballroom.com; 423 N Main St) Rising rockers grace the boards where Bob Wills played Western swing in the '30s and the Sex Pistols caused confusion in 1978 (check out the hole Sid Vicious punched in a wall).

Admiral Twin Drive-In
OUTDOOR CINEMA

(📞 918-878-8099; www.admiraltwindrivein.com; 7355 E Easton St; adult/child $7/3; ⊙ Fri-Sun evenings Mar-Sep) A classic Route 66 drive-in movie theater with two screens playing the latest Hollywood blockbusters. Arrive well before showtime to get a good spot.

🛈 **Getting There & Around**

Greyhound (317 S Detroit Ave) destinations include Oklahoma City ($17, two hours, five daily) and Muskogee ($14, one hour, one daily). Jefferson Lines (www.jeffersonlines.com) buses ply the route to Bartlesville ($20, one hour, one daily).

Buses snake out from the **Tulsa Transit Hub** (www.tulsatransit.org; 319 S Denver Ave; 2hr/1-day pass $1.75/3.75) to the airport and other points in greater Tulsa.

Guthrie

Guthrie likes to call itself 'Offbeat Oklahoma,' a moniker it wears well. The arts-driven community here prides itself on the town's theater and bluegrass music scenes, while galleries and antique shops fill the brick-and-stone Victorian buildings that line its historic core. Some 30 miles north of Oklahoma City, this was the state's first capital.

⊙ **Sights**

Frontier Drugstore Museum
MUSEUM

(📞 405-282-1895; www.drugmuseum.org; 214 W Oklahoma Ave; suggested donation $3; ⊙ 10am-5pm Tue-Sat) A kooky little museum that shows you the intriguing remedies (like jars of leeches) offered at a frontier pharmacy at the turn of the century.

🛏 **Sleeping**

Pollard Inn
HISTORIC HOTEL $$

(📞 405-517-9266; www.guthrieinns.com; 124 W Harrison Ave; r from $150; ❊) Look up at the tin ceilings to check out the bullet holes at this bank-cum-inn, the site of many a frontier times robbery. The 12 rooms are exceedingly spacious and hearken back to Guthrie's heyday. Ask the new owner, Lucy, about the history of the town, as well as her plan to turn the basement into a performance venue.

✕ **Eating & Drinking**

Coffee culture is alive and well in Guthrie with a handful of noteworthy cafes, including the superb **Hoboken Coffee Roasters** (📞 405-760-3034; www.hoboken.coffee; 224½ S Division St; ⊙ 7am-3pm Mon-Fri, 8am-7pm Sat; 🛜). The nightlife doesn't disappoint either, with some charmingly eclectic small-town bars.

Stables Cafe
AMERICAN $

(📞 405-282-0893; www.stablescafe.net; 223 N Division St; mains $6-13; ⊙ 11am-9pm) Let the old road signs and classic advertisements take you back to the Oklahoma of yesteryear at this decent (if a bit greasy) burger and barbecue joint, housed in an 1889 livery stable. Head to the back side of the restaurant and you'll find Tap Room 223, a craft beer, wine and cider bar with two dozen brews on tap.

Boarding House   LOUNGE
(☑405-466-8146; www.theboardinghousellc.com; 124 W Oklahoma Ave; unlimited game play $5; ☺3:30-10:30pm Mon-Thu, to midnight Fri & Sat; ☎) Calling all board-game fanatics: Guthrie has its very own 'table game lounge' where locals gather to rent out classic or modern games and duke it out. Purchase coffee and snacks at the counter, grab a sofa and be prepared for competition.

❶ Getting There & Away

Guthrie is 30 miles north of Oklahoma City via I-35. There is no public transportation between the two cities.

Anadarko

Eight tribal lands are located in this area, and students from many different tribes are enrolled in Anadarko schools. The town regularly hosts powwows and events, and is a fine place to steep yourself in Native American culture.

National Hall of Fame for Famous American Indians   MONUMENT
(☑405-247-5555; 901 E Central Blvd, Hwy 62; ☺site 24hr, visitor center 9am-5pm Mon-Sat, from 1pm Sun) **FREE** A short outdoor walk leads past the bronze busts of well-known Native Americans including Pocahontas, Geronimo and Sitting Bull. The nearby visitor center has a good selection of books on Native Americans from Oklahoma.

Southern Plains Indian Museum   MUSEUM
(☑405-247-6221; www.doi.gov/iacb/southern-plains-indian-museum; 715 E Central Blvd; ☺9am-4:30pm Mon-Fri; ♿) **FREE** Houses a small but diverse collection of Plains Indian clothing, weaponry and musical instruments. There's also a small collection of Native American art.

Anadarko is a little over an hour southwest of Oklahoma City by car. There is no public transportation in the region.

Claremore

This was the setting for the 1931 play *Green Grow the Lilacs*, which became the hugely popular musical *Oklahoma!* The latter chronicles *highly* fictionalized events in 1906.

Born in a log cabin just north of town in 1879, Will Rogers was a cowboy, hilarious homespun philosopher, star of radio and movies, and part Cherokee. The hilltop **Will**

Rogers Memorial Museum (www.willrogers.com; 1720 W Will Rogers Blvd; adult/child $7/3; ☺10am-5pm) is an entertaining tribute to a man good for quotes such as 'We shouldn't elect a president. We should elect a magician' and 'No man is great if he thinks he is.'

Afternoon teatime is big in Claremore and some of the most atmospheric restaurants in town make an art of it. Try **Belvidere Tea Room** (☑918-342-1127; www.belvideremansion.com; 121 N Chickasaw Ave; mains $6-13; ☺10am-3pm Tue-Sat) for a touch of old-world elegance. Claremore also has some decent barbecue and Mexican restaurants.

Claremore is just 30 minutes northeast of Tulsa by car. There is no public transportation between the two cities.

Muskogee

Namesake of Merle Haggard's 1969 hit 'Okie from Muskogee,' this town 49 miles southeast of Tulsa was, and to some degree still is, Creek and Cherokee land. It's an excellent place to learn about Native American culture, especially before the 1800s.

◎ Sights

Fort Gibson   HISTORIC SITE
(907 N Garrison Rd, Fort Sill; adult/child $7/4; ☺10am-5pm Tue-Sat) Built as a frontier fort in 1824, Fort Gibson came to play an integral – and notorious – role in the Trail of Tears. It was home to the removal commission in the 1830s and is where surviving Creek and Seminole Indians were brought after the forced march. From here they were dispatched around the Indian Territory. You can get a good sense of military life 180 years ago at the restored grounds and buildings.

Five Civilized Tribes Museum   MUSEUM
(☑918-683-1701; www.fivetribes.org; 1101 Honor Heights Dr, Agency Hill; adult/student $3/1.50; ☺10am-5pm Mon-Fri, to 2pm Sat) This museum is inside an 1875 Union Indian Agency house. It recalls the cultures of the Native Americans forcibly moved here from America's southeast on the 'Trail of Tears.'

🛏 Sleeping & Eating

Graham-Carroll House   B&B $$
(☑918-683-0100; www.grahamcarrollhouse.com; 501 N 16th St; r $140-160; ❇☎) This grand five-room B&B lies within a banana-yellow English Tudor manor house in the Founder's Place Historic District. Some rooms have

jetted tubs and all stays include a gourmet three-course breakfast. Don't miss the rooftop balcony.

Harmony House BAKERY $

(☑918-687-8653; www.harmonyhouse4lunch.com; 208 S 7th St; mains $8-10; ☺cafe 11am-2:30pm Mon-Sat, bakery 9am-5pm Mon-Fri) With fresh baked cookies waiting for you at the table, pitchers of apricot iced tea and knickknacks aplenty, you may feel as though you've just arrived at your long-lost Oklahoma grandma's house. There are soups, salads and sandwiches, but the main reason to come here is for the bakery's desserts.

ℹ Getting There & Away

Muskogee is 49 miles southeast of Tulsa. Greyhound links the two cities with a daily bus ($14, one hour).

Tahlequah

Tahlequah (tal-*ah*-quaw) has been the Cherokee capital since 1839. The excellent **Cherokee Heritage Center** (☑918-456-6007; www.cherokeeheritage.org; 21192 S Keeler Dr; adult/child $8.50/5; ☺9am-5pm Mon-Sat Jun-Aug, Tue-Sat Sep-May) lies at Park Hill, once known as 'The Athens of Indian Territory.' Meanwhile, the compact downtown area has a youthful energy and vibrant shopping and dining options thanks to Northeastern State University.

🛏 Sleeping & Eating

The best dining options lie on Muskogee Ave between Choctaw and Spring Sts. College students keep the coffee shops and bars along Muskogee Ave jumping from dawn till well after dusk.

Blue Fern B&B B&B $$

(☑918-316-6973; www.bluefernbedandbreakfast. net; 224 W Chickasaw St; r $120-140; ❋⑧⑧) This 1904 Victorian – built before Oklahoma was a state – has been lovingly restored into a colorful B&B. Each of the three rooms has its own gas fireplace and two of them have kitchenettes.

Sam & Ella's Chicken Palace PIZZA $

(☑918-456-1411; 419 N Muskogee Ave; mains $7-11; ☺10am-10pm) Despite the name (and ever-present chicken theme), this funky restaurant is all about hand-tossed pizza pies and submarine sandwiches. Its claim to fame is that country music superstar Carrie Underwood waited tables here while attending Northeastern State University.

ℹ Getting There & Away

Tahlequah is 65 miles southeast of Tulsa. There is no public transportation between the two cities.

Texas

Includes ➜

Austin..........................700
San Antonio &
The Hill Country.........709
Houston......................717
Clear Lake..................723
Padre Island
National Seashore.....728
South Padre Island....728
Dallas..........................730
Fort Worth...................737
Big Bend
National Park.............740
El Paso........................746

Best Places to Eat

➜ Franklin Barbecue (p705)
➜ Javier's (p735)
➜ Pieous (p715)
➜ Killen's Barbecue (p723)
➜ L&J Cafe (p747)

Best Places to Sleep

➜ Hotel Emma (p711)
➜ Indian Lodge (p743)
➜ Hotel Van Zandt (p704)
➜ Hotel ZaZa Houston (p720)
➜ El Cosmico (p744)

Why Go?

Cue the theme music, and make it something epic: Texas is as big and sweeping a state as can be imagined. If it were a country, it would be the world's 40th largest. And as big as it is geographically, it is equally as large in people's imaginations.

Cattle ranches, pickup trucks, cowboy boots and thick Texas drawls – all of those are part of the culture, to be sure. But an Old West theme park it is not. With a state this big there's room for Texas to be whatever you want it to be.

You can find beaches, sprawling national parks, historic towns, citified shopping and nightlife, and a vibrant music scene. And the nearly year-round warm weather makes it ideal for outdoor activities such as hiking, cycling, rock climbing and kayaking. So saddle up for whatever adventure suits you best: the Lone Star state is ready to ride.

When to Go
Austin

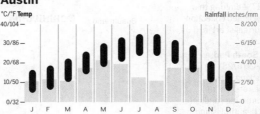

Mar Warm weather during spring break attracts college students and families with kids.

Apr–May Wildflowers line roadsides, festivals are in full swing and summer is yet to swelter.

Oct Crowds have thinned, the heat has broken, but it's still warm enough for shorts.

Texas Highlights

1 **Gruene Hall** (p709) Scooting across the well-worn wooden floor of Texas' oldest dance hall.

2 **River Walk** (p709) Strolling by cafes and riverside restaurants along the promenade in San Antonio.

3 **Austin** (p700) Getting your fill of live music, backyard bars and wildly creative food trucks.

4 **Sixth Floor Museum** (p730) Pondering JFK conspiracy theories at this one-of-a-kind museum in Dallas.

5 **Fort Worth** (p737) Watching longhorn cattle being driven through the dusty streets of this cowboy city.

6 **Big Bend National Park** (p740) Discovering a different kind of rugged Texan beauty.

7 **McDonald Observatory** (p742) Getting a stellar view of the night sky in the Fort Davis Mountains.

8 **Menil Collection** (p717) Admiring this unexpected collection of surrealist art in Houston.

9 **South Padre Island** (p728) Frolicking in the waves and on the shimmering sands of this beautiful island.

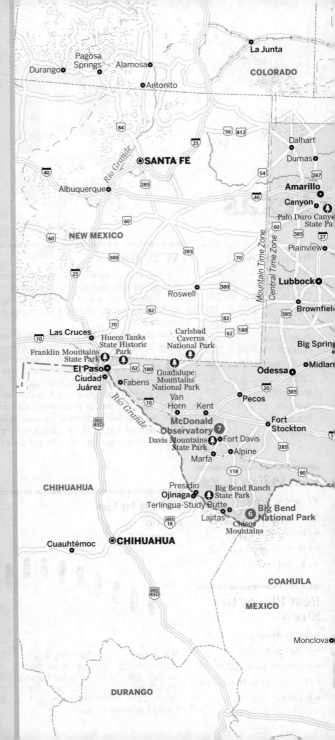

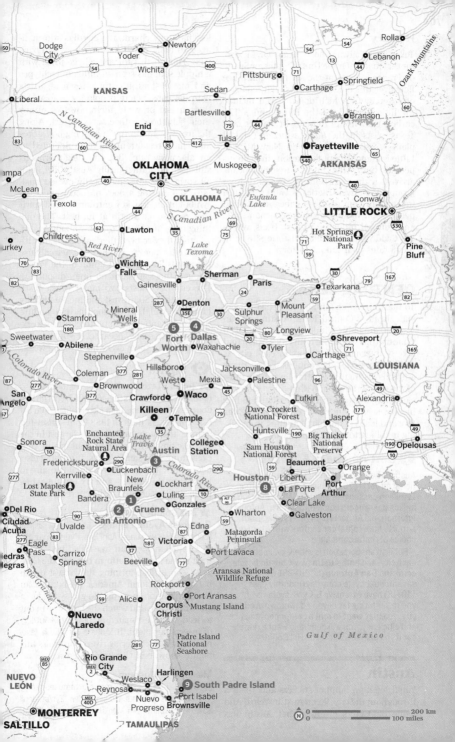

History

Texas hasn't always been Texas. Or Mexico, for that matter. Or the United States, or Spain, or France, or any of the six flags that once flew over this epic state in its eight changes of sovereignty (which doesn't even include the little Republic of the Rio Grande). The earliest evidence of humans in what is now Texas exists in the *llano estacado* ('staked plain') section of Texas and New Mexico. Little is known about the various indigenous peoples, but by the time the first Europeans arrived in the 16th century, several distinct groups of Native Americans were settled in the region. One of these tribes, the Caddo people, still figures strongly as a namesake and cultural influence in east Texas, where the Caddo Mounds State Historic Site commemorates their unique history.

CENTRAL TEXAS

To maximize your fun and for a taste of the state, head to Central Texas. Austin and San Antonio are only 80 miles apart, and the Hill Country rolls west from both cities. You'll find a busy international airport in each city as well as diverse lodging options. Lakes, rivers and hills distinguish Central Texas from most of the rest of the state. Within this region you can enjoy big city nightlife, nation-building history, scenic vineyards, delicious Tex-Mex fare and loads of outdoor activities, from hiking to tubing to wildflower viewing.

❶ Getting There & Away

Austin is home to Austin-Bergstrom International Airport (p707), which serves more than 11 million passengers annually. More than 8.6 million passengers come through San Antonio International Airport (p714) every year. Both airports have rental car centers with a broad choice of rental companies.

Public transportation is widely available within each city, and both **Austin** (www.austin.bcycle. com) and **San Antonio** (📞 210-281-0101; www. sanantonio.bcycle.com; day/monthly pass $10/18) have extensive B-Cycle systems. If you're venturing far beyond downtown in either city, you may want to rent a car for convenience and efficiency. You will definitely want a rental car if you plan to explore the Hill Country.

Austin

You'll see it on bumper stickers and T-shirts throughout the city: 'Keep Austin Weird.' And while old-timers grumble that Austin has lost its funky charm, the city has still managed to hang on to its incredibly laid-back vibe. Though this former college town with a hippie soul has seen an influx of techtypes and movie stars, it's still a town of artists with day jobs, where people try to focus on their music or write their novel or annoy their neighbors with crazy yard art. Along the freeway and in the 'burbs, big box stores and chain restaurants have proliferated at an alarming rate. But the neighborhoods still have an authentically Austin feel, with all sorts of interesting, locally owned businesses, including a flock of food trailers – a symbol of the low-key entrepreneurial spirit that represents Austin at its best. The one thing everyone seems to know about Austin, whether they've been there or not, is that it's a music town, even if they don't actually use the words 'Live Music Capital of the World' (though that's a claim no one's disputing). The city now hosts two major music festivals, South by Southwest and the Austin City Limits festival, but you don't have to endure the crowds and exorbitant hotel prices to experience the scene, because Austin has live music all over town every night of the week.

◉ Sights

★ Texas State Capitol HISTORIC BUILDING

(📞 512-463-5495, tours 512-463-0063; cnr 11th St & Congress Ave; ⊙ 7am-10pm Mon-Fri, 9am-8pm Sat & Sun; 🅿) FREE Built in 1888 from sunset-red granite, this state capitol is the largest in the US, backing up the ubiquitous claim that everything is bigger in Texas. If nothing else, take a peek at the lovely rotunda – be sure to look up at the dome – and try out the whispering gallery created by its curved ceiling.

★ Bat Colony Under Congress Avenue Bridge BRIDGE

(Congress Ave; ⊙ sunset Apr-Nov) Every year up to 1.5 million Mexican free-tailed bats make their home upon a platform beneath the Congress Ave Bridge, forming the largest urban bat colony in North America. It's become an Austin tradition to sit on the grassy banks of Lady Bird Lake and watch the bats swarm out to feed on an estimated 30,000lb (13,500kg) of insects per night. It looks a lot like a fast-moving, black, chittering river. Don't miss this nightly show; best viewing in August.

Mexic-Arte Museum MUSEUM

(📞 512-480-9373; www.mexic-artemuseum.org; 419 Congress Ave; adult/child under 12yr/student $5/1/4; ⊙ 10am-6pm Mon-Thu, to 5pm Fri & Sat,

TEXAS IN TWO WEEKS

So you want to do it all but are short on time? Start with three days in **Dallas**. See the JFK assassination sites downtown and eat in trendy Uptown, then the next day take a trip out to the historic Fort Worth Stockyards. Heading south out of town on day three, stop in cute little Waxahachie for a bite before spending two nights in **Austin** listening to live music and watching the bats fly.

Stop for a night in the Old West–era town of **Gruene** to dance at one of the state's oldest halls, then continue on to **San Antonio**. In two days there you can explore the Alamo and River Walk. From there **Corpus Christi** is just a three-hour drive south; it's a good base to kick back for a couple of nights and hit the beach at **Padre Island National Seashore** or **Port Aransas**.

Afterwards it's time to turn north for three nights in **Houston**. NASA's Space Center Houston is a don't-miss attraction, as is the museum district. For a third day's excursion, history and sunshine lovers should see **Galveston**.

noon-5pm Sun) This wonderful, eclectic downtown museum features works from Mexican and Mexican American artists in exhibitions that rotate every two months. The museum's holdings include carved wooden masks, modern Latin American paintings, historic photographs and contemporary art. Don't miss the back gallery, where new and experimental talent is shown. Admission is free on Sundays.

Bob Bullock Texas
State History Museum   MUSEUM
(☎512-936-8746; www.thestoryoftexas.com; 1800 Congress Ave; adult/child $13/9; ☺9am-5pm Mon-Sat, noon-5pm Sun) This is no dusty historical museum. Big and glitzy, it shows off the Lone Star State's history, from when it used to be part of Mexico up to the present, with high-tech interactive exhibits and fun theatrics. A new permanent exhibit on the 1st floor showcases the history – and the recovered hull – of *La Belle*, a French ship that sank off the Gulf Coast in the 1680s, changing the course of the Texas region's story. Allow a few hours for your visit.

Thinkery   MUSEUM
(☎512-469-6200; www.thinkeryaustin.org; 1830 Simond Ave; adult/child under 2yr $10/free; ☺10am-5pm Tue, Thu & Fri, to 8pm Wed, to 6pm Sat & Sun; ▣) This huge 40,000-sq-ft space north of downtown is an inspiring place for young minds, with hands-on activities in the realms of science, technology and the arts. Kids can get wet learning about fluid dynamics, build LED light structures and explore chemical reactions in the Kitchen Lab, among many other attractions. There's also an outdoor play area with nets and climbing toys. Closed Monday except for Baby Bloomers and other special events.

Contemporary Austin   MUSEUM
(☎512-453-5312; www.thecontemporaryaustin. org; 700 Congress Ave; adult/child under 18yr $5/ free; ☺11am-7pm Tue-Sat, noon-5pm Sun) This two-site museum has a new name and a freshly renovated downtown space. Downtown, the Jones Center features rotating exhibits representing new artists. Don't miss the view of the city from the new Moody Rooftop, an open-air event space. You'll also find temporary exhibits at the museum's original home at Laguna Gloria (3809 W 35th St).

Museum of the Weird   MUSEUM
(☎512-476-5493; www.museumoftheweird.com; 412 E 6th St; adult/child $12/8; ☺10am-midnight) Pay the entrance fee, walk through the gift shop and then step inside Austin's version of a cabinet of curiosities. Or perhaps we should say hallway of curiosities, one lined with shrunken heads, malformed mammals and a range of unusual artifacts. The show stealer? The legendary Minnesota Ice Man – is that a frozen prehistoric man under all that ice? Step up to see for yourself then grab a seat for a live show of amazing physical derring-do.

🏃 Activities

Barton Springs Pool   SWIMMING
(☎512-867-3080; 2201 Barton Springs Rd; adult/ child $8/3; ☺5am-10pm) Hot? Not for long. Even when the temperature hits 100, you'll be shivering in a jiff after you jump into this icy-cold natural-spring pool. Draped with century-old pecan trees, the area around the pool is a social scene in itself, and the place gets packed on hot summer days.

Austin

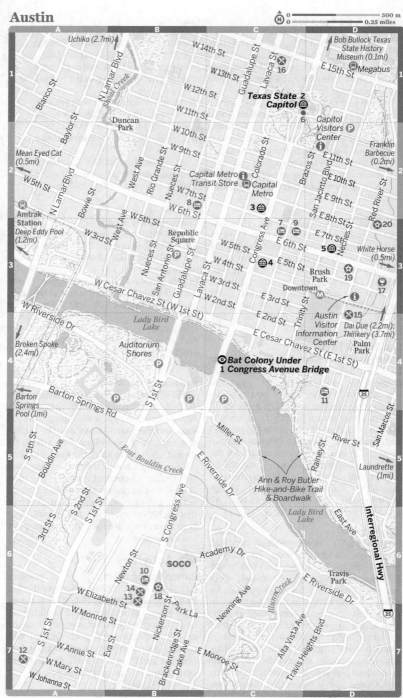

N

0 — 500 m
0 — 0.25 miles

Uchiko (2.7mi)

Bob Bullock Texas State History Museum (0.1mi)

Megabus

W 14th St

W 13th St

W 12th St

W 11th St

W 10th St

W 9th St

Blanco St

Baylor St

N Lamar Blvd

Shoal Creek

Duncan Park

Guadalupe St

Lavaca St

E 15th St

Texas State 2 Capitol 6

Capitol Visitors Center

Franklin Barbecue (0.2mi)

Mean Eyed Cat (0.5mi)

W 5th St

West Ave

Rio Grande St

Nueces St

Colorado St

E 11th St

E 10th St

E 9th St

Brazos St

San Jacinto Blvd

Capital Metro Transit Store

Capital Metro

3

Amtrak Station

Deep Eddy Pool (1.2mi)

N Lamar Blvd

Bowie St

West Ave

W 5th St

W 3rd St

San Antonio St

Guadalupe St

Republic Square

Nueces St

W 7th St

W 6th St

8

7 9

E 8th St

E 7th St

Neches St

5

20

White Horse (0.5mi)

W 5th St

W 4th St

Lavaca St

W 3rd St

W 2nd St

Congress Ave

E 6th St

E 5th St

4

Brush Park

19

17

Downtown

Broken Spoke (2.4mi)

W Cesar Chavez St (W 1st St)

Lady Bird Lake

Auditorium Shores

E 3rd St

E 2nd St

Trinity St

Austin Visitor Information Center

15

Dai Due (2.2mi); Thinkery (3.7mi)

Palm Park

Barton Springs Pool (1mi)

Barton Springs Rd

S 1st St

E Cesar Chavez St (E 1st St)

◉Bat Colony Under 1 Congress Avenue Bridge

11

35

Broken Spoke (2.4mi)

S 5th St

Bouldin Ave

S 2nd St

3rd St

S 1st St

East Bouldin Creek

Miller St

E Riverside Dr

Ann & Roy Butler Hike-and-Bike Trail & Boardwalk

Rainey St

River St

San Marcos St

Lady Bird Lake

East Ave

Laundrette (1mi)

Interregional Hwy

Newton St

S Congress Ave

Academy Dr

SOCO

10

14

13

18

W Elizabeth St

Nickerson St

Park La

Newning Ave

Blunn Creek

Travis Park

E Riverside Dr

W Monroe St

W Annie St

12

W Mary St

W Johanna St

S 1st St

Eva St

Brackenridge St

Drake Ave

E Monroe St

Alta Vista Ave

Travis Heights Blvd

35

Austin

◎ **Top Sights**
  1 Bat Colony Under Congress
      Avenue Bridge.....................................C4
  2 Texas State Capitol C1

◎ **Sights**
  3 Contemporary Austin C2
  4 Mexic-Arte Museum.............................C3
  5 Museum of the Weird...........................D3

◉ **Activities, Courses & Tours**
  6 Historic Walking Tours..........................C1

🛏 **Sleeping**
  7 Driskill Hotel C3
  8 Extended StayAmerica B2
  9 Firehouse Hostel...................................C3

  10 Hotel San José.....................................B6
  11 Hotel Van Zandt...................................D4

✖ **Eating**
  12 Bouldin Creek Coffee House.................A7
  13 Güero's Taco Bar...................................B6
  14 Hopdoddy Burger Bar...........................B6
  15 Moonshine Patio Bar & Grill..................D4
  16 Texas Chili Parlor C1

◉ **Drinking & Nightlife**
  17 Easy Tiger...D3

◉ **Entertainment**
  18 Continental Club...................................B6
  19 Esther's Follies.....................................D3
  20 Stubb's Bar-B-Q D3

Deep Eddy Pool SWIMMING
(☎512-974-1189; www.deepeddy.org; 401 Deep Eddy Ave; adult/child under 11yr/12-17yr $8/3/4; ⊗9am-7:30pm Mon-Fri, 9am-7pm Sat & Sun) With its vintage 1930s bathhouse built as part of the Works Progress Administration, Texas' oldest swimming pool is fed by cold springs and surrounded by cottonwood trees. There are separate areas for waders and lap swimmers.

Lady Bird Lake CANOEING
(☎512-459-0999; www.rowingdock.com; 2418 Stratford Dr; ⊗9am-6pm) Named after former first lady 'Lady Bird' Johnson, Lady Bird Lake looks like a river. And no wonder: it's actually a dammed-off section of the Colorado River that divides Austin into north and south. Get on the water at the rowing dock, which rents kayaks, canoes and stand-up paddle boards from $10 to $20 per hour Monday to Thursday, with higher prices on weekends and during major events.

👉 Tours

Texpert Tours TOURS
(☎512-383-8989; www.texperttours.com; per hr from $100) For an interesting alternative to your stereotypical, run-of-the-mill bus and van tour, try Texpert Tours, led by affable public-radio host Howie Richey (aka the 'Texas Back Roads Scholar'). Historical anecdotes, natural history and environmental tips are all part of the educational experience. A three-hour tour of central Austin takes visitors to the state capitol, the Governor's Mansion and the top of Mt Bonnell.

Historic Walking Tours WALKING
(☎512-474-5171; www.tspb.state.tx.us/plan/tours/tours.html; ⊗9am Tue & Thu-Sat, 11am & 1pm Sun)

FREE One of the best deals around are the free Historic Walking Tours of downtown Austin, which leave from the capitol's south steps. Tours last between 60 and 90 minutes. Make reservations at least 48 hours in advance either online or by phone through the visitor center.

✨ Festivals & Events

South by Southwest MUSIC, FILM
(SXSW; www.sxsw.com; single festival $825-1325, combo pass $1150-1650; ⊗mid-Mar) One of the American music industry's biggest gatherings has now expanded to include film and interactive media. Austin is absolutely besieged with visitors during this two-week window, and many a new resident first came to the city to hear a little live music.

Austin City Limits Music Festival MUSIC
(www.aclfestival.com; 1-/3-day pass $100/250; ⊗Oct) What do music lovers do in autumn? They head to the Austin City Limits Festival, which is not as big as SXSW but has been swiftly gaining on it in terms of popularity. The three-day festival held on eight stages in Zilker Park books more than 100 pretty impressive acts and sells out months in advance.

🛏 Sleeping

Firehouse Hostel HOSTEL **$**
(☎512-201-2522; www.firehousehostel.com; 605 Brazos St; dm $32-40, r $110-170, ste $130-170; ⊗❀🖤🐾) Open since 2013, this hostel in downtown Austin is pretty darn spiffy. In a former firehouse, it still feels fresh, and the downtown location right across from the historic Driskill Hotel is as perfect as you can get.

TEXAS FOR KIDS

San Antonio & Hill Country
Historic sites with activity books, plus theme parks, make San Antonio especially family friendly. In Hill Country, Kerrville and New Braunfels serve as launch points for river inner-tubing.

Gulf Coast & South Texas
Beaches line the southern Gulf Coast: some have diversions, some simply star nature herself. **Galveston Island**, with its organized beaches, pleasure pier, water park and amusements, offers much fun. Corpus Christi is home to the USS Lexington Museum (p726), the huge Texas State Aquarium (p726) and a lovely bayfront promenade.

Houston
The Houston Museum of Natural Science (p717) has popular hands-on exhibits on chemistry, energy and other science disciplines.

Dallas & the Panhandle Plains
Nearby in Arlington, a theme park and water park don't hurt either.

Emma Long Metropolitan Park CAMPGROUND **$**
(☎ 512-346-1831; www.austintexas.gov; 1706 City Park Rd; tent sites with hookups $10-20, RV sites with hookups $20-25, plus entrance fee per car Mon-Thu/Fri-Sun $5/10; ⊙gates open 7am-10pm; 🅿🗩) The only Austin city park with overnight camping, 1000-acre Emma Long Metropolitan Park (aka 'City Park') on Lake Austin, 16 miles northwest of downtown, has good swimming, sunbathing, fishing and boating. Get here early as it fills quickly and doesn't take reservations.

⭐**Hotel San José** BOUTIQUE HOTEL **$$**
(☎ 512-852-2350; www.sanjosehotel.com; 1316 S Congress Ave; r without bath $150, r $215-360, ste $335-500; 🅿🗩🕸🛜🗩) Local hotelier Liz Lambert has revamped a 1930s-vintage motel into a chic SoCo retreat with minimalist rooms in stucco bungalows, a lovely bamboo-fringed pool and a very Austin-esque hotel bar in the courtyard that's known for its celebrity-spotting potential. South Congress has become quite the scene, and this hotel's location puts you right in the thick of it.

Extended StayAmerica BUSINESS HOTEL **$$**
(☎ 512-457-9994, 800-398-7829; www.extendedstayamerica.com; 600 Guadalupe St; ste $160-200; 🅿🗩🕸🛜) This extended-stay hotel has an excellent downtown location, in walking distance to tons of bars and restaurants. Suites are a little on the bland side – and could use some TLC – but include a kitchenette stocked with utensils. Parking is included in the price. It's all a great excuse to hang out in Austin a while.

Lone Star Court HOTEL **$$**
(☎ 512-814-2625; www.lonestarcourt.com; 10901 Domain Dr; r $189-209, ste $399; 🅿🕸🛜🗩🗩) Next door to the Domain shopping mall, this new hotel exudes cowboy cool. Spacious rooms feature stylish barn-style doors and retro refrigerators stocked with local brews. In the courtyard, fire pits await your cowboy beans and trail coffee...oh wait, we meant your modern-day s'mores fixin's. The on-site restaurant offers live music regularly and a tasty hot breakfast.

⭐**Hotel Van Zandt** HOTEL **$$$**
(☎ 512-542-5300; www.hotelvanzandt.com; 605 Davis St; r/ste from $299/499; 🛜🗩🗩) Named for Texas singer-songwriter Townes Van Zandt, this Kimpton property impresses with the details. Touches such as a French horn chandelier above the lobby and leather chairs with low-key buckles give a stylish nod to Austin's cowboy and musical sensibilities. The big-windowed rooms come in a variety of configurations but whatever you do, angle for a view of Lady Bird Lake.

⭐**Driskill Hotel** HISTORIC HOTEL **$$$**
(☎ 512-439-1234; www.driskillhotel.com; 604 Brazos St; r/ste from $299/419; 🅿🗩🕸@🛜🗩) Every city should have a beautiful historic hotel made out of native stone, preferably built in the late 19th century by a wealthy cattle baron. Although it's now owned by the Hyatt, you'll find no generic hotel decor

here; this place is pure Texas, especially the bar with wall-mounted longhorns, leather couches and a stained-glass dome. The elegant rooms are taxidermy free.

✗ Eating

Barbecue and Tex-Mex are the mainstays, but Austin also has many fine-dining restaurants and a broadening array of world cuisines. For hot tips on new restaurants, pick up the free alternative weekly *Austin Chronicle*, published on Thursday. Downtown eateries are a real mixed bag, serving tourists, business folks, politicians, artists and night-owl clubbers. South Austin, Hyde Park and East Austin have lots of interesting choices. Around the UT campus area, prices drop – but often so does quality.

★ **Franklin Barbecue**   BARBECUE **$**
(📞 512-653-1187; www.franklinbarbecue.com; 900 E 11th St; sandwiches $6-10, ribs/brisket per lb $17/20; ⏰ 11am-2pm Tue-Sun) This famous BBQ joint only serves lunch, and only till it runs out – usually well before 2pm. In fact, to avoid missing out, you should join the line – and there will be a line – by 10am (9am on weekends). Just treat it as a tailgating party: bring beer or mimosas to share and make friends. And yes, you do want the fatty brisket.

★ **Hopdoddy Burger Bar**   BURGERS **$**
(📞 512-243-7505; www.hopdoddy.com; 1400 S Congress Ave; burgers $7-13; ⏰ 11am-10pm Sun-Thu, to 11pm Fri & Sat) People line up around the block for the burgers, fries and shakes – and it's not because burgers, fries and shakes are hard to come by in Austin. It's because this place slathers tons of love into everything it makes, from the humanely raised beef to the locally sourced ingredients to the fresh-baked buns. The sleek, modern building is pretty sweet, too.

Texas Chili Parlor   TEX-MEX **$**
(📞 512-472-2828; 1409 Lavaca St; chili $4-9, mains $5-15; ⏰ 11am-2am) Ready for an X-rated meal? When ordering your chili, keep in mind that 'X' is mild, 'XX' is spicy and 'XXX' is melt-your-face-off hot at this Austin institution. There's more than just chili on the menu; there's also Frito pie, which is chili over Fritos. Still not feeling it? There's also burgers, enchiladas and, of course, more chili.

★ **Güero's Taco Bar**   TEX-MEX **$$**
(📞 512-447-7688; www.gueros.com; 1412 S Congress Ave; breakfast $5-7, lunch & dinner $10-34; ⏰ 11am-10pm Mon-Wed, to 11pm Thu & Fri, 8am-11pm Sat, to 10pm Sun) Set in a former feed-and-seed store from the late 1800s, Güero's is an Austin classic and always draws a crowd. It may not serve the best Tex-Mex in town but with its free chips and salsa, refreshing margaritas and convivial vibe, we can almost guarantee a fantastic time. And the food? Try the homemade corn tortillas and chicken tortilla soup.

Laundrette   MODERN AMERICAN **$$**
(📞 512-382-1599; 2115 Holly St; mains $18-24; ⏰ 11am-2:30pm daily, 5-10pm Sun-Thu, to 11pm Fri & Sat) A brilliant repurposing of a former washeteria, Laundrette boasts a stylish, streamlined design that provides a fine backdrop to the delicious Mediterranean-inspired cooking. Among the many hits: crab toast, wood-grilled octopus, brussels sprouts with apple-bacon marmalade, a perfectly rendered brick chicken and whole grilled branzino.

Moonshine Patio Bar & Grill   AMERICAN **$$**
(📞 512-236-9599; www.moonshinegrill.com; 303 Red River St; dinner mains $12-25; ⏰ 11am-10pm Mon-Thu, to 11pm Fri & Sat, 9am-2pm & 5-10pm Sun) Dating from the mid-1850s, this historic building is a remarkably well preserved homage to Austin's early days. Within its exposed limestone walls, you can enjoy upscale comfort food, half-price appetizers at happy hour or a lavish Sunday brunch buffet ($20). Or chill on the patio under the shade of pecan trees.

★ **Uchiko**   JAPANESE **$$$**
(📞 512-916-4808; www.uchikoaustin.com; 4200 N Lamar Blvd; small plates $4-28, sushi rolls $10-16; ⏰ 5-10pm Sun-Thu, to 11pm Fri & Sat) Not content to rest on his Uchi laurels, chef Tyson Cole opened this North Lamar restaurant that describes itself as 'Japanese farmhouse dining.' But we're here to tell you, it's hard to imagine being treated to fantastic and unique delicacies such as these and enjoying this sort of bustling ambience in any Japanese farmhouse. Reservations are highly recommended.

★ **Dai Due**   AMERICAN **$$$**
(📞 512-719-3332; www.daidue.com; 2406 Manor Rd; breakfast & lunch $13-22, dinner $22-84; ⏰ 10am-3pm & 5-10pm Tue-Sun) Even your basic eggs-and-sausage breakfast is a meal to remember at this lauded restaurant, where all the ingredients are from farms, rivers and hunting grounds in Texas, as well as the Gulf of Mexico. Supper Club dinners spotlight limited items like wild game and

foraged treats. Like your cut of meat? See if they have a few pounds to-go at the attached butcher shop.

🍷 Drinking & Nightlife

There are bejillions of bars in Austin. The legendary 6th St bar scene has spilled onto nearby thoroughfares, especially Red River St. Many of the 6th St places are shot bars aimed at college students and tourists, while the Red River establishments retain a harder local edge. A few blocks south, the scene on Rainey St is also jumping, with old bungalows now home to watering holes.

★ Ginny's Little Longhorn Saloon   BAR

(☎512-524-1291; www.thelittlelonghornsaloon. com; 5434 Burnet Rd; ⊙5pm-midnight Tue & Wed, to 1am Thu-Sat, 2-10pm Sun) This funky little cinder-block building is one of those dive bars that Austinites love so very much – and did even before it became nationally famous for chicken-shit bingo on Sunday night. The place gets so crowded during bingo that you can barely see the darn chicken – but, hey, it's still fun. The overflow crowd is out back.

Easy Tiger   BEER GARDEN

(www.easytigeraustin.com; 709 E 6th St; ⊙11am-2am) The one bar on Dirty 6th that all locals love? Easy Tiger, an inside-outside beer garden overlooking Waller Creek. The place welcomes all comers with an upbeat communal vibe. Craft beers are listed on the chalkboard. And the artisanal sandwich-

---

DON'T MISS

BROKEN SPOKE

If you are ready for a little Texas two-steppin', there is only one place you should dream of going: the **Broken Spoke** (www.brokenspokeaustintx.net; 3201 S Lamar Blvd; ⊙11am-11:30pm Tue, to midnight Wed & Thu, to 1:30am Fri & Sat). This is country-and-western nirvana – a totally authentic Texas dance hall that's been in business since 1964. Here you'll find dudes in boots and Wranglers two-stepping around a crowded dance floor alongside hipsters, college students and slackers; many consider it an essential Austin experience. (You'll know you've arrived when you spot a big old oak tree propping up an old wagon wheel out front.)

---

es? They're baked on tasty bread from the bakery upstairs (7am to 2am). The meat is cooked in-house.

White Horse   HONKY-TONK

(☎512-553-6756; www.thewhitehorseaustin.com; 500 Comal St; ⊙3pm-2am) Ladies, you will be asked to dance at this East Austin honky-tonk, where two-steppers and hipsters mingle like siblings in a diverse but happy family. Play pool, take a dance lesson or step outside to sip a microbrew on the patio. Live music nightly, and whiskey on tap. We like this place.

Mean Eyed Cat   BAR

(☎512-920-6645; www.themeaneyedcat.com; 1621 W 5th St; ⊙11am-2am) We're not sure if this watering hole is a legit dive bar or a calculated dive bar (it opened in 2004). Either way, a bar dedicated to Johnny Cash has our utmost respect. Inside, Man in Black album covers, show posters and other knickknackery adorn the walls of this former chainsaw repair shop. A 300-year-old live oak anchors the lively patio.

☆ Entertainment

Austin calls itself the 'Live Music Capital of the World,' and you won't hear any argument from us. Music is the town's leading nighttime attraction, and a major industry as well, with several thousand bands and performers from all over the world plying their trade in the city's clubs and bars. Most bars stay open till 2am, while a few clubs stay hoppin' until 4am.

★ Continental Club   LIVE MUSIC

(☎512-441-2444; www.continentalclub.com; 1315 S Congress Ave; ⊙4pm-2am Mon-Fri, from 3pm Sat & Sun) No passive toe-tapping here; this 1950s-era lounge has a dance floor that's always swinging with some of the city's best local acts. On most Monday nights you can catch local legend Dale Watson and his Lone Stars (10:15pm).

Stubb's Bar-B-Q   LIVE MUSIC

(☎512-480-8341; www.stubbsaustin.com; 801 Red River St; ⊙11am-10pm Mon-Thu, to 11pm Fri & Sat, 10:30am-9pm Sun) Stubb's has live music almost every night, with a great mix of premier local and touring acts from across the musical spectrum. Many warm-weather shows are held out back along Waller Creek. There are two stages, a smaller stage indoors and a larger backyard venue.

LGBTIQ TEXAS

Texas is generally conservative. The larger cities have gay, lesbian, bisexual and transgender communities, but outside of Pride days and Austin in general, you won't see sexual identities being flaunted. In rural areas, displays of affection may draw negative attention from locals.

Gay & Lesbian Yellow Pages (www.glyp.com) Phone directories to Austin, Dallas, Galveston, Houston and San Antonio.

National Gay & Lesbian Task Force (www.thetaskforce.org) Advocacy group with great national news coverage.

This Week in Texas (www.thisweekintexas.com) Statewide publication with business directories and bar guide.

Esther's Follies   COMEDY
(☏512-320-0553; www.esthersfollies.com; 525 E 6th St; reserved seating/general admission $30/25; ☺shows 8pm Thu-Sat, plus 10pm Fri & Sat) Drawing from current events and pop culture, this long-running satire show has a vaudevillian slant, thanks to musical numbers and, yep, even a magician. Good, harmless fun.

ℹ Information

The bulletin boards found outside coffeehouses, cafes and grocery stores are a great source of news about local events, special activities and classified ads.

Austin Visitor Information Center (☏512-478-0098; www.austintexas.org; 602 E 4th St; ☺9am-5pm Mon-Sat, from 10am Sun) Maps, brochures and gift shop downtown.

Capitol Visitors Center (CVC; ☏512-305-8400; www.tspb.texas.gov/prop/tcvc/cvc/cvc.html; 112 E 11th St; ☺9am-5pm Mon-Sat, noon-5pm Sun) Stop here for self-guided tour maps of the capitol and tourist information about Austin and the state.

ℹ Getting There & Away

Austin-Bergstrom International Airport (AUS; www.austintexas.gov/airport) is about 10 miles southeast of downtown. It's served by Air Canada, Alaska Airlines, Allegiant, American, British Airways, Delta, Frontier, JetBlue, Southwest, United and Virgin America.

The **Greyhound bus station** (☏512-458-4463; 916 E Koenig Lane) is 5 miles north of downtown. Capital Metro bus 10-South First/Red River (www.capmetro.org) will deliver you from the station to downtown. Buses leave from here for other major Texas cities frequently.

There is a **Megabus** (☏800-256-2757; www.megabus.com; 1500 San Jacinto Blvd) pick-up and drop-off stop at 1500 San Jacinto Blvd on the northeast corner of the state capitol grounds.

The downtown **Amtrak station** (☏512-476-5684; www.amtrak.com; 250 N Lamar Blvd) is served by the *Texas Eagle,* which extends from Chicago to Los Angeles. There's free parking and an enclosed waiting area but no staff. Fares vary wildly.

ℹ Getting Around

Austin's handy public-transit system is run by **Capital Metro** (CapMetro; ☏512-474-1200, transit store 512-389-7454; www.capmetro.org; transit store 209 W 9th St; ☺transit store 7:30am-5:30pm Mon-Fri). Call for directions to anywhere or stop in at the downtown **Capital Metro Transit Store** (www.capmetro.org; 209 W 9th St; ☺7:30am-5:30pm Mon-Fri) for information. Regular city buses – not including the more expensive express routes – cost $1.25. Children under six years of age are free. There are bicycle racks (where you can hitch your bike for free) on the front of almost all CapMetro buses, including more than a dozen UT shuttle routes.

Uber and Lyft are not available in Austin. For ride sharing, try **Fare** (www.ridefare.com), **Fasten** (www.fasten.com) or the nonprofit **Ride Austin** (www.rideaustin.com).

Around Austin

Northwest of Austin, a series of dams along the Colorado River has blessed the area with the **Highland Lakes**, six lakes with a handsome network of lakeside greenbelts and parks to help you enjoy them. Though recent years have seen serious droughts, when there's water, one of the most popular lakes for recreation is the 19,000-sq-acre **Lake Travis.**

You can rent boats and Jet Skis at the associated marina, let it all hang out – literally – at the nude beach at the county-run **Hippie Hollow park** (https://parks.traviscountytx.gov; 7000 Comanche Trail, Austin; day pass car/

bicycle $15/8; ⊙9am-dusk), or stay overnight at the **Lakeway Resort & Spa** (☑512-261-6600; www.lakewayresortandspa.com; 101 Lakeway Dr, Austin; r from $249; P✳@⊛≋). Feel like splurging? Head for **Lake Austin Spa Resort** (☑512-372-7300; www.lakeaustin.com; 1705 S Quinlan Park Rd, off FM 2222, Austin; 2-night packages from $1425; P✳@⊛≋), one of the premier places to be pampered in the state.

Bastrop

Just 30 miles southeast of Austin lies the quintessential small town of **Bastrop**. With more than 130 buildings listed on the National Register of Historic Places, Bastrop has earned the title of 'Most Historic Small Town in Texas,' but it's the redevelopment of the cute **historic center** (www.bastrop downtown.com) that makes it a fun place to spend a day or two. The happening little burg also has first-Friday **art walks** from 5:30pm to 8:30pm.

Bastrop is also near several family friendly parks, with attractions ranging from dinosaur replicas at **Dinosaur Park** (☑512-321-6262; www.thedinopark.com; 893 Union Chapel Rd, Cedar Creek; $8, child under 2yr free; ⊙10am-4pm Sat & Sun winter, Tue-Sun summer; ⊞) to hiking trails and ziplines at **McKinney Roughs Nature Park** (☑512-303-5073; www.lcra.org; 1884 Texas 71, Cedar Creek; ⊙visitor center 8am-5pm, trails 8am-dusk). There's a 12-mile scenic drive through **Bastrop State Park** (☑512-321-2101; www.tpwd.texas.gov; Hwy 21, Bastrop; adult/under 13yr $5/free), home to a collection of cabins built by the Civilian Conservation Corps (CCC) in the 1930s.

The most interesting accommodations are B&Bs and cabins. It's all about pecans at the **Pecan Street Inn** (☑512-321-3315; www.pecanstreetinn.com; 1010 Pecan St, Bastrop; d $109-119, ste $129-139), which sits under, you guessed it, pecan trees. (The hosts might just mix them into your breakfast pancakes.) Chain hotels and a couple of indie motels line Hwy 21 west of the Colorado River.

Stroll Main St downtown for a mix of bakeries, coffee shops and cafes, plus Mexican food, steaks and pub grub. Meals get charmingly southern at **Maxine's** (☑512-303-0919; www.maxinescafe.com; 905 Main St, Bastrop; mains breakfast $4-20, lunch & dinner $7-19; ⊙7am-3pm Sun-Tue, to 8pm Wed & Thu, to 9pm Fri & Sat), with fried-green tomato BLTs served at lunch.

Contact the **Bastrop Museum & Visitor Center** (☑512-303-0904; www.bastropcounty-historicalsociety.com; 904 Main St, Bastrop; adult/

child under 12yr $5/free; ⊙10am-5pm Mon-Sat, 1-4pm Sun) for more information.

Lockhart

In 1999 the Texas Legislature adopted a resolution naming Lockhart the 'Barbecue Capital of Texas.' Of course, in real terms that means it's the barbecue capital of the *world*. You can eat very well for around $15 or less at any of these places, all of which have been named as one of the top 10 barbecue restaurants in the state by *Texas Monthly* magazine.

 Eating

Smitty's Market   BARBECUE $
(☑512-398-9344; www.smittysmarket.com; 208 S Commerce St; brisket per lb $14.90; ⊙7am-6pm Mon-Fri, to 6:30pm Sat, 9am-6:30pm Sun) The blackened pit room and homely dining room are all original (knives used to be chained to the tables). Ask to have the fat trimmed off the brisket if you're particular about that.

Located a block from the courthouse, Smitty's imbues the entire town square with the nonstop aroma of smoked meat, so if you smell like barbecue before you've even had lunch, you have them to thank.

Black's Barbecue   BARBECUE $
(☑512-398-2712; www.blacksbbq.com; 215 N Main St; sandwiches $10-13, brisket per lb $16.50; ⊙10am-8pm Sun-Thu, to 8:30pm Fri & Sat) This longtime Lockhart favorite has been around and owned by the same family since 1932. The sausage was so good Lyndon Johnson had Black's cater a party at the nation's capital. There's a good selection of salads, veggies and desserts. It's nothing fancy inside, but we found Black's to be the most welcoming of the Lockhart BBQ joints.

Chisholm Trail Bar-B-Q   BARBECUE $
(☑512-398-6027; www.lockhartchisolmtrailbbq.com; 1323 S Colorado St; lunch plates $8-13, brisket per lb $13.50; ⊙8am-8pm Sun-Wed, 6am-9pm Thu-Sat) Chisholm Trail doesn't have much in the way of atmosphere, but it's a favorite among many of the locals. Partly because it's inexpensive, partly because it doesn't skimp on the side dishes and partly because it isn't as much on the radar of out-of-towners.

Kreuz Market   BARBECUE $
(☑512-398-2361; www.kreuzmarket.com; 619 N Colorado St; brisket per lb $16.49; ⊙10:30am-8pm Mon-Sat, to 6pm Sun) Serving Lockhart since 1900, the barn-like Kreuz Market uses a

dry rub – which means you shouldn't insult them by asking for barbecue sauce: Kreuz doesn't serve it, and the meat doesn't need it. Don't ask for a fork, either. But do grab a lot of napkins.

❶ Getting There & Away

Lockhart is 30 miles south of Austin. The quickest route from Austin is I-35 S and TX 130 S. (The latter has tolls, ranging from 48¢ to $1.77 depending on where you enter.)

San Antonio & The Hill Country

Tourism has been good to San Antonio and the sprawling city reciprocates with a wide variety of attractions to keep everyone entertained. In addition to its colorful, European-style River Walk lined with cafes and bars, it rewards visitors with a well-rounded menu of museums, theme parks, outdoor activities and historical sites. The Alamo is a stalwart tourist favorite, and the scene of the most famous battle in the fight for Texas' independence from Mexico. You can find four other beautifully preserved Spanish missions within the city limits.

San Antonio also puts you in close proximity to the Hill Country, a naturally beautiful region known for its wildflower-lined roadways, charming small towns, gorgeous wineries and, yes, hills. Fredericksburg is the most touristy Hill Country town, but the area is more about winding roads and stopping along the way than any particular destination.

San Antonio

San Antonio's selling point these days? Tourists might say they've come for the Alamo and the River Walk. But locals are touting the city's easy diversity, with all races and cultures truly coexisting and supporting each other. Residents are also excited about the ever-growing Pearl District – it may seem like half the city is here on a sunny Saturday afternoon. And we've never seen a place with so many bicycle-share stations, making it easy to explore the Museum Reach and the Mission Reach (the newest sections of the famed River Walk).

The biggest surprise for visitors? The fact that two of the state's most popular destinations – the aforementioned Alamo and River Walk – are smack dab in the middle of downtown, surrounded by historical hotels, tourist attractions and souvenir shops. The rest of the city sprawls out beyond them, never impinging on the tourist trade.

◉ Sights & Activities

★ **River Walk**   WATERFRONT
(www.thesanantonioriverwalk.com) A little slice of Europe in the heart of downtown San Antonio, the 15-mile River Walk is an essential part of the San Antonio experience. This is no ordinary riverfront, but a charming canal and pedestrian street that is the main artery

TEXAS SAN ANTONIO & THE HILL COUNTRY

EXPLORING THE HILL COUNTRY

With so many day-trip destinations so close to San Antonio, it's hard to choose between them, but if you have some time to spare, the following route lets you cover a lot of ground. The entire loop can be driven in 4½ hours, but how long you decide to linger is up to you.

From San Antonio, head northwest on I-10, stopping for a little antique shopping in **Boerne** and **Comfort**. Continue on to **Kerrville** and enjoy cowboy art or swimming in the Guadalupe River. From Kerrville, take Hwy 16 to Fredericksburg (p714), the unofficial capital of the Hill Country, and listen to live music under the trees in tiny Luckenbach (p714).

Continue east to the **LBJ Ranch** (🗷 national park visitor center 830-868-7128, state park visitor center 830-644-2252; www.nps.gov/lyjo; Hwy 290, Stonewall; tour adult/child under 18yr $3/free; ◷ ranch grounds 9am-5:30pm, house tours 10am-4:30pm), then see his childhood home in **Johnson City**. Grab a bite and a beer in **Dripping Springs**, then continue south, passing through **Wimberley** and its giant boots. Next, stop in San Marcos, land of the outlet mall. Don't miss **Texas' oldest dance hall** (🗷 830-606-1281; www.gruenehall. com; 1280 Gruene Rd; ◷ 11am-midnight Mon-Fri, 10am-1am Sat, 10am-9pm Sun) in **Gruene** – a short detour. Just south, **New Braunfels** invites you to float the Guadalupe River, then it's just 32 miles back to San Antonio.

San Antonio

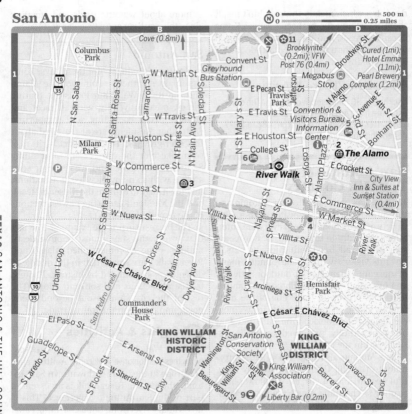

at the heart of San Antonio's tourism efforts. For the best overview, hop on a Rio San Antonio river cruise.

★ **The Alamo**   HISTORIC BUILDING
(☎ 210-225-1391; www.thealamo.org; 300 Alamo Plaza; ⊗ 9am-5:30pm Sep-Feb, to 9pm Mar-Aug) **FREE** Find out why the story of the Alamo can rouse a Texan's sense of state pride like few other things. For many, it's not so much a tourist attraction as a pilgrimage – you might notice some visitors getting downright dewy-eyed at the description of how a few hundred revolutionaries died defending the fort against thousands of Mexican troops.

McNay Art Museum   MUSEUM
(☎ 210-824-5368; www.mcnayart.org; 6000 N New Braunfels Ave; adult/child $10/free, special exhibits extra; ⊗ 10am-4pm Tue, Wed & Fri, to 9pm Thu, to 5pm Sat, noon-5pm Sun, grounds 7am-7pm Mar-Oct, to 6pm Nov-Feb) In addition to seeing

paintings by household names such as Van Gogh, Picasso, Matisse, Renoir, O'Keeffe and Cézanne, half the fun is wandering the spectacular Spanish Colonial revival–style mansion that was the private residence of Marion Koogler McNay. Upon her death in 1950, McNay left her impressive collection of European and American modern art to the city.

San Fernando Cathedral   HISTORIC BUILDING
(☎ 210-227-1297; www.sfcathedral.org; 115 W Main Plaza; ⊗ gift shop 9am-5pm Mon-Fri, to 6:30pm Sat, 8:30am-3:30pm Sun) More than just another pretty church, San Fernando's role in the Battle of the Alamo makes it an important local landmark. In happier times, future Alamo hero James Bowie was married here. But as Bowie defended the Alamo just across the river, Mexican general Santa Anna took over the church as an observation post and raised a flag of 'no quarter' (meaning he would take no prisoners), which began the deadly siege.

San Antonio

◎ Top Sights
1 River Walk C2
2 The Alamo D2

◎ Sights
3 San Fernando Cathedral B2

◎ Activities, Courses & Tours
4 Rio San Antonio Cruises D3

◎ Sleeping
5 Emily Morgan Hotel D2
6 Omni La Mansion del Rio C2

◎ Eating
Las Canarias .... (see 6)
7 Ocho at Hotel Havana C1
8 Rosario's Mexican Cafe C4

◎ Drinking & Nightlife
9 Friendly Spot Ice House C4

◎ Entertainment
10 Magik Children's Theatre D3
San Antonio Symphony .... (see 11)
11 Tobin Center for the
Performing Arts C1

Brackenridge Park PARK
(www.brackenridgepark.org; 3700 N St Marys St; ☉5am-11pm; ☋) North of downtown near Trinity University, this 343-acre park is a great place to spend the day with your family. In addition to the **San Antonio Zoo** (☏210-734-7184; www.sazoo.org; 3903 N St Marys St; adult/child $14.25/11.25; ☉9am-5pm Mon-Fri, to 6pm Sat & Sun; ☋), you'll find the **Kiddie Amusement Park** (☏210-824-4351; www.kiddiepark.com; 3015 Broadway; 1 ticket $2.50, 6 tickets $11.25, day pass $13; ☉10am-7pm Wed-Sun Mar-Aug, 10am-7pm Fri-Sun Sep-Feb; ☋), the *Brackenridge Eagle* miniature train ($3.50), an old-fashioned carousel ($2.50) and the Japanese Tea Gardens.

Witte Museum MUSEUM
(☏210-357-1900; www.wittemuseum.org; 3801 Broadway; adult/child 4-11yr $10/7; ☉10am-5pm Mon & Wed-Sat, to 8pm Tue, noon-5pm Sun; ☋) Older kids will most enjoy this museum on the eastern edge of Brackenridge Park. The Witte (pronounced 'witty') is educational but engaging, with hands-on explorations of natural history, science and Texas history. At press time, the museum was preparing to open the **New Witte**, the result of a 170,000-sq-ft expansion project. Look for a dinosaur gallery, a prehistoric peoples exhibit and immersive wildlife dioramas. A replica of the winged Quetzalcoatlus dinosaur will hang above the foyer.

Japanese Tea Garden GARDENS
(☏210-212-4814; www.sanantonio.gov/ParksAndRec; 3853 N St Marys St; ☉dawn-dusk) FREE Hard to believe that this lovely, tranquil place was just a clever way to hide a hole in the ground. What started out as an eyesore of a quarry nearly 100 years ago was transformed into a Japanese-style strolling garden, with stone bridges, floral displays and a 60ft waterfall. The garden is meant to be enjoyed year-round, but it's especially pretty in spring, when the flowers are in bloom.

Rio San Antonio Cruises CRUISE
(☏210-244-5700; www.riosanantonio.com; 706 River Walk; tour $10, river taxi one way $10, 24hr pass from $12; ☉9am-9pm) These 40-minute narrated cruises give you a good visual overview of the river and a light history lesson. You can buy your tickets online or get them on the waterfront at any of the stops. No reservations are necessary and tours leave every 15 to 20 minutes.

🛌 Sleeping

★ City View Inn & Suites at Sunset Station MOTEL $$
(☏210-222-2220; www.cityviewinnsa.com; 1306 E Commerce St; r $99-109; P☀❋🐾) Just beyond I-37, less than a mile from the Alamo, sits a skinny little three-story building full of clean, new rooms. Amenities are few, but if you're just looking for a place to park your bags, this friendly place is great. It's also just two blocks from the Amtrak station – handy if you're arriving by train.

Emily Morgan Hotel BOUTIQUE HOTEL $$
(☏210-225-5100; www.emilymorganhotel.com; 705 E Houston St; r $219-239, ste $249-750; P☀❋🐾🐶) The name sounds as though it should be awash in floral prints and lace runners, but this historic hotel right behind the Alamo is actually pretty stylish, and is now a Hilton property. The boutique-style rooms are clean, large and enjoy all the luxury amenities.

★ Hotel Emma BOUTIQUE HOTEL $$$
(☏210-448-8300; www.thehotelemma.com; 136 E Grayson St; r/ste from $395/895; P❋🐾🐶) Is steampunk-glam a thing? Going by this new Pearl District hotel, we hope so. Common areas impress with a striking mix of Victorian-era decor and bold industrial

fixtures, which trace back to the building's days as a 19th-century brewhouse. Rooms evoke the charms of a stylish but understated Texas ranch. The nicest amenity? The guests-only library, home to 3700 books.

Omni La Mansion del Rio HISTORIC HOTEL $$$
(210-518-1000; www.lamansion.com; 112 College St; r/ste from $269/799; P❂❄@☎☱) This fabulous downtown property was born out of 19th-century religious school buildings in the Spanish-Mexican hacienda style. It's on a quiet stretch of the River Walk and its discreet oasis attracts stars and other notables. Enjoy in-room spa services, swim in the outdoor heated pool or unwind at the hotel's exceptional restaurant, **Las Canarias** (210-518-1063; www.omnihotels.com; mains breakfast $11-19, lunch $12-21, dinner $27-49; ⏱6:30am-2pm Mon-Sat, 6:30-10am & 11am-2:30pm Sun, 5:30-10pm daily).

✖ Eating

Green Vegetarian Cuisine VEGETARIAN $
(210-320-5865; www.eatatgreen.com; 200 E Grayson St; mains breakfast $4-8, lunch & dinner $8-12; ⏱8am-9pm Mon-Thu, to 8pm Fri, 9am-9pm Sun, closed Sat; 🖋) 🌱 Vegetarians rejoice: San Antonio's first vegetarian restaurant has an appealing location in the Pearl Brewery complex. With dishes like a portabella burger, 'fishless' fish and chips, and enchiladas, it's the kind of place even a meat-eater can enjoy. Not only is it 100% vegetarian, it's also 100% kosher and any meal can be made vegan.

Cove AMERICAN $
(210-227-2683; www.thecove.us; 606 W Cypress St; tacos $4-5, burgers $8-12; ⏱11am-10pm Tue-Thu, to 11pm Fri & Sat, to 8pm Sun; 🖋) This weird, wonderful place is a restaurant, bar, laundromat and car wash. As casual as the restaurant is, the food is top-notch, made from organic, sustainable meat and produce. Sure, it's just tacos, burgers, salads and appetizers, but the food is made with love.

Rosario's Mexican Cafe TEX-MEX $$
(210-223-1806; www.rosariossa.com; 910 S Alamo St; mains lunch $8-11, dinner $10-23; ⏱11am-10pm Mon-Thu, to 11pm Fri & Sat, to 9pm Sun) This lively restaurant is always hopping, with huge windows that let in natural light and wistful glances from hungry onlookers. The Tex-Mex-style food is solid, and the complimentary basket of chips and salsa that show up at your table is better than most.

Ocho at Hotel Havana CUBAN $$
(210-222-2008; www.havanasanantonio.com; 1015 Navarro St; mains breakfast $14-16, lunch & dinner $10-25; ⏱7am-10pm Sun-Thu, to midnight Fri & Sat; 🛜) You're never going to stumble across Ocho while roaming the River Walk or checking out the King William District, but this hidden-away lounge next to Hotel Havana is worth seeking out. The Cuban-inspired menu is not extensive, but it's excellent, serving everything from breakfast to late-night cocktails.

Liberty Bar AMERICAN $$
(210-227-1187; www.liberty-bar.com; 1111 S Alamo St; mains $8-26; ⏱11am-midnight Mon-Fri, from 9am Sat & Sun) The building itself is spectacular: an 1883 home that became a Benedictine convent in 1939 and has now been painted circus-peanut orange. Inside, soaring ceilings and big windows lend an airy vibe, and the menu includes a nice selection of salads, sandwiches and full mains.

★ **Cured** AMERICAN $$$
(210-314-3929; www.curedatpearl.com; 306 Pearl Pkwy; lunch $12-28, dinner $13-35; ⏱11am-3pm & 5-11pm Mon-Fri, 5-11pm Sat, 10am-3pm Sun) Slabs of meat hang smack-dab in the center of the dining room at new-on-the-scene Cured, where the charcuterie platters ($18 to $36) are loaded with meats, spreads, pickles and crackers. At lunch, look for the daily gourmet po'boys and a few salads and sandwiches. Dinner is a carnivore's delight, with pork cheeks, roasted bone marrow, spiced quail and more.

🍷 Drinking & Nightlife

★ **Friendly Spot Ice House** BAR
(210-224-2337; www.thefriendlyspot.com; 943 S Alamo St; ⏱3pm-midnight Mon-Fri, from 11am Sat & Sun; 🖋☱) This place feels like a big neighborhood party where everyone is getting along. And what could be more inviting than a pecan tree–shaded yard filled with colorful metal lawn chairs? Friends (and their dogs) gather to knock back longnecks while the kids amuse themselves in the playground area. More than 250 bottled beers and 76 on tap.

Brooklynite COCKTAIL BAR
(212-444-0707; www.thebrooklynitesa.com; 516 Brooklyn Ave; ⏱5pm-2am) Beer and wine are easy to come by in San Antonio, but head here for a creative, handcrafted cocktail. Vintage wallpaper and wingback chairs

GRUENE & NEW BRAUNFELS: RIVER TUBING

Floating down the Guadalupe in an inner tube is a Texas summer tradition. For the most part, the river is calm, with a few good rapids to make things exciting.

Dozens of local outfitters rent tubes, rafts, kayaks and canoes, then bus you upstream so you can float the three to four hours back to base. Put a plastic cooler full of snacks and beverages (no bottles) in a bottom-fortified tube next to you and make a day of it. Don't forget to bring sunscreen, a hat and drinking water, and also be sure to wear shoes or sandals that you don't mind getting wet. Double-check drinking regulations before buying your supplies to make sure what types of containers and coolers are permitted.

The bottom-fortified tubes cost $2 more than a regular old inner tube, but it's worth the splurge to keep your backside from scraping on the rocks that line the riverbed – and it gets rockier the longer the region goes without rain, which can be for months during summer. Most outfitters offer coupons on their websites that will help defray the cost so you can treat yourself to a luxury ride. The outfitters we list all have current river conditions listed on their website so you'll know what to expect.

You can rent tubes from **Gruene River Company** (☏830-625-2800; www.gruenerivercompany.com; 1404 Gruene Rd; tube rental $20; ⊗10am-2pm Sep-May, 9am-4pm Jun-Aug) and **Rockin' 'R' River Rides** (☏830-629-9999; www.rockinr.com; 1405 Gruene Rd; tube rental $20). Their rental prices include shuttle service, and for an additional fee they can also hook you up with an ice chest for your beverages and a tube to float it on.

give the place a dark, Victorian-esque vibe. Sip away your cares with a gin-based 'Photo Booth Kisses,' with hints of raspberry and rose petals, or a classic old-fashioned – all in a fittingly dignified atmosphere.

VFW Post 76 BAR
(☏210-223-4581; 10 10th St; ⊗4-10:30pm Mon-Thu, to 2am Fri & Sat, noon-10:30pm Sun) We're giving this hidden-away joint near the Pearl development a medal for outstanding service in being a dive bar. But don't get us wrong – it's one of the classiest dives you'll ever visit, where hipsters and old-timers chug longnecks side by side in a two-story Victorian that serves as the oldest Veterans of Foreign Wars post in Texas.

☆ Entertainment

Magik Children's Theatre THEATER
(☏210-227-2751; www.magiktheatre.org; 420 S Alamo St; adult/child 2-17yr $15/12; ⊗box office 9am-5pm Mon-Fri, 10am-7pm Sat, 10am-3pm Sun; ⊕) This merry theater troupe stages adaptations of favorite children's books, hilarious original musicals and modern retellings of Texas legends and classic fairy tales, such as witty (and bilingual!) *La Cinderella*. The theater's regular season starts in September and runs through August, and includes a contemporary play series for adults, too.

Tobin Center for the Performing Arts THEATER
(☏210-223-8624; www.tobincenter.org; 100 Auditorium Circle; ⊗box office 10am-6pm Mon-Fri, to 2pm Sat, plus 1hr before showtime) On the River Walk, San Antonio's performance hall underwent a seven-year renovation project and now hosts performances by **Ballet San Antonio** (www.balletsanantonio.org) and the **San Antonio Symphony** (☏210-223-8624; www.sasymphony.org; tickets from $15). The cutting-edge theater company **Attic Rep** (www.atticrep.org), in residence here, produces shows that are edgy, compelling and current. A fun way to arrive? On a river taxi (p711).

ℹ Information

Convention & Visitors Bureau Information Center (☏800-447-3372; www.visitsantonio.com; 317 Alamo Plaza; ⊗9am-5pm) Well stocked with maps and brochures; its website has loads of information for pre-planning. Staff can answer questions and also sell tour and VIA bus/streetcar passes. Opposite the Alamo.

King William Association (☏210-227-8786; www.ourkwa.org; 122 Madison St; ⊗9am-3pm Mon-Fri) Stop by to pick up a walking-tour map for the King William District. (If the office is closed, there should be a few maps in the box out front.)

San Antonio Conservation Society (☏210-224-6163; www.saconservation.org; 107 King William St; ⊗8:30am-4:30pm Mon-Fri) Has brochures for self-guided walking tours of the King William District (also downloadable from the website).

❶ Getting There & Away

San Antonio International Airport (SAT; ☎ 210-207-3433; www.sanantonio.gov/sat; 9800 Airport Blvd) is about 8 miles north of downtown, just north of the intersection of Loop 410 and US 281. It's served by taxis, public transportation, shuttles and ride services, including Uber and Lyft.

The airport offers frequent flights to destinations in Texas and the rest of the USA, and there are also direct or connecting air services to Mexico. Southwest Airlines is the best airline for short-hop flights around Texas.

Greyhound (☎ 210-270-5868; www.greyhound.com; 500 N St Marys St) has a terminal downtown. **Megabus** (☎ 877-462-6342; www.usmegabus.com; cnr 4th & Broadway Sts) stops downtown and connects to Houston and Austin.

Fredericksburg

Although we highly recommend meandering through the Hill Country, if you're only going to see one town, make it this one. The 19th-century German settlement packs a lot of charm into a relatively small amount of space. There is a boggling array of welcoming inns and B&Bs, and a main street lined with historic buildings that house German restaurants, beer gardens, antique stores and shops. The downtown museums are interesting too.

Many of the shops are typical tourist-town offerings (think T-shirts, fudge and faux-quaint painted signs), but there are enough unique stores to make it fun to wander. Plus, the town is a great base for checking out the surrounding peach orchards, vineyards and getaways, such as Enchanted Rock and Johnson City, as well as little Luckenbach, just 10 miles away.

◉ Sights & Activities

National Museum of the Pacific War   MUSEUM
(☎ 830-997-8600; www.pacificwarmuseum.org; 340 E Main St; adult/child $14/7; ⊙ 9am-5pm) This museum complex consists of three war-centric galleries: the **Admiral Nimitz Museum**, chronicling the life and career of Fredericksburg's most famous son; the **George HW Bush Gallery of the Pacific War**, a large, impressive building housing artifacts and an expansive chronicle of WWII's Pacific campaign; and the revamped **Pacific Combat Zone**, a 2-acre indoor/outdoor exhibit, which spotlights PT (Patrol Torpedo) boats and military vehicles.

Pioneer Museum   HISTORIC SITE
(☎ 830-990-8441; www.pioneermuseum.net; 325 W Main St; adult/child 6-17yr $5/3; ⊙ 10am-5pm Mon-Sat) Find out what life was like for the town's early inhabitants as you wander the 10 historic buildings at the Pioneer Museum. Short audio interpretations begin as you step into each building. If nothing else, this

---

WORTH A TRIP

LUCKENBACH

Come to tiny Luckenbach prepared to relax, get to know some folks, and bask in the small-town atmosphere. Actually, 'small town' doesn't describe it just right: Luckenbach is more like a cluster of buildings than a town, and its permanent structures are outnumbered by the port-a-potties brought in to facilitate weekend visitors. The heart of the, er, action is the old trading post established back in 1849 – now the **Luckenbach General Store** (☎ 830-997-3224; www.luckenbachtexas.com; 412 Luckenbach Town Loop; ⊙ 9am-11pm Sun-Thu, to midnight Fri, to 1am Sat), which also serves as the local post office, saloon and community center.

Despite the lack of amenities, there is a busy music schedule, which you can find on the store's website. Sometimes the picking circle starts at 1pm and sometimes it's 5pm, and there are usually live-music events on the weekends in the old **dance hall** (☎ 830-997-3224; www.luckenbachtexas.com; Luckenbach Town Loop) – a Texas classic. The 4th of July and Labor Day weekends see a deluge of visitors for concerts.

We'd be remiss if we didn't mention that Luckenbach was made famous in a country song by Waylon Jennings – but we figured you already knew that.

To get here from nearby Fredericksburg, take US 290 east, then take FM 1376 south for about three miles.

collection of restored homes and businesses from the late 1800s will help you appreciate the modern conveniences awaiting you at your guesthouse.

Old Tunnel Wildlife Management Area WILDLIFE WATCHING
(☎866-978-2287; http://tpwd.texas.gov/state-parks/old-tunnel; 10619 Old San Antonio Rd; ⊙sunrise-5pm, bat viewing after 5pm Thu-Sun May-Oct) Right around dusk from May to October, you can watch a colony of bats emerging from an abandoned railroad tunnel for their nightly meal. Over three million Mexican free-tailed bats make their home here.

Sleeping & Eating

Cotton Gin Village CABIN **$$**
(☎830-990-8381; www.cottonginlodging.com; 2805 S Hwy 16; cabins $229; P) Rustic on the outside, posh on the inside. Oh yes, we like it here. Just south of town, this cluster of stone-and-timber cabins offers guests a supremely private stay away from both the crowds and the other guests. Cabins come with a stone wood-burning fireplace. Romantic getaway? Start packing.

Fredericksburg Inn & Suites MOTEL **$$**
(☎830-997-0202; www.fredericksburg-inn.com; 201 S Washington St; r $199-219, ste $249; P) Tops in the midpriced-motel category, this place was built to look like the historic house it sits behind, and it succeeds. Property features include a fabulously inviting pool with a water slide, a spacious hot tub, and clean and updated rooms. It's within walking distance of Main St.

★**Vaudeville** CAFE **$$**
(☎830-992-3234; www.vaudeville-living.com; 230 E Main St; lunch mains $15-17, dinner mains $16-36; ⊙10am-4pm Mon, Wed, Thu & Sun, to 9pm Fri & Sat) This dapper underground bistro looks like a soda fountain gone posh. The folks lunching here are as stylish as the decor, but don't worry, you'll find welcoming Hill Country hospitality in these hip digs. The gourmet salads and sandwiches are top-notch – and you do want the pork belly taco. Desserts, coffees, teas and craft beer are also offered.

Information

Fredericksburg Visitor Information Center
(☎830-997-6523, 888-997-3600; www.visitfredericksburgtx.com; 302 E Austin St; ⊙9am-5pm Mon-Sat, 11am-3pm Sun;) Has friendly staff and an attractive building a block off Main St, close to the Pacific War Museum. Lots of parking, too, if you can't find anything on Main St.

LOCAL KNOWLEDGE

GOOD PIZZA IN DRIPPING SPRINGS

Holy moly, this is good pie. Opened just a few years ago, **Pieous** (☎512-394-7041; www.facebook.com/pieous; 12005 W Hwy 290; pizzas $10-15; ⊙11am-2pm & 4-9pm Tue-Fri, 11am-9pm Sat, to 8pm Sun) has earned kudos left and right. The motto here is 'food is our religion,' which gives a nod to the name of the place and to their focus on using fresh and homemade ingredients. The beloved pastrami is cooked in a BBQ smoker out back.

Getting There & Around

Heading west from Austin, US 290 becomes Fredericksburg's Main St. Hwy 16, which runs between Fredericksburg and Kerrville, is S Adams St in town. It isn't easy to get to Fredericksburg without a car; the closest bus station is at Kerrville, but **Greyhound** (☎800-231-2222; www.greyhound.com) will drop you off or pick you up at the **Stripes Shell Station** (2204 Hwy 16 S, Stripes Shell Station) located 2½ miles southwest of downtown.

You can get a shuttle service from the San Antonio Airport through **Stagecoach Taxi and Shuttle** (☎830-385-7722; www.stagecoachtaxiandshuttle.com); the cost is $95 each way for up to four people. However, since driving around the Hill Country is half the fun, your best bet is to drive yourself.

When in town, you can rent bicycles at **Hill Country Bicycle Works** (☎830-990-2609; www.hillcountrybicycle.com; 702 E Main St; rental per day $30-45; ⊙10am-6pm Mon, Tue, Thu & Fri, to 4pm Sat).

Bandera

It's not always easy finding real, live cowboys in Texas, but the pickin's are easy in Bandera, which has branded itself the Cowboy Capital of Texas. There are certainly lots of dude ranches around, and rodeos and horseback riding are easy to come by. Another great reason to come to Bandera? Drinking beer and dancing in one of the many hole-in-the-wall cowboy bars and honky-tonk clubs, where you'll find friendly locals, good live music and a rich atmosphere. Giddy up!

DUDE RANCHES

A dozen or so dude ranches are scattered in and around town, where you can horseback ride for around $35 to $50 an hour. (Note that according to Texas law riders must not weigh more than 240lb.) Some offer packages that include meals in the price, and many take advantage of the **Hill Country State Natural Area**, a park with over 5000 acres. Most of the ranches are within 10 miles of Bandera.

If you'd like to stay longer, these dude ranches offer all-inclusive experiences with horseback riding, meals and a place to hang your hat for the night. Some ranches offer unique features to set themselves apart, but you can generally expect enormous ranch houses set on hundreds of acres. Other amenities might include hayrides, campfires and barbecues.

☉ Sights & Activities

Frontier Times Museum　　　　MUSEUM
(✆830-796-3864; www.frontiertimesmuseum. org; 510 13th St; adult/child 6-17yr/senior $6/2/4; ⊙10am-4:30pm Mon-Sat) To get some historical perspective, stop by this museum's display of Western art, cowboy tchotchkes such as guns, branding irons and cowboy gear, and 'curiosities' collected by the museum's founder, J Marvin Hunter – including the famous two-headed goat.

Silver Spur Guest Ranch　　HORSEBACK RIDING
(✆830-796-3037; www.silverspur-ranch.com; 9266 Bandera Creek Rd; horseback riding nonguests 1hr/2hr $45/80) Day visitors can enjoy one- or two-hour rides, and can throw in lunch or dinner for a small extra fee. For overnight guests, after a long day on the dusty trails, Silver Spur's junior Olympic pool provides a good way to cool off. Also offers hayrides, fossil digging and nightly campfires. Overnight rates ($150) include two horseback rides and three meals daily, plus use of ranch amenities. There is a lower rate ($120 per night) for those who don't want to horseback ride.

🛏 Sleeping & Eating

River Front Motel　　　　CABIN $
(✆800-870-5671, 830-460-3690; www.theriver frontmotel.com; 1103 Maple St; cabins $99, ste $159-179; 🅿❄🖥🐾) This friendly, family-run motel on the south side of town offers 11 cabins by the river, each with a fridge, a coffeemaker and cable TV. It's your best bet for the money. Pet fee is $15 per night.

Sid's Main Street BBQ　　　BARBECUE $
(✆830-796-4227; www.sidsmainstreetbbq.com; 702 Main St; sandwiches $7-10, mains $9-15; ⊙11am-8pm Mon-Sat, to 3pm Sun) Head to Sid's for your barbecue fix. It serves smoky, succulent meat dishes in a former gas station.

① Information

Bandera County Convention & Visitors Bureau (CVB; ✆830-796-3045; www.bandera cowboycapital.com; 126 Hwy 16; ⊙9am-5pm Mon-Fri, 10am-3pm Sat) Offers helpful information and friendly advice. A half block off Main St.

① Getting There & Away

From Kerrville, the most direct route is Hwy 173 (Bandera Hwy). The more pleasant and scenic way – over hill and dale and past Medina – is to take Hwy 16 south. From San Antonio, it's a 50-mile trip to Bandera, on I-10 west followed by Hwy 16 north.

Main St runs roughly north–south through the center of town. At the southern edge of downtown, Cypress St heads east–west along the river, continuing as Hwy 16 at the eastern end of town.

EAST TEXAS

More down-home than Dallas, more buttoned-up than Austin, Houston has money and culture, but wears them like a good ol' country boy come to town. What's that mean? Award-winning, chef-run restaurants where ties are rarely required. Attending world-class museum exhibits followed by cheap beer at patio bars. Enclaves of attractions spread all across the state's largest – and widest – city.

When you get sick of the concrete maze of interstates, it's easy to escape. Within daytrip distance you can visit NASA and the place where Texas won its independence. Washington County entices antique hunters, history buffs and anyone who just loves beautiful, rural countryside. Further afield, northeast Texas *is* the Piney Woods, with towering forests, winding roads, natural attractions and Southern belle historic towns like Jefferson and Nacogdoches.

As you wander the back roads, keep your nose at the ready to follow the scent of superb barbecue and chicken-fried steak.

Houston

Think laid-back, pick-up truck and boot-scooting town meets high-powered, high-cultured and high-heeled metropolis. During the day, chill out in your flip-flops, take in museums and go shopping, then hit happy hour on a leaf-shaded deck. At night, revel in culinary or cultural bliss – the restaurant and entertainment scenes are renowned across the region. Here, starched jeans are de rigueur in all but the very fanciest of restaurants.

Diverse residential neighborhoods and enclaves of restaurants and shops spread far and wide. Where residents of other cities talk about the weather, Houstonians talk about parking. Wealth from oil and energy companies supports luxurious shopping areas but you can also enjoy down-home fun, although don't underestimate the sauna-like summers. Don't forget that one of the town's main attractions – NASA's Space Center Houston in Clear Lake – is outside the city limits, a 30-minute drive down I-45.

⊙ Sights & Activities

★ Houston Museum of Natural Science   MUSEUM
(☑713-639-4629; www.hmns.org; 5555 Hermann Park Dr; adult/child $25/15, free Thu 2-5pm; ☺9am-5pm; ⊞; ⧉Hermann Park/Rice U) World-class traveling exhibits – on everything from prehistoric cave paintings to Mayan civilization – have always been a big part of the attraction at this stellar museum, the most popular in Texas. The permanent collection is no less impressive, with massive dinosaur skeletons (the curator advised on *Jurassic Park*), mummies from ancient Egypt, rare gems (like a 2000-carat blue topaz) and interactive exhibits on the earth's biosphere.

★ Menil Collection   MUSEUM
(☑713-525-9400; www.menil.org; 1533 Sul Ross St; ☺11am-7pm Wed-Sun) FREE The Menil Collection houses over 17,000 artworks and objects, including more than 10,000 works of art, sculpture and archaeological artifacts that John and Dominique de Menil collected during their lives. The modernist

building, designed by Renzo Piano, houses rotating highlights from their extraordinary collection – everything from 5000-year-old antiquities to works by Kara Walker, René Magritte and today's art stars – plus rotating exhibitions. Don't forget to also visit the **Cy Twombly Gallery** (☑713-525-9450; www.menil.org; 1501 Branard St; ☺11am-7pm Wed-Sun) FREE and the serene and meditative Rothko Chapel, annexes of the collection.

★ Rothko Chapel   MUSEUM
(☑713-524-9839; www.rothkochapel.org; 3900 Yupon St at Sul Ross St; ☺10am-6pm) FREE A temple of contemplation, a church or brutalist architecture? The Rothko Chapel and its serene grounds is whatever you want it to be. With 14 large paintings by American abstract expressionist Mark Rothko, it's a perfect place to pause and meditate.

★ Buffalo Bayou Park   PARK
(☑713-752-0314; http://buffalobayou.org; Shepherd Dr to Sabine St, btwn Allen Pkwy & Memorial Dr; ☺dawn-dusk most areas) This newly developed sinuous 160-acre park follows Buffalo Bayou west from downtown. There are numerous parking areas and you can walk here from many points. There are areas for exercise, contemplation, art exhibits and much more. The views back to downtown are striking. Activities here include kayak tours with **Bayou City Adventures** (☑713-538-7433; http://bayoucityadventures.org; 3324 Allen Pkwy; kayak tours from $50; ☺10am-5pm Tue-Sun) and bike rentals with **Bike Barn Bayou Rental** (☑713-955-4455; http://bikebarn.com; 105 Sabine St, Buffalo Bayou Park, Water Works; rentals per hour from $9; ☺10am-dusk daily summer, weekends only other times).

Art Car Museum   MUSEUM
(☑713-861-5526; www.artcarmuseum.com; 140 Heights Blvd; ☺11am-6pm Wed-Sun) FREE The handful of art cars represented here are all wild examples of why you should try to be in town for the Houston Art Car Parade (p719). Check out the quirky-cool rotating exhibits, which have included subjects such as road refuse and bone art but also serious exhibits by noted contemporary artists.

Heritage Society at Sam Houston Park   MUSEUM
(☑713-655-1912; www.heritagesociety.org; 1100 Bagby St; museum free, tours adult/child $15/6; ☺museum 10am-4pm Tue-Sun, tours 10am, 11:30am, 1pm & 2:30pm; ⧉Main St Sq) FREE Take a free tour using your phone around

Central Houston

the 10 historic homes and buildings that have been moved to this park. Among them is the **Yates House** (1870), the home of a freed slave who became a prominent local preacher, and the **Old Place** (1823), a log cabin thought to be the town's oldest. Guided tours get you inside.

Lone Star Flight Museum   MUSEUM
(✆ 346-708-2517; http://lsfm.org; Ellington Airport, 11551 Aerospace Ave) This museum, relocated from Galveston, where the collection was battered by Hurricane Ike in 2008, is south of Houston at the former Ellington

Air Force Base. It should have opened in new $40-million hangars by the time you read this. It will feature over 25 restored warplanes, including an iconic B-17 and B-25 from WWII.

Hermann Park Miniature Train   OUTDOORS
(✆ 713-526-2183; www.hermannpark.org; 6104 Hermann Park Dr, Kinder Station, Lake Plaza; per ride $3.50; ⏱10am-6pm; 🚻; 🚇 Hermann Park/ Rice U) Hop aboard this tiny train for a kid-pleasing 18-minute ride around Hermann Park. You can hop on and off at various stops.

Central Houston

◎ Top Sights
1 Houston Museum of Natural
   Science.. D5
2 Menil Collection.................................... C2
3 Rothko Chapel...................................... C2

◎ Sights
4 Cy Twombly Gallery............................... C3
5 Museum of Fine Arts, Houston............ D4

✈ Activities, Courses & Tours
6 Hermann Park Miniature Train D5

⊟ Sleeping
7 Aloft Houston Downtown E5
8 Hotel Icon... F4
9 Hotel ZaZa Houston D4
10 Houston International Hostel................E4
11 La Maison in Midtown E1
12 Sam Houston Hotel...............................F5

✕ Eating
13 Brennan's of Houston E2
14 Dolce Vita.. D1
15 House of Pies.. A2
16 Hugo's C2
17 Indika..D1
18 Lankford Grocery E1
19 Oh My Gogi! A5
20 Tacos Tierra Caliente........................... B2

⊕ Drinking & Nightlife
21 JR's Bar & Grill......................................D1
22 La Carafe...F4
23 Poison Girl.. C2

⊕ Entertainment
24 AvantGarden E2
25 Cézanne D3
26 Match...E2
27 Rudyard's Pub....................................... C1

⊕ Shopping
28 Brazos Bookstore A4
29 Buffalo Exchange.................................. B2

⌂ Tours

Texana Tours TOURS
(☏ 281-772-9526; www.texanatours.com; rates vary)
To get to grips with Houston in just three
hours, take this fascinating tour with a born-
and-bred Houstonite that takes in most significant neighborhoods and offers a mine of
intriguing city facts. Other tours venture further afield to some of the rural state parks and
NASA. Rates vary depending on group size.

Houston Culinary Tours FOOD & DRINK
(☏ 713-853-8100; www.visithoustontexas.com;
tours from $180) Monthly foodie adventures

are led by local chefs and food celebrities.
Book well in advance.

✾ Festivals & Events

★ Houston Art Car Parade PARADE
(www.thehoustonartcarparade.com; along Smith
St, downtown; ⊙ 2nd Sat Apr) Wacky, arted-out
vehicles (think *Mad Max*, giant gerbils and
more) hit the streets en masse at the city's
top alt event. The parade is complemented
by weekend-long festivities, including concerts and a legendary ball (buy tickets well
in advance).

Juneteenth Emancipation Celebration
CULTURAL

(http://juneteenthfest.com; Emancipation Park, 3018 Dowling St; ⊘mid-Jun) This celebration of African American culture, with plenty of gospel, jazz and blues, takes place at Emancipation Park around June 19 – the day in 1865 when word reached Texas that slaves had been emancipated.

🛏 Sleeping

Houston International Hostel
HOSTEL $

(☎713-523-1009; www.houstonhostel.com; 5302 Crawford St; dm/r from $17/57; P❋@🛜; 🚇Museum District) This hostel attracts a mix of semi-permanent residents and backpackers. A friendly, eccentric staff, worn '70s furnishings and a relaxed attitude to cleanliness and formality lend the place a throwback roadhouse feel. It's in a tree-lined neighborhood and is an easy walk to Houston's major museums and trams.

★La Maison in Midtown
INN $$

(☎713-529-3600; http://lamaisonmidtown.com; 2800 Brazos St; r $170-230; P❋🛜; 🚇McGowen Station) Relaxing on the wraparound porch with skyline views or enjoying a breakfast feast, you'll feel the Southern hospitality at this purpose-built, urban inn. The seven rooms are individually decorated, and all have elevator access. Includes breakfast.

Aloft Houston Downtown
HOTEL $$

(☎713-225-0200; www.alofthoustondowntown.com; 820 Fannin St; r from $150; P❋🛜🏊; 🚇Central Station) Another hotel conversion of a historic commercial building downtown, the Aloft (a Marriott brand) has modishly decorated rooms across 10 floors. It's been much remodelled over the years, so don't expect period charm; rather, look for trendy design details as exemplified by the hipster motif on the delightful rooftop pool.

Sam Houston Hotel
BOUTIQUE HOTEL $$

(☎832-200-8800; www.thesamhoustonhotel.com; 1117 Prairie St; r $110-200; P❋@🛜🏊; 🚇Preston) Sleek yet low-key, the smallish rooms at this historic 1924 10-story property have a contemporary decor done in all-gray. Rooms have luxe features like plush towels, gourmet coffeemakers and more, which are a far cry from its roots as a budget hotel for traveling salesmen. It's part of the Hilton conglomerate.

★Hotel ZaZa Houston
BOUTIQUE HOTEL $$$

(☎713-526-1991; www.hotelzaza.com; 5701 Main St; r from $250; P❋🛜🏊; 🚇Museum District) Hip, flamboyant and fabulous. From the bordello-esque colors to zebra-accent chairs, everything about Hotel ZaZa is good fun – and surprisingly unpretentious. Our favorite rooms are the concept suites such as the eccentric Geisha House, or the space-age 'Houston We Have a Problem.' You can't beat the location overlooking the Museum district's Hermann Park, near the tram.

Hotel Icon
BOUTIQUE HOTEL $$$

(☎713-224-4266; www.hotelicon.com; 220 Main St; r from $290; P❋@🛜; 🚇Preston) You can feel the history in this hotel's ornate red-and-gold lobby. Originally a landmark bank building, there is a 1911 bank-vault reception area, soaring marble columns and coffered ceilings. Take the antique elevator up to modern-chic rooms. It's part of the Marriott empire.

🍴 Eating

Houston's restaurant scene is the city's most vibrant feature. Locals love to eat out and you'll find everything from comforting Tex-Mex to smokin' barbecue to inventive bistros run by top chefs. Most areas of the city have good options. To keep track of the latest, check out the features and listings at *Texas Monthly* as well as www.thrillist.com/houston, www.houston.eater.com and http://houstonfoodblog.com.

★Lankford Grocery
BURGERS $

(☎713-522-9555; 88 Dennis St; mains $5-14; ⊘7am-3pm Mon-Sat) Don't expect to be buying a jar of Tang at this old grocery store that is now dedicated to serving some of Houston's best burgers. Thick, juicy and loaded with your choice of condiments, what more could you want? The interior is shambolic but you're unlikely to notice. Regulars cheerfully razz each other while busy waiters recite the day's specials.

House of Pies
AMERICAN $

(☎713-528-3816; www.houseofpies.com; 3112 Kirby Dr; mains $7-12; ⊘24hr) Classic diner fare served 24/7. The pies are really the thing here: banana cream, lemon ice box, buttermilk, German chocolate, wild blueberry... But the place is also a late-night breakfast hit when the bars turn food-craving masses out onto the streets.

Crawfish & Noodles
VIETNAMESE $

(☎281-988-8098; 11360 Bellaire Blvd; mains $6-15; ⊘3-10pm Mon-Fri, noon-10pm Sat & Sun) Pairing Vietnamese seafood and noodles with

ON THE GO: FOOD TRUCKS

Unlike in some other cities, food trucks in Houston really move. You might see the same one in two or three places on the same day. Check online for their latest locations, but they're often near bars and cafes in Montrose. The Menil Collection (p717) and **Museum of Fine Arts, Houston** (☎713-639-7300; www.mfah.org; 1001 Bissonnet St; adult/child $18/free, Thu free; ⏰10am-5pm Tue & Wed, to 9pm Thu, to 7pm Fri & Sat, 12:15-7pm Sun; 🚇Museum District) parking lots are also frequent stopovers. Note: you'll rarely see them downtown because of parking regulations.

Oh My Gogi! (☎281-694-4644; www.ohmygogi.com; 5555 Morningside Dr; mains $3-8; ⏰9pm-3am Wed-Sat; 🚇Dryden/TMC) A fusion of two local cultures: try Korean barbecue tacos or kimchi quesadillas. This truck is perfectly situated for the Rice University bars.

Tacos Tierra Caliente (☎713-584-9359; 2003 W Alabama St; mains $2-5; ⏰8:30am-11pm Mon-Sat, to 10pm Sun) Some of Houston's best tacos in the city are served piled high from a battered food truck (try the pastor – spicy roast pork). Although there's nowhere to sit, just across the road is the West Alabama Ice House – a fine spot for a taco feast while nursing a few cold ones. At other times you can get Mexican breakfasts.

Waffle Bus (www.thewafflebus.com; mains $3-7) Waffles and waffle sandwiches, with toppings from sweet to savory (cheeseburger, smoked salmon etc). Usually open for lunch, often around the University of Houston.

Cajun flavors was inevitable after Vietnamese immigrants became an important part of the fishing economy along the Gulf. Out here west of the center, there are dozens of strip malls filled with all manner of Asian shops, restaurants and huge supermarkets. This simple storefront is best known for its namesake pairing. Delish!

★**Original Ninfas** MEXICAN $$
(☎713-228-1175; www.ninfas.com; 2704 Navigation Blvd; mains $11-25; ⏰11am-10pm Mon-Fri, 10am-10pm Sat & Sun) Generations of Houstonians have come here since the 1970s for shrimp diablo, *tacos al carbon* (beef cooked over charcoal) and handmade tamales crafted with pride. Great service, seats outside and very fine salsas.

Indika INDIAN $$
(☎713-524-2170; http://indikausa.com; 516 Westheimer Rd; lunch & brunch mains $16-20, dinner mains $17-36; ⏰11am-2pm & 6-10pm Tue-Sat, 11am-3pm Sun) Indika's alluring dining room sets the tone for the sublime Indian food, a fusion of authentic tastes and adventurous preparations, such as crabmeat samosas with papaya-ginger chutney. Great happy hour and Sunday brunch.

Kitchen at The Dunlavy AMERICAN $$
(☎713-360-6477; www.thedunlavy.com; 3422 Allen Pkwy; mains $8-20; ⏰7am-2pm) The creative pick for a fine breakfast, brunch or lunch amid the charms of Buffalo Bayou Park. Order at the counter and then find a table in the high-ceilinged dining rooms, lit by chandeliers. The menu has creative takes on upscale diner fare. Enjoy a fine coffee or drink from the bar.

Dolce Vita ITALIAN $$
(☎713-520-8222; www.dolcevitahouston.com; 500 Westheimer Rd; mains $12-20; ⏰5-10pm Tue-Fri, 11:30am-10pm Sat & Sun) Excellent Italian fare at great prices makes the name Dolce Vita (Sweet Life) highly appropriate! Find a romantic corner on one of two floors of this old house, or choose a table under twinkling lights on the patio. Authentic individual thin-crust pizzas come with Italian flavors like clams, fresh basil, parmesan and more.

★**Brennan's of Houston** CAJUN $$$
(☎713-522-9711; www.brennanshouston.com; 3300 Smith St; ⏰11am-2pm Mon-Sat, from 10am Sun, 5:30-10pm daily) The most famous name in New Orleans cooking runs this refined restaurant in Midtown. It's no mere offshoot but is a culinary temple all of its own. New Orleans flavors are blended with Texas, ingredients are uberfresh and the menu changes with the seasons. Service is excellent and the dining room elegant. Reserve in advance for a table in the beautiful courtyard.

★**Hugo's** MEXICAN $$$
(☎713-524-7744; http://hugosrestaurant.net; 1600 Westheimer Rd; lunch mains $15-22, dinner mains $23-30; ⏰11am-10pm Mon-Thu, to 11pm Fri & Sat,

10am-9pm Sun) Chef Hugo Ortega elevates regional Mexican cooking and street food to high art in this much-celebrated Montrose bodega. You can sample Oaxacan-style dishes and some well-spiced meats. Although many of the items seem familiar, the menu here is much closer to Mexico than Tex-Mex. Brunch is outstanding; the patio alluring. Book ahead.

Drinking & Nightlife

★ La Carafe   BAR
(☑ 713-229-9399; 813 Congress Ave; ⊙ 1pm-2am) Set in Houston's oldest building (1848), La Carafe is the most atmospheric old bar in the city. It's a warmly lit drinking den, with exposed brick, sepia photos on the walls and flickering candles. You'll also find a great jukebox and a friendly, eclectic crowd. On weekends, the upstairs bar room opens, with a 2nd-floor balcony overlooking Market Sq.

★ Moon Tower Inn   BEER GARDEN
(☑ 832-969-1934; www.damngoodfoodcoldass beer.com; 3004 Canal St; ⊙ noon-2am Mon-Sat, to midnight Sun) Moon Tower Inn is a simple shack with a huge yard strung with lights and picnic tables. It draws a lively crowd of young and old who hunker over frothy housemade microbrews plus burgers, weenies and more. It's got an edgy Warehouse District vibe.

Poison Girl   BAR
(☑ 713-527-9929; 1641 Westheimer Rd; ⊙ 4pm-2am) Add a festive back patio with a baby-boomer-friendly Kool Aid man statue to an arty interior with vintage pinball games and you get one very cool, dive-y bar with an eclectic crowd. Lounge outside or find a dark make-out corner inside.

JR's Bar & Grill   GAY
(☑ 713-521-2519; www.jrsbarandgrill.com; 808 Pacific St; ⊙ noon-2am) With a stylish but low-key vibe and cheap drinks, JR's Bar & Grill consistently rates among the best in Houston – especially with reigning drag queen champion Kofi as emcee.

Pearl Houston   CLUB
(☑ 832-740-4933; www.pearlhouston.com; 4216 Washington Ave; ⊙ 5pm-2am Tue-Sun) Start out on the chill back patio at this long-running – and welcoming – women's bar; after midnight when the DJ comes on, migrate to the dance floor where you can show off your moves.

☆ Entertainment

★ Match   LIVE PERFORMANCE
(Midtown Arts and Theater Center Houston; ☑ 713-521-4533; https://matchouston.org; 3400 Main St; 🚍 Ensemble/HCC) A performance space for over 500 Houston cultural groups and organizations that aren't part of the big money Theater District downtown. Opened in 2017, the impressive facility has four spaces that can seat 70 to 350 people for theater, dance, music and more. There are also galleries and meeting spaces. The vibrant calendar is worth a look.

★ Rudyard's Pub   LIVE PERFORMANCE
(☑ 713-521-0521; www.rudyardspub.com; 2010 Waugh Dr; ⊙ 11:30am-2am) Offers live fare many nights, which includes comedy, poetry slams and karaoke, plus a mix of edgy and indie bands. A great selection of microbrews and good pub grub (especially the burgers) make this a great place to hang out, even when there's nothing else on. Good terrace too.

AvantGarden   LIVE PERFORMANCE
(☑ 832-287-5577; www.avantgardenhouston.com; 411 Westheimer Rd; ⊙ noon-6pm Sun) The center for alt-anything in Houston. This old house has a great garden patio and is host to an eclectic mix of performances, from strange theater to poetry readings to live music. On some days you can try your hand at figure modeling. There's a good bar to provide creative lubricants.

Cézanne   JAZZ
(☑ 832-592-7464; www.cezannejazz.com; 4100 Montrose Blvd; ⊙ 9pm-midnight Fri & Sat) Simply Houston's best place to hear jazz (just be sure to get there during its six hours of opening each week). Above the Black Labrador, this classy, intimate venue mixes some of the best Texas and international jazz with a very cool piano bar.

🛍 Shopping

★ Brazos Bookstore   BOOKS
(☑ 713-523-0701; www.brazosbookstore.com; 2421 Bissonnet St; ⊙ 11am-8pm Mon-Sat, noon-6pm Sun) Houston's top independent bookseller since 1974. Browse local titles or meet authors at their many monthly events. Excellent staff recommendations and a fine collection of books by Texans and about Texas.

Buffalo Exchange   CLOTHING
(☑ 713-523-8701; www.buffaloexchange.com; 2901 S Shepherd Dr; ⊙ 10am-9pm Mon-Sat, 11am-8pm

Sun) Houston's outlet of the nationwide chain of selective buy-sell-trade clothing stores is in chic Montrose digs. Yes, they're picky, and that's a good thing.

ⓘ Information

The official **Houston Visitors Center** (☏713-437-5557; www.visithoustontexas.com; 1300 Avenida de las Americas, Hilton Americas; ☉7am-10pm) is as much a giant souvenir shop as an info center; right across from the convention center.

ⓘ Getting There & Away

Houston Airport System has two airports.
George Bush Intercontinental Airport (IAH; ☏281-230-3100; www.fly2houston.com/iah; 2800 N Terminal Rd, off I-59, Beltway 8 or I-45; ☏) is located 22 miles north of the city center. It's a hub for United Airlines, with service by other major airlines to destinations worldwide. The confusing and poorly designed sprawl of gates and terminals can test the fortitude of even veteran travelers.

William P Hobby Airport (HOU; ☏713-640-3000; www.fly2houston.com/hobby; 7800 Airport Blvd, off Broadway or Monroe Sts; ☏) is located 12 miles southeast of town, Hobby Airport is smaller and more manageable than George Bush Intercontinental Airport. It's a major hub for Southwest Airlines and has mostly domestic service.

Long-distance buses depart from the **Greyhound Bus Terminal** (☏713-759-6565; www.greyhound.com; 2121 Main St; 🚇Downtown).

The *Sunset Limited* stops at the **Amtrak Station** (☏800-872-7245; www.amtrak.com; 902 Washington Ave) three times a week en route between New Orleans and Los Angeles; Texas stops also include San Antonio and El Paso.

ⓘ Getting Around

Downtown, metered streetside parking is made easier by numerous vending machines that sell timed tickets that are not site specific. They are plentiful, if not cheap (upwards of $25 a day).

Outside downtown, parking is usually free but can be in short supply. In fact for many Houstonians, the availability of parking is the most important consideration in picking a restaurant. Don't be put off by valet parking at restaurants and malls; if it costs at all, it's cheap, and it can be easier than finding a space.

Clear Lake

Less than 30 miles south of downtown Houston is the greater Clear Lake area, home to the very popular Space Center Houston as well as aquatic diversions of all kinds, including a fun amusement park, and some important historic sites.

To the north where Buffalo Bayou empties into the estuary that flows into the bay, you'll find the industrial town of La Porte with its vital attractions. At Clear Lake's outlet, look out for the communities of Seabrook and Kemah; the latter is an entertaining waterfront village with amusements and eateries. You could definitely visit the whole area as a day trip or on the way to Galveston, but the number of things to do – and the traffic to and from Houston – makes an overnight stop worthwhile.

No matter what your itinerary, don't miss Killen's, the best barbecue in the Houston region.

★ **Space Center Houston**   MUSEUM
(☏281-244-2100; http://spacecenter.org; 1601 NASA Pkwy; adult/child $30/25; ☉10am-5pm, later some weekends & summer) Dream of a moon landing? You can hardly get closer than at the official visitor center and theme park–esque museum next to NASA's Johnson Space Center. The 90-minute tram tour of the center itself includes the historic Mission Control (you know, the 'Houston' as in the *Apollo 13* transmission, 'Houston, we have a problem.').

Rocket Park   HISTORIC SITE
(☏281-244-2100; 1601 Nasa Rd 1, Johnson Space Center; ☉9am-6pm) FREE It's as impressive as it is sad: a surviving example of a never-used Saturn V rocket, which took astronauts to the moon and which was the most powerful rocket ever used by the US, lays on its side in a building that barely encloses it near the Johnson Space Center entrance. The close confines of the structure make it hard to comprehend the 363ft height, but you can still sense the incredible power and technology, which has never been matched since.

★ **Killen's Barbecue**   BARBECUE $$
(☏281-485-2272; www.killensbarbecue.com; 3613 E Broadway St, Pearland; mains $9-24; ☉11am-8pm Tue-Thu & Sun, to 9pm Fri & Sat) This tidy wood restaurant with its grassy site and outdoor patio is a pilgrimage spot for barbecue fans. Ronnie Killen has achieved meaty nirvana with his brisket, ribs, sausages, pulled pork and more. Everything here is superb: in addition to the meat, even often humdrum sides like coleslaw and creamed corn (always made with fresh corn) shine.

The Bay Area Houston Convention & Visitors Bureau (www.visitbayareahouston.com) has information on the welter of areas south of Houston.

GULF COAST & SOUTH TEXAS

America's 'Third Coast,' as it has dubbed itself, is a place of many contrasts. The beach-town scene of Port Aransas is a sea of calm compared with the frenetic hedonism of South Padre Island, for one. There are plenty of reminders of the state's dramatic history, too, from the first shots of the Mexican-American War at the Palo Alto Battlefield National Historic Site to the long and bumpy history of the port city of Galveston.

Along the Rio Grande, border politics affect all aspects of life. In many ways the area forms a cultural border distinct from Mexico and Texas, a unique multicultural and bilingual region that for a short time was even an independent state. The Republic of the Rio Grande may not have survived as a political entity, but its unique history still accents the towns and remote stretches from Brownsville to Laredo and beyond.

Galveston

Part genteel Southern belle, part sunburned beach bunny: Galveston Island is Houston's favorite playmate. The old gal took a pretty severe beating by hurricane Ike in 2008, but she's battled back to normal since. Sitting on a barrier island near the northern end of a 600-mile-long Texas coastline, Galveston may not have the state's favorite beaches, but there's nowhere else boasting such a beautiful combination of sun-drenched historic charms.

History

History and Mother Nature have not always been kind to Galveston Island.

Europeans first arrived in 1528, when a crew of shipwrecked Spanish explorers spent months alternately living with and fleeing from the local Karankawa tribes as they sought out Spanish settlements in present-day Mexico. Jean Lafitte, the notorious pirate, founded the first European settlement here in 1817 (albeit a lawless and bacchanalian one). The party ended when

Lafitte was chased off and the town of nearly 1000 burnt behind him. Needless to say, stories of buried treasure still abound...

Developers arrived in the mid-1830s, and after incorporation in 1839, Galveston quickly became the nation's third-busiest port, a jumping-off point for setters heading west. By the beginning of the 20th century, it was the largest city in Texas, boasting a long list of state firsts: first opera house (1870), first electric lights (1883) etc, etc.

But all that changed with a string of misfortunes that would eventually topple city's dominant place on the Texas coastline. In 1885 a massive fire spread through the Strand District, consuming 42 city blocks and destroying more than 500 buildings and residences. Then on September 8, 1900, a hurricane still known as 'The Great Storm' devastated the island. The town never regained its status, ceding port traffic and population to nearby Houston. The island lost even more with the construction of the Houston Ship Channel in 1914, allowing ocean-going ships to bypass the Port of Galveston and head further inland. It took until the 1970s for the beaches' potential to bring back large-scale investment, but the local economy was humming along again by the 2000s. Then Hurricane Ike hit in September of 2008. It has been a slow journey to rebuild – again – but today the island's industries have once again hit their stride.

⊙ Sights & Activties

★ Bishop's Palace   HISTORIC BUILDING
(☏ 409-762-2475; www.galvestonhistory.org; 1402 Broadway Ave; adult/child $12/9; ⊙10am-5pm Sun-Fri, to 6pm Sat) Built between 1886 and 1893, this ornate stone mansion has hidden back stairs, false-lit stained glass and other fun features. It was constructed by the affluent entrepreneurial Gresham family, though the more colloquial name dates from the 1923 purchase of the building by the Catholic Church when it was the home of the resident bishop for Sacred Heart Church. Self-guided audio tours of the first two floors explain the home's history, and discount coupons and tickets are widely available.

Bryan Museum   MUSEUM
(☏ 409-632-7685; www.thebryanmuseum.org; 1315 21st St; adult/child $12/4; ⊙11am-4pm Thu-Mon) Housed in the 1895 Galveston Orphans' Home, this excellent museum displays a portion of the Bryan family's collection of historical documents and artifacts covering

a range of Texas and Galveston history. After your visit, grab a drink ($2 to $6) from the gift shop and lounge around in the seating scattered across the grounds.

Strand Historical District AREA
(www.galveston.com/downtowntour; btwn 25th & 20th Sts, Strand & Church Sts) Stroll the historic Strand District to get an appreciation of the city's glory days in the late 19th century. The commercial horse-drawn carriages clip-clop over historic trolley tracks and past elaborate brick facades fronting Victorian-era buildings that now contain shops and restaurants. Informative historical markers identify buildings around the district. Look for the Grand 1894 Opera House (p726), which is still in operation.

Galveston Railroad Museum MUSEUM
(☏409-765-5700; www.galvestonrrmuseum.com; 2602 Santa Fe Pl, cnr 25th & Strand Sts; adult/child $7/5, train ride $5; ⏱10am-5pm; 🚂) Housed in the beautiful former Santa Fe Railroad Station, this little museum has exhibits on train history and old rail cars as well as model railroads. Saturday you can all-aboard for a 15-minute train ride on the tracks out back from 11am to 2pm.

★ Artist Boat Kayak Adventures KAYAKING
(☏409-770-0722; www.artistboat.org; 2627 Ave O; per person 2/4hr tours $25/50; ⏱9am-5pm Mon-Fri) Nonprofit Eco-Art organization Artist Boat runs a number of educational programs in Galveston that meld nature and culture, most famously kayaking trips through the island's wetlands. Guides combine science and art during these creative and fascinating kayak tours of the natural sights around Galveston Island; advance reservations required. Ask about discounted tours that support the Coastal Heritage Preserve area off the West Bay.

🛏 Sleeping

Beachcomber Inn MOTEL $
(☏409-744-7133; www.galvestoninn.com; 2825 61st St; r $75-216; 🅿❄🛜🏊) A block from the beach, this basic two-story motel provides a neat-and-clean budget break on weekdays, but weekend upcharges are generally poor value. Minifridges and microwaves in every room.

Hotel Galvez HERITAGE HOTEL $$$
(☏409-765-7721; www.galveston.com/galvez; 2024 Seawall Blvd; r $160-315; ❄🛜🏊) Bask in palm-fringed Spanish-Colonial luxury at this 1911 historic hotel, currently managed by the Wyndham corporation. The full-service spa services – muscle-soaking milk bath or seaweed contour wraps, for example – are renowned, and the pool deck has a lovely gulf view. Ask about special package spa deals.

🍴 Eating

★ Maceo Spice & Import CAJUN $
(☏409-763-3331; www.maceospice.com; 2706 Market St; mains $7-13; ⏱11am-3pm) This excellent importer and spice market also happens to serve the best muffalettas and Cajun food in town at tables crammed between the shelves. The shop stays open till 5pm, but lunch service ends at 3pm.

Star Drug Store DINER $
(☏409-766-7719; http://galvestonstardrug.com; 510 23rd St; mains $6-9; ⏱8:30am-3pm) Not retro, because it just never changed. This 1923 drugstore serves soda-fountain treats and classic diner faves (big breakfasts!). Belly up to the counter and order a banana split.

Gaido's SEAFOOD $$$
(☏409-761-5500; www.gaidos.com; 3802 Seawall Blvd; mains $20-40; ⏱11am-9pm Sun-Thu, to 10pm Fri & Sat) Run by the same family since 1911, Gaido's is a local favorite in Galveston. Expect vast platters of no-compromise seafood (oh, the oysters...) served on white tablecloths and with hushed tones. It has a more casual sister restaurant, Nick's Kitchen & Beach Bar (☏409-762-9625; http://nicksgalveston.com; 3828 Seawall Blvd; mains $11-26; ⏱11am-10pm Mon-Fri, to 10:30pm Sat & Sun), next door.

🍸 Drinking & Entertainment

Spot BAR
(☏409-621-5237; http://thespot.islandfamous.com; 3204 Seawall Blvd; ⏱11am-10pm Sun-Thu, to 11pm Fri & Sat) This boisterous bar complex overlooking the gulf is the best of many competitors. The huge complex has an array of rooms, including a bamboo-filled tiki bar. Head upstairs to the Sideyard for ocean breezes and lawn furniture over Astroturf. Good burgers and tacos help absorb the vast array of fancy cocktails on offer. There's live music on weekends.

Galveston Island Brewing MICROBREWERY
(☏409-740-7000; www.galvestonislandbrewing.com; 8423 Stewart Rd; ⏱3-10pm Mon-Thu, to midnight Fri, noon-midnight Sat, to 9pm Sun) This local icon brews up some excellent quaffs,

including a refreshing half-wheat, half-barley beer (the Tiki Wheat), all of it served out of 11 taps on-site. There's a grassy yard where you can relax (while kids clamber about on the playground), watch the sunset and mingle with a friendly Galveston crowd.

Grand 1894 Opera House THEATER
(☑ 409-765-1894; www.thegrand.com; 2020 Postoffice St; ⊘ box office 9am-5pm Mon-Sat) The beautifully restored 1894 Opera House well illustrates Galveston's turn-of-the-20th-century culture and wealth. Popular concerts, broadway shows and humorous theatrical productions are still staged here. On days when there are no shows or set-up activities underway, self-guided tours are allowed. Check the website for schedules.

❶ Information

The **Galveston Island Visitors Center** (☑ 409-797-5144; www.galveston.com; 2328 Broadway, Ashton Villa; ⊘ 9am-5pm) is full of suggestions for things to do (and places to eat) in Galveston, plus it has details of discount passes for travelers who plan to hit the big tourist sites.

On the south side of the small harbor on Wharf Rd a string of **Fishing Boat Information Booths** (Wharf Rd; ⊘ 6am-7pm) organize fishing trips and party boats, while the head office of the **Galveston Yacht Basin** (☑ 409-765-3000; http://galvestonyachtbasin.com; 715 N Holiday Dr; ⊘ 9am-5pm) can provide contact details for others.

❶ Getting There & Around

From Houston, follow I-45 southeast for 51 miles. On the island, the highway morphs into Broadway Ave and travels toward the historic districts. Turn off onto 61st St to reach Seawall Blvd.

From points east, including Beaumont and Port Arthur, the **Galveston–Port Bolivar Ferry** (☑ 409-795-2230; http://traffic.houston-transtar.org/ferrytimes; 1 Ferry Rd; ⊘ 24hr) connects the long lonely Bolivar Peninsula to the island around the clock via TX 87. Trust us, cruising the peninsula with the waves about 300ft beyond is a much more enjoyable experience than Houston traffic.

Hurricane Ike knocked the Galveston Island Trolley, run by **Island Transit** (☑ 409-797-3900; www.galvestontx.gov; adult/child $1/50¢), off the rails. Until this excellent link between the Strand and Seawall is restored – expected at some point in 2018 – you really need a car to get around. The island's bus service caters to local commuters and students more than tourists.

Corpus Christi

Nicknamed the 'Sparkling City by the Sea,' but known to many simply as Corpus, this city by the placid bay of the same name is a growing and vibrant place. Its attractions are worth a visit and its perpetually sunny location is beguiling.

Spaniards named the bay after the Roman Catholic holy day of Corpus Christi in 1519, when Alonzo Álvarez de Piñeda discovered its calm waters. The town established here in the early 1800s later took the name as well. Growth was slow, however, due to yellow fever in the 19th century and a hurricane in 1919. Construction of Shoreline Blvd and the deepwater port between 1933 and 1941, combined with a boom brought on by WWII migration, caused rapid growth. Although the downtown is sleepy away from the water, the city does good business attracting large conventions and meetings at the vast American Bank Center.

◉ Sights & Activities

★ **Texas State Aquarium** AQUARIUM
(☑ 361-881-1230; www.texasstateaquarium.org; 2710 N Shoreline Blvd, North Beach; adult/child $26/19; ⊘ 9am-5pm, from 10am Sun; 🅿 🕭) You can learn about marine life along the Gulf Coast at this newly renovated space. There are three large handling tanks to get up close to sharks, jellyfish, stingrays and the like, plus exhibits covering the depth of ocean life. The daily schedule of 30-minute presentations includes everything from stingray feeding and raptor flights to otter and diving shows, which change seasonally (so inquire about timings when you arrive).

★ **Art Museum of South Texas** MUSEUM
(☑ 361-825-3500; www.artmuseumofsouthtexas.org; 1902 N Shoreline Blvd; adult/child $8/free; ⊘ 11am-3pm Tue-Fri, from 10am Sat) Rotating exhibits of contemporary art are the main feature at this dramatic museum, across an art-filled plaza from the Museum of Science & History, with selections from the permanent collection of American art. It's free the first Friday of each month.

USS Lexington Museum MUSEUM
(☑ 316-888-4873; www.usslexington.com; 2914 N Shoreline Blvd, North Beach; adult/child $15/10; ⊘ 9am-5pm, to 6pm Jun-Aug) Dominating the Corpus Christi bay is this 900ft-long aircraft carrier moored just north of the ship chan-

nel. The ship served in the Pacific during WWII and was finally retired in 1991. High-tech exhibits give visitors a chance to relive some wartime experiences on any of five self-guided tours. During the evening, the ship is eerily lit with blue lights that recall its WWII nickname: 'the Blue Ghost.' Admission includes a 3-D movie screening in the ship's Mega Theater.

Museum of Science & History   MUSEUM
(☑ 361-826-4667; www.ccmuseum.com; 1900 N Chaparral St; adult/child $11/9; ☺ 10am-5pm Tue-Sat, noon-5pm Sun; ☺) Explore Spanish shipwrecks, Texas' natural history and more at this fun museum. See how native Texas proved to be the doom of French explorer La Salle, and have a look at the peculiar gallery devoted to historical and modern firearms. There's also a huge two-story science center to get kids engaged with the discipline.

North Beach   BEACH
The closest beach to downtown lies across the ship channel to the north. It gets busy in season, but the tight-packed sands and handful of places to eat and drink make for a fun excursion just out of the city.'

🛏 Sleeping

Super 8 Motel – Bayfront   MOTEL $
(☑ 361-884-4815; www.wyndhamhotels.com/super-8; 411 N Shoreline Blvd; r $80-120; ❄☎) No surprises at this chain offering, but you will find decent budget rooms in an excellent downtown location, smack-bang between the T-heads and the nightlife of Water St. The pool is probably more inviting than the limpid waters across the street. Don't confuse this with the other Super 8 in town, which is off I-37 in the industrial quarter.

★ V Boutique Hotel   BOUTIQUE HOTEL $$
(☑ 361-883-9200; www.vhotelcc.com; 701 N Water St, 2nd fl; r $160-210, ste $320; P❄☎) Adored by guests, this small hotel in the heart of downtown offers a high level of service, and you can order room service from the excellent restaurant downstairs. It has eight comfy, well-equipped rooms, all with carpet and a subdued modern design scheme; they range in size from studios to one-bedroom loft suites. Call to book for a 10% discount.

Emerald Beach Hotel   HOTEL $$
(☑ 361-883-5731; www.hotelemeraldbeach.com; 1102 S Shoreline Blvd; r $180-250; P❄@☎) Right on the water at the southern tip of downtown, the Emerald confronts you with tough choices between the sand, the hotel's two bars and its indoor pool. Most rooms have balconies, but 1st-floor rooms in the annex building open directly onto a shared walkway above the beach.

🍴 Eating & Drinking

San Luis   MEXICAN $
(☑ 361-885-0117; 2110 Laredo St; meals $5-9; ☺ 6am-2pm Mon-Sat, 7am-3pm Sun) A dead-simple Mexican diner with the requisite Selena posters, San Luis serves indescribably good food. Breakfast orders start at $1.35, but even if you can't make it by 11am everything about this place is a fantastic value.

Blackbeard's on the Beach   TEX-MEX $
(☑ 361-884-1030; http://blackbeards.restaurant; 3117 E Surfside Blvd, North Beach; mains $7-20; ☺ 11am-9pm Sun-Thu, to 10pm Fri & Sat; ☎) On North Beach, this rollicking place serves up tasty Mexican and American cuisine with a strong seafood focus. Wash it down with cheap margaritas while sitting back for the live music, but watch out for the ghosts that are reputed to haunt the place. Oh, and if it's your birthday? Yours is on the house.

★ Brewster Street Icehouse   BAR
(☑ 361-884-2739; www.brewsterstreet.net; 1724 N Tancahua St; ☺ 11am-2am; ☎☺) The perfect embodiment of the Texas icehouse. Bring the kids for a burger, friends for a beer, or wander over after a game at Whataburger Field for the live music. Thursday nights are Texas Country, but Friday to Sunday run the range of genres. The food is pretty good, too, even the $8 lunch special. You're darn tootin' it's a good deal.

House of Rock   BAR
(☑ 361-882-7625; www.texashouseofrock.com; 511 Starr St; ☺ 11am-2am Mon-Fri, from noon Sat & Sun; ☎) Sort of like an extension of your living room...if only you were cooler and had better taste in music. The bar (21+) and restaurant (all ages) are open daily and there's no cover, but the much larger event space only opens for concerts – of which there are many. Check the website for upcoming shows.

ℹ Information

The friendly staff at the **Corpus Christi Visitor Information Center** (☑ 361-561-2000; www.visitcorpuschristitx.org; 1400 N Shoreline Blvd; ☺ 9am-5pm Mon-Thu, to 6pm Fri-Sun) on the northern stretch of Shoreline Blvd proffer tips on dining, attractions, places to stay, and more.

ℹ Getting There & Away

You'll find **Corpus Christi International Airport** (CRP; ☏ 361-289-0171; www.corpuschristi airport.com; 1000 International Dr) 6 miles west of downtown at International Dr and TX 44. American Eagle serves Dallas–Fort Worth International Airport; Continental Express serves Houston's George Bush International Airport; and Southwest serves Houston's William P Hobby Airport.

Greyhound (☏ 361-226-4393; www.grey hound.com; 602 N Staples St; ⊙ 8am-1:30am) has regular service to Houston ($25, 4½ hours), Brownsville ($14, 3½ hours), San Antonio ($20, 2½ hours) and beyond.

Padre Island National Seashore

The longest stretches of undeveloped barrier island in the world, the southern part of **Padre Island** (☏ 361-949-8068; www.nps.gov/ pais; Park Rd 22; ⊙ park 24hr) is administered by the National Park Service (NPS). Its main feature is 65 miles of white sand and shell beaches, backed by grassy dunes and the very salty Laguna Madre.

The island is home to all the coastal wildlife found elsewhere along the coast and then some. There's excellent birding, of course, plus numerous coyotes, white-tailed deer, sea turtles and more. It offers a delightful day's outing for anyone who wants to try a little natural beauty, or a major adventure for anyone who wants to escape civilization.

The excellent park map is free at the entrance. Besides showing the island in great detail, it has good information about flora, fauna and various activities such as fishing and beachcombing.

Entrance to the park costs $10 per vehicle, which is good for seven days.

The **Malaquite Beach Visitor Center** (☏ 361-949-8068; www.nps.gov/pais; North Padre Island; ⊙ 9am-5pm) is on the beach just before the end of the paved road. It has showers, rest rooms and picnic facilities and offers excellent information. A small store with convenience foods and souvenirs is also here. Check the posted schedule for interpretive walks (there's usually one at 11am along the beach).

There is very little past the visitor center except beautiful beaches and dunes where the only sounds you'll hear are the wind and water, punctuated by the occasional bird's cry.

Corpus Christi's TX 358 turns into PR 22/ South Padre Island Dr (locally known as SPID) as it enters Padre Island, and continues south for 13 miles to the National Seashore entrance gate and another 3½ miles to the Malaquite Beach Visitor Center. From there it's just beaches and dunes for the next 60 miles.

Note that Padre Island National Seashore is separated from South Padre Island by the Mansfield Channel and there is no transport across this gap. South Padre Island, the resort town, is only accessible from the very south of the state.

South Padre Island

Covering the southern 5 miles of South Padre Island, the town of South Padre Island (SPI) works hard to exploit its sunny climate. The water is warm for much of the year, the beaches are clean and the laid-back locals are ready to welcome every tourist who crosses the 2.5-mile Queen Isabella Causeway from the mainland (the permanent population is augmented by 10,000 or more visitors at any given time, more in peak periods).

January and February, when the weather can be either balmy or a bit chilly, are the quietest months to visit SPI (though still popular with winter Texans). The busiest and most expensive periods are spring break (all of March except the first week) and summer, when the moderating gulf breezes make the shore more tolerable than the sweltering inland areas, and the normally chill vibe turns into hedonistic party central for weeks at a time.

◉ Sights & Activities

★ **Sea Turtle, Inc**   WILDLIFE RESERVE
(☏ 956-761-4511; www.seaturtleinc.org; 6617 Padre Blvd; suggested donation adult/child $4/2; ⊙ 10am-4pm Tue-Sun Sep-May, to 5pm Jun-Aug) No, you can't handle the sea turtles. But you can see rescued turtles and learn firsthand about the slow rebirth of critically endangered Kemp's ridley turtle populations. The center serves as a hospital for injured animals, runs educational programs for the public and releases young turtles once they're old enough to face the world on their own. To find out when hatchlings will be released – generally at sunrise in summer – call the Hatchling Hotline (☏ 956-433-5735).

SPRING BREAK ON SPI
....

During the last three weeks of March, more than 100,000 students descend on the island for days of drinking, swimming, sunbathing, frolicking and more, followed by nights of drinking, skinny-dipping, frolicking and more. Major sponsors such as beer and energy-drink companies stage concerts and games on the beaches. MTV is usually there broadcasting live.

During spring break, it's hard to escape the mobs of students cruising the developed part of town. If the idea of spending a week at a beach party with thousands of young people on their first real bender appeals to you, you will have a wonderful time. Otherwise, you should avoid the island for the month.

**South Padre Island
Birding & Nature Center**   NATURE RESERVE
(☑ 956-761-6801; www.southpadreislandbirding.com; 6801 Padre Blvd; adult/child $6/3; ⊙ 9am-5pm) Part of the World Birding Center, this 50-acre nature preserve has boardwalks through the dunes, bird blinds, spotting towers and much more. Learn the differences between a dune meadow, a salt marsh and an intertidal flat in the flashy exhibit hall. Look for butterflies, egrets, alligators, turtles, crabs and much more. There's a blackboard out front listing recent sightings at the reserve. While the visitor center is only open during office hours, ticketed guests can access the boardwalks from dawn to dusk.

North End   BEACH
(Park Rd 100, North End; ⊙ 24hr) **FREE** Padre Blvd ends 12 miles north of Isla Blanca. North of here there's 20 miles of empty sand and dunes all the way to Port Mansfield Pass. Nude sunbathers, anglers, birdwatchers and other outdoorsy types can find a sandy acre to call their own; vehicles can drive on the beach, but be wary of soft sand.

Sandy Feet   SAND CASTLES
(☑ 956-459-2928; www.sandcastleworkshops.com; 117 E Saturn Lane; group lessons from $40; ⊙ by appointment) Everything you've ever wanted to know about building sandcastles, from 30-minute crash courses ($50) up to multi-hour master classes ($150+). It also rents out two condos, with free sandcastle-building lessons for guests.

🛌 Sleeping

⭐ **Palms Resort**   MOTEL $$
(☑ 956-761-1316; www.palmsresortcafe.com; 3616 Gulf Blvd; r $150-230; ❄ 🛜 🏊) This friendly two-story motel has a great location beside the grass-covered dunes on the gulf, and while the rooms themselves don't have

waterfront views the excellent alfresco beachfront restaurant/bar has nothing but. Units are large and tidy with ceramic-tile floors, fridges and microwaves.

Tiki Condominium Hotel   RESORT $$
(☑ 956-761-2694; https://thetikispi.com; 6608 Padre Blvd; r $130-340; ❄ 🛜 🏊 🐾) This Polynesian-themed veteran turns up the tiki clichés at the north end of developed SPI. Units have full kitchens and range in size from one to three bedrooms, but even on the furthest block you're never more than 10 minutes from the beach and even less from the two swimming pools. Two-night minimum. Pet friendly, for a fee ($75).

🍴 Eating & Drinking

Sea Ranch   SEAFOOD $$
(☑ 956-761-1314; http://searanchrestaurant.com; 1 Padre Blvd; mains $20-32; ⊙ 5-9pm Sun-Thu, to 10pm Fri & Sat) A little classier than the beach-bum standard on SPI, Sea Ranch has an impressive menu of wild-caught seafood and Angus steaks. It overlooks the harbor and has an elegant vibe. It doesn't take reservations, but it's worth the wait.

Pier 19   SEAFOOD $$
(☑ 956-761-7437; www.pier19.us; 1 Padre Blvd; mains $9-27; ⊙ 7am-11pm; 🍴) On a pier jutting far out along the water, this rambling eatery has a huge menu of fried seafood, burgers, ceviche, fish tacos, po'boys and much more. If you're just looking for a sundowner, head to the bar all the way out at the end for postcard views.

⭐ **Padre Island
Brewing Company**   MICROBREWERY
(☑ 956-761-9585; www.pibrewingcompany.com; 3400 Padre Blvd; ⊙ 11:30am-10pm, to 11pm Fri & Sat) Although it's not on the beach, this microbrewery is well worth a visit for its changing lineup of local brews. The sampler

($7) is 6oz pours of all five on tap, or if you've already picked a favorite the pitchers are $12.75. Burgers, pizzas and other bar food are popular, and there's a full seafood menu to choose from. Mains are $10 to $26.

Wanna-Wanna Beach Bar & Grill   BAR
(✆956-761-7677; www.wannawanna.com; 5100 Gulf Blvd, Beach Access 19; ⊙11am-10:30pm) A picture-perfect cliché of the laid-back beach bar and restaurant. Lounge barefoot in plastic chairs on the shaded deck and take in the surf and sights. Burgers and other basics ($6 to $14) go down easy, but nothing competes with the large cold drinks. It's tucked out back of the **Wanna Wanna Inn** (✆956-761-7677; r $100-225; ✳🛜).

ℹ️ Information

The **South Padre Island Convention & Visitors Bureau** (✆956-761-4412; www.spichamber. com; 610 Padre Blvd; ⊙9am-5pm) has a selection of brochures detailing tourist services on the island, and a small museum exhibit detailing some of the area's history.

ℹ️ Getting There & Away

No long-range public transit serves the island. The nearest option is the **Greyhound** (✆956-546-7171; www.greyhound.com; 755 International Blvd, Suite H; ⊙4am-midnight) station in Brownsville.

If you can get out to SPI, you won't necessarily need a car. The developed area is fairly compact, easy for walking or cycling, and there's a shuttle around the island and across the causeway to Port Isabel and onward to Brownsville airport.

DALLAS-FORT WORTH

Dallas and Fort Worth may be next-door neighbors, but they're hardly twins – or even kissing cousins. Long regarded as being as divergent as an Escalade-driving sophisticate and a rancher in a dusty pickup truck, these two cities have starkly different facades. Beyond appearances, however, they share a love of high (and low) culture and good old-fashioned Texan fun. In the surrounding area is a plethora of fabulous small towns worthy of a road trip, including Waxahachie and McKinney.

Leave the big smoke behind and you'll find that the Panhandle and Central Plains may be the part of Texas that most typifies the state to outsiders. This is a land of sprawling cattle ranches, where people can still make a living on horseback. The landscape appears endlessly flat, punctuated only by utility poles and windmills, until a vast canyon materializes and seems to plunge into another world.

Dallas

Dallas is Texas' most mythical city, with a past and present rich in the stuff that American legends are made of. The 'Big D' is famous for its contributions to popular culture – notably the Cowboys and their cheerleaders, and *Dallas,* the TV series that once was a worldwide symbol of the USA. An upscale ethos makes for a vaunted dining and shopping scene, where the more conspicuous your consumption, the better.

The museums are not only excellent, but unique – history buffs should not miss the memorials to President John F Kennedy's assassination. The most impressive addition to Dallas' cultural landscape in recent years is the massive 68-acre Arts District.

Pick a neighborhood like Deep Ellum, Lower Greenville or the Bishop Arts District and stake out a space on a patio with a cold beer for the quintessential Dallas experience.

◉ Sights & Activities

⭐**Sixth Floor Museum**   MUSEUM
(✆214-747-6660; www.jfk.org; Book Depository, 411 Elm St; adult/child $16/13; ⊙10am-6pm Tue-Sun, noon-6pm Mon; light rail West End) No city wants the distinction of being the site of an assassination – especially if the victim happens to be President John F Kennedy. But rather than downplay the events that sent the city reeling in 1963, Dallas gives visitors a unique opportunity to delve into the world-altering events unleashed by an assassin in the former Texas School Book Depository. Fascinating multimedia exhibits (plus the included audioguide) give an excellent historical context of JFK's time, as well as his life and legacy.

⭐**Pioneer Plaza**   SQUARE
(cnr S Griffin & Young Sts) For a Texas-sized photo op or just a sight of the largest bronze monument on earth, head to Pioneer Plaza. Its showpiece is a collection of 40 bronze larger-than-life longhorns, amassed as if they were on a cattle drive. There is an unmistakable and compelling power to the tableau.

Dallas–Fort Worth Metroplex

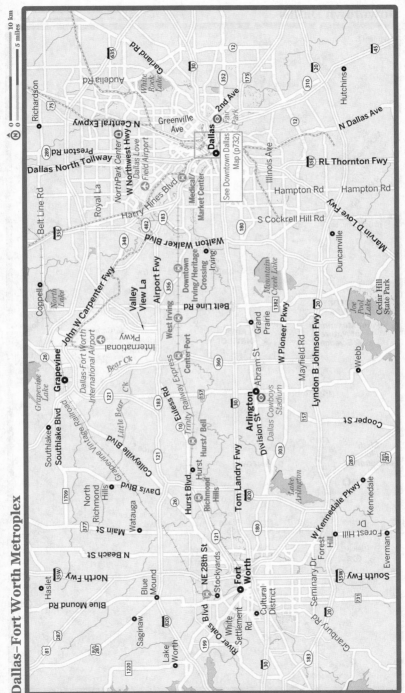

See Downtown Dallas Map (p732)

Downtown Dallas

N 0 — 500 m
0 — 0.25 miles

A **B** **C** **D**

William B. Dean Park

Cosmic Café (0.6mi);
JR's Bar & Grill (0.8mi);
Sue Ellen's (0.8mi)

Abacus (1.6mi);
Highland Park Soda Shop (1.7mi);
Javier's (1.9mi)

Greenwood Cemetery

Fairmount St
Carlisle St
Maple Ave
Wolf St
Randall St
N Pearl St

The Quadrangle ⌖14
⌖13

Howell St · Boll St
Routh St
Boll St
Worthington St
Allen St
Clyde La
State St
Thomas Ave
Clark St

N Hall St
75
Carver Pl
Mc Coy Pl
N Hall St
Griggs Park

McKinnon St
N Harwood St
H Hines Blvd
354
289
Cedar Springs Rd
Crescent Ct
McKinney Ave

UPTOWN

Boll St
Colby St
Guillot St

Flora St
Ross Ave
San Jacinto St
San Liberty St
Allen St

1

2

Meddlesome Moth (0.6mi); Days Inn Market Center Dallas (1mi)

Wichita St
Harry Hines Blvd
Caroline St

Fairmount St

366

12 ✕ One Arts Plaza

Routh St
Fairmount St
Leonard St
Crockett St
Pearl
N Pearl St
N Olive St

Bryan St
N Good Latimer Expwy
N Central Expwy
N Hawkins St

3

Olive St
N Houston St
N Field St
VICTORY PARK
354

Klyde Warren Park
N Harwood St
Flora St
Plaza of the Americas

🏛6 🏛4

Carpenter Plaza
Deep Ellum Green Room (0.2mi)
S Pearl St

M

4

Perot Museum 🏛
of Nature 1
& Science

Victory Ave
McKinney Ave
N Griffin St
Munger Ave
N Munger Ave
N Field St
Laws St
N Lamar St

ARTS DISTRICT

San Jacinto St
N Ervay St
N St Paul St
Heritage Way Park
St Paul M
Aston Park
Live Oak St

AllGood Café (0.4mi)

5

West End Marketplace
Ross Ave

Sixth
Floor 3
Museum 🏛

🏛7

Patterson St
Akard St
WEST END
🏛15 M West End
Founders Plaza
ℹ

Thanks-Giving Square
Pacific Ave
Elm St
Main St
Commerce St

DOWNTOWN

Jackson St
Wood St
9⊙ ⊙11
Akard St

N Harwood St
S St Paul St
Park Ave
S Harwood St
Cadiz St

6

Union Station
🚇
Union M
Reunion Blvd
🏛8
Union

S Houston St
🏛10
Wood St
Lubben Plaza Park
S Record St

Founders Square Park
Pioneer
Plaza
2⊙
Pioneer Cemetery

Young St
City Hall Plaza
Marilla Triangle Park
Marilla St
S Ervay St
S Akard St
Canton St

Park Ave
Corsicana St
Cadiz St
S Louis St

Pioneer 2

Dallas
Convention
Center

Old City Park
⊙5

7

Reunion Park
E Reunion Blvd
Convention Center M
Hotel Dr

S Lamar St
S Griffin St
30
80
67
Griffin St W

Canton St
S Akard St
Griffin St E
Peters St
Wall St
Belleview St
Blakeney St
Browder St
S St Paul St
S Gould St

Sports St
Houston Viaduct
Jefferson Viaduct
S Lamar St
S Austin St

Cedars Station M

A **B** **C** **D**

Downtown Dallas

◉ **Top Sights**
1 Perot Museum of Nature & Science...A4
2 Pioneer Plaza...B6
3 Sixth Floor Museum A5

◉ **Sights**
4 Crow Collection of Asian Art..............C3
5 Dallas Heritage Village......................D7
6 Dallas Museum of Art.........................B3
7 Dealey Plaza & the Grassy Knoll........A5
   Nasher Sculpture Center.............(see 4)
8 Reunion Tower.....................................A6

◎ **Sleeping**
9 Adolphus..C5
10 La Quinta Inns & Suites......................A6
11 Magnolia Hotel....................................C5

◎ **Eating**
   Five Sixty by Wolfgang Puck.......(see 8)
12 Tei-An...C2

◎ **Drinking & Nightlife**
13 Ginger Man B1
14 Two Corks and a Bottle.......................B1

◎ **Shopping**
15 Wild Bill's Western Store A5

★ **Perot Museum
of Nature & Science** MUSEUM
(📞214-428-5555; www.perotmuseum.org; 2201 N Field St; adult/child from $20/13; ⊙10am-5pm Mon-Sat, noon-5pm Sun; 👶; light rail St Paul) A sizable star of the Arts District, this striking museum opened to much acclaim in 2012. It wows both on the outside (thanks to award-winning architect Thom Mayne) and on the inside (there are six floors of wonder). Most of the exhibits are interactive: visitors can design their own bird, journey through the solar system, command robots, commune with dinosaurs and much more.

★ **Dallas Arboretum
& Botanical Gardens** GARDENS
(📞214-515-6615; www.dallasarboretum.org; 8525 Garland Rd; adult/child $15/10; ⊙9am-5pm) On the shores of White Rock Lake, this gorgeous 66-acre arboretum showcases plants and flowers in theme gardens such as the Sunken Garden and the Woman's Garden. Expect to see a lot of wedding parties posing for pictures amid the posies. During the spring wildflower season it gets so mobbed that nearby streets are closed.

Nasher Sculpture Center MUSEUM
(📞214-242-5100; www.nashersculpturecenter.org; 2001 Flora St; adult/child $10/free; ⊙11am-5pm Tue-Sun; light rail St Paul) Modern-art installations shine at the fabulous glass-and-steel Nasher Sculpture Center. The Nashers accumulated what might be one of the greatest privately held sculpture collections in the world, with works by Calder, de Kooning, Rodin, Serra and Miró. The divine sculpture garden is one of the best in the country.

Crow Collection of Asian Art MUSEUM
(📞214-979-6430; www.crowcollection.com; 2010 Flora St; ⊙10am-9pm Tue-Thu, to 6pm Fri & Sat, noon-6pm Sun; light rail St Paul) FREE Enter another world in this calm, pagoda-like oasis of a museum that's nearly as remarkable for its ambience as for its rich collection of artworks from China, Japan, India and Southeast Asia, dating from 3500 BC to the early 20th century. Don't miss the gorgeous sandstone facade from North India. There are free guided tours at 1pm on Saturdays.

Dealey Plaza & the Grassy Knoll PARK
(light rail West End) Now a National Historic Landmark, this rectangular park is south of the former Book Depository. Dealey Plaza was named in 1935 for George Bannerman Dealey, a longtime Dallas journalist, historian and philanthropist. Just steps from here, John F Kennedy was assassinated in November 1963.

Dallas Heritage Village HISTORIC SITE
(📞214-421-5141; www.dallasheritagevillage.org; 1515 S Harwood St; adult/child $9/5; ⊙10am-4pm Tue-Sat, noon-4pm Sun; light rail Cedars) This 13-acre museum of history and architecture, set on a wooded property south of downtown, shows what it was like to live in North Texas from about 1840 to 1910. The modern skyline makes for a striking backdrop for the living history exhibits comprised of 38 historic structures, including a tipi and a Civil War–era farm.

Dallas Museum of Art MUSEUM
(www.dallasmuseumofart.org; 1717 N Harwood St; ⊙11am-5pm Tue-Sun, to 9pm Thu; 👶; light rail St Paul) FREE This museum is a high-caliber world tour of decorative and fine art. Among the many treasures are Edward Hopper's enigmatic *Lighthouse Hill*, Frederic Church's lush masterpiece *The Icebergs* and Rodin's *Sculptor and his Muse*. Other highlights include exquisite pre-Columbian pottery, carvings and tapestries from Oceania, and a

TEXAS DALLAS

villa modeled on Coco Chanel's Mediterranean mansion (where you can see paintings by statesman Winston Churchill).

★ Reunion Tower
LANDMARK

(☎ 214-712-7040; www.reuniontower.com; 300 Reunion Blvd E; adult/child from $17/8; ☺ hours vary by season; light rail Union Station) What's 50 stories high and has a three-level spherical dome with 260 flashing lights? It's Reunion Tower, the unofficial symbol of Dallas. Take the 68-second elevator ride up for a pricey sky-high panoramic view. Or enjoy the view from the celebrity-chef restaurant and lounge **Five Sixty by Wolfgang Puck** (☎ 214-571-5784; www.wolfgangpuck.com; mains from $25; ☺ restaurant 5-10pm Mon-Thu, to 11pm Fri-Sun). An underground pedestrian tunnel connects Reunion Tower with Union Station and the Hyatt Regency Dallas.

★ Katy Trail
WALKING

(☎ 214-303-1180; www.katytraildallas.org; ☺ 5am-midnight) For see-and-be-seen running and cycling, hit the Katy Trail that runs 3.5 miles from the American Airlines center downtown almost all the way to SMU, passing through interesting neighborhoods along the way. The old railway route is tree-lined and at times feels like the country. Planned extensions will link it to other walking routes.

☆☆ Festivals & Events

★ State Fair of Texas
FAIR

(www.bigtex.com; Fair Park, 1300 Cullum Blvd; adult/child $18/14; ☺ late Sep–mid-Oct) This massive fair is the fall highlight for many a Texan. Come ride one of the tallest Ferris wheels in North America, eat corn dogs (it's claimed that this is where they were invented), and browse the prize-winning cows, sheep and quilts.

Martin Luther King Jr Parade
PARADE

(☺ Jan) For the last 30 years Dallas has hosted one of the largest events in the country commemorating Dr King's life. In mid-January, the parade, a festive mix of floats and marching bands, goes from MLK Blvd and Lamar to Fair Park.

🛏 Sleeping

Days Inn Market Center Dallas
MOTEL $

(☎ 214-748-2243; www.daysinn.com; 2026 Market Center Blvd; r from $68; P ❄ 🛜) Sure it's a generic chain hotel, but you won't find a better deal this close – it's about 2.5 miles northeast of downtown. Rooms are clean and simply furnished, and the design district is right around the corner.

★ Hotel Belmont
BOUTIQUE HOTEL $$

(☎ 866-870-8010; www.belmontdallas.com; 901 Fort Worth Ave; r $95-180; P ❄ @ 🛜 ⛱) Just 2 miles west of downtown, this stylish 1940s bungalow hotel is a fabulously low-key antidote to Dallas' flashier digs, with a touch of mid-century-modern design and more than its share of soul. The garden rooms – with soaking tubs, Moroccan-blue tile work, kilim rugs and some city views – are tops.

Magnolia Hotel
BOUTIQUE HOTEL $$

(☎ 214-915-6500; www.magnoliahotels.com; 1401 Commerce St; r from $200; ❄ ❄ @ 🛜 ⛱) Housed in the 1922, 29-story Magnolia Petroleum Company Building, this gracious hotel offers a sumptuous stay. Rooms have period details including wooden blinds and retro furniture. The commodious rooms have fridges, while the suites have kitchenettes.

La Quinta Inns & Suites
HOTEL $$

(☎ 214-761-9090; www.laquintadallasdowntown.com; 302 S Houston St; r from $160; ❄ @ 🛜) One of the better deals downtown, this chain hotel beats the generic blues with a unique design in a 1925 building. Rooms include a small breakfast.

★ Adolphus
HISTORIC HOTEL $$$

(☎ 214-742-8200; www.hoteladolphus.com; 1321 Commerce St; d $270-370; ❄ ❄ @ 🛜 ⛱; light rail Akard) Feel like royalty (yes, Queen Elizabeth has stayed here) the old-fashioned way. The 422-room Adolphus takes us back to the days when gentlemen wore ties and hotels were truly grand, not bastions of ascetic minimalism. Just exploring the 22 floors is an adventure in the 1912 labyrinth. Note that room sizes vary widely. It's part of the Marriott empire.

★ Hotel Lumen
HOTEL $$$

(☎ 214-219-2400; www.hotellumen.com; 6101 Hillcrest Ave; r $240-380; P ❄ @ 🛜) This ultra-modern concrete hotel across from SMU doesn't completely live up to the hype. Yet we love the parade of poodles and shih tzus through the lobby, the video library and the strong coffee in the morning. It has a breezy rooftop lounge.

🍴 Eating

Dining in Dallas sprawls with options much like the city itself. There are several areas worthy of your attention: Deep Ellum, just east of downtown, is your choice for eclectic eats. This area, 'deep' up Elm St, gets its name from the Southern-drawl pronunciation of 'Elm.'

Heading uptown offers myriad choices, especially in the Lower Greenfield neighborhood with its walkable blocks. To the west, the Arts District, University Park and uptown are among the neighborhoods worth exploring for a bite.

Southwest, the Bishop Arts District is dotted with interesting places to eat and drink. It merges hipster and funky – walk off your vittles by window-shopping the idiosyncratic boutiques.

★**Sonny Bryan's Smokehouse** BARBECUE $
(☑ 214-357-7120; www.sonnybryans.com; 2202 Inwood Rd; mains $6-19; ☺24hr) You cannot beat the original location of this Dallas classic. Where some barbecue places serve up their fare for only a few hours a day, this one can sate your smoky fantasies around the clock.

★**AllGood Café** TEX-MEX $
(☑214-742-5362; www.allgoodcafe.com; 2934 Main St; mains $5-9; ☑) A postmodern Deep Ellum cafe with Tex-Mex grace notes and tattooed waitresses, the AllGood is cozy as all get out. Families and rocker types all chow down on King Ranch chicken casserole and other comfort foods. The suppliers are local and listed by name.

Keller's Drive-In FAST FOOD $
(☑214-368-1209; 6537 E Northwest Hwy; mains $4-8; ☺10:30am-10pm) You supply the dining room - your car - at this long-running classic, true, drive-in. The waitresses (yes, all women) have seen it all but still hustle out to take your order as soon as you park. The burgers are remarkably juicy and come with myriad options. The onion rings are a cut above.

Highland Park Soda Shop AMERICAN $
(☑214-521-2126; www.highlandparksodafountain. com; 3229 Knox St; mains $4-8; ☺7am-6pm Mon-Fri, from 8am Sat, 10am-5pm Sun; ☻) Since 1912, this classic soda fountain has been serving up vanilla malts and comfort fare such as grilled-cheese sandwiches to generations of diners. When in doubt, get the root-beer float. It's in Highland Park, about 4 miles north of downtown.

Cosmic Café VEGETARIAN $
(☑214-521-6157; www.cosmiccafedallas.com; 2912 Oak Lawn Ave; mains $5-15; ☺11am-10:30pm; ☑) Cosmic Café serves delicious international

vegetarian fare in wildly colorful surroundings. Amid the wild folk art, beware of service that can falter.

★**Meddlesome Moth** MODERN AMERICAN $$
(☑214-628-7900; www.mothinthe.net; 1621 Oak Lawn Ave; lunch mains $10-15, dinner mains $10-20; ☺11am-midnight Mon-Sat, 10am-10pm Sun) In the Design District, this buzzing gastropub draws small groups of friends who linger over Belgian-style mussels, shrimp and homestead grits, great burgers and beautifully turned out sharing plates. You'll find good cocktails and a superb and rotating selection of craft brews (including 40 on draft). The menu changes by season. It's around 2 miles northwest of downtown.

Kalachandji's VEGETARIAN $$
(☑214-821-1048; www.kalachandjis.com; 5430 Gurley Ave; buffet lunch/dinner $12/15; ☺11:30am-2pm & 5:30-9pm Tue-Sun; ☑) Inside a lavishly decorated Hare Krishna temple, you'll find a small but varied buffet serving basmati rice, curries, mustard greens, *pappadams* and chutneys, *pakora,* tamarind tea and other changing daily specials. It's a fine counterpoint to Texas' many meaty temptations. You can dine in the peaceful, plant-filled courtyard. It's located about 4 miles east of downtown.

Tei-An JAPANESE $$
(☑214-220-2828; www.tei-an.com; One Arts Plaza, 1722 Routh St; mains $12-20; ☺11:30am-2pm Sun & Fri, 6-10:30pm Tue-Sun) The swanky Tei-An specializes in laboriously handmade Japanese soba-noodle dishes. It also has crowd-pleasing *tonkatsu* (delicately fried meats). The dining room is clean-lined and stylish.

Daddy Jack's SEAFOOD $$
(☑214-826-4910; www.daddyjacks.org; 1916 Greenville Ave; mains $14-30; ☺5-10pm) Excellent seafood in relaxed neighborhood surrounds. This restaurant not only does briny denizens well, it does so with praiseworthy service. Casual yet attentive is a quality that never goes out of style. Expect lots of lobster dishes; don't bother coming if you don't order the lobster bisque.

★**Javier's** MEXICAN $$$
(☑214-521-4211; www.javiers.net; 4912 Cole Ave; mains $20-35; ☺5:30-10pm Sun-Thu, to 11pm Fri & Sat) Discard any ideas you have about Tex-Mex at this deeply cultured restaurant that takes the gentrified food of old Mexico City to new levels. The setting is dark, leathery

and quiet, and the food is meaty and pi-quant. Steaks come with a range of Mexican flavors that bring out the best in beef. Get a table under the stars.

It's in Highland Park, about 4 miles north of downtown.

Abacus AMERICAN $$$
(📞 214-559-3111; http://abacus-restaurant.com; 4511 McKinney Ave; mains $35-60, tasting menus from $65; ⏰ 6-10pm Mon-Sat; 🛜) Too many steakhouses in Dallas are part of chains. For the real deal with a contemporary twist, Abacus delivers the beef. Start with sushi or the wildly popular lobster shooters and then make your way through a menu of small, seasonal plates. Then feast on simply superb steaks. The bar is excellent.

🍸 Drinking & Nightlife

⭐ Two Corks and a Bottle LOUNGE
(📞 214-871-9463; www.twocorksandabottle.com; 2800 Routh St; ⏰ noon-7pm Sun & Tue, to 10pm Wed-Thu, to 11pm Fri & Sat) Creative owners make all the difference and the pair behind this cork-sized little uptown wine bar prove it. Besides a fine selection of vino, it has frequent diversions such as acoustic, blues or jazz. That it's romantic is a bonus. Wine flights let you sample widely from the wine list.

⭐ Ginger Man PUB
(📞 214-754-8771; www.thegingerman.com/uptown; 2718 Boll St; ⏰ 1pm-2am) An appropriately spice-colored house is home to this always-busy neighborhood pub. It has multilevel patios, and porches out front and back, plus one of the best beer menus in the city. Great bartenders.

⭐ Green Room BAR
(📞 214-748-7666; www.dallasgreenroom.com; 2715 Elm St; ⏰ 4pm-2am Tue-Sun) In bar-lined Deep Ellum, the Green Room is a go-to spot for rooftop cocktails, a fun crowd and excellent food, from snacks to meals (tacos, burgers, poutine). Pick from three bar areas.

⭐ JR's Bar & Grill GAY
(📞 214-528-1004; www.jrsdallas.com; 3923 Cedar Springs Rd; ⏰ 11am-2am Mon-Sat, from noon Sun) One of the busiest bars in Texas, JR's serves lunch daily and boasts a variety of fun entertainment at night. From the patio you can cheer on Dallas' modest cruising scene. Many Mondays have drag shows. It's 3 miles north of downtown in Oak Lawn.

Sue Ellen's LESBIAN
(📞 214-559-0707; www.sueellensdallas.com; 3014 Throckmorton St; ⏰ 4pm-2am) Chill out in the 'lipstick lounge' or on the dance floor at Dallas' favorite lesbian bar. Good back garden.

☆ Entertainment

High culture, low culture, country culture... Dallas has it in spades.

⭐ Kessler Theater LIVE MUSIC
(📞 214-272-8346; http://thekessler.org; 1230 W Davis St; ⏰ 6pm-midnight) Let the aqua neon outside catch your eye and draw you in to this Oak Cliff landmark. The one-time neighborhood movie house has been transformed into a fairly intimate live music venue. Drink prices are friendly, the bands and acts are good (drag shows!) and the vibe is down-home fun.

⭐ Sons of Hermann Hall LIVE MUSIC
(📞 214-747-4422; www.sonsofhermann.com; 3414 Elm St; ⏰ 7pm-midnight Wed & Thu, to 2am Fri & Sat) For almost 100 years, this classic Texas dancehall has been a chameleon: equal parts pickup bar, live-music venue, honky-tonk and swing-dancing club. A Deep Ellum stalwart. The opening hours can vary; call to find out what's on. Come here and plunge deep into the heart of full-on Big D.

⭐ Granada Theater LIVE MUSIC
(📞 214-824-9933; www.granadatheater.com; 3524 Greenville Ave) This converted movie theater, often praised as the best live-music venue in town, books popular rock and country bands. It's the anchor of Lower Greenwood. Check the website for what's on.

Balcony Club LIVE MUSIC
(📞 214-826-8104; www.balconyclub.com; 1825 Abrams Rd; ⏰ bar 5pm-2am) This mysterious upstairs hideaway feels like a secret, even though it's not. With emerald walls, a tiny stage and a cozy patio nook above the Landmark Theater, this spot draw all ages for nightly live music – mostly jazz – and sassy drinks such as moonlight martinis and three-way tropical punch.

🔒 Shopping

⭐ Wild Bill's Western Store CLOTHING
(📞 214-954-1050; www.wildbillswestern.com; 311 N Market St; ⏰ 10am-7pm Mon & Tue, to 9pm Wed-Sat, noon-6pm Sun; light rail West End) Wild Bill's is a West End treasure chest of Western wear. You'll find Stetsons, snakeskin

boots, oilskin jackets, oversize belt buckles, rhinestone-covered T-shirts, fun kitschy souvenirs, popguns and other toys, country-music CDs and much more. Enjoy a cold beer while you shop.

★ **Highland Park Village** MALL
(☑214-443-9898; www.hpvillage.com; Preston Rd & Mockingbird Lane; ☺ hours vary by store) For an eye-rolling, gasp-inducing and credit-card-maxing experience, head to Spanish Mission–style Highland Park Village in upper-crust Highland Park, which claims to be the oldest suburban shopping center in the world. If Jimmy Choo and Carolina Herrera are among your intimate acquaintances, you'll feel at home.

ℹ Information

Dallas Visitors Center (☑214-571-1316; www.visitdallas.com; Old Red Courthouse, 100 S Houston St; ☺9am-5pm; 🖥) Centrally located. This useful office can answer questions and distribute myriad local guides.

ℹ Getting There & Away

Dallas-Fort Worth International Airport (DFW; ☑972-973-3112; www.dfwairport.com; 2400 Aviation Dr), 16 miles northwest of the city via I-35 E, is a hub for American Airlines. Major airlines provide extensive domestic and international service.

Dallas Love Field Airport (DAL; ☑214-670-6080; www.dallas-lovefield.com; 8008 Herb Kelleher Way), just northwest of downtown, is a hub for Southwest Airlines and has extensive domestic service.

Greyhound buses (www.greyhound.com) make runs to major cities in the region from the **Dallas Bus Station** (☑214-849-6831; 205 S Lamar St).

The **Amtrak** (www.amtrak.com) San Antonio–Chicago *Texas Eagle* train stops at downtown's **Union Station** (☑800-872-7245; www.unionstationdallas.com; 400 S Houston St; light rail Union Station), which is also a hub for local transit.

ℹ Getting Around

DART (Dallas Area Rapid Transit; ☑214-979-1111; www.dart.org; 2-hour ticket $2.50, daypass $5) operates buses and an extensive light-rail system that connects downtown with outlying areas. Tickets are sold on board buses and from vending machines at rail stops. It also operates the Dallas Streetcar, which runs to the southwest from downtown, where it links to bus 723 that serves the Bishop Arts District.

Travel from downtown to uptown on the historic and free **M-Line Trolley** (☑214-855-0006; www.mata.org; ☺7am-10pm Mon-Thu, to 11pm

Fri, 10am-midnight Sat, to 10pm Sun), which runs from the St Paul DART station via the Arts District and up McKinney Ave to City Place/Uptown Station.

Trinity Railway Express (TRE; ☑info 214-979-1111; www.trinityrailwayexpress.org; single ride 1/2 zones $2.50/5, daypass 1/2 zones $5/10; ☺half-hourly 5am-1am Mon-Sat) trains run between Dallas Union Station and Fort Worth (one hour), with a stop at CenterPort/DFW Airport where there is a shuttle-bus connection to the airport.

Fort Worth

Oft-called 'Where the West Begins,' Fort Worth definitely has the cowboy feel.

The city first became famous during the great open-range cattle drives of the late 19th century, when more than 10 million head of cattle tramped through the city on the Chisholm Trail. Today you can see a mini–cattle drive in the morning and a rodeo on Saturday night.

Don't forget to scoot into Billy Bob's, the world's biggest honky-tonk. Down in the Cultural District, tour the Cowgirl Museum and three amazing art collections. Then, after you've meditated on minimalism, Sundance Sq's restaurants and bars call you to the kick-up-your-heels downtown. Whatever you do, don't mistake Fort Worth for being Dallas' sidekick. This city's got a headstrong spirit of its own, and it's a lot more user-friendly than Dallas (not to mention greener and cleaner). Bottom line? There's a lot to do here – without a whole lot of pretense.

◉ Sights

★ **Stockyards** HISTORIC SITE
(☑817-624-4741; www.fortworthstockyards.org; 130 E Exchange Ave) Western-wear stores and knickknack shops, saloons and steakhouses occupy the Old West–era buildings of the Stockyards. Don't miss the twice-daily cattle drive with the Fort Worth Herd, when cowboys drive a small herd of longhorn up E Exchange Ave. Start your visit getting info at the **Fort Worth Stockyards Visitor Center** (☺9am-5pm). It can seem touristy at times but there is a genuine authenticity here.

★ **Fort Worth Herd** HISTORIC SITE
(☑817-336-4373; www.fortworth.com/the-herd; 131 E Exchange Ave; ☺cattle drive 11:30am & 4pm) See the cows for real out behind the

Livestock Exchange Building: the Fort Worth Herd are the longhorns that parade up E Exchange Ave in a re-created cattle drive daily. You can see them in their corral from a viewing area that comes complete with picture-portraits of each – see if you can match names to critters.

★ **Kimbell Art Museum** MUSEUM
(☑ 817-332-8451; www.kimbellart.org; 3333 Camp Bowie Blvd; ⊗ 10am-5pm Tue-Thu & Sat, noon-8pm Fri, noon-5pm Sun) FREE Welcome to one of America's best small museums, with European masterpieces by Caravaggio, El Greco and Cézanne, as well as Michelangelo's first painting, *The Torment of St Anthony*. The architecture is no less stunning. Galleries are spread between an original Louis Kahn building and a more recent edition, designed by celebrated architect Renzo Piano. Admission is charged for special exhibitions.

Bureau of Engraving and Printing MUSEUM
(☑ 817-231-4000; www.moneyfactory.gov; 9000 Blue Mound Rd; ⊗ 8:30am-5:30pm Tue-Fri) FREE Fort Worth is one of two places in the nation where US paper currency is printed, at the Bureau of Engraving and Printing. This US Treasury facility produces this green stuff over which wars are fought, with which engagement rings are purchased, narcotics snorted, bets wagered, waiters tipped and babysitters paid. The bureau suggests allowing 30 minutes to clear security. Tours are self-guided; watch the presses roll! It's eight miles north of the Stockyards.

National Cowgirl Museum MUSEUM
(☑ 817-336-4475; www.cowgirl.net; 1720 Gendy St; adult/child $10/8; ⊗ 10am-5pm Tue-Sat, noon-5pm Sun) This airy, impressive museum explores the myth and the reality of cowgirls in American culture. From rhinestone costumes to rare film footage, this is a fun and educational ride: by the time you walk out, you'll have a whole new appreciation for these tough workers.

🛏 Sleeping

Hotel Texas INN $
(☑ 817-624-2224; www.magnusonhotels.com/hotel/hotel-texas-fort-worth; 2415 Ellis Ave; r $75-100; ◉ ❋ ☎ 🛜) This 1939 'cattleman's home away from home' is a good deal, smack in the center of the Stockyards action. Although the service can be gruff and rooms very basic, it's hard to fault the prices of these simple, clean rooms decorated with framed Western art. Cash only.

★ **Stockyards Hotel** HISTORIC HOTEL $$
(☑ 817-625-6427; www.stockyardshotel.com; 109 E Exchange Ave; r $150-300; ❋ 🛜) First opened in 1907, this 52-room place clings to its cowboy past with Western-themed art, cowboy-inspired rooms and a grand Old West lobby with lots of leather. Hide out in the Bonnie and Clyde room, where the outlaw pair actually stayed while on the lam in 1933 (the faux bullet holes and Bonnie's .38 revolver only add to the mystique).

Hilton Fort Worth HISTORIC HOTEL $$
(☑ 817-870-2100; www.hilton.com; 815 Main St; r from $180; ❋ @ 🛜) Built in 1921 as the Hotel Texas, this landmark hotel has 294 rooms spread across 15 floors. Much renovated through the years, the hotel has a prime central location. A key historical note: this was where John F Kennedy slept the night before he went to Dallas on November 22, 1963.

🍴 Eating

★ **Curly's Frozen Custard** ICE CREAM $
(☑ 817-763-8700; www.curlysfrozencustard.com; 4017 Camp Bowie Blvd; treats from $3; ⊗ 11am-10pm) Creamy frozen custard that you can customize with all sorts of mix-ins to make a 'concrete'. Good any day the temp is above freezing. The patio has a cute fountain.

★ **Heim Barbecue** BARBECUE $
(☑ 817-882-6970; http://heimbbq.com; 1109 W Magnolia Ave; mains $8-18; ⊗ 11am-10pm Wed-Mon) Barbecue for a new age, the family behind this joint brings knowledge and passion to the cause. Sausage, brisket (of course!), turkey, pulled pork and more are smoky and delectable. Note that the meats sell out, so don't delay. It's probably not going to happen, but try to save room for the banana pudding.

★ **Kincaid's** BURGERS $
(☑ 817-732-2881; www.kincaidshamburgers.com; 4901 Camp Bowie Blvd; mains $5-8; ⊗ 11am-8pm Mon-Sat, to 3pm Sun) Sit on picnic tables amid disused grocery shelves at this local institution (never mind the sickly green walls) and wolf down some of the best burgers in the region. They are thick, juicy and come covered in condiments.

Waters SEAFOOD $$$
(☑ 817-984-1100; http://waterstexas.com; 301 Main St; mains $15-50; ⊗ 11am-11pm) This upmarket seafood restaurant is in a restored century-old storefront downtown. Service is

crisp. Fish dishes hit all the favorites. At the lower end of the price range, diners love the New Orleans barbecue shrimp and the lobster mac 'n' cheese.

🍷 Drinking & Nightlife

★ Chimera
BREWERY

(☑ 817-923-8000; www.chimerabrew.com; 1001 W Magnolia Ave; ⊙ 11:30am-midnight Mon-Fri, from 10am Sat, 10am-10pm Sun; 🎤) Fort Worth's top brewery keeps a rotating range of eight beers on tap. The lineup changes regularly. Watch for the bacon special and the wet hop sour among others. Hungry? The pizza is thin-crust Italian and comes in a dozen varieties. Enjoy in the exposed brick dining area or outside on the patio.

★ Lola's Saloon
BAR

(☑ 817-877-0666; www.lolassaloon.com; 2736 W 6th St; ⊙ 2pm-2am Mon-Fri, noon-2am Sat & Sun) Dive into this dive bar for a fairly intimate music experience. Bands (rock, honky-tonk, bluegrass) play many nights to a fun, eclectic crowd. Catch your breath on the small outside patio. On non-show nights, there's a jukebox that's addictive. Regularly voted a favorite bar by readers of *Fort Worth Weekly*.

★ Usual Bar
COCKTAIL BAR

(☑ 817-810-0114; www.facebook.com/theusualbar/; 1408 W Magnolia Ave; ⊙ 4pm-2am Mon-Fri, from 6pm Sat & Sun) Craft-cocktail lust packs hipsters in nightly at this bar that serves up debonair drinks such as the 'Maximillian-aire' and 'the Parlor.' Of course you can be ironic and just have a well-poured Sidecar. Great terrace.

Bird Café
LOUNGE

(☑ 817-332-2473; www.birdinthe.net; 155 E 4th St; ⊙ 11am-midnight Mon-Thu, to 1am Fri & Sat, 10am-10pm Sun) This upscale gastropub serves up locally sourced fare in its main room, but the real charm is up on the roof, where you can have superb drinks while lounging on sofas, enjoying the warmth of a fire pit and gazing down onto the Sundance Sq action.

☆ Entertainment

★ Pearls Dance Hall
LIVE MUSIC

(☑ 817-624-2800; www.pearlsdancehall.com; 302 W Exchange Ave; ⊙ 6pm-2am Wed, from 7pm Fri & Sat) On the edge of the stockyards, this raucous old brothel once owned by Buffalo Bill Cody is an atmospheric place to hear traditional country music with an edge. Texas luminaries are known to rock out here to the strains of the slide guitar and fiddle. Two-steppers hit the floor many nights.

Billy Bob's Texas
LIVE MUSIC

(☑ 817-624-7117; www.billybobstexas.com; 2520 Rodeo Plaza; cover Sun-Thu $2-5, Fri & Sat varies; ⊙ 11am-10pm Mon-Wed, to 2am Thu-Sat, noon-10pm Sun) The 100,000-sq-ft building that is now the world's largest honky-tonk was once a barn housing prize cattle during the Fort Worth Stock Show. Now after a stint as a department store, Billy Bob's can hold more than 6000 people and has 40 bars to serve the thirsty masses. Don't miss the mechanical bull-riding competitions at 9pm and 10pm Friday and Saturday.

Texas Motor Speedway
SPECTATOR SPORT

(☑ 817-215-8500; www.texasmotorspeedway.com; cnr Hwy 114 & I-35, exit 72; tours adult/child $10/8; ⊙ 9am-5pm Mon-Fri, 10am-5pm Sat, noon-5pm Sun) Have yourself a full-on NASCAR experience. The annual stock-car race is in November, but there are races through the year. You can go for a ride with a racer (from $125). The speedway is 20 miles north of downtown, on I-35 W.

ℹ️ Getting There & Away

Dallas-Fort Worth International Airport (p737) is 17 miles east of Fort Worth.

Buses and trains in Fort Worth share the **Intermodal Transportation Center** (1001 Jones St), easing transfers.

The **Amtrak** (☑ 800-872-7245; www.amtrak.com; 1001 Jones St) *Texas Eagle* stops in Fort Worth en route to San Antonio and Chicago. The *Heartland Flyer* serves Oklahoma City.

Trinity Railway Express (p737) trains run between Fort Worth and Dallas Union Station (one hour), with a stop at CenterPort/DFW Airport where there is a shuttle-bus connection to the airport.

Several **Greyhound** (www.greyhound.com; 1001 Jones St) buses a day make the trip ($8 to $10, 45 minutes to one hour) from downtown Fort Worth to Dallas. There's also service to other major Texas cities.

WEST TEXAS

Welcome to the land of wide open spaces. Along I-10 there's not much to look at – just scrub brush and lots of sky – but dip below the interstate and you'll find vistas that are as captivating as they are endless. Sometimes the rugged terrain looks like the backdrop in an old Western movie; other times it looks like an alien landscape, with huge rock formations jutting suddenly out of the desert.

But what is there to do? Plenty. Exploring an enormous national park that's nearly the size of Rhode Island. Stopping in small towns that will surprise you with minimalist art, planet-watching parties or fascinating ghost-town ruins. Checking out the new microbreweries in a reenergized El Paso. Chatting with friendly locals whenever the mood strikes you. And letting the delicious slowness of west Texas get thoroughly under your skin.

Big Bend National Park

Everyone knows Texas is huge. But you can't really appreciate just how big it is until you visit this **national park** (www.nps.gov/bibe; 7-day pass per vehicle $25), which is almost the same size as Rhode Island. When you're traversing Big Bend's 1252 sq miles, you come to appreciate what 'big' really means. It's a land of incredible diversity, vast enough to allow a lifetime of discovery, yet laced with enough well-placed roads and trails to permit short-term visitors to see a lot in two to three days.

Big Bend has one area – the Chisos Basin – that absorbs the overwhelming crunch of traffic. The **Chisos Mountains** are beautiful, and no trip here would be complete without an excursion into the high country. But any visit to Big Bend should also include time in the **Chihuahuan Desert**, home to curious creatures and adaptable plants, and along the **Rio Grande**, a watery border between the US and Mexico.

Park headquarters and the **main visitor center** (432-477-1158; 9am-5pm) are at Panther Junction, which is on the main road 29 miles south of the Persimmon Gap entrance and 22 miles east of the Maverick entrance (near Study Butte). A **gas station** (432-477-2294; Panther Junction; convenience store 7am-6:30pm May-Sep, 8am-5:30pm Jun-Aug, pumps 24hr) here offers fuel, repairs and a small stock of snacks and beverages.

From Panther Junction, it's a (relatively) short 10-mile drive to the Chisos Basin. Sharp curves and steep grades make Chisos Basin Rd unsuitable for recreational vehicles longer than 24ft and trailers longer than 20ft.

Another major road leads 20 miles southeast to Rio Grande Village, where you can find the only other **fuel pumps** (432-477-2293; Rio Grande Village; 8am-7pm Oct-May, to 5pm Jun-Sep) within the park (good to know because you're a long way from anywhere).

The other principal road, the 30-mile Ross Maxwell Scenic Dr, takes off from the main park road west of Panther Junction.

Activities

Big Bend's primitive backpacking routes range from well-traveled desert washes to the truly challenging limestone uplifts of Mesa de Anguila and the Dead Horse Mountains. Rangers say that because of the constantly changing trail and spring conditions, it's pretty much impossible to plan an extended backpacking trip before you actually get to the park. What you can do instead is figure out how much time you have and the distance you'd like to cover – based on that information, park staff will help you plot a trip. Many trails require use of topographical maps and a compass.

Backcountry camping requires a permit ($12). In the Chisos Mountains, 42 designated campsites are available along various trails. Open-zone camping is available outside the mountain area. Pick your zone and find your ideal spot; just stay at least a half-mile from a road and 100yd from trails, historic and archaeological sites, dry creek beds, springs and cliff edges.

With more than 150 miles of trails to explore, it's no wonder hiking is big in Big Bend. There are countless trails and many popular hikes; get specifics from any of the visitor centers.

★ Lost Mine Trail   HIKING

(www.nps.gov/bibe; Chisos Basin Rd) On this Chisos Mountains hike, it's all about the views – which, as you climb over 1000ft in elevation, get better and better. You'll be right up there with **Casa Grande**, **Lost Mine Peak** and, from the highest point, the **Sierra del Carmen**. When you think you've reached the final summit, keep going – the trail's end is a big-whoa drop.

It's 4.8 miles round-trip, but you can get a partial payoff by catching the views from a ridge top about a mile from the trailhead.

Santa Elena Canyon Trail   HIKING

(www.nps.gov/bibe) A hike on this riverside trail is a must if you don't have time to float the Rio Grande. The 1.7-mile round-trip trek from the end of Ross Maxwell Scenic Dr takes hikers upriver into the amazingly steep, narrow Santa Elena Canyon. The trail crosses Terlingua Creek near its start, so bring some old shoes in case you need to wade.

Sleeping

Tent campers or smaller RVs that don't require hookups can use the three main campgrounds; some take reservations but some are first-come, first-served. Sites typically fill up during spring break, Thanksgiving and Christmas. There are also primitive roadside campsites in the backcountry.

There are only three pet-friendly rooms in the Chisos Mountain Lodge complex, and they are found in the cottages, which book out two years in advance.

Chisos Basin Campground CAMPGROUND **$**
(☑ 877-444-6777; www.nps.gov/bibe; tent & RV sites $14) The most centrally located of the main campgrounds, this 60-site place has stone shelters and picnic tables, with bathroom facilities nearby. It's located right near the **Chisos Lodge Restaurant** (Lodge Dining Room; www.chisosmountainlodge. com; Chisos Mountain Lodge; lunch $7-12, dinner $10-22; ☺ 7-10am, 11am-4pm & 5-8pm) and the **Basin Store** (☑ 432-477-2291; ☺ 7am-9pm), as well as several popular trails. Twenty-six sites are available for advance reservations from November 15 through May at www. recreation.gov; the rest are first-come, first-served.

Chisos Mountain Lodge MOTEL **$$**
(☑ 432-477-2291, 877-386-4383; www.chisos mountainslodge.com; lodge & motel r $147-151, cottages $166; [P][❄][🔊]) Run by concession-aire Forever Resorts, the four lodging options in Chisos Basin (collectively known as the Chisos Mountain Lodge) get good, if not great, marks. You can do better if you stay outside the national park, but the scenery here is a lot better, and it's nice to not have to drive 45 minutes to rest after your hike.

❶ Information

In addition to the park headquarters and visitor center at Panther Junction, visitor centers are found in **Chisos Basin** (☑ 432-477-2264; www. nps.gov/bibe; ☺ 8:30am-noon & 1-4pm) and at **Persimmon Gap** (☑ 432-477-2393; www.nps. gov/bibe; ☺ 9-11:30am & 12:30-4pm). There are also seasonal visitor centers open November through April at **Castolon** (☑ 432-477-2222; www.nps.gov/bibe; ☺ 10am-noon & 1-4pm Nov-Apr) and the **Rio Grande Village** (☑ 432-477-2271; www.nps.gov/bibe; ☺ 8:30am-4pm Nov-Apr).

Find out how to make the most of your visit from park rangers, and check bulletin boards for a list of upcoming interpretive activities. You'll also find a variety of free leaflets on special-in-terest topics, including biological diversity, hiking and backpacking, geology, archaeology and dinosaurs.

❶ Dangers & Annoyances

Big Bend National Park is one of the most remote spots in North America, set amid wild country with all kinds of potential hazards. It's not an inherently dangerous place, but you should take precautions.

➜ Don't underestimate the heat; this is the desert, after all. Drink lots of water, and take plenty with you when you hike.

➜ To protect against sunburn, wear a hat, sunscreen, long pants and a long-sleeved shirt.

➜ Do your hiking early in the morning or in the evening, not at midday when the unrelenting sun turns Big Bend into one giant oven.

➜ The poisonous snakes and tarantulas here won't attack unless provoked. Simple rule of thumb? Don't provoke them. Most snakes keep a low profile in daylight, when you're unlikely to see them. Night hikers should stay on the trail and carry a flashlight.

➜ Big Bend's scorpions are not deadly, but you should still get prompt attention if you're stung. Shake out boots or shoes before putting them on.

❶ Getting There & Around

There is no public transportation to, from or within the park. The closest buses and trains run through Alpine, 108 miles northwest of Panther Junction. The nearest major airports are 230 miles northeast in Midland and 325 miles northwest in El Paso (p743).

You'll find gas at the service stations at Panther Junction and Rio Grande Village.

Please note that the border patrol has checkpoints for vehicles coming from Big Bend. If you're not a US citizen, presenting your passport will help avoid delays (ie prove you're not coming from Mexico).

Big Bend Ranch State Park

The 486-sq-mile **Big Bend Ranch State Park** (☑ 432-358-4444; http://tpwd.texas.gov; off Rte 170; adult Nov-Apr/May-Oct $5/3, child under 13yr free) sprawls across the desert between Lajitas and Presidio, reaching north from the Rio Grande into some of the wildest country in North America. As massive as it is, this former ranch is one of the best-kept secrets in Big Bend country. It's full of notable features, most prominently the **Solitario**, a geological formation that sprang up 36 million years ago in a volcanic explosion. The resulting caldera measures 8 miles east to west and 9 miles north to south.

The scenic River Road ribbons across the park beside the Rio Grande on FM 170. Short hiking trails between FM 170 and the river work well for day-trippers who want to stretch their legs and explore a bit of the striking scenery. Rugged hiking and mountain-biking trails crisscross the backcountry. Since the park has few facilities and few visitors, you should come prepared. If you're headed into the backcountry, bring a good map, spare tires, a full tank of gas, a gallon of water per day per person, sunscreen, a hat, mosquito repellent and a well-stocked first-aid kit.

No-frills camping ($5) is available in the backcountry, where there are no designated campsites. You'll find vehicle-accessible sites ($8), with picnic tables, fire pits and pit toilets at the four campgrounds along FM 170. There are also vehicle-accessible sites in the interior of the park. All camping requires reservations (☑ 512-389-8919) and a permit.

To best explore the region, you'll need a car. The **Barton Warnock Visitor Center** (☑ 432-424-3327; http://tpwd.texas.gov; FM 170; adult Nov-Apr/May-Oct $5/3, child under 13yr free; ☺8am-4:30pm), at the east end of the park, is 95 miles south of Alpine. The western entrance, at Fort Leaton State Historic Park, is 63 miles south of Marfa.

A scenic and highly recommended **loop drive** takes in Alpine, Terlingua, River Road/FM 170 through the park, and Marfa. River Road/FM170 stretches 27 miles between Barton Warnock and Fort Leaton.

Central West Texas

The small towns of west Texas have become more than just the gateway to Big Bend National Park. Fort Davis, Marfa, Alpine and Marathon have a sprawling, easy-going charm and plenty of ways to keep a road-tripper entertained. Art enthusiasts will enjoy the galleries and museums in Marfa, while outdoor adventurers can hike and camp in the Davis Mountains, where stargazing at McDonald Observatory is highly recommended. And if you're fond of quirky sights, bars and lodging, well, this region has got you covered. From mystery lights to a white-buffalo bar to tipis, it's all just a bit offbeat.

Fort Davis

More than 5000ft above sea level, Fort Davis has an altitudinal advantage over the rest of Texas, both in terms of elevation and the cooler weather it offers. That makes it a popular oasis during the summer, when west Texans head toward the mountains to escape the searing desert heat. The area is part of both the Chihuahuan Desert and the Davis Mountains, giving it a unique setting where wide-open spaces are suddenly pierced by rock formations springing from the earth.

As for the town itself, it sprang up near the actual fort of the same name, built in 1854 to protect the pioneers and gold rushers who were heading out west from the attacks of Comanche and Apache warriors. The town retains an Old West feel befitting its history.

◉ Sights & Activities

★ **McDonald Observatory** OBSERVATORY (☑ 432-426-3640; www.mcdonaldobservatory.org; 3640 Dark Sky Dr; day pass adult/child 6-12yr/under 6yr $8/7/free; ☺ visitor center 10am-5:30pm; 🖐) Free from the light pollution of big cities, the middle of west Texas has some of the clearest and darkest skies in North America, making it the perfect spot for an observatory. Some of the world's biggest telescopes are here, perched on the peak of **Mt Locke** (6791ft) and so enormous you can spot them from miles away. The popular star parties help you see the night sky in a whole new way.

Davis Mountains State Park STATE PARK, VIEWPOINT (☑ 432-426-3337; www.tpwd.state.tx.us; Hwy 118; adult/child under 13yr $6/free) The majestic sunrises and sunsets at this remote park rival any we've seen – and we've seen plenty. This wonderful place is just a few miles northwest of Fort Davis on Hwy 118, set amid the most extensive mountain range in Texas. Hiking, mountain biking, horseback riding (BYO horse) and stargazing are all big attractions here, as is bird-watching. (You can pick up a bird checklist from park headquarters).

Fort Davis National Historic Site HISTORIC SITE (☑ 432-426-3224; www.nps.gov/foda; Hwy 17; adult/child under 16yr $7/free; ☺ 8am-5pm; 🖐) A remarkably well-preserved frontier military post with an impressive backdrop at the foot of Sleeping Lion Mountain, Fort Davis was established in 1854 and abandoned in 1891. More than 20 buildings remain – five of them restored with period furnishings – as well as 100 or so ruins.

Balmorhea State Park   SWIMMING
(☑ 432-375-2370; www.tpwd.texas.gov; Hwy 17; adult/child under 13yr $7/free; ☺ 8am-7:30pm or sunset) Swimming, scuba diving and snorkeling are the attractions at this 46-acre park, a true oasis in the west Texas desert. The 25ft-deep swimming pool covers 1.75 acres – it's the largest spring-fed swimming facility in the US – and it's about 75°F year-round. The park closes at 7:30pm or at sunset, whichever comes earlier.

🛏 Sleeping & Eating

Local liquor laws mean you can't order an adult beverage with your dinner, but almost every place in town is cheerfully Bring Your Own Bottle (BYOB), with the exception of the **Black Bear Restaurant** (☑ 432-477-2291; www.tpwd.texas.gov; 16453 Park Rd 3, Indian Lodge; breakfast & lunch $7-12; ☺ 7am-2pm Wed-Sun), where it's forbidden. The **Blue Mountain Bistro** (☑ 432-426-3244; www.blue-mountain-bistro.com; 101 Memorial Sq; mains $12-32; ☺ 5-8pm Sun-Tue, to 9pm Fri & Sat, 7:30-10am Sat & Sun) is the only option here with a full bar.

Stone Village Tourist Camp   MOTEL **$**
(☑ 432-426-3941; www.stonevillagetouristcamp.com; 509 N State St; camp r $39, motel r $78-108, ste $108; ☑ 🖥 🐾) This renovated motel is a fun little bargain. The 14 regular rooms are cheery and comfortable, and the six camp rooms are perfect for the budget traveler. Located in the former garages, they have concrete floors, stone walls, a roof, electricity, a sink and even wi-fi. The only catch? One end of the room has a screen and privacy curtain instead of a wall.

★**Indian Lodge**   INN **$$**
(☑ lodge 432-426-3254, reservations 512-389-8982; www.tpwd.texas.gov; Hwy 118; r $95-125, ste 135-$150; ☑ 🖨 🖥 🐾) Located inside Davis Mountains State Park, this historic, 39-room inn is actually its own separate state park. Built by the Civilian Conservation Corps in the 1930s, it has 18in-thick adobe walls, hand-carved cedar furniture and ceilings of pine viga and *latilla* (decorative wood slats) that give it the look of a Southwestern pueblo – that is, one with a swimming pool and gift shop. Reserve early.

Stone Village Market   MARKET, SANDWICHES **$**
(☑ 432-426-2226; www.stonevillagetouristcamp.com; 509 N State St; sandwiches $5-6; ☺ 7am-7pm; 🖥) Looking for the perfect sandwich for your sunset picnic? Then step up to the

deli counter at this welcoming market for the touted cranberry-almond chicken salad. There are plenty of snacks and drinks in the surrounding market to round out your meal.

ℹ Getting There & Away

No regularly scheduled public transportation serves Fort Davis or the Davis Mountains. From El Paso and San Antonio you can get to nearby Alpine (24 miles away) by train or bus, then rent a car.

The closest airports are **Midland International Airport** (about 160 miles away) and **El Paso International Airport** (ELP; ☑ 915-212-0330; www.elpasointernationalairport.com; 6701 Convair Rd; 🖥), 194 miles away.

Marfa

The New York art scene collides with west Texas cowboy culture and Border Patrol formality in tiny, dusty Marfa, where the factions seem to coexist without conflict as they go about their lives. Maybe it's the mysterious Marfa Mystery Lights that keep the vibe more quirky than antagonistic.

Founded in the 1880s, Marfa's two major cultural hallmarks date from the latter part of the 20th century. Its first taste of fame came when Rock Hudson, Elizabeth Taylor and James Dean arrived to film the 1956 film *Giant;* it's since served as a film location for *There Will Be Blood* and *No Country for Old Men.*

As for those New Yorkers: Marfa is a pilgrimage destination for art-lovers, thanks to one of the world's largest installations of minimalist art, which has attracted galleries, quirky lodging options and interesting restaurants. The US Border Patrol has a headquarters here and has noticeably expanded its presence in recent years.

◎ Sights

★**Chinati Foundation Museum**   MUSEUM
(☑ 432-729-4362; www.chinati.org; 1 Calvary Row; adult/student Full Collection Tour $25/10, Selections Tour $20/10; ☺ by guided tour 10am & 2pm Wed-Sun) As you step inside the historic artillery shed, with its enormous windows, sweeping desert views and sun-dappled aluminum boxes, the Marfa hoopla suddenly makes sense. Artist Donald Judd single-handedly put Marfa on the art-world map when he created this museum on the site of a former army post. The grounds and abandoned buildings now house one of the world's largest permanent installations of

WHAT THE...? PRADA & TARGET IN MARFA.

So you're driving along a two-lane highway in dusty west Texas – out in the middle of *nowhere* – when suddenly a small building appears in the distance like a mirage. As you zip past it you glance over and see...a Prada store? Known as the Prada Marfa (although it's really closer to Valentine), this art installation from the Ballroom Marfa folks doesn't sell $1700 handbags, but it does get your attention as a tongue-in-cheek comment on consumerism.

To the east, on Hwy 90 between Alpine and Marathon, the new **Target Marathon** (Hwy 90), a guerrilla art installation that appeared in 2016, seems to be taking a jab at Prada Marfa. What's next? Let us know if you spot anything.

minimalist art. The whole place is an immersive, breathtaking blend of art, architecture and landscape.

Marfa Mystery
Lights Viewing Area   VIEWPOINT
(Hwy 90) Ghost lights, mystery lights...call them what you want, but the Marfa Lights that flicker beneath the Chinati Mountains have captured the imagination of many a traveler over the decades. On many nights, the mystery seems to be whether you're actually just seeing car headlights in the distance. Try your luck at this viewing area about 9 miles east of Marfa on Hwy 90/67.

Ballroom Marfa   GALLERY
(☑432-729-3600; www.ballroommarfa.org; 108 E San Antonio St; suggested donation $5; ☺10am-6pm Wed-Sat, to 3pm Sun) FREE Be sure to find out what's happening at Ballroom Marfa, a nonprofit art space located in a former dance hall. The focus is on offbeat, interesting projects, including film installations and excellent monthly concerts.

🛏 Sleeping

⭐ **El Cosmico**   CAMPGROUND $
(☑432-729-1950; www.elcosmico.com; 802 S Highland Ave; tent sites per person $30, safari tents $95, tipis & yurts $165, trailers $165-210; P ⓟ🐾) One of the funkiest choices in all of Texas, where you can sleep in a stylishly converted travel trailer, tipi, safari tent or even a yurt. It's not for everyone: the grounds are dry and dusty, you might have to shower outdoors, and there's no air-conditioning (luckily, it's cool at night). But when else can you sleep in a tipi?

⭐ **Hotel St George**   BOUTIQUE HOTEL $$$
(☑432-729-3700; www.marfasaintgeorge.com; 105 S Highland Ave; r from $260; ❄@🐾) In a town with a thing for minimalist cubes, this

one is our favorite. The design-minded digs, which opened in 2016, are the brainchild of local resident and Chinati Foundation board member Tim Crowley. Details and decor reflect fine artisanship, regional history and Marfa-sourced creativity, from the eye-catching art to the spare but inviting **Marfa Book Company** (☑432-729-3700; www.marfa bookco.com; 105 S Highland Ave; ☺9am-8pm), which relocated here.

🍴 Eating & Drinking

Food Shark   FOOD TRUCK $
(www.foodsharkmarfa.com; 909 W San Antonio St; mains $6-9; ☺noon-3pm Fri-Sun) See that battered old food trailer near the main road through town? If you do, that means Food Shark is open for business. If you're lucky enough to catch it, you'll find incredibly fresh Greek salad and the specialty, the Marfalafel. Daily specials are excellent, and sell out early.

Cochineal   AMERICAN $$$
(☑432-729-3300; www.cochinealmarfa.com; 107 W San Antonio St; small plates $9-12, mains $22-42; ☺5:30-10pm) Foodies flock to this stylish but minimalist eatery (with outdoor courtyard) for a changing menu that showcases high-quality organic ingredients. Portions are generous, so don't be afraid to share a few small plates – maybe along the lines of brisket tacos, oyster-mushroom risotto or house-made ramen with duck breast – in lieu of a full dinner. Reservations are recommended.

Planet Marfa   BAR
(☑432-386-5099; 200 S Abbott St; ☺2pm-midnight Fri & Sun, to 1am Sun mid-Mar–Nov) Marfa-style nightlife is epitomized in this wonderfully funky open-air bar that's officially open on weekends from spring break to Thanksgiving. There's usually live music at night, and shelters are scattered about to protect you from the elements. If you're lucky, someone will save you a spot inside the tipi.

ℹ Information

Marfa Visitors Center (☏ 432-729-4772; www.visitmarfa.com; 302 S Highland Ave; ◷8am-5pm Mon-Fri, 10am-4pm Sat & Sun except event weekends) Lots of great information on galleries, restaurants and local attractions. The restaurant handout, with detailed opening hours for all the eateries in town, is super helpful, especially if you're visiting during the off-season, or on a Monday or Tuesday.

ℹ Getting There & Away

There's an airport in Marfa, but you can't catch a flight there unless you actually charter one. The closest commercial airports are 156 miles away at Midland and 190 miles away at El Paso.

You can, however, catch a Greyhound. The **bus station** (☏ 432-729-1992; 1412 Berlin St) is on Berlin St, just west of downtown. For train service, Amtrak serves nearby Alpine (26 miles away).

Alpine

Packed tight with hotels and eateries, plus residents who are pretty darn friendly, Alpine works well as a base camp for regional exploring. Centrally located between Fort Davis, Marfa and Marathon, Alpine is about a half-hour drive from any of them. And it's not just a geographical hub: it's the seat of Brewster County and the biggest of the four towns, offering services and amenities the others don't.

As the only city in the area with more than 5000 people, it also has the area's sole four-year college and its only modern hospital. Plus it serves as a transportation center, with Amtrak and Greyhound stations in the heart of downtown.

Hwy 90 through downtown splits into two one-way thoroughfares. Avenue E rolls west while traffic on Holland Ave runs east.

◎ Sights

Museum of the Big Bend   MUSEUM
(☏ 432-837-8143; www.museumofthebigbend.com; 400 N Harrison St; donations accepted; ◷9am-5pm Tue-Sat, 1-5pm Sun) FREE On the campus of Sul Ross State University, this little museum is a great place to delve into the past, with exhibits on marine fossils (a warm shallow sea covered Big Bend 135 million years ago), Native American pictographs, Spanish missionaries, Mexican pioneers, buffalo soldiers (the nickname for the African American soldiers who fought in the Civil War) and – of course – cowboys, with a full-scale chuck wagon on display.

Hancock Hill   VIEWPOINT
(E Ave B) Behind Sul Ross State University, a trail leads up the dusty slopes of Hancock Hill. There are fine views of the area and some curious artifacts here – including a battered school desk that some uni students dragged up in 1981. To reach it, head uphill to the first rock pile and follow the trail to the right; it's about a 20-minute walk. For more information and directions, visit www.sulross.edu/page/1077/desk.

🛏 Sleeping & Eating

Antelope Lodge   CABIN $
(☏ 432-837-2451; www.antelopelodge.com; 2310 W Hwy 90; s $53-75, d $58-80, ste $105-130; ℗⚹ 🛜🐾) You'd think from the name you were getting a hunting lodge, but it's nothing like that. Rustic stucco cottages with Spanish-tile roofs – each one holding two guest rooms – sit sprinkled about a shady lawn. There's a casual, pleasant vibe, and the rooms have kitchenettes.

Ask the geologically minded owner about her **guided rock hunts** (☏ 432-837-2451; www.terismithrockhunts.com).

★ Holland Hotel   HISTORIC HOTEL $$
(☏ 432-837-2800; www.thehollandhoteltexas.com; 209 W Holland Ave; r $150-225, ste $170-250; ⊖⚹🛜🐾) Built in 1928, this beautifully renovated Spanish Colonial building has elegantly furnished rooms set with carved wood furniture, Western-style artwork and sleek modern bathrooms. The lobby, with its stuffed leather chairs and wood-beamed ceiling, is a classy place to unwind; there's a good high-end restaurant, the Century Bar & Grill, attached. Solo traveler on a budget? Try the tiny 'Nina's Room' ($95).

Alicia's Burrito Place   MEXICAN $
(☏ 432-837-2802; 708 E Gallego Ave; mains $5-12; ◷9am-3pm Mon, 8am-3pm Tue-Sun) Alicia's is known for its quick and hot breakfast burritos: eggs, bacon and the like get rolled up in a portable meal you can eat with your hands – known to cure a hangover or two in their time. The Mexican cheeseburger is also a favorite. Drive-through service is available. Cash only.

Reata   STEAK $$
(☏ 432-837-9232; www.reata.net; 203 N 5th St; lunch $10-15, dinner $13-40; ◷11:30am-2pm & 5-10pm Mon-Sat) Named after the ranch in the movie *Giant*, Reata turns on the upscale ranch-style charm – at least in the

front dining room, where the serious diners go. Step back into the lively bar area or onto the shady patio for a completely different vibe, where you can feel free to nibble your way around the menu and enjoy a margarita.

Drinking & Entertainment

Big Bend Brewing Co   MICROBREWERY
(☑ 432-837-3700; www.bigbendbrewing.com; 3401 W Hwy 90; ☺ tap room 4-6pm Wed-Fri, 1-6pm Sat) The taproom is bare bones at this microbrewery on the outskirts of town, but with picnic tables inside and out, chatty beer drinkers all around and wide-open views of the western landscape, you'll hardly notice the lack of frills. Its flagship Tejas lager is an easy-drinking end to your epic afternoon.

Railroad Blues   LIVE MUSIC
(☑ 432-837-3103; www.railroadblues.com; 504 W Holland Ave; ☺ 4pm-2am Mon-Sat) This is the place to go in Alpine for live music and the biggest beer selection in Big Bend Country. The club has hosted an impressive list of musicians, and sometimes draws Austin-based bands heading west on tour. If you'd rather just enjoy some friendly conversation, hit up happy hour (4pm to 7pm).

Information

Alpine Chamber of Commerce (☑ 432-837-2326; www.alpinetexas.com; 106 N 3rd St; ☺ 9am-5pm Mon-Fri, to 2pm Sat) Offers a *Historic Walking Tour* brochure featuring 44 stops in the downtown area.

Getting There & Away

There are no scheduled flights round these parts, but Alpine's airport, north of town along Hwy 118, can accommodate charter flights.

Greyhound (☑ 432-837-5497; www.greyhound.com; KCS Quick Stop, 2305 E Hwy 90; ☺ 6am-10pm) offers bus service to and from El Paso and San Antonio, with a transfer in Fort Stockton. Buy tickets online or at the convenience store where the bus stops.

Rental cars are available from **Alpine Auto Rental** (☑ 432-837-3463; www.alpineautorental.com; 2501 E Hwy 90; ☺ 8am-6pm Mon-Sat).

Amtrak's *Texas Eagle* and *Sunset Limited* routes stop at the **train station** (☑ 800-872-7245; www.amtrak.com; 102 W Holland Ave). Service frequently runs late, so it's important to call Amtrak to get an update before setting out. Check the website for prices and schedules.

El Paso

El Paso has found its cool. Long considered a sleepy western town (it's as far west as you can get in Texas), El Paso moseyed along, keeping its head low while dangerous Ciudad Juarez (just over the Rio Grande) grabbed headlines to the south and New Mexico grabbed tourists to the north. But no more.

A sleek new hotel has opened downtown, luring locals back to the city's core for socializing and dining. A streetcar line linking downtown and the University of Texas at El Paso (UTEP) is under construction. The new Montecillo entertainment and residential district to the west is booming. The city even has a new baseball team, the El Paso Chihuahuas. And the ultimate arbiter of cool? The city's first microbrewery opened in 2015.

Outdoorsy types have it made here: there's cycling and hiking in the largest urban park in the US, and the nearby Hueco Tanks State Park (p748) is ideal for wintertime rock climbing. Prefer the indoors? The city's top museums are free. Best of all is the hospitality of the locals, which makes this city of nearly 700,000 feel a whole lot smaller.

Sights & Activities

El Paso covers 240 sq miles, but much of that space is taken up by Fort Bliss and the enormous Franklin Mountains State Park. The Franklin Mountains divide the city into a west side and an east side, with downtown sitting due south of the mountains, and the I-10 serving as the primary through-route. Just south of downtown is the Rio Grande and, across the river, Juárez, Mexico.

★ **El Paso Museum of Art**   MUSEUM
(☑ 915-212-0300; www.elpasoartmuseum.org; 1 Arts Festival Plaza; ☺ 9am-5pm Tue-Sat, to 9pm Thu, noon-5pm Sun) FREE This thoroughly enjoyable museum is in a former Greyhound station. They'd want us to brag about their Italian *Madonna and Child* (c 1200), but the Southwestern art is terrific, and the engaging modern pieces round out the collection nicely. All this *and* it's free? Well done, El Paso, well done.

El Paso Holocaust Museum   MUSEUM
(☑ 915-351-0048; www.elpasoholocaustmuseum.org; 715 N Oregon St; ☺ 9am-5pm Tue-Fri, 1-5pm Sat & Sun) FREE It may seem a little incongruous in a predominately Hispanic town,

but the Holocaust Museum is as much a surprise inside as out for its thoughtful and moving exhibits, which are imaginatively presented for maximum impact.

Franklin Mountains State Park   PARK

(915-566-6441; www.tpwd.texas.gov; 1331 McKelligon Canyon Rd; adult/child under 13yr $5/free; visitor center 8am-4pm Mon-Fri, Tom Mays Unit 8am-5pm May–mid-Sep, 8am-5pm Mon-Fri, 6:30am-8pm Sat & Sun Apr–mid-Sep) At over 24,000 acres, this is the largest urban park in the US. It's a quick escape from the city to the home of ringtail cats, coyotes and countless other smaller animals and reptiles. There's excellent mountain biking and hiking here, with **North Franklin Peak** (7192ft) looming overhead.

Mission Ysleta   HISTORIC BUILDING

(915-859-9848; www.ysletamission.org; 131 S Zaragoza Rd; 7am-4pm Mon-Sat) **FREE** The parish here is the state's oldest continually active congregation, tracing back to 1680. It was established for Spanish refugees and Tigua Indians fleeing New Mexico after the Pueblo Indian revolt. The original mission on the site was built by the Tigua tribe in 1682; the adobe-brick mission you see today was built in the mid-1800s. The silver-domed **bell tower** was added a few decades later.

Wyler Aerial Tramway   CABLE CAR, VIEWPOINT

(915-566-6622; www.tpwd.texas.gov; 1700 McKinley Ave; adult/child under 13yr $8/4; noon-7pm Fri & Sat, 10am-5pm Sun) Sure, you'd feel a sense of accomplishment if you hiked to the top of the Franklin Mountains. We're not suggesting you take the easy way out (or are we?), but it only takes about four minutes to the top via this gondola system. After gliding 2600ft and gaining 940ft in elevation, you'll reach the viewing platform on top of **Ranger Peak** (5632ft), where you'll enjoy spectacular views of Texas, New Mexico and Mexico.

National Border Patrol Museum   MUSEUM

(915-759-6060; www.borderpatrolmuseum.com; 4315 Transmountain Rd; 9am-5pm Tue-Sat) **FREE** This small but informative museum spotlights the history and activities of the US Border Patrol, which was originally funded in 1924, three days after Congress passed the *National Origins Act,* a law that severely limited immigration based on country-of-origin quotas. The collection of tools and vehicles used to cross the border and elude capture is fascinating, from ladders to boats to motorized hanggliders.

🛏️ Sleeping & Eating

Gardner Hotel   HOTEL, HOSTEL $

(915-532-3661; www.gardnerhotel.com; 311 E Franklin Ave; r $63-70; 🕾) Fresh from a makeover on *Hotel Impossible* in 2016, El Paso's oldest continually operating hotel has a newfound cool. But don't worry history fans, it probably hasn't changed too much since John Dillinger stayed here in the 1930s (hint: room 221 is where the outlaw slept).

Hotel Indigo   BOUTIQUE HOTEL $$

(915-532-5200; www.ihg.com; 325 N Kansas St; r from $196; P❄@🛜🐕🏊) Downtown El Paso has a new spring in its step, thanks in part to this 2016 hotel. From young business travelers passing through to locals sipping cocktails in the glossy bar, the Indigo has become a destination itself. Modern but inviting rooms start above the 5th floor – home to the lobby, the bar and the pool – so views are big.

★ L&J Cafe   MEXICAN $

(915-566-8418; www.landjcafe.com; 3622 E Missouri Ave; mains $8-11; 9am-9pm Sun-Wed, to 10pm Thu-Sat) One of El Paso's best-loved Mexican joints, L&J serves up delicious tacos, fajitas and famous green-chile chicken enchiladas – plus a legendary menudo (tripe stew) on weekends. It's next to the historic Concordia cemetery, and at first glance looks a bit divey. Don't be deterred: it's been open since 1927, and the inside is much more inviting.

★ Crave Kitchen & Bar   AMERICAN $$

(915-351-3677; www.cravekitchenandbar.com; 300 Cincinnati Ave; breakfast mains $8-18, lunch & dinner $9-28; 7am-11pm Mon-Sat, to 6pm Sun) Winning extra points for style – from the cool sign to the cutlery hanging from the ceiling – this hip little eatery serves up creative comfort food: green-chile mac 'n' cheese, juicy burgers with sweet-potato waffle fries and decadent breakfasts. Lots of craft-beer choices on the menu too. There are several locations across town, including one on the **east side** (915-594-7971; 11990 Rojas Dr; breakfast mains $8-18, lunch & dinner $9-28; 7am-11pm Mon-Sat, to 6pm Sun).

Green Ingredient   VEGETARIAN $$

(915-298-1010; www.greeningredienteatery.com; 201 E Main St; breakfast & lunch mains $7-19, dinner $9-19; 8am-4pm Mon-Thu, to 8pm Fri) 🌿 Yes, you can find quality vegan and vegetarian fare in the land of cowboys and beef. You just have to walk into the depths of a

HUECO TANKS STATE HISTORICAL PARK

About 32 miles east of El Paso, 860-acre **Hueco Tanks State Park & Historical Site** (park 915-857-1135, reservations 512-389-8911; www.tpwd.texas.gov; 6900 Hueco Tanks Rd No 1/FM 2775; adult/child under 13yr $7/free; 8am-6pm Mon-Thu, 7am-7pm Fri-Sun May-Sep, 8am-6pm Oct-Apr) contains three small granite mountains that are pocked with depressions (*hueco* is Spanish for 'hollow') that hold rainwater, creating an oasis in the barren desert. The area has attracted humans for as long as 10,000 years, as evidenced by a chipped stone spear point found at the site. Park staff estimate there are more than 2000 **pictographs** here, some dating back 5000 years.

downtown bank building to find it. Step inside this small but airy place for pancakes and omelets in the morning, salads and sandwiches at lunch and smoothies all day.

★ **Cattleman's Steakhouse** STEAK $$$
(915-544-3200; www.cattlemansranch.com; Indian Cliffs Ranch; mains $30-50; 5-10pm Mon-Fri, 12:30-10pm Sat, 12:30-9pm Sun;) This place is 20 miles east of the city, but local folks would drive 200 miles to eat here – the food is good and the scenery is even better. Portions are huge, and for just $6 extra you can share a main and gain full access to the family-style sides.

🍷 Drinking & Entertainment

★ **Hillside Coffee & Donut** COFFEE
(915-474-3453; www.facebook.com/Hillside Coffee; 4935 N Mesa St; 6am-10pm Sun-Wed, to midnight Thu-Sat) We don't know whether to recommend this place for the iced coffee, the gourmet doughnuts or the welcoming service. How about all three? If you're in west El Paso and need a jolt – from caffeine, sugar or a bright, buzzing locale – stop here. The barista's helpful friendliness almost made us cry, as if we'd encountered a unicorn or something.

Ode Brewing Co MICROBREWERY
(915-351-4377; www.odebrewingco.com; 3233 N Mesa St; 11am-11pm Sun-Wed, to midnight Thu-Sat) The craft-beer scene has been slow to ignite in El Paso, but with the opening of the

city's first three microbreweries – all since 2015 – we dare say the scene is on fire. Or maybe smoldering nicely? Ode was first on the scene and keeps drawing imbibers with its easy-drinking ales and lagers. The patio is darn nice too.

Briar Patch/Hyde Patio Bar GAY
(915-577-9555; www.facebook.com/BriaratHyde; 508 N Stanton St; 2pm-2am) You can keep your calendar full at this place: Trivia Mondays, Karaoke Tuesdays, Latin Thursdays and so much more. Don't miss the back patio: it's a nice spot to chill.

McKelligon Canyon Amphitheater LIVE PERFORMANCE
(McKelligon Canyon Rd) The **Viva El Paso!** (915-231-1165; www.viva-ep.org) musical plays here on Friday and Saturday nights, and a handful of Sundays, from June though August.

Abraham Chávez Theatre THEATER
(915-534-0609; www.elpasolive.com; 1 Civic Center Plaza) The sombrero-shaped Abraham Chávez Theatre is host to most of El Paso's major performing organizations – including **El Paso Symphony Orchestra** (915-532-3776; www.epso.org), **Showtime! El Paso** (915-544-2022; www.showtimeelpaso.com) and **El Paso Opera Company** (915-581-5534; www.epopera.org) – and many touring concerts and plays.

ℹ️ Information

El Paso Visitors Center (915-534-0661; www.visitelpaso.com; 400 W San Antonio St; 9am-4pm Mon-Fri, to 2pm Sat)
Franklin Mountains State Park Visitor Center (915-566-6441; www.tpwd.texas.gov; 1331 McKelligon Canyon Rd; 8am-4pm)
Mission Valley Visitors Information Center (http://visitelpasomissiontrail.com; 9065 Alameda Ave; 9am-4pm Mon-Fri, to 3pm Sat & Sun;) The website offers the history of the Mission Trail and a self-guided walking tour of San Elizario.

ℹ️ Dangers & Annoyances

El Paso is among the safest cities of its size in the US, thanks in part to Operation Hold the Line, an effort to crack down on illegal immigration. Green-and-white Border Patrol vehicles are highly visible all along the El Paso side of the Rio Grande, and the police presence has had the side effect of quelling crime.

Crossing over into Mexico is a different story. While El Paso is one of the safest cities, Juárez has become one of the most dangerous, due to gruesome violence – some of it random – resulting from drug wars. For now, just say no.

ℹ Getting There & Away

El Paso International Airport (ELP; ☎ 915-212-0330; www.elpasointernationalairport.com; 6701 Convair Rd; 🛜) is 8 miles northeast of downtown El Paso. It's accessible by bus, taxi and shuttles.

Southwest Airlines is the biggest carrier at El Paso International. Other airlines include American Airlines, Delta, United and Allegiant.

The terminal for **Greyhound** (☎ 915-532-5095; www.greyhound.com; 200 W San Antonio Ave) is four blocks from the center of downtown.

You can catch Amtrak at **Union Depot** (☎ 800-872-7245; www.amtrak.com; 700 W San Francisco Ave), which serves both the *Texas Eagle*, which runs from Los Angeles to Chicago with stops in San Antonio, Austin and Dallas, and the *Sunset Limited*, which runs from Los Angeles to New Orleans with stops in San Antonio and Houston. Check the website for fares and schedules.

Guadalupe Mountains National Park

We won't go so far as to call it Texas' best-kept secret, but even many Texans aren't aware of the **Guadalupe Mountains National Park** (☎ 915-828-3251; www.nps.gov/gumo; US Hwy 62/180; 7-day pass adult/child under 16yr $5/free; ⊙ visitor center 8am-4:30pm). It's just this side of the Texas–New Mexico state line and a long drive from practically everywhere in the state.

Despite its low profile, it's a Texas high spot, both literally and figuratively. At 8749ft, Guadalupe Peak is the highest point in the Lone Star State. The fall foliage in McKittrick Canyon is the best in west Texas, and more than half the park is a federally designated wilderness area.

The NPS has deliberately curbed development to keep the park wild. There are no restaurants or indoor accommodations and only a smattering of services and programs (so plan ahead to keep your gas tank full and your cooler stocked). There are also no paved roads within the park, so whatever you want to see, you're going to have to get there on foot. But the hiking and high-country splendor are top-notch.

Interpretive programs are held on summer evenings in the Pine Springs campground amphitheater, as well as several times a week during the spring. Topics depend on the rangers' interests, but they have included everything from stargazing to geology.

ℹ Information

Information, restrooms and drinking water are available at the **Pine Springs Visitor Center** (☎ 915-828-3251; www.nps.gov/gumo; ⊙ 8am-4:30pm). You'll also find water, restrooms and outdoor exhibits in McKittrick Canyon; the Dog Canyon Ranger Station has information, restrooms and water.

You can also visit the park website to download a map of the park before you visit.

ℹ Getting There & Away

Guadalupe Mountains National Park is on Hwy 62/180, 110 miles east of El Paso and 55 miles southwest of Carlsbad, NM. The closest gas stations are 35 miles in either direction on Hwy 62/180 and the closest services are in Whites City, NM, 45 minutes northeast of the park entrance on Hwy 62/180.

Rocky Mountains

Includes ➔

Colorado 754
Denver 754
Boulder 763
Wyoming 787
Cheyenne 787
Yellowstone
National Park 794
Grand Teton
National Park 799
Glacier
National Park 810
Idaho 812

Best Places to Eat

➔ Root Down (p757)

➔ Loula's (p809)

➔ Sweet Melissa's (p789)

➔ Acorn (p757)

➔ Frasca (p765)

Best Places to Sleep

➔ Curtis (p756)

➔ Nagle Warren Mansion Bed & Breakfast (p788)

➔ Old Faithful Inn (p799)

➔ Crawford Hotel (p756)

➔ Chautauqua Lodge & Cottages (p764)

Why Go?

Adventure has always defined the United States' backbone. Native tribes hunted in the Rocky Mountains, but few stayed. Most white settlers regarded the mountains as obstacles, not destinations. Only a few rugged individuals forayed into the wilderness to explore the hidden valleys and towering peaks – some never came back.

True, today's Rockies are dotted with civilization. And, yes, modern adventurers plan casual expeditions over microbrews and organic burgers. But these lands are far from tamed. Vast mountain ranges remain wild, largely thanks to the USA's brilliant public lands system.

You're likely familiar with the big ones: Yellowstone, Rocky Mountain, Grand Teton and Glacier National Parks, but over half of the total area of Colorado, Wyoming, Montana and Idaho is national forests, monuments and recreation areas, all open for everyone to enjoy. Welcome to America's playground, where there's still plenty of wild places to be wild in.

When to Go

Denver

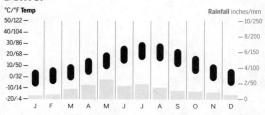

Jun–Aug Long days of sunshine for biking, hiking, farmers markets and summer festivals.

Sep & Oct Fall foliage coincides with terrific lodging deals and far fewer crowds.

Jan–Mar Snow-dusted peaks, powdery slopes and deluxe après-ski parties.

History

When French trappers and Spaniards 'discovered' the Rocky Mountains in the late 18th century, they found the area was already home to several tribes of Native Americans, including the Nez Percé, the Shoshone, the Crow, the Lakota and the Ute. This fact did not slow the European conquest, and countries began claiming, defending, buying and selling what they called 'unclaimed' territory.

A young US government purchased all lands east of the Continental Divide from France in the 1803 Louisiana Purchase. Shortly thereafter it dispatched Meriwether Lewis and William Clark to survey the area and see exactly what they had bought. Their epic survey covered nearly 8000 miles in two-and-a-half years, and tales of what they found urged on other adventurers, setting migration in motion.

Wagon trains voyaged to the Rockies and beyond right into the 20th century, only temporarily slowed by the completion of the Transcontinental Railroad across southern Wyoming in the late 1860s.

To accommodate settlers, the US purged the western frontier of the Spanish, British and, in a truly shameful era, most of the Native American population. The government signed endless treaties to defuse Native American objections to increasing settlement, but always reneged and shunted tribes onto smaller reservations. Gold-miners' incursions into Native American territory in Montana and the building of US Army forts along the Bozeman Trail ignited a series of wars with the Lakota, Cheyenne, Arapaho and others.

Gold and silver mania preceded Colorado's entry to statehood in 1876. Statehood soon followed for Montana (1889), Wyoming (1890) and Idaho (1890). Mining, grazing and timber played major roles in regional economic development, sparking growth in financial and industrial support. The miners, white farmers and ranchers controlled power in the late 19th century, but the boom-and-bust cycles of their industries coupled with unsustainable resource management took their toll on the landscape.

When the economy thrived post-WWII, national parks started attracting vacationers, and a heightened conservation movement flourished. Tourism became a leading industry in all four states, with the military a close second (particularly in Colorado).

Political shifts in recent years have placed many of the Rocky Mountain region's protected areas in jeopardy. Special interest groups continually lobby for increased resource extraction and development on federal lands, which may cut off access for the public.

Land & Climate

Extending from British Columbia, Canada, to northern New Mexico, the Rocky Mountains are North America's longest chain of mountains. Over 100 separate ranges make up the Rockies and most uplifted during the Laramide orogeny, when a chunk of oceanic crust took a shallow dive under the continental plate bumping along just under the surface of the earth. This movement forced the Rockies upwards, sideways and in some cases on top of itself – like at the Lewis Overthrust Fault in Glacier National Park where older rock, miles thick, was pushed some 50 miles (80km) across the top of younger rock. Over time, glaciers and erosion have worn the peaks down to their present form, revealing rock layers that betray their long and chaotic past.

The spring is largely a muddy time as the snow melts and deciduous trees begin to bud. It generally doesn't feel 'summery' in many regions of the mountains until late June. During the brief summer months (typically July through September) all the plants must get on with the business of reproduction at once, and high alpine meadows glow with the colors of the rainbow. All the humans must get on with the business of recreating during this time, too, and trails are flooded with bikers and backpackers – particularly in much of Colorado.

It can snow any time of year in the Rockies, though typically the first flurries fly in early October as the aspen leaves blanket the hillsides with shimmering gold. The days are warm, nights are cool and most of the crowds have gone back to school. This is possibly the best time to visit (but don't tell anyone).

ⓘ Getting There & Around

Denver has the only major international airport (p762) in the Rocky Mountains area. Both Denver and Colorado Springs offer flights on smaller planes to Jackson, WY; Boise, ID; Bozeman, MT; Aspen, CO; and other destinations. Salt Lake City, UT, may be more convenient to destinations in the west and north regions.

Two Amtrak (www.amtrak.com) train routes pass through the region. *California Zephyr*, traveling daily between Emeryville, CA, and Chicago, IL, has six stops in Colorado, including Denver, Fraser-Winter Park, Glenwood Springs and Grand Junction. *Empire Builder* runs daily from Seattle,

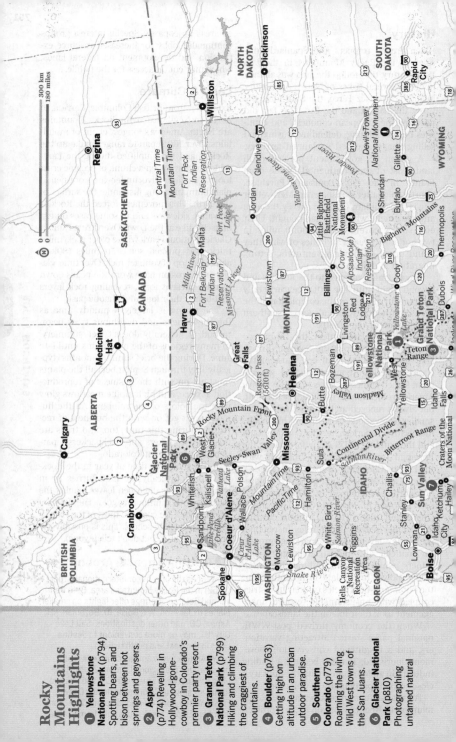

Rocky Mountains Highlights

1 Yellowstone National Park (p794) Spotting bears, and bison between hot springs and geysers.

2 Aspen (p774) Reveling in Hollywood-gone-cowboy in Colorado's premier party resort.

3 Grand Teton National Park (p799) Hiking and climbing the craggiest of mountains.

4 Boulder (p763) Getting high on altitude in an urban outdoor paradise.

5 Southern Colorado (p779) Roaming the living Wild West towns of the San Juans.

6 Glacier National Park (p810) Photographing untamed natural

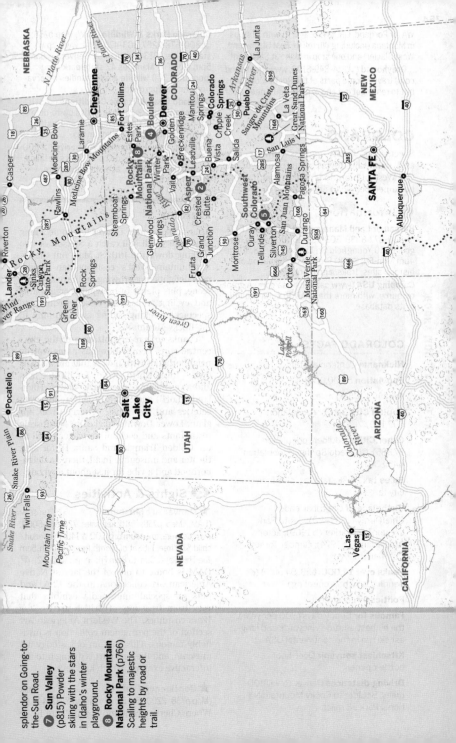

splendor on Going-to-the-Sun Road.

7 Sun Valley
(p815) Powder skiing with the stars in Idaho's winter playground.

8 Rocky Mountain National Park (p766)
Scaling to majestic heights by road or trail.

WA, or Portland, OR, to Chicago, IL, with 12 stops in Montana (including Whitefish, East Glacier and West Glacier) and one stop in Idaho at Sandpoint.

Greyhound (✆214-849-8100; www.greyhound. com) travels some parts of the Rocky Mountains, but to really get out and explore you'll need a car.

COLORADO

Spectacular vistas, endless powder runs and mountain towns with echoes of the Old West – Colorado is a place that has long beckoned people to adventure.

❶ Information

Bureau of Land Management Colorado (BLM; ✆800-877-8339, 303-239-3600; www.co.blm. gov; 2850 Youngfield St, Lakewood; ⏰8:30am-4pm Mon-Fri; ☐28) Provides information on historic sites, trails, and more.

Camping USA (www.camping-usa.com) A great resource, with more than 12,000 campgrounds in its database.

COLORADO FACTS

Nickname Centennial State

Population 5,500,000

Area 104,185 sq miles

Capital City Denver (population 693,100)

Other Cities Boulder (population 97,385), Colorado Springs (population 445,830)

Sales tax 2.9% state tax, plus individual city taxes

Birthplace of Ute tribal leader ChiefOuray (1833–80); South Park creator Trey Parker (b 1969); actor Amy Adams (b 1974); climber Tommy Caldwell (b1978)

Peaks over 14,000ft 53, 54 or 58 (depending on who's counting)

Politics Swing state

Famous for Sunny days (300 per year), the highest-altitude vineyards and longest ski run in the continental USA

Kitschiest souvenir Deer-hoof bottle-opener

Driving distances Denver to Vail 100 miles, Boulder to Rocky Mountain National Park 38 miles

---

Colorado Parks & Wildlife (CPW; Map p758; ✆800-678-2267, 303-470-1144; www.cpw. state.co.us; 1313 Sherman St, Denver; ⏰8am-5pm Mon-Fri) Manages 42 state parks and more than 300 wildlife areas; handles reservations for campgrounds.

Colorado Road & Traffic Conditions (✆511; www.codot.gov; ⏰24hr) Provides up-to-date information on Colorado highway and traffic conditions, including cycling maps.

Colorado Travel & Tourism Authority (✆800-265-6723; www.colorado.com) Offers detailed information on sights, activities and more throughout the state.

Denver

As an urban center, Denver has come a long way. Sure you'll still catch a Stetson or two walking down the 16th St Mall, but the Intermountain West's cosmopolitan capital now delights in a growing culinary and arts scene, plus plenty of brewpubs, great parks and cycling trails, and close proximity to spectacular hiking, skiing and camping in the Rocky Mountains.

Thanks to a re-urbanization of the city's central core, Denver now has name-worthy neighborhoods with flavors that are all their own – River North (RiNo) for hipster bars and eye-catching street art, Lower Highlands (LoHi) and South Broadway for great eateries and live music, Cherry Creek for glam, Lower Downtown (LoDo) for upscale restaurants and cocktail lounges as well as the Golden Triangle and Santa Fe for arts, theater and museums. In all, there's a neighborhood and a vibe for just about anybody.

◉ Sights & Activities

★**Denver Art Museum**   MUSEUM
(DAM; Map p758; ✆ticket sales 720-865-5000; www.denverartmuseum.org; 100 W 14th Ave; adult/child $13/free, 1st Sat of month free; ⏰10am-5pm Tue-Thu, Sat & Sun, to 8pm Fri; 🅿♿; ☐0, 52) ✎ DAM is home to one of the largest Native American art collections in the USA, and puts on special multimedia exhibits that vary from treasures of British art to *Star Wars* costumes. The Western American Art section of the permanent collection is justifiably famous. This isn't an old, stodgy art museum, and the best part is diving into the interactive exhibits, which kids love.

★**Confluence Park**   PARK
(Map p758; 2200 15th St; ♿; ☐10, 28, 32, 44) Where Cherry Creek and South Platte River

meet is the nexus and plexus of Denver's sunshine-loving culture. It's a good place for an afternoon picnic, and there's a short white-water park for kayakers and tubers. Families also enjoy a small beach and shallow water areas for playing.

★ **Clyfford Still Museum** MUSEUM
(Map p758; ☑720-354-4880; www.clyffordstillmuseum.org; 1250 Bannock St; adult/child $10/free; ⊙10am-5pm Tue-Thu, Sat & Sun, to 8pm Fri; ☐0, 52) Dedicated exclusively to the work and legacy of 20th-century American abstract expressionist Clyfford Still, this fascinating museum's collection includes over 2400 pieces – 95% of his work – by the powerful and narcissistic master of bold. In his will, Still insisted that his body of work only be exhibited in a singular space, so Denver built him a museum. Free tours are offered throughout the week; check the website for dates and times.

History Colorado Center MUSEUM
(Map p758; ☑303-447-8679; www.historycolorado center.org; 1200 Broadway; adult/child $12/8; ⊙10am-5pm; ☑⊞; ☐0, 10) Discover Colorado's frontier roots and high-tech modern triumphs at this sharp, smart and charming museum. There are plenty of interactive exhibits, including a Jules Verne–esque 'Time Machine' that you push across a giant map of Colorado to explore seminal moments in the Centennial State's history. Periodically, story times for toddlers and low-sensory morning sessions are offered before the museum opens.

★ **Blair-Caldwell African American Museum** MUSEUM
(Map p758; ☑720-865-2401; https://history.denver library.org/blair; 2401 Welton St, 3rd fl; ⊙noon-8pm Mon & Wed, 10am-6pm Tue, Thu & Fri, 9am-5pm Sat; ☑⊞; ☐43, ☐D) FREE Tucked into the 3rd floor of a public library, this multimedia museum provides an excellent overview of the history of African Americans in the Rocky Mountain region – from their migration and settlement to their discrimination and achievements. Exhibits on Wellington Webb, Denver's first African American mayor, as well as Five Points, Denver's historically black neighborhood, are particularly interesting.

Denver Museum of Nature & Science MUSEUM
(DMNS; ☑303-370-6000; www.dmns.org; 2001 Colorado Blvd; museum adult/child $17/12, IMAX $10/8, Planetarium $5/4; ⊙9am-5pm; ☑⊞; ☐20, 32, 40) The Denver Museum of Nature & Science is a classic natural-science museum with excellent temporary exhibits on topics like the biomechanics of bugs, Pompeii and mythical creatures. Permanent exhibits are equally engaging and include those cool panoramas we all loved as kids. The **IMAX theater** and **Gates Planetarium** are especially fun. Located on the eastern edge of City Park.

★ Festivals & Events

First Friday CULTURAL
(www.rivernorthart.com) FREE On the first Friday of every month, Denverites come out for an art stroll, cruising galleries for free wine and fun conversations in the Santa Fe and RiNo Arts Districts. The event typically runs from 6pm to 10pm.

Five Points Jazz Festival MUSIC
(www.artsandvenuesdenver.com; Welton St; ⊙May; ⊞; ☐12, 28, 43, ☐D) FREE This one-day jazz fest celebrates the historically African American neighborhood of Five Points, which was once home to several jazz clubs. Over 50 bands perform on stages set up on Welton St. Several kid-friendly activities – instrument making, drum circles, face painting – are offered, making it a fun event for all. Held the third Saturday of May.

Great American Beer Festival BEER
(☑303-447-0816; www.greatamericanbeerfestival. com; 700 14th St; $85; ⊙Sep or Oct; ☐1, 8, 19, 48, ☐D, F, H) Colorado has more microbreweries per capita than any other US state, and this hugely popular festival sells out in advance. More than 500 breweries are represented, from the big players to home enthusiasts.

🛏 Sleeping

★ **Hostel Fish** HOSTEL $
(Map p758; ☑303-954-0962; www.hostelfish.com; 1217 20th St; dm/r from $53/185; ❄🛜; ☐38) This swanked-out hostel is an oasis for budget travelers. Stylish, modern and squeaky clean, dorms have themes – Aspen, Graffiti, Vintage Biker – and sleep five to 10 people in bunks. Mattresses are thick, duvets plush and each guest gets a locker and individual charging station. A common kitchen and pub crawls make it easy to make new friends.

Mile High Guest House HOSTEL $
(☑720-531-2898; www.milehighguesthouse.com; 1445 High St; dm $38, r with shared bath $82; 🛜; ☐15) A gorgeous old Denver mansion makes for a cool hostel, and a welcome addition to Denver's budget lodging options. Large

parlor rooms serve as dorms, outfitted with bunk beds (but no lockers, oddly). Private rooms with shared bathrooms are also available, and the friendly staff help organize group outings, like pub crawls, art walks and backyard BBQs. Convenient bus-friendly location.

★ **Queen Anne Bed & Breakfast Inn** B&B $$
(Map p758; ☎ 303-296-6666; www.queenannebnb.com; 2147 Tremont Pl; r/ste from $160/230; P 🅿️❄🐾📶; 🚃28, 32) 🍃 Soft chamber music wafting through public areas, fresh flowers, manicured gardens and evening wine tastings create a romantic ambience at this eco-conscious B&B in two late-1800s Victorian homes. Featuring period antiques, private hot tubs and exquisite hand-painted murals, each room has its own personality.

★ **Crawford Hotel** HOTEL $$$
(Map p758; ☎ 855-362-5098; www.thecrawfordhotel.com; 1701 Wynkoop St, Union Station; r $349-469, ste $589-709; ❄📶🐾; 🚃55L, 72L,120L, FF2, 🅿️A, B, C, E, W) Set in the historic Union Station (p762), the Crawford Hotel is an example of Denver's amazing transformation. Rooms are luxurious and artful, with high ceilings and throwbacks like the art-deco headboards and clawfoot tubs. Service is impeccable, and the station's bar, the Terminal, is a fun hangout. Steps away, there's light-rail service to Denver International Airport (p762).

Curtis HOTEL $$$
(Map p758; ☎ 303-571-0300; www.thecurtis.com; 1405 Curtis St; r $269-449; ❄📶@📶; 🚃9, 10, 15, 20, 28, 32, 38, 43, 44) The Curtis is like stepping into a doo-bop Warhol wonderworld: 13 themed floors, each devoted to a different genre of American pop culture. Rooms are spacious and very mod. Attention to detail – either through the service or the decor – is paramount at the Curtis, a one-of-a-kind hotel in the heart of downtown Denver.

ROCKY MOUNTAINS IN ...

Two Weeks

Start your Rocky Mountain odyssey in the **Denver** area. Go tubing, vintage-clothes shopping or biking in outdoor-mad, boho **Boulder**, then soak up the liberal rays eavesdropping at a sidewalk cafe. Enjoy the vistas of the **Rocky Mountain National Park** before heading west on I-70 to play in the mountains around **Breckenridge**, which also has some of the best beginner slopes in Colorado. Go to ski and mountain-bike mecca **Steamboat Springs** before crossing the border into Wyoming.

Get a taste of prairie-town life in **Laramie**, then stop in **Lander**, rock-climbing destination extraordinaire. Continue north to chic Jackson and the majestic **Grand Teton National Park** before hitting iconic **Yellowstone National Park**. Save at least three days for exploring this geyser-packed wonderland.

Cross the state line into 'big sky country' and slowly make your way northwest through **Montana**, stopping in funky **Bozeman** and lively **Missoula** before visiting **Flathead Lake**. Wrap up your trip in Idaho, exploring Basque culture in up-and-coming **Boise**.

One Month

With a month on your hands, you can really delve into the region's off-the-beaten-path treasures. Follow the two-week itinerary, but dip southwest in **Colorado** – a developing wine region – before visiting **Wyoming**. Ride the 4WD trails around **Ouray**. Be sure to visit **Mesa Verde National Park** and its ancient cliff dwellings.

In **Montana**, you'll want to visit **Glacier National Park** before the glaciers disappear altogether. In Idaho, spend more time playing in **Sun Valley** and be sure to explore the shops, pubs and yummy organic restaurants in delightful little **Ketchum**. With a one-month trip, you also have time to drive along a few of Idaho's fantastically remote scenic byways. Make sure you cruise Hwy 75 from **Sun Valley** north to **Stanley**. Situated on the wide banks of the **Salmon River**, this stunning mountain hamlet is completely surrounded by national forestland and wilderness areas. Stanley is also blessed with world-class trout fishing and mild to wild rafting.

Take Hwy 21 (the **Ponderosa Pine Scenic Byway**) from Stanley to **Boise**. This scenic drive takes you through miles of dense ponderosa forests and past some excellent, solitary riverside camping spots – some of which come with their own natural hot-springs pools.

★**Art – a Hotel** BOUTIQUE HOTEL **$$$**
(Map p758; ☎303-572-8000; www.thearthotel.
com; 1201 Broadway; r $305-348, ste $382-518;
🅿❋@🛜🐾; 🚌0, 6, 10, 52) As the name sug-
gests, this hotel has intriguing artwork in
the guest rooms and common areas, be-
fitting its location, just around the corner
from the Denver Art Museum (p752). Rooms
are sizable and modern, and the large patio
with fire pits and great views is perfect for
happy-hour cocktails. The location close
to downtown restaurants and attractions,
could hardly be better.

🍴 Eating

Denver's food scene is booming, with new
restaurants, cafes and food trucks seemingly
opening every month. Downtown offers the
greatest depth and variety in Denver, though
strollable neighborhoods like LoHi, RiNo,
South Broadway, Uptown and Five Points
hold some of Denver's best eateries. Check
out www.5280.com for new eats.

★**Denver Central Market** FOOD HALL **$**
(Map p758; 2669 Larimer St; ⏱8am-9pm Sun-Thu,
to 10pm Fri & Sat; 🚌44, 48) Set in a repurposed
warehouse, this gourmet market place wows
with its style and breadth of options. Eat a
bowl of handmade pasta or an artisanal
sandwich; consider a wood-fired pizza or
street tacos. Or just grab a cocktail at the
bar, and wander between the fruit stand and
chocolatier. Patrons eat at communal tables
or on the street-side patio.

★**Civic Center Eats** FOOD TRUCK **$**
(Map p758; ☎303-861-4633; www.civiccentercon
servancy.org; cnr Broadway & Colfax Ave, Civic Center
Park; mains $5-10; ⏱11am-2pm Tue-Thu May-Oct;
👶❋; 🚌0, 9, 10, 52) When the weather gets
warm, head to Civic Center Park for lunch.
There are heaps of food trucks – everything
from BBQ and pizza to sushi and Indian – roll
into the park and serve up hearty meals. Ta-
bles are set up, live bands play, office workers
picnic on the grass. It's Denver at its best.

★**Hop Alley** CHINESE **$$**
(Map p758; ☎720-379-8340; www.hopalleyden
ver.com; 3500 Larimer St; mains $10-25; ⏱5:30-
10:30pm Mon-Sat; 🍴; 🚌12, 44) Hop Alley was
a slur used for Denver's hardscrabble Chinatown in the 1880s, until a race riot and
anti-Chinese legislation scattered the community. The moniker was reclaimed for this
small bustling restaurant located in (what
else?) a former soy sauce plant. Come for

authentic yet inventive Chinese dishes, and
equally creative cocktails, named after the
signs of the Chinese zodiac.

★**Acorn** AMERICAN **$$$**
(☎720-542-3721; www.denveracorn.com;
3350 Brighton Blvd, The Source; dishes $14-30;
⏱11:30am-10pm Mon-Sat, 5:30-10pm Sun; 🅿🍴👶;
🚌12, 20, 48) The oak-fired oven and grill are
the shining stars of this superb restaurant,
where small plates of innovative and share-
able eats make up meals. The menu changes
seasonally but dishes like crispy fried pickles,
oak-grilled broccolini and smoked-pork pos-
ole are hits. If dinner is too pricey, consider
a midday meal (2:30pm to 5:30pm) – the
menu is limited but more affordable.

★**Rioja** MODERN AMERICAN **$$$**
(Map p758; ☎303-820-2282; www.riojadenver.com;
1431 Larimer St; mains $19-39; ⏱11:30am-2:30pm
Wed-Fri, 10am-2:30pm Sat & Sun, 5-10pm daily; 🍴;
🚌10, 28, 32, 38, 44) This is one of Denver's most
innovative restaurants. Smart, busy and upscale, yet relaxed and casual – just like Colorado – Rioja features modern cuisine inspired
by Italian and Spanish traditions and powered by modern culinary flavors.

★**Root Down** MODERN AMERICAN **$$$**
(Map p758; ☎303-993-4200; www.rootdowndenver.
com; 1600 W 33rd Ave; small plates $8-19, mains $14-
35; ⏱5-10pm Sun-Thu, 5-11pm Fri & Sat, 11am-2pm
Fri, 10am-2:30pm Sat & Sun; 🍴; 🚌19, 52) 🌿 In a
converted gas station, chef Justin Cucci has
undertaken one of the city's most ambitious
culinary concepts, marrying sustainable 'field-
to-fork' practices, high-concept culinary fu-
sions and a low-impact, energy-efficient ethos.
The menu changes seasonally, but consider
yourself lucky if it includes the sweet-potato
falafel or lamb sliders. Vegetarian, vegan, raw
and gluten-free diets very welcome.

🍸 Drinking & Nightlife

Denver's top nightlife districts include Up-
town for gay bars and a young professional
crowd, LoDo for loud sports bars and heavy
drinking, RiNo for hipsters, LoHi for an ec-
lectic mix, and South Broadway and Colfax
for Old School wannabes.

★**Black Shirt Brewing Co** BREWERY
(☎303-993-2799; www.blackshirtbrewingco.com;
3719 Walnut St; ⏱11am-10pm Sun-Thu, to midnight
Fri & Sat; 👶; 🚌12, 44, 🚆A) Artisanal brewers
create the all-red-ale menu at the popular
BSB; ales take anywhere from two months

ROCKY MOUNTAINS DENVER

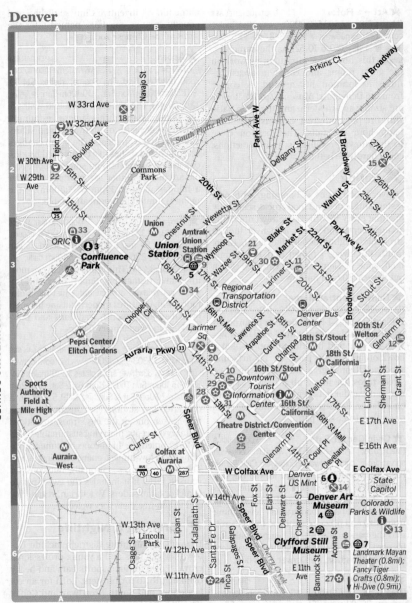

to three years to brew. So careful are they with the handcrafted beers, the brewers developed lopsided glasses to showcase the aromas. Live music is part of the culture here, as is good food. A kitchen offers brick-oven pizzas and gourmet salads.

★ **Williams & Graham** COCKTAIL BAR
(Map p758; ☑303-997-8886; www.williamsandgraham.com; 3160 Tejon St; ☺5pm-1am; ☐32,44) Denver's top speakeasy looks like an old Western bookstore, but ask for a seat and the cashier pushes a wall of books and leads you

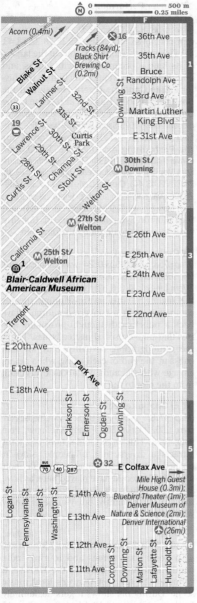

Denver

Top Sights
1 Blair-Caldwell African American Museum E3
2 Clyfford Still Museum D6
3 Confluence Park A3
4 Denver Art Museum D6
5 Union Station B3

Sights
6 Civic Center Park D5
7 History Colorado Center D6

Sleeping
8 Art – a Hotel D6
9 Crawford Hotel B3
10 Curtis C4
11 Hostel Fish C3
12 Queen Anne Bed & Breakfast Inn D4

Eating
13 City O' City D6
14 Civic Center Eats D5
15 Denver Central Market D2
16 Hop Alley F1
17 Rioja B4
18 Root Down B1

Drinking & Nightlife
19 Crema Coffee House E2
20 Crú C4
21 Falling Rock Tap House C3
22 Linger A2
23 Williams & Graham A2

Entertainment
24 Colorado Ballet C6
25 Colorado Convention Center C5
26 Colorado Symphony Orchestra C4
27 Curious Theatre D6
28 Denver Center for the Performing Arts B4
29 Denver Performing Arts Complex C4
30 El Chapultepec C3
31 Ellie Caulkins Opera House C4
32 Ogden Theatre F5
    Opera Colorado .... (see 31)

Shopping
33 REI A3
34 Tattered Cover Bookstore B3

ROCKY MOUNTAINS DENVER

deeper into the era. Polished wood, gleaming brass features, antique lamps, tin ceilings and mixologists in aprons await. Cocktails are creative and artfully prepared – almost too beautiful to drink. Almost.

★ Crema Coffee House   CAFE
(Map p758; ☎720-284-9648; www.cremacoffeehouse.net; 2862 Larimer St; ☺7am-5pm; ☎; ☐44) Noah Price, a clothing-designer-turned-coffee-impresario, takes his job seriously, selecting, brewing and pouring

Denver's absolute-best coffee. The espresso and French-pressed are complete perfection, but it's the oatmeal latte, delicately infused ice teas and spectacularly eclectic menu – Moroccan meatballs to peanut-butter and jelly sandwiches with goat's cheese – that put this place over the top.

Linger LOUNGE
(Map p758; ☑303-993-3120; www.lingerdenver.com; 2030 W 30th Ave; ☉11:30am-2:30pm & 4-10pm Tue-Thu, to 11pm Fri, 10am-2:30pm & 4-11pm Sat, 10am-2:30pm Sun; ☐28, 32, 44) This rambling LoHi complex sits in the former Olinger mortuary. Come nighttime, they black out the 'O' and it just becomes Linger. There's an interesting menu, but most people come for the tony feel and light-up-the-night rooftop bar, which has great views of downtown Denver and even a replica of the RV made famous by the Bill Murray smash *Stripes*.

Falling Rock Tap House BAR
(Map p758; ☑303-293-8338; www.fallingrock taphouse.com; 1919 Blake St; ☉11am-2am; ☐0, 15, 20) High fives and hollers punctuate the scene when the Rockies triumph and beer drinkers file in to forget an afternoon of drinking Co-ors at the ball park. There are – count 'em – 80-plus beers on tap and the bottle list has almost 150. With all the local favorites, this is *the* place to drink beer downtown.

Crú WINE BAR
(Map p758; ☑303-893-9463; www.cruawine bar.com; 1442 Larimer St; glass of wine $10-27; ☉2pm-midnight Mon-Thu, noon-2am Fri & Sat, 10:30am-3pm Sun; ☐10, 28, 32, 38, 44) This classy Larimer Sq wine bar is decked out in wine labels and glassware, with dim lighting and gentle music. It looks so bespoke it's surprising to learn it's a chain (Dallas, Austin). Come for happy hour (4pm to 6:30pm Monday to Friday) when flights of wine are $3 off and light fare includes mussels and goat's cheese beignets.

☆ Entertainment

Denver is bursting with entertainment options. There's live music and theater practically everywhere, from intimate jazz clubs to the amazing multitheater Denver Center for the Performing Arts. Denver is a four-sport town (one of few in the country) and also has professional soccer and lacrosse. Add to that comedy, movies, dance and yearly festivals and there's truly something for everyone.

★ **Denver Performing Arts Complex** PERFORMING ARTS
(Map p758; ☑720-865-4220; www.artscomplex. com; cnr 14th & Champa Sts; ☐9, 15, 28, 32, 38, 43, 44) This massive complex – one of the largest of its kind – occupies four city blocks, and houses 10 major venues, including the historic **Ellie Caulkins Opera House** and the Boettcher Concert Hall. It's also home to the **Colorado Ballet** (☑303-837-8888; www.colo radoballet.org; 1075 Santa Fe Dr; ☉box office 9am-5pm Mon-Fri; ☐1, 9), **Denver Center for the Performing Arts** (☑303-893-4100; www. denvercenter.org; 1101 13th St; ☉box office 10am-6pm Mon-Sat & 1hr before each show; ☐9, 15, 28, 32, 38, 43, 44), **Opera Colorado** (☑303-468-2030; www.operacolorado.org; ☉box office 10am-5pm Mon-Fri; ☐9, 15, 28, 32, 38, 43, 44) and the Colorado Symphony Orchestra. Not sure what you want to do tonight? Come here.

★ **Curious Theatre** THEATER
(Map p758; ☑303-623-0524; www.curioustheatre. org; 1080 Acoma St; tickets from $18; ☉box office 2-7pm Tue-Sat; ☐0, 6, 52) 'No guts, no story' is the tagline of this award-winning theater company, set in a converted church. Plays pack a punch with thought-provoking stories that take on social justice issues. Think race, immigration, sexuality. Stay for talk backs at the end of each show, when actors engage with the audience about everything from the plot to the set.

★ **El Chapultepec** JAZZ
(Map p758; ☑303-295-9126; www.thepeclodo. com; 1962 Market St; ☉7am-1am, music from 9pm; ☐38) This smoky, old-school jazz joint attracts a diverse mix of people. Since it opened in 1951, Frank Sinatra, Tony Bennett and Ella Fitzgerald have played here, as have Jagger and Richards. Local jazz bands take the tiny stage nightly, but you never know who might drop by.

Hi-Dive LIVE MUSIC
(☑303-733-0230; www.hi-dive.com; 7 S Broadway; ☐0) Local rock heroes and touring indie bands light up the stage at the Hi-Dive, a venue at the heart of Denver's local music scene. During big shows it gets deafeningly loud, cheek-to-jowl with hipsters and humid as an armpit. In other words, perfection.

Ogden Theatre LIVE MUSIC
(Map p758; ☑303-832-1874; www.ogdentheatre.com; 935 E Colfax Ave; ☉box office 10am-2pm Sat, 1hr before doors open show days; ☐15) One of Denver's best live-music venues, the Ogden Theatre

has a checkered past. Built in 1917, it was derelict for many years and might have been bulldozed in the early 1990s, but it's now listed on the National Register of Historic Places. Bands such as Edward Sharpe & the Magnetic Zeros and Lady Gaga have played here.

**Colorado Symphony
Orchestra** CLASSICAL MUSIC
(CSO; Map p758; ☑303-623-7876; www.colorado symphony.org; 1000 14th St, Boettcher Concert Hall; ☺box office 10am-6pm Mon-Fri, noon-6pm Sat; ♿; ☐9, 15, 28, 32, 38, 43, 44) The Boettcher Concert Hall in the Denver Performing Arts Complex is home to this renowned symphony orchestra. The orchestra performs an annual 21-week Masterworks season, as well as concerts aimed at a broader audience – think live performances of movie scores during the screening of films.

Bluebird Theater LIVE MUSIC
(☑303-377-1666; www.bluebirdtheater.net; 3317 E Colfax Ave; ♿; ☐15) This medium-sized theater is general admission standing room and has terrific sound and clear sight lines from the balcony. The venue often offers the last chance to catch bands – Denver faves the Lumineers and Devotchka both headlined here – on their way up to the big time.

Landmark Mayan Theater CINEMA
(☑303-744-6799; www.landmarktheatres.com; 110 Broadway; ♿; ☐0) Even without the fancy sound system and enormous screen, this is the best place in Denver to take in a film. The 1930s movie palace is a romantic, historic gem and – bonus! – it serves beer.

🛍 Shopping

★Tattered Cover Bookstore BOOKS
(Map p758; ☑303-436-1070; www.tatteredcover. com; 1628 16th St; ☺6:30am-9pm Mon-Fri, 9am-9pm Sat, 10am-6pm Sun; 🖥♿; ☐10, 19, 28, 32, 44, MallRide) There are plenty of places to curl up with a book in Denver's beloved independent bookstore. Bursting with new and used books, it has a good stock of regional travel guides and nonfiction titles dedicated to the Western states and Western folklore. There's a second smaller location on Colfax near City Park.

★REI SPORTS & OUTDOORS
(Recreational Equipment Incorporated; Map p758; ☑303-756-3100; www.rei.com; 1416 Platte St; ☺9am-9pm Mon-Sat, to 7pm Sun; ♿; ☐10, 28, 32, 44) The flagship store of this outdoor-equipment super supplier is an essential stop if you are heading to the mountains or

LIVE AT RED ROCKS!

Set between 400ft-high red sandstone rocks 15 miles southwest of Denver is **Red Rocks Park & Amphitheatre** (☑303-697-4939; www.redrocksonline. com; 18300 W Alameda Pkwy; ☺5am-11pm; ♿). Acoustics are so good many artists record live albums here. The 9000-seat theater offers stunning views and draws big-name bands all summer. To see your favorite singer go to work on the stage is to witness a performance in one of the most exceptional music venues in the world. For many, it's reason enough for a trip to Colorado.

just cruising through Confluence. In addition to top gear for camping, cycling, climbing and skiing, it has a rental department, maps and the Pinnacle, a 47ft-high indoor structure of simulated red sandstone for climbing and rappelling.

★Fancy Tiger Crafts ARTS & CRAFTS
(☑303-733-3855; www.fancytigercrafts.com; 59 Broadway; ☺10am-7pm Mon & Wed-Sat, to 9pm Tue, 11am-6pm Sun; ♿; ☐0) So you dig crochet and quilting? You knit a mean sweater and have a few too many tattoos? Welcome to Fancy Tiger Crafts, a sophisticated remodel of granny's yarn barn that's ground zero for Denver's crafty hipsters. There are classes in the back (including ones by Jessica, 'mistress of patchwork') and a rad selection of fabric, yarn and books.

ℹ Information

The Tourist Information Center website (www. denver.org) has great information about events.
DIA Information Booth (☑303-317-0629; www. visitdenver.com; Denver International Airport; ☺hours vary; 🖥♿; ☐A) Tourist and airport information is available at this booth on the east end of Denver International Airport's central hall.
ORIC (Outdoor Recreation Information Center; Map p758; ☑REI main line 303-756-3100; www.oriconline.org; 1416 Platte St; ☺hours vary; 🖥; ☐10, 28, 32, 44) Inside REI, this information desk is a must for those looking to get out of town for outdoor adventure. It has maps and expert information on trip planning and safety. The desk is staffed by volunteers, so hours vary wildly, but arriving on a weekend afternoon is a good bet.
Downtown Tourist Information Center (Map p758; ☑303-892-1505; www.denver.org; 1575

WORTH A TRIP

BEST DAY HIKES & RIDES FROM DENVER

There are literally hundreds of day hikes within an hour of Denver.

Jefferson County Open Space Parks (www.jeffco.us/openspace) Jefferson County runs along most of the western edge of Denver, and its open spaces are the best around.

Golden Gate Canyon State Park (☑303-582-3707; www.cpw.state.co.us; 92 Crawford Gulch Rd; entrance $7, camping $20-26; ⊘5am-10pm; 🚹🐾) Located halfway between Golden and Nederland, this massive 12,000-acre park has plenty of hiking trails and rockclimbing.

Staunton State Park (☑303-816-0912; www.parks.state.co.us/parks; 12102 S Elk Creek Rd; ⊘7am-9pm; 🚹🐾) Colorado's newest state park sits on a historic ranch site 40 miles west of Denver. Ranging in elevation from 8100ft to 10,000ft, it has a rich variety of landscapes – from grassy meadows to dramatic granite cliffs.

Waterton Canyon (☑303-634-3745; www.denverwater.org/recreation/watertoncanyon; 11300 Waterton Rd; ⊘30min before dawn-30min after dusk; 🚹) South of Denver, just west of Chatfield Reservoir, this pretty canyon has an easy 6.5-mile trail to the Strontia Springs Dam.

Pike National Forest (☑303-275-5610, campsite reservations only 877-444-6777; www.fs.usda.gov; 19316 Goddard Ranch Ct; ⊘8am-4:30pm Mon-Fri; 🚹) Start exploring this large national forest by picking up information available at the South Platte Ranger Station, about 5 miles from Morrison.

Buffalo Creek Mountain Bike Area (www.frmbp.org; 18268 S Buffalo Creek Rd, Pine; ⊘7am-7pm; 🚹) If you're into singletrack mountain biking, this area has about 40 miles of bike trails, including the sections of the Colorado Trail that permit bikes.

California St; ⊘9am-6pm Mon-Fri, 9am-5pm Sat, 10am-2pm Sun May-Oct, 9am-5pm Mon-Fri, 9am-2pm Sat, 10am-2pm Sun Nov-Apr; 🚌9, 15, 20, MallRide, 🚇D, F, H) When you get to town, make for the largest and most central information center, located just off the 16th St Mall. You can load up on brochures, browse online travel pages and get solid information from knowledgeable staffers.

❶ Getting There & Away

Denver International Airport (DIA; ☑303-342-2000; www.flydenver.com; 8500 Peña Blvd; ⊘24hr; 🛜🚹; 🚇A) is a major air hub and one of the country's busiest facilities. In all, DIA has 53 sq miles of land, making it the biggest airport in the country by area. The facility has an automated subway that links the terminal to three concourses (Concourse C is almost 1 mile from the terminal). Give yourself a little extra time to find your way around.

Greyhound offers frequent buses on routes along the Front Range and on transcontinental routes. All buses stop at the **Denver Bus Center** (Map p758; ☑303-293-6555; 1055 19th St; ⊘6am-midnight; 🛜; 🚌8, 48).

The **Colorado Mountain Express** (CME; ☑800-525-6363; www.coloradomountainexpress.com; 8500 Peña Blvd, Denver International Airport; 🛜🚹; 🚇A) has shuttle services from Denver International Airport (DIA), downtown Denver or Morrison to Summit County, including Breckenridge

and Keystone (adult/child $66/35, 2½ hours) and Vail (adult/child $84/44, three hours).

Amtrak (☑800-872-7245; www.amtrak.com; 1701 Wynkoop St, Union Station; 🚌55L, 72L,120L, FF2, 🚇A, B, C, E, W) runs the *California Zephyr* train service daily between Chicago ($121-325, 19 hours) and San Francisco ($144-446, 33 hours) stopping in Denver's gorgeously renovated **Union Station** (Map p758; ☑303-592-6712; www.unionstationindenver.com; 1701 Wynkoop St; 🅿; 🚌55L, 72L,120L, FF2, 🚇A, B, C, E, W).

❶ Getting Around

TO/FROM THE AIRPORT

An **RTD** (☑303-299-6000; www.rtd-denver.com; per ride $2.60-4.50, day pass $5.20-9; 🚹) light-rail transports people from DIA to downtown Denver (Line A; $9, 45 minutes), servicing Denver suburbs along the way.

BICYCLE

You can get all the information you need on cycling in Denver from Bike Denver (www.bikedenver.org) and City of Denver (www.denvergov.org), both of which have downloadable bike maps for the city.

B-Cycle (☑303-825-3325; www.denverbcycle.com; 1-day membership $9; ⊘5am-midnight; 🚹) This bike-share company has more than 80 stations throughout Denver. The daily rate includes unlimited rides as long as they're under 30 minutes.

CAR & MOTORCYCLE

Street parking can be a pain, but there is a slew of pay garages in downtown and LoDo. Nearly all the major car-rental agencies have counters at Denver International Airport, though only a few have offices in downtown Denver.

Enterprise Rent-A-Car (☑303-293-8644; www.enterprise.com; 2255 Broadway; ☺7am-7pm Mon-Fri, 8am-4pm Sat & Sun; ☑44, 48) is an international car-rental agency with several offices in the Denver metro area.

PUBLIC TRANSPORTATION

Regional Transportation District (RTD; Map p758; ☑303-299-6000; www.rtd-denver.com; 1600 Blake St; ☑10, 19, 28, 32, 44, MallRide) provides public transportation throughout the Denver and Boulder area (local/regional fares $2.60/4.50). The website has schedules, routes, fares and a trip planner.

TAXI

Two major taxi companies offer door-to-door service in Denver:

Metro Taxi (☑303-333-3333; www.metrotaxidenver.com; ☺24hr)

Yellow Cab (☑303-777-7777; www.denveryellowcab.com; ☺24hr)

Boulder

Twenty-five square miles surrounded by reality. That's the joke about Boulder that never goes away. The weather is perfect, the surroundings – stone Flatirons, gurgling creek, ponderosa trails and manicured college campus – beg idylling. And the populace – fit do-gooders with the beta on the best fair-trade coffee and hoppiest home brew – seals the stereotype.

Boulder's mad love of the outdoors was officially legislated in 1967, when it became the first US city to tax itself specifically to preserve open space. Thanks to such vision, people (and dogs) enjoy a number of city parks and open spaces while packs of cyclists whip up and down the Boulder Creek corridor.

For travelers looking for an outdoorsy holiday with the cultural outlets of an urban oasis – gourmet restaurants, lively bars, concerts and theater – Boulder is where it's at.

◎ Sights & Activities

Few towns have this combination of nature and culture. Whether you're climbing the Flatirons (p764), cycling up **Flagstaff** (☑303-441-3440; www.bouldercolorado.gov; Flagstaff Summit Rd; ⓟ🐕), roaming Pearl St (p765) or patrolling CU's campus, there are plenty of sights and activities to keep you and the family smiling. Most sites are fairly centrally located, along W Pearl St or on the Hill, where you'll also find the university.

★**Chautauqua Park** PARK
(☑303-442-3282; www.chautauqua.com; 900 Baseline Rd; ☑HOP 2) This historic landmark park is the gateway to Boulder's most magnificent slab of open space adjoining the iconic Flatirons, and its wide, lush lawn attracts picnicking families, sunbathers, Frisbee folk and students from nearby CU. It also gets copious hikers, climbers and trail runners. It's a popular site so parking can be a hassle. During the summer of 2017, the City of Boulder piloted a free shuttle to several lots around the city to ease the congestion. Check the website for updates.

★**Dairy Arts Center** ARTS CENTER
(☑303-440-7826; www.thedairy.org; 2590 Walnut St; prices vary; ⓟ🐕; ☑HOP) A historic milk-processing-factory-turned-arts-center, the Dairy is one of Boulder's top cultural hubs. Recently renovated, it's a state-of-the-art facility with three stages, four gallery spaces and a 60-seat cinema. There's always something going on – from lectures and plays to modern dance and art exhibits. There's a small cafe and bar on-site too.

★**Boulder Creek** WATER SPORTS
(🐕) An all-time favorite Boulder summer ritual is to tube down Boulder Creek. Most people put in at **Eben G Fine Park** (Boulder Canyon Dr; ⓟ🐕🐾; ☑205, N) and float as far as 30th St, or even 55th St. Be sure to check the water volume, especially early in the season; anything over 200 cu feet per second can be a real rodeo. Rent tubes at **White Water Tube** (☑720-239-2179; www.whitewatertubing.com; 2709 Spruce St; rental per day tube $16-21, kayak $45-50, paddleboard $35; ☺10am-6pm May-Sep; 🐕; ☑205, BOLT, HOP) or **Lolita's Market** (☑303-443-8329; www.facebook.com/lolitasmarket; 800 Pearl St; tube hire $10; ☺market 24hr; 🐕; ☑HOP).

Eldorado Canyon State Park OUTDOORS
(☑303-494-3943; www.cpw.state.co.us; 9 Kneale Rd, Eldorado Springs; $8; ☺dawn-dusk, visitor center 9am-5pm) Among the country's best rock-climbing areas, Eldorado has Class 5.5 to 5.12 climbs. Suitable for all visitors, a dozen miles of hiking trails also link up to Chautauqua Park. A public pool (summer only) offers chilly swims in the canyon's famous spring water. Located 5 miles southwest of town.

ROCKY MOUNTAINS BOULDER

★ Local Table Tours
FOOD & DRINK

(☎303-909-5747; www.localtabletours.com; tours $35-70; ⏰hours vary) Go behind the scenes with one of these fun downtown walking tours presenting a smattering of great local cuisine and inside knowledge on food and wine or coffee and chocolate. The tours also highlight locally owned businesses with regional or sustainable food sources. The cocktail crawl is a hit.

★✦ Festivals & Events

Bolder Boulder
SPORTS

(☎303-444-7223; www.bolderboulder.com; adult/child from $70/55; ⏰Memorial Day; 🖌; 🚌209, STAMPEDE) With over 50,000 runners and pros mingling with costumed racers, live bands and sideline merrymakers, this may be the most fun 10km run in the US, ending at Folsom Field, CU's football stadium.

Boulder Creek Festival
MUSIC, FOOD

(☎303-449-3137; www.bceproductions.com; Canyon Blvd, Central Park; ⏰May; 🖌; 🚌203, 204, 225, AB, B, DASH, DD, DM, GS, SKIP) FREE Billed as the kick-off to summer and capped with the Bolder Boulder, this summer festival is massive. Over 10 event areas feature more than 30 live entertainers and 500 vendors plus a whole carnival ride zone. There's food and drink, entertainment and sunshine. What's not to love?

🛏 Sleeping

★ Chautauqua Lodge & Cottages
HISTORIC HOTEL $$

(☎303-952-1611; www.chautauqua.com; 900 Baseline Rd; r from $103, cottages $196-303; P❄✿🐾🛜🐕; 🚌HOP 2) Adjoining beautiful hiking trails to the Flatirons (900 Baseline Rd, Chautauqua Park; 🚌HOP 2) and in a leafy neighborhood inside Chautauqua Park (p763), this is our top Boulder pick. It has contemporary rooms and one- to three-bedroom cottages with porches and patchwork-quilt beds. It's perfect for families and pets. All have full kitchens, though the wraparound porch of the Chautauqua Dining Hall is a local favorite for breakfast.

★ Boulder Adventure Lodge
HOTEL $$

(A-Lodge; ☎303-444-0882; www.a-lodge.com; 91 Fourmile Canyon Dr; r from $159; P❄✿🐾🐕; 🚌N) You've come to Boulder to get outdoors, so why not stay nearer the action? Located a short distance from town, the A-Lodge has hiking, biking, climbing and fishing right from the property. Rooms are simple but well-appointed, ranging from dorms to suites. There's a pool, fire pit and more, generating a warm esprit de corps among guests and staff alike.

★ St Julien Hotel & Spa
HOTEL $$$

(☎720-406-9696, reservations 877-303-0900; www.stjulien.com; 900 Walnut St; r/ste from $400/650; P❄@🛜🐕; 🚌205, HOP, SKIP) In the heart of downtown, Boulder's finest four-star option is modern and refined, with photographs of local scenery and cork walls that warm the ambience. With fabulous views of the Flatirons, the back patio hosts live world music, jazz concerts and popular Latin dance parties. Rooms are spacious and plush. The on-site spa is considered one of the best around.

🍴 Eating

★ Rayback Collective
FOOD TRUCK $

(☎303-214-2127; www.therayback.com; 2775 Valmont Rd; mains $6-12; ⏰11am-10pm Mon-Fri, to 11pm Sat, to 9pm Sun; 🖌🖌🐕; 🚌205, BOLT) A plumbing-supplies warehouse turned urban oasis, Rayback is a snapshot of Boulder. A place to feel community. A huge outdoor space with fire pit and lawn games. A lounge with cozy chairs and live music. A bar serving up Colorado brews. A food truck park with loads of good eats. Young or old, even furry friends, are welcome here.

★ Rincón Argentino
ARGENTINE $

(☎303-442-4133; www.rinconargentinoboulder. com; 2525 Arapahoe Ave; mains $4-13; ⏰11am-8pm Mon-Thu, to 9pm Fri & Sat; 🖌; 🚌JUMP) Don't be turned off by the shopping plaza setting: Rincón packs a wallop of authentic Argentina. It bakes fresh empanadas – savory, small turnovers filled with spiced meat, or mozzarella and basil – which are perfect with a glass of malbec. It also offers *milanesas*-breaded beef cutlet sandwiches and gourds of yerba maté, a high-octane coffee alternative.

★ Oak at Fourteenth
MODERN AMERICAN $$

(☎303-444-3622; www.oakatfourteenth.com; 1400 Pearl St; mains $13-30; ⏰11:30am-10pm Mon-Sat, 5:30-10pm Sun; 🚌205, 206) Zesty and innovative, locally owned Oak manufactures top-notch cocktails and tasty small plates for stylish diners. Standouts include the grilled bacon-wrapped pork tenderloin and cucumber sashimi drizzled with passion fruit. Portions at this farm-to-table eatery are minimal – when it's this scrumptious you notice. Waiters advise well. The only downside:

it tends to be noisy, so save your intimate confessions.

★ Brasserie Ten Ten BISTRO $$

(☎303-998-1010; www.brasserietenten.com; 1011 Walnut St; mains $15-27; ◷11am-10pm Mon-Thu, 11am-11pm Fri, 9am-11pm Sat, 9am-9pm Sun; ▢203, 204, 225, AB, B) A go-to place for both students and professors, this sunny French bistro has a refined menu and an elegant atmosphere – think fresh flowers, marble high tops and polished brass. Sure, it's fancy, but not too uppity to offer killer happy-hour deals on crepes, sliders, mussels and beer. Don't miss the truffle fries.

Salt MODERN AMERICAN $$

(☎303-444-7258; www.saltthebistro.com; 1047 Pearl St; mains $15-30; ◷11am-9pm Mon-Thu, 11am-11pm Fri & Sat, 10am-9pm Sun; ▮; ▢208, HOP, SKIP) While farm-to-table is ubiquitous in Boulder, this is one spot that delivers and surpasses expectations. The handmade fettuccine with snap peas, radicchio and herb cream is a feverish delight. But Salt also knows meat: local and grass-fed, basted, braised and slow roasted to utter perfection. When in doubt, ask – the waiters really know their stuff.

★ Frasca ITALIAN $$$

(☎303-442-6966; www.frascafoodandwine.com; 1738 Pearl St; mains $35, tasting menus $50-115; ◷5:30-9:30pm Mon-Thu, to 10:30pm Fri, 5-10:30pm Sat; ▮; ▢HOP, 204) Deemed Boulder's finest by many (the wine service earned a James Beard award), Frasca has an impeccable kitchen and only the freshest farm-to-table ingredients. Rotating dishes range from earthy braised pork to housemade gnocchi and grilled quail served with leeks and wilted pea shoots. Reserve days, even weeks in advance. Mondays offer 'bargain' $50 tasting menus with suggested wine pairings.

🍸 Drinking & Entertainment

★ Mountain Sun BREWERY

(☎303-546-0886; www.mountainsunpub.com; 1535 Pearl St; ◷11am-1am; ▮; ▢HOP, 205, 206) Boulder's favorite brewery cheerfully serves a smorgasbord of fine brews and packs in everyone from yuppies to hippies. Best of all is its community atmosphere. The pub grub, especially the burgers and chili, is delicious and it's fully family friendly, with board games and kids' meals. There's often live bluegrass and reggae on Sunday, Monday and Wednesday nights. Cash only.

Avery Brewing Company BREWERY

(☎303-440-4324; www.averybrewing.com; 4910 Nautilus Ct; ◷3-11pm Mon, 11am-11pm Tue-Sun; ▢205) For craft breweries, how big is too big? Avery pushes the limit, with its imposing two-story building, complete with gift shop selling hats and tees. But the 1st-floor patio and tap room are lively and fun, while upstairs has a quieter restaurant feel. One thing's for sure: the beer's outstanding, from Apricot Sour to a devilish Mephistopheles Stout. Guided tours available.

Located about 6 miles northeast of downtown.

Boulder Dushanbe Teahouse TEAHOUSE

(☎303-442-4993; www.boulderteahouse.com; 1770 13th St; mains $8-24; ◷8am-9pm; ▮; ▢203, 204, 205, 206, 208, 225, DASH, JUMP, SKIP) It's impossible to find better ambience than at this incredible Tajik teahouse, a gift from Dushanbe, Boulder's sister city. The elaborate carvings and paintings were reassembled over an eight-year period on the edge of **Central Park**. It's too bad the fusion fare is so lackluster, but it's very worth coming here for a pot of tea.

eTown Hall LIVE MUSIC

(☎303-443-8696; www.etown.org; 1535 Spruce St; from $25; ◷hours vary; ▢HOP) Beautiful, brand-new and solar-powered, this repurposed church is the home of the eTown radio show (heard on National Public Radio). The show features rising and well-known artists and you can get in on it by attending a live taping in its 200-seat theater. Tapings run two hours starting at 7pm, and are typically held on weeknights.

🛍 Shopping

★ Pearl Street Mall AREA

(Pearl St, btwn 9th & 15th Sts; ▮▧; ▢205, 206, 208, HOP, SKIP) The highlight of downtown Boulder is the Pearl Street Mall, a vibrant pedestrian zone filled with kids' climbing boulders and splash fountains, bars, galleries and restaurants. Street performers often come out in force on weekends.

★ Boulder Book Store BOOKS

(☎303-447-2074; www.boulderbookstore.net; 1107 Pearl St; ◷10am-10pm Mon-Sat, to 9pm Sun; ▩▮; ▢208, HOP, SKIP) Boulder's favorite indie bookstore has a huge travel section downstairs, along with all the hottest new fiction and nonfiction. Check the visiting-authors lineup posted at the entry and on its website.

★ **Common Threads** CLOTHING
(☑303-449-5431; www.shopcommonthreads.
com; 2707 Spruce St; ⊘10am-6pm Mon, Tue &
Thu-Sat, to 7pm Wed; ⬚205, BOLT, HOP) Vintage
shopping at its most haute couture, this
fun place is where to go for secondhand
Choos and Prada purses. Prices are higher
than at your run-of-the-mill vintage shop,
but clothes, shoes and bags are always in
good condition, and the designer clothing is
guaranteed authentic. Offers fun classes on
clothes altering and innovating.

ⓘ Information

Boulder Visitor Center (☑303-442-2911;
www.bouldercoloradousa.com; 2440 Pearl St;
⊘8:30am-5pm Mon-Fri; ⬚HOP) Set in the
Boulder Chamber of Commerce, this visitor
center offers basic information, maps and tips
on nearby hiking trails and other activities.
There's a more accessible **tourist information
kiosk** (☑303-417-1365; cnr Pearl & 13th Sts;
⊘10am-8pm; ⬚208, HOP, SKIP) on the Pearl
St Mall in front of the courthouse.

Boulder Ranger District (☑303-541-2500;
2140 Yarmouth Ave; ⊘8:30am-4:30pm Mon-
Fri; ⬚204) This US Forest Service outpost
provides information on the national forests
that surround the Rocky Mountain National
Park, including campgrounds and trails that
cross between the two.

ⓘ Getting There & Around

Located just 45 miles from Boulder, Denver
International Airport (p762) is the main entry
point for travelers arriving by air.

Green Ride (☑303-997-0238; http://greenride
boulder.com; 4800 Baseline Rd, D110; 1-way $28-
38) Serving Boulder and its satellite suburbs, this
Denver International Airport shuttle is cheap and
convenient ($28 to $38), working on an hourly
schedule (3:25am to 11:25pm). The cheapest
service leaves from the depot. Additional travelers in groups are discounted.

SuperShuttle (☑303-444-0808; www.
supershuttle.com; 1-way from $84) Provides a
private van service to the airport (from $84).
The base fare includes up to three people; each
additional person costs $25. Unless you have
loads of luggage, parties of four or more are
better served by a taxi.

RTD (p762) buses travel to Denver, Denver International Airport, Nederland and within Boulder. **Boulder Transit Center** (☑303-299-6000;
www.rtd-denver.com; 1800 14th St; ⬚204, 205,
208, N, DASH, HOP, JUMP, SKIP) is a good place
to pick up maps of the area's bus system, and
offers free public parking on weekends.

Most streets have dedicated bike lanes and the
Boulder Creek Bike Path (⬚) is a must-ride commuter corridor. There are plenty of places to get
your hands on a rental. With rental cruisers stationed all over the city, **Boulder B-Cycle** (☑303-
532-4412; www.boulder.bcycle.com; 24hr rental
$8; ⊘office 9am-5pm Mon-Fri, 10am-3pm Sat) is
a popular citywide program of hourly or daily bike
rentals, but riders must sign up online first. The
downtown area is also pleasantly walkable.

Northern Mountains

With one foot on either side of the continental divide and behemoths of granite in every
direction, Colorado's Northern Mountains offer out-of-this-world alpine adventures, laid-
back skiing, kick-butt hiking and biking, and
plenty of rivers to raft, fish and float.

Rocky Mountain National Park

This **park** (www.nps.gov/romo; vehicle 1/7 days
$20/30, motorcycle, foot & bicycle 1/7 days $10/15,
annual passes $60) is a place of natural spec-
tacle on every scale: from hulking granite
formations, many taller than 12,000ft, some
over 130 million years old, to the delicate
yellow burst of the glacier lily, one of the
dozen alpine wildflowers that explode in
short, colorful life at the edge of receding
snowfields for a few days every spring.

Though it doesn't rank among the largest
national parks in the USA (it's only 265,000
acres), it's rightly among the most popular,
hosting four million visitors every year.

This is a place of natural spectacle on
every scale: from hulking granite formations, many taller than 12,000ft, some over

---

BOULDER COUNTY FARMERS MARKET

This **market** (☑303-910-2236; www.
boulderfarmers.org; 13th St, btwn Canyon
Blvd & Arapahoe Ave; ⊘8am-2pm Sat Apr-
Nov, 4-8pm Wed May-Oct; ☑⬚⬚; ⬚203,
204, 205, 206, 208, 225, DASH, JUMP, SKIP)
is a massive spring and summer sprawl
of colorful, mostly organic local food.
Find flowers and herbs, as well as brain-
sized mushrooms, delicate squash
blossoms, crusty pretzels, vegan dips,
grass-fed beef, raw granola and yogurt.
Prepared food booths offer all sorts of
international taste treats. Live music is
as standard as the family picnics in the
park along Boulder Creek.

130 million years old, to the delicate yellow burst of the glacier lily, one of the dozen alpine wildflowers that explode in short, colorful life at the edge of receding snowfields for a few days every spring.

And though it tops many travelers' itineraries and can get maddeningly crowded, the park has miles of less-beaten paths and the backcountry is a little-explored nature-lovers' wonderland. Excellent hiking trails crisscross alpine fields, skirt the edge of isolated high-altitude lakes and bring travelers to the wild, untamed heart of the Rockies.

⊙ Sights & Activities

With over 300 miles of trail, traversing all aspects of its diverse terrain, the park is suited to every hiking ability. Those with the kids in tow might consider the easy hikes in the Wild Basin to Calypso Falls, or to Gem Lake in the Lumpy Ridge area, while those with unlimited ambition, strong legs and enough trail mix will be lured by the challenge of summiting Longs Peak. Regardless, it's best to spend at least one night at 7000ft to 8000ft prior to setting out to allow your body to adjust to the elevation. Before July, many trails are snowbound and high water runoff makes passage difficult. In the winter, avalanches are a hazard.

★ **Moraine Park Museum**   MUSEUM
(☑ 970-586-1206; Bear Lake Rd; ⊙ 9am-4:30pm Jun-Oct; ➹) FREE Built by the Civilian Conservation Corps in 1923 and once the park's proud visitors lodge, this building has been renovated in recent years to host exhibits on geology, glaciers and wildlife. Kids will like the interactive exhibits and half-mile nature trail out the door.

🛏 Sleeping

Glacier Basin Campground   CAMPGROUND $
(☑ 877-444-6777; www.recreation.gov; off Bear Lake Rd; RV & tent sites summer $26) This developed campground is surrounded by evergreens, offering plenty of sun and shade. It also sports a large area for group camping and accommodates RVs. It is served by the shuttle buses on Bear Lake Rd throughout the summer. Make reservations through the website.

Aspenglen Campground   CAMPGROUND $
(☑ 877-444-6777; www.recreation.gov; State Hwy 34; summer tent & RV sites $26) With only 54 sites, this is the smallest of the park's reservable camping grounds. There are many tent-only sites, including some walk-ins, and

a limited number of trailers are allowed. This is the quietest campground in the park while still being highly accessible (5 miles west of Estes Park on US 34). Make reservations through the website.

Moraine Park Campground   CAMPGROUND $
(☑ 877-444-6777; www.recreation.gov; off Bear Lake Rd; summer tent & RV sites $26, winter $18) In the middle of a stand of ponderosa pine forest off Bear Lake Rd, this is the biggest of the park's campgrounds, approximately 2.5 miles south of the Beaver Meadows Visitor Center and with 245 sites. The walk-in, tent-only sites in the D Loop are recommended if you want quiet. Make reservations through the website.

Olive Ridge Campground   CAMPGROUND $
(☑ 303-541-2500; www.recreation.gov; State Hwy 7; tent sites $26; ⊙ mid-May–Nov) This well-kept USFS campground has access to four trailheads: St Vrain Mountain, Wild Basin, Longs Peak and Twin Sisters. In the summer it can get full; sites are first-come, first-served.

❶ Information

For private vehicles, the park entrance fee is $20 for one day and $30 for seven. Annual passes are $60. Individuals entering the park on foot, bicycle, motorcycle or bus pay $10 each for one day and $15 for seven.

Backcountry permits ($26 for a group of up to seven people for seven days) are required for overnight stays in the 260 designated backcountry camping sites in the park. A bear box to store your food in is required if you are staying overnight in the backcountry between May and October (established campsites already have them).

Alpine Visitor Center (www.nps.gov/romo; Fall River Pass; ⊙ 10:30am-4:30pm late May–mid-Jun, 9am-5pm late Jun-early Sep, 10:30am-4:30pm early Sep–mid-Oct; ➹)

Beaver Meadows Visitor Center (☑ 970-586-1206; www.nps.gov/romo; US Hwy 36; ⊙ 8am-9pm late Jun–late Aug, to 4:30pm or 5pm rest of year; ➹)

Kawuneeche Visitor Center (☑ 970-627-3471; 16018 US Hwy 34; ⊙ 8am-6pm last week May–Labor Day, to 5pm Labor Day–Sep, to 4:30pm Oct-May; ➹)

❶ Getting There & Away

Trail Ridge Rd (US 34) is the only east–west route through the park; the US 34 eastern approach from I-25 and Loveland follows the Big Thompson River Canyon. The most direct route from Boulder follows US 36 through Lyons to the east entrances. Another approach from the south, mountainous Hwy 7, passes by **Enos Mills Cabin** (🖉 970-586-4706; www.enosmills. com; 6760 Hwy 7; $20; ⊙ 11am-4pm Tue & Wed summer, by appointment only; ♿) and provides access to campsites and trailheads on the east side of the divide. Winter closure of US 34 through the park makes access to the park's west side dependent on US 40 at Granby.

There are two entrance stations on the east side: **Fall River** (US 34) and **Beaver Meadows** (US 36). The **Grand Lake Entrance Station** (US 34) is the only entry on the west side. Year-round access is available through Kawuneeche Valley along the Colorado River headwaters to **Timber Creek Campground** (Trail Ridge Rd, US Hwy 34; tent & RV sites $26). The main centers of visitor activity on the park's east side are the Alpine Visitor Center (p767), high on Trail Ridge Rd, and Bear Lake Rd, which leads to campgrounds, trailheads and the Moraine Park Museum (p767).

North of Estes Park, Devils Gulch Rd leads to several hiking trails. Further out on Devils Gulch Rd, you pass through the village of Glen Haven to reach the trailhead entry to the park along the North Fork of the Big Thompson River.

ⓘ Getting Around

A majority of visitors enter the park in their own cars, using the long and winding Trail Ridge Rd (US 34) to cross the Continental Divide. There are options for those without wheels, however. In summer a free shuttle bus operates from the **Estes Park Visitor Center** (🖉 970-577-9900; www.visitestespark.com; 500 Big Thompson Ave; ⊙ 9am-8pm daily Jun-Aug, 8am-5pm Mon-Fri, 9am-5pm Sat & 10am-4pm Sun Sep-May) multiple times daily, bringing hikers to a park-and-ride location where you can pick up other shuttles. The year-round option leaves the Glacier Basin parking area and heads to Bear Lake, in the park's lower elevations.

During the summer peak, a second shuttle operates between Moraine Park campground and the Glacier Basin parking area. The second shuttle runs on weekends only from mid-August through September.

Estes Park

Estes Park is just seconds from one of the US's most popular national parks. The town itself is a jib-jab of T-shirt shops and ice-cream parlors, sidewalks jammed with tourists and streets plugged with RVs. But when the sun reflects just right off Lake Estes, or you spend an afternoon with a lazy coffee on the riverwalk, you might just find a little piece of zen.

🏃 Activities

★ **Colorado Mountain School**   CLIMBING
(🖉 800-836-4008; https://coloradomountain school.com; 341 Moraine Ave; half-day guided climbs per person from $125) Simply put, there's no better resource for climbers in Colorado – this outfit is the largest climbing operator in the region, has the most expert guides and is the only organization allowed to operate within Rocky Mountain National Park. It has a clutch of classes taught by world-class instructors.

🛏 Sleeping

Be warned: lodgings fill up very fast during the peak July and August period, when prices are sky high.

Estes Park KOA   CAMPGROUND $
(🖉 970-586-2888, 800-562-1887; www.estespark koa.com; 2051 Big Thompson Ave; tent sites $27-33, RV sites $38-48, cabins from $75; 🛜) With so much excellent camping just up the road in Rocky Mountain National Park, it's hard to see the allure of this roadside RV-oriented camping spot. But for those in need of a staging day before a big adventure, the proximity to town is appealing.

★ **YMCA of the Rockies – Estes Park Center**   RESORT $$
(🖉 888-613-9622; www.ymcarockies.org; 2515 Tunnel Rd; r & d from $109, cabins from $129; 🅿❄✻🛜🐾) Estes Park Center is not your typical YMCA boarding house. Instead it's a favorite vacation spot with families, boasting upmarket motel-style accommodations and cabins set on hundreds of acres of high alpine terrain. Choose from roomy cabins that sleep up to 10 or motel-style rooms for singles or doubles. Both are simple and practical.

Stanley Hotel   HOTEL $$
(🖉 970-577-4000; www.stanleyhotel.com; 333 Wonderview Ave; r from $200; 🅿🛜✻🐾) The white Georgian Colonial Revival hotel stands in brilliant contrast to the towering peaks of Rocky Mountain National Park that frame the skyline. A favorite local retreat, this best-in-class hotel served as the inspiration for Stephen King's famous cult novel *The Shining*. Rooms are decorated to retain some of the Old West feel while still ensuring all the creature comforts.

Black Canyon   LODGE $$$
(🖉 800-897-3730; www.blackcanyoninn.com; 800 MacGregor Ave; 1-/2-/3-bed r from $150/199/399;

P⊕❄?) A fine place to splurge, this lovely, secluded 14-acre property offers luxury suites and a 'rustic' log cabin (which comes with a Jacuzzi). The rooms are dressed out with stone fireplaces, dark wood and woven tapestries in rich dark colors.

✖ Eating

Self-caterers will make out best by stocking up at the local **Safeway supermarket** (☏970-586-4447; 451 E Wonderview Ave; ☺9am-7pm Mon-Fri, to 6pm Sat, 10am-4pm Sun; P❄) on the way into town to picnic at **Bond Park** (E Elkhorn Ave) or in one of the national park picnic spots up the road.

Ed's Cantina & Grill   MEXICAN $
(☏970-586-2919; www.edscantina.com; 390 E Elkhorn Ave; mains $9-12; ☺11am-late Mon-Fri, 8am-10pm Sat & Sun; ❧) With an outdoor patio right on the river, Ed's is a great place to kick back with a margarita. Serving Mexican and American staples, the restaurant is in a retro woodsy space with leather booth seating and bold primary colors.

**Smokin' Dave's
BBQ & Tap House**   BARBECUE $$
(☏866-674-2793; www.smokindavesbbqand taphouse.com; 820 Moraine Ave; mains $8-20; ☺11am-9pm Sun-Thu, to 10pm Fri & Sat; ❧) Half-assed BBQ joints are all too common in Colorado's mountain towns, but Dave's, situated in a spare dining room, fully delivers. The buffalo ribs and pulled pork come dressed in a slightly sweet, smoky, tangy sauce and the sweet potato fries are crisply fried. Also excellent? The long, well-selected beer list.

ⓘ Getting There & Away

Estes Park Shuttle (☏970-586-5151; www. estesparkshuttle.com; one-way/round-trip $45/85) This shuttle service connects Denver's airport to Estes Park about four times a day. The trip takes two hours.

Steamboat Springs

Sitting on the edge of the Western Slope, Steamboat Springs is an idyllic ski town that's unpretentious, direct, laid-back and just about as Colorado-friendly as you can get.

The ski area here is one of the best in the West, offering terrific skiing for the whole family. Summer is almost as popular as winter, with hiking, backpacking, white-water rafting, mountain biking and a host of other outdoor activities.

🏃 Activities

Steamboat Mountain Resort   SNOW SPORTS
(☏ticket office 970-871-5252; www.steamboat. com; lift tickets adult/child $120/$75; ☺ticket office 8am-5pm) The stats of the Steamboat Ski Area speak volumes for the town's claim as 'Ski Town, USA' – 165 trails, 3668ft vertical and nearly 3000 acres. With excellent powder and trails for all levels, this is the main draw for winter visitors and some of the best skiing in the US. In summer, check out the **Steamboat Bike Park** (www.steamboat.com; Steamboat Mountain Resort; $25; ☺gondola rides 8:30am-4:30pm Jun 10–Aug 28).

⭐**Strawberry Park Hot Springs**   HOT SPRINGS
(☏970-879-0342; www.strawberryhotsprings. com; 44200 County Rd; per day adult/child $15/8; ☺10am-10:30pm Sun-Thu, to midnight Fri & Sat; ❧) ✿ Steamboat's favorite hot springs are actually outside the city limits, and offer great back-to-basics relaxation. The natural pools sit lovingly beside a river. After dark it is adults only and clothing optional (though most people wear swimsuits these days); you'll want a headlamp if you are visiting at this time. On weekends, expect a 15 to 45 minute wait to park.

Orange Peel Bikes   CYCLING
(☏970-879-2957; www.orangepeelbikes.com; 1136 Yampa St; bike rental per day $20-65; ☺10am-6pm Mon-Fri, to 5pm Sat; ❧) In a funky old building at the end of Yampa, this is perfectly situated for renting a bike to ride the trails crisscrossing Howelsen Hill. A staff of serious riders and mechanics can offer tons of information about local trails, including maps. This is the coolest bike shop in town, hands down.

Bucking Rainbow Outfitters RAFTING, FISHING
(☏970-879-8747; www.buckingrainbow.com; 730 Lincoln Ave; inner tubes $18, rafting $50-100, fishing $150-500) This excellent outfitter has fly-fishing, rafting, outdoor apparel and the area's best fly shop, but it's most renowned for its rafting trips on the Yampa and beyond. Rafting trips run from half-day to full-day excursions. Two-hour in-town fly-fishing trips start at $155 per person. It has a tube shack that runs shuttles from Sunpies Bistro on Yampa St.

Old Town Hot Springs   HOT SPRINGS
(☏970-879-1828; www.oldtownhotsprings.org; 136 Lincoln Ave; adult/child $18/11, waterslide $7; ☺5:30am-10pm Mon-Fri, 7am-9pm Sat, 8am-9pm Sun; ❧) Smack dab in the center of town,

the water here is warmer than most other springs in the area. Known by the Utes as the 'medicine springs,' the mineral waters here are said to have special healing powers. Because there's a 230ft waterslide, a climbing wall and plenty of shallow areas, this is your best family-friendly hot springs in town.

🛏 Sleeping & Eating

★ **Vista Verde Guest Ranch**　RANCH $$$
(☏800-526-7433; www.vistaverde.com; 31100 Seedhouse Rd; per week per person from $2700; ❄☏) Simply put, this is the most luxurious of Colorado's top-end guest ranches. Here, you spend the day riding with expert staff, the evening around the fire in an elegantly appointed lodge, and the night in high-thread-count sheets. If you have the means, this is it.

Rex's American Bar & Grill　AMERICAN $
(☏970-870-0438; www.rexsgrill.com; 3190 S Lincoln Ave; mains $11-15; ⊙7am-11pm; P🅿🚻) Grass-fed steaks, elk sausage, bison burgers and other carnivorous delights are the ticket at this place, and they're so good that you'll have to forgive the restaurant's location – attached to the Holiday Inn. By serving until 11pm, it's also the latest dinner you can have in town.

Laundry　AMERICAN $$
(☏970-870-0681; www.thelaundryrestaurant. com; 127 11th St; small plates $10-16, large plates $35-38; ⊙4:30pm-2am) This new-generation Steamboat eatery has some of the best food in town. You'll love creative takes on comfort food, charcuterie boards, big steaks, barbecue, creative presentations and pickled everything. Budget-busters will love sharing small plates – which all go a long way.

ℹ Information

Steamboat Springs Visitor Center (☏970-879-0880; www.steamboat-chamber.com; 125 Anglers Dr; ⊙8am-5pm Mon-Fri, 10am-3pm Sat) This visitor center, facing Sundance Plaza, has a wealth of local information, and its website is also excellent for planning.

USFS Hahns Peak Ranger Office (☏970-879-1870; www.fs.usda.gov; 925 Weiss Dr; ⊙8am-5pm Mon-Sat) Rangers staff this office offering permits and information about surrounding national forests, including Mount Zirkel Wilderness, as well as information on hiking, mountain biking, fishing and other activities in the area.

ℹ Getting There & Away

Greyhound Terminal (☏800-231-2222; www. greyhound.com; 1505 Lincoln Ave) Greyhound's

US 40 service between Denver and Salt Lake City stops here, about half a mile west of town.
Storm Mountain Express (☏877-844-8787; www.stormmountainexpress.com) This shuttle service runs to Yampa Valley Regional Airport ($38 one-way) and beyond, though trips to DIA and Vail get very pricey.

Central Colorado

Colorado's central mountains are well known for their plethora of world-class ski resorts, sky-high hikes and snow-melt rivers. To the southeast are Colorado Springs and Pikes Peak, which anchor the southern Front Range.

Winter Park

Located less than two hours from Denver, unpretentious Winter Park Resort is a favorite with Front Rangers, who drive here to ski fresh tracks each weekend. Beginners can frolic on miles of powdery groomers while experts test their skills on Mary Jane's world-class bumps.

The congenial town is a wonderful base for year-round romping. Most services are found either in the ski village, which is actually south of Winter Park proper, or strung along US 40 (the main drag), which is where you'll find the visitor center. Follow Hwy 40 and you'll get to Fraser – essentially the same town – then Tabernash, and eventually the back of Rocky Mountain National Park.

In addition to downhill and cross-country skiing, Winter Park has some 600 miles of mountain biking trails for all levels. The paved 5.5-mile **Fraser River Trail** runs through the valley from the ski resort to Fraser, connecting to different trail systems. Pick up trail maps at the **visitor center** (☏970-726-4118; www.winterpark-info.com; 78841 Hwy 40; ⊙9am-5pm). You can even bike in winter, too – it's known as fatbiking.

🛏 Sleeping & Eating

There are two first-come, first-served USFS campgrounds off Hwy 40 on the way into Winter Park: **Robber's Roost** (Hwy 40; tent & RV sites $20; ⊙mid-Jun–Aug; 🐾), which has no water, 5 miles from town, and **Idlewild** (Hwy 40; tent & RV sites $20; ⊙late May–Sep; 🐾), 1 mile from town. There's also plenty of free dispersed camping in the surrounding national forest.

★ **Devil's Thumb Ranch**   LODGE $$$
(📞800-933-4339; www.devilsthumbranch.com; 3530 County Rd 83; bunkhouse $119-149, lodge r from $270, cabins from $450; ❋🛜🐾❋) 🦮 The classiest digs in the Winter Park area, this high-altitude ranch is a fantastic base for year-round activities (📞970-726-8231; trail passes adult/child $22/10, horseback riding $95-175; 🐾). Accommodations are plush, but not out of reach. The self-service bunkhouse has the cheapest rates, while the cowboy-chic lodge is a must for a romantic weekend escape. Cabins are a good bet for groups or for more privacy.

★ **Pepe Osaka's Fish Taco**   JAPANESE $
(📞970-726-7159; www.pepeosakas.com; 78707 US Hwy 40; 2 tacos $13-15; ⏰4-9pm daily plus noon-3pm Sat & Sun) You like sushi. You like fish tacos. And as it turns out, you love sushi tacos, because…why not? At this almost-but-not-quite Nikkei eatery (that's Japanese-Peruvian cuisine if you haven't been keeping up), dig in to some outstandingly spicy tuna tacos, ahi *poke* ceviche tacos and blackened mahi-mahi *al pastor* tacos. All served with delish fried plantains and margaritas.

Breckenridge & Around

Set at the foot of the marvelous Tenmile Range, Breck is a sweetly surviving mining town with a vibrant historic district. The down-to-earth vibe is a refreshing change from Colorado's glitzier resorts, and the family-friendly ski runs and gold-nugget history make it Summit County's most atmospheric destination.

⊙ Sights & Activities

Thanks to its endless peaks and adventure opportunities, Breckenridge is easily the highlight of Summit County. Ski groomed runs and high-alpine bowls, snowshoe cross-country, ascend 14,000ft summits, race over miles of mountain-biking trails, go white-water rafting or fish the Blue River.

★ **Barney Ford Museum**   MUSEUM
(www.breckheritage.com; 111 E Washington Ave; suggested donation $5; ⏰11am-3pm Tue-Sun, hours vary seasonally) FREE Barney Ford was an escaped slave who became a prominent entrepreneur and Colorado civil-rights pioneer, and made two stops in Breckenridge (where he ran a 24-hour chopstand serving delicacies such as oysters) over the course of his incredibly rich, tragic and triumphant life. He also owned a restaurant and hotel in Denver. The museum is set in his old home, where he lived from 1882 to 1890.

★ **Breckenridge Ski Area**   SNOW SPORTS
(📞800-789-7669; www.breckenridge.com; lift ticket adult/child $171/111; ⏰8:30am-4pm Nov–mid-Apr; 🚡) Breckenridge spans five mountains, covering 2900 acres and featuring some of the best beginner and intermediate terrain in the state, as well as plenty of exhilarating high-alpine runs and hike-to bowls. There are also four terrain parks and a super pipe.

🎭 Festivals & Events

Ullr Fest   CULTURAL
(www.gobreck.com; ⏰Jan) The Ullr Fest celebrates the Norse god of winter, with a wild parade and four-day festival featuring a fatbike race, a town-wide talent show and a bonfire.

International Snow Sculpture Championship   ART
(www.gobreck.com; ⏰Jan-Feb) The International Snow Sculpture Championship begins in mid-January and lasts for three weeks. It starts with Technical Week, when the snow blocks are made, proceeds with Sculpting Week, when the sculptures are created and then judged by the public, and concludes with Viewing Week, when the sculptures decorate the River Walk.

🛌 Sleeping

★ **Bivvi Hostel**   HOSTEL $
(📞970-423-6553; www.thebivvi.com; 9511 Hwy 9; dm winter/summer from $85/29; 🅿🛜) A modern hostel with a log-cabin vibe, the Bivvi wins points for style, friendliness and affordability. The four- to six-person dorm rooms come with private lockers, en suites and complimentary breakfast; chill out in the funky common room or out on the gorgeous deck, equipped with a gas grill and hot tub. Private rooms are also available.

★ **Abbett Placer Inn**   B&B $$
(📞970-453-6489; www.abbettplacer.com; 205 S French St; r winter/summer from $179/129; 🅿❋@🛜) This violet house has five large rooms decked out with wood furnishings, iPod docks and fluffy robes. It's very low-key. Warm and welcoming hosts cook big breakfasts, and guests can enjoy an outdoor Jacuzzi deck and use of a common kitchenette. The top-floor room has massive views of the peaks from a private terrace. Check-in is from 4pm to 7pm.

✖ Eating & Drinking

★ Breckenridge Distillery — AMERICAN $$

(☑ 970-547-9759; www.breckenridgedistillery.com; 1925 Airport Rd; small plates $10-18; ⏱ 4-9pm Tue-Sat) Served in a big-city-cool dining space, the eclectic menu at this distillery (⏱ 11am-9pm Tue-Sat, to 6pm Sun & Mon) follows the delightful whims of former DC chef Daniel O'Brien, jumping from the sublime *cacio e pepe* (Roman spaghetti and cheese) to chicken-liver profiteroles to dates and marscapone without missing a beat. It's mostly small plates, perfect for sharing over the top-notch cocktails.

★ Crown — CAFE

(☑ 970-453-6022; www.thecrownbreckenridge. com; 215 S Main St; ⏱ 7:30am-8pm; 🛜) Breck's living room might as well be at the Crown, a buzzing cafe-cum-social hub. Grab a mug of Silver Canyon coffee and a sandwich or salad, and catch up on all the latest gossip.

Broken Compass Brewing — BREWERY

(☑ 970-368-2772; www.brokencompassbrewing. com; 68 Continental Ct; ⏱ 11:30am-11pm) Set in an industrial complex at the north end of Airport Road, the Broken Compass is generally regarded as the best brewery in Breckenridge. Fill up with a pint of their Coconut Porter or Chili Pepper Pale and sink back with a couple of friends in the old chairlift. They run a shuttle every two hours between the brewery and town.

ⓘ Information

Visitor Center (☑ 877-864-0868; www.go breck.com; 203 S Main St; ⏱ 9am-6pm; 🛜) Along with a host of maps and brochures, this center has a pleasant riverside museum that delves into Breck's gold-mining past.

ⓘ Getting There & Away

Breckenridge is 80 miles west of Denver via I-70 exit 203, then Hwy 9 south. **Summit Stage** (☑ 970-668-0999; www.summitstage. com). Summit County's free bus service, links Breckenridge with Keystone and A-Basin in winter (Swan Mountain Flyer) and with Frisco year-round.

Vail

Blessed with peaks, graced with blue skies and fresh powder, carved by rivers and groomed with ski slopes and bike trails, Vail is the ultimate Colorado playground. The real draw has always been Vail Mountain, a hulking, domed mass of snow-driven euphoria that offers more terrain than anywhere else in the US: 1500 acres of downhill slopes on the north face and 3500 acres of back-bowl bliss.

Factor in Vail's gourmet offerings, well-coiffed clientele and pretty young powder-fueled staff and you have an adrenaline-addled yuppie utopia.

⊙ Sights & Activities

The draw to Vail is no secret. It's the endless outdoor activities in both winter and summer that make this resort so attractive. Do remember that the mud season (mid-April through May, plus November) holds little attraction for visitors – you can't ski, but you can't really get up into the mountains to hike around either.

★ Vail Mountain — SNOW SPORTS

(☑ 970-754-8245; www.vail.com; lift ticket adult/child $189/130; ⏱ 9am-4pm Nov–mid-Apr; 🅿) Vail Mountain is our favorite in Colorado, with 5289 skiable acres, 195 trails, three terrain parks and (ahem) the highest lift-ticket prices on the continent. If you're a Colorado ski virgin, it's worth experiencing your first time here – especially on a bluebird fresh-powder day. Multiday tickets are good at three other resorts (Beaver Creek, Breck and Keystone).

Vail to Breckenridge Bike Path — CYCLING

(www.summitbiking.org) This paved, car-free bike path stretches 8.7 miles from East Vail to the top of Vail Pass (elevation gain 1831ft), before descending 14 miles into Frisco (it's 9 miles more if you go all the way to Breckenridge). If you're only interested in the downhill, hop on a shuttle from **Bike Valet** (☑ 970-476-7770; www.bikevalet.net; 616 W Lionshead Cir; bike rental per day from $50; ⏱ 9am-6pm; 🅿) and enjoy the ride back to Vail.

🛏 Sleeping

Gore Creek Campground — CAMPGROUND $

(☑ 877-444-6777; www.recreation.gov; Bighorn Rd; tent sites $22; ⏱ mid-May–Sep; 🅿) This campground at the end of Bighorn Rd has 19 tent sites with picnic tables and fire grates nestled in the woods by Gore Creek. There is excellent fishing near here – try the Slate Creek or Deluge Lake trails; the latter leads to a fish-packed lake. The campground is 6 miles east of Vail Village via exit 180 (East Vail) off I-70.

Austria Haus   HOTEL $$$
(☑ 866-921-4050; www.austriahaushotel.com; 242 E Meadow Dr; r winter/summer from $500/280; ⓟ❋⛦🛜🛁) One of Vail's longest-running properties, the Austria Haus offers both hotel rooms and condos (more information at www.austriahausclub.com), so make sure you're clear on what you're signing up for. In the hotel, charming details such as wood-framed doorways, Berber carpet and marble baths make for a pleasant stay. Fuel up at the generous breakfast spread in the morning.

★ **Sebastian Hotel**   HOTEL $$$
(☑ 800-354-6908; www.thesebastianvail.com; 16 Vail Rd; r winter/summer from $800/300; ⓟ❋🛜🛁🐾) Deluxe and modern, this sophisticated hotel showcases tasteful contemporary art and an impressive list of amenities, including a mountainside ski valet, luxury spa and 'adventure concierge.' Room rates dip in the summer, the perfect time to enjoy the tapas bar and spectacular pool area, with hot tubs frothing and spilling over like champagne.

✖ Eating & Drinking

★ **Westside Cafe**   DINER $
(☑ 970-476-7890; www.westsidecafe.net; 2211 N Frontage Rd; mains $9-16; ⊙ 7am-3pm Mon-Wed, to 10pm Thu-Sun; 🛜👶) Set in a West Vail strip mall, the Westside is a local institution. It does terrific all-day-breakfast skillets – like the 'My Big Fat Greek Skillet' with scrambled eggs, gyro, red onion, tomato and feta served with warm pita – along with all the usual high-cal offerings you need before or after a day on the slopes. Also has a grab-and-go counter.

bōl   AMERICAN $$
(☑ 970-476-5300; www.bolvail.com; 141 E Meadow Dr; mains $18-27; ⊙ 2pm-1am; 🛜🐾) Half hip eatery, half space-age bowling alley, bōl is the most unusual hangout in Vail. You can go bowling in the back ($105 to $300 per hour!), but it's the eclectic menu that's the real draw: creations range from lamb lollipops and blue corn–crusted chile rellenos to duck-confit gnocchi.

★ **Game Creek Restaurant**   AMERICAN $$$
(☑ 970-754-4275; www.gamecreekvail.com; Game Creek Bowl; 3-/4-course meal $99/109; ⊙ 5:30-9pm Tue-Sat Dec-Apr, 5:30-8:30pm Thu-Sat & 11am-2pm Sun late Jun–Aug; 🐾👶) This gourmet destination is nestled high in the spectacular Game Creek Bowl. Take the Eagle Bahn Gondola to Eagle's Nest and staff

---

CLIMBING YOUR FIRST FOURTEENER

Known as Colorado's easiest fourteener, **Quandary Peak** (www.14ers.com; County Rd 851) is the state's 15th highest peak at 14,265ft. Though you'll see plenty of dogs and children, 'easiest' may be misleading – the summit remains 3 grueling miles from the trailhead.

It's 6 miles round-trip, taking roughly between seven and eight hours. To get here, take Hwy 9 south from Breckenridge toward Hoosier Pass. Make a right on County Rd 850 and turn right again onto 851. Drive 1.1 miles to the unmarked trailhead. Park parallel on the fire road. Go between June and September.

---

will shuttle you (via snowcat in the winter) to their lodge-style restaurant, which serves an American-French menu with stars like wild boar, elk tenderloin and succulent leg of lamb. Reserve.

★ **Sweet Basil**   AMERICAN $$$
(☑ 970-476-0125; www.sweetbasilvail.com; 193 Gore Creek Dr; mains lunch $18-22, dinner $27-48; ⊙ 11:30am-2:30pm & 6pm-late) 🍴 In business since 1977, Sweet Basil remains one of Vail's top restaurants. The menu changes seasonally, but the eclectic American fare, which usually includes favorites such as Colorado lamb and seared Rocky Mountain trout, is consistently innovative and excellent. The ambience is also fantastic. Reserve.

ⓘ Information

Vail Visitor Center (☑ 970-477-3522; www. vailgov.com; 241 S Frontage Rd; ⊙ 8:30am-5:30pm winter, to 8pm summer; 🛜) Provides maps, last-minute lodging deals and activities and town information. It's located next to the Transportation Center. The larger **Lionshead welcome center** is located at the entrance to the parking garage.

ⓘ Getting There & Around

Eagle County Airport (☑ 970-328-2680; www. flyvail.com; 217 Eldon Wilson Dr, Gypsum) This airport is 35 miles west of Vail and has services to destinations across the country (many of which fly through Denver) and rental-car counters.

Colorado Mountain Express Shuttles to/from Denver International Airport ($92, three hours) and Eagle County Airport ($51, 40 minutes). All buses arrive and depart from the Vail Transportation Center.

Eagle County Regional Transportation Authority (www.eaglecounty.us; per ride $4, to Leadville $7) ECO buses offer affordable transport to Beaver Creek, Minturn and even Leadville. Buses run from roughly 5am to 11pm; check the website for the exact schedule. Buses leave from the **Vail Transportation Center** (☑ 970-476-5137; 241 S Frontage Rd).

Vail Transit (☑ 970-477-3456; www.vailgov. com; ☻ 6:30am-1:30am) Loops through all the Vail resort areas – West Vail (both North and South), Vail Village, Lionshead and East Vail, as well as Ford Park and Sandstone. Most buses have bike and ski racks and all are free.

Aspen

Here's a unique town, unlike anyplace else in the American West. It's a cocktail of cowboy grit, Euro panache, Hollywood glam, Ivy League brains, fresh powder, live music and lots of money. It's the kind of place where no matter the season you can bring on a head rush in countless ways.

☉ Sights & Activities

★ **Aspen Center for Environmental Studies**   OUTDOORS
(ACES; ☑ 970-925-5756; www.aspennature.org; 100 Puppy Smith St, Hallam Lake; ☻ 9am-5pm Mon-Fri; 👶) FREE The Aspen Center for Environmental Studies is a 25-acre wildlife sanctuary that hugs the Roaring Fork River and miles of hiking trails in the Hunter Creek Valley. With a mission to advance environmental conservation, the center's naturalists provide free guided hikes and snowshoe tours, raptor demonstrations (eagles and owls are among the residents) and special programs for youngsters.

★ **Aspen Snowmass Ski Resort**   SNOW SPORTS
(☑ 800-525-6200; www.aspensnowmass.com; 4-mountain lift ticket adult/child $164/105; ☻ 9am-4pm Dec–mid-Apr; 👶) OK, the top winter activity here is pretty much a given: the pursuit of powder, and lots of it. The Aspen Skiing Company runs the area's four resorts – **Snowmass** (☑ 970-923-0560; ☻ late Nov–mid Apr; 👶), best all-around choice, with the most terrain and vertical; **Aspen** (☑ 970-925-1220; 601 E Dean St; ☻ late Nov–mid-Apr), intermediate/expert; the **Highlands** (☑ 970-920-7009; Prospector Rd; ☻ Dec–early Apr), expert; and **Buttermilk** (☑ 970-925-1220; Hwy

82; ☻ Dec–Mar; 👶), beginner/terrain parks – which are spread out through the valley and connected by free shuttles.

★ **Maroon Bells**   HIKING, SKIING
If you have but one day to enjoy a slice of pristine wilderness, spend it in the shadow of Colorado's most iconic mountains: the pyramid-shaped twins of **North Maroon Peak** (14,014ft) and **South Maroon Peak** (14,156ft). Eleven miles southwest of Aspen, it all starts on the shores of **Maroon Lake**, an absolutely stunning spot backed by the towering, striated summits.

Aspen Art Museum   MUSEUM
(☑ 970-925-8050; www.aspenartmuseum.org; 637 E Hyman Ave; ☻ 10am-6pm Tue-Sun) FREE Opening in 2014, the art museum's striking new building features a warm, lattice-like exterior designed by Pritzker Prize winner Shigeru Ban, and contains three floors of gallery space. There's no permanent collection, just edgy, innovative contemporary exhibitions featuring paintings, mixed media, sculpture, video installations and photography by artists such as Mamma Andersson, Mark Manders and Susan Philipsz. Art lovers will not leave disappointed. Head up to the roof for views and a bite to eat at the cool cafe.

🛌 Sleeping

★ **Difficult Campground**   CAMPGROUND $
(☑ 877-444-6777; www.recreation.gov; Hwy 82; tent & RV sites $24-26; ☻ mid-May–Sep; 🐾) The largest campground in the Aspen area, Difficult is one of four sites at the foot of Independence Pass and the only one that takes reservations. Located 5 miles west of town, it also has the lowest altitude (8000ft). Higher up are three smaller campgrounds: **Weller**, **Lincoln Gulch** and **Lost Man**. Water is available, but no electrical hookups for RVs.

Annabelle Inn   HOTEL $$
(☑ 877-266-2466; www.annabelleinn.com; 232 W Main St; r winter/summer from $249/200; P👶@🛜) Personable and unpretentious, the cute and quirky Annabelle Inn resembles an old-school European-style ski lodge in a central location. Rooms are cozy without being too cute, and come with flat-screen TVs and warm duvets. We enjoyed the after-dark ski-video screenings from the upper-deck hot tub (one of two on the property); a good breakfast is included.

★ **Limelight Hotel**   HOTEL **$$$**
(☑ 855-925-3025; www.limelighthotel.com; 355
S Monarch St; r winter/summer from $500/250;
P ✹ 🛜 🐾 🍽) Sleek and trendy, the Lime-
light's brick-and-glass modernism reflects
Aspen's vibe. Rooms are spacious, with
stylish accoutrements: granite washbasins,
leather headboards and mountain views
from the balconies and rooftop terraces. Ad-
ditional perks include shuttles that run to all
the slopes and a fab breakfast.

✗ Eating & Drinking

Justice Snow's   AMERICAN **$$**
(☑ 970-429-8192; www.justicesnows.com; 328
E Hyman Ave; mains lunch $12-18, dinner $17-26;
⏱11am-2am Mon-Fri, 9am-2am Sat & Sun; 🛜🚳)
● Located in the historic **Wheeler Opera
House** (☑ 970-920-5770; www.aspenshowtix.com;
320 E Hyman Ave; ⏱box office noon-5pm Mon-Fri),
Justice Snow's is a retro-fitted old saloon that
marries antique wooden furnishings with a
deft modern touch. Although nominally a
bar – the speakeasy cocktails are the soul of
the place – the affordable and locally sourced
menu (a $12 gourmet burger – in Aspen!) is
what keeps the locals coming back.

★ **Pyramid Bistro**   CAFE **$$**
(☑ 970-925-5338; www.pyramidbistro.com; 221
E Main St; mains lunch $12-18, dinner $19-29;
⏱11:30am-9:30pm; 🚳) ● Set on the top
floor of **Explore Booksellers** (☑ 970-925-
5336; www.explorebooksellers.com; 221 E Main
St; ⏱10am-9pm; 🛜), this gourmet veggie
cafe serves up some delightful creations,
including sweet-potato gnocchi with goat's
cheese, red-lentil sliders and quinoa salad
with avocado, goji berries and sesame vin-
aigrette. Definitely Aspen's top choice for
health-conscious fare.

★ **Matsuhisa**   JAPANESE **$$$**
(☑ 970-544-6628; www.matsuhisarestaurants.
com; 303 E Main St; mains $29-42, 2 pieces sushi
$8-12; ⏱5:30pm-close) The original Colorado
link in Matsuhisa Nobu's iconic global chain
that now wraps around the world, this converted house is more intimate than its Vail
sibling and still turns out spectacular dishes such as miso black cod, Chilean sea bass
with truffle, and flavorful uni (sea urchin)
shooters.

Aspen Brewing Co   BREWERY
(☑970-920-2739; www.aspenbrewingcompany.
com; 304 E Hopkins Ave; ⏱noon-late; 🛜) With
five signature flavors and a sun-soaked balcony facing the mountain, this is definitely
the place to unwind after a hard day's play.
Brews range from the flavorful This Year's
Blonde and high-altitude Independence Pass
Ale (its IPA) to the mellower Conundrum Red
Ale and the chocolatey Pyramid Peak Porter.

Woody Creek Tavern   PUB
(☑970-923-4585; www.woodycreektavern.com; 2
Woody Creek Plaza, 2858 Upper River Rd; ⏱11am-
10pm) Enjoying a 100% agave tequila and
fresh-lime margarita at the late, great gonzo
journalist Hunter S Thompson's favorite watering hole is well worth the 8-mile drive – or
Rio Grande Trail (www.riograndetrail.com; Puppy
Smith St) bike ride – from Aspen. The walls at
this rustic funky tavern, a local haunt since
1980, are plastered with newspaper clippings,
photos of customers and paraphernalia.

ℹ Information

Aspen-Sopris Ranger District (☑ 970-925-
3445; www.fs.usda.gov/whiteriver; 806 W
Hallam St; ⏱8am-4:30pm Mon-Fri) The USFS
Aspen-Sopris Ranger District operates about
20 campgrounds and covers Roaring Fork Val-
ley and from Independence Pass to Glenwood
Springs, including the Maroon Bells Wilderness.
Come here for maps and hiking tips.

Aspen Visitor Center (☑ 970-925-1940;
www.aspenchamber.org; 425 Rio Grande Pl;
⏱8:30am-5pm Mon-Fri) Located across from
Rio Grande Park.

Cooper Street Kiosk (cnr E Cooper Ave & S
Galena St; ⏱10am-6pm) Maps, brochures and
magazines.

ℹ Getting There & Around

Aspen-Pitkin County Airport (☑ 970-920-
5380; www.aspenairport.com; 233 E Airport
Rd; 🛜) Four miles northwest of Aspen on Hwy
82, this spry airport has direct year-round
flights from Denver, as well as seasonal flights
direct to eight US cities, including Los Angeles and Chicago. Several car-rental agencies
operate here. A free bus runs to and from the
airport, departing every 10 to 15 minutes.

Colorado Mountain Express (☑ 800-525-
6363; www.coloradomountainexpress.com;
adult/child to DIA $120/61.50; 🛜) Runs
frequent shuttles to/from the Denver International Airport (four hours).

Roaring Fork Transportation Authority (RFTA;
☑970-925-8484; www.rfta.com; 430 E Durant
Ave, Aspen; ⏱6:15am-2:15am; 🛜) RFTA buses
connect Aspen with the Highlands, Snowmass
and Buttermilk via free shuttles, while the **Ve-
lociRFTA** serves the down-valley towns of Basalt
($4, 25 minutes), Carbondale ($6, 45 minutes)
and Glenwood Springs ($7, one hour).

Salida

Blessed with one of the state's largest historic districts, Salida is not only an inviting spot to explore, it also has an unbeatable location, with the Arkansas River on one side and the intersection of two large mountain ranges on the other. The plan of attack here is to hike, bike or raft during the day, then come back to town to refuel with grilled buffalo ribs and a cold IPA at night.

🏃 Activities

Both bikers and hikers should note that some big-time trails – the **Continental Divide** (www.continentaldividetrail.org), the **Colorado Trail** (www.coloradotrail.org) and the **Rainbow Trail** – are within spitting distance of town. If you don't want to sweat it, a **gondola** (☎719-539-4091; www.monarchcrest. net; adult/child $10/5; ⊙8:30am-5:30pm mid-May–mid-Sep) can haul you from Monarch Pass nearly 1000ft up to the top of the ridge.

★Absolute Bikes
CYCLING

(☎719-539-9295; www.absolutebikes.com; 330 W Sackett Ave; bike rental per day $15-100, tours from $90; ⊙9am-6pm; 🖭) The go-to place for bike enthusiasts, offering maps, gear, advice, rentals (cruisers and mountain bikes) and, most importantly, shuttles to the trailhead. Check out the great selection of guided rides, from St Elmo ghost town to the Monarch Crest.

★Monarch Crest Trail
MOUNTAIN BIKING

One of the most famous rides in all of Colorado, the Monarch Crest is an extreme 20- to 35-mile adventure. It starts off at Monarch Pass (11,312ft), follows the exposed ridge 12 miles to Marshall Pass and then either cuts down to Poncha Springs on an old railroad grade or hooks onto the Rainbow Trail. A classic ride with fabulous high-altitude views.

Arkansas River Tours
RAFTING

(☎800-321-4352; www.arkansasrivertours.com; 19487 Hwy 50; half-/full-day adult $59/109, child $49/99; ⊙May-Aug; 🖭) This outfit runs from Brown's Canyon downstream, specializing in Royal Gorge trips. They have an office in Cotopaxi, 23 miles east of Salida.

🛏 Sleeping

Salida has a good hostel and hotel in town, along with a smattering of generic motels on the outskirts. The **Arkansas Headwaters Recreation Area** (☎719-539-7289; http://cpw. state.co.us; 307 W Sackett Ave; ⊙8am-5pm, closed noon-1pm Sat & Sun) operates six campgrounds (bring your own water) along the river, including **Hecla Junction** (☎719-539-7289; http://coloradostateparks.reserveamerica.com; Hwy 285, Mile 135; tent & RV sites $18, plus daily pass $7; 🐾). Another top campground is **Monarch Park** (☎877-444-6777; www.recreation.gov; off Hwy 50; tent & RV sites $18; ⊙Jun-Sep; 🐾), up by the pass, near the hiking and biking along the Monarch Crest and Rainbow Trails.

★Simple Lodge & Hostel
HOSTEL $

(☎719-650-7381; www.simplelodge.com; 224 E 1st St; dm/d/q $24/60/84; 🅿@🛜🐾) If only Colorado had more spots like this. Run by the super-friendly Mel and Justin, this hostel is simple but stylish, with a fully stocked kitchen and a comfy communal area that feels just like home. It's a popular stopover for touring cyclists following the coast-to-coast Rte 50 – you're likely to meet some interesting folks here.

🍴 Eating

Fritz
TAPAS $

(☎719-539-0364; 113 East Sackett St; tapas $5-10, mains $10-15.50; ⊙11am-9pm; 🛜) This fun and funky riverside watering hole serves up clever American-style tapas: think three-cheese mac with bacon, fries and truffle aioli, seared ahi wontons, and brie ciabatta with date jam. It also does a mean grass-fed beef burger and other salads and sandwiches. Good selection of local beers on tap.

★Amícas
PIZZA $$

(☎719-539-5219; www.amicassalida.com; 127 F St; pizzas & paninis $6.90-13; ⊙11am-9pm Mon-Wed, 7am-9pm Thu-Sun; 🖊🖭) Thin-crust wood-fired pizzas, panini, housemade lasagna and five microbrews on tap? Amícas can do no wrong. This high-ceilinged, laid-back hangout is the perfect spot to replenish all those calories you burned off during the day. Savor a Michelangelo (pesto, sausage and goat cheese) or Vesuvio (artichoke hearts, sun-dried tomatoes, roasted peppers) alongside a cool glass of Headwaters IPA.

ℹ Information

Salida Chamber of Commerce (☎719-539-2068; www.nowthisiscolorado.com; 406 W Rainbow Blvd; ⊙9am-5pm Mon-Fri) General tourist info.

USFS Ranger Office (☎719-539-3591; www. fs.usda.gov; 5575 Cleora Rd; ⊙8am-4:30pm Mon-Fri) Located east of town off Hwy 50, with camping and trail info for the Sawatch and northern Sangre de Cristo Ranges.

❶ Getting There & Away

Located at the 'exit' of the Arkansas River Valley, Salida occupies a prime location at the crossroads of Hwys 285 and 50. Indeed, this used to be a railroad hub, and you'll likely spot an abandoned line or two while exploring the area. Gunnison, Colorado Springs, the Great Sand Dunes and Summit County are all within one to two hours' drive, provided you have your own car.

Colorado Springs

One of the nation's first destination resorts, Colorado Springs is now the state's second-largest city. Its natural beauty and pleasant climate attract visitors from around the globe, who come to ascend majestic Pikes Peak and admire the exquisite sandstone spires of the Garden of the Gods.

Recently, the Springs has come of its own as a year-round adventure and leisure tourism destination, with a bunch of new family-focused attractions adding to the appeal of the Front Range and its existing cache of sights, from the excellent fine-arts museum to the historic Air Force Academy and an up-and-coming restaurant scene.

◎ Sights & Activities

★ Pikes Peak   MOUNTAIN

(📋719-385-7325; www.springsgov.com; highway per adult/child $12/5; ⊙7:30am-8pm Jun-Aug, to 5pm Sep, 9am-3pm Oct-May; ℗) Pikes Peak (14,110ft) may not be the tallest of Colorado's 54 14ers, but it's certainly the most famous. The Ute originally called it the Mountain of the Sun, an apt description for this majestic peak, which crowns the southern Front Range. Rising 7400ft straight up from the plains, over half a million visitors climb it every year.

★ Garden of the Gods   PARK

(www.gardenofgods.com; 1805 N 30th St; ⊙5am-11pm May-Oct, to 9pm Nov-Apr; ℗) FREE This gorgeous vein of red sandstone (about 290 million years old) appears elsewhere along Colorado's Front Range, but the exquisitely thin cathedral spires and mountain backdrop of the Garden of the Gods are particularly striking. Explore the network of paved and unpaved trails, enjoy a picnic and watch climbers test their nerve on the sometimes flaky rock.

★ Colorado Springs
Fine Arts Center   MUSEUM

(FAC; 📋719-634-5583; www.csfineartscenter.org; 30 W Dale St; adult/student $12/5; ⊙10am-5pm Tue-Sun; ℗) Fully renovated in 2007, this expansive museum and 400-seat theater originally opened in 1936. The museum's collection is surprisingly sophisticated, with some terrific Latin American art and photography, and great rotating exhibits that draw from the 23,000 pieces in its permanent collection.

Colorado Springs
Pioneers Museum   MUSEUM

(📋719-385-5990; www.cspm.org; 215 S Tejon St; ⊙10am-5pm Tue-Sat; ℗) FREE Colorado Springs' municipal museum is set in the old El Paso County Courthouse, built in 1903. The collection and exhibition of some 60,000 pieces sums up the region's history. Particularly good is the Native American collection, which features hundreds of items from the Ute, Cheyenne and Arapaho Nations.

US Air Force Academy   SCHOOL

(📋719-333-2025; www.usafa.af.mil; I-25, exit 156B; ⊙visitor center 9am-5pm; ℗) FREE A visit to this campus, one of the highest-profile military academies in the country, offers a limited but nonetheless fascinating look into the lives of an elite group of cadets. The visitor center provides general background on the academy; from here you can walk over to the dramatic chapel (1963) or embark on a driving tour of the expansive grounds.

🛏 Sleeping

Mining Exchange   HOTEL $$

(📋719-323-2000; www.wyndham.com; 8 S Nevada Ave; r from $149; ℗❈🖁) Opened in 2012 and set in the former turn-of-the-century bank where Cripple Creek prospectors traded in their gold for cash (check out the vault door in the lobby), the Mining Exchange takes the prize for Colorado Spring's most stylish hotel. Twelve-foot-high ceilings, exposed brick walls and leather furnishings make for an inviting, contemporary feel.

★ Broadmoor   RESORT $$$

(📋855-634-7711; www.broadmoor.com; 1 Lake Ave; r from $295; ℗❈🖁🏊🐾) One of the top five-star resorts in the US, the 744-room Broadmoor sits in a picture-perfect location against the blue-green slopes of Cheyenne Mountain. Everything here is exquisite: acres of lush grounds and a lake, a glimmering pool, world-class golf, myriad bars and restaurants, an incredible spa and ubercomfortable guest rooms (which, it must be said, are of the 'grandmother' school of design).

★ Garden of the Gods Resort   RESORT $$$

(☑ 719-632-5541; www.gardenofthegodsclub.com; 3320 Mesa Rd; d/ste from $309/459; P❄🐾🏊) Under new management, with ongoing expansion, and having just completed the renovation of all its luxury hotel rooms and suites and the construction of an enormous day-spa facility, the resort wing of the Garden of the Gods Club is giving the competition (known for its historic elegance) a run for its old-money.

✕ Eating & Drinking

Shuga's   CAFE $

(☑ 719-328-1412; www.shugas.com; 702 S Cascade Ave; dishes $8-9; ⏲ 11am-midnight; 🐾) If you thought Colorado Springs couldn't be hip, stroll to Shuga's, a Southern-style cafe with a knack for knockout espresso drinks and hot cocktails. Cuter than a button, this little white house is decked out in paper cranes and red vinyl chairs; there's also patio seating. The food – brie BLT on rosemary toast, Brazilian coconut shrimp soup – comforts and delights. Don't miss vintage-movie Saturdays.

★ Pizzeria Rustica   PIZZA $$

(☑ 719-632-8121; www.pizzeriarustica.com; 2527 W Colorado Ave; pizzas $12-24; ⏲ noon-9pm Tue-Sun; 🚗🐾) Wood-fired pizzas, locally sourced ingredients and a historic Old Colorado City locale make this bustling pizza joint the place to make a beeline for when you have a craving for pie. Its popularity means that it's always smart to make dinner reservations when possible.

★ Uchenna   ETHIOPIAN $$

(☑ 719-634-5070; www.uchennaalive.com; 2501 W Colorado Ave, Suite 105; mains $12-22; ⏲ noon-2pm & 5-8pm Tue-Sun; P🚗🐾) Chef Maya learned her recipes from her mother before she moved to America, and you'll love the homely cooking and family-friendly vibe at this authentic Ethiopian restaurant. Go for well-spiced meat or veg options and mop everything up with the spongy injera.

★ Marigold   FRENCH $$

(☑719-599-4776; www.marigoldcafeandbakery.com; 4605 Centennial Blvd; mains lunch $8-13, dinner

$11-24; ⏲ bistro 11am-2:30pm & 5-9pm, bakery 8am-9pm Mon-Sat) Way out by the Garden of the Gods is this buzzy French bistro and bakery that's easy on both the palate and the wallet. Feast on delicacies such as snapper Marseillaise, garlic-and-rosemary rotisserie chicken, and gourmet salads and pizzas, and be sure to leave room for the double (and triple!) chocolate mousse cake or the lemon tarts.

★ Blue Star   MODERN AMERICAN $$$

(☑ 719-632-1086; www.thebluestar.net; 1645 S Tejon St; mains $21-38; ⏲ 3pm-midnight; P🚗) One of Colorado Springs' most popular gourmet eateries, the Blue Star is in the gentrifying Ivywild neighborhood just south of downtown. The menu at this landmark spot changes regularly, but always involves fresh fish, top-cut steak and inventive chicken dishes, flavored with Mediterranean and Pacific Rim rubs and spices.

Bristol Brewing Co   BREWERY

(☑719-633-2555; www.bristolbrewing.com; 1604 S Cascade Ave; ⏲ 11am-10pm; 🐾) Although a bit out of the way in southern Colorado Springs, this brewery – which in 2013 spearheaded a community market center in the shuttered Ivywild Elementary School – is worth seeking out for its Laughing Lab ale and pub grub from the owner of the gourmet Blue Star.

ⓘ Information

Colorado Springs Convention and Visitors Bureau (☑ 719-635-7506; www.visitcos.com; 515 S Cascade Ave; ⏲ 8:30am-5pm; 🐾) A well-stocked resource for all things Southern Colorado.

ⓘ Getting There & Around

A smart alternative to Denver, **Colorado Springs Airport** (COS; ☑ 719-550-1900; www.flycos.com; 7770 Milton E Proby Pkwy; 🐾) is served principally by United and Delta, with flights to 11 major cities around the country. There is no public transportation into town, however, so you'll have to rent a car or take a cab, about $35 with **Yellow Cab** (☑ 719-777-7777; www.yccos.com).

Up to six **Greyhound** (☑ 800-231-2222; www.greyhound.com) buses a day ply the route between Colorado Springs and Denver (from $10, 90 minutes), departing from the **Colorado Springs Downtown Transit Terminal** (☑ 719-385-7433; 127 E Kiowa St; ⏲ 8am-5pm Mon-Fri).

Reliable **Mountain Metropolitan Transit** (☑ 719-385-7433; www.coloradosprings.gov/department/91; per trip $1.75, day pass $4) buses serve the entire Pikes Peak area.

Southern Colorado

Home to the dramatic San Juan and Sangre de Cristo mountain ranges, Colorado's bottom half is just as pretty as its top.

Crested Butte

Powder-bound Crested Butte has retained its rural character better than most Colorado ski resorts. Ringed by three wilderness areas, this remote former mining village is counted among Colorado's best ski resorts (some say the best). The old town center features beautifully preserved Victorian-era buildings refitted with hip shops and businesses. Two-wheel traffic matches the laidback, happy attitude.

In winter, the scene centers on Mt Crested Butte, the conical ski mountain emerging from the valley floor. But come summer, these rolling hills become the state wildflower capital (according to the Colorado State Senate), and many mountain bikers' fave for sweet alpine singletrack.

◎ Sights & Activities

★ Crested Butte
Center for the Arts   ARTS CENTER

(☑970-349-7487; www.crestedbuttearts.org; 606 6th St; prices vary; ◎10am-6pm; P🚸) With a magnificent recent expansion, the arts center hosts shifting exhibitions of local artists and a stellar schedule of live music and performance pieces. There's always something lively and interesting happening here.

★ Crested Butte Mountain Resort   SKIING

(☑970-349-2222; www.skicb.com; 12 Snowmass Rd; lift ticket adult/child $111/100; 🚸) One of Colorado's best, Crested Butte is known for open tree skiing, deep powder and few crowds. Catering mostly to intermediates and experts, the resort sits 2 miles north of the town at the base of Mt Crested Butte. Surrounded by forests, rugged peaks, and the West Elk, Raggeds and Maroon Bells-Snowmass Wilderness Areas, the scenery is breathtaking.

Alpineer   MOUNTAIN BIKING

(☑970-349-5210; www.alpineer.com; 419 6th St; bike rental per day $25-75) Serves the mountain-biking mecca with maps, information and rentals. There's a great selection of men's and women's clothing. It also rents out skis and hiking and camping equipment.

🛏 Sleeping

Crested Butte International Hostel   HOSTEL $

(☑970-349-0588, toll-free 888-389-0588; www.crestedbuttehostel.com; 615 Teocalli Ave; dm $37, r $104-115; 🕾) For the privacy of a hotel with the lively ambience of a hostel, grab a room here, one of Colorado's nicest hostels. The best private rooms have their own baths. Dorm bunks come with reading lamps and lockable drawers, and the communal area has a stone fireplace and comfortable couches. Rates vary with the season, with winter being high season.

Inn at Crested Butte   BOUTIQUE HOTEL $$

(☑970-349-2111, toll-free 877-343-211; www.innatcrestedbutte.com; 510 Whiterock Ave; d $199-249; P🌣🕾) This refurbished boutique hotel offers intimate lodgings in stylish and luxurious surrounds. With just a handful of rooms, some opening onto a balcony with views over Mt Crested Butte, and all decked out with antiques, flat-screen TVs, coffee-makers and minibars, this is one of Crested Butte's nicest vacation addresses.

★ Ruby of Crested Butte   B&B $$$

(☑800-390-1338; www.therubyofcrestedbutte.com; 624 Gothic Ave; d $149-299, ste $199-499; P🚸🌣🕾) Thoughtfully outfitted, down to the bowls of jellybeans and nuts in the stylish communal lounge. Rooms are brilliant, with heated floors, flat-screen TVs with DVD players and DVD selections, iPod docks and deluxe linens. There's also a Jacuzzi, a library, a ski-gear drying room and use of retro townie bikes. Hosts help with dinner reservations and other services.

🍴 Eating & Drinking

★ Secret Stash   PIZZA $$

(☑970-349-6245; www.thesecretstash.com; 303 Elk Ave; mains $12-18; ◎8am-late; 🚸) With phenomenal food, the funky-casual Stash is adored by locals, who also dig the original cocktails. The sprawling space was once a general store, but now is outfitted with teahouse seating and tapestries. The house specialty is pizza; its Notorious Fig (with prosciutto, fresh figs and truffle oil) won the World Pizza Championship. Start with the salt-and-pepper fries.

Soupçon   FRENCH $$$

(☑970-349-5448; www.soupcon-cb.com; 127 Elk Ave; mains $39-47; ◎6-10:30pm) 🌿 Specializing in seduction, this petite French bistro occupies a characterful old mining cabin with

WORTH A TRIP

RAFTING THE ARKANSAS RIVER

Running from Leadville down the eastern flank of Buena Vista, through Browns Canyon National Monument, and then rocketing through the spectacular Royal Gorge at class V speeds, the Arkansas River is the most diverse, the longest and arguably the wildest river in the state. Brace yourself for yet another icy splash swamping the raft as you plunge into a roaring set of big waves, or surrender to the power of the current as your shouting, thoroughly drenched crew unintentionally spins backwards around a monster boulder. Is this fun? You bet! See p776 for tours.

just a few tables. Chef Jason has worked with big NYC names and keeps it fresh with changing menus of local meat and organic produce. Reserve ahead.

★**Montanya**   BAR
(www.montanyarum.com; 212 Elk Ave; snacks $3-12; ⊙11am-9pm) The Montanya distillery receives wide acclaim for its high-quality rums. Its basiltini, made with basil-infused rum, fresh grapefruit and lime, will have you levitating. There are also tours, free tastings and worthy mocktails.

❶ Information

The **Visitor Center** (☑970-349-6438; www.crestedbuttechamber.com; 601 Elk Ave; ⊙9am-5pm) is just past the entrance to town on the main road and stocks loads of brochures and maps.

❶ Getting There & Away

Crested Butte is about four hours' drive from Denver, and about 3½ hours from Colorado Springs. Head for Gunnison on US 50 and there head north for about 30 minutes to Crested Butte on Hwy 135.

Ouray

With gorgeous icefalls draping the box canyon and soothing hot springs dotting the valley floor, Ouray (you-ray) is privileged, even for Colorado. For ice climbers, it's a world-class destination, but hikers and 4WD fans can also appreciate its rugged and sometimes stunning charms. The town is a well-preserved quarter-mile mining village sandwiched between imposing peaks.

☆ Activities

★**Million Dollar Highway**   SCENIC DRIVE
The whole of US Hwy 550 has been called the Million Dollar Hwy (p39), but more properly it's the amazing stretch south of Ouray through the Uncompahgre Gorge up to Red Mountain Pass at 11,018ft. The alpine scenery is truly awesome and driving south towards Silverton positions drivers on the outside edge of the skinny, winding road, a heartbeat away from free-fall.

★**Ouray Hot Springs**   HOT SPRINGS
(☑970-325-7073; www.ourayhotsprings.com; 1200 Main St; adult/child $18/12; ⊙10am-10pm Jun-Aug, noon-9pm Mon-Fri & 11am-9pm Sat & Sun Sep-May; ⊕) For a healing soak or kiddish fun, try the recently renovated historic Ouray Hot Springs. The natural springwater is crystal-clear and free of the sulphur smells plaguing other hot springs. There's a lap pool, water slides, a climbing wall overhanging a splash pool and prime soaking areas (100°F to 106°F). The complex also offers a gym and massage service.

Ouray Ice Park   CLIMBING
(☑970-325-4061; www.ourayicepark.com; County Rd 361; ⊙7am-5pm mid-Dec–Mar; ⊕) FREE
Enthusiasts from around the globe come to ice climb at the world's first public ice park, spanning a 2-mile stretch of the Uncompahgre Gorge. The sublime (if chilly) experience offers something for all skill levels. Get instruction through a local guide service.

★ Festivals & Events

Ouray Ice Festival   CULTURAL
(☑970-325-4288; www.ourayicefestival.com; donation for evening events; ⊙Jan; ⊕) The Ouray Ice Festival features four days of climbing competitions, dinners, slide shows and clinics. There's even a climbing wall set up for kids. You can watch the competitions for free, but various evening events require a donation to the ice park. Once inside, you'll get free brews from popular Colorado microbrewer New Belgium.

⌂ Sleeping & Eating

**Amphitheater Forest
Service Campground**   CAMPGROUND $
(☑877-444-6777; www.recreation.gov; US Hwy 550; tent sites $20; ⊙Jun-Aug) With great tent sites under the trees, this high-altitude campground is a score. On holiday weekends, a three-night minimum applies. South of town on Hwy 550, take a signposted left-hand turn.

★ Wiesbaden HOTEL $$
(📞970-325-4347; www.wiesbadenhotsprings.com; 625 5th St; r $132-347; 🌐🛜🏊) Quirky, quaint and new age, Wiesbaden even boasts a natural indoor vapor cave, which, in another era, was frequented by Chief Ouray. Rooms with quilted bedcovers are cozy and romantic, but the sunlit suite with a natural rock wall tops all. In the morning, guests roam in thick robes, drinking the free organic coffee or tea, post-soak, or awaiting massages.

Box Canyon Lodge & Hot Springs LODGE $$
(📞800-327-5080, 970-325-4981; www.boxcanyonouray.com; 45 3rd Ave; r $189; 🛜) 🧹 It's not every hotel that offers geothermal heating, not to mention pineboard rooms that are spacious and fresh, and spring-fed barrel hot tubs – perfect for a romantic stargazing soak. With good hospitality that includes free apples and bottled water, it's popular, so book ahead.

Bon Ton Restaurant FRENCH, ITALIAN $$$
(📞970-325-4419; www.bontonrestaurant.com; 426 Main St; mains $16-40; ⏰5:30-11pm Thu-Mon, brunch 9:30am-12:30pm Sat & Sun; 🅿) Bon Ton has been serving supper for a century in a beautiful room under the historic St Elmo Hotel. The French-Italian menu includes specialties like roast duck in cherry peppercorn sauce and tortellini with bacon and shallots. The wine list is extensive and the champagne brunch comes recommended.

ℹ Information

Ouray Visitors Center (📞970-325-4746, 800-228-1876; www.ouraycolorado.com; 1230 Main St; ⏰9am-6pm Mon-Sat, 10am-4pm Sun; 🛜)

ℹ Getting There & Away

Ouray is on Hwy 550, 70 miles north of Durango, 24 miles north of Silverton and 37 miles south of Montrose. There are no bus services in the area and private transportation is necessary.

Telluride

Surrounded on three sides by mastodon peaks, exclusive Telluride is quite literally cut off from the hubbub of the outside world. Once a rough mining town, today it's dirtbag-meets-diva – mixing the few who can afford the real estate with those scratching out a slope-side living for the sport of it. The town center still has palpable old-time charm, though locals often villainize the recently developed Mountain Village,

whose ready-made attractions have a touch of Vegas. Yet idealism remains the Telluride mantra. Shreds of paradise persist with the town's free box – where you can swap unwanted items (across from the post office) – the freedom of luxuriant powder days and the bonhomie of its infamous festivals.

◉ Sights & Activities

You don't have to be a skier to appreciate Telluride, but loving the outdoors is a must. The town is surrounded by epic alpine scenery. Ajax Peak, a glacial headwall, rises up behind the village to form the end of the U-shaped valley. To the right (or south) on Ajax Peak, Colorado's highest waterfall, Bridal Veil Falls, cascades 365ft down; a switchback trail leads to a restored Victorian powerhouse atop the falls. To the south, Mt Wilson reaches 14,246ft among a group of rugged peaks that form the Lizard Head Wilderness Area.

Telluride Ski Resort SNOW SPORTS
(📞970-728-7533, 888-288-7360; www.tellurideskiresort.com; 565 Mountain Village Blvd; adult/child full-day lift ticket $124/73) Known for its steep and deep terrain – with plunging runs and deep powder at the best times, Telluride is a real skier's mountain, but dilettantes love the gorgeous San Juan mountain views and the social town atmosphere. Covering three distinct areas, the resort is served by 16 lifts. Much of the terrain is for advanced and intermediate skiers, but there's still ample choice for beginners.

★ Ashley Boling HISTORY
(📞970-728-6639, cell 970-798-4065; per person $20; ⏰by appointment) Local Ashley Boling has been giving engaging historical walking tours of Telluride for over 20 years. They last over an hour and are offered year-round. Rates are for a minimum of four participants, but he'll cut a reasonable deal for two or more. By reservation.

🎊 Festivals & Events

Telluride Bluegrass Festival MUSIC
(📞800-624-2422; www.planetbluegrass.com; 4-day pass $235; ⏰late Jun) This festival attracts thousands for a weekend of top-notch rollicking alfresco bluegrass. Stalls sell all sorts of food and local microbrews to keep you happy, and acts continue well into the night. Camping out for the four-day festival is very popular. Check out the website for more info.

★ **Mountainfilm** FILM
(www.mountainfilm.org; ☉May) An excellent four-day screening of outdoor adventure and environmental films, with gallery exhibits and talks, held on Memorial Day weekend. Events (some free) are held throughout Telluride and Mountain Village.

🛏 Sleeping

Aside from camping, there's no cheap lodging in Telluride. If staying in the summer or winter peak seasons, or during one of the city's festivals, you'll pay dearly. Off-season rates drop quite a bit, sometimes up to 30%. If you're coming during festival time, contact the festival organizers directly about camping.

★ **Telluride Town Park Campground** CAMPGROUND $
(☎970-728-2173; 500 E Colorado Ave; campsite with/without vehicle space $28/17; ☉mid-May–mid-Oct; 🤝🏊) Right in the center of town, this convenient creekside campground has 43 campsites, along with showers, swimming and tennis. Sites are all on a first-come, first-served basis, unless it is festival time (consult ahead with festival organizers). Fancy some nightlife with your camping? Why not.

New Sheridan Hotel HOTEL $$
(☎800-200-1891, 970-728-4351; www.newsheridan.com; 231 W Colorado Ave; d from $223; ☸🤝) Elegant and understated, this historic brick hotel (erected in 1895) provides a lovely base camp for exploring Telluride. High-ceilinged rooms feature crisp linens and snug flannel throws. Check out the hot-tub deck with mountain views. In the bull's eye of downtown, the location is perfect, but some rooms are small for the price.

Inn at Lost Creek BOUTIQUE HOTEL $$$
(☎970-728-5678; www.innatlostcreek.com; 119 Lost Creek Lane, Mountain Village; r $275-500; ☸🤝) This lush boutique-style hotel in Mountain Village knows cozy. At the bottom of Telluride's main lift, it's also very convenient. Service is personalized, and impeccable rooms have alpine hardwoods, Southwestern designs and molded tin. There are also two rooftop spas. Check the website for packages.

✕ Eating & Drinking

Meals and even groceries can be pricey in Telluride, so check out the food carts and the taco truck on Colorado Ave, with picnic table seating, for quick fixes. There's more good times to be had in Telluride than the rest of southern Colorado combined. Bring your wallet; those drinks aren't free or even close. Live bands liven it up.

Tacos del Gnar MEXICAN $
(☎970-728-7938; www.gnarlytacos.com; 123 S Oak St; mains $7-14; ☉noon-9pm Tue-Sat) The second outlet of a no-nonsense taco shop that puts flavor ahead of frills. Its fusion-style tacos, borrowing from Korean BBQ and Asian flavors, will make your tastebuds sing. Do it.

Oak BARBECUE $$
(The New Fat Alley; ☎970-728-3985; www.oaksteluride.com; 250 San Juan Ave, base of chair 8; mains $11-23; ☉11am-10pm; 🐾) You can pick something off the chalkboard or just take what the other guy has his face in – a cheap and messy delight. Go for the pulled-pork sandwich with coleslaw on top. Do it right by siding it with a bowl of crispy sweet-potato fries. The beer specials are outrageous.

★ **Chop House** MODERN AMERICAN $$$
(☎970-728-4531; www.newsheridan.com; 231 W Colorado Ave, New Sheridan Hotel; mains $26-62; ☉5pm-2am) With superb service and a chic decor of embroidered velvet benches, this is an easy pick for an intimate dinner. Start with a cheese plate, but from there the menu gets Western with exquisite elk shortloin and ravioli with tomato relish and local sheep-milk ricotta. Top it off with a flourless dark chocolate cake in fresh caramel sauce.

New Sheridan Bar BAR
(☎970-728-3911; www.newsheridan.com; 231 W Colorado Ave, New Sheridan Hotel; ☉5pm-2am) It's rush hour for beautiful people, though in low season you'll find real local flavor and opinions. In summertime, beeline for the breezy rooftop. Old bullet holes in the wall testify to the plucky survival of the bar itself, even as the adjoining hotel sold off chandeliers and antiques to pay the heating bills when mining fortunes waned.

☆ Entertainment

Fly Me to the Moon Saloon LIVE MUSIC
(☎970-728-6666; 132 E Colorado Ave; ☉3pm-2am) Let your hair down and kick up your heels to the tunes of live bands at this saloon, the best place in Telluride to party hard.

Sheridan Opera House THEATER

(☑ 970-728-4593; www.sheridanoperahouse.com; 110 N Oak St; ☑) This historic venue has a burlesque charm and is always the center of Telluride's cultural life. It hosts the Telluride Repertory Theater, and frequently has special performances for children.

ℹ Information

Telluride Visitor Center (☑ 888-353-5473, 970-728-3041; www.telluride.com; 230 W Colorado Ave; ⊙10am-5pm winter, to 7pm summer)

ℹ Getting There & Around

In ski season **Montrose Regional Airport** (☑ 970-249-3203; www.montroseairport.com; 2100 Airport Rd), 65 miles north, has direct flights to and from Denver (on United), Houston, Phoenix and limited cities on the east coast.

Commuter aircraft serve the mesa-top **Telluride Airport** (☑ 970-778-5051; www.tellurideairport.com; 1500 Last Dollar Rd), 5 miles east of town – weather permitting. At other times, planes fly into Montrose.

The **Galloping Goose** (☑ 970-728-5700; www.telluride-co.gov; ⊙7am-9pm) has routes downtown and to nearby communities. The **Telluride Express** (☑ 970-728-6000; www.tellurideexpress.com; to Montrose adult/child $53/31) shuttles from town to Telluride Airport, Mountain Village or Montrose airport; call to arrange pickup

---

Silverton

Ringed by snowy peaks and steeped in the sooty tales of a tawdry mining town, Silverton would seem more at home in Alaska than the Lower 48. But here it is. For those into snowmobiling, biking, fly-fishing or just basking in some very high-altitude sunshine, Silverton delivers.

It's a two-street town, but only one is paved. Greene St is where you'll find most businesses (think homemade jerky, fudge and feather art). Still unpaved, notorious Blair St – renamed Empire – runs parallel to Greene. During the silver rush, Blair St was home to thriving brothels and boozing establishments.

🏃 Activities

★ Silverton Railroad Depot RAIL

(☑ 970-387-5416, toll-free 877-872-4607; www.durangotrain.com; 12th St; deluxe/adult/child return from $189/89/55; ⊙departures 1:45pm, 2:30pm & 3pm; ☑) You can buy one-way and return tickets for the brilliant Durango & Silverton Narrow Gauge Railroad (p785) at the Silverton terminus. The Silverton Freight Yard Museum is located at the Silverton depot. The train ticket provides admission two days prior to, and two days following, your ride on the train.

★ Silverton Mountain Ski Area SKIING

(☑ 970-387-5706; www.silvertonmountain.com; State Hwy 110; daily lift ticket $59, all-day guide & lift ticket $159) Not for newbies, this is one of the most innovative ski mountains in the US – a single lift takes advanced and expert backcountry skiers up to the summit of an area of ungroomed ski runs. Numbers are limited and the mountain designates unguided and the more exclusive guided days.

San Juan Backcountry DRIVING

(☑ 970-387-5565, toll-free 800-494-8687; www.sanjuanbackcountry.com; 1119 Greene St; 2hr tour adult/child $60/40; ⊙May-Oct; ☑) ✈ Offering both 4WD tours and rentals, the folks at San Juan Backcountry can get you out and into the brilliant San Juan Mountain wilderness areas around Silverton. The tours take visitors around in modified open-top Chevy Suburbans.

🛏 Sleeping & Eating

Inn of the Rockies at the Historic Alma House B&B $$

(☑ 970-387-5336, toll-free 800-267-5336; www.innoftherockies.com; 220 E 10th St; r $129-173; ☑❄❄) Opened by a local named Alma in 1898, this inn has nine unique rooms furnished with Victorian antiques. The hospitality is first-rate and its New Orleans–inspired breakfasts, served in a chandelier-lit dining room, merit special mention. Cheaper rates are available without breakfast. There's also a garden hot tub for soaking after a long day.

Wyman Hotel B&B $$

(☑ 877-504-5272; www.thewyman.com; 1371 Greene St; d from $175; ⊙closed Nov; ❄❄) A handsome sandstone on the National Register of Historic Places, this just-revamped 1902 building offers sleek rooms with muted colors and a fine-tuned minimalist touch. It's a stylish alternative to the usual bric-a-brac approach. Check out the historic caboose alongside a gravel patio out back.

Grand Restaurant & Saloon AMERICAN $$

(☑ 970-387-5527; 1219 Greene St; mains $8-26; ⊙11am-3pm May-Oct, occasional dinners 5-9pm; ☑) Stick with the burgers and club sandwiches at this atmospheric eatery. The player piano and historic decor are a big draw. The full bar is well serviced by locals and visitors alike.

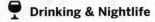 Drinking & Nightlife

★ Rum Bar
BAR

(☑970-769-8551; www.silvertonrumbar.com; 1309 Greene St; mains $6-14; ⊙11am-2am) This regional favorite delivers rum bliss in a spacious minimalist bar on Greene St. On a summer day, score a seat on the rooftop deck. Bartenders here can talk you into anything, crafting exotic cocktails with homemade syrups and award-winning rum. Note: low-season hours change.

❶ Getting There & Away

Silverton is on Hwy 550 midway between Montrose, about 60 miles to the north, and Durango, some 48 miles to the south.

Other than private car, the only way to get to and from Silverton is by using the Durango and Silverton Narrow Gauge Railroad or the private buses that run its return journeys.

Mesa Verde National Park

More than 700 years after its inhabitants disappeared, **Mesa Verde** (☑970 529 4465; www.nps.gov/meve; 7-day car/motorcycle pass Jun-Aug $20/10, Sep-May $15/7; P ⓘ ⬤) ⬤ retains an air of mystery. No one knows for sure why the Ancestral Puebloans left their elaborate cliff dwellings in the 1300s. Anthropologists love it here: Mesa Verde is unique among American national parks in its focus on maintaining this civilization's cultural relics rather than its natural treasures. It's a wonderland for adventurers of all sizes, who can clamber up ladders to carved-out dwellings, see rock art and delve into the mysteries of ancient America.

Mesa Verde National Park occupies 81 sq miles of the northernmost portion of the mesa. Ancestral Puebloan sites are found throughout the park's canyons and mesas, perched on a high plateau south of Cortez and Mancos.

The National Parks Service (NPS) strictly enforces the Antiquities Act, which prohibits the removal or destruction of any antiquities and prohibits public access to many of the 4000 known Ancestral Puebloan sites.

◎ Sights & Activities

If you only have time for a short visit, check out the Chapin Mesa Museum and try a walk through the Spruce Tree House, where you can climb down a wooden ladder into the cool chamber of a kiva.

Mesa Verde rewards travelers who set aside a day or more to take the ranger-led tours of Cliff Palace and Balcony House, explore Wetherill Mesa (the quieter side of the canyon), linger around the museum or participate in one of the campfire programs run at Morefield Campground.

Chapin Mesa Museum
MUSEUM

(☑970-529-4475; www.nps.gov/meve; Chapin Mesa Rd; admission incl with park entry; ⊙8am-6:30pm Apr–mid-Oct, to 5pm mid-Oct–Apr; P ⓘ) The Chapin Mesa Museum has exhibits pertaining to the park and is a good first stop. Staff at the museum provide information on weekends when the park headquarters is closed.

Chapin Mesa
ARCHAEOLOGICAL SITE

The largest concentration of Ancestral Puebloan sites is at Chapin Mesa, where you'll see the densely clustered **Far View Site** and the large **Spruce Tree House**, the most accessible of sites, with a paved half-mile round-trip path.

Wetherill Mesa
ARCHAEOLOGICAL SITE

This is the second-largest concentration of sites. Visitors may enter stabilized surface sites and two cliff dwellings, including the **Long House**, open from late May through August.

Aramark Mesa Verde
HIKING, TOURS

(☑970-529-4421; www.visitmesaverde.com; Mile 15, Far View Lodge; adult $42-48) The park concessionaire offers varied guided private and group tours throughout the park daily from May to mid-October. Book online or at the office in Far View Lodge.

⌷ Sleeping & Eating

There are plenty of accommodation options in nearby Cortez and Mancos, and Mesa Verde can be easily visited as a daytrip from Durango.

Morefield Campground
CAMPGROUND $

(☑970-529-4465; www.visitmesaverde.com; Mile 4; tent/RV site $30/40; ⊙May-early Oct; ⬤) ⬤ The park's camping option, located 4 miles from the entrance gate, also has 445 regular tent sites on grassy grounds conveniently located near Morefield Village. The village has a general store, a gas station, a restaurant, showers and a laundry. It's managed by Aramark. Dry RV campsites (without hookup) cost the same as tent sites.

Far View Lodge
LODGE $$

(📞970-529-4421, toll-free 800-449-2288; www.visit mesaverde.com; Mile 15; r $124-177; ⏰mid-Apr–Oct; 🅿🛗❄🛜🐕) Perched on a mesa top 15 miles inside the park entrance, this tasteful Pueblo-style lodge has 150 Southwestern-style rooms, some with kiva fireplaces. Don't miss sunset over the mesa from your private balcony. Standard rooms don't have air con (or TV) and summer daytimes can be hot.

Metate Room
MODERN AMERICAN $$$

(📞800-449-2288; www.visitmesaverde.com; Mile 15, Far View Lodge; mains $20-36; ⏰7-10am & 5:30-9:30pm Apr–mid-Oct, 5-7:30pm mid-Oct–Mar; 🍴👶) 🌿 With an award in culinary excellence, this upscale restaurant in the Far View Lodge offers an innovative menu inspired by Native American food and flavors. Interesting dishes include stuffed poblano chilies, prickly pear pork belly and cold smoked trout.

ℹ️ Information

The Mesa Verde National Park entrance is off US 160, midway between Cortez and Mancos.

The huge **Mesa Verde Visitor & Research Center** (📞970-529-5034, 800-305-6053; www. nps.gov/meve; ⏰8am-7pm Jun–early Sep, to 5pm early Sep–mid-Oct, closed mid-Oct–May; 🛜👶) has water, wi-fi and bathrooms, in addition to information desks selling tickets for tours of Cliff Palace, Balcony House or Long House. It also displays museum-quality artifacts.

Durango

An archetypal old Colorado mining town, Durango is a regional darling that's nothing short of delightful. Its graceful hotels, Victorian-era saloons and tree-lined streets of sleepy bungalows invite you to pedal around soaking up all the good vibes. There is plenty to do outdoors. Style-wise, Durango is torn between its ragtime past and a cool, cutting-edge future where townie bikes, caffeine and farmers markets rule.

🏃 Activities

⭐ Durango & Silverton Narrow Gauge Railroad
RAIL

(📞970-247-2733; www.durangotrain.com; 479 Main Ave; return adult/child 4-11yr from $89/55; ⏰May-Oct; 👶) Riding the Durango & Silverton Narrow Gauge Railroad is a Durango must. These vintage steam locomotives have been making the scenic 45-mile trip north to Silverton (3½ hours each way) for more than 125 years. The dazzling journey allows two hours for exploring Silverton. This trip operates only from May through October. Check online for different winter options.

Mild to Wild Rafting
RAFTING

(📞970-247-4789, toll-free 800-567-6745; www. mild2wildrafting.com; 50 Animas View Dr; trips from $59; ⏰9am-5pm; 👶) In spring and summer white-water rafting is one of the most popular sports in Durango. Mild to Wild Rafting is one of numerous companies around town offering rafting trips on the Animas River. Beginners should check out the one-hour introduction to rafting, while the more adventurous (and experienced) can run the upper Animas, which boasts Class III to V rapids.

Purgatory
SNOW SPORTS

(📞970-247-9000; www.purgatoryresort.com; 1 Skier Pl; lift tickets adult/child from $89/55; ⏰mid-Nov–Mar; 👶) Durango's winter highlight is 25 miles north on US 550. The resort offers 1200 skiable acres of varying difficulty, boasting 260in of snow per year. Two terrain parks offer plenty of opportunities for snowboarders to catch big air. Check local grocery stores and newspapers for promotions and two-for-one lift tickets and other specials before purchasing directly from the ticket window.

🛏️ Sleeping

General Palmer Hotel
HOTEL $$

(📞970-247-4747, toll-free 800-523-3358; www. generalpalmer.com; 567 Main Ave; d $165-275; ❄@🛜) With turn-of-the century elegance, this 1898 Victorian has a damsel's taste, with pewter four-post beds, floral prints and teddies on every bed. Rooms are small but elegant, and if you tire of TV, there's a collection of board games at the front desk. Check out the cozy library and the relaxing solarium.

⭐ Rochester House
HOTEL $$

(📞970-385-1920, toll-free 800-664-1920; www. rochesterhotel.com; 721 E 2nd Ave; d $169-229; 🛗❄🛜🐕) Influenced by old Westerns (movie posters and marquee lights adorn the hallways), the Rochester is a little bit of old Hollywood in the new West. Rooms are spacious, with high ceilings. Two formal sitting rooms, where you're served cookies, and a breakfast room in an old train car, are other perks at this pet-friendly establishment.

★ Antlers on the Creek B&B $$$

(☑970-259-1565; www.antlersonthecreek.com; 999 Lightner Creek Rd; r from $249; P 🛜) Tuck yourself into this peaceful creekside setting surrounded by sprawling lawns and cottonwoods and you may never want to leave. Between the spacious main house and the carriage house there are seven tasteful rooms with jetted tubs, plush bed linens and gas fireplaces. There's also a decadent three-course breakfast and hot tub in the outdoor gazebo. It's open year-round.

✖ Eating & Drinking

★ James Ranch MARKET $

(☑970-385-9143; www.jamesranch.net; 33800 US Hwy 550; mains $5-18; ☺11am-7pm Mon-Sat) 🍃 A must for those road-tripping the San Juan Skyway, the family-run James Ranch, 10 miles out of Durango, features a market and an outstanding farmstand grill featuring the farm's own organic grass-fed beef and fresh produce. Steak sandwiches and fresh cheese melts with caramelized onions rock. Kids dig the goats.

★ El Moro GASTROPUB $$

(☑970-259-5555; www.elmorotavern.com; 945 Main Ave; mains $10-30; ☺11am-midnight Mon-Fri, 9am-midnight Sat & Sun) There are two reasons to come here: drinking damn good custom cocktails at the bar or dining on some innovative small plates like Korean fried cauliflower, cheeses, housemade sausages and fresh salads. It's ground zero for Durango hipsters but really aims to please all.

Ore House STEAK $$$

(☑970-247-5707; www.orehouserestaurant.com; 147 E College Dr; mains $25-75; ☺5-10pm; 🐾) The best steakhouse in town, with food served in casual and rustic environs. Order a hand-cut aged steak, or try the steak, crab leg and lobster combo known as the Ore House Grubsteak, easily serving two people. The meat is natural and antibiotic free and organic vegetables are the norm. There's also a large wine cellar.

★ Bookcase & the Barber COCKTAIL BAR

(☑970-764-4123; www.bookcaseandbarber.com; 601 E 2nd Ave, suite B; ☺2pm-midnight) This modern speakeasy may be Durango's sexiest nightcap, hidden behind a heavy bookcase, with exquisite cocktails worth the $12 price tag and a dimly-lit allure. Enter via the barbershop, but you'll need the password (found somewhere on their Facebook page).

Try a spicy *paloma celosa* (jealous dove), a perfect tease of tequila, grapefruit and ancho chile.

★ Ska Brewing Company BREWERY

(☑970-247-5792; www.skabrewing.com; 225 Girard St; mains $9-15; ☺9am-9pm Mon-Fri, 11am-9pm Sat, to 7pm Sun) Big on flavor and variety, these are the best beers in town. Although the small, friendly tasting-room bar was once mainly a production facility, over the years it's steadily climbed in the popularity charts. Today it is usually jam-packed with friends meeting for an after-work beer.

ℹ Information

Durango Welcome Center (☑970-247-3500, toll-free 800-525-8855; www.durango.org; 802 Main Ave; ☺9am-7pm Sun-Thu, to 9pm Fri & Sat; 🛜) An excellent information center located downtown. There is a second visitor center south of town, at the Santa Rita exit from US Hwy 550.

ℹ Getting There & Around

Durango-La Plata County Airport (DRO; ☑970-247-8143; www.flydurango.com; 1000 Airport Rd) The regional airport is 18 miles southwest of Durango via US Hwy 160 and Hwy 172. Both United and American Airlines have direct flights to Denver; American flies to Dallas-Fort Worth and Phoenix.

Greyhound Bus Station (☑970 259 2755; www.greyhound.com; 250 E 8th Ave) Serves the region and beyond.

Durango Transit (☑970-259-5438; www.getarounddurango.com; 250 W 8th St; fares $1-2) Runs local bus routes around the city and to nearby destinations.

Great Sand Dunes National Park

For all of Colorado's striking natural sights, the surreal Great Sand Dunes National Park, a veritable sea of sand bounded by jagged peaks and scrubby plains, is a place of stirring optical illusions and where nature's magic is on full display.

🏃 Activities

Stop by the informative **Great Sand Dunes National Park Visitor Center** (☑719-378-6399; www.nps.gov/grsa; 11999 Hwy 150; ☺8:30am-5pm Jun-Aug, 9am-4:30pm Sep-May; 🐾) before venturing out, to learn about the geology and history of the dunes or to chat with a ranger about hiking or backcountry-camping options. A free backcountry permit is required if you're planning on being adventurous, and it pays to let the ranger know where you're going.

Hiking is the main pastime in the park, but there's also mountain biking, dune sandboarding and even inner tubing in late May and early June, as the snowmelt **Medano Creek** flows down from the Sangre de Cristos and along the eastern edge of the dunes.

Hiking

There are no trails through this expansive field of sand, but it's the star attraction for hikers. Two informal hikes afford excellent panoramic views of the dunes. The first is a hike to High Dune (strangely, not the highest dune in the park), which departs from a parking area just beyond the visitor center. It's about 2.5 miles out to the peak and back, but be warned: it's not easy. If you're up for it, try pushing on to the second worthy goal: just west of High Dune is Star Dune (750ft), the tallest in the park.

From the visitor center, a short trail leads to the Mosca Picnic Area next to ankle-deep Medano Creek, which you must ford (when the creek is running) to reach the dunes. Across the road from the visitor center, the Mosca Pass Trail climbs up into the Sangre de Cristo Wilderness. Throughout summer NPS rangers lead interpretive nature walks from the visitor center and hold evening programs at the amphitheater.

🛏 Sleeping & Eating

Although there are limited supplies at the **Great Sand Dunes Oasis** (🖉 719-378-2222; www.greatdunes.com; 5400 Hwy 150; tent/RV sites $25/38, cabins $55, r $100; ☻Apr-Oct; 🅿 @), it's best to buy your groceries in either Alamosa or a larger town outside the San Luis Valley.

★ **Zapata Falls Campground** CAMPGROUND $ (🖉 719-852-7074; www.fs.usda.gov; BLM Rd 5415; tent & RV sites $11; 🐾) Seven miles south of the national park, this campground offers glorious panoramas of the San Luis Valley from its 9000ft perch in the Sangre de Cristos. There are 23 first-come, first-served sites, but note that there is no water and that the 3.6-mile access road is steep and fairly washed out, making for slow going.

Zapata Ranch RANCH $$$ (🖉 719-378-2356; www.zranch.org; 5303 Hwy 150; d with full board $300) Ideal for horseback-riding enthusiasts, this exclusive preserve is a working cattle and bison ranch set amid groves of cottonwood trees. Owned and operated by the Nature Conservancy, the main inn is a refurbished 19th-century log structure, with distant views of the sand dunes.

❶ Getting There & Away

Great Sand Dunes National Park is 33 miles northeast of Alamosa.

WYOMING

You may think of Wyoming as an empty land of windswept plains and sagebrush hills baking under brooding blue skies. And, you'd be right. It is. But not all of it.

The country's least populated state is also home to some of its most dramatic mountains, most diverse wildlife, and most unique geology. From the unspoiled Snowy Range near Laramie to the granite wilderness of the Wind River Range behind Lander, the peaks only become more impressive as you travel across Wyoming toward the archetypal – and truly grand – Teton Range.

❶ Information

Wyoming Road Conditions (🖉 888-996-7623; www.wyoroad.info) Up-to-date info on road conditions and closures.

Wyoming State Parks & Historic Sites (🖉 307-777-6323; http://wyoparks.state.wy.us; day-use $6, historic site $4, campsite $10) Wyoming has 13 state parks and 26 historic sites providing a wide range of boating, biking, hiking, fishing, climbing and camping. Campsite reservations are taken online or over the phone.

Cheyenne

Windy Cheyenne may not wow you with its looks, but like the rough-skinned cowboys you'll meet here, there's good-natured charm once you scratch the surface.

◉ Sights

Frontier Days Old West Museum MUSEUM (🖉 307-778-7290; www.oldwestmuseum.org; 4610 Carey Ave; adult/child $10/free; ☻9am-5pm; 🐾) For a deep dive into Cheyenne's pioneer past and rodeo present, visit this museum year round on the Frontier Days rodeo grounds. It is chock-full of rodeo memorabilia, from saddles to trophies, displays cowboy art and photography, houses a fine collection of horse drawn buggies, and dispenses nuggets of history – like the story of Steamboat, the un-rideable bronco who likely isn't the one depicted on Wyoming's license plates (though many will tell you he is.)

☆☆ Festivals & Events

Cheyenne Frontier Days RODEO
(☑307-778-7222; www.cfdrodeo.com; 4610 Carey Ave; rodeo per day $17-29, concerts $20-70; ☺last full week Jul; 🚼) During the last full week in July, the world's largest outdoor rodeo and celebration of all things Wyoming features 10 days of roping, bucking, riding, singing and dancing between air shows, parades, melodramas, carnivals and chile cook-offs. There's also a lively Frontier Town, Indian village and free morning 'slack' rodeos.

🛏 Sleeping & Eating

★**Nagle Warren**
Mansion Bed & Breakfast B&B $$
(☑307-637-3333; www.naglewarrenmansion. com; 222 E 17th St; r from $163; ✴🛜🐕) This fully-modernized historic mansion is a rare find. The 1888 house still has the original carved leather ceiling, and is decked out with late-19th-century regional antiques in 12 spacious and elegant rooms, all with private baths. The property boasts a hot tub, a reading room tucked into a turret and classic 1954 Schwinn bikes for cruising.

Tasty Bones Barbecue
& Bakery BARBECUE $
(☑307-514-9494; www.tastybonesbarbecue.com; 1719 Central Ave; mains $8-16; ☺10am-9pm Mon-Sat, 11am-4pm Sun) Imagine that a Filipino food truck crashed into a barbecue smoker and fell in love. This mash-up of two distinct menus is the result of a husband and wife team with two very different ideas about what makes good home-cooking. Both are right. The slow-roasted brisket pairs surprisingly well with the miso ramen bowl.

🍷 Drinking & Nightlife

Accomplice Brewing
Company MICROBREWERY
(☑307-632-2337; www.accomplicebeer.com; 115 W 15th, Depot; mains $10-15; ☺2-10pm Mon-Thu, 11am-10pm Fri-Sun; 🛜🐕) Sample as many beers as you like as often as you like at the crowded pour-it-yourself taproom in Cheyenne's latest brewery to occupy the historic Depot building. The drafts are tasty, and food options don't disappoint.

ℹ Information

Cheyenne Visitor Center (☑307-778-3133; www.cheyenne.org; 1 Depot Sq; ☺9am-5pm Mon-Fri, to 3pm Sat, 11am-3pm Sun; 🛜)

ℹ Getting There & Around

For a capital city, Cheyenne is hard to reach. Black Hills Stage Lines/Express Arrow stops at the **bus terminal** (☑307-635-1327; www. greyhound.com; 5401 Walker Rd, Rodeway Inn) on the north end of town with direct service to Denver ($18-33, two hours) as well as anywhere Greyhound travels. Sleepy **Cheyenne Airport** (CYS; ☑307-634-7071; www.cheyenneairport. com; 200 E 8th Ave) will get you to Denver every Thursday.

Once in town, the regular **Cheyenne Transit Program** (☑307-637-6253; 322 W Lincolnway; standard fare $1.50; ☺6am-6pm Mon-Fri, 10am-5pm Sat) will get you around while the **Cheyenne Street Railway Trolley** (☑307-778-3133; www.cheyennetrolley.com; 121 W 15th St, Depot; adult/child $12/6; ☺10am, 11:30am, 1pm, 2:30pm & 4pm May-Sep) will tour you through the most interesting bits of downtown.

Laramie

Not exactly 'in' the mountains, this prairie town definitely feels 'of' the mountains, largely thanks to Wyoming's only four-year university (University of Wyoming), which maintains a constant flow of hip and lively students who re-energize an otherwise sleepy city.

The small historic downtown, with its grid of brick buildings pressed up against the railroad tracks, can occupy an hour of window shopping, and a few museums on the pleasantly green university campus are informative ways to stretch your legs. The real reason to visit, however, is the Wyoming Territorial Prison: a well-preserved piece of frontier past.

◉ Sights

★**Wyoming Territorial Prison** MUSEUM
(☑307-745-3733; www.wyomingterritorialprison. com; 975 Snowy Range Rd; adult/child $5/2.50; ☺8am-7pm May-Sep, 8am-5pm Apr & Oct; 🚼) See the only prison ever to hold Butch Cassidy, who was in for grand larceny from 1894–96, only to emerge a well-connected criminal who fast became one of history's greatest robbers. His story is told in thrilling detail in a back room, while the faces of other 'malicious and desperate outlaws' stare hauntingly

at you as you explore the main cellblocks. Outside, tour the factory where convicts produced over 700 brooms a day – one of the prison's short-lived revenue-generating schemes.

Geological Museum MUSEUM

(☎307-766-2646; www.uwyo.edu/geomuseum; SH Knight Geology Building, University of Wyoming; ◷10am-4pm Mon-Sat) FREE The Morrison Formation – a Jurassic sedimentary rock – stretches from New Mexico to Montana and is centered in Wyoming. This layer has produced many of the world's dinosaurs fossils, an impressive collection of which are on display in this tiny university museum, including a 75ft *Apatosaurus excelsus* (formerly known as the Brontosaurus), and a *Diatryma gigantea* (a 7ft-tall carnivorous bird discovered in Wyoming). Linger at the new 'Prep Lab' and watch researchers liberate brittle fossils from solid rock. Science!

🛏 Sleeping

Find the usual suspects of chain motels along Grand Ave to the east of Laramie and I-80 to the west. Unfortunately the independent offerings near historic downtown are, for the most part, not recommendable.

Gas Lite Motel MOTEL $

(☎307-742-6616; 960 N 3rd St; s/d $49/59; ❉🐾☍🛁) The Gas Lite Motel stands out – more due to the plastic horse and rooster on the roof, and tattered plywood cowboys lounging against the banisters than the modernity of the amenities. However, the rooms are clean if dated, the owners reasonably friendly, and the price is right if variable.

Mad Carpenter Inn B&B $$

(☎307-742-0870; www.madcarpenterinn.net; 353 N 8th St; r $95-125; 🛜) With landscaped gardens, hot breakfast, and comfy, snug wood-trimmed rooms, the Mad Carpenter Inn has warmth and class to spare. A serious game room features billiards and ping-pong while the detached 'Doll House' with its kitchenette and Jacuzzi tub is an absolute steal for a couple looking for a quiet escape.

🍴 Eating & Drinking

Having a university means Laramie has a good spread of culinary offerings. Multiple breweries, sports bars and hangouts pepper Laramie's historic downtown, many of which host local live music.

★ Sweet Melissa's VEGETARIAN $

(☎307-742-9607; www.facebook.com/sweetmelissacafe; 213 S 1st St; mains $9-14; ◷11am-9pm Mon-Thu, till 10pm Fri-Sat; 🛜🍴) Sweet Melissa's makes delicious vegetarian and gluten-free grub, no doubt the healthiest food for miles, like portabello fajitas or gorgonzola-leek mac 'n' cheese. The cauliflower wings are bomber, as is the service.

Coal Creek Coffee Co CAFE

(☎307-745-7737; www.coalcreekcoffee.com; 110 E Grand Ave; mains $5-11; ◷6am-11pm; 🛜) With superlative brews, Coal Creek Coffee is everything you want in a coffee house: modern and stylish, even borderline hipster – but not in a bad way. When the fair-trade beans and expertly prepared lattes start to feel so 10am, roll over to **Coal Creek Tap** in the west wing where you'll find over a dozen draft beers.

ⓘ Getting There & Away

Daily **flights** (☎307-742-4164; www.laramieairport.com; 555 General Brees Rd; ◷5am-7:30pm Mon-Fri, till 5pm Sat-Sun) connect Laramie with Denver ($87, 40 minutes), while **Greyhound** (☎307-745-7394; www.greyhound.com; 1952 N Banner Rd) buses stop at the gas station

---

WYOMING FACTS

Nickname Equality State

Population 586,107

Area 97,914 sq miles

Capital city Cheyenne (population 59,466)

Other cities Laramie (population 30,816), Cody (9689), Jackson (9838)

Sales tax 4%

Birthplace of Artist Jackson Pollock (1912–56)

Home of Women's suffrage, coal mining, geysers, wolves

Politics Conservative to the core (except Teton County)

Famous for Rodeo, ranches, former vice-president Dick Cheney

Tallest mountain Gannett Peak 13,809ft (4209m)

Driving distances Cheyenne to Jackson 432 miles

everyone calls the 'Diamond Shamrock,' and are a good option for regional destinations.

Lander

Nestled against the foothills of the Wind River Range, Lander has always been a frontier town. Originally established as a fort on a spur of the Oregon Trail, it was later the end of the rail line and a frequent haunt of outlaws and horse thieves. It is also the gateway to the Wind River Indian Reservation, where indigenous Eastern Shoshone share 2.2 million acres of land with displaced Northern Arapaho at the base of the state's tallest peak.

This wilderness playground landed on the radar of savvy outdoorspeople when Paul Petzoldt started the renowned National Outdoor Leadership School here in 1965. The epic climbing at Sinks Canyon and nearby Wild Iris brings climbers in droves, while expanding mountain-bike trails diversifies that crowd.

But the town's remoteness means few stay for long, leaving Lander in relative peace, retaining its mellow blend of the Old and New West.

◉ Sights & Activities

Sinks Canyon State Park   PARK
(☑307-332-3077; www.sinkscanyonstatepark.org; 3079 Sinks Canyon Rd; tent & RV nonresident $11; ☺visitor center 9am-6pm Jun-Sep) Beautiful Sinks Canyon State Park, 6 miles southwest of Lander on Hwy 131, centers on a curious feature of the Middle Fork of the Popo Agie River, where the rushing water suddenly turns into a small cave and disappears into the soluble Madison limestone. Although the water bubbles up a quarter-mile downstream, scientists have learned it takes nearly two hours for it to make the subterranean journey before emerging warmer and with more volume.

Fremont County Pioneer Museum   MUSEUM
(☑307-332-3339; www.fremontcountymuseums.com/the-lander-museum; 1445 W Main St; ☺9am-4pm Mon-Sat, to 5pm summer) **FREE** Wyoming's first history museum has been continually updated and overhauled to share the living history of Lander, Fremont County and the state as a whole. Catch the display of Frederic Remington's engravings of frontier life for *Harper's Weekly*, before exploring the cabins and historic buildings out back.

Gannett Peak Sports   MOUNTAIN BIKING
(351b Main St; ☺10am-6pm Mon-Fri, 9am-5pm Sat, 10am-2pm Sun) If you want to check out the single-track trails outside town, head to Gannett Peak Sports for advice, gear and equipment rentals.

🛏 Sleeping

With landscapes this beautiful you'll want to be camping, and fortunately there are a number of options up **Sinks Canyon** (sites $11-15; ☺May-Sep).

★**Outlaw Cabins**   B&B $$
(☑307-332-9655; www.outlawcabins.com; 2411 Squaw Creek Rd; cabins $125) On a working ranch are a pair of real cabins done real nice. The Lawman was built by a county sheriff over 120 years ago, but has been maintained and restored for modern sensibilities. The Outlaw is our favorite, however, on account of its more Wild West vibe. Both are beautifully appointed with quiet porches made for sittin' on.

✕ Eating & Drinking

If you're not swapping stories over a case of beer around a campfire, you should probably be at the Lander Bar. The rest of the town shuts down relatively early.

The Middle Fork   BREAKFAST $
(☑307-335-5035; www.themiddleforklander.com; 351 Main St; mains $6-10; ☺7am-2pm Mon-Sat, 5-9pm Wed-Sat, 9am-2pm Sun; 🛜🎗) A large hall with spartan ambience leaves you free to focus on the food – which is excellent. Homemade baked goods hold court with eggs benedict and in-house corned-beef hash washed down with mimosas.

★**Cowfish**   GRILL $$
(☑307-332-8227; www.cowfishlander.com; 148 Main St; brunch $10-16, dinner $17-35; ☺8am-2pm, 5-10pm; 🛜) Spring for a candlelit dinner of brussels-sprout carbonara or coffee-rubbed rib-eye at Lander's upscale restaurant suitable for date nights. The attached brewery serves the same food in a more casual atmosphere among the mash tuns (steel brewing vessels) that churn out a rotating menu of handcrafted beer-experiments – many of which are excellent (sample a few before committing).

Lander Bar   BAR
(☑307-332-8228; www.landerbar.com; 126 Main St; ☺11am-2am Mon-Sat, noon-10pm Sun; 🛜)

This big, wooden, barn-like watering hole is the place where local and visiting adventurers go to share notes about the day's 'sick lines' on rock or trail well into the night. There's often live music.

Get food from the attached **Gannett Grill** (☑ 307-332-8227; 128 Main St; mains $8-11; ⊙ 11am-9pm).

ⓘ Information

Lander Visitor Center (☑ 307-332-3892; www. landerchamber.org; 160 N 1st St; ⊙ 9am-5pm Mon-Fri)

ⓘ Getting There & Away

Wind River Transportation Authority (☑ 307-856-7118; www.wrtabuslines.com; Shopko; fare one-way $1) provides scheduled Monday-to-Friday services between Riverton and Lander, plus reserved service to Casper or Jackson (prices vary based on number of riders). You'll want a car, however, to access trailheads and climbing crags.

Jackson

Welcome to the other side of Wyoming. Hiding in a verdant valley between some of America's most rugged and wild mountains, Jackson looks similar to other towns in the state – false-front roof lines, covered wooden walkways, saloons on every block – but it ain't quite the same.

Here, hard-core climbers, bikers and skiers (recognizable as sunburned baristas) outnumber cowboys by a wide margin, and you're just as likely to see a celebrity as a moose wandering the urban trails.

Although Jackson being posh and popular does have its downsides for the traveler (the median house price is $1.2 million), it does mean you'll find a lively urban buzz, a refreshing variety of foods and no shortage of things to do – both in town and out.

⊙ Sights & Activities

★ **National Museum of Wildlife Art** MUSEUM
(☑ 307-733-5771; www.wildlifeart.org; 2820 Rungius Rd; adult/child $14/6; ⊙ 9am-5pm May-Oct, from 11am Sun & closed Mon Nov-Apr; ♿) Major works by Bierstadt, Rungius, Remington and Russell, breathe life into their subjects in impressive and inspiring ways – almost better than seeing the animals in the wild. Almost. The outdoor sculptures and building itself (inspired, oddly, by a ruined Scot-

tish castle) are worth stopping by to see even if the museum is closed.

National Elk Refuge WILDLIFE RESERVE
(☑ 307-733-9212; www.fws.gov/refuge/national_elk_refuge; Hwy 89; sleigh ride adult/child $21/15; ⊙ 10am-4pm Dec-Apr) **FREE** This refuge protects Jackson's herd of several thousand elk, offering them a winter habitat from November to May. During summer, ask at the Jackson visitor center for the best places to see elk. An hour-long horse-drawn sleigh ride is the highlight of a winter visit; buy tickets at the visitor center.

★ **Jackson Hole Mountain Resort** SNOW SPORTS
(☑ 307-733-2292; www.jacksonhole.com; adult/child ski pass $140/88, summer tram $34/21; ⊙ Nov-Apr & June-Sep) This mountain is larger than life. Whether tackling Jackson Hole with skis, board, boots or mountain bike, you will be humbled. With more than 4000ft of vertical rise and some of the world's most infamous slopes, Jackson Hole's 2500 acres and average 400in of snow sit at the top of every serious shredder's bucket list.

Summer months are active with a bike park, disc-golf course, climbing wall and a new high alpine *via ferrata* course (starting at $109, two hours) where you tackle mountaineering assisted by cables and ladders. The most popular activity is the scenic tram ($34, 12 minutes) which takes alpine hikers and sightseers to a network of trails at the summit of Rendezvous mountain (10,927ft). Pro-tip: climb up the 7-mile, 4139ft trail to the top, and ride the tram down for free.

Jackson Hole Paragliding PARAGLIDING
(☑ Jackson Hole 307-739-2626, Snow King 605-381-9358; www.jhparagliding.com; tandem flight $345; ⊙ May-Oct) The only thing better than being in the Tetons is to be soaring above the Tetons. Tandem rides with experienced pilots take off from Jackson Hole Mountain Resort in the mornings, or Snow King (402 E Snow King Ave) in the afternoons.

No experience is necessary, but age and weight limits apply.

Snake River Rafting RAFTING
(half-day adult/child from $70/50) You can't swing an oar in Jackson without hitting a rafting company eager to take you down the Snake River. Most offer a mellow 13-mile float through wetlands teeming with wildlife, from the town of Wilson to Hoback

Junction, or the more punchy Snake River canyon with its churning Class III rapids.

Only a few outfits offer trips wholly within Grand Teton National Park – if that's important to you – including Barker-Ewing and Teton Whitewater.

Trips typically include transportation and lunch.

Granite Creek Hot Springs HOT SPRINGS
(☏ 307-690-6323; www.fs.usda.gov/recarea/btnf/recarea/?recid=71639; Granite Creek Road, Hwy 191; adult/child $8/5; ☉10am-6pm summer, 10am-5pm winter) Head 25 miles southeast of Jackson on Hwy 191 and turn east on gravel Granite Creek Road. Continue for 10 miles through alpine meadows and forested hills to the the natural hot springs with killer views of the surrounding peaks.

🎉 Festivals & Events

Grand Teton Music Festival MUSIC
(GTMF; ☏ 307-733-1128; www.gtmf.org; Walk Festival Hall, Teton Village; ☉Jul-Aug) A near-continuous celebration of classical music in a fantastic summer venue. The Festival Orchestra plays every Friday at 8pm and Saturday at 6pm showcasing worldwide musicians and directors. The GTMF Presents program highlights noted talent on most Wednesdays. Free family concerts give you a more informal way to experience the symphony of sound.

🛌 Sleeping

Jackson has plenty of lodging, both in town and at Jackson Hole Mountain Resort (p791), but reservations are still essential in summer and winter high season. Prices, which may double during holidays or weekends, fall precipitously during the spring and fall 'slack' seasons. There are a few camping options scattered in the forest nearby, but most require a long drive, often down poor roads.

The Hostel HOSTEL $
(☏ 307-733-3415; www.thehostel.us; 3315 Village Dr, Teton Village; dm $34-45, r $79-139; @ 🛜 🐾) This skier's favorite has been here so long it doesn't need a name – everybody knows the Hostel. Budget privates and cramped four-person bunk rooms are smack in the middle of everything (meaning you'll only be in them when you're sleeping). The spacious lounge, with fireplace and pool table, foosball and ski waxing station, are all chill places to socialize.

Antler Inn HOTEL $$
(☏ 307-733-2535; www.townsquareinns.com/antler-inn; 43 W Pearl Ave; r $100-260, ste $220-325; ❄ 🛜 🐾) Right in the middle of the Jackson action, this sprawling complex provides clean and comfortable rooms, some with fireplaces and bathtubs. Stepping into the cheaper 'cedar log' rooms feels like you're coming home to a cozy Wyoming cabin, mostly because you are: they were hauled here and attached to the back of the hotel.

★ Wort Hotel HISTORIC HOTEL $$$
(☏ 307-733-2190; www.worthotel.com; 50 N Glenwood St; r from $450; ❄ @ 🛜) A distinctly Wyoming vibe permeates this luxury historic hotel that has only gotten better with age. Knotty pine furniture and handcrafted bedspreads compliment full-size baths and Jacuzzis while the best concierge service in Jackson helps you fill out your itinerary with outdoor adventures. Even if staying here is out of your reach, swing by the antique **Silver Dollar Bar** downstairs.

🍴 Eating

Jackson is home to Wyoming's most sophisticated and diversified food scene. Look for deals dished out for happy hour at many of the bar-restaurant combos.

Persephone BAKERY $
(☏ 307-200-6708; www.persephonebakery.com; 145 E Broadway; mains $8-15; ☉7am-6pm Mon-Sat, to 5pm Sun; 🛜) With rustic breads, oversized pastries and breakfast masterpieces, this tiny white-washed French bakery is worth waiting in line for (and you will). In summer the spacious patio provides more room for lingering with your coffee (though at $0.75 a refill, you might not want to linger for that long – go for a pitcher of Bloody Marys instead).

Lotus FUSION $$
(☏ 307-734-0882; www.theorganiclotus.com; 140 N Cache St; mains $15-26; ☉8am-10pm; 🛜 🐾) 🌿 In a region where steak and potatoes reign supreme, Lotus pushes back with things like plantain torte, vegan burgers and giant grain-and-veg bowls. There's plenty of meat, too – this is Wyoming – but it's all organic.

Gun Barrel STEAK $$
(☏ 307-733-3287; http://jackson.gunbarrel.com; 852 W Broadway; mains $19-36; ☉5:30pm-late) The line stretches out the door for Jackson's best steakhouse, where the buffalo prime rib and elk chop rival the grilled bone-in

ribeye for the title of 'king cut.' For a fun game, try to match the meat with the animal watching you eat it: this place was once the wildlife and taxidermy museum, and many original tenants remain.

Mangy Moose Saloon   PUB FOOD $$
(☑ 307-733-4913; www.mangymoose.com; 3295 Village Drive, Teton Village; lunch mains $9-13, dinner mains $15-32; ☺ food 7am-10pm, saloon 11am-2am; ☎) For more than half a century, Mangy Moose has been the rowdy epicenter for après-ski, big-name bands, slope-side dining and general mountain mischief at Jackson Hole Mountain Resort (p791). The cavernous **pub** cranks out bowls of chile, buffalo burgers and steaks from local farms and offers a decent salad bar, while the **Rocky Mountain Oyster cafe** has your breakfast needs covered.

Thai Me Up   THAI $$
(☑ 307-733-0005; www.thaijh.com; 75 E Pearl Ave; mains $15-20; ☺ from 5pm; ☎) First, the beer. Meet Melvin: the IPA everyone is talking about. He has 19 friends. They're pretty good, too. So is the Thai food. And burgers. And the kung-fu movies work mesmerizingly well with the hip-hop. The reverse-curve bar is a bit cramped, but that's the point. Maybe. Did we mention the tuk-tuk out front? Just check the place out.

🍷 Drinking & Nightlife

From breweries to bars to concerts to theaters, there's no lack of things to fill your evenings in Jackson, especially during the summer and winter high seasons. Consult the Jackson Hole News & Guide (www.jhnewsandguide.com/calendar) for the latest happenings, or just head downtown and follow the sound of laughter.

★ Snake River Brewing Co   MICROBREWERY
(☑307-739-2337; www.snakeriverbrewing.com; 265 S Millward St; pints $4-5, mains $10-22; ☺ 11am-11pm, drinks till late; ☎) With an arsenal of microbrews crafted on the spot (some award-winning), it's no wonder this is a favorite among the younger, outdoor-sports-positive crowd. Food includes wood-fired pizzas, bison burgers and pasta served in a modern-industrial warehouse with two floors and plenty of (but not too many) TVs broadcasting the game.

The Rose   COCKTAIL BAR
(☑ 307-733-1500; www.therosejh.com; 50 W Broadway; cocktails $9-14; ☺ 5:30pm-2am Wed-Sat,

8pm-2am Sun-Tue) Slide into a red-leather booth at this swank little lounge upstairs at the Pink Garter theater and enjoy the best craft cocktails in Jackson. Encouraged by the success of their libations, they now offer multicourse culinary adventures Thursday through Saturday from 6pm to 10pm.

ℹ Information

Jackson Hole Guest Services (☑ 307-739-2753, 888-333-7766; Clock Tower Bldg) Information on activities and tours, located near the tram ticket office in Teton Village.
Jackson Ranger District (☑ 307-739-5450; www.fs.fed.us/btnf; 25 Rosencranz Ln; ☺ 8am-4:30pm Mon-Fri) Side by side with the USFS Bridger-Teton National Forest Headquarters.

ℹ Getting There & Around

Alltrans (Mountain States Express; ☑ 307-733-3135; www.jacksonholealltrans.com) runs a shuttle to Salt Lake (\$75, 5¼ hours) and Grand Targhee ski area (adult/child $114/85 includes ski-lift pass) in the winter, while **Jackson Hole Shuttle** (☑ 307-200-1400; www.jhshuttle.com; ☺ 24hr) provides regular service from the busy airport to your hotel in the town of Jackson or Teton Village.

The free **START Bus** (Southern Teton Area Rapid Transit; ☑ 307-733-4521; www.startbus.com) system gets you anywhere you need to go locally and to Driggs, ID ($3). A bike path runs between Jackson and Jenny Lake in Grand Teton National Park.

Cody

You have a few choices when it comes to getting into Yellowstone National Park, and approaching from the Cody side of life should be top on your list. Not just for the mesmerizing drive along the North Fork of the Shoshone – which Theodore Roosevelt once called the '50 most beautiful miles in America' – but also for the town.

Cody revels in its frontier image, a legacy that started with its founder, William 'Buffalo Bill' Cody: Chief of Scouts for the army, notorious buffalo hunter, and showman who spent years touring the world with his Wild West extravaganza. The town rallies around nightly rodeos, rowdy saloons and a world-class museum that was started by Buffalo Bill's estate and is a worthy destination all by itself.

◉ Sights

★**Buffalo Bill Center of the West** MUSEUM
(☑307-587-4771; www.centerofthewest.org; 720 Sheridan Ave; adult/child $19/12; ⊘open daily Mar-Nov, Thu-Sun Dec-Feb, hours vary; ◈) Do not miss Wyoming's most impressive (constructed) attraction. This sprawling complex of five museums, showcases everything western: from the spectacle of Buffalo Bill's world-famous Wild West shows, to galleries featuring powerful frontier-oriented artwork, to the visually absorbing **Plains Indian Museum** to a fascinating collection of 7000 firearms. Meanwhile, the **Draper Museum of Natural History** explores the Yellowstone region's ecosystem in excruciating, yet enthralling detail. Look for Teddy Roosevelt's saddle, the busy beaver ball, and one of the world's last buffalo tepees.

▣ Sleeping

An unusually high number of independent hotels are found along Cody's Hwy 14. They range widely in cleanliness and amenities, if not in price. Beware that eye-catching exteriors are no guarantee of comfortable rooms. Campgrounds aplenty stretch along Hwys 14, 16 and 20 between Cody and Yellowstone.

Irma Hotel HISTORIC HOTEL $$
(☑307-587-4221; www.irmahotel.com; 1192 Sheridan Ave; r $147-169, ste $197; ❋❞) Built in 1902 by Buffalo Bill as the cornerstone of his planned city, this creaky hotel has old-fashioned charm with a few modern touches. The original high-ceiling historical suites are named after past guests (Annie Oakley, Calamity Jane), while the slightly more modern annex rooms are very similar for $20 cheaper (and still have classic pull-chain toilets).

Big Bear Motel MOTEL $$
(☑307-587-3117; www.codywyomingbigbear.com; 139 W Yellowstone Ave; r $159-209; ❋❞❋❋) This friendly place on the edge of town is close (but not too close) to the Cody Nite Rodeo and offers clean rooms, a laundry, a swimming pool and a distinctly Wyoming take on 'pony rides.' Prices get out of control during high season, but are reasonable in the shoulder months.

✖ Eating

Steak, steak and more steak (and a revolving door of unforgettable Mexican restaurants) sets the tone for dining. A few creative alternatives are trying to buck the trend, and although we appreciate the variety, eating salad almost feels sacrilegious in this Wild West tribute town.

★**The Local** MODERN AMERICAN $$
(☑307-586-4262; www.thelocalcody.com; 1134 13th St; lunch $10-13, dinner $13-38; ⊘espresso from 8:30am, lunch noon-2pm, dinner 5-9pm Tue-Sat; ☑) ✦ When Cody's cowboy cuisine starts to weigh on your arteries, find the antidote in the Local's fresh, organic and locally sourced dishes. Think tempeh and avocado wrap for lunch, or grilled scallops and saffron risotto for dinner.

Cassie's Western Saloon STEAK $$
(☑307-527-5500; www.cassies.com; 214 Yellowstone Ave; steaks $20-45; ⊘food 11am-10pm, drinks to 2am) This classic roadhouse and former house of ill repute hosts heavy swilling, swingin' country-and-western music and the occasional bar fight. Strap on the feedbag at the attached supper club and tackle tender steaks ranging in size from 8oz to 5.25lb, or the triple threat: a 2.25lb burger with five types of cheese and bacon (add a fried egg for $1).

☆ Entertainment

Cody Nite Rodeo SPECTATOR SPORT
(www.codystampederodeo.com; 519 W Yellowstone Ave; adult/child $20/10; ⊘8pm Jun-Aug) Experience a quintessential small-town rodeo at this summer-night Cody tradition going on 80 years old – despite the fact that animal welfare groups often criticize rodeo events as being harmful to animals. Sensitive viewers may find some events disturbing.

❶ Getting There & Away

Cody's small **airport** (COD; ☑307-587-5096; www.flyyra.com; 2101 Roger Sedam Drive) connects this otherwise isolated town with Salt Lake City and Denver, and you can thank Buffalo Bill Cody for the scenic byway that bears his name and connects Cody to Yellowstone – another spectacular approach to the park.

Yellowstone National Park

Teeming with moose, elk, bison, grizzlies and wolves, America's first **national park** (☑307-344-7381; www.nps.gov/yell; Grand Loop Rd, Mammoth, Yellowstone National Park; $30; ⊘north entrance year-round, south entrance May-Oct) also contains some of America's wildest lands just begging to be explored.

Yellowstone is home to over 60% of the world's geysers, alongside myriad Technicolor hot springs and bubbling mud pits. But while these astounding phenomena attract over 4 million people each year, it's the surrounding canyons, mountains and forests that truly astonish.

◉ Sights

Yellowstone is split into five distinct regions, each with unique attractions. Upon entering the national park you'll be given a basic map and a park newspaper detailing the excellent ranger-led talks and walks (well worth attending).

◉ Geyser Country

Geothermal features litter Yellowstone (you're on top of a massive volcano, after all) but only a few places have what it takes to create geysers. The area stretching between Norris and Old Faithful – is the hottest part of the park – is your best bet.

Highlights include Old Faithful (Upper Geyser Basin; ⊘ approx every 90min) FREE and the Upper Geyser Basin, Grand Prismatic Spring and Norris Geyser Basin, especially if Steamboat Geyser is thinking of erupting. The 1-mile hike around Artists Paintpots (southwest of Norris) is an uncrowded delight.

In addition to geyser gazing, the Firehole and Madison Rivers also offer superb fly-fishing and wildlife viewing.

Old Faithful Visitor Education Center   VISITOR CENTER
(☑ 307-545-2751; Old Faithful; ⊘ 8am-8pm Jun-Sep, hours vary spring & fall, 9am-5pm Dec-Mar; ♿) ⊘ This new, improved and environmentally friendly center is all about the thermal features at Yellowstone, exploring the differences between geysers, hot springs, fumaroles and mud pots, and explaining why there are no geysers in Mammoth. Kids will enjoy the hands-on Young Scientist displays, which include a working laboratory geyser. Available information includes standard park maps and itinerary advice, as well as predicted eruption times for a handful of the park's most notorious gushers.

Grand Prismatic Spring   SPRING
(Midway Geyser Basin) At 370ft wide and 121ft deep, Grand Prismatic Spring is the park's largest and deepest hot spring. It's also considered by many to be the most beautiful thermal feature in the park. Boardwalks lead around the multicolored mist of the gorgeous pool and its spectacularly colored rainbow rings of algae. From above, the spring looks like a giant blue eye, weeping exquisite multicolored tears. The features are linked by a 0.5-mile boardwalk; allow for 30 minutes here, after you find parking.

◉ Mammoth Country

The park's first developed area once housed US Army soldiers tasked with stopping vandalism and poaching. Success! The laundry stations have long since been removed from the majestic limestone terraces of Mammoth Hot Springs and herds of elk now placidly wander through the valley.

The peaks of the Gallatin Range rise to the west, towering above the area's lakes, creeks and numerous hiking trails, including beautiful Bunsen Peak (p797).

◉ Tower-Roosevelt Country

The park is rich with wildlife, and one of the best places to see much of it is in Lamar Valley where hundreds of buffalo roam, and the ranges of multiple wolf packs overlap. Tower Fall and the Absaroka Mountains' craggy peaks are the geographical highlights of this area, the park's most remote, scenic and undeveloped region.

◉ Canyon Country

A series of scenic overlooks linked by hiking trails explore the cliffs, precipices and waterfalls of the Grand Canyon of the Yellowstone. Here the river continues to gouge out

WORTH A TRIP

SCENIC DRIVE: THE ROOF OF THE ROCKIES

A contender for the most dramatic route into Yellowstone Park, Beartooth Highway (Hwy 212; www.beartoothhighway.com; ⊘ late May–mid-Oct) connects Red Lodge to Yellowstone's northeast entrance by an incredible 68-mile journey alongside 11,000ft peaks and wildflower-sprinkled alpine tundra. It has been called both America's most scenic drive and its premier motorcycle ride. There are a dozen USFS campgrounds along the highway, four within 12 miles of Red Lodge.

ROCKY MOUNTAINS YELLOWSTONE NATIONAL PARK

Yellowstone National Park

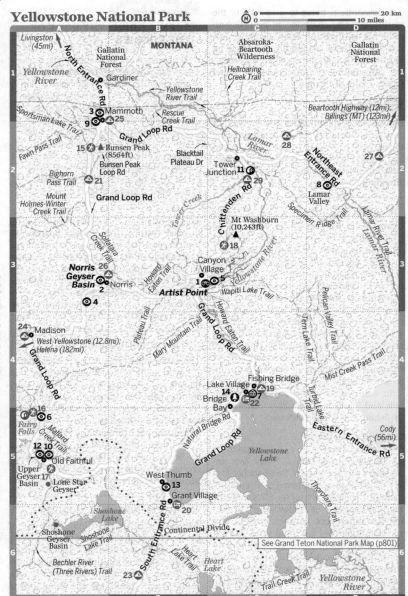

a fault line through an ancient golden geyser basin, most impressively at **Lower Falls**. The **South Rim Drive** leads to the canyon's most spectacular overlook at **Artist Point**, while the **North Rim Drive** accesses the daring precipices of both falls.

Grand Canyon of the Yellowstone   CANYON
(near Canyon Village) This is one of the park's true blockbuster sights. After its placid meanderings north from Yellowstone Lake, the Yellowstone River suddenly plummets over Upper Falls and then the much larger Lower

Yellowstone National Park

⊙ **Top Sights**
1 Artist Point B3
2 Norris Geyser Basin A3

⊙ **Sights**
3 Albright Visitor Center A1
4 Artists Paintpots A3
5 Grand Canyon of the
  Yellowstone C3
6 Grand Prismatic Spring A5
7 Lake Yellowstone Hotel C4
8 Lamar Valley D2
9 Mammoth Hot Springs A2
10 Old Faithful A5
  Old Faithful Visitor
    Education Center .... (see 10)
11 Tower Fall C2
12 Upper Geyser Basin A5
13 West Thumb Geyser Basin B5
14 Yellowstone National Park C4

⊕ **Activities, Courses & Tours**
15 Bunsen Peak & Osprey Falls A2

16 Fairy Falls Trail & Twin Buttes A5
17 Lone Star Geyser Trail A5
18 Mt Washburn C3

⊜ **Sleeping**
19 Fishing Bridge RV Park C4
20 Grant Village B6
21 Indian Creek Campground A2
22 Lake Yellowstone Hotel C4
23 Lewis Lake Campground B6
24 Madison Campground A4
25 Mammoth Campground B1
26 Norris Campground A3
  Old Faithful Inn .... (see 10)
27 Pebble Creek Campground D2
28 Slough Creek Campground C2
29 Tower Fall Campground C2

⊗ **Eating**
  Lake House .... (see 20)
  Lake Yellowstone Hotel
    Dining Room .... (see 22)

Falls, before raging through the 300m-deep (1000ft) canyon. Scenic overlooks and a network of trails along the canyon's rims highlight its beauty from a dozen angles – South Rim Dr leads to the most spectacular overlook at Artist Point.

⊙ Lake Country

Yellowstone Lake, the region's centerpiece, is one of the world's largest alpine lakes. This watery wilderness lined with volcanic beaches is best explored by boat or sea kayak. Rising east and southeast of the lakes, the wild and snowcapped Absaroka Range hides the wildest lands in the lower 48, perfect for epic backpacking or horseback trips.

West Thumb Geyser Basin (west Yellowstone Lake) is good for a short stroll past infamous **Fishing Cone**, while colonial **Lake Yellowstone Hotel** (Lake Village) is a historic place to take an indoor break.

🏃 Activities

Hiking

Hikers can explore Yellowstone's backcountry from more than 92 trailheads that give access to over 1000 miles of hiking trails and 300 primitive campsites. Backcountry permits ($3 per person per night, up to $15) are required for overnight use, and are available at visitor centers and ranger stations up to 48 hours before your departure. Some of the backcountry sites can be reserved in advance by mail and are allotted through a lottery system.

Day hiking on any trail is free and requires no permit, but it does require proper preparation. Be sure to carry extra water, a rain jacket and bear spray on any hike.

⭐ Bunsen Peak & Osprey Falls   HIKING, MOUNTAIN BIKING

(southwest of Mammoth) Bunsen Peak (8564ft) is a popular half-day hike that you can extend to a more demanding day hike by continuing down the mountain's gentler eastern slope to the Bunsen Peak Rd and then *waaay* down (800ft) to the base of seldom-visited Osprey Falls. Better yet, bring a mountain bike and ride the two-track past the falls down to Mammoth (6.3 miles).

Lone Star Geyser Trail   HIKING, CYCLING

This paved and pine-lined hike is an easy stroll along a former service road to one of the park's largest backcountry geysers. It's popular but quite a contrast to the chaotic scene around Old Faithful. Isolated Lone Star erupts every three hours for between two and 30 minutes and reaches 30ft to 45ft in height. It is definitely worth timing your visit with an eruption.

Mt Washburn   HIKING, BIKING

(Tower-Roosevelt) A fairly strenuous uphill hike from Dunraven Pass trailhead to a mountaintop fire tower with 360-degree views over the park and nearby bighorn sheep (6.4 mile round-trip, moderate). Or tackle the climb on a bicycle via the dirt Chittenden Road from the north.

Fairy Falls Trail & Twin Buttes　　HIKING

Tucked away in the northwest corner of the Midway Geyser Basin, Fairy Falls (197ft) is a popular hike. Beyond Fairy Falls the trail continues to a hidden thermal area at the base of the Twin Buttes. The geysers are undeveloped, and you're likely to have them to yourself – a stark contrast to the throngs surrounding Grand Prismatic Spring (p795) below.

Cycling

Cyclists can ride on public roads and a few designated service roads in Yellowstone, but not on the backcountry trails. Every campground (except Slough Creek) has hiker/biker sites that rarely fill.

From mid-March to mid-April the Mammoth–West Yellowstone park road is closed to cars but open to cyclists as plowing allows, offering a long and stress-free ride.

🛏 Sleeping

NPS and private campgrounds, along with cabins, lodges and hotels are all available in the park. Reservations, where possible, are essential in summer. Plentiful accommodations can also be found in the gateway towns of Cody, Gardiner and West Yellowstone.

The best budget options are the seven NPS–run campgrounds in **Mammoth** (tent & RV sites $20; ⊘ year-round), **Tower Fall** (Tower-Roosevelt, near Tower Fall; tent & small RV sites $15; ⊘ mid-May–late Sep), **Indian Creek** (tents & RV sites $15; ⊘ early Jun–mid-Sep), **Pebble Creek** (off Northeast Entrance Rd; tent & RV sites $15; ⊘ mid-Jun–late Sep), **Slough Creek** (Tower-Roosevelt; tent & small RV sites $15; ⊘ mid-Jun–early Oct), Norris Campground and **Lewis Lake** (South Entrance; tent sites $15; ⊘ mid-Jun–Oct), which are first come, first served.

Xanterra (☑ 307-344-7311, 866-439-7375; www.yellowstonenationalparklodges.com) runs five more reservable campgrounds, all with cold-water bathrooms, flush toilets and drinking water. RV sites with full hookups are available at Fishing Bridge.

★ **Norris Campground**　　CAMPGROUND $

(Norris; tent & RV sites $20; ⊘ mid-May–Sep) Nestled in a scenic, open, lodgepole pine forest on a sunny hill overlooking the Gibbon River and meadows, this is one of the park's nicest campgrounds. Sites are given on a first-come basis and the few loop A riverside spots get snapped up quickly. Campfire talks are at 7:30pm and firewood is sold between 7pm and 8:30pm. Generators allowed 8am to 8pm.

Madison Campground　　CAMPGROUND $

(☑ 307-344-7311; www.yellowstonenationalpark lodges.com; Madison, W Entrance Rd; tent & RV sites $24.25; ⊘ May-Oct) The nearest campground to Old Faithful and the West Entrance occupies a sunny, open forest in a broad meadow above the Madison River. Bison and the park's largest elk herd frequent the meadows to its west, making for great wildlife-watching, and it's a fine base for fly-fishing the Madison. You can (and should) reserve your site in advance.

Fishing Bridge RV Park　　CAMPGROUND $

(www.yellowstonenationalparklodges.com; Fishing Bridge; RV sites $47.75; ⊘ late May-late Sep) This is the only campground with full hookups

---

ℹ BEAT THE CROWDS

Yellowstone's wonderland attracts up to 30,000 visitors daily in July and August and tops 4 million gatecrashers annually. Avoid the worst of the crowds with the following advice:

Visit in May or October Services may be limited, but there will be far fewer people.

Hit the trail Most (95%) of visitors never set foot on a backcountry trail; only 1% camp at a backcountry site (permit required).

Bicycle the park Most campgrounds have underutilized hiker/biker sites, and your skinny tires can slip through any traffic jam.

Mimic the wildlife Be active during the golden hours after dawn and before dusk.

Pack a lunch Eat at one of the park's many overlooked scenic picnic areas.

Bundle up Enjoy a private Old Faithful eruption during the winter months.

(water, electric, sewage) and due to heavy bear activity only allows hard-sided trailers or RVs are allowed. The 340 sites are crammed together cheek-to-jowl and have no privacy. Public facilities include a pay laundry and showers. Reservations are essential.

★**Old Faithful Inn**　　　　HOTEL $$
(☎307-344-7311; www.yellowstonenationalpark lodges.com; Old Faithful; old house d with shared/private bath from $119/191, r $236-277; ☺early May-early Oct) The historic log masterpiece of design and engineering rivals Yellowstone's natural beauty. The lobby alone is worth a visit just to sit in front the impossibly large rhyolite fireplace and listen to the pianist upstairs. The cheapest 'Old House' rooms provide the most atmosphere with log walls and original wash basins, but bathrooms are down the hall.

Grant Village　　　　HOTEL $$
(☎307-344-7311; www.yellowstonenationalpark lodges.com; Grant Village; r $242; ☺late May-Sep) The 300 condo-like boxes with standard hotel interiors at Grant Village were once dismissed by author Alston Chase as 'an inner-city project in the heart of primitive America, a wilderness ghetto.' They do happen to be the closest lodging to the Tetons for those getting an early start, and the rooms were completely updated in 2016, which helped increase their comfort (and price).

Lake Yellowstone Hotel　　　　HOTEL $$$
(☎866-439-7375; www.yellowstonenationalpark lodges.com; cabins $157, Sandpiper r $244, hotel r $397-452; ☺mid-May-early Oct; @🐾) Commanding the northern lake shore, this buttercup-yellow colonial behemoth harks back to a bygone era – though the rooms that cost $4 in 1895 have appreciated somewhat. The spacious main-building rooms were upgraded in 2014, with new carpet and the park's only wired internet connections ($4.75 per hour). Lakeside rooms cost extra, sell out first and don't guarantee lake views.

✖ **Eating**

Lake House　　　　CAFETERIA $$
(Grant Village; mains $10-24; ☺6:30-10:30am & 5-9:30pm May-Sep) This quiet lakeshore spot offers casual dining with the best lakeviews in the park. Dinner includes creative items like huckleberry chicken and wild-game meatloaf.

SOUTH RIM TRAIL

Southeast of the Yellowstone Canyon's South Rim, this network of trails meanders through meadows and forests and past several small lakes. This loop links several of these and makes a nice antidote to seeing canyon views framed by the windshield of your car. It's an incredibly varied hike that combines awesome views of the Grand Canyon of the Yellowstone with a couple of lakes and even a backcountry thermal area.

Walk down from the main parking area or marina to the lakeshore. It's closed for lunch.

★**Lake Yellowstone Hotel Dining Room**　　　　AMERICAN $$$
(☎307-344-7311; www.yellowstonenationalpark lodges.com; Lake Village; mains $14-40; ☺6:30-10am, 11:30am-2:30pm & 5-10pm mid-May-Sep; 🍴) Save your one unwrinkled outfit (and an unwrinkled $100 bill) to feast in style at the dining room of the Lake Yellowstone Hotel. Lunch options include trout, a poached-pear salad and sandwiches. Dinner ups the ante with starters of lobster ravioli and mains of bison tenderloin, quail and rack of Montana lamb. Dinner reservations are required.

ⓘ **Information**

The park is open year-round, but most roads close in winter. Park entrance permits (hiker/vehicle $15/30) are valid for seven days. For entry into both Yellowstone and Grand Teton the fee is $50.

Cell service is limited in the park, and wi-fi can only be found at Mammoth's **Albright Visitor Center** (☎307-344-2263; Mammoth; ☺8am-7pm Jun-Sep, 9am-5pm Oct-May).

ⓘ **Getting There & Away**

Most visitors to Yellowstone fly into Jackson, WY, or Bozeman, MT, but it's often more affordable to choose Billings, MT. You will need a car; there is no public transportation to or within Yellowstone National Park.

Grand Teton National Park

The 12 imposing glacier-carved summits, which frame the singular Grand Teton (13,775ft), were designated a **national park**

(☑307-739-3300; www.nps.gov/grte; Teton Park Rd, Grand Teton National Park; entrance per vehicle $30) in 1929. Much of the Snake River Valley was later donated to the park by John D Rockefeller, who acquired it through secret purchases.

The scenery only gets more impressive the further into the mountains you go – make time to take a hike through the fragrant forests past glistening alpine lakes to dramatic canyons blanketed with wildflowers.

◉ Sights & Activities

With almost 250 miles of **hiking trails** you really can't go wrong in Grand Teton. Backcountry-use permits are required for overnight trips.

The Tetons are also known for excellent short-route **rock climbs** as well as classic longer routes to summits like Grant Teton, Mt Moran and Mt Owen. These are best attempted with an experienced guide.

Fishing is another draw, with several species of whitefish and cutthroat, lake and brown trout thriving in local rivers and lakes. Get a license at the **Moose Village store**, Signal Mountain Lodge (p802) or **Colter Bay Marina** (☑307-543-2811; www.gtlc. com/activities/marina; Colter Bay; ⊗8am-5pm).

Cross-country skiing and **snowshoeing** are the best ways to take advantage of park winters. Pick up a brochure detailing routes at Craig Thomas Discovery & Visitor Center.

★Craig Thomas Discovery & Visitor Center
VISITOR CENTER

(☑307-739-3399, backcountry permits 307-739-3309; Teton Park Rd, Moose; ⊗8am-7pm Jun-Aug, hours vary spring & fall, closed Nov-Feb; ♦) **FREE** Your first stop should be this incredibly well-done visitor center, if only for the sighting-lines on the floor that nail down exactly which peaks are staring back at you through the floor-to-ceiling windows. The obligatory raised-relief map helps you focus on where to go while informative kid-friendly interactive displays help you understand what you'll see. A battery of rangers are on hand to help plan your visit, and you can get backcountry permits here, too. Ranger programs include Map-chats and various guided hikes around Moose.

Mormon Row
GHOST TOWN

(Antelope Flats Rd; ℗) Welcome to possibly the most photographed spot in the park – and for good reason. The aged wooden barns and fence rails make a quintessential pastoral scene perfectly framed by the imposing bulk of the Tetons. The barns and houses were built by Mormon settlers in the 1890s who farmed the fertile alluvial soil irrigated via miles of hand-dug ditches.

Oxbow Bend
RIVER

(N Park Rd) One of the most famous scenic spots in Grand Teton National Park for wildlife-watching is Oxbow Bend, with the reflection of Mt Moran as a stunning backdrop. Dawn and dusk are the best times to spot moose, elk, sandhill cranes, ospreys, bald eagles, trumpeter swans, Canada geese, blue herons and white pelicans. The oxbow was created as the river's faster water eroded the outer bank while the slower inner flow deposited sediment.

★Death Canyon Trail
HIKING

Death Canyon remains one of our favorite hikes – both for the challenge and the astounding scenery. The trail ascends a mile to the Phelps Lake overlook before dropping down into the valley bottom and following Death Canyon. For a challenging add-on with impossibly beautiful views, turn right at the historic ranger cabin onto the Alaska Basin Trail and climb another 3000ft to Static Peak Divide (10,792ft) – the highest trail in Grand Teton National Park.

Garnet Canyon
HIKING, CLIMBING

Garnet Canyon is the gateway to the most popular scrambles to Middle and South Teton and the technical ascent of Grand Teton – but you need to know what you're doing and be with someone familiar with the routes. Even if you don't plan to go any higher, the 4-mile hike to the foot of the Tetons is a memorable one.

Grand Teton Multi-Use Bike Path
CYCLING

(www.nps.gov/grte/planyourvisit/bike.htm; Jackson to Jenny Lake) Starting from the excellent **Jackson Vistor Center** (☑307-733-3316; www.jacksonholechamber.com; 532 N Cache Dr; ⊗8am-7pm Jun-Sep, 9am-5pm Oct-May; 🐾) and continuing 20 miles to the **Jenny Lake Ranger Station** (☑307-739-3343; ⊗8am-6pm Jun-Aug), this new mutli-use path is an excellent way to see the park at a slower, more intimate pace. If that's too much of a commitment, rent bikes at **Dornan's** (☑307-733-2415; www.dornans.com; Moose Village; ⊗9am-6pm) in Moose for the 8-mile ride to the lake.

Grand Teton National Park

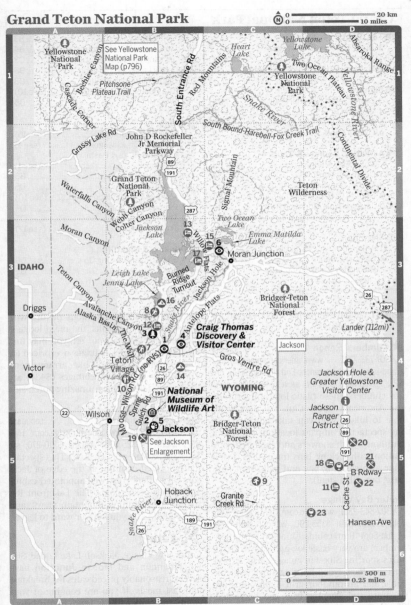

🛏 Sleeping

Demand for lodging and camping in Grand Teton is high from Memorial Day to Labor Day; book lodges well in advance. Most campsites get snatched up before 11am: **Jenny Lake** (Teton Park Rd; tent sites $28;

⊘ May-Sep) fills much earlier; **Gros Ventre** (Gros Ventre Rd; tent/RV sites $24/52; ⊘ late Apr-mid-Oct) usually stays open. **Colter Bay** (☑ 307-543-3100; www.gtlc.com; Hwy 89/191/287; tent/RV sites $30/71; ⊘ mid-May-mid-Sep) and

Grand Teton National Park

◉ Top Sights
1 Craig Thomas Discovery &
   Visitor Center..B4
2 National Museum of Wildlife Art B5

◎ Sights
3 Grand Teton National Park B4
4 Mormon Row B4
5 National Elk Refuge................................B5
6 Oxbow Bend C3

☉ Activities, Courses & Tours
Colter Bay Marina ....(see 13)
7 Death Canyon Trail B4
8 Garnet Canyon B3
9 Granite Creek Hot Springs...................C5
10 Jackson Hole Mountain Resort B4
Jackson Hole Paragliding..............(see 10)

⊕ Sleeping
11 Antler Inn D5
12 Climbers' Ranch B4
Colter Bay Campground &
   RV..(see 13)

13 Colter Bay Village B3
14 Gros Ventre Campground B4
15 Jackson Lake Lodge...............................C3
16 Jenny Lake Campground.......................B3
17 Signal Mountain Lodge B3
The Hostel...(see 10)
18 Wort Hotel... D5

⊗ Eating
Blue Heron Lounge .... (see 15)
Dornan's Chuckwagon....................(see 1)
Dornan's Pizza & Pasta
   Company...(see 1)
19 Gun Barrel... B5
20 Lotus... D5
Mangy Moose Saloon ....(see 10)
21 Persephone D5
22 Thai Me Up.. D5
Trapper Grill .... (see 17)

☕ Drinking & Nightlife
23 Snake River Brewing Co D6
24 The Rose D5

Jenny Lake have tent-only sites reserved for hikers and cyclists.

★ Climbers' Ranch   CABIN $

(☏ 307-733-7271; www.americanalpineclub.org/grand-teton-climbers-ranch; End Highlands Rd; dm $25; ☉ Jun-Sep) Started as a refuge for serious climbers, these rustic log cabins run by the American Alpine Club are now available to hikers who can take advantage of the spectacular in-park location. There is a bathhouse with showers and sheltered cook station with locking bins for coolers. Bring your own sleeping bag and pad (bunks are bare, but still a steal).

Colter Bay Village   CABIN $$

(☏ 307-543-2811; www.gtlc.com; tent cabins $66, cabins with bath $155-290, without bath $85; ☉ Jun-Sep) Tent cabins (June to early September) are very basic log-and-canvas structures sporting Siberian gulag charm. Expect bare bunks, a wood-burning stove, a picnic table and an outdoor grill. Bathrooms are separate and sleeping bags can be rented. The log cabins, some original, are much more comfortable and a better deal, and available late May through September.

★ Jackson Lake Lodge   LODGE $$$

(☏ 307-543-2811; www.gtlc.com; Jackson Lake Lodge Rd; r & cottages from $320; ☉ mid-May–Sep; ☏✿✿) With soft sheets, meandering trails

for long walks and enormous picture windows framing the peaks, the main lodge is the perfect place to woo. Yet, you may find the 348 cinder-block cottages overpriced for their viewless, barracks-like arrangement. The Moose Pond View cottages ($430) are more secluded and have amazing porch-side panoramas.

Signal Mountain Lodge   LODGE $$$

(☏ 307-543-2831; www.signalmtnlodge.com; Hwy 89/191/287; r $253-363, cabins $210-270, ste $363-394; ☉ May–mid-Oct; ☏✿) This spectacularly located complex at the edge of Jackson Lake offers cozy, well-appointed cabins and rather posh rooms. The Lakefront Retreats have stunning mountain views, and the kind of patio you'll never want to leave.

✕ Eating

Colter Bay Village, Jackson Lake Lodge, Signal Mountain and **Moose Junction** have several reasonably priced cafes for breakfast and fast meals. If you are cooking at your camp, remember this is bear country; store and dispose of food properly.

★ Dornan's Pizza & Pasta Company   PIZZA $

(☏ ext 204 307-733-2415; www.dornans.com; Moose; mains $10-13, pizza $9-17; ☉ 11:30am-9pm; ☏) If there is a more ideal place to have pizza and a beer than sitting on Dornan's rooftop deck looking across the Snake River and Menor's Ferry at the towering Tetons, we've yet to find it. The food is almost as good as the view here at one of the only independently owned restaurants in the park.

Blue Heron Lounge BARBECUE $
(☑307-543-2811; www.gtlc.com/dining; Jackson Lake Lodge; mains $11-23; ☺11am-midnight mid-May–Sep) An outdoor casual grill attached to an attractive corner cocktail lounge with knee-to-ceiling windows. Alcohol and appetizers are served from 11am to midnight. Occasionally you'll hit on live music.

Dornan's Chuckwagon BARBECUE $$
(☑ext 203 307-733-2415; www.dornans.com; Moose; breakfast & lunch $7-15, dinner $21-32; ☺7:30am-3pm & 5-9pm Jun-Aug) At this family favorite, breakfast means sourdough pancakes and eggs off the griddle while lunchtime offers light fare and sandwiches. Come dinner, Dutch ovens are steaming. There's beef, ribs or trout, along with a bottomless salad bar. Picnic tables have unparalleled views of the Grand.

Trapper Grill CAFE $$
(☑307-543-2831; www.signalmountainlodge.com; Signal Mountain Lodge; mains $10-19; ☺7am-2:30pm & 4:30-10pm) Sandwiches, burgers and baby-back ribs are among the many choices sure to please each picky member of the family. It's the cheaper of the two restaurants at Signal Mountain Lodge, and it has the better view out over the lake. Breakfast, with sides of ham, bacon or buffalo sausage, are gut busters.

❶ Information

Park permits (hiker/bicycle/vehicle $24/24/30) are valid for seven days. If you are continuing on to Yellowstone, the fee is $50.

MONTANA

It's not just the sky that's big, but everything in Montana is just a little larger than life. The mountains seem just a touch taller, the valleys feel a smidge wider and the lakes are a bit longer than in other mountain states.

❶ Information

Visit Montana (☑800-847-4868; www.visitmt. com) The Office of Tourism website is well-done and informative, with maps, guides and trip suggestions.

Bozeman

Bozeman is what all those formerly-hip, now-overrun Colorado mountain towns used to be like. The laid-back, old-school rancher legacy still dominates over the New West pioneers with their mountain bikes, skis and climbing racks. But that's changing rapidly. It is now one of the fastest-growing towns in America and cost of living is on the rise, but it hasn't turned yet.

◉ Sights & Activities

★**Museum of the Rockies** MUSEUM
(☑406-994-2251; www.museumoftherockies.org; 600 W Kagy Blvd; adult/child $14.50/9.50; ☺8am-6pm Jun-Aug, 9am-5pm Sep-May; ☼) Hands down the most entertaining museum in Montana shouldn't be missed. It has stellar dinosaur exhibits including an *Edmontosaurus* jaw with its incredible battery of teeth, the largest T-Rex skull in the world, and a new full T-Rex (with only a slightly smaller skull). Laser planetarium shows are interesting, as is the living-history outdoors section (closed in winter).

★**Bridger Bowl Ski Area** SNOW SPORTS
(☑406-587-2111; www.bridgerbowl.com; 15795 Bridger Canyon Rd; lift ticket adult/child $60/22; ☺mid-Dec–Apr) As the nation's leading nonprofit ski resort, it's all about the 'cold smoke', not cold, hard cash, at Bridger Bowl. Which means all you'll find at this small (2000 acres) community-owned hill 16 miles north of Bozeman is passionate skiers, reasonable prices, and surprisingly great skiing.

Explore Rentals OUTDOORS
(Phasmid; ☑406-922-0179; www.explore-rentals. com; 32 Dollar Dr; ☺9am-5pm Mon-Sat, 10am-4pm Sun) Imagine stepping off the plane, and there waiting for you is a car complete with luggage box, camping trailer, cook set, sleeping bags, backpacks, tent, bear spray, and full fly-fishing setup – all ready to go for your ultimate outdoor adventure. Or maybe you just forgot your stove. Explore has that and (just about) everything else for rent.

⌷ Sleeping

Most big-box chain motels are north of downtown Bozeman on 7th Ave, near I-90, with a handful of budget options east of downtown. Camping is plentiful in the Gallatin Valley toward Big Sky.

Howlers Inn
B&B $$

(☑406-587-2050; www.howlersinn.com; 3185 Jackson Creek Rd; r $165-170, 2-person cabin $225; ☎) Wolf-watchers will love this beautiful sanctuary 15 minutes outside of Bozeman. Rescued captive-born wolves live in enclosed natural areas on 4 acres, supported by the profits of the B&B. There are three spacious Western-style rooms in the main lodge and a two-bedroom carriage house.

The Lark
MOTEL $$$

(☑406-624-3070; www.larkbozeman.com; 122 W Main St; r $249-279; ❋☎) With a lively yellow palette and modern graphic design, this hip place is a big step up from its former life as a grungy motel. Rooms are fresh and the fine location puts it in walking distance of downtown's bars and restaurants, or hang out by the fire under the decked-out porte cochere, snacking on tacos from next door.

✗ Eating & Drinking

With seven breweries at last count (an eighth is on the way) and an active live music scene, if you're not having fun in Bozeman, you're doing it wrong. Check the Bozone (www.bozone.com) for a good music calendar.

★ Nova Cafe
CAFE $

(☑406-587-3973; www.thenovacafe.com; 312 E Main St; mains $8-13; ☉7am-2pm; ☎) ✐ A helpful map at the entrance shows you where the food you'll be eating comes from at this retro-contemporary locals' favorite. The hollandaise is a bit on the sweet side for our liking, but still excessively delicious – as is everything else.

Community Co-Op
SUPERMARKET $

(☑406-922-2667; www.bozo.coop; 44 E Main St; mains $7-12; ☉8am-8pm Mon-Fri, from 8:30am Sat, 9am-7pm Sun; ☎✐) ✐ This downtown branch of the beloved local market and deli is all about the hot bar, soups, salads and grab-and-go goodies. Fresh sandwiches and smoothies made to order. Eat in or take away.

Bozeman Taproom & Fill Station
BEER GARDEN

(☑406-577-2337; www.bozemantaproom.com; 101 N Rouse Ave; mains $9-13; ☉11am-midnight Sun-Tue, to 1am Fri & Sat) Bozeman's coolest new place to grab a pint and fill a growler has an open-air rooftop beer garden. Their 44 draft brews can be combined in as many ways as you like with the 'build your own flight' program.

Bridger Brewing
MICROBREWERY

(☑406-587-2124; www.bridgerbrewing.com; 1609 11th Ave; pizza $11-21; ☉11:30am-9pm, beer to 8pm; ☎) This well-run and friendly brewpub with central horseshoe bar draws a loyal combination of beer hounds and local MSU students. The Lee Metcalfe Pale Ale is a firm favorite and there are lots of food specials, including great pizza. The not-so-hidden upstairs deck is a great place to hang if you can find a seat.

Happy hour is from 2pm to 4pm.

❶ Information

Custer Gallatin National Forest Bozeman Ranger District (☑406-522-2520; www.fs.usda.gov/gallatin; 3710 Fallon, Suite C; ☉8:30am-4:30pm Mon-Fri) Tricky to find in the west of town, with info on campsites and cabins, plus it sells USGS topo maps.

Bozeman District Office (☑406-522-2520)

❶ Getting There & Away

Bozeman's **airport** (BZN; ☑406-388-8321; www.bozemanairport.com; 850 Gallatin Field Rd) keeps expanding to handle the increase in traffic, which also means more direct flights to more locations including LA, Seattle, Dallas and New York. **Greyhound** (Jefferson Lines; ☑612-499-3468; www.jeffersonlines.com; 1500 North 7th Ave, south side of Walmart; ☉noon-5pm) buses depart daily from a nondescript bus stop on the south side of the Super Walmart near the garden center.

Gallatin & Paradise Valleys

Outdoor enthusiasts could explore the expansive beauty around the Gallatin and Paradise Valleys for days. While they now compete with the likes of the Tetons and Beartooth Pass for title of 'most dramatic approach,' cruising through the pastoral river flats flanked by the Gallatin and Abasaroka Ranges will definitely excite your passion for adventure and exploration. It's not called 'paradise' for nothing.

🏃 Activities

Big Sky Resort
SNOW SPORTS

(☑800-548-4486; www.bigskyresort.com; 50 Big Sky Resort Rd; ski lift $129, bike lift $42) The 4th-largest ski hill in North America is actually four mountains covering 5800 acres of skiable terrain (60% advanced/expert) that get over 400in of powder a year. In short, Big

Sky is big skiing. And when the snow melts, you get over 40 miles of lift-served mountain bike and hiking trails making it a worthy summer destination as well.

Chico Hot Springs HOT SPRINGS
(☏406-333-4933; www.chicohotsprings.com; 163 Chico Road, Pray; cabins $120-135, main lodge r $71-140; ☺7am-11pm; ⊕) The unpretentious and historic Chico Hot Springs has garnered a loyal following of locals, Hollywood celebrities and return travelers. The creaking main lodge and sparkling log cabins are as much a draw as the mineral hot spring itself – which might as well be a heated swimming pool (admission for nonguests is $7.50).

Billings

It's hard to believe laid-back little Billings is Montana's largest city. The friendly oil-and-ranching center is not a must-see but makes for a decent overnight pit stop, or a point of departure for Yellowstone National Park via the breathtaking Beartooth Highway.

🛏 Sleeping

The main knot of chain motels is outside of Billings on I-90, exit 446, but there are a few standout independent options downtown – as well as a few dicey ones.

Dude Rancher Lodge MOTEL $
(☏406-545-6331; www.duderancherlodge.com; 415 N 29th St; d from $96; ❄@🌐🐾) This historic motor lodge looks a little out of place in the downtown area, but has been well maintained, with about half the rooms renovated to good effect. Western touches like tongue-and-groove walls and cattle-brand carpet give it a welcoming rustic feel.

Northern Hotel HOTEL $$
(☏406-867-6767; www.northernhotel.com; 19 N Broadway; r/ste $161/206; ❄🌐) The historic Northern was recently renovated, combining its previous elegance with fresh and modern facilities that are a solid step above generic business hotel. Breakfast or lunch is in the attached 1950s diner, and **Ten restaurant** offers one of best dinners in town.

✗ Eating & Drinking

McCormick Cafe BREAKFAST $
(☏406-255-9555; www.mccormickcafe.com; 2419 Montana Ave; meals $8-10; ☺7am-3pm Mon-Fri, 8am-3pm Sat, 8am-2pm Sun; 🌐) For espresso, granola breakfasts, French-style crepes,

good sandwiches and a lively atmosphere, stop by this downtown favorite that started life as an internet cafe (and even still has a few Windows-XP computers – use at your own risk.)

★**Walkers Grill** MODERN AMERICAN $$
(☏406-245-9291; www.walkersgrill.com; 2700 1st Ave N; tapas $6-12, mains $15-30; ☺5-10pm) Upscale Walkers offers good grill items and fine tapas at the bar (open from 4pm) accompanied by cocktails crafted by expert mixologists. It's an elegant, large-windowed space that would be right at home in Manhattan, though maybe without the barbed-wire light fixtures – or with. You owe it to yourself to try the Korean pork fork fries.

Überbrew MICROBREWERY
(☏406-534-6960; www.facebook.com/uberbrew; 2305 Montana Ave; mains $9-11; ☺11am-9pm, beer til 8pm) The most polished of Billings' half-dozen downtown brewpubs also happens to create award-winning beers that are

---

MONTANA FACTS

Nickname Treasure State, Big Sky Country

Population 1,042,5200

Area 147,040 sq miles

Capital city Helena (population 30,581)

Other cities Billings (population 110,263), Missoula (72,364), Bozeman (45,250)

Sales tax No state sales tax

Birthplace of Movie star Gary Cooper (1901–61), motorcycle daredevil Evel Knievel (1938–2007), actress Michelle Williams (1980)

Home of Crow, Blackfeet, Chippewa, Gros Ventre and Salish Native Americans

Politics Republican ranchers and oil barons generally edge out the Democratic students and progressives of left-leaning Bozeman and Missoula

Famous for Fly-fishing, cowboys and grizzly bears

Random fact Some Montana highways didn't have a speed limit until the 1990s

Driving distances Bozeman to Denver 695 miles, Missoula to Whitefish 133 miles

a noticeable step above the rest. Their food isn't half bad either: wash down a beer-marinated bockwurst with a pint of the White Noise Hefeweizen, which outsells the other drafts three to one.

ⓘ Getting There & Away

Downtown Billings is just off I-90 occupying a wide valley of the Yellowstone river. The **airport** (BIL; ☑ 406-247-8609; www.flybillings.com; N 27th Street) serves major hubs (Salt Lake City, Minneapolis, Denver, Seattle, Portland, Phoenix, Los Angeles, Las Vegas and other Montana destinations) while **Jefferson Lines** (Jefferson Lines; ☑ 406-245-5116; www.jeffersonlines. com; 2502 1st Ave N; ⊙ 9am-8pm & 11pm-6am; 🛜) has service to Bozeman ($39, three hours) and Missoula ($70, seven hours) twice daily, and connects to the larger Greyhound bus system.

Helena

It's pretty easy to overlook diminutive Helena as you zip by on the interstate, but you'd be doing yourself a grave disservice. Penetrate through the drab, utilitarian commerce sprawl toward Last Chance Gulch and old Helena where imposing brick and stone buildings – all arches and angles – portray a resolute commitment to permanence.

🏃 Activities

★ The Trail Rider   HIKING, MOUNTAIN BIKING
(☑ 406-449-2107; www.bikehelena.com/trail-rider; cnr Broadway & Last Chance Gulch; ⊙ Wed-Sun late May-Sep) **FREE** During the summer months a dedicated city bus pulling a bike trailer runs mountain bikers and hikers to one of three trailheads for epic single-track journeys back to town. Destinations include the Mt Helena Ridge Trail, the Mt Ascension trails, and the Continental Divide Trail at MacDonald pass.

🛏 Sleeping & Eating

The Sanders   B&B $$
(☑ 406-442-3309; www.sandersbb.com; 328 N Ewing St; r $145-165; ❀🛜) Located in the old mansion district, this historic B&B once belonged to Wilbur Sanders, a frontier lawyer and Montana's first senator. It now has seven elegant guest rooms, a wonderful old parlor and a breezy front porch. Each bedroom is unique and thoughtfully decorated, and it's run by a relative of the Ringling Brothers Circus family, with appropriate memorabilia.

Murry's   CAFE $
(☑ 406-431-2886; www.murryscafe.com; 438 N Last Chance Gulch; mains $6-11; ⊙ 8am-3pm Mon-Fri, 9am-2pm Sat & Sun; 🛜🍴) From spanakopita to souffle, this little cafe on the south end of downtown offers something a little different from the regular breakfast fare. Things really go off the hook during their Saturday and Sunday brunch when the name of the game is waffles – regular, stuffed, topped or drenched.

★ General Mercantile   COFFEE
(☑ 406-442-6078; www.generalmerc.com; 413 N Last Chance Gulch; ⊙ 8am-5:30pm Mon-Fri, 9am-5pm Sat, 11am-4pm Sun; 🛜) You'll have to weave through all sorts of Montana eclectica for sale – hummingbird feeders, postcards and homemade jam – to get what is widely regarded as the best coffee in the universe. Take your espresso to a private nook where you can contemplate what you'd look like with a mermaid fin and an octopus mustache – both also available.

ⓘ Information

Helena Visitor Center (☑ 406-442-4120; www.helenachamber.com; 225 Cruse Ave; ⊙ 8am-5pm Mon-Fri)

ⓘ Getting There & Away

The **airport** (HNL; ☑ 406-442-2821; www.helenaairport.com; 2850 Mercer Loop) two miles north of downtown Helena connects to regional hubs including Salt Lake City, Seattle, Denver and Minneapolis. The **Salt Lake Express** (www.saltlakeexpress.com; 1415 N Montana Ave; ⊙ 3am-8pm) bus heads south to tie in with the Greyhound system at Butte.

Missoula

Missoulians love to get outside, and summer means an almost endless stream of farmers markets, concerts in the park, outdoor cinema and similar celebrations of community life. Patio seating is the rule not the exception, and an afternoon outing is likely to involve some human-powered activity on the miles of urban and foothills trails. The wandering Clark Fork River is popular with stand-up paddleboarders where it cuts through town, and is a fly-fishing magnet downstream. Stand on its bank for five minutes and you'll understand why the classic novella *A River Runs Through It* was set here.

The University of Montana ensures a continuous lifeblood of young energy that keeps the town vibrant and the music rocking. However, Missoula is also growing fast, which means sprawling development on the outskirts, and increasing traffic during rush hour. Stay downtown.

⊙ Sights

★ Garnet Ghost Town
GHOST TOWN

(☎406-329-3914; www.garnetghosttown.org; Bear Gulch Rd; adult/child $3/free; ⊙9:30am-4:30pm Jun-Sep; 🚗) Over a dozens buildings preserved in a state of 'arrested decay' transport you back to the gold rush days, when cities were built overnight and vanished almost as quickly. Visit the site any time roads are clear, but select structures are opened for exploration during visiting hours.

Smokejumper Visitor Center
MUSEUM

(☎406-329-4934; www.fs.fed.us/fire/people/smokejumpers/missoula; 5765 West Broadway; ⊙8:30am-5pm Jun-Aug) **FREE** The visitor center on this active base for the heroic men and women who parachute into forests to combat raging wildfires has thought-provoking displays about an increasingly hazardous job. The real treat is touring the facility where the crew lives, trains and sews their own parachutes.

🏃 Activities

A Carousel for Missoula
PLAYGROUND

(☎406-549-8382; www.carouselformissoula. com; 101 Carousel Drive, Caras Park; adult/child $2.25/0.75; ⊙11am-5:30pm Sep-May, to 7pm Jun-Aug; 🚗) Hand-carved and individually painted by local artists, every horse that gallops around the classic carousel at Caras Park has a story to tell. But the bigger story is how a community rallied around one man's dream to restore a bit of whimsy to downtown.

Mount Sentinel
HIKING

(Campus Dr) A steep switchback trail from behind the University of Montana football stadium leads up to a concrete whitewashed 'M' (visible for miles around) on 5158ft Mt Sentinel. Tackle it on a warm summer's evening for glistening views of this much-loved city and its spectacular environs.

The trailhead is at Phyllis Washington Park on the east edge of campus.

🛏 Sleeping & Eating

★ Shady Spruce Hostel
HOSTEL $

(☎406-285-1197; www.shadysprucehostel.com; 204 E Spruce St; dm $35-40, s/ste $55/85; 🅿🅿)

We're superexcited to see the resurgence of the hostel in the US, and this clean, bright and spacious new addition to the family nails it in all the right places. Downtown is literally a block away from the converted house, but they have bikes for the walking-averse.

Goldsmith's Bed & Breakfast
B&B $$

(☎406-728-1585; www.missoulabedandbreakfast. com; 809 E Front St; r $144-204; 🅿🅿🅿) Before being moved here in two massive pieces, this inviting riverside B&B was a frat house, and before that, home to the University of Montana president. The modern-Victorian rooms are all comfortable, but we're partial to the Greenough Suite with its writing table and private river-view deck.

The Catalyst
CAFE $

(☎406-542-1337; www.thecatalystcafe.com; 111 N Higgins Ave; mains $8-13; ⊙8am-3pm) A local's favorite breakfast diner serves large portions of chilaquiles that you can drench in their house-made chipotle-coffee hot sauce. Don't miss the buckwheat waffles. There is usually a wait to get into this small space, but service is efficient and everyone leaves happy.

Market on Front
DELI

(☎406-541-0246; www.marketonfront.co; 201 E Front St; ⊙8am-8pm, to 7pm Sun) 🥗 Order a fresh-made sandwich or overflowing breakfast bowl, or take advantage of the gourmet grab-and-go items in the fridge. Shelves of healthy snacks, local teas, organic chocolate and local beer by the six-pack will take your picnic plans to the next level. Or dine in – with all those windows it feels like you're outside anyway.

▼ Drinking & Nightlife

Missoula has a surprisingly high-profile music scene for a smaller town.

Top Hat Lounge   LOUNGE
(www.tophatlounge.com; 134 W Front St; ⊙11:30am-10pm Mon-Wed, to 2am Thu-Sat) Where Missoula goes to get its groove on. This dark venue features live music most weekends in a space large enough to cut a rug, but small enough to feel like the band is playing just for you.

If the headliner is too big for the Hat, you can catch them at the historic **Wilma** theater, another Logjam music venue (www.logjampresents.com).

The Old Post   BAR
(☑406-721-7399; www.facebook.com/oldpostpub; 103 W Spruce St; mains $8-12; ⊙11am-1am Mon-Thu, to 2am Fri, from 9am Sat & Sun) Great beer on tap, friendly servers, decent pub food, and a sombrero-wearing moose – what's not to love about this American Legion Forgotten Warriors Post open to all. It's a comfortable, unpretentious western bar that has a lived-in feel with well-worn booths and a cozy little patio out back.

ⓘ Information

Visitor Center (☑406-532-3250; destinationmissoula.org; 101 E Main St; ⊙8am-5pm Mon-Fri) Destination Missoula has a useful website as well as a walk-in space downtown.

ⓘ Getting There & Away

Though small, Missoula's **airport** (MSO; ☑406-728-4381; www.flymissoula.com; 5225 Hwy 10 W) has regular and usually affordable service to most major hubs including Salt Lake City, Denver, Phoenix, LA, Seattle and Minneapolis, while regular **Greyhound** (☑406-549-2339; www.greyhound.com; 1660 W Broadway; ⊙7:15am-noon & 6-11pm) service connects you to most regional destinations.

Flathead Lake

The largest natural freshwater lake west of the Mississippi, sitting not an hour's drive from Glacier National Park, completes western Montana's embarrassment of natural

splendor. The small postcard community of **Bigfork** does its own artsy things on the north end of the lake while the southern end is anchored by the anywhere-USA town of **Polson**.

You can drive down either side of the lake, each with its own suite of campgrounds and lodges, beaches and hiking trails. Choosing is largely a matter of whether you prefer to watch the sun rise or set over the placid waters.

If you'd rather get away from the crowds, Swan Lake just to the east is a bit more primitive, while the Jewel Basin hiking area at its north draws backpackers from around the country.

Miracle of America Museum   MUSEUM
(☑406-883-6804; www.miracleofamericamuseum.org; 36094 Memory Lane, Polson; adult/child $6/3; ⊙8am-8pm Mon-Sat, reduced hours Sep-May) When Gil Mangels was a soldier on foreign soil, he became acutely aware of how America's freedom allowed for so much innovation and creativity – and he's been trying to collect every last bit of it ever since. At turns baffling and fascinating, these 5 acres are cluttered with the leftovers of American history: old motorcycles, bicycles, snow machines, steam tractors, antique quilts, coins, cast-iron skillets and countless other weird artifacts in a jumbled assortment of displays and piles.

Kwataqnuk Resort   HOTEL $$
(☑406-883-3636; www.kwataqnuk.com; 49708 Hwy 93, Polson; r from $170; ❋🛜🏊🐾) The lakeside Kwataqnuk Resort, run by the Salish and Kootenai tribes, has a boat dock, lakeside patio with lounge chairs, indoor pool and a mellow casino-lounge. The spacious rooms were all updated in 2016, but that unfortunately didn't remove the lingering smoke smell that permeates from the casino downstairs.

★ **Echo Lake Cafe**   CAFE $
(☑406-837-4252; www.echolakecafe.com; 1195 Hwy 83, Bigfork; mains $9-12; ⊙6:30am-2:30pm; 🛜) Go out of your way to stop by this valley favorite that serves an extensive menu of affordable breakfast and lunch creations. Try the Echo Lake crepes for a hearty take on the all-too-ubiquitous Benedict.

The **Swan Rangers** (www.swanrange.org) meet Saturday morning before heading off to clear trail. Join them for the insider scoop on area hiking.

ℹ Information

Swan Lake Ranger District (☑406-837-7500; www.fs.usda.gov/flathead; 200 Ranger Station Rd, Bigfork; ⊙8am-4:30pm Mon-Fri) manages the forest surrounding Flathead Lake and Swan Lake to the east, including the epically scenic Jewel Basin hiking area.

Whitefish

Tiny Whitefish feels on the verge of tipping from an easy-going outdoorsy mountain town to a fur-lined playground for the glitterati. It's not quite there yet, thankfully, but there's something suspiciously refined about this charismatic and caffeinated New West town. It is home to an attractive stash of restaurants, a historic railway station and an underrated ski resort, as well as excellent biking and hiking on a rapidly growing network of trails. Whitefish is well worth a visit – just get here while it's still affordable.

🏃 Activities

Whitefish Legacy Partners   HIKING, MOUNTAIN BIKING

(www.whitefishlegacy.org) Whitefish is surrounded by a growing network of trails ideal for hiking and mountain biking. The driving force behind the development, Whitefish Legacy Partners rallies support for the system with things like guided walks focusing on wildflowers, bears and noxious weeds.

Whitefish Mountain Resort   SKIING

(☑406-862-2900; www.skiwhitefish.com; Big Mountain Rd; ski/bike lift $76/38) Whitefish Mountain Resort at Big Mountain is a laid-back old-school ski hill with 3000 acres of varied terrain that sees 300in of snow a year. The views are unsurpassed (when it's clear).

🛏 Sleeping

★ Whitefish Bike Retreat   HOSTEL $

(☑406-260-0274; www.whitefishbikeretreat.com; 855 Beaver Lake Rd; dm/r $45/95; ❄🖰) Celebrating all things bicycle, this forested compound is a must-stay for two-wheel enthusiasts. The spacious polished-wood house with bunks, private rooms and a communal living area is a great place to hang when you're not hot-lapping the property trails or exploring the excellent **Whitefish Trail** that runs nearby.

The Lodge at Whitefish Lake   RESORT $$$

(☑406-863-4000; www.lodgeatwhitefishlake.com; 1380 Wisconsin Ave; r from $300; ❄🖰🏊) Consistently ranked among the top luxury hotels in Montana, the Lodge exudes refinement and sophistication almost to a fault. It offers a range of rooms, from standards to fully stocked condos, on the sprawling complex. The lakefront **restaurant** and poolside tiki bar are both great places to catch the sunset.

🍴 Eating & Drinking

Whitefish keeps up a lively evening scene, with a handful of bars and breweries, though the latter usually shut early due to Montana's byzantine liquor-licensing laws.

★ Loula's   CAFE $

(☑406-862-5614; www.whitefishrestaurant.com; 300 Second St E, downstairs; mains 9-11; ⊙7am-2pm Mon-Sun & 5-9:30pm Thu-Sun; 🖰) Downstairs in the century-old Masonic temple building, this bustling cafe has local art on the wall and culinary artists in the kitchen. The highly recommended lemon-crème-filled French toast dripping with raspberry sauce is a sinfully delicious breakfast, especially paired with the truffle eggs Benedict.

Buffalo Café   CAFE $$

(☑406-862-2833; www.buffalocafewhitefish.com; 514 3rd St E; mains $12-20; ⊙7am-2pm & 5-9pm Mon-Sat, from 8am Sun) Hopping with neighborly locals, the Buffalo is what you get when a standard chain diner hires someone who actually knows how to cook. For breakfast try the original Buffalo Pie: a mountain of poached eggs and various add-ins (cheese, veggies, bacon) piled atop a wedge of hash browns. You won't leave hungry.

★ Spotted Bear Spirits   DISTILLERY

(☑406-730-2436; www.spottedbearspirits.com; 503 Railway St, Suite A; ⊙noon-8pm; 🖰) Award-winning spirits (vodka, gin, and agave) are paired with secret blends of herbs and spices to create unique, award-winning cocktails you won't find anywhere else. Grab a drink and head to the sofa upstairs for a relaxing break from your day.

Montana Coffee Traders   COFFEE

(☑406-862-7667; www.coffeetraders.com; 110 Central Ave; ⊙7am-6pm Mon-Sat, 8am-4pm Sun; 🖰) Whitefish's home-grown microroaster runs this always-busy cafe and gift shop in the old Skyles building in the center of town. The organic, fair-trade beans are roasted in

ROCKY MOUNTAINS WHITEFISH

an old farmhouse on Hwy 93 that you can tour (10am Friday by reservation).

ℹ Information

Whitefish Visitor Center (www.whitefishvisit.com; 307 Spokane Ave; ⊗9am-5pm Mon-Fri)

ℹ Getting There & Away

Glacier Park International Airport (p812), 11 miles away, has daily service to Denver, Salt Lake and Seattle, but by far the best way to get here is via **Amtrak** (⌑ 406-862-2268; 500 Depot St; ⊗ 6am-1:30pm, 4:30pm-midnight) on the Empire Builder line, which also connects to Glacier National Park via West Glacier ($7.50, 30 minutes) and East Glacier ($16, two hours).

Glacier National Park

Few places on earth are as magnificent and pristine as **Glacier** (www.nps.gov/glac). Protected in 1910 during the first flowering of the American conservationist movement, Glacier ranks with Yellowstone, Yosemite and the Grand Canyon among the United States' most astounding natural wonders.

The glacially carved remnants of an ancient thrust fault have left us a brilliant landscape of towering snowcapped pinnacles laced with plunging waterfalls and glassy turquoise lakes. The mountains are surrounded by dense forests, which host a virtually intact pre-Columbian ecosystem. Grizzly bears still roam in abundance and smart park management has kept the place accessible and authentically wild.

Glacier is renowned for its historic 'parkitecture' lodges, the spectacular Going-to-the-Sun Rd and 740 miles of hiking trails. These all put visitors within easy reach of some 1489 sq miles of the wild and astonishing landscapes found at the crown of the continent.

◉ Sights & Activities

Visitor centers and ranger stations in Glacier National Park sell field guides and hand out hiking maps. Those at Apgar and St Mary are open daily May to October, and Logan Pass Visitor Center is open when the Going-to-the-Sun Rd is open. Many Glacier, Two Medicine and Polebridge Ranger Stations close at the end of September.

Entry to the park (hiker/vehicle $15/30) is valid for seven days.

You do not need a permit to day-hike the park's trails, but overnight backpackers do (May to October only). Half of the permits are available on a first-come-first-serve basis from the **Apgar Backcountry Office** (⌑406-888-7800; www.nps.gov/glac/planyourvisit/backcountry-reservations.htm; Apgar Village; ⊗7am-5pm May–late Oct), **St Mary Visitor Center** (east end of Going-to-the-Sun Road; ⊗8am-6pm mid-Jun–mid-Aug, 8am-5pm early Jun & Sep) and the park's ranger stations. The other half can be reserved in advance online.

Logan Pass Visitor Center   VISITOR CENTER
(⌑406-888-7800; Going-to-the-Sun Rd; ⊗9am-7pm Jun-Aug, 9:30am-4pm Sep) Certainly in the most magnificent setting of all the park's visitor centers, the building has park information, interactive exhibits, and a good gift shop. The **Hidden Lakes Overlook** and Highline trails begin from here.

Check times for ranger talks and guided hikes in the area.

Bird Woman Falls   WATERFALL
(Going-to-the-Sun Rd) Standing at the artificially created Weeping Wall, look across the valley to this distant natural watery spectacle; the spectacular Bird Woman Falls drops 500ft from one of Glacier's many hanging valleys.

Sunrift Gorge   CANYON
(Going-to-the-Sun Rd) Just off the Going-to-the-Sun Rd and adjacent to a shuttle stop lies this narrow canyon carved over millennia by the gushing glacial meltwaters of Baring Creek. Look out for picturesque **Baring Bridge**, a classic example of rustic Going-to-the-Sun Rd architecture, and follow a short, tree-covered trail down to misty **Baring Falls**.

Jackson Glacier Overlook   VIEWPOINT
This popular pull-over, located a short walk from the Gunsight Pass trailhead, offers telescopic views of the park's fifth-largest glacier, which sits close to its eponymous 10,052ft peak – one of the park's highest.

Going-to-the-Sun Road   SCENIC DRIVE
(www.nps.gov/glac/planyourvisit/goingtothesunroad.htm; ⊗mid-Jun–late Sep) A strong contender for the most spectacular road in America, the 50-mile Going-to-the-Sun Rd was built for the express purpose of giving park visitors a way to explore its interior without having to hike. The marvel of engineering is a national historic landmark that crosses Logan Pass (6,646ft) and is flanked by hiking trails, waterfalls and endless views.

★**Highline Trail**   HIKING
(Logan Pass) A Glacier classic, the Highline Trail contours across the face of the famous Garden Wall to **Granite Park Chalet** (☎406-387-5555; www.graniteparkchalet.com; 1st person US$107, extra person US$85; ⊙Jul–mid-Sep) – one of two historic lodges only accessible by trail. The summer slopes are covered with alpine plants and wildflowers while the views are nothing short of stupendous. With only 800ft elevation gain over 7.6 miles, the treats come with minimal sweat.

From Granite Park you have four options: you can retrace your steps back to Logan Pass; continue along the continental divide to Goat Haunt (22 miles); head for Swiftcurrent Pass and the Many Glacier Valley (7 miles); or descend to the Loop (4 miles), where you can pick up a shuttle bus to all points on the Going-to-the-Sun Rd.

Avalanche Lake Trail   HIKING
(north of Lake McDonald) This low-commitment introduction to Glacier hiking pays big dividends in the form of a pristine alpine lake, waterfalls and cascades. The 2.3-mile hike is relatively gentle and easily accessed by the shuttle – and therefore invariably mobbed in peak season with everyone from flip-flop-wearing families to stick-wielding seniors making boldly for the tree line.

Glacier Park Boat Co   BOATING
(☎406-257-2426;   www.glacierparkboats.com) Six historic boats – some dating back to the 1920s – ply five of Glacier's attractive mountain lakes, and some of them combine the float with a short guided hike led by interpretive, often witty, guides. For those more adventurous types, they also rent rowboats, kayaks and paddleboards ($18.30 per hour) at Lake Mary, Many Glacier, and Two Medicine.

🛏 **Sleeping**

There are 13 **NPS campgrounds** (☎518-885-3639; www.recreation.gov; tent & RV sites $10-23) and seven historic lodges in Glacier National Park, which operate between mid-May and the end of September. Lodges invariably require reservations.

Only Fish Creek, St Mary and a few sites at Many Glacier campgrounds can be booked in advance (up to five months). First-come sites fill by mid-morning, particularly in July and August.

About half the two to seven sites at each of the 65 backcountry campgrounds can be

ℹ **FREE PARK SHUTTLE**

See more with less stress by ditching the car and taking the park's free hop-on-hop-off **shuttle service** (www.nps.gov/glac/planyourvisit/shuttles.htm; ⊙9am-7pm July-Aug) 🚌**FREE** that hits all major points along Going-to-the-Sun Rd between Apgar and St. Mary Visitor Centers. Buses run every 15 to 30 minutes depending on traffic, with the last trips down from Logan Pass leaving at 7pm.

Not only does taking the shuttle reduce emissions, but it means you can actually see the scenery instead of worrying about other drivers, and actually go hiking instead of trying to find parking at the trailheads.

reserved, the rest are allotted on a first-come basis the day before you start hiking.

★**Izaak Walton Inn**   HISTORIC HOTEL **$$**
(☎406-888-5700; www.izaakwaltoninn.com; 290 Izaak Walton Inn Rd, Essex; r $109-179, cabins & cabooses $199-249; 🕿) Perched on a hill within snowball-throwing distance of Glacier National Park's southern boundary, this historic mock-Tudor inn was originally built in 1939 to accommodate local railway personnel. It remains a daily flag-stop (request stop) on Amtrak's *Empire Builder* route – a romantic way to arrive. Caboose cottages with kitchenettes are available, along with a historic GN441 locomotive refurbished as a luxury four-person suite ($329).

Many Glacier Hotel   HISTORIC HOTEL **$$**
(☎303-265-7010;   www.glaciernationalparklodges.com; 1 Many Glacier Rd; r $207-322, ste $476; ⊙mid-Jun–mid-Sep; 🕿) Enjoying the most wondrous setting in the park, this massive, Swiss chalet-inspired lodge commands the northeastern shore of Swiftcurrent Lake. It was built by the Great Northern Railway in 1915, and although the comfortable, if rustic, rooms have been updated over the last 15 years, many still suffer from thin walls and antiquated plumbing.

🍴 **Eating**

In summer in Glacier National Park, there are grocery stores with limited camping supplies in Apgar, Lake McDonald Lodge, Rising Sun and at the Swiftcurrent Motor Inn. Most lodges have on-site restaurants. Dining options in West Glacier and St Mary offer mainly hearty hiking fare.

If cooking at a campground or picnic area, be sure to take appropriate bear safety precautions and do not leave food unattended.

★**Serrano's Mexican Restaurant** MEXICAN $
(☏406-226-9392; www.serranosmexican.com; 29 Dawson Ave, East Glacier Park; mains US$13-18; ☉5-9pm May-Sep; ☏) East Glacier Park's most buzzed-about restaurant serves a mean chile relleno. Renowned for its excellent iced margaritas, Serrano's also has economical burritos, enchiladas and quesadillas in the vintage Dawson house log cabin, originally built in 1909. Expect a wait.

★**Belton Chalet Grill
& Taproom** INTERNATIONAL $$$
(☏406-888-5000; www.beltonchalet.com; 12575 US 2, West Yellowstone; mains $24-35; ☉5-9pm, tap room from 3pm) 🌿 A fine option for a fine evening, West Glacier's historic chalet knows how to wine and dine. The sit-down restaurant sports tablecloths, wine glasses and a small menu with items like Montana bison meatloaf wrapped in hickory-smoked bacon.

ⓘ Information

Glacier National Park Headquarters (☏406-888-7800; www.nps.gov/glac; West Glacier; ☉8am-4:30pm Mon-Fri)

ⓘ Getting There & Around

Glacier Park International Airport (FCA; ☏406-257-5994; www.iflyglacier.com; 4170 Highway 2 East, Kalispell) in Kalispell has year-round service to Salt Lake, Minneapolis, Denver, Seattle and Las Vegas, and seasonal service to Atlanta, Oakland, LA, Chicago and Portland.

The **Glacier Park Express** (☏406-253-9192; www.bigmtncommercial.org; Whitefish Library; adult/child round-trip US$10/5; ☉Jul-early Sep) shuttle connects Whitefish to West Glacier.

Amtrak's *Empire Builder* stops daily (year round) at **West Glacier** (www.amtrak.com) and **East Glacier Park** (www.amtrak.com; ☉summer only) (April to October). Xanterra provides a shuttle ($15, 10 to 20 minutes) from West Glacier to their lodges on the west end, and Glacier Park, Inc. shuttles (from $15, one hour) connect East Glacier Park to St Mary.

Glacier National Park runs a free hop-on-hop-off **shuttle bus** (p815) from Apgar to St Mary over Going-to-the-Sun Rd during summer months, that stops at all major trailheads. Xanterra concession operates the classic guided **Red Bus Tours** (☏303-265-7010; www.glacier

nationalparklodges.com/red-bus-tours; adult $34-100, child $17-50).

If driving a personal vehicle, be prepared for narrow winding roads, traffic jams, and limited parking at most stops along Going-to-the-Sun Rd.

IDAHO

Hiding between Montana and Oregon is a rather large chunk of land with some of the most vast and rugged mountains in the lower 48. It's called Idaho (no, not Iowa), and when the federal government was dividing the northern territories into states, it got stuck with the leftovers nobody wanted: those bothersome mountain ranges that you just can't farm in – 114 of them to be precise.

While that may have been a setback for the agriculturally deprived young state, it is a golden opportunity in the modern recreation economy. Over 60% of the state is public land, and with 3.9 million acres of Wilderness, it's the 3rd-most wild state in the union – and mountain lovers are beginning to notice. The outdoor industry now brings six times as much cash into Idaho as do its famous potatoes.

Boise

Refreshingly modern, urban and trendy are not words you usually associate with Idaho towns, but the state's capital (and largest city) isn't really into stereotypes. Boise's lively downtown scene – complete with walking streets, Parisian-style bistros and sophisticated wine bars – would fit in on the East Coast. The network of trails shooting up from town to the forested hills above rivals some of Colorado's best hiking destinations. Floating through the Greenbelt is as good as anything you'll find along Austin, Texas' beloved tubing circuit. Sample a steaming pan of paella in the Basque Block and you might as well be in Bilbao. With so much going on, you won't know what to make of Boise, but Boise will undoubtedly make a lasting impression on you.

◉ Sights & Activities

★**Basque Block** AREA
(www.thebasqueblock.com; Grove St at 6th & Capital) Boise is home to one of the largest Basque populations outside Spain with as many as 15,000 residing here, depending on who you ask. The original émigrés arrived

in the 1910s to work as shepherds when sheep outnumbered people seven to one. Few continue that work today, but many extended families have remained, and the rich elements of their distinct culture are still very much alive – glimpses of which can be seen along Grove St between 6th St and Capitol Blvd.

Boise River Greenbelt
PARK, MUSEUM

(http://parks.cityofboise.org) The glowing emerald of Treasure Valley began as an ambitious plan in the 1960s to prevent development in the Boise River's flood-plain and provide open space in a rapidly growing city. Now, the growing collection of parks and museums along the tree-lined river-way is connected by over 30 miles of multi-use paths, and hosts an insanely popular summer floating scene. A developing $12 million whitewater park, complete with hydraulically controlled waves, promises to be the largest of its kind.

World Center for Birds of Prey
BIRD SANCTUARY

(Peregrine Fund; ☑208-362-8687; www.peregrine fund.org/visit; 5668 W Flying Hawk Lane; adult/child $7/5; ◷10am-5pm Tue-Sun Mar-Oct, to 4pm Nov-Feb) The Peregrine Fund's worldwide raptor conservation programs have brought many species back from the brink of extinction – including the iconic California Condor, successfully bred in captivity here for release in California and the Grand Canyon. A pair of condors reside at the center, along with a dozen other impressive birds including the northern aplomado falcon, whose mating pairs work in tandem to hunt grassland sparrows. Open-air Fall Flights are a must-see (3pm, Friday to Sunday in October).

Boise Art Museum
MUSEUM

(☑208-345-8330; www.boiseartmuseum.org; 670 Julia Davis Dr; adult/child $6/3; ◷10am-5pm Tue-Sat, noon-5pm Sun) Inside 90-acre Julia Davis Park, this small but bright museum displays mostly contemporary art in all media, including the occasional Warhol, and touring exhibitions by some big names. On First Thursdays each month, admission is by donation and the museum stays open until 8pm.

Idaho State Historical Museum
MUSEUM

(☑208-334-2120; https://history.idaho.gov/ida ho-state-historical-museum; 610 N Julia Davis Dr, temporary: 214 Broadway; ◷during renovation: 11am-4pm Mon-Fri) While the main building is under renovations a temporary museum

with a handful of exhibits, including the much-adored two-headed stuffed calf, are on display at 214 Broadway. The re-opening is slated for spring 2018.

Ridge to Rivers Trail System
HIKING

(☑208-493-2531; www.ridgetorivers.org; north-east of Boise; 🖐) Some 190 miles of hiking and mountain-biking trails meander through the foothills above town, crossing grasslands, scrub slopes and tree-lined creeks on their way to the Boise National Forest. The options are literally endless. The most convenient access is via Cottonwood Creek Trailhead east of the capitol building, or Camel's Back Park to the north.

Boise River Float
PARK

(www.boiseriverraftandtube.com; 4049 S Eckert Rd, Barber Park; tube rental $12, ducky $35, raft $45; ♿) There is no better way to spend a sunny summer day in Boise than floating down the river. Rent watercraft – from tubes to six-person rafts – at Barber Park (parking $5 Monday to Thursday, $6 Friday to Sunday) where you'll put in for a self-guided 6-mile, 1½ to three-hour float downstream to Ann Morrison Park. Open June through August depending on river flows.

🛏 Sleeping

Inn at 500
HOTEL $$

(☑208-227-0500; www.innat500.com; 500 S Capitol; r $205-265, ste $295-315; ❉🌐🐾) Finally, a luxury boutique hotel that doesn't give up at the lobby. Fine art, unique dioramas and blown glass – all from local artists – adorn the hallways and rooms, creating warm and inviting spaces a step above your standard high-quality-bed-in-a-box affair. All within walking distance of Boise's buzzing downtown.

★ Boise Guest House
GUESTHOUSE $$

(☑208-761-6798; www.boiseguesthouse.com; 614 North 5th St; ste $99-189; 🌐🐾) A veritable home away from home, this appealing old house has a handful of suites with kitchenettes and living areas comfortably arranged and taste-fully decorated. All rooms have access to the large grill in the relaxing backyard, red-and-white cruiser bikes and laundry.

🍴 Eating

Boise's vibrant downtown hosts a range of dining options from casual to formal. Seek out Basque specialties. The hip Hyde Park region on 13th street is even more laid-back, and a great place to grab a snack after hiking.

★ **Goldy's Breakfast Bistro**   BREAKFAST **$**
(📞208-345-4100; www.goldysbreakfastbistro.
com; 108 S Capitol Blvd; mains $6-20; ⏱6:30am-
2pm Mon-Fri, 7:30am-2pm Sat & Sun) Assuming
an egg is just an egg (regardless of whether
it's sunny-side up, poached or fried) Goldy's
offers 866,320 'Create Your Own Breakfast
Combos.' Check our math – we were already
drunk on hollandaise sauce when we put
pen to napkin. Or go for the frittatas, bennies or massive breakfast burrito.

Fork   MODERN AMERICAN **$$**
(📞207-287-1700; www.boisefork.com; 199 N
8th St; mains $15-28; ⏱11:30am-10pm Mon-Fri,
9:30am-11pm Sat, 9:30am-9pm Sun; 🍴) 🌱 This
cavernous corner restaurant occupying the
old bank building downtown is good an-
ytime, but excels during weekend brunch
when things like the Dungeness crab scram-
ble pair unbelievably well with the local
favorite: asparagus fries. Try the Fork Lem-
onade for a refreshing pickup on a sunny
summer day.

 Drinking & Nightlife

There is no shortage of lively and creative
drinking spots in Boise's urban center,

IDAHO FACTS

Nickname Gem State

Population 1,596,000

Area 83,570 sq miles

Capital city Boise (population 223,154)

Other cities Idaho Falls (population
60,211)

Sales tax 6%

Birthplace of Lewis and Clark guide
Sacagawea (1788–1812); politician
Sarah Palin (b 1964); poet Ezra Pound
(1885–1972)

Home of Star garnet, Sun Valley ski
resort

Politics Reliably Republican with small
pockets of Democrats, eg Sun Valley

Famous for Potatoes, Wilderness, the
world's first chairlift

North America's deepest river gorge
Idaho's Hells Canyon (7900ft deep)

Driving distances Boise to Idaho Falls
280 miles, Lewiston to Coeur d'Alene
116 miles

---

which is hopping even on a Sunday night.
The further from the city center you get, the
more generic the options become.

★ **Bodovino**   WINE BAR
(📞208-336-8466; www.bodovino.com; 404 S 8th
St; ⏱11am-11pm, to 1am Fri-Sat, to 9pm Sun; 🍴)
Whether you're a sommelier or a swiller, the
variety of vintages on tap here is nothing
short of hazardous – especially considering
you're on your own with walls of vending
machines that decant tastes or pours from
144 different wines.

Bardenay   DISTILLERY
(📞208-426-0538; www.bardenay.com; 610 Grove
St; cocktails from $7; ⏱11am-late Mon-Fri, from
10am Sat & Sun) Bardenay was the USA's very
first 'distillery-pub,' and remains a one-of-
a-kind watering hole. Located on Basque
Block (p812), it makse rum in house and
has whiskey ageing for imminent release.
A dizzying array of cocktails are created
from spirits crafted in all three Idaho loca-
tions, including the dizzying Sunday Morn-
ing Paper – a lemon-vodka–Bloody Mary
experience.

ℹ Information

Visitor Center (📞208-344-7777; www.boise.
org; 250 S 5th St, Ste 300; ⏱10am-5pm Mon-
Fri, 10am-2pm Sat Jun-Aug, 9am-4pm Mon-Fri
Sep-May) Boise's tourist-info website has a
useful events calendar.

ℹ Getting There & Around

Although small, **Boise Municipal Airport** (BOI;
📞208-383-3110; www.iflyboise.com; 3201
Airport Way, I-84 exit 53) stays busy and is well
connected, with nonstop flights to a range of
locations including Denver, Las Vegas, Phoenix,
Portland, Salt Lake City, Seattle and Chicago.
Greyhound services depart from the **bus sta-
tion** (www.greyhound.com; 1212 W Bannock
St; ⏱6am-11am, 4pm-11:59pm 6am-11am,
4pm-midnight) with routes fanning out to Spo-
kane, Pendleton and Portland, Twin Falls and
Salt Lake City.

   The **Green Bike** (📞208-345-7433; www.
boise.greenbike.com; per hour $5) system, is by
far the coolest way to get around downtown.

Ketchum & Sun Valley

Occupying one of Idaho's more stunning
natural locations, Sun Valley is a living piece
of ski history. It was the first purpose-built
ski resort in the US (a venture by the Un-

ion Pacific Railroad to boost ridership) and opened in 1936 to much fanfare, thanks to both its luxury showcase lodge and the world's first chairlift.

The ski area and town of Ketchum were popularized early on by celebrities like Ernest Hemingway, Clark Gable and Gary Cooper (who received free trips as a marketing ploy by Averell Harriman – politician, railroad heir and Sun Valley's founder). It has kept a steady stream of swanky Hollywood clientele ever since.

Yet it still remains a pretty and accessible place that's flush with hot springs, hiking trails, fishing, hunting and mountain biking, extending from Galena Pass down to the foothills of Hailey.

🏃 Activities

⭐Galena Lodge
OUTDOORS
(☑208-726-4010; www.galenalodge.com; 15187 Hwy 75; XC ski pass adult/child $17/$5; ⊙lodge 9am-4pm, kitchen 11:30am-3:30pm) Miles of mountain bike and groomed XC ski trails spiderweb out from this cool lodge that rents equipment and serves up lunch to keep you fueled for the day. If you're feeling guilty about leaving your four-legged friend at home, don't worry, they have loaner dogs (most with four legs). It's 23 miles north of Ketchum.

Sun Valley Resort
SNOW SPORTS
(☑888-490-5950; www.sunvalley.com; Ketchum; winter ski ticket $89-139) Sun Valley has been synonymous with luxury skiing ever since they invented the chairlift in 1936. But while you can now sit-to-ski elsewhere, people still flock here for the fluffy powder and celebrity spotting. Two mountains – mellow **Dollar Mountain** with its extensive terrain parks to the east of town and black-and-blue **Bald Mountain** to the west – provide plenty of variety.

Wood River Trail System
HIKING, CYCLING
(www.bcrd.org/wood-river-trail-summer.php) Good things happen when a community rallies behind outdoor activities. This paved urban trail system extends over 32 miles, connecting the major hubs of Sun Valley with the towns of Ketchum, Hailey and Bellevue (20 miles south) following the old Union Pacific Railroad line.

🛏 Sleeping

Ketchum's new hostel means that the free camping on Bureau of Land Management (BLM) and Forest Service lands near town is no longer the only affordable lodging option. Rates vary with the seasons, winter being most expensive.

Hot Water Inn
HOSTEL $
(☑626-484-3021; www.facebook.com/thehoth2oinn; 100 Picabo St; dm $39, r $109, ste $126; ᷰ) Score one for the ski bums. A group of passionate locals have tricked out an old boarding school to become Ketchum's most affordable – and most chill – place to spend the weekend. The bar and stage now occupying the great room host jam sessions many an evening, and Sun Valley's Warm Springs ski lifts are just a bleary-eyed stumble away.

Tamarack Lodge
HOTEL $$
(☑208-726-3344; www.tamaracksunvalley.com; 291 Walnut Ave; r from $169-179, ste $209-249; ❄ᷰᷰᷰ) Rooms are tasteful at this aging but clean downtown lodge that exudes '1970s ski condo' vibe. Some rooms are a bit dark, but many have fireplaces and all have a balcony and use of the Jacuzzi and indoor pool.

Sun Valley Lodge
HOTEL $$$
(☑208-622-2001; www.sunvalley.com; 1 Sun Valley Rd; inn from $349, lodge from $439; ❄᷐@ᷰᷰ) The celebrities already came in droves before the 2015 renovation that spruced up this swank 1930s-era lodge – Sun Valley's first and finest. Standard rooms have the exact same amenities as the higher end picks – including the spacious bathrooms with tub – just less floor space around the bed.

🍴 Eating & Drinking

You'll want to après-ski at **Apple's** (☑208-726-7067; www.facebook.com/applesbarandgrill; 205 Picabo St; ⊙11am-6pm summer & winter) before checking out the valley's regular live-music scene. The more swanky bars are not averse to turning out the riffraff. If you unexpectedly find yourself in that category, the **Casino Club** (☑208-726-9901; 220 N Main St; ⊙11am-2am) has a stool for you.

The Kneadery
BREAKFAST $
(☑208-726-9462; www.kneadery.com; 260 N Leadville Ave; mains $8-13; ⊙8am-2pm) A solid bet for breakfast or lunch, the Kneadery is off the main drag in an old split-log cabin outfitted with large fireplace, western art and a birchbark canoe hanging from the ceiling. The ambience is almost as fine as their pancakes.

Powerhouse PUB FOOD $

(☑208-788-9184; www.powerhouseidaho.com; 411 N Main, Hailey; mains $9-15; ⊙11:30am-10pm) 🖉 We debated whether to classify this as a 'bicycle shop', 'bar' or 'restaurant'. We don't have a category for 'awesome'. With 17 beers on tap, it's a great place to get your two-wheeler wrenched on after a hard day on Sun Valley's trails. Or just hang out and meet local dirt-jockeys. The tacos and burgers are pretty good, too.

★Pioneer Saloon STEAK $$$

(☑208-726-3139; www.pioneersaloon.com; 320 N Main St; mains $15-35; ⊙5-10pm, bar 4pm-late) For the best steak in Ketchum (and, some argue, Idaho) step into the former illicit gambling hall, now an unashamed Western den decorated with deer heads, antique guns (one being Hemingway's) and bullet boards. If red meat isn't your thing, they also have a range of fish options and a tasty mango-chutney and grilled-vegetable chicken kabob.

❶ Information

Sun Valley/Ketchum Visitors Center (☑20 8-726-3423; www.visitsunvalley.com; 491 Sun Valley Rd; ⊙6am-7pm; ☎) Staffed only from 9am to 6pm, but you can still come in and get maps and brochures before and after hours.

❶ Getting There & Around

Friedman Memorial Airport (SUN; ☑208-788-4956; www.iflysun.com; 1616 Airport Circle, Hailey, ID) is located 12 miles south of Ketchum in Hailey, and has daily service to most western-states hubs (LA, San Francisco, Seattle, Salt Lake City and Denver, as well as twice-weekly flights to Portland), though it can sometimes be more economical to fly into Boise and take the three-hour **Sun Valley Express** (Caldwell Transportation; ☑208-576-7381; www.sunvalleyexpress.com; adult/child $85/75) from there.

Mountain Rides (☑208-788-7433; www.mountainrides.org) offers free transportation throughout Ketchum.

Stanley

Barely more than a cluster of rustic log cabins at the base of the jagged Sawtooth mountains, Stanley might be the most scenic small town in America. Its population of 60-odd is dramatically augmented in summer by an influx of white-water rafters, anglers and woodsy folk keen to lose themselves among the foreboding peaks and hidden valleys of the Sawtooths.

🏃 Activities

★Sawtooth National Recreation Area OUTDOORS

(www.fs.usda.gov/recarea/sawtooth/recarea/?recid=5842) You'll find rivers to boat, mountains to climb, animals to hunt, over 300 lakes to fish, and an excess of 700 miles of trails to hike or mountain bike in the dramatic Sawtooth National Recreation Area. It protects 1170 sq miles of America's public lands stretching between Stanley and Ketchum, offering unparalleled opportunities for exploration and recreation.

Middle Fork of the Salmon RAFTING

(☑877-444-6777; www.recreation.gov) Stanley is the jumping-off point for the legendary Middle Fork of the Salmon. Billed as the 'last wild river', it throws over 100 rapids at boaters during the 100-mile, 3000ft run that passes through the ominously named River of No Return Wilderness. This is alpine rafting at its finest, and is accessible through a number of guiding companies.

Kirkham Creek Hot Springs HOT SPRINGS

(Hwy 21, Lowan; ⊙dawn-dusk) FREE These natural hot springs at Kirkham Campground are about 5 miles east of Lowman and 53 miles southwest of Stanley on Hwy 21. Although they can get busy on weekends (parking $5), the cascades and pools of steaming water beside the frigid Payette River are still a relaxing experience.

🛏 Sleeping & Eating

There are about half-a-dozen hotels and lodges in Stanley, and plentiful camping in the surrounding national forest. Dining is limited, even during the short summer season when a few more restaurants open up.

National Forest Campgrounds CAMPGROUND $

(☑877-444-6777; www.fs.usda.gov/activity/sawtooth/recreation/camping-cabins; Stanley District Office; tent & RV sites $12-18) Dozens of established campgrounds provide exceptional opportunities to sleep under the stars throughout the Sawtooth National Recreation Area; many are within an hour drive of Stanley. Some campsites are reservable online (www.recreation.gov) while others are first come, first served.

Sawtooth Hotel
HOTEL $

(208-721-2459; www.sawtoothhotel.com; 755 Ace of Diamonds St; d with/without bath $100/70; mid-May–mid-Oct;) Set in a nostalgic 1931 log motel, the Sawtooth updates the slim comforts of yesteryear, but keeps the hospitality effusively Stanley-esque. Six rooms are furnished old-country style, two with private bathrooms. Don't expect TVs or speedy wi-fi, but count on excellent dining (mains $14 to $26) with vegetarian and gluten-free options and a tiny selection of drinkable wines.

★ Stanley Baking Company
BAKERY, BREAKFAST $

(www.stanleybakingco.com; 250 Wall St; mains $8-13; 7am-2pm May-Oct) Something of a legend, this middle-of-nowhere bakery and brunch spot is a must stop. Operating for five months of the year out of a small log cabin, Stanley Baking Co is the only place in town where you're likely to see a queue. The reason: off-the-ratings-scale homemade baked goods and oatmeal pancakes.

Idaho Panhandle

In many ways northern Idaho feels more like the Pacific Northwest than the Rockies. Perhaps it's the impressively large lakes speckled with sailboats giving it a nautical vibe. Or maybe it's the understated mountains, dense forests and rebounding timber industry. Or it could be as simple as sharing a timezone (the panhandle observes Pacific Standard Time) which makes those lazy days on the lake feel all the longer – encouraging you to linger.

Sandpoint reigns as the panhandle's most interesting destination, and not just because of sprawling Lake Pend Oreille (Idaho's largest) but thanks also to its neat, walkable downtown and local ski resort.

The region's largest town, Coeur d'Alene (population 46,402), is an extension of the Spokane metro area, but manages to retain a rural feel. There's a small boardwalk and a manicured park in front of the landmark resort on the north shore of Lake Coeur d'Alene.

🏃 Activities

Schweitzer Mountain Resort
SNOW SPORTS

(208-263-9555; www.schweitzer.com; 10000 Schweitzer Mountain Rd, Sandpoint; ski lift $77, mountain bike lift $35) Eleven miles northwest of Sandpoint is highly rated Schweitzer Mountain Resort, lauded for its tree-skiing.

Its 2900 acres of terrain gets 300 inches of snowfall. The summer mountain-bike trails are more traditional routes, with natural features than you don't typically find in today's engineered big-drop bike parks.

Trail of the Coeur d'Alenes
CYCLING

(208-682-3814; www.parksandrecreation.idaho. gov/parks/trail-coeur-d-alenes) An excellent rails-to-trails route crosses the Idaho panhandle from Plummer to Mullan, skirting the shore of Lake Coeur d'Alene before connecting to the I-90 corridor through the mountains. The incredibly scenic 72-mile trail is completely paved with a consistent grade, making it accessible to all types of non-motorized travel – including hiking, biking and rollerblading.

🛏 Sleeping & Eating

Flamingo Motel
MOTEL $$

(208-664-2159; www.flamingomotelidaho. com; 718 E Sherman Ave, Coeur d'Alene; s/d/ste $110/120/180;) Channeling the best of the 1950s car-loving, motel-staying, road-tripping culture, this retro motor inn has rooms decked out in various themes – from over-the-top 'Flamingo' to 'Irish' – but with updates like flat-screen TVs and minifridges.

★ Lodge at Sandpoint
BOUTIQUE HOTEL $$$

(208-263-2211; www.lodgeatsandpoint.com; 41 Lakeshore Dr, Sandpoint; d/ste $219/419;) Stealing the best lakeside location on Lake Pend Oreille, this modern lodge raises the bar for rustic-chic. They don't skimp on amenities with a gym, two outdoor hot tubs and beach access.

★ The Garnet Cafe
BREAKFAST $

(208-667-2729; www.garnetcafe.com; 315 E Walnut Ave, Coeur d'Alene; mains $10-14;) 🌿 One foolproof way to be sure your ingredients are organic and sustainably sourced is to own the farm that grows them. Enter the McLane family who personally raise the pigs, ducks and chickens that feed the satisfied customers lining up outside the Garnet Cafe's door.

❶ Getting There & Away

The closest major airport is in Spokane and several companies operate shuttles to Coeur d'Alene ($60, 45 minutes) or Sandpoint ($120, 6½ hours). **Amtrak** (SPT; www.amtrak.com; 450 Railroad Ave, Sandpoint) is another fine, if underutilized, option for getting to Sandpoint from Whitefish, MT ($30, four hours) or Spokane ($13, two hours) on the *Empire Builder* line.

Southwest

Includes ➜

Nevada	822
Las Vegas	822
Arizona	838
Phoenix	839
Grand Canyon National Park	854
Utah	871
Salt Lake City	872
New Mexico	891
Albuquerque	892
Santa Fe	896

Best Places to Eat

➜ Kai Restaurant (p844)

➜ Love Apple (p907)

➜ Hell's Backbone Grill (p888)

➜ Cafe Pasqual's (p900)

➜ Red Iguana (p874)

Best Places to Sleep

➜ Washington School House (p880)

➜ Earthship Rentals (p906)

➜ La Fonda (p898)

➜ El Tovar (p859)

➜ Arizona Biltmore Resort & Spa (p842)

Why Go?

The Southwest is America's untamed playground, luring adventurous travelers with thrilling red-rock landscapes, the legends of shoot-'em-up cowboys and the kicky delights of green chile stew. Reminders of the region's Native American heritage and hardscrabble Wild West heyday dot the landscape, from enigmatic pictographs and abandoned cliff dwellings to crumbling Hispanic missions and rusty mining towns. Today, history making continues, with astronomers and rocket builders peering into star-filled skies while artists and entrepreneurs flock to urban centers and quirky mountain towns. The best part for travelers? A splendid network of scenic drives linking the most beautiful and iconic sites. But remember: it's not just iconic, larger-than-life landscapes that make a trip through the Southwest memorable. Study that saguaro up close; ask a Hopi artist about their craft; savor that green-chile stew. You may just cherish those moments the most.

When to Go
Las Vegas

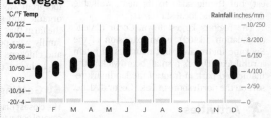

Jan Ski near Taos and Flagstaff. In Park City, hit the slopes and the Sundance Film Festival.

June–Aug High season for exploring national parks in New Mexico, Utah and northern Arizona.

Sep–Nov Hike to the bottom of the Grand Canyon or gaze at bright leaves in northern New Mexico.

History

By about AD 100, three dominant cultures were emerging in the Southwest: the Hohokam of the desert, the Mogollon of the central mountains and valleys, and the Ancestral Puebloans. Archaeologists originally called the Ancestral Puebloans the Anasazi, which comes from a Navajo term meaning 'ancient enemy' and has fallen out of favor.

Francisco Vásquez de Coronado led the first major expedition into North America in 1540. It included 300 soldiers, hundreds of Native American guides and herds of livestock. It also marked the first major violence between Spanish explorers and the native people.

In addition to armed conflict, Europeans introduced smallpox, measles and typhus, to which the Native Americans had no resistance. Pueblo populations were decimated by these diseases, shattering cultures and trade routes and proving a destructive force that far outstripped combat.

Development in the Southwest expanded rapidly during the 19th century, mainly due to railroad and geological surveys. As the US pushed west, the army forcibly removed entire tribes of Native Americans in horrifyingly brutal Indian Wars. Gold and silver mines drew fortune seekers, and the lawless mining towns of the Wild West mushroomed practically overnight. Soon the Santa Fe Railroad was luring a flood of tourists to the West.

Modern settlement is closely linked to water use. Following the Reclamation Act of 1902, huge federally funded dams were built to control rivers and irrigate the desert. Rancorous disagreements over water rights are ongoing, especially with the phenomenal boom in residential development and the extensive recent drought. The other major issue in recent years, especially in southern Arizona, has been illegal immigration across the border from Mexico.

Local Culture

Rugged individuality is the cultural idiom of the Southwest. But the reality? It's a bit more complex. The major identities of the region, centered on a trio of tribes – Anglo, Hispanic and Native American – are as vast and varied as the land that has shaped them. Whether their personal religion involves aliens, art, nuclear fission, slot machines, peyote or Joseph Smith, there's plenty of room for you in this beautiful, barely tamed chunk of America.

ℹ Getting There & Around

Las Vegas' McCarran International Airport (p834) and Phoenix's Sky Harbor International Airport (p847) are the region's busiest airports, with plenty of domestic and international connections. They're followed by those at Salt Lake City and Albuquerque.

Greyhound stops at major cities, but barely serves national parks or off-the-beaten-path

SOUTHWEST

SOUTHWEST IN ...

One Week

Museums and a burgeoning arts scene set an inspirational tone in **Phoenix**. In the morning, follow Camelback Rd into **Scottsdale** for top-notch shopping and gallery-hopping in Old Town. Drive north to **Sedona** for spiritual recharging before pondering the immensity of the **Grand Canyon**. From here, choose either bling or buttes. For bling, detour onto **Route 66**, cross the new bridge beside **Hoover Dam** then indulge your fantasies in **Las Vegas**. For buttes, drive east from the Grand Canyon into Navajo country, cruising beneath the giant rock formations in **Monument Valley Navajo Tribal Park** then stepping back in time at stunning **Canyon de Chelly National Monument**.

Two Weeks

Start in glitzy **Las Vegas** before kicking back in funky **Flagstaff** and peering into the abyss at **Grand Canyon National Park**. Check out collegiate **Tucson** or frolic among forests of cacti at **Saguaro National Park**. Watch the gunslingers in **Tombstone** before settling into offbeat Victorian **Bisbee**. Secure your sunglasses for the blinding dunes of **White Sands National Monument** in New Mexico then sink into **Santa Fe**, a magnet for art-lovers. Explore the pueblo in **Taos** and watch the sunrise at awesome **Monument Valley Navajo Tribal Park**. Head into Utah for the red-rock national parks, **Canyonlands** and **Arches**. Do the hoodoos at **Bryce Canyon** then pay your respects at glorious **Zion**.

Southwest Highlights

1 Grand Canyon National Park (p854)
Finding the rights words isn't easy: sublime, awesome, tremendous.

2 Santa Fe (p896)
Lapping up the culture and diversions of this charismatic of southwest cities.

3 Angels Landing (p890) Hiking through this truly stunning slice of Utah canyonland in Zion National Park.

4 Las Vegas (p822) Finding out it's even more brash, synthetic and irresponsible than you'd hoped!

5 Sedona (p849) Rejoicing that even monetised hippy culture can't tarnish this unique red-rock city.

6 Route 66 (p866) Winding along the 'mother road' through stunning landscapes and time-capsule townships.

7 Moab (p883) Celebrating Christmas early! If you're a mountain biker. Or a hiker. Or a camper. Or ...

8 Monument Valley (p863) Snapping impossibly photogenic brick-red buttes and mesas, the stars of countless Westerns.

towns such as Moab. Amtrak train service is even more limited, although it too links several southwestern cities and offers bus connections to others (including Santa Fe and Phoenix). The *California Zephyr* crosses Utah and Nevada; the *Southwest Chief* stops in Arizona and New Mexico; and the *Sunset Limited* traverses southern Arizona and New Mexico.

Ultimately, this means private vehicles are often the only means to reach out-of-the-way towns, trailheads and swimming spots, and to explore the region in any depth.

NEVADA

Nevada is defined by contrasts and contradictions, juxtaposing arid plains with skyward, snow-capped mountains, while stilettos demand equal suitcase space with ski boots. Many visitors come only for the main event, Las Vegas: Nevada's twinkling desert jewel is a mecca for pleasure-seekers, and where priv-

---

NEVADA FACTS

Nickname Silver State

Population 2.84 million

Area 109,800 sq miles

Capital city Carson City (population 54,080)

Other cities Las Vegas (population 594,294), Reno (233,294)

Sales tax From 8.25%

Birthplace of Andre Agassi (b 1970), Greg LeMond (b 1961)

Home of The slot machine, Burning Man

Politics Nevada has six electoral votes – the state went for Obama in the 2012 presidential election, but it is split evenly in sending elected officials to Washington

Famous for The 1859 Comstock Lode (the country's richest known silver deposit), legalized gambling and prostitution (outlawed in certain counties), and liberal alcohol laws allowing 24-hour bars

Best Las Vegas T-Shirt 'I saw nothing at the Mob Museum.'

Driving distances Las Vegas to Reno 452 miles, Great Basin National Park to Las Vegas 313 miles

---

ilege and poverty collide and three-quarters of the state's population resides.

In this libertarian state, rural brothels coexist with Mormon churches, casinos and cowboys. Isolated ghost towns recall a pioneering past and the promise of a better life – just as Vegas riches lure punters today. But Nevada's rightful drawcard is nature, with Reno's rushing Truckee River, Lake Tahoe's crystal waters and forested peaks, the playas of the Black Rock Desert, where Burning Man's utopia was born, and the expanses of the Great Basin and the 'Loneliest Road in America.'

A place of discovery, Nevada is full of firsts, where there's something for daredevils and dreamers alike.

❶ Information

Prostitution is illegal in Clark County (which includes Las Vegas) and Washoe County (which includes Reno), although there are legal brothels in many of the smaller counties.

Nevada is on Pacific Standard Time. **Nevada Tourism Commission** (☏ 775-687-4322; www. travelnevada.com; 401 N Carson St; ☉ 9am-5pm Mon-Fri) Sends free books, maps and information on accommodations, campgrounds and events. **Nevada Division of State Parks** (☏ 775-684-2770; www.parks.nv.gov; 901 S Stewart St, 5th fl; ☉ 8am-5pm Mon-Fri) Camping in state parks ($10 to $15 per night) is first come, first-served.

Las Vegas

Las Vegas remains the ultimate escape. Where else can you party in ancient Rome, get hitched at midnight, wake up in Egypt and brunch beneath the Eiffel Tower? Double down with the high rollers, browse couture or tacky souvenirs, sip a neon 3ft-high margarita or a frozen vodka martini from a bar made of ice – it's all here for the taking.

Ever notice that there are no clocks inside casinos? Vegas exists outside time, a sequence of never-ending buffets, ever-flowing drinks and adrenaline-fueled gaming tables. In this never-ending desert dreamscape of boom and bust, once-famous signs collect dust in a neon boneyard while the clang of construction echoes over the Strip. After the alarming hiccup of the 2008 recession, the city is once more back on track, attracting well over 40 million visitors per year and bursting with schemes to lure even more in future.

Las Vegas' largest casinos – each one a gigantic and baffling mélange of theme park, gambling den, shopping and dining destination, hotel and theater district – line up along the legendary Strip. Once you've explored those, head to the city's compact downtown to encounter Vegas' nostalgic beginnings, peppered with indie shops and cocktail bars where local culture thrives. Then detour further afield to find intriguing museums that investigate Vegas' gangster, atomic-fueled past.

⊙ Sights

Vegas' sights are primarily concentrated along the 4.2-mile stretch of Las Vegas Blvd anchored by Mandalay Bay to the south (at Russell Rd) and the **Stratosphere** (Map p827; ☑702-380-7777; www.stratospherehotel.com; 2000 S Las Vegas Blvd; tower entry adult/child $20/10, all-day pass incl unlimited thrill rides $40; ⊙casino 24hr, tower & thrill rides 10am-1am Sun-Thu, to 2am Fri & Sat, weather permitting; P★) to the north (at Sahara Ave) and in the Downtown area around the intersection of Las Vegas Blvd (N Las Vegas Blvd at this point) and Fremont St. Note that while the street has the same name, there's an additional 2 miles between Downtown and the northern end of the Strip, with not much of interest in-between. It might look close if you decide to walk between the two, but you'll probably find yourself cursing in the desert heat if you do so. Ride-shares, the Monorail and Deuce bus services are by far the easiest ways to get around this spaced-out (in more ways than one) city.

⊙ The Strip

★ CityCenter   LANDMARK
(Map p827; www.citycenter.com; 3780 S Las Vegas Blvd; P) We've seen this symbiotic relationship before (think giant hotel anchored by a mall 'concept') but the way that this futuristic-feeling complex places a small galaxy of hypermodern, chichi hotels in orbit around the glitzy **Shops at Crystals** (www.crystalsatcitycenter.com; 3720 S Las Vegas Blvd; ⊙10am-11pm Sun-Thu, to midnight Fri & Sat) is a first. The uberupscale spread includes the subdued, stylish **Vdara** (☑702-590-2111; www.vdara.com; 2600 W Harmon Ave; weekday/weekend ste from $129/189; P☻✳@☎☎★) ✎, the hush-hush opulent Mandarin Oriental (p829) and the dramatic architectural showpiece **Aria** (☑702-590-7111; www.aria.com; 3730 S Las Vegas Blvd; ⊙24hr; P), whose sophisticated casino provides a fitting backdrop to its many drop-dead-gorgeous restaurants. CityCenter's hotels have in excess of 6700 rooms!

★ Cosmopolitan   CASINO
(Map p827; ☑702-698-7000; www.cosmopolitanlasvegas.com; 3708 S Las Vegas Blvd; ⊙24hr; P) Hipsters who thought they were too cool for Vegas finally have a place to go where they don't need irony to endure – or enjoy – the aesthetics of the Strip. Like the new Hollywood 'It' girl, the Cosmopolitan casino looks absolutely fabulous at all times. A steady stream of ingenues and entourages parade through the lobby (with some of the coolest design elements we've seen) along with anyone else who adores cart and design.

★ Bellagio   CASINO
(Map p827; ☑888-987-6667; www.bellagio.com; 3600 S Las Vegas Blvd; ⊙24hr; P★) The Bellagio experience transcends its decadent casino floor of high-limit gaming tables and in excess of 2300 slot machines; locals say odds here are less than favorable. A stop on the World Poker Tour, Bellagio's tournament-worthy poker room offers kitchen-to-gaming-table delivery around-the-clock. Most, however, come for the property's stunning architecture, interiors and amenities, including the **Conservatory & Botanical Gardens** (⊙24hr; P★) 〖FREE〗, **Gallery of Fine Art** (☑702-693-7871; adult/child under 12yr $18/free; ⊙10am-8pm, last entry 7:30pm; P★), unmissable **Fountains of Bellagio** (⊙shows every 30min 3-8pm Mon-Fri, noon-8pm Sat, 11am-7pm Sun, every 15min 8pm-midnight Mon-Sat, from 7pm Sun; P★) 〖FREE〗 and the 2000-plus hand-blown glass flowers embellishing the **hotel** lobby.

★ Mandalay Bay   CASINO
(Map p827; ☑702-632-7700; www.mandalaybay.com; 3950 S Las Vegas Blvd; ⊙24hr; P★) Since opening in 1999, in place of the former '50s-era Hacienda, Mandalay Bay has anchored the southern Strip. Its theme may be tropical, but it sure ain't tacky, nor is its 135,000-sq-ft casino. Well-dressed sports fans find their way to the upscale race and sports book near the high-stakes poker room. Refusing to be pigeonholed, the Bay's standout attractions are many and include the multilevel Shark Reef Aquarium (p825), decadent day spas, oodles of signature dining and the unrivaled **Mandalay Bay Beach** (Map p827; ☑877-632-7800; www.mandalaybay.com/en/amenities/beach.html; ⊙pool 8am-5pm, Moorea Beach Club 11am-6pm; ★).

★ LINQ Casino   CASINO
(Map p827; ☑800-634-6441; www.caesars.com/linq; 3535 S Las Vegas Blvd; ⊙24hr; P) With a

fresh, young and funky vibe, one of Vegas' newest casinos benefits from also being one of its smallest with just over 60 tables and around 750 slot machines. There's an airy, spacious feel to the place, tables feature high-backed, ruby-red, patent-vinyl chairs, and when you need to escape, the fun and frivolity of **LINQ Promenade** is just outside the door.

★ **Paris Las Vegas**   CASINO
(Map p827; ☎877-603-4386; www.parislasvegas. com; 3655 S Las Vegas Blvd; ⊙24hr; P) This mini-version of the French capital might lack the charm of the City of Light, but its efforts to emulate Paris' landmarks, including a 34-story Hotel de Ville and facades from the Opera House and Louvre, make it a fun stop for families and anyone yet to see the real thing. Its vaulted casino ceilings simulate sunny skies above myriad tables and slots, while its high-limit authentic French roulette wheels, sans 0 and 00, slightly improve your odds.

★ **Caesars Palace**   CASINO
(Map p827; ☎866-227-5938; www.caesarspalace. com; 3570 S Las Vegas Blvd; ⊙24hr; P) Caesars

Palace claims that its smartly renovated casino floor has more million-dollar slots than anywhere in the world, but its claims to fame are far more numerous than that. Entertainment's heavyweights Celine Dion and Elton John 'own' its custom-built **Colosseum** (www.thecolosseum.com; tickets $55-500) theater, fashionistas saunter around the **Shops at Forum** (www.simon.com/mall/the-forum-shops-at-caesars-palace/stores; ⊙10am-11pm Sun-Thu, to midnight Fri & Sat), while Caesars group hotel guests quaff cocktails in the **Garden of the Gods Pool Oasis**. By night, megaclub **Omnia** (www.omnianightclub.com; cover female/male $20/40; ⊙10pm-4am Tue & Thu-Sun) is the only place to get off your face this side of Ibiza.

★ **Wynn & Encore Casinos**   CASINO
(Map p827; ☎702-770-7000; www.wynnlasvegas. com; 3131 S Las Vegas Blvd; ⊙24hr; P) Steve Wynn's signature casino hotel (literally – his name is emblazoned across the top) **Wynn** (weekday/weekend r from $199/259; P✳@🎔🍴) and its younger sibling **Encore** (☎702-770-7100; r/ste from $199/259; P✳@🎔🍴) are a pair of curvaceous, copper-toned twin towers, whose entrances are obscured by high fences and lush greenery. Each hotel is unique, but their sprawling subterranean casinos converge to form the Strip's second-largest and arguably most elegant gaming floor, whose popular poker rooms lure pros around the clock and labyrinth of slot machines range from a penny to $5000 per pull!

★ **New York–New York**   CASINO
(Map p827; ☎800-689-1797; www.newyork newyork.com; 3790 S Las Vegas Blvd; ⊙24hr; P) Opened in 1997, the mini-megalopolis of New York–New York remains a perennial hit with spring breakers. Tables in the casino's 'Party Pit' are set against a backdrop of go-go dancers and occasional live entertainers, while out front, perspective-warping replicas of the Statue of Liberty, Brooklyn Bridge, and Chrysler and Empire State buildings delight visitors from abroad. Tying it all together, the **Big Apple Arcade** (⊙8am-midnight; P🎔) and **Roller Coaster** (☎702-740-6616; single ride/day pass $15/26; ⊙11am-11pm Sun-Thu, 10:30am-midnight Fri & Sat; P🎔) are timeless hits with kids and big kids alike.

★ **Lucky Dragon**   CASINO
(Map p827; ☎702-889-8018; www.luckydragonlv. com; 300 W Sahara Ave; ⊙24hr) Las Vegas' newest casino hotel, Lucky Dragon opened

THRILLS & SPILLS IN LAS VEGAS

Stratosphere (Map p827; ☑702-383-5210; www.stratospherehotel.com/attractions/thrill-rides; Stratosphere; elevator adult $20, incl 3 thrill rides $35, all-day pass $40; ⊙10am-1am Sun-Thu, to 2am Fri & Sat; ☑Sahara) The world's highest thrill rides await, a whopping 110 stories above the Strip.

Sky Combat Ace (☑888-494-5850; www.skycombatace.com; 1420 Jet Stream Dr #100; experiences $249-1995) A bona-fide fighter pilot takes you through the paces of air-to-air dogfights and extreme acrobatics!

VooDoo ZipLine (Map p827; ☑702-388-0477; http://voodoozipline.com; Rio; $27; ⊙11am-midnight) If you've ever wanted to zip-line between two skyscrapers, here's your chance.

Gravady (☑702-843-0395; www.gravady.com; 7350 Prairie Falcon Rd #120; 1hr flight adult/child $13/10; ⊙9am-9pm Mon-Wed, from 3:30pm Thu, 9am-noon Fri & Sat, 11am-7pm Sun; ☑) Get bouncy with the kids at this high-energy trampoline park in Summerlin.

Speedvegas (☑702-874-8888; www.speedvegas.com; 14200 S Las Vegas Blvd; laps $39-99, experiences $395-995; ⊙10am-4:30pm) Burn serious rubber at the wheel of a sports car on Vegas' only custom-built track.

Richard Petty Driving Experience (☑800-237-3889; www.drivepetty.com; 7000 N Las Vegas Blvd, Las Vegas Motor Speedway; ride-alongs from $109, drives from $499; ⊙hours vary) This is your chance to ride shotgun during a Nascar-style qualifying run.

its doors in December 2016. The majority of front-end staff at the city's first 'authentic' Asian casino, dining and lifestyle experience speak Mandarin or Cantonese. It's the hot ticket for inbound visitors from Asia, and lovers of Asian culture and cuisine alike.

Mirage Volcano LANDMARK
(Map p827; ☑800-374-9000; www.mirage.com; Mirage; ⊙shows 8pm & 9pm daily, also 10pm Fri & Sat) FREE When the Mirage's trademark artificial volcano erupts with a roar out of a 3-acre lagoon, it inevitably brings traffic on the Strip to a screeching halt. Be on the lookout for wisps of smoke escaping from the top, signaling that the fiery Polynesian-style inferno, with a soundtrack by a Grateful Dead drummer and an Indian tabla musician, is about to begin.

Shark Reef Aquarium AQUARIUM
(Map p827; ☑702-632-4555; www.sharkreef.com; 3950 S Las Vegas Blvd, Mandalay Bay; adult/child $25/19; ⊙10am-8pm Sun-Thu, to 10pm Fri & Sat; ☑☑) Mandalay Bay's (p821) unusual walk-through aquarium is home to 2000 submarine beasties, including jellyfish, moray eels, stingrays and 15 species of shark. Scuba-diver caretakers and naturalists are available to chat as you wander around. Better yet, go scuba diving yourself (from $650).

Madame Tussauds MUSEUM
(Map p827; ☑866-841-3739; www.madametussauds.com/lasvegas; 3377 S Las Vegas Blvd #2001; adult/child from $30/20; ⊙10am-8pm Sun-Thu, to 9pm Fri & Sat; ☑) Outside the **Venetian** (Map p827; www.venetian.com; 3355 S Las Vegas Blvd) next to the mock Rialto Bridge is this interactive version of the wax museum many love to loathe. Strike a pose with Elvis, pretend to marry George Clooney, go '4D' with Marvel Super Heroes or don Playboy Bunny ears and sit on Hugh Hefner's lap (be sure to touch him, because Hef's made of silicone – how appropriate!).

⊙ Downtown & Off the Strip

For tourists, the five-block **Fremont Street Experience** (Map p827; ☑702-678-5600; www.vegasexperience.com; Fremont St Mall; ⊙shows hourly dusk-midnight or 1am; ☑Deuce, SDX) FREE is the focal point of Downtown, with its wealth of vintage casinos, where today's Vegas was born – and fear not, they're still going strong. Further south, the **18b Arts District** (www.18b.org) revolves around the **Arts Factory** (☑702-383-9907; www.theartsfactory.com; 107 E Charleston Blvd; ⊙9am-6pm; ☑Deuce, SDX), while heading east on Fremont St will take you to the sweetest little hodgepodge of hip bars and happening restaurants that you could possibly imagine.

★**Mob Museum**   MUSEUM
(Map p827; ☑702-229-2734; www.themobmu
seum.org; 300 Stewart Ave; adult/child $24/14;
⊙9am-9pm; **P**; ☐Deuce) It's hard to say
what's more impressive: the museum's physical location in a historic federal courthouse
where mobsters sat for federal hearings in
1950–51, the fact that the board of directors
is headed up by a former FBI Special Agent,
or the thoughtfully curated exhibits telling
the story of organized crime in America. In
addition to hands-on FBI equipment and
mob-related artifacts, the museum boasts a
series of multimedia exhibits featuring interviews with real-life Tony Sopranos.

★**Neon Museum – Neon Boneyard** MUSEUM
(☑702-387-6366; www.neonmuseum.org; 770 N
Las Vegas Blvd; 1hr tour adult/child $19/15, after
dark $26/22; ⊙tours daily, schedules vary; ☐113)
This nonprofit project is doing what almost
no one else does: saving Las Vegas' history.
Book ahead for a fascinating guided walking
tour of the 'Neon Boneyard,' where irreplace-
able vintage neon signs – Las Vegas' original
art form – spend their retirement. Start exploring at the visitor center inside the salvaged La Concha Motel lobby, a mid-century
modern icon designed by African American
architect Paul Revere Williams. Tours are
usually given throughout the day, but are
most spectacular at night.

★**Container Park**   CULTURAL CENTER
(Map p827; ☑702-359-9982; http://downtowncon
tainerpark.com; 707 Fremont St E; ⊙11am-9pm
Mon-Thu, 10am-10pm Fri & Sat, to 8pm Sun) An
incubator for up-and-coming fashion designers and local artisans, the edgy Container Park stacks pop-up shops on top of one
another. Wander along the sidewalks and
catwalks while searching out handmade
jewelry, contemporary art and clothing at
a dozen or so specialty boutiques, eateries
and art installations. When the sun sets, the
container bars come to life and host regular
themed events and movie nights. It's adults
only (21-plus) after 9pm.

★**National Atomic
Testing Museum**   MUSEUM
(Map p827; ☑702-794-5151; www.nationalatom
ictestingmuseum.org; 755 Flamingo Rd E, Desert Research Institute; adult/child $22/16; ⊙10am-5pm
Mon-Sat, noon-5pm Sun; ☐202) Fascinating multimedia exhibits focus on science, technology
and the social history of the 'Atomic Age,'
which lasted from WWII until atmospheric

bomb testing was driven underground in
1961 and a worldwide ban on nuclear testing
was declared in 1992. View footage of atomic
testing and examine southern Nevada's nuclear past, present and future, from Native
American ways of life to the environmental
legacy of atomic testing. Don't miss the ticket booth (how could you?); it's a Nevada Test
Site guard-station replica.

🏃 Activities

★**Dream Racing**   ADVENTURE SPORTS
(☑702-605-3000; www.dreamracing.com; 7000 N
Las Vegas Blvd, Las Vegas Motor Speedway; 5-lap experiences $199-599; ⊙by appointment; ☀) Ever
wanted to get behind the wheel of a Porsche
911, Lamborghini, Lotus, AMG Mercedes or
McLaren and really let fly? Of course you
have. Well, now you can choose from the
largest selection of insured supercars in the
world, without having to buy one.

★**Qua Baths & Spa**   SPA
(Map p827; ☑866-782-0655; Caesars Palace;
fitness center day pass $25, incl spa facilities $50;
⊙6am-8pm) Qua evokes the ancient Roman
rituals of indulgent bathing. Try a signature
'bath liqueur,' a personalized potion of herbs
and oils poured into your own private tub.
The women's side includes a tea lounge, a
herbal steam room and an Arctic ice room
where artificial snow falls. On the men's
side, there's a barber spa and big-screen
sports TVs.

Desert Adventures   KAYAKING
(☑702-293-5026; www.kayaklasvegas.com; 1647a
Nevada Hwy; full-day Colorado River kayak $179;
⊙9am-6pm Apr-Oct, 10am-4pm Nov-Mar) Would-
be river rats should check in here for guided
kayaking and stand up paddle surfing (SUP)
tours on Lake Mead and the Colorado River.
Experienced paddlers can rent canoes and
kayaks for DIY trips.

🛏 Sleeping

Room rates in Las Vegas rise and fall dramatically each and every day; visiting on
weekdays is almost always cheaper than
weekends. Note that almost every Strip hotel also charges an additional 'resort fee' of
$10 to $30 per day.

🛏 The Strip

SLS   HOTEL $
(Map p827; ☑702-761-7000; www.slslasvegas.com;
2535 S Las Vegas Blvd; d from $79; **P**✳️🛜🏊)

Las Vegas

N 0 ___ 1 km
0 ___ 0.5 miles

Las Vegas Premium
Outlets North (1.3mi)

E Oakey Blvd

Retro Vegas (0.4mi);
Arts Factory (0.5mi);
Downtown Las Vegas
(1mi; see inset)

Downtown Las Vegas
0 ___ 200 m

Mob Museum 15

Neon Museum –
Neon Boneyard (0.3mi)

Stewart Ave

Fremont Street Experience 9

58

Ogden Ave

38

40

DOWNTOWN

25 24

46

54

Fremont St E

51

48

6

Container Park

49

Carson Ave

Meade Ave

Main St

S 1st St

Casino Center Blvd

S 3rd St

S 4th St

Lewis Ave

S Las Vegas Blvd (The Strip)

N Las Vegas Blvd

N 6th St

N 7th St

Stratosphere 19

33

Lucky Dragon 12

W Sahara Ave

E Sahara Ave

SLS 43

Karen Ave

Wynn Golf and Country Club

Westgate

Western Ave

Fairfield Ave

S Las Vegas Blvd (The Strip)

Paradise Rd

Circus Circus Dr

32 35

Circus Circus

Riviera Blvd

57

Convention Center Dr

52

Las Vegas Convention Center

Las Vegas Convention & Visitors Authority

E Desert Inn Rd

39

Las Vegas Convention Center

Sierra Vista Dr

Desert Inn Rd Super-Arterial

Sirius Ave

Polaris Ave

Procyon Ave

Veggie Delight (0.4mi)

I-15

S Highland Dr

S Industrial Rd

Sammy Davis Jr Dr

Spring Mountain Rd

66 65

63 21

45

Wynn & Encore Casinos

Treasure Island

THE STRIP

60

30

29

20

27

67

Palazzo

Sands Ave

E Twain Ave

Cassella Dr

LINQ Casino
LINQ Promenade

69 59

62

Caesars Palace 42

4

34

Rio

Bellagio Conservatory & Botanical Gardens

Palms (0.4mi)

2

Bellagio 8

Fountains of Bellagio

Bellagio

Cosmopolitan 55

44

CityCenter

7

68

22

5

Monte Carlo

CityCenter

Tompkins Ave

W Harmon Ave

Venetian

10 50

Harrah's/
The LINQ

Ida Ave

11

53

64

36

High Roller

Flamingo/
Caesars Palace

Flamingo Wash

E Flamingo Rd

Paris Las Vegas

56 18

Bally's

Bally's/
Paris Las Vegas

Planet Hollywood

E Harmon Ave

National Atomic Testing Museum 16

University of Nevada, Las Vegas (UNLV)

Thomas & Mack Stadium

Tropicana Wash

41

Koval La

Swenson St

Swenson St

Big Apple Roller Coaster

23 17

3

MGM Grand 14

New York–New York

Excalibur

Tropicana

MGM Grand

E Tropicana Ave

E Reno Ave

Gun Store (1.9mi)

W Tropicana Ave

Ali Baba La

26

61

W Hacienda Ave

Mandalay Bay Rd

37 47

Mandalay Bay

31 13

28

E Mandalay Bay Rd

Giles St

S Las Vegas Blvd (The Strip)

McCarran International Airport

Paradise Rd

Swenson St

Las Vegas

◎ Top Sights
1 Bellagio B5
2 Bellagio Conservatory &
   Botanical Gardens B5
3 Big Apple Roller Coaster B6
4 Caesars Palace B5
5 CityCenter B6
6 Container Park B2
7 Cosmopolitan B5
8 Fountains of Bellagio B5
9 Fremont Street Experience A1
10 LINQ Casino B4
11 LINQ Promenade B4
12 Lucky Dragon C1
13 Mandalay Bay B7
14 MGM Grand B6
15 Mob Museum B1
16 National Atomic Testing
   Museum D5
17 New York–New York B6
18 Paris Las Vegas B5
19 Stratosphere C1
20 Venetian B4
21 Wynn & Encore Casinos C3

◎ Sights
22 Aria B6
   Bellagio Gallery of Fine Art .... (see 1)
23 Big Apple Arcade B6
24 El Cortez B2
25 Emergency Arts B2
26 Luxor B7
27 Madame Tussauds B4
28 Mandalay Bay Beach B7
29 Mirage B4
30 Mirage Volcano B4
31 Shark Reef Aquarium B7

◎ Activities, Courses & Tours
32 Adventuredome B2
   Qua Baths & Spa .... (see 4)
33 Stratosphere Thrill Rides C1
34 VooDoo ZipLine A5

◎ Sleeping
   Bellagio .... (see 1)
   Caesars Palace .... (see 4)
35 Circus Circus C2
   Cosmopolitan .... (see 7)
36 Cromwell Las Vegas B5
37 Delano B7
38 El Cortez B1
39 Encore C3
   Four Seasons Hotel .... (see 13)
40 Golden Nugget A1

41 Hard Rock D5
   Mandalay Bay .... (see 13)
   Mandarin Oriental .... (see 5)
42 NOBU Hotel B5
43 SLS C2
44 Vdara A5
45 Wynn B3

◎ Eating
46 Andiamo Steakhouse A2
47 Burger Bar B7
48 Carson Kitchen B2
   Container Park .... (see 6)
49 eat. B2
   Giada .... (see 36)
   Grand Wok .... (see 14)
50 Jaburrito B4
   Jean Philippe Patisserie .... (see 1)
   Joël Robuchon .... (see 14)
51 La Comida B2
   Morimoto .... (see 14)
   Peppermill .... (see 57)
52 Tacos El Gordo C3
53 Virgil's Real BBQ B4

◎ Drinking & Nightlife
54 Beauty Bar B2
55 Chandelier Lounge B5
56 Chateau Nightclub & Gardens B5
   Drai's Beachclub &
   Nightclub .... (see 36)
57 Fireside Lounge C3
   Foundation Room .... (see 13)
58 Gold Spike B1
59 Omnia B4
   Surrender .... (see 39)
   XS .... (see 39)

◎ Entertainment
60 Aces of Comedy B4
61 Blue Man Group B7
62 Colosseum B4
   House of Blues .... (see 13)
63 Le Rêve the Dream B3
64 Legends in Concert B5
   O .... (see 2)
65 Tix 4 Tonight B3

◎ Shopping
66 Fashion Show B3
67 Grand Canal Shoppes at the
   Venetian B4
68 Shops at Crystals B5
69 Shops at Forum B4

You can nab a room at Vegas' SLS (the Starwood Hotel Group's boutique brand) on the north Strip at a crazy rate compared to same-branded properties in other cities. The hotel's quirky style is infectious: you'll have fun with the acronym within minutes.

★**Mandalay Bay** CASINO HOTEL **$$**
(Map p827; ☎702-632-7700; www.mandalaybay.
com; 3950 S Las Vegas Blvd; weekday/weekend r
from $119/229; P✳@🖥🏊) Anchoring the
south Strip, upscale Mandalay Bay's (p821)
same-named hotel has a cache of classy
rooms worthy of your attention in their own
right, not to mention the exclusive **Four
Seasons Hotel** (☎702-632-5000; www.four-
seasons.com/lasvegas; weekday/weekend r from
$229/289; P✳@🖥🏊) and boutique **De-
lano** (☎877-632-7800; www.delanolasvegas.com;
r/ste from $69/129; P✳@🖥🏊) within its
bounds and a diverse range of noteworthy
attractions and amenities, not least of which
is Mandalay Bay Beach (p821).

★**NOBU Hotel** HOTEL **$$**
(Map p827; ☎800-727-4923; www.nobucaesarspal
ace.com; 3570 S Las Vegas Blvd, Caesars Palace; d
from $159) This exclusive boutique hotel with-
in Caesars Palace (p824) is one for lovers of
Japanese design from the traditional to the
modern. Rooms are in high demand and
suites are often the domain of celebrities.

★**Cromwell Las Vegas** BOUTIQUE HOTEL **$$**
(Map p827; ☎702-777-3777; www.caesars.com/
cromwell; 3595 S Las Vegas Blvd; r/ste from
$199/399; P✳🏊) If you're 20- to
30-something, can hold your own with the
cool kids, or you're just effortlessly stylish
whatever your demographic, there are a few
good reasons to choose Cromwell, the best
being its location and frequently excellent
rates on sassy, entry-level rooms. The oth-
ers? You've got your sites set on partying
at **Drai's** (☎702-777-3800; www.draislv.com;
nightclub cover $20-50; ☺nightclub 10pm-5am
Thu-Sun, beach club 11am-6pm Fri-Sun) or dining
downstairs at **Giada** (☎855-442-3271; www.
caesars.com; mains $25-58; ☺8am-11pm).

Caesars Palace CASINO HOTEL **$$**
(Map p827; ☎866-227-5938; www.caesarspalace.
com; 3570 S Las Vegas Blvd; weekday/weekend r from
$109/149; P✳@🖥🏊) In 2016, Caesars cele-
brated turning 50 by (how else?) throwing a
bunch of money into shaking off some gaudy
and making itself look fabulous. Almost 600
rooms in its Roman Tower got a lavish makeover and the tower, a new name: Julius, of
course! Augustus' guest rooms got some style
too: think grey, white-gold and royal blue.

★**Cosmopolitan** CASINO HOTEL **$$$**
(Map p827; ☎702-698-7575, 702-698-7000; www.
cosmopolitanlasvegas.com; 3708 S Las Vegas Blvd;

r/ste from $250/300; P✳@🖥🏊; 🚌Deuce)
With at least eight distinctively different and
equally stylish room types to choose from,
Cosmo's digs are the hippest on the Strip.
Ranging from oversized to decadent, about
2200 of its 2900 or so rooms have balconies
(all but the entry-level category), many sport
sunken Japanese tubs and all feature plush
furnishings and design quirks you'll delight
in uncovering.

★**Mandarin Oriental** HOTEL **$$$**
(Map p827; ☎702-590-8888; www.mandarinori
ental.com; 3752 S Las Vegas Blvd, CityCenter; r/ste
from $239/469; ✳🖥🏊) Part of the CityCenter
(p821) complex, luscious oriental flavors
meet the latest technology in Mandarin
Oriental's 392 slick, state-of-the-art yet effortlessly elegant guest rooms and suites,
undoubtedly some of the finest to be found
on a Strip dripping with gold and shimmering with shiny things. Add a high ratio of
courteous, attentive staff to each guest and
you're on a winning streak.

🛏 **Downtown & Off the Strip**

★**El Cortez** CASINO HOTEL **$**
(Map p827; ☎702-385-5200; www.elcortezhotelca
sino.com; 651 E Ogden Ave; weekday/weekend r from
$40/80; P✳@🖥) A wide range of rooms
with all kinds of vibes are available at this
fun, retro property close to all the action on
Fremont St. Rooms are in the 1980s tower
addition to the heritage-listed 1941 **El Cortez**
(600 Fremont St E; ☺24hr; 🚌Deuce) casino and
the modern, flashier El Cortez Suites, across
the street. Rates offered are generally great
value, though don't expect the earth.

★**Hard Rock** CASINO HOTEL **$**
(Map p827; ☎702-693-5000; www.hardrockhotel.
com; 4455 Paradise Rd; weekday/weekend r from
$45/89; P✳@🖥🏊) Sexy, oversized rooms
and HRH suites underwent a bunch of re-
furbishments in 2016 and 2017, making this
party palace for music lovers a great alternative to staying on the Strip – there's even a
free shuttle to take you there and bring you
back.

★**Golden Nugget** CASINO HOTEL **$**
(Map p827; ☎702-385-7111; www.goldennugget.
com; 129 Fremont St E; weekday/weekend r from
$45/85; P✳@🖥) Pretend to relive the
fabulous heyday of Vegas in the 1950s at this
swank Fremont St address. Rooms in the
Rush Tower are the best in the house.

✖ Eating

The Strip has been studded with celebrity chefs for years. All-you-can-eat buffets and $10 steaks still exist, but today's high-rolling visitors demand ever more sophisticated dining experiences, with meals designed – although not personally prepared – by famous taste-makers.

✖ The Strip

★ Jaburrito   SUSHI $

(Map p827; ☎702-901-7375; www.jaburritos.com; LINQ Promenade; items $7-14; ⊙11am-11pm Sun-Thu, to midnight Fri & Sat) It's simple: hybridize a nori (seaweed) sushi roll with a burrito. What could go wrong? Nothing actually... they're awesome!

★ Tacos El Gordo   MEXICAN $

(Map p827; ☎702-251-8226; www.tacoselgordobc. com; 3049 S Las Vegas Blvd; small plates $3-12; ⊙10am-2am Sun-Thu, to 4am Fri & Sat; Ｐ🅿🚻; 🚌Deuce, SDX) This Tijuana-style taco shop from SoCal is just the ticket when it's way late, you've got almost no money left and you're desperately craving *carne asada* (beef) or *adobada* (chile-marinated pork) tacos in hot, hand-made tortillas. Adventurous eaters order the authentic *sesos* (beef brains), *cabeza* (roasted cow's head) or tripe (intestines) variations.

Jean Philippe Patisserie   BAKERY $

(Map p827; www.jpchocolates.com; Bellagio; snacks & drinks $4-11; ⊙6am-11pm Mon-Thu, to midnight Fri-Sun; 🚻) As certified by the *Guinness Book of World Records,* the world's largest chocolate fountain cascades inside the front windows of this champion pastry-maker's shop, known for its fantastic sorbets, gelati, pastries and chocolate confections. Coffee and espresso are above the Strip's low-bar average.

★ Grand Wok   CHINESE $$

(Map p827; ☎702-891-7879; www.mgmgrand.com/ en/restaurants.html; MGM Grand; mains $12-28; ⊙11am-10pm Sun-Thu, to 11pm Fri & Sat) Come to Grand Wok, in business for over 25 years serving some of the best pan-Asian dishes you'll find this side of the Far East. Try the garlic shrimp fried rice with dried scallops. Sensational.

★ Burger Bar   AMERICAN $$

(Map p827; ☎702-632-9364; www.burger-bar. com; Shoppes at Mandalay Place; mains $10-60;

⊙11am-11pm Sun-Thu, to 1am Fri & Sat; Ｐ❋🚻) Since when can a hamburger be worth $60? When it's built with Kobe beef, sautéed foie gras and truffle sauce: it's the Rossini burger, the signature sandwich of chef Hubert Keller. Most menu options are more down-to-earth – diners select their own gourmet burger toppings and pair them with skinny fries and a liquor-spiked milkshake or beer float.

★ Virgil's Real BBQ   BARBECUE $$

(Map p827; ☎702-389-7400; www.virgilsbbq.com/ locations/las-vegas; LINQ Promenade; mains $10-24; ⊙10am-2am) If you've never tried real-deal Southern cooking, and you're not shy of chunks of mouthwatering smoky meats, baby back ribs, cheesy grits and sugary caramelized sides, you simply must make a bee-line for Virgil's and you will be converted. Hallelujah!

★ Joël Robuchon   FRENCH $$$

(Map p827; ☎702-891-7925; www.joel-robuchon. com/en; MGM Grand; tasting menus $120-425; ⊙5-10pm) The acclaimed 'Chef of the Century' leads the pack in the French culinary invasion of the Strip. Adjacent to the **MGM Grand's** (Map p827; ☎877-880-0880; www. mgmgrand.com; 3799 S Las Vegas Blvd; ⊙24hr; Ｐ🚻) high-rollers' gaming area, Robuchon's plush dining rooms, done up in leather and velvet, feel like a dinner party at a 1930s Paris mansion. Complex seasonal tasting menus promise the meal of a lifetime – and they often deliver.

★ Morimoto   FUSION $$$

(Map p827; ☎702-891-1111; www.mgmgrand.com; MGM Grand; mains $24-75; ⊙5-10pm) Iron Chef Masaharu Morimoto's latest Vegas incarnation is in his eponymous showcase restaurant, which pays homage to his Japanese roots and the cuisine of this city that has propelled him to legend status around the world. Dining here is an experience in every possible way and, we think, worth every penny.

✖ Downtown & off the Strip

★ eat.   BREAKFAST $

(Map p827; ☎702-534-1515; http://eatdtlv.com; 707 Carson Ave; mains $7-14; ⊙8am-3pm Mon-Fri, to 2pm Sat & Sun; 🚻) 🍴 Community spirit and creative cooking provide reason enough to venture off Fremont St to find this cafe. With a concrete floor and spare decor, it can get loud as folks chow down on truffled egg sandwiches, cinnamon biscuits with strawberry compote, shrimp po'boy sandwiches and bowls of New Mexican green-chili chicken *posole*.

Container Park
FAST FOOD $

(Map p827; ☑702-359-9982; www.downtown containerpark.com; 707 Fremont St; items $3-12; ☺11am-11pm Mon-Thu, to 1am Fri & Sat, 10am-11pm Sun; ☑; ☑Deuce) With food-truck-style menus, outdoor patio seating and late-night hours, food vendors inside the cutting-edge Container Park (p826) sell something to satisfy everyone's appetite. When we last stopped by, the ever-changing lineup included **Pinches Tacos** for Mexican flavors, Southern-style **Big Ern's BBQ**, raw-food and healthy vegan cuisine from **Simply Pure**, and salads and panini at **Bin 702** wine bar.

★Carson Kitchen
AMERICAN $$

(Map p827; ☑702-473-9523; www.carsonkitchen.com; 124 S 6th St; tapas & mains $8-22; ☺11:30am-11pm Thu-Sat, to 10pm Sun-Wed; ☑Deuce) This tiny eatery with an industrial theme of exposed beams, bare bulbs and chunky share tables hops with downtowners looking to escape the mayhem of Fremont St or the Strip's high prices. Excellent shared plates include rainbow cauliflower, watermelon and feta salad and decadent mac 'n' cheese, and there's a creative 'libations' menu.

★Andiamo Steakhouse
STEAK $$$

(Map p827; ☑702-388-2220; www.thed.com; 301 Fremont St E, The D; mains $24-79; ☺5-11pm; ☑Deuce, SDX) Of all the old-school steakhouses inside Downtown's carpet joints, the current front-runner is Joe Vicari's Andiamo Steakhouse. Upstairs from the casino, richly upholstered half-moon booths and impeccably polite waiters set the tone for a classic Italian steakhouse feast of surf-and-turf platters and housemade pasta, followed by a rolling dessert cart. Extensive Californian and European wine list. Reservations recommended.

La Comida
MEXICAN $$

(Map p827; ☑702-463-9900; www.lacomidalv.com; 100 6th St; mains $13-22; ☺noon-10:30pm Tue-Thu, to midnight Fri & Sat, to 11pm Sun) Meaning 'family meal,' La Comida's emphasis is on simple, culturally authentic dishes (soups, salads, tacos, enchiladas), presented in a warm, convivial environment to be shared with family. Why not throw some tequila into the mix (the restaurant has more varieties than it does seats), straight up or

in sweet and salty margaritas, and get your Downtown evening started right?

Drinking & Nightlife

The Strip

★Fireside Lounge
LOUNGE

(Map p827; ☑702-735-7635; www.peppermill laslasvegas.com; 2985 S Las Vegas Blvd, Peppermill; ☺24hr; ☑Deuce) Don't be blinded by the outlandishly bright neon outside. The Strip's most spellbinding retro hideaway awaits at the pint-sized **Peppermill** (mains $8-32; ☺24hr) casino. Courting couples adore the sunken fire pit, fake tropical foliage and 64oz goblet-sized 'Scorpion' cocktails served by waiters in black evening gowns.

★Chandelier Lounge
COCKTAIL BAR

(Map p827; ☑702-698-7979; www.cosmopolitan laslasvegas.com/lounges-bars/chandelier; Cosmopolitan; ☺24hr; ☑Deuce) Towering high in the center of Cosmopolitan (p821), this ethereal cocktail bar is inventive yet beautifully simple, with three levels connected by romantic curved staircases, all draped with glowing strands of glass beads. The second level is headquarters for molecular mixology (order a martini made with liquid nitrogen), while the third specializes in floral and fruit infusions.

★Chateau Nightclub & Gardens
BAR

(Map p827; ☑702-776-7770; www.chateaunights.com; Paris Las Vegas; ☺10pm-4am Wed, Fri & Sat) Hip-hop prevails at this rooftop venue landscaped to look like Parisian gardens. Views over the Strip are divine from tiered outdoor terraces while, back inside, go-go dancers do their thing above a small dance floor, which can be half empty even on weekends. Sometimes on summer days, the lounge space on the open-air deck doubles as a beer garden.

Downtown & off the Strip

Want to chill out with the locals? Loads of new and interesting bars and cafes are opening along E Fremont St, making it the number-one alternative to the Strip.

★Beauty Bar
BAR

(Map p827; ☑702-598-3757; www.thebeautybar.com; 517 Fremont St E; cover free-$10; ☺9pm-4am; ☑Deuce) Swill a cocktail or just chill with the cool kids inside the salvaged innards of a 1950s New Jersey beauty salon. DJs and live bands rotate nightly, spinning everything from tiki lounge tunes, disco and '80s hits to punk, metal, glam and indie rock. Check the website for special events like 'Karate Karaoke.' There's often no cover charge.

★ Gold Spike
BAR
(Map p827; ☏702-476-1082; www.goldspike.com; 217 N Las Vegas Blvd; ⏰24hr) Gold Spike, with its playroom, living room and backyard, is many things: bar, nightclub, performance space, work space; sometime host of roller derbies, discos, live bands or dance parties; or just somewhere to soak up the sun with a relaxed crew and escape mainstream Vegas.

☆ Entertainment

There's always plenty going on in Las Vegas, and Ticketmaster (www.ticketmaster.com) sells tickets for pretty much everything. Tix 4 Tonight (Map p827; ☏877-849-4868; www.tix4to night.com; 3200 S Las Vegas Blvd, Fashion Show Mall; ⏰10am-8pm) offers half-price tickets for a limited lineup of same-day shows, plus smaller discounts on 'always sold-out' shows.

Nightclubs & Live Music
Nightclubs are serious businesses in Las Vegas. Admission prices vary wildly, according to the mood of door staff, male-to-female ratio, the acts that night and how crowded the club may be. Avoid waiting in line by booking ahead with the club VIP host. Most bigger clubs have someone working the door in the late afternoon and early evening. Hotel concierges often have free passes for clubs, or can at least make reservations. Bottle service usually waives cover charges and waiting in line, but is hugely expensive.

BUFFET ALL THE WAY

Extravagant all-you-can-eat buffets are a Sin City tradition. Here are three of the best:

Bacchanal Buffet (3570 Las Vegas Blvd S, Caesars Palace; $40-58 per adult, 8am-10pm)

Wicked Spoon Buffet (3708 Las Vegas Blvd S, Cosmopolitan; $28-52 per adult, 8am-9pm)

Buffet at Bellagio (3600 Las Vegas Blvd S; Bellagio; $39-54 per adult, 7am-10pm)

Legends in Concert
LIVE MUSIC
(Map p827; ☏702-777-2782; www.legendsincon cert.com; Flamingo; adult/child from $58/36; ⏰shows 4pm, 7:30pm & 9:30pm) Vegas' top pop-star impersonator show features real singing and dancing talent mimicking famous performers such as the Beatles, Elvis, Madonna, James Brown, Britney Spears, Shania Twain and many more.

★ Foundation Room
CLUB
(Map p827; ☏702-632-7601; www.houseofblues. com; Mandalay Bay; cover usually $30; ⏰5pm-2am) House of Blues' (☏702-632-7600; ⏰box office 9am-9pm) sophisticated nightclub hosts nightly DJ parties and special events in a stylish space that's half Gothic mansion, half Hindu temple. The expansive views of the Strip are just as impressive as the decor. Look for club promoters around the casino passing out two-for-one drink and free-entry tickets. Dress code enforced.

★ XS
CLUB
(Map p827; ☏702-770-0097; www.xslasvegas.com; Encore; cover $20-50; ⏰10pm-4am Fri & Sat, from 9:30pm Sun, from 10:30pm Mon) XS is the hottest nightclub in Vegas – at least for now. Its extravagantly gold-drenched decor and over-the-top design mean you'll be waiting in line for cocktails at a bar towered over by ultra-curvaceous, larger-than-life golden statues of female torsos. Famous-name electronica DJs make the dancefloor writhe, while high rollers opt for VIP bottle service at private poolside cabanas.

★ Surrender
CLUB
(Map p827; ☏702-770-7300; www.surrendernight club.com; Encore; cover $20-40; ⏰10:30pm-4am Wed, Fri & Sat) Even the club-averse admit that this is an audaciously gorgeous place to hang out, with its saffron-colored silk walls, mustard banquettes, bright yellow patent leather entrance and a shimmering wall-art snake coiled behind the bar. Play blackjack or just hang out by the pool after dark during summer. EDM and hip-hop DJs and musicians pull huge crowds.

Production Shows
There are hundreds of shows to choose from in Vegas. Any Cirque du Soleil offering tends to be an unforgettable experience.

★ Le Rêve the Dream
THEATER
(Map p827; ☏702-770-9966; http://boxoffice. wynnlasvegas.com; Wynn; tickets $105-205; ⏰shows at 7pm & 9:30pm Fri-Tue) Underwater

acrobatic feats by scuba-certified performers are the centerpiece of this intimate 'aqua-in-the-round' theater, which holds a one-million-gallon swimming pool. Critics call it a less-inspiring version of Cirque's *O*, while devoted fans find the romantic underwater tango, thrilling high dives and visually spectacular adventures to be superior. Beware: the cheapest seats are in the 'splash zone.'

★ O   THEATER

(Map p827; ☑888-488-7111; www.cirquedusoleil.com; Bellagio; tickets $99-185; ⊙7pm & 9:30pm Wed-Sun) Phonetically speaking, it's the French word for water (*eau*). With a lithe international cast performing in, on and above water, Cirque du Soleil's *O* tells the tale of theater through the ages. It's a spectacular feat of imagination and engineering, and you'll pay dearly to see it – it's one of the Strip's few shows that rarely sells discounted tickets.

★ Blue Man Group   LIVE PERFORMANCE

(Map p827; ☑702-262-4400; www.blueman.com; Luxor; tickets $80-190; ⊙shows at 7pm & 9:30pm; ♿) Art, music and technology combine with a dash of comedy in one of Vegas' most popular, family-friendly shows at **Luxor** (☑702-262-4000; www.luxor.com; 3900 S Las Vegas Blvd; ⊙24hr; ℗).

★ Aces of Comedy   COMEDY

(Map p827; ☑702-792-7777; www.mirage.com; Mirage; tickets $40-100; ⊙schedules vary, box office 10am-10pm Thu-Mon, to 8pm Tue & Wed) You'd be hard pressed to find a better A-list collection of famous stand-up comedians than this year-round series of appearances at the **Mirage** (☑702-791-7111; 3400 S Las Vegas Blvd; ⊙24hr; ℗), which delivers the likes of Jay Leno, Kathy Griffin and Lewis Black to the Strip. Buy tickets in advance online or by phone, or go in person to the Mirage's **Cirque du Soleil** (☑877-924-7783; www.cirquedusoleil.com/las-vegas; discount tickets from $49, full-price from $69) box office.

🛍 Shopping

★ Las Vegas Premium
Outlets North   MALL

(☑702-474-7500; www.premiumoutlets.com/vegasnorth; 875 S Grand Central Pkwy; ⊙9am-9pm Mon-Sat, to 8pm Sun; ♿; ◻SDX) Vegas' biggest-ticket outlet mall features 120 mostly high-end names such as Armani, Brooks Brothers, Diane Von Furstenberg, Elle Tahari, Kate Spade, Michael Kors, Theory and

Tory Burch, alongside casual brands like Banana Republic and Diesel.

Retro Vegas   VINTAGE

(☑702-384-2700; www.retro-vegas.com; 1131 S Main St; ⊙11am-6pm Mon-Sat, noon-5pm Sun; ◻108, Deuce) Near Downtown's 18b Arts District, this flamingo-pink-painted antiques shop is a primo place for picking up mid-20th-century modern and swingin' 1960s and '70s gems, from artwork to home decor.

Fashion Show   MALL

(Map p827; ☑702-369-8382; www.thefashion-show.com; 3200 S Las Vegas Blvd; ⊙10am-9pm Mon-Sat, 11am-7pm Sun; ♿) Nevada's largest shopping mall is an eye-catcher: topped off by 'the Cloud,' a silver multimedia canopy resembling a flamenco hat, Fashion Show harbors more than 250 chain shops and department stores. Hot European additions to the mainstream lineup include British clothier Topshop (and Topman for men). Live runway shows happen hourly from noon to 5pm on Friday, Saturday and Sunday.

Grand Canal Shoppes
at the Venetian   MALL

(Map p827; ☑702-414-4525; www.grandcanalshoppes.com; 3377 S Las Vegas Blvd, Venetian; ⊙10am-11pm Sun-Thu, to midnight Fri & Sat) Wandering, painted minstrels, jugglers and laughable living statues perform in Piazza San Marco, while gondolas float past in the canals and mezzo-sopranos serenade shoppers. In this airy Italianate mall adorned with frescoes and cobblestone walkways, strut past Burberry, Godiva, Sephora and 85 more luxury shops.

ℹ Information

EMERGENCY & MEDICAL SERVICES

Police ☑911 (in emergencies) or ☑702-828-3111
Sunrise Hospital & Medical Center (☑702-731-8000; http://sunrisehospital.com; 3186 S Maryland Pkwy; ⊙24hr) Specialized children's trauma services available at a 24-hour emergency room.
University Medical Center (UMC; ☑702-383-2000; www.umcsn.com; 1800 W Charleston Blvd; ⊙24hr) Southern Nevada's most advanced trauma center has a 24-hour ER.

INTERNET ACCESS & MEDIA

Most casino hotels charge a fee of up to $15 per 24 hours (sometimes only wired access is available). Free wi-fi hot spots are more common off-Strip. Cheap internet cafes hide inside souvenir shops on the Strip and along Maryland Pkwy opposite the UNLV campus.

SOUTHWEST LAS VEGAS

Newspapers & magazines *Las Vegas Review Journal* (www.reviewjournal.com), *Las Vegas Weekly* (www.lasvegasweekly.com), *Las Vegas Life* (www.lvlife.com).

Radio National Public Radio (NPR), lower end of FM dial.

TV PBS (public broadcasting); cable: CNN (news), ESPN (sports), HBO (movies), Weather Channel.

DVDs Coded for region 1 (USA and Canada) only.

POST

Post Office (Map p827; ☑702-382-5779; www.usps.com; 201 S Las Vegas Blvd; ☺9am-5pm Mon-Fri)

TOURIST INFORMATION

Websites offering travel information and booking services include www.lasvegas.com and www.vegas.com.

Las Vegas Convention & Visitors Authority (LVCVA; Map p827; ☑702-892-7575; www.lasvegas.com; 3150 Paradise Rd; ☺8am-5:30pm Mon-Fri; Las Vegas Convention Center)

✪ Getting There & Around

Vegas is served by **McCarran International Airport** (LAS; Map p827; ☑702-261-5211; www.mccarran.com; 5757 Wayne Newton Blvd; ☎), near the south end of the Strip. A free, wheelchair-accessible tram links outlying gates, while free shuttle buses link Terminals 1 and 3 and serve the **McCarran Rent-a-Car Center** (☑702-261-6001; www.mccarran.com/go/rentalcars.aspx; 7135 Gillespie St; ☺24hr).

Shuttle buses run to Strip hotels from $7 one-way, and from $9 to Downtown and off-Strip hotels. You'll pay at least $20 plus tip for a taxi to the Strip – tell your driver to use surface streets, not the I-15 Fwy airport connector tunnel ('long-hauling').

Greyhound runs long-distance buses connecting Las Vegas with Reno ($81, 9½ hours) and Salt Lake City (from $48, eight hours), as well as regular discounted services to/from Los Angeles (from $11, five to eight hours). You'll disembark at a downtown station just off the Fremont Street Experience. To reach the Strip, catch a southbound **SDX** bus (two-hour pass $6).

Day passes on the 24-hour **Deuce** and faster (though not 24-hour and not servicing all casinos) **SDX** buses are an excellent way to get around.

Around Las Vegas

Lake Mead and **Hoover Dam** are the most visited sites within the **Lake Mead National Recreation Area** (☑info desk 702-293-8906, visitor center 702-293-8990; www.nps.gov/lake; Lakeshore Scenic Dr; 7-day entry per vehicle $10;

☺24hr; ☎), which encompasses 110-mile-long Lake Mead, 67-mile-long Lake Mohave and many miles of desert around the lakes. The excellent **Visitor Center** (Alan Bible Visitor Center; ☑702-293-8990; www.nps.gov/lake; Lakeshore Scenic Dr, off US Hwy 93; ☺9am-4:30pm), on Hwy 93 halfway between Boulder City and Hoover Dam, has information on recreation and desert life. From there, North Shore Rd winds around the lake and makes a great scenic drive.

Straddling the Arizona–Nevada border, the graceful curve and art-deco style of the 726ft **Hoover Dam** (☑702-494-2517, 866-730-9097; www.usbr.gov/lc/hooverdam; off Hwy 93; admission visitor center incl parking $10; ☺9am-6pm Apr-Oct, to 5pm Nov-Mar; ☎) contrasts superbly with the stark landscape. Don't miss a stroll over the **Mike O'Callaghan-Pat Tillman Memorial Bridge** (Hwy 93), which features a pedestrian walkway with perfect views upstream of Hoover Dam.

For a relaxing lunch or dinner break, head to nearby downtown Boulder City, where **Milo's** (☑702-293-9540; www.milosbouldercity.com; 534 Nevada Hwy; mains $9-14; ☺11am-10pm Sun-Thu, to 11pm Fri & Sat) serves fresh sandwiches, salads and gourmet cheese plates at sidewalk tables outside the wine bar.

Western Nevada

The state's western corner, carved by the conifer-clad Sierra Nevada, drops off near Genoa. It's a vast treeless steppe of sagebrush, unfurling itself like a plush green-gray carpet across the undulating plains of the Great Basin. From Lake Tahoe's sandy shores to the historic hamlet of Virginia City, the enduring gentility of Carson City, little Reno, Burning Man, Black Rock and beyond, Western Nevada's has plenty to entice you.

Reno

In downtown Reno you can gamble at one of two-dozen casinos in the morning then walk down the street and shoot rapids at the Truckee River Whitewater Park. That's what makes 'The Biggest Little City in the World' so interesting – it's holding tight to its gambling roots but also earning kudos as a top-notch basecamp for outdoor adventure. The Sierra Nevada Mountains and Lake Tahoe are less than an hour's drive away, and the region teems with lakes, trails and ski resorts. Wedged between the I-80 and the

Truckee River, downtown's N Virginia St is casino central; south of the river it continues as S Virginia St.

◉ Sights

★ National Automobile Museum MUSEUM
(☎775-333-9300; www.automuseum.org; 10 S Lake St; adult/child 6-18yr $10/4; ⊘9:30am-5:30pm Mon-Sat, 10am-4pm Sun) Stylized street scenes illustrate a century's worth of automobile history at this engaging car museum. The collection is enormous and impressive, with one-of-a-kind vehicles – including James Dean's 1949 Mercury from *Rebel Without a Cause*, a 1938 Phantom Corsair and a 24-karat gold-plated DeLorean – and rotating exhibits with all kinds of souped-up and fabulously retro rides.

★ Atlantis CASINO
(☎775-825-4700; www.atlantiscasino.com; 3800 S Virginia St; ⊘24hr) Looking like it's straight out of a 1970s B-grade flick on the outside, Atlantis is all fun on the inside, modeled on the legendary underwater city, with a mirrored ceiling and tropical flourishes like indoor waterfalls and palm trees. It's one of Reno's most popular offerings, though not downtown.

★ Discovery MUSEUM
(Terry Lee Wells Nevada Discovery Museum; ☎775-786-1000; www.nvdm.org; 490 S Center St; entry $10, Wed $5 after 4pm; ⊘10am-5pm Tue, Thu-Sat, to 8pm Wed, noon-5pm Sun; Ⓟ▥) Since opening its doors in 2011 as a children's museum, the Discovery rapidly grew in popularity and expanded its focus to become a world-class, hands-on center for 'science, technology, engineering, art and math' (STEAM) learning, with 11 permanent, participatory exhibitions designed to inspire kids and young adults to have fun and develop an interest in these disciplines.

Nevada Museum of Art MUSEUM
(☎775-329-3333; www.nevadaart.org; 160 W Liberty St; adult/child 6-12yr $10/1; ⊘10am-5pm Wed & Fri-Sun, to 8pm Thu) In a sparkling building inspired by the geological formations of the Black Rock Desert north of town, a floating staircase leads to galleries showcasing temporary exhibits and eclectic collections on the American West, labor and contemporary landscape photography. In 2016 the museum opened its $6.2-million Sky Room function area. Visitors are free to explore and enjoy the space – essentially a fabulous rooftop penthouse and patio with killer views – providing it's not in use.

VALLEY OF FIRE STATE PARK

It's about 50 miles from the Fremont Street Experience (p825) to the visitor center at the **Valley of Fire State Park** (☎702-397-2088; www.parks.nv.gov/parks/valley-of-fire; 29450 Valley of Fire Hwy, Overton; per vehicle $10; ⊘visitor center 8:30am-4:30pm, park 7am-7pm). Make this your first port of call to find out how best to tackle this masterpiece of Southwest desert scenery containing 40,000 acres of red Aztec sandstone, petrified trees and ancient Native American petroglyphs (at Atlatl Rock). Dedicated in 1935, the park was Nevada's first designated state park. Its psychedelic landscape has been carved by wind and water over thousands of years.

Silver Legacy CASINO
(☎775-329-4777; www.silverlegacyreno.com; 407 N Virginia St; ⊘24hr) A Victorian-themed place, the Silver Legacy is easily recognized by its white landmark dome, where a giant mock mining rig periodically erupts into a fairly tame sound-and-light spectacle. The casino's hotel tower is usually lit emerald green at night and looks like something out of *The Wizard of Oz*.

Galena Creek Recreation Area NATURE RESERVE
(☎775-849-4948; www.galenacreekvisitorcenter.org/trail-map.html; 18250 Mt Rose Hwy) Just 19 miles from downtown Reno, a complex network of scenic hiking trails beginning at this recreation area within the Humboldt-Toiyabe National Forest gets you right into the heart of the wilderness. Check in with the **Galena Creek Visitor Center** when you arrive for the latest conditions and friendly advice.

🏃 Activities

Reno is a 30- to 60-minute drive from Tahoe ski resorts, and many hotels and casinos offer special stay-and-ski packages.

Mere steps from the casinos, the Class II and III rapids at the city-run Truckee River Whitewater Park (www.reno.gov) are gentle enough for kids riding inner tubes, yet also sufficiently challenging for professional freestyle kayakers. Two courses wrap around Wingfield Park, a small river island that hosts free concerts in summertime. **Tahoe Whitewater Tours** (☎775-787-5000; www.gowhitewater.com; 400 Island Ave; 2hr kayak rental/tour from $48/68) and **Sierra Adventures** (☑ 866-323-8928, 775-323-8928; www.wildsierra.com; Truckee River Lane; kayak rental from $22) offer kayak trips and lessons.

🛏 Sleeping

Lodging rates vary widely, day by day. Sunday through Thursday are generally the best; Friday is more expensive and Saturday can be as much as triple the midweek rate.

In summer there's gorgeous high-altitude camping at **Mt Rose** (☑ 877-444-6777; www.recreation.gov; Mt Rose Hwy/Hwy 431; RV & tent sites $20-50; ⊙ mid-Jun–Sep; P ⊠).

Sands Regency   HOTEL $
(☑ 775-348-2200; www.sandsregency.com; 345 N Arlington Ave; r from $49 Sun-Thu, from $89 Fri & Sat; P❋🛜⊠🐾) The Sands Regency has some of the largest standard digs in town. Its rooms are decked out in a cheerful tropical palette of upbeat blues, reds and greens – a visual relief from typical motel decor. Empress Tower rooms are best. The 17th-floor gym and Jacuzzi are perfectly positioned to capture the drop-dead panoramic mountain views, and an outdoor pool opens in summer.

Peppermill   CASINO HOTEL $
(☑ 775-826-2121; www.peppermillreno.com; 2707 S Virginia St; r from $69 Sun-Thu, from $149 Fri & Sat; P❋@🛜⊠) 🐾 With a dash of Vegas-style opulence, the ever-popular Peppermill boasts Tuscan-themed suites in its newest 600-room tower, and plush remodeled rooms throughout the rest of the property. The two sparkling pools (one indoors) are dreamy, with a full spa on hand. Geothermal energy powers the resort's hot water and heat. The nightly resort fee is $20.

★ **Whitney Peak**   DESIGN HOTEL $$
(☑ 775-398-5400; www.whitneypeakhotel.com; 255 N Virginia St; d from $129; P❋🛜) 🐾 What's not to love about this independent, inventive, funky, friendly, non-smoking, non-gambling downtown hotel? Spacious guest rooms have a youthful, fun vibe celebrating the great outdoors and don't skimp on designer creature comforts. With an executive-level concierge lounge, free use of the climbing wall, a noteworthy on-site restaurant and friendly, professional staff, Whitney Peak is hard to beat.

🍴 Eating

★ **Gold 'n Silver Inn**   DINER $
(☑ 775-323-2696; www.goldnsilverreno.com; 790 W 4th St; mains $6-20; ⊙ 24hr) A Reno insti-

tution for over 50 years, this slightly divey but superfriendly 24-hour diner has a huge menu of homestyle American favorites such as meatloaf, plated dinners, all-day breakfasts and burgers, not to mention seriously incredible caramel milkshakes.

★ **Old Granite Street Eatery**   AMERICAN $$
(☑ 775-622-3222; www.oldgranitestreeteatery.com; 243 S Sierra St; dinner mains $12-29; ⊙ 11am-10pm Mon-Thu, to 11pm Fri, 10am-11pm Sat, to 3pm Sun; 🐾) A lovely well-lit place for organic and local comfort food, old-school artisanal cocktails and craft beers, this antique-strewn hot spot enchants diners with its stately wooden bar, water served in old liquor bottles and lengthy seasonal menu. Forgot to make a reservation? Check out the iconic rooster and pig murals and wait at a communal table fashioned from a barn door.

Louis' Basque Corner   BASQUE $$
(☑ 775-323-7203; www.louisbasquecorner.com; 301 E 4th St; dinner menu $12-29; ⊙ 11am-9:30pm Tue-Sat, 4-9:30pm Sun & Mon) Get ready to dine on lamb, rabbit, sweetbreads and more lamb at a big table full of people you've never met before. A different set-course menu is offered every day and posted in the window.

★ **Wild River Grille**   GRILL $$
(☑ 775-847-455; www.wildrivergrille.com; 17 S Virginia St; mains lunch $11-16, dinner $21-37; ⊙ 11am-9pm; 🐾) At the Wild River Grille you'll love the smart-casual dining and the varied menu of creative cuisine, from the Gruyère croquettes to the lobster ravioli, but most of all the wonderful patio overlooking the lovely Truckee River: it's also the best spot in town for a drink on a balmy summer's evening and a great place to take a date.

🍷 Drinking & Nightlife

★ **Pignic**   BAR
(☑ 775-376-1948; www.renoriver.org/pignic-pub-patio; 235 Flint St; ⊙ 3-11pm) This awesome little place gets points for originality: occupying what was formerly a private home, the concept is simple. You bring your own food and barbecue it here, and buy your drinks at the bar. It's participatory, friendly and speaks to the importance of friends, family and community. Lots of fun.

☆ Entertainment

The free weekly *Reno News & Review* (www.newsreview.com) is your best source for listings.

Knitting Factory LIVE MUSIC
(☑ 775-323-5648; http://re.knittingfactory.com;
211 N Virginia St) This midsized music venue
books mainstream and indie favorites.

ⓘ Information

**Reno-Sparks Convention & Visitors Author-
ity Visitor Center** (☑ 775-682-3800; www.
visitrenotahoe.com; 135 N Sierra St; ⊙ 9am-
6pm)

ⓘ Getting There & Around

About 5 miles southeast of downtown, **Reno-
Tahoe International Airport** (RNO; www.
renoairport.com; ☎) is served by most major
airlines, with connections throughout the US to
international routes.

The **North Lake Tahoe Express** (☑ 866-216-
5222; www.northlaketahoeexpress.com; one
way $49) operates a shuttle (six to eight daily,
3:30am to midnight) to and from the airport
to multiple North Shore Lake Tahoe locations.
The **South Tahoe Airporter** (☑ 866-898-2463;
www.southtahoeairporter.com; adult/child one
way $29.75/16.75, round-trip $53/30.25) operates several daily shuttle buses from the airport
to Stateline casinos. Casino hotels usually offer
frequent free airport shuttles for their guests.

Greyhound (☑ 800-231-2222; www.grey
hound.com) offers up to five direct buses a day
to Reno from San Francisco (from $8, from five
hours): book well in advance for these lowest
fares.

The **Amtrak** (☑ 800-872-7245; www.amtrak.
com) *California Zephyr* train makes one daily
departure from Emeryville/San Francisco ($52,
6¾ hours) to Reno.

The local **RTC Washoe** (☑ 775-348-0400;
www.rtcwashoe.com) RTC Ride buses blanket
the city, and most routes converge at the RTC
4th St station downtown (between Lake St and
Evans Ave).

Carson City

An easy drive from Reno or Lake Tahoe, this
underrated town is a perfect stop for lunch
and a stroll around the quiet, old-fashioned
downtown.

The **Kit Carson Blue Line Trail** passes
pretty historic buildings on pleasant treelined
streets. Pick up a trail map at the visitor
center (p820), a mile south of downtown.

The 1870 **Nevada State Capitol** (☑ 775-
684-5670; 101 North Carson St; ⊙ 8am-5pm Mon-
Fri) FREE anchors downtown; you might
spot the governor himself chatting with a
constituent. Train buffs shouldn't miss the
Nevada State Railroad Museum (☑ 775-

ⓘ RENO AREA TRAIL INFORMATION

For information on regional hiking and
mountain-biking trails, including the Mt
Rose summit trail and Tahoe-Pyramid
Bikeway, download the *Truckee Meadows Trails Guide* (www.washoecounty.
us/parks/trails/trail_challenge.php).

687-6953; http://nvdtca.org/nevadastaterailroad
museumcarsoncity; 2180 S Carson St; adult/child
under 18 yr $6/free; ⊙ 9am-5pm Thu-Mon), which
displays train cars and locomotives from the
1800s to the early 1900s.

Grab lunch at fetching **Comma Coffee**
(☑ 775-883-2662; www.commacoffee.com; 312
S Carson St; meals $7-12; ⊙ 7am-8pm Mon-Sat;
☎☑) and eavesdrop on the politicians, or
spend the evening in an English-style pub,
the **Firkin & Fox** (☑ 775-883-1369; www.fox
brewpub.com; 310 S Carson St; ⊙ 11am-midnight
Sun-Thu, to 2am Fri & Sat).

Hwy 395/Carson St is the main drag. For
hiking and camping information, stop by
the Nevada Division of State Parks (p820).

Virginia City

The discovery of the legendary Comstock
Lode in 1859 sparked a silver bonanza in
the mountains 25 miles south of Reno. During the 1860s gold rush, Virginia City was
a high-flying, rip-roaring Wild West boom-
town. Newspaperman Samuel Clemens, ali-
as Mark Twain, spent time here during its
heyday, and described the mining life in his
book *Roughing It*.

The high-elevation town is a National Historic Landmark, with a main street of Victorian buildings, wooden sidewalks and some
hokey but fun museums. To see how the
mining elite lived, stop by the **Mackay Mansion** (☑ 775-847-0373; www.uniquitiesmackay
mansion.com; 291 S D St; adult/child $5/free;
⊙ 10am-6pm) and the Castle (B St).

Locals agree that **Cafe del Rio** (www.cafe
delriovc.com; 394 S C St; mains $11-17; ⊙ 11am-
8pm Wed-Sat, 10am-7pm Sun) serves the town's
best food – a nice blend of nuevo Mexican
and good cafe meals, including breakfast.
Wet your whistle at the longtime family-run
Bucket of Blood Saloon (www.bucketofblood
saloonvc.com; 1 S C St; ⊙ 10am-7pm), which
serves up beer and 'bar rules' at its antique
wooden bar ('If the bartender doesn't laugh,
you are not funny'). The **visitor center**

(☎ 775-847-7500, 800-718-7587; www.visitvirginia
citynv.com; 86 S C St; ⊘ 9am-5pm Mon-Sat, 10am-
4pm Sun) is on the main drag, C St.

The Great Basin

A trip across Nevada's Great Basin is a serene, almost haunting experience. Anyone seeking the 'Great American Road Trip' will relish the historic towns and quirky diversions tucked away along lonely desert highways.

Along I-80

The culture of the American West is diligently cultivated in **Elko**, almost 300 miles along I-80 northeast of Reno. Aspiring cowboys and cowgirls should visit the **Western Folklife Center** (☎ 775-738-7508; www.westernfolklife.org; 501 Railroad St; adult/child 6-18yr $5/1; ⊘ 10am-5:30pm Mon-Fri, 10am-5pm Sat), which offers art and history exhibits, musical jams, and dance nights, and hosts the **Cowboy Poetry Gathering** each January. Elko also holds a **National Basque Festival** every July 4, with games, traditional dancing and a 'Running of the Bulls'. If you've never sampled Basque food, the best place for your inaugural experience is the **Star Hotel** (☎ 775-753-8696; www.eatdrinkandbebasque.com; 246 Silver St; lunch $8-14, dinner $16-38; ⊘ 11am-2pm & 5-9pm Mon-Fri, 4:30-9:30pm Sat), a family-style supper club located in a circa-1910 boarding house for Basque sheepherders.

Along Highway 50

The transcontinental Hwy 50 cuts across the heart of Nevada, connecting Carson City in the west to Great Basin National Park in the east. Better known here by its nickname, 'The Loneliest Road in America,' it once formed part of the Lincoln Hwy, and follows the route of the Overland Stagecoach, the Pony Express and the first transcontinental telegraph line. Towns are few, and the only sounds are the hum of the engine or the whisper of wind.

About 25 miles southeast of Fallon, the **Sand Mountain Recreation Area** (☎ 775-885-6000; www.blm.gov/nv; 7-day permit $40, entry free Tue & Wed; ⊘ 24hr; P) is worth a stop for a look at its 600ft sand dune and the ruins of a Pony Express station. Just east, enjoy a juicy burger at an old stagecoach stop, **Middlegate Station** (☎ 775-423-7134; www.facebook.com/middlegate.station; 42500 Austin Hwy, cnr Hwys 50 & 361; mains $6-17; ⊘ 6am-2am) then toss your sneakers onto the new **Shoe Tree** on the north side of Hwy 50 just ahead (the old one was cut down).

A fitting reward for surviving Hwy 50 is the awesome, uncrowded **Great Basin National Park** (☎ 775-234-7331; www.nps.gov/grba; ⊘ 24hr) `FREE`. Near the Nevada–Utah border, it's home to 13,063ft Wheeler Peak, which rises abruptly from the desert. Hiking trails near the summit take in superb country with glacial lakes, ancient bristlecone pines and even a permanent ice field. Admission is free; in summer, you can get oriented at the **Lehman Caves Visitor Center** (☎ 775-234-7331, tour reservations 775-234-7517; www.nps.gov/grba; 5500 NV-488, Baker; adult $8-10, child $4-5; ⊘ 8am-4:30pm, tours 8:30am-4pm), just north of Baker.

Along Highways 375 & 93

Hwy 375 is dubbed the 'Extraterrestrial Hwy', both for its huge number of UFO sightings and because it intersects Hwy 93 near top secret **Area 51**, part of Nellis Air Force Base, supposedly a holding area for captured UFOs. Some people may find Hwy 375 more unnerving than the Loneliest Road; it's a desolate stretch of pavement where cars are few and far between. In the tiny town of Rachel, on Hwy 375, **Little A'Le' Inn** (☎ 775-729-2515; www.littlealeinn.com; 9631 Old Mill St, Rachel; RV sites with hookups $15, r $50-165; ⊘ restaurant 8am-10pm; ❀ 🎧 🐾) accommodates earthlings and aliens alike, and sells extraterrestrial souvenirs. Probings not included.

ARIZONA

Arizona is made for road trips. Yes, the state has its showstoppers – Monument Valley, the Grand Canyon, Cathedral Rock – but you'll remember the long, romantic miles under endless skies for as long as you do the icons in between. Each drive reveals a little more of the state's soul: for a dose of mom-and-pop friendliness, follow Route 66 into Flagstaff; to understand the sheer will of Arizona's mining barons, take a twisting drive through rugged Jerome; and American Indian history becomes contemporary as you drive past mesatop Hopi villages dating back 1000 years.

History

American Indian tribes and their ancestors inhabited Arizona for millennia before Francisco Vásquez de Coronado, leading an expedition from Mexico City in 1540, became the first European to clap eyes on the Grand Canyon and Colorado River. Settlers and missionaries followed in his wake, and by the mid-19th century the US acquired Arizona from Mexico by conquest and purchase. The Indian Wars, in which the US Army battled American Indians to protect settlers and claim land for the government, officially ended in 1886 with the surrender of Apache warrior Geronimo.

Railroad and mining expansion followed and people started arriving in ever larger numbers. After President Theodore Roosevelt visited Arizona in 1903 he supported the damming of its rivers to provide year-round water for irrigation and drinking, thus paving the way to statehood: in 1912 Arizona became the last of the 48 contiguous US states to be admitted to the Union.

The state shares a 250-mile border with Mexico. Although it was traditionally a gateway for illegal immigration, far stricter controls have seen the number of people entering through the state plummet since 2005. However, after the mysterious murder of a popular rancher near the border in 2010, the legislature passed a controversial law requiring police officers to ask for identification from anyone they suspect of being in the country illegally. While the constitutionality of the request for immigration papers was upheld, key provisions of the law, known as SB 1070, were struck down by the US Supreme Court.

ⓘ Information

Although Arizona is on Mountain Standard Time, it's the only western state that does not observe daylight saving time from spring to early fall – except for on the Navajo Reservation. Generally speaking, lodging rates in southern Arizona (including Phoenix, Tucson and Yuma) are much higher in winter and spring, considered to be the 'high season', so great deals can befound in the hotter areas in summer.

Arizona Office of Tourism (☑ 602-364-3700; www.arizonaguide.com) Free state information.

Arizona State Parks (☑ 877-697-2757, 602-542-4174; www.azstateparks.com) Sixteen of the state's parks have campgrounds, open to online reservations.

Public Lands Interpretative Association (www.publiclands.org) Information about USFS, NPS, Bureau of Land Management (BLM) and state lands and parks.

WORTH A TRIP

BURNING MAN

For a week in August, 'Burners' from around the world descend on **Burning Man** (www.burningman.com; entry $425; ☉Aug) in the Black Rock Desert to build the temporary Black Rock City, only to tear it all down again and set fire to an effigy of man. In between, there's peace, love, music, art, nakedness, drugs, sex and frivolity in a safe space where attendees uphold the principles of the festival.

Phoenix

Phoenix is Arizona's indubitable cultural and economic powerhouse, a thriving desert metropolis boasting some of the best Southwestern and Mexican food you'll find anywhere. And with more than 300 days of sunshine a year, exploring the 'Valley of the Sun' is an agreeable proposition (except in the sapping heat from June to August).

Culturally, it offers an opera, a symphony, several theaters and three of the state's finest museums – the Heard, Phoenix Art and Musical Instrument Museums – while the Desert Botanical Garden is a stunning introduction to the region's flora and fauna. For sports fans, there are professional baseball, football, basketball and ice-hockey teams, and more than 200 golf courses.

⊙ Sights

Greater Phoenix consists of several distinct cities. Phoenix, the largest, combines a business-like demeanor with top-notch museums, a burgeoning cultural scene and great sports facilities. Southeast of here, lively, student-flavored Tempe (tem-pee), hugs 2-mile-long Tempe Town Lake, while suburban Mesa, further east, holds a couple of interesting museums. Two ritzy enclaves lie northeast of Phoenix – Scottsdale, known for its cutesy old town, galleries and lavish resorts, and the largely residential Paradise Valley.

⊙ Phoenix

★**Heard Museum** MUSEUM
(Map p844; ☑ 602-252-8848; www.heard.org; 2301 N Central Ave; adult $18, child 6-17yr & student $7.50, senior $13.50; ☉9:30am-5pm Mon-Sat, 11am-5pm Sun; ⓟ⊕) This extraordinary museum spotlights the history, life, arts and culture of

American Indian tribes in the Southwest. Visitors will find art galleries, ethnographic displays, films, a get-creative kids exhibit and an unrivaled collection of Hopi kachinas (elaborate spirit dolls, many gifted by Presidential nominee Barry Goldwater). The Heard emphasizes quality over quantity and is one of the best museums of its kind in America.

★ **Musical Instrument Museum**　MUSEUM
(☑480-478-6000; www.themim.org; 4725 E Mayo Blvd; adult/teen/child 4-12yr $20/15/10; ☺9am-5pm; P) From Uganda thumb pianos to Hawaiian ukuleles to Indonesian boat lutes, the ears have it at this lively museum that celebrates the world's musical instruments. More than 200 countries and territories are represented within five regional galleries, with wireless recordings bringing many to life as you get within 'earshot' (headsets are provided). You can also bang a drum in the Experiences Gallery and listen to Taylor Swift or Elvis Presley rock out in the Artist Gallery.

★ **Desert Botanical Garden**　GARDENS
(Map p844; ☑480-941-1225; www.dbg.org; 1201 N Galvin Pkwy; adult/senior/student 13-18yr/child 3-12yr $22/20/12/10; ☺8am-8pm Oct-Apr, 7am-8pm May-Sep) Blue bells and Mexican gold poppies are just two of the colorful showstoppers blooming from March to May along the Desert Wildflower Loop Trail at this well-nurtured botanical garden, a lovely place to reconnect with nature while learning about desert plant life. Looping trails lead past a profusion of desert denizens, arranged by theme (including a Sonoran Desert nature loop and an edible desert garden). It's pretty dazzling year-round, but the flowering spring season is the busiest and most colorful.

Phoenix Art Museum　MUSEUM
(Map p844; ☑602-257-1880; www.phxart.org; 1625 N Central Ave; adult/senior/student/child 6-17yr $18/15/13/9; ☺10am-5pm Tue & Thu-Sat, 10am-9pm Wed, noon-5pm Sun; P⊞) Arizona's premier repository of fine art includes works by Claude Monet, Diego Rivera and Georgia O'Keeffe. Make a beeline for the Western Gallery, to see how the astonishing Arizona landscape has inspired everyone from the early pioneers to modernists. Got kids? Pick up a Kidpack at Visitor Services, examine the ingeniously crafted miniature period Thorne Rooms or visit the PhxArtKids Gallery.

◉ Scottsdale

For a list of permanent and temporary public art displays, visit www.scottsdalepublic art.org.

Old Town Scottsdale　AREA
(Map p844; http://downtownscottsdale.com) Tucked among Scottsdale's malls and bistros is its Old Town, a Wild West–themed enclave filled with cutesy buildings, covered sidewalks and stores hawking mass-produced 'Indian' artifacts. There's also a museum, public sculptures, saloons, a few galleries stocking genuine American Indian art.

Taliesin West　ARCHITECTURE
(☑480-860-2700; www.franklloydwright.org; 12621 N Frank Lloyd Wright Blvd; tours from $26; ☺8:30am-6pm Oct-May, shorter hours Jun-Sep, closed Tue & Wed Jun-Aug) Taliesin West was the desert home and studio of Frank Lloyd Wright, one of America's greatest 20th-century architects. A prime example of organic architecture, with buildings incorporating elements and structures found in surrounding nature, it was built between 1938 and 1940, and is still home to an architecture school. It's now a National Historical

---

ARIZONA FACTS

Nickname Grand Canyon State

Population 6.9 million

Area 113,637 sq miles

Capital city Phoenix (population 1,563,025)

Other cities Tucson (population 531,641), Flagstaff (70,320), Sedona (10,388)

Sales tax 5.6%

Birthplace of Cesar Chavez (1927–93), singer Linda Ronstadt (b 1946)

Home of The OK Corral, mining towns turned art colonies

Politics Majority vote Republican

Famous for Grand Canyon, saguaro cacti

Best souvenir Pink cactus-shaped neon lamp from roadside stall

Driving distances Phoenix to Grand Canyon Village 235 miles, Tucson to Sedona 230 miles

Monument, open to the public for informative guided tours.

Tempe

Founded in 1885 and home to around 50,000 students, **Arizona State University** (ASU; Map p844; ☎ 480-965-2100; www.asu.edu) is the heart and soul of Tempe. The **Gammage Auditorium** (Map p844; ☎ box office 480-965-3434, tours 480-965-6912; www.asugammage.com; 1200 S Forest Ave, cnr Mill Ave & Apache Blvd; entry free, performances from $20; ⊙ box office 10am-5pm Mon-Thu in summer, 10am-6pm Mon-Fri rest of year) was Frank Lloyd Wright's last major building. Easily accessible by light-rail from downtown Phoenix, **Mill Avenue**, Tempe's main drag, is packed with restaurants, themed bars and other collegiate hangouts. You could also check out **Tempe Town Lake** (Map p844; www.tempe.gov/lake), an artificial lake with boat rides and hiking paths.

Mesa

★ Arizona Museum of Natural History   MUSEUM
(☎ 480-644-2230; www.azmnh.org; 53 N MacDonald St; adult/child 3-12yr/student/senior $12/7/8/10; ⊙ 10am-5pm Tue-Fri, 11am-5pm Sat, 1-5pm Sun; ⊕) Even if you're not staying in Mesa, this museum is worth a trip, especially if your kids are into dinosaurs (and aren't they all?). In addition to the multilevel Dinosaur Mountain, there are loads of life-sized casts of the giant beasts plus a touchable apatosaurus thighbone. Other exhibits highlight the Southwest's pre-conquest past, and that of the Americas more broadly, from a prehistoric Hohokam village to an entire hall on ancient Mesoamerican cultures.

🏃 Activities

Camelback Mountain   HIKING
(Map p844; ☎ 602-261-8318; www.phoenix.gov; ⊙ sunrise-sunset) This 2704ft twin-humped mountain sits smack in the center of the Phoenix action. Two trails, the Cholla Trail (6131 E Cholla Lane) and the Echo Canyon Trail (4925 E McDonald Dr), climb about 1200ft to the summit. The newly renovated Echo Canyon Trail is extremely popular in spring and winter – the car park fills very early, even with 135 spots.

Salt River Recreation   WATER SPORTS
(☎ 480-984-3305; www.saltrivertubing.com; 9200 N Bush Hwy; tubes & shuttle $17; ⊙ 8:30am-6pm

---

CATHEDRAL GORGE

Fifteen miles north of Caliente, just past the turn-off to Panaca, **Cathedral Gorge State Park** (☎ 775-728-4460; http://parks.nv.gov/parks/cathedral-gorge; Hwy 93, Pioche; $7; ⊙ visitor center 9am-4:30pm, park 24hr; ℗ ⊕) is one of those magical out-of-the-way places that you never regret traveling all that way for. Wandering among its wind- and water-eroded shapes, you get the feeling that you've stepped into a magnificent, many-spired cathedral, albeit one whose dome is the blue sky above. Head to the **Miller Point Overlook** for sweeping views and easy hikes into narrow side canyons.

May-late Sep, hours vary after Labor Day; ⊕) With Salt River Recreation you can float in an inner tube on the Lower Salt River through the stark Tonto National Forest. The launch is in northeast Mesa, about 15 miles north of Hwy 60 on Power Rd. Floats are two, three or five hours long, including the shuttle-bus ride back. Cash only.

Cactus Adventures   MOUNTAIN BIKING
(☎ 480-688-4743; www.cactusadventures.com; 8000 S Arizona Grand Pkwy; half-day rental $60; ⊙ phone line 8am-8pm) Based at Arizona Grand Resort, Cactus Adventures rents bikes for use at South Mountain and offers guided hiking and biking tours at various parks. For rentals, they will meet you at the trailhead; guided tours start from $155 per person (minimum two people).

Ponderosa Stables   HORSEBACK RIDING
(☎ 602-268-1261; www.arizona-horses.com; 10215 S Central Ave; 1/2/3hr rides $40/60/80, minimum 2 riders for 3hr rides; ⊙ 9am-8pm Mon-Sat; ⊕) This outfitter leads breakfast, lunch, dinner and sunset rides through South Mountain Park. Reservations required for most trips. The stables are around 7 miles south of downtown Phoenix, directly down Central Ave.

✦ Festivals & Events

First Fridays   ART
(www.artlinkphoenix.com; ⊙ 6-10pm first Fri of month) Up to 20,000 people hit the streets of downtown Phoenix on the first Friday of every month for this self-guided 'art walk,' held across more than 70 galleries and performance spaces. Free shuttles radiating

out from the Phoenix Art Museum ferry the cognoscenti from venue to venue.

Arizona State Fair FAIR
(☑ 602-252-6771; www.azstatefair.com; 1826 W McDowell Rd; adult/child 5-13yr $10/5; ☺ Oct) This fair lures over a million folks to the Arizona State Fairgrounds every October, with a rodeo, rides and amusements, livestock displays, a pie-eating contest and plenty of live performances.

🛏 Sleeping

🛏 Phoenix

HI Phoenix Hostel HOSTEL $
(Map p844; ☑ 602-254-9803; www.phxhostel.org; 1026 N 9th St; dm/r from $24/37; ☀@☎) Fall in love with backpacking again at this small hostel with fun owners who know Phoenix and want to enjoy it with you. The 22-bed hostel sits in an up-and-coming working-class neighborhood and has relaxing garden nooks. The 'talking table' – at which laptops and other devices are banned from 8am to 10am and 5pm to 10pm each day – is a very sociable innovation.

Maricopa Manor BOUTIQUE HOTEL $$
(Map p844; ☑ 602-264-9200, 800-292-6403; www.maricopamanor.com; 15 W Pasadena Ave; ste from $149; P☎☀) This small, Spanish-ranch-style place right near busy Central Ave has six individually appointed suites, many with French doors onto a deck overlooking the pool, garden and fountain areas. Although Maricopa Manor is central, it's well supplied with shady garden nooks, and privacy is easily achieved.

⭐**Arizona Biltmore Resort & Spa** RESORT $$$
(Map p844; ☑ 800-950-0086, 602-955-6600; www.arizonabiltmore.com; 2400 E Missouri Ave; d from $480; P☀@☎☀☀) With architecture inspired by Frank Lloyd Wright and past guests including Irving Berlin, Marilyn Monroe and every president from Hoover to Bush the younger, the Biltmore is perfect for connecting to the magic of yesterday. A landmark, lending its name to much in the surrounding area, it boasts over 700 beautifully appointed units, two golf courses, several pools and endless luxe touches.

Royal Palms Resort & Spa RESORT $$$
(Map p844; ☑ 602-840-3610; www.royalpalms hotel.com; 5200 E Camelback Rd; r/ste from $499/519; P☀☎☀☀) Camelback Mountain is the photogenic backdrop for this posh and intimate resort, built as the winter retreat of New York industrialist Delos Cook in 1929. Today, it's a hushed and elegant place, dotted with Spanish Colonial villas, flower-lined walkways and palms imported from Egypt. Pets can go Pavlovian for soft beds, personalized biscuits and walking services.

Palomar Phoenix HOTEL $$$
(Map p844; ☑ 602-253-6633, reservations 877-488-1908; www.hotelpalomar-phoenix.com; 2 E Jefferson St; r/ste from $449/509; P☀☎☀☀) Shaggy pillows, antler-shaped lamps and portraits of blue cows. Yep, the 242 rooms of the Palomar are whimsical, and we like it. Larger than average and popping with fresh, modern style, the rooms come with yoga mats, animal-print robes and Italian Frette linens. There's a nightly wine reception, and Phoenix's major baseball and basketball stadiums are just around the corner.

🛏 Scottsdale

⭐**Bespoke Inn, Cafe & Bicycles** B&B $$$
(Map p844; ☑ 480-664-0730; www.bespokeinn. com; 3701 N Marshall Way; d incl brunch from $349; P☀☎☀☀) A small slice of 'European' hospitality in downtown Scottsdale, this breezy B&B offers guests chocolate scones to nibble in the chic cafe, an infinity pool to loll in and Pashley city bikes to roam the neighborhood on. Rooms are plush, with handsome touches like handcrafted furniture and nickel bath fixtures. Gourmet brunch is served at the on-site restaurant Virtu. Book early.

Boulders RESORT $$$
(☑ 480-488-9009; www.theboulders.com; 34631 N Tom Darlington Dr, Scottsdale; casitas/villas from $239/391; P☀☎@☎☀☀) Tensions evaporate upon arrival at this desert oasis that blends into a landscape of natural rock formations – and that's before you've put in a session at the on-site spa or settled in at one of the four pools. Basically, everything here is calculated to make life better.

⭐**Hotel Valley Ho** BOUTIQUE HOTEL $$$
(Map p844; ☑ 480-376-2600; www.hotelvalleyho. com; 6850 E Main St; r/ste $409/532; P☀@☎☀☀) Everything's swell at the Valley Ho, where midcentury modern gets a 21st-century twist. This jazzy joint once bedded Bing Crosby, Natalie Wood and Janet Leigh, and today it's a top pick for movie stars filming on location in Phoenix. Bebop music, up-

beat staff and eye magnets like the 'ice fire-place' recapture the Rat Pack vibe, and the theme travels well to the balconied rooms.

 Tempe

Sheraton Wild Horse
Pass Resort & Spa
RESORT $$$

(☎602-225-0100; www.wildhorsepassresort.com; 5594 W Wild Horse Pass Blvd, Chandler; r/ste from $339/534; P❋🛜🏊) At sunset, scan the lonely horizon for the eponymous wild horses silhouetted against the South Mountains. Owned by the Gila River tribe and nestled on their sweeping reservation south of Tempe, this 500-room resort is a stunning alchemy of modern luxury and American Indian tradition. The domed lobby is a mural-festooned roundhouse, and rooms reflect the traditions of local tribes.

🍴 Eating

🍴 Phoenix

★Desoto Central Market
MARKET $

(Map p844; ☎602-680-7747; http://desotocentralmarket.com; 915 N Central Ave; mains $11-15; ⊘7am-10pm Mon-Wed, 7am-midnight Thu-Sat, 8am-9pm Sun) Making great use of a sensitively restored 1920s DeSoto dealership, this indoor 'market' is really a collective of inventive kitchens, slinging their goods together under the one roof. Special mention goes to New Southern affair the Larder and the Delta, whose shrimp 'n' grits (with smoked andouille sausage and hot sauce) or chili-garlic glazed baby back ribs will leave you gasping.

★Phoenix Public Market
CAFE $

(Map p844; ☎602-253-2700; www.phxpublicmarket.com; 14 E Pierce St; mains $9-10; ⊘7am-10pm; 🛜🍽) This buzzing barn of a place – the onsite cafe for Arizona's largest farmers market – attracts a dedicated clientele of Arizona State University (ASU) students, local professionals at lunch, vegetarians and food lovers of all stripes. The housemade bagels and flame-roasted chicken are fantastic, while inventive daily specials, community dinners and happy hours keep the cognoscenti coming at all hours.

Green New
American Vegetarian
VEGAN, VEGETARIAN $

(Map p844; ☎602-258-1870; www.greenvegetarian.com; 2022 N 7th St; mains $8-10; ⊘11am-9pm Mon-Sat; 🍽) Your expectations of vegan food will be forever raised after dining at this hip cafe, where chef Damon Brasch stirs up savory vegan and vegetarian dishes. Made with mock meats, the burgers, po'boys and Asian-style bowls taste as good, if not better, than their carnivorous counterparts. Order at the counter then take a seat in the garage-style digs.

Barrio Café
MEXICAN $$

(Map p844; ☎602-636-0240; www.barriocafe.com; 2814 N 16th St; mains $12-29; ⊘11am-10pm Tue-Sat, to 9pm Sun; 🍽) Barrio's staff wear T-shirts emblazoned with *comida chingona,* which translates as 'fucking good food,' and they don't lie. This is Mexican food at its most creative: how many menus have you seen featuring guacamole spiked with pomegranate seeds, buttered corn with chipotle, aged cheese, cilantro and lime or goat's-milk-caramel-filled churros? Drinks are half price from 2pm to 5pm daily.

★Dick's Hideaway
NEW MEXICAN $$$

(Map p844; ☎602-265-5886; http://richardsonsnm.com; 6008 N 16th St; breakfast $15-16, mains $25-27; ⊘8am-11pm Sun-Wed, to midnight Thu-Sat) At this pocket-sized ode to New Mexican cuisine, grab a small table beside the bar or settle in at the communal table in the side room and prepare for hearty servings of savory, chile-slathered New Mexican fare, from enchiladas to tamales to rellenos. We especially like the Hideaway for breakfast, when the Bloody Marys arrive with a shot of beer.

House of Tricks
AMERICAN $$$

(Map p844; ☎480-968-1114; www.houseoftricks.com; 114 E 7th St, Tempe; lunch $12-13, dinner $27-30; ⊘11am-10pm Mon-Sat) No, they don't do magic, but Robin and Robert Trick will still wow you with their eclectic, contemporary American menu that borrows influences from the Southwest, the Med and Asia. The trellised garden patio usually buzzes with regulars and drop-ins, but the tables inside the vintage cottages are equally charming.

🍴 Scottsdale

★The Mission
MEXICAN $$

(Map p844; ☎480-636-5005; www.themissionaz.com; 3815 N Brown Ave; lunch $14-18, dinner $14-30; ⊘11am-3pm & 5-10pm) With its dark interior and glowing votives, we'll call this *nuevo* Latin spot sexy – although our exclamations about the food's deliciousness may ruin the sultry vibe. The Tecate-marinated steak taco with lime and avocado is superb and makes

Phoenix

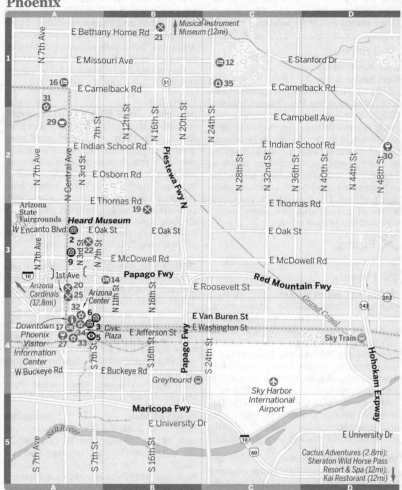

for a satisfying light lunch. The guacamole is made table-side, and wins raves. Margaritas and mojitos round out the fun.

Herb Box   AMERICAN **$$**
(Map p844; ☑ 480-289-6160; www.theherbbox. com; 7134 E Stetson Dr; brunch $13-15, lunch $14-17, dinner $17-22; ⊙ 11am-9pm Mon-Thu, 11am-10pm Fri, 9am-10pm Sat, 9am-4pm Sun; 🛜 🖉) It's not just about sparkle and air kisses at this chi-chi bistro in the heart of Old Town Scottsdale's Southbridge. It's also about fresh regional ingredients, artful presentation and attentive service. For a light, healthy lunch,

settle in on the patio and toast your good fortune with a blackberry mojito.

✖ Tempe

★**Kai Restaurant**   AMERICAN INDIAN **$$$**
(☑ 602-225-0100; www.wildhorsepassresort.com; 5594 W Wild Horse Pass Blvd, Chandler; mains $48-54, tasting menus $145-$245; ⊙ 5:30-9pm Tue-Sat) American Indian cuisine – based on traditional crops grown along the Gila River – soars to new heights at Kai ('seed'). Expect creations such as grilled buffalo tenderloin with smoked corn puree and cholla buds, or

tion Headquarters, this stylish seating-only cocktail bar shakes up some serious mixes and slings some delicious food to keep drinkers upright. Particularly lip-smacking is the dragon dumpling burger – pork and beef with Sichuan pickle and dumpling sauce.

Lux Central Coffeebar CAFE
(Map p844; ☑ 602-327-1396; www.luxcoffee.com; 4402 N Central Ave; ⊙ 6am-midnight Sun-Thu, to 2am Fri & Sat; ☞) MacBooks, tatts and hipster looks are de rigueur at this cafe-bar. The staff are adept and welcoming, the coffee is hand-roasted and the vibe is lively – everything you need to while away an hour over mid-morning coffee, dinner or a cocktail.

Four Peaks Brewing Company BREWERY
(Map p844; ☑ 480-303-9967; www.fourpeaks. com; 1340 E 8th St; ⊙ 11am-midnight Mon-Wed, 11am-1am Thu & Fri, 9am-midnight Sat & Sun; ☞) Hipsters, families, craft-beer obsessives and the plain thirsty congerate happily in this 1890s brick brewhouse, filling growlers of Kilt Lifter or Pitchfork Pale from the tap, or just chatting over a pint or two. There's also toothsome pub grub, tasting tours ($10 per head), a gift shop, and further locations in Tempe, Scottsdale and Phoenix Sky Harbor.

☆ Entertainment

Check *Arizona Republic Calendar* (www. azcentral.com/thingstodo/events) and *Phoenix New Times* (www.phoenixnewtimes. com) for listings.

The **Phoenix Symphony** (Map p844; ☑ administration 602-495-1117, box office 602-495-1999; www.phoenixsymphony.org; 75 N 2nd St) performs at **Symphony Hall** (Map p844; ☑ 602-262-6225; www.phoenixconventioncenter.com; 75 N 2nd St) and other local venues, while the **Arizona Opera** (Map p844; ☑ 602-266-7464; www. azopera.com; 75 N 2nd St) is based at an opera hall across the street from the Phoenix Art Museum (p840). The **Arizona Diamondbacks** (Map p844; ☑ 602-462-6500; http://arizona.diamondbacks.mlb.com; 401 E Jefferson St) play baseball at downtown's air-conditioned **Chase Field** (☑ tours 602-462-6799; www. mlb.com/ari/ballpark; adult/senior/child $7/5/3; ⊙ tours 9:30am, 11am, 12:30pm Mon-Sat, additional tours on game days), while the men's basketball team, the **Phoenix Suns** (Map p844; ☑ 602-379-7900; www.nba.com/suns; 201 E Jefferson St), and the women's team, the **Phoenix Mercury** (☑ 602-252-9622; www.wnba.com/mercury), are also downtown, at **Talking Stick Resort Arena**. The **Arizona Cardinals**

wild scallops with mesquite-smoked caviar and tepary-bean crackling. The unobtrusive service is flawless, the wine list expertly curated and the room decorated with American Indian art.

Kai is at the Sheraton Wild Horse Pass Resort & Spa (p843) on the Gila River Indian Reservation. Book ahead and dress nicely.

🍸 Drinking & Nightlife

★ **Bitter & Twisted** COCKTAIL BAR
(Map p844; ☑ 602-340-1924; https://bitterandtwistedaz.com; 1 W Jefferson St; ⊙ 4pm-2am Tue-Sat) Housed in the former Arizona Prohibi-

Phoenix

⊙ Top Sights
1 Desert Botanical Garden......................E3
2 Heard Museum...A3

⊙ Sights
3 Arizona Science Center.......................A4
4 Arizona State University F5
5 Chase Field..A4
6 Children's Museum of Phoenix A4
7 Gammage Auditorium...........................F5
8 Old Town Scottsdale F2
9 Phoenix Art Museum A3
10 Tempe Town Lake...................................F4

✪ Activities, Courses & Tours
11 Camelback Mountain..............................E1

🛌 Sleeping
12 Arizona Biltmore Resort & Spa C1
13 Bespoke Inn, Cafe & Bicycles................F2
14 HI Phoenix Hostel...................................B3
15 Hotel Valley Ho F2
16 Maricopa Manor A1
17 Palomar Phoenix A4
18 Royal Palms Resort & Spa E1

✴ Eating
19 Barrio Café B3
20 Desoto Central Market A3

21 Dick's Hideaway.......................................B1
22 Green New American Vegetarian A3
23 Herb Box F2
24 House of Tricks F5
25 Phoenix Public Market A3
26 The Mission F2

⊙ Drinking & Nightlife
27 Bitter & Twisted A4
28 Four Peaks Brewing Company F5
29 Lux Central Coffeebar...........................A2
30 OHSO Brewery & Distillery....................D2

✪ Entertainment
Arizona Diamondbacks.................(see 5)
Arizona Opera ....(see 34)
31 Char's Has the Blues..............................A1
32 Herberger Theater Center.....................A4
Phoenix Mercury...........................(see 33)
33 Phoenix Suns...A4
34 Phoenix Symphony A4
Symphony Hall.............................(see 34)

🛍 Shopping
35 Biltmore Fashion Park.............................C1
Heard Museum Shop &
Bookstore ....(see 2)
Phoenix Public Market ....(see 25)

(☑602-379-0101; www.azcardinals.com; 1 Cardinals Dr) play football in Glendale at the **University of Phoenix Stadium**.

Herberger Theater Center　　　THEATER
(Map p844; ☑602-252-8497; www.herbergertheat er.org; 222 E Monroe St; ☺box office 10am-5pm Mon-Fri, from noon Sat & Sun & 1hr before performances) Housing several theater companies and three stages, the Herberger also plays host to visiting troupes and productions. The predominant fare is drama and musicals, but you can also catch dance, opera and exhibitions of local art here.

Char's Has the Blues　　　BLUES
(Map p844; ☑602-230-0205; www.charshas theblues.com; 4631 N 7th Ave; cover $3 Thu-Sun; ☺8pm-1am) Dark and intimate – but very welcoming – this shabby-fronted blues and R&B shack packs 'em in with solid acts most nights of the week, but somehow still manages to feel like a well-kept secret.

🔒 Shopping

Phoenix Public Market　　　MARKET
(Map p844; ☑602-625-6736; https://phxpublic market.com; 721 N Central Ave; ☺8am-1pm Sat

Oct-Apr, 8am-noon Sat May-Sep) The largest farmers market in Arizona brings the state's best produce, both fresh and pre-made, together in one open-air jamboree of good tastes. Alongside spanking-fresh fruit and veg, you can find indigenous foods, wonderful bread, spices, paste and salsas, organic meat, BBQ trucks and plenty more to eat on the spot. Jewelry, textiles and body products also make appearances.

Heard Museum Shop & Bookstore　　　ARTS & CRAFTS
(Map p844; ☑602-252-8344; www.heardmuseum shop.com; 2301 N Central Ave; ☺9:30am-5pm Mon-Sat, 11am-5pm Sun; 🎧) This museum store has a top-notch collection of American Indian original arts and crafts; the variety and quality of kachina dolls alone is mind-boggling. Jewelry, pottery, American Indian books and a broad selection of fine arts can also be found, while the bookstore sells a wide array of books about the American Indian cultures of the Southwest.

Biltmore Fashion Park　　　MALL
(Map p844; ☑602-955-8400; www.shopbiltmore. com; 2502 E Camelback Rd; ☺10am-8pm Mon-Sat, noon-6pm Sun) Packed with high-end fashion

retailers, this exclusive mall preens from her perch on Camelback just south of the Arizona Biltmore Resort. Parking for under two hours is free, with validation.

ℹ️ Information

EMERGENCY & MEDICAL SERVICES

Police (☎ emergency 911, non-emergency 602-262-6151; http://phoenix.gov/police; 620 W Washington St)

Both **Banner – University Medical Center Phoenix** (☎ 602-839-2000; www.bannerhealth. com; 1111 E McDowell Rd) and **St Joseph's Hospital & Medical Center** (☎ 602-406-3000; www.stjosephs-phx.org; 350 W Thomas Rd) have 24-hour emergency rooms.

INTERET RESOURCES & MEDIA

KJZZ 91.5 FM (http://kjzz.org) National Public Radio (NPR).

Wi-fi is ubiquitous throughout Phoenix, or you can use the free internet at **Burton Barr Central Library** (☎ 602-262-4636; www.phoenixpub liclibrary.org; 1221 N Central Ave; ⊙ 9am-5pm Mon, Fri & Sat, 9am-9pm Tue-Thu, 1-5pm Sun; 🛜); see the website for additional locations.

POST

Downtown Post Office (Map p844; ☎ 602-253-9648; www.usps.com; 522 N Central Ave; ⊙ 9am-5pm Mon-Fri) Housed in a beautiful 1930s federal building.

TOURIST INFORMATION

Downtown Phoenix Visitor Information Center (Map p844; ☎ 877-225-5749; www. visitphoenix.com; 125 N 2nd St, Suite 120; ⊙ 8am-5pm Mon-Fri) The Valley's most complete source of tourist information. Located across from the Hyatt Regency.

Experience Scottsdale (Map p844; ☎ 480-421-1004, 800-782-1117; www.experience scottsdale.com; 7014 E Camelback Rd; ⊙ 9am-6pm Mon-Sat, 10am-5pm Sun) In the Food Court of Scottsdale Fashion Square.

Mesa Convention & Visitors Bureau (☎ 480-827-4700, 800-283-6372; www.visitmesa.com; 120 N Center St; ⊙ 8am-5pm Mon-Fri)

Tempe Tourism Office (Map p844; ☎ 800-283-6734, 480-894-8158; www.tempetourism. com; 222 S Mill Ave, Suite 120; ⊙ 8:30am-5pm Mon-Fri)

ℹ️ Getting There & Around

Sky Harbor International Airport (Map p844; ☎ 602-273-3300; http://skyharbor.com; 3400 E Sky Harbor Blvd; 🛜) is 3 miles southeast of downtown Phoenix and served by airlines including United, American, Delta and British Airways. Its three terminals (Terminals 2, 3 and 4; Terminal 1 was demolished in 1990) and the parking lots are linked by free shuttles and the **Phoenix Sky Train** (www.skyharbor.com/phxskytrain).

Greyhound (Map p844; ☎ 602-389-4200; www.greyhound.com; 2115 E Buckeye Rd) runs buses to Tucson ($18, two hours, six daily), Flagstaff ($25, three hours, five daily), Albuquerque ($70 to $87, 9½ hours, three daily) and Los Angeles ($46, 7½ hours, seven daily). Valley Metro's No 13 bus links the airport and the Greyhound station; tell the driver your destination is the station.

For shared rides from the airport, the citywide door-to-door shuttle service provided by **Super Shuttle** (☎ 602-244-9000, 800-258-3826; www.supershuttle.com) costs about $13 to downtown Phoenix, $15 to Tempe, $17 to Old Town Scottsdale and $21 to Mesa.

Valley Metro (☎ 602-253-5000; www.val leymetro.org) operates buses all over the Valley and a 20-mile light-rail line linking north Phoenix with downtown Phoenix, Tempe/ASU and downtown Mesa. Fares for both light-rail and bus are $2 per ride (no transfers) or $4 for a day pass. Buses run daily at intermittent times.

Central Arizona

North of Phoenix, the wooded, mountainous and much cooler Colorado Plateau is draped with scenic sites and attractions. You

---

PHOENIX FOR KIDS

Wet 'n' Wild Phoenix (☎ 623-201-2000; www.wetnwildphoenix.com; 4243 W Pinnacle Peak Rd, Glendale; over/under 42in tall $43/33, senior $33; ⊙ 10am-8pm Sun-Thu, to 10pm Fri & Sat Jun & Jul, shorter hours & weeks Mar-May & Aug-Oct; 🐾) This water park has pools, tube slides, wave pools, waterfalls and floating rivers. It's in Glendale, 2 miles west of I-17 at exit 217.

Children's Museum of Phoenix (Map p844; ☎ 602-253-0501; http://childrensmuseumof phoenix.org; 215 N 7th St; entry $11; ⊙ 9am-4pm Tue-Sun; 🐾) A tactile, climbable, paintable wonderland of interactive (and surreptitiously educational) exhibits.

Arizona Science Center (Map p844; ☎ 602-716-2000; www.azscience.org; 600 E Washington St; adult/child $18/13; ⊙ 10am-5pm; 🐾) A high-tech temple of discovery; there are more than 300 hands-on exhibits and a planetarium.

848

ARIZONA'S BEST SCENIC DRIVES

Oak Creek Canyon A thrilling plunge past swimming holes, rockslides and crimson canyon walls on Hwy 89A between Flagstaff and Sedona.

Hwy 89/89A Wickenburg to Sedona The Old West meets the New Weston on this lazy drive past dude ranches, mining towns, art galleries and stylish wineries.

Patagonia–Sonoita Scenic Road This one's for the birds, and those who like to track them, in Arizona's southern wine country on Hwys 82 and 83.

Kayenta–Monument Valley Star in your own Western on an iconic loop past cinematic red rocks in Navajo country.

Vermilion Cliffs Scenic Road A solitary drive on Hwy 89A through the Arizona Strip linking condor country, the North Rim and Mormon hideaways.

can channel your inner goddess at a vortex, hike through ponderosa-perfumed canyons, admire ancient Native American dwellings and delve into Old West history.

The main hub, Flagstaff, is a lively and delightful college town that's the gateway to the Grand Canyon South Rim. Summer, spring and fall are the best times to visit. On I-17, you can drive the 145 miles between Phoenix and Flagstaff in just over two hours. Opt for the more leisurely Hwy 89 and you'll be rewarded with beautiful landscapes and intriguing diversions.

Prescott

With its historic Victorian-era downtown and colorful Wild West heritage, Prescott feels like the Midwest-meets-cowboy country. Boasting more than 500 buildings on the National Register of Historic Places, it's the home of the world's oldest rodeo, while the infamous strip of old saloons known as Whiskey Row still plies its patrons with booze.

Just south of downtown, the winningly retro **Motor Lodge** (📞928-717-0157; www.themotorlodge.com; 503 S Montezuma St; r/ste/apt from $109/129/139; 🅿🛜) welcomes guests with 12 snazzy bungalows arranged around a central driveway – it's indie lodging at its best. For breakfast, mosey into the friendly

Local (📞928-237-4724; 520 W Sheldon St; mains $11-12; ⏰7am-2.30pm; 🛜), where home baking and a classic Southwestern breakfast can be counted on. Cajun and Southwest specialties spice up the menu at delightful **Iron Springs Cafe** (📞928-443-8848; www.ironspringscafe.com; 1501 Iron Springs Rd; brunch & lunch $11-13, dinner $16-20; ⏰11am-8pm Wed-Sat, 9am-2pm Sun), which sits inside an old train station 3 miles northwest of downtown.

On Whiskey Row, the **Palace** (📞928-541-1996; www.historicpalace.com; 120 S Montezuma St; ⏰11am-10pm Sun-Thu, to 11pm Fri & Sat) is an atmospheric place to drink; you enter through swinging saloon doors into a big room anchored by a Brunswick bar. The **visitor center** (📞800-266-7534, 928-445-2000; https://prescott.org; 117 W Goodwin St; ⏰9am-5pm Mon-Fri, 10am-2pm Sat & Sun) has tourist information, while **Arizona Shuttle** (📞928-226-8060, 800-888-2749; www.arizonashuttle.com) runs buses to/from Phoenix airport.

Jerome

This resurrected ghost town was known as the 'Wickedest Town in the West' during its late-1800s mining heyday, but its historic buildings have now been restored to hold galleries, restaurants, B&Bs and wine-tasting rooms.

Feeling brave? Stand on the glass platform covering the 1910ft mining shaft at **Audrey Headframe Park** (www.jeromehistoricalsociety.com; 55 Douglas Rd; ⏰8am-5pm) **FREE** – it's deeper than the Empire State Building by 650ft! Just ahead, the excellent **Jerome State Historic Park** (📞928-634-5381; www.azstateparks.com; 100 Douglas Rd; adult/child 7-13yr $7/4; ⏰8:30am-5pm) preserves the 1916 mansion of mining mogul Jimmy 'Rawhide' Douglas.

A community hospital in the mining era, the **Jerome Grand Hotel** (📞928-634-8200; www.jeromegrandhotel.com; 200 Hill St; r/ste $225/325; 🅿🛜) plays up its past with medical relics in the hallways and an entertaining ghost tour kids will enjoy. The adjoining **Asylum Restaurant** (📞928-639-3197; www.asylumrestaurant.com; 200 Hill St; lunch $12-14, dinner $26-28), with its sweeping views, is a breathtaking spot for a fine meal and glass of wine.

Downtown, the **Spirit Room Bar** (📞928-634-8809; www.spiritroom.com; 166 Main St; ⏰11am-1am) is a lively watering hole. Step into the **Flatiron Café** (📞928-634-2733; www.theflatironjerome.com; 416 Main St; breakfast $8-10, lunch $11-13; ⏰8:30am-3:30pm Wed-Mon) at the Y intersection for a gourmet breakfast or lunch; the specialty coffees are delicious. For information, call in at the **chamber of commerce** (☑ 928-634-2900; www.jeromechamber. com; 310 Hull Ave; ⊙ 11am-3pm Thu-Mon).

Sedona

Nestled amid striking red sandstone formations at the south end of the 16-mile Oak Creek Canyon, Sedona attracts spiritual seekers, artists and healers, as well as day-trippers from Phoenix trying to escape the oppressive heat. Many New Age types believe that this area is the center of vortexes (not 'vortices' here in Sedona) that radiate the earth's power, and you'll find all sorts of alternative medicines and practices on display. More tangibly, the surrounding canyons offer outstanding hiking, biking, swimming and camping.

⊙ Sights & Activities

New Agers believe Sedona's rocks, cliffs and rivers radiate Mother Earth's mojo. The four best-known vortexes are **Bell Rock** near the Village of Oak Creek east of Hwy 179; **Cathedral Rock** near Red Rock Crossing; **Airport Mesa** (Airport Rd) along Airport Rd; and **Boynton Canyon**. Airport Rd is also a great location for watching the Technicolor sunsets.

★ **Red Rock State Park**   PARK
(☑ 928-282-6907;   https://azstateparks.com/red-rock; 4050 Red Rock Loop Rd; adult $7, child 7-13yr $4, 6yr & under free; ⊙ 8am-5pm, visitor center 9am-4:30pm; ⊛) Not to be confused with Slide Rock State Park, this 286-acre park includes an environmental education center, picnic areas and 5 miles of well-marked, interconnecting trails in a riparian environment amid gorgeous red-rock country. Trails range from flat creekside saunters to moderate climbs to scenic ridges. Ranger-led activities include nature and bird walks. Swimming in the creek is prohibited. It's 9 miles west of downtown Sedona off Hwy 89A, on the eastern edge of the 15-mile Lime Kiln Trail.

★ **Slide Rock State Park**   SWIMMING
(☑ 928-282-3034, information line 602-542-0202; www.azstateparks.com/parks/slro; 6871 N Hwy 89A, Oak Creek Canyon; per car Jun-Sep $20, Oct-May $10; ⊙ 8am-7pm Jun-Aug, shorter hours rest of the year; ⊛) One of Sedona's most popular and most crowded destinations, this state park 7 miles north of town features an 80ft sandstone chute that whisks swimmers

through Oak Creek. Short trails ramble past old cabins, farming equipment and an apple orchard, but the park's biggest draw is the set of wonderful natural rock slides.

★ **Pink Jeep Tours**   DRIVING
(☑ 800-873-3662, 928-282-5000; www.pinkjeep-tours.com; 204 N Hwy 89A; ⊙ 6am-10pm; ⊛) It seems like this veteran of Sedona's tour industry has jeeps everywhere, buzzing around like pink flies. But once you join a tour, laughing and bumping around, you'll see why they're so popular. Pink runs 15 thrilling, bone-rattling off-road and adventure tours around Sedona, with most lasting from about two hours (adult/child from $59/54) to four hours (from $154/139).

🛏 Sleeping

Sedona and nearby Oak Creek Canyon host many beautiful B&Bs, creekside cabins, motels and full-service resorts. Dispersed camping is not permitted in Red Rock Canyon. The Forest Service runs campgrounds, without hookups, in the woods of Oak Creek Canyon, just off Hwy Alt 89. It costs $18 to camp, and you don't need a Red Rock Pass. All campgrounds except Pine Flat East accept reservations. Six miles north of town, Manzanita has 19 sites, showers and is open year round; 11.5 miles north, Cave Springs has 82 sites, and showers; Pine Flat East and Pine Flat West, 12.5 miles north, together have 58 sites, 18 of which can be reserved.

Cozy Cactus   B&B $$
(☑ 800-788-2082, 928-284-0082; www.cozycactus.com; 80 Canyon Circle Dr, Village of Oak Creek; d from $210; ⊛ 🐾) This five-room B&B, run by Carrie and Mark, works well for adventure-loving types – the Southwest-style house bumps up against Agave Trail, and is just around the bend from cyclist-friendly Bell Rock Pathway. Post-adventuring, get comfy beside the firepit on the back patio, perfect for wildlife watching and stargazing, and enjoy the three-course breakfast that awaits you the next morning.

★ **El Portal**   B&B $$$
(☑ 928-203-9405, 800-313-0017; www.elportal sedona.com; 95 Portal Lane; d from $300; 🐾⊛) ⏀ This discreet little inn is a beautiful blend of Southwestern and Craftsman style. It's a pocket of relaxed luxury tucked away in a corner across from the galleries and restaurants of Tlaquepaque, and marvelously removed from the chaos of Sedona's tourist-heavy

downtown. The look is rustic but sophisticated, incorporating reclaimed wood, Navajo rugs, river rock and thick adobe walls.

Eating

Sedona's restaurants are clustered around Uptown and strung along Highways 89A and 179. Pick up groceries and picnic ingredients at **Whole Foods** (📞928-282-6311; 1420 W Hwy 89A; ⏰8am-9pm Mon-Sat, to 8pm Sun; 🅿) or **Bashas'** (📞928-282-5351; 160 Coffee Pot Dr; ⏰6am-11pm).

Sedona Memories   DELI **$**
(📞928-282-0032; 321 Jordan Rd; sandwiches $8.50; ⏰10am-2pm Mon-Fri) This tiny local spot assembles gigantic sandwiches on slabs of homemade bread. A great choice for a picnic, as they pack 'em tight to-go, so there's less mess. You can also nosh on their quiet porch. If you call in your order, they'll toss in a free cookie. Cash only.

★ Elote Cafe   MEXICAN **$$$**
(📞928-203-0105; www.elotecafe.com; Arabella Hotel, 771 Hwy 179; mains $22-28; ⏰5-10pm Tue-Sat) Come here for some of the best, most authentic Mexican food in the region. Elote Cafe serves unusual and traditional dishes you won't find elsewhere, like the namesake *elote* (fire-roasted corn with spicy mayo, lime and cotija cheese) or smoked chicken in guajillo chiles. Reservations are not accepted and the line can be off-putting: come early, bring a book, order a margarita.

Dahl & DiLuca Ristorante   ITALIAN **$$$**
(📞928-282-5219; www.dahlanddiluca.com; 2321 Hwy 89A; mains $27-38; ⏰5-10pm) Though this lovely Italian place fits perfectly into the groove and color scheme of Sedona, at the same time it feels like the kind of place

you'd find in a small Italian seaside town. It's a bustling, welcoming spot serving excellent, authentic Italian food. Try the pork chop and asparagus from the grill or the four-cheese ravioli in truffle cream.

ℹ Information

Red Rock Country Visitor Center (📞928-203-2900; www.redrockcountry.org; 8375 Hwy 179; ⏰9am-4:30pm) Get a Red Rock Pass here, as well as hiking guides, maps and local national forest information.

Sedona Chamber of Commerce Visitor Center (📞928-282-7722, 800-288-7336; www.visitsedona.com; 331 Forest Rd; ⏰8:30am-5pm) Located in the pedestrian center of Uptown Sedona; pick up free maps and buy a Red Rock Pass.

ℹ Getting There & Around

Ace Xpress (📞800-336-2239, 928-649-2720; www.acexshuttle.com; one-way/round-trip adult $68/109, child $35/55; ⏰office hours 7am-8pm Mon-Fri, 8am-8pm Sat & Sun) and **Arizona Shuttle** (📞800-888-2749, 928-282-2066; www.arizonashuttle.com) run shuttle services between Sedona and Phoenix's Sky Harbor International Airport.

Amtrak (📞800-872-7245; www.amtrak.com) and **Greyhound** (📞800-231-2222; www.greyhound.com) both stop in nearby Flagstaff.

Barlow Jeep Rentals (📞928-282-8700, 800-928-5337; www.barlows.us; 3009 W Hwy 89A; half-/1-/3-day jeep rental $250/350/576; ⏰8am-6pm) is great for rough-road exploring. Free maps and trail information are provided. **Bob's Taxi** (📞982-282-1234; www.bobstaxisedona.com) is a good local operator, while rental cars are available at **Enterprise** (📞928-282-2052; www.enterprise.com; 2090 W Hwy 89A; per day from $50; ⏰8am-6pm Mon-Fri, 9am-2pm Sat & Sun).

Flagstaff

Flagstaff's laid-back charms are many, from a pedestrian-friendly historic downtown crammed with eclectic vernacular architecture and vintage neon, to hiking and skiing in the country's largest ponderosa pine forest. And the locals are a happy, athletic bunch, skewing more toward granola than gunslinger: buskers play bluegrass on street corners while cycling culture flourishes. Northern Arizona University (NAU) gives Flag its college-town flavor, while its railroad history still figures firmly in the town's identity. Throw in a healthy appreciation for craft beer, freshly roasted coffee beans and

---

RED ROCK PASS

To park on National Forest land around Sedona and Oak Creek Canyon, you'll need to buy a Red Rock Pass, which is available at ranger stations, visitor centers and vending machines at most trailheads and picnic areas. Passes cost $5 per day or $15 per week and must be displayed under the windshield of your car. You don't need a pass if you're just stopping briefly for a photograph or to enjoy a viewpoint, or if you have one of the Federal Interagency Passes.

VERDE VALLEY WINE TRAIL

Vineyards, wineries and tasting rooms are increasingly thick on the ground in the well-watered valley of the Verde River. Bringing star power is Maynard James Keenan, lead singer of the band Tool and owner of Caduceus Cellars and Merkin Vineyards. His 2010 documentary *Blood into Vine* takes a no-holds-barred look at the wine industry.

In Cottonwood, drive or float to **Alcantara Vineyards** (☑928-649-8463; www.alcantaravineyard.com; 3445 S Grapevine Way, Cottonwood; wine tasting $10-15; ☺11am-5pm) on the Verde River, then stroll through Old Town where **Arizona Stronghold** (☑928-639-2789; www.azstronghold.com; 1023 N Main St; wine tasting $9; ☺noon-7pm Sun-Thu, to 9pm Fri & Sat), **Merkin Vineyards Osteria** (☑928-639-1001; http://merkinvineyardsosteria.com; 1001 N Main St; ☺11am-9pm; 🛜) and **Pillsbury Wine Company** (☑928-639-0646; www.pillsburywine.com; 1012 N Main St; wine tasting $10-12; ☺11am-6pm Sun-Thu, to 9pm Fri & Sat) are three of the best wine-tasting rooms on oenophile-friendly Main St.

In Jerome, start at **Cellar 433** (☑928-634-7033; www.cellar433.com; 240 Hull Ave; ☺11am-6pm Thu-Sun, to 5pm Mon-Wed) near the visitor center. From there, stroll up to Keenan's **Caduceus Cellars** (☑928-639-9463; www.caduceus.org; 158 Main St; ☺11am-6pm Sun-Thu, to 8pm Sat), near the Connor Hotel.

Three wineries with tasting rooms hug a scrubby stretch of Page Springs Rd east of Cornville: bistro-housing **Page Springs Cellars** (☑928-639-3004; http://pagespringscellars.com; 1500 Page Springs Rd, Cornville; tours $10; ☺11am-7pm Sun-Wed, to 9pm Thu-Sat), the welcoming **Oak Creek Vineyards** (☑928-649-0290; www.oakcreekvineyards.net; 1555 N Page Springs Rd, Cornville; wine tasting $10; ☺10am-6pm) and the mellow-rock-playing **Javelina Leap Vineyard** (☑928-649-2681; www.javelinaleapwinery.com; 1565 Page Springs Rd, Cornville; tasting per wine $2-3; ☺11am-5pm Sun-Thu, to 6pm Fri & Sat).

For a wine-trail map and more details about the wineries, visit www.vvwinetrail.com.

---

an all-around good time and you have the makings of the perfect northern Arizonan escape.

☉ Sights

★**Lowell Observatory**   OBSERVATORY
(☑main phone 928-774-3358, recorded information 928-233-3211; www.lowell.edu; 1400 W Mars Hill Rd; adult/senior/child 5-17yr $15/14/8; ☺10am-10pm Mon-Sat, to 5pm Sun; ♿) Sitting atop a hill just west of downtown, this national historic landmark – famous for the first sighting of Pluto, in 1930 – was built by Percival Lowell in 1894. Weather permitting, visitors can stargaze through on-site telescopes, including the famed 1896 Clark Telescope, the impetus behind the now-accepted theory of an expanding universe. Kids will love the paved Pluto Walk, which meanders through a scale model of our solar system.

★**Museum of Northern Arizona**   MUSEUM
(☑928-774-5213; www.musnaz.org; 3101 N Fort Valley Rd; adult/senior/child 10-17yr $12/10/8; ☺10am-5pm Mon-Sat, noon-5pm Sun; ♿) Housed in an attractive Craftsman-style stone building amid a pine grove, this small but excellent museum spotlights local American Indian archaeology, history and culture, as well as geology, biology and

the arts. Intriguing permanent collections are augmented by exhibitions on subjects such as John James Audubon's paintings of North American mammals. On the way to the Grand Canyon it makes a wonderful introduction to the human and natural history of the region.

**Riordan Mansion
State Historic Park**   HISTORIC SITE
(☑928-779-4395; https://azstateparks.com/riordan-mansion; 409 W Riordan Rd; tour adult/child 7-13yr $10/5; ☺9:30am-5pm May-Oct, 10:30am-5pm Thu-Mon Nov-Apr) Having made a fortune from their Arizona Lumber Company, brothers Michael and Timothy Riordan built this sprawling duplex in 1904. The Craftsman-style design was the brainchild of architect Charles Whittlesey, who also designed El Tovar in Grand Canyon Village. The exterior features hand-split wooden shingles, log-slab siding and rustic stone. Filled with Edison, Stickley, Tiffany and Steinway furniture, the interior is a shrine to arts and crafts.

🏃 Activities

Absolute Bikes   CYCLING
(☑928-779-5969; www.absolutebikes.net; 202 E Rte 66; bike rentals per day from $39; ☺9am-7pm

Mon-Fri, 9am-6pm Sat, 10am-4pm Sun Apr-Thanks-giving, shorter hours Dec-Mar) Visit these super-friendly gearheads for the inside track on the local mountain-biking scene, and to hire wheels for the surrounding trails.

Arizona Snowbowl SKIING
(☑ 928-779-1951; www.arizonasnowbowl.com; 9300 N Snowbowl Rd; lift ticket adult $75, youth 13-17yr $64, child 8-12yr $42; ☺ 9am-4pm mid-Nov–mid-Apr; ▣) About 14 miles north of down-town Flagstaff, Arizona Snowbowl is small but lofty, with eight lifts that service 40 ski runs between 9200ft and 11,500ft. The sea-son normally runs from November to April.

🛏 Sleeping

Unlike in southern Arizona, summer is high season here.

★Motel Dubeau HOSTEL $
(☑ 928-774-6731; www.modubeau.com; 19 W Phoe-nix Ave; dm/r from $27/53; ▣ ▣ @ ▣) Built in 1929 as Flagstaff's first motel, this independ-ent hostel offers the same friendly service and clean, well-run accommodations as its sister property, Grand Canyon Internation-al Hostel. The private rooms are similar to basic, but handsome, hotel rooms, with re-frigerators, cable TV and private bathrooms. On-site Nomads serves beer, wine and light snacks. There are also kitchen and laundry facilities.

Flagstaff KOA CAMPGROUND $
(☑ 928-526-9926, reservations 800-562-3524; www.flagstaffkoa.com; 5803 N Hwy 89; tent/RV site $33/38, cabins & tipis from $65; ▣ ▣ ▣) This big ponderosa-shaded campground lies a mile north of I-40 off exit 201, 5 miles northeast of downtown Flagstaff. A path leads from the campground to trails at Mt Elden, and it's family friendly, with banana-bike rentals, summer barrel-train rides, weekend movies and a splash park. The four one-room cabins sleep four, but bedding isn't supplied.

★Hotel Monte Vista HISTORIC HOTEL $$
(☑ 928-779-6971; www.hotelmontevista.com; 100 N San Francisco St; r/ste from $115/145; ▣ ▣) A huge, old-fashioned neon sign towers over this 1926 landmark hotel, hinting at what's inside: feather lampshades, vintage furni-ture, bold colors and eclectic decor. Rooms are named for the movie stars who stayed here, including the 'Humphrey Bogart,' with dramatic black walls, yellow ceiling and gold-satin bedding. Several resident ghosts supposedly make regular appearances.

★Inn at 410 B&B $$
(☑ 928-774-0088; www.inn410.com; 410 N Leroux St; r from $185; ▣ ▣ ▣) This fully renovated 1894 house offers 10 spacious, beautiful-ly decorated and themed bedrooms, each with a fridge and bathroom, and many with four-poster beds and delightful views. A short stroll from downtown, the inn has a shady orchard-garden and a cozy dining room, where a full gourmet breakfast and afternoon snacks are served.

🍴 Eating

Flagstaff's college population and general dedication to living well translate into one of the best dining scenes in the state. Self-caterers can try **Bashas'** (☑ 928-774-3882; www.bashas.com; 2700 S Woodlands Village Blvd; ☺ 6am-11pm), a good local chain supermarket with a respectable selection of organic foods. For healthy food, there's **Whole Foods Mar-ket** (☑ 928-774-5747; www.wholefoodsmarket.com; 320 S Cambridge Lane; ☺ 7am-9pm; ▣).

★Macy's CAFE $
(☑ 928-774-2243; www.macyscoffee.net; 14 S Beaver St; breakfast/lunch $6/7; ☺ 6am-6pm; ▣ ▣) The delicious coffee at this Flagstaff institution – house roasted in the original, handsome, fire-engine-red roaster in the corner – has kept local students and caf-feine devotees buzzing since the 1980s. The vegetarian menu includes many vegan choices, along with traditional cafe grub like pastries, steamed eggs, waffles, yogurt and granola, salads and veggie sandwiches.

Diablo Burger BURGERS $
(☑ 928-774-3274; www.diabloburger.com; 120 N Leroux St; mains $11-14; ☺ 11am-9pm Sun-Wed, 11am-10pm Thu-Sat; ▣) This locally focused gourmet-burger joint slings hefty burgers on English-muffin buns and delicious Herbes de Provence seasoned fries. The cheddar-topped Blake gives a nod to New Mexico with Hatch-chile mayo and roasted green chiles. The place is tiny, so come early or sit outside and people-watch. Beer and wine are also served.

★Criollo Latin Kitchen FUSION $$
(☑ 928-774-0541; www.criollolatinkitchen.com; 16 N San Francisco St; mains $17-20; ☺ 11am-9pm Mon-Fri, 9am-9pm Sat & Sun) ⌀ Sister to Brix Restaurant & Wine Bar and **Proper Meats + Provisions** (☑ 928-774-9001; www.propermeats.com; 110 S San Francisco St; sandwiches $12-13; ☺ 10am-7pm) ⌀, this on-trend Latin-fusion

restaurant gives similar encouragement to local producers, sourcing ingredients from Arizona wherever possible. Set up your day with the Haitian brunch of slow-roasted pork with over-easy eggs, pinto beans and Ti-Malice hot sauce, or come back at happy hour (3pm to 6pm Monday to Friday) for fish tacos and $4 margaritas.

★ **Brix Restaurant**
& Wine Bar   INTERNATIONAL **$$$**
(☑ 928-213-1021; www.brixflagstaff.com; 413 N San Francisco St; mains $30-32; ⊗ 5-9pm Sun & Tue-Thu, to 10pm Fri & Sat; ☑) Brix offers seasonal, locally sourced and generally top-notch fare in a handsome room with exposed brick walls and an intimate copper bar. Sister business Proper Meats + Provisions, supplies charcuterie, free-range pork and other fundamentals of lip-smacking dishes. The wine list is well curated, and reservations are recommended.

★ **Coppa Cafe**   CAFE **$$$**
(☑ 928-637-6813; www.coppacafe.net; 1300 S Milton Rd; lunch & brunch $11-15, mains $28-31; ⊗ 3-9pm Wed-Fri, 11am-3pm & 5-9pm Sat, 10am-3pm Sun; ☎) Brian Konefal and Paola Fioravanti, who met at an Italian culinary school, are the husband-and-wife team behind this friendly, art-strewn bistro with egg-yolk-yellow walls. Expect ingredients foraged from nearby woods (and further afield in Arizona) in dishes such as slow-roasted top loin with wild-flower butter, or clay-baked duck's egg with a 'risotto' of Sonoran wheat and wild herbs.

♟ **Drinking & Entertainment**

For details about festivals and music programs, call the Visitor Center or check www.flagstaff365.com. On Friday and Saturday nights in summer, people gather on blankets for free music and family movies at Heritage Sq. The fun starts at 5pm.

On Thursdays pick up a free copy of *Flagstaff Live!* (www.flaglive.com) for current shows and happenings around town.

★ **Hops on Birch**   PUB
(☑ 928-774-4011; www.hopsonbirch.com; 22 E Birch Ave; ⊗ 1:30pm-12:30am Mon-Thu, to 2am Fri, noon-2am Sat, noon-12.30am Sun) Simple and handsome, Hops on Birch has 34 rotating beers on tap, live music five nights a week and a friendly local-crowd vibe. In classic Flagstaff style, dogs are as welcome as humans.

DON'T MISS

WALNUT CANYON

The Sinagua cliff dwellings at **Walnut Canyon** (☑ 928-526-3367; www.nps.gov/waca; I-40 exit 204; adult/child under 16yr $8/free; ⊗ 8am-5pm Jun-Oct, 9am-5pm Nov-May, trails close 1hr earlier; ℗) are set in the nearly vertical walls of a small limestone butte amid this stunning forested canyon. The mile-long Island Trail steeply descends 185ft (more than 200 stairs), passing 25 rooms built under the natural overhangs of the curvaceous butte. A shorter, wheelchair-accessible Rim Trail affords several views of the cliff dwelling from across the canyon.

Monte Vista Cocktail Lounge   BAR
(☑ 928-779-6971; www.hotelmontevista.com; 100 N San Francisco St, Hotel Monte Vista; ⊗ 4pm-2am Mon-Sat) With a prime corner spot in downtown Flagstaff, complete with broad windows for people-watching, this former speakeasy in the historic Hotel Monte Vista has a pressed-tin ceiling, pool table, live music three nights a week, plus a Sunday quiz, karaoke and all-day 'happy hour' on Mondays.

ⓘ **Information**

USFS Flagstaff Ranger Station (☑ 928-526-0866; www.fs.usda.gov; 5075 N Hwy 89; ⊗ 8am-4pm Mon-Fri) Provides information on the Mt Elden, Humphreys Peak and O'Leary Peak areas north of Flagstaff.

Visitor Center (☑ 800-842-7293, 928-213-2951; www.flagstaffarizona.org; 1 E Rte 66; ⊗ 8am-5pm Mon-Sat, 9am-4pm Sun) Located inside the Amtrak station, the visitor center has a great Flagstaff Discovery map and tons of information on things to do.

ⓘ **Getting There & Around**

Greyhound (☑ 928-774-4573, 800-231-2222; www.greyhound.com; 880 E Butler Ave; ⊗ 10am-6.30am) stops in Flagstaff en route to/from Albuquerque, Las Vegas, Los Angeles and Phoenix. **Arizona Shuttle** (p848) and **Flagstaff Shuttle & Charter** (☑ 888-215-3105; www.flagshuttle.com) have shuttles that run between Flagstaff, Grand Canyon National Park, Williams, Sedona and Phoenix's Sky Harbor International Airport.

Operated by **Amtrak** (☑ 800-872-7245, 928-774-8679; www.amtrak.com; 1 E Rte 66; ⊗ 3:30am-10:30pm), the *Southwest Chief* stops at Flagstaff on its daily run between Chicago and Los Angeles.

Mountain Line Transit (📞 928-779-6624; www.mountainline.az.gov; one-way adult/child $1.25/0.60) has several fixed bus routes daily; pick up a user-friendly map at the visitor center. Buses are equipped with ramps for passengers in wheelchairs.

If you need a taxi, call **Action Cab** (📞 928-774-4427) or **Sun Taxi** (📞 928-774-7400; www.suntaxi andtours.com). Several major car-rental agencies operate from the airport and downtown.

Williams

Affable Williams, 60 miles south of Grand Canyon Village and 35 miles west of Flagstaff, is a gateway town with character. Classic motels and diners line Route 66, and the old-school homes and train station give a nod to simpler times.

Most tourists visit to ride the turn-of-the-20th-century **Grand Canyon Railway** (📞 reservations 800-843-8724; www.thetrain.com; 233 N Grand Canyon Blvd, Railway Depot; round-trip adult/child from $79/47) to the Canyon's South Rim, which departs Williams 9:30am and returns at 5:45pm. Even if you're not a train buff, a trip is a scenic stress-free way to visit the Grand Canyon. Characters in period costumes provide historical and regional narration, and banjo folk music sets the tone.

The **Red Garter Inn** (📞 928-635-1484; www.redgarter.com; 137 W Railroad Ave; d from $170; ❄🛜) is an 1897 bordello turned B&B where the ladies used to hang out the windows to flag down customers. The four rooms have nice period touches and the downstairs bakery has good coffee. The funky little **Grand Canyon Hotel** (📞 928-635-1419; www.thegrand canyonhotel.com; 145 W Route 66; dm/r from $33/87; ⊗ Mar-Nov; ❄🛜) has small themed rooms, a six-bed dorm and no TVs. You can also sleep inside a 1929 Santa Fe caboose or a Pullman railcar at the **Canyon Motel & RV Park** (📞 928-635-9371, 800-482-3955; www.the canyonmotel.com; 1900 E Rodeo Rd; tent/RV sites from $31/44, cottages/cabooses from $90/180; ❄🛜🏊🐾), just east of downtown.

Grand Canyon National Park

No matter how much you read about the **Grand Canyon** (📞 928-638-7888; www.nps. gov/grca; 20 South Entrance Rd; ⊗ 7-day entry per car/individual $30/15), or how many photographs you've seen, nothing really prepares you for the sight of it. The sheer immensity of the canyon grabs you first, followed by the dramatic layers of rock, which pull you in for a closer look. Next up are the artistic details – rugged plateaus, crumbly spires, maroon ridges – that flirt and catch your eye as shadows flicker across the rock.

Snaking along its floor are 277 miles of the Colorado River, which has carved the canyon over the past six million years and exposed rocks up to two billion years old – half the age of the earth. The two rims of the Grand Canyon offer quite different experiences; they lie more than 200 miles apart by road and are rarely visited on the same trip. Most visitors choose the South Rim with its easy access, wealth of services and vistas that don't disappoint. The quieter North Rim has its own charms; at 8200ft elevation (1000ft higher than the South Rim), its cooler temperatures support wildflower meadows and tall, thick stands of aspen and spruce.

June is the driest month, July and August the wettest. January has average overnight lows of 13°F (-11°C) to 20°F (-7°C) and daytime highs around 40°F (4°C). Summer temperatures inside the canyon regularly soar above 100°F (38°C). While the South Rim is open year-round, most visitors come between late May and early September. The North Rim is open from mid-May to mid-October.

ℹ Information

The most developed area in the Grand Canyon National Park is **Grand Canyon Village**, 6 miles north of the South Rim Entrance Station. The North Rim has one entrance, which is 30 miles south of Jacob Lake on Hwy 67; continue another 14 miles south to the actual rim. The North and South Rims are 215 miles apart by car, 21 miles on foot through the canyon, or 10 miles as the condor flies

The park entrance ticket is valid for seven days and can be used at both rims. All overnight hikes and backcountry camping in the park require a permit. The **Backcountry Information Center** (📞 928-638-7875; www.nps.gov/grca; Grand Canyon Village; ⊗ 8am-noon & 1-5pm, phone staffed 8am-5pm Mon-Fri; 🖥 Village) accepts applications for backpacking permits ($10, plus $8 per person per night) starting four months before the proposed month. Your chances are decent if you apply early and provide alternative hiking itineraries. Reservations are accepted in person or by mail or fax, not by phone or email. For more information see www.nps.gov/grca/planyourvisit/backcountry-permit.htm.

If you arrive at the South Rim without a permit, head to the backcountry office, by **Maswik**

Lodge (☎ 888-297-2757, ext 6784, front desk & reservations within 48hr 928-638-2631; www.grandcanyonlodges.com; Grand Canyon Village; r South/North $107/205; ⓟ ✳ @ ☎; ☐ Village), to join the waiting list. As a conservation measure, the park no longer sells bottled water. Fill your flask at water filling stations along the rim or at **Canyon Village Market** (p859).

South Rim

If you don't mind bumping elbows with other travelers, you'll be fine on the South Rim, where you'll find an entire village worth of lodging, restaurants, bookstores, libraries, a supermarket and a deli. Museums and historic stone buildings illuminate the park's human history, and rangers lead daily programs on subjects from geology to resurgent condors. In summer, when day-trippers converge en masse, escaping the crowds can be as easy as taking a day hike below the rim or merely tramping a hundred yards away from a scenic overlook.

 Activities

Driving & Hiking

A **scenic route** follows the rim on the west side of Grand Canyon Village along Hermit Rd. Closed to private vehicles March through November, the 7-mile road is serviced by free park shuttle buses; cycling is encouraged because of the relatively light traffic. Stops offer spectacular views, and interpretive signs explain canyon features.

Desert View Drive starts east of Grand Canyon Village and follows the canyon rim for 26 miles to Desert View, the east entrance of the park. Pullouts offer tremendous views.

Hiking trails along the South Rim include options for every skill level. The **Rim Trail** is the most popular, and easiest, walk in the park. It dips in and out of the scrubby pines of Kaibab National Forest to connect scenic points and historical sights over 13 miles. Portions are paved, and every viewpoint is accessed by one of the three shuttle routes. Along the **Trail of Time**, bordering the Rim Trail just west of Yavapai Geology Museum, every meter represents one million years of geologic history.

Hiking down into the canyon itself is a serious undertaking; most visitors are content with short day hikes. Bear in mind that the climb back out of the canyon is much harder than the descent into it, and do not attempt to hike all the way to the Colorado River and

SUNSET CRATER VOLCANO NATIONAL MONUMENT

Around AD 1064 a volcano erupted on this spot, spewing ash across 800 sq miles, spawning the Kana-A lava flow and forcing farmers to vacate lands tilled for 400 years. Now the 8029ft **Sunset Crater Volcano National Monument** (☎928-526-0502; www.nps.gov/sucr; Park Loop Rd 545; car/motorcycle/bicycle or pedestrian $20/15/10; ⊗9am-5pm Nov-May, from 8am Jun-Oct) is quiet, and mile-long trails wind through the Bonito lava flow (formed c 1180), and up Lenox Crater (7024ft). More ambitious hikers and bikers can ascend O'Leary Peak (8965ft; 8 miles round-trip), or there's a gentle, 0.3-mile, wheelchair-accessible loop overlooking the petrified flow.

Sunset Crater is 19 miles northeast of Flagstaff. Access fees include entry to nearby **Wupatki National Monument** (☎928-679-2365; www.nps.gov/wupa; Park Loop Rd 545; car/motorcycle/bicycle or pedestrian $20/15/10; ⊗ visitor center 9am-5pm, trails sunrise-sunset; ⓟ ♿), and are valid for seven days.

back in a single day. On the most popular route, the beautiful **Bright Angel Trail**, the scenic 8-mile drop to the river is punctuated with four logical turnaround spots. Summer heat can be crippling; day hikers should either turn around at one of the two resthouses (a 3- or 6-mile round-trip) or hit the trail at dawn to safely make the longer hikes to **Indian Garden** and **Plateau Point** (9.2- and 12.2-mile round-trips, respectively).

The steeper and much more exposed **South Kaibab Trail** is one of the park's prettiest routes, combining stunning scenery and unobstructed 360-degree views with every step. Hikers overnighting at **Phantom Ranch** generally descend this way, and return the next day via the Bright Angel. Summer ascents can be dangerous, and during this season rangers advise day hikers to turn around at **Cedar Ridge** (about 3 miles round-trip).

Cycling

Bright Angel Bicycles & Cafe at Mather Point   CYCLING
(☎928-814-8704, 928-638-3055; www.bikegrandcanyon.com; 10 S Entrance Rd, Visitor Center Plaza; 24hr rental adult/child 16yr & under $40/30, 5hr

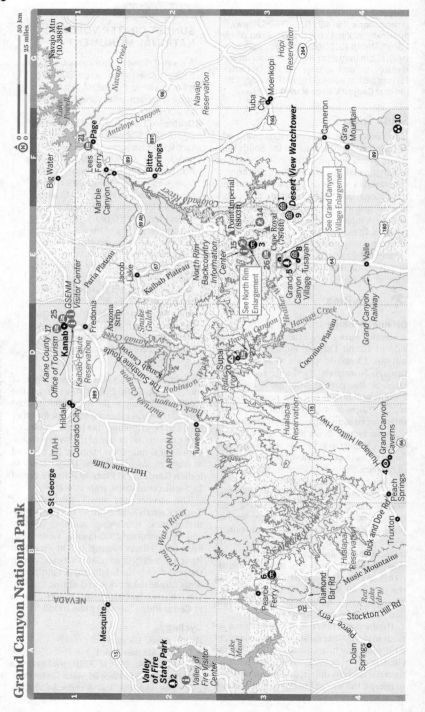

Grand Canyon National Park

SOUTHWEST GRAND CANYON NATIONAL PARK

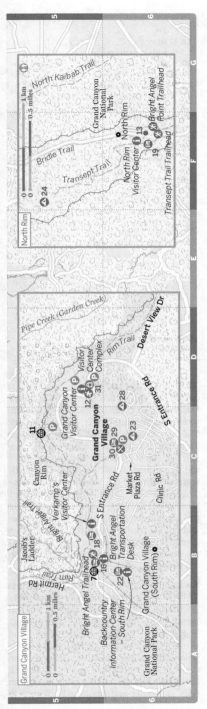

rental $30/20, wheelchair $10, s/d stroller up to 8hr $18/27; ⊘7am-5pm Mar-Oct; 🚌Village, 🚌Kaibab/ Rim) Half-or full-day bicycle rentals, with helmets and an add-on pull-along trailer option, can be reserved in advance online or by phone. With the exception of the peak stretch from July through mid-August, however, walk-ins can usually be accommodated. Hermit Rd bicycle-shuttle packages allow you to ride past overlooks going one way, and hop on one of their private shuttles the other.

👉 Tours

⭐**Canyon Vistas Mule Rides**   TOURS
(☑888-297-2757, same day/next day reservations 928-638-3283; www.grandcanyonlodges.com; Bright Angel Lodge; 3hr mule ride $135, 1-/2-night mule ride incl meals & accommodation $552/788; ⊘rides available year-round, hours vary) This outfit takes groups of up to 20 mules 4 miles along the East Rim Trail. If you want to descend into the canyon, the only option is an overnight trip to Phantom Ranch. These trips follow the Bright Angel Trail 10.5 miles (5½ hours) down, spend one or two nights at Phantom Ranch, and return 7.8 miles (five hours) along the South Kaibab Trail.

🛏 Sleeping

The South Rim's six lodges are operated by **Xanterra** (☑888-297-2757, 303-297-2757, 928-638-3283; www.grandcanyonlodges.com). Contact them to make advance reservations (essential in summer), although it's best to call Phantom Ranch, down beside the Colorado River, directly. For same-day reservations or to reach a guest, call the South Rim **switchboard** (☑928-638-2631). If you can't find accommodations in the national park, try Tusayan (at South Rim Entrance Station), Valle (31 miles south), Cameron (53 miles east), Williams (about 60 miles south) or Flagstaff (80 miles southeast). All campgrounds and lodges are open year-round except Desert View.

Phantom Ranch   CABIN $
(☑888-297-2757, same day or next-day reservations 928-638-3283; www.grandcanyonlodges.com; dm $49, cabin d $142; ❄) Bunks at this camplike complex on the canyon floor are spread across cozy private cabins sleeping up to four people and single-sex dorms for 10 people. Rates include bedding, liquid soap and towels, but meals are extra and must be reserved when booking your bunk. Phantom

Grand Canyon National Park

⊙ Top Sights
1 Desert View Watchtower F3
2 Valley of Fire State Park A2

◎ Sights
3 Bright Angel Point E3
4 Grand Canyon Caverns & Inn C4
5 Grand Canyon National Park E3
6 Grand Canyon West (West Rim) B3
7 Kolb Studio B5
8 National Geographic Visitor
   Center & IMAX Theater E3
9 Tusayan Museum & Ruins E3
10 Wupatki National Monument F4
11 Yavapai Geology Museum C5

☺ Activities, Courses & Tours
12 Bright Angel Bicycles & Cafe at
   Mather Point D5
13 Canyon Trail Rides F6
   Canyon Vistas Mule Rides .... (see 7)
14 Cape Final Trail E3
15 North Kaibab Trail E3
   Roger Ekis' Antelope
   Canyon Tours .... (see 21)

🛏 Sleeping
16 Bright Angel Lodge B5
17 Canyons Lodge D1
   Desert View Campground .... (see 1)

18 El Tovar B5
19 Grand Canyon Lodge F6
20 Havasu Campground D3
21 Lake Powell Motel F1
22 Maswik Lodge B6
23 Mather Campground C6
24 North Rim Campground F5
25 Parry Lodge D1
26 Phantom Ranch E3
27 Supai Lodge D3
28 Trailer Village D6
29 Yavapai Lodge C6

⊗ Eating
   Arizona Room .... (see 16)
   Big John's Texas BBQ .... (see 21)
   Bright Angel Ice-Cream
   Fountain .... (see 16)
30 Canyon Village Market C6
   El Tovar Dining Room &
   Lounge .... (see 18)
   Grand Canyon Lodge Dining
   Room .... (see 19)
   Ranch House Grille .... (see 21)
   Rocking V Cafe .... (see 25)
   Sego Restaurant .... (see 17)
   Yavapai Lodge Restaurant .... (see 29)

⊙ Shopping
31 Visitor Center Plaza Park Store D5

is only accessible by mule trip, on foot or via raft on the Colorado River.

Desert View Campground   CAMPGROUND $
(www.nps.gov/grca; Desert View; campsites $12; ☺mid-Apr–mid-Oct) In a forest near the East Entrance, this first-come, first-served 50-site NPS campground is quieter than campgrounds in the Village, with a spread-out design that ensures a bit of privacy. The best time to secure a spot is mid-morning, when people are breaking camp. It usually fills by midafternoon. Facilities include toilets and drinking water, but no showers or hookups.

Trailer Village   CARAVAN PARK $
(☑877-404-4611, same-day booking 928-638-1006; www.visitgrandcanyon.com; Trailer Village Rd; hookups $45; ☺year-round; 🖵Village) A trailer park with RVs lined up tightly at paved pull-through sites on a rather barren patch of ground. You'll find picnic tables, barbecue grills and full hookups, but coin-operated showers and laundry are a quarter-mile away at Mather Campground (☑877-444-6777, late arrival 928-638-7851; www.recreation.gov; 1 Mather Campground Rd; sites $18; ☺year-round; 🛜; 🖵Village).

★ Bright Angel Lodge   LODGE $$
(☑888-297-2757, ext 6285, front desk & reservations within 48hr 928-638-2631; www.grandcanyonlodges.com; Village Loop Dr; r with/without bath $110/89, cabins/ste $197/426; 🅿🛜; 🖵Village) This 1935 log-and-stone lodge on the canyon ledge delivers simple historic charm by the bucketload. Small public spaces bustle with activity, and the transportation desk (☑928-638-3283; Bright Angel Lodge; ☺5am-8pm summer; 🖵Village) in the lobby is the central contact for hiking services, mule rides and guided trips. Though the lodges are an excellent economy option, historic cabins are brighter, airier and have tasteful Western character.

Yavapai Lodge   MOTEL $$
(☑877-404-4611, reservations within 48hr 928-638-6421; www.visitgrandcanyon.com; 11 Yavapai Lodge Rd; r from $153; ☺year-round; 🅿✳@🛜🐾; 🖵Village) Basic one- and two-story motel-style lodgings cluster in the piñon and juniper forest about a mile from the rim. Air-conditioned rooms at Yavapai East sleep four to six, and offer two queen beds or a king and bunk beds. Rooms in

Yavapai West sleep up to four and do not have air-conditioning.

★ El Tovar — LODGE $$$

(☏888-297-2757, ext 6380, front desk & reservations within 48hr 928-638-2631; www.grandcanyon lodges.com; Village Loop Dr; r/ste from $187/381; ⊗year-round; 🅿❄🛜; 🚻Village) Stuffed mounts. Thick pine walls. Sturdy fireplaces. Is this the fanciest hotel on the South Rim or a backcountry hunting lodge? Despite renovations, this rambling 1905 wooden lodge hasn't lost a lick of its genteel historic patina, or its charm.

✖ Eating & Drinking

Grand Canyon Village has all the eating options you need, whether it's picking up picnic sandwiches at **Canyon Village Market** (☏928-638-2262; Market Plaza; ⊗6:30am-9pm May 19–Sep 13, shorter hours rest of year; 🚻Village), an après-hike ice-cream cone at **Bright Angel Ice-Cream Fountain** (☏928-638-2631; www.grandcanyonlodges.com; Bright Angel Lodge; mains $4-6; ⊗11am-6pm May-Sep, shorter hours rest of year; 👶; 🚻Village) or a sit-down celebratory dinner at El Tovar Dining Room.

Yavapai Lodge Restaurant — AMERICAN $

(☏928-638-6421; www.visitgrandcanyon.com; 11 Yavapai Lodge Rd, Yavapai Lodge; breakfast $7-9, lunch & dinner $13-16; ⊗6am-10pm May-Sep, shorter hours rest of year; 👶; 🚻Village) The restaurant at the Yavapai Lodge serves barbecue and sandwiches as well as beer and wine. Place your order, pick up your drinks, and your number will get called when the food is ready.

★ El Tovar Dining Room & Lounge — AMERICAN $$$

(☏928-638-2631; www.grandcanyonlodges.com; National Historic Landmark District; mains $20-30; ⊗restaurant 6-10:30am, 11am-2pm & 4:30-10pm, lounge 11am-11pm; 👶; 🚻Village) Dark-wood tables are set with china and white linen, eye-catching murals spotlight American Indian tribes and huge windows frame views of the Rim Trail and canyon beyond. Breakfast options include El Tovar's pancake trio (buttermilk, blue cornmeal and buckwheat pancakes with pine-nut butter and prickly pear syrup), and blackened trout with two eggs.

Arizona Room — AMERICAN $$$

(☏928-638-2631; www.grandcanyonlodges.com; 9 Village Loop Dr, Bright Angel Lodge; lunch $13-16, dinner $22-28; ⊗11:30am-3pm & 4:30-10pm Jan-Oct; 👶; 🚻Village) Antler chandeliers hang from the ceiling and picture windows overlook the Rim Trail and canyon beyond. Try to get on the waitlist when the doors open at 4:30pm, because by 4:40pm you may have an hour's wait – reservations are not accepted. Agave and citrus-marinated chicken, oven-roasted squash and ribs with chipotle barbecue give a Western vibe.

ⓘ Information

SOUTH RIM VISITOR CENTERS

Grand Canyon Visitor Center (☏928-638-7888; www.nps.gov/grca; Visitor Center Plaza, Grand Canyon Village; ⊗9am-5pm; 🚻Village, 🚻Kaibab/Rim) Three hundred yards behind Mather Point, a large plaza holds the visitor center and the **Visitor Center Plaza Park Store** (☏800-858-2808; www.grandcanyon. org; Visitor Center Plaza; ⊗8am-8pm Jun-Aug, shorter hours rest of year; 🚻Village, Kaibab/Rim). Outdoor bulletin boards display information about trails, tours, ranger programs and the weather.

National Geographic Visitor Center (☏928-638-2203; www.explorethecanyon.com; 450 Hwy 64; adult/child $14/11; ⊗visitor center 8am-10pm Mar-Oct, 10am-8pm Nov-Feb, theater 8:30am-8:30pm Mar-Oct, 9:30am-6:30pm Nov-Feb; 🚻Tusayan) In Tusayan, 7 miles south of Grand Canyon Village; pay your $30 vehicle entrance fee here to spare yourself a potentially long wait at the park entrance. The IMAX theater screens the terrific film *Grand Canyon – The Hidden Secrets*. In addition to the visitor centers already mentioned, information is available inside the park:

Desert View Watchtower (www.nps.gov/grca; Desert View, East Enrance; ⊗8am-sunset mid-May–Aug, 9am-6pm Sep–mid-Oct, 9am-5pm mid-Oct–Feb, 8am-6pm Mar–mid-May)

Kolb Studio (☏928-638-2771; www.nps.gov/grca; National Historic Landmark District; ⊗8am-7pm Mar-May & Sep-Nov, to 6pm Dec-Feb, to 8pm Jun-Aug; 🚻Village)

Tusayan Museum & Ruins (www.nps.gov/grca; Desert View Dr; ⊗9am-5pm)

Verkamp's Visitor Center (☏928-638-7888; www.nps.gov/grca; Rim Trail; ⊗8am-8pm Jun-Aug, shorter hrs rest of year; 🚻Village)

Yavapai Geology Museum (☏928-638-7890; www.nps.gov/grca; Grand Canyon Village; ⊗8am-7pm Mar-May & Sep-Nov, to 6pm Dec-Feb, to 8pm Jun-Aug; 👶; 🚻Kaibab/Rim)

ⓘ Getting There & Around

Most people arrive at the canyon in private vehicles or on a tour. Parking can be a chore in Grand Canyon Village. Once inside the park, free park shuttles operate along three routes: around

Grand Canyon Village, west along Hermits Rest Route and east along Kaibab Trail Route. Buses typically run every 15 minutes, from one hour before sunset to one hour afterward. In summer a free shuttle from Bright Angel Lodge, the Hiker's Express, has early-morning pickups at the Backcountry Information Center and Grand Canyon Visitor Center, and then heads to the South Kaibab trailhead.

North Rim

Solitude reigns supreme on the North Rim. There are no shuttles or bus tours, no museums, shopping centers, schools or garages. In fact, there isn't much of anything here beyond a classic rimside national park lodge, a campground, a motel, a general store and miles of trails carving through sunny meadows thick with wildflowers, willowy aspen and towering ponderosa pines

The entrance to the North Rim is 24 miles south of **Jacob Lake** on Hwy 67; Grand Canyon Lodge lies another 20 miles beyond. At 8000ft, it's about 10°F (6°C) cooler here than the South Rim – even on summer evenings you'll need a sweater. All facilities on the North Rim are closed from mid-October to mid-May, although you can drive into the park and stay at the campground until snow closes the road from Jacob Lake.

🏃 Activities

The short and easy paved trail (0.5 miles) to **Bright Angel Point** (www.nps.gov; North Rim) is a canyon must. Beginning from the back porch of Grand Canyon Lodge, it goes to a narrow finger of an overlook with fabulous views.

The **North Kaibab Trail**, the North Rim's only maintained rim-to-river trail, connects with trails to the South Rim in the Phantom Ranch (p858) area. The first 4.7 miles are the steepest, dropping 3050ft to **Roaring Springs** – a popular all-day hike. If you prefer a shorter day hike below the rim, walk just 0.75 miles down to **Coconino Overlook**, or 2 miles to the **Supai Tunnel** to get a taste of steep inner-canyon hiking. The 28-mile round-trip to the Colorado River is a multiday affair.

For a short hike up on the rim, which works well for families, try the 4-mile round-trip **Cape Final Trail**, on the **Walhalla Plateau** east of Grand Canyon Lodge, which leads through ponderosa pines to sweeping views of the eastern Grand Canyon area.

Canyon Trail Rides TOURS
(📞 435-679-8665; www.canyonrides.com; North Rim; 1hr/half-day mule ride $45/90; ⊙ schedules vary mid-May–mid-Oct) You can make reservations anytime for the upcoming year, but, unlike mule trips on the South Rim, you can usually book a trip upon your arrival at the park; just duck inside the Grand Canyon Lodge to the Mule Desk. Rides don't reach the Colorado River, but the half-day trip gives a taste of life below the rim.

🛏 Sleeping

North Rim Campground CAMPGROUND $
(📞 877-444-6777, 928-638-7814; www.recreation. gov; tent sites $18, RV sites $18-25; ⊙ by reservation May 15-Oct 15, first-come, first-served Oct 16-31; 🐾) Operated by the National Park Service, this campground, 1.5 miles north of the Grand Canyon Lodge, offers shaded sites on level ground blanketed in pine needles. Sites 11, 14, 15, 16 and 18 overlook the Transept (a side canyon) and cost $25. There's water, a store, a snack bar, coin-operated showers and laundry facilities, but no hookups. Make reservations online.

⭐ **Grand Canyon Lodge** HISTORIC HOTEL $$
(📞 advance reservations 877-386-4383, reservations outside USA 480-337-1320, same-day reservations 928-638-2611; www.grandcanyonlodgenorth.com; r/ cabins from $130/143; ⊙ May 15-Oct 15) 🌿 Walk through the front door of the lodge, and here, framed by picture windows, is the canyon in all its glory. Built in 1937 with wood, Kaibab limestone and glass, the lodge features a spacious rimside dining room and sun porches lined with Adirondack chairs. Guest rooms are not in the lodge itself – most accommodations are cozy log cabins nearby.

🍴 Eating

⭐ **Grand Canyon
Lodge Dining Room** AMERICAN $$
(📞 May-Oct 928-638-2611, Nov-Apr 928-645-6865; www.grandcanyonforever.com; breakfast $8-11, lunch $10-13, dinner $18-28; ⊙ 6:30-10:30am, 11:30am-2:30pm & 4:30-9:30pm May 15-Oct 15; 🌿♿) Although seats beside the window are wonderful, views from the dining room are so huge it really doesn't matter where you sit. While the solid dinner menu includes buffalo steak, western trout and several vegetarian options, don't expect great culinary memories – the view is the thing. Make reservations in advance of your arrival to guarantee a spot for dinner.

ℹ Information

North Rim Backcountry Information Center
(☑ 928-638-7875; www.nps.gov/grca; Administrative Bldg; ⊘ 8am-noon & 1-5pm May 15-Oct 15) Backcountry permits for overnight camping on and below the rim, at Tuweep Campground, or camping anytime between November 1 and May 14.

North Rim Visitor Center (☑ 928-638-7888; www.nps.gov/grca; ⊘ 8am-6pm May 15-Oct 15) Beside Grand Canyon Lodge, this is the place to get information on the park, and the starting point for ranger-led nature walks.

ℹ Getting There & Away

The only access road to the Grand Canyon North Rim is Hwy 67, which closes with the first snowfall and reopens in spring after the snowmelt (exact dates vary).

Although only 11 miles from the South Rim as the crow flies, it's a grueling 215-mile, four- to five-hour drive on winding desert roads between here and Grand Canyon Village. You can drive yourself or take the **Trans-Canyon Shuttle** (☑ 928-638-2820, 877-638-2820; www.trans-canyonshuttle.com; one-way rim to rim $90, one-way South Rim to Marble Canyon $80). Reserve at least two weeks in advance.

Around the Grand Canyon

Havasupai Canyon

In a hidden side canyon off the Colorado River, complete with stunning, spring-fed waterfalls and azure swimming holes, this beautiful spot is hard to reach, but the hike down and back up makes the trip unique – and an amazing adventure.

Located on the Havasupai Indian Reservation, Havasu Canyon is just 35 miles directly west of the South Rim, but it's more like 195 miles by road. The four falls lie 10 miles below the rim, accessed via a moderately challenging hiking trail that starts from Hualapai Hilltop, and is reached by following a 62-mile road that leaves Route 66 7 miles east of Peach Springs.

All trips require an overnight stay, which must be reserved in advance, and there's a $50 entrance fee for all guests.

The village of Supai, 8 miles along the trail, is home to **Supai Lodge** (☑ 928-448-2201, 928-448-2111; www.havasuwaterfalls.net; Supai; r for up to 4 people $145; ✳), where basic motel-style rooms have nothing to recom-

mend them bar the location. Check in by 5pm, when the lobby closes. A village cafe serves meals and accepts credit cards.

The **Havasu Campground** (☑ 928-448-2180, 928-448-2141, 928-448-2121, 928-443-2137; www.havasuwaterfalls.net; Havasu Canyon; sites per person per night $25), 2 miles beyond, has primitive campsites along a creek; every camper must pay an additional $10 environmental fee. Continue deeper into Havasu Canyon to reach the waterfalls and blue-green swimming holes. If you don't want to hike to Supai, call the lodge or campground to arrange for a mule or horse (one-way/round-trip to Lodge $121/242) to carry you there.

Hualapai Reservation

Run by the Hualapai Nation, around 215 driving miles west of the South Rim or 70 miles northeast of Kingman, the remote site known as Grand Canyon West is not part of Grand Canyon National Park. The rough road out here is partly unpaved, and unsuitable for RVs (though Joshua-tree forests and other scenic delights make it worth the effort).

Grand Canyon West (West Rim) VIEWPOINT
(☑ 888-868-9378, 928-769-2636; www.grandcanyonwest.com; Hualapai Reservation; per person $44-81; ⊘ 7am-7pm Apr-Sep, 8am-5pm Oct-Mar) Nowadays, the only way to visit Grand Canyon West, the section of the Grand Canyon overseen by the Hualapai Nation, is to purchase a package tour. These include a hop-on, hop-off shuttle ride, which loops to scenic points along the rim. Tours can include lunch, cowboy activities at an ersatz Western town and informal American Indian performances.

Northern & Eastern Arizona

Between the brooding buttes of Monument Valley, the blue waters of Lake Powell and the fossilized logs of the Petrified Forest National Park are photogenic lands locked in ancient history. Inhabited by Native Americans for centuries, this region is dominated by the Navajo reservation – widely known as the Navajo Nation – which spills into surrounding states. The Hopi reservation is here as well, completely surrounded by Navajo land.

Lake Powell

The country's second-largest artificial reservoir, Lake Powell, stretches north from Arizona into Utah. Set amid striking red-rock formations, sharply cut canyons and dramatic desert scenery, and part of the **Glen Canyon National Recreation Area** (☎928-608-6200; www.nps.gov/glca; 7-day pass per vehicle $25, per pedestrian or cyclist $12), it's water-sports heaven

The lake was created by the construction of Glen Canyon Dam, 2.5 miles north of what's now the region's central town, Page. The Carl Hayden Visitor Center is located beside the dam.

To visit other-worldly **Antelope Canyon**, a stunning sandstone slot canyon, you must join a Navajo-led tour. Several tour companies offer trips into **Upper Antelope Canyon**, which is easier to navigate. Expect a bumpy ride and a bit of a cattle call; try **Roger Ekis' Antelope Canyon Tours** (☎928-645-9102; www.antelopecanyon.com; 22 S Lake Powell Blvd; adult/child 5-12yr from $45/35). The more strenuous **Lower Antelope Canyon** sees much smaller crowds.

A deservedly popular hike is the 1.5 mile round-trip to **Horseshoe Bend**, where the Colorado wraps around a dramatic stone outcropping to form a perfect U on a jaw-dropping scale. The trailhead is south of Page off Hwy 89, across from mile marker 541.

Chain hotels line Page's main strip, Hwy89, but there are independent alternatives along 8th Ave. The revamped **Lake Powell Motel** (☎480-452-9895; www.lakepowellmotel.net; 750 S Navajo Dr; ste from $99, r with kitchen from $139; ☉Apr-Oct; ❈🐾) was originally built to house workers building the Glen Canyon Dam; four of its units have kitchens, and book up quickly, while a fifth, smaller room is usually held for walk-ins.

For breakfast in Page, the **Ranch House Grille** (☎928-645-1420; www.ranchhousegrille.com; 819 N Navajo Dr; mains $9-14; ☉6am-3pm) has good food, huge portions and fast service. If you're in need of a more substantial feed, later in the day, **Big John's Texas BBQ** (☎928-645-3300; www.bigjohnstexasbbq.com; 153 S Lake Powell Blvd; mains $13-18; ☉11am-10pm; 🐾) is an unabashed celebration of meat and smoke.

Navajo Nation

The Navajo Nation is vast: at 27,000 sq miles it's bigger than some US states, and spreads across the junction of Arizona, New Mexico, Colorado and Utah. It also contains natural beauty of staggering richness, and, of course, the living culture, language, institutions, farms and homes of the Diné (Navajo). America's largest Indian nation.

Unlike the rest of Arizona, the Navajo Nation observes mountain daylight saving time. During summer, the reservation is one hour ahead of Arizona. For details about hiking and camping, and required permits, visit www.navajonationparks.org.

CAMERON

Cameron, a historic settlement that serves as the gateway to the east entrance of the Grand Canyon's South Rim, is one of the few worthwhile stops on Hwy 89 between Flagstaff and Page. The Cameron Trading Post, just north of the Hwy 64 turnoff to the Grand Canyon, offers food, lodging, a gift shop and a post office.

NAVAJO NATIONAL MONUMENT

The sublimely well-preserved Ancestral Puebloan cliff dwellings of Betatakin and Keet Seel are protected within the **Navajo National Monument** (☎928-672-2700; www.nps.gov/nava; Hwy 564; ☉visitor center 8am-5:30pm Jun-early Sep, 9am-5pm early Sep-May) **FREE** and can only be reached on foot. This walk in the park is no walk in the park, but there's truly something magical about approaching these ancient stone villages in relative solitude, among the piñon and juniper. The National Park Service controls access to the site and maintains the visitor center, which is informative and has excellent staff.

During summer months the park observes daylight saving time.

CANYON DE CHELLY NATIONAL MONUMENT

The many-fingered Canyon De Chelly (duh-shay) contains several beautiful Ancestral Puebloan sites, including ancient cliff dwellings. For centuries, though, it has been home to Navajo farmers, who winter on the rims then move to hogans (traditional roundhouses) on the canyon floor in spring and summer. The canyon is private Navajo property administered by the NPS. Enter hogans only with a guide and don't photograph people without their permission.

The only lodging in the park is **Thunderbird Lodge** (☎928-674-5842, 800-679-2473; http://thunderbirdlodge.com; Rural Rte 7; d/ste $100/110; ❈🐾❈), just outside the canyon itself. It has comfortable rooms and an inexpensive cafeteria serving Navajo and American meals. The nearby Navajo-run campground has about 90 sites on a first-come, first-served basis ($10), with water but no showers.

The Canyon de Chelly **visitor center** (✆928-674-5500; www.nps.gov/cach; ☺8am-5pm) is 3 miles off Rte 191, beyond the small village of Chinle, near the mouth of the canyon. Two scenic drives follow the canyon's rim, but you can only explore the canyon floor on a guided tour. Stop by the visitor center, or check the park website, for a list of tour companies. The only unguided hiking trail you can follow in the park is a short but very spectacular round-trip route that descends to the amazing **White House Ruin**.

MONUMENT VALLEY NAVAJO TRIBAL PARK

When Monument Valley rises into sight from the desert floor, you realize you've always known it. Its brick-red spindles, sheer-walled mesas and grand buttes, stars of countless films, TV commercials and magazine ads, are part of the modern consciousness. And Monument Valley's epic beauty is only heightened by the barren landscape surrounding it: one minute you're in the middle of sand, rocks and infinite sky, then suddenly you're transported to a fantasyland of crimson sandstone towers, thrusting up to 1200ft skyward.

For up-close views of the towering formations, visit the **Monument Valley Navajo Tribal Park** (✆435-727-5870; www.navajo nationparks.org; per 4-person vehicle $20; ☺drive 6am-7pm Apr-Sep, 8am-4:30pm Oct-Mar, visitor center 6am-8pm Apr-Sep, 8am-5pm Oct-Mar; P), where a rough and unpaved scenic driving loop covers 17 miles of stunning valley views. You can drive it yourself, or arrange a tour through one of the kiosks in the parking lot, which will take you to areas where private vehicles can't go (1½ hours $75; two-hour trail ride $98).

Inside the tribal park, the sandstone-colored **View Hotel** (✆435-727-5555; www.monumentvalleyview.com; Indian Rte 42; r/ste from $247/349; ❄@✆) blends naturally with its surroundings, and most of the 96 rooms have private balconies facing the monuments. The Navajo-accented food at the adjoining restaurant (mains $11 to $15, no alcohol) aren't life-changing, but the vista makes up for all.

The peerlessly-situated **View Campground** (✆435-727-5802; http://monument valleyview.com/campground; Indian Rte 42; tent/RV sites $20/40) is a cheaper option, while historic **Goulding's Lodge** (✆435-727-3231; www.gouldings.com; Monument Valley, Utah; d/ste from $184/199; P❄✆✆❄), just over the road in Utah, offers basic rooms, camping and small cabins. Book early for summer. Kayenta, 20 miles south, has a handful of acceptable motels and borderline-acceptable restaurants; try the **Wetherill Inn** (✆928-697-3231; www.wetherill-inn.com; 1000 Main St/Hwy 163; r $149; ❄✆❄) if everything in Monument Valley is booked.

RAFTING THE COLORADO

A boat trip down the Colorado is an epic, adrenaline-pumping adventure, which will take you beyond contact with civilization for several nights. The biggest single drop at Lava Falls plummets 37ft in just 300yd. But the true highlight is experiencing the Grand Canyon by looking up, not down from the rim. Its human history comes alive in ruins, wrecks and rock art. Commercial trips run from three days to three weeks and vary in the type of watercraft used.

Arizona Raft Adventures (✆800-786-7238, 928-526-8200; www.azraft.com; 6-day Upper Canyon hybrid/paddle trips $2097/2197, 10-day Full Canyon motor trips $3160) This multigenerational-family-run outfit offers motor, paddle, oar and hybrid (with opportunities for both paddling and floating) trips. Music fans can join one of the folk and bluegrass trips, with professional pickers and banjo players providing background music.

Arizona River Runners (✆602-867-4866, 800-477-7238; www.raftarizona.com; 6-day Upper Canyon oar trip $1984, 8-day Full Canyon motor trip $2772) At their game since 1970, this outfit offers oar-powered and motorized trips. Arizona River Runners specializes in family trips as well as 'Hiker's Special' trips that take place over six to 12 days in the cooler temperatures of April. The company also caters to travelers with special needs, offering departures for people with disabilities.

Petrified Forest National Park

Home not only to an extraordinary array of fossilized logs that predate the dinosaurs but also the multicolored sandscape of the Painted Desert, this **national park** (928-524-6228; www.nps.gov/pefo; vehicle $20, walk-in/bicycle/motorcycle $10; ⊙7am-7pm Mar-Sep, shorter hours Oct-Feb) is a compulsory spectacle. The park straddles I-40 at exit 311, 25 miles east of **Holbrook**. Its **visitor center** (928-524-6228; www.nps.gov; 1 Park Rd, Petrified Forest National Park; ⊙8am-5pm), just half a mile north of I-40, holds maps and information on guided tours, while the 28-mile paved park road beyond offers a splendid scenic drive. There are no campsites, but a number of short trails, ranging from less than a mile to 2 miles, pass through the stands of petrified trees and ancient Native American dwellings. Those prepared for rugged backcountry camping need to pick up a free permit at the visitor center.

Western Arizona

The Colorado River is alive with sun worshippers at Lake Havasu City, while Route 66 offers well-preserved stretches of classic highway near Kingman. Much further south, beyond I-10 towards Mexico, the wild, empty landscape is among the most barren in the West. If you're already here, there are some worthwhile sites, but there's nothing worth planning an itinerary around unless you're a Route 66 or boating fanatic.

Kingman & Around

Among Route 66 aficionados, Kingman is known as the main hub of the longest uninterrupted stretch of the historic highway, running from Topock to Seligman. Among its early-20th-century buildings is the former Methodist church at 5th and Spring Sts where Clark Gable and Carole Lombard eloped in 1939. Hometown hero Andy Devine had his Hollywood breakthrough as the perpetually befuddled driver of the eponymous *Stagecoach* in John Ford's Oscar-winning 1939 movie.

Pick up maps and brochures at the historic **Kingman Visitor Center** (866-427-7866, 928-753-6106; www.gokingman.com; 120 W Andy Devine Ave; ⊙8am-5pm), housed in an old powerhouse and entailing a small but engaging Route 66 museum and a display of electric cars.

A cool neon sign draws road-trippers to the **Hilltop Motel** (928-753-2198; www.hilltopmotelaz.com; 1901 E Andy Devine Ave; r from $44; ❈@🖳🖥🖥) on Route 66. Rooms are basic-but-comfortable (thanks to a heritage grant) but the views, retro style and price can't be beaten. Pets (dogs only) stay for $5. There's tasty pit-smoked meats at **Floyd & Co Real Pit BBQ** (928-757-8227; www.rednecksouthernpitbbq.com; 420 E Beale St; mains $9-13; ⊙11am-8pm Tue-Sat; 🖩) and commendable coffee at **Beale Street Brews** (928-753-1404; www.bealestreetbrews.net; 510 E Beale St; ⊙6am-6pm; 🖥).

Southern Arizona

This is a land of Stetsons and spurs, where cowboy ballads are sung around the campfire under starry, black-velvet skies and thick steaks sizzle on the grill. Anchored by the bustling college town of Tucson, it's a vast region, where long, dusty highways slide past rolling vistas and steep, pointy mountain ranges. Majestic saguaro cacti, the symbol of the region, stretch out as far as the eye can see.

Tucson

A college town with a long history, Tucson (*too*-sawn) is attractive, fun-loving and one of the most culturally invigorating places in the Southwest. Set in a flat valley hemmed in by snaggletoothed mountains and swathes of saguaro, Arizona's second-largest city smoothly blends American Indian, Spanish, Mexican and Anglo traditions. Distinct neighborhoods and 19th-century buildings give a rich sense of community and history not found in the more modern, sprawling Phoenix. The eclectic shops toting vintage garb, scores of funky restaurants and dive bars don't let you forget Tucson is a college town at heart, home turf to the 40,000-strong University of Arizona.

⊙ Sights & Activities

Downtown Tucson and the historic district lie east of I-10 exit 258. The University of Arizona campus is a mile northeast of downtown; 4th Ave, the main drag here, is packed with cafes, bars and interesting shops. Many of Tucson's most fabulous treasures lie on the periphery, or even beyond town.

Presidio Historic District   AREA
(www.nps.gov/nr/travel/amsw/sw7.htm) The Tucson Museum of Art (p865) is part of this low-key neighborhood, bounded by W 6th St, W Alameda St, N Stone Ave and Granada Ave, and embracing the site of the original Spanish fort and upmarket 'Snob Hollow.' This is one of the oldest continually inhabited places in North America: the Spanish **Presidio de San Augustín del Tucson** dates back to 1775, but the fort itself was built over a Hohokam site that has been dated to AD 700 to 900.

Barrio Histórico
District (Barrio Viejo)   AREA
This compact neighborhood was an important business district in the late 19th century. Today it's home to funky shops and galleries in brightly painted adobe houses. The barrio is bordered by I-10, Stone Ave and Cushing and 17th Sts.

★ **Arizona-Sonora Desert Museum**   MUSEUM
(520-883-2702; www.desertmuseum.org; 2021 N Kinney Rd; adult/senior/child 3-12yr $20.50/18.50/8; 8:30am-5pm Oct-Feb, 7:30am-5pm Mar-Sep, incl 10pm Sat Jun-Aug) Home to cacti, coyotes and palm-sized hummingbirds, this 98-acre ode to the Sonoran Desert is one-part zoo, one-part botanical garden and one-part museum – a trifecta that'll entertain young and old for easily half a day. Desert denizens, from precocious coatis to playful prairie dogs, inhabit natural enclosures, the grounds are thick with desert plants, and docents give demonstrations. Strollers and wheelchairs are available, and there's a gift shop, an art gallery, a restaurant and a cafe.

Arizona State Museum   MUSEUM
(520-621-6302; www.statemuseum.arizona.edu; 1013 E University Blvd; adult/child 17yr & under $5/ free; 10am-5pm Mon-Sat) To learn more about the history and culture of the region's American Indian tribes, visit the Arizona State Museum, the oldest and largest anthropology museum in the Southwest. The exhibit covering the tribes' cultural history is extensive but easy to navigate, and should appeal to newbies and history buffs alike. These galleries are complemented by much-envied collections of minerals and Navajo textiles.

Reid Park Zoo   ZOO
(520-791-3204; https://reidparkzoo.org; 3400 E Zoo Ct; adult/senior/child 2-14yr $11/8.50/6.50; 9am-4pm Oct-May, 8am-3pm Jun-Sep;) At the compact Reid Park Zoo, a global menagerie, including grizzly bears, jaguars, giant anteaters and pygmy hippos, delights young and old. Cap a visit with a picnic in the surrounding park, which also has playgrounds and a pond with paddleboat rentals.

Old Tucson Studios   FILM LOCATION
(520-883-0100; www.oldtucson.com; 201 S Kinney Rd; adult/child 4-11yr $19/11; 10am-5pm daily Feb-Apr, 10am-5pm Fri-Sun May, 10am-5pm Sat & Sun Jun-early Sep;) Nicknamed 'Hollywood in the Desert,' this old movie set of Tucson in the 1860s was built in 1939 for the filming of *Arizona*. Hundreds of flicks followed, bringing in movie stars from Clint Eastwood to Leonardo DiCaprio. Now a Wild West theme park, it's all about shoot-outs, stagecoach rides, stunt shows and dancing saloon girls. Closed from early September to the end of January, it does open for 'Nightfall' after-dark ghost tours in October.

Tucson Museum of Art   MUSEUM
(520-624-2333; www.tucsonmuseumofart.org; 140 N Main Ave; adult $12, senior & student $10, child 13-17yr $7; 10am-5pm Tue-Sat, noon-5pm

---

HOPI INDIAN RESERVATION

Direct descendants of the Ancestral Puebloans, the Hopi have arguably changed less in the last five centuries than any other Native American group. Their village of Old Oraibi may be the oldest continuously inhabited settlement in North America. Hopi land is surrounded on all sides by the Navajo Nation. Hwy 264 runs past the three mesas (First, Second and Third Mesa) that form the heart of the reservation.

On Second Mesa, 8 miles west of First Mesa, the **Hopi Cultural Center Restaurant & Inn** (928-734-2401; www.hopiculturalcenter.com; Hwy 264, Mile 379; r $115; restaurant 7am-9pm summer, to 8pm winter) is as visitor-oriented as things get on the Hopi reservation. It provides food and lodging, and holds the small **Hopi Museum** (928-734-6650; Hwy 264, Mile 379; adult/child 12yr & under $3/1; 8am-5pm Mon-Fri, 9am-3pm Sat;), filled with historic photographs and cultural exhibits.

Photographs, sketching and recording are not allowed anywhere on the reservation.

Sun) For a small city, Tucson boasts an impressive art museum. There's a respectable collection of American, Latin American and modern art, and the permanent exhibition of pre-Columbian artifacts will awaken your inner Indiana Jones. The special exhibits are varied and interesting, there's a superb gift shop, and the block surrounding the building holds a number of notable historic homes. The museum stays open to 8pm on the first Thursday of the month; when admission is free from 5pm.

Tucson Children's Museum MUSEUM
(☑520-792-9985; www.childrensmuseumtucson. org; 200 S 6th Ave; $8; ☺9am-5pm Tue-Fri, 10am-5pm Sat & Sun; 🖽) Parents sing the praises of the Tucson Children's Museum, which has plenty of engaging, hands-on exhibits – from Dinosaur World to Wee World (as in tiny) and an aquarium.

⭐ Festivals & Events

Tucson Gem & Mineral Show CULTURAL
(☑520-332-5773; www.tgms.org; ☺Feb) The most famous event on the city's calendar, held on the second full weekend in February, this is the largest gem and mineral show in the world. An estimated 250 retail dealers who trade in minerals, crafts and fossils take over the Tucson Convention Center.

Fiesta de los Vaqueros RODEO
(Rodeo Week; ☑520-741-2233; www.tucsonrodeo. com; 4823 S 6th Ave, Tucson Rodeo Grounds; tickets $15-70; ☺last week of Feb) Held in the last week of February for nearly a century, the Fiesta de los Vaqueros brings world-famous cowboys to town and features a spectacular parade with Western-themed floats and buggies, historical horse-drawn coaches, folk dancers and marching bands.

🛏 Sleeping

Lodging prices vary considerably, with lower rates in summer and fall. To sleep under the stars and saguaros, try **Gilbert Ray Campground** (☑520-724-5000; www.pima.gov; 8451 W McCain Loop Rd; tent/RV sites $10/20; 🐾) near the western district of Saguaro National Park.

⭐**Hotel Congress** HISTORIC HOTEL **$$**
(☑800-722-8848, 520-622-8848; www.hotel congress.com; 311 E Congress St; d from $109; 🅿❄🛜🐾) Perhaps Tucson's most famous hotel, this is where infamous bank robber John Dillinger and his gang were captured during their 1934 stay, when a fire broke out. Built in 1919 and beautifully restored, this charismatic place feels very modern, despite period furnishings such as rotary phones and wooden radios (but no TVs). There's a popular cafe, bar and club on-site.

ROADSIDE ATTRACTIONS ON ROUTE 66

Route 66 enthusiasts will find 400 miles of America's Highway stretching across Arizona, including the longest uninterrupted portion of old road left in the country, between Seligman and Topock. The **Mother Road** (www.azrt66.com) connects the dots between gun-slinging Oatman, Kingman's mining settlements, Williams' 1940s-vintage downtown and Winslow's windblown streets, with plenty of kitschy sights, listed here from west to east, along the way.

Wild burros of Oatman Feral mules, the progeny of mining days, beg for treats in the middle of the road.

Grand Canyon Caverns & Inn (☑928-422-3223, 855-498-6969; www.grandcanyoncav erns.com; Mile 115, Rte 66; tour adult/child from $16/11; ☺8am-6pm May-Sep, call for off-season hours) A guided tour 21 stories underground loops past mummified bobcats, civil-defense supplies and an $800 motel room (or cave).

Burma Shave signs Red-and-white ads from a bygone era between Grand Canyon Caverns and Seligman.

Snow Cap Drive-In (☑928-422-3291; 301 Rte 66; mains $5-6.50; ☺10am-6pm Mar-Nov) Prankish burger and ice-cream joint open in Seligman since 1953.

Meteor Crater (☑800-289-5898, 928-289-5898; www.meteorcrater.com; Meteor Crater Rd; adult/senior/child 6-17yr $18/16/9; ☺7am-7pm Jun–mid-Sep, 8am-5pm mid-Sep–May; 🅿🖽) A 550ft-deep pockmark that's nearly 1 mile across, 38 miles east of Flagstaff.

Wigwam Motel (☑928-524-3048; www.galerie-kokopelli.com/wigwam; 811 W Hopi Dr; r $56-62; ❄) Concrete wigwams with hickory logpole furniture in Holbrook.

SOUTHWEST SOUTHERN ARIZONA

⭐ **Desert Trails B&B**   B&B **$$**
(📞 520-885-7295; www.deserttrails.com; 12851
E Speedway Blvd; r/guesthouse from $140/175;
🅿️🛜❄️) Outdoorsy types who want a per-
sonable B&B close to Saguaro National
Park (Rincon Mountain District) have their
answer at Desert Trails on Tucson's eastern
fringe. Rooms are comfy with all the latest
amenities. John Higgins, an avid backpack-
er, was a fireman for Saguaro National Park
for six years and is glad to share his knowl-
edge about the park's trails.

Aloft Tucson   HOTEL **$$**
(📞 520-908-6800; www.starwoodhotels.com;
1900 E Speedway Blvd; d from $145; 🅿️🛜) Tucson
is surprisingly light on for stylish hotels. The
new Aloft, near the university, isn't an indie
property, but it is a slick operation catering
to tech-minded, style-conscious travelers.
Rooms and common areas pop with bright,
spare, yet inviting decor, there's an on-site
bar, and 24-hour grab 'n' go food is available
beside the lobby.

⭐ **Hacienda del Sol**   RANCH **$$$**
(📞 520-299-1501; www.haciendadelsol.com; 5501
N Hacienda del Sol Rd; d/ste from $209/339;
🅿️@🛜❄️) An elite hilltop girls' school
built in the 1920s, this relaxing refuge has
artist-designed Southwest-style rooms and
teems with unique touches like carved
ceiling beams and louvered exterior doors
to catch the courtyard breeze. The Haci-
enda del Sol has sheltered Spencer Tracy,
Katharine Hepburn, John Wayne and other
legends, so you'll be sleeping with history.
Its restaurant, the Grill, is fabulous too.

❌ **Eating**

Diablo Burger   BURGERS **$**
(📞 520-882-2007; www.diabloburger.com; 312 E
Congress St; burgers $10-12; ⏲️ 11am-9pm Sun-
Wed, to 10pm Thu-Sat) This satellite of Flag-
staff's popular burger joint does a mean
patty of open-range, locally sourced beef.
Try the Big Daddy Kane, with sharp ched-
dar, pickles and special sauce. The herby
'Belgian-style' fries are salty, but so good.

⭐ **Lovin' Spoonfuls**   VEGAN **$**
(📞 520-325-7766; www.lovinspoonfuls.com; 2990
N Campbell Ave; breakfast $6-9, lunch $5.25-8,
dinner $7.25-11.25; ⏲️ 9:30am-9pm Mon-Sat, 10am-
3pm Sun; 🍴) Burgers, country-fried chicken
and club sandwiches – the menu reads like
one at your typical diner but there's a big
difference: no animal products will ever find

their way into this vegan haven. Outstand-
ingly creative choices include the Old Pueblo
bean burrito and Buddha's Delight – a gin-
gery stir-fry of cabbage, shiitake and other
goodies over brown rice.

⭐ **Cafe Poca Cosa**   MEXICAN **$$**
(📞 520-622-6400; www.cafepocacosatucson.
com; 110 E Pennington St; lunch $13-15, dinner
$20-24; ⏲️ 11am-9pm Tue-Thu, to 10pm Fri &
Sat) Chef Suzana Davila's award-winning
nuevo-Mexican bistro is a must for fans of
Mexican food in Tucson. A Spanish-English
blackboard menu circulates between tables
because dishes change twice daily – it's all
freshly prepared, innovative and beautifully presented. The undecided can't go wrong
by ordering the 'Plato Poca Cosa' and letting
Suzana decide what's best. Great margaritas,
too.

El Charro Café   MEXICAN **$$**
(📞 520-622-1922; www.elcharrocafe.com; 311 N
Court Ave; lunch $10-12, dinner $16-20; ⏲️ 10am-
9pm) This rambling, buzzing hacienda has
been making great Mexican food on this
site since 1922. It's particularly famous for
the *carne seca,* sundried lean beef that's
been reconstituted, shredded and grilled
with green chile and onions. The fabulous
margaritas pack a burro-stunning punch,
and help while away the time as you wait
for your table.

🍷 **Drinking & Entertainment**

Congress St in downtown and 4th Ave near
the University of Arizona are both busy par-
ty strips.

⭐ **Che's Lounge**   BAR
(📞 520-623-2088; http://cheslounge.com; 350
N 4th Ave; ⏲️ noon-2am) This slightly grungy
but hugely popular watering hole does
cheap Pabst Blue Ribbon and features a
huge wraparound bar and fantastic murals
by local artist (and bartender) Donovan. A
popular college hangout, Che's rocks with
live music most Saturday nights and on the
patio on Sunday afternoons (4pm to 7pm) in
the summer.

IBT's   GAY
(📞 520-882-3053; www.ibtstucson.com; 616 N 4th
Ave; ⏲️ noon-2am) At Tucson's most sizzling
gay fun house, the theme changes night-
ly – from drag shows to karaoke – plus the
monthly Sunday 'Fun Day,' with karaoke,
DJs and drink specials all day. Chill on the

MINI TIME MACHINE OF MUSEUM OF MINIATURES

Divided into the Enchanted Realm, Exploring the World and the History Gallery, this delightful **museum** (☑520-881-0606; www.theminitimemachine.org; 4455 E Camp Lowell Dr; adult/senior/child 4-17yr $9/8/6; ⊙9am-4pm Tue-Sat, noon-4pm Sun; ⊕) of miniatures presents dioramas fantastical, historical and plain intriguing. You can also walk over a snow-globe-y Christmas village, peer into tiny homes constructed in the 1700s and 1800s, and search for the little inhabitants of a magical tree. The museum grew from a personal collection in the 1930s. Parents may find themselves having more fun than their kids.

patio, check out the bods or sweat it out on the dance floor.

Thunder Canyon Brewery　　MICROBREWERY
(☑520-396-3480; www.thundercanyonbrewery. com; 220 E Broadway Blvd; ⊙11am-11pm Sun-Thu, to midnight Fri & Sat) This cavernous microbrewery, within walking distance of the Hotel Congress, has more than 40 beers on tap, serving up its own creations as well as handcrafted beers from across the US. There's now a second location at 1234 N Williams St.

Club Congress　　LIVE MUSIC
(☑520-622-8848; www.hotelcongress.com; 311 E Congress St; ⊙live music from 7pm, club nights from 10pm) Skinny jeansters, tousled hipsters, aging folkies, dressed-up hotties – the crowd at Tucson's most happening club inside the grandly aging Hotel Congress defines the word eclectic. And so does the musical lineup, which usually features the finest local and regional talent, and DJs some nights. And for a no-fuss drink, there's the Lobby Bar for cocktails, or the Tap Room, open since 1919.

ⓘ Information

General information on Tucson is available from the **Tucson Visitor Center** (☑800-638-8350, 520-624-1817; www.visittucson.org; 811 N Euclid Ave; ⊙9am-5pm Mon-Fri, to 4pm Sat & Sun), while specific information on access and camping in the Coronado National Forest can be found at the downtown **Coronado National Forest Supervisor's Office** (☑520-388-8300; www.fs.usda.gov/coronado; 300 W Congress St, Federal Bldg; ⊙8am-4:30pm Mon-Fri).

ⓘ Getting There & Around

Tucson International Airport (☑520-573-8100; www.flytucson.com; 7250 S Tucson Blvd; 🛜) is 15 miles south of downtown and served by six airlines, with nonstop flights to destinations including Atlanta, Denver, Las Vegas, Los Angeles and San Francisco.

Greyhound (☑520-792-3475; www.grey hound.com; 471 W Congress St) runs seven buses to Phoenix (from $10, two hours), among other destinations.

The *Sunset Limited*, operated by **Amtrak** (☑800-872-7245, 520-623-4442; www.amtrak. com; 400 N Toole Ave), comes through on its way west to Los Angeles (10 hours, three weekly) and east to New Orleans (36 hours, three weekly).

The **Ronstadt Transit Center** (215 E Congress St, at 6th Ave) is the main hub for the public buses with **Sun Tran** (☑520-792-9222; www. suntran.com) that serve the entire metro area. Single/day fares are $1.50/4 using the SunGo smart card. The same fares apply on the new streetcar line **SunLink**.

Around Tucson

All the places listed here are less than 1½ hours' drive from Tucson, and make great day trips.

Saguaro National Park

Saguaros (sah-wah-ros) are icons of the American Southwest, and an entire cactus army of these majestic, ribbed sentinels is protected in this desert **playground** (☑Rincon 520-733-5153, Tucson 520-733-5158, park information 520-733-5100; www.nps.gov/sagu; 7-day pass per vehicle/bicycle $10/5; ⊙sunrise-sunset). Or, more precisely, playgrounds: the park is divided into east and west units, separated by 30 miles and Tucson itself. Both sections – the Rincon Mountain District in the east and Tucson Mountain District in the west – are filled with trails and desert flora; if you only visit one, make it the spectacular western half.

The larger section is the **Rincon Mountain District**, about 15 miles east of downtown. The **Red Hills Visitor Center** (☑520-733-5158; www.nps.gov/sagu; 2700 N Kinney Rd; ⊙9am-5pm) has information on day hikes, horseback riding and backcountry camping. The camping requires a permit ($8 per site per day) and must be obtained by noon on the day of your hike. The meandering 8-mile **Cactus Forest Scenic Loop Drive**, a paved road open to cars and bicycles, provides access to picnic areas, trailheads and viewpoints.

Hikers pressed for time should follow the 1-mile round-trip **Freeman Homestead Trail** to a grove of massive saguaro. For a full-fledged desert adventure, head out on the steep and rocky Tanque Verde Ridge Trail, which climbs to the summit of Mica Mountain (8666ft) and back in 20 miles (backcountry camping permit required for overnight use). If you'd rather someone (or something) else did the hard work, family-run **Houston's Horseback Riding** (☎520-298-7450; www.tucsonhorsebackriding.com; 12801 E Speedway Blvd; per person 2hr tour $60) offers trail rides in the eastern section of the Park.

West of town, the **Tucson Mountain District** has its own branch of the Red Hills Visitor Center. The **Scenic Bajada Loop Drive** is a 6-mile graded dirt road through cactus forest that begins 1.5 miles north of the visitor center. Two quick, easy and rewarding hikes are the 0.8-mile **Valley View Overlook** (awesome at sunset) and the half-mile **Signal Hill Trail** to scores of ancient petroglyphs. For a more strenuous trek we recommend the 7-mile **King Canyon Trail**, which starts 2 miles south of the visitor center, near the Arizona-Sonora Desert Museum. The 0.5-mile informative **Desert Discovery Trail**, which is one mile northwest of the visitor center, is wheelchair accessible. Distances for all four hikes are round-trip.

As for the park's namesake cactus, don't refer to the limbs of the saguaro as branches. As park docents will quickly tell you, the mighty saguaro grows arms, not lowly branches – a distinction that makes sense when you consider their human-like features.

Saguaros grow slowly, taking about 15 years to reach a foot in height, 50 years to reach 7ft and almost a century before they begin to take on their typical many-armed appearance. The best time to visit is April, when the cacti begin blossoming with lovely white blooms – Arizona's state flower. By June and July, the flowers give way to ripe red fruit that local American Indians use for food. Their foot soldiers are the spidery ocotillo, the fluffy teddy bear cactus, the green-bean-like pencil cholla and hundreds of other plant species. It is illegal to damage or remove saguaros.

Note that trailers longer than 35ft and vehicles wider than 8ft are not permitted on the park's narrow scenic loop roads.

HOT DIGGITY DOG

The Sonoran hot dog is a local specialty, a palm-held heart attack comprising a bacon-wrapped hot dog layered with tomatillo salsa, pinto beans, shredded cheese, mayo, ketchup, mustard, chopped tomatoes and onions. They may not be for everyone, but the curious should head to where they're done best – **El Guero Canelo** (☎520-295-9005; www.elguerocanelo.com; 5201 S 12th Ave; hot dogs $3-4, mains $7-9; ☉10am-10pm Sun-Thu, 8:30am-midnight Fri & Sat).

West of Tuscon

You want wide solitude? Follow Hwy 86 west from Tuscon into some of the emptiest parts of the Sonoran Desert – except for the ubiquitous green-and-white border-patrol trucks. The lofty **Kitt Peak National Observatory** (☎520-318-8726; www.noao.edu/kpno; Hwy 86; tours adult/child $9.75/3.25; ☉9am-4pm; ♿) **FREE**, about a 75-minute drive from Tucson, features the largest collection of optical telescopes in the world. Guided tours (adult/child $10/3.25, at 10am, 11:30am and 1:30pm) last about an hour. Book two to four weeks in advance for the worthwhile nightly observing program (adult $50; no programs from mid-July through August).

Clear, dry skies equal an awe-inspiring glimpse of the cosmos. Dress warmly, buy gas in Tucson (the nearest gas station is 30 miles from the observatory) and note that children under eight years of age are not allowed at the evening program. The picnic area draws amateur astronomers at night

If you truly want to get away from it all, you can't get much further off the grid than the huge and exotic **Organ Pipe Cactus National Monument** (☎520-387-6849; www.nps.gov/orpi; Hwy 85; per vehicle $12; ☉visitor center 8:30am-5pm) along the Mexican border. It's a gorgeous, forbidding land that supports an astonishing number of animals and plants, including 28 species of cacti, first and foremost its namesake organ-pipe. A giant columnar cactus, it differs from the more prevalent saguaro in that its branches radiate from the base.

The 21-mile **Ajo Mountain Drive** takes you through a spectacular landscape of steep-sided, jagged cliffs and rock tinged a faintly hellish red. There are 208 first-come, first-served sites at **Twin Peaks Campground** (☑520-387-6849, ext 7302; www.nps.gov/orpi; 10 Organ Pipe Dr; tent & RV sites $16) by the visitor center.

South of Tuscon

South of Tucson, I-19 is the main route to Nogales and Mexico. Along the way are several interesting stops.

The magnificent **Mission San Xavier del Bac** (☑520-294-2624; www.patronatosanxavier.org; 1950 W San Xavier Rd; donations appreciated; ⊙museum 8:30am-4:30pm, church 7am-5pm), on the San Xavier reservation 9 miles south of downtown Tucson, is Arizona's oldest Hispanic-era building still in use. Completed in 1797, it's a graceful blend of Moorish, Byzantine and late-Mexican Renaissance architecture, with an unexpectedly ornate interior.

At exit 69, 16 miles south of the mission, the **Titan Missile Museum** (☑520-625-7736; www.titanmissilemuseum.org; 1580 Duval Mine Rd, Sahuarita; adult/senior/child 7-12yr $9.50/8.50/6; ⊙9:45am-5pm Sun-Fri, 8:45am-5pm Sat, last tour 3:45pm) features an underground launch site for Cold War–era intercontinental ballistic missiles. Tours are chilling, informative and should be booked ahead.

If history or shopping for crafts interest you, head 48 miles south of Tucson to the small village of Tubac (www.tubacaz.com), with more than 100 galleries, studios and shops clustered around a Spanish colonial-era Presidio.

Patagonia & the Mountain Empire

This lovely riparian region, sandwiched between the Mexican border and the Santa Rita and Patagonia Mountains, is one of the shiniest gems in Arizona's jewel box. It's a tranquil destination for bird-watching and wine tasting. Bird-watchers and nature-lovers wander the gentle trails at the **Patagonia-Sonoita Creek Preserve** (☑520-394-2400; www.nature.org/arizona; 150 Blue Heaven Rd; $6; ⊙6:30am-4pm Wed-Sun Apr-Sep, 7:30am-4pm Wed-Sun Oct-Mar), an enchanting creekside willow and cottonwood forest managed by the Nature Conservancy. The peak migratory seasons are April through May, and late August to September.

For a leisurely afternoon of wine tasting, head to the villages and surrounding wineries of **Sonoita** and **Elgin**, north of Patagonia. If you're in Patagonia for dinner, try the satisfying gourmet pizzas at **Velvet Elvis** (☑520-394-2102; www.velvetelvispizza.com; 292 Naugle Ave, Patagonia; mains $8-24; ⊙11:30am-8pm; ⏸). Then salute the Old West and its simple charms at the **Stage Stop Inn** (☑520-394-2211; www.stagestophotelpatagonia.com; 303 McKeown Ave, Patagonia; d/ste from $99/149; ⏸⏸⏸), where rooms surround a central courtyard and pool. The stage coach did indeed stop here on the Butterfield Trail, and a small **visitor center** (☑520-394-7750, 888-794-0060; www.patagoniaaz.com; 299 McKeown Ave, Patagonia; ⊙10am-4pm daily Oct-May, Fri-Sun Jun-Sep) now provides information.

Southeastern Arizona

Chockablock with places that loom large in Wild West folklore, southern Arizona is home to the wonderfully preserved mining town of Bisbee, the OK Corral in Tombstone, and a wonderland of stone spires at Chiricahua National Monument.

Kartchner Caverns State Park

This wonderland of spires, shields, pipes, columns, soda straws and other ethereal formations has been five million years in the making, but miraculously wasn't discovered until 1974. In fact, its very location was kept secret for another 25 years in order to prepare for its opening as **Kartchner Caverns State Park** (☑information 520-586-4100, reservations 877-697-2757; http://azstateparks.com/kartchner; 2980 Hwy 90; park entrance per vehicle/bicycle $7/3, tours adult/child $23/13; ⊙park 7am-6pm, visitor center 8am-6pm late Dec-May, shorter hours rest of year; ⓟ⏸). Two tours are available, both about 90 minutes long and equally impressive.

The Big Room tour closes to the public around mid-April, when a colony of migrating female cave myotis bats starts arriving from Mexico to roost and give birth to pups in late June. Mom and baby bats hang out until mid-September before flying off to their wintering spot. While a bat nursery, the cave is closed to the public.

There's a campground (with cabins) and the entrance is 9 miles south of I-10, off Hwy 90, exit 302.

Tombstone

In Tombstone's 19th-century heyday as a booming mining town, the whiskey flowed and six-shooters blazed over disputes large and small, most famously at the OK Corral.

Now a National Historic Landmark, it attracts hordes of tourists to its old Western buildings, stagecoach rides and gunfight reenactments.

And yes, you must visit the **OK Corral** (☑ 520-457-3456; www.ok-corral.com; Allen St, btwn 3rd & 4th Sts; entry $10, without gunfight $6; ⊙ 9am-5pm), site of the legendary gunfight where the Earps and Doc Holliday took on the McLaurys and Billy Clanton on October 26, 1881. The McClaurys, Clanton and many other casualties of those violent days now rest at the **Boothill Graveyard** (☑ 520-457-3300; www.boothillgiftshop.com; 408 Hwy 80; adult/child 15yr & under $3/free; ⊙ 8am-6pm) FREE on Hwy 80 north of town.

Also make time for the dusty **Bird Cage Theater** (☑ 520-457-3421; www.tombstonebird cage.com; 517 E Allen St; adult/senior/child 8-18yr $10/9/8; ⊙ 9am-6pm), a one-time dance hall, saloon and bordello crammed with historic odds and ends. And a merman. The **Visitor Center** (☑ 520-457-3929, 888-457-3929; www. tombstonechamber.com; 395 E Allen St, at 4th St; ⊙ 9am-4pm Mon-Thu, to 5pm Fri-Sun) has walking maps.

Bisbee

Oozing untidy, unforced old-world charm, Bisbee is a former copper-mining town that's now a delightful mix of aging bohemians, elegant buildings, sumptuous restaurants and charming hotels. Most businesses are in the Historic District (Old Bisbee), along Subway and Main Sts.

To burrow under the earth in a tour led by the retirees who once mined here, take the **Queen Mine Tour** (☑ 520-432-2071; www. queenminetour.com; 478 Dart Rd, off Hwy 80; adult/ child 4-12yr $13/5.50;). The Queen Mine Building, just south of downtown, also holds the local **visitor center** (☑ 866-224-7233, 520-432-3554; www.discoverbisbee.com; 478 Dart Rd; ⊙ 8am-5pm Mon-Fri, 10am-4pm Sat & Sun), and is the obvious place to start exploring. Right outside of town, check out the **Lavender Pit**, an ugly yet impressive testament to strip mining.

Rest your head at **Shady Dell RV Park** (☑ 520-432-3567; www.theshadydell.com; 1 Douglas Rd, Lowell; trailers from $85; ⊙ closed high summer & winter;), a deliciously retro trailer park where meticulously restored Airstream trailers are neatly fenced off and kitted out with fun furnishings. Swamp coolers provide cold air. You can sleep in a covered wagon at the quirky but fun **Bisbee Grand Hotel**

(☑ 520-432-5900; www.bisbeegrandhotel.com; 61 Main St; d/ste from $99/135; ❀), which brings the Old West to life with Victorian-era decor and a kick-up-your spurs saloon.

For good food, stroll up Main St and pick a restaurant – you can't go wrong. For fine American food, try stylish **Cafe Roka** (☑ 520-432-5153; www.caferoka.com; 35 Main St; dinner $20-30; ⊙ 5-9pm Thu-Sat, 3-8pm Sun), where four-course dinners include salad, soup, sorbet and a rotating choice of crowd-pleasing mains. Continue up Main St for wood-fired pizzas and punk-rock style at **Screaming Banshee** (☑ 520-432-1300; www.screamingbansheepizza.net; 200 Tombstone Canyon Rd; pizzas $14-16; ⊙ 4-9pm Tue & Wed, 11am-10pm Thu-Sat, 11am-9pm Sun). Bars cluster in the aptly-named Brewery Gulch, at the south end of Main St.

Chiricahua National Monument

The towering rock spires at remote but mesmerizing **Chiricahua National Monument** (☑ 520-824-3560; www.nps.gov/chir; 12856 E Rhyolite Creek Rd; ⊙ visitor center 8:30am-4:30pm; ❀) FREE in the Chiricahua Mountains sometimes rise hundreds of feet high and often look like they're on the verge of tipping over. The **Bonita Canyon Scenic Drive** takes you 8 miles to Massai Point (6870ft) where you'll see thousands of spires positioned on the slopes like some petrified army. There are numerous hiking trails, but if you're short on time, hike the **Echo Canyon Trail** at least half a mile to the Grottoes, an amazing 'cathedral' of giant boulders where you can lie still and enjoy the wind-caressed silence. The monument is 36 miles southeast of Willcox off Hwy 186/181.

UTAH

Welcome to nature's most perfect playground. From red-rock mesas to skinny slot canyons, powder-bound slopes and slick rock trails, Utah's diverse terrain will stun you. The biking, hiking and skiing are world-class. And with more than 65% of the state lands public, including 13 national parks and monuments, the access is simply superb.

Southern Utah is defined by red-rock cliffs, sorbet-colored spindles and seemingly endless sandstone desert. The pine-forested and snow-covered peaks of the Wasatch Mountains dominate northern Utah. Interspersed are old pioneer remnants, ancient rock art and ruins, and traces of dinosaurs.

Mormon-influenced rural towns can be quiet and conservative, but the rugged beauty has attracted outdoorsy progressives as well. Salt Lake City (SLC) and Park City, especially, have vibrant nightlife and dining scenes. So pull on your boots and stock up on water: Utah's wild and scenic hinterlands await.

History

Traces of the Ancestral Puebloan and Fremont peoples, this land's earliest human inhabitants, remain in the rock art and ruins they left behind. But the modern Ute, Paiute and Navajo tribes were living here when settlers of European heritage arrived in large numbers. Led by Brigham Young (second president of the Mormon church), Mormons fled to this territory to escape religious persecution starting in the late 1840s. They set out to settle every inch of their new land, no matter how inhospitable, which resulted in skirmishes with Native Americans – and more than one abandoned ghost town.

For nearly 50 years after the United States acquired the Utah Territory from Mexico, petitions for statehood were rejected due to the Mormon practice of polygamy (taking multiple wives). Tension and prosecutions grew until 1890, when Mormon leader Wilford Woodruff had a divine revelation and the church officially discontinued the practice. Utah became the 45th state in 1896. The modern Mormon church, now called the Church of Jesus Christ of Latter-Day Saints (LDS), continues to exert a strong influence.

❶ Information

Utah Office of Tourism (☑ 800-200-1160; www.utah.com) Publishes the free *Utah Travel Guide* and runs several visitor centers statewide. The website has links in six languages.

Utah State Parks & Recreation Department (☑ 801-538-7220; www.stateparks.utah.gov) Produces a great guide to the 40-plus state parks; available online and at visitor centers.

❶ Getting There & Around

International flights land in Salt Lake City. Larger cities and tourist hubs have car-rental offices.

Utah is not a large state, but it is largely rural – so unless you're staying in Salt Lake City or Park City, you'll need a car. If you're headed to the parks in southern Utah, your cheapest bet may be to fly into Las Vegas, and rent a ride there.

Salt Lake City

Sparkling Salt Lake, with its bluebird skies and powder-dusted mountains, is Utah's capital city. The only Utah city with an international airport, it still manages to emanate a small-town feel. Downtown is easy to get around and fairly quiet come evening. It's hard to grasp that 1.2 million people live in the metro area. While it's the Mormon equivalent of Vatican City, and the LDS owns a lot of land, less than half the population are church members. The university and excellent outdoor access have attracted a wide range of residents. A liberal spirit permeates the coffeehouses and yoga classes, where elaborate tattoos are the norm. Foodies find much to love among the multitude of international and organic dining options. And when the trail beckons, it's a scant 45 minutes from the Wasatch Mountains' brilliant hiking and skiing. Friendly people, great food and outdoor adventure – what could be better?

◉ Sights

Mormon Church–related sights cluster mostly near the town center point for SLC addresses: the intersection of Main and South Temple Sts. (Streets are so wide – 132ft – because they were originally built so that four oxen pulling a wagon could turn around.) The downtown hub underwent a renaissance with the development of City Creek. To the east, the University-Foothills District has most of the museums and kid-friendly attractions.

◉ Temple Square Area

Temple Square PLAZA
(www.visittemplesquare.com; cnr S Temple & N State Sts; ⊙grounds 24hr, visitor centers 9am-9pm) FREE The city's most famous sight occupies a 10-acre block surrounded by 15ft-high walls. LDS docents give free, 30-minute tours continually, leaving from the visitor centers at the two entrances on South and North Temple Sts. Sisters, brothers and elders are stationed every 20ft or so to answer questions. (Don't worry, no one is going to try to convert you – unless you express interest.) In addition to the noteworthy sights, there are administrative buildings and two theater venues.

Museum of Church History & Art   MUSEUM
(www.churchhistorymuseum.org; 45 N West Temple St; ⊙9am-9pm Mon-Fri, 10am-7pm Sat & Sun) FREE Adjoining Temple Sq, this museum has impressive exhibits of pioneer history and fine art.

Salt Lake Temple   RELIGIOUS SITE
(Temple Sq) Lording over Temple Sq is the impressive 210ft-tall Salt Lake Temple. Atop the tallest spire stands a statue of the angel Moroni, who appeared to LDS founder Joseph Smith. Rumor has it that when the place was renovated, cleaners found old bullet marks in one of the gold-plated surfaces. The temple and ceremonies are private, open only to LDS members in good standing.

Tabernacle   CHRISTIAN SITE
(www.mormontabernaclechoir.org; Temple Sq; ⊙9am-9pm) FREE The domed, 1867 auditorium – with a massive 11,000-pipe organ – has incredible acoustics. A pin dropped in the front can be heard in the back, almost 200ft away. Free daily organ recitals are held at noon Monday through Saturday, and at 2pm Sunday.

Beehive House   HISTORIC SITE
(☏801-240-2671; www.visittemplesquare.com; 67 E South Temple St; ⊙9:30am-8:30pm Mon-Sat) FREE Brigham Young lived with one of his wives and families in the Beehive House during much of his tenure as governor and church president in Utah. The required tours vary; some offer historic house details over religious education, depending on the LDS docent.

⊙ Greater Downtown

Utah State Capitol   HISTORIC BUILDING
(www.utahstatecapitol.utah.gov; 350 N State St; ⊙7am-8pm Mon-Fri, 8am-6pm Sat & Sun, visitor center 8:30am-5pm Mon-Fri) FREE The grand, 1916 State Capitol is set among 500 cherry trees on a hill north of Temple Sq. Inside, colorful Works Progress Administration (WPA) murals of pioneers, trappers and missionaries adorn part of the building's dome. Free guided tours (hourly, 9am to 5pm, Monday to Friday) start at the 1st-floor visitor center; self-guided tours are available from the visitor center.

Clark Planetarium   MUSEUM
(☏385-468-7827; www.clarkplanetarium.org; 110 S 400 W; adult/child $9/7; ⊙10am-10pm Sun-Thu, to 11pm Fri & Sat) You'll be seeing stars at Clark Planetarium, home to the latest and greatest 3D sky shows and Utah's only IMAX theater. There are free science exhibits, too. The planetarium is on the edge of the Gateway (www.shopthegateway.com; 200 S to 50 N, 400 W to 500 W; ⊙10am-9pm Mon-Sat, noon-6pm Sun), a combination indoor-outdoor shopping complex anchored by the old railway depot.

⊙ University-Foothill District & Beyond

★ Natural History Museum of Utah   MUSEUM
(http://nhmu.utah.edu; 301 Wakara Way; adult/child 3-12yr $15/10; ⊙10am-5pm Thu-Tue, to 9pm Wed) Rio Tinto Center's stunning architecture forms a multistory indoor 'canyon' that showcases exhibits to great effect. Walk up through the layers as you explore both indigenous peoples' cultures and natural history. Past Worlds paleontological displays are the most impressive – an incredible perspective from beneath, next to and above a vast collection of dinosaur fossils offers the full breadth of prehistory.

This is the Place Heritage Park   HISTORIC SITE
(www.thisistheplace.org; 2601 E Sunnyside Ave; adult/child $13/9; ⊙9am-5pm Mon-Sat, 10am-5pm Sun; ⊕) Dedicated to the 1847 arrival of the Mormons, this heritage park covers 450 acres. The centerpiece is a living-history village where, June through August, costumed docents depict mid-19th-century life. Admission includes a tourist-train ride and activities. The rest of the year, access is limited to varying degrees at varyingly reduced prices; you'll at least be able to wander around the exterior of the 41 buildings. Some are replicas, but some are originals, such as Brigham Young's farmhouse.

Red Butte Garden   GARDENS
(www.redbuttegarden.org; 300 Wakara Way; adult/child $12/7; ⊙9am-9pm May-Aug) Both landscaped and natural gardens cover a lovely 150 acres, with access to trails in the Wasatch foothills. Check online to see who's playing at the popular, outdoor summer concert series also held here. Daylight hours in low season.

🛏 Sleeping

Downtown chain properties cluster around S 200 West near 500 South and 600 South; there are more in Mid-Valley (off I-215) and near the airport. At high-end hotels rates are lowest on weekends. Parking downtown is often not included. Look for camping and alternative lodging in the Wasatch Mountains.

Wildflowers B&B
B&B $

(☎385-419-2301; http://wildflowersbb.com; 936 E 1700 S; r $90-125) Quaint to the core, this old-fashioned B&B revels in stained glass and period furnishings. Cheaper than most B&Bs in town, it's probably worth it for the breakfast alone. It sits in a characterful neighborhood of Salt Lake with plenty of shops and restaurants.

★ Engen Hus
B&B $$

(☎801-450-6703; http://engenhusutah.com; 2275 6200 S; r $125-140; 🛜) Ideally positioned for mountain jaunts, this lovely home features four rooms with handmade quilts on log beds and flat-screen TVs. Hosts are knowledgeable about local hiking. The cozy quotient is high, with board games, a hot-tub deck and DIY laundry. Dig the buffet breakfast with the likes of caramel French toast. Has a room that's accessible to travelers in wheelchairs.

★ Inn on the Hill
INN $$

(☎801-328-1466; www.inn-on-the-hill.com; 225 N State St; r $155-240; P❄@🛜) Exquisite woodwork and Maxfield Parrish Tiffany glass adorn this sprawling, 1906 Renaissance Revival mansion-turned-inn. Guest rooms

---

UTAH FACTS

Nickname Beehive State

Population 2.9 million

Area 82,169 sq miles

Capital city Salt Lake City (population 186,440), metro area (1,153,340)

Other cities St George (population 82,318

Sales tax from 4.7%

Birthplace of Entertainers Donny (b 1957) and Marie (b 1959) Osmond, beloved bandit Butch Cassidy (1866–1908)

Home of 2002 Winter Olympic Games

Politics Mostly conservative

Famous for Mormons, red-rock canyons, polygamy

Best souvenir Wasatch Brewery T-shirt:'Polygamy Porter – Why Have Just One?'

---

are classically comfortable, not stuffy, with Jacuzzi tubs and some fireplaces and balconies. Great shared spaces include patios, a billiard room, a library and a dining room where chef-cooked breakfasts are served.

Hotel Monaco
BOUTIQUE HOTEL $$

(☎801-595-0000; www.monaco-saltlakecity.com; 15 W 200 S; r $229-279; P❄@🛜🐾) Subdued with a dollop of funk, rich colors and plush prints create a whimsical vibe at this boutique chain. Here, pampered-guest pets receive special treatment, and the front desk will loan you a goldfish if you need company. Evening wine receptions are free, as are cruiser bicycles; parking is extra.

Hotel RL
HOTEL $$

(☎801-521-7373; www.redlion.com/salt-lake; 161 W 600 S; r from $239; P❄@🛜🐾) Sleek comfort in a remodeled Red Lion hotel with almost 400 rooms, which feature black-and-white wall murals and flat-screen TVs. There's a classic diner attached, a modern-woodsy design lounge, 24-hour gym and outdoor pool and Jacuzzi. As big box hotels go, this one delivers.

✖ Eating

★ Red Iguana
MEXICAN $

(www.rediguana.com; 736 W North Temple St; mains $10-18; ⏱11am-10pm Mon-Thu, to 11pm Fri, 10am-11pm Sat, 10am-9pm Sun) Mexico at its most authentic, aromatic and delicious – no wonder the line is usually snaking out the door at this family run restaurant. Ask for samples of the mole to decide on one of seven chili- and chocolate-based sauces. The incredibly tender *cochinita pibil* (shredded roast pork) tastes like it's been roasting for days.

★ Tosh's Ramen
RAMEN $

(☎801-466-7000; 1465 State St; mains $9-11; ⏱11:30am-3pm & 5-9pm Tue-Sat) Ecstasy by the steaming oversized bowl, Tosh's ramen comes with silken broth and crunchy sprouts, topped with a poached egg if you like it that way. It couldn't get more authentic. Try to carve out some room for an order of spicy wings. Everyone is drawn to this happy place in a nondescript strip mall, so go early.

Caputo's Deli
DELI $

(☎801-486-6615; 1516 S 1500 E; mains $5-15; ⏱7am-8pm Mon-Sat) Stock up on gorgeous cheeses, marinated peppers, fresh sandwiches and pastries at this deli counter and gourmet store.

Del Mar al Lago
PERUVIAN $$

(📞801-467-2890; 310 Bugatti Ave S; mains $16-24; ⊙11am-4pm & 6-9pm Mon-Thu, 11am-10pm Fri & Sat) Get ready for a treat. The Peruvian patrons tell you it's authentic. Chef Wilmer from Trujillo cooks up the country's best dishes, including ceviche (fish marinated in lime), yucca fries and whipped potato *causas* with jalapeño aioli.

Takashi
JAPANESE $$

(📞801-519-9595; 18 W Market St; rolls $10-18, mains $10-19; ⊙11:30am-2pm & 5:30-10pm Mon-Sat) Who wouldn't be tempted by 'sex on rice'? The best of a number of surprisingly good sushi restaurants here in landlocked Salt Lake, and often packed. Even LA restaurant snobs rave about the innovative rolls at this ever-so-chic establishment.

★Avenues Bistro on Third
BISTRO $$$

(📞801-831-5409; http://avenuesbistroonthird.com; 564 E 3rd Ave; mains $16-37; ⊙11am-10pm Wed-Fri, 9am-3pm & 5pm-close Sat & Sun) 🍴 An intimate, food-first experience. Enter the tiny house in the Avenues to a handful of tables around an open grill. The owner is seating guests and chatting up neighbors. The fare: fresh greens with Utah trout, trumpet mushrooms brushed in honey lavender and homemade fig newtons all melt in your mouth.

🍷 Drinking & Nightlife

Pubs and bars that also serve food are mainstays of SLC's nightlife, and no one minds if you mainly drink and nibble. A complete schedule of local bar music is available in the *City Weekly* (www.cityweekly.net).

★Beer Bar
PUB

(www.beerbarslc.com; 161 E 200 S; ⊙11am-2am Mon-Sat, 10am-2am Sun) With shared wooden tables and over 140 beers and 13 sausage styles, Beer Bar is a little slice of Bavaria in Salt Lake City. The crowd is diverse and far more casual than at Bar X next door (a linked venue). A great place to meet friends and make friends, but it gets pretty loud.

Bar X
COCKTAIL BAR

(155 E 200 S; ⊙4pm-2am Mon-Fri, 6pm-2am Sat, 7pm-2am Sun) So low-lit and funky, it's hard to believe you're down the street from Temple Sq (p872). Cozy up to the crowded bar with a Moscow Mule and listen to Motown or funk (or the guy at the next table saying to his date, 'Your voice is pretty').

MUSEUM OF ANCIENT LIFE

A family-friendly **museum** (📞801-768-2300; www.thanksgivingpoint.org; 3003 N Thanksgiving Way, Lehi; all-attraction pass adult/child $25/20, museum adult/child $15/12; ⊙10am-8pm Mon-Sat; 🚗) at Thanksgiving Point. Prehistoric life is on display with exhibits on dinosaurs and aquatic life, lots of interactive exhibits for kids and a 3D theater.

★Jack Mormon Coffee Co
CAFE

(www.jackmormoncoffee.com; 82 E St; ⊙10am-6pm Mon-Sat) Utah's finest roaster also serves mean espresso drinks. When the temps rise, locals binge on a Jack Frost.

Gracie's
BAR

(www.graciesslc.com; 326 S West Temple St; ⊙11am-2am Mon-Sat, 10am-2am Sun) Even with two levels and four bars, Gracie's trendy bar-restaurant still gets crowded. The two sprawling patios are the best place to kick back. Live music or DJs most nights.

☆ Entertainment

We wouldn't say the nightlife here is all that hot; major dance clubs change frequently and few are open more than a couple of nights a week. See the *City Weekly* (www.cityweekly.net) for listings. Classical entertainment options, especially around Temple Sq (p872), are plentiful.

Music

★Mormon Tabernacle Choir
LIVE MUSIC

(📞801-570-0080, 801-240-4150; www.mormontabernaclechoir.org) Hearing the world-renowned Mormon Tabernacle Choir is a must-do on any SLC bucket list. A live choir broadcast goes out every Sunday at 9:30am. September through November, and January through May, attend in person at the Tabernacle (p873). Free public rehearsals are held here from 8pm to 9pm Thursday.

Theater

The Salt Lake City Arts Council provides a complete cultural events calendar on its website (www.slcgov.com/city-life/ec). Local venues include the **Gallivan Center** (www.thegallivancenter.com; 200 S, btwn State & Main Sts), **Depot** (📞801-355-5522; www.smithstix.com; 400 W South Temple St), and the **Rose Wagner Performing Arts Center**

THE BOOK OF MORMON, THE MUSICAL

Singing and dancing Mormon missionaries? You betcha...at least on Broadway. In the spring of 2011, *The Book of Mormon* musical opened to critical acclaim at the Eugene O'Neill Theatre in New York. The light-hearted satire about LDS missionaries in Uganda came out of the comic minds that also created the musical *Avenue Q* and the animated TV series *South Park*. No wonder people laughed them all the way to nine Tony Awards.

The LDS church's official response? Actually quite measured, avoiding any direct criticism – though it was made clear that their belief is that while 'the Book, the musical' can entertain you, the scriptures of the actual Book of Mormon can change your life.

(https://artsaltlake.org; 138 W 300 S); you can reserve through **ArtTix** (☑ 801-355-2787, 888-451-2787; https://artsaltlake.org).

Eccles Theatre
THEATER
(☑ 385-468-1010; www.eccles.theatersaltlakecity. com; 131 Main St) Opened in 2016, this gorgeous building has two theaters (one seating 2500 people), showing Broadway shows, concerts and other entertainment.

Sports

Utah Jazz
BASKETBALL
(☑ 801-325-2500; www.nba.com/jazz; 301 W South Temple St) Utah Jazz, the men's professional basketball team, plays at the **Vivint Smart Home Arena** (www.vivintarena.com; 301 W South Temple St), where concerts are also held.

Real Salt Lake
SOCCER
(☑ 844-732-5849; www.rsl.com; 9256 State St, Rio Tinto Stadium; ☺ Mar-Oct) Salt Lake's winning Major League Soccer team (*ree*-al) has a loyal local following and matches are fun to take in at the **Rio Tinto Stadium**.

🛍 Shopping

An interesting array of boutiques, antiques and cafes line up along Broadway Ave (300 South), between 100 and 300 East. Drawing on Utah pioneer heritage, SLC has quite a few crafty shops and galleries scattered around; a few can be found on the 300 block of W Pierpont Ave. Many participate in the one-day Craft Salt Lake expo in August.

Utah Artist Hands
ARTS & CRAFTS
(www.utahhands.com; 163 E Broadway; ☺ noon-6pm Mon-Fri, to 5pm Sat) Local artists' work, all made in-state, runs the gamut from fine art and photography to scarves and pottery.

🛈 Information

EMERGENCY & MEDICAL SERVICES
Local Police (☑ 801-799-3000; 315 E 200 S)
Salt Lake Regional Medical Center (☑ 801-350-4111; www.saltlakeregional.com; 1050 E South Temple St; ☺ 24hr emergency)
University Hospital (☑ 801-581-2121; 50 N Medical Dr)

TOURIST INFORMATION
Public Lands Information Center (☑ 801-466-6411; www.publiclands.org; 3285 E 3300 S, REI Store; ☺ 10:30am-5:30pm Mon-Fri, 9am-1pm Sat) Recreation information for nearby public lands (state parks, BLM, USFS), including the Wasatch-Cache National Forest.
Visit Salt Lake (☑ 801-534-4900; www. visitsaltlake.com; 90 S West Temple St, Salt Palace Convention Center; ☺ 9am-6pm Mon-Fri, to 5pm Sat & Sun) Publishes a free visitor-guide booklet; large gift shop onsite at the visitor center.

🛈 Getting There & Around

Five miles northwest of downtown, **Salt Lake City International Airport** (SLC; ☑ 801-575-2400; www.slcairport.com; 776 N Terminal Dr; ☎) has mostly domestic flights, though you can fly direct to Canada and Mexico. **Express Shuttle** (☑ 801-596-1600; www.xpressshuttleutah. com; to downtown $17) run shared van services to the airport.

Greyhound (☑ 800-231-2222; www.grey hound.com; 300 S 600 W; ☎) has buses to nationwide destinations and the **Union Pacific Rail Depot** (340 S 600 W) is serviced daily by **Amtrak** (☑ 800-872-7245; www.amtrak.com) trains heading to Denver and California.

Utah Transit Authority (UTA; www.rideuta. com; one way $2.50; ☎) runs light-rail services to the international airport and downtown area. Bus 550 travels downtown from the parking structure between Terminals 1 and 2.

Park City & Wasatch Mountains

Utah offers some of North America's most awesome skiing, with fabulous low-density, low-moisture snow – between 300in and 500in annually – and thousands of acres of high-altitude terrain. The Wasatch Mountain Range, which towers over SLC, holds numerous ski resorts, abundant hiking, camping and mountain biking – not to mention chichi Park City, with its upscale amenities and famous film festival.

Salt Lake City Resorts

Because of Great Salt Lake–affected snow patterns, these resorts receive almost twice as much snow as Park City. The four resorts east of Salt Lake City sit 30 to 45 miles from the downtown core at the end of two canyons. In summer, access the numerous hiking and biking trails that lead off from both canyons.

🏃 Activities

⭐ Alta   SNOW SPORTS
(✆801-359-1078, 888-782-9258; www.alta.com; Little Cottonwood Canyon; day lift-pass adult/child $96/50) Dyed-in-the-wool skiers make a pilgrimage to Alta, at the top of the valley. No snowboarders are allowed here, which keeps the snow cover from deteriorating, especially on groomers. Wide-open powder fields, gullies, chutes and glades, such as **East Greeley**, **Devil's Castle** and **High Rustler**, have helped make Alta famous. Warning: you may never want to ski anywhere else.

⭐ Snowbird   SNOW SPORTS
(✆800-232-9542; www.snowbird.com; Hwy 210, Little Cottonwood Canyon; day lift-ticket adult/child $116/55) The biggest and busiest of all the Salt Lake City resorts, with all-round great snow riding – think steep and deep. Numerous lift-assist summer hiking trails; aerial tramway runs year-round.

Solitude   SNOW SPORTS
(✆801-534-1400; www.skisolitude.com; 12000 Big Cottonwood Canyon Rd; day lift-ticket adult/child $83/53) Exclusive, European-style village surrounded by excellent terrain. The **Nordic Center** (http://skisolitude.com/winter-activities/nordic-skiing-nordic-center; day pass adult/child $18/free; ⊙8:30am-4:40pm Dec-Mar & Jun-Aug) has cross-country skiing in winter and nature trails in summer.

Brighton   SNOW SPORTS
(✆801-532-4731, 800-873-5512; www.brightonresort.com; Big Cottonwood Canyon Rd; day lift-ticket adult/child $79/free; 🚻) Slackers, truants and bad-ass boarders rule at Brighton. But don't be intimidated: the low-key resort where many Salt Lake residents first learned to ski remains a good first-timers' spot, especially if you want to snowboard. Thick stands of pines line sweeping groomed trails and wide boulevards, and from the top, the views are gorgeous.

Park City

With a dusting of snow, the century-old buildings on main street create a snow globe scene come to life. A one-time silver boom-and-bust town, pretty Park City is now lined

---

SALT LAKE CITY FOR KIDS

Salt Lake is a child-friendly city if ever there was one. The wonderful hands-on exhibits at the **Discovery Gateway** (www.discoverygateway.org; 444 W 100 S; $8.50; ⊙10am-6pm Mon-Thu, to 7pm Fri & Sat, noon-6pm Sun; 🚻) stimulate imaginations and senses.

Kids can help farmhands milk cows, churn butter and feed animals at **Wheeler Historic Farm** (✆385-468-1755; www.wheelerfarm.com; 6351 S 900 E, South Cottonwood Regional Park; hay ride $3, house tour adult/child $4/2; ⊙daylight hours; 🚻) FREE, which dates from 1886. There's also blacksmithing, quilting and hay rides in summer.

More than 800 animals inhabit zones such as the Asian Highlands on the landscaped 42-acre grounds at **Hogle Zoo** (www.hoglezoo.org; 2600 E Sunnyside Ave; adult/child $15/11; ⊙9am-6pm; 🚻). Daily animal encounter programs help kids learn more about their favorite species.

Tracy Aviary (www.tracyaviary.org; 589 E 1300 S; adult/child $8/5; ⊙9am-4pm; 🚻) lets little ones toss fish to the pelicans as one of its interactive programs and performances. More than 400 winged creatures from around the world call this bird park home.

With 55 acres of gardens, a full-scale working and petting farm, golf course, giant movie theater, museum, dining, shopping and ice-cream parlor, what doesn't Thanksgiving Point, located in Lehi, have? The on-site Museum of Ancient Life (p875) is one of the highest-tech and most hands-on dinosaur museums in the state. Kids can dig for their own bones, dress up a dinosaur or play in a watery Silurian reef. Lehi is 28 miles south of downtown SLC; to get there take exit 287 off I-15.

CAN I GET A DRINK IN UTAH?

Absolutely. Although a few unusual liquor laws remain, in recent years they've been relaxed and private club membership bars are no more. Some rules to remember:

➡ Few restaurants have full liquor licenses: most serve beer and wine only. You have to order food to drink.

➡ Minors aren't allowed in bars.

➡ Mixed drinks and wine are available only after midday; 3.2% alcohol beer can be served starting at 10am.

➡ Mixed drinks cannot contain more than 1.5oz of a primary liquor, or 2.5oz total including secondary alcohol. Sorry, no Long Island Iced Teas or double shots.

➡ Packaged liquor can only be sold at state-run liquor stores; grocery and convenience stores can sell 3.2% alcohol beer and malt beverages. Sales are made from Monday through Saturday only.

with condos and mansions in the valleys. Utah's premier ski village boasts fabulous restaurants and cultural offerings. It recently annexed the adjacent Canyons Resort to become the largest ski resort in North America.

Park City first shot to international fame when it hosted the downhill, jumping and sledding events at the 2002 Winter Olympics. Today it's the permanent home base for the US Ski Team. There's usually snow through mid-April.

Come summer, more residents than visitors gear up for hiking and mountain biking among the nearby peaks. June to August, temperatures average in the 70s; nights are chilly. Spring and fall can be wet and boring; resort services, limited in summer compared with winter, shut down entirely between seasons.

◉ Sights

★ **Utah Olympic Park**   AMUSEMENT PARK
(☑ 435-658-4200; www.utaholympiclegacy.com; 3419 Olympic Pkwy; museum free, activity day pass adult/child $70/45; ☺ 10am-6pm, tours 11am-4pm)
Visit the site of the 2002 Olympic ski jump-

ing, bobsledding, skeleton, Nordic combined and luge events, which continues to host national competitions. There are 10m, 20m, 40m, 64m, 90m and 120m Nordic ski-jumping hills as well as a bobsled-luge run. The US Ski Team practices here year-round – in summer, the freestyle jumpers land in a bubble-filled jetted pool, and the Nordic jumpers on a hillside covered in plastic. Call for a schedule; it's free to observe.

★ **Park City Museum**   MUSEUM
(www.parkcityhistory.org; 528 Main St; adult/child $10/4; ☺ 10am-7pm Mon-Sat, noon-6pm Sun) A well-staged interactive museum touches on the highlights of the town's history as a mining boomtown, hippie hangout and premier ski resort. There are fascinating exhibits on the world's first underground ski lift, a real dungeon in the basement and a 3D map of mining tunnels under the mountain.

🏃 Activities

Skiing is the big area attraction, but there are activities enough to keep you more than busy in both summer and winter. Most are based out of the three resorts: Canyons, Park City Mountain and Deer Valley.

Deer Valley   SNOW SPORTS, ADVENTURE SPORTS
(☑ 435-649-1000, snowmobiling 435-645-7669; www.deervalley.com; Deer Valley Dr; day lift ticket adult/child $128/80, round-trip gondola ride $17; ☺ snowmobiling 9am-5pm) Want to be pampered? Deer Valley, a resort of superlatives, has thought of everything – from tissue boxes at the base of slopes to ski valets. Slalom, mogul and freestyle-aerial competitions in the 2002 Olympics were held here, but the resort is just as famous for its superb dining, white-glove service and uncrowded slopes as meticulously groomed as the gardens of Versailles.

Canyons Village at Park City   SNOW SPORTS, ADVENTURE SPORTS
(☑ 435-649-5400; www.thecanyons.com; 4000 Canyons Resort Dr; lift ticket adult/child $134/86) Bolstered by tens of millions of dollars in improvements, and now merged with Park City Resorts, Canyons seeks novelty with the first North American 'bubble' lift (an enclosed, climate-controlled lift), expanded services, 300 new acres of advanced trails and an increased snow-making capability. The resort currently sprawls across nine aspen-covered peaks 4 miles outside of town, near the freeway.

Park City

Mountain Resort   SNOW SPORTS, ADVENTURE SPORTS
(☑ 435-649-8111; www.parkcitymountainresort.
com; 1310 Lowell Ave; lift ticket adult/child $134/86;
🚠) From boarder dudes to parents with tots,
everyone skis Park City Mountain Resort,
host of the Olympic snowboarding and giant
slalom events. The awesome terrain couldn't
be more family friendly – or more accessible,
rising as it does right over downtown.

✦✦ Festivals & Events

Sundance Film Festival   FILM
(☑ 888-285-7790; www.sundance.org/festival) Independent films and their makers, and movie stars and their fans, fill the town to bursting for 10 days in late January. Passes, ticket
packages and the few individual tickets sell
out well in advance – plan ahead.

🛏 Sleeping

Mid-December through mid-April is winter
high season, with minimum stays required;
rates rise during Christmas, New Year's and
the Sundance Film Festival. Off-season rates

drop 50% or more. For better nightlife, stay
in the old town.

Chateau Apres Lodge   HOSTEL **$**
(☑ 435-649-9372; www.chateauapres.com; 1299
Norfolk Ave; dm $50, r $140-165; 🛜) The only
budget-oriented accommodation in town
is this basic, 1963 lodge – with a 1st-floor
dorm – near the town ski lift. Reserve ahead,
as it's very popular with groups and seniors.

★**Old Town Guest House**   B&B **$$**
(☑ 435-649-2642; www.oldtownguesthouse.com;
1011 Empire Ave; r $169-229; ❀@🛜) Grab the
flannel robe, pick a paperback off the shelf
and snuggle under a quilt on your lodgepole
bed or kick back on the large deck at this
comfy in-town B&B. The host will gladly give
you the lowdown on the great outdoors, guid-
ed ski tours, mountain biking and the rest.

Park City Peaks   HOTEL **$$**
(☑ 435-649-5000; www.parkcitypeaks.com; 2121
Park Ave; d/ste $219/319; ❀@🛜🏊) Comfort-
able, contemporary rooms include access to
a heated outdoor pool, hot tub, restaurant

BEARS EARS NATIONAL MONUMENT

Protecting 1.35 million acres filled with ancient cliff dwellings, ponderosa forests, five-thousand-year-old petroglyphs, mesas, canyons and red rock, **Bears Ears National Monument** (www.fs.fed.us/visit/bears-ears-national-monument) is the newest addition to the awesome collection of American parks.

Some notable landmarks within the monument include the **Bears Ears Buttes**, **Cedar Mesa**, **White Canyon**, **San Juan River**, **Indian Creek**, **Comb Ridge** and **Valley of the Gods**. Their treasures, described by David Roberts' *In Search of the Old Ones*, are nothing short of exquisite.

Archaeological sites dating back 8500 years have been threatened by vandalism and destruction over recent years. The Navajo, Hopi, Zuni, Ute Mountain and Ute Indian tribes led the Bears Ears proposal, and will have a strong stake in the management of the monument, a status that makes this area's conservation approach unique among the Utah parks.

The designation has been plagued by controversy. Protecting this vast area goes against energy leasing and development interests that are very strong in the state. Governor Gary Herbert's vocal support to remove protection for the monument to promote fossil fuel development was met by the Outdoor Retailer show pulling out of holding its annual gathering in Salt Lake City.

Patagonia's founder, Yvon Chouinard, spearheaded the boycott with an editorial letter arguing that outdoor recreation brings $12 billion in consumer spending in Utah and supports 122,000 jobs – three times the number of positions that the fossil fuel industry offers in Utah.

As the Trump administration rallies to increase jobs in the fossil fuel sector and ease environmental protections on public lands, the status of Bears Ears remains precarious. Only this designation protects Lockhart Basin bordering Canyonlands, considered Utah's Serengeti for its pronghorn antelope and mountain lions, from future energy leasing.

No park infrastructure has been created yet, though parts of the monument feature trails, information centers and campgrounds already. For updates on the site, its highlights and its status, check out www.bearsearscoalition.org.

ANTELOPE ISLAND STATE PARK

White-sand beaches, birds and buffalo are what attract people to the pretty, 15-mile-long **Antelope Island State Park** (☑801-773-2941; http://stateparks. utah.gov; Antelope Dr; day use per vehicle $10, tent & RV sites without hookups $15; ◷7am-10pm Jul-Sep, to 7pm Oct-Jun). That's right, the largest island in the Great Salt Lake is home to a 600-strong herd of American bison (buffalo). The November roundup, for veterinary examination, is a thrilling wildlife spectacle. Hundreds of thousands of migratory birds stop to feast on tiny brine shrimp along the Great Salt Lake's shore en route to distant lands during fall and spring migrations.

and bar. Great deals off-season. December through April, breakfast is included.

★**Washington School House** BOUTIQUE HOTEL $$$
(☑435-649-3800; www.washingtonschoolhouse. com; 543 Park Ave; r $405; ❄🗜🖥) Architect Trip Bennett oversaw the restoration that turned an 1898 limestone schoolhouse on a hill into a luxurious boutique hotel with 12 suites. How did the children ever concentrate when they could gaze out at the mountains through 9ft-tall windows instead?

✕ Eating

Park City is well known for exceptional upscale eating – a reasonably priced meal is harder to find. The ski resorts have numerous eating options in season. Dinner reservations are required at all top-tier places in winter. From April through November restaurants reduce opening hours variably, and may take extended breaks, especially in May.

★**Vessel Kitchen** CAFE $
(☑435-200-8864; www.vesselkitchen.com; 1784 Uinta Way; mains $7-13; ◷8am-9pm; 🖋🖘) Locals in the know head to this gourmet cafeteria in the shopping plaza for fast value eats. With kombucha on tap, avocado toast and lovely winter salads and stews, there's something for everyone. Even kids. Breakfasts shine with skillets of *shakshuka* (poached eggs in tomato sauce) and sweet-potato hash.

Good Karma INDIAN, FUSION $$
(www.goodkarmarestaurants.com; 1782 Prospector Ave; breakfast $8-13, mains $12-25; ◷7am-10pm; 🖋) 🖉 Whenever possible, local and organic ingredients are used in the Indo-Persian meals at Good Karma. Start the day with Punjabi eggs and dine on curries and grilled meats. You'll recognize the place by the Tibetan prayer flags flapping out front.

★**Riverhorse on Main** AMERICAN $$$
(☑435-649-3536; www.riverhorseparkcity.com; 540 Main St; dinner mains $38-60; ◷5-10pm Mon-Thu, to 11pm Fri & Sat, 11am-2:30pm & 5-10pm Sun; 🖋) A fine mix of the earthy and exotic, with cucumber quinoa salad, polenta fries and macadamia-crusted halibut. There's a separate menu for vegetarians. A wall-sized window and the sleek modern design creates a stylish atmosphere. Reserve ahead: this is a longtime, award-winning restaurant.

★**J&G Grill** AMERICAN $$$
(☑435-940-5760; www.jggrilldeercrest.com; 2300 Deer Valley Drive E, Deer Valley Resort; lunch mains $17-31, dinner mains $33-65; ◷7am-9pm) A favorite of locals, who love the tempura onion rings and seared scallops with sweet chili sauce. The bold flavors of meat and fish star here at one of celebrity chef Jean-Georges Vongerichten's collaborative projects. The mid-mountain **St Regis** (☑435-940-5700; www.stregisdeervalley.com; 2300 Deer Valley Dr E; r from $446; ❄@🗜🖥) setting is spectacular.

Wahso ASIAN $$$
(☑435-615-0300; www.wahso.com; 577 Main St; mains $30-56; ◷5:30-10pm Wed-Sun, closed mid-Apr–mid-Jun) Park City's cognoscenti flock to this modern pan-Asian phenomenon, where fine-dining dishes may include lamb vindaloo or Malaysian snapper. The sake martinis pack a punch. Expect to see and be seen.

🍷 Drinking & Nightlife

Main St is where it's at. In winter there's action nightly; weekends are most lively off-season. For listings, see www.thisweekinpark city.com. Several restaurants, such as **Bistro 412** (☑435-649-8211; www.bistro412.com; 412 Main St; mains $13-34; ◷11am-2:30pm & 5pm-1am) 🖉, **Squatters** (☑435-649-9868; www.squatters. com; 1900 Park Ave; burgers $10-15, mains $10-23; ◷8am-10pm Sun-Thu, to 11pm Fri & Sat; 🖋) and **Wasatch Brew Pub** (☑435-649-0900; www. wasatchbeers.com; 250 Main St; lunch & sandwiches $10-15, dinner $10-30; ◷11am-10pm Mon-Fri, 10am-10pm Sat & Sun), also have good bars.

★ **High West Distillery** BAR
(☑435-649-8300; www.highwest.com; 703 Park
Ave; ⊙11am-9pm Sun-Thu, to 10pm Fri & Sat, tours
3pm & 4pm) This former livery and Model A–
era garage is now home to Park City's most
happenin' nightspot. The ski-in distillery
was founded by a biochemist whose homemade rye whiskey fuels a spicy lemonade
bound to kill the strongest colds.

Spur BAR
(☑435-615-1618; www.thespurbarandgrill.com;
350 Main St; ⊙10am-1am) What an upscale
Western bar should be: rustic walls, leather
couches, roaring fire. Good grub, too. Live
music on weekends in summer or daily in
ski season.

ⓘ Information

Visitor Information Center (☑435-658-9616;
www.visitparkcity.com; 1794 Olympic Pkwy;
⊙9am-6pm; 🛜) Vast visitor center with a
coffee bar, a terrace and incredible views of
the mountains at **Olympic Park** (p878). Visitor
guides available online.

ⓘ Getting There & Around

Downtown Park City is 5 miles south of I-80
exit 145, 32 miles east of Salt Lake City and 40
miles from **Salt Lake City International Airport** (p876). Hwy 190 (closed October through
March) crosses over Guardsman Pass between
Big Cottonwood Canyon and Park City. In addition to public buses, a number of van services go
to the airport and other mountain destinations:

All Resort Express (☑435-649-3999; www.
allresort.com; one-way $39)

Canyon Transportation (☑800-255-1841;
www.canyontransport.com; shared van $39)

Park City Transportation (☑435-649-8567;
www.parkcitytransportation.com; shared
van $39)

Powder for the People (☑435-649-6648)

Utah Transit Authority (www.rideuta.com;
one-way $4.50)

The excellent **public transit system** (www.
parkcity.org; 558 Swede Alley; ⊙8am-11pm
winter) covers most of Park City, including the
three ski resorts, and makes it easy not to need
a car to get around.

Northeastern Utah

Northeastern Utah is high-wilderness terrain, much of which is more than a mile
above sea level. Most travelers come to see
Dinosaur National Monument, but you'll
also find other dino dig sites and museums,
as well as Fremont Indian rock art and ruins
in the area. Up near the Wyoming border,
the Uinta Mountains and Flaming Gorge attract trout fishers and wildlife lovers alike.

Vernal

As the closest town to Dinosaur National
Monument, it's not surprising that Vernal
welcomes you with a large pink allosaurus.
The informative film, interactive exhibits,
video clips and giant fossils at the **Utah Field
House of Natural History State Park Museum** (☑435-789-3799; http://stateparks.utah.
gov; 496 E Main St; ⊙9am-7pm Apr-Aug, to 5pm
low season; ♿) 【FREE】 make a great all-round
introduction to Utah's dinosaurs.

Don Hatch River Expeditions (☑435-
789-4316, 800-342-8243; www.donhatchriver
trips.com; 221 N 400 E; one-day tour adult/child
$105/85) offers rapid-riding and gentler float
trips on the nearby Green and Yampa Rivers.

Chain motels are numerous along Main
St, but they book up with local workers –
so don't expect a price break. **Holiday Inn
Express & Suites** (☑800-315-2621, 435-789-
4654; www.holidayinn.com/vernal; 1515 W Hwy
40; r $119-176; ❄🛜🐾) and **Landmark Inn
& Suites** (☑435-781-1800, 888-738-1800; www.
landmark-inn.com; 301 E 100 S; r from $90; 🛜)
offer a few upscale touches. For dinner, try
the excellent pub food at **Vernal Brewing
Company** (☑435-781-2337; www.vernalbrew
ingco.com; 55 S 500 E; mains $11-20; ⊙11:30am-
9pm Mon-Sat), or go Mexican at **Don Pedro's**
(☑435-789-3402; http://klcyads.com/don-pedros;
3340 N Vernal Ave; dishes $8-15; ⊙11am-2pm
& 5-10pm).

**SCENIC DRIVE: MIRROR LAKE
HIGHWAY**

This alpine route, also known as Hwy
150, begins about 12 miles east of
Park City in **Kamas** and climbs to
elevations of more than 10,000ft as
it covers the 65 miles into Wyoming.
The highway provides breathtaking
mountain vistas, passing by scores of
lakes, campgrounds and trailheads in
the **Uinta-Wasatch-Cache National
Forest** (www.fs.usda.gov/uwcnf). Note
that sections may be closed to traffic
well into spring due to heavy snowfall;
check online first.

Dinosaur National Monument

Straddling the Utah-Colorado state line, **Dinosaur National Monument** (www.nps.gov/dino; off Hwy 40, Vernal; 7-day passes per vehicle $20; ⊙24hr) protects a huge dinosaur fossil bed, discovered in 1909. Both states' sections are beautiful, but Utah has the bones. Don't miss the **Quarry Exhibit** (www.nps.gov/dino; per vehicle $20; ⊙8am-7pm Memorial Day–Labor Day, to 4:30pm rest of year), an enclosed, partially excavated wall of rock with more than 1600 bones protruding. In summer, shuttles run to the Quarry itself, 15 miles northeast of Vernal's **Quarry Visitor Center** (⊙8am-6pm mid-May–late Sep, 9am-5pm late Sep–mid-May) on Hwy 149; out of season you drive there in a ranger-led caravan. Follow the Fossil Discovery Trail from below the parking lot (2.2 miles round-trip) to see a few more giant femurs sticking out of the rock. The rangers' interpretive hikes are highly recommended.

In Colorado, the **Canyon Area** – 30 miles further east, outside Dinosaur, CO, and home to the monument's main **visitor center** (☑970-374-3000; 4545 E Hwy 40; ⊙8am-5pm May-Sep, 9am-5pm Sep-May) – holds some stunning overlooks, but thanks to its higher elevation is closed by snow until late spring. Both sections have numerous hiking trails, interpretive driving tours, Green or Yampa river access and campgrounds ($18 per tent and RV site).

Flaming Gorge National Recreation Area

Named for its fiery red sandstone formations, this gorge-ous park has 375 miles of reservoir shoreline, part of the Green River system. Resort activities at **Red Canyon Lodge** (☑435-889-3759; www.redcanyonlodge.com; 790 Red Canyon Rd, Dutch John; 2-/4-person cabin from $155/165; ☎☀) include fly-fishing, rowing, rafting and horseback riding; its pleasantly rustic cabins have no TVs but there's wi-fi in the decent restaurant. **Nine Mile Bunk & Breakfast** (☑435-637-2572; http://9mileranch.com; r $70-85, cabin $50-80, campsite $15) offers themed rooms, a log cabin and campgrounds, and can organise canyon tours.

Contact the **USFS Flaming Gorge Headquarters** (☑435-784-3445; www.fs.usda.gov/ashley; 25 W Hwy 43, Manila; park day use $5; ⊙8am-5pm Mon-Fri) for the public camping

lowdown. The area's 6040ft elevation ensures pleasant summers.

Moab & Southeastern Utah

Experience the earth's beauty at its most elemental in this rocky-and-rugged desert corner of the Colorado Plateau. Beyond the few pine-clad mountains, there's little vegetation to hide the impressive handiwork of time, water and wind: the thousands of red-rock spans in Arches National Park, the sheer-walled river gorges from Canyonlands to Lake Powell, and the stunning buttes and mesas of Monument Valley. The town of Moab is the best base for adventure, with as much four-wheeling, white-knuckle rafting, outfitter-guided fun as you can handle. Or you can lose the crowd while looking for Ancestral Puebloan rock art and dwellings in miles of isolated and undeveloped lands.

Green River

The 'World's Watermelon Capital,' the town of Green River offers a good base for river running on the Green and Colorado Rivers. The legendary one-armed Civil War veteran, geologist and ethnologist John Wesley Powell first explored these rivers in 1869 and 1871. Learn about his amazing travels at the **John Wesley Powell River History Museum** (☑435-564-3427; www.jwprhm.com; 885 E Main St; adult/child $6/2; ⊙9am-7pm Mon-Sat, noon-5pm Sun Apr-Oct, 9am-5pm Nov-Mar), which doubles as the local visitor center.

Holiday River Expeditions (☑800-624-6323, 435-564-3273; www.holidayexpeditions.com; 10 Holiday River St; day trip $190) run one-day rafting trips in Westwater Canyon, as well as multiday excursions. Family-owned, clean and cheerful, **Robbers Roost Motel** (☑435-564-3452; www.rrmotel.com; 325 W Main St; r from $58; ❋☎☀) is a motorcourt budget-gem. Otherwise, there's the **Green River State Park campground** (☑800-322-3770; http://utahstateparks.reserveamerica.com; tent/RV sites $21/30, cabins $60), or numerous chain motels where W Main St (Business 70) connects with I-70.

Residents and rafters alike flock to **Ray's Tavern** (☑435-564-3511; 25 S Broadway; dishes $8-27; ⊙11am-9:30pm), the local beer joint, for hamburgers and fresh-cut French fries. Green River is 182 miles southeast of Salt Lake City and 52 miles northwest of Moab, and is a stop on the daily California Zephyr train, run by **Amtrak** (☑ 800-872-7245; www.amtrak.com; 250 S Broadway) to Denver, CO (from $59, 10¾ hours).

Moab

Doling out hot tubs and pub grub after a dusty day on the trail, Moab is southern Utah's adventure base camp. Mobs arrive to play in Utah's recreation capital. From the hiker to the four-wheeler, the cult of recreation borders on fetishism.

The town becomes overrun from March through October. The impact of all those feet, bikes and 4WDs on the fragile desert is a serious concern. People here love the land, even if they don't always agree about how to protect it. If the traffic irritates you, just remember – you can disappear into the vast desert in no time.

🏃 Activities

★ **Canyonlands Field Institute**   TOURS
(☑ 435-259-7750; www.cfimoab.org; 1320 S Hwy 191; ☺ May-Oct) This nonprofit operation uses proceeds from guided tours to create youth outdoor-education programs and train local guides. It offers occasional workshops and seminars throughout the summer. Top tours include the Rock Art Tour (8am Friday to Sunday), the geology-focused Arches Sunset Tour (4pm Friday to Sunday) and customized river trips.

★ **Rim Cyclery**   MOUNTAIN BIKING
(☑ 435-259-5333; www.rimcyclery.com; 94 W 100 N; ☺ 8am-6pm) Moab's longest-running family owned bike shop not only does rentals and repairs, it also has a museum of mountain-bike technology, and rents cross-country skis in the winter.

Moab Desert Adventures   OUTDOORS
(☑ 804-814-3872; www.moabdesertadventures.com; 415 N Main St; ☺ 7am-7pm) Top-notch climbing tours scale area towers and walls; the 140ft arch rappel is especially exciting. Canyoneering trips are also available.

Sheri Griffith Expeditions   RAFTING
(☑ 800-332-2439; www.griffithexp.com; 2231 S Hwy 191; ☺ 8am-6pm) Operating since 1971, this rafting specialist has a great selection of river trips on the Colorado, Green and San Juan Rivers – from family floats to Cataract Canyon rapids, and from a couple of hours to a couple of weeks.

ROBERT REDFORD'S SUNDANCE RESORT

Robert Redford's **ski resort** (☑ reservations 801-223-4849; 8841 Alpine Loop Scenic Byway; day lift-ticket adult/child $70/43) could not be more idyllic. There are four chairlifts and a beginner area. Most terrain is intermediate and advanced, climbing 2150ft up the northeast slope of Mt Timpanogos. It hosts the independent Sundance Film Festival (p879) and the nonprofit Sundance Institute.

🛏 Sleeping

Prices drop by as much as 50% outside March to October; some smaller places close November through March. Most lodgings have hot tubs and mini-refrigerators, and motels have laundries. Cyclists should ask whether a property provides *secure* bike storage, not just an unlocked closet.

Though there's a huge number of motels, they are often booked out. Reserve as far ahead as possible. For a full lodging list, see www.discovermoab.com.

Individual **BLM campsites** (☑ 435-259-2100; www.blm.gov; Hwy 128; tent sites $15; ☺ year-round) in the area are first-come, first-served. In peak season, check with the Moab Information Center (p884) to see which sites are full.

Kokopelli Lodge   MOTEL $
(☑ 435-259-7615; www.kokopellilodge.com; 72 S 100 E; r $79-149; ❄ ⊛ 🐾) Retro styling meets with desert chic at this great-value budget motel. Amenities include a hot tub, a BBQ grill and secure bike storage.

★ **Cali Cochitta**   B&B $$
(☑ 435-259-4961, 888-429-8112; www.moabdreaminn.com; 110 S 200 E; cottages $155-190; ❄ ⊛) Charming and central, these adjoining brick cottages offer snug rooms fitted with smart decor. A long wooden table on the patio makes a welcome setting for communal breakfasts. You can also take advantage of the porch chairs, hammock or backyard hot tub in the Zen garden.

Pack Creek Ranch   LODGE $$
(☑ 888-879-6622; www.packcreekranch.com; off La Sal Mountain Loop; cabins $175-235; ⊛ 🐾) This hidden Shangri-la's log cabins are tucked beneath mature cottonwoods and

willow trees in the La Sal Mountains, 2000ft above Moab. Most feature fireplaces; all have kitchens and gas grills (bring groceries). No TV or phones. Edward Abbey is among the artists and writers who came here for inspiration. Amenities include horseback riding and an indoor hot tub and sauna.

★ Sunflower Hill Inn   INN $$$
(☑ 435-259-2974; www.sunflowerhill.com; 185 N 300 E; r $208-293; ❄ 🛜 ≋) Wow! This is one of the best bets in town. A top-shelf B&B, Sunflower Hill offers 12 rooms in a quaint country setting. Grab a room in the cozier cedar-sided early-20th-century home over the annex rooms. All rooms come with quilt-piled beds and antiques – some even have jetted tubs.

Sorrel River Ranch   LODGE $$$
(☑ 877-317-8244; www.sorrelriver.com; Mile 17, Hwy 128; r from $529; ❄ @ ≋) Southeast Utah's only full-service luxury resort and gourmet restaurant was originally an 1803 homestead. The lodge and log cabins sit on 240 lush acres, with riding areas and alfalfa fields along the Colorado River. Details strive for rustic perfection, with bedroom fireplaces, handmade log beds, copper-top tables and Jacuzzi tubs.

✖ Eating

There's no shortage of places to fuel up in Moab, from backpacker coffeehouses to gourmet dining rooms. Pick up the *Moab Menu Guide* (www.moabmenuguide.com) at area lodgings. Some restaurants close or operate on variable days, from December through March.

★ Milt's   BURGERS $
(☑ 435-259-7424; 356 Mill Creek Dr; mains $4-9; ☺11am-8pm Mon-Sat) Meet greasy goodness. A triathlete couple bought this classic 1954 burger stand and smartly changed nothing. Heaven is one of their honest burgers made from grass-fed wagyu beef, jammed with pickles, fresh lettuce, a side of fresh-cut fries and creamy butterscotch milkshake. Be patient: the line can get long. It's near the **Slickrock Trail** (Sand Flats Recreation Area; www.discovermoab.com/sandflats.htm; car/cyclist $5/2).

Sabaku Sushi   SUSHI $$
(☑ 435-259-4455; www.sabakusushi.com; 90 E Center St; rolls $6-11, mains $13-19; ☺5pm-midnight Tue-Sun) The ocean is about a million miles away, but with overnight delivery from Hawaii, you still get a creative selection of fresh rolls, catches of the day and a few Utah originals at this small hole-in-the-wall sushi joint. Go for happy hour (5pm to 6pm on Wednesdays and Thursdays) for discounts on rolls.

Twisted Sistas   CAFE $$
(☑ 435-355-0088; 11 E 100 N; lunch $11-13, mains $16-30; ☺noon-3pm & 5-9pm Fri-Tue, 5-9pm Thu; 🍴) For a calm alternative to the breweries, this low-lit cafe delivers warm ambience, attentive service and tasty food inspired by global flavors. For lighter fare, try the tapas, such as stuffed piquillo peppers and lollipop chicken. There's also a full bar. Check out the rooftop patio.

★ Desert Bistro   SOUTHERN US $$$
(☑ 435-259-0756; www.desertbistro.com; 36 S 100 W; mains $20-60; ☺5:30-11pm Wed-Sun) Stylized preparations of game and fresh, flown-in seafood are the specialty at this welcoming white-tablecloth restaurant inside an old house. Think smoked elk in a huckleberry glaze, pepper-seared scallops and jicama salad with crisp pears. Everything is made onsite, from freshly baked bread to delicious pastries. Great wine list, too.

❶ Information

Moab Information Center (www.discover moab.com; 25 E Center St; ☺8am-7pm; 🛜) Excellent source of information on area parks, trails, activities, camping and weather. Extensive bookstore and knowledgeable staff. Walk-in only.

❶ Getting There & Around

Moab is 235 miles southeast of Salt Lake City, 150 miles northeast of Capitol Reef National Park, and 115 miles southwest of Grand Junction, CO.

Canyonlands Airport (CNY; www.moabairport. com; off Hwy 191), 16 miles north of town, receives flights from Salt Lake City. Major car-rental agencies, such as **Enterprise** (☑ 435-259-8505; N Hwy 191, Mile 148; ☺8am-5pm Mon-Fri, to 2pm Sat), have representatives at the airport.

Boutique Air (☑ 855-268-8478; www.bou tiqueair.com) flies to Salt Lake City and Denver.

There are also limited bus and shuttle van services, including **Elevated Transit** (☑ 888-353-8283; www.elevatedtransit.com; Moab to Salt Lake City airport $70) and **Moab Luxury Coach** (☑ 435-940-4212; www.moabluxury coach.com; 3320 E Fairway Loop), to get you to Salt Lake City, Grand Junction, Colorado and regional destinations.

A private vehicle is pretty much a requirement to get around Moab and the parks. Vehicle traffic is heavy in high season. There's a number of bike paths in and around town; the Moab Information Center can offer a map guide.

Coyote Shuttle (☎ 435-259-8656; www.coyoteshuttle.com) and **Roadrunner Shuttle** (☎ 435-259-9402; www.roadrunnershuttle.com) travel on-demand to Canyonlands Airport and do hiker-biker and river shuttles.

Arches National Park

Stark, exposed, and unforgettably spectacular, **Arches National Park** (www.nps.gov/arch; 7-day pass per vehicle/motorcycle/bike $25/15/10; ☺9am-4pm) boasts the world's greatest concentration of sandstone arches – more than 2000, ranging from 3ft to 300ft wide at last count. Nearly one million visitors make the pilgrimage here each year; it's just 5 miles north of Moab, and small enough for you to see most of it within a day. Many noteworthy arches are easily reached by paved roads and relatively short hiking trails. To avoid crowds, consider a moonlight exploration, when it's cooler and the rocks feel ghostly.

Highlights along the park's main scenic drive include **Balanced Rock**, precariously perched beside the main park road, and, for hikers, the moderate-to-strenuous, 3-mile round-trip trail that ascends the slick rock to reach the unofficial state symbol, **Delicate Arch** (best photographed in the late afternoon).

Further along the road, the spectacularly narrow canyons and maze-like fins of the **Fiery Furnace** must be visited on three-hour, ranger-led hikes, for which advance reservation is usually necessary. It's not easy: be prepared to scramble up and over boulders, chimney down between rocks and navigate narrow ledges.

The scenic drive ends 19 miles from the visitor center at **Devils Garden**. The trailhead marks the start of a 2- to 7.7-mile round-trip hike that passes at least eight arches, though most hikers only go the relatively easy 1.3 miles to Landscape Arch, a gravity-defying, 290ft-long behemoth. For stays between March and October, advance reservations are a must for the **Devils Garden Campground** (☎877-444-6777; www.recreation.gov; tent & RV sites $25). No showers, no hookups.

Because of water scarcity and heat, few visitors backpack, though it is allowed with free permits (available from the visitor center).

ⓘ LOCAL PASSPORTS

Southeastern Utah national parks sell a **Southeast Utah Parks Pass** (per vehicle $50) that's good for a year's entry to Arches and Canyonlands National Parks, plus Hovenweep and Natural Bridges National Monuments. **National Park Service Passes** (www.nps.gov/findapark/passes.htm; per vehicle adult/senior $80/10), available online and at parks, allow year-long access to all federal recreation lands in Utah and beyond – and are a great way to support the Southwest's amazing parks.

Canyonlands National Park

Red-rock fins, bridges, needles, spires, craters, mesas, buttes – **Canyonlands National Park** (www.nps.gov/cany; per vehicle 7 days $25, tent & RV sites without hookups $15-20; ☺24hr) is a crumbling, decaying beauty, a vision of ancient earth. Roads and rivers make inroads into this high-desert wilderness stretching 527 sq miles, but much of it is still untamed. You can hike, raft and 4WD here but be sure that you have plenty of gas, food and water.

The canyons of the Colorado and Green Rivers divide the park into several entirely separate areas. The appropriately named **Island in the Sky** district, just over 30 miles northwest of Moab, consists of a 6000ft-high flat-topped mesa that provides astonishing long-range vistas. Starting from the **visitor center** (☎435-259-4712; www.nps.gov/cany; Hwy 313; ☺8am-6pm Mar-Oct, 9am-4:30pm Nov-Feb), a scenic drive leads past numerous overlooks and trailheads, ending after 12 miles at **Grand View Point**, where a sinuous trail runs for a mile along the very lip of the mesa. Our favorite short hike en route is the half-mile loop to oft-photographed **Mesa Arch**, a slender, cliff-hugging span that frames a magnficent view of Washer Woman Arch. Seven miles from the visitor center, the first-come, first served, 12-site **Willow Flat Campground** (www.nps.gov/cany/planyourvisit/islandinthesky.htm; Island in the Sky; tent & RV sites $15; ☺year-round) has vault toilets but no water, and no hookups.

Named for the spires of orange-and-white sandstone jutting skyward from the desert floor, the wild and remote **Needles** district is ideal for backpacking and off-roading. To reach the **visitor center** (☎435-259-4711;

Hwy 211; ☺8am-6pm Mar-Oct, 9am-4:30pm Nov-Feb), follow Hwy 191 south for 40 miles from Moab, then take Hwy 211 west. This area is much more about long, challenging hikes than roadside overlooks. The awesome **Chesler Park/Joint Trail Loop** is an 11-mile route across desert grasslands, past towering red-and-white-striped pinnacles, and through deep, narrow slot canyons, at times just 2ft across. Elevation changes are moderate, but the distance makes it an advanced day hike. The first-come, first-served, 27-site **Squaw Flat Campground** (www.nps.gov/cany; Needles; tent & RV sites $15; ☺year-round), 3 miles west of the visitor center, fills up every day, spring to fall. It has flush toilets and running water, but no showers or hookups.

In addition to normal entrance fees, advance-reservation permits from the **NPS Backcountry Permits Office** (☑reservations 435-259-4351; https://canypermits.nps.gov/index.cfm; 2282 SW Resource Blvd, Moab; permits $10-30; ☺8:30am-noon Mon-Fri) are required for backcountry camping, mountain biking, 4WD trips and river trips. Remoter areas west of the rivers, only accessible southwest of the town of Green River, include **Horseshoe Canyon**, where determined hikers are rewarded with extraordinary ancient rock art, and the **Maze**.

Dead Horse Point State Park

Tiny but stunning **Dead Horse Point State Park** (www.stateparks.utah.gov; Hwy 313; park day use per vehicle $15, tent & RV sites $35; ☺park 6am-10pm, visitor center 8am-6pm Mar-Oct, 9am-4pm Nov-Feb) has been the setting for numerous movies, including the climactic scenes of *Thelma & Louise*. It's not a hiking destination, but mesmerizing views merit the short detour off Hwy 313 en route to the Island in the Sky in Canyonlands National Park: look out at red-rock canyons rimmed with white cliffs, the Colorado River, Canyonlands and the distant La Sal Mountains. The excellent **visitor center** (http://stateparks.utah.gov/parks/dead-horse; ☺8am-6pm mid-Mar–mid-Oct, 9am-5pm mid-Oct–mid-Mar) has exhibits, on-demand videos, books and maps, along with ranger-led walks and talks in summer. To the south, the 21-site **campground** (☑800-322-3770; www.stateparks.utah.gov; sites $30, yurts $90) has limited water (bring your own if possible); no showers, no hookups. Reserve ahead.

Bluff

One hundred miles south of Moab, this little community (population 320) makes a comfortable, laid-back base for exploring Utah's desolately beautiful southeastern corner. Founded by Mormon pioneers in 1880, Bluff sits surrounded by red rock and public lands near the junction of Hwys 191 and 162, along the San Juan River. Other than a trading post and a couple of places to eat or sleep, there's not much town.

For backcountry tours that access rock art and ruins, join **Far Out Expeditions** (☑435-672-2294; www.faroutexpeditions.com; day tours $295) on a day or multiday hike into the remote region. A rafting trip along the San Juan with **Wild Rivers Expeditions** (☑800-422-7654; www.riversandruins.com; half-day trip adult/child $89/69), a history and geology-minded outfitter, also includes ancient site visits.The hospitable **Recapture Lodge** (☑435-672-2281; www.recapturelodge.com; Hwy 191; d $98; ❉@⊛☎⊛) is a rustic, cozy place to stay. Owners sell maps and know the region inside and out. You might also get off-grid at **Valley of the Gods B&B** (☑970-749-1164; http://valleyofthegodsbandb.com; off Hwy 261; s/d $145/175, cabins $195) ✐, one of the original ranches in the area.

Artsy **Comb Ridge Bistro** (☑435-485-5555; http://combridgebistro.com; 680 S Hwy 191; breakfast mains $5-7, dinner mains $10-17; ☺8am-3pm & 5-9pm Tue-Sun; ☎☑) serves standout single-pour coffee, blue-corn pancakes and breakfast sandwiches loaded with peppers and eggs, inside a timber and adobe cafe, while the Western-themed **Cottonwood Steakhouse** (☑435-672-2282; www.cottonwoodsteakhouse.com; Hwy 191, cnr Main & 4th East Sts; mains $18-27; ☺5:30-9:30pm Mar-Nov) serves substantial portions of barbecued steak and beans.

Hovenweep National Monument

Beautiful, little-visited **Hovenweep** (www.nps.gov/hove; Hwy 262; tent & RV sites $10; ☺park dusk-dawn, visitor center 8am-6pm Jun-Sep, 9am-5pm Oct-May) FREE, meaning 'deserted valley' in the Ute language, showcases several neighboring Ancestral Puebloan sites, where impressive towers and granaries stand in shallow desert canyons. The Square Tower Group is accessed near the **ranger station** (☑970-562-4282; www.nps.gov/hove; McElmo Rte; ☺8am-6pm Apr-Sep, to 5pm Oct-Mar; ♿); other sites require long hikes. The **campground** (tent & RV sites $10) has 31 basic, first-come, first-served sites (no showers, no hookups). The main access is east of Hwy 191 on Hwy 262 via Hatch Trading Post, more than 40 miles northeast of Bluff.

Natural Bridges National Monument

Fifty-five miles northwest of Bluff, the ultra-remote **Natural Bridges National Monument** (www.nps.gov/nabr; Hwy 275; 7-day pass per vehicle $10, tent & RV sites $10; ⊘24hr, visitor center 8am-6pm May-Sep, 9am-5pm Oct-Apr) protects a white sandstone canyon (it's not red!) containing three impressive and easily accessible natural bridges. The oldest, **Owachomo Bridge**, spans 180ft but is only 9ft thick. The flat 9-mile Scenic Drive loop is ideal for overlooking. The campground offers 13 basic sites on a first-come, first served basis; no showers, no hookups. There is some primitive overflow camping space, but be aware that the nearest services are in Blanding, 40 miles east.

Zion & Southwestern Utah

Wonder at the deep-crimson canyons of Zion National Park; hike among the delicate pink-and-orange minarets at Bryce Canyon; drive past the swirling grey-white-and-purple mounds of Capitol Reef. Southwestern Utah is so spectacular that the vast majority of the territory has been preserved as national park or forest, state park or BLM wilderness. The whole area is ripe for outdoor exploration, with narrow slot canyons to shoulder through, pink sand dunes to scale and wave-like sandstone formations to seek out.

Capitol Reef National Park

Not as crowded as its fellow parks but equally scenic, **Capitol Reef** (☑ext 4111 435-425-3791; www.nps.gov/care; cnr Hwy 24 & Scenic Dr; admission free, 7-day scenic drive per vehicle $10, tent & RV sites $20; ⊘24hr, visitor center & scenic drive 8am-6pm Apr-Oct, to 4:30pm Nov-Mar) contains much of the 100-mile Waterpocket Fold, created 65 million years ago when the earth's surface buckled up and folded, exposing a cross-section of geologic history that is painterly in its colorful intensity.

Hwy 24 cuts grandly through the park, but make sure you head south on the **Capitol Reef Scenic Drive** (7-day pass per vehicle/

person $5/3), a paved, dead-end 9-mile road that passes through orchards – a legacy of Mormon settlement. In season you can freely pick cherries, peaches and apples, as well as stop by the historic **Gifford Farmhouse** (⊘8am-5pm Mar-Oct) to see an old homestead and buy fruit-filled mini-pies. Great walks en route include the **Grand Wash** and **Capitol Gorge** trails, each following the level floor of a separate slender canyon; if you're in the mood for a more demanding hike, climb the **Golden Throne Trail** instead. The shady, green **campground** (www.nps.gov/care; Scenic Dr; sites $20) has no showers, no hookups and is first-come, first served; it fills early spring through fall.

Torrey

Just 15 miles west of Capitol Reef, the small pioneer town of Torrey serves as the base for most national-park visitors. In addition to a few Old West–era buildings, there are a dozen or so restaurants and motels.

Flirting with cowboy style, **Capitol Reef Resort** (☑435-425-3761; www.capitolreefresort.com; 2600 E Hwy 24; r $139-179, cabins & tipis from $249; P❄🐾🛜) is one of the closest to the national park of the same name. Dressed with country elegance, each airy room at the 1914 **Torrey Schoolhouse B&B** (☑435-633-4643; www.torreyschoolhouse.com; 150 N Center St; r $120-160; ⊘Apr-Oct; ❄🛜) has a story to tell. (Butch Cassidy may have attended a town dance here.) After consuming the gourmet breakfast, laze in the garden or the huge 1st-floor lounge.

Thanks to its outstanding, highly stylized Southwestern cooking, **Cafe Diablo** (☑435-425-3070; www.cafediablo.net; 599 W Main St; lunch $10-14, dinner mains $22-40; ⊘11:30am-10pm mid-Apr–Oct; ☑) ranks highly among the finest restaurants in southern Utah.

Boulder

Though the tiny outpost of **Boulder** (www.boulderutah.com; population 222) is just 32 miles south of Torrey on Hwy 12, you have to cross Boulder Mountain to reach it. From here, the attractive **Burr Trail Rd** heads east across the northeastern corner of the Grand Staircase-Escalante National Monument, eventually winding up on a gravel road that leads either up to Capitol Reef or down to Bullfrog Marina on Lake Powell.

The small **Anasazi State Park Museum** (www.stateparks.utah.gov; Main St/Hwy 12; $5;

ℹ ELEVATION MATTERS

Southern Utah is generally warmer than northern Utah. But before you go making any assumptions about weather, check the elevation of your destination. Places less than an hour apart may have several thousand feet of elevation – and 20°F (10°C) temperature – difference.

➡ St George (3000ft)

➡ Zion National Park – Springdale entrance (3900ft)

➡ Cedar Breaks National Monument (10,000ft)

➡ Bryce National Park Lodge (8100ft)

➡ Moab (4026ft)

➡ Salt Lake City (4226ft)

➡ Park City (7100ft)

⊙8am-6pm Mar-Oct, 9am-5pm Nov-Feb) curates artifacts and a Native American site inhabited from AD 1130 to 1175. Rooms at **Boulder Mountain Lodge** (☑435-335-7460; www.boulder-utah.com; 20 N Hwy 12; r $140-175, ste $325, apt $230; ❋@🛜🐾) are plush, but it's the 15-acre wildlife sanctuary setting that's unsurpassed. An outdoor hot tub with mountain views is a soothing spot to bird-watch. The lodge's destination restaurant, **Hell's Backbone Grill** (☑435-335-7464; www.hellsbackbonegrill.com; ⊙7.30-11.30am & 5-9.30pm Mar-Nov; breakfast $10-12, lunch $9-17, dinner $17-36) serves soulful, earthy preparations of regionally inspired and sourced cuisine – book ahead – while the nearby **Burr Trail Grill & Outpost** (☑435-335-7511; cnr Hwy 12 & Burr Trail Rd; dishes $8-18; ⊙grill 11:30am-9:30pm, outpost 8:30am-6pm Mar-Oct; 🛜) offers organic vegetable tarts, eclectic burgers and scrumptious homemade desserts.

Grand Staircase-Escalante National Monument

The 2656-sq-mile **Grand Staircase-Escalante National Monument** (GSENM; ☑435-826-5499; www.blm.gov; ⊙24hr) **FREE**, a waterless region so inhospitable that it was the last to be mapped in the continental US, covers more territory than Delaware and Rhode Island combined. The nearest services, and GSENM visitor centers, are in Boulder and Escalante on Hwy 12 in the north, and Kanab on US 89 in the south. Otherwise, infrastructure is minimal, leaving a vast, uninhabited

canyonland full of 4WD roads that call to adventurous travelers who have the time, equipment and knowledge to explore.

The most accessible and most used trail in the monument is the 6-mile round-trip hike to the magnificent multicolored waterfall on **Lower Calf Creek** (Hwy 12, Mile 75; day use $5; ⊙day use dawn-dusk), between Boulder and Escalante. The 14 sought-after creekside sites at **Calf Creek Campground** (www.blm.gov/ut; Hwy 12; tent & RV sites $15), just off Hwy 12, fill fast; no showers, no hookups, and no reservations taken.

Escalante

This national-monument gateway town of 800 souls is the closest thing to a metropolis for many a lonely desert mile. Thirty slow and winding miles from Boulder, and 65 from Torrey, it's a good place to base yourself before venturing into the adjacent Grand Staircase-Escalante National Monument. The **Escalante Interagency Visitor Center** (☑435-826-5499; www.ut.blm.gov/monument; 775 W Main St; ⊙8am-4:30pm daily Apr-Sep, Mon-Fri Oct-Mar) is a superb resource center with complete information on nearby monument and forest-service lands.

Escalante Outfitters (☑435-826-4266; www.escalanteoutfitters.com; 310 W Main St; natural history tours $45; ⊙7am-9pm) is a traveler's oasis: the bookstore sells maps, guides, camping supplies – and liquor(!) – while the pleasant cafe serves homemade breakfast, pizzas and salads. It also rents out tiny, rustic cabins (from $50) and mountain bikes (from $35 per day). Long-time area outfitter **Excursions of Escalante** (☑800-839-7567; www.excursionsofescalante.com; 125 E Main St; all-day canyoneering $175; ⊙8am-6pm) leads canyoneering, climbing and photo hikes.

Other fine lodgings in town include **Canyons B&B** (☑435-826-4747, 866-526-9667; www.canyonsbnb.com; 120 E Main St; d $160; ⊙Mar-Oct; ❋🛜) with upscale cabin-rooms that surround a shady courtyard, and **Escalante Grand Staircase B&B** (☑435-826-4890; www.escalantebnb.com; 280 W Main St; d $142; ❋🛜), where you can get a spacious room and plenty of local information.

Bryce Canyon National Park

The Grand Staircase, a series of uplifted rock layers that climb in clearly defined 'steps' north from the Grand Canyon, culminates in the Pink Cliffs formation at this deservedly popular **national park** (📞435-834-5322; www.nps.gov/brca; Hwy 63; 7-day pass per vehicle $30; ⏰24hr, visitor center 8am-8pm May-Sep, to 4:30pm Oct-Apr). Not actually a 'canyon', but an amphitheater eroded from the cliffs, it's filled with wondrous sorbet-colored pinnacles and points, steeples and spires, and totem-pole-shaped 'hoodoos'. The park is 50 miles southwest of Escalante; from Hwy 12, turn south on Hwy 63.

Rim Road Scenic Drive (8000ft) travels 18 miles, roughly following the canyon rim past the **visitor center** (📞435-834-5322; www.nps.gov/brca; Hwy 63; ⏰8am-8pm May-Sep, 8am-6pm Oct & Apr, 8am-4:30pm Nov-Mar; 📶), the lodge, incredible overlooks – don't miss **Inspiration Point** – and trailheads, ending at **Rainbow Point** (9115ft). From early May through early October, a free shuttle bus runs (8am until at least 5:30pm) from a staging area just north of the park to as far south as **Bryce Amphitheater**.

The park has two camping areas, both of which accept some reservations through the park website. **Sunset Campground** (📞877-444-6777; www.recreation.gov; Bryce Canyon Rd; tent/RV site $20/30; ⏰Apr-Sep) is bit more wooded, but is not open year-round. Coin-op laundry and showers are available at the general store near **North Campground** (📞877-444-6777; www.recreation.gov; Bryce Canyon Rd; tent/RV sites $20/30). During summer, remaining first-come sites fill before noon.

The 1920s **Bryce Canyon Lodge** (📞877-386-4383, 435-834-8700; www.brycecanyonforever.com; Hwy 63; r & cabins $208-270; ⏰Apr-Oct; @📶) exudes rustic mountain charm. Rooms are in modern hotel-style units, with up-to-date furnishings, and thin-walled duplex cabins with gasfire places and front porches. No TVs. The lodge **restaurant** (📞435-834-5361; Bryce Canyon Rd; breakfast & lunch $10-20, dinner $10-35; ⏰7am-10pm Apr-Oct) 🍴 is excellent, if expensive, while **Bryce Canyon Pines Restaurant** (📞435-834-5441; Hwy 12; breakfast & lunch $5-14, dinner mains $12-24; ⏰6:30am-9:30pm Apr-Oct) is a diner classic.

Just north of the park boundaries, **Ruby's Inn** (www.rubysinn.com; 1000 S Hwy 63) is a resort complex with multiple motel lodging options, plus a campground. You can also dine at several restaurants, admire Western art, wash laundry, shop for groceries, fill up with gas, and take a helicopter ride.

Eleven miles east on Hwy 12, the small-town of **Tropic** (www.brycecanyoncountry.com) has additional food and lodging.

NEWSPAPER ROCK STATE HISTORIC MONUMENT

This tiny recreation area showcases a single large sandstone rock panel packed with more than 300 petroglyphs attributed to Ute and Ancestral Puebloan groups during a 2000-year period. The many red rock figures etched out of a black 'desert varnish' surface make for great photos. It's located 50 miles south of Moab, east of Canyonlands National Park (p885) on Hwy 211.

Kanab

At the southern edge of Grand Staircase-Escalante National Monument, vast expanses of rugged desert surround remote Kanab (population 4500). Western filmmakers made dozens of movies here from the 1920s to the 1970s, and the town still has an Old West feel.

John Wayne and Gregory Peck are among Hollywood notables who slumbered at the somewhat dated **Parry Lodge** (📞888-289-1722, 435-644-2601; www.parrylodge.com; 89 E Center St; r $119-149; ❄📶♨🐾). The renovated, **Canyons Lodge** (📞435-644-3069, 800-644-5094; www.canyonslodge.com; 236 N 300 W; r $169-179; ❄@📶♨🐾) 🍴 motel has an art-house Western feel; rooms feature original artwork. Stay there, then eat downtown at **Rocking V Cafe** (📞435-644-8001; www.rockingvcafe.com; 97 W Center St; lunch $8-18, dinner $18-48; ⏰11:30am-10pm; 🍴) or the classy **Sego** (📞435-644-5680; 190 N 300 W, Canyons Boutique Hotel; mains $14-23; ⏰5-9pm Tue-Sat), where you can expect gorgeous eats such as foraged mushrooms with goat's cheese and noodles with red-crab curry.

The **Kanab GSENM Visitor Center** (📞435-644-1300; www.ut.blm.gov/monument; 745 E Hwy 89; ⏰8am-4:30pm) provides monument information; **Kane County Office of Tourism** (📞435-644-5033, 800-733-5263; www.visitsouthernutah.com; 78 S 100 E; ⏰8:30am-6pm Mon-Fri, to 4pm Sat) focuses on town and movie sites.

Zion National Park

Get ready for an overdose of awesome. **Zion National Park** (www.nps.gov/zion; Hwy 9; 7-day pass per vehicle $30; ⏰24hr, visitor center 8am-7:30pm Jun-Aug, closes earlier Sep-May) abounds in amazing experiences: gazing up at the red-and-white cliffs of **Zion Canyon**, soaring high over the **Virgin River**; peering beyond **Angels Landing** after a 1400ft ascent; or hiking downriver through the notorious **Narrows**. But it also holds more delicate beauties: weeping rocks, tiny grottoes, hanging gardens and meadows of mesa-top wildflowers. Lush vegetation and low elevation give the magnificent rock formations a far lusher feel than the barren parks in the east.

Most visitors enter the park along Zion Canyon floor; even the most challenging hikes become congested May through September (shuttle required). If you've time for only one activity, the 6-mile **Scenic Drive**, which pierces the heart of Zion Canyon, is the one. From mid-March through early-November, you have to take a free shuttle from the **visitor center** (☑ 435-586-0895; www.nps.gov/zion; Kolob Canyons Rd; ⊗ 8am-7.30pm late May-Sep, to 5pm rest of year), but you can hop off and on at any of the scenic stops and trailheads along the way.

Of the easy-to-moderate trails, the paved, mile-long **Riverside Walk** at the end of the road is a good place to start. The **Angels Landing Trail** is a much more strenuous,

5.4-mile vertigo-inducer (1400ft elevation gain, with sheer drop-offs), but the canyon views are phenomenal. Allow four hours round-trip.

The most famous backcountry route is the unforgettable **Narrows**, a 16-mile journey into skinny canyons along the Virgin River's north fork (June through October). Plan on getting wet: at least 50% of the 12-hour hike is in the river. Split the hike into two days, reserving an overnight camping spot in advance, or finish it in time to catch the last park shuttle. A trailhead shuttle is necessary for this one-way trip.

Heading eastwards, Hwy 9 climbs out of Zion Canyon in a series of six tight switchbacks to reach the 1.1-mile Zion-Mt Carmel Tunnel, a 1920s engineering marvel. It then leads quickly into dramatically different terrain – a landscape of etched multicolor slickrock, culminating at the mountainous **Checkerboard Mesa**.

Reserve far ahead and request a riverside site in the canyon's cottonwood-shaded **Watchman Campground** (☑ reservations 877-444-6777; www.recreation.gov; Hwy 9, Zion National Park; tent sites $20, RV sites with hookups $30; ⊗ year-round; ▣); adjacent **South Campground** (☑ 435-772-3256; Hwy 9; tent & RV sites $20; ⊗ year-round; ▣) is first-come, first-served only. Smack in the middle of the scenic drive, rustic **Zion Lodge** (☑ 435-772-7700, 888-297-2757; www.zionlodge.com; Zion Canyon Scenic Dr; cabins/r $227/217; ▣ @ ☎) has basic motel rooms and cabins with gas fireplaces. All have wooden porches with stellar red-rock cliff views, but no TVs. The lodge's full-service dining room, **Red Rock Grill** (☑ 435-772-7760; Zion Canyon Scenic Dr, Zion Lodge; breakfast & sandwiches $6-15, dinner $16-30; ⊗ 6:30-10am, 11:30am-2:30pm & 5-9pm Mar-Oct, hours vary Nov-Feb), has similarly amazing views. Just outside the park, the town of Springdale offers many more services.

Note that you must pay the park entrance fee to drive on public Hwy 9 in the park, even if you are just passing through.

Springdale

Positioned at the main, south entrance to Zion National Park, Springdale is a perfect little park town. Stunning red cliffs form the backdrop to eclectic cafes, restaurants are big on organic ingredients, and galleries are interspersed with indie motels and B&Bs.

In addition to hiking trails in the national park, you can take outfitter-led climbing,

NEW MEXICO FACTS

Nickname Land of Enchantment

Population 2.1 million

Area 121,599 sq miles

Capital city Santa Fe (population 69,976)

Other cities Albuquerque (population 556,500), Las Cruces (101,643)

Sales tax 5% to 9%

Birthplace of John Denver (1943–97), Smokey Bear (1950–76)

Home of International UFO Museum & Research Center (Roswell), Julia Roberts

Politics A 'purple' state, with a more liberal north and conservative south

Famous for Ancient pueblos, the first atomic bomb (1945), where Bugs Bunny should have turned left

State question 'Red or green?' (chili sauce, that is)

Highest/Lowest points Wheeler Peak (13,161ft) / Red Bluff Reservoir (2842ft)

Driving distances Albuquerque to Santa Fe 50 miles, Santa Fe to Taos 71 miles

canyoneering, mountain biking and 4WD trips (from $140 per person, per half-day) on adjacent BLM lands. **Zion Adventure Company** (☑435-772-1001; www.zionadventures.com; 36 Lion Blvd; canyoneering day from $177; ☺8am-8pm Mar-Oct, 9am-noon & 4-7pm Nov-Feb) offers excellent excursions, Narrows outfitting, hiker-biker shuttles and river tubing, while **Zion Cycles** (☑435-772-0400; www.zioncycles.com; 868 Zion Park Blvd; half-/full-day rentals from $30/40, car racks from $15; ☺9am-7pm Feb-Nov) is the most helpful bike shop in town.

Desert Pearl Inn (☑888-828-0898, 435-772-8888; www.desertpearl.com; 707 Zion Park Blvd; r from $239; ❋@☎☀) offers the most stylish digs in town, while **Red Rock Inn** (☑435-772-3139; www.redrockinn.com; 998 Zion Park Blvd; cottages $199-259; ❋☎) has five romantic country-contemporary cottages

Zion Canyon B&B (☑435-772-9466; www.zioncanyonbnb.com; 101 Kokopelli Circle; r $159-199; ❋☎) is the most traditional local B&B, with full gourmet breakfasts and mini-spa. The owners' creative collections of art and artifacts enliven the 1930s bungalow that is **Under the Eaves Inn** (☑435-772-3457; www.undertheeaves.com; 980 Zion Park Blvd; r $109-189; ❋☎); the morning meal is a coupon for a local restaurant.

For a coffee and *trés bonnes crepes* – both sweet and savory – make **MeMe's Cafe** (☑435-772-0114; www.memescafezion.com; 975 Zion Park Blvd; mains $10-14; ☺7am-9pm) your first stop of the day. It also serves paninis and waffles, and for dinner, beef brisket and pulled pork. In the evening, the Mexican-tiled patio with twinkly lights at **Oscar's Cafe** (www.cafeoscars.com; 948 Zion Park Blvd; mains $12-18, breakfast $6-12; ☺8am-9pm) and the rustic **Bit & Spur Restaurant & Saloon** (www.bitandspur.com; 1212 Zion Park Blvd; mains $13-28; ☺5-11pm daily Mar-Oct, 5-10pm Thu-Sat Nov-Feb; ☎) are local-favored places to hang out, eat and drink. Resere ahead for the excellent hotel-restaurant **King's Landing** (☑435-772-7422; www.klbzion.com; 1515 Zion Park Blvd, Driftwood Lodge; mains $16-38; ☺5-9pm) ✐.

NEW MEXICO

They call this the Land of Enchantment for a reason. Maybe it's the drama of sunlight and shadow playing out across juniper-speckled hills, or the traditional mountain villages of horse pastures and adobe homes. Maybe it's the centuries-old towns on the northern plateaus, overlooked by the magnificent Sangre de Cristos, or the volcanoes, canyons and vast desert plains spread beneath an even vaster sky. The beauty casts a powerful spell. Mud-brick churches filled with sacred art, ancient Indian pueblos, real-life cowboys and legendary outlaws, chile-smothered enchiladas – all add to the pervasive sense of otherness that often makes New Mexico feel like a foreign country.

Maybe the state's all-but-indescribable charm is best expressed in the iconic paintings of Georgia O'Keeffe. The artist herself exclaimed, on her very first visit: 'Well! Well! Well!... This is wonderful! No one told me it was like this.'

But seriously, how could they?

History

Ancestral Puebloan civilization first began to flourish in the 8th century AD, and the impressive structures at Chaco Canyon were begun not long after. By the time Francisco Vasquez de Coronado got here in the 16th century, many Pueblo Indians had migrated to the Rio Grande Valley and were the dominant presence. After Santa Fe was established as the Spanish colonial capital in around 1610, Spanish settlers fanned out across northern New Mexico and Catholic missionaries began their often violent efforts to convert the Puebloans. Following the Pueblo Revolt of 1680, Native Americans occupied Santa Fe until 1692, when Don Diego de Vargas recaptured the city.

The US took control of New Mexico in 1846 during the Mexican-American War, and it became a US Territory in 1850. Native American wars with the Navajo, Apache and Comanche further transformed the region, and the arrival of the railroad in the 1870s prompted an economic boom.

Painters and writers set up art colonies in Santa Fe and Taos in the early 20th century, and New Mexico became the 47th state in 1912. A top-secret scientific community descended on Los Alamos in 1943 and developed the atomic bomb. Some say that four years later, aliens crashed outside of Roswell...

ⓘ Information

For information on the New Mexico stretch of Route 66, visit www.rt66nm.org.

New Mexico State Parks (www.emnrd.state.nm.us) Info on state parks, with a link to campsite reservations.

New Mexico Tourism (www.newmexico.org) Information on destination planning, activities and events.

Recreation.gov (www.recreation.gov) Reservations for national park and forest campsites and tours.

Albuquerque

Albuquerque: it's the pink hues of the Sandia Mountains at sunset, the Rio Grande's cottonwood bosque, Route 66 diners and the hometown of Walter White and Jesse Pinkman. It's a bustling desert crossroads and the largest city in the state, yet you can still hear the howls of coyotes when the sun goes down.

Often passed over by travelers on their way to Santa Fe, Albuquerque has plenty of understated appeal beneath its gritty urban facade. Good hiking and mountain-biking trails abound just outside of town, while the city's modern museums explore Pueblo culture, New Mexican art and space. Take the time to let your engine cool as you take a walk among the desert petroglyphs or order up a plate of red chile enchiladas and a local beer.

◉ Sights

◉ Old Town

From its foundation in 1706 until the arrival of the railroad in 1880, the plaza, centering on the diminutive 1793 **San Felipe de Neri Church** (www.sanfelipedeneri.org; Old Town Plaza; ⊙7am-5:30pm daily, museum 9:30am-5pm Mon-

Sat), was the hub of Albuquerque. Today Old Town is the city's most popular tourist area.

★American International Rattlesnake Museum   MUSEUM

(☑505-242-6569; www.rattlesnakes.com; 202 San Felipe St NW; adult/child $5/3; ⊙10am-6pm Mon-Sat, 1-5pm Sun Jun-Aug, 11:30am-5:30pm Mon-Fri, 10am-6pm Sat, 1-5pm Sun Sep-May) Anyone charmed by snakes and all things slithery will find this museum fascinating; for ophidiophobes, it's a complete nightmare, filled with the world's largest collection of different rattlesnake species. You'll also find snake-themed beer bottles and postmarks from every town named 'Rattlesnake' in the US.

★Albuquerque Museum of Art & History   MUSEUM

(☑505-242-4600; www.cabq.gov/museum; 2000 Mountain Rd NW; adult/child $4/1; ⊙9am-5pm Tue-Sun) With a great Albuquerque history gallery that's imaginative, interactive and easy to digest, as well as a permanent New Mexico art collection that extends to 20th-century masterpieces from Taos, this showpiece museum should not be missed. There's free admission on Saturday afternoons and Sunday mornings, and free guided walking tours of Old Town at 11am (March to mid-December).

◉ Around Town

★Indian Pueblo Cultural Center   MUSEUM

(IPCC; ☑505-843-7270; www.indianpueblo.org; 2401 12th St NW; adult/child $8.40/5.40; ⊙9am-5pm) Collectively run by New Mexico's 19

ALBUQUERQUE FOR KIDS

Albuquerque has lots on offer for kids, from hands-on museums to cool hikes.

¡Explora! (☑505-224-8300; www.explora.us; 1701 Mountain Rd NW; adult/child $8/4; ⊙10am-6pm Mon-Sat, noon-6pm Sun; ⬛) From the lofty high-wire bike to the mind-boggling Light, Shadow, Color area, this gung-ho museum holds a hands-on exhibit for every type of child (don't miss the elevator). Not traveling with kids? Check the website to see if you're around for the 'Adult Night.' Hosted by an acclaimed local scientist, it's one of the hottest tickets in town.

New Mexico Museum of Natural History & Science (☑505-841-2800; www.nmnaturalhistory.org; 1801 Mountain Rd NW; adult/child $8/5; ⊙9am-5pm Wed-Mon; ⬛) Dinosaur-mad kids are certain to love this huge modern museum, on the northeastern fringes of Old Town. From the T Rex in the main atrium onwards, it's crammed with ferocious ancient beasts. The emphasis throughout is on New Mexico, with dramatic displays on the state's geological origins and details of the impact of climate change; there's also a planetarium and large-format 3D movie theater (both of which have additional admission fees).

Pueblos, this cultural center is an essential stop-off during even the shortest Albuquerque visit. The museum downstairs holds fascinating displays on the Pueblos' collective history and individual artistic traditions, while the galleries above offer changing temporary exhibitions. They're arrayed in a crescent around a plaza that's regularly used for dances and crafts demonstrations, and as well as the recommended **Pueblo Harvest Cafe** (☑505-724-3510; lunch $12-16, dinner $13-28; ☺7am-9pm Mon-Sat, 7am-4pm Sun; ☑🖶) there's also a large gift shop and retail gallery.

Petroglyph National Monument   ARCHAEOLOGICAL SITE
(☑505-899-0205; www.nps.gov/petr; 6001 Unser Blvd NW; ☺visitor center 8am-5pm) **FREE** The lava fields preserved in this large desert park, west of the Rio Grande, are adorned with more than 23,000 ancient petroglyphs (1000 BC–AD 1700). Several trails are scattered far and wide: **Boca Negra Canyon** is the busiest and most accessible (parking $1/2 weekday/weekend); **Piedras Marcadas** holds 300 petroglyphs; while **Rinconada Canyon** is a lovely desert walk (2.2 miles round-trip), but with fewer visible petroglyphs.

Sandia Peak Tramway   CABLE CAR
(☑505-856-7325; www.sandiapeak.com; 30 Tramway Rd NE; adult/youth 13-20yr/child $25/20/15, parking $2; ☺9am-9pm Jun-Aug, 9am-8pm Wed-Mon, from 5pm Tue Sep-May) The United States' longest aerial tram climbs 2.7 miles from the desert floor in the northeast corner of the city to the summit of 10,378ft Sandia Crest. The views are spectacular at any time, though sunsets are particularly brilliant. The complex at the top holds gift shops and a **cafeteria** (☑505-243-0605; www.sandiacresthouse.com; Hwy 536; mains $5.50-14; ☺10am-5pm, weekends only winter), while hiking trails lead off through the woods, and there's also a small **ski area** (☑505-242-9052; www.sandiapeak.com; lift tickets adult/child $55/40; ☺9am-4pm Fri-Sun mid-Dec–Mar). If you plan on hiking down (or up), a one-way ticket costs $15.

🏃 Activities

The omnipresent Sandia Mountains and the less-crowded Manzano Mountains offer outdoor activities, including hiking, skiing (downhill and cross-country), mountain biking, rock climbing and camping.

Cycling is the ideal way to explore Albuquerque under your own steam. In addition to cycling lanes throughout the city, moun-

SCENIC DRIVE: HIGHWAY 12

Arguably Utah's most diverse and stunning route, **Hwy 12 Scenic Byway** (www.scenicbyway12.com) winds through rugged canyonland on a 124-mile journey west of Bryce Canyon to near Capitol Reef. The section between Escalante and Torrey traverses a moonscape of sculpted slickrock, crosses narrow ridge backs and climbs over 11,000ft Boulder Mountain. Pretty much everything between Torrey and Panguitch is on or near Hwy 12.

tain bikers will dig the foothills trails east of town and the scenic **Paseo del Bosque** (☺dawn-dusk), alongside the Rio Grande. For details of the excellent network of cycling lanes (slated to reach 50 interconnected miles in 2018), see www.bikeabq.org.

Elena Gallegos Open Space   HIKING, MOUNTAIN BIKING
(www.cabq.gov; Simms Park Rd; weekday/weekend parking $1/2; ☺7am-9pm Apr-Oct, closes 7pm Nov-Mar) The western foothills of the Sandias are Albuquerque's outdoor playground, and the high desert landscape here is sublime. As well as several picnic areas, this section holds trailheads for hiking, running and mountain biking; some routes are wheelchair-accessible. Come early, before the sun gets too hot, or late, to enjoy the panoramic views at sunset amid the lonesome howls of coyotes.

🎉 Festivals & Events

Friday's *Albuquerque Journal* (www.abqjournal.com) includes exhaustive listings of festivals and activities.

Gathering of Nations Powwow   CULTURAL
(www.gatheringofnations.com; ☺Apr) Dance competitions, displays of Native American arts and crafts, and the 'Miss Indian World' contest. Held in late April.

⭐ **International Balloon Fiesta**   BALLOON
(www.balloonfiesta.com; ☺early Oct) The largest balloon festival in the world. You simply haven't lived until you've seen a three-story-tall Tony the Tiger land in your hotel courtyard, and that's exactly the sort of thing that happens during the festival, which features mass dawn take-offs on each of its nine days, overlapping the first and second weekends in October.

🛏 Sleeping

Route 66 Hostel
HOSTEL $

(☏ 505-247-1813; http://route66hostel.com; 1012 Central Ave SW; dm $25, r from $30; 🅿@🛜) This pastel-lemon hostel, in a former residence a few blocks west of downtown, holds male and female dorms plus simple private rooms, some of which share bathrooms. The beds are aging, but there's a welcoming atmosphere, with common facilities including a library and a kitchen offering free self-serve breakfasts. Voluntary chores; no check-ins between 1:30pm and 4:30pm.

⭐ Andaluz
BOUTIQUE HOTEL $$

(☏ 505-242-9090; www.hotelandaluz.com; 125 2nd St NW; r from $174; 🅿🌀@🛜🐾) Albuquerque's finest historic hotel, built in the heart of downtown in 1939, has been comprehensively modernized while retaining period details like its stunning central atrium, where cozy arched nooks hold tables and couches. Rooms feature hypoallergenic bedding and carpets, the **Más Tapas Y Vino** (☏ 505-923-9080; www.hotelandaluz.com; 125 2nd St NW; tapas $6-16, mains $26-36; ⊙ 7am-2pm & 5-9:30pm) restaurant is notable, and there's a rooftop bar. Reserve 30 days in advance for the best rates.

Böttger Mansion
B&B $$

(☏ 505-243-3639; www.bottger.com; 110 San Felipe St NW; r $115-159; 🅿🌀@🛜) The friendly proprietor gives this well-appointed B&B, built in 1912 and one minute's walk from the plaza, an edge over tough competition. Three of its seven themed, antique-furnished rooms have pressed-tin ceilings, one has a Jacuzzi tub, and sumptuous breakfasts are served in a honeysuckle-lined courtyard loved by bird-watchers. Past guests include Elvis, Janis Joplin and Machine Gun Kelly.

⭐ Los Poblanos
B&B $$$

(☏ 505-344-9297; www.lospoblanos.com; 4803 Rio Grande Blvd NW; r $230-450; 🅿🌀@🛜🐾) This amazing 20-room B&B, on a 1930s rural ranch that's a National Historic Place, is five minutes' drive north of Old Town. Close to the Rio Grande, it's set amid 25 acres of gardens, lavender fields (blooming mid-June through July) and an organic farm. The gorgeous rooms feature kiva fireplaces, while produce from the farm is served for breakfast.

✕ Eating

⭐ Pop Fizz
MEXICAN $

(☏ 505-508-1082; www.pop-fizz.net; 1701 4th St SW, National Hispanic Cultural Center; mains $5-7.50; ⊙ 11am-8pm; 🛜🍴) These all-natural *paletas* (popsicles) straight-up rock: cool off with flavors such as cucumber chile lime, mango or pineapple habanero – or perhaps you'd rather splurge on a cinnamon-churro ice-cream taco? Not to be outdone by the desserts, the kitchen also whips up all sorts of messy goodness, including carne asada fries, Sonoran dogs and Frito pies.

⭐ Golden Crown Panaderia
BAKERY $

(☏ 505-243-2424; www.goldencrown.biz; 1103 Mountain Rd NW; mains $7-20; ⊙ 7am-8pm Tue-Sat, 10am-8pm Sun) Who doesn't love a friendly neighborhood cafe-bakery? Especially one in a cozy old adobe, with gracious staff, oven-fresh bread and pizza (with green chile or blue-corn crusts), fruity empanadas, smooth espresso coffees and cookies all round? Call ahead to reserve a loaf of quick-selling green chile bread – then eat it hot, out on the patio.

Slate Street Cafe & Wine Loft
MODERN AMERICAN $$

(☏ 505-243-2210; www.slatestreetcafe.com; 515 Slate St; breakfast $7.50-15, lunch $10-15, dinner $11-27; ⊙ 7:30am-3pm Mon-Fri, 9am-2pm Sat & Sun, 5-9pm Tue-Thu, 5-10pm Fri & Sat; 🍴) A popular downtown rendezvous, the cafe downstairs is usually packed with people enjoying imaginative comfort food, from green chile mac-and-cheese to herb-crusted pork chops, while the upstairs wine loft serves 25 wines by the glass and offers regular tasting sessions. It's off 6th St NW, just north of Lomas Blvd.

⭐ Artichoke Cafe
MODERN AMERICAN $$$

(☏ 505-243-0200; www.artichokecafe.com; 424 Central Ave SE; lunch mains $12-19, dinner mains $16-39; ⊙ 11am-2:30pm & 5-9pm Mon-Fri, 5-10pm Sat) Elegant and unpretentious, this popular bistro prepares creative gourmet cuisine with panache and is always high on foodies' lists of Albuquerque's best. It's on the eastern edge of downtown, between the bus station and I-40.

🍷 Drinking & Entertainment

Popejoy Hall (☏ 505-925-5858; www.popejoypresents.com; 203 Cornell Dr) and the historic **KiMo Theatre** (☏ 505-768-3544; www.cabq.gov/kimo; 423 Central Ave NW) are the primary venues for big-name national acts, local opera, symphony and theater. **Launch Pad**

SOUTHWEST ALBUQUERQUE

(☑505-764-8887; www.launchpadrocks.com; 618 Central Ave SW) is best for local acts.

Java Joe's
CAFE

(☑505-765-1514; www.downtownjavajoes.com; 906 Park Ave SW; ⊗6:30am-3:30pm; ☗🐾) Best known these days for its explosive cameo role in *Breaking Bad*, this comfy coffee shop still makes a great stop-off for a java jolt or a bowl of the hottest chile in town.

★Anodyne
BAR

(☑505-244-1820; 409 Central Ave NW; ⊗4pm-1:30am Mon-Sat, 7-11:30pm Sun) An excellent spot for a game of pool, Anodyne is a huge space with book-lined walls, wood ceilings, plenty of overstuffed chairs, more than 100 bottled beers and great people-watching.

★Marble Brewery
BREWERY

(☑505-243-2739; www.marblebrewery.com; 111 Marble Ave NW; ⊗noon-midnight Mon-Sat, to 10:30pm Sun) Popular downtown brew-pub, attached to its namesake brewery, with a snug interior for winter nights and a beer garden where local bands play early-evening gigs in summer. Be sure to try its Red Ale.

❶ Information

EMERGENCY & MEDICAL SERVICES

Police (☑505-242-2677; www.apdonline.com; 400 Roma Ave NW)

Presbyterian Hospital (☑505-841-1234; www. phs.org; 1100 Central Ave SE; ⊗emergency 24hr)

UNM Hospital (☑505-272-2411; 2211 Lomas Blvd NE; ⊗emergency 24hr)

POST

Post Office (☑800-275-8777; 201 5th St SW; ⊗9am-4:30pm Mon-Fri)

TOURIST INFORMATION

Old Town Information Center (☑505-243-3215; www.visitalbuquerque.org; 303 Romero Ave NW; ⊗10am-5pm Oct-May, to 6pm Jun-Sep)

UNM Welcome Center (☑505-277-1989; 2401 Redondo Dr; ⊗8am-5pm Mon-Fri)

USEFUL WEBSITES

Albuquerque Journal (www.abqjournal.com) Local news, events and sports.

City of Albuquerque (www.cabq.gov) Public transportation and area attractions.

Gil's Thrilling (And Filling) Blog (www.nmgastronome.com) Local foodie eats his way across ABQ, Santa Fe and the rest of the state.

❶ Getting There & Around

AIR

New Mexico's largest airport, **Albuquerque International Sunport** (ABQ; ☑505-244-7700; www. abqsunport.com; 🛜), is 5 miles southeast of downtown and served by multiple airlines. Free shuttles connect the terminal building with the Sunport Car Rental Center at 3400 University Blvd SE, home to all the airport's car-rental facilities.

The **Sunport Shuttle** (☑505-883-4966; www.sunportshuttle.com) runs from the airport to local hotels and other destinations.

BUS

The **Alvarado Transportation Center** (100 1st St SW, cnr Central Ave) is home to **Greyhound** (☑800-231-2222, 505-243-4435; www. greyhound.com; 320 1st St SW), which serves destinations throughout the state and beyond, though not Santa Fe or Taos.

ABQ Ride (☑505-243-7433; www.cabq.gov/ transit; 100 1st St SW; adult/child $1/0.35, day pass $2) is a public bus system covering most of Albuquerque on weekdays and major tourist spots daily.

TRAIN

Amtrak's *Southwest Chief* stops at Albuquerque's **Amtrak Station** (☑800-872-7245; www. amtrak.com; 320 1st St SW), which is part of the Alvarado Transportation Center. Trains head east to Chicago (from $117, 26 hours) or west to Los Angeles (from $66, 16½ hours), once daily in each direction.

A commuter light rail line, the **New Mexico Rail Runner Express** (www.nmrailrunner.com), shares the station. It makes several stops in the Albuquerque metropolitan area, but more importantly for visitors it runs all the way north to Santa Fe (one-way $10, 1¾ hours), with eight departures on weekdays and four on weekends.

Along I-40

Although you can zip between Albuquerque and Flagstaff, AZ, in less than five hours, the national monuments and pueblos along the way are well worth a visit. For a scenic loop, take Hwy 53 southwest from Grants, which leads to all the following sights except Acoma. Hwy 602 brings you north to Gallup.

Acoma Pueblo

The dramatic mesa-top 'Sky City' sits 7000ft above sea level and 367ft above the surrounding plateau. One of the oldest continuously inhabited settlements in North America, this place has been home to pottery-making

Pueblo peoples since the 11th century. Guided tours leave from the **cultural center** (☏800-747-0181; www.acomaskycity.org; Rte 38; tours adult/child $25/17; ☺hourly tours 8:30am-3:30pm Mar-Oct, 9:30am-2:30pm Sat & Sun Nov-Feb) at the foot of the mesa and take two hours, or one hour just to tour the historic mission. From I-40, take exit 102, which is about 60 miles west of Albuquerque, then drive 12 miles south. Check ahead to make sure it's not closed for ceremonial or other reasons.

El Morro National Monument

The 200ft sandstone outcropping at the El **Morro National Monument** (☏505-783-4226; www.nps.gov/elmo; Hwy 53; ☺9am-6pm Jun-Aug, to 5pm Sep-May) FREE, also known as 'Inscription Rock,' has been a travelers' oasis for millennia. Thousands of carvings – from petroglyphs in the pueblo at the top (c 1275) to elaborate inscriptions by Spanish conquistadors and Anglo pioneers – offer a unique historical record. It's about 38 miles southwest of Grants via Hwy 53.

Zuni Pueblo

The Zuni are known for their delicately inlaid silverwork, which is sold in stores lining Hwy 53. Check in at the **Zuni Tourism Office** (☏505-782-7238; www.zunitourism. com; 1239 Hwy 53; tours $15; ☺8:30am-5:30pm Mon-Fri, 10:30am-4pm Sat, noon-4pm Sun) for information, photo permits and tours of the pueblo, which lead you among stone houses and beehive-shaped adobe ovens to the massive **Our Lady of Guadalupe Mission**, featuring impressive kachina (spirit) murals. The **A:shiwi A:wan Museum & Heritage Center** (☏505-782-4403; www.ashiwi-muse um.org; Ojo Caliente Rd; admission by donation; ☺9am-5pm Mon-Fri) displays early photos and other tribal artifacts.

The friendly, eight-room **Inn at Halona** (☏505-782-4547; www.halona.com; 23b Pia Mesa Rd; r from $75; P🛜), decorated with local Zuni arts and crafts, is the only place to stay on the pueblo. Its breakfasts rank with the best in the state.

Santa Fe

Welcome to 'the city different,' a place that makes its own rules without ever forgetting its long and storied past. Walking through its adobe neighborhoods, or around the busy Plaza that remains its core, there's no denying that Santa Fe has a timeless, earthy soul. Indeed, its artistic inclinations are a principal attraction – there are more quality museums and galleries here than you could possibly see in just one visit.

At over 7000ft above sea level, Santa Fe is also the nation's highest state capital. Sitting at the foot of the Sangre de Cristo range, it makes a fantastic base for hiking, mountain biking, backpacking and skiing. When you come off the trails, you can indulge in chile-smothered local cuisine, buy turquoise and silver directly from Native American jewelers in the Plaza, visit remarkable churches, or simply wander along centuries-old, cottonwood-shaded lanes and daydream about one day moving here.

◉ Sights

★**Georgia O'Keeffe Museum**　MUSEUM
(Map p900; ☏505-946-1000; www.okeeffemu seum.org; 217 Johnson St; adult/child $12/free; ☺10am-5pm Sat-Thu, to 7pm Fri) With 10 beautifully lit galleries in a rambling 20th-century adobe, this museum boasts the world's largest collection of O'Keeffe's work. She's best known for her luminous New Mexican landscapes, but the changing exhibitions here range through her entire career, from her early years through to her time at Ghost Ranch. Major museums worldwide own her most famous canvases, so you may not see familiar paintings, but you're sure to be bowled over by the thick brushwork and transcendent colors on show.

★**Meow Wolf**　MUSEUM
(☏505-395-6369; https://meowwolf.com; 1352 Rufina Circle; adult/child $18/12; ☺10am-8pm Sun, Mon, Wed, Thu, to 10pm Fri & Sat) If you've been hankering for a trip to another dimension but have yet to find a portal, the House of Eternal Return by Meow Wolf could be the place for you. The premise is quite ingenious: visitors get to explore a re-created Victorian house for clues related to the disappearance of a California family, following a narrative that leads deeper into fragmented bits of a multiverse (often via secret passages), all of which are unique, interactive art installations.

Wheelwright Museum of the American Indian　MUSEUM
(☏505-982-4636; www.wheelwright.org; 704 Camino Lejo; adult/child $8/free, 1st Sun of month free; ☺10am-5pm) Mary Cabot established this museum in 1937 to showcase Nava-

CANYON ROAD GALLERIES

Originally a Pueblo Indian footpath and later the main street through a Spanish farming community, Santa Fe's most famous art avenue embarked on its current incarnation in the 1920s, when artists led by Los Cinco Pintores (five painters who fell in love with New Mexico's landscape) moved in to take advantage of the cheap rent.

Today Canyon Rd is a top attraction, holding more than a hundred of Santa Fe's 300-plus galleries. The epicenter of the city's vibrant art scene, it offers everything from rare Native American antiquities to Santa Fe School masterpieces and in-your-face modern work. If gallery-hopping seems a bit overwhelming, don't worry, just wander.

Friday nights are particularly fun: that's when the galleries put on glittering openings, starting around 5pm. Not only are these great social events, but you can also browse while nibbling on cheese, sipping Chardonnay or sparkling cider, and chatting with the artists.

The following is just a sampling of some Canyon Rd (and around) favorites. For more, pick up the handy, free *Collector's Guide* map, or check out www.santafegalleryassociation.org. More contemporary galleries around the Railyard are also worth checking out.

Adobe Gallery (Map p900; ☑505-955-0550; www.adobegallery.com; 221 Canyon Rd; ⊙10am-5pm Mon-Sat)

Economos/Hampton Galleries (Map p900; ☑505-982-6347; 500 Canyon Rd; ⊙9:30am-4pm, closed Wed & Sun)

Gerald Peters Gallery (Map p900; ☑505-954-5700; www.gpgallery.com; 1005 Paseo de Peralta; ⊙10am-5pm Mon-Sat)

GF Contemporary (☑505-983-3707; www.gfcontemporary.com; 707 Canyon Rd; ⊙10am-5pm Mon-Sat, noon-5pm Sun)

Marc Navarro Gallery (Map p900; ☑505-986-8191; 520 Canyon Rd; ⊙11am-4pm)

Morning Star Gallery (Map p900; ☑505-982-8187; www.morningstargallery.com; 513 Canyon Rd; ⊙9am-5pm Mon-Sat)

Nedra Matteucci Galleries (Map p900; ☑505-982-4631; www.matteucci.com; 1075 Paseo de Peralta; ⊙9am-5pm Mon-Sat)

jo ceremonial art, and its major strength is Navajo and Zuni jewellery, in particular silverwork. The first gallery hosts temporary exhibits, showcasing Native American art from across North America. The gift store, known as the Case Trading Post, sells museum-quality rugs, jewelry, kachinas and crafts.

🏃 Activities

The **Pecos Wilderness** and **Santa Fe National Forest**, east of town, have more than 1000 miles of hiking and biking trails, several of which lead to 12,000ft peaks. Contact the Public Lands Information Center for maps and details, and check weather reports for advance warnings of frequent summer storms.

Mellow Velo (Map p900; ☑505-995-8356; www.mellowvelo.com; 132 E Marcy St; mountain bikes per day from $40; ⊙10am-6pm Mon-Sat) rents mountain bikes and provides trail information. Operators including **New Wave**

Rafting Co (☑800-984-1444; www.newwaverafting.com; adult/child from $57/51; ⊙mid-Apr–Aug) offer white-water rafting adventures through the Rio Grande Gorge, the wild Taos Box and the Rio Chama Wilderness.

Dale Ball Trails MOUNTAIN BIKING, HIKING
(www.santafenm.gov/trails_1) Over 20 miles of shared mountain biking and hiking trails, with fabulous desert and mountain views. The 9.7-mile Outer Limits trail is a classic ride here, combining fast singletrack in the north section with the more technical central section. Hikers should check out the 4-mile round-trip trail to Picacho Peak, with a steep but accessible 1250ft elevation gain.

Ski Santa Fe SKIING
(☑505-982-4429, snow report 505-983-9155; www.skisantafe.com; lift ticket adult/teen/child $75/60/52; ⊙9am-4pm Dec-Mar) Often overlooked for its more famous cousin outside Taos, the smaller Santa Fe ski area boasts the same dry powder (though not quite

as much), with a higher base elevation (10,350ft). It caters to families and expert skiers, who come for the glades, steep bump runs and long groomers a mere 16 miles from town.

Santa Fe School of Cooking   COOKING
(Map p900; 505-983-4511; www.santafeschoolof cooking.com; 125 N Guadalupe St; 2/3hr class $78/98; 9:30am-5:30pm Mon-Fri, 9:30am-5pm Sat, 10:30am-3:30pm Sun) Sign up for green or red chile workshops to master the basics of Southwestern cuisine, or try your hand at rellenos, tamales or more sophisticated flavors such as mustard mango habanero sauce. It also offers several popular restaurant walking tours.

🎎 Festivals & Events

⭐ **International Folk Art Market**   CULTURAL
(505-992-7600; www.folkartalliance.org; mid-Jul) The world's largest folk art market draws around 150 artists from 50 countries to the Folk Art Museum for a festive weekend of craft shopping and cultural events in July.

⭐ **Santa Fe Indian Market**   CULTURAL
(505-983-5220; www.swaia.org; Aug) Over a thousand artists from 100 tribes and Pueblos show work at this world-famous juried show, held the weekend after the third Thursday in August. Around 100,000 visitors converge on the Plaza, at open studios, gallery shows and the Native Cinema Showcase. Come Friday or Saturday to see pieces competing for the top prizes; wait until Sunday before trying to bargain.

⭐ **Santa Fe Fiesta
& Burning of Zozobra**   CULTURAL
(505-913-1517; www.santafefiesta.org; early Sep) This 10-day celebration of the 1692 resettlement of Santa Fe following the 1680 Pueblo Revolt includes concerts, a candlelit procession and the much-loved Pet Parade. Everything kicks off with the unmissable Friday-night torching of **Zozobra** (https:// burnzozobra.com) – a 50ft-tall effigy of 'Old Man Gloom' – before some 40,000 people in Fort Marcy Park.

🛏 Sleeping

Silver Saddle Motel   MOTEL $
(505-471-7663; www.santafesilversaddlemotel. com; 2810 Cerrillos Rd; r from $62; 🅿❄@🛜🐾) This old-fashioned, slightly kitschy Route 66 motel compound offers the best budget val-

ue in town. Some rooms have pleasant tiled kitchenettes, while all have shady wooden arcades outside and cowboy-inspired decor inside – get the Kenny Rogers or Wyatt Earp rooms if you can. It's located 3 miles southwest of the Plaza on busy Cerillos Rd.

Black Canyon Campground   CAMPGROUND $
(877-444-6777; www.recreation.gov; Hwy 475; tent & RV sites $10; May–mid-Oct) A mere 8 miles from the Plaza is this gorgeous and secluded spot, complete with 36 sites and hiking and biking trails nearby. Water is available, but no hookups. If it's full, Hyde Memorial State Park is just up the road, while the Big Tesuque and Aspen Basin campgrounds (free, but no potable water) are closer to the ski area.

⭐ **El Paradero**   B&B $$
(Map p900; 505-988-1177; www.elparadero.com; 220 W Manhattan Ave; r from $155; 🅿❄@🛜) Each room in this 200-year-old adobe B&B, south of the river, is unique and loaded with character. Two have their own bathrooms across the hall, the rest have en suites; our favorites are rooms 6 and 12. The full breakfasts satisfy, and rates also include afternoon tea. A separate casita holds two kitchenette suites that can be combined into one.

⭐ **Santa Fe Motel & Inn**   HOTEL $$
(Map p900; 505-982-1039; www.santafemotel. com; 510 Cerrillos Rd; r from $149, casitas from $169; 🅿❄@🛜🐾) Even the motel rooms in this downtown option, close to the Railyard and a real bargain in low season, have the flavor of a Southwestern B&B, with colorful tiles, clay sunbursts and tin mirrors. The courtyard casitas cost a little more and come with kiva fireplaces and little patios. Rates include a full hot breakfast, served outdoors in summer.

⭐ **La Fonda**   HISTORIC HOTEL $$$
(Map p900; 800-523-5002; www.lafondasan tafe.com; 100 E San Francisco St; r from $259; 🅿❄@🛜🐾🐾) Long renowned as the 'Inn at the end of the Santa Fe Trail,' Santa Fe's loveliest historic hotel sprawls through an old adobe just off the Plaza. Retaining its beautiful folk-art windows and murals, it's both classy and cozy, with some wonderful top-floor luxury suites, and superb sunset views from the rooftop **Bell Tower Bar** (Map p900; 100 E San Francisco St; 3pm-sunset Mon-Thu, 2pm-sunset Fri-Sun May-Oct).

THE MUSEUM OF NEW MEXICO

The Museum of New Mexico administers four excellent museums in Santa Fe. Two are at the Plaza, two are on Museum Hill, 2 miles southwest.

Palace of the Governors & New Mexico History Museum (Map p900; ☑505-476-5100; www.palaceofthegovernors.org; 105 W Palace Ave; adult/child $12/free; ☺10am-5pm, closed Mon Oct-May) The oldest public building in the US, this low-slung adobe complex started out as home to New Mexico's first Spanish governor in 1610. It was occupied by Pueblo Indians following their revolt in 1680, and after 1846 became the seat of the US Territory's earliest governors. It now holds fascinating displays on Santa Fe's multifaceted past, and some superb Hispanic religious artwork – join a free tour if possible.

New Mexico Museum of Art (Map p900; ☑505-476-5072; www.nmartmuseum.org; 107 W Palace Ave; adult/child $12/free; ☺10am-5pm Tue-Sun) Built in 1917 and a prime early example of Santa Fe's Pueblo Revival architecture, the New Mexico Museum of Art has spent a century collecting and displaying works by regional artists. A treasure trove of works by the great names who put New Mexico on the cultural map, from the Taos Society of Artists to Georgia O'Keeffe, it's also a lovely building in which to stroll around, with a cool garden courtyard. Constantly changing temporary exhibitions ensure its continuing relevance.

Museum of International Folk Art (☑505-827-6344; www.internationalfolkart.org; 706 Camino Lejo; adult/child $12/free; ☺10am-5pm, closed Mon Nov-Apr) Santa Fe's most unusual and exhilarating museum centers on the world's largest collection of folk art. Its huge main gallery displays whimsical and mind-blowing objects from more than 100 different countries. Tiny human figures go about their business in fully realized village and city scenes, while dolls, masks, toys and garments spill across the walls. Changing exhibitions in other wings explore vernacular art and culture worldwide.

Museum of Indian Arts & Culture (☑505-476-1250; www.indianartsandculture.org; 710 Camino Lejo; adult/child $12/free; ☺10am-5pm, closed Mon Sep-May) This top-quality museum sets out to trace the origins and history of the various Native American peoples of the entire Southwest, and explain and illuminate their widely differing cultural traditions. Pueblo, Navajo and Apache interviewees describe the contemporary realities each group now faces, while a truly superb collection of ceramics, modern and ancient, is complemented by stimulating temporary displays.

SOUTHWEST SANTA FE

✕ Eating

★**La Choza** NEW MEXICAN $
(☑505-982-0909; www.lachozasf.com; 905 Alarid St; lunch $9-13, dinner $10.50-18; ☺11:30am-2pm & 5-9pm Mon-Sat; P ☷) Blue-corn burritos, a festive interior and an extensive margarita list make La Choza a perennial (and colorful) favorite among Santa Fe's discerning diners. Of the many New Mexican restaurants in Santa Fe, this one always seems to be reliably excellent. As with the Shed, its sister restaurant, arrive early or reserve.

Tia Sophia's NEW MEXICAN $
(Map p900; ☑505-983-9880; www.tiasophias.com; 210 W San Francisco St; mains $7-12; ☺7am-2pm Mon-Sat, 8am-1pm Sun; ☷☷) Local artists and visiting celebrities outnumber tourists at this longstanding and always packed Santa Fe favorite. Breakfast is the meal of choice, with fantastic burritos and other Southwestern dishes, but lunch is pretty damn tasty too; try the perfectly prepared *chile rellenos* (stuffed chile peppers), or the rota of daily specials. The shelf of kids' books helps little ones pass the time.

★**Jambo Cafe** AFRICAN $$
(☑505-473-1269; www.jambocafe.net; 2010 Cerrillos Rd; mains $9-17; ☺11am-9pm Mon-Sat) Hidden within a shopping center, this African-flavored cafe is hard to spot from the road; once inside, though, it's a lovely spot, always busy with locals who love its distinctive goat, chicken and lentil curries, veggie sandwiches and roti flatbreads, not to mention the reggae soundtrack.

Dr Field Goods NEW MEXICAN $$
(☑505-471-0043; http://drfieldgoods.com; 2860 Cerrillos Rd, Suite A1; mains $13.50-18;

Santa Fe

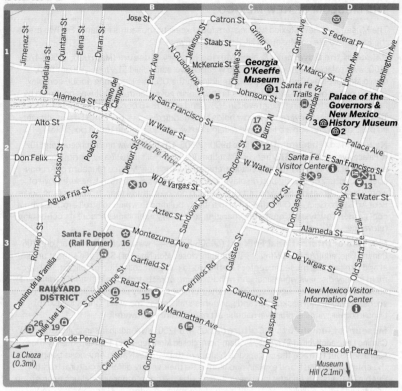

⊙11am-9pm) This locavore deli has a dedicated following, and for good reason – it's a top pick for a casual bite out on Cerrillos Rd. Diners can choose between free-range buffalo enchiladas, goat tortas with honey habanero sauce, grilled fish tostadas and green chile–pulled pork sandwiches, among other delicacies. A butcher shop and bakery is a few doors down.

★**Cafe Pasqual's**　　　NEW MEXICAN $$$
(Map p900; ☑505-983-9340; www.pasquals.com; 121 Don Gaspar Ave; breakfast & lunch $14-18.75, dinner $15-39; ⊙8am-3pm & 5:30-10pm; ☑🖶)
🖉 Whatever time you visit this exuberantly colorful, utterly unpretentious place, the food, most of which has a definite south-of-the-border flavor, is worth every penny of the high prices. The breakfast menu is famous for dishes such as *huevos motuleños*, made with sautéed bananas, feta cheese and

more; later on, the meat and fish mains are superb. Reservations taken for dinner only.

★**La Plazuela**　　　NEW MEXICAN $$$
(Map p900; ☑505-982-5511; www.lafondasantafe.com; 100 E San Francisco St, La Fonda de Santa Fe; lunch $11-22, dinner $15-39; ⊙7am-2pm & 5-10pm Mon-Fri, 7am-3pm & 5-10pm Sat & Sun) One of Santa Fe's greatest pleasures is a meal in the Fonda's irresistible see-and-be-seen central atrium, with its excited bustle, colorful decor and high-class New Mexican food, with contemporary dishes sharing menu space with standards like fajitas and tamales.

Joseph's Culinary Pub　　　FRENCH $$$
(Map p900; ☑505-982-1272; www.josephsofsantafe.com; 428 Agua Fria St; mains $24-42; ⊙5:30-10pm, closed Mon Nov-Mar) This romantic old adobe, open for dinner only, is best seen as a fine-dining restaurant rather than a pub. Order from the shorter, cheaper bar menu

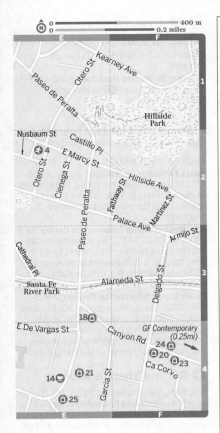

Santa Fe

◎ Top Sights
1 Georgia O'Keeffe Museum.................C1
2 Palace of the Governors & New
   Mexico History Museum.................D2

◎ Sights
3 New Mexico Museum of Art...............D2

◆ Activities, Courses & Tours
4 Mellow Velo...............................E2
5 Santa Fe School of Cooking...............C1

◉ Sleeping
6 El Paradero................................B4
7 La Fonda..................................D2
8 Santa Fe Motel & Inn B4

◎ Eating
9 Cafe Pasqual's............................D2
10 Joseph's Culinary Pub.....................B2
11 La Plazuela...............................D2
12 Tia Sophia's..............................C2

◎ Drinking & Nightlife
13 Bell Tower Bar............................D2
14 Kakawa Chocolate House....................E4
15 Santa Fe Spirits..........................B4

◎ Entertainment
16 Jean Cocteau Cinema.......................B3
17 Lensic Performing Arts Center.........C2

◎ Shopping
18 Adobe Gallery.............................E3
19 Blue Rain.................................A4
20 Economos/Hampton Galleries...........F4
21 Gerald Peters Gallery.....................E4
22 Kowboyz...................................B4
23 Marc Navarro Gallery......................F4
24 Morning Star Gallery......................F4
25 Nedra Matteucci Galleries.................E4
26 Santa Fe Farmers Market..................A4

SOUTHWEST SANTA FE

if you'd rather, but it's worth lingering in the warm-hued dining room to savor rich, hybrid French dishes with a modern twist: think campfire cassoulet with housemade sausage or sweet and spicy duck confit.

♥ Drinking & Entertainment

★ Kakawa Chocolate House   CAFE
(Map p900; ☑505-982-0388; https://kakawachocolates.com; 1050 Paseo de Peralta; ☺10am-6pm Mon-Sat, noon-6pm Sun) Chocolate addicts simply can't miss this loving ode to the sacred bean. This isn't your mom's marshmallow-laden hot chocolate, though – these rich elixirs are based on historic recipes and divided into two categories: European (eg 17th-century France) and Meso-American (Mayan and Aztec). Bonus: it also sells sublime chocolates (prickly pear mescal) and spicy chili caramels.

★ Santa Fe Spirits   DISTILLERY
(Map p900; ☑505-780-5906; https://santafespirits.com; 308 Read St; ☺3-8:30pm Mon-Thu, to 10pm Fri & Sat) The local distillery's $10 tasting flight includes an impressive amount of liquor, including shots of Colkegan single malt, Wheeler's gin and Expedition vodka. Leather chairs and exposed rafters make the in-town tasting room an intimate spot for an aperitif; fans can reserve a spot on the hourly tours of the distillery.

★ Santa Fe Opera   OPERA
(☑505-986-5900; www.santafeopera.org; Hwy 84/285, Tesuque; backstage tours adult/child $10/ free; ☺Jun-Aug, backstage tours 9am Mon-Fri

Jun-Aug) Many visitors flock to Santa Fe for the opera alone: the theater is a marvel, with 360-degree views of sandstone wilderness crowned with sunsets and moonrises, while at center stage the world's finest talent performs magnificent masterworks. It's still the Wild West, though; you can even wear jeans. Shuttles run to and from Santa Fe ($24) and Albuquerque ($39); reserve online.

Lensic Performing Arts Center
PERFORMING ARTS

(Map p900; 505-988-7050; www.lensic.com; 211 W San Francisco St) A beautifully renovated 1930 movie house, the theater hosts touring productions and classic films as well as seven different performance groups, including the Aspen Santa Fe Ballet and the Santa Fe Symphony Orchestra & Chorus.

Jean Cocteau Cinema
CINEMA

(Map p900; 505-466-5528; www.jeancocteau cinema.com; 418 Montezuma Ave) Revived by George RR Martin in 2013, this is the top cinema in town for indie flicks; also has book signings, occasional live concerts and an in-theater bar.

🛍 Shopping

★ Santa Fe Farmers Market
MARKET

(Map p900; 505-983-4098; www.santafefarm ersmarket.com; Paseo de Peralta & Guadalupe St; 7am-1pm Sat year-round, 7am-1pm Tue & 4-8pm Wed May-Nov; 🐾) Local produce, much of it heirloom and organic, is on sale at this spacious indoor-outdoor market, alongside homemade goodies, inexpensive food, natural body products and arts and crafts.

★ Blue Rain
ART

(Map p900; 505-954-9902; www.blueraingallery. com; 544 S Guadalupe St; 10am-6pm Mon-Sat) This large space in the Railyard district is the top gallery in town representing contemporary Native American and regional artists. There are generally several shows on at once, encompassing everything from modern pottery and sculpture to powerful landscapes and portraits.

Kowboyz
CLOTHING

(Map p900; 505-984-1256; www.kowboyz.com; 345 W Manhattan Ave; 10am-5:30pm) Secondhand shop selling everything you need to cowboy up. Shirts are a great deal; the amazing selection of boots, however, demands top dollar. Movie costumers in search of authentic Western wear often come here.

ℹ Information

EMERGENCY & MEDICAL SERVICES

Police (505-428-3710; 2515 Camino Entrada)

Christus St Vincent Hospital (505-983-3361; www.stvin.org; 455 St Michaels Dr; 24hr emergency)

POST

Post Office (Map p900; 120 S Federal Pl; 8am-5:30pm Mon-Fri, 9am-4pm Sat)

TOURIST INFORMATION

Santa Fe Visitor Center (Map p900; 800-777-2489; www.santafe.org; 66 E San Francisco St, Suite 3, Plaza Galeria; 10am-6pm) Pop into the Plaza Galeria center for maps and brochures.

New Mexico Visitor Information Center (Map p900; 505-827-7336; www.newmexico.org; 491 Old Santa Fe Trail; 8am-5pm Mon-Fri, 8am-4pm Sat & Sun) Housed in the historic 1878 Lamy Building, this friendly place offers helpful advice and free coffee.

Public Lands Information Center (505-954-2002; www.publiclands.org; 301 Dinosaur Trail; 8:30am-4pm Mon-Fri) Staff at this hugely helpful office have maps and information on public lands throughout New Mexico, and can talk you through all the hiking options.

ℹ Getting There & Around

Daily flights to/from Denver, Dallas, and Phoenix serve the small **Santa Fe Municipal Airport** (SAF; 505-955-2900; www.santafenm.gov/airport; 121 Aviation Dr), 10 miles southwest of downtown.

The **Sandia Shuttle Express** (888-775-5696; www.sandiashuttle.com; $30) connects Santa Fe with the Albuquerque Sunport.

North Central Regional Transit (505-629-4725; www.ncrtd.org) provides free shuttle bus service from downtown Santa Fe to Española on weekdays, where you can transfer to shuttles to Taos, Los Alamos, Ojo Caliente and other northern destinations. Pick-up/drop-off is by the Santa Fe Trails bus stop on Sheridan St, a block northwest of the Plaza.

On weekends, the **Taos Express** (866-206-0754; www.taosexpress.com; one way $5; Sat & Sun) runs north to Taos from the corner of Guadalupe and Montezuma Sts, by the Railyard.

The **Rail Runner** (www.nmrailrunner.com; adult/child $10/5) commuter train offers eight daily connections (four on weekends) with Albuquerque from its terminus in the Railyard and the South Capitol Station, a mile southwest. The trip takes about 1¾ hours. Arriving passengers can make use of the free Santa Fe Trails bus network.

Amtrak ([📞] 800-872-7245; www.amtrak.com) serves Lamy station, 17 miles southeast, with 30-minute bus connections to Santa Fe.

If driving between Santa Fe and Albuquerque, try to take Hwy 14 (the Turquoise Trail), which passes through the old mining town (now arts colony) of Madrid, 28 miles south of Santa Fe.

Santa Fe Trails (Map p900; [📞] 505-955-2001; www.santafenm.gov; one way adult/child $1/free, day pass $2) operates buses from the Downtown Transit Center, with routes M, to Museum Hill, and 2, along Cerrillos Rd, being the most useful for visitors. If you need a taxi, call **Capital City Cab** ([📞] 505-438-0000; www.capitalcitycab.com).

Around Santa Fe

Santa Fe Area Pueblos

The region north of Santa Fe remains the heartland of New Mexico's Pueblo Indian peoples. Eight miles west of Pojoaque along Hwy 502, the ancient **San Ildefonso Pueblo** ([📞] 505-455-2273; www.sanipueblo.org; Hwy 502; per vehicle $10, camera/video/sketching permits $10/20/25; ⊗ 8am-5pm) was the home of Maria Martinez, who in 1919 revived a distinctive traditional black-on-black pottery style. Stop to browse the shops of the exceptional potters (including Maria's direct descendants) who work in the pueblo today.

Just north of San Ildefonso, on Hwy 30, **Santa Clara Pueblo** ([📞] 505-753-7330) is home to the **Puyé Cliff Dwellings**, where you can visit Ancestral Puebloan cliffside and mesa-top ruins.

Las Vegas

Not to be confused with Nevada's glittery gambling megalopolis, this Las Vegas is one of the loveliest towns in New Mexico, and the largest and oldest community east of the Sangre de Cristo Mountains. Its eminently strollable downtown has a pretty Old Town Plaza and holds some 900 Southwestern and Victorian buildings listed in the National Register of Historic Places.

Built in 1882 and carefully remodeled a century later, the elegant **Plaza Hotel** ([📞] 505-425-3591; http://plazahotellvnm.com; 230 Old Town Plaza; r $89-149; [❄][@][📶][🐾]) is Las Vegas' most celebrated lodging, as seen in the movie *No Country For Old Men*. Choose between Victorian-style, antique-filled rooms in the original building or bright, modern rooms in a newer adjoining wing. You can

get your caffeine fix at **World Treasures Traveler's Cafe** ([📞] 505-426-8638; 1814 Plaza St; salads & sandwiches $6-8.50; ⊗ 7am-7pm Mon-Sat; [📶]), right on the plaza, and great modern American fare at **El Fidel** ([📞] 505-425-6659; 510 Douglas Ave; sandwiches $8-13, pasta $11-14, dinner mains $16-24; ⊗ 11am-3pm & 5-9pm Mon-Fri, 5-9pm Sat, 11am-2pm Sun).

Los Alamos

When the top-secret Manhattan Project sprang to life in 1943, it turned the sleepy mesa-top village of Los Alamos into a busy laboratory of secluded brainiacs. Here, in the 'town that didn't exist,' the first atomic bomb was developed in almost total secrecy. Today you'll encounter a fascinating dynamic in which souvenir T-shirts emblazoned with atomic explosions and 'La Bomba' wine are sold next to books on pueblo history and wilderness hiking.

While you can't visit the **Los Alamos National Laboratory**, where classified cutting-edge research still takes place, the interactive **Bradbury Science Museum** ([📞] 505-667-4444; www.lanl.gov/museum; 1350 Central Ave; ⊗ 10am-5pm Tue-Sat, 1-5pm Sun & Mon) [FREE] covers atomic history in fascinating detail. The small but interesting **Los Alamos Historical Museum** ([📞] 505-662-6272; www.losalamoshistory.org; 1050 Bathtub Row; ⊗ 9:30am-4:30pm Mon-Fri, 11am-4pm Sat & Sun) [FREE] is on the nearby grounds of the former Los Alamos Ranch School – an outdoorsy school for boys that closed when the scientists arrived. Grab a bite with a boffin at the **Blue Window Bistro** ([📞] 505-662-6305; www.labluewindowbistro.com; 813 Central Ave; lunch $10-12.50, dinner $11.25-28.50; ⊗ 11am-2:30pm Mon-Fri, 5-8:30pm Mon-Sat).

Bandelier National Monument

Ancestral Puebloans dwelt in the cliffsides of beautiful Frijoles Canyon, now preserved within **Bandelier** ([📞] 505-672-3861; www.nps.gov/band; Hwy 4; per vehicle $20; ⊗ dawn-dusk; [♿]). The adventurous can climb ladders to reach ancient caves and kivas (chambers) used until the mid-1500s. Backcountry camping (restricted to mesa tops from July to mid-September because of flood danger) requires a free permit, or there are around 100 sites at Juniper Campground, set among the pines near the monument entrance.

Note that between 9am and 3pm, from May 14 to October 15, you have to take a shuttle bus to Bandelier from the **White Rock Visitor Center** (Hwy 4) 8.5 miles north on Hwy 4.

Abiquiu

The Hispanic village of Abiquiu (sounds like 'barbecue'), on Hwy 84 about 45 minutes' drive northwest of Santa Fe, is famous because artist Georgia O'Keeffe lived and painted here from 1949 until her death in 1986. With the Chama River flowing through farmland and spectacular rock landscape, this ethereal setting continues to attract artists. O'Keeffe's adobe house is open for limited visits, with one-hour **tours** (☑505-685-4539; www.okeeffemuseum.org; tours $35-65; ☉Tue-Sat mid-Mar–mid-Nov) offered at least three days per week, but often booked months in advance.

Set amid 21,000 Technicolor acres 15 miles northwest, **Ghost Ranch** (☑505-685-1000; www.ghostranch.org; US Hwy 84; day pass adult/child $5/3; 👪) is a retreat center where O'Keeffe stayed many times. Besides fabulous hiking trails, it holds a **dinosaur museum** and offers basic **lodging** (tent & RV sites $25, dm $69, r with/without bath from $119/109; 🅿☉) plus horseback rides (from $50).

The lovely **Abiquiú Inn** (☑505-685-4378; www.abiquiuinn.com; US Hwy 84; r from $110, casitas from $120; 🅿☎) is a sprawling collection of shaded faux-adobes. Its spacious casitas have kitchenettes, and the menu at the on-site restaurant, **Cafe Abiquiú** (☑505-685-4378; www.abiquiuinn.com; Abiquiú Inn; lunch $10-14, dinner $21-26; ☉7am-8pm; ☎), includes the usual array of New Mexico specialties.

Ojo Caliente

At 140 years old, **Ojo Caliente Mineral Springs Resort & Spa** (☑505-583-2233; www.ojospa.com; 50 Los Baños Rd; r $189, cottages $229, ste $299-399, tent & RV $40; 🌣☎) is one of the country's oldest health resorts – and Pueblo Indians have used the springs for centuries! Fifty miles north of Santa Fe on Hwy 285, it offers 10 soaking pools with several combinations of minerals. In addition to the pleasant, if nothing special, historic hotel rooms, the resort has several plush, boldly colored suites with kiva fireplaces and private soaking tubs, and New Mexican–style cottages. Its **Artesian Restaurant** (www.ojospa.com; Hwy 285; lunch $11-16, dinner $16-32; ☉7:30am-11am, 11:30am-2:30pm &

5-9pm; ☎🍴) ☝ prepares organic and local ingredients with aplomb.

Taos

A magical spot even by the standards of this Land of Enchantment, Taos remains forever under the spell of the powerful landscape that surrounds it: 12,300ft snowcapped peaks rise behind town, while a sage-speckled plateau unrolls to the west before plunging 800ft straight down into the Rio Grande Gorge. The sky can be a searing sapphire blue or an ominous parade of rumbling thunderheads so big they dwarf the mountains. And then there are the sunsets...

Taos Pueblo, a marvel of adobe architecture, ranks among the oldest continuously inhabited communities in the US, and stands at the root of a long history that also extends from conquistadors to mountain men to artists. The town itself is a relaxed and eccentric place, with classic mud-brick buildings, fabulous museums, quirky cafes and excellent restaurants. Its 5700 residents include bohemians and hippies, alternative-energy aficionados and old-time Hispanic families. It's both rural and worldly, and a little bit otherworldly.

◉ Sights

★**Millicent Rogers Museum**   MUSEUM
(☑575-758-2462; www.millicentrogers.org; 1504 Millicent Rogers Rd; adult/child $10/2; ☉10:10am-5pm Apr-Oct, closed Mon Nov-Mar) Rooted in the private collection of model and oil heiress Millicent Rogers, who moved to Taos in 1947, this superb museum, 4 miles northwest of the Plaza, ranges from Hispanic folk art to Navajo weaving, and even modernist jewelry designed by Rogers herself. The principal focus, however, is on Native American ceramics, and especially the beautiful black-on-black pottery created during the 20th century by Maria Martínez from San Ildefonso Pueblo.

Martínez Hacienda   MUSEUM
(☑575-758-1000; www.taoshistoricmuseums.org; 708 Hacienda Way, off Lower Ranchitos Rd; adult/child $8/4, Blumenschein Museum joint ticket $12; ☉10am-5pm Mon-Sat, noon-5pm Sun Apr-Oct, closed Wed & Thu rest of the year) Set amid the fields 2 miles southwest of the Plaza, this fortified adobe homestead was built in 1804. It served as a trading post, first for merchants venturing north from Mexico City along the Camino Real, and then west along

the Santa Fe Trail. Its 21 rooms, arranged around a double courtyard, are furnished with the few possessions that even a wealthy family of the era would have been able to afford. Cultural events are held here regularly.

Harwood Foundation Museum   MUSEUM
([icon]575-758-9826; www.harwoodmuseum.org; 238 Ledoux St; adult/child $10/free; [clock]10am-5pm Mon-Sat, noon-5pm Sun Apr-Oct, closed Mon & Tue Nov-Mar) Attractively displayed in a gorgeous and very spacious mid-19th-century adobe compound, the paintings, drawings, prints, sculpture and photographs here are predominantly the work of northern New Mexican artists, both historical and contemporary. Founded in 1923, the Harwood is the second-oldest museum in New Mexico, and is as strong on local Hispanic traditions as it is on Taos' 20th-century school.

**Taos Art Museum
& Fechin Institute**   MUSEUM
([icon]575-758-2690;   www.taosartmuseum.org; 227 Paseo del Pueblo Norte; adult/child $10/free; [clock]10am-5pm Tue-Sun May-Oct, to 4pm Nov-Apr) Russian artist Nicolai Fechin moved to Taos in 1926, aged 46, and adorned the interior of this adobe home with his own distinctly Russian woodcarvings between 1928 and 1933. Now a museum, it displays Fechin's paintings and sketches along with his private collection and choice works by members of the Taos Society of Artists, and also hosts occasional chamber music performances in summer.

San Francisco de Asís Church   CHURCH
([icon]575-751-0518; St Francis Plaza, Ranchos de Taos; [clock]9am-4pm Mon-Fri) Just off Hwy 68 in Ranchos de Taos, 4 miles south of Taos Plaza, this iconic church was completed in 1815. Famed for the rounded curves and stark angles of its sturdy adobe walls, it was repeatedly memorialized by Georgia O'Keeffe in paint, and Ansel Adams with his camera. Mass is celebrated at 6pm the first Saturday of the month, and usually at 7am, 9am and 11:30am every Sunday.

Blumenschein Home & Museum   MUSEUM
([icon]575-758-0505;   www.taoshistoricmuseums.org; 222 Ledoux St; adult/child $8/4, Martínez Hacienda joint ticket $12; [clock]10am-5pm Mon-Sat, noon-5pm Sun Apr-Oct, closed Wed & Thu rest of year) Wonderfully preserved adobe residence, dating originally from 1797, which provides a vivid glimpse of life in Taos' artistic community during the 1920s. Ernest L Blumenschein, founder member of the Taos Society of Artists, lived here with his wife and daughter, Mary and Helen Greene Blumenschein, both also artists, and every room remains alive with their artworks and personal possessions.

Earthships   ARCHITECTURE
([icon]575-613-4409; www.earthship.com; US Hwy 64; self-guided tours $7; [clock]9am-5pm Jun-Aug, 10am-4pm Sep-May) [icon] Numbering 70 Earthships, with capacity for 60 more, Taos' pioneering community was the brainchild of architect Michael Reynolds. Built with recycled materials such as used car tires and cans, and buried on three sides, Earthships heat and cool themselves, make their own electricity and catch their own water; dwellers grow their own food. Stay overnight (p906) if possible; the 'tour' is a little disappointing. The visitor center is 1.5 miles west of the Rio Grande Gorge Bridge on US Hwy 64.

[icon] Activities

During summer, white-water rafting is popular in the Taos Box, the steep-sided cliffs that frame the Rio Grande. There are also plenty of excellent hiking and mountain biking trails. With a peak elevation of 11,819ft and a 3274ft vertical drop, **Taos Ski Valley** ([icon]866-968-7386; www.skitaos.org; lift ticket

---

CHIMAYÓ

The so-called 'Lourdes of America' – the extraordinarily beautiful two-towered adobe chapel of **El Santuario de Chimayó** ([icon]505-351-9961; www.elsantuariodechimayo.us; [clock]9am-6pm May-Sep, to 5pm Oct-Apr) **FREE** – nestles amid the hills of the 'High Road' east of Hwy 84, 28 miles north of Santa Fe. It was built in 1826, on a site where the earth was said to have miraculous healing properties. Even today, the faithful come to rub the *tierra bendita* (holy dirt) from a small pit inside the church on whatever hurts. During Holy Week, about 30,000 pilgrims walk to Chimayó from Santa Fe, Albuquerque and beyond, in the largest Catholic pilgrimage in the USA. The artwork in the santuario is worth a trip on its own. Stop at **Rancho de Chimayó** ([icon]505-984-2100; www.ranchodechimayo.com; County Rd 98; mains $7-10.75, dinner $10.25-25; [clock]11:30am-9pm, closed Mon Nov-Apr) afterward for lunch or dinner.

DON'T MISS

TAOS PUEBLO

Centered on twin five-story adobe complexes, set either side of the Río Pueblo de Taos, against the stunning backdrop of the Sangre de Cristos mountains, **Taos Pueblo** (☑ 575-758-1028; www. taospueblo.com; Taos Pueblo Rd; adult/ child $16/free; ⊙ 8am-4:30pm Mon-Sat, 8:30am-4:30pm Sun, closed mid-Feb–mid-Apr) are quintessential examples of ancient Pueblo architecture. They're thought to have been completed by around 1450 AD. Modern visitors are thus confronted by the same staggering spectacle as New Mexico's earliest Spanish explorers, though a small and very picturesque Catholic mission church now stands nearby.

Residents lead guided walking tours of the Pueblo (by donation) and explain some of the history. You'll also have the chance to buy fine jewelry, pottery and other arts and crafts, and sample flatbread baked in traditional bee-hive-shaped adobe ovens. Note that the Pueblo closes for 10 weeks around February through April, and at other times for ceremonies and events; call ahead or check the website for dates.

adult/teen/child $98/81/61; ⊙ 9am-4pm) offers some of the most challenging skiing and boarding in the US and yet remains low-key and relaxed.

Los Rios River Runners　　　RAFTING
(☑ 575-776-8854; www.losriosriverrunners.com; 1033 Paseo del Pueblo Sur; adult/child half-day from $54/44; ⊙ late Apr-Aug) Half-day trips on the Racecourse – in one- and two-person kayaks if you prefer – full-day trips on the Box (minimum age 12), and multinight expeditions on the scenic Chama. On its 'Native Cultures Feast and Float' you're accompanied by a Native American guide and have lunch homemade by a local Pueblo family. Rates rise slightly at weekends.

🛏 Sleeping

Sun God Lodge　　　MOTEL $
(☑ 575-758-3162; www.sungodlodge.com; 919 Paseo del Pueblo Sur; r from $55; P 🛜 🐾) The hospitable folks at this well-run two-story motel can fill you in on local history and point you to a restaurant to match your mood. Rooms

are clean – if a bit dark – and decorated with low-key Southwestern flair. The highlight is the lush-green courtyard dappled with twinkling lights, a scenic spot for a picnic or enjoying the sunset. It's 1.5 miles south of the Plaza.

★**Doña Luz Inn**　　　B&B $$
(☑ 575-758-9000; www.stayintaos.com; 114 Kit Carson Rd; r $119-209; ✳ @ 🛜 🐾) Funky and fun, this central B&B is a labor of love by owner Paul Castillo. Rooms are decorated in colorful themes from Spanish colonial to Native American, with abundant art, murals and artifacts plus adobe fireplaces, kitchenettes and hot tubs. The cozy La Luz room is the best deal in town, and there are also sumptuous larger suites.

★**Earthship Rentals**　　　BOUTIQUE HOTEL $$
(☑ 575-751-0462; www.earthship.com; US Hwy 64; earthship $185-410; 🛜 🐾) 🌿 How about an off-grid night in a boutique-chic, solar-powered dwelling? Part Gaudí-esque visions, part space-age fantasy, these futuristic structures are built using recycled tires and aluminum cans, not that those components are visible. Set on a beautiful mesa across the river 14 miles northwest, they offer a unique experience, albeit rather different to staying in Taos itself. Drop-ins welcome.

★**Historic Taos Inn**　　　HISTORIC HOTEL $$
(☑ 575-758-2233; www.taosinn.com; 125 Paseo del Pueblo Norte; r from $119; P ✳ 🛜) Lovely and always lively old inn, where the 45 characterful rooms have Southwest trimmings such as heavy-duty wooden furnishings and adobe fireplaces (some functioning, some for show). The famed Adobe Bar spills into the cozy central atrium, and features live music every night – for a quieter stay, opt for one of the detached separate wings – and there's also a good **restaurant** (☑ 575-758-1977; breakfast & lunch $7-15, dinner $15-28; ⊙ 11am-3pm & 5-9pm Mon-Fri, 7:30am-2:30pm & 5-9pm Sat & Sun).

★**Mabel Dodge Luhan House**　　　INN $$
(☑ 505-751-9686; www.mabeldodgeluhan.com; 240 Morada Lane; r from $116; P) Every inch of this rambling compound, once home to Mabel Dodge Luhan, the so-called Patroness of Taos, exudes elegant-meets-earthy beauty. Sleep where Georgia O'Keeffe, Willa Cather or Dennis Hopper once laid their heads, or even use a bathroom decorated by DH Lawrence. It also runs arts, crafts, spiritual and

creative workshops. Rates include buffet breakfast. Wi-fi in public areas only.

✗ Eating

Michael's Kitchen NEW MEXICAN $

(☑ 575-758-4178; www.michaelskitchen.com; 304c Paseo del Pueblo Norte; mains $8-13.50; ⊗ 7am-2:30pm Mon-Thu, to 8pm Fri-Sun; ⏲) Locals and tourists alike converge on this old favorite because the menu is long, the food's reliably good, it's an easy place for kids, and the in-house bakery produces goodies that fly out the door. Plus, it serves the best damn breakfast in town. You just may spot a Hollywood celebrity or two digging into a chile-smothered breakfast burrito.

★ Love Apple NEW MEXICAN $$$

(☑ 575-751-0050; www.theloveapple.net; 803 Paseo del Pueblo Norte; mains $17-29; ⊗ 5-9pm Tue-Sun) A real 'only in New Mexico' find, from the setting in the converted 19th-century adobe Placitas Chapel, to the delicious, locally sourced and largely organic food. Everything – from the local beefburger with red chile and blue cheese, via the tamales with mole sauce, to the wild boar tenderloin – is imbued with regional flavors, and the understated rustic-sacred atmosphere enhances the experience. Reserve; cash only.

★ Lambert's MODERN AMERICAN $$$

(☑ 505-758-1009; www.lambertsoftaos.com; 123 Bent St; lunch $11-14, dinner $23-38; ⊗ 11:30am-close; ⏲⏲) Consistently hailed as the 'Best of Taos,' this charming old adobe just north of the Plaza remains what it's always been – a cozy, romantic local hangout where patrons relax and enjoy sumptuous contemporary cuisine, with mains ranging from lunchtime's barbecue pork sliders to dinner dishes such as chicken mango enchiladas or Colorado rack of lamb.

♟ Drinking & Entertainment

Adobe Bar BAR

(☑ 575-758-2233; Historic Taos Inn, 125 Paseo del Pueblo Norte; ⊗ 11am-11pm, music 6:30-10pm) There's something about the Adobe Bar. Everyone in Taos seems to turn up at some point each evening, to kick back in the comfy covered atrium, enjoying no-cover live music from bluegrass to jazz, and drinking the famed Cowboy Buddha margaritas. If you decide to stick around, you can always order food from the well-priced bar menu.

Caffe Tazza CAFE

(☑ 575-758-8706; 122 Kit Carson Rd; ⊗ 7am-6pm) For a taste of how Taos used to be, back when hippies stalked the earth – or just to enjoy some great coffee – call in at Tazza, which now caters mostly to the crunchy-hipster-tattooed crowd. It's not everyone's cup of tea, but there's plenty of space to kick back, and most evenings see open mics or live music.

KTAOS Solar Center LIVE MUSIC

(☑ 575-758-5826; www.ktao.com; 9 Ski Valley Rd; ⊗ bar 4-9pm Mon-Thu, to 11pm Fri & Sat) Taos' best live-music venue, at the start of Ski Valley Rd, shares its space with much-loved radio station KTAOS 101.9FM. Local and touring acts stop by to rock the house; when there's no show, watch the DJs in the booth at the 'world's most powerful solar radio station' while hitting happy hour at the bar.

⭑ Shopping

Taos has historically been a mecca for artists, demonstrated by the huge number of galleries and studios in and around town. Indie stores and galleries line the **John Dunn Shops** (www.johndunnshops.com) pedestrian walkway linking Bent St to Taos Plaza.

Just east of the Plaza, pop into **El Rincón Trading Post** (☑ 575-758-9188; 114 Kit Carson Rd; ⊗ 10am-5pm) for classic Western memorabilia.

ⓘ Information

Taos Visitor Center (☑ 575-758-3873; http://taos.org; 1139 Paseo del Pueblo Sur; ⊗ 9am-5pm; ☎) This excellent visitor center stocks information of all kinds on northern New Mexico and doles out free coffee; everything, including the comprehensive *Taos Vacation Guide*, is also available online.

ⓘ Getting There & Away

From Santa Fe, take either the scenic 'High Road' along Hwys 76 and 518, with galleries, villages and sites worth exploring, or follow the lovely unfolding Rio Grande landscape on Hwy 68.

Greyhound buses do not serve Taos, but on weekdays, **North Central Regional Transit** (☑ 866-206-0754; www.ncrtd.org) provides free shuttle service to Española, where you can transfer to Santa Fe and other northern destinations; pick-up/drop-off is at the Taos County offices off Paseo del Pueblo Sur, a mile south of the Plaza.

Taos Express has shuttle service to Santa Fe on Saturday and Sunday (one-way adult/child $5/free), connecting with RailRunner trains to and from Albuquerque.

Northwestern New Mexico

New Mexico's wild northwest is home to wide-open, empty spaces. It's still dubbed Indian Country, and for good reason: huge swaths of land fall under the aegis of the Navajo, Zuni, Acoma, Apache and Laguna. This portion of New Mexico showcases remarkable ancient sites alongside modern, solitary Native American settlements. And when you've had your fill of culture, you can ride a historic narrow-gauge railroad through the mountains, hike around some trippy badlands or cast for huge trout.

Farmington & Around

The largest town in northwest New Mexico, Farmington makes a convenient base from which to explore the Four Corners area. The **visitors bureau** (☏505-326-7602; www. farmingtonnm.org; 3041 E Main St; ☉8am-5pm Mon-Sat) has more information. **Shiprock**, a 1700ft-high volcanic plug that rises eerily over the landscape to the west, was a landmark for the Anglo pioneers and is a sacred site to the Navajo.

Fourteen miles northeast of Farmington, the 27-acre **Aztec Ruins National Monument** (☏505-334-6174; www.nps.gov/azru; 84 Ruins Rd; adult/child $5/free; ☉8am-5pm Sep-May, to 6pm Jun-Aug) features the largest reconstructed kiva in the country, with an internal diameter of almost 50ft. A few steps away, let your imagination wander as you stoop through low doorways and dark rooms inside the West Ruin.

About 35 miles south of Farmington along Hwy 371, the undeveloped **Bisti Badlands & De-Na-Zin Wilderness** is a trippy, surreal landscape of strange, colorful rock formations, especially spectacular in the hours before sunset; desert enthusiasts shouldn't miss it. The Farmington **BLM office** (☏505-564-7600; www.blm.gov/nm; 6251 College Blvd; ☉7:45am-4:30pm Mon-Fri) has information.

The lovely, three-room **Silver River Adobe Inn B&B** (☏505-325-8219; www.silveradobe. com; 3151 W Main St; r $115-205; ▣☎) offers a peaceful respite among the trees along the San Juan River. Managing to be both trendy

and kid-friendly, the hippish **Three Rivers Eatery & Brewhouse** (☏505-324-2187; www. threeriversbrewery.com; 101 E Main St; mains $9-27, pizza $7.50-13.50; ☉11am-9pm; ☎▣) has good steaks, pub grub and its own microbrews. It's the best restaurant in town by a mile.

Chaco Culture National Historical Park

Featuring massive Ancestral Puebloan buildings set in an isolated high-desert environment, intriguing **Chaco** (☏505-786-7014; www.nps.gov/chcu; per vehicle $20; ☉7am-sunset) contains evidence of 5000 years of human occupation.

In its prime, the community at Chaco Canyon was a major trading and ceremonial hub for the region – and the city the Puebloan people created here was masterly in its layout and design. **Pueblo Bonito** is four stories tall and may have had 600 to 800 rooms and kivas. As well as driving the self-guided loop tour, you can hike various backcountry trails. For stargazers, there are evening astronomy presentations in summer. The park is in a remote area approximately 80 miles south of Farmington, far beyond the reach of any public transport. **Gallo Campground** (☏877-444-6777; www. recreation.gov; tent & RV sites $15) is 1 mile east of the visitor center. No RV hookups.

Northeastern New Mexico

East of Santa Fe, the lush Sangre de Cristo Mountains give way to high and vast rolling plains. Dusty grasslands stretch to infinity and beyond – or at least to Texas. Cattle and dinosaur prints dot a landscape punctuated by volcanic cones. Ranching is an economic mainstay, and on many stretches of road you'll see more cattle than cars – and quite possibly herds of bison too.

The Santa Fe Trail, along which early traders rolled in wagon trains, ran from Missouri to New Mexico. You can still see the wagon ruts in some places off I-25 between Santa Fe and Raton. For a bit of the Old West without a patina of consumer hype, this is the place.

Cimarron

Cimarron once ranked among the rowdiest of Wild West towns; its name even means 'wild' in Spanish. According to local lore, murder was such an everyday occurrence in the 1870s that peace and quiet was newsworthy, one paper going so far as to report: 'Everything is quiet in Cimarron. Nobody has been killed in three days.'

Today, the town really is quiet, luring nature-minded travelers who want to enjoy the great outdoors. Driving to or from Taos, you'll pass through gorgeous **Cimarron Canyon State Park**, a steep-walled canyon with several hiking trails, excellent trout fishing and camping.

You can stay or dine at what's reputed to be one of the most haunted hotels in the USA, the 1872 **St James** (☑ 575-376-2664; www.exstjames.com; 617 Collison St; r $85-135; ❄ ☎) – one room is so spook-filled that it's never been rented out! Many legends of the West stayed here, including Buffalo Bill, Annie Oakley, Wyatt Earp and Jesse James, and the front desk has a long list of who shot whom in the hotel bar.

Capulin Volcano National Monument

Rising 1300ft above the surrounding plains, **Capulin** (☑ 575-278-2201; www.nps.gov/cavo/; vehicle $7; ☉ 8am-5pm Jun-Aug, to 4:30pm Sep-May) is the most accessible of several volcanoes in the area. A 2-mile road spirals up the mountain to a parking lot at the rim (8182ft), where trails lead around and into the crater. The entrance is 3 miles north of Capulin village, which itself is 30 miles east of Raton on Hwy 87.

Southwestern New Mexico

The Rio Grande Valley unfurls from Albuquerque down to the bubbling hot springs of funky Truth or Consequences and on toward Mexico and Texas. En route, it feeds one of New Mexico's agricultural treasures: Hatch, the so-called chile capital of the world. East of the river, the desert is so dry it's been known since Spanish times as the Jornada del Muerto, which literally translates as the 'day-long journey of the dead man.' Pretty appropriate that this area was chosen for the detonation of the first atomic bomb, at what's now Trinity Site.

Away from Las Cruces, the state's second-largest city, residents in these parts are few and far between. To the west, the rugged Gila National Forest is wild with backcountry adventure, while the Mimbres Valley is rich with archaeological treasures.

Truth or Consequences & Around

An offbeat joie de vivre permeates the funky little town of Truth or Consequences ('T or C'), which was built on the site of natural hot springs in the 1880s. Originally, called, sensibly enough, Hot Springs, it changed its name in 1950, after a then-popular radio game show called, you guessed it, Truth or Consequences. Publicity these days comes courtesy of Virgin Galactic CEO Richard Branson and other space-travel visionaries driving the development of nearby **Spaceport America**, where wealthy tourists are expected to launch into orbit sometime soon.

About 60 miles north, sandhill cranes and Arctic geese winter in the 90 sq miles of fields and marshes at **Bosque del Apache National Wildlife Refuge** (www.fws.gov/refuge/bosque_del_apache; Hwy 1; per vehicle $5; ☉ dawn-dusk).

🛏 Sleeping & Eating

★ **Riverbend Hot Springs**   BOUTIQUE HOTEL **$$**
(☑ 575-894-7625; www.riverbendhotsprings.com; 100 Austin St; r $97-218, RV sites $60; ❄ ☎ ☎)
This delightful place, occupying a fantastic perch beside the Rio Grande, is the only T or C hotel to feature outdoor, riverside hot tubs – tiled, decked and totally irresistible. Accommodation, colorfully decorated by local artists, ranges from motel-style rooms to a three-bedroom suite. Guests can use the public pools for free, and private tubs for $10. No children under 12 years.

Blackstone Hotsprings   BOUTIQUE HOTEL **$$**
(☑ 575-894-0894; www.blackstonehotsprings.com; 410 Austin St; r $85-175; ℗ ❄ ☎) Blackstone embraces the T or C spirit with an upscale wink, decorating each of its ten rooms in the style of a classic TV show, from *The Jetsons* to *The Golden Girls* to *I Love Lucy*. Best part? Each room comes with its own oversized tub or waterfall fed from the hot springs. No children under 12.

Passion Pie Cafe   CAFE **$**
(☑ 575-894-0008; www.deepwaterfarm.com; 406 Main St; breakfast & lunch mains $4.25-9.50; ☉ 7am-3pm; ☎) Watch T or C get its morning groove on through the windows of this espresso cafe, and set yourself up with a breakfast waffle; the Elvis (with peanut butter) or

the Fat Elvis (with bacon too) should do the job. Later on there are plenty of healthy salads and sandwiches.

Las Cruces & Around

Las Cruces and her older and smaller sister city, Mesilla, sit at the edge of a broad basin beneath the fluted Organ Mountains, at the crossroads of two major highways, I-10 and I-25. An eclectic mix of old and young, Las Cruces is home to New Mexico State University (NMSU), whose 18,000 students infuse it with a healthy dose of youthful liveliness, while at the same time its 350 days of sunshine and numerous golf courses are turning it into a popular retirement destination.

◉ Sights

For many, a visit to neighboring **Mesilla** (aka Old Mesilla) is the highlight of their time in Las Cruces. Wander a few blocks off Old Mesilla's plaza to gather the essence of a mid-19th-century Southwestern town of Hispanic heritage.

★ New Mexico Farm & Ranch Heritage Museum   MUSEUM
(☑ 575-522-4100; www.nmfarmandranchmuseum. org; 4100 Dripping Springs Rd; adult/child $5/3; ☺ 9am-5pm Mon-Sat, noon-5pm Sun; 🐾) This terrific museum doesn't just display engaging exhibits on the state's agricultural history – it's got livestock too. Enclosures on the working farm alongside hold assorted breeds of cattle, along with horses, donkeys, sheep and goats. The taciturn cowboys who tend the animals proffer little extra information, but they add color, and you can even buy a pony if you have $450 to spare. There are daily milking demonstrations plus weekly displays of blacksmithing, spinning and weaving, and heritage cooking.

White Sands Missile Test Center Museum   MUSEUM
(☑ 575-678-3358; www.wsmr-history.org; ☺ 8am-4pm Mon-Fri, 10am-3pm Sat) **FREE** Explore New Mexico's military technology history with a visit to this museum, 25 miles east of Las Cruces along Hwy 70. It represents the heart of the White Sands Missile Range, a major testing site since 1945. There's a missile garden, a real V-2 rocket and a museum with lots of defense-related artifacts. Visitors have to park outside the Test Center gate and check in at the office before walking in.

🛏 Sleeping

★ Best Western Mission Inn   MOTEL $
(☑ 575-524-8591; www.bwmissioninn.com; 1765 S Main St; r from $71; ❋ 🐾 📶 ❄) A truly out-of-the-ordinary accommodation option: yes it's a roadside chain motel, but the rooms are beautifully kitted out with attractive tiling, stonework and colorful stenciled designs; they're sizable and comfortable; and the rates are great.

★ Lundeen Inn of the Arts   B&B $$
(☑ 505-526-3326; www.innofthearts.com; 618 S Alameda Blvd, Las Cruces; r/ste $125/155; 🅿 ❋ 📶 ❄) Each of the 20 guest rooms in this large and very lovely century-old Mexican Territorial–style inn is unique and decorated in the style of a New Mexico artist. Check out the soaring pressed-tin ceilings in the great room. Owners Linda and Jerry offer the kind of genteel hospitality you seldom find these days.

✕ Eating

★ Chala's Wood-Fired Grill   NEW MEXICAN $
(☑ 575-652-4143; 2790 Ave de Mesilla, Mesilla; mains $5-10; ☺ 8am-9pm Mon-Sat, to 8pm Sun) With house-smoked carnitas and turkey, housemade bacon and chile-pork sausage, plus *calabacitas* (squash and corn), quinoa salad and organic greens, this place rises well above the standard New Mexican diner fare. Located at the southern end of Mesilla, it's kick-back casual and the price is right.

Double Eagle Restaurant   STEAK $$$
(☑ 575-523-6700; www.double-eagle-mesilla.com; 308 Calle de Guadalupe, Mesilla; mains $24-45; ☺ 11am-10pm Mon-Sat, 11am-9pm Sun) A glorious melange of Wild West opulence, all dark wood and velvet hangings, and featuring a fabulous old bar, this Plaza restaurant is on the National Register of Historic Places. The main dining room offers continental and Southwestern cuisine, especially steaks, while the less formal **Peppers** (mains $7 to $15) occupies the verdant courtyard.

ℹ Information

Las Cruces Visitors Bureau (☑ 575-541-2444; www.lascrucescvb.org; 211 N Water St; ☺ 8am-5pm Mon-Fri)

Mesilla Visitor Center (☑ 575-524-3262; www. oldmesilla.org; 2231 Ave de Mesilla; ☺ 9:30am-4:30pm Mon-Sat, 11am-3pm Sun)

ⓘ Getting There & Away

Greyhound (☑575-523-1824; www.greyhound. com; 800 E Thorpe Rd, Chucky's Convenience Store) Buses run to all major destinations in the area, including El Paso, Albuquerque and Tucson. The bus stop is about 7 miles north of town.

Las Cruces Shuttle Service (☑575-525-1784; www.lascrucesshuttle.com) Runs eight to 10 vans daily to the El Paso International Airport ($49 one-way, $33 each additional person), and to Deming, Silver City and other destinations on request.

Silver City & Around

The spirit of the Wild West still hangs in the air in Silver City, 113 miles northwest of Las Cruces, as if Billy the Kid himself – who grew up here – might amble past at any moment. But things are changing, as the mountain-man/cowboy vibe succumbs to the charms of art galleries, coffee houses and gelato.

Silver City is also the gateway to outdoor activities in the **Gila National Forest**, which is rugged country suitable for remote cross-country skiing, backpacking, camping, and fishing. Two hours north of town, up a winding 42-mile road, is **Gila Cliff Dwellings National Monument** (☑575-536-9461; www.nps.gov/gicl; Hwy 15; adult/child $5/free; ⊙trail 9am-4pm, visitor center to 4:30pm), occupied in the 13th century by the Mogollon people. Mysterious and relatively isolated, these remarkable cliff dwellings are easily accessed from a 1-mile loop trail and look very much as they would have at the turn of the first millennium. For pictographs, stop by the **Lower Scorpion Campground** and walk a short distance along the marked trail.

Weird rounded monoliths make the **City of Rocks State Park** an intriguing playground, with great **camping** (☑575-536-2800; www.nmparks.com; Hwy 61; tent/RV sites $10/18) among the formations; there are tables and fire pits. For a rock-lined gem of a spot, check out campsite 43, the Lynx. Head 33 miles southeast of Silver City along Hwy 180 and Hwy 61.

For a smattering of Silver City's architectural history, overnight in the 22-room **Palace Hotel** (☑575-388-1811; www.silvercitypalacehotel.com; 106 W Broadway; r incl breakfast $58-94; ❉🐾). Exuding a low-key, turn-of-the-19th-century charm (no air-con, older fixtures), the Palace is a great choice for those tired of cookie-cutter chains.

Downtown eating options range from the comfy, come-as-you-are **Javalina** (☑575-388-1350; 201 N Bullard St; ⊙6am-6pm Sun-Thu, to 9pm Fri & Sat; 🐾) coffee shop to the gastronomically adventurous **1zero6** (☑575-313-4418; http://1zero6-jake.blogspot.com; 106 N Texas St; mains $19-24; ⊙5pm-10pm Fri-Sun). For a taste of local culture, head 7 miles north to Pinos Altos and the atmospheric **Buckhorn Saloon** (☑575-538-9911; www.buckhornsaloonandoperahouse.com; 32 Main St, Pinos Altos; mains $11-49; ⊙4-10pm Mon-Sat), where the specialty is steak and there's live music most nights. Call for reservations.

ⓘ Information

Visitor Center (☑575-538-5555; www.silvercitytourism.org; 201 N Hudson St; ⊙9am-5pm Mon-Sat, 10am-2pm Sun) This helpful office can provide everything you need to make the most of Silver City.

Gila National Forest Ranger Station (☑575-388-8201; www.fs.fed.us/r3/gila; 3005 E Camino del Bosque; ⊙8am-4pm Mon-Fri)

Southeastern New Mexico

Two extraordinary natural wonders are tucked away in New Mexico's arid southeast: the mesmerizing White Sands National Monument and the magnificent Carlsbad Caverns National Park. This region also swirls with some of the state's most enduring legends: aliens in Roswell, Billy the Kid in Lincoln, and Smokey Bear in Capitan. Most of the lowlands are covered by hot, rugged Chihuahuan Desert – once submerged under the ocean – but you can always escape to the cooler climes around the popular forest resorts of Cloudcroft or Ruidoso.

White Sands National Monument

Slide, roll and slither through brilliant, towerings and hills. Sixteen miles southwest of Alamogordo (15 miles southwest of Hwy82/70), gypsum covers 275 sq miles to create a dazzling white landscape at this crisp, stark **monument** (☑575-479-6124; www.nps.gov/whsa; adult/under 16yr $5/free; ⊙7am-9pm Jun-Aug, to sunset Sep-May). These captivating windswept dunes, which doubled as David Bowie's space-alien home planet in *The Man Who Fell To Earth*, are a highlight of any trip to New Mexico. Don't forget your sunglasses – the sand is as bright as snow!

PEERING INTO THE COSMIC UNKNOWN

Beyond the town of Magdalena on Hwy 60, 130 miles southwest of Albuquerque, the amazing **Very Large Array** (VLA; 505-835-7000; www.nrao.edu; off Hwy 52; adult/child $6/free; 8:30am-sunset) radio telescope consists of 27 huge antenna dishes sprouting like giant mushrooms in the high plains. Watch a short film at the visitor center, then take a self-guided walking tour with a window peek into the control building.

Spring for a $15 plastic saucer at the visitor center gift store then sled one of the backdunes. It's fun, and you can sell the disc back for $5 at day's end. Check the park calendar for sunset strolls and occasional moonlight bicycle rides (adult/child $5/2.50). Backcountry campsites, with no water or toilet facilities, are a mile from the scenic drive. Pick up a permit ($3, issued first-come, first-served) in person at the visitor center at least one hour before sunset.

Alamogordo & Around

In Alamogordo, a desert outpost famous for its space- and atomic-research programs, the four-story **New Mexico Museum of Space History** (575-437-2840; www.nmspacemuseum.org; 3198 Hwy 2001; adult/child $7/5; 10am-5pm Wed-Sat & Mon, noon-5pm Sun;) has excellent exhibits on space research and flight, and shows outstanding science-themed films in its adjoining **New Horizons Dome Theater** (adult/child $7/5).

Motels stretch along White Sands Blvd, including a decent branch of **Super 8** (575-434-4205; www.wyndhamhotels.com; 3204 N White Sands Blvd; r incl breakfast from $60;). If you'd rather camp, hit **Oliver Lee State Park** (575-437-8284; www.nmparks.com; 409 Dog Canyon Rd; tent/RV sites $8/14), 12 miles south of Alamogordo. Grab some good Mexican grub at the brisk **Rizo's** (575-434-2607; 1480 White Sands Blvd; $8.75-15; 9am-9pm Tue-Sat, to 6pm Sun;).

Cloudcroft

Situated high in the mountains, little Cloudcroft provides welcome relief from the lowlands heat. With turn-of-the-19th-century buildings, it offers lots of outdoor recreation, is a good base for exploration and has a low-key feel. **High Altitude** (575-682-1229; 310 Burro Ave; rentals per day from $30; 10am-5:30pm Mon-Thu, to 6pm Fri & Sat, to 5pm Sun) rents mountain bikes and has maps of local fat-tire routes.

The **Lodge Resort & Spa** (800-395-6343; www.thelodgeresort.com; 601 Corona Pl; r $125-235;) is one of the Southwest's finest historic hotels. Rooms in the main Bavarian-style hotel are furnished with period and Victorian pieces, while the great-value **Cloudcroft Mountain Park Hostel** (575-682-0555; www.cloudcrofthostel.com; 1049 Hwy 82; dm $19, r with shared bath $35-60;) sits on 28 wooded acres west of town. **Rebecca's** (575-682-3131; Lodge Resort, 601 Corona Pl; lunch $9-15, dinner $22-38; 7-10am, 11:30am-2pm & 5:30-9pm) offers the best food in town.

Ruidoso

Perched on the eastern slopes of Sierra Blanca Peak (11,981ft), Ruidoso is a year-round resort town that's downright bustling in the summer, attracts skiers in winter, has a lively arts scene, and is also home to a renowned racetrack. Neighboring Texans and locals escaping the summer heat of Alamogordo and Roswell are happy campers here (or more precisely, happy cabiners). The lovely Rio Ruidoso, a small creek with good fishing, runs through town.

Sights & Activities

To stretch your legs, try the easily accessible forest trails on Cedar Creek Rd just west of Smokey Bear Ranger Station. Choose from the USFS Fitness Trail or the meandering paths at the Cedar Creek Picnic Area. Longer day hikes and backpacking routes abound in the White Mountain Wilderness, north of town. Always check fire restrictions around here – the forest closes during dry spells.

Hubbard Museum of the American West   MUSEUM
(575-378-4142; www.hubbardmuseum.org; 26301 Hwy 70; adult/child $7/2; 9am-5pm Thu-Mon;) This town-run museum focuses on local history, with a wonderful gallery of old photos, and also displays Native American kachinas, war bonnets, weapons and pottery. Traces of its original incarnation as

the Museum of the Horse linger in various horse-related exhibits – and be sure to check out the fascinating, if completely irrelevant, history of toilets in the restrooms.

Ski Apache
SKIING

(📞 575-464-3600; www.skiapache.com; 1286 Ski Run Rd; lift ticket adult/child $68/48) Unlikely as it sounds, Ski Apache, 18 miles northwest of Ruidoso on the slopes of Sierra Blanca Peak, really is owned by the Apache. Potentially it's the finest ski area south of Albuquerque, a good choice for affordability and fun. Snowfall down here can be sporadic, though – check conditions ahead.

🛏 Sleeping & Eating

Rental cabins are a big deal in Ruidoso. Most have kitchens and grills, and often fireplaces and decks. Some cabins in town are cramped, while newer ones are concentrated in the Upper Canyon. There's also free primitive camping along the forest roads on the way to the ski area; for campsite specifics, ask at the **ranger station** (📞 575-257-4095; www.fs.usda.gov/lincoln; 901 Mechem Dr; ⊙8am-4pm Mon-Fri, plus Sat in summer).

Sitzmark Chalet
HOTEL $

(📞 575-257-4140; www.sitzmark-chalet.com; 627 Sudderth Dr; r from $87; ❇🛜) This ski-themed chalet offers 17 simple but nice rooms. Picnic tables, grills and an eight-person hot tub are welcome perks.

Upper Canyon Inn
LODGE $$

(📞 575-257-3005; www.uppercanyoninn.com; 215 Main Rd; r & cabins from $149; ❇🛜🐾) Rooms and cabins here range from simple good values to rustic-chic luxury. Bigger doesn't necessarily mean more expensive, so look at a few options. The pricier cabins have some fine interior woodwork and Jacuzzi tubs.

⭐Cornerstone Bakery
CAFE $

(📞 575-257-1842; www.cornerstonebakerycafe. com; 1712 Sudderth Dr; mains $5.50-11; ⊙7am-3pm Mon-Fri, to 4pm Sat & Sun; 🐾) Totally irresistible, hugely popular local bakery and cafe, where everything, from the breads, pastries and espresso to the omelets and croissant sandwiches, is just the way it should be. Stick around long enough and the Cornerstone may become your morning touchstone.

⭐ Entertainment

Ruidoso Downs Racetrack
SPORTS GROUND

(📞 575-378-4431; www.raceruidoso.com; 26225 Hwy 70; grandstand seats free; ⊙Fri-Mon late May-early Sep) National attention focuses on the Ruidoso Downs racetrack on Labor Day for the world's richest quarter-horse race, the All American Futurity, which has a purse of $2.4 million. The course is also home to the Racehorse Hall of Fame, and the small Billy the Kid Casino.

Flying J Ranch
LIVE MUSIC

(📞 575-336-4330; www.flyingjranch.com; 1028 Hwy 48; adult/child $27/15; ⊙from 5:30pm Mon-Sat late May-early Sep, Sat only early Sep–mid-Oct; 🐾) Families with little ones will love this 'Western village,' 1.5 miles north of Alto, as it delivers a full night of entertainment, with gunfights, pony rides and Western music, to go with its cowboy-style chuckwagon dinner.

ℹ Information

Visitor Center (📞 575-257-7395; www.rui dosonow.com; 720 Sudderth Dr; ⊙8am-5pm Mon-Fri, 9am-3pm Sat)

Lincoln & Capitan

Fans of Western history won't want to miss little Lincoln. Twelve miles east of Capitan along the **Billy the Kid National Scenic Byway** (www.billybyway.com), this is where the gun battle known as the Lincoln County War turned Billy the Kid into a legend. The whole town is beautifully preserved in close to original form, with its unspoiled main street designated as the **Lincoln Historic Site** (📞 575-653-4082; www.nmmonuments.org/ lincoln; adult/child $7/free; ⊙Apr-Oct).

Buy tickets to the historic town buildings at the **Anderson-Freeman Visitors Center**, where you'll also find exhibits on Buffalo soldiers, Apaches and the Lincoln County War. Make the fascinating **Courthouse Museum**, the well-marked site of Billy's most daring – and violent – escape, your last stop. For overnighters, the **Wortley Hotel** (📞 575-653-4300; www.wortleyhotel.com; Hwy 380; r $110) has been a fixture since 1874.

Like Lincoln, cozy Capitan is surrounded by the beautiful mountains of Lincoln National Forest. The main reason to come is so the kids can visit **Smokey Bear Historical Park** (📞 575-354-2748; 118 W Smokey Bear Blvd; adult/child $2/1; ⊙9am-4:30pm), where the original Smokey is buried.

Roswell

If you believe 'The Truth Is Out There', then the Roswell Incident is already filed away in your memory bank. In 1947 a mysterious object crashed at a nearby ranch. No one would have skipped any sleep over it, but the military made a big to-do of hushing it up, and for a lot of folks, that sealed it: the aliens had landed! International curiosity and local ingenuity have transformed the city into a quirky extraterrestrial-wannabe zone. Bulbous white heads glow atop the downtown streetlamps and busloads of tourists come to find good souvenirs.

Believers and kitsch-seekers must check out the **International UFO Museum & Research Center** (☑575-625-9495; www.roswell ufomuseum.com; 114 N Main St; adult/child $5/2; ☻9am-5pm), while the annual **Roswell UFO Festival** (www.roswellufofestival.com) beams down in early July.

Ho-hum chain motels line N Main St. About 36 miles south of Roswell, the **Heritage Inn** (☑575-748-2552; www.artesiaheri tageinn.com; 209 W Main St, Artesia; r incl breakfast from $99; ✸@☎) in Artesia is the nicest lodging in the area.

For simple, dependable New Mexican fare, try Martin's **Capitol Cafe** (☑575-624-2111; 110 W 4th St; mains $6-12; ☻6am-8:30pm Mon-Sat); for American eats, **Big D's Downtown Dive** (☑575-627-0776; 505 N Main St; mains $7-13; ☻11am-9pm) has the best salads, sandwiches and burgers in town.

Pick up local information at the **visitors bureau** (☑575-624-6700; www.seeroswell.com; 912 N Main St; ☻8:30am-5:30pm Mon-Fri, 10am-3pm Sat & Sun; ☎); **Greyhound** (☑575-622-2510; www.greyhound.com; 1100 N Virginia Ave) has buses to Las Cruces.

Carlsbad

Carlsbad is the closest town to Carlsbad Caverns National Park and the Guadalupe Mountains. To the northwest **Living Desert State Park** (☑575-887-5516; www.nmparks. com; 1504 Miehls Dr N, off Hwy 285; adult/child $5/3; ☻8am-5pm Jun-Aug, 9am-5pm Sep-May, last zoo entry 3:30pm) is a great place to see and learn about desert plants and wildlife. There's a good 1.3-mile trail that showcases different habitats of the Chihuahuan Desert, with live antelopes, wolves, roadrunners and more.

However, a recent boom in the oil industry means that even the most ordinary motel room in Carlsbad is liable to cost well over $200 per night, so it makes much more sense to visit on a long day-trip from, say, Roswell or Alamogordo. The best room rates, oddly enough, tend to be at the appealing **Trinity Hotel** (☑575-234-9891; www.thetrinityhotel.com; 201 S Canal St; r $149-209; ✸☎), originally the First National Bank. The sitting room of one suite is inside the old vault, and the restaurant is Carlsbad's classiest.

The perky **Blue House Bakery & Cafe** (☑575-628-0555; 609 N Canyon St; ☻6am-noon Mon-Sat) brews the best coffee in these parts, while the lip-smackin' **Red Chimney Pit Barbecue** (☑575-885-8744; www.redchimney bbq.com; 817 N Canal St; mains $6.50-16; ☻11am-2pm & 4:30-8:30pm Tue-Fri, 11am-8:30pm Sat) serves succulent Southern-style meats.

Greyhound (☑575-628-0768; www.grey hound.com; 3102 National Parks Hwy) buses depart from Food Jet South, 2 miles south of downtown. Destinations include El Paso, TX, and Las Cruces.

California

Includes ➜
Los Angeles 918
Disneyland &
Anaheim. 943
Palm Springs. 958
Santa Barbara. 965
San Francisco 977
Sacramento. 1016
Sierra Nevada 1021
Yosemite National
Park 1022

Best Places to Eat

➜ Benu (p994)

➜ Rich Table (p995)

➜ Otium (p937)

➜ Chez Panisse (p1005)

➜ SingleThread (p1010)

Best Places to Sleep

➜ Post Ranch Inn (p971)

➜ Inn of the Spanish Garden (p967)

➜ Chateau Marmont (p935)

➜ Jabberwock (p974)

➜ Hotel del Coronado (p955)

Why Go?

With bohemian spirit and high-tech savvy, not to mention a die-hard passion for the good life – whether that means cracking open a bottle of old-vine Zinfandel, climbing a 14,000ft peak or surfing the Pacific – California soars beyond any expectations sold on Hollywood's silver screens.

More than anything, California is iconic. It was here that the hurly-burly gold rush kicked off in the mid-19th century, where poet-naturalist John Muir rhapsodized about the Sierra Nevada's 'range of light,' and where Jack Kerouac and the Beat Generation defined what it really meant to hit the road.

California's multicultural melting pot has been cookin' since this bountiful promised land was staked out by Spain and Mexico. Today, waves of immigrants from around the world still look to find their own American dream on these palm-studded Pacific shores.

Come see the future in the making here in the Golden State.

When to Go
Los Angeles

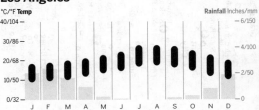

Jun–Aug Mostly sunny weather, occasional coastal fog; summer vacation crowds.

Apr–May & Sep–Oct Cooler nights, many cloudless days; travel bargains galore.

Nov–Mar Peak tourism at ski resorts and in SoCal's warm deserts.

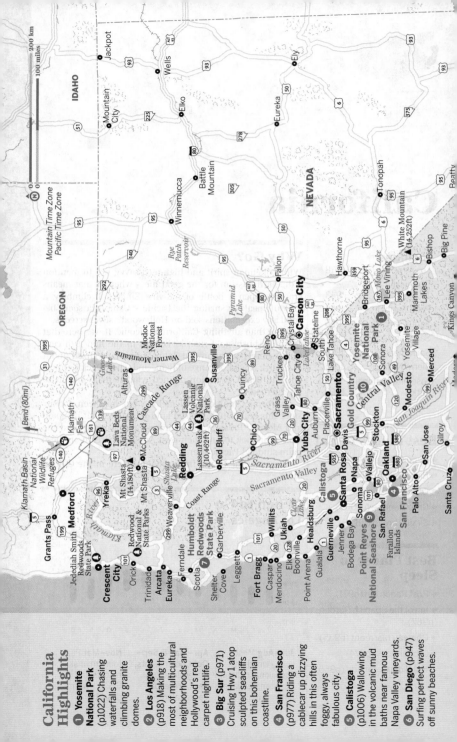

California Highlights

1 Yosemite National Park
(p1022) Chasing waterfalls and climbing granite domes.

2 Los Angeles
(p918) Making the most of multicultural neighborhoods and Hollywood's red carpet nightlife.

3 Big Sur (p971)
Cruising Hwy 1 atop sculpted seacliffs on this bohemian coastline.

4 San Francisco
(p977) Riding a cablecar up dizzying hills in this often foggy, always fabulous city.

5 Calistoga
(p1006) Wallowing in the volcanic mud baths near famous Napa Valley vineyards.

6 San Diego (p947)
Surfing perfect waves off sunny beaches.

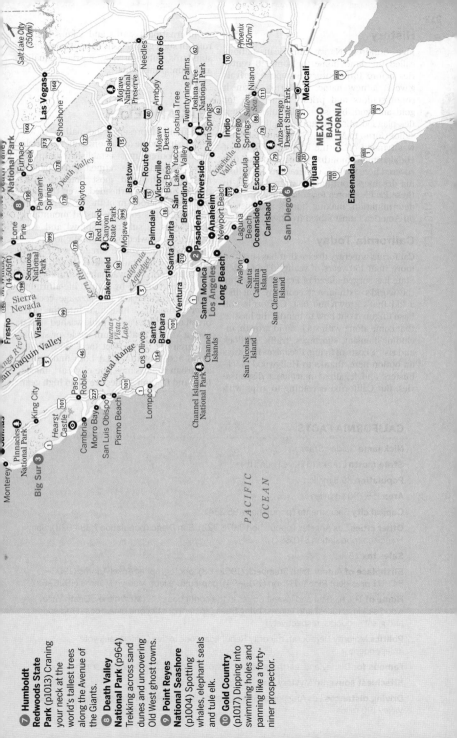

7 Humboldt Redwoods State Park (p1013) Craning your neck at the world's tallest trees along the Avenue of the Giants.

8 Death Valley National Park (p964) Trekking across sand dunes and uncovering Old West ghost towns.

9 Point Reyes National Seashore (p1004) Spotting whales, elephant seals and tule elk.

10 Gold Country (p1017) Dipping into swimming holes and panning like a forty-niner prospector.

History

Five hundred Native American nations called this land home for some 18 centuries before 16th-century European arrivals gave it a new name: California. Spanish conquistadors and priests came here for gold and god, but soon relinquished their flea-plagued missions and ill-equipped presidios (forts) to Mexico. The unruly territory was handed off to the US in the Treaty of Hidalgo mere months before gold was discovered here in 1848. Generations of California dreamers continue to make the trek to these Pacific shores for gold, glory and self-determination, making homes and history on America's most fabled frontier.

California Today

California is a crazy dream that has survived more than 150 years of reality. The Golden State has surged ahead of France to become the world's sixth-largest economy. But like a kid that's grown too fast, California still hasn't figured out how to handle the hassles that come along with such rapid growth, including housing shortages, traffic gridlock and rising costs of living. Escapism is always an option here, thanks to Hollywood blockbusters and legalized marijuana dispensaries. But California is coming to grips with its international status and taking leading roles in such global issues as environmental standards, online privacy, marriage equality and immigrant rights.

LOS ANGELES

LA County represents the nation in extremes. Its people are among America's richest and poorest, most established and most newly arrived, most refined and roughest, most beautiful and most botoxed, most erudite and most airheaded. Even the landscape is a microcosm of the USA: from cinematic beaches to snow-dusted mountains, skyscrapers to suburban sprawl and even wilderness prowled by mountain lions.

If you think you've already got LA figured out – celebutantes, smog, traffic, bikini babes and pop-star wannabes – think again. LA is best defined by simple life-affirming moments: a cracked-ice, jazz-age cocktail after midnight, a hike high into the sagebrush of Griffith Park, a pink-washed sunset over a Venice Beach drum circle, or simply a search for the perfect taco. With Hollywood and Downtown LA both undergoing an urban renaissance, the city's art, music, food and fashion scenes are all in high gear.

CALIFORNIA FACTS

Nickname Golden State

State motto Eureka ('I Have Found It')

Population 39.5 million

Area 155,780 sq miles

Capital city Sacramento (population 495,234)

Other cities Los Angeles (population 3,976,322), San Diego (population 1,394,928), San Francisco (population 870,887)

Sales tax 7.5%

Birthplace of Author John Steinbeck (1902–68), photographer Ansel Adams (1902–84), US president Richard Nixon (1913–94), pop-culture icon Marilyn Monroe (1926–62)

Home of The highest and lowest points in the contiguous US (Mt Whitney, Death Valley), world's oldest, tallest and biggest living trees (ancient bristlecone pines, coast redwoods and giant sequoias, respectively)

Politics Majority Democrat, minority Republican, one in five Californians vote independent

Famous for Disneyland, earthquakes, Hollywood, hippies, Silicon Valley, surfing

Kitschiest souvenir 'Mystery Spot' bumper sticker

Driving distances Los Angeles to San Francisco 380 miles, San Francisco to Yosemite Valley 190 miles

CALIFORNIA IN...

One Week

California in a nutshell: start in beachy **Los Angeles**, detouring to **Disneyland**. Head up the breezy **Central Coast**, stopping in **Santa Barbara** and **Big Sur**, before getting a dose of big-city culture in **San Francisco**. Head inland to nature's temple, **Yosemite National Park**, then zip back to LA.

Two Weeks

Follow the one-week itinerary above, but at a saner pace. Add jaunts to NorCal's **Wine Country**; **Lake Tahoe**, perched high in the Sierra Nevada; the bodacious beaches of Orange County and laid-back **San Diego**; or **Joshua Tree National Park**, near the chic desert resort of **Palm Springs**.

One Month

Do everything described above, and more. From San Francisco, head up the foggy **North Coast**, starting in Marin County at **Point Reyes National Seashore**. Stroll Victorian-era **Mendocino** and **Eureka**, find yourself on the **Lost Coast** and ramble through fern-filled **Redwood National & State Parks**. Inland, snap a postcard-perfect photo of **Mt Shasta**, drive through **Lassen Volcanic National Park** and ramble in California's historic **Gold Country**. Trace the backbone of the **Eastern Sierra** before winding down into other-worldly **Death Valley National Park**.

Chances are, the more you explore, the more you'll love 'La-La Land.'

History

The hunter-gatherer existence of the area's Gabrielino and Chumash peoples ended with the arrival of Spanish missionaries and colonists in the late 18th century. Spain's first civilian settlement, El Pueblo de Nuestra Señora la Reina de Los Ángeles del Río de Porciúncula, remained an isolated farming outpost for decades after its founding in 1781. The city wasn't officially incorporated until 1850.

LA's population repeatedly swelled after the collapse of the California gold rush, the arrival of the transcontinental railroad, the growth of the citrus industry, the discovery of oil, the launch of the port of LA, the birth of the movie industry and the opening of the California Aqueduct. After WWII, the city's population doubled from nearly two million in 1950 to around four million today.

◉ Sights

A dozen miles inland from the Pacific, Downtown LA combines history and high-brow arts and culture. Hip-again Hollywood awaits northwest of Downtown, while urban-designer chic and gay pride rule West Hollywood. South of WeHo, Museum Row is Mid-City's main draw. Further west are ritzy Beverly Hills, Westwood near the University of California, Los Angeles (UCLA) campus and West LA. Beach towns include kid-friendly Santa Monica, boho Venice, star-powered Malibu and busy Long Beach. Leafy Pasadena lies northeast of Downtown.

◉ Downtown

Downtown is divided into numerous areas. Bunker Hill is home to major modern-art museums and the **Walt Disney Concert Hall**. To the east is **City Hall** and, further east still, **Little Tokyo**. Southeast of Little Tokyo lies the trendy **Arts District**. Broadway is flanked by glorious heritage buildings, while the city's oldest colonial buildings flank Olvera St, north of City Hall and the 101 freeway. Further north still is **Chinatown**.

★**Hauser & Wirth**　　　　GALLERY
(Map p924; ☑213-943-1620; www.hauserwirth losangeles.com; 901 E 3rd St; ⊙11am-6pm Wed & Fri-Sun, to 8pm Thu) **FREE** The LA outpost of internationally acclaimed gallery Hauser & Wirth has art fiends in a flurry with its museum-standard exhibits of modern and contemporary art. It's a huge space, occupying 116,000 square feet of a converted flour mill complex in the Arts District. Past exhibits have showcased the work of luminaries such as Louise Bourgeois, Eva Hesse and Jason Rhoades. The complex is also home to a superlative art bookshop.

CALIFORNIA LOS ANGELES

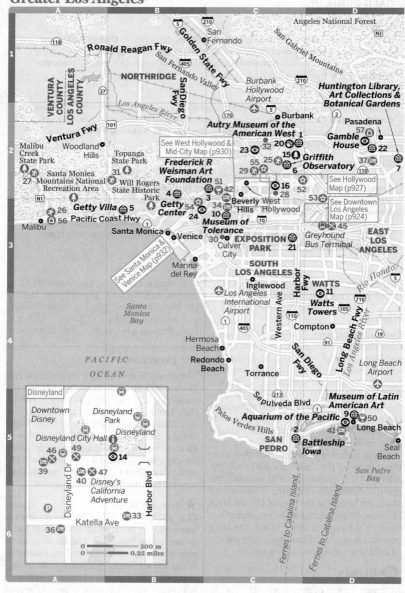

Bradbury Building

HISTORIC BUILDING

(Map p924; www.laconservancy.org; 304 S Broadway; ⊙lobby usually 9am-5pm; Ⓜ Red/Purple Lines to Pershing Sq) Debuting in 1893, the Bradbury is one of the city's undisputed architectural jewels. Behind its robust Romanesque facade lies a whimsical galleried atrium that wouldn't look out of place in New Orleans. Inky filigree grillwork, rickety birdcage elevators and yellow-brick walls

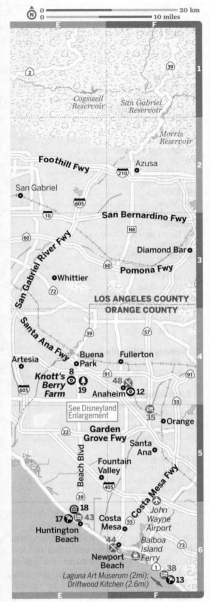

glisten golden in the afternoon light, which filters through the peaked glass roof. Such striking beauty hasn't been lost on Hollywood – the building's star turn came in the cult sci-fi flick *Blade Runner*.

El Pueblo de Los Angeles & Around

Compact, colorful and car free, this historic district immerses you in LA's Spanish-Mexican roots. Its spine is festive **Olvera St** (Map p924; www.calleolvera.com;), where you can snap up handmade folkloric trinkets, then chomp on tacos and sugar-sprinkled churros. 'New' **Chinatown** (Map p924; www.chinatownla.com) is about a half mile north along Broadway and Hill St, crammed with dim-sum parlors, herbal apothecaries, curio shops and Chung King Rd's edgy art galleries.

LA Plaza   MUSEUM
(La Plaza de Cultura y Artes; Map p924; ☎213-542-6200; www.lapca.org; 501 N Main St; ◷noon-5pm Mon, Wed & Thu, to 6pm Fri-Sun; ⊕) **FREE** This museum offers snapshots of the Mexican American experience in Los Angeles, from Spanish colonization in the late 18th century and the Mexican–American War (when the border crossed the original *pueblo*), to the Zoot Suit Riots, activist César Chávez and the Chicana movement. Exhibitions include a re-creation of 1920s Main St as well as rotating showcases of modern and contemporary art by LA-based Latino artists.

Avila Adobe   MUSEUM
(Map p924; ☎213-628-1274; www.elpueblo.lacity. org; 10 Olvera St; ◷9am-4pm) **FREE** The oldest surviving house in LA was built in 1818 by wealthy ranchero and one-time LA mayor Francisco José Avila. After subsequent lives as a boarding house and restaurant, the abode was restored to offer a glimpse into domestic LA life circa 1840. Rooms are filled with period furniture and furnishings, including a handful of items that belonged to the Avila family. Among these is the sewing machine. The house is open for self-guided tours.

Union Station   NOTABLE BUILDING
(Map p924; www.amtrak.com; 800 N Alameda St; ℗) Built on the site of LA's original Chinatown, Union Station opened in 1939 as America's last grand rail station. It's a glamorous exercise in Mission Revival style with art-deco and American Indian accents. The marble-floored main hall, with cathedral ceilings, original leather chairs and 3000-pound chandeliers, is breathtaking. The station's Traxx Bar was once the telephone room, complete with operator to place customers' calls. The LA Conservancy

Greater Los Angeles

◎ Top Sights

1 Autry Museum of the American
  West..C2
2 Battleship Iowa..............................C5
3 Frederick R Weisman Art
  Foundation................................C2
4 Getty Center.................................B2
5 Getty Villa....................................B3
6 Griffith Observatory......................C2
7 Huntington Library, Art
  Collections & Botanical
  Gardens...................................D2
8 Knott's Berry Farm.......................E4
9 Museum of Latin American Art.....D5
10 Museum of Tolerance....................C3
11 Watts Towers...............................D3

◎ Sights

12 Anaheim Packing District..............F4
  California Science Center.........(see 21)
  Center Street Anaheim.............(see 12)
13 Crystal Cove State Park...............F6
14 Disneyland Resort.........................B5
15 Griffith Park.................................C2
  Hammer Museum....................(see 24)
16 Hollywood Forever Cemetery........C2
17 Huntington City Beach..................E6
18 International Surfing Museum.........E6
19 Knott's Soak City.........................E4
20 Los Angeles Zoo & Botanical
  Gardens...................................C2
21 Natural History Museum of Los
  Angeles...................................C3
22 Norton Simon Museum..................D2
  Rose Garden...........................(see 21)
23 Universal Studios Hollywood.........C2
24 Westwood Village Memorial
  Park Cemetery........................B3

◎ Activities, Courses & Tours

25 Bronson Canyon............................C2
26 Malibu Canyon..............................A3
27 Malibu Creek State Park...............A2
28 Paramount Pictures.......................C2
29 Runyon Canyon.............................C2

30 Sony Pictures Studios....................C3
31 Topanga Canyon State Park...........B2
32 Warner Bros Studio Tour...............C2

◎ Sleeping

33 Alpine Inn.....................................B6
34 Avalon Hotel.................................C3
35 Ayres Hotel Anaheim....................F5
36 Best Western Plus Stovall's Inn.....A6
37 Bissell House B&B.........................D2
38 Crystal Cove Beach Cottages........F6
39 Disneyland Hotel...........................A5
40 Disney's Grand Californian
  Hotel & Spa.............................A5
41 Hotel Maya...................................D5
42 Montage.......................................C2
43 Paséa..E6

◎ Eating

44 Bear Flag Fish Company................F6
45 Bestia..D3
46 Earl of Sandwich..........................A5
  Fourth & Olive........................(see 9)
  Lot 579..................................(see 43)
47 Napa Rose....................................A5
48 Pour Vida.....................................F4
  Ración....................................(see 22)
49 Ralph Brennan's New Orleans
  Jazz Kitchen...........................A5

◎ Drinking & Nightlife

50 Pike...D5
51 Polo Lounge.................................C2

◎ Entertainment

52 Cavern Club Theater.....................C2
53 Dodger Stadium...........................D2
54 Geffen Playhouse.........................B3
55 Hollywood Bowl............................C2

◎ Shopping

56 Malibu Country Mart.....................A3
  Pacific City.............................(see 43)
57 Rose Bowl Flea Market..................D2

runs 2½-hour walking tours of the station on Saturdays at 10am (book online).

◎ Civic Center & Cultural Corridor

★ **Broad**   MUSEUM
(Map p924; ☏ 213-232-6200; www.thebroad.
org; 221 S Grand Ave; ⊙ 11am-5pm Tue & Wed, to
8pm Thu & Fri, 10am-8pm Sat, to 6pm Sun; P ⚐;
M Red/Purple Lines to Civic Center/Grand Park)
FREE From the instant it opened in September 2015, the Broad (rhymes with 'road') be-

came a must-visit for contemporary-art fans. It houses the world-class collection of local philanthropist and billionaire real-estate honcho Eli Broad and his wife Edythe, with more than 2000 postwar pieces by dozens of heavy hitters, including Cindy Sherman, Jeff Koons, Andy Warhol, Roy Lichtenstein, Robert Rauschenberg, Keith Haring and Kara Walker.

★ **Walt Disney Concert Hall**   NOTABLE BUILDING
(Map p924; ☏ 323-850-2000; www.laphil.org;
111 S Grand Ave; ⊙ guided tours usually noon &
1:15pm Thu-Sat, 10am & 11am Sun; P; M Red/

Purple Lines to Civic Center/Grand Park) FREE A molten blend of steel, music and psychedelic architecture, this iconic concert venue is the home base of the Los Angeles Philharmonic, but has also hosted contemporary bands such as Phoenix and classic jazz musicians such as Sonny Rollins. Frank Gehry pulled out all the stops: the building is a gravity-defying sculpture of heaving and billowing stainless steel.

★**MOCA Grand**   MUSEUM
(Museum of Contemporary Art; Map p924; ☎213-626-6222; www.moca.org; 250 S Grand Ave; adult/child $15/free, 5-8pm Thu free; ⊙11am-6pm Mon, Wed & Fri, to 8pm Thu, to 5pm Sat & Sun) MOCA's superlative art collection focuses mainly on works created from the 1940s to the present. There's no shortage of luminaries, among them Mark Rothko, Dan Flavin, Willem de Kooning, Joseph Cornell and David Hockney. Their creations are housed in a post-modern building by award-winning Japanese architect Arata Isozaki. Galleries are below ground, yet sky-lit bright.

La Placita   CHURCH
(Map p924; www.laplacita.org; 535 N Main St; ⊙6am-8:30pm) Founded as la Iglesia de Nuestra Señora la Reina de Los Ángeles (Our Lady the Queen of the Angels Church) in 1781, and now affectionately known as 'Little Plaza.' Head inside for a peek at the gilded altar and painted ceiling.

◉ **Little Tokyo**

Little Tokyo swirls with shopping arcades, Buddhist temples, traditional gardens, authentic sushi bars and noodle shops, and a provocative branch of **MOCA** (Map p924; ☎213-625-4390; www.moca.org; 152 N Central Ave; adult/student/child under 12yr $15/8/free, 5-8pm Thu free; ⊙11am-6pm Mon, Wed & Fri, to 8pm Thu, to 5pm Sat & Sun; Ⓜ Gold Line to Little Tokyo/Arts District).

Japanese American National Museum   MUSEUM
(Map p924; ☎213-625-0414; www.janm.org; 100 N Central Ave; adult/child $10/6, 5-8pm Thu & all day 3rd Thu of month free; ⊙11am-5pm Tue, Wed & Fri-Sun, noon-8pm Thu; ➹; Ⓜ Gold Line to Little Tokyo/Arts District) A great first stop in Little Tokyo, this is the country's first museum dedicated to the Japanese immigrant experience. The 2nd floor is home to the permanent 'Common Ground' exhibition, which explores the evolution of Japanese-American culture since the late 19th century and offers moving insight into the painful chapter of America's WWII internment camps. Afterwards relax in the tranquil garden and browse the well-stocked gift shop.

◉ **South Park**

South Park isn't actually a park but an emerging Downtown LA neighborhood around **LA Live** (Map p924; ☎866-548-3452, 213-763-5483; www.lalive.com; 800 W Olympic

---

LOS ANGELES IN...

Distances are ginormous in LA, so allow extra time for traffic and don't try to pack too much into a day.

One Day
Fuel up for the day at the **Original Farmers Market**, then go star-searching on the **Hollywood Walk of Fame** along Hollywood Blvd. Up your chances of spotting actual celebs by hitting the fashion-forward boutiques on paparazzi-infested **Robertson Boulevard**, or get a dose of nature at **Griffith Park**. Then drive west to the lofty **Getty Center** or head out to the **Venice Boardwalk** to see the seaside sideshow. Catch a Pacific sunset in **Santa Monica**.

Two Days
Explore rapidly evolving **Downtown LA**. Dig up the city's roots at **El Pueblo de Los Angeles**, then catapult to the future at dramatic **Walt Disney Concert Hall** topping Grand Ave's **Cultural Corridor**. Walk off lunch ambling between Downtown's historic buildings, **Arts District** galleries and **Little Tokyo**. At South Park's glitzy **LA Live** entertainment center, romp through the multimedia **Grammy Museum**, then join real-life celebs cheering on the LA Lakers next door at the **Staples Center**. After dark, hit the dance floor at clubs in **Hollywood**.

Downtown Los Angeles

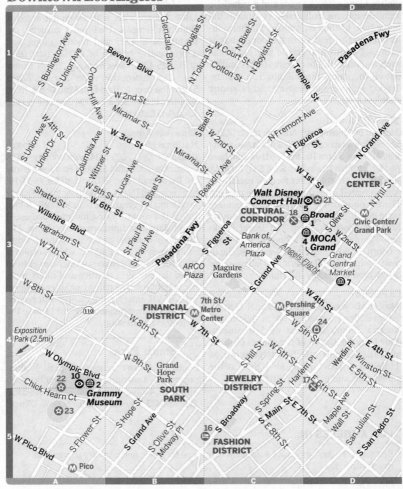

Blvd; P 🚻), a dining and entertainment hub where you'll find the Staples Center (p941) and **Microsoft Theater** (Map p924; ☎213-763-6020; www.microsofttheater.com; 777 Chick Hearn Ct).

★**Grammy Museum**   MUSEUM
(Map p924; ☎213-765-6800; www.grammymuseum.org; 800 W Olympic Blvd; adult/child $13/11; ⏰10:30am-6:30pm Mon-Fri, from 10am Sat & Sun; P 🚻) It's the highlight of LA Live (p923). Music-lovers will get lost in interactive exhibits, which define, differentiate and link musical genres. Spanning three levels, the

museum's rotating exhibitions might include threads worn by the likes of Michael Jackson, Whitney Houston and Beyonce, scribbled words from the hands of Count Basie and Taylor Swift and instruments once used by rock deities. Inspired? Interactive sound chambers allow you to try your own hand at singing, mixing and remixing.

⦿ Exposition Park & Around

Just south of the University of Southern California (USC) campus, this park has a full day's worth of kid-friendly museums.

Downtown Los Angeles

◎ Top Sights
1 Broad	D3
2 Grammy Museum	A4
3 Hauser & Wirth	F4
4 MOCA Grand	D3
5 Walt Disney Concert Hall	D3

◎ Sights
6 Avila Adobe	E2
7 Bradbury Building	D3
8 Chinatown	E1
9 Japanese American National Museum	E4
10 LA Live	A4
11 La Placita	E2
12 LA Plaza	E2
13 MOCA Geffen	E3
14 Olvera Street	E2
15 Union Station	F3

⊟ Sleeping
16 Ace Hotel	C5

⊗ Eating
17 Cole's	D4
18 Otium	C3
19 Sushi Gen	E4

◎ Drinking & Nightlife
20 Angel City Brewery	E4

✪ Entertainment
LA Clippers	(see 23)
LA Lakers	(see 23)
21 Los Angeles Philharmonic	D3
22 Microsoft Theater	A4
23 Staples Center	A5

ⓐ Shopping
24 Last Bookstore in Los Angeles	D4
25 Raggedy Threads	E4

Outdoor landmarks include the **Rose Garden** (Map p920; ☎213-763-0114; www.laparks.org/expo/garden; 701 State Dr, Exposition Park; ☉8:30am-sunset Mar 16–Dec 31; ℗; ⓂExpo Line to Exposition Park/USC) FREE and the Los Angeles Memorial Coliseum, site of the 1932 and 1984 Summer Olympic Games. Parking costs around $10. From Downtown, take the Metro Expo Line or DASH minibus F.

California Science Center MUSEUM
(Map p920; ☎film schedule 213-744-2019, info 323-724-3623; www.californiasciencecenter.org; 700 Exposition Park Dr, Exposition Park; IMAX movie adult/child $8.50/5.25; ☉10am-5pm; 🅿) FREE
Top billing at the Science Center goes to the Space Shuttle Endeavour, one of only four space shuttles nationwide, but there's plenty else to see at this large, multistory, multimedia museum filled with buttons to push, lights to switch on and knobs to pull. A simulated earthquake, baby chicks hatching and a giant techno-doll named Tess bring out the kid in everyone. Admission is free, but special exhibits, experiences and IMAX movies cost extra.

★**Watts Towers** LANDMARK
(Map p920; ☎213-847-4646; www.wattstowers.us; 1761-1765 E 107th St, Watts; adult/child 13-17yr & senior/child under 13yr $7/3/free; ☉tours

11am-3pm Thu & Fri, 10:30am-3pm Sat, noon-3pm Sun; P; M Blue Line to 103rd St) The three Gothic spires of the fabulous Watts Towers rank among the world's greatest monuments of folk art. In 1921 Italian immigrant Simon Rodia set out 'to make something big' and then spent 33 years cobbling together this whimsical free-form sculpture from concrete, steel and a motley assortment of found objects: green 7Up bottles, sea shells, tiles, rocks and pottery.

Natural History Museum of Los Angeles
MUSEUM

(Map p920; ☑213-763-3466; www.nhm.org; 900 Exposition Blvd, Exposition Park; adult/student & senior/child $12/9/5; ☺9:30am-5pm; P; M Expo Line to Expo/Vermont) Dinos to diamonds, bears to beetles, hissing roaches to African elephants – this museum will take you around the world and back, through millions of years in time. It's all housed in a beautiful 1913 Spanish Renaissance–style building that stood in for Columbia University in the first Toby McGuire *Spider-Man* movie – yup, this was where Peter Parker was bitten by the radioactive arachnid. There's enough to see here to fill several hours.

👁 Hollywood

Just as aging movie stars get the occasional face-lift, so has Hollywood. While it still hasn't recaptured its mid-20th-century 'Golden Age' glamour, its contemporary seediness is disappearing. The **Hollywood Walk of Fame** (Map p927; www.walkoffame. com; Hollywood Blvd; M Red Line to Hollywood/ Highland) honors more than 2400 celebrities with stars embedded in the sidewalk.

The Metro Red Line stops beneath **Hollywood & Highland** (Map p927; www.hollywood andhighland.com; 6801 Hollywood Blvd; ☺10am-10pm Mon-Sat, to 7pm Sun; 🛗; M Red Line to Hollywood/Highland), a multistory mall with nicely framed views of the hillside Hollywood sign, erected in 1923 as an advertisement for a land development called Hollywoodland. Two-hour validated mall parking costs $2 (daily maximum $15).

★ Hollywood Museum
MUSEUM

(Map p927; ☑323-464-7776; www.thehollywood museum.com; 1660 N Highland Ave; adult/child $15/5; ☺10am-5pm Wed-Sun; M Red Line to Hollywood/Highland) For a taste of Old Hollywood, do not miss this musty temple to the stars, its four floors crammed with movie

and TV costumes and props. The museum is housed inside the Max Factor Building, built in 1914 and relaunched as a glamorous beauty salon in 1935. At the helm was Polish-Jewish businessman Max Factor, Hollywood's leading authority on cosmetics. And it was right here that he worked his magic on Hollywood's most famous screen queens.

★ Grauman's Chinese Theatre
LANDMARK

(TCL Chinese Theatres; Map p927; ☑323-461-3331; www.tclchinesetheatres.com; 6925 Hollywood Blvd; guided tour adult/senior/child $16/13.50/8; 🛗; M Red Line to Hollywood/Highland) Ever wondered what it's like to be in George Clooney's shoes? Just find his footprints in the forecourt of this world-famous movie palace. The exotic pagoda theater – complete with temple bells and stone heaven dogs from China – has shown movies since 1927 when Cecil B DeMille's *The King of Kings* first flickered across the screen.

Hollywood Forever Cemetery
CEMETERY

(Map p920; ☑323-469-1181; www.hollywood forever.com; 6000 Santa Monica Blvd; ☺usually 8:30am-5pm, flower shop 9am-5pm Mon-Fri, to 4pm Sat & Sun; P) Paradisiacal landscaping, vainglorious tombstones and epic mausoleums set an appropriate resting place for some of Hollywood's most iconic dearly departed. Residents include Cecil B DeMille, Mickey Rooney, Jayne Mansfield, and punk rockers Johnny and Dee Dee Ramone. Valentino lies in the Cathedral Mausoleum (open from 10am to 2pm), while Judy Garland rests in the Abbey of the Psalms.

Dolby Theatre
THEATER

(Map p927; ☑323-308-6300; www.dolbytheatre. com; 6801 Hollywood Blvd; tours adult/child, senior & student $23/18; ☺10:30am-4pm; P; M Red Line to Hollywood/Highland) The Academy Awards are handed out at the Dolby Theatre, which has also hosted the *American Idol* finale, the Excellence in Sports Performance Yearly (ESPY) Awards and the Daytime Emmy Awards. The venue is home to the annual PaleyFest, the country's premier TV festival, held in March. Guided tours of the theater will have you sniffing around the auditorium, admiring a VIP room and nosing up to an Oscar statuette.

👁 Griffith Park

America's largest urban **park** (Map p920; ☑323-644-2050; www.laparks.org; 4730 Crystal Springs Dr; ☺5am-10pm, trails sunrise-sunset;

Hollywood

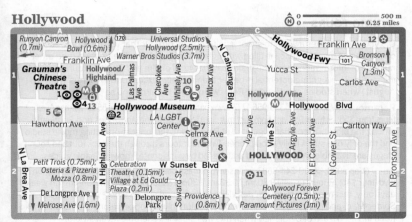

P🚻) **FREE** is five times the size of New York's Central Park, with an outdoor theater, zoo, observatory, museum, merry go-round, antique and miniature trains, children's playgrounds, golf, tennis and over 50 miles of hiking paths, including to the original Batman TV series cave.

★**Griffith Observatory** MUSEUM
(Map p920; ☎213-473-0890; www.griffithobser vatory.org; 2800 E Observatory Rd; admission free, planetarium shows adult/child $7/3; ⊙noon-10pm Tue-Fri, from 10am Sat & Sun; P🚻; 🚇DASH Observatory) **FREE** LA's landmark 1935 observatory opens a window onto the universe from its perch on the southern slopes of Mt Hollywood. Its planetarium claims the world's most advanced star projector, while its astronomical touch displays explore some mind-bending topics, from the evolution of the telescope and the ultraviolet x-rays used to map our solar system to the cosmos itself. Then, of course, there are the views, which (on clear days) take in the entire LA Basin, surrounding mountains and Pacific Ocean.

★**Autry Museum
of the American West** MUSEUM
(Map p920; ☎323-667-2000; www.autrynational center.org; 4700 Western Heritage Way, Griffith Park; adult/senior & student/child $14/10/6, 2nd Tue each month free; ⊙10am-4pm Tue-Fri, to 5pm Sat & Sun; P🚻) Established by singing cowboy Gene Autry, this expansive, underrated museum offers contemporary perspectives on the history and people of the American West, as well as their links to the region's contemporary culture. Permanent exhibitions explore everything from Native American traditions

Hollywood

◎ **Top Sights**
1 Grauman's Chinese Theatre...............A1
2 Hollywood Museum B1

◎ **Sights**
3 Dolby Theatre A1
4 Hollywood Walk of Fame.....................A1

🛏 **Sleeping**
5 Hollywood Roosevelt Hotel.................A1
6 Mama Shelter B2
7 USA Hostels Hollywood B2

🍴 **Eating**
8 Life Food Organic...............................C2

🍷 **Drinking & Nightlife**
9 Dirty Laundry B1
10 No Vacancy.......................................B1

🎭 **Entertainment**
11 ArcLight Cinemas C2
12 Upright Citizens Brigade
Theatre...D1

🛍 **Shopping**
13 Hollywood & Highland A1

to the cattle drives of the 19th century and daily frontier life; look for the beautifully carved vintage saloon bar. You'll also find costumes and artifacts from famous Hollywood westerns such as *Annie Get Your Gun*, as well as rotating art exhibitions.

Los Angeles Zoo & Botanical Gardens ZOO
(Map p920; ☎323-644-4200; www.lazoo.org; 5333 Zoo Dr, Griffith Park; adult/senior/child $20/17/15; ⊙10am-5pm, closed Christmas Day; P🚻) Home

STUDIO TOURS

Did you know it takes a week to shoot a half-hour sitcom? Or that you rarely see ceilings on shows because the space is filled with lights and lamps? You'll learn these and other nuggets of information about the make-believe world of film and TV while touring a working studio. Star-sighting potential is better than average, except during 'hiatus' (May to August) when studios are deserted. Reservations are required and so is photo ID.

Paramount (Map p920; ☑ 323-956-1777; www.paramountstudiotour.com; 5555 Melrose Ave; tours from $55; ☺ tours 9:30am-5pm, last tour 3pm) *Star Trek*, *Indiana Jones* and *Shrek* are among the blockbusters that originated at Paramount, the longest-operating movie studio and the only one still in Hollywood proper. Two-hour tours through the back lots and sound stages are available daily year-round and are led by passionate, knowledgeable guides.

Sony (Map p920; ☑ 310-244-8687; www.sonypicturesstudiostours.com; 10202 W Washington Blvd; tour $45; ☺ tours usually 9:30am, 10:30am, 1:30pm & 2:30pm Mon-Fri) Running on weekdays only, this two-hour tour includes visits to the sound stages where *Men in Black*, *Spider-Man*, and *Charlie's Angels* were filmed. Munchkins hopped along the Yellow Brick Road in *The Wizard of Oz*, filmed when this was still the venerable MGM studio.

Warner Bros (Map p920; ☑ 877-492-8687, 818-972-8687; www.wbstudiotour.com; 3400 W Riverside Dr, Burbank; tours adult/child 8-12yr from $62/52; ☺ 8:30am-3:30pm, extended hours Jun-Aug; ⬚ 155, 222, 501 stop about 400yd from tour center) This tour offers the most fun and authentic look behind the scenes of a major movie studio. Consisting of a two-hour guided tour and a self-guided tour of Studio 48, the adventure kicks off with a video of WB's greatest film hits – among them *Rebel Without a Cause* and *La La Land* – before a tram whisks you to sound stages, back-lot sets and technical departments, including props, costumes and the paint shop. Tours run daily, usually every half-hour.

---

to 1100 finned, feathered and furry friends from more than 250 species, the LA Zoo rarely fails to enthrall the little ones. Adults who have been to bigger zoos, however, may find the place a little average. To save time, purchase tickets online. To save money, bring your own food and drinks as the offerings at the zoo are expectantly overpriced.

⊙ West Hollywood & Mid-City

In WeHo, rainbow flags fly proudly over Santa Monica Blvd, while celebs keep gossip rags happy by misbehaving at clubs on the fabled Sunset Strip. Boutiques along Robertson Blvd and Melrose Ave purvey sassy and ultrachic fashions for Hollywood royalty and celebutantes. WeHo's also a hotbed of cutting-edge interior design, fashion and art, particularly in the **West Hollywood Design District** (http://westhollywooddesigndistrict. com). Further south, some of LA's best museums line Mid-City's Museum Row along Wilshire Blvd east of Fairfax Ave.

★ **Los Angeles County
Museum of Art**   MUSEUM
(LACMA; Map p930; ☑ 323-857-6000; www.lacma. org; 5905 Wilshire Blvd, Mid-City; adult/child $15/ free, 2nd Tue each month free; ☺ 11am-5pm Mon, Tue & Thu, to 8pm Fri, 10am-7pm Sat & Sun; ℗; ⬚ Metro lines 20, 217, 720, 780 to Wilshire & Fairfax) The depth and wealth of the collection at the largest museum in the western US is stunning. LACMA holds all the major players – Rembrandt, Cézanne, Magritte, Mary Cassatt, Ansel Adams – plus millennia's worth of Chinese, Japanese, pre-Columbian and ancient Greek, Roman and Egyptian sculpture. Recent acquisitions include massive outdoor installations such as Chris Burden's *Urban Light* (a surreal selfie backdrop of hundreds of vintage LA streetlamps) and Michael Heizer's *Levitated Mass,* a surprisingly inspirational 340-ton boulder perched over a walkway.

La Brea Tar Pits & Museum   MUSEUM
(Map p930; www.tarpits.org; 5801 Wilshire Blvd, Mid-City; adult/student & senior/child $12/9/5, 1st Tue of month Sep-Jun free; ☺ 9:30am-5pm; ℗ ⬚) Mammoths, saber-toothed cats and dire wolves used to roam LA's savannah in prehistoric times. We know this because of an archaeological trove of skulls and bones unearthed here at the La Brea Tar Pits, one of the world's most fecund and famous fossil sites. A museum has been built here, where generations of young dino hunters have come to seek out fossils and learn about

paleontology from docents and demonstrations in on-site labs.

Beverly Hills & the Westside

The major cultural sight here is the **Getty Center**, located in the hills of Brentwood. Westwood is home to the well-tended UCLA campus, the contemporary-art-focused **Hammer Museum** (Map p920; 310-443-7000; www.hammer.ucla.edu; 10899 Wilshire Blvd, Westwood; 11am-8pm Tue-Fri, to 5pm Sat & Sun; P) FREE and the star-studded **Westwood Village Memorial Park Cemetery** (Map p920; 310-474-1579; 1218 Glendon Ave, Westwood; 8am-6pm, P), all three of which are within walking distance of each other. Beverly Hills claims Rodeo Dr, a prime people-watching spot. Guided tours of celebrity homes depart from Hollywood.

★ **Getty Center**   MUSEUM
(Map p920; 310-440-7300; www.getty.edu; 1200 Getty Center Dr, off I-405 Fwy; 10am-5:30pm Tue-Fri & Sun, to 9pm Sat; P 734, 234) FREE In its billion-dollar, in-the-clouds perch, high above the city grit and grime, the Getty Center presents triple delights: a stellar art collection (everything from medieval triptychs to baroque sculpture and impressionist brushstrokes), Richard Meier's cutting-edge architecture, and the visual splendor of seasonally changing gardens. Admission is free, but parking is $15 ($10 after 3pm).

★ **Museum of Tolerance**   MUSEUM
(Map p920; reservations 310-772-2505; www.museumoftolerance.com; 9786 W Pico Blvd; adult/senior/student $15.50/12.50/11.50, Anne Frank Exhibit adult/senior/student $15.50/13.50/12.50; 10am-5pm Sun-Wed & Fri, to 9:30pm Thu, to 3:30pm Fri Nov-Mar; P) Run by the Simon Wiesenthal Center, this deeply moving museum uses interactive technology to engage visitors in discussion and contemplation around racism and bigotry. Particular focus is given to the Holocaust, with a major basement exhibition that examines the social, political and economic conditions that led to the Holocaust as well as the experience of the millions persecuted. On the museum's 2nd floor, another major exhibition offers an intimate look into the life and effect of Anne Frank.

★ **Frederick R Weisman Art Foundation**   MUSEUM
(Map p920; 310-277-5321; www.weismanfoundation.org; 265 N Carolwood Dr; 90min guided tours 10:30am & 2pm Mon-Fri, by appointment only) FREE The late entrepreneur and philanthropist Frederick R Weisman had an insatiable passion for art, a fact confirmed when touring his former Holmby Hills home. From floor to ceiling, the mansion (and its manicured grounds) bursts with extraordinary works from visionaries such as Picasso, Kandinsky, Miró, Magritte, Rothko, Warhol, Rauschenberg and Ruscha. There's even a motorcycle painted by Keith Haring. Tours should be reserved at least a few days ahead.

Malibu

The beach is king, of course, and whether you find a sliver of sand among the sandstone rock towers and topless sunbathers at El Matador or enjoy the wide loamy blonde beaches of Zuma and Westward, you'll have a special afternoon. Many A-listers have homes here and can sometimes be spotted shopping at the village-like **Malibu Country Mart** (Map p920; 310-456-7300; www.malibucountrymart.com; 3835 Cross Creek Rd, Malibu; 10am-midnight Mon-Sat, to 10pm Sun; MTA line 534).

One of Malibu's natural treasures is canyon-riddled **Malibu Creek State Park** (Map p920; 818-880-0367; www.malibucreekstatepark.org; 1925 Las Virgenes Rd, Cornell; parking $12; dawn-dusk), a popular movie and TV filming location with hiking trails galore (parking $12). A string of famous Malibu beaches include aptly named Surfrider near Malibu Pier, secretive El Matador, family fave Zuma Beach and wilder Point Dume (beach parking $3 to $12.50).

★ **Getty Villa**   MUSEUM
(Map p920; 310-430-7300; www.getty.edu; 17985 Pacific Coast Hwy, Pacific Palisades; 10am-5pm Wed-Mon; P line 534 to Coastline Dr) FREE Stunningly perched on an ocean-view hillside, this museum in a replica 1st-century Roman villa is an exquisite, 64-acre showcase for Greek, Roman and Etruscan antiquities. Dating back 7000 years, they were amassed by oil tycoon J Paul Getty. Galleries, peristiles, courtyards and lushly landscaped gardens ensconce all manner of friezes, busts and mosaics, millennia-old cut, blown and colored glass and brain-bending geometric configurations in the Hall of Colored Marbles. Other highlights include the Pompeii fountain and Temple of Herakles.

West Hollywood & Mid-City

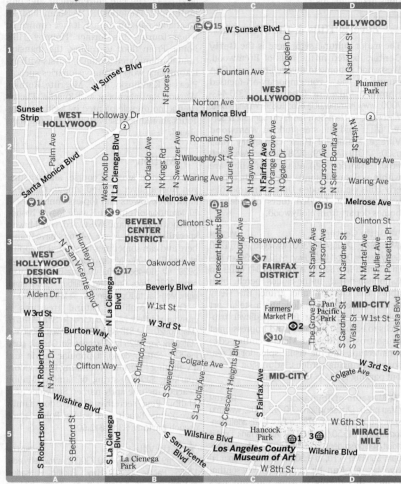

◉ Santa Monica

The belle by the beach mixes urban cool with a laid-back vibe. Tourists, teens and street performers throng car-free, chain-store-lined Third Street Promenade. For more local flavor, shop posh **Montana Avenue** or eclectic **Main Street**, backbone of the neighborhood once nicknamed 'Dogtown,' – the birthplace of skateboard culture. There's free 90-minute parking in most public garages downtown.

★ **Santa Monica Pier**   LANDMARK
(Map p932; ☎310-458-8901; www.santamonicapier.org; 🚶) Once the very end of Route 66 and still the object of a tourist love affair, the Santa Monica Pier dates back to 1908 and is the city's most compelling landmark. There are arcades, carnival games, a vintage carousel, a Ferris wheel, a roller coaster and an aquarium, and the pier comes alive with free concerts (Twilight Dance Series) and outdoor movies in the summertime.

West Hollywood & Mid-City

◎ Top Sights
1 Los Angeles County Museum of Art	C5

◎ Sights
2 Grove	C4
3 La Brea Tar Pits & Museum	D5
4 Village at Ed Gould Plaza	E2

🛏 Sleeping
5 Chateau Marmont	B1
6 Palihotel	C3

✕ Eating
7 Canter's	C3
8 Catch LA	A3
9 EP & LP	B3
10 Original Farmers Market	C4
11 Osteria & Pizzeria Mozza	E3
12 Petit Trois	E3
13 Providence	F3

◎ Drinking & Nightlife
14 Abbey	A3
15 Bar Marmont	C1

✪ Entertainment
16 Celebration Theatre	F2
17 Largo at the Coronet	B3

🛍 Shopping
18 Fred Segal	C3
19 Melrose Avenue	D3

a genteel escape among funky to modernist homes around the waterways that lent the neighborhood its name. For a quieter beach scene, head down the Marina Del Rey peninsula (one of America's largest pleasure-boat harbors is just inland), or head around the Ballona Wetlands to the wide open beaches of Playa del Rey.

◉ Venice

Be it beach, canal or wetlands, you're never far from water in these oceanside communities. Prepare for sensory overload on Venice's Boardwalk, a one-of-a-kind experience. Buff bodybuilders brush elbows with street performers and sellers of sunglasses, string bikinis, Mexican ponchos and medical marijuana, all while cyclists and rollerbladers whiz by on the bike path and skateboarders and graffiti artists get their own domains. A few blocks away, the Venice Canals offer

◉ Long Beach

Long Beach stretches along LA County's southern flank, harboring the world's third-busiest container port after Singapore and Hong Kong. Its industrial edge has been worn smooth downtown – Pine Ave is chockablock with restaurants and bars – and along the restyled waterfront. The Metro Blue Line connects Downtown LA with Long Beach in under an hour. Passport (www.lbtransit.com) minibuses shuttle around major tourist sights for free.

Santa Monica & Venice

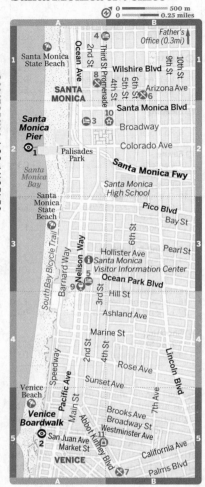

0 — 500 m
0 — 0.25 miles

Santa Monica & Venice

⊙ Top Sights
1 Santa Monica Pier A2
2 Venice Boardwalk A5

⊟ Sleeping
3 HI Los Angeles-Santa Monica A2
4 Palihouse A1
5 Sea Shore Motel A3

⊗ Eating
6 Cassia B1
7 Gjelina B5
8 Santa Monica Farmers Markets A1

⊙ Drinking & Nightlife
9 Basement Tavern A3

⊛ Entertainment
10 Harvelle's B2

⊝ Shopping
11 Waraku A5

which churned out 8000 hot meals a day during WWII.

★**Aquarium of the Pacific**   AQUARIUM
(Map p920; ☑tickets 562-590-3100; www.aqua riumofpacific.org; 100 Aquarium Way, Long Beach; adult/senior/child $30/27/19; ⊙9am-6pm; P⊞) Long Beach's most mesmerizing experience, the Aquarium of the Pacific is a vast, high-tech indoor ocean where sharks dart, jelly-fish dance and sea lions frolic. More than 11,000 creatures inhabit four re-created habitats: the bays and lagoons of Baja California, the frigid northern Pacific, tropical coral reefs and local kelp forests.

★**Museum of Latin American Art**   MUSEUM
(Map p920; ☑562-437-1689; www.molaa.org; 628 Alamitos Ave, Long Beach; adult/senior & student/child $10/7/free, Sun free; ⊙11am-5pm Wed, Thu, Sat & Sun, to 9pm Fri; P) This gem of a museum is the only one in the US to present art created since 1945 in Latin America and in Latino communities in the US, in important temporary and traveling exhibits. Blockbuster shows have recently included Caribbean art and the works of LA's own Frank Romero.

⊙ Pasadena

Below the lofty San Gabriel Mountains, this city drips with wealth and gentility, feeling a world apart from urban LA. It's known for its early 20th-century arts-and-crafts archi-

★**Battleship Iowa**   MUSEUM, MEMORIAL
(Map p920; ☑877-446-9261; www.pacificbattle ship.com; Berth 87, 250 S Harbor Blvd, San Pedro; adult/senior/child $20/17/12; ⊙10am-5pm, last entry 4pm; P⊞; ⊟ Metro Silver Line) This WWII to Cold War–era battleship is now permanently moored in San Pedro Bay and open to visitors as a museum. It's massive – 887ft long (that's 5ft longer than *Titanic*) and about as tall as an 18-story building. Step onto the gangway and download the app to take a self-guided audio tour of everything from the stateroom where FDR stayed to missile turrets and the enlisted men's galley,

tecture and the Tournament of Roses Parade on New Year's Day. Amble on foot around the shops, cafes, bars and restaurants of Old Town Pasadena, along Colorado Blvd east of Pasadena Ave. Metro Gold Line trains connect Pasadena and Downtown LA (20 minutes).

★ Huntington Library, Art Collections & Botanical Gardens
MUSEUM, GARDEN

(Map p920; ☑ 626-405-2100; www.huntington. org; 1151 Oxford Rd, San Marino; adult weekday/ weekend & holidays $23/25, child $10, 1st Thu each month free; ⊙ 10am-5pm Wed-Mon; P) One of the most delightful, inspirational spots in LA, the Huntington is rightly a highlight of any trip to California thanks to a world-class mix of art, literary history and over 120 acres of themed gardens (any one of which would be worth a visit on its own), all set amid stately grounds. There's so much to see and do that it's hard to know where to begin; allow three to four hours for even a basic visit.

★ Gamble House
ARCHITECTURE

(Map p920; ☑ info 626-793-3334, tickets 844-325-0712; www.gamblehouse.org; 4 Westmoreland Pl, Pasadena; tours adult/child $15/free; ⊙ tours 11:30am-3pm Thu & Fri, noon-3pm Sat & Sun Sep-May, 11am-3pm Thu-Sat, noon-3pm Sun Jun-Aug, bookstore 11am-2pm Tue, 10am-5pm Thu-Sun; P) This mansion in northwest central Pasadena has been called one of the 10 most architecturally significant homes in America, a 1908 masterpiece of California arts-and-crafts architecture built by Charles and Henry Greene for Procter & Gamble heir David Gamble. Incorporating 17 woods, art glass and subdued light, the entire home is a work of art, with its foundation, furniture and fixtures all united by a common design and theme inspired by its Southern California environs and Japanese and Chinese architecture.

Norton Simon Museum
MUSEUM

(Map p920; www.nortonsimon.org; 411 W Colorado Blvd, Pasadena; adult/child $12/free; ⊙ noon-5pm Mon, Wed & Thu, 11am-8pm Fri & Sat, 11am-5pm Sun; P) Rodin's *The Burghers of Calais* standing guard by the entrance is only a mind-teasing overture to the full symphony of art in store at this exquisite museum. Norton Simon (1907–93) was an entrepreneur with a Midas touch and a passion for art who parlayed his millions into an admirable collection of Western art and Asian sculpture. Meaty captions really help tell each piece's story.

☆ Activities

Despite spending a lot of time jammed on freeways, Angelenos love to get physical. Theirs is a city made for pace-quickening thrills, with spectacular mountain hikes, one of the country's largest urban nature reserves and surf-pounded beach. Add to this almost 300 days of sunshine and you'll forgive the locals for looking so, so good.

Hiking

If hiking doesn't feel like an indigenous LA activity to you, you need to reassess. This town is hemmed in and defined by two mountain ranges and countless canyons. In the **San Gabriel Mountains**, trails wind from Mt Wilson into granite peak wilderness, once the domain of the Gabrielino people and the setting for California's last grizzly-bear sighting. The Chumash roamed the **Santa Monica Mountains** (www.nps.gov/ samo/index.htm), which are smaller, but still offer spectacular views of chaparral-draped peaks with stark drops into the Pacific. The **Backbone Trail** spans the range, but our favorite hike is to Sandstone Peak. Day hikes in **Topanga Canyon State Park** (Map p920; ☑ 310-455-2465; www.parks.ca.gov; 20828 Entrada Rd, Topanga; per vehicle $10; ⊙ 8am-dusk), **Malibu Canyon** (Map p920; Malibu Canyon Rd, Malibu), Point Mugu and **Leo Carrillo** (☑ 310-457-8143; www.parks.ca.gov; 35000 W Pacific Coast Hwy, Malibu; per car $12; ⊙ 8am-10pm; P ⊞) state parks are also recommended. If you only have an hour or two, check out **Runyon** (Map p920; www.runyoncanyonhike.com; 2000 N Fuller Ave; ⊙ dawn-dusk) or **Bronson** (Map p920; ☑ 818-243-1145; www.laparks.org; 3200 Canyon Dr; ⊙ 5am-10:30pm) canyons in Hollywood. For more advice about trails in and around Southern California check out www. trails.com, or buy any of *Afoot and Afield: Los Angeles County: A Comprehensive Hiking Guide* (Wilderness Press; 2009), *Secret Walks: A Walking Guide to the Hidden Trails of Los Angeles* (Santa Monica Press; 2015) or *60 Hikes Within 60 Miles* (Menasha Ridge Press; 2009).

Cycling & In-line Skating

Get scenic exercise pedaling or skating along the paved **South Bay Bicycle Trail**, which parallels the beach for most of the 22 miles between Santa Monica and Pacific Palisades. Rental shops are plentiful in busy beach towns. Warning: it's crowded on weekends.

Surfing & Swimming

Top beaches for swimming are Malibu's Leo Carrillo State Park, Santa Monica State Beach and the South Bay's Hermosa Beach. Malibu's Surfrider Beach is a legendary surfing spot. Parking rates vary seasonally. 'Endless summer' is, sorry to report, a myth – much of the year you'll want a wetsuit in the Pacific. Water temperatures become tolerable by June and peak just under 70°F (21°C) in August. Water quality varies – check the 'Beach Report Card' at http://brc.healthebay.org.

Tours

★ Esotouric
BUS

(☑ 213-915-8687; www.esotouric.com; tours $58) Discover LA's lurid and fascinating underbelly on these offbeat, insightful and entertaining walking and bus tours themed around famous crime sites (Black Dahlia anyone?), literary lions (Chandler to Bukowski) and more.

★ Los Angeles Conservancy
WALKING

(☑ 213-623-2489; www.laconservancy.org; adult/child $15/10) Downtown LA's intriguing historical and architectural gems – from an art-deco penthouse to a beaux-arts ballroom and a dazzling silent-movie theater – are revealed on this nonprofit group's 2½-hour walking tours. To see some of LA's grand historic movie theaters from the inside, the conservancy also offers the Last Remaining Seats film series, screening classic movies in gilded theaters.

Dearly Departed
BUS

(☑ 855-600-3323; www.dearlydepartedtours.com; tours $50-85) This long-running, occasionally creepy, frequently hilarious tour will clue you in on where celebs kicked the bucket, George Michael dropped his trousers, Hugh Grant received certain services and the Charles Manson gang murdered Sharon Tate. Not for kids.

★ Festivals & Events

First Friday
STREET CARNIVAL

(www.abbotkinneyfirstfridays.com; ☉ 5-11pm 1st Fri each month) Businesses along Abbot Kinney Blvd stay open late and the street is filled with food trucks at this monthly street fair.

Academy Awards
FILM

(www.oscars.org) Ogle your favorite film stars from the Dolby Theatre's red-carpet-adjacent bleachers. Apply in November or December for one of around 700 lucky spots. Held in late February or early March.

Rose Parade
PARADE

(www.tournamentofroses.com; ☉ Jan) This cavalcade of flower-festooned floats snakes through Pasadena on New Year's Day. Get close-ups during post-parade viewing at Victory Park. Avoid traffic and take the Metro Rail Gold Line to Memorial Park.

West Hollywood Halloween Carnaval
CARNIVAL

(www.visitwesthollywood.com/halloween-carnaval) This rambunctious street fair brings 500,000 revelers – many in over-the-top and/or X-rated costumes – out for a day of dancing, dishing and flirting on Halloween. In late October.

🛏 Sleeping

For seaside life, base yourself in Santa Monica, Venice or Long Beach. Cool-hunters and party people will be happiest in Hollywood or WeHo; culture vultures should go to Downtown LA. Prices do not include lodging taxes (12% to 14%).

🛏 Downtown

Ace Hotel
HOTEL $$$

(Map p924; ☑ 213-623-3233; www.acehotel.com/losangeles; 929 S Broadway; lofts from $400; P ✻ @ ⓢ ☒) The ever-hip, buzzy, 182-room Ace is big on quirky details: Haas Brothers murals in the lobby and restaurant, whimsically themed cocktails at the rooftop bar and retro-inspired rooms with boxer-style robes, blank music sheets and, in many cases, record players or guitars. Small rooms can feel tight, so consider opting for a medium. Valet parking is $36 a night.

🛏 Hollywood

USA Hostels Hollywood
HOSTEL $

(Map p927; ☑ 800-524-6783, 323-462-3777; www.usahostels.com; 1624 Schrader Blvd; dm $38-49, r with bath from $120; ✻ @ ⓢ; M Red Line to Hollywood/Vine) This sociable hostel puts you within steps of the Hollywood party circuit. Private rooms are a bit cramped, but making new friends is easy during staff-organized barbecues, comedy nights and various walking tours. Freebies include wi-fi and a cook-your-own-pancake breakfast. It has cushy lounge seating on the front porch and free beach shuttles, too.

LOCAL KNOWLEDGE

LA INSIDER MOVES

Classic movies on Broadway What better place to enjoy cult-status films than in one of Broadway's old movie palaces? Throughout the year, Cinespia (http://cinespia.org) runs special film screenings in historic Downtown theaters usually not open to the public. Many of the films are screened in 35mm. Check the Cinespia website for upcoming movies.

City Hall Farmers Market City Hall's South Lawn transforms into a mouthwatering farmers market on Thursday mornings. You'll find everything from organic fruit and vegetables to fresh seafood, meats, specialty food producers and ready-to-eat-food stalls. Best of all, 10% of sales goes to neighborhood nonprofit LARABA (Los Angeles River Artists and Business Association).

Run, yoga and beer If you feel like really earning your beer, join Angel City Brewery (p939) on its weekly Sunday morning exercise and beer-drinking combo ($15). The session begins with a 30-minute warm-up run through Downtown before a Vinyasa Flow yoga session (bring your own mat). Sweaty and centered, it's time for your well-deserved draft. Sign up online at www.brew-yoga.com.

★**Mama Shelter**　　　　BOUTIQUE HOTEL **$$**
(Map p927; ☑323-785-6666; www.mamashel ter.com; 6500 Selma Ave; r from $179; ❄@🕾; Ⓜ Red Line to Hollywood/Vine) Hip, affordable Mama Shelter keeps things playful with its lobby gumball machines, foosball table and live streaming of guests' selfies and videos. Standard rooms are small but cool, with quality beds and linen and subway-tiled bathrooms with decent-sized showers. Quirky in-room touches include movie scripts, masks and Apple TVs with free Netflix. The rooftop bar is one of LA's best.

★**Hollywood**
Roosevelt Hotel　　　　HISTORIC HOTEL **$$$**
(Map p927; ☑323-856-1970; www.thehollywood roosevelt.com; 7000 Hollywood Blvd; d from $282; Ⓟ❄@🕾🏊; Ⓜ Red Line to Hollywood/Highland) Roosevelt heaves with Hollywood lore: Shirley Temple learned to tap dance on the stairs off the lobby, Marilyn Monroe shot her first print ad by the pool (later decorated by David Hockney) and the ghost of actor Montgomery Clift can still be heard playing the bugle. Poolside rooms channel a modernist, Palm Springs vibe, while those in the main building mix contemporary and 1920s accents.

▨ West Hollywood & Mid-City

★**Palihotel**　　　　BOUTIQUE HOTEL **$$**
(Map p930; ☑323-272-4588; www.pali-hotel.com; 7950 Melrose Ave, Mid-City; r from $195; Ⓟ@🕾) We love the rustic wood-panelled exterior, the polished-concrete floor in the lobby, the elemental Thai massage spa, and the 32 contemporary rooms with two-tone paint jobs, a wall-mounted flat-screen TV, and enough room for a sofa. Some have terraces. Terrific all-around value.

★**Chateau Marmont**　　　　HOTEL **$$$**
(Map p930; ☑323-656-1010; www.chateaumar mont.com; 8221 W Sunset Blvd, Hollywood; r $450, ste from $820; Ⓟ🐾❄🍴🕾🏊) The French-flavored indulgence may look dated, but this faux castle has long lured A-listers with its hilltop perch, five-star mystique and legendary discretion. Howard Hughes used to spy on bikini beauties from the same balcony suite that became the favorite of U2's Bono. If nothing else, it's worth stopping by for a cocktail at **Bar Marmont** (Map p930; ☑323-650-0575; 8171 Sunset Blvd, Hollywood; ☻6pm-2am).

▨ Beverly Hills

Avalon Hotel　　　　HOTEL **$$$**
(Map p920; ☑844-328-2566, 310-277-5221; www. avalon-hotel.com/beverly-hills; 9400 W Olympic Blvd, Beverly Hills; r from $289; Ⓟ❄@🕾🏊🐾) Mid-century modern gets a 21st-century spin at this fashion-crowd fave, which was Marilyn Monroe's old pad in its days as an apartment building. Funky retro rooms are all unique, but most have arched walls, marble slab desks and night stands, as well as playful art and sculpture. Perks include a sexy hourglass-shaped pool. Call it affordable glamor.

★**Montage**　　　　HOTEL **$$$**
(Map p920; ☑888-860-0788; www.montagebev erlyhills.com; 225 N Canon Dr, Beverly Hills; r/ste from $695/1175; Ⓟ@🕾🏊) Drawing on-point eye candy and serious wealth, the 201-room Montage balances elegance with warmth

and affability. Models and moguls lunch by the gorgeous rooftop pool, while the property's sprawling five-star spa is a Moroccan-inspired marvel, with both single-sex and unisex plunge pools. Rooms are classically styled, with custom Sealy mattresses, dual marble basins, spacious showers and deep-soaking tubs.

Santa Monica

HI Los Angeles – Santa Monica HOSTEL $
(Map p932; ☎310-393-9913; www.hilosangeles.
org; 1436 2nd St; dm low season $27-45, May-Oct $40-55, r with shared bath $109-140, with private bath $160-230; ❋❁@✆; Ⓜ Expo Line to Downtown Santa Monica) Near the beach and Promenade, this hostel has an enviable location and recently modernized facilities that rival properties charging many times more. Its approximately 275 beds in single-sex dorms are clean and safe, private rooms are decorated with hipster chic and public spaces (courtyard, library, TV room, dining room, communal kitchen) let you lounge and surf.

Sea Shore Motel MOTEL $$
(Map p932; ☎310-392-2787; www.seashoremo
tel.com; 2637 Main St; r $125-175, ste $200-300; ❗❋✆) The friendly, family-run lodgings at this comfy 25-unit motel put you just a Frisbee toss from the beach on happening Main St (quadruple-pane windows help cut street noise). The tiled, rattan-decorated rooms are basic, but 2nd-floor rooms have high ceilings and families can stretch out in the suites (basically full apartments) with kitchen and balcony a few doors down.

★**Palihouse** BOUTIQUE HOTEL $$$
(Map p932; ☎310-394-1279; www.palihousesanta
monica.com; 1001 3rd St; r/studios from $315/350;

❗❋@✆☻) LA's grooviest hotel brand (not named Ace) occupies the 38 rooms, studios and one-bedroom apartments of the 1927 Spanish Colonial Embassy Hotel, with antique-meets-hipster-chic style. Each comfy room is slightly different, but look for picnic-table-style desks and wallpaper with intricate sketches of animals. Most rooms have full kitchens (and we love the coffee mugs with lifelike drawings of fish).

Long Beach

★**Hotel Maya** BOUTIQUE HOTEL $$
(Map p920; ☎562-435-7676; www.hotelmayalong
beach.com; 700 Queensway Dr, Long Beach; r from $179; ❗❋@✆☻☼) West of the *Queen Mary*, this boutique property hits you with hip immediately upon entering the rusted-steel, glass and magenta-paneled lobby. The feel continues in the 199 rooms (coral tile, river-rock headboards, Mayan-icon accents), set in four 1970s-era hexagons with views of downtown Long Beach that are worth the upcharge.

Pasadena

★**Bissell House B&B** B&B $$
(Map p920; ☎626-441-3535; www.bissellhouse.
com; 201 S Orange Grove Ave, South Pasadena; r from $159; ❗❋✆) Antiques, hardwood floors and a crackling fireplace make this secluded Victorian (1887) B&B on 'Millionaire's Row' a bastion of warmth and romance. The hedge-framed garden feels like a sanctuary, and there's a pool for cooling off on hot summer days. The Prince Albert room has gorgeous wallpaper and a claw-foot tub. All seven rooms have private baths.

LA FOR CHILDREN

Keeping kids happy is child's play in LA. The sprawling Los Angeles Zoo (p927) in family-friendly Griffith Park (p926) is a sure bet. Dino fans will dig the La Brea Tar Pits (p928) and the Natural History Museum (p926), while budding scientists crowd the Griffith Observatory (p927) and California Science Center (p925). For under-the-sea creatures, head to the Aquarium of the Pacific (p932) in Long Beach. The amusement park at Santa Monica Pier (p930) is fun for all ages. Activities for younger kids are more limited at tween-teen-oriented **Universal Studios Hollywood** (Map p920; ☎800-864-8377; www.universalstudioshollywood.com; 100 Universal City Plaza, Universal City; admission from $99, child under 3yr free; ☺daily, hours vary; ❗❸; Ⓜ Red Line to Universal City). In neighboring Orange County, Disneyland (p943) and Knott's Berry Farm (p944) are the first and last word in theme parks.

✗ Eating

Bring an appetite. A big one. LA's cross-cultural make up is reflected at its table, which is an epic global feast. And while there's no shortage of just-like-the-motherland dishes – from Cantonese *xiao long bao* to Ligurian *farinata* – it's the takes on tradition that really thrill. Ever tried Korean-Mexican tacos? Or a vegan cream-cheese donut with jam, basil and balsamic reduction? LA may be many things, but a culinary bore isn't one of them.

✗ Downtown

Cole's   SANDWICHES $
(Map p924; ☎213-622-4090; http://213hospitality.com/project/coles; 118 E 6th St; sandwiches $10-13.50; ◷11am-midnight Sun-Wed, to 2am Thu-Sat; 🛜) An atmospheric old basement tavern with vintage vinyl booths, original glass lighting and historic photos, Cole's is known for originating the French Dip sandwich way back in 1908, when those things cost a nickel. You know the drill – French bread piled with sliced lamb, beef, turkey, pork or pastrami, dipped once or twice in *au jus*.

★ Sushi Gen   JAPANESE $$$
(Map p924; ☎213-617-0552; www.sushigen.org; 422 E 2nd St; sushi $11-23; ◷11:15am-2pm & 5:30-9:45pm Tue-Fri, 5-9:45pm Sat; 🅿; Ⓜ Gold Line to Little Tokyo/Arts District) Come early to grab a table at this classic sushi spot, where bantering Japanese chefs carve thick slabs of melt-in-your-mouth salmon, buttery *toro* (tuna belly), Japanese snapper and more. At lunch, perch yourself at the sushi counter for à la carte options, or queue for a table in the dining room, where the sashimi lunch special ($17) is a steal.

★ Otium   MODERN AMERICAN $$$
(Map p924; ☎213-935-8500; http://otiumla.com; 222 S Hope St, Downtown; dishes $15-45; ◷11:30am-2:30pm & 5:30-10pm Tue-Thu, 11:30am-2:30pm & 5:30-11pm Fri, 11am-2:30pm & 5:30-11pm Sat, 11am-2:30pm & 5:30-10pm Sun; 🛜) In a modernist pavilion beside the Broad is this fun, of-the-moment hot spot helmed by chef Timothy Hollingsworth. Prime ingredients conspire in unexpected ways, from the crunch of wild rice and amaranth in an eye-candy salad of avocado, beets and pomegranate, to a twist of lime and sake in flawlessly al dente whole-wheat bucatini with Dungeness crab.

★ Bestia   ITALIAN $$$
(Map p920; ☎213-514-5724; www.bestiala.com; 2121 7th Pl; pizzas $16-19, pasta $19-29, mains $28-120; ◷5-11pm Sun-Thu, to midnight Fri & Sat; 🅿) Years on, this loud, buzzing, industrial dining space remains the most sought-after reservation in town (book at least a week ahead). The draw remains its clever, produce-driven take on Italian flavors, from charred pizzas topped with housemade 'nduja (a spicy Calabrian paste), to a sultry stinging-nettle raviolo with egg, mixed mushrooms, hazelnut and ricotta. The wine list celebrates the boutique and obscure.

✗ Hollywood & Griffith Park

Life Food Organic   VEGETARIAN $
(Map p927; ☎323-466-0927; www.lifefoodorganic.com; 1507 N Cahuenga Ave; dishes $7-14; ◷7:30am-9pm; 🛜) 🌱 If you're done with the tacos and cocktails, detox at this little health shop and eatery. Slurp on an almond-milk chocolate shake and fill up on the likes of turmeric-and-quinoa salads, veggie chili burgers and chocolate-cream pie. Some of it might sound naughty, but everything on the menu is raw, vegetarian and nutritious.

★ Petit Trois   FRENCH $$
(Map p930; ☎323-468-8916; http://petittrois.com; mains $14-36; ◷noon-10pm Sun-Thu, to 11pm Fri & Sat; 🅿) Good things come in small packages...like tiny, no-reservations Petit Trois! Owned by acclaimed TV chef Ludovic Lefebvre, its two long counters (the place is too small for tables) are where food-lovers squeeze in for smashing, honest, Gallic-inspired grub, from a ridiculously light Boursin-stuffed omelette to a showstopping double cheeseburger served with a standout foie gras–infused red-wine bordelaise.

★ Providence   MODERN AMERICAN $$$
(Map p930; ☎323-460-4170; www.providencela.com; 5955 Melrose Ave; lunch mains $40-45, tasting menus $120-250; ◷noon-2pm & 6-10pm Mon-Fri, 5:30-10pm Sat, 5:30-9pm Sun; 🅿) The top restaurant pick by preeminent LA food critic Jonathan Gold for four years running, this two-starred Michelin darling turns superlative seafood into arresting, nuanced dishes that might see abalone paired with eggplant, turnip and nori, or spiny lobster conspire decadently with macadamia nut and earthy black truffle.

★ **Osteria & Pizzeria Mozza**   ITALIAN $$$
(Map p930; ☑osteria 323-297-0100, pizzeria 323-297-0101; http://la.osteriamozza.com; 6602 Melrose Ave; pizzas $11-25, osteria mains $29-38; ☺pizzeria noon-midnight, osteria 5:30-11pm Mon-Fri, 5-11pm Sat, 5-10pm Sun; ℗) Osteria Mozza crafts fine cuisine from market-fresh, seasonal ingredients, but being a Mario Batali joint, you can expect adventure – think squid-ink *chitarra freddi* with Dungeness crab, sea urchin and jalapeño – and consistent excellence. Reservations are recommended. Next door, Pizzeria Mozza is more laid-back and cheaper, its gorgeous thin-crust pies topped with combos such as squash blossoms, tomato and creamy *burrata*.

✖ West Hollywood & Mid-City

Original Farmers Market   MARKET $
(Map p930; ☑323-933-9211; www.farmersmarketla.com; 6333 W 3rd St; mains $6-12; ☺9am-9pm Mon-Fri, to 8pm Sat, 10am-7pm Sun; ℗🚻) The Farmers Market is a great spot for a casual meal any time of day, especially if the rug rats are tagging along. There are lots of options here, from gumbo and diner food to Singapore-style noodles and tacos, sit-down or takeout. Before or afterwards, go check out the **Grove** (Map p930; www.thegrovela.com; 189 The Grove Dr, Los Angeles; ℗🚻; 🚌MTA lines 16, 17, 780 to Wilshire & Fairfax), next door.

Canter's   DELI $$
(Map p930; ☑323-651-2030; www.cantersdeli.com; 419 N Fairfax Ave, Mid-City; ☺24hr; ℗) As old-school delis go, Canter's is hard to beat. A fixture in the traditionally Jewish Fairfax district since 1931, it serves up the requisite pastrami, corned beef and matzo-ball soup with a side of sass by seen-it-all waitresses, in a rangy room with deli and bakery counters up front.

EP & LP   SOUTHEAST ASIAN $$
(Map p930; ☑310-855-9955; http://eplosangeles.com; 603 N La Cienega Blvd, West Hollywood; small plates $10-18, large plates $20-34; ☺5pm-2am Mon-Fri, from noon Sat & Sun) Louis Tikaram, Australia's Chef of the Year in 2014, has brought the creative, bold flavors of his Fijian-Chinese heritage – *kakoda* (Fijian-style ceviche), Chiang Mai larb (spiced salmon stands in for meat), and crispy chicken with black vinegar, chili and lemon – to some of LA's most enviable real estate, at the corner of Melrose and La Cienega.

★ **Catch LA**   FUSION $$$
(Map p930; ☑323-347-6060; http://catchrestaurants.com/catchla; 8715 Melrose Ave, West Hollywood; shared dishes $11-31, dinner mains $28-41; ☺11am-3pm Sat & Sun, 5pm-2am daily; ℗) An LA-scene extraordinaire. You may well find sidewalk paparazzi stalking celebrity guests and a doorman to check your reservation, but all that's forgotten once you're up in this 3rd-floor rooftop restaurant/bar above WeHo. The Pacific Rim–inspired menu features creative cocktails and shared dishes such as truffle sashimi and black-cod lettuce wraps.

✖ Santa Monica & Venice

★ **Santa Monica Farmers Markets**   MARKET $
(Map p932; www.smgov.net/portals/farmersmarket; Arizona Ave, btwn 2nd & 3rd Sts; ☺Arizona Ave 8:30am-1:30pm Wed, 8am-1pm Sat, Main St 8:30am-1:30pm Sun; 🚻) 🍴 You haven't really experienced Santa Monica until you've explored one of its weekly outdoor farmers markets stocked with organic fruits, vegetables, flowers, baked goods and freshly shucked oysters. The mack daddy is the Wednesday market, around the intersection of 3rd and Arizona – it's the biggest and arguably the best for fresh produce, and often patrolled by local chefs.

★ **Gjelina**   AMERICAN $$$
(Map p932; ☑310-450-1429; www.gjelina.com; 1429 Abbot Kinney Blvd, Venice; veggies, salads & pizzas $10-18, large plates $15-45; ☺8am-midnight; 🚻; 🚌Big Blue Bus line 18) If one restaurant defines the new Venice, it's this. Carve out a slip on the communal table between the hipsters and yuppies, or get your own slab of wood on the elegant stone terrace, and dine on imaginative small plates (raw yellowtail spiced with chili and mint and drenched in olive oil and blood orange) and sensational thin-crust, wood-fired pizza.

★ **Cassia**   SOUTHEAST ASIAN $$$
(Map p932; ☑310-393-6699; 1314 7th St; appetizers $12-24, mains $18-77; ☺5-10pm Sun-Thu, to 11pm Fri & Sat; ℗) Ever since it opened in 2015, open, airy Cassia has made about every local and national 'best' list of LA restaurants. Chef Bryant Ng draws on his Chinese-Singaporean heritage in dishes such as *kaya* toast (with coconut jam, butter and a slow-cooked egg), 'sunbathing' prawns, and the encompassing Vietnamese pot-au-feu: short-rib stew, veggies, bone marrow and delectable accompaniments.

Long Beach

★ Fourth & Olive
ALSATIAN $$

(Map p920; ☑ 562-269-0731; www.4thandolive. com; 743 E 4th St, East Village, Long Beach; mains $15-29; ⊗ 4:30-10pm Mon & Tue, 11am-10pm Wed, Thu & Sun, 11am-11pm Fri & Sat) There's much to love about this new Cal-French bistro: farmers-market produce, small-farm-raised beef and pork, housemade sausages, classic dishes such as *steak frites* and *choucroute garnie,* and low-key service, all under a high-raftered roof with generous windows to watch the world go by. *And* many of its staff are disabled veterans, so you're doing good while eating well.

Pasadena

Ración
SPANISH $$$

(Map p920; ☑ 626-396-3090; www.racionrestau rant.com; 119 W Green St, Pasadena; small plates $4-14, mains $20-58; ⊗ 6-10pm Mon-Thu, 11:30am-3pm & 6-10:30pm Fri, 11:30am-3pm & 5:30-10:30pm Sat, 5:30-10pm Sun; Ⓜ Gold Line to Memorial Park or Del Mar) A foodie favorite, this minimalist, Basque-inspired spot offers tapas such as *conservas* (pâté), chicken croquettes and seared prawns in salsa verde. Its house cures yellowfin tuna in anchovy vinaigrette and offers larger plates *(raciónes)* ranging from a wild market fish with heirloom beans to duck breast with date jam and slow-braised lamb belly.

🍷 Drinking & Nightlife

Whether you're after an organic Kurimi espresso, a craft cocktail made with peanut-butter-washed Campari, or a saison brewed with Chinatown-sourced Oolong tea, LA pours on cue. From post-industrial coffee roasters and breweries to mid-century lounges, classic Hollywood martini bars and cocktail-pouring bowling alleys, LA serves its drinks with a generous splash of wow. So do the right thing and raise your glass to America's finest town.

Angel City Brewery
MICROBREWERY

(Map p924; ☑ 213-622-1261; www.angelcitybrewery. com; 216 S Alameda St; ⊗ 4pm-1am Mon-Thu, to 2am Fri, noon-2am Sat, noon-1am Sun) Where suspension cables were once manufactured, craft brews are now made and poured. Located on the edge of the Arts District, it's a popular spot to knock back an Indian pale ale or chai-spiced Imperial stout, listen to some tunes and chow down some food-truck tacos.

★ No Vacancy
BAR

(Map p927; ☑ 323-465-1902; www.novacancyla. com; 1727 N Hudson Ave; ⊗ 8pm-2am; Ⓜ Red Line to Hollywood/Vine) If you prefer your cocktail sessions with plenty of wow factor, make a reservation online, style up (no sportswear, shorts or logos) and head to this old shingled Victorian. A vintage scene of dark timber panels and elegant banquettes, it has bars in nearly every corner, tended by clever barkeeps while burlesque dancers and a tightrope walker entertain the droves of party people.

★ Dirty Laundry
BAR

(Map p927; ☑ 323-462-6531; http://dirtylaun drybarla.com; 1725 N Hudson Ave; ⊗ 10pm-2am Tue-Sat; Ⓜ Red Line to Hollywood/Vine) Under a cotton-candy-pink apartment block of no particular import is this funky den of musty odor, low ceilings, exposed pipes and good times. There's fine whiskey, funkalicious tunes on the turntables and plenty of eye-candy peeps with low inhibitions. Alas, there are also velvet-rope politics at work here, so reserve a table to make sure you slip through.

★ Abbey
GAY & LESBIAN

(Map p930; ☑ 310-289-8410; www.theabbey weho.com; 692 N Robertson Blvd, West Hollywood; ⊗ 11am-2am Mon-Thu, from 10am Fri, from 9am Sat & Sun) It's been called the best gay bar in the world, and who are we to argue? Once a humble coffee house, the Abbey has expanded into WeHo's bar/club/restaurant of record. It has so many different-flavored martinis and mojitos that you'd think they were invented here, plus a full menu of upscale pub food (mains $14 to $21).

★ Polo Lounge
COCKTAIL BAR

(Map p920; ☑ 310-887-2777; www.dorchestercol lection.com/en/los-angeles/the-beverly-hills-hotel; Beverly Hills Hotel, 9641 Sunset Blvd, Beverly Hills; ⊗ 7am-1:30am) For a classic LA experience, dress up and swill martinis in the Beverly Hills Hotel's legendary bar. Charlie Chaplin had a standing lunch reservation at booth 1 and it was here that HR Haldeman and John Ehrlichman learned of the Watergate break-in in 1972. There's a popular Sunday jazz brunch (adult/child $75/35).

★ Basement Tavern
BAR

(Map p932; www.basementtavern.com; 2640 Main St; ⊗ 5pm-2am) A creative speakeasy, housed in the basement of the Victorian, and our favorite well in Santa Monica. We love it for its craftsman cocktails, cozy booths, island bar and nightly live-music calendar that features blues, jazz, bluegrass and rock bands. It gets way too busy on weekends for our taste, but weeknights can be special.

★ Pike   BAR

(Map p920; ☑ 562-437-4453; www.pikelongbeach. com; 1836 E 4th St, Long Beach; ⊙11am-2am Mon-Fri, from 9am Sat & Sun; ☐line 22) Adjacent to Retro Row, this nautical-themed dive bar, owned by Chris Reece of the band Social Distortion, brings in the cool kids for live music acts every night – with no cover, thank you – and serves beer by the pitcher or bottle and cocktails such as the Mezcarita and Greenchelada (a *michelada* with cucumber, jalapeño and lime).

★ Entertainment

For discounted and half-price tickets, check Goldstar (www.goldstar.com) or LA StageTix (www.lastagetix.com), the latter strictly for theater.

★ Hollywood Bowl   CONCERT VENUE

(Map p920; ☑323-850-2000; www.hollywoodbowl. com; 2301 N Highland Ave; rehearsals free, performance costs vary; ⊙Jun-Sep) Summers in LA just wouldn't be the same without alfresco melodies under the stars at the Bowl, a huge natural amphitheater in the Hollywood Hills. Its annual season – which usually runs from June to September – includes symphonies, jazz bands and iconic acts such as Blondie, Bryan Ferry and Angélique Kidjo. Bring a sweater or blanket as it gets cool at night.

LGBTIQ LA

LA is one of the country's gayest cities and has made a number of contributions to gay culture. Your gaydar may well be pinging throughout the county, but the rainbow flag flies especially proudly in Boystown, along Santa Monica Blvd in West Hollywood, which is flanked by dozens of high-energy bars, cafes, restaurants, gyms and clubs. Most cater to gay men, although there's plenty for lesbians and mixed audiences. Thursday through Sunday nights are prime time.

Beauty reigns supreme among the buff, bronzed and styled of Boystown. Elsewhere the scene is considerably more laid back and less body conscious. The crowd in Silver Lake is more mixed age and runs from cute hipsters to leather-and-Levi's, while Downtown's burgeoning scene is an equally eclectic mix of hipsters, East LA Latinos, general counterculture types and business folk. Venice and Long Beach have the most relaxed, neighborly scenes.

If nightlife isn't your scene, there are plenty of other ways to meet, greet and engage. Outdoor options include the **Frontrunners** (www.lafrontrunners.com) running club and the **Great Outdoors** (www.greatoutdoorsla.org) hiking club. The latter runs day and night hikes, as well as neighborhood walks. For insight into LA's fascinating queer history, book a walking tour with **Out & About Tours** (www.thelavendereffect.org/tours; tours from $30).

There's gay theater all over town, but the **Celebration Theatre** (Map p930; ☑323-957-1884; www.celebrationtheatre.com; 6760 Lexington Ave, Hollywood) ranks among the nation's leading stages for LGBT plays. The **Cavern Club Theater** (Map p920; www.cavernclubtheater.com; 1920 Hyperion Ave, Silver Lake) pushes the envelope, particularly with uproarious drag performers; it's downstairs from Casita del Campo restaurant. If you're lucky enough to be in town when the **Gay Men's Chorus of Los Angeles** (www.gmcla.org) is performing, don't miss out: this amazing group has been doing it since 1979.

The **LA LGBT Center** (Map p927; ☑323-993-7400; www.lalgbtcenter.org; 1625 Schrader Blvd; ⊙9am-9pm Mon-Fri, to 1pm Sat) is a one-stop service and health agency, and its affiliated **Village at Ed Gould Plaza** (Map p930; ☑323-993-7400; https://lalgbtcenter.org; 1125 N McCadden Pl, Hollywood; ⊙6-10pm Mon-Fri, 9am-5pm Sat; ℗) offers art exhibits, theater and film screenings throughout the year.

The festival season kicks off in mid- to late May with the **Long Beach Pride Celebration** (☑562-987-9191; www.longbeachpride.com; 450 E Shoreline Dr, Long Beach; parade free, festival admission adult/child & senior $25/free; ⊙mid-May) and continues with the three-day **LA Pride** (www.lapride.org) in mid-June with a parade down Santa Monica Blvd. On Halloween (October 31), the same street brings out 500,000 outrageously costumed revelers of all persuasions.

★**Upright Citizens
Brigade Theatre** COMEDY
(Map p927; ☏323-908-8702; http://franklin.ucbthe
atre.com; 5919 Franklin Ave; tickets $5-12) Origin-
ally founded in New York by *Saturday Night
Live* alums Amy Poehler and Ian Roberts
along with Matt Besser and Matt Walsh.
With nightly shows spanning anything from
stand-up comedy to improv and sketch, it's
arguably the best comedy hub in town. Valet
parking costs $7.

★**Geffen Playhouse** THEATER
(Map p920; ☏310-208-5454; www.geffenplay
house.com; 10886 Le Conte Ave, Westwood) American magnate and producer David Geffen
forked over $17 million to get his Mediter-
ranean-style playhouse back into shape.
The center's season includes both American
classics and freshly minted works, and it's
not unusual to see well-known film and TV
actors treading the boards.

**Largo at the
Coronet** LIVE MUSIC, PERFORMING ARTS
(Map p930; ☏310-855-0530; www.largo-la.com; 366
N La Cienega Blvd, Mid-City) Ever since its early
days on Fairfax Ave, Largo has been progen-
itor of high-minded pop culture (it nurtured
Zach Galifianakis to stardom). Now part of
the Coronet Theatre complex, it features edgy
comedy, such as Sarah Silverman and Nick
Offerman, and nourishing night music such
as the Preservation Hall Jazz Band.

ArcLight Cinemas CINEMA
(Map p927; ☏323-464-1478; www.arclightcin
emas.com; 6360 W Sunset Blvd; Ⓜ Red Line to
Hollywood/Vine) Assigned seats, exceptional
celeb-sighting potential and a varied program that covers mainstream and art-house
movies make this 14-screen multiplex the
best around. If your taste dovetails with its
schedule, the awesome 1963 geodesic Ciner-
ama Dome is a must.

★**Los Angeles Philharmonic** CLASSICAL MUSIC
(Map p924; ☏323-850-2000; www.laphil.org; 111 S
Grand Ave) The world-class LA Phil performs
classics and cutting-edge works at the Walt
Disney Concert Hall, under the baton of
Venezuelan phenom Gustavo Dudamel.

★**Harvelle's** BLUES
(Map p932; ☏310-395-1676; www.harvelles.com;
1432 4th St; cover $5-15) This dark blues grot-
to has been packing 'em in since 1931, but
somehow still manages to feel like a well-
kept secret. There are no big-name acts here,

but the quality is usually high. Sunday's To-
ledo Show mixes soul, jazz and cabaret, and
Wednesday night brings the always-funky
House of Vibe All-Stars.

★**Dodger Stadium** BASEBALL
(Map p920; ☏866-363-4377; www.dodgers.com;
1000 Vin Scully Ave) Few clubs can match the
Dodgers when it comes to history, success
and fan loyalty. The club's newest owners
bought the organization for roughly $2 bil-
lion, an American team-sports record.

Staples Center STADIUM
(Map p924; ☏213-742-7100; www.staplescenter.
com; 1111 S Figueroa St) South Park got its first
jolt in 1999 with the opening of this sau-
cer-shaped sports and entertainment arena.
It's home court for the Los Angeles **Lakers**
(Map p924; ☏888-929-7849; www.nba.com/
lakers; tickets from $30), **Clippers** (Map p924;
☏213-204-2900; www.nba.com/clippers; tickets
from $20) and Sparks basketball teams, and
home ice for the LA Kings. Parking costs $10
to $30, depending on the event.

🛍 **Shopping**

Consider yourself a disciplined shopper?
Get back to us after your trip. LA is a pro
at luring cards out of wallets. After all, how
can you *not* bag that super-cute vintage-fab-
ric frock? Or that tongue-in-cheek tote? And
what about that mid-century-modern lamp,
the one that perfectly illuminates that rare,
signed Hollywood film script you scored?
Creativity and whimsy drive this town, right
down to its racks and shelves.

★**Raggedy Threads** VINTAGE
(Map p924; ☏213-620-1188; www.raggedythreads.
com; 330 E 2nd St; ⊙noon-8pm Mon-Sat, to 6pm
Sun; Ⓜ Gold Line to Little Tokyo/Arts District) A tremendous vintage Americana store just off the
main Little Tokyo strip. There's plenty of beautifully ragged denim, with a notable collection
of pre-1950s workwear from the US, Japan
and France. You'll also find a good number of
Victorian dresses, soft T-shirts and a wonderful turquoise collection at decent prices.

★**Last Bookstore in Los Angeles** BOOKS
(Map p924; ☏213-488-0599; www.lastbookstorela.
com; 453 S Spring St; ⊙10am-10pm Mon-Thu, to
11pm Fri & Sat, to 9pm Sun) What started as a
one-man operation out of a Main St storefront is now California's largest new-and-
used bookstore, spanning two levels of an
old bank building. Eye up the cabinets of

rare books before heading upstairs, home to a horror-and-crime book den, a book tunnel and a few art galleries to boot. The store also houses a terrific vinyl collection.

Melrose Avenue FASHION & ACCESSORIES
(Map p930) A popular shopping strip as famous for its epic people-watching as it is for its consumer fruits. You'll see hair (and people) of all shades and styles, and everything from Gothic jewels to custom sneakers to medical marijuana to stuffed porcupines available for a price.

★ **Fred Segal** FASHION & ACCESSORIES
(Map p930; ☑ 323-651-4129; www.fredsegal.com; 8100 Melrose Ave, Mid-City; ⊙ 10am-7pm Mon-Sat, noon-6pm Sun) Celebs and beautiful people circle for the very latest from Babakul, Aviator Nation and Robbi & Nikki at this warren of high-end boutiques under one impossibly chic but slightly snooty roof. The only time you'll see bargains (sort of) is during the two-week blowout sale in September.

Waraku SHOES
(Map p932; ☑ 310-452-5300; www.warakuusa.com; 1225 Abbot Kinney Blvd, Venice; ⊙ 10am-7pm; ☐ Big Blue Bus line 18) Waraku is a compact, Japanese-owned shop for shoe-lovers. It blends Far East couture with mainstream street brands such as Puma and Converse. Some 60% of the shoes are imported from Japan; the rest are domestic limited editions.

★ **Rose Bowl Flea Market** MARKET
(Map p920; www.rgcshows.com; 1001 Rose Bowl Dr, Pasadena; admission from $9; ⊙ 9am-4:30pm 2nd Sun each month, last entry 3pm, early admission from 5am) Every month since the 1960s, the Rose Bowl football field has hosted 'America's Marketplace of Unusual Items,' with rummaging hordes seeking the next great treasure. Over 2500 vendors and some 20,000 buyers converge here, and it's a great time.

NAVIGATING THE FASHION DISTRICT

∙∙∙

Bargain hunters love the frantic, 100-block warren of fashion in southwestern Downtown that is the Fashion District. Deals can be amazing, but first timers are often bewildered by the district's size and immense selection. For orientation, check out www.fashiondistrict.org.

---

❶ Information

DANGERS & ANNOYANCES

Despite its seemingly apocalyptic list of dangers – guns, violent crime, earthquakes – Los Angeles is a reasonably safe place to visit. The greatest danger is posed by car accidents (buckle up – it's the law), while the biggest annoyance is city traffic.

MEDIA

➜ **KCRW 89.9 FM** (www.kcrw.com) LA's cultural pulse, the best radio station in the city.

➜ **KPFK 90.7 FM** (www.kpfk.org) Part of the Pacifica radio network; news and progressive talk.

➜ **LA Weekly** (www.laweekly.com) Free alternative news, live music and entertainment listings.

➜ **Los Angeles Times** (www.latimes.com) Major, center-left daily newspaper.

MEDICAL SERVICES

Cedars-Sinai Medical Center (☑ 310-423-3277; http://cedars-sinai.edu; 8700 Beverly Blvd) 24-hour emergency room skirting West Hollywood.

Keck Medicine of USC (☑ 323-226-2622; www.keckmedicine.org; 1500 San Pablo St) 24-hour emergency department just east of Downtown.

Ronald Reagan UCLA Medical Center (☑ 310-825-9111; www.uclahealth.org; 757 Westwood Plaza, Westwood) 24-hour emergency room on the UCLA campus.

TOURIST INFORMATION

Downtown LA Visitor Center (Map p924; www.discoverlosangeles.com; Union Station, 800 N Alameda St; ⊙ 9am-5pm; Ⓜ Red/Purple/Gold Lines to Union Station)

Hollywood Visitor Information Center (Map p927; ☑ 323-467-6412; www.discoverlosangeles.com; Hollywood & Highland, 6801 Hollywood Blvd; ⊙ 8am-10pm Mon-Sat, 9am-7pm Sun; Ⓜ Red Line to Hollywood/Highland)

Santa Monica Visitor Information Center (Map p932; ☑ 800-544-5319; www.santamonica.com; 2427 Main St)

❶ Getting There & Away

AIR

The main LA gateway is **Los Angeles International Airport** (LAX; Map p920; www.lawa.org/welcomeLAX.aspx; 1 World Way). Its nine terminals are linked by the free LAX Shuttle A, leaving from the lower (arrival) level of each terminal. Cabs and hotel and car-rental shuttles stop here as well. A free minibus for travelers with disabilities can be ordered by calling ☑ 310-646-6402.

Some domestic flights also arrive at **Burbank Hollywood Airport** (BUR, Bob Hope Airport;

Map p920; www.burbankairport.com; 2627 N Hollywood Way), while to the south the small **Long Beach Airport** (Map p920; www.lgb. org; 4100 Donald Douglas Dr) is convenient for Disneyland.

BUS

The main bus terminal for **Greyhound** (Map p920; ☎213-629-8401; www.greyhound.com; 1716 E 7th St) is in an industrial part of Downtown, so try not to arrive after dark.

CAR

The usual international car-rental agencies have branches at LAX airport and throughout LA.

TRAIN

Amtrak (www.amtrak.com) trains roll into Downtown's historic **Union Station** (☎800-872-7245; www.amtrak.com; 800 N Alameda St). Interstate trains stopping in LA are the daily *Coast Starlight* to Seattle, the daily *Southwest Chief* to Chicago and the thrice-weekly *Sunset Limited* to New Orleans. The *Pacific Surfliner* travels numerous times daily between San Diego, Santa Barbara and San Luis Obispo via LA.

ℹ️ Getting Around

TO/FROM THE AIRPORT

LAX FlyAway (☎866-435-9529; www.lawa. org/FlyAway) runs to Union Station (Downtown), Hollywood, Van Nuys, Westwood Village near UCLA, and Long Beach. A one-way ticket costs $9.75. For scheduled bus services, catch the free shuttle bus from the airport toward parking lot C. It stops by the LAX City Bus Center hub for buses serving all of LA County.

Taxis are readily available outside the terminals. The flat rate to Downtown LA is $47. Expect to pay around $30 to $35 to Santa Monica, $40 to West Hollywood and $50 to Hollywood. These rates exclude the $4 LAX airport surcharge.

CAR & MOTORCYCLE

Driving in LA doesn't need to be a hassle, but be prepared for some of the worst traffic in the country during weekday rush hours (roughly 7am to 10am and 3pm to 7pm). Self-parking at motels is usually free; most hotels charge from $10 to $45. Valet parking at restaurants, hotels and nightspots is common, with average rates of $5 to $10.

PUBLIC TRANSPORTATION

Most public transportation is handled by **Metro** (☎323-466-3876; www.metro.net), which offers maps, schedules and trip-planning help through its website.

To ride Metro trains and buses, buy a reusable TAP card. Available from TAP vending machines at Metro stations with a $1 surcharge, the cards allow you to add a preset cash value or day passes. The regular base fare is $1.75 per boarding, or $7 for a day pass with unlimited rides. Both single-trip tickets and TAP cards loaded with a day pass are available on Metro buses (ensure you have the exact change). When using a TAP card, tap the card against the sensor at station entrances and aboard buses.

TAP cards are accepted on DASH and municipal bus services and can be reloaded at vending machines or online on the TAP website (www. taptogo.net).

TAXI

Because of LA's size and heavy traffic, getting around by cab will cost you. Metered taxis charge $2.85 at flagfall, then $2.70 per mile. Except for taxis lined up outside airports, train stations and major hotels, it's best to phone for a cab.

SOUTHERN CALIFORNIAN COAST

Disneyland & Anaheim

The mother of all West Coast theme parks, aka the 'Happiest Place on Earth,' **Disneyland** (Map p920; ☎714-781-4636; www.disneyland.com; 1313 Harbor Blvd; adult/child 3-9yr 1-day pass from $97/91, 2-day park-hopper pass $244/232; ⊙ open daily, seasonal hr vary) is a parallel world that's squeaky clean, enchanting and wacky all at once. It's an 'imagineered' hyper-reality where the employees – called 'cast members' – are always upbeat and there are parades every day of the year. More than 16 million kids, grandparents, honeymooners and international tourists stream through the front gates annually.

Disneyland opened to great fanfare in 1955 and the workaday city of Anaheim grew up around it. Today the Disneyland Resort comprises the original Disneyland Park and newer Disney California Adventure park. And Anaheim itself has developed some surprising pockets of cool that have nothing to do with the Mouse House.

👁️ Sights & Activities

Spotless, wholesome **Disneyland Park** is still laid out according to Walt's original plans. It's here you'll find plenty of rides and some of the attractions most associated with the Disney name – Main Street, U.S.A., Sleeping Beauty Castle and Tomorrowland.

Disneyland Resort's larger but less crowded park, **Disney California Adventure**, celebrates the natural and cultural glories

KNOTT'S BERRY FARM

What, Disney's not enough for you? Find even more thrill rides and cotton candy at **Knott's Berry Farm** (Map p920; 714-220-5200; www.knotts.com; 8039 Beach Blvd, Buena Park; adult/child 3-11yr $75/42; from 10am, closing hours vary 5-11pm; P). This Old West–themed amusement park teems with packs of speed-crazed adolescents testing their mettle on a line-up of rides. Gut-wrenchers include the Boomerang 'scream machine,' wooden GhostRider and 1950s-themed Xcelerator. Younger kids will enjoy tamer action at Camp Snoopy. From late September through October, the park transforms at night into Halloween-themed 'Knott's Scary Farm.'

When summer heat waves hit, jump next door to **Knott's Soak City** (Map p920; 714-220-5200; www.soakcityoc.com; 8039 Beach Blvd, Buena Park; adult/child 3-11yr $43/38; 10am-5pm, 6pm or 7pm mid-May–mid-Sep; P) water park. Save time and money by buying print-at-home tickets for either park online. All-day parking is $18.

of the Golden State but lacks the original's density of attractions and depth of imagination. The best rides are Soarin' Around the World, a virtual hang glide, and Guardians of the Galaxy – Mission: BREAKOUT! that drops you 183ft down an elevator chute.

Going on all the rides at both theme parks requires at least two days, as queues for top attractions can be an hour or more. To minimize wait times, arrive midweek (especially during summer) before the gates open, buy print-at-home tickets online and take advantage of the parks' FASTPASS system, which preassigns boarding times at select rides and attractions. For seasonal park hours and schedules of parades, shows and fireworks, check the official website.

While of course Disneyland Resort dominates Anaheim tourism, it's worth visiting the redeveloped neighborhoods around city hall, the **Anaheim Packing District** (Map p920; www.anaheimpackingdistrict.com; S Anaheim Bl) and **Center Street** (Map p920; www.centerstreetanaheim.com; W Center St). By the latter is the Frank Gehry–designed hockey rink where the Anaheim Ducks practice; it's open to the public.

Sleeping

While the Disney resorts have their own hotels, there are a number of other worthwhile hotels just offsite or a few miles away, and every stripe of chain hotel you can imagine. Generally Anaheim's hotels are good value relative to those in the OC beach towns.

Alpine Inn MOTEL $
(Map p920; 714-535-2186, 800-772-4422; www.alpineinnanaheim.com; 715 W Katella Ave; r $99-149; P) Connoisseurs of kitsch will hug their Hummels over this 42-room,

snow-covered chalet facade on an A-frame exterior and icicle-covered roofs – framed by palm trees, of course. Right on the border of Disney California Adventure, the inn also has Ferris-wheel views. It's circa 1958, and air-con rooms are well kept. Simple grab 'n' go breakfast served in the lobby.

Best Western Plus Stovall's Inn MOTEL $$
(Map p920; 714-778-1880, ext 3 800-854-8175; www.bestwestern.com; 1110 W Katella Ave; r $99-175; P) Generations of guests have been coming to this 289-room motel about 15 minutes' walk to Disneyland. Around the side are two pools, two Jacuzzis, fitness center, kiddie pool and a garden of topiaries (for real). The remodeled sleek and modern design rooms sparkle; all have air-con, a microwave and minifridge. Rates include a hot breakfast and there's a guest laundry.

Ayres Hotel Anaheim HOTEL $$
(Map p920; 714-634-2106; www.ayreshotels.com/anaheim; 2550 E Katella Ave; r incl breakfast $139-219; P) This well-run minichain of business hotels delivers solid-gold value. The 133 recently renovated rooms have microwaves, minifridges, safes, wet bars, pillow-top mattresses and design inspired by the Californian arts-and-crafts movement. Fourth-floor rooms have extrahigh ceilings. Rates include a full breakfast and evening social hours Monday to Thursday with beer, wine and snacks.

★**Disney's Grand Californian Hotel & Spa** RESORT $$$
(Map p920; info 714-635-2300, reservations 714-956-6425; https://disneyland.disney.go.com/grand-californian-hotel; 1600 S Disneyland Dr; d from $360; P) Soaring timber beams rise above the cathedral-like lobby

of the six-story Grand Californian, Disney's homage to the arts-and-crafts architectural movement. Cushy rooms have triple-sheeted beds, down pillows, bathrobes and all-custom furnishings. Outside there's a faux-redwood waterslide into the pool. At night, kids wind down with bedtime stories by the lobby's giant stone hearth.

✕ Eating & Drinking

From stroll-and-eat Mickey-shaped pretzels ($4) and jumbo turkey legs ($10) to deluxe, gourmet dinners (sky's the limit), there's no shortage of eating options, though mostly pretty expensive and targeted to mainstream tastes. Phone **Disney Dining** (☎ 714-781-3463; http://disneyland.disney.go.com/dining) to make reservations up to 60 days in advance.

If you want to steer clear of Mickey Mouse food, drive to the Anaheim Packing District (3 miles northeast), Old Towne Orange (7 miles southeast), Little Arabia (3 miles west) or Little Saigon (8 miles southwest).

★ **Pour Vida**   MEXICAN $
(Map p920; ☎ 657-208-3889; www.pourvidalatin flavor.com; 185 W Center St Promenade; tacos $2-8; ⊙10am-7pm Mon, to 9pm Tue-Thu, to 10pm Fri, 9am-10pm Sat, 9am-7pm Sun) Chef Jimmy has worked in some of LA's top kitchens but returned to his Mexican roots to make some of the most gourmet tacos we've ever seen: pineapple skirt steak, tempura oyster, heirloom cauliflower...*caramba*! Even the tortillas are special, made with squid ink, spinach and a secret recipe. It's deliberately informal, all brick and concrete with chalkboard walls.

Earl of Sandwich   SANDWICHES $
(Map p920; ☎ 714-817-7476; www.earlofsandwich usa.com; Downtown Disney; mains $4.50-7.50; ⊙8am-11pm Sun-Thu, to midnight Fri & Sat; ⊛) This counter-service chain near the **Disneyland Hotel** (Map p920; ☎ 714-778-6600; www.disneyland.com; 1150 Magic Way, Anaheim; r $210-395; P@🛇☰) serves grilled sandwiches that are both kid- and adult-friendly. The 'original 1762' is roast beef, cheddar and horseradish, or look for chipotle chicken with avocado or holiday turkey. There are also pizza, salad and breakfast options.

Ralph Brennan's
New Orleans Jazz Kitchen   CAJUN $$
(Map p920; ☎ 714-776-5200; http://rbjazzkitchen. com; Downtown Disney; mains lunch/dinner $14-19/$24.50-38.50; ⊙8am-10pm Sun-Thu, to 11pm Fri & Sat; ⊛) Hear live jazz combos on the weekends and piano weeknights at this resto-bar with NOLA-style Cajun and Creole dishes: gumbo, po-boy sandwiches, jambalaya, plus a (less adventurous) kids' menu and specialty cocktails. There's breakfast and lunch express service if you don't have time to linger.

★ **Napa Rose**   CALIFORNIAN $$$
(Map p920; ☎ 714-300-7170; https://disneyland.dis ney.go.com/dining; Disney's Grand Californian Hotel & Spa; mains $38-48, 4-course prix-fixe dinner from $100; ⊙5:30-10pm; ⊛) High-back arts-and-crafts-style chairs, leaded-glass windows and towering ceilings befit Disneyland Resort's top-drawer restaurant. On the plate, seasonal 'California Wine Country' (read: NorCal) cuisine is as impeccably crafted as the Sleeping Beauty Castle. Kids menu available. Reservations essential. Enter the hotel from Disney California Adventure or Downtown Disney.

ℹ Information

Disneyland's **City Hall** (Map p920; ☎ 714-781-4565; Main Street, U.S.A.) offers foreign-currency exchange. In Disney California Adventure, head to the guest relations lobby. Multiple ATMs are found in both theme parks and at Downtown Disney.

For information or help inside the parks, just ask any cast member or visit Disneyland's City Hall or Disney California Adventure's guest relations lobby.

ℹ Getting There & Around

Disneyland and Anaheim can be reached by car (off the I-5 Fwy) or Amtrak or Metrolink trains at Anaheim's **ARTIC** (Anaheim Regional Transportation Intermodal Center; 2150 E Katella Ave, Anaheim) transit center. From here it's a short taxi, ride share or **Anaheim Resort Transportation** (ART; ☎ 888-364-2787; www.rideart.org; adult/child fare $3/1, day pass $5.50/2, multiple-day passes available) shuttle to Disneyland proper. The closest airport is Orange County's **John Wayne Airport** (SNA; Map p920; www.ocair. com; 18601 Airport Way, Santa Ana).

The miniature biodiesel Disneyland Railroad chugs in a clockwise circle around Disneyland, stopping at Main Street USA, New Orleans Square, Mickey's Toontown and Tomorrowland, taking about 20 minutes to make a full loop.

Orange County Beaches

If you've seen *The OC* or *The Real Housewives*, you might imagine you already know what to expect from this giant quilt of suburbia connecting LA and San Diego, lolling beside 42 miles of glorious coastline. In

LAGUNA'S FESTIVAL OF ARTS

The **Festival of Arts** (www.foapom.com; 650 Laguna Canyon Rd; admission $7-10; ⊙ usually 10am-11:30pm Jul & Aug; ♿) is a two-month celebration of original artwork in almost all its forms. About 140 exhibitors display works ranging from paintings and handcrafted furniture to scrimshaw; there are also kid-friendly art workshops and live music and entertainment daily.

reality, Hummer-driving hunks and Botoxed beauties mix it up with hang-loose surfers and beatnik artists to give each of Orange County's beach towns a distinct vibe.

Just across the LA–OC county line, old-fashioned **Seal Beach** is refreshingly noncommercial, with a quaint walkable downtown. Less than 10 miles further south along the Pacific Coast Hwy (Hwy 1), **Huntington Beach** – aka 'Surf City, USA' – epitomizes SoCal's surfing lifestyle. Fish tacos and happy-hour specials abound at bars and cafes along downtown HB's Main St, not far from a shortboard-sized **surfing museum** (Map p920; ☎ 714-960-3483; www.surfingmuseum.org; 411 Olive Ave; adult/child $2/1; ⊙ noon-5pm Tue-Sun).

Next up is the ritziest of the OC's beach communities: yacht-filled **Newport Beach**. Families and teens steer toward **Balboa Peninsula** for its beaches, vintage wooden pier and quaint amusement center. From near the 1906 Balboa Pavilion, **Balboa Island Ferry** (Map p920; www.balboaislandferry.com; 410 S Bay Front; adult/child $1/50¢, car incl driver $2; ⊙ 6:30am-midnight Sun-Thu, to 2am Fri & Sat) shuttles across the bay to Balboa Island for strolls past historic beach cottages and boutiques along Marine Ave.

Continuing south, Hwy 1 zooms past the wild beaches of **Crystal Cove State Park** (Map p920; ☎ 949-494-3539; www.parks.ca.gov; 8471 N Coast Hwy; per car $15; ⊙ 6am-sunset; P ♿) ✈ before winding downhill into **Laguna Beach**, the OC's most cultured seaside community. Secluded beaches, glassy waves and eucalyptus-covered hillsides create a Riviera-like feel. Art galleries dot the narrow streets of the 'village' and the coastal highway, where the **Laguna Art Museum** (☎ 949-494-8971; www.lagunaartmuseum.org; 307 Cliff Dr; adult/student & senior/child under 13yr $7/5/free, 5-9pm 1st Thu of month free; ⊙ 11am-

5pm Fri-Tue, to 9pm Thu) exhibits modern and contemporary Californian works. Soak up the natural beauty right in the center of town at **Main Beach**.

Another 10 miles south, detour inland to **Mission San Juan Capistrano** (☎ 949-234-1300; www.missionsjc.com; 26801 Ortega Hwy; adult/child $9/6; ⊙ 9am-5pm; ♿), one of California's most beautifully restored Spanish Colonial missions, with flowering gardens, a fountain courtyard and the charming 1778 Serra Chapel.

🛏 Sleeping & Eating

⭐ **Crystal Cove Beach Cottages** CABIN $$ (Map p920; ☎ reservations 800-444-7275; www.crystalcovealliance.org; 35 Crystal Cove, Crystal Cove State Park Historic District; r with shared bath $35-140, cottages $171-249; ⊙ check-in 4-9pm; P) Right on the beach, these two dozen preserved cottages (circa 1930s to '50s) now host guests for a one-of-a-kind stay. Each cottage is different, sleeping between two and eight people in a variety of private or dorm-style accommodations. To snag one, book on the first day of the month seven months before your intended stay – or pray for cancellations.

⭐ **Paséa** RESORT $$$ (Map p920; ☎ 888-674-3634; http://meritagecollection.com/paseahotel; 21080 Pacific Coast Hwy; r from $359; P ⊛ ❄ @ 🛜 🏊) This hotel is slick and serene, with tons of light and air. Floors are themed for shades of blue from denim to sky and each of its 250 shimmery, minimalist, high-ceilinged rooms has an ocean-view balcony. As if the stunning pool, gym and Balinese-inspired spa weren't enough, it also connects to **Pacific City** (www.gopacificcity.com; 21010 Pacific Coast Hwy; ⊙ hours vary).

⭐ **Lot 579** FOOD HALL $ (Map p920; www.gopacificcity.com/lot-579; Pacific City, 21010 Pacific Coast Hwy; ⊙ hours vary; P 🛜 ♿) The food court at HB's stunning new ocean-view mall offers some unique and fun restaurants for pressed sandwiches (Burnt Crumbs – the spaghetti grilled cheese is so Instagrammable), Aussie meat pies (Pie Not), coffee (Portola) and ice cream (Han's). For best views, take your takeout to the deck, or eat at American Dream (brewpub) or Bear Flag Fish Company.

⭐ **Bear Flag Fish Company** SEAFOOD $ (Map p920; ☎ 949-673-3474; www.bearflagfishco.com; 3421 Via Lido; mains $10-16; ⊙ 11am-9pm Tue-Sat, to 8pm Sun & Mon; ♿) This is *the* place for generously sized, grilled and *panko*-breaded fish tacos, ahi burritos, spankin' fresh ceviche and oysters. Pick out what you want from the ice-cold display cases, then grab a picnic-table seat. About the only way this seafood could be any fresher is if you caught and hauled it off the boat yourself!

★ **Driftwood Kitchen** AMERICAN $$$
(☑949-715-7700; www.driftwoodkitchen.com; 619 Sleepy Hollow Lane; mains lunch $15-36, dinner $24-39; ⊙9-10:30am & 11am-2:30pm Mon-Fri, 5-9:30pm Sun-Thu, to 10:30pm Fri & Sat, 9am-2:30pm Sat & Sun) Ocean views and ridonkulous sunsets alone ought to be enough to bring folks in, but gourmet Driftwood steps up the food with seasonal menus centered around fresh, sustainable seafood, plus options for landlubbers. Inside it's all beachy casual, whitewashed and pale woods. And the cocktails are smart and creative.

San Diego

San Diego calls itself 'America's Finest City' and its breezy confidence and sunny countenance filter down to folks you encounter every day on the street. It feels like a collection of villages each with its own personality, but it's the nation's eighth-largest city and we're hard-pressed to think of a more laid-back place.

◉ Sights

San Diego's **Downtown** is the region's main business, financial and convention district. Whatever intense urban energy Downtown generally lacks, it makes up for in spirited shopping, dining and nightlife in the historic **Gaslamp Quarter** and the hipster havens of **East Village** and **North Park**. The waterfront **Embarcadero** is great for a stroll; in the northwestern corner of Downtown, vibrant **Little Italy** is full of good eats, and **Old Town** is the seat of local history.

The city of **Coronado**, with its landmark 1888 Hotel del Coronado (p955) and top-rated beach, sits across San Diego Bay from Downtown. At the entrance to the bay, **Point Loma** has sweeping views across sea and city from the Cabrillo National Monument (p953). **Mission Bay**, northwest of Downtown, has lagoons, parks and recreation from waterskiing to camping. The nearby coast – Ocean, Mission and Pacific Beaches – epitomizes the SoCal beach scene.

◉ Downtown & Embarcadero

Downtown once harbored a notorious strip of saloons, gambling joints and bordellos known as Stingaree. These days, Stingaree has been beautifully restored and rechristened the **Gaslamp Quarter**, a heart-thumping playground of restaurants, bars, clubs, boutiques and galleries. At downtown's northern edge, **Little Italy** has evolved into one of the city's hippest neighborhoods to live, eat and shop in.

USS Midway Museum MUSEUM
(Map p950; ☑619-544-9600; www.midway.org; 910 N Harbor Dr; adult/child $20/$10; ⊙10am-5pm, last admission 4pm; P▣) The giant aircraft carrier USS *Midway* was one of the navy's flagships from 1945 to 1991, last playing a combat role in the First Gulf War. On the flight deck of the hulking vessel, walk right up to some 29 restored aircraft including an F-14 Tomcat and F-4 Phantom jet fighter. Admission includes an audio tour along the narrow confines of the upper decks to the bridge, admiral's war room, brig and 'pri-fly' (primary flight control; the carrier's equivalent of a control tower). Parking costs $10.

★ **Maritime Museum** MUSEUM
(Map p950; ☑619-234-9153; www.sdmaritime.org; 1492 N Harbor Dr; adult/child $16/8; ⊙9am-9pm late May-early Sep, to 8pm early Sep-late May; ▣) This museum is easy to find: look for the 100ft-high masts of the iron-hulled square-rigger *Star of India*. Built on the Isle of Man and launched in 1863, the ship plied the England–India trade route, carried immigrants to New Zealand, became a trading ship based in Hawaii and, finally, ferried cargo in Alaska. It's a handsome vessel, but don't expect anything glamorous on board.

Museum of Contemporary Art MUSEUM
(MCASD Downtown; Map p950; ☑858-454-3541; www.mcasd.org; 1001 Kettner Blvd; adult/child under 25yr/senior $10/free/$5, free 5-8pm 3rd Thu each month; ⊙11am-5pm Thu-Tue, to 8pm 3rd Thu each month) This Financial District museum has brought an ever-changing variety of innovative artwork to San Diegans since the 1960; check the website for exhibits. Tickets are valid for seven days.

◉ Coronado

Technically a peninsula, Coronado Island is joined to the mainland by a 2.2-mile-long bridge. The peninsula's main draw is the

Greater San Diego

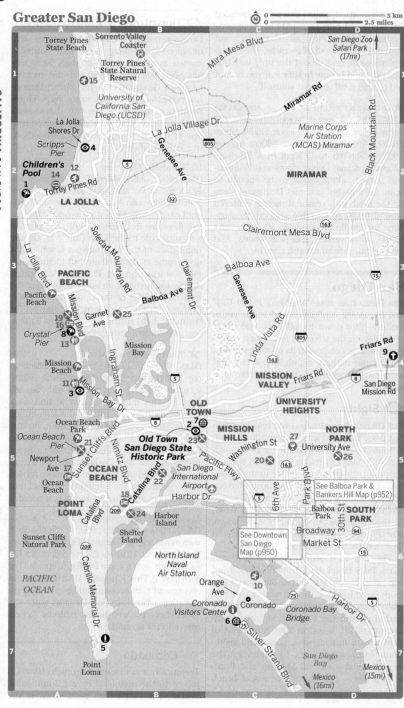

Greater San Diego

⊚ **Top Sights**
1 Children's Pool A2
2 Old Town San Diego State
   Historic Park.. B5

⊚ **Sights**
3 Belmont Park.. A4
4 Birch Aquarium at Scripps A2
5 Cabrillo National Monument A7
6 Hotel del Coronado................................. C7
7 Junípero Serra Museum........................ B5
8 Mission & Pacific Beaches.................... A4
9 Mission Basilica San Diego de
   Alcalá D4

⊕ **Activities, Courses & Tours**
10 Bikes & Beyond C6
11 Flowrider A4
12 Hike, Bike, Kayak San Diego................. A2
13 Pacific Beach Surf Shop....................... A4

14 San Diego-La Jolla Underwater Park... A2
15 Torrey Pines Gliderport A1

⊟ **Sleeping**
16 Crystal Pier Hotel & Cottages.............. A4
   Hotel del Coronado ....(see 6)
17 Inn at Sunset Cliffs A5
18 Pearl... B5

⊗ **Eating**
19 Dirty Birds... A4
20 Hash House a Go Go C5
21 Hodad's A5
22 Liberty Public Market............................ B5
23 Old Town Mexican Café......................... B5
24 Point Loma Seafoods............................. B6
25 The Patio on Lamont............................. B4
26 Urban Solace... D5

⊜ **Drinking & Nightlife**
27 Gossip Grill.. C5

Hotel del Coronado (p955), known for its seaside Victorian architecture and illustrious guestbook, which includes Thomas Edison, Babe Ruth and Marilyn Monroe (its exterior stood in for a Miami hotel in the classic flick *Some Like it Hot*).

The hourly **Coronado Ferry** (Map p950; ☑800-442-7847; www.flagshipsd.com; 990 N Harbor Dr; 1 way $4.75; ☺9am-10pm) departs from the Embarcadero's **Broadway Pier** (1050 N Harbor Dr) and from downtown's convention center. All ferries arrive on Coronado at the foot of 1st St, where **Bikes & Beyond** (Map p948; ☑619-435-7180; www.bikes-and-beyond. com; 1201 1st St, Coronado; per hr/day from $8/30; ☺9am-sunset) rents cruisers and tandems, perfect for pedaling past Coronado's white-sand beaches sprawling south along the Silver Strand.

◉ Balboa Park

Balboa Park is an urban oasis brimming with more than a dozen museums, gorgeous gardens and architecture, performance spaces and a zoo. Early 20th-century beaux arts and Spanish Colonial Revival–style buildings (the legacy of world's fairs) are grouped around plazas along east–west ElPrado promenade.

The free **Balboa Park Tram** bus makes a continuous loop around the park; however, it's most enjoyable to walk, past the 1915 **Spreckels Organ Pavilion** (Map p952; ☑619-702-8138; http://spreckelsorgan.org; Balboa Park)

FREE, the shops and galleries of the **Spanish Village Art Center** (Map p952; ☑619-233-9050; http://spanishvillageart.com; 1770 Village Place, Balboa Park; ☺11am-4pm) **FREE** and the international themed exhibition cottages by the **United Nations Building**.

★ **San Diego Zoo**   ZOO
(Map p952; ☑619-231-1515; http://zoo.san diego.org; 2920 Zoo Dr; 1-day pass adult/child from $52/42; 2-visit pass to zoo &/or safari park adult/child $83.25/73.25; ☺9am-9pm mid-Jun–early Sep, to 5pm or 6pm early Sep–mid-Jun; 🅿🚹) ✐ This justifiably famous zoo is one of SoCal's biggest attractions, showing more than 3000 animals representing more than 650 species in a beautifully landscaped setting, typically in enclosures that replicate their natural habitats. Its sister park is **San Diego Zoo Safari Park** (☑760-747-8702; www.sdzsafari park.org; 15500 San Pasqual Valley Rd, Escondido; 1-day adult/child $52/42, 2-visit pass to zoo and/or safari park adult/child $83.25/73.25; ☺8am-6pm, to 7pm late Jun–mid-Aug; 🅿🚹) in northern San Diego County.

★ **Mingei International Museum** MUSEUM
(Map p952; ☑619-239-0003; www.mingei.org; 1439 El Prado; adult/youth/child $10/7/free; ☺10am-5pm Tue-Sun; 🚹) A diverse collection of folk art, costumes, toys, jewelry, utensils and other handmade objects of traditional cultures from around the world, plus changing exhibitions covering beads to surfboards. Check the website to find out what's on.

Downtown San Diego

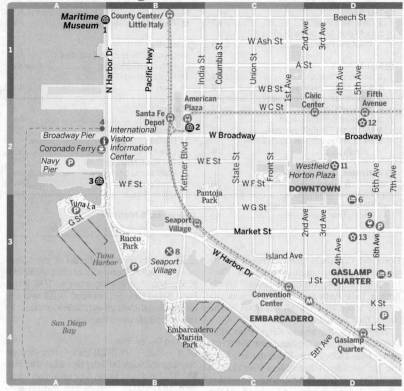

Reuben H Fleet Science Center MUSEUM
(Map p952; ☏ 619-238-1233; www.rhfleet.org; 1875 El Prado; adult/child 3-12 years incl IMAX $20/17; ☉10am-5pm Mon-Thu, to 6pm Fri-Sun; ⊞) One of Balboa Park's most popular venues, this hands-on science museum features interactive displays and a toddler room. Look out for opportunities to build gigantic structures with Keva planks and visit the **Gallery of Illusions and Perceptions**. The biggest draw is the **Giant Dome Theater**, which screens several different films each day. The hemispherical, wraparound screen and 152-speaker state-of-the-art sound system create sensations ranging from pretty cool to mind-blowing.

San Diego Natural History Museum MUSEUM
(Map p952; ☏ 877-946-7797; www.sdnhm.org; 1788 El Prado; adult/youth 3-17/child under 2 $19/12/free; ☉10am-5pm; ⊞) The 'Nat' houses 7.5 million specimens, including rocks, fossils and taxidermied animals, as well as an impressive dinosaur skeleton and a California fault-line exhibit, all in beautiful spaces. Kids love the movies about the natural world in the giant-screen cinema; the selections change frequently. Children's programs are held most weekends. Special exhibits (some with an extra charge) span pirates to King Tut. The museum also arranges field trips and nature walks in Balboa Park and further afield.

San Diego Museum of Man MUSEUM
(Map p952; ☏ 619-239-2001; www.museumofman. org; Plaza de California, 1350 El Prado; adult/child/ teen $13/6/8; ☉10am-5pm; ⊞) This is the county's only anthropological museum, with exhibits spanning ancient Egypt, the Mayans and local indigenous Kumeyaay people as well as human evolution and the human life cycle. Recent temporary exhibits have covered everything from cannibalism to beer. The basket and pottery collections are especially fine and the museum shop sells handicrafts from Central America and elsewhere.

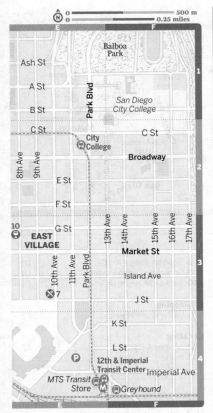

Downtown San Diego

◎ **Top Sights**
1 Maritime Museum................................A1

◎ **Sights**
2 Museum of Contemporary Art..........B2
3 USS Midway Museum A2

◈ **Activities, Courses & Tours**
4 Flagship Cruises................................A2

◔ **Sleeping**
5 Hotel Solamar....................................D3
6 USA Hostels San Diego......................D3

✖ **Eating**
7 Basic E3
Neighborhood............................(see 10)
8 Puesto at the Headquarters..............B3

◔ **Drinking & Nightlife**
9 Bang Bang..D3
10 Noble Experiment E3

◉ **Entertainment**
Arts Tix ....(see 11)
11 Balboa Theatre..................................D2
12 House of Blues..................................D2
13 Prohibition Lounge............................D3

important traveling exhibits. The sculpture garden has works by Alexander Calder and Henry Moore.

San Diego Air & Space Museum   MUSEUM
(Map p952; ☑619-234-8291; www.sandiegoairand space.org; 2001 Pan American Plaza; adult/youth/ child under 2 $19.75/$10.75/free; ⊙10am-4:30pm; ▣) The round building at the southern end of the plaza houses an excellent museum with extensive displays of aircraft throughout history – originals, replicas, models – plus memorabilia from legendary aviators, including Charles Lindbergh and astronaut John Glenn. Catch films in the 3D/4D theater.

⊙ Old Town & Mission Valley

Mission & Pacific Beaches   BEACH
(Map p948) FREE Central San Diego's best beach scene is concentrated in a narrow strip of land between the ocean and Mission Bay. There's amazing people-watching on the **Ocean Front Walk**, the boardwalk that connects the two beaches. From South Mission Jetty to Pacific Beach Point, it's crowded with joggers, in-line skaters and cyclists any time of the year. On warm summer weekends, oiled bodies, packed like

Timken Museum of Art   MUSEUM
(Map p952; ☑619-239-5548; www.timkenmuse um.org; 1500 El Prado; ⊙10am-4:30pm Tue-Sat, from noon Sun) FREE Don't skip the Timken, home of the Putnam collection, a small but impressive group of paintings, including works by Rembrandt, Rubens, El Greco, Cézanne and Pissarro, plus a wonderful selection of Russian icons. Built in 1965, the building stands out for *not* being in imitation-Spanish style.

San Diego Museum of Art   MUSEUM
(SDMA; Map p952; ☑619-232-7931; www.sdmart. org; 1450 El Prado; adult/child $15/free; ⊙10am-5pm Mon, Tue & Thu-Sat, from noon Sun) The SDMA is the city's largest art museum. The permanent collection has works by a number of European masters from the renaissance to the modernist eras (though no renowned pieces), American landscape paintings and several fantastic pieces in the Asian galleries; the museum also often has

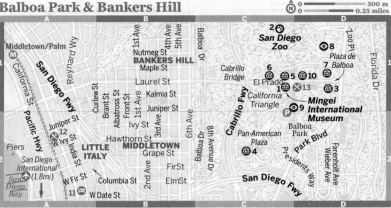

Balboa Park & Bankers Hill

⊚ **Top Sights**
1 Mingei International Museum C1
2 San Diego Zoo C1

⊚ **Sights**
3 Reuben H Fleet Science Center D1
4 San Diego Air & Space Museum C2
5 San Diego Museum of Art C1
6 San Diego Museum of Man C1
7 San Diego Natural History
    Museum... D1

8 Spanish Village Art Center D1
9 Spreckels Organ Pavilion........................D1
10 Timken Museum of Art D1

⊟ **Sleeping**
11 La Pensione Hotel....................................A2

⊗ **Eating**
12 Juniper & Ivy A2
13 Prado D1

sardines, cover the beach from end to end and cheer the setting sun.

★ Old Town San Diego State Historic Park
HISTORIC SITE

(Map p948; ☎ 619-220-5422; www.parks.ca.gov; 4002 Wallace St; ☺ visitor center & museums 10am-5pm daily; P ♿) FREE This park has an excellent history museum in the **Robinson-Rose House** at the southern end of the plaza. You'll also find a diorama depicting the original pueblo at the park's **visitor center**, where you can pick up a copy of the *Old Town San Diego State Historic Park Tour Guide & Brief History* ($3), or a presentation tour (free) at 11am and 2pm daily.

Mission Basilica San Diego de Alcalá
CHURCH

(Map p948; ☎ 619-281-8449; www.missionsandiego.com; 10818 San Diego Mission Rd; adult/child/under 5 $5/2/free; ☺ 9am-4:30pm; P ♿) Although the site of the first California mission (1769) was on Presidio Hill by present-day Old Town, in 1774 Padre Junípero Serra moved it about 7

miles upriver, closer to water and more arable land, to what is now the Mission Basilica San Diego de Alcalá. In 1784 missionaries built a solid adobe-and-timber church, which was destroyed by an earthquake in 1803. The church was promptly rebuilt, and at least some of it still stands on a slope overlooking Mission Valley.

Junípero Serra Museum
MUSEUM

(Map p948; ☎ 619-232-6203; www.sandiegohistory.org/serra_museum; 2727 Presidio Dr; by donation; ☺ 10am-4pm Fri-Sun early Jun-early Sep, 10am-5pm Sat & Sun early Sep-early Jun; P ♿) Located at one of the most important sites in the city, the Junípero Serra Museum stands atop Presidio Hill, the place where California first began. In 1769, the first mission, known as the Mission San Diego de Alcalá, was established here before it was moved 7 miles upriver.. The current Presidio building is Spanish Revival in style and houses a small but interesting collection of artifacts and pictures from San Diego's Mission and rancho periods.

⊙ Point Loma

On maps Point Loma looks like an elephant's trunk guarding the entrance to San Diego Bay. Highlights are the **Cabrillo National Monument** (Map p948; ☑619-557-5450; www. nps.gov/cabr; 1800 Cabrillo Memorial Dr; per car $10; ☺9am-5pm; P🚹) 🅿 at the end of the trunk, the shopping and dining of **Liberty Public Market** (Map p948; ☑619-487-9346; http://libertypublicmarket.com; 2820 Historic Decatur Rd; ☺7am-10pm) at its base and seafood meals around **Shelter Island**.

⊙ Mission Bay & Beaches

San Diego's big three beach towns all have ribbons of hedonism where armies of tanned, taut bodies frolic in the sand. West of amoeba-shaped Mission Bay, surf-friendly **Mission Beach** and its northern neighbor, **Pacific Beach** (aka 'PB'), are connected by car-free **Ocean Front Walk**, which swarms with skaters, joggers and cyclists year-round.

South of Mission Bay, bohemian **Ocean Beach** (OB) has a fishing pier, beach volleyball and good surf. Its main drag, **Newport Avenue**, is chockablock with scruffy bars, flip-flop eateries and shops selling surf gear, tattoos, vintage clothing and antiques.

Belmont Park   AMUSEMENT PARK
(Map p948; ☑858-228-9283; www.belmontpark. com; 3146 Mission Blvd; per ride $3-6, all-day pass adult/child $30/20; ☺from 11am daily, closing times vary; P) This old-style family-amusement park at the southern end of Mission Beach has been here since 1925. There's a large indoor pool, known as the **Plunge**, and a classic wooden roller coaster named the **Giant Dipper**, plus adventure golf, a new escape-room game, a carousel and other classics. More modern attractions include wave machines like **Flowrider** (Map p948; ☑858-228-9283; www.belmontpark.com/flow/; WaveHouse Beach Club, 3125 Ocean Front Walk; wave-riding per hour $30) FREE, for simulated surfing. Even if it sits on dry land, Belmont is to San Diego what the Santa Monica Pier amusement park is to LA.

⊙ La Jolla

Facing one of SoCal's loveliest sweeps of coastline, wealthy La Jolla (Spanish for 'the jewel,' pronounced la-hoy-ah) possesses shimmering beaches and an upscale downtown filled with boutiques and cafes. Oceanfront diversions include the **Children's Pool** (La Jolla seals; Map p948; 850 Coast Blvd) – no longer for swimming, it's now home to barking sea lions – kayaking, exploring sea caves at **La Jolla Cove** and snorkeling at **San Diego-La Jolla Underwater Park** (Map p948).

Torrey Pines State
Natural Reserve   STATE PARK
(☑858-755-2063; www.torreypine.org; 12600 N Torrey Pines Rd; ☺7:15am-sunset, visitor center 10am-4pm Oct-Apr, 9am-6pm May-Sep; P🚹) 🅿 FREE Between N Torrey Pines Rd and the ocean, and from the **Torrey Pines Glider-port** (Map p948; ☑858-452-9858; www.flytorrey. com; 2800 Torrey Pines Scenic Dr; 20min paragliding $175, hang-gliding tandem flight per person $225) to Del Mar, this reserve preserves the last mainland stands of the Torrey pine (*Pinus torreyana*), a species adapted to sparse rainfall and sandy, stony soils. Steep sandstone gullies have eroded into wonderfully textured surfaces, and the views over the ocean and north, including whale-watching, are superb. Volunteers lead nature walks on weekends and holidays. Several trails wind through the reserve and down to the beach.

Birch Aquarium at Scripps   AQUARIUM
(Map p948; ☑858-534-3474; www.aquarium.ucsd. edu; 2300 Expedition Way; adult/child $18.50/14; ☺9am-5pm; P🚹) 🅿 Marine scientists were working at the Birch Aquarium at Scripps Institution of Oceanography (SIO) as early as 1910 and, helped by donations from the ever-generous Scripps family, the institute has grown to be one of the world's largest marine research institutions. It is now a part of University of California (UC) San Diego. Off N Torrey Pines Rd, the aquarium has brilliant displays. The **Hall of Fishes** has more than 60 fish tanks, simulating marine habitats from the Pacific Northwest to tropical seas.

🏃 Activities

There are plenty of hikes in San Diego, but most outdoor activities involve the ocean. These waters are a dream for surfers, paddleboarders, kayakers and boaters. Call ☑619-221-8824 for surf reports.

Pacific Beach Surf Shop   SURFING
(Map p948; ☑858-373-1138; www.pbsurfshop.com; 4150 Mission Blvd; group surfing lessons from $75; ☺store 9am-6pm (winter), 9am-7pm (summer)) This shop provides instruction through its Pacific Beach Surf School. It has friendly

SURFING IN SAN DIEGO

A good number of residents moved to San Diego just for the surfing, and boy, is it good. Even beginners will understand why it's so popular.

Fall brings strong swells and offshore Santa Ana winds. In summer swells come from the south and southwest, and in winter from the west and northwest. Spring brings more frequent onshore winds, but the surfing can still be good. For the latest beach, weather and surf reports, call **San Diego County Lifeguard Services** (☏619-221-8824).

Beginners should head to Mission or Pacific Beach (p951), for beach breaks (soft-sand bottomed). North of Crystal Pier, **Tourmaline Surfing Park** is a crowded, but good, improvers spot for those comfortable surfing reef.

Rental rates vary depending on the quality of the equipment, but figure on soft boards from around \$15/45 per hour/full day; wetsuits cost \$7/28. Packages are available.

service and also rents wetsuits and both soft (foam) and hard (fiberglass) boards. Call ahead for lessons, offered hourly until 3pm in winter and 5pm in summer.

Hike, Bike, Kayak San Diego　　　ADVENTURE SPORTS
(Map p948; ☏858-551-9510; www.hikebikekayak. com; 2222 Avenida de la Playa; kayak rental from \$28, tours from \$50) Join a kayak tour to La Jolla's cove and caves or opt for a coastal biking tour. Rentals also available.

Flagship Cruises　　　BOATING
(Map p950; ☏619-234-4111; www.flagshipsd.com; 990 N Harbor Dr; tours adult/child from \$24/12; ▣) Harbor tours and seasonal whale-watching cruises from the Embarcadero, from one to several hours long.

🛌 Sleeping

We list high-season (summer) rates for single- or double-occupancy rooms. Prices drop significantly between September and June, but whatever time of year, ask about specials, suites and package deals. San Diego Tourism runs a **room-reservation line** (☏800-350-6205; www.sandiego.org).

🛌 Downtown & Around

★ USA Hostels San Diego　　　HOSTEL \$
(Map p950; ☏800-438-8622, 619-232-3100; www. usahostels.com; 726 5th Ave; dm/r with shared bath from \$32/80; ❄@🛜) Lots of charm and color at this convivial hostel in a former Victorian-era hotel with cheerful rooms, a full kitchen and a communal lounge. Rates include linens, lockers and bagels for breakfast. Surrounded by bars, it's smack-bang in the middle of Gaslamp's nightlife scene, so bring earplugs if you're a light sleeper.

★ La Pensione Hotel　　　BOUTIQUE HOTEL \$\$
(Map p952; ☏619-236-8000, 800-232-4683; www.lapensionehotel.com; 606 W Date St; r from \$145-200; ▣❄🛜) Despite the name, Little Italy's La Pensione isn't a pension but an intimate, friendly, recently renovated hotel of 67 rooms with queen-size beds and private bathrooms. It's set around a frescoed courtyard and is just steps to the neighborhood's dining, cafes and galleries, and walking distance to most Downtown attractions. There's an attractive cafe downstairs, and a recently introduced spa. Parking is \$20.

★ Hotel Solamar　　　BOUTIQUE HOTEL \$\$
(Map p950; ☏619-819-9500; www.hotelsolamar. com; 435 6th Ave; r \$169-299; ▣❄@🛜🏊) A great compromise in the Gaslamp: hip style that needn't break the bank. A new pool bar is set to open in 2017, with cabanas, outdoor games (like corn hole) and skyscraper views. Rooms have sleek lines and nautical blue and neo-rococo accents for a touch of fun. There's a fitness center, in-room yoga kit, free loaner bikes and a nightly complimentary wine hour. Parking costs \$47.

🛌 Beaches

Pearl　　　MOTEL \$\$
(Map p948; ☏877-732-7573, 619-226-6100; www. thepearlsd.com; 1410 Rosecrans St; r \$125-199; ▣❄🛜🏊) The mid-century-modern Pearl feels more Palm Springs than San Diego. The 23 rooms in its 1959 shell have soothing blue hues, trippy surf motifs and fishbowls. There's a lively pool scene (including **'dive-in' movies** on Wednesday nights), or you can play Jenga or Parcheesi in the groovy, shag-carpeted lobby. Light sleepers: request a room away from busy street traffic.

Inn at Sunset Cliffs　　　　　INN $$

(Map p948; ☎619-222-7901, 866-786-2453; www.
innatsunsetcliffs.com; 1370 Sunset Cliffs Blvd; r/
ste from $175/289; P❄❀@☎❄) At the south
end of Ocean Beach, wake up to the sound of
surf crashing onto the rocky shore. This low-
key 1950s charmer wraps around a flower-
bedecked courtyard with a small heated
pool. Its 24 breezy rooms are compact, but
most have attractive stone-and-tile bath-
rooms, and some suites have full kitchens.

★**Hotel del Coronado**　　LUXURY HOTEL $$$

(Map p948; ☎800-468-3533, 619-435-6611; www.
hoteldel.com; 1500 Orange Ave; r from $297; P❄
❀@☎❄❄) San Diego's iconic hotel provides the essential Coronado experience:
over a century of history, a pool, full-service
spa, shops, restaurants, manicured grounds,
a white-sand beach and an ice-skating rink
during Christmas season. Even the basic
rooms have luxurious marbled bathrooms.
Note: half the accommodations are not in the
main Victorian-era hotel (368 rooms) but in
an adjacent seven-story building constructed
in the 1970s. For a sense of place, book a room
in the original hotel. Self-parking is $39.

Crystal Pier Hotel & Cottages　　COTTAGE $$$

(Map p948; ☎800-748-5894; www.crystalpier.
com; 4500 Ocean Blvd, Pacific Beach; d $185-525;
P❄❀☎) Charming, wonderful and unlike
any other place in San Diego, Crystal Pier
has cottages built right on the pier above the
water. Almost all 29 cottages have full ocean
views and kitchens; most date from the
1930s. Newer, larger cottages sleep up to six.
Book eight to 11 months in advance for sum-
mer reservations. Minimum-stay require-
ments vary by season. No air-conditioning.
Rates include parking.

✖ Eating

San Diego has a thriving dining culture,
with an emphasis on Mexican, Californian
and seafood.

✖ Downtown & Around

★**Puesto at the
Headquarters**　　　　　MEXICAN $$

(Map p950; ☎610-233-8880; www.eatpuesto.com;
789 W Harbor Dr, The Headquarters; mains $11-19;
☺11am-10pm) This eatery serves Mexican
street food that knocked our *zapatos* off:
innovative takes on traditional tacos like
chicken (with hibiscus, chipotle, pineapple
and avocado) and some out-there fillings

like zucchini and cactus. Other highlights:
crab guacamole, the lime-marinated shrimp
ceviche, and the grilled Baja striped bass.

★**Old Town Mexican Café**　　MEXICAN $$

(Map p948; ☎619-297-4330; www.oldtownmex
cafe.com; 2489 San Diego Ave; mains $5-17; ☺7-
11pm weekdays, to midnight weekends; ⛟) Oth-
er restaurants come and go, but this place
has been in this busy adobe with hardwood
booths since the 1970s. While you wait to
be seated, watch the staff turn out tortillas.
Then enjoy *machaca* (shredded beef with
eggs, onions and peppers), carnitas and
Mexican ribs. For breakfast: *chilaquiles*
(tortilla chips with salsa or mole, broiled or
grilled with cheese).

Basic　　　　　　　　PIZZA $$

(Map p950; ☎619-531-8869; www.barbasic.com;
410 10th Ave; small/large pizzas from $14/32;
☺11:30am-2am) East Village hipsters feast on
fragrant thin-crust, brick-oven-baked pizzas
under Basic's high ceiling (it's in a former
warehouse). Small pizzas have a large footprint but are pretty light. Toppings span the
usual to the newfangled, like the mashed
pie with mozzarella, mashed potatoes and
bacon. Wash them down with beers (craft,
naturally) or one of several cocktails.

★**Juniper & Ivy**　　　CALIFORNIAN $$$

(Map p952; ☎619-269-9036; www.juniperandivy.
com; 2228 Kettner Blvd; small plates $10-23, mains
$19-45; ☺5-10pm Sun-Thu, to 11pm Fri & Sat) The
menu changes daily at chef Richard Blais'
highly rated San Diego restaurant, opened
in 2014. The molecular gastronomy includes
dishes in the vein of lobster congee, Hawai-
ian snapper with Valencia Pride mango, ahi
(yellowfin tuna) with creamed black trum-
pets, and pig-trotter *totelloni*. It's in a rock-
in' refurbished warehouse.

✖ Balboa Park & Around

★**Hash House a Go Go**　　AMERICAN $$

(Map p948; ☎619-298-4646; www.hashhouse
agogo.com; 3628 5th Ave, Hillcrest; breakfast $10-
22, dinner mains $15-29; ☺7.30am-2.30pm Mon,
7:30am-2pm & 5:30-9pm Tue-Thu, to 2:30pm and
9:30pm Fri-Sun; ⛟) This buzzing bungalow
makes biscuits and gravy straight outta
Indiana, towering Benedicts, large-as-your-
head pancakes and – wait for it – hash seven
different ways. Eat your whole breakfast,
and you won't need to eat the rest of the day.
It's worth coming back for the equally mas-

sive burgers, sage-fried chicken and award-winning meatloaf sandwich. No wonder it's called 'twisted farm food.'

★ **Urban Solace**　CALIFORNIAN $$
(Map p948; ☑619-295-6464; www.urbansolace.net; 3823 30th St, North Park; mains lunch $12-22, dinner $14-27; ☺11am-9pm Mon-Tue, to 9:30pm Wed-Thu, to 10:30pm Fri, 10:30am-10:30pm Sat, 9:30am-2:30pm & 4-9pm Sun) North Park's young hip gourmets revel in creative comfort food here: quinoa-veg burger; 'not your mama's' meatloaf of ground lamb, fig, pine nuts and feta; 'duckaroni' (mac 'n' cheese with duck confit); and pulled chicken and dumplings. The setting's surprisingly chill for such great eats, maybe because of the creative cocktails.

★ **Prado**　CALIFORNIAN $$$
(Map p952; ☑619-557-9441; www.pradobalboa.com; 1549 El Prado; lunch $8-19, dinner $8-37; ☺11:30am-3pm Mon, 11am-10pm Tue-Thu, 11:30am-9:30pm Sat, 11am-9pm Sun; ⊞) In one of San Diego's more beautiful dining rooms, feast on Cal-eclectic cooking by one of San Diego's most renowned chefs: bakery sandwiches, lobster bucatini, and thyme-roasted Jidori half-chicken. Go for a civilized lunch on the verandah or for afternoon cocktails and appetizers in the bar.

✕ Beaches

★ **Dirty Birds**　AMERICAN $
(Map p948; www.dirtybirdsbarandgrill.com; 4656 Mission Blvd; 5 wings for $7.50/20 for $26; ☺11am-12pm Sun-Wed, 11am-2am Thu-Sat) Come to this sports bar–slash–surf hangout for its award-winning chicken wings. On the menu are 37 different flavors including classic buffalo, plus weird and wonderful concoctions like salt and vinegar, apple bourbon chipotle and chicken enchilada. Wash them down with 10 rotating draft brews.

★ **Point Loma Seafoods**　SEAFOOD $
(Map p948; ☑619-223-1109; www.pointlomaseafoods.com; 2805 Emerson St; mains $7-16; ☺9am-7pm Mon-Sat, 10am-7pm Sun; Ｐ⊞) For off-the-boat-fresh seafood sandwiches, salads, sashimi, fried dishes and icy-cold beer, order at the counter at this fish-market-cum-deli and grab a seat at a picnic table on the up-stairs harbor-view deck. It also does great sushi and takeout dishes from ceviche to clam chowder.

★ **Hodad's**　BURGERS $
(Map p948; ☑619-224-4623; www.hodadies.com; 5010 Newport Ave; dishes $4-15; ☺11am-10pm) Since the flower-power days of 1969, OB's legendary burger joint has served great shakes, massive baskets of onion rings and succulent hamburgers wrapped in paper. The walls are covered in license plates; grunge/surf-rock plays (loud!) and your bearded, tattooed server might sidle into your booth to take your order. No shirt, no shoes, no problem, dude.

★ **The Patio on Lamont**　AMERICAN $$
(Map p948; ☑858-412-4648; www.thepatioonlamont.com; 4445 Lamont St; dishes $7-26; ☺9am-midnight) Popular local hangout serving beautifully prepared New American small plates and cocktails. Try the crab and ahi tower or crispy artichoke with goat's cheese in a cozy fairy-lit patio area (with outside heaters in winter). Daily happy hours on selected beers and cocktails ($5/6) run from 3pm to 6pm and 10pm to midnight.

🍷 Drinking & Nightlife

San Diego's bar scene is diverse, ranging from live-music pubs and classic American pool bars to beach bars with tiki cocktails, gay clubs offering drag shows, and even a few hidden speakeasies. It's easy to find a local craft beer in town, or you can venture out to one of the 100 breweries or vineyards in the Temecula area.

★ **Bang Bang**　BAR
(Map p950; ☑619-677-2264; www.bangbangsd.com; 526 Market St; cocktails $14-26; ☺5-10:30pm Wed-Thu, to 2am Fri & Sat) Beneath lantern light, the Gaslamp's hottest new spot brings in local and world-renowned DJs and serves sushi and Asian small plates like dumplings and *panko*-crusted shrimp to accompany the imaginative cocktails (some in giant goblets meant for sharing with your posse). Plus, the bathrooms are shrines to Ryan Gosling and Hello Kitty: in a word, awesome.

Noble Experiment　BAR
(Map p950; ☑619-888-4713; http://nobleexperimentsd.com; 777 G St; ☺7pm-2am Tue-Sun) This place is literally a find. Open a secret door and enter a contemporary speakeasy with miniature gold skulls on the walls, classical paintings on the ceilings and inventive cocktails on the list (from $12). The hard part: getting in. Text for a reservation, and they'll tell you if your requested time

is available and how to find the place. It's also possible to turn up to the bar upstairs, **Neighborhood** ([☑] 619-446-0002; www.neighborhoodsd.com; ⊙ noon-midnight), and put your name on a waiting list.

Gossip Grill LESBIAN
(Map p948; [☑] 619-260-8023; www.thegossipgrill. com; 1220 University Ave; ⊙ noon-2am Mon-Fri, 10am-2am Sat & Sun) They pour the drinks strong at San Diego's premier lesbian bar. It has a full patio, restaurant and dance floor, decorated with plants, chandeliers and two fire pits. The menu includes wings, sliders, flatbreads, soups, salads and sandwiches (mains from $9). There are often themed events, DJs and weekly drinks offers.

☆ Entertainment

Check out the San Diego *City Beat* or *UT San Diego* for the latest movies, theater, galleries and music gigs around town. **Arts Tix** (Map p950; [☑] 858-437-9850; www.sdartstix.com; 28 Horton Plaza, next to Balboa Theatre; ⊙ 10am-4pm Tue-Thu, to 6pm Fri & Sat, to 2pm Sun), in a kiosk near Westfield Horton Plaza, has half-price tickets for same-day evening or next-day matinee performances; it also offers discounted tickets to other events. **Ticketmaster** ([☑] 800-653-8000; www.ticketmaster. com) and **House of Blues** (Map p950; [☑] 619-299-2583; www.houseofblues.com/sandiego; 1055 5th Ave; ⊙ 4-11pm) sell tickets to other gigs around the city.

Prohibition Lounge LIVE MUSIC
(Map p950; http://prohibitionsd.com; 548 5th Avenue; ⊙ 8:00pm-1:30am Wed-Sat) Find the unassuming doorway on 5th Ave with 'Eddie O'Hare's Law Office' on it, then flip the light switch on to alert the doorman, who'll guide you into a dimly lit basement serving craft cocktails, with patrons enjoying live jazz (music from 9:30pm). Come early as it gets busy fast; at weekends expect to put your name on a list.

Balboa Theatre THEATER
(Map p950; [☑] 619-570-1100; http://sandiegotheatres.org; 868 4th Ave; from $35) Built in 1924, this building has a colorful past: in the '30s it screened films from Mexico City to San Diego's growing Latino audience. During World War II, it was turned into US Navy bachelor quarters. It was later closed, before a recent $26 million refurbishment. Since 2008, this fabled stage has hosted everything from comedy to movies and operas.

ⓘ Information

MEDIA
➡ Free listings magazines *Citybeat* (http://sdcitybeat.com) and *San Diego Reader* (www.sdreader.com), cover the active music, art and theater scenes. Find them in shops and cafes.
➡ KPBS 89.5 FM (www.kpbs.org) National Public Radio station.
➡ *San Diego Magazine* (www.sandiego magazine.com) Glossy monthly.
➡ *UT San Diego* (www.utsandiego.com) The city's major daily.

MEDICAL SERVICES
Scripps Mercy Hospital ([☑] 619-294-8111; www.scripps.org; 4077 5th Ave; ⊙ 24hr) has a 24-hour emergency room. There are also 24-hour drugstores around the city, including CVS stores in Pacific Beach, Gas Lamp and Adams Ave.

TOURIST INFORMATION
Coronado Visitor Center (Map p948; [☑] 866-599-7242, 619-437-8788; www.coronadovisitorcenter.com; 1100 Orange Ave; ⊙ 9am-5pm Mon-Fri, 10am-5pm Sat & Sun)
International Visitor Information Center (Map p950; [☑] 619-236-1242; www.sandiego. org; 1140 N Harbor Dr; ⊙ 9am-5pm Jun-Sep, to 4pm Oct-May) Across from the B St Cruise Ship Terminal, helpful staff offer very detailed neighborhood maps, sell discounted tickets to attractions and maintain a hotel-reservation hotline.

USEFUL WEBSITES
Gaslamp Quarter Association (http://gaslamp.org) Everything you need to know about the bustling Gaslamp Quarter, including parking secrets.
San Diego Tourism (www.sandiego.org) Search hotels, sights, dining, rental cars and more, and make reservations.

ⓘ Getting There & Away

Most flights to **San Diego International Airport** (SAN; Map p948; [☑] 619-400-2404; www.san. org; 3325 N Harbor Dr; 🛜) are domestic.

Greyhound (Map p950; [☑] 619-515-1100, 800-231-2222; www.greyhound.com; 1313 National Ave; ⊙ ticket office 5am-11:59pm) serves San Diego from cities across North America from its Downtown location.

Amtrak ([☑] 800-872-7245; www.amtrak.com; 1050 Kettner Blvd) runs the *Pacific Surfliner* several times daily to Anaheim (two hours), Los Angeles (2¾ hours) and Santa Barbara (6½ hours) from the historic **Union Station** (Santa Fe Depot; [☑] 800-872-7245; 1050 Kettner Blvd; ⊙ 3am-11:59pm).

All the big-name car-rental companies have desks at the airport; smaller agencies, such as **West Coast Rent a Car** (☑ 619-544-0606; http://westcoastrentacar.net; 834 W Grape St; ☺ 9am-6pm Mon-Sat, to 5pm Sun), in Little Italy, may be cheaper.

❶ Getting Around

MTS (Metropolitan Transit System) bus 992 'The Flyer' ($2.25) runs every 10 to 15 minutes between the airport and Downtown with stops along Broadway. Airport shuttles like **Super Shuttle** (☑ 800-258-3826; www.supershuttle. com) charge from around $10 to downtown; book in advance. An airport taxi to downtown averages $12 to $18, plus tip.

City buses ($2.25 to $2.50) and trolleys ($2.50), including routes to the Mexico border, are operated by MTS, whose **Transit Store** (Map p950; ☑ 619-234-1060; www.sdmts.com; 1255 Imperial Ave; ☺ 8am-5pm Mon-Fri) sells regional passes (or purchase one-day passes on board buses). Taxi fares vary, but plan on about $12 for a 3-mile journey.

PALM SPRINGS & THE DESERTS

From swanky Palm Springs to desolate Death Valley, Southern California's desert region swallows up 25% of the entire state. At first what seems harrowingly barren may eventually be transformed in your mind's eye to perfect beauty: weathered volcanic peaks, booming sand dunes, purple-tinged mountains, cactus gardens, tiny wildflowers pushing up from hard-baked soil in spring, lizards scurrying beside colossal boulders, and in the night sky, uncountable stars. California's deserts are serenely spiritual, surprisingly chic and ultimately irresistible, whether you're a bohemian artist, movie star, rock climber or 4WD adventurer.

Palm Springs

The Rat Pack is back, baby, or at least its hangout is. In the 1950s and '60s, Palm Springs, some 100 miles east of LA, was the swinging getaway of Sinatra, Elvis and other Hollywood stars. Once the Rat Pack packed it in, though, Palm Springs surrendered to golfing retirees. However, in the mid-1990s new generations discovered the city's retro-chic vibe and elegant mid-century modern structures built by famous architects. Today, retirees and snowbirds mix comfortably with hipsters, hikers and a sizeable LGBTIQ community, on getaways from LA or from across the globe.

◉ Sights & Activities

Palm Springs is the principal city of the Coachella Valley, a string of desert towns ranging from ho-hum Cathedral City to glamtastic Palm Desert and Coachella, home of the star-studded music festival, all linked by Hwy 111.

★**Palm Springs Aerial Tramway** CABLE CAR (☑ 760-325-1391, 888-515-8726; www.pstramway. com; 1 Tram Way, Palm Springs; adult/child $26/17, parking $5; ☺ 1st tram up 10am Mon-Fri, 8am Sat & Sun, last tram down 9:45pm daily, varies seasonally; **P** ♿) This rotating cable car climbs nearly 6000 vertical feet and covers five different vegetation zones, from the Sonoran desert floor to pine-scented Mt San Jacinto State Park, in 10 minutes during its 2.5-mile journey. From the mountain station (8561ft), which is 30°F to 40°F (up to 22°C) cooler than the desert floor, you can enjoy stupendous views, dine in two restaurants (ask about ride 'n' dine passes), explore over 50 miles of trails or visit the natural-history museum.

★**Palm Springs Art Museum** MUSEUM (☑ 760-322-4800; www.psmuseum.org; 101 Museum Dr, Palm Springs; adult/student $12.50/free, all free 4-8pm Thu; ☺ 10am-5pm Sun-Tue & Sat, noon-9pm Thu & Fri; **P**) Art fans should not miss this museum which presents changing exhibitions drawn from its stellar collection of international modern and contemporary painting, sculpture, photography and glass art. The permanent collection includes works by Henry Moore, Ed Ruscha, Mark di Suvero, Frederic Remington and many more heavy hitters. Other highlights are glass art by Dale Chihuly and William Morris and a collection of pre-Columbian figurines.

★**Sunnylands Center & Gardens** GARDENS (☑ 760-202-2222; www.sunnylands.org; 37977 Bob Hope Dr, Rancho Mirage; tours $20-45, center & gardens free; ☺ 9am-4pm Thu-Sun, closed early Jun–mid-Sep; **P**) Sunnylands is the mid-century modern winter retreat of Walter and Leonore Annenberg, one of America's 'first families.' It was here that they entertained seven US presidents, royalty, Hollywood celebrities and heads of state. The only way to get inside is on a guided 90-minute tour ($45) which must be booked far in advance via the website. No reservations are required to see the film and exhibits at the new visitor center, surrounded by magnificent desert gardens.

★ Living Desert Zoo & Gardens ZOO
(☑ 760-346-5694; www.livingdesert.org; 47900 Portola Ave, Palm Desert; adult/child $20/10; ◷ 9am-5pm Oct-May, 8am-1:30pm Jun-Sep; 🅿 ♿) ◢ This amazing animal park showcases desert plants and animals alongside exhibits on regional geology and Native American culture. Highlights include a walk-through wildlife hospital and an African-themed village with a fair-trade market and storytelling grove. Camel rides, giraffe feeding, a spin on the endangered species carousel, and a hop-on, hop-off shuttle cost extra. It's educational, fun and worth the 15-mile drive down-valley.

★ Indian Canyons HIKING
(☑ 760-323-6018; www.indian-canyons.com; 38520 S Palm Canyon Dr, Palm Springs; adult/child $9/5, 90min guided hike $3/2; ◷ 8am-5pm Oct-Jun, Fri-Sun only Jul-Sep) Streams flowing from the San Jacinto Mountains sustain rich plant varieties in oases around Palm Springs. Home to Native American communities for centuries, these canyons are a hiker's delight. Follow the Palm Canyon trail to the world's largest oasis of fan-palm trees, the Murray Canyon trail to a seasonal waterfall or the Andreas Canyon trail to rock formations along a year-round creek.

Smoke Tree Stables HORSEBACK RIDING
(☑ 760-327-1372; www.smoketreestables.com; 2500 S Toledo Ave, Palm Springs; 1/2hr guided ride $50/120; ◷ 1hr rides hourly 8am-3pm, 2hr rides 9am, 11am & 1pm; ♞) Near the Indian Canyons, this outfit offers public one-hour guided horse rides along the base of the mountains and two-hour tours into palm-lined Murray Canyon. Both are geared toward novice riders. Reservations are not needed but call to confirm departure times. Private tours are available by arrangement.

🛏 Sleeping

Palm Springs and the Coachella Valley offer an astonishing variety of lodging, including fine vintage-flair boutique hotels, full-on luxury resorts and chain motels. Some places don't allow children. Campers should head to Joshua Tree National Park or into the San Jacinto Mountains (via Hwy 74).

Caliente Tropics MOTEL $$
(☑ 800-658-6034, 760-327-1391; www.caliente tropics.com; 411 E Palm Canyon Dr, Palm Springs; r $99-225; 🅿 ❄ 🛜 🏊 ♿) Elvis and the Rat Pack once frolicked poolside at this premier budget pick, a nicely spruced-up 1964 tiki-style motor lodge. Drift off to dreamland on quality mattresses in spacious rooms dressed in warm colors.

★ Arrive Hotel BOUTIQUE HOTEL $$
(☑ 760-507-1650; www.arrivehotels.com; 1551 N Palm Canyon Dr, Palm Springs; studio from $179; 🅿 ♿ ❄ 🛜 🏊) ◢ Ecofriendly rusted steel, wood and concrete are the main design ingredients of this new adult-only lair where the bar doubles as the reception. The 32 rooms (some with patio) tick all the requisite hipster boxes such as rain shower, Apple TV and fancy bath products. The poolside restaurant, coffee shop, ice-cream parlor and craft-beer bar score high among locals.

★ L'Horizon BOUTIQUE HOTEL $$
(☑ 760-323-1858; http://lhorizonpalmsprings.com; 1050 E Palm Canyon Dr, Palm Springs; r $169-249; 🅿 ❄ 🛜 🏊) The intimate William F Cody-designed retreat that saw Marilyn Monroe and Betty Grable lounging poolside has been rebooted as sleek and chic adult-only desert resort with 25 bungalows scattered across generous grounds for maximum privacy. Treat yourself to alfresco showers, a chemical-free swimming pool and private patio.

★ El Morocco Inn & Spa BOUTIQUE HOTEL $$
(☑ 888-288-9905, 760-288-2527; http://elmo roccoinn.com; 66810 4th St, Desert Hot Springs; r $199-219; 🅿 ❄ 🛜 🏊) Heed the call of the casbah at this drop-dead gorgeous hideaway where the scene is set for romance. Twelve exotically furnished rooms wrap around

---

WORLD'S BIGGEST DINOSAURS

West of Palm Springs, you may do a double take when you glimpse 'Dinny the Dinosaur' and 'Mr Rex' from the I-10. Claude K Bell, a sculptor for Knott's Berry Farm, spent over a decade in the 1980s crafting the concrete behemoths at World's Biggest Dinosaurs (☑ 951-922-8700; www.cabazondinosaurs.com; 50770 Seminole Dr, Cabazon; adult/child $10/9; ◷ 10am-4:30pm Mon-Fri, 9am-6:30pm Sat & Sun; 🅿 ♿). Today you can pan for dino fossils, climb inside Rex's mouth, marvel at dozens of dinosaur models and stock up on dino souvenirs in the gift shop.

WORTH A TRIP

PIONEERTOWN

Looking like an 1870s frontier town, Pioneertown (www.pioneertown.com; P 🚼) FREE was actually built in 1946 as a Hollywood Western movie set. Gene Autry and Roy Rogers were among the original investors, and more than 50 movies and several TV shows were filmed here in the 1940s and '50s. These days, it's fun to stroll around the old buildings and drop into the local honky-tonk for refreshments. Mock gunfights take place on 'Mane St' at 2:30pm every second and fourth Saturday, April to October.

Within staggering distance is the atmospheric **Pioneertown Motel** (☑ 760-365-7001; www.pioneertown-motel.com; 5040 Curtis Rd, Pioneertown; r from $155; P ❄ 🛜 🐾), where yesteryear's silver-screen stars once slept during filming, and whose rooms are now filled with eccentric Western-themed memorabilia; some rooms have kitchenettes.

a pool deck where your enthusiastic hosts serve free 'Morocco-tinis' during happy hour. The on-site spa offers such tempting massages as 'Moroccan Rain' using an essential oil to purge the body of toxins.

Hacienda at Warm Sands   BOUTIQUE HOTEL **$$$**
(☑ 760-327-8111; www.thehacienda.com; 586 Warm Sands Dr, Palm Springs; r $309-439; P ❄ @ 🛜 🐾) With Indonesian teak furnishings, this 10-suite gay male resort raises the bar for luxury with its pillow menu, flawless landscaping, two pools and Jacuzzi with fireplace. The genial innkeepers are happy to customize stays with everything from in-room massages to arranging a personal shopper.

🍴 Eating

A new line-up of zeitgeist-capturing restaurants has seriously elevated the level of dining in Palm Springs. The most exciting newcomers, including several with eye-catching design, flank N Palm Canyon Dr in the Uptown design district.

★**Cheeky's**   CALIFORNIAN **$**
(☑ 760-327-7595; www.cheekysps.com; 622 N Palm Canyon Dr, Palm Springs; mains $9-14; ⊙ 8am-2pm Thu-Mon, last seating 1:30pm; ❄) Waits can be long and service only so-so at this breakfast

and lunch spot, but the farm-to-table menu dazzles with witty inventiveness. The kitchen tinkers with the menu on a weekly basis but perennial faves such as custardy scrambled eggs and grass-fed-beef burger with pesto fries keep making appearances.

Trio   CALIFORNIAN **$$**
(☑ 760-864-8746; www.triopalmsprings.com; 707 N Palm Canyon Dr, Palm Springs; mains lunch $13-16, dinner $15-30; ⊙ 11am-10pm Sun-Thu, to 11pm Fri & Sat; 🛜) The winning formula in this '60s modernist space: updated American comfort food (awesome Yankee pot roast!) amid eye-catching artwork and picture windows. The $19 prix-fixe three-course dinner (served until 6pm) is a steal, and the all-day daily happy hour lures a rocking after-work crowd with bar bites and cheap drinks.

★**Workshop Kitchen + Bar**   AMERICAN **$$$**
(☑ 760-459-3451; www.workshoppalmsprings.com; 800 N Palm Canyon Dr, Palm Springs; mains $26-45; ⊙ 5-10pm Mon-Sun, 10am-2pm Sun; ❄) Hidden away in the back of the ornate 1920s El Paseo building, a large patio with olive trees leads to this starkly beautiful space centered on a lofty concrete tunnel flanked by mood-lit booths. The kitchen crafts market-driven American classics reinterpreted for the 21st century and the bar is among the most happening in town.

🍷 Drinking & Nightlife

Arenas Rd, east of Indian Canyon Dr, is gay-and-lesbian-nightlife central.

★**Bootlegger Tiki**   COCKTAIL BAR
(☑ 760-318-4154; www.bootleggertiki.com; 1101 N Palm Canyon Dr, Palm Springs; ⊙ 4pm-2am) Crimson light bathes even pasty-faced hipsters into a healthy glow, as do the killer crafted cocktails at this teensy speakeasy with blowfish lamps and rattan walls. The entrance is via the Ernest coffee shop.

Birba   BAR
(☑ 760-327 5678; www.birbaps.com; 622 N Palm Canyon Dr, Palm Springs; ⊙ 5-11pm Sun & Wed-Thu, to midnight Fri & Sat; 🛜) On a balmy night, Birba's hedge-fringed patio with twinkle lights and sunken fire pit is perfect for unwinding with a glass of wine or smooth libations like the tequila-based Heated Snake. Get a plate of *cicchetti* (Italian bar snacks) to stave off the blur or order modern pizza or pasta from the full menu.

🛍 Shopping

For art galleries, modern design stores and fashion boutiques, including fabulous **Trina Turk** (✓760-416-2856; www.trinaturk.com; 891 N Palm Canyon Dr, Palm Springs; ⊙10am-6pm Mon-Sat, 11am-5pm Sun), head 'Uptown' to North Palm Canyon Dr. If you're riding the retro wave, uncover treasures in thrift, vintage and consignment shops scattered around downtown and along Hwy 111. For a local version of Rodeo Dr, drive down-valley to Palm Desert's El Paseo.

ℹ Information

Palm Springs Historical Society (✓760-323-8297; www.pshistoricalsociety.org; 221 S Palm Canyon Dr, Palm Springs; ⊙10am-4pm Mon & Wed-Sat, noon-3pm Sun) Volunteer-staffed nonprofit organization. Maintains two museums and offers guided tours focusing on local history, architecture and celebrities.

Palm Springs Visitor Center (✓800-347-7746, 760-778-8418; www.visitpalmsprings.com; 2901 N Palm Canyon Dr, Palm Springs; ⊙9am-5pm) Well-stocked and well-staffed visitor center in a 1965 Albert Frey–designed gas station at the Palm Springs Aerial Tram turnoff, 3 miles north of downtown.

ℹ Getting There & Around

Palm Springs International Airport (PSP; ✓760-318-3800; www.palmspringsairport.com; 3400 E Tahquitz Canyon Way, Palm Springs) connects year-round to destinations throughout North America. Ask if your hotel provides free airport transfers. Otherwise, a taxi to downtown Palm Springs costs about $12 to $15, including a $2.50 airport surcharge.

The Sunset Limited operated by **Amtrak** (www.amtrak.com) comes through three times weekly on its route between New Orleans and Los Angeles.

SunLine (✓800-347-8628; www.sunline.org; ticket $1, day pass $3) alternative-fuel-powered public buses travel around the valley, albeit slowly.

Joshua Tree National Park

Taking a page from a Dr Seuss book, the whimsical Joshua trees (actually tree-sized yuccas) welcome visitors to this 794,000-acre park at the transition zone of two deserts: the low and dry Colorado and the higher, moister and slightly cooler Mojave.

Rock climbers know 'JT' as one of the best places to climb in California; hikers seek out hidden, shady, desert fan-palm oases fed by natural springs and small streams; and mountain bikers are hypnotized by the desert vistas.

👁 Sights & Activities

Dominating the north side of the **park** (✓760-367-5500; www.nps.gov/jotr; 7-day entry per car $25; ⊙24hr; 🅿 👣) 🖊, the epic **Wonderland of Rocks** calls to climbers, as does **Hidden Valley**. Sunset-worthy **Keys View** overlooks the San Andreas Fault and on clear days, you can see as far as Mexico. For pioneer history, tour **Keys Ranch** (✓760-367-5500; www.nps.gov/jotr; tour adult/child $10/5; ⊙tour schedules vary; 🅿 👣). Hikers seek out native desert fan-palm oases like **49 Palms Oasis** (3-mile round-trip) and **Lost Palms Oasis** (7.2-mile round-trip). Kid-friendly nature trails include **Barker Dam** (1.1-mile loop), which passes Native American petroglyphs; **SkullRock** (1.7-mile loop); and **Cholla Cactus Garden** (0.25-mile loop). For a scenic 4WD route, tackle bumpy 18-mile **Geology Tour Road**, also open to mountain bikers.

🛏 Sleeping

Of the park's eight campgrounds, only **Cottonwood** (✓760-367-5500; www.nps.gov/jotr; Pinto Basin Rd; per site $20) and **Black Rock** (✓760-367-5500, reservations 877-444-6777; www.nps.gov/jotr; Joshua Lane; per site $20; 🅿) have potable water, flush toilets and dump stations. **Indian Cove** (✓760-367-5500, reservations 877-444-6777; www.nps.gov/jotr; Indian Cove Rd; per site $20) and Black Rock accept reservations from October through May. The others are first-come, first-served and have pit toilets, picnic tables and fire grates. None have showers, but there are some at **Coyote Corner** (✓760-366-9683; www.jtcoyotecorner.com; 6535 Park Blvd; ⊙9am-6pm) in Joshua Tree. Details are available at www.nps.gov/jotr or ✓760-367-5500.

Budget and midrange motels line Hwy 62. Twentynine Palms and Yucca Valley have mostly national chain motels, while pads in Joshua Tree have plenty of charm and character.

Harmony Motel　　　　　　　　　　MOTEL $
(✓760-367-3351, 760-401-1309; www.harmonymotel.com; 71161 29 Palms Hwy/Hwy 62, Twentynine Palms; r $65-85; 🅿👄❄🛜🏊) This well-kept 1950s motel, run by the charming Ash, was where U2 stayed while working on the *Joshua Tree* album. It has a small pool and seven

large, cheerfully painted rooms (some with kitchenette) set around a tidy desert garden with serenely dramatic views. A light breakfast is served in the communal guest kitchen.

★ **Kate's Lazy Desert**　　　　INN $$
(☑ 845-688-7200; www.lazymeadow.com; 58380 Botkin Rd, Landers; Airstream $175 Mon-Thu, $200 Fri & Sat; P🅿❋🐾🛏) Owned by Kate Pierson of the B-52s, this desert camp has a coin-sized pool (May to October) and half a dozen Airstream trailers to sleep inside. Each is kitted out with matching fantasia-pop design and a double bed and kitchenette.

★ **Sacred Sands**　　　　B&B $$$
(☑ 760-424-6407; www.sacredsands.com; 63155 Quail Springs Rd, Joshua Tree; north/west r $329/359, 2-night minimum; P🅿❋🐾) 🐾 In an isolated, pin-drop-quiet spot, these two desert-chic suites are the ultimate romantic retreat, each with a private outdoor shower, hot tub, sundeck and sleeping terrace under the stars. There are astounding views across the desert hills and into the National Park. Owners Scott and Steve are gracious hosts and killer breakfast cooks.

✖ Eating

There's no food available inside the park itself. Nearby **Crossroads Cafe** (☑ 760-366-5414; www.crossroadscafejtree.com; 61715 29 Palms Hwy/Hwy 62, Joshua Tree; mains $6-12; ⏰ 7am-9pm Mon-Sat, to 8pm Sun; P🅿) is a JT institution. It's the go-to place for carb-loaded breakfast, dragged-through-the-garden salad and fresh sandwiches that make both omnivores and vegans happy.

★ **La Copine**　　　　AMERICAN $
(www.lacopinekitchen.com; 848 Old Woman Rd, Flamingo Heights; mains $10-16; ⏰ 9am-3pm Thu-Sun; P🅿❋) It's a long road from Philadelphia to the high desert, but that's where Nikki and Claire decided to take their farm-to-table brunch cuisine from pop-up to brick and mortar. Their roadside bistro serves zeitgeist-capturing dishes such as the signature salad with smoked salmon and poached egg, homemade crumpets and gold milk turmeric tea. Expect a wait on weekends.

ℹ Information

Pick up park information at NPS visitor centers at **Joshua Tree** (www.nps.gov/jotr; 6554 Park Blvd, Joshua Tree; ⏰ 8am-5pm; 🐾 🅿), **Oasis** (www. nps.gov/jotr; 74485 National Park Dr, Twentynine Palms; ⏰ 8:30am-5pm; 🅿) and **Cottonwood** (www.nps.gov/jotr; Cottonwood Springs; ⏰ 8:30am-4pm; 🅿). There are no park facilities aside from restrooms, so bring all the drinking water and food you'll need. Get gas and stock up in the three towns linked by the Twentynine Palms Hwy (Hwy 62) along the park's northern boundary: Yucca Valley, with the most services (banks, supermarkets etc); beatnik Joshua Tree, where outdoor outfitters and shops offering internet access cluster; and Twentynine Palms.

Anza-Borrego Desert State Park

Shaped by an ancient sea and tectonic forces, Anza-Borrego is the USA's largest state park outside Alaska. Cradling the park's only commercial hub – tiny Borrego Springs (pop 3429) – are more than 600,000 acres of mountains, canyons and badlands; a fabulous variety of plants and wildlife; and intriguing historical relics of Native American tribes, Spanish explorers and gold-rush pioneers. Early spring wildflower blooms bring the biggest crowds, while in summer, Hades-like heat makes daytime exploring dangerous.

👁 Sights & Activities

Two miles west of Borrego Springs, the park **visitor center** (☑ 760-767-4205; www.parks. ca.gov; 200 Palm Canyon Dr, Borrego Springs; ⏰ 9am-5pm daily mid-Oct–mid-May, Sat, Sun & holidays only mid-May–mid-Oct) has natural-history exhibits, information handouts and updates on road conditions. Driving through the park is free, but if you camp, hike or picnic, a day-use parking fee ($5 per car) applies. You'll need a 4WD to tackle the 500 miles of backcountry dirt roads. If you're hiking, always bring extra water.

Park highlights include **Fonts Point** desert lookout, **Clark Dry Lake** for birding, the **Elephant Tree Discovery Trail** near Split Mountain's wind caves, and **Blair Valley**, with its Native American pictographs and pioneer traces. Further south, soak in concrete hot-spring pools at **Agua Caliente Regional Park** (☑ 760-765-1188; www.sdparks. org; 39555 Great Southern Overland Stage Route of 1849/County Rte S2; per car $3; ⏰ 9:30am-5pm Mon-Fri, to sunset weekends Sep-May).

🛏 Sleeping & Eating

A handful of seasonally open motels and hotels cluster in and around Borrego Springs. Otherwise, camping is the go (free backcountry camping is permitted anywhere).

OFF THE BEATEN TRACK

SALTON SEA & SALVATION MOUNTAIN

East of Anza-Borrego and south of Joshua Tree awaits a most unexpected sight: the **Salton Sea** (☎760-393-3052; www.parks.ca.gov; 100-225 State Park Rd, North Shore; car $7; ☺visitor center 10am-4pm Oct-May, Fri-Sun only Jun-Sep; 🅿), California's largest lake in the middle of its biggest desert. After the Colorado River flooded in 1905, it took 1500 workers and half a million tons of rock to put it back on course. With no natural outlet, the artificial lake's surface is 220ft below sea level and its waters 50% saltier than the Pacific – an environmental nightmare that's yet to be cleaned up.

An even stranger sight near the lake's eastern shore is **Salvation Mountain** (www.salvationmountain.us), a 100ft-high hill of hand-mixed clay slathered in colorful acrylic paint and found objects, and inscribed with Christian messages. This creation of folk artist Leonard Knight (1931–2014) is in Niland, about 3 miles east of Hwy 111, via Main St/Beal Rd.

Borrego Palm Canyon Campground

CAMPGROUND $

(☎800-444-7275; www.reserveamerica.com; 200 Palm Canyon Dr, Borrego Springs; tent/RV sites $25/35; 🅿🐾) Near the Anza-Borrego Desert State Park visitor center, this campground has award-winning toilets, campsites that are close together and an amphitheater with ranger programs.

Palm Canyon Hotel & RV Resort

HOTEL $$

(☎760-767-5341; www.palmcanyonrvresort.com; 221 Palm Canyon Dr, Borrego Springs; incl tax d $128-177, RV with full hook-up $48-56, trailers $70-150; ☺Oct-May; 🅿🛜🐾) About a mile west of the park's visitor center, this modern property has spacious rooms, some with Jacuzzi; for a memorable experience, stay in one of the vintage Airstream trailers. Upstairs rooms have nice mountain views, and there are two pools and a restaurant-saloon. Two-night-minimum weekends September to June.

★ La Casa del Zorro

RESORT $$$

(☎760-767-0100; www.lacasadelzorro.com; 3845 Yaqui Pass Rd; r $224-350; 🅿❄🛜🐾) After a top-to-bottom facelift, this venerable 1937 resort is again the region's grandest stay. The ambience exudes desert romance in 67 elegantly rustic poolside rooms and family-sized casitas sporting vaulted ceilings and marble bathtubs. A staggering 28 pools and Jacuzzi are scattered across the 42 landscaped acres, and there's a spa, five tennis courts, fun bar and gourmet restaurant.

❶ Information

Borrego Springs has banks with ATMs, gas stations, a supermarket, a post office and a public library with free wi-fi and internet terminals, all on Palm Canyon Dr. Call the **Wildflower Hotline** (☎760-767-4684) for information on seasonal blooms.

Mojave National Preserve

If you're on a quest for the 'middle of nowhere,' you may find it in **Mojave National Preserve** (☎760-252-6100; www.nps.gov/moja; btwn I-15 & I-40) FREE a 1.6-million-acre jumble of sand dunes, Joshua trees, volcanic cinder cones and habitat for endangered desert tortoises. Warning: no gas is available here.

Southeast of Baker and the I-15 Fwy, Kelbaker Rd crosses a ghostly landscape of cinder cones before arriving at **Kelso Depot**, a 1920s Mission Revival–style railroad station. It now houses the park's main **visitor center** (☎760-252-6108; www.nps.gov/moja; Kelbaker Rd, Kelso; ☺10am-5pm), which has excellent natural-and-cultural history exhibits, and an old-fashioned lunch counter. It's another 11 miles southwest to 'singing' **Kelso Dunes**. When wind conditions are right, they emanate low-pitched vibrations caused by shifting sands – running downhill can jump-start the effect. From Kelso Depot, Kelso–Cima Rd takes off northeast. After 19 miles, Cima Rd slingshots northwest toward I-15 around **Cima Dome**, a 1500ft-high hunk of granite with lava outcroppings, the slopes of which are home to the world's largest **Joshua tree forest**. For close-ups, summit **Teutonia Peak** (3 miles round-trip); the trailhead is 6 miles northwest of Cima.

🛏 Sleeping & Eating

Camping is the only way to overnight in the preserve. Baker, on the northwestern edge along I-15, has plenty of cheap, charmless motels. Coming from the north, the casino hotels in Primm on the Nevada border offer slightly better options. If you're traveling on the I-40, Needles is the closest town to spend the night.

The only place in the park to get a bite is at the old-fashioned lunch counter in the Kelso Visitor Center. Baker is the closest town with restaurants and grocery stores.

Death Valley National Park

The very name evokes all that is harsh, hot and hellish – a punishing, barren and lifeless place of Old Testament severity. Yet closer inspection reveals that in Death Valley nature is putting on a truly spectacular show: singing sand dunes, water-sculpted canyons, boulders moving across the desert floor, extinct volcanic craters, palm-shaded oases, stark mountains rising to 11,000ft and plenty of endemic wildlife.

This is a land of superlatives, holding the US records for hottest temperature (134°F/57°C), lowest point (Badwater, 282ft below sea level) and largest national park outside Alaska (over 5000 sq miles).

👁 Sights & Activities

In summer, stick to paved roads, limit your exertions outdoors to early morning hours and night, and visit higher-elevation areas of the park. From **Furnace Creek**, the central hub of the **park** (☎760-786-3200; www.nps.gov/deva; 7-day-pass per car $25; ⏰24hr; P🚻) 🖊, drive southeast up to **Zabriskie Point** for spectacular sunset views across the valley and golden badlands eroded into waves, pleats and gullies. Twenty miles southeast at **Dante's View**, you can simultaneously spot

RHYOLITE

Just outside the Death Valley eastern park boundary, four miles west of Beatty, NV, look for the turnoff to the ghost town of **Rhyolite** (off Hwy 374; P) **FREE**, which epitomizes the hurly-burly, boom-and-bust story of so many Western gold-rush mining towns. Don't miss the 1906 'bottle house' or the skeletal remains of a three-story bank. Next door is the bizarre **Goldwell Open Air Museum** (☎702-870-9946; www.goldwellmuseum.org; off Hwy 374; ⏰park 24hr, visitor center 10am-4pm Mon-Sat, to 2pm summer; P) **FREE** of trippy art installations begun by Belgian artist Albert Szukalski in 1984.

the highest (Mt Whitney,14,505ft) and lowest (Badwater) points in the contiguous USA.

Badwater itself, a timeless landscape of crinkly salt flats, is 17 miles south of Furnace Creek. Along the way, **Golden Canyon** and **Natural Bridge** are easily explored on short hikes. A 9-mile detour along **Artists Drive** through a narrow canyon is best in late afternoon when the eroded hillsides erupt in fireworks of color.

Northwest of Furnace Creek, near Stovepipe Wells Village, trek across Saharanesque **Mesquite Flat** sand dunes – magical under a full moon – and scramble along the smooth marble walls of **Mosaic Canyon**.

About 55 miles northwest of Furnace Creek at whimsical **Scotty's Castle** (☎760-786-3200; www.nps.gov/deva; ⏰closed); tour guides in historical character dress bring to life the Old West tales of con man 'Death Valley Scotty' (reservations advised). Five miles west of Grapevine junction, circumambulate volcanic **Ubehebe Crater** and its younger sibling.

🛏 Sleeping & Eating

Camping is plentiful but if you're looking for a place with a roof, in-park options are limited, pricey and often booked solid in springtime. Alternative bases are the gateway towns of Beatty (40 miles from Furnace Creek), Lone Pine (40 miles), Death Valley Junction (30 miles) and Tecopa (70 miles). Options a bit further afield include Ridgecrest (120 miles) and Las Vegas (140 miles).

Mesquite Springs Campground   CAMPGROUND $
(☎760-786-3200; www.nps.gov/deva; Hwy 190; per site $14) In the northern reaches of the park, this first-come, first-served campground has only 40 spaces and is a handy base for Ubehebe Crater and Racetrack Rd. At an elevation of 1800ft, it's also a lot cooler than the desert floor. Sites come with fire pits and tables, and there's water and flush toilets.

Ranch at Furnace Creek   RESORT $$
(☎760-786-2345; www.furnacecreekresort.com; Hwy 190, Furnace Creek; cabin/r from $140/180; P🐾❄🐕📶🐕) Tailor-made for families, this rambling resort with multiple, motel-style buildings has received a vigorous facelift, resulting in spiffy rooms swathed in desert colors, updated bathrooms and French doors leading to porches with comfortable patio furniture. The grounds encompass a

playground, spring-fed swimming pool, tennis courts, golf course, restaurants, shops and the **Borax Museum** (⊙ 9am-9pm Oct-May, variable summer; P ⚐) **FREE**.

Inn at Furnace Creek
HOTEL $$$

(☎760-786-2345; www.furnacecreekresort.com; Hwy 190; d from $450; ⊙mid-Oct–mid-May; P ⊙ ❄@⚐≋) Roll out of bed and count the colors of the desert as you pull back the curtains in your room at this 1927 Spanish Mission–style hotel. After a day of sweaty touring, enjoy languid valley views while lounging by the spring-fed swimming pool, cocktail in hand. It's the classiest place in Death Valley, but rooms would benefit from updating.

Amargosa Opera House Cafe
CAFE $$

(☎760-852-4432; www.amargosacafe.org; Death Valley Junction; mains $9-19, pie per slice $5; ⊙8am-3pm Mon, Fri, Sat & Sun, 6:30-9pm Sat; P ❄) 🥢 This charmer in the middle of nowhere gets you ready for a day in Death Valley with hearty breakfasts or healthy sandwiches, but truly shows off its farm-to-table stripes at dinnertime on Saturdays. Combine with a tour of (or show at) the late Marta Becket's kooky opera house. Excellent coffee to boot.

❶ Information

Park entry permits ($25 per vehicle) are valid for seven days and available from self-service pay stations at the park's access roads and at the **Furnace Creek Visitor Center** (☎760-786-3200; www.nps.gov/deva; ⊙8am-5pm; ⚐ ⚐). This modern visitor center has engaging exhibits on the park's ecosystem and the indigenous tribes as well as a gift shop, clean toilets, (slow) wi-fi and friendly rangers to answer questions and help you plan your day.

CENTRAL COAST

Too often forgotten or dismissed as 'flyover' country between San Francisco and LA, this fairy-tale stretch of California coast is packed with wild beaches, misty redwood forests that hide hot springs, and rolling golden hills of fertile vineyards and farm fields.

Santa Barbara

Perfect weather, beautiful buildings, excellent bars and restaurants, and activities for all tastes and budgets make Santa Barbara a great place to live (as the locals will proudly tell you) and a must-see place for visitors to Southern California. Check out the Spanish Mission church first, then just see where the day takes you.

⦿ Sights

★MOXI
MUSEUM

(Wolf Museum of Exploration + Innovation; ☎805-770-5000; www.moxi.org; 125 State St; adult/child $14/10; ⊙10am-5pm; ⚐) Part of the regeneration of this neglected strip of State St, Moxi's three floors filled with hands-on displays covering science, arts and technology themes will tempt families in, even when it's not raining outside. If all that interactivity gets too much, head to the roof terrace for views across Santa Barbara and a nerve-challenging walk across a glass ceiling.

★Santa Barbara County Courthouse
HISTORIC BUILDING

(☎805-962-6464; http://sbcourthouse.org; 1100 Anacapa St; ⊙8am-5pm Mon-Fri, 10am-5pm Sat & Sun) **FREE** Built in Spanish-Moorish Revival style in 1929, the courthouse features hand-painted ceilings, wrought-iron chandeliers and tiles from Tunisia and Spain. On the 2nd floor, step inside the hushed mural room depicting Spanish-colonial history, then head up to El Mirador, the 85ft clock tower, for arch-framed panoramas of the city, ocean and mountains.

★Mission Santa Barbara
CHURCH

(☎805-682-4713; www.santabarbaramission.org; 2201 Laguna St; adult $9, child 5-17yr $4; ⊙9am-5pm, last entry 4:15pm; P ⚐) California's 'Queen of the Missions' reigns above the city on a hilltop perch over a mile north of downtown. Its imposing Ionic facade, an architectural homage to an ancient Roman chapel, is topped by an unusual twin-bell tower. Inside the mission's 1820 stone church, notice the striking Chumash artwork. In the cemetery the elaborate mausoleums of early California settlers stand out, while the graves of thousands of Chumash lie largely forgotten.

Santa Barbara Maritime Museum
MUSEUM

(☎805-962-8404; www.sbmm.org; 113 Harbor Way; adult $8, child 6-17yr $5; ⊙10am-5pm Thu-Tue; P ⚐) On the harborfront, this jam-packed, two-story exhibition hall celebrates the town's briny history with nautical artifacts, memorabilia and hands-on exhibits, including a big-game fishing chair from which you can 'reel in' a trophy marlin. Take a virtual trip through the Santa Barbara Channel,

CHANNEL ISLANDS NATIONAL PARK

Remote, rugged **Channel Islands National Park** (☑ 805-658-5730; www.nps.gov/chis) 🏄 FREE earns the nickname 'California's Galápagos' for its unique wildlife. These islands offer superb snorkeling, scuba diving and sea kayaking. Spring, when wildflowers bloom, is a gorgeous time to visit; summer and fall are bone-dry, but the latter brings the calmest water and winds; winter can be stormy.

Anacapa, an hour's boat ride from the mainland, is the best island for day-tripping, with easy hikes and unforgettable views. **Santa Cruz**, the biggest island, is for overnight camping excursions, kayaking and hiking. Other islands require longer channel crossings and multiday trips. **San Miguel** is often shrouded in fog. Tiny **Santa Barbara** supports seabird and seal colonies. So does **Santa Rosa**, which also protects Torrey pine trees.

Boats leave from Ventura Harbor, 32 miles south of Santa Barbara on Hwy 101, where the park's **visitor center** (☑ 805-658-5730; www.nps.gov/chis; 1901 Spinnaker Dr, Ventura; ◷ 8:30am-5pm) has info and maps. The main tour-boat operator is Island Packers (☑ 805-642-1393; www.islandpackers.com; 1691 Spinnaker Dr, Ventura; 3hr cruise adult/child 3-12yr from $36/26); book ahead. Primitive island campgrounds require reservations; book through Recreation.gov and bring food and water.

stand on a surfboard or watch deep-sea-diving documentaries in the theater. There's 90 minutes of free parking in the public lot or take the **Lil' Toot water taxi** (☑ 805-465-6676; www.celebrationsantabarbara.com; 1-way fare adult/child $5/1; ◷ usually noon-6pm Apr-Oct, hours vary Nov-Mar; 👪) from Stearns Wharf.

🏃 Activities

Overlooking busy municipal beaches, 1872 **Stearns Wharf** (www.stearnswharf.org; ◷ open daily, hours vary; 🅿 👪) FREE is the West's oldest continuously operating wooden pier, strung with touristy shops and restaurants. Outside town off Hwy 101, bigger palm-fringed **state beaches** await at Carpinteria, 12 miles east, and El Capitan and Refugio, more than 20 miles west.

Wheel Fun Rentals   CYCLING
(☑ 805-966-2282; http://wheelfunrentalssb.com; 23 E Cabrillo Blvd; ◷ 8am-8pm; 👪) Hourly rentals of beach cruisers ($9.95), mountain bikes ($10.95) and two-/four-person surreys ($28.95/38.95), with discounted half-day and full-day rates. A second, seasonal branch is in the Fess Parker Double Tree Hotel at 633 E Cabrillo Blvd.

Santa Barbara Sailing Center   CRUISE, SAILING
(☑ 805-962-2826; www.sbsail.com; Marina 4, off Harbor Way; ◷ 9am-6pm, to 5pm winter; 👪) Climb aboard the *Double Dolphin,* a 50ft sailing catamaran, for a two-hour coastal or sunset cruise ($35). Seasonal whale-watching trips ($40) and quick half-hour spins around the harbor to view marine life ($18)

are more kid-friendly. It also offers kayak and SUP rentals and tours.

Condor Express   CRUISE
(☑ 805-882-0088; www.condorcruises.com; 301 W Cabrillo Blvd; 2½/4½hr cruises adult from $50/99, child 5-12yr from $30/50; 👪) Take a whale-watching excursion aboard the high-speed catamaran *Condor Express.* Whale sightings are guaranteed, so if you miss out the first time, you'll get a free voucher for another cruise.

🛏 Sleeping

Hello, sticker shock: even basic motel rooms can command over $200 in summer. Less expensive motels line upper State St, north of downtown, and Hwy 101.

★ Santa Barbara

Auto Camp   CAMPGROUND $$
(☑ 888-405-7553; http://autocamp.com/sb; 2717 De La Vina St; d $175-215; 🅿 ❄ 🛜 🐕) 🏄 Ramp up the retro chic and bed down with vintage style in one of five shiny metal Airstream trailers parked near upper State St, north of downtown. All five architect-designed trailers have unique perks, such as a clawfoot tub or extra twin-size beds for kiddos, as well as full kitchen and complimentary cruiser bikes to borrow.

Agave Inn   MOTEL $$
(☑ 805-687-6009; www.agaveinnsb.com; 3222 State St; r from $119; 🅿 ❄ 🛜) While it's still just a motel at heart, this boutique-on-a-budget property's 'Mexican pop meets modern' motif livens things up with a color palette from a Frida Kahlo painting. Flat-screen TVs,

microwaves, minifridges and air-con make it a standout option. Family-sized rooms have a kitchenette and pullout sofa beds.

Harbor House Inn MOTEL $$
(☎805-962-9745; www.harborhouseinn.com; 104 Bath St; r from $180; P❄✳🐾) Down by the harbor, this friendly, converted motel offers brightly lit studios with hardwood floors and a beachy design scheme. Most have a full kitchen and one has a fireplace. Rates include a welcome basket of breakfast goodies (with a two-night minimum stay) and beach towels, chairs, umbrellas and three-speed bicycles to borrow.

★ **Inn of the Spanish Garden** BOUTIQUE HOTEL $$$
(☎805-564-4700; www.spanishgardeninn.com; 915 Garden St; r from $309; P❄✳@🐾🏊) At this Spanish Colonial–style inn, casual elegance, first-rate service and a romantic central courtyard will have you lording about like the don of your own private villa. Rooms have a balcony or patio, beds have luxurious linens and bathrooms have oversized tubs. The concierge service is top-notch. Chill by the small outdoor pool, or unwind with a massage in your room.

✖ Eating

★ **La Super-Rica Taqueria** MEXICAN $
(☎805-963-4940; 622 N Milpas St; ⊙11am-9pm Thu-Mon) It's small, there's usually a line and the decor is basic, but all that's forgotten once you've tried the most authentic Mexican food in Santa Barbara. The fish tacos, tamales and other Mexican staples have been drawing locals and visitors here for decades, and were loved by TV chef and author Julia Child.

★ **Mesa Verde** VEGAN $$
(☎805-963-4474; http://mesaverderestaurant. com; 1919 Cliff Dr; mains $15-21; ⊙11am-9pm; 🥗) 🍷 Perusing the menu is usually a quick job for vegetarians – but not at Mesa Verde. There are so many delicious, innovative all-vegan dishes on offer here (the tacos with jackfruit are a highlight) that meat-avoiding procrastinators will be in torment. If in doubt, pick a selection and brace yourself for flavor-packed delights. Meat-eaters welcome (and possibly converted).

★ **Lark** CALIFORNIAN $$$
(☎805-284-0370; www.thelarksb.com; 131 Anacapa St; shared plates $7-17, mains $19-48; ⊙5-10pm Tue-Sun, bar to midnight) 🍷 There's no better place in Santa Barbara County to taste the bountiful farm and fishing goodness of this stretch of SoCal coast. Named after an antique Pullman railway car, this chef-run restaurant in the Funk Zone morphs its menu with the seasons, presenting unique flavor combinations such as crispy Brussels sprouts with dates or harissa-and-honey chicken. Make reservations.

🍷 Drinking & Nightlife

Nightlife orbits lower State St and the Funk Zone. Ramble between a dozen wine-tasting rooms along the city's Urban Wine Trail (www.urbanwinetrailsb.com). Check the free alt-weekly *Santa Barbara Independent* (www.independent.com) for an entertainment calendar.

★ **Figueroa Mountain Brewing Co** BAR
(☎805-694-2252; www.figmtnbrew.com; 137 Anacapa St; ⊙11am-11pm Sun-Thu, to midnight Fri & Sat) Father and son brewers have brought their gold-medal-winning hoppy IPA, Danish red lager and double IPA from Santa Barbara's Wine Country to the Funk Zone. Knowledgeable staff will help you choose before you clink glasses on the taproom's open-air patio while acoustic acts play. Enter on Yanonali St.

ℹ Information

Santa Barbara Visitors Center (☎805-568-1811, 805-965-3021; www.santabarbaraca. com; 1 Garden St; ⊙9am-5pm Mon-Sat, 10am-5pm Sun, closes 1hr earlier Nov-Jan) Pick up maps and brochures while consulting with the helpful but busy staff.

ℹ Getting There & Around

Amtrak (☎800-872-7245; www.amtrak.com; 209 State St) trains run south to LA ($31, 2½ hours) via Carpinteria, Ventura and Burbank's airport, and north to San Luis Obispo ($22, 2¾ hours) and Oakland ($43, 8¾ hours), with stops in Paso Robles, Salinas and San Jose.

Greyhound (☎805-965-7551; www.greyhound. com; 224 Chapala St) operates a few direct buses daily to LA ($15, three hours), Santa Cruz ($42, six hours) and San Francisco ($40, nine hours).

Local buses operated by the **Metropolitan Transit District** (MTD; ☎805-963-3366; www. sbmtd.gov) cost $1.75 per ride (exact change, cash only). Equipped with front-loading bike racks, these buses travel all over town and to adjacent communities.

Santa Barbara to San Luis Obispo

You can speed up to San Luis Obispo in less than two hours along Hwy 101, or take all day detouring to wineries, historical missions and hidden beaches.

A scenic backcountry drive north of Santa Barbara follows Hwy 154, where you can go for the grape in the wine country (www.sbcountywines.com) of the Santa Ynez and Santa Maria Valleys. Ride along with **Sustainable Vine** (☑805-698-3911; www.sustainablevinewinetours.com; tours from $150) ✆, or just follow the pastoral **Foxen Canyon Wine Trail** (www.foxencanyonwinetrail.com) north to discover cult winemakers' vineyards. In the town of **Los Olivos**, where two dozen more wine-tasting rooms await, **Los Olivos Wine Merchant & Café** (☑805-688-7265; www.winemerchantcafe.com; 2879 Grand Ave; mains breakfast $9-12, lunch & dinner $13-29; ☉11:30am-8:30pm daily, also 8-10:30am Sat & Sun) is a charming Cal-Mediterranean bistro with a wine bar.

Further south, the Danish-immigrant village of **Solvang** (www.solvangusa.com) abounds with windmills and fairy-tale bakeries. Fuel up on breakfast biscuits, buttermilk fried-chicken sandwiches and farm-fresh salads at **Succulent Café** (☑805-691-9444; www.succulentcafe.com; 1555 Mission Dr; mains breakfast & lunch $5-15, dinner $16-36; ☉10am-3pm & 5-9pm Mon & Wed-Sun, from 8:30am Sat & Sun; ✆🐾) ✆. For a picnic lunch or BBQ takeout, swing into **El Rancho Market** (☑805-688-4300; http://elranchomarket.com; 2886 Mission Dr; ☉6am-11pm; 🐾), east of Solvang's 19th-century Spanish Colonial **mission** (☑805-688-4815; www.missionsantaines.org; 1760 Mission Dr; adult $5, child under 12yr free; ☉9am-4:30pm; P🐾).

Follow Hwy 246 about 15 miles west of Hwy 101 to **La Purísima Mission State Historic Park** (☑805-733-3713; www.lapurisimamission.org; 2295 Purísima Rd, Lompoc; per car $6; ☉9am-5pm, tours at 1pm Wed-Sun & public holidays Sep-Jun, daily Jul & Aug; P🐾) ✆. It's one of California's most evocative Spanish Colonial missions, with flowering gardens, livestock pens and adobe buildings. South of Lompoc off Hwy 1, Jalama Rd travels 14 twisting miles to windswept **Jalama Beach County Park** (☑recorded info 805-736-3616; www.countyofsb.org/parks/jalama; Jalama Beach Rd, Lompoc; per car $10). Book ahead for its crazy-popular **campground** (☑805-568-2460; www.countyofsb.org/parks/jalama.sbc; 9999 Jalama Rd, Lompoc; tent/RV sites from $25/40, cabins $120-220; P🐾), where simple cabins have kitchenettes.

Where Hwy 1 rejoins Hwy 101, **Pismo Beach** is a long, lazy stretch of sand with a **butterfly grove** (☑805-773-5301; www.monarchbutterfly.org; Hwy 1; ☉sunrise-sunset; 🐾) ✆**FREE**, where migratory monarchs perch in eucalyptus trees from late October until February. Adjacent **North Beach Campground** (☑reservations 800-444-7275; www.reserveamerica.com; 399 S Dolliver St; tent & RV sites $40; 🐾) offers beach access and hot showers. Dozens of motels and hotels stand by the ocean and along Hwy 101, but rooms fill quickly, especially on weekends. **Pismo Lighthouse Suites** (☑805-773-2411; www.pismolighthousesuites.com; 2411 Price St; ste from $239; P🐾@🛜🐾🐾) has everything vacationing families need, including a life-sized outdoor chessboard; ask about off-season discounts. Near Pismo's seaside pier, **Old West Cinnamon Rolls** (☑805-773-1428; www.oldwestcinnamonrolls.com; 861 Dolliver St; snacks $3-6; ☉6:30am-5:30pm; 🐾) offers gooey goodness. Uphill at the **Cracked Crab** (☑805-773-2722; www.crackedcrab.com; 751 Price St; mains $16-59; ☉11am-9pm Sun-Thu, to 10pm Fri & Sat; 🐾), make sure you don a plastic bib before a fresh bucket o' seafood gets dumped on your butcher-paper-covered table.

The nearby town of **Avila Beach** has a sunny waterfront promenade, an atmospherically creaky wooden fishing pier and a historical **lighthouse** (☑guided hike reservations 805-528-8758, trolley tour reservations 805-540-5771; www.pointsanluislighthouse.org; lighthouse $5, incl trolley tour adult/child 3-12yr $20/15; ☉guided hikes 8:45am-1pm Wed & Sat, trolley tours noon & 1pm Wed & Sat). Back toward Hwy 101, pick juicy fruit and feed the goats at **Avila Valley Barn** (☑805-595-2816; www.avilavalleybarn.com; 560 Avila Beach Dr; ☉9am-6pm mid-Mar–late Dec, to 5pm Thu-Mon Jan–mid-Mar; 🐾) farmstand, then do some stargazing from a private redwood hot tub at **Sycamore Mineral Springs** (☑805-595-7302; www.sycamoresprings.com; 1215 Avila Beach Dr; 1hr per person $15-20; ☉8am-midnight).

San Luis Obispo

Halfway between LA and San Francisco, San Luis Obispo is normally a low-key place. Cal Poly college students inject a healthy dose of hubbub into the streets, bars and cafes, especially during the weekly **farmers market** (☑805-541-0286; www.downtownslo.com; Higuera

St; ⏱6-9pm Thu; 🖊🍴) 🌿, which turns downtown's Higuera St into a party with live music and sidewalk BBQs.

Like several other California towns, SLO grew up around a Spanish Catholic **mission** (☎805-543-6850; www.missionsanluisobispo.org; 751 Palm St; suggested donation $5; ⏱9am-5pm late Mar-Oct, to 4pm Nov–mid-Mar; 🍴), founded in 1772 by Junípero Serra. These days, SLO is just a grape's throw from thriving Edna Valley wineries (www.slowine.com), known for crisp chardonnay and subtle pinot noir.

🛏 Sleeping

Motels cluster off Hwy 101 in San Luis Obispo, especially off Monterey St northeast of downtown and around Santa Rosa St (Hwy 1).

HI Hostel Obispo HOSTEL $
(☎805-544-4678; www.hostelobispo.com; 1617 Santa Rosa St; dm $32-39, r from $65, all with shared bath; ⏱check in 4:30-10pm; @🛜) 🌿 On a tree-lined street near SLO's train station, this solar-powered, avocado-colored hostel inhabits a converted Victorian, which gives it a bit of a B&B feel. Amenities include a kitchen, bike rentals (from $10 per day) and complimentary sourdough pancakes and coffee for breakfast. BYOT (bring your own towel).

Madonna Inn HOTEL $$
(☎805-543 3000; www.madonnainn.com; 100 Madonna Rd; r $209-329; ❄@🛜🏊) The fantastically campy Madonna Inn is a garish confection visible from Hwy 101. Japanese tourists, vacationing Midwesterners and irony-loving hipsters adore the 110 themed rooms – including Yosemite Rock, Caveman and hot-pink Floral Fantasy (check out photos online). The urinal in the men's room is a bizarre waterfall. But the best reason to stop here? Old-fashioned cookies from the storybook bakery.

🍴 Eating & Drinking

Downtown in SLO, Higuera St is littered with college-student-jammed bars, and craft-beer fans have plenty to look forward to.

Luna Red FUSION $$
(☎805-540-5243; www.lunaredslo.com; 1023 Chorro St; shared plates $6-20, mains $20-39; ⏱11:30am-9:30pm Mon-Thu, to midnight Fri, 9am-11:30pm Sat, to 9pm Sun; 🖊) 🌿 Local bounty from the land and sea, artisan cheeses and farmers-market produce pervade the chef's Californian, Asian and Mediterranean

small-plates menu. Cocktails and glowing lanterns enhance a sophisticated ambience indoors and there is a mission-view garden patio where you can linger over brunch.

Guiseppe's Cucina Rustica ITALIAN $$
(☎805-541-9922; www.giuseppesrestaurant.com; 849 Monterey St; pizza & sandwiches $13-16, mains $21-36; ⏱11:30am-11pm) 🌿 Visit Guiseppe's for a leisurely downtown lunch of excellent salad, pizza and antipasti, or to grab a take-out meatball or Caprese sandwich from the deli counter out the front. Out the back, the facade of the heritage Sinsheimer Brothers building looks over a shaded courtyard that's equally suited to long dinners of slow-roasted chicken and SLO County wines.

Luis Wine Bar WINE BAR
(☎805-762-4747; www.luiswinebar.com; 1021 Higuera St; ⏱3-11pm Sun-Thu, to midnight Fri-Sat) Evincing style and sophistication, this downtown wine bar has wide-open seating, a strong craft-beer list of more than 70 brews, and small plates including cheese and charcuterie platters. Welcome to an urbane but unpretentious alternative to SLO's more raucous student-heavy bars and pubs.

ℹ Information

San Luis Obispo Visitor Center (☎805-781-2777; www.visitslo.com; 895 Monterey St; ⏱10am-5pm Sun-Wed, to 7pm Thu-Sat) Free maps and tourist brochures.

ℹ Getting There & Away

Amtrak (☎800-872-7245; www.amtrak.com; 1011 Railroad Ave) runs daily Seattle–LA *Coast Starlight* and twice-daily SLO–San Diego *Pacific Surfliner* trains. Both routes head south to Santa Barbara ($35, 2¾ hours) and Los Angeles ($57, 5½ hours). The *Coast Starlight* connects north via Paso Robles to Salinas ($28, 3 hours) and Oakland ($41, six hours). Several daily Thruway buses link to more regional trains.

San Luis Obispo Regional Transit Authority (RTA; ☎805-541-2228; www.slorta.org; single-ride fares $1.50-3, day pass $5) operates daily county-wide buses with limited weekend services. All buses are equipped with bicycle racks. Lines converge on downtown's **transit center** (cnr Palm & Osos Sts).

SLO Transit (☎805-541-2877; www.slocity.org) runs local city buses ($1.25), plus a trolley (50¢) that loops around downtown every 20 minutes between 5pm and 9pm on Thursdays year-round, on Fridays from June to early September and on Saturdays from April through October.

Morro Bay to Hearst Castle

A dozen miles northwest of San Luis Obispo via Hwy 1, Morro Bay is a sea-sprayed fishing town where **Morro Rock**, a volcanic peak jutting up from the ocean floor, is your first hint of the coast's upcoming drama. (Never mind those power-plant smokestacks obscuring the views.) Hop aboard boat cruises or rent kayaks along the **Embarcadero**, which is packed with touristy shops. A classic seafood shack, **Giovanni's** (☏877-521-4467; www.giovannisfishmarket.com; 1001 Front St; mains $5-15; ◷market 9am-6pm, restaurant from 11am; ♠) cooks killer garlic fries and fish-and-chips. Midrange motels cluster uphill off Harbor and Main Sts and along Hwy 1.

Nearby are fantastic state parks for coastal hikes and **camping** (☏reservations 800-444-7275; www.reserveamerica.com; tent & RV sites $25-50; ❀). South of the Embarcadero, **Morro Bay State Park** (☏805-772-2694; www.parks.ca.gov; 60 State Park Rd; park entry free, museum adult/child under 17yr $3/free; ◷museum 10am-5pm; P♠) has a natural-history museum for kids. Further south in Los Osos, west of Hwy 1, wilder **Montaña de Oro State Park** (☏805-528-0513; www.parks.ca.gov; 3550 Pecho Valley Rd, Los Osos; ◷6am-10pm; P♠) ✍ FREE features coastal bluffs, tide pools, sand dunes, peak hiking and mountain-biking trails. Its Spanish name (which means 'mountain of gold') comes from native California poppies that blanket the hillsides in spring.

Heading north of downtown Morro Bay along Hwy 1, surfers love the Cal-Mexican **Taco Temple** (☏805-772-4965; www.tacotemple.com; 2680 Main St; mains $10-16; ◷11am-9pm; ♠), a cash-only joint, and **Ruddell's Smokehouse** (☏805-995-5028; www.smokerjim.com; 101 D St; dishes $4-13; ◷11am-6pm; ♠❀), serving smoked-fish tacos by the beach in Cayucos. Vintage motels on Cayucos' Ocean Ave include the cute, family-run **Seaside Motel** (☏805-995-3809; www.seasidemotel.com; 42 S Ocean Ave; d $80-170; ☎). You can fall asleep to the sound of the surf at the ocean-view **Shoreline Inn on the Beach** (☏805-995-3681; www.cayucosshorelineinn.com; 1 N Ocean Ave; r $159-249; ❀).

North of Harmony (population: just 18 souls), Hwy 46 leads east into the vineyards of **Paso Robles wine country** (www.pasowine.com). Tired of wine? Off Hwy 101 in Paso Robles, **Firestone Walker Brewing Company** (☏805-225.5913; www.firestonebeer.

com; 1400 Ramada Dr; ◷tasting room & restaurant 10am-9pm, tours 10:30am-3:30pm) offers brewery tours ($3; reservations recommended), or just stop by the taproom for samples.

Further north along Hwy 1, quaint **Cambria** has lodgings along unearthly-pretty Moonstone Beach, where the **Blue Dolphin Inn** (☏805-927-3300; www.cambriainns.com; 6470 Moonstone Beach Dr; r from $188; ☎❀) embraces modern rooms with romantic fireplaces. Inland, **Bridge Street Inn** (☏805-215-0724; www.bsicambria.com; 4314 Bridge St; r $50-90, vans $30; ☎) sleeps like a hostel but feels like a B&B, while the retro **Cambria Palms Motel** (☏805-927-4485; www.cambriapalmsmotel.com; 2662 Main St; r from $109; ◷check-in 3-9pm; ☎❀) has clean-lined rooms and cruiser bicycles to borrow. An artisan cheese and wine shop, **Indigo Moon** (☏805-927-2911; www.indigomooncafe.com; 1980 Main St; lunch $9-14, dinner $14-35; ◷10am-9pm; ♠) ✎ has breezy bistro tables and market-fresh salads and sandwiches at lunch. With a sunny patio and takeout counter, **Linn's Easy as Pie Cafe** (☏805-927-0371; www.linnsfruitbin.com; 4251 Bridge St; dishes $6-12; ◷10am-7pm Mon-Thu, to 8m Fri-Sat; ♠) is famous for its olallieberry pie.

About 10 miles north of Cambria, hilltop **Hearst Castle** (☏info 805-927-2020, reservations 800-444-4445; www.hearstcastle.org; 750 Hearst Castle Rd; tours adult/child 5-12yr from $25/12; ◷from 9am; P♠) is California's most famous monument to wealth and ambition. Newspaper magnate William Randolph Hearst entertained Hollywood stars and royalty at this fantasy estate dripping with European antiques, accented by shimmering pools and surrounded by flowering gardens. Try to make tour reservations in advance or show up early in the day.

Across Hwy 1, overlooking a historic whaling pier, **Sebastian's** (☏805-927-3307; www.facebook.com/SebastiansSanSimeon; 442 SLO–San Simeon Rd; mains $9-14; ◷11am-4pm Tue-Sun) sells Hearst Ranch beef burgers and giant sandwiches for impromptu beach picnics. Five miles back south along Hwy 1, past a forgettable row of budget and midrange motels in San Simeon, **Hearst San Simeon State Park** (☏reservations 800-444-7275; www.reserveamerica.com; Hwy 1; tent & RV sites $25) offers primitive and developed creekside campsites.

Heading north, Point Piedras Blancas is home to an enormous **elephant seal colony** that breeds, molts, sleeps, frolics and, occasionally, goes aggro on the beach. Keep your distance from these wild animals who move faster on the sand than you can. The sign-posted vista point, about 4.5 miles north of Hearst Castle, has interpretive panels. Seals haul out year-round, but the frenzied birthing and mating season runs from January through March. Nearby, the 1875 **Piedras Blancas Light Station** (☑805-927-7361; www.piedrasblancas.gov; off Hwy 1; tours adult/child 6-17yr $10/5; ☺tours 9:45am Mon-Tue & Thu-Sat mid-Jun–Aug, 9:45am Tue, Thu & Sat Sep–mid-Jun) is an outstandingly scenic spot; call ahead to confirm tour schedules (no reservations) and directions to the meet-up point.

Big Sur

Much ink has been spilled extolling the raw beauty and energy of this 100-mile stretch of craggy coastline sprawling south of Monterey Bay. More a state of mind than a place you can pinpoint on a map, Big Sur has no traffic lights, banks or strip malls. When the sun goes down, the moon and stars are the only illumination – if summer fog hasn't extinguished them, that is.

Lodging, food and gas are all scarce and pricey in Big Sur. Demand for rooms is high year-round, especially on weekends, so book ahead. The free Big Sur Guide (www.bigsurcalifornia.org), an info-packed newspaper, is available at roadside businesses. The day use parking fee (per car $10) charged at Big Sur's state parks is valid for same-day entry to all except Limekiln.

It's about 25 miles from Hearst Castle to blink-and-you-miss-it Gorda, home of **Treebones Resort** (☑877-424-4787; www.treebonesresort.com; 71895 Hwy 1; campsites $95, d with shared bath from $320; ☺☎☒), which offers back-to nature clifftop yurts. Basic United States Forest Service (USFS) campgrounds are just off Hwy 1 at shady **Plaskett Creek** (☑reservations 877-477-6777; www.recreation.gov; Hwy 1; tent & RV sites $35) and oceanside **Kirk Creek** (☑reservations 877-444-6777; www.recreation.gov; Hwy 1; tent & RV sites $35).

Ten miles north of Lucia is new-agey **Esalen Institute** (☑831-667-3000; www.esalen.org; 55000 Hwy 1), famous for its esoteric workshops and ocean-view hot springs. By reservation only (call ☑831-667-3047 between 9am and noon daily), you can frolic nekkid in the baths from 1am to 3am nightly ($30, credit cards only). It's surreal.

Another 3 miles north, **Julia Pfeiffer Burns State Park** (☑831-667-2315; www.parks.ca.gov; Hwy 1; per car $10; ☺30min before

PINNACLES NATIONAL PARK

A study in geological drama, **Pinnacles National Park's** (☑831-389-4486; www.nps.gov/pinn; per car $15; ☐☒) ☞craggy monoliths, sheer-walled canyons and twisting caves are the result of millions of years of erosion. Besides hiking and rock climbing, the park's biggest attractions are endangered California condors and talus caves where bats live. It's best visited during spring or fall; summer's heat is too extreme.

sunrise-30min after sunset; ☐☒) ☞ hides 80ft-high McWay Falls, one of California's only coastal waterfalls.

Over 7 miles further north, the beatnik **Henry Miller Memorial Library** (☑831-667-2574; www.henrymiller.org; 48603 Hwy 1; ☺10am-5pm & longer hours for specific events; ☎) is the art and soul of Big Sur bohemia, with a jam-packed bookstore, live-music concerts, open-mic nights and outdoor film screenings. Opposite, food takes a backseat to dramatic panoramic views at clifftop **Nepenthe** (☑831-667-2345; www.nepenthebigsur.com; 48510 Hwy 1; mains $18-50; ☺11:30am-4:30pm & 5-10pm; ☒☒), meaning 'island of no sorrow.'

Heading north, rangers at **Big Sur Station** (☑831-667-2315; www.bigsurcalifornia.org/contact.html; 47555 Hwy 1; ☺9am-4pm) have information on area camping and hiking, including the popular 10-mile one-way hike to **Sykes Hot Springs**. On the opposite side of Hwy 1 just south, turn onto Sycamore Canyon Rd, which drops two narrow, twisting miles to crescent-shaped **Pfeiffer Beach** (☑831-667-2315; www.fs.usda.gov/lpnf; end of Sycamore Canyon Rd; per car $10; ☺9am-8pm; ☐☒☒), with a towering offshore sea arch. Strong currents make it too dangerous for swimming. Dig down into the sand – it's purple!

Next up, **Pfeiffer Big Sur State Park** (☑831-667-2315; www.parks.ca.gov; 47225 Hwy 1; per car $10; ☺30min before sunrise-30min after sunset; ☐☒) ☞ is crisscrossed by sun-dappled trails through redwood forests. Make **campground** (☑reservations 800-444-7275; www.reserveamerica.com; 47225 Hwy 1; tent & RV sites $35-50; ☐☒) reservations or ramp up the luxury and watch the surf break far below from your private deck at the delightful **Post Ranch Inn** (☑831-667-2200; www.postranchinn.com; 47900 Hwy 1; d from $925; ☐☒☀@☎☒).

Most of Big Sur's commercial activity is concentrated just north along Hwy 1, including private campgrounds with rustic cabins, motels, restaurants, gas stations and shops. **Glen Oaks Motel** (📞831-667-2105; www.glenoaksbigsur.com; 47080 Hwy 1; d $300-475; 🅿😊🛜) 🍴 is a redesigned 1950s redwood-and-adobe motor lodge with romantic, woodsy cabins and cottages. Nearby, the Big Sur River Inn's **general store** (📞831-667-2700; www.bigsurriverinn.com; 46840 Hwy 1; breakfast & lunch $15-20, dinner $15-40; 🕐8am-9pm; 🛜🛗) hides a burrito and fruit-smoothie bar at the back, while **Maiden Publick House** (📞831-667-2355; Village Center Shops, Hwy 1; 🕐3pm-2am Mon-Thu, from 1pm Fri & from 11am Sat-Sun) offers an encyclopedic beer menu and live-music. Back south by the post office, put together a picnic at **Big Sur Deli** (📞831-667-2225; www.bigsurdeli.com; 47520 Hwy 1; snacks $2-12; 🕐7am-8pm), attached to the laid-back **Big Sur Taphouse** (📞831-667-2225; www.bigsurtaphouse.com; 47520 Hwy 1; 🕐noon-10pm Mon-Fri, 10am-midnight Sat, to 10pm Sun; 🛜), a beer-centric bar with board games and pub grub.

Heading north again, don't skip **Andrew Molera State Park** (📞831-667-2315; www.parks.ca.gov; Hwy 1; per car $10; 🕐30min before sunrise-30min after sunset; 🅿🛗) 🍴, a gorgeous trail-laced pastiche of grassy meadows, waterfalls, ocean bluffs and rugged beaches. Learn all about endangered California condors at the park's **Discovery Center** (📞831-624-1202; www.ventanaws.org/discovery_center; Andrew Molera State Park; 🕐10am-4pm Sat & Sun late May–early Sep; 🅿🛗) 🍴 **FREE**. From the dirt parking lot, a 0.3-mile trail leads to a primitive, no-reservations **campground** (www.parks.ca.gov; Hwy 1; tent sites $25).

Six miles before the landmark **Bixby Creek Bridge**, you can go on a tour (includ-

ing a seasonal moonlight walk) of the 1889 lighthouse at **Point Sur Historic Park** (📞831-625-4419; www.pointsur.org; off Hwy 1; adult/child 6-17yr from $12/5; 🕐tours usually at 1pm Wed, 10am Sat & Sun Oct-Mar; 10am & 2pm Wed & Sat, 10am Sun Apr-Sep, also 10am Thu Jul & Aug) **FREE**. Check online or call for tour schedules and directions to the meeting point. Arrive early since space is limited (no reservations).

Carmel

With borderline-fanatical devotion to its canine citizens, quaint Carmel has the well-manicured feel of a country club. Watch the parade of behatted ladies toting fancy-label shopping bags to lunch and dapper gents driving top-down convertibles along Ocean Ave, the village's slow-mo main drag.

👁 Sights & Activities

Escape downtown Carmel's harried shopping streets and stroll tree-lined neighborhoods on the lookout for domiciles charming and peculiar. The Hansel and Gretel houses on Torres St, between 5th and 6th Avenues, are just how you'd imagine them. Another eye-catching house in the shape of a ship, made from local river rocks and salvaged ship parts, is on Guadalupe St near 6th Ave.

★ Mission San Carlos Borromeo de Carmelo   CHURCH
(📞831-624-1271; www.carmelmission.org; 3080 Rio Rd; adult/child 7-17yr $6.50/2; 🕐9:30am-7pm; 🛗) Monterey's original mission was established by Franciscan friar Junípero Serra in 1770, but poor soil and the corrupting influence of Spanish soldiers forced the move to Carmel two years later. Today this is one of California's most strikingly beautiful missions, an oasis of solemnity bathed in flowering gardens. The mission's adobe chapel was later replaced with an arched basilica made of stone quarried in the Santa Lucia Mountains. Museum exhibits are scattered throughout the meditative complex.

★ Point Lobos State Natural Reserve   STATE PARK
(📞831-624-4909; www.pointlobos.org; Hwy 1; per car $10; 🕐8am-7pm, to 5pm early Nov–mid-Mar; 🅿🛗) 🍴 They bark, they bathe and they're fun to watch – sea lions are the stars here at Punta de los Lobos Marinos (Point of the Sea Wolves), almost 4 miles south of Carmel, where a dramatically rocky coastline offers

---

ℹ **DRIVING HIGHWAY 1**

Driving this narrow two-lane highway through Big Sur and beyond is very slow going. Allow about three hours to cover the distance between the Monterey Peninsula and San Luis Obispo, and much more if you want to explore the coast. Traveling after dark can be risky and, more to the point, it's futile, because you'll miss out on the seascapes. Watch out for cyclists and make use of signposted roadside pullouts to let faster-moving traffic pass.

excellent tide-pooling. The full perimeter hike is 6 miles, but shorter walks take in wild scenery too, including **Bird Island**, shady cypress groves, the historical **Whaler's Cabin** and the **Devil's Cauldron**, a whirlpool that gets splashy at high tide.

🛏 Sleeping

Shockingly overpriced boutique hotels, inns and B&Bs fill up quickly in Carmel-by-the-Sea, especially in summer. Ask the **chamber of commerce** (☑831-624-2522; www.carmelcalifornia.org; San Carlos St, btwn 5th & 6th Aves; ⊙10am-5pm) about last-minute deals. For better-value lodgings, head north to Monterey.

🍴 Eating & Drinking

Winery tasting rooms dot Carmel's compact and well-kept centre, and the best option for late-night drinks is the cool and energetic scene at **Barmel** (☑831-626-2095; www.facebook.com/BarmelByTheSea; San Carlos St, btwn Ocean & 7th Aves; ⊙2pm-2am Mon-Fri, 1pm-2am Sat-Sun).

Cultura Comida y Bebida   MEXICAN $$
(☑831-250-7005; www.culturacarmel.com; Dolores St btwn 5th & 6th Aves; mains $19-32; ⊙11:30am-midnight Thu-Sun, 5pm-midnight Mon-Tue) Located near art galleries in a brick-lined courtyard, Cultura Comida y Bebida is a relaxed bar and eatery inspired by the food of Oaxaca in Mexico. Pull up a seat at the elegant bar and sample a vertical tasting of mezcal, or partner Monterey squid tostadas and oak-roasted trout with cilantro, lime and garlic with Californian and French wines.

Mundaka   TAPAS $$
(☑831-624-7400; www.mundakacarmel.com; San Carlos St, btwn Ocean & 7th Aves; small plates $8-15; ⊙5-9pm Sun-Thu, to 10pm Fri-Sat) This stone courtyard hideaway is a svelte escape from Carmel's stuffy 'newly wed and nearly dead' crowd. Taste Spanish tapas and housemade sangria while world beats spin. Partner the garlic prawns or grilled octopus with a chilled glass of local wine.

Monterey

Working-class Monterey is all about the sea. What draws many visitors is a world-class aquarium overlooking **Monterey Bay National Marine Sanctuary**, which protects dense kelp forests and a sublime variety of marine life, including seals and sea lions, dolphins and whales. The city itself possesses the best-preserved historical evidence of California's Spanish and Mexican periods, with many restored adobe buildings. An afternoon's wander through downtown's historic quarter promises to be more edifying than time spent in the tourist ghettos of Fisherman's Wharf and Cannery Row.

👁 Sights

⭐**Monterey Bay Aquarium**   AQUARIUM
(☑info 831-648-4800, tickets 866-963-9645; www.montereybayaquarium.org; 886 Cannery Row; adult/child 3-12yr/youth 13-17yr $50/30/40; ⊙10am-6pm; ⬛) 🎫 Monterey's most mesmerizing experience is its enormous aquarium, built on the former site of the city's largest sardine cannery. All kinds of aquatic creatures are featured, from kid-tolerant sea stars and slimy sea slugs to animated sea otters and surprisingly nimble 800lb tuna. The aquarium is much more than an impressive collection of glass tanks – thoughtful placards underscore the bay's cultural and historical contexts.

⭐**Monterey State Historic Park**   HISTORIC SITE
(☑info 831-649-7118; www.parks.ca.gov) `FREE` Old Monterey is home to an extraordinary assemblage of 19th-century brick and adobe buildings, administered as Monterey State Historic Park and all found along a 2-mile self-guided walking tour portentously called the 'Path of History.' You can inspect dozens of buildings, many with charming gardens; expect some to be open while others not, according to a capricious schedule dictated by unfortunate state-park budget cutbacks.

Cannery Row   HISTORIC SITE
(⬛) John Steinbeck's novel *Cannery Row* immortalized the sardine-canning business that was Monterey's lifeblood for the first half of the 20th century. A bronze **bust** of the Pulitzer Prize–winning writer sits at the bottom of Prescott Ave, just steps from the unabashedly touristy experience that the famous row has devolved into. The historical **Cannery Workers Shacks** at the base of flowery Bruce Ariss Way provide a sobering reminder of the hard lives led by Filipino, Japanese, Spanish and other immigrant laborers.

🏃 Activities

You can spot whales off the coast of Monterey Bay year-round. The season for blue and humpback whales runs from April to early December, while gray whales pass by from mid-December through March. Tour boats depart from Fisherman's Wharf and **Moss Landing** (🔗info 831-917-1042, tickets 888-394-7810; www.sanctuarycruises.com; 7881 Sandholdt Rd; tours $45-55; 🖰) 🔗. Reserve trips at least a day in advance; be prepared for a bumpy, cold ride.

Monterey Bay Whale Watch   BOATING

(🔗831-375-4658; www.montereybaywhalewatch.com; 84 Fisherman's Wharf; 3hr tour adult/child 4-12yr from $44/29; 🖰) Morning and afternoon departures; young children and well-behaved dogs are welcome on board.

Adventures by the Sea   CYCLING, KAYAKING

(🔗831-372-1807; www.adventuresbythesea.com; 299 Cannery Row; rental per day kayak or bicycle $35, SUP set $50, kayak tours from $60; ⏱9am-5pm, to 8pm in summer; 🖰) Beach cruisers, electric bikes and watersports gear rentals and tours available at multiple locations on Cannery Row and **downtown** (🔗831-372-1807; www.adventuresbythesea.com; 210 Alvarado St; ⏱9am-5pm, to 8pm in summer; 🖰).

Monterey Bay Dive Charters   DIVING

(🔗831-383-9276; www.mbdcscuba.com; scuba-gear rental $75, shore/boat dives from $65/85) Arrange shore or boat dives and rent a full scuba kit with wetsuit from this well-reviewed outfitter.

🛏 Sleeping

Book ahead for special events, on weekends and in summer. To avoid the tourist congestion and jacked-up prices of Cannery Row, look to Pacific Grove. Cheaper motels line Munras Ave, south of downtown, and N Fremont St, east of Hwy 1.

HI Monterey Hostel   HOSTEL $

(🔗831-649-0375; www.montereyhostel.org; 778 Hawthorne St; dm with shared bath $30-40; ⏱check in 4-10pm; @🛜) Four blocks from Cannery Row and the aquarium, this simple, clean hostel houses single-sex and mixed dorms, as well as private rooms accommodating up to five people. Budget backpackers stuff themselves silly with make-your-own-pancake breakfasts. Reservations strongly recommended. Take MST bus 1 from downtown's Transit Plaza.

Monterey Hotel   HISTORIC HOTEL $$

(🔗831-375-3184; www.montereyhotel.com; 406 Alvarado St; r $131-275; 🛜) In the heart of downtown and a short walk from Fisherman's Wharf, this 1904 edifice harbors smallish but renovated rooms and suites with Victorian-styled furniture and plantation shutters. No elevator. A recently added boutique spa offers massage and beauty treatments.

★ Jabberwock   B&B $$$

(🔗831-372-4777; www.jabberwockinn.com; 598 Laine St; r $249-339; @🛜) Barely visible through a shroud of foliage, this 1911 arts-and-crafts house hums a playful *Alice in Wonderland* tune through seven immaculate rooms, a few with fireplaces and Jacuzzis. Over afternoon tea and cookies or evening wine and hors d'oeuvres, ask the genial hosts about the house's many salvaged architectural elements. Weekends are more expensive and have a two-night minimum.

🍴 Eating

Uphill from Monterey's Cannery Row, Lighthouse Ave features casual, budget-friendly eateries including Hawaiian barbecue and Thai flavors, through to sushi and Middle Eastern kebabs. Downtown around Alvarado St also features cafes and pub dining.

Zab Zab   NORTHERN THAI $

(🔗831-747-2225; www.zabzabmonterey.com; 401 Lighthouse Ave; mains $11-15; ⏱11am-2:30pm & 5-9pm Tue-Fri, noon-9pm Sat-Sun; 🔗) Our pick of Lighthouse Ave's ethnic eateries, Zab Zab channels the robust flavors of northeast Thailand. The bijou cottage interior is perfect in cooler weather, but during summer the best spot is on the deck surrounded by a pleasantly overgrown garden. For fans of authentic Thai heat, go for the Kai Yang grilled chicken. Lunch boxes ($11 to $13) are good value.

LouLou's Griddle in the Middle   AMERICAN $$

(🔗831-372-0568; www.loulousgriddle.com; Municipal Wharf 2; mains $8-17; ⏱7:30am-4pm Sun, Mon, Wed & Thu, to 6pm Fri-Sat, closed Tue; 🖰🐾) Stroll down the municipal wharf to this zany diner, best for breakfasts of ginormous pancakes and omelettes with Mexican *pico de gallo* salsa, or fresh seafood for lunch. Breezy outdoor tables are dog-friendly, or secure a spot at the counter and chat with the friendly chefs.

Montrio Bistro   CALIFORNIAN $$$

(🔗831-648-8880; www.montrio.com; 414 Calle Principal; shared plates $12-30, mains $25-44; ⏱4:30-10pm Sun-Thu, to 11pm Fri & Sat) 🔗 Inside a 1910 firehouse, Montrio combines leather walls and iron trellises, and the tables have butcher paper and crayons for kids. The eclectic seasonal menu mixes local, organic fare with Californian, Asian and European flair, including tapas-style shared plates and mini desserts. Well-priced bar snacks and happy-hour prices from 4:30pm daily are a fine end-of-the-day option.

ℹ️ Information

Monterey Visitor Center (☑️831-657-6400; www.seemonterey.com; 401 Camino el Estero; ⏰9am-6pm Mon-Sat, to 5pm Sun, closes 1hr earlier Nov-Mar) Ask for a *Monterey County Literary & Film Map*. Also a handy accommodation-booking service.

ℹ️ Getting There & Away

Monterey-Salinas Transit (MST; ☑️888-678-2871; www.mst.org; Jules Simmoneau Plaza; single-ride fares $1.50-3.50, day pass $10) operates local and regional buses; routes converge on downtown's Transit Plaza (cnr Pearl & Alvarado Sts), including routes to Pacific Grove, Carmel and Big Sur. From late May until early September, MST's free trolley loops around downtown, Fisherman's Wharf and Cannery Row between 10am and 7pm or 8pm daily.

Santa Cruz

Santa Cruz is a city of madcap fun, with a vibrant but chaotic downtown. On the waterfront is the famous beach boardwalk, and in the hills redwood groves embrace the University of California Santa Cruz (UCSC) campus. Plan at least half a day here, but to appreciate the aesthetic of jangly skirts, crystal pendants and Rastafarian dreadlocks, stay longer and plunge headlong into the rich local brew of surfers, students, punks and eccentric characters.

◎ Sights & Activities

One of the best things to do in Santa Cruz is simply stroll, shop and watch the sideshow along **Pacific Ave** downtown. A 15-minute walk away is the beach and **Municipal Wharf**, where seafood restaurants, gift shops and barking sea lions compete for attention. Ocean-view **West Cliff Dr** follows the waterfront southwest of the wharf, paralleled by a paved recreational path.

★ Santa Cruz
Beach Boardwalk   AMUSEMENT PARK
(☑️831-423-5590; www.beachboardwalk.com; 400 Beach St; per ride $4-7, all-day pass $37-82; ⏰daily Apr-early Sep, seasonal hours vary; P♿) The West Coast's oldest beachfront amusement

park, this 1907 boardwalk has a glorious old-school Americana vibe. The smell of cotton candy mixes with the salt air, punctuated by the squeals of kids hanging upside down on carnival rides. Famous thrills include the **Giant Dipper**, a 1924 wooden roller coaster, and the 1911 **Looff carousel**, both National Historic Landmarks. During summer, catch free midweek movies and Friday-night concerts by rock veterans you may have thought were already dead.

★ Seymour Marine
Discovery Center   MUSEUM
(☑️831-459-3800; http://seymourcenter.ucsc.edu; 100 Shaffer Rd; adult/child 3-16yr $8/6; ⏰10am-5pm Tue-Sun; P♿) 🌿 By Natural Bridges State Beach, this kids educational center is part of UCSC's Long Marine Laboratory. Interactive natural-science exhibits include tidal touch pools and aquariums, while outside you can gawk at the world's largest blue-whale skeleton. Guided one-hour tours happen at 1pm, 2pm and 3pm daily, with a special 30-minute tour for families with younger children at 11am; sign up for tours in person an hour in advance (no reservations).

Santa Cruz Surfing Museum   MUSEUM
(☑️831-420-6289; www.santacruzsurfingmuseum.org; 701 W Cliff Dr; by donation; ⏰10am-5pm Wed-Mon Jul 4-early Sep, noon-4pm Thu-Mon early Sep-Jul 3; ♿) A mile southwest of the wharf along the coast, this tiny museum inside an old lighthouse is packed with memorabilia, including vintage redwood surfboards. Fittingly, Lighthouse Point overlooks two popular surf breaks.

Natural Bridges State Beach   BEACH
(☑️831-423-4609; www.parks.ca.gov; 2531 W Cliff Dr; per car $10; ⏰8am-sunset; P♿) Best for sunsets, this family favorite has lots of sand, tide pools and monarch butterflies from mid-October through mid-February. It's at the far western end of W Cliff Dr.

O'Neill Surf Shop   SURFING
(☑️831-475-4151; www.oneill.com; 1115 41st Ave; wetsuit/surfboard rental from $15/25; ⏰9am-8pm Mon-Fri, from 8am Sat & Sun) Head east toward Pleasure Point to worship at this internationally renowned surfboard-maker's flagship store, with branches on the beach boardwalk and downtown.

★ Santa Cruz Food Tour   FOOD
(☑️866-736-6343; www.santacruzfoodtour.com; per person $59; ⏰2:30-6pm Fri & Sat) Combining

Afghan flavors, a farm-to-table bistro, vegan cupcakes and artisan ice cream, these highly recommended walking tours also come with a healthy serving of local knowledge and interesting insights into Santa Cruz history, culture and architecture. Sign up for a tour when you first arrive in town to get your bearings in the tastiest way possible.

Richard Schmidt Surf School   SURFING
(☑ 831-423-0928; www.richardschmidt.com; 849 Almar Ave; 2hr group/1hr private lesson $90/120; ☑) Award-winning, time-tested surf school can get you out there, all equipment included. Summer surf camps hook adults and kids alike.

🛏 Sleeping

Santa Cruz does not have enough beds to satisfy demand: expect high prices at peak times for nothing-special rooms. Places near the beach boardwalk range from friendly to frightening. For a decent motel, cruise Ocean St inland or Mission St (Hwy 1). Several new hotels scheduled to open from late 2017 will improve the city's accommodations options. Contact the visitor center for details.

**California State Park
Campgrounds**   CAMPGROUND $
(☑ reservations 800-444-7275; www.reserveameri ca.com; tent & RV sites $35-65) Book well ahead to camp at state beaches off Hwy 1 south of Santa Cruz or up in the foggy Santa Cruz Mountains off Hwy 9. Family-friendly campgrounds include Henry Cowell Redwoods State Park in Felton and New Brighton State Beach in Capitola.

HI Santa Cruz Hostel   HOSTEL $
(☑ 831-423-8304; www.hi-santacruz.org; 321 Main St; dm $28-31, r $85-140, all with shared bath; ☑ check in 5-10pm; @ ☜) Budget overnighters dig this cute hostel at the century-old Carmelita Cottages, just two blocks from the beach. Cons: midnight curfew, daytime lockout (11am to 5pm) and three-night maximum stay. Reservations essential. Street parking costs $2.

★ Adobe on Green B&B   B&B $$
(☑ 831-469-9866; www.adobeongreen.com; 103 Green St; r $179; ℗ ☺ ☜) Peace and quiet are the mantras at this place, a short walk from Pacific Ave. The hosts are practically invisible, but their thoughtful touches are everywhere, from boutique-hotel amenities in spacious, solar-powered rooms to breakfast spreads from their organic gardens.

✖ Eating

Downtown Santa Cruz is packed with casual cafes. If you're looking for seafood, wander the wharf's takeout counter joints. Mission St, near UCSC, and 41st Ave offer cheaper eats.

Akira   JAPANESE $
(☑ 831-600-7093; www.akirasantacruz.com; 1222 Soquel Ave; sushi & sashimi $10-15; ☑ 11am-11pm; ☑) Head northeast of downtown Santa Cruz to Soquel Ave's restaurant strip for Akira's modern take on sushi, sashimi and other Japanese flavors. Combining sake, craft brews and a surf-town ambience, Akira's menu harnesses briny-fresh tuna, salmon, eel and shellfish for a huge variety of sushi. Bento boxes for lunch ($10 to $14) are good value, and there's a wide range of vegetarian options.

★ Assembly   CALIFORNIAN $$
(☑ 831-824-6100; www.assembly.restaurant; 1108 Pacific Ave; brunch & lunch $12-16, dinner mains $22-28; ☑ 11:30am-9pm Mon & Wed-Thu, to 10pm Fri, 10am-10pm Sat-Sun; ☑) Farm-to-table and proudly regional flavors feature at this excellent bistro in downtown Santa Cruz. Assembly's Californian vibe belies real culinary nous in the kitchen, and the seasonal menu could include dishes such as chicken breast with crispy pancetta or a truffle-laced asparagus risotto. Don't miss trying the Scotch olives and meatballs with a tasting flight of local craft beers.

Soif   BISTRO $$
(☑ 831-423-2020; www.soifwine.com; 105 Walnut Ave; small plates $5-17, mains $19-25; ☑ 5-9pm Sun-Thu, to 10pm Fri & Sat; ☑) Following a recent makeover, one of Santa Cruz's more established restaurants is now better than ever, and the chic and cosmopolitan decor showcases a stunning wine list – including tasting flights ($20.50) of local Santa Cruz varietals – and a well-curated menu with standouts like slow-roasted pork and scallops wrapped in bacon. Wine-matching suggestions are available for all dishes.

🍷 Drinking & Nightlife

Santa Cruz's downtown overflows with bars, lounges and coffee shops. Heading west on Mission St (Hwy 1), craft breweries and wine-tasting rooms fill the raffish industrial ambience of the Smith St and Ingalls St courtyards.

Verve Coffee Roasters   CAFE

(☑ 831-600-7784; www.vervecoffee.com; 1540 Pacific Ave; ☺ 6:30am-9pm; 🛜) To sip finely roasted artisan espresso or a cup of rich pour-over coffee, join the surfers and hipsters at this industrial-zen cafe. Single-origin brews and house blends rule. It's been so successful around their home patch that it's also opened satellite cafes in Los Angeles and Tokyo.

Lupulo Craft Beer House   CRAFT BEER

(☑ 831-454-8306; www.lupulosc.com; 233 Cathcart St; ☺ 11:30am-10pm Sun-Thu, to 11:30pm Fri-Sat) Named after the Spanish word for hops, Lupulo Craft Beer House is an essential downtown destination for traveling beer fans. Modern decor combines with an ever-changing taplist – often including seasonal brews from local California breweries – and good bar snacks such as empanadas, tacos and charcuterie plates. Almost 400 bottled and canned beers create delicious panic for the indecisive drinker.

ⓘ Information

Santa Cruz Visitor Center (☑ 831-425-1234; www.santacruzca.org; 303 Water St; ☺ 9am-noon & 1-4pm Mon-Fri, 11am-3pm Sat & Sun) Free public internet terminal, maps and brochures.

ⓘ Getting There & Around

Santa Cruz is 75 miles south of San Francisco via coastal Hwy 1 or Hwy 17, a nail-bitingly narrow, winding mountain road. Monterey is about an hour's drive further south via Hwy 1.

Santa Cruz Airport Shuttles (☑ 831-421-9883; www.santacruzshuttles.com) runs shared shuttles to/from the airports at San Jose ($50), San Francisco ($80) and Oakland ($80), with a $5 cash discount; the second passenger pays $10.

   Greyhound (☑ 800-231-2222; www.greyhound. com; Metro Center, 920 Pacific Ave) has a few daily buses to San Francisco ($16, three hours), Salinas ($15, one hour), Santa Barbara ($53, six hours) and Los Angeles ($59, nine hours).

   Santa Cruz Metro (☑ 831-425-8600; www. scmtd.com; 920 Pacific Ave; single-ride/day pass $2/6) operates local and countywide bus routes that converge on downtown's **Metro Center** (920 Pacific Ave). Hwy 17 express buses link Santa Cruz with San Jose's Amtrak/CalTrain station ($5, 50 minutes, once or twice hourly).

   From late May through early September, the **Santa Cruz Trolley** (www.santacruztrolley.com; per ride 25¢) shuttles between downtown and the beach from 11am until 9pm daily.

SAN FRANCISCO & THE BAY AREA

San Francisco

Grab your coat and a handful of glitter, and enter the land of fog and fabulousness. So long, inhibitions; hello, San Francisco.

History

Native Californians had found gold in California long before 1849 – but it hardly seemed worth mentioning, as long as there were oysters for lunch and venison for dinner. Once word circulated, San Francisco was transformed almost overnight from bucolic trading backwater to gold-rush metropolis. Over 160 years of booms, busts, history-making high jinks and lowdown dirty dealings later, SF remains the wildest city in the west.

◉ Sights

Most major museums are downtown, though Golden Gate Park is home to the de Young Museum and the California Academy of Sciences. The city's most historic districts are the Mission, Chinatown, North Beach and the Haight. Galleries are clustered downtown and in North Beach, the Mission, Potrero Flats and Dogpatch. You'll find hilltop parks citywide, but Russian, Nob and Telegraph Hills are the highest and most panoramic.

◎ Embarcadero

★ **Ferry Building**   LANDMARK

(Map p982; ☑ 415-983-8030; www.ferrybuilding marketplace.com; cnr Market St & the Embarcadero; ☺ 10am-7pm Mon-Fri, 8am-6pm Sat, 11am-5pm Sun; ♿; ☑ 2, 6, 9, 14, 21, 31, Ⓜ Embarcadero, Ⓑ Embarcadero) Hedonism is alive and well at this transit hub turned gourmet emporium, where foodies happily miss their ferries over Sonoma oysters and bubbly, SF craft beer and Marin-raised beef burgers, or locally roasted coffee and just-baked cupcakes. Star chefs are frequently spotted at the farmers market (p994) that wraps around the building all year.

★ **Exploratorium**   MUSEUM

(Map p982; ☑ 415-528-4444; www.explorati um.edu; Pier 15; adult/child $30/20, 6-10pm Thu $15; ☺ 10am-5pm Tue-Sun, over 18yr only 6-10pm Thu; Ⓟ ♿; Ⓜ E, F) 🖋 Is there a science to

CALIFORNIA SAN FRANCISCO

skateboarding? Do toilets really flush counterclockwise in Australia? At San Francisco's hands-on science museum, you'll find out things you wished you learned in school. Combining science with art and investigating human perception, the Exploratorium nudges you to question how you perceive the world around you. The setting is thrilling: a 9-acre, glass-walled pier jutting straight into San Francisco Bay, with large outdoor portions you can explore free of charge, 24 hours a day.

Union Square & Civic Center

Bordered by high-end department stores, **Union Square** (Map p982; btwn Geary, Powell, Post & Stockton Sts; 🚋 Powell-Mason, Powell-Hyde, Ⓜ Powell, Ⓑ Powell) was named for pro-Union Civil War rallies held here 150 years ago. People-watch with espresso from **Emporio Rulli** (Map p982; 📞 415-433-1122; www.rulli.com; Union Sq; pastries $4-8; ⏲ 8am-7pm; 🚻; Ⓜ Powell, Ⓑ Powell) cafe.

★ **Asian Art Museum**   MUSEUM
(Map p982; 📞 415-581-3500; www.asianart.org; 200 Larkin St; adult/student/child $15/10/free, 1st Sun of month free; ⏲ 10am-5pm Tue, Wed & Fri-Sun, to 9pm Thu; 🚻; Ⓜ Civic Center, Ⓑ Civic Center) Imaginations race from ancient Persian miniatures to cutting-edge Japanese minimalism across three floors spanning 6000 years of Asian art. Besides the largest collection outside Asia – 18,000 works – the museum offers excellent programs for all ages, from shadow-puppet shows and tea tastings

with star chefs to mixers with cross-cultural DJ mash-ups.

Powell St Cable Car Turnaround   LANDMARK
(Map p982; www.sfmta.com; cnr Powell & Market Sts; 🚋 Powell-Mason, Mason-Hyde, Ⓜ Powell, Ⓑ Powell) Peek through the passenger queue at Powell and Market Sts to spot cable-car operators leaping out, gripping the chassis of each trolley and slooowly turning the car atop a revolving wooden platform. Cable cars can't go in reverse, so they need to be turned around by hand here at the terminus of the Powell St lines. Riders queue up midmorning to early evening here to secure a seat, with raucous street performers and doomsday preachers on the sidelines as entertainment.

Chinatown

Since 1848, this community has survived riots, bootlegging gangsters and earthquakes.

★ **Chinatown Alleyways**   AREA
(Map p982; btwn Grant Ave, Stockton St, California St & Broadway; 🚌 1, 30, 45, 🚋 Powell-Hyde, Powell-Mason, California) The 41 historic alleyways packed into Chinatown's 22 blocks have seen it all since 1849: gold rushes and revolution, incense and opium, fire and icy receptions. In clinker-brick buildings lining these narrow backstreets, temple balconies jut out over bakeries, laundries and barbers – there was nowhere to go but up in Chinatown after 1870, when laws limited Chinese immigration, employment and housing. **Chinatown**

SAN FRANCISCO IN ...

One Day

Since the Gold Rush, San Francisco adventures have started in Chinatown, where you can still find hidden fortunes – in cookies, that is. After dining on dim sum, beat it to **City Lights Bookstore** to revel in Beat poetry. Stroll past the Italian streetside cafes of **North Beach** to climb **Coit Tower** for 360-degree city and bay views. Then head to Civic Center's **Asian Art Museum**, where art transports you across centuries and oceans within an hour. Have an early dinner at the **Ferry Building** before taking a spooky night tour of **Alcatraz**. Make your escape from the island prison in time to hit the dance floor in **SoMa** clubs.

Two Days

Start your day in the **Mission** amid mural-covered garage doors lining **Balmy Alley**, then step inside meditative **Mission Dolores**. Break for burritos before hoofing it to the **Haight** for flashbacks at vintage boutiques and the Summer of Love site: **Golden Gate Park**. Glimpse bay views atop the **de Young Museum**, take a walk on the empirical side at the **California Academy of Sciences** and brave howling winds on the **Golden Gate Bridge**.

San Francisco & the Bay Area

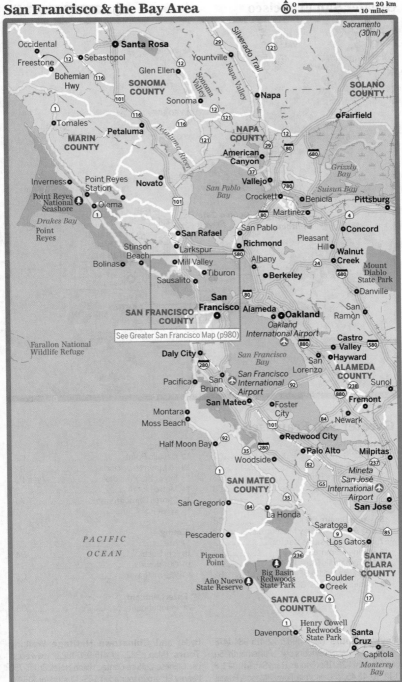

Greater San Francisco

Greater San Francisco

◎ Top Sights
1 Alcatraz	C2
2 Crissy Field	C3
3 Golden Gate Bridge	C3
4 Point Bonita Lighthouse	B3

◎ Sights
5 Alamo Square Park	C3
6 Bay Area Discovery Museum	C2
7 Bay Model Visitors Center	B2
8 Marine Mammal Center	B2
9 Mt Tamalpais State Park	A1
10 Nike Missile Site SF-88	B2
11 Presidio Officers' Club	C3

⬤ Sleeping
12 Cavallo Point	C2
13 HI Marin Headlands	B2
Inn at the Presidio	(see 11)
14 Metro Hotel	C3
15 Pantoll Campground	A1
16 West Point Inn	A1

⊗ Eating
17 A16	C3
18 Ichi Sushi	C4
19 Outerlands	B4
20 Warming Hut	C3

✹ Entertainment
21 Independent	C3

Alleyway Tours (Map p982; ☎ 415-984-1478; www.chinatownalleywaytours.org; Portsmouth Sq; adult/student $26/16; ⊗ tours 11am Sat; 🚼; 🚌 1, 8, 10, 12, 30, 41, 45, 🚋 California, Powell-Mason, Powell-

Hyde) and **Chinatown Heritage Walking Tours** (Map p982; ☎ 415-986-1822; www.cccsf. us; Chinese Culture Center, Hilton Hotel, 3rd fl, 750 Kearny St; group tour adult $25-30, student $15-20, private tour (1-4 people) $60; ☉ tours 10am, noon & 2pm Tue-Sat; 🚼; 🚃1, 8, 10, 12, 30, 41, 45, 🚋California, Powell-Mason, Powell-Hyde) offer community-supporting, time-traveling strolls through defining moments in American history.

Chinese Historical
Society of America
MUSEUM

(CHSA; Map p982; ☎415-391-1188; www.chsa.org; 965 Clay St; adult/student/child $15/10/free; ☉11am-4pm Wed-Sun; 🚼; 🚃1, 8, 30, 45, 🚋California, Powell-Mason, Powell-Hyde) **FREE** Picture what it was like to be Chinese in America during the gold rush, transcontinental railroad construction or Beat heyday in this 1932 landmark, built as Chinatown's YWCA by Julia Morgan (chief architect of Hearst Castle). CHSA historians unearth fascinating artifacts, from 1920s silk *qipao* dresses to Chinatown miniatures created by set designer Frank Wong. Exhibits reveal once-popular views of Chinatown, including the sensationalist opium-den exhibit at San Francisco's 1915 Panama-Pacific International Expo inviting fairgoers to 'Go Slumming' in Chinatown.

◎ North Beach

★City Lights Books
CULTURAL CENTER

(Map p982; ☎415-362-8193; www.citylights.com; 261 Columbus Ave; ☉10am-midnight; 🚼; 🚃8, 10, 12, 30, 41, 45, 🚋Powell-Mason, Powell-Hyde) Free speech and free spirits have flourished here since 1957, when City Lights founder and poet Lawrence Ferlinghetti and manager Shigeyoshi Murao won a landmark ruling defending their right to publish Allen Ginsberg's magnificent epic poem *Howl*. Celebrate your freedom to read freely in the designated Poet's Chair upstairs overlooking Jack Kerouac Alley, load up on zines on the mezzanine and entertain radical ideas downstairs in the new Pedagogies of Resistance section.

Beat Museum
MUSEUM

(Map p982; ☎800-537-6822; www.kerouac.com; 540 Broadway; adult/student $8/5, walking tours $25; ☉museum 10am-7pm, walking tours 2-4pm Sat; 🚃8, 10, 12, 30, 41, 45, 🚋Powell-Mason) The closest you can get to the complete Beat experience without breaking a law. The 1000-plus artifacts in this museum's literary-ephemera collection include the sublime (the banned edition of Ginsberg's *Howl*, with the author's own annotations) and the ridiculous (those Kerouac bobblehead dolls are definite head-shakers). Downstairs, watch Beat-era films in ramshackle theater seats

redolent with the odors of literary giants, pets and pot. Upstairs, pay your respects at shrines to individual Beat writers.

◎ Russian Hill & Nob Hill

★Lombard Street
STREET

(Map p982; 🚋Powell-Hyde) You've seen the eight switchbacks of Lombard St's 900 block in a thousand photographs. The tourist board has dubbed it 'the world's crookedest street,' which is factually incorrect: Vermont St in Potrero Hill deserves that award, but Lombard is much more scenic, with its redbrick pavement and lovingly tended flowerbeds. It wasn't always so bent; before the arrival of the car it lunged straight down the hill.

★Cable Car Museum
HISTORIC SITE

(Map p982; ☎415-474-1887; www.cablecarmuseum.org; 1201 Mason St; donations appreciated; ☉10am-6pm Apr-Sep, to 5pm Oct-Mar; 🚼; 🚋Powell-Mason, Powell-Hyde) **FREE** Hear that whirring beneath the cable-car tracks? That's the sound of the cables that pull the cars, and they all connect inside the city's long-functioning cable-car barn. Grips, engines, braking mechanisms… if these warm your gearhead heart, you'll be besotted with the Cable Car Museum.

Diego Rivera Gallery
GALLERY

(Map p982; ☎415-771-7020; www.sfai.edu; 800 Chestnut St; ☉9am-7pm; 🚃30, 🚋Powell-Mason) **FREE** Diego Rivera's 1931 *The Making of a Fresco Showing the Building of a City* is a trompe l'oeil fresco within a fresco, showing the artist himself, pausing to admire his work, as well as the work in progress that is San Francisco. The fresco covers an entire wall in the Diego Rivera Gallery at the San Francisco Art Institute.

◎ Fisherman's Wharf

★Maritime National
Historical Park
HISTORIC SITE

(Map p982; ☎415-447-5000; www.nps.gov/safr; 499 Jefferson St, Hyde St Pier; 7-day ticket adult/child $10/free; ☉9:30am-5pm Oct-May, to 5:30pm Jun-Sep; 🚼; 🚃19, 30, 47, 🚋Powell-Hyde, Ⓜ F) Four historic ships are floating museums at this maritime national park, Fisherman's Wharf's most authentic attraction. Moored along Hyde St Pier are the 1891 schooner *Alma*, which hosts guided sailing trips in summer; 1890 steamboat *Eureka*; paddlewheel tugboat *Eppleton Hall*; and iron-hulled *Balclutha*.

Downtown San Francisco

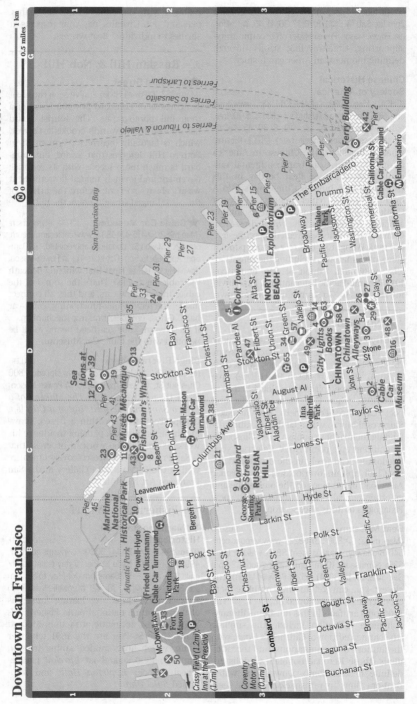

San Francisco Bay

Ferries to Tiburon & Vallejo
Ferries to Sausalito
Ferries to Larkspur

Aquatic Park

Maritime National Historical Park

Pier 45

Sea Lions at Pier 39

Musée Mécanique

Fisherman's Wharf

Pier 43

Pier 41

Pier 39

Pier 35

Pier 33

Pier 31

Pier 29

Pier 27

Pier 23

Pier 19

Pier 17

Pier 15

Pier 9

Pier 7

Pier 3

Pier 1

Pier 2

Ferry Building

The Embarcadero

Exploratorium

Coit Tower

NORTH BEACH

Powell-Mason Cable Car Turnaround

Powell-Hyde (Friedel Klussmann) Cable Car Turnaround

Victoria Park

McDowell Ave

Fort Mason

Crissy Field (1.2mi); Inn at the Presidio (1.7mi)

Coventry Motor Inn (0.1mi)

Lombard St

RUSSIAN HILL

George Sterling Park

Lombard Street

CHINATOWN

Chinatown Alleyways

City Lights Books

Cable Car Museum

NOB HILL

The Embarcadero

Broadway

Drumm St

Commercial St

California St

Cable Car Turnaround

Embarcadero

Washington St

Jackson St

Pacific Ave

Walton Park

Clay St

Stone St

John St

Taylor St

Ina Coolbrith Park

Aladdin Tce

Filbert St

Valparaiso St

Columbus Ave

Hyde St

Larkin St

Jones St

Polk St

Leavenworth St

Bergen Pl

North Point St

Beach St

Bay St

Francisco St

Chestnut St

Lombard St

Stockton St

Union St

Green St

Vallejo St

Pacific Ave

Jackson St

Broadway

Franklin St

Gough St

Octavia St

Laguna St

Buchanan St

Polk St

Franklin St

Van Ness

Alta St

Pardee Al

August Al

Filbert St

Green St

Vallejo St

Union St

Chestnut St

Francisco St

Greenwich St

Filbert St

San Francisco

0   1 km
0   0.5 miles

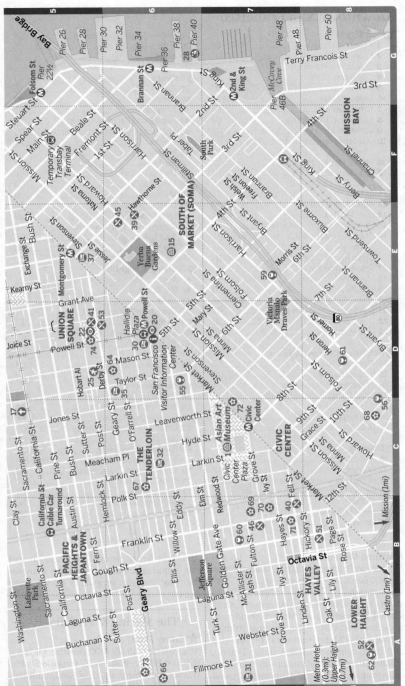

Downtown San Francisco

◎ **Top Sights**
1 Asian Art Museum C7
2 Cable Car Museum D4
3 Chinatown Alleyways..............................D4
4 City Lights Books D4
5 Coit Tower...D3
6 Exploratorium..E3
7 Ferry Building F4
8 Fisherman's Wharf..................................C2
9 Lombard Street..C3
10 Maritime National Historical
    Park...B2
11 Musée Mécanique....................................C2
12 Sea Lions at Pier 39 ....D1

◎ **Sights**
13 Aquarium of the Bay...............................D2
14 Beat Museum D4
15 Children's Creativity Museum E6
16 Chinese Historical Society of
    America..D4
    Diego Rivera Gallery ....(see 21)
17 Grace Cathedral.......................................C5
18 Maritime Museum....................................B2
19 Pier 39 ....D1
20 Powell St Cable Car Turnaround..........D6
21 San Francisco Art Institute....................C3
22 Union Square..D5
23 USS Pampanito...C1

◎ **Activities, Courses & Tours**
24 Alcatraz Cruises......................................E2
25 Blazing Saddles..D5
26 Chinatown Alleyway Tours E4
27 Chinatown Heritage Walking
    Tours...E4
28 City Kayak...G6
29 Drag Me Along Tours..............................D4

◎ **Sleeping**
30 Axiom...D6
31 Chateau Tivoli..A7
32 HI San Francisco City Center C6
33 HI San Francisco Fisherman's
    Wharf..A2
34 Hotel Bohème...D3
35 Marker D6

36 Pacific Tradewinds Hostel.....................E4
37 Palace Hotel E5
38 San Remo Hotel.......................................C2

◎ **Eating**
39 Benu...E6
40 Cala..B7
41 Emporio Rulli D5
42 Ferry Plaza Farmers Market..................F4
43 Fisherman's Wharf Crab Stands C2
44 Greens...A2
45 In Situ..E6
46 Jardinière..B7
47 Liguria Bakery..D3
48 Mister Jiu's...D4
49 Molinari D3
50 Off the Grid A2
51 Rich Table...B8
52 Rosamunde Sausage Grill A8
53 Tout Sweet..D5
54 Z & Y..D4

◎ **Drinking & Nightlife**
55 Aunt Charlie's Lounge.............................D6
56 Bar Agricole C8
57 Caffe Trieste D3
58 Comstock Saloon D4
59 EndUp..E7
60 Smuggler's Cove.......................................B7
61 Stud..D8
62 Toronado...A8
63 Vesuvio..D4

◎ **Entertainment**
64 American Conservatory Theater...........D6
65 Beach Blanket Babylon............................D3
66 Fillmore Auditorium A6
67 Great American Music Hall.....................C6
68 Oasis..C8
69 San Francisco Ballet...............................B7
    San Francisco Opera.....................(see 69)
70 San Franciso Symphony..........................B7
71 SFJAZZ Center...B7
72 Strand Theater...C7
73 Sundance Kabuki Cinema A6
74 TIX Bay Area...D5

Maritime Museum　　　　　　　　MUSEUM
(Aquatic Park Bathhouse; Map p982; www.maritime.
org; 900 Beach St; ◎10am-4pm; ⛟; ☐19, 30, 47,
☐ Powell-Hyde) FREE A monumental hint to
sailors in need of a scrub, this restored, ship-
shaped 1939 Streamline Moderne landmark
is decked out with Works Progress Administration (WPA) art treasures: playful seal
and frog sculptures by Beniamino Bufano,
Hilaire Hiler's surreal underwater dreamscape murals, and recently uncovered wood
reliefs by Richard Ayer. Acclaimed African
American artist Sargent Johnson created
the stunning carved green slate marquee
doorway and the verandah's mesmerizing
aquatic mosaics.

◎ The Marina & Presidio

★**Crissy Field**　　　　　　　　　　PARK
(Map p980; ☑415-561-4700; www.crissyfield.org;
1199 East Beach; ⓟ🐾; ☐30, PresidiGo Shuttle)
War is for the birds at Crissy Field, a military
airstrip turned waterfront nature preserve

with knockout Golden Gate views. Where military aircraft once zoomed in for landings, bird-watchers now huddle in the silent rushes of a reclaimed tidal marsh. Joggers pound beachside trails and the only security alerts are raised by puppies suspiciously sniffing surfers. On foggy days, stop by the certified-green **Warming Hut** (☑415-561-3042; www.parksconservancy.org/visit/eat/warming-hut.html; 983 Marine Dr; items $4-9; ⊘9am-5pm; P; 🚌PresidiGo shuttle) ✐ to browse regional-nature books and warm up with fair-trade coffee.

Presidio Officers' Club　　HISTORIC BUILDING
(Map p980; ☑415-561-4165; www.presidio.gov/officers-club-internal; 50 Moraga Ave; ⊘10am-6pm Tue, Wed, Sat & Sun, to 8pm Thu & Fri; 🚌PresidiGo shuttle) FREE The Presidio's oldest building dates to the late 1700s, and was fully renovated in 2015, revealing gorgeous Spanish-Moorish adobe architecture. The free **Heritage Gallery** shows the history of the Presidio, from Native American days to the present. Moraga Hall – the former officers'-club lounge – is a lovely spot to sit fireside and also has free wi-fi. Thursday and Friday evenings the club hosts a dynamic lineup of events and lectures; check the website.

★**Musée Mécanique**　　AMUSEMENT PARK
(Map p982; ☑415-346-2000; www.museemechanique.org; Pier 45, Shed A; ⊘10am-8pm; 🚻; 🚌47, 🚋Powell-Mason, Powell-Hyde, Ⓜ E, F) A flashback to penny arcades, the Musée Mécanique houses a mind-blowing collection of vintage mechanical amusements. Sinister, freckle-faced Laughing Sal has creeped out kids for over a century, but don't let this manic mannequin deter you from the best arcade west of Coney Island. A quarter lets you start brawls in Wild West saloons, peep at belly dancers through a vintage Mutoscope and even learn a cautionary tale about smoking opium.

★**Sea Lions at Pier 39**　　SEA LIONS
(Map p982; www.pier39.com; Pier 39, cnr Beach St & the Embarcadero; ⊘24hr; 🚻; 🚌15, 37, 49, Ⓜ E, F) Beach bums took over San Francisco's most coveted waterfront real estate in 1990 and have been making a public display of themselves ever since. Naturally these unkempt squatters have become San Francisco's favorite mascots, and since California law requires boats to make way for marine mammals, yacht owners have to relinquish valuable slips to accommodate as many as 1300 sea

lions. These giant mammals 'haul out' onto the docks between January and July, and whenever else they feel like sunbathing.

★**Baker Beach**　　BEACH
(Map p988; ☑10am-5pm 415-561-4323; www.nps.gov/prsf; ⊘sunrise-sunset; P; 🚌29, PresidiGo Shuttle) Picnic amid wind-sculpted pines, fish from craggy rocks or frolic nude at mile-long Baker Beach, with spectacular views of the Golden Gate. Crowds come weekends, especially on fog-free days; arrive early. For nude sunbathing (mostly straight girls and gay boys), head to the north. Families in clothing stick to the south, nearer parking. Mind the currents and the c-c-cold water.

⊙ The Mission & the Castro

★**Balmy Alley**　　PUBLIC ART
(Map p986; ☑415-285-2287; www.precitaeyes.org; btwn 24th & 25th Sts; 🚌10, 12, 14, 27, 48, 🅱24th St Mission) Inspired by Diego Rivera's 1930s San Francisco murals and provoked by US foreign policy in Central America, 1970s Mission *muralistas* (muralists) led by Mia Gonzalez set out to transform the political landscape, one mural-covered garage door at a time. Today, Balmy Alley murals span three decades, from an early memorial for El Salvador activist Archbishop Óscar Romero to a homage to Frida Kahlo, Georgia O'Keeffe and other trailblazing female modern artists.

Mission Dolores　　CHURCH
(Misión San Francisco de Asís; Map p986; ☑415-621-8203; www.missiondolores.org; 3321 16th St; adult/child $5/3; ⊘9am-4pm Nov-Apr, to 4:30pm May-Oct; 🚌22, 33, 🅱16th St Mission, Ⓜ J) The city's oldest building and its namesake, whitewashed adobe Misión San Francisco de Asís was founded in 1776 and rebuilt from 1782 with conscripted Ohlone and Miwok labor – a graveyard memorial hut commemorates 5000 Ohlone and Miwok laborers who died in mission measles epidemics in the early 19th century. Today the modest adobe structure is overshadowed by the ornate adjoining 1913 basilica, featuring stained-glass windows depicting California's 21 missions.

★**Dolores Park**　　PARK
(Map p986; http://sfrecpark.org/destination/mission-dolores-park; Dolores St, btwn 18th & 20th Sts; ⊘6am-10pm; 🚻🧒; 🚌14, 33, 49, 🅱16th St Mission, Ⓜ J) Semiprofessional tanning and taco picnics: welcome to San Francisco's sunny side. Dolores Park has something for everyone,

The Mission & The Castro

from street ball and tennis to the Mayan-pyramid playground (sorry, kids: no blood sacrifices allowed). Political protests and other favorite local sports happen year-round, and there are free movie nights and mime troupe performances in summer. Climb to the upper southwestern corner for superb views of downtown, framed by palm trees.

★ **Women's Building** NOTABLE BUILDING
(Map p986; ☎415-431-1180; www.womensbuild ing.org; 3543 18th St; ♿; ☒14, 22, 33, 49, Ⓑ16th St Mission, ⓂJ) The nation's first women-owned-and-operated community center has quietly done good work with 170 women's organizations since 1979, but the 1994 addition of the *Maestrapeace* mural showed the Women's Building for the landmark it truly is. An all-star team of *muralistas* covered the building with images of cross-cultural goddesses and women trailblazers, including Nobel Prize winner Rigoberta Menchú, poet

Audre Lorde, artist Georgia O'Keeffe and former US Surgeon General Dr Joycelyn Elders.

◎ The Haight & Around

★ **Haight Street** STREET
(Map p988; Haight St, btwn Fillmore & Stanyan Sts; ☒7, 22, 33, 43, ⓂN) Was it the fall of 1966 or the winter of '67? As the Haight saying goes, if you can remember the Summer of Love, dude, you probably weren't there. The fog was laced with pot, sandalwood incense and burning draft cards, entire days were spent contemplating Day-Glo Grateful Dead posters, and the corner of **Haight and Ashbury Sts** (Map p988; ☒6, 7, 33, 37, 43) became the turning point for an entire generation.

Alamo Square Park PARK
(Map p980; www.sfparksalliance.org/our-parks/ parks/alamo-square; cnr Hayes & Steiner Sts; ☺sunrise-sunset; ♿☂; ☒5, 21, 22, 24) Hippie communes and Victorian bordellos, jazz

The Mission & The Castro

◎ **Top Sights**
1 Balmy Alley D3
2 Dolores Park B2
3 Women's Building C2

◎ **Sights**
4 Mission Dolores B1

◔ **Activities, Courses & Tours**
5 Precita Eyes Mission Mural
   Tours D3

◔ **Sleeping**
6 Inn San Francisco C2
7 Parker Guest House B2

◍ **Eating**
8 Al's Place C4

9 Commonwealth C2
10 Craftsman & Wolves C2
11 La Taqueria C4

◔ **Drinking & Nightlife**
12 %ABV B1
13 Blackbird B1
14 Cafe Flore A1
15 El Rio C4
16 HiTops A1

◎ **Entertainment**
17 Roxie Cinema C1

◍ **Shopping**
18 Aggregate Supply C2
19 Betabrand C2

greats and opera stars, earthquakes and Church of Satan services: these genteel **'Painted Lady' Victorian mansions** have hosted them all since 1857, and survived elegantly intact. Pastel Postcard Row mansions along Alamo Sq's eastern side pale in comparison with the colorful characters along the northwestern end of this hilltop park. The northern side features Barbary Coast baroque mansions at their most bombastic, bedecked with fish-scale shingles and gingerbread trim dripping from peaked roofs.

◉ Golden Gate & Around

In 1865 the city voted to turn more than 1000 acres of sand dunes into Golden Gate Park. At the park's western end is **Ocean Beach** (Map p988; ☎415-561-4323; www.parksconservancy.org; Great Hwy; ☉sunrise-sunset; ℗♿☻; ☐5,18,31,ⓂN), where **Cliff House** (Map p988; ☎415-386-3330; www.cliffhouse.com; 1090 Point Lobos Ave; ☉9am-11pm Sun-Thu, to midnight Fri & Sat; ☐5,18,31,38) **FREE** overlooks the splendid ruin of **Sutro Baths** (Map p988; www.nps.gov/goga/historyculture/sutro-baths.htm; 680 Point Lobos Ave, visitor center 9am-5pm; ℗; ☐5,31,38) **FREE**. Follow the partly paved hiking trail around **Lands End** for shipwreck sightings and **Golden Gate Bridge** (Map p980; ☎toll information 877-229-8655; www.goldengatebridge.org/visitors; Hwy 101; northbound free, southbound $6.50-7.50; ☐28, all Golden Gate Transit buses) views. On Sundays, when JFK Drive is closed to cars, rent your own wheels from **Golden Gate Park Bike & Skate** (Map p988; ☎415-668-1117; www.goldengateparkbikeandskate.com; 3038 Fulton St; skates

per hour $5-6, per day $20-24, bikes per hour $3-5, per day $15-25, tandem bikes per hour/day $15/75, discs $6/25; ☉10am-6pm Mon-Fri, to 7pm Sat & Sun; ♿; ☐5, 21, 31, 44).

★**Golden Gate Park**   PARK
(Map p988; www.golden-gate-park.com; btwn Stanyan St & Great Hwy; ℗♿☻; ☐5, 7, 18, 21, 28, 29, 33, 44, ⓂN) ✿**FREE** When San Franciscans refer to 'the park,' there's only one that gets the definite article: Golden Gate Park. Everything San Franciscans hold dear is here: free spirits, free music, redwoods, Frisbee, protests, fine art, bonsai and buffalo. Thanks to SF's mystical microclimates and natural eccentricity, the park is filled with flora from around the world and extraordinary sights, including the **de Young Museum** (☎415-750-3600; http://deyoung.famsf.org; 50 Hagiwara Tea Garden Dr; adult/child $15/free, 1st Tue of month free; ☉9:30am-5:15pm Tue-Sun, to 8:45pm Fri Apr-Nov; ♿; ☐5, 7, 44, ⓂN), California Academy of Sciences (p993), **San Francisco Botanical Garden** (Strybing Arboretum; ☎415-661-1316; www.strybing.org; 1199 9th Ave; adult/child $8/2, before 9am daily & 2nd Tue of month free; ☉7:30am-7pm Mar-Sep, to 6pm Oct–mid-Nov & Feb, to 5pm mid-Nov–Jan, last entry 1hr before closing, bookstore 10am-4pm; ♿; ☐6, 7, 44, ⓂN) ✿, **Japanese Tea Garden** (☎415-752-1171; www.japaneseteagardensf.com; 75 Hagiwara Tea Garden Dr; adult/child $8/2, before 10am Mon, Wed & Fri free; ☉9am-6pm Mar-Oct, to 4:45pm Nov-Feb; ℗♿; ☐5, 7, 44, ⓂN), **Conservatory of Flowers** (☎info 415-831-2090; www.conservatoryofflowers.org; 100 John F Kennedy Dr; adult/student/child $8/6/2, 1st Tue of month free; ☉10am-4pm Tue-Sun; ♿; ☐5, 7, 21, 33, ⓂN) and **Stow**

CALIFORNIA SAN FRANCISCO

The Richmond, The Haight & Golden Gate Park

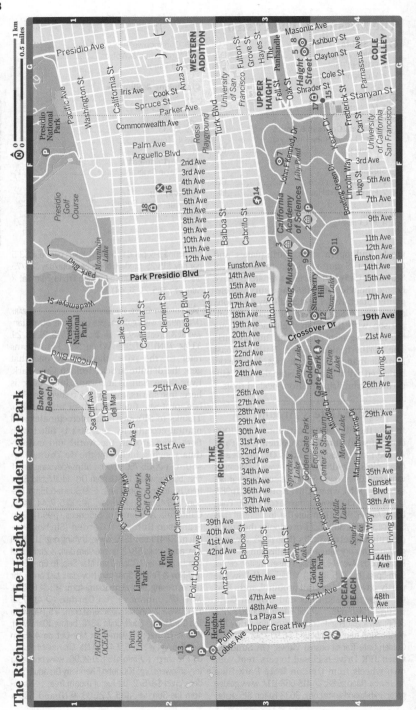

The Richmond, The Haight & Golden Gate Park

◎ **Top Sights**
1 Baker Beach.............................D1
2 California Academy of Sciences E3
3 de Young Museum E3
4 Golden Gate Park D4
5 Haight Street G3

◎ **Sights**
6 Cliff House..A2
7 Conservatory of Flowers F3
8 Haight & Ashbury G3
9 Japanese Tea Garden.............................E3
10 Ocean Beach...A4
11 San Francisco Botanical Garden...........E4

12 Stow Lake D4
13 Sutro Baths A2

◐ **Activities, Courses & Tours**
14 Golden Gate Park Bike & Skate F3
15 Haight-Ashbury Flower Power
         Walking Tour G4

◾ **Eating**
16 Burma Superstar F2

◐ **Shopping**
17 Amoeba Music G4
18 Green Apple Books...................................F2

Lake (www.sfrecpark.org; ☺sunrise-sunset; ♿; ⊟7, 44, Ⓜ N).

🏃 Activities

Blazing Saddles
CYCLING

(Map p982; ☎415-202-8888; www.blazingsaddles.com; 433 Mason St; bike hire per hour $8-15, per day $32-88, electric bikes per day $48-88; ☺8am-8pm; ⊟Powell-Hyde, Powell-Mason, Ⓑ Powell, Ⓜ Powell) Rent bicycles near Union Sq to cover downtown in a day – just mind the traffic. Reserve online for 20% off rates.

City Kayak
KAYAKING

(Map p982; ☎415-294-1050, 888-966-0953; www.citykayak.com; Pier 40, South Beach Harbor; kayak rentals per hour $35-125, 3hr lesson & rental $49, tours $59-75; ☺rentals noon-3pm, return by 5pm Thu-Mon; ⊟30, 45, Ⓜ N, T) You haven't seen San Francisco until you've seen it from the water. Newbies to kayaking can take lessons and paddle calm waters near the Bay Bridge; experienced paddlers can rent kayaks to brave currents near the Golden Gate (conditions permitting; get advice first). Sporty romantics: twilight tours past the Bay Bridge lights are ideal for proposals. Check website for details.

🧭 Tours

★Precita Eyes
Mission Mural Tours
WALKING

(Map p986; ☎415-285-2287; www.precitaeyes.org; 2981 24th St; adult $15-20, child $3; ♿; ⊟12, 14, 48, 49, Ⓑ24th St Mission) Muralists lead weekend walking tours covering 60 to 70 Mission murals within a six- to 10-block radius of mural-bedecked Balmy Alley (p985). Tours last 90 minutes to two hours and 15 minutes (for the more in-depth Classic Mural Walk).

Proceeds fund mural upkeep at this community arts nonprofit.

Drag Me Along Tours
WALKING

(Map p982; ☎415-857-0865; www.dragmealongtours.com; Portsmouth Sq; $20; ☺tours usually 11am-1pm Sun; ⊟1, 8, 10, 12, 30, 41, 45, ⊟California, Powell-Mason, Powell-Hyde) Explore San Francisco's bawdy Barbary Coast with a bona-fide legend: gold-rush burlesque star Countess Lola Montez, reincarnated in drag by SF historian Rick Shelton. Her Highness leads you through Chinatown alleyways where Victorian ladies made and lost reputations, and past North Beach saloons where sailors were shanghaied. Barbary Coast characters gambled, loved and lived dangerously. Adult content; reservations required; cash only.

Haight-Ashbury
Flower Power Walking Tour
WALKING

(Map p988; ☎415-863-1621; www.haightashburytour.com; adult/under 10yr $20/free; ☺10:30am Tue & Sat, 2pm Fri; ♿; ⊟6, 7, Ⓜ N) Take a long, strange trip through 12 blocks of hippie history, following in the steps of Jimi, Jerry and Janis – if you have to ask for last names, you seriously need this tour, dude. Tours meet at the corner of Stanyan and Waller Sts and last about two hours; reservations required.

🎊 Festivals & Events

Bay to Breakers
SPORTS

(www.baytobreakers.com; race registration from $65; ☺3rd Sun May) Run costumed or in not much at all from the Embarcadero to Ocean Beach; joggers dressed as salmon run upstream.

SF Pride Celebration
LGBT

(☺Jun) A day isn't enough to do SF proud: June begins with the **San Francisco LGBTQ Film Festival** (www.frameline.org; tickets $10-35;

Alcatraz

A HALF-DAY TOUR

Book a ferry from Pier 33 and ride 1.5 miles across the bay to explore America's most notorious former prison. The trip itself is worth the money, providing stunning views of the city skyline. Once you've landed at the ❶ **Ferry Dock & Pier**, you begin the 580-yard walk to the top of the island and prison; if you need assistance to reach the top, there's a twice-hourly tram.

As you climb toward the ❷ **Guardhouse**, notice the island's steep slope; before it was a prison, Alcatraz was a fort. In the 1850s, the military quarried the rocky shores into near-vertical cliffs. Ships could then only dock at a single port, separated from the main buildings by a sally port (a drawbridge and moat in what became the guardhouse). Inside, peer through floor grates to see Alcatraz' original prison.

Volunteers tend the brilliant ❸ **Officer's Row Gardens** an orderly counterpoint to the overgrown rose bushes surrounding the burned-out shell of the ❹ **Warden's House**. At the top of the hill, by the front door of the ❺ **Main Cellhouse**, beautiful shots unfurl all around, including a view of the ❻ **Golden Gate Bridge**. Above the main door of the administration building, notice the ❼ **historic signs & graffiti**, before you step inside the dank, cold prison to find the ❽ **Frank Morris cell**, former home to Alcatraz' most notorious jail-breaker.

TOP TIPS

➡ Book at least one month prior for self-guided daytime visits, longer for ranger-led night tours. For info on garden tours, see www.alcatraz gardens.org.

➡ Be prepared to hike; a steep path ascends from the ferry landing to the cell block. Most people spend two to three hours on the island. You need only reserve for the outbound ferry; take any ferry back.

➡ There's no food (just water) but you can bring your own; picnicking is allowed at the ferry dock only. Dress in layers as weather changes fast and it's usually windy.

Historic Signs & Graffiti
During their 1969–71 occupation, Native Americans graffitied the water tower: 'Home of the Free Indian Land.' Above the cellhouse door, examine the eagle-and-flag crest to see how the red-and-white stripes were changed to spell 'Free.'

Warden's House
Fires destroyed the warden's house and other structures during the Indian Occupation. The government blamed the Native Americans; the Native Americans blamed agents provocateurs acting on behalf of the Nixon Administration to undermine public sympathy.

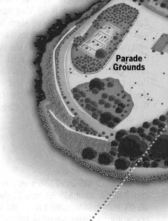

Parade Grounds

Officer's Row Gardens
In the 19th century soldiers imported topsoil to beautify the island with gardens. Well-trusted prisoners later gardened – Elliott Michener said it kept him sane. Historians, ornithologists and archaeologists choose today's plants.

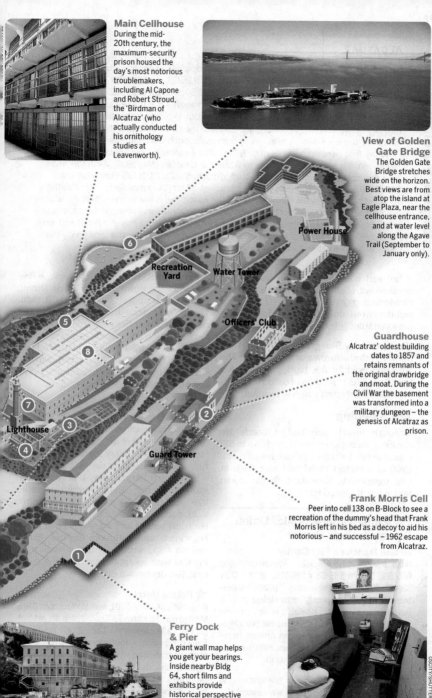

Main Cellhouse
During the mid-20th century, the maximum-security prison housed the day's most notorious troublemakers, including Al Capone and Robert Stroud, the 'Birdman of Alcatraz' (who actually conducted his ornithology studies at Leavenworth).

View of Golden Gate Bridge
The Golden Gate Bridge stretches wide on the horizon. Best views are from atop the island at Eagle Plaza, near the cellhouse entrance, and at water level along the Agave Trail (September to January only).

Power House

Recreation Yard

Water Tower

Officers' Club

Guardhouse
Alcatraz' oldest building dates to 1857 and retains remnants of the original drawbridge and moat. During the Civil War the basement was transformed into a military dungeon – the genesis of Alcatraz as prison.

Lighthouse

Guard Tower

Frank Morris Cell
Peer into cell 138 on B-Block to see a recreation of the dummy's head that Frank Morris left in his bed as a decoy to aid his notorious – and successful – 1962 escape from Alcatraz.

Ferry Dock & Pier
A giant wall map helps you get your bearings. Inside nearby Bldg 64, short films and exhibits provide historical perspective on the prison and details about the Indian Occupation.

FRANCKREPORTER/GETTY IMAGES ©

OSGITY/SHUTTERSTOCK ©

ALCATRAZ

For more than 150 years, the name **Alcatraz** (Map p980; ☑ Alcatraz Cruises 415-981-7625; www.nps.gov/alcatraz; tours adult/child 5-11yr day $37.25/23, night $44.25/26.50; ☺ call center 8am-7pm, ferries depart Pier 33 half-hourly 8:45am-3:50pm, night tours 5:55pm & 6:30pm; ⓐ) has given the innocent chills and the guilty cold sweats. Over the decades, it's been the nation's first military prison, a forbidding maximum-security penitentiary and disputed territory between Native American activists and the FBI. No wonder that first step you take onto 'the Rock' seems to cue ominous music: dunh-dunh-dunnnnh!

Today, first-person accounts of daily life in the Alcatraz lockup are included on the award-winning audio tour provided by **Alcatraz Cruises** (Map p982; ☑ 415-981-7625; www.alcatrazcruises.com; tours day adult/child/family $37.25/23/112.75, night adult/child $44.25/26.50; Ⓜ E, F). But take your headphones off for just a moment and notice the sound of carefree city life traveling across the water: this is the torment that made perilous escapes into riptides worth the risk. Though Alcatraz was considered escape-proof, in 1962 the Anglin brothers and Frank Morris floated away on a makeshift raft and were never seen again. Security and upkeep proved prohibitively expensive, and finally the island prison was abandoned to the birds in 1963.

☺ Jun) and goes out in style over the last weekend with Saturday's **Dyke March** (www.thedykemarch.org) to the Castro's Pink Party and the joyous, million-strong **Pride Parade** (www.sfpride.org; ☺ last Sun Jun) on Sunday.

Hardly Strictly Bluegrass　　MUSIC
(www.hardlystrictlybluegrass.com; ☺ Oct) The West goes wild for free bluegrass at Golden Gate Park, with three days of concerts by 100-plus bands and seven stages of headliners.

🛏 Sleeping

Although hostels and budget hotels are cheapest, rooms are never truly cheap in SF: expect to pay $100 for a private hostel room, $200 at a budget motel and over $300 at midrange hotels. Note the hefty 15% room tax on top of quoted rates.

🛏 Embarcadero, SoMa, Union Square & Civic Center

HI San Francisco City Center　　HOSTEL $
(Map p982; ☑ 415-474-5721; www.sfhostels.org; 685 Ellis St; dm $33-52, r $90-155; @ 🛜; 🚌 19, 38, 47, 49) The seven-story, 1920s Atherton Hotel was recently remodeled into a better-than-average hostel, with private baths in all rooms. All-you-can-eat pancakes or eggs cost $1 and there's an on-site bar – though dive bars and bargain eats are the main selling point of this location.

★**Axiom**　　BOUTIQUE HOTEL $$
(Map p982; ☑ 415-392-9466; www.axiomhotel. com; 28 Cyril Magnin St; d $189-342; @ 🛜 🖶;

🚋 Powell-Mason, Powell-Hyde, Ⓑ Powell, Ⓜ Powell) Of all the downtown SF hotels aiming for high-tech appeal, this one gets it right. The lobby is razzle-dazzle LED, marble and riveted steel, but the game room looks like a start-up HQ, with arcade games and foosball. Guest rooms have king platform beds, dedicated routers for high-speed wireless streaming to Apple/Google/Samsung devices, and Bluetooth-enabled everything.

★**Marker**　　BOUTIQUE HOTEL $$
(Map p982; ☑ 844-736-2753, 415-292-0100; http://themarkersanfrancisco.com; 501 Geary St; r from $209; 🌀@🛜🖶; 🚌 38, 🚋 Powell-Hyde, Powell-Mason) 🍃 Snazzy Marker gets details right, with guest-room decor in bold colors – lipstick-red lacquer, navy-blue velvet and shiny purple silk – and thoughtful amenities like high-thread-count sheets, ergonomic workspaces, digital-library access, multiple electrical outlets and ample space in drawers, closets and bathroom vanities. Extras include a spa with a Jacuzzi, a small gym, evening wine reception and bragging rights to stylish downtown digs.

★**Palace Hotel**　　HOTEL $$$
(Map p982; ☑ 415-512-1111; www.sfpalace.com; 2 New Montgomery St; r from $300; 🌀@🛜🖶; Ⓜ Montgomery, Ⓑ Montgomery) The 1906 landmark Palace remains a monument to turn-of-the-century grandeur, with 100-year-old Austrian-crystal chandeliers and Maxfield Parrish paintings. Cushy (if staid) accommodations cater to expense-account travelers, but prices drop at weekends. Even if you're not staying

here, visit the opulent Garden Court to sip tea beneath a glass ceiling. There's also a spa; kids love the big pool.

North Beach

Pacific Tradewinds Hostel
HOSTEL $

(Map p982; ☏ 415-433-7970; www.san-francis co-hostel.com; 680 Sacramento St; dm $35-45; ⊙ front desk 8am-midnight; ⊜@🛜; 🚊1, 🚡 California, 🚇 Montgomery) San Francisco's smartest all-dorm hostel has a blue-and-white nautical theme, a fully equipped kitchen (free peanut butter and jelly sandwiches all day!), spotless glass-brick showers, a laundry (free sock wash!), luggage storage and no lockout time. Bunks are bolted to the wall, so there's no bed-shaking when bunkmates roll. No elevator means hauling bags up three flights – but it's worth it. Great service; fun staff.

San Remo Hotel
HOTEL $

(Map p982; ☏ 800-352-7366, 415-776-8688; www. sanremohotel.com; 2237 Mason St; r without bath $119-159; @🛜🐾; 🚊30, 47, 🚡Powell-Mason) One of the city's best-value stays, the San Remo was built in 1906, right after the Great Earthquake. More than a century later, this upstanding North Beach boarding house still offers Italian *nonna* (grandma)-styled rooms with mismatched turn-of-the-century furnishings and shared bathrooms. The least expensive rooms have windows onto the corridor, not outdoors. Family suites accommodate up to five. No elevator.

★ Hotel Bohème
BOUTIQUE HOTEL $$

(Map p982; ☏ 415-433-9111; www.hotelboheme. com; 444 Columbus Ave; r $235–295; ⊜@🛜;

🚊10, 12, 30, 41, 45) Eclectic, historic and unabashedly poetic, this quintessential North Beach boutique hotel has jazz-era color schemes, pagoda-print upholstery and photos from the Beat years on the walls. The vintage rooms are smallish, some face noisy Columbus Ave (quieter rooms are in back) and bathrooms are teensy, but novels beg to be written here – especially after bar crawls.

Fisherman's Wharf, the Marina & Presidio

★ HI San Francisco Fisherman's Wharf
HOSTEL $

(Map p982; ☏ 415-771-7277; www.sfhostels.com; Fort Mason, Bldg 240; dm $30-53, r $116-134; 🅿@🛜; 🚊28, 30, 47, 49) Trading downtown convenience for a glorious park-like setting with million-dollar waterfront views, this hostel occupies a former army-hospital building, with bargain-priced private rooms and dorms (some co-ed) with four to 22 beds (avoid bunks one and two – they're by doorways). Huge kitchen. No curfew, but no heat during daytime: bring warm clothes. Limited free parking.

★ Inn at the Presidio
HOTEL $$

(Map p980; ☏ 415-800-7356; www.innatthepresid io.com; 42 Moraga Ave; r $295-380; 🅿⊜@🛜🐾; 🚊43, PresidiGo Shuttle) 🌿 Built in 1903 as bachelor quarters for army officers, this three-story, redbrick building in the Presidio was transformed in 2012 into a spiffy national-park lodge, styled with leather, linen and wood. Oversized rooms are plush, including feather beds with Egyptian-cotton sheets. Suites have gas fireplaces. Nature surrounds

---

SAN FRANCISCO FOR CHILDREN

Although it has almost the fewest children per capita of any US city – there are more canines than kids in town – San Francisco is packed with family-friendly attractions, including the **California Academy of Sciences** (Map p988; ☏415-379-8000; www.calacademy.org; 55 Music Concourse Dr; adult/student/child $35/30/25; ⊙9:30am-5pm Mon-Sat, from 11am Sun; 🅿👶; 🚊5, 6, 7, 21, 31, 33, 44, 🚇N) 🌿 in Golden Gate Park and the waterfront Exploratorium (p977), Crissy Field (p984), Musée Mécanique (p985) and **Pier 39** (Map p982; ☏415-705-5500; www.pier39.com; cnr Beach St & the Embarcadero; 🅿👶; 🚊47, 🚡Powell-Mason, 🚇E, F), with its barking sea lions and hand-painted Italian carousel.

The **Children's Creativity Museum** (Map p982; ☏415-820-3320; http://creativity. org/; 221 4th St; $12; ⊙10am-4pm Wed-Sun; 👶; 🚊14, 🚇Powell, 🚈Powell) in SoMa has technology that's too cool for school: robots, live-action video games and 3D animation workshops. At the **Aquarium of the Bay** (Map p982; ☏415-623-5300; www.aquariumofthebay. org; Pier 39; adult/child/family $24.95/14.95/70; ⊙9am-8pm late May-early Sep, shorter hours low season; 👶; 🚊49, 🚡Powell-Mason, 🚇E, F) on Pier 39, wander through underwater glass tubes as sharks circle overhead, then let tots gently touch tide-pool critters.

you, with hiking trailheads out back, but taxis downtown cost $25. Free parking.

🛏 The Mission & the Castro

Inn San Francisco
B&B **$$**

(Map p986; 📞 415-641-0188, 800-359-0913; www.innsf.com; 943 S Van Ness Ave; r $195-255, without bath $165-225, cottages $365-475; 🅿️😊@🛜🐾; 📺14, 49) 🏊 An elegant 1872 Italianate-Victorian mansion has become a stately Mission District inn, impeccably maintained and packed with antiques. All rooms have fresh-cut flowers and sumptuous mattresses with feather beds; some have Jacuzzis. Outside there's an English garden and a redwood hot tub open 24 hours – a rarity in SF. Limited parking; reserve. No elevator.

★ Parker Guest House
B&B **$$**

(Map p986; 📞 888-520-7275, 415-621-3222; www.parkerguesthouse.com; 520 Church St; r $219-279, without bath $179-99; @🛜; 📺33, 🅼J) The Castro's stateliest gay digs occupy two side-by-side Edwardian mansions. Details are elegant and formal, never froufrou. Rooms feel like they belong more to a swanky hotel than to a B&B, with super-comfortable beds and down duvets. The garden is ideal for a lovers' tryst – as is the steam room. No elevator.

🛏 The Haight

Metro Hotel
HOTEL **$**

(Map p980; 📞 415-861-5364; www.metrohotelsf.com; 319 Divisadero St; r $107; @🛜; 📺6, 24, 71) The Metro Hotel has a prime position – some rooms overlook the garden patio of top-notch Ragazza Pizzeria. Rooms are cheap and clean, if bland – if possible, get the one with the SF mural. Some have two double beds. The hotel's handy to the Haight and has 24-hour reception; no elevator.

★ Chateau Tivoli
B&B **$$**

(Map p982; 📞 800-228-1647, 415-776-5462; www.chateautivoli.com; 1057 Steiner St; r $195-300, without bath $150-200; 🛜; 📺5, 22) The source of neighborhood gossip since 1892, this gilded and turreted mansion once hosted Isadora Duncan, Mark Twain and (rumor has it) the ghost of a Victorian opera diva – and now you too can be Chateau Tivoli's guest. Nine antique-filled rooms and suites set the scene for romance; most have claw-foot bathtubs, though two share a bathroom. No elevator; no TVs.

✖ Eating

✖ Embarcadero & SoMa

★ Ferry Plaza Farmers Market
MARKET **$**

(Map p982; 📞 415-291-3276; www.cuesa.org; cnr Market St & the Embarcadero; street food $3-12; ⏰10am-2pm Tue & Thu, from 8am Sat; 🍴👶; 📺2, 6, 9, 14, 21, 31, 🅼Embarcadero, 🅱Embarcadero) 🦪 The pride and joy of SF foodies, the Ferry Building market showcases 50 to 100 prime purveyors of California-grown organic produce, pasture-raised meats and gourmet prepared foods at accessible prices. On Saturdays, join top chefs early for prime browsing, and stay for eclectic bayside picnics of Namu Korean tacos, RoliRoti porchetta, Dirty Girl tomatoes, Nicasio cheese samples, and Frog Hollow fruit turnovers.

★ In Situ
CALIFORNIAN, INTERNATIONAL **$$**

(Map p982; 📞 415-941-6050; http://insitu.sfmoma.org; SFMOMA, 151 3rd St; mains $14-34; ⏰11am-3:30pm Mon & Tue, 11am-3:30pm & 5-9pm Thu-Sun; 📺5, 6, 7, 14, 19, 21, 31, 38, 🅱Montgomery, 🅼Montgomery) The landmark gallery of modern cuisine attached to SFMOMA also showcases avant-garde masterpieces – but these ones you'll lick clean. Chef Corey Lee collaborates with star chefs worldwide, scrupulously recreating their signature dishes with California-grown ingredients so that you can enjoy Harald Wohlfahrt's impeccable anise-marinated salmon, Hiroshi Sasaki's decadent chicken thighs and Albert Adrià's gravity-defying cocoa-bubble cake in one unforgettable sitting.

★ Benu
CALIFORNIAN, FUSION **$$$**

(Map p982; 📞 415-685-4860; www.benusf.com; 22 Hawthorne St; tasting menu $285; ⏰6-9pm seatings Tue-Sat; 📺10, 12, 14, 30, 45) SF has pioneered Asian fusion cuisine for 150 years, but the pan-Pacific innovation chef-owner Corey Lee brings to the plate is gasp-inducing: foie-gras soup dumplings – what?! Dungeness crab and truffle custard pack such outsize flavor into Lee's faux–shark's fin soup, you'll swear Jaws is in there. A Benu dinner is an investment, but don't miss star sommelier Yoon Ha's ingenious pairings ($185).

✖ Union Square, Civic Center & Hayes Valley

★ Tout Sweet
BAKERY **$**

(Map p982; 📞 415-385-1679; www.toutsweetsf.com; Macy's, 3rd fl, cnr Geary & Stockton Sts; baked goods $2-8; ⏰11am-6pm Sun-Wed, to 8pm Thu-Sat; 🛜♿; 🚌2, 38, 🚋Powell-Mason, Powell-Hyde, 🚋Powell) Mango with Thai chili or peanut butter and jelly? Choosing your favorite California-French macaron isn't easy at Tout Sweet, where *Top Chef Just Desserts* champion Yigit Pura keeps outdoing his own inventions – he's like the love child of Julia Child and Steve Jobs. Chef Pura's sweet retreat on Macy's 3rd floor offers unbeatable views overlooking Union Sq, excellent teas and free wi-fi.

★**Rich Table** CALIFORNIAN $$
(Map p982; ☎415-355-9085; http://richtablesf.com; 199 Gough St; mains $17-36; ⏰5:30-10pm Sun-Thu, to 10:30pm Fri & Sat; 🚌5, 6, 7, 21, 47, 49, Ⓜ Van Ness) 🍴 Impossible cravings begin at Rich Table, inventor of porcini dough-nuts, miso-marrow-stuffed pasta and fried-chicken madeleines with caviar. Mar-ried co-chefs and owners Sarah and Evan Rich playfully riff on seasonal California fare, freestyling with whimsical off-menu amuse-bouches like trippy beet marshmal-lows or the Dirty Hippie: nutty hemp atop silky goat-buttermilk *pannacotta*, as offbeat and entrancing as Hippie Hill drum circles.

★**Cala** MEXICAN, CALIFORNIAN $$$
(Map p982; ☎415-660-7701; www.calarestaurant.com; 149 Fell St; ⏰5-10pm Mon-Wed, to 11pm Thu-Sat, 11am-3pm Sun, taco bar 11am-2pm Mon-Fri; 🚌6, 7, 21, 47, 49, Ⓜ Van Ness) Like discovering a long-lost twin, Cala's Mexico Norte cuisine is a revelation. San Francisco's Mexican-rancher roots are deeply honored here: silky bone-marrow salsa and fragrant herit-age-corn tortillas grace a sweet potato slow-cooked in ashes. Brace yourself with mezcal margaritas for the ultimate California surf and turf: sea urchin with beef tongue. Orig-inal and unforgettable, even before Ma-yan-chocolate gelato with amaranth brittle.

🍴 Chinatown & North Beach

★**Liguria Bakery** BAKERY $
(Map p982; ☎415-421-3786; 1700 Stockton St; focaccia $4-6; ⏰8am-1pm Tue-Fri, from 7am Sat; ✏️♿; 🚌8, 30, 39, 41, 45, 🚋Powell-Mason) Bleary-eyed art students and Italian grandmothers are in line by 8am for cinnamon-raisin focac-cia hot out of the 100-year-old oven, leaving 9am dawdlers a choice of tomato or classic rosemary and garlic, and 11am stragglers out of luck. Take yours in waxed paper or boxed

DON'T MISS

COIT TOWER

The exclamation mark on San Francis-co's skyline is **Coit Tower** (Map p982; ☎415-249-0995; www.sfrecpark.org; Telegraph Hill Blvd; nonresident elevator fee adult/child $8/5; ⏰10am-6pm Apr-Oct, to 5pm Nov-Mar; 🚌39), with 360-degree views of downtown and wraparound 1930s Works Progress Administration (WPA) murals glorifying SF workers. Initially denounced as communist, the murals are now a national landmark. For a wild-parrot's panoramic view of San Francisco 210ft above the city, take the elevator to the tower's open-air plat-form. To glimpse seven recently restored murals up a hidden stairwell on the 2nd floor, join the 11am tour Wednesday or Saturday (free; donations welcome).

for picnics – but don't kid yourself that you're going to save some for later. Cash only.

★**Molinari** DELI $
(Map p982; ☎415-421-2337; www.molinarisalame.com; 373 Columbus Ave; sandwiches $10-13.50; ⏰9am-6pm Mon-Fri, to 5:30pm Sat; 🚌8, 10, 12, 30, 39, 41, 45, 🚋Powell-Mason) Observe quasi-religious North Beach noontime rituals: en-ter Molinari, and grab a number and a crusty roll. When your number's called, wisecrack-ing staff pile your roll with heavenly fixings: milky buffalo mozzarella, tangy sun-dried tomatoes, translucent sheets of prosciutto di Parma, slabs of legendary house-cured sala-mi, drizzles of olive oil and balsamic. Enjoy hot from the panini press at sidewalk tables.

★**Mister Jiu's** CHINESE $$
(Map p982; ☎415-857-9688; http://misterjius.com; 28 Waverly Pl; mains $14-45; ⏰5:30-10:30pm Tue-Sat; 🚌30, 🚋California) Ever since the gold rush, San Francisco has craved Chinese food, powerful cocktails and hyperlocal specialties – and Mister Jiu's satisfies on all counts. Build your own banquet of Chinese classics with California twists: chanterelle chow mein, Dungeness-crab rice noodles, quail and Mission-fig sticky rice. Cocktail pairings are equally inspired – try jasmine-infused-gin Happiness ($13) with tea-smoked Sonoma-duck confit.

★**Z & Y** CHINESE $$
(Map p982; ☎415-981-8988; www.zandyrestaurant.com; 655 Jackson St; mains $9-20; ⏰11am-9:30pm

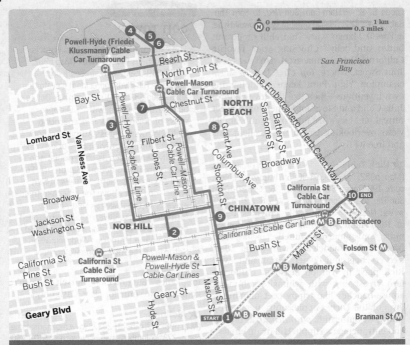

🏃 City Walk
SF by Cable Car

START POWELL ST CABLE CAR
TURNAROUND
END FERRY BUILDING
LENGTH 2 MILES; 2 HOURS WITH STOPS

At the **1 Powell St Cable Car Turnaround** (p978), you'll see operators turn the car atop a revolving wooden platform and a vintage kiosk where you can buy an all-day Muni Passport for $21, instead of paying $7 per ride. Board the red-signed Powell-Hyde cable car and begin your 338ft ascent of Nob Hill.

As your cable car lurches uphill, you can imagine horses struggling up this slippery crag. Nineteenth-century city planners were skeptical of inventor Andrew Hallidie's 'wire-rope railway' – but Hallidie's cable cars even survived the 1906 earthquake and fire that destroyed 'Snob Hill' mansions, returning the faithful to the rebuilt **2 Grace Cathedral** – hop off to say hello to SF's gentle patron, St Francis.

Back on the Powell-Hyde car, enjoy Bay views as you careen past crooked, flower-lined **3 Lombard Street** (p981) toward **4 Fish-erman's Wharf**. The waterfront terminus is named for Friedel Klussmann, who saved cable cars from mayoral modernization plans in 1947. She did the math: cable cars brought in more tourism dollars than they cost in upkeep. For her funeral in 1986, cable cars citywide were draped in black.

At the wharf, emerge from the submarine **5 USS Pampanito** to glimpse SF as sailors used to. Witness Western saloon brawls in vintage arcade games at the **6 Musée Mécanique** (p985) before hitching the Powell-Mason cable car to North Beach.

Hop off to see Diego Rivera's 1934 city-scape at the **7 San Francisco Art Institute**, or follow your rumbling stomach directly to **8 Liguria Bakery** (p995). Stroll through North Beach and Chinatown alleyways, or take the Powell-Mason line to time-travel through the **9 Chinese Historical Society of America** (p981). Nearby, catch a ride on the city's oldest line: the California St cable car. The terminus is near the **10 Ferry Building** (p977), where champagne-and-oyster happy hour awaits.

Sun-Thu, to 11pm Fri & Sat; 🚋 8, 10, 12, 30, 45, 🚋 Powell-Mason, Powell-Hyde) Graduate from hohum sweet-and-sour and middling *mu-shu* to sensational Szechuan dishes that go down in a blaze of glory. Warm up with spicy pork dumplings and heat-blistered string beans, take on the housemade *tantan* noodles with peanut-chili sauce, and leave lips buzzing with fish poached in flaming chili oil and buried under red Szechuan chili peppers. Go early; worth the inevitable wait.

✖ Fisherman's Wharf, the Marina & Presidio

★ Off the Grid FOOD TRUCK $
(Map p982; www.offthegridsf.com; Fort Mason Center, 2 Marina Blvd; items $6-14; ⏱ 5-10pm Fri Apr-Oct; 🚻; 🚌 22, 28) Spring through fall, some 30 food trucks circle their wagons at SF's largest mobile-gourmet hootenannies on Friday night at Fort Mason Center, and 11am to 4pm Sunday for **Picnic at the Presidio** on the Main Post lawn. Arrive early for the best selection and to minimize waits. Cash only.

Fisherman's Wharf Crab Stands SEAFOOD $
(Map p982; Taylor St; mains $5-15; Ⓜ F) Brawny men stir steaming cauldrons of Dungeness crab at several side-by-side takeout crab stands at the foot of Taylor St, the epicenter of Fisherman's Wharf. Crab season typically runs winter through spring, but you'll find shrimp and other seafood year-round.

★ Greens VEGETARIAN, CALIFORNIAN $$
(Map p982; 📞 415-771-6222; www.greensrestaurant. com; Fort Mason Center, 2 Marina Blvd, Bldg A; mains lunch $16-19, dinner $20-28; ⏱ 11:45am-2:30pm & 5:30-9pm; 🚗🚻; 🚌 22, 28, 30, 43, 47, 49) 🌱 Career carnivores won't realize there's zero meat in the hearty black-bean chili, or in Greens' other flavor-packed vegetarian dishes, made using ingredients from a Zen farm in Marin. And, oh, what views! The Golden Gate rises just outside the window-lined dining room. The on-site cafe serves to-go lunches, but for sit-down meals, including Sunday brunch, reservations are essential.

★ A16 ITALIAN $$$
(Map p980; 📞 415-771-2216; www.a16pizza.com; 2355 Chestnut St; pizzas $18-21, mains $22-36; ⏱ lunch 11:30am-2:30pm Wed-Sun, dinner 5:30-10pm Mon-Thu, 5-11pm Fri & Sat, 5-10pm Sun; 🚌 28, 30, 43) Even before A16 won a James Beard Award, it was hard to book, but persevere:

the housemade mozzarella *burrata*, blister-crusted pizzas from the wood-burning oven and 12-page Italian wine list make it worth your while. Skip the spotty desserts and instead double up on adventurous appetizers, including house-cured *salumi* platters and delectable marinated tuna.

✖ The Mission & the Castro

★ La Taqueria MEXICAN $
(Map p986; 📞 415-285-7117; 2889 Mission St; items $3-11; ⏱ 11am-9pm Mon-Sat, to 8pm Sun; 🚻; 🚌 12, 14, 48, 49, Ⓑ 24th St Mission) SF's definitive burrito has no saffron rice, spinach tortilla or mango salsa – just perfectly grilled meats, slow-cooked beans and tomatillo or mesquite salsa wrapped in a flour tortilla. They're purists at James Beard Award–winning La Taqueria. You'll pay extra to go without beans, because they add more meat – but spicy pickles and *crema* (sour cream) bring burrito bliss. Worth the wait, always.

★ Craftsman & Wolves BAKERY, CALIFORNIAN $
(Map p986; 📞 415-913-7713; http://crafts man-wolves.com; 746 Valencia St; pastries $3-8; ⏱ 7am-6pm Mon-Fri, from 8am Sat & Sun; 🚌 14, 22, 33, 49, Ⓑ 16th St Mission, Ⓜ J) Breakfast routines are made to be broken by the infamous Rebel Within: a sausage-spiked Asiago-cheese muffin with a silken soft-boiled egg baked inside. SF's surest pick-me-up is a Highwire macchiato with *matcha* (green tea) cookies; a Thai coconut-curry scone enjoyed with pea soup and rosé is lunch perfected. Exquisite hazelnut cube-cakes and vanilla-violet cheesecakes are ideal for celebrating unbirthdays and imaginary holidays.

★ Ichi Sushi SUSHI $$
(Map p980; 📞 415-525-4750; www.ichisushi.com; 3369 Mission St; sushi $4-8; ⏱ 11:30am-2pm & 5:30-10pm Mon-Thu, to 11pm Fri & Sat, 5:30-9:30pm Sun; 🚌 14, 24, 49, Ⓑ 24th St Mission, Ⓜ J) 🌱 Alluring on the plate and positively obscene on the tongue, Ichi Sushi is a sharp cut above other seafood joints. Chef Tim Archuleta slices silky, sustainably sourced fish with a jeweler's precision, balances it atop well-packed rice, and tops it with tiny but powerfully tangy dabs of gelled *yuzu* and microscopically cut spring onion and chili daikon that make soy sauce unthinkable.

★ Al's Place CALIFORNIAN $$
(Map p986; 📞 415-416-6136; www.alsplacesf.com; 1499 Valencia St; share plates $15-19; ⏱ 5:30-10pm

Wed-Sun; ☒; ⬜12, 14, 49, Ⓜ J, Ⓑ 24th St Mission) 🍴 The Golden State dazzles on Al's plates, featuring homegrown heirloom ingredients, pristine Pacific seafood, and grass-fed meat on the side. Painstaking preparation yields sun-drenched flavors and exquisite textures: crispy-skin cod with frothy preserved-lime dip, grilled peach melting into velvety foie gras. Dishes are half the size but thrice the flavor of mains elsewhere – get two or three, and you'll be California dreaming.

Commonwealth CALIFORNIAN **$$$**
(Map p986; ☒415-355-1500; www.common-wealthsf.com; 2224 Mission St; small plates $15-22; ⏲5:30-10pm Sun-Thu, to 11pm Fri & Sat; ☒; ⬜14, 22, 33, 49, Ⓑ16th St Mission) Wildly imaginative farm-to-table dining where you'd least expect it: in a converted cinder-block Mission dive. Chef Jason Fox serves adventurous dishes like *uni* and bone-marrow cream with nasturtiums, and lamb with beets and seaweed. Try the six-course tasting menu ($80) knowing that a portion benefits local charities.

✖ The Haight & Fillmore

Rosamunde Sausage Grill FAST FOOD **$**
(Map p982; ☒415-437-6851; http://rosamunde sausagegrill.com; 545 Haight St; sausages $8-8.50; ⏲11:30am-10pm Sun-Wed, to 11pm Thu-Sat; ⬜6, 7, 22, Ⓜ N) Impress a dinner date on the cheap: load up Coleman Farms pork Brats or free-range duck links with complimentary roasted peppers, grilled onions, whole-grain mustard and mango chutney, and enjoy with your choice of 45 seasonal draft brews at Toronado (p1000) next door. To impress a local lunch date, call ahead or line up by 11:30am Tuesday for massive $6 burgers.

★ Jardinière CALIFORNIAN **$$**
(Map p982; ☒415-861-5555; www.jardiniere.com; 300 Grove St; mains $20-36; ⏲5-9pm Sun-Thu, to 10:30pm Fri & Sat; ⬜5, 21, 47, 49, Ⓜ Van Ness) 🍴 *Iron Chef* winner, *Top Chef Masters* finalist and James Beard Award–winner Traci Des Jardins champions sustainable, salacious California cuisine. She has a way with California's organic produce, sustainable meats and seafood, slathering sturgeon with buttery chanterelles and lavishing root vegetables with truffles and honey from Jardinière's rooftop hives. Mondays bring $55 three-course dinners with wine pairings.

✖ Golden Gate Park & Around

★ Outerlands CALIFORNIAN **$$**
(Map p980; ☒415-661-6140; www.outerlandssf.com; 4001 Judah St; sandwiches & small plates $8-14, mains $15-27; ⏲9am-3pm & 5-10pm; ☒👶; ⬜18, Ⓜ N) 🍴 When windy Ocean Beach leaves you feeling shipwrecked, drift into this beach-shack bistro for organic Californian comfort food. Brunch demands Dutch pancakes in iron skillets with housemade ricotta, lunch brings cast-iron-grilled artisan cheese on house-baked levain bread with citrusy Steely Dan–themed beach cocktails, and dinner means creative coastal fare like hazelnut-dusted California salmon with black-eyed peas. Reserve.

Burma Superstar BURMESE **$$**
(Map p988; ☒415-387-2147; www.burmasuperstar.com; 309 Clement St; mains $11-28; ⏲11:30am-3:30pm & 5-9:30pm Sun-Thu, to 10pm Fri & Sat; ☒; ⬜1, 2, 33, 38, 44) Yes, there's a wait, but do you see anyone walking away? Blame it on fragrant *moh hinga* (catfish curry), tangy vegetarian *samusa* soup, and traditional Burmese green-tea salads tarted up with lime and fried garlic. Reservations aren't accepted – ask the host to call you so you can browse Burmese cookbooks at **Green Apple Books** (Map p988; ☒415-742-5833; www.greenapplebooks.com; 506 Clement St; ⏲10am-10:30pm; ⬜2, 38, 44) while you wait.

🍷 Drinking & Nightlife

For a pub crawl, start with North Beach saloons or Mission bars around Valencia and 16th Sts. The Castro has historic gay bars; SoMa adds dance clubs. Downtown and around Union Square mix dives with speakeasies. Haight bars draw mixed alternacrowds.

★ Bar Agricole BAR
(Map p982; ☒415-355-9400; www.baragricole.com; 355 11th St; ⏲5-11pm Mon-Thu, 5pm-12am Fri & Sat, 10am-2pm & 6-9pm Sun; ⬜9, 12, 27, 47) 🍴 Drink your way to a history degree with well-researched cocktails: Whiz Bang with house bitters, whiskey, vermouth and absinthe scores high, but El Presidente with white rum, farmhouse curaçao and California-pomegranate grenadine takes top honors. This overachiever wins James Beard Award nods for spirits and eco-savvy design, plus popular acclaim for $1 oysters and $5 aperitifs during happy hour (5pm to 6pm, Monday to Sunday).

LGBTIQ SF

Doesn't matter where you're from, who you love or who your daddy is: if you're here, and queer, welcome home. The Castro is the heart of the gay cruising scene, but South of Market (SoMa) has leather bars and thump-thump clubs. The Mission is the preferred 'hood for many women and has a diverse transgender community.

Bay Area Reporter (aka BAR; www.ebar.com) covers community news and listings. *San Francisco Bay Times* (www.sfbaytimes.com) focuses on LGBTIQ perspectives and events. Free *Gloss Magazine* (www.glossmagazine.net) locks down nightlife.

Over 1.5 million people come out for SF Pride (p989) parades and parties in late June. For weekly roving dance parties, check Honey Soundsystem (http://hnysndsystm.tumblr.com).

Blackbird (Map p986; ☑415-503-0630; www.blackbirdbar.com; 2124 Market St; ⊗3pm-2am Mon-Fri, from 2pm Sat & Sun; MChurch St) Castro's first-choice lounge offers craft cocktails, billiards and everyone's favorite: a photo booth.

HiTops (Map p986; http://hitopssf.com; 2247 Market St; ⊗11:30am-midnight Mon-Wed, to 2am Thu & Fri, 10am-2am Sat & Sun; MCastro St) Castro's prime-time sports bar for friendly guys, big-screen TVs, shuffleboard and pub grub.

Cafe Flore (Map p986; ☑415-621-8579; www.cafeflore.com; 2298 Market St; ⊗10am-10pm Mon-Fri, 9am-10pm Sat & Sun; ☎; MCastro St) You haven't done the Castro till you've lollygagged on the sundrenched patio here.

Stud (Map p982; www.studsf.com; 399 9th St; $5-8; ⊗noon-2am Tue, 5pm-3am Thu-Sat, 5pm-midnight Sun; ☐12, 19, 27, 47) Rocking SoMa's gay scene since 1966. Anything goes here, especially on 'Club Some Thing' Fridays.

Oasis (Map p982; ☑415-795-3180; www.sfoasis.com; 298 11th St; tickets $15-35; ☐9, 12, 14, 47, MVan Ness) SoMa drag shows so fearless and funny, you'll laugh till it hurts. Afterwards, shake it on the dance floor.

EndUp (Map p982; ☑415-646-0999; www.facebook.com/theendup; 401 6th St; $10-25; ⊗11pm Fri-8am Sat, 10pm Sat-4am Mon; ☐12, 19, 27, 47) A mixed gay/straight crowd and marathon dance parties that don't end with sunrise over the 101 freeway ramp.

Aunt Charlie's Lounge (Map p982; ☑415-441-2922; www.auntcharlieslounge.com; 133 Turk St; free-$5; ⊗noon-2am Mon-Fri, from 10am Sat, 10am-midnight Sun; ☐27, 31, MPowell, BPowell) Tenderloin drag dive bar for fabulously seedy glamour and a vintage pulp fiction vibe.

★**Caffe Trieste**   CAFE
(Map p982; ☑415-392-6739; www.caffetrieste.com; 601 Vallejo St; ⊗6:30am-10pm Sun-Thu, to 11pm Fri & Sat; ☎; ☐8, 10, 12, 30, 41, 45) Poetry on bathroom walls, opera on the jukebox, live accordion jams and sightings of Beat poet-laureate Lawrence Ferlinghetti: this is North Beach at its best, since the 1950s. Linger over espresso and scribble your screenplay under the Sardinian fishing mural just as young Francis Ford Coppola did. Perhaps you've heard of the movie: *The Godfather*. Cash only.

★**Comstock Saloon**   BAR
(Map p982; ☑415-617-0071; www.comstocksaloon.com; 155 Columbus Ave; ⊗4pm-midnight Sun-Mon, to 2am Tue-Thu & Sat, noon-2am Fri; ☐8, 10, 12, 30, 45, ☐Powell-Mason) Relieving yourself in the marble trough below the bar is no longer advisable – Emperor Norton is watching from above – but otherwise this 1907 Victorian saloon brings back the Barbary Coast's glory days with authentic pisco punch and martini-precursor Martinez (gin, vermouth, bitters, maraschino liqueur). Reserve booths or back-parlor seating to hear on nights when ragtime-jazz bands play.

★**El Rio**   CLUB
(Map p986; ☑415-282-3325; www.elriosf.com; 3158 Mission St; cover free-$8; ⊗1pm-2am; ☐12, 14, 27, 49, ☐24th St Mission) Work it all out on the dance floor with SF's most down and funky crowd – the full rainbow spectrum of colorful characters is here to party. Calendar highlights include Salsa Sunday, free oysters from 5:30pm Friday, drag-star DJs, backyard bands and ping-pong. Expect knockout margaritas and shameless flirting on a patio that's seen it all since 1978. Cash only.

★ %ABV
COCKTAIL BAR

(Map p986; ☑ 415-400-4748; www.abvsf.com; 3174 16th St; ☺ 2pm-2am; ☐ 14, 22, Ⓑ 16th St Mission, Ⓜ J) As kindred spirits will deduce from the name (the abbreviation for 'percent alcohol by volume'), this bar is backed by cocktail crafters who know their Rittenhouse rye from their Japanese malt whisky. Top-notch hooch is served promptly and without pretension, including excellent Cali wine and beer on tap and original historically inspired cocktails.

★ Vesuvio
BAR

(Map p982; ☑ 415-362-3370; www.vesuvio.com; 255 Columbus Ave; ☺ 8am-2am; ☐ 8, 10, 12, 30, 41, 45, ☐ Powell-Mason) Guy walks into a bar, roars and leaves. Without missing a beat, the bartender says to the next customer, 'Welcome to Vesuvio, honey – what can I get you?' Jack Kerouac blew off Henry Miller to go on a bender here and, after you've joined neighborhood characters on the stained-glass mezzanine for microbrews or Kerouacs (rum, tequila and OJ), you'll see why.

★ Smuggler's Cove
BAR

(Map p982; ☑ 415-869-1900; www.smugglerscovesf.com; 650 Gough St; ☺ 5pm-1:15am; ☐ 5, 21, 47, 49, Ⓜ Civic Center, Ⓑ Civic Center) Yo-ho-ho and a bottle of rum...wait, make that a Dead Reckoning (Nicaraguan rum, port, pineapple and bitters), unless you'll split the flaming Scorpion Bowl? Pirates are bedeviled by choice at this Barbary Coast–shipwreck tiki bar, hidden behind tinted-glass doors. With 550 rums and 70-plus cocktails gleaned from rum-running around the world – and $2 off 5pm to 6pm daily.

★ Toronado
PUB

(Map p982; ☑ 415-863-2276; www.toronado.com; 547 Haight St; ☺ 11:30am-2am; ☐ 6, 7, 22, Ⓜ N) Glory hallelujah, beer-lovers: your prayers are answered. Genuflect before the chalkboard altar that lists 40-plus beers on tap and hundreds more bottled, including sensational microbrews. Bring cash for all-day happy hours and score sausages from Rosamunde (p998) to accompany ale made by Trappist monks. It sometimes gets too loud to hear your date talk, but you'll hear angels sing.

☆ Entertainment

At Union Square, **TIX Bay Area** (Map p982; http://tixbayarea.org; 350 Powell St; ☐ Powell-Mason, Powell-Hyde, Ⓑ Powell, Ⓜ Powell) sells last minute theater tickets for half-price.

★ San Francisco Symphony
CLASSICAL MUSIC

(Map p982; ☑ box office 415-864-6000, rush-ticket hotline 415-503-5577; www.sfsymphony.org; Grove St, btwn Franklin St & Van Ness Ave; tickets $20-150; ☐ 21, 45, 47, Ⓜ Van Ness, Ⓑ Civic Center) From the moment conductor Michael Tilson Thomas bounces up on his toes and raises his baton, the audience is on the edge of their seats for another thunderous performance by the Grammy-winning SF Symphony. Don't miss signature concerts of Beethoven and Mahler, live symphony performances with such films as *Star Trek*, and creative collaborations with artists from Elvis Costello to Metallica.

★ SFJAZZ Center
JAZZ

(Map p982; ☑ 866-920-5299; www.sfjazz.org; 201 Franklin St; tickets $25-120; ☐; ☐ 5, 6, 7, 21, 47, 49, Ⓜ Van Ness) ⊘ Jazz legends and singular talents from Argentina to Yemen are showcased at North America's newest, largest jazz center. Hear fresh takes on classic jazz albums and poets riffing with jazz combos in the downstairs Joe Henderson Lab, and witness extraordinary main-stage collaborations ranging from Afro-Cuban All Stars to roots legends Emmylou Harris, Rosanne Cash and Lucinda Williams.

★ San Francisco Opera
OPERA

(Map p982; ☑ 415-864-3330; www.sfopera.com; War Memorial Opera House, 301 Van Ness Ave; tickets $10-350; ☐ 21, 45, 47, 49, Ⓑ Civic Center, Ⓜ Van Ness) Opera was SF's gold-rush soundtrack – and SF Opera rivals the Met, with world premieres of original works ranging from Stephen King's *Dolores Claiborne* to *Girls of the Golden West*, filmmaker Peter Sellars' collaboration with composer John Adams. Expect haute couture costumes and radical sets by painter David Hockney. Score $10 same-day standing-room tickets at 10am; check website for Opera Lab pop-ups.

★ Independent
LIVE MUSIC

(Map p980; ☑ 415-771-1421; www.theindependentsf.com; 628 Divisadero St; tickets $12-45; ☺ box office 11am-6pm Mon-Fri, to 9:30pm show nights; ☐ 5, 6, 7, 21, 24) Bragging rights are earned with breakthrough shows at the small but mighty Independent, featuring indie dreamers (Magnetic Fields, Death Cab for Cutie), legends (Steel Pulse, Guided by Voices), alt-pop (the Killers, Imagine Dragons) and international bands (Tokyo Chaotic, Australia's Airbourne). Ventilation is poor in this max-capacity-800 venue, but the sound is stellar, drinks reasonable and bathrooms improbably clean.

★ **American Conservatory Theater** THEATER
(ACT; Map p982; ☑ 415-749-2228; www.act-sf.
org; 405 Geary St; ☺ box office 10am-6pm Mon, to
curtain Tue-Sun; ☑ 8, 30, 38, 45, ☑ Powell-Mason,
Powell-Hyde, B Powell, M Powell) Breakthrough
shows launch at this turn-of-the-century
landmark, which has hosted ACT's productions of Tony Kushner's *Angels in America*
and Robert Wilson's *Black Rider*, with William S Burroughs' libretto and music by Tom
Waits. Major playwrights like Tom Stoppard,
Dustin Lance Black, Eve Ensler and David
Mamet premiere work here, while the ACT's
new **Strand Theater** (Map p982; ☑ 415-749-
2228; www.act-sf.org/home/box_office/strand.
html; 1127 Market St; ☑ F, B Civic Center, M Civic
Center) stages experimental works.

San Francisco Ballet DANCE
(Map p982; ☑ tickets 415-865-2000; www.sfballet.
org; War Memorial Opera House, 301 Van Ness Ave;
tickets $22-141; ☺ ticket sales 10am-4pm Mon-Fri;
☑ 5, 21, 47, 49, M Van Ness, B Civic Center) The
USA's oldest ballet company is looking sharp
in more than 100 shows annually, from *The
Nutcracker* (the US premiere was here) to
modern originals. Performances are mostly
at the War Memorial Opera House from January to May, and occasionally at the Yerba
Buena Center for the Arts. Score $15-to-$20
same-day standing-room tickets at the box
office (from noon Tuesday to Friday, 10am
weekends).

★ **Beach Blanket Babylon** CABARET
(BBB; Map p982; ☑ 415-421-4222; www.beach
blanketbabylon.com; 678 Green St; $25-130;
☺ shows 8pm Wed, Thu & Fri, 6pm & 9pm Sat, 2pm
& 5pm Sun; ☑ 8, 30, 39, 41, 45, ☑ Powell-Mason)
Snow White searches for Prince Charming
in San Francisco: what could possibly go
wrong? The Disney-spoof musical-comedy
cabaret has been running since 1974, but
topical jokes keep it outrageous as wigs
remain big and parade floats gasp-worthy.
Spectators must be over 21 to handle racy
humor, except at cleverly sanitized Sunday
matinees. Reservations essential; arrive one
hour early for best seats.

Fillmore Auditorium LIVE MUSIC
(Map p982; ☑ 415-346-6000; http://thefillmore.
com; 1805 Geary Blvd; tickets from $20; ☺ box of-
fice 10am-3pm Sun, plus 30min before doors open
to 10pm show nights; ☑ 22, 38) Jimi Hendrix,
Janis Joplin, the Doors – they all played the
Fillmore. Now you might catch the Indigo
Girls, Willie Nelson or Tracy Chapman in the

historic 1250-capacity, standing-room-only
theater (if you're polite and lead with the
hip, you might squeeze up to the stage).
Don't miss the priceless collection of psychedelic posters in the upstairs gallery.

★ **Great American Music Hall** LIVE MUSIC
(Map p982; ☑ 415-885-0750; www.gamh.com; 859
O'Farrell St; shows $20-45; ☺ box office 10:30am-
6pm Mon-Fri & show nights; ☜; ☑ 19, 38, 47, 49)
Everyone busts out their best sets at this
opulent 1907 bordello turned all-ages venue – indie rockers like the Band Perry throw
down, international legends such as Salif
Keita grace the stage, and John Waters hosts
Christmas extravaganzas. Pay $25 extra for
dinner with prime balcony seating to watch
shows comfortably, or rock out with the
standing-room scrum downstairs.

★ **Roxie Cinema** CINEMA
(Map p986; ☑ 415-863-1087; www.roxie.com; 3117
16th St; regular screening/matinee $11/8; ☑ 14,
22, 33, 49, B 16th St Mission) This vintage 1909
cinema is a neighborhood nonprofit with
an international reputation for distributing
documentaries and showing controversial
films banned elsewhere. Tickets to film-
festival premieres, rare revivals and raucous
Oscars telecasts sell out – get tickets online
– but if the main show's packed, discover
riveting documentaries in teensy next-door
Little Roxy instead. No ads, plus personal
introductions to every film.

Sundance Kabuki Cinema CINEMA
(Map p982; ☑ 415-346-3243; www.sundancecine
mas.com; 1881 Post St; adult $11-16.50; ☑ 2, 3, 22,
38) ✐ Cinema-going at its best. Reserve a
stadium seat, belly up to the bar and order
wine and surprisingly good food to enjoy
during the film. A multiplex initiative by
Robert Redford's Sundance Institute, Kabuki features big-name flicks and festivals
– and it's green, with recycled-fiber seating,
reclaimed-wood decor and local chocolates
and booze (hence the 21-plus designation
most shows). Validated parking.

🛍 Shopping

★ **Aggregate Supply** CLOTHING, HOMEWARES
(Map p986; ☑ 415-474-3190; www.aggregatesup
plysf.com; 806 Valencia St; ☺ 11am-7pm Mon-Sat,
noon-6pm Sun; ☑ 14, 33, 49, B 16th St Mission)
Wild West modern is the look at Aggregate
Supply, purveyors of California-cool fashion
and home decor. Local designers and indie
makers get pride of place, including vintage

SAN FRANCISCO'S BEST SHOPPING AREAS

All those rustic-chic dens, well-stocked cupboards and fabulous outfits don't just pull themselves together – San Franciscans scoured their city for it all. Here's where to find what:

Ferry Building Local food, wine and kitchenware.

Hayes Valley Independent fashion designers, housewares, gifts.

Valencia Street Bookstores, local design collectives, art galleries, vintage whatever.

Haight Street Head shops, music, vintage, skate and surf gear.

Union Square Department stores, megabrands, discount retail, Applestore.

Russian Hill and the Marina Date outfits, urban accessories, housewares, gifts.

Grant Avenue From Chinatown souvenirs to funky North Beach boutiques.

Heath stoneware mugs, Turk+Taylor's plaid shirt-jackets, and SF artist Tauba Auerbach's 24-hour clocks. Souvenirs don't get more authentically local than Aggregate Supply's own op-art California graphic tee and NorCal-forest-scented organic soaps.

★ **Amoeba Music**   MUSIC
(Map p988; ☑ 415-831-1200; www.amoeba.com; 1855 Haight St; ⊙11am-8pm; 🚌6, 7, 33, 43, Ⓜ N) 🔖 Enticements are hardly necessary to lure the masses to the West Coast's most eclectic collection of new and used music and video, but Amoeba offers listening stations, free zines with uncannily accurate staff reviews, and a free concert series that recently starred the Violent Femmes, Kehlani, Billy Bragg and Mike Doughty – plus a foundation that's saved one million acres of rainforest.

Betabrand   CLOTHING
(Map p986; ☑ 415-400-9491; www.betabrand.com; 780 Valencia St; ⊙11am-7pm Mon-Fri, to 8pm Sat, noon-6pm Sun; 🚌14, 22, 33, 49, Ⓑ16th St Mission) Crowdsource fashion choices at Betabrand, where experimental designs are put to an online vote and winners are produced in limited editions. Recent approved designs include office-ready dress yoga pants, disco-ball windbreakers and sundresses with a smiling-poo-emoji print. Some styles are clunkers – including the 'chillmono,' a kimono-style down puffer jacket – but at these prices you can afford to take fashion risks.

❶ Information

DANGERS & ANNOYANCES

Keep your city smarts and wits about you, especially at night in the Tenderloin, South of Market (SoMa) and the Mission.

MEDICAL SERVICES

San Francisco General Hospital (Zuckerberg San Franciso General Hospital and Trauma Center; ☑ emergency 415-206-8111, main hospital 415-206-8000; www.sfdph.org; 1001 Potrero Ave; ⊙24hr; 🚌9, 10, 33, 48) Best ER for serious accidents.

TOURIST INFORMATION

SF Visitor Information Center (Map p982; ☑ 415-391-2000; www.sftravel.com/visitor-information-center; lower level, Hallidie Plaza, cnr Market & Powell Sts; ⊙9am-5pm Mon-Fri, to 3pm Sat & Sun, closed Sun Nov-Apr; 🚋 Powell-Mason, Powell-Hyde, Ⓜ Powell, Ⓑ Powell) Muni Passports, activities deals, culture and event calendars.

USEFUL WEBSITES

SFGate.com (www.sfgate.com)

SFist (www.sfist.com)

7x7 (www.7x7.com)

❶ Getting There & Away

AIR

San Francisco International Airport (SFO; www.flysfo.com; S McDonnell Rd) is 14 miles south of downtown, off Hwy 101 and accessible by Bay Area Rapid Transit (BART). Serving primarily domestic destinations, **Oakland International Airport** (OAK; www.oaklandairport. com; 1 Airport Dr; 🚇; Ⓑ Oakland International Airport) is a 40-minute BART ride across the Bay, while **Mineta San José International Airport** (SJC; ☑ 408-392-3600; www.flysanjose.com; 1701 Airport Blvd) is 45 miles south via Hwy 101.

BUS

Until the new terminal is complete in late 2017, SF's intercity hub remains the **Temporary Transbay Terminal** (Map p982; cnr Howard & Main Sts; 🚌5,38,41,71). From here you can catch the following buses:

AC Transit (☑ 510-891-4777; www.actransit. org) Buses to the East Bay.

Greyhound (☑ 800-231-2222; www.greyhound. com) Buses leave daily for Los Angeles ($39 to $90, eight to 12 hours), Truckee near Lake Tahoe ($35 to $46, 5½ hours) and other major destinations.

Megabus (☑ 877-462-6342; http://us.mega bus.com) Low-cost bus service to San Francisco from Los Angeles, Sacramento and Reno.

SamTrans (☑ 800-660-4287; www.samtrans. com) Southbound buses to Palo Alto and the Pacific coast.

TRAIN

Amtrak (☑ 800-872-7245; www.amtrakcali fornia.com) serves San Francisco via stations in Oakland and Emeryville (near Oakland), with free shuttle-bus connections to San Francisco's Ferry Building and Caltrain station, and Oakland's Jack London Sq.

Caltrain (www.caltrain.com; cnr 4th & King Sts) connects San Francisco with Silicon Valley hubs and San Jose.

❶ Getting Around

TO/FROM SAN FRANCISCO INTERNATIONAL AIRPORT

From SFO's **BART** (Bay Area Rapid Transit; www. bart.gov) station, connected to the International Terminal, it's a 30-minute ride to downtown SF. A taxi to downtown SF from SFO costs $40 to $55, plus tip. Airport shuttles (one way $17 to $20 plus tip) depart from *upper-level* ticketing areas (not lower-level baggage claim); anticipate 45 minutes to most SF locations. **SuperShuttle** (☑ 800-258-3826; www.supershuttle.com) offers shared van rides for $17 per person.

BOAT

San Francisco Bay Ferry (☑ 415-705-8291; http://sanfranciscobayferry.com) Operates from both Pier 41 and the Ferry Building to Oakland/Alameda. Fares are $6.60.

CAR & MOTORCYCLE

If you can, avoid driving in San Francisco: heavy traffic is a given, street parking is harder to find than true love, and meter readers are ruthless.

PUBLIC TRANSPORTATION

When San Franciscans aren't pressed for time, most walk, bike or ride **Muni** (San Francisco Municipal Transportation Agency) instead of taking a car or cab. For Bay Area transit options, departures and arrivals, call 511 or check www.511.org. A detailed Muni Street & Transit Map is available free online.

Cable cars Frequent, slow and scenic, from 6am to 12:30am daily. Single rides cost $7; for frequent use, get a Muni Passport ($21 per day).

Muni streetcar and bus Reasonably fast, but schedules vary wildly by line; infrequent after 9pm. Fares are $2.50.

BART High-speed transit to East Bay, Mission St, SF airport and Millbrae, where it connects with Caltrain.

TAXI

Fares are about $2.75 per mile; meters start at $3.50. Hailing a cab in the street can be difficult. Download the mobile app Flywheel (http://fly wheel.com) for prompt service.

Marin County

Majestic redwoods cling to tawny coastal headlands just across the Golden Gate Bridge in laid-back Marin. The southernmost town, **Sausalito** (www.sausalito.org), is a tiny bayfront destination for cycling trips over the bridge (take the ferry back to San Francisco). Near the harbor, where picturesque bohemian houseboats are docked, the **Bay Model Visitors Center** (Map p980; ☑ 415-332-3871; www.spn.usace.army.mil/mis sions/recreation/baymodelvisitorcenter.aspx; 2100 Bridgeway Blvd; ⊙9am-4pm Tue-Sat, extended summer hours 10am-5pm Sat & Sun; P ⊞) FREE houses a giant hydraulic re-creation of the entire bay and delta.

Marin Headlands

These windswept, rugged headlands are laced with hiking trails, providing panoramic bay and city views. To find the **visitor center** (Map p980; ☑ 415-331-1540; www.nps. gov/goga/marin-headlands.htm; Bunker Rd, Fort Barry; ⊙9:30am-4:30pm), take the Alexander Ave exit after crossing north over the Golden Gate Bridge, turn left under the freeway and follow the signs.

Attractions west of Hwy 101 include **Point Bonita Lighthouse** (Map p980; ☑ 415-331-1540; www.nps.gov/goga/pobo.htm; ⊙12:30-3:30pm Sat-Mon; P) FREE, Cold War–era **Nike Missile Site SF-88** (Map p980; ☑ 415-331-1540; www.nps.gov/goga/nike-missile-site.htm; Field Rd; ⊙12:30-3:30pm Sat; P) FREE and the educational **Marine Mammal Center** (Map p980; ☑ 415-289-7325; www.marinemammal center.org; 2000 Bunker Rd; by donation, audio tour adult/child $9/5; ⊙10am-4pm; P ⊞) 🚶 uphill from **Rodeo Beach** (Map p980; www.parks conservancy.org/visit/park-sites/rodeo-beach. html; off Bunker Rd; P ⊞). East of Hwy 101 at Fort Baker, the interactive **Bay Area Discovery Museum** (Map p980; ☑ 415-339-3900;

www.baykidsmuseum.org; 557 McReynolds Rd; $14, 1st Wed each month free; ☉9am-4pm Tue-Fri, to 5pm Sat & Sun, also 9am-4pm some Mon; P ♿) is awesome for kids.

Near the visitor center, HI Marin Headlands Hostel (Map p980; ☑415-331-2777; www. norcalhostels.org/marin; Fort Barry, Bldg 941; r with shared bath $105-135, dm $31-40; ☉reception 7:30am-11:30pm; P ☕ @ ✿) ⌀ occupies two 1907 military buildings on a forested hill. For historical luxury, book a fireplace room with bay views at Fort Baker's LEED-certified Cavallo Point (Map p980; ☑415-339-4700; www.cavallopoint.com; 601 Murray Circle; r from $399; P ☕ ✳ @ ✿ ☂ ☎) ⌀ lodge.

Mt Tamalpais State Park

Majestic Mt Tam (2572ft) is a woodsy playground for hikers and mountain bikers. Mt Tamalpais State Park (Map p980; ☑415-388-2070; www.parks.ca.gov; per car $8; ☉7am-sunset; P ♿) ⌀ encompasses 6300 acres of parklands and over 200 miles of trails. Don't miss driving up to East Peak Summit lookout. Panoramic Hwy passes through the park, connecting Muir Woods with Stinson Beach, a coastal town with a sandy crescent-shaped beach on Hwy 1.

Park headquarters are Pantoll Station (Map p980; ☑415-388-2070; www.parks.ca.gov; 801 Panoramic Hwy; ☉hours vary; ☎), the nexus of many trails, with a first-come, first-served campground (Map p980; ☑info 415-388-2070; www.parks.ca.gov; Panoramic Hwy; tent sites $25; P ☎). Book far ahead for a rustic cabin (no electricity or running water) or walk-in campsite at Steep Ravine (☑reservations 800-444-7275; www.reserveamerica.com; tent sites $25, cabins $100; ☉Nov-Sep; P), off Hwy 1 south of Stinson Beach. Or hike in with a sleeping bag, towel and food to off-the-grid West Point Inn (Map p980; ☑info 415-388-9955, reservations 415-646-0702; www.westpointinn.com; 100 Old Railroad Grade, San Anselmo; r with shared bath per adult/child $50/25, linen rental $10; ☕) ⌀; reservations required.

Point Reyes National Seashore

The windswept peninsula of Point Reyes National Seashore (☑415-654-5100; www.nps.gov/pore; P ♿) ⌀FREE juts 10 miles out to sea on an entirely different tectonic plate, protecting over 100 sq miles of beaches, lagoons and forested hills. A mile west of Olema, Bear Valley Visitor Center (☑415-464-5100; www.nps.gov/pore; 1 Bear Valley Rd, Point Reyes Station; ☉10am-

5pm Mon-Fri, 9am-5pm Sat & Sun; ♿) has maps, information and natural-history displays. The 0.6-mile Earthquake Trail, which crosses the San Andreas Fault zone, starts nearby.

Crowning the peninsula's westernmost tip, Point Reyes Lighthouse (☑415-669-1534; www.nps.gov/pore; end of Sir Francis Drake Blvd; ☉10am-4:30pm Fri-Mon, lens room 2:30-4pm Fri-Mon) is ideal for winter whale-watching. Off Pierce Point Rd, the 10-mile round-trip Tomales Point Trail rolls atop blustery bluffs past herds of tule elk to the peninsula's northern tip. To paddle out into Tomales Bay, Blue Waters Kayaking (☑415-669-2600; www.bluewaterskayaking.com; 12944 Sir Francis Drake Blvd; rentals/tours from $60/68; ☉usually 9am-5pm, last rental 2pm; ♿) launches from Inverness and Marshall.

Nature-lovers bunk at the only in-park lodging, HI Point Reyes Hostel (☑415-663-8811; www.norcalhostels.org/reyes; 1390 Limantour Spit Rd; r with shared bath $105-130, dm $29-38; ☉reception 7:30-10:30am & 4:30-10pm; P ☕ @) ⌀, 8 miles inland from the visitor center. In the coastal town of Inverness, the Cottages at Point Reyes Seashore (☑415-669-7250; www.cottagespointreyes.com; 13275 Sir Francis Drake Blvd; r $129-269; P ☕ ✿ ☂ ☎) is a family-friendly place tucked away in the woods. The West Marin Chamber of Commerce (☑415-663-9232; www.pointreyes.org) checks availability at more cozy inns, cottages and B&Bs.

Two miles north of Olema, the tiny town of Point Reyes Station has bakeries, cafes and restaurants. Gather a picnic lunch at Cowgirl Creamery at Tomales Bay Foods (☑415-663-9335; www.cowgirlcreamery.com; 80 4th St; deli items $3-10; ☉10am-6pm Wed-Sun; ☝♿) ⌀ or head 10 miles north of town for an oyster feast at Hog Island Oyster Company (☑415-663-9218; https://hogislandoysters.com; 20215 Hwy 1, Marshall; 12 oysters $13-16, picnic per person $5; ☉shop 9am-5pm daily, picnic area from 10am, cafe 11am-5pm Fri-Mon).

Berkeley

As the birthplace of the free-speech and disability-rights movements and the home of the hallowed halls of the University of California, Berkeley (aka 'Cal'), it is no bashful wallflower. A national hot spot of (mostly left-of-center) intellectual discourse and one of the most vocal activist populations in the country, this infamous college town has an interesting mix of graying progressives and idealistic undergrads.

⊙ Sights & Activities

Leading to the campus's south gate, **Telegraph Avenue** is a youthful street carnival, packed with cheap cafes, music stores, streethawkers and buskers.

University of California, Berkeley
UNIVERSITY

(☎ 510-642-6000; www.berkeley.edu; P; B Downtown Berkeley) 'Cal' is one of the country's top universities, California's oldest university (1866), and home to 40,000 diverse, politically conscious students. Next to **California Memorial Stadium** (www.californiamemorial stadium.com), the **Koret Visitor Center** (☎ 510-642-5215; http://visit.berkeley.edu; 2227 Piedmont Ave; ⊙ 8:30am-4:30pm Mon-Fri, 9am-1pm Sat & Sun; ☐ AC Transit 36) has information and maps, and leads free campus walking tours (reservations required). Cal's landmark is the 1914 **Campanile** (Sather Tower; ☎ 510-642-6000; http://campanile.berkeley.edu; adult/child $3/2; ⊙ 10am-3:45pm Mon-Fri, 10am-4:45pm Sat, to 1:30pm & 3-4:45pm Sun; ♿; B Downtown Berkeley), with elevator rides ($3) to the top and carillon concerts. The **Bancroft Library** (☎ 510-642-3781; www.lib.berkeley.edu/libraries/bancroft-library; University Dr; ⊙ archives 10am-4pm or 5pm Mon-Fri; B Downtown Berkeley) FREE displays the small gold nugget that started the California gold rush in 1848.

☷ Sleeping

Lodging rates spike during special university events such as graduation (mid-May) and home football games. A number of older, less expensive motels along University Ave can be handy during peak demand, as can chain motels and hotels off I-80 in Emeryville or Vallejo.

Hotel Shattuck Plaza
HOTEL $$

(☎ 510-845-7300; www.hotelshattuckplaza.com; 2086 Allston Way; r from $200; P❀❄@☎; B Downtown Berkeley) Following a $15-million renovation and greening of this 100-year-old downtown jewel, a foyer of red Italian glass lighting, flocked Victorian-style wallpaper – and yes, a peace sign tiled into the floor – leads to comfortable rooms with down comforters and an airy, columned restaurant serving all meals.

★ Claremont Resort & Spa
RESORT $$$

(☎ 510-843-3000; www.fairmont.com/claremont-berkeley; 41 Tunnel Rd; r from $240; P❀❄@☎❄☷) The East Bay's classy crème de la crème, this Fairmont-owned historic hotel is a glamorous white 1915 building with elegant restaurants, a fitness center, swimming pools, tennis courts and a full-service spa. The bay-view rooms are superb. It's located at the foot of the Berkeley Hills, off Hwy 13 (Tunnel Rd) near the Oakland border. Parking is $30.

✖ Eating & Drinking

Ippuku
JAPANESE $$

(☎ 510-665-1969; www.ippukuberkeley.com; 2130 Center St; shared plates $5-20; ⊙ 5-10pm Tue-Thu, to 11pm Fri & Sat; B Downtown Berkeley) Japanese expats gush that Ippuku reminds them of *izakaya* (Japanese gastropubs) back in Tokyo. Choose from a menu of yakitori (skewered meats and vegetables) and handmade soba noodles as you settle in at one of the traditional tatami tables (no shoes, please) or cozy booth perches. Order *shōchū*, a distilled alcohol usually made from rice or barley. Reservations essential.

★ Chez Panisse
CALIFORNIAN $$$

(☎ cafe 510-548-5049, restaurant 510-548-5525; www.chezpanisse.com; 1517 Shattuck Ave; cafe dinner mains $22-35, restaurant prix-fixe dinner $75-125; ⊙ cafe 11:30am-2:45pm & 5-10:30pm Mon-Thu, 11:30am-3pm & 5-11:30pm Fri & Sat, restaurant seatings 5:30pm & 8pm Mon-Sat; ✐; ☐ AC Transit 7) ✐ Foodies come to worship here at the church of Alice Waters, inventor of California cuisine. It's in a lovely arts-and-crafts house in Berkeley's 'Gourmet Ghetto,' and you can choose to pull out all the stops with a prix-fixe meal downstairs, or go less expensive and a tad less formal in the upstairs cafe. Reservations accepted one month ahead.

Jupiter
PUB

(☎ 510-843-8277; www.jupiterbeer.com; 2181 Shattuck Ave; ⊙ 11:30am-12:30am Mon-Thu, to 1:30am Fri, noon-1:30am Sat, noon-11:30pm Sun; B Downtown Berkeley) This downtown pub has loads of regional microbrews, a beer garden, decent pizza and live bands most nights. Sit upstairs for a bird's-eye view of bustling Shattuck Ave.

☆ Entertainment

Berkeley Repertory Theatre
THEATER

(☎ 510-647-2949; www.berkeleyrep.org; 2025 Addison St; tickets $40-100; ⊙ box office noon-7pm Tue-Sun; B Downtown Berkeley) This highly respected company has produced bold versions of classical and modern plays since 1968. Most shows have half-price tickets for patrons under 30.

Freight & Salvage Coffeehouse LIVE MUSIC
(☎510-644-2020; www.thefreight.org; 2020 Addison St; tickets $5-45; ⊙shows daily; ♿; Ⓑ Downtown Berkeley) This legendary club has almost 50 years of history and is conveniently located in the downtown arts district. It features great traditional folk, country, bluegrass and world music and welcomes all ages, with half-price tickets for patrons under 21.

ⓘ Getting There & Around

To get to Berkeley, catch a Richmond-bound train to one of three **BART** (Bay Area Rapid Transit; www.bart.gov) stations: Ashby, Downtown Berkeley or North Berkeley. Fares between Berkeley and San Francisco cost $4.10 to $4.40, between Berkeley and downtown Oakland $1.95.

NORTHERN CALIFORNIA

The Golden State goes wild in Northern California, with coast redwoods swirled in fog, Wine Country vineyards and hidden hot springs. Befitting this dramatic meeting of land and water is an unlikely mélange of local residents: timber barons and hippie tree huggers, dreadlocked Rastafarians and biodynamic ranchers, pot farmers and political radicals of every stripe. Come for the scenery, but stay for the top-notch wine and farm-to-fork restaurants, misty hikes among the world's tallest trees and rambling conversations that begin with 'Hey, dude!' and end hours later.

Wine Country

America's premier viticulture region has earned its reputation among the world's best. Despite hype about Wine Country style, it's from the land that all Wine Country lore springs. Rolling hills, dotted with century-old oaks, turn the color of lion's fur under the summer sun and swaths of vineyards carpet hillsides as far as the eye can see. Where they end, redwood forests follow serpentine rivers to the sea.

ⓘ Getting There & Around

Either Napa or Sonoma is a 90-minute drive north of San Francisco via Hwy 101 or I-80. Getting to and around the valleys by public transportation (mainly buses, perhaps in combination with BART trains or ferries) is slow and complicated, but just possible – consult http://511.org for trip planning and schedules.

Rent bicycles from **Wine Country Cyclery** (☎707-966-6800; www.winecountrycyclery.com; 262 W Napa St; bicycle rental per day $30-75; ⊙10am-6pm), **Napa Valley Bike Tours** (☎707-944-2953; www.napavalleybiketours.com; 6500 Washington St, Yountville; bicycle rental per day $45-75, tours $109-124; ⊙8:30am-5pm), **Calistoga Bike Shop** (☎707-942-9687; http://calistogabikeshop.com; 1318 Lincoln Ave; bicycle rental from $28, guided tours from $149; ⊙10am-6pm) or **Spoke Folk Cyclery** (☎707-433-7171; www.spokefolk.com; 201 Center St; hybrid bicycle rental per hour/day from $14/38; ⊙10am-6pm Mon-Fri, to 5pm Sat & Sun).

Napa Valley

More than 200 wineries crowd 30-mile-long Napa Valley along three main routes. Traffic-jammed on weekends, **Highway 29** is lined with blockbuster wineries. Running parallel, **Silverado Trail** moves faster, passing boutique winemakers, bizarre architecture and cult-hit Cabernet Sauvignon. Heading west toward Sonoma, **Carneros Highway** (Hwy 121) winds by landmark vineyards specializing in sparkling wines and Pinot Noir.

At the southern end of the valley, **Napa** – the valley's workaday hub – lacks rusticity, but has trendy restaurants and tasting rooms downtown. Stop by the **Napa Valley Welcome Center** (☎855-847-6272, 707-251-5895; www.visitnapavalley.com; 600 Main St; ⊙9am-5pm; ♿) for wine-tasting passes and winery maps.

Heading north on Hwy 29, the former stagecoach stop of tiny **Yountville** has more Michelin-starred eateries per capita than San Francisco. Another 10 miles north, traffic snarls in charming **St Helena**, where there's genteel strolling and shopping – if you can find parking. At the valley's northern end, folksy **Calistoga** is home to hot-springs spas and mud-bath emporiums using volcanic ash from nearby Mt St Helena.

◉ Sights & Activities

Many Napa wineries require reservations. Plan to visit no more than a few tasting rooms each day.

★**Hess Collection** WINERY, GALLERY
(☎707-255-1144; www.hesscollection.com; 4411 Redwood Rd, Napa; museum free, tasting $25 & $35, tours free; ⊙10am-5:30pm, last tasting 5pm) Art-lovers: don't miss Hess Collection, whose galleries display mixed-media and large-canvas works, including pieces by Francis Bacon and Robert Motherwell. In

the elegant stone-walled tasting room, find well-known Cabernet Sauvignon and Chardonnay, but also try the Viognier. There's garden service in the warmer months, which is lovely, as Hess overlooks the valley. Make reservations and be prepared to drive a winding road. Bottles are $30 to $100. Public tour 10:30am.

★ **Frog's Leap** WINERY
(☎707-963-4704; www.frogsleap.com; 8815 Conn Creek Rd, Rutherford; tasting $20-25, incl tour $25; ⏲10am-4pm by appointment only; P♿🐾) ✿ Meandering paths wind through magical gardens and fruit-bearing orchards surrounding an 1884 barn and farmstead with cats and chickens. The vibe is casual and down-to-earth, with a major emphasis on *fun*. Sauvignon Blanc is its best-known wine but the Merlot merits attention. There's also a dry, restrained Cabernet, atypical of Napa.

★ **Tres Sabores** WINERY
(☎707-967-8027; www.tressabores.com; 1620 South Whitehall Lane, St Helena; tour & tasting $40; ⏲10:30am-3pm, by appointment; 🐾) ✿ At the valley's westernmost edge, where sloping vineyards meet wooded hillsides, Tres Sabores is a portal to old Napa – no fancy tasting room, no snobbery, just great wine in a spectacular setting. Bucking the Cabernet custom, Tres Sabores crafts elegantly structured, Burgundian-style Zinfandel and spritely Sauvignon Blanc, which the *New York Times* dubbed a top 10 of its kind in California. Reservations are essential.

Castello di Amorosa WINERY, CASTLE
(☎707-967-6272; www.castellodiamorosa.com; 4045 Hwy 29, Calistoga; entry & tasting $25-35, incl guided tour $40-85; ⏲9:30am-6pm Mar-Oct, to 5pm Nov-Feb; P♿) It took 14 years to build this perfectly replicated, 13th-century Italian castle, complete with moat, hand-cut stone walls, ceiling frescoes by Italian artisans, Roman-style cross-vault brick catacombs, and a torture chamber with period equipment. You can taste without an appointment, but this is one tour worth taking. Oh, the wine? Some respectable Italian varietals, including a velvety Tuscan blend and a Merlot that goes great with pizza. Bottles are $20 to $98.

🛏 Sleeping

Pricey and fabulous hotels are scattered throughout Napa Valley, with the most opulent stays perched in and around St Helena and Yountville. Calistoga is a bit more relaxed and affordable, and the best budget option, without question, is a yurt (or campsite) in Bothe-Napa Valley State Park.

★ **El Bonita** MOTEL $$
(☎707-963-3216, 800-541-3284; www.elbonita. com; 195 Main St; r $140-325; P♿❄@🛜🏊🐾) Book in advance to secure this sought-after motel, with up-to-date rooms (quietest are in the back), attractive grounds, a heated pool, hot tub and sauna.

Napa Valley Railway Inn INN $$
(☎707-944-2000; www.napavalleyrailwayinn.com; 6523 Washington St; r $215-295; P♿❄@🛜🏊) Sleep in a converted railroad car, part of two short trains parked at a central platform. They've little privacy, but are moderately priced compared with the competition. Bring earplugs.

Las Alcobas BOUTIQUE HOTEL $$$
(☎707-963-7000; www.lasalcobasnapavalley.com; 1915 Main St; r from $600-2500; ❄🛜🏊) A newcomer with a sister property in Mexico City, this boutique has already secured its place among Napa Valley's finest stays. The plush, modern rooms offer both vineyard vista and proximity to some of the region's best dining, shopping and wine tasting. That's if you attempt to pry yourself from the delicious hotel-restaurant Acacia, heated pool and relaxing spa.

🍴 Eating

The $400-per-person, 12-course meals are procured in Yountville where Thomas Keller and his French Laundry reign, and St Helena, home of equally fabulous Meadowwood. For the less indulgent, the valley has a delicious array of midrange options and country stores offering picnic items and gourmet sandwiches. At wineries, charcuterie plates and food pairings are popular; show up hungry.

★ **Oxbow Public Market** MARKET $
(☎707-226-6529; www.oxbowpublicmarket.com; 610 & 644 1st St; items from $3; ⏲9am-9pm; 🛜🐾) ✿ Graze at this gourmet market and plug into the Northern California food scene. Standouts: **Hog Island Oyster Co**; comfort cooking at celeb-chef Todd Humphries' **Kitchen Door**; great Cal-Mexican tacos at **C Casa & Taco Lounge**; the India pale ales (IPAs) and sour beers at **Fieldwork Brewing Company**; espresso from **Ritual Coffee**; and **Three Twins** certified-organic ice cream.

Bouchon Bakery   BAKERY $
(☏ 707-944-2253; www.bouchonbakery.com; 6528
Washington St; items from $3; ☉ 7am-7pm; ☝)
Bouchon makes as-good-as-in-Paris French
pastries and strong coffee. There's always a
line and rarely a seat: get it to go.

Gott's Roadside   AMERICAN $$
(☏ 707-963-3486; http://gotts.com; 933 Main St;
mains $8-16; ☉ 10am-10pm May-Sep, to 9pm Oct-
Apr; ☝) ☝ Wiggle your toes in the grass and
feast on quality burgers – beef, turkey, ahi or
veggie – plus Cobb salads and fish tacos at
this classic roadside drive-in. Avoid weekend
waits by phoning ahead or ordering online.
There's another at Oxbow Public Market.

★French Laundry   CALIFORNIAN $$$
(☏ 707-944-2380;   www.thomaskeller.com/tfl;
6640 Washington St; prix-fixe dinner $310; ☉ seat-
ings 11am-12:30pm Fri-Sun, 5-9pm daily) The pinnacle of California dining, Thomas Keller's
French Laundry is epic, a high-wattage culinary experience on par with the world's best.
Book one month ahead on the online app
Tock, where tickets are released in groupings. This is the meal you can brag about the
rest of your life.

Sonoma Valley

We have a soft spot for Sonoma's folksy
ways. Unlike fancy Napa, nobody cares if
you drive a clunker and vote Green. Locals
call it 'Slow-noma.' Anchoring the bucolic 17-mile-long valley, the town of Sonoma
makes a great jumping-off point for exploring Wine Country – it's an hour from San
Francisco – and has a marvelous sense of
place, with storied 19th-century historical
sights surrounding the state's largest town
square.

◉ Sights & Activities

Downtown Sonoma was once the capital
of the short-lived Bear Flag Republic. Today Sonoma Plaza – the state's largest town
square – is bordered by historic hotels, busy
restaurants, chic shops and a **visitor center**
(☏ 866-966-1090; www.sonomavalley.com; 453 1st
St E; ☉ 9am-5pm Mon-Sat, 10am-5pm Sun).

★Gundlach-Bundschu Winery   WINERY
(☏ 707-938-5277; www.gunbun.com; 2000 Denmark St, Sonoma; tasting $20-30, incl tour $30-
60; ☉ 11am-5:30pm May-Oct, to 4:30pm Nov-Apr;
P) ☝ California's oldest family-run winery
looks like a castle but has a down-to-earth

vibe. Founded in 1858 by a Bavarian immigrant, its signatures are Gewürztraminer
and Pinot Noir, but 'Gun-Bun' was the first
American winery to produce 100% Merlot.
Down a winding lane, it's a terrific bike-
to winery with picnicking, hiking, a lake
and frequent concerts, including a two-
day folk-music festival in June. Tour the
1800-barrel cave by reservation only. Bottles
are $20 to $50.

Bartholomew Park   PARK
(☏ 707-938-2244;   www.bartholomewpark.org;
1000 Vineyard Lane; ☉ 10am-4:30pm; P ☝)
FREE The top near-town outdoors destination is 375-acre Bartholomew Park, off Castle
Rd, where you can picnic beneath giant oaks
and hike 2 miles of trails, with hilltop vistas to San Francisco. The **Palladian Villa**, at
the park's entrance, is a re-creation of Count
Haraszthy's original Pompeian residence,
open noon to 3pm Saturdays and Sundays.
There's also a good **winery**, independently
operated. Last entry is at 4:30pm.

Jack London State Historic Park   PARK
(☏ 707-938-5216; www.jacklondonpark.com; 2400
London Ranch Rd, Glen Ellen; per car $10, cottage
adult/child $4/2; ☉ 9:30am-5pm; P ☝) ☝ Napa
has Robert Louis Stevenson, but Sonoma has
Jack London. This 1400-acre park frames
that author's last years; don't miss the excellent on-site **museum**. Miles of **hiking
trails** (some open to mountain bikes) weave
through oak-dotted woodlands, between
600ft and 2300ft elevations; an easy 2-mile
loop meanders to **London Lake**, great for
picnicking. On select summer evenings, the
park transforms into a theater for 'Broadway
Under the Stars.' Be alert for poison oak.

Benziger   WINERY
(☏ 888-490-2739, 707-935-3000; www.benziger.
com; 1883 London Ranch Rd, Glen Ellen; tasting
$20-40, tours $25-50; ☉ 10am-5pm; P ☝) ☝
If you're new to wine, make Benziger your
first stop for Sonoma's best crash course
in winemaking. The worthwhile tour
(11am–3:30pm; reservations recommended)
includes an open-air tram ride (weather permitting) through biodynamic vineyards and
a five-wine tasting. Great picnicking, excellent for families. The large-production wine
is OK (head for the reserves); the tour's the
thing. Bottles are $20 to $80.

Kunde   WINERY
(☏ 707-833-5501; www.kunde.com; 9825 Hwy
12, Kenwood; tasting $15-50, cave tours free;

⊙10:30am-5pm; P) 🚗 This family-owned winery on a historic ranch has vineyards that are more than a century old. It offers mountaintop tastings with impressive valley views and seasonal guided hikes (advance reservations recommended), though you can also just stop for a tasting and a tour. Elegant, 100% estate-grown wines include crisp Chardonnay and unfussy red blends, all made sustainably. Bottles $17 to $100.

Cline Cellars   WINERY
(☎707-940-4030; www.clinecellars.com; 24737 Arnold Dr, Hwy 121; tasting free-$20; ⊙tasting room 10am-6pm, museum to 4pm) 🚗 Balmy days are for pondside picnics and rainy ones for fireside tastings of old-vine Zinfandel and Mourvèdre inside an 1850s farmhouse. Stroll out back to the **California Mission Museum**, housing 1930s miniature replicas of California's original 21 Spanish Colonial missions.

🛏 Sleeping

The most sensible bases for exploring this valley are historic downtown Sonoma and lush, romantic Glen Ellen. Kenwood also has one sumptuous inn.

★Windhaven Cottage   COTTAGE $$
(☎707-938-2175, 707-483-1856; www.windhaven cottage.com; 21700 Pearson Ave; cottages $165-175; ❋🛜) Great-bargain Windhaven has two units: a hideaway cottage with vaulted wooden ceilings and fireplace, and a handsome 800-sq-ft studio. We prefer the romantic cottage. Both have hot tubs. Bicycles and barbecues sweeten the deal.

Beltane Ranch   B&B $$
(☎707-833-4233; www.beltaneranch.com; 11775 Hwy 12, Glen Ellen; d $185-375; P😊🛜) 🚗 Surrounded by horse pastures and vineyards, Beltane is a throwback to 19th-century Sonoma. The cheerful 1890s ranch house has double porches lined with swinging chairs and white wicker. Though it's technically a B&B, each country-Americana-style room and the cottage has a private entrance – nobody will make you pet the cat. No phone or TV means zero distraction from pastoral bliss.

🍴 Eating & Drinking

★Fremont Diner   AMERICAN, SOUTHERN $$
(☎707-938-7370; www.thefremontdiner.com; 2698 Fremont Dr; mains $9-22; ⊙8am-3pm Mon-Wed, to 9pm Thu-Sun; 🚸) 🚗 Lines snake out the door at peak times at this farm-to-table roadside diner. We prefer the indoor tables but will happily accept a picnic table to feast on buttermilk pancakes with homemade cinnamon-vanilla syrup, chicken and waffles, oyster po'boys, finger-licking barbecue and skillet-baked cornbread.

Fig Cafe & Winebar   FRENCH, CALIFORNIAN $$
(☎707-938-2130; www.thefigcafe.com; 13690 Arnold Dr, Glen Ellen; mains $12-24, 3-course dinner $36; ⊙10am-2:30pm Sat & Sun, 5-9pm Sun-Thu, 5-9:30pm Fri & Sat) The Fig's earthy California-Provençal comfort food includes flash-fried calamari with spicy lemon aioli, fig and arugula salad and *steak frites*. Good wine prices and weekend brunch give reason to return. No reservations; complimentary corkage.

Hopmonk Tavern   PUB FOOD $$
(☎707-935-9100; www.hopmonk.com; 691 Broadway; mains $11-23; ⊙11:30am-9pm Sun-Thu, to 10pm Fri & Sat) This happening gastropub and beer garden takes its brews seriously with over a dozen of its own and guest beers on tap, served in type-appropriate glassware. Live music Friday through Sunday, open mike on Wednesday starting at 8pm.

★Cafe La Haye   CALIFORNIAN $$$
(☎707-935-5994; www.cafelahaye.com; 140 E Napa St; mains $19-25; ⊙5:30-9pm Tue-Sat) 🚗 One of Sonoma's top tables for earthy New American cooking, La Haye only uses produce sourced from within 60 miles. Its dining room gets packed cheek-by-jowl and service can border on perfunctory, but the clean simplicity and flavor-packed cooking make it many foodies' first choice. Reserve well ahead.

Russian River Valley

Redwoods tower over small wineries in the Russian River Valley, about 75 miles northwest of San Francisco (via Hwys 101 and 116), in western Sonoma County. Famous for its apple orchards and farm tour trails, **Sebastopol** has a new-age spiritual aura, with downtown bookshops, art galleries and boutiques, and antiques stores further south. Wander around the **Barlow** (☎707-824-5600; www.thebarlow.net; cnr Sebastopol & Morris Sts; ⊙hours vary; P🚸) 🚗, an indoor market of food producers, winemakers, coffee roasters, spirit distillers and indie chefs. Or go straight to the source by driving or cycling local farm trails (www.farmtrails.org).

Guerneville is the main river beach town, buzzing with Harleys and gay-friendly honky-tonks. Explore old-growth redwoods at **Armstrong Redwoods State Reserve** (info 707-869-2015, visitor center 707-869-2958; www.parks.ca.gov; 17000 Armstrong Woods Rd; per car $8; 8am-1hr after sunset;), next to no-reservations **Bullfrog Pond Campground** (707-869-2015; www.stewardscr.org; sites reserved/nonreserved $35/25;). Paddle downriver with **Burke's Canoe Trips** (707-887-1222; www.burkescanoetrips.com; 8600 River Rd, Forestville; canoe/kayak rental incl shuttle $68/$45, cash only). Head southeast to sip sparkling wines at hilltop **Iron Horse Vineyards** (707-887-1507; www.ironhorsevineyards.com; 9786 Ross Station Rd, off Hwy 116, Sebastopol; tasting $25, incl tour $50; 10am-4:30pm, last tasting 4pm;); reserve tours in advance.

Other excellent wineries, many known for award-winning pinot noir, scatter along rural **Westside Road**, which follows the river toward Healdsburg. Guerneville's **visitor center** (707-869-9000; www.russianriver.com; 16209 1st St; 10am-5pm Mon-Sat, plus to 3pm Sun May-Oct) offers winery maps and lodging info. It's worth the wait for a table at California-smart **Boon Eat + Drink** (707-869-0780; http://eatatboon.com; 16248 Main St; mains lunch $15-18, dinner $15-26; 11am-3pm Thu-Tue, 5-9pm Sun-Thu, to 10pm Fri & Sat;), which also manages boutique **Boon Hotel + Spa** (707-869-2721; www.boonhotels.com; 14711 Armstrong Woods Rd; tents $175-225, r $225-425;), a minimalist oasis with a saline pool.

The aptly named Bohemian Hwy winds 10 miles south of the river to tiny **Occidental**, where **Howard Station Cafe** (707-874-2838; www.howardstationcafe.com; 3611 Bohemian Hwy; mains $8-14; 7am-2:30pm Mon-Fri, to 3pm Sat & Sun;) serves hearty breakfasts like blueberry cornmeal pancakes (cash only), and **Barley & Hops Tavern** (707-874-9037; www.barleynhops.com; 3688 Bohemian Hwy; 4-9pm Mon-Thu, 1-9:30pm Fri-Sun) pours craft beers. It's another few miles south to Freestone, home of the phenomenal bakery **Wild Flour Bread** (707-874-2938; www.wildflourbread.com; 140 Bohemian Hwy, Freestone; items from $3; 8:30am-6:30pm Fri-Mon;) and invigorating cedar-enzyme baths at **Osmosis** (707-823-8231; www.osmosis.com; 209 Bohemian Hwy, Freestone; packages from $219; by appointment 9am-8pm) spa.

Healdsburg & Around

More than 100 wineries dot the valleys within a 20-mile radius of Healdsburg, where upscale eateries, wine-tasting rooms and stylish hotels surround a leafy plaza. For tasting passes and maps, drop by the **visitor center** (800-648-9922, 707-433-6935; www.healdsburg.com; 217 Healdsburg Ave; 10am-4pm Mon-Fri, to 3pm Sat & Sun). Dine with California-chic locavores at the **Shed** (707-431-7433; www.healdsburgshed.com; 25 North St; dinner mains $15-30; 8am-9pm Wed-Mon, to 6pm Tue;) or **SingleThread** (707-723-4646; www.singlethreadfarms.com; 131 North St; tasting menu per person $293; 5:30-11pm Tue-Sun), or grab lunch near the vineyards at country-style **Dry Creek General Store** (707-433-4171; www.drycreekgeneralstore1881.com; 3495 Dry Creek Rd; sandwiches $10-13; 7am-5pm Mon-Fri, to 5:30 Sat & Sun). Afterward bed down at old-fashioned **L&M Motel** (707-433-6528; www.landmmotel.com; 70 Healdsburg Ave; r $175-195;) or romantic **Healdsburg Modern Cottages** (707-395-4684; www.healdsburgcottages.com; 425 Foss St; d $340-575;).

Picture-perfect farmstead wineries await discovery in Dry Creek Valley, west of Hwy 101 and Healdsburg. Pedal a bicycle out to taste citrusy Sauvignon Blanc and peppery Zinfandel at biodynamic **Preston Vineyards** (707-433-3372; www.prestonvineyards.com; 9282 W Dry Creek Rd; tasting/tours $10/25; 11am-4:30pm;) and **Quivira Vineyards** (707-431-8333, 800-292-8339; www.quivirawine.com; 4900 W Dry Creek Rd; tasting $15-30, incl tour $40, tour & estate tasting by reservation only; 11am-4pm, 10am-4:30pm Apr-Oct;). Motor toward the Russian River and **Porter Creek Vineyards** (707-433-6321; www.portercreekvineyards.com; 8735 Westside Rd; tasting $15; 10:30am-4:30pm;) for forest-floor Pinot Noir and fruity Viognier poured at a bar made from a bowling-alley lane.

Northwest of Healdsburg off Hwy 101, follow Hwy 128 through the **Anderson Valley**, known for its fruit orchards and family-owned wineries like **Navarro** (707-895-3686; www.navarrowine.com; 5601 Hwy 128, Philo; 8am-6pm Mon-Fri, to 5pm Sat & Sun;) FREE and **Husch** (707-462-5370; www.huschvineyards.com; 4400 Hwy 128, Philo; 10am-6pm, to 5pm Nov-Mar;) FREE. Outside Boonville, which has roadside cafes, bakeries and delis, brake for disc-golf and beer at solar-powered **Anderson Valley Brewing Company** (707-895-2337; www.avbc.com; 17700 Hwy 253, Boonville; tasting from $2, tours & disc-golf course free; 11am-6pm Sat-Thu, to 7pm Fri;).

North Coast

This is not the legendary California of the Beach Boys' song – there are very few surfboards and no palm-flanked beaches. The jagged edge of the continent is wild, scenic and even slightly foreboding: spectral fog and an outsider spirit have fostered the world's tallest trees, most potent weed and a string of idiosyncratic two-stoplight towns.

Coastal Highway 1 to Mendocino

Often winding precariously atop ocean cliffs, this serpentine slice of Hwy 1 passes salty fishing harbors and hidden beaches. Use roadside pullouts to scan the Pacific horizon for migrating whales or to amble coves bounded by startling rock formations and relentlessly pounded by the surf. The 110-mile stretch from Bodega Bay to Fort Bragg takes at least three hours of nonstop driving; at night or in the fog, it takes steely nerves and much, much longer.

Bodega Bay, the first pearl in a string of sleepy fishing villages, was the setting for Hitchcock's terrifying 1963 psycho-horror flick *The Birds*. Today the skies are free from bloodthirsty gulls, but you'd best keep an eye on that picnic basket as you explore the arched rocks, blustery coves and wildflower-covered bluffs of **Sonoma Coast State Park** (www.parks.ca.gov; per car $8), with beaches rolling beyond Jenner, 10 miles north. **Bodega Bay Sportfishing Center** (☑707-875-3495; www.bodegacharters.com; 1410b Bay Flat Rd; fishing trips $135, whale-watching adult/child $50/35; ⊛) runs winter whale-watching trips (adult/child $50/35). Landlubbers hike Bodega Head or saddle up at **Chanslor Ranch** (☑707-875-3333, 707-875-2721; www.horsenaroundtrailrides.com; 2660 N Hwy 1; rides from $125; ⊙10am-5pm; ⊛).

Where the wide, lazy Russian River meets the Pacific, you'll find **Jenner,** a cluster of shops and restaurants dotting coastal hills. Informative volunteers protect the resident colony of harbor seals at the river's mouth during pupping season, between March and August. **Water Treks Ecotours** (☑707-865-2249; www.watertreks.com; kayak rental from $30; ⊙hours vary) rents kayaks on Hwy 1; reservations recommended.

Twelve miles north of Jenner, the salt-weathered structures of **Fort Ross State Historic Park** (☑707-847-3437; www.fortross.org; 19005 Hwy 1; per car $8; ⊙10am-4:30pm) preserve an 1812 trading post and Russian Orthodox church. It's a quiet place, but the history is riveting: this was once the southernmost reach of Tsarist Russia's North-American trading expeditions. The small, wood-scented museum offers historical exhibits and respite from the windswept cliffs.

Several miles further north, **Salt Point State Park** (☑707-847-3221; www.parks.ca.gov; 25050 Hwy 1; per car $8; ⊙park sunrise-sunset, visitor center 10am-3pm Sat & Sun Apr-Oct; ℗) abounds with hiking trails and tide pools and has two **campgrounds** (☑800-444-7275; www.reserveamerica.com; tent/RV sites $25/35; ℗). At neighboring **Kruse Rhododendron State Natural Reserve**, pink blooms spot the misty greenwoods between April and June. Cows graze the fields on the bluffs heading north to **Sea Ranch** (www.tsra.org), where public-access hiking trails lead downhill from roadside parking lots (per car $7) to pocket beaches.

Two miles north of Point Arena town, detour to wind-battered **Point Arena Lighthouse** (☑707-882-2809; www.pointarenalighthouse.com; 45500 Lighthouse Rd; adult/child $7.50/1; ⊙10am-3:30pm mid-Sep–mid-May, to 4:30pm mid-May–mid-Sep; ℗), built in 1908. Ascend 145 steps to inspect the flashing Fresnel lens and get jaw-dropping coastal views. Eight miles north of the Little River crossing at Hwy 128 is **Van Damme State Park** (☑707-937-5804; www.parks.ca.gov; 8001 N Hwy 1, Little River; per car $8; ⊙8am-9pm; ℗), where the popular 5-mile round-trip **Fern Canyon Trail** passes through a lush river canyon with young redwoods, continuing another mile each way to a pygmy forest. The park's **campground** (☑800-444-7275; www.reserveamerica.com; 8001 Hwy 1, Little River; tent/RV sites $25/35; ℗⊛) has coin-op hot showers.

In **Mendocino**, a historical village perched on a gorgeous headland, baby boomers stroll around New England saltbox and water-tower B&Bs, quaint shops and art galleries. Wilder paths pass berry brambles, wildflowers and cypress trees standing guard over rocky cliffs and raging surf at **Mendocino Headlands State Park** (www.parks.ca.gov). The **Ford House Museum & Visitor Center** (☑707-537-5397; www.mendoparks.org; 45035 Main St; ⊙11am-4pm) is nearby.

Just south of town, paddle your way up the Big River with **Catch a Canoe & Bicycles, Too** (☑707-937-0273; www.catchacanoe.com; 44850 Comptche-Ukiah Rd, Stanford Inn by the Sea; 3hr kayak, canoe or bicycle rental adult/child $28/14; ⊙9am-5pm; ♿). North of town, 1909 **Point Cabrillo Light Station** (☑707-937-6123; www.pointcabrillo.org; 45300 Lighthouse Rd; ⊙park sunrise-sunset, lighthouse 11am-4pm) FREE is a perfect winter whale-watching perch.

🛏 Sleeping

Standards are high in stylish Mendocino and so are prices; two-day minimums often crop up on weekends. Fort Bragg, 10 miles north, has cheaper lodgings. All B&B rates include breakfast; only a few places have TVs. For a range of cottages and B&Bs, contact **Mendocino Coast Reservations** (☑707-937-5033; www.mendocinovacations.com; 45084 Little Lake St; ⊙9am-5pm).

Gualala Point Regional Park　CAMPGROUND **$**
(☑707-567-2267; http://parks.sonomacounty.ca.gov; 42401 Hwy 1, Gualala; tent & RV sites $35; P) Shaded by a stand of redwoods and fragrant California bay laurel trees, a short trail connects this creekside campground to the windswept beach. The quality of sites, including several secluded hike-in spots, makes it the best drive-in camping on this part of the coast.

Andiron Seaside Inn & Cabins　CABIN **$$**
(☑707-937-1543; http://theandiron.com; 6051 N Hwy 1, Little River; d $109-299; P❤🛜📺) 🅟 Styled with hip vintage decor, this cluster of 1950s roadside cottages is a refreshingly playful option amid the cabbage-rose and lace aesthetic of Mendocino. Each cabin houses two rooms with complementing themes: 'Read' has old books, comfy vintage chairs and retro eyeglasses, while the adjoining 'Write' features a huge chalkboard and a ribbon typewriter.

⭐**Alegria**　B&B **$$$**
(☑707-937-5150; www.oceanfrontmagic.com; 44781 Main St; r $239-299; ❤🛜) A perfect romantic hideaway: beds have views over the coast, decks have ocean views and all rooms have wood-burning fireplaces; outside, a gorgeous path leads to a big, amber-gray beach. Ever-so-friendly innkeepers whip up amazing breakfasts served in the sea-view dining area. Less expensive rooms are available across the street at bright and simple **Raku House** (☑800-780-7905; www.rakuhouse.com; 998 Main St; r $109-139; P❤🛜).

⭐**Mar Vista Cottages**　CABIN **$$$**
(☑707-884-3522; www.marvistamendocino.com; 35101 Hwy 1, Anchor Bay; cottages $190-310;

P❤🛜📺) 🅟 These elegantly renovated 1930s fishing cabins offer a simple, stylish seaside escape with a vanguard commitment to sustainability. The harmonious environment is the result of pitch-perfect details: linens are line-dried over lavender, guests browse the organic vegetable garden to harvest their own dinner and chickens cluck around the grounds laying the next morning's breakfast. It often requires two-night stays.

🍴 Eating & Drinking

Even tiny coastal towns usually have a bakery, deli, natural-foods market and a couple of roadside cafes and restaurants.

Franny's Cup & Saucer　BAKERY **$**
(☑707-882-2500; www.frannyscupandsaucer.com; 213 Main St; cakes from $2; ⊙8am-4pm Wed-Sat) The cutest patisserie on this stretch of coast is run by Franny and her mother, Barbara (a veteran of Chez Panisse in Berkeley). The fresh berry tarts and creative housemade chocolates seem too beautiful to eat, until you take the first bite and immediately want to order another. Once a month they pull out all the stops for a farmhouse dinner ($28).

Spud Point Crab Company　SEAFOOD **$**
(☑707-875-9472; www.spudpointcrab.com; 1860 Westshore Rd; mains $6.75-12; ⊙9am-5pm; P♿) In the classic tradition of dockside crab shacks, Spud Point serves salty-sweet crab sandwiches and *real* clam chowder (that consistently wins local culinary prizes). You can also buy a crab to take home if you fancy. Eat at picnic tables overlooking the marina. Take Bay Flat Rd to get here.

Mendocino Cafe　CALIFORNIAN, FUSION **$$**
(☑707-937-6141; www.mendocinocafe.com; 10451 Lansing St; lunch mains $12-16, dinner mains $21-33; ⊙11:30am-8pm; 🛜🍴) One of Mendocino's few fine dinner spots also serves lovely alfresco lunches on its ocean-view deck surrounded by roses. Try the Thai burrito or the 'Healing Bowl' of soba noodles, miso, shitake mushrooms and choice of meat or seafood. At dinner there's grilled steak and seafood.

⭐**Café Beaujolais**　CALIFORNIAN **$$$**
(☑707-937-5614; www.cafebeaujolais.com; 961 Ukiah St; lunch mains $10-18, dinner mains $23-38; ⊙11:30am-2:30pm Wed-Sun, dinner from 5:30pm daily; P) 🅟 Mendocino's iconic, beloved country-Cal–French restaurant occupies an 1893 farmhouse restyled into a monochromatic urban-chic dining room, perfect for holding hands by candlelight. The refined,

inspired cooking draws diners from San Francisco, who make this the centerpiece of their trip. The locally sourced menu changes with the seasons, but the Petaluma duck confit is a gourmand's delight.

955 Ukiah Street CALIFORNIAN $$$
(☎707-937-1955; www.955restaurant.com; 955 Ukiah St; mains $18-37; ☺from 6pm Thu-Sun) One of those semi-secret institutions, the menu here changes with what's available locally. When we visited, that meant wondrous things such as a roasted cauliflower, feta and caramelized-onion appetizer. The dimly lit, bohemian setting overlooks rambling gardens. Check the website for the excellent-value, three-course meal with wine for $25 every Thursday, and other events.

Dick's Place BAR
(☎707-937-6010; 45080 Main St; ☺11:30am-2am) A bit out of place among the fancy-pants shops downtown, but an excellent spot to check out the *other* Mendocino and do shots with rowdy locals. And don't miss the retro experience of dropping 50¢ in the jukebox to hear that favorite tune.

ⓘ Getting There & Around

The **Mendocino Transit Authority** (MTA; ☎800-696-4682, 707-462-1422; www.mendocinotransit.org; 241 Plant Rd, Ukiah; most 1-way fares $1.50-6) operates bus 65, which travels between Willits, Ukiah and Santa Rosa daily, with an afternoon return ($26.25, three hours, four daily). Bus 95 runs between Point Arena (Hwy 1) and Santa Rosa daily, via Jenner and Bodega Bay with an afternoon return ($8.25, 3¼ hours, one daily). The North Coast route 60 goes north between Navarro River junction and Albion, Little River, Mendocino and Fort Bragg, Monday to Friday ($2.25, 1½ hours, two daily). Route 75 connects Gualala with the Navarro River Junction and continues to Ukiah ($6.75 2¾ hours, daily).

Along Highway 101 to Avenue of the Giants

To get into the most remote and wild parts of the North Coast behind the 'Redwood Curtain' on the quick, eschew winding Hwy 1 for inland Hwy 101, which occasionally pauses under the traffic lights of small towns. Diversions along the way include bountiful redwood forests past Leggett and the abandoned wilds of the Lost Coast.

Although **Ukiah** is mostly a place to gas up or grab a bite downtown, it's worth a 30-minute meandering mountain drive

west to soak at clothing-optional **Orr Hot Springs** (☎707-462-6277; www.orrhotsprings. org; 13201 Orr Springs Rd; day-use adult/child $30/25; ☺by appointment 10am-10pm).

Just north of tiny **Leggett** on Hwy 101, take a dip in the Eel River at **Standish-Hickey State Recreation Area** (☎707-925-6482; www.parks.ca.gov; 69350 Hwy 101; per car $8; ▦), where hiking trails traipse through virgin and second-growth redwoods. South of **Garberville** on Hwy 101, **Richardson Grove State Park** (☎707-247-3318; www.parks.ca.gov; 1600 Hwy 101, Garberville; per car $8) also protects old-growth redwood forest beside the river. Both parks have developed **campgrounds** (☎reservations 800-444-7275; www.reserveameri-ca.com; 1600 Hwy 101; tent & RV sites $35; ⓟ).

The **Lost Coast** tempts hikers with the most rugged coastal backpacking in California. It became 'lost' when the state's highway bypassed the mountains of the King Range, which rises over 4000ft within a few miles of the ocean. From Garberville, it's 23 steep, twisting miles along a paved road to **Shelter Cove**, the main supply point but little more than a seaside subdivision with a general store, cafes and none-too-cheap ocean-view lodgings.

Along Hwy 101, 82-sq-mile **Humboldt Redwoods State Park** (☎707-946-2409; www. parks.ca.gov; Hwy 101; ⓟ▦) ✅**FREE** protects some of California's oldest redwoods, including more than half of the world's tallest 100 trees. Magnificent groves rival those in Redwood National Park, a long drive further north. If you don't have time to hike, at least drive the awe-inspiring **Avenue of the Giants**, a 31-mile, two-lane road parallel to Hwy 101. Book ahead for **campsites** (☎information 707-946-2263, reservations 800-444-7275; www. reserveamerica.com; tent & RV sites $20-35; ⓟ▦).

🛏 Sleeping & Eating

Main motel chains are well represented on Hwy 101, particularly in and around Ukiah and Clear Lake, while midrange options and some memorable B&Bs can be found in and around the Anderson Valley.

★**Old West Inn** MOTEL $
(☎707-459-4201; www.theoldwestinn.com; 1221 S Main St; r $79; ⓟ🐾❄🌐) The facade looks like a mock-up of an Old West main street and each room has a theme, from the 'Stable' to the 'Barber Shop.' The decor is simple and comfy with just enough imagination to make it interesting. Besides that this is the

cleanest, friendliest and most highly recommended place in town.

⭐ **Lakeport English Inn** B&B $$
(☎707-263-4317; www.lakeportenglishinn.com; 675 N Main St, Lakeport; r $185-210, cottages $210; P✆❀❄🔊) The finest B&B at Clear Lake is an 1875 Carpenter Gothic with 10 impeccably furnished rooms, styled with a nod to the English countryside and with such quaint names as the Prince of Wales or (wait for it) Roll in the Hay. Weekends take high tea (nonguests welcome by reservation), with scones and real Devonshire cream.

⭐ **Boonville Hotel** BOUTIQUE HOTEL $$$
(☎707-895-2210; www.boonvillehotel.com; 14050 Hwy 128, Boonville; d $295-365; P❀❄🔊) Decked out in a contemporary American country feel with sea-grass flooring, pastel colors and fine linens, this historic hotel's rooms and suites are safe for urbanites who refuse to abandon style just because they've gone to the country. The rooms are all different and there are agreeable extras, including hammocks and fireplaces.

Jyun Kang Vegetarian Restaurant VEGETARIAN $
(☎707-462-0939; www.cttbusa.org; 4951 Bodhi Way; mains $8-12; ⊙11:30am-3pm Wed-Mon; ✎) Vegetarians (and vegans) will be swooning at the superb Asian-influenced dishes at this lunchtime restaurant located at the site of the **City of Ten Thousand Buddhas** (☎707-462-0939; www.cttbusa.org; 4951 Bodhi Way; ⊙8am-6pm; P).

⭐ **Saucy Ukiah** PIZZA $$
(☎707-462-7007; www.saucyukiah.com; 108 W Standley St; pizzas $14-19, mains $13-19; ⊙11:30am-9pm Mon-Thu, to 10pm Fri, noon-10pm Sat) Yes there are arty pizzas with toppings like organic fennel pollen and almond basil pesto but there are also amazing soups, salads, pastas and starters – Nana's meatballs are to die for and the 'kicking' minestrone lives up to its name. The small-town ambience is mildly chic but fun and informal at the same time.

ℹ️ **Getting There & Around**

Mendocino Transit Authority (☎707-462-1422; www.mendocinotransit.org; 241 Plant Rd) operates bus 65, which travels between Willits, Ukiah and Santa Rosa daily, with an afternoon return ($26.25, three hours, four daily). Bus 75 heads north every weekday from Gualala to the Navarro River junction at Hwy 128, then runs inland

through the Anderson Valley to Ukiah, returning in the afternoon ($6.75, 2½ hours, daily).

Highway 101 from Eureka to Crescent City

Past the strip malls sprawling around its edges, the heart of Eureka is Old Town, abounding with fine Victorians buildings, antique shops and restaurants. Cruise the harbor aboard the blue-and-white 1910 **Madaket** (Madaket Cruises; ☎707-445-1910; www.humboldtbaymaritimemuseum.com; 1st St; narrated cruises adult/child $22/18; ⊙1pm, 2:30pm & 4pm Wed-Sat, 1pm & 2:30pm Sun-Tue mid-May–mid-Oct; 🚻) – 75-minute cruises cost adults $22 and depart from the foot of C St, while sunset cocktail cruises ($10) serve from the state's smallest licensed bar. The **visitor center** (www.fws.gov/refuge/humboldt_bay/visit/visitor center.html; 1020 Ranch Rd, Loleta; ⊙8am-5pm) is on Hwy 101, south of downtown.

On the north side of Humboldt Bay, **Arcata** is a patchouli-dipped hippie haven of radical politics. Biodiesel-fueled trucks drive in for the Saturday **farmers market** (www.humfarm.org; 9am-2pm Apr-Nov, from 10am Dec-Mar) on the central plaza, surrounded by art galleries, shops, cafes and bars. Make reservations to soak at **Finnish Country Sauna & Tubs** (☎707-822-2228; http://cafe mokkaarcata.com; 495 J St; per 30min adult/child $9.75/2; ⊙noon-11pm Sun-Thu, to 1am Fri & Sat; 🚻). Northeast of downtown stands eco-conscious, socially responsible **Humboldt State University** (HSU; ☎707-826-3011; www.humboldt.edu; 1 Harpst Dr; P) ✎.

Sixteen miles north of Arcata, **Trinidad** sits on a bluff overlooking a breathtakingly beautiful fishing harbor. Stroll sandy beaches or take short hikes around Trinidad Head after meeting tide-pool critters at the **HSU Telonicher Marine Laboratory** (☎707-826-3671; www.humboldt.edu/marinelab; 570 Ewing St; $1; ⊙9am-4:30pm Mon-Fri year-round, plus 10am-5pm Sat & Sun mid-Sep–mid-May; P🚻) ✎. Heading north of town, Patrick's Point Dr is dotted with forested campgrounds, cabins and lodges. **Patrick's Point State Park** (☎707-677-3570; www.parks.ca.gov; 4150 Patrick's Point Dr; per car $8; ⊙sunrise-sunset; P🚻) ✎ has stunning rocky headlands, beachcombing, an authentic reproduction of a Yurok village and a **campground** (☎information 707-677-3570, reservations 800-444-7275; www.re serveamerica.com; 4150 Patrick's Point Dr; tent/RV sites $35/45; P🐾) with coin-op hot showers.

Heading north, Hwy 101 passes Redwood National Park's **Thomas H Kuchel Visitor Center** ([📞]707-465-7765; www.nps.gov/redw; Hwy 101, Orick; ⊙9am-5pm Apr-Oct, to 4pm Nov-Mar; [♿]). Together, the national park and three state parks – Prairie Creek, Del Norte and Jedediah Smith – are a World Heritage site containing more than 40% of the world's remaining old-growth redwood forests. The national park is free, while state parks have an $8 day-use parking fee and developed campgrounds (p1013). This patchwork of state- and federally managed land stretches all the way north to the Oregon border, interspersed with several towns. Furthest south, you'll encounter **Redwood National Park**, where a 1-mile nature trail winds through Lady Bird Johnson Grove.

Six miles north of Orick, the 10-mile Newton B Drury Scenic Parkway runs parallel to Hwy 101 through **Prairie Creek Redwoods State Park**. Roosevelt elk graze in the meadow outside the **visitor center** ([📞]707-488-2039; www.parks.ca.gov; Newton B Drury Scenic Pkwy; ⊙9am-5pm May-Sep, to 4pm Wed-Sun Oct-Apr; [♿]), where sunlight-dappled hiking trails begin. Three miles back south, mostly unpaved Davison Rd heads northwest to Gold Bluffs Beach, dead-ending at the trailhead for unbelievably lush **Fern Canyon**.

North of tiny Klamath, Hwy 101 passes the **Trees of Mystery** ([📞]707-482-2251; www.treesofmystery.net; 15500 Hwy 101; museum free, gondola adult/child $16/8; ⊙8:30am-6:30pm Jun-Aug, 9am-6pm Sep & Oct, 9:30am-4:30pm Nov-May; [P][♿]), a kitschy roadside attraction. Next up, Del Norte Coast Redwoods State Park preserves virgin redwood groves and unspoiled coastline. The 4.5-mile round-trip **Damnation Creek Trail** careens over 1000ft downhill past redwoods to a hidden rocky beach, best visited at low tide. Find the trailhead at a parking turnout near mile-marker 16 on Hwy 101.

Backed by a fishing harbor and bay, Crescent City is drab because, after more than half the town was destroyed by a tidal wave in 1964, it was rebuilt with utilitarian architecture. When the tide's out, you can walk across to the 1856 **Battery Point Lighthouse** ([📞]707-467-3089; www.delnortehistory.org; South A St; adult/child $3/1; ⊙10am-4pm Wed-Sun Apr-Sep) from the south end of A St.

Beyond Crescent City, **Jedediah Smith Redwoods State Park** is the northernmost park in the system. The redwood stands here are so dense that there are few trails, but a couple of easy hikes start near riverside swimming holes along Hwy 199 and rough, unpaved Howland Hill Rd, a 10-mile scenic drive. The Redwood National & State Parks' **Crescent City Information Center** ([📞]707-465-7335; www.nps.gov/redw; 1111 2nd St; ⊙9am-5pm Apr-Oct, to 4pm Nov-Mar) has maps and info.

🛏 Sleeping

A mixed bag of budget and midrange motels is scattered along Hwy 101, including in Eureka, Arcata and Crescent City.

Curly Redwood Lodge   MOTEL **$**
([📞]707-464-2137; www.curlyredwoodlodge.com; 701 Hwy 101 S; r $79-107; [P][❄][🌐]) The motel is a marvel: it's entirely built and paneled from a single curly redwood tree that measured over 18ft thick in diameter. Progressively restored and polished into a gem of mid-20th-century kitsch, the inn is like stepping into a time capsule and a delight for retro junkies. Rooms are clean, large and comfortable (request one away from the road).

⭐ **Historic Requa Inn**   HISTORIC HOTEL **$$**
([📞]707-482-1425; www.requainn.com; 451 Requa Rd; r $119-199; [P][🐾][🌐]) 🌿 A woodsy country lodge on bluffs overlooking the mouth of the Klamath, the creaky and bright 1914 Requa Inn is a North Coast favorite and – even better – it's a carbon-neutral facility. Many of the charming, old-timey Americana rooms have mesmerizing views over the misty river, as does the dining room, which serves locally sourced, organic New American cuisine.

Carter House Inns   B&B **$$$**
([📞]707-444-8062; www.carterhouse.com; 301 L St; r $184-384; [P][🐾][🌐]) Constructed in period style, this aesthetically remodeled hotel is a Victorian lookalike. Rooms have all modern amenities and top-quality linens; suites have in-room Jacuzzis and marble fireplaces. The same owners operate four other sumptuously decorated lodgings: a single-level house, two honeymoon hideaway cottages and a replica of an 1880s San Francisco mansion, which the owner built himself, entirely by hand.

🍴 Eating & Drinking

Arcata has the biggest variety of dining options, from organic juice bars and vegan cafes to Californian and world-fusion bistros.

Wildberries Marketplace   MARKET, DELI **$**
([📞]707-822-0095; www.wildberries.com; 747 13th St, Arcata; sandwiches $4-10; ⊙7am-midnight;

P ✐) Wildberries Marketplace is Arcata's best grocery, with natural foods, a good deli, a bakery and a juice bar.

★ **Cafe Nooner** MEDITERRANEAN **$**
(☑ 707-443-4663; www.cafenooner.com; 409 Opera Alley; mains $10-14; ⊙ 11am-4pm Sun-Wed, to 8pm Thu-Sat; 🖪) Exuding a cozy bistro-style ambience with red-and-white checkered tablecloths, this perennially popular restaurant serves natural, organic and Med-inspired cuisine with choices that include a Greek-style *meze* platter, plus kebabs, salads and soups. There's a healthy kids menu, as well.

★ **Brick & Fire** CALIFORNIAN **$$**
(☑ 707-268-8959; www.brickandfirebistro.com; 1630 F St, Eureka; dinner mains $14-23; ⊙ 11:30am-9pm Mon & Wed-Fri, 5-9pm Sat & Sun; 🛜) Eureka's best restaurant is in an intimate, warm-hued, bohemian-tinged setting that is almost always busy. Choose from thin-crust pizzas, delicious salads (try the pear and blue cheese) and an ever-changing selection of appetizers and mains that highlight local produce and wild mushrooms. There's a weighty wine list and servers are well-versed in pairings.

★ **Six Rivers Brewery** MICROBREWERY
(☑ 707-839-7580; www.sixriversbrewery.com; 1300 Central Ave, McKinleyville; ⊙ 11:30am-11:30pm Sun & Tue-Thu, to 12:30am Fri & Sat, from 4pm Mon) One of the first female-owned breweries in California, the 'brew with a view' kills it in every category: great beer, amazing community vibe, occasional live music and delicious hot wings. The spicy chili-pepper ale is amazing. At first glance the menu might seem like ho-hum pub grub, but portions are fresh and huge. They also make a helluva pizza.

🛈 Getting There & Away

Arcata's **Greyhound** (☑ 800-231-2222; www. greyhound.com; 🛜) depot has daily buses to San Francisco ($57, seven hours) via Eureka, Garberville, Ukiah and Santa Rosa. Several daily **Redwood Transit System** (☑ 707-443-0826; www.redwoodtransit.org) buses stop in Eureka and Arcata on the Hwy 101 (Trinidad–Scotia) route ($3, 2½ hours).

Sacramento

Sacramento is a city of contrasts. It's a former cow town where state legislators' SUVs go bumper-to-bumper with farmers' muddy, half-ton pickups at rush hour. It has sprawling suburbs, but also new lofts and upscale

boutiques squeezed between aging mid-century storefronts.

The people of 'Sac' are a resourceful lot that have fostered small but thriving food, art and nightlife scenes. They rightfully crow about **Second Saturday**, the monthly Midtown gallery hop that is the symbol of the city's cultural awakening. Their ubiquitous farmers markets, farm-to-fork fare and craft beers are another point of pride.

⊙ Sights

★ **Golden 1 Center** STADIUM
(☑ 916-701-5400; www.golden1center.com; 500 David J Stern Walk; 🖪) 🖉 Welcome to the arena of the future. This gleaming home to the Sacramento Kings is one of the most advanced sports facilities in the country. Made to the highest sustainability standard, it's built from local materials, powered by solar and cooled by five-story airplane hangar doors that swing open to capture the Delta breeze.

★ **California Museum** MUSEUM
(☑ 916-653-0650; www.californiamuseum.org; 1020 O St; adult/child $9/6.50; ⊙ 10am-5pm Tue-Sat, from noon Sun; 🖪) This modern museum is home to the California Hall of Fame and so the only place to simultaneously encounter César Chávez, Mark Zuckerberg and Amelia Earhart. The *California Indians* exhibit is a highlight, with artifacts and oral histories of more than 10 tribes.

Crocker Art Museum MUSEUM
(☑ 916-808-7000; https://crockerartmuseum.org; 216 O St; adult/child $10/5; ⊙ 10am-5pm Tue, Wed & Fri-Sun, to 9pm Thu) Housed in the ornate Victorian mansion of a railroad baron, this museum has an excellent collection. Works by California painters and European masters hang beside an enthusiastically curated collection of contemporary art.

★ **California**
State Capitol HISTORIC BUILDING
(☑ 916-324-0333; http://capitolmuseum.ca.gov; 1315 10th St; ⊙ 8am-5pm Mon-Fri, from 9am Sat & Sun; 🖪) FREE The gleaming dome of the California State Capitol is Sacramento's most recognizable structure. A painting of Arnold Schwarzenegger in a suit hangs in the West Wing along with the other governors' portraits. Some will find Capitol Park, the 40 acres of gardens and memorials surrounding the building, more interesting than what's inside. Tours run hourly until 4pm.

🛏 Sleeping

Hotels cater to business travelers, so look for weekend bargains. The freeways and suburbs around the city are glutted with budget and midrange chain lodgings.

HI Sacramento Hostel HOSTEL $
(☑ 916-443-1691; http://norcalhostels.org/sac; 925 H St; dm $30-33, r from $86, without bath from $58; ☺ reception 2-10:30pm; P ❀ @ 🛜) In a grand Victorian mansion, this hostel offers impressive trimmings at rock-bottom prices. It's within walking distance of the capitol, Old Sac and the train station, and has a piano in the parlor and large dining room. It attracts an international crowd often open to sharing a ride to San Francisco or Lake Tahoe.

★ Citizen Hotel BOUTIQUE HOTEL $$
(☑ 877-829-2429, 916-442-2700; www.thecitizen hotel.com; 926 J St; r from $180; P ❄ ❀ @ 🛜 🛎) After an elegant, ultra-hip upgrade, this long-vacant 1927 beaux-arts tower became Downtown's coolest place to stay. The details are spot-on: luxe linens, wide-striped wallpaper and a rooftop patio with a great view of the city. There's an upscale farm-to-fork **restaurant** (☑ 916-492-4450; www.grange sacramento.com; 926 J St; mains $19-39; ☺ 6:30-10:30am, 11:30am-2pm & 5:30-10pm Mon-Thu, to 11pm Fri, 8am-2pm & 5:30-11pm Sat, to 10pm Sun; 🛜) on the ground floor.

Greens Hotel BOUTIQUE HOTEL $$
(www.thegreenshotel.com; 1700 Del Paso Blvd.; r from $127; P ❄ ❀ @ 🛜 🛎) This stylishly updated motel is one of Sacramento's hippest places to stay. Although the neighborhood is a bit rough around the edges, the Greens' secure parking, pool and spacious grounds make it an ideal place for families to stop en route to or from Tahoe. The chic rooms are also classy enough for a romantic getaway.

🍴 Eating & Drinking

Skip the overpriced fare in Old Sacramento or by the capitol and head Midtown or to the Tower District.

La Bonne Soupe Cafe DELI $
(☑ 916-492-9506; 920 8th St; items $5-8; ☺ 11am-3pm Mon-Sat) Divine soup and sandwiches assembled with such care that the line of Downtown lunchers snakes out the door. If you're in a hurry, skip it. This humble lunch counter is focused on quality that predates drive-through haste.

★ Empress Tavern NEW AMERICAN $$$
(☑ 916-662-7694; www.empresstavern.com; 1013 K St; mains $13-40; ☺ 11:30am-9pm Mon-Thu, to 10pm Fri, 5-10pm Sat) In the catacombs under the historic Crest Theater, this gorgeous restaurant hosts a menu of creative, meat-focused dishes. The space itself is just as impressive; the arched brick ceilings and glittering bar feel like a speakeasy supper club from a bygone era.

★ Fieldwork Brewing Company BREWERY
(☑ 916-329-8367; www.fieldworkbrewing.com; 1805 Capitol Ave; ☺ 11am-9pm Sun-Thu, to 11pm Fri & Sat) Bustling with activity, this ultra-hip brewpub has over a dozen rotating taps of excellent, fresh beer. Playful variations of hoppy IPAs are the specialty (like the peachy Hammer Pants IPA), but it does lighter seasonal brews like the Salted Watermelon Gose. It also has board games – making it an easy place to linger when the weather is sweltering.

ℹ Getting There & Around

Sacramento International Airport is one of the nearest options for those traveling to Yosemite National Park.

The regional **Yolobus** (☑ 530-666-2877; www.yolobus.com) route 42B costs $2 and runs hourly between the airport and downtown; it also goes to West Sacramento, Woodland and Davis. Local **Sacramento Regional Transit buses** (RT; ☑ 916-321-2877; www.sacrt.com; fare $2.75) run around town; RT also runs a trolley between Old Sacramento and Downtown, as well as Sacramento's light-rail system.

Sacramento is also a fantastic city to cruise around by bike; rent them from **City Bicycle Works** (www.citybicycleworks.com; 2419 K St; per hour/day from $5/20; ☺ 10am-7pm Mon-Fri, to 6pm Sat, 11am-5pm Sun).

Gold Country

The miner forty-niners are gone, but a ride along Hwy 49 through sleepy hill towns, past clapboard saloons and oak-lined byways, is a journey back to the wild ride that was modern California's founding: umpteen historical markers tell tales of gold-rush violence and banditry.

Hwy 50 divides the Northern and Southern Mines. Winding Hwy 49, which connects everything, provides plenty of vistas of the famous hills. The **Gold Country Visitors Association** (www.calgold.org) has many more touring ideas.

❶ Getting There & Around

You can reach the region by train on the transcontinental line that links Sacramento and Truckee/Reno and has a stop in Auburn. Auburn is the main entry point of the area, a short hop on the I-80 from Sacramento. From Auburn pick up Hwy 49, the classic route through the Gold Country.

Northern Mines

Known as the 'Queen of the Northern Mines,' the narrow streets of Nevada City gleam with lovingly restored buildings, tiny theaters, art galleries, cafes and shops. The **visitor center** (☑530-265-2692; www.nevada citychamber.com; 132 Main St; ☯9am-5pm Mon-Fri, 11am-4pm Sat, 11am-3pm Sun) dispenses information and self-guided walking-tour maps. On Hwy 49, the **Tahoe National Forest Headquarters** (☑530-265-4531; www. fs.usda.gov/tahoe; 631 Coyote St; ☯8am-4:30pm Mon-Fri) provides camping and hiking information and wilderness permits.

Just over a mile east of utilitarian **Grass Valley** and Hwy 49, **Empire Mine State Historic Park** (☑530-273-8522; www.empire mine.org; 10791 Empire St; adult/child $7/3; ☯10am-5pm; Ⓟ⊞) marks the site of one of the richest mines in California. From 1850 to 1956 it produced almost 6 million ounces of gold – over $6 billion in today's market.

If it's hot, one of the best swimming holes in the area is at **Auburn State Recreation Area** (☑530-885-4527; www.parks.ca.gov; per car $10; ☯7am-sunset). It's just east of Auburn, an I-80 pit stop about 25 miles south of Grass Valley.

Coloma is where California's gold rush started. Riverside **Marshall Gold Discovery State Historic Park** (☑530-622-3470; www. parks.ca.gov; Hwy 49, Coloma; per car $8; ☯8am-8pm late May-early Sep, to 5pm early Sep-late May; Ⓟ⊞☀) pays tribute to James Marshall's riot-inducing discovery, with restored buildings and gold-panning opportunities.

🛏 Sleeping & Eating

Nevada City has the biggest spread of restaurants and historical B&Bs. Motels speckle Hwy 49 in Grass Valley and I-80 in Auburn.

★ Outside Inn   INN, COTTAGE $$
(☑530-265-2233; http://outsideinn.com; 575 E Broad St; d $79-210; Ⓟ⊞❄🔊☀❄) The best option for active explorers, this is an unusually friendly and fun inn, with 12 rooms and three cottages maintained by staff who love the outdoors. Some rooms have a patio over-

looking a small creek; all have nice quilts and access to BBQ grills. It's a 10-minute walk from downtown.

★ Broad Street Inn   INN $$
(☑530-265-2239; www.broadstreetinn.com; 517 W Broad St; r $119-134; ❄🔊☀) 🥾 This six-room inn in the heart of town is a favorite because it keeps things simple. (No weird old dolls, no yellowing lace doilies.) The good-value rooms are modern, brightly but soothingly furnished and elegant. No breakfast served.

★ Argonaut Farm to Fork Cafe   AMERICAN $
(☑530-626-7345; www.argonautcafe.com; 331 Hwy 49, Coloma; items $3-10; ☯8am-4pm; 🔊☀⊞) Truly delicious soups, sandwiches, baked goods and coffee from well-known Sacramento and local purveyors find their way to this little wooden house in Marshall Gold Discovery State Historic Park. Crowds of schoolkids waiting for gelato can slow things down.

★ New Moon Cafe   CALIFORNIAN $$$
(☑530-265-6399; www.thenewmooncafe.com; 203 York St; dinner mains $23-38; ☯11:30am-2pm Tue-Fri, 5-8:30pm Tue-Sun) 🥾 Pure elegance, Peter Selaya's organic- and local-ingredient menu changes with the seasons. If you visit during spring or summer, go for the line-caught fish or the house-made, moon-shaped fresh ravioli. The wine list is excellent.

Southern Mines

The towns of the Southern Mines – from Placerville to Sonora – receive less traffic and their dusty streets have a whiff of Wild West, today evident in the motley crew of Harley riders and gold prospectors (still!) who populate them. Some, like **Plymouth** (ol' Pokerville), **Volcano** and **Mokelumne Hill**, are virtual ghost towns, slowly crumbling into photogenic oblivion. Others, like **Sutter Creek**, **Murphys** and **Angels Camp**, are gussied-up showpieces of Victorian Americana. Get off the beaten path at family-run vineyards and subterranean caverns, where geological wonders reward those who first navigate the touristy gift shops above ground.

A short detour off Hwy 49, **Columbia State Historic Park** (☑209-588-9128; www.parks.ca.gov; Main St; ☯most businesses 10am-5pm; Ⓟ⊞) 𝗙𝗥𝗘𝗘 preserves blocks of authentic 1850s buildings complete with shopkeepers and street musicians in period costumes. Also near Sonora, **Railtown 1897**

State Historic Park (☎209-984-3953; www.railtown1897.org; 10501 Reservoir Rd, Jamestown; adult/child $5/3, incl train ride $15/10; ⊙9:30am-4:30pm Apr-Oct, 10am-3pm Nov-Mar, train rides 10:30am-3pm Sat & Sun Apr-Oct; ℗🚻) offers excursion trains through the surrounding hills where Hollywood Westerns including *High Noon* have been filmed.

🛏 Sleeping & Eating

Lacy B&Bs, cafes and ice-cream parlors are found in nearly every town. Sonora, about an hour's drive from Yosemite National Park, and Placerville have the most motels.

★ Imperial Hotel   B&B $$
(☎209-267-9172; www.imperialamador.com; 14202 Hwy 49, Amador City; r $110-155, ste $125-195; ❋🖥) Built in 1879, this is one of the area's most inventive updates to the typical antique-cluttered hotel, with sleek art-deco touches accenting the warm red brick, a genteel bar and a very good, seasonally minded restaurant (dinner mains $14 to $30). On weekends and holidays, expect a two-night minimum.

Union Inn   HISTORIC HOTEL $$
(☎209-296-7711; www.volcanounion.com; 21375 Consolation St; r $130-150; ℗➗❋🖥) The more comfortable of the two historic hotels in Volcano: there are four lovingly updated rooms with crooked floors, two with street-facing balconies. Flat-screen TVs and modern touches are a bit incongruous in the old building, but it's a cozy place to stay. The on-site **Union Pub** (☎209-296-7711; www.volcanounion.com; 21375 Consolation St; mains $10-30; ⊙5-8pm Mon & Thu, to 9pm Fri, noon-9pm Sat, noon-8pm Sun) has the best food in town and a lovely patio garden.

City Hotel   HISTORIC HOTEL $$
(☎information 209-532-1479, reservations 800-444-7275; www.reserveamerica.com; 22768 Main St; r $85-115; ℗➗❋🖥) Among a handful of restored Victorian hotels in the area, City Hotel is the most elegant, with rooms that overlook a shady stretch of Main St. Adjoining the on-site restaurant Christopher's at the City Hotel (mains $10 to $30), What Cheer Saloon is an atmospheric Gold Country joint with oil paintings of lusty ladies and striped wallpaper.

Farm Table Restaurant   MEDITERRANEAN $$
(☎530-295-8140; https://ourfarmtable.com; 311 Main St; sandwiches from $8, mains from $14; ⊙11am-5pm Mon, 11am-8pm Wed, 11am-9pm Thu-Sat, 9am-5pm Sun; 🥗) A lovely deli-style place dishing up well-cooked farm-fresh food with a Mediterranean feel, alongside homespun fare such as rabbit pot pie. It specializes in charcuterie and preserving, and has plenty of gluten-free and veggie options on the menu too.

California's Northern Mountains

Remote, empty and eerily beautiful, these are some of California's least visited wild lands, an endless show of geological wonders, clear lakes, rushing rivers and high desert. The major peaks – Lassen, Shasta and the Trinity Alps – have few geological features in common, but all offer backcountry camping under starry skies.

Redding to Mt Shasta

Much of the drive north of Redding is dominated by Mt Shasta, a 14,180ft snowcapped goliath at the southern end of the volcanic Cascades Range. It arises dramatically, fueling the anticipation felt by mountaineers who seek to climb its slopes.

Don't believe the tourist brochures: Redding, the region's largest city, is a snooze. The best reason to detour off I-5 is the **Sundial Bridge**, a glass-bottomed pedestrian marvel designed by Spanish neofuturist architect Santiago Calatrava. It spans the Sacramento River at **Turtle Bay Exploration Park** (☎800-887-8532; www.turtlebay.org; 844 Sundial Bridge Dr; adult/child $16/12, after 3:30pm $11/7; ⊙9am-5pm Mon-Sat, from 10am Sun, closes 1hr earlier Nov–mid-Mar; 🚼), a kid-friendly science and nature center with botanical gardens. Six miles west of Redding along Hwy 299, explore a genuine gold-rush town at **Shasta State Historic Park** (☎520-243-8194; www.parks.ca.gov; 15312 CA 299; museum entry adult/child $3/2; ⊙10am-5pm Thu-Sun). Two miles further west, **Whiskeytown National Recreation Area** (☎530-246-1225; www.nps.gov/whis; Hwy 299 at JFK Memorial Dr, Whiskeytown; ⊙10am-4pm) harbors **Whiskeytown Lake**, with sandy beaches, waterfall hikes and watersports and camping opportunities. In sleepy **Weaverville**, another 35 miles further west, **Joss House State Historic Park** (☎530-623-5284; www.parks.ca.gov; 630 Main St; tour adult/child $4/2; ⊙tours hourly 10am-4pm Thu-Sun; ℗) preserves an ornate 1874 Chinese immigrant temple.

North of Redding, I-5 crosses deep-blue **Shasta Lake**, California's biggest reservoir, formed by colossal **Shasta Dam** ([📞]530-275-4463; www.usbr.gov/mp/ncao/shasta-dam.html; 16349 Shasta Dam Blvd; [⊙]visitor center 8am-5pm, tours 9am, 11am, 1pm & 3pm; [P][♿]) **FREE** and ringed by houseboat marinas and RV campgrounds. High in the limestone megaliths on the lake's northern side are prehistoric **Lake Shasta Caverns** ([📞]530-238-2341, 800-795-2283; www.lakeshastacaverns.com; 20359 Shasta Caverns Rd, Lakehead; 2hr tour adult/child 3-15yr $26/15; [⊙]tours every 30min 9am-4pm late May-early Sep, hourly 9am-3pm Apr-late May & early-late Sep,10am, noon & 2pm Oct-Mar; [P][♿]), where tours include a catamaran ride.

Another 35 miles north on I-5, **Dunsmuir** is a teeny historic railroad town with vibrant art galleries inhabiting a quaint downtown district. Six miles south off I-5, **Castle Crags State Park** ([📞]530-235-2684; www.parks.ca.gov; per car $8; [⊙]sunrise-sunset) shelters forested **campsites** ([📞]reservations 800-444-7275; www.reserveamerica.com; tent & RV sites $15-30). Be awed by stunning views of Mt Shasta from the top of the park's hardy 5.6-mile round-trip **Crags Trail**.

Nine miles north of Dunsmuir, **Mt Shasta city** lures climbers, new-age hippies and back-to-nature types, all of whom revere the majestic mountain looming overhead. Usually open and snow-free beyond Bunny Flat from June until October, **Everitt Memorial Hwy** ascends the mountain to a perfect sunset-watching perch at almost 8000ft – simply head east from town on Lake St and keep going. For experienced mountaineers, climbing the peak above 10,000ft requires a Summit Pass ($25), available from **Mt Shasta Ranger Station** ([📞]530-926-4511; www.fs.usda.gov/stnf; 204 W Alma St; [⊙]8am-4:30pm Mon-Fri), which has weather reports and sells topgraphic maps. Stop by downtown's **Fifth Season** ([📞]530-926-3606; http://thefifthseason.com; 300 N Mt Shasta Blvd; [⊙]9am-6pm Mon-Fri, from 8am Sat, 10am-5pm Sun) outdoor-gear shop for equipment rentals. **Shasta Mountain Guides** ([📞]530-926-3117; http://shasta guides.com; 2-day climbs from $625 per person) offers mountaineering trips (from $550).

🛏 Sleeping

Roadside motels are abundant, including in Mt Shasta city. Redding has the most chain lodgings, clustered near major highways. Campgrounds are abundant, especially on public lands.

⭐**Shasta MountInn**   B&B $$
([📞]530-926-1810; www.shastamountinn.com; 203 Birch St; r $150-175; [P][♿][🐾][📶]) Only antique on the outside, this bright Victorian 1904 farmhouse is all relaxed minimalism, bold colors and graceful decor on the inside. Each airy room has a great bed and exquisite views of the luminous mountain. Enjoy the expansive garden, wraparound deck, outdoor hot tub and sauna. Not relaxed enough yet? Chill on the perfectly placed porch swings.

⭐**McCloud River Mercantile Hotel**   INN $$
([📞]530-964-2330; www.mccloudmercantile.com; 241 Main St; r $129-250; [P][♿][📶]) Stroll upstairs to the 2nd floor of McCloud's central Mercantile Hotel and try not to fall in love; it's all high ceilings, exposed brick and a perfect marriage of preservationist class and modern panache. Antique-furnished rooms have open-floor plans. Guests are greeted with fresh flowers and can drift to sleep on feather beds after soaking in claw-foot tubs.

Railroad Park Resort   INN, CAMPGROUND $$
([📞]530-235-4440; www.rrpark.com; 100 Railroad Park Rd; tent/RV sites from $29/37, d $135-165; [❄][📶][🏊][🐾]) About 2 miles south of town, off I-5, visitors can stay in refitted vintage railroad cars and cabooses. The grounds are fun for kids, who can run around the engines and plunge in a centrally situated pool. The deluxe boxcars are furnished with antiques and claw-foot tubs.

🍴 Eating & Drinking

⭐**Dunsmuir Brewery Works**   PUB FOOD $
([📞]530-235-1900; www.dunsmuirbreweryworks.com; 5701 Dunsmuir Ave; mains $9-13; [⊙]11am-10pm May-Sep, to 9pm Tue-Sun Oct-Apr; [📶]) It's hard to describe this little microbrew pub without veering into hyperbole. Start with the beer: the crisp ales and porter are perfectly balanced and the IPA is apparently pretty good too, because patrons are always drinking it dry. Soak it up with awesome bar food: a warm potato salad, bratwurst, or a thick Angus or perfect veggie nut burger.

Berryvale Grocery   MARKET, CAFE $
([📞]530-926-1576; www.berryvale.com; 305 S Mt Shasta Blvd; cafe items from $5; [⊙]store 8am-8pm, cafe to 7pm; [🐾][♿]) 🌱 This market sells groceries and organic produce to health-conscious eaters. The excellent cafe serves good coffee, fresh juices and an array of tasty – mostly veggie – salads, sandwiches and wraps.

★ **Café Maddalena** EUROPEAN, NORTH AFRICAN **$$**
(☑ 530-235-2725; www.cafemaddalena.com; 5801
Sacramento Ave; mains $15-26; ☺ 5-9pm Thu-Sun
Feb-Dec) Simple and elegant, this cafe put
Dunsmuir on the foodie map. The menu
was designed by chef Brett LaMott (of Trin-
ity Cafe fame) and changes seasonally to
feature dishes from southern Europe and
northern Africa. Some highlights include
pan-roasted king salmon with basil cream,
wild mushroom soup or sautéed rabbit with
carrots and morel sauce.

Seven Suns Coffee & Cafe CAFE
(1011 S Mt Shasta Blvd; ☺ 5:30am-7pm; 🛜) This
snug little hangout serves organic, locally
roasted coffee, light meals (around $10) and
is consistently busy. There's live acoustic
music some evenings.

❶ Getting There & Around

Greyhound (www.greyhound.com) buses head-
ing north and south on I-5 stop at the depot (628
S Weed Blvd) in Weed, 8 miles north of Mt Shas-
ta city on I-5. Services include Redding ($15, one
hour and 20 minutes, three daily), Sacramento
($40, 5½ hours, three daily) and San Francisco
($50, 10½ hours, two or three times daily).

The **STAGE bus** (☑ 530-842-8295; www.
co.siskiyou.ca.us; 914 Pine St; fares $2.50-8)
includes Mt Shasta City in its local I-5 corridor
route (fares $2.50 to $8, depending on dis-
tance), which also serves McCloud, Dunsmuir,
Weed and Yreka several times each weekday.
Other buses connect at Yreka.

Northeast Corner

Site of California's last major Native Amer-
ican conflict and a half-million years of
volcanic destruction, **Lava Beds National
Monument** (☑ 530-667-8113; www.nps.gov/
labe; 1 Indian Well HQ, Tulelake; 7-day entry per car
$15; 🅿 🚻) 🏞 is a peaceful monument to cen-
turies of turmoil. This park's got it all: lava
flows, cinder and spatter cones, volcanic cra-
ters and amazing lava tubes. It was the site
of the Modoc War, and ancient Native Amer-
ican petroglyphs are etched into rocks and
pictographs painted on cave walls. Pick up
info and maps at the **visitor center** (☑ 530-
667-8113; www.nps.gov/labe; Tulelake; ☺ 8am-6pm
late May-early Sep, to 5pm mid-Sep–mid-May),
which sells basic spelunking gear (borrow
flashlights for free). Nearby is the park's ba-
sic **campground** (www.nps.gov/labe/planyour
visit/campgrounds.htm; tent & RV sites $10; 🚻),
where drinking water is available.

Over 20 miles northeast of the park, the
dusty town of **Tulelake** off Hwy 139 has
basic motels, roadside diners and gas. Com-
prising six separate refuges in California and
Oregon, **Klamath Basin National Wildlife
Refuge Complex** is a prime stopover on the
Pacific Flyway and an important wintering
site for bald eagles. When the spring and fall
migrations peak, more than a million birds
can fill the sky. The **visitor center** (☑ 530-
667-2231; www.klamathbasinrefuges.fws.gov; 4009
Hill Rd, Tulelake; ☺ 8am-4:30pm Mon-Fri, 9am-4pm
Sat & Sun) is off Hwy 161, about 4 miles south
of the Oregon border. Self-guided 10-mile
auto tours of the Lower Klamath and Tule
Lake refuges provide excellent birding op-
portunities. Paddle the Upper Klamath ref-
uge's 9.5-mile canoe trail by launching from
Rocky Point Resort (☑ 541-356-2287; 28121
Rocky Point Rd, Klamath Falls, OR; canoe & kayak
rental per hour/half-day/day $20/45/60; ☺ Apr-
Oct; 🚻 🛜). For gas, food and lodging, drive
into Klamath Falls, OR, off Hwy 97.

Quietly impressive **Lassen Volcanic Na-
tional Park** (☑ 530-595-4480; www.nps.gov/
lavo; 38050 Hwy 36 E, Mineral; 7-day entry per
car mid-Apr–Nov $20, Dec–mid-Apr $10; 🅿 🚻)
🏞 has hydrothermal sulfur pools, boiling
mud pots and steaming pools, as glimpsed
from the **Bumpass Hell** boardwalk. Tackle
Lassen Peak (10,457ft), the world's largest
plug-dome volcano, on a strenuous, but
non-technical 5-mile roundtrip trail. The
park has two entrances: an hour's drive east
of Redding off Hwy 44, near popular **Man-
zanita Lake Campground** (☑ reservations
877-444-6777; www.recreation.gov; tent & RV sites
$15-24; 🚻); and a 40-minute drive northwest
of Lake Almanor off Hwy 89, by the **Kom
Yah-mah-nee Visitor Facility** (☑ 530-595-
4480; www.nps.gov/lavo; ☺ 9am-5pm, closed Mon
& Tue Nov-Mar; 🚻) 🏞 Hwy 89 through the
park is typically snow free and open to cars
from June though October.

SIERRA NEVADA

The mighty Sierra Nevada – baptized the
'Range of Light' by poet-naturalist John
Muir – is California's backbone. This 400-mile
phalanx of craggy peaks, chiseled and gouged
by glaciers and erosion, both welcomes and
challenges outdoor-sports enthusiasts. Cra-
dling three national parks (Yosemite, Sequoia
and Kings Canyon), the Sierra is a spellbind-
ing wonderland of superlative wilderness,

boasting the contiguous USA's highest peak (Mt Whitney), North America's tallest waterfall (Yosemite Falls) and the world's oldest and biggest trees.

Yosemite National Park

There's a reason why everybody's heard of it: the granite-peak heights are dizzying, the mist from thunderous waterfalls drenching, the Technicolor wildflower meadows amazing and the majestic silhouettes of El Capitan and Half Dome almost shocking against a crisp blue sky. It's a landscape of dreams, surrounding oh-so-small people on all sides.

Crowds can be an issue in summer holidays: try to go in a shoulder season, start early and walk to escape the throng.

◎ Sights

There are four main entrances to the park ($25-30 per vehicle, depending on the season): South Entrance (Hwy 41), Arch Rock (Hwy 140), Big Oak Flat (Hwy 120 W) and Tioga Pass (Hwy 120 E). Hwy 120 traverses the park as Tioga Rd, connecting Yosemite Valley with the Eastern Sierra.

◎ Yosemite Valley

From the ground up, this dramatic valley cut by the meandering Merced River is song inspiring: rippling green meadow-grass; stately pines; cool, impassive pools reflecting looming granite monoliths; and cascading ribbons of glacially-cold white water. Often overrun and traffic-choked, **Yosemite Village** is home to the park's main **visitor center** (209-372-0200; 9035 Village Dr; 9am-5pm;), **museum** (www.nps.gov/yose; 9037 Village Dr; 9am-5pm summer, 10am-4pm rest of year, often closed noon-1pm) FREE, photography gallery, movie theater, general store and many more services. Curry Village is another valley hub, offering public showers and outdoor-equipment rental and sales, including camping gear.

Spring snowmelt turns the valley's famous waterfalls into thunderous cataracts; most are reduced to a mere trickle by late summer. **Yosemite Falls** is North America's tallest, dropping 2425ft in three tiers. A wheelchair-accessible trail leads to the bottom of this cascade or, for solitude and different perspectives, you can trek the grueling trail to the top (6.8 miles round-trip). No less impressive are other waterfalls around the valley. A strenuous granite staircase beside **Vernal Fall** leads you, gasping, right to the waterfall's edge for a vertical view – look for rainbows in the clouds of mist.

You can't ignore the valley's monumental **El Capitan** (7569ft), an El Dorado for rock climbers. Toothed **Half Dome** (8842ft) soars above the valley as Yosemite's spiritual centerpiece. The classic panoramic photo op is at **Tunnel View** on Hwy 41 as you drive into the valley.

◎ Glacier Point

Rising over 3000ft above the valley floor, dramatic Glacier Point (7214ft) practically puts you at eye level with Half Dome. It's at least an hour's drive from Yosemite Valley up Glacier Point Rd (usually open from May into November) off Hwy 41, or a strenuous hike along the **Four Mile Trail** (actually 4.6 miles, one way) or the less-crowded, waterfall-strewn **Panorama Trail** (8.5 miles one way). To hike one way downhill from Glacier Point, reserve a seat on the **Glacier Point Hikers' Bus** (888-413-8869; 1 way/return $25/49; mid-May–Oct).

◎ Wawona

At Wawona, an hour's drive south of Yosemite Valley, is the **Pioneer Yosemite History Center** (rides adult/child $5/4; 24hr, rides Wed-Sun Jun-Sep;), with its covered bridge, historic buildings and horsedrawn stagecoach rides. Further south the towering **Mariposa Grove** is home to the Grizzly Giant and other giant sequoia trees. Free shuttle buses usually run to the grove from spring through fall.

◎ Tuolumne Meadows

A 90-minute drive from Yosemite Valley, high-altitude Tuolumne Meadows (pronounced *twol*-uh-mee) draws hikers, backpackers and climbers to the park's northern wilderness. The Sierra Nevada's largest subalpine meadow (8600ft) is a vivid contrast to the valley, with wildflower fields, azure lakes, ragged granite peaks, polished domes and cooler temperatures. Hikers and climbers have a paradise of options, and lake swimming and picnicking are also popular. Access is via scenic Tioga Rd (Hwy 120), which is only open seasonally. West of Tuolumne Meadows and **Tenaya Lake**, stop at **Olmsted Point** for epic vistas of Half Dome.

Hetch Hetchy

A 40-mile drive northwest of Yosemite Valley, it's the site of perhaps the most controversial dam in US history. Despite not existing in its natural state, Hetch Hetchy Valley remains pretty and mostly crowd free. A 5.4-mile round-trip hike across the dam and through a tunnel to the base of **Wapama Falls** lets you get thrillingly close to an avalanche of water crashing down into the sparkling reservoir.

Activities

With more than 800 miles of varied hiking trails, you're spoiled for choice. Easy valley-floor routes can get jammed – escape the teeming masses by heading up. Other diversions include rock climbing, cycling, trail rides, swimming, rafting and cross-country skiing.

For overnight backpacking trips, wilderness permits (from $10) are required year round. A quota system limits the number of hikers leaving daily from each trailhead. Make reservations up to 26 weeks in advance, or try your luck at the **Yosemite Valley Wilderness Center** (☏209-372-0745; Yosemite Village; ⊙8am-5pm May-Oct) or another permit-issuing station, starting at 11am on the day before you aim to hike.

Yosemite Mountaineering School CLIMBING (☏209-372-8344; www.travelyosemite.com; Half Dome Village; ⊙Apr-Oct) Offers top-flight instruction for novice to advanced climbers, plus guided climbs, equipment rental and bouldering instruction. Operating since the 1960s.

Sleeping

Camping, even if it's car camping in a campground near busy Yosemite Village, enhances the being-out-in-nature feeling. Backcountry wilderness camping is for the prepared and adventurous. All non-camping reservations within the park are handled by **Aramark/Yosemite Hospitality** (☏888-413-8869; www.travelyosemite.com) and can be made up to 366 days in advance; reservations are critical from May to early September. Rates – and demand – drop from October to April.

★**Majestic Yosemite Hotel** HISTORIC HOTEL $$$ (☏reservations 888-413-8869; www.travelyosemite.com; 1 Ahwahnee Dr, Yosemite Valley; r/ste from $480/590; P⊛⊜@⊚⊠⊠) The crème de la crème of Yosemite's lodging, this sumptuous historic property (formerly called the Ahwahnee) dazzles with soaring ceilings and atmospheric lounges with mammoth stone fireplaces. Classic rooms have inspiring views of Glacier Point and (partial) Half Dome. For high season and holidays, book a year in advance.

Yosemite Valley Lodge MOTEL $$$ (☏reservations 888-413-8869; www.travelyosemite.com; 9006 Yosemite Lodge Dr, Yosemite Valley; r from $260; P⊛@⊚⊠⊠) ✦ Situated a short

---

CAMPING IN YOSEMITE

From mid-March through mid-October or November, many park campgrounds accept or require reservations, which are available starting five months in advance. Campsites routinely sell out online within minutes. All campgrounds have bear-proof lockers and campfire rings; most have potable water.

In summer most campgrounds are noisy and booked to bulging, especially **North Pines** (tent & RV sites $26; ⊙Apr-Oct; ⊠), **Lower Pines** (www.nps.gov/yose; tent & RV sites $26; ⊙Apr-Oct; ⊠) and **Upper Pines** (www.nps.gov/yose; tent & RV sites $26; ⊙year-round; ⊠) in Yosemite Valley; **Tuolumne Meadows** (www.nps.gov/yose; Tioga Rd; tent & RV sites $26; ⊙Jul-Sep; ⊠) off Tioga Rd; and riverside **Wawona** (www.nps.gov/yose; tent & RV sites $26; ⊙year-round; ⊠).

Year-round the following are all first-come, first served: **Camp 4** (www.nps.gov/yose; shared tent sites per person $6; ⊙year-round), a rock climber's hangout in the valley; **Bridalveil Creek** (www.nps.gov/yose; tent & RV sites $18; ⊙Jul-early Sep; ⊠), off Glacier Point Rd; and **White Wolf** (www.nps.gov/yose; tent & RV sites $18; ⊙Jul-early Sep; ⊠), off Tioga Rd. They often fill before noon, especially on weekends.

Looking for a quieter, more rugged experience? Try the primitive campgrounds (no potable water) off Tioga Rd at **Tamarack Flat** (Old Big Oak Flat Rd; tent sites $12; ⊙late Jun-Sep; ⊠), **Yosemite Creek** (www.nps.gov/yose; tent sites $12; ⊙Jul-early Sep; ⊠) and **Porcupine Flat** (www.nps.gov/yose; tent & RV sites $12; ⊙Jul–mid-Oct; ⊠), all first-come, first-served.

walk from Yosemite Falls, this large complex contains eateries, a lively bar, a big pool and handy amenities. The rooms, spread over 15 buildings, feel somewhat lodge-like, with wooden furniture and nature photography. All have cable TV, telephone, fridge and coffeemaker, and patio or balcony panoramas.

May Lake High Sierra Camp CABIN $$$
(☑888-413-8869; www.travelyosemite.com; adult/child $175/90) Because it's the easiest of the High Sierra camps to access, May Lake is also the best for children – at least those who'll be untroubled by the mile-plus hike to get there. Views of Mt Hoffman are quite stunning. Breakfast and dinner included in rates.

🏨 Outside Yosemite

Gateway towns that have a mixed bag of motels, hotels, lodges and B&Bs include Fish Camp, Oakhurst, El Portal, Midpines, Mariposa, Groveland and, in the Eastern Sierra, Lee Vining.

★Yosemite Bug Rustic Mountain Resort HOSTEL, CABIN $
(☑209-966-6666; www.yosemitebug.com; 6979 Hwy 140, Midpines; dm $30, tent cabins from $65, r with/without bath from $165/95; P☕@🛜) This folksy oasis is tucked away on a forested hillside about 25 miles west of Yosemite. A wide range of accommodations types lines the narrow ridges; some require more walking from parking areas and bathrooms than others. The **June Bug Cafe** (☑206-966-6666; www.yosemitebug.com/cafe.html; mains $8-22; ☕7-10am, 11am-2pm & 6-9pm; 🍴♿) is highly recommended. Also available are yoga lessons, massages and a spa with hot tub.

🛈 TIOGA PASS

Hwy 120 is the only road connecting Yosemite National Park with the Eastern Sierra, climbing through Tioga Pass (9945ft). Most maps mark this road 'closed in winter' which, while literally true, is also misleading. Tioga Rd is usually closed from the first heavy snowfall in October or November, not reopening until May or June. Call ☑209-372-0200 or check www.nps.gov/yose/planyourvisit/conditions.htm for current road conditions.

★Evergreen Lodge CABIN $$$
(☑209-379-2606; www.evergreenlodge.com; 33160 Evergreen Rd, Groveland; tents $90-125, cabins $180-415; ☕usually closed Jan–mid-Feb; P☕❄@🛜🐾) Outside Yosemite National Park near the entrance to Hetch Hetchy, this classic, nearly century-old resort consists of lovingly decorated and comfy cabins (each with its own cache of board games) spread among the trees. Accommodations run from rustic to deluxe, and all cabins have private porches without distracting phone or TV. Roughing-it guests can cheat with comfy, prefurnished tents.

🛈 Information

Yosemite's entrance fee is $30 per vehicle or $15 for those on a bicycle or on foot and is valid for seven consecutive days. Passes are sold (you can use cash, checks, traveler's checks or credit/debit cards) at the various entrance stations, as well as at visitor centers in Oakhurst, Groveland, Mariposa and Lee Vining.

Yosemite Valley Visitor Center (p1022) Park's busiest information desk. Shares space with bookstore run by Yosemite Conservancy and part of the museum complex in the center of Yosemite Village.

🛈 Getting There & Around

Greyhound buses and **Amtrak** trains serve Merced, west of the park, where they are met by buses operated by the **Yosemite Area Regional Transportation System** (YARTS; ☑877-989-2787; www.yarts.com); you can buy Amtrak tickets that include the YARTS segment all the way into the park. One-way tickets to Yosemite Valley are $13 ($9 child and senior, three hours) from Merced and $18 ($15 child and senior, 3½ hours) from Mammoth Lakes; fares include the park-entrance fee, making them a super bargain, and drivers accept credit cards.

The free, air-conditioned **Yosemite Valley Shuttle Bus** (www.nps.gov/yose) is a comfortable and efficient way of traveling around the park. Buses operate year-round at frequent intervals and stop at 21 numbered locations, including parking lots, campgrounds, trailheads and lodges.

Bicycling is an ideal way to take in Yosemite Valley. You can rent a wide-handled cruiser (per hour/day $11.50/32) or a bike with an attached child trailer (per hour/day $19/59) at the **Yosemite Valley Lodge** or **Half Dome Village** (per hour/day $12.50/30.50; ☕9am-6pm Mar-Oct). Strollers and wheelchairs are also rented here.

Valley visitors are advised to park and take advantage of the Yosemite Valley Shuttle Bus. Even so, traffic in the valley can feel like rush hour in LA. Glacier Point and Tioga Rds are closed in winter.

Sequoia & Kings Canyon National Parks

In these neighboring parks, giant sequoia trees are bigger – up to 27 stories high! – and more numerous than anywhere else in the Sierra Nevada. Tough and fire-charred, they'd easily swallow two freeway lanes each. Giant, too, are the mountains – including Mt Whitney (14,505ft), the tallest peak in the lower 48 states. Finally, there is the deep Kings Canyon, carved out of granite by ancient glaciers and a powerful river. For quiet, solitude and close-up sightings of wildlife, including black bears, hit the trails and lose yourself in this stunning wilderness.

◉ Sights

The two **parks** (☎559-565-3341; www.nps.gov/seki; 7-day entry per car $30; ▣⛽) ✦, though distinct, are operated as one unit with a single admission fee; for 24-hour recorded information, including road conditions, call the number listed or visit the parks' comprehensive website. At either entrance station (Big Stump or Ash Mountain), you'll receive an NPS map and a copy of the parks' *Guide* newspaper, with information on seasonal activities, camping and special programs, including those in the surrounding national forests and the **Giant Sequoia National Monument** (www.fs.usda.gov). It's easy enough to explore sections of both parks in a single day.

◉ Sequoia National Park

We dare you to try hugging the trees in Giant Forest, a 3-sq-mile grove protecting gargantuan specimens – the world's largest is the **General Sherman Tree**. With sore arms and sticky sap fingers, lose the crowds on a network of forested hiking trails (bring a map).

Worth a detour is **Mineral King Valley**, a late-19th-century mining and logging camp ringed by craggy peaks and alpine lakes. The 25-mile one-way scenic drive – navigating almost 700 white-knuckle hairpin turns – is usually open from late May until late October.

Giant Forest Museum   MUSEUM
(☎559-565-4480; www.nps.gov/seki; cnr Generals Hwy & Crescent Meadow Rd; ⊙9am-4:30pm; ▣⛽) ✦FREE For a primer on the intrigu-

ing ecology and history of giant sequoias, this pint-sized modern museum will entertain both kids and adults. Hands-on exhibits teach about the life stages of these big trees, which can live for over 3000 years, and the fire cycle that releases their seeds and allows them to sprout on bare soil. The museum is housed in a historic 1920s building designed by Gilbert Stanley Underwood, famed architect of the Majestic Yosemite (formerly Ahwahnee) Hotel.

Crystal Cave   CAVE
(www.explorecrystalcave.com; Crystal Cave Rd; tours adult/child/youth from $16/5/8; ⊙May-Sep; ▣⛽) ✦ Discovered in 1918 by two parks employees who were going fishing, this unique cave was carved by an underground river and has marble formations estimated to be 10,000 years old. Tickets for the 50-minute introductory tour are only sold online in advance or, during October and November, at the Giant Forest Museum and Foothills Visitor Center, *not* at the cave. Bring a jacket.

◉ Kings Canyon National Park & Scenic Byway

Just north of Grant Grove Village, **General Grant Grove** brims with majestic giants. Beyond, Hwy 180 begins its 30-mile descent into Kings Canyon, serpentining past chiseled rock walls laced with waterfalls. The road meets the **Kings River**, its roar ricocheting off granite cliffs soaring over 8000ft high, making this one of North America's deepest canyons.

At the bottom of the canyon, **Cedar Grove** is the last outpost before the rugged grandeur of the Sierra Nevada backcountry begins. A popular day hike climbs 4.6 miles one way to gushing **Mist Falls** from Roads End. A favorite of birders, an easy 1.5-mile nature trail loops around **Zumwalt Meadow**, just west of Roads End. Watch for lumbering black bears and springy mule deer.

The scenic byway past Hume Lake to Cedar Grove Village is usually closed from mid-November to late April.

Boyden Cavern   CAVE
(☎209-736-2708, 866-762-2837; www.caverntours.com/BoydenRt.htm; Hwy 180; tours adult/child from $17.50/9.50; ⊙late Apr–Sep; ⛽) Touring the beautiful and fantastical formations here requires no advance tickets: just show up for the basic 45-minute tour, which

departs hourly from 10am to 5pm during peak summer season. Reaching the entrance requires a short walk up a steep, paved grade. The cavern was closed for much of 2016 and 2017 because of fire damage to a footbridge; check before you visit to make sure it's open.

Activities

With over 850 miles of marked trails, the parks are a backpacker's dream. Cedar Grove and Mineral King offer the best backcountry access. Trails are usually open by mid- to late May.

For overnight backcountry trips you'll need a wilderness permit (per group $15), which is subject to a quota system in summer; outside the quota season, permits are free and available by self-registration. About 75% of spaces can be reserved, while the rest are available in person on a first-come, first-served basis. Reservations can be made from March 1 until two weeks before your trip. For details, see www.nps.gov/seki/planyourvisit/wilderness_permits.htm. There's also a dedicated wilderness desk at the Lodgepole Visitor Center.

All ranger stations and visitor centers carry topo maps and hiking guides. Note that you need to store your food in park-approved bear-proof canisters, which can be rented at markets and visitor centers (from $5 per trip).

🛏 Sleeping & Eating

Camping is the best and most affordable way to experience the parks, though of course sites fill up fast in high season. Sequoia National Forest and other wilderness areas that border the parks offer alternatives. Sequoia has only one official in-park lodging option: **Wuksachi Lodge** (ℹ️ information 866-807-3598, reservations 317-324-0753; www.visitsequoia.com; 64740 Wuksachi Way; r $215-290; P❄🐾📶🎿). The gateway town of Three Rivers, just outside the park entrance, offers the most accommodations. Kings Canyon has lodges in Grant Grove and Cedar Grove villages.

The few park lodges – Wuksachi, **John Muir** (ℹ️866-807-3598; www.visitsequoia.com; Grant Grove Village; r from $225; P❄📶) and Cedar Grove – have restaurants, as do a couple of spots in the adjoining Sequoia National Forest. Three Rivers, just south of Sequoia, is a good place to fill up.

NPS & USFS
Campgrounds ACCOMMODATION SERVICES $
(ℹ️877-444-6777, 518-885-3639; www.recreation.gov) Reservation service for many of the campgrounds in the parks.

DNC Parks &
Resorts ACCOMMODATION SERVICES $$
(ℹ️866-807-3598, 801-559-4930; www.visitsequoia.com) Delaware North is the concessionaire operating lodges and other services in Sequoia and Kings Canyon National Parks.

⭐ Sequoia High Sierra Camp CABIN $$
(ℹ️866-654-2877; www.sequoiahighsierracamp.com; tent cabins without bath incl all meals adult/child $250/150; ⏰mid-Jun–mid-Sep) A mile's hike deep into the Sequoia National Forest, this off-the-grid, all-inclusive resort is nirvana for those who don't think luxury camping is an oxymoron. Canvas bungalows are spiffed up with pillow-top mattresses, feather pillows and cozy wool rugs. Restrooms and a shower house are shared. Reservations are required, and there's usually a two-night minimum stay.

Cedar Grove Lodge LODGE $$
(ℹ️559-565-3096; www.visitsequoia.com; 86724 Hwy 180, Cedar Grove Village; r from $130; ⏰mid-May–mid-Oct; P❄🐾📶) The only indoor sleeping option in the canyon, this riverside lodge offers 21 unexciting motel-style rooms. A recent remodel has updated some of the frumpy decor. Three ground-floor rooms with shady furnished patios have spiffy river views and kitchenettes.

ℹ Information

Lodgepole Village and Grant Grove Village are the parks' main commercial hubs. Both have visitor centers, post offices, markets, ATMs, a coin-op laundry and public showers (summer only). Expensive gas is available at Hume Lake (year-round) and Stony Creek (closed in winter) outside the parks on national-forest land.

The following visitor centres are open year-round:

Kings Canyon Visitor Center (ℹ️559-565-4307; Hwy 180, Grant Grove Village; ⏰9am-5pm) In the Grant Grove Village of Kings Canyon.

Lodgepole Visitor Center (ℹ️559-565-4436; Lodgepole Village; ⏰7am-5pm late Apr-early Oct, to 7pm peak season) Located in the heart of Sequoia.

ℹ Getting There & Around

You can use Fresno to connect to Grant Grove in Kings Canyon with **Big Trees Transit** (📞 800-325-7433; www.bigtreestransit.com; round-trip incl park entry fee $15; ☉ late May-early Sep), or the **Sequoia Shuttle** (📞 877-287-4453; www.sequoiashuttle.com; ☉ late May-late Sep) (summer only) to get between Visalia and the Giant Forest area of Sequoia.

Sequoia and Kings Canyon are both accessible by car only from the west, via Hwy 99 from Fresno or Visalia.

Sequoia National Park has five free shuttle routes within the park; Kings Canyon has no shuttles.

Eastern Sierra

Vast, empty and majestic, here jagged peaks plummet down into the desert, a dramatic juxtaposition that creates a potent scenery cocktail. Hwy 395 runs the entire length of the eastern side of the Sierra Nevada, with turnoffs leading to pine forests, wildflower-strewn meadows, placid lakes, hot springs and glacier-gouged canyons. Hikers, backpackers, mountain bikers, fishers and skiers all find escapes here.

At **Bodie State Historic Park** (📞 760-647-6445; www.parks.ca.gov/bodie; Hwy 270; adult/child $8/4; ☉ 9am-6pm mid-Mar–Oct, to 4pm Nov–mid-Mar; 🅿 ♿), the weathered buildings of a gold-rush boomtown sit frozen in time on a dusty, windswept plain. To get there, head east for 13 miles (the last three unpaved) on Hwy 270, about 7 miles south of Bridgeport. Snow usually closes the access road in winter and early spring.

Further south at **Mono Lake** (www.monolake.org), unearthly tufa towers rise from the alkaline water like drip sand castles. Off Hwy 395, **Mono Basin Scenic Area Visitor Center** (📞 760-647-3044; www.fs.usda.gov/inyo; 1 Visitor Center Dr; ☉ generally 8am-5pm Apr-Nov; ♿) has excellent views and educational exhibits, but the best photo ops are from the mile-long nature trail at the **South Tufa Area** (adult/child $3/free). From the nearby town of Lee Vining, Hwy 120 heads west into Yosemite National Park via seasonal Tioga Pass.

Continuing south on Hwy 395, detour along the scenic 16-mile **June Lake Loop** or push on to **Mammoth Lakes**, a popular four-seasons resort guarded by 11,053ft **Mammoth Mountain** (📞 800-626-6684, 760-934-2571, 24hr snow report 888-766-9778; www.

mammothmountain.com; adult/13-18yr/7-12yr $125/98/35; ♿), a top-notch skiing area. The slopes morph into a mountain-bike park in summer, when scenic gondola rides run. There's also camping and day hiking around Mammoth Lakes Basin and Reds Meadow, the latter near the 60ft-high basalt columns of **Devils Postpile National Monument** (📞 760-934-2289; www.nps.gov/depo; shuttle day pass adult/child $7/4; ☉ late May-Oct), formed by volcanic activity. Hot-springs fans can soak in primitive pools off Benton Crossing Rd or view the geysering water at **Hot Creek Geological Site**, both off Hwy 395 southeast of town. The in-town **Mammoth Lakes Welcome Center & Ranger Station** (📞 760-924-5500, 888-466-2666; www.visitmammoth.com; 2510 Hwy 203; ☉ 9am-5pm) has helpful maps and information.

Further south, Hwy 395 descends into the Owens Valley. In frontier-flavored **Bishop**, **Mountain Light Gallery** (📞 760-873-7700; www.mountainlight.com; 106 S Main St; ☉ 10am-5pm Mon-Sat, 11am-4pm Sun) FREE and the historical **Laws Railroad Museum** (📞 760-873-5950; www.lawsmuseum.org; Silver Canyon Rd; donation $5; ☉ 10am-4pm; ♿) are minor attractions. A gateway for packhorse trips, Bishop accesses the Eastern Sierra's best fishing and rock climbing. Budget a half-day for the thrilling drive up to the **Ancient Bristlecone Pine Forest**. These gnarled, otherworldly looking trees – the world's oldest – are found above 10,000ft on the slopes of the White Mountains. The road (closed by snow in winter and early spring) is paved to the **Schulman Grove Visitor Center** (📞 760-873-2500; www.fs.usda.gov/inyo; White Mountain Rd; per person/car $3/6; ☉ 10am-4pm Fri-Mon mid-May–early Nov), where hiking trails await. From Hwy 395 in Big Pine, take Hwy 168 east for 12 miles, then follow White Mountain Rd uphill for 10 miles.

Hwy 395 barrels south to **Manzanar National Historic Site** (📞 760-878-2194; www.nps.gov/manz; 5001 Hwy 395; ☉ 9am-5:30pm Apr–mid-Oct, 10am-4:30pm mid-Oct–Mar; 🅿 ♿) ✏FREE, which memorializes the camp where some 10,000 Japanese Americans were unjustly interned during WWII. Further south in Lone Pine, you'll finally glimpse Mt Whitney (14,505ft), the highest mountain in the lower 48 states. The heart-stopping, 12-mile scenic drive up **Whitney Portal Road** (closed in winter and early spring) is spectacular. Climbing the peak is hugely popular, but requires a permit (per person $15) awarded via annual lottery. Just south of town, the **Eastern Sierra Interagency Visitor Center** (✆760-876-6222; www.fs.fed.us/r5/inyo; cnr Hwys 395 & 136; ☺8am-5pm) issues wilderness permits, dispenses outdoor-recreation info and sells books and maps.

West of Lone Pine, the bizarrely shaped boulders of the Alabama Hills have enchanted filmmakers of Hollywood Westerns. Peruse vintage memorabilia and movie posters back in town at the **Museum of Western Film History** (✆760-876-9909; www.museumofwesternfilmhistory.org; 701 S Main St; adult/under 12yr $5/free; ☺10am-6pm Mon-Wed, to 7pm Thu-Sat, to 4pm Sun Apr-Oct, 10am-5pm Mon-Sat, to 4pm Sun Nov-Mar; P 🚸).

🛏 Sleeping

The Eastern Sierra is freckled with campgrounds; backcountry camping requires a wilderness permit, available at ranger stations. Bishop, Lone Pine and Bridgeport have the most motels. Mammoth Lakes has a few motels and hotels and dozens of inns, B&Bs, condos and vacation rentals. Reservations are essential everywhere in summer.

★**Whitney Portal**
Hostel & Hotel   HOSTEL, MOTEL $
(✆760-876-0030; www.whitneyportalstore.com; 238 S Main St; dm/d $25/85; ❄🛜🐾) A popular launchpad for Mt Whitney trips and a locus of posthike washups (public showers are available), the Whitney has the cheapest beds in town – reserve dorms months ahead for July and August. There's no common space, just well-maintained single-sex bunkbed rooms, though amenities include towels, TVs, in-room kitchenettes and coffeemakers.

★**Inn at Benton Hot Springs**   INN $$
(✆866-466-2824, 760-933-2287; www.historicbentonhotsprings.com; Hwy 120, Benton; tent & RV sites for 2 people $40-50, d with/without bath $129/109; ❄🛜🐾) Soak in your own hotsprings tub and snooze beneath the moonlight at Benton Hot Springs, a small, historic resort in a 150-year-old former silver-mining town nestled in the White Mountains. Choose from nine well-spaced camp sites with private tubs or themed, antique-filled B&B rooms with semi-private tubs. Daytime dips ($10 per person per hour) are available. Reservations essential.

Dow Hotel & Dow Villa Motel   HOTEL, MOTEL $$
(✆760-876-5521; www.dowvillamotel.com; 310 S Main St; hotel r with/without bath from $89/70, motel r $117-158; P🚿❄@🛜♨🐾) John Wayne and Errol Flynn are among the stars who have stayed at this venerable hotel. Built in 1922, the place has been restored but retains much of its rustic charm. The rooms in the newer motel section have air-con and are more comfortable and bright, but also more generic.

Tamarack Lodge   LODGE, CABIN $$
(✆800-626-6684, 760-934-2442; www.tamaracklodge.com; 163 Twin Lakes Rd; r with/without bath from $199/149, cabins from $169; P🚿@🛜) 🌿 In business since 1924, this charming year-round resort on Lower Twin Lake has a cozy fireplace lodge, a bar and excellent restaurant, 11 rustic-style rooms and 35 cabins. The cabins range from very simple to simply deluxe, and come with full kitchen, private bathroom, porch and wood-burning stove. Some can sleep up to 10 people. Daily resort fee $20.

🍴 Eating & Drinking

Alabama Hills Cafe   DINER $
(✆760-876-4675; 111 W Post St; mains $8-14; ☺7am-2pm; 🛜🍴🚸) At everyone's favorite breakfast joint, the portions are big, the bread is freshly baked, and the hearty soups, sandwiches and fruit pies make lunch an attractive option too. You can also plan your drive through the **Alabama Hills** with the help of the map on the menu.

Mammoth Tavern   GASTROPUB $$
(✆760-934-3902; www.mammothtavern.com; 587 Old Mammoth Rd; mains $13-28; ☺4-11pm Tue-Sun) Mammoth Tavern hits the spot with comfort food like shepherd's pie, oysters, fondue and garlic-turkey meatballs. Gorgeous salads too. Warm lighting, wood-paneled walls rising to a circular ceiling, and drop-dead-gorgeous views of the snow-capped Sherwin Range mean the big-screen TVs are an unnecessary distraction. Drinks include tasty house cocktails, local drafts, interesting whiskeys and over two dozen wines by the glass.

★**Skadi**   NORWEGIAN $$$
(✆760-914-0962; www.skadirestaurant.com; 94 Berner St; mains $30-38; ☺5-11pm Wed-Mon) Considering its more-than-mundane location in an industrial strip, Skadi comes as a surprise. The Swiss Alps decor and innovative menu are the creation of chef Ian Algerøen, inspired by his Norwegian heritage and training in European fine-dining techniques. On the menu you'll find house-smoked trout with horserad-

ish cream, Canadian duck breast with arctic lingonberries and pan-seared day-boat scallops. Reservations required.

★ **June Lake Brewing** MICROBREWERY
(www.junelakebrewing.com; 131 S Crawford Ave; ☺11am-8pm Wed-Mon, to 9pm Fri & Sat; ☻) A top regional draw, June Lake Brewing's open tasting room serves 10 drafts, including a 'SmoKin' Porter, Deer Beer Brown Ale and some awesome IPAs. Brewers swear the June Lake water makes all the difference.

Mammoth Brewing Company BREWERY
(☎760-934-7141; www.mammothbrewingco.com; 18 Lake Mary Rd; ☺10am-9:30pm Sun-Thu, to 10:30pm Fri & Sat) You be the judge whether beer is brewed best at high altitude. Boasting the highest West Coast brewery, at 8000ft, Mammoth Brewing Company offers more than a dozen brews on tap (flights $5 to $7) – including special seasonal varieties not found elsewhere. Tasty bar food's available, and you can pick up some IPA 395 or Double Nut Brown to go.

Lake Tahoe

Shimmering in myriad shades of blue and green, Lake Tahoe is the USA's second-deepest lake and, at 6255ft high, it is also one of the highest-elevation lakes in the country. Driving around the spellbinding 72-mile scenic shoreline will give you quite a workout behind the wheel. Generally, the north shore is quiet and upscale; the west shore, rugged and old-timey; the east shore, undeveloped; the south shore, busy and tacky, with aging motels and flashy casinos; and nearby Reno, the biggest little city in the region.

ℹ Information

Lake Tahoe Visitors Authority (☎800-288-2463; www.tahoesouth.com; 169 Hwy 50, Stateline, NV; ☺9am-5pm Mon-Fri) A full range of tourist information.

North Lake Tahoe Visitors Bureaus (☎800-468-2463; www.gotahoenorth.com) Help with accommodations and outdoor-activity bookings.

ℹ Getting There & Around

Greyhound buses from Reno, Sacramento and San Francisco run to Truckee, and you can also get the daily Zephyr train here from the same destinations. From Truckee, take the **Truckee Transit** (☎530-587-7451; www.laketahoetransit.com; single/day pass $2.50/5) to Donner Lake, or **Tahoe Area Rapid Transit** (TART;

☎530-550-1212; www.laketahoetransit.com; 10183 Truckee Airport Rd; single/day pass $2/4) (TART) buses to the north, west and east shore of the lake.

The winter **Bay Area Ski Bus** (☎925-680-4386; www.bayareaskibus.com) connects San Francisco and Sacramento with Tahoe's slopes.

TART runs buses along the north shore as far as Incline Village, down the western shore to Ed Z'berg Sugar Pine Point State Park, and north to Squaw Valley and Truckee via Hwy 89. The main routes typically depart hourly from about 6am until 6pm daily.

South Lake Tahoe & West Shore

With retro motels and eateries lining busy Hwy 50, South Lake Tahoe gets crowded. Gambling at Stateline's casino hotels, just across the Nevada border, attracts thousands, as does the world-class ski resort of **Heavenly** (☎775-586-7000; www.skiheavenly.com; 4080 Lake Tahoe Blvd; adult/child 5-12yr/youth 13-18yr $135/79/113; ☺9am-4pm Mon-Fri, from 8:30am Sat, Sun & holidays; ☻). In summer a trip up Heavenly's gondola (adult/child $42/20) guarantees fabulous views of the lake and the **Desolation Wilderness**, with its raw granite peaks, glacier-carved valleys and alpine lakes favored by hikers. Get maps, information and wilderness permits (per adult $5 to $10) from the **USFS Taylor Creek Visitor Center** (☎530-543-2674; www.fs.usda.gov/ltbmu; Visitor Center Rd, off Hwy 89; ☺8am-5pm late May-Sep, to 4pm Oct). It's 3 miles north of the 'Y' intersection of Hwys 50/89, at **Tallac Historic Site** (www.tahoeheritage.org; Tallac Rd; optional tour adult/child $10/5; ☺10am-4pm daily mid-Jun–Sep, Fri & Sat late May–mid-Jun; ☻) **FREE**, preserving swish early-20th-century vacation estates.

From sandy, swimmable **Zephyr Cove** (☎775-589-4901; www.zephyrcove.com; 760 Hwy 50; per car $10; ☻) across the Nevada border or the in-town Ski Run Marina, **Lake Tahoe Cruises** (☎800-238-2463; www.zephyrcove.com; 900 Ski Run Blvd; adult/child from $55/20; ☻) plies the 'Big Blue' year round. Paddle under your own power with **Kayak Tahoe** (☎530-544-2011; www.kayaktahoe.com; 3411 Lake Tahoe Blvd; kayak single/double 1hr $25/35, 1 day $65/85, lessons & tours from $40; ☺9am-5pm Jun-Sep). Back on shore, boutique-chic motels include the **Alder Inn** (☎530-544-4485; www.alderinn.com; 1072 Ski Run Blvd; r $89-149; P☺☺☺) and the hip **Basecamp Hotel** (☎530-208-0180; www.basecamphotels.com; 4143 Cedar Ave; d $109-229, 8-person bunk room

$209-299, pet fee $40; (🐾🛏️🌀) 🐾, which has a rooftop hot tub, or pitch a tent at lakeside **Fallen Leaf Campground** (☎info 530-544-0426, reservations 877-444-6777; www.recreation. gov; 2165 Fallen Leaf Lake Rd; tent & RV sites $33-35, yurts $84; ☀mid-May–mid-Oct; 🛏️). Fuel up at vegetarian-friendly **Sprouts** (www.sprouts cafetahoe.com; 3123 Harrison Ave; mains $7-10; ☀8am-9pm; 🍴🛏️) natural-foods cafe, or with a peanut-butter-topped burger and garlic fries at the **Burger Lounge** (☎530-542-2010; 717 Emerald Bay Rd; dishes $4-10; ☀10am-8pm Jun-Sep, 11am-7pm Thu-Mon Oct-May; 🛏️).

Hwy 89 threads northwest along the thickly forested west shore to **Emerald Bay State Park** (☎530-541-6498; www.parks. ca.gov), where granite cliffs and pine trees frame a sparkling fjordlike inlet. A 1-mile trail leads steeply downhill to **Vikingsholm Castle** (http://vikingsholm.com; tour adult/child 7-17yr $10/8; ☀10:30am-3:30pm or 4pm late May–Sep; 🅿🛏️), a 1920s Scandinavian-style mansion. From there, the **Rubicon Trail** ribbons 4.5 miles north along the lakeshore past petite coves to **DL Bliss State Park** (☎530-525-7277; www.parks.ca.gov; per car $10; ☀late May–Sep; 🅿🛏️) 🐾, offering sandy beaches. Further north, **Tahoma Meadows B&B Cottages** (☎530-525-1553; www.tahomamea dows.com; 6821 W Lake Blvd; cottages $119-239, pet fee $20; 🅿⊖🌀🛏️) rents country cabins.

North & East Shores

A busy commercial hub, **Tahoe City** is great for grabbing food and supplies and renting outdoor-sports gear. It's not far from **Squaw Valley USA** (☎530-452-4331; www.squaw.com; 1960 Squaw Valley Rd, off Hwy 89, Olympic Valley; adult/child 5-12yr/youth 13-22yr $124/75/109; ☀9am-4pm Mon-Fri, from 8:30am Sat, Sun & holidays; 🛏️), a huge ski resort. Après-ski crowds gather at **Bridgetender Tavern & Grill** (www.tahoebridgetender.com; 65 W Lake Blvd; ☀11am-11pm, to midnight Fri & Sat) back in town. In the morning, gobble eggs Benedict with house-smoked salmon at down-home **Fire Sign Cafe** (www.firesigncafe.com; 1785 W Lake Blvd; mains $7-13; ☀7am-3pm; 🍴🛏️), 2 miles further south.

In summer, swim or kayak at **Tahoe Vista** or **Kings Beach**. Overnight at **Cedar Glen Lodge** (☎530-546-4281; www.tahoecedarglen. com; 6589 N Lake Blvd; r, ste & cottages $139-350, pet fee $30; @🌀🛏️🐾), where rustic-themed cottages and rooms have kitchenettes, or well-kept, compact **Hostel Tahoe** (☎530-546-3266; www.hosteltahoe.com; 8931 N Lake Blvd;

dm/d/q $33/60/80; @🌀) 🐾. East of Kings Beach's casual lakeside eateries, Hwy 28 barrels into Nevada. Catch a live-music show at a just-over-the-border casino, or for more happening bars and bistros, drive further to Incline Village.

With pristine beaches, lakes and miles of multi-use trails, **Lake Tahoe-Nevada State Park** is the east shore's biggest draw. Summer crowds splash in the turquoise waters of **Sand Harbor**. The 13-mile **Flume Trail**, a mountain biker's holy grail, ends further south at **Spooner Lake**. Back in Incline Village, **Flume Trail Bikes** (http://flumetrailtahoe. com) offers bicycle rentals and shuttles.

Truckee & Around

North of Lake Tahoe off I-80, Truckee is not in fact a truck stop but a thriving mountain town, with coffee shops, trendy boutiques and dining in downtown's historical district. Ski bums have several resorts to pick from, including glam **Northstar California** (☎530-562-1010; www.northstarcalifornia.com; 5001 Northstar Dr, off Hwy 267; adult/child 5-12yr/youth 13-18yr $130/77/107; ☀8am-4pm; 🛏️); kid-friendly **Sugar Bowl** (☎530-426-9000; www.sugarbowl.com; 629 Sugar Bowl Rd, off Donner Pass Rd, Norden; adult/child 6-12yr/youth 13-22yr $85/35/76; ☀9am-4pm; 🛏️); and **Royal Gorge** (☎530-426-3871; www.royalgorge.com; 9411 Pahatsi Rd, off I-80 exit Soda Springs/Norden, Soda Springs; adult/youth 13-22yr $32/25; ☀9am-5pm during snow season; 🛏️🌀), paradise for cross-country skiers.

West of Hwy 89, **Donner Summit** is where the infamous Donner Party became trapped during the fierce winter of 1846–47. Fewer than half survived – some by cannibalizing their dead friends. The grisly tale is chronicled at the museum inside **Donner Memorial State Park** (☎530-582-7892; www. parks.ca.gov; Donner Pass Rd; per car $8; ☀10am-5pm; 🅿🛏️), which offers **camping** (☎530-582-7894, reservations 800-444-7275; www. reserveamerica.com; tent & RV sites $35; ☀late May-late Sep). Nearby **Donner Lake** is popular with swimmers and paddlers.

On the outskirts of Truckee, green-certified **Cedar House Sport Hotel** (☎530-582-5655; www.cedarhousesporthotel.com; 10918 Brockway Rd; r $170-295; 🅿⊖@🌀🛏️) 🐾 offers stylish boutique rooms and an outstanding restaurant. Down pints of Donner Party Porter at **Fifty Fifty Brewing Co** (www.fiftyfifty-brewing.com; 11197 Brockway Rd; ☀11:30am-9pm Sun-Thu, to 9:30pm Fri & Sat).

Pacific Northwest

Includes →

Washington 1035
Seattle 1035
San Juan Islands 1055
North Cascades 1057
South Cascades 1060
Oregon 1063
Portland 1063
Willamette Valley 1073
Columbia
River Gorge 1075
Oregon Cascades 1076
Oregon Coast 1080

Best Places to Eat

→ Ned Ludd (p1070)
→ Chow (p1079)
→ Ox (p1070)
→ Sitka & Spruce (p1045)

Best Places to Sleep

→ Timberline Lodge (p1077)
→ Crater Lake Lodge (p1080)
→ Hotel Monaco (p1043)
→ Olympic Lights B&B (p1055)
→ Historic Davenport Hotel (p1059)

Why Go?

As much a state of mind as a geographical region, the northwest corner of the US is a land of subcultures and new trends, where evergreen trees frame snow-dusted volcanoes, and inspired ideas scribbled on the back of napkins become tomorrow's start-ups. You can't peel off the history in layers here, but you *can* gaze wistfully into the future in fast-moving, innovative cities such as Seattle and Portland, which are sprinkled with food carts, streetcars, microbreweries, green belts, coffee connoisseurs and weird urban sculpture.

Ever since the days of the Oregon Trail, the Northwest has had a hypnotic lure for risk-takers and dreamers; the metaphoric carrot still dangles. There's the air, so clean they ought to bottle it; the trees, older than many of Rome's Renaissance palaces; and the end-of-the-continent coastline, holding back the force of the world's largest ocean. Cowboys take note: it doesn't get much more 'wild' or 'west' than this.

When to Go
Seattle

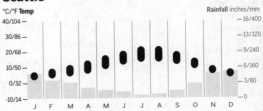

Jan–Mar Most reliable snow cover for skiing in the Cascades and beyond.

May Festival season: Portland Rose and International Film Festival and more.

Jul–Sep The best hiking months, between the spring snowmelt and the first fall flurries.

Pacific Northwest Highlights

1 San Juan Islands (p1055) Cycling and kayaking around the quieter corners.

2 Oregon Coast (p1080) Exploring this gorgeous region, from scenic Astoria to balmy Port Orford.

3 Olympic National Park (p1050) Admiring trees older than Europe's Renaissance castles.

4 Pike Place Market (p1036) Watching the greatest outdoor show in the Pacific Northwest.

5 Portland (p1063) Walking the green and serene neighborhoods, energized by beer, coffee and food-cart treats.

6 Crater Lake National Park (p1080) Witnessing the impossibly deep-blue waters and scenic panoramas.

7 Bend (p1078) Going mountain biking, rock climbing or skiing in this outdoor mecca.

8 Walla Walla (p1062) Tasting sumptuous reds and whites in the surrounding wine regions.

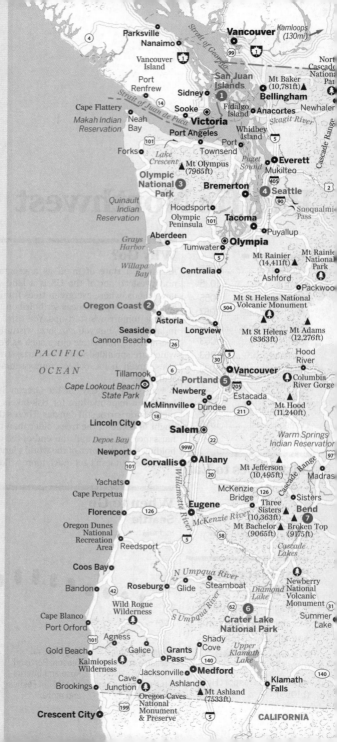

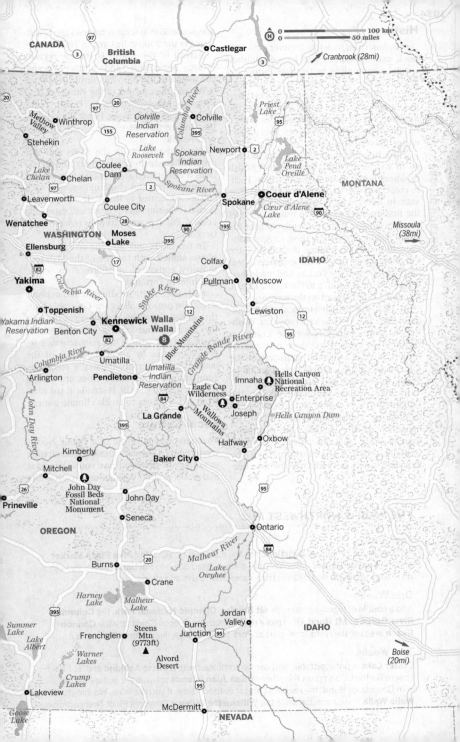

History

Native American societies, including the Chinook and the Salish, had long-established coastal communities by the time Europeans arrived in the Pacific Northwest in the 18th century. Inland, on the arid plateaus between the Cascades and the Rocky Mountains, the Spokane, Nez Percé and other tribes thrived on seasonal migration between river valleys and temperate uplands.

Three hundred years after Columbus landed in the New World, Spanish and British explorers began probing the northern Pacific coast, seeking the fabled Northwest Passage. In 1792 Captain George Vancouver was the first explorer to sail the waters of Puget Sound, claiming British sovereignty over the entire region. At the same time, an American, Captain Robert Gray, found the mouth of the Columbia River. In 1805 the explorers Lewis and Clark crossed the Rockies and made their way down the Columbia to the Pacific Ocean, extending the US claim on the territory.

In 1824 the British Hudson's Bay Company established Fort Vancouver in Washington as headquarters for the Columbia region. This opened the door to waves of settlers, but had a devastating impact on the indigenous cultures, which were assailed by European diseases and alcohol.

In 1843 settlers at Champoeg, on the Willamette River south of Portland, voted to organize a provisional government independent of the Hudson's Bay Company, thereby casting their lot with the US, which formally acquired the territory from the British by treaty in 1846. Over the next decade, some 53,000 settlers came to the Northwest via the 2000-mile Oregon Trail.

Arrival of the railroads set the region's future. Agriculture and lumber became the pillars of the economy until 1914, when WWI and the opening of the Panama Canal brought increased trade to Pacific ports. Shipyards opened along Puget Sound, and the Boeing aircraft company set up shop near Seattle.

Big dam projects in the 1930s and '40s provided cheap hydroelectricity and irrigation. WWII offered another boost for aircraft manufacturing and shipbuilding, and agriculture continued to thrive. In the postwar period, Washington's population, especially around Puget Sound, grew to twice that of Oregon.

In the 1980s and '90s, the economic emphasis shifted with the rise of the high-tech industry, embodied by Microsoft in Seattle and Intel in Portland.

Hydroelectricity production and massive irrigation projects along the Columbia have threatened the river's ecosystem in the past few decades, and logging has also left its scars. But the region has reinvigorated its eco-credentials by attracting some of the country's most environmentally conscious companies, and its major cities are among the greenest in the US. It stands at the forefront of US efforts to tackle climate issues.

Local Culture

The stereotypical image of a Pacific Northwesterner is a casually dressed latte-sipping urbanite who drives a Prius, votes Democrat and walks around with an unwavering diet

---

THE PACIFIC NORTHWEST IN ...

Four Days

Hit the ground running in **Seattle** to see the main sights, including **Pike Place Market** and the **Seattle Center**. After a couple of days, head down to **Portland**, where you can do like the locals do and cycle to bars, cafes, food carts and shops.

One Week

Add a couple of highlights such as **Mt Rainier**, **Olympic National Park**, the **Columbia River Gorge** or **Mt Hood**. Or explore the spectacular Oregon Coast (try the **Cannon Beach** area) or the historic seaport of **Port Townsend** on the Olympic Peninsula.

Two Weeks

Crater Lake is unforgettable, and can be combined with a trip to **Ashland** and its Shakespeare Festival. Don't miss the ethereal **San Juan Islands** up near the watery border with Canada, or **Bend**, the region's biggest outdoor draw. If you like wine, Washington's **Walla Walla** is your mecca, while the **Willamette Valley** is Oregon's Pinot Noir paradise.

of Nirvana-derived indie rock programmed into their iPod. But, as with most fleeting regional generalizations, the reality is far more complex.

Noted for their sophisticated cafe culture and copious microbrew pubs, the urban hubs of Seattle and Portland are the Northwest's most emblematic cities. But head east into the region's drier and less verdant interior, and the cultural affiliations become increasingly more traditional. Here, strung along the Columbia River Valley or nestled amid the arid steppes of southeastern Washington, small towns host raucous rodeos, tourist centers promote cowboy culture, and a cup of coffee is served 'straight up' with none of the chai lattes and frappés that are par for the course in the bigger cities.

In contrast to the USA's hardworking eastern seaboard, life out west is more casual and less frenetic. Ideally, Westerners would rather work to live than live to work. Indeed, with so much winter rain, the citizens of the Pacific Northwest will dredge up any excuse to shun the nine-to-five treadmill and hit the great outdoors a couple of hours (or even days) early. Witness the scene in late May and early June, when the first bright days of summer prompt a mass exodus of hikers and cyclists to make enthusiastically for the national parks and wilderness areas for which the region is justly famous.

❶ Getting There & Around

AIR

Seattle-Tacoma International Airport, aka 'Sea-Tac,' and Portland International Airport are the main airports for the region, serving many North American and several international destinations.

BOAT

Washington State Ferries (www.wsdot.wa.gov/ferries) links Seattle with Bainbridge and Vashon Islands. Other WSF routes cross from Whidbey Island to Port Townsend on the Olympic Peninsula, and from Anacortes through the San Juan Islands to Sidney, BC. Victoria Clipper (www.clippervacations.com) operates services from Seattle to Victoria, BC; ferries to Victoria also operate from Port Angeles. Alaska Marine Highway ferries (www.dot.state.ak.us/amhs) go from Bellingham, WA, to Alaska.

BUS

Greyhound (www.greyhound.com) provides service along the I-5 corridor from Bellingham in northern Washington down to Medford in southern Oregon, with connecting services across the US and Canada. East–west routes fan out toward Spokane, Yakima, the Tri-Cities (Kennewick, Pasco and Richland in Washington), Walla Walla and Pullman in Washington, and Hood River and Pendleton in Oregon. Private bus companies service most of the smaller towns and cities across the region, often connecting to Greyhound or Amtrak.

CAR

Driving your own vehicle is by far the most convenient way of touring the Pacific Northwest. Major and minor rental agencies are commonplace throughout the region. I-5 is the major north–south artery. In Washington I-90 heads east from Seattle to Spokane and into Idaho. In Oregon I-84 branches east from Portland along the Columbia River Gorge to link up with Boise in Idaho.

TRAIN

Amtrak (www.amtrak.com) runs train services north (to Vancouver, Canada) and south (to California), linking Seattle, Portland and other major urban centers with the *Cascades* and *Coast Starlight* routes. The famous *Empire Builder* heads east to Chicago from Seattle and Portland (joining up in Spokane).

WASHINGTON

Washington state is the heart of the Pacific Northwest. With that title comes everything you'd hope for, from the lush, green Olympic Peninsula to the white peaks of the Cascade Mountains and the crisp, whale-surrounded San Juan Islands. Head east and you'll see another side of the state that's more cowboy than boutique, where the world gets much of its apples and the skies go on forever. The biggest urban jolt is Seattle, but other corners such as Spokane, Bellingham and Olympia are gaining sophistication by the day.

Seattle

Combine the brains of Portland, OR, with the beauty of Vancouver, BC, and you'll get something approximating Seattle. It's hard to believe that the Pacific Northwest's largest metropolis was considered a 'secondary' US city until the 1980s, when a combination of bold innovation and unabashed individualism turned it into one of the dot-com era's biggest trendsetters, spearheaded by an unlikely alliance of coffee-sipping computer geeks and navel-gazing musicians.

WASHINGTON FACTS

Nickname Evergreen State

Population 7.3 million

Area 71,362 sq miles

Capital city Olympia (population 49,218)

Other cities Seattle (population 668,342), Spokane (population 212,052), Bellingham (population 83,365)

Sales tax 6.5%

Birthplace of Singer and actor Bing Crosby (1903–77), guitarist Jimi Hendrix (1942–70), computer geek Bill Gates (b 1955), political commentator Glen Beck (b 1964), musical icon Kurt Cobain (1967–94)

Home of Mt St Helens, Microsoft, Starbucks, Amazon.com, Evergreen State College

Politics Democrat governors since 1985

Famous for Grunge rock, coffee, *Grey's Anatomy*, *Twilight*, volcanoes, apples, wine, precipitation

State vegetable Walla Walla sweet onion

Driving distances Seattle to Portland,174 miles; Spokane to Port Angeles, 365 miles

Surprisingly elegant in places and coolly edgy in others, Seattle is notable for its strong neighborhoods, top-rated university, monstrous traffic jams and proactive city mayors who harbor green credentials. Although it has fermented its own pop culture in recent times, it has yet to create an urban mythology befitting Paris or New York, but it does have 'the Mountain.' Better known as Rainier, Seattle's unifying symbol is a 14,411ft mass of rock and ice, which acts as a perennial reminder to the city's huddled masses that raw wilderness, and potential volcanic catastrophe, are never far away.

⊙ Sights

◎ Downtown

★ Pike Place Market   MARKET

(Map p1038; www.pikeplacemarket.org; 85 Pike St; ⊗9am-6pm Mon-Sat, to 5pm Sun; ⓡWestlake) ⊘
A cavalcade of noise, smells, personalities, banter and urban theater sprinkled liberally around a spatially challenged waterside strip, Pike Place Market is Seattle in a bottle. In operation since 1907 and still as soulful today as it was on day one, this wonderfully local experience highlights the city for what it really is: all-embracing, eclectic and proudly unique. A brand-new expansion of the market infrastructure adds vendor space, weather-protected common areas, extra parking, and housing for low-income seniors.

★ Seattle Art Museum   MUSEUM

(SAM; Map p1038; ☑206-654-3210; www.seattle artmuseum.org; 1300 1st Ave; adult/student $24.95/14.95; ⊗10am-5pm Wed & Fri-Sun, to 9pm Thu; ⓡUniversity St) While not comparable with the big guns in New York and Chicago, Seattle Art Museum is no slouch. Always re-curating its art collection with new acquisitions and imported temporary exhibitions, it's known for its extensive Native American artifacts and work from the local Northwest school, in particular by Mark Tobey (1890–1976). Modern American art is also well represented, and the museum gets some exciting traveling exhibitions (including Yayoi Kusama's infinity mirrors).

★ Olympic
Sculpture Park   PARK, SCULPTURE

(Map p1038; 2901 Western Ave; ⊗sunrise-sunset; ⓠ13) **FREE** This smart urban-renewal project and outpost of the Seattle Art Museum was inaugurated in 2007 to widespread local approval. The terraced park is landscaped over railway tracks and overlooks Puget Sound with the distant Olympic Mountains winking on the horizon. Joggers and dog walkers meander daily through its zigzagging paths, enjoying over 20 pieces of modern sculpture.

International District

**Wing Luke Museum of
the Asian Pacific American
Experience**   MUSEUM

(Map p1038; ☑206-623-5124; www.wingluke.
org; 719 S King St; adult/child $17/10; ☺10am-
5pm Tue-Sun; ☒7th & Jackson/Chinatown) The
beautifully unique Wing Luke examines
Asia Pacific–American culture, focusing on
prickly issues such as Chinese settlement in
the 1880s and Japanese internment camps
during WWII. Recent temporary exhibits include 'A Day in the Life of Bruce Lee.' There
are also art exhibits and a preserved immigrant apartment. Guided tours are available;
the first Thursday of the month is free (with
extended hours until 8pm).

Seattle Center

Seattle Center   LANDMARK

(Map p1038; ☑206-684-8582; www.seattlecenter.
com; 400 Broad St; ☒Seattle Center) The remnants of the futuristic 1962 World's Fair
hosted by Seattle and subtitled Century
21 Exposition are still visible over 50 years
later at the Seattle Center. The fair was a
major success, attracting 10 million visitors,
running a profit (rare for the time) and inspiring a skin-crawlingly kitsch Elvis movie, *It Happened at the World's Fair* (1963).
Thanks to regular upgrades, the complex
has retained its luster and contains Seattle's
highest concentration of A-list sights.

★Space Needle   LANDMARK

(Map p1038; ☑206-905-2100; www.spaceneedle.
com; 400 Broad St; adult/child $29/18; ☺9:30am-
11pm Mon-Thu, to 11:30pm Fri & Sat, 9am-11pm
Sun; ☒Seattle Center) This streamlined, mod-
ern-before-its-time tower built for the 1962
World's Fair has been the city's defining symbol for over 50 years. The needle anchors the
complex now called the Seattle Center and
draws over one million annual visitors to
its flying saucer-like observation deck and
pricey rotating restaurant. Purchase a combination ticket with Chihuly Garden & Glass
for $49.

★Museum of Pop Culture   MUSEUM

(Map p1038; ☑206-770-2700; www.mopop.org;
325 5th Ave N; adult/child $25/16; ☺10am-7pm
Jun-Aug, to 5pm Sep-May; ☒Seattle Center) The
Museum of Pop Culture (formerly EMP, the
'Experience Music Project') is an inspired
marriage between super-modern architecture and legendary rock-and-roll history
that sprang from the imagination (and pocket) of Microsoft co-creator Paul Allen. Inside
its avant-garde frame, designed by Canadian
architect Frank Gehry, you can tune into the
famous sounds of Seattle (with an obvious
bias toward Jimi Hendrix and grunge) or
attempt to imitate the masters in the Interactive Sound Lab.

★Chihuly Garden & Glass   MUSEUM

(Map p1038; ☑206-753-4940; www.chihulygarden
andglass.com; 305 Harrison St; adult/child $24/14;
☺10am-8pm Sun-Thu, to 9pm Fri & Sat; ☒Seattle
Center) Opened in 2012 and reinforcing Seattle's position as the Venice of North America,
this exquisite exposition of the life and work
of dynamic local sculptor Dale Chihuly is
possibly the finest collection of curated glass
art you'll ever see. It shows off Chihuly's
creative designs in a suite of interconnected
dark and light rooms before depositing you
in an airy glass atrium and – finally – a landscaped garden in the shadow of the Space
Needle. Glassblowing demonstrations are a
highlight.

Capitol Hill

Millionaires mingle with goth musicians in
Capitol Hill, a well-heeled but liberal neighborhood rightly renowned for its fringe
theater, alternative music scene, indie coffee
bars and vital gay and lesbian culture. You
can take your dog for a herbal bath here, go
shopping for ethnic crafts on Broadway, or
blend in (or not) with the young punks and
old hippies on the eclectic Pike–Pine corridor. The junction of Broadway and E John

> **ⓘ SEATTLE CITYPASS**
>
> If you're going to be in Seattle for a
> while and plan on seeing its premier
> attractions, consider buying a **Seattle
> CityPASS** (www.citypass.com/seattle;
> $144/97 per adult/child aged four to 12).
> Good for nine days, the pass gets you
> entry into five sights: the Space Needle,
> Seattle Aquarium, Argosy Cruises Seat-
> tle Harbor Tour, Museum of Pop Culture
> *or* Woodland Park Zoo, Pacific Science
> Center *or* Chihuly Garden & Glass. You
> wind up saving about 45% on admission
> costs and you never have to stand in
> line. You can buy one at any of the ven-
> ues or online.

PACIFIC NORTHWEST SEATTLE

Seattle

500 m
0.25 miles

13th Ave E
12th Ave E
E Mercer St
E Republican St
E Harrison St
E Thomas St

E John St
Capitol Hill
CAPITOL HILL
Capitol Hill

E Olive St
E Howell St
Cascina
Spinasse (0.1mi)
34

45
11th Ave
10th Ave
E Pine St
E Union St
E Madison St
46
42

Broadway E
E Denny Way
Nagle Pl
Broadway
& Pine

Harvard Ave E
Harvard Ave
Boylston Ave E
Boylston Ave
Belmont Ave E
Belmont Ave
E Pine St
E Pike St
Boylston Ave

Summit Ave E
Summit Ave
E Howell St
E Union St
University St

Bellevue Ave E
Bellevue Ave
Boren Ave

Melrose Ave E
Melrose Ave
31
Terry Ave

Lake Union (0.3mi);
U District (3.5mi);
University of
Washington (3.5mi)

Eastlake Ave E
Yale Ave N
Yale Ave
E Olive Way

Pontius Ave N
Minor Ave N
Minor Ave
9th Ave
8th Ave

Mercer St
Fairview Ave N
Boren Ave
Terry Ave
9th Ave
Quick
Shuttle
17
Visit
Seattle

EASTLAKE
Lake Union
Park
Terry &
Mercer
Republican St
Harrison St
Thomas St
Terry &
Thomas
Denny Way
Howell St
Olive Way
Virginia St
Stewart St
Westlake Hub
Westlake
Center
Westlake Center

Northwest
Outdoor
Center (1mi)
Terry Ave N
Westlake Ave N
Westlake
& Mercer
Westlake &
Thomas
Westlake
& 9th
Westlake
& 7th
Lenora St
South Lake Union Street Car

Fremont (2mi);
Green Lake (3mi);
Ballard (5mi)
9th Ave N
8th Ave N
John St
Denny
Park
8th Ave
7th Ave
6th Ave
Virginia St
25

Dexter Ave N
6th Ave N
Denny Way
5th Ave
22
DENNY
TRIANGLE
Blanchard St
33

Aurora Ave N
Taylor Ave N
Bell St
3rd
Ave
20
40

Roy St
Mercer St
5th Ave N
4th Ave N
Broad St
Battery St
Wall St
Vine St
Cedar St
4th Ave
21
32
2nd Ave
1st Ave
Western Ave
19

Toulouse Petit (0.1mi);
SIFF Cinema Uptown (0.2mi);
On the Boards (0.2mi)
24
41
14
Museum of
Pop Culture
3
Monorail
Space
Needle
7
Chihuly
Garden
& Glass
11
Clay St
Cedar St
Vine St
BELLTOWN
Elliott Ave
Alaskan Way
39

McCaw
Hall
SEATTLE
CENTER
Memorial
Stadium
Seattle
Center
1
43
Key
Arena
44
2nd Ave N
Warren Ave N
Eagle St
Broad St
Clay St
4
Olympic
Sculpture
Park
Pier 69
Victoria
Clipper
Pier 67

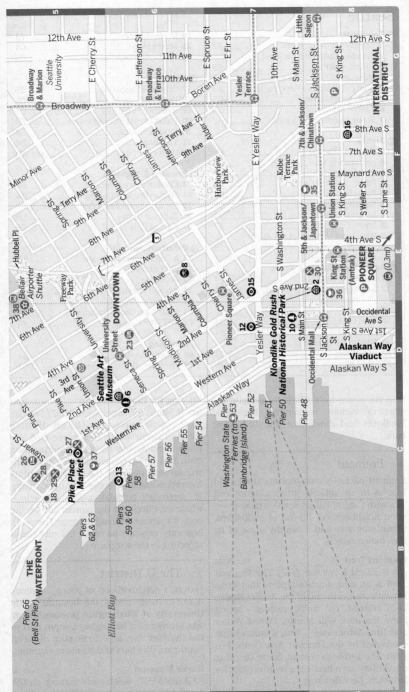

Seattle

◎ Top Sights

1 Chihuly Garden & Glass A2
2 Klondike Gold Rush National
    Historical Park E8
3 Museum of Pop Culture B2
4 Olympic Sculpture Park A3
5 Pike Place Market C5
6 Seattle Art Museum D6
7 Space Needle A2

◎ Sights

8 Columbia Center E6
9 Hammering Man C6
10 Occidental Park D7
11 Pacific Science Center A3
12 Pergola D7
13 Seattle Aquarium C6
14 Seattle Center A1
15 Smith Tower E7
16 Wing Luke Museum of the Asian
    Pacific American Experience F8

◑ Activities, Courses & Tours

17 Seattle Cycling Tours D4
18 Seattle Free Walking Tours C5

⬒ Sleeping

19 Ace Hotel B4
20 Belltown Inn B4
21 City Hostel Seattle B4
22 Hotel Five C3
23 Hotel Monaco D6
24 Maxwell Hotel A1
25 Moore Hotel C4
26 Thompson Seattle C5

⊗ Eating

27 Crumpet Shop C5
28 Le Pichet C5
29 Piroshky Piroshky C5
30 Salumi Artisan Cured Meats E8
31 Sitka & Spruce E4
32 Tavolàta B4
    Upper Bar Ferdinand .... (see 45)

◒ Drinking & Nightlife

33 Clouburst Brewing B4
34 Elysian Brewing Company G4
35 Panama Hotel Tea & Coffee House F8
36 Zeitgeist Coffee E8
37 Zig Zag Café C5

◒ Entertainment

38 A Contemporary Theatre D5
39 Big Picture A4
40 Crocodile B4
41 Intiman Theatre Festival A1
42 Neumo's G4
43 Seattle Children's Theater A2
44 SIFF Film Center A1

◒ Shopping

45 Chophouse Row G4
46 Elliott Bay Book Company G4

St is the nexus from which to navigate the quarter's various restaurants, brewpubs, boutiques and dingy (but not dirty) dive bars.

◉ Fremont

Fremont pitches young hipsters among old hippies in an unlikely urban alliance and vies with Capitol Hill as Seattle's most irreverent neighborhood. It's full of junk shops, urban sculpture and a healthy sense of its own ludicrousness.

Fremont Troll   SCULPTURE
(cnr N 36th St & Troll Ave; 🚌62) The Fremont Troll is an outlandish sculpture that lurks beneath the north end of the Aurora Bridge at N 36th St. The troll's creators – artists Steve Badanes, Will Martin, Donna Walter and Ross Whitehead – won a competition sponsored by the Fremont Arts Council in 1990. The 18ft-high cement figure snacking on a Volkswagen Beetle is a favorite place for late-night beer drinking.

Waiting for the Interurban   MONUMENT
(cnr N 34th St & Fremont Ave N; 🚌62) Seattle's most popular piece of public art, *Waiting for the Interurban*, is cast in recycled aluminum and depicts six people waiting for a train that never comes. Occasionally locals will lovingly decorate the people in outfits corresponding to a special event, the weather, someone's birthday, a Mariners win – whatever. Check out the human face on the dog; it's Armen Stepanian, once Fremont's honorary mayor, who made the mistake of objecting to the sculpture.

◉ The U District

U-dub, a neighborhood of young, studious out-of-towners, places the beautiful, leafy **University of Washington** (www.washington. edu; 🚉 University of Washington) campus next to the shabbier 'Ave,' an eclectic strip of cheap boutiques, dive bars and ethnic restaurants.

Burke Museum   MUSEUM
(📞206-543-5590; www.burkemuseum.org; cnr 17th Ave NE & NE 45th St; adult/child $10/7.50, 1st Thu of

month free; ⊙10am-5pm, to 8pm 1st Thu of month; 🖾70) An interesting hybrid museum covering both natural history and indigenous cultures of the Pacific Rim. On the entry-level floor is, arguably, Washington's best natural-history collection, focusing on the geology and evolution of the state. It guards an impressive stash of fossils, including a 20,000-year-old saber-toothed cat. Downstairs is the 'Pacific Voices' exhibition, with cultural artifacts amassed from around the Pacific Rim. The centerpiece is an excellent Pacific Northwest collection with some dramatic Kwakwaka'wakw masks from British Columbia.

◎ Ballard

A former seafaring community with a strong Scandinavian heritage, Ballard still feels like a small town engulfed by a bigger city. Traditionally gritty, no-nonsense and uncommercial, it's slowly being condo-ized, but remains a good place to down a microbrew or see a live band.

★**Hiram M Chittenden Locks**   CANAL
(3015 NW 54th St; ⊙7am-9pm; 🖾40) **FREE**
Seattle shimmers like an impressionist painting on sunny days at the Hiram M Chittenden Locks. Here, the freshwaters of Lake Washington and Lake Union drops 22ft into saltwater Puget Sound. You can stand inches away and watch the boats rise or sink (depending on direction). Construction of the canal and locks began in 1911; today 100,000 boats pass through them annually. You can view fish-ladder activity through underwater glass panels, stroll through botanical gardens and visit a small museum.

🏃 Activities

Cycling

Despite frequent rain and hilly terrain, cycling is still a major form of both transportation and recreation in the Seattle area.

In the city, commuter bike lanes are painted green on many streets, city trails are well maintained and the friendly and enthusiastic cycling community is happy to share the road. The wildly popular 20-mile **Burke-Gilman Trail** winds from Ballard to Log Boom Park in Kenmore on Seattle's Eastside. There, it connects with the 11-mile-long **Sammamish River Trail**, which winds past the Chateau Ste Michelle winery in Woodinville before terminating at Redmond's Marymoor Park.

Other good places to cycle are around Green Lake (congested), at Alki Beach (sublime) or, closer to downtown, through scenic Myrtle Edwards Park.

Anyone planning on cycling in Seattle should pick up a copy of the *Seattle Bicycling Guide Map*, available online and at bike shops.

For bicycle rentals and tours, try **Recycled Cycles** (📞206-547-4491; www.recycled cycles.com; 1007 NE Boat St; rental per day from $40; ⊙10am-7pm Mon-Fri, to 8pm Thu, 10am-6pm Sat & Sun; 🖾70) or **Seattle Cycling Tours** (Map p1038; 📞206-356-5803; www.seattle-cy cling-tours.com; 714 Pike St; tours from $55; 🖾10).

Watersports

Seattle is not just on a network of cycling trails. With Venice-like proportions of downtown water, it is also strafed with kayak-friendly marine trails. The **Lakes to Locks Water Trail** links Lake Sammamish with Lake Washington, Lake Union and – via the Hiram M Chittenden Locks – Puget Sound. For launching sites and maps, check the website of the Washington Water Trails Association (www.wwta.org).

Northwest Outdoor Center   KAYAKING
(📞206-281-9694; www.nwoc.com; 2100 Westlake Ave N; rental per hour kayak/SUP $16/18; ⊙10am-8pm Mon-Fri, 9am-6pm Sat & Sun Apr-Sep, closed Mon & Tue Oct-Mar; 🖾62) Located on the west side of Lake Union, this place rents kayaks and stand-up paddleboards (SUPs) and offers tours and instruction in sea and white-water kayaking.

👉 Tours

★**Seattle Free Walking Tours**   WALKING
(Map p1038; www.seattlefreewalkingtours.org) **FREE** A nonprofit set up by a couple of world travelers and Seattle residents in 2012 who were impressed with the free walking tours offered in various European cities. An intimate two-hour walk takes in Pike Pl, the waterfront and Pioneer Square. Each tour has different starting times and meeting places; check online.

Seattle by Foot   WALKING
(📞206-508-7017; www.seattlebyfoot.com; per person from $30) Runs a handful of tours, including the practically essential (this being Seattle) Coffee Crawl, which will ply you with caffeine while explaining the nuances of latte art and dishing the inside story of the rise (and rise) of Starbucks. The tour

costs $30 including samples; registration starts at 9:50am Thursday to Sunday at the **Hammering Man** (Map p1038; 🚆 University St) outside the Seattle Art Museum.

Festivals & Events

Seattle International Film Festival FILM

(SIFF; www.siff.net; 🕒 May-Jun) Held over three weeks from mid-May to early June, this prestigious film festival uses a half-dozen cinemas to screen more than 400 movies. Major venues include the Egyptian Cinema in Capitol Hill, the **SIFF Cinema Uptown** (☎ 206-285-1022; 511 Queen Anne Ave N; 🚌 13) in Lower Queen Anne and its own dedicated **SIFF Film Center** (Map p1038; ☎ 206-324-9996; Northwest Rooms; [S] Seattle Center) in the Seattle Center.

Seafair FAIR

(www.seafair.com; 🕒 Jun-Aug) Huge crowds attend this festival, held on the water from mid-June to mid-August, with a pirate's landing, a torchlight parade, an air show, a music marathon and even a Milk Carton Derby (look it up!).

Bumbershoot PERFORMING ARTS

(www.bumbershoot.com; 3-day pass from $249; 🕒 Sep) A fair few people – Seattleites or otherwise – would say that this is Seattle's finest festival, with major arts and cultural events at the Seattle Center on the Labor Day weekend in September. Bank on live music, comedy, theater, visual arts and dance, but also bank on crowds and hotels stuffed to capacity. Book well in advance!

Sleeping

Reserve ahead in summer, when hotels book up and prices tend to skyrocket.

City Hostel Seattle HOSTEL $

(Map p1038; ☎ 206-706-3255; www.hostelseattle.com; 2327 2nd Ave; dm/d from $33/99; 🚭 @ 📶; 🚆 Westlake) This well-located, boutique 'art hostel' has colorful murals painted by local artists splashed on the walls of every room. There's also a common room, hot tub, in-house movie theater and all-you-can-eat breakfast. Dorms have four or six beds and some are female only. There are also several private rooms, some with shared bathroom.

Ace Hotel HOTEL $$

(Map p1038; ☎ 206-448-4721; www.acehotel.com; 2423 1st Ave; r with shared/private bath from $129/239; [P] 🚭 ❄ 📶 🐾; 🚌 13) The original locale of the highly stylized Ace Hotel chain, this place sports nouveau-industrial decor, sliding-barn-door bathrooms and Pendleton wool blankets. True to its original ethos, the hotel is economical but trendy, especially if you don't mind sharing a bathroom. Enhancing the hipster appeal, some rooms come with record players.

Hotel Five BOUTIQUE HOTEL $$

(Map p1038; ☎ 206-448-0924; www.hotelfiveseattle.com; 2200 5th Ave; r from $212; [P] 🚭 ❄ 📶; 🚌 13) This trendy hotel mixes retro '70s furniture with sharp color accents to produce something dazzlingly modern. The ultra-comfortable beds are a valid cure for insomnia, while the large reception area invites lingering, especially when they lay out the complimentary cupcakes and coffee in the late afternoon.

SEATTLE FOR CHILDREN

Make a beeline for the Seattle Center, preferably on the monorail, where food carts, street entertainers, fountains and green spaces will make the day fly by. One essential stop is the **Pacific Science Center** (Map p1038; ☎ 206-443-2001; www.pacificsciencecenter.org; 200 2nd Ave N; exhibits only adult/child $19.75/14.75; 🕒 10am-5pm Mon-Fri, to 6pm Sat & Sun; 👪; [S] Seattle Center), which entertains and educates with virtual reality exhibits, laser shows, holograms, an Imax theater and a planetarium. Parents won't be bored either.

Downtown on Pier 59, **Seattle Aquarium** (Map p1038; ☎ 206-386-4300; www.seattleaquarium.org; 1483 Alaskan Way; adult/child $24.95/16.95; 🕒 9:30am-5pm; 👪; 🚆 University St) is a fun way to learn about the natural world of the Pacific Northwest. Even better is **Woodland Park Zoo** (☎ 206-548-2500; www.zoo.org; 5500 Phinney Ave N; adult/child May-Sep $20.95/12.95, Oct-Apr $14.95/9.95; 🕒 9:30am-6pm May-Sep, to 4pm Oct-Apr; 👪; 🚌 5) in the Green Lake neighborhood, one of Seattle's greatest tourist attractions and consistently rated as one of the top 10 zoos in the country.

Belltown Inn
HOTEL $$

(Map p1038; ☑206-529-3700; www.belltown-inn. com; 2301 3rd Ave; r from $206; ⊜❄@☎; ☐Westlake) The reliable Belltown Inn is a popular midrange place to stow your suitcase – good on the basics, if a little light on embellishments. That said, there's a roof terrace, free bike rentals and some rooms have kitchenettes. Both downtown and the Seattle Center are within easy walking distance.

Moore Hotel
HOTEL $$

(Map p1038; ☑206-448-4851; www.moorehotel. com; 1926 2nd Ave; d with shared/private bath from $99/117; ☎; ☐Westlake) Old-world and allegedly haunted, the hip and whimsical Moore is undoubtedly central Seattle's most reliable bargain, offering fixed annual prices for its large stash of simple but cool rooms. Bonuses – aside from the dynamite location – are the cute ground-floor cafe, and zebra- and leopard-skin patterned carpets.

★Hotel Monaco
BOUTIQUE HOTEL $$$

(Map p1038; ☑206-621-1770; www.monaco-seat tle.com; 1101 4th Ave; d/ste $339/399; ℗@☎❋; ☐University St) ✿ Whimsical and with dashes of European elegance, the downtown Monaco is a classic Kimpton hotel whose rooms live up to the hints given off in the illustrious lobby. Bed down amid the bold, graphic decor and reap the perks (complimentary bikes, fitness center, free wine tasting, inroom yoga mats).

★Maxwell Hotel
BOUTIQUE HOTEL $$$

(Map p1038; ☑206-286-0629; www.themaxwell hotel.com; 300 Roy St; r from $319; ℗❄@☎❋; ☐Rapid Ride D-Line) Located in Lower Queen Anne, the Maxwell has a huge designer-chic lobby with a floor mosaic and funky furnishings that welcomes you with aplomb. Upstairs the slickness continues in 139 gorgeously modern rooms with hardwood floors and Scandinavian bedding. There's a small pool, a gym, free bike rentals and complimentary cupcakes.

Thompson Seattle
HOTEL $$$

(Map p1038; ☑206-623-4600; www.thompson hotels.com/hotels/thompson-seattle; 110 Stewart St; d $309; bus, light rail University Street Station) The Thompson Hotel has been a hot spot among tourists and locals alike since it opened early in the summer of 2016. Designed by the famed local Olson Kundig architects, the boutique hotel is sleek and modern, and offers expansive views of Puget Sound.

HIGHER THAN THE SPACE NEEDLE

Everyone rushes for the iconic Space Needle, but it's not the tallest Seattle viewpoint. That honor goes to the sleek **Columbia Center** (Map p1038; ☑20 6-386-5564; www.skyviewobservatory.com; 701 5th Ave; adult/child $14.75/9; ⊘10am-8pm; ☐Pioneer Sq) at 932ft high with 76 floors. An elevator in the lobby takes you up to the free-access 40th floor, where there's a Starbucks. From here you must take another elevator to the plush Sky View Observatory on the 73rd floor, from where you can look down on ferries, cars, islands, roofs and – ha, ha – the Space Needle!

✕ Eating

The best budget meals are to be found in Pike Place Market (p1036). Take your pick from fresh produce, baked goods, deli items and takeout ethnic foods.

★Salumi Artisan Cured Meats
SANDWICHES $

(Map p1038; ☑206-621-8772; www.salumicured meats.com; 309 3rd Ave S; sandwiches $10-14; ⊘11am-1:30pm Mon for takeout only, to 3:30pm Tue-Fri; ☐International District/Chinatown) With a shopfront as wide as a smart car and a following as large as the Seattle Mariners, Salumi is a well-known vortex of queues. But it's worth the wait for the legendary Italian-quality salami and cured-meat sandwiches (grilled lamb, pork shoulder, meatballs) that await you at the counter. Grab one and go! Fresh homemade gnocchi is available most Tuesdays.

★Piroshky Piroshky
BAKERY $

(Map p1038; www.piroshkybakery.com; 1908 Pike Pl; snacks $3-6; ⊘8am-6pm; ☐Westlake) Piroshky knocks out its delectable sweet and savory Russian pies and pastries in a space about the size of a walk-in closet. Get the savory smoked-salmon pâté or the sauerkraut with cabbage and onion, and follow it with the chocolate-cream hazelnut roll or a fresh rhubarb piroshki.

★Fonda la Catrina
MEXICAN $

(☑206-767-2787; www.fondalacatrina.com; 5905 Airport Way S; mains $9-14; ⊘11am-10pm Mon-Thu, to 11pm Fri, 10am-11pm Sat, 10am-10pm Sun;

DON'T MISS

PIONEER SQUARE

Pioneer Sq is Seattle's oldest quarter, which isn't saying much if you're visiting from Rome or London. Most of the buildings here date from just after the 1889 fire (a devastating inferno that destroyed 25 city blocks, including the entire central business district), and are referred to architecturally as Richardsonian Romanesque, a redbrick revivalist style in vogue at the time. In the early years, the neighborhood's boom-bust fortunes turned its arterial road, Yesler Way, into the original 'skid row' – an allusion to the skidding logs that were pulled downhill to Henry Yesler's pier-side mill. When the timber industry fell on hard times, the road became a haven for the homeless and its name subsequently became a byword for poverty-stricken urban enclaves countrywide.Thanks to a concerted public effort, the neighborhood avoided being laid to waste by the demolition squads in the 1960s and is now protected in the Pioneer Sq–Skid Rd Historic District.

The quarter today mixes the historic with the seedy, harboring art galleries, cafes and nightlife. Its most iconic building is the 42-story **Smith Tower** (Map p1038; ☑ 20 6-622-4004; www.smithtower.com; 506 2nd Ave; observatory tickets from $12; ⊗ 10am-10pm; ⑬ Pioneer Sq), completed in 1914 and, until 1931, the tallest building west of the Mississippi. Other highlights include the 1909 **Pergola** (Map p1038; cnr Yesler Way & James St; ⑬ Pioneer Sq), a decorative iron shelter reminiscent of a Parisian Metro station, and **Occidental Park** (Map p1038; btwn S Washington & S Main Sts; ⑯ Occidental Mall), containing totem poles carved by Chinook artist Duane Pasco.

The **Klondike Gold Rush National Historical Park** (Map p1038; ☑ 206-553-3000; www.nps.gov/klse; 319 2nd Ave S; ⊗ 10am-5pm; ⑯ Occidental Mall) **FREE** is a city-based visitor-center outpost. It shows off exhibits, photos and news clippings from the 1897 Klondike gold rush, when a Seattle-on-steroids acted as a fueling depot for prospectors bound for the Yukon in Canada.

☐124) The search to find a decent Mexican restaurant in Seattle comes to an end in Georgetown in the busy confines of Fonda la Catrina, where Day of the Dead iconography shares digs with Diego Rivera–like murals and – more importantly – fabulous food. Offering way beyond the standard taco-burrito-enchilada trilogy, this place puts soul into its Latino cooking.

The highlight? One of the best *moles poblanos* this side of the Rio Grande.

Crumpet Shop   BAKERY **$**
(Map p1038; ☑ 206-682-1598; www.thecrumpet shop.com; 1503 1st Ave; crumpets $3-6; ⊗ 7am-3pm Mon, Wed & Thu, to 4pm Fri-Sun; ⑭ Westlake) ✐ The treasured British crumpet has been given a distinct American twist with lavish toppings such as pesto, wild salmon or lemon curd at this casual Pike Place Market eatery, family owned and operated for 40 years. Organic ingredients make it very Pacific Northwest, though there's Marmite for homesick Brits.

★ **Tavolàta**   ITALIAN **$$**
(Map p1038; ☑ 206-838-8008; 2323 2nd Ave; pasta dishes $17-21, mains $24-28; ⊗ 5-11pm; ☐ 13) Owned by top Seattle chef Ethan Stowell, Ta-

volàta is a dinner-only, Italian-inspired eatery emphasizing homemade pasta dishes. Keeping things simple with venison-stuffed ravioli and *linguine nero* (clams with black pasta), the results are as good as those found in Italy – and there's no praise finer than that!

★ **Toulouse Petit**   CAJUN, CREOLE **$$**
(☑ 206-432-9069; www.toulousepetit.com; 601 Queen Anne Ave N; dinner mains $17-45; ⊗ 9am-2am Mon-Fri, from 8am Sat & Sun; ☐ 13) Hailed for its generous happy hours, cheap brunches and rollicking atmosphere, this perennially busy Queen Anne eatery has the common touch. The menu is large and varied, offering choices such as blackened rib-eye steak, freshwater gulf prawns and house-made gnocchi with artichoke hearts.

Le Pichet   FRENCH **$$**
(Map p1038; ☑ 206-256-1499; www.lepichet seattle.com; 1933 1st Ave; dinner mains $21-24; ⊗ 8am-midnight; ⑭ Westlake) Say *bonjour* to Le Pichet, just up from Pike Place Market, a cute and very French bistro with pâtés, cheeses, wine, *chocolat* and a refined Parisian feel. Dinner features delicacies such as wild-boar shoulder or foie gras with duck

eggs. The specialty is a roast chicken ($45) – just know that there's an hour's wait when you order one.

Revel
KOREAN, AMERICAN $$

(☑206-547-2040; www.revelseattle.com; 403 N 36th St; small plates $11-18; ⏰11am-2pm & 5-10pm Mon-Fri, 10am-2pm & 5-10pm Sat & Sun; ☐40) This modern Korean-American crossover restaurant (with a bit of French influence thrown in) has quickly established itself as a big name on the Seattle eating scene thanks, in part, to its simple, shareable plates. Of note are the pork-belly pancakes, the short-rib dumplings and the various seasonal hot pots, all of which go down well with a cocktail or two.

★Sitka & Spruce
MODERN AMERICAN $$$

(Map p1038; ☑206-324-0662; www.sitkaand spruce.com; 1531 Melrose Ave; plates $15-35; ⏰11:30am-2pm & 5-10pm Mon-Fri, 10am-2pm & 5-11pm Sat, 10am-2pm & 5-9pm Sun; ☑; ☐10) The king of all locavore restaurants, Sitka & Spruce was the pilot project of celebrated Seattle chef Matt Dillon. It's since become something of an institution and a trend-setter, with its small country-kitchen decor and a constantly changing menu concocted with ingredients from Dillon's own Vashon Island farm. Sample items include house-made charcuterie, conica morels or roasted-asparagus-and-liver parfait.

Cascina Spinasse
ITALIAN $$$

(☑206-251-7673; www.spinasse.com; 1531 14th Ave; mains $26-45; ⏰5-10pm Sun-Thu, to 11pm Fri & Sat; ☐11) Successfully re-creating the feel of an Italian trattoria, Spinasse specializes in the cuisine of northern Italy's Piedmont region. This means dishes like *agnolotti* (veal-stuffed pasta pockets) in beef broth, veal in tuna sauce, and top-notch risotto (from the region famous for its arborio rice). The finely curated wine list includes the kings and queens of Piedmontese reds: Barolo and Barbaresco.

Upper Bar Ferdinand
AMERICAN $$$

(Map p1038; ☑206-693-2434; www.barferdinand seattle.com; 1424 11th Ave; mains $45; ⏰4-11pm Tue-Fri, 1-11pm Sat) Homey, rustic, cozy, charming and classic all at once, Ferdinand serves locally sourced, Asian-inspired food cooked by fire and paired with a carefully curated wine selection. Located a few blocks from the original Bar Ferdinand bottle shop and wine bar, Upper Bar Ferdinand sits in Chop-house Row (p1048) and offers a unique take on a wine bar with its innovative food.

🍷 Drinking & Nightlife

It's hard to complain too much about Seattle's crappy weather when the two best forms of rainy-day solace – coffee and beer – are available in such abundance. No doubt about it, Seattle's an inviting place to enjoy a drink, whatever your poison. Adding fresh flavors to an already complex brew is a new obsession with micro-distilleries and cider houses.

★Fremont Brewing Company
BREWERY

(☑206-420-2407; www.fremontbrewing.com; 3409 Woodland Park Ave N; ⏰11am-9pm; ☑☑; ☐62) 🍴 This relatively new microbrewery, in keeping with current trends, sells its wares via an attached tasting room rather than a full-blown pub. Not only is the beer divine (try the seasonal bourbon barrel-aged Abominable), the industrial-chic tasting room and 'urban beer garden' are highly inclusive spaces, where pretty much everyone in the 'hood comes to hang out at communal tables.

★Zeitgeist Coffee
CAFE

(Map p1038; ☑206-583-0497; www.zeitgeistcof fee.com; 171 S Jackson St; ⏰6am-7pm Mon-Fri, 7am-7pm Sat, 8am-6pm Sun; ☑; ☐Occidental Mall) Possibly Seattle's best (if also busiest) indie coffee bar, Zeitgeist brews smooth *doppio macchiatos* to go with its sweet almond croissants and other luscious baked goods. The atmosphere is trendy industrial, with brick walls and large windows for people-watching. Soups, salads and sandwiches are also on offer.

★Blue Moon
BAR

(☑206-675-9116; www.bluemoonseattle.word press.com; 712 NE 45th St; ⏰2pm-2am Mon-Fri, noon-2am Sat & Sun; ☐74) A legendary counterculture dive that first opened in 1934 to celebrate the repeal of Prohibition, Blue Moon makes much of its former literary patrons – including Dylan Thomas and Allen Ginsberg. The place is agreeably gritty and unpredictable, with graffiti carved into the seats and punk poets likely to stand up and start pontificating at any moment. Frequent live music.

Noble Fir
BAR

(☑206-420-7425; www.thenoblefir.com; 5316 Ballard Ave NW; ⏰4pm-midnight Tue-Thu, to 1am Fri &

Sat, 1-9pm Sun; 🚌40) Almost qualifying as a travel bookstore as well as a bar, Noble Fir's highly curated, hops-heavy beer list might fill you with enough liquid courage to plan that hair-raising trip into the Amazon, or even just a trek around Ballard. The bright, laid-back bar has a nook given over to travel books and maps with packing cases on which to rest your drinks.

Elysian Brewing Company

MICROBREWERY

(Map p1038; ☑206-860-1920; www.elysianbrew ing.com; 1221 E Pike St; ⊙11:30am-2am Mon-Fri, noon-2am Sat & Sun; 🚌Broadway & Pine) Elysian Brewing's Immortal IPA personifies the strong, bitter 'hop-forward' beers that have become part of craft-beer folklore in the Pacific Northwest, and at 6.3% alcohol by volume, it won't take many to liberally loosen your tongue. Despite being bought out by Anheuser-Busch in January 2015, Elysian maintains several popular Seattle pubs, including this one (its 1996 original) in Capitol Hill.

Zig Zag Café

COCKTAIL BAR

(Map p1038; ☑206-625-1146; www.zigzagseattle. com; 1501 Western Ave; cocktails from $10; ⊙5pm-2am; 🚌University St) If you're writing a research project on Seattle's culinary history, you'll need to reserve a chapter for the Zig Zag Café. For serious cocktails, this place is legendary – this is the bar that repopularized gin-based Jazz Age cocktail 'The Last Word' in the early 2000s. The drink went viral and the Zig Zag's nattily attired mixers were rightly hailed as the city's finest alchemists.

Cloudburst Brewing

MICROBREWERY

(Map p1038; ☑206-602-6061; www.cloudburst brew.com; 2116 Western Ave; ⊙2-10pm Wed-Fri, noon-10pm Sat, to 8pm Sun) The brainchild of former experimental brewer at Elysian Brewing, Steve Luke, Cloudburst Brewing has become a Seattle favorite. Replicating the success of Luke's past brewing creations, Cloudburst Brewing features hoppy beers with sassy names, and the bare-bones tasting room is always packed to the gills with beer fans who want to support craft beer in Seattle.

Panama Hotel Tea & Coffee House

CAFE

(Map p1038; ☑206-515-4000; www.panama hotel.net; 607 S Main St; tea from $5; ⊙8am-9pm; 🚌5th & Jackson/Japantown) The intensely atmospheric teahouse inside the historic Panama Hotel has such a thoroughly back-in-time feel that you'll be reluctant to pull out your laptop (although there is wi-fi). It's in a National Treasure–designated 1910 building containing the only remaining Japanese bathhouse in the US, and doubles as a memorial to the neighborhood's Japanese residents forced into internment camps during WWII.

GRUNGE – PUNK'S WEST COAST NIRVANA

Synthesizing Generation X angst with a questionable approach to personal hygiene, the music popularly categorized as 'grunge' first dive-bombed onto Seattle's scene in the early 1990s like a clap of thunder on a typically wet and overcast afternoon. The anger had been fermenting for years – not purely in Seattle but also in its sprawling satellite towns and suburbs. Some said it was inspired by the weather, others cited the Northwest's geographic isolation. It didn't matter which. Armed with dissonant chords and dark, sometimes ironic lyrics, a disparate collection of bands stepped sneeringly up to the microphone to preach a new message from a city that all of the touring big-name rock acts serially chose to ignore. There were Screaming Trees from collegiate Ellensburg, the Melvins from rainy Montesano, Nirvana from the timber town of Aberdeen, and the converging members of Pearl Jam from across the nation.

What should have been grunge's high point came in October 1992, when Nirvana's second album, the hugely accomplished *Nevermind*, knocked Michael Jackson off the number-one spot, but the kudos ultimately killed it. After several years of railing against the mainstream, Nirvana and grunge had been incorporated into it. The media blitzed in, grunge fashion spreads appeared in Vanity Fair and half-baked singers from Seattle only had to cough to land a record contract. Many recoiled, most notably Nirvana vocalist and songwriter Kurt Cobain, whose drug abuse ended in suicide in his new Madison Park home in 1994. Other bands soldiered on, but the spark – which had burnt so brightly while it lasted – was gone. By the mid-1990s, grunge was officially dead.

☆ Entertainment

Consult *The Stranger*, *Seattle Weekly* or the daily papers for listings. Tickets for big events are available at TicketMaster (www. ticketmaster.com).

★ Crocodile
LIVE MUSIC

(Map p1038; ☑ 206-441-4618; www.thecrocodile. com; 2200 2nd Ave; ☐13) Nearly old enough to be called a Seattle institution, the Crocodile is a clamorous 560-capacity music venue that first opened in 1991, just in time to grab the coattails of the grunge explosion. Everyone who's anyone in Seattle's alt-music scene has since played here, including a famous occasion in 1992 when Nirvana appeared unannounced, supporting Mudhoney.

★ A Contemporary Theatre
THEATER

(ACT; Map p1038; ☑ 206-292-7676; www.actthe atre.org; 700 Union St; ☐ University St) One of the three big theater companies in the city, the ACT fills its $30-million home at Kreielsheimer Pl with performances by Seattle's best thespians and occasional big-name actors. Terraced seating surrounds a central stage and the interior has gorgeous architectural embellishments.

Big Picture
CINEMA

(Map p1038; ☑ 206-256-0566; www.thebigpicture. net; 2505 1st Ave; ⊙2pm-midnight) It's easy to miss **Big Picture** when exploring Seattle's Belltown neighborhood. For those in the know, it's an 'underground' cinema experience with affordable tickets of first-run screenings in an intimate setting. Order a cocktail from the bar, and pay for another to be delivered mid-screening. You can also linger in the cozy bar area before or after your showing.

Neumo's
LIVE MUSIC

(Map p1038; ☑ 206-709-9442; www.neumos.com; 925 E Pike St; ☐Broadway & Pine) This punk, hip-hop and alternative-music joint is, along with the Crocodile in Belltown, one of Seattle's most revered small music venues. Its storied list of former performers is too long to include, but, if they're cool and passing through Seattle, they've probably played here. The audience space can get hot and sweaty, and even smelly, but that's rock and roll.

Tractor Tavern
LIVE MUSIC

(☑206-789-3599; www.tractortavern.com; 5213 Ballard Ave NW; tickets $8-20; ⊙8pm-2am; ☐40)

DISCOVERY PARK

Hard to beat on a sunny spring day, this former military installation has been transformed into a wild coastal park, laced with walking trails and offering glimpses of the Olympic mountains across the water. **Discovery Park** (www.seattle.gov/parks/environment/ discovery.htm; ⊙4am-11:30pm; Ⓟ ⊞ ☎; ☐33) wasn't inaugurated until 1973 and the American military only left the area in 2012. It's the largest green space in the city, with 534 acres of forest, meadows, sand dunes and beaches, providing a welcome escape for locals and a vital corridor for wildlife.

One of Seattle's premier venues for folk and acoustic music, the Tractor books local songwriters and regional bands, plus quality touring acts. Music runs toward country, rockabilly, folk, bluegrass and old-time. It's an intimate place with a small stage and great sound; occasional square dancing is frosting on the cake.

On the Boards
DANCE, THEATER

(☑206-217-9888; www.ontheboards.org; 100 W Roy St; ☐13) *The* place for avant-garde performance art, the nonprofit On the Boards makes its home at the intimate Behnke Center for Contemporary Performance and showcases some innovative and occasionally weird dance and music.

Intiman Theatre Festival
THEATER

(Map p1038; ☑206-441-7178; www.intiman.org; 201 Mercer St; tickets $20-50; ⓗ; Ⓢ Seattle Center) Beloved theater company based at the Cornish Playhouse in the Seattle Center. Artistic director Andrew Russell curates magnificent stagings of Shakespeare and Ibsen as well as work by emerging artists. Productions run from July to October.

Seattle Children's Theater
THEATER

(Map p1038; ☑206-441-3322; www.sct.org; 201 Thomas St; tickets from $22; ⊙Thu-Sun Sep-May; ⓗ; Ⓢ Seattle Center) This highly esteemed theater group has two auditoriums in its Seattle Center campus. Friday and Saturday matinees and evening performances run September through May. There's also a Drama School summer season.

Shopping

The city's tour de force are its bookstores and record stores, surely some of the best in the nation. The main big-name shopping area is downtown between 3rd and 6th Aves and University and Stewart Sts. Pike Place Market is a maze of arts-and-crafts stalls, galleries and small shops. Pioneer Sq and Capitol Hill have locally owned gift and thrift shops.

★ **Elliott Bay Book Company**   BOOKS
(Map p1038; ☑206-624-6600; www.elliottbaybook.com; 1521 10th Ave; ⊙10am-10pm Mon-Thu, to 11pm Fri & Sat, to 9pm Sun; ☒Broadway & Pine) Seattle's most beloved bookstore offers over 150,000 titles in a large, airy, wood-beamed space with cozy nooks that can inspire hours of serendipitous browsing. Bibliophiles will be further satisfied with regular book readings and signings.

Chophouse Row   FOOD & DRINKS
(Map p1038; 1424 11th Ave; 6am to 11:30pm; ☒Capitol Hill, light rail Capitol Hill) Hidden among the historical and modern architecture of Capitol Hill, Chophouse Row feels like a locals-only secret. This new-in-2016 establishment features independent shops like Niche Outside, a charming garden shop; farmstead ice cream at Kurt Farm Shop and cocktail and wine bar Upper Bar Ferdinand.

Information

EMERGENCY & MEDICAL SERVICES

Seattle Police (☑206-625-5011; www.seattle.gov/police)

Harborview Medical Center (☑206-744-3000; www.uwmedicine.org/harborview; 325 9th Ave; ☒Broadway & Terrace) Full medical care, with emergency room.

MEDIA

KEXP 90.3 FM (stream at http://kexp.org) Legendary independent music and community station.

Seattle Times (www.seattletimes.com) The state's largest daily paper.

The Stranger (www.thestranger.com) Irreverent and intelligent free weekly, formerly edited by Dan Savage of 'Savage Love' fame.

POST

Post Office (Map p1038; ☑206-748-5417; www.usps.com; 301 Union St; ⊙8:30am-5:30pm Mon-Fri; ☒Westlake)

TOURIST INFORMATION

Visit Seattle (Map p1038; ☑206-461-5800; www.visitseattle.org; Washington State Convention Center, cnr Pike St & 7th Ave; ⊙9am-5pm daily Jun-Sep, Mon-Fri Oct-May; ☒Westlake) Information desk inside the Washington State Convention Center. You can pick up leaflets even when the desk is closed.

Getting There & Away

AIR

Sea-Tac International Airport (SEA; ☑206-787-5388; www.portseattle.org/sea-tac; 17801 International Blvd; ☎) Located 13 miles south of downtown Seattle, Sea-Tac has flights all over the US and to some international destinations. Amenities include restaurants, money changers, baggage storage, car-rental agencies, a cell-phone waiting area (for drivers waiting to pick up arriving passengers) and free wi-fi.

BOAT

The **Victoria Clipper** (Map p1038; ☑206-448-5000; www.clippervacations.com; 2701 Alaskan Way, Pier 69) ferry from Victoria, BC, docks at Pier 69 just south of the Olympic Sculpture Park in Belltown. **Washington State Ferries** (Map p1038) services from Bremerton and Bainbridge Island use Pier 52.

BUS

Various inter-city coaches serve Seattle and there is more than one drop-off point – it all depends on which company you are using.

Bellair Airporter Shuttle (Map p1038; ☑866-235-5247; www.airporter.com) Runs buses to Yakima, Bellingham and Anacortes and stops at King Street Station (for Yakima) and the Washington State Convention Center (for Bellingham and Anacortes).

Cantrail (www.cantrail.com) Amtrak's bus connector runs four daily services to Vancouver (one way $42) and picks up and drops off at King Street Station.

Greyhound (☑206-628-5526; www.greyhound.com; 503 S Royal Brougham Way; ☒Stadium) Connects Seattle with cities all over the country, including Chicago (from $195 one way, two days, two daily), Spokane ($39, eight hours, three daily), San Francisco ($100, 20 hours, three daily) and Vancouver (Canada; $23, four hours, five daily). The company has its own terminal just south of King Street Station in SoDo, accessible on the Central Link light rail (stadium station).

Quick Shuttle (Map p1038; ☑800-665-2122; www.quickcoach.com; ☎) Fast and efficient, with five to six daily buses to Vancouver ($43). Picks up at the Best Western Executive Inn in

Taylor Ave N near the Seattle Center. Grab the monorail or walk to downtown.

TRAIN

King Street Station (206-296-0100; www. amtrak.com; 303 S Jackson St) Amtrak serves Seattle's King Street Station. Three main routes run through town: the *Amtrak Cascades* (connecting Vancouver, BC, Seattle, and Portland and Eugene in Oregon); the very scenic *Coast Starlight* (connecting Seattle to Oakland and Los Angeles in California) and the *Empire Builder* (a cross-continental to Chicago, IL).

① Getting Around

TO/FROM THE AIRPORT

There are a number of options for making the 13-mile trek from the airport to downtown Seattle. The most efficient is the light-rail service run by **Sound Transit** (www.soundtransit.org). It runs every 10 to 15 minutes between 5am and midnight; the ride between Sea-Tac Airport and downtown (Westlake Center) takes 36 minutes. There are additional stops in Pioneer Sq and the International District; the service was extended to Capitol Hill and the U District in 2016.

Shuttle Express (425-981-7000; www. shuttleexpress.com) has a pickup and drop-off point on the 3rd floor of the airport garage; it charges approximately $18 and is handy if you have a lot of luggage.

Taxis are available at the parking garage on the 3rd floor. Fares to downtown start at $39.

CAR & MOTORCYCLE

Seattle traffic is disproportionately heavy and chaotic for a city of its size, and parking is scarce and expensive. Add to that the city's bizarrely cobbled-together mishmash of skewed grids, the hilly terrain and the preponderance of one-way streets and it's easy to see why driving downtown is best avoided if at all possible.

PUBLIC TRANSPORTATION

Buses are operated by **King County Metro Transit** (206-553-3000; http://kingcounty. gov/depts/transportation/metro.aspx), part of the King County Department of Transportation. The website prints schedules and maps and has a trip planner.

To make things simple, all bus fares within Seattle city limits are a flat $2.75 at peak hours (6am to 9am and 3pm to 6pm weekdays). Off-peak rates are $2.50. Those aged six to 18 pay $1.50, kids under six are free, and seniors and travelers with disabilities pay $1. Most of the time you pay or show your transfer when you board. Your transfer ticket is valid for three hours from time of purchase. Most buses can carry two to three bikes.

Monorail (206-905-2620; www.seattlemonorail.com; 7:30am-11pm Mon-Fri, 8:30am-11pm Sat & Sun) This cool futuristic train, built for the 1962 World's Fair, travels only between two stops: Seattle Center and Westlake Center. Fares are $2.25/1 per adult/child.

Seattle Streetcar (www.seattlestreetcar.org) Two lines. One runs from downtown Seattle (Westlake) to South Lake Union; the other goes from Pioneer Square via the International District, the Central District and First Hill to Capitol Hill. Stops allow connections with numerous bus routes. Trams run approximately every 15 minutes throughout the day. The fare is $2.25.

TAXI

All Seattle taxi cabs operate at the same rate, set by King County: $2.60 at meter drop, then $2.70 per mile.

Seattle Orange Cab (206-522-8800; www. orangecab.net)

Seattle Yellow Cab (206-622-6500; www. seattleyellowcab.com)

STITA Taxi (206-246-9999; www.stitataxi. com)

Olympia

Small in size but big in clout, Washington state capital Olympia is a political, musical and outdoor powerhouse that punches well above its 49,000-strong population. Look no further than the street-side buskers on 4th Ave, the smartly attired bureaucrats marching across the lawns of the resplendent state legislature or the Gore-Tex–clad outdoor fiends overnighting before rugged sorties into the Olympic Mountains. Truth is, despite its Classical Greek–sounding name, creative, out-of-the-box Olympia is anything but ordinary. Progressive Evergreen college has long lent the place an artsy turn (creator of *The Simpsons* Matt Groening studied here), while the dive bars and secondhand-guitar shops of downtown provided an original pulpit for riot-grrrl music and grunge.

◉ Sights & Activities

Washington State Capitol LANDMARK
(360-902-8880; 416 Sid Snyder Ave SW; 7am-5:30pm Mon-Fri, 11am-4pm Sat & Sun) FREE Olympia's capitol complex is set in a 30-acre park overlooking Capitol Lake with the Olympic Mountains glistening in the background. The campus' crowning glory is the magnificent **Legislative Building**. Completed in 1927, it's a dazzling display of craning

columns and polished marble, topped by a 287ft dome that is only slightly smaller than its namesake in Washington, DC. Tours are available.

Olympia Farmers Market MARKET
(☑360-352-9096; www.olympiafarmersmarket. com; 700 N Capitol Way; ⊙10am-3pm Thu-Sun Apr-Oct, Sat & Sun Nov & Dec, Sat Jan-Mar) ◢ Second only to Seattle's Pike Place in size and character, Olympia's local market is a great place to shop for organic herbs, vegetables, flowers, baked goods and the famous specialty: oysters.

🛏 Sleeping & Eating

Fertile Ground Guesthouse GUESTHOUSE $$
(☑360-352-2428; www.fertileground.org; 311 9th Ave SE; s/d $110/120; 🛜) Surrounded by a lush and leafy organic garden, this comfortable, homey guesthouse offers three lovely rooms, one en suite and two with shared bath. Breakfast is made mostly from organic and locally sourced ingredients. There's a sauna on the premises. More rooms (including a dorm) are available at other locations; check the website for details.

**Traditions Cafe
& World Folk Art** HEALTH FOOD $
(☑360-705-2819; www.traditionsfairtrade.com; 300 5th Ave SW; mains $6-12; ⊙9am-6pm Mon-Fri, 10am-6pm Sat, 11am-5pm Sun; ☑🐾) ◢ This comfortable hippie enclave at the edge of Heritage Park offers fresh salads and tasty, healthy sandwiches (lemon-tahini, smoked salmon etc), coffee drinks, herbal teas, local ice cream, beer and wine. Posters advertise community-action events, and in the corner is a 'Peace and Social Justice Lending Library.' It's attached to an eclectic folk-art store.

❶ Information

State Capitol Visitor Center (☑360-902-8881; http://olympiawa.gov/community/vis iting-the-capitol.aspx; 103 Sid Snyder Ave SW; ⊙10am-3pm Mon-Fri, 11am-3pm Sat & Sun) Offers information on the capitol campus, the Olympia area and Washington state. Note the limited opening hours.

Olympic Peninsula

Surrounded on three sides by sea and exhibiting many of the characteristics of a full-blown island, the remote Olympic Peninsula is about as 'wild' and 'west' as America gets.

What it lacks in cowboys it makes up for in rare, endangered wildlife and dense primeval forest. The peninsula's roadless interior is largely given over to the notoriously wet Olympic National Park, while the margins are the preserve of loggers, Native American reservations and a smattering of small but interesting settlements, most notably Port Townsend. Equally untamed is the western coastline, America's isolated end point, where tempestuous ocean and misty old-growth Pacific rainforest meet in aqueous harmony.

Olympic National Park

Declared a national monument in 1909 and a national park in 1938, the 1406-sq-mile **Olympic National Park** (www.nps.gov/olym; 7-day access per vehicle $25, pedestrian/cyclist $10, 1yr unlimited entry $50) shelters a unique rainforest, copious glaciated mountain peaks and a 57-mile strip of Pacific coastal wilderness that was added to the park in 1953. One of North America's great wilderness areas, most of it remains relatively untouched by human habitation. Opportunities for independent exploration in this huge back-country region abound, be they for hiking, fishing, kayaking or skiing.

EASTERN ENTRANCES

The graveled Dosewallips River Rd follows the river from US 101 (turnoff approximately 1km north of Dosewallips State Park) for 15 miles to **Dosewallips Ranger Station**, where hiking trails begin; call 360-565-3130 for road conditions. Even hiking smaller portions of the two long-distance paths, including the 14.9 mile Dosewallips River Trail, with views of glaciated **Mt Anderson**, is reason enough to visit the valley. Another eastern entry for hikers is the **Staircase Ranger Station** (☑360-877-5569; ⊙May-Oct), just inside the national-park boundary, 15 miles from Hoodsport on US 101. Two campgrounds along the eastern edge of the national park are popular: **Dosewallips State Park** (☑888-226-7688; http://parks.state.wa.us/499/dosewallips; 306996 Hwy 101; tent sites $12-35, RV sites $30-45) and **Skokomish Park Lake Cushman** (☑360-877-5760; www.skokomishpark.com; tent sites from $28, RV sites from $34; ⊙late May-early Sep). Both have running water, flush toilets and some RV hookups. Reservations are accepted.

NORTHERN ENTRANCES

The park's easiest – and hence most popular – entry point is at **Hurricane Ridge**, 18 miles south of Port Angeles. At the road's end, an interpretive center gives a stupendous view of Mt Olympus (7965ft) and dozens of other peaks. The 5200ft altitude can mean you'll hit inclement weather, and the winds here (as the name suggests) can be ferocious. Aside from various summer trekking opportunities, the area maintains the small, family-friendly **Hurricane Ridge Ski & Snowboard Area** (www.hurricaneridge.com; all-lift day pass $34; ☉10am-4pm Sat & Sun mid-Dec–Mar; 🚗).

Popular for boating and fishing is **Lake Crescent**, the site of the park's oldest and most reasonably priced **lodge** (☑888-896-3818; www.olympicnationalparks.com; 416 Lake Crescent Rd; lodge r from $123, cabins from $292; ☉May-Dec, limited availability winter; 🅿⊠🛜⛵). Sumptuous Northwestern-style food is served in the lodge's ecofriendly restaurant. From **Storm King Ranger Station** (☑360-928-3380; 343 Barnes Point Rd; ☉May-Sep) on the lake's south shore, a 1-mile hike climbs through old-growth forest to Marymere Falls.

Along the Sol Duc River, the **Sol Duc Hot Springs Resort** (☑360-327-3583; www.olympicnationalparks.com; 12076 Sol Duc Hot Springs Rd, Port Angeles; park entrance fee $25, tent/RV sites $20/40, cabins from $179; ☉Mar-Oct; ⊠⛵) 🌿 has lodging, dining, massage and, of course, hot-spring pools, as well as great day hikes.

WESTERN ENTRANCES

Isolated by distance and home of one of the country's rainiest microclimates, the Pacific side of the Olympics remains the wildest. Only US 101 offers access to its noted temperate rainforests and untamed coastline. The **Hoh River Rainforest**, at the end of the 19-mile Hoh River Rd, is a Tolkienesque maze of dripping ferns and moss-draped trees. The **Hoh Rain Forest Visitor Center** (☑360-374-6925; ☉9am-4:30pm Sep-Jun, to 6pm Jul & Aug) has information on guided walks and longer backcountry hikes. The attached **campground** (☑360-374-6925; www.nps.gov/olym/planyourvisit/camping.htm; campsites $20) has no hookups or showers, and it's first-come, first-served.

A little to the south lies **Lake Quinault**, a beautiful glacial lake surrounded by forested peaks. It's popular for fishing, boating and swimming, and is surrounded by some of the nation's oldest trees. **Lake Quinault Lodge** (☑360-288-2900; www.olympicnationalparks.com; 345 S Shore Rd; r $219- 450; ⊠🛜⛵), a luxury classic of 1920s 'parkitecture,' has a massive fireplace, a manicured cricket-pitch-quality lawn and a dignified lakeview restaurant serving upscale American cuisine. For a cheaper sleep nearby, try the ultrafriendly **Quinault River Inn** (☑360-288-2237; www.quinaultriverinn.com; 8 River Dr; r $159; ⊠⊠🛜⛵) in Amanda Park, a favorite with anglers.

A number of short hikes begin just outside the Lake Quinault Lodge, or you cantry the longer **Enchanted Valley Trail**, a medium-grade 13-miler that begins from the Graves Creek Ranger Station at the end of South Shore Rd and climbs up to a large meadow resplendent with wildflowers and copses of alder trees.

ⓘ Information

The park entry fee is $10/25 per person/vehicle, valid for one week and payable at park entrances. Many park visitor centers double as United States Forestry Service (USFS) ranger stations, where you can pick up permits for wilderness camping ($8).

Olympic National Park Visitor Center (☑360-565-3100; www.nps.gov/olym; 3002 Mt Angeles Rd; ☉8am-6pm Jul & Aug, to 4pm Sep-Jun)

USFS Headquarters (☑360-956-2402; www.fs.fed.us/r6/olympic; 1835 Black Lake Blvd SW; ☉8am-4:30pm Mon-Fri)

Forks Chamber of Commerce (☑360-374-2531; www.forkswa.com; 1411 S Forks Ave; ☉10am-5pm Mon-Sat, 11am-4pm Sun; 🛜)

Port Townsend

Inventive eateries, elegant *fin de siècle* hotels and an unusual stash of year-round festivals make Port Townsend an Olympic Peninsula rarity: a weekend vacation that doesn't require hiking boots. Cut off from the rest of the area by eight bucolic miles of US 101, this is not the spot to base yourself for national-park exploration unless you don't mind driving a lot. Instead, settle in and enjoy one of the prettiest towns in the state.

⊙ Sights

Fort Worden State Park   PARK
(☑360-344-4412; http://parks.state.wa.us/511/fort-worden; 200 Battery Way; ☉6:30am-dusk

Apr-Oct, 8am-dusk Nov-Mar) FREE This attractive park located within Port Townsend's city limits is the remains of a large fortification system constructed in the 1890s to protect the strategically important Puget Sound area from outside attack – supposedly from the Spanish during the 1898 war. Sharp-eyed film buffs might recognize the area as the backdrop for the movie *An Officer and a Gentleman*.

Visitors can arrange tours of the **Commanding Officer's Quarters** (☏360-385-1003; Fort Worden State Park, 200 Battery Way; adult/child $2/free; ☉tours by appointment), a 12-bedroom mansion. You will also find the **Puget Sound Coast Artillery Museum** (adult/child $4/2; ☉11am-4pm, longer weekend hours Jun-Aug), which tells the story of early Pacific coastal fortifications.

Hikes lead along the headland to **Point Wilson Lighthouse Station** and some wonderful windswept beaches. On the park's fishing pier is the **Port Townsend Marine Science Center** (www.ptmsc.org; 532 Battery Way; adult/child $5/3; ☉noon-5pm Fri-Sun Apr-Oct), featuring four touch tanks and daily interpretive programs. There are also several camping and lodging possibilities.

🛌 Sleeping & Eating

Waterstreet Hotel HOTEL $
(☏360-385-5467; www.watersthotel.com; 635 Water St; r with shared bath $50-70, with private bath $75-175; ❋🛜) Homey and friendly, the Waterstreet offers great-value rooms in a naturally aged Victorian flophouse. If you're a family or group, go for suite 5 or 15 – essentially apartments, with a loft, a full kitchen and a big back porch right on Puget Sound. Reception is in the Native American gift shop next door to the hotel.

★Palace Hotel HISTORIC HOTEL $$
(☏360-385-0773; www.palacehotelpt.com; 1004 Water St; r $109-159, higher on festival weekends; 🛜🐾) Built in 1889, this beautiful Victorian building was once a brothel run by the locally notorious Madame Marie. It's been reincarnated as an attractive, character-filled period hotel with antique furnishings (plus all the modern amenities). Pleasant common spaces; kitchenettes available. The cheapest rooms share a bathroom.

Waterfront Pizza PIZZA $$
(☏360-379-9110; 951 Water St; slices $4, large pizzas $16-28; ☉11am-8pm Sun-Thu, to 9pm Fri & Sat) If you're craving a quick snack, grab a delicious, crispy, thin-crust slice downstairs – just be prepared for lines in the walk-in closet-sized dining room. For more relaxed, sit-down service, climb the stairs and sample the pies, topped with treats such as Cajun sausage, feta cheese, artichoke hearts and pesto.

★Sweet Laurette Cafe & Bistro FRENCH $$
(www.sweetlaurette.com; 1029 Lawrence St; mains $10-20, brunch $9-15; ☉8am-9pm, closed Tue; 🐾) This French shabby-chic cafe serves breakfast, lunch and dinner in the bistro and delicious coffee and pastries between mealtimes. The food is made with sustainable and mostly local ingredients – try a breakfast *croque madame* with honey-baked ham and Gruyère on French bread for breakfast, or Whidbey Island mussels in a white-wine cream sauce or Cape Cleare king salmon for dinner.

ℹ Information

Visitor Center (☏360-385-2722; www.ptchamber.org; 2409 Jefferson St; ☉9am-5pm Mon-Fri) Pick up a useful walking-tour map and guide to the downtown historic district here.

ℹ Getting There & Away

Washington State Ferries (☏206-464-6400; www.wsdot.wa.gov/ferries) operates up to 15 trips daily (depending on the season) to Coupeville on Whidbey Island from the downtown terminal (car and driver/passenger $14.05/3.30, 35 minutes).

Port Angeles

Despite the name, there's nothing Spanish or particularly angelic about Port Angeles, propped up by the lumber industry and backed by the steep-sided Olympic Mountains. Rather than visiting to see the town per se, many come here to catch a ferry for Victoria, BC, or to plot an outdoor excursion into the nearby Olympic National Park.

🏃 Activities

The **Olympic Discovery Trail** (www.olympicdiscoverytrail.com) is a 30-mile off-road hiking and cycling trail between Port Angeles and Sequim, starting at the end of Ediz Hook, the sand spit that loops around the bay. Bikes can be rented at **Sound Bikes & Kayaks** (www.soundbikeskayaks.com; 120 E Front St; bike rental per hour/day $10/45, kayak rental per day $50; ☉10am-6pm Mon-Sat, 11am-4pm Sun).

🛏 Sleeping & Eating

Downtown Hotel HOTEL **$**
(☑ 360-565-1125; www.portangelesdowntownhotel.
com; 101 E Front St; d with shared/private bath from
$45/65; 😊 📶) Nothing special on the outside
but surprisingly spacious and tidy within,
this no-frills, family-run place down by the
ferry launch is Port Angeles' secret bargain.
Bright rooms are decked out in wicker and
wood, and several have water views. The
cheapest rooms share a bathroom in the
hallway. The soundproofing isn't great, but
the location is tops.

Olympic Lodge HOTEL **$$**
(☑ 360-452-2993; www.olympiclodge.com; 140
Del Guzzi Dr; r from $139; 🌐 @ 📶 🏊) This is the
most comfortable place in town, offering
gorgeous rooms, on-site bistro, swimming
pool with hot tub, and complimentary cook-
ies and soup in the afternoon. Prices vary
widely depending on day and month.

Bella Italia ITALIAN **$$**
(☑ 360-457-5442; www.bellaitaliapa.com; 118 E
1st St; dinner mains $10-34; ☉ 4-9pm) Bella Ita-
lia has been around a lot longer than Bella, the heroine of the *Twilight* saga, but its
mention in the book as the site of Bella and
Edward's first date has turned what was
already a popular restaurant into an icon.
Try the clam linguine or the smoked duck
breast, or have what Bella ordered: mush-
room ravioli.

Wash it down with an outstanding wine
from a list with 500 selections.

ℹ Information

Port Angeles Visitor Center (☑ 360-452-
2363; www.portangeles.org; 121 E Railroad Ave;
☉ 9:30am-5:30pm Mon-Fri, 10am-5:30pm Sat,
noon-3pm Sun May-Sep, 10am-5pm Mon-Sat,
noon-3pm Sun Oct-Apr) Adjacent to the ferry
terminal. Open later in summer if volunteers
are available.

ℹ Getting There & Away

Clallam Transit (☑ 360-452-4511; www.
clallamtransit.com) Buses go to Forks and Se-
quim, where they link up with other transit buses
that circumnavigate the Olympic Peninsula.

Olympic Bus Lines (www.olympicbuslines.
com; Gateway Transit Center, 123 E Front St)
Runs twice daily to Seattle.

Coho Vehicle Ferry (☑ 888-993-3779; www.
cohoferry.com) Runs to/from Victoria, BC (1½
hours, $128 round-trip).

Northwest Peninsula

Several Native American reservations cling
to the extreme northwest corner of the continent and are welcoming to visitors. The
small weather-beaten settlement of **Neah
Bay** on Hwy 112 is home to the Makah Indian Reservation, whose **Makah Museum**
(☑ 360-645-2711; www.makahmuseum.com; 1880
Bayview Ave; adult/child $6/5; ☉ 10am-5pm) dis-
plays artifacts from one of North America's
most significant archaeological finds, the
500-year-old Makah village of Ozette. Several miles beyond the museum, a short boardwalk trail leads to stunning **Cape Flattery**,
a 300ft promontory that marks the most
northwesterly point in the lower 48 states.

Convenient to the Hoh River Rainforest
and the Olympic coastline is **Forks**, a one-
horse lumber town that's now more famous
for its *Twilight* paraphernalia. It's a central
town for exploring Olympic National Park;
a good accommodation choice is the **Miller
Tree Inn** (☑ 360-374-6806; www.millertreeinn.
com; 654 E Division St; r from $175; 📶 🏊).

Northwest Washington

Wedged between Seattle, the Cascades and
Canada, northwest Washington draws influences from three sides. Its urban hub is
collegiate Bellingham, while its outdoor
highlight is the pastoral San Juan Islands,
an extensive archipelago that glimmers like
a sepia-toned snapshot from another era.
Anacortes is the main hub for ferries to the
San Juan Islands and Victoria, BC.

Whidbey Island

While not as detached (there's a bridge connecting it to adjacent Fidalgo Island at its
northernmost point) or nonconformist as
the San Juans, life is almost as slow, quiet
and pastoral on Whidbey Island. Having six
state parks is a bonus, along with a plethora
of B&Bs, two historic fishing villages (Lang-
ley and Coupeville), famously good clams
and a thriving artist's community.

Deception Pass State Park (☑ 360-
675-2417; 41229 N State Hwy 20) straddles the
eponymous steep-sided strait that flows
between Whidbey and Fidalgo Islands, and
incorporates lakes, islands, campsites and
38 miles of hiking trails.

**Ebey's Landing National Historical Re-
serve** (☑ 360-678-6084; www.nps.gov/ebla; 162

Cemetery Rd) comprises 17,400 acres encompassing working farms, sheltered beaches, two state parks and the town of **Coupeville**. This small settlement is one of Washington's oldest towns and has an attractive seafront, antique stores and a number of old inns, including the **Captain Whidbey Inn** (☑ 360-678-4097; www.captainwhidbey.com; 2072 W Captain Whidbey Inn Rd; r/cabins from $103/210; ☎), a forest-clad log-built inn dating to 1907. For the famous fresh local clams, head to **Christopher's** (☑ 360-678-5480; www.christopher sonwhidbey.com; 103 NW Coveland St; lunch mains $12-16, dinner mains $16-26; ☺ 11:30am-2pm & 5pm-close, closed Tue).

❶ Getting There & Around

Regular **Washington State Ferries** (WSF; ☑ 888-808-7977; www.wsdot.wa.gov/ferries) link Clinton to Mukilteo and Coupeville to Port Townsend. Free **Island Transit** (☑ 360-678-7771; www.islandtransit.org) buses run the length of Whidbey every hour daily, except Sundays, from the Clinton ferry dock.

Bellingham

Welcome to a green, liberal and famously livable settlement that has taken the libertine, nothing-is-too-weird ethos of Oregon's 'City of Roses' and given it a peculiarly Washingtonian twist. Mild in both manners and weather, the 'city of subdued excitement,' as a local mayor once dubbed it, is an unlikely alliance of espresso-sipping students, venerable retirees, all-weather triathletes and placard-waving peaceniks. Publications such as *Outside Magazine* have consistently lauded it for its abundant outdoor opportunities.

◉ Sights & Activities

Bellingham offers outdoor sights and activities by the truckload. **Whatcom Falls Park** is a natural wild region that bisects Bellingham's eastern suburbs. The change in elevation is marked by four sets of waterfalls, including **Whirlpool Falls**, a popular summer swimming hole.

Fairhaven Bike & Mountain Sports   CYCLING
(☑ 360-733-4433; www.fairhavenbike.com; 1103 11th St; rental per 4hr $25-40; ☺ 9:30am-6pm Mon-Sat, 11am-5pm Sun) Bellingham is one of the most bike-friendly cities in the Northwest, with a well-maintained intra-urban trail going as far south as **Larrabee State Park** (www.parks. wa.gov; Chuckanut Dr; ☺ dawn-dusk; ⊞). This outfit rents bikes and has maps on local routes.

San Juan Cruises   CRUISE
(☑ 360-738-8099; www.whales.com; 355 Harris Ave; cruises $39-109; ☺ 8am-6pm) Runs cruises around Bellingham Bay with beer or wine tasting, plus whale-watching around the San Juan Islands and more.

🛏 Sleeping & Eating

Larrabee State Park   CAMPGROUND $
(☑ 360-676-2093; http://parks.state.wa.us/536/ larrabee; Chuckanut Dr; tent/RV sites from $12/30) Seven miles south of Bellingham, along scenic Chuckanut Dr, these campsites sit among Douglas firs and cedars with access to Chuckanut Bay and 12 miles of hiking and biking trails.

★ **Hotel Bellwether**   BOUTIQUE HOTEL $$
(☑ 360-392-3100; www.hotelbellwether.com; 1 Bellwether Way; r from $198; ❄ @ ☎ ☎) Bellingham's finest and most charismatic hotel lies on the waterfront and offers views of Lummi Island. Standard rooms come with Italian furnishings and Hungarian-down duvets, but the finest stay is the 900-sq-ft lighthouse suite (from $525), a converted three-story lighthouse with a wonderful private lookout. Spa and restaurant on premises.

Old Town Cafe   CAFE $
(☑ 360-671-4431; www.theoldtowncafe.com; 316 W Holly St; mains $6-10; ☺ 6:30am-3pm Mon-Sat, 8am-2pm Sun) Very popular for its casual, artsy atmosphere, this bohemian breakfast joint cooks up tasty dishes such as custom omelets, egg tortillas and whole-wheat French toast. There's also homemade granola, gluten-free hotcakes, organic tofu scrambles, garden salads and 10 kinds of sandwiches.

Mount Bakery   BREAKFAST $
(www.mountbakery.com; 308 W Champion St; brunch $6-16; ☺ 8am-3:30pm; ☎) This is where you go on Sunday mornings with a Douglas fir–sized copy of the *New York Times* for Belgian waffles, crepes and organic eggs done any way you like. Plenty of gluten-free options. There's a second location in Fairhaven.

❶ Information

Downtown Info Center (☑ 360-671-3990; www.bellingham.org; 1306 Commercial St; ☺ 11am-3pm Tue-Sat)

❶ Getting There & Away

Bellingham is the terminal for **Alaska Marine Highway** (AMHS; ☑ 800-642-0066; www.dot. state.ak.us/amhs; 355 Harris Ave) ferries, which travel weekly up the Inside Passage to Juneau, Skagway and other southeast Alaskan ports.

The **Bellair Airporter Shuttle** (www.airporter.com; 1200 Iowa St) runs around the clock to Sea-Tac Airport (round-trip $74) and Anacortes (round-trip $35).

San Juan Islands

There are 172 landfalls in this expansive archipelago, but unless you're rich enough to charter your own yacht or seaplane, you'll be restricted to seeing the big four – San Juan, Orcas, Shaw and Lopez Islands – all served daily by Washington State Ferries. Communally, the islands are famous for their tranquility, whale-watching opportunities, sea kayaking and seditious nonconformity.

A great way to explore the San Juans is by sea kayak or bicycle. Cycling-wise, Lopez is flat and pastoral and San Juan is worthy of an easy day loop, while Orcas offers the challenge of undulating terrain and a steep 5-mile ride to the top of Mt Constitution.

ⓘ Getting There & Around

Two airlines have scheduled flights from the mainland to the San Juans. **Kenmore Air** (☑ 866-435-9524; www.kenmoreair.com) flies from Lake Union and Lake Washington to Lopez, Orcas and San Juan Islands daily on three- to 10-person seaplanes. Fares start at $155 one way. **San Juan Airlines** (☑ 800-874-4434; www.sanjuanairlines.com) flies from Anacortes and Bellingham to the three main islands (one way $89).

Washington State Ferries leave Anacortes for the San Juans; some continue to Sidney, BC, near Victoria. Ferries run to Lopez Island (45 minutes), Orcas Landing (60 minutes) and Friday Harbor on San Juan Island (75 minutes). Fares vary by season; the cost of the entire round-trip is collected on westbound journeys only (except those returning from Sidney, BC).

Shuttle buses ply Orcas and San Juan Island between May and October.

San Juan Island

San Juan Island is the archipelago's unofficial capital, a harmonious mix of low forested hills and small rural farms that resonates with a dramatic and unusual 19th-century history. The only real settlement is Friday Harbor, home to the visitor center and **Chamber of Commerce** (☑ 360-378-5240; www.sanjuanisland.org; 165 1st St S, Friday Harbor; ⊘ 10am-5pm).

◉ Sights

San Juan Island National Historical Park   HISTORIC SITE
(☑ 360-378-2240; www.nps.gov/sajh; ⊘ visitor center 8:30am-5pm Jun-Aug, to 4:30pm Sep-May) 🆓 Known more for their scenery than their history, the San Juans nonetheless hide one of the 19th century's oddest political confrontations, the so-called 'Pig War' between the USA and Britain. This curious standoff is showcased in two separate historical parks at either end of the island, which once housed opposing **American** (☑ 360-378-2240; www.nps.gov/sajh; ⊘ grounds 8:30am-11pm) 🆓 and **English** military encampments.

Lime Kiln Point State Park   PARK
(☑ 360-902-8844; http://parks.state.wa.us/540/lime-kiln-point; 1567 Westside Rd; ⊘ 8am-dusk) 🌿 Clinging to the island's rocky west coast, this beautiful park overlooks the deep Haro Strait and is reputedly one of the best places in the world to view whales from the shoreline. The word is out, however, so the view areas are often packed with hopeful picnickers. There's a small **interpretive center** (☑ 360-378-2044; ⊘ 11am-4pm Jun–mid-Sep) in the park, along with trails, a restored lime kiln and the landmark **Lime Kiln Lighthouse**, built in 1919.

🛏 Sleeping & Eating

There are hotels, B&Bs and resorts scattered around the island, but Friday Harbor has the highest concentration.

Wayfarer's Rest   HOSTEL $
(☑ 360-378-6428; www.hostelssanjuan.com; 35 Malcolm St, Friday Harbor; dm $40, r from $70, cabins from $85; 🅿❄🐾) A short walk from the ferry terminal, this pleasant hostel is located in a homey house with comfortable dorms and affordable private rooms. The main kitchen overlooks the grassy backyard, and there's also a suite that sleeps six ($245). Reserve two months ahead in summer.

★ Olympic Lights B&B   B&B $$
(☑ 360-378-3186; www.olympiclights.com; 146 Starlight Way; r $165-185; 🅿) Once the centerpiece of a 320-acre estate, this splendidly restored 1895 farmhouse now hosts an equally formidable B&B that stands on an open bluff facing the snow-coated Olympic Mountains. The four rooms are imaginatively named Garden, Ra, Heart and Olympic; sunflowers adorn the garden and the

hearty breakfasts include homemade buttermilk biscuits. Two-night minimum.

Market Chef
DELI $

(☑ 360-378-4546; 225 A St, Friday Harbor; sandwiches from $9; ⊘ 10am-4pm Mon-Fri) 🥢 Super popular and famous for its delicious sandwiches, including its signature curried-egg salad with roasted peanuts and chutney, or roast beef and rocket. Salads are also available; local ingredients are used. If you're in town on a Saturday in summer, visit Market Chef at the San Juan Island Farmers Market (10am to 1pm).

Backdoor Kitchen
FUSION $$$

(☑ 360-378-9540; www.backdoorkitchen.com; 400 A St, Friday Harbor; mains $30-37; ⊘ 11:30am-2:30pm Mon, 5-9pm Wed-Sun) One of San Juan Island's finest restaurants, Backdoor Kitchen uses fresh local ingredients to serve up creative multi-ethnic dishes such as Spanish-style pork with wild-prawn stew and East Indian spiced lentils with spinach cake. Dine in the pretty garden in summer. Reserve.

Orcas Island

More rugged than Lopez yet less crowded than San Juan, Orcas has struck a delicate balance between friendliness and frostiness, development and preservation, tourist dollars and priceless privacy – for the time being, at least. The ferry terminal is at Orcas Landing, 8 miles south of the main village, Eastsound.

On the island's eastern lobe is **Moran State Park** (☑ 360-376-6173; 3572 Olga Rd; Discover Pass required at some parking lots $10; ⊘ 6:30am-dusk Apr-Sep, 8am-dusk Oct-Mar), dominated by Mt Constitution (2409ft), with 40 miles of trails and an amazing 360-degree mountaintop view. **Camping** (☑ 360-376-2326; http://moranstatepark.com; campsites from $25) is a great option here.

🛏 Sleeping

★ Golden Tree Hostel
HOSTEL $

(☑ 360-317-8693; www.goldentreehostel.com; 1159 North Beach Rd, Eastsound; dm/d with shared bath $45/115; @🅿🛜🐾) Located in an 1890s-era heritage house, this hip hostel offers cozy rooms and pleasant common spaces, along with a hot tub and sauna in the grassy garden. There's even a separate recreation building with pool, Foosball, shuffleboard

and darts. Bicycle rentals are $20. Friday pizza nights. Reserve in summer.

Doe Bay Village Resort & Retreat
HOSTEL $

(☑ 360-376-2291; www.doebay.com; 107 Doe Bay Rd, Olga; campsites from $60, cabins from $100, yurts from $80; 🛜🐾) 🥢 One of the least expensive resorts in the San Juans, Doe Bay has the atmosphere of an artists' commune combined with a hippie retreat. Accommodations include sea-view campsites and various cabins and yurts, some with views of the water.

Outlook Inn
HOTEL $$

(☑ 360-376-2200; www.outlookinn.com; 171 Main St, Eastsound; r with shared/private bath from $89/159; @🅿🛜🐾) Eastsound's oldest and most eye-catching building, the Outlook Inn (1888) is an island institution. Budget rooms are cozy and neat (try for room 30), while the luxurious suites have fireplaces, Jacuzzi tubs and stunning water views from their balconies. Excellent attached cafe.

🍴 Eating & Drinking

★ Brown Bear Baking
BAKERY $

(cnr Main St & North Beach Rd, Eastsound; pastries $7; ⊘ 8am-5pm, closed Tue) No one wants to pay $7 for a pastry, but the trouble is that once you start eating the baked goods here, nothing else will do. Options include croissants *aux amandes*, quiche using fresh Orcas Island eggs and roast veggies, caramel sticky buns and fruit pie. Balance the nutritional ledger with one of the hearty soups or sandwiches.

★ Inn at Ship Bay
SEAFOOD $$$

(☑ 877-276-7296; www.innatshipbay.com; 326 Olga Rd; mains $21-30; ⊘ 5:30-10pm Tue-Sat) 🥢 Locals unanimously rate this place as the best fine-dining experience on the island. The chefs work overtime preparing everything from scratch using the freshest island ingredients. Seafood is the specialty and it's served in an attractive 1860s orchard house a couple of miles south of Eastsound. There's also an on-site 11-room hotel (doubles from $195).

Island Hoppin' Brewery
BREWERY $

(www.islandhoppinbrewery.com; 33 Hope Lane, Eastsound; ⊘ noon-9pm Tue-Sun) The location just off Mt Baker Rd near the airport makes this tiny brewery hard to find, but the locals sure know it's there – this is *the* place to go to enjoy local brews on tap. Don't come hungry – only snacks are served. Happy hour runs from 7pm to 9pm Sunday to Thursday, while a ping-pong table adds some action.

Lopez Island

If you're going to Lopez – or 'Slow-pez,' as locals prefer to call it – take a bike. With its undulating terrain and salutation-offering residents (who are famous for their three-fingered 'Lopezian wave'), this is the ideal cycling isle. A leisurely pastoral spin can be tackled in a day, with good overnight digs available next to the marina in the **Lopez Islander Resort** (☑360-468-2233; www.lopezfun.com; 2864 Fisherman Bay Rd; r from $129; ⊛⊠). For something more upscale, try the **Edenwild Inn** (☑360-468-3238; www.edenwildinn.com; Lopez Rd, Lopez Village; r $115-225; ☎), a Victorian mansion set in lovely formal gardens.

If you arrive cycleless, call up **Village Cycles** (☑360-468-4013; www.villagecycles.net; 214 Lopez Rd; rental per hour $7-16), which can deliver a bicycle to the ferry terminal for you.

North Cascades

Dominated by Mt Baker and – to a lesser extent – the more remote Glacier Peak, the North Cascades is made up of a huge swath of protected forests, parks and wilderness areas that dwarf even the expansive Rainier and St Helens parks to the south. The crème de la crème is the North Cascades National Park, a primeval stash of old-growth rainforest, groaning glaciers and untainted ecosystems whose savage beauty is curiously missed by all but 2500 or so annual visitors who penetrate its rainy interior.

Mt Baker

Rising like a ghostly sentinel above the sparkling waters of upper Puget Sound, Mt Baker has been mesmerizing visitors to the Northwest for centuries. A dormant volcano that last belched smoke in the 1850s, this haunting 10,781ft peak shelters 12 glaciers, and in 1999 registered a record-breaking 95ft of snow in one season.

Well-paved Hwy 542, known as the Mt Baker Scenic Byway, climbs 5100ft to **Artist Point**, 56 miles from Bellingham. Near here you'll find the **Heather Meadows Visitor Center** (Mt Baker Hwy, Mile 56; ⊗8am-4:30pm mid-Jul–late Sep) and a plethora of varied hikes, including the 7.5-mile **Chain Lakes Loop** that leads you around a half-dozen lakes surrounded by huckleberry meadows.

Receiving more annual snow than any ski area in North America, the **Mt Baker Ski Area** (☑360-734-6771; www.mtbaker.us; lift tickets adult/child $60/40) has 38 runs, eight lifts and a vertical rise of 1500ft. The resort has gained something of a cult status among snowboarders, who have been coming here for the Legendary Baker Banked Slalom every January since 1985.

On your way up the mountain, stop for a bite at authentic honky-tonk bar and restaurant **Graham's** (☑360-599-9883; 9989 Mt Baker Hwy; mains $6-18; ⊗noon-9pm Mon-Fri, 8-11am & noon-9pm Sat & Sun) and grab trail munchies at **Wake & Bakery** (☑360-599-1658; www.getsconed.com; 6903 Bourne St, Glacier; snacks from $4; ⊗7:30am-5pm), both in the town of **Glacier**.

Leavenworth

Blink hard and rub your eyes. This isn't some strange Germanic hallucination. This is Leavenworth, a former lumber town that underwent a Bavarian makeover back in the 1960s after the re-routing of the cross-continental railway threatened to put it permanently out of business. Swapping wood for tourists, Leavenworth today has successfully reinvented itself as a traditional *Romantische Strasse* village, right down to the beer, sausages and lederhosen-loving locals (25% of whom are of German descent). The classic *Sound of Music* mountain setting helps, as does the fact that Leavenworth serves as the main activity center for sorties into the nearby Alpine Lakes Wilderness.

The **Leavenworth Chamber of Commerce** (www.leavenworth.org; 940 Hwy 2; ⊗8am-5pm Mon-Thu, 8am-6pm Fri & Sat, 10am-4pm Sun) can advise on the local outdoor activities. Highlights include the best climbing in the state at **Castle Rock** in Tumwater Canyon, about 3 miles northwest of town off US 2.

The **Devil's Gulch** is a popular off-road mountain-bike trail (25 miles, four to six hours). Local outfitters **Der Sportsmann** (☑509-548-5623; www.dersportsmann.com; 837 Front St; 1-day cross-country ski/snowshoe rentals $15/12; ⊗9am-6pm) rents mountain bikes.

🛏 Sleeping & Eating

Hotel Pension Anna HOTEL **$$**
(☑509-548-6273; www.pensionanna.com; 926 Commercial St; r from $179, ste from $300; ☎) The most authentic Bavarian hotel in town

is also spotless and incredibly friendly. Each room is kitted out in imported Austrian decor and the European-inspired breakfasts (included) may induce joyful yodels. A recommended room is the double with hand-painted furniture, but the spacious suite in the adjacent St Joseph's chapel is perfect for families.

Enzian Inn   HOTEL **$$**
(☑509-548-5269; www.enzianinn.com; 590 Hwy 2; d from $140; ☎❧☲) At this Leavenworth classic the day starts with a blast on an alpenhorn before breakfast. If that doesn't send you running for your lederhosen, consider the free putting green (with resident grass-trimming goats), the indoor and outdoor swimming pools, and the nightly pianist pounding out requests in the Bavarian lobby.

München Haus   GERMAN **$**
(☑509-548-1158; www.munchenhaus.com; 709 Front St; brats $5-7; ☉11am-9pm) The Haus is 100% alfresco, meaning that the hot German sausages and pretzels are essential stomach warmers in winter, while the Bavarian brews will cool you down in summer. The casual beer-garden atmosphere is complemented by an aggressively jaunty accordion soundtrack, laid-back staff, a kettle of cider relish and an epic mustard bar. Hours vary outside summer.

Lake Chelan

Long, slender Lake Chelan is central Washington's watery playground. The town of Chelan, at the lake's southeastern tip, is the primary base for accommodations and services, and has a **USFS Ranger Station** (☑509-682-4900; 428 W Woodin Ave).

Lake Chelan State Park (☑509-687-3710; https://washington.goingtocamp.com/lakechelanstatepark; 7544 S Lakeshore Rd; primitive/standard sites from $20/25) has 144 campsites; a number of lakeshore campgrounds are accessible only by boat. If you'd rather sleep in a real bed, try the great-value **Midtowner Motel** (☑800-572-0943; www.midtowner.com; 721 E Woodin Ave; r $45-130; ❃@❧☲) or the delightful **Riverwalk Inn** (☑509-682-2627; www.riverwalkinnchelan.com; 205 E Wapato St; d $79-119, f $89-189; ❧☲), both in town.

Several wineries have also opened in the area and many have excellent restaurants. Try **Tsillan Cellars** (☑509-682-9463; www.tsillancellars.com; 3875 Hwy 97A; ☉noon-6pm) or the swanky Italian **Sorrento's Ristorante**

(☑509-682-5409; mains $22-36; ☉5pm-late Wed-Fri, noon-late Sat, 10am-late Sun).

Link Transit (☑509-662-1155; www.linktransit.com) buses connect Chelan with Wenatchee and Leavenworth ($2.50 one way).

Beautiful **Stehekin**, on the northern tip of Lake Chelan, is accessible only by **boat** (www.ladyofthelake.com; 1418 W Woodin Ave, Chelan; round-trip $61), or a long hike across Cascade Pass, 28 miles from the lake. You'll find lots of information about hiking, campgrounds and cabin rentals at www.stehekin.com. Most facilities are open from mid-June to mid-September.

Methow Valley

The Methow's combination of powdery winter snow and abundant summer sunshine has transformed this valley into one of Washington's primary recreation areas. You can bike, hike and fish in summer, and cross-country ski on the second-biggest snow trail network in the US in winter.

The 200km of trails are maintained by the nonprofit **Methow Valley Sport Trails Association** (MVSTA; ☑509-996-3287; www.methowtrails.org; 309 Riverside Ave, Winthrop; ☉9am-3:30pm Mon-Fri) ✎, which in winter provides the most comprehensive network of hut-to-hut (and hotel-to-hotel) skiing in North America. An extra blessing is that few people seem to know about it. For classic accommodations and easy access to the skiing, hiking and cycling trails, decamp at the exquisite **Sun Mountain Lodge** (☑509-996-2211; www.sunmountainlodge.com; 604 Patterson Lake Rd, Winthrop; r from $205, cabins from $405; ❃❧☲), 10 miles west of the town of Winthrop. Winthrop is also the locus of the area's best eating: try the fine-dining **Arrowleaf Bistro** (☑509-996-3920; www.arrowleafbistro.com; 253 Riverside Ave; mains $22-28; ☉5-10pm Wed-Sun).

North Cascades National Park

Even the names of the lightly trodden, dramatic mountains in **North Cascades National Park** (www.nps.gov/noca) sound wild and untamed: Desolation Peak, Jagged Ridge, Mt Despair and Mt Terror. Not surprisingly, the region offers some of the best backcountry adventures outside of Alaska.

The **North Cascades Visitor Center** (☑206-386-4495, ext 11; 502 Newhalem St, Newhalem; ☉9am-5pm daily Jun-Sep, Sat & Sun May & Oct) ✎, in the small settlement of

Newhalem on Hwy 20, is the best orientation point for visitors and is staffed by expert rangers who can enlighten you on the park's highlights.

Built in the 1930s for loggers working in the valley (which was soon to be flooded by Ross Dam), the floating cabins at the **Ross Lake Resort** (⌨ 206-386-4437; www.rosslakeresort.com; 503 Diablo St, Rockport; cabins $195-370; ⊙ mid-Jun–late Oct; ⊜) on the eponymous lake's west side are the state's most unique accommodations. There's no road in – guests can either hike the 2-mile trail from Hwy 20 or take the resort's tugboat-taxi-and-truck shuttle from the parking area near Diablo Dam.

Northeastern Washington

Spokane

Washington's second-biggest population center is one of the state's latent surprises and a welcome break after the treeless monotony of the eastern scablands. Situated at the nexus of the Pacific Northwest's so-called 'Inland Empire,' this understated yet confident city sits on the banks of the Spokane River, close to where British fur traders founded a short-lived trading post in 1810. Though rarely touted in national tourist blurbs, Spokane hosts one of the world's largest mass-participation running events (May's annual Bloomsday).

⊙ Sights

Riverfront Park   PARK
(www.spokaneriverfrontpark.com; ⊞) The site of the 1974 World's Fair and Exposition, this park has numerous highlights, including a 17-point **Sculpture Walk** (Riverfront Park) and the scenic **Spokane Falls**. A short gondola ride, the **Spokane Falls SkyRide** (Riverfront Park) takes you directly above the falls, as does the equally spectacular **Monroe Street Bridge** (Monroe St), built in 1911 and still one of the largest concrete arches in the USA. An ongoing renovation project means parts of the park are inaccessible and most attractions are closed until fall 2017.

Northwest Museum
of Arts & Culture   MUSEUM
(MAC; ⌨ 509-456-3931; www.northwestmuseum.org; 2316 W 1st Ave; adult/child $15/10; ⊙ 10am-5pm Tue-Sun, to 8pm Wed; ⊞) In a striking state-of-the-art building in the historic Browne's Addition neighborhood, this museum has – arguably – one of the finest collections of indigenous artifacts in the Northwest. Leading off a plush glass foyer overlooking the Spokane River are four galleries showcasing Spokane's history, as well as a number of roving exhibitions that change every three to four months.

🛏 Sleeping & Eating

Hotel Ruby   MOTEL $
(⌨ 509-747-1041; www.hotelrubyspokane.com; 901 W 1st Ave; r from $78; 🅿 ❉ 🛜 ⊜) An arty redesign of a formerly basic motel, the Ruby has a '70s feel, with cool original art on the walls, funky light fixtures and a sleek cocktail lounge attached to the lobby. Rooms have minifridge and microwave, and you can use the gym at the nearby sister hotel, Ruby 2. It's an easy walk to bars and restaurants.

★**Historic**
Davenport Hotel   HISTORIC HOTEL $$
(⌨ 800-899-1482;   www.thedavenporthotel.com; 10 S Post St; r from $188; ❉ 🛜 ⊜) This historic landmark (opened in 1914) is considered one of the best hotels in the country. Even if you're not staying here, linger in the exquisite lobby or have a drink in the Peacock Lounge. The adjacent, modern Davenport Tower sports a safari-themed lobby and bar.

Mizuna   FUSION $$
(⌨ 509-747-2004; www.mizuna.com; 214 N Howard St; dinner mains $20-36; ⊙ 11am-10pm Mon-Sat, 4-10pm Sun; 🖉) Located in an antique brick building, the simply furnished Mizuna is well known for its specialties, such as quinoa meatloaf and pan-roasted organic chicken, as well as an extensive vegetarian menu. Wash dinner down with an exquisite wine for a memorable experience.

🍷 Drinking & Entertainment

From opera and cocktail bars to billiards and craft breweries, Spokane has the best nighttime entertainment and drinking scene east of the Cascades.

NoLi Brewhouse   BREWERY
(⌨ 509-242-2739; www.nolibrewhouse.com; 1003 E Trent Ave; mains $12-16; ⊙ 11am-10pm Sun-Wed, to 11pm Thu-Sat) A student hangout near Gonzaga University, Spokane's best microbrewery serves some weird and wonderful flavors, including a tart cherry ale and an imperial stout with coffee, chocolate and brown-sugar tones. Food-wise, check out the

cod and chips cooked in batter made with the brewery's own pale ale.

Mootsy's   BAR
(☑ 509-838-1570; 406 W Sprague Ave; ☺ 2pm-2am) This popular dive bar is the hub of the nightlife and alternative-music scene that hops all along this block between Stevens and Washington Sts. Cheap Pabst Blue Ribbon during happy hour keeps its customer base loyal.

Bing Crosby Theater   THEATER
(☑ 509-227-7638;   www.bingcrosbytheater.com; 901 W Sprague Ave) Yes, Bing Crosby hailed from Spokane, and now his namesake venue the 'Bing' presents concerts, plays and festivals in a fairly intimate setting.

ℹ Information

Spokane Area Visitor Information Center
(☑ 888-776-5263; www.visitspokane.com; 808 W Main Ave; ☺ 8am-5pm Mon-Sat, 11am-6pm Sun) Has plenty of pamphlets and maps.

ℹ Getting There & Away

Spokane International Airport (www.spokaneairports.net) Flights to Seattle, Portland, OR, and Boise, ID.

Spokane Intermodal Center (221 W 1st Ave) Buses and trains depart from this station.

South Cascades

More rounded and less hemmed in than their saw-toothed cousins to the north, the South Cascades are nonetheless higher. Their pinnacle in more ways than one is 14,411ft Mt Rainier, the fifth-highest mountain in the lower 48 and arguably one of the most dramatic stand-alone mountains in the world. Further south, fiery Mt St Helens needs zero introduction, while unsung Adams glowers way off to the east like a sulking middle child.

Mt Rainier National Park

The USA's fifth-highest peak outside Alaska, majestic Mt Rainier is also one of its most beguiling. Encased in a 368-sq-mile national park, the mountain's snowcapped summit and forest-covered foothills boast numerous hiking trails, huge swaths of flower-carpeted meadows, and an alluring conical peak that presents a formidable challenge for aspiring climbers.

Mt Rainier National Park (www.nps.gov/ mora; car $25, pedestrian & cyclist $10, under 17yr free, 1yr pass $50) has four entrances. Call 800-695-7623 for road conditions. The National Park Service (NPS) website includes downloadable maps and descriptions of dozens of park trails. The most famous is the hardcore, 93-mile-long Wonderland Trail that completely circumnavigates Mt Rainier and takes around 10 to 12 days to tackle.

Campgrounds located in the park have running water and toilets, but no showers or RV hookups. Reservations at park campsites (☑ 800-365-2267; www.nps.gov/ mora; campsites $20) are strongly advised during summer and can be made up to two months in advance by phone or online. For overnight backcountry trips, you'll need a wilderness permit – check the NPS website for details.

NISQUALLY ENTRANCE
The busiest and most convenient gate to Mt Rainier National Park, Nisqually lies on Hwy 706 via Ashford, near the park's southwest corner. It's open year-round. Longmire, 7 miles inside the Nisqually entrance, has a **museum and information center** (☑ 360-569-6575; Hwy 706; ☺ 9am-4:30pm May-Jul), a number of important trailheads, and the rustic **National Park Inn** (☑ 360-569-2275; Hwy 706; r with shared/private bath from $126/177; ✷), complete with an excellent restaurant.

More hikes and interpretive walks can be found 12 miles further east at loftier **Paradise**, which is served by the informative **Henry M Jackson Visitor Center** (☑ 360-569-6571; Paradise; ☺ 10am-5pm daily May-Oct, Sat & Sun Nov-Apr), and the vintage **Paradise Inn** (☑ 360-569-2275; r with shared/private bath from $123/182; ☺ May-Oct; ☺☎), a historical 'parkitecture' inn constructed in 1916. Climbs to the top of Rainier leave from the inn; excellent four-day guided ascents are led by **Rainier Mountaineering Inc** (☑ 888-892-5462; www.rmiguides.com; 30027 Hwy 706 E, Ashford; 4-day climb $1087).

OTHER ENTRANCES
The three other entrances to Mt Rainier National Park are **Ohanapecosh**, accessed via Hwy 123 and the town of Packwood, where lodging is available; **White River**, off Hwy 410, which literally takes the highroad (6400ft) to the beautiful viewpoint at the **Sunrise Lodge Cafeteria** (snacks $6-9; ☺ 10am-7pm Jul & Aug); and remote **Carbon River** in the northwest corner, which gives access to the park's inland rainforest.

Mt St Helens National Volcanic Monument

What it lacks in height, Mt St Helens makes up for in fiery infamy – 57 people perished on the mountain when it erupted with a force of 1500 atomic bombs on May 18, 1980. The cataclysm began with an earthquake measuring 5.1 on the Richter scale, which sparked the biggest landslide in recorded history and buried 230 sq miles of forest under millions of tons of volcanic rock and ash. Today it's a fascinating landscape of recovering forests, new river valleys and ash-covered slopes. There's an $8 per person fee to enter the National Monument.

NORTHEASTERN ENTRANCE

From the main northeast entrance on Hwy 504, your first stop should be the **Silver Lake Visitor Center** (www.mtsthelensinfo.com/visitor_centers/silver_lake; 3029 Spirit Lake Hwy; adult/child $5/2.50; 9am-5pm May-Sep, to 4pm Oct-Apr;), which has films, exhibits and free information about the mountain (including trail maps). For a closer view of the destructive power of nature, venture to the **Johnston Ridge Observatory** (360-274-2140; 24000 Spirit Lake Hwy; day use $8; 10am-6pm mid-May–Oct), situated at the end of Hwy 504, which looks directly into the mouth of the crater. A welcome stop in an accommodations-light area, the **Eco Park Resort** (360-274-7007; www.ecoparkresort.com; 14000 Spirit Lake Hwy, Toutle; campsites $25, cabins $140-150;) offers campsites and RV hookups, and basic two- or four-person cabins.

SOUTHEASTERN & EASTSIDE ENTRANCES

The southeastern entrance via the town of **Cougar** on Hwy 503 holds some serious lava terrain, including the 2-mile-long Ape Cave lava tube, which you can explore year round; be prepared for the chill as it remains a constant 41°F (5°C). Bring two light sources per adult or rent lanterns at **Apes' Headquarters** (360-449-7800; 10am-5pm mid-Jun–early Sep) for $5 each.

The eastside entrance is the most remote, but the harder-to-reach **Windy Ridge** viewpoint on this side gives you a palpable, if eerie, sense of the destruction from the blast. It's often closed until June. A few miles down the road you can descend 600ft on the 1-mile-long Harmony Trail (hike 224) to **Spirit Lake**.

Central & Southeastern Washington

The sunny, dry, near-California-looking central and southeastern parts of Washington harbor one not-so-secret weapon: wine. The fertile land that borders the Nile-like Yakima and Columbia River Valleys is awash with enterprising new wineries producing quality grapes that now vie with the Napa and Sonoma Valleys for recognition. Yakima and its more attractive cousin Ellensburg once held the edge, but nowadays the real star is Walla Walla.

Yakima & Ellensburg

The main reason to stop in Yakima is to visit one of the numerous wineries that lie between here and Benton City; pick up a map at

---

WORTH A TRIP

GRAND COULEE DAM

While the more famous Hoover Dam (conveniently located between Las Vegas and the Grand Canyon) gets around 1.6 million visitors per year, the four-times-larger and arguably more significant **Grand Coulee Dam** FREE (inconveniently located far from everything) gets only a trickle of tourism. If you're in the area, don't miss it – it's one of the country's most spectacular displays of engineering and you'll get to enjoy it crowd-free.

The **Grand Coulee Dam Visitor Center** (509-633-9265; www.usbr.gov/pn/grandcoulee/visit; 8:30am-11pm Jun & Jul, to 10:30pm Aug, to 9:30pm Sep, 9am-5pm Oct-May) details the history of the dam and surrounding area with movies, photos and interactive exhibits. Free guided tours of the facility run on the hour 10am to 5pm May to September, and at 11am and 2pm the rest of the year, and involve taking a glass-walled elevator 465ft down into the Third Power Plant, where you can view the generators from an observation deck.

the **visitor center** (☑ 800-221-0751; www.visit yakima.com; 101 N 8th St; ⊙ 9am-5pm Mon-Sat, 10am-4pm Sun Jun-Aug, reduced hours Sep-May).

A better layover is Ellensburg, a diminutive settlement 36 miles to the northwest that juxtaposes the state's largest rodeo (each Labor Day) with a town center that has more coffee bars per head than anywhere else in the world (allegedly). Grab your latte at local roaster **D&M Coffee** (☑ 509-962-9333; www.dmcoffee.com; 323 N Pearl St; mains $5-7; ⊙ 7am-10pm Mon-Sat, to 8pm Sun) and eat at the unconventional **Yellow Church Cafe** (☑ 509-933-2233; www.theyellow churchcafe.com; 111 S Pearl St; dinner mains $17-27; ⊙ 11am-9pm Mon-Thu, 8am-9pm Fri-Sun).

Greyhound services both cities, with buses to Seattle, Spokane and points in between.

Walla Walla

Walla Walla has converted itself into the hottest wine-growing region outside of California. While venerable Marcus Whitman College is the town's most obvious cultural attribute, you'll also find zany coffee bars, cool wine-tasting rooms, fine Queen Anne architecture, and one of the state's freshest and most vibrant farmers markets.

⊙ Sights & Activities

You don't need to be sloshed on wine to appreciate Walla Walla's historical and cultural heritage. Its Main St has won countless historical awards, and to bring the settlement to life, the local **chamber of commerce** (☑ 509-525-0850; www.wallawalla.org; 29 E Sumach St; ⊙ 8:30am-5pm Mon-Fri) has concocted some interesting walking tours. Main St and environs are also crammed with tasting rooms. Expect tasting fees of $5 to $10.

Fort Walla Walla Museum   MUSEUM
(☑ 509-525-7703; www.fwwm.org; 755 Myra Rd; adult/child $8/3; ⊙ 10am-5pm Mar-Oct, to 4pm Nov-Feb; ▣) This is a pioneer village of 17 historic buildings. There are collections of farm implements, ranching tools and what could be the world's largest plastic replica of a mule team.

Waterbrook Wine   WINE
(☑ 509-522-1262; www.waterbrook.com; 10518 W US 12; tastings $5-10; ⊙ 11am-5pm Sun-Thu, to 6pm Fri & Sat Oct-Apr, 11am-7pm May-Sep) About 10 miles west of town, this large winery has a pond-side patio that's a great place to imbibe a long selection of wines on a sunny day. Food served Thursday to Sunday.

Amavi Cellars   WINE
(☑ 509-525-3541; www.amavicellars.com; 3796 Peppers Bridge Rd; ⊙ 10am-4pm) South of Walla Walla, amid a scenic spread of grape and apple orchards, you can sample some of the most talked about wines in the valley (try the Syrah and Cabernet Sauvignon). The classy yet comfortable patio has views of the Blue Mountains.

🛏 Sleeping & Eating

Walla Walla Garden Motel   MOTEL $
(☑ 509-529-1220; www.wallawallagardenmotel. com; 2279 Isaacs Ave; r from $72; ▣ 🕸) A simple family-run motel halfway to the airport, the Garden Motel (formerly the Colonial) is welcoming and bike friendly, with safe bike storage and plenty of local maps.

Marcus Whitman Hotel   HOTEL $$
(☑ 509-525-2200; www.marcuswhitmanhotel.com; 6 W Rose St; r from $149; ▣🕸🛜🍽) Walla Walla's best-known landmark is also the town's only tall building, impossible to miss with its distinctive rooftop turret. In keeping with the settlement's well-preserved image, the red-brick 1928 beauty has been elegantly renovated and decorated, with ample rooms in rusts and browns, embellished with Italian-crafted furniture, huge beds and great views over the nearby Blue Mountains. Its restaurant, the **Marc** (mains $15-40; ⊙ from 5:30pm), is one of the town's fanciest eating joints.

Graze   CAFE $
(☑ 509-522-9991; 5 S Colville St; sandwiches $8-12; ⊙ 10am-7:30pm Mon-Sat, to 3:30pm Sun; ☑) Amazing sandwiches are packed for your picnic or (if you can get a table) eaten in at this simple cafe. Try the turkey and pear panini with provolone and blue cheese or the flank-steak torta with pickled jalapeños, avocado, tomato, cilantro and chipotle dressing. There are plenty of vegetarian options.

**Saffron Mediterranean
Kitchen**   MEDITERRANEAN $$$
(☑ 509-525-2112; www.saffronmediterraneankitch en.com; 125 W Alder St; mains $26-42; ⊙ 2-10pm Tue-Sat, to 9pm Sun May-Oct, 2-9pm Tue-Sun Nov-Apr) This place isn't about cooking, it's about alchemy: Saffron takes seasonal, local ingredients and turns them into pure gold. The Med-inspired menu lists dishes such as bison rib eye and nettle pappardelle with duck ragù. Then there are the intelligently paired wines – and beers. Reserve.

ℹ️ Getting There & Away

Alaska Airlines has two daily flights to Seattle-Tacoma International Airport from the **Walla Walla Regional Airport** (www.wallawallaairport.com), northeast of town off US 12.

Greyhound buses run once daily to Seattle ($47, seven hours) via Pasco, Yakima and Ellensburg; change buses in Pasco for Spokane.

OREGON

It's hard to slap a single characterization onto Oregon's geography and people. Its landscape ranges from rugged coastline and thick evergreen forests to barren, fossil-strewn deserts, volcanoes and glaciers. As for its denizens, you name it – Oregonians run the gamut from pro-logging conservatives to tree-hugging liberals. What they have in common is an independent spirit, a love of the outdoors and a fierce devotion to where they live.

It doesn't usually take long for visitors to feel a similar devotion. Who wouldn't fall in love with the spectacle of glittering Crater Lake, the breathtaking colors of the Painted Hills in John Day or the hiking trails through deep forests and over stunning mountain passes? And then there are the towns: you can eat like royalty in funky Portland, see top-notch dramatic productions in Ashland or sample an astounding number of brewpubs in Bend.

OREGON FACTS

Nickname Beaver State

Population 4,028,977

Area 98,466 sq miles

Capital city Salem (population 160,614)

Other cities Portland (population 632,309), Eugene (population 160,561), Bend (population 87,014)

Sales tax Oregon has no sales tax

Birthplace of Former US president Herbert Hoover (1874–1964), actor and dancer Ginger Rogers (1911–95), writer Ken Kesey (1935–2001), filmmaker Gus Van Sant (b 1952), *The Simpsons* creator Matt Groening (b 1954)

Home of Oregon Shakespeare Festival, Nike, Crater Lake

Politics Democrat governors since 1987

Famous for Forests, rain, microbrews, coffee, Death with Dignity Act

State beverage Milk (dairy's big here)

Driving You can't pump your own gas in Oregon; Portland to Eugene, 110 miles; Portland to Astoria, 96 miles

Portland

Oregon's largest city used to seem like a well-kept secret: it had all the cultural advantages of a major city but the feel and affordability of a small town. But little old Stumptown is growing up, in many ways.

Most of the changes happening in Portland are for the better. Sure, parking might be a little harder, and grubby dive bars are now pretty scarce, but on the other hand, there's a coffee roastery and a craft brewery on just about every block. And the food carts – more and better than ever.

Portland has an almost unfair abundance of natural beauty – perfect parks, leafy trees, vibrantly flowering shrubs lining pretty residential streets, the Willamette River meandering through town, and Mt Hood on the horizon. And the open-minded, appealingly off-kilter vibe of the place – that whole 'Keep Portland Weird' thing – certainly hasn't changed. These days, there's just more to love.

👁️ Sights

👁️ Downtown

⭐ **Tom McCall Waterfront Park**   PARK
(Map p1064; Naito Parkway) This popular riverside park, which lines the west bank of the Willamette River, was finished in 1978 after four years of construction. It replaced an old freeway with 1.5 miles of paved sidewalks and grassy spaces, and attracts heaps of joggers, in-line skaters, strollers and cyclists. During summer the park is perfect for hosting large outdoor events such as the Oregon Brewers Festival (p1068). Walk over the Steel and Hawthorne bridges to the **Eastbank Esplanade**, making a 2.6-mile loop.

⭐ **Pioneer**
Courthouse Square   LANDMARK
(Map p1064; www.thesquarepdx.org; 🚇 Red, Blue, Green) The heart of downtown Portland, this brick plaza is nicknamed 'Portland's living room' and is the most-visited public

Portland

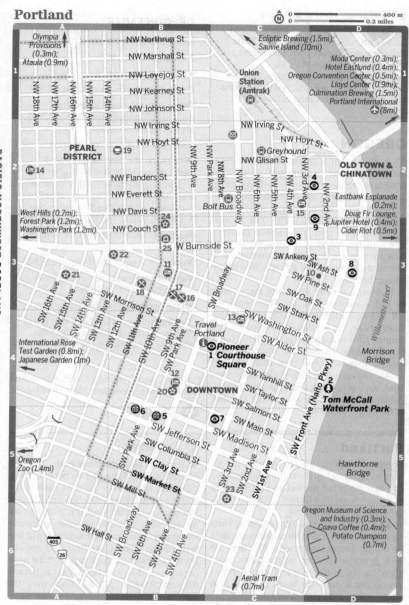

space in the city. When it isn't full of Hacky Sack players, sunbathers or office workers lunching, the square hosts concerts, festivals, rallies, farmers markets, and even summer Friday-night movies (aka 'Flicks on the Bricks').

Portland Building LANDMARK

(Map p1064; cnr SW 5th Ave & SW Main St) This controversial 15-story building (1982) was designed by Michael Graves and catapulted the postmodern architect to celebrity status. But the blocky, pastel-colored edifice has

Portland

◎ Top Sights
- 1 Pioneer Courthouse Square C4
- 2 Tom McCall Waterfront Park D4

◎ Sights
- 3 Chinatown Gates C3
- 4 Lan Su Chinese Garden D2
- 5 Oregon Historical Society B5
- 6 Portland Art Museum B5
- 7 Portland Building C5
- 8 Saturday Market D3
- 9 Shanghai Tunnels D3

◎ Activities, Courses & Tours
- 10 Pedal Bike Tours D3

◎ Sleeping
- 11 Ace Hotel B3
- 12 Heathman Hotel B4
- 13 Hotel Monaco C4
- 14 Northwest Portland Hostel A2

- 15 Society Hotel C2

◎ Eating
- 16 Bing Mi! B3
  - Clyde Common .... (see 11)
- 17 Nong's Khao Man Gai B3
- 18 Tasty n Alder B3

◎ Drinking & Nightlife
- 19 Barista B2

◎ Entertainment
- 20 Arlene Schnitzer Concert Hall B4
- 21 Artists Repertory Theatre A3
- 22 Crystal Ballroom B3
- 23 Keller Auditorium C5
- 24 Portland Center Stage B3

◎ Shopping
- 25 Powell's City of Books B3

never been popular with the people who work inside it, and in recent years the city has found structural problems that mean the building will need massive reconstruction in order to stay standing. At least it's been made somewhat green: an eco-roof was installed in 2006.

Oregon Historical Society MUSEUM
(Map p1064; ☑503-222-1741; www.ohs.org; 1200 SW Park Ave; adult/child $11/5; ☉10am-5pm Mon-Sat, noon-5pm Sun; ☒Red, Blue) Along the tree-shaded **South Park Blocks** sits the state's primary history museum, which dedicates most of its space to the story of Oregon and the pioneers who featured in it. There are interesting sections on various immigrant groups, Native American tribes and the travails of the Oregon Trail. Temporary exhibits furnish the downstairs space.

Portland Art Museum MUSEUM
(Map p1064; ☑503-226-2811; www.portlandartmuseum.org; 1219 SW Park Ave; adult/child $19.99/free; ☉10am-5pm Tue-Sun, to 8pm Thu & Fri; ☒6, 38, 45, 55, 58, 68, 92, 96, ☒NS Line, A-Loop) Alongside the South Park Blocks, the art museum's excellent exhibits include Native American carvings, Asian and American art, photography and English silver. The museum also houses the Whitsell Auditorium, a first-rate theater that frequently screens rare or international films and that is part of the Northwest Film Center and school.

◎ Old Town & Chinatown

The core of rambunctious 1890s Portland, once-seedy Old Town had a reputation as the lurking ground of unsavory characters. Now it's home to some lovely historic buildings, plus Waterfront Park, Saturday Market and a few good pockets of nightlife.

Old Town is generally lumped together with the city's historic Chinatown – no longer the heart of the Chinese community (that's moved to outer Southeast) but still home to the ornate **Chinatown Gates** (Map p1064; cnr W Burnside St & NW 4th Ave; ☒20), tranquil **Lan Su Chinese Garden** (Map p1064; ☑503-228-8131; www.lansugarden.org; 239 NW Everett St; adult/child $10/7; ☉10am-7pm mid-Apr–mid-Oct, to 5pm mid-Oct–mid-Apr; ☒4, 8, 16, 35, 44, 77, ☒Blue, Red) and the so-called **Shanghai Tunnels** (Map p1064; ☑503-622-4798; www.shanghaitunnels.info; 120 NW 3rd Ave; adult/child $13/8; ☒12, 19, 20, ☒Blue, Red), some of which can be toured.

Saturday Market MARKET
(Map p1064; ☑503-222-6072; www.portlandsaturdaymarket.com; 2 SW Naito Parkway; ☉10am-5pm Sat, 11am-4:30pm Sun Mar-Dec; ☒; ☒12, 16, 19, 20, ☒Red, Blue) The best time to walk along the Portland Waterfront is on a weekend, when you can catch this famous market showcasing arts and crafts, street entertainers and food booths.

◉ The Pearl District & Northwest

When Portlanders talk about 'Northwest,' they're usually referring to the attractive neighborhood surrounding NW 21st and 23rd Aves, north of W Burnside St. The residential heart of late-19th-century Portland, this area later became the city's upper-crust commercial strip, but it's struggled a bit in recent years as the dining-and-shopping buzz has spread eastward. Still, it's a pleasant and scenic strolling neighborhood, anchored by vintage apartment buildings and one of the city's best art-house cinemas. Parking is tough but not impossible; you can also take the streetcar (or just walk) from downtown.

Just east of Northwest, the **Pearl District** is an old industrial precinct that has been transformed into Portland's swankiest neighborhood. Warehouses have been converted to fancy lofts commanding some of the highest real-estate prices in Oregon. It's a great place to walk around and check out upscale boutiques, trendy restaurants and art galleries.

◉ West Hills

Forest Park   PARK
(✆503-223-5449; www.forestparkconservancy. org) Abutting the more manicured Washington Park to the south (to which it is linked by various trails) is the far wilder 5100-acre Forest Park, a temperate rainforest that harbors plants and animals and hosts an avid hiking fraternity. The **Portland Audubon Society** (✆503-292-6855; www.audubonport land.org; 5151 NW Cornell Rd; ◷9am-5pm, nature store 10am-6pm Mon-Sat, to 5pm Sun; 🚌20) **FREE** maintains a bookstore, a wildlife-rehabilitation center and 4.5 miles of trails within its Forest Park sanctuary.

Washington Park   PARK
(www.washingtonparkpdx.org; 🚇; 🚊Blue, Red) Tame and well-tended Washington Park contains several key attractions within its 400 acres of greenery. The **International Rose Test Garden** (www.rosegardenstore. org; 400 SW Kingston Ave; ◷7:30am-9pm; 🚌63) **FREE** is the centerpiece of Portland's famous rose blooms; there are 400 types on show here, plus great city views. Further uphill is the **Japanese Garden** (✆503-223-1321; www. japanesegarden.com; 611 SW Kingston Ave; adult/child $14.95/10.45; ◷noon-7pm Mon, 10am-7pm

Tue-Sun mid-Mar–Sep, noon-4pm Mon, 10am-4pm Tue-Sun Oct–mid-Mar; 🚌63), another oasis of tranquility. If you have kids, the **Oregon Zoo** (✆503-226-1561; www.oregonzoo.org; 4001 SW Canyon Rd; adult/child $14.95/9.95; ◷9:30am-6pm Jun-Aug, reduced hours Sep-May; 🚇; 🚌63, 🚊Blue, Red) and **Portland Children's Museum** (✆503-233-6500; www.portlandcm.org; 4015 SW Canyon Rd; $10.75, 4-7pm 1st Fri of month free; ◷9am-5pm; 🚇; 🚌63, 🚊Red, Blue) should be on your docket.

◉ Northeast & Southeast

Across the Willamette River from downtown is the **Lloyd Center** (✆503-282-2511; www.lloydcenter.com; 2201 Lloyd Center; ◷10am-9pm Mon-Sat, 11am-6pm Sun; 🚊Red, Blue, Green), Oregon's largest shopping mall and where notorious ice-queen Tonya Harding first learned to skate. A few blocks to the southwest are the unmissable glass towers of the **Oregon Convention Center** (www.oregoncc. org; 777 NE Martin Luther King Jr Blvd; 🚊Red, Blue, Green, Yellow), and nearby is the **Moda Center** (✆503-235-8771; www.rosequarter.com/ venue/moda-center; 1 N Center Court St; 🚊Yellow), home of professional basketball team the Trailblazers.

Further up the Willamette, **N Mississippi Ave** used to be full of run-down buildings, but is now a hot spot of trendy shops and eateries. Northeast is artsy **NE Alberta St**, a long ribbon of art galleries, boutiques and cafes (don't miss the **Last Thursday** (www. lastthursdayonalberta.com) street-art event here, taking place the last Thursday of each month). **SE Hawthorne Blvd** (near SE39th Ave) is affluent hippy territory, with gift stores, cafes, coffeeshops and two branches of Powell's bookstores. One leafy mile to the south, **SE Division St** has become a foodie destination, with plenty of excellent restaurants, bars and pubs. The same is true of **E Burnside at NE 28th Ave**, though it has a more concentrated and upscale feel.

🏃 Activities

Hiking

Portland boasts the 5000-acre Forest Park within city limits, which will keep avid hikers busy for a while. There's also a network of trails in **Hoyt Arboretum** (✆503-865-8733; www.hoytarboretum.org; 4000 Fairview Blvd; ◷trails 5am-9:30pm, visitor center 9am-4pm Mon-Fri, 11am-3pm Sat & Sun; 🚊Washington Park) **FREE**, easily reached by light rail, and more

PORTLAND FOR CHILDREN

Washington Park has the most to offer families with young kids. Here you'll find the world-class Oregon Zoo, which is set in a beautiful natural environment parents will also enjoy. Next door is the Portland Children's Museum and **World Forestry Center** (☑ 503-228-1367; www.worldforestry.org; 4033 SW Canyon Rd; adult/child $7/5; ☉ 10am-5pm, closed Tue & Wed Labor Day-Memorial Day; ☑; ☑ 63, ☒ Blue, Red), both offering fun learning activities and exhibits.

On the other side of the **Willamette River**, the **Oregon Museum of Science and Industry** (OMSI; ☑ 503-797-4000; www.omsi.edu; 1945 SE Water Ave; adult/child $14/9.75; ☉ 9:30am-5:30pm Jun-Aug, closed Mon Sep-May; ☑; ☑ 9, 17, ☒ A Loop, B Loop, ☒ Orange) is a top-notch destination with a theater, planetarium and even a submarine to explore. And finally, further south is **Oaks Amusement Park** (☑ 503-233-5777; www.oakspark.com; 7805 SE Oaks Park Way; ride bracelets $15-31, individual rides $3.75, skating $6.60-7.50; ☉ hours vary; ☑; ☑ 35, 99), home to pint-size roller coasters, miniature golf and carnival games.

to explore at **Tryon Creek State Natural Area** (☑ 503-636-9886; www.oregonstateparks. org; 11321 SW Terwilliger Blvd).

If that's not enough, the hiking wonderlands of Mt Hood (p1076) and the Columbia River Gorge (p1075) are each less than an hour's drive away.

Cycling

Portland often tops lists of the USA's most bike-friendly cities.

Look for pleasant paths along the **Willamette River** downtown, or try the 21-mile **Springwater Corridor**, which heads out to the suburb of Boring.

Mountain bikers can head to **Leif Erikson Dr**, or for single-track and technical trails, **Hood River** and **Mt Hood** (both about an hour's drive away) have great options.

For scenic farm country, head to **Sauvie Island** (www.sauvieisland.org; Hwy 30; daily parking pass $10), 10 miles northwest of downtown Portland.

Snag a free *Portland by Bicycle* or $6 *Bike There!* map from a visitor center or a bike shop.

Everybody's Bike Rentals & Tours CYCLING
(☑ 503-358-0152; www.pdxbikerentals.com; 305 NE Wygant St; tours per person from $69, rentals per hour $8-15; ☉ 10am-3pm; ☑ 6) It's true that Portland is best seen by bicycle, and this company offers low-key, fun tours of the city and its surroundings – whether you're into food and farms or beer and parks. Bicycle rentals are also available.

Kayaking

Situated close to the confluence of the Columbia and Willamette Rivers, Portland has miles of navigable waterways.

Portland Kayak Company KAYAKING
(☑ 503-459-4050; www.portlandkayak.com; 6600 SW Macadam Ave; rental per hour from $14; ☉ 10am-5pm; ☑ 43) Kayaking rentals (minimum two hours), instruction and tours – notably a three-hour circumnavigation of Ross Island on the Willamette River ($49), available at 10am and 2pm daily and at sunset (starts 6pm) May through September.

☞ Tours

Pedal Bike Tours CYCLING
(Map p1064; ☑ 503-243-2453; www.pedal biketours.com; 133 SW 2nd Ave; tours $59-199; ☉ 10am-6pm; ☑ 12, 19, 20, ☒ Blue, Red) Offers all sorts of themes – history, food carts, beer – and even a Pot Tour through Portland ($69), where you spend three hours touring the city through the lens of the new retail pot industry. Learn about Oregon's history with hemp, visit dispensaries and head shops, and get the lowdown on what's legal in terms of buying and smoking. Vegan munchies available!

Portland Walking Tours WALKING
(☑ 503-774-4522; www.portlandwalkingtours.com; tours per person $20-79) Food, chocolate, underground and even ghost-hunting tours are available daily. A new tour of 'makers and their spaces' offers a glimpse behind the scenes of Portland's indie-creative side, from crafts and woodworking to leather goods and a brewery. Each tour meets at a different location; reservations recommended.

✵✵ Festivals & Events

Portland Rose Festival CULTURAL
(www.rosefestival.org; ☉ late May–mid-Jun) Rose-covered floats, dragon-boat races,

a riverfront carnival, fireworks, roaming packs of sailors and the crowning of a Rose Queen all make this Portland's biggest celebration. The evening Starlight Parade and the Grand Floral Parade (mid-June) are the highlights.

Oregon Brewers Festival   BEER
(www.oregonbrewfest.com; Tom McCall Waterfront Park; admission free, tasting glass $7, per taste $1; ☉late Jul) In the last full weekend in July you can quaff microbrews from near and far in Waterfront Park – everyone's happy and even nondrinkers have fun. There are also food stalls and other beer-focused vendors in the park.

Bite of Oregon   FOOD & DRINK
(www.biteoforegon.com; tickets $6; ☉early Sep) Bite of Oregon features all the food (and beer) you could think of consuming, much of it from great local restaurants – and some of it from Portland's famous food carts. You'll find good microbrews too. The festival benefits Special Olympics Oregon. Dates and location vary by year; check online.

🛏 Sleeping

Tariffs listed are for the summer season, when reservations are a good idea. Prices at top-end hotels are highly variable depending on occupancy and day of the week.

Hawthorne Portland Hostel   HOSTEL $
(☑503-236-3380; www.portlandhostel.org; 3031 SE Hawthorne Blvd; dm $34-37, d with shared bath $74; ✳@🛜; ☐14) ☞ This ecofriendly hostel has a great Hawthorne location. The two private rooms are good and the dorms are spacious. There are summertime open-mike nights in the grassy backyard, and bicycle rentals (and a fix-it station) are available. The hostel composts and recycles, harvests rainwater for toilets, and has a nice eco-roof. Discounts are offered to those who are bicycle touring.

Northwest Portland Hostel   HOSTEL $
(Map p1064; ☑503-241-2783; www.nwportland hostel.com; 425 NW 18th Ave; dm $34-40, d with shared bath from $89; ✳@🛜; ☐77) Perfectly located between the Pearl District and NW 21st and 23rd Aves, this friendly and clean hostel takes up four old buildings and features plenty of common areas (including a small deck) and discounted bicycle rentals. Dorms are spacious and private rooms can be as nice as those in hotels, though all share

outside bathrooms. Non-HI members pay $3 extra.

★**Kennedy School**   HOTEL $$
(☑503-249-3983; www.mcmenamins.com/ken nedyschool; 5736 NE 33rd Ave; d from $155; 🛜; ☐70) This former elementary school is now home to a hotel (sleep in old classrooms!), a restaurant with a great garden courtyard, several bars, a microbrewery and a movie theater. Guests can use the soaking pool for free. The whole school is decorated in the McMenamins' distinctive art style – mosaics, fantasy paintings and historical photographs.

★**Ace Hotel**   BOUTIQUE HOTEL $$
(Map p1064; ☑503-228-2277; www.acehotel. com; 1022 SW Stark St; d with shared/private bath from $175/245; P⏻✳@🛜🐾; ☐20) A well-established brand, the Ace fuses industrial, minimalist and retro styles to great effect. From the photo booth in its lobby to the recycled fabrics and salvaged-wood furniture in its rooms, the hotel feels very chic and very Portland. There's a Stumptown coffee shop and underground bar on-site and **Clyde Common bistro** (Map p1064; ☑503-228-3333; www.clydecommon.com; 1014 SW Stark St; mains $9-29; ☉11:30am-midnight Mon-Fri, 3pm-midnight Sat, 3-11pm Sun) adjoins the lobby. The location can't be beat.

★**Society Hotel**   HOTEL $$
(Map p1064; ☑503-445-0444; www.thesocietyho tel.com; 203 NW 3rd Ave; bunks $55, d from $129; 🛜; ☐4, 8, 16, 35, 44, 77, 🚈Red, Blue, Green) A newcomer and the only place to stay in Old Town-Chinatown, this pretty hotel in the historic 1881 Mariners Building – originally a lodging house for sailors – has impeccable fashion sense. Options include dorms as well as private rooms. There's a lively bar and rooftop deck. Some corner rooms have huge windows designed to catch sunlight.

Jupiter Hotel   MOTEL $$
(☑503-230-9200; www.jupiterhotel.com; 800 E Burnside St; d from $143; ✳🛜🐾; ☐20) This slick motel is within walking distance of downtown and attached to the Doug Fir (p1071), a top-notch live-music venue. Standard rooms are tiny – go for the Metro rooms instead – and ask for a pad away from the bar patio if you're not into staying up late. Bicycle rentals are available; walk-ins after midnight get a discount if there are vacancies.

Caravan BOUTIQUE HOTEL **$$**

(📞503-288-5225; www.tinyhousehotel.com; 5009 NE 11th Ave; r $165-175; 📶; 🅿72) The tiny-house trend is, ironically, huge these days. Get a taste of what it's like to live in one of these adorable minuscule dwellings (84 to 170 sq ft – smaller than most hotel rooms – complete with kitchen and bathroom) at this hotel in the artsy Alberta neighborhood. Free s'mores nightly and live music some nights. Book way ahead in summer.

Heathman Hotel HOTEL **$$$**

(Map p1064; 📞503-241-4100; www.heathman hotel.com; 1001 SW Broadway; d from $265; 🅿✳@📶📶; 🅿15, 17, 35, 51) A Portland institution, the Heathman has top-notch services and a newly reopened seafood restaurant run by beloved chef Vitaly Paley. Rooms are elegant, stylish and luxurious, and the location is central. It hosts high tea in the afternoons, plays jazz Wednesday to Saturday evenings and has a library stocked with 2700 signed books by authors who have stayed here.

Hotel Eastlund HOTEL **$$$**

(📞503-235-2100; www.hoteleastlund.com; 1021 NE Grand Ave; r from $249; 🅿📶📶; 🅿6) This shiny new hotel in the Lloyd District replaced what was the Red Lion. From the lobby on up, it's all ultra-modern furniture, huge art, bright colors and open spaces. Rooms have one king or two queen beds; suites are not huge but include kitchenettes and floor-to-ceiling windows. The restaurant upstairs, Altabira (📞503-963-3600; www.altabira.com; 1021 NE Grand Ave; mains $17-28; ⏰11:30am-11pm), has a long beer list and a great patio.

🍴 Eating

Portland has become nationally recognized for its food scene, with dozens of young, top-notch chefs pushing the boundaries of ethnic and regional cuisines and making the most of locally sourced, sustainably raised ingredients.

Nong's Khao Man Gai FOOD TRUCK **$**

(Map p1064; 📞971-255-3480; www.khaomangai. com; cnr SW 10th Ave & SW Alder St; mains from $9; ⏰10am-4pm Mon-Sat; 🅿NS Line, A Loop, 🅿Red, Blue) This widely adored food cart dishes out tender poached chicken with rice in a magical sauce. That's it – and that's plenty. There are bricks-and-mortar locations at 411 SW College St and 609 SE Ankeny St, both of which have a more extensive menu.

Bing Mi! FOOD TRUCK **$**

(Map p1064; www.bingmiportland.com; cnr SW 9th Ave & SW Alder St; crepes $6; ⏰7:30am-3pm Mon-Fri, 11am-4pm Sat; 🅿Red, Blue) This downtown food cart – a critics' fave – serves savory *jian bing* (grilled crepes from Northern China, stuffed with scrambled egg, pickled vegetables, fried crackers, black-bean paste and chili sauce). That's all you get, and that's all you'll need.

⭐ Stammtisch GERMAN **$$**

(📞503-206-7983; www.stammtischpdx.com; 401 NE 28th Ave; small plates $4-9, mains $12-23; ⏰3pm-1:30am Mon-Fri, 11am-1:30am Sat & Sun; 🦽; 🅿19) Dig into serious German food – with a beer list to match – at this dark and cozy neighborhood pub. Don't miss the *Maultaschen* (a gorgeous pasta pocket filled with leek fondue in a bright, lemony wine sauce), the mussels in nettle broth, or the paprika-spiced roast chicken.

PACIFIC NORTHWEST PORTLAND

PORTLAND'S FOOD CARTS

Some of Portland's most amazing food comes from humble little kitchens-on-wheels. Found all over town clumped together in parking lots or otherwise unoccupied spaces, food carts offer hungry wanderers a chance to try unusual dishes at low prices, and they often have covered seating areas if you don't like to walk while you eat. A few to try:

Holy Mole (https://www.facebook.com/holymolepdx)

Nong's Khao Man Gai

Potato Champion (📞503-683-3797; www.potatochampion.tumblr.com; 1207 SE Hawthorne Blvd; mains $3-11; ⏰11am-1am Tue-Thu & Sun, to 3am Fri & Sat; 🚹)

Bing Mi!

Viking Soul Food (📞971-506-5579; www.vikingsoulfood.com; 4255 SE Belmont St; mains $3-10; ⏰noon-8pm Sun-Thu, to 9pm Fri & Sat; 🅿15)

Ken's Artisan Pizza
PIZZA **$$**

(☑ 503-517-9951; www.kensartisan.com; 304 SE 28th Ave; pizzas $13-18; ⊘ 5-9:30pm Mon-Thu, 5-10pm Fri, 4-10pm Sat, 4-9pm Sun; 🚇 20) Glorious wood-fired, thin-crust pizzas with toppings such as prosciutto, fennel sausage and green garlic. Super-cool atmosphere, with huge sliding windows that open to the street on warm nights. Expect a long wait – no reservations taken.

Olympia Provisions
FRENCH **$$**

(☑ 503-894-8136; www.olympiaprovisions.com; 1632 NW Thurman St; charcuterie $14-18, sandwiches $11-15, mains $22-35; ⊘ 11am-10pm Mon-Fri, 9am-10pm Sat & Sun; 🚇 16) French-inspired rotisserie bistro serving up charcuterie and cheese boards, gourmet sandwiches, salads and deli items, and main plates such as rotisserie chicken and steamed clams. It also does delicious eggs Benedict for brunch. There's another branch at 107 SE Washington St.

Paadee
THAI **$$**

(☑ 503-360-1453; www.paadeepdx.com; 6 SE 28th Ave; mains $12-19; ⊘ 11:30am-3pm & 5-10pm; 🚇 20) Located on a strip of 28th Ave dubbed 'Restaurant Row' is this beautiful dining room with birdcages as lampshades, inspired by the owner's childhood in Thailand. Bright, fresh flavors come alive in plates such as the steak salad or *gra prao muu grob* (crispy pork belly with basil and chili). Tasty cocktails are available, too.

People's Pig
BARBECUE **$$**

(☑ 503-282-2800; www.peoplespig.com; 3217 N Williams Ave; sandwiches $10-12, mains $14-25; ⊘ 11am-9pm Sun-Thu, to 10pm Fri & Sat; 🚇 4, 24, 44) The smoked fried-chicken sandwich at the People's Pig, with jalapeño jelly and spicy mayo, occupies the top position on many Portlanders' lists of favorite sandwiches. It comes with one side: get the collard greens. You can also have it as a plate, with extra sides – or opt for the pork shoulder, ribs, lamb or brisket. It's all good.

Tasty n Sons
AMERICAN **$$**

(☑ 503-621-1400; www.tastynsons.com; 3808 N Williams Ave; small plates $2-13, mains $12-30; ⊘ 9am-2:30pm & 5-10pm Sun-Thu, to 11pm Fri & Sat; 🚇 44) Superb small plates in a high-ceilinged, industrial-feel dining room along a suddenly wildly hip stretch of Portland's bicycle-commuter highway. Share delicacies such as bacon-wrapped dates, grilled quail with couscous or lamb souvlaki – don't skip the Burmese stew if it's available. A wait is guaranteed at brunch. Compare and contrast with its sibling, **Tasty n Alder** (Map p1064; ☑ 503-621-9251; www.tastynalder.com; 580 SW 12th Ave; mains $16-27; ⊘ 9am-2pm & 5:30-10pm Sun-Thu, to 11pm Fri & Sat; 🚇 15, 51).

★ Ava Gene's
ITALIAN **$$$**

(☑ 971-229-0571; www.avagenes.com; 3377 SE Division St; mains $20-36; ⊘ 5-10pm Mon-Thu, 5-11pm Fri, 4:30-11pm Sat, 4:30-10pm Sun; 🚇 4) This renowned trattoria-inspired eatery – owned by Duane Sorenson, who founded Stumptown Coffee – serves rustic Italian cuisine, with exquisite pasta and vegetable dishes as highlights. Exceptional ingredients, a great wine list and cocktails, and outstanding service make it a swoon-worthy dining experience worth seeking out. Reserve.

★ Ned Ludd
AMERICAN **$$$**

(☑ 503-288-6900; www.nedluddpdx.com; 3925 NE Martin Luther King Jr Blvd; small plates $4-15, mains $25-32; ⊘ 5-10pm; 🚇 6) 🖋 Quintessentially Portland, this offbeat, upscale joint exudes thick artisan vibes, from its rustic-peasant decor to the prominent brick wood-fired oven where all dishes are cooked. The beautifully presented small plates are rotated daily. This is not a place to simply fill your tummy but one in which to sample eclectic 'American craft' delicacies.

★ Ox
STEAK **$$$**

(☑ 503-284-3366; www.oxpdx.com; 2225 NE Martin Luther King Jr Blvd; mains $13-52; ⊘ 5-10pm Sun-Thu, to 11pm Fri & Sat; 🚇 6) One of Portland's most popular restaurants is this upscale, Argentine-inspired steakhouse. Start with the smoked bone-marrow clam chowder, then go for the gusto: the grass-fed beef rib eye. If there's two of you, the *asado* (barbecue grill; $80) is a good choice, allowing you to try several different cuts. Reserve.

Ataula
SPANISH **$$$**

(☑ 503-894-8904; www.ataulapdx.com; 1818 NW 23rd Pl; tapas $8-17, paella dishes $34-40; ⊘ 4:30-10pm Tue-Sat; 🚇 15, 77) This critically acclaimed Spanish tapas restaurant offers outstanding cuisine. If these are on the menu, try the *nuestras bravas* (sliced, fried potatoes in milk aioli), *croquetas* (salt-cod fritters), *xupa-xup* (chorizo lollipop) and *ataula montadito* (salmon with mascarpone yogurt and black-truffle honey). Great cocktails, too. Be sure to reserve.

🍷 Drinking & Nightlife

Drinking, whether it's coffee or a craft brew, cider or kombucha, is practically a sport in Portland. In winter it's a reason to hunker down and escape the rain; in summer, an excuse to sit on a patio or deck and soak up the long-awaited sunshine. Whatever you like to drink, there's bound to be a hand-crafted, artisan version of it here.

★ **Barista**   COFFEE
(Map p1064; ☑503-274-1211; www.baristapdx. com; 539 NW 13th Ave; ⊙6am-6pm Mon-Fri, 7am-6pm Sat & Sun; ☐4, 6, 10, 14, 15, 30, 51) One of Portland's best coffee shops, this tiny, stylish shop is owned by award-winning barista Billy Wilson. Beans are sourced from specialty roasters. Three other locations in town.

Coava Coffee   COFFEE
(☑503-894-8134; www.coavacoffee.com; 1300 SE Grand Ave; ⊙6am-6pm Mon-Fri, 7am-6pm Sat & Sun; 🎧; ☐6, 15, ☐B Loop) The decor takes the concept of 'neo-industrial' to extremes, but it works – and Coava delivers where it matters. The pour-over makes for a fantastic cup of java, and the espressos are exceptional, too. Also at 2631 SE Hawthorne Blvd.

Stumptown Coffee Roasters   COFFEE
(☑503-230-7702; www.stumptowncoffee.com; 4525 SE Division St; ⊙6am-7pm Mon-Fri, 7am-7pm Sat & Sun; 🎧; ☐4) Stumptown was the first micro-roaster to put Portland on the coffee map and this small, narrow space is where it all started.

Breakside Brewery   BREWERY
(☑503-719-6475; www.breakside.com; 820 NE Dekum St; ⊙11:30am-10pm Sun-Thu, to 11pm Fri & Sat; ☐8) Over 20 taps of some of the most experimental, tasty beer you'll ever drink, laced with fruits, vegetables and spices (try the hoppy Breakside IPA). Past beers have included a Meyer lemon kölsch, a mango IPA and a beet beer with ginger. For dessert, pray they have the salted-caramel stout. Good food and nice outdoor seating, too.

Culmination Brewing   MICROBREWERY
(www.culminationbrewing.com; 2117 NE Oregon St; plates $5-13; ⊙noon-9pm Sun-Thu, to 10pm Fri & Sat; ☐12) At this comfortable tasting room in a refurbished old warehouse, you'll find some of the city's best beers (including the top-notch Phaedrus IPA plus a whole array of limited-edition seasonals) and a brief but unusually ambitious food menu. If the *pêche*

is available, try it, even if you don't normally like 'fruit' beers.

Ecliptic Brewing   BREWERY
(☑503-265-8002; www.eclipticbrewing.com; 825 N Cook St; ⊙11am-10pm Sun-Thu, to 11pm Fri & Sat; ☐4) It's in kind of a chilly industrial space, but the beer speaks for itself – Ecliptic was founded by John Harris, who previously brewed for McMenamins, Deschutes and Full Sail. The brewery's astronomically named creations (such as the Craft Beer medal-winning Spica Pilsner) are ambitious and wildly successful. Food includes a roast-lamb sandwich, razor clams and sauteed kale.

Cider Riot   BREWERY
(www.ciderriot.com; 807 NE Couch St; ⊙4-11pm Mon & Wed-Fri, noon-11pm Sat & Sun; ☐12, 19, 20) Portland's best cider company now has its very own pub and tasting room, so you can sample Everybody Pogo, Never Give an Inch or Plastic Paddy at the source of the goodness. Ciders here are dry and complex, made with regional apples and hyper-regional attitude.

Hopworks Urban Brewery   BREWERY
(HUB; ☑503-232-4677; www.hopworksbeer.com; 2944 SE Powell Blvd; ⊙11am-11pm Sun-Thu, to midnight Fri & Sat; 👶; ☐9) 🍴 All-organic beers made with local ingredients, served in an ecofriendly building with bicycle frames above the bar. Try the IPA or the Survival Stout, made with Stumptown coffee. There's a good selection of food and a family-friendly atmosphere, and the back deck can't be beat on a warm day. There's another branch at 3947 N Williams Ave.

☆ Entertainment

For current guides to what's on around town, check the two local weekly papers and their websites: *Willamette Week* (www. wweek.com), which comes out on Wednesday, and the *Portland Mercury* (www.port landmercury.com), out on Thursday.

Live Music

Doug Fir Lounge   LIVE MUSIC
(☑503-231-9663; www.dougfirlounge.com; 830 E Burnside St; ☐20) Combining futuristic elements with a rustic log-cabin aesthetic, this venue has helped transform the LoBu (lower Burnside) neighborhood from seedy to slick. Doug Fir books great bands and the sound quality is usually tops. Crowds range from tattooed youth to suburban yuppies. Its

PACIFIC NORTHWEST PORTLAND

DON'T MISS

POWELL'S

One of the USA's largest independent bookstores, **Powell's City of Books** (Map p1064; ☎800-878-7323; www.powells.com; 1005 W Burnside St; ⏰9am-11pm; 🚌20) has a whole city block of new and used titles and a well-attended series of readings. There's another branch at 3723 SE Hawthorne Blvd (with a Home and Garden bookstore next door), and one at the airport.

upstairs restaurant has long hours. Find it next door to the after-party-friendly Jupiter Hotel (p1068).

Crystal Ballroom LIVE MUSIC
(Map p1064; ☎503-225-0047; www.mcmenamins.com; 1332 W Burnside St; 🚌20) This large, historic ballroom has hosted some major acts, including James Brown and Marvin Gaye in the early '60s. The bouncy, 'floating' dance floor makes dancing almost effortless.

Mississippi Studios LIVE MUSIC
(☎503-288-3895; www.mississippistudios.com; 3939 N Mississippi Ave; 🚌4) This intimate bar is good for checking out budding acoustic talent along with more established musical acts. Excellent sound system, and good restaurant-bar with patio (and awesome burgers) next door. Located right on busy N Mississippi Ave.

Performing Arts

Portland Center Stage THEATER
(Map p1064; ☎503-445-3700; www.pcs.org; 128 NW 11th Ave; tickets from $25; 🚌4, 8, 44, 77) The city's main theater company now performs in the Portland Armory – a renovated Pearl District landmark with state-of-the-art features.

Arlene Schnitzer Concert Hall CLASSICAL MUSIC
(Map p1064; ☎503-248-4335; www.portland5.com; 1037 SW Broadway; 🚌10, 14, 15, 35, 36, 44, 54, 56) This beautiful, if not acoustically brilliant, downtown venue, built in 1928, hosts a wide range of shows, lectures, concerts and other performances.

Artists Repertory Theatre THEATER
(Map p1064; ☎503-241-1278; www.artistsrep.org; 1515 SW Morrison St; tickets preview/regular $25/50; 🚌15, 51) Some of Portland's

best plays, including regional premieres, are performed in two intimate theaters here.

Keller Auditorium PERFORMING ARTS
(Map p1064; ☎503-248-4335; www.portland5.com; 222 SW Clay St; 🚌38, 45, 55, 92, 96) Built in 1917 and formerly known as the Civic Auditorium, Keller hosts a wide range of performers, from big-name musicians (Sturgill Simpson) to the Portland Opera and the Oregon Ballet Theatre, along with some Broadway productions.

Shopping

Portland's downtown shopping district extends in a two-block radius from Pioneer Courthouse Sq and hosts all of the usual suspects. The Pearl District is dotted with high-end galleries, boutiques and home decor shops. On weekends, you can visit the quintessential Saturday Market by the Skidmore Fountain. For a pleasant, upscale shopping street, head to NW 23rd Ave.

Eastside has lots of trendy shopping streets that also host restaurants and cafes. SE Hawthorne Blvd is the biggest, N Mississippi Ave is the newest and NE Alberta St is the most artsy and funkiest. Down south, Sellwood is known for its antique shops.

ℹ️ Information

EMERGENCY & MEDICAL SERVICES
Portland Police Bureau (☎503-823-0000; www.portlandoregon.gov/police; 1111 SW 2nd Ave) Police and emergency services.

Legacy Good Samaritan Medical Center (☎503-413-7711; www.legacyhealth.org; 1015 NW 22nd Ave) Convenient to downtown.

MEDIA
KBOO 90.7 FM (www.kboo.fm) Progressive local station run by volunteers; alternative news and views.

Portland Mercury (www.portlandmercury.com) Free **local sibling of Seattle's** The Stranger.

Willamette Week (www.wweek.com) Free weekly covering local news and culture.

POST
Post Office (Map p1064; ☎503-525-5398; www.usps.com; 715 NW Hoyt St; ⏰8am-6:30pm Mon-Fri, 8:30am-5pm Sat)

TOURIST INFORMATION
Travel Portland (Map p1064; ☎503-275-8355; www.travelportland.com; 701 SW 6th Ave; ⏰8:30am-5:30pm Mon-Fri, 10am-4pm Sat Nov-Apr, plus 10am-2pm Sun May-Oct; 🚋Red,

Blue, Green, Yellow) Super-friendly volunteers staff this office in Pioneer Courthouse Sq. There's a small theater with a 12-minute film about the city, and Tri-Met bus and light-rail offices inside.

Getting There & Away

AIR

Portland International Airport (PDX; ☑ 503-460-4234; www.flypdx.com; 7000 NE Airport Way; ☎; ☐ red) Award-winning Portland International Airport has daily flights all over the US, as well as to several international destinations. It's situated just east of I-5 on the banks of the Columbia River (20 minutes' drive from downtown).

BUS

Greyhound (Map p1064; ☑ 503-243-2361; www.greyhound.com; 550 NW 6th Ave; ☐ green, orange, yellow) Greyhound connects Portland with cities along I-5 and I-84. Destinations beyond Oregon include Chicago, Denver, San Francisco, Seattle and Vancouver, BC.

Bolt Bus (Map p1064; ☑ 877-265-8287; www.boltbus.com) Connects Portland with Seattle (from $25), Bellingham ($40), Eugene ($15) and Vancouver, BC ($50), among other cities. Buses leave from the corner of NW 8th Ave and NW Everett St.

TRAIN

Amtrak (☑ 800-872-7245; www.amtrak.com; 800 NW 6th Ave; ☐17, ☐ green, yellow) Amtrak serves Chicago, Oakland, Seattle and Vancouver, BC. Departures are from Union Station.

Getting Around

TO/FROM THE AIRPORT

Tri-Met's light-rail MAX red line takes about 40 minutes to get from downtown to the airport (adult/child $2.50/1.25). If you prefer a bus, **Blue Star** (☑ 503-249-1837; www.bluestarbus.com) offers shuttle services between PDX and several downtown stops.

Taxis charge around $35-40 (not including tip) from the airport to downtown.

BICYCLE

Clever Cycles (☑ 503-334-1560; www.clevercycles.com; 900 SE Hawthorne Blvd; rentals per day $30, cargo bikes $60; ☺11am-6pm Mon-Fri, to 5pm Sat & Sun; ☐10, 14) Rents folding, family and cargo bikes.

PUBLIC TRANSPORTATION

Portland has a good public-transportation system, which consists of local buses, streetcars and the MAX light rail. All are run by TriMet, which has an **information center** (☑ 503-238-7433, 503-725-9005; www.trimet.org; 701 SW 6th Ave; ☺8:30am-5:30pm Mon-Fri; ☐ blue, red, green, yellow) at Pioneer Courthouse Sq.

Tickets for the transportation systems are completely transferable within 2½ hours of the time of purchase. Buy tickets for local buses from fare machines as you enter; for streetcars, you can buy tickets at streetcar stations or on the streetcar itself. Tickets for the MAX must be bought from ticket machines at MAX stations (*before* you board); there is no conductor or ticket seller on board (but there *are* enforcers).

If you're a night owl, be aware that there are fewer services at night, and most stop running at 1am; check the website for details on a specific line.

CAR

Most major car-rental agencies have outlets both downtown and at Portland's airport. Many of these agencies have added hybrid vehicles to their fleets. **Car 2 Go** (www.car2go.com/en/portland; membership fee $5, rental per hour from $15) and **Zipcar** (www.zipcar.com; membership fee per month from $7, rental per hour $8-10) are two popular car-sharing options.

CHARTER SERVICE

For custom bus or van charters and tours, try **EcoShuttle** (☑ 503-548-4480; www.ecoshuttle.net). Its vehicles run on 100% biodiesel.

TAXI

Cabs are available 24 hours by phone. Downtown, you can sometimes flag them down, and some bartenders will call you a cab on request.

Broadway Cab (☑ 503-333-3333; www.broadwaycab.com)

Radio Cab (☑ 503-227-1212; www.radiocab.net)

Willamette Valley

The Willamette Valley, a fertile 60-mile wide agricultural basin, was the Holy Grail for Oregon Trail pioneers who headed west more than 170 years ago. Today it's the state's breadbasket, producing more than 100 kinds of crops – including renowned Pinot Noir grapes. Salem, Oregon's capital, is about an hour's drive from Portland at the northern end of the valley, and most of the other attractions in the area make easy day trips as well. Toward the south is Eugene, a dynamic college town worth a day or two of exploration.

Salem

Oregon's legislative center is renowned for its cherry trees, art-deco capitol building and Willamette University.

WORTH A TRIP

HOT SPRINGS

Wine isn't the only liquid indulgence to be had in the Willamette Valley – it's also known for its many natural hot springs. Three are easily accessible from Salem and Eugene.

Bagby Hot Springs (www.bagbyhotsprings.org; $5; ☉24hr) is a rustic hot spring with various wooden tubs in semi-private bathhouses. It's a couple of hours' drive east of Salem, accessible via a lovely 1.5-mile hiking trail.

Enjoy salubrious climes at **Breitenbush Hot Springs** (☑503-854-3320; www.breitenbush.com; 53000 Breitenbush Rd, Detroit; day use per person $18-32; ☉office 9am-4pm Mon-Sat), a fancy spa with massages, yoga and the like. Day-use activities include the hot springs and sauna, yoga and meditation, massage, hiking trails, and a library; you can also stay the night here. Reservations are required, including for day use.

About 40 miles east of Eugene, **Terwilliger Hot Springs** (Cougar Hot Springs; $6) is a beautiful cluster of terraced outdoor pools framed by large rocks. The springs are rustic but well maintained, with the hottest on top. From the parking lot, walk a quarter-mile to the springs. To get here, turn south onto Aufderheide Scenic Byway from Hwy 126 and drive 7.5 miles. Clothing is optional, no alcohol is allowed and it's day use only.

The University's **Hallie Ford Museum of Art** (☑503-370-6855; www.willamette.edu/arts/hfma; 700 State St; adult/child $6/free, Tue free; ☉10am-5pm Tue-Sat, 1-5pm Sun) showcases the state's best collection of Pacific Northwest art, including an impressive Native American gallery.

The **Oregon State Capitol** (☑503-986-1388; www.oregonlegislature.gov; 900 Court St NE; ☉8am-5pm Mon-Fri; **FREE**), built in 1938, looks like a background prop from a lavish Cecil B DeMille movie; free tours are offered. Rambling 19th-century **Bush House** (☑503-363-4714; www.salemart.org; 600 Mission St SE; adult/child $6/3; ☉park 10am-5pm Tue-Fri, noon-5pm Sat & Sun, tours 1-4pm Wed-Sun Mar-Dec) is an Italianate mansion now preserved as a museum with historical accents, including original wallpapers and marble fireplaces.

You can get oriented at the **Visitors Information Center** (☑503-581-4325; www.travelsalem.com; 181 High St NE; ☉9am-5pm Mon-Fri, 10am-4pm Sat). Salem is served daily by **Greyhound** (☑503-362-2428; www.greyhound.com; 500 13th St SE) buses and **Amtrak** (☑503-588-1551; www.amtrak.com; 500 13th St SE) trains.

Eugene

'Track Town' offers a great art scene, exceptionally fine restaurants, boisterous festivals, miles of riverside paths and several lovely parks. Its location at the confluence of the Willamette and McKenzie Rivers, just west of the Cascades, means there's plenty of outdoor recreation on offer – especially around the McKenzie River region, the Three Sisters Wilderness and Willamette Pass.

◉ Sights

Alton Baker Park   PARK
(100 Day Island Rd) This popular 400-acre riverside park, which provides access to the **Ruth Bascom Riverbank Trail System**, a 12-mile bikeway that flanks both sides of the Willamette, is heaven for cyclists and joggers. There's good downtown access via the DeFazio Bike Bridge.

University of Oregon   UNIVERSITY
(☑541-346-1000; www.uoregon.edu; 1585 E 13th Ave) Established in 1872, the University of Oregon is the state's foremost institution of higher learning, with a focus on the arts, sciences and law. The campus is filled with historic ivy-covered buildings and includes a **Pioneer Cemetery**, with tombstones that give a vivid insight into life and death in the early settlement. Campus tours are held in summer.

🛏 Sleeping

Prices can rise sharply during key football games (September to November) and at graduation (mid-June).

Eugene Whiteaker International Hostel   HOSTEL **$**
(☑541-343-3335; www.eugenehostel.org; 970 W 3rd Ave; dm from $35, r from $50; ☜@☎) This casual hostel in an old, rambling house has an artsy vibe, nice front and back patios to hang out on, and a free simple breakfast. Towels and bedding are included in the price.

C'est La Vie Inn

B&B $$

(☑541-302-3014; www.cestlavieinn.com; 1006 Taylor St; r from $160; ☻✻@⛱) This gorgeous Victorian house, run by a friendly French woman and her American husband, is a neighborhood showstopper. Beautiful antique furniture fills the living and dining areas, while the four tastefully appointed rooms (each named for a French artist) offer comfort and luxury. Hosts provide a full breakfast, as well as afternoon port and other nice touches.

Eating & Drinking

Kiva

HEALTH FOOD $

(☑541-342-8666; www.kivagrocery.com; 125 W 11th Ave; sandwiches $4-9; ⊙8am-8pm Mon-Fri, 9am-8pm Sat & Sun) An exceptional natural-food grocery store, Kiva stocks all-organic and mostly local produce. There are sandwiches and soups available too.

Papa's Soul Food Kitchen

SOUTHERN US $

(☑541-342-7500; www.papassoulfoodkitchen. com; 400 Blair Blvd; mains $9-14; ⊙noon-2pm & 5-10pm Tue-Fri, 2-10pm Sat) This popular Southern-food spot grills up awesome jerk chicken, pulled-pork sandwiches, crawfish jambalaya and fried okra. The best part is the live blues music that keeps the joint open late on Friday and Saturday nights. Nice back patio, too.

★ Beppe & Gianni's Trattoria

ITALIAN $$

(☑541-683-6661; www.beppeandgiannis.net; 1646 E 19th Ave; mains $15-26; ⊙5-9pm Sun-Thu, to 10pm Fri & Sat) One of Eugene's most beloved restaurants, Beppe & Gianni's serves up homemade pastas and excellent desserts. Expect a wait, especially on weekends.

Board

AMERICAN $$

(☑541-343-3023; www.boardrestaurant.com; 394 Blair Blvd; mains $10-19; ⊙4-11pm Tue, Thu & Sun, to 10pm Wed, to 1am Fri & Sat) The menu sounds fancy, but the atmosphere in this low-ceilinged neighborhood joint – the former home of Eugene's oldest and diviest bar, Tiny's Tavern – is comfy, soothing and completely unpretentious. Rough-hewn wood and copper accents give everything a warm glow; the cocktails don't hurt, either. The food is top notch. Try the burger (perfect), anything with lamb, or shrimp and grits.

Ninkasi Brewing Company

BREWERY

(☑541-344-2739; www.ninkasibrewing.com; 272 Van Buren St; ⊙noon-9pm Sun-Wed, to 10pm Thu-Sat) Head to this tasting room to sample some of Oregon's most distinctive and innovative microbrews at the source. There's a sweet patio with snacks available, and a rotating lineup of food carts. Brewery tours start at 4pm daily, plus 2pm Thursday to Monday and 12:30pm Saturday and Sunday.

ⓘ Information

Visitor Center (☑541-484-5307; www.eugene cascadescoast.org; 754 Olive St; ⊙8am-5pm Mon-Fri) This center is open weekdays. On weekends, stop by the visitor center at 3312 Gateway St in Springfield for information.

ⓘ Getting There & Around

Eugene Airport (☑541-682-5544; www. flyeug.com; 28801 Douglas Dr) is about 7 miles northwest of the center. **Greyhound** (☑541-344-6265; www.greyhound.com; 987 Pearl St) provides long-distance services to Salem, Corvallis, Portland, Medford, Grants Pass, Hood River, Newport and Bend.

Trains leave from the **Amtrak station** (☑541-687-1383; www.amtrak.com; 433 Willamette St) for Portland, Seattle, WA, and Vancouver, BC (among other places).

Local bus service is provided by **Lane Transit District** (☑541-687-5555; www.ltd.org). For bike rentals, head to **Paul's Bicycle Way of Life** (☑541-344-4105; www.bicycleway.com; 556 Charnelton St; rentals per day $24-48; ⊙9am-7pm Mon-Fri, 10am-5pm Sat & Sun).

Columbia River Gorge

The fourth-largest river in the US by volume, the mighty Columbia runs 1243 miles from Alberta, Canada, into the Pacific Ocean just west of Astoria. For the final 309 miles of its course, the heavily dammed waterway delineates the border between Washington and Oregon and cuts though the Cascade Mountains via the spectacular Columbia River Gorge. Sheltering numerous ecosystems, waterfalls and magnificent vistas, the land bordering the river is protected as a National Scenic Area and is a popular sporting nexus for windsurfers, cyclists, anglers and hikers.

Not far from Portland, **Multnomah Falls** is a huge tourist draw, while **Vista House** offers stupendous gorge views. And if you want to stretch your legs, the **Eagle Creek Trail** is the area's premier tromping ground – provided you don't get vertigo!

Hood River & Around

Famous for its surrounding fruit orchards and wineries, the small town of Hood River – 63 miles east of Portland on I-84 – is also a huge mecca for windsurfing and kiteboarding. Premier wineries have also taken hold in the region, providing good wine-tasting opportunities.

Sights & Activities

Mt Hood Railroad   RAIL
(☑ 800-872-4661; www.mthoodrr.com; 110 Railroad Ave; excursions adult/child from $35/30) Built in 1906, the railroad once transported fruit and lumber from the upper Hood River Valley to the main railhead in Hood River. The vintage trains now transport tourists beneath Mt Hood's snowy peak and past fragrant orchards. The line is about 21 miles long and ends in pretty Parkdale. See the website for schedules and fares. Reserve.

Cathedral Ridge Winery   WINE
(☑ 800-516-8710; www.cathedralridgewinery.com; 4200 Post Canyon Dr; tastings from $10; ☺ 11am-6pm) This attractive winery in pretty farm country at the edge of town has signature red blends and a slew of awards on display. In nice weather, sit outdoors and take in the awesome view of Mt Hood. Tours and tastings at various levels are available.

Hood River Waterplay   WATER SPORTS
(☑ 541-386-9463; www.hoodriverwaterplay.com; I-84 exit 64; 3hr windsurfing course $119, SUP lessons per hour from $48; ☺ May-Oct) Interested in windsurfing, kayaking, SUP, catamaran sailing and so on? Contact this company, with a location right on the water.

Discover Bicycles   CYCLING
(☑ 541-386-4820; www.discoverbicycles.com; 210 State St; rentals per day $30-80; ☺ 10am-6pm Mon-Sat, to 5pm Sun) This shop rents road, hybrid and mountain bikes and can give advice on area trails.

Sleeping & Eating

Hood River Hotel   HISTORIC HOTEL $$
(☑ 541-386-1900; www.hoodriverhotel.com; 102 Oak St; d from $91, ste from $169; ☻✳☎☺) Located right in the heart of downtown, this fine 1913 hotel offers comfortable, old-fashioned rooms with four-poster or sleigh beds, some with tiny bathrooms. The suites have the best amenities and views. Kitchen-

ettes are also available, and there's a restaurant and a sauna on the premises.

Columbia Gorge Hotel   HOTEL $$$
(☑ 800-345-1921; www.columbiagorgehotel.com; 4000 Westcliff Dr; r $149-329; ☻✳@☎☺) Hood River's most famous place to stay is this historic Spanish-style hotel, set high on a cliff above the Columbia. The atmosphere is classy and the grounds lovely, and there's a fine restaurant on the premises. Rooms have antique beds and furnishings. River-view rooms cost more but are worth it.

pFriem Tasting Room   GASTROPUB $
(☑ 541-321-0490; www.pfriembeer.com; 707 Portway Ave; mains $10-18; ☺ 11:30am-9pm) The highly regarded beers at this brewery are matched by a meat-heavy menu that is definitely not run-of-the-mill: think mussels and *frites*, beef tongue, pork terrine, and a stew made with braised lamb and duck confit. It's located near the waterfront along a stretch of industrial-chic new development.

Information

Chamber of Commerce (☑ 541-386-2000; www.hoodriver.org; 720 E Port Marina Dr; ☺ 9am-5pm Mon-Fri, 10am-4pm Sat & Sun Apr-Oct, 9am-5pm Mon-Fri Nov-Mar) Visitor information for Hood River and the surrounding area.

Getting There & Away

Greyhound (☑ 541-386-1212; www.greyhound.com; 110 Railroad Ave) Hood River is connected to Portland by daily Greyhound buses (three daily, one hour, from $15).

Oregon Cascades

The Oregon Cascades offer plenty of dramatic volcanoes that dominate the skyline for miles around. Mt Hood, overlooking the Columbia River Gorge, is the state's highest peak, and has year-round skiing plus a relatively straightforward summit ascent. Tracking south you'll pass Mt Jefferson and the Three Sisters before reaching Crater Lake, the ghost of erstwhile Mt Mazama that collapsed in on itself after blowing its top approximately 7000 years ago.

Mt Hood

The state's highest peak, 11,240ft Mt Hood pops into view over much of northern Oregon whenever there's a sunny day, exerting an almost magnetic tug on skiers, hikers and sightseers. In summer, wildflowers bloom on the mountainsides and hidden ponds shimmer in blue, making for some unforgettable hikes; in winter, downhill and cross-country skiing dominates people's minds and bodies.

Mt Hood is accessible year-round on Hwy 26 from Portland (56 miles), and from Hood River (44 miles) on Hwy 35. Together with the Columbia River Hwy, these routes comprise the Mt Hood Loop, a popular scenic drive. Government Camp, the center of business on the mountain, is at the pass over Mt Hood.

🏃 Activities

Skiing

Hood is rightly revered for its skiing. There are six ski areas on the mountain, including Timberline, which lures snow-lovers with the only year-round skiing in the US. Closer to Portland, **Mt Hood SkiBowl** (☑503-272-3206; www.skibowl.com; Hwy 26; lift tickets $51, night skiing $37) is no slacker either. It's the nation's largest night-ski area and popular with city slickers who ride up for an evening of powder play from the metro zone. The largest ski area on the mountain is **Mt Hood Meadows** (☑503-337-2222; www.skihood.com; lift tickets adult/child $89/44), where the best conditions usually prevail.

Hiking

The Mt Hood National Forest protects an astounding 1200 miles of trails. A Northwest Forest Pass ($5 per day) is required at most trailheads.

One popular trail loops 7 miles from near the village of Zigzag to beautiful **Ramona Falls**, which tumble down mossy columnar basalt. Another heads 1.5 miles up from US 26 to **Mirror Lake**, continues 0.5 miles around the lake, then tracks 2 miles beyond to a ridge.

The 41-mile **Timberline Trail** circumnavigates Mt Hood through scenic wilderness. Noteworthy portions include the hike to McNeil Point and the short climb to Bald Mountain. From Timberline Lodge, Zigzag Canyon Overlook is a 4.5-mile round-trip.

Climbing Mt Hood should be taken seriously, as deaths do occur, though dogs have made it to the summit and the climb can be done in a long day. Contact **Timberline Mountain Guides** (☑541-312-9242; www.timberlinemtguides.com; 2-day summit per person $645) for guided climbs.

🛏 Sleeping & Eating

Most area **campsites** (☑877-444-6777; www.recreation.gov; sites $16-39) have drinking water and vault toilets. Reserve on busy weekends, though some walk-in sites are usually set aside. For more information, contact a nearby ranger station.

Huckleberry Inn　　　　　　　INN $$
(☑503-272-3325; www.huckleberry-inn.com; 88611 E Government Camp Loop; r $90-150, 10-bed dm $160; ☺🛜) Simple and comfortably rustic rooms are available here, along with bunk rooms that sleep up to 10. It's in a great central location in Government Camp. The casual restaurant (which doubles as the hotel's reception) serves good breakfasts. Peak holiday rates are higher.

⭐**Timberline Lodge**　　　　LODGE $$$
(☑800-547-1406; www.timberlinelodge.com; 27500 Timberline Rd; bunk r $145-195, d from $255; ☺🛜🏊) As much a community treasure as a hotel, this gorgeous **historic lodge** (☑800-547-1406; www.timberlinelodge.com; 27500 Timberline Rd) offers a variety of rooms, from dorms that sleep up to 10 to deluxe fireplace rooms. There's a heated outdoor pool, and the **ski lifts** (☑503-272-3158; www.timberlinelodge.com; Government Camp; lift tickets adult/child $68/46) are close by. Enjoy awesome views of Mt Hood, nearby hiking trails, two bars and a good dining room. Rates vary widely.

Mt Hood Brewing Co　　　PUB FOOD $$
(☑503-272-3172; www.mthoodbrewing.com; 87304 E Government Camp Loop, Government Camp; mains $12-20; ☺11am-10pm) Government Camp's only brewery-restaurant offers a friendly, family-style atmosphere and pub fare including hand-tossed pizzas, sandwiches and short ribs.

**Rendezvous Grill
& Tap Room**　　　　　　AMERICAN $$
(☑503-622-6837; http://thevousgrill.com; 67149 E Hwy 26, Welches; mains $12-29; ☺11:30am-8pm Tue-Sun, to 9pm Fri & Sat) In a league of its own is this excellent restaurant with outstanding dishes such as wild salmon with caramelized shallots and artichoke hash or chargrilled pork chop with rhubarb chutney. Lunch means gourmet sandwiches, burgers and salads on the patio. Bonus: excellent cocktails.

ℹ Information

For maps, permits and information, contact regional ranger stations. If you're approaching from Hood River, visit the **Hood River Ranger Station** (☑541-352-6002; 6780 OR 35, Parkdale; ⊙8am-4:30pm Mon-Fri). The **Zigzag Ranger Station** (☑503-622-3191; 70220 E Hwy 26; ⊙7:45am-4:30pm Mon-Sat) is more handy for Portland arrivals. Mt Hood **Information Center** (☑503-272-3301; 88900 E Hwy 26; ⊙9am-5pm) is in Government Camp. The weather changes quickly here; carry chains in winter.

❶ Getting There & Away

From Portland, Mt Hood is one hour (56 miles) by car along Hwy 26. Alternatively, you can take the prettier and longer approach via Hwy 84 to Hood River, then Hwy 35 south (1¾ hours, 95 miles).

The **Central Oregon Breeze** (☑800-847-0157; www.cobreeze.com) shuttle between Bend and Portland stops briefly at Government Camp, 6 miles from the Timberline Lodge. **Sea to Summit** (☑503-286-9333; www.seatosummit.net; round-trip from $59) runs regular shuttles from Portland to the ski areas during the winter.

Sisters

Once a stagecoach stop and trade town for loggers and ranchers, today Sisters is a bustling tourist destination whose main street is lined with boutiques, art galleries and eateries housed in Western-facade buildings. Visitors come for the mountain scenery, spectacular hiking, fine cultural events and awesome climate – there's plenty of sun and little precipitation here.

At the southern end of Sisters, the **city park** (Creekside Campground; ☑541-323-5220; S Locust St; tent/RV sites $20/40; ⊙May-Oct) has camp sites, but no showers. For ultra comfort, bag a room in the luxurious **Five Pine Lodge** (☑866-974-5900; www.fivepinelodge.com; 1021 Desperado Trail; d from $159, cabins from $179; ☻❋@�413☷). Or there's **Blue Spruce** (☑888-328-9644; www.bluesprucebnb.com; 444 S Spruce St; d $149-189; ☻❋�413), a fine B&B with fireplaces and jettubs in each room.

For refined French food you might not expect out here, head to **Cottonwood Cafe** (☑541-549-2699; www.intimatecottagecuisine.com; 403 E Hood Ave; breakfast $9-13, lunch mains $9-13), while **Three Creeks Brewing** (☑541-549-1963; www.threecreeksbrewing.com; 721 Desperado Ct; mains $11-21, pizzas $11-26; ⊙11:30am-9pm Sun-Thu, to 10pm Fri & Sat) is the place for home brew and pub grub.

❶ Information

Chamber of Commerce (☑541-549-0251; www.sisterscountry.com; 291 E Main Ave; ⊙10am-4pm Mon-Sat)

❶ Getting There & Away

Valley Retriever (☑541-265-2253; www.kokkola-bus.com/VRBSchedule) Buses connect Sisters with Bend, Newport, Corvallis, Salem, McMinnville and Portland; the buses stop at the corner of Cascade and Spruce Sts.

Bend

Bend is where all lovers of the outdoors should live – it's an absolute paradise. You can ski fine powder in the morning, paddle a kayak in the afternoon and play golf into the evening. Or would you rather go mountain biking, hiking, mountaineering, stand-up paddleboarding, fly-fishing or rock climbing? It's all close by and top drawer. Plus, you'll probably be enjoying it all in great weather, as the area gets nearly 300 days of sunshine each year.

◉ Sights

★**High Desert Museum**   MUSEUM
(☑541-382-4754; www.highdesertmuseum.org; 59800 Hwy 97; adult/child $12/7; ⊙9am-5pm May-Oct, 10am-4pm Nov-Apr; ☷) This excellent museum, about 3 miles south of Bend, charts the exploration and settlement of the West, using reenactments of a Native American camp, a hard-rock mine and an old Western town. The region's natural history is also explored; kids love the live snake, tortoise and trout exhibits, and watching the birds of prey and otters is always fun. Guided walks and other programs are well worth attending – don't miss the raptor presentation.

Smith Rock State Park   STATE PARK
(☑800-551-6949; www.oregonstateparks.org; 9241 NE Crooked River Dr; day use $5) Best known for its glorious rock climbing, Smith Rock State Park boasts rust-colored 800ft cliffs that tower over the pretty Crooked River. Nonclimbers have several miles of fine hiking trails, some of which involve a little simple rock scrambling. Nearby Terrebonne has a climbing store, along with some restaurants and grocery stores. There's **camping** right next to the park, or at **Skull Hollow** (no water; campsites $5), 8 miles east. The nearest motels are a few miles south in Redmond.

🏃 Activities

Smith Rock
Climbing Guides Inc CLIMBING
(☑ 541-788-6225; www.smithrockclimbingguides.
com; Terrebonne; half-day per person from $65)
This company offers a variety of climbing
instruction (basic, lead, trad, multipitch, aid
and self-rescue), along with guided climbs
to famous routes at Smith Rock State Park.
Gear is included. Prices depend on the number in your group. Open by appointment.

Mt Bachelor Ski Resort SKIING
(☑ 800-829-2442; www.mtbachelor.com; lift tickets adult/child $92/52, cross-country day pass
$19/12; ⊙ Nov-May, depending on snowfall; 🚠)
Bend hosts some of Oregon's best skiing 22
miles southwest of town at Mt Bachelor Ski
Resort, famous for its 'dry' powdery snow,
long season and ample terrain (it's the largest ski area in the Pacific Northwest). The resort has long advocated cross-country skiing
in tandem with downhill and it maintains
35 miles of groomed trails.

Mountain Biking

Bend is a mountain-biking paradise, with
hundreds of miles of awesome trails to explore. The good Bend Area Trail Map ($12;
www.adventuremaps.net/shop/product/
product/bend-area-trail-map) is available at
the Visit Bend tourist office and elsewhere.

The king of Bend's mountain biking trails
is **Phil's Trail** network, which offers a variety
of excellent fast single-track forest trails just
minutes from town. If you want to catch air,
don't miss the **Whoops Trail**.

Cog Wild CYCLING
(☑ 541-385-7002; www.cogwild.com; 255 SW Century Dr, Suite 201; half-day tours from $60, rentals
$30-80; ⊙ 9am-6pm) This adventure-oriented
company offers tours and shuttles out to the
best trailheads. You can also arrange to rent
bikes, either directly from Cog or through
other local shops.

🛏️ Sleeping

There's an endless supply of cheap motels,
hotels and services on 3rd St (US 97). Because of festivals and events, Bend's lodging
rates head north most weekends, and booking ahead is recommended.

Mill Inn INN $
(☑ 541-389-9198; www.millinn.com; 642 NW Colorado Ave; d $100-170; ⊛🤶) A 10-room bou-
tique hotel with small, classy rooms decked

out with velvet drapes and comforters; four
share outside bathrooms. Full breakfast and
hot-tub use are included, and there are nice
small patios on which to hang out.

★ McMenamins Old
St Francis School HOTEL $$
(☑ 541-382-5174; www.mcmenamins.com; 700 NW
Bond St; r from $155; ⊛❋🤶) One of McMe-
namins' best venues, this old schoolhouse
has been remodeled into a classy 19-room
hotel – two rooms even have side-by-side
clawfoot tubs. A recent expansion has added
41 new rooms. The fabulous tiled saltwater
Turkish bath alone is worth the stay, though
nonguests can soak for $5. A restaurant-pub,
three bars, a movie theater and artwork
complete the picture.

★ Oxford Hotel BOUTIQUE HOTEL $$$
(☑ 541-382-8436; www.oxfordhotelbend.com; 10
NW Minnesota Ave; r from $249; ⊛❋🤶🐾) 🐾
Bend's premier boutique hotel is deservedly
popular. The smallest rooms are still huge
(470 sq ft) and are decked out with ecofriendly features such as soy-foam mattresses and
cork flooring. High-tech aficionados will love
the iPod docks and smart-panel desks. Suites
(with kitchen and steam shower) are available, and the basement restaurant is slick.

🍴 Eating

★ Chow AMERICAN $
(☑ 541-728-0256; www.chowbend.com; 1110 NW
Newport Ave; mains $8-15; ⊙ 7am-2pm) 🐾 The
signature poached-egg dishes here are spectacular and beautifully presented, coming
with sides such as crab cakes, house-cured
ham and cornmeal-crusted tomatoes (don't
miss the house-made hot sauces). Gourmet
sandwiches and salads, some with an Asian
influence, are served for lunch. Much of the
produce is grown in the garden, and there
are good cocktails, too.

10 Barrel Brewing Co AMERICAN $
(☑ 541-678-5228; www.10barrel.com; 1135 NW Galveston Ave; mains $11-15, pizzas $15-20; ⊙ 11am-
11pm Sun-Thu, to midnight Fri & Sat) Located in
a charming house, this popular brewery-
restaurant has a great patio for warm nights.
The tasty pub-food menu includes starters
such as fried brussels sprouts and steak
and gorgonzola nachos, while mains run
the gamut from elk burgers to coconut-lime
mussels. Sports lovers should head to the
bar in the back.

Sparrow Bakery
BAKERY **$**

(☎541-330-6321; www.thesparrowbakery.net; 50 SE Scott St; breakfasts $5-9; ⊗7am-2pm Mon-Sat, 8am-2pm Sun) This bakery is famous for its Ocean Rolls, a delicious cardamom-laced sweet pastry – but the breakfast sandwiches, including an outstanding cream cheese and lox bagel, are also great.

Victorian Café
BREAKFAST **$$**

(1404 NW Galveston Ave; mains $13-25; ⊗7am-2pm) One of Bend's best breakfast spots, the Victorian Café is especially awesome for its eggs Benedict (nine kinds). It's also good for sandwiches, burgers and salads. There's really nice outdoor seating in summer. Be ready to wait for a table, especially on weekends.

Zydeco
AMERICAN **$$$**

(☎541-312-2899; www.zydecokitchen.com; 919 NW Bond St; dinner mains $12-32; ⊗11:30am-2:30pm & 5-9pm Mon-Fri, 5-9pm Sat & Sun) Zydeco is one of Bend's most acclaimed restaurants, and with good reason. Start with the duck fries (french fries fried in duck fat) or tricolored beet salad with goat cheese, then move on to your main course: pan-roasted steelhead, crawfish jambalaya or roasted duck with mushroom gravy. Reserve.

ℹ Information

Visit Bend (☎541-382-8048; www.visitbend. com; 750 NW Lava Rd; ⊗9am-5pm Mon-Fri, 10am-4pm Sat & Sun) Great information, plus maps, books and recreation passes available for purchase.

ℹ Getting There & Around

Central Oregon Breeze (☎541-389-7469; www.cobreeze.com) offers transport to Portland two or more times daily ($52 one-way, reserve ahead).

High Desert Point (☎541-382-4193; http:// oregon-point.com/highdesert-point) buses link Bend with Chemult, where the nearest train station is located (65 miles south). It also has bus services to Eugene, Ontario and Burns.

Cascades East Transit (☎541-385-8680; www.cascadeseasttransit.com) is the regional bus company in Bend, covering La Pine, Mt Bachelor, Sisters, Prineville and Madras. It also provides bus transport within Bend.

Newberry National Volcanic Monument

Showcasing 400,000 years of dramatic seismic activity is **Newberry National Volcanic Monument** (☎541-593-2421; Hwy 97; day use $5; ⊗May-Sep). Start your visit at the **Lava Lands Visitor Center** (☎541-593-2421; 58201 S Hwy 97; ⊗9am-5pm late May-Sep, closed Nov-May), 13 miles south of Bend. Nearby attractions include **Lava Butte**, a perfect cone rising 500ft, and **Lava River Cave**, Oregon's longest lava tube. Four miles west of the visitor center is **Benham Falls**, a good picnic spot on the Deschutes River.

Newberry Crater was once one of the most active volcanoes in North America, but after a large eruption a caldera was born. Close by are **Paulina Lake** and **East Lake**, deep bodies of water rich with trout, while looming above is 7985ft **Paulina Peak**.

Crater Lake National Park

It's no exaggeration: **Crater Lake** (☎541-594-3000; www.nps.gov/crla; 7-day vehicle pass $15) is so blue, you'll catch your breath. And if you get to see it on a calm day, the surrounding cliffs are reflected in those deep waters like a mirror. It's a stunningly beautiful sight. Crater Lake is Oregon's only national park.

The classic tour is the 33-mile rim drive (open from approximately June to mid-October), but there are also exceptional hiking and cross-country skiing opportunities. Note that because the area receives some of the highest snowfalls in North America, the rim drive and north entrance are sometimes closed up until early July.

You can stay from late May to mid-October at the **Cabins at Mazama Village** (☎888-774-2728; www.craterlakelodges.com; d $160; ⊗late May–mid-Oct; ⚲) or the majestic **Crater Lake Lodge** (☎888-774-2728; www. craterlakelodges.com; r from $220; ⊗late May–mid-Oct; ⚲🛜), opened in 1915. Campers head to **Mazama Campground** (☎888-774-2728; www.craterlakelodges.com; tent/RV sites from $22/31; ⊗Jun–mid-Oct; 🛜🐾). For more information, head to **Steel Visitor Center** (☎541-594-3000; ⊗9am-5pm May-Oct, 10am-4pm Nov-Apr).

Oregon Coast

This magnificent littoral is paralleled by US 101, a scenic highway that winds its way through towns, resorts, state parks (more than 70 of them) and wilderness areas. Everyone from campers to gourmets will find a plethora of ways to enjoy this exceptional region, which is especially popular in summer (reserve accommodations in advance).

Astoria

Named after America's first millionaire, John Jacob Astor, Astoria sits at the 5-mile-wide mouth of the Columbia River and was the first US settlement west of the Mississippi. The city has a long seafaring history and has seen its old harbor, once home to poor artists and writers, attract fancy hotels and restaurants in recent years. Inland are many historical houses, including lovingly restored Victorians – a few converted into romantic B&Bs.

◎ Sights

Adding to the city's scenery is the 4.1-mile **Astoria-Megler Bridge**, the longest continuous truss bridge in North America, which crosses the Columbia River into Washington state. See it from the **Astoria Riverwalk**, which follows the trolley route. **Pier 39** is an interesting covered wharf with an informal cannery museum and a couple of places to eat.

**Columbia River
Maritime Museum**   MUSEUM
(☑503-325-2323; www.crmm.org; 1792 Marine Dr; adult/child $14/5; ◎9:30am-5pm; ⦿) Astoria's seafaring heritage is well interpreted at this wave-shaped museum. It's hard to miss the retired Coast Guard boat, frozen mid-rescue, through a huge outside window. Other exhibits highlight the salmon-packing industry and the Chinese immigrants who made up the bulk of its workforce; the river's commercial history; and the crucial job of the bar pilot. You get a keen sense of the treacherous conditions that define this area, known for good reason as the 'Graveyard of the Pacific.'

Flavel House   HISTORIC BUILDING
(☑503-325-2203; www.cumtux.org; 441 8th St; adult/child $6/2; ◎11am-4pm Oct-Apr, 10am-5pm May-Sep) The extravagant Flavel House was built by Captain George Flavel, one of Astoria's leading citizens during the 1880s. The Queen Anne house has been repainted in its original colors and the grounds have been returned to Victorian-era landscaping; it has great views of the Columbia River, too.

Fort Stevens State Park   PARK
(☑ext 21 503-861-3170; www.oregonstateparks. org; 100 Peter Iredale Rd, Hammond; day use $5) Ten miles west of Astoria, this park holds the historic military installation that once guarded the mouth of the Columbia River. Near the **Military Museum** (☑503-861-2000; http://visitftstevens.com; day-use fee $5; ◎10am-6pm May-Sep, to 4pm Oct-Apr) **FREE** are gun batteries dug into sand dunes – interesting remnants of the fort's mostly demolished military stations (truck and walking tours available). There's a popular **beach** at the small *Peter Iredale* 1906 shipwreck, and good ocean views from parking lot C. There's also camping and 12 miles of paved **bike trails**.

🛏 Sleeping & Eating

Fort Stevens State Park   CAMPGROUND $
(☑503-861-1671; www.oregonstateparks.org; 100 Peter Iredale Rd, Hammond; tent/RV sites $22/32, yurts/cabins $46/90) About 560 sites (most for RVs) are available at this popular campground 10 miles west of Astoria. Great for families; reserve in summer. Entry off Pacific Dr.

Commodore Hotel   BOUTIQUE HOTEL $$
(☑503-325-4747;   www.commodoreastoria. com; 258 14th St; d with shared/private bath from $79/154; ⦿⦿) Hip travelers should make a

---

LEWIS & CLARK: JOURNEY'S END

In November 1805 William Clark and his fellow explorer Meriwether Lewis of the Corps of Discovery staggered, with three dozen others, into a sheltered cove on the Columbia River, 2 miles west of the present-day Astoria-Megler Bridge, completing what was indisputably the greatest overland trek in American history.

After the first truly democratic ballot in US history (in which a woman and a black slave both voted), the party elected to make their bivouac 5 miles south of Astoria at Fort Clatsop, where the Corps spent a miserable winter in 1805–06. Today this site is called the **Lewis and Clark National Historical Park** (☑503-861-2471; www.nps.gov/lewi; 92343 Fort Clatsop Rd; adult/child $5/free; ◎9am-6pm mid-Jun–Aug, to 5pm Sep–mid-Jun). Here you'll find a reconstructed Fort Clatsop, along with a visitor center and historical reenactments in summer.

beeline for this stylish hotel, which offers attractive but small, minimalist rooms. Choose a room with bathroom or go Euro style (sink in room, bathroom down the hall; 'deluxe' rooms have better views). There's a lounge-style lobby with cafe, free samples of local microbrews from 5pm to 7pm, an impressive movie library and record players to borrow.

Bowpicker
SEAFOOD $

(☑ 503-791-2942; www.bowpicker.com; cnr 17th & Duane St; dishes $8-10; ⊙ 11am-6pm Wed-Sun) On just about every list of great seafood shacks is this adorable place in a converted 1932 gillnet fishing boat, serving beer-battered chunks of albacore and steak fries and that's it.

Fort George Brewery
PUB FOOD $

(☑ 503-325-7468; www.fortgeorgebrewery.com; 1483 Duane St; mains $7-16, pizzas $13-25; ⊙ 11am-11pm, noon-11pm Sun) Fort George has established itself as one of the state's best and most reliable craft brewers. Its atmospheric brewery-restaurant is in a historic building that was the original settlement site of Astoria. Apart from the excellent beer, you can get gourmet burgers, house-made sausages, salads and, upstairs, wood-fired pizza.

Astoria Coffeehouse & Bistro
AMERICAN $$

(☑ 503-325-1787; www.astoriacoffeehouse.com; 243 11th St; dinner mains $12-25; ⊙ 7am-9pm Sun, to 10pm Mon-Thu, to 11pm Fri & Sat) 🍽 Small, popular cafe with attached bistro offering an eclectic menu – things like Peruvian root-vegetable stew, wasabi wonton prawns, chili-relleno burger, fish tacos, pad Thai and mac 'n' cheese. Everything is made in-house, even the ketchup. There's sidewalk seating and excellent cocktails. Expect a wait at dinner and Sunday brunch.

❶ Getting There & Away

Northwest Point (☑ 503-484-4100; http://oregon-point.com/northwest-point) Daily buses head to Seaside, Cannon Beach and Portland; check the website for schedules.

Pacific Transit (☑ 360-642-9418; www.pacifictransit.org) Buses to Washington.

Cannon Beach

Charming Cannon Beach is one of the most popular beach towns on the Oregon coast. Several premier hotels here cater to a fancier clientele, as do the town's many boutiques and art galleries. In summer the streets are ablaze with flowers. Lodging is expensive, and the streets are jammed: on a warm, sunny Saturday, you'll spend a good chunk of time just finding a parking spot.

◉ Sights & Activities

Photogenic **Haystack Rock**, a 295ft seastack, is the most spectacular landmark on the Oregon coast and is accessible from the beach at low tide. Birds cling to its ballast cliffs and tide pools ring its base.

The coast to the north, protected inside **Ecola State Park** (☑ 503-436-2844; www.oregonstateparks.org; day use $5), is the Oregon you may have already visited in your dreams: sea stacks, crashing surf, hidden beaches and gorgeous pristine forest. The park is 1.5 miles from town and is crisscrossed by paths, including part of the **Oregon Coast Trail**, which leads over Tillamook Head to the town of Seaside.

The Cannon Beach area is good for surfing, though not the beach itself. The best spots are **Indian Beach** in Ecola State Park, 3 miles to the north, and **Oswald West State Park**, 10 miles south. **Cleanline Surf Shop** (☑ 503-738-2061; www.cleanlinesurf.com; 171 Sunset Blvd; board/wet-suit rentals from $20/15; ⊙ 10am-6pm Sun-Fri, 9am-6pm Sat) is a friendly local shop that rents out boards and mandatory wetsuits.

🛌 Sleeping

Cannon Beach is pretty exclusive; for budget choices head 7 miles north to Seaside. For vacation rentals, check out www.visitcb.com.

★ Ocean Lodge
HOTEL $$$

(☑ 888-777-4047, 503-436-2241; www.theoceanlodge.com; 2864 S Pacific St; d $219-369; ☻❄🛜🐾) This gorgeous place has some of Cannon Beach's most luxurious rooms, most with ocean view and all with fireplace and kitchenette. A complimentary continental breakfast, an 800-DVD library and pleasant sitting areas are available to guests. Located on the beach at the southern end of town.

🍴 Eating & Drinking

Here you'll find everything from coffee shops to a coffee shop that doubles as a fine restaurant. If you're just after a warm cup of buttery clam chowder with a view, stop in at **Mo's** (www.moschowder.com).

★ Irish Table
IRISH $$$

(☑ 503-436-0708; 1235 S Hemlock St; mains $20-30; ⊙ 5:30-9pm Fri-Tue) 🍽 Excellent restaurant hidden at the back of the Sleepy Monk coffee shop, serving a fusion of Irish and Pacific Northwest cuisine made with local and seasonal ingredients. The menu is small and simple, but the choices are tasty; try the vegetarian shepherd's pie, lamb-loin chops or seared Piedmontese flat-iron steak. If the curried mussels are on the menu, don't hesitate.

Sleepy Monk Coffee COFFEE
(☎503-436-2796; www.sleepymonkcoffee.com; 1235 S Hemlock St; drinks & snacks $2-7; ⊙8am-3pm Mon, Tue & Thu, to 4pm Fri-Sun) 🍴 For organic, certified-fair-trade coffee, try this little coffee shop on the main street. Sit on an Adirondack chair in the tiny front yard and enjoy the rich brews, all tasty and roasted on the premises. Good homemade pastries, too.

ℹ Information

Chamber of Commerce (☎503-436-2623; www.cannonbeach.org; 207 N Spruce St; ⊙10am-5pm) Has good local information, including tide tables.

ℹ Getting There & Around

Northwest Point (☎541-484-4100; www. oregon-point.com/northwest-point) Twice-daily routes between Portland and the coast. Buy tickets online, at Portland's Union Station, or at the Astoria Transit Center. The one-way fare from Portland to Astoria is $18.

Cannon Beach Shuttle (☎503-861-7433; www.ridethebus.org) Buses between Cannon Beach and Astoria, plus other coastal stops. The Cannon Beach bus runs the length of Hemlock St to the end of Tolovana Beach; the schedule varies depending on day and season.

Tillamook County Transportation (The Wave; ☎503-815-8283; www.tillamookbus.com) Buses between Astoria and Newport, with stops all along the coast.

Newport

Home to Oregon's largest commercial fishing fleet, Newport is a lively tourist city with several fine beaches and a world-class aquarium. In 2011 it became the host of NOAA (the National Oceanic and Atmospheric Administration). Good restaurants – along with some tacky attractions, gift shops and barking sea lions – abound in the historic bayfront area, while bohemian Nye Beach offers art galleries and a friendly village atmosphere. The area was first explored in the 1860s by fishing crews who found oyster beds at the upper end of Yaquina Bay.

◉ Sights

The world-class **Oregon Coast Aquarium** (☎541-867-3474; www.aquarium.org; 2820 SE Ferry Slip Rd; adult/3-12yr/13-17yr $22.95/14.95/19.95; ⊙10am-6pm Jun-Aug, to 5pm Sep-May; 🅿) is an unmissable attraction, featuring a sea-otter pool, surreal jellyfish tanks and Plexiglas tunnels through a shark tank. Nearby, the **Hatfield Marine Science Center** (☎541-867-0100; www.hmsc.oregonstate.edu; 2030 SE Marine Science Dr; ⊙10am-5pm Jun-Aug, to 4pm Thu-Mon Sep-May; 🅿) FREE is much smaller, but still worthwhile. For awesome tidepooling and views, don't miss the **Yaquina Head Outstanding Natural Area** (☎541-574-3100; 750 NW Lighthouse Dr; vehicle fee $7; ⊙8am-sunset, interpretive center 10am-6pm) FREE, site of the coast's tallest lighthouse and an interesting interpretive center.

🛏 Sleeping & Eating

Campers can head to large and popular **South Beach State Park** (☎541-867-4715; www.oregonstateparks.org; tent/RV sites $21/29, yurts $44; 🐾), two miles south on US101. Book-lovers can stay at the **Sylvia Beach Hotel** (☎541-265-5428; www.sylviabeachhotel.com; 267 NW Cliff St; d $135-235; ❄) and nautical and romantic types at the shipshape **Newport Belle** (☎541-867-6290; http://newportbelle.com; 2126 SE Marine Science Dr, South Beach Marina, H Dock; d $165-175; ⊙Feb-Oct; ❄🛜).

For crab po'boys, pan-fried oysters and other tasty seafood, head to **Local Ocean Seafoods** (☎541-574-7959; www.localocean.net; 213 SE Bay Blvd; mains $16-28; ⊙11am-9pm, to 8pm winter) – it's especially great on warm days, when the glass walls open to the port area.

ℹ Information

Visitor Center (☎541-265-8801; www. newportchamber.org; 555 SW Coast Hwy; ⊙8:30am-5pm Mon-Fri)

Yachats & Around

One of the Oregon coast's best-kept secrets is the neat and friendly little town of Yachats (ya-*hots*). Lying at the base of massive Cape Perpetua, Yachats offers the memorable scenery of a rugged and windswept land. People come here to get away from it all, which isn't hard to do along this relatively undeveloped stretch of coast.

Lining the town is the 804 Coast Trail, providing a lovely walk and access to tide pools and fabulous ocean vistas. It hooks up with the Amanda trail to the south, eventually arriving at Cape Perpetua Scenic Area.

★ **Cape Perpetua Scenic Area**   PARK
(Hwy 101; day-use fee $5) Located 3 miles south of Yachats, this volcanic remnant was sighted and named by England's Captain James Cook in 1778. Famous for dramatic rock formations and crashing surf, the area contains numerous trails that explore ancient shell middens, tide pools and old-growth forests. Views from the cape are incredible, taking in coastal promontories from Cape Foulweather to Cape Arago.

For spectacular ocean views, head up Overlook Rd to the **Cape Perpetua** day-use area.

Deep fractures in the old volcano allow waves to erode narrow channels into the headland, creating effects such as **Devil's Churn**, about a half-mile north of the visitor center. Waves race up this chasm, shooting up the 30ft inlet to explode against the narrowing sides of the channel. For an easy hike, take the paved **Captain Cook Trail** (1.2 miles round-trip) down to tide pools near **Cooks Chasm**, where at high tide the geyser-like spouting horn blasts water out of a sea cave. (There's also parking along Hwy 101 at Cooks Chasm.)

The **Giant Spruce Trail** (2 miles round-trip) leads up Cape Creek to a 500-year-old Sitka spruce with a 15ft diameter. The **Cook's Ridge–Gwynn Creek Loop Trail** (6.5 miles round-trip) heads into deep old-growth forests along Gwynn Creek; follow the Oregon Coast Trail south and turn up the Gwynn Creek Trail, which returns via Cook's Ridge.

The **visitor center** (☑ 541-547-3289; www.fs.usda.gov/siuslaw; 2400 Hwy 101; vehicle fee $5; ☺ 9:30am-4:30pm Jun-Aug, 10am-4pm Sep-May) details human and natural histories, and has displays on the Alsi tribe.

Heceta Head Lighthouse   LIGHTHOUSE
(☑ 541-547-3416;   Heceta.h.lighthouse@oregon. gov; day use $5; ☺ 11am-3pm, to 2pm winter) Built in 1894 and towering precipitously above the churning ocean, this lighthouse, 13 miles south of Yachats on Hwy 101, is supremely photogenic and still functioning. Tours are available; hours may be erratic, especially in winter, so call ahead. Park at Heceta Head State Park for views.

Sea Lion Caves   CAVE
(☑ 541-547-3111; www.sealioncaves.com; 91560 Hwy 101, Florence; adult/child $14/8; ☺ 9am-5pm) Fifteen miles south of Yachats is an enormous sea grotto that's home to hundreds of Steller sea lions. An elevator descends 208ft to a dark interpretive area, and an observation window lets you watch the sea lions jockeying for the best seat on the rocks. There are also outside observation areas, as usually from late September to November there are no sea lions in the cave. There are lots of interesting coastal birds to look for.

Ya'Tel Motel   MOTEL $
(☑ 541-547-3225; www.yatelmotel.com; cnr Hwy 101 & 6th St; d $74-119; ☺ @ ☎ ☎ ☎) This eight-room motel has personality, along with large, clean rooms, some with kitchenette. A large room that sleeps six is also available ($119). Look for the (changeable) sign out front, which might say something like, 'Always clean, usually friendly.'

Green Salmon Coffee House   CAFE $
(☑ 541-547-3077; www.thegreensalmon.com; 220 Hwy 101; coffee drinks $2-5; ☺ 7:30am-2:30pm; ☑) ☕ Organic and fair trade are big words at this eclectic cafe, where locals meet for tasty breakfast items (pastries, lox bagels, homemade oatmeal). The inventive list of hot beverages ranges from regular drip coffee to organic chocolate chai latte to lavendar rosemary cocoa. Vegan menu available, plus a used-book exchange.

Oregon Dunes National Recreation Area

Stretching for 50 miles between Florence and Coos Bay, the Oregon Dunes form the largest expanse of coastal dunes in the USA. They tower up to 500ft and undulate inland as far as three miles to meet coastal forests, harboring curious ecosystems that sustain an abundance of wildlife, especially birds. The area inspired Frank Herbert to pen his epic sci-fi *Dune* novels. Hiking trails, bridle paths, and boating and swimming areas are available, but avoid the stretch south of Reedsport as noisy dune buggies dominate. Find out more at the **Oregon Dunes National Recreation Area Visitor Center** (☑ 541-271-6000; www.fs.usda.gov/siuslaw; 855 Hwy 101; ☺ 8am-4:30pm Mon-Sat Jun-Aug, Mon-Fri Sep-May) in Reedsport.

State parks with camping include popular **Jessie M Honeyman** (☑ 800-452-5687, 541-997-3641; www.oregonstateparks.org; 84505 Hwy 101 S; tent/RV sites $21/29, yurts $44; ☎), 3 miles south of Florence, and pleasant, wooded **Umpqua Lighthouse** (☑ 541-271-4118; www.oregonstateparks.org; 460 Lighthouse Rd;

tent/RV sites $19/26, yurts/deluxe yurts $41/80; 🐾), 4 miles south of Reedsport. There's plenty of other camping in the area, too.

Port Orford

Occupying a rare natural harbor and guarding plenty of spectacular views, the scenic hamlet of Port Orford sits on a headland wedged between two magnificent state parks. **Cape Blanco State Park** (☎541-332-2973; www.oregonstateparks.org; Cape Blanco Rd) **FREE**, nine miles to the north, is the second-most-westerly point in the continental US, and the promontory is often lashed by fierce 100mph winds. As well as hiking, visitors can tour the **Cape Blanco Lighthouse** (☎541-332-2207; www.oregonstateparks.org; 91814 Cape Blanco Rd; tour adult/child $2/free; ⊙10am-3:15pm Wed-Mon Apr-Oct) – built in 1870, it's the oldest and highest operational lighthouse in Oregon.

Six miles south of Port Orford, in **Humbug Mountain State Park** (☎541-332-6774), mountains and sea meet in aqueous disharmony, generating plenty of angry surf. You can climb the 1750ft peak on a 3-mile trail through old-growth cedar groves.

For an affordable stay try **Castaway-by-the-Sea Motel** (☎541-332-4502; www.castawaybythesea.com; 545 W 5th St; d $75-135, ste $115-165; ❅@🐾); for a more luxurious cabin, **Wildspring Guest Habitat** (☎866-333-9453; www.wildspring.com; 92978 Cemetery Loop; d $298-328; ❅@🔾). Eating well in this fishing village means a visit to slick **Redfish** (☎541-366-2200; www.redfishportorford.com; Hawthorne Gallery, 517 Jefferson St; mains $18-34; ⊙11am-9pm Mon-Fri, 10am-9pm Sat & Sun) 🍴 for the freshest seafood in town.

Southern Oregon

With a warm, sunny and dry climate that belongs in nearby California, Southern Oregon, the state's 'banana belt,' is an exciting place to visit. Rugged and remote landscapes are entwined with a number of designated 'wild and scenic' rivers, which are famous for their challenging white-water rafting, world-class fly-fishing and excellent hiking.

Ashland

This pretty city is the cultural center of Southern Oregon thanks to its internationally renowned Oregon Shakespeare Festival (OSF), which runs for nine months of the year and attracts hundreds of thousands of theatergoers from all over the world. The festival is so popular that it's Ashland's main attraction, packing it out in summer and bringing in steady cash flows for the town's many fancy hotels, upscale B&Bs and fine restaurants.

Even without the OSF, however, Ashland is still a pleasant place whose trendy downtown streets buzz with well-heeled shoppers and youthful bohemians. In late fall and early winter – those few months when the festival doesn't run – folks come to ski at nearby Mt Ashland. And wine-lovers, take note: the area has several good wineries worth seeking out.

◎ Sights & Activities

Lithia Park PARK
(59 Winburn Way) Adjacent to Ashland's three splendid theaters lies what is arguably the loveliest city park in Oregon, the 93 acres of which wind along Ashland Creek above the center of town. Unusually, the park is in the National Register of Historic Places. It is embellished with fountains, flowers, gazebos and an ice-skating rink (winter only), plus a playground and woodsy trails.

Schneider Museum of Art MUSEUM
(☎541-552-6245; http://sma.sou.edu; 1250 Siskiyou Blvd; suggested donation $5; ⊙10am-4pm Mon-Sat) If you like contemporary art, check out this Southern Oregon University museum, where new exhibitions go up every month or so. The university also puts on theater and opera performances, along with classical concerts.

Siskiyou Cyclery CYCLING
(☎541-482-1997; www.siskiyoucyclery.com; 1729 Siskiyou Blvd; half-/full-day rental $30/45; ⊙10am-6pm Mon-Sat) Rent a bicycle and explore the countryside on Bear Creek Greenway, a 21-mile bike path between Ashland and the town of Central Point.

🛏 Sleeping

From May to October, try to arrive with reservations. Rooms are cheaper in Medford, 12 miles north of Ashland.

Ashland Hostel HOSTEL $
(☎541-482-9217; www.theashlandhostel.com; 150 N Main St; dm $29, s/d from $45/55; ❅✳@🔾) his is a central and somewhat upscale hostel (shoes off inside!) in a bungalow on the National Registry. Most private rooms share

DON'T MISS

OREGON SHAKESPEARE FESTIVAL

As a young town, Ashland was included in the Methodist Church's cultural education program. By the 1930s, one of the venues had deteriorated to a dilapidated wooden shell. Angus Bowmer, a drama professor at the local college, noted the resemblance of the roofless structure to drawings of Shakespeare's Globe Theatre. He convinced the town to sponsor two performances of Shakespeare's plays and a boxing match (the Bard would have approved) as part of its 1935 July 4 celebration. The plays proved a great success, and the **Oregon Shakespeare Festival** (OSF; ☑ 541-482-4331; www.osfashland.org; cnr Main & Pioneer Sts; tickets $30-136; ⊙ Tue-Sun Feb-Oct) was off and running. Performances sell out quickly, but the box office sometimes has rush tickets an hour before showtime.

Check with the **OSF Welcome Center** (76 N Main St; ⊙ 11am-5pm Tue-Sun) for other events, including scholarly lectures, play readings, concerts and pre-show talks.

bathrooms; some can be connected to dorms. Hangout spaces include the cozy basement living room and the shady front porch. No pets, and no alcohol or smoking; call ahead, as reception times are limited.

Palm   BOUTIQUE HOTEL **$$**
(☑ 541-482-2636; www.palmcottages.com; 1065 Siskiyou Blvd; d $75-249; ❂❋☎☒❀) Fabulous small motel remodeled into 16 charming garden-cottage rooms and suites (some with kitchens). It's an oasis of green on a busy avenue, complete with grassy lawns and a saltwater pool. A house nearby harbors three large suites (from $249). No breakfast, but it's right next to the popular Morning Glory cafe.

🍴 Eating & Drinking

Morning Glory   CAFE **$**
(☑ 541-488-8636; 1149 Siskiyou Blvd; mains $9.50-15; ⊙ 8am-1:30pm) This colorful, casual cafe is one of Ashland's best breakfast joints. Creative dishes include the Alaskan-crab omelet, vegetarian hash with roasted chilies, and shrimp cakes with poached eggs. For lunch there's gourmet salad and sandwiches. Go early or late to avoid a long wait.

Agave   MEXICAN **$**
(☑ 541-488-1770; www.agavetaco.net; 5 Granite St; tacos $3.75-5; ⊙ 11am-8pm Sun-Thu, to 9pm Fri & Sat, later in summer) Tasty and creative tacos are cooked up at this popular restaurant. There's the regular stuff such as *carnitas* (little meats) and grilled chicken, but for something more exotic go for the shredded duck or sautéed lobster ($9.95). There's ceviche, salads and tamales, too.

Caldera Brewing   BREWPUB **$$**
(☑ 541-482-4677; www.calderabrewing.com; 590 Clover Lane; mains $13-23; ⊙ 11am-10pm; ⊛) This bright, airy brewery-restaurant just off I-5

has pleasant outdoor seating and views of the countryside. It's kid friendly until 10pm and serves pizza, fancy pasta, burgers and good salads. Wash it all down with one of the 40 beers on tap. Also located at 31 Water St on the river with more of a cozy pub atmosphere.

Greenleaf   DINER **$$**
(☑ 541-482-2808; www.greenleafrestaurant.com; 49 N Main St; mains $10-21; ⊙ 8am-8pm; ☑) ❧ This casual diner, with booths as well as counter seating, focuses on sustainable ingredients in innovative combinations. There are lots of vegetarian options, and the specials board is well worth checking out, although the regular menu is so massive that you might not ever need to venture that far. There's a whole gluten-free menu, too.

Amuse   FRENCH **$$$**
(☑ 541-488-9000; www.amuserestaurant.com; 15 N 1st St; mains $26-38; ⊙ 5:30-9pm Wed-Sun) Amuse is a fine French bistro serving dishes like Parisian gnocchi, pan-seared scallops and truffle-roasted game hen. Dessert means bittersweet chocolate-truffle cake and warm beignets with crème anglaise. Reserve.

🛈 Information

Ashland Chamber of Commerce (☑ 541-482-3486; www.ashlandchamber.com; 110 E Main St; ⊙ 9am-5pm Mon-Fri)

Jacksonville

This small but endearing ex-gold-prospecting town is the oldest settlement in southern Oregon and a National Historic Landmark. The main drag is lined with well-preserved buildings dating from the 1880s, now converted into boutiques and galleries. Music lovers shouldn't miss the September **Britt Festival** (☑ 541-773-6077; www.brittfest.org; cnr

1st & Fir Sts; ⊙ Jun-Sep), a world-class musical experience with top-name performers. Seek more enlightenment at the **Chamber of Commerce** (✆ 541-899-8118; www.jacksonville oregon.org; 185 N Oregon St; ⊙ 10am-3pm daily May-Oct, to 2pm Mon-Sat Nov-Apr).

Jacksonville is full of fancy B&Bs; for budget motels head 6 miles east to Medford. The **Jacksonville Inn** (✆ 541-899-1900; 175 E California St; r $159-325; ❀❋🐾🖥) is the most pleasant abode, shoehorned downtown in an 1863 building with regal antique-stuffed rooms. There's a fine restaurant on-site.

North Umpqua River

This 'Wild and Scenic' river boasts world-class fly-fishing, fine hiking and serene camping. The 79-mile **North Umpqua Trail** begins near Idleyld Park, 3 miles east of Glide, and passes through Steamboat en route to the Pacific Crest Trail. A popular sideline is pretty **Umpqua Hot Springs**, east of Steamboat near Toketee Lake. Not far away, stunning, two-tiered **Toketee Falls** (113ft) flows over columnar basalt, while **Watson Falls** (272ft) is one of the highest waterfalls in Oregon. For information, stop by Glide's **Colliding Rivers Information Center** (✆ 541-496-3532; 18782 N Umpqua Hwy, Glide; ⊙ 9am-5pm May-Sep). Adjacent is the **North Umpqua Ranger District** (✆ 541-496-3532; 18782 N Umpqua Hwy, Glide; ⊙ 8am-4:30pm Mon-Fri).

Between Idleyld Park and Diamond Lake are dozens of riverside campgrounds; these include lovely **Susan Creek** and primitive **Boulder Flat** (no water). Area accommodations fill up quickly in summer; try the log cabin–like rooms at **Dogwood Motel** (✆ 541-496-3403; www.dogwoodmotel.com; 28866 N Umpqua Hwy, Idleyld Park; s/d from $60/70; ❀❋🐾🖥).

Oregon Caves National Monument & Preserve

This very popular cave (singular) lies 19 miles east of Cave Junction on Hwy 46. Three miles of passages are explored via 90-minute cave tours that include 520 rocky steps and dripping chambers running along the River Styx. Dress warmly, wear shoes with good traction and be prepared to get dripped on.

Cave Junction, 28 miles south of Grants Pass on US 199 (Redwood Hwy), provides the region's services – though one of the best accommodations in the area is **Out 'n' About Treesort** (✆ 541-592-2208; www.

treehouses.com; 300 Page Creek Rd, Takilma; tree houses $150-330; ❀) – super-fun treehouses in Katilma, 12 miles south. For fancy lodgings right at the cave there's the impressive **Oregon Caves Chateau** (✆ 541-592-3400; www.oregoncaveschateau.com; 20000 Caves Hwy; r $117-212; ⊙ May-Oct; ❀) – grab a milkshake at the old-fashioned soda fountain here.

Eastern Oregon

Oregon east of the Cascades bears little resemblance to its wetter western cohort, either physically or culturally. Few people live here – the biggest town, Pendleton, numbers only 17,000 – and the region holds high plateaus, painted hills, alkali lake-beds and the country's deepest river gorge.

John Day Fossil Beds National Monument

Within the soft rocks and crumbly soils of John Day country lies one of the world's greatest fossil collections, laid down between six and 50 million years ago. The national monument includes 22 sq miles at three different units: Sheep Rock Unit, Painted Hills Unit and Clarno Unit. Each has hiking trails and interpretive displays.

Visit the excellent **Thomas Condon Paleontology Center** (✆ 541-987-2333; www. nps.gov/joda; 32651 Hwy 19, Kimberly; ⊙ 10am-5pm) **FREE**, 2 miles north of US 26 at the **Sheep Rock Unit**. Displays include a three-toed horse and petrified dung-beetle balls, along with many other fossils and geologic history exhibits. If you feel like walking, take the short hike up the Blue Basin Trail.

The **Painted Hills Unit**, near the town of Mitchell, consists of low-slung, colorfully banded hills formed about 30 million years ago. Ten million years older is the **Clarno Unit**, which exposes mud flows that washed over an Eocene-era forest and eroded into distinctive, sheer white cliffs topped with spires and turrets of stone.

Rafting is popular on the John Day River, the longest free-flowing river in the state. **Oregon River Experiences** (✆ 800-827-1358; www.oregonriver.com; 4/5/9-day trips per person $635/735/1195; ⊙ May-Jun) offers trips of up to five days. There's also good fishing for smallmouth bass and rainbow trout; find out more at the Oregon Department of Fish & Wildlife (www.dfw.state.or.us).

Most towns in the area have at least one hotel; these include the atmospheric **Historic Oregon Hotel** (☑541-462-3027; www.the oregonhotel.net; 104 E Main St, Mitchell; dm $20, d $50-110; 🛱) in Mitchell. The town of John Day has most of the district's services and there are several public campgrounds in the area (sites $5), including Lone Pine and Big Bend, both on Hwy 402.

Wallowa Mountains Area

The Wallowa Mountains, with their glacier-hewn peaks and crystalline lakes, are among the most beautiful natural areas in Oregon. The only drawback is the large number of visitors who flock here in summer, especially to the pretty Wallowa Lake area.

Escape them all on one of several long hikes into the nearby **Eagle Cap Wilderness**, such as the 6-mile one-way jaunt to **Aneroid Lake** or the 8-mile trek on the **Ice Lake Trail**.

Just north of the mountains, in the Wallowa Valley, **Enterprise** is a homely backcountry town with several motels – try the **Ponderosa** (☑541-426-3186; 102 E Greenwood St; s/d from $69/75; ✳🛱✳). If you like beer and good food, don't miss the town's microbrewery, **Terminal Gravity Brewing** (☑541-426-3000; www.terminalgravitybrewing.com; 803 SE School St; mains $9-14; ⊙11am-9pm Sun, Mon & Wed, to 10pm Thu-Sat). Just 6 miles south is Enterprise's fancy cousin, the upscale town of **Joseph**. Expensive bronze galleries and artsy boutiques line the main strip, along with some good eateries.

Hells Canyon

The mighty Snake River has taken 13 million years to carve its path through the high plateaus of eastern Oregon to its present depth of 8000ft, creating Aerica's deepest gorge.

For perspective, drive 30 miles northeast from Joseph to Imnaha, where a slow-going 24-mile gravel road leads up to **Hat Point**. From here you can see the Wallowa Mountains, Idaho's Seven Devils, the Imnaha River and the wilds of the canyon itself. This road is open from late May until snowfall; give yourself two hours each way for the drive.

For white-water action and spectacular scenery, head down to **Hells Canyon Dam**, 25 miles north of the small community of Oxbow. A few miles past the dam, the road ends at the **Hells Canyon Visitors Center** (Hells Canyon Rd, Hells Canyon Dam; ⊙8am-4pm May-Oct), which has good advice on the area's campgrounds and hiking trails. Beyond here, the Snake River drops 1300ft through wild rapids accessible only by jet boat or raft. **Hells Canyon Adventures** (☑800-422-3568; www.hellscanyonadventures.com; jet-boat tours adult/child from $75/38; ⊙May-Sep) is the main operator running raft trips and jet-boat tours (reservations required).

The area has many campgrounds and more solid lodgings. Just outside Imnaha is the beautiful **Imnaha River Inn** (☑541-577-6002; www.imnahariverinn.com; 73946 Rimrock Rd; s/d from $70/130), a B&B replete with Hemingway-esque animal trophies. For more services, head to the towns of Enterprise, Joseph and Halfway.

Steens Mountain & Alvord Desert

The highest peak in southeastern Oregon, Steens Mountain (9773ft) is part of a massive, 30-mile-long fault-block range that was formed about 15 million years ago.

Beginning in Frenchglen, the gravel 59-mile **Steens Mountain Loop Rd** is Oregon's highest road, offers the range's best sights, and has access to camping and hiking trails. You'll see sagebrush, bands of juniper and aspen forests, and finally fragile rocky tundra at the top. **Kiger Gorge Viewpoint**, 25 miles up from Frenchglen, is especially stunning. It takes about three hours all the way around if you're just driving through, but you'll want to see the sights, so give yourself much more time. You can also see the eastern side of the Steens via the **Fields-Denio Rd**, which goes through the Alvord Desert between Hwys 205 and 78. Take a full tank of gas and plenty of water, and be prepared for weather changes at any time of year.

Frenchglen, with a population of roughly 12, nonetheless supports the historic **Frenchglen Hotel** (☑541-493-2825; www.frenchglenhotel.com; 39184 Hwy 205; r with shared bath $75-82, Drovers' Inn s/d $115/135; ⊙mid-Mar–Oct; ⊝✳✳), with eight small rooms, huge meals (reserve for dinners), a small store with a seasonal gas pump and not much else. There are camping options on the Steens Mountain Loop Rd, such as the BLM's pretty **Page Springs** ($8 per vehicle, open year-round). A few other campgrounds further into the loop are very pleasant, but accessible in summer only. Water is available at all of these campgrounds. Free backcountry camping is also allowed in the Steens.

Alaska

Includes ➡

Anchorage	1091
Wrangell	1095
Sitka	1096
Juneau	1098
Haines	1100
Skagway	1101
Glacier Bay National Park & Preserve	1103
Ketchikan	1104
Fairbanks	1105

Best Places to Eat

➡ Snow City Café (p1093)

➡ Pel'Meni (p1099)

➡ Rustic Goat (p1093)

➡ Bar Harbor Restaurant (p1105)

➡ Ludvig's Bistro (p1098)

Best Places to Sleep

➡ Gustavus Inn (p1103)

➡ Copper Whale Inn (p1092)

➡ Ultima Thule Lodge (p1096)

➡ Inn at Creek Street – New York Hotel (p1105)

➡ Mendenhall Lake Campground (p1099)

Why Go?

Pure, raw, unforgiving and humongous in scale, Alaska is a place that arouses basic instincts and ignites what Jack London termed the 'call of the wild.' Yet, unlike London and his gutsy, gold-rush companions, visitors today will have a far easier time penetrating the region's vast, feral wilderness. Indeed, one of the beauties of the 49th state is its accessibility. Nowhere else in North America is it realistically possible to climb an unclimbed mountain, walk where – quite conceivably – no human foot has trodden before, or sally forth into a national park that gets fewer annual visitors than the International Space Station.

With scant phone coverage and a dearth of hipster-friendly coffee bars to plug in your iPad, Alaska is a region for 'doing' rather than observing. Whether you go it alone with bear spray and a backpack, or place yourself in the hands of an experienced 'sourdough' (Alaskan old-timer), the rewards are immeasurable.

When to Go
Anchorage

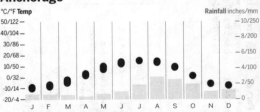

Jun Enjoy summer solstice festivals and 20-hour days. Stay up and play outdoors.

Jul Salmon runs, with millions of spawning fish choking streams, hit their peaks.

Late Sep The mystical northern lights begin to appear in the night skies.

Alaska Highlights

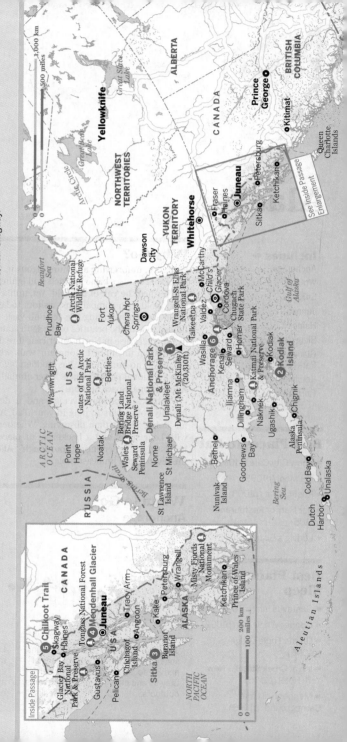

1 Denali National Park & Preserve (p1106) Gawking at the hulking, icy mass of Mt McKinley (Denali).

2 Kodiak Island (p1095) Viewing the world's largest bears feasting on salmon on this emerald-green island.

3 Sitka National Historical Park (p1097) Uncovering Russia's history in Alaska.

4 Mendenhall Glacier (p1098) Hiking alongside Alaska's most popular river of ice.

5 Chilkoot Trail (p1102) Following in the footsteps of the Klondike stampeders of 1898, near Skegway.

6 Anchorage Museum (p1091) Exploring Alaska's history and culture, in Anchorage.

History

Indigenous Alaskans – Athabascans, Aleuts and Inuit, and the coastal tribes Tlingits and Haidas – migrated over the Bering Strait land bridge 20,000 years ago. In the 18th century waves of Europeans arrived: first British and French explorers, then Russian whalers and fur traders, naming land formations, taking otter pelts and leaving the cultures of the Alaska Native peoples in disarray.

With the Russians' finances badly over extended by the Napoleonic Wars, US Secretary of State William H Seward was able to purchase the territory from them for $7.2 million– less than 2¢ an acre – in 1867. There was uproar over 'Seward's Folly,' but the land's riches soon revealed themselves: whales initially, then salmon, gold and finally oil. After Japan bombed and occupied the Aleutian Islands in WWII, the military built the famous Alcan (Alaska–Canada) Hwy, which connected the territory with the rest of the USA. The 1520-mile Alcan contributed greatly to post-war Alaska becoming a state in 1959.

The Good Friday earthquake in 1964 left Alaska in a shambles, but recovery was boosted when oil was discovered under Prudhoe Bay, resulting in the construction of a 789-mile pipeline to Valdez. For most Alaskans, the abundant oil made it hard to see beyond the gleam of the oil dollar.

In 1989 the *Exxon Valdez*, a 987ft Exxon oil supertanker, rammed Bligh Reef a few hours out of the port of Valdez, spilling almost 11 million gallons of crude oil into Prince William Sound. The spill eventually contaminated 1567 miles of shoreline and killed an estimated 100,000 to 250,000 birds and 2800 sea otters and decimated fish populations. The fisheries are just now recovering from the spill, as are animal populations, though you can still find oil just below the sand on many beaches.

In 2006 Sarah Palin, a former mayor of Wasilla, stunned the political world by beating the incumbent governor to become Alaska's first female governor as well as its youngest at 42. Two years later presidential candidate John McCain named her as his running mate on the Republican ticket. Commanding a little less international attention was Republican Senator Ted Stevens who, when he left office in 2009, had served the state for a record 41 years.

Land & Climate

It's one thing to be told Denali is the tallest mountain in North America; it's another to see it crowning the sky in Denali National Park. It's a mountain so tall, so massive and so overwhelming it has visitors stumbling off the park buses. As a state, Alaska is the same, a place so huge, so wild and so unpopulated it's incomprehensible to most people until they arrive.

🛈 Getting There & Away

Whether you're from the US or overseas, traveling to Alaska is like traveling to a foreign country. By sea it takes almost a week on the Alaska Marine Highway ferry to reach Whittier in Prince William Sound from the lower 48. By land a motorist in the Midwest needs 10 days to drive straight to Fairbanks.

If you're coming from the US mainland, the quickest and least expensive way to reach Alaska is to fly nonstop from a number of cities. If you're coming from Asia or Europe, it's almost impossible to fly directly to Alaska as few international airlines maintain a direct service to Anchorage, except for seasonal flights from Frankfurt on **Condor Airlines** (☏ 800-524-6975; www.condor.com). Most international travelers come through the gateway cities of Seattle, Portland, Minneapolis or Denver.

Flights, cars and tours can be booked online at lonelyplanet.com/bookings.

ANCHORAGE

Locals like to say that Anchorage is only 30 minutes from Alaska: wedged between 5000ft peaks and an inlet filled with salmon and whales, the Big Apple of the north is unlike any other city.

At first glance the traffic, strip malls and suburban sprawl can feel off-putting. But inside those strip malls are top-notch restaurants serving fresh seafood and locally grown produce, and the two roads that lead in and out of town spool right into some of the most majestic wilderness in the world. This is a city where bears are seen wandering bike paths, moose munch on neighborhood gardens, and locals pull salmon from a creek within blocks of hotels and office buildings.

Dive into this city of parks, museums and restaurants and you'll see why almost half the state's population calls it home.

◎ Sights

★ **Anchorage Museum**   MUSEUM
(www.anchoragemuseum.org; 625 C St; adult/child $15/7; ⊙ summer 9am-6pm; 🚻) This world-class facility is Anchorage's cultural jewel. The West Wing, a four-story, shimmering, mirrored facade, adds 80,000 sq ft to what

was already the largest museum in the state, and a new wing was under construction at the time of writing. The museum's flagship exhibit is the **Smithsonian Arctic Studies Center** – with more than 600 Alaska Native objects, such as art, tools, masks and household implements – which was previously housed in Washington, DC.

★ **Alaska Native Heritage Center**   CULTURAL CENTER
(☑ 907-330-8000; www.alaskanative.net; 8800 Heritage Center Dr; adult/child $25/17; ☺ 9am-5pm) If you can't travel to the Bush region to experience Native Alaska culture first-hand, visit this 26-acre center and see how humans survived – and thrived – before central heating. This is much more than just a museum: it represents a knowledge bank of language, art and culture that will survive no matter how many sitcoms are crackling through the Alaskan stratosphere.

Alaska Zoo   ZOO
(www.alaskazoo.org; 4731 O'Malley Rd; adult/child $15/7; ☺ 9am-9pm; ⊞) The unique wildlife of the Arctic is on display at this zoo, the only one in North America that specializes in northern animals, including snow leopards, Amur tigers and Tibetan yaks. Alaskan native species, from wolverines and moose to caribou and Dall sheep, are abundant. What kids will love watching, however, are the bears. The zoo has all Alaskan species, but the polar bears are clearly the star attraction.

Alaska Native Medical Center   GALLERY
(www.anmc.org; 4315 Diplomacy Dr; ☺ 24hr) **FREE** This hospital has a fantastic collection of Alaska Native art and artifacts: take the elevator to the top floor and wind down the staircase past dolls, basketry and tools from all over Alaska. It's an informal presentation but a worthy visit.

Ship Creek Viewing Platform   VIEWPOINT
FREE From mid- to late summer, king, coho and pink salmon spawn up Ship Creek, the historical site of Tanaina Indian fish camps. At the overlook you can cheer on those love-starved fish humping their way toward destiny, and during high tide see the banks lined with anglers trying to hook them in what has to be one of the greatest urban fisheries anywhere in the USA. Take C St north, cross Ship Creek Bridge and turn right on Whitney Rd.

Alaska Aviation Heritage Museum   MUSEUM
(www.alaskaairmuseum.org; 4721 Aircraft Dr; adult/child $15/8; ☺ 9am-5pm) On the south shore of Lake Hood, the world's busiest floatplane lake, this museum is a tribute to Alaska's colorful Bush pilots and their faithful planes. Housed within are 25 planes along with historic photos and displays of pilots' achievements, from the first flight to Fairbanks (1913) to the early history of Alaska Airlines.

⌖ **Tours**

★ **Alaska Railroad**   RAIL
(☑ 907-265-2494; www.akrr.com; 411 W 1st Ave) Has many one-day tours from Anchorage that begin with a train ride. Its nine-hour Spencer Glacier Float Tour (per person $242) trundles to Spencer Lake and includes a gentle raft trip among icebergs. The Glacier Quest Cruise ($223) rumbles to Whittier and includes a four-hour boat cruise in Prince William Sound; watch glaciers calve while feasting on king crab cakes.

Ghost Tours of Anchorage   HISTORY
(☑ 907-274-4678; www.ghosttoursofanchorage. com; per person $15; ☺ 7:30pm Tue-Sun) This excellent and quirky 90-minute downtown walk takes place nightly (rain or shine) in summer. To join, just show up in front of Snow City Café at 4th Ave and L St – site of perhaps the most notorious murder in Anchorage's history.

🛏 **Sleeping**

Bent Prop Inn Midtown   HOSTEL $
(☑ 907-222-5220; www.bentpropinn.com; 3104 Eide St; dm $30-35; ☎) The microdorms here are the best deal in town: in converted one-bedroom apartments, these come with four beds, a private kitchen and a living room – it's like dorms meet the suite life. Regular dorms are co-ed and have six beds. There are two kitchens, coin-operated laundry and big-screen TV. The one private apartment goes for $149.

★ **Copper Whale Inn**   INN $$
(☑ 907-258-7999; www.copperwhale.com; cnr W 5th Ave & L St; r $199-240, ste $279; @☎) An ideal downtown location and a bright and elegant interior make this inn one of the best midrange places in Anchorage. The suite has a full kitchen. Two relaxing waterfall courtyards make it easy to consume that novel, while many rooms and the breakfast lounge give way to views of Cook Inlet.

Anchorage Grand Hotel   LUXURY HOTEL $$
(☑ 907-929-8888; www.anchoragegrand.com; 505 W 2nd Ave; r $199; @☎) This converted apartment building rests on a quiet street with 31 spacious suites that include full kitchens

and separate living and bedroom areas. Many overlook Ship Creek and Cook Inlet, and its downtown location is convenient to everything.

Hotel Captain Cook HOTEL **$$$**

(☏907-276-6000; www.captaincook.com; 939 W 5th Ave; s/d $295/315; @🛜🏊) The grand dame of Anchorage accommodations still has an air of an Alaskan aristocrat, right down to the finely dressed doormen. There are plenty of plush services and upscale shops: hot tubs, a fitness club, beauty salon, jewelry store and four restaurants, including the famed Crow's Nest bar on the top floor.

🍴 Eating

★Snow City Café CAFE **$**

(☏907-272-2489; www.snowcitycafe.com; 1034 W 4th Ave; breakfast $8-15, lunch $10-15; ☉6:30am-3pm Mon-Fri, to 4pm Sat & Sun; 🛜) Consistently voted best breakfast by *Anchorage Press* readers, this busy cafe serves healthy grub to a clientele that ranges from the tattooed to the up-and-coming. For breakfast, skip the usual eggs and toast and try a 'crabby' omelet or a sockeye smoked salmon Benedict.

Red Chair Cafe BREAKFAST **$**

(www.theredchaircafe.com; 337 E 4th Ave; breakfast $12-16; ☉7am-3pm Tue-Sun) The best and worst thing about eating in this steampunk-decorated cafe is choosing which brunch dish. The hollandaise sauce is made fresh daily, as are the muffins. Or should you go for the stuffed poblano pepper, the lemon poppyseed pancakes or the kale baked skillet?

Fromagio's Artisan Cheese SANDWICHES **$**

(www.fromagioscheese.com; 3555 Arctic Blvd; sandwiches $11; ☉11am-6pm Tue-Sat, noon-5pm Sun) A cheesemonger that serves gourmet sandwiches. Stop in for lunch, sample some exotic cheeses and then grab some for a picnic while on your hike.

★Rustic Goat BISTRO **$$**

(☏907-334-8100; www.rusticgoatak.com; 2800 Turnagain St; pizzas $14-16, mains $18-32; ☉6am-10pm Mon-Thu, to 11pm Fri, 7am-11pm Sat, to 10pm Sun) This sweet little bistro is in the suburban Turnagain neighborhood, but it feels like a city loft. Old-growth timbers support two stories of windows that look out to the Chugach Mountains. The assorted menu includes wood-fired pizzas, steaks and salads. In the morning it's a casual coffee shop.

🍷 Drinking & Nightlife

Williwaw BAR

(www.williwawsocial.com; 609 F St; ☉11am-late) It almost feels like you're in the big city when you spend a sunny evening at the rooftop bar surrounded by Anchorage's downtown buildings. A hidden speakeasy mixes upscale drinks (entry requires a password – note the payphone in the lobby), and there's live musical acts every weekend on the 1st floor. By day, a coffee shop serves up espressos.

Bernie's Bungalow Lounge LOUNGE

(www.bernieslounge.com; 626 D St; ☉11am-1am Mon-Fri, 2pm-2:30am Sat & Sun) Pretty people, pretty drinks: this is the place to see and be seen. Its outdoor patio, complete with a water-spewing serpent, is the best in Anchorage, and on summer weekends it rocks late into the night with DJs up in the VIP room.

☆ Entertainment

★Cyrano's Theatre Company THEATER

(☏907-274-2599; www.cyranos.org; 413 D St) This small off-center playhouse is the best live theater in town, staging everything from *Hamlet* to *Archy and Mehitabel* (comic cockroach and a cat characters), Mel Brooks' jazz musical based on the poetry of Don Marquis and an ever-changing lineup of original shows. Shows typically run Thursday to Sunday.

LGBTIQ ALASKA

The gay community in Alaska is far smaller and much less open than in major US cities, and Alaskans in general are not as tolerant to diversity. In 1998 Alaska passed a constitutional amendment banning same-sex marriages. However, attitudes are slowly changing. A 2014 poll found 47% of Alaskan voters in favor of same-sex marriage.

In Anchorage, the only city in Alaska of any real size, there is **Identity Inc** (☏907-929-4528; www.identityinc.org), which has a gay and lesbian helpline, a handful of openly gay clubs and bars, and a weeklong PrideFest (http://alaskapride.org) in mid-June. The Southeast Alaska Gay & Lesbian Alliance (www.seagla.org) is based in Juneau and offers links and travel lists geared to gay visitors. The list is short, however, because most towns do not have an openly active gay community. In rural Alaska, same-sex couples should exercise discretion.

Alaska Center for the Performing Arts

PERFORMING ARTS

([✓] tickets 907-263-2787; www.myalaskacenter.
com; 621 W 6th Ave) Impresses tourists with
the 40-minute film *Aurora: Alaska's Great
Northern Lights* (adult/child $13/7), screened
on the hour from 9am to 9pm during summer in its Sydney Laurence Theatre. It's also
home to the **Anchorage Opera** ([✓] 907-279-
2557; www.anchorageopera.org), **Anchorage
Symphony Orchestra** ([✓] 907-274-8668; www.
anchoragesymphony.org), **Anchorage Concert
Association** ([✓] 907-272-1471; www.anchorage
concerts.org) and **Alaska Dance Theatre**
([✓] 907-277-9591; www.alaskadancetheatre.org).

Chilkoot Charlie's

LIVE MUSIC

(www.koots.com; 2435 Spenard Rd; ⏱ 11:45am-
2:30am Mon-Thu, 10:30am-3am Fri & Sat, to 2:30am
Sun) More than just Anchorage's favorite
meat market, 'Koots,' as the locals call it, is
a landmark. The sprawling, wooden edifice
has 10 bars, four dance floors and a sawdust-strewn floor. Many live acts perform
here and there's at least one fun thing happening every night of the week.

ℹ️ Information

Alaska Public Lands Information Center
([✓] 907-644-3661; www.alaskacenters.gov;
605 W 4th Ave, Suite 105; ⏱ 9am-5pm) In
the Federal Building (you'll need photo ID).
The center has handouts for hikers, mountain
bikers, kayakers, fossil hunters and just about
everyone else, on almost every wilderness area
in the state. There are also excellent wildlife
displays, free movies, fun dioramas, and
ranger-led walks (11am and 3:15pm).

Anchorage Convention & Visitors Bureau
([✓] 907-276-4118; www.anchorage.net) Has a
useful website. Ring before your trip and ask to
be posted a guide.

Log Cabin & Downtown Information Center
([✓] 907-257-2363; www.anchorage.net; 524 W
4th Ave; ⏱ 8am-7pm) Has pamphlets, maps,
bus schedules, city guides in several languages
and a lawn growing on its roof.

Visitors Center ([✓] 907-266-2437; Anchorage
International Airport; ⏱ 9am-4pm) Two visitor-
center kiosks are located in the baggage-claim
areas of both airport terminals.

ℹ️ Getting There & Away

AIR

Ted Stevens Anchorage International Airport
(ANC; www.dot.state.ak.us/anc; 📶; 🚌 7) The
vast majority of visitors to Alaska, land here, at Alaska's
biggest airport.

BUS

Anchorage is a hub for various small passenger
and freight lines that make daily runs between
specific cities. Always call first; Alaska's volatile
bus industry is as unstable as an Alaska Peninsula volcano.

Alaska Park Connection ([✓] 800-266-8625;
www.alaskacoach.com) Offers daily service
from Anchorage north to Talkeetna ($65, 2½
hours) and Denali National Park ($90, six
hours), and south to Seward ($65, three hours).

Alaska/Yukon Trails ([✓] 907-479-2277, 907-
888-5659; www.alaskashuttle.com) Runs a bus
up the George Parks Hwy to Denali ($75, six
hours) and Fairbanks ($99, nine hours).

Homer Stage Lines ([✓] 907-868-3914; http://
stagelineinhomer.com) Will take you to Homer
($90, 4½ hours) and points in between.

Interior Alaska Bus Line ([✓] 800-770-6652;
www.interioralaskabusline.com) Has regular services between Anchorage and Glennallen ($70,
three hours), Tok ($115, eight hours) and Fair-
banks ($160, 17 hours), and points in between.

Seward Bus Line ([✓] 907-563-0800; www.
sewardbuslines.net) Runs between Anchorage
and Seward ($40, three hours) twice daily in
summer. For an extra $5, you can arrange an
airport pickup/drop off.

CAR

Avoid renting a car at the Anchorage airport if
possible, as you will be hit with an extra 11.11%
airport rental tax. Rental agencies within Anchorage will tack on only an 18% tax and generally have cheaper rates. And while they can't
pick you up at the airport, if you drop the car off
during business hours some rental places will
provide you with a ride to the airport.

Also keep in mind that if you can rent a vehicle
in May or September as opposed to June, July or
August, you will usually save an additional 30%.

TRAIN

Alaska Railroad ([✓] 800-544-0552; www.akrr.
com) From its downtown depot, the Alaska
Railroad sends its *Denali Star* north daily to
Talkeetna (adult/child $101/51), Denali National
Park ($167/84) and Fairbanks ($239/120). The
Coastal Classic stops in Girdwood ($80/40) and
Seward ($89/45), while the *Glacial Discovery*
connects to Whittier ($105/53). You can save
20% to 30% traveling in May and September.

SOUTHEAST ALASKA

Southeast Alaska is so *un-Alaska*. While
much of the state is a treeless expanse of
land with a layer of permafrost, the Panhandle is a slender, long rainforest that stretches
540 miles from Icy Bay, near Yakutat, south
to Portland Canal and is filled with ice-blue

WORTH A TRIP

THE WILDS OF KODIAK ISLAND

Kodiak is the island of plenty. Consider its famous brown bears, the second-largest ursine creatures in the world (after the polar bear). Thanks to an unblemished ecosystem and an unlimited diet of rich salmon that spawn in Kodiak's lakes and rivers, adult male bears can weigh up to 1400lb.

Part of the wider Kodiak Archipelago and the second-largest island in the US after Hawaii's Big Island, Kodiak acts as a kind of ecological halfway house between the forested Alaskan Panhandle and the treeless Aleutian Islands. Its velvety green mountains and sheltered, ice-free bays were the site of the earliest Russian settlement in Alaska and are still home to one of the US's most important fishing fleets.

The island's main attraction – beyond its bears – is its quiet Alaskan authenticity. Only a small northeastern section of Kodiak is populated. The rest is roadless wilderness protected in the Kodiak National Wildlife Refuge.

Most travelers arriving on Kodiak Island come via plane or boat through Kodiak town.

glaciers, rugged snowcapped mountains, towering Sitka spruce and a thousand islands known as the Alexander Archipelago.

Before WWII, the Southeast was Alaska's heart and soul, and Juneau was not only the capital but the state's largest city. Today the region is characterized by big trees and small towns. Each community here has its own history and character: from Norwegian-influenced Petersburg to Russian-tinted Sitka. You can feel the gold fever in Skagway and see a dozen glaciers near Juneau. Each town is unique and none of them is connected to another by road. Jump on the state ferry or book a cruise and discover the idiosyncrasies.

Wrangell

Wrangell is Southeast Alaska's rough, gruff coastal outpost, a small boom-bust fishing community colored by centuries of native Tlingit settlement and more recent incursions by the Russians and British. Posh it isn't. Lacking the fishing affluence of Petersburg or the cruise-ship-oriented economy of Ketchikan, the town nurtures a tough outback spirit more familiar to Alaska's frigid north than its drizzly Panhandle. A collapse in the lumber industry in the 1990s hit the town hard, a blow from which it has only recently recovered.

If people stop in Wrangell at all, it's normally as a launchpad for excursions to the Anan bear-watching observatory and the incredible Stikine River delta nearby. However, the countryside around town, a mishmash of boggy 'muskeg' and tree-covered mountains, offers fine hiking, a fact not lost on Scottish American naturalist John Muir, who decamped here in 1879 on the first of four Alaska visits.

⊙ Sights & Activities

★ **Wrangell Museum**   MUSEUM
(☎907-874-3770; 296 Campbell Dr; adult/child/family $5/2/12; ⊙10am-5pm Mon-Sat late Apr–mid-Sep, 1-5pm Tue-Sat mid-Sep–late Apr) This impressive museum is what the colorful history and characters of Wrangell deserve. As you stroll through the many rooms, an audio narration automatically comes on and explains each chapter of Wrangell's history, from Tlingit culture and the gold-rush era to the time Hollywood arrived in 1972 to film the movie *Timber Tramps*. You can marvel at a collection of Alaskan art that includes a Sidney Laurence painting or be amused that this rugged little town has had two presidential visits.

Petrolyph Beach   ARCHAEOLOGICAL SITE
(Evergreen Ave; 🚗) **FREE** Thought Alaska's history started with the Klondike gold rush? Not so. Historians and anthropologists should home in on this state historic park on Wrangell's north side, where you can see primitive rock carvings believed to be at least 1000 years old, plus a viewing deck with interpretive displays and replicas. Turn right and walk north on the beach about 50yd. Before you reach the wrecked fishing vessels, look for faint carvings on the large rocks, many of them resembling spirals and faces.

★ **Anan Creek Wildlife Observatory**   WILDLIFE WATCHING
(☎1-800-877-444-6777; www.fs.usda.gov/recarea/tongass/recreation/natureviewing; permits $10) Thirty miles southeast of Wrangell on the mainland, Anan Creek is the site of one of the largest pink-salmon runs in Southeast Alaska. Here you can watch eagles, harbor seals, black bears and brown bears chowing down on the spawning humpies. This is one of the few places in Alaska where black and

brown bears coexist – or at least put up with each other – at the same run. Permits are required from early July through August.

🛏 Sleeping & Eating

Wrangell Hostel
HOSTEL $

(☎907-874-3534; 220 Church St; dm $20; ⊙ Jun-Sep) The First Presbyterian Church doubles up as a basic hostel, with single-sex dorm rooms with inflatable mattresses, showers and a large kitchen and dining room. It has no curfew and will graciously let you hang out here during an all-day rain. There's no sign, just knock or push on the church door.

★ Ultima Thule Lodge
LUXURY HOTEL $$$

(☎907-854-4500; www.ultimathulelodge.com; 4-night 4-day package per person $7950) 🍴 Located in the lonely backcountry of Wrangell-St Elias National Park on the Chitina River, over 100 miles from the nearest road, this fabulously luxurious lodge is the last thing you expect in such an inhospitable environment. But far from being just another expensive resort, Ultima Thule is elegant, tasteful, unpretentious and as beautiful as the land that envelops it.

★ Stikine Inn Restaurant
AMERICAN $$

(107 Stikine Ave; mains lunch $14-18, dinner $16-30; ⊙11am-8pm) It's not hard being the best restaurant in Wrangell, but the Stikine goes above and beyond the call of duty with dishes like rockfish tacos, and a lobster po'boy that manage to be decadent without a decadent price. Everything's made a little more hunky dory by the view (water and fishing boats) and service (small-town Alaska friendly).

ℹ Information

USFS Office (☎907-874-2323; 525 Bennet St; ⊙8am-4:30pm Mon-Fri) Located 0.75 miles north of town; has information on regional USFS cabins, trails and campgrounds.

Wrangell Visitor Center (☎907-874-3901; www.wrangell.com; 293 Campbell Dr; ⊙10am-5pm Mon-Sat) In the plush Nolan Center, it stocks the free *Wrangell Guide* and shows a 10-minute film on the area in a small theater.

ℹ Getting There & Away

Daily northbound and southbound flights are available with Alaska Airlines (p1107) on the so-called 'Milk Run' serving Seattle, Ketchikan, Petersburg, Juneau and Anchorage. Many claim the flight north to Petersburg is the world's shortest jet flight – around nine minutes on a good day with fabulous views to boot.

The **airport** (☎907-874-3107) is just over a mile from the town center; an easy walk with light luggage.

Sitka

It's not always easy to uncover reminders of Alaska's 135-year-long dalliance with the Russian Empire – until you dock in Sitka. This sparkling gem of a city, which kisses the Pacific Ocean on Baranof Island's west shore, is one of the oldest non-native settlements in the state and the former capital of Russian Alaska (when it was known as New Archangel).

The bonus for visitors is that Sitka mixes wonderfully preserved history with outstanding natural beauty. Looming on the horizon, across Sitka Sound, is impressive Mt Edgecumbe, an extinct volcano with a graceful cone similar to Japan's Mt Fuji. Closer in, myriad small, forested islands

---

ALASKA FOR KIDS

The best that Alaska has to offer cannot be found in stuffy museums or amusement parks filled with heart-pounding rides. It's outdoor adventure, wildlife and scenery on a grand scale, attractions and activities that will intrigue the entire family – whether you're a kid or a parent.

Pioneer Park (☎907-459-1087; Airport Way; ⊙stores & museums noon-8pm late May-early Sep, park 5am-midnight; 🅿🚻) Train rides, salmon bakes and genuine pioneer history entertain the offspring in Fairbanks.

Mendenhall Glacier (p1098) Fascinating and easily accessible natural feature that's capable of dropping the jaws of any age group.

Sitka Sound (☎907-752-0660; www.kayaksitka.com) Sheltered waters, plenty of wooded islands and a good local guiding company make this one of Alaska's best family sea-kayaking spots.

Petroglyph Beach (p1095) Search for ancient rock carvings and sea life at low tide in Wrangell.

turn into beautiful ragged silhouettes at sunset, competing for attention with the snowcapped mountains and sharp granite peaks flanking Sitka to the east. And in town picturesque remnants of Sitka's Russian heritage are tucked around every corner. It's like Skagway but with less tourists.

◎ Sights & Activities

★ Sitka National Historical Park
HISTORIC SITE
(www.nps.gov; Lincoln St; ◎6am-10pm) FREE
This mystical juxtaposition of tall trees and totems is Alaska's smallest national park and the site where the Tlingits were finally defeated by the Russians in 1804.

The mile-long **Totem Trail** winds it way past 18 totems first displayed at the 1904 Louisiana Exposition in St Louis and then moved to the park. These intriguing totems, standing in a thick rainforest setting by the sea and often enveloped in mist, have become synonymous with the national park and, by definition, the city itself.

★ Russian Bishop's House
HISTORIC BUILDING
(☏907-747-0135; Lincoln St; ◎9am-5pm) FREE
East of downtown along Lincoln St, the Russian Bishop's House is the oldest intact Russian building in Sitka. Built in 1843 by Finnish carpenters out of Sitka spruce, the two-story log house is one of only four surviving examples of Russian colonial architecture in North America. The National Park Service (NPS) has restored the building to its 1853 condition, when it served as a school and residence for the Russian bishop, Innocent (Ivan Veniaminov).

Sitka Sound Science Center
AQUARIUM
(www.sitkascience.org; 801 Lincoln St; $5; ◎9am-4pm; 🚼) Sitka's best children's attraction is this hatchery and science center. Outside, the facade is being restored to its original appearance. Inside the science center are five aquariums, including the impressive 800-gallon 'Wall of Water' and three touch tanks where kids can get their hands wet handling anemones, sea cucumbers and starfish.

Whale Park
PARK
(Sawmill Creek Rd) If you can't afford a wildlife cruise, try Whale Park, 4 miles south of downtown, which has a boardwalk and free spotting scopes overlooking the ocean. Best of all is listening to whale songs over the 'hydrophone.' Fall is the best time to sight cetaceans; as many as 80 whales – mostly humpbacks – can gather between mid-September and year's end.

Alaska Raptor Center
WILDLIFE RESERVE
(☏907-747-8662; www.alaskaraptor.org; 101 Sawmill Creek Rd; adult/child $12/6; ◎8am-4pm; P🚼) 🦅 This is no zoo, or bird show for gawping kids. Rather, think of it more as a raptor hospital and rehab center – and a good one at that. The 17-acre center treats 200 injured birds a year, with its most impressive facility being a 20,000-sq-ft flight-training center that helps injured eagles, owls, falcons and hawks regain their ability to fly.

🛏 Sleeping

Sitka International Hostel
HOSTEL $
(☏907-747-8661; www.sitkahostel.org; 109 Jeff Davis St; dm/d $24/65; 🛜) Sitka's typically bohemian hostel is downtown in the historic Tillie Paul Manor, which once served as the town's hospital. The charismatic building crammed with all sorts of information and mementos features a men's room with its own kitchen and several women's rooms, along with a family room, another small kitchen and a lovely sun porch with a mountain view.

Cascade Creek Inn
INN $$
(☏907-747-6804; www.cascadecreekinnandcharters.com; 2035 Halibut Point Rd; r $130-160; 🛜) Perched right above the shoreline, all 10 rooms in this handsome wooden inn face the ocean and have a private balcony overlooking it. There are four top-floor rooms with kitchenettes. Sure, you're 2.5 miles north of town, but the inn's oceanfront deck is worth the ride on the downtown bus.

Aspen Suites Hotel
HOTEL $$$
(www.aspenhotelsak.com/sitka; 210 Lake St; ste $259-269; P@🛜) This new chain has infiltrated several Alaskan cities in the last couple of years, Juneau and Haines among them. The new Sitka offering opened in the summer of 2017 with Aspen's characteristic selection of businesslike suites complete with kitchenettes, sofas and large bathrooms. There's also an on-site gym and a surgical level of cleanliness (and newness) throughout.

🍴 Eating & Drinking

★ Grandma Tillie's Bakery
BAKERY $
(www.grandmatilliesbakery.com; Sawmill Creek Rd; baked goods $3-8; ◎6:30am-2pm Wed-Sat) Pink drive-through bakery located 1 mile east of the town center that is – frankly – worth the walk, let alone the drive, courtesy of its sponge-y fresh savory rolls and rich chewy cookies. We'll stick our neck out and

announce that these are, possibly, the best baked goods in Southeast Alaska.

★ **Ludvig's Bistro** MEDITERRANEAN $$$
(☑ 907-966-3663; www.ludvigsbistro.com; 256 Katlian St; mains $28-40; ⊙ 4:30-9:30pm Mon-Sat) Sophistication in the wilderness! Sitka's boldest restaurant has only seven tables, and a few stools at its brass-and-blue-tile bar. Described as 'rustic Mediterranean fare,' almost every dish is local, even the sea salt. If seafood paella is on the menu, order it. The traditional Spanish rice dish comes loaded with whatever fresh seafood the local boats have netted that day.

★ **Baranof Island Brewing Co** BREWERY
(www.baranofislandbrewing.com; 1209 Sawmill Creek Rd; ⊙ 2-8pm; ⊛) Encased in a handsome new taproom since July 2017, the Baranof is a local legend providing microbrews for every pub and bar in town. For the real deal, however, the taproom's the place. Line up four to six tasters and make sure you include a Halibut Point Hefeweisen and a Redoubt Red Ale.

❶ Information

Sitka Information Center (☑ 907-747-5940; www.sitka.org; 104 Lake St; ⊙ 9am-4:30pm Mon-Fri) Ultra-helpful office opposite the Westmark hotel downtown. Also staffs a desk at the **Harigan Centennial Hall** (☑ 907-747-3225; 330 Harbor Dr; ⊙ 9am-5pm) when there's a cruise ship in town.

USFS Sitka Ranger District Office (☑ 907-747-6671, recorded information 907-747-6685; 2108 Halibut Point Rd; ⊙ 8am-4:30pm Mon-Fri) Has information about local trails, camping and USFS cabins. It's 2 miles north of town. More central is the visitor center at Sitka National Historical Park (p1097).

❶ Getting There & Away

Alaska Airlines (p1107) Flights to/from Juneau (45 minutes) and Ketchikan (one hour).
Harris Aircraft Services (☑ 907-966-3050; www.harrisair.com; Airport Rd) Floatplane air-taxi service to small communities and USFS cabins as well as larger Southeast towns such as Juneau.
Sitka Airport (SIT; ☑ 907-966-2960) On Japonski Island, 1.5 miles, or a 20-minute walk, west of downtown. The Ride Sitka green line bus runs to the island but stops short of the airport.

Juneau

Juneau is a capital of contrasts and conflicts. It borders a waterway that never freezes but lies beneath an ice field that never melts. It was the first community in the Southeast to slap a head tax on cruise-ship passengers but still draws more than a million a year. It's the state capital but since the 1980s Alaskans have been trying to move it. It doesn't have any roads that go anywhere, but half its residents and its mayor opposed a plan to build one that would.

Welcome to America's strangest state capital. In the winter it's a beehive of legislators, their loyal aides and lobbyists locked in political struggles. In summer it's a launchpad for copious outdoor adventures. Superb hiking starts barely 10 minutes from downtown, a massive glacier calves into a lake 12 miles up the road, and boats and seaplanes take off from the waterfront bound for nearby bear-viewing, ziplining and whale-watching.

◉ Sights & Activities

★ **Mendenhall Glacier** GLACIER
Going to Juneau and not seeing the Mendenhall is like visiting Rome and skipping the Colosseum. The most famous of Juneau's ice floes, and the city's most popular attraction, flows 13 miles from its source, the Juneau Icefield, and has a half-mile-wide face. It ends at **Mendenhall Lake**, the reason for all the icebergs.

Alaska State Museum MUSEUM
(☑ 907-465-2901; www.museums.state.ak.us; 395 Whittier St; adult/child $12/free; ⊙ 9am-5pm; ⊛) Demolished and rebuilt in a snazzy new $140-million complex in 2016, the result is impressive. Sometimes called SLAM (State Library, Archives and Museum), the museum shares digs with the state archives along with a gift store, the Raven Cafe, an auditorium, a research room and a historical library. The beautifully curated displays catalogue the full historical and geographic breadth of the state, from native canoes to the oil industry.

Mt Roberts Tramway CABLE CAR
(www.mountrobertstramway.com; 490 S Franklin St; adult/child $33/16; ⊙ 11am-9pm Mon, 8am-9pm Tue-Sun; ⊛) As far as cable cars go, this tramway is rather expensive for a five-minute ride. But from a marketing point of view its location couldn't be better. It whisks you right from the cruise-ship dock up 1750ft to the timberline of Mt Roberts, where you'll find a restaurant, gift shops, a small raptor center and a theater with a film on Tlingit culture.

BEARS OF ADMIRALTY ISLAND & PACK CREEK

Just 15 miles south of Juneau is Admiralty Island National Monument, a 1493-sq-mile preserve, of which 90% is designated wilderness. The monument has a wide variety of wildlife – from Sitka black-tailed deer and nesting bald eagles to harbor seals, sea lions and humpback whales – but more than anything else, Admiralty Island is known for bears. The 96-mile-long island has one of the highest populations of bears in Alaska, with an estimated 1500 brown bears, more than all the lower 48 states combined. It's the reason the Tlingit called Admiralty Kootznoowoo, 'the Fortress of Bears.'

The monument's main attraction for visitors is **Pack Creek** (permits adult $25-50, child $10-25), which flows from 4000ft mountains before spilling into Seymour Canal on the island's east side. The extensive tide flats at the mouth of the creek draw a large number of bears in July and August to feed on salmon. This, and its proximity to Juneau, make it a favorite spot for observing and photographing the animals.

Admiralty Air Service (907-796-2000; www.admiraltyairservice.com) offers charter flights to Pack Creek and elsewhere for $450 an hour (up to four people).

Alaska Seaplanes (907-789-3331; www.flyalaskaseaplanes.com) has three daily flights from Juneau to Angoon ($144, 35 minutes).

★ **Alaska Zipline Adventures**   ADVENTURE SPORTS
(907-321-0947; www.alaskazip.com; adult/child $149/99) Possibly Alaska's most adrenaline-laced zip, these nine lines and two sky bridges are located at beautiful Eaglecrest Ski Area on Douglas Island, from where they zigzag across Fish Creek Valley. Transportation (usually a boat) from the cruise-ship dock is included.

✦ Festivals & Events

★ **Celebration**   CULTURAL
(⊙ Jun) In June of even-numbered years, Southeast Alaska's three main tribal groups, the Tlingit, Haida and Tsimshian, gather for the aptly named 'Celebration,' the largest native cultural event in Alaska. The festival's sentiment is as simple as its name: to celebrate and revitalize ancient traditions in native dance, music and art which, by the early 20th century, were in danger of extinction.

🛏 Sleeping

★ **Mendenhall Lake Campground**   CAMPGROUND $
(518-885-3639, reservations 877-444-6777; www.recreation.gov; Montana Creek Rd; tent sites $10, RV sites $28) One of Alaska's most beautiful USFS campgrounds. The 69-site area (17 sites with hookups) is on Montana Creek Rd, off Mendenhall Loop Rd, and has a separate seven-site walk-in area. The campsites are alongside Mendenhall Lake, and many have spectacular views of the icebergs or even the glacier that discharges them.

All the sites are well spread out in the woods, and 20 can be reserved in advance.

Alaskan Hotel   HOTEL $
(907-586-1000; www.thealaskanhotel.com; 167 S Franklin St; r with/without private bath $90/80; 🐾) Welcome to a quintessential gold-boom hotel, with heavily patterned wallpaper clashing with the heavily patterned carpet, lots of wood paneling and walls that would probably relate some lewd erstwhile antics could they talk (it's the oldest operating hotel in Alaska, dating from 1913).

★ **Silverbow Inn**   BOUTIQUE HOTEL $$$
(907-586-4146; www.silverbowinn.com; 120 2nd St; r $199-244; @🐾) A swanky (for Alaska) boutique inn with 11 rooms. The 100-year-old building emanates a retro-versus-modern feel with antiques and rooms with private baths, king and queen beds and flat-screen TVs. A 2nd-floor deck features a hot tub with a view of Douglas Island's mountains. Breakfast is served in the morning and there's a cocoa and cookies 'happy hour' in the afternoon.

🍴 Eating

★ **Pel'Meni**   DUMPLINGS $
(Merchant's Wharf, Marine Way; dumplings $7; ⊙11:30am-1:30am Sun-Thu, to 3:30am Fri & Sat) Juneau was never part of Russia's Alaskan empire, but that hasn't stopped the city succumbing to a silent invasion of pelmeni (homemade Russian dumplings), filled with either potato or beef, spiced with hot sauce, curry and cilantro, and tempered with a little optional sour cream and rye bread on the side.

★ **Saffron** INDIAN $$

(☑ 907-586-1036; www.saffronalaska.com; 112 N Franklin St; mains $8-19; ⊙ 11:30am-9pm Mon-Fri, 5-9pm Sat & Sun; 🖉) Juneau flirts with *nuevo* Indian food at Saffron and the results are commendable. There are plenty of delicate breads to go with the aromatic curries with a strong bias toward vegetarian dishes (including a good spinach paneer). For lunch it offers *thalis* (small taster-sized plates). Everything is made from scratch and the exotic cooking smells lure you in from the street.

Tracy's King Crab Shack SEAFOOD $$

(www.kingcrabshack.com; 406 S Franklin St; crab $13-45; ⊙ 10am-8pm) The best of the food shacks along the cruise-ship berths is Tracy's. On a boardwalk surrounded by a beer shack and a gift shop, she serves up outstanding crab bisque, mini crab cakes and 3lb buckets of king-crab pieces ($110). Grab a friend or six and share.

🍷 Drinking & Nightlife

Alaskan Brewing Company BREWERY

(www.alaskanbeer.com; 5429 Shaune Dr; ⊙ 11am-6pm) Established in 1986 (ancient history in craft-brewing years), Alaska's largest brewery has always been a pioneer. Its amber ale (along with many other concoctions) is ubiquitous across the state and rightly so. Note: this is not a brewpub but a tasting room with tours. It isn't located downtown, either, but 5 miles to the northwest in Lemon Creek.

❶ Information

Alaska Division of Parks (☑ 907-465-4563; www.dnr.state.ak.us/parks; 400 Willoughby Ave; ⊙ 8am-4:30pm Mon-Fri) Head to the 5th floor of the Natural Resources Building for state-park information, including cabin rentals.

Juneau Visitor Center (☑ 907-586-2201; www.traveljuneau.com; 470 S Franklin St; ⊙ 8am-5pm) The visitor center is on the cruise-ship terminal right next to the Mt Roberts Tramway and has all the information you need to explore Juneau, find a trail or book a room. The center also maintains smaller booths at the airport, at the marine ferry terminal and **downtown** (Marine Way; ⊙ hours vary) near the library.

USFS Juneau Ranger District Office (☑ 907-586-8800; 8510 Mendenhall Loop Rd; ⊙ 8am-4:30pm Mon-Fri) This impressive office is in Mendenhall Valley and is the place for questions about cabins, trails, kayaking and Pack Creek bear-watching permits. It also serves as the USFS office for Admiralty Island National Monument.

❶ Getting There & Away

Juneau International Airport is located 9 miles northwest of downtown. There is a bus link.

Alaska Airlines (p1107) offers scheduled jet service to Seattle (two hours), all major Southeast cities, Glacier Bay (30 minutes), Anchorage (two hours) and Cordova (2½ hours) daily in summer.

Alaska Seaplanes (☑ 907-789-3331; www.flyalaskaseaplanes.com) flies daily floatplanes from Juneau to Angoon ($144), Gustavus ($115), Pelican ($180) and Tenakee Springs ($144).

Haines

The first thing you notice about Haines is that it *isn't* Skagway, the tourist showpiece situated 33 nautical miles to the north. Instead, this is a quiet, independent, unprepossessing town of native artists, outdoor-adventure lovers and 100% Alaskans hooked on the tranquil life. People come here to see bald eagles in the wild, dissect one thousand years of Chilkat-Tlingit culture, ponder the remains of an old military barracks and enjoy the best drinking scene in an American town of this size.

After logging fell on hard times in the 1970s, Haines swung its economy toward tourism; not so much cruise ships (Haines receives a mere 40,000 cruisers per season), but more independent travelers. Haines is particularly popular with RVers in summer and heli-skiers in winter. As a result, the businesses here are uniquely Hainesian, and most likely the person behind the counter is the one who owns the store.

◉ Sights & Activities

★ **Jilkaat Kwaan Cultural Heritage & Bald Eagle Preserve Visitor Center** CULTURAL CENTRE

(☑ 907-767-5485; www.jilkaatkwaanheritagecenter.org; Mile 22, Haines Hwy; $15; ⊙ 10am-4pm Mon-Fri, noon-3pm Sat, closed Oct-Apr) Part of a welcome renaissance in Tlingit art and culture in Alaska, this new heritage center is located in the ancient native village of Klukwan, 22 miles north of Haines. The center includes some of the most prized heirlooms of Alaska Native culture, namely four elaborate house posts and a rain screen (the legendary 'whale house collection') carved by a Tlingit Michelangelo over 200 years ago and only recently made available for public viewing.

Fort Seward HISTORIC SITE

Alaska's first permanent military post is reached by heading uphill (east) at the Front

St–Haines Hwy junction. Built in 1903 and decommissioned after WWII, the fort is now a national historical site, with a handful of restaurants, lodges and art galleries in the original buildings. A walking-tour map of the fort is available at the visitor center, or you can just wander around and read the historical panels that have been erected there.

Fjord Express BOATING
(☎ 800-320-0146; www.alaskafjordlines.com; Small-Boat Harbor; adult/child $169/139) Don't have time to make it to Juneau? The Fjord Express zips you down Lynn Canal in a catamaran (will stop for whales, sea lions and other marine wildlife), and then rumbles around Juneau's top sights in a motorcoach before dropping you back in Haines. A light breakfast and dinner are included. It departs Haines at 8:30am and returns at 7:30pm.

🛏 Sleeping

Bear Creek Cabins & Hostel HOSTEL $
(☎ 907-766-2259; www.bearcreekcabinsalaska. com; Small Tract Rd; dm/cabins $20/68; 🛜) A rare Southeastern Alaska hostel of sorts, this place is a 20-minute walk from town – follow Mud Bay Rd and when it veers right, continue straight onto Small Tract Rd for 1½ miles. The complex consists of eights cabins (most sleep four) clustered around a grassy common area.

Aspen Suites Hotel HOTEL $$
(☎ 907-766-2211; www.aspenhotelsak.com/haines; 409 Main St; r $179; P✳@🛜) One of six Aspen hotels in Alaska, this slick new building offers rooms more akin to studio apartments, all equipped with kitchenettes and comfortable sofas. There's coffee on tap at reception, a small fitness room and a clean, polished sheen to the whole operation.

🍴 Eating & Drinking

Big Al's SEAFOOD $
(Mile 0, Haines Hwy; mains $10-13; ⊙11am-7pm) Run by a local fisherman, this merry food truck serves seafood which is all locally caught, probably that day. There are three kinds of fish and chips: halibut, rockfish and salmon. Get a combo and sample them all.

★Fireweed Restaurant BISTRO $$
(37 Blacksmith St; pizzas $14-30, salads $10-19; ⊙4:30-9pm Tue-Sat; 🥢) This clean, bright and laid-back bistro is in an old Fort Seward building and its copious salads are an ideal antidote to the Southeast's penchant for grease. A quick scroll down the menu will reveal words like 'organic,' 'veggie' and 'grilled' as opposed to 'deep fried' and 'captain's special.'

★Haines Brewing Company BREWERY
(☎ 907-766-3823; www.hainesbrewing.com; Main St, cnr 4th Ave; ⊙noon-7pm Mon-Sat) Surely one of the finest small breweries in America, this Haines operation, founded in 1999, has recently opened a lovely new tasting room in what passes for downtown Haines. The beautiful wood and glass structure serves all of the locally brewed favorites, including Spruce Tip Ale, Elder Rock Red and the potent Black Fang stout (8.2% alcohol content).

ℹ Information

Alaska Division of Parks (☎ 907-766-2292; 219 Main St, Suite 25; ⊙8am-5pm Mon-Fri) For information on state parks and hiking; above Howser's IGA (there's no sign).

Haines Convention & Visitors Bureau (☎ 907-766-2234; www.haines.ak.us; 122 2nd Ave; ⊙8am-5pm Mon-Fri, 9am-4pm Sat & Sun) Has restrooms, free coffee and racks of free information for tourists. There is also a lot of information on Canada's Yukon for those heading up the Alcan.

ℹ Getting There & Away

There is no jet service to Haines, but **Alaska Seaplanes** (☎ 907-766-3800, 907-789-3331; www. flyalaskaseaplanes.com) will take you to Juneau seven times a day ($125). The airport is 3 miles northwest of town just off the Haines Hwy.

Skagway

At first sight, Skagway appears to be solely an amusement park for cruise-ship daytrippers, a million of whom disgorge onto its sunny boardwalks every summer. But, haunted by Klondike ghosts and beautified by a tight grid of handsome false-fronted buildings, this is no northern Vegas. Skagway's history is very real.

During the 1898 gold rush, 40,000 stampeders passed through the nascent settlement, a sometimes unsavory cast of characters who lived against a backdrop of brothels, gunfights and debauched entertainment wilder than the Wild West. Today, the main actors are seasonal workers, waitstaff posing in period costume and storytelling National Park rangers. Indeed, most of the town's important buildings are managed by the National Park Service and this, along with Skagway's location on the cusp of a burly wilderness with trails (including the legendary Chilkoot) leading off in all directions, has saved it from overt Disneyfication. Dive in and join the show.

DON'T MISS

CHILKOOT TRAIL

The **Chilkoot Trail** (☎907-983-9234; www.nps.gov; Broadway St, Skagway), the epic trek undertaken by over 30,000 gold-rush stampeders in 1897–8, is sometimes known as the 'Last Great Adventure.' or the 'Meanest 33 Miles in America.' Its appeal is legendary and, consequently, more than 3000 people spend three to five days following the historic route every summer. If you're planning to trek the trail, stop off at the Trail Center the day before.

⊙ Sights & Activities

★ **Klondike Gold Rush National Historical Park Museum & Visitor Center**   MUSEUM
(☎907-983-9200; www.nps.gov/klgo; Broadway St, at 2nd Ave; ⊙8:30am-5:30pm May-Sep) FREE The recently improved NPS center is in the original 1898 White Pass & Yukon Route depot. The center is spread over two interconnecting buildings. One contains a small museum, explaining some of the Klondike background with an emphasis on the two routes out of Skagway: Chilkoot Pass and White Pass. The other space is a visitor center staffed by park rangers.

Skagway Museum   MUSEUM
(☎907-983-2420; cnr 7th Ave & Spring St; adult/child $2/1; ⊙9am-5pm Mon-Sat, 1-4pm Sun) Skagway Museum is not only one of the finest in a town filled with museums, but it's one of the finest in the Southeast. It occupies the 1st floor of the venerable century-old McCabe Building, a former college, and is devoted to various aspects of local history, including Alaska Native baskets, beadwork and carvings, and, of course, the Klondike Gold Rush.

★ **White Pass & Yukon**
Route Railroad   RAIL
(☎800-343-7373; www.wpyr.com; 231 2nd Ave; ⊙May-Sep) This epic gold-rush-era railroad has departures from Skagway, AK; Fraser, British Columbia; and Carcross and Whitehorse, Yukon. The line was built across White Pass between 1898 and 1900 just in time to catch the coattails of the gold rush. In WWII it was used to transport troops to Whitehorse in Canada.

Skagway Float Tours   RAFTING
(☎907-983-3688; www.skagwayfloat.com; 209 Broadway St; ⊙9am-6:30pm Mon-Sat, to 4pm Sun) Fancy some bliss on the river? Try the three-hour tour of Dyea that includes a 45-minute float down the placid Taiya River (adult/child $75/55); there are two per day at 9am and 1:30pm. The Hike & Float Tour ($95/75) is a four-hour outing that includes hiking 2 miles of the Chilkoot Trail then some floating back; there are several per day.

🛏 Sleeping

Morning Wood Hotel   HOTEL $
(☎907-983-3200; 444 4th Ave; r with shared/private bath $90/150; 🛜) A buoyant new hotel with a handsome, if typical, false-fronted wooden exterior. Inside, the rooms (located at the rear) aren't fancy, but at least they're spanking new and come with deluxe bathroom accessories and sharp color accents. There's an affiliated restaurant and bar.

Skagway Inn   INN $$
(☎907-983-2289; www.skagwayinn.com; Broadway St, at 7th Ave; r $149-249; @🛜) In a restored 1897 Victorian building that was originally one of the town's brothels – what building still standing in Skagway wasn't? – this beautiful downtown inn features 10 rooms, four with shared baths. All are small but filled with antique dressers, iron beds and chests, and named after the 'ladies' who worked here. Breakfast is included, as are ferry/airport/train transfers.

🍴 Eating & Drinking

Woadie's South East Seafood   SEAFOOD $$
(☎907-983-3133; State St & 4th Ave; mains $14-19; ⊙11:30am-7pm Mon-Thu, noon-6pm Fri & Sat) A food cart with its own deck and awning, equipped with picnic tables, delivers the town's best fish at a lightning pace. Report to the window and place your order for fresh oysters, crab or halibut. It's under new dynamic ownership and allows BYO booze.

Skagway Fish Company   SEAFOOD $$$
(☎907-983-3474; Congress Way; mains $18-52; ⊙11am-9pm) Overlooking the harbor, with crab traps on the ceiling, this is a culinary homage to fish. You can feast heartily on halibut stuffed with king crab, shrimp and veggies, or king-crab bisque, but surprisingly, what many locals rave about are its baby back ribs. Its bar has the best view in town.

ℹ Information

Klondike Gold Rush National Historical Park Museum & Visitor Center For general info on Skagway's historical sites, museums and free walking tours. Run by the National Park Service.

Skagway Convention & Visitors Bureau

(☑907-983-2854; www.skagway.com; cnr Broadway St & 2nd Ave; ☺8am-6pm Mon-Fri, to 5pm Sat & Sun) For information on lodging, tours, restaurant menus and what's new, visit this bureau housed in the can't-miss Arctic Brotherhood Hall – think driftwood.

Trail Center

(☑907-983-9234; www.nps. gov/klgo; Broadway St, btwn 5th & 6th Aves; ☺8am-5pm Jun-Sep) If you're stampeding to the Chilkoot Trail, you'll need to stop off here the day before to pick up trail passes, get the latest trail and weather conditions, and watch a mandatory bear-awareness video. Expert rangers from both the US NPS and Parks Canada are there to answer any questions.

❶ Getting There & Away

Yukon-Alaska Tourist Tours (☑866-626-7383, Whitehorse 867-668-5944; www.yukon-alaskatouristtours.com) offers a bus service to Whitehorse (one way $70), departing the train depot in Skagway at 2pm daily.

Glacier Bay National Park & Preserve

Glacier Bay is the crowning jewel of the cruise-ship industry and a dreamy destination for anybody who has ever paddled a kayak. Seven tidewater glaciers spill out of the mountains and fill the sea with icebergs of all shapes, sizes and shades of blue, making Glacier Bay National Park and Preserve an icy wilderness renowned worldwide.

Apart from its high concentration of tidewater glaciers, Glacier Bay is a dynamic habitat for humpback whales. Other wildlife seen at Glacier Bay includes porpoises, sea otters, brown and black bears, wolves, moose and mountain goats.

The park is an expensive side trip, even by Alaskan standards. Plan on spending at least $400 for a trip from Juneau. Of the 500,000 annual visitors, more than 95% arrive aboard a ship and never leave it. The rest are a mixture of tour-group members, who head straight for the lodge, and backpackers, who gravitate toward the free campground.

◉ Sights

Gustavus   TOWN

(www.gustavusak.com) About nine miles from Bartlett Cove is the small settlement of Gustavus, an interesting backcountry community. The town's 400 citizens include a mix of professional people – doctors, lawyers, former government workers and artists – who

decided to drop out of the rat race and live on their own in the middle of the woods. Electricity only arrived in the early 1980s and in some homes you must pump water at the sink or build a fire before you can have a hot shower.

Spirit Walker Expeditions   KAYAKING

(☑907-697-2266; www.seakayakalaska.com; 1 Grandpa's Farm Rd) Kayaking specialist Spirit Walker runs paddling trips to Point Adolphus where humpback whales congregate during the summer. Trips begin with a short boat ride pulling the kayaks across Icy Strait to Point Adolphus and run $439 for a day paddle ($379 per person for four or more) and $1099 for a three-day paddle.

🛏 Sleeping & Eating

Bartlett Cove Campground   CAMPGROUND $

(free) This NPS facility 0.25 miles south of Glacier Bay Lodge is set in a lush forest just off the shoreline, and camping is free. There's no need for reservations; there always seems to be space. It's a walk-in campground, so no RVs.

Glacier Bay Lodge   LODGE $$

(☑888-229-8687; www.visitglacierbay.com; 199 Bartlett Cove Rd; r $219-249; ☺May-Sep) This is essentially a national park lodge and the only accommodations in the park itself. Located at Bartlett Cove, 8 miles northwest of Gustavus, the self-contained lodge has 55 rooms, a crackling fire in a huge stone fireplace and a dining room that usually hums in the evening with an interesting mixture of park employees, backpackers and locals from Gustavus.

★Gustavus Inn   INN $$$

(☑907-697-2254; www.gustavusinn.com; Mile 1, Gustavus Rd; r per person all-incl $250; P🐾🐾) 🐾 This longtime Gustavus favorite is a charming family homestead lodge mentioned in every travel book on Alaska, with good reason. It's thoroughly modern and comfortable, without being sterile or losing its folksy touch. The all-inclusive inn is well known for its gourmet dinners, which feature homegrown vegetables and fresh local seafood served family style.

Sunnyside Market   CAFE $

(☑907-697-3060; 3 State Dock Rd; sandwiches $7-10; ☺9am-6pm; 🐾) 🐾 This bright market and cafe is your one-stop choice for organic sundries, deli sandwiches and breakfast burritos. There are two tables inside and plenty outside under a sunny overhang. On Saturday there's an artsy market.

ℹ Information

Glacier Bay National Park Visitor Center
(☎ 907-697-2661; www.nps.gov/glba; ◷11am-8pm) On the 2nd floor of Glacier Bay Lodge (p1103), this center has exhibits, a bookstore and an information desk. There are also daily guided walks from the lodge, park films and slide presentations.

Gustavus Visitors Association
(☎ 907-697-2454; www.gustavusak.com) Has loads of information on its website.

Visitor Information Station
(☎ 907-697-2627; ◷7am-8pm May-Sep) Campers, kayakers and boaters can stop at the park's Visitor Information Station at the foot of the public dock in Bartlett Cove for backcountry and boating permits, logistical information and a 20-minute orientation video.

ℹ Getting There & Away

The cheapest way to reach Gustavus is via the **Alaska Marine Highway** (☎ 800-642-0066; www.ferryalaska.com). Several times a week the MV *LeConte* makes the round-trip run from Juneau to Gustavus (one way $44, 4½ hours) along a route that often features whale sightings. **TLC Taxi** (☎ 907-697-2239) meets most ferry arrivals and also charges $15 per person for a trip to Bartlett Cove.

Alaska Airlines (p1107) Offers the only jet service, with a daily 25-minute trip from Juneau to Gustavus.

Alaska Seaplanes (☎ 907-789-3331; www.flyalaskaseaplanes.com) Has up to five flights per day between Gustavus and Juneau for $115 one way.

Ketchikan

Close to Alaska's southern tip, where the Panhandle plunges deep into British Columbia, lies rainy Ketchikan, the state's fourth-largest city, squeezed onto a narrow strip of coast on Revillagigedo Island abutting the Tongass Narrows. Ketchikan is known for its commercial salmon fishing and indigenous Haida and Tlingit heritage – there is no better place in the US to see totem poles in all their craning, colorful glory. Every year between May and September, Ketchikan kowtows to around one million cruise-ship passengers, a deluge that turns the town into something of a tourist circus. Some cruisers stay in town, ferrying between souvenir shops and Ketchikan's emblematic totems. Others jump on boats or seaplanes bound for the Gothic majesty of Misty Fiords National Monument, a nearby wilderness area.

Despite the seasonal frenzy, Ketchikan retains a notable historical heritage exemplified by the jumbled clapboard facades of **Creek Street**, perched on stilts above a river.

◉ Sights

★Saxman Native Village & Totem Park
HISTORIC SITE
(☎ 907-225-4421; www.capefoxtours.com; $5; ◷8am-5pm) On South Tongass Hwy, 2.5 miles south of Ketchikan, is this incorporated Tlingit village of 475 residents. It's best known for Saxman Totem Park, which holds 24 totem poles from abandoned villages around the Southeast, restored or recarved in the 1930s. Among them is a replica of the Lincoln Pole (the original is in the Alaska State Museum in Juneau), which was carved in 1883, using a picture of Abraham Lincoln, to commemorate the first sighting of white people.

Southeast Alaska Discovery Center
MUSEUM
(www.alaskacenters.gov; 50 Main St; adult/child $5/free; ◷8am-4pm; ♿) Three large totems greet you in the lobby of this NPS-run center, while a school of silver salmon suspended from the ceiling leads you toward a slice of re-created temperate rainforest. Upstairs, the exhibit hall features sections on Southeast Alaska's ecosystems and Alaska Native traditions.

🛏 Sleeping

Last Chance Campground
CAMPGROUND $
(Ward Lake Rd; tent & RV sites $10) In a beautiful area north of Ketchikan, a couple of miles beyond Ward Lake, with four scenic lakes, 19 drive-in sites and three trails that run through the lush rainforest.

Ketchikan Hostel
HOSTEL $
(☎ 907-225-3319; www.ketchikanhostel.com; 400 Main St; dm $20; ◷May-Sep) In common with several other Alaskan towns, Ketchikan's 'hostel' is located inside a church (a Methodist one) with no street signage. The facility includes a large kitchen, three small common areas and single-sex dorm rooms. It's clean, but no-frills and doors are locked after curfew (11pm). Reservations are recommended in July.

★**Inn at Creek Street –
New York Hotel** BOUTIQUE HOTEL **$$**
(☑ 907-225-0246; www.thenewyorkhotel.com; 207
Stedman St; r $89-149, ste $119-289; 🐾) A historic boutique hotel that walks a delicate balance between old-world ambience and modern comfort. The eight rooms have a 1920s period feel without seeming 'olde', with soft quilts, flat-screen TVs, refrigerators and private baths.

✗ Eating

Burger Queen BURGERS **$**
(518 Water St; burgers $7-10; ⊗ 11am-7pm Tue-Sat, to 3pm Sun & Mon) Ketchikan's favorite burger joint is definitely not a chain. Ten varieties, including one with a Polish sausage *and* a hamburger patty, plus 30 flavors of milkshake are served out of a small space just north of the road tunnel. It's something of a local legend.

Alaska Fish House FISH & CHIPS **$$**
(☑ 907-225-4055; 3 Salmon Landing; mains $13-23; ⊗ 10am-9pm) Take your pick of fish – cod, salmon or halibut – and then your coating – in batter or a bun. The chips are default. And all this before the menu gets down to the crab: whole or just the legs. For those lacking seafood taste buds there are burgers.

★**Bar Harbor
Restaurant** MODERN AMERICAN **$$$**
(☑ 907-225-2813; 55 Schoenbar Ct, Berth 4; mains $22-42; ⊗ 11am-2pm & 5-8pm Tue-Fri, 9am-2pm & 5-8pm Sat, 9am-2pm Sun) This slightly pricey fish-biased restaurant, usually touted among locals as the best in town, opened for the 2017 season in a new cruise-dock location on Berth 4. Expect larger than normal crowds descending on its modern ocean-themed interior to feast on creative seafood and chowder renditions.

ⓘ Information

Ketchikan Visitor Center Substation (Berth 3; ⊗ 8am-5pm May-Sep) Smaller overflow visitor center near the road tunnel; only opens in the spring/summer.

Ketchikan Visitor Information & Tour Center (☑ 907-225-6166; www.visit-ketchikan.com; 131 Front St, City Dock; ⊗ 7am-6pm) Vast modern building on the cruise-ship dock with brochures, free maps, courtesy phones and toilets. Adjoining it is a huge tour center complete with up to 20 booths where various activity companies set up desks in the summer to catch the cruise-ship trade. Reservations for most activities can be made here.

Southeast Alaska Discovery Center (☑ 907-228-6220; www.fs.fed.us/r10/tongass/districts/discoverycenter; 50 Main St; ⊗ 8:30am-4pm) You don't need to pay the admission fee to get recreation information at this Alaska Public Lands Information Center. Park passes are also sold here.

ⓘ Getting There & Away

Ketchikan's **Alaska Marine Highway Ferry Terminal** (☑ 907-225-6182; www.dot.state.ak.us/amhs; 3501 Tongass Ave) is 2 miles north of the city center. Northbound ferries leave almost daily in summer, heading for Wrangell ($53, six hours), Petersburg ($72, 9½ hours), Sitka ($109, 25 hours), Juneau ($126, 24 hours) and Haines ($155, 26 hours). Heading south, there's at least one departure a week for Bellingham, WA ($310, 40 hours) and also Prince Rupert in Canada ($63, 7½ hours).

Inter-Island Ferry Authority (☑ 907-225-4838; www.interislandferry.com) vessels are capable of holding vehicles and depart Ketchikan's ferry terminal at 3:30pm daily, bound for Hollis on Prince of Wales Island (one way adult/child $49/22.50, three hours). Rates for the ferry vary and are based on your vehicle's length; a subcompact one way costs $50.

FAIRBANKS

Fairbanks is the only 'city' in the interior, and the largest settlement for hundreds of miles, but it has many characteristics of a small town. Everyone seems to know everyone, and 'everyone' includes some truly fascinating characters – sled-dog breeders, crusading environmentalists, college students, gun nuts, military personnel, outdoor enthusiasts, bush pilots, and the rest of the usual Alaska cast of oddities. Because the city sits at the nexus of some truly epic routes – north to the Arctic, east to Canada and south to Denali – you'll almost inevitably end up spending time here, and that time is rarely boring.

This is a spread-out burg that's admittedly heavy on ugly strip malls, but the residential streets of compact downtown are pretty as a picture, and during winter, this is ground zero for viewing the aurora borealis.

◉ Sights & Activities

★**University of Alaska
Museum of the North** MUSEUM
(☑ 907-474-7505; www.uaf.edu/museum; 907 Yukon Dr; adult/child $12/7; ⊗ 9am-7pm) In an architecturally abstract, igloo- and aurora-inspired edifice sits one of Alaska's

ALASKA FAIRBANKS

DENALI NATIONAL PARK & PRESERVE

In our collective consciousness, Alaska represents the concept of the raw wilderness. But that untamed perception can be as much a deterrent as a draw. For many travelers, in-depth exploration of this American frontier is a daunting task.

Enter **Denali National Park & Preserve** (☎ 907-683-9532; www.nps.gov/dena; George Parks Hwy; $10; ⓟ ♿) ◢ : a parcel of land both primeval and easily accessible. Here, you can peer at a grizzly bear, moose, caribou, or even wolves, all from the comfort of a bus. On the other hand, if independent exploration is your thing, you can trek into 6 million acres of tundra, boreal forest and ice-capped mountains – a space larger than Massachusetts. This all lies in the shadow of Denali, once known as Mt McKinley and to native Athabascans as the Great One. Denali is North America's highest peak, rightly celebrated as an icon of all that is awesome and wild in a state where those adjectives are ubiquitous.

Consider making reservations at least six months in advance for a park campsite during the height of summer, and at least three months ahead for accommodations outside the park. The park entrance fee is $10 per person, good for seven days.

There's only one road through the park: the 92-mile unpaved Park Rd, which is closed to private vehicles after Mile 15 in summer. Shuttle buses run from the middle of May until September past Mile 15. Sometimes, if the snow melts early in April, visitors will be allowed to proceed as far as Mile 30 until the shuttle buses begin operation. The park entrance area, where most visitors congregate, extends a scant 4 miles up Park Rd. It's here you'll find the park headquarters, visitor center and main campground, as well as the **Wilderness Access Center** (WAC; ☎ 907-683-9532; Mile 0.5, Park Rd; ⏰ 5am-7pm late May–mid-Sep), where you pay your park entrance fee and arrange campsites and shuttle-bus bookings to take you further into the park. Across the lot from the WAC sits the **Backcountry Information Center** (BIC; ☎ 907-683-9532/90; Mile 0.5, Park Rd; ⏰ 9am-6pm late May–mid-Sep), where backpackers get backcountry permits and bear-proof food containers.

There are few places to stay within the park, excluding campgrounds, and only one restaurant. The majority of visitors base themselves in the nearby communities of Canyon, McKinley Village, Carlo Creek and Healy.

From May 15 to June 1, park services are just starting up and access to the backcountry is limited. Visitor numbers are low but shuttle buses only run as far as **Toklat River** (Mile 53, Park Rd; ⏰ 9am-7pm late May–mid-Sep) ◢ FREE. From June 1 to 8, access increases and the shuttle buses run as far as **Eielson Visitor Center** (☎ 907-683-9532; www.nps.gov/dena/planyourvisit/the-eielson-visitor-center.htm; Mile 66, Park Rd; ⏰ 9am-7pm Jun–mid-Sep) FREE. After June 8, the park is in full swing till late August.

Shuttle buses stop running after the second Thursday after Labor Day in September. Following a few days in which lottery winners are allowed to take their private vehicles as far along Park Rd as weather allows, the road closes to all traffic until the following May.

While most area lodges close, **Riley Creek Campground** (www.nps.gov/dena; Mile 0.25, Park Rd; tent sites $24, RV sites $24-30) ◢ stays open in winter and camping is free, though the water and sewage facilities don't operate. If you have the equipment, you can use the unplowed Park Rd and the rest of the park for cross-country skiing, snowshoeing or dog sledding.

finest museums, with artifact-rich exhibits on the geology, history, culture and trivia of each region of the state. You are greeted by an 8ft 9in, 1250lb stuffed bear and signposted around very well laid-out exhibits, which examine the state's regions as geographic *and* cultural units.

**Morris Thompson
Cultural & Visitors Center**   CULTURAL CENTER
(☎ 907-459-3700; www.morristhompsoncenter. org; 101 Dunkel St; ⏰ 8am-9pm late May–early Sep, to 5pm mid-Sep–mid-May; ⓟ) There are a few contenders for 'best visitor center in Alaska' but this one, an ingenious mix of museum, info point and cultural center, has to be in the running. Inside are exhibits on Alaskan history and Alaska Native culture, as well as daily movies and cultural performances.

Outside, on the grounds, don't miss the historic cabin and moose-antler arch.

☞ Tours

Northern Alaska Tour Co   SCENIC FLIGHTS
(☏907-474-8600; www.northernalaska.com) The Arctic Circle may be an imaginary line, but it's become one of Fairbanks' biggest draws, with small air-charter companies doing booming business flying travelers on sightseeing excursions across it. This company offers flights to the Dalton Hwy (starting from around $480), day flights to Barrow ($900) and van tours across the Arctic Circle ($220), among many other options.

🛏 Sleeping

Sven's Basecamp Hostel   HOSTEL, CAMPGROUND $
(☏907-456-7836; www.svenshostel.com; 3505 Davis Rd; tent sites $9, tipis/tents/cabins/treehouses $30/35/75/100; P🐾) Sven, from Switzerland, welcomes all kinds of travelers and vagabonds to this fine, multifarious hostel. This is where you'll meet some of Alaska's most intrepid, sweatiest explorers and hear plenty of travel tales. Accommodations are in cabins, shared tents, a plush treehouse or your own tent. Showers are coin-operated and there's table football, books, a movie room and kitchen.

Springhill Suites   HOTEL $$$
(☏907-451-6552; www.marriott.com; 575 1st Ave; r from $254; P@🐾🏊) A northerly branch of the Marriott empire, Springhill Suites is recently renovated and boasts clean, bland rooms spiced up with local artwork. You can't beat the location on the Chena River smack downtown for convenience. Amenities include an indoor pool and fitness center.

✕ Eating & Drinking

Big Daddy's BBQ & Banquet Hall   BARBECUE $$
(☏907-452-2501; www.bigdaddysbarb-q.com; 107 Wickersham St; mains $9-19; ⊙11am-10pm Mon-Sat, noon-9pm Sun) This must be, as the owners claim, the northernmost Southern barbecue in the USA, and if you like slow-smoked ribs, juicy brisket, bowls of baked beans and creamy mac 'n' cheese, it does not disappoint. Wash it all down with one of the cold beers on tap, and roll yourself out the door when you finish.

Pike's Landing   AMERICAN $$$
(☏907-479-6500; 4438 Airport Way; mains $18-36; ⊙11am-11pm) For fine dining riverfront style, head to this restaurant, which has a cozy-cabin main dining room, a huge deck that looks out over the water and solid American-Alaskan mains: prime-rib sandwiches, roasted salmon, coconut shrimp and the like. Reservations for dinner are a good idea.

The Big I   BAR
(☏907-456-6437; 122 Turner St; ⊙10am-2am Sun-Thu, to 3:30am Fri, 9am-2am Sat; 🐾) This excellent dive has a large outdoor drinking area, sassy bartenders, grizzled locals and lots of bush kitsch lining the walls, which look like they haven't been scrubbed since the time of the Bering land bridge. Live music acts liven up the scene on some nights.

ℹ Information

Alaska Public Lands Information Center
(☏907-456-0527; www.alaskacenters.gov; 101 Dunkel St; ⊙8am-6pm) Encased in the Morris Thompson Cultural & Visitors Center, this is the place to head if you're planning on visiting any state or national parks and reserves in the region. Pick up one of its detailed free brochures on the Steese, Elliot, Taylor and Denali Hwys.

Department of Fish & Game Office (☏907-459-7206; 1300 College Rd)

Fairbanks Convention & Visitors Bureau
(☏907-456-5774; www.explorefairbanks.com; 101 Dunkel St; ⊙8am-9pm late May-early Sep, to 5pm late Sep-mid-May)

ℹ Getting There & Away

Alaska Airlines (☏800-426-0333; www.alaskaair.com) flies direct to Anchorage, where there are connections to the rest of Alaska, the lower 48 and overseas, on a daily basis. There are also handy direct flights to Seattle with Delta and Alaska. For travel into the Bush, try **Ravn Alaska** (www.flyravn.com), **Warbelow's Air Ventures** (☏907-474-0518; www.warbelows.com; 3758 University Ave S) or **Wright Air Service** (☏907-474-0502; www.wrightairservice.com; 3842 University Ave).

Alaska Railroad (☏907-458-6025; www.alaskarailroad.com) leaves Fairbanks daily at 8:15am from mid-May to mid-September. The train gets to Denali National Park & Preserve (adult/child $73/37) at noon, Talkeetna (adult/child $141/71) at 4:40pm, Wasila (adult/child $239/120) at 6:15pm and Anchorage (adult/child $239/120) at 8pm. The **station** (☏907-458-6025; www.alaskarailroad.com; 1031 Alaska Railroad Depot Road; ⊙6:30am-3pm) is at the southern end of Danby St. **MACS** (Metropolitan Area Commuter Service; ☏907-459-1010; http://fnsb.us/transportation/Pages/MACS.aspx) Red Line buses run to and from the station.

Hawaii

Includes ➜

O'ahu.................................. 1110
Honolulu........................... 1110
Waikiki.............................. 1113
Hawai'i, the
Big Island 1117
Kailua-Kona 1117
Hilo 1121
Maui 1123
Lahaina 1123
Kaua'i 1126

Best Places to Eat

➜ Alan Wong's (p1112)

➜ Hy's Steakhouse (p1115)

➜ KCC Farmers Market (p1115)

➜ Umekes (p1118)

➜ Frida's Mexican Beach House (p1124)

Best Places to Sleep

➜ Halekulani (p1114)

➜ Four Seasons Resort Hualalai (p1120)

➜ Royal Grove Hotel (p1114)

➜ Hanalei Dolphin Cottages (p1128)

➜ Pineapple Inn Maui (p1125)

Why Go?

Truth: this string of emerald islands in the cobalt blue Pacific, more than 2000 miles from any continent, takes work to get to. And besides, aren't the beaches totally crushed by sunbaked tourists and cooing honeymooners? Cue the galloping *Hawaii Five-0* theme music and lei-draped beauties dancing hula beneath wind-rustled palms.

Hawaii, as tourist bureaus and Hollywood constantly remind us, is 'paradise.' Push past the hype and you may find they're not far wrong. Hawaii is diving into coral-reef cities in the morning and listening to slack key guitar at sunset. It's biting into juicy *liliko'i* (passion fruit) with hibiscus flowers in your hair. These Polynesian islands show off nature's diversity at its most divine, from fiery volcanoes to lacy rainforest waterfalls to crystal-clear aquamarine bays.

Locals know Hawaii isn't always paradise, but on any given day it can sure feel like it.

When to Go
Honolulu

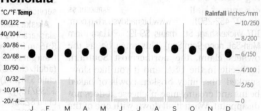

Dec–Apr Slightly cooler, wetter weather; peak season for tourism, surfing and whale-watching.	**May–Sep** Mostly sunny, cloudless days; summer vacation keeps beaches and resorts busy.	**Oct–Nov** Hotter, humid weather; fewer visitors mean cheaper accommodations.

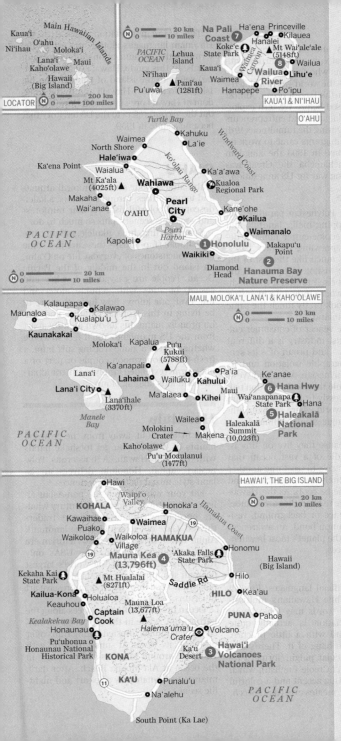

Hawaii Highlights

1 **Honolulu**
(p1110) Exploring multicultural Honolulu with its eye-popping museums and ethnic eats.

2 **Hanauma Bay Nature Preserve**
(p1116) Snorkeling with tropical fish and sea turtles.

3 **Hawai'i Volcanoes National Park** (p1122) Witnessing the eruptions of a living volcano.

4 **Mauna Kea**
(p1120) Stargazing atop Hawaii's highest mountain on the Big Island.

5 **Haleakalā National Park**
(p1123) Catching dawn over the 'house of the rising sun.'

6 **Maui** (p1123) Driving the twisting seaside Hana Hwy past black-sand beaches and jungle waterfalls.

7 **Kaua'i** (p1126) Trekking the sculpted sea cliffs of the dramatic Na Pali Coast.

8 **Wailua River**
(p1126) Kayaking this sacred river to waterfall swimming holes.

History

Hawaii's discovery and colonization is one of humanity's great epic tales, starting with ancient Polynesians who found their way to these tiny islands – the world's most isolated – in the midst of Earth's largest ocean. Almost a millennium passed before Western explorers, whalers, missionaries and entrepreneurs arrived on ships. During the tumultuous 19th century, global immigrants came to work on Hawaii's plantations. In 1893 the kingdom founded by Kamehameha the Great was overthrown, making way for US annexation.

Local Culture

Hawaii may be a Polynesian paradise, but it's one with shopping malls, landfills and industrial parks, cookie-cutter housing developments and sprawling military bases. In many ways, it's much like the rest of the USA. A first-time visitor stepping off the plane may be surprised to find a thoroughly modern place where interstate highways and McDonald's look pretty much the same as back on 'da mainland.'

Underneath the veneer of consumer culture and the tourist industry is a different world, defined by – and proud of – its separateness, its geographic isolation and its unique blend of Polynesian, Asian and Western traditions. While those cultures don't always merge seamlessly in Hawaii, there are few places in the world where so many ethnicities, with no single group commanding a majority, get along.

Perhaps it's because they live on tiny islands in the middle of a vast ocean that Hawaii residents strive to treat one another with aloha, act politely and respectfully, and 'make no waves' (ie be cool). As the Hawaiian saying goes, 'We're all in the same canoe.' No matter their race or background, residents share a common bond: an awareness of living in one of the planet's most bewitchingly beautiful places.

Language

Hawaii has two official languages: English and Hawaiian. While Hawaiian's multisyllabic, vowel-heavy words may look daunting, the pronunciation is actually quite straightforward and with a little practice, you'll soon get the hang of it. There's also an unofficial vernacular, pidgin (formerly referred to as Hawai'i Creole English), which has a laid-back, lilting accent and a colorful vocabulary that permeates everyday speech.

The 'okina punctuation mark (') is the Hawaiian language's glottal stop, which determines the pronunciation and meaning of words. In this guide, Hawai'i (with the 'okina) refers to the island of Hawai'i (the Big Island), to ancient Hawai'i and to the Kingdom of Hawai'i pre-statehood. Hawaii (without the 'okina) refers to the US territory that became a state in 1959.

O'AHU

O'ahu attacks your senses. Tropical aromas and temperatures, turquoise waters, a kaleidoscope of colorful fish, verdant rainforest and sensuous scenery, plus so much to do.

Spam, surfing, hula, ukulele, pidgin, rubbah slippah (flip-flops) – these are just some of the touchstones of everyday life on O'ahu, an island out in the middle of the Pacific Ocean. People are easygoing, low-key and casual, bursting with genuine aloha and fun. Everyone knows how lucky they are to be living in this tropical paradise and O'ahu proudly maintains its own identity apart from the US mainland. You'll feel welcome whether you're a globe-trotting surf bum, a fresh-faced honeymoon couple or part of a big 'ohana (extended family) with grandparents and kids tagging along.

Honolulu

Here in Honolulu, away from the crowded haunts of Waikiki, you get to shake hands with the real Hawaii. A boisterous Polynesian capital, Honolulu delivers an island-style mixed plate of experiences.

Eat your way through the pan-Asian alleys of Chinatown, where 19th-century whalers once brawled and immigrant traders thrived. Gaze out to sea atop the landmark Aloha Tower, then sashay past Victorian-era brick buildings, including the USA's only royal palace. Browse at the world's largest open-air shopping center at Ala Moana, then poke your nose into the city's impressive art museums.

Ocean breezes rustle palm trees along the harborfront, while in the cool, mist-shrouded Ko'olau Range, forested hiking trails offer postcard city views. At sunset, cool off with an amble around Magic Island or splash in the ocean at Ala Moana Beach. After dark, migrate to Chinatown's edgy art and nightlife scene.

HAWAII IN...

Four Days

Anyone on a trans-Pacific stopover will land at **Honolulu**, so spend the few days you have on **O'ahu**. In between surfing and sunning on **Waikiki Beach**, check out Honolulu's museums and wander **Chinatown**, summit **Diamond Head** and snorkel **Hanauma Bay**. In winter admire gargantuan waves on the **North Shore**.

One Week

With a week, fit in another island – say, **Maui**. Explore the old whaling town of **Lahaina**, head to **Haleakalā National Park** to see sunrise at the volcano's summit, take a whale-watching cruise, snorkel or dive **Molokini** crater, drive the serpentine **Hana Hwy** and swim in waterfall pools at **Ohe'o Gulch**.

Two Weeks

With two weeks, tack on a third island. On **Hawai'i, the Big Island**, lounge on golden beaches in **North Kona** and **South Kohala**; visit coffee farms in **South Kona**; summit Hawaii's highest peak, **Mauna Kea**; and say aloha to the goddess Pele at **Hawai'i Volcanoes National Park**. If you choose **Kaua'i**, kayak the **Wailua River** to take a dip in a jungle waterfall, hike in spectacular **Waimea Canyon** and **Koke'e State Park**, hang 10 at **Hanalei Bay**, and trek or paddle past towering sea cliffs on the **Na Pali Coast**.

⊙ Sights & Activities

Honolulu's compact downtown is just a lei's throw from the harborfront. Nearby, the buzzing streets of Chinatown are packed with food markets, antiques shops, art galleries and hip bars. Between downtown and Waikiki, Ala Moana has Hawaii's biggest mall and the city's best beach. The University of Hawai'i campus is a gateway to the Manoa Valley. A few outlying sights, including the Bishop Museum, are worth putting into your schedule.

★**Bishop Museum**   MUSEUM
(☎808-847-3511; www.bishopmuseum.org; 1525 Bernice St; adult/child $23/15; ⊙9am-5pm; 🅿🚼)
🖉 Like Hawaii's version of the Smithsonian Institute in Washington, DC, the Bishop Museum showcases a remarkable array of cultural and natural history exhibits. It is often ranked as the finest Polynesian anthropological museum in the world. Founded in 1889 in honor of Princess Bernice Pauahi Bishop, a descendant of the Kamehameha dynasty, it originally housed only Hawaiian and royal artifacts. These days it honors all of Polynesia. Book online for reduced admission rates.

★**Chinatown Markets**   MARKET
(www.chinatownnow.com; ⊙8am-6pm)   The commercial heart of Chinatown revolves around its markets and food shops. Noodle factories, pastry shops and produce stalls line the narrow sidewalks, always crowded with cart-pushing grandmothers and errand-running families. An institution since 1904, the **O'ahu Market** sells everything a Chinese cook needs: ginger root, fresh octopus, quail eggs, jasmine rice, slabs of tuna, long beans and salted jellyfish. You owe yourself a bubble tea if you spot a pig's head among the stalls.

★**'Iolani Palace**   PALACE
(☎808-522-0832; www.iolanipalace.org; 364 S King St; grounds free, basement galleries adult/child $7/3, self-guided audio tour $15/6, guided tour $22/6; ⊙9am-4pm Mon-Sat) No other place evokes a more poignant sense of Hawaii's history. The palace was built under King David Kalakaua in 1882. At that time, the Hawaiian monarchy observed many of the diplomatic protocols of the Victorian world. The king traveled abroad meeting with leaders around the globe and received foreign emissaries here. Although the palace was modern and opulent for its time, it did little to assert Hawaii's sovereignty over powerful US-influenced business interests, who overthrew the kingdom in 1893.

Blue Hawaiian Helicopters   SCENIC FLIGHTS
(☎808-831-8800; www.bluehawaiian.com; 99 Kaulele Pl; 45min flight per person $240) This may well be the most exciting thing you do on O'ahu. The 45-minute Blue Skies of O'ahu flight takes in Honolulu, Waikiki, Diamond Head, Hanauma Bay and the whole of the Windward Coast, then the North Shore, central O'ahu and Pearl Harbor. Everything you need to know, including video clips, is on the website. Book well ahead.

LGBT HAWAII

The state of Hawaii has strong minority protections and a constitutional guarantee of privacy that extends to sexual behavior between consenting adults. Same-sex couples have the right to marry.

Locals tend to be private about their personal lives, so you will not see much public hand-holding or open displays of affection, either same-sex or opposite-sex. Everyday LGBTQ life is low-key – it's more about picnics and potlucks, not nightclubs. Even in Waikiki, the laid-back gay scene comprises just a half dozen or so bars, clubs and restaurants. That said, Hawaii is a popular destination for LGBTQ travelers, who are served by a small network of gay-owned and gay-friendly B&Bs, guesthouses and hotels. For more info on recommended places to stay, beaches, events and more, check out the following resources:

Out Traveler (www.outtraveler.com/hawaii) Hawaii travel articles free online.

Pride Guide Hawaii (www.gogayhawaii.com) Free island visitor guides for gay-friendly activities, accommodations, dining, nightlife, shopping, festivals, weddings and more.

Hawai'i LGBT Legacy Foundation (http://hawaiilgbtlegacyfoundation.com) News, resources and a community calendar of LGBTQ events, mostly on O'ahu.

Gay Hawaii (http://gayhawaii.com) Short listings of LGBTQ-friendly businesses, beaches and community resources on O'ahu, Maui, Kaua'i and Hawai'i, the Big Island.

Purple Roofs (www.purpleroofs.com) Online directory of gay-owned and gay-friendly B&Bs, vacation rentals, guesthouses and hotels.

🛏 Sleeping

Hostelling International (HI) Honolulu
HOSTEL $

(☑ 808-946-0591; www.hostelsaloha.com; 2323a Seaview Ave, University Area; dm/r $25/60; ⏺ reception 8am-noon & 4pm-midnight; P@🛜) Along a quiet residential side street near the UH Manoa campus, this tidy, low-slung house just a short bus ride from Waikiki has same-sex dorms and basic private rooms kept cool by the tradewinds. Some students crash here while looking for apartments, so it's often full. It has a kitchen, a laundry room, lockers and two free parking spaces.

Aston at the Executive Centre Hotel
HOTEL $$

(☑ 855-945-4090; www.astonexecutivecentre.com; 1088 Bishop St, Downtown; rooms from $209; ⏺@🛜🏊) Honolulu's only downtown hotel is geared for business travelers and extended stays. Large, modern suites with floor-to-ceiling windows get kitchenettes, while one-bedroom condos add a full kitchen and washer/dryer. A fitness center, heated lap pool and complimentary continental breakfast round out the executive-class amenities. Convenient to the restaurants of Downtown and Chinatown.

🍴 Eating

⭐ Tamura's Poke
SEAFOOD $

(☑ 808-735-7100; www.tamurasfinewine.com/pokepage.html; 3496 Wai'alae Ave, Kaimuki; ⏺ 11am-8:45pm Mon-Fri, 9:30am-8:45pm Sat, 9:30am-7:45pm Sun; P) Arguably the best *poke* on the island is up on Wai'alae Rd in undistinguished-looking Tamura's Fine Wines & Liquors. Head inside, turn right, wander down to *poke* corner and feast your eyes. The 'spicy ahi' and the smoked marlin are to die for. Ask for tasters before you buy.

Agu Ramen Bistro
JAPANESE $$

(☑ 808-797-2933; www.aguramen.com; 925 Isenberg St, University area; ramen from $13; ⏺ 11am-11pm Mon-Thu, to midnight Fri-Sun) A sturdy range of delicious ramen noodle options with chicken- or pork-based broth is backed up by delicious small plates such as *ban ban ji kurage* (crunchy jellyfish), *ikageso* (deep-fried squid legs) and fried *mimiga* (pig ears). Japanese beer, sake, shochu, Okinawan *awamori* and Kenzo Estate wines from California are also on offer. Parking out front.

⭐ Alan Wong's
HAWAII REGIONAL $$$

(☑ 808-949-2526; www.alanwongs.com; 1857 S King St, Ala Moana & Around; mains from $35; ⏺ 5-10pm) 🌿 One of O'ahu's big-gun chefs, Alan Wong offers his creative interpretations of Hawaii Regional Cuisine (HRC; Hawaii's homegrown cuisine) with a menu inspired by the state's diverse ethnic cultures. Emphasis is on fresh seafood and local produce. Order Wong's time-tested signature dishes such as ginger-crusted *onaga* (red snapper), steamed shellfish bowl, and twice-cooked *kalbi* (short ribs). Make reservations weeks in advance.

🍷 Drinking & Nightlife

⭐ La Mariana Sailing Club
BAR

(☑ 808-848-2800; www.lamarianasailingclub.com; 50 Sand Island Access Rd, Greater Honolulu; ⊙ 11am-9pm) Time warp! Who says all the great tiki bars have gone to the dogs? Irreverent and kitschy, this 1950s joint by the lagoon is filled with yachties and long-suffering locals. Classic mai tais are as killer as the other tropical potions. Grab a waterfront table and dream of sailing to Tahiti.

⭐ Tea at 1024
TEAHOUSE

(☑ 808-521-9596; www.teaat1024.net; 1024 Nu'uanu Ave, Chinatown; ⊙ 11am-2pm Tue-Fri, to 3pm Sat & Sun) Tea at 1024 takes you back in time to another era. Cutesy sandwiches, scones and cakes accompany your choice of tea as you relax by the window and watch the Chinatown crowd rush by. They even have bonnets for you to don to add to the ambience. Set menus run from $22.95 per person and reservations are recommended.

ℹ️ Information

There are staffed tourist-information desks in the airport arrivals areas. While you're waiting for your bags to appear on the carousel, you can peruse racks of free tourist brochures and magazines, which contain discount coupons for activities, tours, restaurants etc.

For pre-trip planning in several languages, browse the information-packed website of the Hawaii Visitors & Convention Bureau (www.gohawaii.com).

ℹ️ Getting There & Around

Most visitors to O'ahu arrive via Honolulu International Airport. Flights, cars and tours can be booked online at lonelyplanet.com/bookings.

Honolulu is the gateway to Hawaii. It has flights from major North American cities as well as Asia and Australia. It is also a hub of interisland service for flights serving the neighboring islands.

Honolulu International Airport (HNL; ☑ 808-836-6411; http://hawaii.gov/hnl; 300 Rodgers Blvd; 🛜), O'ahu's main commercial airport, is about 6 miles northwest of Downtown Honolulu and 9 miles northwest of Waikiki. The airport is run by the local government, which gives it a certain throwback character: shopping is limited and food concessions are paltry but gate areas have restful seat areas that haven't been replaced by commerce. It even has a beautiful and mostly secret outdoor tropical garden near gate 49. Wait for your flight sniffing plumeria rather than fast food.

The public transit system is comprehensive and convenient. You can get a bus to most parts of O'ahu, but to explore thoroughly and reach off-the-beaten-path sights, you'll need your own wheels.

Waikiki

Once a Hawaiian royal retreat, Waikiki revels in its role as a retreat for the masses. This famous strand of sand moves to a rhythm of Hawaiian music at beachfront high-rises and resorts. In this pulsing jungle of modern hotels and malls, you can, surprisingly, still hear whispers of Hawaii's past, from the chanting of hula troupes at Kuhio Beach to the legacy of Olympic gold medalist Duke Kahanamoku.

Take a surfing lesson from a bronzed instructor, then spend a lazy afternoon lying on Waikiki's golden sands. Before the sun sinks below the horizon, hop aboard a catamaran and sail off toward Diamond Head. Sip a sunset mai tai and be hypnotized by the lilting harmonies of slack key guitar, then mingle with the colorful locals, many of whom have made this their lifetime playground, who come here to party after dark too.

👁 Sights

Yes, the beach is the main sight, but Waikiki also has historic hotels, evocative public art, amazing artifacts of Hawaiian history, and even a zoo and aquarium.

⭐ Royal Hawaiian Hotel
HISTORIC BUILDING

(☑ 808-923-7311; www.royal-hawaiian.com; 2259 Kalakaua Ave; ⊙ tours 1pm Tue & Thu) **FREE** With its Moorish-style turrets and archways, this gorgeously restored 1927 art-deco landmark, dubbed the 'Pink Palace,' is a throwback to the era when Rudolph Valentino was *the* romantic idol and travel to Hawaii was by Matson Navigation luxury liner. Its guest list reads like a who's-who of A-list celebrities, from royalty to Rockefellers, along with luminaries such as Charlie Chaplin and Babe Ruth. Today, historic tours explore the architecture and lore of this grande dame.

Kuhio Beach Park
BEACH

(🛝) If you're the kind of person who wants it all, this beach offers everything from protected swimming to outrigger-canoe rides, and even a free sunset-hula and Hawaiian-music show. You'll find restrooms, outdoor showers, a snack bar and beach-gear-rental stands at **Waikiki Beach Center** (off Kalakaua Ave), near the police substation. Also here is the **Kuhio Beach Surfboard Lockers** (off Kalakaua Ave, Kuhio Beach Park), an iconic storage area for local surfers. World-famous **Canoes** (Pops) surf break is right offshore – you can spend hours watching surfers of all types riding the curls.

HAWAII FOR KIDS

There's not too much to worry about when visiting Hawaii with kids, as long as you keep them covered in sunblock. Here, coastal temperatures rarely drop below 65°F and driving distances are relatively short. Just don't try to do or see too much, especially not if it's your first trip to Hawaii. Slow down and hang loose!

Travel with Children (Lonely Planet) Loaded with valuable tips and amusing tales, especially for first-time parents.

Lonelyplanet.com Ask questions and get advice from other travelers in the Thorn Tree's online 'Kids to Go' and 'USA' forums.

Go Hawaii (www.gohawaii.com) The state's official tourism site lists family-friendly activities, special events and more – easily search the site using terms such as 'kids' or 'family.'

★ **Queen's Surf Beach** BEACH
(Wall's; off Kalakaua Ave, Kap'iolani Beach Park; 🅿) Just south of Kuhio Beach, the namesake beach for the famous surf break is a great place for families as the waves are rarely large when they reach shore but they are still large enough for bodyboarding, which means older kids can frolic for hours. At the south end of the beach, the area in front of the beach pavilion is popular with the local gay community.

★ **Wizard Stones of Kapaemahu** STATUE
(off Kalakaua Ave, Kuhio Beach Park) Near the police substation at Waikiki Beach Center (p1113), four ordinary-looking boulders are actually the legendary Wizard Stones of Kapaemahu, said to contain the mana (spiritual essence) of four wizards who came to O'ahu from Tahiti around AD 400. According to ancient legend, the wizards helped the island residents by relieving their aches and pains, and their fame became widespread. As a tribute when the wizards left, the islanders placed the four boulders where the wizards had lived.

🏃 Activities

★ **O'ahu Diving** DIVING
(☑ 808-721-4210; www.oahudiving.com; 2-dive trips for beginners $130) Specializes in first-time experiences for beginner divers without certification, as well as deep-water boat dives offshore and PADI refresher classes if you're already certified and have some experience under your diving belt. Trips depart from various locations near Waikiki.

★ **Snorkel Bob's** SNORKELING
(☑ 808-735-7944; www.snorkelbob.com; 700 Kapahulu Ave; snorkel set rental per week from $9; ☺ 8am-5pm) A top spot to get your gear. Rates vary depending on the quality of the snorkeling gear and accessories packages, but excellent weekly discounts are available

and online reservations taken. You can even rent gear on O'ahu, then return it to a Snorkel Bob's location on another island.

🛏 Sleeping

Waikiki's main beachfront strip, along Kalakaua Ave, is lined with hotels and sprawling resorts. Some of them are true beauties with either historic or boutique atmosphere. Most are aimed at the masses, however. Further from the sand, look for inviting small hotels on Waikiki's backstreets. Many are quite affordable year-round. And don't forget the hundreds of condos, time-shares and apartments on offer on Airbnb (www.airbnb.com) and HomeAway (www.homeaway.com) etc.

★ **Royal Grove Hotel** HOTEL $
(☑ 808-923-7691; www.royalgrovehotel.com; 161 Uluniu Ave; r per night/week from $90/550; 🅿 @ ➷) No frills but plenty of aloha characterize this kitschy, candy-pink, six-story hotel that attracts so many returning snowbirds it's nearly impossible to get a room in winter without reservations. Retro motel-style rooms in the main wing are basic but do have balconies. All rooms have kitchenettes. Inquire about discounted weekly off-season rates. Great budget option.

Waikiki Prince Hotel HOTEL $$
(☑ 808-922-1544; www.waikikiprince.com; 2431 Prince Edward St; r from $120; 🅿 🅿 ➷) Forget about ocean views and never mind the cramped check-in office at this six-story, 1970s-era apartment complex on an anonymous side street. Inside this standout budget option are 29 compact yet cheery rooms with kitchenettes that feel fresh and modern after a 2017 renovation. Weekly rates are available year-round. A good budget option.

★ **Halekulani** RESORT $$$
(☑ 808-923-2311; www.halekulani.com; 2199 Kalia Rd; r from $490; 🅿 🅿 @ ➷ ➷) Evincing mod-

ern sophistication, this family-owned resort lives up to its name, which means 'House Befitting Heaven.' It's an all-encompassing experience of gracious living, not merely a place to crash. Meditative calm washes over you immediately as you step onto the lobby's cool stone tiles. The design focuses on the blue Pacific, and the hubbub of Waikiki is walled away. There's no resort fee.

**Surfjack Hotel
& Swim Club**   BOUTIQUE HOTEL $$$

(☑808-923-8882; www.surfjack.com; 412 Lewers St; r from $275; ❄ 🛜 🏊) If the Don Draper fantasy still sizzles years after *Mad Men*, then you'll love this retro-chic 10-story hotel that recreates a posh early 1960s world that may not have existed but which would have been cool if it had. Rooms in this vintage building encircle a courtyard pool. All have balconies and reimagined mid-century furniture your parents would have thrown out.

✕ Eating

★ Rainbow Drive-In   HAWAIIAN $

(☑808-737-0177; www.rainbowdrivein.com; 3308 Kanaina Ave; meals $4-9; ⊙7am-9pm; 🏄) If you only hit one classic Hawaiian plate-lunch joint, make it this one. Wrapped in rainbow-colored neon, this famous drive-in is a throwback to another era. Construction workers, surfers and gangly teens order all their down-home favorites such as burgers, mixed-plate lunches, *loco moco* and Portuguese sweet-bread French toast from the takeout counter. Many love the hamburger steak.

Tonkatsu Ginza Bairin   JAPANESE $$

(☑808-926-8082; www.pj-partners.com/bairin/; 255 Beach Walk; mains $18-24; ⊙11am-9:30pm Sun-Thu, to midnight Fri & Sat) Why go to Tokyo for perfect pork *tonkatsu* when you can enjoy the lightly breaded bits of deep-fried pork goodness right here in Waikiki? Since 1927 the family behind this restaurant has been serving *tonkatsu* at a Ginza restaurant. At this far-flung expansion, nothing has been lost. Besides the namesake there is great sushi, rice bowls and more.

MAC 24/7   AMERICAN $$

(☑808-921-5564; http://mac247waikiki.com; 2500 Kuhio Ave, Hilton Waikiki Beach; mains $9-25; ⊙24hr) If it's 3am and you're famished, skip the temptation for a cold $25 burger from room service (*if* you have room service) and drop by Waikiki's best all-night diner. The dining room has a bold style palette and by day has a lovely garden view. Food (and prices) are a cut above.

★ Hy's Steakhouse   STEAK $$$

(☑808-922-5555; http://hyswaikiki.com; 2440 Kuhio Ave; mains $30-80; ⊙6-10pm) Hy's is so old-school that you expect to find inkwells on the tables. This traditional steakhouse has a timeless old leather and wood interior. But ultimately, it's not whether you expect to see Frank and Dean at a back table; rather, it's the steak at Hy's that is superb.

🍷 Drinking & Entertainment

★ Beach Bar   BAR

(☑808-922-3111; www.moana-surfrider.com; 2365 Kalakaua Ave, Moana Surfrider; ⊙10:30am-11:30pm) Waikiki's best beach bar is right on an especially lovely stretch of beach. The atmosphere comes from the historic **Moana Surfrider** (⊙tours 11am Mon, Wed & Fri) hotel and its vast banyan tree. The people-watching of passersby, sunbathers and surfers is captivating day and night. On an island of mediocre mai tais, the version here is one of O'ahu's best. Although it's always busy, turnover is quick so you won't wait long for a table. There's live entertainment much of the day.

★ Hula's Bar & Lei Stand   GAY

(☑808-923-0669; www.hulas.com; 134 Kapahulu Ave, 2nd fl, Waikiki Grand Hotel; ⊙10am-2am; 🛜) This friendly, open-air bar is Waikiki's legendary gay venue and a great place to make new friends, boogie and have a few drinks. Hunker down at the pool table, or gaze at the spectacular vista of Diamond Head. The breezy balcony-bar also has views of Queen's Surf Beach, a prime destination for a sun-worshipping LGBTQ crowd.

ℹ Getting There & Around

Waikiki is a district of the city of Honolulu, so much of the transport information applies to both.

SATURDAY FARMERS MARKET

At **KCC Farmers Market** (http://hfbf.org/markets; parking lot C, Kapi'olani Community College, 4303 Diamond Head Rd; ⊙7:30-11am Sat; 🅿), O'ahu's premier gathering of farmers and their fans, everything sold is locally made or grown and has a loyal following, from Nalo greens to Kahuku shrimp and corn. Restaurants and vendors sell all kinds of tasty takeout meals, with Hawaii coffee brewed fresh and cold coconuts cracked open on demand. Get there early for the best of everything.

Honolulu International Airport (p1113) is about 9 miles northwest of Waikiki.

A bus in a crude disguise, the **Waikiki Trolley** (☑ 808-593-2822; www.waikikitrolley.com; 1-day passes $25-45, 4 days from $59) runs five color-coded lines designed for tourists that shuttle around Waikiki and serve major shopping areas and tourist sights in Diamond Head, Honolulu and Pearl Harbor. The passes, good for unlimited use, aren't cheap but can be purchased from any hotel activity desk or at a discounted rate online.

Pearl Harbor

The WWII-era rallying cry 'Remember Pearl Harbor!' that once mobilized a nation dramatically resonates on O'ahu. It was here that the surprise Japanese attack on December 7, 1941, hurtled the US into war in the Pacific. Every year about 1.6 million tourists visit Pearl Harbor's unique collection of war memorials and museums, all clustered around a quiet bay where oysters were once farmed.

The iconic offshore shrine at the sunken USS *Arizona* doesn't tell the only story. Nearby are two other floating historical sites: the USS *Bowfin* submarine, aka the 'Pearl Harbor Avenger,' and the battleship USS *Missouri*, where General Douglas MacArthur accepted the Japanese surrender at the end of WWII. Together, for the US, these military sites represent the beginning, middle and end of the war. To visit all three, as well as the Pacific Aviation Museum, dedicate at least a day.

ℹ Getting There & Away

The entrance to the Valor in the Pacific Monument and the other Pearl Harbor historic sites is off the Kamehameha Hwy (Hwy 99), southwest of Aloha Stadium. From Honolulu or Waikiki, take H-1 west to exit 15A (Arizona Memorial/Stadium), then follow the highway signs for the monument, not the signs for Pearl Harbor (which lead onto the US Navy base). There's plenty of free parking.

From Waikiki, bus 42 ('Ewa Beach) is the most direct, running twice hourly between 6am and 3pm, taking just over an hour each way. The 'Arizona Memorial' stop is right outside the main entrance to the National Park site.

Diamond Head

A dramatic backdrop for Waikiki Beach, Diamond Head is one of the best-known landmarks in Hawaii. Ancient Hawaiians called it Leʻahi, and at its summit they built a *luakini* heiau, a temple dedicated to the war god Ku and used for human sacrifices. Ever since 1825, when British sailors found calcite crystals sparkling in the sun and mistakenly thought they'd struck it rich, the sacred peak has been called Diamond Head.

The coast is an easy walk from Waikiki and there are some good beaches below the cliffside road and viewpoints.

★ **Diamond Head**
State Monument   STATE PARK
(☑ 800-464-2924; www.hawaiistateparks.org; off Diamond Head Rd btwn Makapu'u & 18th Aves; per pedestrian/car $1/5; ⊙ 6am-6pm, last trail entry 4:30pm; ♿) The extinct crater of Diamond Head is now a state monument, with picnic tables and a spectacular hiking trail up to the 761ft-high summit. The trail was built in 1908 to service military observation stations located along the crater rim.

★ **Diamond Head Lookout**   VIEWPOINT
(3483 Diamond Head Rd) From this small parking area, there are fine views over **Kuilei Cliffs Beach Park** (3450 Diamond Head Rd) and up the coast toward Kahala. On the east side of the parking area, look for the Amelia Earhart Marker, which recalls her 1935 solo flight from Hawaii to California. It's an enjoyable 1.4-mile walk beyond **Kaimana Beach** (Sans Souci Beach) in Waikiki.

The Diamond Head area is a pretty 2-mile walk from Waikiki. Bus routes 14 and 22 follow Diamond Head Rd along the beaches and coast, and then continue along Kahala Ave.

Hanauma Bay

This wide, curved bay of turquoise waters protected by a coral reef and backed by palm trees is a gem, especially for snorkelers. You come here for the scenery, you come here for the beach, but above all you come here to snorkel – and if you've never been snorkeling before, it's a perfect place to start.

The bay is a park and a nature preserve. It is hugely popular; to beat the crowds, arrive as soon as the park opens.

★ **Hanauma Bay Nature Preserve**   PARK
(☑ 808-396-4229; www.honolulu.gov; off Kalaniana'ole Hwy; adult/child under 13yr $7.50/free; ⊙ 6am-6pm Wed-Mon Nov-Mar, to 7pm Wed-Mon Apr-Oct; ♿) From an overlook, you can peer into the translucent waters and see the outline of the 7000-year-old coral reef that stretches across the width of the bay. You're bound to see schools of glittering silver fish, the bright-blue flash of parrotfish and perhaps sea turtles so used to snorkelers they're ready to go eyeball-to-mask with you. Feeding the fish is strictly prohibited, to preserve the delicate ecological balance of the bay. Despite its protected status as a marine-life

conservation district, this beloved bay is still a threatened ecosystem, constantly in danger of being loved to death.

★ **Marine Educational Center**   MUSEUM
(☏808-397-5840; http://hbep.seagrant.soest.hawaii.edu; 100 Hanauma Bay Rd; ⊗8am-4pm Wed-Mon; ♿) ✐ Past the park's entrance ticket windows is an excellent educational center run by the University of Hawai'i. Interactive, family-friendly displays teach visitors about the unique geology and ecology of the bay. Everyone should watch the informative 12-minute video about environmental precautions before snorkeling. Visit the website for links to a great app that covers snorkeling in the bay.

Bus 22 runs between Waikiki and Hanauma Bay (50 minutes, every 30 to 60 minutes). Buses leave Waikiki between 8am and 4pm (4:45pm on weekends and holidays). Buses back to Waikiki pick up at Hanauma Bay from 10:50am until 5:20pm (5:50pm on weekends and holidays). Shuttle buses and tours to the bay are also heavily marketed to tourists.

Kailua & Windward Coast

Welcome to O'ahu's lushest, most verdant coast, where turquoise waters and light-sand beaches share the dramatic backdrop of misty cliffs in the Ko'olau Range. Cruise over the *pali* (mountains) from Honolulu (only 20 minutes) and you first reach Kailua, a pleasant place with an extraordinary beach.

Many repeat visitors make this laid-back community their island base, whether they intend to kayak, stand up paddle (SUP), snorkel, dive, drive around the island or just laze on the sand. To the south, more beautiful beaches (and good food) await in Waimanalo. North up the coast, Kamehameha Hwy narrows into a winding two-lane road with a dramatic oceanfront on one side and small rural farms, towns and frequent sheer cliffs on the other.

The coast is the main part of the round-island drive that also circles through the North Shore.

HAWAI'I, THE BIG ISLAND

Indulge your spirit of adventure on the biggest Hawaiian island. It's still a vast frontier, full of unexpected wonders.

Less than a million years old, Hawai'i is a baby in geological terms. Here you'll find the Hawaiian Islands' tallest, largest and only active volcanic mountains. Kilauea, on the eastern side, is the world's most active volcano, spewing molten lava continuously since 1983. If you see glowing, red-hot lava, you are witnessing Earth in the making, a thrilling and humbling experience. At 33,000ft tall when measured from the ocean floor, Mauna Kea is the world's tallest mountain, and its significance cannot be overstated – as a sacred place to Hawaiians and a top astronomical site to scientists.

ⓘ Getting There & Around

Virtually all visitors arrive on the Big Island by air, mostly from Honolulu International Airport on O'ahu. Travelers must then catch an interisland flight to one of the Big Island's two primary airports: Kona International Airport at Keahole or Hilo International Airport. Flights, cars and tours can be booked online at lonelyplanet. com/bookings. Renting a car is the only way to explore all of the Big Island. The island is divided into six districts: Kona, Kohala, Waimea, Hilo, Puna and Ka'u. The Hawai'i Belt Rd circles the island, connecting the main towns and sights. A 4WD vehicle will be handy for off-the-beaten-track adventures, but for basic sightseeing it's unnecessary. Public transit by bus is available, but service is limited and you'll probably find it way too time-consuming.

Kailua-Kona

Kailua-Kona, also known as 'Kailua,' 'Kona Town' and sometimes just 'Town,' is a love-it-or-leave-it kind of place. On the main drag of Ali'i Dr, along the shoreline, Kailua works hard to evoke the nonchalance of a sun-drenched tropical getaway, but in an injection-molded, bargain-priced way.

But we like it. Spend enough time here and you'll scratch past the souvenirs to an oddball identity built from a collision of two seemingly at-odds forces: mainlanders who want to wind down to Hawaiian time, and ambitious Big Islanders who want to make it in one of the few local towns worthy of the title. Somehow, this marriage works. Kailua-Kona can be tacky, but it's got character.

At the end of the day, Kailua is a convenient base from which to enjoy the Kona Coast's beaches, snorkeling, water sports and ancient Hawaiian sites.

⊙ Sights & Activities

★ **Magic Sands Beach**   BEACH
(La'aloa Beach Park; Ali'i Dr; ⊗ sunrise-sunset; 🅿♿) This small but gorgeous beach (also

DON'T MISS

KONA COFFEE FARMS

Many coffee-farm tours are perfunctory 15-minute affairs. The **Kona Coffee Living History Farm** (☑ 808-323-3222; www.konahistorical.org; 82-6199 Mamalahoa Hwy; 1hr tour adult/child 5-12yr $15/5; ☺10am-2pm Mon-Fri; Ⓟ) tour, run by the Kona Historical Society, an affiliate of the Smithsonian Institute, is different and deep. More than just an exploration of how coffee is grown and harvested, it's a look at rural Japanese immigrant life in South Kona throughout several decades of the 20th century. Restored to Hawai'i's pre-statehood era, this 5.5-acre working coffee farm once belonged to the Uchida family, who lived here until 1994.

called White Sands and, officially, La'aloa Beach) has turquoise water, great sunsets, little shade and possibly the best bodysurfing and bodyboarding on the Big Island. Waves are consistent and just powerful enough to shoot you across the water into a sandy bay (beware: the north side of the bay has more rocks). During high winter surf the beach can vanish literally overnight, earning the nickname 'Magic Sands.' The park is about 4 miles south of central Kailua-Kona.

Three Ring Ranch Exotic Animal Sanctuary   WILDLIFE RESERVE
(☑ 808-331-8778; www.threeringranch.org; 75-809 Keaolani Sbd, Kailua-Kona; minimum donation $50 per person; ☺tours by reservation) ⚐ Dr Ann Goody runs this animal sanctuary on five lovely acres in upland Kona. This isn't a zoo, or even a conventional sanctuary; instead, Dr Goody cares for and genuinely communicates with her charges, which include flamingos, zebras, tortoises and more. Guests are invited to wander the grounds on guided tours, but at all times, you are aware this is a place dedicated to education and animal healing, as opposed to viewing. You must call or email for reservations.

Jack's Diving Locker   DIVING
(☑ 808-329-7585; www.jacksdivinglocker.com; 75-5813 Ali'i Dr, Coconut Grove Marketplace, Bldg H; manta snorkel/dive from $105/155; ☺8am-8pm Mon-Sat, 8am-6pm Sun; ④) ⚐ With top-notch introductory dives and courses, plus extensive programs for kids, this eco-conscious dive outfitter has a 5000-sq-ft facility with a store, classrooms, tank room and Hawaii's only 12ft-deep indoor dive pool. Sign up for

a boat or shore dive, as well as a night manta-ray dive. Snorkelers are welcome on many dive-boat trips.

🛏 Sleeping

My Hawaii Hostel   HOSTEL $
(☑ 808-374-2131; www.myhawaiihostel.com; 76-6241 Ali'i Drive; dm/rm $40/80; Ⓟ❄🛜) This simple, clean hostel is a welcome addition to the slim pickings that are the Kailua-Kona budget accommodations scene. While $40 is a bit steep for the dorm rooms, the private chambers are about as good value for money as you'll find. Note that it's located about 2 miles south of downtown Kailua-Kona.

Kona Tiki Hotel   HOTEL $$
(☑ 808-329-1425; www.konatikihotel.com; 75-5968 Ali'i Dr; r $99-199; Ⓟ🛜🌊) You can find affordable oceanfront views at this retro three-story hotel, a quirky, well-kept complex south of downtown Kailua-Kona with very friendly owners. The motel-style rooms are basic, but all have a fridge and enchanting lanai. Book well ahead.

🍴 Eating & Drinking

★**Umekes**   HAWAII REGIONAL $
(☑ 808-329-3050; www.umekespoke808.com; 75-143 Hualalai Rd; mains $5-14; ☺10am-7pm Mon-Sat; ⚐④) Umekes takes island-style food to the next level. Local ingredients such as ahi tuna, spicy crab salad and salted Waimea beef are served plate-lunch style with excellent, innovative sides such as seasoned seaweed and cucumber kimchi (along with heaping scoops of rice). It's some of the best-value grinds on the island. There's another location at 74-5563 Kaiwi St.

Jackie Rey's Ohana Grill   HAWAII REGIONAL $$
(☑ 808-327-0209; www.jackiereys.com; 75-5995 Kuakini Hwy; mains lunch $13-19, dinner $16-35; ☺11am-9pm Mon-Fri, 5-9pm Sat & Sun; Ⓟ④) Jackie Rey's is a casual, family-owned grill with a delightfully retro-kitsch Hawaii vibe. Haute versions of local *grinds* include guava-glazed ribs, wasabi-seared ahi and *mochiko* (rice flour–battered) fish with Moloka'i purple sweet potatoes.

Kona Brewing Company   AMERICAN $$
(☑ 808-334-2739; http://konabrewingco.com; 75-5629 Kuakini Hwy; mains $13-25; ☺11am-10pm; ④) ⚐ Expect a madhouse crowd at this sprawling, eco-sustainable brewpub, with tiki torch-lit outdoor seating and laid-back waitstaff. Pizza toppings verge on gourmet, but crusts can be soggy; BBQ sandwich-

es and fish tacos are better bets. Enter the parking lot off Kaiwi St.

ⓘ Getting There & Around

Both the public Hele-On Bus and privately operated Keauhou and Kona Trolley make stops within Kailua-Kona. The drive from Kailua-Kona to Hilo is 75 miles and takes at least 1¾ hours via Saddle Rd, 95 miles (two hours) via Waimea and 125 miles (three hours) via Ka'u and Volcano.

To avoid snarly commuter traffic on Hwy 11 leading into and away from Kailua-Kona, try the Mamalahoa Hwy Bypass Rd. It connects Ali'i Dr in Keauhou with Haleki'i St in Kealakekua, between Miles 111 and 112 on Hwy 11.

South Kona Coast

South Kona, more than any other district of Hawai'i, embodies the many strands that make up the geo-cultural tapestry of the Big Island. There is both the dry lava desert of the Kohala Coast and the wet, misty jungles of Puna and Hilo; fishing villages inhabited by country-living locals next to hippie art galleries established by counterculture exiles from the US mainland, next to condos plunked down by millionaire land developers.

In addition, the dozen or so miles heading south from Kailua-Kona to Kealakekua Bay are among Hawai'i's most action-packed, historically speaking. It's here that ancient Hawaiian *ali'i* (royalty) secretly buried the bones of their ancestors, *kapu* (taboo)

breakers braved shark-infested waters to reach the *pu'uhonua* (place of refuge), and British explorer Captain Cook and his crew fatally first stepped ashore in Hawaii.

ⓘ Getting There & Away

The Belt Rd that rings the island becomes Hwy 11 in South Kona, and it's a twisty, sometimes treacherous route – while there aren't many hairpin turns, folks who are used to flatland driving will need to acclimate themselves to driving in the mountains.

In some places the highway is quite narrow; while cycling is relatively common, make sure to wear reflective gear and sport good lighting on your rig. Note that mile markers decrease as you head further south; this may seem weird given that mile markers decrease going *north* in North Kona, but you're technically on Hwy 11, as opposed to Hwy 19, down here. The Hele-On Bus (www.heleonbus.org) passes through the area sporadically, mainly in the morning and early evening, taking commuters to and from resorts; it can also drop travelers off along the way.

North Kona Coast

If you thought the Big Island was all jungle mountains and white-sand beaches, the severe North Kona Coast and its beige deserts and black-and-rust lava fields will come as a shock. Yet always, at the edge of your eyesight, is the bright blue Pacific, while bits of green are sprinkled like jade flecks amid the dry. Turn off the Queen Ka'ahumanu

HAWAII SOUTH KONA COAST

DON'T MISS

BEACHES OF NORTH KONA

If what you're after is an almost deserted, postcard-perfect scoop of soft, white-sand beach cupping brilliant blue-green waters (got your attention?), head to **Makalawena Beach**. Although popular, this string of idyllic coves absorbs crowds so well you'll still feel like you've found paradise. The northernmost cove is sandier and gentler, while the southernmost cove is (illegally) a naked sunbathing spot. Swimming is splendid, but beware of rough surf and rocks in the water. Bodyboarding and snorkeling are other possibilities.

This crescent-shaped white-sand beach of **Kua Bay** (Manini'owali Beach; www.hawaii stateparks.org; ⊙8am-7pm; P 🚻) is fronted by sparkling turquoise waters that offer first-rate swimming and bodyboarding, and good snorkeling on the north side of the bay (by the large rock outcroppings) when waters are calm. A paved road leads right up to it, and thus the beach, also known as Manini'owali, draws major crowds, especially on weekends. Arrive late and cars will be parked half a mile up the road. The parking area has bathrooms and showers.

Beautiful, hook-shaped **Honokohau Beach** (⊙daylight hours; 🚻) has a mix of black lava, white coral and wave-tossed shells, the water is usually too cloudy for snorkeling, but just standing on shore you'll see *honu* (green sea turtles). You may spot more *honu* munching on *limu* (seaweed) around the ancient **'Ai'opio fishtrap**, bordered by a Hawaiian **heiau** at the beach's southern end. Inland are **anchialine ponds** – pools of brackish water that make unique habitats for marine and plant life.

Hwy and make your way across the eerie lava fields to snorkel with sea turtles, bask on almost deserted black-sand beaches and catch an iconic Kona sunset. On clear days, gaze *mauka* (inland) at panoramas of Mauna Kea and Mauna Loa volcanoes, both often snow-dusted in winter, and in the foreground between the two, Mt Hualalai.

North Kona technically runs 33 miles along Queen Ka'ahumanu Hwy (Hwy 19) from Kailua-Kona up the Kona Coast to Kawaihae. Honokohau Harbor is an easy 2-mile drive from downtown Kailua.

🛏 Sleeping

This sparsely populated area is light on accommodations options; it's far easier to find resorts further north (South Kohala) or guesthouses, rentals and the like further south (Kailua-Kona and South Kona). Either way, you won't be more than a 30-minute drive from North Kona's best sights.

Four Seasons Resort Hualalai RESORT $$$ (☑ 888-340-5662, 808-325-8000; www.four-seasons.com/hualalai; 72-100 Ka'upulehu Dr; r/ ste from $695/1595; P❉@🛜🏊❉) Earns its accolades with top-flight service and lavish attention to detail like fresh orchids in every room, embracing lush gardens and an oceanview infinity pool. Some poolside rooms have rejuvenating lava-rock garden outdoor showers. The golf course and spa are both outstanding, or snorkel with 75 species of tropical fish in the King's Pond.

❶ Getting There & Away

The Hele-On Bus (www.heleonbus.org) runs at least one daily line out to the resorts at Kohala that pass through North Kona. Otherwise, North Kona is an easy drive north of Kailua-Kona; just be aware of heavy traffic conditions around the airport during rush hour (7am to 9am and 3:30pm to 6pm). You can also cycle out here (bring water); this is one of the few areas of the Belt Rd with a wide shoulder. Note that mile markers *decrease* as you head north.

South Kohala Coast

The Queen Ka'ahumanu Hwy (Hwy 19) cuts through stark fields of lava, but as you head toward the ocean, rolling emerald golf course slopes edge onto condo complexes and electric teal pools. This is the Gold Coast of the Big Island, and whatever your feelings are on resorts, this is where you'll find some of the area's best beaches.

Oddly enough, South Kohala also contains numerous ancient Hawaiian sights. This coast was more populated at the time of their creation than it is now, and the region is packed with village sites, heiau, fishponds, petroglyphs and historic trails – areas that are often preserved for visitors.

The waters off the coast in South Kohala are pristine and teeming with marine life – and they're relatively uncrowded. The reef drops off more gradually here than along the Kona Coast, so you might see sharks, dolphins, turtles and manta rays.

This is resort country, and the accommodations are pricey. Modern amenities and plush digs are the norm. Note that many units within resorts are owner-occupied condos, which are often rented to short-term visitors via the usual rental website booking engines. Whole house rentals are the norm in Puako, and there are some camping options on Kohala beaches. Check out www.waikoloahawaii vacations.com, www.2papayas.com and www.hawaiis4me.com for rentals in the area.

❶ Getting There & Away

The resorts and sights of South Kohala are located north of Kailua-Kona off Hwy 19 – depending on which resort you're going to, they're located about 25 to 35 miles from town.

The Pahala–South Kohala Hele-On Bus plies this route three times a day Monday to Saturday, and once a day on Sundays.

Traffic jams around KOA airport during rush hours can eat up your travel time.

Mauna Kea

Mauna Kea (White Mountain) is called Mauna O Wakea (Mountain of Wakea) by Hawaiian cultural practitioners. While all of the Big Island is considered the first-born child of Wakea (Sky Father) and Papahānaumoku (Earth Mother), Mauna Kea has always been the sacred *piko* (navel) connecting the land to the heavens. For the scientific world, it all began in 1968 when the University of Hawai'i (UH) began observing the universe from atop the mountain. The summit is so high, dry, dark and pollution-free that it allows investigation of the furthest reaches of the observable universe.

Many Hawaiians are opposed to the summit 'golf balls' – the white observatories now dotting the skyline. While not antiscience, they believe unchecked growth threatens the mountain's *wahi pana* (sacred places), including heiau (temples) and burial sites. Litter, vandalism and pollution (including toxic mercury spills) have been a problem. Visit with respect, and pack out your trash.

★ **Mauna Kea Visitor Information Station** TOURIST INFORMATION
(MKVIS; ☎808-961-2180; www.ifa.hawaii.edu/info/vis; ☺9am-10pm) FREE Modestly sized MKVIS packs a punch with astronomy and space-exploration videos and posters galore, and information about the mountain's history, ecology and geology. Budding scientists of all ages revel in the gift shop, while knowledgeable staff help you pass the time acclimatizing to the 9200ft altitude. Check the website for upcoming special events, such as lectures about science and Hawaiian culture, typically held on Saturday nights.

Excellent free stargazing programs happen from 6pm until 10pm nightly, weather permitting.

ⓘ Getting There & Away

Coming from Waimea or Kona take Saddle Road (Hwy 200) or the new Daniel K Inouye reroute. From Hilo, drive *mauka* (inland) on Kaumana Dr (Hwy 200) or Puainako Extension (Hwy 2000), both of which become Saddle Road. Start with a full tank of gas – there are no service stations out here. The Visitor Information Station (MKVIS) and the summit beyond are on Mauna Kea Access Rd, near Mile 28 on Saddle Road. MKVIS is 6 miles uphill from Saddle Road; the summit is another 8 miles beyond that. Call ☎808-935-6268 for current road conditions.

Hamakua Coast

Stretching from Waipi'o Valley to Hilo, the Hamakua Coast combines rugged beauty and bursting fertility. Here you'll find rocky shores and pounding surf, tropical rainforests and thunderous waterfalls. The color green takes on new meaning, especially in Waipi'o Valley, which you can explore on horseback or by a steep, exhilarating hike.

On the slopes of Mauna Kea, farmers grow vanilla, tea, mushrooms and other boutique crops, modernizing and diversifying island agriculture. Visit these small-scale farms for a close-up look at island life (and to sample its delicious bounty). Sugarcane once ruled the Hamakua Coast, with acres of plantations and massive trains chugging along the coast and across towering bridges spanning the tremendous gulches. Stop at old-time museums and delve into the rich history here. Pause to imagine the 'old plantation days.' Go slow, explore the back roads and step back in time.

WORTH A TRIP

KOHALA MOUNTAIN ROAD

Arguably the Big Island's best scenic drive, Kohala Mountain Rd (Hwy 250) affords stupendous views of the Kohala–Kona coastline and three majestic volcanic mountains: Mauna Kea, Mauna Loa and Hualalai. Start from Waimea, climb past an overlook, and then follow the spine of the peninsula through green pastures until you finally descend to the sea at Hawi. The name changes to Hawi Rd close to that town.

A car is essential to navigate the Hamakua Coast along Hwy 19. Honoka'a, the biggest town along the Hamakua Coast, is approximately 50 miles from Kailua-Kona and 40 miles from Hilo. Expect the drive to take 75 minutes from Kona and an hour from Hilo.

The **Hele-On Bus** (☎808-961-8744; www.heleonbus.org; per trip adult/senior & student $2/1) route between Kona and Hilo stops at various towns along the coast, including Honoka'a, Pa'auilo, Laupahoehoe, Hakalau, Honomu and Papaikou. Buses run between Kona and Hilo three times daily. Service between Hilo and Honoka'a is more frequent. Check the website for schedules.

Hilo

Kailua-Kona may host more visitors, but Hilo is the beating heart of Hawai'i Island. Hidden beneath its daily drizzle lies deep soil and soul, from which sprouts a genuine community and aloha spirit. Hilo's demographics still mirror its sugar-town roots, with a diverse mix of Native Hawaiians, Japanese, Filipinos, Portuguese, Puerto Ricans, Chinese and Caucasians. People might seem low-key, but they're a resilient lot. Knocked down by two tsunamis, threatened with extinction by Mauna Loa lava flows, deluged with the highest annual rainfall in the USA and always battling for its share of tourist dollars, Hilo knows how to survive and to thrive.

Hilo had a life before tourism, and it remains refreshingly untouristy. Yet it offers many attractions: compelling museums, a walkable downtown, two thriving farmers markets and dozens of indie restaurants. Hilo is an ideal base for exploring Hawai'i Volcanoes National Park, Mauna Kea, Puna and the Hamakua Coast.

◉ Sights & Activities

★ Lili'uokalani Park
PARK

(189 Lihiwai St; 🖫) Savor Hilo's simple pleasures with a picnic lunch in scenic Japanese gardens overlooking the bay. Named for Hawaii's last queen (r 1891–93), the 30-acre county park features soaring trees, sprawling lawns and quaint footbridges over shallow ponds. At sunrise or sunset, join the locals jogging or power walking the perimeter, or simply admire the Mauna Kea view.

★ Pacific Tsunami Museum
MUSEUM

(🖰 808-935-0926; www.tsunami.org; 130 Kamehameha Ave; adult/child $8/4; ⊙10am-4pm Tue-Sat) You cannot understand Hilo without knowing its history as a two-time tsunami survivor (1946 and 1960). This seemingly modest museum is chock-full of riveting information, including a section on the Japanese tsunami of 2011, which damaged Kona. Allow enough time to experience the multimedia exhibits, including chilling computer simulations and heart-wrenching first-person accounts.

★ 'Imiloa Astronomy Center of Hawai'i
MUSEUM

(🖰 808-969-9700; www.imiloahawaii.org; 600 'Imiloa Pl; adult/child 6-17yr $17.50/9.50; ⊙9am-5pm Tue-Sun; 🖫) 'Imiloa, which means 'exploring new knowledge,' is a $28 million museum and planetarium complex with a twist: it juxtaposes modern astronomy on Mauna Kea with ancient Polynesian ocean voyaging. It's a great family attraction and the natural complement to a summit tour. One planetarium show is included with admission. On Friday catch special evening programs, including a mind-blowing Led Zeppelin planetarium rock show.

🛌 Sleeping

★ Arnott's Lodge
HOSTEL, CAMPGROUND $

(🖰 808-339-0921; www.arnottslodge.com; 98 Apapane Rd; camping per person $16, dm from $30, r with/without bath $90/70, ste from $100; 🄿 🖭 ❋ 🖥) Hilo's longest-running hostel remains solid value, with a dizzying variety of lodging options close to Onekahakaha Beach. All rooms and dorms are clean, safe and comfortably furnished. The Deluxe Suite ($110) is especially pleasant, with an airy high ceiling and private kitchenette. Camping is also available.

★ Dolphin Bay Hotel
HOTEL $$

(🖰 808-935-1466, 877-935-1466; www.dolphinbayhotel.com; 333 Iliahi St; studio $110-160, ste $180-200; 🄿 🖭 🖥) This family-owned, two-story hotel attracts countless loyal, repeat guests – which is no surprise. Its 18 apartment-style

units are spotless and reasonably priced and all include full kitchen. Welcoming staffers are generous with island advice and provide free coffee, fruit and banana bread for breakfast. The property is conveniently located within a five-minute walk of downtown Hilo.

✖ Eating & Drinking

★ Suisan Fish Market
SEAFOOD $

(🖰 808-935-9349; 93 Lihiwai St; takeout poke $10-12, poke per lb $18; ⊙8am-6pm Mon-Fri, to 4pm Sat, 10am-4pm Sun) For a fantastic variety of freshly made *poke* (sold by the pound), Suisan is a must. Buy a bowl of takeout *poke* and rice and eat outside the shop or across the street at Lili'uokalani Park.

★ Restaurant Kenichi
JAPANESE $

(🖰 808-969-1776; www.restaurantkenichi.com; 684 Kilauea Ave; mains $13-15; ⊙10am-2pm & 5-9pm Mon-Sat; 🖫) For delicious, untouristy dining, Kenichi has it all: Japanese comfort food, high-volume flavor, cheerful staff and a simple dining room crowded with locals. Favorites include ramen bowls made with house *dashi* (broth), succulent grilled *saba* (mackerel), boneless Korean chicken and rib-eye steak.

Bayfront Kava Bar
BAR

(🖰 808-345-1698; www.bayfrontkava.com; 264 Keawe St; cup of kava $5; ⊙4-10pm Mon-Sat) If you're curious about kava ('awa in Hawaiian), try a cup at this minimalist bar. Friendly bar staff serve freshly brewed, locally grown kava root in coconut shells. Get ready for tingling taste buds and a calm buzz. Live music and art exhibitions kick off on a regular basis.

ℹ Getting There & Away

The drive from Hilo to Kailua-Kona (via Waimea) along Hwy 19 is 95 miles and takes about 2½ hours. Driving along Saddle Road can cut travel time by about 15 minutes.

Hawai'i Volcanoes National Park

From the often-snowy summit of Mauna Loa, the world's most massive volcano, to the boiling coast where lava pours into the sea, Hawai'i Volcanoes National Park is a micro-continent of thriving rainforests, volcano-induced deserts, high-mountain meadows, coastal plains and plenty of geological marvels in between.

At the heart of it all is Kilauea – the earth's youngest and most active shield volcano. Since 1983 Kilauea's East Rift Zone has been erupting almost nonstop from the Pu'u

'O'o vent, adding nearly 500 acres of new land to the island.

The national park staff excel at managing this chaotic landscape. Their education programs deftly blend modern science with ancient beliefs and customs, and their outreach feels boundless. Ample interpretive signs, unusually informative trail guides, a slew of well-thought-out ranger-led hikes, living history programs and a weekly lecture series all provide visitors with a solid connection to the park and the people of Hawai'i.

The park's two vehicle-accessible campgrounds are relatively uncrowded outside of summer months. Nights can be crisp and cool and wet. Campsites are first-come, first-served (with a seven-night limit). Nearby Volcano Village has the most variety for those who prefer a roof over their heads.

★Kilauea Visitor
Center & Museum   MUSEUM
(☑808-985-6000; www.nps.gov/havo; Crater Rim Dr; ⊙9am-5pm, film screenings hourly 9am-4pm; 🅿) 🖊 Stop here first. Extraordinarily helpful (and remarkably patient) rangers and volunteers can advise you about volcanic activity, air quality, road closures, hiking-trail conditions and how best to spend however much time you have. Interactive museum exhibits are small but family friendly, and will teach even science-savvy adults about the park's delicate ecosystem and Hawaiian heritage. All of the rotating movies are excellent. Pick up fun junior ranger program activity books for your kids before leaving.

❶ Information

Air Quality (www.hawaiiso2network.com) Air-quality updates from nine monitoring stations throughout the park.

Hawai'i County Civil Defense (www.hawaii-county.gov/civil-defense) Information on lava flows and volcanic activity.

Trail & Road Closures (www.nps.gov/havo/closed_areas.htm) Updated information on trail and road closings.

USGS Hawaiian Volcano Observatory (http://hvo.wr.usgs.gov) Kilauea Volcano eruption updates, current earthquake and atmospheric conditions, and webcams.

❶ Getting There & Around

The park is 30 miles (45 minutes) from Hilo and 95 miles (2¾ hours) from Kailua-Kona via Hwy 11. The turnoffs for Volcano village are a couple of miles east of the main park entrance. Hwy 11 is prone to flooding, washouts and closures during rainstorms. Periods of drought may close Mauna Loa Rd and Hilina Pali Rd due to wildfire hazards.

The public **Hele-On Bus** (☑808-961-8744; www.heleonbus.org; adult one-way $2) departs Monday through Saturday (no service Sunday) from Hilo, arriving at the park visitor center ($5 surcharge) about 1¼ hours later. One bus continues to Ka'u. There is no public transportation once you get inside the park, and hitchhiking is illegal in all national parks.

Cyclists are permitted on paved roads, and a handful of dirt ones, including the Escape Rd but not on any trails – pavement or no.

MAUI

According to some, you can't have it all. Perhaps those folks haven't been to Maui, which consistently lands atop travel-magazine reader polls as one of the world's most romantic islands. And why not? With its sandy beaches, deluxe resorts, gourmet cuisine, fantastic luau, whale-watching, surfing, snorkeling and hiking, it leaves most people more in love than when they arrived.

❶ Getting There & Away

Maui has a large number of nonstop flights to/from cities on the mainland, including Los Angeles, San Diego, San Francisco, Seattle, Dallas, Chicago and Vancouver, BC. Otherwise it's common to connect through Honolulu.

Kahului International Airport (OGG; ☑808-872-3830; http://hawaii.gov/ogg; 1 Kahului Airport Rd) All trans-Pacific flights to Maui arrive in Kahului, the island's main airport. There's a staffed Visitor Information Desk in the baggage claim area that's open 7:45am to 10pm daily. There are racks of local travel brochures beside the desk. A huge new rental-car facility and monorail will make the terminal area a construction site through 2019.

Kapalua Airport (JHM; ☑808-665-6108; www.hawaii.gov/jhm; 4050 Honoapiilani Hwy) Off Hwy 30, south of Kapalua in West Maui, this regional airport has flights with **Mokulele Airlines** (☑866-260-7070; www.mokuleleairlines.com) to Moloka'i and Honolulu.

Lahaina

With its weathered storefronts, narrow streets and bustling harbor, plus a few chattering mynahs, Hawaii's most historic town looks like a port-of-call for Captain Ahab. Is this the 21st century, or an 1850s whaling village? In truth, it offers a mix of both.

Tucked between the West Maui Mountains and a tranquil sea, Lahaina has long been a popular convergence point. Ancient Hawaiian royals were the first to gather here, followed by missionaries, whalers and

DON'T MISS

BIG BEACH

The crowning glory of Makena State Park, the untouched **Big Beach** (Oneloa Beach; http://dlnr.hawaii.gov/dsp/parks/maui; Makena Rd; ⊙ 6am-6pm; P) is arguably the finest on Maui. In Hawaiian it's called Oneloa, literally 'Long Sand.' And indeed the golden sands stretch for the better part of a mile and are as broad as they come. The waters are a beautiful turquoise. When they're calm you'll find kids boogie-boarding here, but at other times the shorebreaks can be dangerous, suitable for experienced bodysurfers only.

sugar plantation workers. Today it's a base for creative chefs, passionate artists and dedicated surf instructors.

Near the harbor, storefronts that once housed saloons, dance halls and brothels now teem with art galleries, souvenir shops and, well, still plenty of watering holes. As for the whalers, they've been replaced by a new kind of leviathan hunter: whale-watchers as dedicated as Ahab in their hunt. Between January and March, they don't have to look hard.

◉ Sights & Activities

★ Banyan Tree Square   PARK
(cnr Front & Hotel Sts) A leafy landmark (the largest tree in Hawaii) stands in the center of Lahaina. Remarkably, it sprawls across the entire square. Planted as a seedling on April 24, 1873, to commemorate the 50th anniversary of missionaries in Lahaina, the tree has become a virtual forest unto itself, with 16 major trunks and scores of horizontal branches reaching across the better part of an acre. The square was recently given a major restoration.

★ Wo Hing Museum   MUSEUM
(www.lahainarestoration.org/wo-hing-museum; 858 Front St; adult/child $7/free; ⊙10am-4pm) This temple, built in 1912 as a meeting hall for the benevolent society Chee Kung Tong, provided Chinese immigrants with a place to preserve their cultural identity, celebrate festivities and socialize in their native tongue. After WWII, Lahaina's ethnic Chinese population spread far and wide and the temple fell into decline. Now restored and turned into a cultural museum, it houses ceremonial instruments, a teak medicine cabinet c 1900, jade pieces dating back thousands of years and a Taoist shrine.

★ Trilogy Excursions   BOATING
(☑808-874-5649, 888-225-6284; www.sailtrilogy.com; 207 Kupuohi St; 4hr snorkel trip adult/child from $120/60; ⊙8:30am-4pm Mon- Fri, noon-3pm Sun) Offering snorkeling tours in Maui for more than 40 years, this family-run operation specializes in catamaran tours. There's a variety of trips, including ones to the reef at Olowalu and the much-loved islet of Molokini. In season there are whale-watching trips as wells as dinner and sunset cruises.

🛏 Sleeping & Eating

★ Ilikahi   BOUTIQUE HOTEL $$
(☑808-662-8780; www.theilikahi.com; 441 Ilikahi St; r $170-220; P✳🛜) 🍃 Serenity is the word at this tropical escape that combines design cues from Hawaii and Bali. The four rooms are large and private, and each has modern conveniences and lanais (balconies) as well as king beds or four-poster queens. The Ginger Suite has a beautiful terrace. Ecofriendly touches include solar power.

★ Frida's Mexican
Beach House   MEXICAN $$$
(☑808-661-1287; http://fridasmaui.com; 1287 Front St; mains $20-40; ⊙11am-9:30pm) Not your cheap taco joint, Frida's (with plenty of imagery from its namesake Frida Kahlo) has a superb waterfront location, with a large open dining area on a terrace that will have your blood pressure falling minutes after arriving. Steaks and seafood with a Latin flair feature on the upscale menu. Cocktails are creative; yes, there are margaritas!

🍸 Drinking & Nightlife

★ Fleetwood's on Front St   BAR
(☑808-669-6425; www.fleetwoodsonfrontst.com; 744 Front St; ⊙2-10pm) With its comfy pillows, cushy lounges and ornate accents, this rooftop oasis – owned by Fleetwood Mac drummer Mick Fleetwood – evokes Morocco. But views of the Pacific and the West Maui Mountains keep you firmly rooted in Hawaii. At sunset, a conch-shell blast announces a tiki-lighting ceremony that's followed by a bagpipe serenade – from a kilt-wearing Scot.

★ Down the Hatch   BAR
(☑808-661-4900; www.dthmaui.com; 658 Front St, Wharf Cinema Center; ⊙11am-2am) Lahaina's best late-night bar is on the lower level of the mall. All open-air, its fountains are drowned out by the raucous revelry of the mixed crowd of locals and visitors. There's a long happy hour (3pm to 7pm) when you can enjoy the long list of drinks at big discounts.

❶ Getting There & Away

It takes about one hour to drive between Lahaina and the airport in Kahului.

Hawaii Executive Transportation (☑808-669-2300; www.hawaiiexecutivetransportation.com; 1/2/3/4 passengers $51/59/64/66; ⊙reservations 7am-11pm) provides van service between the airport and Lahaina, and serves most addresses in town. A taxi between Lahaina and the airport costs about $80.

The **Maui Bus** (☑808-871-4838; www.mauicounty.gov/bus; single ride $2, day pass $4) runs the Lahaina Islander route 20 between Kahului bus hub and Lahaina (one hour), stopping at Ma'alaea Harbor, where a connection can be made to Kihei (various stops) via the Kihei Villager bus service. Another route, the Ka'anapali Islander, connects Lahaina and Ka'anapali (30 minutes). Both Islander routes depart from the Wharf Cinema Center hourly from 6:30am to 8:30pm.

The **Expeditions Ferry** (☑808-661-3756; www.go-lanai.com; Lahaina Harbor; adult/child one way $30/20) to Lana'i uses the **Ferry Dock** (off Wharf St) in Lahaina Harbor. The Moloka'i ferry no longer runs.

Kihei

Two reasons to visit Kihei? The beaches and your budget. Yes, it's overrun with strip malls and traffic, but with 6 miles of easy-to-access beaches, loads of affordable accommodations and a variety of dining options, it offers everything you need for an enjoyable beach vacation. An energetic seaside town, Kihei also works well for short-trip vacationers seeking reliable sunshine – on average Kihei is sunny 276 days per year. It's also home to the island's busiest bar scene.

To zip from one end of Kihei to the other, take the Pi'ilani Hwy (Hwy 31). It runs parallel to and bypasses the stop-start traffic of S Kihei Rd. Well-marked crossroads connect these two routes.

❂ Sights

★**Keawakapu Beach** BEACH
(☑808-879-4364; www.mauicounty.gov/Facilities; ℗) From break of day to twilight, this sparkling stretch of sand is a showstopper. Extending from south Kihei to Wailea's Mokapu Beach, Keawakapu is set back from the main road and is less visible than Kihei's main roadside beaches just north. It's also less crowded, and is a great place to settle in and watch the sunset.

🛏 Sleeping

★**Pineapple Inn Maui** INN $$
(☑808-298-4403, 877-212-6284; www.pineappleinnmaui.com; 3170 Akala Dr; r $179-189, cottage $255; ℗❄🐾🛜) The Pineapple Inn may be the best deal going in South Maui. This inviting boutique property offers style and functionality with a personal touch, and it's less than a mile from the beach. The four rooms, which have ocean-view lanai and private entrances, are as attractive as those at the exclusive resorts, but at a fraction of the cost. Rooms have kitchenettes, and the two-bedroom cottage comes with a full kitchen.

DON'T MISS

HALEAKALĀ NATIONAL PARK

Haleakalā National Park (☑808-572-4400; www.nps.gov/hale; Summit District: Haleakalā Hwy, Kipahulu District: Hana Hwy; 3-day pass car $20, motorcycle $15, individual on foot or bicycle $10; ℗♿) has two distinct sections, and if you have just one day to visit, head to the summit. Whether you make a pre-dawn haul up the mountain to watch the sunrise, or mosey up after breakfast, begin your explorations here. Not only is the **visitor center** (www.nps.gov/hale; Haleakalā Hwy; ⊙sunrise-3pm; ℗) the ideal perch for crater views, it's also a fine starting point for jaunts into the crater.

Next, burn off the morning chill with an invigorating hike on the sun-warmed cinders of the unearthly **Keonehe'ehe'e (Sliding Sands) Trail**. Once you've completed your lunar-like crater hike, continue your road trip to Maui's highest point, **Pu'u'ula'ula (Red Hill) Overlook**. Admire the 'ahinahina (silversword) garden and take in a ranger talk.

It's time to head back down the mountain. Make your way to the **Kalahaku Overlook** lookout, a crater rim-hugger with an eye-popping, wide-angle view of the cinder cones dotting the crater floor.

You've seen the starkly barren side of Haleakalā. Now make acquaintance with its lush green face by taking a half-mile walk along the **Hosmer Grove Trail**, in forest brimming with birdsong. Like many animals in the park, some of these birds are found nowhere else.

This leg covers 17 miles.

Kohea Kai Resort BOUTIQUE HOTEL $$$
(☑ 808-879-1261; www.koheakai.com; 551 S Kihei
Rd; r $219-253, ste $279-479; P✳@♠) With
new owners and a name change, the former
Maui Sunseeker is now the new kid in the
neighborhood. Except it's adults only. Inti-
mate, smart, progressive and inclusive, this
breezy property sprawls across five buildings
in North Kihei, across the street from Mai
Poina 'Oela'u Beach. The low-key tropical de-
cor outshines other places in this price range.

✖ Eating & Drinking

★ **Café O'Lei** HAWAIIAN $$
(☑ 808-891-1368; www.cafeoleirestaurants.com;
2439 S Kihei Rd, Rainbow Mall; lunch $8-16, dinner
$17-29; ☺ 10:30am-3:30pm & 4:30-9:30pm) This
strip-mall bistro looks ho-hum at first blush.
But step inside: the sophisticated atmosphere,
innovative Hawaii Regional Cuisine, honest
prices and excellent service knock Café O'Lei
into the fine-dining big league. For a tangy
treat, order the blackened mahimahi with
fresh papaya salsa. Look for unbeatable lunch
mains, with salads, for under $10, and a sushi
chef after 4:30pm (Tuesday to Saturday).

★ **5 Palms** COCKTAIL BAR
(☑ 808-879-2607; www.5palmsrestaurant.com;
2960 S Kihei Rd, Mana Kai Maui; ☺ 8am-11pm, happy hour 3-7pm & 9-11pm) For sunset cocktails
beside the beach, this is the place. Arrive an
hour before the sun goes down because the
patio bar, just steps from stunning Keawakapu Beach, fills quickly. During happy hour,
sushi and an array of delicious appetizers
are half price, with a one drink minimum,
while mai tais and margaritas are $5.75. Pop-
ular with tourists and locals.

❶ Getting There & Away

The **Maui Bus** (☑ 808-871-4838; www.mau-
icounty.gov/bus; single ride $2, day pass $4)
serves Kihei with two routes. One route, the Kihei
Islander, connects Kihei with Wailea and Kahalui;
stops include Kama'ole Beach Park III, Pi'ilani
Village shopping center, and Uwapo at South Kihei
Rd. The other route, the Kihei Villager, primarily
serves the northern half of Kihei, with a half-dozen
stops along South Kihei Rd and at Pi'ilani Village
shopping center and Ma'alaea. Both routes operate hourly from around 6am to 8pm and cost $2.

KAUA'I

Emerald mountains, weeping waterfalls, red-
rock canyons, jaw-dropping beaches, clear
seas and big waves. Kaua'i's natural gifts are
unparalleled in Hawaii, the USA, the world.

Tourist information kiosks aren't really a
thing on Kaua'i, but the local tourist board,
Kaua'i Visitors Bureau (☑ 808-245-3971; www.
gohawaii.com/kauai; 4334 Rice St, Suite 101; ☺ 8am-
4:30pm Mon-Fri), does have a useful website.

❶ Getting There & Around

Getting here is easy, especially from the mainland USA and Canada, with numerous flights
daily. Often, flights will get here with layovers
in Honolulu. There are no ferry services here.
Flights, cars and tours can be booked online at
lonelyplanet.com/bookings.

Renting a car is highly recommended unless
you're on a very tight budget. Well-maintained
highways provide access to most of the island
and free parking is widely available.

Lihu'e

The island's commercial center is strip-mall
plain, but there's an abundance of economical eateries and shops along with a down-to-
earth, workaday atmosphere that's missing
in resort areas. While Kalapaki Beach is a
charmer, Lihu'e is more a place to stock up
on supplies after arrival at the airport before
heading out on your island adventure.

Lihu'e arose as a plantation town back
in 1849 when sugar was king, and its massive sugar mill (still standing south of town
along Kaumuali'i Hwy) was Kaua'i's largest.
The mill closed in 2000, ending more than a
century of operations. It left behind an ethnic
melting pot of Asian, European and Hawaiian
traditions that make the town what it is today.

Activities tend to center on Kalapaki
Beach with a few top golf courses and cool
beaches nearby. This is the kickoff point for
helicopter tours and a few fun excursions to
waterfalls.

Wailua

To ancient Hawaiians, the Wailua River was
among the most sacred places across the islands. The river basin, near its mouth, was one
of the island's two royal centers (the other was
Waimea) and home to the high chiefs. Here,
you can find the remains of many important
heiau (ancient stone temples); together they
now form a national historic landmark.

Long and narrow **Hikina'akala Heiau** (Rising of the Sun Temple) sits south of the Wailua
River mouth, which is today the north end of
Lydgate Beach Park. In its heyday, the temple
(built around AD 1300) was aligned directly north to south, but only a few remaining
boulders outline its original massive shape.

Neighboring **Hauola Pu'uhonua** (meaning 'the place of refuge of the dew of life') is marked by a bronze plaque. Ancient Hawaiian *kapu* (taboo) breakers were assured safety from persecution if they made it inside.

Believed to be the oldest *luakini* (temple dedicated to the war god Ku, often a place for human sacrifice) on the island, **Holoholoku Heiau** is a quarter-mile up Kuamo'o Rd on the left. It's believed to be Kaua'i's oldest heiau. Toward the west, against the flat-backed birthstone marked by a plaque reading **Pohaku Ho'ohanau** (Royal Birthstone), queens gave birth to future royals. Only a male child born here could become king of Kaua'i.

Perched high on a hill overlooking the meandering Wailua River, well-preserved **Poli'ahu Heiau**, another *luakini*, is named after the snow goddess Poli'ahu, one of the sisters of the volcano goddess Pele. The heiau is immediately before **'Opaeka'a Falls Lookout**, on the opposite side of the road.

Although Hawaiian heiau were originally imposing stone structures, most now lie in ruins, covered with scrub. But they are still considered powerful vortices of mana (spiritual essence) and should be treated with respect. For a compelling history of the Wailua River's significance to ancient Hawaiians, read Edward Joesting's *Kauai: the Separate Kingdom*.

ⓘ Getting There & Around

Don't look for a town center. Most attractions are scattered along coastal Kuhio Hwy (Hwy 56) or Kuamo'o Rd (Hwy 580) heading *mauka* (inland).

Driving north, Kapa'a Bypass runs from just north of the Wailua River to beyond Kapa'a, usually skipping the Waipouli and Kapa'a gridlock.

Hanalei

There are precious few towns with the majestic natural beauty and barefoot soul of Hanalei. The bay is the thing, of course. Its half-dozen surf breaks are legendary, partly because local surf gods such as the late Andy Irons cut their teeth here. Even if you aren't here for the waves, the beach will demand your attention with its wide sweep of cream-colored sand and magnificent jade mountain views.

So will the pint-sized town where you may take a yoga class, snack on sushi, shop for chic beach gear, vintage treasures and stunning art, or duck into a world-class dive bar. Sure, Hanalei has more than its share of adults with Peter Pan syndrome, and you'll see as many men in their sixties waxing their surfboards as you will groms with 'guns' (big-wave surfboards). Which begs the query: why grow up at all when you can grow old in Hanalei?

◉ Sights & Activities

★ **Black Pot Beach Park (Hanalei Pier)**   BEACH
This small section of Hanalei Bay near the Hanalei River mouth usually offers the calmest surf among the wild North Shore swells. Also known as Hanalei Pier for its unmistakable landmark, the sand is shaded by ironwood trees and is popular mainly

HAWAII HANALEI

DON'T MISS

WAIMEA CANYON STATE PARK

Of all Kaua'i's unique wonders, none can touch Waimea Canyon for grandeur. Few would expect to find a gargantuan chasm of ancient lava rock, 10 miles long and over 3500ft deep. It's so spectacular that it has been popularly nicknamed 'the Grand Canyon of the Pacific'. Flowing through the canyon is Waimea River, Kaua'i's longest, fed by tributaries that bring reddish-brown waters from Alaka'i Swamp's mountaintop.

Waimea Canyon was formed when Kaua'i's original shield volcano, Wai'ale'ale, slumped along an ancient fault line. The horizontal striations along the canyon walls represent successive volcanic eruptions. The red colors indicate where water has seeped through the rocks, creating mineral rust from the iron ore inside.

Drives here on a clear day are phenomenal. Don't be disappointed by rain, as that's what makes the waterfalls gush. Sunny days following rain are ideal for prime views, though slick mud makes hiking challenging at these times.

The southern boundary of Waimea Canyon State Park is about 6 miles uphill from Waimea. You can reach the park by two roads: more scenic Waimea Canyon Dr (Hwy 550), which starts in Waimea just past Mile 23, or Koke'e Rd (Hwy 552), starting in Kekaha off Mana Rd. The two roads merge between Miles 6 and 7.

with novice surfers. In summer, swimming and snorkeling are decent, as is kayaking and SUP.

Hanalei Beach Park
BEACH

With its sweeping views, this makes a great place for a picnic, sunset or lazy day at the beach. Ideally located, its downside is the parking, which can be a challenge. Park along Weke Rd if you have to, as the public lot gets crowded. Facilities include restrooms and outdoor showers. Camping is allowed only with an advance county permit.

★ Ho'opulapula Haraguchi Rice Mill & Taro Farm Tours
TOURS

(☎ 808-651-3399; www.haraguchiricemill.org; tours incl lunch adult/child 5-12yr $87/52; ⊙ tours usually 9:45am Wed, by reservation only) 🖋 Learn about cultivating taro on Kaua'i at this sixth-generation family-run nonprofit farm and rice mill (the last remaining in the Hawaiian Islands). On farmer-guided tours, which take you out into the *lo'i kalo* (Hawaiian wet taro fields), you'll get a glimpse of the otherwise inaccessible Hanalei National Wildlife Refuge and learn about Hawaii's immigrant history.

🛏 Sleeping & Eating

★ Hanalei Dolphin Cottages
COTTAGE $$$

(☎ 808-826-1675; www.hanaleicottages.com; 5-5016 Kuhio Hwy; 2-bedroom cottage $260; 🐾) Launch a canoe, kayak or SUP board right from your backyard on the Hanalei River. A lazy walk from the heart of Hanalei town, each of the four cottages is styled similarly, with bamboo furniture, a full kitchen, BBQ grill, private outdoor (and indoor) showers, front-of-house bedrooms and airy quasi-lounge areas facing the river. Cleaning fee $130.

Chicken in a Barrel
BARBECUE $

(☎ 808-826-1999; www.chickeninabarrel.com; Ching Young Village, 5-5190 Kuhio Hwy; meals $10-17; ⊙ 11am-8pm Mon-Sat, to 7pm Sun; 🅼) Using a custom-made 50-gallon barrel drum smoker, this island BBQ joint is all about the bird. Grab a heaping plate of chicken or a hoagie sandwich with chili-cheese fries. It does ribs and pulled pork too. Whichever you choose, you won't have to eat again all day. There's a second location in **Kapa'a** (☎ 808-823-0780; 4-1586 Kuhio Hwy; meals $12-16; ⊙ 11am-8:30pm Mon-Sat, to 7pm Sun).

★ BarAcuda Tapas & Wine
MEDITERRANEAN $$$

(☎ 808-826-7081; www.restaurantbaracuda.com; Hanalei Center, 5-5161 Kuhio Hwy; shared plates $7-26; ⊙ 5:30-10pm, kitchen closes at 9:30pm) 🖋 This is the most chef-driven spot in Hanalei and its best kitchen. The wine list is expertly curated, and the tapas-style plates, featuring local beef, fish, pork and veg, are meant to be shared.

❶ Getting There & Away

There's one road into and out of Hanalei. During heavy rains (common in winter), the Hanalei Bridge occasionally closes due to flooding and those on either side are stuck until it reopens.

Parking in town can be a headache and absent-minded pedestrians even more so. Everything in Hanalei is walkable. Otherwise, do as the locals do and hop on a bicycle.

If you opted not to rent a car, the **North Shore Shuttle** (☎ 808-826-7019; www.kauai.gov/NorthShoreShuttle; one way $4) links Hanalei to Ke'e with multiple stops in Waniha and Haena along the way.

Po'ipu & South Shore

Po'ipu is the nexus of South Shore tourism... and with good reason. This is one of the sunniest spots on the island – with notably less rain (and less green) than other spots to the north. There are amazing sun-kissed beaches, plenty of top-end resorts and vacation rental condos, plus some of Kaua'i's best restaurants.

While most vacations here center on the beaches and waterborne activities such as surfing, diving, snorkeling, paddle boarding or just beach bumming, the South Shore also has two world-renowned botanical gardens that showcase beautiful collections of endemic species. The undeveloped Maha'ulepu Coast has lithified sand-dune cliffs and pounding surf that make for an unforgettable walk. And in between, you have the lasting remnants of the sugar-plantation area, with friendly art galleries, intimate restaurants and interesting historic perspectives in the cozy centers of Koloa and Kalaheo.

❶ Getting There & Around

Navigating is easy, with just two main roads: Po'ipu Rd (along eastern Po'ipu) and Lawa'i Rd (along western Po'ipu). You'll need a car, scooter or bike to go anywhere here besides the beach. It's possible to walk along the roads, but the vibe is more suburbia than surf town.

The **Kaua'i Bus** (☎ 808-246-8110; www.kauai.gov/Bus; 3220 Ho'olako St, Lihu'e; one-way fare adult/senior & child 7-18yr $2/1) runs through Koloa into Po'ipu, stopping along Po'ipu Rd at the turnoff to Po'ipu Beach Park and also by the Hyatt. It's an option for getting here from other towns, but not very useful as transport around the resort area.

Understand USA

USA TODAY 1130

Changing cityscapes, greener futures and a nation divided by its controversial president... and still more guns.

HISTORY 1133

The people and events that have shaped a nation: from Native Americans, colonists, revolutionaries and reconstructionists to New Dealers and civil rights fighters.

THE WAY OF LIFE 1145

Lifestyles, immigration, religion, sports and politics.

NATIVE AMERICANS 1150

Overview of some Native American tribes, plus the lowdown on crafts and iconic texts.

ARTS & ARCHITECTURE 1152

Providing a window into the American identity – literature, painting, theater and architecture.

THE MUSIC SCENE 1161

The great American sound in all its beauty and dissonance, from blues and jazz to country, folk, rock and hip-hop.

THE LAND & WILDLIFE 1164

Geology, natural disasters, environmentalism and the iconic creatures of the American landscape.

USA Today

The controversial result of the 2016 election, which saw businessman Donald Trump lose the popular vote but win the presidency, thrust the US into an uncertain future, dividing the nation across hot-topic issues such as immigration and health care, and sparking waves of protests, with those on the left resisting the nation's sudden (and sharp) turn to the right. Meanwhile, recreational marijuana gains increasing acceptance, cities blossom, and the divide between rich and poor grows ever wider.

Best on Film

Singin' in the Rain (1952) Among the best in the era of musicals, with an exuberant Gene Kelly.

Annie Hall (1977) Woody Allen's brilliant romantic comedy, with New York City playing a starring role.

North by Northwest (1959) Alfred Hitchcock thriller with Cary Grant on the run across America.

The Godfather (1972–90) Famed trilogy looking at American society through the lens of immigrants and organized crime.

Boyhood (2014) Richard Linklater's coming-of-age tale, shot over the course of 12 years.

Best in Print

On the Road (Jack Kerouac; 1957) A journey through post–WWII America.

The Great Gatsby (F Scott Fitzgerald; 1925) A powerful Jazz Age novel.

Beloved (Toni Morrison; 1987) A Pulitzer Prize–winning novel set during the post–Civil War years.

Adventures of Huckleberry Finn (Mark Twain; 1884) A moving tale of journey and self-discovery.

Blue Highways (William Least Heat-Moon; 1982) A classic of travel writing.

The Underground Railroad (Colson Whitehead; 2016) Pulitzer Prize–winning novel chronicling a young slave's bid for freedom.

Changing Cityscapes

Cities are booming in America, growing at a faster rate than the rest of the country. Far from being the burned-out hulls of decades past, American cities are safer, and have wide-ranging appeal (in the realms of culture, food, nightlife and livability). Yet with more people moving from the suburbs and the exurbs to city centers, this has brought many challenges – particularly in terms of housing and transportation. Creating affordable housing is one of the biggest challenges facing American cities. In many places rent and housing prices have skyrocketed. In particular, middle-class families – whose incomes aren't rising fast enough to meet the price increases – are feeling the pinch. Nationally, more than half of all renters are spending over 30% of their income on rent. And low-income families spend more than half their income on rent.

To meet the growing demand, housing units are being built across the country, though often these new units cater to the luxury market, doing little to diminish demand. Some mayors, such as Bill de Blasio of New York City and Ed Lee of San Francisco, have launched ambitious programs to create more affordable housing. De Blasio stated that unless New York acted boldly, the city risked becoming a gated community of exclusivity rather than opportunity. The same could be said for many American cities.

A Divided Nation

Speaking of exclusivity, the income gap continues to widen in the US. The top 1% of the population earns more than 20% of the income (up from 9% in 1976). Meanwhile, the poor are getting poorer: the median wage earner takes home 2.5% less than in 1999. Unfortunately, it isn't just the income gap that is widening. Rich people in America are living longer than poor people:

the wealthy lived 2.7 years longer than the poor in the 1980s. Today, the life expectancy gap between the richest and poorest Americans has ballooned to 15 years. And privileged children are outpacing their peers by bigger margins (the gap in test scores between rich and poor is over 30% wider than it was two decades ago). The challenge: how to fix the problem. A potential solution – raising taxes on the rich – is considered political suicide, and both strengthening unions and creating universal pre-kindergarten programs have received little traction in the current political climate. There is one silver lining: states from California and Washington across to New York plan to raise minimum wages to as high as $15 in the coming years in an attempt to lift their poorest citizens out of poverty.

Greener Futures

With more people moving to urban areas, cities have also grappled with transportation. Building more roads has never helped alleviate traffic congestion – as engineers have known since the 1960s. The answer has been greater investment in public transit. Cities, once deeply married to the automobile (Houston, we're looking at you), have greatly expanded public transportation options, with new light-rail lines, express bus lanes and dedicated bus lanes.

Bike-sharing programs have also exploded across the country, with nearly 120 cities offering easy rental (usually by the day and week) for residents and visitors. The benefits – fewer cars on the streets, a bit of exercise for commuters, less carbon in the atmosphere – are obvious, though critics worry about injuries (since no bike-sharing programs provide helmets), as well as the long-term financial viability of these often expensive programs.

Gun Culture

In the USA there have been scores of mass shootings over the past 30 years, and sadly the trend has continued with recent high-profile attacks. In 2017, a heavily armed gunman in Las Vegas, NV, fired down on a country music festival from his hotel room on The Strip, killing 58 people, while in 2016 a man opened fire on a LGBT nightclub in Orlando, FL, killing 49 people. Other devastating incidents include the 2015 race-related killing of nine members of a bible study group at an African American Baptist church in Charleston, SC, and the 2012 Newtown, CT, massacre, which claimed the lives of 20 young children and six adults.

On average, 32 Americans are murdered by people with firearms every day and another 216 are wounded. Add to this accidental shootings and suicides and some 34,000 Americans are killed each year by guns. Despite evidence (including a 2013 study published in the *American Journal of Medicine*) that more guns equals more murders, and the comparatively

POPULATION: 324 MILLION

GDP PER CAPITA: $57,300

UNEMPLOYMENT: 4.8%

POPULATION BELOW THE POVERTY LINE: 14.5%

if USA were 100 people

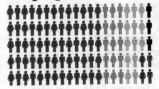

65 would be white
15 would be Hispanic
13 would be African American
4 would be Asian American
3 would be other

belief systems
(% of population)

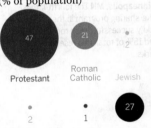

47 — Protestant
21 — Roman Catholic
2 — Jewish
2 — Mormon
1 — Muslim
27 — Other

population per sq mile

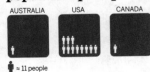

AUSTRALIA   USA   CANADA

≈ 11 people

Best in Music

America (Simon & Garfunkel; 1968)
Young lovers hitchhiking in search of America.

Cowboy Take Me Away (Dixie Chicks; 1999) Classic country music at its best.

Smells Like Teen Spirit (Nirvana; 1991) The Gen-X grunge-rock anthem.

Gangsta's Paradise (Coolio; 1995) A hip-hop classic lamenting the cyclical nature of violence.

Born This Way (Lady Gaga; 2011)
A gay anthem for a new era in LGBT rights.

Alright (Kendrick Lamar; 2015) The song against injustice chanted at Black Lives Matter protests.

Greenest Cities

Portland, OR Huge parks, 350 miles of bike lanes, a walkable city center and an eco-mad populace.

San Francisco, CA Abundant green markets, organic restaurants and ecofriendly buildings. Biking, walking and public transit rule.

New York City, NY Bike-sharing programs, waterfront parks and green spaces, with 100,000 trees planted each year. Plus no need for a car – ever.

Minneapolis, MN The fourth-largest bike-sharing program in the nation, a wildly successful green roofs initiative and 15% of total area reserved for parks.

low rates of death by firearms in countries with strict gun laws, American legislators have been unwilling to enact even modest gun-control laws. The reason in part: gun lobbies such as the National Rifle Association (NRA) wield incredible power, contributing over $35 million annually to state and national political campaigns. But Americans are also enamored of their guns: a recent Pew Research poll found that 52% of Americans said it was more important to protect the right of Americans to own guns versus 46% who said that it was more important to control gun ownership (ie have stricter hand-gun laws).

The 'Green Rush'

Only 32% of Americans favored legalizing marijuana for recreational use in 2006. Today, that figure is fast approaching 60%. Attitudes toward the drug have changed dramatically over the past decade, thanks in no small part to Colorado, which legalized recreational use for adults aged 21 and older in 2012 and went on to develop the nation's first true cannabis industry, with pot shops, weed tours and cannabis-friendly lodgings.

While the drug remains illegal under federal law, one in five Americans now lives in a state where it's considered legal to smoke marijuana without a doctor's prescription. Meanwhile, the weed industry is in the midst of a so-called 'green rush,' with legal sales expected to surpass $20 billion by 2021. Proponents of the movement say it's an economic boon that takes money out of the hands of drug cartels and puts it to good use as tax revenue. Opponents argue that legalization normalizes drug use, spurs dependency and can have adverse effects on teens and impoverished communities. The debate rages on. Meanwhile, new states legalize the drug each year and the federal government turns a blind eye.

History

From its early days as an English colony to its rise to number one on the world stage in the 20th century, American history has been anything but dull. War against the British, westward expansion, slavery and its abolishment, Civil War and Reconstruction, the Great Depression, the post-war boom, and more recent conflicts in the 21st century – they've all played a part in shaping the nation's complicated identity.

Turtle Island

According to oral traditions and sacred myths, indigenous peoples have always lived on the North American continent, which some called Turtle Island. When Europeans arrived, approximately two to 18 million Native American people occupied the turtle's back north of present-day Mexico and spoke more than 300 languages.

Among North America's most significant prehistoric cultures were the Mound Builders, who inhabited the Ohio and Mississippi River valleys from around 3500 BC to AD 1400. In Illinois, Cahokia was once a metropolis of 20,000 people, the largest in pre-Columbian North America.

In the Southwest, Ancestral Puebloans occupied the Colorado Plateau from around AD 100 to AD 1300, until warfare, drought and scarcity of resources likely drove them out. You can still see their cliff dwellings at Colorado's Mesa Verde National Park and desert adobe pueblos at New Mexico's Chaco Culture National Historical Park.

It was the Great Plains cultures that came to epitomize 'Indians' in the popular American imagination, in part because these tribal peoples put up the longest fight against the USA's westward expansion. Oklahoma is rich in sites that interpret Native American life before Europeans arrived, including at Anadarko and along the Trail of Tears.

Enter the Europeans

In 1492 Italian explorer Christopher Columbus, backed by Spain, voyaged west – looking for the East Indies. He found the Bahamas. With visions of gold, Spanish explorers quickly followed: Cortés conquered much of today's Mexico; Pizarro conquered Peru; Ponce de León wandered through Florida looking for the fountain of youth. Not to be left

In 1502 Italian explorer Amerigo Vespucci used the term Mundus Novus (New World) to describe his discoveries. His reward? In 1507 new maps labeled the western hemisphere 'America.'

TIMELINE	20,000–40,000 BC	8000 BC	7000 BC–AD 100
	The first peoples to the Americas arrive from Central Asia by migrating over a wide land bridge between Siberia and Alaska (when sea levels were lower than today).	Widespread extinction of ice-age mammals including the woolly mammoth, due to cooperative hunting by humans and a warming climate. Indigenous peoples begin hunting smaller game and gathering native plants.	'Archaic period' marked by nomadic hunter-gatherer lifestyle. By the end of this period, corn, beans and squash (the agricultural 'three sisters') and permanent settlements are well established.

out, the French explored Canada and the Midwest, while the Dutch and English cruised North America's eastern seaboard.

European explorers left in their wake diseases to which indigenous peoples had no immunity. More than any other factor – war, slavery or famine – disease epidemics devastated Native American populations by anywhere from 50% to 90%. By the 17th century, indigenous North Americans numbered only about a million, and many of the continent's once-thriving societies were in turmoil and transition.

In 1607 English noblemen established North America's first permanent European settlement in Jamestown. Earlier settlements had ended badly, and Jamestown almost did, too: the English chose a swamp, planted their crops late and died from disease and starvation. Some despairing colonists ran off to live with the local tribes, who provided the settlement with enough aid to survive.

For Jamestown and America, 1619 proved a pivotal year: the colony established the House of Burgesses, a representative assembly of citizens to decide local laws, and it received its first boatload of 20 African slaves.

The next year was equally momentous, as a group of radically religious Puritans pulled ashore at what would become Plymouth, MA. The Pilgrims were escaping religious persecution under the 'corrupt' Church of England, and in the New World they saw a divine opportunity to create a new society that would be a religious and moral beacon. The Pilgrims signed a 'Mayflower Compact,' one of the seminal texts of American democracy, to govern themselves by consensus.

The People: Indians of the American Southwest (1993), by Stephen Trimble, is a diverse account of indigenous history and contemporary culture as related by Native Americans themselves.

Colonial Sights

Williamsburg (Virginia)

Jamestown (Virginia)

Plymouth (Massachusetts)

North End (Boston)

Philadelphia (Pennsylvania)

Annapolis (Maryland)

Charleston (South Carolina)

Capitalism & Colonialism

For the next two centuries, European powers competed for position and territory in the New World, extending European politics into the Americas. As Britain's Royal Navy came to rule Atlantic seas, England increasingly profited from its colonies and eagerly consumed the fruits of their labors – sweet tobacco from Virginia, sugar and coffee from the Caribbean.

Over the 17th and 18th centuries, slavery in America was slowly legalized into a formal institution to support this plantation economy. By 1800, one out of every five persons was a slave.

Meanwhile, Britain mostly left the American colonists to govern themselves. Town meetings and representative assemblies, in which local citizens (that is, white men with property) debated community problems and voted on laws and taxes, became common.

However, by the end of the Seven Years' War in 1763, Britain was feeling the strains of running an empire: it had been fighting France for a century and had colonies scattered all over the world. It was time to clean up bureaucracies and share financial burdens.

The colonies, however, resented English taxes and policies. Public outrage soon culminated in the 1776 Declaration of Independence. With

1492	1607	1620	1675
Italian explorer Christopher Columbus 'discovers' America, making three voyages throughout the Caribbean. He names the indigenous people 'Indians,' mistakenly thinking he has reached the Indies.	The English found the first English colony, the Jamestown settlement, on marshland in present-day Virginia. The first few years are hard, with many dying from sickness and starvation.	The *Mayflower* lands at Plymouth with 102 English Pilgrims, who have come to the New World to escape religious persecution. The Wampanoag tribe saves them from starvation.	For decades, the Pilgrims and local tribes live fairly cooperatively, but deadly conflict erupts in 1675. King Philip's War lasts 14 months and kills over 5000 people (mostly Native Americans).

this document, the American colonists took many of the Enlightenment ideas then circulating worldwide – of individualism, equality and freedom; of John Locke's 'natural rights' of life, liberty and property – and fashioned a new type of government to put them into practice.

Frustrations came to a head with the Boston Tea Party in 1773, after which Britain clamped down hard, shutting Boston's harbor and increasing its military presence. In 1774 representatives from 12 colonies convened the First Continental Congress in Philadelphia's Independence Hall to air complaints and prepare for the inevitable war ahead.

Revolution & The Republic

In April 1775 British troops skirmished with armed colonists in Massachusetts, and the Revolutionary War began. George Washington, a wealthy Virginia farmer, was chosen to lead the American army. Trouble was, Washington lacked gunpowder and money (the colonists resisted taxes even for their own military), and his troops were a motley collection of poorly armed farmers, hunters and merchants, who regularly quit and returned to their farms due to lack of pay. On the other side, the British 'Redcoats' represented the world's most powerful military. The inexperienced General Washington had to improvise constantly, sometimes wisely retreating, sometimes engaging in 'ungentlemanly' sneak attacks. During the winter of 1777–78, the American army nearly starved at Valley Forge.

Meanwhile, the Second Continental Congress tried to articulate what exactly they were fighting for. In January 1776 Thomas Paine published the wildly popular *Common Sense*, which passionately argued for independence from England. Soon, independence seemed not just logical, but noble and necessary, and on July 4, 1776, the Declaration of Independence was finalized and signed. Largely written by Thomas Jefferson, it elevated the 13 colonies' particular gripes against the monarchy into a universal declaration of individual rights and republican government.

However, to succeed on the battlefield, General Washington needed help, not just patriotic sentiment. In 1778 Benjamin Franklin persuaded France (always eager to trouble England) to ally with the revolutionaries, and they provided the troops, material and sea power that helped win the war. The British surrendered at Yorktown, VA, in 1781, and two years later the Treaty of Paris formally recognized the 'United States of America.'

At first, the nation's loose confederation of fractious, squabbling states was hardly 'united.' So the founders gathered again in Philadelphia, and in 1787 drafted a new-and-improved Constitution: the US government was given a stronger federal center, with checks and balances between its three major branches; and to guard against the abuse of centralized power, a citizen's Bill of Rights was approved in 1791.

Authoritative and sobering, *Bury My Heart at Wounded Knee* (1970), by Dee Brown, tells the story of the late 19th-century Indian Wars from the perspective of Native Americans.

1756–63	1773	1775	1776
In the Seven Years' War (or the 'French and Indian War'), France loses to England and withdraws from Canada. Britain now controls most territory east of the Mississippi River.	To protest a British tax on tea, Bostonians dress as Mohawks, board East India Company ships and toss their tea overboard during what would be named the Boston Tea Party.	Paul Revere rides from Boston to warn colonial 'Minutemen' that the British are coming. The next day, 'the shot heard round the world' is fired at Lexington, starting the Revolutionary War.	On July 4, the colonies sign the Declaration of Independence. Famous figures who helped create this document include John Hancock, Samuel Adams, John Adams, Benjamin Franklin and Thomas Jefferson.

TECUMSEH'S CURSE

According to legend, a curse spanning more than 100 years hung over every president elected in a year ending in zero (every 20 years). It all began with future president William Henry Harrison, who in 1811 led a battle against the Shawnee, which devastated the hopes of Tecumseh (Native American chief of the Shawnee) for a pan-Indian alliance. After the bitter defeat, Tecumseh placed a curse, uttering something along the lines of 'Harrison will die, and after him every great chief chosen 20 years thereafter will also die. And when each dies, let everyone remember the death of my people.'

According to legend, George Washington was so honest that after chopping down his father's cherry tree when he was just a child, he admitted, 'I cannot tell a lie. I did it with my little hatchet.'

With the Constitution, the scope of the American Revolution solidified to a radical change in government, and the preservation of the economic and social status quos. Rich landholders kept their property, which included their slaves; Native Americans were excluded from the nation; and women were excluded from politics. These blatant discrepancies and injustices, which were widely noted, were the results of both pragmatic compromise (eg to get slave-dependent Southern states to agree) and also widespread beliefs in the essential rightness of things as they were.

Westward, Ho!

As the 19th century dawned on the young nation, optimism was the mood of the day. With the invention of the cotton gin in 1793 – followed by threshers, reapers, mowers and later combines – agriculture was industrialized, and US commerce surged. The 1803 Louisiana Purchase doubled US territory, and expansion west of the Appalachian Mountains began in earnest.

Relations between the US and Britain – despite lively trade – remained tense, and in 1812 the US declared war on England again. The two-year conflict ended without much gain by either side, although the British abandoned their forts, and the US vowed to avoid Europe's 'entangling alliances.'

In the 1830s and 1840s, with growing nationalist fervor and dreams of continental expansion, many Americans came to believe it was 'Manifest Destiny' that all the land should be theirs. The 1830 *Indian Removal Act* aimed to clear one obstacle, while the building of the railroads cleared another hurdle, linking Midwestern farmers with East Coast markets.

In 1836 a group of Texans fomented a revolution against Mexico. (Remember the Alamo?) Ten years later, the US annexed the Texas Republic, and when Mexico resisted, the US waged war for it – and while they were at it, took California, too. In 1848 Mexico was soundly defeated and ceded this territory to the US. This completed the USA's continental expansion.

By a remarkable coincidence, only days after the 1848 treaty with Mexico was signed, gold was discovered in California. By 1849 surging rivers of wagon trains were creaking west filled with miners, pioneers, entrepreneurs, immigrants, outlaws and prostitutes, all seeking their fortunes.

1787	1791	1803	1804–6
The Constitutional Convention in Philadelphia draws up the US Constitution. Power is balanced between the presidency, Congress and judiciary.	Bill of Rights adopted as constitutional amendments outlining citizens' rights, including free speech, assembly, religion and the press; the right to bear arms; and prohibition of 'cruel and unusual punishments.'	France's Napoleon sells the Louisiana Territory to the US for just $15 million, thereby extending the boundaries of the new nation from the Mississippi River to the Rocky Mountains.	President Thomas Jefferson sends Meriwether Lewis and William Clark west. Guided by the Shoshone tribeswoman Sacagawea, they trailblaze from St Louis, MO, to the Pacific Ocean and back.

This made for exciting, legendary times, but throughout loomed a troubling question: as new states joined the USA, would they be slave states or free states? The nation's future depended on the answer.

The Civil War

The US Constitution hadn't ended slavery, but it had given Congress the power to approve (or not) slavery in new states. Public debates raged constantly over the expansion of slavery, particularly since this shaped the balance of power between the industrial North and the agrarian South.

Since the founding, Southern politicians had dominated government and defended slavery as 'natural and normal', which an 1856 *New York Times* editorial called 'insanity'. The Southern proslavery lobby enraged Northern abolitionists. But even many Northern politicians feared that ending slavery would be ruinous. Limit slavery, they reasoned, and in the competition with industry and free labor, slavery would wither without inciting a violent slave revolt – a constantly feared possibility. Indeed, in 1859 radical abolitionist John Brown tried unsuccessfully to spark just that at Harpers Ferry.

The economics of slavery were undeniable. In 1860 there were more than four million slaves in the US, most held by Southern planters – who grew 75% of the world's cotton, accounting for more than half of US exports. Thus, the Southern economy supported the nation's economy, and it required slaves. The 1860 presidential election became a referendum on this issue, and the election was won by a young politician who favored limiting slavery: Abraham Lincoln.

In the South, even the threat of federal limits was too onerous to abide, and as President Lincoln took office, 11 states eventually seceded from the union and formed the Confederate States of America. Lincoln faced the nation's greatest moment of crisis. He had two choices: let the Southern states secede and dissolve the union or wage war to keep the union intact. He chose the latter, and war soon erupted.

It began in April 1861, when the Confederacy attacked Fort Sumter in Charleston, SC, and raged on for the next four years – in the most gruesome combat the world had ever known until that time. By the end, as many as 750,000 soldiers, nearly an entire generation of young men, were dead; Southern plantations and cities (most notably Atlanta) lay sacked and burned. The North's industrial might provided an advantage, but its victory was not preordained; it unfolded battle by bloody battle.

As fighting progressed, Lincoln recognized that if the war didn't end slavery outright, victory would be pointless. In 1863 his Emancipation Proclamation expanded the war's aims and freed all slaves. In April 1865, Confederate General Robert E Lee surrendered to Union General Ulysses S Grant in Appomattox, VA. The Union had been preserved, but at a staggering cost.

You can follow the Lewis and Clark expedition on its extraordinary journey west to the Pacific and back again online at www.pbs.org/lewisandclark, which features historical maps, photo albums and journal excerpts.

HISTORY THE CIVIL WAR

James McPherson is a pre-eminent Civil War historian, and his Pulitzer Prize–winning *Battle Cry of Freedom* (1988) somehow gets the whole heartbreaking saga between two covers.

1812	1823	1849	1861–65
The War of 1812 begins with battles against the British and Native Americans in the Great Lakes region. Even after the 1814 Treaty of Ghent, fighting continues along the Gulf Coast.	President Monroe articulates the Monroe Doctrine, seeking to end European military interventions in America. Roosevelt later extends it to justify US interventions in Latin America.	After the 1848 discovery of gold near Sacramento, an epic cross-country gold rush sees 60,000 'forty-niners' flock to California's Mother Lode. San Francisco's population explodes from 850 to 25,000.	American Civil War erupts between North and South (delineated by the Mason–Dixon line). The war's end on April 9, 1865, is marred by President Lincoln's assassination five days later.

FIGHTING FOR CHANGE: FIVE WHO SHAPED HISTORY

American history is littered with larger-than-life figures who brought dramatic change through bold deeds, sometimes at great personal cost. While presidents tend to garner all the attention, there are countless lesser-known visionaries who have made enormous contributions to civic life.

Rachel Carson (1907–64) An eloquent writer with a keen scientific mind, Carson helped spawn the environmental movement. Her pioneering work *Silent Spring* illustrated the ecological catastrophe unleashed by pesticides and unregulated industry. The ensuing grassroots movement spurred the creation of the Environmental Protection Agency.

Cesar Chavez (1927–93) A second-generation Mexican American who grew up in farm labor camps (where entire families labored for $1 a day), Chavez was a charismatic and inspiring figure – Gandhi and Martin Luther King Jr were among his role models. He gave hope, dignity and a brighter future to thousands of poor migrants by creating the United Farm Workers.

Harvey Milk (1930–78) California's first openly gay public servant was a tireless advocate in the fight against discrimination, encouraging gays and lesbians to 'come out, stand up and let the world know... Only that way will we start to achieve our rights.' Milk, along with San Francisco mayor George Moscone, was assassinated in 1978.

Betty Friedan (1921–2006) Founder of the National Organization for Women (NOW), Friedan was instrumental in leading the feminist movement of the 1960s. Friedan's groundbreaking book *The Feminine Mystique* inspired millions of women to envision a life beyond mere 'homemaker.'

Ralph Nader (b 1934) The frequent presidential contender (in 2008, Nader received 738,000 votes) is one of America's staunchest consumer watchdogs. The Harvard-trained lawyer has played a major role in insuring Americans have safer cars, cheaper medicines and cleaner air and water.

Great Depression, The New Deal & World War II

In October 1929, investors, worried over a gloomy global economy, started selling stocks, and seeing the selling, everyone panicked until they had sold everything. The stock market crashed, and the US economy collapsed like a house of cards.

Thus began the Great Depression. Frightened banks called in their dodgy loans, people couldn't pay, and the banks folded. Millions lost their homes, farms, businesses and savings, and as much as 25% of the American workforce became unemployed. The droughts of the Dust Bowl further exacerbated problems, prompting the largest migration in

1870	1880–1920	1882	1896
Freed black men are given the right to vote, but the South's segregationist 'Jim Crow' laws (which remain until the 1960s) effectively disenfranchise blacks from every meaningful sphere of daily life.	Millions of immigrants flood in from Europe and Asia, fueling the age of cities. New York, Chicago and Philadelphia swell in size, becoming global centers of industry and commerce.	Racist sentiment, particularly in California (where over 50,000 Chinese immigrants have arrived since 1848) leads to the Chinese Exclusion Act, the only US immigration law to exclude a specific race.	In Plessy v Ferguson, the US Supreme Court rules that 'separate but equal' public facilities for blacks and whites are legal, arguing that the Constitution addresses only political, not social, equality.

American history as three million people moved out of the Great Plains states toward California in search of work.

In 1932 Democrat Franklin D Roosevelt was elected president on the promise of a 'New Deal' to rescue the US from its crisis, which he did with resounding success. When war once again broke out in Europe in 1939, the isolationist mood in America was as strong as ever. However, the extremely popular President Roosevelt, elected to an unprecedented third term in 1940, understood that the US couldn't sit by and allow victory for fascist, totalitarian regimes. Roosevelt sent aid to Britain and persuaded a skittish Congress to go along with it.

Then, on December 7, 1941, Japan launched a surprise attack on Hawaii's Pearl Harbor, killing more than 2000 Americans and sinking several battleships. As US isolationism transformed overnight into outrage, Roosevelt suddenly had the support he needed. Germany also declared war on the US, and America joined the Allied fight against Hitler and the Axis powers. From that moment, the US put almost its entire will and industrial prowess into the war effort.

Initially, neither the Pacific nor European theaters went well for the US. In the Pacific, fighting didn't turn around until the US unexpectedly routed the Japanese navy at Midway Island in June 1942. Afterward, the US drove Japan back with a series of brutal battles recapturing Pacific islands.

In Europe, the US dealt the fatal blow to Germany with its massive D-Day invasion of France on June 6, 1944: unable to sustain a two-front war (the Soviet Union was savagely fighting on the eastern front), Germany surrendered in May 1945.

Nevertheless, Japan continued fighting. Newly elected President Harry Truman – ostensibly worried that a US invasion of Japan would lead to unprecedented carnage – chose to drop experimental atomic bombs on Hiroshima and Nagasaki in August 1945. Created by the government's top-secret Manhattan Project, the bombs devastated both cities, killing over 200,000 people. Japan surrendered days later. The nuclear age was born.

Hidden Figures, a biopic about three real-life mathematicians – Katherine Johnson, Dorothy Vaughn and Mary Jackson – whose talents were integral to the NASA space launch despite the limitations placed on them as black women in the 1960s, was Fox's second-highest-grossing movie of 2016 and earned three Oscar nominations.

The Red Scare, Civil Rights & the Wars in Asia

The US enjoyed unprecedented prosperity in the decades after WWII, but little peace.

Formerly wartime allies, the communist Soviet Union and the capitalist USA soon engaged in a running competition to dominate the globe. The superpowers engaged in proxy wars – notably the Korean War (1950–53) and Vietnam War (1954–75) – with only the mutual threat of nuclear annihilation preventing direct war. Founded in 1945, the UN couldn't overcome this worldwide ideological split and was largely ineffectual in preventing Cold War conflicts.

HISTORY THE RED SCARE, CIVIL RIGHTS & THE WARS IN ASIA

1898	1906	1908	1914
Victory in the Spanish-American War gives US control of the Philippines, Puerto Rico and Guam, and indirect control of Cuba. But the Philippines' bloody war for independence deters future US colonialism.	Upton Sinclair publishes *The Jungle*, an exposé of Chicago's unsavory meatpacking industry. Many workers suffer through poverty and dangerous, even deadly, conditions in choking factories and sweatshops.	The first Model T (aka 'Tin Lizzie') car is built in Detroit, MI. Assembly-line innovator Henry Ford is soon selling one million automobiles annually.	US wins the right to build and run the Panama Canal, linking the Atlantic and Pacific Oceans, by inciting a Panamanian revolt over independence from Colombia.

THE AFRICAN AMERICAN EXPERIENCE: THE STRUGGLE FOR EQUALITY

It's impossible to properly grasp American history without taking into account the great struggles and hard-won victories of African Americans who come from all spheres of life.

Slavery

From the early 17th century until the 19th century, an estimated 600,000 slaves were brought from Africa to America. Those who survived the horrific transport on crowded ships (which sometimes had 50% mortality rates) were sold in slave markets (African males cost $27 in 1638). The majority of slaves ended up in Southern plantations where conditions were usually brutal – whipping and branding were commonplace.

All (White) Men are Created Equal

Many of the founding fathers – George Washington, Thomas Jefferson and Benjamin Franklin – owned slaves, though privately expressed condemnation for the abominable practice. The abolition movement, however, wouldn't pick up steam until the 1830s, long after the appearance of the rousing but ultimately hollow words 'all men are created equal' on the Declaration of Independence.

Free at Last

While some revisionist historians describe the Civil War as being about states' rights, most scholars agree that the war was really about slavery. Following the Union victory at Antietam, Lincoln drafted the Emancipation Proclamation, which freed all blacks in occupied territories. African Americans joined the Union effort, with more than 180,000 serving by war's end.

Jim Crow Laws

During Reconstruction (1865–77) federal laws provided civil rights protection for newly freed blacks. Southern bitterness, however, coupled with centuries of prejudice, fueled a backlash. By the 1890s, the Jim Crow laws (named after a derogatory character in a minstrel show) appeared. African Americans were effectively disenfranchised, and America became a deeply segregated society.

Civil Rights Movement

Beginning in the 1950s, a movement was underway in African American communities to fight for equality. Rosa Parks, who refused to give up her seat to a white passenger, inspired the Montgomery bus boycott. There were sit-ins at lunch counters where blacks were excluded; massive demonstrations led by Martin Luther King Jr in Washington, DC; and harrowing journeys by 'freedom riders' that aimed to end bus segregation. The work of millions paid off: in 1964 President Johnson signed the Civil Rights Act, which banned discrimination and racial segregation.

Meanwhile, with its continent unscarred and its industry bulked up by WWII, the American homeland entered an era of growing affluence. In the 1950s, a mass migration left the inner cities for the suburbs, where

1917	1920s	1941–45	1948–51
President Woodrow Wilson enters US into WWI. The US mobilizes 4.7 million troops, and suffers around 116,000 of the war's 11 million military deaths.	Spurred by African American migration to northern cities, the Harlem Renaissance inspires an intellectual flowering of literature, art and music. Important figures include WEB Du Bois and Langston Hughes.	WWII: America deploys 16 million troops and suffers 400,000 deaths. Overall, civilian deaths outpace military deaths two to one, and total 50 to 70 million people from over 50 countries.	The US-led Marshall Plan funnels $12 billion in material and financial aid to help Europe recover from WWII. The plan also aims to contain Soviet influence and reignite America's economy.

affordable single-family homes sprang up. Americans drove cheap cars using cheap gas over brand-new interstate highways. They relaxed with the comforts of modern technology, swooned over TV, and got busy, giving birth to a 'baby boom.'

Middle-class whites did, anyway. African Americans remained segregated, poor and generally unwelcome at the party. Echoing 19th-century abolitionist Frederick Douglass, the Southern Christian Leadership Conference (SCLC), led by African American preacher Martin Luther King Jr, aimed to end segregation and 'save America's soul': to realize color-blind justice, racial equality and fairness of economic opportunity for all.

Beginning in the 1950s, King preached and organized nonviolent resistance in the form of bus boycotts, marches and sit-ins, mainly in the South. White authorities often met these protests with water hoses and batons, and demonstrations sometimes dissolved into riots, but with the 1964 Civil Rights Act, African Americans spurred a wave of legislation that swept away racist laws and laid the groundwork for a more just and equal society.

Meanwhile, the 1960s saw further social upheavals: rock and roll spawned a youth rebellion, and the 1967 Summer of Love in San Francisco's Haight-Ashbury neighborhood catapulted hippie culture into mainstream America.

President John F Kennedy was assassinated in Dallas in 1963, followed by the assassinations in 1968 of his brother, Senator Robert Kennedy, and of Martin Luther King Jr. Americans' faith in their leaders and government was further shocked by the bombings and brutalities of the Vietnam War, as seen on TV, which led to widespread student protests.

Yet President Richard Nixon, elected in 1968 partly for promising an 'honorable end to the war,' instead escalated US involvement and secretly bombed Laos and Cambodia. Then, in 1972, the Watergate scandal broke: a burglary at Democratic Party offices was, through dogged journalism, tied to 'Tricky Dick,' who, in 1974, became the first US president to resign from office.

The tumultuous 1960s and '70s also witnessed the sexual revolution, women's liberation, struggles for gay rights, energy crises over the supply of crude oil from the Middle East and, with the 1962 publication of Rachel Carson's *Silent Spring*, the realization that the USA's industries had created a polluted, diseased environmental mess.

Reagan, Clinton & Bush

In 1980 Republican California governor and former actor Ronald Reagan campaigned for president by promising to make Americans feel good about America again. The affable Reagan won easily, and his election marked a pronounced shift to the right in US politics.

In *The Souls of Black Folk* (1903), WEB Du Bois, who helped found the National Association for the Advancement of Colored People (NAACP), eloquently describes the racial dilemmas of politics and culture facing early 20th-century America.

HISTORY REAGAN, CLINTON & BUSH

1963	1964	1965–75	1969
On November 22, President John F Kennedy is publicly assassinated by Lee Harvey Oswald while riding in a motorcade through Dealey Plaza in Dallas, TX.	Congress passes the Civil Rights Act, outlawing discrimination on basis of race, color, religion, sex or national origin. First proposed by Kennedy, it was one of President Johnson's crowning achievements.	US involvement in the Vietnam War tears the nation apart as 58,000 Americans die, along with four million Vietnamese and 1.5 million Laotians and Cambodians.	American astronauts land on the moon, fulfilling President Kennedy's unlikely 1961 promise to accomplish this feat within a decade and culminating in the 'space race' between the US and USSR.

Reagan wanted to defeat communism, restore the economy, deregulate business and cut taxes. To tackle the first two, he launched the biggest peacetime military buildup in history, and dared the Soviets to keep up. They went broke trying, and the USSR collapsed.

Military spending and tax cuts created enormous federal deficits, which hampered the presidency of Reagan's successor, George HW Bush. Despite winning the Gulf War – liberating Kuwait in 1991 after an Iraqi invasion – Bush was soundly defeated in the 1992 presidential election by Southern Democrat Bill Clinton. Clinton had the good fortune to catch the Silicon Valley–led high-tech internet boom of the 1990s, which seemed to augur a 'new economy' based on white-collar telecommunications. The US economy erased its deficits and ran a surplus, and Clinton presided over one of America's longest economic booms.

In 2000 and 2004, George W Bush, the eldest son of George HW Bush, won the presidential elections so narrowly that the divided results seemed to epitomize an increasingly divided nation. 'Dubya' had the misfortune of being president when the high-tech bubble burst in 2000, but he nevertheless enacted tax cuts that returned federal deficits even greater than before. He also championed the right-wing conservative 'backlash' that had been building since Reagan.

On September 11, 2001, Islamic terrorists flew hijacked planes into New York's World Trade Center and the Pentagon in Washington, DC. This catastrophic attack united Americans behind their president as he vowed revenge and declared a 'war on terror.' Bush soon attacked Afghanistan in an unsuccessful hunt for Al-Qaeda terrorist cells, then he attacked Iraq in 2003 and toppled its anti-US dictator, Saddam Hussein. Meanwhile, Iraq descended into civil war.

Following scandals and failures – torture photos from Abu Ghraib, the federal response in the aftermath of Hurricane Katrina and the inability to bring the Iraq War to a close – Bush's approval ratings reached historic lows in the second half of his presidency.

Obama

In 2008, hungry for change, Americans elected political newcomer, Barack Obama, America's first African American president. He certainly had his work cut out for him. These were, after all, unprecedented times economically, with the US in the largest financial crisis since the Great Depression. What started as a collapse of the US housing bubble in 2007 spread to the banking sector, with the meltdown of major financial institutions. The shock wave quickly spread across the globe, and by 2008 many industrialized nations were experiencing a recession in one form or another.

As Americans tried to look toward the future, many found it difficult to leave the past behind. This was not surprising since wars in Afghanistan and Iraq, launched a decade prior, continued to simmer on the back

Suspicious of political factoids? Factcheck.org is a nonpartisan, self-described 'consumer advocate' that monitors the accuracy of statements made by US politicians during debates, speeches, interviews and in campaign ads. It's a great resource for separating truth from bombast and is particularly handy during election cycles.

1973	1980s	1989	1990s
In Roe v Wade, the Supreme Court legalizes abortion. Today this decision remains controversial and divisive, pitting 'right to choose' advocates against the 'right to life' anti-abortion lobby.	New Deal–era financial institutions, deregulated under President Reagan, gamble with their customers' savings and loans, and fail, leaving the government with the bill: $125 billion.	The 1960s-era Berlin Wall is torn down, marking the end of the Cold War between the US and the USSR (now Russia). The USA becomes the world's last remaining superpower.	The World Wide Web debuts in 1991. Silicon Valley, CA, leads a high-tech internet revolution, remaking communications and media, and overvalued tech stocks drive the massive boom (and subsequent bust).

burner of the ever-changing news cycle until 2011, when, in a subterfuge operation vetted by President Obama, Navy Seals raided Osama bin Laden's Pakistan hideout. This brought an end to the mastermind behind Al-Qaeda and America's greatest public enemy.

Following his sober announcement describing the raid, Obama saw his approval ratings jump by 11%. The president, for his part, certainly needed a boost. The economy remained in bad shape, and the ambitious $800-billion stimulus package passed by Congress in 2009 hadn't born much fruit in the eyes of many Americans – even though economists estimated that the stimulus did soften the blow of the recession, which would have been much worse without it.

With lost jobs, overvalued mortgages and little relief in sight, millions of Americans found themselves adrift, gathering in large numbers to voice their anger. This, in turn, gave birth to the Tea Party, a wing of politically conservative Republicans who believed that Obama was leaning too far to the left, and that government handouts would destroy the economy and, thus, America. High federal spending and government bailouts (of the banking and auto industries) roused their ire, as did Obama's landmark 2010 health-care reform (derisively named 'Obamacare').

Obamacare was a major victory for the president. It brought healthcare coverage to more Americans, lowered costs and closed loopholes that allowed insurance companies to deny coverage to individuals based on preexisting conditions. Yet, when Obama returned to the White House in 2013 for his second term, he did so without the same hope and optimism that once surrounded him. Times had changed, and America, like much of the world, had struggled through tough years since the global economic crisis erupted in 2007.

Obama did manage to get unemployment rates back under 5% by 2016, but he had mixed success spurring the sluggish economy. As his presidency came to a close, he turned his focus to liberal and globally minded causes that stoked resentment on the populist right, including climate change, environmental protections, LGBT rights and the negotiation of rapprochements with Iran and Cuba. By the time Obama left office, America was a starkly divided nation of those who believed strongly in his progressive ideals, and others who felt increasingly left behind by the global economy.

The 2016 Election & The Trump Presidency

When Donald J Trump, real estate magnate and former host of TV's reality game-show *The Apprentice,* announced he was running for President in June 2015, many around the world thought it was a publicity stunt. What ensued could only be described as a media circus: coverage of the protracted campaign, which eventually pitted Trump, with no prior political experience, against Hillary Clinton, former First Lady and then

Great Presidential Reads

Washington (Ron Chernow)

Thomas Jefferson (RB Bernstein)

Lincoln (David Herbert Donald)

Mornings on Horseback (David McCullough)

The Bridge (David Remnick)

2001	2003	2005	2008–9
On September 11, Al-Qaeda terrorists hijack four commercial airplanes, flying two into NYC's twin towers, and one into the Pentagon (the fourth crashes in Pennsylvania); nearly 3000 people are killed.	After citing evidence that Iraq possesses weapons of mass destruction, President George W Bush launches a preemptive war that will cost over 4000 American lives and some $3 trillion.	On August 29, Hurricane Katrina hits the Mississippi and Louisiana coasts, rupturing poorly maintained levees and flooding New Orleans. Over 1800 people die, and cost estimates exceed $110 billion.	Barack Obama becomes the first African American president. The stock market crashes due to mismanagement by major American financial institutions. The crisis spreads worldwide.

If history is a partisan affair, Howard Zinn makes his allegiance clear in *A People's History of the United States* (1980 and 2005), which tells the often-overlooked stories of laborers, minorities, immigrants, women and radicals.

Secretary of State (2009–13), was relentless. Trump's pithy soundbites and no-holds-barred insults stood out in a crowded Republican primary field and made for irresistible headlines, while the primary contest on the Democratic side was winnowed down to Clinton and populist candidate Bernie Sanders early on.

Once the Trump and Clinton lineup was announced, a contentious campaign followed. Trump refused to release his tax records, a common practice among presidential candidates. On October 7 *Access Hollywood* tapes leaked in which Trump admitted to assaulting women. On Clinton's side, opponents invoked Benghazi, and her ties to Wall Street. A week before the election, FBI head James Comey stoked the conspiracy theories around Hillary Clinton by announcing in a letter to Congress that her emails, which she stored on a private server against security recommendations, were still under investigation. Still, polls gave Clinton a strong lead, and on election night, the country prepared to celebrate the election of the first female President of the United States. Clinton did win the popular vote, but the Electoral College math was not in her favor. She conceded to Donald Trump in the early hours of November 9 with an emotional speech that reminded 'all the little girls who are watching this, never doubt that you are valuable, and powerful, and deserving of every chance and opportunity in the world to pursue and achieve your own dreams.'

In his victory speech, Trump declared 'I will be president for all Americans,' though to many, Trump's definition of what it means to be an American remains unclear. Uncertainty, in fact, seems to be the defining quality of the Trump presidency. Scandal and controversy surrounded the administration in its first 100 days, during which the nation's democratic integrity was challenged by conflicts of interest between public office and private enterprise. Public protest quickly became a defining feature of the sociopolitical landscape, starting with the Women's March the day after the inauguration, the largest single-day demonstration in recorded US history, with an estimated four million participants in some 653 cities around the country.

2012	2013	2015	2016
Hurricane Sandy devastates the East Coast, becoming the second-costliest hurricane ($65 billion) in American history. Over 100 Americans die (plus 200 more in other countries).	Huge scandal erupts when former National Security Agency contractor Edward Snowden leaks classified information about a US intelligence program that monitors communication between US citizens and its allies.	In a historic decision, the US Supreme Court legalizes same-sex marriage, giving gay couples in all 50 states the right to marry.	Political outsider Donald Trump rides a populist wave into the White House in a surprise victory over opponent Hillary Clinton, who wins the popular vote by nearly three million, but loses to Trump in the Electoral College.

The Way of Life

One of the world's great melting pots, America boasts an astonishing variety of cultures and creeds. The country's diversity was shaped by its rich history of immigration, though today regional differences (East Coast, South, West Coast and Midwest) play an equally prominent role in defining American identity. Religion, sport, politics and, of course, socioeconomic backgrounds are also pivotal in creating the complicated American portrait.

Multiculturalism

From the get-go, America was called a 'melting pot,' which presumed that newcomers came and blended into the existing American fabric. The country hasn't let go of that sentiment completely. On one hand, diversity is celebrated (Cinco de Mayo, Martin Luther King Jr Day and Chinese New Year all get their due), but on the other hand, many Americans are comfortable with the status quo.

Immigration is at the crux of the matter. Immigrants currently make up around 13% of the population. Nearly 1.4 million foreign-born individuals move to the US legally each year, with the majority from India, China and Mexico. Another 10.9 million or so are in the country illegally. This is the issue that makes Americans edgy, especially as it gets politicized.

'Immigration reform' has been a Washington buzzword for nearly two decades. Some people believe the nation's current system deals with illegal immigrants too leniently – that higher walls should be built on the border, immigrants who are here unlawfully should be deported and employers who hire them should be fined. Other Americans think those rules are too harsh – that immigrants who have been here for years working, contributing to society and abiding by the law deserve amnesty. Perhaps they could pay a fine and fill out the paperwork to become citizens while continuing to live here with their families. Despite several attempts, Congress has not been able to pass a comprehensive package addressing illegal immigration, though it has put through various measures to beef up enforcement.

Age has a lot to do with Americans' multicultural tolerance. When asked in a survey if immigration strengthens the nation, less than half of older Americans said yes, whereas more than 75% of 18- to 35-year-olds said yes, according to the Pew Research Center. In a similar survey, those aged 65 and older were asked if it's acceptable for whites and African Americans to marry each other: 30% said no, but that dropped to 4% when asked of Americans aged 30 and younger.

Many people point to the election of President Barack Obama as proof of America's multicultural achievements. It's not just his personal story (white mother, black father, Muslim name, has lived among the diverse cultures of Hawaii, Indonesia and Chicago, among others), or that he's the first African American to hold the nation's highest office (in a country where as recently as the 1960s African Americans couldn't even vote in certain regions), it's that Americans of all races and creeds voted overwhelmingly to elect the self-described 'mutt' and embrace his message of diversity and change.

The US holds the world's second-largest Spanish-speaking population, behind Mexico and just ahead of Spain. Latino people are also the fastest-growing minority group in the nation.

Religion

When the Pilgrims (early settlers to the US who fled their European homeland to escape religious persecution) came ashore, they were adamant that their new country would be one of religious tolerance. They valued the freedom to practice religion so highly they refused to make their Protestant faith official state policy. What's more, they forbade the government from doing anything that might sanction one religion or belief over another. Separation of church and state became the law of the land.

Today Protestants are on the verge of becoming a minority in the country they founded. According to the Pew Research Center, Protestant numbers have declined steadily to under 50%. Meanwhile, other faiths have held their own or seen their numbers increase.

The country is also in a period of exceptional religious fluidity. Forty-four percent of American adults have left the denomination of their childhood for another denomination, another faith or no faith at all, according to Pew. A unique era of 'religion shopping' has been ushered in. As for the geographic breakdown: the USA's most Catholic region is shifting from the Northeast to the Southwest; the South is the most evangelical; and the West is the most unaffiliated.

All that said, America's biggest schism isn't between religions or even between faith and skepticism. It's between fundamentalist and progressive interpretations within each faith. Most Americans don't care much if you're Catholic, Episcopalian, Buddhist or atheist. What they do care about are your views on abortion, contraception, LGBT rights, stem-cell research, teaching of evolution, school prayer and government displays of religious icons. The country's Religious Right (the oft-used term for evangelical Christians) has pushed these issues onto center stage, and the group has been effective at using politics to codify its conservative beliefs into law. This effort has prompted a slew of court cases, testing the nation's principles on separation of church and state. The split remains one of America's biggest culture wars, and it almost always plays a role in politics, especially during elections.

Americans are increasingly defining their spiritual beliefs outside of organized religion. The proportion of those who say they have 'no religion' is now around 21%. Some in this catch-all category disavow religion altogether (around 7%), but the majority sustain spiritual beliefs that simply fall outside the box.

Lifestyle

The USA has one of the world's highest standards of living. The median household income is around $56,500, though it varies by region (with higher earnings in the Mid-Atlantic, Northeast and West and lower earn-

---

KNOW YOUR GENERATIONS

American culture is often stratified by age groups. Here's a quick rundown to help you tell Generation X from Z, and then some.

Baby Boomers Those born from 1946 to 1964. After American soldiers came home from WWII, they got busy with the ladies, and the birthrate exploded (hence the term 'baby boom'). Youthful experimentation, self-expression and social activism was often followed by midlife affluence.

Generation X Those born between 1965 and the early 1980s. Characterized by their rejection of Baby Boomer values, skepticism and alienation.

Millennials Those born from the early 1980s to the late 1990s. Known for being brash and self-confident, they were the first to grow up with the internet. Weaned on iPods, instant messaging and social-networking websites, they are a work in progress, and also the largest living generation in the US.

Generation Z Those born in the 2000s. Call them the 'selfie generation' or 'generation like.' These are the kids of today who have never known a world without the internet and who often interact more on social media than face to face.

ings in the South). Wages also vary by ethnicity, with African Americans and Latinos earning less than whites and Asians ($37,000 and $45,000 respectively, versus $63,000 and $77,000, according to the most recent census data). Likewise the wage gap between men and women continues to persist, with women earning roughly 80% of what men earn.

About 90% of Americans are high-school graduates, while some 34% go on to graduate from college with a four-year bachelor's degree.

More often than not there are two married parents in an American household, and both of them work. Single parents head 23% of households. More than half of all full-time employees work more than 40 hours per week. Divorce is common – some 40% of first marriages go kaput – but both divorce and marriage rates have declined over the last three decades. Despite the high divorce rate, Americans spend more than $55 billion annually on weddings. The average number of children in an American family is two.

While many Americans hit the gym or walk, bike or jog regularly, over 50% don't exercise at all during their free time, according to the Centers for Disease Control (CDC). Health researchers speculate this lack of exercise and Americans' fondness for sugary and fatty foods have led to rising obesity and diabetes rates. More than two-thirds of Americans are overweight, with one-third considered obese, the CDC says.

About 25% of Americans volunteer their time to help others or help a cause. This is truer in the Midwest, followed by the West, South and Northeast, according to the Corporation for National and Community Service. Eco-consciousness has entered the mainstream: over 75% of Americans recycle at home, and most big-chain grocery stores – including Walmart – now sell organic foods.

Americans tend to travel close to home. Just over one-third of Americans have passports, so most people take vacations within the 50 states. According to the US Department of Commerce's Office of Travel and Tourism Industries, Mexico and Canada are the top countries for international getaways, followed by the UK, Dominican Republic, France, Italy and Germany. America's reputation as the 'no-vacation nation,' with many workers having only five to 10 paid annual vacation days, contributes to this stay-at-home scenario.

NPR radio host Terry Gross interviews Americans from all walks of life, from rock stars to environmental activists to nuclear scientists. Listen online at www. npr.org/freshair.

Sports

What really draws Americans together, sometimes slathered in blue body paint or with foam-rubber cheese wedges on their heads, is sports. It provides a social glue, so whether a person is conservative or liberal, married or single, Mormon or pagan, chances are come Monday at the office they'll be chatting about the weekend performance of their favorite team.

The fun and games go on all year long. In spring and summer there's baseball nearly every day. In fall and winter a weekend or Monday night doesn't feel right without a football game on, and through the long days and nights of winter there's plenty of basketball to keep the adrenaline going. Those are the big three sports. Car racing has revved up interest in recent years. Major League Soccer (MLS) is attracting an ever-increasing following. And ice hockey, once favored only in northern climes, is popular nationwide, with five Stanley Cup winners since 2000 hailing from either California or the South.

Key Sports Sites

Baseball
(www.mlb.com)

Football
(www.nfl.com)

Basketball
(www.nba.com)

Car Racing
(www.nascar.com)

Baseball

Despite high salaries and its biggest stars being dogged by steroid rumors, baseball remains America's pastime. It may not command the same TV viewership (and subsequent advertising dollars) as football, but baseball has 162 games over a season versus 16 for football.

THE WAY OF LIFE SPORTS

STATES & TRAITS

Regional US stereotypes now have solid data behind them, thanks to a study titled *The Geography of Personality*. Researchers processed more than a half-million personality assessments collected from individual US citizens, then looked at where certain traits stacked up on the map. Turns out 'Minnesota nice' is for real – the most 'agreeable' states cluster in the Great Lakes, Great Plains and South. These places rank highest for friendliness and cooperation. The most neurotic states? They line up in the Northeast. But New York didn't place number one, as you might expect; that honor goes to West Virginia. Many of the most 'open' states lie out West. California, Nevada, Oregon and Washington all rate high for being receptive to new ideas, although they lag behind Washington, DC, and New York. The most dutiful and self-disciplined states sit in the Great Plains and Southwest, led by New Mexico. Go figure.

Even college and high-school football games enjoy an intense amount of pomp and circumstance, with cheerleaders, marching bands, mascots, songs and mandatory pre- and post-game rituals, especially the tailgate – a full-blown beer-and-barbecue feast that takes place over portable grills in ball-ground parking lots.

Besides, baseball isn't about seeing it on TV, it's all about the live version: being at the ballpark on a sunny day, sitting in the bleachers with a beer and hot dog, and indulging in the seventh-inning stretch, when the entire park erupts in a communal singalong of 'Take Me Out to the Ballgame.' The playoffs, held every October, still deliver excitement and unexpected champions. The New York Yankees, Boston Red Sox and Chicago Cubs continue to be America's favorite teams, even when they're abysmal.

Tickets are relatively inexpensive – the cheap seats average about $15 at most stadiums – and are easy to get for most games. Minor-league baseball games cost half as much, and can be even more fun, with lots of audience participation, stray chickens and dogs running across the field, and wild throws from the pitcher's mound. For info, click to www.milb.com.

Football

Football is big, physical and rolling in dough. With the shortest season and least number of games of any of the major sports, every match takes on the emotion of an epic battle, where the results matter and an unfortunate injury can deal a lethal blow to a team's play-off chances.

Football is also the toughest because it's played in fall and winter in all manner of rain, sleet and snow. Some of history's most memorable matches have occurred at below-freezing temperatures. Green Bay Packers fans are in a class by themselves when it comes to severe weather. Their stadium in Wisconsin, known as Lambeau Field, was the site of the infamous Ice Bowl, a 1967 championship game against the Dallas Cowboys where the temperature plummeted to –13°F – mind you, that was with a wind-chill factor of –48°F.

The rabidly popular Super Bowl is pro football's championship match, held in late January or early February. The bowl games (such as Rose Bowl and Orange Bowl) are college football's title matches, held on and around New Year's Day.

Basketball

The teams bringing in the most fans these days include the Chicago Bulls (thanks to the lingering Michael Jordan effect), Detroit Pistons (a rowdy crowd in which riots have broken out), Cleveland Cavaliers, the San Antonio Spurs and, last but not least, the Los Angeles Lakers, which won five championships between 2000 and 2010. Small-market teams such as Sacramento and Portland have true-blue fans, and such cities can be great places to take in a game.

College-level basketball also draws millions of fans, especially every spring when March Madness rolls around. This series of college play-off games culminates in the Final Four, when the four remaining teams compete for a spot in the championship game. The Cinderella stories and unexpected outcomes rival the pro league for excitement. The games are widely televised – and bet on. This is when Las Vegas bookies earn their keep.

Politics

There's nothing quite like a good old-fashioned discussion of politics to throw a bucket of cold water onto a conversation. Many Americans have fairly fixed ideas when it comes to political parties and ideologies, and bridging the Republican–Democratic divide can often seem as insurmountable as leaping over the Grand Canyon. Here's a quick cheat sheet on the dominant American parties and where they stand on the major topics of the day.

Republicans

Known as the GOP (Grand Old Party), Republicans believe in a limited role of federal government. They also prescribe to fiscal conservatism: lower taxes, privatization and reduced government spending constitute the path toward prosperity. Historically, Republicans were strong supporters of the environment: Theodore Roosevelt was a notable conservationist who helped create the National Parks system, and Nixon established the Environmental Protection Agency in 1970. More recently, however, Republicans have sided with business over environmental regulation, particularly under the Trump administration. Climate change remains a hot topic: more than 55% of Congressional Republicans and 70% of Republican Senators deny its basic tenets. This includes James Inhofe, a veteran lawmaker from Oklahoma and senior member of the Environment and Public Works Committee – he is the author of the book *The Greatest Hoax: How the Global Warming Conspiracy Threatens Your Future*. There's also a fundamentalist wing in the party that believes in creationism and a literal interpretation of the Bible. Republicans also believe in social conservatism, promoting family and church values, and are often opposed to same-sex marriage, abortion and transgender rights. The Republican Party is most successful in the South and Great Plains.

Democrats

The Democratic Party is liberal and progressive. The role model for most Democrats is Franklin Roosevelt, whose New Deal policies (namely creating government jobs for the unemployed and regulating Wall Street) are credited with partially ending the Great Depression. Democrats believe government should take an active role in regulating the economy to help keep inflation and unemployment low, and in a progressive tax structure to reduce economic inequality. They also have a strong social agenda, endorsing the government to take an active role in providing poverty relief, maintaining a social safety net, creating a health-care system for all and ensuring civil and political rights. By and large, Democrats support abortion rights and same-sex marriage, and believe in subsidizing alternative energy sources to help combat climate change, which most party members accept as indisputable. The Democratic Party is strongest in big cities and in the Northeast.

The Super Bowl costs America $1 billion dollars in lost workplace productivity as employees gossip about the game, make bets and shop for new TVs online. It's still less than the $2.1 billion estimate for March Madness when many folks get caught up in the NCAA basketball tournament.

Some 3.5 million Americans tune in every week to the old-timey radio show *A Prairie Home Companion*, currently hosted by mandolinist Chris Thile; listen to the live music, sketches and storytelling online at www.prairie home.org.

THE WAY OF LIFE POLITICS

Native Americans

Although the population is a fraction of its pre-Columbian size, there are more than three million Native Americans from 562 tribes, speaking some 175 languages and residing in every region of the United States. Not surprisingly, North America's indigenous people are an extremely diverse bunch, with unique customs and beliefs, molded in part by the landscapes they inhabit – from the Inuit living in the frozen tundra of Alaska, to the many tribes of the arid, mountainous Southwest.

Always observe reservation etiquette. Most tribes ban alcohol. Ask before taking pictures or drawing; if granted permission, a tip is polite and often expected. Treat ceremonies like religious services; watch respectfully, and wear modest clothing. Ask before discussing religion and respect each person's boundaries. Silent listening shows respect.

The Tribes

The Cherokee, Navajo, Chippewa and Sioux are the largest tribal groupings in the lower 48 (ie excluding Alaska and Hawaii). Other well-known tribes include the Choctaw (descendants of a great mound-building society originally based in the Mississippi Valley), the Apache (a nomadic hunter-gatherer tribe that fiercely resisted forced relocation) and the Hopi (a Pueblo people with Southwest roots dating back 2000 years).

Culturally speaking, America's tribes today grapple with questions about how to prosper in contemporary America while protecting their traditions from erosion and their lands from further exploitation, and how to lift their people from poverty while maintaining their sense of identity and the sacred.

Cherokee

The Cherokee (www.cherokee.org) originally lived in an area of more than 80 million acres, covering a huge swath of the South (including Tennessee, Virginia, the Carolinas and Kentucky). However, in 1830 they were forcibly relocated east of the Mississippi and today reside largely in Oklahoma (home to more than 200,000 Cherokee). Tahlequah has been the Cherokee capital since 1839.

NATIVE AMERICAN ART & CRAFTS

It would take an encyclopedia to cover the myriad artistic traditions of America's tribal peoples, from pre-Columbian rock art to the contemporary multimedia scene.

What ties such diverse traditions together is that Native American art and crafts are not just functional for everyday life, but can also serve ceremonial purposes and have social and religious significance. The patterns and symbols are woven with meanings that provide a window into the heart of Native American peoples. This is as true of Zuni fetish carvings as it is of patterned Navajo rugs, Southwestern pueblo pottery, Sioux beadwork, Inuit sculptures and Cherokee and Hawaiian wood carvings, to name just a few examples.

In addition to preserving their culture, contemporary Native American artists have used sculpture, painting, textiles, film, literature and performance art to reflect and critique modernity since the mid-20th century, especially after the civil rights activism of the 1960s and cultural renaissance of the '70s. *Native North American Art* by Berlo and Phillips offers an introduction to North America's varied indigenous art.

Many tribes run craft outlets and galleries, usually in the main towns of reservations. The Indian Arts & Crafts Board (www.iacb.doi.gov) lists Native American–owned galleries and shops state-by-state online (click on 'Source Directory').

Cherokee society was originally matrilineal, with bloodlines traced through the mother. Like some other native tribes, the Cherokee recognize seven cardinal directions: north, south, east and west along with up, down and center (or within).

Navajo

The Navajo Reservation (www.discovernavajo.com) is by far the largest and most populous in the US. Also called the Navajo Nation and Navajoland, it covers 17.5 million acres (over 27,000 sq miles) in Arizona and parts of New Mexico and Utah.

The Navajo were feared nomads and warriors who both traded with and raided the Pueblos and who fought settlers and the US military. They also borrowed generously from other traditions: they acquired sheep and horses from the Spanish, learned pottery and weaving from the Pueblos, and picked up silversmithing from Mexico. Today, the Navajo are renowned for their woven rugs, pottery and inlaid silver jewelry, as well as for their intricate sandpainting, which is used in healing ceremonies.

Chippewa

Although Chippewa, or Ojibwe, is the commonly used term for this tribe, members prefer to be called Anishinabe. They are based in Minnesota, Wisconsin and Michigan. According to legend, the Chippewa once lived on the Atlantic coast and gradually migrated west over 500 years. They traditionally survived by fishing, hunting, and farming corn and squash. They also harvested (by canoe) wild rice, which remains an essential Chippewa tradition.

Sioux

Like the Iroquois, the Sioux is not one tribe, but a consortium of three major tribes (and various sub-branches) speaking different dialects but sharing a common subculture. Prior to European arrival they lived in the northeast of present-day North America but slowly migrated to the Great Plains by 1800. The Sioux were fierce defenders of their lands, and fought many battles to preserve them, although the slaughter of the buffalo (on whom they had survived) did more to remove them from their lands than anything else. Today, they live in Minnesota, Nebraska, North Dakota and South Dakota – the latter contains the 2-million-acre Pine Ridge Reservation, the nation's second largest.

TIMELINE

NATIVE AMERICANS THE TRIBES

700–1400

North America's largest ancient city outside Mesoamerica, Cahokia, supports a population of 10,000 to 20,000 at its peak. By 1400 it is mysteriously abandoned.

750–1300

Ancestral Pueblo peoples living near Chaco Canyon flourish. This advanced desert civilization develops adobe dwellings in enormous complexes.

1831

Following the 1830 *Indian Removal Act*, Cherokee and other tribes are forced to abandon homelands to areas west of the Mississippi. Thousands die on the 1000-mile Trail of Tears.

1876

Lakota chief Sitting Bull defeats Custer at the Battle of Little Big Horn, one of the last military victories by Native Americans in the effort to protect their lands.

1968

The American Indian Movement (AIM) is founded. Through protests, marches and demonstrations, AIM brings attention to marginalized peoples.

1975

President Nixon passes the *Indian Self-Determination Act*, empowering Native Americans to control how federal money is spent on native matters.

2011

FNX, the first Native American TV network, launches. It presents Native American films, documentaries, children's programs and more.

2016

Standing Rock Indian Reservation files an injunction to stop the building of the 1172-mile Dakota Access Pipeline.

Arts & Architecture

The American people's love of entertainment is evident to anyone who's ever been to a touring Broadway musical or lavish Hollywood film. From its biggest entertainers to its eccentric artists, reclusive novelists, postmodern dancers and rule-breaking architects, Americans have had an outsized influence on arts scenes the world over. Geography and race are the key elements that join together to inspire the varied regionalism at the core of each discipline.

Film

Hollywood and American film are virtually inseparable. No less an American icon than the White House itself, Hollywood is increasingly the product of an internationalized cinema and film culture. This evolution is partly pure business: Hollywood studios are the showpieces of multinational corporations, and funding flows to talent that brings the biggest grosses, regardless of nationality.

But this shift is also creative. It's Hollywood's recognition that if the studios don't incorporate the immense filmmaking talent emerging worldwide, they will be made irrelevant by it. Co-option is an old Hollywood strategy, used most recently to subvert the challenge posed by the independent film movement of the 1990s that kicked off with daring homegrown films like *Sex, Lies, and Videotape* and *Reservoir Dogs,* and innovative European imports. That said, for the most part, mainstream American audiences remain steadfastly indifferent to foreign films.

Top US Photographers

Ansel Adams

Walker Evans

Man Ray

Alfred Stieglitz

Richard Avedon

Robert Frank

Dorothea Lange

Cindy Sherman

Edward Weston

Diane Arbus

Lee Friedlander

Television

In the 20th century, it could be argued that TV was the defining medium of the modern age. In its brief history, TV has proved to be one of the most passionately contested cultural battlegrounds in American society, blamed for a whole host of societal ills, from skyrocketing obesity to plummeting attention spans and school test scores. The average American still watches loads of TV a week (34 hours if you believe the commonly touted figure), but they are watching differently, often streaming their favorite shows via providers such as Netflix and Amazon Prime.

For many decades, critics sneered that TV was lowbrow, and movie stars wouldn't be caught dead on it. But well-written, thought-provoking shows have existed almost since the beginning. In the 1950s, the original *I Love Lucy* show was groundbreaking: shot on film before a live audience and edited before airing, it pioneered syndication. It established the sitcom ('situation comedy') formula, and showcased a dynamic female comedian, Lucille Ball, in an interethnic marriage.

Indeed, 'good' American TV has been around for a long time, whether through artistic merit or cultural and political importance. The 1970s comedy *All in the Family* aired an unflinching examination of prejudice, as embodied by bigoted patriarch Archie Bunker, played by Carroll O'Connor. Similarly, the sketch-comedy show *Saturday Night Live,* which debuted in 1975, pushed social hot buttons with its subversive, politically charged humor.

WOMEN ON SCREEN

After years of being dominated by men, the TV and film industries are finally making space for female-led projects. Creative talents such as Lena Dunham, Mindy Kaling and Rachel Bloom are starring in and producing stellar TV projects, while the all-female (and African American) stars of *Hidden Figures* drew flocks of eager moviegoers. Perhaps the ultimate expression of this change is the emergence of the female superhero, from TV's Supergirl and Jessica Jones to *Wonder Woman*, the first female-directed film to make more than $100 million in North America on an opening weekend.

In the 1980s, videotapes brought movies into American homes, blurring the distinction between big and small screens, and the stigma Hollywood attached to TV slowly faded. The decade also saw the rise of shows such as *The Golden Girls*, a humorous sitcom that explored themes like aging and mortality (as well as more taboo topics such as sexuality among the elderly). It starred four retired women living in Miami and was both critically acclaimed and a commercial success.

In the 1990s, TV audiences embraced the unformulaic, no-holds-barred-weird cult show *Twin Peaks*, leading to a slew of provocative idiosyncratic series such as *The X-Files*.

These days, the most popular shows are a mix of edgier, long-narrative serial dramas, as well as cheap-to-produce, 'unscripted' reality TV: what *Survivor* started in 2000, the contestants and 'actors' of *The Voice, Dancing with the Stars, Project Runway* and *Keeping up with the Kardashians* keep alive today, for better or for worse.

As cable TV has emerged as the frontier for daring and innovative programming, some of the TV shows of the past decade have proved as riveting and memorable as anything American viewers (and the scores of people around the world who watch American TV) have ever seen. Streaming services such as Netflix, Amazon and Hulu, and niche networks such as AMC and HBO have created numerous lauded series, including *Mad Men* (which followed the antics of 1960s advertising execs in NYC), *Portlandia* (a satire of Oregonian subcultures) and *Breaking Bad* (about a terminally ill high-school teacher who starts cooking meth to safeguard his family's financial future). More recent favorites include *Transparent* (about a family coming to terms with having a transgender parent), *Atlanta* (a comedy-drama starring Donald Glover), *Stranger Things* (a supernatural saga set in the 1980s that recalls *The Goonies*) and *The Handmaid's Tale* (a near-future dystopia based on Margaret Atwood's 1985 novel). A number of previously canceled series have also returned from the dead with mixed results, including *Gilmore Girls, Twin Peaks, Full House* and *The X-Files*.

Literature

America first articulated a vision of itself through its literature. Until the American Revolution, the continent's citizens identified largely with England, but after independence, an immediate call went out to develop an American national voice. Not until the 1820s, however, did writers take up the two aspects of American life that had no counterpart in Europe: the untamed wilderness and the frontier experience.

James Fenimore Cooper is credited with creating the first truly American literature with *The Pioneers* (1823). In Cooper's 'everyman' humor and individualism, Americans first recognized themselves.

In his essay *Nature* (1836), Ralph Waldo Emerson articulated similar ideas, but in more philosophical and spiritual terms. Emerson claimed that nature reflected God's instructions for humankind as plainly as the

Bible did, and that individuals could understand these through rational thought and self-reliance. Emerson's writings became the core of the transcendentalist movement, which Henry David Thoreau championed in *Walden; or, Life in the Woods* (1854).

Literary highlights of this era include Herman Melville's ambitious *Moby Dick* (1851) and Nathaniel Hawthorne's examination of the dark side of conservative New England in *The Scarlet Letter* (1850). Canonical poet Emily Dickinson wrote haunting, tightly structured poems, which were first published in 1890, four years after her death.

Civil War & Beyond

The celebration of common humanity and nature reached its apotheosis in Walt Whitman, whose poetry collection *Leaves of Grass* (1855) signaled the arrival of an American literary visionary. In Whitman's informal, intimate, rebellious free verse were songs of individualism, democracy, earthy spirituality, taboo-breaking sexuality and joyous optimism that encapsulated the heart of a throbbing new nation.

But not everything was coming up roses. Abolitionist Harriet Beecher Stowe's controversial novel *Uncle Tom's Cabin* (1852) depicted African American life under slavery with Christian romanticism, but also enough realism to inflame passions on both sides of the 'great debate' over slavery, which would shortly plunge the nation into civil war.

After the Civil War (1861–65), two enduring literary trends emerged: realism and regionalism. Regionalism was especially spurred by the rapid late 19th-century settlement of the West; novelist Jack London serialized his adventures for popular magazines such as the *Saturday Evening Post*.

However, it was Samuel Clemens (aka Mark Twain) who came to define American letters. In *Adventures of Huckleberry Finn* (1884), Twain made explicit the quintessential American narrative of an individual journey of self-discovery. The image of Huck and Jim – a poor white teenager and a runaway black slave – standing outside society's norms and floating together toward an uncertain future down the Mississippi River challenges American society still. Twain wrote in the vernacular, loved 'tall tales' and reveled in satirical humor and absurdity, while his folksy, 'anti-intellectual' stance endeared him to everyday readers.

Disillusionment & Diversity

With the dramas of world wars and a newly industrialized society for artistic fodder, American literature came into its own in the 20th century.

Dubbed the 'Lost Generation,' many US writers, most famously Ernest Hemingway, became expats in Europe. Hemingway's novels exemplified the era, and his spare, stylized realism has often been imitated, yet never bettered. Other notable American figures at Parisian literary salons included modernist writers Gertrude Stein and Ezra Pound, and iconoclast Henry Miller, whose semiautobiographical novels were published in Paris, only to be banned for obscenity and pornography in the USA until the 1960s.

F Scott Fitzgerald eviscerated East Coast society life with his fiction, while John Steinbeck became the great voice of rural working poor in the West, especially during the Great Depression. William Faulkner examined the South's social rifts in dense prose riddled with bullets of black humor.

Between the world wars, the Harlem Renaissance also flourished, as African American intellectuals and artists took pride in their culture and undermined racist stereotypes. Among the most well known writers were poet Langston Hughes and novelist Zora Neale Hurston.

Books Once Banned in America

Are You There, God? It's Me, Margaret (Judy Blume)

Lord of the Flies (William Golding)

1984 (George Orwell)

The Catcher in the Rye (JD Salinger)

Adventures of Huckleberry Finn (Mark Twain)

The Color Purple (Alice Walker)

After WWII, American writers delineated ever-sharper regional and ethnic divides, pursued stylistic experimentation and often caustically repudiated conservative middle-class American values. Writers of the 1950s Beat Generation, such as Jack Kerouac, Allen Ginsburg and Lawrence Ferlinghetti, threw themselves like Molotov cocktails onto the profusion of smug suburban lawns. Meanwhile, novelists JD Salinger and Ken Kesey, Russian immigrant Vladimir Nabokov and poet Sylvia Plath darkly chronicled descents into madness by characters who struggled against stifling social norms.

The South, always ripe with paradox, inspired masterful short-story writers and novelists Flannery O'Connor and Eudora Welty and novelist Dorothy Allison. The mythical romance and modern tragedies of the West have found their champions in Chicano writer Rudolfo Anaya, Larry McMurtry and Cormac McCarthy, whose characters poignantly tackle the rugged realities of Western life.

As the 20th century ended, American literature became ever more personalized, starting with the 'me' decade of the 1980s. Narcissistic, often nihilistic narratives by writers such as Jay McInerney and Bret Easton Ellis, catapulted the 'Brat Pack' into pop culture.

Since the 1990s, an increasingly diverse, multiethnic panoply of voices reflects the kaleidoscopic society Americans live in. Ethnic identity (especially that of immigrant cultures), regionalism and narratives of self-discovery remain at the forefront of American literature, no matter how experimental. The quarterly journal *McSweeney's,* founded by Dave Eggers, publishes titans of contemporary literature such as Joyce Carol Oates and Michael Chabon, as well as inventive humor pieces from new voices. Watch out for emerging writers such as Emma Cline, Brit Bennett, Roxane Gay, Yaa Gyasi and Nathan Hill.

For a sweeping, almost panoramic look at American society, read Jonathan Franzen's *The Corrections* (2001). More recent literary hits include Phil Klay's powerful *Redeployment* (2014), a series of 12 short stories set during the US war in Iraq and Afghanistan. Angela Flournoy's 2015 National Book Award–winning debut, *The Turner House,* traces the history of a Detroit family through three generations. Paul Beatty's electric satire about race in America, *The Sellout* (2015) made him the first US author to win Britain's Man Booker Prize. And Paulette Jiles' spare historical novel, *News of the World* (2016), explores the little-remembered role of traveling newsreaders in the American West.

Painting & Sculpture

An ocean away from Europe's aristocratic patrons, religious commissions and historic art academies, colonial America was not exactly fertile ground for the visual arts. Since then, thankfully, times have changed: once a swampy Dutch trading post, New York is the red-hot center of the art world, and its make-or-break influence shapes tastes across the nation and around the globe.

Shaping a National Identity

Artists played a pivotal role in the USA's 19th-century expansion, disseminating images of far-flung territories and reinforcing the call to Manifest Destiny. Thomas Cole and his colleagues in the Hudson River School translated European romanticism to the luminous wild landscapes of upstate New York, while Frederic Remington offered idealized, often stereotypical portraits of the Western frontier.

After the Civil War and the advent of industrialization, realism increasingly became prominent. Eastman Johnson painted nostalgic scenes of rural life, as did Winslow Homer, who later became renowned for watercolor seascapes.

Art in Out-of-the-Way Places

Marfa (Texas)

Santa Fe (New Mexico)

Traverse City (Michigan)

Lucas (Kansas)

Bellingham (Washington)

Beacon (New York)

Provincetown (Massachusetts)

AMERICA DANCES

America fully embraced dance in the 20th century. New York City has always been the epicenter for dance innovation and the home of many premier dance companies, but every major city supports resident and touring troupes, both ballet and modern.

Modern ballet is said to have begun with Russian-born choreographer George Balanchine's *Apollo* (1928) and *Prodigal Son* (1929). With these, Balanchine invented the 'plotless ballet' – in which he choreographed the inner structure of music, not a panto-mimed story – and thereby created a new, modern vocabulary of ballet movement. In 1934, Balanchine founded the School of American Ballet; in 1948 he founded the New York City Ballet, turning it into one of the world's foremost ballet companies. Jerome Robbins took over that company in 1983, after achieving fame choreographing huge Broadway musicals such as *West Side Story* (1957). Broadway remains an important venue for dance today. National companies elsewhere, such as San Francisco's Lines Ballet, keep evolving contemporary ballet.

The pioneer of modern dance, Isadora Duncan, didn't find success until she began performing in Europe at the turn of the 20th century. Basing her ideas on ancient Greek myths and concepts of beauty, she challenged the strictures of classical ballet and sought to make dance an intense form of self-expression.

Martha Graham founded the Martha Graham School for Contemporary Dance in 1926 after moving to New York, and many of today's major American choreographers developed under her tutelage. In her long career she choreographed more than 140 works and developed a new dance technique, now taught worldwide, aimed at expressing inner emotion and dramatic narrative. Her most famous work was *Appalachian Spring* (1944).

Merce Cunningham, Paul Taylor and Twyla Tharp succeeded Graham as leading exponents of modern dance; they all have companies that are active today. In the 1960s and '70s, Cunningham explored abstract expressionism in movement, collaborating famously with musician John Cage. Taylor experimented with everyday movements and expressions, while Tharp is known for incorporating pop music, jazz and ballet.

Another student of Martha Graham, Alvin Ailey, was part of the post-WWII flowering of African American culture. He made his name with *Revelations* (1960), two years after he founded the still-lauded Alvin Ailey American Dance Theater in New York City.

Other celebrated postmodern choreographers include Mark Morris and Bill T Jones. Beyond New York, San Francisco, Los Angeles, Chicago, Minneapolis and Philadelphia are noteworthy for modern dance.

An American Avant-Garde

New York's Armory Show of 1913 introduced the nation to European modernism and changed the face of American art. It showcased impressionism, fauvism and cubism, including the notorious 1912 *Nude Descending a Staircase, No. 2* by Marcel Duchamp, a French artist who later became an American citizen. The show was merely the first in a series of exhibitions evangelizing the radical aesthetic shifts of European modernism, and it was inevitable that American artists would begin to grapple with what they had seen. Alexander Calder, Joseph Cornell and Isamu Noguchi produced sculptures inspired by surrealism and constructivism, while the precisionist paintings of Charles Demuth, Georgia O'Keeffe and Charles Sheeler combined realism with a touch of cubist geometry.

In the 1930s, the Federal Art Project of the Works Progress Administration (WPA), part of Franklin D Roosevelt's New Deal, commissioned murals, paintings and sculptures for public buildings nationwide. WPA artists borrowed from Soviet social realism and Mexican muralists to forge a socially engaged figurative style with regional flavor.

Abstract Expressionism

In the wake of WWII, American art underwent a sea change at the hands of New York School painters such as Franz Kline, Jackson Pollock and Mark Rothko. Moved by surrealism's celebration of spontaneity and the unconscious, these artists explored abstraction and its psychological potency through imposing scale and the gestural handling of paint. The movement's 'action painter' camp went extreme; Pollock, for example, made his drip paintings by pouring and splattering pigments over large canvases.

Having stood the test of time, abstract expressionism is widely considered to be the first truly original school of American art.

Art + Commodity = Pop

Once established in America, abstract expressionism reigned supreme. However, stylistic revolts had begun much earlier, in the 1950s. Most notably, Jasper Johns came to prominence with thickly painted renditions of ubiquitous symbols, including targets and the American flag, while Robert Rauschenberg assembled artworks from comics, ads and even – à la Duchamp – found objects (a mattress, a tire, a stuffed goat). Both artists helped break down traditional boundaries between painting and sculpture, opening the field for pop art in the 1960s.

America's postwar economic boom also influenced pop. Not only did artists embrace representation, they drew inspiration from consumer images such as billboards, product packaging and media icons. Employing mundane mass-production techniques to silkscreen paintings of movie stars and Coke bottles, Andy Warhol helped topple the myth of the solitary artist laboring heroically in the studio. Roy Lichtenstein combined newsprint's humble Benday dots with the representational conventions of comics. Suddenly, so-called 'serious' art could be political, bizarre, ironic and fun – and all at once.

Pop-art icon Andy Warhol turned the art world on its head in the early 1960s with his celebrity portraits of figures such as Marilyn Monroe and Jackie Onassis. His works were both a comment on celebrity and commercial culture, while also showing these legendary figures in a startling new light.

Minimalism

What became known as minimalism shared pop's interest in mass production, but all similarities ended there. Like the abstract expressionists, artists such as Donald Judd, Agnes Martin and Robert Ryman eschewed representational subject matter; their cool, reductive works of the 1960s and '70s were often arranged in gridded compositions and fabricated from industrial materials.

The '80's & Beyond

By the 1980s, civil rights, feminism and AIDS activism had made inroads in visual culture; artists not only voiced political dissent through their work, but embraced a range of once-marginalized media, from textiles and graffiti to video, sound and performance. The decade also ushered in the so-called Culture Wars, which commenced with tumult over photographs by Robert Mapplethorpe and Andres Serrano. Break-out artists Futura 2000, Keith Haring and Jean-Michel Basquiat moved from the subways and the streets to the galleries, and soon to the worlds of fashion and advertising.

To get the pulse of contemporary art in the US, check out works by artists such as Cindy Sherman, Kara Walker, Chuck Close, Kerry James Marshall, Eddie Martinez and Josh Smith.

Theater

American theater is a three-act play of sentimental entertainment, classic revivals and urgent social commentary. From the beginning, Broadway musicals (www.livebroadway.com) have aspired to be 'don't-miss-this-show!' tourist attractions. And today, they continue to be one of NYC's biggest draws. Broadway shows earn over a billion dollars in revenue from ticket sales each year, with top shows pulling in a cool $2 million a week. The most successful Broadway shows, including the hip-hop hit *Hamilton* (which re-imagines the life of Founding Father

Alexander Hamilton), often go on to even greater earnings worldwide. (Gross worldwide earnings of *The Phantom of the Opera* has now topped an astounding $6 billion.) Meanwhile, long-running classics such as *The Lion King* and *Wicked* continue to play before sold-out houses.

Independent theater arrived in the 1920s and '30s, with the Little Theatre Movement, which emulated progressive European theater and developed into today's 'off-Broadway' scene. Always struggling and scraping, and mostly surviving, the country's 2000 nonprofit regional theaters are breeding grounds for new plays and fostering new playwrights. Some also develop Broadway-bound productions, while others sponsor festivals dedicated to the Bard himself, William Shakespeare.

Eugene O'Neill – the first major US playwright, and still widely considered the best – put American drama on the map. After WWII, American playwrights joined the nationwide artistic renaissance. Two of the most famous were Arthur Miller, who famously married Marilyn Monroe and wrote about everything from middle-class male disillusionment to the dark psychology of the mob mentality of the Salem witch trials, and the prolific Southerner Tennessee Williams.

As in Europe, absurdism and the avant-garde marked American theater in the 1960s. Few were more scathing than Edward Albee, who started provoking bourgeois sensibilities. Neil Simon arrived at around the same time; his ever-popular comedies kept Broadway humming for 40 years.

Other prominent, active American dramatists emerging in the 1970s include David Mamet, Sam Shepard and innovative 'concept musical' composer Stephen Sondheim. August Wilson created a monumental 10-play 'Pittsburgh Cycle' dissecting 20th-century African American life.

Today, American theater is evolving in its effort to remain a relevant communal experience in an age of ever-isolating media. Shows including *Breakfast with Mugabe* explore the trauma of the past, while *Avenue Q*, with its trash-talking, love-making puppets, presents a hilarious send-up of life on *Sesame Street*. More immersive experiences such as *Sleep No More* put theater-goers inside the play to wander freely among wildly decorated rooms – including a graveyard, stables, a psychiatric ward and a ballroom – as the drama (loosely based on *Macbeth*) unfolds around them.

Architecture

In the 21st century, computer technology and innovations in materials and manufacturing allow for curving, asymmetrical buildings once considered impossible, if not inconceivable. Architects are being challenged to 'go green,' and the creativity unleashed is riveting, transforming skylines and changing the way Americans think about their built environments. The public's architectural taste remains conservative, but never mind: avant-garde 'starchitects' are revising urban landscapes with radical visions that the nation will catch up with – one day.

The Colonial Period

Perhaps the only lasting indigenous influence on American architecture has been the adobe dwellings of the Southwest. In the 17th and 18th centuries, Spanish colonists incorporated elements of what they called the Native American *pueblo* (village). It reappeared in late 19th- and early 20th-century architecture in both the Southwest's Pueblo Revival style and Southern California's Mission Revival style.

Elsewhere until the 20th century, immigrant Americans mainly adopted English and continental European styles and followed their trends. For most early colonists in the eastern US, architecture served necessity rather than taste, while the would-be gentry aped grander English homes, a period well preserved in Williamsburg, VA.

After the Revolutionary War, the nation's leaders wanted a style befitting the new republic and adopted neoclassicism. Virginia's capitol, designed by Thomas Jefferson, was modeled on an ancient Roman temple, and Jefferson's own private estate, Monticello, sports a Romanesque rotunda.

Professional architect Charles Bulfinch helped develop the more monumental federal style, which paralleled the English Georgian style. The grandest example is the US Capitol in Washington, DC, which became a model for state legislatures nationwide. As they moved into the 19th century, Americans, mirroring English fashions, gravitated toward the Greek and Gothic Revival styles, still seen today in many churches and college campuses.

Building the Nation

Meanwhile, small-scale architecture was revolutionized by 'balloon-frame' construction: a light frame of standard-milled timber joined with cheap nails. Easy and economical, balloon-frame stores and houses made possible swift settlement of the expanding west and, later, the surreal proliferation of the suburbs. Home-ownership was suddenly within reach of average middle-class families, making real the enduring American Dream.

After the Civil War, influential American architects studied at Paris' École des Beaux-Arts, and American buildings began to show increasing refinement and confidence. Major examples of the beaux-arts style include Richard Morris Hunt's Biltmore Estate in North Carolina and New York's Public Library.

In San Francisco and other cities across America, Victorian architecture appeared as the 19th century progressed. Among well-to-do classes, larger and fancier private houses added ever more adornments: balconies, turrets, towers, ornately painted trim and intricate 'gingerbread' wooden millwork.

In a reaction against Victorian opulence, the Arts and Crafts movement arose after 1900 and remained popular until the 1930s. Its modest bungalows, such as the Gamble House in Pasadena, CA, featured locally handcrafted wood and glasswork, ceramic tiles and other artisan details.

Reaching for the Sky

By the 1850s, internal iron-framed buildings had appeared in Manhattan, and this freed up urban architectural designs, especially after the advent of Otis hydraulic elevators in the 1880s. The Chicago School of architecture transitioned beyond beaux-arts style to produce the skyscraper – considered the first truly 'modern' architecture, and America's most prominent architectural contribution to the world at that time.

In the 1930s, the influence of art deco – which became instantly popular in the US after the Paris Exposition of 1925 – meant that urban high-rises soared, becoming fitting symbols of America's technical achievements, grand aspirations, commerce and affinity for modernism.

Modernism & Beyond

When the Bauhaus school fled the rise of Nazism in Germany, architects such as Walter Gropius and Ludwig Mies van der Rohe brought their pioneering modern designs to American shores. Van der Rohe landed in Chicago, where Louis Sullivan, considered to be the inventor of the modern skyscraper, was already working on a simplified style of architecture in which 'form ever follows function.' This evolved into the International style, which favored glass 'curtain walls' over a steel frame. IM Pei, who designed Cleveland's Rock and Roll Hall of Fame, is considered the last living high-modernist architect in America.

ARTS & ARCHITECTURE ARCHITECTURE

Art deco architecture simultaneously appeared nationwide in the design of movie houses, train stations and office buildings across the country, and in neighborhoods such as downtown Detroit and Miami's South Beach. Remarkable examples of art-deco skyscrapers include NYC's Chrysler Building and Empire State Building.

In the mid-20th century, modernism transitioned into America's suburbs, especially in Southern California. Mid-century modern architecture was influenced not only by the organic nature of Frank Lloyd Wright's homes, but also the spare, geometric, clean-lined designs of Scandinavia. Post-and-beam construction allowed for walls of sheer glass that gave the illusion of merging indoor and outdoor living spaces. Today, a striking collection of mid-century modern homes and public buildings by Albert Frey, Richard Neutra and other luminaries can be found in Palm Springs, CA.

Rejecting modernism's 'ugly boxes' later in the 20th century, postmodernism reintroduced decoration, color, historical references and whimsy. In this, architects such as Michael Graves and Philip Johnson took the lead. Another expression of postmodernism is the brash, mimetic architecture of the Las Vegas Strip, which Pritzker Prize–winning architect Robert Venturi held up as the triumphant antithesis of modernism (he sardonically described the latter as 'less is a bore').

Today, aided and abetted by digital tools, architectural design favors the bold and the unique. Leading this plunge into futurama has been Frank Gehry; his Walt Disney Concert Hall in Los Angeles is but one example. Other notable contemporary architects include Richard Meier (Los Angeles' Getty Center), Thom Mayne (San Francisco's Federal Building) and Daniel Libeskind (San Francisco's Contemporary Jewish Museum and the Denver Art Museum's Hamilton Building).

Even as the recession crippled the American economy in 2008 and stalled new construction, several phenomenal new examples of visionary architecture have burst upon the scene in American cities. Notable examples include Jeanne Gang's Aqua Building in Chicago, Santiago Calatrava's soaring World Trade Center transportation hub in New York City, Renzo Piano's California Academy of Sciences in San Francisco, David Adjaye's shimmering National Museum of African American History and Culture in Washington, DC, and Norman Foster's spaceship-like Apple Park in Cupertino, CA.

The Music Scene

American popular music is the nation's heartbeat and its unbreakable soul. It's John Lee Hooker's deep growls and John Coltrane's passionate cascades. It's Hank Williams' yodel and Elvis' pout. It's Beyoncé and Bob Dylan, Duke Ellington and Patti Smith. It's a feeling as much as a form – always a foot-stomping, defiant good time, whether folks are boot scooting to bluegrass, sweating to zydeco, jumping to hip-hop or stage-diving to punk rock.

Blues

The South is the mother of American music, most of which has roots in the frisson and interplay of black-white racial relations. The blues developed after the Civil War, out of the work songs, or 'shouts', of black slaves and out of black spiritual songs and their 'call and response' pattern, both of which were adaptations of African music.

Improvisational and intensely personal, the blues remain at heart an immediate expression of individual pain, suffering, hope, desire and pride. Nearly all subsequent American music has tapped this deep well.

At the turn of the 20th century, traveling blues musicians, and particularly female blues singers, gained fame and employment across the South. Early pioneers included Robert Johnson, WC Handy, Ma Rainey, Huddie Ledbetter (aka Lead Belly) and Bessie Smith, who some consider the best blues singer who ever lived. At the same time, African American Christian choral music evolved into gospel, the greatest singer of which, Mahalia Jackson, came to prominence in the 1920s.

After WWII, blues from Memphis and the Mississippi Delta dispersed northward, particularly to Chicago, in the hands of a new generation of musicians such as Muddy Waters, Buddy Guy, BB King, John Lee Hooker and Etta James.

Today's generation of blues players include the likes of Bonamassa, Warren Haynes (a longtime player for the Allman Brothers), Seasick Steve, Tedeschi Trucks Band, Alabama Shakes and the sometimes-blues players The Black Keys.

Jazz

Down in New Orleans, Congo Sq – where slaves gathered to sing and dance from the late 18th century onward – is considered the birthplace of jazz. There, ex-slaves adapted the reed, horn and string instruments used by the city's often French-speaking, multiracial Creoles – who themselves preferred formal European music – to play their own African-influenced music. This fertile cross-pollination produced a steady stream of innovative sounds.

The first variation was ragtime, so-called because of its 'ragged,' syncopated African rhythms. Beginning in the 1890s, ragtime was popularized by musicians such as Scott Joplin, and was made widely accessible through sheet music and player-piano rolls.

Dixieland jazz, centered on New Orleans' infamous Storyville redlight district, soon followed. In 1917 Storyville shut down and New Orleans' jazz musicians dispersed. In 1919 bandleader King Oliver moved to Chicago, and his star trumpet player, Louis Armstrong, soon

One of rock music's most phenomenal success stories, Prince, was born Prince Rogers Nelson in 1950s Minneapolis. He originally tried out for the high-school basketball team, but being too short at 5ft 2in, he was cut. His back-up hobby? He took up the guitar.

followed. Armstrong's distinctive vocals and talented improvisations led to the solo becoming an integral part of jazz throughout much of the 20th century. The 1920s and '30s are known as the Jazz Age, but music was just part of the greater flowering of African American culture during New York's Harlem Renaissance. Swing – an urbane, big-band jazz style – swept the country, led by innovative bandleaders Duke Ellington and Count Basie. Jazz singers Ella Fitzgerald and Billie Holiday combined jazz with its Southern sibling, the blues.

After WWII, bebop (aka bop) arose, reacting against the smooth melodies and confining rhythms of big-band swing. A new crop of musicians came of age, including Charlie Parker, Dizzy Gillespie and Thelonious Monk. Critics at first derided such 1950s and '60s permutations as cool jazz, hard-bop, free or avant-garde jazz, and fusion (which combined jazz and Latin or rock music) – but there was no stopping the postmodernist tide deconstructing jazz. Pioneers of this era include Miles Davis, Dave Brubeck, Chet Baker, Charles Mingus, John Coltrane, Melba Liston and Ornette Coleman.

Country

Early Scottish, Irish and English immigrants brought their own instruments and folk music to America, and what emerged over time in the secluded Appalachian Mountains was fiddle-and-banjo hillbilly, or 'country,' music. In the Southwest, steel guitars and larger bands distinguished 'western' music. In the 1920s, these styles merged into 'country and western' music and became centered on Nashville, TN, especially once the *Grand Ole Opry* began its radio broadcasts in 1925. Country musicians who are now 'classics' include Hank Williams, Johnny Cash, Willie Nelson, Patsy Cline, Loretta Lynn and Dolly Parton.

Country music influenced rock and roll in the 1950s, while rock-flavored country was dubbed 'rockabilly.' In the 1980s, country and western achieved new levels of popularity with stars like Garth Brooks. Today, country-music stations dominate other genres. Musicians with record-breaking success include Shania Twain, Dwight Yoakam, Tim McGraw, Carrie Underwood and Taylor Swift. Occupying the eclectic 'alt country' category are Lucinda Williams and Lyle Lovett.

Folk

The tradition of American folk music was crystallized by Woody Guthrie, who traveled the country during the Depression singing politically conscious songs. In the 1940s, Pete Seeger emerged as a tireless preserver of America's folk heritage. Folk music experienced a revival during 1960s protest movements, but then-folkie Bob Dylan ended it almost single-handedly when he plugged in an electric guitar to shouts of 'traitor!'

Folk has seen a resurgence in the 21st century, particularly in the Pacific Northwest. Iron and Wine's mournful tunes channel pop, blues and rock, while Joanna Newsom, with her extraordinary voice and unusual instrumentation (she plays the harp), adds a new level of complexity to folk. Indie folk singers making waves in recent years (and expanding the boundaries of the genre) include Edward Sharpe and the Magnetic Zeros, Laura Gibson, Lord Huron, Father John Misty and Angel Olsen.

Rock & Roll

Most say rock and roll was born in 1954 the day Elvis Presley walked into Sam Phillips' Sun Studio and recorded 'That's All Right.' Initially, radio stations weren't sure why a white country boy was singing black music, or whether they should play it. Two years later Presley scored his first big breakthrough with 'Heartbreak Hotel.'

Musically, rock and roll was a hybrid of guitar-driven blues, black rhythm and blues (R&B), and white country-and-western music. R&B evolved in the 1940s out of swing and the blues and was then known as 'race music.' With rock and roll, white performers and some African

The American Soundtrack

'America,' Simon & Garfunkel (1968)

'Respect,' Aretha Franklin (1967)

'Like a Prayer,' Madonna (1989)

'Fast Car,' Tracy Chapman (1988)

'Push it,' Salt-N-Pepa (1987)

'Born to Run,' Bruce Springsteen (1975)

'I've Been Everywhere,' Johnny Cash (1996)

'Carolina in My Mind,' James Taylor (1968)

'West Coast,' Coconut Records (2007)

'City of New Orleans,' Arlo Guthrie (1972)

'Jolene,' Dolly Parton (1973)

'Home,' Edward Sharpe & the Magnetic Zeros (2010)

'Summertime,' Ella Fitzgerald (1968)

'Nikes,' Frank Ocean (2016)

American musicians transformed 'race music' into something that white youths could embrace freely – and oh, did they.

Rock and roll instantly abetted a social revolution even more significant than its musical one: openly sexual, as it celebrated youth and dancing freely across color lines, rock scared the nation. Authorities worked diligently to control 'juvenile delinquents' and to sanitize and suppress rock and roll, which might have withered if not for the early 1960s 'British invasion,' in which the Beatles and the Rolling Stones, emulating Chuck Berry, Little Richard and others, shocked rock and roll back to life.

The 1960s witnessed a full-blown youth rebellion, epitomized by the drug-inspired psychedelic sounds of the Grateful Dead and Jefferson Airplane, and the electric wails of Janis Joplin and Jimi Hendrix. Ever since, rock has been about music *and* lifestyle, alternately torn between hedonism and seriousness, commercialism and authenticity.

Punk arrived in the late 1970s, led by the Ramones and the Dead Kennedys, as did the working-class rock of Bruce Springsteen and Tom Petty. As the counterculture became the culture in the 1980s, critics prematurely pronounced 'rock is dead.' Rock was saved (by the Talking Heads, REM, Nirvana, Sonic Youth, Pavement and Pearl Jam among others) as it always has been: by splintering and evolving, whether it's called new wave, heavy metal, grunge, indie rock, world beat, skate punk, hardcore, goth, emo or electronica.

In the early 2000s guitar groups The Killers, The Strokes, the Yeah Yeah Yeahs and The White Stripes were dubbed the saviors of rock for their stripped-back sound that saw the genre established as the commercial mainstream.

Today, while American rock music may be waiting for its next big revival, bands such as Imagine Dragons, pop-rockers Haim, and various incarnations by Jack White ensure it's not going anywhere soon.

The country that spawned the world's most successful recording industry also popularized the technology accused of killing it. From the emergence of file-sharing to Apple's iTunes and more recent music-streaming services like Spotify, it's no surprise that the American music industry is under stress – though from its ability to evolve, you'd hardly know it.

Hip-Hop

From the ocean of sounds coming out of the early 1970s – funk, soul, Latin, reggae, and rock and roll – young DJs from the Bronx in NYC began to spin a groundbreaking mixture of records together in an effort to drive dance floors wild. And so hip-hop was born. Groups such as Grandmaster Flash and the Furious Five were soon taking the party from the streets to the trendy clubs of Manhattan and mingling with punk and new wave bands including the Clash and Blondie.

As groups like Run-DMC, Public Enemy and the Beastie Boys sold millions, the sounds and styles of the growing hip-hop culture rapidly diversified. The confrontational 'gangsta rap' of Niggaz With Attitude came out of Los Angeles, and the group got both accolades and bad press for its daring sounds and social commentary – which critics called battle cries for violence – on racism, drugs, sex and urban poverty.

Come the turn of the millennium, what started as some raggedy kids playing their parents' funk records at illegal block parties had evolved into a multibillion-dollar business. Russell Simmons and P Diddy stood atop media empires, and stars Queen Latifah and Will Smith were Hollywood royalty. A white rapper from Detroit, Eminem, sold millions of records, and hip-hop overtook country as America's second-most-popular music behind pop rock.

Today, many view hip-hop as a vapid wasteland of commercial excess – glorifying consumerism, misogyny, homophobia, drug use and a host of other social ills. But just as the hedonistic days of arena rock and roll gave birth to the rebel child of punk, the evolving offspring of hip-hop and DJ culture are constantly breaking the rules to create something new and even more energizing. Major players of the moment include Jay-Z, Kanye West, Nicki Minaj, Drake and the more experimental and feel-good hip-hop duo of Macklemore & Ryan Lewis. Drawing critical acclaim are rising stars such as Danny Brown, Anderson Paak and Kamaiyah.

The Land & Wildlife

The USA is home to creatures both great and small, from the ferocious grizzly to the industrious beaver, with colossal bison, snowy owls, soaring eagles, howling coyotes and doe-eyed manatees all part of the great American menagerie. The nation's varied geography – coastlines along two oceans, mountains, deserts, rainforests, and massive bay and river systems – harbor ecosystems where an extraordinary array of plant and animal life can flourish.

Geography

High in the White Mountains (east of California's Sierra Nevada) stand the oldest single living plant species on earth. Known as bristlecone pines *(Pinus longaeva)*, these bare and dramatically twisted trees date back more than 4000 years and have long mystified scientists with their extraordinary longevity.

The USA is big, no question. Covering nearly 3.8 million sq miles, it's the world's third-largest country, trailing only Russia and Canada, its friendly neighbor to the north. The continental USA is made up of 48 contiguous states ('the lower 48'), while Alaska, its largest state, is northwest of Canada, and the volcanic islands of Hawaii, the 50th state, are 2300 miles southwest of the mainland in the Pacific Ocean.

It's more than just size, though. America feels big because of its incredibly diverse topography, which began to take shape around 50 to 60 million years ago.

In the contiguous USA, the east is a land of temperate, deciduous forests and contains the ancient Appalachian Mountains, a low range that parallels the Atlantic Ocean. Between the mountains and the coast lies the country's most populated, urbanized region, particularly in the corridor between Washington, DC, and Boston, MA.

To the north are the Great Lakes, which the USA shares with Canada. These five lakes, part of the Canadian Shield, are the greatest expanse of fresh water on the planet, constituting nearly 20% of the world's supply.

Going south along the East Coast, things get wetter and warmer till you reach the swamps of southern Florida and make the turn into the Gulf of Mexico, which provides the USA with a southern coastline.

West of the Appalachians are the vast interior plains, which lie flat all the way to the Rocky Mountains. The eastern plains are the nation's breadbasket, roughly divided into the northern 'corn belt' and the southern 'cotton belt.' The plains, an ancient sea bottom, are drained by the mighty Mississippi River, which together with the Missouri River forms the world's fourth-longest river system, surpassed only by the Nile, Amazon and Yangtze Rivers. Going west, farmland slowly gives way to cowboys and ranches in the semiarid, big-sky Great Plains.

The young, jagged Rocky Mountains are a complex set of tall ranges that run all the way from Mexico to Canada, providing excellent skiing. West of these mountains are the Southwestern deserts, an arid region of extremes that has been cut to dramatic effect by the Colorado River system. This land of eroded canyons leads to the unforgiving Great Basin as you go across Nevada. Also an ancient sea bottom, the Great Basin is used as a training ground and a test range by the US military. It's also where the USA plans to bury its nuclear waste.

Then you reach America's third major mountain system: the southern, granite Sierra Nevada and the northern, volcanic Cascades, which both parallel the Pacific Coast. California's Central Valley is one of the most fertile places on earth, while the coastline from San Diego to Seattle is celebrated in folk songs and Native American legends – a stretch of sandy beaches and old-growth forests, including coast redwoods.

But wait, there's more. Northwest of Canada, Alaska reaches the Arctic Ocean and contains tundra, glaciers, an interior rainforest and the lion's share of federally protected wilderness. Hawaii, in the Pacific Ocean, is a string of tropical island idylls.

Land Mammals

Nineteenth-century Americans did not willingly suffer competing predators, and federal eradication programs nearly wiped out every single wolf and big cat and many of the bears in the continental US. Almost all share the same story of abundance, precipitous loss and, today, partial recovery.

The grizzly bear, a subspecies of brown bear, is one of North America's largest land mammals. Male grizzlies can stand 7ft tall, weigh up to 850lb and consider 500 sq miles home. At one time, as many as 100,000 grizzlies roamed the West, but by 1975 fewer than 1000 remained. Conservation efforts, particularly in the Greater Yellowstone Region, have increased the population in the lower 48 states to between 1200 and 1400 today. By contrast, Alaska remains chock-full of grizzlies, with upwards of 30,000. Despite a decline in numbers, black bears survive nearly everywhere. Smaller than grizzlies, these opportunistic, adaptable and curious animals can survive on very small home ranges.

Another extremely adaptable creature is the coyote, which looks similar to a wolf but is about half the size, ranging from 15lb to 45lb. An icon of the Southwest, coyotes are found all over, even in cities. The USA has one primary big-cat species, which goes by several names: mountain lion, cougar, puma and panther. In the east, a remnant population of panthers is found within Everglades National Park. In the west, mountain lions are common enough for human encounters to be on the increase. These powerful cats are about 150lb of pure muscle, with short tawny fur, long tails and a secretive nature.

Wilderness Films

Wild
(Jean-Marc Vallée)

Winged Migration
(Jacques Perrin)

Grizzly Man
(Werner Herzog)

Into the Wild
(Sean Penn)

Jeremiah Johnson
(Sydney Pollack)

The Revenant
(Alejandro González Iñárritu)

THE LAND & WILDLIFE LAND MAMMALS

RETURN OF THE WOLF

The wolf is a potent symbol of America's wilderness. This smart, social predator is the largest species of canine – averaging more than 100lb and reaching nearly 3ft at the shoulder. An estimated 400,000 once roamed the continent from coast to coast, from Alaska to Mexico.

Wolves were not regarded warmly by European settlers. The first wildlife legislation in the British colonies was a wolf bounty. As 19th-century Americans tamed the West, they slaughtered the once-uncountable herds of bison, elk, deer and moose, replacing them with domestic cattle and sheep, which wolves found equally tasty.

To stop wolves from devouring the livestock, the wolf's extermination soon became official government policy. Up until 1965, for $20 to $50 an animal, wolves were shot, poisoned, trapped and dragged from dens until in the lower 48 states only a few hundred gray wolves remained in northern Minnesota and Michigan.

In 1944 naturalist Aldo Leopold called for the return of the wolf. His argument was ecology, not nostalgia. His studies showed that wild ecosystems need their top predators to maintain a healthy biodiversity; in complex interdependence, all animals and plants suffered with the wolf gone.

Despite dire predictions from ranchers and hunters, gray wolves were reintroduced to the Greater Yellowstone region in 1995–96 and Mexican wolves to Arizona in 1998.

Protected and encouraged, wolf populations have made a remarkable recovery, with more than 5700 now counted in the continental US, and around 8000 in Alaska.

AMERICA'S WORST NATURAL DISASTERS

Earthquakes, wildfires, tornadoes, hurricanes and blizzards – the US certainly has its share of natural disasters. A few of the more infamous events that have shaped the national consciousness:

Johnstown Flood In 1889 torrential rains overwhelmed the South Fork dam that stood high on the Little Conemaugh River in Central Pennsylvania. When the dam broke, some 20 million tons of water and debris quickly inundated nearby Johnstown, killing over 2200 people and destroying 1600 homes.

Galveston Hurricane In 1900 Galveston – then known as 'the jewel of Texas' – was practically obliterated by a category-4 hurricane. Fifteen-foot waves destroyed buildings and at one point the entire island was submerged. More than 8000 perished, making it America's deadliest natural disaster.

1906 San Francisco Earthquake A powerful earthquake (estimated to be around an 8 on the Richter scale) leveled the city, followed by even more devastating fires. The quake was felt as far away as Oregon and Central Nevada. An estimated 3000-plus died, while more than 200,000 people (of a population of 410,000) were left homeless.

Dust Bowl During a prolonged drought of the 1930s, the overworked topsoil of the Great Plains dried up, turned to dust and billowed eastward in massive windstorm-fueled 'black blizzards,' reaching all the way to NYC and Washington, DC. Millions of acres of crops were destroyed and more than 500,000 people were left homeless. The great exodus westward by stricken farmers and migrants was immortalized in John Steinbeck's *The Grapes of Wrath*.

Hurricane Katrina August 29, 2005, is not a day easily forgotten in New Orleans. A massive category-5 hurricane swept across the Gulf of Mexico and slammed into Louisiana. As levees failed, floods inundated more than 80% of the city. The death toll reached 1836, with more than $100 billion in estimated damages.

Hurricane Sandy In 2012 this hurricane affected some 24 states, with New Jersey and New York among the hardest hit. More than 100 died in the USA, and estimated damages amounted to more than $65 billion. It was also the largest Atlantic hurricane ever recorded, with storm winds spanning over 1100 miles.

Hurricane Irma On September 10, 2017, one of the largest hurricanes ever recorded barreled over Florida, causing flooding and destruction. Hurricane Irma made landfall in the Florida Keys as a category 4 storm the width of Texas. Homes and businesses in Everglades City were left battered and mud-soaked after an 8-foot storm surge; in the Keys, a FEMA survey reported that 25% of buildings had been destroyed, with another 65% damaged.

The story of the great American buffalo is a tragic one. These massive herbivores numbered as many as 65 million in 1800 – in herds so thick they 'darkened the whole plains,' as explorers Lewis and Clark wrote. They were killed for food, hides, sport and to impoverish Native Americans, who depended on them for survival. By the 20th century, only a few hundred bison remained. Overcoming near extinction, new herds arose from these last survivors, so that one of America's noblest animals can again be admired in its gruff majesty – among other places, in Yellowstone, Grand Teton and Badlands National Parks.

Marine Mammals & Fish

Perhaps no native fish gets more attention than salmon, whose spawning runs up Pacific Coast rivers provide famous spectacles. However, both Pacific and Atlantic salmon are considered endangered; hatcheries release millions of young every year, but there is debate about whether this practice hurts or helps wild populations.

As for marine life, gray, humpback and blue whales migrate annually along the Pacific Coast, making whale-watching very popular. Alaska and Hawaii are important breeding grounds for whales and marine mammals, and Washington's San Juan Islands are visited by orcas. The Pacific Coast is also home to ponderous elephant seals, playful sea lions and endangered sea otters.

In California, Channel Islands National Park and Monterey Bay preserve unique, highly diverse marine worlds. For coral reefs and tropical fish, Hawaii and the Florida Keys are the prime destinations. The coast of Florida is also home to the unusual, gentle manatee, which moves between freshwater rivers and the ocean. Around 10ft long and weighing on average 1000lb, these agile, expressive creatures number around 6600 today, and may once have been mistaken for mermaids.

The Gulf of Mexico is another vital marine habitat, perhaps most famously for endangered sea turtles, which nest on coastal beaches.

Birds

Birding is the most popular wildlife-watching activity in the US, and little wonder – all the hemisphere's migratory songbirds and shorebirds rest here at some point, and the USA consequently claims some 800 native avian species.

The bald eagle was adopted as the nation's symbol in 1782. It's the only eagle unique to North America, and perhaps half a million once ruled the continent's skies. By 1963, habitat destruction and, in particular, poisoning from DDT had caused the population to plummet to 487 breeding pairs in the lower 48 states. By 2006, however, bald eagles had recovered so well, increasing to almost 9800 breeding pairs across the continent (plus 50,000 in Alaska), that they've now been removed from the endangered species list.

Another impressive bird is the endangered California condor, a prehistoric, carrion-eating bird that weighs about 20lb and has a wingspan of over 9ft. Condors were virtually extinct by the 1980s (reduced to just 22 birds), but they have been successfully bred and reintroduced in California and northern Arizona, where they can sometimes be spotted soaring above the Grand Canyon.

Unusual Wildlife Reads

Rats (Robert Sullivan)

Pigeons (Andrew Blechman)

Secret Life of Lobsters (Trevor Corson)

American Buffalo (Steven Rinella)

The Beast in the Garden (David Baron)

The Environmental Movement

The USA is well known for its political and social revolutions, but it also birthed environmentalism. The USA was the first nation to make significant efforts to preserve its wilderness, and US environmentalists often spearhead preservation efforts worldwide.

America's Protestant settlers believed that civilization's Christian mandate was to bend nature to its will. Not only was wilderness deadly and difficult, it was also a potent symbol of humanity's godless impulses, and the Pilgrims set about subduing both with gusto.

Then, in the mid-19th century, taking their cue from European Romantics, the USA's transcendentalists claimed that nature was not fallen, but holy. In *Walden; or, Life in the Woods* (1854), iconoclast Henry David Thoreau described living for two years in the woods, blissfully free of civilization's comforts. He persuasively argued that human society was harmfully distant from nature's essential truths. This view marked a profound shift toward believing that nature, the soul and God were one.

John Muir & National Parks

The continent's natural wonders – vividly captured by America's 19th-century landscape painters – had a way of selling themselves, and rampant nationalism led to a desire to promote them. In the late 1800s, US presidents began setting aside land for state and national parks.

USA'S ENDANGERED SPECIES

Currently, more than 1650 plants and animals are listed in the USA as either endangered or threatened. Although all endangered species are vital to the ecosystem, if it's brag-worthy animals that you're keen to see (and photograph), here are the places to spot them before it's too late:

California condor Big Sur, CA, and Grand Canyon National Park, AZ

Desert tortoise Mojave National Preserve, CA

Florida panther Everglades National Park, FL

Hawaiian goose Haleakalā National Park, HI

Manatee Everglades National Park, FL

Mexican long-nosed bat Big Bend National Park, TX

Whooping cranes Aransas National Wildlife Refuge, TX, and Bosque del Apache National Wildlife Refuge, NM

One of the most fascinating theories about the planet is James Lovelock's Gaia hypothesis, which proposes that the earth is a living, complex, self-regulating organism. Read about Lovelock's mind-blowing ideas in *The Ages of Gaia*.

Scottish naturalist John Muir soon emerged to champion wilderness for its own sake. Muir considered nature superior to civilization, and he spent much of his life wandering the Sierra Nevada mountain range and passionately advocating on its behalf. Muir was the driving force behind the USA's emerging conservation movement, which had its first big victory in 1890 when Yosemite National Park was established. Muir founded the Sierra Club in 1892 and slowly gained national attention.

Environmental Laws & Climate Change

As the 19th century drew to a close and in the decades that followed, the USA passed a series of landmark environmental and wildlife laws that resulted in significant improvements in the nation's water and air quality, and the partial recovery of many near-extinct plants and animals. The movement's focus steadily broadened – to preserving entire ecosystems, not just establishing parks – as it confronted devastation wrought by pollution, overkill of species, habitat destruction through human impact and the introduction of nonnative species.

Today environmentalism is a worldwide movement, one that understands that each nation's local problems also contribute to a global threat: climate change. In the USA, the dangers of global warming are inspiring an environmental awareness as widespread as at any time in US history. Whether or not average Americans believe God speaks through nature, they're increasingly disturbed by the messages they are hearing.

Survival Guide

DIRECTORY A–Z . . . 1170

Accommodations 1170
Customs
Regulations 1171
Discount Cards 1172
Electricity 1172
Embassies &
Consulates 1172
Food & Drink 1173
Health 1173
Insurance 1173
Internet Access 1174
Legal Matters 1174
LGBTIQ Travelers 1175
Money 1175
Opening Hours 1176
Post 1176
Public Holidays 1176
Safe Travel 1176
Telephone 1177
Time 1178
Toilets 1178
Tourist
Information 1178
Travelers with
Disabilities 1178
Visas 1179
Volunteering 1181
Women Travelers 1181
Work 1182

TRANSPORTATION . . 1183

GETTING
THERE & AWAY 1183
Entering the Country 1183
Air 1183
Land 1184
Sea 1184
Tours 1185
GETTING AROUND 1185
Air 1185
Bicycle 1185
Boat 1186
Bus 1186
Car & Motorcycle 1187
Local Transportation 1187
Train 1187

DRIVING IN
THE USA 1190

Automobile
Associations 1190
Bring Your Own Vehicle . . . 1190
Drive-Away Cars 1190
Driver's License 1190
Insurance 1190
Purchase 1191
Rental 1191
Road Conditions
& Hazards 1193
Road Rules 1193

Directory A–Z

Accommodations

For all but the cheapest places and the slowest seasons, reservations are advised. In tourist hot spots, book accommodations at least three months ahead in high season (June to August for summer resort areas, January to February for ski destinations) – or up to a year ahead in popular national parks such as the Grand Canyon, Yosemite and Yellowstone.

Many hotels offer specials on their websites, while low-end chains sometimes give a slightly better rate over the phone. Chain hotels also offer frequent-flier mileage deals and other rewards programs; ask when booking.

Online travel booking, bidding and comparison websites are a good way to find discounted hotel rates – but are usually limited to chain hotels; check out Hotels. com, Hotwire (www.hotwire. com) and Booking.com. If you have a smartphone, each of these sites has a free app – which are often great for finding good last-minute deals. Hotel Tonight (www. hoteltonight.com) is another good app for booking rooms on the fly, and includes boutique hotels and historic properties.

Many campsites, including those in national and state parks, can also be booked online (and it's wise to do so if coming in peak season) – the two leading sites are www.reserveamerica.com and www.recreation.gov.

B&Bs

In the USA, many B&Bs are high-end romantic retreats in restored historic homes that are run by personable, independent innkeepers who serve gourmet breakfasts. These B&Bs often take pains to evoke a theme – Victorian, rustic, Cape Cod and so on – and amenities range from merely comfortable to indulgent. Rates normally top $120, and the best run are $200 to $300. Some have minimum-stay requirements, and most exclude young children.

European-style B&Bs also exist: these may be rooms in someone's home, with plainer furnishings, simpler breakfasts, shared bathrooms and cheaper rates. These often welcome families.

B&Bs can close out of season, and reservations are essential, especially for top-end places. To avoid surprises, always ask about bathrooms (whether shared or private). Recommended B&B agencies:

Bed & Breakfast Inns Online (www.bbonline.com)

BedandBreakfast.com (www. bedandbreakfast.com)

BnB Finder (www.bnbfinder.com)

Select Registry (www.select registry.com)

Camping & Holiday Parks

Most federally managed public lands and many state parks offer camping. First-

---

SLEEPING PRICE RANGES

In this book, the following price ranges refer to a double room in high season, excluding taxes (which can add 10% to 15%).

$ less than $100

$$ $100–$250

$$$ more than $250

For New York City, San Francisco and Washington, DC, the following price ranges are used:

$ less than $150

$$ $150–$350

$$$ more than $350

come, first-served 'primitive' campgrounds offer no facilities; overnight fees range from free to less than $10. 'Basic' sites usually provide toilets (flush or pit), drinking water, fire pits and picnic tables; they cost $8 to $20 a night, and some or all may be reserved in advance. 'Developed' campgrounds, usually in national or state parks, have nicer facilities and more amenities: showers, barbecue grills, RV sites with hookups etc. These are $18 to $50 a night, and many can be reserved in advance.

Camping on most federal lands – including national parks, national forests and Bureau of Land Management land – can be reserved through Recreation.gov (www.recreation.gov). Camping is limited to 14 days and can be reserved up to six months in advance. For some state park campgrounds, you can make bookings through ReserveAmerica (www.reserveamerica.com). Both websites let you search for campground locations and amenities, check availability, reserve a site, view maps and get driving directions.

Private campgrounds tend to cater to RVs and families (tent sites may be few and lack atmosphere). Facilities may include playgrounds, convenience stores, wi-fi access, swimming pools and other activities. Some rent camping cabins, ranging from canvas-sided wooden platforms to log-frame structures with real beds, heating and private bathrooms. Kampgrounds of America (www.koa.com) is a national network of private campgrounds with a full range of facilities. You can browse its comprehensive campground listings and make bookings online.

Hostels

Hostels are mainly found in urban areas, in the northeast, the Pacific Northwest, California and the Southwest.

HOUSE & APARTMENT RENTALS

To rent a house or apartment from locals, visit Airbnb (www.airbnb.com), which has thousands of listings across the country. Budget travelers can also rent a room – a great way to connect with locals if you don't mind sharing facilities.

Hostelling International USA (www.hiusa.org) runs more than 50 hostels in the US. Most have gender-segregated dorms, a few private rooms, shared bathrooms and a communal kitchen. Overnight fees for dorm beds range typically from $25 to $45 (though in NYC, a dorm bed can cost upwards of $75). HI-USA members are entitled to small discounts. Reservations are accepted (you can book online) and advised during high season, when there may be a three-night maximum stay.

The USA has many independent hostels not affiliated with HI-USA. For online listings, check Hostels.com, Hostelworld.com or Hostelz.com.

Hotels

Hotels in all categories typically include in-room phones, cable TV, private bathrooms, wi-fi and a simple continental breakfast. Many midrange properties provide minibars, microwaves, hairdryers, internet access, air-conditioning and/or heating, swimming pools and writing desks, while top-end hotels add concierge services, fitness and business centers, spas, restaurants, bars and higher-end furnishings.

Even if hotels advertise that children 'sleep free,' cots or rollaway beds may cost extra. Always ask about the hotel's policy for telephone calls; all charge an exorbitant amount for long-distance and international calls, but some also charge for dialing local and toll-free numbers.

Motels

Motels – distinguishable from hotels by having rooms that open onto a parking lot – tend to cluster around interstate exits and on main routes into town. Some remain smaller, less-expensive 'mom-and-pop' operations; breakfast is rarely included, and amenities might be a phone and TV (maybe with cable); most also have free wi-fi. Motels often have a few rooms with simple kitchenettes.

Although many motels are of the bland, cookie-cutter variety, these can be good for discount lodging or when other options fall through.

Don't judge a motel solely on looks. Facades may be faded and tired, but the proprietor may keep rooms spotlessly clean. Of course, the reverse could also be true. Try to see your room before you commit.

Customs Regulations

For a complete list of US customs regulations, visit the official portal for US Customs and Border Protection (www.cbp.gov).

Duty-free allowance per person is as follows:

➜ 1L of liquor (provided you are at least 21 years old)

➜ 100 cigars and 200 cigarettes (if you are at least 18 years)

➜ $200 worth of gifts and purchases ($800 if you're a returning US citizen)

BOOK YOUR STAY ONLINE

For more accommodations reviews by Lonely Planet authors, check out http://lonelyplanet.com/hotels/. You'll find independent reviews, as well as recommendations on the best places to stay. Best of all, you can book online.

➡ If you arrive with $10,000 or more in US or foreign currency, it must be declared.

There are heavy penalties for attempting to import illegal drugs. Forbidden items include drug paraphernalia, lottery tickets, items with fake brand names, and most goods made in North Korea, Cuba, Iran, Syria and Sudan. Fruit, vegetables and other food or plant material must be declared or left in the arrival-area bins.

Discount Cards

The following passes can net you savings on museums, accommodations and some transport:

American Association of Retired Persons (AARP; www. aarp.org) For US travelers aged 50 and older.

International Student Identity Card (ISIC; www.isic.org) Discount card for full-time students 12 years and older; similar cards available for full-time teachers and for youth 30 years and under.

Student Advantage Card (www. studentadvantage.com) For US and foreign students.

Membership in the **American Automobile Association** (AAA; www.aaa.com) and reciprocal clubs in the UK, Australia and elsewhere can also earn discounts.

Electricity

AC 120V is standard; buy adapters to run most non-US electronics.

Type A
120V/60Hz

Type B
120V/60Hz

Embassies & Consulates

In addition to the following foreign embassies in Washington, DC (see www. embassy.org for a complete list), most countries have an embassy for the UN in New York City. Some countries have consulates in other large cities – check online, look under 'Consulates' in the *Yellow Pages*, or call local directory assistance.

Australian Embassy (☑20 2-797-3000; www.usa.embassy. gov.au; 1601 Massachusetts Ave NW; ☺8:30am-5pm Mon-Fri; ⓜRed Line to Farragut North)

Canadian Embassy (☑20 2-682-1740; www.can-am. gc.ca; 501 Pennsylvania Ave NW; ☺8:30am-4:40pm Mon-Fri; ⓜGreen, Yellow Lines to Archives)

French Embassy (☑202-944-6000; www.franceintheus. org; 4101 Reservoir Rd NW; ☺8:45am-12:30pm & 2:30-3:30pm Mon-Fri; ⓠD6)

German Embassy (☑202-298-4000; www.germany.info; 4645 Reservoir Rd NW; ☺8-11:45am & 1-2:30pm Mon-Thu, 8am-noon Fri; ⓠD6)

Irish Embassy (☑202-462-3939; www.embassyofireland. org; 2234 Massachusetts Ave NW; ☺9am-1pm & 2-4pm Mon-Fri; ⓜRed Line to Dupont Circle)

Mexican Embassy (☑202-728-1600; https://embamex.sre. gob.mx/eua; 1911 Pennsylvania Ave NW; ☺9am-6pm Mon-Fri; ⓜOrange, Silver, Blue Lines to Farragut West)

Netherlands Embassy (☑20 2-244-5300; www.netherlands worldwide.nl/countries/united-states; 4200 Linnean Ave NW; ☺8:30am-4:30pm Mon-Fri; ⓜRed Line to Van Ness-UDC)

New Zealand Embassy (☑20 2-328-4800; www.mfat.govt. nz/usa; 37 Observatory Circle NW; ☺8:30am-5pm Mon-Fri; ⓜRed Line to Dupont Circle then bus N2 or N4)

UK Embassy (☎202-588-6500; www.gov.uk/government/world/usa; 3100 Massachusetts Ave NW; ◷9am-4pm Mon-Fri; Ⓜ Red Line to Dupont Circle then bus N2 or N4)

Food & Drink

In a country of such size and regional variation, you could spend a lifetime eating your way across America and barely scratch the surface. Owing to such scope, dining American-style could mean many things: from munching on pulled-pork sandwiches at an old roadhouse to feasting on sustainably sourced seafood in a waterfront dining room.

Health

The USA offers excellent health care. The problem is that, unless you have good insurance, it can be prohibitively expensive. It's essential to purchase travel health insurance if your regular policy doesn't cover you when you're abroad.

Bring any medications you may need in their original containers, clearly labeled. A signed, dated letter from your physician that describes all medical conditions and medications, including generic names, is also a good idea.

Insurance

Health-care costs in the USA are extremely high. All travelers are advised to carry a valid health-insurance policy. Without insurance you may be billed the full cost of any care you receive. Costs can easily rise into the thousands of dollars, especially for emergency-room visits.If your health insurance doesn't cover you for medical expenses abroad, consider supplemental insurance. Find out in advance if your insurance plan will make payments directly to providers or reimburse you later for overseas health expenditures.

Medical Checklist

Recommended items for a medical kit:

➡ acetaminophen (Tylenol) or aspirin

➡ antibacterial ointment (eg Bactroban) for cuts and abrasions

➡ antihistamines (for hay fever and allergic reactions)

➡ anti-inflammatory drugs (eg ibuprofen)

➡ bandages, gauze, gauze rolls

➡ sunblock

➡ insect repellent for the skin

Resources

The World Health Organization publishes regular international health advisories for travelers, along with the book *International Travel and Health,* available free online at www.who.int/ith/en.

It's usually a good idea to consult your government's travel-health website before departure:

Australia (www.smartraveller.gov.au)

Canada (www.hc-sc.gc.ca, www.travel.gc.ca)

UK (www.travelhealthpro.org.uk)

Vaccinations

No vaccinations are currently recommended or required for temporary visitors to the USA. For the most up-to-date information, see the Centers for Disease Control website (www.cdc.gov).

Availability & Cost of Health Care

In general, if you have a medical emergency your best bet is to find the nearest hospital and go to its emergency room. If the problem isn't urgent, you can call a nearby hospital and ask for a referral to a local physician, which is usually much cheaper than a trip to the emergency room. Stand-alone, for-profit, urgent-care centers can be convenient, but may perform large numbers of expensive tests, even for minor illnesses.

Pharmacies are abundantly supplied, but you may find that some medications that are available over the counter in your home country (such as Ventolin, for asthma) require a prescription in the USA and, as always, if you don't have insurance to cover the cost of prescriptions, they can be shockingly expensive.

Tap Water

Tap water is drinkable virtually everywhere in the USA.

Insurance

No matter how long or short your trip, make sure you have adequate travel insurance, purchased before departure. At a minimum, you need coverage for medical emergencies and treatment, including hospital stays and an emergency flight home if necessary. Medical treatment in the USA is of the highest caliber, but the expense could bankrupt you.

PRACTICALITIES

Newspapers & Magazines The *New York Times*, *Wall Street Journal* and *USA Today* are the national newspapers; *Time* and *Newsweek* are the mainstream news magazines.

Radio & TV National Public Radio (NPR) can be found at the lower end of the FM dial. The main TV broadcasting channels are ABC, CBS, NBC, FOX and PBS (public broadcasting); the major cable channels are CNN (news), ESPN (sports), HBO (movies), Weather Channel.

DVDs DVDs are coded for Region 1 (US and Canada only).

Weights & Measures Weights are measured in ounces (oz), pounds (lb) and tons; liquids in fluid ounces (fl oz), pints, quarts and gallons (gal); and distance in feet (ft), yards (yd) and miles (mi).

You should also consider getting coverage for luggage theft or loss and trip cancellation. If you already have a home-owner's or renter's policy, see what it will cover and consider getting supplemental insurance to cover the rest. If you have prepaid a large portion of your trip, cancellation insurance is a worthwhile expense. A comprehensive travel-insurance policy that covers all these things can cost up to 10% of the total outlay of your trip.

If you will be driving, it's essential that you have liability insurance. Car-rental agencies offer insurance that covers damage to the rental vehicle and separate liability insurance, which covers damage to people and other vehicles.

Worldwide travel insurance is available at www.lonelyplanet.com/travel-insurance. You can buy, extend and claim online anytime – even if you're already on the road.

Internet Access

Travelers will have few problems staying connected in tech-savvy USA. Most hotels, guesthouses, hostels and motels have wi-fi (usually free, though luxury hotels are more likely to charge for access); ask when reserving.

Across the US, most cafes offer free wi-fi. Some cities have wi-fi-connected parks and plazas. If you're not packing a laptop or other web-accessible device, try the public library – most have public terminals (though they have time limits) in addition to wi-fi. Occasionally out-of-state residents are charged a small fee.

If you're not from the US, remember that you will need an AC adapter for your laptop, plus a plug adapter for US sockets; both are available at larger electronics shops, such as Best Buy.

Legal Matters

In everyday matters, if you are stopped by the police, bear in mind that there is no system of paying traffic or other fines on the spot. Attempting to pay a fine to an officer is frowned upon at best and may result in a charge of bribery. For traffic offenses, the police officer or highway patrol will explain the options to you. There is usually a 30-day period to pay a fine. Most matters can be handled by mail.

If you are arrested, you have a legal right to an attorney, and you are allowed to remain silent. There is no legal reason to speak to a police officer if you don't wish to, but never walk away from an officer until given permission to do so. Anyone who is arrested is legally allowed to make one phone call. If you can't afford a lawyer, a public defender will be appointed to you free of charge. Foreign visitors who don't have a lawyer, friend or family member to help them should call their embassy; the police will provide the number upon request.

As a matter of principle, the US legal system presumes a person innocent until proven guilty. Each state has its own civil and criminal laws, and what is legal in one state may be illegal in others.

Drinking

Bars and stores often ask for photo ID to prove you're of legal drinking age (21 years or over). Being 'carded' is standard practice; don't take it personally. The sale of liquor is subject to local government regulations – some counties prohibit liquor sales on Sunday, after midnight or before breakfast. In 'dry' counties, liquor sales are banned altogether.

Driving

In all states, driving under the influence of alcohol or drugs is a serious offense, subject to stiff fines and even imprisonment. A blood alcohol level of 0.08% or higher is illegal in all jurisdictions.

Marijuana & Other Substances

The states have quite different laws regarding the use of marijuana, and what's legal in one state may be illegal in others. As of mid-2017, recreational use of small amounts of marijuana (generally up to 1oz/28g) was legal in Alaska, California, Colorado, Maine, Massachusetts, Nevada, Oregon, Washington and the

District of Columbia. Another 13 states have decriminalized marijuana (treating recreational use as a civil violation similar to a minor traffic infraction), while others continue to criminalize non-medical use, punishing possession of small amounts as a misdemeanor and larger amounts as a felony. Thus, it's essential to know the local laws before lighting up – see http://norml.org/laws for a state-by-state breakdown.

Aside from marijuana, recreational drugs are prohibited by federal and state laws. Possession of any illicit drug, including cocaine, ecstasy, LSD, heroin and hashish, is a felony potentially punishable by a lengthy jail sentence. For foreigners, conviction of any drug offense is grounds for deportation.

LGBTIQ Travelers

It's never been a better time to be gay in the USA. GLBT travelers will find lots of places where they can be themselves without thinking twice. Beaches and big cities typically are the most gay-friendly destinations.

Hot Spots

Manhattan has loads of great gay bars and clubs, especially in Hells Kitchen, Chelsea and the West Village. A few hours away (by train and ferry) is Fire Island, the sandy gay mecca on Long Island. Other East Coast cities that flaunt it are Boston, Philadelphia, Washington, DC, Massachusetts' Provincetown on Cape Cod and Delaware's Rehoboth Beach. Even Maine brags a gay beach destination: Ogunquit.

In the South, there's always steamy 'Hotlanta', and Texas gets darn-right gay-friendly in Austin and parts of Houston and Dallas. In Florida, Miami and the 'Conch Republic' of Key West support thriving gay communities, though Fort Lauderdale attracts bronzed boys and girls, too. New Orleans has a lively gay scene.

In the Great Lakes region, seek out Chicago and Minneapolis. Further west, you'll find San Francisco, probably the happiest gay city in America. There's also Los Angeles and Las Vegas, where pretty much anything goes. When LA or Vegas gets to be too much, flee to the desert resorts of Palm Springs.

Lastly, for an island idyll, Hawaii is generally gay-friendly, especially in Waikiki.

Attitudes

Most major US cities have a visible and open GLBT community that is easy to connect with. Same-sex marriage was legalized nationwide by the US Supreme Court in 2015, and a 2016 Pew Research survey showed a majority of Americans (55%) supporting same-sex marriage, with millennials (71%) leading the way.

The level of acceptance varies nationwide. In some places, there is absolutely no tolerance whatsoever, and in others acceptance is predicated on GLBT people not 'flaunting' their sexual preference or identity. Bigotry still exists. In rural areas and conservative enclaves, it's unwise to be openly out, as violence and verbal abuse can sometimes occur. When in doubt, assume locals follow a 'don't ask, don't tell' policy.

Resources

The Queerest Places: A Guide to Gay and Lesbian Historic Sites by Paula Martinac is full of juicy details and history, and covers the country. Visit her blog at www.queerestplaces.com.

Advocate (www.advocate.com) Gay-oriented news website reports on business, politics, arts, entertainment and travel.

Damron (www.damron.com) Publishes the classic gay travel guides, but they're advertiser-driven and sometimes outdated.

Gay & Lesbian National Help Center (www.glnh.org) Counseling, information and referrals.

Gay Travel (www.gaytravel.com) Online guides to dozens of US destinations.

National LGBTQ Task Force (www.thetaskforce.org) National activist group's website covers news, politics and current issues.

Out Traveler (www.outtraveler.com) Gay-oriented travel articles.

Purple Roofs (www.purpleroofs.com) Lists gay-owned and gay-friendly B&Bs and hotels.

Money

ATMs

ATMs are available 24/7 at most banks, and in shopping centers, airports, grocery stores and convenience shops. Most ATMs charge a service fee of $2.50 or more per transaction and your home bank may impose additional charges. Withdrawing cash from an ATM using a credit card usually incurs a hefty fee; check with your credit-card company first.

For foreign visitors, ask your bank or credit-card company for exact information about using its cards in stateside ATMs. If you will be relying on ATMs (not a bad strategy), bring more than one card and carry them separately. The exchange rate on ATM transactions is usually as good as you'll get anywhere. Before leaving home, notify your bank and credit-card providers of your upcoming travel plans. Otherwise, you may trigger fraud alerts with atypical spending patterns, which may result in your accounts being temporarily frozen.

Credit Cards

Major credit cards are almost universally accepted. In fact, it's almost impossible to rent a car or make phone reservations without one (some airlines require your credit-card billing address to be in the USA – a hassle if you're booking domestic flights once in the country). It's highly recommended that you carry at least one credit card, if only for emergencies. Visa and MasterCard are the most widely accepted.

Money Changers

Banks are usually the best places to exchange foreign currencies. Most large city banks offer currency exchange, but banks in rural areas may not. Currency-exchange counters at the airport and in tourist centers typically have the worst rates; ask about fees and surcharges first. Travelex (www.travelex.com) is a major currency-exchange company, but American Express (www.americanexpress.com) travel offices may offer better rates.

Taxes

Five states (Alaska, Delaware, Montana, New Hampshire and Oregon) do not impose a statewide sales tax. Elsewhere, sales tax varies by state and county, and ranges from 5% to 10%. Hotel taxes vary by city from about 10% to more than 18% (in NYC).

Tipping

Tipping is *not* optional; only withhold tips in cases of outrageously bad service.

Airport & hotel porters $2 per bag, minimum per cart $5

Bartenders 15% to 20% per round, minimum per drink $1

Hotel maids $2 to $4 per night, left under the card provided

Restaurant servers 15% to 20%, unless a gratuity is already charged on the bill

Taxi drivers 10% to 15%, rounded up to the next dollar

Valet parking attendants At least $2 when handed back the keys

Opening Hours

Typical normal opening times are as follows:

Banks 8:30am–4:30pm Monday to Thursday, to 5:30pm Friday (and possibly 9am–noon Saturday)

Bars 5pm–midnight Sunday to Thursday, to 2am Friday and Saturday

Nightclubs 10pm–4am Thursday to Saturday

Post offices 9am–5pm Monday to Friday

Shopping malls 9am–9pm

Stores 9am–6pm Monday to Saturday, noon–5pm Sunday

Supermarkets 8am–8pm, some open 24 hours

Post

For postal information, including post-office locations and hours, contact the US Postal Service (www.usps.com), which is reliable and inexpensive.

For sending urgent or important letters and packages either domestically or internationally, FedEx (www.fedex.com) and UPS (www.ups.com) offer more expensive door-to-door delivery services.

Public Holidays

On the following national public holidays, banks, schools and government offices (including post offices) are closed, and transportation, museums and other services operate on a Sunday schedule. Holidays falling on a weekend are usually observed the following Monday.

New Year's Day January 1

Martin Luther King Jr Day Third Monday in January

Presidents' Day Third Monday in February

Memorial Day Last Monday in May

Independence Day July 4

Labor Day First Monday in September

Columbus Day Second Monday in October

Veterans' Day November 11

Thanksgiving Fourth Thursday in November

Christmas Day December 25

During spring break, high school and college students get a week off from school so they can overrun beach towns and resorts. This occurs throughout March and April. For students of all ages, summer vacation runs from June to August.

Safe Travel

Despite its seemingly apocalyptic list of dangers – violent crime, riots, earthquakes, tornadoes – the USA is actually a pretty safe country to visit. The greatest danger for travelers is posed by car accidents (buckle up – it's the law).

Crime

For the traveler it's not violent crime but petty theft that is the biggest concern. When possible, withdraw money from ATMs during the day, or in well-lit, busy areas at night. When driving, don't pick up hitchhikers, and lock

SMOKING

As of 2017, 24 states, the District of Columbia and many municipalities across the US were entirely smoke-free in restaurants, bars and workplaces; an additional 11 states had enacted 100% public smoking bans in at least one of these venues. You may still encounter smoky lobbies in chain hotels and budget-minded inns, but most other accommodations are smoke-free. For more detailed state-by-state info on smoking laws, see www.cdc.gov and www.no-smoke.org.

valuables in the trunk of your car before arriving at your destination. In hotels, you can secure valuables in your room or hotel safes.

Scams

Pack your street smarts. In big cities, don't forget that three-card-monte card games are always rigged, and that expensive electronics, watches and designer items sold on the cheap from sidewalk tables are either fakes or stolen.

Natural Disasters

Most areas with predictable natural disturbances – tornadoes on the Great Plains, tsunamis in Hawaii, hurricanes in the South, earthquakes in California – have an emergency-siren system to alert communities to imminent danger. These sirens are tested periodically at noon, but if you hear one and suspect trouble, turn on a local TV or radio station, which will be broadcasting safety warnings and advice. Incidentally, hurricane season runs from June to November.

The US Department of Health and Human Services (www.phe.gov) has preparedness advice, news and information on all the ways your vacation could go horribly, horribly wrong. But relax: it probably won't.

Telephone

The US phone system comprises regional service providers, competing long-distance carriers and several cell-phone and pay-phone companies. Overall, the system is very efficient, but it can be expensive. Avoid making long-distance calls on a hotel phone or on a pay phone. It's usually cheaper to use a regular landline or cell phone. Most hotels allow guests to make free local calls.

Telephone books can be handy resources: some list community services, public

transportation and things to see and do as well as phone and business listings. Online phone directories include www.411.com and www.yellowpages.com.

Cell/Mobile Phones

Tri- or quad-band phones brought from overseas will generally work in the USA. However, you should check with your service provider to see if roaming charges apply, as these will turn even local US calls into pricey international calls.

It's often cheaper to buy a compatible prepaid SIM card for the USA, such as those sold by AT&T, which you can insert into your international cell phone to get a local phone number and voicemail. Telestial (www.telestial.com) offers these services, as well as cell-phone rentals.

If you don't have a compatible phone, you can buy inexpensive, no-contract (prepaid) phones with a local number and a set number of minutes, which can be topped up at will. Virgin Mobile, T-Mobile, AT&T and other providers offer phones starting around $20, with a package of minutes starting around $20 for 400 minutes, or $30 monthly for unlimited minutes. Electronics stores such as Radio Shack and Best Buy sell these phones.

Huge swathes of rural America, including many national parks and recreation areas, don't pick up a signal. Check your provider's coverage map.

Dialing Codes

All phone numbers within the USA consist of a three-digit area code followed by a seven-digit local number.

In some locations, local calls only require you to dial the seven-digit number; in others, you will need to dial the entire 10-digit number.

If you're calling long distance, dial ☑1 plus the area code plus the phone number.

If you're not sure whether the number is local or long distance (new area codes are added all the time, confusing even residents), try one way – if it's wrong, usually a recorded voice will correct you.

Toll-free numbers begin with ☑800, 888, 877, 866, 855 and 844, and when dialing are preceded by 1. Most can only be used within the USA, some only within the state, and some only from outside the state. You won't know until you try dialing. The ☑900 series of area codes, and a few other prefixes, are for calls charged at a premium per-minute rate – phone sex, horoscopes, jokes etc.

➡ 1 is the international country code for the USA if calling from abroad (the same as Canada, but international rates apply between the two countries).

➡ Dial ☑011 to make an international call from the USA (followed by country code, area code and phone number).

➡ Dial ☑00 for assistance making international calls.

➡ Dial ☑411 for directory assistance nationwide.

➡ ☑800-555-1212 is directory assistance for toll-free numbers.

Phonecards

If you're traveling without a cell phone or in a region with limited cell service, a prepaid phonecard is an alternative solution. Phonecards typically come precharged with a fixed number of minutes that can be used on any phone, including landlines. You'll generally need to dial an 800 number and enter a PIN (personal identification number) before placing each call.

Phonecards are available from online retailers such as amazon.com and at some convenience stores. Be sure to read the fine print, as many cards contain hidden charges such as 'activation fees' or per-call 'connection fees' in addition to the per-minute rates.

Time

The USA uses daylight saving time (DST). At 2am on the second Sunday in March, clocks are set one hour ahead ('spring forward'). Then on the first Sunday of November, clocks are turned back one hour ('fall back'). Just to keep you on your toes, Arizona (except the Navajo Nation) and Hawaii don't follow DST.

The US date system is written as month/day/year. Thus, 8 June 2015 becomes 6/8/15.

Toilets

Toilets in the USA are universally of the sit-down variety and generally of high standard. Most states have rest areas with free toilets along major highways; alternatively, you can seek out toilets at gas stations, coffee shops and chain restaurants – technically these are for the use of paying customers, but you may be able to use them free of charge by asking or discreetly entering. Public buildings such as airports, train and bus stations, librar-

ies and museums usually have free toilet facilities for public use. Some towns and cities also provide public toilets, though these are not widespread.

Tourist Information

For links to the official tourism websites of every US state and most major cities, see www.visit-usa.com. The similarly named www.visit theusa.com is jam-packed with itinerary planning ideas and other useful info.

Any tourist office worth contacting has a website, where you can download free travel e-guides. They also field phone calls; some local offices maintain daily lists of hotel-room availability, but few offer reservation services. All tourist offices have self-service racks of brochures and discount coupons; some also sell maps and books.

State-run 'welcome centers,' usually placed along interstate highways, tend to have free state road maps, brochures and other travel planning materials. These offices are usually open longer hours, including weekends and holidays.

Many cities have an official convention and visitors bureau (CVB). These sometimes double as tourist bureaus, but since their main focus is drawing the business trade, CVBs can be less useful for independent travelers.

Keep in mind that in smaller towns where the local chamber of commerce runs the tourist bureau, its lists of hotels, restaurants and services usually mention only chamber members; the town's cheapest options may be missing.

Similarly in prime tourist destinations, some private 'tourist bureaus' are really agents that book hotel rooms and tours on commission. They may offer excellent

service and deals, but you'll get what they're selling and nothing else.

Travelers with Disabilities

If you have a physical disability, the USA can be an accommodating place. The Americans with Disabilities Act (ADA) requires that all public buildings, private buildings built after 1993 (including hotels, restaurants, theaters and museums) and public transit be wheelchair accessible. However, call ahead to confirm what is available. Some local tourist offices publish detailed accessibility guides.

Telephone companies offer relay operators, available via teletypewriter (TTY) numbers, for the hearing impaired. Most banks provide ATM instructions in Braille and via earphone jacks for hearing-impaired customers. All major airlines, Greyhound buses and Amtrak trains will assist travelers with disabilities; just describe your needs when making reservations at least 48 hours in advance. Service animals (guide dogs) are allowed to accompany passengers, but bring documentation.

Some car-rental agencies, such as Budget and Hertz, offer hand-controlled vehicles and vans with wheelchair lifts at no extra charge, but you must reserve them well in advance. **Wheelchair Getaways** (www.wheel chairgetaways.com) rents accessible vans throughout the USA. In many cities and towns, public buses are accessible to wheelchair riders and will 'kneel' if you are unable to use the steps; just let the driver know that you need the lift or ramp.

Most cities have taxi companies with at least one accessible van, though you'll have to call ahead. Cities with underground transport have varying levels of facilities such as elevators for passengers needing assistance – DC has the best network (every station has an elevator), while NYC has elevators in about a quarter of its stations.

Many national and some state parks and recreation areas have wheelchair-accessible paved, graded-dirt or boardwalk trails. US citizens and permanent residents with permanent disabilities are entitled to a free 'America the Beautiful' Access Pass. Go online (www.nps.gov/findapark/passes.htm) for details.

For tips on travel and thoughtful insight on traveling with a disability, check out online posts by Lonely Planet's Accessible Travel Manager: twitter.com/martin_heng.

Some helpful resources for travelers with disabilities:

Disabled Sports USA (www.disabledsportsusa.org) Offers sport, adventure and recreation programs for those with disabilities. Also publishes *Challenge* magazine.

Flying Wheels Travel (www.flyingwheelstravel.com) A full-service travel agency, highly recommended for those with mobility issues or chronic illness.

Mobility International USA (www.miusa.org) Advises USA-bound disabled travelers on mobility issues, and promotes the global participation of people with disabilities in international exchange and travel programs.

Visas

Visitors from Canada, the UK, Australia, New Zealand, Japan and many EU countries don't need visas for stays of less than 90 days. Citizens of other nations should check http://travel.state.gov.

Be warned that all visa information is highly subject to change. US entry requirements keep evolving as national security regulations change. All travelers should double-check current visa and passport regulations *before* coming to the USA.

The US State Department (www.travel.state.gov) maintains the most comprehensive visa information, providing downloadable forms, lists of US consulates abroad and even visa wait times calculated by country.

Visa Applications

Apart from most Canadian citizens and those entering under the Visa Waiver Program, all foreign visitors will need to obtain a visa from a US consulate or embassy abroad. Most applicants must schedule a personal interview, to which you must bring all your documentation and proof of fee payment. Wait times for interviews vary, but afterward, barring problems, visa issuance takes from a few days to a few weeks.

➡ Your passport must be valid for the entirety of your intended stay in the USA, and sometimes six months longer, depending on your country of citizenship. You'll need a recent photo (2in by 2in) and you must pay a nonrefundable $160 processing fee, plus in a few cases an additional visa-issuance reciprocity fee. You'll also need to fill out the online DS-160 nonimmigrant visa electronic application.

➡ Visa applicants are required to show documents of financial stability (or evidence that a US resident will provide financial support), a round-trip or

VISA WAIVER PROGRAM

Currently under the Visa Waiver Program (VWP), citizens of the following countries may enter the USA without a visa for stays of 90 days or less: Andorra, Australia, Austria, Belgium, Brunei, Chile, Czech Republic, Denmark, Estonia, Finland, France, Germany, Greece, Hungary, Iceland, Ireland, Italy, Japan, Latvia, Liechtenstein, Lithuania, Luxembourg, Malta, Monaco, the Netherlands, New Zealand, Norway, Portugal, San Marino, Singapore, Slovakia, Slovenia, South Korea, Spain, Sweden, Switzerland, Taiwan and the UK.

If you are a citizen of a VWP country, you do not need a visa *only if* you have a passport that meets current US standards *and* you have gotten approval from the Electronic System for Travel Authorization (ESTA) in advance. Register online with the Department of Homeland Security at https://esta.cbp.dhs.gov/esta at least 72 hours before arrival; once travel authorization is approved, your registration is valid for two years. The fee, payable online, is $14.

Visitors from VWP countries must still produce at the port of entry all the same evidence as for a nonimmigrant visa application. They must demonstrate that their trip is for 90 days or less, and that they have a round-trip or onward ticket, adequate funds to cover the trip and binding obligations abroad.

In addition, the same 'grounds for exclusion and deportation' apply, except that you will have no opportunity to appeal or apply for an exemption. If you are denied under the Visa Waiver Program at a US point of entry, you will have to use your onward or return ticket on the next available flight.

onward ticket and 'binding obligations' that will ensure their return home, such as family ties, a home or a job. Because of these requirements, those planning to travel through other countries before arriving in the USA are generally better off applying for a US visa while they're still in their home country, rather than while on the road.

→ The most common visa is a nonimmigrant visitor's visa: type B-1 for business purposes, B-2 for tourism or visiting friends and relatives. A visitor's visa is good for multiple entries over one or five years, and specifically prohibits the visitor from taking paid employment in the USA. The validity period depends on what country you are from. The actual length of time you'll be allowed to stay in the USA is determined by US immigration at the port of entry.

→ If you're coming to the USA to work or study, you will need a different type of visa, and the company or institution to which you are going should make the arrangements.

→ Other categories of nonimmigrant visas include an F-1 visa for students attending a course at a recognized institution; an H-1, H-2 or H-3 visa for temporary employment; and a J-1 visa for exchange visitors in approved programs.

Grounds for Exclusion & Deportation

If on your visa application form you admit to being a subversive, smuggler, prostitute, drug addict, terrorist or an ex-Nazi, you may be excluded. You can also be refused a visa or entry to the USA if you have a 'communicable disease of public health significance' or a criminal record, or if you've

ever made a false statement in connection with a US visa application. However, if any of these last three apply, you're still able to request an exemption; many people are granted them and then given visas.

Communicable diseases include tuberculosis, the Ebola virus, gonorrhea, syphilis, infectious leprosy and any disease deemed subject to quarantine by Presidential Executive Order. US immigration doesn't test people for disease, but officials at the point of entry may question anyone about his or her health. They can exclude anyone whom they believe has a communicable disease, perhaps because they are carrying medical documents, prescriptions or medicine. Being an IV drug user is also grounds for exclusion. Visitors may be deported if US immigration finds out they have HIV but did not declare it. Being HIV-positive is no longer grounds for deportation, but failing to provide accurate information on the visa application is.

The US immigration department has a very broad definition of a criminal record. If you've ever been arrested or charged with an offense, that's a criminal record, even if you were acquitted or discharged without conviction. Don't attempt to enter through the VWP if you have a criminal record of any kind; assume US authorities will find out about it.

Often United States Citizenship and Immigration Services (USCIS) will grant an exemption (a 'waiver of ineligibility') to a person who would normally be subject to exclusion, but this requires referral to a regional immigration office and can take some time (allow at least two months). If you're tempted to conceal something, remember that US immigration is strictest of all about false statements. It will often view favorably an applicant who admits to an old criminal

charge or a communicable disease, but it is extremely harsh on anyone who has ever attempted to mislead it, even on minor points. After you're admitted to the USA, any evidence of a false statement to US immigration is grounds for deportation.

Prospective visitors to whom grounds of exclusion may apply should consider their options *before* applying for a visa.

Entering the USA

→ Everyone arriving in the US needs to fill out the US customs declaration. US and Canadian citizens, along with eligible foreign nationals participating in the Visa Waiver Program, can complete this procedure electronically at an APC (Automated Passport Control) kiosk upon disembarking. All others must fill out a paper customs declaration, which is usually handed out on the plane. Have it completed before you approach the immigration desk. For the question, 'US Street Address,' give the address where you will spend the first night (a hotel address is fine).

→ No matter what your visa says, US immigration officers have an absolute authority to refuse admission to the country, or to impose conditions on admission. They may ask about your plans and whether you have sufficient funds; it's a good idea to list an itinerary, produce an onward or round-trip ticket and have at least one major credit card.

→ The Department of Homeland Security's registration program, called Office of Biometric Identity Management, includes every port of entry and nearly every foreign visitor to the USA. For most visitors (excluding, for now, most Canadian and some Mexican citizens), registration consists of having a digital photo and electronic (inkless) fingerprints taken; the process takes less than a minute.

Visa Extensions

To stay in the USA longer than the date stamped on your passport, go to a local USCIS (www.uscis.gov) office to apply for an extension well before the stamped date. If the date has passed, your best chance will be to bring a US citizen with you to vouch for your character, and to produce lots of other verification that you are not trying to work illegally and have enough money to support yourself. However, if you've overstayed, the most likely scenario is that you will be deported. Travelers who enter the USA under the VWP are ineligible for visa extensions.

Short-Term Departures & Re-Entry

➡ It's temptingly easy to make trips across the border to Canada or Mexico, but on return to the USA, non-Americans will be subject to the full immigration procedure.

➡ Always take your passport when you cross the border.

➡ If your immigration card still has plenty of time on it, you will probably be able to re-enter using the same one, but if it has nearly expired, you will have to apply for a new card, and border control may want to see your onward air ticket, sufficient funds and so on.

➡ Traditionally, a quick trip across the border has been a way to extend your stay in the USA without applying for an extension at a USCIS office. Don't assume this still works. First, make sure you hand in your old immigration card to the immigration authorities when you leave the USA, and when you return make sure you have all the necessary application documentation from when you first entered the country. US immigration will be very suspicious of anyone who leaves for a few days and returns immediately hoping for a new six-month stay; expect to be questioned closely.

➡ Citizens of most Western countries will not need a visa to visit Canada, so it's really not a problem at all to cross to the Canadian side of Niagara Falls, detour up to Québec, or pass through on the way to Alaska.

➡ Travelers entering the USA by bus from Canada may be closely scrutinized. A round-trip ticket that takes you back to Canada will most likely make US immigration feel less suspicious.

➡ Mexico has a visa-free zone along most of its border with the USA, including the Baja Peninsula and border towns such as Tijuana and Ciudad Juárez. As of 2017, residents of the US, Canada, the UK, Japan, and Schengen countries (Europe) no longer need a tourist visa anywhere in Mexico. Others may need a Mexican visa or tourist card to travel beyond the border zone.

Volunteering

Volunteer opportunities abound in the USA, and they can be a great way to break up a long trip. They can also provide truly memorable experiences: you'll get to interact with people, society and the land in ways you never would by just passing through.

Casual, drop-in volunteer opportunities are plentiful in big cities, where you can socialize with locals while helping out nonprofit organizations. Check weekly alternative newspapers for calendar listings, or browse the free classified ads online at Craigslist (www.craigslist.org). The public website Serve.gov and private websites Idealist.org and VolunteerMatch (www.volunteermatch.org) offer free searchable databases of short- and long-term volunteer opportunities nationwide.

More formal volunteer programs, especially those designed for international travelers, typically charge a hefty fee of $250 to $1000, depending on the length of the program and what amenities are included (eg housing, meals). None cover the costs of travel to the USA.

Recommended volunteer organizations:

Habitat for Humanity (www.habitat.org) Focuses on building affordable housing for those in need.

Sierra Club (www.sierraclub.org) 'Volunteer vacations' restore wilderness areas and maintain trails, including in national parks and nature preserves.

Volunteers for Peace (www.vfp.org) Grassroots, multiweek volunteer projects emphasize manual labor and international exchange.

Wilderness Volunteers (www.wildernessvolunteers.org) Weeklong trips helping maintain national-park lands and outdoor recreation areas.

World Wide Opportunities on Organic Farms USA (www.wwoofusa.org) Represents more than 2000 organic farms in all 50 states that host volunteer workers in exchange for meals and accommodations, with opportunities for both short- and long-term stays.

Women Travelers

Women traveling alone or in groups should not expect to encounter any particular problems in the USA. The community website www.journeywoman.com facilitates women exchanging travel tips, and has links to other helpful resources. The booklet *Her Own Way*, published by the Canadian government, is filled with general travel advice, useful for any woman; click to travel.gc.ca/travelling/publications/her-own-way to download the PDF or read it online.

Some women carry a whistle, mace or cayenne-pepper spray in case of assault. If you purchase a spray, contact a police station to find out about local regulations. Laws regarding sprays vary from state to state, and federal law prohibits them being carried on planes.

If you're assaulted, consider calling a rape-crisis hotline before calling the police, unless you are in immediate danger, in which case you should call 911. But be aware that not all police have as much sensitivity training or experience assisting sexual-assault survivors, whereas staff at rape crisis centers will tirelessly advocate on your behalf and act as a link to other community services, including hospitals and the police. Telephone books have listings of local rape-crisis centers, or contact the 24-hour National Sexual Assault Hotline on ☎800-656-4673. Alternatively, go straight to a hospital emergency room.

National advocacy groups that may be useful:

National Organization for Women (www.now.org) A grassroots movement fighting for women's rights.

Planned Parenthood (www.plannedparenthood.org) Offers referrals to women's health clinics throughout the country.

Work

If you are a foreigner in the USA with a standard non-immigrant visitor's visa, you are expressly forbidden to partake in paid work and will be deported if you're caught working illegally. Employers are required to establish the bona fides of their employees or face fines, making it much tougher than it once was for a foreigner to get work.

To work legally, foreigners need to apply for a work visa before leaving home. A J-1 visa, for exchange visitors, is issued to young people (age limits vary) for study, student vacation employment, work in summer camps and short-term traineeships with a specific employer. One organization that can help arrange international student exchanges, work placements and J-1 visas is International Exchange Programs (IEP), which operates in Australia (www.iep.com.au) and New Zealand (www.iep.co.nz).

For nonstudent jobs, temporary or permanent, you need to be sponsored by a US employer, who will have to arrange an H-category visa. These are not easy to obtain, since the employer has to prove that no US citizen or permanent resident is available to do the job.

Seasonal work is possible in national parks and at tourist attractions and ski resorts. Contact park concessionaire businesses, local chambers of commerce and ski-resort management. Lonely Planet's *Gap Year Book* has more ideas on how best to combine work and travel.

Au Pair in America (www.aupairinamerica.com) Find a job as an au pair in the USA.

Camp America (www.campamerica.co.uk) Offers opportunities to work in a youth summer camp.

Council on International Educational Exchange (www.ciee.org) CIEE helps international visitors find USA-based jobs through its four work-exchange programs (Work & Travel USA, Internship USA, Professional Career Training USA and Camp Exchange USA).

InterExchange (www.interexchange.org) Camp, au pair and other work-exchange programs.

Transportation

GETTING THERE & AWAY

Flights, cars and tours can be booked online at lonely planet.com/bookings.

Entering the Country

If you're flying to the US, the first airport that you land in is where you must go through immigration and customs, even if you're continuing on the flight to another destination. Upon arrival, all international visitors must register with the Department of Homeland Security's Office of Biometric Identity Management program, which entails having your fingerprints scanned and a digital photo taken.

Once you go through immigration, you collect your baggage and pass through customs. If you have nothing to declare, you'll probably

clear customs without a baggage search, but don't assume this. If you're continuing on the same plane or connecting to another one, it's your responsibility to get your bags to the right place. There are usually airline representatives just outside the customs area who can help you.

If you're a single parent, grandparent or guardian traveling with anyone under 18 years of age, carry proof of legal custody or a notarized letter from the non-accompanying parent(s) authorizing the trip. This isn't required, but the USA is concerned with thwarting child abduction, and not having authorizing papers could cause delays or even result in being denied admittance to the country.

Passports

Every visitor entering the USA from abroad needs a passport. Visitors from most countries only require

a passport valid for their intended period of stay in the USA. However, nationals of certain countries require a passport valid for at least six months longer than their intended stay. For a country-by-country list, see the latest 'Six-Month Club Update' from US Customs and Border Protection. If your passport does not meet current US standards, you'll be turned back at the border. All visitors wishing to enter the USA under the Visa Waiver Program must have an e-Passport with a digital photo and an integrated RFID chip containing biometric data.

Air

Airports

The USA has more than 375 domestic airports, but only a baker's dozen form the main international gateways. Many other airports are called

---

CLIMATE CHANGE & TRAVEL

Every form of transport that relies on carbon-based fuel generates CO_2, the main cause of human-induced climate change. Modern travel is dependent on airplanes, which might use less fuel per mile per person than most cars but travel much greater distances. The altitude at which aircraft emit gases (including CO_2) and particles also contributes to their climate change impact. Many websites offer 'carbon calculators' that allow people to estimate the carbon emissions generated by their journey and, for those who wish to do so, to offset the impact of the greenhouse gases emitted with contributions to portfolios of climate-friendly initiatives throughout the world. Lonely Planet offsets the carbon footprint of all staff and author travel.

'international' but may have only a few flights from other countries – typically Mexico or Canada. Even travel to an international gateway sometimes requires a connection in another gateway city (eg London–Los Angeles flights may involve transferring in Houston).

The USA does not have a national air carrier. The largest USA-based airlines are American, Delta, United and Southwest.

International gateway airports in the USA:

Atlanta Hartsfield-Jackson International Airport (ATL, Atlanta;☏800-897-1910; www.atl.com)

Boston Logan International Airport (BOS;☏800-235-6426; www.massport.com/logan)

Chicago O'Hare International Airport (ORD;☏800-832-6352; www.flychicago.com)

Dallas-Fort Worth International Airport (DFW;☏972-973-3112; www.dfwairport.com; 2400 Aviation Dr)

Honolulu International Airport (HNL;☏808-836-6411; http:// hawaii.gov/hnl; 300 Rodgers Blvd; ☎)

Houston George Bush Intercontinental Airport (IAH;☏281-230-3100; www.fly2houston. com/iah; 2800 N Terminal Rd, off I-59, Beltway 8 or I-45; ☎)

Los Angeles International Airport (LAX; www.lawa.org/ welcomeLAX.aspx; 1 World Way)

Miami International Airport (MIA;☏305-876-7000; www. miami-airport.com; 2100 NW 42nd Ave)

New York JFK International Airport (JFK;☏718-244-4444; www.kennedyairport.com; ☒A to Howard Beach or E, J/Z to Sutphin Blvd-Archer Ave then, ☒JFK Airtrain)

Newark Liberty International Airport (EWR;☏973-961-6000; www.panynj.gov)

San Francisco International Airport (SFO; www.flysfo.com; S McDonnell Rd)

Seattle-Tacoma International Airport (SEA;☏206-787-5388; www.portseattle.org/Sea-Tac; 17801 International Blvd; ☎)

Washington Dulles International Airport (IAD;☏703-572-2700; www.flydulles.com)

Land

Border Crossings

CANADA

Bus

Greyhound has direct connections between main cities in Canada and the northern USA, but you may have to transfer to a different bus at the border. Book through Greyhound USA (www.greyhound.com) or Greyhound Canada (www.greyhound.ca).

Car & Motorcycle

If you're driving into the USA from Canada, bring the vehicle's registration papers, proof of liability insurance and your home driver's license. Canadian driver's licenses and auto insurance are typically valid in the USA, and vice versa.

If your papers are in order, taking your own car across the US–Canadian border is usually fast and easy, but occasionally the authorities of either country decide to search a car *thoroughly*. On weekends and holidays, especially in summer, traffic at the main border crossings can be heavy and waits long.

Train

Amtrak (www.amtrak.com) and VIA Rail Canada (www. viarail.ca) operate daily services between Montreal and New York, Toronto and New York (via Niagara Falls), and Vancouver and Seattle. Customs inspections occur at the border.

MEXICO

Bus

Greyhound USA (www.greyhound.com) and Greyhound México (www.greyhound.

com.mx) operate direct bus routes between main towns in Mexico and the USA.

For connections to smaller destinations south of the border, there are numerous domestic Mexican bus companies.

Car & Motorcycle

If you're driving into the USA from Mexico, bring the vehicle's registration papers, proof of liability insurance and your driver's license from your home country. Mexican driver's licenses are valid, but it's worth having an International Driving Permit (IDP).

Very few car-rental companies will let you take a car from the US into Mexico. US auto insurance is not valid in Mexico, so even a short trip into Mexico's border region requires you to buy Mexican car insurance, available for around \$25 per day at most border crossings, as well as from AAA (www.aaa.com).

For a longer driving trip into Mexico (25km or more beyond the border), you'll need a Mexican *permiso de importación temporal de vehículos* (temporary vehicle import permit), available at the border for \$60 or online from Banjercito (www.banjercito. com.mx/registroVehiculos) for \$53.

Sea

If you're interested in taking a cruise ship to America, as well as to other interesting ports of call, a good specialized travel agency is Cruise Web (www.cruiseweb.com).

You can also travel to and from the USA on a freighter, though it will be much slower and less cushy than a cruise. Nevertheless, freighters aren't spartan (some advertise cruise-ship-level amenities), and they are much cheaper (sometimes by half). Trips range from a week to two months; stops at interim ports are usually quick.

For more information, try Cruise and Freighter Travel Association (www.travltips.com), which has listings for freighter cruises and other boat travel.

Tours

Group travel can be an enjoyable way to get to and tour around the USA.Reputable tour companies:

American Holidays (www.amer icanholidays.com) Ireland-based company specializes in tours to North America.

Contiki (www.contiki.com) Party-hardy sightseeing tour-bus vacations for 18 to 35 year olds.

North America Travel Service (www.northamericatravelservice. co.uk) UK-based tour operator arranges luxury US trips.

Trek America (www.trekamerica. com) Active outdoor adventures for 18 to 38 year olds.

GETTING AROUND

Air

When time is tight, book a flight. The domestic air system is extensive and reliable, with dozens of competing airlines, hundreds of airports and thousands of flights daily. Flying is usually more expensive than traveling by bus, train or car, but it's the way to go when you're in a hurry.

Main 'hub' airports in the USA include all international gateways plus many other large cities. Most cities and towns have a local or county airport, but you usually have to travel via a hub airport to reach them.

Airlines in the USA

Overall, air travel in the USA is very safe (much safer than driving out on the nation's highways); for comprehensive details by carrier, check out airsafe.com.

The main domestic carriers:

Alaska Airlines (www.alaskaair.com) Has direct flights to Anchorage from Seattle, Chicago, Los Angeles and Denver. It also flies between many towns within Alaska, including daily northbound and southbound flights year-round through southeast Alaska, with stops at all main towns, including Ketchikan and Juneau.

American Airlines (www.aa.com) Nationwide service.

Delta Air Lines (www.delta.com) Nationwide service.

Frontier Airlines (www.flyfrontier.com) Denver-based airline with service across the continental USA.

Hawaiian Airlines (www.hawaiianairlines.com) Nonstop flights between the Hawaiian islands and various spots on the mainland.

JetBlue Airways (www.jetblue.com) New York City–based airline serving many East Coast cities, plus other destinations across the USA.

Southwest Airlines (www.southwest.com) Dallas-based budget airline with service across the continental USA.

Spirit Airlines (www.spirit.com) Florida-based budget airline; serves many US gateway cities.

United Airlines (www.united.com) Nationwide service.

Virgin America (www.virginamerica.com) California-based airline serving over two dozen cities, from Honolulu to Boston.

Air Passes

International travelers who plan on doing a lot of flying might consider buying a North American air pass. Passes are normally available only to non–North American citizens, and they must be purchased in conjunction with an international ticket. Conditions and cost structures can be complicated, but all passes include a certain number of domestic flights (from as few as two to as many

as 16, depending on airline network) that typically must be used within a 60-day period. Often you must plan your itinerary in advance, but sometimes dates (and even destinations) can be left open. Talk with a travel agent to determine if an air pass will save you money. Networks offering air passes include Star Alliance (www.staralliance.com), One World (www.oneworld.com) and Skyteam (www.skyteam.com).

Bicycle

Regional bicycle touring is popular. It means coasting along winding backroads (because bicycles are often not permitted on freeways) and calculating progress in miles per day, not miles per hour. Cyclists must follow the same rules of the road as automobiles, but don't expect drivers to respect your right of way. Better World Club (www.betterworldclub.com) offers a bicycle roadside-assistance program.

For epic cross-country journeys, get the support of a tour operator; it's about two months of dedicated pedaling coast to coast.

For advice, route maps, guided tours and lists of local bike clubs and repair shops, browse the websites of Adventure Cycling (www.adventurecycling.org) and the League of American Bicyclists (www.bikeleague.org). If you're bringing your own bike to the USA, be sure to call around to check oversize luggage prices and restrictions. Amtrak trains and Greyhound buses will transport bikes within the USA, sometimes charging extra.

It's not hard to buy a bike once you're here and resell it before you leave. Every city and town has bike shops; if you prefer a cheaper, used bicycle, try garage sales, bulletin boards at hostels and colleges, or the free classified ads at Craigslist (craigslist.org). These are also the best places to sell your bike, though stores selling used bikes may also buy from you.

Long-term bike rentals are also easy to find. Rates run from $100 per week and up, and a credit-card authorization for several hundred dollars is usually necessary as a security deposit.

Some cities are more amenable to bicycles than others, but most have at least a few dedicated bike lanes and paths, and bikes can usually be carried on public transportation.

Boat

There is no river or canal public-transportation system in the USA, but there are many smaller, often state-run, coastal ferry services, which provide efficient, scenic links to the many islands off both coasts. Most larger ferries will transport private cars, motorcycles and bicycles.

The most spectacular coastal ferry runs are on the southeastern coast of Alaska and along the Inside Passage. The Great Lakes have several islands that can be visited only by boat, such as Mackinac Island, MI; the Apostle Islands, off Wisconsin; and remote Isle Royale National Park, MI. Off the Pacific coast, ferries serve the scenic San Juan Islands in Washington and Catalina Island in California.

Bus

To save money, travel by bus, particularly between major towns and cities. Middle-class Americans prefer to fly or drive, but buses let you see the countryside and meet folks along the way. As a rule, buses are reliable, cleanish and comfortable, with air-conditioning, barely reclining seats, lavatories and no smoking.

Greyhound (www.greyhound.com) is the major long-distance bus company, with routes throughout the USA and Canada. To improve efficiency and profitability, Greyhound has discontinued service to many small towns; routes generally trace major highways and stop at larger population centers. To reach country towns on rural roads, you may need to transfer to local or county bus systems; Greyhound can usually provide their contact information. Greyhound often has excellent online fares – web-only deals will net you substantial discounts over buying at a ticket counter.

Competing with Greyhound are the 75-plus franchises of Trailways (www.trailways.com). Trailways may not be as useful as Greyhound for long trips, but fares can be competitive. Other long-distance bus lines that offer decent fares and free wi-fi (that doesn't always work) include Megabus (www.megabus.com) and BoltBus (www.boltbus.com).

Both operate routes along the East and West Coasts, with Megabus also offering service in Texas and the Great Lakes region.

Most baggage has to be checked in; label it loudly and clearly to avoid it getting lost. Larger items, including skis, surfboards and bicycles, can be transported, but there may be an extra charge. Call to check.

The frequency of bus services varies widely, depending on the route. Despite the elimination of many tiny destinations, non-express Greyhound buses still stop every 50 to 100 miles to pick up passengers, and long-distance buses will stop for meal breaks and driver changes.

Many bus stations are clean and safe, but some are in dodgy areas. If you arrive in the evening, it's worth spending the money on a taxi. Some towns have just a flag stop. If you are boarding at one of these, pay the driver with exact change.

Most cities and larger towns have dependable local bus systems, though they are often designed for commuters and provide limited service in the evening and on weekends. Costs range from free to between $1 and $4 per ride.

Costs

For lower fares on Greyhound, purchase tickets ahead of time (purchasing 14 or more days in advance usually nets the best bar-

BUS FARES

Some sample standard one-way adult fares and trip times on Greyhound:

SERVICE	PRICE ($)	DURATION (HR)
Boston–Philadelphia	31-58	7
Chicago–New Orleans	89-164	24
Los Angeles–San Francisco	24-48	8
New York–Chicago	56-102	18
New York–San Francisco	139-318	72
Washington, DC–Miami	72-145	25

gains). Special promotional fares are regularly offered on Greyhound's website, especially for online bookings (see www.greyhound.com/promos for details).

As for other Greyhound discounts: tickets for children aged two to 16 are discounted 20% during non-peak periods; seniors over 62 years get a whopping 5% off; and students get 10% off if they have purchased the $23 Student Advantage Discount Card (www.studentadvantage.com).

Reservations

Tickets for most trips on Greyhound, Trailways, Megabus and BoltBus can be bought online. You can print all tickets at home or in the case of Megabus or BoltBus, simply show ticket receipts through an email on a smartphone. Greyhound also allows customers to pick up tickets at the terminal using 'Will Call' service.

Seating is normally first-come, first-served. Greyhound recommends arriving an hour before departure to get a seat.

Car & Motorcycle

For information on driving, see the Driving in the USA chapter (p1190) and the Road Trips & Scenic Drives chapter (p40).

Local Transportation

Except in large US cities, public transportation is rarely the most convenient option for travelers, and coverage can be sparse to outlying towns and suburbs. However, it is usually cheap, safe and reliable.

More than two-thirds of the states in the nation have adopted 511 as an all-purpose local-transportation help line.

TRAIN FARES

Sample standard, one-way, adult coach-class fares and trip times on Amtrak's long-distance routes:

SERVICE	PRICE ($)	DURATION (HR)
Chicago–New Orleans	133	20
Los Angeles–San Antonio	151	29
New York–Chicago	108	19
New York–Los Angeles	232	63
Seattle–Oakland	109	23
Washington, DC–Miami	147	23

Subway

The largest systems are in New York, Chicago, Boston, Washington, DC, the San Francisco Bay Area, Philadelphia, Los Angeles and Atlanta. Other cities have small, one- or two-line rail systems that mainly serve downtown areas.

Taxis & Ride Sharing Services

Taxis are metered, with flag-fall charges of around $3 to start, plus $2 to $3 per mile. They charge extra for waiting and handling baggage, and drivers expect a 10% to 15% tip. Taxis cruise the busiest areas in large cities; otherwise, it's easiest to phone and order one.

Ride-sharing companies such as Uber (www.uber.com) and Lyft (www.lyft.com) have seen a recent surge in popularity as an alternative to taxis.

Train

Amtrak (www.amtrak.com) has an extensive rail system throughout the USA, with Amtrak's Thruway buses providing connections to and from the rail network to some smaller centers and national parks. Compared with other modes of travel, trains are rarely the quickest, cheapest, timeliest or most convenient option, but they turn the journey into a

relaxing, social and scenic all-American experience, especially on western routes, where double-decker Superliner trains boast spacious lounge cars with panoramic windows.

Amtrak has several long-distance lines traversing the nation east to west, and even more running north to south. These connect all of America's biggest cities and many of its smaller ones. Long-distance services (on named trains) mostly operate daily on these routes, but some run only three to five days per week. See Amtrak's website for detailed route maps.

Commuter trains provide faster, more frequent services on shorter routes, especially the northeast corridor from Boston, MA, to Washington, DC. Amtrak's high-speed Acela Express trains are the most expensive, and rail passes are not valid on these trains. Other commuter rail lines include those serving the Lake Michigan shoreline near Chicago, IL, major cities on the West Coast and the Miami, FL, area.

Classes & Costs

Amtrak fares vary according to the type of train and seating. On long-distance lines, you can travel in coach seats (reserved or unreserved), business class, or 1st class, which includes all sleeping compartments. Sleeping

ALL ABOARD!

Who doesn't enjoy the steamy puff and whistle of a mighty locomotive as glorious scenery streams by? Dozens of historic narrow-gauge railroads still operate today as attractions, rather than as transportation. Most trains only run in the warmer months, and they can be extremely popular – so book ahead.

Here are some of the best:

1880 Train (605-574-2222; www.1880train.com; 222 Railroad Ave; adult/child round-trip $29/14; mid-May–Dec) Classic steam train running through rugged Black Hills country.

Cass Scenic Railroad (www.cassrailroad.com) Nestled in the Appalachian Mountains in West Virginia.

Cumbres & Toltec Scenic Railroad Depot (888-286-2737; www.cumbrestoltec.com; 5234 Hwy 285; trips from adult/child $99/59) Living, moving museum from Chama, NM, into Colorado's Rocky Mountains.

Durango & Silverton Narrow Gauge Railroad (970-247-2733; www.durangotrain.com; 479 Main Ave; return adult/child 4-11yr from $89/55; May-Oct) Ends at historic mining town Silverton in Colorado's Rocky Mountains.

Great Smoky Mountains Railroad (800-872-4681; www.gsmr.com; 226 Everett St; Nantahala Gorge trip adult from $55, child 2-12yr from $31) Rides from Bryson City, NC, through the Great Smoky Mountains.

Mt Hood Railroad (800-872-4661; www.mthoodrr.com; 110 Railroad Ave; excursions adult/child from $35/30) Winds through the scenic Columbia River Gorge outside Portland, OR.

Skunk Train (707-964-6371; www.skunktrain.com; 100 W Laurel St; adult/child $84/42; 9am-3pm) Runs between Fort Bragg, CA, on the coast and Willits further inland, passing through redwoods.

White Pass & Yukon Route Railroad (800-343-7373; www.wpyr.com; 231 2nd Ave; May-Sep) Klondike gold-rush-era railroad has departures from Skagway, AK, and Fraser (British Columbia), and Carcross and Whitehorse (Yukon) in Canada.

Also worth riding are the vintage steam and diesel locomotives of Arizona's **Grand Canyon Railway** (reservations 800-843-8724; www.thetrain.com; 233 N Grand Canyon Bvd, Railway Depot; round-trip adult/child from $79/47), New York State's **Delaware & Ulster Railroad** (800-225-4132; www.durr.org; 43510 Rte 28, Arkville; adult/child $18/12; Sat & Sun Jul-Oct) and Colorado's **Pikes Peak Cog Railway** (719-685-5401; www.cograilway.com; 515 Ruxton Ave; round-trip adult/child $40/22; 8am-5:20pm May-Oct, reduced hours Nov-Apr).

cars include simple bunks (called 'roomettes'), bedrooms with en-suite facilities and suites sleeping four with two bathrooms. Sleeping-car rates include meals in the dining car, which offers everyone sit-down meal service (pricey if not included). Food service on commuter lines, when it exists, consists of sandwich and snack bars. Bringing your own food and drink is recommended on all trains.

Various one-way, round-trip and touring fares are available from Amtrak, with discounts of 15% for students with a valid ID and

seniors aged 62 and over, and 50% for children aged two to 12 when accompanied by a paying adult. AAA members get 10% off. Web-only 'SmartFares' offer 30% discounts on certain undersold routes (destinations change weekly; see www.aaa.com for details).

Generally the earlier you book, the lower the price. To get many of the standard discounts, you need to reserve at least three days in advance. If you want to take an Acela Express or Metroliner train, avoid peak commute times and aim for weekends.

Amtrak Vacations (www.amtrakvacations.com) offers vacation packages that include car rental, hotels, tours and attractions. Air-Rail packages let you travel by train in one direction, then return by plane the other way.

Reservations

Reservations can be made any time from 11 months in advance up to the day of departure. Space on most trains is limited, and certain routes can be crowded, especially during summer and holiday periods, so it's a good idea to book as far in advance as you can. This also gives you the best chance of fare discounts.

Rail Passes

Amtrak's USA Rail Pass offers coach-class travel for 15 ($459), 30 ($689) or 45 ($899) days, with travel limited to eight, 12 or 18 one-way 'segments,' respectively. A segment is *not* the same as a one-way trip. If reaching your destination requires riding more than one train (for example, getting from New York to Miami with a transfer in Washington, DC), that one-way trip will actually use two segments of your pass.

Present your pass at an Amtrak office to pick up your ticket(s) for each trip. Reservations should be made by phone (call ☎800-872-7245, or ☎215-856-7953 from outside the USA). Book desired dates as far in advance as possible, as seats allocated for USA Rail Pass holders are limited. At some rural stations, trains will only stop if there's a reservation. Tickets are not for specific seats,

but a conductor on board may allocate you a seat. Business-class, 1st-class and sleeper accommodations cost extra and must be reserved separately.

All travel must be completed within 330 days of purchasing your pass. Passes are not valid on the Acela Express, Auto Train, Thruway motorcoach connections, or the Canadian portion of Amtrak routes operated jointly with Via Rail Canada.

Driving in the USA

For maximum flexibility and convenience, and to explore rural America and its wide-open spaces, a car is essential. Although gas prices are high, you can often score fairly inexpensive rentals (NYC excluded), with rates as low as $20 per day.

Automobile Associations

The American Automobile Association (AAA; www. aaa.com) has reciprocal membership agreements with several international auto clubs (check with AAA and bring your membership card from home). For its members, AAA offers travel insurance, tour books, diagnostic centers for used-car buyers and a wide-ranging network of regional offices. AAA advocates politically for the auto industry.

A more ecofriendly alternative, the Better World Club (www.betterworldclub.com) donates 1% of revenue to assist environmental cleanup, offers ecologically sensitive choices for every service it provides and advocates politically for environmental causes.

With these organizations, the primary member benefit is 24-hour emergency roadside assistance anywhere in the USA. Both also offer trip planning, free travel maps, travel-agency services, car insurance and a range of travel discounts (eg on hotels, car rentals, attractions).

Bring Your Own Vehicle

It's possible to drive your own car over the border from Canada (p1184) or Mexico (p1184). Unless you're moving to the USA, don't even think about freighting your car from overseas.

Drive-Away Cars

'Drive-away cars' refers to the business of driving cars across the country for people who are moving or otherwise can't transport their own vehicles. For flexible travelers, they can be a dream come true: you can cover the long distances between A and B for the price of gas. Timing and availability are key.

To be a driver you must be at least 23 years old with a valid driver's license (non-US citizens should have an International Driving Permit). You'll also need to provide a $350 deposit – sometimes requested in cash – which is refunded upon safe delivery of the car, a printout of your 'clean' driving record from home, a major credit card and a passport (or three other forms of identification).

The drive-away company provides insurance; you pay for gas. The stipulation is that you must deliver the car to its destination within a specified time and mileage, which usually requires that you drive no more than eight hours and about 400 miles a day along the shortest route (ie no sightseeing). Availability depends on demand.

One major company is Auto Driveaway (www.auto driveaway.com/driver), which has more than 40 offices nationwide.

Driver's License

Foreign visitors can legally drive a car in the USA for up to 12 months using their home driver's license. However, an International Driving Permit (IDP) will have more credibility with US traffic police, especially if your home license doesn't have a photo or isn't in English. Your automobile association at home can issue an IDP, valid for one year, for a small fee. Always carry your home license together with the IDP.

To ride a motorcycle in the USA, you will need either a valid US state motorcycle license or an IDP specially endorsed for motorcycles.

Insurance

Don't put the key into the ignition if you don't have insurance, which is legally required. You risk financial ruin and legal consequences if there's an accident. If you already have auto insurance, or if you buy travel insurance that covers car rentals, make sure your policy has adequate liability coverage for where you will be driving, as different states specify different minimum levels of coverage.

Car-rental companies will provide liability insurance, but most charge extra. Rental companies almost never include collision-damage insurance for the vehicle. Instead, they offer an optional Collision Damage Waiver (CDW) or Loss Damage Waiver (LDW), usually with an initial deductible cost of between $100 and $500. For an extra premium, you can usually get this deductible covered as well. Paying extra for some or all of this insurance increases the cost of a rental car by as much as $30 a day.

Many credit cards offer free collision damage coverage for rental cars if you rent for 15 days or less and charge the total rental to your card. This is a good way to avoid paying extra fees to the rental company, but note that if there's an accident, sometimes you must pay the car-rental company first and then seek reimbursement from the credit-card company. There may be exceptions that are not covered, too, such as 'exotic' rentals (eg 4WD Jeeps or convertibles). Check your credit-card policy.

Purchase

Buying a car is usually much more hassle than it's worth, particularly for foreign visitors and for trips of less than four months. Foreigners will have the easiest time arranging this if they have stateside friends or relatives who can provide a fixed address for registration, licensing and insurance.

Once purchased, the car's transfer of ownership papers must be registered with the

FUELING UP

Many gas stations in the USA have fuel pumps with automated credit-card pay screens. Some machines ask for your ZIP code after you swipe your card. For foreign travelers, or those with cards issued outside the US, you'll have to pay inside before fueling up. Just indicate how much you'd like to put on the card. If there's still credit left over after you fuel up, pop back inside and the attendant will put the difference back on your card.

state's Department of Motor Vehicles (DMV) within 10 days – you'll need the bill of sale, the title (or 'pink slip') and proof of insurance. Some states also require a 'smog certificate.' This is the seller's responsibility, so don't buy a car without a current certificate. A dealer will submit all necessary paperwork to the DMV for you.

For foreigners, independent liability insurance is difficult to virtually impossible to arrange without a US driver's license. A car dealer or AAA may be able to suggest an insurer who will do this. Even with a local license, insurance can be expensive and difficult to obtain if you don't have evidence of a good driving record. Bring copies of your home auto-insurance policy if it helps establish that you are a good risk. All drivers under 25 years will have problems getting insurance.

Finally, selling a car can become a desperate business. Selling to dealers gets you the worst price, but involves a minimum of paperwork. Otherwise, fellow travelers and college students are the best bets – but be sure the DMV is properly notified about the sale, or you may be on the hook for someone else's traffic tickets later on.

Rental

Car

Car rental is a competitive business in the USA. Most rental companies require

that you have a major credit card, be at least 25 years old and have a valid driver's license. Some major national companies may rent to drivers between the ages of 21 and 24 for an additional charge of around $25 per day. Those under 21 years are usually not permitted to rent at all.

Car-rental prices vary wildly, so shop around. The average daily rate for a small car ranges from around $20 to $75, or $125 to $500 per week. If you belong to an auto club or frequent-flier program, you may get a discount (or earn rewards points or miles).

Some other things to keep in mind: most national agencies make 'unlimited mileage' standard on all cars, but independents might charge extra for this. Tax on car rental varies by state and agency location; always ask for the total cost *including* all taxes and fees. Most agencies charge more if you pick the car up in one place and drop it off in another, and usually only national agencies offer this option. Be careful about adding extra days or turning in a car early – extra days may be charged at a premium rate, or an early return may jeopardize any weekly or monthly discounts you originally arranged.

Some major national companies, including Avis, Budget and Hertz, offer 'green' fleets of hybrid rental cars (eg Toyota Priuses and Honda Civics), though you'll

Driving Distances & Times

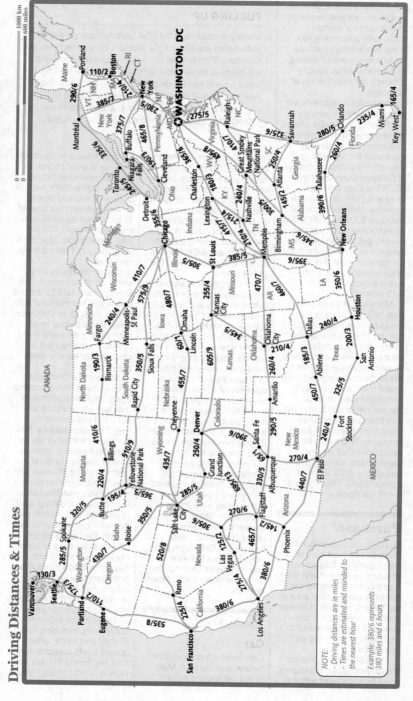

NOTE:
- Driving distances are in miles
- Times are estimated and rounded to the nearest hour

Example: 380/6 represents 380 miles and 6 hours

usually have to pay quite a bit more to rent a hybrid. Some independent local agencies, especially on the West Coast, also offer hybrid-vehicle rentals. Try Southern California's Simply RAC (www.simplyrac.com) and Hawaii's Bio-Beetle (www.bio-beetle.com).

Motorcycle & RV

If you dream of cruising across America on a Harley, EagleRider (www.eaglerider.com) rents motorcycles in major cities nationwide. If a recreational vehicle (RV) is more your style, places such as www.usarvrentals.com and www.cruiseamerica.com can help. Beware that rental and insurance fees for these vehicles are expensive.

Road Conditions & Hazards

America's highways are thought of as legendary ribbons of unblemished asphalt, but that's not always the case. Road hazards include potholes, city commuter traffic, wandering wildlife and cell-phone-wielding, kid-distracted and enraged drivers. Caution, foresight, courtesy and luck usually gets you past them. For nationwide traffic and road-closure information, click to www.fhwa.dot.gov/trafficinfo.

In places where winter driving is an issue, many cars are fitted with steel-studded snow tires, while snow chains can sometimes be required in mountain areas. Driving off-road, or on dirt roads, is often forbidden by car-rental companies, and it can be very dangerous in wet weather.

In deserts and range country, livestock sometimes graze next to unfenced roads. These areas are signed as 'Open Range' or with the silhouette of a steer. Where deer and other wild animals frequently appear roadside, you'll see signs with the silhouette of a leaping deer. Take these signs seriously, particularly at dusk and dawn.

Road Rules

In the USA, cars drive on the right-hand side of the road. The use of seat belts is required in every state except New Hampshire, and child safety seats are required in every state. Most car-rental agencies rent child safety seats for $10 to $14 per day, but you must reserve them when booking. In some states, motorcyclists are required to wear helmets.

On interstate highways, the speed limit is sometimes raised to 75mph. Unless otherwise posted, the speed limit is generally 55mph or 65mph on highways, 25mph to 35mph in cities and towns, and as low as 15mph in school zones (strictly enforced during school hours).

It's forbidden to pass a school bus when its lights are flashing.

Unless signs prohibit it, you may turn right at a red light after first coming to a full stop – note that turning right on red is illegal in NYC. At four-way stop signs, cars should proceed in order of arrival; when two cars arrive simultaneously, the one on the right has the right of way. When in doubt, just politely wave the other driver ahead. When emergency vehicles (ie police, fire or ambulance) approach from either direction, pull over safely and get out of the way.

In many states, it's illegal to talk on a handheld cell phone while driving; use a hands-free device instead.

The maximum legal blood-alcohol concentration for drivers is 0.08%. Penalties are very severe for 'DUI' – driving under the influence of alcohol and/or drugs. Police can give roadside sobriety checks to assess if you've been drinking or using drugs. If you fail, they'll require you to take a breath test, urine test or blood test to determine the level of alcohol or drugs in your body. Refusing to be tested is treated the same as if you'd taken the test and failed.

In some states it's illegal to carry 'open containers' of alcohol in a vehicle, even if they're empty.

Behind the Scenes

SEND US YOUR FEEDBACK

We love to hear from travelers – your comments keep us on our toes and help make our books better. Our well-traveled team reads every word on what you loved or loathed about this book. Although we cannot reply individually to your submissions, we always guarantee that your feedback goes straight to the appropriate authors, in time for the next edition. Each person who sends us information is thanked in the next edition – the most useful submissions are rewarded with a selection of digital PDF chapters.

Visit **lonelyplanet.com/contact** to submit your updates and suggestions or to ask for help. Our award-winning website also features inspirational travel stories, news and discussions.

Note: We may edit, reproduce and incorporate your comments in Lonely Planet products such as guidebooks, websites and digital products, so let us know if you don't want your comments reproduced or your name acknowledged. For a copy of our privacy policy visit lonelyplanet.com/privacy.

OUR READERS

Many thanks to the travelers who used the last edition and wrote to us with helpful hints, useful advice and interesting anecdotes: Adrienne Nielsen, Antonio Dutra, Ashley Turner, Bella Wang, Hugo Gundewall, Jo Evans, Katie Mitchell, Luna Soo, Meghan Hagedorn, Michael Greene, Nuria Guilayn, Paul Jeffries, Pete Reilich, Peter Marshall, Sagar Wadgaonkar, Susanna Locke

WRITER THANKS
Benedict Walker

First and foremost, I'm forever grateful to Alex Howard, my destination editor on the other side of the planet, who found a space for me on this gig, knowing I loved the mountains, and who dealt with some weird challenges I threw at him with an air of calm and an absence of judgement that few of today's young men could muster. Thanks to Brad, my beautiful friend from Missoula, who reminded me that while many men wage wars, some put out fires, and some paint pictures with words. And thanks to the aliens of Nevada and Colorado for pushing me out of my comfort zone. It's a beautiful world out there, whatever we choose to focus on. And there is always more...

Kate Armstrong

La'Vell Brown: thank you for your magic wand, plus your passion, knowledge and insights of Disney World, and for transforming me from the Beastess into Cinderella herself. Thanks to Cory O'Born, Visit Orlando; Nathalia Romano and Ashlynn Webb, Universal Orlando; Jessica Savage, Greater Fort Lauderdale Convention & Visitors Bureau; and to Chris, for your flexibility, patience and everything (except holding my hand on the Hogwarts Express). Finally, thank you to Lauren Keith and Trisha Ping for their understanding and helping to put out a few nothing-but-Disney fireworks.

Brett Atkinson

Thanks to everyone who made my exploration of California's Central Coast so enjoyable, especially Christina Glynn in Santa Cruz. Thanks also to Margaret Leonard for travel inspiration beyond the borders of Monterey Bay. The staff at the region's visitor centers were all uniformly helpful, and at Lonely Planet, huge thanks to Cliff Wilkinson for the opportunity to return to Big Sur. Across the vast South Pacific in Auckland, thanks to Carol and my family for their support.

Carolyn Bain

My warmest thanks to all the chatty innkeepers, bartenders and barflies I had the good fortune to spend time with – who else would you ask for tips on the region's best beach/trail/lobster roll/craft brew etc? Sincerest thanks to the people of Nantucket for welcoming me back into your fold and embracing my nostalgia – especially to Roselyne Hatch and Tania Jones. Special mention goes to Emily Golin, Carla Tracy, Thomas Masters, and Kimberly and Barry Hunter for their kindnesses.

Amy C Balfour

I had a blast checking out my regional neighborhood. Special thanks to the following folks who shared their favorite places: Dave Dekema, Sketchy, Barbra Byington, Ed & Melissa Reid, Lynn Neumann, Lori Jarvis, Andrew McRoberts, Tom Fleming, Melissa & Mary Peeler, Erin Stolle, Alicia Hay Matthai, Liz Smith Robinson, Alice Merchant Dearing, Severn Miller, James Foley, John Park, Suzie Lublin Tiplitz, Sharon Nicely, Eone Moore Beck, Kendall Sims Hunt, Lee Bagby Ceperich, Justin Shephard, Tim Stinson, Trish Mullen and Steve Bruce.

Ray Bartlett

This project couldn't have happened without the awesome love and support of my family, including my extended family out in Pennsylvania, who offered to put me up and show me around as I was researching. Many thanks too to the numerous guides, hotel receptionists, waiters and waitresses, and museum curators who took time to share their info and views with me. A lovely part of the planet, and one I hope to visit again soon. Readers, you're in for a treat.

Loren Bell

To all of my family and friends on the way who provided hot tips, cold beer and warm support: thank you – your friendships make this all worthwhile. To Kari: I don't know how you put up with me during these projects, but your patience must be deeper than Grand Prismatic Spring – your beauty certainly is. Finally, to Hawkeye: I know you can't read, but having you by my side was the highlight of the trip. You're a good boy.

Greg Benchwick

This book wouldn't be possible without the support and love of my family. First and foremost, there's little Violeta 'Monkey Face' Benchwick, who continues to research the world with her wayward daddy. Thanks too to Sarah for making the trip to Estes and beyond, and to the lovely editors, writers and big thinkers at Lonely Planet.

Andrew Bender

Thanks to Denise Lengyeltoti, Christie Bacock, Melissa Perez, Jackie Alvarez, Jennifer Tong, Erin Ramsauer, Michael Ramirez, Jenny Wedge, Ashley Johnson and the many information center, hotel and restaurant staffers who gave me way more of their time than I deserved. In house, thanks especially to Clifton Wilkinson, Sarah Stocking, Anita Isalska, Judith Bamber and Kathryn Rowan.

Sara Benson

Thank you to editors Cliff Wilkinson and Alex Howard for guidance and long-distance support. A big thank you to Jonathan Hayes for driving thousands of miles with me through Gold Country, Wine Country, the Sierra Nevada and all around the Bay Area. PS Hi, Beth!

Alison Bing

Thanks to Cliff Wilkinson, Sarah Sung, Lisa Park, DeeAnn Budney, PT Tenenbaum and, above all, Marco Flavio Marinucci, for making a Muni bus ride into the adventure of a lifetime.

Catherine Bodry

Guidebook projects are never solo, and I'm grateful for the help and support of many. Thanks to Steph Johnson, Emily Mechtenberg, Jenny Miller and Josh Kelly for friendship and companionship. Thanks to Michael and Micheley for the Homer homestead cabin and Seward retreat. To the Lonely Planet staff: thanks for always being responsive and patient with my luddite questions. Finally, thanks to the authors before me who've paved the way; Lonely Planet was my first guide to Alaska back in 1999.

Cristian Bonetto

A heartfelt thank you to the many Angelenos (and New Yorkers) who shared their LA secrets and insights with me, especially John-Mark Horton, Michael Amato, Andy Bender, Norge Yip, Calvin Yeung, Douglas Levine, Daphne Barahona, Nicholas Maricich, David Singleman, William J Brockschmidt, Richard Dragisic and Andy Walker. Thanks also to fellow Aussies in SoCal, Mary-ann Gardner and Natalie Yanoulis. At Lonely Planet, much gratitude to Cliff Wilkinson.

Celeste Brash

Thanks to my Aunt Kem and Uncle Ken for Susanville roots, Gerad in Mt Shasta City for great beer and info, countless friends and family for tips and suggestions, and my husband and kids for being the best people to come home to. Last but not least, big love to the glorious state of California, where my heart will always live.

Jade Bremner

Thanks to editor Clifton Wilkinson for his support and endless knowledge about Lonely Planet guidebooks, plus everyone working their socks off behind the scenes – Cheree Broughton, Dianne Schallmainer, Jane Grisman, Neill Coen, Evan Godt and Helen Elfer. Last, but not least, thanks to the friendly staff at Fig Tree Cafe for making those marvelous egg Bennies, which often set me up for the day.

Nate Cavalieri

Many thanks to my partner Florence, who is always game for a last-minute road trip to Bakersfield. Thanks to Cliff, Daniel, Jane, Dianne and the staff at Lonely Planet for all the support and to my colleague Alison Bing, who inspired me to get back in the travel writing game after a long and ill-advised hiatus.

Gregor Clark

Sincere thanks to the many Bostonians who so generously shared their love of city, particularly Aaron Miller at HI Boston, Dave O'Donnell at GBCVB, Joanne Chang at Myers & Chang, Ayr Muir at Clover Food Lab and Maria Cole at NPS. Special thanks to fellow Lonely Planet author Mara Vorhees, whose superb work on previous editions made my job immeasurably more enjoyable. Finally, hugs to my wife Gaen and daughters Meigan and Chloe for helping test-taste cannoli in the North End.

Michael Grosberg

Thanks especially to Carly, Rosie and Booney for keeping the home fires burning; and Carly especially for sharing her experiences as a forest ranger in Mammoth Lakes and Mono Lake all those years ago. Thanks also to Peter Bartelme of Yosemite Conservancy; Lisa Cesaro from Aramark; Joe Juszkiewicz at Rush Creek Lodge; Lauren Burke in Mammoth; Tawni Thompson in Bishop; and Julie Wright for help in Sequoia.

Ashley Harrell

Thanks to: editors Lauren and Trisha, and co-authors Adam, Kate and Regis, for your support. Josie, Nora and Ashley Guttuso for having me at the fort. Tiffany Grandstaff for the upgrade. Alex Pickett for existing. Trevor, Malissa and Soraya Aaronson for being my surrogate family. Tom Francis for finally coming. Alanna Bjork for dog-sitting and the cozy shack. Beanie Guez for destroying me in shuffleboard and Elodie Guez for bringing wine (and glasses). Andy Lavender for showing up in Sarasota, and in general.

Alexander Howard

A huge thanks to the barkeeps, B&B owners, restaurant staff and all the Alaskans that kept me out of trouble in bear country. Thanks also to my co-writers Catherine Bodry, Adam Karlin and Brendan Sainsbury for their advice, input and hard work that they put into this book. Huge thanks to Evan Godt, for pulling strings. Thanks to my parents, for their support and adventurousness, and to Danielle for forever making the road a lot less lonely.

Mark Johanson

A big thanks to my parents for dragging me across America on road trips as a kid and inspiring me to appreciate different landscapes and cultures. Thanks to my partner Felipe for allowing me to spend so much time away from my current home in South America to explore the bowels of my native country. I'm grateful for the help, warm meals and inspiration along the way from JP Bumby, Jamie Thomas and all the welcoming Great Plains folks.

Adam Karlin

Thanks y'all: to Lauren Keith and Trisha Ping, editors extraordinaire, to my brother in arms on Southern roadtrips, Kevin Raub, to the parks workers and bartenders and baristas and service industry folks who showed me how much there is to discover in my own backyard, to mom and dad, for their constant support, to Karen Shacham and Michelle Putnam (and Lior!), the best hosts Atlanta could provide, and Rachel and Sanda, for both joining me on the road and tolerating my absences.

Brian Kluepfel

Paula Zorrilla, my guiding light and co-pilot. I couldn't have done it without you. Trisha Ping, Greg Benchwick, Jane Grisman and Dianne Schallmeiner at Lonely Planet for moral and technical support. Tom Kluepfel, honorary mayor of Hoboken and 'mutz' maven. Laura Collins, Rebecca Rozen and her dog Gizmo, for Hamptons knowledge and good cheer. Stacey Borelli and Peggy Watson at Siemens for holding the fort. The Ocean Grove cop who didn't give me that ticket. June McPartland for selling me that car.

Stephen Lioy

Many thanks to many people, but specifically to the following: Aileen for the thousand tips, Anthony for the copilot miles and company, Jess and Kevin for always being there, Kalli and Tonie for helping me enjoy inefficiency, Shane for tips and time and sometimes beer, Cindy/Payton/Pres for being so bad at Catan, Dav and Nan and UpChuck for the very many nights and meals and help, and Jack for being Jack. Hey Tonie...you wanna be frieeeeeends?

Carolyn McCarthy

My many thanks go out to the Utah tourism office and friends Drew and Zinnia, Francisco Kjolseth and Meg and Dave. Thanks also to my co-writers, especially Chris Pitts. Utah worked its magic once more. Also, many thanks to the fine people of southern Colorado whose help and hospitality in mud season is highly appreciated. My gratitude goes out to Dave and Lyn in Telluride, Angela and Jim in Ouray, and Katie in Durango. *Gracias* to Sandra for her contributions to the hiking portion of the trip. *Hasta la próxima*, Colorado!

Craig McLachlan

A huge and hearty mahalo to my on-the-road assistants, my exceptionally beautiful wife,

Yuriko, and our son, Riki. And cheers to Alex at Lonely Planet, co-author Ryan, Paul and Nezia, Phil and Liwei and everyone else who helped us out.

Hugh McNaughtan

My sincere thanks to everyone who helped me through an epic research trip through Arizona – Tas and my girls, editor Alex, the ever-helpful support crew at Lonely Planet, and the kind people of the Grand Canyon State. And Matt for the mescal.

Becky Ohlsen

Thanks to dad for being the greatest research assistant thus far, and to all the various park rangers and campground officials who talked about the weather and gave reassurances about road conditions, Paul Bracke for over-the-top intel on Spokane, the previous authors of this chapter, and ace editor Alex Howard.

Christopher Pitts

Thanks to the inordinately kind people of New Mexico, in particular Michael Benanav in Dixon, John Feins and Cynthia Delgado in Santa Fe, and all the rangers at the national parks – especially the guy who led the incredible Carlsbad Cave tour – keep up the great work! At the writing desk, thanks to co-authors Carolyn McCarthy, Benedict Walker and Hugh McNaughtan for suggestions, and Alex Howard for keeping the whole project on track. Also, huge thanks to Debbie Lew for her Summit County connections, Melissa Wisenbaker in Aspen, Sara Stookey in Snowmass, and Sally Gunter in Vail.

Liza Prado

Sincere thanks to the extraordinary Lonely Planet team, especially Alex Howard and my coauthors. Special thanks to my Coloradan friends Meghan Howes, Alexia Eslan, Samantha Lentz, Kate McGoldrick, Paisley Johnson, Darin Pitts and Rob Roberts for the inside scoop on some of your favorite places. *Mil gracias* to Mom, Dad, Joe, Elyse and Susan for your loving help with the kids. Big thanks to Eva and Leo for waiting so patiently for family movie night. And to Gary: thank you for your boundless love and support – you make my world turn.

Josephine Quintero

Thanks to Cliff Wilkinson for the opportunity of researching this fabulous region of California. Also to my road trip buddy, Robin Chapman and my good local resident pals who invaluably assisted me: Janice Crowe and Linda Sinclair. Also thanks to the helpful folk in the various visitor centers and, last but not least, those at the SPP help desk when I had a serious technical glitch!

Kevin Raub

Thanks to my wife, Adriana Schmidt Raub, who shockingly sticks around despite my travels! Lauren Keith, Trisha Ping, MaSovaida Morgan and all my partners-in-crime at Lonely Planet. On the road, Jana Clauser, Kristi Amburgey, Susan Dallas, Dawn Przystal, Niki Heichelbech-Goldey, Erin Hilton, Courtney McKinney, Brian Mansfield, Alison Duke, Erin Donovan, Liz Beck, Eleanor Talley, Dodie Stephens, Sarah Lowery, Anne Fitten Glenn, Kaitlin Sheppard, Heather Darnell, Scott Peacock, Doug Warner, Halsey Perrin, Charlie Clark, Kim Jamieson and Jeff Hulett.

Simon Richmond

Many thanks to Van Vahle, Tonny Wong and Curtis Maxwell Perrin for insights, assistance and hospitality along the way.

Brendan Sainsbury

Thanks to all the pilots, ferry captains, chefs, travel guides, hoteliers, National Park rangers and innocent bystanders who helped me – unwittingly or otherwise – during this research. Special thanks to my nephew, Matt and my son, Kieran for their company on the road in Juneau and Sitka.

Andrea Schulte-Peevers

Big heartfelt thankyous go to the following people for their invaluable tips, insights and hospitality (in no particular order): Valerie Summers, Kristin Schmidt, Joyce Kiehl, Andrew Bender, Abigail Wines, Bruce Moore, Susan Witty, Brandy Marino and Mona Spicer.

Adam Skolnick

Much aloha and *mahalo* to Taj Jure and Marc-Andre Gagnon, Jeffrey Courson, Susan Dierker, Camille Page and her whole lovely family, Derek Pellin, Gary Hooser, Andrea Brower, Michelle Marsh, Josh Meneley, John Moore and Jacklynn Evans. Thanks also to Alexander Howard, Greg Benchwick and the entire Lonely Planet team for the collaboration. And many *mahalos* to the Garden Island itself. You are home.

Helena Smith

Many thanks to everyone who offered warm hospitality in the Gold Country and Lake Tahoe, most especially Naomi Terry for keeping us company, and Anna and her family for hospitality and local expertise. King was a great road-trip buddy, and so was Art Terry, who drove and DJed me round California, and made every exploration a joy.

Regis St Louis

Countless people helped along the way, and I'm grateful to national park guides, lodging hosts, restaurant servers, barkeeps and baristas who shared tips and insight throughout South Florida. Big thanks to Adam Karlin who

THIS BOOK

This 10th edition of Lonely Planet's *USA* guidebook was researched and written by Benedict Walker, Kate Armstrong, Brett Atkinson, Carolyn Bain, Amy C Balfour, Robert Balkovich, Ray Bartlett, Loren Bell, Greg Benchwick, Andrew Bender, Sara Benson, Alison Bing, Catherine Bodry, Cristian Bonetto, Celeste Brash, Jade Bremner, Nate Cavalieri, Gregor Clark, Michael Grosberg, Ashley Harrell, Alexander Howard, Mark Johanson, Adam Karlin, Brian Kluepfel, Stephen Lioy, Carolyn McCarthy, Craig McLachlan, Hugh McNaughtan, Becky Ohlsen, Christopher Pitts, Liza Prado, Josephine Quintero, Kevin Raub, Simon Richmond, Brendan Sainsbury, Andrea Schulte-Peevers, Adam Skolnick, Helena Smith, Regis St Louis, Ryan Ver Berkmoes, John A Vlahides, Mara Vorhees, Clifton Wilkinson, Luci Yamamoto and Karla Zimmerman. This guidebook was produced by the following:

Destination Editors
Alexander Howard, Evan Godt, Lauren Keith, Trisha Ping, Sarah Stocking, Clifton Wilkinson

Product Editors Carolyn Boicos, Kate Mathews

Senior Cartographer Alison Lyall

Book Designer Jessica Rose

Assisting Editors Sarah Bailey, James Bainbridge, Judith Bamber, Imogen Bannister, Michelle Bennett, Nigel Chin, Michelle Coxall, Melanie Dankel, Andrea Dobbin, Carly Hall, Jennifer Hattam, Gabrielle Innes, Anita Isalska, Kellie Langdon, Ali Lemer, Jodie Martire, Rosie Nicholson, Kristin Odijk, Charlotte Orr, Monique Perrin, Christopher Pitts, Sarah Reid, Saralinda Turner, Amanda Williamson, Simon Williamson

Cover Researcher Naomi Parker

Thanks to William Allen, Sasha Drew, Bailey Freeman, Shona Gray, Paul Harding, Elizabeth Jones, Kate Kiely, Indra Kilfoyle, Rachel Rawling, Valerie Stimac, Greg Thilmont, Tony Wheeler

did such an outstanding job on previous editions. I'd also like to thank Cassandra and our daughters, Magdalena and Genevieve, who made the Miami trip all the more worthwhile.

Ryan Ver Berkmoes

Fond thanks to those many people who were so helpful in Texas two decades ago and again this time. And fond love to Alexis Ver Berkmoes, who is proof that as some things fade away, other things just get better.

John A Vlahides

Thanks to commissioning editor Clifton Wilkinson and my coauthor Alison Bing, with whom it's always lovely to work. And most of all, thanks to you, dear reader – you make my life so joyful and I'm grateful for the honor of being your guide through the cool gray city of love.

Mara Vorhees

Thanks to friends and neighbors who have taught me so much about New England over the years. I am grateful to my faithful travel companions, Shay and Van: it's always more fun to travel – though more difficult to write – when you're along for the ride. And thank you, Jerz, for going along with the sunrise thing, all 19 times (and counting).

Clifton Wilkinson

Thanks to the Santa Barbara County tourism people (Karna, Danielle, Chrisie) who provided excellent recommendations, including my favorite meal of the whole update. Thanks too to all the inhouse Lonely Planet team, especially colleagues who listened patiently to all my pre-trip plans. And final thanks to the weather, which mostly played along with my research – except for all the mud on Santa Cruz Channel Island.

Luci Yamamoto

Mahalo to Alex Howard for an opportunity to explore my home island again. To island residents, both locals and transplants, thanks for talking story and sharing your lives with me. To David Bock, Derek Kurisu and Bobby Camara, I appreciate your singular insights about Hawai'i. Most of all, endless thanks to my parents, wonderful assistants and true *kama'aina*.

Karla Zimmerman

Many thanks to Lisa Beran, Lisa DiChiera, Ruggero Fatica, Cathy McKee, Chuck Palmer, Keith Pandolfi, Tamara Robinson, Susan Hayes Stephan, Hannah Stephan and Mark Wallace for taking the time to share their favorite local spots. Thanks most to Eric Markowitz, the world's best partner-for-life, who indulges my beer- and donut-filled ramblings with an endless supply of good humor.

ACKNOWLEDGEMENTS

Climate map data adapted from Peel MC, Finlayson BL & McMahon TA (2007) 'Updated World Map of the Köppen-Geiger Climate Classification', *Hydrology and Earth System Sciences*, 11, 163344.

Cover photograph: Bison grazing in Yellowstone National Park, Maciej Bledowski/Shutterstock ©

Illustrations pp98–9 and pp276–7 by Javier Martinez Zarracina, pp990–1 by Michael Weldon.

Index

18b Arts District 825
360° Chicago 540
10,000 Islands 497

A
Abilene 688
Abingdon 339-40
Abiquiu 904
Acadia National Park 19, 263, 633, **632**
accommodations 24, 1170-1, *see also individual locations*
Acoma Pueblo 895-6
activities 31-4, 47-54, *see also individual activities*
Adirondacks, the 154-7
Admiralty Island National Monument 1099
African American Civil War Memorial 281
air travel 1183-4, 1185
Ajo Mountain Drive 869-70
Alabama 426-32
Alamogordo 912
Alaska 72, 640, 1089-107
accommodations 1089
climate 1089, 1091
food 1089
geography 1091
highlights 1090, **1090**
travel seasons 1089, 1091
travel to/from 1091
Albany 154-5
Albuquerque 892-5
Alcatraz 990-1, 992, **990-1, 990, 991**
Alexandria 318-21
Alexandria Bay 157-8
Alpine 745-6
Alvord Desert 1088
Amana Colonies 662
Amelia Island 510-11
Amherst 219-20
Amish Country 570, 576-7

Map Pages **000**
Photo Pages **000**

amusement parks 27
Belmont Park 953
Busch Gardens 512
Carousel Gardens Amusement Park 450
Casino Pier 165
Cedar Point Amusement Park 574
Dinosaur Kingdom II 336
Disneyland 943-5
Dollywood 398
Knott's Berry Farm 944
Musée Mécanique 985
Orlando Eye 519
Santa Cruz Beach Boardwalk 975
SeaWorld 519
Silver Dollar City 654
SkyWheel 377
Steel Pier 166
Stratosphere 825
Trimpers Rides 307-8
Universal Orlando Resort 523-4
Utah Olympic Park 878
Valleyfair 615
Walt Disney World® Resort 521-3
Wet 'n' Wild Phoenix 847
Anadarko 695
Anaheim 943-5
Anchorage 1091-4
Ancient Bristlecone Pine Forest 1027
Andrew Molera State Park 972
Angels Camp 1018
Angels Landing 890
animals 1165-7, 1168, *see also individual species*
Ann Arbor 592-3
Annapolis 303-6
Antelope Canyon 862
Antelope Island State Park 880
Antietam National Battlefield 309-10
Anza-Borrego Desert State Park 942
Apalachicola National Forest 526

Apollo Theater 101
Apostle Islands 612-13
Appalachian Trail 265, 335, 338, 342-3, 366
Appomattox Court House National Historic Park 332-3
aquariums
Aquarium of the Bay 993
Aquarium of the Pacific 932
Birch Aquarium at Scripps 953
Echo Leahy Center for Lake Champlain 247
Florida Aquarium 512
Monterey Bay Aquarium 973
Mystic Aquarium & Institute for Exploration 234
National Aquarium 298-9
Newport Aquarium 580
Oregon Coast Aquarium 1083
Seattle Aquarium 1042
Seymour Marine Discovery Center 975
Shark Reef Aquarium 825
Shedd Aquarium 535
Sitka Sound Science Center 1097
Texas State Aquarium 726
Virginia Aquarium & Marine Science Center 330
Arcata 1014
Arches National Park 637, 885, **636-7**
architecture 29, 1158-60
Area 51 838
area codes 1177
Arizona 838-71
Arkansas 438-45
Arlington 317-18
Armstrong Redwoods State Reserve 1010
art museums & galleries, *see also* museums
Adobe Gallery 897

Albright-Knox Art Gallery 159
Albuquerque Museum of Art & History 892
American Visionary Art Museum 300
Andy Warhol Museum 181
Art Institute of Chicago 534
Art Museum of Texas 726
Arts Factory 825
Asian Art Museum 978
Aspen Art Museum 774
Bakehouse Art Complex 478
Ballroom Marfa 744
Balmy Alley 985
Birmingham Museum of Art 428
Boise Art Museum 813
Brattleboro Museum & Art Center 240
Broad Art Museum 593
Carnegie Museums 181
Center for Photography at Woodstock 151
Chazen Museum of Art 607-8
Chihuly Garden & Glass 1037
Chrysler Museum of Art 329
Cincinnati Art Museum 580
Clark Art Institute 222
Cleveland Museum of Art 571
Colorado Springs Fine Arts Center 777
Contemporary Arts Center 580
Cooper-Hewitt National Design Museum 100-1
Crocker Art Museum 1016
Crow Collection of Asian Art 733
Cummer Museum of Art & Gardens 508-9
Dallas Museum of Art 733-4
de Young Museum 987
Delaware Art Museum 313

art museums & galleries
continued
Delaware Center for the
Contemporary Arts 313
Detroit Institute of Arts
585
Dia: Beacon 146
Diego Rivera Gallery 981
District of Columbia Arts
Center 282
Economos/Hampton
Galleries 897
El Paso Museum of
Art 746
Empire State Plaza 154
Eskenazi Museum of
Art 566
Figge Art Museum 661
Florence Griswold
Museum 235
Frederick R Weisman Art
Foundation 929
Freer-Sackler Museums
of Asian Art 278
Frick Art & Historical
Center 181
Frick Collection 100
Frist Center for the Visual
Arts 390
Gallery of Fine Art 823
Georgia O'Keeffe
Museum 896
Gerald Peters Gallery 897
Getty Center 929
Getty Villa 929
GF Contemporary 897
Gibbes Museum of
Art 370
Grand Rapids Art
Museum 594
Guggenheim Museum
100
Hallie Ford Museum of
Art 1074
Hammer Museum 929
Harvard Art Museums
197
Harwood Foundation
Museum 905
Hauser & Wirth 919
Herbert F Johnson
Museum of Art 152
High Museum of Art 410
Hunter Museum of
American Art 396
Hyde Collection Art
Museum 155
Indianapolis Museum of
Art 562
Institute of
Contemporary Art 195

Map Pages **000**
Photo Pages **000**

International Center of
Photography 82
Intuit: The Center for
Intuitive & Outsider
Art 542
Isabella Stewart Gardner
Museum 197
Jepson Center for the
Arts 421
Kaufman Arts District
107
Kimbell Art Museum 738
Laguna Art Museum 946
Lexington Art League at
Loudoun House 402
Los Angeles County
Museum of Art 928
LSU Museum of Art 461
Lyme Academy of Fine
Arts 235
Marc Navarro Gallery 897
Margulies Collection at
the Warehouse 478
MASS MoCA 223
McNay Art Museum 710
Metropolitan Museum of
Art 100
Milwaukee Art Museum
603-4
Minneapolis Institute of
Arts 615
Mississippi Museum of
Art 435
MOCA Grand 923
MoMA PS1 106
Morning Star Gallery 897
Museum of Church
History & Art 873
Museum of Contemporary
Art (Chicago) 540
Museum of Contemporary
Art (Detroit) 585
Museum of Contemporary
Art Jacksonville 509
Museum of Contemporary
Art North Miami 479
Museum of Contemporary
Art (San Diego) 947
Museum of Contemporary
Photography 538-9
Museum of Fine Arts 197
Museum of International
Folk Art 899
Museum of Latin
American Art 932
Museum of Modern
Art 91
National Gallery of
Art 271
National Museum of
Mexican Art 542
Nedra Matteucci
Galleries 897
Nelson-Atkins Museum of
Art 655
Neue Galerie 101

Nevada Museum of
Art 835
New Mexico Museum of
Art 899
New Museum of
Contemporary Art 84
New Orleans Museum of
Art 450
New York State Museum
154
Norman Rockwell
Museum 221
North Carolina Museum
of Art 356
Norton Simon Museum
933
Ogden Museum of
Southern Art 451
Palm Springs Art
Museum 958
Parrish Art Museum 142
Philadelphia Museum of
Art 169-71
Philbrook Museum of
Art 692
Phillips Collection 282
Phoenix Art Museum 840
Pollock-Krasner House
142
Portland Art Museum 1065
Provincetown Art
Association & Museum
212
Renwick Gallery 280
Reynolds Center for
American Art &
Portraiture 280-1
RISD Museum of Art 224
Rodin Museum 172
Rubin Museum of Art 87
RW Norton Art Gallery
467
Salvador Dalí Museum
514
San Diego Museum of
Art 951
SCAD Museum of Art 421
Schneider Museum of
Art 1085
Seattle Art Museum 1036
Shelburne Museum 247
Smith College Museum of
Art 219
Spencer Museum of
Art 686
St Louis Art Museum 647
Strawbery Banke
Museum 249
Studio Museum in
Harlem 102
Taos Art Museum &
Fechin Institute 905
Taubman Museum of
Art 338
Timken Museum of
Art 951

Torpedo Factory Art
Center 319
Tucson Museum of Art
865-6
University of Michigan
Museum of Art 592
Virginia Museum of
Contemporary Art 330
Virginia Museum of Fine
Arts 322
Wadsworth Atheneum
231
Walker Art Center 614
Walters Art Museum 299
Weisman Art Museum
615
Whitney Museum of
American Art 86-7
Williams College Museum
of Art 222
Yale Center for British
Art 236-7
Yale University Art
Gallery 237
arts 1150, 1157-8
Asbury Park 164-5
Asheville 363-6
Ashland 1085-6
Aspen 21, 774-5, **21**
Assateague Island 308
Astoria 1081-2
Athens (Georgia) 418-20
Athens (Ohio) 583
Atlanta 407-17, **408-9**
accommodations 411-12
activities 407-11
drinking & nightlife
415-16
entertainment 416-17
festivals & events 411
food 412-15
sights 407-11
travel to/from 417
travel within 417
Atlantic City 166-7
Atlantic Coast 503-11
ATMs 1175
Auburn 570
Auburn State Recreation
Area 1018
Aurora 153
Austin 700-7, **702**
Avenue of the Giants 1013
Avila Beach 968
Aztec Ruins National
Monument 908

B
Badlands National Park
635, 669-70, **672-3**
Badwater 964
Balmy Alley 985
Baltimore 298-303

Bandelier National Monument 903-4
Bandera 715-16
Banner Elk 361
Bar Harbor 264-5
Barataria Preserve 460
Barnegat Peninsula 165-6
Bartlesville 693
baseball 1147-8
basketball 1148-9
Bass Islands 574-5
Bastrop 708
Bath 261-2
bathhouses 107
bathrooms 1178
Baton Rouge 461-2
Battleship Iowa 932
Battleship North Carolina 355
beaches 27
  Aquinnah Public Beach 216
  Baker Beach 985
  Balboa Peninsula 946
  Belleayre Beach 150
  Big Beach 1124
  Black Pot Beach Park 1127-8
  Boardwalk 473
  Cannon Beach 1082
  Chicago 545
  Echo Lake Beach 253
  Fort Lauderdale 487
  Hanalei Beach Park 1128
  Huntington Beach 946
  Inlet Beach 165
  Keawakapu Beach 1125
  Kuhio Beach Park 1113
  Laguna Beach 946
  Magic Sands Beach 1117-18
  Miami 469, 478
  Mission Beach 951-2, 953
  Natural Bridges State Beach 975
  Newport 227
  Newport Beach 946
  North Beach 727
  North End 729
  North Kona 1119-20
  Ocean Beach 987
  Ogunquit Beach 258
  Oneloa 1124
  Orange County 945-7
  Orient Beach State Park 145
  Oval Beach 595
  Pacific Beach 951-2, 953
  Pfeiffer Beach 971
  Point Pleasant Beach 165
  Queen's Surf Beach 1114
  Race Point Beach 213
  Rodeo Beach 1003
  San Diego 951-2
  South Beach 472
  St Augustine Beach 507-8
  Stinson Beach 1004
  Waikiki 1113
  West Beach 568
Beale Street Music Festival 384
bears 1095, 1099, **633**
Bears Ears National Monument 26, 879
Beartooth Highway 795
Beaufort 354, 375-7
beer 30, 62-3, 365
Bellingham 1054-5
Bemidji 626
Bend 1078-80
Bennington 241-2
Berkeley 1004-6
Berkeley Springs 343
Berkshires, the 220-4
Berlin 306-7
Bethel 265
bicycling 48-9, 1131, 1185-6, see also mountain biking
  Abingdon 339
  Albuquerque 893
  Bellingham 1054
  C&O Canal National Historic Park 342
  Cape Cod Rail Trail 212
  Chicago 544-5
  Cumberland 310
  Fayetteville 345
  Grand Canyon National Park 855, 857
  Grand Teton National Park 800
  Harbor Country 595
  Indiana Dunes 568
  Indianapolis 562
  Kelleys Island 575
  Los Angeles 933
  Martha's Vineyard 217
  Miami 480
  Monterey 974
  Mt Rogers National Recreation Area 339
  New York City 107, 108
  Norwottuck Rail Trail 219
  Olympic Discovery Trail 1052
  Portland 1067
  Province Lands Bike Trail 213
  Richmond 324
  San Francisco 989
  Santa Barbara 966
  St Louis 647
  Steamboat Springs 769
  Sun Valley 815
  Tallahassee 524
Trail of the Coeur d'Alenes 817
Vail 772
Washington, DC 283
Yellowstone National Park 797-8
Big Island (Hawai'i) 1117-123
Big Sur 971-2
Billings 805-6
Billy the Kid National Scenic Byway 913
Biltmore Estate 364
birds 1167
bird-watching 465
  Bosque del Apache National Wildlife Refuge 909
  Cape May Bird Observatory 167-8
  Felix Neck Wildlife Sanctuary 216
  Klamath Basin National Wildlife Refuge Complex 1021
  Patagonia-Sonoita Creek Preserve 870
  Pinnacles National Park 971
  VINS Nature Center 243
  Wellfleet Bay Wildlife Sanctuary 211
  World Center for Birds of Prey 813
Birmingham 427-9
Bisbee 871
Biscayne National Park 494-5
Bishop 1027
Bismarck 666
Bisti Badlands & De-Na-Zin Wilderness 908
Bixby Creek Bridge 972
Black Hills 670-7, **672-3**
Black Hills National Forest 675
Block Island 229
Bloomington 566
Blowing Rock 361-3
Blue Ridge Highlands 338-41
Blue Ridge Parkway 43-5, 339, 362
Bluegrass Country 402-4
Bluff 886
boat travel 1184-5, 1186
boat trips
  Bellingham 1054
  Boston 199
  Brewster 210
  Burlington 247
  Chicago 545
  Essex 236
  Eureka 1014
  Glacier National Park 811
Hannibal 653
Juneau 1101
Lahaina 1124
Lake George 155
Monterey 974
Mystic 234
New York City 107, 108
Niagara Falls 161
Portland 260
Portsmouth 250
Rockland 263
San Antonio 711
San Diego 954
Santa Barbara 966
St Louis 647
Staten Island Ferry 107
Tilghman Island 306
Washington, DC 283
Weirs Beach 251
Bodega Bay 1011
Bodie State Historic Park 1027
Bogue Banks 354
Boise 812-14
Bonnaroo Music Festival 394
Book of Mormon, The 876
books 1130, 1143, 1153-5
Boone 363
Boothbay Harbor 262
border crossings 1184
Boston 185-205, **188-9**, **192-3**
  accommodations 200
  activities 199
  drinking & nightlife 203-4
  entertainment 204
  festivals & events 200
  food 200-3
  shopping 204-5
  sights 190-9
  tourist information 205
  tours 199
  travel to/from 205
  travel within 205
  walking tour 198, **198**
Boulder (Colorado) 763-6
Boulder (Utah) 887-8
Boulder Creek 763
Boundary Waters 625
Bourbon Trail 405
Bozeman 803-4
Bradbury Building 920-1
Brandywine Valley 313-14
Branson 654-5
Brattleboro 240-1
Breckenridge 771-2
Bretton Woods 254-5
breweries & microbreweries 30, 63
Brewster 210
Brooklyn Bridge 75

INDEX B-C

Brunswick 424-5
Bryce Canyon National Park 637, 888-9, **636**
budget 23, 25
Buffalo 158-60
Buffalo National River 445
Burlington 246-9
Burning Man 839
bus travel 1186-7
business hours 23, 61, 1176

C

C&O Canal National Historic Park 310
cable cars
  Cannon Mountain Aerial Tramway 253
  El Paso 747
  Palm Springs Aerial Tramway 958
  Powell St Cable Car Turnaround 978
  Sandia Peak Tramway 893
Cahokia Mounds State Historic Site 560
Cajun Country 463-7
Cajun culture 447
Cajun Prairie 466-7
Cajun Wetlands 465-6
California 72, 915-1030, **916-17**
  accommodations 915
  climate 915
  food 59, 915
  highlights 916-17
  itineraries 919
Cambria 970
Camden 263
Cameron 862
Canada, travel to/from 1184
Canaveral National Seashore 504
Cannon Beach 1082-3
canoeing, see kayaking & canoeing
Canyon de Chelly National Monument 862-3
Canyonlands National Park 885-6
Cape Cod 207-14, **209**
Cape Cod National Seashore 214
Cape Flattery 1053
Cape Hatteras National Seashore 351
Cape May 167-8
Cape Perpetua Scenic Area 1084

Map Pages **000**
Photo Pages **000**

Capital Region 70, 266-345, **268-9**
Capitan 913
Capitol Reef National Park 887
Captiva Island 516-17
Capulin Volcano National Monument 909
car travel 1190-3, **1192**
Carboro 359-60
Carhenge 678
Carlsbad 914
Carlyle House 319
Carmel 972-3
Carnegie Hall 131
Carson City 837
Carson, Rachel 1138
Cash, Johnny 390
casinos 823-5, 835
Castillo de San Marcos National Monument 507
castles 157, 235, 495
Cathedral Gorge State Park 841
cathedrals, see churches & cathedrals
Catskills 149-52
caves
  Blanchard Springs Caverns 443
  Boyden Cavern 1025-6
  Crystal Cave 1025
  Jewel Cave National Monument 671
  Kartchner Caverns State Park 870
  Lake Shasta Caverns 1020
  Luray Caverns 333
  Marengo Cave 567
  Oregon Caves National Monument & Preserve 1087
  Skyline Caverns 333
  Wind Cave National Park 677
Cedar Valley 664-5
cell phones 1177
cemeteries
  Arlington National Cemetery 317
  Boothill Graveyard 871
  Granary Burying Ground 191
  Hollywood Cemetery 324
  Hollywood Forever Cemetery 926
  Lafayette Cemetery No 1 452
  Lake View Cemetery 571
  Mt Moriah Cemetery 674
  Sleepy Hollow Cemetery 206

Westwood Village Memorial Park Cemetery 929
Woodlawn Cemetery 105
Central Park 96-7, 98-9, **94-5, 98-9**, 98, 99
Chaco Culture National Historical Park 908
Chamberlain 668
Channel Islands National Park 966
Chapel Hill 359-60
Charleston 369-73
Charleston County Sea Islands 374-5
Charlevoix 597-8
Charlotte 360-1
Charlottesville 331-2
Chase County 688
Chatham 210-11
Chattanooga 396-7
Chavez, Cesar 1138
Chequamegon National Forest 613
Cherokee peoples 1150-1
Cheyenne 787-8
Chicago 18, 26, 532-57, **533, 536-7,** 18
  accommodations 546-8
  activities 544-5
  drinking & nightlife 552-3
  entertainment 553-6
  festivals & events 546
  food 548-52
  itineraries 534
  shopping 556
  sights 532-44
  tours 545-6
  travel to/from 557
  travel within 557
  walking tour 543, **543**
Chicago Blues Festival 32
children, travel with 66-8
  Alaska 1096
  Albuquerque 892
  Atlanta 413
  Baltimore 301
  Boston 196
  Chicago 544
  Hawaii 1114
  Las Vegas 824
  Los Angeles 936
  Miami 479
  New Orleans 454
  New York City 108
  Phoenix 847
  Salt Lake City 877
  San Francisco 993
  Seattle 1042
  Texas 704
childrens museums
  Boston Children's Museum 195

Brooklyn Children's Museum 103
Chicago Children's Museum 539
Children's Creativity Museum 993
Children's Museum of Atlanta 413
Children's Museum of Indianapolis 562
Children's Museum of Memphis 383
Children's Museum of Phoenix 847
Louisiana Children's Museum 454
Miami Children's Museum 479
Portland Children's Museum 1066
Tucson Children's Museum 866
Chippewa National Forest 626
Chippewa peoples 1151
Chiricahua National Monument 871
Chrysler Building 92
Chua Bo De Temple 462
churches & cathedrals
  16th Street Baptist Church 428
  Abyssinian Baptist Church 102
  Cathedral Church of St John the Divine 101
  El Santuario de Chimayó 905
  First Ebenezer Baptist Church 411
  Full Gospel Tabernacle Church 383
  La Placita 923
  Mary Queen of Vietnam Church 462
  Mission Basilica San Diego de Alcalá 952
  Mission Dolores 985
  Mission San Carlos Borromeo de Carmelo 972
  Mission Santa Barbara 965
  Old North Church 195
  San Francisco de Asís Church 905
  St Andrew's Dune Church 143
  St Augustine's Church 450
  St John's Episcopal Church 322
  St John's Lutheran Church 369
  St Louis Cathedral 446
  St Patrick's Cathedral 93

St Philip's Church 369
Thorncrown Chapel 444
Washington National Cathedral 283
Churchill Downs 399
Cimarron 908-9
Cincinnati 579-82
City Island 105
City Lights Books 981
CityCenter 823
Civil Rights movement 416, 429, 1139-41
Civil Rights Memorial Center 429
Claremore 695
Clark, William 1081
Clarksdale 433-4
Clear Lake 723-4
Cleveland 570-3
climate 22, 31, 32, 33, 34
climbing 52-3
Cloudcroft 912
CNN Center 407
cocktails 62, 64
Cody 793-4
coffee 64-5
Coit Tower 995
Coloma 1018
Colorado 754-87
Colorado Springs 777-8
Columbia Center 1043
Columbia River Gorge 1075-6
Columbia State Historic Park 1018
Columbus 565, 577-8
comedy 134, 295, 555
Concord 206
Coney Island 102
Congaree National Park 376
Connecticut 230-8
consulates 1172-3
Corolla 350
Corpus Christi 726-8
costs 23, 1170, 1173, 1176
Cougar 1061
Coupeville 1054
Crater Lake National Park 1080
Crawford Notch 254-5
Crazy Horse Memorial 676
credit cards 1175-6
Creole culture 447, 456
Crested Butte 779-80
crime 1131-2, 1176-7
Crisfield 298
Crooked Road, the 340-1
cruises 1184-5
Crystal Coast 354-5
culture 1145-9
Cumberland 310-11
Cumberland Island

National Seashore 425
currency 22
customs regulations 1171-2
cycling, see bicycling

D
Dagom Gaden Tensung Ling Monastery 566
Dahlonega 417-18
Dallas 730-7, **731**, **732**
dance 1156
dangers, see safety
Daniel Boone National Forest 404-6
Davenport 661
Dayton 578-9
Daytona Beach 505-6
Daytona International Speedway 505
Dead Horse Point State Park 886
Deadwood 674-5
Dealey Plaza & the Grassy Knoll 733
Dearborn 591-2
Death Valley National Park 638, 964-5, **639**
Delaware 311-15
Delaware Water Gap National Recreation Area 165
Denali National Park & Preserve 1106, **640**
Denver 754-63, **758-9**
accommodations 755-7
drinking & nightlife 757-60
entertainment 760-1
festivals & events 755
food 757
shopping 761
sights 754-5
travel to/from 762
travel within 762-3
Des Moines 660-1
Desolation Wilderness 1029
Detroit 26, 584-91, **586**
Devils Postpile National Monument 1027
Diamond Head 1116
Dickinson, Emily 220
Dinosaur National Monument 882
disabilities, travelers with 1178-9
Disneyland 943-5
distilleries
Boot Hill Distillery 686
Breckenridge Distillery 772
Jack Daniel's Distillery 385

Kentucky 405
Maker's Mark 403
Ole Smoky Moonshine Holler 398
Santa Fe Spirits 901
Sarasota 515
Straitsville Special Moonshine Distillery 583
Tom's Town 657-8
Wigle Whiskey 183
diving 53-4
Dodge City 686
Dolby Theatre 926
Dollywood 398
Donner Summit 1030
Door County 611-12
Douglas 595-6
Dover 314-16
drinking 62-5, 1173, 1174
driving, see car travel
drugs 1174-5
Dubuque 663-4
Duck 350
Duluth 622-4
Dunsmuir 1020
Duquesne Incline 181
Durango 785-6
Durham 357-9
DVDs 1174
Dylan, Bob 623

E
earthquakes 1166
Earthships 905
East Bay 229-31
East Hampton 142
Eastern Panhandle 342-3
Eastern Shore 306-7
economy 1130-1
Edisto Island 374
El Morro National Monument 896
El Paso 746-9
electricity 1172
Elko 838
Ellensburg 1061-2
Ellis Island 78
Embassy Row 281
embassies 1172-3
Emerald Mound 436
emergencies 23
Empire Mine State Historic Park 1018
Empire State Building 92
environmental issues 1131, 1167-8
Erie Lakeshore 573-5
Escalante 888
Essex 235-40
Estes Park 768-9
etiquette 25, 59, 1150

Eugene 1074-5
Eureka Springs 443-5
Evanston 558
events 31-4, see also individual events, locations
Everglades City 496-7
Everglades National Park 20, 493-4, 633, **20**, **632**
exchange rates 23

F
Fairbanks 1105-7
Fairmount 564-5
Fakahatchee Strand Preserve 496
Falmouth 208
Faneuil Hall 194
Fargo 665-6
farmers markets, see also markets
Arcata 1014
Boulder County 766
Los Angeles 935, 938
Madison 607
New York 90
Olympia 1050
Phoenix 846
San Francisco 994
Santa Fe 902
Waikiki 1115
Farmington 908
Fayetteville 345
Ferry Building 977
ferry travel 1186
festivals 31-4, see also individual events, locations
Fifth Avenue 91
film 1130, 1152
studios & tours 406, 407, 928
Finger Lakes 152-4
Fire Island National Seashore 141
Flagstaff 850-4
Flaming Gorge National Recreation Area 882
Flathead Lake 808-9
Flatiron Building 87
Florida 70, 468-527, **470-1**
accommodations 468
climate 468
food 468
highlights 470-1
travel seasons 468
Florida City 495-6
Florida Keys 498-504
Florida Panhandle 524-7
Floyd 340-1
Folly Beach 374

food 25, 27-8, 55-65,
    see also individual
    locations
  barbecue 56, 58, 359
  blue crabs 307
  buffets 832
  costs 1173
  customs 61-2
  food trucks 291, 721
  glossary 65
  local specialties 56-9, 549
  Mexican & Tex-Mex 56
  opening hours 61
  pizza 56
  seafood 57, 59
  Slow Food movement
    55-6
  vegetarian restaurants 58
football 1148, 1149
Forks 1053
Fort Adams 227
Fort Davis 742-3
Fort Holmes 599
Fort Lauderdale 487-90
Fort Mackinac 599
Fort Raleigh National
    Historic Site 351
Fort Ross State Historic
    Park 1011
Fort Seward 1100-1
Fort Sumter National
    Monument 370
Fort Totten 106
Fort Worden State Park
    1051-2
Fort Worth 737-9, **731**
Franconia Notch State Park
    253-4
Frank Lloyd Wright Home &
    Studio 558
Franklin 393
Franklin Delano Roosevelt
    Memorial 278
Frederick 309-10
Fredericksburg 321-2,
    714-15
Fredericksburg &
    Spotsylvania National
    Military Park 321
Freeport 261
Fremont Street Experience
    825
Friedan, Betty 1138
Front Royal 333-4
fuel 1191

G
Galax 341
Galena 558-9

Gallatin Valley 804-5
galleries, see art museums
    & galleries
Galveston 724-6
Gamble House 933
gardens, see parks &
    gardens
Garnet Ghost Town 807
Gatlinburg 398-9
gay travelers, see LGBTIQ
    travelers
General Sherman Tree 1025
geography 1164-5
geology 30
George Washington
    Memorial Parkway 317
Georgetown 282-3
Georgia 406-26
Gila Cliff Dwellings National
    Monument 911
Gila National Forest 911
Glacier National Park 20,
    635, 810-12, **20**, **634-5**
Going-to-the-Sun Road 810
Gold Coast 594-8
Gold Country 1017-19
Golden Gate Bridge 987
Golden Gate Park 987
Graceland 383
Grand Canyon National
    Park 12, 637, 854-61,
    856-7, **12**, **628**
Grand Coulee Dam 1061
Grand Island 681
Grand Rapids 593-4
Grand Staircase-Escalante
    National Monument
    888
Grand Teton National Park
    799-803, **801**
Grass Valley 1018
Great Barrington 220-1
Great Basin National
    Park 838
Great Lakes 70, 528-626,
    530-1
  accommodations 528
  climate 528
  food 58, 528
  highlights 530-1
  itineraries 529
  travel seasons 528
Great Plains 71, 641-96,
    642-3
  accommodations 641
  climate 641
  food 58, 641
  highlights 642-3
  itineraries 644
  travel seasons 641
Great River Road 45-6, 664
Great Sand Dunes National
    Park 786-7

Great Smoky Mountains
    National Park 366-9,
    633, **631**
Green Bay 611
Green County 607
Green River 882-3
Greenport 145
Greenville 378-9
Gruene 709
Guadalupe Mountains
    National Park 749
Guerneville 1009-10
Guggenheim Museum 100
Gulf Coast (Mississippi)
    437-8
Gulf Coast (Texas) 724-30
Gulf Islands National
    Seashore 526
Gullah culture 374
gun culture 1131-2
Gustavus 1103
Guthrie 694-5

H
Haines 1100-1
Haleakalā National Park
    1125, **631**
Hamakua coast 1121
Hampton Roads 328-9
Hamptons, the 142-3
Hanalei 1127-8
Hanauma Bay 1116-17
Hannibal 652-3
Hanover 255-8
Harbor Country 594-5
Harley-Davidson Plant 603
Harpers Ferry 342-3
Hartford 231-2
Harvard University 197
Hatteras Island 350
Havasupai Canyon 861
Hawaii 72, 640, 1108-128,
    631
  accommodations 1108
  climate 1108
  food 59, 1108
  highlights 1109, **1109**
  itineraries 1111
  language 1110
  travel seasons 1108
Hawai'i (the Big Island)
    1117-123
Hawai'i Volcanoes National
    Park 18, 1122-3, **18**
Healdsburg 1010
health 1173
Hearst Castle 970
Helena 806
Hells Canyon 1088
Hemingway House 501
Highway 2 680
Highway 13 612

Highway 61 625
hiking 28-9, 47-8, 49
  Abingdon 339
  Albuquerque 893
  Appalachian Trail 342-3
  Boise 813
  C&O Canal National
    Historic Park 342
  Camelback Mountain 841
  Canyonlands National
    Park 885-6
  Cape Perpetua Scenic
    Area 1084
  Capitol Reef National
    Park 887
  Chilkoot Trail 1102
  Chiricahua National
    Monument 871
  Cimarron Canyon State
    Park 909
  Crater Lake National
    Park 1080
  Crawford Notch State
    Park 254
  Denver 762
  Eldorado Canyon State
    Park 763
  Fayetteville 345
  Flume Gorge & the Basin
    253
  Galena Creek Recreation
    Area 835
  Garden of the Gods 777
  George S Mickelson
    Trail 675
  Gile Mountain 255
  Glacier National Park 811
  Golden Gate Canyon
    State Park 762
  Grand Canyon National
    Park 855, 860
  Grand Teton National
    Park 800
  Grandfather Mountain
    362
  Great Sand Dunes
    National Park 787
  Great Smoky Mountains
    National Park 366-9,
    633, **631**
  Indian Canyons 959
  Jack London State
    Historic Park 1008
  Jefferson County Open
    Space Parks 762
  Joshua Tree National
    Park 961
  Keonehe'ehe'e (Sliding
    Sands) Trail 1125
  Kings Canyon National
    Park 1026
  Lansing River Trail 593
  Lassen Volcanic National
    Park 1021
  Lincoln Woods Trail 252
  Los Angeles 933

Lost Mine Trail 740
Marginal Way 258
Maroon Bells 774
Monadnock State Park 253
Moran State Park 1056
Mount Sentinel 807
Mt Baker 1057
Mt Hood 1077
Mt Rainier National Park 1060
Mt Rogers National Recreation Area 339
Mt Washington 254
North Umpqua Trail 1087
Olympic Discovery Trail 1052
Olympic National Park 1050-1
Pike National Forest 762
Pikes Peak 777
Portland 1066-7
Rocky Mountain National Park 635, 766-8, **634**
Saguaro National Park 868-9
Santa Elena Canyon Trail 740
Santa Fe 897
Sawtooth National Recreation Area 816
Shenandoah National Park 335, 633, **632-3**
Sleeping Bear Dunes National Lakeshore 596
Standish-Hickey State Recreation Area 1013
Staunton State Park 762
Sun Valley 815
Sunset Crater Volcano National Monument 855
Superior Hiking Trail 624
Wallowa Mountains Area 1088
Washington, DC 283
Waterton Canyon 762
Whitefish 809
Yellowstone National Park 797-8
Yosemite National Park 1023
Zion National Park 889-90
Hill City 675-6
Hill Country 709-17
Hilo 1121-2
Historic RCA Studio B 391
historic sites 29-30
Historic Triangle 325-8
history 1133-44
  African American 1140
  American Revolution 1135-6
Boston Tea Party 1135
Bush eras 1142
Civil Rights movement 416, 429, 1139-41
civil war 1137
Clinton era 1142
colonialism 1134-5
continental expansion 1136
Declaration of Independence 1134-5
European settlement 1133-4
Great Depression 1138-9
Native American 1133
Obama era 1142-3
Reagan era 1141-2
slavery 1134-5, 1137
Trump presidency 1143-4
WWII 1138-9
Hoboken 162
Hocking Hills Scenic Byway 583
holidays 1176
Homestead 495-6
Honolulu 1110-13
Hood River 1076
Hoover Dam 834
horseback riding 54
  Mad River Valley 244
  Palm Springs 959
  Phoenix 841
  Saguaro National Park 868-9
Hot Springs (Arkansas) 440-1
Hot Springs (South Dakota) 677
hot springs & spas
  Agua Caliente Regional Park 962
  Chico Hot Springs 805
  Devils Postpile National Monument 1027
  Esalen Institute 971
  Granite Creek Hot Springs 792
  Kirkham Creek Hot Springs 816
  Ojo Caliente Mineral Springs Resort & Spa 904
  Ouray 780
  Qua Baths & Spa 826
  Staten Island 107
  Steamboat Springs 769-70
  Sykes Hot Springs 971
  Truth or Consequence 909
  Umpqua Hot Springs 1087
  Willamette Valley 1074
Houston 717-23, **718-19**

Hovenweep National Monument 886
Hualapai Reservation 861
Hudson Valley 145-9
Humboldt Redwoods State Park 1013
hurricanes 1166
Hyannis 208-10

I
ice climbing 780
Idaho 812-17
Idaho Panhandle 817
Illinois 529-61
immigration 1145, 1180-1, 1183
Independence 658-9
Independence Day 33
Independence Hall 169
Indiana 561-70
Indiana Dunes 568-9
Indianapolis 561-4
Indianola 434
Institute Woods 163
insurance 1173-4, 1190-1
internet access 1174
internet resources 23, 1147, 1173
Iowa 660-5
Iowa City 662
Islamorada 499-500
Isle of Palms 373
Isle Royale National Park 601-2
Ithaca 152-3
itineraries 35-9, **35**, **36**, **37**, **39**, see also individual locations

J
Jackson (Mississippi) 435-6, 791-3
Jackson (Wyoming) 791-3
Jacksonville (Florida) 508-10
Jacksonville (Oregon) 1086-7
Jalama Beach County Park 968
James Island 374
Jamestown 327-8
Jedediah Smith Redwoods State Park 1015, **14**
Jefferson Memorial 275
Jekyll Island 425-6
Jenner 1011
Jerome 848-9
Jersey Shore 163-9
John Day Fossil Beds National Monument 1087-8

Joshua Tree National Park 638, 961-2, **639**
Juneau 1098-100

K
Kaaterskill Falls 150
Kailua-Kona 1117-19
Kanab 889
Kancamagus Highway 252
Kansas 684-8
Kansas City 655-8
Kartchner Caverns State Park 870
Kaua'i 1126-8
kayaking & canoeing 51
  Amelia Island 510
  Austin 703
  Bar Harbor 264
  Bass Islands 574
  Bethel 265
  Boundary Waters 625
  Brandywine Valley 314
  Buffalo National River 445
  Everglades 495, 497
  Fort Lauderdale 487-8
  Galveston 725
  Glacier Bay National Park & Preserve 1103
  Harpers Ferry 343
  Hood River 1076
  James River 336
  Jekyll Island 426
  Key Largo 499
  Lake Dardanelle 442
  Lake Tahoe 1029
  Las Vegas 826
  Lewes 312
  Marquette 601
  Monterey 974
  New York City 108
  North Shore 624
  Ocracoke Island 353
  Ohio River 567
  Point Reyes National Seashore 1004
  Portland 1067
  Richmond 324
  San Diego 954
  San Francisco 989
  Seattle 1041
  Tarpon Bay 516
  Truckee River Whitewater Park 835-6
  Valentine 682
  Voyageurs National Park 626
Kearney 681
Kelleys Island 575
Kenai Fjords 640, **640**
Kennebunks, the 259
Kennedy Space Center 504

Kentucky 399-406
Ketchikan 1104-5
Ketchum 814-16
Key Largo 498-9
Key West 501-3
Kiawah Island 374
Kihei 1125-6
Kill Devil Hills 350
Killington 244
King, Martin Luther 411, 416
Kingman 864
Kings Canyon National Park 1025-7
Kitty Hawk 350
Klamath Basin National Wildlife Refuge Complex 1021
Knoxville 397-8
Kodiak Island 1095
Kohala Mountain Road 1121

L

La Purísima Mission State Historic Park 968
Lafayette 464-5
Lahaina 1123-5
Lake Chelan 1058
Lake George 155
Lake Mead 834
Lake of the Clouds 602
Lake Placid 156-7
Lake Powell 862
Lake Tahoe 1029-30
Lake Waramaug 233
Lakes Region 250-1
Lander 790-1
Lansing 593
Laramie 788-90
Las Cruces 910-11
Las Vegas (Nevada) 19, 26, 822-34, **827**, 19
    accommodations 826-9
    activities 826
    drinking & nightlife 831-2
    entertainment 832-3
    food 830-1
    shopping 833
    sights 823-6
    tourist information 834
    travel to/from 834
    travel within 834
Las Vegas (New Mexico) 903
Lassen Volcanic National Park 1021
Lava Beds National Monument 1021

Map Pages **000**
Photo Pages **000**

Lawrence 685-7
Lead 675
Leavenworth 1057-8
Leesburg 337
legal matters 65, 1174-5
Lenox 221-2
lesbian travelers, see LGBTIQ travelers
Lewes 311-12
Lewis, Meriwether 1081
Lexington (Kentucky) 402-4
Lexington (Massachusetts) 205-6
Lexington (Virginia) 335-7
LGBTIQ travelers 1175
    Alaska 1093
    Atlanta 415
    Boston 202
    Chicago 554
    Fort Lauderdale 489
    Los Angeles 940
    Miami 485
    Minneapolis 618
    New Orleans 458
    New York City 126
    San Francisco 999
    Texas 707
    Washington, DC 294
libraries
    Billy Graham Library 360
    FDR Presidential Library & Museum 148
    Folger Shakespeare Library 279
    James Monroe Museum & Memorial Library 321
    Library of Congress 279
    Lincoln Presidential Library & Museum 559
    Mary Baker Eddy Library & Mapparium 196
    Morgan Library & Museum 92
    National Sporting Library 337
    New York Public Library 92
    Providence Athenaeum 224
    Provincetown Public Library 213
    Sanborn Library 255
    Woodrow Wilson Presidential Library 334
lighthouses
    Cape May Lighthouse 167
    Horton Point Lighthouse 145
    Martha's Vineyard 217
    Portland Head Light 260
    Rockland Breakwater Lighthouse 262-3
    Saugerties Lighthouse 151

Lincoln (Nebraska) 680-1
Lincoln (New Hampshire) 252-3
Lincoln (New Mexico) 913
Lincoln, Abraham 559-60
Lincoln Center 97
Lincoln Memorial 270
Litchfield 232-3
literature 1130, 1143, 1153-5
Little Bighorn Battlefield National Monument 807
Little Rock 438-40
Living Desert State Park 914
Lockhart 708-9
Logan 583
Lombard Street 981
Long Island 141-5
Lopez Island 1057
Los Alamos 903
Los Angeles 20, 918-43, **920-1**, 20
    accommodations 934-6
    activities 933-4
    Beverly Hills 929, 935-6
    Downtown 919-21, 934, 937, **924-5**
    drinking & nightlife 939-40
    El Pueblo de Los Angeles 921-2
    entertainment 940-1
    festivals & events 934
    food 937-9
    Griffith Park 926-8, 937-8
    Hollywood 926, 927, 928-9, 934-5, 937-8, **930-1**
    itineraries 923
    Long Beach 931-2, 936, 939
    Malibu 929
    Mid-City 928-9, 938, **930-1**
    Pasadena 932-3, 936, 939
    Santa Monica 930, 936, 938, **932**
    shopping 941-2
    sights 919-33
    South Park 923-4
    tourist information 942
    tours 934
    travel to/from 942
    travel within 943
    Venice 931, 938
Los Olivos 968
Lost Coast 1013
Louisiana 445-67
Louisville 399-402
Lowcountry 374-7
Lower Hudson Valley 146-7
Lower Keys 500-1
Luckenbach 714
Luray 333-4

M

Mackinac Island 599-600
Mackinaw City 598
Mad River Valley 244-5
Madison 607-9
Madison County 661
magazines 1174
Maine 256-65, **257**
Mall of America 620
Mammoth Cave National Park 406, 633, **629**
Mamou 466
Manassas National Battlefield Park 317
Manchester 242
Manitou Islands 596
Mansfield 180
Manteo 350
Marathon 500
Mardi Gras 31, 452
Marfa 743-5
marijuana 1132, 1174-5
Marin County 1003-4
Maritime National Historical Park 981
markets, see also farmers markets
    Ann Arbor 592
    Davenport 661
    Detroit 585
    Indianapolis 563
    Kidron 576
    Milwaukee 605
    New Orleans 451
    New York 87, 135, 136
    O'ahu 1111
    Pittsburgh 182
    Seattle 1036
Marquette 601
Martha's Vineyard 217-18, **209**
Martin House Complex 159
Martin Luther King Jr Memorial 271
Maryland 297-311
Mashomack Nature Preserve 145
Massachusetts 185-223
Massachusetts State House 190
Maui 1123-6
Mauna Kea 1120-1
measures 1174
medical services 1173
Medicine Park 690
Memorial to Peace & Justice 26
Memphis 26, 379-87, **379**, **382**
    accommodations 384
    drinking & entertainment 387
    festivals & events 383-4

food 385-6
sights 381-3
tours 384
travel to/from 387
travel within 387
Mendocino 1011
Menemsha 216
Meow Wolf 26
Mesa Verde National Park 635, 784-5, **16**, **634**
Methow Valley 1058
Mexico, travel to/from 1184
Miami 469-87, **474**, **476**
accommodations 481-3
activities 480
drinking & nightlife 484-5
festivals & events 480-1
food 483-4
itineraries 472
sights 469-80
tours 480
travel to/from 486
travel within 486-7
walking tour 482, **482**
Michigan 583-602
microbreweries, see breweries & microbreweries
Middleburg 337
Milk, Harvey 1138
Million Dollar Highway 780
Milwaukee 603-6
Minneapolis 614-20, **616-17**
Minnesota 613-26
Mission San Xavier del Bac 870
Mississippi 432-8
Mississippi Delta 433-5
Missoula 806-8
Missouri 644-60
Moab 883-5
Mobile 431-2
mobile phones 1177
Mojave National Preserve 963-4
Mokelumne Hill 1018
money 22, 23, 25, 1172, 1175-6
Mono Lake 1027
Monona Terrace 607
Monongahela National Forest 344
Montana 803-12
Montauk 143-4
Monterey 973-5
Montgomery 429-30
Monticello 331
Montpelier (Vermont) 245
Montpelier (Virginia) 331
Monument Valley Navajo Tribal Park 863
Morehead City 354

Morro Bay State Park 970
motor sports 378, 505
motorcycle travel 1190-3, **1192**
Motown Records 590
Mount Magazine State Park 441
Mount Vernon 318-19
mountain biking 50, see also bicycling
Bend 1079
Buffalo Creek 762
Crested Butte 779
Duluth 624
Flagstaff 851-2
Helena 806
Lander 790
Leavenworth 1057
Moab 883
Monarch Crest Trail 776
Phoenix 841
Portland 1067
Santa Fe 897
Stanley 816
Whitefish 809
Winter Park 770-1
Mountain View 442-3
Mt Airy 309-10
Mt Baker 1057
Mt Baldhead 595
Mt Equinox Skyline Drive 242
Mt Hood 1076-8
Mt Pleasant 373-4
Mt Rainier National Park 638, 1060, **630-1**
Mt Rogers National Recreation Area 339
Mt Rushmore 676
Mt Shasta 1020
Mt St Helens National Volcanic Monument 1061
Mt Tamalpais State Park 1004
Mt Vernon 662-3
Mt Washington 254
Mt Washington Valley 254-5
Murphys 1018
museums 30, see also art museums & galleries, childrens museums
4-H Tidelands Nature Center 426
Abbe Museum 264
Acadian Cultural Center 464
Acadian Village 464
Adler Planetarium 535
Aiken-Rhett House 370
Air Mobility Command Museum 315
Akta Lakota Museum & Cultural Center 668

Alaska Aviation Heritage Museum 1092
Alaska State Museum 1098
Allegany Museum 310
Amelia Island Museum of History 510
American Civil War Museum: Historic Tredegar 322-3
American International Rattlesnake Museum 892
American Jazz Museum 656
American Museum of Natural History 97
American Revolution Museum at Yorktown 328
American Sign Museum 579-80
Amstel House 314
Anchorage Museum 1091-2
Arabia Steamboat Museum 656
Arizona Museum of Natural History 841
Arizona Science Center 847
Arizona-Sonora Desert Museum 865
Arizona State Museum 865
Art Car Museum 717
Art Deco Museum 472-3
Atlantic City Historical Museum 166
Auburn Cord Duesenberg Museum 570
Auburn Mansion 437
Automotive Hall of Fame 592
Autry Museum of the American West 927
Avila Adobe 921
Backstreet Cultural Museum 447
Baker Museum 517
Barnes Foundation 169
Barney Ford Museum 771
Bay Area Discovery Museum 1003-4
BB King Museum and Delta Interpretive Center 434
Beat Museum 981
Benjamin Franklin Museum 172
Bennington Museum 241
Billings Farm & Museum 243
Birmingham Civil Rights Institute 427
Bishop Museum 1111

Black Voices 342
Blaine Kern's Mardi Gras World 451
Blair-Caldwell African American Museum 755
Blumenschein Home & Museum 905
Bob Bullock Texas State History Museum 701
Bonnet House 487
Boston Tea Party Ships & Museum 195-6
Bradbury Science Museum 903
Broad 922
Brooklyn Museum 103
Brown v Board of Education National Historic Site 687
Brunswick Visitor Center 309
Bryan Museum 724-5
Buffalo Bill Center of the West 794
Bureau of Engraving and Printing 738
Burke Museum 1040-1
Cabildo 446
Cable Car Museum 981
Cajun Music Hall of Fame & Museum 466
California Academy of Sciences 993
California Museum 1016
California Science Center 925
Cape Cod Museum of Natural History 210
Carnegie Museums 181
Carolina Basketball Museum 359
Carter Center 411
Center for Civil & Human Rights 407
Center for PostNatural History 181
Center in the Square 338
Chapin Mesa Museum 784
Charleston Museum 370
Chesapeake Bay Maritime Museum 306
Chicago History Museum 541
Chinati Foundation Museum 743-4
Chinese Historical Society of America 981
Cincinnati Museum Center 579
City Museum 645
Clark Planetarium 873
Cloisters Museum & Gardens 102
Clyfford Still Museum 755

museums *continued*

College Basketball Experience 655

College Football Hall of Fame 407

Colonial Quarter 507

Colonial Williamsburg 326

Colorado Springs Pioneers Museum 777

Columbia River Maritime Museum 1081

Connecticut River Museum 236

Contemporary Austin 701

Cooper-Hewitt National Design Museum 100-1

Country Music Hall of Fame & Museum 390

Cranberry Mountain Nature Center 344

Da Yoopers Tourist Trap and Museum 601

Dahlonega Courthouse Gold Museum 417

Dallara IndyCar Factory 561

DEA Museum 318

Delaware History Museum 313

Delta Blues Museum 433

Denver Museum of Nature & Science 755

Design Museum Boston 194-5

Dexter Avenue Parsonage 429

Discovery 835

Discovery World at Pier Wisconsin 604

Doo Wop Experience 167

Dumbarton Oaks 282

Durham Museum 679

Dutch House 314

East Hampton Town Marine Museum 142

Eastern State Penitentiary 173

Edgar Allan Poe House & Museum 299

Eisenhower Presidential Center 688

El Paso Holocaust Museum 746-7

Emily Dickinson Museum 220

Empire State Railway Museum 149

Eric Carle Museum of Picture Book Art 220

Eudora Welty House 435

Evergreen Museum 300

Exploration Place 684-5

Exploratorium 977-8

Fairmount Historical Museum 564

Field Museum of Natural History 535

First State Heritage Park Welcome Center & Galleries 315

Five Civilized Tribes Museum 695

Flagler Museum 490

Florida Keys History of Diving Museum 499

Florida Museum of Photographic Arts 512

Ford Piquette Avenue Plant 585

Ford's Theatre Center for Education and Leadership 280

Fort William Henry Museum 155

Frazier History Museum 400

Freedom House Museum 319

Fremont County Pioneer Museum 790

Frontier Culture Museum 334

Frontier Days Old West Museum 787-8

Frontier Drugstore Museum 694

Frontier Times Museum 716

Galaxy Connection 440

Galveston Railroad Museum 725

Gangster Museum of America 440

Geological Museum 789

Georgia Museum of Art 418

Gerald R Ford Museum 594

Giant Forest Museum 1025

Gilcrease Museum 692

Glore Psychiatric Museum 659

Gold Coast Railroad Museum 480

Graceland 383

Grammy Museum 924

Grand Ole Opry House 391

Graveyard of the Atlantic Museum 351

Great Lakes Science Center 571

Greater Ridgewood Historic Society 106-7

Green Bay Packers Hall of Fame 611

Greenfield Village 591-2

Griffith Observatory 927

Gulf Coast Exploreum 431

Hammond Harwood House 304

Harley-Davidson Museum 603

Harriet Beecher-Stowe Center 231

Harrison Museum of African American Culture 338

Harvard Museum of Natural History 197, 199

Heard Museum 839-40

Hemingway House 501

Henry Ford Museum 591

Heritage Museums & Gardens 207

Heritage Society at San Houston Park 717-18

High Desert Museum 1078

Hirshhorn Museum 275

Historic New Orleans Collection 447

Historic Pensacola Village 526

Historic Village at Allaire 164

History Colorado Center 755

HistoryMiami 475

Hoboken Historical Museum 162

Hollywood Museum 926

Hopi Museum 865

House on the Rock 610

Houston Museum of Natural Science 717

Hubbard Museum of the American West 912-13

Huntington Library, Art Collections & Botanical Gardens 933

Idaho State Historical Museum 813

Illinois Holocaust Museum 558

'Imiloa Astronomy Center of Hawai'i 1122

Immigration Museum (Ellis Island) 78

Indian Pueblo Cultural Center 892-3

Indiana Medical History Museum 562

Indianapolis Motor Speedway 561

International Museum of Muslim Cultures 435

International Spy Museum 281

International Tennis Hall of Fame 227-8

Intrepid Sea, Air & Space Museum 93

J Millard Tawes Historical Museum 298

James Dean Gallery 564

James Monroe Museum & Memorial Library 321

Japanese American National Museum 923

Jewish Museum 101

Jewish Museum of Maryland 299

John Brown House 224

John Brown Museum 342

John Dickinson Plantation 315

John F Kennedy Hyannis Museum 208

John Wesley Powell River History Museum 882

Johnny Cash Museum & Store 390

Joseph Manigault House 370

Joslyn Art Museum 679

Journey Museum & Learning Center 671-2

Junípero Serra Museum 952

Kansas Cosmosphere & Space Center 685

Kansas Museum of History 687

Kennedy Space Center 504

Kentucky Derby Museum 399-400

Kentucky Horse Park 402

Kentucky Science Center 400

Kilauea Visitor Center & Museum 1123

King Center for Non-Violent Social Change 411

Klondike Gold Rush National Historical Park Museum & Visitor Center 1102

Kurt Vonnegut Museum & Library 562

La Brea Tar Pits & Museum 928-9

LA Plaza 921

Landis Valley Museum 179

Landmark Center 620

Laura Ingalls Wilder Museum 610-11

Levine Museum of the New South 360

Lewis & Clark Boathouse & Nature Center 651

Lewis & Clark Information Center 668

Lighthouse Museum 425

Lightner Museum 507

Lincoln Presidential Library & Museum 559

Litchfield History Museum 232

Lone Star Flight Museum 718

Los Alamos Historical Museum 903

Louisiana Universities Marine Consortium 465-6

Louisville Slugger Museum & Factory 400

Lower East Side Tenement Museum 83

Lower Mississippi River Museum 435

Lowndes County Interpretive Center 431

Madame Tussauds 825

Maine Maritime Museum 262

Margaret Mitchell House & Museum 410

Marine Educational Center 1117

Maritime Museum (San Diego) 947

Maritime Museum (San Francisco) 984

Maritime Visitor Center 623

Mark Twain Boyhood Home & Museum 653

Mark Twain House & Museum 231

Martin Luther King Jr Birthplace 411

Martin Luther King Jr National Historic Site 411

Martínez Hacienda 904-5

Maryland Historical Society 299-300

Maryland Science Center 301

Memphis Rock 'n' Soul Museum 381

Menil Collection 717

Mennello Museum of American Art 518

Meow Wolf 896

Mercer-Williams House 420

Mexic-Arte Museum 700-1

Mill City Museum 614

Millicent Rogers Museum 904

Mingei International Museum 949

Mini Time Machine of Museum of Miniatures 868

Miracle of America Museum 808

Missouri History Museum 647

MIT Museum 197

Mob Museum 826

Moraine Park Museum 767

Morgan Library & Museum 92

Morven Museum & Garden 163

Motown Historical Museum 585

MOXI 965

Muhammad Ali Center 400

Museum at Eldridge Street Synagogue 84-5

Museum of Ancient Life 875

Museum of Art & History at the Custom House 501

Museum of Arts & Design 93

Museum of Chinese in America 83

Museum of Discovery 438-9

Museum of Discovery & Science 487

Museum of Indian Arts & Culture 899

Museum of Jewish Heritage 78

Museum of Natural Science 435

Museum of Northern Arizona 851

Museum of Pop Culture 1037

Museum of Science 195

Museum of Science & History 727

Museum of Science & Industry 542

Museum of Sex 93

Museum of the American Revolution 169

Museum of the Big Bend 745

Museum of the City of New York 101

Museum of the Everglades 497

Museum of the Moving Image 105

Museum of the Rockies 803

Museum of the Shenandoah Valley 333

Museum of the Weird 701

Museum of Tolerance 929

Museum of Transportation 647

Museum of Western Film History 1028

Musical Instrument Museum 840

Mütter Museum 171-2

Mystery Hole 345

Mystic Seaport Museum 233

Nantucket Whaling Museum 215

NASCAR Hall of Fame 360

Nasher Sculpture Center 733

Nathaniel Russell House 370

National Air and Space Museum 270-1

National Atomic Testing Museum 826

National Automobile Museum 835

National Automotive and Truck Museum 570

National Blues Museum 646

National Border Patrol Museum 747

National Civil Rights Museum 381

National Cowboy & Western Heritage Museum 689

National Cowgirl Museum 738

National Frontier Trails Museum 659

National Geographic Museum 282

National Great Blacks in Wax Museum 299

National Inventors Hall of Fame & Museum 319

National Mississippi River Museum & Aquarium 663

National Museum of African American History and Culture 271

National Museum of American History 274

National Museum of Civil War Medicine 309

National Museum of Natural History 274

National Museum of the American Indian 75, 278

National Museum of the Pacific War 714

National Museum of the US Air Force 578

National Museum of Toys & Miniatures 656

National Museum of Wildlife Art 791

National Mustard Museum 609

National Naval Aviation Museum 526

National Postal Museum 279

National Railroad Museum 611

National Toy Train Museum 179

National Underground Railroad Freedom Center 579

National Voting Rights Museum 430-1

National Women's Hall of Fame 153

National WWI Museum 655

National WWII Museum 451

Natural History Museum of Los Angeles 926

Natural History Museum of Utah 873

Nauticus 329

Naval Station Norfolk 329

Negro Leagues Baseball Museum 655-6

Neon Museum – Neon Boneyard 826

Nevada State Railroad Museum 837

New Mexico Farm & Ranch Heritage Museum 910

New York City Fire Museum 82-3

New York Hall of Science 106

New York Transit Museum 103

New-York Historical Society 97, 100

Newseum 280

North Carolina Maritime Museum 354

North Carolina Museum of History 356

North Carolina Museum of Natural Sciences 357

North Dakota Heritage Center 666

Northwest Museum of Arts & Culture 1059

Norton Museum of Art 492

Ocean City Life-Saving Station Museum 307

Okhaloma City National Memorial Museum 689

Okhaloma History Center 689

Oklahoma Jazz Hall of Fame 692

Old Capitol Museum 435, 662

Old Court House 314

museums *continued*
Old Courthouse Museum 668
Old Cowtown Museum 684
Old Rhinebeck Aerodrome 149
Old Slave Mart Museum 369
Old Town San Diego State Historic Park 952
Oregon Historical Society 1065
Osborn-Jackson House 142
Oscar Getz Museum of Whiskey History 405
Owens-Thomas House 420-1
Pacific Science Center 1042
Pacific Tsunami Museum 1122
Palace of the Governors & New Mexico History Museum 899
Park City Museum 878
Parris Island Museum 376
Parthenon 390
Patricia & Phillip Frost Museum of Science 475, 476
Patriot's Point Naval & Maritime Museum 374
Peabody Museum of Archaeology & Ethnology 199
Peggy Notebaert Nature Museum 544
Penn Center 376
Pérez Art Museum Miami 475
Perot Museum of Nature & Science 733
Pilgrim Monument & Provincetown Museum 212-13
Pioneer Museum 714-15
Plains Art Museum 665
Poe Museum 323
Pony Express National Museum 659
Prairie Acadian Cultural Center 466
Prairie Village Museum 667
Presbytère 446-7
Queens Museum 106
Railroad Museum of Pennsylvania 179
RE Olds Transportation Museum 593

Red Cloud Heritage Center 670
Reuben H Fleet Science Center 950
Rhythm! Discovery Center 562
Ringling Museum Complex 515
Ripley's Believe it or Not! 166
Rock & Roll Hall of Fame & Museum 571
Rosa Parks Museum 430
Rothko Chapel 717
Route 66 689
Sag Harbor Whaling & Historical Museum 142
San Diego Air & Space Museum 951
San Diego Museum of Man 950
San Diego Natural History Museum 950
Santa Barbara Maritime Museum 965-6
Science Museum of Minnesota 621
Scott & Zelda Fitzgerald Museum 429-30
Selma Interpretive Center 431
Seymour Marine Discovery Center 975
Shaker Village at Pleasant Hill 404
Shore Line Trolley Museum 237
Sixth Floor Museum 730
Skagway Museum 1102
Skeletons: Museum of Osteology 690
Skyscraper Museum 78
Slave Haven Underground Railroad Museum/ Burkle Estate 381
Songbirds 396
South Dakota Cultural Heritage Center 668
South Florida Science Center & Aquarium 492
Southampton Historical Museum 143
Southeast Alaska Discovery Center 1104
Southeast Museum of Photography 505
Southern Plains Indian Museum 695
Space Center Houstin 723
St Louis Science Center 647
St Petersburg Museum of Fine Arts 514
Star-Spangled Banner Flag House & 1812 Museum 299

Stax Museum of American Soul Music 383
Story of Wounded Knee 669
Strategic Air Command & Aerospace Museum 679
Studebaker National Museum 569
Stuhr Museum of the Prairie Pioneer 681
Tallahassee Automobile & Collectibles Museum 524
Tallahassee Museum of History & Natural Science 524
Telfair Academy of Arts & Sciences 421
Textile Museum 280
Thinkery 701
Titan Missile Museum 870
Titanic the Experience 519
Truman Presidential Museum & Library 658-9
Tudor Place 283
Union Pacific Railroad Museum 678
United States Holocaust Memorial Museum 278-9
University of Alaska Museum of the North 1105-6
University of Mississippi Museum 432
USS *Alabama* 431
USS *Albacore* 250
USS *Lexington* Museum 726-7
USS *Midway* Museum 947
Utah Field House of Natural History State Park Museum 881
Vermilionville 464
Villa Zorayda Museum 507
Virginia Historical Society 322
Vizcaya Museum & Gardens 479
WC Handy House Museum 381
Western Folklife Center 838
Wheelwright Museum of the American Indian 896-7
White House Visitor Center 280
White Sands Missile Test Center Museum 910

William J Clinton Presidential Center 438
Willie Nelson & Friends Museum Showcase 391
Wing Luke Museum of the Asian Pacific American Experience 1037
Witte Museum 711
Wo Hing Museum 1124
Wolfsonian-FIU 472
Women's Basketball Hall of Fame 397
Women's Rights National Historical Park 153
Woody Guthrie Center 692
World of Coca-Cola 407
Wrangell Museum 1095
Wright Brothers National Memorial 350-1
Wyoming Territorial Prison 788-9
Ybor City Museum State Park 512
Zwaanendael Museum 311
music 16, 30, 1046, 1132, 1161-3
Muskogee 695-6
Myrtle Beach 377-8
Mystic 233-4

N
Nader, Ralph 1138
Nags Head 350
Nantucket 215-16, **209**
Napa Valley 1006-8
Naples 517-18
Nashville 387-96, **388-9**
Natchez 436-7
National Archives 280
National Cherry Blossom Festival 31
National Mall 13, 267, 270-8, **676-7**, 13, **276**, **277**
national parks 627-40, 1167-8, *see also* parks & gardens, state parks, wildlife reserves
Acadia National Park 19, 263, 633, **632**
Arches National Park 637, 885, **636-7**
Badlands National Park 635, 669-70, **672-3**
Big Bend National Park 740-1
Biscayne National Park 494-5
Bryce Canyon National Park 637, 888-9, **636**
Canyonlands National Park 885-6

Capitol Reef National Park 887

Channel Islands National Park 966

Congaree National Park 376

Crater Lake National Park 1080

Death Valley National Park 638, 964-5, **639**

Denali National Park & Preserve 1106, **640**

Everglades National Park 493-4, 633, **20**, **632**

Glacier Bay National Park & Preserve 1103-4

Glacier National Park 20, 635, 810-12, **20**, **634-5**

Grand Canyon National Park 12, 637, 854-61, **856-7**, **12**, **628**

Grand Teton National Park 799-803, **801**

Great Basin National Park 838

Great Sand Dunes National Park 786-7

Great Smoky Mountains National Park 366-9, 633, **631**

Haleakalā National Park 1125, **631**

Hanauma Bay Nature Preserve 1116-17

Hawai'i Volcanoes National Park 18, 1122-3, **18**

Hot Springs National Park 440

Isle Royale National Park 601-2

Joshua Tree National Park 638, 961-2, **639**

Kenai Fjords 640, **640**

Kings Canyon National Park 1025-7

Lassen Volcanic National Park 1021

Mammoth Cave National Park 406, 633, **629**

Mesa Verde National Park 635, 784-5, **16**, **634**

Mt Rainier National Park 638, 1060, **630-1**

North Cascades National Park 1058-9

Olympic National Park 638, 1050-1, **629**

Petrified Forest National Park 864

Redwood National Park 638, 1015, **638**

Rocky Mountain National Park 635, 766-8, **634**

Saguaro National Park 637, 868-9

Sequoia National Park 1025

Shenandoah National Park 335, 633, **632-3**

Sitka National Historical Park 1097

Theodore Roosevelt National Park 666-7

Voyageurs National Park 626

Wind Cave National Park 677

Yellowstone National Park 11, 635, 794-9, **796**, **11**, **635**

Yosemite National Park 13, 638, 1022-5, **13**, **639**

Zion National Park 637, 889-90, **637**

National September 11 Memorial 75

National WWII Memorial 275

Native American people & culture 16, 29, 1150-1

Native American sites

Acoma Pueblo 895-6

Aztec Ruins National Monument 908

Bandelier National Monument 903-4

Bears Ears National Monument 879

Cahokia Mounds State Historic Site 560

Canyon de Chelly National Monument 862-3

Chaco Culture National Historical Park 908

El Morro National Monument 896

Gila Cliff Dwellings National Monument 911-14

Hopewell Culture National Historical Park 582

Hovenweep National Monument 886-7

Inscription Rock Petroglyphs 575

Lava Beds National Monument 1021

Mesa Verde National Park 784

Monument Valley 863

Navajo National Monument 862

Newspaper Rock State Historic Monument 889

Petroglyph National Monument 893

Puyé Cliff Dwellings 903

San Ildefonso Pueblo 903

Serpent Mound 582

Taos Pueblo 906

Valley of Fire State Park 835

Walnut Canyon 853

Natural Bridges National Monument 887

Navajo Nation 862-3

Navajo National Monument 862

Navajo peoples 1151

Neah Bay 1053

Nebraska 677-83

Nebraska Panhandle 682-3

Nevada 822-38

New Castle 314

New England 15, 69, 184-265, **186-7**, **15**

accommodations 184

climate 184

food 57, 184

highlights 186-7

travel seasons 184

New Hampshire 249-56, **239**

New Harmony 567

New Haven 236-8

New Jersey 69, 162-8, **76-7**

New London 234-5

New Mexico 891-914

New Orleans 14, 446-60, **448-9**

accommodations 452-5

drinking & nightlife 457

entertainment 457-8

festivals & events 452

food 455-7

shopping 458

sights 446-52

tours 452

travel to/from 459

travel within 459-60

walking tour 453, **453**

New Paltz 147-8

New River Gorge National River 344-5

New York City 11, 75-140, **79**, **10-11**

accommodations 74, 109-13

activities 107-8

Bronx, the 103-5, 123

Brooklyn 102-3, 112, 121-3, 129-30, 135

Central Park 96-7, 98-9, **94-5**, **98-9**, **98**, **99**

Chelsea 85-7, 110-11, 116-17, 126-7, **88-9**

Chinatown 81-3, 110, 114-24, 125, **80-1**

climate 74

Downtown 135-6

drinking & nightlife 124-31

East Village 83-5, 115-16, 126, **84-5**

entertainment 131-5

festivals & events 109

Fifth Avenue 91

Financial District 75, 78, 81, 109, 113-14, 124-5

Flatiron District 87, 90-1, 111, 117-18, 127-8

food 56-7, 74, 113-24

Gramercy 87, 90-1, 111, 117-18, 127-8

Harlem 101-2, 112, 121, 129

highlights 76-7, **76-7**

internet access 136-7

itineraries 83

Little Italy 82

Lower East Side 83-5, 115-16, 126

Lower Manhattan 75, 78, 81, 109, 113-14, 124-5

Meatpacking District 85-7, 110-11, 116-17, 126-7

Midtown 91-3, 111, 118-20, 128-9, 136, **88-9**

Queens 105-7, 112-13, 123-4, 130-1

shopping 135-41

sights 75-107

SoHo 81-3, 110, 114-5, 125

Staten Island 107

Times Square 91, **88-9**

tourist information 137

tours 108-9

travel seasons 74

travel to/from 137-9

travel within 139-40

Union Square 87, 90-1, 111, 117-18, 127-8

Upper East Side 100-1, 112, 120-1, 129

Upper Manhattan 101-2, 112, 121, 129

Upper West Side 93, 96-7, 100, 111-12, 120, 129

Uptown 136, **94-5**

walking tour 104, **104**

West Village 85-7, 110-11, 116-17, 126-7, **84-5**

New York State 69, 140-62

Newberry National Volcanic Monument 1080

Newport 226-9, 1083

Newspaper Rock State Historic Monument 889

newspapers 1174

Niagara Falls 160-2

Nike Missile Site SF-88 1003

Norfolk 328-9

North Adams 223
North Carolina 347-68
North Cascades 1057-9
North Dakota 665-7
North Fork 144-5
North Platte 681-2
North Umpqua River 1087
North Woodstock 252-3
Northampton 218-19

O
O'ahu 1110-17
Oak Park 557
Obama, Barack 1142-3
observatories
    Griffith Observatory 927
    Kitt Peak National
        Observatory 869
    Lowell Observatory 851
    McDonald Observatory
        742
    Very Large Array 912
Ocean City 307-9
Ocean Grove 164-5
Ocracoke Island 350, 353-4
Ogunquit 258-9
Ohio 570-83
Ohio River 566-7
Ojo Caliente 904
OK Corral 871
Oklahoma 688-96
Oklahoma City 689-91
Old Lyme 235
Old State House (Boston)
    191
Olympia 1049-50
Olympic National Park 638,
    1050-1, 629
Olympic Peninsula 1050-3
Omaha 678-80
One World Observatory 75
opening hours 23, 61, 1176
Orange County 945-7
Orcas Island 1056-7
Oregon 1063-88
Oregon Cascades 1076-80
Oregon Caves National
    Monument & Preserve
    1087
Oregon Dunes National
    Recreation Area 1084-5
Organ Pipe Cactus National
    Monument 869
Orlando 518-21, 520
Ouray 780-1
Outer Banks 350-3
Oxford 432-3
Ozark Mountains 442-6
Ozarks, the 653-5

Map Pages 000
Photo Pages 000

P
Pacific Coast Highway
    14, 42-3
Pacific Northwest 72, 1031-
    88, 1032-3
    accommodations 1031
    climate 1031
    food 59, 1031
    highlights 1032-3
    itineraries 1034
    travel seasons 1031
    travel to/from 1035
    travel within 1035
Padre Island National
    Seashore 728
painting 1155-7
Palm Beach 490-1
Palm Springs 958-61
Paradise Valley 804-5
paragliding 791
Park City 876-81
parks & gardens, see
    also national parks,
    state parks, wildlife
    reserves
    Airlie Gardens 355
    Alamo Square Park 986-7
    Alton Baker Park 1074
    Ashland 402
    Atlanta Botanical Garden
        410
    Audrey Headframe Park
        848
    Banyan Tree Square 1124
    Bartholomew Park 1008
    Battery & White Point
        Gardens 370
    Battery Park 81
    Belle Isle 323
    Boise River Float 813
    Boise River Greenbelt 813
    Boscobel House &
        Gardens 146
    Boston Common 190
    Brackenridge Park 711
    Brookgreen Gardens 377
    Brooklyn Botanic Garden
        103
    Brooklyn Bridge Park 102
    Bryant Park 93
    Buffalo Bayou Park 717
    Campus Martius Park
        585
    Cave Point County
        Park 611
    Central Park 96-7, 98-9,
        94-5, 98-9, 98, 99
    Chautauqua Park 763
    Chicago Botanic Garden
        558
    Confluence Park 754-5
    Coolidge Park 396
    Cornell Botanic Gardens
        152
    Crescent Park 451
    Crissy Field 984-5
    Dallas Arboretum &
        Botanical Gardens 733
    Desert Botanical Garden
        840
    Discovery Park 1047
    Dolores Park 985-6
    Dumbarton Oaks 282
    Elizabethan Gardens 351
    Fairchild Tropical Gardens
        478
    Forest Park (Portland)
        1066
    Forest Park (St Louis)
        645
    Forsyth Park 420
    Fort Williams Park 259-60
    Frederik Meijer Gardens
        593
    Garden of the Gods 777
    Gardens of the American
        Rose Center 467
    Georgetown Waterfront
        Park 282
    Golden Gate Park 987-9
    Gramercy Park 91
    Griffith Park 926-7
    Harriet Island 621
    Heritage Museums &
        Gardens 207
    High Line 86
    Hudson River Park 87
    Huntington Botanical
        Gardens 933
    Independence National
        Historic Park 169
    Island Park 515
    Japanese Tea Garden 711
    Lake Leatherwood City
        Park 444
    Lili'uokalani Park 1122
    Lincoln Park 541
    Lithia Park 1085
    Los Angeles Botanical
        Gardens 927-8
    Louis Armstrong Park
        450
    Maggie Daley Park 535
    Marsh-Billings-
        Rockefeller National
        Historical Park 243
    Mary Ann Brown Preserve
        463
    Mary Ross Waterfront
        Park 424
    Máximo Gómez Park
        477
    McKinney Roughs Nature
        Park 708
    Millennium Park 532, 534
    Minneapolis Sculpture
        Garden 614
    Minute Man National
        Historic Park 206
    Missouri Botanical
        Garden 647
    Mohonk Preserve 147
    Mud Island 381
    Naples Botanical Gardens
        517
    National Sculpture
        Garden 271
    New Haven Green 237
    New York Botanical
        Garden 105
    Northerly Island 535
    Olympic Sculpture Park
        1036-7
    Opus 40 Sculpture Park
        & Museum 151
    Pappajohn Sculpture
        Park 660
    Piedmont Park 410
    Presque Isle Park 601
    Prospect Park 103
    Public Garden (Boston)
        191
    Railroad Park 427
    Red Butte Garden 873
    Riverside Park 100
    Roanoke Star & Mill
        Mountain Park 338
    Roger Williams Park 225
    Rose Garden 925
    Rose Kennedy Greenway
        194
    San Francisco Botanical
        Garden 987
    Scotts Bluff National
        Monument 683
    Shofuso Japanese House
        & Garden 172
    State Botanical Garden of
        Georgia 418
    Sunnylands Center &
        Gardens 958-9
    Tom McCall Waterfront
        Park 1063
    Tompkins Square Park 84
    Vulcan Park 427
    Walkway Over the
        Hudson 148
    Washington Park 1066
    Washington Square
        Park 87
passports 1179-80, 1183
Patagonia-Sonoita Creek
    Preserve 870
Paul Revere House 195
Peanut Island 492
Pearl Harbor 1116
Pelee Island 575
Pennsylvania 69, 168-83
Pennsylvania Dutch
    Country 178-9
Pennsylvania Wilds 179-80
Pensacola 525-7
Pentagon 317
Petoskey 597-8

Petroglyph Beach 1095
Petroglyph National Monument 893
Pfeiffer Big Sur State Park 971
Philadelphia 169-78, **170-1, 174**
accommodations 173-5
activities 169-73
drinking & nightlife 176-7
entertainment 177
festivals & events 173
food 175-6
shopping 177-8
sights 169-73
tourist information 178
travel to/from 178
travel within 178
Phoenecia 149-50
Phoenix 839-47, **844-5**
phonecards 1178
Pictured Rocks National Lakeshore 600-3
Piedmont, the 330-3
Pierre 668-9
Pike Place Market 1036
Pine Ridge Indian Reservation 670
Pinnacles National Park 971
Pioneer Square 1044
Pioneertown 960
Pittsburgh 180-3
planning
budgeting 23, 25, 1170, 1173
calendar of events 31-4
children, travel with 66-8
eating & drinking 55-65
first-time travelers 24-5
internet resources 23
itineraries 35-9
repeat visitors 26
travel seasons 22, 31, 32, 33, 34
USA basics 22-3
USA's regions 69-72
plantations
Berkeley Plantation 326
Boone Hall Plantation 373
Drayton Hall 371
John Dickinson Plantation 315
Laura Plantation 460
Magnolia Plantation 371
Middleton Place 371
Myrtles Plantation 463
Oak Alley Plantation 460-1
Oakley Plantation & Audubon State Historic Site 463
Oatlands Plantation 337

Shirley Plantation 326
Whitney Plantation 460
Plymouth 207, 1018
Point Lobos State Natural Reserve 972-3
Point Reyes National Seashore 1004
Point Sur Historic Park 972
Po'ipu 1128
politics 1132, 1149
population 1130-1, 1145, 1146-7, 1148
Port Angeles 1052-3
Port Orford 1085
Port Townsend 1051-2
Portland (Maine) 259-61
Portland (Oregon) 16, 1063-73, **1064, 16**
accommodations 1068-9
activities 1066-7
drinking & nightlife 1071
entertainment 1071-2
festivals & events 1067-8
food 1069-70
shopping 1072
sights 1063-6
tourist information 1072-3
tours 1067
travel to/from 1073
travel within 1073
Portsmouth 249-50
postal services 1176
Poughkeepsie 148
Powell St Cable Car Turnaround 978
Prescott 848
Princeton 162-3
Providence 224-6
Provincetown 212-14
public holidays 1176

Q
Quechee 243-4
Queens 26, 105-7, 112-13, 123-4, 130-1

R
Racine 606-7
radio 1147, 1149, 1174
railways
Delaware & Ulster Railroad 149
Durango & Silverton Narrow Gauge Railroad 785
Essex 236
Grand Canyon Railway 854
Mount Washington Cog Railway 254
Mt Hood Railroad 1076
Strasburg Railroad 179

Western Maryland Scenic Railroad 310
Winnipesaukee Scenic Railroad 251
Raleigh 356-7
Rapid City 671-4
Red Rock State Park 849
Red Rocks Park & Amphitheatre 761
Red Wing 622
Redwood National Park 638, 1015, **638**
Rehoboth Beach 312-13
religion 1131, 1146
Reno 834-7
responsible travel 631
Rhinebeck 148-9
Rhode Island 223-30
Rhyolite 964
Richmond 322-5
ride sharing 1187
River Road 460-1
road trips 40-6, **43**
Roanoke 338-9
Roanoke Island 350
Robie House 542
rock climbing 52-3
City of Rocks State Park 911
Colorado Mountain School 768
Eldorado Canyon State Park 763
Garden of the Gods 777
Grand Teton National Park 800
Joshua Tree National Park 961
Moab 883
Mohonk Preserve 147
Mt Rainier National Park 1060
Pinnacles National Park 971
Smith Rock State Park 1078-9
Yosemite National Park 1023
Rockbridge County 335-7
Rockefeller Center 91-2
Rockland 262-3
Rocky Mountain National Park 635, 766-8, **634**
Rocky Mountains 21, 71, 750-817, **21**
accommodations 750
climate 750
food 750
highlights 752-3, **752-3**
itineraries 756
travel seasons 750
travel to/from 751, 754
travel within 751, 754

Roosevelt, Franklin D 148
Roswell 914
Route 66 19, 40-2, 652, 687, 689, 866, **19**
Rugby 667
Ruidoso 912-13
Russian River Valley 1009-10
Ryman Auditorium 390

S
Sacramento 1016-17
safety 1176-7
road 1193
Sag Harbour 142
Saguaro National Park 637, 868-9
Sainte Genevieve 654
Salem (Massachusetts) 206-7
Salem (Oregon) 1073-4
Salida 776-7
Salt Lake City 872-6
Salt River Recreation Area 841
Salton Sea 963
Salvation Mountain 963
San Antonio 21, 709-17, **710, 21**
San Diego 947-58, **948, 950-1, 952**
accommodations 954-5
activities 953-4
drinking & nightlife 956-7
entertainment 957
food 955-6
sights 947-53
tourist information 957
travel to/from 957-8
travel within 958
San Francisco 12, 977-1003, **979, 980, 982-3, 988, 12**
accommodations 992-4
activities 989
Castro, the 985-6, 994, 997-8, **986**
Chinatown 978-81, 995-7
Civic Center 978, 992-3, 994-5
drinking & nightlife 998-1000
Embarcadero 977-8, 992-3, 994
entertainment 1000-1
festivals & events 989-92
Fisherman's Wharf 981-4
food 994-8
Haight, the 986-7, 994, 998
itineraries 978
Mission, the 985-6, 994, 997-8

INDEX S-S

San Francisco continued
  North Beach 981, 993, 995-7
  Presidio 984-5, 993-4, 997
  shopping 1001-2
  sights 977-89
  SoMa 992-3, 994
  tourist information 1002
  tours 989
  travel to/from 1002-3
  travel within 1003
  Union Square 978, 992-3, 994-5
  walking tour 996, **996**
San Ildefonso Pueblo 903
San Juan Islands 1055-7
San Luis Obispo 968-9
Sand Mountain Recreation Area 838
Sandwich 207-8
Sandy Hook Gateway National Recreation Area 168
Sanibel Island 516-17
Santa Barbara 965-7
Santa Clara Pueblo 903
Santa Cruz 975-7
Santa Fe 15, 896-903, **900-1**
Saranac Lake 157
Sarasota 515-16
Saugatuck 595-6
Saugerties 151
Sault Ste Marie 600
Savannah 17, 420-4, **422, 17**
sculpture 1155-7
Seattle 1035-49, **1038-9**
  accommodations 1042-3
  activities 1041
  drinking & nightlife 1045-6
  entertainment 1047
  festivals & events 1042
  shopping 1048
  sights 1036-41
  tourist information 1048
  tours 1041-2
  travel to/from 1048-9
  travel within 1049
Sebastopol 1009
Sedona 849-50
Selma 430-1
Seneca Falls 153-4
senior travelers 1172
Senoia 406
Sequoia National Park 1025
Shasta Dam 1020

Shawnee National Forest 561
Shelter Island 144-5
Shenandoah National Park 335, 633, **632-3**
Shenandoah Valley 333-7
Shiprock 908
Shreveport 467
Sierra Nevada 1021-30
Silver City 911
Silverton 783-4
Sioux Falls 667-8
Sioux peoples 1151
Sisters 1078
Sitka 1096-8
Skagway 1101-3
skiing & snowboarding 51-2
  Alta 877
  Arizona Snowbowl 852
  Aspen 774
  Big Sky Resort 804-5
  Breckenridge 771-2
  Bridger Bowl Ski Area 803
  Brighton 877
  Canyons Village at Park City 878
  Crater Lake National Park 1080
  Crested Butte 779
  Deer Valley 878
  Heavenly 1029
  Hunter Mountain 150
  Hurricane Ridge Ski & Snowboard Area 1051
  Jackson Hole 791
  Killington Resort 244
  Mad River Glen 244
  Mammoth Mountain 1027
  Methow Valley 1058
  Mt Bachelor Ski Resort 1079
  Mt Baker 1057
  Mt Hood 1077
  Northstar California 1030
  Park City Mountain Resort 879
  Porcupine Mountain Ski Area 602
  Purgatory 785
  Royal Gorge 1030
  Schweitzer Mountain Resort 817
  Silverton 783
  Ski Apache 913
  Ski Santa Fe 897-8
  Snowbird 877
  Solitude 877
  Spirit Mountain 623
  Squaw Valley USA 1030
  Steamboat Mountain Resort 769
  Stowe 246

Sugar Bowl 1030
  Sun Valley Resort 815
  Sundance Resort 883
  Taos 905-6
  Telluride 781
  Vail 772
  Whiteface Mountain 156
  Whitefish 809
  Winter Park 770-1
Sleeping Bear Dunes National Lakeshore 596-7
Slide Rock State Park 849
Smith Island 298
smoking 1176
snorkeling 53-4
snowboarding, see skiing & snowboarding
Solvang 968
Sonoma Coast State Park 1011
Sonoma Valley 1008-9
South, the 70, 346-467
  accommodations 346
  climate 346
  food 346
  highlights 348-9, **348-9**
  itineraries 350
  travel seasons 346
South Bend 569-70
South by Southwest 32
South Carolina 368-79
South Cascades 1060-1
South Dakota 667-77
South Padre Island 728-30
Southwest, the 71, 818-914
  accommodations 818
  climate 818
  food 59, 818
  highlights 820-1, **820-1**
  itineraries 819
  travel seasons 818
  travel to/from 819, 822
  travel within 819, 822
Southampton 142-3
Space Coast 504-5
Space Needle 1037
spas, see hot springs & spas
Sperryville 337
Spokane 1059-60
sports 47-54, 1147-9, see also individual sports
Spring Green 609
Springdale 890-1
Springfield 559-60
St Augustine 506-8
St Charles 651-2
St Francisville 463
St Helena Island 375
St Ignace 598-9
St Joseph 659-60
St Louis 645-51, **646, 648**

St Michaels 306
St Paul 620-2
St Petersburg 513-15
St Simons Island 425
Staatsburg State Historic Site 148-9
Stagecoach Trail 559
Standish-Hickey State Recreation Area 1013
Stanley 816-17
Staten Island 107
state parks, see also national parks, parks & gardens, wildlife reserves
  Amicalola Falls State Park 417
  Antelope Island State Park 880
  Anza-Borrego Desert State Park 962-3
  Assateague State Park 308
  Babcock State Park 345
  Bastrop State Park 708
  Baxter State Park 265
  Beartown State Forest 220
  Berkeley Springs State Park 343
  Big Bend Ranch State Park 741-2
  Bill Baggs Cape Florida State Park 479
  Blackwater Falls State Park 344
  Brandywine Creek State Park 313
  Brown County State Park 565
  Cape Henlopen State Park 311
  Cape May Point State Park 167
  Cathedral Gorge State Park 841
  Cherry Springs State Park 180
  Chicot State Park 466
  Cimarron Canyon State Park 909
  City of Rocks State Park 911
  Clifty Falls State Park 567
  Colt State Park 229
  Crawford Notch State Park 254
  Crystal Cove State Park 946
  Custer State Park 676-7
  Cypremont Point State Park 466
  Davis Mountains State Park 742
  Dead Horse Point State Park 886

Deception Pass State Park 1053
Echo Bluff State Park 653
Ecola State Park 1082
Eldorado Canyon State Park 763
Falls of the Ohio State Park 567
First Landing State Park 330
Fort Adams State Park 227
Fort Clinch State Park 510
Fort Robinson State Park 683
Fort Stevens State Park 1081
Fort Worden State Park 1051-2
Franconia Notch State Park 253-4
Franklin Mountains State Park 747
Golden Gate Canyon State Park 762
Grafton Notch State Park 265
Hammonasset Beach State Park 235-6
Hawks Nest State Park 345
Hocking Hills State Park 583
Hueco Tanks State Park & Historical Site 748
Humboldt Redwoods State Park 1013
Hunting Island State Park 376
Indiana Dunes State Park 568
Island Beach State Park 165
Jack London State Historic Park 1008
Jedediah Smith Redwoods State Park 1015
Jerome State Historic Park 848
John Bryan State Park 578
John Pennekamp Coral Reef State Park 498
Johnson's Shut-Ins State Park 653
Judge CR Magney State Park 624
Julia Pfeiffer Burns State Park 971
Kartchner Caverns State Park 870
Kelleys Islands State Park 575
Lake Chelan State Park 1058

Lake Dardanelle State Park 442
Leonard Harrison State Park 180
Lime Kiln Point State Park 1055
Living Desert State Park 914
Malibu Creek State Park 929
Mississippi Palisades State Park 559
Monadnock State Park 253
Montauk Point State Park 144
Moran State Park 1056
Morro Bay State Park 970
Mount Magazine State Park 441
Mount Nebo State Park 441
Mt Tamalpais State Park 1004
Natural Bridge State Park 336
Natural Bridge State Resort Park 405-6
Newport State Park 611
Old Town San Diego State Historic Park 952
Oliver Lee State Park 912-14
Orient Beach State Park 145
Ozark Folk Center State Park 443
Patrick's Point State Park 1014
Petit Jean State Park 441
Pfeiffer Big Sur State Park 971
Point Lobos State Natural Reserve 972-3
Point Sur Historic Park 972
Porcupine Mountains Wilderness State Park 602
Prairie Creek Redwoods State Park 1015
Red Rock State Park 849
Richardson Grove State Park 1013
Riordan Mansion State Historic Park 851
Robert H Treman State Park 152
Robert Moses State Park 141
Route 66 State Park 652
Salt Point State Park 1011
Sinks Canyon State Park 790
Slide Rock State Park 849

Smith Rock State Park 1078
Sonoma Coast State Park 1011
South Bass Island State Park 574
Split Rock Lighthouse State Park 624
Staunton State Park 762
Table Rock State Park 378
Tahquamenon Falls State Park 601
Topanga Canyon State Park 933
Torrey Pines State Natural Reserve 953
Unicoi State Park 419
Valley of Fire State Park 835
Vogel State Park 419
Waimea Canyon State Park 1127
Warren Dunes State Park 594-5
Wellesley Island State Park 158
Whirlpool State Park 161
White River State Park 561
Worthington State Forest 165
Statue of Liberty 78
Staunton 334-5
Steamboat Springs 769-70
Steens Mountain 1088
Stillwater 622
Stockbridge 221
Stowe 246
Straits of Mackinac 598-600
Sturgis 674
Sullivan's Island 373
Sun Studio 381
Sun Valley 814-16
Sundance Film Festival 879
Sundial Bridge 1019
Sunken Forest 141-2
Sunset Crater Volcano National Monument 855
surfing 49-50, 480
  Barnegat Peninsula 165
  Hawaii 1113-4, 1117-8
  Los Angeles 934
  San Diego 954
  Santa Cruz 975-6
  Surfrider Beach 934
  Wellfleet 211
Sutter Creek 1018
synagogues 370

T
Tahlequah 696
Tahoe City 1030
Taliesin 610
Taliesin West 840-1

Tallahassee 524-5
Tallulah Gorge 419
Tamiami Trail 496
Tampa 511-13
Tannersville 150-1
Taos 15, 904-8, **15**
Taos Pueblo 906
taxes 1176
taxis 1187
telephone services 1177-8
Telluride 781-3
Tennessee 379-99
Texas 71, 697-749, **698-9**
  accommodations 697
  climate 697
  food 697
  highlights 698-9
  itineraries 701
  travel seasons 697
theater 1157-8
theme parks, see amusement parks
Thousand Islands 157-8
Tilghman Island 306
time 23, 1178
Times Square 91
tipping 25, 65, 1176
toilets 1178
Tombstone 870-1
Top of the Rock 92
Topeka 687
tornadoes 684
Torrey 887
Torrey Pines State Natural Reserve 953
tourist information 1178
tours 1185
train travel 1187-9
travel to/from USA 1183-5
travel within USA 1131, 1185-9
Traverse City 597
Treaty Oak 509
Tree Snail Hammock Nature Trail 496
trekking, see hiking
Triangle, the 356-60
Trinidad 1014
Tri-Peaks Region 441-2
Truckee 1030
Trump, Donald 1143-4
Truth or Consequences 909-11
Tucson 864-8
Tulelake 1021
Tulsa 692-4
TV 1152-3, 1174
Twain, Mark 231

U
Ukiah 1013
United Nations 92-3
Unity Temple 558

Universal Orlando Resort 523-4
universities
Arizona State University 841
Brown University 224
Dartmouth College 255
Georgetown University 282
Harvard University 197
Humboldt State University 1014
Johns Hopkins University 300
Princeton University 163
University of California, Berkeley 1005
University of Chicago 544
University of Oregon 1074
University of Virginia 331
University of Washington 1040
US Naval Academy 304
Virginia Military Institute 336
Washington & Lee University 336
Yale University 236
Up Island 216
Upper Peninsula 600-3
US *Capitol* 278
USS *Midway* Museum 947
Utah 871-91

V
vacations 1176
Vail 772-4
Valentine 682
Valley of Fire State Park 835
vegetarian & vegan travelers 58
Vermont 15, 238-49, **239**, 15
Vernal 881
Very Large Array telescope 912
Vicksburg 434-5
Vietnam Veterans Memorial 271
Virginia 316-41
Virginia Beach 329-30
Virginia City 837-8
visas 1179-81
Volcano 1018
volunteering 1181
Voyageurs National Park 626

Map Pages **000**
Photo Pages **000**

W
Waikiki 1113-17
Waimea Canyon State Park 1127
walking, *see* hiking
walking tours
Boston 198, **198**
Chicago 543, **543**
Miami 482, **482**
New Orleans 453, **453**
New York City 104, **104**
San Francisco 996, **996**
Washington, DC 284, **284**
Wall 669
Walla Walla 1062-3
Wallowa Mountains Area 1088
Walnut Canyon 853
Walt Disney World® Resort 17, 521-3, **17**
Warhol, Andy 181, 1157
Wasatch Mountains 876-81
Washington (state) 1035-63
Washington, DC 70, 266, 267-97, **272-3**
accommodations 266, 285-7
activities 283
climate 266
drinking & nightlife 292-5
entertainment 295-7
festivals & events 285
food 266, 287-92
highlights 268-9, **268-9**
itineraries 270
sights 267-83
tourist information 296
tours 283, 285
travel seasons 266
travel within 296-7
walking tours 284, **284**
Washington, George 1135
Washington Monument 271
water, drinking 1173
weather 22, 31, 32, 33, 34
websites, *see* internet resources
Weedon Island Preserve 514
weights 1174
Weirs Beach 251
Wellfleet 211-12
Wellsboro 180
West Palm Beach 491-3
West Virginia 341-5
whale-watching
Monterey 973-4
Provincetown 213
Whidbey Island 1053-4
Whiskeytown National Recreation Area 1020
White House 279-80

White Mountains 251-5
White Pass & Yukon Route Railroad 1102
White Sands National Monument 911-12
Whiteface Veteran's Memorial Highway 156
Whitefish 809-10
white-water rafting 51
Arkansas River 780
Bluff 886
Colorado River 863
Durango 785
Fayetteville 345
Gauley River 344
Green River 882-3
Harpers Ferry 343
Jackson 791-2
John Day River 1087
Middle Fork of the Salmon 816
Moab 883
Salida 776
Santa Fe 897
Snake River 1088
Steamboat Springs 769
Taos 905-6
Vernal 881
Wichita 684-5
wi-fi 1174
wildfires 367
wildlife 1165-7, 1168, *see also individual species*
wildlife reserves
Alaska Raptor Center 1097
Back Bay National Wildlife Refuge 330
Bear Country USA 672-3
Bombay Hook National Wildlife Refuge 315
Bosque del Apache National Wildlife Refuge 909
Chincoteague National Wildlife Refuge 308
Cypress Creek National Wildlife Refuge 560
Everglades Outpost 495
Felix Neck Wildlife Sanctuary 216
Fort Niobrara National Wildlife Refuge 682
Georgia Sea Turtle Center 426
JN 'Ding' Darling National Wildlife Refuge 516
Laura Quinn Wild Bird Sanctuary 498
Manatee Viewing Center 512
Merritt Island National Wildlife Refuge 504
Old Tunnel Wildlife Management Area 715

Pea Island National Wildlife Refuge 351
Sea Turtle, Inc 728
South Padre Island Birding & Nature Center 729
Three Ring Ranch Exotic Animal Sanctuary 1118
VINS Nature Center 243
Wellfleet Bay Wildlife Sanctuary 211
World Center for Birds of Prey 813
wildlife-watching
Admiralty Island National Monument 1099
Anan Creek Wildlife Observatory 1095-6
Antelope Island State Park 880
Denali National Park & Preserve 1106
Grand Teton National Park 800
Monterey 973-4
National Elk Refuge 791
Pack Creek 1099
Point Lobos State Natural Reserve 972-3
Point Piedras Blancas 970-1
Provincetown 213
San Francisco 985
Sitka 1097
Yellowstone National Park 795
Whale Park 1097
Wildwood 167
Willamette Valley 1073-5
Williams 854
Williamsburg 326-7
Williamstown 222-3
Wilmington (Delaware) 313
Wilmington (North Carolina) 355-6
Windley Key Fossil Reef Geological State Site 499
windsurfing 478, 1076
wine 26, 27, 63-4
wine regions
Healdsburg 1010
Napa Valley 1006-8
Paso Robles 970
Russian River Valley 1009-10
Santa Maria Valley 968
Santa Ynez Valley 968
Sonoma Valley 1008-9
Verde Valley 851
Walla Walla 1062-3
Wingspread 607
Winter Park 770-1
Wisconsin 603-13

Wizard Stones of
  Kapaemahu 1114
Wolfeboro 251
wolves 1165
women travelers 1181-2
Woodstock 151, 243-4
work 1182
Wormsloe Plantation
  Historic Site 420
Wrangell 1095-6
Wright, Frank Lloyd 1160
Wynwood Walls 477-8
Wyoming 787-803

Y
Yachats 1083-4
Yakima 1061-2
Yale University 236
Yankee Stadium 105
Yellow Springs 578
Yellowstone National Park
  11, 635, 794-9, **796**,
  11, 635
Yorktown 328
Yosemite National Park 13,
  638, 1022-5, **13, 639**

Z
Zion National Park 637,
  889-90, **637**
ziplining 150, 345, 825, 1099
zoos
  Alaska Zoo 1092
  Bronx Zoo 105
  Cape Fear Serpentarium
    355
  Duke Lemur Center 357
  Henry Doorly Zoo 678
  Jungle Island 479
  Lincoln Park Zoo 541
  Living Desert Zoo &
    Gardens 959
  Los Angeles Zoo 927-8
  Maryland Zoo in
    Baltimore 301
  Minnesota Zoo 615
  Monkey Jungle 479
  National Zoo 283
  Oregon Zoo 1066
  Reid Park Zoo 865
  San Diego Zoo 949
  St Louis Zoo 646-7
  Woodland Park Zoo 1042
  Zoo Miami 479
Zuni Pueblo 896

INDEX W-Z

Map Legend

Sights

- Beach
- Bird Sanctuary
- Buddhist
- Castle/Palace
- Christian
- Confucian
- Hindu
- Islamic
- Jain
- Jewish
- Monument
- Museum/Gallery/Historic Building
- Ruin
- Shinto
- Sikh
- Taoist
- Winery/Vineyard
- Zoo/Wildlife Sanctuary
- Other Sight

Activities, Courses & Tours

- Bodysurfing
- Diving
- Canoeing/Kayaking
- Course/Tour
- Sento Hot Baths/Onsen
- Skiing
- Snorkeling
- Surfing
- Swimming/Pool
- Walking
- Windsurfing
- Other Activity

Sleeping

- Sleeping
- Camping

Eating

- Eating

Drinking & Nightlife

- Drinking & Nightlife
- Cafe

Entertainment

- Entertainment

Shopping

- Shopping

Information

- Bank
- Embassy/Consulate
- Hospital/Medical
- Internet
- Police
- Post Office
- Telephone
- Toilet
- Tourist Information
- Other Information

Geographic

- Beach
- Gate
- Hut/Shelter
- Lighthouse
- Lookout
- Mountain/Volcano
- Oasis
- Park
- Pass
- Picnic Area
- Waterfall

Population

- Capital (National)
- Capital (State/Province)
- City/Large Town
- Town/Village

Transport

- Airport
- BART station
- Border crossing
- Boston T station
- Bus
- Cable car/Funicular
- Cycling
- Ferry
- Metro/Muni station
- Monorail
- Parking
- Petrol station
- Subway/SkyTrain station
- Taxi
- Train station/Railway
- Tram
- Underground station
- Other Transport

Note: Not all symbols displayed above appear on the maps in this book

Routes

- Tollway
- Freeway
- Primary
- Secondary
- Tertiary
- Lane
- Unsealed road
- Road under construction
- Plaza/Mall
- Steps
- Tunnel
- Pedestrian overpass
- Walking Tour
- Walking Tour detour
- Path/Walking Trail

Boundaries

- International
- State/Province
- Disputed
- Regional/Suburb
- Marine Park
- Cliff
- Wall

Hydrography

- River, Creek
- Intermittent River
- Canal
- Water
- Dry/Salt/Intermittent Lake
- Reef

Areas

- Airport/Runway
- Beach/Desert
- Cemetery (Christian)
- Cemetery (Other)
- Glacier
- Mudflat
- Park/Forest
- Sight (Building)
- Sportsground
- Swamp/Mangrove

Robert Balkovich

New York Robert was born and raised in Oregon, but has called New York City home for almost a decade. When he was a child and other families were going to theme parks and grandma's house, he went to Mexico City and toured Eastern Europe by train. He's now a writer and travel enthusiast seeking experiences that are ever so slightly out of the ordinary to report back on. Instagram: @oh_balky

Ray Bartlett

Pennsylvania Ray is a travel writer specializing in Japan, Korea, Mexico and the United States. He's worked on many different Lonely Planet titles, starting with Japan in 2004 and going through to the present.

Loren Bell

Hawaii, Idaho, Montana, Rocky Mountains, Wyoming When Loren first back-packed through Europe, he was in the backpack. That memorable experience corrupted his six-month-old brain, ensuring he would never be happy sitting still. When he's not demystifying destinations for Lonely Planet, Loren writes about science and conservation news.

Greg Benchwick

Colorado A long-time Lonely Planet travel writer, Greg has rumbled in the jungles of Bolivia, trekked across Spain on the Camino de Santiago, interviewed presi-dents and grammy-award winners, dodged flying salmon in Alaska and climbed mountains (big and small) in between.

Andrew Bender

California Award-winning travel and food writer Andrew has written three doz-en Lonely Planet guidebooks (from Amsterdam to Los Angeles, Germany to Taiwan and more than a dozen titles about Japan), plus numerous articles for lonelyplanet.com.

Sara Benson

Hawaii, California The author of more than 70 travel and non-fiction books, Sara's writing has featured in national and international newspapers and magazines, in-cluding numerous Lonely Planet titles, CNN and National Geographic Adventure, as well as on popular travel websites such as Jetsetter.

Alison Bing

California Over 10 guidebooks and 20 years in San Francisco, author Alison has spent more time on Alcatraz than some inmates, become an aficionado of drag and burritos, and willfully ignored Muni signs warning that safety requires avoid-ing unnecessary conversation.

Catherine Bodry

Alaska Catherine is based in Anchorage, Alaska, but spends much time in South-east Asia. As a writer, she's covered Alaska, Thailand and China, among other destinations. A lover of mountains, she spends as much time as possible in or near hills, whether it's running, hiking, camping, berry picking, rafting or just gazing at them.

Cristian Bonetto

California Cristian has contributed to more than 30 Lonely Planet guides, while his musings on travel, food, culture and design appear in numerous publications around the world. When not on the road, you'll find the reformed playwright and TV scriptwriter slurping espresso in his beloved hometown, Melbourne.

OUR STORY

A beat-up old car, a few dollars in the pocket and a sense of adventure. In 1972 that's all Tony and Maureen Wheeler needed for the trip of a lifetime – across Europe and Asia overland to Australia. It took several months, and at the end – broke but inspired – they sat at their kitchen table writing and stapling together their first travel guide, *Across Asia on the Cheap*. Within a week they'd sold 1500 copies. Lonely Planet was born.

Today, Lonely Planet has offices in Franklin, London, Melbourne, Oakland, Dublin, Beijing and Delhi, with more than 600 staff and writers. We share Tony's belief that 'a great guidebook should do three things: inform, educate and amuse'.

OUR WRITERS

Benedict Walker

Curator, Connecticut, Rhode Island, Colorado, Nevada Ben had a suburban upbringing in Newcastle, Australia, and spent his weekends and long summers by the beach, whenever possible. Although he's drawn magnetically to the kinds of mountains he encountered in the Rockies and the Japan and Swiss Alps, beach life is in his blood. To date he has contributed to Lonely Planet's *Australia, Canada, Germany, Japan, Sweden, Switzerland, USA* and *Vietnam* guidebooks. Ben also wrote the Plan Your Trip, Understand and Survival Guide sections.

Kate Armstrong

Florida Kate has spent much of her adult life traveling and living around the world. A full-time freelance travel journalist, she has contributed to around 40 Lonely Planet guides and trade publications and is regularly published in Australian and worldwide publications. She is the author of several books and children's educational titles.

Brett Atkinson

California Based in New Zealand, but frequently on the road for Lonely Planet, Brett's a full-time travel and food writer specializing in adventure travel, unusual destinations, and surprising angles on more well-known destinations. Craft beer and street food are Brett's favorite reasons to explore places.

Carolyn Bain

Maine, Massachusetts A travel writer and editor for more than 20 years, Carolyn has lived, worked and studied in various corners of the globe, including Denmark, London, St Petersburg and Nantucket. Carolyn writes about travel and food for a range of publishers; see carolynbain.com.au for more.

Amy C Balfour

Delaware, Maryland, Virginia, West Virginia, Hawaii, Texas Amy grew up in Richmond, Virginia, and now lives in the Shenandoah Valley in the foothills of the Blue Ridge Mountains. A few of her favorite places between the Atlantic and the Appalachians include Sharp Top Mountain, Lexington, VA, Berlin, MD, and the New River Gorge. Amy has authored or co-authored more than 30 books for Lonely Planet, including *USA, Eastern USA* and *Florida & the South's Best Trips*. Her stories have appeared in *Backpacker, Sierra, Southern Living* and *Women's Health*.

OVER PAGE | MORE WRITERS

Published by Lonely Planet Global Limited
CRN 554153
10th edition – Apr 2018
ISBN 978 1 78657 448 0
© Lonely Planet 2018 Photographs © as indicated 2018
10 9 8 7 6 5 4 3 2 1
Printed in Singapore

Celeste Brash

California, Washington Celeste has been writing guidebooks for Lonely Planet since 2005 and her travel articles have appeared in publications from BBC Travel to National Geographic. She's currently writing a book about her five years on a remote pearl farm in the Tuamotu.

Jade Bremner

California Jade has been a journalist for more than a decade, and has edited travel magazines and sections for *Time Out* and *Radio Times*, and worked as a correspondent for the *Times*, CNN and the *Independent*. She feels privileged to share tales from this wonderful planet we call home and is always looking for the next adventure.

Nate Cavalieri

California A writer and musician based in California, Nate has authored over a dozen titles for Lonely Planet, including *Epic Bike Rides of the World*. He's cycled across China and Southern Africa as a guide with Tour d'Afrique and played third chair percussion in an Orlando theme park.

Gregor Clark

Connecticut, Maine, Massachusetts, New Hampshire, Vermont, Rhode Island Gregor is a US-based writer whose love of foreign languages and curiosity about what's around the next bend have taken him to dozens of countries on five continents. Chronic wanderlust has also led him to visit all 50 states and most Canadian provinces on countless road trips through his native North America. Since 2000, Gregor has regularly contributed to Lonely Planet guides.

Michael Grosberg

California, New York Michael has worked on over 45 Lonely Planet guidebooks. Whether covering Myanmar or New Jersey, each project has added to his rich and complicated psyche and taken years from his (still?) relatively young life. Prior to his freelance writing career, other international work included development on the island of Rota in the western Pacific; South Africa where he investigated and wrote about political violence and helped train newly elected government representatives; and Quito, Ecuador to teach. He received a Masters in Comparative Literature and taught literature and writing as an adjunct professor at several New York City area colleges.

Ashley Harrell

Florida After a brief stint selling day spa coupons door-to-door in South Florida, Ashley decided she'd rather be a writer. She went to journalism grad school, convinced a newspaper to hire her, and starting covering wildlife, crime and tourism, sometimes all in the same story. Fueling her zest for storytelling and the unknown, she traveled widely and moved often, from a tiny NYC apartment to a vast California ranch to a jungle cabin in Costa Rica, where she started writing for Lonely Planet.

Alexander Howard

Alaska Alexander is the managing editor of the US edition of Lonely Planet Magazine. He began his work at Lonely Planet as a guidebook editor (and eventually writer) covering the Western US and Canada, a job that frequently took him on adventures including trekking into the lava fields of Hawai'i, piloting an aerobatic plane in Vegas and (until recently) being afraid of grizzlies.

Mark Johanson

Missouri, Iowa, North Dakota, South Dakota, Nebraska, Kansas, Oklahoma Mark grew up in Virginia and has called five different countries home over the last decade. His travel-writing career began as something of a quarter-life crisis, and he's happily spent the past eight years circling the globe reporting for Australian travel magazines (like *Get Lost*), British newspapers (like the *Guardian*), American lifestyles (like *Men's Journal*) and global media outlets (like CNN and BBC). When not on the road, you'll find him gazing at the Andes from his home in Santiago, Chile. Follow the adventure at www.markjohanson.com.

Adam Karlin

Florida, Alabama, Arkansas, Georgia, Louisiana, Mississippi, Alaska, Hawaii Adam has contributed to dozens of Lonely Planet guidebooks, covering an alphabetical spread that ranges from the Andaman Islands to the Zimbabwe Border. As a journalist, he has written on travel, crime, politics, archeology and the Sri Lankan Civil War. Adam is based out of New Orleans, which helps explain his love of wetlands, food and good music. Learn more at http://walkonfine.com.

Brian Kluepfel

New Jersey, New York Brian has worked for Lonely Planet across the Americas since 2006. He's been the editor of the *Bolivian Times* in La Paz, a correspondent for Major League Soccer and a contributor to Frontier Airlines inflight magazine. His Lonely Planet adventures have taken him to Venezuela, Bolivia and even the pine barrens of New Jersey. His stories on Sleepy Hollow Cemetery and the mines of Potosi, Bolivia will feature in the Lonely Planet title *Amazing Secret Marvels*.

Stephen Lioy

Texas Stephen is a photographer, writer, hiker and travel blogger. A 'once in a lifetime' Euro trip and post-university move to China set the stage for what would eventually become a semi-nomadic lifestyle. When Stephen isn't at home in Kyrgyzstan, which is more often than not, he can usually be found leading very large tour groups of very small children or, in between work periods, out in the mountains sleeping in a tent and eating the sort of things your stomach warns you about. Follow Stephen's travels at www.monkboughtlunch.com.

Carolyn McCarthy

Colorado, Rocky Mountains, Utah Carolyn specializes in travel, culture and adventure in the Americas. She has written for *National Geographic, Outside, BBC Magazine, Boston Globe* and other publications. She has contributed to over 30 guidebooks for Lonely Planet, including for *Colorado, Argentina, Chile, Panama, Peru* and the *Trekking in the Patagonian Andes* guide. For more information, visit www.carolynmccarthy.org or follow her Instagram travels at @masmerquen.

Craig McLachlan

Hawaii Craig has covered destinations all over the globe for Lonely Planet for two decades. Based in Queenstown, New Zealand for half the year, he runs an outdoor activities company and a sake brewery, then moonlights overseas for the other half, leading tours and writing for Lonely Planet. Describing himself as a 'freelance anything', Craig has an MBA from the University of Hawai'i and is also a Japanese interpreter, pilot, photographer, hiking guide, tour leader, karate instructor and budding novelist. Check out www.craigmclachlan.com.

Hugh McNaughton

Arizona A former English lecturer, Hugh decided visa applications beat grant applications, and turned his love of travel into a full-time thing. Having also done a bit of restaurant reviewing in his home town (Melbourne, Australia), he's now eaten his way across Europe and North America, and found the best way to work up an appetite for the USA's great, gut-busting food is spending all day cycling through its stunning landscapes.

Becky Ohlsen

Oregon, Washington Becky is a freelance writer, editor and critic based in Portland, Oregon. She writes guidebooks and travel stories about Scandinavia, Portland and elsewhere for Lonely Planet. When she's not covering ground for Lonely Planet, Becky is working on a book about motorcycles and the paradoxical appeal of risk.

Christopher Pitts

Colorado, New Mexico Chris's first expedition in life ended in failure when he tried to dig from Pennsylvania to China at the age of six. He went on to study Chinese in university, living for several years in China. He spent more than a decade in Paris with his wife and two children before the lure of Colorado's sunny skies and outdoor adventure proved too great to resist.

Liza Prado

Colorado Liza has been a travel writer since 2003, when she made a move from corporate lawyering to travel writing. She's written dozens of guidebooks and articles to destinations throughout the Americas. She lives very happily in Denver, Colorado, with her husband and fellow writer, Gary Chandler, and their two kids.

Josephine Quintero

California Josephine first got her taste of not-so-serious travel when she slung a guitar on her back and traveled in Europe in the early '70s, along the way working on a kibbutz in Israel and meeting her husband. She primarily covers Spain and Italy for Lonely Planet.

Kevin Raub

Great Smoky Mountains National Park, Kentucky, North Carolina, South Carolina, Tennessee Kevin grew up in Atlanta and started his career as a music journalist in New York, working for *Men's Journal* and *Rolling Stone* magazines. A Georgia boy gone AWOL, he always appreciates coming home to the South for barbecue and brews. Follow him on Twitter and Instagram (@RaubOnTheRoad). To learn more about Kevin, check out www.lonelyplanet.com/members/kraub.

Simon Richmond

New York Journalist and photographer Simon has specialized as a travel writer since the early 1990s and first worked for Lonely Planet in 1999 on the Central Asia guide. He's long since stopped counting the number of guidebooks he's researched and written for the company, but countries covered including Australia, China, India, Iran, Japan, Korea, Malaysia, Mongolia, Myanmar (Burma), Russia, Singapore, South Africa and Turkey. For Lonely Planet's website he's penned features on topics from the world's best swimming pools to the joys of Urban Sketching.

Brendan Sainsbury

Alaska Originally from Hampshire, England, Brendan has traveled all over Alaska from Ketchikan in the south to Deadhorse in the north by bus, train, kayak, bicycle, ferry, airplane and his own two feet. Memorable moments have included taking a bus up the Dalton Highway from Fairbanks to the Arctic Ocean, catching a ferry through the off-the-grid Alaskan peninsula to the Aleutian Islands and running the Chilkoot trail in the footsteps of the Klondike 'stampeders' in a day. Brendan has contributed to over 50 Lonely Planet guides including six editions of *Cuba*.

Andrea Schulte-Peevers

California Born and raised in Germany and educated in London and at UCLA, Andrea has traveled the distance to the moon and back in her visits to some 75 countries. She has earned her living as a professional travel writer for more than two decades and authored or contributed to nearly 100 Lonely Planet titles.

Adam Skolnick

Hawaii Adam's travel obsession bloomed while working as an environmental activist in the mid '90s. These days he's an award-winning journalist and travel writer who writes about travel, culture, human rights, sports and the environment for a variety of publications, including the *New York Times, Playboy, Outside,* BBC. com, *Wired,* ESPN.com, and *Men's Health,* and he's authored or co-authored over 35 Lonely Planet guidebooks. He lives in Malibu, California.

Helena Smith

California Helena is an award-winning writer and photographer covering travel, outdoors and food. Helena is from Scotland but was partly brought up in Malawi, so Africa always feels like home. She also enjoys living in multicultural Hackney and wrote, photographed and published Inside Hackney.

Regis St Louis

Florida Regis grew up in a small town in the American Midwest – the kind of place that fuels big dreams of travel – and he developed an early fascination with foreign dialects and world cultures. He spent his formative years learning Russian and a handful of Romance languages, which served him well on journeys across much of the globe. Regis has contributed to more than 50 Lonely Planet titles, covering destinations across six continents. Follow him on www.instagram.com/regisstlouis.

Ryan Ver Berkmoes

Hawaii, Texas Ryan has written more than 110 guidebooks for Lonely Planet. He grew up in Santa Cruz, California, which he left at age 17 for college in the Midwest, where he first discovered snow. All joy of this novelty soon wore off. Since then he has been traveling the world, both for pleasure and for work – which are often indistinguishable. He has covered everything from wars to bars. He definitely prefers the latter. Ryan calls New York City home. Read more at ryanverberkmoes.com and at @ryanvb.

John A Vlahides

California John has been a cook in a Parisian bordello, luxury-hotel concierge, television host, safety monitor in a sex club, French–English interpreter and is one of Lonely Planet's most experienced guidebook authors. When not talking travel, John sings with the San Francisco Symphony and spends free time in the Sierra Nevada.

Mara Vorhees

Massachusetts Born and raised in St Clair Shores, Michigan, Mara traveled the world (if not the universe) before settling in the Hub. The pen-wielding traveler covers destinations as diverse as Belize and Russia, as well as her home of New England. She lives in a pink house in Somerville, Massachusetts with her husband, two kiddies and two kitties.

Clifton Wilkinson

California Clifton has been in love with California since first visiting in 1995. Christmases spent near Sacramento, bike rides across the Golden Gate Bridge and hiking in Yosemite National Park have all reinforced Clifton's opinion that the Golden State is the best state in the whole US, and Santa Barbara is one of its most beautiful corners. Having worked for Lonely Planet for more than 11 years, he's now based in the London office, but hoping for the call back to CA's Sideways country and the chance to show that Merlot isn't all that bad.

Luci Yamamoto

Hawaii A fourth-generation native of Hawai'i, Luci is unfazed by rain, pidgin and long Hawaiian words. When she left law to be a writer, she heard the old adage: write what you know. For Lonely Planet she thus targeted the Hawaiian Islands. To her surprise, her kama'aina background was only a launchpad – and she discovered extraordinary new people and places on her home island. Currently a writer, editor, Iyengar yoga teacher, and blogger (www.yogaspy.com) in Vancouver, she regularly returns to Hawai'i and recharges her local 'cred.' Even more than papayas and poke, she loves the Big Island's aloha spirit.

Karla Zimmerman

Illinois; Indiana; Michigan; Minnesota; Virginia; Ohio; Washington, DC; Wisconsin Karla lives in Chicago, where she eats doughnuts, yells at the Cubs, and writes stuff for books, magazines and websites when she's not doing the first two things. She has contributed to 40-plus guidebooks and travel anthologies covering destinations in Europe, Asia, Africa, North America and the Caribbean – all of which are a long way from the early days, when she wrote about gravel for a construction magazine and got to trek to places like Fredonia, Kansas. To learn more, follow her on Instagram and Twitter (@karlazimmerman).

Contributing Writers: Laura Pearson, Illinois; Trisha Ping, Michigan